Common English Bible

Concise Concordance

COMMON
ENGLISH
BIBLE

Nashville

The Common English Bible publishing staff thanks Glenn Weaver and BibleWorks Software for their invaluable assistance designing and creating this concordance.

Library of Congress Cataloging-in-Publication Data

CEB Bible concordance.
p. cm.
ISBN 978-1-60926-064-4 (trade pbk. : alk. paper) 1. Bible--Concordances, English.

BS425.C43 2011
220.5'208--dc23

2011043214

Printed in China

1 2 3 4 5 6 7 8 9 10 – 15 14 13 12 11

Contents

Introduction iv
Concordance 1
- A 1
- B 30
- C 54
- D 88
- E 125
- F 142
- G 172
- H 190
- I 218
- J 230
- K 244
- L 256
- M 306
- N 336
- O 356
- P 379
- Q 460
- R 462
- S 515
- T 631
- U 679
- V 685
- W 694
- X .... (no entries)
- Y 757
- Z 762

Abbreviations 764

Introduction

The *CEB Concise Concordance* is an index to Common English Bible translation of the 66 canonical books of the Bible. It does not index all the words in the Bible or every occurrence of the words that have been chosen. The words, phrases, and references included in this concordance have been chosen because they are the most useful for exploring and studying the Bible.

There are two different types of references in the *CEB Concise Concordance*, word entries and phrase entries.

The **word entries** are alphabetically arranged keywords—including names and places—followed by Bible references (book, chapter, and verse) and a brief context line that shows the words immediately surrounding the keyword in that particular verse. These context lines are meant to help you find the reference you are seeking. We have tried to make them useful, but very short lines like these are frequently misleading, often saying the opposite of what the full context says in the Bible. Always check the verse in the Bible.

The **phrase entries** are alphabetically arranged by the first word in the phrase, but they are also indicated by cross references from keywords that appear in the phrase. For instance, the key word *hearts* is followed by an arrow pointing to the phrase *change your hearts and lives*. The same is true of the key words *change* and *lives*. These phrases are particularly useful, because the Common English Bible frequently uses phrases for important concepts and titles. *Change your hearts and lives*, for instance, replaces the traditional *repent*. The phrase entries are followed by a list of references without context lines. The index for each phrase entry is exhaustive.

Aa

AARON → AARON AND HIS SONS, AARON THE PRIEST, AARON'S SONS
Exodus
4:16 ***A*** will speak for you to the people.
4:27 The LORD said to ***A***, "Go into the
7:1 and your brother ***A*** will be your
32:35 did with the bull calf that ***A*** made.
39:1 holy clothes for ***A*** as the LORD had
Leviticus
9:8 ***A*** went to the altar and slaughtered the
Numbers
17:6 and the staff of ***A*** was with their
33:39 ***A*** was 123 years old when he died on
Psalms
77:20 sheep under the care of Moses and ***A***.
99:6 Moses and ***A*** were among his priests,
106:16 jealous too of ***A***, the LORD's holy
115:10 the LORD, house of ***A***! God is their
115:12 Israel; God will bless the house of ***A***;
Luke
1:5 wife Elizabeth was a descendant of ***A***.
Acts
7:40 They told ***A***, 'Make us gods that will
Hebrews
7:11 than one according to the order of ***A***?

AARON AND HIS SONS
Ex 27:21; 28:1, 4, 43; 29:4, 9, 10, 15, 19, 20, 24, 27, 28, 32, 35, 44; 30:19, 30; 39:27; 40:12, 31; Lv 2:3; 2:10; 6:9, 16, 20, 25; 7:31, 35; 8:2, 6, 14, 18, 22, 31, 36; 10:6; 22:2; 24:9; Nm 3:9; 3:10, 38, 48, 51; 4:5, 15, 19, 27; 6:23; 8:13, 19, 22; 1Ch 6:49

AARON THE PRIEST
Ex 31:10; 35:19; Lv 1:7; 7:34; 21:21; Nm 3:6; 3:32; 4:16, 28, 33; 18:28; 26:64; 33:38; Josh 21:4; 21:13

AARON'S DESCENDANTS
Lv 6:18; Nm 16:40; 1Ch 24:31; 2Ch 13:10; 26:18; 31:19; 35:14

AARON'S SONS
Ex 28:1; 28:40; Lv 1:5; 1:8, 11; 2:2; 3:2, 5, 8, 13; 6:14, 22; 7:10; 8:13, 24, 30; 9:1, 9, 12, 18; 10:1; 21:1; Nm 3:2; 3:3; 10:8; 2Ch 13:9; 29:21

ABANDON
Numbers
32:15 away again to ***a*** Israel in the
Nehemiah
9:19 mercy, didn't ***a*** them in the
Psalms
89:30 his children ever ***a*** my Instruction,
94:14 he will not ***a*** his very own
Proverbs
4:2 teach you well. Don't ***a*** my instruction.
9:6 ***A*** your simplistic ways and live; walk
15:10 for those who ***a*** the way; those
28:4 Those who ***a*** Instruction praise the
Isaiah
1:28 alike; those who ***a*** the LORD will be
41:17 I, the God of Israel, won't ***a*** them.
58:2 that didn't ***a*** their God. They
65:11 But you who ***a*** the LORD, who forget my
Jeremiah
2:19 bitter it is to ***a*** the LORD your God
9:19 to leave the land and ***a*** our homes!"
47:3 wheels, parents ***a*** children, so
Lamentations
5:20 why do you ***a*** us for such a
Ezekiel
18:31 ***A*** all of your repeated sins. Make
Acts
2:27 because you won't ***a*** me to the grave,
27:30 sailors tried to ***a*** the ship by
Hebrews
13:5 said, I will never leave you or ***a*** you.

ABANDONED → ABANDONED THE LORD
Exodus
23:29 the land won't be ***a*** and the wild
32:8 They've already ***a*** the path that I
Deuteronomy
28:20 the evil acts by which you have ***a*** him.
29:25 those people ***a*** the covenant of
Judges
6:13 now the LORD has ***a*** us and allowed
1 Kings
11:33 because they have ***a*** me and worshipped
19:10 Israelites have ***a*** your covenant.
1 Chronicles
10:7 were dead, they ***a*** their towns and
Ezra
9:9 our God hasn't ***a*** us in our
9:10 this? We have ***a*** your commandments,
Psalms
9:10 you have not ***a*** any who seek you,
71:11 God has ***a*** him! Pursue him! Grab him
74:1 God, why have you ***a*** us forever? Why
78:60 God ***a*** the sanctuary at Shiloh, the tent
119:87 Meanwhile, I haven't ***a*** your precepts!
Isaiah
2:6 You have ***a*** your people, house of Jacob.
62:12 Sought After—A City That Is Not ***A***.
Jeremiah
5:19 Just as you have ***a*** me and served
9:13 because they have ***a*** my Instruction
51:5 forces, hasn't ***a*** Israel and Judah,
Ezekiel
8:12 see us; the LORD has ***a*** the land."

Luke
13:35 your house is ***a***. I tell you, you
Acts
2:31 that he wasn't ***a*** to the grave, nor
7:21 After he was ***a***, Pharaoh's daughter
Romans
1:24 So God ***a*** them to their hearts' desires,

ABANDONED THE LORD
1Sa 12:10; 2Ch 7:22; 21:10; 24:20, 24; 28:6; Is 1:4; Jer 17:13

ABEDNEGO
Daniel
1:7 Mishael "Meshach," and Azariah "***A***."
2:49 Meshach, and ***A*** to administer the
3:12 Meshach, and ***A***—who have ignored

ABEL
Genesis
4:2 to Cain's brother ***A***. Abel cared for
4:4 while ***A*** presented his flock's oldest
4:8 to his brother ***A***, "Let's go out to
Matthew
23:35 righteous man ***A*** to the blood of
Luke
11:51 prophet—from ***A*** to Zechariah—who
Hebrews
11:4 By faith ***A*** offered a better sacrifice

ABIATHAR
1 Samuel
22:22 David told ***A***, "That day, when Doeg the
30:7 to the priest ***A***, Ahimelech's son,
2 Samuel
15:24 chest down, and ***A*** offered
15:35 priests Zadok and ***A*** will be with you
1 Kings
1:7 from the priest ***A***. They assisted
Mark
2:26 the time when ***A*** was high priest,

ABIGAIL
1 Samuel
25:3 wife's name was ***A***. She was an
2 Samuel
2:2 from Jezreel and ***A***, Nabal's widow,
1 Chronicles
2:16 were Zeruiah and ***A***. Zeruiah's

ABIHU
Exodus
6:23 birth to Nadab, ***A***, Eleazar, and
Leviticus
10:1 Now Nadab and ***A***, two of Aaron's sons,
Numbers
3:2 the oldest, and ***A***, Eleazar, and
26:61 Nadab and ***A*** died when they made an
1 Chronicles
6:3 family: Nadab, ***A***, Eleazar, and

ABIJAH
1 Samuel
8:2 of the second was ***A***. They served as
1 Kings
14:1 time, Jeroboam's son ***A*** became sick.
Nehemiah
10:7 Meshullam, ***A***, Mijamin
12:4 Iddo, Ginnethon, ***A***
12:17 of ***A***, Zichri; of Miniamin, of Moadiah,
Matthew
1:7 was the father of ***A***. Abijah was the
Luke
1:5 division of ***A***. His wife

ABIMELECH
Genesis
20:2 sister." So King ***A*** of Gerar took her
26:1 and toward King ***A*** of the
Judges
8:31 bore him a son, and he named him ***A***.
2 Samuel
11:21 Jerubbaal's son ***A***? didn't a woman
Psalms
34:1 be crazy before ***A***, who banished him

ABINADAB
1 Samuel
16:8 Jesse called for ***A***, who presented
17:13 Eliab the oldest, ***A*** the second
31:2 his sons Jonathan, ***A***, and Malchishua.
1 Chronicles
2:13 his oldest son, ***A*** his second,

ABISHAI
1 Samuel
26:6 Joab's brother ***A***, Zeruiah's son,
2 Samuel
2:18 the battle: Joab, ***A***, and Asahel.
20:6 David told ***A***, "Bichri's son Sheba will
1 Chronicles
2:16 Zeruiah's family: ***A***, Joab, and Asahel-

ABLE → ABLE TO STAND
Genesis
16:1 had not been ***a*** to have children.
Leviticus
25:49 or they may be ***a*** to afford their
27:20 it is no longer ***a*** to be bought back.
Numbers
5:28 she will be immune and ***a*** to conceive.
1 Samuel
9:6 Maybe he'll be ***a*** to tell us which
17:9 If he is ***a*** to fight me and kill me,
1 Kings
5:3 David wasn't ***a*** to build a temple
13:4 Jeroboam wasn't ***a*** to bend it back
Psalms
64:5 Who will be ***a*** to see them? they
Proverbs
22:27 should they be ***a*** to take your bed
Isaiah
19:15 nor reed will be ***a*** to do anything
46:2 They aren't ***a*** to rescue the
47:11 you won't be ***a*** to dispel.
47:12 Maybe you will be ***a*** to succeed. Maybe
Jeremiah
10:23 that we're not ***a*** to direct our
11:11 they won't be ***a*** to escape. They
44:14 of Egypt will be ***a*** to return to the
Ezekiel
3:26 You won't be ***a*** to correct them,
7:13 won't even be ***a*** to hang on to

46:11 whatever one is ***a*** to give for each
Daniel
2:47 because you were ***a*** to reveal this
3:17 one we serve—is ***a*** to rescue us from
4:18 me. But you are ***a*** to do it because
4:37 and he is ***a*** to humble all who
11:16 no one will be ***a*** to oppose him. He
Amos
7:10 The land isn't ***a*** to cope with
Micah
2:3 you will not be ***a*** to remove your
Zephaniah
1:18 gold won't be ***a*** to deliver them
Matthew
3:9 you that God is ***a*** to raise up
11:5 were blind are ***a*** to see. Those who
22:46 Nobody was ***a*** to answer him. And from
26:53 that I'm not ***a*** to ask my Father
Luke
1:64 Zechariah was ***a*** to speak again,
John
9:10 asked him, "How are you now ***a*** to see?"
16:16 Soon you won't be ***a*** to see me; soon
Acts
5:39 God, you won't be ***a*** to stop them.
20:32 grace, which is ***a*** to build you up
Romans
11:23 because God is ***a*** to graft them in
1 Corinthians
14:13 should pray to be ***a*** to interpret.
Hebrews
2:18 He's ***a*** to help those who are being
James
1:21 very word that is ***a*** to save you.
Jude
1:24 To the one who is ***a*** to protect you from

ABLE TO STAND

Dt 7:24; 11:25; Josh 1:5; 7:13; Jdg 2:14; Est 9:2; Mt 16:18; Rev 6:17

ABNER

1 Samuel
14:50 his general was ***A***, Ner's son,
20:25 him while ***A*** sat beside Saul.
2 Samuel
3:6 David's house, ***A*** was gaining power
1 Kings
2:5 of Israel, ***A***, Ner's son, and
2:32 with the sword: ***A***, Ner's son and
1 Chronicles
26:28 Saul, Kish's son; ***A***, Ner's son; and

ABOVE → ABOVE THE EARTH

Genesis
1:7 from the waters ***a*** the dome. And it
27:39 far away from the showers of the sky ***a***.
49:25 from the skies ***a*** and blessings
Exodus
12:23 blood on the beam ***a*** the door and on
Deuteronomy
26:19 to set you high ***a*** all the other
Esther
3:1 by promoting him ***a*** all the officials
Psalms
18:48 lifted me high ***a*** my adversaries;
50:4 out to the skies ***a*** and to the earth
103:11 high as heaven is ***a*** the earth, that's
Ecclesiastes
12:5 afraid of things ***a*** and of terrors
Isaiah
2:2 It will be lifted ***a*** the hills;
Jeremiah
31:37 If the heavens ***a*** could be measured
Matthew
27:37 They placed ***a*** his head the charge
Mark
2:4 part of the roof ***a*** where Jesus was.
John
3:31 who comes from ***a*** is above all
8:23 below; I'm from ***a***. You are from
19:11 given to you from ***a***. That's why the
Philippians
2:9 him and gave him a name ***a*** all names,
James
1:17 gift, comes from ***a***. These gifts come
3:15 comes down from ***a***. Instead, it is
3:17 the wisdom from ***a***? First, it is

ABOVE THE EARTH

Gn 1:20; 7:17; Ps 103:11; Eze 1:19; 1:21; 10:16

ABRAHAM → ABRAHAM, ISAAC, AND JACOB; ABRAHAM'S CHILDREN; ABRAHAM'S DESCENDANTS

Genesis
17:5 name will no longer be Abram but ***A***.
18:11 Now ***A*** and Sarah were both very old.
19:29 God remembered ***A*** and sent Lot away
25:8 ***A*** took his last breath and died after a
Leviticus
26:42 my covenant with ***A***. And I will
Ezekiel
33:24 land are saying, "***A*** was just one man,
Micah
7:20 faithful love to ***A***, as you swore to
Matthew
1:1 Jesus Christ, son of David, son of ***A***:
3:9 to yourselves, ***A*** is our father. I
22:32 I'm the God of ***A***, the God of Isaac,
Luke
16:24 shouted, 'Father ***A***, have mercy on
John
8:39 Our father is ***A***." Jesus
8:58 Jesus replied, "before ***A*** was, I Am."
Romans
4:9 was credited to ***A*** as righteousness."
2 Corinthians
11:22 Are they descendants of ***A***? So am I.
Galatians
3:7 who believe are the children of ***A***.
4:22 It's written that ***A*** had two sons, one
Hebrews
11:8 By faith ***A*** obeyed when he was called to
James
2:21 What about ***A***, our father? Wasn't he

ABRAHAM, ISAAC, AND JACOB

Ex 2:24; 6:3, 8; 33:1; Nm 32:11; Dt 1:8; 6:10; 9:5, 27; 29:13; 30:20; 34:4; 2Ki 13:23; Jer 33:26; Ac 3:13; 7:32

ABRAHAM'S CHILDREN

Mt 3:9; Lk 3:8; Jn 8:33; 8:37, 39; Ro 9:7

ABRAHAM'S DESCENDANTS
Lk 1:55; Ro 4:16; 9:7; Ga 3:29; Heb 2:16

ABRAM
Genesis
12:1 The LORD said to ***A***, "Leave your land,
12:7 LORD appeared to ***A*** and said, "I give
17:5 name will no longer be ***A*** but Abraham.
1 Chronicles
1:27 and ***A***, that is, Abraham
Nehemiah
9:7 the one who chose ***A***. You brought him

ABSALOM
2 Samuel
13:1 sister of ***A***, who was also
13:30 came to David: "***A*** has killed all of
14:24 see my face." So ***A*** went straight to
15:10 But ***A*** sent secret agents throughout the
19:4 Oh, my son ***A***! Oh, Absalom, my
1 Kings
1:6 was very handsome and was born after ***A***.
2:7 from your brother ***A***, they came to me.
2:28 hadn't supported ***A***. Joab ran to the
1 Chronicles
3:2 the third ***A*** son of Maacah, the daughter
Psalms
3:1 fled from his son ***A***.] LORD, I have so

ABUNDANCE
Genesis
41:29 years of great ***a*** are now coming
Deuteronomy
33:19 on the sea's ***a***; they are
Jeremiah
31:14 the priests with ***a*** and shower my
33:6 them with an ***a*** of peace and
Acts
4:33 Jesus, and an ***a*** of grace was at
11:29 ministry according to each person's ***a***.

ABUSE
Judges
19:24 out, and you can ***a*** them and do
Psalms
74:10 enemies going to ***a*** your name forever?
89:50 your servant's ***a***, my Lord!
89:51 ones they use to ***a*** every step your
94:5 LORD! They ***a*** your very own
Isaiah
43:28 Jacob to destruction and Israel to ***a***.
51:7 and don't be upset when they ***a*** you.
Ezekiel
23:32 Appointed for ***a*** and scorn, it
Matthew
13:21 distress or ***a*** because of the
24:9 will arrest you, ***a*** you, and they
Mark
4:17 distress or ***a*** because of the
Acts
7:6 enslave them and ***a*** them for four
2 Corinthians
6:8 and with verbal ***a*** and good
1 Timothy
6:4 conflict, verbal ***a***, and evil
2 Timothy
3:11 physical ***a*** and ordeals in
Hebrews
10:33 to insults and ***a*** in public. Other

ACACIA WOOD
Ex 25:5; 25:28; 35:7, 24; 37:1, 4, 10, 15, 25, 28; 38:1, 6; Dt 10:3

ACCEPT
Numbers
35:31 You may not ***a*** a ransom for the life of
1 Samuel
2:15 roast. He won't ***a*** boiled meat from
Psalms
15:5 who won't ***a*** a bribe against
50:9 I won't ***a*** bulls from your house or
119:108 Please, LORD, ***a*** my spontaneous gifts of
Proverbs
2:1 My son, ***a*** my words and store up my
6:35 He won't ***a*** compensation; he'll refuse
19:20 to advice and ***a*** instruction, so
Ecclesiastes
5:19 to enjoy it, to ***a*** their place in
Hosea
8:13 the LORD doesn't ***a*** them. Now he will
John
5:34 Although I don't ***a*** human testimony, I
5:41 I don't ***a*** praise from people
Acts
7:59 prayed, "Lord Jesus, ***a*** my life!"
18:14 would have reason to ***a*** your complaint.
22:18 they won't ***a*** your testimony
1 Corinthians
2:14 unspiritual don't ***a*** the things from
16:16 So ***a*** the authority of people like them
1 Timothy
5:11 But don't ***a*** younger widows for the
2 Timothy
2:3 ***A*** your share of suffering like a good
1 Peter
5:5 who are younger: ***a*** the authority of

ACCEPTABLE
Leviticus
22:19 for it to be ***a*** on your behalf, it must
Ecclesiastes
5:1 house. It's more ***a*** to listen than to
Romans
14:20 food. All food is ***a***, but it's a bad
2 Corinthians
5:9 our goal is to be ***a*** to him, whether

ACCOMPLISHED
Mark
6:2 about the powerful acts ***a*** through him?
Luke
18:31 Human One by the prophets will be ***a***.
Acts
14:27 that God had ***a*** through their
Romans
3:27 law? With what we have ***a*** under the Law?
Ephesians
3:11 of time that he ***a*** through Christ
James
5:11 what the Lord has ***a***, for the Lord is

Revelation
10:7 purpose will be ***a***, fulfilling the

ACCOUNT
Genesis
2:4 This is the ***a*** of the heavens and the
Matthew
10:22 will hate you on ***a*** of my name. But
Luke
1:1 of compiling an ***a*** of the events
Philippians
4:17 a profit that accumulates in your ***a***.

ACHISH
1 Samuel
21:10 from Saul. He went to ***A***, Gath's king.
27:3 at Gath with ***A***. Each man had his

ACKNOWLEDGE
Deuteronomy
21:17 Instead, he must ***a*** the unloved wife's
Daniel
4:25 you, until you ***a*** that the Most
11:32 the people who ***a*** their God will
11:38 worship a god his fathers did not ***a***.
Matthew
10:32 I also will ***a*** before my Father
Luke
12:8 Human One will ***a*** before God's
John
12:42 but they wouldn't ***a*** their faith

ACROSS → ACROSS THE JORDAN, ACROSS THE JORDAN RIVER
Genesis
50:1 Joseph fell ***a*** his father's body, wept
Numbers
21:13 and camped ***a*** the Arnon in the
Judges
19:28 So he lay her ***a*** a donkey, and the
2 Chronicles
3:4 ***A*** the front of the temple was a porch
Psalms
78:26 east wind moving ***a*** the skies and
106:27 the nations, casting them ***a*** many lands.
Jonah
3:3 enormous city, a three days' walk ***a***.)
Luke
8:26 land, which is ***a*** the lake from
John
6:1 this Jesus went ***a*** the Galilee Sea
Revelation
20:9 They came up ***a*** the whole earth and

ACROSS THE JORDAN
Gn 32:10; Nm 22:1; 32:19, 32; 34:15; 35:14; Dt 1:1; 3:20; 4:46, 47, 49; 11:30; Josh 7:7; 1Sa 10:27; 31:7; 2Sa 19:15; 19:41; Mt 4:15; Jn 1:28; 3:26; 10:40

ACROSS THE JORDAN RIVER
Dt 1:1; 3:20; 4:46, 47, 49; 11:30; 1Sa 10:27; 2Sa 19:41

ACT
Genesis
18:25 judge of all the earth not ***a*** justly?"
Leviticus
19:15 You must not ***a*** unjustly in a legal
Deuteronomy
12:4 Don't ***a*** like they did toward the LORD
Judges
19:23 such an evil ***a***, given that this
1 Samuel
1:14 long will you ***a*** like a drunk?
Psalms
15:4 those who ***a*** wickedly, but who
37:5 way to the LORD! Trust him! He will ***a***
64:9 will announce the ***a*** of God, will
109:21 LORD, my Lord!—***a*** on my behalf for
119:124 ***A*** toward your servant according to your
Proverbs
13:16 The prudent all ***a*** intelligently, but
21:7 for they refuse to ***a*** with justice.
Isaiah
3:8 way they talk and ***a*** in word and deed
16:3 carefully, ***a*** justly; at high
Jeremiah
14:9 warrior unable to ***a***? Yet you are in
15:15 Remember me and ***a*** on my behalf.
Hosea
4:13 your daughters ***a*** like prostitutes,
7:4 They all ***a*** like adulterers; they are
John
8:4 was caught in the ***a*** of committing
Romans
5:18 the righteous ***a*** of one person,
1 Corinthians
9:20 I ***a*** like a Jew to the Jews, so I can
Ephesians
6:6 people, but ***a*** like slaves of
Colossians
4:5 ***A*** wisely toward outsiders, making the
1 Peter
3:16 good conscience. ***A*** in this way so
1 John
1:6 we are lying and do not ***a*** truthfully.
3:4 sin commits an ***a*** of rebellion, and

ACTED
Exodus
13:3 because the LORD ***a*** with power to
Judges
8:33 once again ***a*** unfaithfully by
9:16 So now, if you ***a*** faithfully and
1 Samuel
14:48 He ***a*** heroically, defeating the
Nehemiah
9:10 that they had ***a*** arrogantly
Job
42:9 and the LORD ***a*** favorably toward
Psalms
18:21 ways. I haven't ***a*** wickedly against
39:9 won't open my mouth because you have ***a***.
52:9 because you have ***a***. In the presence
73:22 and ignorant. I ***a*** like nothing but
105:22 sure his princes ***a*** according to his
106:6 done what is wrong. We've ***a*** wickedly.
118:24 the day the LORD ***a***; we will rejoice
Isaiah
38:15 he himself has ***a***. I will wander my
40:13 LORD's spirit and ***a*** as God's advisor?
58:2 a nation that ***a*** righteously, that

ACTED [cont.]

Jeremiah
2:20 tree, you have ***a*** like a prostitute.
Luke
24:28 to Emmaus, he ***a*** as if he was
Acts
3:17 I know you ***a*** in ignorance. So
1 Timothy
1:13 mercy because I ***a*** in ignorance and

ACTIONS

Proverbs
20:11 known by their ***a***, whether their
John
3:19 than the light, for their ***a*** are evil.
Romans
1:27 shameful ***a*** with males, and
4:6 God credits righteousness apart from ***a***:
12:17 for their evil ***a*** with evil
13:12 get rid of the ***a*** that belong to
2 Corinthians
4:2 and shameful ***a***. We don't use
Colossians
1:21 minds, which was shown by your evil ***a***.
James
2:18 apart from your ***a***? Instead, I'll
2:20 faith without ***a*** has no value at
3:13 Show that your ***a*** are good with a
Revelation
2:23 to each of you what your ***a*** deserve.
22:12 to repay all people as their ***a*** deserve.

ADAM

Genesis
4:1 The man ***A*** knew his wife Eve intimately.
5:5 In all, ***A*** lived 930 years, and he died
Joshua
3:16 off, just below ***A***, which is the
1 Chronicles
1:1 ***A***, Seth, Enosh
Job
15:7 born the first ***A***, brought forth
31:33 like ***A***, concealing my
Hosea
6:7 But like ***A*** they broke the covenant;
Luke
3:38 Enos son of Seth son of ***A*** son of God.
Romans
5:14 death ruled from ***A*** until Moses, even
1 Corinthians
15:22 everyone dies in ***A***, so also everyone
15:45 The first human, ***A***, became a living
1 Timothy
2:13 ***A*** was formed first, and then Eve
2:14 ***A*** wasn't deceived, but rather his wife
Jude
1:14 generations after ***A***, prophesied about

ADD

Deuteronomy
4:2 Don't ***a*** anything to the word that I am
12:32 care! Don't ***a*** anything to it or
2 Kings
20:6 I will ***a*** fifteen years to your life. I
Ecclesiastes
3:14 impossible to ***a*** to it or take
Isaiah
38:5 tears. I will ***a*** fifteen years to
Jeremiah
7:21 of Israel, says: ***A*** your entirely
30:19 of thanks. I will ***a*** to their numbers
Ezekiel
5:16 I will ***a*** to your famine
Matthew
6:27 by worrying can ***a*** a single moment
Luke
12:25 by worrying can ***a*** a single moment
Revelation
22:18 to them, God will ***a*** to that person

ADONIJAH

2 Samuel
3:4 the fourth was ***A***, by Haggith; the
1 Kings
1:5 ***A***, Haggith's son, bragged about
1:18 But now, look, ***A*** has become king, and
1:50 ***A*** was afraid of Solomon, so he got up
1 Chronicles
3:2 Talmai; the fourth ***A***, Haggith's son;
2 Chronicles
17:8 Jehonathan, ***A***, Tobijah, and Tob-
Nehemiah
10:16 ***A***, Bigvai, Adin

ADULTERY → COMMIT ADULTERY, COMMITS ADULTERY

Isaiah
57:3 offspring of ***a*** and prostitution!
Jeremiah
3:9 and committing ***a*** with stone and
13:27 I have seen your ***a*** and lust, your
Ezekiel
16:38 convict you of ***a*** and murder, and I
Hosea
2:2 her presence, and ***a*** from between her
3:1 is involved in ***a***, just as the LORD
4:2 with stealing and ***a*** are common;
Matthew
5:28 has already committed ***a*** in his heart.
15:19 murders, ***a***, sexual sins,
John
8:3 a woman caught in ***a***. Placing her in
Romans
2:22 If you say, "No ***a***," do you commit
7:3 she's committing ***a***. But if her

ADVANTAGE

Deuteronomy
24:14 Don't take ***a*** of poor or needy workers,
28:29 and taken ***a*** of without any
Ecclesiastes
6:8 What ***a*** do the wise have over the
7:11 inheritance—an ***a*** for those who see
Jeremiah
7:6 you stop taking ***a*** of the immigrant,
Hosea
12:7 hands; he loves to take ***a*** of others.
Luke
9:25 What ***a*** do people have if they gain the
Romans
3:1 So what's the ***a*** of being a Jew? Or
2 Corinthians
2:11 we won't be taken ***a*** of by Satan,
7:2 anyone. We didn't take ***a*** of anyone.

ADVERSARY
Numbers
22:22 messenger stood in the road as his ***a***.
22:32 out here as an ***a***, because you took
1 Chronicles
21:1 A heavenly ***A*** arose against Israel and
Job
1:6 the LORD, and the ***A*** also came among
2:1 the LORD. The ***A*** also came among
Zechariah
3:1 the LORD, and the ***A*** was standing by
3:2 LORD said to the ***A***: "The LORD
Luke
18:3 me justice in this case against my ***a***.'

ADVICE
Genesis
41:37 This ***a*** seemed wise to Pharaoh and all
Exodus
18:19 me give you some ***a***. And may God be
33:7 who wanted ***a*** from the LORD
Numbers
31:16 on Balaam's ***a***, made the
1 Kings
1:7 He took ***a*** from Joab, Zeruiah's son, and
12:8 ignored the ***a*** the elders gave
Job
29:21 to me and waited, were silent for my ***a***.
Psalms
1:1 follow wicked ***a***, doesn't stand on
73:24 me with your ***a***; later you will
81:12 hearts; they followed their own ***a***.
106:13 had done! They wouldn't wait for his ***a***.
Proverbs
1:25 ignored all my ***a***, and you didn't
8:14 I have ***a*** and ability, as well as
12:15 way as right, but the wise listen to ***a***.
13:10 of pride; those who take ***a*** are wise.
19:20 Listen to ***a*** and accept instruction, so
20:5 ***A*** comes from the deep waters of the
20:18 are firmed up by ***a***; wage wars with
21:30 understanding, or ***a*** can stand up
22:20 thirty sayings full of ***a*** and knowledge?
27:9 of friends comes from their ***a***.
Hosea
4:12 My people take ***a*** from a piece of wood,

AFFLICTED
Leviticus
13:44 the person is ***a*** with skin disease; they
2 Kings
15:5 Now the LORD ***a*** the king with a skin
Job
30:11 my bowstring and ***a*** me, they throw
34:28 reach him, he hears the cry of the ***a***.
Psalms
69:29 And me? I'm ***a***. I'm full of pain. Let
69:32 Let the ***a*** see it and be glad! You who
74:19 the lives of your ***a*** people forever!
88:15 young I've been ***a***, I've been dying.
90:15 of time that you ***a*** us—for the same

AFFORD
Leviticus
5:7 If you can't ***a*** an animal from the
12:8 the mother cannot ***a*** a sheep, she can
14:22 whatever they can ***a***—one as a purifica
1 Corinthians
16:2 whatever you can ***a*** from what you

AFRAID
Genesis
3:10 the garden; I was ***a*** because I was
15:1 vision, "Don't be ***a***, Abram. I am your
Exodus
2:14 Then Moses was ***a*** when he realized:
3:6 face because he was ***a*** to look at God.
14:13 people, "Don't be ***a***. Stand your
Deuteronomy
1:17 or not. Don't be ***a*** of anyone because
2:4 They will be ***a*** of you, so watch
31:8 abandon you. So don't be ***a*** or scared!"
Joshua
8:1 Joshua, "Don't be ***a*** or terrified.
10:2 people were very ***a***, because Gibeon
11:6 Joshua, "Don't be ***a*** of them. By this
2 Kings
6:16 Don't be ***a***," Elisha said, "because
Ezra
3:3 because they were ***a*** of the
4:4 people of Judah, made them ***a*** to build,
Esther
9:2 way because everyone was ***a*** of the Jews.
Psalms
3:6 I won't be ***a*** of thousands of people
27:3 my heart won't be ***a***. If war comes up
49:5 Why should I be ***a*** in times of trouble,
56:3 whenever I'm ***a***, I put my trust in you-
56:4 God; I won't be ***a***. What can mere
56:11 God; I won't be ***a***. What can anyone
78:53 they were not ***a***! But the sea
91:5 Don't be ***a*** of terrors at night, arrows
118:6 me—I won't be ***a***. What can anyone
Ecclesiastes
9:2 pledges and those who are ***a*** to swear.
12:5 when people are ***a*** of things above and
Isaiah
12:2 and won't be ***a***. Yah, the LORD,
41:23 bad! Then we will all be ***a*** and fearful.
51:13 were continually ***a***, all day long, on
Jeremiah
1:8 Don't be ***a*** of them, because I'm with
3:8 Judah was not ***a*** but kept on
Ezekiel
2:6 one, don't be ***a*** of them or their
3:9 stone. Don't be ***a*** of them or shrink
Matthew
1:20 David, don't be ***a*** to take Mary as
Mark
5:36 leader, "Don't be ***a***; just keep
John
6:19 approaching the boat and they were ***a***.
12:15 Don't be ***a***, Daughter Zion. Look! Your
20:19 because they were ***a*** of the Jewish
Acts
5:26 because they were ***a*** the people would
9:26 but they were all ***a*** of him. They
18:9 vision, "Don't be ***a***. Continue
27:24 said, 'Don't be ***a***, Paul! You must
27:29 ***A*** that we might run aground somewhere
1 Corinthians
16:10 no reason to be ***a*** while he's with

Philippians
1:28 way, you won't be ***a*** of anything your
Hebrews
11:23 and they weren't ***a*** of the king's
1 John
4:18 The person who is ***a*** has not been made
Revelation
1:17 said, "Don't be ***a***. I'm the first
2:10 Don't be ***a*** of what you are going to
18:10 because they are ***a*** of the pain she

AGAG
Numbers
24:7 be higher than ***A***, and his kingdom
1 Samuel
15:9 the troops spared ***A*** along with the
15:33 Then Samuel cut ***A*** to pieces in the

AGE
Genesis
18:13 and say, 'Me give birth? At my ***a***?'
Joshua
13:1 had reached old ***a***. The LORD said to
Job
5:26 your grave in old ***a*** as bundles of
12:12 In old ***a*** is wisdom; understanding in a
Psalms
71:9 me off in old ***a***. Don't abandon me
71:18 even in my old ***a*** with gray hair,
91:16 you full with old ***a***. I'll show you my
Proverbs
20:29 gray hair is the splendor of old ***a***.
29:21 from a young ***a***, and later on
Matthew
12:32 not in this ***a*** or in the age
13:39 of the present ***a***. The harvesters
13:40 it will be at the end of the present ***a***.
13:49 of the present ***a***. The angels will
24:3 of your coming and the end of the ***a***?"
28:20 day until the end of this present ***a***."

AGREE
Deuteronomy
27:15 All the people will reply: "We ***a***!"
Matthew
18:19 if two of you ***a*** on earth about
Acts
15:15 prophets' words ***a*** with this; as it
Romans
7:22 I gladly ***a*** with the Law on the inside
1 Corinthians
1:10 Jesus Christ: ***a*** with each other

AGREED
Matthew
3:15 So John ***a*** to baptize Jesus.
20:2 After he ***a*** with the workers to pay them
26:5 But they ***a*** that it shouldn't happen
Mark
14:2 But they ***a*** that it shouldn't happen
Luke
22:6 He ***a*** and began looking for an
23:51 He hadn't ***a*** with the plan and actions
Acts
15:22 entire church, ***a*** to send some

AGREEMENT
Genesis
26:28 there be a formal ***a*** between us and
Nehemiah
9:38 are making a firm ***a*** in writing, with
Proverbs
6:1 or shake hands in ***a*** with a stranger,
Daniel
11:6 they will make an ***a*** together. The
11:17 He will make an ***a*** with him and will
11:23 they make an ***a*** with him, he will
2 Corinthians
6:16 What ***a*** can there be between God's
1 John
5:8 blood—and the three are united in ***a***.
5:14 for anything in ***a*** with his will, he

AGRIPPA
Acts
25:13 had passed, King ***A*** and Bernice
26:1 ***A*** said to Paul, "You may speak for
26:2 King ***A***, I consider myself especially
26:32 ***A*** said to Festus, "This man could have

AHAB
1 Kings
18:2 to appear before ***A***. Now the famine
18:45 a huge rainstorm. ***A*** was already
21:2 ***A*** ordered Naboth, "Give me your
21:18 Israel's King ***A*** in Samaria. He is
2 Kings
1:1 After ***A*** died, Moab rebelled against
21:3 as Israel's King ***A*** had done. He
2 Chronicles
18:1 allied himself with ***A*** through marriage.
21:13 as the house of ***A*** did, and because
Jeremiah
29:21 concerning ***A***, Kolaiah's son,
29:22 like Zedekiah and ***A***, who were burned
Micah
6:16 of the house of ***A***; you have

AHASUERUS
Ezra
4:6 In the rule of ***A***, at the beginning of
Esther
1:1 back when ***A*** lived, the very

AHAZ
2 Kings
16:1 ***A***, Jotham's son, became king of Judah
16:7 ***A*** sent messengers to Assyria's King
1 Chronicles
3:13 his son ***A***, his son Hezekiah, his son
2 Chronicles
27:9 City. His son ***A*** succeeded him as
29:19 the items King ***A*** threw out during
Isaiah
7:10 Again the LORD spoke to ***A***
Hosea
1:1 Uzziah, Jotham, ***A***, and Hezekiah,
Micah
1:1 Kings Jotham, ***A***, and Hezekiah,
Matthew
1:9 was the father of ***A***. Ahaz was the

AHAZIAH
1 Kings
22:40 His son ***A*** succeeded him as
22:53 ***A*** served Baal and worshipped him. He
2 Kings
1:2 ***A*** fell out the window of his
1 Chronicles
3:11 son Joram, his son ***A***, his son Joash,
2 Chronicles
20:35 Israel's King ***A***, which caused him

AHIJAH
1 Samuel
14:3 including ***A***, the son of Ahitub, who
14:18 Saul said to ***A***, "Bring the priestly
1 Kings
11:30 ***A*** tore his new garment into twelve
14:18 through his servant the prophet ***A***.
15:29 by the LORD's servant ***A*** of Shiloh.
1 Chronicles
2:25 his oldest, Bunah, Oren, Ozem, and ***A***.
11:36 the Mecherathite; ***A*** the Pelonite;
2 Chronicles
9:29 the prophecies of ***A*** from Shiloh, and
10:15 God delivered through ***A*** from Shiloh.

AHIMAAZ
2 Samuel
15:27 sons, your son ***A*** and Abiathar's
18:30 the king said. So ***A*** stepped aside and
1 Kings
4:15 ***A*** in Naphtali, who also took Solomon's
1 Chronicles
6:8 Ahitub of Zadok, Zadok of ***A***
6:9 ***A*** of Azariah, Azariah of Johanan
6:53 his son Zadok, and his son ***A***

AHIMELECH
1 Samuel
21:1 came to Nob where ***A*** was priest.
22:16 will be executed, ***A***—you and all of yo
22:20 of the sons of ***A***, Ahitub's son,
26:6 David asked ***A*** the Hittite and Joab's
1 Chronicles
18:16 Abiathar's son ***A***, were priests;
24:3 family and ***A*** from Ithamar's
24:6 Zadok the priest; ***A***, Abiathar's son;
24:31 David, Zadok, ***A***, and the heads of

AHITHOPHEL
2 Samuel
16:23 days, the advice ***A*** gave was like
1 Chronicles
27:33 ***A*** was the king's counselor, and Hushai
27:34 After ***A*** came Benaiah's son Jehoiada,

AI
Genesis
12:8 on the west and ***A*** on the east.
Joshua
7:4 But they fled from the men of ***A***.
8:26 population of ***A*** as something

AIJALON
Joshua
10:12 at Gibeon! and Moon, at the ***A*** Valley!"

AIR
Psalms
39:5 life is nothing but a puff of ***a***! Selah
39:11 a human life is just a puff of ***a***! Selah
78:27 were dust in the ***a***; he rained as
144:4 like a puff of ***a***; their days go by
Song of Songs
1:12 king close by my perfume filled the ***a***.
1 Corinthians
14:10 speaking into the ***a***! There are
1 Thessalonians
4:17 the Lord in the ***a***. That way we will

ALERT
Matthew
24:42 Therefore, stay ***a***! You don't know what
25:13 Therefore keep ***a*** because you don't
26:38 dying. Stay here and keep ***a*** with me."
26:40 Couldn't you stay ***a*** one hour with me?
Luke
12:38 whom he finds ***a***, even if he comes
21:36 Stay ***a*** at all times, praying that you
Acts
20:31 Stay ***a***! Remember that for three years
Ephesians
6:18 the time. Stay ***a*** by hanging in
1 Peter
5:8 clearheaded. Keep ***a***. Your accuser,

ALIVE
Genesis
6:19 into the ark with you to keep them ***a***.
45:26 Joseph's still ***a***! He's actually
Job
19:25 my redeemer is ***a*** and afterward
Psalms
23:3 he keeps me ***a***. He guides me in proper
63:4 as long as I'm ***a***; I will lift up
104:33 praises to my God while I'm still ***a***.
Ecclesiastes
4:2 than the living, who are still ***a***.
9:3 while they are ***a***, and afterward
Jeremiah
10:14 their images are shams; they aren't ***a***.
Mark
16:11 that Jesus was ***a*** and that Mary had
Luke
15:32 was dead and is ***a***. He was lost and
24:23 vision of angels who told them he is ***a***.
Acts
1:3 them that he was ***a*** with many
20:10 then said, "Don't be alarmed. He's ***a***!"
Romans
6:11 dead to sin but ***a*** for God in Christ
7:2 Law while he is ***a***. But if her
1 Corinthians
7:39 as her husband is ***a***. But if her
Philippians
1:25 this: I will stay ***a*** and remain with
Colossians
2:13 God made you ***a*** with Christ and
Hebrews
9:17 while the one who made the will is ***a***.
1 Peter
3:18 as a human, but made ***a*** by the Spirit.

ALIVE [cont.]

Revelation

1:18 but look! Now I'm ***a*** forever and

19:20 them were thrown ***a*** into the fiery

ALL DAY

1Sa 28:20; Ps 25:5; 32:3; 35:28; 38:6, 12; 44:15; 52:1; 56:1, 2, 5; 71:8, 15, 24; 72:15; 73:14; 74:22; 86:3; 88:17; 89:16; 102:8; Is 21:8; 51:13; 52:5; 62:6; 65:2, 5; Lam 2:18; 3:3, 14; Hos 12:1; Mt 20:6; Ro 8:36; 10:21; 1Co 15:30

ALL DAY LONG

Ps 25:5; 32:3; 35:28; 38:6, 12; 44:15; 52:1; 56:1, 2, 5; 71:8, 15, 24; 72:15; 73:14; 74:22; 86:3; 88:17; 89:16; 102:8; Is 51:13; 52:5; Lam 3:3; 3:14; Hos 12:1; Mt 20:6; Ro 8:36; 10:21

ALL GENERATIONS

Ex 3:15; Ps 49:11; 145:13; Is 51:8; 60:15; Jl 3:20; Eph 3:21

ALL GOD'S PEOPLE

Ps 116:14; 116:18; Eph 1:15; 3:8; Phi 4:21; 4:22; Col 1:4; Phm 1:5

ALL HIS WAYS

Dt 10:12; 11:22; 32:4; Josh 22:5; 1Ki 8:58; Job 34:27; Ps 145:17; Hos 9:8

ALL HUMANITY

Is 40:5; 66:16, 23; Jer 45:5; Lk 3:6

ALL ISRAEL

Ex 18:25; Dt 1:1; 5:1; 11:6; 13:11; 21:21; 27:9; 29:2; 31:1, 7, 11; 32:45; Josh 3:7; 3:17; 4:14; 7:24, 25; 8:15, 21, 24, 33; 10:15, 29, 31, 34, 36, 38, 43; 23:2; Jdg 8:27; 1Sa 3:20; 4:1, 5; 7:5; 11:2; 12:1; 13:4; 14:40; 17:11; 19:5; 24:2; 25:1; 28:3, 4; 2Sa 2:9; 3:12, 19, 21, 37; 4:1; 5:5; 8:15; 10:17; 12:12; 16:18, 21, 22; 17:10, 13; 1Ki 1:20; 2:15; 3:28; 4:1, 7; 8:62, 63, 65; 11:42; 12:1, 16, 18, 20; 14:13, 18; 15:27, 33; 18:19; 22:17; 2Ki 3:6; 1Ch 9:1; 11:4, 10; 12:38; 13:5, 6, 8; 14:8; 15:3, 28; 18:14; 19:17; 21:4, 5; 28:4; 29:23, 25, 26; 2Ch 1:2; 7:6, 8; 9:30; 10:1, 3, 16; 11:3, 13; 12:1; 13:4, 15; 18:16; 24:5; 28:23; 29:24; 30:1, 5, 6; 35:3; Ezr 2:70; 6:17; 8:25, 35; 10:5; Neh 7:73; 12:47; 13:26; Dn 9:7; 9:11; Mal 4:4; Ac 2:36; Ro 11:26

ALL LIVING THINGS

Gn 6:19; Nm 16:22; 27:16; Ps 65:2; 136:25; Jer 32:27; Dn 4:12

ALL MY HEART

Ps 9:1; 86:12; 111:1; 119:10, 34, 58, 69, 145; 138:1; Song 1:7; 3:1, 2, 3, 4; Jer 32:41; Lk 1:46

ALL NATIONS

Dt 28:1; 29:24; Ps 22:28; 46:10; 67:4; 82:8; 97:6; Is 25:7; 66:18, 20; Jer 3:17; 15:4; 26:6; 27:7; 29:18; 33:9; 34:17; Hab 2:5; Mt 24:9; 28:19; Mk 11:17; Lk 21:24; 24:47; Rev 15:4

ALL NATIONS ON EARTH

Dt 28:1; Jer 15:4; 26:6; 29:18; 33:9; 34:17

ALL OF THE PEOPLE

Gn 26:11; 35:6; Josh 7:3; Jdg 7:1; 2Ki 23:3; 1Ch 16:43; Ezr 3:11; 10:9; Neh 8:5; 8:6, 9, 11, 12

ALL OTHER GODS

1Ch 16:25; 2Ch 2:5; Ps 95:3; 96:4; 97:9; 135:5; 138:1

ALL PEOPLE

Gn 11:1; Jdg 9:28; 1Ch 16:8; 16:24; Ps 9:8; 9:11; 47:3, 9; 64:9; 96:3, 10, 13; 98:9; 102:22; 105:1; 107:8, 15, 21, 31; 115:16; Ecc 3:13; Jer 25:31; Dn 6:26; Mt 13:41; Lk 2:10; Jn 1:4; 1:9; 2:24; Ac 2:17; 24:16; Ro 11:32; 12:18; 1Co 7:7; 9:19, 22; Phi 4:5; Col 3:11; 1Ti 2:1; 2:4, 6; 4:10; 2Ti 2:24; Ti 2:11; 1Pt 1:17; Rev 22:12

ALL PEOPLES

Dt 33:17; Est 3:14; Ps 44:14; 77:14; Is 25:6; 25:7; 56:7; Dn 5:19; 7:14; Hab 2:5; Lk 2:31

ALL THE DAYS

Dt 6:2; Josh 24:31; 1Ki 4:21; 8:40; 2Ki 23:22; 2Ch 6:31; Job 14:14; 15:20; Ps 23:6; 27:4; Prv 15:15; 31:12; Ecc 9:9; Is 38:20; Jer 32:39

ALL THE EARTH

Gn 1:26; 11:4, 9; 18:25; Josh 23:14; 1Ch 16:23; 16:30; Ps 33:8; 57:5, 11; 66:1, 4; 72:19; 83:18; 96:1, 9; 97:9; 98:4; 100:1; 108:5; Is 6:3; 12:5; 14:7, 26; 54:5; Jer 51:49; Lam 2:15; Eze 34:6; Dn 2:39; Mi 4:13; Hab 2:20; Zep 3:8; Zec 4:14; 6:5

ALL YOUR ENEMIES

Ex 23:27; Dt 6:19; 12:10; Jdg 5:31; 2Sa 7:9; 7:11; 1Ch 17:8; 17:10; Ps 21:8; Lam 2:16; Mi 5:9

ALLOWED

Leviticus

7:29 the LORD, you are ***a*** to bring your

18:6 No one is ***a*** to approach any blood

21:1 None of you are ***a*** to make

22:10 No layperson is ***a*** to eat the holy

25:44 that you are ***a*** to have: You can

Deuteronomy

12:17 you are not ***a*** to eat any of the

14:4 animals you are ***a*** to eat: ox,

15:3 You are ***a*** to demand payment from

17:15 You are not ***a*** to appoint over

18:8 he is ***a*** to eat equal portions, despite

20:20 tree, you are ***a*** to destroy it,

21:14 You are not ***a*** to sell her for

22:29 her. He is never ***a*** to divorce her.

Psalms

106:46 God ***a*** them to receive compassion from

Matthew

12:4 which only the priests were ***a*** to eat.

19:8 replied, "Moses ***a*** you to divorce

Luke

12:39 he wouldn't have ***a*** his home to be

1 Corinthians

14:34 They are not ***a*** to talk. Instead,

ALMIGHTY → GOD ALMIGHTY, LORD GOD ALMIGHTY
Genesis
49:25 you, by the ***A*** who blesses you
Job
6:14 or do they stop fearing the ***A***?
8:3 or does the ***A*** distort what is
22:3 Does the ***A*** delight in your innocence?
35:13 cry; the ***A*** doesn't pay
Psalms
68:14 When the ***A*** scattered the kings there,
Matthew
26:64 right side of the ***A*** and coming on the
Revelation
1:8 who is and was and is coming, the ***A***."
16:14 battle on the great day of God the ***A***.

ALTAR → ALTAR TO THE LORD, BUILD AN ALTAR, BUILT AN ALTAR, INCENSE ALTAR
Exodus
20:24 Make for me an ***a*** from fertile soil on
21:14 killer from my ***a*** and put him to
24:6 of the blood he threw against the ***a***.
27:4 Make for the ***a*** a grate made of copper
28:43 they approach the ***a*** to minister as
38:30 the copper ***a***, its copper
39:38 the gold ***a***, the anointing oil, and the
40:5 Place the gold ***a*** for burning incense in
40:6 Put the ***a*** for entirely burned offerings
Leviticus
1:5 every side of the ***a*** at the meeting
2:2 portion on the ***a*** as a food gift of
3:2 the blood against every side of the ***a***.
4:7 the horns of the ***a*** of perfumed
5:9 the side of the ***a***. The rest of the
9:8 Aaron went to the ***a*** and slaughtered
16:25 of the purification offering on the ***a***.
Deuteronomy
12:27 LORD your God's ***a***. The blood from
Judges
6:25 your father's ***a*** to Baal and cut
13:20 flame from the ***a*** went up toward
1 Kings
16:32 He made an ***a*** for Baal in the Baal
18:26 dance around the ***a*** that had been set
2 Kings
16:10 Ahaz noticed the ***a*** that was in
18:22 worship before this ***a*** in Jerusalem'?
23:9 up on the LORD's ***a*** in Jerusalem,
Ezra
3:2 to rebuild the ***a*** of Israel's God
3:3 They set up the ***a*** on its foundations,
7:17 offer them on the ***a*** of God's house in
Nehemiah
10:34 to burn on the ***a*** of the LORD our
Psalms
26:6 I walk all around your ***a***, LORD,
43:4 me come to God's ***a***—let me come to G
51:19 will again be sacrificed on your ***a***.
118:27 all the way to the horns of the ***a***.
Isaiah
6:6 he had taken from the ***a*** with tongs.
Matthew
5:23 your gift to the ***a*** and there
23:18 swear by the ***a***, it's nothing.
Luke
1:11 to the right of the ***a*** of incense.
11:51 between the ***a*** and the holy
Acts
17:23 I even found an ***a*** with this
Hebrews
7:13 ever served at the ***a*** from that tribe.
9:4 It had the gold ***a*** for incense and the
13:10 We have an ***a***, and those who serve as
James
2:21 when he offered his son Isaac on the ***a***?
Revelation
6:9 I saw under the ***a*** those who had
8:3 and stood at the ***a***, and he held a
8:5 fire from the ***a***. He threw it down
9:13 horns of the gold ***a*** that is before
11:1 God's temple, the ***a***, and those who
14:18 came out from the ***a***. He said in a
16:7 And I heard the ***a*** say, "Yes, Lord God

ALTAR TO THE LORD
Gn 8:20; 12:8; 13:18; Jdg 6:26; 1Sa 7:17; 14:35; 2Sa 24:18; 24:21; 1Ch 21:22; Is 19:19

AMALEK
Genesis
36:12 she gave birth to ***A*** for Eliphaz.
36:16 Gatam, and Chief ***A***. These are the
Exodus
17:8 ***A*** came and fought with Israel at
Numbers
24:20 He looked at ***A*** and raised his voice and
Deuteronomy
25:17 after all, what ***A*** did to you on
2 Samuel
8:12 Philistines, and ***A***, including the
1 Chronicles
1:36 Zephi, Gatam, Kenaz, Timna, and ***A***.
18:11 the Ammonites, the Philistines, and ***A***.
Psalms
83:7 Gebal, Ammon, ***A***, Philistia along with

AMALEKITE
Judges
12:15 land of Ephraim, in the ***A*** highlands.
1 Samuel
15:5 advanced on the ***A*** city and laid an
15:8 captured Agag the ***A*** king alive, but
15:20 captured Agag the ***A*** king, and I put
15:32 me Agag the ***A*** king," Samuel
30:13 the slave of an ***A***. My master
2 Samuel
1:8 he asked, and I told him, 'I'm an ***A***.'
1:13 of an immigrant," he answered. "An ***A***."
1:15 servant struck the ***A*** down, and he died.
1:16 David said to the ***A***, "because your

AMALEKITES
Genesis
14:7 territory of the ***A***, as well as the
Numbers
13:29 The ***A*** live in the land of the arid

AMARIAH
1 Chronicles
6:7 Meraioth of ***A***, Amariah of Ahitub

AMARIAH [cont.]

2 Chronicles
19:11 ***A*** the chief priest will be in charge of
31:15 Jeshua, Shemaiah, ***A***, and Shecaniah
Ezra
7:3 son of ***A*** son of Azariah son of Meraiot
10:42 Shallum, ***A***, and Joseph
Nehemiah
10:3 Pashhur, ***A***, Malchijah
11:4 Zechariah son of ***A*** son of Shephatiah
12:2 ***A***, Malluch, Hattush
12:13 of Ezra, Meshullam; of ***A***, Jehohanan

AMASA

2 Samuel
17:25 Absalom had put ***A*** in charge of the army
20:10 But ***A*** didn't notice the sword in Joab's
20:12 ***A*** was writhing in blood in the middle
20:13 Once ***A*** was moved out of the road,
1 Kings
2:5 Ner's son, and ***A***, Jether's son. He
2:32 general, and ***A***, Jether's son and
1 Chronicles
2:17 gave birth to ***A***, whose father was
2 Chronicles
28:12 and Hadlai's son ***A***—confronted those

AMAZED

Job
17:8 right thing are ***a*** at this; the
Psalms
40:3 of this and be ***a***; they will trust
Matthew
7:28 the crowds were ***a*** at his teaching
8:27 The people were ***a*** and said, "What kind
9:33 The crowds were ***a*** and said,
12:23 the crowds were ***a*** and said, "This
15:31 So the crowd was ***a*** when they saw those
21:20 saw it, they were ***a***. "How did the fig
27:14 word. So the governor was greatly ***a***.
Acts
2:7 surprised and ***a***, saying, "Look,
3:11 them at Solomon's Porch, completely ***a***.
3:12 why are you ***a*** at this? Why are
Galatians
1:6 I'm ***a*** that you are so quickly deserting
Revelation
13:3 whole earth was ***a*** and followed the
17:7 me, "Why are you ***a***? I will tell you
17:8 was made, will be ***a*** when they see the

AMAZIAH

2 Kings
12:21 City. His son ***A*** succeeded him as
14:2 ***A*** was 25 years old when he became king,
15:3 eyes, just as his father ***A*** had done.
1 Chronicles
3:12 his son ***A***, his son Azariah, his son
4:34 Meshobab, Jamlech, Joshah son of ***A***
6:45 of Hashabiah son of ***A*** son of Hilkiah
2 Chronicles
24:27 kings. His son ***A*** succeeded him as
25:1 ***A*** was 25 years old when he became king,
Amos
7:10 Then ***A***, the priest of Bethel, reported

AMBUSH

Job
38:40 in their den, lie in ***a*** in their lair.
Psalms
10:8 place perfect for ***a***; from their
56:6 and set an ***a***—they are watchin
59:3 how they lie in ***a*** for my life!
Proverbs
1:11 set up a deadly ***a***. Let's secretly
Jeremiah
51:12 prepare an ***a***, because the LORD
Acts
23:16 heard about the ***a*** and he came to
23:21 are waiting to ***a*** him. They have
25:3 were planning to ***a*** and kill him

AMEN

Nehemiah
5:13 assembly said, "***A***," and praised the
8:6 people answered, "***A***! Amen!" while
Psalms
41:13 from forever to forever! ***A*** and Amen!
106:48 the people say, "***A***!" Praise the LORD!
Isaiah
65:16 by the God called ***A***; those who make a
1 Corinthians
14:16 language say "***A***!" to your
2 Corinthians
1:20 is why we say ***A*** through him to
Revelation
3:14 the words of the ***A***, the faithful and
5:14 creatures said, "***A***," and the elders
19:4 throne, and they said, "***A***. Hallelujah!"
22:20 I'm coming soon." ***A***. Come, Lord Jesus!

AMMINADAB

Ruth
4:19 the father of Ram, Ram the father of ***A***,
4:20 ***A*** the father of Nahshon, Nashon the
1 Chronicles
2:10 was the father of ***A***, and Amminadab
Luke
3:33 son of ***A*** son of Admin son of Arni son

AMMON

1 Kings
14:21 mother's name was Naamah from ***A***.
14:31 was Naamah from ***A***. His son Abijam
2 Chronicles
12:13 His mother's name was Naamah from ***A***.
Nehemiah
13:23 married women of Ashdod, ***A***, and Moab.
Psalms
83:7 Gebal, ***A***, Amalek, Philistia along with
Jeremiah
27:3 of Edom, Moab, ***A***, Tyre, and Sidon
40:11 living in Moab, ***A***, Edom, and in
40:14 King Baalis of ***A*** has sent Ishmael,
Ezekiel
25:5 for camels and ***A*** a resting place
25:10 And so ***A*** will no longer be

AMMONITES

Genesis
19:38 He is the ancestor of today's ***A***.

Numbers
21:24 as far as the ***A***, for the border

AMNON
2 Samuel
3:2 oldest son was ***A***, by Ahinoam from
13:21 to punish his son ***A*** because he loved
13:22 never spoke to ***A***, good word or
13:32 been killed—only ***A*** is dead. This has
13:33 are dead, because only ***A*** is dead,
1 Chronicles
3:1 the oldest ***A***, with Ahinoam the
4:20 Shimon's family: ***A***, Rinnah, Ben-hanan,

AMONG THE GENTILES
Mt 10:5; Ac 15:12; 21:19, 21; Ro 15:9; 1Co 5:1; Col 1:27

AMONG THE ISRAELITES
Ex 28:1; 29:45; Lv 24:10; 25:33; Nm 2:33; 8:17, 18; 13:3; 18:20, 23, 24; 25:8; 26:62; 35:34; Josh 18:2; 1Ki 6:13; 14:24; Eze 43:7; 44:9

AMONG THE NATIONS
Lv 26:33; 26:38; Nm 23:9; 24:20; Dt 4:27; 1Ch 16:24; 16:35; Neh 6:6; Ps 44:11; 57:9; 79:10; 96:3; 106:27; 108:3; 126:2; Is 61:9; 66:19; Jer 3:19; 18:13; 43:5; 49:14; 50:23; 51:27, 41; Lam 1:3; 2:9; 4:20; Eze 4:13; 11:16; 12:15, 16; 16:14; 20:23; 22:15; 25:10; 29:12, 13; 30:23, 26; 31:17; 32:2; 36:21, 22, 23, 30; 37:21; 39:21, 28; Hos 8:8; 9:17; Jl 2:17; 2:19; 3:2, 9; Obad 1:1; 1:2; Mi 5:8; Hab 1:5; Zec 8:13; Mal 1:11; 1:14

AMONG THE PEOPLE
Nm 16:47; 21:6; Josh 8:9; Jdg 5:9; 16:2; 21:12; 1Sa 10:24; 2Sa 24:21; 1Ki 14:7; 1Ch 21:22; 2Ch 19:4; Jer 11:9; 37:4; 39:14; Hos 7:8; Hg 1:12; Mt 4:23; 26:5; Mk 14:2; Lk 7:1; 19:47; Ac 4:17; 5:12; 6:8; 2Pt 2:1

AMORITE
Numbers
21:21 sent messengers to Sihon the ***A*** king:

ANAKIM
Deuteronomy
2:10 and numerous and tall—just like the ***A***.
2:11 Rephaim, like the ***A*** were. But the
2:21 just like the ***A***. But the LORD
9:2 are the ***A***. You know and
Joshua
11:21 and wiped out the ***A*** from the
11:22 The ***A*** no longer remained in the land of
14:12 day. True, the ***A*** are there with
14:15 greatest of the ***A***.) Then the land

ANANIAS
Acts
5:1 a man named ***A***, along with his
9:10 disciple named ***A***. The Lord spoke
23:2 The high priest ***A*** ordered those

ANATHOTH
Jeremiah
29:27 Jeremiah of ***A***, who pretends to

ANCESTOR
Genesis
17:4 you; you will be the ***a*** of many nations.
19:37 Moab. He is the ***a*** of today's
36:9 of Esau, the ***a*** of Edom, which
1 Kings
15:3 with all his heart like his ***a*** David.
Isaiah
43:27 Your first ***a*** sinned, and your officials
Mark
11:10 kingdom of our ***a*** David! Hosanna in
Luke
1:73 he made to our ***a*** Abraham. He has
Acts
4:25 through our ***a*** David, your
7:2 appeared to our ***a*** Abraham while he
Romans
4:1 Abraham is our ***a*** on the basis of

ANCESTORS
Genesis
15:15 will join your ***a*** in peace and be
25:8 old man, and he was placed with his ***a***.
35:29 buried with his ***a*** after a long,
Exodus
3:13 The God of your ***a*** has sent me to
13:5 promised your ***a*** to give to you, a
Deuteronomy
4:31 the covenant that he swore to your ***a***.
Joshua
1:6 which I pledged to give to their ***a***.
24:6 I brought your ***a*** out of Egypt, and you
Ezra
4:15 records of your ***a***. You will
5:12 But because our ***a*** angered the God of
Psalms
22:4 Our ***a*** trusted you—they trusted you
39:12 with you, just like all my ***a*** were.
Proverbs
19:14 from one's ***a***, but an
22:28 marker that your ***a*** established.
Isaiah
65:7 the sins of your ***a*** as well, says the
Jeremiah
2:5 wrong did your ***a*** find in me that
3:18 that I gave their ***a*** as an inheritance.
Hosea
9:10 tree, I saw your ***a***. But they came to
Micah
7:20 as you swore to our ***a*** a long time ago.
Zechariah
1:2 LORD was terribly angry with your ***a***.
8:14 you when your ***a*** angered me, says
Malachi
2:10 to make the covenant of our ***a*** impure?
Matthew
1:1 A record of the ***a*** of Jesus Christ, son
23:32 Go ahead, complete what your ***a*** did
Luke
11:47 to the prophets, whom your ***a*** killed.
John
4:20 Our ***a*** worshipped on this mountain,
6:31 Our ***a*** ate manna in the wilderness, just
Acts
3:13 God of our ***a***—has glorified his
3:25 made with your ***a*** when he told

5:30 The God of our ***a*** raised Jesus from the
7:11 came with it. Our ***a*** had nothing to
7:12 he sent our ***a*** there for the
7:15 down to Egypt, where he and our ***a*** died.
7:19 and abused our ***a***. He even forced
7:32 the God of your ***a***, the God of
7:38 with our ***a*** and with the
7:39 the one whom our ***a*** refused to obey.
7:44 was with our ***a*** in the
7:45 the tent, our ***a*** carried it with
7:51 the Holy Spirit, just like your ***a*** did.
7:52 prophet your ***a*** didn't harass?
13:17 Israel chose our ***a***. God made them a
13:32 good news. What God promised to our ***a***,
13:36 buried with his ***a***. He experienced
15:10 that neither we nor our ***a*** could bear?
22:14 The God of our ***a*** has selected you
24:14 the God of our ***a*** and believe
26:6 the hope in the promise God gave our ***a***.
28:17 customs of our ***a***, I'm a prisoner

1 Corinthians
10:1 the fact that our ***a*** were all under

Galatians
1:14 militant about the traditions of my ***a***.

2 Timothy
1:3 conscience as my ***a*** did. I constantly

Hebrews
1:1 prophets to our ***a*** in many times and
3:9 is where your ***a*** challenged and
8:9 I made with their ***a*** on the day I took

1 Peter
1:18 lifestyle you inherited from your ***a***.

2 Peter
3:4 creation, nor even since the ***a*** died."

ANDREW

Matthew
4:18 called Peter, and ***A***, throwing fishing

Mark
1:16 Simon and ***A***, throwing fishing
1:29 and John went home with Simon and ***A***.
3:18 and ***A***; Philip; Bartholomew; Matthew;
13:3 James, John, and ***A*** asked him

Luke
6:14 his brother ***A***; James; John;

John
1:40 Jesus was ***A***, the brother of
1:44 Bethsaida, the hometown of ***A*** and Peter.
6:8 of his disciples, ***A***, Simon Peter's
12:22 Philip told ***A***, and Andrew and Philip

Acts
1:13 John, James, and ***A***; Philip and

ANGEL → ANGEL BLEW HIS TRUMPET, ANGEL FROM THE LORD, ANGEL OF THE CHURCH, ANGEL POURED HIS BOWL

Matthew
2:20 Get up," the ***a*** said, "and take the
28:5 But the ***a*** said to the women, "Don't be

Luke
1:12 Zechariah saw the ***a***, he was startled
1:19 The ***a*** replied, "I am Gabriel. I stand
22:43 Then a heavenly ***a*** appeared to him and

John
12:29 Others said, "An ***a*** spoke to him."

Acts
7:30 years later, an ***a*** appeared to Moses
10:4 he stared at the ***a*** and replied,
12:15 to say, "It must be his guardian ***a***."
27:24 The ***a*** said, 'Don't be afraid, Paul! You

2 Corinthians
11:14 disguises himself as an ***a*** of light.

Galatians
1:8 or a heavenly ***a*** should ever

1 Thessalonians
4:16 shout by the head ***a*** and a blast on

Revelation
1:1 it through his ***a*** to his servant
10:1 another powerful ***a*** coming down from
14:6 I saw another ***a*** flying high
18:21 Then a powerful ***a*** picked up a stone
22:1 Then the ***a*** showed me the river of
22:16 have sent my ***a*** to bear witness

ANGEL BLEW HIS TRUMPET

Rev 8:7; 8:8, 10, 12; 9:1, 13; 11:15

ANGEL FROM THE LORD

Mt 1:20; 2:13, 19; 28:2; Lk 1:11; Ac 5:19; 8:26; 12:7, 23

ANGEL OF THE CHURCH

Rev 2:1; 2:8, 12, 18; 3:1, 7, 14

ANGEL POURED HIS BOWL

Rev 16:2; 16:3, 4, 8, 10, 12, 17

ANGELS → GOD'S ANGELS

Job
4:18 and levels a charge against his ***a***,

Matthew
4:6 I will command my ***a*** concerning you,
13:39 present age. The harvesters are the ***a***.
16:27 Father with his ***a***. And then he will
18:10 to you that their ***a*** in heaven are
22:30 Instead, they will be like ***a*** from God.
24:31 He will send his ***a*** with the sound of a
24:36 not the heavenly ***a*** and not the Son.
25:31 and all his ***a*** are with him, he
26:53 twelve battle groups of ***a*** right away?

Mark
1:13 animals, and the ***a*** took care of him.
13:27 he will send the ***a*** and gather
13:32 come, not the ***a*** in heaven and not

Luke
2:15 When the ***a*** returned to heaven, the
4:10 will command his ***a*** concerning you,
9:26 glory of the Father and of the holy ***a***.
16:22 was carried by ***a*** to Abraham's
20:36 they are like ***a*** and are God's
24:23 seen a vision of ***a*** who told them he

John
20:12 She saw two ***a*** dressed in white, seated
20:13 The ***a*** asked her, "Woman, why are you

Acts
7:53 the Law given by ***a***, but you haven't

Romans
8:38 or life, not ***a*** or rulers, not

1 Corinthians
4:9 in the world, both to ***a*** and to humans.
6:3 we will judge ***a***? Why not ordinary
11:10 over her head, because of the ***a***.

13:1 beings and of ***a*** but I don't have
Galatians
3:19 in place through ***a*** by the hand of a
Colossians
2:18 and worship ***a*** rob you of the
2 Thessalonians
1:7 from heaven with his powerful ***a***.
1 Timothy
3:16 Spirit, seen by ***a***, preached to
5:21 and the elect ***a*** to follow these
Hebrews
1:4 such as ***a***, that he received
1:5 say to any of the ***a***: You are my Son.
1:7 talks about the ***a***: He's the one who
2:2 was spoken by ***a*** was reliable, and
12:22 to countless ***a*** in a festival
13:2 been hosts to ***a*** without knowing
1 Peter
1:12 which even ***a*** long to examine,
3:22 he rules over all ***a***, authorities, and
2 Peter
2:4 didn't spare the ***a*** when they sinned
2:11 yet ***a***, who are stronger and more
Jude
1:6 you too of the ***a*** who didn't keep
1:8 reject authority, and slander the ***a***.
Revelation
1:20 stars are the ***a*** of the seven
3:5 in the presence of my Father and his ***a***.
5:11 the sound of many ***a*** surrounding the
7:1 this I saw four ***a*** standing at the
8:2 I saw the seven ***a*** who stand before
9:14 Release the four ***a*** who are bound at
12:7 Michael and his ***a*** fought the
14:10 presence of the holy ***a*** and the Lamb.
15:1 There were seven ***a*** with seven
16:1 say to the seven ***a***, "Go and pour out
17:1 one of the seven ***a*** who had the seven
21:12 gates were twelve ***a***, and on the gates

ANGER → GOD'S ANGER

Exodus
15:7 send out your hot ***a***; it burns them up
32:12 down your fierce ***a***. Change your mind
Leviticus
10:6 die and bring ***a*** upon the whole
26:28 oppose you—with ***a***! I will punish
Job
5:2 Surely ***a*** can kill the foolish; fury can
9:5 are unaware; who overthrows them in ***a***?
9:13 won't retract his ***a***; the helpers of
40:11 your raging ***a***; look on all the
Psalms
2:12 because his ***a*** ignites in an
30:5 His ***a*** lasts for only a second, but his
102:10 because of your ***a*** and wrath, because
106:23 and turned God's destructive ***a*** away.
106:40 So the LORD's ***a*** burned against his
119:53 I'm seized with ***a*** because of the
119:139 ***A*** consumes me because my enemies
Proverbs
12:16 reveal their ***a*** right away, but
14:31 the powerless ***a*** their maker,
15:1 but an offensive word stirs up ***a***.
16:14 The king's ***a*** is a messenger of death;
19:11 restrain their ***a***; their glory is
20:2 growl. Those who ***a*** him may lose
21:14 secret gift calms ***a***, and a hidden
22:24 controlled by ***a***; don't associate
24:18 and he will turn his ***a*** from them.
27:4 is cruel and ***a*** is a flood, but
29:8 city on fire, but the wise turn back ***a***.
29:11 show all their ***a***, but the wise
30:33 and stirring up ***a*** produces strife.
Isaiah
1:24 I will vent my ***a*** against my foes;
5:25 is why the LORD's ***a*** burned against
66:15 to repay in hot ***a***, to rebuke with
Jeremiah
2:35 he will turn his ***a*** away from me."
Ezekiel
5:13 My ***a*** will be complete. I will exhaust
Daniel
9:16 turn your raging ***a*** from Jerusalem,
11:20 broken, though not by ***a*** and not by war.
Hosea
5:10 will pour out my ***a*** like water upon
Amos
1:11 kept his ***a*** alive, and fueled
Jonah
4:4 responded, "Is your ***a*** a good thing?"
4:9 Jonah, "Is your ***a*** about the shrub a
Habakkuk
3:8 Or was your ***a*** directed against
3:12 the earth; in ***a*** you tread the
Zephaniah
2:2 the burning ***a*** of the LORD comes
2:3 be hidden on the day of the LORD's ***a***.
3:8 the heat of my ***a***. In the fire of
Acts
19:28 themselves with ***a*** and began to
Ephesians
4:26 Don't let the sun set on your ***a***.
1 Timothy
2:8 that are holy, without ***a*** or argument.

ANGERED THE LORD

Dt 9:8; Jdg 2:12; 1Ki 15:30; 22:53; 2Ch 29:8

ANGRY

Genesis
4:5 Cain became very ***a*** and looked
18:30 said, "Don't be ***a*** with me, my Lord,
30:2 Jacob was ***a*** at Rachel and said, "Do you
31:36 Jacob was ***a*** and complained to Laban,
40:2 Pharaoh was ***a*** with his two officers,
Exodus
4:14 Then the LORD got ***a*** at Moses and said,
Numbers
16:15 Moses became very ***a*** and he said to the
22:27 Balaam became ***a*** and beat the
25:3 and the LORD was ***a*** at the Israelites.
Judges
2:14 the LORD became ***a*** with Israel, and
1 Samuel
20:30 At that, Saul got ***a*** at Jonathan. "You
Psalms
2:12 he will become ***a***, and your way
6:1 me when you are ***a***; don't discipline
7:6 Get up, LORD; get ***a***! Stand up against
18:15 LORD, at the ***a*** blast of air
60:1 us. You've been so ***a***. Now restore us!

76:7 can stand before you when you are ***a***?
85:4 us, restore us! Stop being ***a*** with us!
103:9 play the judge; he won't be ***a*** forever.
106:29 They made God ***a*** by what they did, so a
Proverbs
19:19 ***A*** people must pay the penalty; if you
21:19 a house with a contentious and ***a*** woman.
25:23 who plots quietly provokes ***a*** faces.
29:22 ***A*** people stir up conflict; hotheads
Jeremiah
3:5 will you stay ***a*** forever? Will you
Jonah
4:1 was utterly wrong, and he became ***a***.
Matthew
2:16 him, he grew very ***a***. He sent soldiers
3:7 escape from the ***a*** judgment that is
5:22 everyone who is ***a*** with their
Mark
10:14 saw this, he grew ***a*** and said to them,
John
3:36 see life, but the ***a*** judgment of God
7:23 Law, why are you ***a*** with me because I
Galatians
5:26 make each other ***a***, or be jealous of
Ephesians
4:26 Be ***a*** without sinning. Don't let the sun
Hebrews
3:10 So I was ***a*** with them. I said, "Their
3:17 with whom was God ***a*** for forty years?
James
1:19 slow to speak, and slow to grow ***a***.

ANIMAL

Genesis
7:2 From every clean ***a***, take seven pairs,
37:20 we'll say a wild ***a*** devoured him.
Job
39:15 crush them or a wild ***a*** trample them.
Psalms
50:10 every forest ***a*** already belongs
73:22 acted like nothing but an ***a*** toward you.
104:11 for every wild ***a***—the wild donkeys
104:20 is night, when every forest ***a*** prowls.
135:8 oldest offspring—both human and ***a***!
Jeremiah
51:62 -neither human nor ***a***; that it will
Hosea
13:8 a lion, as a wild ***a*** would eat them.
Jonah
3:7 Neither human nor ***a***, cattle nor
Malachi
1:8 you bring a blind ***a*** to sacrifice,
Hebrews
12:20 If even a wild ***a*** touches the

ANIMALS

Genesis
1:21 the great sea ***a*** and all the tiny
2:19 land all the wild ***a*** and all the birds
3:1 of all the wild ***a*** that the LORD God
8:1 and all the ***a*** with him in the
Exodus
8:17 both people and ***a***. All the land's
8:18 do it. There were lice on people and ***a***.
Psalms
8:7 sheep and all cattle, the wild ***a*** too,
36:6 sea. LORD, you save both humans and ***a***.
49:12 they're just like the ***a*** that pass away.
49:20 they're just like the ***a*** that pass away.
68:30 Rebuke the wild ***a*** of the marshland, the
74:19 your dove to wild ***a***! Don't forget the
79:2 faithful to the wild ***a*** of the earth.
147:9 gives food to the ***a***—even to the baby
148:10 Do the same, you ***a***—wild or tame—
Proverbs
9:2 slaughtered her ***a***, mixed her wine,
Ecclesiastes
3:18 them to show them that they are but ***a***
3:19 human beings and ***a*** share the same
Isaiah
23:13 it for wild ***a***: they raised up
Jeremiah
7:33 birds and wild ***a***, with no one to
5:22 look at your offerings of well-fed ***a***.
Habakkuk
2:17 destruction of ***a*** will terrify you,
Zephaniah
2:15 for the wild ***a***. All those who
Zechariah
8:10 for people or ***a***; there was no
Mark
1:13 among the wild ***a***, and the angels
Acts
10:12 of four-legged ***a***, reptiles, and
Romans
1:23 mortal humans: birds, ***a***, and reptiles.
1 Corinthians
15:32 if I fought wild ***a*** in Ephesus? If
Hebrews
13:11 The blood of the ***a*** is carried into the
2 Peter
2:12 like irrational ***a***, mere creatures
Jude
1:10 as though they were irrational ***a***.
Revelation
6:8 disease, and the wild ***a*** of the earth.

ANNOUNCE

Matthew
4:17 Jesus began to ***a***, "Change your
10:27 hear whispered, ***a*** from the rooftops.
12:18 him, and he'll ***a*** judgment to the
Romans
10:15 the feet of those who ***a*** the good news.
Hebrews
2:12 I will publicly ***a*** your name to my
1 John
1:1 We ***a*** to you what existed from the

ANNOUNCED

Genesis
41:25 dream. God has ***a*** to Pharaoh what
45:26 They ***a*** to him, "Joseph's still alive!
Psalms
76:8 You have ***a*** judgment from heaven. The
Jonah
3:7 Then he ***a***, "In Nineveh, by decree of
Matthew
4:23 synagogues. He ***a*** the good news of
26:13 this good news is ***a***, what she's done
Mark
1:7 He ***a***, "One stronger than I am is

Luke
12:3 the house will be ***a*** from the rooftops.
Ephesians
2:17 When he came, he ***a*** the good news of
Hebrews
2:3 It was first ***a*** through the Lord,

ANOINT
1 Samuel
9:16 You will ***a*** him as leader of
15:1 LORD sent me to ***a*** you king over his
16:3 do. You will ***a*** for me the person
16:12 LORD said, "That's the one. Go ***a*** him."
Daniel
9:24 vision, and to ***a*** the most holy
Micah
6:15 but you don't ***a*** with oil; you
Mark
16:1 they could go and ***a*** Jesus' dead body.
Luke
7:46 You didn't ***a*** my head with oil, but she

ANOINTED → ANOINTED ONE, LORD'S ANOINTED
2 Samuel
5:17 David had been ***a*** king over Israel,
1 Kings
1:39 from the tent and ***a*** Solomon. They
2 Kings
11:12 made him king and ***a*** him, as everyone
23:30 Josiah's son, ***a*** him, and made him
Psalms
45:7 your God, has ***a*** you with the oil
89:20 servant David. I ***a*** him with my holy
Isaiah
45:1 LORD says to his ***a***, to Cyrus, whom I
61:1 the LORD has ***a*** me. He has sent
Habakkuk
3:13 salvation of your ***a*** you smashed the
Mark
6:13 demons, and they ***a*** many sick people
14:8 could. She has ***a*** my body ahead of
Luke
4:18 the Lord has ***a*** me. He has sent
John
11:2 was the Mary who ***a*** the Lord with
12:3 of pure nard. She ***a*** Jesus' feet with
Acts
4:27 your holy servant Jesus, whom you ***a***.
10:38 whom God ***a*** with the Holy
2 Corinthians
1:21 us with you in Christ and who ***a*** us.
Hebrews
1:9 your God, has ***a*** you with oil

ANOINTED ONE
1Sa 2:10; 2:35; 12:5; 2Sa 22:51; 2Ch 6:42; Ps 2:2; 18:50; 20:6; 28:8; 84:9; 89:38, 51; 132:10, 17; Dn 9:26

ANOINTING → ANOINTING OIL
Exodus
40:15 as priests. Their ***a*** is to the
James
5:14 pray over them, ***a*** them with oil in
1 John
2:20 But you have an ***a*** from the holy one,

ANOINTING OIL
Ex 25:6; 29:7, 21; 30:25, 31; 31:11; 35:8, 15, 28; 37:29; 39:38; 40:9; Lv 8:2; 8:10, 12, 30; 10:7; 21:10, 12; Nm 4:16

ANSWER
Exodus
19:19 and God would ***a*** him with thunder.
Deuteronomy
18:22 Here's the ***a***: The prophet who speaks
Judges
14:14 they couldn't tell the ***a*** to the riddle.
18:5 him, "Ask for an ***a*** from God so we
1 Samuel
8:18 but on that day the LORD won't ***a*** you."
28:6 the LORD didn't ***a*** him—not by dreams
Psalms
4:1 psalm of David.] ***A*** me when I cry
13:3 Look at me! ***A*** me, LORD my God!
18:41 to the LORD, but he wouldn't ***a*** them.
20:9 the king! Let him ***a*** us when we cry
22:2 but you don't ***a***; even at
38:15 you, LORD! You will ***a***, my Lord, my God!
69:13 faithful love, ***a*** me with your
69:16 ***A*** me, LORD, for your faithful love is
69:17 I'm in deep trouble. ***A*** me quickly!
86:1 closely to me and ***a*** me because I am
86:7 I cry out to you because you will ***a*** me.
91:15 out to me, I'll ***a***. I'll be with you
102:2 Listen to me! ***A*** me quickly as I
108:6 by your power and ***a*** me so that the
119:145 my heart: "Lord, ***a*** me so I can guard
143:1 Because of your righteousness, ***a*** me!
143:7 ***A*** me, LORD—and quickly! My breath is
Proverbs
1:28 me, but I won't ***a***; they will seek
15:1 A sensitive ***a*** turns back wrath, but an
15:23 an appropriate ***a*** is a joy; how
16:1 heart, but the ***a*** of the tongue
18:13 Those who ***a*** before they listen are
18:23 for help, but the wealthy ***a*** harshly.
21:13 themselves call out but receive no ***a***.
26:4 Don't ***a*** fools according to their folly,
26:5 ***A*** fools according to their folly, or
26:16 wiser than seven people who ***a*** sensibly.
27:11 glad, so I can ***a*** those who insult
Ecclesiastes
5:20 God gives an ***a*** in their hearts'
Matthew
12:36 will have to ***a*** on Judgment Day
Mark
7:29 Good ***a***!" he said. "Go on home. The
11:29 you. Give me an ***a***, then I'll tell
11:30 of heavenly or of human origin? ***A*** me."
13:11 about what to ***a*** or say. Instead,
14:61 silent and didn't ***a***. Again, the high
15:4 you going to ***a***? What about all
Luke
20:26 Astonished by his ***a***, they were
22:68 if I ask you a question, you won't ***a***.
John
1:22 need to give an ***a*** to those who sent
18:22 how you would ***a*** the high priest?"
19:9 Where are you from?" Jesus didn't ***a***.
Hebrews
4:13 the one to whom we have to give an ***a***.

ANSWERED
Genesis
22:1 him, "Abraham!"Abraham ***a***, "I'm here."
1 Samuel
4:17 The messenger ***a***, "Israel has fled from
10:16 been found," Saul ***a***. But Saul didn't
12:4 anything from anyone," the people ***a***.
12:20 But Samuel ***a*** the people, "Don't be
2 Kings
3:11 of Israel's king ***a***, "Elisha,
Nehemiah
8:6 all of the people ***a***, "Amen! Amen!"
Job
1:7 The Adversary ***a*** the LORD, "From
Isaiah
49:8 the right time, I ***a*** you; on a day of
50:2 call when no one ***a***? Is my hand too
66:4 called and no one ***a***. I spoke and no
Ezekiel
4:15 He ***a*** me: "Then I'll let you use cow
Matthew
3:15 Jesus ***a***, "Allow me to be baptized now.
15:28 Jesus ***a***, "Woman, you have great faith.
17:17 Jesus ***a***, "You faithless and crooked
19:4 Jesus ***a***, "Haven't you read that at the
21:11 The crowds ***a***, "It's the prophet Jesus
26:25 is it, Rabbi?" Jesus ***a***, "You said it."
26:66 think?" And they ***a***, "He deserves to
Mark
7:28 But she ***a***, "Lord, even the dogs under
8:29 that I am?" Peter ***a***, "You are the
9:12 He ***a***, "Elijah does come first to
9:19 Jesus ***a*** them, "You faithless
Luke
3:11 He ***a***, "Whoever has two shirts must
9:20 that I am?" Peter ***a***, "The Christ sent
9:41 Jesus ***a***, "You faithless and crooked
10:28 to him, "You have ***a*** correctly. Do
10:41 The Lord ***a***, "Martha, Martha, you are
20:39 responded, "Teacher, you have ***a*** well."
22:67 tell us!" He ***a***, "If I tell you,
John
1:21 Are you the prophet?" John ***a***, "No."
1:26 John ***a***, "I baptize with water. Someone
3:3 Jesus ***a***, "I assure you, unless someone
4:17 I don't have a husband'," Jesus ***a***.
7:20 The crowd ***a***, "You have a demon. Who
10:33 Jewish opposition ***a***, "We don't stone
14:6 Jesus ***a***, "I am the way, the truth, and
Acts
4:8 the Holy Spirit, ***a***, "Leaders of the
22:8 I ***a***, 'Who are you, Lord?' 'I am Jesus

ANTIOCH
Acts
11:26 he brought him to ***A***. They were there
13:1 The church at ***A*** included prophets and
Galatians
2:11 Cephas came to ***A***, I opposed him to

APART → SET APART
Judges
14:6 he tore the lion ***a*** with his bare
1 Kings
13:5 The altar broke ***a***, and the ashes
13:28 the body, nor had it torn the donkey ***a***.
18:23 Let them cut it ***a*** and set it on the
19:11 and broke ***a*** the stones before
Nehemiah
4:19 and we are far ***a*** from each other
Job
7:9 A cloud breaks ***a*** and moves on—like
Psalms
7:2 they will rip me ***a***, dragging me off
16:2 You are my Lord. ***A*** from you, I have
22:14 bones have fallen ***a***. My heart is like
46:2 the world falls ***a***, when the
60:2 its cracks because it's shaking ***a***!
139:14 marvelously set ***a***. Your works are
Proverbs
18:18 conflicts and keep strong opponents ***a***.
Isaiah
7:6 Judah, tear it ***a***, capture it for
45:6 there is nothing ***a*** from me. I am the
Jeremiah
52:17 Babylonians broke ***a*** the bronze
Matthew
12:25 or house torn ***a*** by divisions will
14:19 broke the loaves ***a*** and gave them to
19:6 must not pull ***a*** what God has put
Romans
3:21 has been revealed ***a*** from the Law,
3:28 by faith, ***a*** from what is
2 Corinthians
12:4 in the body or ***a*** from the body.
James
2:18 I see your faith ***a*** from your

APOLLOS
Acts
18:24 certain Jew named ***A*** arrived in
19:1 While ***A*** was in Corinth, Paul took a
1 Corinthians
3:6 I planted, ***A*** watered, but God made it

APOSTLE → APOSTLE OF JESUS CHRIST
Romans
1:1 called to be an ***a*** and set apart for
11:13 that I'm an ***a*** to the Gentiles,
1 Corinthians
9:1 free? Am I not an ***a***? Haven't I seen
15:9 to be called an ***a***, because I
2 Corinthians
1:1 From Paul, an ***a*** of Christ Jesus by
12:12 The signs of an ***a*** were performed among
Galatians
1:1 From Paul, an ***a*** who is not sent from
2:8 to become an ***a*** to the
Ephesians
1:1 From Paul, an ***a*** of Christ Jesus by
Colossians
1:1 From Paul, an ***a*** of Christ Jesus by
1 Timothy
2:7 be a preacher and ***a*** of this testimony-
2 Timothy
1:1 From Paul, an ***a*** of Christ Jesus by
1:11 a messenger, ***a***, and teacher of
Hebrews
3:1 about Jesus, the ***a*** and high priest

APOSTLE OF JESUS CHRIST
1Co 1:1; 1Ti 1:1; Ti 1:1; 1Pt 1:1; 2Pt 1:1

APOSTLES → APOSTLES AND THE ELDERS

Matthew
10:2 of the twelve ***a***: first, Simon,
Mark
3:14 and called them ***a***. He appointed
Luke
6:13 chose twelve of them whom he called ***a***:
17:5 The ***a*** said to the Lord, "Increase our
22:14 at the table, and the ***a*** joined him.
24:10 them who told these things to the ***a***.
24:11 words struck the ***a*** as nonsense, and
Acts
1:2 Jesus instructed the ***a*** he had chosen.
1:26 Matthias. He was added to the eleven ***a***.
2:14 the other eleven ***a***. He raised his
2:37 and the other ***a***, "Brothers, what
2:43 many wonders and signs through the ***a***.
4:2 incensed that the ***a*** were teaching the
4:13 that these ***a*** were uneducated
4:33 The ***a*** continued to bear powerful
4:35 authority of the ***a***. Then it was
4:36 Joseph, whom the ***a*** nicknamed Barnabas
4:37 care and under the authority of the ***a***.
5:2 care and under the authority of the ***a***.
5:12 The ***a*** performed many signs and wonders
5:18 They seized the ***a*** and made a public
5:21 to have the ***a*** brought before
5:26 and brought the ***a*** back. They didn't
5:27 The ***a*** were brought before the council
5:29 Peter and the ***a*** replied, "We must obey
5:33 furious and wanted to kill the ***a***.
5:40 After calling the ***a*** back, they had them
5:41 The ***a*** left the council rejoicing
6:6 seven to the ***a***, who prayed and
8:1 except the ***a*** was scattered
8:14 word reached the ***a*** in Jerusalem that
8:25 After the ***a*** had testified and
9:27 Saul to the ***a*** and told them the
11:1 The ***a*** and the brothers and sisters
11:18 Once the ***a*** and other believers heard
Romans
1:5 appointment to be ***a***. This was to
16:7 among the ***a***, and they were in
1 Corinthians
4:9 has shown that we ***a*** are at the end of
9:5 the rest of the ***a***, the Lord's
12:28 appointed first ***a***, second prophets,
12:29 All aren't ***a***, are they? All aren't
15:7 appeared to James, then to all the ***a***,
15:9 important of the ***a***. I don't deserve
2 Corinthians
8:23 are the churches' ***a*** and an honor to
11:13 people are false ***a*** and dishonest
Galatians
1:17 the men who were ***a*** before me either,
1:19 any other of the ***a*** except James the
Ephesians
2:20 foundation of the ***a*** and prophets with
3:5 to his holy ***a*** and prophets
4:11 He gave some ***a***, some prophets, some
1 Thessalonians
2:7 as Christ's ***a***. Instead, we were
2 Peter
3:2 and savior commanded through your ***a***.
Jude
1:17 beforehand by the ***a*** of our Lord Jesus
Revelation
2:2 who say they are ***a*** but are not, and
18:20 saints, ***a***, and prophets—bec
21:14 twelve names of the Lamb's twelve ***a***.

APOSTLES AND THE ELDERS

Ac 15:2; 15:4, 6, 22, 23

APPEAR

Exodus
4:1 say to me, 'The LORD didn't ***a*** to you!'"
4:21 sure that you ***a*** before Pharaoh
Leviticus
9:4 because today the LORD will ***a*** to you.'"
9:6 glorious presence will ***a*** to you."
1 Samuel
3:21 LORD continued to ***a*** at Shiloh because
Psalms
21:9 When you ***a***, LORD, you will light them
Isaiah
40:5 LORD's glory will ***a***, and all humanity
42:9 Before they even ***a***, I tell you about
60:2 upon you; God's glory will ***a*** over you.
Jeremiah
12:6 even if they ***a*** to be on your
Ezekiel
1:20 the wind would ***a*** to go, the wind
6:13 when their slain ***a*** among their idols
13:11 flooding rains ***a*** and I send
Zechariah
9:14 The LORD will ***a*** above them; his arrow
Matthew
24:11 prophets will ***a*** and deceive many
24:30 Human One will ***a*** in the sky. At
Mark
13:22 prophets will ***a***, and they will
Luke
17:24 Human One will ***a*** on his day in the
19:11 God's kingdom would ***a*** right away.
Acts
19:30 Paul wanted to ***a*** before the assembly,
2 Corinthians
5:10 We all must ***a*** before Christ in court so
Hebrews
9:28 people. He will ***a*** a second time,

APPEARANCE

1 Samuel
16:7 no regard for his ***a*** or stature,
Job
14:20 you change their ***a*** and send them
Isaiah
52:14 inhuman, his ***a*** unlike that of
Ezekiel
1:16 The ***a*** and composition of the wheels
10:9 creature, and the ***a*** of the wheels was
2 Thessalonians
2:8 Lord comes, his ***a*** will put an end
2 Timothy
1:10 through the ***a*** of our savior,
4:8 set their heart on waiting for his ***a***.
Titus
2:13 and the glorious ***a*** of our great God
Revelation
1:16 sword. His ***a*** was like the sun

APPEARED
Genesis
1:3 Let there be light." And so light ***a***.
2:5 any wild plants ***a*** on the earth, and
12:7 The LORD ***a*** to Abram and said, "I give
Exodus
3:2 LORD's messenger ***a*** to him in a flame
6:3 I ***a*** to Abraham, Isaac, and Jacob as God
16:10 presence of the LORD ***a*** in the cloud.
Numbers
9:15 the cloud ***a*** with lightning
14:10 the LORD's glory ***a*** in the meeting
Deuteronomy
31:15 The LORD ***a*** in the tent in a pillar of
Judges
6:12 LORD's messenger ***a*** to him and said,
1 Kings
3:5 The LORD ***a*** to Solomon at Gibeon in a
2 Chronicles
1:7 That night God ***a*** to Solomon and said,
Daniel
5:5 of a human hand ***a*** and wrote on the
Matthew
1:20 from the Lord ***a*** to him in a dream
2:7 the time when the star had first ***a***.
2:13 from the Lord ***a*** to Joseph in a
17:3 Moses and Elijah ***a*** to them, talking
Mark
9:4 Elijah and Moses ***a*** and were talking
16:9 of the week, he ***a*** first to Mary
John
21:1 Jesus himself ***a*** again to his
21:14 third time Jesus ***a*** to his disciples
1 Corinthians
15:5 He ***a*** to Cephas, then to the Twelve
15:8 last of all he ***a*** to me, as if I
Hebrews
9:11 But Christ has ***a*** as the high priest of
9:26 he has now ***a*** once at the end
1 John
2:18 antichrists have ***a***. This is how we
3:8 God's Son ***a*** for this purpose:
Revelation
8:7 mixed with blood ***a***, and was thrown
11:19 his covenant ***a*** in his temple.
12:1 Then a great sign ***a*** in heaven: a woman
12:3 Then another sign ***a*** in heaven: it was a
13:3 One of its heads ***a*** to have been slain
15:2 Then I saw what ***a*** to be a sea of glass
16:2 and terrible sore ***a*** on the people who

APPEARS
Genesis
9:14 the earth and the bow ***a*** in the clouds,
Proverbs
21:29 The wicked person ***a*** brash, but the
27:25 away, new growth ***a***, and the plants

APPOINT
Numbers
3:10 You will ***a*** Aaron and his sons to be
Deuteronomy
17:14 might say: "Let's ***a*** a king over us,
1 Samuel
10:19 by saying, 'No! ***A*** a king over us!'
Psalms
2:6 I hereby ***a*** my king on Zion, my holy
45:16 fathers; you will ***a*** them as princes
109:6 ***A*** a wicked person to be against this
Isaiah
49:6 I will also ***a*** you as light to
Jeremiah
1:10 This very day I ***a*** you over nations and
Zechariah
11:16 I am about to ***a*** a shepherd in the
Acts
13:2 Spirit said, "***A*** Barnabas and Saul

APPOINTED → APPOINTED TIME
Genesis
39:4 his assistant; he ***a*** Joseph head of
Psalms
18:43 many people; you ***a*** me the leader of
Ecclesiastes
10:6 Fools are ***a*** to high posts, while the
Mark
3:14 He ***a*** twelve and called them apostles.
Luke
7:8 I'm also a man ***a*** under authority, with
John
15:16 I chose you and ***a*** you so that you
Romans
4:17 written: I have ***a*** you to be the
Hebrews
3:2 to the one who ***a*** him just like
5:10 He was ***a*** by God to be a high priest
7:28 after the Law, ***a*** a Son who has
8:3 high priest is ***a*** to offer gifts
1 Peter
2:8 this is the end to which they were ***a***.

APPOINTED TIME
Ex 13:10; 23:15; Nm 9:2; 9:3, 7, 13; 28:2; Dt 31:10; 1Sa 13:11; Jer 10:15; Dn 8:19; Hab 2:3

APPOINTED TIMES
Lv 23:2; 23:4, 37, 44; Nm 29:39; Ezr 10:14; Neh 10:34; 13:31; Ac 17:26

ARABIA
Jeremiah
25:24 all the kings of ***A*** and the nomadic
Ezekiel
27:21 ***A*** and all the princes of Kedar traded
30:5 Put, and Lud, all ***A*** and Cub, and the
Galatians
1:17 I went away into ***A*** and I returned
4:25 is Mount Sinai in ***A***, and she

ARAM
Genesis
10:22 Elam, Asshur, Arpachshad, Lud, and ***A***.
Numbers
23:7 address: "From ***A*** Balak led me, the
Judges
10:6 as the gods of ***A***, Sidon, Moab, the
Matthew
1:3 of Hezron. Hezron was the father of ***A***.

ARAMAIC
2 Kings
18:26 your servants in ***A*** because we
Ezra
4:7 letter was written in ***A*** and translated.

John
20:16 said to him in ***A***, "Rabbouni"
Acts
6:1 accused the ***A***-speaking disciples
21:40 were quiet, he addressed them in ***A***.

ARAMEAN
Genesis
31:20 Laban the ***A*** by not sending
Deuteronomy
26:5 was a starving ***A***. He went down to
2 Kings
7:6 Lord had made the ***A*** camp hear the

ARAMEANS
2 Samuel
8:6 forts among the ***A*** of Damascus. And
2 Kings
8:28 where the ***A*** wounded Joram.

ARGUE
Genesis
26:22 but they didn't ***a*** about it, so he
Judges
6:31 is a god, let him ***a*** for himself,
6:32 Let Baal ***a*** with him,"
Job
15:3 Will they ***a*** with a word that has no
16:3 what bothers you that you must ***a***?
23:7 the upright can ***a*** with him; I could
Psalms
35:23 justice for me; ***a*** my case, my Lord
43:1 for me, God! ***A*** my case against
119:154 ***A*** my case and redeem me. Make me live
Isaiah
50:8 is near. Who will ***a*** with me? Let's
Micah
6:2 his people; with Israel he will ***a***.
Matthew
12:19 He won't ***a*** or shout, and nobody will
Mark
8:11 up and began to ***a*** with Jesus. To
Luke
22:23 They began to ***a*** among themselves about
Romans
14:1 not in order to ***a*** about differences
1 Corinthians
11:16 someone wants to ***a*** about this, we

ARK
Genesis
6:14 so make a wooden ***a***. Make the ark with
Matthew
24:38 until the day Noah entered the ***a***.
Luke
17:27 Noah entered the ***a*** and the flood
Hebrews
11:7 yet. He built an ***a*** to deliver his
1 Peter
3:20 Noah built an ***a*** in which a few

ARM
Job
31:22 may my ***a*** fall from my shoulder, my
40:9 Or do you have an ***a*** like God; can you
Psalms
44:3 strong hand, your ***a***, and the light of
71:18 about your mighty ***a***, tell all who are
77:15 With your mighty ***a*** you redeemed your
79:11 your powerful ***a*** spare those who
83:8 are the strong ***a*** for Lot's
89:10 your enemies with your strong ***a***.
89:13 have a powerful ***a***; your hand is
89:21 him—yes, my ***a*** will strengthen
98:1 and his own holy ***a*** have won the
136:12 and outstretched ***a***—God's faithful l
Isaiah
30:30 his crushing ***a*** in furious anger,
44:12 with his strong ***a***. He even becomes
52:10 bared his holy ***a*** in view of all
62:8 hand and strong ***a***: I will never
63:12 with his glorious ***a***; who split the
Jeremiah
21:5 hand and strong ***a*** in fierce anger
27:5 and outstretched ***a***, I have made the
32:17 and outstretched ***a***; nothing is too
32:21 an outstretched ***a***, and with awesome
48:25 is cut off; its ***a*** is broken,
Ezekiel
4:7 With your ***a*** stretched out, face the
17:9 need a strong ***a*** or a mighty army
20:33 an outstretched ***a***, and with wrath
20:34 an outstretched ***a*** and with wrath
30:21 I've broken the ***a*** of Pharaoh,
Zechariah
11:17 will strike his ***a*** and his right
Luke
1:51 strength with his ***a***. He has scattered
John
12:38 To whom is the ***a*** of the Lord fully
1 Peter
4:1 you should also ***a*** yourselves with

ARMIES
Joshua
10:5 up with all their ***a***, camped against
Judges
7:11 outpost of the ***a*** that were in the
1 Kings
20:10 left in Samaria for the ***a*** under me!"
20:29 The two ***a*** camped opposite each other
Psalms
33:16 strength of their ***a***; warriors aren't
44:9 us. You no longer accompany our ***a***.
60:10 God, you no longer accompany our ***a***.
68:12 The kings of ***a*** are on the run! The
108:11 You, God, no longer accompany our ***a***.
Isaiah
34:2 with all their ***a***. God is about to
Jeremiah
4:16 it to Jerusalem! ***A*** are approaching
18:22 suddenly bring ***a*** against them.
35:11 and Aramean ***a***.' That's why
46:22 away is Egypt as ***a*** approach in
51:48 north destroying ***a*** will come to
51:53 the destroying ***a*** will still come
Ezekiel
7:11 others or their ***a*** or their
Luke
21:20 surrounded by ***a***, then you will
Hebrews
11:34 mighty in war, and routed foreign ***a***.

ARMIES [cont.]

Revelation
19:14 Heaven's ***a***, wearing fine linen that
19:19 earth and their ***a*** had gathered to

ARMOR

Judges
9:54 who carried his ***a***, "Draw your sword
1 Samuel
14:1 said to his young ***a***-bearer, "Come on!
16:21 much, and David became his ***a***-bearer.
17:39 sword on over the ***a***, but he couldn't
Nehemiah
4:16 bows, and body ***a***. Meanwhile, the
Psalms
35:2 Grab a shield and ***a***; stand up and help
Isaiah
59:17 righteousness as ***a*** and a helmet of
Jeremiah
46:4 on! Polish your spears; put on your ***a***!
51:3 prepare their ***a***. Show no mercy to
Luke
11:22 takes away the ***a*** he had trusted
Ephesians
6:11 Put on God's ***a*** so that you can make a
6:13 pick up the full ***a*** of God so that
1 Thessalonians
5:8 as a piece of ***a*** that protects our
Revelation
9:9 seemed to be iron ***a*** upon their

ARMS

Genesis
27:22 voice, but the ***a*** are Esau's arms."
Isaiah
40:11 lambs in his ***a*** and lift them
49:22 sons in their ***a***, and will carry
Daniel
2:32 its chest and ***a*** were made from
10:6 torches. His ***a*** and feet looked
Matthew
23:5 bands for their ***a*** and long tassels
Luke
2:28 took Jesus in his ***a*** and praised God.

ARMY

Exodus
14:17 Pharaoh, all his ***a***, his chariots,
15:4 chariots and his ***a*** he hurled into
Deuteronomy
11:4 to the Egyptian ***a***, to its horses
20:9 the troops, the ***a*** commanders will
Judges
4:2 commander of his ***a*** was Sisera, and
Psalms
27:3 If an ***a*** camps against me, my heart
136:15 Pharaoh and his ***a*** into the Reed Sea-
Jeremiah
6:22 proclaims: An ***a*** is on the move
22:25 King Nebuchadnezzar and his ***a***.
Ezekiel
1:24 the sound of an ***a*** camp. When they
29:19 it, and it will be the wages for his ***a***.
38:4 you and all your ***a***, horses and
38:13 assembled your ***a*** to take silver
38:15 horses, a great assembly, a mighty ***a***.
Joel
2:5 like a powerful ***a*** ready for battle.
1 Corinthians
9:7 Who joins the ***a*** and pays their own way?
Revelation
19:19 the rider on the horse and his ***a***.

ARNON

Numbers
21:13 camped across the ***A*** in the desert
Joshua
12:1 This ran from the ***A*** Valley as far as
Jeremiah
48:20 Tell it by the ***A*** River: Moab's

AROER

Numbers
32:34 The Gadites built Dibon, Ataroth, ***A***
Isaiah
17:2 The villages of ***A*** are abandoned
Jeremiah
48:6 your lives! Be like ***A*** in the desert.
48:19 inhabitants of ***A***. Ask the men who

ARREST

1 Samuel
19:14 messengers to ***a*** David, but she
Matthew
21:46 were trying to ***a*** him, but they
24:9 They will ***a*** you, abuse you, and they
26:4 were plotting to ***a*** Jesus by cunning
26:48 given them a sign: "***A*** the man I kiss."
26:55 and clubs to ***a*** me, like a thief?
John
7:32 and Pharisees sent guards to ***a*** him.
7:44 Some wanted to ***a*** him, but no one
11:57 should report it, so they could ***a*** him.
Acts
9:14 chief priests to ***a*** everyone who

ARRESTED

Matthew
4:12 that John was ***a***, he went to
14:3 Herod had ***a*** John, bound him, and put
26:50 they came and grabbed Jesus and ***a*** him.
26:57 Those who ***a*** Jesus led him to Caiaphas
Acts
1:16 became a guide for those who ***a*** Jesus.
12:3 the Jews, he ***a*** Peter as well.
21:13 not only to be ***a*** but even to die
22:5 those who were ***a*** to Jerusalem so
24:6 the temple. That's when we ***a*** him.

ARROGANT

Deuteronomy
8:14 don't become ***a***, forgetting the LORD
Psalms
5:5 ***A*** people won't last long in your sight;
36:11 let the feet of ***a*** people walk all
73:3 I envied the ***a***; I observed how
75:4 I said to the ***a***, "Don't be arrogant!"
86:14 The ***a*** rise up against me, God. A gang
94:2 Pay back the ***a*** exactly what they
94:4 They spew ***a*** words; all the evildoers
101:5 who has proud eyes or an ***a*** heart.

119:21 You rebuke the ***a***, accursed people who
119:51 The ***a*** make fun of me to no end, but I
138:6 but God keeps his distance from the ***a***.
140:5 ***A*** people have laid a trap for me with
Proverbs
15:25 snatches away the ***a*** one's house, but
16:5 all who are ***a***; they surely
21:4 Prideful eyes, an ***a*** heart, and the lamp
30:13 are those—how ***a*** are their eyes;
30:32 been foolish and ***a***, if you've been
Isaiah
9:9 But with a proud and ***a*** heart they said,
10:12 Assyrian king's ***a*** actions and the
Jeremiah
13:15 closely, don't be ***a***, for the LORD has
43:2 son, and all the ***a*** men said to
50:31 against you, you ***a*** one, declares the
Ezekiel
31:10 reach up among the clouds, it became ***a***.
Daniel
5:20 when he became ***a***, acting in
Habakkuk
2:5 wine betrays an ***a*** man. He doesn't
Malachi
3:15 we consider the ***a*** fortunate.
4:1 an oven. All the ***a*** ones and all
Luke
1:51 those with ***a*** thoughts and
1 Corinthians
4:6 you will become ***a*** by supporting one
4:18 Some have become ***a*** as if I'm not coming
4:19 on what these ***a*** people say, but
8:1 makes people ***a***, but love builds
13:4 jealous, it doesn't brag, it isn't ***a***,
Galatians
5:26 Let's not become ***a***, make each other
Colossians
2:18 unjustifiably ***a*** by their selfish
1 John
2:16 eyes see and the ***a*** pride in one's
Jude
1:16 They speak ***a*** words and they

ARROW
1 Samuel
20:20 I will shoot an ***a*** to the side of
20:21 Go retrieve the ***a***.' If I yell to
2 Kings
9:24 in the back. The ***a*** went through his
2 Chronicles
18:33 randomly shot an ***a*** that struck
Psalms
7:12 will bend his bow, will string an ***a***.
64:3 They aim their ***a***—a cruel word—
64:7 them with an ***a***! Without warning,
Proverbs
7:23 until an ***a*** pierces his liver, like a
25:18 like a club, sword, and sharpened ***a***.
Isaiah
37:33 shoot a single ***a*** here. He won't
49:2 me a sharpened ***a***, and concealed me
Jeremiah
9:8 is a lethal ***a***; their words are
Ezekiel
39:9 buckler, bow and ***a***, spear and lance.
Zechariah
9:14 above them; his ***a*** will go forth

ARROWS
Genesis
27:3 bow and quiver of ***a***, go out to the
49:23 and fired ***a***; the archers
Job
6:4 The Almighty's ***a*** are in me; my spirit
39:23 a quiver of ***a*** flies by him, flashing
41:28 ***A*** can't make him flee; slingstones he
Psalms
7:13 change; he gets his flaming ***a*** ready!
11:2 strung their ***a***; they are ready
18:14 God shot his ***a***, scattering the enemy;
38:2 Your ***a*** have pierced me; your fist has
45:5 May your sharp ***a*** pierce the hearts
57:4 are spears and ***a***; their tongues
58:7 bow, let their ***a*** be like headless
77:17 thunder; your ***a*** were flying all
91:5 terrors at night, ***a*** that fly in
120:4 sharpened ***a***, coupled with
127:4 is young are like ***a*** in the hand of a
144:6 enemy! Shoot your ***a*** and defeat them!
Proverbs
26:18 crazy person shooting deadly flaming ***a***
Isaiah
5:28 their ***a*** are sharp; all their bows
7:24 with bows and ***a*** will go there,
Jeremiah
50:9 captured. Their ***a*** are like those of
50:14 save none of your ***a***, because she's
51:11 Sharpen your ***a***; prepare your shields.
Lamentations
3:12 bow, made me a shooting target for ***a***.
3:13 He shot the ***a*** of his quiver into my
Ezekiel
5:16 launch my deadly ***a*** of famine against
21:21 He shakes the ***a***, consults the
39:3 and make your ***a*** fall from your
Habakkuk
3:9 curses for the ***a***. Selah With
3:11 the light, your ***a*** shoot, your spear
Ephesians
6:16 the flaming ***a*** of the evil one.

ARTAXERXES
Ezra
4:7 In the days of ***A***, Bishlam, Mithredath,
7:12 ***A***, king of kings, to Ezra the priest,
Nehemiah
2:1 year of King ***A***, the king was
13:6 to Babylon's King ***A*** in the thirty-seco

ASA
1 Kings
15:9 King Jeroboam, ***A*** became king of
1 Chronicles
3:10 Abijah, his son ***A***, his son
9:16 Berechiah son of ***A*** son of Elkanah,
2 Chronicles
14:1 City. His son ***A*** succeeded him as
20:32 way of his father ***A*** and didn't turn
Jeremiah
41:9 the one that King ***A*** had made to

ASAHEL

2 Samuel
2:18 Abishai, and ***A***. Asahel was as
23:24 the Thirty were: ***A***, Joab's brother;
1 Chronicles
2:16 Abishai, Joab, and ***A***—three in all.
11:26 mighty warriors: ***A***, Joab's brother;

ASAPH

1 Chronicles
6:39 His relative was ***A***, who stood on his
25:9 lot fell for ***A*** to Joseph; the
2 Chronicles
20:14 of the line of ***A***, as he stood in
29:30 and the seer ***A***. They did so
Ezra
2:41 The singers: The family of ***A*** 1
3:10 the sons of ***A*** with cymbals,
Nehemiah
2:8 issue a letter to ***A*** the keeper of the
Psalms
50:1 [A psalm of ***A***.] From the rising of the
Matthew
1:7 of Abijah. Abijah was the father of ***A***.
1:8 ***A*** was the father of Jehoshaphat.

ASHAMED

Psalms
6:10 enemies will be ***a*** and completely
22:5 they trusted you and they weren't ***a***.
34:5 will shine; their faces are never ***a***.
37:19 They won't be ***a*** in troubling times, and
70:2 seek my life be ***a*** and humiliated!
119:6 I wouldn't be ***a*** when I examine
127:5 They won't be ***a*** when arguing with
129:5 who hates Zion be ***a***, thoroughly
Isaiah
1:29 You will be ***a*** of the oaks you once
49:23 the one who hopes in me won't be ***a***.
Jeremiah
2:26 of Israel are ***a***—their kings, off
6:10 hear. They are ***a*** of the LORD's
9:19 We're so ***a***! We have to leave
12:13 They will be ***a*** of their harvest
14:3 with empty jars, ***a***, bewildered, and
15:9 day; she will be ***a*** and disgraced. I
Ezekiel
16:52 than you. Be ***a***, and bear the
16:61 your ways and be ***a***, when in spite of
36:32 known to you! Be ***a*** and be humiliated
Daniel
9:7 Lord! But we are ***a*** this day—we, the
9:8 LORD, we are ***a***—we, our kings, our
Hosea
4:19 they will be ***a*** of their
10:6 Israel will be ***a*** of his own idol.
Micah
3:7 visions will be ***a***, and the diviners
7:16 will see and be ***a*** of all their
Zephaniah
3:11 day, you won't be ***a*** of all your deeds
Zechariah
10:5 with them. All the cavalry will be ***a***.
13:4 prophets will be ***a*** of his vision
Mark
8:38 Whoever is ***a*** of me and my words in this
Romans
1:16 I'm not ***a*** of the gospel: it is God's
2 Corinthians
10:8 I wouldn't be ***a*** of it. The Lord
11:21 I'm ***a*** to say that we have been weak in
2 Timothy
1:8 So don't be ***a*** of the testimony about
1:12 I do, but I'm not ***a***. I know the one
1:16 and he wasn't ***a*** of my
2:15 need to be ***a*** but is one who
Titus
2:8 opponent will be ***a*** because they
Hebrews
2:11 why Jesus isn't ***a*** to call them
11:16 God isn't ***a*** to be called
1 Peter
3:16 in Christ may be ***a*** when they slander
4:16 But don't be ***a*** if you suffer as one who
1 John
2:28 and not be ***a*** in front of him

ASHDOD

Joshua
13:3 for Gaza, ***A***, Ashkelon, Gath,
1 Samuel
5:1 they brought it from Ebenezer to ***A***.
Nehemiah
13:23 married women of ***A***, Ammon, and Moab.

ASHER

Genesis
30:13 call me happy." So she named him ***A***.
Luke
2:36 to the tribe of ***A***. She was very
Revelation
7:6 from the tribe of ***A***, twelve thousand;

ASHERAH

Judges
6:25 and cut down the ***A*** that is beside it.
1 Kings
15:13 made an image of ***A***. Asa cut down her
18:19 prophets of ***A*** who eat at
2 Kings
21:7 set up the carved ***A*** image he had made
23:4 made for Baal, ***A***, and all the
2 Chronicles
15:16 made an image of ***A***. Asa cut down her

ASHES

Exodus
9:8 Take handfuls of ***a*** from a furnace
27:3 for removing its ***a*** and its shovels,
Numbers
4:13 will remove the ***a*** from the altar
16:37 and scatter the ***a*** about, because
19:9 will gather the ***a*** of the cow and
2 Samuel
13:19 Tamar put ***a*** on her head and tore the
Esther
4:1 clothes, and put ***a*** on his head. Then
Job
2:8 himself and sat down on a mound of ***a***.
30:19 mud; I'm a cliché, like dust and ***a***.
Psalms
102:9 I've been eating ***a*** instead of bread.

147:16 wool; God scatters frost like it was ***a***;
Isaiah
44:20 He's feeding on ***a***; his deluded mind
58:5 clothing and ***a***? Is this what you
61:3 crown in place of ***a***, oil of joy in
Jeremiah
6:26 and roll in ***a***; weep and wail as
31:40 by corpses and ***a***, and all the
51:58 vain; nations toil for nothing but ***a***!
Lamentations
3:16 gravel; he pressed me down into the ***a***.
Ezekiel
27:30 heads and cover themselves with ***a***.
Daniel
9:3 with fasting, mourning clothes, and ***a***.
Jonah
3:6 with mourning clothes, and sat in ***a***.
Matthew
11:21 funeral clothes and ***a*** a long time ago.
Luke
10:13 sat around in funeral clothes and ***a***.
Hebrews
9:13 and the sprinkled ***a*** of cows made
2 Peter
2:6 reducing them to ***a*** as a warning to

ASHKELON
Judges
14:19 he went down to ***A***. He killed thirty
Zechariah
9:5 ***A*** will look and be afraid. Gaza will

ASIA
Acts
2:9 Judea, and Cappadocia, Pontus and ***A***,
6:9 Cilicia, and ***A*** entered into
16:6 speaking the word in the province of ***A***.
19:10 the province of ***A***—both Jews and
21:27 the province of ***A*** saw Paul in the
24:19 the province of ***A***. They should be
27:2 the province of ***A***. So we put out to
Romans
16:5 was the first convert in ***A*** for Christ.

ASLEEP
Judges
4:21 Sisera was sound ***a*** from exhaustion,
1 Samuel
26:7 Saul lying there, ***a*** in the camp, with
1 Kings
3:20 side while I was ***a***. She laid him on
Psalms
4:8 lie down and fall ***a*** in peace because
121:3 Your protector won't fall ***a*** on the job.
Jeremiah
51:39 will fall fast ***a***. They will sleep
Matthew
8:24 over the boat. But Jesus was ***a***.
9:24 isn't dead but is ***a***"; but they
Mark
14:37 Simon, are you ***a***? Couldn't you
Luke
8:23 sailing, he fell ***a***. Gale-force winds
22:45 He found them ***a***, overcome by
Acts
12:6 Peter was ***a*** between two
20:9 When he was sound ***a***, he fell from the
1 Thessalonians
5:10 we are awake or ***a***, we will live

ASSEMBLY → ASSEMBLY OF ISRAEL
Exodus
16:3 to starve this whole ***a*** to death."
Numbers
10:7 To gather the ***a***, blow a long blast,
16:3 exalt yourselves above the LORD's ***a***?"
Deuteronomy
5:22 to your entire ***a*** with a loud voice
Joshua
8:35 of the entire ***a*** of Israel. This
Psalms
1:5 will sinners in the ***a*** of the righteous.
35:18 you in the great ***a***; I will praise
40:9 in the great ***a***. I didn't hold
40:10 and trustworthiness from the great ***a***.
89:5 too—in the ***a*** of the holy ones.
107:32 and praise God in the ***a*** of the elders.
149:1 God's praise in the ***a*** of the faithful!
Ecclesiastes
1:1 Teacher of the ***A***, David's son,
Joel
1:14 request a special ***a***. Gather the
Luke
2:13 Suddenly a great ***a*** of the heavenly
23:1 The whole ***a*** got up and led Jesus to
Acts
7:38 who was in the ***a*** in the wilderness
15:12 The entire ***a*** fell quiet as they
19:30 appear before the ***a***, but the
23:7 and Sadducees, and the ***a*** was divided.
Hebrews
2:12 will praise you in the middle of the ***a***.

ASSEMBLY OF ISRAEL
Lv 16:17; Dt 31:30; Josh 8:35; 1Ki 8:14; 2Ch 6:3; 6:13

ASSHUR
Genesis
10:22 sons: Elam, ***A***, Arpachshad, Lud,
1 Chronicles
1:17 family: Elam, ***A***, Arpachshad, Lud,

ASSIGNED
Genesis
40:4 the royal guard ***a*** Joseph to assist
Exodus
38:8 ranks of women ***a*** to the meeting
Leviticus
10:17 holy, and it was ***a*** to you for
Numbers
3:9 They have been ***a*** as a gift to him
3:36 Merarites were ***a*** responsibility
4:49 load. Each was ***a*** just as the LORD
Joshua
9:27 That day Joshua ***a*** them as woodcutters
13:32 Moses ***a*** these territories when he was
14:1 of the Israelite tribes ***a*** them.
14:2 Their legacy was ***a*** by lot, exactly as
19:51 Israelite tribes ***a*** by lot at Shiloh.
Judges
18:1 had been ***a*** to them among the
1 Kings
11:18 its king. Pharaoh ***a*** him a home, food,

14:27 shields and ***a*** them to the
1 Chronicles
9:22 Samuel the seer ***a*** them to their
23:24 who carried out ***a*** tasks in the
25:8 lots for their ***a*** duties, small as
26:15 Obed-edom was ***a*** the South Gate, and
26:16 Hosah was ***a*** the West Gate, that is, the
2 Chronicles
12:10 shields and ***a*** them to the
23:18 that David had ***a*** to the LORD's
31:19 cities, men were ***a*** to distribute
35:2 He ***a*** the priests to their posts,
Nehemiah
9:22 and peoples, and ***a*** to them every
Ezekiel
32:23 who were ***a*** graves in the deepest region
Luke
2:34 This boy is ***a*** to be the cause
1 Corinthians
7:17 that the Lord ***a*** when he called
2 Corinthians
10:13 area that God has ***a*** to us.

ASSYRIA
Genesis
2:14 flowing east of ***A***; and the name of
25:18 on the road to ***A***. He died among
2 Kings
15:29 He sent the people into exile to ***A***.
18:11 into exile to ***A***. He settled them
Ezra
6:22 of the king of ***A*** toward them so
Nehemiah
9:32 the time of the kings of ***A*** until today.
Psalms
83:8 ***A*** too has joined them—they are the
Isaiah
10:5 Doom to ***A***, rod of my anger, in whose
Jeremiah
50:18 land, just as I punished the king of ***A***.
Hosea
14:3 ***A*** won't save us; we won't ride upon
Nahum
3:18 asleep, king of ***A***! Your officials
Zephaniah
2:13 and will cause ***A*** to perish. Let
Zechariah
10:10 collect them from ***A***. I will bring
10:11 up. The pride of ***A*** will be brought

ASSYRIANS
2 Kings
18:10 three years the ***A*** captured the
19:18 The ***A*** burned the gods of those nations
Isaiah
37:19 The ***A*** burned the gods of those nations
Ezekiel
23:5 me and lusted after her lovers the ***A***

ASTARTES
Judges
2:13 the LORD and served Baal and the ***A***.
10:6 the Baals and the ***A***, as well as the
1 Samuel
7:3 gods and the ***A*** you have. Set
7:4 the Baals and the ***A*** and worshipped
12:10 the Baals and the ***A***. But now deliver

ATHALIAH
2 Kings
8:26 mother's name was ***A***; she was the
11:20 at peace now that ***A*** had been executed
1 Chronicles
8:26 family: Shamsherai, Shehariah, ***A***,
2 Chronicles
22:2 mother's name was ***A***; she was the
23:21 at peace now that ***A*** had been executed
24:7 Now wicked ***A*** and her followers had

ATTACHED
Genesis
32:32 eat the tendon ***a*** to the thigh
Exodus
25:31 and petals should all be ***a*** to it.
28:7 shoulder pieces ***a*** to its two edges
28:8 belt should be ***a*** to it and made in
30:2 Its horns should be permanently ***a***.
39:4 pieces for it ***a*** to its two edges
2 Chronicles
9:18 a gold footrest ***a***. Two lions stood
Romans
12:8 with no strings ***a***. The leader

ATTACK
Deuteronomy
20:12 makes war against you, you may ***a*** it.
28:7 any enemies who ***a*** you. They will
28:52 That nation will ***a*** you in all your
Joshua
10:19 your enemies and ***a*** them from the
11:7 a surprise ***a*** against them at
24:9 son, set out to ***a*** Israel. He
1 Samuel
7:7 rulers went up to ***a*** Israel. When the
14:14 In the first ***a***, Jonathan and his
15:3 So go! ***A*** the Amalekites; put everything
17:48 moved closer to ***a*** David, and David
22:17 to lift a hand to ***a*** the LORD's
2 Samuel
5:19 LORD, "Should I ***a*** the Philistines?
12:28 of the troops, ***a*** the city, and
15:14 destroy us, and ***a*** the city with the
17:2 I will ***a*** him while he is tired and
Esther
8:7 pole because he planned to ***a*** the Jews.
Job
30:21 are cruel to me, ***a*** me with the
Psalms
60:4 can rally around it, safe from ***a***. Selah
62:3 will all of you ***a*** others; how long
109:3 surround me; they ***a*** me for no reason.
139:21 you? Don't I despise those who ***a*** you?
Jeremiah
1:19 They will ***a*** you, but they won't defeat
5:6 the forest will ***a*** them; a wolf from
Daniel
3:8 seizing a chance to ***a*** the Jews.
11:13 passed, he will ***a*** with a large and
Zechariah
14:13 neighbors; neighbors will ***a*** each other.
Matthew
7:6 the pearls, then turn around and ***a*** you.

Luke
19:43 encircle you, and ***a*** you from all
1 Thessalonians
5:3 destruction will ***a*** them, like labor
1 Timothy
1:13 against him, ***a*** his people, and I

ATTACKED

Genesis
4:8 the field, Cain ***a*** his brother Abel
Joshua
10:5 camped against Gibeon, and ***a*** it.
10:9 Joshua quickly ***a*** them, having come up
19:47 Dan went up and ***a*** Leshem and
24:8 the Jordan. They ***a*** you, but I gave
24:11 of Jericho ***a*** you. They were
1 Samuel
13:3 Jonathan ***a*** the Philistine fort at Geba,
13:4 that Saul had ***a*** the Philistine
15:2 Israel: how they ***a*** the Israelites as
22:18 Edomite went and ***a*** the priests,
27:9 When David ***a*** an area, he wouldn't leave
30:1 Ziklag. They had ***a*** Ziklag and burned
31:1 the Philistines ***a*** the Israelites,
2 Samuel
5:24 for God has ***a*** in front of you
11:17 came out and ***a*** Joab, some of the
20:15 men arrived and ***a*** Sheba at Abel of
1 Kings
2:25 son. He ***a*** Adonijah, and
9:16 Egypt's king, had ***a*** and captured
14:25 King Shishak of Egypt ***a*** Jerusalem.
15:17 King Baasha ***a*** Judah and
16:7 was also about how the Lord ***a*** Baasha.
16:10 Zimri came, ***a***, and killed Elah in the
20:21 king went out and ***a*** the horses and
22:29 King Jehoshaphat ***a*** Ramoth-gilead.
Esther
8:11 and province that ***a*** them, along with
Psalms
53:5 of those who ***a*** you. You will put
55:20 My friend ***a*** his allies, breaking his
124:2 been for us, when those people ***a*** us,
129:1 have constantly ***a*** me—let Israel no
129:2 have constantly ***a*** me—but they have
Hosea
6:5 Therefore, I have ***a*** them by the
Jonah
4:7 at dawn, and it ***a*** the shrub so that
Zechariah
14:16 the nations who ***a*** Jerusalem will go
Matthew
11:12 is violently ***a*** as violent people
Acts
17:5 in the city. They ***a*** Jason's house,
1 Corinthians
4:13 our reputation is ***a***, we are

ATTENTION

Exodus
3:16 been paying close ***a*** to you and to
23:21 Pay ***a*** to him and do as he says. Don't
Numbers
16:15 the LORD, "Pay no ***a*** to their
Deuteronomy
4:5 So pay ***a***! I am teaching all of you the
11:26 Pay ***a***! I am setting blessing and curse
32:1 Heaven! Pay ***a*** and I will speak; Earth!
Judges
20:48 turned their ***a*** to the rest of
Ruth
1:6 the LORD had paid ***a*** to his people by
2 Samuel
20:17 Pay close ***a*** to the words of
1 Kings
17:18 to me to call ***a*** to my sin and
22:28 he added, "Pay ***a***, every last one
Esther
3:4 but he paid no ***a*** to them. So they
Job
13:6 teaching and pay ***a*** to the arguments
35:13 cry; the Almighty doesn't pay ***a*** to it.
Psalms
5:2 Pay ***a*** to the sound of my cries, my king
8:4 human beings that you pay ***a*** to them?
17:1 right, LORD; pay ***a*** to my cry! Listen
40:4 LORD, who pay no ***a*** to the proud or
41:1 who pay close ***a*** to the poor are
45:10 daughter; pay ***a***, and listen
49:4 I will pay close ***a*** to a proverb; I will
54:3 me dead. They pay no ***a*** to God. Selah
55:2 Pay ***a***! Answer me! I can't sit still
61:1 listen to my cry; pay ***a*** to my prayer!
78:56 God; they didn't pay ***a*** to his warnings.
84:9 God; pay close ***a*** to the face of
86:6 LORD; pay close ***a*** to the sound of
107:43 is wise will pay ***a*** to these things,
130:2 ears pay close ***a*** to my request for
142:4 See? No one pays ***a*** to me. There's no
142:6 Pay close ***a*** to my shouting because I've
Proverbs
1:24 out my hand to you, but you paid no ***a***.
4:1 instruction; pay ***a*** to gain
4:20 My son, pay ***a*** to my words. Bend your
5:1 My son, pay ***a*** to my wisdom. Bend your
6:22 you awake, they will occupy your ***a***.
7:24 listen to me, and pay ***a*** to my speech.
17:4 An evildoer pays ***a*** to guilty lips; a
27:23 your flock well; pay ***a*** to your herds,
Ecclesiastes
8:9 of this as I paid ***a*** to all that
Isaiah
28:23 hear my voice; pay ***a*** and hear my word:
Jeremiah
6:10 I get someone's ***a***? Their ears are
6:18 Therefore, pay ***a***, nations; take
7:24 listen or pay ***a***. They followed
27:14 Pay no ***a*** to the words of the prophets
29:8 you. Don't pay ***a*** to your dreams.
34:14 didn't obey or pay any ***a*** to me.
44:5 listen or pay ***a*** or turn from
Ezekiel
18:6 or give their ***a*** to the idols of
33:5 If they had paid ***a*** to the warning,
44:5 one, pay close ***a***! Use your eyes
Daniel
9:19 My Lord, pay ***a*** and act! Don't
11:19 he will turn his ***a*** to the walled
Matthew
6:1 to draw their ***a***. If you do, you
22:5 But they paid no ***a*** and went away—

ATTENTION [cont.]

Mark
4:9 has ears to listen should pay ***a***!"
Luke
8:8 Everyone who has ears should pay ***a***."
14:35 Whoever has ears to hear should pay ***a***."
Acts
8:6 and they gave him their undivided ***a***.
23:22 anyone that you brought this to my ***a***."
26:26 have escaped his ***a***. This didn't
1 Corinthians
3:10 needs to pay ***a*** to the way they
7:34 His ***a*** is divided. A woman who isn't
15:1 want to call your ***a*** to the good news
1 Timothy
1:4 shouldn't pay ***a*** to myths and
4:1 They will pay ***a*** to spirits that
2 Timothy
3:10 But you have paid ***a*** to my teaching,
Titus
1:9 They must pay ***a*** to the reliable message
1:14 shouldn't pay ***a*** to Jewish myths
3:8 give careful ***a*** to doing good.
Hebrews
2:1 us to pay more ***a*** to what we have
James
4:13 Pay ***a***, you who say, "Today or tomorrow
5:1 Pay ***a***, you wealthy people! Weep and
2 Peter
1:19 do well to pay ***a*** to it, just as

AUTHORITIES → JEWISH AUTHORITIES

Luke
12:11 rulers,and ***a***, don't worry
Acts
16:20 the legal ***a***, they said,
16:22 and Silas, so the ***a*** ordered that they
16:23 beaten, the ***a*** threw them into
16:35 morning the legal ***a*** sent the police
16:36 him, "The ***a*** sent word that
16:38 this to the legal ***a***, who were alarmed
Romans
13:1 from God, and the ***a*** that are there
13:3 The ***a*** don't frighten people who are
13:6 because the ***a*** are God's
Ephesians
6:12 against rulers, ***a***, forces of cosmic
Colossians
1:16 or rulers or ***a***, all things were
2:15 the rulers and ***a***, he exposed them
Titus
3:1 to rulers and ***a***. They should be
1 Peter
3:22 rules over all angels, ***a***, and powers.

AUTHORITY

Genesis
41:33 man and give him ***a*** over the land of
41:41 I've given you ***a*** over the entire
Ecclesiastes
8:4 king's word has ***a***, no one can say
Isaiah
9:6 given to us, and ***a*** will be on his
Daniel
7:6 had four heads. ***A*** was given to it.
Matthew
7:29 like someone with ***a*** and not like
8:9 I'm a man under ***a***, with soldiers under
9:6 the Human One has ***a*** on the earth to
10:1 and gave them ***a*** over unclean
12:27 out demons by the ***a*** of Beelzebul,
20:25 show off their ***a*** over them and
21:23 What kind of ***a*** do you have for
28:18 received all ***a*** in heaven and on
Mark
1:22 them with ***a***, not like the
1:27 new teaching with ***a***! He even commands
11:33 you what kind of ***a*** I have to do
Luke
4:32 he delivered his message with ***a***.
5:24 the Human One has ***a*** on the earth to
7:8 appointed under ***a***, with soldiers
9:1 them power and ***a*** over all demons
10:19 I have given you ***a*** to crush snakes
11:15 demons with the ***a*** of Beelzebul, the
12:5 killed, has the ***a*** to throw you into
19:17 you will have ***a*** over ten cities.'
20:2 us: What kind of ***a*** do you have for
22:25 and those in ***a*** over them are
John
2:18 him, "By what ***a*** are you doing
5:27 He gives the Son ***a*** to judge, because he
17:2 You gave him ***a*** over everyone so that he
19:10 know that I have ***a*** to release you
19:11 would have no ***a*** over me if it had
Acts
1:7 that the Father has set by his own ***a***.
4:35 and under the ***a*** of the apostles.
5:2 care and under the ***a*** of the apostles.
8:19 Give me this ***a*** too so that
9:14 He's here with ***a*** from the chief priests
25:11 no one has the ***a*** to hand me over
26:10 prison under the ***a*** of the chief
26:12 with the full ***a*** of the chief
Romans
13:1 under the ***a*** of the
13:2 who opposes the ***a*** is standing
13:5 the government's ***a***, not only to
1 Corinthians
7:4 wife doesn't have ***a*** over her own
11:10 woman should have ***a*** over her head,
15:24 of rule, every ***a*** and power to an
16:16 So accept the ***a*** of people like them and
2 Corinthians
10:8 to brag about our ***a***, I wouldn't be
13:10 you by using the ***a*** that the Lord
Galatians
1:1 sent from human ***a*** or commissioned
Ephesians
1:21 every ruler and ***a*** and power and
Colossians
2:10 who is the head of every ruler and ***a***.
1 Thessalonians
4:8 rejecting a human ***a***. They are
5:27 By the Lord's ***a***, I order all of you to
1 Timothy
1:9 obeying any ***a***. They are the
2:2 who is in ***a*** so that we can
Titus
2:15 with complete ***a***. Don't let anyone
1 Peter
2:18 by accepting the ***a*** of your masters
3:5 accepting the ***a*** of their own
3:6 Abraham's ***a*** when she called

5:5 accept the ***a*** of the elders.
2 Peter
2:10 defy the Lord's ***a***. These reckless,
Jude
1:6 their position of ***a*** but deserted
1:8 reject ***a***, and slander the
1:25 power, and ***a***, before all time,
Revelation
2:26 end, I will give ***a*** over the nations—
2:28 as I received ***a*** from my Father. I
6:8 They were given ***a*** over a fourth of
12:10 our God, and the ***a*** of his Christ
13:2 gave it his power, throne, and great ***a***.
13:4 the beast its ***a***. They worshipped
13:5 and it was given ***a*** to act for forty
13:7 It was given ***a*** over every tribe,
13:12 exercises all the ***a*** of the first
17:12 receive royal ***a*** for an hour,
17:13 give their power and ***a*** to the beast.
18:1 He had great ***a***, and the earth

AWESOME → AWESOME DEEDS, AWESOME GOD, GREAT AND AWESOME
Genesis
28:17 sacred place is ***a***. It's none other
31:42 Abraham and the ***a*** one of Isaac—
Exodus
34:10 because I will do an ***a*** thing with you.
Deuteronomy
4:34 arm, or ***a*** power like all
28:58 by fearing the ***a*** and glorious name
29:3 witnessed, those ***a*** signs and wonders!
1 Samuel
12:16 Look at this ***a*** thing the LORD is
2 Samuel
7:23 doing great and ***a*** things for them,
1 Chronicles
16:25 of praise. He is ***a*** beyond all other
17:21 doing great and ***a*** things, by
Nehemiah
4:14 LORD is great and ***a***! Fight for your
Esther
1:4 He showed off the ***a*** riches of his
Job
10:16 me; you would do ***a*** things to me
37:22 golden light, the ***a*** splendor of God.
Psalms
47:2 LORD Most High is ***a***, he is the great
66:3 Say to God: "How ***a*** are your works!
66:5 his works for human beings are ***a***:
71:19 you've done ***a*** things! Who can
76:7 You! You are ***a***! Who can stand before
86:10 because you are ***a*** and a wonder worker.
92:5 How ***a*** are your works, LORD! Your
96:4 of praise. He is ***a*** beyond all other
99:3 your great and ***a*** name. He is holy!
106:22 the land of Ham, ***a*** deeds at the Reed
111:9 last forever. Holy and ***a*** is God's name!
145:6 the power of your ***a*** deeds; I will
Jeremiah
32:21 arm, and with ***a*** power, yes, with
Mark
13:1 look! What ***a*** stones and
2 Corinthians
4:7 pots so that the ***a*** power belongs to

AWESOME DEEDS
Ex 15:11; Dt 6:22; Ps 45:4; 65:5; 106:22; 145:6

AWESOME GOD
Dt 7:21; 10:17; Neh 9:32; Ps 68:35; Dn 9:4

AZARIAH
1 Kings
4:2 officials: the priest ***A***, Zadok's son;
4:5 ***A***, Nathan's son, who was in charge of
2 Kings
14:21 of Judah took ***A*** and made him king
15:8 of Judah's King ***A***. He ruled for six
15:27 of Judah's King ***A***. Pekah ruled for
Ezra
7:1 son of Seraiah son of ***A*** son of Hilkiah
7:3 son of Amariah son of ***A*** son of Meraiot
Nehemiah
3:23 After them, ***A***, Maaseiah's son
3:24 from the house of ***A*** to the Angle and
7:7 Jeshua, Nehemiah, ***A***, Raamiah,
8:7 Maaseiah, Kelita, ***A***, Jozabad, Hanan,
10:2 Seraiah, ***A***, Jeremiah
12:33 along with ***A***, Ezra, Meshullam
Jeremiah
43:2 ***A***, Hoshaiah's son, and Johanan,
Daniel
1:6 were Daniel, Hananiah, Mishael, and ***A***.
1:7 Mishael "Meshach," and ***A***"Abednego."

Bb

BAAL
Numbers
25:3 attached to the ***B*** of Peor, and the
Deuteronomy
4:3 concerning the ***B*** of Peor. The LORD
Judges
2:13 the LORD and served ***B*** and the Astartes.
6:25 father's altar to ***B*** and cut down the
1 Kings
16:31 Sidonians. He served and worshipped ***B***.
16:32 made an altar for ***B*** in the Baal
18:19 fifty prophets of ***B*** and the four
2 Kings
10:18 Ahab served ***B*** a little. Jehu
10:19 planned for ***B***. Anyone who
10:20 a holy assembly for ***B***, and it was done.
10:23 There should be only ***B*** worshippers."
23:4 objects made for ***B***, Asherah, and all
23:5 burned incense to ***B***, to the sun, to
1 Chronicles
4:33 towns as far as ***B***. These were their
5:5 son Micah, his son Reaiah, his son ***B***,
2 Chronicles
17:3 ways of his father by not seeking ***B***.
Jeremiah
2:8 in the name of ***B***, going after what
7:9 sacrifice to ***B*** and go after
Hosea
2:8 silver, and gold that they used for ***B***.
13:1 he became guilty through ***B*** and died.
Zephaniah
1:4 what's left of ***B*** from this place
Romans
11:4 who haven't bowed their knees to ***B***.

BAAL-ZEBUB
2 Kings
1:2 to Ekron's god ***B***, and ask if I
1:3 are going to question Ekron's god ***B***?
1:6 Ekron's god ***B***? Because of this
1:16 Ekron's god ***B***? Is there no God

BAASHA
1 Kings
15:16 and Israel's King ***B*** throughout their
16:12 entire house of ***B*** in agreement with
2 Kings
9:9 like the dynasty of ***B***, Ahijah's son.
2 Chronicles
16:1 Israel's King ***B*** attacked Judah
16:6 and timber that ***B*** was using to
Jeremiah
41:9 Israel's King ***B***. Ishmael,

BABIES
Deuteronomy
28:57 pushed out or the ***b*** she bore, because
Job
3:16 infant, like ***b*** who never see
Psalms
8:2 mouths of nursing ***b*** you have laid a
17:14 they have leftovers enough for their ***b***.
Isaiah
65:20 No more will ***b*** live only a few days, or
Lamentations
2:11 children and ***b*** are fainting in
2:20 own beautiful ***b***? Should priest
Ezekiel
9:6 men and women, ***b*** and mothers. Only
Hosea
13:16 will fall—their ***b*** will be dashed,
Matthew
11:25 intelligent and have shown them to ***b***.
21:16 the mouths of ***b*** and infants
Luke
10:21 and shown them to ***b***. Indeed, Father,
18:15 were bringing ***b*** to Jesus so that
Acts
7:19 their newly born ***b*** so they would die.
1 Corinthians
3:1 unspiritual people, like ***b*** in Christ.
14:20 think. Well, be ***b*** when it comes to
Hebrews
5:13 of righteousness, because they are ***b***.

BABY
Exodus
1:17 Instead, they let the ***b*** boys live.
1 Kings
3:21 my son—not the ***b*** I had birthed."
12:10 say to them: 'My ***b*** finger is thicker
2 Chronicles
10:10 say to them, 'My ***b*** finger is thicker
Luke
1:44 greeting, the ***b*** in my womb jumped
2:6 the time came for Mary to have her ***b***.
2:12 find a newborn ***b*** wrapped snugly
2:16 Joseph, and the ***b*** lying in the
1 Peter
2:2 like a newborn ***b***, desire the pure

BABYLON
2 Kings
20:17 be carried off to ***B***. Not a single
24:1 Nebuchadnezzar of ***B*** attacked.
1 Chronicles
9:1 into exile in ***B*** because of their
2 Chronicles
33:11 chains, and carried him off to ***B***.

36:6 with bronze chains, and took him to ***B***.
Psalms
137:8 Daughter ***B***, you destroyer, a blessing
Isaiah
13:1 An oracle about ***B***, which Isaiah,
47:1 virgin Daughter ***B***! Sit on the
Jeremiah
20:6 be deported to ***B*** where you will
39:9 Babylonians, and deported them to ***B***.
40:1 and Judah who were being sent off to ***B***.
50:8 wander far from ***B***. Get out of that
51:24 I will repay ***B*** and all its inhabitants
51:55 is destroying ***B*** and silencing her
51:64 In the same way, ***B*** will sink and
Ezekiel
1:3 in the land of ***B*** at the Chebar
32:11 of the king of ***B*** is coming against
Daniel
2:24 out the sages of ***B***! Bring me before
4:30 Isn't this ***B***, the magnificent
Micah
4:10 you will go to ***B***. There you will
Zechariah
2:7 Flee, you who dwell with Daughter ***B***!
6:10 who came from ***B***, from Heldai,
Matthew
1:11 This was at the time of the exile to ***B***.
1:12 the exile to ***B***: Jechoniah was
1:17 to the exile to ***B***, and fourteen
Acts
7:43 will send you far away, farther than ***B***.
1 Peter
5:13 church in ***B*** greets you, and
Revelation
14:8 fallen is ***B*** the great! She
16:19 God remembered ***B*** the great so that
17:5 on her forehead: "***B*** the great, the
18:2 fallen is ***B*** the great! She
18:10 Oh, the horror! ***B***, you great city,
18:21 the great city of ***B*** will be thrown

BABYLONIAN
Joshua
7:21 robe in the ***B*** style, two
2 Kings
17:30 The ***B*** people made the god
2 Chronicles
32:31 sent from ***B*** officials to find
36:17 God brought the ***B*** king against
Jeremiah
32:2 the army of the ***B*** king had
52:34 The ***B*** king provided him daily

BALAAM
Numbers
22:20 God came to ***B*** in the night and said to
22:29 ***B*** said to the donkey, "Because you've
24:3 The oracle of ***B***, Beor's son; the
Deuteronomy
23:4 they hired ***B***, Beor's son, from
23:5 in listening to ***B***. The LORD your
Joshua
13:22 fortune-teller ***B***, Beor's son, with
24:9 He summoned ***B***, Beor's son, to
24:10 to listen to ***B***, so he actually
Nehemiah
13:2 but instead hired ***B*** against them to
Micah
6:5 planned, and how ***B***, Beor's son,
2 Peter
2:15 the way of ***B*** son of Bosor, who
Revelation
2:14 teaching. ***B*** had taught Balak

BALAK
Numbers
22:10 God, "Moab's King ***B***, Zippor's son,
23:30 ***B*** did just as Balaam said. He offered a
Joshua
24:9 Then Moab's King ***B***, Zippor's son, set
Judges
11:25 than Moab's King ***B***, Zippor's son?
Micah
6:5 what Moab's King ***B*** had planned, and
Revelation
2:14 Balaam had taught ***B*** to trip up the

BAPTISM
Mark
10:38 I drink or receive the ***b*** I receive?"
11:30 Was John's ***b*** of heavenly or of human
Luke
12:50 I have a ***b*** I must experience. How I am
20:4 Was John's ***b*** of heavenly or of human
Acts
10:37 in Galilee after the ***b*** John preached.
13:24 the Israelites a ***b*** to show they were
18:25 aware only of the ***b*** John proclaimed
19:3 he said, "What ***b*** did you receive,
19:4 baptized with a ***b*** by which people
Romans
6:4 with him through ***b*** into his death,
Ephesians
4:5 There is one Lord, one faith, one ***b***
Colossians
2:12 with him through ***b*** and raised with
James
2:7 good name spoken over you at your ***b***?
1 Peter
3:21 ***B*** is like that. It saves you now—not

BAPTIZE
Matthew
3:11 I ***b*** with water those of you who have
21:25 his authority to ***b***? Did he get it
John
1:25 Why do you ***b*** if you aren't the
1:33 who sent me to ***b*** with water said
Acts
11:16 words: 'John will ***b*** with water, but
1 Corinthians
1:14 God that I didn't ***b*** any of you,
1:17 didn't send me to ***b*** but to preach the

BAPTIZED
Matthew
3:14 I need to be ***b*** by you, yet you
3:16 When Jesus was ***b***, he immediately came up
Mark
1:4 for people to be ***b*** to show that they

16:16 believes and is ***b*** will be saved,
John
3:23 were coming to him and being ***b***.
10:40 where John had ***b*** at first, and he
Acts
1:5 John ***b*** with water, but in only a few
2:38 of you must be ***b*** in the name of
8:12 Christ, both men and women were ***b***.
9:18 could see again. He got up and was ***b***.
10:47 them from being ***b*** with water, can
11:16 but you will be ***b*** with the Holy
16:15 household were ***b***, she urged, "Now
18:8 believed and were ***b*** after listening
19:5 Paul, they were ***b*** in the name of
22:16 for? Get up, be ***b***, and wash away
Romans
6:3 that all who were ***b*** into Christ Jesus
1 Corinthians
1:13 for you, or were you ***b*** in Paul's name?
10:2 All were ***b*** into Moses in the cloud and
12:13 We were all ***b*** by one Spirit into one
15:29 who are getting ***b*** for the dead
Galatians
3:27 of you who were ***b*** into Christ have

BARABBAS
Matthew
27:16 a well-known prisoner named Jesus ***B***.
27:26 Then he released ***B*** to them. He had
Mark
15:7 A man named ***B*** was locked up with the
15:11 to have him release ***B*** to them instead.
15:15 so he released ***B*** to them. He had
Luke
23:18 Away with this man! Release ***B*** to us."
23:19 (***B*** had been thrown into prison because
John
18:40 this man! Give us ***B***!" (Barabbas was

BARAK
Judges
4:6 She sent word to ***B***, Abinoam's son,
4:22 Just then, ***B*** arrived after chasing
1 Samuel
12:11 sent Jerubbaal, ***B***, Jephthah, and
Hebrews
11:32 you about Gideon, ***B***, Samson,

BARNABAS
Acts
4:36 nicknamed ***B*** (that is, "one
1 Corinthians
9:6 is it only I and ***B*** who don't have
Galatians
2:1 again with ***B***, and I took Titus
2:13 so that even ***B*** got carried away

BARTHOLOMEW
Matthew
10:3 Philip; and ***B***; Thomas; and Matthew the
Mark
3:18 Andrew; Philip; ***B***; Matthew; Thomas;
Luke
6:14 brother Andrew; James; John; Philip; ***B***;
Acts
1:13 and Thomas; ***B*** and Matthew;

BARUCH
Nehemiah
3:20 After him, ***B***, Zabbai's son, thoroughly
Jeremiah
32:16 the documents to ***B***, Neriah's son, I
36:8 ***B***, Neriah's son, did everything the
36:10 Then ***B*** read Jeremiah's words from the

BASES
Exodus
26:19 make forty silver ***b*** to go under the

BASHAN
Numbers
21:33 the road of ***B***. Og, Bashan's
Joshua
13:30 Mahanaim, all ***B***, the whole
22:7 of Manasseh in ***B***. But Joshua
Nehemiah
9:22 Heshbon and the land of King Og of ***B***.
Psalms
22:12 me; mighty bulls from ***B*** encircle me.
Amos
4:1 word, you cows of ***B***, who are on Mount
Micah
7:14 Let them graze in ***B*** and Gilead, as a
Zechariah
11:2 Scream, oaks of ***B***, for the deep

BASKET
Exodus
2:3 she took a reed ***b*** and sealed it up
Amos
8:1 God showed me: a ***b*** of summer fruit.
Matthew
5:15 put it under a ***b***. Instead, they
Acts
9:25 lowered him in a ***b*** through an
2 Corinthians
11:33 lowered in a ***b*** through a window

BATHE
Exodus
2:5 came down to ***b*** in the river,
Ruth
3:3 You should ***b***, put on some perfume,
Psalms
23:5 my enemies. You ***b*** my head in oil;

BATHSHEBA
2 Samuel
11:3 Eliam's daughter ***B***, the wife of
12:24 his wife ***B***. He went to her
1 Kings
1:28 Bring me ***B***." She came and
2:19 So ***B*** went to King Solomon to talk with
Psalms
51:1 he had been with ***B***.] Have mercy on

BATTLE
Exodus
13:18 out of the land of Egypt ready for ***b***.
Leviticus
26:7 and they will fall before you in ***b***.
26:8 your enemies will fall before you in ***b***.
Joshua
4:13 to the plains of Jericho, ready for ***b***.

8:14 to meet Israel in ***b***. They moved out
11:19 They captured every single one in ***b***.
Psalms
18:29 I can charge into ***b***; with my God I
24:8 and powerful! The LORD—powerful in ***b***!
76:3 the sword—even the ***b*** itself! Selah
78:9 with bows, retreated on the day of ***b***.
89:43 his sword and didn't support him in ***b***.
110:3 on your day of ***b***. "In holy
140:7 protected my head on the day of ***b***.
144:1 who taught my fingers how to do ***b***!
Proverbs
21:31 for the day of ***b***, but victory
28:4 those who follow Instruction ***b*** them.
Ecclesiastes
9:11 swift, nor the ***b*** to the mighty,
Ezekiel
13:5 withstand the ***b*** on the day of the
Hosea
10:14 on the day of ***b***, when mothers
Matthew
26:53 more than twelve ***b*** groups of angels
1 Corinthians
14:8 then who will prepare for ***b***?
Revelation
9:7 horses ready for ***b***. On their heads
16:14 gather them for ***b*** on the great day
20:8 gather them for ***b***. Their number is

BEAR → BEAR FRUIT, BEAR THEIR GUILT
Genesis
3:16 in pain you will ***b*** children. You
Deuteronomy
21:15 Both wives ***b*** children, but the
Ruth
1:12 and even more, if I were to ***b*** sons—
1 Samuel
17:34 ever a lion or a ***b*** came and carried
2 Samuel
17:8 as a wild ***b*** robbed of her
Job
9:9 made the ***B*** and Orion, Pleiades and the
38:32 proper times, lead the ***B*** with her cubs?
Proverbs
9:12 are cynical, you will ***b*** it all alone.
17:12 Safer to meet a ***b*** robbed of her cubs
28:15 like a growling lion or a prowling ***b***.
Isaiah
11:7 The cow and the ***b*** will graze. Their
Lamentations
3:10 He is a ***b*** lurking for me, a lion in
Daniel
7:5 one, like a ***b***. It was raised on
Matthew
11:30 yoke is easy to ***b***, and my burden is
13:23 understand, and ***b*** fruit and produce-
21:19 never again ***b*** fruit!" The fig
Mark
4:20 embrace it. They ***b*** fruit, in one
Romans
7:4 dead so that we can ***b*** fruit for God.
Galatians
6:17 me because I ***b*** the marks of
1 Peter
4:16 honor God as you ***b*** Christ's name.

BEAR FRUIT
2Ki 19:30; Ps 92:14; Is 37:31; 45:8; Jer 12:2; 17:8; Eze 17:8; 17:23; 34:27; Mt 13:23; 21:19; Mk 4:20; Lk 8:15; Ro 7:4

BEAR THEIR GUILT
Is 53:11; Eze 14:10; 44:10, 12; Hos 10:2

BEARS
1 Samuel
17:36 both lions and ***b***. This
17:37 of both lions and ***b***, will rescue me
2 Kings
2:24 name. Then two ***b*** came out of the

BEAST
Daniel
7:5 I saw another ***b***, a second one,
Revelation
11:7 witnessing, the ***b*** that comes up
13:1 and I saw a ***b*** coming up out of the sea.
14:9 any worship the ***b*** and its image,
15:2 victory over the ***b***, its image, and
17:3 on a scarlet ***b*** that was covered
18:2 lair for every unclean and disgusting ***b***
19:19 I saw that the ***b*** and the kings of
20:4 worshipped the ***b*** or its image, who

BEASTS
Job
4:10 of the king of ***b***—yet the teeth of
Ezekiel
8:10 form of loathsome ***b*** and creeping
38:20 in the sky, the ***b*** of the field, all
Daniel
7:3 Four giant ***b*** emerged from the sea, each
Zephaniah
1:3 humanity and the ***b***; I will destroy
Haggai
1:11 on humanity, on ***b***, and upon
Acts
11:6 wild ***b***

BEAT
Exodus
9:25 The hail ***b*** down everything that was in
Deuteronomy
24:20 when you ***b*** the olives off
Isaiah
2:4 Then they will ***b*** their swords into
Joel
3:10 ***B*** the iron tips of your plows into
Jonah
4:8 wind, and the sun ***b*** down on Jonah's
Micah
4:3 away. They will ***b*** their swords into
Matthew
26:67 in his face and ***b*** him. They hit him
Luke
10:30 him naked, ***b*** him up, and left
22:63 custody taunted him while they ***b*** him.

BEATEN
Exodus
5:16 are being ***b***! Your own people
Acts
16:22 of their clothes and ***b*** with a rod.

2 Corinthians
11:23 often. I've been ***b*** more times than I
11:25 I was ***b*** with rods three times. I was

BEAUTIFUL

Genesis
2:9 God grew every ***b*** tree with edible
12:14 the Egyptians saw how ***b*** his wife was.
29:17 but Rachel had a ***b*** figure and was
Exodus
2:2 was healthy and ***b***, so she hid him
2 Samuel
11:2 a woman bathing; the woman was very ***b***.
13:1 with Tamar the ***b*** sister of
Esther
1:4 his kingdom and ***b*** treasures as
2:2 a search made for ***b*** young women who
2:3 bring all the ***b*** young women
2:7 The girl had a ***b*** figure and was
Job
42:15 the land were as ***b*** as Job's
Psalms
16:11 celebration. ***B*** things are always
48:2 is a ***b*** summit, the joy of the whole
135:3 praises to God's name because it is ***b***!
147:1 it is a pleasure to make ***b*** praise!
Proverbs
11:22 a pig's nose is a ***b*** woman who lacks
Song of Songs
1:8 your way, most ***b*** of women, then
4:1 Look at you—so ***b***, my dearest! Look at
5:9 who are the most ***b*** of women? How is
6:1 who are the most ***b*** of women? Which
7:6 You are so ***b***, so lovely—my love,
Isaiah
52:7 How ***b*** upon the mountains are the feet
Jeremiah
3:19 and give you a ***b*** land, an
Lamentations
2:20 their own ***b*** babies? Should
Ezekiel
16:39 take your ***b*** jewels, and they
27:4 and it's your builders who made you ***b***.
31:7 It became ***b*** in its greatness and in its
Daniel
4:12 Its leaves were ***b***, its fruit abundant;
8:9 the south, the east, and the ***b*** country.
11:16 his place in the ***b*** country, and he
Amos
8:13 On that day the ***b*** young women and the
Matthew
23:27 tombs. They look ***b*** on the outside.
Acts
3:2 gate known as the ***B*** Gate so he could
3:10 at the temple's ***B*** Gate asking for
Romans
10:15 is written, How ***b*** are the feet of
1 Corinthians
14:17 You may offer a ***b*** prayer of
Hebrews
11:23 the child was ***b*** and they weren't
1 Peter
3:4 make yourselves ***b*** on the inside, in

BEAUTY

Esther
1:11 to show off her ***b*** both to the
2:3 he might provide ***b*** treatments for
Psalms
26:8 I love the ***b*** of your house, LORD; I
27:4 seeing the LORD's ***b*** and constantly
37:20 like the ***b*** of a meadow—in
45:11 king desire your ***b***. Because he is
50:2 Zion, perfect in ***b***, God shines
96:6 him; strength and ***b*** are in his
Proverbs
6:25 Don't desire her ***b*** in secret; don't let
31:30 is deceptive and ***b*** fleeting, but a
Hosea
14:6 spread out; his ***b*** will be like the
James
1:11 fall and its ***b*** is lost. Just
1 Peter
3:4 This type of ***b*** is very precious

BED

Leviticus
15:4 Any ***b*** on which someone with an emission
15:5 touches such a ***b*** must wash their
Deuteronomy
3:11 the Rephaim. His ***b*** was made of iron.
1 Samuel
9:25 to the town, a ***b*** was made for Saul
19:13 laid it in the ***b***, putting some
2 Samuel
4:7 was lying on the ***b*** in his bedroom.
1 Kings
17:19 was staying. Elijah laid him on his ***b***.
2 Chronicles
24:25 killed him in his ***b***. He died and was
Job
7:13 comfort me," my ***b*** will diminish my
17:13 my dwelling, lay out my ***b*** in darkness,
33:15 humans, during their slumber on a ***b***,
33:19 by pain while in ***b***, bones ever aching
Psalms
4:4 about it in your ***b*** and weep over it!
6:6 I drench my ***b*** with tears; I
36:4 while resting in ***b***! They commit
41:3 they are lying in ***b***, sick. You will
63:6 ponder you on my ***b***, whenever I
132:3 enter my house, won't get into my ***b***.
Proverbs
7:16 I've spread my ***b*** with luxurious covers,
22:27 they be able to take your ***b*** from you?
Song of Songs
1:16 Yes, our ***b*** is lush and green!
3:1 Upon my ***b***, night after night, I looked
3:7 Picture Solomon's ***b***—sixty heroic men
Amos
3:12 the corner of a ***b***, and those in
Micah
2:1 when they are in ***b***. By the light of
Matthew
8:14 mother-in-law lying in ***b*** with a fever.
Mark
1:30 was in ***b***, sick with a
2:9 Get up, take up your ***b***, and walk'?
Luke
8:16 puts it under a ***b***. Instead, they
11:7 and I are in ***b***. I can't get up
17:34 be in the same ***b***: one will be

Acts
9:33 been confined to his ***b*** for eight years.
9:34 up and make your ***b***." At once he got

BEELZEBUL
Matthew
10:25 head of the house ***B***, it's certain
12:24 the authority of ***B***, the ruler of the
Mark
3:22 possessed by ***B***. He throws out
Luke
11:15 the authority of ***B***, the ruler of
11:18 throw out demons by the authority of ***B***.
11:19 the authority of ***B***, then by whose

BEER-SHEBA → DAN TO BEER-SHEBA
Genesis
21:31 of that place is ***B*** because there
26:33 the city's name has been ***B*** until today.
Judges
20:1 from Dan to ***B***, as well as from
1 Samuel
3:20 from Dan to ***B*** knew that Samuel
2 Samuel
3:10 over Judah, from Dan all the way to ***B***!"

BEGINNING
Mark
1:1 The ***b*** of the good news about Jesus
10:6 At the ***b*** of creation, God made them
Luke
1:3 from the ***b***, I have also
John
1:1 In the ***b*** was the Word and the Word was
Hebrews
1:10 in the ***b***, and the heavens
7:3 family. He has no ***b*** or end of life,
1 John
1:1 existed from the ***b***, what we have
Revelation
21:6 the Omega, the ***b*** and the end. To
22:13 first and the last, the ***b*** and the end.

BELIEVE → BELIEVE HIM, BELIEVE IN HIM
Job
9:16 me, I couldn't ***b*** that he heard my
29:24 they couldn't ***b*** it. They never
Proverbs
14:15 The naive ***b*** anything, but the prudent
26:25 graciously, don't ***b*** them, for seven
Jeremiah
28:15 is persuading these people to ***b*** a lie.
Habakkuk
1:5 days that you wouldn't ***b*** even if told.
Matthew
9:28 to them, "Do you ***b*** I can do this?"
18:6 little ones who ***b*** in me to trip and
24:23 or 'He's over here,' don't ***b*** it.
Mark
16:11 news, they didn't ***b*** that Jesus was
Luke
22:67 answered, "If I tell you, you won't ***b***.
24:11 nonsense, and they didn't ***b*** the women.
John
1:7 him everyone would ***b*** in the light.
1:50 answered, "Do you ***b*** because I told
3:12 and you don't ***b***, how will you
5:38 because you don't ***b*** the one whom he
8:45 I speak the truth, you don't ***b*** me.
9:18 leaders didn't ***b*** the man had been
9:35 said, "Do you ***b*** in the Human One?"
9:38 said, "Lord, I ***b***." And he
10:38 and you don't ***b*** me, believe the
11:15 so that you can ***b***. Let's go to him."
11:27 Yes, Lord, I ***b*** that you are the
11:40 you that if you ***b***, you will see
17:20 for those who ***b*** in me because of
17:21 that the world will ***b*** that you sent me.
19:35 has testified so that you also can ***b***.
20:25 put my hand into his side, I won't ***b***."
20:31 so that you will ***b*** that Jesus is the
Acts
8:12 they came to ***b*** Philip, who
8:13 himself came to ***b*** and was baptized.
11:21 number came to ***b*** and turned to the
13:12 place, he came to ***b***, for he was
16:34 in his household had come to ***b*** in God.
17:12 Many came to ***b***, including a number
18:8 household came to ***b*** in the Lord. Many
18:27 those who had come to ***b*** through grace.
19:2 when you came to ***b***?" They replied,
19:4 whom they were to ***b***. This one is
28:24 what he said, but others refused to ***b***.
Romans
2:3 this: Do you ***b*** that you will
8:18 I ***b*** that the present suffering is
15:31 Judea who don't ***b***. Also, pray that
1 Corinthians
1:21 to save those who ***b*** through the
3:5 who helped you to ***b***. Each one had a
7:12 wife who doesn't ***b***, and she agrees
11:18 divisions among you, and I partly ***b*** it.
14:22 those who don't ***b***, not for those
2 Corinthians
6:14 people who don't ***b***. What does
6:15 in common with someone who doesn't ***b***?
Galatians
3:7 those who ***b*** are the children of
3:9 those who ***b*** are blessed
1 Thessalonians
4:14 Since we ***b*** that Jesus died and rose, so
Hebrews
11:6 near to God must ***b*** that he exists
James
2:19 good that you ***b*** that God is one.
1 Peter
2:7 honors you who ***b***. For those who
2:8 they refuse to ***b*** in the word, they
3:1 of them refuse to ***b*** the word, they
4:17 those who refuse to ***b*** God's good news?
1 John
3:23 that we ***b*** in the name of
4:1 friends, don't ***b*** every spirit.
5:10 one who doesn't ***b*** God has made God
5:13 things to you who ***b*** in the name of

BELIEVE HIM
2Ch 32:15; Mt 21:25; 21:32; Mk 11:31; Lk 20:5

BELIEVE IN HIM

Mt 27:42; Jn 3:18; 6:29, 40; 7:5; 8:30; 9:36; 11:48; 12:37; 1Ti 1:16

BELIEVED → BELIEVED IN HIM

Exodus
4:31 The people ***b***. When they heard that the
14:31 LORD, and they ***b*** in the LORD and
Jonah
3:5 people of Nineveh ***b*** God. They
Matthew
8:13 just as you have ***b***." And his servant
9:29 happen for you just as you have ***b***."
21:32 and prostitutes ***b*** him. Yet even
Luke
1:45 Happy is she who ***b*** that the Lord would
John
1:12 him, those who ***b*** in his name, he
2:11 his glory, and his disciples ***b*** in him.
4:39 in that city ***b*** in Jesus because
4:41 Many more ***b*** because of his word
4:50 lives." The man ***b*** the word that
4:53 he and his entire household ***b*** in Jesus.
5:46 If you ***b*** Moses, you would believe me,
7:31 from that crowd ***b*** in Jesus. They
8:31 to the Jews who ***b*** in him, "You are
10:42 Many ***b*** in Jesus there
11:45 Mary and saw what Jesus did ***b*** in him.
12:38 Lord, who has ***b*** through our
12:42 so, many leaders ***b*** in him, but they
12:43 They ***b***, but they loved human praise
16:27 have loved me and ***b*** that I came from
17:8 from you, and they ***b*** that you sent me.
20:8 first, also went inside. He saw and ***b***.
Acts
8:20 you because you ***b*** you could buy
11:17 he gave us who ***b*** in the Lord Jesus
13:48 who was appointed for eternal life ***b***,
14:1 a huge number of Jews and Greeks ***b***.
14:9 and saw that he ***b*** he could be
18:8 Many Corinthians ***b*** and were baptized
1 Corinthians
15:2 unless somehow you ***b*** it for nothing.
15:11 we preach and this is what you have ***b***.
Galatians
2:16 We ourselves ***b*** in Christ Jesus
3:6 way that Abraham "***b*** God and it was
3:9 blessed together with Abraham who ***b***.
Ephesians
1:13 Holy Spirit because you ***b*** in Christ.
Philippians
1:5 from the time you first ***b*** it until now.
2 Thessalonians
1:10 everyone who has ***b***—and our testimony
1 Timothy
3:16 the nations, ***b*** in around the
Hebrews
11:11 because she ***b*** that the one who
James
2:23 says, Abraham ***b*** God, and God
1 John
4:16 known and have ***b*** the love that God
5:10 that one has not ***b*** the testimony

BELIEVED IN HIM

Jn 2:11; 7:39, 48; 8:31; 11:45; 12:42

BELIEVERS → FELLOW BELIEVERS

John
17:25 you, and these ***b*** know that you
Acts
1:15 the family of ***b*** was a company of
2:42 The ***b*** devoted themselves to the
4:4 the word became ***b*** and their number
4:32 The community of ***b*** was one in heart
5:14 more and more ***b*** in the Lord,
6:8 out among the ***b*** for the way God's
8:15 that the new ***b*** would receive the
9:30 the family of ***b*** learned about
10:23 together with some of the ***b*** from Joppa.
10:45 The circumcised ***b*** who had come with
12:12 as Mark.) Many ***b*** had gathered
15:1 the family of ***b***, "Unless you are
16:4 Gentile ***b*** to keep the
17:6 Jason and some ***b*** before the city
21:12 we and the local ***b*** urged Paul not to
1 Corinthians
6:5 wise enough to pass judgment between ***b***?
8:6 However, for us ***b***, There is one God
14:22 is a sign for ***b***, not for those
2 Corinthians
11:9 things. The ***b*** who came from
Ephesians
1:18 of God's glorious inheritance among ***b***,
1:19 working among us ***b***. This power is
3:18 height and depth, together with all ***b***.
5:4 acceptable for ***b***. Instead, there
6:18 hanging in there and praying for all ***b***.
1 Thessalonians
1:7 to all the ***b*** in Macedonia and
2:10 and blameless we were toward you ***b***.
2:13 it continues to work in you who are ***b***.
1 Timothy
3:6 shouldn't be new ***b*** so that they
4:6 things out to the ***b***, you will be a
4:12 example for the ***b*** through your
6:2 masters who are ***b*** shouldn't look
Titus
1:10 some of those who are Jewish ***b***.
Hebrews
10:25 with other ***b***, which some
1 Peter
1:22 for your fellow ***b***, love each other
2:17 the family of ***b***. Have respectful
3:8 of your fellow ***b***, compassionate,
5:9 that your fellow ***b*** are enduring the

BELIEVES → BELIEVES IN HIM, WHOEVER BELIEVES

Mark
11:23 doesn't waver but ***b*** that what is said
16:16 Whoever ***b*** and is baptized will be
John
3:36 Whoever ***b*** in the Son has eternal life.
5:24 hears my word and ***b*** in the one who
11:25 the life. Whoever ***b*** in me will live,
12:44 shouted, "Whoever ***b*** in me doesn't
14:12 you that whoever ***b*** in me will do the
Acts
13:39 everyone who ***b*** is put in right

Romans
12:17 for what everyone else ***b*** is good.
14:2 One person ***b*** in eating everything,
1 Corinthians
9:5 with a wife who ***b*** like the rest of
1 John
5:1 Everyone who ***b*** that Jesus is the Christ
5:5 it the one who ***b*** that Jesus is
5:10 The one who ***b*** in God's Son has the

BELIEVES IN HIM
Jn 3:15; 3:16, 18; Ac 10:43; 1Pt 2:6

BELLY
Genesis
3:14 animals. On your ***b*** you will crawl,
Leviticus
11:42 that moves on its ***b*** or anything that
Job
10:19 existed, taken from the ***b*** to the grave.
Jonah
1:17 Jonah was in the ***b*** of the fish for
2:1 LORD his God from the ***b*** of the fish:
Matthew
12:40 in the whale's ***b*** for three days

BELONG → BELONG TO CHRIST, BELONG TO HIM, BELONG TO THE LORD
Genesis
40:8 interpretations ***b*** to God? Describe
Deuteronomy
21:17 The oldest male's rights ***b*** to that son.
Ruth
2:5 To whom does this young woman ***b***?"
Psalms
47:9 earth's guardians ***b*** to God; God is
50:12 and everything in it already ***b*** to me.
104:18 high mountains ***b*** to the mountain
Proverbs
16:1 To people ***b*** the plans of the heart, but
Luke
16:8 People who ***b*** to this world are
Acts
27:23 the God to whom I ***b*** and whom I
Romans
14:8 whether we live or die, we ***b*** to God.
1 Corinthians
1:12 of you says, "I ***b*** to Paul," "I

BELONG TO CHRIST
Mk 9:41; 1Co 1:12; 3:23; 15:23; 2Co 10:7; Ga 5:24

BELONG TO HIM
Ps 95:4; 100:3; Hab 2:6; 3:6; Ro 8:9; 1Co 8:6; 1Ti 6:16; 2Ti 2:19

BELONG TO THE LORD
Ex 13:12; Lv 27:30; 1Sa 2:8; 2Ki 11:17; Zec 9:1; Mal 3:3; 1Co 10:26

BELOW
Genesis
6:16 side. In the hold ***b***, make the second
Exodus
20:4 or on the earth ***b*** or in the waters
John
8:23 You are from ***b***; I'm from above.
Acts
2:19 on the earth ***b***, blood and fire
Romans
10:7 into the region ***b***?"

BELSHAZZAR
Daniel
5:1 King ***B*** threw a huge party for a
7:1 of Babylon's King ***B***, Daniel had a

BELT
Exodus
28:8 The vest's ***b*** should be attached to it
1 Samuel
18:4 well as his sword, his bow, and his ***b***.
Daniel
10:5 a brilliant gold ***b*** around his waist,
Matthew
3:4 with a leather ***b*** around his waist.
Acts
21:11 us, took Paul's ***b***, tied his own
Ephesians
6:14 So stand with the ***b*** of truth around

BELTESHAZZAR
Daniel
1:7 He named Daniel "***B***," Hananiah
2:26 (whose name was ***B***), "Can you really
4:8 who is called ***B*** after the name of
5:12 the king named ***B***—possesses an extraordinary spirit
10:1 who was called ***B***. The message was

BEN-HADAD
1 Kings
15:18 to Aram's King ***B***, Tabrimmon's son
20:34 ***B*** said to the king, "I will return the
2 Kings
6:24 that Aram's King ***B*** gathered all his
13:24 died. His son ***B*** succeeded him as
2 Chronicles
16:2 to Aram's King ***B*** who ruled in
16:4 ***B*** agreed with King Asa and sent his
Jeremiah
49:27 it will burn up the fortresses of ***B***.
Amos
1:4 it will devour the palaces of ***B***.

BENAIAH
2 Samuel
8:18 Jehoiada's son ***B*** was in command of the
23:22 Jehoiada's son ***B*** did. He made a
1 Kings
1:8 Jehoiada's son ***B***, the prophet
4:4 the general ***B***, Jehoiada's son; the
1 Chronicles
4:36 Jeshohaiah, Asaiah, Adiel, Jesimiel, ***B***,
11:22 ***B***, Jehoiada's son from Kabzeel, was a
27:6 This ***B*** was a warrior of the Thirty and
2 Chronicles
20:14 Zechariah son of ***B*** son of Jeiel son
31:13 Mahath, and ***B*** served as
Ezra
10:25 Mijamin, Eleazar, Hashabiah, and ***B***.

BENEFIT
2 Samuel
21:3 so you can ***b*** from the LORD's
Job
35:3 What does it ***b*** you? What have I
Proverbs
9:12 it is to your ***b***; if you are
Ecclesiastes
5:11 what do owners ***b*** from such goods,
Romans
3:1 a Jew? Or what's the ***b*** of circumcision?

BENJAMIN
Genesis
35:18 Ben-oni, but his father named him ***B***.
Exodus
1:3 Issachar, Zebulun, and ***B***
Numbers
1:36 descendants of ***B***, registered by
Deuteronomy
27:12 Levi, Judah, Issachar, Joseph, and ***B***.
33:12 He said to ***B***: "The LORD's dearest one
Joshua
21:4 the tribes of Judah, Simeon, and ***B***.
21:17 From the tribe of ***B***: Gibeon and its
Ezra
1:5 of Judah and ***B***, and the priests
Psalms
68:27 There's ***B*** leading them, though he's
80:2 before Ephraim, ***B***, and Manasseh!
Jeremiah
1:1 priests from Anathoth in the land of ***B***.
6:1 Escape, people of ***B***, get out of
Ezekiel
48:22 of Judah and the boundary of ***B***.
Acts
13:21 from the tribe of ***B***, and he served as
Romans
11:1 of Abraham, from the tribe of ***B***.
Philippians
3:5 and the tribe of ***B***. I am a Hebrew of
Revelation
7:8 from the tribe of ***B***, twelve thousand

BETH-HORON
Joshua
10:10 on the way up to ***B*** and struck them

BETH-SHEAN
Joshua
17:11 and in Asher were ***B*** and its dependent

BETH-SHEMESH
Joshua
15:10 went down to ***B***, and passed by

BETHANY
Matthew
21:17 of the city to ***B*** and spent the
26:6 When Jesus was at ***B*** visiting the house
Mark
11:1 to Bethphage and ***B*** at the Mount of
11:11 he returned to ***B*** with the Twelve.
11:12 day, after leaving ***B***, Jesus was hungry.
14:3 Jesus was at ***B*** visiting the house of
Luke
19:29 to Bethphage and ***B*** on the Mount of
24:50 out as far as ***B***, where he lifted
John
1:28 the Jordan in ***B*** where John was
11:1 ill. He was from ***B***, the village of
11:18 ***B*** was a little less than two miles from
12:1 Jesus came to ***B***, home of Lazarus,

BETHEL
Genesis
12:8 mountains east of ***B***, and pitched his
28:19 that sacred place ***B***, though Luz was
31:13 I am the God of ***B***, where you anointed
35:8 and was buried at ***B*** under the oak,
Joshua
8:9 stayed between ***B*** and Ai, to the
Judges
20:18 marched up to ***B*** to ask for
1 Samuel
7:16 traveled between ***B***, Gilgal, and
1 Kings
12:29 put one calf in ***B***, and the other he
2 Kings
2:2 has sent me to ***B***." But Elisha
10:29 the gold calves that were in ***B*** and Dan.
23:15 altar that was in ***B***. That was the
Amos
4:4 Come to ***B***—and commit a crime;
7:10 the priest of ***B***, reported to

BETHLEHEM
Ruth
1:1 sons went from ***B*** of Judah to dwell
2:4 Boaz arrived from ***B***. He said to the
4:11 and may you preserve a name in ***B***.
1 Samuel
16:1 you to Jesse of ***B*** because I have
20:28 David begged my permission to go to ***B***.
2 Samuel
2:32 father's tomb in ***B***. Then Joab and
Micah
5:2 As for you, ***B*** of Ephrathah, though you
Matthew
2:1 Jesus was born in ***B*** in the territory
2:5 They said, "In ***B*** of Judea, for this is
2:6 You, ***B***, land of Judah, by no means are
2:8 He sent them to ***B***, saying, "Go and
2:16 male children in ***B*** and in all the
Luke
2:4 to David's city, called ***B***, in Judea.
2:15 go right now to ***B*** and see what's
John
7:42 family and from ***B***, David's village?"

BETHSAIDA
Matthew
11:21 will be for you, ***B***! For if the
Mark
6:45 the lake, toward ***B***, while he
8:22 disciples came to ***B***. Some people
Luke
9:10 withdrew privately to a city called ***B***.
10:13 will be for you, ***B***. If the miracles
John
1:44 Philip was from ***B***, the hometown of
5:2 the Aramaic name ***B***. It had five

12:21 who was from ***B*** in Galilee, and

BETHUEL
Genesis
22:23 ***B*** became the father of Rebekah. These
24:15 of ***B*** the son of Milcah
28:5 to Laban son of ***B*** the Aramean and

BETRAY
Psalms
89:33 from him. I won't ***b*** my faithfulness.
Matthew
26:21 assure you that one of you will ***b*** me."
Luke
22:48 Judas, would you ***b*** the Human One
John
6:64 believe and the one who would ***b*** him.
6:71 one of the Twelve, was going to ***b*** him.
13:2 Simon Iscariot's son, to ***b*** Jesus.
21:20 him, "Lord, who is going to ***b*** you?"

BETTER
Exodus
14:12 would have been ***b*** for us to work
Numbers
11:18 to eat? It was ***b*** for us in Egypt."
Proverbs
3:14 Her profit is ***b*** than silver, and her
8:11 Wisdom is ***b*** than pearls; nothing is
16:16 wisdom is much ***b*** than gold, and
21:9 ***B*** to live on the edge of a roof than
21:19 ***B*** to live in a wilderness than in a
25:24 ***B*** to live on the edge of a roof than to
27:5 correction is ***b*** than hidden love.
28:6 ***B*** to be poor and walk in innocence
Ecclesiastes
3:19 Humans are no ***b*** off than animals
3:22 there was nothing ***b*** for human beings
8:15 there's nothing ***b*** for people to do
Jonah
4:3 it would be ***b*** for me to die
Matthew
5:29 it away. It's ***b*** that you lose a
11:22 and Sidon will be ***b*** off on Judgment
11:24 that it will be ***b*** for the land of
18:6 sin, it would be ***b*** for them to have
18:8 it away. It's ***b*** to enter into
18:9 it away. It's ***b*** to enter into
19:10 his wife, then it's ***b*** not to marry."
25:9 yours. We have a ***b*** idea. You go to
26:24 would have been ***b*** for him if he had
Mark
9:43 chop it off. It's ***b*** for you to enter
Luke
5:39 but says, 'The well-aged wine is ***b***.'"
John
4:52 started to get ***b***. And they said,
11:50 see that it is ***b*** for you that one
16:7 you that it is ***b*** for you that I go
18:14 that it was ***b*** for one person to
Romans
11:18 brag like you're ***b*** than the other
1 Corinthians
7:9 because it's ***b*** to marry than to
Philippians
1:21 serves Christ and dying is even ***b***.
Hebrews
11:4 Abel offered a ***b*** sacrifice to God
1 Peter
3:17 It is ***b*** to suffer for doing good (if
2 Peter
2:21 It would be ***b*** for them never to have

BEYOND THE JORDAN
Dt 1:5; 3:8; Mt 4:25; Mk 3:8; 10:1

BEYOND THE RIVER
Ezr 4:10; 4:11, 16, 17, 20; 5:3, 6; 6:6, 8, 13; 7:21, 25; 8:36; Neh 2:7; 2:9; 3:7

BIG
Exodus
29:20 hands, and on the ***b*** toes of their
Leviticus
8:23 right thumb, and on his right ***b*** toe.
14:14 and the right ***b*** toe of the person

BILDAD
Job
2:11 -Eliphaz of Teman, ***B*** of Shuah, and
8:1 ***B*** from Shuah responded
18:1 ***B*** from Shuah answered
25:1 ***B*** from Shuah replied
42:9 from Teman, ***B*** from Shuah, and

BILHAH
Genesis
29:29 given his servant ***B*** to his daughter
30:3 my servant ***B***. Sleep with her,
35:22 and slept with ***B*** his father's
35:25 The sons of ***B***, Rachel's servant, were
1 Chronicles
4:29 ***B***, Ezem, Tolad

BIRD
Genesis
6:20 From each kind of ***b***, from each kind of
Leviticus
1:17 then tear the ***b*** open by its
Deuteronomy
14:11 You are allowed to eat any clean ***b***
Psalms
11:1 say to me, "Flee to the hills like a ***b***
50:11 every mountain ***b***; even the insects
102:7 I'm all alone like a ***b*** on a roof.
124:7 We escaped like a ***b*** from the hunters'
Proverbs
1:17 to cast a net in the sight of a ***b***.
6:5 a hunter, like a ***b*** from the hand of
7:23 his liver, like a ***b*** hurrying to the
27:8 Like a ***b*** wandering from its nest, so is
Daniel
7:6 four wings like ***b*** wings. This beast
Revelation
18:2 for every unclean ***b***, and a lair for

BIRDS
Psalms
8:8 the ***b*** in the sky, the fish of the
104:17 where the ***b*** make their nests, where the
148:10 that creep along and you ***b*** that fly!
Isaiah
16:2 are like orphaned ***b*** pushed from the

BIRDS [cont.]

Matthew
6:26 Look at the ***b*** in the sky. They don't
Luke
8:5 crushed, and the ***b*** in the sky came
9:58 have dens and the ***b*** in the sky have
12:24 You are worth so much more than ***b***!
Revelation
19:17 said to all the ***b*** flying high

BIRTH → BIRTH TO A SON

Ecclesiastes
3:2 a time for giving ***b*** and a time for
Matthew
1:18 This is how the ***b*** of Jesus Christ took
19:12 been eunuchs from ***b***. And there are
Luke
2:7 She gave ***b*** to her firstborn child, a
John
9:1 he saw a man who was blind from ***b***.
Acts
3:2 crippled since ***b*** was being carried
22:28 Paul said, "I'm a citizen by ***b***."
1 Peter
1:3 has given us new ***b***. You have been
1:23 been given new ***b***—not from the type
Revelation
12:13 who had given ***b*** to the male child.

BIRTH TO A SON

Gn 4:25; 16:11, 15; 17:19; 19:37, 38; 21:2, 7; 24:36; 29:32, 33, 34, 35; 30:5, 10, 23; 38:3, 4; Ex 2:2; 2:22; Lv 12:2; Jdg 13:3; 13:5, 7, 24; Ru 4:13; 1Sa 1:20; 4:20; 2Sa 12:24; 2Ki 4:17; 1Ch 7:16; 7:23; Is 7:14; 8:3; Hos 1:8; Mt 1:21; 1:23, 25; Lk 1:31; Rev 12:5

BITTER

Exodus
12:8 with unleavened bread and ***b*** herbs.
Numbers
9:11 lamb with unleavened bread and ***b*** herbs.
Isaiah
5:20 make bitterness sweet and sweetness ***b***.
Revelation
8:11 from the water, because it became so ***b***.

BITTERNESS

Numbers
5:18 The water of ***b*** that brings the
Hebrews
12:15 that no root of ***b*** grows up that

BLAME

Psalms
15:2 who lives free of ***b***, does what is
101:6 who walks without ***b*** will work for me.
Romans
9:19 why does he still ***b*** people? Who has
2 Corinthians
7:11 yourselves of ***b***, such
Colossians
1:22 who are holy, faultless, and without ***b***.

BLAMELESS

Job
9:21 I'm ***b***, yet don't know myself; I reject
Psalms
19:13 be completely ***b***; I'll be innocent
119:1 whose way is ***b***—who walk in the
Luke
1:6 before God, ***b*** in their
1 Corinthians
1:8 that you will be ***b*** on the day of our
Ephesians
1:4 to be holy and ***b*** in God's presence
Philippians
1:10 be sincere and ***b*** on the day of
2:15 that you may be ***b*** and pure,
3:6 to righteousness under the Law, I'm ***b***.
Jude
1:24 to present you ***b*** and rejoicing
Revelation
14:5 lie came from their mouths; they are ***b***.

BLESS → BLESS GOD, BLESS THE LORD, BLESS YOU, I WILL BLESS YOU

Genesis
12:3 I will ***b*** those who bless you, those who
28:3 God Almighty will ***b*** you, make you
Exodus
20:24 come to you and ***b*** you in every
23:25 the LORD will ***b*** your bread and
Numbers
6:24 The LORD ***b*** you and keep you
Ruth
9:5 Stand up and ***b*** the LORD your
Job
1:21 the LORD has taken; ***b*** the LORD's name."
Psalms
5:12 you, LORD, ***b*** the righteous.
26:12 ground. I will ***b*** the LORD in the
28:9 your people, God! ***B*** your possession!
29:11 Let the LORD ***b*** his people with
62:4 their mouths they ***b***, but inside they
65:10 it with rain showers; you ***b*** its growth.
67:1 us grace and ***b*** us; let God make
67:7 God continue to ***b*** us; let the far
96:2 Sing to the LORD! ***B*** his name! Share the
109:28 curse—but you, ***b*** me! If they rise
115:12 us and will ***b*** us: God will
118:26 is blessed; we ***b*** all of you from
128:5 May the LORD ***b*** you from Zion. May
132:15 most certainly ***b*** its food supply;
145:1 true king. I will ***b*** your name forever
145:2 I will ***b*** you every day. I will praise
145:21 living thing will ***b*** God's holy name
Proverbs
11:26 grain, but they ***b*** those who sell it.
20:21 quickly at first won't ***b*** later on.
30:11 their father and don't ***b*** their mother.
31:28 Her children ***b*** her; her husband praises
Isaiah
19:25 this blessing: ***B*** Egypt my people;
Mark
10:13 so that he would ***b*** them. But the
Luke
1:68 ***B*** the Lord God of Israel because he
6:28 ***B*** those who curse you. Pray for those
18:15 so that he would ***b*** them. When the
Romans
12:14 ***B*** people who harass you—bless and

1 Corinthians
10:16 blessing that we ***b*** a sharing in the
Ephesians
1:3 ***B*** the God and Father of our Lord Jesus
James
3:9 With it we both ***b*** the Lord and Father

BLESS GOD

2Sa 22:47; Ps 18:46; 66:20; 68:26, 35; 134:1

BLESS THE LORD

Gn 9:26; 24:27; Ex 18:10; Dt 8:10; Jdg 5:2; 5:9; 1Sa 25:32; 25:39; 2Sa 18:28; 1Ki 10:9; 1Ch 16:36; 29:20; 2Ch 2:12; 6:4; 9:8; Ezr 7:27; Ps 16:7; 26:12; 28:6; 31:21; 34:1; 41:13; 68:19, 26; 72:18; 89:52; 103:1, 2, 20, 21, 22; 104:1, 35; 106:48; 115:18; 124:6; 134:1, 2; 135:19, 20, 21; 144:1; Lk 1:68; Jas 3:9

BLESS YOU

Gn 12:2; 12:3; 22:17; 26:3, 24; 27:4, 7, 10, 25, 29; 28:3; Ex 20:24; Nm 6:24; Dt 1:11; 7:13; 12:15; 14:24, 29; 15:4, 18; 16:15; 24:13; 28:8; 30:16; Jdg 17:2; Ru 2:4; 1Sa 15:13; 23:21; 25:33; 26:25; 2Sa 2:5; Ps 63:4; 128:5; 129:8; 134:3; 145:2, 10; Jer 31:23; Hg 2:19; Ac 3:26; Heb 6:14

BLESSED

→ BLESSED BY THE LORD, BLESSED FOREVER, BLESSED THE LORD, YOU WILL BE BLESSED

Genesis
1:22 Then God ***b*** them: "Be fertile and
2:3 God ***b*** the seventh day and made it holy,
5:2 and female. He ***b*** them and called
9:1 God ***b*** Noah and his sons and said to
12:3 of earth will be ***b*** because of you."
14:19 and he ***b*** him, "Bless Abram by El Elyon,
18:18 nations will be ***b*** because of him.
22:18 the earth will be ***b*** because of your
24:1 older, the LORD ***b*** Abraham in every
27:23 hairy like Esau's arms, so he ***b*** him.
Exodus
20:11 is why the LORD ***b*** the Sabbath day
39:43 the LORD had commanded, Moses ***b*** them.
Numbers
22:6 you bless is ***b*** and whomever you
23:11 curse my enemy. But now you've ***b*** him."
23:20 blessing, and he ***b***. I can't take it
24:9 you will be ***b***, and the one
Deuteronomy
2:7 LORD your God has ***b*** you in all that
7:14 You will be more ***b*** than any other group
12:7 because the LORD your God has ***b*** you.
15:6 LORD your God has ***b*** you, exactly as
15:14 with which the LORD your God has ***b*** you.
28:3 You will be ***b*** in the city and blessed
33:13 that his land is ***b*** by God: with
Nehemiah
8:6 Then Ezra ***b*** the LORD, the great God,
11:2 The people ***b*** those who agreed to live
Job
1:10 all he has—and ***b*** the work of his
Psalms
37:22 Those ***b*** by God will possess the land,
49:18 themselves ***b*** during their
72:15 for always! Let him be ***b*** all day long!
72:17 the nations be ***b*** through him and
112:2 of those who do right will be ***b***;
113:2 LORD's name be ***b*** from now until
115:15 May you be ***b*** by the LORD, the maker of
118:26 LORD's name is ***b***; we bless all of
119:12 LORD, are to be ***b***! Teach me your
128:4 who honors the LORD: they will be ***b***!
Proverbs
5:18 your spring be ***b***. Rejoice in the
16:20 those who trust the LORD are ***b***.
Isaiah
3:10 the righteous how ***b*** they are; they
Jeremiah
20:14 my mother gave birth to me not be ***b***.
Matthew
14:19 up to heaven, ***b*** them and broke
19:15 Then he ***b*** the children and went away
26:26 Jesus took bread, ***b*** it, broke it, and
Romans
1:25 of the creator, who is ***b*** forever. Amen.
9:5 who is God, and who is ***b*** forever. Amen.
14:22 God. People are ***b*** who don't convict
James
1:12 testing are ***b***. They are tried
1:25 They will be ***b*** in whatever they
1 Peter
1:3 Jesus Christ be ***b***! On account of
4:14 name, you are ***b***, for the Spirit

BLESSED BY THE LORD

Gn 26:29; Ru 2:20; 3:10; Ps 115:15; Is 61:9; 65:23

BLESSED FOREVER

2Sa 7:29; 1Ch 17:27; Ro 1:25; 9:5; 2Co 11:31

BLESSED THE LORD

Gn 24:48; 1Ch 29:10; 29:20; 2Ch 20:26; 31:8; Neh 8:6

BLESSING

Genesis
12:2 name respected, and you will be a ***b***.
Psalms
3:8 LORD! May your ***b*** be on your
37:26 and generous. Their children are a ***b***.
109:17 care much for ***b***, let it be far
129:8 May the LORD's ***b*** be on you! We
133:3 has commanded the ***b***: everlasting life.
137:8 you destroyer, a ***b*** on the one who
137:9 A ***b*** on the one who seizes your children
Proverbs
10:7 righteous is a ***b***, but the name of
10:22 The LORD's ***b*** makes a person rich, and
11:11 is honored by the ***b*** of the virtuous;
24:25 them. A rich ***b*** will come to them.
Zechariah
8:13 you will be a ***b***. Don't fear, but
Malachi
3:10 and empty out a ***b*** until there is
Matthew
10:13 give it your ***b*** of peace. But if
Mark
8:7 fish. He said a ***b*** over them, then

Acts
15:33 sent back with a ***b*** of peace from the
Romans
4:6 also pronounces a ***b*** on the person to
15:29 will come with the fullest ***b*** of Christ.
1 Corinthians
4:12 we respond with a ***b***; when we are
10:16 Isn't the cup of ***b*** that we bless a

BLIND

Leviticus
19:14 in front of a ***b*** person that would
21:18 anyone who is ***b***, crippled,
2 Kings
6:18 LORD struck them ***b***, just as Elisha
Psalms
146:8 who makes the ***b*** see. The LORD:
Proverbs
28:27 those who turn a ***b*** eye will be
Matthew
9:27 departed, two ***b*** men followed him,
11:5 Those who were ***b*** are able to see. Those
12:22 man who was ***b*** and unable to
15:14 alone. They are ***b*** people who are
20:30 When two ***b*** men sitting along the road
21:14 People who were ***b*** and lame came to
23:16 will be for you ***b*** guides who say,
Mark
8:22 people brought a ***b*** man to Jesus and
8:23 Taking the ***b*** man's hand, Jesus led him
10:46 sizable crowd, a ***b*** beggar named
Luke
4:18 of sight to the ***b***, to liberate the
6:39 them a riddle. "A ***b*** person can't lead
7:21 he gave sight to a number of ***b*** people.
14:13 invite the poor, crippled, lame, and ***b***.
18:35 a certain ***b*** man was sitting
John
5:3 who were sick, ***b***, lame, and
9:1 he saw a man who was ***b*** from birth.
9:2 that he was born ***b***, this man or his
10:21 heal the eyes of people who are ***b***?"
11:37 of the man born ***b***. Couldn't he have
12:40 made their eyes ***b*** and closed their
Acts
9:9 three days he was ***b*** and neither ate
13:11 you. You will be ***b*** for a while,
Romans
2:19 a guide for the ***b***; a light to those
2 Peter
1:9 shortsighted and ***b***, forgetting that
Revelation
3:17 pathetic, poor, ***b***, and naked.

BLOOD → BLOOD OF THE COVENANT

Genesis
4:10 of your brother's ***b*** is crying to me
9:6 sheds human ***b***, by a human his
Exodus
4:9 will turn into ***b*** on the dry
7:17 in my hand, and it will turn into ***b***.
12:13 The ***b*** will be your sign on the houses
24:8 then took the ***b*** and threw it over
Leviticus
1:5 will present the ***b*** and toss it
3:17 live: you must not eat any fat or ***b***.
17:11 life is in the ***b***. I have provided
17:14 life, its ***b*** is its life. That
Numbers
35:19 for the ***b*** of the dead is
35:33 you live, for the ***b*** pollutes the
Deuteronomy
12:23 any of the ***b***, because blood is
1 Samuel
14:32 devoured them with the ***b*** still in them.
1 Kings
21:19 up Naboth's ***b***, they will lick
2 Kings
9:33 Some of her ***b*** splattered
Psalms
50:13 I eat bulls' meat? Do I drink goats' ***b***?
72:14 violence; their ***b*** is precious in
78:44 their rivers into ***b***; they couldn't
79:3 poured out the ***b*** of the faithful
79:10 for the spilled ***b*** of your servants
94:21 the righteous. They condemn innocent ***b***.
105:29 their waters into ***b*** and killed their
106:38 shed innocent ***b***, the blood of
Proverbs
1:16 run to evil; they hurry to spill ***b***.
6:17 tongue, hands that spill innocent ***b***,
Isaiah
1:11 I don't want the ***b*** of bulls, lambs,
9:5 garment rolled in ***b*** will be burned,
34:6 covered with ***b***; it is soaked
66:3 offers swine's ***b***; the one who
Joel
2:31 and the moon to ***b*** before the great
Zechariah
9:11 Moreover, by the ***b*** of your covenant, I
Matthew
27:8 called "Field of ***B***" to this very day.
27:24 of this man's ***b***," he said. "It's
27:25 replied, "Let his ***b*** be on us and on
John
1:13 born not from ***b*** nor from human desire
6:53 One and drink his ***b***, you have no life
19:34 and immediately ***b*** and water came
Acts
1:19 language Hakeldama, or "Field of ***B***.")
2:20 be changed into ***b***, before the great
1 Corinthians
10:16 a sharing in the ***b*** of Christ? Isn't
11:25 covenant in my ***b***. Every time you
15:50 flesh and ***b*** can't inherit the
Hebrews
2:14 in flesh and ***b***, he also shared
9:7 does this without ***b***, which he offers
10:4 for the ***b*** of bulls and
11:28 the sprinkling of ***b***, in order that
12:4 yet to the point of shedding ***b***,
1 Peter
1:19 by the precious ***b*** of Christ, like
1 John
5:6 came by water and ***b***: Jesus Christ.
Revelation
1:5 us and freed us from our sins by his ***b***,
5:9 and by your ***b*** you purchased for
6:12 and the entire moon turned red as ***b***.
7:14 and made them white in the Lamb's ***b***.
8:8 the sea. A third of the sea became ***b***,
11:6 to turn them into ***b***, and to strike
12:11 on account of the ***b*** of the Lamb and

14:20 the city, and the ***b*** came out of the
16:3 sea turned into ***b***, like the blood
17:6 was drunk on the ***b*** of the saints and
18:24 the ***b*** of prophets, of saints, and of
19:13 a robe dyed with ***b***, and his name was

BLOOD OF THE COVENANT

Ex 24:8; Mt 26:28; Mk 14:24; Heb 9:20; 10:29

BLOW

Exodus
10:13 made an east wind ***b*** over the land all
Numbers
10:5 When you ***b*** a series of short blasts,
Joshua
6:5 Have them ***b*** a long blast on the ram's
Judges
7:18 When I ***b*** the trumpet, along with all
1 Kings
1:34 king over Israel. ***B*** the ram's horn
Psalms
81:3 ***B*** the horn on the new moon, at the full
147:18 makes his winds ***b***; the water flows
Matthew
6:2 the poor, don't ***b*** your trumpet as
Acts
27:13 wind began to ***b***, they thought
Revelation
7:1 no wind would ***b*** against the
8:6 the seven trumpets got ready to ***b*** them.
8:13 that the three angels are about to ***b***!"

BLUE

Exodus
25:4 ***b***, purple, and deep red yarns; fine
Numbers
4:6 a whole cloth of ***b*** over it, and they
Esther
8:15 presence in a ***b*** and white royal
Jeremiah
10:9 Clothed in ***b*** and purple, all
Ezekiel
23:6 dressed in fine ***b*** cloth, governors
27:7 was made of ***b*** and purple cloth
Revelation
9:17 fiery red, dark ***b***, and yellow as

BOAT

Isaiah
33:21 streams where no ***b*** will go, no
Matthew
4:21 They were in a ***b*** with Zebedee
8:23 Jesus got into a ***b***, his disciples
9:1 Boarding a ***b***, Jesus crossed to the
13:2 he climbed into a ***b*** and sat down. The
14:13 he withdrew in a ***b*** to a deserted
15:39 got into the ***b*** and came to the
Mark
1:19 sons, in their ***b*** repairing the
3:9 to get a small ***b*** ready for him so
4:1 he climbed into a ***b*** there on the
4:38 the rear of the ***b***, sleeping on a
5:2 got out of the ***b***, a man possessed
6:32 departed in a ***b*** by themselves for
6:51 He got into the ***b***, and the wind
8:14 had only one loaf with them in the ***b***.
Luke
5:3 down and taught the crowds from the ***b***.
8:22 boarded a ***b***. He said to them,
John
6:17 They got into a ***b*** and were crossing the
21:3 They set out in a ***b***, but throughout

BOAZ

Ruth
4:13 So ***B*** took Ruth, and she became his
4:21 the father of ***B***, Boaz the father
1 Kings
7:21 Jachin. The north column he named ***B***.
1 Chronicles
2:11 of Salma, Salma was the father of ***B***,
2:12 ***B*** was the father of Obed, and Obed was
2 Chronicles
3:17 and the one on the north he named ***B***.
Matthew
1:5 was the father of ***B***, whose mother was
Luke
3:32 of Obed son of ***B*** son of Sala son

BODIES → HEAVENLY BODIES

Leviticus
11:8 touch their dead ***b***; they are unclean
21:5 their beards or make gashes in their ***b***.
21:11 go near any dead ***b*** and cannot make
Deuteronomy
4:19 all the heavenly ***b***, and be led
Jeremiah
9:22 LORD says: Dead ***b*** will lie like
41:7 them and threw their ***b*** into a cistern.
Mark
13:25 and other heavenly ***b*** will be shaken.
John
19:31 didn't want the ***b*** to remain on the
Acts
7:16 Their ***b*** were brought back to Shechem
Romans
1:24 degrading their own ***b*** with each other.
2:28 are outwardly circumcised on their ***b***.
12:1 to present your ***b*** as a living
1 Corinthians
6:15 know that your ***b*** are parts of
6:18 commit sin against their own ***b***.
15:52 be raised with ***b*** that won't decay,

BODY

Genesis
25:23 emerge from your ***b***. One people will
Leviticus
15:7 who touches the ***b*** of the one with
Ecclesiastes
12:12 Studying too much wearies the ***b***.
Isaiah
17:4 dwindle; his sleek ***b*** will waste away.
50:6 I gave my ***b*** to attackers, and
Matthew
5:29 a part of your ***b*** than that your
6:22 the lamp of the ***b***. Therefore, if
10:28 who kill the ***b*** but can't kill
26:26 and said, "Take and eat. This is my ***b***."
27:59 Joseph took the ***b***, wrapped it in a
28:13 and stole his ***b*** while you were
Mark
14:8 has anointed my ***b*** ahead of time for

14:22 them, and said, "Take; this is my ***b***."
16:1 they could go and anoint Jesus' dead ***b***.
Luke
11:34 the lamp of your ***b***. When your eye is
12:4 who can kill the ***b*** but after that
23:52 went to Pilate and asked for Jesus' ***b***.
John
2:21 Jesus was talking about was his ***b***.
Romans
6:12 let sin rule your ***b***, so that you do
7:25 but I'm a slave to sin's law in my ***b***.
8:10 but the ***b*** is dead because
12:5 of us, we are one ***b*** in Christ, and
1 Corinthians
6:13 with both. The ***b*** isn't for sexual
11:24 said, "This is my ***b***, which is for
12:12 like the human ***b***—a body is a unit
12:13 Spirit into one ***b***, whether Jew or
2 Corinthians
7:1 contaminates our ***b*** or spirit so that
Galatians
2:20 I now live in my ***b***, I live by faith,
6:13 they can boast about your physical ***b***.
Colossians
1:18 the head of the ***b***, the church, who
1 Peter
2:24 in his own ***b*** on the cross the

BONES
Genesis
50:25 you must bring up my ***b*** out of here."
Exodus
12:46 house, and you shouldn't break the ***b***.
13:19 with him Joseph's ***b*** just as Joseph
Joshua
24:32 brought up the ***b*** of Joseph from
2 Kings
13:21 touched Elisha's ***b***, the man came to
Psalms
22:14 water. All my ***b*** have fallen
22:17 I can count all my ***b***! Meanwhile, they just stare
34:20 all their ***b***; not even one
Ezekiel
37:1 of a certain valley. It was full of ***b***.
37:3 one, can these ***b*** live again?" I
37:11 Human one, these ***b*** are the entire
Micah
3:2 off them, and the flesh off their ***b***,
3:3 skin, break their ***b*** in pieces, and
Matthew
23:27 are full of dead ***b*** and all kinds of
Luke
24:39 have flesh and ***b*** like you see I
John
19:36 They won't break any of his ***b***.

BORN
Exodus
1:22 every baby boy ***b*** to the Hebrews
Deuteronomy
23:8 Children ***b*** to them are permitted to
Job
3:1 spoke up and cursed the day he was ***b***.
5:7 Surely humans are ***b*** to distress, just
15:7 Were you ***b*** the first Adam, brought
Psalms
22:31 to those not yet ***b***, telling them
51:5 Yes, I was ***b*** in guilt, in sin, from the
78:6 children not yet ***b*** will know these
89:27 make him the one ***b*** first—I'll make
90:2 mountains were ***b***, before you
127:4 The children ***b*** when one is young are
Isaiah
9:6 A child is ***b*** to us, a son is given to
Jeremiah
1:5 before you were ***b*** I set you apart;
Matthew
1:16 of whom Jesus was ***b***, who is called
2:1 After Jesus was ***b*** in Bethlehem in the
2:4 them where the Christ was to be ***b***.
26:24 better for him if he had never been ***b***."
Luke
2:11 Your savior is ***b*** today in David's city.
John
3:3 unless someone is ***b*** anew, it's not
9:2 so that he was ***b*** blind, this man
11:37 eyes of the man ***b*** blind. Couldn't
1 Peter
1:3 You have been ***b*** anew into a

BOTH JEWS AND GREEKS
Ac 18:4; 19:10; 20:21; Ro 3:9; 1Co 1:24

BOUGHT
Genesis
33:19 He ***b*** the section of the field where he
Exodus
12:44 who has been ***b*** may eat it after
21:8 must let her be ***b*** back by her
Leviticus
25:24 must allow for the land to be ***b*** back.
27:33 will be holy and cannot be ***b*** back.
Matthew
13:44 sold everything and ***b*** that field.
Acts
1:18 In fact, he ***b*** a field with the payment
1 Corinthians
6:20 You have been ***b*** and paid for, so honor

BOUND
Daniel
3:24 throw three men, ***b***, into the fire?"
4:15 in the earth, ***b*** with iron and
Matthew
14:3 arrested John, ***b*** him, and put him
27:2 They ***b*** him, led him away, and turned
Mark
15:1 a plan. They ***b*** Jesus, led him
Luke
8:29 so he would be ***b*** with leg irons
13:16 of Abraham, ***b*** by Satan for
John
11:44 out, his feet ***b*** and his hands
18:12 took Jesus into custody. They ***b*** him
18:24 Annas sent him ***b*** to Caiaphas the
Acts
12:6 two soldiers and ***b*** with two chains,
21:33 ordered him to be ***b*** with two chains.
22:29 he realized he had ***b*** a Roman citizen.
Revelation
9:14 angels who are ***b*** at the great

20:2 and Satan, and ***b*** him for a

BOW (N.)
Genesis
9:13 I have placed my ***b*** in the clouds; it
2 Samuel
1:18 the Song of the ***B***.
Psalms
7:12 will bend his ***b***, will string an
18:34 for war so my arms can bend a bronze ***b***.
21:12 when you aim your ***b*** straight at their
44:6 won't trust in my ***b***; my sword won't
46:9 breaking the ***b*** and shattering
58:7 they bend the ***b***, let their arrows
76:3 shafts of the ***b***, the shield, the
78:57 they twisted away like a defective ***b***.

BOW (V.) → BOW DOWN AND WORSHIP
Exodus
20:5 Do not ***b*** down to them or worship them,
23:24 don't ***b*** down to their gods, worship
Deuteronomy
5:9 Do not ***b*** down to them or worship them
32:43 All you gods: ***b*** down to the Lord!
Psalms
5:7 love; I will ***b*** down at your holy
29:2 due his name! ***B*** down to the LORD
72:11 Let all the kings ***b*** down before him;
81:9 you. You must not ***b*** down to any
95:6 let's worship and ***b*** down! Let's kneel
96:9 ***B*** down to the LORD in his holy
97:7 to shame. All gods ***b*** down to the Lord!
99:5 LORD, our God! ***B*** low at his
99:9 the LORD our God! ***B*** low at his holy
138:2 I ***b*** toward your holy temple and thank
Romans
14:11 every knee will ***b*** to me, and every
Philippians
2:10 on earth, and under the earth might ***b***
Revelation
3:9 them come and ***b*** down at your feet

BOW DOWN AND WORSHIP
Dn 3:5; 3:6, 10, 15; Mt 4:9

BOWED DOWN
Gn 24:26; 33:6; 37:7; 42:6; 43:28; Ex 4:31; 12:27; 18:7; 32:8; Ru 2:10; 2Sa 12:20; 1Ki 1:16; 1:31, 53; 18:42; 19:18; 2Ki 17:16; 21:3; 1Ch 29:20; 2Ch 20:18; 25:14; 29:29, 30; 33:3; Neh 8:6; Dn 3:7; Mt 27:29

BOWED DOWN AND WORSHIPPED
Ex 4:31; 12:27; 1Ch 29:20; Neh 8:6; Dn 3:7

BOWING
Genesis
37:9 and eleven stars were ***b*** down to me."
Matthew
20:20 with her sons. ***B*** before him, she
John
19:30 is completed." ***B*** his head, he gave

BOWL → ANGEL POURED HIS BOWL
Exodus
12:22 that is in the ***b***, and touch the
Numbers
7:14 one gold ***b*** weighing ten shekels full of
Proverbs
19:24 their hand in the ***b***; they won't even
26:15 hand into the ***b***, too tired to
Ecclesiastes
12:6 and the gold ***b*** shatters; the jar
Isaiah
22:24 every little dish, every ***b***, every jar.
Ezekiel
4:9 Put them in a ***b*** and make your
Zechariah
4:2 of gold. It has a ***b*** on top. The bowl
4:3 the right of its ***b*** and one to the
9:15 be filled like a ***b***, like the corners
Matthew
26:23 who dips his hand with me into this ***b***.
Mark
14:20 is dipping bread with me into this ***b***.
Luke
8:16 covers it with a ***b*** or puts it under
John
13:26 dipped into the ***b***." Then he dipped
2 Timothy
2:21 as a "special ***b***." They will be
Revelation
8:3 he held a gold ***b*** for burning
16:2 angel poured his ***b*** on the earth, and

BOWLS
Revelation
5:8 a harp and gold ***b*** full of incense,
15:7 angels seven gold ***b*** full of the anger
16:1 out the seven ***b*** of God's anger on
17:1 who had the seven ***b*** spoke with me.
21:9 who had the seven ***b*** full of the seven

BOY
Exodus
1:16 born, if it's a ***b***, kill him. But if
1:22 Throw every baby ***b*** born to the
2:6 the child. The ***b*** was crying, and
1 Samuel
1:11 Give her a ***b***! Then I'll give
1:25 the bull, then brought the ***b*** to Eli.
1:28 now I give this ***b*** back to the LORD.
Ecclesiastes
10:16 whose king is a ***b*** and whose princes
Isaiah
7:16 Before the ***b*** learns to reject evil and
Matthew
17:17 up with you? Bring the ***b*** here to me."
Luke
1:57 have her child, she gave birth to a ***b***.
2:43 home, but the ***b*** Jesus stayed
18:21 all of these things since I was a ***b***."

BRAG
Romans
2:23 If you ***b*** about the Law, do you shame
4:2 had a reason to ***b***, but not in front
11:18 then don't ***b*** like you're better than
15:17 in Christ Jesus I ***b*** about things that

BRAG [cont.]

1 Corinthians
1:29 no human being can ***b*** in God's presence.
1:31 The one who brags should ***b*** in the Lord!
2 Corinthians
10:17 one who brags, should ***b*** in the Lord.
1 Thessalonians
2:19 crown that we can ***b*** about in front of
James
4:16 now you boast and ***b***, and all such

BRANCH

Isaiah
11:1 stump of Jesse; a ***b*** will sprout from
Jeremiah
1:11 I said, "A ***b*** of an almond
33:15 up a righteous ***b*** from David's
Daniel
11:7 A ***b*** from her roots will rise up in his
Matthew
24:32 tree. After its ***b*** becomes tender
Mark
13:28 tree. After its ***b*** becomes tender
John
15:2 and he trims any ***b*** that produces
15:4 remain in you. A ***b*** can't produce
15:6 will be like a ***b*** that is thrown
Romans
11:17 were a wild olive ***b***, and you were

BRANCHES

Daniel
4:12 nested in its ***b***. All living
Matthew
13:32 in the sky come and nest in its ***b***."
21:8 Others cut palm ***b*** off the trees and
Mark
4:32 such large ***b*** that the birds in
11:8 others spread ***b*** cut from the
Luke
13:19 the birds in the sky nested in its ***b***."
John
12:13 They took palm ***b*** and went out to meet
Romans
11:16 a root is holy, the ***b*** will be holy too.
Revelation
7:9 robes and held palm ***b*** in their hands.

BREAD → BERAD OF THE PRESENCE, FESTIVAL OF UNLEAVENED BREAD

Exodus
8:3 and even into your ovens and ***b*** pans.
34:28 He didn't eat any ***b*** or drink any
Deuteronomy
8:3 don't live on ***b*** alone. No, they
Psalms
37:25 seen their children begging for ***b***.
53:4 they are eating ***b*** but never calling
78:25 person ate the ***b*** of the powerful
80:5 You've fed them ***b*** made of tears;
102:9 ashes instead of ***b***. I've been mixing
Proverbs
6:26 costs a loaf of ***b***, but a married
20:17 Stolen ***b*** is sweet, but afterward the
Ecclesiastes
11:1 Send your ***b*** out on the water
Matthew
4:3 Son, command these stones to become ***b***."
4:4 live only by ***b***, but by every
6:11 Give us the ***b*** we need for today
7:9 children a stone when they ask for ***b***?
14:17 except five loaves of ***b*** and two fish."
15:26 the children's ***b*** and toss it to
15:36 seven loaves of ***b*** and the fish.
26:26 Jesus took ***b***, blessed it,
Mark
14:20 who is dipping ***b*** with me into this
Luke
22:19 After taking the ***b*** and giving thanks,
John
6:11 Jesus took the ***b***. When he had
6:35 I am the ***b*** of life. Whoever
13:18 one who eats my ***b*** has turned
21:9 there, with fish on it, and some ***b***.
Acts
27:35 things, he took ***b***, gave thanks to
1 Corinthians
5:7 to be unleavened ***b***. Christ our
11:23 he was betrayed, the Lord Jesus took ***b***.
11:26 time you eat this ***b*** and drink this

BREAD OF THE PRESENCE

Ex 25:30; 35:13; 39:36; 1Sa 21:6; 1Ki 7:48; 2Ch 4:19; Mt 12:4; Mk 2:26; Lk 6:4

BREAK → BREAK MY COVENANT

Exodus
12:46 house, and you shouldn't ***b*** the bones.
13:13 it, you must ***b*** its neck. You
Judges
2:1 I will never ***b*** my covenant with
Psalms
58:6 God, ***b*** their teeth out of their mouths!
65:13 they shout for joy; they ***b*** out in song!
89:34 I won't ***b*** my covenant. I won't renege
Proverbs
25:15 and a tender tongue can ***b*** a bone.
Hosea
1:5 that day I will ***b*** the bow of Israel
10:2 The LORD will ***b*** down their altars
Matthew
6:19 and where thieves ***b*** in and steal them.
15:3 Why do you ***b*** the command of
24:43 allow the thief to ***b*** into his house.
John
19:33 already dead so they didn't ***b*** his legs.
1 Corinthians
10:16 of bread that we ***b*** a sharing in the

BREAK MY COVENANT

Jdg 2:1; Ps 89:34; Jer 33:20; 33:25; Zec 11:10

BREAST

Exodus
29:26 Take the ***b*** of the ram for Aaron's
29:27 Make holy the ***b*** that was lifted for the
Leviticus
7:30 the fat with the ***b*** so that the
7:31 altar, but the ***b*** will go to Aaron
7:34 I have taken the ***b*** of the uplifted
8:29 Moses took the ***b*** from the ram for
10:14 You must eat the ***b*** for the uplifted

10:15 the gift and the ***b*** for the uplifted
Numbers
6:20 priest, with the ***b*** of the uplifted
11:12 them at the ***b***, as a nurse
18:18 yours just as the ***b*** of the uplifted
Ruth
4:16 held him to her ***b***, and she became
Job
24:9 stolen from the ***b***; the infant of
Song of Songs
8:1 at my mother's ***b***. I would find you
Isaiah
28:9 those who have hardly outgrown the ***b***?
Lamentations
4:3 jackals offer the ***b***; they nurse their

BREASTS

Job
3:12 knees receive me and ***b*** let me nurse?
Psalms
22:9 placing me safely at my mother's ***b***.
Song of Songs
1:13 to me, lying all night between my ***b***.
4:5 Your two ***b*** are like two fawns, twins of
7:3 Your two ***b*** are like two fawns, twins of
7:8 fruit!" May your ***b*** be now like grape
8:8 small; she has no ***b***. What will we do
Isaiah
32:12 beating your ***b*** for the pleasant fields,
60:16 nurse at royal ***b***. You will know
66:11 her comforting ***b***, that you may
Lamentations
2:12 draining away at their own mother's ***b***.
Ezekiel
16:7 endowed. Your ***b*** were firm, your
23:3 young and nubile ***b*** to be touched and
23:34 and tear off your ***b***, for I have
Hosea
2:2 and adultery from between her ***b***,
9:14 miscarries and ***b*** that are dried up.
Nahum
2:7 moan like doves, beating their ***b***.
Luke
23:29 birth, and the ***b*** that never nursed

BREATH

Genesis
2:7 and blew life's ***b*** into his
25:17 He took his last ***b*** and died, and was
49:33 took his last ***b***, and joined his
Exodus
15:8 With the ***b*** of your nostrils the waters
1 Kings
10:5 the LORD's temple, it took her ***b*** away.
Psalms
62:9 are nothing but a ***b***. Human beings are
78:39 just flesh, just ***b*** that passes and
104:29 take away their ***b***, they die and
135:17 No, there's no ***b*** in their lungs!
Proverbs
20:27 The ***b*** of a person is the lamp of the
Song of Songs
7:8 and the scent of your ***b*** like apples!
Isaiah
33:11 to stubble; your ***b*** is a fire that
40:7 when the LORD's ***b*** blows on it.
42:5 the one who gave ***b*** to its people and
57:13 them all; one ***b*** will take them
Jeremiah
4:31 Zion, gasping for ***b***, her arms
Lamentations
4:20 one, the very ***b*** in our lungs, was
Hosea
13:15 will come—the ***b*** of God rising
Habakkuk
2:19 silver, but there is no ***b*** within it.
Acts
17:25 who gives life, ***b***, and everything
2 Thessalonians
2:8 him with the ***b*** from his mouth.
Revelation
13:15 allowed to give ***b*** to the beast's

BRIDE

Jeremiah
2:2 as a young ***b***, how you followed
7:34 as the voice of ***b*** and bridegroom in
16:9 the voices of the bridegroom and the ***b***.
25:10 the voices of the ***b*** and the
Joel
2:16 leave his room and the ***b*** her chamber.
Revelation
18:23 a bridegroom and ***b*** will never be
19:7 has come, and his ***b*** has made herself
21:2 made ready as a ***b*** beautifully
21:9 will show you the ***b***, the Lamb's wife."
22:17 Spirit and the ***b*** say, 'Come!' Let

BROKE

1 Samuel
4:18 gate. His neck ***b***, and he died
1 Kings
13:5 The altar ***b*** apart, and the ashes
Psalms
76:3 was there that he ***b*** the fiery shafts
102:23 God ***b*** my strength in midstride, cutting
106:29 did, so a plague ***b*** out against them.
Jeremiah
2:20 Long ago I ***b*** your yoke; I shattered
28:10 the prophet Jeremiah's neck and ***b*** it.
34:11 afterward they ***b*** their promise,
Matthew
12:4 God's house and ***b*** the law by eating
14:19 blessed them and ***b*** the loaves apart
15:36 gave thanks, he ***b*** them into pieces
26:26 blessed it, ***b*** it, and gave it
Mark
5:4 chains, but he ***b*** the chains and
14:3 of pure nard. She ***b*** open the vase and
14:22 blessed it, ***b*** it, and gave it
14:72 three times." And he ***b*** down, sobbing.
John
19:32 soldiers came and ***b*** the legs of the
Acts
27:35 of them all, then ***b*** it and began to
1 Corinthians
11:24 giving thanks, he ***b*** it and said,
Ephesians
2:14 With his body, he ***b*** down the barrier

BROKEN

Genesis
17:14 from his people. He has ***b*** my covenant."

2 Kings
18:21 nothing but a ***b*** reed! It will
Nehemiah
1:3 Jerusalem is ***b*** down, and its
Psalms
22:15 like a piece of ***b*** pottery. My
34:20 their bones; not even one will be ***b***.
51:17 A ***b*** spirit is my sacrifice, God. You
Proverbs
18:14 person, but who can bear a ***b*** spirit?
Ecclesiastes
12:6 the jar is ***b*** at the spring and
Jeremiah
33:21 before me be ***b***; only then would
Daniel
11:4 kingdom will be ***b***, divided to the
Hosea
8:1 because they have ***b*** my covenant, and
Luke
12:39 have allowed his home to be ***b*** into.
John
19:31 those crucified ***b*** and the bodies
Acts
27:41 and the stern was ***b*** into pieces by
Romans
11:17 the branches were ***b*** off, and you were
11:19 Branches were ***b*** off so that I
11:20 Fine. They were ***b*** off because they

BRONZE

Numbers
16:39 priest took the ***b*** censers presented
21:9 Moses made a ***b*** snake and placed it on a
Deuteronomy
28:23 be as hard as ***b***; the earth under
Judges
16:21 bound him with ***b*** chains, and he
1 Samuel
17:5 He had a ***b*** helmet on his head and wore
17:6 He had ***b*** plates on his shins, and a
17:38 on him and a ***b*** helmet on his
2 Samuel
8:8 a large amount of ***b*** from Tebah and
8:10 silver, gold, and ***b*** objects with him.
21:16 shekels of ***b***, and he was
22:35 for war so my arms can bend a ***b*** bow.
Job
6:12 my strength that of rocks, my flesh ***b***?
20:24 an iron weapon, a ***b*** bow pierces them.
40:18 bones are like ***b*** tubes, his limbs
41:27 treats iron as straw, ***b*** as rotten wood.
Psalms
18:34 for war so my arms can bend a ***b*** bow.
107:16 God has shattered ***b*** doors and split
Isaiah
45:2 I will shatter ***b*** doors; I will cut
48:4 made of iron, and your forehead is ***b***.
60:17 Instead of ***b*** I will bring gold; instead
Ezekiel
1:7 and they shone like burnished ***b***.
9:2 came in and stood beside the ***b*** altar,
27:13 They gave you ***b*** vessels for these
40:3 He appeared to be ***b***, and he had a
Daniel
2:32 its abdomen and hips were made of ***b***.
2:35 clay, ***b***, silver, and
4:15 with iron and ***b*** in the field
5:4 of gold, silver, ***b***, iron, wood, and
7:19 iron teeth and ***b*** claws. As it ate
10:6 like polished ***b***. When he spoke,
Micah
4:13 will make out of ***b***. You will crush
Zechariah
6:1 the mountains were made of ***b***.
Revelation
9:20 of gold, silver, ***b***, stone, and wood—
18:12 ivory, fine wood, ***b***, iron, and marble;

BROTHER → BROTHER OR SISTER

Genesis
4:9 Where is your ***b*** Abel?" Cain said,
9:5 a man for his ***b***, I will demand
27:11 Rebekah, "My ***b*** Esau is a hairy
36:6 land of Canaan and from his ***b*** Jacob.
42:4 send Joseph's ***b*** Benjamin along
48:19 But his younger ***b*** will be greater
Exodus
4:14 What about your ***b*** Aaron the Levite?
Ruth
4:3 field that belonged to our ***b*** Elimelech.
2 Samuel
1:26 for you, my ***b*** Jonathan! You
13:4 Tamar, the sister of my ***b*** Absalom."
13:12 to him, "No, my ***b***! Don't rape me.
14:7 who killed his ***b*** so we can execute
1 Kings
1:10 David's veterans, or his ***b*** Solomon.
2:7 away from your ***b*** Absalom, they
Job
30:29 I have become a ***b*** to jackals, a
Psalms
35:14 a friend or a ***b***. I was weighed
Song of Songs
8:1 you were as my ***b***—the one who nurs
Malachi
1:2 Esau Jacob's ***b***? says the LORD. I
Matthew
4:21 Zebedee and his ***b*** John. They were
5:22 angry with their ***b*** or sister will be
7:4 you say to your ***b*** or sister, 'Let
10:2 and Andrew his ***b***; James the son of
12:50 in heaven is my ***b***, sister, and
14:3 Herodias, the wife of Herod's ***b*** Philip.
17:1 and John his ***b***, and brought them
22:24 dies, his ***b*** must marry his
22:25 no children he left his widow to his ***b***.
22:26 with the second ***b*** and the third,
John
1:40 Jesus was Andrew, the ***b*** of Simon Peter.
1:41 found his own ***b*** Simon and said to
11:21 had been here, my ***b*** wouldn't have
11:23 told her, "Your ***b*** will rise again."
Acts
9:17 Saul and said, "***B*** Saul, the Lord
12:2 had James, John's ***b***, killed with a
1 Corinthians
5:11 calls themselves "***b***" or "sister" who
Galatians
1:19 except James the ***b*** of the Lord.
1 Peter
5:12 to be a faithful ***b***. In these lines I

2 Peter
3:15 dear friend and ***b*** Paul wrote to you
1 John
3:12 and murdered his ***b***. And why did he
Jude
1:1 Jesus Christ and ***b*** of James. To
Revelation
1:9 I, John, your ***b*** who shares with you in

BROTHER OR SISTER
Nm 6:7; Jer 34:9; Mt 5:22; 5:23, 24; 7:4; 18:15, 21, 35; Lk 6:42; 17:3; Ro 14:10; 14:13, 15, 21; 1Co 5:11; 6:6; 7:15; 8:11, 13; 1Th 4:6; 2Th 3:6; 3:15; Heb 8:11; Jas 2:15; 4:11; 1Jn 2:9; 2:11; 3:10, 15, 17; 4:20; 5:16

BROTHERS → BROTHERS AND SISTERS
Genesis
37:11 His ***b*** were jealous of him, but his
45:1 when he revealed his identity to his ***b***.
45:3 said to his ***b***, "I'm Joseph! Is
Exodus
1:6 Joseph, his ***b***, and everyone in
Psalms
69:8 to my own ***b***, an immigrant to
Proverbs
17:2 will divide an inheritance with the ***b***.
18:9 are lazy in their work are ***b*** to thugs.
Song of Songs
1:6 gaze. My own ***b*** were angry with
Hosea
12:3 oldest of twin ***b***; as an adult he
Matthew
1:2 was the father of Judah and his ***b***.
4:18 Sea, he saw two ***b***, Simon, who is
4:21 another set of ***b***, James the son of
12:48 Who is my mother? Who are my ***b***?"
22:25 there were seven ***b*** among us. The
28:10 Go and tell my ***b*** that I am going
John
2:12 his mother, his ***b***, and his
Acts
1:14 Mary the mother of Jesus, and his ***b***.
7:2 responded, "***B*** and fathers,
7:13 Joseph told his ***b*** who he was, and
7:26 saying, 'You are ***b***! Why are you
22:1 ***B*** and fathers, listen now to my
23:6 in the council, "***B***, I'm a Pharisee
2 Corinthians
8:23 about our ***b***, they are the
9:3 I'm sending the ***b*** so that our
1 Timothy
5:1 father; treat younger men like your ***b***,
6:2 because they are ***b***. Instead, they

BROTHERS AND SISTERS
Josh 2:13; Est 10:3; Ps 22:22; Mt 5:47; 10:21; 23:8; 25:40; Mk 3:32; 13:12; Lk 14:12; 14:26; 21:16; 22:32; Jn 20:17; 21:23; Ac 1:16; 2:29; 3:17; 4:23; 6:3; 11:1, 29; 12:17; 13:38; 15:3, 22, 23, 32, 33, 36, 40; 16:2, 40; 17:10, 14; 18:18, 27; 21:7, 17; 28:14, 15; Ro 1:13; 7:1, 4; 8:12, 29; 9:3; 10:1; 11:25; 12:1; 15:14, 30; 16:14, 17; 1Co 1:10; 1:11, 26; 2:1; 3:1; 4:6; 6:8; 7:24, 29; 8:12; 10:1; 11:33; 12:1; 14:6, 20, 26, 39; 15:1, 6, 31, 50, 58; 16:11, 12, 15, 20; 2Co 1:8; 8:1; 11:26; 13:11; Ga 1:2; 1:11; 2:4; 3:15; 4:12, 28, 31; 5:11, 13; 6:1, 18; Eph 6:23; Phi 1:12; 1:14; 3:1, 13, 17; 4:1, 8, 21; Col 1:2; 4:15; 1Th 1:4; 2:1, 9, 14, 17; 3:7; 4:1, 9, 10, 13; 5:1, 4, 12, 14, 25, 26, 27; 2Th 1:3; 2:1, 13, 15; 3:1, 6, 13; 2Ti 4:21; Heb 2:11; 2:12, 17; 3:1, 12; 6:9; 7:5; 10:19; 13:22; Jas 1:2; 1:9, 16, 19; 2:1, 5, 14; 3:1, 10, 12; 4:11; 5:7, 9, 10, 12, 19; 2Pt 1:10; 1Jn 3:13; 3:14, 16; 3Jn 1:3; 1:5, 10; Rev 6:11; 12:10; 19:10; 22:9

BUILD → BUILD A TEMPLE, BUILD AN ALTAR, BUILD THE LORD'S TEMPLE, BUILD THE TEMPLE, BUILD UP
Ezra
1:2 commanded me to ***b*** him a house at
Nehemiah
4:3 on whatever they ***b***, their wall of
4:6 We continued to ***b*** the wall. All of it
Psalms
104:3 You ***b*** your lofty house on the waters;
Proverbs
17:19 those who ***b*** a high doorway
24:27 the field; then you can ***b*** your house.
Hosea
2:6 and I will ***b*** a wall against
Matthew
16:18 Peter. And I'll ***b*** my church on this
23:29 Hypocrites! You ***b*** tombs for the
Mark
14:58 three days I will ***b*** another, one not
Luke
11:48 the prophets, and you ***b*** memorials!
12:18 down my barns and ***b*** bigger ones.
14:28 of you wanted to ***b*** a tower, wouldn't
19:43 your enemies will ***b*** fortifications
Acts
7:49 of house will you ***b*** for me,' says the
20:32 which is able to ***b*** you up and give
Romans
14:19 and the things that ***b*** each other up.
15:2 for their good in order to ***b*** them up.
1 Corinthians
3:10 pay attention to the way they ***b*** on it.
10:23 but everything doesn't ***b*** others up.
2 Corinthians
13:10 so that I could ***b*** you up, not tear

BUILD A TEMPLE
2Sa 7:13; 1Ki 5:3; 5:5; 8:17, 18; 1Ch 22:6; 22:7, 8, 10; 28:2, 3, 10; 2Ch 2:1; 2:4, 12; 6:7, 8; 36:23

BUILD AN ALTAR
Gn 35:1; 35:3; Dt 27:5; Jdg 6:26; 2Sa 24:18; 24:21; 1Ch 21:22

BUILD THE LORD'S TEMPLE
1Ki 9:15; 1Ch 22:5; 2Ch 3:1; Zec 6:12; 6:13, 15

BUILD THE TEMPLE
2Sa 7:5; 1Ki 5:5; 8:19; 1Ch 17:4; 22:11; 29:19; 2Ch 3:3; 6:9

BUILD UP
Dt 25:9; Jdg 9:29; 2Ch 14:7; Ps 89:4; 1Co 14:4; 14:26

BUILD YOU UP
Jer 31:4; 42:10; Ac 20:32; 2Co 10:8; 12:19; 13:10

BUILT AN ALTAR
Gn 8:20; 12:7, 8; 13:18; 22:9; 26:25; 35:7; Ex 17:15; 24:4; 32:5; Josh 8:30; 22:10, 11; Jdg 6:24; 21:4; 1Sa 7:17; 14:35; 2Sa 24:25; 1Ch 21:26

BUILDING
Exodus
36:1 for the work of ***b*** the sanctuary do
Joshua
22:19 in rebellion by ***b*** an altar for
1 Kings
3:1 until he finished ***b*** his royal palace,
Nehemiah
2:20 we will start ***b***. But you will
Ecclesiastes
3:3 for tearing down and a time for ***b*** up,
Micah
7:11 A day for the ***b*** of your walls! On that
Luke
6:48 like a person ***b*** a house by
17:28 buying, selling, planting, and ***b***.
Romans
15:20 that I won't be ***b*** on someone else's
1 Corinthians
3:9 and you are God's field, God's ***b***.
3:10 someone else is ***b*** on top of it.
2 Corinthians
5:1 down, we have a ***b*** from God. It's a
5:2 ourselves with our ***b*** from heaven—
Ephesians
2:21 The whole ***b*** is joined together in him,
4:12 of serving and ***b*** up the body of
1 Thessalonians
5:11 each other and ***b*** each other up,

BULL
Genesis
49:22 Joseph is a young ***b***, a young bull by a
Exodus
29:1 Take a young ***b*** and two flawless
32:4 metal image of a ***b*** calf, and the
Leviticus
1:5 slaughter the ***b*** before the LORD.
4:3 LORD a flawless ***b*** from the herd as
8:2 anointing oil, a ***b*** for the
9:2 Take a young ***b*** from the herd as
16:3 follows: with a ***b*** from the herd as
23:18 old lambs, one ***b*** from the herd,
Deuteronomy
33:17 A firstborn ***b***—that's how majestic he
Psalms
29:6 like a young ***b***, makes Sirion
69:31 than a young ***b*** with full horns
106:20 for an image of a ***b*** that eats grass.
Proverbs
14:4 there is a strong ***b***, there is
Ezekiel
43:19 provide a young ***b*** as a purification
45:18 a flawless young ***b*** from the herd,
46:6 a flawless young ***b*** from the herd,
Amos
6:4 the flock, and ***b*** calves from the

BULLS
1 Kings
7:29 Lions, ***b***, and winged otherworldly
18:23 Give us two ***b***. Let Baal's prophets
2 Kings
16:17 from the bronze ***b*** that were under
1 Chronicles
15:26 they sacrificed seven ***b*** and seven rams.
29:21 LORD—a thousand ***b***, a thousand rams,
Job
42:8 now, take seven ***b*** and seven rams,
Psalms
22:12 Many ***b*** surround me; mighty bulls from
50:9 I won't accept ***b*** from your house or
51:19 offerings. Then ***b*** will again be
66:15 I will offer both ***b*** and goats. Selah
68:30 the herd of ***b*** among the calves
Isaiah
1:11 want the blood of ***b***, lambs, and goats.
34:7 with mighty ***b***, and their land
Jeremiah
50:27 Destroy all her ***b***; prepare them for
52:20 the twelve bronze ***b*** that held it up,
Ezekiel
39:18 lambs, goats, ***b***, all fattened
45:23 seven flawless ***b*** and seven
Hosea
12:11 they sacrifice ***b***, so their altars
14:2 good. Instead of ***b***, let us offer
Acts
14:13 the city, brought ***b*** and wreaths to
Hebrews
9:13 of goats and ***b*** and the sprinkled
10:4 for the blood of ***b*** and goats to take

BURDEN
Matthew
11:30 is easy to bear, and my ***b*** is light."
Acts
15:10 God by placing a ***b*** on the shoulders

BURIAL
Genesis
23:4 property for a ***b*** plot among you so
49:30 Ephron the Hittite as a ***b*** property.
50:13 had purchased as ***b*** property from
2 Chronicles
22:9 given a decent ***b***, however, because
Isaiah
14:20 join them in ***b***, for you
57:2 paths will find rest on their ***b*** beds.
Jeremiah
22:19 him a donkey's ***b***, dragging him
25:33 their bodies for ***b***. They will become
26:23 was thrown into the common ***b*** ground.
34:5 death. As ***b*** incense was
Mark
14:8 anointed my body ahead of time for ***b***.
John
12:7 for my ***b***, and this is how

BURIED

Genesis
25:10 Sarah were both ***b*** in the field
50:13 of Canaan and ***b*** him in the cave
Deuteronomy
34:6 The Lord ***b*** him in a valley in Moabite
Joshua
24:30 They ***b*** him within the border of his own
Ruth
1:17 there I will be ***b***. May the LORD do
Job
3:16 wasn't I like a ***b*** miscarried
16:15 over my skin and ***b*** my dignity in the
27:15 survivors will be ***b*** with the dead;
Jeremiah
13:5 So I went and ***b*** it at the Euphrates, as
Matthew
14:12 took his body and ***b*** it. Then they
25:18 in the ground and ***b*** his master's
26:12 over my body she's prepared me to be ***b***.
27:7 field where strangers could be ***b***.
Mark
15:47 the mother of Joses saw where he was ***b***.
Luke
16:22 side. The rich man also died and was ***b***.
23:53 rock, in which no one had ever been ***b***.
Acts
2:29 He died and was ***b***, and his tomb is
5:6 his body, carried him out, and ***b*** him.
8:2 Some pious men ***b*** Stephen and deeply
13:36 he died and was ***b*** with his
Romans
6:4 Therefore we were ***b*** together with him
1 Corinthians
15:4 he was ***b***, and he rose on the third day
Colossians
2:12 You were ***b*** with him through baptism and

BURN

Exodus
3:2 bush was in flames, but it didn't ***b*** up.
29:14 ***B*** the rest of the meat of the bull, its
Leviticus
1:9 then completely ***b*** all of it on the
Numbers
16:40 approach to ***b*** incense in the
Deuteronomy
6:15 God's anger will ***b*** against you, and
7:4 the LORD's anger ***b*** against you, and
Joshua
7:15 death by burning. ***B*** everything that
11:6 their horses! ***B*** their chariots!"
11:13 But Israel didn't ***b*** any of the cities
Nehemiah
10:34 every year, to ***b*** on the altar of
Psalms
79:5 How long will your anger ***b*** like fire?
89:46 How long will your wrath ***b*** like fire?
Jeremiah
4:4 wildfire. It will ***b***, with no one to
34:2 king of Babylon, and he will ***b*** it down.
34:22 capture it, and ***b*** it down along
36:25 the king not to ***b*** the scroll, but
Hosea
7:6 it continues to ***b*** like a flaming
Amos
5:6 The fire will ***b*** up Bethel, with
Obadiah
1:18 straw; they will ***b*** them up
Malachi
1:10 so that you don't ***b*** something on my
4:1 coming day will ***b*** them, says the
Matthew
3:12 barn. But he will ***b*** the husks with a
13:40 gather weeds and ***b*** them in the fire,
Luke
1:9 the Lord's sanctuary and ***b*** incense.
3:17 barn. But he will ***b*** the husks with a
1 Corinthians
7:9 better to marry than to ***b*** with passion.

BURNED → BURNED OFFERING, BURNED OFFERINGS

Matthew
13:30 in bundles to be ***b***. But bring the
John
15:6 gathered up, thrown into a fire, and ***b***.
Acts
19:19 sorcery texts and ***b*** them publicly.
Romans
1:27 with females, and ***b*** with lust for
Hebrews
6:8 to being cursed. It ends up being ***b***.
13:11 their bodies are ***b*** outside the camp.
Revelation
8:7 of the earth was ***b*** up. A third of
16:9 The people were ***b*** by intense heat, and

BURNED OFFERING

Gn 22:2; 22:3, 6, 7, 8, 13; Ex 18:12; 29:18, 25, 42; 30:9; 40:29; Lv 1:3; 1:4, 6, 9, 10, 13, 14, 17; 3:5; 4:24, 33; 5:7, 10; 6:9, 10, 12, 25; 7:2, 8, 37; 8:18, 21, 28; 9:2, 3, 7, 12, 13, 14, 16, 17, 22, 24; 12:6, 8; 14:13, 19, 20, 22, 31; 15:15, 30; 16:3, 5; 17:8; 22:18; 23:12, 18; Nm 6:11; 6:14; 7:15, 21, 27, 33, 39, 45, 51, 57, 63, 69, 75, 81, 87; 8:12; 15:3, 5, 8, 24; 23:3, 6, 15, 17; 28:3, 6, 10, 11, 13, 14, 15, 19, 23, 24, 27, 31; 29:2, 6, 8, 11, 13, 16, 19, 22, 25, 28, 31, 34, 36, 38; Dt 13:16; 33:10; Josh 22:23; 22:26, 29; Jdg 6:26; 11:31; 13:16, 23; 1Sa 6:14; 7:9, 10; 13:9, 10, 12; 2Sa 24:22; 2Ki 3:27; 10:25; 16:13, 15; 1Ch 21:24; 21:26; 2Ch 7:1; 29:18, 27, 28, 29; Ezr 8:35; Neh 10:33; Job 42:8; Ps 51:16; Is 40:16; 43:23; Eze 40:38; 40:42; 45:17, 23; 46:4, 12, 13, 15

BURNED OFFERINGS

Gn 8:20; Ex 10:25; 20:24; 24:5; 30:28; 31:9; 32:6; 35:16; 38:1; 40:6, 10, 29; Lv 4:7; 4:10, 18, 25, 29, 30, 34; 10:19; 16:24; 23:37; Nm 6:16; 10:10; 29:39; Dt 12:6; 12:11, 13, 14; Josh 8:31; 22:27, 28; Jdg 20:26; 21:4; 1Sa 6:15; 10:8; 15:22; 2Sa 6:17; 6:18; 24:24, 25; 1Ki 3:4; 3:15; 8:64; 9:25; 10:5; 2Ki 5:17; 10:24; 16:15; 1Ch 6:49; 16:1, 2, 40; 21:23, 26, 29; 22:1; 23:31; 29:21; 2Ch 1:6; 2:4; 4:6; 7:7; 8:12; 9:4; 13:11; 24:14; 29:7, 31, 32, 34, 35; 30:15; 31:2, 3; 35:12, 14, 16; Ezr 3:2; 3:3, 4, 5, 6; 6:9; 8:35; Job 1:5; Ps 20:3; 40:6; 50:8; 51:19; 66:13, 15; Is 1:11; 56:7; Jer 6:20; 7:21, 22; 14:12; 17:26; 33:18; Eze 40:39; 43:18, 24, 27;

44:11; 45:15, 17, 25; 46:2; Hos 4:13; 6:6; Am 5:22; Mi 6:6; Mk 12:33; Heb 10:6; 10:8

BURNING → BURNING COALS, BURNING INCENSE
Exodus
3:3 and find out why the bush isn't ***b*** up.
29:18 ram into smoke by ***b*** it on the altar.
Leviticus
6:12 fire must be kept ***b***; it must not go
16:12 pan full of ***b*** coals from the
24:2 the lamp, to keep a light ***b*** constantly.
Numbers
19:6 them into the fire where the cow is ***b***.
Joshua
7:15 put to death by ***b***. Burn everything
Job
20:23 unleash his ***b*** anger on them,
Psalms
38:7 My insides are ***b*** up; there's nothing in
46:9 the spear, ***b*** chariots with
69:24 on them—let your ***b*** fury catch them.
78:49 God unleashed his ***b*** anger against
85:3 you've turned away from your ***b*** anger.
97:3 before him, ***b*** up his enemies on
118:12 extinguished like ***b*** thorns. I cut
124:3 up whole with their rage ***b*** against us!
Daniel
10:6 eyes were like ***b*** torches. His arms
Malachi
4:1 day is coming, ***b*** like an oven. All
Matthew
13:42 throw them into a ***b*** furnace. People
18:9 to be cast into a ***b*** hell with two
Mark
12:26 passage about the ***b*** bush, how God
John
5:35 John was a ***b*** and shining lamp, and, at
Acts
7:30 in the flame of a ***b*** bush in the
Hebrews
10:27 judgment and of a ***b*** fire that's going
Revelation
1:12 seven oil lamps ***b*** on top of seven
8:8 a huge mountain ***b*** with fire was
8:10 and a great star, ***b*** like a torch,
18:9 her when they see the smoke from her ***b***.
18:18 smoke from her ***b*** and said, 'What

BURNING COALS
Lv 16:12; Ps 120:4; 140:10; Prv 25:22; Ro 12:20

BURNING INCENSE
Ex 30:1; 40:5; 1Ki 13:1; 2Ki 12:3; 14:4; 15:4; 18:4; 23:8; 2Ch 28:3; 28:25; 29:7; Is 65:3; Jer 44:8; 44:18; Rev 8:3

BURNS
Job
19:11 His anger ***b*** against me; he considers me
Isaiah
13:13 heavenly forces on the day his anger ***b***.
Joel
2:3 them a flame ***b***. Land ahead of
Amos
6:10 someone who ***b*** the dead, picks
Habakkuk
1:16 to his net; he ***b*** incense to his
Zechariah
10:3 My anger ***b*** hot against the shepherds; I
Revelation
11:5 their mouth and ***b*** up their enemies.
19:20 into the fiery lake that ***b*** with sulfur.
21:8 in the lake that ***b*** with fire and

BURY
Psalms
79:3 and there's no one left to ***b*** them.
Matthew
8:21 first let me go and ***b*** my father."
8:22 me, and let the dead ***b*** their own dead."
Luke
9:59 first let me go and ***b*** my father."
9:60 Let the dead ***b*** their own dead.

BUSINESS
Deuteronomy
25:16 all who do ***b*** dishonestly, are
Job
20:18 won't enjoy the wealth from their ***b***.
Ecclesiastes
5:14 is lost in a bad ***b*** venture so that
Jeremiah
17:21 day or conduct ***b*** at the gates of
Luke
19:13 He said, 'Do ***b*** with this until I
John
2:16 make my Father's house a place of ***b***."
Acts
19:24 temple, and his ***b*** generated a lot
19:25 we make an easy living from this ***b***.
2 Corinthians
11:17 my confidence in this ***b*** of bragging.
Philippians
2:21 put their own ***b*** ahead of Jesus
1 Thessalonians
4:11 mind your own ***b***, and earn your
2 Thessalonians
3:11 they are meddling in other people's ***b***.

BUY
Exodus
21:2 When you ***b*** a male Hebrew slave, he will serve you for six
Leviticus
27:13 maker wishes to ***b*** it back, they
Deuteronomy
2:6 Of course you may ***b*** food from them with money
Ruth
4:8 said to Boaz, "***B*** it for yourself,"
Ezra
7:17 be careful to ***b*** bulls, rams, and
Nehemiah
10:31 Sabbath, we won't ***b*** it from them on
Proverbs
23:23 ***B*** truth and don't sell it; buy wisdom,
Jeremiah
6:20 offerings won't ***b*** your pardon; your
19:1 proclaims: Go ***b*** a clay jar from a

Matthew
27:7 to use it to ***b*** the potter's
Mark
6:36 and villages and ***b*** something to eat
6:37 we go off and ***b*** bread worth
Luke
9:13 —unless we go and ***b*** food for all
22:36 must sell their clothes and ***b*** one.
John
4:8 gone into the city to ***b*** him some food.
6:5 Where will we ***b*** food to feed
13:29 told him, "Go, ***b*** what we need for
Acts
8:20 you could ***b*** God's gift with
22:28 a lot of money to ***b*** my citizenship."

Cc

CAESAR
Matthew
22:17 allow people to pay taxes to **C** or not?"
22:21 he said, "Give to **C** what belongs to
Luke
2:1 In those days **C** Augustus declared that everyone
Acts
25:8 Law, against the temple, or against **C**."
25:11 hand me over to them. I appeal to **C**!"
26:32 released if he hadn't appealed to **C**."
27:24 must stand before **C**! Indeed, God has
28:19 to appeal to **C**. Don't think I

CAESAREA
Matthew
16:13 to the area of **C** Philippi, he
Mark
8:27 the villages near **C** Philippi. On the
Acts
10:1 was a man in **C** named Cornelius,
12:19 Judea in order to spend some time in **C**.
25:4 keeping Paul in **C**, since he was to

CAIN
Genesis
4:2 the flocks, and **C** farmed the
4:8 **C** said to his brother Abel, "Let's go
4:9 The LORD said to **C**, "Where is your
Hebrews
11:4 to God than **C**, which showed
1 John
3:12 Don't behave like **C**, who belonged to
Jude
1:11 the footsteps of **C**. For profit they

CAKES
Exodus
12:39 baked unleavened ***c*** from the dough
Numbers
11:8 and make it into ***c***. It tasted like
2 Samuel
13:6 of heart-shaped ***c*** in front of me so
1 Kings
14:3 loaves of bread, ***c***, and a bottle of
1 Chronicles
9:31 was entrusted with baking the flat ***c***.
12:40 of flour, fig ***c***, clusters of
23:29 bread, the ***c*** made on the
Song of Songs
2:5 me with raisin ***c***, strengthen me
Isaiah
16:7 for the raisin ***c*** of Kir-hareseth.
Jeremiah
7:18 make sacrificial ***c*** for the Queen of
44:19 when we make ***c*** in her image and
Hosea
3:1 turn to other gods and love raisin ***c***."

CALEB
Numbers
13:6 the tribe of Judah, **C**, Jephunneh's son;
34:19 the tribe of Judah, **C**, Jephunneh's son;
Deuteronomy
1:36 only exception is **C**, Jephunneh's son.
Joshua
14:6 Joshua. **C** son of Jephunneh
15:16 **C** said, "I will give Achsah my daughter
15:17 captured it, and **C** gave him Achsah
15:18 off her donkey, **C** asked her, "What
21:12 areas to **C**, Jephunneh's son,
Judges
1:12 **C** said, "I'll give my daughter Achsah
1:13 captured it; so **C** gave him his
1:20 gave Hebron to **C**, just as Moses
1 Samuel
30:14 southern plain of **C**. We also burned
1 Chronicles
2:18 **C**, Hezron's son, had children with his

CALF
Exodus
32:4 image of a bull ***c***, and the people
Deuteronomy
9:16 made yourselves a ***c***, an idol made of
Nehemiah
9:18 an image of a ***c*** for themselves,
Isaiah
11:6 young goat; the ***c*** and the young
Hosea
8:5 Your ***c*** is rejected, Samaria. My anger
Luke
15:23 the fattened ***c*** and slaughter it.
Acts
7:41 in the shape of a ***c***, offered a

CALL → CALL OUT, CALL UPON
Genesis
17:15 will no longer ***c*** her Sarai. Her
Deuteronomy
4:26 I ***c*** heaven and earth as my witnesses
Ruth
1:20 to them, "Don't ***c*** me Naomi, but
1 Samuel
3:5 me?" "I didn't ***c*** you," Eli
1 Kings
18:24 all of you will ***c*** on the name of
1 Chronicles
16:8 to the LORD, ***c*** on his name; make
Psalms
18:6 for help, and my ***c*** reached his ears.

72:17 be blessed through him and ***c*** him happy.
80:18 us so that we can ***c*** on your name.
116:13 salvation. I'll ***c*** on the LORD's
116:17 to you, and I'll ***c*** on the LORD's
Proverbs
1:28 Then they will ***c*** me, but I won't
Ecclesiastes
11:9 this: God will ***c*** you to account
Isaiah
5:20 Doom to those who ***c*** evil good and good
12:4 Thank the LORD; ***c*** on God's name;
55:6 still be found; ***c*** him while he is
60:14 feet. They will ***c*** you The LORD's
65:24 Before they ***c***, I will answer; while
Jeremiah
33:3 ***c*** to me and I will answer and reveal to
Lamentations
3:21 I ***c*** all this to mind—therefore, I
Hosea
2:16 LORD, you will ***c*** me, "My husband,"
Jonah
1:6 deeply? Get up! ***C*** on your god!
Matthew
9:13 I didn't come to ***c*** righteous people,
23:9 Don't ***c*** anybody on earth your father,
Mark
10:18 Why do you ***c*** me good? No one
Luke
6:46 Why do you ***c*** me 'Lord, Lord' and don't do what I say
John
13:13 You ***c*** me 'Teacher' and 'Lord,' and you
15:15 I don't ***c*** you servants any longer,
Romans
9:25 in Hosea, I will ***c*** "my people"those
1 Thessalonians
4:7 God didn't ***c*** us to be immoral but to be
Hebrews
2:11 isn't ashamed to ***c*** them brothers and
James
5:14 sick, they should ***c*** for the elders of
2 Peter
1:10 to confirm your ***c*** and election. Do

CALL OUT

Job 5:1; Ps 55:16; 57:2; 116:2; 145:18; Prv 2:3; 21:13; Is 40:6; 43:22; Jer 31:7; Lam 3:8; Eze 8:18; Zec 1:17

CALL UPON

1Sa 12:17; Ps 105:1; Jer 11:12; Hos 7:7; 7:11; Am 5:16; Jon 3:8; 1Co 1:2; 1Pt 1:17

CALLED

→ CALLED OUT, CALLED TOGETHER, CALLED YOU

Genesis
2:23 flesh.She will be ***c*** a woman because
3:9 The LORD God ***c*** to the man and said to
21:17 God's messenger ***c*** to Hagar from
Exodus
3:4 to look, God ***c*** to him out of the
16:31 Israelite people ***c*** it manna. It was
19:3 to God. The LORD ***c*** to him from the
1 Samuel
3:4 The LORD ***c*** to Samuel. "I'm here," he
1 Kings
18:26 prepared it and ***c*** on Baal's name
1 Chronicles
21:26 sacrifices. He ***c*** on the LORD, who
Psalms
116:4 So I ***c*** on the LORD's name: "LORD,
Isaiah
1:26 this you will be ***c*** Righteous City,
4:3 Jerusalem will be ***c*** holy, everyone
49:1 away. The LORD ***c*** me before my
65:12 because I ***c*** and you didn't
Hosea
11:1 loved him, and out of Egypt I ***c*** my son.
Matthew
1:16 Jesus was born, who is ***c*** the Christ.
2:15 prophet: I have ***c*** my son out of
2:23 settled in a city ***c*** Nazareth so that
5:9 because they will be ***c*** God's children.
5:19 the same will be ***c*** the lowest in the
21:13 My house will be ***c*** a house of
23:8 you shouldn't be ***c*** Rabbi, because
Luke
1:32 and he will be ***c*** the Son of the
1:35 will be holy. He will be ***c*** God's Son.
1:76 child, will be ***c*** a prophet of the
15:19 deserve to be ***c*** your son. Take me
John
19:17 out to a place ***c*** Skull Place
1 Corinthians
1:9 and you were ***c*** by him to
1:24 to those who are ***c***—both Jews and Greeks
7:17 assigned when he ***c*** each one. This is
Galatians
5:13 You were ***c*** to freedom, brothers and
Colossians
3:15 which you were ***c*** in one body. And
2 Thessalonians
2:14 God ***c*** all of you through our good news
1 Timothy
6:12 life—you were ***c*** to it, and you
2 Timothy
1:9 one who saved and ***c*** us with a holy
Hebrews
9:15 those who are ***c*** might receive the
11:16 ashamed to be ***c*** their God—he has
James
2:23 is more, Abraham was ***c*** God's friend.
1 Peter
3:9 return. You were ***c*** to do this so
5:10 the one who ***c*** you into his
2 Peter
1:3 of the one who ***c*** us by his own
1 John
3:1 that we should be ***c*** God's children,
Jude
1:1 To those who are ***c***, loved by God the
Revelation
1:9 was on the island ***c*** Patmos because of
6:16 They ***c*** to the mountains and the rocks,
11:8 is spiritually ***c*** Sodom and Egypt,
12:9 old snake, who is ***c*** the devil and
16:16 the place that is ***c*** in Hebrew,
17:14 with him are ***c***, chosen, and
18:2 He ***c*** out with a loud voice, saying,
19:11 Its rider was ***c*** Faithful and
19:13 and his name was ***c*** the Word of God.

CALLED OUT
Gn 22:11; 22:15; Dt 5:1; 22:27; Josh 8:16; Jdg 7:20; 7:23, 24; 9:7; 10:17; 15:18; 16:9, 12, 14, 20, 28; 18:23; 1Sa 15:4; 2Sa 18:25; 18:28; 1Ki 17:10; 20:39; 2Ki 7:10; Song 5:6; Is 21:8; Eze 9:1; 38:8; Dn 6:20; 8:16; Jon 2:2; Zec 1:14; 6:8; Lk 8:8; 8:54; Rev 10:3; 18:2; 19:17

CALLED TOGETHER
Ex 4:29; 7:11; 12:21; 19:7; 36:2; Mk 15:16; Lk 6:13; 19:13; 23:13; Jn 11:47

CALLED YOU
Is 42:6; 43:1; 45:4; Jer 7:13; Jn 1:48; 1Co 7:15; Ga 1:6; Eph 4:4; 1Pt 1:15; 2:9; 5:10

CALLING → CALLING OUT
1 Samuel
3:8 that it was the LORD who was ***c*** the boy.
Matthew
27:47 standing there said, "He's ***c*** Elijah."
Mark
10:49 Be encouraged! Get up! He's ***c*** you."
John
11:28 teacher is here and he's ***c*** for you."
Romans
11:29 God's gifts and ***c*** can't be taken back
2 Timothy
1:9 us with a holy ***c***. This wasn't
Hebrews
3:1 in the heavenly ***c***, think about

CALLING OUT
Ps 50:1; 88:9; Mt 11:16; Lk 7:32; Ac 10:18

CALLS
Isaiah
64:7 No one ***c*** on your name; no one bothers
Joel
2:32 But everyone who ***c*** on the LORD's name
Micah
6:9 voice of the LORD ***c*** out to the city;
Matthew
22:45 If David ***c*** him Lord, how can he be
John
10:3 to his voice. He ***c*** his own sheep by
Acts
2:21 And everyone who ***c*** on the name of the
Romans
4:17 to the dead and ***c*** things that don't
Revelation
2:20 Jezebel, who ***c*** herself a
13:18 This ***c*** for wisdom. Let the one who
17:9 This ***c*** for an understanding mind. The

CALM
Psalms
65:7 you ***c*** the roaring seas; calm the
Jonah
1:12 sea will become ***c*** around you. I
Matthew
8:26 and the lake, and there was a great ***c***.

CALVES
1 Kings
12:28 made two gold ***c***. He said to the
2 Kings
10:29 the gold ***c*** that were in
Hosea
13:2 these," they say. People are kissing ***c***!
Micah
6:6 burned offerings, with year-old ***c***?
Malachi
4:2 and jump about like ***c*** in the stall.
Hebrews
9:12 blood of goats or ***c***, securing our

CAMELS
Genesis
24:14 I will give your ***c*** water too,' may

CANAAN
Genesis
9:25 said, "Cursed be **C**: the lowest
13:12 in the land of **C**, and Lot settled
42:5 the famine had spread to the land of **C**.
Exodus
6:4 them the land of **C** where they lived
Numbers
13:2 the land of **C**, which I'm giving
34:2 enter the land of **C**, this is the land
Deuteronomy
32:49 at the land of **C**, which I'm giving
Judges
4:2 to King Jabin of **C**, who reigned in
1 Chronicles
16:18 you the land of **C** as your allotted
Psalms
105:11 you the land of **C** as your allotted
Zephaniah
2:5 is against you, **C**, land of the
Acts
13:19 in the land of **C** and gave the

CANAANITE
Genesis
28:1 these orders: "Don't marry a **C** woman.
Matthew
15:22 A **C** woman from those territories came

CANAANITES
Genesis
12:6 oak of Moreh. The **C** lived in the land
Exodus
3:8 a place where the **C**, the Hittites,
33:2 drive out the **C**, the Amorites,
Joshua
16:10 didn't remove the **C** who lived in
17:12 cities, and the **C** were determined
Judges
1:1 first to fight for us against the **C**?"
1:27 villages. The **C** were determined
3:5 lived among the **C**, Hittites,

CAPERNAUM
Matthew
4:13 and settled in **C**, which lies
8:5 Jesus went to **C**, a centurion
11:23 And you, **C**, will you be honored by
17:24 When they came to **C**, the people who
John
4:46 into wine. In **C** there was a
6:59 he was teaching in the synagogue in **C**.

CAPTIVE

Ezra
2:1 —from among those ***c*** exiles whom
Nehemiah
4:4 and make them like plunder in a ***c*** land.
Psalms
78:61 his power be held ***c***, let his glory go
Isaiah
52:2 bonds from your neck, ***c*** Daughter Zion!
Jeremiah
48:46 off; your daughters have been taken ***c***.
51:41 whole earth taken ***c***! How Babylon has
52:30 Altogether, 4,600 were taken ***c***.
Lamentations
1:5 have gone away, ***c*** before the enemy.

CAPTIVES

Deuteronomy
21:11 you see among the ***c*** a beautiful
Psalms
68:18 leading away your ***c***, receiving
69:33 to the needy and doesn't despise his ***c***.
Isaiah
14:2 land, making ***c*** of their captors
20:4 Assyria lead the ***c*** of Egypt and the
49:24 from warriors? Can a tyrant's ***c*** escape?
Jeremiah
33:7 bring back the ***c*** of Judah and
49:39 bring back the ***c*** of Elam, declares
Ezekiel
39:25 bring back the ***c*** of Jacob. I will
Habakkuk
1:9 the desert. He takes ***c*** like sand.
Luke
21:24 be taken away as ***c*** among all

CAPTIVITY

Ezra
3:8 had come from the ***c*** to Jerusalem—made a beginning
Nehemiah
1:2 and survived the ***c***, and about
Isaiah
46:2 burden, but they themselves go into ***c***.
Jeremiah
20:6 will go into ***c***. You will be
Lamentations
2:14 to prevent your ***c***. Instead, they
Nahum
3:10 she went into ***c***. Indeed, her
Revelation
13:10 then into ***c*** they will go. If

CAPTURE

Genesis
43:18 can overpower us, ***c*** us, make slaves
1 Samuel
4:21 referring to the ***c*** of God's chest
Isaiah
7:6 tear it apart, ***c*** it for ourselves,
Jeremiah
18:22 have dug a pit to ***c*** me, set traps for
32:24 are about to ***c*** it by war,
Ezekiel
17:15 he overturn the agreement and escape ***c***?
17:18 these things, and he won't escape ***c***.
2 Corinthians
10:5 of God. They ***c*** every thought to
11:32 the city of Damascus in order to ***c*** me,

CAPTURED

1 Samuel
4:19 chest had been ***c*** and that her
2 Kings
17:6 the Assyrian king ***c*** Samaria. He sent

CARE

Genesis
2:15 of Eden to farm it and to take ***c*** of it.
Exodus
3:1 Moses was taking ***c*** of the flock for his
30:7 morning when he takes ***c*** of the lamps.
Numbers
23:12 I have to take ***c*** to speak whatever
Judges
19:20 but let me take ***c*** of all your
1 Samuel
7:1 son, to ***c*** for the LORD's
2 Samuel
9:8 that you should ***c*** about a dead dog
18:22 to Joab, "I don't ***c*** what happens,
18:23 I don't ***c*** what happens, I want to go,"
20:3 had left to take ***c*** of the palace and
1 Kings
1:2 the king and take ***c*** of him by laying
2:4 will take ***c*** to walk before me
12:16 Why should we ***c*** about David? We
17:9 ordered a widow there to take ***c*** of you.
Ezra
8:33 house into the ***c*** of the priest
Nehemiah
2:18 my God had taken ***c*** of me, and also
Psalms
77:20 sheep under the ***c*** of Moses and
Proverbs
12:10 The righteous ***c*** about their livestock's
13:18 those who don't ***c*** about
Daniel
2:38 into your ***c*** human beings,
Zechariah
1:14 forces says: I ***c*** passionately
Matthew
4:11 him, and angels came and took ***c*** of him.
23:3 you must take ***c*** to do everything
25:36 sick and you took ***c*** of me. I was in
28:14 we will take ***c*** of it with him so
Luke
10:34 took him to an inn, and took ***c*** of him.
21:34 Take ***c*** that your hearts aren't dulled
John
21:16 said to him, "Take ***c*** of my sheep."
1 Corinthians
4:3 I couldn't ***c*** less if I'm judged by you
2 Corinthians
8:19 we are taking ***c*** of for the sake
Ephesians
5:29 it and takes ***c*** of it just like
1 Timothy
3:5 how can they take ***c*** of God's church?
5:16 she should take ***c*** of them and not
Hebrews
2:6 the human being that you ***c*** about them?

CARE [cont.]

James
1:27 is this: to ***c*** for orphans and
1 Peter
3:7 of the gracious ***c*** of life. Do this
5:3 entrusted to your ***c***, but become
1 John
3:17 person doesn't ***c***—how can the love
Jude
1:12 reverence. They ***c*** only for
Revelation
12:6 she will be taken ***c*** of for one
12:14 would be taken ***c*** of—out of the sna

CARMEL
1 Samuel
15:12 Saul went to ***C***, where he is
1 Kings
18:20 He gathered the prophets at Mount ***C***.
Nahum
1:4 Bashan and ***C*** wither; the bud

CARVED
Leviticus
26:1 not place any ***c*** stone in your
Numbers
33:52 destroy all their ***c*** figures. You will
Deuteronomy
10:3 acacia wood and ***c*** two stone tablets
Judges
3:19 back at the ***c*** stones near
3:26 had passed the ***c*** stones and
Psalms
144:12 be like pillars ***c*** to decorate a
Proverbs
9:1 house; she has ***c*** out her seven
Ezekiel
23:14 She saw men ***c*** in wall reliefs,
41:25 main hall were ***c*** with winged
Amos
5:11 built houses of ***c*** stone, but you
Nahum
1:14 I will remove ***c*** idol and cast
Matthew
27:60 which he had ***c*** out of the rock.
Mark
15:46 that had been ***c*** out of rock. He
Luke
23:53 laid it in a tomb ***c*** out of the rock,
2 Corinthians
3:7 brought death was ***c*** in letters on

CASE LAWS
Ex 21:1; 24:3; Nm 35:24; 35:29; 36:13; Dt 4:1; 4:5, 8, 14, 45; 5:1, 31; 6:1, 20; 7:11, 12; 8:11; 11:1, 32; 12:1; 26:16, 17; 30:16; 33:10; 1Ki 9:4; 2Ki 17:34; 17:37; 1Ch 22:13; 28:7; 2Ch 7:17; 19:10; 33:8; Eze 5:6; 5:7, 10, 15; 11:12, 20; 18:9, 17; 20:11, 13, 16, 18, 19, 21, 24, 25; 36:27; 37:24; 44:24

CAST → CAST LOTS
Exodus
25:12 ***C*** four gold rings for it and put them
Leviticus
19:4 or make gods of ***c*** metal for
Numbers
33:52 destroy all their ***c*** images. You will
Deuteronomy
9:12 themselves an idol out of ***c*** metal."
1 Kings
7:15 He ***c*** two bronze pillars. Each one was
Psalms
55:22 ***C*** your burden on the LORD—he will
71:9 Don't ***c*** me off in old age. Don't
Isaiah
19:8 lament; all who ***c*** fishhooks in the
44:10 form a god or ***c*** an idol that does
Jeremiah
7:15 I will ***c*** you out of my sight, just as I
Ezekiel
19:8 against him. They ***c*** their nets over
Hosea
14:5 the lily, he will ***c*** out his roots
Matthew
18:9 eye than to be ***c*** into a burning
Mark
6:13 They ***c*** out many demons, and they
16:9 from whom he had ***c*** out seven demons.
Luke
10:15 No, you will be ***c*** down to the place
12:49 I came to ***c*** fire upon the earth. How I
John
19:24 tear it. Let's ***c*** lots to see who
21:6 He said, "***C*** your net on the right side
Revelation
18:23 by the spell you ***c***, and because
21:8 who use drugs and ***c*** spells, the

CAST LOTS
Lv 16:8; Josh 18:10; 1Ch 24:31; 25:8; 26:13, 14; Neh 10:34; 11:1; Ps 22:18; Jl 3:3; Obad 1:11; Jon 1:7; Na 3:10; Jn 19:24; Ac 1:26

CATCH
Matthew
17:27 first fish you ***c***. When you open
Luke
5:6 nets and their ***c*** was so huge that
5:8 Peter saw the ***c***, he fell at
Acts
27:40 the foresail to ***c*** the wind and made

CATTLE
Psalms
50:10 to me, as do the ***c*** on a thousand
104:14 grass grow for ***c***; you make plants
144:14 so that our ***c*** can be loaded with
Ecclesiastes
2:7 great herds of ***c*** and sheep, more
Matthew
22:4 and the fattened ***c***. Now everything's
John
2:14 who were selling ***c***, sheep, and

CAUSE
Psalms
7:16 The trouble they ***c*** will come back on
35:19 enemies without ***c*** celebrate over
119:161 me without ***c***, but my heart
Proverbs
13:10 The empty-headed ***c*** conflict out of
29:22 up conflict; hotheads ***c*** much offense.
Isaiah
1:23 and the widow's ***c*** never reaches

34:8 a year of payback for Zion's **c**.
Lamentations
3:59 look at my mistreatment; judge my **c**.
Luke
17:2 necks than to **c** one of these
1 Corinthians
8:13 or else I may **c** my brother or
Philemon
1:1 prisoner for the **c** of Christ Jesus,
Revelation
13:15 even speak and **c** anyone who didn't

CAVALRY
Exodus
14:9 chariots, his **c**, and his army,
15:19 chariots, and **c** went into the
1 Samuel
8:11 chariots and his **c** and as runners
13:5 six thousand **c**, and as many
1 Kings
9:19 chariots and **c** and whatever he
9:22 those in charge of his chariots and **c**.
1 Chronicles
18:4 seven thousand **c**, and twenty
19:6 hire chariots and **c** for themselves
2 Chronicles
8:6 for chariots and **c**—along with everything else
8:9 the commanders of his chariots and **c**.
Ezra
8:22 of soldiers and **c** to help us in
Nehemiah
2:9 officers of the army and **c** with me.
Nahum
3:3 Charging **c**, flashing sword, and
Zechariah
10:5 with them. All the **c** will be ashamed.
Revelation
9:16 The number of **c** troops was two hundred

CAVE
Genesis
19:30 he and his two daughters lived in a **c**.
23:9 give me his own **c** in Machpelah at
25:9 buried him in the **c** in Machpelah,
49:29 ancestors in the **c** that's in the
50:13 buried him in the **c** in the field of
Joshua
10:16 fled and hid in the **c** at Makkedah.
Psalms
57:1 Saul into the **c**.] Have mercy on
142:1 he was in the **c**. A prayer.] I cry
John
11:38 tomb. It was a **c**, and a stone

CEDAR
Numbers
24:6 has planted, like **c** trees next to
2 Samuel
7:2 I'm living in a **c** palace, but God's
Job
40:17 his tail like a **c**; the tendons in
Psalms
92:12 will grow strong like a **c** of Lebanon.
Song of Songs
8:9 will barricade her with a panel of **c**.
Isaiah
41:19 in the desert **c**, acacia, myrtle,
Ezekiel
17:3 and took the top branch of the **c**.
31:3 Assyria, a **c** of Lebanon:
31:8 No **c** was its equal in God's garden. The
Amos
2:9 was as tall as **c** trees, and whose

CELEBRATE
Leviticus
23:4 which you will **c** at their
23:39 crops, you will **c** the LORD's
23:41 You will **c** this festival to the LORD
25:2 the land must **c** a sabbath rest to
Numbers
29:12 work. You will **c** a festival to the
Deuteronomy
16:14 **C** your festival: you, your sons, your
26:11 Then **c** all the good things the LORD
Nehemiah
12:27 to Jerusalem to **c** the dedication
Psalms
35:27 shout for joy and **c**! Let them
96:11 Let heaven **c**! Let the earth rejoice!
107:42 right see it and **c**, but every wicked
149:5 Let the faithful **c** with glory; let them
Zechariah
14:16 forces, and to **c** the Festival of
Matthew
25:21 in charge of much. Come, **c** with me.'
26:18 I'm going to **c** the Passover with
John
4:36 and those who harvest can **c** together.
5:35 you were willing to **c** in his light.
Acts
7:41 it, and began to **c** what they had
1 Corinthians
5:8 so let's **c** the feast with the
Revelation
11:10 them. They will **c** and give each
19:7 us rejoice and **c**, and give him the

CELEBRATED → CELEBRATED THE FESTIVAL
Ezra
6:16 exiles, joyfully **c** the dedication of
Psalms
35:15 I stumbled, they **c** and gathered
Luke
1:58 and relatives **c** with her because

CELEBRATED THE FESTIVAL
2Ch 7:8; 7:9; 30:21; Ezr 3:4; 6:22

CELEBRATION
Deuteronomy
16:8 day will be a **c** for the LORD your
1 Samuel
11:15 the Israelites held a great **c** there.
18:7 The women sang in **c**: "Saul has killed
Nehemiah
8:12 to have a great **c**, because they
Psalms
16:11 presence is total **c**. Beautiful things
45:15 palace, they are led in with **c** and joy.
51:8 me hear joy and **c** again; let the

81:3 at the full moon, for our day of ***c***!
100:2 the LORD with ***c***! Come before him
145:7 They will rave in ***c*** of your abundant
Luke
12:36 from a wedding ***c***, who can
John
2:2 disciples were also invited to the ***c***.

CENSUS
Exodus
30:12 When you take a ***c*** of the Israelites to
Numbers
1:2 Take a ***c*** of the entire Israelite
26:2 Take a ***c*** of the entire Israelite
2 Samuel
24:2 and take a ***c*** of the people so
Acts
5:37 the time of the ***c***, Judas the

CENTURION
Matthew
8:5 went to Capernaum, a ***c*** approached,
27:54 When the ***c*** and those with him who were
Mark
15:39 When the ***c***, who stood facing Jesus,
Acts
10:1 Cornelius, a ***c*** in the Italian
22:25 Paul said to the ***c*** standing there,

CHAINS
Exodus
28:14 along with two ***c*** of pure gold, twisted
1 Kings
6:21 He placed gold ***c*** in front of the
Psalms
2:3 off their ropes and throw off their ***c***!"
Lamentations
3:7 I couldn't escape; he made my ***c*** heavy.
Mark
5:4 leg irons and ***c***, but he broke the
Acts
8:23 poisoned you and evil has you in ***c***."
12:7 Get up!" The ***c*** fell from his
16:26 flew open and everyone's ***c*** came loose.
Ephesians
6:20 an ambassador in ***c*** for the sake of
Colossians
4:3 plan of Christ—which is why I'm in ***c***.
Hebrews
11:36 they were even put in ***c*** and in prison.
2 Peter
2:4 committed them to ***c*** of darkness,
Jude
1:6 them in eternal ***c*** in the underworld

CHALDEA
Isaiah
48:14 Babylon and with the descendants of ***C***."
Ezekiel
23:15 of Babylonians whose native land is ***C***.

CHALDEAN
Ezra
5:12 the ***C***, who destroyed
Daniel
5:30 Belshazzar the ***C*** king was killed.

CHALDEANS
Genesis
11:31 left Ur of the ***C*** for the land of
15:7 out of Ur of the ***C*** to give you this
2 Kings
25:4 garden. The ***C*** were surrounding
Nehemiah
9:7 out of Ur of the ***C*** and gave him the
Ezekiel
23:14 images of ***C*** outlined in
Daniel
2:2 diviners, and ***C*** to explain his
Habakkuk
1:6 to rouse the ***C***, that bitter and
Acts
7:4 the land of the ***C*** and settled in

CHAMBERS
Proverbs
7:27 grave, going down to the ***c*** of death.
Song of Songs
1:4 me into his ***c***, saying, "Let's
Jeremiah
22:13 and his upper ***c*** with injustice,

CHANGE THEIR HEARTS AND LIVES
1Ki 8:33; Mt 11:20; 13:15; Mk 6:12; Lk 5:32; 15:7; 16:30; 17:3; Ac 11:18; 17:30; 20:21; 26:20; 28:27; 2Pt 3:9; Rev 2:22; 9:20; 16:9

CHANGE YOUR HEARTS AND LIVES
Mt 3:2; 4:17; 21:32; Mk 1:15; Lk 13:3; 13:5; Ac 2:38; 3:19; 2Co 7:9; Rev 2:5; 2:16; 3:3, 19

CHANGED → CHANGED HIS MIND, CHANGED THEIR HEARTS AND LIVES
Genesis
31:7 cheated me and ***c*** my payment ten
Exodus
14:5 and his officials ***c*** their minds about
32:14 Then the LORD ***c*** his mind about the
Numbers
13:16 the land. Moses ***c*** the name of
2 Samuel
12:20 himself, and ***c*** his clothes. He
1 Chronicles
21:15 LORD looked and ***c*** his mind about
Job
42:10 Then the LORD ***c*** Job's fortune when he
Psalms
30:11 You ***c*** my mourning into dancing. You
85:1 your land; you've ***c*** Jacob's
105:25 whose hearts God ***c*** so they hated his
106:45 faithful love he has, God ***c*** his mind.
126:1 When the LORD ***c*** Zion's
Jeremiah
15:7 because they haven't ***c*** their ways.
20:3 The LORD has ***c*** your name from
Daniel
4:16 mind is to be ***c***: it will be given
5:6 The king's mood ***c*** immediately, and he
6:15 the king has issued, cannot be ***c***."
Matthew
3:8 shows you have ***c*** your hearts and
3:11 of you who have ***c*** your hearts and
12:41 because they ***c*** their hearts and

Mark
6:52 hearts had been ***c*** so that they
Luke
3:8 shows you have ***c*** your hearts and
9:29 of his face ***c*** and his clothes
Acts
2:20 The sun will be ***c*** into darkness, and
28:6 to him, they ***c*** their minds and
Romans
2:25 circumcised has ***c*** into not being
1 Corinthians
15:51 of us won't die, but we will all be ***c***—
2 Corinthians
7:10 produces a ***c*** heart and life
Hebrews
1:12 They will be ***c*** like a person
6:4 restore people to ***c*** hearts and lives
2 Peter
3:4 all, nothing has ***c***—not since the beg

CHANGED HIS MIND
Ex 32:14; 2Ki 24:1; 1Ch 21:15; Ps 106:45; Mt 21:29

CHANGED THEIR HEARTS AND LIVES
Zec 1:6; Mt 11:21; 12:41; Lk 10:13; 11:32; 2Co 12:21

CHARGE
Genesis
1:26 they may take ***c*** of the fish of
24:2 who was in ***c*** of everything he
41:40 You will be in ***c*** of my kingdom, and all
Exodus
22:25 be a creditor and ***c*** them interest.
Deuteronomy
23:19 Don't ***c*** your fellow Israelites
Esther
2:3 king's eunuch in ***c*** of the women so
Psalms
18:29 With you I can ***c*** into battle; with my
Joel
2:4 horses, and like warhorses they ***c***,
Matthew
24:45 master puts in ***c*** of giving food at
25:21 I'll put you in ***c*** of much. Come,
27:37 his head the ***c*** against him. It
Mark
15:26 of the formal ***c*** against him was
John
18:29 and asked, "What ***c*** do you bring
Romans
8:33 Who will bring a ***c*** against God's elect
1 Corinthians
9:18 good news free of ***c***. That's why I
2 Corinthians
11:7 the gospel of God to you free of ***c***?
Philemon
1:18 or owes you money, ***c*** it to my account.

CHARIOT
Genesis
41:43 put Joseph on the ***c*** of his second-in-c
Judges
4:15 got down from his ***c*** and fled on foot.
1 Kings
7:33 wheels resembled ***c*** wheels. The
22:33 When the ***c*** officers realized that he
2 Kings
2:11 suddenly a fiery ***c*** and fiery horses
1 Chronicles
28:18 of the ***c***—with the gold win
2 Chronicles
1:17 would import a ***c*** from Egypt for
Psalms
76:6 Jacob's God, both ***c*** and horse were
Song of Songs
6:12 she had set me in an official's ***c***!
Ezekiel
26:10 of the charioteers and ***c*** wheels.

CHARIOTS
Exodus
14:28 and covered the ***c*** and the cavalry,
15:4 Pharaoh's ***c*** and his army he hurled into the sea
Joshua
11:4 There were very many horses and ***c***.
17:18 they have iron ***c*** and are strong."
Judges
4:3 nine hundred iron ***c*** and had oppressed
2 Samuel
8:4 one thousand ***c***, seven hundred
1 Kings
4:26 stalls for his ***c*** and twelve
2 Kings
6:17 horses and fiery ***c*** surrounding
Psalms
20:7 people trust in ***c***, others in
68:17 God's ***c*** are twice ten thousand—
Song of Songs
1:9 dearest, as a mare among Pharaoh's ***c***!
Isaiah
36:9 are relying on Egypt for ***c*** and riders?
Daniel
11:40 against him with ***c*** and horses and
Joel
2:5 the rumbling of ***c***. They leap on the
Nahum
2:3 ironwork of the ***c*** flashes like fire
Zechariah
6:1 and saw four ***c*** coming out from
Revelation
9:9 the sound of many ***c*** and horses racing

CHASE
Leviticus
26:7 You will ***c*** your enemies, and they will
26:8 Five of you will ***c*** away a hundred, and
Psalms
7:1 Save me from all who ***c*** me! Rescue me!
7:5 my enemy not only ***c*** but catch me,

CHASED
Deuteronomy
1:44 in battle. They ***c*** you like bees
Psalms
18:37 I ***c*** my enemies and caught them! I
Lamentations
4:19 eagles. They ***c*** us up the
John
2:15 from ropes and ***c*** them all out of
Revelation
12:13 to the earth, he ***c*** the woman who had

CHASING
Psalms
35:6 messenger be the one who does the ***c***!
143:3 The enemy is ***c*** me, crushing my life in
Ecclesiastes
1:14 is pointless, a ***c*** after wind.
2:11 was pointless—a ***c*** after wind.
6:9 This too is pointless, just wind ***c***.

CHEMOSH
Numbers
21:29 people of ***C***! He gave his sons
1 Kings
11:7 built a shrine to ***C*** the detestable
2 Kings
23:13 Sidonian god, for ***C***, the monstrous
Jeremiah
48:7 will be captured. ***C*** will go into

CHEST → CHEST CONTAINING THE COVENANT, COVENANT CHEST, GOD'S CHEST

CHEST CONTAINING THE COVENANT
Ex 25:22; 26:33, 34; 30:6, 26; 31:7; 39:35; 40:3, 5, 21; Nm 4:5; 7:89; 10:33; 14:44; 17:4, 10; Josh 3:3; 8:33; 1Sa 4:4; Heb 9:4

CHIEF PRIEST
2Ki 25:18; 1Ch 27:5; 2Ch 19:11; 24:6; 26:20; 31:10; Ezr 7:5; Hg 2:2; Jn 18:19; Ac 19:14

CHIEF PRIESTS
Mt 2:4; 16:21; 20:18; 21:15, 23, 45; 26:3, 14, 47, 59; 27:1, 3, 6, 12, 20, 41, 62; 28:11; Mk 8:31; 10:33; 11:18, 27; 14:1, 10, 43, 53, 55; 15:1, 3, 10, 11, 31; Lk 9:22; 19:47; 20:1, 19, 20; 22:2, 4, 52, 66; 23:4, 10, 13; 24:20; Jn 7:32; 7:45; 11:47, 57; 12:10; 18:3, 35; 19:6, 15, 21; Ac 4:23; 5:24; 9:14, 21; 22:30; 23:14; 25:2, 15; 26:10, 12

CHIEF PRIESTS AND ELDERS
Mt 21:23; 26:3, 47; 27:3, 12; Ac 4:23; 23:14; 25:15

CHIEF PRIESTS AND PHARISEES
Jn 7:32; 7:45; 11:47, 57; 18:3

CHIEFS
Genesis
36:15 are the tribal ***c*** from Esau's sons.
Exodus
15:15 Edom's tribal ***c*** were terrified;
Numbers
1:44 and the twelve ***c*** of Israel, each
3:32 chief over the ***c*** of the Levites
4:34 Aaron, and the ***c*** of the community
4:46 Aaron, and the ***c*** of Israel
7:2 The ***c*** of Israel, the leaders of their
17:6 and each of their ***c*** gave him a staff,
Deuteronomy
5:23 all the ***c*** of your tribes
2 Samuel
23:13 of the thirty ***c*** went down and

CHILD
Genesis
4:25 given me another ***c*** in place of Abel
15:4 be your very own biological ***c***."
17:17 or a 99-year-old woman have a ***c***?
44:20 his mother's only ***c***. But his father
Exodus
2:3 tar. She put the ***c*** in the basket and
11:5 Every oldest ***c*** in the land of Egypt
Ruth
4:16 Naomi took the ***c*** and held him to her
1 Kings
3:25 Cut the living ***c*** in two! Give half
Psalms
58:8 woman's stillborn ***c***, let them never
86:16 strength; save this ***c*** of your servant!
131:2 like a weaned ***c*** on its mother;
Proverbs
10:1 Solomon: A wise ***c*** makes a father
23:26 My ***c***, give your mind to me and let
24:13 My ***c***, eat honey, for it is good. The
Isaiah
9:6 A ***c*** is born to us, a son is given to
11:6 and a little ***c*** will lead them.
11:8 A nursing ***c*** will play over the snake's
Jeremiah
1:6 how to speak because I'm only a ***c***."
Ezekiel
18:19 Why doesn't the ***c*** bear his parent's
Amos
8:10 loss of an only ***c***, and the end of
Matthew
2:8 carefully for the ***c***. When you've
2:9 stood over the place where the ***c*** was.
18:2 called a little ***c*** over to sit among
18:5 welcomes one such ***c*** in my name
23:15 become twice the ***c*** of hell you are.
Mark
2:5 the paralytic, "***C***, your sins are
5:39 crying about? The ***c*** isn't dead. She's
7:30 she found the ***c*** lying on the bed
10:15 kingdom like a ***c*** will never enter
Luke
1:41 greeting, the ***c*** leaped in her
1:59 to circumcise the ***c***. They wanted to
John
16:21 But when the ***c*** is born, she no
Acts
7:5 even though Abraham had no ***c***.
Romans
9:12 to her: The older ***c*** will be a slave
1 Corinthians
13:11 When I was a ***c***, I used to speak like a
1 Timothy
1:2 Timothy, my true ***c*** in the faith.
Hebrews
11:11 ability to have a ***c***, though she
1 John
5:1 parent loves the ***c*** born to the
Revelation
12:4 she gave birth, he might devour her ***c***.
12:5 to a son, a male ***c*** who is to rule
12:13 who had given birth to the male ***c***.

CHILDREN → ABRAHAM'S CHILDREN
Genesis
3:16 you will bear ***c***. You will desire

30:1 bear Jacob no ***c***, Rachel became
Exodus
2:6 This must be one of the Hebrews' ***c***."
12:26 And when your ***c*** ask you, 'What does
20:5 God. I punish ***c*** for their
Deuteronomy
4:9 them to your ***c*** and your
6:7 them to your ***c***. Talk about them
11:19 them to your ***c***, by talking about
14:1 are the LORD's ***c***. Don't cut
24:16 of what their ***c*** have done;
29:29 to us and to our ***c*** forever: to keep
Joshua
4:6 the future your ***c*** may ask, 'What do
1 Samuel
1:2 Peninnah had ***c***, but Hannah
2:5 has birthed seven ***c***, but the mother
Ezra
8:21 ourselves, our ***c***, and all our
10:44 women, some of whom had borne ***c***.
Nehemiah
13:24 Half of their ***c*** spoke the language of
Psalms
34:11 Come, ***c***, listen to me. Let me teach
37:25 never seen their ***c*** begging for bread.
78:5 our ancestors to teach them to their ***c***.
82:6 You are gods, ***c*** of the Most High—
103:13 for their ***c***—that's how the L
149:2 maker; let Zion's ***c*** rejoice in their
Proverbs
7:24 Now, ***c***, listen to me, and pay
13:24 rod hate their ***c***, but the one who
14:26 confidence and refuge for one's ***c***.
17:6 and the glory of ***c*** is their parents.
19:18 Discipline your ***c*** while there is hope,
20:7 happy are their ***c*** who come after
22:6 Train ***c*** in the way they should go; when
23:13 instruction from ***c***; if you strike
28:7 Intelligent ***c*** follow instruction, but
31:28 Her ***c*** bless her; her husband praises
Isaiah
30:1 you, rebellious ***c***, says the LORD,
49:20 again hear the ***c*** who were born
54:13 All your ***c*** will be disciples of the
Jeremiah
4:22 are thoughtless ***c*** without
31:15 crying for her ***c***; she refuses to
Lamentations
1:5 wrong acts. Her ***c*** have gone away,
4:2 Zion's precious ***c***, once valued as pure
4:4 mouth, thirsty. ***C*** ask for bread,
Ezekiel
5:10 will eat their ***c***, and children
23:37 even took their ***c*** whom they had
Daniel
6:24 their wives and ***c***. They hadn't even
Hosea
1:2 and have ***c*** of prostitution,
1:10 be said to them, "***C*** of the living
2:4 compassion on her ***c*** because they are
Joel
1:3 Tell it to your ***c***, and have your
Zechariah
10:7 wine. Their ***c*** will watch and be
Matthew
2:16 kill all the male ***c*** in Bethlehem and
2:18 weeping for her ***c***, and she did not
3:7 to them, "You ***c*** of snakes! Who
7:9 will give your ***c*** a stone when they
12:34 ***C*** of snakes! How can you speak good
19:14 Allow the ***c*** to come to me," Jesus
23:33 You snakes! You ***c*** of snakes! How will
24:19 and for women who are nursing their ***c***.
27:25 Let his blood be on us and on our ***c***."
John
1:12 name, he authorized to become God's ***c***,
13:33 Little ***c***, I'm with you for a little
21:5 called to them, "***C***, have you caught
Romans
8:15 adopted as his ***c***. With this
8:16 with our spirit, that we are God's ***c***.
9:8 isn't the natural ***c*** who are God's
9:26 will be called "the living God's ***c***."
1 Corinthians
14:20 don't be like ***c*** in the way you
2 Corinthians
12:14 up for their parents but parents for ***c***.
Galatians
3:26 You are all God's ***c*** through faith in
4:28 sisters, you are ***c*** of the promise
Ephesians
2:3 so that you were ***c*** headed for
6:1 As for ***c***, obey your parents in the
6:4 provoke your ***c*** to anger, but
Philippians
2:15 pure, innocent ***c*** of God surrounded
Colossians
3:20 ***C***, obey your parents in everything,
3:21 provoke your ***c*** in a way that
1 Thessalonians
2:7 a nursing mother caring for her own ***c***.
1 Timothy
3:4 see that their ***c*** are obedient with
3:12 and manage their ***c*** and their own
5:10 good: raising ***c***, providing
Titus
1:6 and have faithful ***c*** who can't be
2:4 women to love their husbands and ***c***,
Hebrews
2:13 I am with the ***c*** whom God has
12:23 God's firstborn ***c*** who are
1 Peter
1:14 you were ignorant. But, as obedient ***c***,
1 John
3:1 be called God's ***c***, and that is what
3:10 This is how God's ***c*** and the devil's
2 John
1:1 and her ***c***, whom I truly
3 John
1:4 to hear that my ***c*** are living

CHOICE

Romans
8:20 not by its own ***c***—it was the choice
9:11 continue because it was based on his ***c***.
11:5 group by the ***c*** of God's grace.
11:28 to God's ***c***, they are loved
Colossians
3:12 as God's ***c***, holy and loved,

CHOOSE

Joshua
9:27 God would ***c***. That is still
24:15 the LORD, then ***c*** today whom you

CHOOSE [cont.]

Job
7:15 I would ***c*** strangling and death instead
34:4 Let's ***c*** for us what's right; let's
34:33 sin, for you must ***c***, not I; declare
Psalms
65:4 is the one you ***c*** to bring close,
78:67 Joseph and didn't ***c*** the tribe of
Proverbs
1:29 and didn't ***c*** the fear of the
3:31 violent people or ***c*** any of their ways,
Isaiah
7:15 and learn to reject evil and ***c*** good.
14:1 Jacob, will again ***c*** Israel, and will
58:6 this the fast I ***c***: releasing wicked
Matthew
27:15 one prisoner, whomever they might ***c***.
John
6:70 Didn't I ***c*** you twelve? Yet
15:16 You didn't ***c*** me, but I chose you and
Romans
9:15 on whomever I ***c*** to have mercy,

CHOSE

Genesis
13:11 So Lot ***c*** for himself the entire Jordan
Deuteronomy
4:37 ancestors and ***c*** their descendants
33:21 He ***c*** the best part for himself because
1 Samuel
2:28 I ***c*** your father from all of Israel's
17:40 his staff and ***c*** five smooth
Psalms
78:68 Instead, he ***c*** the tribe of Judah, the
78:70 And God ***c*** David, his servant, taking
132:13 Because the LORD ***c*** Zion; he wanted it for his home
Isaiah
65:12 evil, and ***c*** what I didn't
Ezekiel
20:5 On the day I ***c*** Israel, I swore a
Mark
13:20 the ones whom God ***c***, he has cut short
Luke
6:13 his disciples. He ***c*** twelve of them
John
15:16 choose me, but I ***c*** you and appointed
Acts
15:40 Paul ***c*** Silas and left, entrusted by the
1 Corinthians
1:27 But God ***c*** what the world considers
Ephesians
1:4 God ***c*** us in Christ to be holy and
2 Thessalonians
2:13 is because he ***c*** you from the
James
1:18 He ***c*** to give us birth by his true word,

CHOSEN → CHOSEN ONE, CHOSEN ONES, CHOSEN YOU

Joshua
24:22 that you have ***c*** to serve the
Judges
10:14 the gods you've ***c***. Let them rescue
1 Kings
8:44 the city you have ***c*** and toward this
Nehemiah
1:9 place that I have ***c*** as a dwelling for
Psalms
33:12 that God has ***c*** as his
89:19 up someone specially ***c*** from the people.
119:30 I've ***c*** the way of faithfulness; I'm set
119:173 help me because I have ***c*** your precepts.
Isaiah
41:8 whom I have ***c***, offspring of
42:1 one I uphold; my ***c***, who brings me
Matthew
22:14 are invited, but few people are ***c***."
John
13:18 those whom I've ***c***. But this is to
Romans
11:7 Those who were ***c*** found it, but the
Titus
1:1 faith of God's ***c*** people and a
James
2:5 Hasn't God ***c*** those who are
1 Peter
2:6 in Zion, ***c***, valuable. The
2:9 But you are a ***c*** race, a royal
Revelation
17:14 with him are called, ***c***, and faithful."

CHOSEN ONE

Ps 89:3; 106:23; Lam 4:20; Lk 9:35; 23:35

CHOSEN ONES

1Ch 16:13; Ps 105:6; 105:43; 106:5; Is 43:20; 65:9, 15; Mt 24:31; Mk 13:20

CHOSEN YOU

1Ch 28:10; 2Ch 29:11; Is 49:7; Hg 2:23; Jn 15:19; 1Th 1:4

CHRIST → CHRIST JESUS OUR LORD, CHRIST OUR LORD

Matthew
1:1 of Jesus **C**, son of David,
16:16 You are the **C**, the Son of the
16:20 not to tell anybody that he was the **C**.
27:22 who is called **C**?" They all said,
Mark
1:1 the good news about Jesus **C**, God's Son,
8:29 I am?" Peter answered, "You are the **C**."
Luke
2:11 in David's city. He is **C** the Lord.
2:26 die before he had seen the Lord's **C**.
4:41 they recognized that he was the **C**.
9:20 Peter answered, "The **C** sent from God."
20:41 do they say that the **C** is David's son?
22:67 If you are the **C**, tell us!" He
23:2 and claiming that he is the **C**, a king."
23:35 he really is the **C** sent from God,
24:26 necessary for the **C** to suffer these
24:46 is written: the **C** will suffer and
John
1:17 truth came into being through Jesus **C**.
11:27 that you are the **C**, God's Son, the
Acts
2:36 whom you crucified, both Lord and **C**."
Romans
1:1 Paul, a slave of **C** Jesus, called to
10:4 **C** is the goal of the Law, which leads
16:27 to him through Jesus **C** forever! Amen.

1 Corinthians
1:23 but we preach **C** crucified, which is a
1:30 that you are in **C** Jesus. He became
4:10 We are fools for **C**, but you are wise
2 Corinthians
5:19 himself through **C**, by not counting
13:5 that Jesus **C** is in you?
13:13 of the Lord Jesus **C**, the love of God,
Galatians
1:1 through Jesus **C** and God the
2:19 for God. I have been crucified with **C**
2:20 longer live, but **C** lives in me. And
Ephesians
5:2 the example of **C**, who loved us and
6:6 like slaves of **C** carrying out
Philippians
2:5 Adopt the attitude that was in **C** Jesus
4:7 your hearts and minds safe in **C** Jesus.
Colossians
2:2 of the secret plan of God, namely **C**.
3:11 nor free, but **C** is all things and
3:15 The peace of **C** must control your
4:12 He's a slave of **C** Jesus who always
1 Thessalonians
3:2 good news about **C**. We sent him to
2 Thessalonians
2:14 possess the honor of our Lord Jesus **C**.
3:12 By the Lord Jesus **C**, we command and
1 Timothy
1:15 full acceptance: "**C** Jesus came into
1:16 mercy, so that **C** Jesus could show
6:14 the appearance of our Lord Jesus **C**.
2 Timothy
1:1 an apostle of **C** Jesus by God's
1:2 God the Father and **C** Jesus our Lord.
2:3 like a good soldier of **C** Jesus.
3:15 through faith that is in **C** Jesus.
4:1 of God and of **C** Jesus, who is
Titus
1:1 apostle of Jesus **C**. I'm sent to
1:4 God the Father and **C** Jesus our savior.
2:13 of our great God and savior Jesus **C**.
3:6 generously through Jesus **C** our savior.
Philemon
1:8 confidence in **C** to command you to
1:9 and now also a prisoner for **C** Jesus—
Hebrews
9:11 But **C** has appeared as the high priest
13:8 Jesus **C** is the same yesterday, today,
13:21 him through Jesus **C**. To him be the
1 Peter
4:1 Therefore, since **C** suffered as a human,
4:11 through Jesus **C**. To him be honor
4:16 who belongs to **C**. Rather, honor
1 John
2:22 that Jesus is the **C**? This person is
5:6 and blood: Jesus **C**. Not by water
Revelation
11:15 our Lord and his **C**, and he will rule
12:10 authority of his **C** have come. The
20:4 and ruled with **C** for one thousand
20:6 of God and of **C**, and will rule

CHRIST JESUS OUR LORD
Ro 6:23; 8:38; 1Co 15:31; Eph 3:11; 1Ti 1:2; 1:12; 2Ti 1:2

CHRIST OUR LORD
Ro 1:4; 5:21; 7:25; 1Co 1:9; Jud 1:25

CHURCH → ANGEL OF THE CHURCH, GOD'S CHURCH
Matthew
16:18 And I'll build my **c** on this rock. The
18:17 report it to the **c**. If they won't
Acts
8:3 havoc against the **c**. Entering one
15:22 with the entire **c**, agreed to send
Romans
16:5 say hello to the **c** that meets in
16:23 and to the whole **c**, says hello to
1 Corinthians
1:2 To God's **c** that is in Corinth: To those
4:17 way as I teach everywhere in every **c**.
6:4 judges who aren't respected by the **c**?
11:18 together as a **c**, I hear that
12:28 In the **c**, God has appointed first
14:4 those who prophesy build up the **c**.
14:5 them so that the **c** might be built up.
Ephesians
1:22 made him head of everything in the **c**,
1:23 His body, the **c**, is the fullness
5:23 is head of the **c**, that is, the
5:24 like the **c** submits to Christ.
5:25 Christ loved the **c** and gave himself
Philippians
3:6 I harassed the **c**. With respect to
4:15 Macedonia how no **c** shared in
Colossians
1:18 of the body, the **c**, who is the
1:24 the sake of his body, which is the **c**.
1:25 a servant of the **c** by God's
1 Thessalonians
1:1 Thessalonians' **c** that is in God
2 Thessalonians
1:1 Timothy: To the **c** of the
1 Timothy
3:1 supervisor in the **c**, they want a good
3:5 how can they take care of God's **c**?
3:7 those outside the **c** so that they
3:8 servants in the **c** should be
3:11 servants in the **c** should be
3:15 It is the **c** of the living God
5:16 not burden the **c** so that it can
Philemon
1:2 soldier, and the **c** that meets in
James
5:14 the elders of the **c**, and the elders
1 Peter
5:13 The fellow-elect **c** in Babylon greets
3 John
1:6 in front of the **c**. You all would do
1:9 something to the **c**, but Diotrephes,
1:10 so and even throws them out of the **c**!

CHURCHES → ALL THE CHURCHES
Acts
15:41 Syria and Cilicia, strengthening the **c**.
16:5 So the **c** were strengthened in the faith
1 Corinthians
7:17 one. This is what I teach in all the **c**.
11:16 have such a custom, nor do God's **c**.
11:22 down on God's **c** and humiliate
16:1 I have directed the **c** in Galatia to do.

16:19 The ***c*** in the province of Asia greet
2 Corinthians
8:1 that was given to the ***c*** of Macedonia.
8:19 is chosen by the ***c*** to be our
8:24 in such a way that the ***c*** can see it.
11:8 I robbed other ***c*** by taking a salary
12:13 than the other ***c***, except that I
Galatians
1:2 sisters with me. To the ***c*** in Galatia.
1:22 personally by the Christian ***c*** in Judea.
1 Thessalonians
2:14 imitators of the ***c*** of God in Judea,
2 Thessalonians
1:4 you in God's ***c***. We tell about
Revelation
1:4 to the seven ***c*** that are in Asia:
3:6 to what the Spirit is saying to the ***c***.
22:16 things for the ***c***. I'm the root and

CIRCUMCISED
Genesis
17:12 must be ***c***, including those
17:26 day Abraham and his son Ishmael were ***c***.
21:4 Abraham ***c*** his son Isaac when he was
34:17 to us and become ***c***, we will take our
34:24 able-bodied male in the city was ***c***.
Leviticus
12:3 flesh of the boy's foreskin must be ***c***.
Joshua
5:3 for himself. He ***c*** the Israelites at
Jeremiah
9:25 deal with everyone who is physically ***c***:
Luke
2:21 Jesus' parents ***c*** him and gave him
John
7:23 If a man can be ***c*** on the Sabbath
Acts
7:8 birth, Abraham ***c*** him. Isaac did
10:45 The ***c*** believers who had come with Peter
11:2 to Jerusalem, the ***c*** believers
15:1 Unless you are ***c*** according to the
15:5 Gentiles must be ***c***. They must be
16:3 with him, so he ***c*** him. This was
Romans
2:25 status of being ***c*** has changed into
3:30 one who makes the ***c*** righteous by
4:9 only for the ***c*** or is it also for
15:8 of those who are ***c*** for the sake of
1 Corinthians
7:18 If someone was ***c*** when called, he
Galatians
2:3 who was a Greek, was required to be ***c***.
5:2 have yourselves ***c***, having Christ
6:12 to get you to be ***c***, but only so they
Ephesians
2:11 by Jews who are physically ***c***.
Philippians
3:5 I was ***c*** on the eighth day. I am from
Colossians
2:11 You were also ***c*** by him. This wasn't
3:11 Greek nor Jew, ***c*** nor

CISTERN
Genesis
37:24 him into the ***c***, an empty cistern
Proverbs
5:15 from your own ***c***, gushing water
Jeremiah
37:16 was put in a ***c***, which was like a
38:7 Jeremiah into the ***c***. Since the king

CITIES → FORTIFIED CITIES, REFUGE CITIES
Genesis
13:12 settled near the ***c*** of the valley and
19:25 destroyed these ***c***, the entire
Exodus
1:11 to build storage ***c*** named Pithom and
Leviticus
25:32 in the levitical ***c*** that are part of
Numbers
35:11 for yourselves ***c*** to be refuge
35:12 The ***c*** will be for you a place of refuge
35:13 establish six refuge ***c*** for yourselves.
35:15 These six ***c*** will be refuge for
Joshua
20:4 to one of these ***c***, stand at the
Psalms
9:6 torn down their ***c***—even the memory
69:35 rebuild Judah's ***c*** so that God's
Isaiah
6:11 God said, "Until ***c*** lie ruined with
64:10 Your holy ***c*** have become a wilderness;
Jeremiah
51:14 to fill your ***c*** with soldiers
Lamentations
2:2 down the walled ***c*** of Daughter
5:11 in Zion, young women in Judah's ***c***.
Zechariah
1:17 proclaims: My ***c*** will again
Mark
5:20 in the Ten ***C*** all that Jesus
7:31 Sea through the region of the Ten ***C***.
Luke
2:3 went to their own ***c*** to be enrolled.
2 Peter
2:6 God condemned the ***c*** of Sodom and
Revelation
16:19 parts, and the ***c*** of the nations

CITIZEN
Leviticus
24:22 you, immigrant or ***c*** alike, because I
Acts
21:39 in Cilicia, a ***c*** of an important
22:25 whip a Roman ***c*** who hasn't been
22:27 me! Are you a Roman ***c***?" He said, "Yes."

CITIZENS
Acts
16:38 learn that Paul and Silas were Roman ***c***.
Ephesians
2:19 you are fellow ***c*** with God's

CITY → FORTIFIED CITY, REFUGE CITY
Genesis
4:17 Cain built a ***c*** and named the
2 Samuel
5:7 of Zion—which became David's ***C***.
5:9 renamed David's ***C***. David built a
Ezra
4:13 king that if this ***c*** is rebuilt and
4:21 people: this ***c*** is not to be

Psalms
31:21 to me when I was like a ***c*** under siege!
46:4 gladden God's ***c***, the holiest
46:5 God is in that ***c***. It will never
48:1 In the ***c*** belonging to our
48:2 far north, is the ***c*** of the great king.
48:8 ourselves in the ***c*** of the LORD of
69:12 who sit at the ***c*** gate muttered
87:3 are said about you, the ***c*** of God! Selah
101:8 all evildoers from the LORD's ***c***.
108:10 me to a fortified ***c***! I wish someone
Matthew
2:23 He settled in a ***c*** called Nazareth so
4:5 him into the holy ***c*** and stood him at
Hebrews
11:10 forward to a ***c*** that has
11:16 God—he has prepared a ***c*** for them.
Revelation
3:12 the name of the ***c*** of my God, the
21:2 I saw the holy ***c***, New Jerusalem,

CLAIM
Psalms
9:4 for me and my ***c***, because you rule
Ezekiel
28:2 seas!" Though you ***c*** to have the mind
Amos
2:10 to lay ***c*** to the land of
Acts
6:11 some people to ***c***, "We heard him
28:6 minds and began to ***c*** that he was a god.
Titus
1:16 They ***c*** to know God, but they deny God
James
1:26 If those who ***c*** devotion to God don't
2:18 Someone might ***c***, "You have faith and I
1 John
1:6 If we ***c***, "We have fellowship with
4:21 him: Those who ***c*** to love God ought

CLANS
Genesis
10:5 and their ***c*** within their
10:32 These are the ***c*** of Noah's sons
Joshua
7:17 He made the ***c*** of Judah come forward.
1 Samuel
10:19 before the LORD by your tribes and ***c***."
Psalms
83:6 They are the ***c*** of Edom and the

CLAY
Numbers
5:17 holy water in a ***c*** jar, and taking
Job
4:19 in houses of ***c***, whose
38:14 turn it over like ***c*** for a seal, so it
Proverbs
26:23 heart are like silver coating on ***c***.
Isaiah
41:25 like mud, as a potter treads ***c***.
Jeremiah
18:6 the LORD? Like ***c*** in the potter's
19:1 Go buy a ***c*** jar from a potter
Lamentations
4:2 no more than ***c*** pots made by a
Daniel
2:33 its feet were a mixture of iron and ***c***.
Romans
9:20 to God? Does the ***c*** say to the
2 Corinthians
4:7 this treasure in ***c*** pots so that the

CLEAN
Genesis
7:2 From every ***c*** animal, take seven pairs,
8:20 took some of the ***c*** large animals and
Leviticus
10:10 and between the unclean and the ***c***,
20:25 separate between ***c*** and unclean
Deuteronomy
14:11 You are allowed to eat any ***c*** bird
2 Kings
5:10 skin will be restored and become ***c***."
Psalms
24:4 Only the one with ***c*** hands and a pure
51:7 and I will be ***c***; wash me and I
Jeremiah
49:32 those who are ***c***-shaven, and I will
Ezekiel
36:25 I will sprinkle ***c*** water on you, and you
Zechariah
3:5 He said, "Put a ***c*** turban upon his
Matthew
8:2 Lord, if you want, you can make me ***c***."
23:25 Hypocrites! You ***c*** the outside of
27:59 body, wrapped it in a ***c*** linen cloth,
Luke
11:41 who you are and you will be ***c*** all over.
John
13:10 are completely ***c***. You disciples
1 Corinthians
5:7 ***C*** out the old yeast so you can be a new
Hebrews
10:22 are sprinkled ***c*** from an evil

CLEANSE
Deuteronomy
32:43 hate him; he will ***c*** his people's land.
Proverbs
20:30 evil; beatings ***c*** the inner parts.
Jeremiah
4:11 my people, not merely to winnow or ***c***.
4:14 ***C*** your heart of evil, Jerusalem, that
Daniel
12:10 Many will purify, ***c***, and refine
Zechariah
13:1 will open to ***c*** the sin and
2 Corinthians
7:1 promises, let's ***c*** ourselves from
Titus
2:14 behavior, and ***c*** a special people
1 John
1:9 us our sins and ***c*** us from

CLEANSED
Joshua
22:17 we still haven't ***c*** ourselves from
Daniel
11:35 purified, and ***c***—until an end time
Matthew
8:3 Instantly his skin disease was ***c***.

CLEANSED [cont.]

11:5 skin diseases are ***c***. Those who were
Luke
4:27 none of them were ***c***. Instead, Naaman
Hebrews

CLOSED

Genesis
2:21 of his ribs and ***c*** up the flesh over
19:6 the entrance, ***c*** the door behind
Numbers
16:33 and the earth ***c*** over them. They
Joshua
6:1 Now Jericho was ***c*** up tightly because of the Israelites
Judges
3:22 stomach, the fat ***c*** over the blade,
Isaiah
48:8 your ears are ***c***, because I knew
Jeremiah
38:16 Jeremiah behind ***c*** doors, "As the
John
12:40 eyes blind and ***c*** their minds so
20:19 were behind ***c*** doors because
Acts
19:9 Some people had ***c*** their minds, though.
21:30 temple. Immediately the gates were ***c***.
2 Corinthians
3:14 their minds were ***c***. Right up to the
Ephesians
4:18 of their ignorance and their ***c*** hearts.

CLOTH

Numbers
4:6 spread a whole ***c*** of blue over it,
Job
16:15 I've sewed rough ***c*** over my skin and
Song of Songs
3:10 its covering, ***c*** of gold, its
Isaiah
19:10 Makers of ***c*** will be crushed; all who
38:12 like woven ***c***; God cuts me off
Matthew
6:28 out with work, and they don't spin ***c***.
9:16 of new, unshrunk ***c*** on old clothes
27:59 body, wrapped it in a clean linen ***c***,
John
11:44 covered with a ***c***. Jesus said to
20:7 also saw the face ***c*** that had been on
Acts
16:14 dealer in purple ***c***. As she listened,

CLOTHED

Genesis
25:25 out red all over, ***c*** with hair, and
1 Samuel
2:18 was a young boy, ***c*** in a linen
2 Chronicles
6:41 LORD God, be ***c*** with salvation;
Ezra
3:10 the priests ***c*** in their vests
Job
8:22 hate you will be ***c*** with shame, and
10:11 You ***c*** me with skin and flesh, wove me
29:14 justice, and it ***c*** me, righteousness
Psalms
93:1 LORD is robed, ***c*** with strength.
104:1 you are! You are ***c*** in glory and
Isaiah
61:10 because he has ***c*** me with clothes
Jeremiah
10:9 of a goldsmith. ***C*** in blue and
Ezekiel
10:2 said to the man ***c*** in linen: Go in
10:6 the man ***c*** in linen to take
10:7 palm of the one ***c*** in linen. He took
16:10 I ***c*** you with colorful garments, put
16:18 fine garments and ***c*** them. You set my
23:12 warriors richly ***c***, charioteers and
26:16 They will be ***c*** only in terror as
Daniel
10:5 saw a man ***c*** in linen in front
12:6 said to the man ***c*** in white linen,
Luke
9:31 They were ***c*** with heavenly splendor and
16:19 rich man who ***c*** himself in purple
1 Corinthians
15:53 body to be ***c*** with what can't
15:54 body has been ***c*** in what can't
Galatians
3:27 into Christ have ***c*** yourselves with
Revelation
3:4 will walk with me ***c*** in white because
12:1 heaven: a woman ***c*** with the sun,
15:6 temple. They were ***c*** in pure bright
16:15 stay awake and ***c*** so that they

CLOTHES

Genesis
37:34 Jacob tore his ***c***, put a simple
41:14 shaved, changed ***c***, and appeared
49:11 He washes his ***c*** in wine, his
Deuteronomy
8:4 forty years, your ***c*** didn't wear out
29:5 now; neither the ***c*** on your back nor
2 Samuel
1:11 David grabbed his ***c*** and ripped them—a
1 Kings
21:27 he tore his ***c*** and put mourning
2 Kings
5:7 he ripped his ***c***. He said, "What?
11:14 ripped her ***c*** and screamed,
Nehemiah
4:23 took off our ***c***, even when they
Esther
4:1 done, he tore his ***c***, dressed in
Psalms
22:18 themselves; they cast lots for my ***c***.
30:11 off my funeral ***c*** and dressed me up
Proverbs
6:27 into his lap and his ***c*** not get burned?
Isaiah
37:1 he ripped his ***c***, covered himself
Jeremiah
52:33 his prison ***c*** and ate his meals
Jonah
3:5 put on mourning ***c***, from the
Zechariah
3:3 wearing filthy ***c*** and standing
Matthew
3:4 John wore ***c*** made of camel's hair, with
17:2 the sun, and his ***c*** became as white
27:35 divided up his ***c*** among them by
Luke
23:11 Jesus in elegant ***c*** and sent him back

John
19:24 They divided my ***c*** among themselves,
20:7 with the other ***c*** but was folded up

CLOTHING

Exodus
3:22 as well as their ***c***. Then you will
12:35 and gold jewelry as well as their ***c***.
21:10 reduce her food, ***c***, or marital
Numbers
15:38 the edges of your ***c*** for all time.
Deuteronomy
10:18 immigrants, giving them food and ***c***.
Psalms
102:26 wear out like ***c***; you change them
104:6 like a piece of ***c***; the waters were
Proverbs
31:22 fine linen and purple are her ***c***.
31:25 and honor are her ***c***; she is confident
Mark
6:56 the hem of his ***c***. Everyone who
John
19:24 cast lots for my ***c***. That's what the
1 Timothy
2:9 appearance with ***c*** that is modest
Revelation
3:4 stained their ***c***. They will walk
3:5 will wear white ***c*** like this. I
17:4 and scarlet ***c***, and she

CLOUD → COLUMN OF CLOUD

Exodus
14:20 camp. The ***c*** remained there,
16:10 presence of the LORD appeared in the ***c***.
19:9 to you in a thick ***c*** in order that the
24:15 mountain, and the ***c*** covered the
34:5 came down in the ***c*** and stood there
40:34 the ***c*** covered the meeting tent and the
Leviticus
16:2 I am present in the ***c*** above the cover.
Numbers
9:15 was erected, the ***c*** covered the
10:11 second year, the ***c*** ascended from the
11:25 descended in a ***c***, spoke to him,
12:10 When the ***c*** went away from over the
14:14 Your ***c*** stands over them.
16:42 that moment the ***c*** covered it, and
Deuteronomy
1:33 taking, and in ***c*** during the
4:11 sky, with darkness, ***c***, and thick smoke!
5:22 of the fire, the ***c***, and the thick
Judges
20:38 sent up a big ***c*** of smoke from the
1 Kings
8:10 holy place, the ***c*** filled the LORD's
8:11 duties due to the ***c*** because the
8:12 said that he would live in a dark ***c***,
18:44 I see a small ***c*** the size of a
2 Chronicles
5:13 forever! Then a ***c*** filled the LORD's
5:14 on account of the ***c*** because the
6:1 said that he would live in a dark ***c***;
Nehemiah
9:12 With a pillar of ***c*** you led them by day
Job
3:5 claim it and a ***c*** linger over it;
Psalms
18:11 covering was dark water and dense ***c***.
78:14 led them with the ***c*** by day; by the
Proverbs
16:15 favor is like a ***c*** that brings
Isaiah
4:5 its assembly a ***c*** by day and smoke
44:22 rebellions like a ***c***, and your sins
60:8 who fly like a ***c***, like doves to
Lamentations
2:1 Zion under a ***c***; he threw
3:44 yourself up in a ***c***; prayers can't
Ezekiel
1:4 north, a great ***c*** flashing fire,
8:11 and the scent of the incense ***c*** rose up.
10:3 went in, and the ***c*** filled the inner
30:18 proud strength. A ***c*** will cover it,
32:7 the sun with a ***c***, and the moon
38:16 Israel like a ***c*** covering the
Hosea
6:4 is like a morning ***c***, like the dew
Matthew
17:5 look, a bright ***c*** overshadowed
Luke
9:35 a voice from the ***c*** said, "This is my
12:54 When you see a ***c*** forming in the
21:27 One coming on a ***c*** with power and
Acts
1:9 lifted up and a ***c*** took him out of
2:19 below, blood and fire and a ***c*** of smoke.
1 Corinthians
10:1 all under the ***c*** and they all went
10:2 into Moses in the ***c*** and in the sea.
Hebrews
12:1 have such a great ***c*** of witnesses
Revelation
10:1 was robed with a ***c***, with a rainbow
11:12 up to heaven in a ***c***, while their
14:14 there was a white ***c***. On the cloud was
14:15 one seated on the ***c***: "Use your sickle
14:16 one seated on the ***c*** swung his sickle

CLOUDS

Genesis
9:13 my bow in the ***c***; it will be the
Deuteronomy
33:26 you, rides majestically through the ***c***.
Judges
5:4 poured down, the ***c*** poured down water.
Job
20:6 heaven and their heads touch the ***c***,
22:13 God know? Can he judge through thick ***c***?
22:14 ***C*** conceal him so he can't see while he
26:8 up water in his ***c***, yet they didn't
35:5 and see; scan the ***c*** high over you.
36:28 the ***c*** pour moisture and drip
37:11 He also fills ***c*** with moisture; his
37:12 the circling ***c***; by his guidance
37:15 commands them, his ***c*** produce lightning?
37:16 of the ***c***, the amazing
37:21 wind has passed and cleared away the ***c***.
38:9 when I made the ***c*** its garment, the
38:34 an order to the ***c*** so their abundant
38:37 to count the ***c***, and who can tilt

Psalms
18:12 God's **c** went ahead of the brightness
36:5 skies; your faithfulness reaches the **c**.
57:10 your faithfulness reaches the **c**.
68:4 one who rides the **c**! The LORD is his
68:34 over Israel; his strength is in the **c**.
77:17 The **c** poured water, the skies cracked
97:2 **C** and thick darkness surround God. His
104:3 you make the **c** your chariot,
105:39 God spread out **c** as a covering; gave
108:4 your faithfulness reaches the **c**.
135:7 God forms **c** at the far corners of the
147:8 the skies with **c**; God makes rain
Proverbs
8:28 he thickened the **c** above, when he
25:14 given are like **c** and wind that
Ecclesiastes
11:3 If **c** fill up, they will empty out rain
12:2 too, before the **c** return after the
Isaiah
5:6 I will command the **c** not to rain on it.
45:8 and let the **c** flow with
Jeremiah
4:13 like the **c**; his chariots
10:13 He raises the **c** from the ends of
51:16 God raises the **c** from the ends of
Ezekiel
19:11 up between the **c**. Because of her
30:3 comes, a day of **c**: the nations'
31:3 indeed, its top went up between the **c**.
34:12 the time of **c** and thick
38:9 you, will be like **c** covering the
Daniel
7:13 with the heavenly **c**. He came to the
Joel
2:2 light, a day of **c** and thick
Nahum
1:3 and storm; **c** are the dust of
Zephaniah
1:15 a day of **c** and deep darkness,
Matthew
24:30 in the heavenly **c** with power and
26:64 Almighty and coming on the heavenly **c**."
1 Thessalonians
4:17 with them in the **c** to meet with the
Jude
1:12 are waterless **c** carried along by
Revelation
1:7 coming with the **c**! Every eye will

COALS → BURNING COALS
Psalms
11:6 will rain fiery **c** and sulfur on the
18:8 fire; flaming **c** blazed out in
18:12 him; hail and **c** of fire went too.
18:13 voice heard with hail and **c** of fire.
Proverbs
6:28 man walks on hot **c**, don't his feet
25:22 will heap burning **c** on their heads,
Isaiah
44:12 works it over **c**, and shapes it
44:19 bread on its **c**, and roasted meat
Ezekiel
1:13 like blazing **c**, like torches.
10:2 hands with fiery **c** from between the
24:11 empty on its **c** until it's so hot
Romans
12:20 will pile burning **c** of fire upon his

COAT
Deuteronomy
22:12 for the four corners of the **c** you wear.
24:12 not allowed to sleep in their pawned **c**.
1 Samuel
17:38 gear, putting a **c** of armor on him
Job
29:14 me, righteousness as my **c** and turban;
Psalms
109:18 curses like a **c**, let them seep
109:29 let them wear their disgrace like a **c**.
Zechariah
13:4 put on a shaggy **c** in order to
Matthew
5:40 your shirt, let them have your **c** too.
27:28 him and put a red military **c** on him.
Luke
6:29 takes your **c**, don't withhold
John
21:7 he wrapped his **c** around himself

COLLECT
Nehemiah
10:37 the Levites who **c** the tenth-part gif
Matthew
6:20 Instead, **c** treasures for yourselves in
17:25 do earthly kings **c** taxes, from their
21:34 to the tenant farmers to **c** his fruit.
Luke
3:13 He replied, "**C** no more than you are
Ecclesiastes
12:11 -tipped prods; the **c** sayings of the
Matthew
15:37 The disciples **c** seven baskets
17:24 the people who **c** the half-shekel te

COLUMN → COLUMN OF CLOUD, COLUMN OF LIGHTNING
Judges
20:40 But then the **c** of smoke began to rise
1 Kings
7:21 named the south **c** Jachin. The north
Jeremiah
52:21 Each **c** was about twenty-seven feet high
52:22 it. The second **c** was the same

COLUMN OF CLOUD
Ex 13:21; 13:22; 14:19; 33:9, 10; Nm 12:5; 14:14; Neh 9:19

COLUMN OF LIGHTNING
Ex 13:21; 13:22; 14:24; Nm 14:14; Neh 9:12; 9:19

COLUMNS
1 Kings
7:2 rows of cedar **c** with cedar
2 Kings
25:13 the bronze **c**, the stands, and
Joel
2:30 earth—blood and fire and **c** of smoke.

COMFORT

Job
2:11 come so they could console and ***c*** him.
21:34 How empty is your ***c*** to me; only deceit
Psalms
71:21 increase my honor and ***c*** me all around.
119:50 My ***c*** during my suffering is this: your
119:76 faithful love ***c*** me, according to
119:82 your word. "When will you ***c*** me?" I ask,
Ecclesiastes
4:1 have no one to ***c*** them. Their
Isaiah
40:1 ***C***, comfort my people! says your God
Zechariah
10:2 and provide empty ***c***. Therefore, they
Luke
6:24 you have already received your ***c***.
John
11:19 Jews had come to ***c*** Martha and Mary
1 Corinthians
14:3 and giving them encouragement and ***c***.
2 Thessalonians
2:16 gave us eternal ***c*** and a good hope.

COMFORTED

Psalms
77:2 numb; my whole being refuses to be ***c***.
86:17 you, LORD, have helped me and ***c*** me.
119:52 your ancient rules, I'm ***c***, LORD.
Matthew
2:18 not want to be ***c***, because they
Luke
16:25 Lazarus is being ***c*** and you are in
Acts
20:12 away alive, and they were greatly ***c***.

COMMAND

Genesis
41:40 will obey your ***c***. Only as the
Exodus
7:2 everything that I ***c*** you, and your
25:22 to you all that I ***c*** you concerning
34:11 to obey what I ***c*** you today. I'm
Numbers
9:18 At the LORD's ***c***, the Israelites would
14:41 disobey the LORD's ***c***? It won't succeed.
Deuteronomy
2:4 ***C*** the people as follows: You are about
34:5 of Moab, according to the LORD's ***c***.
Joshua
1:13 Remember the ***c*** that Moses the LORD's
Job
39:27 Or at your ***c*** does the eagle soar, the
Psalms
7:6 up, my God; you ***c*** that justice be
17:4 violent ways by the ***c*** from your lips.
68:11 My Lord gives the ***c***—many messengers
147:15 God issues his ***c*** to the earth—God's
148:5 God gave the ***c*** and they were
Proverbs
6:20 your father's ***c***; don't abandon
8:29 go beyond his ***c***, when he marked
Ecclesiastes
8:5 Whoever keeps a ***c*** will meet no harm,
Isaiah
5:6 grow up. I will ***c*** the clouds not to
23:11 The LORD gave the ***c*** to destroy
Jeremiah
1:17 every word I ***c*** you. Don't be
Daniel
2:13 So the ***c*** went out: The sages were to be
Matthew
4:3 are God's Son, ***c*** these stones to
15:3 do you break the ***c*** of God by keeping
19:7 why did Moses ***c*** us to give a
Mark
9:25 deaf spirit, I ***c*** you to come out
John
15:14 are my friends if you do what I ***c*** you.
Acts
16:18 Jesus Christ, I ***c*** you to leave
Romans
16:26 based on the ***c*** of the eternal
2 Thessalonians
3:6 and sisters, we ***c*** you in the name
2 John
1:5 I'm writing a new ***c*** to you, but it's
Revelation
3:10 you kept my ***c*** to endure, I will

COMMANDED

Genesis
2:16 The LORD God ***c*** the human, "Eat your
3:11 the tree, which I ***c*** you not to eat?"
21:4 eight days old just as God had ***c*** him.
Exodus
5:6 same day Pharaoh ***c*** the people's
7:6 and Aaron did just as the LORD ***c*** them.
19:7 these words that the LORD had ***c*** him.
32:8 the path that I ***c***. They have made a
40:32 just as the LORD had ***c*** Moses.
Leviticus
8:36 everything the LORD ***c*** through Moses.
10:1 the LORD, which he had not ***c*** them.
Deuteronomy
6:24 Then the LORD ***c*** us to perform all these
18:20 that I haven't ***c*** him to speak, or
34:9 they did exactly what the LORD ***c*** Moses.
Joshua
1:7 Moses my servant ***c*** you. Don't
1:16 you have ***c*** us and go
22:2 LORD's servant ***c*** you. You have
2 Kings
17:13 that I ***c*** your ancestors
21:8 everything I have ***c*** them-keeping all
2 Chronicles
33:8 everything I have ***c*** them—keeping all
Psalms
33:9 it happened! When he ***c***, there it was!
105:8 the word he ***c*** to a thousand
111:9 his people; God ***c*** that his covenant
119:138 The laws you ***c*** are righteous,
119:166 your saving help. I do what you've ***c***.
133:3 that the LORD has ***c*** the blessing:
Isaiah
13:3 I have ***c*** my holy ones; I have called my
Amos
2:12 drink wine, and ***c*** the prophets,
Matthew
Luke
8:29 Jesus had already ***c*** the unclean
John
14:31 as the Father has ***c*** me. Get up. We're

COMMANDED [cont.]

Acts
10:42 He ***c*** us to preach to the people and to
1 Corinthians
9:14 way, the Lord ***c*** that those who
1 John
3:23 Christ, and love each other as he ***c*** us.
2 John
1:4 just as we had been ***c*** by the Father.

COMMANDER

Joshua
5:14 Neither! I'm the ***c*** of the LORD's
5:15 The ***c*** of the LORD's heavenly force said to Joshua

COMMANDERS

Numbers
31:14 angry with the ***c*** of the army, the
Deuteronomy
1:15 There were ***c*** over thousands,

COMMANDING

Deuteronomy
4:40 commandments. I'm ***c*** them to you today
30:8 commandments that I'm ***c*** you right now.
30:16 that I'm ***c*** you right now by
Jonah
3:2 it the proclamation that I am ***c*** you."

COMMANDMENT

Deuteronomy
7:11 keep the ***c***, the regulations,
30:11 This ***c*** that I'm giving you right now is
Joshua
22:5 to carry out the ***c*** and Instruction
Psalms
119:96 has a limit, but your ***c*** is boundless.
Proverbs
6:23 The ***c*** is a lamp and instruction a
19:16 who keep the ***c*** preserve their
Matthew
22:36 what is the greatest ***c*** in the Law?"
22:38 This is the first and greatest ***c***
Mark
7:8 You ignore God's ***c*** while holding on to
12:31 No other ***c*** is greater than
Luke
23:56 on the Sabbath in keeping with the ***c***.
John
13:34 I give you a new ***c***: Love each other.
Romans
7:8 and used this ***c*** to produce all
7:13 more thoroughly sinful through the ***c***.
Ephesians
6:2 The ***c*** Honor your father and mother is
Hebrews
7:5 of priest have a ***c*** under the Law to
2 Peter
2:21 back from the holy ***c*** entrusted to them.
1 John
2:7 not writing a new ***c*** to you, but an
3:23 This is his ***c***, that we believe in the
4:21 This ***c*** we have from him: Those who

COMMANDMENTS

Genesis
26:5 my orders, my ***c***, my statutes, and
Exodus
20:6 of those who love me and keep my ***c***.
Numbers
36:13 These are the ***c*** and the case laws that
Deuteronomy
4:13 to do—the Ten ***C***—and wrote them
10:4 set: the Ten ***C*** that the LORD
11:27 LORD your God's ***c*** that I am giving
28:13 LORD your God's ***c*** that I'm
30:16 LORD your God's ***c*** that I'm
2 Kings
17:16 deserted all the ***c*** of the LORD their
Ezra
9:10 after this? We have abandoned your ***c***,
Nehemiah
1:5 to those who love you and keep your ***c***.
Psalms
112:1 who adore God's ***c***, are truly happy!
119:10 Don't let me stray from any of your ***c***!
Ecclesiastes
12:13 and keep God's ***c*** because this is
Matthew
19:17 to enter eternal life, keep the ***c***."
Mark
10:19 You know the ***c***: Don't commit murder.
Luke
1:6 of all the Lord's ***c*** and regulations.
18:20 You know the ***c***. Don't commit adultery.
John
14:15 If you love me, you will keep my ***c***
15:10 If you keep my ***c***, you will remain in
Romans
13:9 The ***c***, Don't commit adultery, don't
1 John
2:3 that we know him: if we keep his ***c***.
3:22 we keep his ***c*** and do what
5:2 God: when we love God and keep God's ***c***.
Revelation
12:17 who keep God's ***c*** and hold firmly
14:12 who keep God's ***c*** and keep faith

COMMANDS

Genesis
44:1 Joseph gave ***c*** to his household manager:
Leviticus
27:34 These are the ***c*** that the LORD gave
Numbers
15:22 obey all these ***c*** that the LORD
36:6 that the LORD ***c*** to Zelophehad's
Deuteronomy
4:2 Instead, keep the ***c*** of the LORD your
5:15 the LORD your God ***c*** you to keep the
6:17 LORD your God's ***c*** along with the
Joshua
1:18 obey any of your ***c*** will be put to
1 Samuel
13:13 have broken the ***c*** the LORD your God
2 Kings
17:19 didn't keep the ***c*** of the LORD their
Job
9:7 Who ***c*** the sun, and it does not rise,
36:10 discipline and ***c*** them to turn from

37:12 everything he **c** over the entire
37:15 that when God **c** them, his clouds
Psalms
19:8 heart. The LORD's **c** are pure, giving
42:8 By day the LORD **c** his faithful love; by night his song
103:18 covenant and remember to keep his **c**.
Proverbs
2:1 son, accept my words and store up my **c**.
3:1 instruction. Let your heart guard my **c**
4:4 on to my words: Keep my **c** and live.
7:1 my words; store up my **c** within you.
7:2 Keep my **c** and live, and my instruction
10:8 mind accepts **c**, but a foolish
Isaiah
48:18 attention to my **c**, your well-being w
Daniel
9:4 to all who love him and keep his **c**:
Matthew
5:19 least of these **c** and teaches
22:40 the Prophets depend on these two **c**."
Luke
8:25 Who is this? He **c** even the winds

COMMIT → COMMIT ADULTERY, COMMIT MURDER
Genesis
20:9 What sin did I **c** against you that
Exodus
32:21 you led them to **c** such a terrible
Judges
19:23 please don't **c** such an evil act,
Psalms
7:16 the violence they **c** will come down on
36:4 in bed! They **c** themselves to a
37:5 **C** your way to the LORD! Trust him! He
Proverbs
16:3 **C** your work to the LORD, and your plans
Ecclesiastes
8:12 Wrongdoers may **c** a hundred crimes but
Jeremiah
26:19 We are about to **c** a huge mistake
Amos
4:4 to Bethel—and **c** a crime; multiply
Zephaniah
3:13 from Israel won't **c** injustice; they
1 Corinthians
6:18 sexual immorality **c** sin against their
1 Peter
4:19 God's will should **c** their lives to a

COMMIT ADULTERY
Ex 20:14; Dt 5:18; Jer 7:9; 23:14; Hos 4:13; 4:14; Mt 5:27; 5:32; 19:18; Mk 10:19; Lk 18:20; Ro 2:22; 13:9; Jas 2:11; 2Pt 2:14

COMMIT MURDER
Eze 11:6; Mt 5:21; 19:18; Mk 10:19; Jas 2:11; 4:2

COMMITS ADULTERY
Lv 20:10; Prv 6:32; Eze 33:26; Mt 5:32; 19:9; Mk 10:11; 10:12; Lk 16:18; Heb 13:4

COMMITTED → COMMITTED ADULTERY
Exodus
32:30 people, "You've **c** a terrible sin.
Leviticus
4:3 offering for the sin he has **c**.
4:14 the sin that they **c** becomes known,
Deuteronomy
9:18 sin that you had **c** by doing such
22:26 woman. She hasn't **c** any capital crime-
Judges
20:6 because they had **c** a disgraceful act
Nehemiah
1:6 which we have **c** against you. Both
Psalms
22:8 He **c** himself to the LORD, so let God
51:4 alone. I've **c** evil in your
Jeremiah
2:13 My people have **c** two crimes: They have
Ezekiel
18:14 that his father **c**. He becomes
Mark
15:7 rebels who had **c** murder during an
Luke
2:19 Mary **c** these things to memory and
Hebrews
9:7 for the sins the people **c** in ignorance.
9:15 from the offenses **c** under the first

COMMITTED ADULTERY
Jer 3:2; 5:7; Eze 23:37; Mt 5:28; Rev 2:22

COMMUNAL SACRIFICE
Lv 3:1; 3:3, 6, 9; 4:10, 26, 31, 35; 7:11, 12, 16, 17, 20, 21, 29, 32, 37; 9:18; 17:8; 19:5; 22:21, 29; 23:19

COMMUNAL SACRIFICES
Lv 7:34; 10:14; 17:5, 7; 23:37; Eze 40:42

COMMUNITY
Joshua
22:12 entire Israelite **c** assembled at
Judges
21:10 The **c** dispatched twelve thousand
1 Samuel
6:19 people, and the **c** grieved because
Proverbs
5:14 of utter ruin in the assembled **c**."
Zechariah
13:7 for my **c**, says the LORD of
Acts
2:41 thousand people into the **c** on that day.
2:42 teaching, to the **c**, to their shared
2:47 daily to the **c** those who were

COMPANIONS
Job
6:15 My **c** are treacherous like a stream in
Psalms
45:7 the oil of joy more than all your **c**!
88:18 my loved ones and **c** distant. My only
Ecclesiastes
4:8 alone, with no **c**, not even a child
Isaiah
1:23 are rebels, **c** of thieves.
Luke
6:3 David and his **c** did when they

COMPANIONS [cont.]

6:4 also gave some of the bread to his ***c***."
24:33 eleven and their ***c*** gathered together.
Acts
13:13 Paul and his ***c*** sailed from Paphos to
16:6 Paul and his ***c*** traveled throughout the
19:29 Paul's traveling ***c*** from the province
20:34 for those of my ***c*** with my own hands.
22:9 My traveling ***c*** saw the light, but they
26:13 and my traveling ***c***. That light was
Hebrews
1:9 you with oil instead of your ***c***.

COMPARE

Deuteronomy
32:31 their rocks can't ***c*** to our rock! Our
2 Samuel
7:22 God! No one can ***c*** to you, no god
Job
28:17 nor glass can ***c*** with it; she
Psalms
35:10 LORD, who could ***c*** to you? You
40:5 us—no one can ***c*** with you! If I
71:19 awesome things! Who can ***c*** to you, God?
86:8 is nothing that can ***c*** to your works!
89:6 the sky who could ***c*** to the LORD? Who among the gods
113:5 could possibly ***c*** to the LORD our
Proverbs
3:15 all you desire can't ***c*** with her.
Matthew
11:16 To what will I ***c*** this generation? It
Luke
13:20 said, "To what can I ***c*** God's kingdom?

COMPASSION

Exodus
33:19 and I will have ***c*** to whomever I
2 Samuel
12:6 he did this and because he had no ***c***."
2 Chronicles
36:15 because he had ***c*** on his people and
Job
33:24 so that God has ***c*** on that person and
Psalms
25:6 remember your ***c*** and faithful love-
40:11 back any of your ***c*** from me. Let your
51:1 wrongdoings according to your great ***c***!
69:16 is good! Turn to me in your great ***c***!
72:13 He has ***c*** on the weak and the needy; he
77:9 Has he angrily stopped up his ***c***?" Selah
79:8 let your ***c*** hurry to meet us
86:15 are a God of ***c*** and mercy; you
90:13 quick! Have some ***c*** for your servants!
102:13 up—you'll have ***c*** on Zion because
103:4 crowns you with faithful love and ***c***,
103:13 a parent feels ***c*** for their
106:46 them to receive ***c*** from all their
111:4 works. The LORD is full of mercy and ***c***.
119:77 Let your ***c*** come to me so I can live
119:156 You have so much ***c***, LORD—make me
135:14 people and has ***c*** on those who
145:9 everything; God's ***c*** extends to all
Proverbs
12:10 but even the ***c*** of the wicked is
Isaiah
49:10 one who has ***c*** for them will
Jeremiah
12:15 I will again have ***c*** on them and
21:7 to the sword without pity, mercy, or ***c***.
33:26 the captives and have ***c*** on them.
Ezekiel
5:11 tear. You will have no ***c***, even from me.
24:14 have any pity or ***c***. Your punishments
39:25 I will have ***c*** on the whole
Hosea
1:6 Name her No ***C***, because I will
2:1 My People, and to your sister, ***C***:
2:23 and I will have ***c*** on No Compassion,
11:8 within me; my ***c*** grows warm and
13:14 your destruction? ***C*** is hidden from my
14:3 our hands. In you the orphan finds ***c***."
Matthew
9:36 crowds, he had ***c*** for them because
18:27 The master had ***c*** on that servant,
20:34 Jesus had ***c*** on them and touched their
Romans
9:15 and I'll show ***c*** to whomever I
James
5:11 for the Lord is full of ***c*** and mercy.

COMPASSIONATE → MERCIFUL AND COMPASSIONATE

Deuteronomy
4:31 your God is a ***c*** God. He won't let
13:17 anger and is ***c*** to you, showing
2 Chronicles
30:9 is merciful and ***c***. He won't
Nehemiah
9:17 merciful and ***c***, very patient,
Psalms
78:38 But God, being ***c***, kept forgiving their
103:8 The LORD is ***c*** and merciful, very
112:4 They are merciful, ***c***, and righteous.
116:5 mericful and righteous; our God is ***c***.
145:8 is merciful and ***c***, very patient,
Joel
2:13 is merciful and ***c***, very patient,
Jonah
4:2 a merciful and ***c*** God, very
Luke
6:36 Be ***c*** just as your Father is
Acts
9:36 good works and ***c*** acts on behalf of
2 Corinthians
1:3 He is the ***c*** Father and God of
Ephesians
4:32 Be kind, ***c***, and forgiving to each
1 Peter
3:8 fellow believers, ***c***, and modest in

COMPENSATION OFFERING

Lv 5:15; 5:16, 18, 19; 6:6, 17; 7:1, 2, 5, 7, 37; 14:12, 13, 14, 17, 21, 24, 25, 28; 19:21, 22; Nm 6:12; 1Sa 6:4; 6:8, 17; Ezr 10:19; Prv 14:9; Eze 42:13

COMPENSATION OFFERINGS

Nm 18:9; Ps 40:6; Eze 40:39; 44:29; 46:20

COMPLETE

Matthew
5:48 Father is ***c*** in showing love
19:21 you want to be ***c***, go, sell what

23:32 Go ahead, **c** what your ancestors did
Luke
13:32 and on the third day I will **c** my work.
14:28 whether you have enough money to **c** it?
14:30 began construction and couldn't **c** it!'
John
3:29 voice. Therefore, my joy is now **c**.
5:36 so that I might **c** them. These works
16:24 receive, so that your joy will be **c**.
Acts
3:16 Jesus gave him **c** health right
4:29 to speak your word with **c** confidence.
28:31 and with **c** confidence, he
2 Corinthians
7:1 make our holiness **c** in the fear of
10:6 your obedience is **c**, we are ready to
13:9 pray for this: that you will be made **c**.
Philippians
1:6 stay with you to **c** the job by the
Colossians
1:25 me for you, in order to **c** God's word.
4:12 fully mature and **c** in the entire
4:17 to it that you **c** the ministry that
1 Thessalonians
3:10 in person and to **c** whatever you
1 Timothy
2:2 peaceful life in **c** godliness and
3:4 children are obedient with **c** respect,
Titus
2:15 and correct with **c** authority. Don't
3:2 kind, and show **c** courtesy toward
James
1:4 this endurance **c** its work so that
2:22 faith was made **c** by his faithful
1 John
1:4 these things so that our joy can be **c**.
2 John
1:12 face-to-face, so that our joy can be **c**.
Revelation
3:2 are far from **c** in the eyes of my

COMPLETED

Genesis
2:2 sixth day God **c** all the work that
29:28 Jacob did. He **c** the celebratory
Leviticus
8:33 ordination is **c**, because your
12:4 until her time of purification is **c**.
Numbers
6:13 as a nazirite is **c**, the person will
Job
1:5 feast had been **c**, Job would send
Daniel
11:36 until the doom is **c**, because what is
Luke
1:23 When he **c** the days of his priestly
2:39 and Joseph had **c** everything
12:50 How I am distressed until it's **c**!
John
19:28 was already **c**, in order to
19:30 said, "It is **c**." Bowing his
Acts
14:26 God's grace to the work they had now **c**.
Romans
15:19 Spirit. So I've **c** the circuit of
Hebrews
4:3 God's works were **c** at the foundation

CONCEIVED

1 Samuel
1:20 of time, Hannah **c** and gave birth to
2 Samuel
11:5 The woman **c** and sent word to David.
2 Kings
4:17 But the woman **c** and gave birth to a son
1 Chronicles
7:23 his wife, and she **c** and gave birth to
Job
3:3 night someone said, "A boy has been **c**."
Psalms
51:5 in sin, from the moment my mother **c** me.
Song of Songs
3:4 to the chamber of the one who **c** me.
Isaiah
59:13 muttering lying words **c** in our minds.
Hosea
2:5 she who **c** them has behaved
Matthew
1:20 she carries was **c** by the Holy
Luke
1:36 Elizabeth has **c** a son. This woman
Romans
9:10 but also Rebecca **c** children with one
Galatians
4:23 slave woman was **c** the normal way,

CONDEMN

Psalms
5:10 **C** them, God! Let them fail by their own
94:21 the righteous. They **c** innocent blood.
109:31 to save them from any who would **c** them.
Proverbs
24:24 will curse them. Nations will **c** them.
Isaiah
50:9 help me. Who will **c** me? Look, they
Matthew
12:41 generation and **c** it as guilty,
Mark
10:33 They will **c** him to death and
Luke
6:22 insult you, and **c** your name as evil
John
8:11 Neither do I **c** you. Go, and from
Acts
7:7 And I will **c** the nation they serve as
Romans
2:1 any excuse. You **c** yourself when you
1 John
3:20 if our hearts **c** us, God is
3:21 our hearts don't **c** us, we have

CONDEMNED

Matthew
5:22 danger of being **c** by the governing
12:7 you wouldn't have **c** the innocent.
27:3 that Jesus was **c** to die, he felt
John
16:11 because this world's ruler stands **c**.
Romans
8:3 selfishness. God **c** sin in the body

CONDEMNED [cont.]

James
5:6 You have **c** and murdered the righteous
2 Peter
2:6 God **c** the cities of Sodom and Gomorrah
Revelation
18:20 God has **c** her as she

CONDUCT

Deuteronomy
4:15 So watch your **c** closely, because you
Job
4:6 integrity of your **c**, the source of
Psalms
112:5 as are those who **c** their affairs
Proverbs
20:11 whether their **c** is pure and
21:24 their name! Their **c** involves
Ecclesiastes
6:8 by knowing how to **c** themselves before
Jeremiah
4:18 Your own **c**, your own deeds have done
7:3 Improve your **c** and your actions,
17:21 Sabbath day or **c** business at the
17:24 LORD, and don't **c** business at the
17:27 your loads and **c** your business at
Luke
23:14 in this man's **c** that provides a
2 Corinthians
12:20 gossip, conceit, and disorderly **c**.
Ephesians
4:2 **C** yourselves with all humility,
2 Timothy
3:10 to my teaching, **c**, purpose,
1 Peter
1:17 you should **c** yourselves with

CONFESS

Isaiah
45:23 knee will bow and every tongue will **c**;
Romans
10:9 Because if you **c** with your mouth "Jesus
15:9 of this I will **c** you among the
Philippians
2:11 and every tongue **c** that Jesus Christ is
2 Timothy
2:22 with those who **c** the Lord with a
Hebrews
13:15 fruit from our lips that **c** his name.
James
5:16 For this reason, **c** your sins to each
1 John
1:9 But if we **c** our sins, he is faithful
4:3 that doesn't **c** Jesus is not from
4:15 If any of us **c** that Jesus is the God's
2 John
1:7 world who do not **c** that Jesus Christ

CONFIDENCE

Proverbs
3:26 LORD will be your **c**; he will guard
10:9 walk with **c**, but those on
11:13 but a trustworthy person keeps a **c**.
14:26 LORD is strong **c** and refuge for
Luke
1:4 want you to have **c** in the soundness
Acts
4:13 surprise by the **c** with which Peter
4:29 to speak your word with complete **c**.
9:27 them about the **c** with which Saul
18:26 speaking with **c** in the synagogue.
28:31 and with complete **c**, he continued to
Ephesians
6:20 will give me the **c** to say what I
Philippians
1:14 have had more **c** through the Lord
3:3 We don't put our **c** in rituals
3:4 have this kind of **c**. If anyone else
1 Timothy
1:7 they are talking about with such **c**.
3:13 and considerable **c** in the faith that
Philemon
1:8 I have enough **c** in Christ to
Hebrews
3:6 we hold on to the **c** and the pride
4:16 of favor with **c** so that we can
10:35 throw away your **c**—it brings a great
1 John
2:28 we can have **c** and not be

CONFLICT

Proverbs
10:12 Hate stirs up **c**, but love covers all
13:10 cause **c** out of pride;
Ezekiel
44:24 in cases of civil **c**. They must
Titus
3:10 more to do with a person who causes **c**,
James
4:1 is the source of **c** among you? What

CONGREGATION

Ezra
10:8 be separated from the **c** of the exiles.
Psalms
22:22 praise you in the very center of the **c**!
22:25 in the great **c** because of you; I
26:12 I will bless the LORD in the great **c**.
68:26 God in the great **c**; bless the LORD
74:2 Remember your **c** that you took as your own
107:32 exalt God in the **c** of the people and
111:1 of those who do right, in the **c**.

CONSCIENCE → GOOD CONSCIENCE

Job
27:6 it; my **c** will never blame
Acts
23:1 altogether clear **c** right up to this
24:16 a clear **c** before God and
Romans
9:1 not lying, as my **c** assures me with
13:5 but also for the sake of your **c**.
1 Corinthians
8:7 until now. Their **c** is weak because
8:10 with a weak **c** be encouraged to
10:25 questions about it because of your **c**.
10:27 asking questions because of your **c**.
10:28 one who told you and for the sake of **c**.
10:29 Now when I say "**c**" I don't mean yours
2 Corinthians
1:12 and our **c** confirms this. We
4:2 to everyone's **c** in the sight of
Titus
1:15 their mind and **c** are corrupted.

Hebrews
9:9 can't perfect the **c** of the one who is
10:22 from an evil **c** and our bodies
13:18 we have a good **c**, and we want to

CONSIDER

Exodus
23:7 I will not **c** innocent those
Leviticus
19:23 tree, you must **c** its fruit off
Psalms
5:1 Hear my words, LORD! **C** my groans!
32:2 the LORD doesn't **c** guilty—in whose
49:18 Though they **c** themselves blessed during their lives
50:22 So **c** this carefully, all you who forget
74:20 **C** the covenant! Because the land's dark
144:3 are human beings that you even **c** them?
Proverbs
3:7 Don't **c** yourself wise. Fear the LORD
23:1 ruler, carefully **c** what is in front
26:12 see people who **c** themselves wise?
Ecclesiastes
7:13 **C** God's work! Who can straighten what
7:14 times are bad, **c**: God has made the
Matthew
12:33 Either **c** the tree good and its fruit
13:18 **C** then the parable of the farmer
Mark
4:31 **C** a mustard seed. When scattered on the
Romans
3:28 law of faith. We **c** that a person is
6:11 you also should **c** yourselves dead
12:16 **C** everyone as equal, and don't think
14:16 let something you **c** to be good be
2 Corinthians
11:5 I don't **c** myself as second-rate in any

CONSIDERED

Deuteronomy
6:25 more, we will be **c** righteous if we
24:13 and you will be **c** righteous before
Job
18:3 Why are we **c** beasts, ignorant in your
32:2 Job because he **c** himself more
Psalms
44:22 you that we are **c** sheep ready for
88:4 I am **c** as one of those plummeting into the pit
106:31 why Phinehas is **c** righteous,
119:59 I've **c** my ways and turned my feet back
Ecclesiastes
9:1 So I **c** all of this carefully, examining
Isaiah
32:5 honorable, nor a villain **c** respectable.
65:12 You did what I **c** evil, and chose
Ezekiel
47:22 among you are **c** full citizens
Mark
10:42 the ones who are **c** the rulers by the
Luke
1:66 heard about this **c** it carefully.
2:19 things to memory and **c** them carefully.
20:35 But those who are **c** worthy to
1 Corinthians
1:28 low-life—what is **c** to be nothing—to
Galatians
2:9 and John, who are **c** to be key
2 Thessalonians
1:5 that you will be **c** worthy of God's
1 Timothy
1:12 because he **c** me faithful. So
Philemon
1:13 I **c** keeping him with me so that he

CONSTANTLY

1 Thessalonians
1:2 when we mention you **c** in our prayers.
2:13 We also thank God **c** for this: when you
2:16 Their sins are **c** pushing the
2 Thessalonians
1:11 We are **c** praying for you for this: that
2 Timothy
1:3 ancestors did. I **c** remember you in

CONSUME

Leviticus
7:26 You must not **c** any blood
Ecclesiastes
5:11 so do those who **c** them. But what do
Luke
9:54 call fire down from heaven to **c** them?"

CONSUMED

2 Peter
3:10 elements will be **c** by fire, and the
Revelation
18:8 She will be **c** by fire because
20:9 fire came down from heaven and **c** them.

CONTEMPT

Genesis
3:15 I will put **c** between you and the woman,
Job
12:5 a torch of **c** to one who is idle, a
Psalms
31:18 against the righteous with pride and **c**!
107:40 God pours **c** on their leaders, making
119:22 their insults and **c** away from me
Proverbs
12:8 insight, but a warped mind leads to **c**.
12:16 away, but the shrewd hide their **c**.
18:3 arrive, so does **c**; with shame comes
Luke
16:13 the one and have **c** for the other.
23:11 Jesus with **c**. Herod mocked him
Romans
2:4 Or do you have **c** for the riches of

CONTINUE

Ruth
2:13 She said, "May I **c** to find favor in
Psalms
4:2 How long will you **c** to love what is
27:3 against me, I will **c** to trust in this:
67:7 Let God **c** to bless us; let the far ends
Ecclesiastes
1:7 the rivers flow, there they **c** to flow.
Hosea
4:18 drinking, they **c** to behave like
Acts
18:9 Don't be afraid. **C** speaking. Don't

23:32 let the horsemen **c** on with Paul
Romans
6:1 to say? Should we **c** sinning so grace
1 Thessalonians
5:11 So **c** encouraging each other and
1 Timothy
2:15 if they both **c** in faith, love,

CONTROL

Genesis
45:1 could no longer **c** himself in front
1 Corinthians
7:37 own will under **c**, he does right if
1 Thessalonians
4:4 and learn how to **c** your own body in a

CONVINCED

Luke
18:9 people who had **c** themselves that
20:6 because they are **c** that John was a
Acts
5:39 The council was **c** by his reasoning.
17:4 Some were **c** and joined Paul and Silas,
Romans
4:21 He was fully **c** that God was able to do
8:38 I'm **c** that nothing can separate us from God's love

COPPER

Luke
21:2 in two small **c** coins worth a

CORDS

2 Samuel
22:6 The **c** of the grave surrounded me;
Psalms
18:4 Death's **c** were wrapped around me;
Hosea
11:4 kindness, with **c** of love. I

CORNER

1 Samuel
24:4 up and cut off a **c** of Saul's robe.
Daniel
4:11 be seen from every **c** of the earth.
Amos
3:12 escape with the **c** of a bed, and
Zechariah
14:10 gate, to the **C** Gate, and from

CORNERS

Deuteronomy
22:12 for the four **c** of the coat you
1 Samuel
2:10 He judges the far **c** of the earth! May
Psalms
2:8 the far **c** of the earth will
48:10 to the far **c** of the earth.
135:7 clouds at the far **c** of the earth. God
Matthew
6:5 and on the street **c** so that people
24:31 from the four **c** of the earth,
Acts
10:11 lowered to the earth by its four **c**.
Romans
10:18 gone out to the **c** of the inhabited
Revelation
7:1 at the four **c** of the earth.

CORRECT

Deuteronomy
17:9 They will announce to you the **c** ruling.
Job
6:26 Do you intend to **c** my words, to treat
Psalms
141:5 let the faithful **c** me! Let my head
Proverbs
1:23 respond when I **c** you. Look, I'll
1:25 and you didn't want me to **c** you.
8:6 things that are **c**; from my lips
9:8 Don't **c** the impudent, or they will hate
15:12 like those who **c** them. They won't
19:25 become clever; **c** someone with
28:23 Those who **c** someone will, in the end,
30:6 words, or he will **c** you and show you
Matthew
16:22 him, began to **c** him: "God forbid,
18:15 you, go and **c** them when you are
1 Timothy
5:1 Don't **c** an older man but encourage him
2 Timothy
2:25 and should **c** opponents with gentleness.
Revelation
3:19 I **c** and discipline those whom I love.

CORRUPT

Genesis
6:11 earth had become **c** and was filled
Psalms
14:1 no God. They are **c** and do evil
101:4 A **c** heart will be far from me. I won't
Philippians
2:15 are crooked and **c**. Among these
2 Peter
2:10 follow after the **c** cravings of the

COUNCIL

Genesis
49:6 never enter their **c**. May my honor
Job
15:8 listen in God's **c**; is wisdom
Psalms
82:1 in the divine **c**; he gives
89:7 respected in the **c** of the holy ones;
Jeremiah
23:18 in the LORD's **c** to listen to
23:22 had stood in my **c**, they would have
Ezekiel
13:9 in my people's **c**, or recorded in
Matthew
5:22 by the governing **c**. And if they say,
26:59 and the whole **c** were looking for
Mark
15:43 was a prominent **c** member who also
Luke
22:66 and Jesus was brought before their **c**.
Acts
4:13 The **c** was caught by surprise by the
5:21 the Jerusalem **C**, that is, the
17:33 At that, Paul left the **c**

COUNT

Genesis
13:16 If someone could **c** the bits of dust
15:5 up at the sky and **c** the stars if you

COUNTRIES

Isaiah
36:20 gods from those **c** has rescued their
Ezekiel
11:16 for them in the **c** to which they've
20:34 you from the **c** where you've been
Daniel
11:40 He will invade **c**, sweeping over
11:42 power into other **c**. Even Egypt won't

COUNTRY

Exodus
8:2 a plague of frogs over your whole **c**.
18:27 and Jethro went back to his own **c**.
2 Samuel
15:19 foreigner and an exile from your own **c**.
24:8 the entire **c**, they came back
1 Kings
16:4 Birds will eat any who die in the **c**.
Job
5:10 surface, sends water to the open **c**,
39:4 up in the open **c**, leave and never
Isaiah
1:7 Your **c** is deserted, your cities burned
Jonah
1:8 from? What's your **c** and of what
Matthew
2:12 back to their own **c** by another route.
8:28 the lake in the **c** of the Gadarenes,
John
4:44 prophets have no honor in their own **c**.
Acts
13:17 great power, he led them out of that **c**.
Hebrews
11:15 about the **c** that they had
11:16 for a better **c**, that is, a

COURAGE

Joshua
2:11 work up their **c**. This is because
5:1 They lost all **c** because of the
2 Samuel
2:7 So now take **c** and be brave—yes, your master Saul
Psalms
27:14 your heart take **c**! Hope in the LORD!
31:24 be strong and let your heart take **c**.
40:12 than hairs on my head—my **c** leaves me.
107:26 The sailors' **c** melted at this
Isaiah
41:6 each saying to the other, "Take **c**!"
Daniel
11:25 his strength and **c** against the
Philippians
1:20 hope with daring **c** that Christ's
1:28 faithfulness and **c** are a sign of
1 Thessalonians
2:2 we had the **c** through God to

COURT

Genesis
41:46 he left Pharaoh's **c** and traveled
Psalms
1:5 standing in the **c** of justice—neith
Jeremiah
2:9 will take you to **c** and charge even
38:7 the Cushite, a **c** official in the
Daniel
2:49 Daniel himself remained at the royal **c**.
7:10 to serve him! The **c** sat in session;
Matthew
5:25 on the way to **c**. Otherwise, they
5:40 to haul you to **c** and take your
Luke
12:58 you are going to **c** with your
Acts
18:12 Paul and brought him before the **c**.
22:25 who hasn't been found guilty in **c**?"
25:17 my seat in the **c** and ordered that
1 Corinthians
4:3 or by any human **c**; I don't even
6:1 to take it to **c** to be judged by
2 Corinthians
5:10 before Christ in **c** so that each
1 Timothy
1:10 testimonies in **c**, and those who do
2 Timothy
4:16 side at my first **c** hearing. Everyone
James
2:6 they the ones who drag you into **c**?
Revelation
11:2 don't measure the **c** outside the

COVENANT

→ BLOOD OF THE COVENANT, BREAK MY COVENANT, CHEST CONTAINING THE COVENANT, COVENANT CHEST, COVENANT DOCUMENT, COVENANT TABLETS, COVENANT WITH YOU, ENDURING COVENANT, GOD'S COVENANT, NEW COVENANT

Genesis
6:18 I will set up my **c** with you. You
9:13 the symbol of the **c** between me and
15:18 the LORD cut a **c** with Abram: "To
17:2 I will make a **c** between us and I will
31:44 let's make a **c**, you and me, and
Exodus
2:24 remembered his **c** with Abraham,
6:5 into slaves, and I've remembered my **c**.
19:5 stay true to my **c**, you will be my
Leviticus
26:42 will remember my **c** with Jacob. I
Deuteronomy
4:13 LORD declared his **c** to you, which he
29:1 the words of the **c** the LORD
Psalms
25:10 for those who keep his **c** and laws.
44:17 haven't forgotten you or broken your **c**.
50:5 those who made a **c** with me by
78:10 didn't keep God's **c**; they refused to
Proverbs
2:17 youth; she even forgets her **c** with God.
Luke
1:72 ancestors, and remembered his holy **c**,
22:20 cup is the new **c** by my blood,
Acts
3:25 prophets and the **c** that God made

COVENANT [cont.]

Romans
11:27 This is my **c** with them, when I take
1 Corinthians
11:25 cup is the new **c** in my blood.
Revelation
11:19 containing his **c** appeared in his

COVENANT CHEST

Josh 3:6; 3:8, 11, 14, 17; 4:7, 9, 18; 6:6, 8; Ps 132:8; Jer 3:16

COVENANT DOCUMENT

Ex 16:34; 25:16, 21; 27:21; 30:6, 36; 40:20; Lv 16:13; 24:3

COVENANT TABLETS

Ex 31:18; 32:15; 34:29; Dt 9:9; 9:11, 15

COVENANT WITH YOU

Gn 6:18; 9:9, 11; 17:7; Ex 34:27; Lv 26:9; Jdg 2:1; 1Sa 20:8; 2Sa 3:13; 3:21; Is 55:3; Eze 16:8; 16:60, 62

COVENANTS

Exodus
23:32 Don't make any **c** with them or their
Deuteronomy
7:2 Don't make any **c** with them, and
Ezekiel
16:59 solemn pledges and breaking **c**.
Hosea
10:4 when making **c**; so judgment
Romans
9:4 the glory, the **c**, the giving of
Galatians
4:24 the women are two **c**. One is from
Ephesians
2:12 strangers to the **c** of God's promise.

COVER

Genesis
6:14 places and **c** it inside and out
Exodus
21:33 a pit and doesn't **c** it and an ox or a
22:27 only blanket to **c** himself. What
Leviticus
13:45 their hair, **c** their upper lip,
Numbers
4:5 and they will **c** the chest
4:8 them a red cloth, **c** it with fine
7:89 from above the **c** that was on the
19:15 without a sealed **c** on it is unclean.
Job
14:17 is sealed in a bag; you would **c** my sin.
15:27 They **c** their face with grease and make
Psalms
5:12 righteous. You **c** them with favor
79:9 Deliver us and **c** our sins for the
83:16 **C** their faces with shame, LORD, so that
104:9 so they'll never again **c** the earth.
119:69 The arrogant **c** me with their lies, but
Proverbs
10:6 Blessings **c** the head of the righteous,
26:26 They may **c** their hatred with trickery,
Ezekiel
1:23 also had two wings to **c** their bodies.
12:6 out in the dark. **C** your face so that
27:30 their heads and **c** themselves with
Hosea
2:9 cloth, which were to **c** her nakedness.
10:8 the mountains, "**C** us," to the
1 Corinthians
11:6 a woman doesn't **c** her head, then
1 Peter
2:16 using your freedom as a **c**-up for evil.

COVERED

Genesis
7:19 the earth; they **c** all of the
8:9 waters still **c** the entire earth.
Job
7:5 My flesh is **c** with worms and crusted
Matthew
13:44 else found and **c** up. Full of joy,
Acts
7:57 they shrieked and **c** their ears.
Romans
4:7 Law are forgiven, and whose sins are **c**.
1 Corinthians
11:4 with his head **c** shames his head.
11:6 then she should keep her head **c**.
11:7 have his head **c**, because he is

COWS

1 Samuel
6:7 with two nursing **c** that have never
Job
21:10 their **c** give birth and
Amos
4:1 this word, you **c** of Bashan, who
Hebrews
9:13 ashes of **c** made spiritually

CREATE

Genesis
1:1 When God began to **c** the heavens and the earth
Nehemiah
4:8 Jerusalem and to **c** a disturbance in
Psalms
51:10 **C** a clean heart for me, God; put a new,
Proverbs
6:14 to do evil; they **c** controversies all
13:5 but the wicked **c** disgust and scorn.
Isaiah
4:5 the LORD will **c** over the whole
8:10 **C** a plan, but be frustrated! Speak a
45:7 I form light and **c** darkness, make
45:18 it, who didn't **c** it a wasteland
57:19 I will **c** reason for praise: utter
63:12 water for them to **c** an enduring
66:9 LORD. Will I, who **c** life, close the
Acts
15:19 that we shouldn't **c** problems for
Romans
16:17 for people who **c** divisions and
Ephesians
2:15 so that he could **c** one new person
Jude
1:19 These people **c** divisions. Since they

CREATED → GOD CREATED

Genesis
2:4 when they were **c**. On the day the

5:2 and **c** them male and female. He blessed
6:7 race that I've **c**: from human
Exodus
15:17 the sanctuary, LORD, that your hand **c**.
Deuteronomy
4:32 the day God first **c** human beings on
1 Chronicles
16:26 idols, but it is the LORD who **c** heaven!
Psalms
89:12 and south—you **c** them! The
89:47 life is! Have you **c** humans for no
96:5 idols, but it is the LORD who **c** heaven!
102:18 people not yet **c** will praise the
104:30 breath, they are **c**, and you make the
139:13 are the one who **c** my innermost
148:5 God gave the command and they were **c**!
Proverbs
8:22 The LORD **c** me at the beginning of his
Isaiah
14:27 forces has **c** a plan; who can
40:26 and consider: Who **c** these? The one
41:20 and the holy one of Israel has **c** it.
42:5 the one who **c** the heavens, the
43:1 the one who **c** you, Jacob, the
43:7 name and whom I **c** for my glory,
45:8 well. I, the LORD, have **c** these things.
45:12 the earth, and **c** humans upon it.
45:18 LORD said, who **c** the heavens, who
48:7 They are **c** now, not long ago; before
54:16 Look, I myself **c** the metalworker who
Jeremiah
1:5 Before I **c** you in the womb I knew you;
13:11 to the body, so I **c** the people of
31:22 The LORD has **c** something new on
31:36 If the **c** order should vanish from my
32:17 LORD God, you **c** heaven and earth by
Ezekiel
21:30 where you were **c**, in the land of
28:13 day that you were **c**, finely crafted
28:15 the day you were **c** until injustice
Malachi
2:10 us, one God who **c** us? Why does
Mark
2:27 The Sabbath was **c** for humans;
7:8 on to rules **c** by humans and
John
17:5 shared with you before the world was **c**.
Acts
4:24 are the one who **c** the heaven, the
17:26 one person God **c** every human
Romans
8:39 or depth, or any other thing that is **c**.
1 Corinthians
11:9 and man wasn't **c** for the sake of the
Ephesians
2:10 accomplishment, **c** in Christ Jesus
3:9 of time by God, who **c** everything.
4:24 the new person **c** according to
Colossians
1:16 all things were **c** by him: both in
3:10 to the image of the one who **c** it.
1 Timothy
4:3 foods that God **c**—and he intended t
4:4 that has been **c** by God is good,
Hebrews
1:2 of everything and **c** the world through
11:3 universe has been **c** by a word from
James
1:18 from the harvest of everything he **c**.
Revelation
4:11 because you **c** all things. It is
10:6 and always, who **c** heaven and what is in it

CREATION

Genesis
2:3 it God rested from all the work of **c**.
Numbers
16:30 an act of **c**, and the ground
Jeremiah
51:48 Then all **c** will rejoice over Babylon,
Mark
10:6 the beginning of **c**, God made them
John
17:24 you loved me before the **c** of the world.
Romans
1:20 Ever since the **c** of the world, God's
8:19 The whole **c** waits breathless with
2 Corinthians
5:17 part of the new **c**. The old things
Galatians
6:15 mean anything. What matters is a new **c**.
Ephesians
1:4 presence before the **c** of the world.
Colossians
1:15 God, the one who is first over all **c**,
1:23 throughout all **c** under heaven. And
Hebrews
4:4 seventh day of **c**: God rested on
12:27 are part of this **c**—so that what
1 Peter
1:20 chosen before the **c** of the world, but
2 Peter
3:4 the beginning of **c**, nor even since
Revelation
3:14 and true witness, the ruler of God's **c**.

CREATURE

Genesis
1:25 and every kind of **c** that crawls on
7:15 the ark, two of every **c** that breathes.
Exodus
25:19 winged heavenly **c** at one end and
Leviticus
5:2 unclean swarming **c**—but the fact goes unknown
Deuteronomy
14:20 Any clean winged **c** can be eaten,
1 Kings
6:24 the first winged **c** were each seven
6:25 The second winged **c** also measured
Ecclesiastes
10:20 some winged **c** could report what
Mark
16:15 and proclaim the good news to every **c**.
Hebrews
4:13 No **c** is hidden from it, but rather
Revelation
4:7 The first living **c** was like a lion. The
5:13 And I heard every **c** in heaven and on
6:3 heard the second living **c** say, "Come!"
6:5 the third living **c** say, "Come!" So I
6:7 of the fourth living **c** say, "Come!"

CREATURES → ALL CREATURES, HEAVENLY CREATURES

Genesis
3:24 stationed winged ***c*** wielding flaming
9:17 set up between me and all ***c*** on earth."
Leviticus
11:2 These are the ***c*** that you are
Proverbs
30:25 Ants as ***c*** aren't strong, but they store
30:26 Badgers as ***c*** aren't powerful, but they
Isaiah
6:2 Winged ***c*** were stationed around him.
37:16 on the winged ***c***. You alone are
Ezekiel
1:5 of four living ***c***. This was what
9:3 above the winged ***c*** where he had been
10:1 of the winged ***c***. It appeared
11:22 Then the winged ***c*** raised their wings.
25:13 all living ***c***, and make it a
38:20 field, all the ***c*** crawling on the
41:18 carved winged ***c*** and palm trees.
2 Peter
2:12 animals, mere ***c*** of instinct, born
Revelation
4:6 were four living ***c*** encircling the
5:6 the four living ***c*** and among the
6:1 the four living ***c*** say in a voice
7:11 the four living ***c***. They fell
8:9 a third of the ***c*** living in the sea
14:3 the four living ***c***, and the elders.
15:7 the four living ***c*** gave the seven
19:4 the four living ***c*** fell down and

CRIED

Genesis
21:16 at a distance, ***c*** out in grief, and
23:2 and Abraham ***c*** out in grief and
Numbers
11:2 When the people ***c*** out to Moses, Moses
Deuteronomy
1:45 came back, you ***c*** before the LORD,
26:7 So we ***c*** out for help to the LORD, our
Joshua
24:7 Then they ***c*** for help to the LORD. So he
Judges
2:4 raised their voices and ***c*** out loud.
Esther
4:1 of the city and ***c*** out loudly and
Job
29:12 the weak who ***c*** out, the orphans
31:38 If my land has ***c*** out against me, its
Psalms
18:3 praiseworthy, I ***c*** out to the LORD,
22:5 they ***c*** out to you and they were saved;
30:2 LORD, my God, I ***c*** out to you for help,
107:6 So they ***c*** out to the LORD in their
Isaiah
33:7 those in Ariel ***c*** out in the
Jonah
1:5 and each one ***c*** out to his god.
2:2 the underworld I ***c*** out for help; you
3:4 one day, and he ***c*** out, "Just forty
Matthew
8:29 They ***c*** out, "What are you going to do
26:75 Peter went out and ***c*** uncontrollably.
27:46 about three Jesus ***c*** out with a loud
27:50 Again Jesus ***c*** out with a loud shout.
Mark
9:24 the boy's father ***c*** out, "I have
15:34 At three, Jesus ***c*** out with a loud
John
19:12 Jewish leaders ***c*** out, saying, "If
Acts
20:37 They ***c*** uncontrollably as everyone
Revelation
6:10 They ***c*** out with a loud voice, "Holy and
18:19 heads, and they ***c*** out, weeping and

CRIME

Genesis
31:36 and what's my ***c*** that you've
Numbers
35:31 of a capital ***c***, for he must
Deuteronomy
19:15 someone in any ***c***, wrongdoing, or
21:22 of a capital ***c***, and they are
22:26 any capital ***c***—rather, this
Joshua
22:20 wasn't the only one to die for his ***c***.'"
1 Samuel
20:1 done? What is my ***c***? How have I
Job
31:11 for that's a ***c***; it's a punishable
Proverbs
28:24 say, "It's not a ***c***," are friends of
Isaiah
58:1 my people their ***c***, to the house of
Hosea
4:2 common; bloody ***c*** followed by
10:10 they are punished for their double ***c***.
Amos
4:4 commit a ***c***; multiply crimes
Micah
1:5 this is for the ***c*** of Jacob and the
6:7 child for my ***c***; the fruit of my
Acts
16:37 us guilty of a ***c***, and they threw
24:20 here declare what ***c*** they found when I

CRIMES

Psalms
64:6 try to expose our ***c***! We've devised a
Proverbs
29:16 numerous, so do ***c***; the righteous
Ecclesiastes
8:12 commit a hundred ***c*** but still live
Isaiah
1:4 weighed down with ***c***, evildoing
53:5 because of our ***c***. He bore the
53:6 but the LORD let fall on him all our ***c***.
Jeremiah
2:13 committed two ***c***: They have
5:6 of their many ***c*** and countless
Hosea
12:14 will bring his ***c*** down on him and
Acts
25:18 him with any of the ***c*** I had expected.

CROOKED

27:2 the people continued their ***c*** practices.
Psalms
18:26 pure, but toward the ***c***, you are tricky.
Proverbs
6:12 guilty people go around with ***c*** talk.

8:8 nothing in them is twisted or ***c***.
10:9 but those on ***c*** paths will be
11:20 LORD detests a ***c*** heart, but he
14:2 those who take a ***c*** path despise him.
17:20 Those with ***c*** hearts won't prosper, and
22:5 the path of the ***c***; those who guard
28:6 than to be on ***c*** paths and wealthy.

Ecclesiastes
1:15 What's ***c*** can't be straightened; what
7:13 Who can straighten what God has made ***c***?

Isaiah
59:8 make their roads ***c***; no one who walks

Lamentations
3:9 with stonework; he made my routes ***c***.

Matthew
17:17 faithless and ***c*** generation, how

Luke
3:5 be leveled. The ***c*** will be made
9:41 faithless and ***c*** generation, how

Acts
13:10 straight ways of the Lord into ***c*** paths?

Philippians
2:15 by people who are ***c*** and corrupt.

CROSS

Matthew
16:24 take up their ***c***, and follow me.
27:32 Cyrene. They forced him to carry his ***c***.
27:40 are God's Son, come down from the ***c***."
27:42 down from the ***c*** now. Then we'll

John
19:17 Carrying his ***c*** by himself, he went out
19:19 and posted on the ***c***. It read "Jesus
19:25 and Mary Magdalene stood near the ***c***.
19:31 to remain on the ***c*** on the Sabbath,

Acts
2:23 had Jesus killed by nailing him to a ***c***.
13:29 him down from the ***c*** and laid him in a

1 Corinthians
1:17 so that Christ's ***c*** won't be emptied
1:18 message of the ***c*** is foolishness to

Galatians
5:11 the offense of the ***c*** would be canceled.
6:12 won't be harassed for the ***c*** of Christ.
6:14 except for the ***c*** of our Lord Jesus

Ephesians
2:16 to God by the ***c***, which ended the

Philippians
2:8 the point of death, even death on a ***c***.
3:18 many people live as enemies of the ***c***.

Colossians
1:20 peace through the blood of his ***c***.
2:14 He canceled it by nailing it to the ***c***.

Hebrews
12:2 He endured the ***c***, ignoring the

1 Peter
2:24 own body on the ***c*** the sins we

CROWD

Psalms
35:18 will praise you in a huge ***c*** of people.
42:4 songs—a huge ***c*** celebrating the
55:14 we entered God's house with the ***c***.
106:17 Dathan, and covering over Abiram's ***c***.
109:30 among a great ***c*** I will praise God!

Proverbs
1:21 Above the noisy ***c***, she calls out. At

Isaiah
13:4 that of a great ***c***. Listen! An

Jeremiah
26:17 got up and addressed the whole ***c***:
44:15 with the great ***c*** of women who were

Ezekiel
7:12 because wrath overcomes the whole ***c***.
7:13 the whole ***c***. It won't be
7:14 because my wrath overcomes the whole ***c***.
23:42 sound of a noisy ***c*** was around her.

Daniel
10:6 spoke, it sounded like the roar of a ***c***.

Joel
2:8 They don't ***c*** each other; each keeps to
3:14 ***C*** after crowd fills the valley of

Matthew
8:18 Jesus saw the ***c***, he ordered his
14:5 he feared the ***c*** because they
15:10 Jesus called the ***c*** near and said to
17:14 they came to the ***c***, a man met Jesus.
20:29 out of Jericho a large ***c*** followed him.
21:8 Now a large ***c*** spread their clothes on
22:33 Now when the ***c*** heard this, they were
26:47 him was a large ***c*** carrying swords
27:15 to release to the ***c*** one prisoner,

John
5:3 and a ***c*** of people who were sick, blind,
5:13 slipped away from the ***c*** gathered there.
6:2 A large ***c*** followed him, because they
6:5 and saw the large ***c*** coming toward
6:9 what good is that for a ***c*** like this?"
6:24 When the ***c*** saw that neither Jesus nor
7:20 The ***c*** answered, "You have a demon. Who wants to kill you?
8:9 woman were left in the middle of the ***c***.
11:42 benefit of the ***c*** standing here so
12:12 day the great ***c*** that had come for

Acts
2:6 this sound, a ***c*** gathered. They
2:37 When the ***c*** heard this, they were deeply
14:11 had done, the ***c*** shouted in the
16:22 The ***c*** joined in the attacks against
17:8 This provoked the ***c*** and the city
19:32 and most of the ***c*** didn't know why
21:27 threw the whole ***c*** into confusion by
22:22 The ***c*** listened to Paul until he said
24:12 or stirring up a ***c***, whether in the
24:18 There was no ***c*** and no

Revelation
7:9 there was a great ***c*** that no one could
19:1 like a huge ***c*** in heaven. They
19:6 like a huge ***c***, like rushing

CROWDS

Matthew
4:25 Large ***c*** followed him from Galilee, the
5:1 Jesus saw the ***c***, he went up a
7:28 these words, the ***c*** were amazed at
8:1 the mountain, large ***c*** followed him.
9:8 When the ***c*** saw what had happened, they were afraid
9:33 to talk. The ***c*** were amazed and
11:7 spoke to the ***c*** about John: "What
12:15 from there. Large ***c*** followed him, and

12:23 All the **c** were amazed and said, "This
12:46 speaking to the **c**, his mother and
13:2 Such large **c** gathered around him that
14:13 himself. When the **c** learned this,
15:30 Large **c** came to him, including those
19:2 Large **c** followed him, and he healed
21:9 The **c** in front of him and behind him
23:1 Jesus spoke to the **c** and his disciples,
26:55 Jesus said to the **c**, "Have you come
27:20 persuaded the **c** to ask for
Mark
10:1 region of Judea. **C** gathered around
John
7:12 The **c** were murmuring about him. "He's a good man
Acts
8:6 The **c** were united by what they heard
14:19 and won the **c** over. They stoned
17:13 were upsetting and disturbing the **c**.
Revelation
17:15 are peoples, **c**, nations, and

CROWN
Exodus
29:6 and place the holy **c** on the turban.
39:30 for the holy **c** out of pure gold.
Deuteronomy
33:16 head, on the **c** of that prince
2 Samuel
1:10 that. I took the **c** that was on his
12:30 took Milcom's **c** off his head. It
Esther
1:11 wearing the royal **c**. She was
2:17 placed the royal **c** on her head and
8:15 a large gold **c** and a white and
Job
19:9 from me, removed the **c** from my head,
Psalms
21:3 to him; you put a **c** of pure gold on
65:11 You **c** the year with your goodness; your
89:19 I placed a **c** on a strong man.
89:39 You've thrown his **c** in the dirt.
132:18 in shame, but the **c** he wears will
Proverbs
4:9 head; she will give you a glorious **c**."
12:4 strong woman is a **c** to her husband,
14:24 Wealth is the **c** of the wise, and the
16:31 Gray hair is a **c** of glory; it is found
17:6 are the **c** of the elderly,
27:24 forever, nor a **c** generation after
Matthew
27:29 together a **c** of thorns and put
1 Corinthians
9:25 do this to get a **c** of leaves that
Philippians
4:1 are my joy and **c**, stand firm in
1 Thessalonians
2:19 our hope, joy, or **c** that we can brag
1 Peter
5:4 will receive an unfading **c** of glory.
Revelation
2:10 and I will give you the **c** of life.
3:11 you have so that no one takes your **c**.
6:2 and was given a **c**. And he went
12:1 her feet and a **c** of twelve stars
13:1 with a royal **c**, and on its heads
14:14 He had a gold **c** on his head and a

CRUCIFIED
Matthew
20:19 tortured, and **c**. But he will be
26:2 Human One will be handed over to be **c**."
27:26 whipped, then handed him over to be **c**.
28:5 you are looking for Jesus who was **c**."
Mark
15:15 whipped, then handed him over to be **c**.
16:6 Nazareth, who was **c**. He has been
John
19:16 Jesus over to be **c**. The soldiers
19:41 where Jesus was **c**, and in the
Acts
2:36 Jesus, whom you **c**, both Lord and
4:10 you **c** but whom God
Romans
6:6 we used to be was **c** with him in order
1 Corinthians
1:23 we preach Christ **c**, which is a
2:8 would never have **c** the Lord of glory!
2 Corinthians
13:4 Certainly he was **c** because of weakness,
Galatians
2:19 live for God. I have been **c** with Christ
3:1 put on display as **c** before your eyes!
5:24 Christ Jesus have **c** self with its
6:14 world has been **c** to me through
Revelation
11:8 and Egypt, where also their Lord was **c**.

CRUCIFIED HIM
Mt 27:35; Mk 15:24; 15:25; Lk 23:33; 24:20; Jn 19:18

CRUCIFY
Matthew
23:34 you will kill and **c**. And some you
Mark
15:20 on him. Then they led him out to **c** him.
Luke
23:21 shouting out, "**C** him! Crucify him!"
John
19:10 to release you and also to **c** you?"

CRUCIFY HIM
Mt 27:22; 27:23, 31; Mk 15:13; 15:14, 20; Lk 23:21; Jn 19:6; 19:15

CRUEL
Exodus
1:14 them to do all kinds of other **c** work.
Deuteronomy
32:33 is snake poison, venom from a **c** cobra.
2 Samuel
7:10 be disturbed. **C** people will no
1 Chronicles
17:9 be disturbed. **C** people will no
Job
30:21 You are **c** to me, attack me with the
Psalms
64:3 They aim their arrow—a **c** word—
73:8 scoff and talk so **c**; from their
Proverbs
5:9 to others, your years to a **c** person.
11:17 themselves, but **c** people harm
12:10 even the compassion of the wicked is **c**.

17:11 only rebellion; a **c** messenger will be
27:4 Wrath is **c** and anger is a flood, but
28:16 is a **c** oppressor, but
Isaiah
13:9 is coming with **c** rage and burning
Jeremiah
6:23 spear, they are **c**; they show no
50:42 spear, they are **c** and show no
Lamentations
4:3 people has become **c**, like desert

CRY
Exodus
2:23 out, and their **c** to be rescued
Judges
10:14 Go **c** out to the gods you've chosen. Let
1 Kings
8:28 and hear the **c** and prayer that
Psalms
3:4 I **c** out loud to the LORD, and he
34:17 the righteous **c** out, the LORD
40:1 to me; he listened to my **c** for help.
119:146 I **c** out to you, "Save me so I can keep
130:1 song.] I **c** out to you from
147:9 to the baby ravens when they **c** out.
Proverbs
2:3 for insight, and **c** aloud for
Isaiah
3:7 Someone else will **c** out on that day,
42:2 He won't **c** out or shout aloud or make
Jeremiah
4:31 I hear the **c** of a woman in labor, the
Lamentations
2:18 **C** out to my Lord from the heart, you
Hosea
7:14 They don't **c** to me from the heart, but
Habakkuk
1:2 you not listen? I **c** out to you,
Mark
15:37 But Jesus let out a loud **c** and died
Romans
8:15 With this Spirit, we **c**, "Abba, Father."
James
4:9 **C** out in sorrow, mourn, and weep! Let

CRYING
Genesis
4:10 blood is **c** to me from the
Psalms
69:3 I am tired of **c**. My throat is hoarse.
9:27 men followed him, **c** out, "Show us
Mark
5:38 with people **c** and wailing
Galatians
4:6 Son into our hearts, **c**, "Abba, Father!"
Revelation
21:4 be no mourning, **c**, or pain anymore,

CUP
Genesis
40:11 Pharaoh's **c** was in my hand, so I took
44:2 Put my **c**, the silver cup, on top of
2 Samuel
12:3 drink from his **c**—even sleep in his
1 Kings
7:26 was shaped like a **c** or an open lily
Psalms
23:5 head in oil; my **c** is so full it
75:8 Indeed, there's a **c** in the LORD's hand
Proverbs
23:31 sparkles in the **c**, going down
Isaiah
51:22 I have taken the **c** of reeling, the
Jeremiah
25:15 this seething **c** of wine from my
Lamentations
4:21 of Uz. But this **c** will pass over to
Ezekiel
23:31 so I have put her **c** into your hand.
Habakkuk
2:16 and stagger. The **c** of the LORD's
Matthew
10:42 who gives even a **c** of cold water to
20:22 drink from the **c** that I'm about to
23:25 outside of the **c** and plate, but
23:26 the inside of the **c** so that the
26:27 He took a **c**, gave thanks, and gave it
26:39 take this **c** of suffering away
Mark
9:41 gives you a **c** of water to drink
10:38 Can you drink the **c** I drink or
14:23 He took a **c**, gave thanks, and gave it
Luke
11:39 outside of the **c** and platter, but
22:17 After taking a **c** and giving thanks, he
22:20 way, he took the **c** after the meal
22:42 will, take this **c** of suffering away
John
18:11 not to drink the **c** the Father has
1 Corinthians
10:16 Isn't the **c** of blessing that we bless a
10:21 can't drink the **c** of the Lord and
11:25 thing with the **c**, after they had
11:26 and drink this **c**, you broadcast
11:27 or drink the **c** of the Lord
11:28 bread and drink from the **c** in that way.
Revelation
14:10 strength into the **c** of his wrath.
16:19 gave her the wine **c** of his furious
17:4 she held a gold **c** full of the vile
18:6 has done. In the **c** that she has

CUPS
Exodus
25:33 will have three **c** shaped like
Psalms
11:6 the wicked; their **c** will be filled
Isaiah
65:11 fortune, and fill **c** of mixed wine for
Jeremiah
35:5 with several **c**, and I said to
Nahum
1:10 in their **c**. They are
Mark
7:4 as the washing of **c**, jugs, pans, and

CURSE
Genesis
8:21 I will not **c** the fertile land
12:3 you, those who **c** you I will curse;
27:13 to him, "Your **c** will be on me, my
Exodus
22:28 Don't say a **c** against God, and don't

CURSE [cont.]

Numbers
5:18 that brings the **c** will be in the
22:12 with them. Don't **c** the people,
Deuteronomy
11:26 blessing and **c** before you right
11:28 but the **c** if you don't obey the LORD
11:29 Gerizim and the **c** on Mount Ebal. (
21:23 day because God's **c** is on those who
Joshua
24:9 summoned Balaam, Beor's son, to **c** you.
2 Samuel
16:9 this dead dog **c** my master the
Job
1:11 He will certainly **c** you to your face."
2:5 he will definitely **c** you to your face."
2:9 to your integrity? **C** God, and die."
Psalms
109:28 Let them **c**—but you, bless me! If they
Proverbs
3:33 The LORD's **c** is on the house of the
20:20 Those who **c** their father or mother—
30:11 are those who **c** their father and
Lamentations
3:65 a tortured mind—put your **c** on them!
Malachi
2:2 I will send a **c** among you. I will
4:6 will come and strike the land with a **c**.
Luke
6:28 Bless those who **c** you. Pray for those
Romans
12:14 who harass you—bless and don't **c** them.
Galatians
3:10 Law are under a **c**, because it is
3:13 us from the **c** of the Law by
James
3:9 and Father and **c** human beings made
2 Peter
2:14 in greed. They are under God's **c**.
Revelation
22:3 no longer be any **c**. The throne of

CURSED

Genesis
3:14 you are the one **c** out of all the
3:17 not eat from it,' **c** is the ground
4:11 You are now **c** from the ground that
9:25 He said, "**C** be Canaan: the lowest
Numbers
22:6 blessed and whomever you curse is **c**."
23:8 whom God hasn't **c**? How can I
24:9 and the one cursing you will be **c**."
Deuteronomy
27:15 **C** is anyone who makes an idol or an
28:16 You will be **c** in the city and cursed in
Joshua
6:26 Jericho will be **c** before the LORD.
1 Samuel
17:43 sticks?" And he **c** David by his gods.
2 Samuel
16:7 Shimei said as he **c** David: "Get out
1 Kings
21:13 people, "Naboth **c** God and king!" So
2 Kings
2:24 at them and **c** them in the
9:34 Deal with this **c** woman and bury
Nehemiah
13:25 scolded them and **c** them, and beat
Job
1:5 sinned and then **c** God in their
3:1 Job spoke up and **c** the day he was
Psalms
37:22 land, but those **c** by God will be
Proverbs
28:27 who turn a blind eye will be greatly **c**.
Ecclesiastes
7:22 that you've often **c** others yourself!
Isaiah
9:1 earlier time, God **c** the land of
65:20 falling short of a hundred will seem **c**.
Jeremiah
11:3 of Israel, says: **C** are those who
17:5 LORD proclaims: **C** are those who
Malachi
3:9 You are being **c** with a curse, and you,
Matthew
26:74 Then he **c** and swore, "I don't know the
Mark
11:21 how the fig tree you **c** has dried up."
14:71 But he **c** and swore, "I don't know this
Romans
9:3 I wish I could be **c**, cut off from
1 Corinthians
12:3 says, "Jesus is **c**!" when speaking
Galatians
3:10 Everyone is **c** who does not keep
3:13 Everyone who is hung on a tree is **c**.
Hebrews
6:8 close to being **c**. It ends up being
Revelation
16:9 heat, and they **c** the name of the
16:11 and they **c** the God of heaven because of their pains
16:21 the people. They **c** God for the

CURSES

Exodus
21:17 Anyone who **c** their father or mother
Leviticus
20:9 If anyone **c** their father or mother,
Psalms
10:7 are filled with **c**, dishonesty,
59:12 pride. For the **c** and lies they
109:18 Since he wore **c** like a coat, let them
Jeremiah
15:10 lent or borrowed, still everyone **c** me.
15:17 upon me and you had filled me with **c**.
Habakkuk
3:9 bow, uttering **c** for the arrows.

CURSING

Psalms
10:3 the greedy reject the LORD, **c**.
62:4 bless, but inside they are **c**. Selah
Ecclesiastes
7:21 so you don't hear your servant **c** you.
Jeremiah
25:18 horror, shock, and **c**, as it is today;
Romans
3:14 mouths are full of **c** and bitterness.
James
3:10 Blessing and **c** come from the same

CURTAIN

Exodus
26:2 Each **c** should be forty-two feet long

26:12 that is, the half **c** that remains,
Leviticus
4:17 before the LORD toward the inner **c**.
Matthew
27:51 Look, the **c** of the sanctuary was torn
Mark
15:38 The **c** of the sanctuary was torn in two
Luke
23:45 shining. Then the **c** in the sanctuary
Hebrews
6:19 enters the sanctuary behind the **c**.
9:3 behind the second **c** called the holy
10:20 us through the **c**, which is his

CURTAINS

Exodus
26:1 dwelling with ten **c** of fine twisted
Numbers
4:26 the **c** of the courtyard, the screen of
Esther
1:6 White linen **c** and purple hangings were

CUSH

Genesis
2:13 It flows around the entire land of **C**.
10:6 Ham's sons: **C**, Egypt, Put, and Canaan

CUSHITE

Numbers
12:1 on account of the **C** woman whom he had married
2 Samuel
18:21 Joab said to a **C**, "Go tell the

CUT

Exodus
4:25 flint stone and **c** off her son's
Leviticus
1:6 will be skinned and **c** up into pieces.
8:20 He **c** up the ram into pieces, and then
Deuteronomy
7:5 sacred stones, **c** down their sacred
19:5 an axe to **c** down the tree,
Judges
1:6 captured him, and **c** off his thumbs
1 Samuel
5:4 his hands were **c** off and lying on
11:7 He took two oxen, **c** them into pieces,
15:33 Then Samuel **c** Agag to pieces in
17:51 off. Then David **c** off the
24:4 snuck up and **c** off a corner of
31:9 They **c** off Saul's head and stripped off
1 Chronicles
18:4 Then David **c** the hamstrings of
Psalms
12:3 Let the LORD **c** off all slick-talking
118:10 me, but I **c** them down in the
118:11 side, but I **c** them down in the
118:12 burning thorns. I **c** them down in the
129:4 righteous—God **c** me free from the
Proverbs
2:22 wicked will be **c** off from the
10:27 years of the wicked will be **c** short.
10:31 but the twisted tongue will be **c** off.
23:18 a future, and your hope won't be **c** off.
24:14 is a future. Your hope won't be **c** off.
Jeremiah
6:6 forces proclaims: **C** down her trees,
7:29 **C** off your hair and cast it away;
Lamentations
2:3 burning rage, he **c** off each of
Daniel
2:34 until a stone was **c**, but not by
Matthew
21:8 the road. Others **c** palm branches off
24:22 God chose that time will be **c** short.
24:51 He will **c** them in pieces and put them
26:51 high priest's slave, he **c** off his ear.
Mark
6:27 went to the prison, **c** off John's head,
14:47 high priest's slave and **c** off his ear.
Luke
12:46 The master will **c** them into pieces
13:7 never found any. **C** it down! Why
13:9 year; if not, then you can **c** it down.'"
John
18:26 ear Peter had **c** off, said to him,
Romans
9:3 could be cursed, **c** off from Christ
11:22 otherwise you could be **c** off too.
11:23 those who were **c** off will be
11:24 tree and you were **c** off from it, and
1 Corinthians
11:6 have her hair **c** off. If it is
Revelation
14:18 sharp sickle to **c** the clusters in
14:19 the earth, and **c** the vineyard of

CYPRUS

Isaiah
23:1 returning from **C**, they heard about
23:12 up and head to **C**; even there you
Jeremiah
2:10 as the shores of **C** and to the east
Ezekiel
27:6 ivory, of boxwood from the coasts of **C**.
Acts
4:36 who encourages"), was a Levite from **C**.
11:19 far as Phoenicia, **C**, and Antioch.
11:20 some people from **C** and Cyrene. They
13:4 Seleucia. From there they sailed to **C**.
15:39 Barnabas took Mark and sailed to **C**.
21:3 We spotted **C**, but passed by it on our
21:16 He was from **C** and had been a
27:4 off. We passed **C**, using the island

CYRENE

Matthew
27:32 Simon, a man from **C**. They forced him

CYRUS

2 Chronicles
36:23 Persia's King **C** says: The LORD,
Ezra
1:1 year of King **C** of Persia's rule,
Isaiah
44:28 who say about **C**, "My shepherd—he
Daniel
1:21 service until the first year of King **C**.
6:28 and during the rule of **C** the Persian.
10:1 of Persia's King **C**, a message was

Dd

DAGON
Judges
16:23 to their god ***D*** and to hold a
1 Samuel
5:2 Dagon's temple and set it next to ***D***.
5:3 there was ***D***, fallen facedown
5:4 there was ***D*** again, fallen
5:7 hard against us and against our god ***D***."
1 Chronicles
10:10 his skull on a pole in the temple of ***D***.

DAILY
Exodus
5:13 you make the same ***d*** quota as when you had the straw
5:19 Don't reduce your ***d*** quota of bricks."
2 Chronicles
31:16 also distributed ***d*** rations to those
Proverbs
8:34 to me, watching ***d*** at my doors,
Daniel
1:5 these young men ***d*** allotments from
Luke
9:23 take up their cross ***d***, and follow me.
19:47 was teaching ***d*** in the temple.
Acts
2:47 The Lord added ***d*** to the community
6:1 being overlooked in the ***d*** food service.
19:9 and continued his ***d*** interactions in
2 Corinthians
11:28 there's my ***d*** stress because
James
1:11 midst of their ***d*** lives, the

DAILY SACRIFICE
Dn 8:11; 8:12, 13; 11:31; 12:11

DAMASCUS
2 Samuel
8:5 the Arameans of ***D*** came to help
2 Kings
8:7 had gone to ***D*** when Aram's King
16:10 King Ahaz went to ***D*** to meet up with
Isaiah
7:8 chief of Aram is ***D***; the chief of
17:1 An oracle about ***D***. Look! Damascus is
Jeremiah
49:23 Concerning ***D***: Hamath and Arpad lose
Amos
1:3 three crimes of ***D***, and for four, I
Acts
9:3 as he approached ***D***, suddenly a light
22:6 as I approached ***D***, suddenly a
Galatians
1:17 into Arabia and I returned again to ***D***.

DAN → DAN TO BEER-SHEBA
Genesis
14:14 and went after them as far as ***D***.
30:6 given me a son." So she named him ***D***.
Exodus
31:6 from the tribe of ***D***. To all who are
Judges
18:29 renamed the city ***D***, after their
2 Kings
10:29 gold calves that were in Bethel and ***D***.

DAN TO BEER-SHEBA
Jdg 20:1; 1Sa 3:20; 2Sa 17:11; 24:2, 15; 1Ch 21:2

DANIEL
1 Chronicles
3:1 the second ***D***, with Abigail the
Ezra
8:2 of Ithamar, ***D***; of David,
Nehemiah
10:6 ***D***, Ginnethon, Baruch
Ezekiel
14:20 If Noah, ***D***, and Job lived there, as
28:3 wiser than ***D***; no secrets are
Daniel
1:9 loyalty between ***D*** and the chief
6:3 spirit, ***D*** soon surpassed
6:16 and they brought ***D*** and hurled him
Matthew
24:15 thing that ***D*** talked about

DANITE
Numbers
26:42 These are the ***D*** clans according
Joshua
19:40 seventh for the clans of the ***D*** tribe.
19:48 legacy for the clans of the ***D*** tribe.
Judges
13:2 Zorah, from the ***D*** clan, whose name
18:11 men from the ***D*** clan at Zorah and
18:30 priests for the ***D*** tribe until the

DANITES
Numbers
34:22 the tribe of the ***D***, a chief, Bukki,
Judges
18:2 The ***D*** sent five men from their whole

DARIUS
Ezra
4:5 until the rule of Persia's King ***D***.
6:1 Then King ***D*** made a decree, and they
Nehemiah
12:22 families in the rule of ***D*** the Persian.

Daniel
5:31 ***D*** the Mede received the kingdom at the
11:1 the first year of ***D*** the Mede's rule,
Haggai
1:1 year of King ***D***, in the sixth
1:15 month in the second year of ***D*** the king.
2:10 second year of ***D***, the LORD's word
Zechariah
1:1 second year of ***D***, the LORD's word

DARK

Genesis
1:2 or form, it was ***d*** over the deep
Nehemiah
13:19 it began to grow ***d*** at the gates of
Job
3:9 stars stay ***d***; may it wait in
12:25 their way in the ***d*** without light; he
16:16 from crying, and ***d*** gloom hangs on my eyelids
18:6 tent becomes ***d***, and their lamp
24:16 In the ***d*** they break into houses; they
29:3 head, I walked by his light in the ***d***;
30:28 I walk in the ***d***, lacking sunshine; I
Psalms
18:11 his covering was ***d*** water and dense
74:20 the land's ***d*** places are full
82:5 around in the ***d***. All the earth's
105:28 and it became ***d***, but the
112:4 They shine in the ***d*** for others who do
137:7 on Jerusalem's ***d*** day: "Rip it
139:12 isn't too ***d*** for you!
143:3 me to live in the ***d*** like those who've
Proverbs
20:20 will be snuffed out when it becomes ***d***.
Ecclesiastes
11:8 will also be many ***d*** days. Everything
12:2 the light grow ***d***, the moon and the
Isaiah
13:10 The sun will be ***d*** when it rises;
Jeremiah
4:28 the heavens grow ***d*** because I have
Matthew
4:16 who lived in the ***d*** have seen a great
24:29 sun will become ***d***, and the moon
27:45 in the afternoon the whole earth was ***d***.
John
6:17 already getting ***d*** and Jesus hadn't
20:1 it was still ***d***, Mary Magdalene
Acts
17:10 As soon as it was ***d***, the brothers and
1 Corinthians
4:5 are hidden in the ***d*** to light, and he
Ephesians
4:18 they are in the ***d*** in their
2 Peter
1:19 lamp shining in a ***d*** place, until the
Revelation
8:12 of them became ***d***. The day lost a
9:17 were fiery red, ***d*** blue, and yellow

DARKNESS

Genesis
1:4 God separated the light from the ***d***.
15:12 terrifying and deep ***d*** settled over him.
Joshua
24:7 LORD. So he set ***d*** between you and
1 Samuel
2:9 the wicked die in ***d*** because no one
Job
3:4 day—let it be ***d***; may God above
5:14 They encounter ***d*** during the day, and at
10:21 don't return to a land of deepest ***d***,
11:17 than noon; ***d*** will be like
12:22 deep secrets of ***d***, makes utter
17:12 day; light is near because of the ***d***.
17:13 as my dwelling, lay out my bed in ***d***,
Psalms
18:9 came down; thick ***d*** was beneath his
18:11 God made ***d*** cloak him; his covering was
18:28 lamp—the LORD my God illumines my ***d***.
44:19 live, covering us with deepest ***d***.
88:12 in the land of ***d***, your
88:18 distant. My only friend is ***d***.
97:2 Clouds and thick ***d*** surround God. His
104:20 You bring on the ***d*** and it is night,
105:28 God sent ***d***, and it became dark, but
107:10 been sitting in ***d*** and deep gloom;
107:14 them out from the ***d*** and deep gloom;
139:11 If I said, "The ***d*** will definitely hide
139:12 even then the ***d*** isn't too dark for you!
Proverbs
4:19 is like deep ***d***; they don't know
7:9 evening, at the onset of night and ***d***.
Ecclesiastes
2:13 as light is more beneficial than ***d***.
5:17 constantly eat in ***d***, with much
6:4 passes away in ***d***. Darkness covers
Lamentations
3:2 away, forced me to walk in ***d*** not light.
Daniel
2:22 what hides in ***d***; light lives with
Joel
2:2 a day of ***d*** and no light, a day of
2:31 will be turned to ***d***, and the moon to
Amos
4:13 makes the morning ***d***, and moves over
5:8 and turns deep ***d*** into the morning,
Micah
3:6 vision, only ***d*** without
7:8 rise; if I sit in ***d***, the LORD is my
Nahum
1:8 place and pursue his enemies into ***d***.
Zephaniah
1:15 a day of ***d*** and gloominess, a
Luke
1:79 are sitting in ***d*** and in the shadow
12:3 have said in the ***d*** will be heard in
22:53 But this is your time, when ***d*** rules."
23:44 about noon, and ***d*** covered the whole
John
1:5 shines in the ***d***, and the darkness
3:19 and people loved ***d*** more than the
8:12 me won't walk in ***d*** but will have the
12:35 the light so that ***d*** doesn't overtake
Acts
2:20 be changed into ***d***, and the moon
26:18 can turn from ***d*** to light and from
Romans
2:19 blind; a light to those who are in ***d***;
13:12 belong to the ***d*** and put on the
2 Corinthians
4:6 shine out of the ***d***. He is the same

6:14 relationship does light have with ***d***?
Ephesians
5:8 You were once ***d***, but now you are light
5:11 actions of ***d***. Instead you
6:12 forces of cosmic ***d***, and spiritual
Colossians
1:13 the control of ***d*** and transferred
1 Thessalonians
5:4 But you aren't in ***d***, brothers and
5:5 the day. We don't belong to night or ***d***.
Hebrews
12:18 a burning fire, ***d***, shadow, a
1 Peter
2:9 called you out of ***d*** into his amazing
2 Peter
2:4 them to chains of ***d***, keeping them
1 John
1:5 light and there is no ***d*** in him at all."
2:8 you, because the ***d*** is passing away
2:9 brother or sister is in the ***d*** even now.
2:11 sister is in the ***d*** and lives in the
Jude
1:13 for whom the ***d*** of the underworld
Revelation
16:10 throne, and ***d*** covered its

DAUGHTER → DAUGHTER BABYLON, DAUGHTER JERUSALEM, DAUGHTER ZION

Genesis
34:5 defiled his ***d*** Dinah; but his
Judges
11:35 said, "Oh no! My ***d***! You have brought
11:40 story of the Gileadite, Jephthah's ***d***.
19:24 Here's my ***d***, the young woman, and his
21:1 us will allow his ***d*** to marry a
Ruth
1:22 the Moabite, her ***d***-in-law, returned w
2:2 Naomi replied to her, "Go, my ***d***."

DAUGHTER BABYLON

Ps 137:8; Is 47:1; Jer 50:42; 51:33; Zec 2:7

DAUGHTER JERUSALEM

2Ki 19:21; Is 37:22; Lam 2:13; 2:15; Zep 3:14; Zec 9:9

DAUGHTER ZION

2Ki 19:21; Ps 9:14; Is 1:8; 16:1; 37:22; 52:2; 62:11; Jer 4:31; 6:2, 23; Lam 1:6; 2:1, 13, 18; 4:22; Mi 1:13; 4:8, 10, 13; Zep 3:14; Zec 2:10; 9:9; Mt 21:5; Jn 12:15

DAUGHTERS

Genesis
19:8 I've got two ***d*** who are virgins. Let me
19:36 Both of Lot's ***d*** became pregnant by
29:16 Now Laban had two ***d***: the older was
Exodus
2:16 who had seven ***d***. The daughters
Leviticus
10:14 and your sons and ***d***. These things are
Ezra
9:12 do not give your ***d*** to their sons in
Psalms
106:37 their own sons and ***d*** to demons!
106:38 own sons and ***d***—the ones they
144:12 so that our ***d*** can be like
Hosea
4:13 Therefore, your ***d*** act like
Joel
2:28 sons and your ***d*** will prophesy,
Amos
7:17 sons and your ***d*** will fall by the
Luke
23:28 women and said, "***D*** of Jerusalem,
Acts
2:17 Your sons and ***d*** will prophesy.

DAVID → SON OF DAVID

Ruth
4:22 of Jesse, and Jesse the father of ***D***.
1 Samuel
16:23 affected Saul, ***D*** would take the
17:12 Now ***D*** was Jesse's son, an Ephraimite
17:50 And that's how ***D*** triumphed over the
18:1 As soon as ***D*** had finished talking with
18:12 was afraid of ***D*** because the LORD
19:18 So ***D*** fled and escaped. When he reached
2 Samuel
2:4 and anointed ***D*** king over the
3:1 and drawn out. ***D*** kept getting
6:12 King ***D*** was told, "The LORD has blessed
12:13 the LORD!" ***D*** said to Nathan.
24:25 ***D*** built an altar there for the LORD and
1 Kings
1:1 King ***D*** had become very old. His
1:31 May my master King ***D*** live forever!"
1:32 King ***D*** said, "Bring me Zadok the
1:37 than the throne of my master King ***D***."
1:43 Our master King ***D*** has made Solomon
15:5 This was because ***D*** did the right thing
Mark
2:25 ever read what ***D*** did when he was
11:10 of our ancestor ***D***! Hosanna in the
Acts
1:16 through ***D*** had to be
4:25 our ancestor ***D***, your servant:
7:45 in the land until the time of ***D***.
13:22 him, he raised up ***D*** to be their king.
Romans
1:3 His Son was descended from ***D***.
4:6 In the same way, ***D*** also pronounces a
11:9 And ***D*** says, Their table should become a
2 Timothy
2:8 descended from ***D***. This is my good
Hebrews
4:7 he says through ***D*** much later,
11:32 Samson, Jephthah, ***D***, Samuel, and the
Revelation
3:7 has the key of ***D***. Whatever he
5:5 the Root of ***D***, has emerged
22:16 and descendant of ***D***, the bright

DAWN

Genesis
19:15 When ***d*** broke, the messengers urged Lot,
32:24 a man wrestled with him until ***d*** broke.
Job
7:4 and restless thoughts fill me until ***d***.
24:5 they go forth at ***d*** searching for
38:12 morning, informed the ***d*** of its place
Psalms
22:1 of ***D***. A psalm of

37:6 shine like the ***d***, your justice
57:8 and lyre! I will wake the ***d*** itself!
108:2 and lyre! I will wake the ***d*** itself!
139:9 on the wings of ***d***, stopping to rest

Daniel
6:19 At ***d***, at the first sign of light, the

Hosea
6:3 as certain as the ***d***; who will come to
10:15 wickedness. At ***d***, the king of

Jonah
4:7 the next day at ***d***, and it attacked

Matthew
28:1 the Sabbath, at ***d*** on the first day

Luke
1:78 compassion, the ***d*** from heaven will
12:38 he comes at midnight or just before ***d***.

DAY → ALL DAY, DAY OF RECONCILIATION, DAY OF THE LORD, JUDGMENT DAY, SABBATH DAY

Genesis
1:5 named the light ***D*** and the darkness

Exodus
20:10 but the seventh ***d*** is a Sabbath to the

Matthew
6:34 itself. Each ***d*** has enough
20:19 But he will be raised on the third ***d***."
24:36 knows when that ***d*** or hour will
24:42 don't know what ***d*** the Lord is

Mark
4:27 wakes night and ***d***. The seed sprouts

John
11:24 in the resurrection on the last ***d***."

Romans
2:5 will be revealed on the ***d*** of wrath.

1 Corinthians
1:8 blameless on the ***d*** of our Lord Jesus

2 Corinthians
3:14 up to the present ***d*** the same veil

DAY OF RECONCILIATION

Lv 23:27; 23:28; 25:9; Ac 27:9

DAY OF THE LORD

Is 13:6; 13:9; Eze 13:5; 30:3; Jl 1:15; 2:1, 11, 31; 3:14; Am 5:18; 5:20; Obad 1:15; Zep 1:7; 1:14; Mal 4:5; Ac 2:20; 1Co 5:5; 1Th 5:2; 2Th 2:2; 2Pt 3:10

DAYS → ALL THE DAYS

DEAD → DEAD SEA, RESURRECTION FROM THE DEAD, RESURRECTION OF THE DEAD, RISE FROM THE DEAD

DEAD SEA

Gn 14:3; Nm 34:3; 34:12; Dt 3:17; 4:49; Josh 3:16; 12:3; 15:2, 5; 18:19; 2Ki 14:25; Eze 47:8; 47:18; Zec 14:8

DEADLY

Exodus
5:3 will give us a ***d*** disease or
9:3 will send a very ***d*** disease on your
9:15 people with a ***d*** disease so that

1 Samuel
5:11 there was a ***d*** panic throughout

Psalms
7:13 God has ***d*** weapons in store for those
17:9 me, away from my ***d*** enemies who are
91:3 the hunter's trap and from ***d*** sickness.
109:16 even the brokenhearted—with ***d*** intent!

Proverbs
1:11 Let's set up a ***d*** ambush. Let's
1:18 sinners set up a ***d*** ambush; they lie
26:18 crazy person shooting ***d*** flaming arrows

Jeremiah
5:16 Its weapons are ***d***; its warriors are

Ezekiel
5:16 When I launch my ***d*** arrows of famine
21:14 times! It's a ***d*** sword, a great

James
3:8 is a restless evil, full of ***d*** poison.

Revelation
13:3 killed, but its ***d*** wound was healed.

DEAR

Deuteronomy
13:6 daughter or your ***d*** spouse or best
28:54 or his own ***d*** wife, or the last
28:56 scowl at her own ***d*** husband, her son,

2 Samuel
1:26 You were so ***d*** to me! Your love

Proverbs
1:22 their mocking ***d***, and fools hate

Song of Songs
5:1 and my milk. Eat, ***d*** friends! Drink

Jeremiah
31:20 I still hold him ***d***. I yearn for him

Acts
15:25 along with our ***d*** friends Barnabas

Romans
12:19 yourselves, my ***d*** friends, but
16:5 to Epaenetus, my ***d*** friend, who was
16:8 to Ampliatus, my ***d*** friend in the
16:9 in Christ, and my ***d*** friend Stachys.
16:12 Say hello to my ***d*** friend Persis,

1 Corinthians
10:14 So then, my ***d*** friends, run away from

2 Corinthians
7:1 My ***d*** friends, since we have these
12:19 and in Christ. ***D*** friends,

2 Timothy
1:2 To Timothy, my ***d*** child. Grace, mercy,

James
1:16 be misled, my ***d*** brothers and
1:19 Know this, my ***d*** brothers and sisters:
2:5 My ***d*** brothers and sisters, listen!

1 Peter
2:11 ***D*** friends, since you are immigrants and
4:12 ***D*** friends, don't be surprised about the

2 Peter
3:1 My ***d*** friends, this is now my second
3:8 your notice, ***d*** friends, that
3:14 Therefore, ***d*** friends, while you are
3:15 just as our ***d*** friend and
3:17 Therefore, ***d*** friends, since you have

1 John
2:7 ***D*** friends, I'm not writing a new
3:2 ***D*** friends, now we are God's children,
3:21 ***D*** friends, if our hearts don't condemn
4:1 ***D*** friends, don't believe every spirit.
4:7 ***D*** friends, let's love each other,
4:11 ***D*** friends, if God loved us this way, we

2 John
1:5 Now, ***d*** friends, I am requesting that we
3 John
1:1 the elder. To my ***d*** friend Gaius,
1:2 ***D*** friend, I'm praying that all is well
1:5 ***D*** friend, you act faithfully in
1:11 ***D*** friend, don't imitate what is bad but
Jude
1:3 ***D*** friends, I wanted very much to write
1:17 But you, ***d*** friends, remember the words
1:20 But you, ***d*** friends: build each other up

DEARLY LOVED

Ecc 9:9; Is 22:4; Ro 1:7; Eph 5:1; Col 4:7; 4:9, 14; Phm 1:1; 1:16; 2Pt 1:17

DEATH

Leviticus
16:1 After the ***d*** of Aaron's two sons, which
19:20 not be put to ***d*** because she had
Deuteronomy
34:8 mourned Moses' ***d*** for thirty days.
Joshua
1:18 will be put to ***d***. Be brave and
Ruth
1:17 more so if even ***d*** separates me from
2:11 your husband's ***d*** has been reported
1 Samuel
2:6 LORD! He brings ***d***, gives life,
2 Samuel
1:1 After Saul's ***d***, when David had
1 Kings
12:18 stoned him to ***d***. King Rehoboam
Psalms
9:13 brings me back from the very gates of ***d***
13:3 Otherwise, I'll sleep the sleep of ***d***,
22:15 you've set me down in the dirt of ***d***.
33:19 their lives from ***d*** and keep them
40:2 out of the pit of ***d***, out of the mud
49:14 for the grave. ***D*** will be their
55:15 Let ***d*** devastate my enemies; let them go
56:6 are watching my steps, hoping for my ***d***.
56:13 my life from ***d***, saved my feet
68:20 from certain ***d*** come through God
78:50 save them from ***d***, but delivered
89:48 without seeing ***d***? Who is ever
102:20 to set free those condemned to ***d***,
116:8 delivered me from ***d***, my eyes from
116:15 The ***d*** of the LORD's faithful is a
118:18 me, but he didn't hand me over to ***d***.
Proverbs
2:18 sinks down to ***d***, and her paths go
5:5 feet go down to ***d***; her steps lead
7:27 grave, going down to the chambers of ***d***.
8:36 all those who hate me love ***d***.
10:2 righteousness rescues people from ***d***.
11:4 but righteousness rescues from ***d***.
11:19 but those who pursue evil, toward ***d***.
12:28 but the detestable path leads to ***d***.
14:12 but in the end it is a path to ***d***.
14:32 the righteous find refuge even in ***d***.
16:14 is a messenger of ***d***; the wise will
16:25 but in the end it is the path of ***d***.
18:21 ***D*** and life are in the power of the
21:6 are like a drifting fog, leading to ***d***.
24:11 taken off to ***d***; and from those
Ecclesiastes
7:1 and the day of ***d*** better than the
7:26 more bitter than ***d***: she who is a
8:8 over the day of ***d***. There's no
Song of Songs
8:6 is as strong as ***d***, passionate love
Hosea
9:16 I will put to ***d*** their much loved
13:14 death's hold? ***D***, where are your
Amos
9:5 in it are sick to ***d***. All of it rises
Jonah
2:5 to the point of ***d***; the deep
4:9 anger is good—even to the point of ***d***!"
Matthew
4:16 lived in the region and in shadow of ***d***.
20:18 experts. They will condemn him to ***d***.
21:35 killed. Some of them they stoned to ***d***.
26:24 One goes to his ***d*** just as it is
26:59 Jesus so that they could put him to ***d***.
27:1 the decision to have Jesus put to ***d***.
John
5:24 but has passed from ***d*** into life.
11:13 but Jesus had spoken about Lazarus' ***d***.
11:19 and Mary after their brother's ***d***.
21:19 show the kind of ***d*** by which Peter
Acts
2:24 was impossible for ***d*** to hang on to him.
22:4 this Way to their ***d***, arresting and
23:29 charge deserving of ***d*** or imprisonment.
25:11 that deserves ***d***, then I won't try
26:10 were condemned to ***d***, I voted against
28:18 find any reason for putting me to ***d***.
Romans
1:32 practices deserve ***d***, they not only
5:10 God through the ***d*** of his Son while
5:12 one person, and ***d*** came through sin,
6:3 Christ Jesus were baptized into his ***d***?
7:5 our body, so that we bore fruit for ***d***.
7:10 was intended to give life brought ***d***.
8:2 set you free from the law of sin and ***d***.
1 Corinthians
3:22 the world, life, ***d***, things in the
4:9 sentenced to ***d***, because we have
11:26 you broadcast the ***d*** of the Lord until
15:21 Since ***d*** came through a human being, the
15:26 ***D*** is the last enemy to be brought to an
15:31 Jesus our Lord, I'm facing ***d*** every day.
15:54 will happen: ***D*** has been
15:55 is your victory, ***D***? Where is your
2 Corinthians
1:9 we had gotten the ***d*** penalty. This was
1:10 from a terrible ***d***, and he will
3:7 that brought ***d*** was carved in
4:10 carry Jesus' ***d*** around in our
4:11 handed over to ***d*** for Jesus' sake
4:12 So ***d*** is at work in us, but life is at
7:10 the influence of the world produces ***d***.
11:23 I can count. I've faced ***d*** many times.
Philippians
2:8 to the point of ***d***, even death on a
2:27 on me because his ***d*** would have caused
3:10 It includes being conformed to his ***d***
Colossians
1:22 body through ***d***, to present you
3:5 So put to ***d*** the parts of your life that

2 Timothy
1:10 He destroyed ***d*** and brought life
4:6 to God, and the time of my ***d*** is near.
Hebrews
2:9 suffering of his ***d***. He suffered
2:14 the power over ***d***—the devil—by
2:15 their entire lives by their fear of ***d***.
5:7 to save him from ***d***. He was heard
7:23 numerous because ***d*** prevented them
9:15 the basis of his ***d***. His death
9:16 to confirm the ***d*** of the one who
9:17 only after a ***d***, since it's not
10:28 they were put to ***d*** without mercy on
11:5 he didn't see ***d***, and he wasn't
11:37 were stoned to ***d***, they were cut in
James
1:15 when sin grows up, it gives birth to ***d***.
5:20 save them from ***d*** and will bring
1 Peter
3:18 Christ was put to ***d*** as a human, but
2 Peter
1:15 to remember these things after my ***d***.
1 John
3:14 transferred from ***d*** to life, because
5:16 not result in ***d***, they should
5:17 is a sin that does not result in ***d***.
Revelation
1:18 I have the keys of ***D*** and the Grave.
2:10 to the point of ***d***, and I will give
2:11 won't be hurt by the second ***d***.
2:23 her children to ***d*** with disease.
3:2 on the brink of ***d***, for I've found
6:8 rider's name was ***D***, and the Grave
9:6 people will seek ***d***, but they won't
13:15 the beast's image to be put to ***d***.
20:6 The second ***d*** has no power over
20:13 were in it, and ***D*** and the Grave
20:14 Then ***D*** and the Grave were thrown into
21:4 from their eyes. ***D*** will be no more.
21:8 fire and sulfur. This is the second ***d***."

DECEIT
Job
13:7 for God, speak ***d*** on his behalf?
15:35 to sorrow; their belly establishes ***d***.
21:34 to me; only ***d*** remains in your
27:4 wickedness; my tongue will mumble no ***d***.
31:5 frauds or my feet have hurried to ***d***,
Proverbs
12:20 ***D*** is in the heart of those who plan
Isaiah
59:4 and speaking ***d***, they conceive
Jeremiah
8:5 me? They cling to ***d*** and refuse to
9:6 in a world of ***d***, and in their
14:14 predictions, and ***d*** they have made up
29:23 wives and ***d*** spoken in my
Daniel
8:25 succeed by using ***d***. In his own mind,
Nahum
3:1 of bloodshed—all ***d***, full of plunder:
Zephaniah
1:9 of their master with violence and ***d***.
Mark
7:22 evil actions, ***d***, unrestrained
12:15 recognized their ***d***, he said to them,
John
1:47 Israelite in whom there is no ***d***."
1 Peter
2:1 ill will and all ***d***, pretense, envy,

DECEIVE
Leviticus
19:11 not steal nor ***d*** nor lie to each
Proverbs
24:28 without reason; don't ***d*** with your lips.
26:19 are those who ***d*** their neighbor and say,
Isaiah
37:10 the God you trust ***d*** you by saying,
Hosea
7:1 Samaria; for they ***d*** and steal, a
Amos
8:5 the shekel, and ***d*** with false
Habakkuk
2:3 end; it does not ***d***. If it delays,
Zechariah
13:4 put on a shaggy coat in order to ***d***.
Malachi
3:8 Should a person ***d*** God? Yet you deceive
Matthew
7:5 You ***d*** yourself! First take the log out
24:5 the Christ.' They will ***d*** many people.
24:11 prophets will appear and ***d*** many people.
24:24 in order to ***d***, if possible,
Mark
13:6 I'm the one!' They will ***d*** many people.
13:22 in order to ***d***, if possible,
Luke
6:42 your own eye? You ***d*** yourselves! First
Romans
16:18 feelings. They ***d*** the hearts of
Ephesians
5:6 Nobody should ***d*** you with stupid ideas.
2 Thessalonians
2:3 Don't let anyone ***d*** you in any way. That
1 Timothy
4:1 to spirits that ***d*** and to the
2 Timothy
3:13 worse, as they ***d*** others while
1 Peter
2:22 did he ever speak in ways meant to ***d***.
1 John
1:8 have any sin," we ***d*** ourselves and the
2:26 those who are attempting to ***d*** you.
Revelation
19:20 used the signs to ***d*** people into
20:3 continuing to ***d*** the nations until
20:8 He will go out to ***d*** the nations that

DECEIVED
Genesis
31:20 Moreover, Jacob ***d*** Laban the Aramean by not sending word
31:26 done? You have ***d*** me and taken off
Joshua
9:22 Why have you ***d*** us by saying, 'We
Job
12:16 the deceiver and the ***d*** are his.
Jeremiah
4:10 You have utterly ***d*** this people and
37:9 let yourself be ***d*** into thinking
38:22 you; they have ***d*** you; now that

49:16 on others has ***d*** you, as has your
Lamentations
1:19 lovers, but they ***d*** me. My priests
Jonah
2:8 Those ***d*** by worthless things lose their
Malachi
3:8 say, "How have we ***d*** you?" With your
Luke
21:8 that you aren't ***d***. Many will come
John
7:47 replied, "Have you too been ***d***?
Romans
7:11 the commandment, ***d*** me, and killed me.
1 Corinthians
6:9 kingdom? Don't be ***d***. Those who are
15:33 Don't be ***d***, bad company corrupts good
2 Corinthians
11:3 way as the snake ***d*** Eve with his
1 Timothy
2:14 Adam wasn't ***d***, but rather his wife
2 Timothy
3:13 others while being ***d*** themselves.
Titus
3:3 disobedient, ***d***, and slaves to
Revelation
18:23 the nations were ***d*** by the spell you
20:10 devil, who had ***d*** them, was thrown

DECEPTION

Numbers
25:18 after you by the ***d*** they devised for
Psalms
52:2 it's like a sharpened razor, causing ***d***.
62:4 they delight in ***d***. With their
144:8 strong hand is a strong hand of ***d***!
144:11 strong hand is a strong hand of ***d***,
Proverbs
26:24 their lips, keeping their ***d*** within.
Daniel
8:23 He will be stern and a master of ***d***.
Micah
1:14 have become a ***d*** for the kings of
Matthew
27:64 dead.' This last ***d*** will be worse
Luke
20:23 recognized their ***d***, he said to them,
Romans
1:29 murder, fighting, ***d***, and malice. They
2 Corinthians
4:2 We don't use ***d***, and we don't
Colossians
2:8 and foolish ***d***, which conform to
1 Thessalonians
2:3 information, the wrong motives, or ***d***.
2 Thessalonians
2:10 sort of wicked ***d*** of those who are
Hebrews
3:13 insensitive to God because of sin's ***d***.
Revelation
22:15 and all who love and practice ***d***.

DECISION

Numbers
27:21 for him the ***d*** by lot before the
Deuteronomy
1:17 favoritism in a ***d***. Hear both sides
19:15 sufficient. The ***d*** must stand by two
Joshua
9:14 didn't ask for any ***d*** from the LORD.
Ezra
5:17 to send us his ***d*** about this matter.
Psalms
2:7 the LORD's ***d***: He said to me,
Daniel
2:5 Chaldeans: "My ***d*** is final: If you
2:8 because you see that my ***d*** is final
4:17 decree; this ***d*** is the holy ones'
6:12 replied, "The ***d*** is absolutely
Zephaniah
2:2 before the ***d*** is made—the day vanishes
Matthew
27:1 reached the ***d*** to have Jesus put
Luke
23:24 Pilate issued his ***d*** to grant their
Acts
15:25 reached a united ***d*** to select some
15:28 has led us to the ***d*** that no burden
25:21 custody pending a ***d*** from His Majesty
Romans
1:32 they know God's ***d*** that those who
1 Corinthians
7:37 firm in his ***d***, and doesn't feel
Hebrews
10:26 If we make the ***d*** to sin after we

DECLARE

Exodus
19:3 household and ***d*** to the Israelites:
Leviticus
13:3 this, he will ***d*** the person
14:7 seven times and ***d*** that they are
14:48 the priest will ***d*** the house clean
23:2 which you will ***d*** to be holy
Deuteronomy
4:10 to me. I will ***d*** my words to them
Joshua
1:18 opposes what you ***d*** and doesn't obey
Judges
17:2 you led you to ***d*** a curse and even
1 Chronicles
16:24 ***D*** God's glory among the nations;
Job
9:28 I know that you won't ***d*** me innocent.
10:2 say to God, Don't ***d*** me guilty; tell
15:17 you; what I've seen, I will ***d*** to you;
32:17 state my piece; I too will ***d*** my view,
33:23 of a thousand to ***d*** one's integrity
34:33 must choose, not I; ***d*** what you know.
Psalms
9:14 so I can ***d*** all your praises, so I can
22:22 I will ***d*** your name to my brothers and
78:2 a proverb. I'll ***d*** riddles from days
82:6 I hereby ***d***, "You are gods, children of
96:3 ***D*** God's glory among the nations;
107:22 sacrifices and ***d*** what God has done
118:17 I will live and ***d*** what the LORD has
119:13 I will ***d*** out loud all the rules you
119:172 Let my tongue ***d*** your word because all
145:6 deeds; I will ***d*** your great
Ecclesiastes
4:2 So I ***d*** that the dead, who have already
Song of Songs
6:9 women see her and ***d*** her fortunate;

Isaiah
12:4 the peoples; ***d*** that God's name
40:27 say, Jacob, and ***d***, Israel, "My way
42:12 LORD glory and ***d*** God's praise in
50:8 The one who will ***d*** me innocent is near.
66:19 glory. They will ***d*** my glory among
Jeremiah
1:16 I will ***d*** my judgment against them for
5:20 ***D*** this to the people of Jacob, announce
9:22 ***D*** what the LORD says: Dead bodies will lie
22:1 the king of Judah and ***d*** this message:
23:28 who has a dream ***d*** it, but let the
26:7 heard Jeremiah ***d*** these words in
51:10 defense, so let's ***d*** in Zion what the
Ezekiel
3:18 If I ***d*** that the wicked will die but you
38:19 blazing anger I ***d***: On that day, a
Daniel
2:11 No one could ***d*** the dream to the
Jonah
3:2 great city, and ***d*** against it the
Micah
3:8 and might, to ***d*** to Jacob his
Zechariah
9:12 hope. Moreover, ***d*** today that I will
Matthew
13:35 in parables; I'll ***d*** what has been
Acts
24:20 who are here ***d*** what crime they
Revelation
3:5 of life, but will ***d*** their names in

DECLARED

Genesis
14:2 ***d*** war on Sodom's King Bera, Gomorrah's
45:1 attendants, so he ***d***, "Everyone, leave
Exodus
32:4 and the people ***d***, "These are your
32:8 to it and ***d***, 'These are your
Numbers
14:17 be as great as you ***d*** when you said,
Deuteronomy
4:13 The LORD ***d*** his covenant to you, which
Judges
6:36 rescue Israel through me as you have ***d***,
6:37 Israel through me, as you have ***d***."
1 Chronicles
16:12 marvelous works, and the justice he ***d***—
2 Chronicles
7:16 this temple and ***d*** it holy so that
Esther
2:18 and courtiers. He ***d*** a public holiday
Psalms
40:10 only to myself. I ***d*** your faithfulness
75:1 is near. Your marvelous deeds are ***d***.
102:21 name may be ***d*** in Zion and his
105:5 marvelous works, and the justice he ***d***—
Jeremiah
4:28 because I have ***d*** my plan and will
23:35 the LORD said?" What has the LORD ***d***?"
23:37 said to you?" What has the LORD ***d***?"
36:29 scroll because it ***d*** that the king of
40:2 LORD your God ***d*** that a great
48:8 because the LORD has ***d*** it so.
51:62 say, "LORD, you ***d*** that this place
Ezekiel
3:21 sin, they will be ***d*** righteous. Their
7:20 Therefore, I've ***d*** it an unclean
18:5 People are ***d*** innocent when they act
18:20 do right will be ***d*** innocent, and the
20:8 idols. So I ***d*** that I would pour
20:13 my sabbaths. So I ***d*** that I would pour
20:21 my sabbaths. So I ***d*** that I would pour
Daniel
2:47 The king ***d*** to Daniel, "No doubt about
3:28 Nebuchadnezzar ***d***: "May the God of
4:19 him. The king ***d***, "Don't let the
4:30 The king ***d***, "Isn't this Babylon, the
5:10 hall and ***d***, "Long live the
Mark
7:19 this, Jesus ***d*** that no food
Luke
2:1 Caesar Augustus ***d*** that everyone
Acts
2:14 his voice and ***d***, "Judeans and
9:20 synagogues. "He is God's Son," he ***d***.
17:3 from the dead. He ***d***, "This Jesus whom
18:13 to worship God unlawfully," they ***d***.
24:2 against him. He ***d***, "Under your
26:22 the Prophets and Moses ***d*** would happen:
26:24 defense, Festus ***d*** with a loud
1 Timothy
3:16 as a human, ***d*** righteous by the
Hebrews
2:6 Instead, someone ***d*** somewhere, What is

DECORATED

Exodus
26:36 fine twisted linen, ***d*** with needlework.
27:16 twisted linen, ***d*** with needlework.
28:39 linen. Make a sash ***d*** with needlework.
36:37 fine twisted linen, ***d*** with needlework.
38:18 twisted linen, ***d*** with needlework.
39:28 fine linen, the ***d*** turbans of fine
39:29 crimson yarns, ***d*** with needlework,
2 Samuel
1:24 with jewels; he ***d*** your clothes with
2 Kings
25:17 second pillar was ***d*** with lattices
2 Chronicles
3:5 fine gold, and ***d*** them with palm
Ezekiel
40:16 The arches were ***d*** with palm trees.
40:31 courtyard. Palms ***d*** its arches, and
40:34 Palm trees ***d*** its arches on
40:37 Palm trees ***d*** its arches on
41:26 and palm trees ***d*** both sides of the
Matthew
12:44 the place vacant, cleaned up, and ***d***.
Luke
11:25 it finds the house cleaned up and ***d***.
21:5 how it was ***d*** with beautiful
Revelation
13:1 of its horns was ***d*** with a royal
21:19 foundations were ***d*** with every kind

DECREE

Joshua
6:26 Joshua made this ***d***: "Anyone who
2 Chronicles
36:22 his kingdom, along with a written ***d***:

Ezra
4:21 is not to be rebuilt until I make a ***d***.
5:13 Cyrus issued a ***d*** to rebuild this
5:17 had issued a ***d*** to rebuild this
6:1 Darius made a ***d***, and they
6:3 King Cyrus made a ***d***: Concerning God's
6:8 I also issue a ***d*** about what you should
6:11 I also ***d*** that if anyone disobeys this
7:13 I ***d*** that any of the people of Israel or
7:21 King Artaxerxes, ***d*** to all of the
Job
22:28 If you ***d*** something, it will stand;
28:26 when he made a ***d*** for the rain, a path
Psalms
81:5 He made it a ***d*** for Joseph when he went
Isaiah
50:1 mother's divorce ***d***, with which I
Ezekiel
23:46 against them, and ***d*** terror and
Daniel
3:29 I now issue a ***d*** to every people,
4:17 by the watchers' ***d***; this decision is
6:25 the following ***d***: To all the
Jonah
3:7 In Nineveh, by ***d*** of the king and

DEDICATED → DEDICATED TO THE LORD

Leviticus
22:3 Israelites have ***d*** to the LORD while
Numbers
6:2 nazirite in order to be ***d*** to the LORD,
8:17 the land of Egypt, I ***d*** them to myself.
18:6 a gift to you, ***d*** to the LORD to
Deuteronomy
20:5 but hasn't yet ***d*** it? He can leave
26:14 nor have I ***d*** any of it to the
1 Samuel
7:1 hill. Then they ***d*** Eleazar,
2 Samuel
8:11 King David ***d*** these to the LORD, along
1 Kings
7:51 father David had ***d*** and put them in
8:63 and all Israel ***d*** the LORD's temple.
9:7 the temple that I ***d*** for my name.
15:15 equipment that he and his father had ***d***.
2 Kings
12:18 that had been ***d*** by his ancestors
23:11 Judah's kings had ***d*** to the sun. They
1 Chronicles
6:48 the Levites were ***d*** to all the
18:11 King David ***d*** these to the LORD along
26:20 and the treasuries of the ***d*** gifts:
26:26 of the gifts ***d*** by King David, by
26:27 They had ***d*** some of the valuable objects
26:28 that was ***d*** by Samuel the
28:12 temple and the ***d*** gifts would be
29:3 temple, I have ***d*** my own private
2 Chronicles
5:1 father David had ***d*** and put them in
7:5 king and all the people ***d*** God's temple.
7:7 Solomon also ***d*** the middle of the
7:9 They had ***d*** the altar for
15:18 objects that he and his father had ***d***.
29:31 that you have ***d*** yourselves to the
31:6 that had been ***d*** to the LORD their
31:12 gifts, and the ***d*** things. Conaniah,
31:14 reserved for the LORD and the ***d*** gifts.
36:14 temple that God had ***d*** in Jerusalem.
Nehemiah
3:1 Sheep Gate. They ***d*** it and set up its
Ezekiel
44:29 offerings. Every ***d*** thing in Israel
Hosea
2:13 her for the days ***d*** to the Baals,
Luke
2:23 firstborn male will be ***d*** to the Lord.")
21:5 and ornaments ***d*** to God. Jesus
1 Corinthians
7:34 that she can be ***d*** to God in both
16:15 Achaia. They have ***d*** themselves to the
Ephesians
2:21 up into a temple that is ***d*** to the Lord.
1 Thessalonians
4:3 your lives are ***d*** to him. This
4:7 us to be immoral but to be ***d*** to him.
5:23 to be completely ***d*** to him; and may

DEDICATED TO THE LORD

Lv 22:3; Nm 6:2; 18:6; 2Ch 31:6; Lk 2:23; Eph 2:21

DEDICATION

Exodus
28:3 for Aaron for his ***d*** to serve me as a
Numbers
6:5 the period of ***d*** to the LORD is
6:6 The period of ***d*** to the LORD also
6:7 the sign of their ***d*** to God on their
7:10 for the ***d*** of the altar on
7:11 their offering for the ***d*** of the altar.
7:84 provided for the ***d*** of the altar on
7:88 old. This was the ***d*** offering for the
1 Kings
9:4 with complete ***d*** and honesty, and
Ezra
6:16 celebrated the ***d*** of this house of
6:17 At the ***d*** of this house of God, they
Nehemiah
12:27 was time for the ***d*** of Jerusalem's
Psalms
30:1 for the temple ***d***. Of David.] I
Daniel
3:2 and come for the ***d*** of the statue
3:3 assembled for the ***d*** of the statue
John
10:22 the Festival of ***D*** in Jerusalem. It
2 Thessalonians
2:13 through your ***d*** to God by the

DEED

Leviticus
4:13 and the ***d*** escapes the
Ruth
2:12 you for your ***d***. May you receive
2 Samuel
2:5 doing this loyal ***d*** for your master
Job
33:17 turn them from a ***d*** and to smother
Psalms
137:8 pays you back the very ***d*** you did to us!
Ecclesiastes
3:17 a time for every matter and every ***d***.
12:14 bring every ***d*** to judgment,

Isaiah
3:8 act in word and ***d*** insults the LORD,
28:21 rage to do his ***d***—strange is his de
Jeremiah
32:10 I signed the ***d***, sealed it, had it
32:11 Then I took the ***d*** of purchase—the
32:12 named in the ***d***, as well as
32:14 sealed ***d*** of purchase along
50:29 her back for her ***d*** do to her what
Acts
4:9 sick person, a good ***d*** that healed him?
Jude
1:15 every ungodly ***d*** they have

DEEDS → AWESOME DEEDS, EVIL DEEDS, RIGHTEOUS DEEDS

DEEP

Genesis
1:2 was dark over the ***d*** sea, and God's
2:21 the human into a ***d*** and heavy sleep,
7:11 springs of the ***d*** sea erupted, and
8:2 springs of the ***d*** sea and the skies
15:12 A terrifying and ***d*** darkness settled
43:28 they bowed down again with ***d*** respect.
49:25 from the ***d*** sea below,
Exodus
15:5 The ***d*** sea covered them; they sank into
15:8 a great wave; the ***d*** waters foamed in
Deuteronomy
33:13 above, with the ***d*** waters stretching
Isaiah
7:11 God. Make it as ***d*** as the grave or
29:10 you a spirit of ***d*** sleep, and has
Ezekiel
23:32 God proclaims: ***D*** and wide is your
Daniel
9:9 Compassion and ***d*** forgiveness belong to
Hosea
5:2 they have sunk ***d*** into corruption;
Amos
5:8 Orion, and turns ***d*** darkness into the
7:4 the great ***d*** and was eating up
Jonah
1:5 vessel to lie down and was ***d*** in sleep.
2:5 of death; the ***d*** surrounds me.
Habakkuk
3:10 through. The ***d*** utters its voice;
Matthew
13:5 immediately because the soil wasn't ***d***.
24:26 he's in the rooms ***d*** inside the
27:3 to die, he felt ***d*** regret. He
John
4:11 and the well is ***d***. Where would you
11:13 Lazarus was in a ***d*** sleep, but Jesus
Acts
20:9 sinking into a ***d*** sleep as Paul
24:3 we acknowledge this with ***d*** gratitude.
27:28 twenty feet ***d***. After proceeding
Romans
11:33 knowledge are so ***d***! They are as
Philippians
3:18 and now say with ***d*** sadness, many
1 Thessalonians
1:5 Spirit and with ***d*** conviction. You
James
1:21 the word planted ***d*** inside you—the ve
2 Peter
2:8 them he felt ***d*** distress every
Revelation
2:24 the so-called "***d*** secrets" of Satan-
17:1 prostitute, who is seated on ***d*** waters.

DEFEAT

Genesis
32:25 that he couldn't ***d*** Jacob, he grabbed
Exodus
32:18 of a song of ***d***. The sound of
Deuteronomy
1:4 was after the ***d*** of Sihon, the
28:7 The LORD will ***d*** any enemies who attack
Judges
6:16 with you, you'll ***d*** the Midianites as
11:33 great ***d***; he defeated
20:39 had begun to ***d*** some of the
1 Samuel
4:3 Why did the LORD ***d*** us today before
4:10 It was a massive ***d***: thirty thousand
4:17 a massive ***d***. Also, your own
14:30 the Philistine ***d*** isn't as thorough
2 Samuel
5:24 front of you to ***d*** the Philistine
8:10 on his battle and ***d*** of Hadadezer,
2 Kings
13:19 it is, you will ***d*** them only three
16:5 Ahaz, but they weren't able to ***d*** him.
1 Chronicles
14:15 front of you to ***d*** the Philistine
18:10 his battle and ***d*** of Hadadezer,
2 Chronicles
28:9 Judah and let you ***d*** them? But look
Job
32:13 wisdom; God, not a person, will ***d*** him."
Psalms
54:7 My eyes have seen my enemies' ***d***.
92:11 seen my enemies' ***d***; my ears have
112:8 they will witness their enemies' ***d***.
144:6 enemy! Shoot your arrows and ***d*** them!
Jeremiah
1:19 but they won't ***d*** you, because I am
48:15 will go down in ***d***, declares the
Lamentations
1:7 her. Enemies saw her, laughed at her ***d***.
Daniel
7:24 previous ones. He will ***d*** three kings.
Obadiah
1:13 the day of their ***d***; you shouldn't
1:14 over his survivors on the day of ***d***.
Acts
18:28 would vigorously ***d*** Jewish arguments
Romans
11:12 world, and their ***d*** brings riches to
12:21 defeated by evil, but ***d*** evil with good.
Hebrews
7:1 returned from the ***d*** of the kings, and

DEFEATED

Psalms
6:10 they will be ***d*** and ashamed
60:1 Joab returned and ***d*** Edom, killing
Jeremiah
46:2 king, which was ***d*** by Babylon's
49:28 Nebuchadnezzar ***d***, the LORD
50:10 Babylon will be ***d***; its attackers will

51:41 Sheshach has been ***d***, the pride of the
Daniel
7:21 war against the holy ones and ***d*** them,
Romans
12:21 Don't be ***d*** by evil, but defeat evil
1 John
4:4 and you have ***d*** these people
5:4 victory that has ***d*** the world: our

DEFEND

2 Kings
19:34 I will ***d*** this city and save it for my
20:6 king. I will ***d*** this city for my
Esther
8:11 join together and ***d*** their lives. The
9:2 King Ahasuerus to ***d*** themselves
9:16 together to ***d*** their lives. They
Psalms
54:1 me by your name; ***d*** me by your might!
Proverbs
31:9 and to ***d*** the needy and the
Isaiah
1:17 the oppressed; ***d*** the orphan; plead
1:23 gifts. They don't ***d*** the orphan, and
37:35 I will ***d*** this city and save it for my
38:6 the Assyrian king. I will ***d*** this city.
Jeremiah
5:28 reluctant to ***d*** the rights of the
33:4 were torn down to ***d*** against the siege
39:18 I will ***d*** you; you won't die in battle.
41:9 Asa had made to ***d*** against Israel's
50:34 He will surely ***d*** their cause and
51:36 I'm going to ***d*** your cause; I'll
Ezekiel
39:25 house of Israel and ***d*** my holy name.
Luke
12:11 about how to ***d*** yourself or what
1 Peter
3:15 speak of your hope, be ready to ***d*** it.

DEFENSE

Numbers
14:9 our prey. Their ***d*** has deserted
2 Chronicles
11:5 but he built cities for Judah's ***d***
Isaiah
43:9 witnesses as a ***d***; let them hear
Jeremiah
51:10 has come to our ***d***, so let's declare
Luke
21:14 minds not to prepare your ***d*** in advance.
Acts
19:33 wanted to offer a ***d*** before the
22:1 and fathers, listen now to my ***d***."
24:10 many years, so I gladly offer my own ***d***.
25:8 In his own ***d***, Paul said, "I've done
25:16 to offer a ***d*** against the
26:1 gestured with his hand and began his ***d***.
26:2 as I offer my ***d*** concerning all
26:24 point in Paul's ***d***, Festus declared
Romans
2:15 accuse them, or even make a ***d*** for them,
1 Corinthians
9:3 This is my ***d*** against those who
2 Corinthians
10:5 and every ***d*** that is raised up to oppose
Philippians
1:7 prison and in the ***d*** and support of
1:16 I'm put here to give a ***d*** of the gospel;

DEFILED

Genesis
34:5 that Shechem ***d*** his daughter
2 Kings
23:8 to Beer-sheba, he ***d*** the shrines where
23:10 Josiah ***d*** the Topheth in the Ben-hinnom
23:13 The king then ***d*** the shrines facing
Nehemiah
13:29 because they have ***d*** the priesthood
Psalms
74:7 the ground; they ***d*** the dwelling
79:1 God! They've ***d*** your holy temple.
106:38 so the land was ***d*** by the bloodshed.
Ezekiel
7:24 and their sanctuaries will be ***d***.
Hosea
5:3 acted like a prostitute; Israel is ***d***.
Micah
4:11 say, "Let her be ***d***," or "Let our
Zephaniah
3:1 one, the ***d*** one, the violent
Acts
21:28 the temple and ***d*** this holy place."
Revelation
14:4 They weren't ***d*** with women, for these

DELIVER

Exodus
25:22 covenant, I will ***d*** to you all that I
1 Samuel
4:8 doomed! Who will ***d*** us from the grip
7:3 Then he will ***d*** you from the
12:10 Astartes. But now ***d*** us from the power
17:17 loaves of bread. ***D*** them quickly to
26:24 and may he ***d*** me from all
2 Samuel
14:16 will agree to ***d*** his servant from
1 Chronicles
16:35 Gather us! ***D*** us from among the
2 Chronicles
12:7 them. I will ***d*** them in a little
20:17 is with you, will ***d*** you, Judah and
25:15 couldn't even ***d*** their own people
Ezra
7:19 You will ***d*** the equipment that has been
Job
5:19 he will ***d*** you; from seven
22:30 He will ***d*** the guilty; they will be
Psalms
6:4 back to me, LORD! ***D*** me! Save me for
22:8 him; let God ***d*** him because God
22:20 ***D*** me from the sword. Deliver my life
25:20 protect my life! ***D*** me! Don't let me
31:2 closely to me! ***D*** me quickly; be a
33:19 to ***d*** their lives from death and keep
39:8 ***D*** me from all my sins; don't make me
40:13 me, LORD, and ***d*** me! LORD, come
50:15 trouble; I will ***d*** you, then you
50:22 rip you to pieces with no one to ***d*** you:
51:14 ***D*** me from violence, God, God of my
59:1 him.] Oh, my God, ***d*** me from my
59:2 ***D*** me from evildoers; save me from the

70:1 Hurry, God, to ***d*** me; hurry, LORD,
71:2 ***D*** me and rescue me by your
71:11 Grab him because no one will ***d*** him!"
74:19 Don't ***d*** the life of your dove to wild
79:9 of your name! ***D*** us and cover our
82:4 and the needy. ***D*** them from the
109:21 of your name; ***d*** me because your
119:153 my suffering and ***d*** me because I
119:170 come before you; ***d*** me according to
120:2 Lord, ***d*** me from lying lips and a
142:6 down so low! ***D*** me from my
143:9 ***D*** me from my enemies, LORD! I seek
144:7 Rescue me and ***d*** me from deep
144:11 Rescue me and ***d*** me from the power of

Ecclesiastes
8:8 wickedness won't ***d*** those who

Isaiah
33:22 the LORD is our king—he will ***d*** us.

Jeremiah
13:12 So ***d*** this word to them: The LORD the
14:17 So ***d*** this word to them: My eyes well up
15:9 disgraced. I will ***d*** the survivors to
15:13 belongings I will ***d*** as plunder,
21:7 the LORD, I will ***d*** Judah's King
23:31 who carelessly ***d*** oracles, declares
30:10 Israel. I will ***d*** you from faraway
31:11 of Jacob and ***d*** them from the
46:27 Israel. I will ***d*** you from a

Ezekiel
3:17 you hear a word from me, ***d*** my warning.
7:19 their gold won't ***d*** them on the day
34:27 of their yoke and ***d*** them from those
37:23 I will ***d*** them from all the

Micah
5:8 and tears to pieces with no one to ***d***.

Habakkuk
1:2 to you, "Violence!" but you don't ***d*** us.

Zephaniah
1:18 won't be able to ***d*** them on the day
3:19 that time. I will ***d*** the lame; I will

Zechariah
8:7 I'm about to ***d*** my people from
8:13 so now I will ***d*** you; you will be
9:16 their God will ***d*** them on that day
10:6 of Judah and ***d*** the house of
12:7 LORD will first ***d*** the tents of

Matthew
27:43 God, so let God ***d*** him now if he

Romans
7:24 being. Who will ***d*** me from this dead

Galatians
1:4 sins, so he could ***d*** us from this

Hebrews
11:7 built an ark to ***d*** his household.

DELIVERED

Joshua
22:31 LORD. Now you've ***d*** the Israelites

Judges
6:9 I ***d*** you from the power of the Egyptians
8:34 God, who had ***d*** them from the

1 Samuel
10:18 of Egypt, and I ***d*** you from the
12:11 Samson, and he ***d*** you from the

2 Samuel
12:7 over Israel and ***d*** you from Saul's
18:28 your God, who has ***d*** up the men who
19:9 saying, "The king ***d*** us from our
22:1 after the LORD ***d*** him from the
22:44 You ***d*** me from struggles with many
22:49 adversaries; you ***d*** me from violent

1 Kings
12:15 the promise he ***d*** through Ahijah

1 Chronicles
21:19 Gad had ***d*** in the LORD's

2 Chronicles
10:15 son, which God ***d*** through Ahijah
16:8 on the LORD, he ***d*** them into your
34:9 Hilkiah, they ***d*** the money that

Ezra
8:36 They also ***d*** the king's orders to the

Job
8:4 him, then he ***d*** them into the
40:14 you, for your strong hand has ***d*** you.

Psalms
18:1 after the LORD ***d*** him from the
18:43 You ***d*** me from struggles with many
18:48 adversaries; you ***d*** me from violent
34:4 answered me. He ***d*** me from all my
54:7 because God has ***d*** me from every
78:48 God ***d*** their cattle over to disease,
78:50 from death, but ***d*** their lives over
78:62 God ***d*** his people up to the sword; he
106:43 God ***d*** them numerous times, but they
107:6 distress, and God ***d*** them from their
116:8 You, God, have ***d*** me from death, my eyes from tears

Isaiah
39:8 word that you ***d*** is good," since
66:7 her pangs came upon her, she ***d*** a boy.

Jeremiah
20:15 be the one who ***d*** the news to my
21:10 LORD; it will be ***d*** to the king of
25:3 to me. I have ***d*** it to you
27:12 I ***d*** the same message to Judah's King
29:3 It was ***d*** to Babylon by Elasah,
30:7 Jacob. But they will be ***d*** from it.
34:6 prophet Jeremiah ***d*** this message to
44:30 him, just as I ***d*** Judah's King

Daniel
2:38 God has ***d*** into your care human beings,
4:24 of the Most High, ***d*** to my master the
7:25 of time, they will be ***d*** into his power.

Amos
1:9 because they have ***d*** up entire

Matthew
17:22 is about to be ***d*** over into human
24:13 one who endures to the end will be ***d***.

Mark
9:31 Human One will be ***d*** into human hands.

Luke
1:68 has come to help and has ***d*** his people.
4:32 because he ***d*** his message with
8:36 how the demon-possessed man had been ***d***.
9:44 One is about to be ***d*** into human hands."

Acts
15:30 the believers and ***d*** the letter.
23:33 entered Caesarea, ***d*** the letter to the

Romans
15:28 and have safely ***d*** the final amount

1 Corinthians
1:30 us righteous and holy, and he ***d*** us.

DELIVERED [cont.]

2 Corinthians
3:3 Christ's letter, ***d*** by us. You
Jude
1:3 for the faith ***d*** once and for all

DEMON

Isaiah
34:14 hyenas, the goat ***d*** will call to his
Matthew
9:33 thrown out the ***d***, the man who
11:18 drinking, and they say, 'He has a ***d***.'
15:22 suffering terribly from ***d*** possession."
17:18 harshly to the ***d***. And it came out
17:19 Why couldn't we throw the ***d*** out?"
Mark
1:25 harshly to the ***d***. "Come out of
7:26 to throw the ***d*** out of her
7:29 Go on home. The ***d*** has already left
7:30 child lying on the bed and the ***d*** gone.
Luke
4:33 spirit of an unclean ***d***. He screamed,
4:35 harshly to the ***d***. "Come out of
7:33 wine, and you say, 'He has a ***d***.'
8:29 and the ***d*** would force him
9:42 was coming, the ***d*** threw him down
11:14 throwing out a ***d*** that causes
John
7:20 You have a ***d***. Who wants to
8:48 a Samaritan and have a ***d***, weren't we?"
8:49 I don't have a ***d***," Jesus replied.
8:52 that you have a ***d***. Abraham and the
10:20 said, "He has a ***d*** and has lost his
10:21 someone who has a ***d***. Can a demon heal

DEMON-POSSESSED

Matthew
8:16 many who were ***d***. He threw the
8:28 two men who were ***d*** came from among
8:33 that had happened to the ***d*** men.
9:32 him a man who was ***d*** and unable to
12:22 to Jesus a ***d*** man who was blind
Mark
1:32 to Jesus those who were sick or ***d***.
5:15 who used to be ***d***. They saw the
5:16 happened to the ***d*** man told the
5:18 one who had been ***d*** pleaded with
Luke
8:36 told them how the ***d*** man had been

DEMONS → THROW OUT DEMONS

Leviticus
17:7 to the goat ***d*** that they follow
Deuteronomy
32:17 sacrificed to ***d***, not to God, to
Psalms
106:37 their own sons and daughters to ***d***!
Isaiah
13:21 there, and goat ***d*** will dance there.
Matthew
4:24 possessed by ***d***, those with
7:22 name and expel ***d*** in your name and
8:31 The ***d*** pleaded with him, "If you throw
8:32 he said to the ***d***, "Go away," and
9:34 He throws out ***d*** with the
12:24 man throws out ***d*** only by the
Luke
4:41 ***D*** also came out of many people. They
8:2 (from whom seven ***d*** had been thrown
8:27 was possessed by ***d***. For a long time,
8:30 because many ***d*** had entered him.
8:32 the hillside. The ***d*** begged Jesus to
8:33 and the ***d*** left the man and entered the
8:35 man from whom the ***d*** had gone. He was
8:38 man from whom the ***d*** had gone begged
9:1 over all ***d*** and to heal
10:17 Lord, even the ***d*** submit themselves
13:32 I'm throwing out ***d*** and healing
1 Corinthians
10:20 is sacrificed to ***d*** and not to God. I
10:21 and the cup of ***d***; you can't
1 Timothy
4:1 that deceive and to the teaching of ***d***.
James
2:19 one. Ha! Even the ***d*** believe this, and
Revelation
9:20 stop worshipping ***d*** and idols made of
18:2 become a home for ***d*** and a lair for

DENIED

Genesis
39:9 and he hasn't ***d*** me anything
Numbers
24:11 you, but the LORD has ***d*** you any honor."
Job
6:10 for I've not ***d*** the words of the
22:7 ***d*** water to the thirsty, withheld bread
31:16 If I have ***d*** what the poor wanted, made a widow's
34:5 I'm innocent; God has ***d*** my just cause;
Psalms
21:2 you haven't ***d*** what his lips
Ezekiel
22:29 They've oppressed and ***d*** justice.
Amos
1:11 with the sword, ***d*** all compassion,
Matthew
26:70 But he ***d*** it in front of all of them,
26:72 solemn pledge, he ***d*** it again, saying,
Mark
14:68 But he ***d*** it, saying, "I don't know what
14:70 But he ***d*** it again. A short time later,
Luke
8:45 When everyone ***d*** it, Peter said,
22:34 before you have ***d*** three times that
22:57 But Peter ***d*** it, saying, "Woman, I don't
John
18:25 disciples?" Peter ***d*** it, saying, "I'm
18:27 Peter ***d*** it again, and immediately a
Acts
3:13 handed over and ***d*** in Pilate's
1 Timothy
5:8 they have ***d*** the faith. They
Revelation
3:8 kept my word and haven't ***d*** my name.

DENY

Leviticus
16:29 month, you must ***d*** yourselves. You
16:31 you, and you will ***d*** yourselves. This
23:27 for you. You must ***d*** yourselves and
23:29 who does not ***d*** themselves on
23:32 you, and you must ***d*** yourselves. You
Numbers
29:7 for you. You will ***d*** yourselves and

Proverbs
30:9 I'll be full and ***d*** you, and say,
Ezekiel
22:7 immigrants and ***d*** the rights of
Matthew
10:33 I also will ***d*** before my Father
22:23 Sadducees, who ***d*** that there is a
26:34 tonight, you will ***d*** me three times."
26:35 you, I won't ***d*** you." All the
26:75 crows you will ***d*** me three times."
Mark
12:18 Sadducees, who ***d*** that there is a
14:30 twice, you will ***d*** me three times."
14:31 you, I won't ***d*** you." And they
14:72 twice, you will ***d*** me three times."
Luke
20:27 Sadducees, who ***d*** that there's a
22:61 today, you will ***d*** me three times."
John
1:20 (he didn't ***d*** but confessed),
13:38 you that you will ***d*** me three times
Acts
4:16 obvious to everyone and we can't ***d*** it.
2 Timothy
2:12 together. If we ***d*** him, he will also
3:5 are religious but ***d*** God's power.
Titus
1:16 God, but they ***d*** God by the things
James
2:1 favoritism you ***d*** the faithfulness
3:14 and living in ways that ***d*** the truth.
2 Peter
2:1 opinions and ***d*** the master who
Jude
1:4 immorality and ***d*** our only master

DEPARTED

1 Samuel
16:14 LORD's spirit had ***d*** from Saul, and an
1 Kings
13:24 The man of God ***d***, and a lion found him
19:19 So Elijah ***d*** from there and found
2 Kings
10:15 Jehu ***d*** from there and encountered
19:36 King Sennacherib ***d***, returning to
25:26 army officers, ***d*** for Egypt because
Job
2:7 The Adversary ***d*** from the LORD's
23:12 his lips and not ***d***, valued the words
Isaiah
6:7 Your guilt has ***d***, and your sin is
Ezekiel
31:12 earth's peoples ***d*** from its shade
Matthew
2:13 When the magi had ***d***, an angel from the
9:27 As Jesus ***d***, two blind men followed
13:53 Jesus finished these parables, he ***d***.
22:22 this they were astonished, and they ***d***.
Mark
6:32 They ***d*** in a boat by themselves for a
Luke
4:13 the devil ***d*** from him until
9:6 They ***d*** and went through the villages
Acts
21:5 to an end, we ***d***. All of them,

DEPTHS

Exodus
15:8 deep waters foamed in the ***d*** of the sea.
Deuteronomy
32:22 will blaze to the ***d*** of the grave; it
Nehemiah
9:11 pursuers into the ***d***, as a stone into
Job
28:3 to the furthest ***d***, into stone in
41:31 He causes the ***d*** to churn like a boiling
Psalms
16:7 I am instructed in the ***d*** of my mind.
68:22 will bring them back from the ocean's ***d***
69:14 who hate me and from these watery ***d***!
71:20 more. From the ***d*** of the earth, you
77:16 you and reeled! Even the deep ***d*** shook!
95:4 The earth's ***d*** are in his hands; the
107:24 his wondrous works in the ***d*** of the sea.
107:26 down to the ***d***. The sailors'
130:1 I cry out to you from the ***d***, LORD—
148:7 you sea monsters and all you ocean ***d***!
Proverbs
3:20 the watery ***d*** burst open, and
8:24 were no watery ***d***, I was brought
9:18 her guests are in the ***d*** of the grave.
25:3 heavens and the ***d*** of the earth, so
Isaiah
14:15 you are brought, to the ***d*** of the pit.
44:23 has acted; shout, ***d*** of the earth!
44:27 say to the ocean ***d***, "Dry up; I will
51:10 cross through the ***d*** of the sea, a
63:13 them through the ***d***? Like a horse in
Jeremiah
4:18 is, piercing into the ***d*** of your heart.
Lamentations
3:55 your name, LORD, from the ***d*** of the pit.
Ezekiel
27:4 is in the ***d*** of the sea, and
27:26 an east wind sank you into the sea's ***d***.
27:34 company, are sunk into the water's ***d***.
Jonah
2:3 cast me into the ***d*** in the heart of
Micah
7:19 all our sins into the ***d*** of the sea.
Zechariah
10:11 waves. All the ***d*** of the river will
Luke
1:47 In the ***d*** of who I am I rejoice in God
1 Corinthians
2:10 everything, including the ***d*** of God.
2:11 knows a person's ***d*** except their own

DESCENDANT

Genesis
21:13 nation too, because he is also your ***d***."
Leviticus
21:21 No ***d*** of Aaron the priest who has an
22:3 to them: If any ***d*** of yours should
22:4 Any ***d*** of Aaron who is afflicted with
25:47 guest, or to a ***d*** of a foreigner,
2 Samuel
7:12 raise up your ***d***—one of your very
14:7 without name or ***d*** on the earth."
21:16 Ishbi-benob, a ***d*** of the Raphah, planned
21:18 Hushah killed Saph, a ***d*** of the Raphah.
1 Chronicles
17:11 I will raise up a ***d*** of yours after

DESCENDANT [cont.]

26:24 Shebuel, a ***d*** of Gershom, Moses' son,
Jeremiah
23:5 up a righteous ***d*** from David's
33:21 no longer have a ***d*** to rule on his
35:19 always have a ***d*** that stands
Luke
1:5 His wife Elizabeth was a ***d*** of Aaron.
1:27 named Joseph, a ***d*** of David's house.
Acts
23:6 a Pharisee and a ***d*** of Pharisees. I
Romans
11:1 an Israelite, a ***d*** of Abraham, from
Galatians
3:16 and to his ***d***. It doesn't say,
3:19 until the ***d*** would come to
Revelation
22:16 I'm the root and ***d*** of David, the

DESCENDANTS → AARON'S DESCENDANTS, ABRAHAM'S DESCENDANTS

Genesis
9:9 up my covenant with you, with your ***d***,
15:18 Abram: "To your ***d*** I give this land,
Exodus
28:43 for him and for his ***d*** after him.
Deuteronomy
4:37 and chose their ***d*** after them, God
2 Samuel
22:51 to David and to his ***d*** forever.
Ezra
9:2 and the holy ***d*** have become mixed
Psalms
18:50 one—to David and to his ***d*** forever.
112:2 Their ***d*** will be strong throughout the
Isaiah
44:3 spirit upon your ***d*** and my blessing
Acts
2:30 to seat one of his ***d*** on his throne.

DESCENDED

Numbers
11:25 The LORD ***d*** in a cloud, spoke to him,
Joshua
21:19 of the priests ***d*** from Aaron:
Romans
1:3 scriptures. His Son was ***d*** from David.
9:5 and the Christ ***d*** from those
9:6 Not all who are ***d*** from Israel are
2 Timothy
2:8 from the dead and ***d*** from David. This
Hebrews
7:5 though they also are ***d*** from Abraham.

DESERT

Genesis
37:22 him into this ***d*** cistern, but
Exodus
3:1 the edge of the ***d***, and he came to
3:18 journey into the ***d*** so that we can
4:27 Go into the ***d*** to meet Moses."
14:12 the Egyptians than to die in the ***d***."
Job
1:19 came from the ***d*** and struck the
6:15 a stream in the ***d***, like channels
21:33 The soil near the ***d*** streambed is sweet
22:24 from Ophir on a rock in a ***d*** streambed.
24:5 donkeys in the ***d***; they go forth at
38:26 to uninhabited land, a ***d*** with no human
39:6 whom I gave the ***d*** as home, his
Psalms
55:7 so far away! I'd live in the ***d***. Selah
63:1 was in the Judean ***d***.] God! My God!
65:12 Even the ***d*** pastures drip with it, and
72:9 Let the ***d*** dwellers bow low before him;
74:14 You gave it to the ***d*** dwellers for food!
78:17 against the Most High in the ***d***.
78:40 wilderness and distressed him in the ***d***!
102:6 owl—like some screech owl in the ***d***.
105:41 flowing like a river through the ***d***!
106:9 the deeps like they were a dry ***d***.
106:14 craving in the ***d***; they tested God
106:26 them, making them fall in the ***d***,
107:4 wandered into the ***d***, into the
107:33 turns rivers into ***d***, watery springs
107:35 can also turn the ***d*** into watery
126:4 like dry streams in the ***d*** waste!
136:16 through the ***d***—God's faithful l
Proverbs
27:10 Don't ***d*** your friend or a friend of your
Song of Songs
1:14 love to me in the ***d*** gardens of En-gedi
Matthew
3:1 appeared in the ***d*** of Judea
24:26 he's in the ***d***,' don't go out.
Acts
8:26 Jerusalem to Gaza." (This is a ***d*** road.)
21:38 terrorists into the ***d*** some time ago?"
2 Corinthians
11:26 the city, in the ***d***, on the sea, and
Hebrews
3:8 the day when they tested me in the ***d***.
3:17 who sinned, whose bodies fell in the ***d***?
Revelation
12:6 fled into the ***d***, where God has
12:14 her place in the ***d***. There she would
17:3 trance to a ***d***. There I saw a

DESERVE

Genesis
32:10 I don't ***d*** how loyal and truthful you've
Exodus
23:6 that your poor ***d*** in their lawsuits.
Judges
9:16 and have treated him as his actions ***d***—
Ezra
9:13 our iniquities ***d*** and have allowed
Psalms
28:4 Give back to them exactly what they ***d***!
94:2 back the arrogant exactly what they ***d***!
Ecclesiastes
8:14 what the wicked ***d***, and the wicked
Jeremiah
17:10 what they ***d***, the consequences
17:18 disaster, as they ***d***; destroy them
26:16 This man doesn't ***d*** to die, for he
30:11 I will discipline you as you ***d***.
46:28 I will discipline you as you ***d***.
Matthew
8:8 Lord, I don't ***d*** to have you come
10:9 Workers ***d*** to be fed, so don't gather
Luke
7:6 bothered. I don't ***d*** to have you come
10:7 you, for workers ***d*** their pay. Don't
15:19 I no longer ***d*** to be called your son.

15:21 you. I no longer ***d*** to be called your
17:10 say, 'We servants ***d*** no special
Romans
1:32 in such practices ***d*** death, they not
3:8 that, but these people ***d*** criticism.)
4:4 but rather on the basis of what they ***d***.
1 Corinthians
9:12 you, don't we ***d*** them all the
15:9 apostles. I don't ***d*** to be called an
15:19 life, then we ***d*** to be pitied more
2 Corinthians
11:15 Their end will be what their actions ***d***.
1 Timothy
5:18 treads grain, and Workers ***d*** their pay.
Hebrews
11:38 The world didn't ***d*** them. They wandered
Revelation
2:23 to each of you what your actions ***d***.
16:6 given them blood to drink. They ***d*** it!"
22:12 to repay all people as their actions ***d***.

DESIRE

Genesis
3:16 You will ***d*** your husband, but
Exodus
20:17 Do not ***d*** your neighbor's house. Do not
34:24 No one will ***d*** and try to take
Numbers
16:28 deeds and that it wasn't my own ***d***.
Deuteronomy
5:21 Do not ***d*** and try to take your
7:25 their gods. Don't ***d*** the silver or the
12:20 you have the ***d*** to do so), feel
Joshua
6:18 so that you don't ***d*** and take some of
2 Samuel
13:39 Then the king's ***d*** to go out after
19:38 do for you anything you ***d*** from me."
23:5 and brings my every ***d*** to pass.
1 Kings
11:37 that you could ***d***. You will be king
Esther
5:8 my wish and my ***d***, I'd like the
7:3 lives of my people too. That's my ***d***.
9:12 you. What is your ***d***? I'll do it this
Psalms
45:11 Let the king ***d*** your beauty. Because he
62:4 The only ***d*** of this people is to bring
73:25 nothing on earth I ***d*** except you.
111:2 they are treasured by all who ***d*** them.
119:40 Look how I ***d*** your precepts! Make me
145:16 satisfying the ***d*** of every living
Proverbs
3:15 pearls; all you ***d*** can't compare
6:25 Don't ***d*** her beauty in secret; don't let
10:24 the righteous ***d*** will be given to
13:19 A ***d*** fulfilled is pleasant, but fools
19:2 Ignorant ***d*** isn't good; rushing feet
21:10 Wicked people ***d*** evil; their neighbors
21:26 The lazy ***d*** things constantly, but the
Ecclesiastes
6:2 lack nothing they ***d***. But God doesn't
Isaiah
13:17 pay no mind to silver, no ***d*** for gold.
56:4 choose what I ***d***, and remain loyal
Jeremiah
2:24 Those who ***d*** her need not give
17:14 be saved, for you are my heart's ***d***.
Ezekiel
24:21 Your heart's ***d***, the sons and
Hosea
6:6 I ***d*** faithful love and not sacrifice,
Amos
5:18 Doom to those who ***d*** the day of the
Micah
4:11 or "Let our eyes look with ***d*** at Zion."
7:1 to eat, no ripe fig that I might ***d***.
Matthew
6:33 Instead, ***d*** first and foremost God's
Mark
4:19 wealth, and the ***d*** for more things
Luke
12:31 Instead, ***d*** his kingdom and these things
John
1:13 nor from human ***d*** or passion, but
Acts
18:15 I have no ***d*** to sit in
Romans
7:7 have known the ***d*** for what others
7:18 in my body. The ***d*** to do good is
9:16 on a person's ***d*** or effort. It
10:1 my heart's ***d*** is for Israel's
13:9 steal, don't ***d*** what others have,
2 Corinthians
7:7 us about your ***d*** to see me, how
7:11 what a ***d*** to clear
8:19 himself, and to show our ***d*** to help.
Colossians
3:5 lust, evil ***d***, and greed (which
1 Thessalonians
2:17 effort in our ***d*** to see you again
2 Thessalonians
1:11 every good ***d*** and faithful work
1 Peter
2:2 a newborn baby, ***d*** the pure milk of
4:3 what unbelievers ***d***—living in their u

DESIRES

1 Samuel
2:35 my thoughts and ***d***. I will build a
2 Samuel
3:21 your heart ***d***." At that, David
Job
17:11 my goals are destroyed, my heart's ***d***.
23:13 who can reverse it? What he ***d***, he does.
Psalms
10:17 listen to the ***d*** of those who
21:2 what his heart ***d***; you haven't
27:12 me over to the ***d*** of my enemies,
63:1 for you! My body ***d*** you in a dry and
Proverbs
10:3 but he rejects the ***d*** of the wicked.
11:6 are caught by their own ***d***.
11:23 The ***d*** of the righteous end up well, but
13:4 lazy have strong ***d*** but receive
21:25 The ***d*** of the lazy will kill them
Song of Songs
2:7 rouse, don't arouse love until it ***d***.
3:5 rouse, don't arouse love until it ***d***.
8:4 rouse, never to arouse love until it ***d***.
Habakkuk
2:4 Some people's ***d*** are truly audacious;
Acts
1:24 thoughts and ***d***. Show us clearly

DESIRES [cont.]

7:39 thoughts and ***d***, returned to
13:22 man who shares my ***d***. Whatever my will
15:8 thoughts and ***d***, confirmed this
15:9 deepest thoughts and ***d*** through faith.
Romans
1:24 to their hearts' ***d***, which led to the
7:8 all kinds of ***d*** in me. Sin is
13:14 don't plan to indulge your selfish ***d***.
Galatians
5:16 and you won't carry out your selfish ***d***.
5:17 person's selfish ***d*** are set against
5:24 self with its passions and its ***d***.
Ephesians
4:22 once were, corrupted by deceitful ***d***.
1 Timothy
5:11 their physical ***d*** distract them
2 Timothy
3:6 with sins and driven by all kinds of ***d***.
Titus
2:12 ungodly lives and the ***d*** of this world.
3:3 and slaves to our ***d*** and various
1 Peter
1:14 to your former ***d***, those that
2:11 you avoid worldly ***d*** that wage war
4:2 by human ***d*** but in ways
Jude
1:16 to their own ***d***. They speak
1:18 according to their own ungodly ***d***."

DESPISE

Leviticus
26:11 among you, and I will not ***d*** you.
26:15 my rules and ***d*** my regulations,
26:30 bodies of your idols. I will ***d*** you.
26:44 reject them or ***d*** them to the point
Job
19:18 Even the young ***d*** me; I get up, and they rail
19:19 closest friends ***d*** me; the ones I
Psalms
22:24 Because he didn't ***d*** or detest the
51:17 God. You won't ***d*** a heart, God,
69:33 the needy and doesn't ***d*** his captives.
102:17 impoverished; he won't ***d*** their prayers.
119:163 I absolutely ***d***, what is false,
139:21 you? Don't I ***d*** those who attack
Proverbs
1:7 LORD, but fools ***d*** wisdom and
3:11 LORD, my son; don't ***d*** his correction.
6:30 People don't ***d*** a thief if he steals to
8:7 the truth; my lips ***d*** wickedness."
13:13 come on those who ***d*** a word, but those
14:2 those who take a crooked path ***d*** him.
14:21 Those who ***d*** their neighbors are
15:20 to a father, but fools ***d*** their mothers.
15:32 refuse discipline ***d*** themselves, but
23:22 you life; don't ***d*** your elderly
Ezekiel
22:8 You ***d*** my holy things and degrade my
Zechariah
4:10 Those who ***d*** a time of little things
Malachi
1:6 you priests who ***d*** my name. So you

DESPISED

Leviticus
26:43 rejected my regulations and ***d*** my rules.
Judges
9:38 these the men you ***d***? Now march out
1 Samuel
10:27 save us?" They ***d*** Saul and didn't
15:9 anything that was ***d*** or of no value
2 Samuel
12:9 Why have you ***d*** the LORD's word by doing what is evil
12:10 that, because you ***d*** me and took the
Nehemiah
4:4 God; we are ***d***! Turn their
Psalms
22:6 insulted by one person, ***d*** by another.
36:2 their guilt ever being found out and ***d***.
89:38 have rejected and ***d*** him. You've
95:10 For forty years I ***d*** that generation; I
106:40 his people; he ***d*** his own
Proverbs
5:12 instruction! How my heart ***d*** correction!
Ecclesiastes
9:16 of commoners is ***d*** and their words
Isaiah
1:4 the LORD, ***d*** the holy one of
5:24 forces, and have ***d*** the word of
49:7 one, says to one ***d***, rejected by
52:5 continually all day long my name is ***d***.
53:3 He was ***d*** and avoided by others; a man
60:14 to you; all who ***d*** you will bow down
Lamentations
1:11 take notice: I am most certainly ***d***."
1:15 My Lord has ***d*** my mighty warriors. He
Ezekiel
16:5 for you. You were ***d*** on the day of
Obadiah
1:2 the nations; you will be totally ***d***.
Malachi
1:6 So you say, "How have we ***d*** your name?"
1:7 say, "The table of the LORD can be ***d***."
1:12 polluted. Its fruit, its food, is ***d***."
2:9 I have made you ***d*** and humiliated in

DESTROY → COMPLETELY DESTROY

Genesis
6:13 I am now about to ***d*** them along with
9:11 never again be a flood to ***d*** the earth."
18:28 fifty? Will you ***d*** the whole city
Deuteronomy
7:16 You will ***d*** all the peoples that the
1 Samuel
15:6 Otherwise, I'll ***d*** you right along
2 Kings
8:19 wasn't willing to ***d*** Judah. The LORD
1 Chronicles
21:15 to Jerusalem to ***d*** it. But just as
Esther
3:9 be sent out to ***d*** them, and I will
9:24 had planned to ***d*** the Jews. He had
Job
10:8 made me; yet you want to ***d*** me utterly.
14:19 carry away soil; you ***d*** a people's hope.
21:19 children. Let him ***d*** them so they know.
30:13 ***d*** my road, profit from my fall, with no
Psalms
143:12 faithful love. ***D*** everyone who
Isaiah
11:9 won't harm or ***d*** anywhere on my
65:8 says, "Don't ***d*** it, for there is

65:25 won't hurt or ***d*** at any place on
Jeremiah
1:10 and pull down, to ***d*** and demolish, to
Hosea
11:9 I won't return to ***d*** Ephraim; for I am
Zechariah
1:21 them and to ***d*** the horns of the
Matthew
10:28 the one who can ***d*** both body and
26:61 man said, 'I can ***d*** God's temple and
Mark
14:58 saying, 'I will ***d*** this temple,
Luke
4:34 Have you come to ***d*** us? I know who
John
10:10 steal, kill, and ***d***. I came so that
1 Corinthians
1:19 scripture: I will ***d*** the wisdom of the
3:17 temple, God will ***d*** that person,
James
4:12 to save and to ***d***. But you who
1 John
3:8 this purpose: to ***d*** the works of the
Revelation
11:18 and great, and to ***d*** those who destroy

DESTROYED → COMPLETELY DESTROYED
Genesis
13:10 before the LORD ***d*** Sodom and
Exodus
10:7 Don't you get it? Egypt is being ***d***!"
2 Samuel
1:27 how the weapons of war have been ***d***!
Job
4:7 those who do the right thing been ***d***?
16:7 me out. You have ***d*** my entire group,
17:11 my goals are ***d***, my heart's
30:14 as if through a ***d*** wall; they roll
Psalms
1:6 but the way of the wicked is ***d***.
37:38 will be ***d*** all together; the
105:33 God ***d*** their vines and their fig trees;
Hosea
4:6 My people are ***d*** from lack of knowledge.
Joel
1:7 It has ***d*** my vines, splintered my fig
Mark
2:22 and the wineskins ***d***. But new wine is
Hebrews
7:16 that can't be ***d***, rather than a
10:39 and end up being ***d***. We're the sort
James
5:2 have rotted. Moths have ***d*** your clothes.

DESTRUCTION
Deuteronomy
28:22 and drought; with ***d*** and disease for
32:35 the day of their ***d*** is just around
2 Kings
23:13 the Mountain of ***D***. Solomon the king
Esther
4:7 was in exchange for the ***d*** of the Jews.
Job
5:21 and you won't fear ***d*** when it comes.
5:22 You will laugh at ***d*** and hunger; you
28:22 ***D*** and Death have said, "We've heard a
31:3 for the wicked, ***d*** for workers of
Psalms
5:9 inside them is ***d***. Their throats
52:2 tongue devises ***d***: it's like a
52:7 sought refuge in it—to their own ***d***!"
57:1 shadow of your wings until ***d*** passes by.
78:38 kept avoiding ***d***; he took back his
91:6 in the dark, ***d*** that ravages at
Proverbs
16:30 their eye plot ***d***; those who purse
26:28 crushes; a flattering mouth causes ***d***.
Daniel
8:25 he will bring ***d*** on many, opposing
Micah
2:10 it destroys and the ***d*** is horrific.
6:16 you a sign of ***d***, your inhabitants
Matthew
7:13 that leads to ***d*** is broad and the
John
17:12 was destined for ***d***, so that
Romans
9:22 were designed for ***d***, because he
2 Corinthians
2:15 and to those who are on the road to ***d***.

DETESTABLE → YOUR DETESTABLE PRACTICES
Leviticus
11:10 creatures in the water—is ***d*** to you
18:22 would with a woman; it is a ***d*** practice.
20:13 done something ***d***. They must be
20:25 Do not become ***d*** through some
Deuteronomy
7:25 by it. That is ***d*** to the LORD your
12:31 gods that are ***d*** to the LORD,
13:14 true that this ***d*** thing was done in
14:3 Don't eat any ***d*** thing
17:1 because that is ***d*** to the LORD your
18:9 to imitate the ***d*** things those
20:18 you to do all the ***d*** things they did
22:5 such things is ***d*** to the LORD your
23:18 these things are ***d*** to the LORD your
25:16 dishonestly, are ***d*** to the LORD your
27:15 an image—things ***d*** to the LORD, made
32:16 gods, aggravated him with ***d*** things.
Hosea
9:10 they became ***d*** like the thing
Malachi
2:11 Judah cheated—a ***d*** thing was done in
Titus
1:16 they do. They are ***d***, disobedient, and

DEVASTATED
Leviticus
26:33 Your land will be ***d*** and your cities
Deuteronomy
29:23 vegetation, as ***d*** as Sodom and
Judges
16:24 the very one who ***d*** our land and
1 Samuel
6:5 mice that have ***d*** the land. Honor
Psalms
69:25 Let their camp be ***d***; let no one dwell
73:19 quickly they are ***d***, utterly
Isaiah
6:11 without people and the land is left ***d***."
15:1 Moab. Ar was ***d*** in a night; Moab
24:3 The earth will be ***d***, totally

60:12 will perish; such nations will be ***d***.
Jeremiah
4:30 And you, ***d*** one, why dress up in
9:19 from Zion: "We're ***d***! We're so
12:11 They have ***d*** her; desolate, she cries
51:43 Her towns are ***d***; her land is scorched
Lamentations
1:13 He left me ***d***, constantly sick.
Ezekiel
29:12 cities the most ***d*** of ruined cities.
Joel
1:10 The fields are ***d***, the ground mourns;
Obadiah
1:5 —how you've been ***d***!—wouldn't they
Nahum
3:7 Nineveh has been ***d***! Who will lament
Zechariah
7:14 The land was ***d*** behind them, with
11:2 ones have been ***d***. Scream, oaks of
11:3 majesty has been ***d***. The sound of

DEVASTATION

Psalms
46:8 deeds, what ***d*** he has imposed on
Isaiah
51:19 —destruction and ***d***, famine and sword-
60:18 your land, nor ***d*** or destruction
Jeremiah
4:6 disaster from the north, massive ***d***.
6:1 looms from the north, massive ***d***.
16:10 such massive ***d*** against us? What
48:3 Horonaim: "Destruction and massive ***d***!"
50:22 of war in the land and enormous ***d***.
51:54 signs of massive ***d*** in the land,
Ezekiel
23:33 sadness. A cup of ***d*** and dismay is the
Daniel
9:18 and look at our ***d***. Look at the city
Obadiah
1:12 the day of their ***d***; you shouldn't
Nahum
2:10 Destruction and ***d***; the city is laid
Habakkuk
1:3 anguish so that ***d*** and violence are
Zephaniah
1:15 of desolation and ***d***, a day of
2:9 salt pits, and ***d*** forever. The few
Galatians
6:8 will harvest ***d*** from their

DEVIATE

Deuteronomy
5:32 God commands you. Don't ***d*** even a bit!
17:11 to you. Don't ***d*** even a bit from
28:14 Don't ***d*** even a bit from any of these
Joshua
1:7 you. Don't ***d*** even a bit from
11:15 that. He didn't ***d*** a bit from any
23:6 from Moses. Don't ***d*** a bit from it
2 Samuel
14:19 king, no one can ***d*** a bit from
1 Kings
15:5 David didn't ***d*** from anything the
2 Kings
3:3 to commit. He didn't ***d*** from them.
10:29 Jehu didn't ***d*** from the sins
10:31 heart. He didn't ***d*** from the sins
13:2 to commit. He didn't ***d*** from them.
13:6 But they didn't ***d*** from the sins that
13:11 eyes. He didn't ***d*** from all the sins
14:24 eyes. He didn't ***d*** from all the sins
15:9 done. He didn't ***d*** from the sins
15:18 life, he didn't ***d*** from the sins
15:24 eyes. He didn't ***d*** from the sins
15:28 eyes. He didn't ***d*** from the sins
17:22 Jeroboam did. They didn't ***d*** from them,
2 Chronicles
8:15 They didn't ***d*** in any way from the
Proverbs
4:27 Don't ***d*** a bit to the right or the left;
5:7 to me, and don't ***d*** from the words of

DEVIL

Matthew
4:1 so that the ***d*** might tempt him.
4:5 After that the ***d*** brought him into the
4:8 Then the ***d*** brought him to a very high
4:11 The ***d*** left him, and angels came and
13:39 them is the ***d***. The harvest is
25:41 been prepared for the ***d*** and his angels.
Luke
4:2 forty days by the ***d***. He ate nothing
4:3 The ***d*** said to him, "Since you are God's
4:5 Next the ***d*** led him to a high place and
4:6 The ***d*** said, "I will give you this whole
4:9 The ***d*** brought him into Jerusalem and
4:13 temptation, the ***d*** departed from him
8:12 but then the ***d*** comes and steals
John
6:70 you twelve? Yet one of you is a ***d***."
8:44 father is the ***d***. You are his
13:2 evening meal. The ***d*** had already
Acts
10:38 oppressed by the ***d*** because God was
13:10 trickster! You ***d***! You attack
Ephesians
4:27 Don't provide an opportunity for the ***d***
6:11 a stand against the tricks of the ***d***.
Hebrews
2:14 the power over death—the ***d***—by dying.
James
4:7 God. Resist the ***d***, and he will run
1 Peter
5:8 Your accuser, the ***d***, is on the prowl
1 John
3:8 belongs to the ***d***, because the
Jude
1:9 argued with the ***d*** about Moses'
Revelation
2:10 suffer. Look! The ***d*** is going to throw
12:9 who is called the ***d*** and Satan, the
12:12 and sea! The ***d*** has come down to
20:2 snake, who is the ***d*** and Satan, and
20:10 Then the ***d***, who had deceived them, was

DEVOUR

Genesis
25:30 starving! Let me ***d*** some of this red
Deuteronomy
28:39 the grapes because worms will ***d*** them.
28:51 That nation will ***d*** your livestock's
1 Kings
21:23 this: Dogs will ***d*** Jezebel in the

2 Kings
9:10 The dogs will ***d*** her in the area
9:36 Tishbe: Dogs will ***d*** Jezebel's flesh
Job
5:5 The hungry ***d*** their crops; it's taken
22:20 off; fire will ***d*** what's left of
Ezekiel
19:3 he learned to tear flesh and ***d*** humans.
25:4 residence, ***d*** your fruit, and
32:4 all the beasts of the earth to ***d*** you.
34:28 will no longer ***d*** them. They will
36:14 will no longer ***d*** human beings or
Daniel
7:5 It was told: "Get up! ***D*** much flesh!"
7:23 It will ***d*** the entire earth,
Hosea
5:7 the new moon will ***d*** them along with
8:7 it were to yield, strangers would ***d*** it.
8:14 cities, and it will ***d*** his fortresses.
13:8 hearts. I will ***d*** them like a lion,
Amos
1:4 Hazael; it will ***d*** the palaces of
1:7 wall of Gaza; it will ***d*** Gaza's palaces.
1:10 wall of Tyre; it will ***d*** their palaces.
1:12 on Teman; it will ***d*** the fortresses of
1:14 the fire will ***d*** its palaces, with
2:2 on Moab; it will ***d*** the palaces of
2:5 and it will ***d*** the palaces of
Micah
3:3 who ***d*** the flesh of my people, tear off
6:14 You ***d***, but you aren't satisfied; a
Nahum
2:13 the sword will ***d*** your young lions;
Habakkuk
1:8 They fly in to ***d***, swiftly, like an
Zephaniah
1:18 His jealousy will ***d*** the entire land
Zechariah
9:15 them. They will ***d*** and subdue like
11:1 so that fire will ***d*** your cedars.
11:9 who are left ***d*** the flesh of
11:16 Instead, he will ***d*** the flesh of the
12:6 grain. They will ***d*** all the
Malachi
3:11 one who wants to ***d*** you so that it
Galatians
5:15 if you bite and ***d*** each other, be
Hebrews
10:27 fire that's going to ***d*** God's opponents.
1 Peter
5:8 a roaring lion, seeking someone to ***d***.•
Revelation
12:4 she gave birth, he might ***d*** her child.
17:16 bare. They will ***d*** her flesh and

DEW

Exodus
16:13 was a layer of ***d*** all around the
Psalms
110:3 strength is like the ***d*** itself."

DIE

Genesis
2:17 the day you eat from it, you will ***d***!"
3:3 and don't touch it, or you will ***d***.'"
3:4 snake said to the woman, "You won't ***d***!
Exodus
7:18 Nile are going to ***d***, the Nile will
14:12 the Egyptians than to ***d*** in the desert."
20:19 don't let God speak to us, or we'll ***d***."
Deuteronomy
4:22 I will ***d*** here in this land. I won't
33:6 lives, doesn't ***d***, though his
Joshua
22:20 the only one to ***d*** for his crime.'"
Judges
6:23 Peace! Don't be afraid! You won't ***d***."
Ruth
1:17 Wherever you ***d***, I will die, and there
1 Samuel
18:25 that David would ***d*** at the hands of
2 Samuel
12:13 Nathan replied to David. "You won't ***d***.
1 Kings
1:52 any evil is found in him, he will ***d***."
13:31 his sons, "When I ***d***, bury me in the
1 Chronicles
17:11 comes for you to ***d***, I will raise up
2 Chronicles
21:19 causing him to ***d*** in horrible pain.
Esther
4:14 your family will ***d***. But who knows?
4:16 and if I am to ***d***, then die I will."
9:28 of Purim won't ***d*** out among the
Job
2:9 to your integrity? Curse God, and ***d***."
Psalms
79:11 arm spare those who are destined to ***d***.
83:17 forever. Let them ***d*** in disgrace.
92:9 how your enemies ***d***, how all
104:29 breath, they ***d*** and return to
118:17 I won't ***d***—no, I will live and declare
141:8 I take refuge in you; don't let me ***d***!
146:4 that very same day, their plans ***d*** too.
Proverbs
1:32 The immature will ***d*** because they turn
5:23 instruction will ***d***, misled by their
10:21 but fools who lack sense will ***d***.
11:7 When the wicked ***d***, their hope
15:10 way; those who hate correction will ***d***.
19:16 those who disregard their ways will ***d***.
23:13 strike them with a rod, they won't ***d***.
30:7 don't keep them from me before I ***d***:
Ecclesiastes
2:16 How can the wise ***d*** just like the
7:17 a fool, or you may ***d*** before your time.
9:3 they are alive, and afterward they ***d***.
Isaiah
22:2 by the sword; they didn't ***d*** in battle.
22:13 Eat and drink! Tomorrow we will ***d***!"
Ezekiel
3:18 the wicked will ***d*** but you don't
Daniel
2:18 friends wouldn't ***d*** with the rest of
11:41 of thousands will ***d***. But Edom, Moab,
Jonah
4:3 be better for me to ***d*** than to live."
Matthew
16:28 here won't ***d*** before they see
26:35 Even if I must ***d*** alongside you, I
26:66 And they answered, "He deserves to ***d***!"
27:3 was condemned to ***d***, he felt deep

DIE [cont.]

Mark
5:23 is about to ***d***. Please, come and
14:64 all condemned him. "He deserves to ***d***!"
John
4:47 his son, for his son was about to ***d***.
6:50 that whoever eats from it will never ***d***.
12:33 this to show how he was going to ***d***.)
19:7 Law he ought to ***d*** because he made
21:23 disciple wouldn't ***d***. However, Jesus
Acts
7:19 newly born babies so they would ***d***.
13:41 marvel and ***d***. I'm going to do
Romans
2:12 the Law will also ***d*** outside the Law,
5:7 that someone will ***d*** for a righteous
6:9 and he will never ***d*** again. Death no
8:13 you are going to ***d***. But if you put
14:7 ourselves and we don't ***d*** for ourselves.
14:8 Lord, and if we ***d***, we die for the
Hebrews
7:8 by people who ***d***, and in the other
9:27 are destined to ***d*** once and then
James
1:10 because they will ***d*** off like
Revelation
9:6 They will want to ***d***, but death will
12:11 own lives didn't make them afraid to ***d***.
14:13 are the dead who ***d*** in the Lord from

DIES

Ecclesiastes
3:19 same fate. One ***d*** just like the
Mark
12:19 a man's brother ***d***, leaving a widow
John
4:49 to him, "Lord, come before my son ***d***."
12:24 the earth and ***d***, it can only be a
Romans
7:2 if her husband ***d***, she is released
1 Corinthians
7:39 if her husband ***d***, she is free to

DIFFICULT

Genesis
18:14 Is anything too ***d*** for the LORD? When I
Mark
10:24 Children, it's ***d*** to enter God's
Acts
27:7 days of slow and ***d*** sailing, we
Hebrews
5:11 topic, and it's ***d*** to explain,
James
2:6 wealthy make life ***d*** for you? Aren't
1 John
5:3 God's commandments are not ***d***,

DINNER

Genesis
43:16 the men will have ***d*** with me at noon."
43:31 together, and said, "Set out the ***d***."
Psalms
63:5 as with a rich ***d***. My mouth speaks
78:19 Can God set a ***d*** table in the
Matthew
26:7 Jesus' head while he was sitting at ***d***.
Mark
6:22 Herod and his ***d*** guests. The king
14:3 disease. During ***d***, a woman came in
Luke
14:12 host a lunch or ***d***, don't invite
14:15 When one of the ***d*** guests heard Jesus'
14:16 hosted a large ***d*** and invited many
14:17 was time for the ***d*** to begin, he sent
14:24 who were invited will taste my ***d***.'"
17:8 instead, 'Fix my ***d***. Put on the
John
12:2 sisters hosted a ***d*** for him. Martha
Revelation
3:20 and will have ***d*** with them, and

DIRECTION

Genesis
24:48 me in the right ***d*** to choose the
Exodus
38:21 under the ***d*** of Ithamar, Aaron
Numbers
9:19 the LORD's ***d*** and they wouldn't
9:23 the LORD's ***d*** according to the
Deuteronomy
28:7 you from one ***d*** but will run for
28:25 them by one ***d***, but you will run
Joshua
2:7 after them in the ***d*** of the Jordan up
7:4 went up in that ***d***. But they fled
8:15 them. They fled in the ***d*** of the desert.
12:3 southward in the ***d*** of Beth-jeshimoth
Judges
3:28 the Jordan in the ***d*** of Moab, allowing
9:37 is coming from the ***d*** of Elon-meonenim."
20:18 Bethel to ask for ***d*** from God. They
20:42 Israelites in the ***d*** of the desert,
1 Kings
1:6 never given him ***d***; he never
2 Kings
3:20 flowing from the ***d*** of Edom. The land
1 Chronicles
25:2 was under Asaph's ***d*** and prophesied by
25:3 father Jeduthun's ***d***, prophesying with
25:6 their father's ***d*** when singing in
Nehemiah
12:31 the right, in the ***d*** of the Dung Gate.
Job
24:13 acknowledge its ***d***, don't dwell in
Psalms
32:8 you about the ***d*** you should go.
Ezekiel
10:11 they moved in that ***d*** without swerving.
16:33 From every ***d*** you even bribed
46:8 of the gate and goes out in the same ***d***.
47:15 and goes in the ***d*** of Hethlon toward
Mark
1:38 head in the other ***d***, to the nearby

DIRT

Genesis
26:15 and filled with ***d*** all of the wells
Exodus
8:16 hit the land's ***d*** so that lice
8:17 hit the land's ***d***, and lice
Leviticus
17:13 its blood out and cover it with ***d***.
Deuteronomy
28:24 into dust. Only ***d*** will fall down on

1 Samuel
4:12 were torn, and ***d*** was on his head.
2 Samuel
1:2 clothes torn and ***d*** on his head. When
15:32 were ripped, and ***d*** was on his head.
16:13 he went, throwing rocks and ***d*** at him.
2 Kings
13:7 them, trampling them as if they were ***d***.
Nehemiah
9:1 clothing, and had ***d*** on their heads.
Job
38:38 dust becomes mud and clods of ***d*** adhere?
Psalms
7:5 laying my reputation in the ***d***. Selah
17:11 make their plans to put me in the ***d***.
22:15 you've set me down in the ***d*** of death.
89:31 my statutes like ***d***, stop keeping my
89:39 You've thrown his crown in the ***d***.
102:14 stones; they show mercy even to her ***d***.
107:34 into unproductive ***d***, when its
113:7 the poor from the ***d*** and raises up the
119:25 is stuck in the ***d***. Now make me live
143:3 my life in the ***d***, forcing me to
143:6 being is like dry ***d***, thirsting for
147:6 but throws the wicked down on the ***d***!
Lamentations
3:29 his mouth in the ***d***—perhaps there is
Ezekiel
24:7 be covered with ***d***, but she spread
26:4 off all its ***d*** and make it into
Amos
9:9 as one sifts ***d*** with a screen,
Habakkuk
1:10 then he piles up ***d*** and takes it.
1 Peter
3:21 it removes ***d*** from your body

DISASTER

Genesis
19:29 Lot away from the ***d*** that overtook the
Exodus
8:15 saw that the ***d*** was over, he
10:17 to take this deathly ***d*** away from me."
11:1 bring one more ***d*** on Pharaoh and on
Deuteronomy
29:21 them out for ***d*** in compliance
32:23 throw on them ***d*** after disaster;
Joshua
7:25 You have brought ***d*** to us! May the
Judges
20:34 realize that ***d*** was almost on
20:41 recognized that ***d*** had fallen on
1 Samuel
6:9 this great ***d*** on us. If the
2 Samuel
17:14 that the LORD could bring ***d*** on Absalom.
24:16 doing this ***d*** and said to the
1 Kings
9:9 the LORD brought all this ***d*** on them."
14:10 going to bring ***d*** on Jeroboam's
22:23 LORD who has pronounced ***d*** against you!"
2 Kings
6:33 said, "Look, this ***d*** is the LORD's
14:10 home. Why invite ***d*** when both you and
21:12 such a great ***d*** that the ears of
22:16 am about to bring ***d*** on this place and
22:20 experience the ***d*** I am about to
1 Chronicles
21:12 bringing ***d*** in every part of
2 Chronicles
7:22 is why God brought all this ***d*** on them.
18:22 LORD who has pronounced ***d*** against you!"
25:19 home! Why invite ***d*** when both you and
34:24 am about to bring ***d*** on this place and
34:28 experience the ***d*** I am about to
Job
2:11 about all this ***d*** that had happened
6:30 or can my mouth not recognize ***d***?
21:17 wicked flicker or ***d*** come upon them,
21:30 On the day of ***d*** the wicked are spared;
31:3 Isn't it ***d*** for the wicked, destruction
42:11 all the ***d*** the LORD had
Psalms
35:8 Let ***d*** come to them when they don't
54:5 He will bring ***d*** on my opponents. By
55:3 they bring ***d*** on me and harass
55:11 ***D*** lives inside it; oppression and fraud
Proverbs
1:26 laugh at your ***d***; I'll make fun of
1:27 and your ***d*** comes in like a
6:15 Therefore, sudden ***d*** will come upon
16:18 comes before ***d***, and arrogance
17:5 who rejoice in ***d*** won't go
18:12 comes before a ***d***, but humility
19:13 foolish son is a ***d*** to his father; a
24:22 ***D*** comes suddenly from them. Who can
27:10 house when ***d*** strikes. Better a
Ecclesiastes
11:2 don't know what ***d*** may come upon the
Isaiah
10:3 punishment when ***d*** comes from far
13:11 I will bring ***d*** upon the world for its
31:2 how to bring ***d***; he has not taken
Jeremiah
2:3 it became guilty; ***d*** overtook them,
4:6 I'm bringing ***d*** from the north,
4:15 someone proclaims ***d*** from the
4:20 ***D*** follows disaster; the whole land is
5:12 do nothing! ***D*** won't come upon
6:1 for ***d*** looms from the
6:15 when I bring ***d***, declares the
6:19 I'm bringing ***d*** upon my people,
8:12 and stumble when ***d*** arrives, declares
11:11 bring upon them a ***d*** from which they
11:12 they won't save them when ***d*** strikes.
11:17 you has announced ***d*** for you, because
11:23 I will bring ***d*** upon the men of
17:16 urge you to bring ***d***; I didn't want
17:17 me; you are my refuge in time of ***d***.
17:18 them the time of ***d***, as they deserve;
18:11 preparing a ***d*** for you; I'm
18:17 their enemy. When ***d*** strikes them, I
19:3 to bring such ***d*** upon this place
19:15 towns every ***d*** that I have
23:12 I will bring ***d*** upon them, when
25:6 hands. Then I won't bring ***d*** upon you."
25:7 do and bringing ***d*** upon yourselves,
25:29 I'm bringing ***d*** upon the city
25:32 proclaims: Look! ***D*** travels from
28:8 prophesied war, ***d***, and disease

29:11 for peace, not ***d***, to give you a
32:23 them. So you brought upon them this ***d***.
32:42 this great ***d*** on this people,
35:17 in Jerusalem the ***d*** I pronounced
36:3 hear about every ***d*** I intend to bring
36:31 of Judah, every ***d*** I pronounced
40:2 that a great ***d*** would overtake
42:10 I grieve over the ***d*** I have brought
42:17 will escape the ***d*** that I will bring
43:11 those marked for ***d***, to disaster, and
44:2 You have seen the ***d*** I brought on
44:11 to bring ***d*** on you, to
45:5 I'm bringing ***d*** on all humanity,
46:21 The day of ***d*** has come to haunt
49:8 I'm bringing ***d*** on Esau: its day
49:32 and I will bring ***d*** on them from
49:37 I will bring ***d*** upon them, my
51:2 They will surround her on the day of ***d***.
51:64 because of the ***d*** I'm bringing

Ezekiel
7:5 God proclaims: ***D***! A singular
7:25 ***D***! It has come! They seek peace, but
7:26 One ***d*** comes after another, and rumor

Amos
3:6 tremble? If ***d*** falls on a city,

Obadiah
1:13 on the day of his ***d***; you shouldn't

Habakkuk
1:13 unable to look at ***d***. Why would you

DISCIPLE

Matthew
13:52 been trained as a ***d*** for the kingdom
27:57 Arimathea who had become a ***d*** of Jesus.

Mark
14:51 One young man, a ***d***, was wearing

Luke
14:26 even one's own life—cannot be my ***d***.
14:27 own cross and follow me cannot be my ***d***.
14:33 up all of your possessions can be my ***d***.

John
9:28 him: "You are his ***d***, but we are
13:25 Jesus, this ***d*** asked, "Lord, who
18:15 Peter and another ***d*** followed Jesus.
18:16 Then the other ***d*** (the one known to
19:26 mother and the ***d*** whom he loved
19:27 he said to the ***d***, "Here is your
19:38 Joseph was a ***d*** of Jesus, but a
20:2 and the other ***d***, the one whom
20:3 and the other ***d*** left to go to the
20:4 but the other ***d*** ran faster than
20:8 Then the other ***d***, the one who arrived
21:7 Then the ***d*** whom Jesus loved said to
21:20 and saw the ***d*** whom Jesus loved
21:21 Peter saw this ***d***, he said to
21:23 sisters that this ***d*** wouldn't die.
21:24 This is the ***d*** who testifies concerning

Acts
9:10 was a certain ***d*** named Ananias.
9:26 They didn't believe he was really a ***d***.
9:36 Joppa there was a ***d*** named Tabitha (in
16:1 where there was a ***d*** named Timothy.
21:16 Cyprus and had been a ***d*** a long time.

DISCIPLES → JESUS AND HIS DISCIPLES, JESUS' DISCIPLES, JOHN'S DISCIPLES

Isaiah
8:16 seal up the teaching among my ***d***.

Matthew
9:11 they said to his ***d***, "Why does your
10:1 called his twelve ***d*** and gave them
12:1 the Sabbath. His ***d*** were hungry so
26:56 Then all the ***d*** left Jesus and
28:19 go and make ***d*** of all nations,

Mark
3:7 left with his ***d*** and went to the
7:5 Why are your ***d*** not living
9:18 I spoke to your ***d*** to see if they
14:14 can eat the Passover meal with my ***d***?"

Luke
6:13 together his ***d***. He chose twelve
11:1 one of his ***d*** said, "Lord,
22:45 he went to the ***d***. He found them

John
2:11 his glory, and his ***d*** believed in him.
6:66 this, many of his ***d*** turned away and
8:31 You are truly my ***d*** if you remain
9:28 are his disciple, but we are Moses' ***d***.
12:16 His ***d*** didn't understand these things at
13:35 that you are my ***d***, when you love
15:8 in this way prove that you are my ***d***.
18:17 one of this man's ***d***?" "I'm not," he
20:20 side. When the ***d*** saw the Lord,

Acts
6:1 the number of ***d*** continued to
9:1 the Lord's ***d***. He went to the
11:26 Antioch where the ***d*** were first
13:52 their lives, the ***d*** were overflowing
14:22 strengthened the ***d*** and urged them to
18:23 of Phrygia, strengthening all the ***d***.

DISCIPLINE

Leviticus
26:23 do not accept my ***d*** and continue to

Deuteronomy
4:36 voice in order to ***d*** you. On earth he
11:2 LORD your God's ***d***, his power, his
21:18 when the parents ***d*** him, he won't

2 Samuel
7:14 wrong, I will ***d*** him with a human

Job
36:10 their ears with ***d*** and commands them

Psalms
6:1 are angry; don't ***d*** me when you are
38:1 are mad; don't ***d*** me when you are
39:11 You ***d*** people for their sin, punishing
50:17 You hate ***d***, and you toss my words
94:12 The people you ***d***, LORD, are truly
141:5 let the righteous ***d*** me; let the

Proverbs
1:2 teach wisdom and ***d***, to help one
12:1 Those who love ***d*** love knowledge, and
13:1 listens to the ***d*** of his father,
13:24 but the one who loves them applies ***d***.
15:10 ***D*** is severe for those who abandon the
15:32 Those who refuse ***d*** despise themselves,
19:18 ***D*** your children while there is hope,
19:27 stop listening to ***d***, you will wander
22:15 child's heart; the rod of ***d*** removes it.

Jeremiah
5:3 have ignored your ***d***. They make their

30:11 I will ***d*** you as you
46:28 I will ***d*** you as you
Zephaniah
3:2 she accepted no ***d***. She didn't trust
Ephesians
6:4 raise them with ***d*** and instruction
Colossians
2:5 happy to see the ***d*** and stability of
1 Timothy
5:20 ***D*** those who are sinning in front of
Hebrews
12:5 of the Lord's ***d*** or give up when
12:7 for the sake of ***d***. God is treating
12:8 don't experience ***d***, which happens to
12:11 No ***d*** is fun while it lasts, but it
Revelation
3:19 I correct and ***d*** those whom I love. So

DISEASE
Exodus
4:6 his hand had a skin ***d*** flaky like snow.
Leviticus
13:2 infection of skin ***d*** on their skin,
Psalms
78:48 cattle over to ***d***, their herds to
78:50 but delivered their lives over to ***d***.
91:10 happen to you; no ***d*** will come close
Matthew
4:23 and healed every ***d*** and sickness
9:35 and healing every ***d*** and every
Mark
1:40 A man with a skin ***d*** approached Jesus,
5:34 you; go in peace, healed from your ***d***."
14:3 who had a skin ***d***. During dinner, a
Revelation
2:23 to death with ***d***. Then all the
6:8 by sword, famine, ***d***, and the wild
18:8 day—deadly ***d***, grief, and

DISEASES
Jeremiah
16:4 die of horrible ***d***. No one will
Hosea
13:14 where are your ***d***? Grave, where is
Mark
1:34 with all kinds of ***d***, and he threw out
Luke
6:18 healed from their ***d***, and those
7:22 People with skin ***d*** are cleansed.
17:12 ten men with skin ***d*** approached him.
Acts
19:12 sick, and their ***d*** were cured and

DISGRACE
Job
19:5 on me and use my ***d*** to criticize me,
Psalms
44:15 All day long my ***d*** confronts me, and
69:19 my shame and my ***d***. All my
71:13 downfall be dressed in insults and ***d***!
78:66 foes; he made them an everlasting ***d***.
83:17 terrified forever. Let them die in ***d***.
109:29 let them wear their ***d*** like a coat.
1 Corinthians
11:14 a man has long hair, it is a ***d*** to him;

DISTANCE
Ezra
3:13 The sound was heard at a great ***d***.
Job
2:12 looked up from a ***d*** and didn't
30:10 me, keep their ***d***, don't withhold
36:25 him; people can observe at great ***d***.
Psalms
38:11 keep their ***d*** from me in my
138:6 but God keeps his ***d*** from the arrogant.
Proverbs
22:5 who guard their lives keep their ***d***.
31:14 merchant ships, bringing food from a ***d***.
Jeremiah
31:3 to them from a ***d***: I have loved you
Ezekiel
23:40 came from a great ***d***. No sooner than a
43:14 inches wide. The ***d*** from the lower to
Matthew
8:30 Far off in the ***d*** a large herd of pigs
26:39 he went a short ***d*** farther and fell
26:58 him from a ***d*** until he came to
27:55 watching from a ***d***. They had
Luke
5:3 row out a little ***d*** from the shore.
16:23 saw Abraham at a ***d*** with Lazarus at
17:12 him. Keeping their ***d*** from him,
18:13 stood at a ***d***. He wouldn't even
22:54 house. Peter followed from a ***d***.
23:49 stood at a ***d*** observing these
Acts
5:38 in this case: ***D*** yourselves from
2 Corinthians
13:2 I'm at a safe ***d***: if I come again,
Hebrews
11:13 promises from a ***d*** and welcomed

DISTRESS
Deuteronomy
4:30 In your ***d***, when all these things
Judges
10:14 them rescue you in the time of your ***d***."
2 Samuel
16:12 LORD will see my ***d***; perhaps the LORD
22:7 In my ***d*** I cried out to the LORD; I
22:19 very day of my ***d***, but the LORD was
2 Kings
19:3 Today is a day of ***d***, punishment, and
2 Chronicles
20:9 out to you in our ***d***, and you will
33:12 During his ***d***, Manasseh made peace with
Ezra
10:1 around him. The people also wept in ***d***.
Nehemiah
9:37 with our livestock. We are in great ***d***.
Job
5:6 dust, nor does ***d*** sprout from the
5:7 are born to ***d***, just as sparks
27:9 hear their cries when ***d*** comes to them;
30:24 in ruins if in ***d*** he cries out to
36:16 place without ***d***; your table is
36:19 your rescue from ***d*** or from all your
38:23 for a time of ***d***, for a day of
Psalms
6:7 grief; it's weak because of all my ***d***.
18:6 In my ***d*** I cried out to the LORD; I

18:18 very day of my ***d***, but the LORD was
25:17 getting bigger—set me free from my ***d***!
31:7 intimately acquainted with my deep ***d***.
54:7 me from every ***d***. My eyes have
78:49 indignation, ***d***, a troop of evil
81:7 In ***d*** you cried out, so I rescued you. I
88:3 is filled with ***d***; my life is at
106:44 But God saw their ***d*** when he heard their
107:6 the LORD in their ***d***, and God
107:13 the LORD in their ***d***, and God saved
107:19 the LORD in their ***d***, and God saved
107:28 the LORD in their ***d***, and God brought
116:3 bound me; the ***d*** of the grave
142:2 before God; I announce my ***d*** to him.
143:11 Bring me out of ***d*** because of your

Proverbs
1:27 a tornado, when ***d*** and oppression
11:8 are saved from ***d***, and the wicked
12:13 lips, but the righteous escape from ***d***.
14:10 knows its own ***d***; another person
24:10 weak on a day of ***d***, your strength is

Isaiah
5:7 but there was a cry of ***d***!
8:22 will see only ***d*** and darkness,
9:1 those who were in ***d*** won't be
15:8 Eglaim, a cry of ***d***, as far as Beer-el
25:4 for the needy in ***d***, a hiding place
26:16 LORD, in ***d*** they sought you out; they
30:6 Through a land of ***d*** and danger,
30:20 you the bread of ***d*** and the water of
33:2 morning, our salvation in times of ***d***.
37:3 Today is a day of ***d***, punishment, and
46:7 It can't save people from their ***d***.
63:9 During all their ***d***, God also was

Jeremiah
4:31 in labor, the ***d*** of one delivering
6:24 panic-stricken; ***d*** overwhelms us,
11:14 cry out to me on account of their ***d***.
12:11 out to me in ***d***: "The whole land
15:8 I will bring ***d*** and terror upon
15:11 your enemies in time of trouble and ***d***?
50:43 panic-stricken; ***d*** overwhelms him,

Lamentations
1:3 her—right in the middle of her ***d***.
1:21 heard about my ***d***; they were

Ezekiel
35:5 the time of their ***d***, during their

Hosea
5:15 seek me. In their ***d***, they will beg

Joel
1:18 of cattle are in ***d*** because there is

Obadiah
1:13 his possessions on the day of his ***d***.

Jonah
2:2 to the LORD in my ***d***, and he answered

Nahum
1:7 haven in a day of ***d***. He acknowledges
1:9 can annihilate! ***D*** will not arise

Habakkuk
3:16 for the day of ***d*** to come against

Zephaniah
1:15 of fury, a day of ***d*** and anxiety, a

Zechariah
8:10 no relief from ***d*** about going out
10:11 the sea of ***d*** and strike the

Matthew
13:21 they experience ***d*** or abuse because

Mark
4:17 they experience ***d*** or abuse because

John
16:21 remembers her ***d*** because of her
16:33 world you have ***d***. But be

Acts
3:20 relief from the ***d*** of this age and

Romans
2:9 be trouble and ***d*** for every human
8:35 by trouble, or ***d***, or harassment,

Philippians
4:14 you have done well to share my ***d***.

1 Thessalonians
3:7 in all our ***d*** and trouble

1 Timothy
5:10 helping those in ***d***, and dedicating

2 Peter
2:8 them he felt deep ***d*** every day on

DIVIDE

Genesis
49:7 relentless. I'll ***d*** them up within

Exodus
12:4 You should ***d*** the lamb in
15:9 overtake, I'll ***d*** the spoils of
21:35 the live ox and ***d*** its price. They

Numbers
31:27 and ***d*** the valuable property between the
33:54 You will ***d*** up the land by lot according

Deuteronomy
19:3 roads to them and ***d*** the regions of
31:7 the one who will ***d*** up the land for

Joshua
13:7 So now ***d*** up this land as a legacy for
18:5 They will ***d*** up the land among
22:8 much clothing. ***D*** the spoil taken

2 Samuel
19:29 order you and Ziba to ***d*** the property."

Job
27:17 it; the innocent will ***d*** the silver.
41:6 him; will they ***d*** him among traders?

Psalms
60:6 celebrate as I ***d*** up Shechem and
68:12 run! The women back home ***d*** the spoil.
108:7 celebrate as I ***d*** up Shechem and

Proverbs
16:19 the needy than to ***d*** plunder with the
17:2 son and will ***d*** an inheritance

Isaiah
9:3 as those who ***d*** plunder rejoice.
18:2 oppressive, whose land the rivers ***d***.
18:7 land the rivers ***d***, to the place of
53:12 and he will ***d*** the spoil with

Ezekiel
5:1 beard. Then use scales to ***d*** the hair.

Luke
12:13 my brother to ***d*** the inheritance

DIVIDED

Genesis
10:5 were ***d*** into their own
10:25 the earth was ***d***. His brother's
14:15 and his servants ***d*** themselves up
32:7 trapped, so he ***d*** the people with
33:1 men. Jacob ***d*** the children

Leviticus
11:3 animal that has ***d*** hoofs, completely
11:4 food and have ***d*** hoofs you must
11:5 it does not have ***d*** hoofs, so it is
11:6 it does not have ***d*** hoofs, so it is
11:7 it has completely ***d*** hoofs, it does
11:26 animals that have ***d*** hoofs, but they
Numbers
31:42 that Moses ***d*** from those who
Deuteronomy
14:6 any animal with a ***d*** hoof—the hoof bei
14:7 or have hooves ***d*** in two parts that
14:8 —because it has a ***d*** hoof but doesn't
32:8 God Most High ***d*** up the nations—w
Joshua
14:5 The Israelites ***d*** up the land exactly as
18:10 There Joshua ***d*** up the shares of
Judges
7:16 He ***d*** the three hundred men into three units
9:43 he took his men, ***d*** them into three
1 Samuel
30:24 with the supplies will be ***d*** equally."
1 Kings
18:6 To search, they ***d*** the land between
2 Kings
2:8 the water was ***d*** in two! Both of
2:14 hit the water, it ***d*** in two! Then
1 Chronicles
1:19 days the land was ***d***; and his
23:6 Then David ***d*** them into three groups
24:3 Ithamar's family, ***d*** them according to
24:4 family, they ***d*** them so that
24:5 They ***d*** both groups by lots because
2 Chronicles
35:12 Next they ***d*** the entirely burned
Nehemiah
9:11 You ***d*** the sea before them so that they
Job
38:24 where light is ***d*** up; the east wind
Psalms
12:2 talk with slick speech and ***d*** hearts.
Isaiah
33:23 spoil will be ***d***; even the lame
Ezekiel
37:22 will no longer be ***d*** into two kingdoms.
Daniel
2:41 that signifies a ***d*** kingdom; but it
5:28 your kingship is ***d*** and given to the
11:4 will be broken, ***d*** to the four winds
Joel
3:2 among the nations. They have ***d*** my land,
Amos
7:17 be measured and ***d*** up; you yourself
Zechariah
14:1 plundered from you will be ***d*** among you.
Matthew
27:35 him, they ***d*** up his clothes
Mark
3:26 himself and is ***d***, then he can't
6:41 people. He also ***d*** the two fish
15:24 him. They ***d*** up his clothes,
Luke
12:52 of five will be ***d***—three against two
15:12 Then the father ***d*** his estate
John
7:43 So the crowd was ***d*** over Jesus
9:16 signs like these?" So they were ***d***.
19:23 his sandals, and ***d*** them into four
19:24 scripture, They ***d*** my clothes among
Acts
14:4 of the city were ***d***—some siding with
23:7 and Sadducees, and the assembly was ***d***.
1 Corinthians
1:10 and don't be ***d*** into rival
1:13 Has Christ been ***d***? Was Paul crucified
7:34 His attention is ***d***. A woman who isn't
Ephesians
2:14 down the barrier of hatred that ***d*** us.

DIVINE → DIVINE BEINGS, DIVINE IMAGES

Genesis
1:27 own image, in the ***d*** image God created
30:27 discovered by a ***d*** sign that the
31:19 the household's ***d*** images that
48:16 may the ***d*** messenger who protected me
Exodus
31:3 him with the ***d*** spirit, with
35:31 him with the ***d*** spirit that will
Leviticus
26:1 do not set up any ***d*** image or sacred
1 Samuel
19:13 the household's ***d*** image and laid it
2 Samuel
22:32 really, who is ***d*** except the LORD?
24:16 But when the ***d*** messenger stretched out his hand
Ezra
7:25 based on the ***d*** wisdom that you
Job
38:7 in unison and all the ***d*** beings shouted?
Psalms
8:5 less than ***d***, crowning them
18:31 really, who is ***d*** except the LORD?
45:6 Your ***d*** throne is eternal and
50:23 path that I will show ***d*** salvation."
82:1 his stand in the ***d*** council; he gives
103:20 You ***d*** messengers, bless the LORD! You
127:3 the fruit of the womb is a ***d*** reward.
Song of Songs
8:6 Its darts are darts of fire—***d*** flame!
Isaiah
31:3 is human and not ***d***; their horses are
35:4 vengeance; with ***d*** retribution God
Ezekiel
8:3 heaven, and in a ***d*** vision it brought
11:24 a vision with a ***d*** wind. When the
28:2 mind of a god, you are mortal, not ***d***.
28:9 killers' hands, you are mortal, not ***d***.
Hosea
3:4 a priestly vest or household ***d*** images.
Malachi
2:13 there is still no ***d*** favor for your
Acts
6:8 endowment with ***d*** power, was doing
Romans
1:20 eternal power and ***d*** nature—have been
1 Peter
4:6 by the Spirit according to ***d*** standards.
2 Peter
1:3 By his ***d*** power the Lord has given us
1:4 you may share the ***d*** nature and escape

DIVINE BEINGS
Gn 6:2; 6:4; Job 1:6; 2:1; 38:7; 41:25; Ps 29:1

DIVINE IMAGES
Gn 31:19; 31:32, 34, 35; Jdg 17:5; 18:14, 17, 18, 20; 2Sa 5:21; 1Ch 14:12; Eze 21:21; Hos 3:4; Zec 10:2

DIVINERS
Deuteronomy
18:14 sign readers and ***d***, but the LORD
1 Samuel
6:2 priests and the ***d***. "What should we
6:4 The priests and ***d*** replied: "Five
28:3 banned all mediums and ***d*** from the land.
28:9 all mediums and ***d*** from the land.
2 Kings
21:6 used mediums and ***d***. He did much evil
2 Chronicles
33:6 used mediums and ***d***. He did much evil
Isaiah
44:25 the omens of ***d*** and makes a
Jeremiah
27:9 to your prophets, ***d***, dreamers,
29:8 the prophets and ***d*** in your midst
50:36 sword against its ***d*** so that they
Ezekiel
13:9 nothingness and ***d*** of lies. They
Daniel
2:2 enchanters, ***d***, and Chaldeans to
2:27 interpreters, and ***d*** can't explain to
4:7 Chaldeans, and ***d*** came. I told them
5:7 and the ***d***. The king told
5:11 Chaldeans, and ***d***. Yes, your father
Micah
3:7 ashamed, and the ***d*** disgraced; they
5:12 you perform; you will have no more ***d***!
Zechariah
10:2 idolatry, and ***d*** see lies. They

DIVISION
Luke
1:5 to the priestly ***d*** of Abijah. His
1:8 God because his priestly ***d*** was on duty.
12:51 you, I have come instead to bring ***d***.
John
10:19 There was another ***d*** among the Jews
1 Corinthians
12:25 there won't be ***d*** in the body and

DIVORCE
Deuteronomy
22:19 his wife; he is never allowed to ***d*** her.
22:29 her. He is never allowed to ***d*** her.
24:1 So he writes up ***d*** papers, hands
24:3 her, writes up ***d*** papers, hands
Isaiah
50:1 your mother's ***d*** decree, with
Jeremiah
3:8 Israel away with ***d*** papers because of
Malachi
2:16 because he hates ***d***, says the LORD God
Matthew
5:31 wife must give her a ***d*** certificate.'
19:3 allow a man to ***d*** his wife for just
19:7 us to give a ***d*** certificate and
19:8 allowed you to ***d*** your wives
Mark
10:2 the Law allow a man to ***d*** his wife?"
10:4 a man to write a ***d*** certificate and
1 Corinthians
7:11 And a man shouldn't ***d*** his wife.
7:12 live with him, then he shouldn't ***d*** her.
7:13 with her, then she shouldn't ***d*** him.
7:27 don't get a ***d***. If you are

DIVORCED
Leviticus
21:7 marry a woman ***d*** from her husband,
21:14 marry a widow, a ***d*** woman, or a woman
22:13 is a widow or ***d*** and has no
Numbers
30:9 of a widow or a ***d*** woman who makes a
Deuteronomy
24:4 who originally ***d*** this woman is not
1 Chronicles
8:8 of Moab after he ***d*** his wives Hushim
Ezekiel
44:22 marry widows or ***d*** women, but only
Matthew
5:32 whoever marries a ***d*** woman commits
Luke
16:18 marries a woman ***d*** from her husband
1 Corinthians
7:27 If you are ***d***, don't try to

DIVORCES
Jeremiah
3:1 If a man ***d*** his wife, and after she
Matthew
5:31 said, 'Whoever ***d*** his wife must
5:32 you that whoever ***d*** his wife except
19:9 you that whoever ***d*** his wife, except
Mark
10:11 to them, "Whoever ***d*** his wife and
10:12 and if a wife ***d*** her husband and marries
Luke
16:18 Any man who ***d*** his wife and marries

DIVORCES HIS WIFE
Jer 3:1; Mt 5:31; 5:32; 19:9; Mk 10:11; Lk 16:18

DO EVIL
Dt 31:29; 1Sa 12:25; Job 34:10; Ps 14:1; 28:3; 34:16; 50:19; Prv 4:16; 6:14; 10:29; 21:15; Ecc 8:11; Mk 3:4; Lk 6:9; Ro 3:8; Phi 3:2; 1Pt 3:12

DO GOOD
Dt 8:16; 30:5; 2Ch 19:11; Est 10:3; Ps 34:14; 37:3, 27; 51:18; 119:68; 125:4; Ecc 7:20; Is 1:17; 41:23; Jer 13:23; Zep 1:12; Zec 8:15; Mk 3:4; Lk 6:9; 6:27, 33, 35; Ro 7:18; Eph 2:10; 4:28; 1Ti 6:18; Ti 2:14; Heb 10:24; 13:16; 1Pt 3:6; 3:11

DO RIGHT
Nm 23:10; 1Ki 8:59; Ps 33:1; 49:14; 107:42; 111:1; 112:2, 4; 140:13; Prv 11:6; 12:6; 14:9, 11; 15:8, 19; 16:17; 21:8; 28:10; Is 26:10; 64:5; Eze 18:20; Am 3:10; Ro 6:13

DO THE RIGHT THING
Gn 4:7; Job 4:7; 8:6; 17:8; Eze 18:24; 18:26; 23:45; Mi 7:4; Hab 2:4; 2Co 13:7; Phm 1:8; Heb 13:18

DO WRONG
Ex 23:2; 23:21; 1Sa 17:29; Ps 37:1; Prv 28:21; Is 26:10; 31:2; Eze 33:13; 33:18; Mt 7:23; Ro 6:13; Rev 22:11

DOGS
Exodus
22:31 the field. Throw it to the ***d*** instead.
1 Kings
14:11 ***D*** will eat any of Jeroboam's family who die in town
16:4 ***D*** will eat any of Baasha's family who
21:19 place where the ***d*** licked up
21:23 LORD says this: ***D*** will devour
21:24 ***D*** will eat anyone of Ahab's family who
22:38 of Samaria. The ***d*** licked up the
2 Kings
9:10 for Jezebel: The ***d*** will devour her
9:36 from Tishbe: ***D*** will devour
Psalms
22:16 ***D*** surround me; a pack of evil people
59:6 growling like ***d***, prowling around
59:14 growling like ***d***, prowling around
Isaiah
56:10 They are all mute ***d*** that can't bark,
56:11 But the ***d*** have monstrous appetites.
Jeremiah
9:11 a den for wild ***d***. I will make the
10:22 of Judah to ruins, a den for wild ***d***.
14:6 like thirsty ***d***; they go blind
15:3 soldiers to kill, ***d*** to drag off, and
49:33 a den for wild ***d***, a wilderness
51:37 a den of wild ***d***, a wasteland with
Matthew
7:6 holy things to ***d***, and don't throw
15:26 the children's bread and toss it to ***d***."
15:27 But even the ***d*** eat the crumbs
Mark
7:27 children's bread and toss it to the ***d***."
7:28 Lord, even the ***d*** under the table
Luke
16:21 table. Instead, ***d*** would come and
Philippians
3:2 out for the "***d***." Watch out for
Revelation
22:15 Outside are the ***d***, the drug users and

DOING EVIL
1Ki 16:19; 21:20, 25; Neh 9:28; Prv 2:14; Jer 1:16; 13:23; Mi 7:3; Mal 2:17; 3:15; 4:1; 1Pt 2:12; 2:14; 3:17

DOING GOOD
Dt 28:63; 30:9; Ps 36:3; Ac 10:38; Ga 6:9; 1Ti 2:10; 5:10; Ti 3:8; 3:14; 1Pt 2:14; 2:15; 3:17

DOING WHAT IS RIGHT
Dt 13:18; 1Ki 11:33; 2Ki 10:30; Dn 4:27; 2Th 3:13; 1Pt 4:19; Rev 22:11

DOING WRONG
Jer 4:22; 9:5; Ro 13:3; 1Co 6:8; 2Pt 2:15

DONKEY
Genesis
22:3 harnessed his ***d***, and took two of
Joshua
15:18 got down off her ***d***, Caleb asked her,
1 Samuel
12:3 taken someone's ***d***? Have I ever
2 Samuel
17:23 he saddled his ***d*** and went home to
19:26 Saddle a ***d*** for me so I can
2 Kings
4:24 She saddled the ***d***, then said to her
Job
6:5 Does a ***d*** bray over grass or an ox
24:3 off an orphan's ***d***, take a widow's
39:5 freed the wild ***d***, loosed the ropes
Proverbs
26:3 a bridle for a ***d***, and a rod for
Isaiah
1:3 its owner, and a ***d*** its master's
21:7 of horsemen, ***d*** riders, camel
32:20 happy, sending out ox and ***d*** to graze.
Jeremiah
2:24 a wild ***d*** in the wilderness, lustfully
Zechariah
9:9 ass, on a colt, the offspring of a ***d***.
Matthew
21:2 you will find a ***d*** tied up and a
21:5 and riding on a ***d***, and on a colt
21:7 They brought the ***d*** and the colt and
Luke
10:34 man on his own ***d***, took him to an
13:15 untie your ox or ***d*** from its stall
John
12:14 found a young ***d*** and sat on it,
2 Peter
2:16 his wrongdoing. A ***d***, which has no

DOOM
Job
10:15 If I were guilty, ***d*** to me; I'm
21:20 witness their ***d***. Let them drink
Psalms
81:15 me, and their ***d*** would last
Isaiah
1:4 ***D***! Sinful nation, people weighed down
3:9 sins in public. ***D*** to them, for they
5:8 ***D*** to those who acquire house after
8:22 and the anguish and ***d*** of banishment.
10:1 ***D*** to those who pronounce wicked
17:12 ***D*** to the raging of many peoples; like
18:1 ***D*** to the land of winged ships, beyond
29:15 ***D*** to those who hide their plan deep,
30:1 ***D*** to you, rebellious children, says the
31:1 ***D*** to those going down to Egypt for
33:1 ***D*** to the destroyer left undestroyed,
45:7 and create ***d***; I am the LORD,
45:9 ***D*** to the one who argues with the
45:10 ***D*** to one who says to a father, "What
Jeremiah
8:14 and meet our ***d*** there. The LORD
Ezekiel
13:3 God proclaims: ***D*** to the foolish
Daniel
8:19 the time of ***d*** that is coming,
11:36 succeed until the ***d*** is completed,

DOOM [cont.]

Hosea
7:13 ***D*** to them, for they have strayed from
9:12 no one is left. ***D*** to them indeed
Amos
5:7 ***D*** to you who turn justice into poison,
5:18 ***D*** to those who desire the day of the
6:1 ***D*** to those resting comfortably in Zion
6:3 ***D*** to those who ignore the evil day and
Micah
2:1 ***D*** to those who devise wickedness, to
Nahum
3:1 ***D***, city of bloodshed—all deceit, full
Habakkuk
2:6 They will say: ***D*** to the one who
2:9 ***D*** to the one making evil gain for his
2:15 ***D*** to the one who makes his companions
2:19 ***D*** to the one saying to the tree, "Wake
Zephaniah
2:5 ***D***, inhabitants of the seacoast, nation
3:1 ***D***, obstinate one, the defiled one, the
Zechariah
11:17 ***D***, foolish shepherd who forsakes the

DOOR

Exodus
12:7 the beam over the ***d*** of the houses in
21:6 bring him to the ***d*** or the doorpost.
1 Kings
6:8 The ***d*** to the stairs was at the south
6:33 He made the ***d*** of the main hall with
Nehemiah
3:20 the Angle to the ***d*** of the house of
3:21 section from the ***d*** to the back of
Psalms
141:3 close watch over the ***d*** that is my lips.
Proverbs
26:14 As a ***d*** turns on its hinge, so do lazy
Matthew
7:7 Knock, and the ***d*** will be opened to
24:33 that the Human One is near, at the ***d***.
27:60 stone at the ***d*** of the tomb, he
Acts
5:9 are at the ***d***. They will carry
18:7 and went next ***d*** to the home of
Colossians
4:3 God would open a ***d*** for the word so
James
5:9 Look! The judge is standing at the ***d***!
Revelation
3:8 of you an open ***d*** that no one can
3:20 standing at the ***d*** and knocking. If
4:1 and there was a ***d*** that had been

DOORS

John
20:19 behind closed ***d*** because they were
20:26 Even though the ***d*** were locked,
Acts
5:19 opened the prison ***d*** during the night
5:23 standing at the ***d***, but when we
16:26 foundations. The ***d*** flew open and
16:27 and saw the open ***d*** of the prison, he

DOVE

Genesis
8:8 he sent out a ***d*** to see if the
8:9 but the ***d*** found no place to set its
8:10 days and sent the ***d*** out from the ark
8:11 The ***d*** came back to him in the evening,
8:12 and sent out the ***d***, but it didn't
15:9 ram, a ***d***, and a young
Psalms
55:6 had wings like a ***d***! I'd fly away and
56:1 Silent ***D*** of Distant
68:13 are wings of a ***d*** covered with
74:19 the life of your ***d*** to wild animals!
Song of Songs
2:14 My ***d***—in the rock crevices, hidden in
5:2 my dearest, my ***d***, my perfect one!
6:9 but my ***d***, my perfect one, is one of a
Isaiah
38:14 I moan like a ***d***. My eyes have
Jeremiah
8:7 seasons, and the ***d***, swallow, and
48:28 Moab. Hide like a ***d*** that nests in the
Hosea
7:11 has become like a ***d***, silly and
11:11 bird, and like a ***d*** from the land of
Matthew
3:16 down like a ***d*** and resting on
Mark
1:10 Spirit, like a ***d***, coming down on
Luke
3:22 form like a ***d***. And there was a
John
1:32 heaven like a ***d***, and it rested on
2:16 He said to the ***d*** sellers, "Get these

DOWN FROM HEAVEN

2Ch 7:1; Ps 14:2; 33:13; 53:2; 80:14; 85:11; Is 63:15; Dn 4:13; 4:23; Mt 28:2; Lk 9:54; 17:29; Jn 1:32; 3:13; 6:33, 38, 41, 42, 50, 51, 58; 1Th 4:16; Rev 10:1; 13:13; 16:21; 18:1; 20:1, 9

DOWN TO EGYPT

Gn 26:2; 37:25; 39:1; 43:15; 46:3, 4; Nm 20:15; Dt 10:22; 26:5; Josh 24:4; Is 30:2; 31:1; Ac 7:15

DRAW

Genesis
24:11 when women come out to ***d*** water.
Psalms
37:14 The wicked ***d*** their swords and bend
Proverbs
20:5 those with understanding can ***d*** it out.
Isaiah
12:3 You will ***d*** water with joy from the
34:1 ***D*** near, you nations, to hear; and
Jeremiah
30:21 me, and he will ***d*** near. Who would
50:29 Babylon, all who ***d*** the bow! Surround
51:3 Let the archers ***d*** their bows; let them
Ezekiel
4:1 front of you and ***d*** the city of
Joel
3:9 all the soldiers ***d*** near, let them
Amos
6:3 evil day and make violent rule ***d*** near:
Nahum
3:14 ***D*** water for yourself to prepare for
Zephaniah
3:2 LORD, nor did she ***d*** near to her God.

Zechariah
1:4 listen; they didn't ***d*** near to me.
Malachi
3:5 I will ***d*** near to you for judgment. I
John
2:8 told them, "Now ***d*** some from them
4:7 to the well to ***d*** water. Jesus said
12:32 the earth, I will ***d*** everyone to me."
2 Timothy
2:1 So, my child, ***d*** your strength from the
Hebrews
4:16 Finally, let's ***d*** near to the throne of
7:19 through which we ***d*** near to God.
10:1 who are trying to ***d*** near to God

DREAD

Genesis
9:2 will fear you and ***d*** you—all the birds
Exodus
1:12 at the Israelites with disgust and ***d***.
Deuteronomy
7:21 Don't ***d*** these nations because the LORD
Esther
7:8 before covering Haman's face with ***d***.
Job
4:14 fear and ***d*** struck me; all of my bones
13:11 scare you and ***d*** of him fall on
21:9 houses safe from ***d***, God's punishing
22:10 you; sudden ***d*** brings panic to
41:25 The divine beings ***d*** his rising; they
Psalms
105:38 left because the ***d*** of Israel had
119:39 insults that I ***d*** because your
Proverbs
1:26 make fun of you when ***d*** comes over you,
1:33 securely, untroubled by the ***d*** of harm."
10:24 What the wicked ***d*** will come on them,
Isaiah
7:16 the two kings you ***d*** will be abandoned.
19:17 the Egyptians ***d***; whenever anyone
21:4 turned my evening of pleasure into ***d***—
57:11 Whom did you ***d*** and fear so that you
Jeremiah
22:25 you, those you ***d***, even Babylon's
23:4 be afraid or ***d*** harm, nor will
39:17 won't be handed over to those you ***d***.
42:16 the famine you ***d*** will hunt you
Micah
7:17 LORD our God; they will ***d*** and fear you!
Mark
16:8 with terror and ***d***, they fled from
Acts
5:11 Trepidation and ***d*** seized the whole

DREAM

Genesis
20:3 that night in a ***d*** and said to him,
20:6 to him in the ***d***, "I know that
31:10 up and saw in a ***d*** that the male
31:11 In the ***d***, God's messenger said to me,
31:24 the Aramean in a ***d*** and said, "Be
37:5 Joseph had a ***d*** and told it to his
37:6 said to them, "Listen to this ***d*** I had.
37:9 had another ***d*** and described it
40:5 and each man's ***d*** had its own
40:9 described his ***d*** to Joseph: "In my
40:16 for me. In my ***d***, there were three
41:5 and had a second ***d***, in which seven
41:7 woke up and realized it was a ***d***.
41:12 giving us an interpretation for each ***d***.
41:15 Joseph, "I had a ***d***, but no one could
41:17 to Joseph, "In my ***d*** I was standing on
41:22 and saw in my ***d*** seven full and
41:25 actually had one ***d***. God has
41:26 are seven years. It's actually one ***d***.
41:32 The ***d*** occurred to Pharaoh twice because
Deuteronomy
13:1 if a prophet or a ***d*** interpreter
13:3 that prophet's or ***d*** interpreter's
13:5 That prophet or ***d*** interpreter must be
Judges
7:13 friend about a ***d***. He said, "Get
7:15 telling of the ***d*** and its meaning,
1 Kings
3:5 at Gibeon in a ***d*** at night. God
3:15 realized it was a ***d***. He went to
Job
20:8 disappear like a ***d***, and none will
33:15 In the ***d***, a vision of the night, when
Psalms
73:20 As quickly as a ***d*** departs from someone
90:5 away like a ***d***, like grass that
Isaiah
29:7 will be like a ***d***, a vision of the
Jeremiah
23:25 I've had a ***d***; I've had a
23:28 prophet who has a ***d*** declare it, but
23:32 the prophets who ***d*** up lies and then
Daniel
1:17 of every type of vision and ***d***.
1:20 above all the ***d*** interpreters and
2:2 king summoned the ***d*** interpreters,
2:3 to them: "I had a ***d***, and I'm anxious
2:4 your servants the ***d***, and we will
2:5 can't tell me the ***d*** and its meaning,
2:6 do explain the ***d*** and its meaning,
2:7 his servants the ***d***. We will then
2:9 can't tell me the ***d***, your fate is
2:10 a thing of any ***d*** interpreter,
2:11 could declare the ***d*** to the king but
2:26 tell me the ***d*** that I saw, as
2:27 enchanters, ***d*** interpreters, and
2:28 Now this was your ***d***—this was the visi
2:36 This was the ***d***. Now we will tell the
2:45 the future. The ***d*** is certain. Its
4:5 had a terrifying ***d***. My thoughts
4:7 So the ***d*** interpreters, enchanters,
4:8 of the holy gods! I told Daniel the ***d***:
4:9 chief of the ***d*** interpreters, I
4:18 This is the ***d*** that I, King
4:19 Don't let the ***d*** and its meaning
5:11 as chief over the ***d*** interpreters,
5:15 the sages and the ***d*** interpreters were
7:1 Daniel had a ***d***—a vision in his
Joel
2:28 your old men will ***d*** dreams, and your
Matthew
1:20 to him in a ***d*** and said, "Joseph
2:12 were warned in a ***d*** not to return to
2:13 to Joseph in a ***d*** and said, "Get
2:19 appeared in a ***d*** to Joseph in
2:22 been warned in a ***d***, he went to the
27:19 much today in a ***d*** because of him."

Acts
2:17 see visions. Your elders will ***d*** dreams.

DREAMS

Genesis
37:8 more because of the ***d*** he told them.
37:10 What kind of ***d*** have you dreamed?
37:20 we will see what becomes of his ***d***!"
40:5 in the jail—had ***d*** one night, and
40:8 We've both had ***d***, but there's no
40:22 when he interpreted their ***d*** for them.
41:8 described his ***d*** to them, but they
41:11 and each of our ***d*** had its own
41:12 We described our ***d*** to him, and he
42:9 remembered the ***d*** he had dreamed
Numbers
12:6 to him in visions. I speak to him in ***d***.
1 Samuel
28:6 him—not by ***d***, not by the Urim,
28:15 by prophets or by ***d***. So I have called
Job
7:14 You scare me with ***d***, frighten me with
Ecclesiastes
5:3 Remember: ***D*** come with many cares, and the voice of fools
5:7 Remember: When ***d*** multiply, so do
Isaiah
29:8 a hungry person ***d*** of eating but
Jeremiah
23:27 me by their ***d*** that people tell
29:8 you. Don't pay attention to your ***d***.
Daniel
2:1 rule, he had many ***d***. The dreams made
2:2 to explain his ***d*** to him. They came
5:12 the meaning of ***d***. He can explain
Joel
2:28 men will dream ***d***, and your young
Zechariah
10:2 They interpret ***d*** falsely and
Acts
2:17 see visions. Your elders will dream ***d***.

DRESS

Exodus
40:13 ***D*** Aaron in the holy clothes. Anoint him
40:14 bring his sons and ***d*** them in tunics.
Leviticus
6:10 The priest will ***d*** in his linen robe,
6:11 off his clothes, ***d*** in a different
16:4 Aaron must ***d*** in a holy linen tunic and
16:24 a holy place and ***d*** in his priestly
21:10 is ordained to ***d*** in the priestly
1 Samuel
2:4 stumbling now ***d*** themselves in
2 Samuel
14:2 be in mourning. ***D*** in mourning
1 Kings
10:5 the function and ***d*** of his
2 Chronicles
9:4 the function and ***d*** of his
Psalms
76:10 praise when you ***d*** yourself with
132:16 I will ***d*** its priests in salvation, and
132:18 I will ***d*** his enemies in shame, but the
Jeremiah
2:32 bride her wedding ***d***? Yet you have
4:30 one, why ***d*** up in scarlet,
Joel
1:13 ***D*** for a funeral and grieve, you
Luke
7:25 Look, those who ***d*** in fashionable
12:37 arrives, he will ***d*** himself to serve,
Romans
13:14 Instead, ***d*** yourself with the Lord Jesus
2 Corinthians
5:2 We really want to ***d*** ourselves with

DRESSED

Genesis
3:21 his wife leather clothes and ***d*** them.
41:42 Joseph's hand, he ***d*** him in linen
Exodus
12:11 it. You should be ***d***, with your
Leviticus
8:7 around him, and ***d*** him in the robe.
8:13 sons forward, ***d*** them in tunics,
1 Samuel
17:38 Then Saul ***d*** David in his own gear,
2 Samuel
1:24 over Saul! He ***d*** you in crimson
6:14 David, ***d*** in a linen priestly vest,
20:8 them. Joab was ***d*** in his soldier's
1 Kings
22:10 on their thrones, ***d*** in their royal
1 Chronicles
21:16 and the elders, ***d*** in mourning
2 Chronicles
5:12 relatives—were ***d*** in fine linen and
18:9 on their thrones ***d*** in their royal
28:15 the captives and ***d*** everyone who was
Ezra
5:8 being built with ***d*** stone and with
6:4 three layers of ***d*** stones and one
Esther
4:1 tore his clothes, ***d*** in mourning
Psalms
30:11 my funeral clothes and ***d*** me up in joy
35:26 over me be ***d*** up in shame and
45:9 at your right, ***d*** in the gold of
45:13 royal princess, ***d*** in pearls, her
65:6 your strength; you are ***d*** in raw power;
65:12 it, and the hills are ***d*** in pure joy.
71:13 my downfall be ***d*** in insults and
109:29 my accusers be ***d*** in shame; let
132:9 your priests be ***d*** in righteousness;
Proverbs
7:10 approaches him, ***d*** like a prostitute
31:21 because they are all ***d*** in warm clothes.
Isaiah
63:1 this splendidly ***d*** one, striding
Ezekiel
9:2 man who was ***d*** in linen and had
9:3 the man who was ***d*** in linen with the
9:11 the man who was ***d*** in linen with the
23:6 warriors ***d*** in fine blue cloth,
38:4 handsomely ***d***, all of them, a
Daniel
3:21 were bound, still ***d*** in all their
5:29 that Daniel be ***d*** in a purple robe,
Hosea
2:13 to them and ***d*** herself up with
Joel
1:8 like a woman ***d*** in funeral

Nahum
2:3 his soldiers are ***d*** in crimson. The
Zechariah
3:5 head, and they ***d*** him in garments
Matthew
6:29 splendor wasn't ***d*** like one of these.
7:15 They come to you ***d*** like sheep, but
11:8 out to see? A man ***d*** up in refined
Mark
5:15 there fully ***d*** and completely
15:17 They ***d*** him up in a purple robe and
Luke
7:25 out to see? A man ***d*** up in refined
8:35 feet, fully ***d*** and completely
12:27 splendor wasn't ***d*** like one of these.
12:35 Be ***d*** for service and keep your lamps
John
19:2 on his head, and ***d*** him in a purple
20:12 saw two angels ***d*** in white, seated
Acts
12:8 continued, "Get ***d***. Put on your
12:21 day Herod ***d*** himself in royal
2 Corinthians
5:4 We want to be ***d*** not undressed, so
James
2:2 the other is poor, ***d*** in filthy rags.
Revelation
4:4 The elders were ***d*** in white clothing
21:2 a bride beautifully ***d*** for her husband.

DRIED

Genesis
8:7 waters over the entire earth had ***d*** up.
8:13 month, the waters ***d*** up from the
47:13 land of Canaan ***d*** up from the
Numbers
6:3 or eat grapes, whether fresh or ***d***.
Joshua
2:10 how the LORD ***d*** up the water of
4:23 the LORD your God ***d*** up the water of
5:1 that the LORD had ***d*** up the water of
9:12 But now here it is, ***d*** up and crumbly.
Judges
16:7 that aren't ***d*** out, I'll become
16:8 that weren't ***d*** out, and she tied
1 Kings
17:7 a while the brook ***d*** up because there
2 Kings
19:24 my own feet, I ***d*** up all of Egypt's
Psalms
22:15 My strength is ***d*** up like a piece of
90:6 but come evening it withers, all ***d*** up.
102:4 is smashed like ***d***-up grass. I even
102:11 soon gone. I'm ***d*** up like dead
106:9 Reed Sea, and it ***d*** right up; he led
119:83 like a bottle ***d*** up by smoke,
Isaiah
5:13 so many of them are ***d*** up with thirst.
37:25 my own feet, I ***d*** up all of Egypt's
Jeremiah
9:10 They are ***d*** up and deserted;
48:34 Even the waters of Nimrim are ***d*** up.
Ezekiel
19:12 The east wind ***d*** her out and
31:15 sea against it. I ***d*** up its rivers and
37:11 Our bones are ***d*** up, and our hope
Hosea
9:14 miscarries and breasts that are ***d*** up.
9:16 their root is ***d*** up, they will
13:15 fountain will be ***d*** up. It will strip
Joel
1:12 The grapevine is ***d*** up; the fig tree
1:17 are in ruin because the grain has ***d*** up.
1:20 the streams have ***d*** up; the fire has
2:20 drive it into a ***d***-up and desolate la
Amos
4:7 on, and the field ***d*** up where it
Nahum
1:10 like stubble that is entirely ***d*** up.
Zechariah
9:5 her hope has ***d*** up. The king will
Matthew
13:6 plants, and they ***d*** up because they
21:19 bear fruit!" The fig tree ***d*** up at once.
Mark
4:6 plants; and they ***d*** up because they
11:21 how the fig tree you cursed has ***d*** up."
Luke
8:6 As it grew, it ***d*** up because it had
Revelation
16:12 Its water was ***d*** up so that the

DRINK → DRINK OFFERING, DRINK OFFERINGS

Genesis
24:45 her, 'Please give me something to ***d***.'
Ruth
2:9 to the jugs and ***d*** from what the
Isaiah
22:13 of wine: "Eat and ***d***! Tomorrow we will die
56:12 some wine! Let's ***d*** beer! Tomorrow
Jeremiah
22:15 father eat and ***d*** and still do what
Daniel
1:10 are to eat and ***d***. What will happen
Matthew
27:34 with vinegar to ***d***. But after
27:48 on a pole. He offered it to Jesus to ***d***.
Luke
1:15 eyes. He must not ***d*** wine and liquor.
22:18 now on I won't ***d*** from the fruit of
John
4:7 said to her, "Give me some water to ***d***."
6:53 the Human One and ***d*** his blood, you
18:11 away! Am I not to ***d*** the cup the
Acts
23:12 wouldn't eat or ***d*** until they had
23:21 not to eat or ***d*** until they have
Romans
12:20 give him a ***d***. By doing this,
14:21 to eat meat or ***d*** wine or to do
1 Corinthians
3:2 gave you milk to ***d*** instead of solid
10:21 You can't ***d*** the cup of the Lord and the
Revelation
14:8 all the nations ***d*** the wine of her
14:10 will also ***d*** the wine of God's
16:6 them blood to ***d***. They deserve it!"

DRINK OFFERING

Ex 29:40; 29:41; 30:9; Lv 23:13; Nm 4:7; 6:15, 17; 15:5, 7, 10, 24; 28:7, 8, 9, 10, 15,

DRINK OFFERING [cont.]

24; 29:16, 22, 25, 28, 33, 34, 38; 2Ki 16:13; Is 57:6; Jl 1:9; 1:13; 2:14; Phi 2:17

DRINK OFFERINGS

Ex 25:29; 37:16; Lv 23:18; 23:37; Nm 28:14; 28:31; 29:6, 11, 18, 19, 21, 24, 27, 30, 31, 37, 39; 2Ki 16:15; 1Ch 29:21; 2Ch 29:35; Ezr 7:17; Jer 7:18; 19:13; 32:29; 44:17, 18, 19, 25; Eze 20:28; 45:17

DRINKING

Genesis
24:22 had finished ***d***, the man took out
Exodus
7:24 had to dig for ***d*** water along the
Deuteronomy
11:11 where your ***d*** water will be
Judges
19:4 days, eating, ***d***, and spending the
Ruth
3:3 man until he has finished eating and ***d***.
1 Samuel
1:9 after eating and ***d*** in Shiloh, Hannah
30:16 eating, ***d***, and celebrating
1 Kings
1:25 are eating and ***d*** with him, and
10:21 of King Solomon's ***d*** cups were made of
20:12 other kings were ***d*** in their tents.
1 Chronicles
12:39 days, eating and ***d***, while their
2 Chronicles
9:20 King Solomon's ***d*** cups were made of
Job
1:13 were eating and ***d*** wine in their
1:18 were eating and ***d*** wine in their
Proverbs
26:6 off one's feet or ***d*** down violence.
Isaiah
21:5 cloth, eating, ***d***. "Arise,
22:13 of meat and ***d*** of wine: "Eat and
29:8 person dreams of ***d*** but wakes up and
Ezekiel
4:11 water by measure, ***d*** a sixth of a hin
34:18 good pasture or ***d*** clear water such
Hosea
4:18 they have stopped ***d***, they continue to
Jonah
3:7 anything! No grazing and no ***d*** water!
Zechariah
7:6 weren't you the ones eating and ***d***?
10:7 as if they were ***d*** wine. Their
Matthew
11:18 eating nor ***d***, and they say,
11:19 came eating and ***d***, and they say,
24:38 were eating and ***d***, marrying and
Luke
5:33 disciples are always eating and ***d***."
7:33 eating bread nor ***d*** wine, and you
7:34 came eating and ***d***, and you say,
10:7 house, eating and ***d*** whatever they set
17:27 were eating, ***d***, marrying, and
17:28 were eating, ***d***, buying, selling,
21:34 aren't dulled by ***d*** parties,
John
2:10 the guests are ***d*** freely. You kept
Romans
14:17 eating food and ***d*** but about
1 Corinthians
11:29 are eating and ***d*** their own
Colossians
2:16 about eating or ***d*** or about a
Titus
2:3 being gossips or addicted to heavy ***d***.

DRINKS

Genesis
44:5 the cup my master ***d*** from and uses to
Numbers
23:24 eats the prey and ***d*** the blood of the
Esther
1:7 They served the ***d*** in cups made of gold,
1:8 rule about the ***d*** was "No limits!"
5:12 king for food and ***d*** that she has
Job
6:4 in me; my spirit ***d*** their poison, and
34:7 a man like Job? He ***d*** mockery like water
Psalms
102:9 bread. I've been mixing tears into my ***d***
110:7 God ***d*** from a stream along the way, then
Isaiah
5:22 warriors, mighty at mixing ***d***,
24:9 No one ***d*** wine or sings; beer is bitter
Jeremiah
51:39 feast and mix the ***d***! But after their
Amos
4:1 husbands, "Bring ***d***, so we can get
Luke
5:39 No one who ***d*** a well-aged wine wants new wine
John
4:13 Everyone who ***d*** this water will
4:14 but whoever ***d*** from the water that I
6:54 eats my flesh and ***d*** my blood has
6:56 eats my flesh and ***d*** my blood remains
Hebrews
6:7 from God when it ***d*** up the rain that

DRIVE

Exodus
6:1 go that he'll ***d*** them out of his
23:30 I'll ***d*** them out before you little by
Numbers
33:52 you will ***d*** out all the inhabitants of
Judges
1:19 they didn't ***d*** out those who
James
3:4 are needed to ***d*** them. But pilots

DRIVEN

Genesis
4:14 Now that you've ***d*** me away from the
Exodus
12:39 because they were ***d*** out of Egypt and
Joshua
24:18 The LORD has ***d*** out all the nations
Psalms
68:2 Like smoke is ***d*** away, drive them away!
109:10 begging, ***d*** out of their
Daniel
4:25 You will be ***d*** away from other humans
John
6:19 When the wind had ***d*** them out for about three or four

Acts
28:3 poisonous snake, ***d*** out by the heat,
2 Timothy
3:6 with sins and ***d*** by all kinds of
2 Peter
2:17 water, mists ***d*** by the wind. The

DRUNK

Genesis
9:21 the wine, became ***d***, and took off his
Deuteronomy
29:6 eaten bread nor ***d*** wine or beer
1 Samuel
1:13 was silent, so Eli thought she was ***d***.
1:14 you act like a ***d***? Sober up!" Eli
25:36 mood and very ***d***, so Abigail
30:12 eaten any food or ***d*** any water for
2 Samuel
11:13 and David got him ***d***. In the evening
1 Kings
16:9 Tirzah, getting ***d*** at the house of
20:16 with him were getting ***d*** in their tents.
2 Kings
19:24 dug wells, have ***d*** waters in foreign
Psalms
107:27 like they were ***d***. None of their
Proverbs
5:19 all the time; always be ***d*** on her love.
23:20 those who get ***d*** on wine or those
26:9 in the hand of a ***d***, so is a proverb
Song of Songs
5:1 my honey; I have ***d*** my wine and my
Isaiah
19:14 does, just as a ***d*** stumbles in his
24:20 trembles like a ***d*** and shudders like
29:9 be blind! Be ***d***, but not on wine;
34:5 When my sword has ***d*** its fill in the
37:25 dug wells, have ***d*** water in foreign
49:26 they will be ***d***, so that all
51:21 one, who is ***d***, but not from
63:6 and made them ***d*** on my wrath; I
Jeremiah
13:13 that makes them ***d***, including the
23:9 I stagger like a ***d*** who has had too
25:27 of wine and get ***d***. Vomit and
35:14 day they have not ***d*** wine, obeying
48:26 Get Moab ***d***, because it has exalted
51:7 the whole earth ***d***. The nations
51:57 leaders and sages ***d***, her governors,
Lamentations
4:21 too. You will get ***d*** on it. You will
Ezekiel
39:19 fat, and get ***d*** on their blood,
Amos
4:1 Bring drinks, so we can get ***d***!"
Obadiah
1:16 Just as you have ***d*** on my holy mountain,
Nahum
3:11 you will become ***d***; you will have to
Habakkuk
2:15 his companions ***d***, pouring out your
2:16 You have ***d*** your fill of dishonor rather
Haggai
1:6 not enough to get ***d***. There is
Matthew
11:19 a glutton and a ***d***, a friend of tax
Luke
7:34 a glutton and a ***d***, a friend of tax
12:45 women, and to eat, drink, and get ***d***.
Acts
2:15 people aren't ***d***, as you suspect;
Romans
13:13 and getting ***d***, not in sleeping
1 Corinthians
5:11 abusive person, a ***d***, or a swindler.
11:21 person goes hungry while another is ***d***.
Ephesians
5:18 Don't get ***d*** on wine, which produces
1 Thessalonians
5:7 people who get ***d*** get drunk at
Revelation
17:2 earth have become ***d*** with the wine of
17:6 the woman was ***d*** on the blood of

DRY

Genesis
1:9 place so that the ***d*** land can appear."
1:10 God named the ***d*** land Earth, and he
Exodus
4:9 pour it out on ***d*** ground. The water
14:16 can go into the sea on ***d*** ground.
14:29 walked on ***d*** ground through
Jonah
1:9 made the sea and the ***d*** land."
2:10 and it vomited Jonah onto the ***d*** land.
John
12:3 wiped his feet ***d*** with her hair.

DUST

Genesis
3:14 will crawl, and ***d*** you will eat
13:16 like the ***d*** of the earth. If
28:14 become like the ***d*** of the earth; you
Numbers
5:17 jar, and taking ***d*** from the floor of
23:10 Who can count the ***d*** of Jacob, or number
Deuteronomy
9:21 it was as fine as ***d***. Then I dumped
28:24 on your land into ***d***. Only dirt will
32:24 after them, venom from ***d*** crawlers too.
Joshua
7:6 evening. They put ***d*** on their heads.
1 Samuel
2:8 the poor from the ***d***, lifts up the
2 Samuel
22:43 crushed them like ***d*** on the ground; I
1 Kings
16:2 you up from the ***d*** and made you a
18:38 stones, and the ***d***. It even licked
20:10 even a handful of ***d*** left in Samaria
2 Kings
23:6 it, ground it to ***d***, and threw the
23:12 and threw their ***d*** into the Kidron
23:15 grinding it into ***d***. Then he burned
2 Chronicles
1:9 a people as numerous as the earth's ***d***.
34:4 grinding them to ***d*** and scattering
34:7 the idols to ***d***, and smashed all
Job
2:12 and scattered ***d*** above his head
4:19 are in ***d***, and who are
5:6 doesn't come from ***d***, nor does

7:21 lie down in the ***d***; you would search
8:19 joy, for from the ***d*** other plants
10:9 from clay, and you will return me to ***d***.
14:8 the ground and its stump dies in the ***d***,
16:15 my skin and buried my dignity in the ***d***.
17:16 will we descend together to the ***d***?
19:25 and afterward he'll rise upon the ***d***.
20:11 and now sleeps with them in the ***d***.
21:26 together in the ***d*** and worms cover
22:24 possession in the ***d***, your gold from
27:16 up silver like ***d***, amass clothing
28:6 lapis lazuli; there is gold ***d*** in it.
30:19 mud; I'm a cliché, like ***d*** and ashes.
34:15 together, and humans would return to ***d***.
38:38 so that ***d*** becomes mud and clods of dirt
39:14 on the earth, lets them warm in the ***d***,
40:13 together in the ***d***; bind their faces
42:6 relent and find comfort on ***d*** and ashes.

Psalms
1:4 They are like ***d*** that the wind
18:42 crushed them like ***d*** blown away by the
22:29 descending to the ***d*** will kneel before
30:9 the pit? Does ***d*** thank you? Does
35:5 Let them be like ***d*** on the wind—and
44:25 going down to the ***d***; our stomachs are
72:9 before him; let his enemies lick the ***d***.
78:27 as if it were ***d*** in the air; he
90:3 return people to ***d***, saying, "Go
103:14 we're made, God remembers we're just ***d***.
104:29 their breath, they die and return to ***d***.

Ecclesiastes
3:20 all are from the ***d***; all return to
12:7 before ***d*** returns to the earth as it was

Isaiah
2:10 yourself in the ***d*** from the terror
2:19 and holes in the ***d*** before the terror
5:24 blossoms turn to ***d***, for they have
25:12 be brought down to the earth, to the ***d***.
26:5 the earth; he will bring it down to ***d***.
26:19 who dwell in the ***d*** will shout for
29:4 from low in the ***d*** your speech will
29:5 will be like fine ***d***, the terrible
34:9 into pitch, its ***d*** into sulfur, and
40:12 the earth's ***d*** up in a measuring
40:15 and valued as ***d*** on a scale. Look,
41:2 making them like ***d*** with his sword,
47:1 and sit in the ***d***, virgin Daughter
49:23 will lick the ***d*** from your feet.
52:2 Shake the ***d*** off yourself; rise up; sit
65:25 —its food will be ***d***. They won't hurt

Jeremiah
25:34 out. Roll in the ***d***, you masters of
48:18 and sit in the ***d***, you inhabitants

Lamentations
2:10 mourn. They throw ***d*** on their heads;

Ezekiel
26:10 The ***d*** from all his horses will cover
27:30 and they put ***d*** on their heads
28:18 turn you into ***d*** on the earth in

Amos
2:7 the poor into the ***d*** of the earth, and

Micah
1:10 Beth-le-aphrah, roll yourself in the ***d***!
7:17 They will lick ***d*** like the snake, like

Nahum
1:3 storm; clouds are the ***d*** of his feet.

Zephaniah
1:17 poured out like ***d*** and their

Zechariah
9:3 up silver like ***d*** and gold like mud

Malachi
4:3 they will be like ***d*** beneath the soles

Matthew
10:14 words, shake the ***d*** off your feet as

Mark
6:11 leave, shake the ***d*** off your feet as

Luke
9:5 city, shake the ***d*** off your feet as
10:11 we brush off the ***d*** of your city that

Acts
13:51 shook the ***d*** from their feet
18:6 him, he shook the ***d*** from his clothes
22:23 garments, and flinging ***d*** into the air,

1 Corinthians
15:47 earth made from ***d***; the second human is from heaven
15:48 person made of ***d*** is shared by
15:49 looked like the person made from ***d***.

Revelation
18:19 They threw ***d*** on their heads, and they

DUTIES

Exodus
29:9 that the ***d*** of priesthood

Numbers
3:7 They will perform ***d*** for him and for the entire community
3:8 tent and the ***d*** on behalf of the
3:28 who would perform ***d*** for the
3:32 performing the ***d*** of the sanctuary.
3:38 who performed the ***d*** of the sanctuary
4:27 All the ***d*** of the Gershonites for
7:5 to the Levites according to their ***d***.
8:24 performing the ***d*** for the meeting
8:25 They will perform their ***d*** no longer.
18:3 perform their ***d*** for you and the
18:4 will perform the ***d*** of the meeting
18:5 will perform the ***d*** of the sanctuary
18:7 must perform the ***d*** of your
31:30 who carry out the ***d*** of the LORD's
31:47 who carry out the ***d*** of the LORD's

Deuteronomy
24:5 any related ***d*** be placed on him.

1 Kings
8:11 carry out their ***d*** due to the cloud

1 Chronicles
6:32 They carried out their usual ***d***.
24:3 them according to their appointed ***d***.
25:8 their assigned ***d***, small as well as

2 Chronicles
5:14 carry out their ***d*** on account of the
19:11 Carry out your ***d*** with confidence,
31:16 out their daily ***d*** as their

Nehemiah
13:30 with specific ***d*** for each person.

Romans
13:7 you owe, pay the ***d*** you are charged,

Hebrews
10:2 their religious ***d*** had been

DUTY

Genesis
38:8 wife, do your ***d*** as her brother-in-
Numbers
4:24 This is the ***d*** of the Gershonite clans
4:33 This is the ***d*** of the Merarite clans for
7:7 he gave to the Gershonites for their ***d***.
7:8 for their ***d*** under the
7:9 because their ***d*** concerned the
Deuteronomy
25:5 according to the brother-in-law's ***d***.
25:7 the brother-in-law's ***d*** with me."
1 Samuel
2:36 to some priestly ***d*** so I can have a
2 Samuel
18:24 The watchman on ***d*** went up on the
2 Kings
11:5 coming on sabbath ***d*** will guard the
11:7 usually go off ***d*** on the Sabbath
11:9 men reporting for ***d*** on the Sabbath as
1 Chronicles
9:27 they had guard ***d*** and were
9:33 because they were on ***d*** day and night.
24:19 their appointed ***d*** and by the
27:1 and they were on ***d*** for a month at a
2 Chronicles
23:4 coming on sabbath ***d*** will guard the
23:6 or Levites on ***d*** can do that. They
23:8 men reporting for ***d*** on the Sabbath,
Ezra
10:4 for it is your ***d*** to deal with this
Nehemiah
7:3 are still on ***d***, have them shut
10:39 the priests on ***d***, the gatekeepers,
Psalms
127:1 the city, the guard on ***d*** is pointless.
Matthew
27:65 for guard ***d***. Go and make it
Luke
1:8 because his priestly division was on ***d***.
17:10 praise. We have only done our ***d***.'"

DWELL

Deuteronomy
12:12 the Levites who ***d*** in your cities
Ruth
1:1 of Judah to ***d*** in the territory
1 Chronicles
16:9 praises to him; ***d*** on all his
Job
4:19 less those who ***d*** in houses of
11:14 don't let injustice ***d*** in your tents,
24:13 its direction, don't ***d*** in its paths.
39:28 They ***d*** on an outcropping of rock, their
Psalms
15:1 LORD? Who can ***d*** on your holy
48:9 We ***d*** on your faithful love, God, in
65:8 Those who ***d*** on the far edges stand in
68:6 but the rebellious ***d*** in a parched land.
69:25 let no one ***d*** in their tents.
69:36 those who love God's name will ***d*** there.
71:16 I will ***d*** on your mighty acts, my Lord.
74:2 remember Mount Zion, where you ***d***.
105:2 to the Lord; ***d*** on all his
Proverbs
1:33 who obey me will ***d*** securely,
2:21 integrity will ***d*** in the land; the
8:12 I, Wisdom, ***d*** with prudence; I have
10:30 but the wicked won't ***d*** in the land.
Isaiah
26:19 and those who ***d*** in the dust will
65:9 possession; my servants will ***d*** there.
Jeremiah
7:3 and I will ***d*** with you in this
7:7 only then will I ***d*** with you in this
7:12 I let my name ***d*** at first, and see
31:24 its towns will ***d*** together with
35:7 you are always to ***d*** in tents so you
46:26 Egypt will ***d*** like it did a
49:18 will live there; no human will ***d*** in it.
49:33 will live there; no human will ***d*** in it.
Ezekiel
43:7 where I will ***d*** among the
43:9 me, and I will ***d*** among them
Micah
4:10 the city and ***d*** in the open
5:4 God. They will ***d*** secure, because
Nahum
1:5 him—the world and all who ***d*** in it.
Haggai
1:4 time for you to ***d*** in your own
Zechariah
2:7 Flee, you who ***d*** with Daughter
2:10 about to come and ***d*** among you, says
2:11 and I will ***d*** among you so you
8:4 women will again ***d*** in the plazas of
8:8 back so they will ***d*** in Jerusalem.
9:6 child will ***d*** in Ashdod; I will
12:6 Jerusalem will ***d*** again in its
14:11 People will ***d*** in it; it will never
Revelation
12:12 and you who ***d*** in them. But oh!
13:6 place (that is, those who ***d*** in heaven).
21:3 He will ***d*** with them, and

DWELLING

Leviticus
26:11 I will place my ***d*** among you, and I will
Joshua
22:19 That's where the ***d*** of the LORD
22:29 LORD our God that stands before his ***d***!"
1 Samuel
2:29 commanded for my ***d*** place? Why do you
2:32 see trouble in my ***d*** place, though all
Ezra
7:15 God of Israel whose ***d*** is in Jerusalem,
Nehemiah
1:9 that I have chosen as a ***d*** for my name.'
Psalms
27:5 me in his own ***d*** during troubling
33:14 From his ***d*** place God observes all who
43:3 to your holy mountain, to your ***d*** place.
46:4 city, the holiest ***d*** of the Most High.
68:16 desired for his ***d***, the mountain
68:18 rebel against the LORD God's ***d*** there.
74:7 they defiled the ***d*** place of your
76:2 His ***d*** place became Salem; his
84:1 lovely is your ***d*** place, LORD of

132:5 for the LORD, a ***d*** place for the
132:7 Let's enter God's ***d*** place; let's

Proverbs
24:15 the righteous. Don't destroy their ***d***.

Ezekiel
37:27 My ***d*** will be with them, and I will be

Acts
7:46 might provide a ***d*** place for the God

1 Peter
1:17 the time of your ***d*** in a strange land.

DYING

Ecclesiastes
3:2 and a time for ***d***, a time for

John
11:37 Couldn't he have kept Lazarus from ***d***?"

2 Corinthians
6:9 well known, as ***d***—and look, we are

Philippians
1:21 serves Christ and ***d*** is even better.

Hebrews
2:14 the power over death—the devil—by ***d***.

Ee

EAGLE
Deuteronomy
32:11 Like an **e** protecting its nest, hovering
Proverbs
23:5 wings like an **e** and flies
30:19 the way of an **e** in the sky, the way of
Jeremiah
48:40 who soars like an **e** and spreads its
Ezekiel
10:14 of a lion, and the fourth that of an **e**.
17:3 The great **e** with great wings,
17:7 was another great **e** with great wings
Obadiah
1:4 you soar like the **e**, though your nest
Revelation
4:7 creature was like an **e** in flight.
8:13 and I heard an **e** flying high
12:14 of the great **e** so that she could

EAR
Exodus
21:6 will pierce his **e** with a pointed
Deuteronomy
15:17 and pierce his **e** with it into the
1 Samuel
18:23 things in David's **e**. But David said,
2 Kings
19:16 LORD, turn your **e** this way and hear!
Nehemiah
1:6 Let your **e** be attentive and your eyes
1:11 LORD, let your **e** be attentive to the
Job
12:11 Doesn't the **e** test words and the palate
13:1 seen it all; my **e** has heard and
29:11 Indeed, the **e** that heard blessed me;
34:3 for the **e** tests words like the palate
Psalms
71:2 Bend your **e** toward me and
88:2 reach you! Turn your **e** to my outcry
94:9 one who made the **e**, can't he hear?
Proverbs
2:2 Turn your **e** toward wisdom, and stretch
4:20 to my words. Bend your **e** to my speech.
5:1 my wisdom. Bend your **e** to what I know,
15:31 The **e** that listens to life-giving
18:15 knowledge; the **e** of the wise seeks
22:17 Turn your **e** and hear the words of the
23:12 instruction, your **e** to knowledgeable
25:12 correction to an **e** that listens is
Ecclesiastes
1:8 neither is the **e** filled up by
Song of Songs
1:10 adorned with **e** hoops; your neck,
Isaiah
37:17 LORD, turn your **e** this way and hear!
50:4 God awakens my **e** in the morning to
50:5 God opened my **e**; I didn't rebel;
64:4 one has heard, no **e** has perceived, no
Lamentations
3:56 Don't close your **e** to my need for
Amos
3:12 the piece of an **e** from the mouth of
Matthew
26:51 high priest's slave, he cut off his **e**.
Mark
14:47 high priest's slave and cut off his **e**.
Luke
22:50 servant, cutting off his right **e**.
22:51 touched the slave's **e** and healed him.
John
18:10 off his right **e**. (The servant's
18:26 of the one whose **e** Peter had cut
1 Corinthians
2:9 eye has seen, or **e** has heard, or
12:16 If the **e** says, "I'm not part of the
12:17 body were an **e**, what would

EARLY
Psalms
127:2 that you get up **e** and stay up late,
Proverbs
27:14 with a loud voice **e** in the morning
Isaiah
5:11 those who wake up **e** in the morning to
28:4 will be like an **e** fig before the
Luke
24:22 They went to the tomb **e** this morning

EARS
Genesis
35:4 rings in their **e**, and Jacob buried
41:5 in which seven **e** of grain, full
41:6 Just then, seven **e** of grain, scrawny
41:7 and the scrawny **e** swallowed up the full
41:22 full and healthy **e** of grain growing
41:23 hard and thin **e** of grain,
41:24 and the thin **e** swallowed up the healthy
41:26 the seven healthy **e** of grain are
41:27 The seven thin **e** of grain,
Exodus
9:31 the barley had **e** of grain and the
32:2 rings from the **e** of your wives,
32:3 rings from their **e** and brought them
Deuteronomy
23:25 you can pluck **e** by hand, but you
29:4 understand, eyes to see, or **e** to hear.
Ruth
2:2 glean among the **e** of grain behind
1 Samuel
3:11 will make the **e** of all who hear
15:14 of sheep in my **e** and mooing of
2 Samuel
7:22 as we have always heard with our own **e**.

22:7 temple; my cry for help reached his ***e***.
2 Kings
19:28 has reached my ***e***, I will put my
21:12 disaster that the ***e*** of anyone who
1 Chronicles
17:20 just as we have heard with our own ***e***.
2 Chronicles
6:40 be open and your ***e*** attentive to the
7:15 be open and my ***e*** will pay
Job
4:12 up on me; my ***e*** caught a hint of
13:17 so that my remarks will be in your ***e***.
15:21 pierces their ***e***; when safe,
33:16 he opens people's ***e***, scares them with
36:10 He opens their ***e*** with discipline and
36:15 opens their ***e*** through
42:5 My ***e*** had heard about you, but now my
Psalms
17:6 me. So tilt your ***e*** toward me now—
18:6 for help, and my call reached his ***e***.
34:15 righteous, his ***e*** listen to their
40:6 offerings—but you have given me ***e***!
44:1 God, with our own ***e***; our ancestors
58:4 a deaf cobra's—one that shuts its ***e***
78:1 tilt your ***e*** toward the words
92:11 defeat; my ***e*** have heard the
115:6 They have ***e***, but they can't hear. They
130:2 voice! Let your ***e*** pay close
135:17 They have ***e***, but they can't listen.
Proverbs
20:12 ***E*** to hear and eyes to see—the LORD
21:13 who close their ***e*** to the cries of
23:9 speak in the ***e*** of fools, for
26:17 Like yanking the ***e*** of a dog, so is one
28:9 who turn their ***e*** from hearing
Isaiah
6:10 dull. Make their ***e*** deaf and their
32:3 be blind, the ***e*** of those who can
35:5 opened, and the ***e*** of the deaf will
37:29 has reached my ***e***, I will put my
42:20 keep watch. With ***e*** open, you don't
43:8 have eyes, the deaf ones who have ***e***.
48:8 in ages past your ***e*** are closed,
59:1 save, nor are his ***e*** too dull to hear,
Jeremiah
5:21 but don't see and ***e*** but don't hear.
6:10 attention? Their ***e*** are shut tight,
Ezekiel
12:2 they don't see, ***e*** to hear but they
16:12 earrings in your ***e***, and a beautiful
23:25 off your nose and ***e***, and those who
44:5 Use your eyes and ***e*** and listen to all
Daniel
9:18 Open your ***e***, my God, and listen! Open
Micah
7:16 their mouths; their ***e*** will be deaf.
Matthew
11:15 Let the person who has ***e***, hear
13:9 Everyone who has ***e*** should pay
13:15 hear with their ***e*** or understand
13:16 Happy are your ***e*** because they hear.
13:43 kingdom. Those who have ***e*** should hear."
Mark
4:9 Whoever has ***e*** to listen should
4:23 Whoever has ***e*** to listen should pay
7:33 in the man's ***e***. Then he spit and
7:35 At once, his ***e*** opened, his twisted
8:18 Don't you have ***e***? Why can't you
Luke
8:8 Everyone who has ***e*** should pay
14:35 away. Whoever has ***e*** to hear should
Acts
7:57 and covered their ***e***. Together, they
28:27 hear with their ***e*** or understand
Romans
11:8 not see and their ***e*** not hear, right
James
5:4 have reached the ***e*** of the Lord of
1 Peter
3:12 righteous and his ***e*** are open to their
Revelation
13:9 Whoever has ***e*** must listen

EARTH

→ ABOVE THE EARTH, ALL NATIONS ON EARTH, ALL THE EARTH, ENDS OF THE EARTH, HEAVEN AND EARTH, HEAVEN AND ON EARTH, HEAVENS AND THE EARTH

Genesis
1:1 began to create the heavens and the ***e***—
7:4 send rain on the ***e*** for forty days
Matthew
5:5 because they will inherit the ***e***.
5:13 the salt of the ***e***. But if salt
9:6 authority on the ***e*** to forgive sins"—
10:34 peace to the ***e***. I haven't come
24:35 Heaven and ***e*** will pass away, but my
27:45 in the afternoon the whole ***e*** was dark.
28:18 all authority in heaven and on ***e***.
John
1:51 and down to ***e*** on the Human One.
3:31 who is from the ***e*** belongs to the
Revelation
21:1 heaven and a new ***e***, for the former

EAST

Genesis
2:8 in Eden in the ***e*** and put there the
3:24 the human. To the ***e*** of the garden of
4:16 down in the land of Nod, ***e*** of Eden.
Job
1:3 greater than all the people of the ***e***.
Psalms
48:7 or like the ***e*** wind when it smashes the
75:6 come from the ***e*** or west; it's not
78:26 God set the ***e*** wind moving across the
103:12 As far as ***e*** is from west—that's how
107:3 countries, from ***e*** and west, north
Isaiah
2:6 from the ***e*** and fortune-teller
Daniel
8:9 the south, the ***e***, and the
Matthew
2:1 magi came from the ***e*** to Jerusalem.
2:2 his star in the ***e***, and we've come
Mark
16:9 out, from the ***e*** to the west, the
Luke
13:29 will come from ***e*** and west, north
Revelation
7:2 up from the ***e***, holding the seal
16:12 way was ready for the kings from the ***e***.

21:13 gates on the ***e***, three gates on

EAT → EAT THE PASSOVER, EAT THE PASSOVER MEAL

Genesis
2:16 the human, "***E*** your fill from
2:17 but don't ***e*** from the tree of the
3:1 you shouldn't ***e*** from any tree in
3:2 snake, "We may ***e*** the fruit of the
3:11 naked? Did you ***e*** from the tree,
27:10 father, he will ***e***, and then he will
27:25 here and let me ***e*** some of my son's
Exodus
2:20 man? Invite him to ***e*** a meal with us."
10:12 land of Egypt and ***e*** all of the land's
12:9 Don't ***e*** any of it raw or boiled in
12:15 You will ***e*** unleavened bread for seven
12:43 the Passover. No foreigner may ***e*** it.
16:25 day Moses said, "***E*** it today, because
Leviticus
3:17 live: you must not ***e*** any fat or blood.
Ecclesiastes
2:24 beings than to ***e***, drink, and
Song of Songs
4:16 garden, let him ***e*** its luscious
5:1 wine and my milk. ***E***, dear friends!
Daniel
1:13 the young men who ***e*** the king's food.
Matthew
6:19 moth and rust ***e*** them and where
8:11 and sit down to ***e*** with Abraham and
9:11 does your teacher ***e*** with tax
25:35 gave me food to ***e***. I was thirsty
26:26 said, "Take and ***e***. This is my body."
John
4:31 spoke to Jesus, saying, "Rabbi, ***e***."
4:32 I have food to ***e*** that you don't
6:31 He gave them bread from heaven to ***e***. "
Acts
7:11 it. Our ancestors had nothing to ***e***.
Romans
14:3 Those who ***e*** must not look down on the
1 Corinthians
8:13 sister, I won't ***e*** meat ever again,
9:4 Don't we have the right to ***e*** and drink
9:7 and doesn't ***e*** its fruit? Who
11:26 Every time you ***e*** this bread and drink

EAT THE PASSOVER

Nm 9:11; Mt 26:17; Mk 14:12; 14:14; Lk 22:8; 22:11; Jn 18:28

EAT THE PASSOVER MEAL

Mt 26:17; Mk 14:12; 14:14; Lk 22:8; 22:11

EATING

Matthew
11:18 John came neither ***e*** nor drinking, and
11:19 Human One came ***e*** and drinking, and
Mark
2:15 and sinners were ***e*** with Jesus and
14:22 While they were ***e***, Jesus took bread,
John
21:15 they finished ***e***, Jesus asked
Revelation
2:20 immorality and ***e*** food sacrificed

EATS

Exodus
12:15 anyone who ***e*** leavened bread
Leviticus
7:18 the person who ***e*** of it will be
11:40 Anyone who ***e*** from the dead body must wash
17:15 or immigrant, who ***e*** an animal that
19:8 Anyone who ***e*** it will be liable to
22:14 If someone ***e*** a holy offering
Numbers
22:4 us, as an ox ***e*** up the grass in
23:24 lie down until it ***e*** the prey and
John
6:54 Whoever ***e*** my flesh and drinks my blood
Romans
14:2 the weak person ***e*** only vegetables.
1 Corinthians
11:21 goes ahead and ***e*** a private meal.

EBER

Genesis
11:17 Peleg was born, ***E*** lived 430 years;
Numbers
24:24 they will attack ***E***, and even he will
Luke
3:35 Reu son of Peleg son of ***E*** son of Shelah

EDOM

Genesis
36:8 So Esau, that is ***E***, lived in the
2 Kings
8:20 Jehoram's rule ***E*** rebelled against
Psalms
60:8 throw my shoe at ***E***. I shout in
60:9 I wish someone would lead me to ***E***!"
108:9 throw my shoe at ***E***. I shout in
Isaiah
34:6 a great slaughter in the land of ***E***.
63:1 this coming from ***E***, from Bozrah in
Amos
9:12 what is left of ***E***, as well as all
Obadiah
1:1 concerning ***E***: We have heard a
1:8 the wise from ***E*** and understanding
Malachi
1:4 ***E*** may say, "We are beaten down, but we will rebuild

EGYPT → DOWN TO EGYPT

Genesis
12:10 went down toward ***E*** to live as an
37:28 silver, and they brought Joseph to ***E***.
42:3 brothers went down to buy grain in ***E***.
Exodus
1:8 came to power in ***E*** who didn't know
3:11 and to bring the Israelites out of ***E***?"
11:5 in the land of ***E*** will die, from
Numbers
11:18 better for us in ***E***." The LORD will
14:4 pick a leader and let's go back to ***E***."
Deuteronomy
6:21 slaves in ***E***. But the LORD

Psalms
78:12 in the land of ***E***, in the field of
80:8 a vine out of ***E***. You drove out
Lamentations
5:6 out a hand to ***E*** and to Assyria,
Ezekiel
29:2 against him and against all of ***E***.
30:4 will come into ***E***, and trembling
Hosea
11:1 him, and out of ***E*** I called my son.
Matthew
2:15 prophet: I have called my son out of ***E***.

EGYPTIAN

Genesis
16:1 Since she had an ***E*** servant named
Exodus
1:17 didn't obey the ***E*** king's order.
1:19 women aren't like ***E*** women. They're
Deuteronomy
11:4 God did to the ***E*** army, to its
Isaiah
19:2 I will stir up ***E*** against Egyptian, and
Ezekiel
20:8 abandoned their ***E*** idols. So I
23:27 lewdness and your ***E***-styled promiscuity
Acts
7:22 everything ***E*** wisdom had to

EGYPTIANS

Exodus
1:12 much so that the ***E*** started to look
3:22 daughters, and you will rob the ***E***.'"
12:36 sure that the ***E*** were kind to the
14:4 his army, and the ***E*** will know that I
15:26 I brought on the ***E***. I am the LORD
Numbers
14:13 to the LORD, "The ***E*** will hear, for
Jeremiah
9:26 whether they are ***E*** or Judeans, Edomites
Ezekiel
16:26 yourself with the ***E***, your neighbors
Hebrews
11:29 but when the ***E*** tried it, they

EHUD

Judges
3:15 for them, ***E***, Gera's son, a
4:1 After ***E*** had died, the Israelites again
1 Chronicles
7:10 Jeush, Benjamin, ***E***, Chenaanah,

EKRON

Joshua
13:3 as far as the ***E*** territory is
1 Samuel
5:10 God's chest to ***E***, but as soon as
6:17 Ashkelon, one for Gath, and one for ***E***.
Amos
1:8 my hand against ***E***, and the

ELAM

1 Chronicles
1:17 Shem's family: ***E***, Asshur, Arpachshad,
Isaiah
21:2 destroys. Go up, ***E***! Lay siege,

ELDERS → APOSTLES AND ELDERS, CHIEF PRIESTS AND ELDERS, PRIESTS AND ELDERS

Exodus
3:16 and get Israel's ***e*** together and say
17:6 Moses did so while Israel's ***e*** watched.
18:12 all of Israel's ***e*** to eat a meal
19:7 the people's ***e***, and set before
Deuteronomy
5:23 chiefs of your tribes and your ***e*** came—
2 Samuel
3:17 word to Israel's ***e***. "You've wanted
17:4 to Absalom and the Israelite ***e***.
1 Kings
8:1 Israel's ***e***, all the tribal
20:8 All of the ***e*** and the people said to
21:8 sent them to the ***e*** and officials who
Ezra
5:5 looked after the ***e*** of the Jews, and
6:14 So the ***e*** of the Jews built and
Psalms
107:32 praise God in the assembly of the ***e***.
119:100 than the ***e*** because I guard
Proverbs
31:23 when he sits with the ***e*** of the land.
Ezekiel
8:11 The seventy ***e*** of the house of Israel
Joel
1:2 Hear this, ***e***, pay attention, everyone
Mark
7:3 the rules handed down by the ***e***.
Luke
7:3 sent some Jewish ***e*** to Jesus to ask
John
8:9 with the ***e***. Finally, only
Acts
2:17 see visions. Your ***e*** will dream dreams.
1 Timothy
4:14 prophecy when the ***e*** laid hands on you.
James
5:14 call for the ***e*** of the church,
Revelation
4:4 with twenty-four ***e*** seated upon them,
5:5 Then one of the ***e*** said to me, "Don't
7:11 and around the ***e*** and the four
11:16 the twenty-four ***e***, who were seated
14:3 and the ***e***. And no one could
19:4 The twenty-four ***e*** and the four living

ELEAZAR

Exodus
6:25 Aaron's son ***E*** married one of Putiel's
Leviticus
10:6 and his sons, ***E*** and Ithamar,
Numbers
3:4 have any sons. ***E*** and Ithamar
Deuteronomy
10:6 buried. His son ***E*** succeeded him in
Joshua
14:1 land of Canaan. ***E*** the priest,
24:33 ***E*** son of Aaron died. They buried him at
1 Samuel
7:1 they dedicated ***E***, Abinadab's son,
2 Samuel
23:9 in command was ***E***, Dodo's son and
23:10 then returned to ***E***, but only to
1 Chronicles
6:3 family: Nadab, Abihu, ***E***, and Ithamar.

24:28 from Mahli: ***E***, who had no sons
Ezra
7:5 Phinehas son of ***E*** son of Aaron the
Nehemiah
12:42 Shemaiah, ***E***, Uzzi, Jehohanan,
Matthew
1:15 was the father of ***E***. Eleazar was the

ELEVEN
Matthew
28:16 Now the ***e*** disciples went to Galilee, to
Mark
16:14 appeared to the ***e*** while they were
Luke
24:9 things to the ***e*** and all the
24:33 They found the ***e*** and their
Acts
1:26 He was added to the ***e*** apostles.
2:14 with the other ***e*** apostles. He

ELI
1 Samuel
1:9 the LORD. (Now ***E*** the priest was
4:18 of God's chest, ***E*** fell backward off
Matthew
27:46 a loud shout, "***E***, Eli, lama

ELIAB
Numbers
1:9 from Zebulun, ***E***, Helon's son
Deuteronomy
11:6 descendants of ***E*** the Reubenite,
1 Samuel
16:6 Samuel looked at ***E*** and thought, that
17:13 Their names were ***E*** the oldest,
17:28 oldest brother ***E*** heard him talking
1 Chronicles
2:13 was the father of ***E*** his oldest son,
2 Chronicles
11:18 and Abihail daughter of ***E***, Jesse's son.

ELIAKIM
2 Kings
18:18 Hilkiah's son ***E***, who was the
19:2 He sent ***E*** the palace administrator,
23:34 Pharaoh Neco made ***E***, Josiah's son,
2 Chronicles
36:4 brother ***E*** king of Judah and
Nehemiah
12:41 were the priests ***E***, Maaseiah,
Isaiah
22:20 will call my servant ***E***, Hilkiah's son.
37:2 He sent ***E*** the palace administrator,
Matthew
1:13 was the father of ***E***. Eliakim was the
Luke
3:30 son of Joseph son of Jonam son of ***E***

ELIASHIB
1 Chronicles
3:24 family: Hodaviah, ***E***, Pelaiah, Akkub,
24:12 the eleventh to ***E***, the twelfth to
Ezra
10:24 Of the singers: ***E***. Of the gatekeepers:
Nehemiah
3:1 Then ***E*** the high priest set to work with
3:20 door of the house of the high priest ***E***.

ELIEZER
Genesis
15:2 my household is ***E***, a man from
Exodus
18:4 other was named ***E*** because he said,
1 Chronicles
7:8 Zemirah, Joash, ***E***, Elioenai, Omri,
2 Chronicles
20:37 ***E***, Dodavahu's son from Mareshah,
Ezra
8:16 So I called for ***E***, Ariel, Shemaiah,
Luke
3:29 of Joshua son of ***E*** son of Jorim son

ELIJAH
1 Kings
17:1 ***E*** from Tishbe, who was one of the
18:46 strengthened ***E***. He gathered up
2 Kings
2:11 two of them. Then ***E*** went to heaven in
Malachi
4:5 I am sending ***E*** the prophet to
Matthew
11:14 to accept it, he is ***E*** who is to come.
16:14 Baptist, others ***E***, and still others
17:3 Moses and ***E*** appeared to them, talking
17:4 for you, one for Moses, and one for ***E***."
17:10 experts say that ***E*** must first come?"
17:11 Jesus responded, "***E*** does come first and will restore
17:12 I tell you that ***E*** has already come,
27:47 standing there said, "He's calling ***E***."
27:49 Let's see if ***E*** will come and
Mark
6:15 saying, "He is ***E***." Still others
8:28 Baptist, others ***E***, and still others
9:4 ***E*** and Moses appeared and were talking
9:5 for you, one for Moses, and one for ***E***."
9:11 experts say that ***E*** must come first?"
9:12 He answered, "***E*** does come first to
9:13 I tell you that ***E*** has come, but
15:35 there said, "Look! He's calling ***E***!"
15:36 Let's see if ***E*** will come to take
Luke
1:17 and power of ***E***. He will turn the
4:26 Yet ***E*** was sent to none of them but only
9:8 others that ***E*** had appeared, and still
9:19 Baptist, others ***E***, and still others
9:30 men, Moses and ***E***, were talking
9:33 and one for ***E***"—but he didn't kn
John
1:21 are you? Are you ***E***?" John said, "I'm
1:25 the Christ, nor ***E***, nor the prophet?"
Romans
11:2 in the case of ***E***, when he pleads
James
5:17 ***E*** was a person just like us. When he

ELIPHAZ
Genesis
36:4 gave birth to ***E*** for Esau,
1 Chronicles
1:35 Esau's family: ***E***, Reuel, Jeush, Jalam,
Job
4:1 Then ***E***, a native of Teman, responded

ELISHA
1 Kings
19:16 and anoint ***E*** from Abel-meholah,
19:19 there and found ***E***, Shaphat's son.
19:20 ***E*** immediately left the oxen and ran
19:21 ***E*** turned back from following Elijah,
2 Kings
2:15 has settled on ***E***!" So they came
8:4 about all the great things ***E*** has done."
13:20 So ***E*** died, and he was buried. Sometimes
Luke
4:27 of the prophet ***E***, but none of them

ELISHAMA
Numbers
1:10 from Ephraim, ***E***, Ammihud's son;
2 Samuel
5:16 ***E***, Eliada, and Eliphelet
1 Chronicles
2:41 and Jekamiah was the father of ***E***.
2 Chronicles
17:8 and by the priests ***E*** and Jehoram.
Jeremiah
36:12 meeting together: ***E*** the scribe;
36:20 in the room of ***E*** the scribe, they
36:21 from the room of ***E*** the scribe. Then

ELIZABETH
Luke
1:5 Abijah. His wife ***E*** was a descendant
1:41 When ***E*** heard Mary's greeting, the child

ELKANAH
Exodus
6:24 Korahites: Assir, ***E***, and Abiasaph.
1 Samuel
1:19 home to Ramah. ***E*** had sex with his
1 Chronicles
6:23 his son ***E***, his son Ebiasaph, his son
2 Chronicles
28:7 Azrikam, and ***E***, the king's

ELYON
Genesis
14:18 the priest of El ***E*** had brought bread
14:19 Abram by El ***E***, creator of
14:20 bless El ***E***, who gave you the victory
14:22 the LORD, El ***E***, creator of

EMISSION
Leviticus
15:2 man has a genital ***e***, that emission is
22:4 a dead body, or who has an ***e*** of semen,
Deuteronomy
23:10 to a nighttime ***e***, he must exit the

EN-GEDI
1 Samuel
23:29 there and lived at the ***E*** fortresses.
24:1 that David was in the ***E*** wilderness.

ENCOURAGE
Deuteronomy
3:28 him, and ***e*** him because he's
2 Samuel
11:25 the city and destroy it!' ***E*** Joab!"
19:7 up! Go out and ***e*** your followers! I
Psalms
64:5 They ***e*** themselves with evil words. They
Jeremiah
23:14 tell lies. They ***e*** evildoers so that
27:14 the prophets who ***e*** you not to serve
Lamentations
1:16 who might ***e*** me is nowhere
Romans
1:12 we can mutually ***e*** each other while
12:1 God's mercies, I ***e*** you to present
1 Corinthians
1:10 Now I ***e*** you, brothers and sisters, in
4:16 so I ***e*** you to follow my example
16:15 and sisters, I ***e*** you to do
2 Corinthians
2:8 So I ***e*** you to show your love for this
9:5 was necessary to ***e*** the brothers to
Ephesians
4:1 for the Lord, I ***e*** you to live as
Colossians
4:8 about us and so he can ***e*** your hearts.
1 Thessalonians
3:2 to strengthen and ***e*** you in your
4:1 we ask and ***e*** you in the Lord
4:10 Macedonia. Now we ***e*** you, brothers and
4:18 So ***e*** each other with these words
2 Thessalonians
2:17 May he ***e*** your hearts and give you
3:12 we command and ***e*** such people to
1 Timothy
5:1 an older man but ***e*** him like he's
6:2 are loved. Teach and ***e*** these things.
2 Timothy
4:2 confront, and ***e*** with patience and
Titus
1:9 so that they can ***e*** people with
2:6 Likewise, ***e*** the younger men to be
2:15 these things. ***E*** and correct with
Hebrews
3:13 Instead, ***e*** each other every day, as
10:25 doing. Instead, ***e*** each other,

END
Genesis
6:13 to Noah, "The ***e*** has come for all
Psalms
19:6 It rises in one ***e*** of the sky; its
39:4 Let me know my ***e***, LORD. How many days do I have
46:9 wars to an ***e*** in every corner
77:8 to a complete ***e***? Is his promise
112:8 afraid. In the ***e***, they will
Proverbs
5:4 but in the ***e*** she is bitter as gall,
5:10 hard work will ***e*** up in a
11:23 of the righteous ***e*** up well, but the
14:12 but in the ***e*** it is a path to
16:25 but in the ***e*** it is the path of
21:5 of the diligent ***e*** up in profit, but
22:8 rod of their fury will come to an ***e***.
23:32 In the ***e***, it bites like a snake and
28:23 will, in the ***e***, find more favor
Ecclesiastes
3:11 what God has done from beginning to ***e***.
7:8 The ***e*** of something is better than its
12:13 So this is the ***e*** of the matter; all has

Isaiah
1:16 from my sight. Put an ***e*** to such evil;
5:26 to them from the ***e*** of the earth—now
7:3 at the ***e*** of the channel of
10:22 will return. The ***e*** is announced,
13:11 wicked. I will ***e*** the pride of the
16:10 I have brought the cheers to an ***e***.
21:2 Media! Put an ***e*** to all her
23:15 one king. At the ***e*** of seventy years,
43:6 my daughters from the ***e*** of the earth,
66:17 will meet their ***e*** together, says
Jeremiah
2:32 you have forgotten me days without ***e***!
51:64 against it." Jeremiah's words ***e*** here.
Lamentations
4:18 our streets. Our ***e*** had drawn near;
Jonah
2:6 held me with no ***e*** in sight. But you
Matthew
10:22 stands firm until the ***e*** will be saved.
Luke
1:33 and there will be no ***e*** to his kingdom."
Acts
1:8 Samaria, and to the ***e*** of the earth."
12:20 then appealed for an ***e*** to hostilities.
13:47 bring salvation to the ***e*** of the earth."
19:21 had come to an ***e***, Paul, guided by
1 Corinthians
1:8 Christ until the ***e*** so that you will
Hebrews
1:12 years of your life won't come to an ***e***.
3:14 we had in the beginning until the ***e***.
Jude
1:18 to you, "In the ***e*** time scoffers
Revelation
2:26 until the ***e***, I will give
22:13 and the last, the beginning and the ***e***.

ENDS OF THE EARTH

Dt 28:49; 33:17; Job 28:24; Ps 19:4; 59:13; 61:2; 67:7; 72:8; Prv 30:4; Is 24:16; 40:28; 41:5, 9; 42:10; 45:22; 52:10; Jer 6:22; 10:13; 16:19; 25:32; 31:8; 50:41; 51:16; Zec 9:10

ENDURANCE

Jeremiah
31:16 because your ***e*** will be rewarded,
Jonah
2:7 When my ***e*** was weakening, I remembered
Romans
5:3 we know that trouble produces ***e***,
5:4 ***e*** produces character, and character
15:4 have hope through ***e*** and through the
15:5 May the God of ***e*** and encouragement give you
2 Corinthians
1:6 the experience of ***e*** while you go
6:4 with our great ***e*** through problems,
12:12 with continuous ***e*** through signs,
2 Thessalonians
1:4 tell about your ***e*** and faithfulness
3:5 to express God's love and Christ's ***e***.
1 Timothy
6:11 faithfulness, love, ***e***, and gentleness.
2 Timothy
3:10 faithfulness, patience, love, and ***e***.
James
1:3 the testing of your faith produces ***e***.
1:4 Let this ***e*** complete its work so that
5:11 have practiced ***e***. You have heard
1 Peter
2:21 to this kind of ***e***, because Christ
2 Peter
1:6 to self-control, ***e***; and to
Revelation
1:9 kingdom, and ***e*** that we have in
2:2 labor, and your ***e***. I also know that
2:3 You have shown ***e*** and put up with a lot
2:19 your service and ***e***. I also know that
13:10 This calls for ***e*** and faithfulness
14:12 calls for the ***e*** of the saints,

ENDURE

Genesis
49:4 waters, you won't ***e***, for you went up
Exodus
18:23 will be able to ***e***. And all these
Numbers
11:15 then don't let me ***e*** this wretched
Job
20:21 their food, so their riches will not ***e***.
31:23 to me; I couldn't ***e*** his splendor.
Psalms
72:17 Let his name ***e*** as long as the
119:91 Your rules ***e*** to this day because
147:17 crumbs—who can ***e*** God's freezing
Proverbs
12:7 but the family of the righteous will ***e***.
12:19 Truthful lips ***e*** forever, but a lying
Isaiah
30:8 in the future it will ***e*** as a witness.
51:6 my salvation will ***e*** forever, and my
66:22 I'm making will ***e*** before me, says
Jeremiah
10:10 quakes; the nations can't ***e*** his rage.
Ezekiel
22:14 and courage ***e*** when I deal with
36:15 of the nations or ***e*** the scorn of the
36:29 abundantly so that you won't ***e*** famine.
36:30 will never again ***e*** the shame of
Daniel
11:25 war, but he won't ***e*** because they will
Joel
2:11 it stirs up great fear—who can ***e*** it?
Habakkuk
1:4 justice does not ***e*** because the
Zephaniah
2:15 no one else, will ***e*** forever. How she
Malachi
3:2 Who can ***e*** the day of his coming? Who
Matthew
12:26 himself. How then can his kingdom ***e***?
Mark
3:26 then he can't ***e***. He's done for.
Luke
11:18 will his kingdom ***e***? I ask this
1 Corinthians
10:13 out so that you will be able to ***e*** it.
Philippians
4:13 I can ***e*** all these things through the
Colossians
1:11 might so that you ***e*** everything and

2 Timothy
2:10 This is why I ***e*** everything for the sake
2:12 If we ***e***, we will also rule together.
4:5 circumstances. ***E*** suffering, do the
Hebrews
10:36 You need to ***e*** so that you can receive
1 Peter
2:19 someone should ***e*** pain through
2:20 it? But if you ***e*** steadfastly when
Revelation
3:10 my command to ***e***, I will keep you

ENDURING → ENDURING COVENANT
Genesis
17:8 of Canaan, as an ***e*** possession. And I
48:4 following you as an ***e*** possession.'
Joshua
4:7 stones will be an ***e*** memorial for the
1 Samuel
15:29 What's more, the ***e*** one of Israel
25:28 make an ***e*** dynasty for my
Proverbs
8:18 me, as well as ***e*** wealth and
Isaiah
55:13 stature, an ***e*** reminder that
56:5 give to them an ***e*** name that won't
Jeremiah
23:40 of disgrace and ***e*** shame that no one
1 Peter
1:4 have a pure and ***e*** inheritance that
1:23 seed is God's life-giving and ***e*** word.
2:20 praise comes from ***e*** patiently when
3:4 hearts, with the ***e*** quality of a
5:9 believers are ***e*** the same

ENDURING COVENANT
Gn 9:16; 17:7, 13, 19; Is 61:8

ENEMIES → ALL YOUR ENEMIES
Genesis
14:20 victory over your ***e***." Abram gave
49:8 the neck of your ***e***; your father's
Exodus
1:10 will join our ***e***, fight against
23:22 an enemy to your ***e*** and fight those
Joshua
5:13 Are you on our side or that of our ***e***?"
Judges
2:14 defeated by their ***e*** around them, so
2 Samuel
7:1 him rest from all his surrounding ***e***,
Esther
9:5 down all their ***e*** with sword blows,
Psalms
23:5 in front of my ***e***. You bathe my
110:1 until I make your ***e*** a footstool for
Proverbs
16:7 LORD, even their ***e*** are at peace with
Jeremiah
12:7 the one I love into the power of her ***e***.
Daniel
4:19 you and its meaning to be for your ***e***!
Hosea
5:11 pressure from its ***e***; Ephraim's rights
Amos
9:4 before their ***e***, there I will
Micah
7:6 the ***e*** of a man are
Matthew
5:44 to you, love your ***e*** and pray for
Mark
12:36 until I turn your ***e*** into your
Luke
6:35 love your ***e***, do good, and
20:43 until I make your ***e*** a footstool for
Acts
2:35 until I make your ***e*** a footstool for
Romans
5:10 we were still ***e***, now that we have
1 Corinthians
15:25 until he puts all ***e*** under his feet.
Ephesians
6:12 against human ***e*** but against
Philippians
3:18 many people live as ***e*** of the cross.
Hebrews
1:13 until I put your ***e*** under your feet
10:13 waiting until his ***e*** are made into a
Revelation
11:5 burns up their ***e***. So if anyone
11:12 in a cloud, while their ***e*** watched them.

ENEMY
Exodus
15:6 your strong hand, LORD, shatters the ***e***!
23:22 then I'll be an ***e*** to your enemies
Deuteronomy
33:27 He drove out the ***e*** before you. He
1 Samuel
18:29 Saul was David's ***e*** for the rest of
2 Samuel
22:18 from my powerful ***e***, saved me from my
Esther
3:10 the Agagite's son, ***e*** of the Jews.
7:6 man who hates, an ***e***—this wicked Haman
9:24 son, the ***e*** of all the Jews,
Psalms
18:17 from my powerful ***e***, saved me from my
74:3 to all that the ***e*** destroyed in the
Proverbs
27:6 excessive are the kisses of an ***e***.
Jeremiah
30:14 with you as an ***e*** would, because
Lamentations
2:5 become like an ***e***. He devoured
Micah
2:8 rose up as an ***e***. You strip off
Matthew
5:43 love your neighbor and hate your ***e***.
13:39 The ***e*** who planted them is the devil.
1 Corinthians
15:26 Death is the last ***e*** to be brought to an
James
4:4 with the world makes you an ***e*** of God?

ENLISTED
Numbers
1:19 Moses ***e*** them in the Sinai desert just
1:46 All those ***e*** were 603,550
1:47 tribe, weren't ***e*** along with them.

ENOCH
Genesis
4:17 and gave birth to ***E***. Cain built a
5:22 ***E*** walked with God. After Methuselah's
5:24 ***E*** walked with God and disappeared
1 Chronicles
1:3 ***E***, Methuselah, Lamech
Luke
3:37 Methuselah son of ***E*** son of Jared son
Hebrews
11:5 By faith ***E*** was taken up so that he
Jude
1:14 ***E***, who lived seven generations after

ENROLLMENT
Luke
2:2 This first ***e*** occurred when Quirinius

ENTER → ENTER GOD'S KINGDOM
Exodus
12:23 let the destroyer ***e*** your houses to
12:25 When you ***e*** the land that the LORD has
40:35 Moses couldn't ***e*** the meeting tent
Deuteronomy
11:10 you are about to ***e*** and possess is
11:31 Jordan River to ***e*** and possess the
18:9 Once you ***e*** the land that the LORD your
24:10 neighbor, don't ***e*** their house to
32:52 of the river, but you won't ***e*** there."
Proverbs
2:10 Wisdom will ***e*** your mind, and knowledge
Matthew
7:13 road wide, so many people ***e*** through it.
18:8 It's better to ***e*** into life
19:17 If you want to ***e*** eternal life,
19:23 a rich person to ***e*** the kingdom of
John
3:4 impossible to ***e*** the mother's womb
10:1 whoever doesn't ***e*** into the sheep
18:28 leaders wouldn't ***e*** the palace;
Hebrews
3:11 I swore: "They will never ***e*** my rest!"
10:19 that we can ***e*** the holy of
Revelation
21:27 unclean will ever ***e*** it, nor anyone
22:14 of life and may ***e*** the city by the

ENTER GOD'S KINGDOM
Mt 19:24; Mk 9:47; 10:23, 24, 25; Lk 18:24; 18:25; Jn 3:5; Ac 14:22

ENTERED
Exodus
24:18 Moses ***e*** the cloud and went up the
33:9 When Moses ***e*** the tent, the column of
Leviticus
9:23 and Aaron then ***e*** the meeting tent.
16:23 wearing when he ***e*** the inner holy
Psalms
55:14 when together we ***e*** God's house with
69:2 bottom! I have ***e*** deep water; the
73:17 until I ***e*** God's sanctuary and
Obadiah
1:11 and foreigners ***e*** his gates and
1:13 shouldn't have ***e*** the gate of my
Matthew
21:10 And when Jesus ***e*** Jerusalem, the whole
21:23 When Jesus ***e*** the temple, the chief
John
13:27 the bread, Satan ***e*** into him. Jesus
18:1 He and his disciples ***e*** a garden there.
20:26 locked, Jesus ***e*** and stood among
Romans
5:12 same way that sin ***e*** the world through
Hebrews
4:10 The one who ***e*** God's rest also rested
9:12 He ***e*** the holy of holies once for all by

ENTERS
Leviticus
14:46 Anyone who ***e*** the house during the
Psalms
118:26 The one who ***e*** in the LORD's name is
Mark
7:18 the outside that ***e*** a person has the
14:14 Wherever he ***e***, say to the owner of the
John
10:2 The one who ***e*** through the gate is the
10:10 The thief ***e*** only to steal, kill, and

ENTHRONED
Genesis
41:40 Only as the ***e*** king will I be
1 Samuel
4:4 forces, who sits ***e*** on the winged
2 Samuel
6:2 forces, who sits ***e*** on the winged
1 Kings
22:19 I saw the LORD ***e*** with all the
2 Kings
19:15 Israel, you sit ***e*** on the winged
1 Chronicles
13:6 LORD, who sits ***e*** on the winged
2 Chronicles
18:18 I saw the LORD ***e*** with all the
Psalms
22:3 are the holy one, ***e***. You are Israel's
29:10 The LORD sits ***e*** over the floodwaters;
55:19 God, who is ***e*** from ancient days, will
61:7 Let him be ***e*** forever before God!
80:1 You, who are ***e*** upon the winged
99:1 shake! He sits ***e*** on the winged
Isaiah
37:16 Israel: you sit ***e*** on the winged
52:2 rise up; sit ***e***, Jerusalem. Loose
Ezekiel
27:3 Tyre, who sits ***e*** at the entrance

ENTRANCE
Genesis
18:1 he sat at the ***e*** of his tent in
28:17 than God's house and the ***e*** to heaven.
Numbers
3:25 screen for the ***e*** of the meeting
Deuteronomy
31:15 the cloud pillar stood at the tent's ***e***.
Psalms
84:10 stand outside the ***e*** of my God's house
Mark
15:46 a stone against the ***e*** to the tomb.

John
11:38 was a cave, and a stone covered the ***e***.

EPHAH
Genesis
25:4 sons were ***E***, Epher, Enoch,
Exodus
16:36 An omer is one-tenth of an ***e***.

EPHESUS
Acts
18:19 they arrived in ***E***, he left
19:1 and came to ***E***, where he found
20:17 sent a message to ***E*** calling for the
1 Corinthians
15:32 wild animals in ***E***? If the dead
Ephesians
1:1 faithful people in Christ Jesus in ***E***.
Revelation
2:1 of the church in ***E***: These are the

EPHRAIM
Genesis
41:52 named the second ***E***, "because," he
48:20 God make you like ***E*** and Manasseh.'"
Psalms
60:7 Manasseh is mine; ***E*** is my helmet;
78:9 The children of ***E***, armed with bows,
78:67 and didn't choose the tribe of ***E***.
80:2 before ***E***, Benjamin, and Manasseh!
108:8 Manasseh is mine; ***E*** is my helmet,
John
11:54 to a city called ***E***, where he stayed

EPHRAIMITE
Joshua
16:8 legacy for the clans of the ***E*** tribe.
1 Samuel
17:12 Jesse's son, an ***E*** from Bethlehem in

EPHRON
Genesis
23:8 listen to me and ask ***E***, Zohar's son,
50:13 as burial property from ***E*** the Hittite.
Joshua
15:9 cities of Mount ***E***. The border
2 Chronicles
13:19 Jeshanah, and ***E***, along with their

EQUIPMENT
Exodus
25:9 you for the dwelling and for all its ***e***.
27:3 trays. Make all its ***e*** out of copper.
30:27 table and all its ***e***, the lampstand
Leviticus
8:11 altar and all its ***e***, as well as the
Numbers
1:50 to all its ***e***, and to
3:8 for all the ***e*** of the meeting
4:10 place it and its ***e*** in a covering of
7:1 it holy. All its ***e***, as well as the
18:3 approach the holy ***e*** of the sanctuary
31:6 the sanctuary ***e*** and the trumpets
1 Kings
7:45 bowls. All the ***e*** that Hiram made
7:48 also made all the ***e*** for the LORD's
8:4 and all the holy ***e*** that was in the
15:15 silver and gold ***e*** that he and his
19:21 them. Then with ***e*** from the oxen,
2 Kings
7:15 with garments and ***e*** that the Arameans
Ezra
1:6 them with silver ***e***, with gold, with
5:14 gold and silver ***e*** from God's house
Nehemiah
10:39 the sanctuary ***e*** is kept, and
13:5 incense, and the ***e***, together with
13:9 back the temple ***e***, along with the
Daniel
1:2 with some of the ***e*** from God's house.
5:2 gold and silver ***e*** that his father
11:8 silver and gold ***e***. For years he

ESAU
Genesis
25:27 men grew up, ***E*** became an
25:34 So Jacob gave ***E*** bread and lentil stew.
27:11 My brother ***E*** is a hairy man,
Joshua
24:4 I gave Jacob and ***E***. I gave Mount
1 Chronicles
1:34 father. Isaac's family: ***E*** and Israel.
Jeremiah
49:8 disaster on ***E***: its day of
49:10 me? I will strip ***E*** bare. I will
Obadiah
1:6 How ***E*** has been looted, his treasures
1:8 Edom and understanding from Mount ***E***?
1:9 from Mount ***E*** will be
1:18 and the house of ***E*** straw; they will
1:19 possess Mount ***E***, and those of the
1:21 to rule Mount ***E***, and the kingdom
Malachi
1:2 loved us?" Wasn't ***E*** Jacob's brother?
1:3 but I rejected ***E***. I turned Esau's
Romans
9:13 written, I loved Jacob, but I hated ***E***.
Hebrews
11:20 blessed Jacob and ***E*** concerning their
12:16 or ungodly like ***E***. He sold his

ESCAPE
Genesis
7:7 entered the ark to ***e*** the floodwaters.
27:43 to me: Get up and ***e*** to my brother
Exodus
1:10 against us, and then ***e*** from the land."
Psalms
68:20 of salvation, and ***e*** from certain
71:3 I can always ***e***. You commanded
88:8 to them. I can't ***e***. I'm trapped!
139:7 Where could I go to ***e*** your presence?
142:4 to me. There's no ***e*** for me. No one
Proverbs
11:21 the children of the righteous will ***e***.
12:13 but the righteous ***e*** from distress.
19:5 go unpunished, and a liar won't ***e***.
Matthew
2:13 his mother and ***e*** to Egypt. Stay
3:7 Who warned you to ***e*** from the angry
10:23 you in one city, ***e*** to the next,

23:33 you be able to ***e*** the judgment of
24:16 those in Judea must ***e*** to the mountains.

Romans
2:3 believe that you will ***e*** God's judgment?

ESTABLISH

Numbers
35:13 You will ***e*** six refuge cities for

Deuteronomy
8:18 in order to ***e*** the covenant he
32:6 creator? Didn't he make you and ***e*** you?

Ezekiel
16:60 young, and I will ***e*** an everlasting
16:62 I myself will ***e*** my covenant with you,

Mark
7:9 commandment in order to ***e*** these rules.

Romans
10:3 and they try to ***e*** their own

Hebrews
10:9 an end to the first to ***e*** the second.

1 Peter
5:10 restore,empower, strengthen, and ***e*** you.

ESTABLISHED

1 Kings
2:12 David, and his royal power was well ***e***.

Ezra
6:12 the God who has ***e*** his name there

Psalms
9:4 because you have ***e*** justice for me and
74:16 night too! You ***e*** both the moon and

Proverbs
8:27 was there when he ***e*** the heavens, when
12:3 No one is ***e*** by wicked acts, but the
22:28 boundary marker that your ancestors ***e***.
24:3 is built; by understanding it is ***e***.
25:5 his throne will be ***e*** in righteousness.
29:14 honestly, his throne will be ***e*** forever.
30:4 garment? Who has ***e*** all the ends of

Isaiah
16:5 a throne will be ***e*** based on goodness,

Matthew
18:16 every word may be ***e*** by the mouth of

Acts
2:23 with God's ***e*** plan and
3:1 in the afternoon, the ***e*** prayer time.

Romans
13:2 what God has ***e***. People who take

Colossians
1:23 to remain well ***e*** and rooted in
2:7 up in him, be ***e*** in faith, and

1 Timothy
1:9 the Law isn't ***e*** for a righteous

Hebrews
9:20 of the covenant that God ***e*** for you.

ESTHER

Esther
2:7 (that is, ***E***), though she was
9:31 the Jew and Queen ***E*** had made. The

ETERNAL

Genesis
49:26 blessings of the ***e*** mountains, the

Deuteronomy
33:15 mountains, with the gifts of ***e*** hills;
33:27 of safety; the ***e*** arms are a

2 Samuel
23:5 He has made an ***e*** covenant with me,

Psalms
45:6 divine throne is ***e*** and everlasting.
49:11 graves are their ***e*** homes, the place
93:2 firm for a very long time. You are ***e***!
105:10 for Jacob, as an ***e*** covenant for
139:24 way in me, then lead me on the ***e*** path!

Matthew
18:8 thrown into the ***e*** fire with two
19:16 good thing must I do to have ***e*** life?"
25:46 will go away into ***e*** punishment. But

John
3:15 who believes in him will have ***e*** life.
4:14 of water that bubbles up into ***e*** life."
5:24 who sent me has ***e*** life and won't
6:27 that endures for ***e*** life, which the
10:28 I give them ***e*** life. They will never
12:50 commandment is ***e*** life. Therefore
17:2 he could give ***e*** life to everyone

Acts
13:46 to receive ***e*** life, we will
13:48 who was appointed for ***e*** life believed,

Romans
1:20 qualities—God's ***e*** power and divine
2:7 he will give ***e*** life to those who
5:21 leading to ***e*** life through
6:22 a holy life, and the outcome is ***e*** life.
6:23 but God's gift is ***e*** life in Christ
16:26 based on the command of the ***e*** God.

Galatians
6:8 will harvest ***e*** life from the

2 Thessalonians
1:9 the penalty of ***e*** destruction away
2:16 grace gave us ***e*** comfort and a

1 Timothy
1:16 are going to believe in him for ***e*** life.
6:12 Grab hold of ***e*** life—you were
6:16 him. Honor and ***e*** power belong to

2 Timothy
2:10 salvation in Christ Jesus with ***e*** glory.

Titus
1:2 on the hope of ***e*** life that God,
3:7 we can inherit the hope for ***e*** life."

Hebrews
6:2 the dead, and ***e*** judgment—all over
9:14 God through the ***e*** Spirit as a
9:15 promise of the ***e*** inheritance on
13:20 dead by the blood of the ***e*** covenant,

1 Peter
5:10 you into his ***e*** glory in Christ

1 John
1:2 to you the ***e*** life that was
2:25 that he himself gave us: ***e*** life.
3:15 no murderer has ***e*** life residing in
5:11 God gave ***e*** life to us, and
5:13 that you can know that you have ***e*** life.
5:20 This is the true God and ***e*** life.

Jude
1:6 has kept them in ***e*** chains in the
1:7 the punishment of ***e*** fire, they serve
1:21 Jesus Christ, who will give you ***e*** life.

EUNUCH
Esther
2:3 Hegai the king's ***e*** in charge of the
2:14 He was the king's ***e*** in charge of the
2:15 Hegai the king's ***e*** in charge of the
Isaiah
56:3 And don't let the ***e*** say, "I'm just a
Jeremiah
52:25 city, he took a ***e*** who was appointed
Acts
8:27 worship. He was a ***e*** and an official
8:34 The ***e*** asked Philip, "Tell me, about
8:36 some water. The ***e*** said, "Look!
8:38 Philip and the ***e*** went down to the
8:39 Philip away. The ***e*** never saw him

EUNUCHS
2 Kings
20:18 They will become ***e*** in the palace of
Esther
1:10 Carcas, the seven ***e*** who served King
1:12 through the ***e***. The king was
1:15 Ahasuerus ordered her through the ***e***?"
2:21 Gate, two royal ***e***, Bigthan and
4:4 servants and ***e*** came and told her
4:5 one of the royal ***e*** whose job it was
6:2 the two royal ***e*** among the guards
6:14 several royal ***e*** arrived. They
7:9 one of the ***e*** serving the king,
Isaiah
39:7 taken to become ***e*** in the king of
56:4 LORD says: To the ***e*** who keep my
Jeremiah
34:19 Jerusalem, the ***e*** and priests, and
Matthew
19:12 For there are ***e*** who have been eunuchs

EUPHRATES
Genesis
2:14 the name of the fourth river is the ***E***.
15:18 from Egypt's river to the great ***E***,
Deuteronomy
11:24 and from the ***E*** River all the way
2 Kings
24:7 the border of Egypt to the ***E*** River.
Jeremiah
13:4 go at once to the ***E*** and put it under
Revelation
9:14 who are bound at the great river ***E***."

EVENING
Genesis
1:5 Night. There was ***e*** and there was
3:8 that day's cool ***e*** breeze, they
Exodus
12:18 month, from the ***e*** of the fourteenth
Leviticus
11:24 dead bodies will be unclean until ***e***,
14:46 is quarantined will be unclean until ***e***.
15:5 in water, and will be unclean until ***e***.
17:15 be unclean until ***e***. At that time,
22:6 be unclean until ***e***. He must not eat
Numbers
19:22 the unclean will be unclean until ***e***.
Ezra
3:3 both the morning and the ***e*** offerings.
Esther
2:14 In the ***e*** she would go in, and the next
Matthew
8:16 That ***e*** people brought to Jesus many who were demon—
16:2 he replied, "At ***e*** you say, 'It will
27:57 That ***e*** a man named Joseph came. He was a rich man
Luke
24:29 us. It's nearly ***e***, and the day is
John
6:16 When ***e*** came, Jesus' disciples went down to the lake
13:2 were sharing the ***e*** meal. The devil
20:19 of the week. That ***e***, while the
Acts
4:3 until the next day. (It was already ***e***.)
28:23 morning until ***e***, he explained and

EVERLASTING
Nehemiah
9:5 your God. From ***e*** to everlasting
Psalms
45:6 is eternal and ***e***. Your royal
78:66 his foes; he made them an ***e*** disgrace.
133:3 has commanded the blessing: ***e*** life.
Ezekiel
16:60 will establish an ***e*** covenant with you.
Daniel
2:44 will raise up an ***e*** kingdom that will
7:14 His rule is an ***e*** one—it will neve
7:27 kingship is an ***e*** one; every
Habakkuk
3:6 the nations. The ***e*** mountains
2 Peter
1:11 welcome into the ***e*** kingdom of our

EVIL
→ DO EVIL, DOING EVIL, EVIL ACTIONS, EVIL DEEDS, EVIL IN THE LORD'S EYES, EVIL ONE, EVIL PEOPLE, EVIL SPIRIT, EVIL SPIRITS, EVIL THING, EVIL THINGS, EVIL WAYS, GOOD AND EVIL
Genesis
2:9 tree of the knowledge of good and ***e***.
Numbers
20:5 bring us to this ***e*** place without
Job
1:1 integrity; he feared God and avoided ***e***.
Psalms
5:4 wickedness; ***e*** doesn't live with
22:16 me; a pack of ***e*** people circle me
37:8 get upset—it will only lead to ***e***.
37:27 Turn away from ***e***! Do good! Then you
51:4 I've committed ***e*** in your sight.
97:10 the LORD, hate ***e***! God guards the
Proverbs
3:7 Fear the LORD and turn away from ***e***.
4:27 the left; turn your feet away from ***e***.
8:13 LORD is to hate ***e***. I hate pride and
11:19 but those who pursue ***e***, toward death.
14:16 careful and avoid ***e***, but fools become
14:22 those who plan ***e*** go astray? Those
16:6 the fear of the LORD turns away ***e***.
17:13 ***E*** will never depart from the house of
20:30 bruises remove ***e***; beatings cleanse
24:20 no future for the ***e***; the lamp of the
26:26 but their ***e*** will be revealed

Isaiah
5:20 to those who call ***e*** good and good
13:11 the world for its ***e***, and bring their
Jeremiah
4:14 your heart of ***e***, Jerusalem, that
18:8 turns from its ***e***, then I'll relent
Lamentations
1:22 Let all their ***e*** come before you. Then
Ezekiel
33:13 They will die because of their ***e*** deeds.
Amos
5:13 silent in that time; it is an ***e*** time.
5:14 Seek good and not ***e***, that you may
Jonah
3:8 stop their ***e*** behavior and the
Matthew
5:37 more than this comes from the ***e*** one.
9:4 do you fill your minds with ***e*** things?
12:39 he replied, "An ***e*** and unfaithful
25:26 replied, 'You ***e*** and lazy servant!
Mark
1:23 a person with an ***e*** spirit screamed,
3:4 do good or to do ***e***, to save life or
3:11 Whenever the ***e*** spirits saw him, they
John
3:19 the light, for their actions are ***e***.
7:7 because I testify that its works are ***e***.
17:15 that you keep them safe from the ***e*** one.
Acts
23:5 will not speak ***e*** about a ruler of
Galatians
1:4 from this present ***e*** age, according to
Philippians
3:2 for people who do ***e*** things. Watch out
1 Thessalonians
5:22 Avoid every kind of ***e***
James
3:9 Don't pay back ***e*** for evil or insult for

EVIL ACTIONS
Is 43:24; Mk 7:22; Ro 12:17; Col 1:21; 3:25; 2Jn 1:11

EVIL DEEDS
1Sa 24:13; Ezr 9:13; Ps 28:4; Jer 4:4; 5:28; 11:15; 21:12; 33:5; Eze 33:13; Mi 3:4; Zec 1:4; Lk 3:20

EVIL IN THE LORD'S EYES
Nm 32:13; Dt 31:29; 1Sa 15:19; 2Sa 11:27; 1Ki 11:6; 14:22; 15:26, 34; 16:7, 19, 25, 30; 21:20, 25; 22:52; 2Ki 3:2; 8:18, 27; 13:2, 11; 14:24; 15:9, 18, 24, 28; 17:2, 17; 21:2, 6, 16, 20; 23:32, 37; 24:9, 19; 2Ch 21:6; 22:4; 33:2, 6, 22; 36:5, 9; Jer 52:2

EVIL ONE
Mt 5:37; 6:13; 13:19, 38; Jn 17:15; 1Co 5:13; Eph 6:16; 2Th 3:3; 1Jn 2:13; 2:14; 3:12; 5:18, 19

EVIL PEOPLE
Ex 23:1; 2Sa 4:11; Job 34:36; Ps 22:16; 140:1; Prv 4:14; 14:19; 17:11; 24:1, 19; 28:5; Mt 12:35; 13:49; 2Th 3:2; 2Ti 3:13

EVIL SPIRIT
1Sa 16:14; 16:15, 16, 23; 18:10; 19:9; Mk 1:23; 3:30; 5:2; Ac 19:15; 19:16

EVIL SPIRITS
Mk 3:11; Lk 7:21; 8:2; Ac 19:12; 19:13

EVIL THING
Gn 19:7; Dt 13:11; 17:5; 19:20; Neh 13:17

EVIL THINGS
1Sa 25:3; 2Ki 17:11; Ps 14:1; 140:2; 141:4; Lam 3:38; Hos 4:8; 6:9; Mt 9:4; 12:35; Mk 7:23; Ro 3:8; 1Co 10:6; Phi 3:2; Jas 4:11

EVIL WAYS
2Sa 3:25; 1Ki 13:33; 2Ki 17:13; Jer 18:11; 23:22; 25:5; 26:3; 35:15; 36:3, 7; 44:3, 5; Eze 13:22; 36:31; Zec 1:4; Ac 3:26

EVILDOERS
1 Samuel
24:13 deeds come from ***e***!' but I won't
Job
34:22 darkness, where ***e*** can hide
Psalms
5:5 long in your sight; you hate all ***e***;
6:8 from me, all you ***e***, because the LORD
14:4 dumb, all these ***e***, devouring my
14:6 You ***e*** may humiliate the plans of those
26:5 the company of ***e***, and I don't sit
27:2 When ***e*** come at me trying to eat me up—
36:12 is where the ***e*** have fallen,
37:1 get upset over ***e***; don't be jealous
37:9 Because ***e*** will be eliminated, but those
53:4 they dumb—these ***e***—devouring my peo
59:2 Deliver me from ***e***; save me from the
64:2 people; hide me from the schemes of ***e***
92:7 grass and all ***e*** seem to blossom,
92:9 die, how all ***e*** are scattered
94:4 arrogant words; all the ***e*** are bragging.
94:16 the wicked? Who will help me against ***e***?
101:8 to eliminate all ***e*** from the LORD's
119:115 away from me, you ***e***; I want to guard
125:5 off with other ***e***! Peace be on
141:4 things with ***e***, so I don't taste
141:9 protect me from the snares of the ***e***.
Isaiah
31:2 the house of ***e*** and against the
53:9 his tomb with ***e***, though he had
Jeremiah
12:1 enjoy success? Why are ***e*** so happy?
20:13 the needy from the clutches of ***e***.
23:14 They encourage ***e*** so that no one
Ezekiel
30:12 sell the land to ***e***. With the help of
Hosea
14:9 walk in them, but ***e*** will stumble in
Luke
13:27 are from. Go away from me, all you ***e***!'
18:11 else—crooks, ***e***, adulterers—or
Colossians
3:25 But ***e*** will receive their reward

EXAMINE

Genesis
18:21 go down now to ***e*** the cries of
Leviticus
13:3 The priest will ***e*** the infection on the
13:5 priest will again ***e*** the infection. If
13:6 the priest will ***e*** it again. If the
13:17 The priest will ***e*** it. If the infection
13:25 the priest will ***e*** it. If the hair has
13:27 priest will again ***e*** it. If it has
13:30 the priest will ***e*** it. If it appears to
13:32 the priest will ***e*** the infection
13:34 priest will again ***e*** the scabies. If
13:36 the priest must ***e*** it again. If the
13:43 The priest must ***e*** it. If the swelling
13:50 The priest will ***e*** the infection and
13:51 day he will ***e*** the infection
14:36 he comes to ***e*** it so that
1 Chronicles
29:17 my God, that you ***e*** the mind and take
Ezra
10:16 month they sat down to ***e*** the matter.
Job
5:24 secure. You will ***e*** your home and
Psalms
26:2 ***E*** me, LORD; put me to the test! Purify
48:13 ***E*** its defenses closely; tour its
119:6 be ashamed when I ***e*** all your
119:15 your precepts and ***e*** all your paths.
119:18 my eyes so I can ***e*** the wonders of
139:23 ***E*** me, God! Look at my heart! Put me to
Isaiah
14:16 at you; they will ***e*** you closely: "Is
Jeremiah
6:27 of metals, to ***e*** my people to know
Lamentations
3:40 must search and ***e*** our ways; we must
John
5:39 ***E*** the scriptures, since you think that
Acts
22:29 who were about to ***e*** him stepped away.
23:15 that you want to ***e*** his case more
2 Corinthians
13:5 ***E*** yourselves to see if you are in the
1 Thessalonians
2:4 God, who continues to ***e*** our hearts.
5:21 but ***e*** everything carefully and hang on
1 Peter
1:12 angels long to ***e***, have now been

EXAMPLE

Judges
2:17 commands, and didn't follow their ***e***.
Psalms
71:7 I've become an ***e*** to many people because
Ecclesiastes
9:13 the following ***e*** of wisdom under
Joel
2:17 a disgrace, an ***e*** of failure among
John
13:15 have given you an ***e***: just as I have
1 Corinthians
4:16 so I encourage you to follow my ***e***
10:11 to them as an ***e*** and were written
11:1 Follow my ***e***, just like I follow
Galatians
3:15 I'll use an ***e*** from human
Ephesians
5:2 following the ***e*** of Christ, who
5:22 For ***e***, wives should submit to their
1 Thessalonians
1:7 you became an ***e*** to all the
2 Thessalonians
3:9 to give you an ***e*** to imitate, not
1 Timothy
1:16 of all. So I'm an ***e*** for those who are
4:12 Instead, set an ***e*** for the believers
Hebrews
4:11 following the same ***e*** of disobedience,
6:12 but follow the ***e*** of the ones who
James
5:10 of the Lord as an ***e*** of patient
1 Peter
2:21 He left you an ***e*** so that you might
3:6 For ***e***, Sarah accepted Abraham's

EXECUTE

Leviticus
20:4 to Molech and do not ***e*** such a person,
Numbers
31:3 Midian and ***e*** the LORD's just
35:19 When he meets him, he will ***e*** him.
Deuteronomy
13:9 Instead, you must ***e*** them. Your own hand must be
Judges
20:13 so that we can ***e*** them and remove
2 Samuel
14:7 brother so we can ***e*** him for murdering
1 Kings
1:51 that he won't ***e*** his servant with
2:8 Surely I won't ***e*** you with the
3:28 was in him so he could ***e*** justice.
Isaiah
13:3 my proud, jubilant ones, to ***e*** my wrath.
Jeremiah
26:19 else in Judah ***e*** him? Didn't he
26:24 and wouldn't let the people ***e*** him.
Ezekiel
11:9 foreigners, and ***e*** judgments against
16:41 your houses and ***e*** judgments against
25:11 I'll ***e*** judgments in Moab, and they will
25:14 I will ***e*** my vengeance in Edom through
25:17 When I ***e*** my vengeance
28:26 in safety. When I ***e*** judgments against
30:14 fire to Zoan, and ***e*** judgments in
30:19 I will ***e*** judgments in Egypt, and they
44:24 They must ***e*** judgments according to my
Luke
21:16 and friends. They will ***e*** some of you.
Jude
1:15 to ***e*** judgment on everyone and to

EXECUTED

Leviticus
20:2 to Molech must be ***e***. The common
20:9 they must be ***e***. They have cursed
20:10 adulterer and the adulteress must be ***e***.
20:11 of them must be ***e***; their blood is
20:12 of them must be ***e***. They have acted
20:13 They must be ***e***; their blood is
20:15 he must be ***e*** and you must kill

20:16 They must be ***e***; their blood is
20:27 they must be ***e***. They will be
24:16 name must be ***e***. The whole
24:17 kills another person, they must be ***e***.
24:21 whoever kills a human being must be ***e***.
27:29 can be bought back; they must be ***e***.
Numbers
33:4 The LORD also ***e*** judgments against
35:30 another will be ***e*** on the evidence
Deuteronomy
13:5 must be ***e*** because he
17:6 No one may be ***e*** on the basis of
19:12 to the blood avenger, and he will be ***e***.
21:22 and they are ***e***, and you then
24:16 shouldn't be ***e*** because of what
33:21 together. Gad ***e*** the LORD's
1 Samuel
11:13 No one will be ***e*** because today the
14:39 person will be ***e***." Not one of the
14:45 rescued Jonathan, and he wasn't ***e***.
19:6 as the LORD lives, David won't be ***e***."
19:15 his bed," he ordered, "so he can be ***e***."
20:32 should David be ***e***? What has he
22:16 You will be ***e***, Ahimelech—you an
2 Samuel
21:9 time. They were ***e*** in the first days
1 Kings
2:24 he promised—Adonijah will be ***e*** today."
2 Kings
11:15 She must not be ***e*** in the LORD's
11:16 at the royal palace. She was ***e*** there.
11:18 into pieces. They ***e*** Mattan, Baal's
11:20 that Athaliah had been ***e*** at the palace.
14:5 his kingdom, he ***e*** the officials who
14:6 shouldn't be ***e*** because of what
21:24 of the land then ***e*** all those who had
2 Chronicles
22:9 to Jehu and ***e***. He was given a
23:14 She must not be ***e*** in the LORD's
23:15 at the royal palace. She was ***e*** there.
23:17 into pieces. They ***e*** Baal's priest
23:21 that Athaliah had been ***e*** at the palace.
25:3 his kingdom, he ***e*** the officials who
25:4 shouldn't be ***e*** because of what
33:25 of the land then ***e*** all those who had
Ezekiel
28:22 in you. When I've ***e*** judgment against
39:21 judgments that I ***e*** and the power
Matthew
10:21 other over to be ***e***. A father will
Mark
13:12 against their parents and have them ***e***.
Luke
23:32 two other criminals to be ***e*** with Jesus.
Acts
12:19 and had them ***e***. Afterward, Herod
13:28 they asked Pilate to have him ***e***.

EXHAUSTED

Judges
8:4 over, they were ***e*** but still giving
8:5 because they're ***e***, but I'm chasing
8:15 we give food to your ***e*** men now?'"
1 Samuel
14:28 doomed.' That's why the troops are ***e***."
14:31 Aijalon, the troops were completely ***e***.
30:10 stayed there, too ***e*** to cross the
30:21 men who were too ***e*** to follow him and
2 Samuel
16:2 for those who get ***e*** in the
16:14 the Jordan River ***e***, and he rested
Psalms
69:3 My eyes are ***e*** with waiting for
Proverbs
5:11 the end when your body and flesh are ***e***,
30:1 tired, God; I'm tired, God, and I'm ***e***.
Isaiah
9:1 distress won't be ***e***. At an earlier
40:29 power to the tired and reviving the ***e***.
57:16 their spirit is ***e***—I gave them
Jeremiah
49:4 Your strength is ***e***, you rebellious
Ezekiel
24:13 until I have ***e*** my anger against

EXILE

Judges
18:30 tribe until the land went into ***e***.
2 Samuel
15:19 foreigner and an ***e*** from your own
2 Kings
15:29 He sent the people into ***e*** to Assyria.
16:9 its citizens into ***e*** to Kir. He also
17:6 sent Israel into ***e*** to Assyria,
17:11 LORD sent into ***e*** before them. They
17:26 you sent into ***e*** and resettled in
18:11 sent Israel into ***e*** to Assyria. He
25:27 year of the ***e*** of King
1 Chronicles
5:6 carried away into ***e***. He was a chief
5:22 place of the inhabitants until the ***e***.
5:26 of Manasseh into ***e***, and brought them
8:6 Geba, who were sent into ***e*** to Manahath.
8:7 sent them into ***e*** and was the
9:1 was carried into ***e*** in Babylon
Ezra
6:21 had returned from ***e***, together with
Nehemiah
7:6 had taken into ***e***. They all
Esther
2:6 been taken into ***e*** away from
Psalms
144:14 in the walls, no ***e***, no outcries in
Isaiah
5:13 my people go into ***e*** since they didn't
Jeremiah
1:3 people of Jerusalem were taken into ***e***.
13:17 flock will be dragged off into ***e***.
13:19 be taken into ***e***; everyone will be
15:2 and those marked for ***e***—to exile.
20:4 Babylon, who will ***e*** some to Babylon
22:22 taken off to ***e***. Then you will be
29:7 sent you into ***e***. Pray to the LORD
29:14 after your long ***e***, declares the
29:16 those among you who didn't go into ***e***:
30:10 the land of their ***e***. My people Jacob
30:16 you will go into ***e***. Those who rob
43:11 those marked for ***e***, to exile. and
46:27 the land of their ***e***. My people Jacob
48:7 will go into ***e***, together with
48:11 been taken into ***e***. Therefore, its
49:3 surely go into ***e***, together with
52:27 Judah went away from its land into ***e***.

EXILE [cont.]

52:31 had been in ***e*** for thirty-seven y
Ezekiel
12:3 for going into ***e***. In the daytime
12:4 as if for ***e***. At twilight
12:11 them. They will go into captivity in ***e***.
25:3 when the house of Judah went into ***e***;
33:21 month of our ***e***, a survivor from
39:23 Israel went into ***e*** because of their
39:28 made them go into ***e*** among the
40:1 year of our ***e***, on the tenth day
Amos
5:5 will go into ***e***, and Bethel will
Micah
1:16 for they have gone from you into ***e***.
Nahum
2:7 She is sent into ***e***, carried away,
3:10 was destined for ***e***; she went into
Zechariah
14:2 go forth into ***e***, but what is left
Matthew
1:11 was at the time of the ***e*** to Babylon.
1:12 After the ***e*** to Babylon: Jechoniah was
1:17 from David to the ***e*** to Babylon, and

EXILED

2 Kings
17:23 So Israel was ***e*** from its land to
17:27 priests that you ***e*** from there. He
17:28 who had been ***e*** from Samaria went
17:33 the nations from which they had been ***e***.
24:14 Nebuchadnezzar ***e*** all of Jerusalem:
24:15 Nebuchadnezzar ***e*** Jehoiachin to Babylon;
24:16 king also ***e*** seven thousand
25:11 of the guard ***e*** the people who
25:21 Hamath. So Judah was ***e*** from its land.
1 Chronicles
6:15 Jerusalem to be ***e*** by Nebuchadnezzar.
2 Chronicles
36:20 Finally, he ***e*** to Babylon anyone who
Esther
2:6 King Nebuchadnezzar ***e*** to Babylon.)
Isaiah
24:11 dusk; happiness is ***e*** from the earth.
49:21 and desolate, ***e*** and sent off. So
Jeremiah
22:12 where he's been ***e*** and never see
Lamentations
1:3 Judah was ***e*** after suffering and hard

EXILES

2 Kings
24:14 thousand ***e***-as well as all the
Ezra
1:11 of these when the ***e*** went up from
2:1 those captive ***e*** whom Babylon's
4:1 that the returned ***e*** were building a
6:16 of the returned ***e***, joyfully
6:19 the returned ***e*** celebrated the
6:20 all the returned ***e***, their fellow
8:35 the returned ***e***, offered as
9:4 of the returned ***e*** while I remained
10:6 because of the unfaithfulness of the ***e***.
10:7 all the returned ***e*** should gather in
10:8 from the congregation of the ***e***.
10:16 Then the returned ***e*** did so. Ezra the
Nehemiah
7:6 of those ***e*** whom Babylon's
Psalms
147:2 Jerusalem, gathering up Israel's ***e***.
Isaiah
20:4 of Egypt and the ***e*** of Cush, both
45:13 city and set my ***e*** free, not for a
Jeremiah
24:5 kindly the Judean ***e*** that I have sent
28:4 with all the ***e*** from Judah who
28:6 temple and all the ***e*** to this place.
29:1 elders among the ***e***, to the priests
29:4 to all the ***e*** I have carried
29:20 But now, all you ***e*** I deported from
29:22 all the Judean ***e*** in Babylon will
29:31 word to all the ***e***: The LORD
Ezekiel
1:1 I was with the ***e*** at the Chebar
3:11 Then go to the ***e***, to your people's
3:15 and I came to the ***e*** who lived beside
11:24 brought me to the ***e*** in Chaldea,
11:25 I spoke to the ***e*** about everything the
Daniel
2:25 from the Judean ***e*** who will tell the
5:13 Daniel from the ***e*** that my father
6:13 of the Judean ***e***, Daniel, has
Zechariah
6:10 and gold from the ***e*** who came from

EXPERTS

→ PHARISEES AND LEGAL EXPERTS, PRIESTS AND LEGAL EXPERTS, RELIGIOUS EXPERTS

EXPLAIN

Exodus
13:8 You should ***e*** to your child on that day,
Deuteronomy
1:5 Moses began to ***e*** this Instruction.
Daniel
2:2 and Chaldeans to ***e*** his dreams to
5:15 me, but they couldn't ***e*** its meaning.
Matthew
13:36 to him and said, "***E*** to us the parable
15:15 Peter spoke up, "***E*** this riddle to

EXPOSED

Exodus
20:26 your genitals won't be ***e*** by doing so."
Leviticus
20:18 with her, he has ***e*** the source of her
Deuteronomy
22:30 his father's private matters are not ***e***.
2 Samuel
22:16 The seabeds were ***e***; the earth's
Psalms
18:15 The seabeds were ***e***; the earth's
Isaiah
47:3 nakedness will be ***e***, and your
Jeremiah
8:2 and ***e*** to the sun, the moon, and the
36:30 be cast out and ***e*** to the heat of
Ezekiel
16:36 of arousal and ***e*** yourself when you
16:57 wickedness was ***e***. You are now the
21:24 treacheries are ***e***, your sins can be
23:18 and her nakedness ***e***, I recoiled from
23:29 betrayal, and seductions will be ***e***.

Hosea
7:1 of Ephraim are ***e***, and the wicked
Luke
8:17 that won't be ***e***. Nor is anything
John
3:20 their actions will be ***e*** to the light.
Romans
7:13 that sin would be ***e*** as sin. That way
Ephesians
5:13 But everything ***e*** to the light is
Colossians
2:15 authorities, he ***e*** them to public
Hebrews
4:13 is naked and ***e*** to the eyes of
10:33 you were ***e*** to insults and
James
2:9 same law you are ***e*** as a lawbreaker.
2 Peter
3:10 and all the works done on it will be ***e***.
Revelation
3:18 be shamefully ***e***, and ointment to
16:15 don't go around naked and ***e*** to shame.)

EYE
Exodus
21:24 an ***e*** for an eye, a tooth for a tooth, a
21:26 and blinds the ***e*** of a male or
Deuteronomy
19:21 life for life, ***e*** for eye, tooth
2 Kings
9:30 she put on her ***e*** shadow and
Psalms
17:8 pupil of your ***e***! Hide me in the
32:8 I'll advise you and keep my ***e*** on you.
66:7 keeps a good ***e*** on the nations.
94:9 The one who formed the ***e***, can't he see?
Proverbs
7:2 instruction like the pupil of your ***e***.
10:10 Those who wink an ***e*** bring trouble;
16:30 who wink their ***e*** plot destruction;
28:27 who turn a blind ***e*** will be greatly
30:17 An ***e*** that mocks a father and rejects
Ecclesiastes
1:8 to speak. The ***e*** isn't satisfied
Matthew
5:29 And if your right ***e*** causes you to fall
5:38 it was said, An ***e*** for an eye and a
6:22 The ***e*** is the lamp of the body.
6:23 But if your ***e*** is bad, your whole body
7:3 or sister's ***e***, but don't notice
18:9 If your ***e*** causes you to fall into sin,
19:24 through the ***e*** of a needle than
1 Corinthians
2:9 love him that no ***e*** has seen, or ear
12:16 I'm not an ***e***," does that mean
15:52 the blink of an ***e***, at the final
Revelation
1:7 the clouds! Every ***e*** will see him,

EYES → EVIL IN THE LORD'S EYES
Matthew
9:30 Their ***e*** were opened. Then Jesus sternly
13:16 Happy are your ***e*** because they see.
21:42 done this, and it's amazing in our ***e***?
26:43 sleeping. Their ***e*** were heavy with
Mark
8:18 Don't you have ***e***? Why can't you see?
8:25 on the man's ***e*** again. He looked
14:40 keep their ***e*** open, and they
John
4:35 you: open your ***e*** and notice that
9:6 and smeared the mud on the man's ***e***.
9:17 he healed your ***e***?" He replied,
9:21 who healed his ***e***. Ask him. He's
9:32 a healing of the ***e*** of someone born
10:21 a demon heal the ***e*** of people who are
11:37 He healed the ***e*** of the man born
12:40 He made their ***e*** blind and closed their
Acts
9:18 fell from Saul's ***e*** and he could see
1 Peter
3:4 of beauty is very precious in God's ***e***.
3:12 The Lord's ***e*** are on the righteous and
Revelation
1:14 snow—and his ***e*** were like a fiery
2:18 God's Son, whose ***e*** are like a fiery
3:2 far from complete in the ***e*** of my God.
5:6 horns and seven ***e***, which are God's
7:17 wipe away every tear from their ***e***."
19:12 His ***e*** were like a fiery flame, and on
21:4 tear from their ***e***. Death will be no

EZRA
Ezra
7:10 ***E*** had determined to study and perform
Nehemiah
8:1 Gate. They asked ***E*** the scribe to

Ff

FACE

Genesis

3:19 the sweat of your ***f*** you will eat
17:3 Abram fell on his ***f***, and God said to
17:17 Abram fell on his ***f*** and laughed. He
30:40 the flock to ***f*** the striped and
32:30 I've seen God ***f***-to-face, and my
33:10 gift. Seeing your ***f*** is like seeing
38:15 because she had covered her ***f***.
43:31 He washed his ***f***, came back, pulled
44:23 with you, you'll never see my ***f*** again.'
46:30 after seeing your ***f***. You are really
48:11 I'd see your ***f***, but now God has
48:12 he bowed low with his ***f*** to the ground.

Exodus

3:6 Moses hid his ***f*** because he was
10:28 you never see my ***f*** again, because
10:29 said it! I'll never see your ***f*** again!"
13:17 have to fight and ***f*** war, they will
25:20 creatures should ***f*** each other toward
33:11 to speak to Moses ***f***-to-face, like two
33:20 you can't see my ***f*** because no one
33:23 my back, but my ***f*** won't be visible."
34:29 the skin of his ***f*** shown brightly
34:30 skin of Moses' ***f*** shining brightly,
34:33 with them, he put a veil over his ***f***.
34:35 skin of Moses' ***f*** was shining

Leviticus

20:3 I will set my own ***f*** against such a
20:5 I will set my own ***f*** against such a
26:9 I will turn my ***f*** to you, will make you
26:17 I will turn my ***f*** against you: you will

Numbers

6:25 The LORD make his ***f*** shine on you and be gracious
6:26 LORD lift up his ***f*** to you and grant
12:8 I speak with him ***f***-to-face, visibly,
12:14 had spit in her ***f***, would she not be
14:14 appear to them ***f***-to-face. Your clou
16:4 Moses heard this, he fell on his ***f***.

Deuteronomy

5:4 spoke with you ***f***-to-face on the mou
25:9 and spit in his ***f***. Then she will
31:17 I'll hide my ***f*** from them. They
31:18 I will hide my ***f*** at that time
32:20 I will hide my ***f*** from them—I will
34:10 Israel; Moses knew the LORD ***f***-to-face!

Joshua

5:14 fell flat on his ***f*** and worshipped.
7:10 do you lie flat on your ***f*** like this?

Judges

6:22 seen the LORD's messenger ***f***-to-face!"
9:33 marching out to ***f*** you, you can do

Ruth

2:10 she bowed down, ***f*** to the ground,

1 Samuel

17:48 ran quickly to the front line to ***f*** him.
17:49 and he fell ***f*** down on the
20:41 and fell down, ***f*** on the ground,

2 Samuel

2:22 I look your brother Joab in the ***f***?"
14:24 must not see my ***f***." So Absalom went
14:28 years without ever seeing the king's ***f***.
14:32 me see the king's ***f***. If I'm guilty,
19:4 king covered his ***f*** and cried out in

1 Kings

1:16 bowed down on her ***f*** before the king.
1:23 the king and bowed his ***f*** to the ground.
1:31 down with her ***f*** to the ground.
18:7 he fell on his ***f***. "My master!" he
18:42 ground and put his ***f*** between his knees.
19:13 he wrapped his ***f*** in his coat. He
21:4 and turned his ***f*** away. He wouldn't

2 Kings

4:29 reply. Put my staff on the boy's ***f***."
4:31 the young boy's ***f***, but there was no
8:15 over Ben-hadad's ***f*** until he died.
20:2 turned his ***f*** to the wall and

1 Chronicles

16:11 and his strength; seek his ***f*** always!
21:21 to David with his ***f*** to the ground.

2 Chronicles

7:14 pray, seek my ***f***, and turn from
20:17 out tomorrow and ***f*** them. The LORD
20:18 down with his ***f*** to the ground,

Ezra

9:6 to lift up my ***f*** to you. Our
9:15 though no one can ***f*** you because of

Esther

7:8 before covering Haman's ***f*** with dread.

Job

1:11 He will certainly curse you to your ***f***."
2:5 will definitely curse you to your ***f***."
4:15 swept by my ***f***; the hair of my
6:28 Now look at me—would I lie to your ***f***
9:27 put on a different ***f*** so I can smile,"
11:15 will lift up your ***f*** without blemish;
13:15 I will surely prove my way to his ***f***.
13:20 to me, then I won't hide from your ***f***.
13:24 Why hide your ***f*** from me and consider me your enemy
15:27 They cover their ***f*** with grease and make
16:16 My ***f*** is red from crying, and dark gloom
22:26 in the Almighty; lift up your ***f*** to God.
24:15 can see me, and puts a mask over his ***f***.
26:9 hid the ***f*** of the full moon, spreading
30:10 don't withhold spit from my ***f***.
34:29 if he hides his ***f***, who can see him?

Psalms

4:6 The light of your ***f*** has left us,
10:11 has hidden his ***f***. God never sees

11:7 whose heart is right will see God's ***f***.
13:1 How long will you hide your ***f*** from me?
17:15 I will see your ***f*** in righteousness;
22:24 didn't hide his ***f*** from me. No, he
24:6 that seeks the ***f*** of Jacob's God.
27:8 says, seek God's ***f***. LORD, I do seek
31:16 Shine your ***f*** on your servant; save me
34:16 But the LORD's ***f*** is set against those
42:2 God. When will I come and see God's ***f***?
44:3 the light of your ***f*** because you were
44:15 confronts me, and shame covers my ***f***
44:24 you hiding your ***f***, forgetting our
50:21 it all out, right in front of your ***f***.
51:9 Hide your ***f*** from my sins; wipe away all
61:3 of strength in the ***f*** of the enemy.
67:1 let God make his ***f*** shine on us, Selah
69:7 because of you. Shame covers my ***f***.
69:17 Don't hide your ***f*** from me, your
80:3 God! Make your ***f*** shine so that we
80:7 forces! Make your ***f*** shine so that we
80:19 forces! Make your ***f*** shine so that we
84:9 attention to the ***f*** of your anointed
88:14 LORD? Why do you hide your ***f*** from me?
90:8 hidden faults in the light from your ***f***.
102:2 Don't hide your ***f*** from me in my time of
104:15 which makes the ***f*** shine, and bread,
104:29 you hide your ***f***, they are
105:4 and his strength; seek his ***f*** always!
116:3 found me—I came ***f***-to-face with troub
119:87 wiped me off the ***f*** of the earth!
119:135 Shine your ***f*** on your servant, and teach
143:7 Don't hide your ***f*** from me or I'll

Proverbs
7:13 kisses him. Her ***f*** is brazen as she
15:13 brightens one's ***f***, but a troubled
16:15 of the king's ***f***. His favor is
27:19 reflects the ***f***, so the heart

Ecclesiastes
7:3 because a sad ***f*** may lead to a
8:1 it changes the hardness of someone's ***f***.

Song of Songs
2:14 in the cliff ***f***—let me catch sig
4:3 the curve of your ***f*** behind the veil
6:7 the curve of your ***f*** behind the veil

Isaiah
8:17 has hidden his ***f*** from the house of
24:1 will twist its ***f*** and scatter its
25:8 tears from every ***f***; he will remove
29:22 now, and his ***f*** won't grow pale
38:2 turned his ***f*** to the wall and
50:6 I didn't hide my ***f*** from insults and
50:7 I set my ***f*** like flint, and
54:8 of rage, I hid my ***f*** from you for a
59:2 have hidden his ***f*** from you so that
65:3 provoke me to my ***f*** continually,

Jeremiah
13:26 skirt over your ***f*** and expose your
18:17 I will show them my back, not my ***f***.
21:10 I have set my ***f*** against this city for
28:16 off the ***f*** of the earth!
33:5 anger. I hid my ***f*** from the people

Ezekiel
1:10 four had a human ***f***, with a lion's
1:28 it, I fell on my ***f***. I heard the
3:8 now hardened your ***f*** so that you can
3:23 the Chebar River, and I fell on my ***f***.
4:3 you and the city. ***F*** it directly. When
4:7 stretched out, ***f*** the siege of
6:2 Human one, ***f*** Israel's mountains, and
7:18 them. On every ***f***, shame; on all
7:22 When I hide my ***f*** from my people,
9:8 I fell on my ***f***, and I cried out,
10:14 faces. The first ***f*** was that of a
11:13 I fell on my ***f***, and I wailed and
12:6 dark. Cover your ***f*** so that you can't
12:12 he will cover his ***f*** so that his eyes
13:17 You, human one, ***f*** the daughters of your people
20:35 and there I will judge you ***f***-to-face.
20:46 Human one, ***f*** Teman, preach against the south
21:2 Human one, ***f*** Jerusalem, preach against
25:2 Human one, ***f*** the Ammonites and prophesy
28:9 When you ***f*** your murderers, will you
28:21 Human one, ***f*** Sidon, prophesy against
29:2 Human one, ***f*** Pharaoh, Egypt's king, and prophesy
35:2 Human one, ***f*** Mount Seir, and prophesy
38:2 Human one, ***f*** Gog in the land of Magog,
39:23 me, I hid my ***f*** from them. When I
39:24 transgressions and hid my ***f*** from them.
39:29 I won't hide my ***f*** from them again.
41:19 A human ***f*** turned toward one palm tree,
42:13 chambers that ***f*** the building and
43:3 the Chebar River, and I fell on my ***f***.
44:4 the LORD's temple, and I fell on my ***f***.

Daniel
3:19 rage, and his ***f*** twisted beyond
5:9 drained from his ***f***, and his princes
8:17 I fell with my ***f*** to the ground.
8:18 into a trance. My ***f*** was still on the
9:3 I then turned my ***f*** to my Lord God,
9:17 help. Shine your ***f*** on your ruined
10:6 like topaz. His ***f*** was like a flash
10:9 into a trance with my ***f*** on the ground.
10:15 me, I turned my ***f*** to the ground and
11:18 He will turn his ***f*** to the coastlands,

Hosea
7:2 who they are, right in front of my ***f***.

Amos
9:6 them out upon the ***f*** of the earth—the
9:8 it from the ***f*** of the earth.

Micah
3:4 He will hide his ***f*** from them at that

Nahum
3:5 skirts over your ***f***; I will show

Matthew
6:16 put on a sad ***f*** like the
6:17 fast, brush your hair and wash your ***f***.
17:2 of them. His ***f*** shone like the
18:10 looking into the ***f*** of my Father who
26:39 and fell on his ***f*** and prayed, "My
26:67 they spit in his ***f*** and beat him.
28:3 Now his ***f*** was like lightning and his

Mark
14:65 Some covered his ***f*** and hit him,

Luke
5:12 he fell on his ***f*** and begged,
9:29 appearance of his ***f*** changed and his
17:16 He fell on his ***f*** at Jesus' feet and
21:35 who lives on the ***f*** of the whole

John
11:44 tied, and his ***f*** covered with a
18:22 Jesus in the ***f***. "Is that how you
19:3 Jews!" And they slapped him in the ***f***.
20:7 He also saw the ***f*** cloth that had been
Acts
6:15 they saw that his ***f*** was radiant, just
1 Corinthians
13:12 then we will see ***f***-to-face. Now I kno
2 Corinthians
3:7 long at Moses' ***f*** because his face
3:13 a veil over his ***f*** so that the
4:6 God's glory in the ***f*** of Jesus Christ.
11:20 you or if someone hits you in the ***f***.
Galatians
2:11 him to his ***f***, because he was
Philippians
1:30 that you saw me ***f*** and now hear that
1 Thessalonians
2:17 our desire to see you again ***f***-to-face.
3:4 we were going to ***f*** problems exactly
1 Timothy
5:24 the people must ***f*** judgment, but the
Hebrews
9:27 to die once and then ***f*** judgment.
2 John
1:12 and talk with you ***f***-to-face, so that o
3 John
1:14 you soon, and we will speak ***f***-to-face.
Revelation
4:7 creature had a ***f*** like a human
6:16 hide us from the ***f*** of the one seated
10:1 his head. His ***f*** was like the sun,
20:11 on it. Before his ***f*** both earth and
22:4 They will see his ***f***, and his name will

FACED

Exodus
37:9 creatures ***f*** each other toward
2 Samuel
19:7 that you've ***f*** from your youth
1 Kings
7:4 sets of window frames ***f*** each other.
17:5 Cherith Brook that ***f*** the Jordan River.
Ezekiel
10:11 the leading one ***f***, they moved in
40:13 openings that ***f*** each other. From
40:31 Its porch ***f*** the outer courtyard. Palms
40:34 Its porch ***f*** the outer courtyard. Palm
40:37 Its porch ***f*** the outer courtyard. Palm
40:44 the North Gate ***f*** south, and the
47:1 (the temple ***f*** east). The water
Daniel
6:10 open windows that ***f*** Jerusalem. Daniel
Luke
8:42 moved forward, he ***f*** smothering crowds.
Acts
25:16 before they have ***f*** their accusers
27:12 its harbor, which ***f*** southwest and
2 Corinthians
11:23 I can count. I've ***f*** death many times.
11:26 many journeys. I ***f*** dangers from
11:27 I ***f*** these dangers with hard work and

FACES

Genesis
42:6 down to him, their ***f*** to the ground.
Numbers
14:5 fell on their ***f*** before the
16:22 fell on their ***f*** and said, "God,
16:45 in an instant. They fell on their ***f***,
20:6 fell on their ***f***. Then the LORD's
33:7 hahiroth, which ***f*** Baal-zephon, and
Deuteronomy
34:1 slope, which ***f*** Jericho. The LORD
Joshua
7:6 lay flat on their ***f*** before the LORD's
15:2 Dead Sea, from the bay that ***f*** south.
1 Samuel
26:1 hill, which ***f*** Jeshimon," they
2 Samuel
2:24 of Ammah, which ***f*** Giah on the road
1 Kings
17:3 Cherith Brook that ***f*** the Jordan River.
18:39 and fell on their ***f***. "The LORD is the
1 Chronicles
21:16 in mourning clothes, fell on their ***f***;
2 Chronicles
7:3 with their ***f*** to the ground,
Nehemiah
8:6 the LORD with their ***f*** to the ground.
Job
9:24 he covers the ***f*** of its judges. If
17:6 proverb; I'm like spit in people's ***f***.
21:31 behavior to their ***f***; they act, and
40:13 dust; bind their ***f*** in a hidden place.
Psalms
21:12 you aim your bow straight at their ***f***!
34:5 will shine; their ***f*** are never ashamed.
83:16 Cover their ***f*** with shame, LORD, so that
Proverbs
25:23 who plots quietly provokes angry ***f***.
27:17 so friends sharpen each other's ***f***.
Isaiah
3:15 and grind the ***f*** of the poor? says
6:2 they veiled their ***f***, with two their
13:8 at each other aghast, their ***f*** blazing.
49:23 nursemaids. With ***f*** to the ground
53:3 people hid their ***f***, he was despised,
Jeremiah
2:27 me and not their ***f***. Yet in their
5:3 They make their ***f*** harder than rock
32:33 me and not their ***f***; and though I
50:5 turning their ***f*** toward it. They
Ezekiel
1:6 though each had four ***f*** and four wings
1:8 All four creatures had ***f*** and wings, and
1:10 the form of their ***f***: each of the four
1:15 to all four ***f*** of the creatures.
9:2 Upper Gate that ***f*** north. All of
10:14 creature had four ***f***. The first face
10:21 Each had four ***f*** and four wings, with
10:22 forms of their ***f*** were the same
27:35 on end; their ***f*** betray their
41:18 and each winged creature had two ***f***.
43:17 is twenty-one inches. Its ramp ***f*** east.
44:1 gate that ***f*** east. It was
Daniel
1:10 if he sees your ***f*** looking thinner
Joel
2:6 with fear; all ***f*** turn red with
Nahum
2:10 in every groin; all the ***f*** grow pale.
Habakkuk
1:9 with all their ***f*** set toward the

Malachi
2:3 feces on your ***f***, the feces of
Matthew
6:16 distort their ***f*** so people will
17:6 fell on their ***f***, filled with awe.
Luke
24:5 and bowed their ***f*** toward the
24:17 along?" They stopped, their ***f*** downcast.
1 Corinthians
14:25 fall on their ***f*** and worship God,
2 Corinthians
3:18 with unveiled ***f*** at the glory of
James
1:23 those who look at their ***f*** in a mirror.
Revelation
9:7 crowns. Their ***f*** were like human
11:16 fell on their ***f*** and worshipped

FACING

Genesis
15:10 laid the halves ***f*** each other, but
Exodus
27:13 on the front, ***f*** east should be
28:26 pendant on its inside edge ***f*** the vest.
38:13 The front side ***f*** east was seventy-five
39:19 pendant, on its inside edge ***f*** the vest.
Joshua
8:33 chest. They were ***f*** the levitical
2 Samuel
15:21 the king may be, ***f*** death or facing
1 Kings
7:5 were rectangular, ***f*** each other in
7:25 the center, three ***f*** north, three
22:35 up in the chariot ***f*** the Arameans. But
2 Kings
23:13 the shrines ***f*** Jerusalem, south
2 Chronicles
3:13 stood on their feet ***f*** the main room.
4:4 the center, three ***f*** north, three
18:34 up in his chariot ***f*** the Arameans. But
Ezra
8:22 to help us in ***f*** enemies on the
Nehemiah
8:3 ***F*** the area in front of the Water Gate,
Esther
5:1 of the palace, ***f*** the palace
Job
10:15 my head, full of shame and ***f*** my misery.
Ezekiel
8:16 twenty-five men ***f*** toward the east
40:6 entered the gate ***f*** east. He went up
40:20 the one ***f*** north at the outer courtyard.
40:24 there was a gate ***f*** south. He
40:45 me: "The chamber ***f*** south is for the
40:46 and the chamber ***f*** north is for the
41:11 free space, one ***f*** north, the other
41:12 The structure ***f*** the yard on the west
42:7 to the chambers ***f*** the outer
42:8 as the chambers ***f*** the outer
46:12 the gate ***f*** east will be
46:19 the holy chambers ***f*** north. There was
Mark
15:39 who stood ***f*** Jesus, saw how he
1 Corinthians
15:31 Jesus our Lord, I'm ***f*** death every day.
Philippians
1:30 me face and now hear that I'm still ***f***.

FAIL

Leviticus
26:16 make the eyes ***f*** and drain life
Deuteronomy
28:40 oil because your olive trees will ***f***.
1 Samuel
3:19 not allowing any of his words to ***f***.
1 Kings
2:4 will never ***f*** to be on the
8:25 You will never ***f*** to have a
9:5 You will never ***f*** to have a
2 Kings
10:10 dynasty will ***f*** to come true. The
2 Chronicles
6:16 You will never ***f*** to have a
7:18 You will never ***f*** to have a
Ezra
6:9 be given to them day by day without ***f***
Job
14:7 still sprouting and its shoots don't ***f***,
17:5 for gain, and his children's eyes ***f***.
Psalms
5:10 God! Let them ***f*** by their own
21:11 a wicked plan—but they will ***f***!
73:26 body and my heart ***f***, but God is my
Proverbs
15:22 Plans ***f*** with no counsel, but with many
Isaiah
19:3 spirit will ***f*** from within; I
26:10 wrong, and they ***f*** to see the LORD's
32:10 harvest will ***f***; the vintage
45:23 and won't ***f***. Surely every
49:15 nursing child, ***f*** to pity the child
65:20 days, or the old ***f*** to live out their
Jeremiah
4:9 his princes will ***f***, the priests will
17:8 the time of drought or ***f*** to bear fruit.
18:18 instruction won't ***f***, nor will the
32:5 against the Babylonians, you will ***f***.'"
42:5 against us if we ***f*** to do everything
Lamentations
1:14 makes my strength ***f***. My Lord has
Daniel
11:14 to support the vision, but they will ***f***.
Hosea
9:2 feed them; the new wine will ***f*** them.
Luke
22:32 your faith won't ***f***. When you have
2 Corinthians
13:5 you? Unless, of course, you ***f*** the test.
13:6 will realize that we don't ***f*** the test.
13:7 right thing, even if we appear to ***f***.
2 Peter
3:5 But they ***f*** to notice that, by God's

FAILED

Genesis
45:26 heart nearly ***f***, and he didn't
48:10 eyesight had ***f*** from old age and
Joshua
8:35 that Joshua ***f*** to read aloud in
21:45 house of Israel ***f***. Every promise
23:14 about you has ***f***. They were all
1 Samuel
25:37 Nabal's heart ***f*** inside him, and
2 Kings
3:26 through to Edom's king. But they ***f***.
22:13 our ancestors ***f*** to obey the words

FAILED [cont.]

2 Chronicles
13:20 Jeroboam **f** to regain power during the
24:22 King Jehoash **f** to remember the loyalty
30:3 the priests had **f** to make
34:21 our ancestors **f** to obey the
Ezra
10:8 All those who **f** to appear within three
Jeremiah
3:3 the showers have **f** and the spring
10:21 is why they have **f** and their flock
Lamentations
4:17 eyes continually **f**, looking for some
Romans
9:6 God's word has **f**. Not all who are

FAITH → FAITH HAS HEALED YOU, FAITH IN GOD, THROUGH FAITH, YOU HAVE FAITH

Deuteronomy
1:32 But you had no **f** in the LORD your God
Psalms
27:13 But I have sure **f** that I will
33:4 right, his every act is done in good **f**.
78:22 they had no **f** in God, because
78:32 and had no **f** in God's wondrous
Isaiah
26:2 nation enter, a nation that keeps **f**.
Matthew
6:30 more for you, you people of weak **f**?
8:10 in Israel I haven't found **f** like this.
9:22 daughter. Your **f** has healed you."
14:31 You man of weak **f**! Why did you
15:28 you have great **f**. It will be just
16:8 people of weak **f**! Why are you
17:20 you have little **f**," he said. "I
21:21 that if you have **f** and don't doubt,
21:22 If you have **f**, you will receive
23:23 peace, and **f**. You ought to
Mark
9:24 out, "I have **f**; help my lack of
John
12:42 acknowledge their **f** because they
Acts
3:16 is, because of **f** in Jesus' name,
6:5 with exceptional **f**, Philip,
14:27 opened a door of **f** for the Gentiles.
Romans
1:16 to all who have **f** in God, to the
1:17 faithfulness for **f**, as it is
3:30 righteous by **f** will also make
4:3 say? Abraham had **f** in God, and it
4:9 We say, "**F** was credited to
6:8 Christ, we have **f** that we will also
9:30 the righteousness that comes from **f**.
10:4 for all who have **f** in God.
12:6 prophesy in proportion to your **f**.
Galatians
1:23 now preaches the **f** that he once
2:20 body, I live by **f**, indeed, by the
3:8 on the basis of **f**, scripture
5:6 Christ Jesus, but **f** working through
Ephesians
6:16 the shield of **f** so that you can
1 Thessalonians
1:3 that comes from **f**, your effort that
Hebrews
10:38 one will live by **f**, and my whole
11:1 **F** is the reality of what we hope for,
James
1:3 testing of your **f** produces
2:26 body is dead, so **f** without actions

FAITH HAS HEALED YOU

Mt 9:22; Mk 5:34; 10:52; Lk 8:48; 17:19; 18:42

FAITH IN GOD

Ps 78:22; Mk 11:22; Ac 27:25; Ro 1:16; 4:3, 5, 11; 10:4; Heb 6:1

FAITHFUL → FAITHFUL LOVE, FAITHFUL LOVE LASTS FOREVER, FAITHFUL ONES

Genesis
24:49 you're loyal and **f** to my master,
Deuteronomy
7:9 God! He is the **f** God, who keeps
32:4 right! He's the **f** God, never
33:8 your Urim to your **f** one—the one you
1 Samuel
2:9 the feet of his **f** ones, but the
2 Samuel
20:19 the peaceful and **f** in Israel, but
1 Chronicles
16:34 good, because his **f** love endures
16:41 LORD, because his **f** love endures
17:13 never withdraw my **f** love from him as
Psalms
4:3 care of the **f**. The LORD will
12:1 are all gone; the **f** have completely
16:10 won't let your **f** follower see the
19:7 LORD's laws are **f**, making naive
30:4 You who are **f** to the LORD, sing praises
32:6 why all the **f** should pray to
37:28 never leave his **f** all alone. They
50:5 Bring my **f** to me, those who made a
51:10 God; put a new, **f** spirit deep
78:8 firm and whose spirit wasn't **f** to God.
78:37 on him; they weren't **f** to his covenant.
79:2 the flesh of your **f** to the wild
79:3 the blood of the **f** like water all
85:7 Show us your **f** love, LORD! Give us your
89:19 a vision to your **f** servants: I
89:37 like the moon, a **f** witness in the
93:5 Your laws are so **f**. Holiness decorates
101:6 on those who are **f** in the land, to
116:15 of the LORD's **f** is a costly loss
132:9 let your **f** shout out with
141:5 me; let the **f** correct me! Let
145:17 in all his ways, **f** in all his deeds.
149:9 for all God's **f** people. Praise
Isaiah
1:21 This **f** town has become a prostitute!
Daniel
1:9 had established **f** loyalty between
9:4 and truly **f** to all who love
Matthew
24:45 Who then are the **f** and wise servants
John
8:31 if you remain **f** to my teaching.
Hebrews
2:17 a merciful and **f** high priest in
3:2 Jesus was **f** to the one who appointed
3:5 Moses was **f** in all God's house as a
3:6 But Jesus was **f** over God's house as a
11:11 that the one who promised was **f**.

James
2:17 when it doesn't result in ***f*** activity.
Revelation
1:5 Jesus Christ—the ***f*** witness, the
2:10 for ten days. Be ***f*** even to the point
3:14 of the Amen, the ***f*** and true witness,
17:14 with him are called, chosen, and ***f***."
19:11 rider was called ***F*** and True, and he

FAITHFUL LOVE

2Sa 7:15; 9:1, 7; 22:51; 1Ch 16:34; 16:41; 17:13; 2Ch 5:13; 7:3, 6; 20:21; Ps 5:7; 6:4; 13:5; 17:7; 18:50; 21:7; 23:6; 25:6, 7; 26:3; 31:7, 16, 21, 23; 32:10; 33:5, 18, 22; 36:7, 10; 42:8; 44:26; 48:9; 51:1; 52:1, 8; 57:10; 59:16; 62:12; 63:3; 66:20; 69:13, 16; 77:8; 85:7, 10; 86:5, 13, 15; 88:11; 90:14; 94:18; 101:1; 103:4, 8, 11, 17; 106:1, 7, 45; 107:1, 8, 15, 21, 31, 43; 108:4; 109:12, 16, 21, 26; 117:2; 118:1, 2, 3, 4, 29; 119:41, 64, 76, 88, 124, 149, 159; 130:7; 136:1, 2, 3, 4, 5, 6, 7, 8, 9, 10, 11, 12, 13, 14, 15, 16, 17, 18, 19, 20, 21, 22, 23, 24, 25, 26; 138:8; 143:8, 12; 145:8; 147:11; Is 54:10; Lam 3:22; Hos 4:1; 6:6; 10:12; 12:6; Jl 2:13; Jon 4:2; Mi 6:8; 7:18, 20

FAITHFUL LOVE LASTS FOREVER

2Ch 5:13; 7:3, 6; 20:21; Ps 107:1; 118:1, 2, 3, 4, 29; 136:1, 2, 3, 4, 5, 6, 7, 8, 9, 10, 11, 12, 13, 14, 15, 16, 17, 18, 19, 20, 21, 22, 23, 24, 25, 26; 138:8

FAITHFUL ONES

1Sa 2:9; Ps 85:8; 97:10; 145:10; 148:14; Mi 7:2

FAITHFULLY

Exodus
19:5 So now, if you ***f*** obey me and stay true
Deuteronomy
4:6 Keep them ***f*** because that will show your
Joshua
2:14 deal loyally and ***f*** with you when the
22:3 Israelites. You ***f*** obeyed the
24:14 him honestly and ***f***. Put aside the
Judges
9:15 If you're acting ***f*** in anointing me
9:16 now, if you acted ***f*** and innocently
9:19 if you've acted ***f*** and innocently
Ruth
1:8 May the LORD deal ***f*** with you, just as
3:10 acted even more ***f*** than you did at
1 Samuel
12:24 and serve him ***f*** with all your
2 Samuel
22:26 You deal ***f*** with the faithful; you show
1 Kings
2:4 to walk before me ***f***, with all their
6:12 all my commands ***f***, then I will
1 Chronicles
17:15 Nathan ***f*** reported all that he had seen
2 Chronicles
31:15 and Shecaniah ***f*** assisted him
31:18 they had ***f*** made themselves
Nehemiah
9:32 are the one who ***f*** keeps the
9:33 you have acted ***f***, and we have done
10:29 and to observe ***f*** all the
Psalms
18:25 You deal ***f*** with the faithful; you show
Isaiah
10:20 they will ***f*** depend on the
16:5 someone will sit ***f*** on it in David's
61:8 I will ***f*** give them their
Jeremiah
23:28 word proclaim it ***f***. What a
32:41 them in this land ***f*** and with all my
Ezekiel
18:9 laws, and act ***f***. Such people are
1 Timothy
6:2 serve them more ***f***, because the
Titus
3:15 those who love us ***f***. Grace be with
3 John
1:5 friend, you act ***f*** in whatever you

FAITHFULNESS → LOVE AND FAITHFULNESS, LOYAL LOVE AND FAITHFULNESS

FALL → FALL AWAY, FALL INTO SIN

Exodus
9:18 heaviest hail to ***f*** on Egypt that has
Numbers
11:9 the night, the manna would ***f*** with it.
14:3 to this land to ***f*** by the sword? Our
1 Chronicles
21:13 Gad. "I'd rather ***f*** into the hands of
2 Chronicles
21:15 will cause your intestines to ***f*** out."
Psalms
72:6 Let him ***f*** like rain upon fresh-cut
91:7 thousand people ***f*** dead next to you,
106:26 them, making them ***f*** in the desert,
140:10 Let burning coals ***f*** on them! Let them
Proverbs
7:26 many corpses to ***f***; she has killed
11:5 but the wicked ***f*** in their
17:20 twisted tongues will ***f*** into trouble.
28:10 an evil path will ***f*** into their own
Isaiah
3:25 Your men will ***f*** by the sword, your
Jeremiah
4:31 I'm about to ***f*** into the hands of
Hosea
7:16 officials will ***f*** by the sword
Amos
3:5 Will a bird ***f*** into a trap on the ground
Matthew
5:29 eye causes you to ***f*** into sin, tear it
24:29 The stars will ***f*** from the sky and
26:31 you will all ***f*** away because of
Luke
10:18 I saw Satan ***f*** from heaven like
Romans
3:23 have sinned and ***f*** short of God's
1 Corinthians
8:13 I may cause my brother or sister to ***f***.
James
1:11 that its flowers ***f*** and its beauty is

FALL AWAY

Mt 13:21; 13:41; 24:10; 26:31; Mk 4:17; Lk 8:13; Jn 16:1

FALL INTO SIN

Mt 5:29; 5:30; 18:6, 7, 8, 9; Mk 9:42; 9:43, 45, 47; Lk 17:1; 17:2

FALLEN

2 Samuel
1:19 Look how the mighty warriors have ***f***!
Psalms
9:15 The nations have ***f*** into the hole they
16:6 lines have ***f*** beautifully for
22:14 All my bones have ***f*** apart. My heart
36:12 evildoers have ***f***, pushed down,
69:9 of those who insult you have ***f*** on me!
Isaiah
3:8 and Judah has ***f***, because the way
21:9 up and said, "***F***, fallen is
Revelation
9:1 a star that had ***f*** from heaven to
14:8 and said, "***F***, fallen is

FALLS

Genesis
49:17 horse's heels, so its rider ***f*** backward.
Exodus
21:33 and an ox or a donkey ***f*** into the pit,
Job
4:13 of night, when deep sleep ***f*** on people,
33:15 when deep sleep ***f*** upon humans,
Psalms
11:3 bottom of things ***f*** out, what can a
46:2 when the world ***f*** apart, when the
Ecclesiastes
11:3 earth. If a tree ***f***, whether to the
Matthew
12:11 has a sheep that ***f*** into a pit on the
17:15 for he often ***f*** into the fire or
21:44 Whoever ***f*** on this stone will be
1 Peter
1:24 grass dries up and its flower ***f*** off,

FALSE → FALSE GODS, FALSE PROPHETS, FALSE TEACHERS, FALSE TESTIMONY, FALSE WITNESS, FALSE WITNESSES

FALSE GODS

Ps 106:36; 106:38; Is 10:11; Jer 14:22; 1Co 5:10; 5:11; 6:9; 8:4, 10; 10:7, 14; 12:2

FALSE PROPHETS

Mt 7:15; 24:11, 24; Mk 13:22; Lk 6:26; 2Pt 2:1; 1Jn 4:1

FALSE TEACHERS

2Pt 2:1; 2:2, 12, 17, 19

FALSE TESTIMONY

Dt 19:18; Mt 19:18; 26:59; Mk 10:19; 14:56; Lk 18:20

FALSE WITNESS

Prv 6:19; 12:17; 14:5; 19:5; Mk 14:57

FALSE WITNESSES

Ps 27:12; Prv 19:9; Mt 26:60; Ac 6:13; 1Co 15:15

FAMILIES

Genesis
8:19 ground, came out of the ark by their ***f***.
12:3 curse; all the ***f*** of earth will be
36:40 to their ***f***, their locations,
Exodus
12:21 flock for your ***f***, and slaughter
Leviticus
25:45 their extended ***f*** that are with
Deuteronomy
11:6 them, their ***f***, their tents, and
12:7 of you and your ***f***, in the LORD your
Joshua
14:1 the heads of the ***f*** of the Israelite
19:51 the heads of the ***f*** of the Israelite
21:1 of the levitical ***f*** approached
1 Samuel
9:21 littlest of the ***f*** in the tribe of
10:21 forward by its ***f***, and the family
1 Chronicles
6:33 served and their ***f*** were: Kohath's
16:28 to the LORD, all ***f*** of the nations—g
2 Chronicles
5:12 and their ***f*** and relatives—wer
31:17 by their ***f***, and to Levites
35:4 yourselves by ***f*** according to your
35:12 by their ***f*** to sacrifice to
Ezra
1:5 the heads of the ***f*** of Judah and
2:68 the heads of the ***f*** brought
3:12 and heads of ***f***, who had seen the
4:2 the heads of the ***f*** and said to them,
4:3 the heads of the ***f*** in Israel
8:1 the heads of the ***f***, and this is the
8:29 the heads of the ***f*** of Israel, within
10:16 men, heads of ***f***, each
Nehemiah
4:13 the people by ***f***, and they had
4:14 Fight for your ***f***, your sons, your
7:5 be registered by ***f***. I found the
7:70 of the heads of ***f*** made a donation
7:71 of the heads of ***f*** gave 20,000
8:13 the heads of the ***f*** of all the
10:34 God's house by ***f*** at the appointed
11:13 heads of ***f***: 242. There was
12:12 of the priestly ***f*** in the days of
12:22 as heads of ***f*** in the rule of
12:23 who were heads of ***f*** were recorded in
Psalms
96:7 to the LORD, all ***f*** of the nations—
107:41 he makes their ***f*** as numerous as
133:1 it is when ***f*** live together as
Isaiah
7:17 and upon your ***f*** days unlike any
Jeremiah
2:4 of Judah, all you ***f*** of the Israelite
31:1 God of all the ***f*** of Israel, and
33:24 rejected the two ***f*** that he had
Ezekiel
47:22 you and raise ***f*** among you are
Amos
3:2 deeply of all the ***f*** of the earth.
Zechariah
14:17 Whoever among the ***f*** of the earth
Acts
3:25 all the ***f*** on earth will be

1 Corinthians
14:10 many language **f** in the world, and
1 Timothy
5:7 so that the **f** will be without

FAMILY → AARON'S FAMILY
1 Samuel
18:18 neither is my **f** or my father's
Psalms
22:27 the LORD; every **f** among all the
122:8 the sake of my **f** and friends, I
Proverbs
11:29 who trouble their **f** will inherit the
Luke
2:4 David's house and **f** line, he went up
John
7:42 from David's **f** and from
Hebrews
7:3 or mother or any **f**. He has no
13:1 Keep loving each other like **f**
1 Peter
2:17 Love the **f** of believers.

FAMINE
Genesis
12:10 When a **f** struck the land, Abram went down toward Egypt
26:1 When a **f** gripped the land, a different
41:27 by the east wind, are seven years of **f**.
43:1 The **f** was severe in the land
45:6 had two years of **f** in the land, and
47:20 field when the **f** worsened. So the
Deuteronomy
28:48 you—during **f**, drought,
Ruth
1:1 there was a **f** in the land.
2 Samuel
21:1 There was a **f** for three years in a row
24:13 three years of **f** come on your
1 Kings
8:37 there is a **f** or plague in the
18:2 Ahab. Now the **f** had become
2 Kings
4:38 there was a **f** in the land.
Psalms
33:19 death and keep them alive during a **f**.
37:19 in a period of **f** they will eat
105:16 God called for a **f** in the land,
Isaiah
51:19 and devastation, **f** and sword—who
Jeremiah
5:12 come upon us; we won't see war or **f**."
11:22 their sons and daughters will die by **f**.
Lamentations
4:9 those stabbed by **f**—those who bled a
5:10 oven because of the burning heat of **f**.
Ezekiel
5:12 and waste away by **f** among you. One-third will fall
Amos
4:6 I have sent a **f** in all your cities, and
Acts
7:11 A **f** came upon all Egypt and Canaan, and a great hardship
11:28 that a severe **f** would overtake
Romans
8:35 or harassment, or **f**, or nakedness, or
Revelation
6:8 to kill by sword, **f**, disease, and the

FARMERS
2 Kings
25:12 behind to work the vineyards and be **f**.
Psalms
129:3 my back like **f**; they made their
Isaiah
61:5 will be your **f** and vinedressers.
Jeremiah
14:4 lack of rain, the **f** too are ashamed;
31:5 hills of Samaria; **f** will plant and
31:24 dwell together with **f** and shepherds.
51:23 you I will crush **f** and oxen. With
Joel
1:11 Be shocked, you **f**; howl, you
Amos
5:16 call upon the **f** to wail, and
Matthew
21:33 rented it to tenant **f** and took a trip.
Mark
12:1 rented it to tenant **f** and took a trip.
12:7 But those tenant **f** said to each other,
Luke
20:9 it to tenant **f**, and went on a

FARMLAND
Genesis
47:18 for my master is our corpses and our **f**.
47:19 eyes, we and our **f** too? Buy us and
47:20 all of Egypt's **f** for Pharaoh
47:22 he didn't buy the **f** of the priests
47:23 you and your **f** for Pharaoh,
47:26 from Egypt's **f**. Only the
Exodus
34:26 produce of your **f** to the LORD your
2 Kings
8:3 to the king for her house and her **f**.
8:5 her house and her **f**. Gehazi said,
8:6 that the **f** has produced,
Isaiah
10:18 forest and **f** will be finished
16:10 from the **f**, and in the
29:17 Lebanon become **f** once again, and
32:15 desert turns into **f**, and the farmland

FAST
Psalms
18:36 let me walk **f** and safe, without
35:13 I kept a strict **f**. When my prayer
37:2 they will fade **f**, like grass; they
147:15 to the earth—God's word speeds off **f**!
Proverbs
28:22 try to get rich **f**, unaware that
Matthew
6:16 And when you **f**, don't put on a sad
9:14 frequently **f**, but your

FASTING
Nehemiah
1:4 mourned for days, **f** and praying
Psalms
109:24 are weak from **f**; my body is skin
Jeremiah
36:6 the next day of **f**, and read the

FASTING [cont.]

Daniel
9:3 and with **f**, mourning
Joel
2:12 your hearts, with **f**, with weeping,
Matthew
6:16 know they are **f**. I assure you
Acts
13:2 the Lord and **f**, the Holy Spirit
14:23 With prayer and **f**, they committed

FAT

Judges
3:17 King Eglon, who was a very **f** man.
3:22 his stomach, the **f** closed over the
Ezekiel
34:3 you slaughter the **f** animals, but you

FATHER → GOD OUR FATHER, GOD THE FATHER, HEAVENLY FATHER, YOUR HEAVENLY FATHER

Genesis
2:24 a man leaves his **f** and mother and
5:3 he became the **f** of a son in his
Exodus
20:12 Honor your **f** and your mother so that
Deuteronomy
5:16 Honor your **f** and your mother, exactly as the LORD
Ruth
2:11 left behind your **f**, your mother, and
Proverbs
3:12 just like a **f** who treats his
4:3 I was a son to my **f**, tender and my
10:1 child makes a **f** glad, but a
13:1 discipline of his **f**, but a mocker
15:20 brings joy to a **f**, but fools
17:21 there's no joy for a scoundrel's **f**.
17:25 irritating to his **f** and bitter to her
19:13 a disaster to his **f**; a contentious
19:26 who assault their **f** and drive out
20:20 who curse their **f** or mother—their
23:22 Listen to your **f**, who gave you life;
23:24 The **f** of the righteous will be very
23:25 Your **f** and your mother will rejoice;
28:24 steal from their **f** and mother, and
29:3 wisdom makes his **f** rejoice, but one
30:11 who curse their **f** and don't bless
30:17 eye that mocks a **f** and rejects
Matthew
1:2 Abraham was the **f** of Isaac. Isaac was
3:9 Abraham is our **f**. I tell you that
6:1 no reward from your **F** who is in heaven.
6:15 neither will your **F** forgive your sins.
10:37 Those who love **f** or mother more than
15:4 said, Honor your **f** and your mother,
15:5 If you tell your **f** or mother,
25:34 things from my **F**. Inherit the
Mark
13:32 and not the Son. Only the **F** knows.
14:36 He said, "Abba, **F**, for you all things
John
3:35 The **F** loves the Son and gives
15:23 Whoever hates me also hates the **F**
16:15 that the **F** has is mine.
Acts
1:4 wait for what the **F** had promised. He
7:4 After Abraham's **f** died, God had him
Romans
1:7 from God our **F** and the Lord
4:16 of Abraham, who is the **f** of all of us.
Ephesians
5:31 will leave his **f** and mother and be
6:2 Honor your **f** and mother is the
Hebrews
1:5 have become your **F**? Or, even, I will
5:5 are my Son. Today I have become your **F**,
7:3 He is without **f** or mother or any
7:4 was! Abraham, the **f** of the people,
12:7 isn't disciplined by his or her **f**?
12:9 we submit to the **F** of spirits and
James
1:17 down from the **F**, the creator of

FATHER-IN-LAW

Genesis
38:13 was told, "Your **f** is now on his way
Exodus
3:1 the flock for his **f** Jethro, Midian's
4:18 went back to his **f** Jethro and said
18:1 priest and Moses' **f**, heard about
Numbers
10:29 son and Moses' **f**, "We're marching
Judges
1:16 of Moses' **f** the Kenite went
4:11 of Hobab, Moses' **f**, and had settled
15:6 it, because his **f** gave his wife in
19:4 Since his **f**, the young woman's father,
John
18:13 Annas. He was the **f** of Caiaphas, the

FAVOR

Genesis
19:19 You've done me a **f** and have been so
Numbers
11:11 haven't I found **f** in your eyes, for
Deuteronomy
29:18 LORD our God in **f** of going to serve
Ruth
2:2 eyes I might find **f**." Naomi replied
Ezra
9:8 our God has shown **f** in leaving us
Esther
2:15 kept winning the **f** of everyone who
Psalms
5:12 You cover them with **f** like a shield.
30:5 a second, but his **f** lasts a lifetime.
40:13 **F** me, LORD, and deliver me! LORD, come quickly
45:12 of all, will seek your **f** with gifts,
51:18 for Zion by your **f**. Rebuild
82:2 by granting **f** to the wicked?
83:3 they plot against the people you **f**.
84:11 shield; God is **f** and glory. The
89:17 strength. By your **f** you make us strong
106:4 LORD, with the **f** you show your
119:58 I've sought your **f** with all my heart;
145:19 God shows **f** to those who honor him,
Proverbs
3:4 you will find **f** and approval in
3:12 a father who treats his son with **f**.
3:34 mockers, but he shows **f** to the humble.
8:35 find life; they gain **f** from the LORD.
11:27 for good find **f**, but those who

13:15 insight brings ***f***, but the way of
14:9 offering, but ***f*** is with those who
16:7 path draws ***f*** from the LORD,
16:13 Kings ***f*** those with righteous lips; they
16:15 king's face. His ***f*** is like a cloud
18:22 what is good, gaining ***f*** from the LORD.
19:6 Many seek ***f*** from rulers; everyone
19:12 like a lion; his ***f*** is like the dew
28:23 end, find more ***f*** than those with

Ecclesiastes
9:11 intelligent, nor ***f*** to the

Matthew
20:20 before him, she asked a ***f*** of him.

Luke
1:25 He has shown his ***f*** to me by removing

Hebrews
4:16 to the throne of ***f*** with confidence

Revelation
2:6 have this in your ***f***: you hate what
20:4 given in their ***f***. They were the

FEAR

→ FEAR GOD, FEAR OF GOD, FEAR OF THE LORD, FEAR THE LORD, FEAR YOUR GOD

Mark
5:33 woman, full of ***f*** and trembling,

Philippians
2:12 own salvation with ***f*** and trembling.

1 John
4:18 There is no ***f*** in love, but perfect love

FEAR GOD

Dt 25:18; Ecc 5:7; 8:12; Lk 18:4; 23:40; Rev 14:7

FEAR OF GOD

2Sa 23:3; 2Ch 20:29; 26:5; Ps 36:1; Ro 3:18; 2Co 7:1; 1Pt 2:17

FEAR OF THE LORD

1Sa 11:7; Ps 111:10; Prv 1:7; 1:29; 2:5; 9:10; 10:27; 14:26, 27; 15:16, 33; 16:6; 19:23; 22:4; Is 11:2; 33:6

FEAR THE LORD

Dt 6:2; 14:23; 1Sa 12:14; 12:24; Prv 3:7; 14:2; 24:21; Jer 5:24; 26:19; Am 3:8; 2Co 5:11

FEAR YOUR GOD

Lv 19:14; 19:32; 25:17, 36, 43

FEAST

Deuteronomy
12:7 You will have a ***f*** there, each of you
12:15 can join in the ***f***, as they would if
12:22 who are purified can ***f*** on it together.
14:26 Then you should ***f*** there and
14:29 will come and ***f*** until they are

Judges
14:10 Samson put on a ***f*** there, as was the
14:12 seven days of the ***f***, I'll give you
14:17 seven days of the ***f***. Finally, on the

1 Samuel
20:5 the king at the ***f***. Instead, let me
20:24 came, the king sat at the ***f*** to eat.

2 Kings
6:23 gave them a great ***f***, and they ate and

Esther
1:3 rule he hosted a ***f*** for all his
1:5 held a seven-day ***f*** for everyone in
1:9 Vashti held a ***f*** for women in King
2:18 lavish ***f***, "the feast of
5:4 Haman for the ***f*** that I have
5:5 Haman came to the ***f*** that Esther had
5:8 come to another ***f*** that I will
5:14 the king to the ***f*** in a happy mood."
6:14 Haman off to the ***f*** that Esther had

Job
1:4 his sons hosted a ***f*** in his own house
1:5 the days of the ***f*** had been

Psalms
36:8 They ***f*** on the bounty of your house; you

Proverbs
15:15 but a happy heart has a continual ***f***.

Ecclesiastes
5:11 goods, except to ***f*** their eyes on
10:16 boy and whose princes ***f*** in the morning.
10:17 and whose princes ***f*** at the right time

Isaiah
25:6 peoples a rich ***f***, a feast of

Jeremiah
12:9 gather all the wild animals for the ***f***.
51:39 I'll prepare the ***f*** and mix the

Lamentations
1:15 He called a ***f*** for me—in order

Amos
6:7 away, and the ***f*** of those who

Matthew
26:5 happen during the ***f*** so there wouldn't

Mark
6:21 he had prepared a ***f*** for his high-

Luke
14:15 are those who will ***f*** in God's kingdom."

John
13:29 we need for the ***f***," or that he

1 Corinthians
5:8 celebrate the ***f*** with the

Jude
1:12 dangerous. They ***f*** with you without

FEED

1 Samuel
17:44 David, "and I'll ***f*** your flesh to the
17:46 Today I will ***f*** your dead body

2 Kings
4:43 said, "How can I ***f*** one hundred men

Matthew
25:37 you hungry and ***f*** you, or thirsty

Luke
15:15 who sent him into his fields to ***f*** pigs.

John
6:5 will we buy food to ***f*** these people?"
21:15 you." Jesus said to him, "***F*** my lambs."
21:17 you." Jesus said to him, "***F*** my sheep.

Romans
12:20 enemy is hungry, ***f*** him; if he is

FEEL

Genesis
18:5 bread so you will ***f*** stronger, and

Exodus
10:21 of Egypt, a darkness that you can ***f***."

Deuteronomy
12:20 desire to do so), ***f*** free to do so

Judges
16:26 me where I can ***f*** the pillars that
1 Samuel
16:16 you, and then you'll ***f*** better."
16:23 would relax and ***f*** better, and the
2 Samuel
16:11 can only ***f*** the same—only
2 Kings
9:15 is the way you ***f***, then don't let
18:19 King says: Why do you ***f*** so confident?
Job
12:25 They ***f*** their way in the dark without
14:22 They only ***f*** the pain of their body, and
Psalms
58:9 Before your pots ***f*** the thorns, whether
94:18 Whenever I ***f*** my foot slipping, your
115:7 but they can't ***f***. They have feet,
Proverbs
23:35 Though hit, I ***f*** no pain; though beaten
Isaiah
36:4 says this: Why do you ***f*** so confident?
Ezekiel
16:54 that you've done to make them ***f*** better.
36:31 and you will ***f*** disgust for
43:11 When they ***f*** humiliated by all that they have done
Matthew
15:32 and said, "I ***f*** sorry for the
26:37 sons, he began to ***f*** sad and anxious.
Mark
8:2 I ***f*** sorry for the crowd because they
14:33 him. He began to ***f*** despair and was
1 Corinthians
7:37 and doesn't ***f*** the pressure, but
13:3 my own body to ***f*** good about what
2 Corinthians
6:12 affection that we ***f*** for you. You are
7:3 this to make you ***f*** guilty. I've
9:5 don't want you to ***f*** like you are
Philippians
1:8 my witness that I ***f*** affection for all

FEET

Leviticus
11:20 walks on four ***f*** is detestable to
Joshua
10:24 forward. Put your ***f*** on the necks of
Psalms
2:12 kiss his ***f*** or else he will become
9:15 made! Their ***f*** are caught in the
17:5 on your paths; my ***f*** haven't slipped.
47:3 us, subdues all people beneath our ***f***.
66:9 living; he didn't let our ***f*** slip a bit.
110:1 your enemies a footstool for your ***f***!"
Song of Songs
5:3 I have bathed my ***f***—why should I get
7:1 are your sandaled ***f***, willing woman!
Isaiah
49:23 dust from your ***f***. You will know
52:7 mountains are the ***f*** of a messenger
Daniel
2:33 of iron, and its ***f*** were a mixture of
2:34 the statue's ***f*** of iron and clay
Malachi
4:3 the soles of your ***f*** on the day that I
Matthew
10:14 the dust off your ***f*** as you leave that
Mark
3:11 fell down at his ***f*** and shouted, "You
5:22 When he saw Jesus, he fell at his ***f***
6:11 the dust off your ***f*** as a witness
7:25 right away. She came and fell at his ***f***.
Luke
20:43 your enemies a footstool for your ***f***.'
John
11:2 oil and wiped his ***f*** with her hair.
13:6 Lord, are you going to wash my ***f***?"
13:8 never wash my ***f***!" Jesus replied,
13:10 to have their ***f*** washed, because
13:12 the disciples' ***f***, he put on his
Acts
2:35 your enemies a footstool for your ***f***.'
Ephesians
1:22 under Christ's ***f*** and made him head
6:15 put shoes on your ***f*** so that you are
Hebrews
1:13 enemies under your ***f*** like a footstool?
James
2:3 over there"; or, "Here, sit at my ***f***."
Revelation
1:13 down to his ***f***, and he had a
22:8 to worship at the ***f*** of the angel who

FELL

Genesis
17:3 Abram ***f*** on his face, and God said to
17:17 Abram ***f*** on his face and laughed. He
44:14 there, and they ***f*** to the ground in
Exodus
10:22 intense darkness ***f*** on the whole land
Deuteronomy
9:18 Then I ***f*** before the LORD as I had done
22:8 your hands because someone ***f*** off of it.
Joshua
5:14 Then Joshua ***f*** flat on his face
2 Kings
1:2 Ahaziah ***f*** out the window of his
Matthew
7:25 The rain ***f***, the floods came, and the
13:5 Other seed ***f*** on rocky ground where the
17:6 the disciples ***f*** on their faces,
Mark
1:40 approached Jesus, ***f*** to his knees, and
9:20 into a fit. He ***f*** on the ground and
Luke
14:5 your child or ox ***f*** into a ditch on
16:21 the crumbs that ***f*** from the rich
James
5:17 rain, no rain ***f*** for three and a

FELLOW → FELLOW BELIEVERS

FELLOW BELIEVERS

Ac 15:7; 15:13; 1Pt 1:22; 3:8; 5:9

FEMALE

Genesis
1:27 them, male and ***f*** God created them.
5:2 them male and ***f***. He blessed them
6:19 a pair, male and ***f***, into the ark
Exodus
20:10 your male or ***f*** servants, your
Ecclesiastes
2:7 male servants and ***f*** servants; I even

2:8 acquired male and *f* singers for
Joel
2:29 out my spirit on the male and *f* slaves.
Matthew
19:4 the creator made them male and *f*?
Mark
10:6 of creation, God made them male and *f*.
14:69 The *f* servant saw him and began a
Acts
12:13 the outer gate, a *f* servant named
Galatians
3:28 is there male and *f*, for you are all

FERTILE

Genesis
1:22 blessed them: "Be *f* and multiply and
2:6 earth and watered all of the *f* land—
35:11 am El Shaddai. Be *f* and multiply. A
Malachi
3:11 the fruit of your *f* land, and so that

FESTIVAL

→ CELEBRATED THE FESTIVAL, FESTIVAL OF BOOTHS, FESTIVAL OF UNLEAVENED BREAD
Exodus
5:1 they can hold a *f* for me in the
13:6 The seventh day is a *f* to the LORD.
1 Samuel
20:18 Tomorrow is the *f* of the new moon,"
Psalms
42:4 songs—a huge crowd celebrating the *f*!
118:27 us! So lead the *f* offering with
Matthew
27:15 during the *f* for the governor
Mark
14:2 happen during the *f*; otherwise, there
15:6 During the *f*, Pilate released one
John
1 Corinthians
16:8 in Ephesus until the ***F*** of Pentecost.
Colossians
2:16 or about a *f*, a new moon

FESTIVAL OF BOOTHS

Lv 23:34; Dt 16:13; 16:16; 31:10; Ezr 3:4; Zec 14:16; 14:18, 19; Jn 7:2

FESTIVAL OF UNLEAVENED BREAD

Ex 12:17; 23:15; 34:18; Lv 23:6; Dt 16:16; 2Ch 30:13; 30:21; 35:17; Ezr 6:22; Mt 26:17; Mk 14:1; 14:12; Lk 22:1; Ac 12:3; 20:6

FESTIVALS

1 Chronicles
23:31 new moons, and *f*, a designated
2 Chronicles
2:4 month, and the *f* of the LORD our
8:13 new moon *f*, and the three
31:3 new moons, and *f*, as written in
Nehemiah
10:33 and the appointed *f*, for the holy
Isaiah
1:14 moons and your *f*. They've become a
29:1 Year by year, let the *f* come around—
Lamentations
1:4 one comes to the *f*. All her gates
2:6 his place for *f*. The LORD made
Ezekiel
36:38 Jerusalem at its *f*, the ruined
44:24 regarding all my *f*. They must keep
45:17 offerings for the *f*, new moons, and
46:9 presence for the *f*, those who enter
46:11 At the *f* and appointed gatherings, the
Hosea
2:11 celebrations, her *f*, her new moons,
Amos
5:21 I reject your *f*; I don't enjoy
Nahum
1:15 Celebrate your *f*, Judah! Fulfill
Malachi
2:3 the feces of your *f*. Then I will lift

FESTUS

Acts
25:4 But ***F*** responded by keeping Paul in
25:14 for many days, ***F*** discussed the
26:25 most honorable ***F***! I'm speaking

FIELD

Genesis
4:8 go out to the *f*." When they were
Deuteronomy
5:21 neighbor's house, *f*, male or female
Job
5:23 the stones of the *f*; and the beasts
24:6 their food in the *f*, glean in
Psalms
78:12 in the land of Egypt, in the *f* of Zoan.
78:43 his marvelous works in the *f* of Zoan.
Proverbs
24:27 in the *f*; then you can
24:30 happened upon the *f* of a lazy person,
31:16 She surveys a *f* and acquires it; from
Ecclesiastes
5:9 be for everyone if the *f* is cultivated.
Isaiah
40:6 loyalty is like the flowers of the *f*.
43:20 The beasts of the *f*, the jackals and
Jeremiah
32:7 tell you: "Buy my *f* in Anathoth, for
Matthew
6:28 the lilies in the *f* grow. They don't
6:30 grass in the *f* so beautifully,
13:36 us the parable of the weeds in the *f*."
24:18 Those in the *f* shouldn't come back to
27:8 That's why that *f* is called "Field of
27:10 for the potter's *f*, as the Lord
Acts
1:18 fact, he bought a *f* with the payment

FIERY

2 Kings
2:11 when suddenly a *f* chariot and fiery
6:17 of horses and *f* chariots
Job
41:19 his mouth; like *f* sparks they fly
Psalms
11:6 God will rain *f* coals and sulfur on the
29:7 The LORD's voice unleashes *f* flames
76:3 that he broke the *f* shafts of the
88:16 Your *f* anger has overwhelmed me; your
Isaiah
66:15 in hot anger, to rebuke with *f* flames.

FIERY [cont.]

Ezekiel
10:2 your hands with ***f*** coals from
Matthew
5:22 they will be in danger of ***f*** hell.
1 Peter
4:12 about the ***f*** trials that have
Revelation
1:14 snow—and his eyes were like a ***f*** flame.
2:18 eyes are like a ***f*** flame, and whose
6:4 another horse, ***f*** red. Its rider
9:17 that were ***f*** red, dark blue,
10:1 sun, and his feet were like ***f*** pillars.
12:3 it was a great ***f*** red dragon, with
19:12 eyes were like a ***f*** flame, and on his
19:20 alive into the ***f*** lake that burns
20:14 thrown into the ***f*** lake. This, the
20:15 of life was thrown into the ***f*** lake.

FIG

Genesis
3:7 So they sewed ***f*** leaves together
Judges
9:10 trees said to the ***f*** tree, 'You come
Psalms
105:33 vines and their ***f*** trees; shattered
Proverbs
27:18 Those who tend a ***f*** tree will eat its
Isaiah
28:4 be like an early ***f*** before the summer
Hosea
2:12 her vines and her ***f*** trees, of which
9:10 fruit on the ***f*** tree, I saw your
Joel
1:7 splintered my ***f*** trees, stripped
1:12 is dried up; the ***f*** tree withers.
2:22 its fruit; the ***f*** tree and
Amos
4:9 devoured your ***f*** treesand your
Micah
4:4 under their own ***f*** trees. There will
7:1 to eat, no ripe ***f*** that I might
Nahum
3:12 are ***f*** trees with ripe
21:19 He saw a ***f*** tree along the road, but
24:32 parable from the ***f*** tree. After its
Mark
11:13 he noticed a ***f*** tree in leaf, so
13:28 parable from the ***f*** tree. After its
Luke
13:6 A man owned a ***f*** tree planted in
21:29 Look at the ***f*** tree and all the
John
1:48 you, I saw you under the ***f*** tree."
James
3:12 sisters, can a ***f*** tree produce
Revelation
6:13 to the earth as a ***f*** tree drops its

FIGHT

1 Samuel
19:8 David went out to ***f*** the Philistines,
Nehemiah
4:20 where we are. Our God will ***f*** for us!"
Psalms
35:1 argue with me, ***f*** with those who
110:3 the dawn's womb, ***f***! Your youthful
144:1 my hands how to ***f***, who taught my
Proverbs
20:3 back off from a ***f***, but fools jump
26:17 gets involved in another person's ***f***.
Isaiah
29:8 of nations who ***f*** against Mount
Matthew
24:7 and kingdoms will ***f*** against each
Luke
22:49 Lord, should we ***f*** with our swords?"
1 Corinthians
9:26 goal in sight. I ***f*** like a boxer in
1 Timothy
6:12 in the good ***f*** of faith. Grab
2 Timothy
4:7 fought the good ***f***, finished the
James
4:2 you struggle and ***f***. You don't have
Jude
1:3 to urge you to ***f*** for the faith
Revelation
13:4 the beast, and who can ***f*** against it?"

FIGS

Numbers
13:23 They also took pomegranates and ***f***.
20:5 without grain, ***f***, vines, or
2 Samuel
16:1 one hundred ***f***, and a jar of
2 Kings
20:7 a bandage made of ***f***." They did so and
Nehemiah
13:15 as wine, grapes, ***f***, and every kind
Isaiah
38:21 a salve made from ***f***, put it on the
Jeremiah
8:13 on the vine, no ***f*** on the tree, only
24:1 me two baskets of ***f*** set in front of
29:17 them like rotten ***f*** that are too
40:10 summer fruits and ***f***, and then store
Matthew
7:16 weeds, or do they get ***f*** from thistles?
Mark
11:13 since it wasn't the season for ***f***.
Luke
6:44 don't gather ***f*** from thorny
James
3:12 grapevine produce ***f***? Of course not,

FIND

Genesis
18:26 LORD said, "If I ***f*** fifty innocent
Job
3:22 who are thrilled when they ***f*** a grave?
Psalms
4:6 say, "We can't ***f*** goodness
10:13 to themselves that you won't ***f*** out?
50:20 own siblings; you ***f*** fault with the
62:5 Oh, I must ***f*** rest in God only because
69:20 for comforters, but couldn't ***f*** any.
119:176 a sheep, lost. ***F*** your servant
Proverbs
8:17 love me; those who seek me will ***f*** me.
8:35 Those who ***f*** me find life; they gain
11:27 who look for good ***f*** favor, but those
31:10 how does one ***f*** her? Her value is
Ecclesiastes
2:23 hearts don't ***f*** rest. This too is

5:18 eat, drink, and ***f*** enjoyment in all
11:1 the course of time, you may ***f*** it again.
Amos
2:14 Fast runners will ***f*** no refuge; the
Matthew
7:7 and you will ***f***. Knock, and the
10:39 Those who ***f*** their lives will lose them,
17:27 mouth, you will ***f*** a shekel coin.
21:2 enter, you will ***f*** a donkey tied up
Mark
13:36 weren't expecting and ***f*** you sleeping.
Luke
2:12 for you: you will ***f*** a newborn baby
John
7:34 me, but you won't ***f*** me, and where I
18:38 and said, "I ***f*** no grounds for
Acts
4:21 they couldn't ***f*** a way to punish
Hebrews
8:8 But God did ***f*** fault with them, since he

FINDS

Matthew
7:8 Whoever seeks, ***f***. And to everyone
Luke
12:37 whom the master ***f*** waiting up when
15:4 search for the lost one until he ***f*** it?

FINEST

Genesis
18:6 seahs of the ***f*** flour and make
24:53 and to her mother he gave the ***f*** gifts.
Deuteronomy
32:14 along with the ***f*** wheat—and for
2 Samuel
10:9 some of Israel's ***f*** warriors and
1 Kings
5:17 stones of the ***f*** quality in order
2 Kings
8:9 of Damascus' ***f*** goods as a gift.
1 Chronicles
19:10 some of Israel's ***f*** warriors and
Psalms
81:16 feed you with the ***f*** wheat. I would
Song of Songs
5:11 His head is ***f*** gold; his wavy hair,
Isaiah
22:7 Your ***f*** valleys were filled with
Jeremiah
22:7 to cut down your ***f*** cedars and hurl
Lamentations
4:5 who wore the ***f*** purple clothes
Ezekiel
16:13 were made of the ***f*** linen and
20:40 offerings, their ***f*** gifts, and all
27:17 trading the ***f*** wheat, millet,
27:22 exchanged the ***f*** spices, every

FINGER

Leviticus
4:6 will dip his ***f*** into the blood
8:15 and, using his ***f***, put it on all of
9:9 and he dipped his ***f*** into the blood
14:16 dip his right ***f*** into the oil and
16:19 altar with his ***f*** seven times. In
Numbers
19:4 blood with his ***f*** and sprinkle it
Deuteronomy
9:10 written by God's ***f***, and on them were
1 Kings
12:10 to them: 'My baby ***f*** is thicker than
2 Chronicles
10:10 to them, 'My baby ***f*** is thicker than
Esther
3:10 ring from his ***f*** and handed it to
Isaiah
58:9 among you, the ***f***-pointing, the wick
Luke
11:46 refuse to lift a single ***f*** to help them.
15:22 Put a ring on his ***f*** and sandals on
16:24 the tip of his ***f*** in water and cool
John
8:6 and wrote on the ground with his ***f***.
20:25 his hands, put my ***f*** in the wounds
20:27 Thomas, "Put your ***f*** here. Look at my

FINISHED

2 Timothy
4:7 the good fight, ***f*** the race, and

FIRE

Genesis
22:6 He took the ***f*** and the knife in
Exodus
3:2 him in a flame of ***f*** in the middle of
Leviticus
1:7 light the altar and lay wood on the ***f***.
1 Kings
18:38 Then the LORD's ***f*** fell; it consumed the
2 Kings
1:10 a man of God, may ***f*** come down from
Job
1:16 said: "A raging ***f*** fell from the sky
41:19 Shafts of ***f*** shoot from his mouth; like
Psalms
18:8 came a devouring ***f***; flaming coals
18:12 him; hail and coals of ***f*** went too.
18:13 voice heard with hail and coals of ***f***.
46:9 the spear, burning chariots with ***f***.
50:3 A devouring ***f*** is before him; a
66:12 been through ***f*** and water. But
68:2 melting before ***f***, let the wicked
74:7 They set ***f*** to your sanctuary, burned it
78:21 became furious. A ***f*** was ignited
78:63 ***F*** devoured his young men, and his young women
79:5 How long will your anger burn like ***f***?
80:16 It is burned with ***f***. It is chopped
83:14 Just like a ***f*** consumes a forest, just
89:46 How long will your wrath burn like ***f***?
97:3 ***F*** proceeds before him, burning up his
104:4 you make ***f*** and flame your
106:18 ***F*** blazed throughout that whole group;
120:4 with burning coals from a wood ***f***!
148:8 Do the same, ***f*** and hail, snow and
Jeremiah
5:14 your mouth as a ***f***; it will consume
Ezekiel
8:2 that looked like ***f***. Below what
Daniel
3:6 thrown into a furnace of flaming ***f***."
7:9 of flame; its wheels were blazing ***f***.
7:10 A river of ***f*** flowed out from his
7:11 handed over to be burned with ***f***.

Joel
2:3 front of them a ***f*** consumes; and
2:30 earth—blood and ***f*** and columns of
Amos
1:4 I will send down ***f*** on the house of
Zechariah
2:5 will be a wall of ***f*** around it, says
12:6 a pot on a wood ***f*** and like a
13:9 part into the ***f***. I will refine
Malachi
3:2 the refiner's ***f*** or the cleaner's
Matthew
3:10 be chopped down and tossed into the ***f***.
3:11 you with the Holy Spirit and with ***f***.
John
15:6 up, thrown into a ***f***, and burned.
21:9 they saw a ***f*** there, with fish
Acts
2:3 flames of ***f*** alighting on each
Romans
12:20 pile burning coals of ***f*** upon his head.
1 Corinthians
3:13 be revealed with ***f***—the fire will tes
James
3:5 flame can set a whole forest on ***f***.
3:6 a small flame of ***f***, a world of evil
5:3 your flesh like ***f***. Consider the
Revelation
3:18 been purified by ***f*** so that you may
20:10 into the lake of ***f*** and sulfur, where

FIRM → STAND FIRM

2 Chronicles
17:5 The LORD gave him ***f*** control over the
Ezekiel
16:7 Your breasts were ***f***, your hair

FIRST

Genesis
1:5 and there was morning: the ***f*** day.
Deuteronomy
18:4 the priest the ***f*** portions of your
Job
15:7 Were you born the ***f*** Adam, brought forth
40:19 He is the ***f*** of God's acts; only his
Psalms
68:25 ***F*** came the singers, then the musicians;
69:4 what I didn't steal in the ***f*** place?
88:13 prayer meets you ***f*** thing in the
89:27 him the one born ***f***—I'll make him th
119:160 The ***f*** thing to know about your word is
Proverbs
3:9 and with the ***f*** of all your crops.
8:26 the fields or the ***f*** of the dry land.
18:17 The ***f*** person to testify seems innocent,
20:21 gained quickly at ***f*** won't bless later
Matthew
7:5 deceive yourself! ***F*** take the log out
17:10 experts say that Elijah must ***f*** come?"
20:10 when those hired ***f*** came, they
20:16 are last will be ***f***. And those who
20:27 wants to be ***f*** among you will be
22:38 This is the ***f*** and greatest commandment
Mark
13:10 ***F***, the good news must be proclaimed to
John
20:4 Peter and was the ***f*** to arrive at the
Acts
1:1 Theophilus, the ***f*** scroll I wrote
Romans
1:16 God, to the Jew ***f*** and also to the
1 Corinthians
12:28 God has appointed ***f*** apostles, second
15:47 The ***f*** human was from the earth made
Hebrews
2:3 salvation? It was ***f*** announced through
7:2 His name means ***f*** "king of
9:1 So then the ***f*** covenant had regulations
9:18 So not even the ***f*** covenant was put into
Revelation
1:17 be afraid. I'm the ***f*** and the last,
20:5 were over. This is the ***f*** resurrection.
22:13 the omega, the ***f*** and the last, the

FISH

Genesis
1:26 charge of the ***f*** of the sea, the
Exodus
7:18 The ***f*** in the Nile are going to die, the
Numbers
11:5 We remember the ***f*** we ate in Egypt for
Psalms
8:8 in the sky, the ***f*** of the ocean,
105:29 waters into blood and killed their ***f***.
Hosea
4:3 the sky, even the ***f*** of the sea are
Jonah
1:17 provided a great ***f*** to swallow Jonah.
2:1 LORD his God from the belly of the ***f***:
Matthew
4:19 I'll show you how to ***f*** for people."
7:10 give them a snake when they ask for ***f***?
13:47 the lake and gathered all kinds of ***f***.
14:17 except five loaves of bread and two ***f***."
15:34 responded, "Seven loaves and a few ***f***."
17:27 take the first ***f*** you catch. When
John
21:11 was full of large ***f***, one hundred
21:13 it to them. He did the same with the ***f***.
1 Corinthians
15:39 kind of flesh, and ***f*** have another kind.

FIVE

1 Samuel
17:40 staff and chose ***f*** smooth stones
21:3 with you? Give me ***f*** loaves of bread
Matthew
14:17 here except ***f*** loaves of bread
14:19 He took the ***f*** loaves of bread
16:9 you remember the ***f*** loaves that fed
20:6 Around ***f*** in the afternoon he went and
25:2 Now ***f*** of them were wise, and the other
25:15 To one he gave ***f*** valuable coins, and to
Mark
6:38 they said, "***F*** loaves of bread
6:41 He took the ***f*** loaves and the two fish,
Luke
1:24 kept to herself for ***f*** months, saying,
9:13 have no more than ***f*** loaves of bread
9:16 He took the ***f*** loaves and the two fish,
12:6 Aren't ***f*** sparrows sold for two small
12:52 a household of ***f*** will be divided—

John
4:18 You've had ***f*** husbands, and the man you
6:9 A youth here has ***f*** barley loaves and
1 Corinthians
14:19 I'd rather speak ***f*** words in my right
Revelation
17:10 ***F*** kings have fallen, the one is, and

FLAME

Genesis
15:17 with a fiery ***f*** passed between
Exodus
3:2 to him in a ***f*** of fire in the
Judges
13:20 as the ***f*** from the altar went up toward
Psalms
104:4 you make fire and ***f*** your ministers.
Joel
2:3 and behind them a ***f*** burns. Land ahead of them is like
2:5 of a fire's ***f***, devouring the
Obadiah
1:18 house of Joseph a ***f***, and the house of Esau straw
Luke
16:24 because I'm suffering in this ***f***.'
Acts
7:30 to Moses in the ***f*** of a burning bush
James
3:5 this: a small ***f*** can set a whole
3:6 tongue is a small ***f*** of fire, a world
Revelation
1:14 snow—and his eyes were like a fiery ***f***.
2:18 are like a fiery ***f***, and whose feet
19:12 were like a fiery ***f***, and on his head

FLAMES

Exodus
3:2 the bush was in ***f***, but it didn't
Psalms
29:7 The LORD's voice unleashes fiery ***f***
83:14 forest, just like ***f*** set mountains
106:18 that whole group; ***f*** burned up the
Isaiah
29:6 tempest, and ***f*** of devouring fire.
47:14 from the powerful ***f***. This is no
64:11 has gone up in ***f***; all that we
66:15 in hot anger, to rebuke with fiery ***f***.
Jeremiah
21:14 on fire; the ***f*** will engulf
48:45 in Heshbon, ***f*** from the house of
Ezekiel
22:20 to fan the ***f*** under them and
22:21 you, fan the ***f*** of my wrath under
Joel
1:19 wilderness; and ***f*** have burned all
Acts
2:3 to be individual ***f*** of fire alighting
1 Corinthians
3:15 work goes up in ***f***, they'll lose it.
Hebrews
1:7 and who uses ***f*** of fire as
James
3:6 itself is set on fire by the ***f*** of hell.
2 Peter
3:12 the elements will melt away in the ***f***.

FLAMING

Genesis
3:24 wielding ***f*** swords to guard
2 Samuel
22:9 a devouring fire; ***f*** coals blazed out
Psalms
7:13 change; he gets his ***f*** arrows ready!
18:8 a devouring fire; ***f*** coals blazed out
Proverbs
26:18 a crazy person shooting deadly ***f*** arrows
Lamentations
2:3 Jacob like a ***f*** fire that ate up
Daniel
3:6 thrown into a furnace of ***f*** fire."
3:11 be thrown into a furnace of ***f*** fire.
3:15 the furnace of ***f*** fire. Then what
3:17 the furnace of ***f*** fire and from
3:20 throw them into the furnace of ***f*** fire.
3:21 thrown into the furnace of ***f*** fire.
3:23 bound, into the furnace of ***f*** fire.
3:26 of the furnace of ***f*** fire and said,
Hosea
7:6 it continues to burn like a ***f*** fire.
Nahum
2:4 They look like ***f*** torches; they
Ephesians
6:16 extinguish the ***f*** arrows of the
Revelation
4:5 throne were seven ***f*** torches, which

FLAWLESS

Exodus
12:5 lamb should be a ***f*** year-old male. You
29:1 Take a young bull and two ***f*** rams.
1 Peter
1:19 like that of a ***f***, spotless lamb.

FLEECE

Judges
6:37 putting a wool ***f*** on the threshing
6:38 and squeezed the ***f***, he wrung out
6:39 test with the ***f***: now let only the
6:40 night. Only the ***f*** was dry, but

FLESH

Genesis
2:21 his ribs and closed up the ***f*** over it.
2:24 his wife, and they become one ***f***.
17:14 male whose ***f*** of his foreskin
29:14 Yes, you are my ***f*** and blood." After
Judges
9:2 remember that I'm your ***f*** and blood!"
1 Samuel
17:44 I'll feed your ***f*** to the wild birds
2 Kings
9:36 devour Jezebel's ***f*** in the area of
Job
2:5 his bones and ***f***. Then he will
Psalms
56:4 be afraid. What can mere ***f*** do to me?
78:39 they were just ***f***, just breath that
79:2 they've left the ***f*** of your faithful
Proverbs
5:11 end when your body and ***f*** are exhausted,
Ecclesiastes
4:5 fold their hands and eat their own ***f***.

Isaiah
9:20 They devoured the *f* of their own
Jeremiah
19:9 to eating the *f* of their sons and
Matthew
19:5 his wife, and the two will be one *f*.'
26:41 spirit is eager, but the *f* is weak."
Luke
24:39 doesn't have *f* and bones like
John
1:14 The Word became *f* and made his home
3:6 is born of the *f* is flesh, and
6:53 you eat the *f* of the Human One
6:54 Whoever eats my *f* and drinks my blood
Romans
7:14 but I'm made of *f* and blood, and
9:3 who are my *f*-and-blood relative
1 Corinthians
6:16 says, The two will become one *f*.
15:39 All *f* isn't alike. Humans have one kind
15:50 and sisters: *f* and blood can't
Hebrews
2:14 children share in *f* and blood, he
James
5:3 It will eat your *f* like fire.
Revelation
17:16 will devour her *f* and burn her with
19:18 Come and eat the *f* of kings, the flesh
19:21 the birds ate their fill of their *f*.

FLOCK

Genesis
21:28 seven female lambs from the *f*.
1 Samuel
17:15 shepherd his father's *f* in Bethlehem.
Ezra
10:19 was a ram of the *f* for their guilt.
Psalms
78:52 them like a *f* in the wilderness.
Proverbs
27:23 Know your *f* well; pay attention to your
Song of Songs
1:7 you pasture your *f*, where do you
4:1 hair is like a *f* of goats as they
6:6 teeth are like a *f* of ewes as they
Ezekiel
34:8 a shepherd, my *f* became prey. My
34:22 I will rescue my *f* so that they will
43:25 and a ram from the *f*, both flawless.
Amos
6:4 lambs from the *f*, and bull calves
7:15 shepherding the *f*, and the LORD
Zechariah
9:16 that day as the *f* of his people;
11:4 Shepherd the *f* intended for
11:7 I shepherded the *f* intended for
11:11 afflicted of the *f* knew that it was
11:17 who forsakes the *f*. A sword will
13:7 to scatter the *f*! I will turn my
Matthew
26:31 the sheep of the *f* will go off in
Luke
12:32 be afraid, little *f*, because your
John
10:16 there will be one *f*, with one
Acts
20:28 and the whole *f*, in which the
20:29 in among you and won't spare the *f*.
1 Corinthians
9:7 Who shepherds a *f* and doesn't drink
1 Peter
5:2 tend the *f* of God among you.
5:3 care, but become examples to the *f*.

FLOOD

Genesis
7:17 The *f* remained on the earth for forty
9:11 never again be a *f* to destroy the
2 Chronicles
20:9 calamity, sword, *f*, plague, or
Job
36:27 of water that distill rain from his *f*;
Psalms
32:6 so that a great *f* of water won't
69:2 deep water; the *f* has swept me up.
Isaiah
14:4 has ceased! How the *f* has receded!
28:15 the overflowing *f* passes through,
28:18 The rushing *f*: when it passes
Jeremiah
47:2 into a raging *f*. They will engulf
Lamentations
2:18 run down like a *f* all day and
Ezekiel
43:2 sound of a mighty *f*, and the earth
Daniel
9:26 will come in a *f*, but devastations
11:10 an overwhelming *f*. And they will
Jonah
2:3 the seas, and the *f* surrounds me. All
Nahum
1:8 With a rushing *f*, he will utterly
Habakkuk
3:10 you and writhe. A *f* of water rushes
Matthew
24:38 days before the *f*, people were
1 Peter
4:4 with the same *f* of unrestrained
2 Peter
2:5 when he brought a *f* on the world of

FLOOR

Genesis
50:10 at the threshing *f* of Atad on the
Ruth
3:2 be winnowing barley at the threshing *f*.
1 Samuel
19:22 at the threshing *f* that was on the
Isaiah
21:10 on my threshing *f*, what I heard
Jeremiah
51:33 is like a thrhing *f* ready to be
Ezekiel
37:2 on the valley *f*, and they were
Hosea
9:2 Threshing *f* and wine vat won't feed
13:3 the threshing *f*, or like smoke
Micah
4:12 them like grain to the threshing *f*!
Acts
20:9 he fell from the third *f* and died.

FLOUR

Genesis
18:6 of the finest *f* and make some

Luke
13:21 a bushel of wheat ***f*** until the yeast
Revelation
18:13 wine, oil, fine ***f***, and wheat;

FLOW
Leviticus
12:7 from her blood ***f***. This is the
15:3 his emission to ***f*** or blocks the
Psalms
63:10 Let their blood ***f*** by the sword! Let
78:16 God made streams ***f*** from the rock, made water
104:10 riverbeds. They ***f*** between the
Ecclesiastes
1:7 All streams ***f*** to the sea, but the sea
Joel
3:18 the hills will ***f*** with milk, and
Amos
9:13 wine, and all the hills will ***f*** with it.
John
7:38 living water will ***f*** out from within
James
3:12 water doesn't ***f*** from a saltwater

FLOWER
Exodus
25:33 each with a ***f*** and petals, and
39:30 They made the ***f*** ornament for the holy crown
8:4 its base to its ***f*** it was hammered.
Job
14:2 Like a ***f***, we bloom, then wither, flee
Song of Songs
6:11 the vine was in ***f***, whether the
Isaiah
28:1 and the fading ***f*** of its splendid
28:4 The withered ***f***, which is a thing of
40:7 dries up and the ***f*** withers when the
1 Peter
1:24 glory is like a ***f*** in a field. The

FOES
2 Samuel
22:18 saved me from my ***f***, who were too
Psalms
7:6 the fury of my ***f***! Wake up, my God;
8:2 because of your ***f***, in order to stop
10:5 for them. They snort at all their ***f***.
13:4 say, "I won!" My ***f*** will rejoice over
18:17 saved me from my ***f***, who were too
18:40 turn tail from me; I destroyed my ***f***.
27:2 it's they, my ***f*** and my enemies,
42:10 bones crushed, my ***f*** make fun of me,
44:5 We've pushed our ***f*** away by your help;
44:7 saved us from our ***f***, you who put
74:10 long, God, will ***f*** insult you? Are
78:66 God beat back his ***f***; he made them an
81:14 I would turn my hand against their ***f***.
89:23 crush all his ***f*** in front of him.
92:11 have heard the downfall of my evil ***f***.
106:11 over their ***f***—not one of them
Isaiah
1:24 anger against my ***f***; I will take it
9:11 raised up their ***f*** against them, and
59:18 wrath to his ***f***, retribution to
Micah
5:9 lifted over your ***f***; all your enemies
Nahum
1:2 against his ***f***; he rages against

FOLLOW OTHER GODS
Dt 6:14; 8:19; 13:2; 1Ki 11:10; Hos 4:12

FOLLOWED → FOLLOWED JESUS
Genesis
24:61 the camels, and ***f*** the man. So the
Exodus
15:20 All the women ***f*** her playing
Deuteronomy
4:3 everyone who ***f*** the Baal of Peor,
Joshua
6:8 trumpets. The LORD's covenant chest ***f***.
Matthew
4:20 away, they left their nets and ***f*** him.
4:22 the boat and their father and ***f*** him.
8:1 from the mountain, large crowds ***f*** him.
9:9 Follow me," and he got up and ***f*** him.
9:27 two blind men ***f*** him, crying out,
12:15 Large crowds ***f*** him, and he
14:13 this, they ***f*** him on foot from
19:2 Large crowds ***f*** him, and he healed them
19:27 everything and ***f*** you. What will we
19:28 you who have ***f*** me that, when
20:29 out of Jericho a large crowd ***f*** him.
26:58 Peter ***f*** him from a distance until he
27:55 They had ***f*** Jesus from
John
6:2 A large crowd ***f*** him, because they had
11:31 and leave, they ***f*** her. They assumed
21:8 other disciples ***f*** in the boat,
Acts
21:36 The mob that ***f*** kept screaming, "Away
26:5 testify that I ***f*** the way of life
1 Timothy
4:6 good teaching that you've carefully ***f***.
Revelation
13:3 whole earth was amazed and ***f*** the beast.
14:8 a second one, ***f*** and said,
14:9 a third one, ***f*** them and said in

FOLLOWED JESUS
Mt 27:55; Lk 5:11; 23:27; Jn 1:37; 1:40; 18:15

FOLLOWERS
Exodus
11:8 you and all your ***f***!' After that I'll
2 Samuel
19:7 encourage your ***f***! I swear to the
Matthew
12:27 authority do your ***f*** throw them out?
13:38 seeds are the ***f*** of the kingdom.
Mark
1:21 Jesus and his ***f*** went into Capernaum.
2:15 Indeed, many of them had become his ***f***.
3:20 for him and his ***f*** even to eat.
9:30 Jesus and his ***f*** went through
10:46 Jesus and his ***f*** came into Jericho. As
11:1 Jesus and his ***f*** approached
Luke
9:49 because he isn't in our group of ***f***."
11:19 authority do your ***f*** throw them out?
Acts
4:13 that they had been ***f*** of Jesus.
5:36 all of his ***f*** scattered, and

5:37 too, and all his ***f*** scattered far and
20:30 the word in order to lure ***f*** after them.

FOLLOWING THE LORD

Josh 22:16; 22:18, 23, 29; 1Sa 12:20

FOLLY

Proverbs
9:13 Woman ***F*** is noisy; she's stupid and
14:24 the wise, and the ***f*** of fools is folly.
15:14 seeks knowledge; but fools feed on ***f***.
15:21 ***F*** is joy to those who lack sense, but
16:22 the instruction of the foolish is ***f***.
17:12 of her cubs than fools in their ***f***.
19:3 People's own ***f*** corrupts their way, but
22:15 ***F*** is bound up in a child's heart; the
26:4 to their ***f***, or you will
26:5 to their ***f***, or they will
27:22 the grain, their ***f*** won't be driven
Ecclesiastes
1:17 madness and ***f***, I realized that
2:3 and by embracing ***f***—with wisdom still
7:25 is foolishness and ***f*** is madness.
10:1 oil, so a little ***f*** outweighs wisdom
Isaiah
32:6 Fools speak ***f***; their minds devise
44:25 wise and turns their knowledge into ***f***.

FOOD → FOOD GIFT, FOOD GIFT OF SOOTHING, FOOD GIFTS

Genesis
1:29 seeds within it. These will be your ***f***.
6:21 every kind of ***f*** and stow it as
9:3 will be your ***f***. Just as I gave
Exodus
12:39 time to prepare any ***f*** for themselves.
Deuteronomy
10:18 immigrants, giving them ***f*** and clothing.
14:6 —and that rechews ***f*** among the various
15:14 from your flock, ***f***, and wine. You
16:13 collected the ***f*** and drink you
Joshua
5:11 they ate ***f*** produced in the
5:12 when they ate ***f*** produced in the
Judges
8:6 Why should we give ***f*** to your army now?"
Ruth
1:6 to his people by providing ***f*** for them.
Job
6:6 Is tasteless ***f*** eaten without salt, or
Psalms
41:9 who shared my ***f***, has kicked me
42:3 have been my ***f*** both day and
59:15 roam about for ***f***, and if they
63:10 sword! Let them be ***f*** for wild jackals!
65:11 your paths overflow with rich ***f***.
69:21 me poison for ***f***. To quench my
74:14 gave it to the desert dwellers for ***f***!
76:4 than the mountains that give ***f***.
78:18 hearts, demanded ***f*** for their
78:30 even with the ***f*** still in their
79:2 bodies as ***f*** for the birds;
102:4 grass. I even forget to eat my ***f***
104:14 in order to get ***f*** from the ground,
104:21 their prey, seeking their ***f*** from God.
104:27 for you to give them their ***f*** on time.
105:16 the land, destroying every source of ***f***,
105:40 filled them full with ***f*** from heaven.
106:15 for; he sent ***f*** to satisfy their
107:18 no appetite for ***f***; they had arrived
111:5 God gives ***f*** to those who honor him. God
124:6 hand us over like ***f*** for our enemies'
132:15 bless its ***f*** supply; I will
136:25 one who provides ***f*** for all living
144:13 all kinds of ***f***; so that our
145:15 you give them their ***f*** right on time,
147:9 God gives ***f*** to the animals—even to
Proverbs
6:8 so, it gets its ***f*** in summer;
9:5 Come, eat my ***f***, and drink the wine I
9:17 water is sweet; ***f*** eaten in secret
12:9 than to be conceited and lack ***f***.
13:23 produce much ***f***, but it is
22:9 they give some of their ***f*** to the poor.
23:3 the ruler's delicacies; the ***f*** misleads.
23:6 Don't eat ***f*** with stingy people; don't
27:27 milk for your ***f***, for the food of
28:3 the needy are rain that washes away ***f***.
30:8 or wealth; give me just the ***f*** I need.
30:22 king and fools when they are full of ***f***;
30:25 they store away their ***f*** in the summer.
31:14 ships, bringing ***f*** from a distance.
31:15 night, providing ***f*** for her
31:27 she doesn't eat the ***f*** of laziness.
Ecclesiastes
9:7 Go, eat your ***f*** joyfully and drink your
9:11 the mighty, nor ***f*** to the wise, nor
Hosea
9:3 and in Assyria they will eat unclean ***f***.
Matthew
6:25 life more than ***f*** and the body more
25:35 and you gave me ***f*** to eat. I was
John
6:55 My flesh is true ***f*** and my blood is true
Romans
14:15 is upset by your ***f***, you are no
14:17 about eating ***f*** and drinking but
14:20 done because of ***f***. All food is
1 Corinthians
3:2 instead of solid ***f***, because you
10:3 All ate the same spiritual ***f***
1 Timothy
6:8 we'll be happy with ***f*** and clothing
Hebrews
5:12 where you need milk instead of solid ***f***.
5:14 But solid ***f*** is for the mature, whose
9:10 are only about ***f***, drink, and
13:9 rather than by ***f***. Food doesn't
Revelation
2:14 they would eat ***f*** sacrificed to

FOOD GIFT

Ex 29:18; 29:25; 30:20; Lv 1:9; 1:13, 17; 2:2, 9, 11, 16; 3:3, 5, 9, 11, 14, 16; 7:5, 25; 8:21, 28; 22:22, 27; 23:13, 18, 25, 27, 36; 24:7; Nm 15:3; 15:10, 13, 14, 25; 28:2, 3, 6, 8, 13, 19, 24; 29:6, 13, 36

FOOD GIFT OF SOOTHING

Lv 1:9; 1:13, 17; 2:2, 9; 3:5; 23:18

FOOD GIFTS

Lv 2:3; 2:10; 4:35; 5:12; 6:17, 18; 7:30, 35; 10:12, 13, 15; 21:6, 21; 23:8, 36, 37; 24:9; Est 9:22

FOOL

Genesis
31:28 good-bye. Now you've acted like a ***f***,
Judges
16:10 You made a ***f*** out of me and
16:13 you've made a ***f*** out of me and
16:15 now you've made a ***f*** out of me and not
1 Samuel
25:25 His name means ***f***, and he is
2 Samuel
3:33 Should Abner have died like a ***f*** dies?
13:13 become like some ***f*** in Israel!
Job
13:9 you, or can you ***f*** him as you fool
Proverbs
10:14 but the mouth of a ***f*** brings on ruin.
11:29 the wind. The ***f*** will be servant
14:3 in the mouth of a ***f***, but the lips of
15:2 the mouth of a ***f*** gushes with
15:5 A ***f*** doesn't like a father's
17:7 isn't right for a ***f***; even less so
17:10 person than a hundred lashes to a ***f***.
17:16 Why should a ***f*** have money to pay for
17:21 Having a ***f*** for a son brings grief;
19:1 than to have dishonest lips and be a ***f***.
19:10 fitting for a ***f***; even less so for
26:1 so honor isn't appropriate for a ***f***.
26:6 messages with a ***f*** is like cutting
26:8 a sling, so is giving respect to a ***f***.
26:10 so is one who hires a ***f*** or a passerby.
26:11 its vomit, so a ***f*** repeats foolish
26:12 is more hope for a ***f*** than for them.
Ecclesiastes
2:15 happens to the ***f*** will also happen
2:16 How can the wise die just like the ***f***?
7:17 and don't be a ***f***, or you may die
10:2 but the mind of the ***f*** toward the left.
Isaiah
32:5 Then a ***f*** will no longer be called
36:18 let Hezekiah ***f*** you by saying,
Hosea
9:7 The prophet is a ***f***, the spiritual
Matthew
5:22 if they say, 'You ***f***,' they will be in
7:26 will be like a ***f*** who built a house
Luke
12:20 God said to him, '***F***, tonight you will
1 Corinthians
3:18 Don't ***f*** yourself. If some of you think
15:36 Look, ***f***! When you put a seed into the
2 Corinthians
11:1 I act like a ***f***. Well, in fact,
11:16 take me for a ***f***. But if you do,
11:17 it like I'm a ***f***. I'm putting my
12:6 I wouldn't make a ***f*** of myself because
12:11 I've become a ***f***! You made me do it.

FOOLISH

1 Samuel
25:25 fool, and he is ***f***! But I myself,
2 Samuel
15:31 LORD, make Ahithophel's advice ***f***."
24:10 because I have done something very ***f***."
1 Chronicles
21:8 because I have done something very ***f***."
Job
2:10 talking like a ***f*** woman. Will we
5:2 can kill the ***f***; fury can kill
5:3 I've seen the ***f*** take root and promptly
Psalms
39:8 don't make me some ***f*** person's joke.
49:10 too, just like ***f*** and stupid people
49:13 for those who are ***f***, as well as for
85:8 ones. Don't let them return to ***f*** ways.
Proverbs
10:1 glad, but a ***f*** child brings
10:8 commands, but a ***f*** talker is ruined.
14:1 house, while a ***f*** woman tears hers
16:22 but the instruction of the ***f*** is folly.
17:25 A ***f*** son is irritating to his father and
18:13 they listen are ***f*** and disgraceful.
19:13 A ***f*** son is a disaster to his father; a
24:7 Wisdom is beyond ***f*** people. They don't open their mouths
26:11 vomit, so a fool repeats ***f*** mistakes.
29:9 against the ***f***, the fools shout,
30:32 If you've been ***f*** and arrogant, if
Ecclesiastes
2:16 any more than the ***f***, because everyone
2:19 will be wise or ***f***? Either way, that
4:13 than an old and ***f*** king, who no
6:8 have over the ***f***? Or what do the
7:4 mourns, but the ***f*** heart is in the
Jeremiah
4:22 My people are ***f***. They don't even know
5:21 Listen, you ***f*** and senseless people who
10:8 But they are both ***f*** and silly; they
10:14 Everyone is too ***f*** to understand; every
51:17 Everyone is too ***f*** to understand; every
Ezekiel
13:3 Doom to the ***f*** prophets who
23:43 I thought, For a ***f*** woman they become
Zechariah
11:15 again the equipment of a ***f*** shepherd
11:17 Doom, ***f*** shepherd who forsakes the
Matthew
23:17 You ***f*** and blind people! Which is
25:2 were wise, and the other five were ***f***.
25:3 The ***f*** ones took their lamps but didn't
25:8 But the ***f*** bridesmaids said to the wise
Luke
11:40 ***F*** people! Didn't the one who made the
24:25 to them, "You ***f*** people! Your dull
Acts
25:27 all, it would be ***f*** to send a
Romans
1:14 Greek, both to the wise and to the ***f***.
1:21 and their ***f*** hearts were
2:20 educator of the ***f***; a teacher of
1 Corinthians
1:20 God made the wisdom of the world ***f***?
1:27 world considers ***f*** to shame the
3:18 should become ***f*** so that they can
Colossians
2:8 philosophy and ***f*** deception, which
2 Timothy
2:23 Avoid ***f*** and thoughtless discussions,
Titus
3:3 We were once ***f***, disobedient, deceived,

FOOLISH [cont.]

1 Peter
2:15 silence the ignorant talk of **f** people.

FOOLS

Psalms
14:1 **F** say in their
53:1 **F** say in their
74:18 how unbelieving **f** have abused your
74:22 how unbelieving **f** insult you all
92:6 don't know—**f** don't understand
94:8 quickly. You **f**—when will you ge
107:17 the redeemed were **f** because of their
Proverbs
1:7 of the LORD, but **f** despise wisdom
1:22 mocking dear, and **f** hate knowledge?
1:32 turn away; smugness will destroy **f**.
3:35 wise gain respect, but **f** receive shame.
8:5 are naive. Take this to heart, you **f**.
10:18 and those who spread slander are **f**.
10:21 many people, but **f** who lack sense
10:23 **F** enjoy vile deeds, but those with
12:15 **F** see their own way as right, but the
12:16 **F** reveal their anger right away, but
12:23 but the heart of **f** proclaims their
13:16 but **f** display their
13:19 is pleasant, but **f** find deviating
13:20 wise; befriend **f** and get in
14:7 Stay away from **f**, for you won't learn
14:8 but the stupidity of **f** deceives them.
14:9 **F** mock a compensation offering, but
14:16 avoid evil, but **f** become excited
14:24 the wise, and the folly of **f** is folly.
14:33 heart, but it's not known in **f**.
15:7 but the hearts of **f** have none.
15:14 seeks knowledge; but **f** feed on folly.
15:20 to a father, but **f** despise their
17:12 of her cubs than **f** in their folly.
17:24 but the eyes of **f** are off to the
17:28 **F** who keep quiet are deemed wise; those who shut their lips
18:2 **F** find no pleasure in understanding,
18:6 The lips of **f** make accusations; their
18:7 The mouth of **f** is their ruin; their
19:29 mockers, and blows for the backs of **f**.
20:3 off from a fight, but **f** jump right in.
21:20 of the wise, but **f** swallow them up.
23:9 in the ears of **f**, for they will
24:9 The scheming of **f** is sin; people detest
26:3 a donkey, and a rod for the back of **f**.
26:4 Don't answer **f** according to their
26:5 Answer **f** according to their folly, or
26:7 so does a proverb in the mouth of **f**.
26:9 so is a proverb in the mouth of **f**.
27:3 the nuisance of **f** is heavier than
27:22 Even if you grind **f** in a mortar, even
28:26 own reasoning are **f**, but those who
29:9 the foolish, the **f** shout, they laugh-
29:11 **F** show all their anger, but the wise
29:20 There is more hope for **f** than for them.
30:22 becomes king and **f** when they are
Ecclesiastes
2:14 their head, but **f** walk around in
10:14 **F** talk too much! No one knows what will happen
10:15 The hard work of **f** tires them out
Romans
1:22 to be wise, they made **f** of themselves.
1 Corinthians
4:10 We are **f** for Christ, but you are wise
2 Corinthians
11:19 so wise, are happy to put up with **f**.

FOOT

Psalms
38:16 themselves over me when my **f** slips,"
66:6 the river on **f**. Right there we
91:12 so you don't bruise your **f** on a stone.
121:3 won't let your **f** slip. Your
Proverbs
3:23 on your path, and your **f** won't stumble.
7:12 She has one **f** in the street, one foot
25:19 like having a bad tooth or a wobbly **f**.
Matthew
4:6 that you won't hit your **f** on a stone."
18:8 your hand or your **f** causes you to
John
20:12 been, one at the head and one at the **f**.
1 Corinthians
12:15 If the **f** says, "I'm not part of the
Revelation
10:2 He put his right **f** on the sea and

FORCES → GOD OF HEAVENLY FORCES, HEAVENLY FORCES, LORD OF HEAVENLY FORCES

FOREHEAD

Genesis
49:26 head, on the **f** of the one set
Exodus
13:9 reminder on your **f** so that you will
13:16 a symbol on your **f** that the LORD
28:38 be on Aaron's **f**, and Aaron will
Leviticus
13:41 the sides of the **f**, the person has a
Numbers
24:17 smashing Moab's **f**, the head of all
Deuteronomy
6:8 They should be on your **f** as a symbol.
11:18 They should be on your **f** as a symbol.
1 Samuel
17:49 Philistine on his **f**. The stone
2 Chronicles
26:19 erupted on his **f** in the presence
26:20 disease on his **f**, they rushed him
Isaiah
48:4 is made of iron, and your **f** is bronze.
Ezekiel
3:9 I've made your **f** like a diamond, harder
Revelation
13:16 put on their right hand or on their **f**.
17:5 written on her **f**: "Babylon the
20:4 the mark on their **f** or hand. They

FOREIGN → FOREIGN GODS

Genesis
35:2 Get rid of the **f** gods you have
35:4 Jacob all of the **f** gods they had, as
Exodus
2:22 been an immigrant living in a **f** land."
12:45 No temporary **f** resident or day laborer
18:3 been an immigrant living in a **f** land."
21:8 to sell her to a **f** people since he

Leviticus
22:10 offerings. No **f** guest or hired
25:6 laborers and **f** guests who live
25:23 just immigrants and **f** guests of mine.
25:35 an immigrant or **f** guest so that
25:40 hired laborer or **f** guest to you.
25:45 buy them from the **f** guests who live
25:47 an immigrant or **f** guest prospers
Deuteronomy
32:12 alone led Israel; no **f** god assisted.
Joshua
24:20 LORD and serve **f** gods, then he
24:23 now put aside the **f** gods that are
Judges
10:16 They put away the **f** gods from among
1 Samuel
7:3 rid of all the **f** gods and the
1 Kings
11:1 loved many **f** women, including
11:8 same for all his **f** wives, who burned
2 Kings
19:24 drunk waters in **f** lands. With my
2 Chronicles
14:3 He removed the **f** altars and shrines,
33:15 He removed the **f** gods and the idol from
Ezra
10:2 God by marrying **f** women from the
10:10 by marrying **f** women and adding
10:11 peoples and from the **f** wives."
10:14 who have taken **f** wives come at
10:17 of all the men who had married **f** women.
10:18 who had married **f** women—of the fami
10:44 men had married **f** women, some of
Nehemiah
13:26 all Israel. Yet **f** wives led even
13:27 toward our God by marrying **f** women?"
13:30 of everything **f** and established
Psalms
81:9 There must be no **f** god among you. You
137:4 sing the LORD's song on **f** soil?
Proverbs
2:16 woman, from the **f** woman with her
5:20 and embrace the breasts of a **f** female?
6:24 the flattering tongue of the **f** woman.
7:5 woman, from the **f** woman who
23:27 a deep pit, and a **f** woman is a narrow
Isaiah
28:11 speech and a **f** tongue, he will
28:21 And to work his work—**f** is his work!
37:25 drunk water in **f** lands. With my
Jeremiah
2:25 in love with **f** gods, and I must
5:19 me and served **f** gods in your
7:18 pour out drink offerings to **f** gods.
8:19 their images, with pointless **f** gods?
Daniel
11:39 the help of a **f** god. He will heap
Zephaniah
1:4 and the names of the priestsof **f** gods,
1:8 sons, and all those wearing **f** clothes.
Malachi
2:11 and married the daughter of a **f** god.
Acts
17:18 a proclaimer of **f** gods." (They said
26:11 as I pursued them, even to **f** cities.
1 Corinthians
14:21 this people with **f** languages and
Hebrews
11:34 mighty in war, and routed **f** armies.

FOREIGN GODS

Gn 35:2; 35:4; Josh 24:20; 24:23; Jdg 10:16; 1Sa 7:3; 2Ch 33:15; Jer 2:25; 5:19; 7:18; 8:19; Zep 1:4; Ac 17:18

FOREIGNERS

Genesis
17:12 and those purchased with silver from **f**.
17:27 with silver from **f**, were circumcised
31:15 he think of us as **f** since he sold us
Deuteronomy
14:21 can sell it to **f**. Don't cook a
15:3 payment from **f**, but whatever is
23:20 You can charge **f** interest, but not your
29:22 after you, or **f** from distant
Judges
19:12 into a city of **f** who aren't
2 Samuel
22:45 **F** grovel before me; after hearing about
22:46 **F** lose their nerve; they come trembling
Nehemiah
9:2 from all of the **f**, they stood to
Psalms
18:44 me, they obey me; **f** grovel before me.
18:45 **F** lose their nerve; they come trembling
Isaiah
1:7 It's a wasteland, as when **f** raid.
25:2 the fortress of **f** into a city no
25:5 the roar of **f**. Like heat shaded
60:10 **F** will rebuild your walls, and their
61:5 **F** will stay and shepherd your sheep,
62:8 for your enemies. **F** won't drink your
Jeremiah
25:20 including the **f** living there; all the
30:8 their shackles. **F** will no longer
Lamentations
5:2 to strangers; our houses belong to **f**.
Ezekiel
7:21 hand it over to **f** as loot taken in
7:22 from my people, **f** will defile my
11:9 hand you over to **f**, and execute
28:7 I'll bring **f**, the most ruthless
28:10 at the hands of **f**. I have spoken.
30:12 With the help of **f** I will lay waste
31:12 **F**, the worst of the nations, cut it
44:7 into my sanctuary **f** who were
44:9 God proclaims: **F** who are
Obadiah
1:11 his wealth, and **f** entered his gates
Acts
17:21 as well as the **f** who live in
1 Corinthians
14:11 it, and they will be like **f** to me.

FOREST

Deuteronomy
19:5 goes into the **f** with a neighbor
Joshua
17:15 So go up to the **f** and clear ground
17:18 Because it is a **f**, you can clear
1 Samuel
22:5 So David left and went to Hereth **f**.

2 Samuel
18:6 The battle was fought in the Ephraim ***f***.
18:8 and the ***f*** devoured more
18:17 a big pit in the ***f***. They piled over
1 Kings
7:2 He built the ***F*** of Lebanon Palace one
10:17 these in the ***F*** of Lebanon Palace.
10:21 the items in the ***F*** of Lebanon Palace
2 Kings
19:23 most remote lodging place, its best ***f***.
1 Chronicles
16:33 the trees of the ***f*** will shout out
2 Chronicles
9:16 these in the ***F*** of Lebanon palace.
9:20 the items in the ***F*** of Lebanon palace
Nehemiah
2:8 of the king's ***f***, directing him to
Psalms
50:10 because every ***f*** animal already belongs
80:13 any boar from the ***f*** can tear it up,
83:14 a fire consumes a ***f***, just like flames
96:12 the trees of the ***f*** too will shout
104:20 is night, when every ***f*** animal prowls.
Isaiah
7:2 as the trees of a ***f*** shake when there
56:9 come and eat, all you beasts of the ***f***!
Jeremiah
5:6 a lion from the ***f*** will attack them;
10:3 a tree from the ***f*** is chopped down
12:5 you survive in the ***f*** along the Jordan?
46:23 destroy her dense ***f***, though it is
Ezekiel
15:2 the wood of all the trees in the ***f***?
34:25 live in the desert and sleep in the ***f***.
39:10 trees from the ***f***, because they
Hosea
2:12 them into a ***f***, and the wild
Amos
3:4 lion roar in the ***f***, when it has no
Micah
5:8 creatures of the ***f***, like a young
7:14 alone in a ***f*** in the midst of
Zechariah
11:2 of Bashan, for the deep ***f*** has fallen.
James
3:5 small flame can set a whole ***f*** on fire.

FOREVER → BLESSED FOREVER, FAITHFUL LOVE LASTS FOREVER, LIVE FOREVER, LOVE LASTS FOREVER

FORGET
Genesis
41:51 has helped me ***f*** all of my
Deuteronomy
4:9 so that you don't ***f*** the things your
4:23 yourselves! Don't ***f*** the covenant that
1 Samuel
1:11 me! Don't ***f*** your servant!
Proverbs
3:1 My son, don't ***f*** my instruction. Let
Isaiah
44:21 are my servant! I won't ***f*** you, Israel.
Hebrews
13:16 Don't ***f*** to do good and to share what
James
1:24 and immediately ***f*** what they were
1:25 listen and then ***f***, but they put it

FORGIVE → FORGIVE SINS, I WILL FORGIVE
Genesis
50:17 Joseph. "Please, ***f*** your brothers'
Deuteronomy
5:11 the LORD won't ***f*** anyone who uses
Matthew
6:12 ***F*** us for the ways we have wronged you,
6:14 If you ***f*** others their sins, your
9:6 on the earth to ***f*** sins"—he said to
18:21 times should I ***f*** my brother or
John
20:23 If you ***f*** anyone's sins, they are
Colossians
3:13 against anyone, ***f*** each other. As
1 John
1:9 and just to ***f*** us our sins and

FORGIVEN → SINS ARE FORGIVEN, YOU WILL BE FORGIVEN, YOUR SINS ARE FORGIVEN
Matthew
9:2 encouraged, my child, your sins are ***f***."
12:32 Human One will be ***f***. But whoever
26:28 for many so that their sins may be ***f***.
Mark
2:5 paralytic, "Child, your sins are ***f***!"
John
20:23 sins, they are ***f***; if you don't
Romans
4:7 the Law are ***f***, and whose sins
2 Corinthians
2:10 And whatever I've ***f*** (if I've forgiven
James
5:15 if they have sinned, they will be ***f***.
1 John
2:12 sins have been ***f*** through Jesus'

FORM
Genesis
1:2 without shape or ***f***, it was dark over
Numbers
12:8 sees the LORD's ***f***. So why aren't
Deuteronomy
4:12 didn't see any ***f***. There was only a
Job
4:16 its visible ***f***, although a
Jeremiah
4:23 without shape or ***f***; at the heavens
Ezekiel
1:5 like: Each had the ***f*** of a human being,
8:10 and I saw every ***f*** of loathsome
10:1 moment I saw a ***f*** of a throne in
Mark
16:12 in a different ***f*** to two of them
Luke
3:22 on him in bodily ***f*** like a dove. And
Acts
14:11 have taken human ***f*** and come down to
1 Corinthians
7:31 world in its present ***f*** is passing away.
15:24 he brings every ***f*** of rule, every
Philippians
2:6 he was in the ***f*** of God, he did
2:7 by taking the ***f*** of a slave and by
James
1:13 tempted by any ***f*** of evil, nor does

FORMED
Genesis
2:7 the LORD God ***f*** the human from the
Exodus
14:22 The waters ***f*** a wall for them
2 Samuel
10:8 marched out and ***f*** a battle line at
Jeremiah
10:16 because God has ***f*** all things,
Galatians
4:19 pains again until Christ is ***f*** in you.
1 Timothy
2:13 Adam was ***f*** first, and then Eve

FORMER
Malachi
3:4 LORD as in ancient days and in ***f*** years.
Acts
6:9 Synagogue of ***F*** Slaves. Members
Ephesians
4:22 change the ***f*** way of life that was part
1 Peter
1:14 conformed to your ***f*** desires, those
Revelation
21:1 earth, for the ***f*** heaven and the
21:4 anymore, for the ***f*** things have

FORTIFIED → FORTIFIED CITIES, FORTIFIED CITY
Numbers
21:24 for the border of the Ammonites was ***f***.
Deuteronomy
3:5 these towns was ***f*** with high walls,
1 Kings
12:25 Jeroboam ***f*** Shechem at Mount Ephraim and
Isaiah
2:15 every tall tower; against every ***f*** wall;
Ezekiel
36:35 and razed are now ***f*** and inhabited.
Amos
1:5 I will break the ***f*** gates of Damascus,

FORTIFIED CITIES
Nm 32:17; 32:36; Josh 10:20; 14:12; 19:35; 1Sa 6:18; 2Sa 20:6; 2Ki 17:9; 18:13; 19:25; 2Ch 11:10; 12:4; 14:6; 17:2, 19; 19:5; 21:3; 32:1; 33:14; Neh 9:25; Is 36:1; 37:26

FORTIFIED CITY
Josh 19:29; 2Ki 10:2; 18:8; 2Ch 11:23; Ps 60:9; 108:10; Is 27:10

FORTRESS
1 Samuel
22:1 to Adullam's ***f***. When David's
2 Samuel
5:7 did capture the ***f*** of Zion—which
1 Chronicles
11:5 the mountain ***f*** of Zion, which
Job
39:28 of rock, their ***f*** on rock's edge.
Psalms
18:2 my solid rock, my ***f***, my rescuer. My
27:1 The LORD is a ***f*** protecting my
28:8 strength; he is a ***f*** of protection for
31:2 me; be a strong ***f*** that saves me!
31:3 my rock and my ***f***. Guide me and
31:4 for me because you are my protective ***f***.
43:2 my protective ***f***! Why have you
71:3 saved because you are my rock and my ***f***.
94:22 the LORD is my ***f***; my God is my
144:2 my loyal one, my ***f***, my place of
150:1 Praise God in his ***f***, the sky!
Isaiah
23:4 has spoken; the ***f*** of the sea has
23:14 of Tarshish, for your ***f*** is destroyed!
25:2 into a ruin, the ***f*** of foreigners
29:7 on her and her ***f*** and besiege her,
Jeremiah
48:1 and shamed; the ***f*** is disgraced,
49:16 you live in a ***f*** and occupy the

FORTY
Genesis
7:4 on the earth for ***f*** days and forty
8:6 After ***f*** days, Noah opened the window of
50:3 mourned for him ***f*** days because that
Exodus
16:35 ate manna for ***f*** years, until they
26:19 Then make ***f*** silver bases to go under
Numbers
13:25 from exploring the land after ***f*** days.
14:33 in the desert for ***f*** years. They will
Deuteronomy
2:7 Throughout these ***f*** years the LORD
1 Samuel
4:18 Eli had judged Israel for ***f*** years.
2 Samuel
5:4 became king, and he ruled for ***f*** years.
Psalms
95:10 For ***f*** years I despised that generation;
Jonah
3:4 cried out, "Just ***f*** days more and
Matthew
4:2 had fasted for ***f*** days and forty
Acts
1:3 over a period of ***f*** days, speaking to

FOUGHT
Joshua
10:14 a human voice. The LORD ***f*** for Israel.
2 Timothy
4:7 I have ***f*** the good fight, finished the
Revelation
12:7 and his angels ***f*** the dragon. The

FOUNDATION
1 Kings
5:17 lay the temple's ***f*** with carefully
6:37 Solomon laid the ***f*** of the LORD's temple
Psalms
8:2 laid a strong ***f*** because of your
87:1 A song.] God's ***f*** is set on the
118:22 the builders is now the main ***f*** stone!
Isaiah
28:16 a sure ***f***: the one who
Luke
6:48 and laying the ***f*** on bedrock. When
Romans
15:20 won't be building on someone else's ***f***.
1 Corinthians
3:10 I laid a ***f*** like a wise master builder

FOUNDATION [cont.]

Ephesians
2:20 are built on the ***f*** of the apostles
1 Timothy
6:19 that is a good ***f*** for the future.
2 Timothy
2:19 God's solid ***f*** is still standing with
Hebrews
4:3 were completed at the ***f*** of the world.
6:1 Let's not lay a ***f*** of turning away
9:26 times since the ***f*** of the world.
Jude
1:20 other up on the ***f*** of your most holy
Revelation
21:19 jewel. The first ***f*** was jasper, the

FOUNDATIONS

2 Samuel
22:8 shook; the sky's ***f*** trembled and
Ezra
3:3 the altar on its ***f***, because they
Psalms
18:15 the earth's ***f*** were laid bare at
82:5 in the dark. All the earth's ***f*** shake.
102:25 laid the earth's ***f*** long ago; the
104:5 the earth on its ***f*** so that it will
137:7 All the way to its ***f***!" they yelled.
Proverbs
3:19 The LORD laid the ***f*** of the earth with
8:29 when he marked out the earth's ***f***.
Isaiah
24:18 open, and the earth's ***f*** will quake.
Amos
9:1 pillars until the ***f*** shake, shatter
Acts
16:26 the prison's ***f***. The doors flew
Hebrews
1:10 laid the earth's ***f*** in the beginning,
11:10 a city that has ***f***, whose architect
Revelation
21:14 wall had twelve ***f***, and on them were

FOUNTAIN OF LIFE

Prv 10:11; 13:14; 14:27; 16:22; 2Co 2:16

FOUR

Ezekiel
1:5 were forms of ***f*** living creatures.
Daniel
7:2 night I saw the ***f*** winds of heaven
Zechariah
1:18 Then I looked up and saw ***f*** horns
2:6 you like the ***f*** winds of heaven,
6:1 up again and saw ***f*** chariots coming
Revelation
4:6 the throne, were ***f*** living creatures
5:6 throne and the ***f*** living creatures
6:1 heard one of the ***f*** living creatures
7:1 After this I saw ***f*** angels standing at
9:13 a voice from the ***f*** horns of the gold
9:14 Release the ***f*** angels who are
14:3 the throne, the ***f*** living creatures,
15:7 Then one of the ***f*** living creatures gave the seven angels
19:4 elders and the ***f*** living creatures
20:8 that are at the ***f*** corners of the

FOXES

Song of Songs
2:15 Catch ***f*** for us—those little foxes
Matthew
8:20 Jesus replied, "***F*** have dens, and the

FREE

Genesis
24:8 you, you will be ***f*** from this
Exodus
6:6 I'll set you ***f*** with great power
23:5 to help set it ***f***, you must help
Leviticus
16:26 who set the goat ***f*** for Azazel must
Numbers
5:31 The man will be ***f*** from guilt, but the
Job
3:19 there; a servant is ***f*** from his masters.
12:14 he ties a person up, he can't be set ***f***.
Psalms
4:1 God! Set me ***f*** from my troubles!
15:2 person who lives ***f*** of blame, does
25:15 because he will ***f*** my feet from the
44:2 peoples, but you set our ancestors ***f***.
50:19 set your mouth ***f*** to do evil, then
68:6 he sets prisoners ***f*** with happiness,
81:6 your hands are ***f*** of the brick
102:20 groans, to set ***f*** those condemned
105:20 and set him ***f***; the ruler of
129:4 God cut me ***f*** from the ropes of
Proverbs
6:5 Get yourself ***f*** like a gazelle from a
Jeremiah
40:4 I'm setting you ***f*** from the chains
Ezekiel
13:20 and I will set ***f*** the lives that
41:9 The space left ***f*** between the
Luke
13:12 you are set ***f*** from your
John
8:32 truth, and the truth will set you ***f***."
8:36 the Son makes you ***f***, you really will
Romans
5:15 But the ***f*** gift of Christ isn't like
6:18 you have been set ***f*** from sin, you
7:3 dies, she's ***f*** from the Law, so
8:2 Jesus has set you ***f*** from the law of
1 Corinthians
7:21 able to be ***f***, take advantage
7:39 dies, she is ***f*** to marry whomever
9:1 Am I not ***f***? Am I not an apostle?
9:18 the good news ***f*** of charge. That's
9:19 Although I'm ***f*** from all people, I make
12:13 or slave or ***f***, and we all were
2 Corinthians
11:7 the gospel of God to you ***f*** of charge?
Galatians
3:28 neither slave nor ***f***; nor is there
5:1 Christ has set us ***f*** for freedom.
Ephesians
6:8 that person is a slave or a ***f*** person.
Colossians
1:14 He set us ***f*** through the Son and forgave
3:11 slave nor ***f***, but Christ is
1 Timothy
2:6 to set all people ***f***. This was a

Hebrews
2:15 He set ***f*** those who were held in slavery
9:15 to set them ***f*** from the offenses
13:5 of life should be ***f*** from the love of
1 Peter
2:16 and yet also as ***f*** people, not using
Revelation
6:15 slave and ***f***, hid themselves
13:16 and poor, the ***f*** and slaves—to
19:18 of all, both ***f*** and slave, both

FREEDOM

Leviticus
19:20 or given her ***f***, there must be a
25:10 holy, proclaiming ***f*** throughout the
Psalms
66:12 and water. But you brought us out to ***f***!
Acts
24:23 to give Paul some ***f***, and his friends
Romans
8:21 into the glorious ***f*** of God's children.
1 Corinthians
6:12 I have the ***f*** to do anything, but not
8:9 out or else this ***f*** of yours might be
10:29 Why should my ***f*** be judged by
2 Corinthians
3:17 where the Lord's Spirit is, there is ***f***.
Galatians
2:4 in to spy on our ***f***, which we have in
5:1 set us free for ***f***. Therefore stand
5:13 were called to ***f***, brothers and
James
1:25 law, the law of ***f***, and continue to
2:12 who will be judged by the law of ***f***.
1 Peter
2:16 not using your ***f*** as a cover-up for
2 Peter
2:19 teachers promise ***f***, but they

FRESH

Genesis
26:19 and found a well there with ***f*** water.
Numbers
6:3 or eat grapes, whether ***f*** or dried.
Song of Songs
4:15 spring, a well of ***f*** water, streams
Ezekiel
47:8 enter the sea, its water becomes ***f***.
47:11 won't be made ***f*** (they are left
Hosea
2:8 new wine, and the ***f*** oil, and that I
8:7 grain, but no ***f*** growth; it will
Joel
2:19 new wine, and ***f*** oil, and you will
2:24 will overflow with new wine and ***f*** oil.
James
3:11 Both ***f*** water and salt water don't come

FRIEND

Exodus
32:27 brother, your ***f***, and your
Deuteronomy
13:6 spouse or best ***f*** entices you
Judges
7:13 a man telling his ***f*** about a dream. He
7:14 His ***f*** replied, "Can this be anything
1 Samuel
15:28 will give it to a ***f*** of yours, someone
28:17 hands and has given it to your ***f*** David.
2 Samuel
12:11 give them to your ***f***, and he will have
13:3 But Amnon had a ***f*** named Jonadab,
15:37 So David's ***f*** Hushai went into
16:16 Then David's ***f*** Hushai, who was from
16:17 love to your ***f***? Why didn't you
1 Kings
4:5 Nathan's son, a priest and royal ***f***;
16:11 on a wall, whether relative or ***f***.
20:35 group said to his ***f***: "Please strike
20:36 So he said to his ***f***, "Because you
2 Chronicles
20:7 descendants of your ***f*** Abraham forever.
Job
6:27 over an orphan, barter away your ***f***?
16:20 my go-between, my ***f***. While my eyes
16:21 being, like a person pleads for a ***f***.
Psalms
7:4 I have repaid a ***f*** with evil or
15:3 does no harm to a ***f***, doesn't insult a
35:14 I was grieving a ***f*** or a brother. I
41:9 Even my good ***f***, the one I trusted, who
55:13 equal, my close companion, my good ***f***!
55:20 My ***f*** attacked his allies, breaking his
88:18 distant. My only ***f*** is darkness.
119:63 I'm a ***f*** to everyone who honors you and
Proverbs
7:4 are my sister"; call understanding "***f***,"
17:18 on a deal, securing a loan for a ***f***.
22:11 is gracious, and the king is their ***f***.
27:6 the bruises of a ***f***; excessive are
27:10 Don't desert your ***f*** or a friend of your
Jeremiah
3:4 to me, "My father, my ***f*** since youth,
6:21 them; neighbor and ***f*** alike will perish.
9:4 and every ***f*** traffics in
Micah
7:5 Don't rely on a ***f***; put no trust in a
Matthew
11:19 and a drunk, a ***f*** of tax collectors
20:13 to one of them, '***F***, I did you no
22:12 He said to him, '***F***, how did you get in
26:50 said to him, "***F***, do what you came
Luke
5:20 faith, he said, "***F***, your sins are
7:34 and a drunk, a ***f*** of tax collectors
11:5 one of you has a ***f*** and you go to
11:6 because a ***f*** of mine on a journey has
11:8 up and give his ***f*** whatever he needs
14:10 he will say, '***F***, move up here to
John
3:29 married. The ***f*** of the groom
11:11 continued, "Our ***f*** Lazarus is
19:12 man, you aren't a ***f*** of the emperor!
Acts
13:1 (a childhood ***f*** of Herod the
Romans
16:5 my dear ***f***, who was the
16:8 to Ampliatus, my dear ***f*** in the Lord.
16:9 in Christ, and my dear ***f*** Stachys.
16:12 hello to my dear ***f*** Persis, who has
Philippians
4:3 asking you, loyal ***f***, to help these

FRIEND [cont.]

James
2:23 is more, Abraham was called God's **f**.
2 Peter
3:15 just as our dear **f** and brother Paul
3 John
1:1 elder. To my dear **f** Gaius, whom I
1:2 Dear **f**, I'm praying that all is well
1:5 Dear **f**, you act faithfully in whatever
1:11 Dear **f**, don't imitate what is bad but

FRIGHTENED

Genesis
18:15 because she was **f**. But he said,
43:18 the men were **f** and said, "We've
Deuteronomy
1:21 you. Don't be afraid! Don't be **f**!
1 Samuel
21:12 and became very **f** of Achish, Gath's
23:3 to him, "Look how **f** we are here in
2 Samuel
6:9 David was **f** by the LORD that day. "How
2 Kings
19:26 power. They are **f** and ashamed.
1 Chronicles
13:12 David was **f** by God that day. "How will
2 Chronicles
20:3 **F**, Jehoshaphat decided to seek the
Job
4:5 it has struck you, and you are **f**.
23:16 my mind; the Almighty has **f** me.
31:34 clan's contempt **f** me; I was quiet
Psalms
27:1 my life. Should I be **f** of anything?
48:5 stunned; they panicked and ran away **f**.
112:7 They won't be **f** at bad news. Their
Isaiah
31:4 by their noise or **f** by their roar. So
37:27 power; they are **f** and dismayed.
Jeremiah
1:17 you. Don't be **f** before them, or I
51:46 be distracted or **f** by the rumors you
Daniel
4:19 he thought about **f** him. The king
5:9 was really **f**. All the color
5:10 Don't be so disturbed. Don't be so **f**.
Matthew
14:26 a ghost!" They were so **f** they screamed.
14:30 wind, he became **f**. As he began to
Mark
4:40 Why are you **f**? Don't you have
Luke
24:5 The women were **f** and bowed their faces

FRUIT → BEAR FRUIT, GOOD FRUIT, PRODUCE FRUIT, PRODUCE GOOD FRUIT, YOUR FRUIT

Genesis
3:3 but not the **f** of the tree in the middle
Exodus
10:15 of the orchards' **f** that the hail had
23:16 gather your crop of **f** from the field.
Leviticus
19:23 and plant any **f** tree, you must
Nehemiah
9:25 and a great many **f** trees. They ate
9:36 to enjoy its **f** and its good
10:35 and the early **f** from all trees
10:37 the **f** of every tree,
Psalms
80:12 all who come along can pluck its **f**,
92:14 They will bear **f** even when old and
Proverbs
1:31 will eat from the **f** of their way, and
8:19 My **f** is better than gold, even fine
11:30 The **f** of the righteous is a tree of
12:14 From the **f** of their speech, people are
13:2 eat well from the **f** of their words,
18:20 satisfied by the **f** of the mouth;
18:21 those who love it will eat its **f**.
27:18 tree will eat its **f**, and those who
Ecclesiastes
2:5 planting every kind of **f** tree in them.
Amos
8:1 God showed me: a basket of summer **f**.
Matthew
7:18 can't produce bad **f**. And a rotten
Mark
4:19 and choke the word, and it bears no **f**.
Romans
7:5 our body, so that we bore **f** for death.
Ephesians
5:9 Light produces **f** that consists of every
Philippians
1:11 filled with the **f** of righteousness,
Colossians
1:6 has been bearing **f** and growing among
James
5:7 forward to the precious **f** of the earth.
Revelation
6:13 tree drops its **f** when shaken by a
18:14 The **f** your whole being craved has gone
22:2 twelve crops of **f**, bearing its

FULFILL

Numbers
15:3 or a sacrifice to **f** a solemn promise,
15:8 or a sacrifice to **f** a solemn promise,
2 Samuel
15:7 Hebron so I can **f** a promise I made
1 Kings
2:27 in order to **f** the LORD's word
2 Chronicles
34:31 in order to **f** the words of the
35:2 them to **f** their
Job
22:27 you; you will **f** your solemn
Psalms
20:4 is in your heart and **f** all your plans.
20:5 God. Let the LORD **f** all your requests!
22:25 of you; I will **f** my promises in
50:14 of thanksgiving! **F** the promises you
56:12 I will **f** my promises to you, God. I
Ecclesiastes
5:4 a promise to God, **f** it without delay
Matthew
3:15 is necessary to **f** all
5:17 to do away with them but to **f** them.
13:35 This was to **f** what the prophet spoke:
21:4 this happened to **f** what the prophet
Luke
1:45 the Lord would **f** the promises he
John
12:38 This was to **f** the word of the prophet

13:18 But this is to ***f*** the scripture,
19:24 it." This was to ***f*** the scripture,
Galatians
6:2 and so you will ***f*** the law of Christ.
James
2:8 when you really ***f*** the royal law

FULFILLED

Joshua
21:45 of Israel failed. Every promise was ***f***.
Psalms
111:8 forever: they are ***f*** with truth and
Proverbs
7:14 today I ***f*** my solemn
13:12 sick; longing ***f*** is a tree of life.
13:19 A desire ***f*** is pleasant, but fools find
Matthew
1:22 spoken through the prophet would be ***f***:
2:15 Herod died. This ***f*** what the Lord had
4:14 This ***f*** what Isaiah the prophet said
8:17 said would be ***f***: He is the one
12:17 through Isaiah the prophet might be ***f***:
26:54 the scriptures be ***f*** that say this
27:9 This ***f*** the words of Jeremiah the
Mark
14:49 me. But let the scriptures be ***f***."
Luke
1:1 the events that have been ***f*** among us.
4:21 has been ***f*** just as you heard
22:16 eat it until it is ***f*** in God's kingdom."
22:37 scripture must be ***f*** in relation to
24:44 Prophets, and the Psalms must be ***f***."
John
17:12 so that scripture would be ***f***.
18:9 spoken might be ***f***: "I didn't lose
Romans
8:4 the Law might be ***f*** in us. Now the
13:8 loves another person has ***f*** the Law.
Galatians
5:14 the Law has been ***f*** in a single
James
2:23 the scripture was ***f*** that says,

FUN

Genesis
27:12 thinks I'm making ***f*** of him? I will be
Judges
8:15 You made ***f*** of me because of
9:27 ate, drank, and made ***f*** of Abimelech.
1 Samuel
1:6 rival would make ***f*** of her
1:7 would make ***f*** of her. Then she
1 Kings
18:27 started making ***f*** of them: "Shout
2 Chronicles
30:10 But they were laughed at and made ***f*** of.
36:16 But they made ***f*** of God's messengers,
Nehemiah
2:19 mocked and made ***f*** of us. "What are
Psalms
2:4 heaven laughs; my Lord makes ***f*** of them.
22:7 who see me make ***f*** of me—they gape,
42:10 my foes make ***f*** of me, constantly
44:16 of those who make ***f*** of me and bad-mouth me
69:11 funeral clothes, people made ***f*** of me.
80:6 neighbors; our enemies make ***f*** of us.
102:8 my enemies make ***f*** of me; those who
119:51 The arrogant make ***f*** of me to no end,
Proverbs
1:11 wait for the innocent just for ***f***.
1:26 I'll make ***f*** of you when dread
8:30 I was having ***f***, smiling before
Isaiah
22:13 instead there was ***f*** and frivolity,
Hosea
7:16 in Egypt they will make ***f*** of them.
Habakkuk
1:10 He makes ***f*** of kings; rulers are
Matthew
27:41 elders, were making ***f*** of him, saying,
Mark
15:31 were making ***f*** of him among
Hebrews
12:11 No discipline is ***f*** while it lasts, but

FUNERAL

Leviticus
11:32 cloth, skin, or ***f*** clothing—any such
2 Samuel
1:17 David sang this ***f*** song for Saul and
3:31 and put on ***f*** clothes! Mourn
Psalms
30:11 You took off my ***f*** clothes and
69:11 When I wore ***f*** clothes, people made fun
Isaiah
50:3 and cover them with ***f*** clothing.
Jeremiah
4:8 So put on ***f*** clothing. Weep and wail,
6:26 My people, put on ***f*** clothes and roll in
49:3 of Rabbah; put on ***f*** clothing, cry
Joel
1:8 woman dressed in ***f*** clothing, one who
Amos
5:1 Hear this word—a ***f*** song—that I am
8:10 singing into a ***f*** song; I will make
Matthew
11:17 dance. We sang a ***f*** song and you
Luke
7:32 dance. We sang a ***f*** song and you
10:13 have sat around in ***f*** clothes and ashes.
Revelation
6:12 became black as ***f*** clothing, and the

FURIOUS

Genesis
27:41 Esau was ***f*** at Jacob because his father
Deuteronomy
9:7 the LORD your God ***f*** in the
9:20 But the LORD was ***f*** with Aaron—he was
Joshua
7:1 So the LORD was ***f*** with the
23:16 the LORD will be ***f*** with you. You
2 Kings
22:13 The LORD must be ***f*** with us because
2 Chronicles
28:11 because the LORD is ***f*** with you."
34:21 The LORD must be ***f*** with us because
Esther
1:12 The king was ***f***, his anger
7:7 ***F***, the king got up and left the
Job
36:13 hearts become ***f***; they don't cry

Psalms
6:1 don't discipline me when you are ***f***.
38:1 don't discipline me when you are ***f***.
78:21 this, he became ***f***. A fire was
85:3 stopped being ***f***; you've turned
Proverbs
14:35 servant, but is ***f*** at a shameful one.
21:14 and a hidden bribe removes ***f*** wrath.
Isaiah
30:30 crushing arm in ***f*** anger, with a
Jeremiah
3:5 continue to be ***f***?" This is what
37:15 who were ***f*** with him. They beat him and
Ezekiel
22:31 on them. With my ***f*** fire I've
Daniel
2:12 exploded in a ***f*** rage and ordered
Matthew
18:34 His master was ***f*** and handed him over to the guard
Luke
6:11 They were ***f*** and began talking with each other about
15:28 the older son was ***f*** and didn't want
Acts
5:33 this, they became ***f*** and wanted to
12:20 Herod had been ***f*** with the people of
2 Corinthians
11:29 led astray without me being ***f*** about it?
Revelation
12:17 So the dragon was ***f*** with the woman, and
16:19 gave her the wine cup of his ***f*** anger.

FURNACE

Isaiah
48:10 I have tested you in the ***f*** of misery.
Daniel
3:6 thrown into a ***f*** of flaming fire."
Matthew
6:30 thrown into the ***f***, won't God do
13:42 into a burning ***f***. People there
Luke
12:28 thrown into the ***f***, how much more
Revelation
1:15 purified in a ***f***, and his voice
9:2 smoke from a huge ***f***. The sun and air

FURY

Exodus
32:10 me alone! Let my ***f*** burn and devour
32:11 why does your ***f*** burn against your
Deuteronomy
29:28 wrath, and great ***f***. He threw them
Joshua
7:26 away from his ***f***. So he named that
Job
5:2 kill the foolish; ***f*** can kill the
9:34 from me, so his ***f*** wouldn't frighten
21:17 them, with its ***f*** inflicting pain
21:30 on the day of ***f*** they are rescued.
Psalms
2:5 then he terrifies them with his ***f***:
7:6 up against the ***f*** of my foes! Wake
69:24 them—let your burning ***f*** catch them.
78:49 against them—***f***, indignation,
90:9 because of your ***f***; we finish up our
Proverbs
22:8 the rod of their ***f*** will come to an
Isaiah
10:5 in whose hand is the staff of my ***f***!
13:5 of his ***f***, to destroy the
26:20 in a little while the ***f*** will be over.
30:27 lips are full of ***f***; his tongue is
42:25 his anger and the ***f*** of battle. It
66:14 servants, but his ***f*** among his enemies.
Jeremiah
4:26 in ruins before the LORD, before his ***f***.
Lamentations
4:11 let loose his ***f***; he poured out
Ezekiel
5:15 and overflowing ***f***. I, the LORD,
8:17 to provoke my ***f***. Look at them!
13:13 proclaims: In my ***f*** I will make a
13:15 I will exhaust my ***f*** on the wall and on
14:19 and pour out my ***f*** on it. With great
16:38 hand you over in bloody ***f*** and zeal.
25:14 to my anger and ***f***, and they will
36:6 my passion and ***f*** lead me to speak.
36:18 I poured out my ***f*** on them for all
Nahum
1:6 the heat of his ***f***? His wrath pours
Habakkuk
3:8 Or was your ***f*** directed against
3:12 In ***f***, you stride the earth; in anger
Zephaniah
1:15 day is a day of ***f***, a day of
1:18 day of the LORD's ***f***. His jealousy

FUTURE

Genesis
9:12 you, on behalf of every ***f*** generation.
Exodus
13:14 When in the ***f*** your child asks you,
Leviticus
3:17 rule for your ***f*** generations,
24:3 rule throughout your ***f*** generations.
Deuteronomy
6:20 In the ***f***, your children will ask you,
Joshua
4:6 among you. In the ***f*** your children may
4:21 In the ***f*** your children
22:24 happen. In the ***f*** your children
22:27 So in the ***f*** your children
22:28 If in the ***f*** they ever say
2 Samuel
7:19 dynasty in the ***f*** and the
1 Chronicles
17:17 spoken about the ***f*** of your servant's
Job
8:7 ordinary, your ***f*** will be
Psalms
22:30 ***F*** descendants will serve him;
31:15 My ***f*** is in your hands. Don't hand me
37:37 right because the ***f*** belongs to
37:38 all together; the ***f*** of the wicked
48:13 so that you may tell ***f*** generations:
77:8 Is his promise over for ***f*** generations?
90:2 past to forever in the ***f***, you are God.
Proverbs
19:20 so you might grow wise in the ***f***.
23:18 you will have a ***f***, and your hope
24:14 it, there is a ***f***. Your hope won't
24:20 there is no ***f*** for the evil; the

25:8 you do in the ***f*** when your
31:25 clothing; she is confident about the ***f***.
Ecclesiastes
10:14 one can say what will happen in the ***f***.
Daniel
2:29 happen in the ***f***. The revealer of
8:26 because it is for days far in the ***f***."
9:26 The army of a ***f*** leader will
10:14 people in the ***f***, because there is
Acts
16:16 to predict the ***f***. She made a lot
Romans
8:38 present things or ***f*** things, not powers
1 Corinthians
3:22 things in the ***f***—everything belong
2 Corinthians
8:14 so that in the ***f*** their surplus can
Ephesians
1:21 be named not only now but in the ***f***.
2:7 did this to show ***f*** generations the
1 Timothy
6:19 for the ***f***. That way they
Hebrews
11:20 Jacob and Esau concerning their ***f***.

Gg

GABRIEL

Daniel

8:16 It called out: "***G***, help this person
8:17 ***G*** approached me, and I was terrified
8:18 the ground. Then ***G*** touched me and
9:21 prayer, the man ***G*** approached me at

Luke

1:19 replied, "I am ***G***. I stand in God's
1:26 sent the angel ***G*** to Nazareth, a

GAD

Genesis

30:11 What good luck!" So she named him ***G***.

Exodus

1:4 Dan and Naphtali, ***G*** and Asher

Deuteronomy

27:13 cursing: Reuben, ***G***, Asher, Zebulun,

Joshua

4:12 the people of ***G***, and half the

GAIN

Genesis

37:26 What do we ***g*** if we kill our

Psalms

119:36 my heart to your laws, not to greedy ***g***.

Proverbs

1:5 those with understanding ***g*** guidance.
8:35 find life; they ***g*** favor from the
11:16 gains honor; violent men ***g*** only wealth.
15:6 but the ***g*** of the wicked
15:27 things unjustly ***g*** trouble for their
15:32 listen to correction ***g*** understanding.
19:25 and they will ***g*** knowledge.
21:6 Those who ***g*** treasure with lies are like
28:16 one who hates unjust ***g*** will live long.
29:23 but those of humble spirit ***g*** honor.

Ecclesiastes

1:3 What do people ***g*** from all the hard work
5:16 What then do they ***g*** from working so
6:8 what do the poor ***g*** by knowing how to
6:11 is pointless. What do people ***g*** by it?

Matthew

16:26 Why would people ***g*** the whole world but lose their lives

Luke

21:19 By holding fast, you will ***g*** your lives

Philippians

3:8 sewer trash, so that I might ***g*** Christ

GALATIA

Acts

16:6 of Phrygia and ***G*** because the Holy
18:23 in the region of ***G*** and the district

1 Corinthians

16:1 have directed the churches in ***G*** to do.

Galatians

1:2 sisters with me. To the churches in ***G***.

2 Timothy

4:10 has gone to ***G***, and Titus has

1 Peter

1:1 live in Pontus, ***G***, Cappadocia,

GALILEAN

Matthew

26:69 him, "You were also with Jesus the ***G***."

Mark

14:70 one of them, because you are also a ***G***."

Luke

22:59 been with him, because he is a ***G*** too."
23:6 this, Pilate asked if the man was a ***G***.

Acts

5:37 census, Judas the ***G*** appeared and got

GALILEANS

Luke

13:1 Jesus about the ***G*** whom Pilate had
13:2 of these ***G*** proves that they

John

4:45 to Galilee, the ***G*** welcomed him

Acts

1:11 They said, "***G***, why are you standing
2:7 who are speaking ***G***, every one of

GALILEE

Isaiah

9:1 the Jordan, and the ***G*** of the nations.

Matthew

3:13 Jesus came from ***G*** to the Jordan
4:15 across the Jordan, ***G*** of the Gentiles,
21:11 the prophet Jesus from Nazareth in ***G***."
26:32 raised up, I'll go before you to ***G***."
28:10 I am going into ***G***. They will see me

Luke

23:49 followed him from ***G***, stood at a

John

2:1 in Cana of ***G***. Jesus' mother
7:41 The Christ can't come from ***G***, can he?

GAMALIEL

Numbers

1:10 son; from Manasseh, ***G***, Pedahzur's son;

Acts

5:34 of the Law named ***G***, well-respected by

GARDEN

Genesis

2:8 God planted a ***g*** in Eden in the
3:1 shouldn't eat from any tree in the ***g***?"
3:3 the middle of the ***g***. God said, 'Don't
3:24 the east of the ***g*** of Eden, he

Nehemiah
3:15 of the King's ***G***, as far as the
Esther
1:5 met in the walled ***g*** of the royal
Song of Songs
4:12 An enclosed ***g*** is my sister, my bride;
4:15 You are a ***g*** spring, a well of fresh
4:16 Blow upon my ***g***; let its perfumes
5:1 I have come to my ***g***, my sister, my
6:2 gone down to his ***g***, to the fragrant
Isaiah
1:30 leaves, like a ***g*** without water.
51:3 like the LORD's ***g***. Happiness and
58:11 be like a watered ***g***, like a spring of
61:11 growth, and as a ***g*** grows its seeds,
Jeremiah
31:12 be like a lush ***g***; they will grieve
Lamentations
2:6 own booth like a ***g***; he destroyed his
Ezekiel
28:13 in Eden, God's ***g***. You were covered
31:8 equal in God's ***g***. The fir trees
31:9 envied it, all that were in God's ***g***.
36:35 become like the ***g*** of Eden." And the
Hosea
14:7 flourish like a ***g***; they will
Joel
2:3 is like Eden's ***g***, but they leave
John
18:1 He and his disciples entered a ***g*** there.
19:41 There was a ***g*** in the place where Jesus

GARMENT

Genesis
39:12 She grabbed his ***g***, saying, "Lie down
Job
2:12 Each one tore his ***g*** and scattered
Proverbs
20:16 Take the ***g*** of the person who secures a
25:20 like taking off a ***g*** on a cold day or
27:13 Take the ***g*** of the person who secures a
30:4 the waters in a ***g***? Who has
Isaiah
9:5 and every ***g*** rolled in blood
Jeremiah
13:10 like this linen ***g***—good for nothing!
Ezekiel
5:3 a few strands and hide them in your ***g***.
Haggai
2:12 the hem of one's ***g*** and that hem
Malachi
2:16 one covering his ***g*** with violence,
Luke
5:36 patch from a new ***g*** to patch an old

GATE

Genesis
19:1 sitting at the ***g*** of Sodom, saw
Deuteronomy
22:15 to the city's elders at the city ***g***.
25:7 at the city ***g***, informing them:
Judges
16:2 night at the city ***g***. They kept quiet
16:3 doors of the city ***g*** and the two
1 Samuel
4:18 chair beside the ***g***. His neck broke,
Nehemiah
2:13 the Valley ***G*** past the Dragon's
3:1 built the Sheep ***G***. They dedicated
8:1 of the Water ***G***. They asked Ezra
12:31 right, in the direction of the Dung ***G***.
Esther
2:19 working for the king at the King's ***G***.
Psalms
69:12 sit at the city ***g*** muttered things
118:20 is the LORD's ***g***; those who are
127:5 arguing with their enemies in the ***g***.
Matthew
7:13 the narrow ***g***. The gate that
John
10:2 through the ***g*** is the shepherd
10:7 you that I am the ***g*** of the sheep.
10:9 I am the ***g***. Whoever enters through me
Acts
3:2 him at the temple ***g*** known as the
12:13 at the outer ***g***, a female servant
Hebrews
13:12 outside the city ***g*** to make the

GATEKEEPERS

2 Kings
7:10 called out to the ***g***, telling them,
7:11 The ***g*** shouted out the news, and it was
1 Chronicles
9:17 The ***g***: Shallum, Akkub, Talmon, and
15:18 and Obed-edom and Jeiel the ***g***.
16:38 Jeduthun's son, and Hosah served as ***g***.
23:5 4,000 ***g***, and 4,000 praising the LORD
26:1 divisions of the ***g***: from the
2 Chronicles
8:14 as well as the ***g*** in their
34:9 by the levitical ***g*** from Manasseh,
Ezra
2:42 The family of the ***g***: of Shallum, Ater,
Nehemiah
7:1 the doors, the ***g***, singers, and
10:28 the Levites, the ***g***, the singers, the
11:19 The ***g***: Akkub, Talmon, and their
12:25 and Akkub were ***g*** standing guard by
12:45 singers and the ***g***, according to the

GATES

Nehemiah
7:3 to them, "The ***g*** of Jerusalem
11:19 who guarded the ***g*** totaled 172.
Psalms
9:13 brings me back from the very ***g*** of death
9:14 salvation in the ***g*** of Daughter Zion.
24:7 Mighty ***g***: lift up your heads! Ancient
24:9 Mighty ***g***: lift up your heads! Ancient
87:2 LORD loves Zion's ***g*** more than all of
100:4 Enter his ***g*** with thanks; enter his
107:18 food; they had arrived at death's ***g***.
118:19 Open the ***g*** of righteousness for me so I
122:2 feet are standing in your ***g***, Jerusalem!
147:13 the bars on your ***g***, God blesses the
Proverbs
1:21 of the city ***g***, she has her say:
14:19 people are at the ***g*** of the righteous.
31:23 known in the city ***g*** when he sits with
31:31 let her deeds praise her in the city ***g***.
Jeremiah
7:2 who enter these ***g*** to worship the

Matthew
16:18 on this rock. The **g** of the underworld
Acts
9:24 watch at the city **g** around the clock
14:13 to the city **g**. Along with the
21:30 temple. Immediately the **g** were closed.
Revelation
21:12 wall with twelve **g**. By the gates
22:14 life and may enter the city by the **g**.

GATH

1 Samuel
5:8 The people of **G** said, "Let the
2 Samuel
1:20 talk about it in **G**; don't bring news
Micah
1:10 In **G** tell it not; no need to weep

GATHER

Exodus
5:7 them go out and **g** the straw for
Ezra
10:7 returned exiles should **g** in Jerusalem.
Nehemiah
1:9 skies, I will **g** them from there
4:20 sound, come and **g** where we are. Our
12:44 They were to **g** into them the
Job
24:6 They **g** their food in the field, glean
34:14 to do it—to **g** his spirit and
39:12 your grain to **g** into your
Psalms
26:9 Don't **g** me up with the sinners, taking
104:22 sun rises, they **g** together and lie
104:28 it to them, they **g** it up; when you
106:47 our God, save us! **G** us back together
119:23 Even if rulers **g** and scheme against me,
142:7 righteous will **g** all around me
Song of Songs
6:2 graze in the gardens, to **g** the lilies.
Lamentations
5:4 for a price; we **g** our own wood—but
Zephaniah
2:1 **G** together and assemble yourselves,
3:8 when I decide to **g** nations, to
3:19 the lame; I will **g** the outcast. I
3:20 the time when I **g** you. I will give
Matthew
6:26 harvest grain or **g** crops into barns.
10:9 be fed, so don't **g** gold or silver or
12:30 and whoever doesn't **g** with me scatters.
Luke
6:44 People don't **g** figs from thorny
John
6:12 his disciples, "**G** up the leftover
18:20 all the Jews **g**. I've said

GATHERING

Exodus
23:16 field, and the **G** Festival at the
34:22 harvest, and the **G** Festival at the
Numbers
15:32 they found a man **g** wood on the
15:33 who found him **g** wood brought him
Deuteronomy
30:3 on you, **g** you up from all
1 Samuel
13:11 and the Philistines were **g** at Michmash.
2 Chronicles
7:9 day there was a **g**. They had
Psalms
147:2 Jerusalem, **g** up Israel's
Ecclesiastes
3:5 and a time for **g** stones, a time
Jeremiah
17:11 Like a partridge **g** a brood that is not
Ezekiel
22:19 product, I'm now **g** you into the
38:8 from the sword, a **g** from many peoples
Daniel
11:10 ready for war, **g** massive forces.
Matthew
22:41 the Pharisees were **g**, Jesus asked them,
Mark
14:60 the middle of the **g** and examined
Luke
8:4 a great crowd was **g** and people were
15:1 and sinners were **g** around Jesus to
John
4:36 their pay and **g** fruit for eternal
Acts
10:27 inside and found a large **g** of people.
19:40 since we can't justify this unruly **g**."
Hebrews
12:22 to countless angels in a festival **g**,

GAVE

Genesis
2:19 them. The human **g** each living being
3:6 ate it, and also **g** some to her
28:4 immigrants, the land God **g** to Abraham."
35:12 The land I **g** to Abraham and to Isaac
Exodus
31:18 Mount Sinai, God **g** him the two
32:24 it off!' So they **g** it to me, I threw
Deuteronomy
2:12 of, which the LORD **g** to them.)
3:12 at that time. I **g** some of it, from
9:10 The LORD **g** me the two stone tablets,
26:9 to this place and **g** us this land—a la
31:9 down and **g** it to the priests-
Joshua
11:23 Moses. Joshua **g** it as a legacy to
13:14 of Levi that he **g** no legacy. Their
15:13 to him, Joshua **g** a portion among
19:49 the Israelites **g** to Joshua, Nun's
21:44 The LORD **g** them rest from surrounding
24:13 I **g** you land on which you hadn't toiled
1 Samuel
27:6 So Achish **g** the town of Ziklag to David
2 Samuel
8:6 tribute. The LORD **g** David victory
12:8 I **g** your master's house to you, and
1 Kings
4:29 And God **g** Solomon wisdom and very great understanding
5:11 return, Solomon **g** an annual gift to
Ezra
2:69 their means, they **g** to the building
Nehemiah
9:15 were hungry, you **g** them bread from
9:20 You **g** your good spirit to teach them.

Nehemiah (cont.)

9:22 You ***g*** them kingdoms and peoples, and
9:27 are merciful, you ***g*** them saviors who
9:34 and the warnings that you ***g*** them.
Psalms
69:21 They ***g*** me poison for food. To quench my
78:23 God ***g*** orders to the skies above, opened
105:44 God ***g*** them the lands of other nations;
106:15 God ***g*** them what they asked for; he sent food
115:16 the LORD, but he ***g*** the earth to all
Ecclesiastes
2:20 I then ***g*** myself up to despair, as I
12:7 life-breath returns to God who ***g*** it.
Daniel
1:7 chief official ***g*** them new names.
1:17 And God ***g*** knowledge, mastery of all
Matthew
25:35 hungry and you ***g*** me food to eat. I
26:26 it, broke it, and ***g*** it to the
Mark
6:7 out in pairs. He ***g*** them authority
11:28 these things? Who ***g*** you this
John
3:16 the world that he ***g*** his only Son, so
17:4 by finishing the work you ***g*** me to do.
17:6 to the people you ***g*** me from this
19:30 Bowing his head, he ***g*** up his life.
Acts
11:17 If God ***g*** them the same gift he gave us
Romans
8:32 his own Son but ***g*** him up for us
2 Corinthians
8:3 you that they ***g*** what they could
8:5 because they ***g*** themselves to the
Ephesians
4:8 prisoners, and he ***g*** gifts to people.
4:11 He ***g*** some apostles, some prophets, some evangelists
5:2 who loved us and ***g*** himself for us.
5:25 loved the church and ***g*** himself for her.

GAZA

Judges
16:1 traveled to ***G***. While there, he
1 Samuel
6:17 Ashdod, one for ***G***, one for
Amos
1:6 three crimes of ***G***, and for four, I
Acts
8:26 from Jerusalem to ***G***."

GEDALIAH

2 Kings
25:22 put ***G***, Ahikam's son and
25:25 and they struck ***G***, and he died.
1 Chronicles
25:3 and his family: ***G***, Izri, Jeshaiah,
25:9 the second to ***G***, his relatives,
Ezra
10:18 Maaseiah, Eliezer, Jarib, and ***G***.
Jeremiah
38:1 Mattan's son; ***G***, Pashhur's son;
39:14 entrusted him to ***G***, Ahikam's son and
40:15 son, met with ***G*** secretly at

GEHAZI

2 Kings
4:12 to his servant ***G***, "Call this
4:29 Elisha said to ***G***, "Get ready, take my
5:20 ***G***(who was the servant of Elisha the

GENERATION

Genesis
6:9 In his ***g***, Noah was a moral
17:12 male in every ***g*** must be
Numbers
32:13 until the entire ***g*** had died, which
Judges
2:7 the next ***g*** of elders who
2:10 When that whole ***g*** had passed away,
2 Samuel
7:19 the future and the ***g*** to come, LORD God!
1 Chronicles
7:9 family records by ***g***, as heads of
Job
8:8 Ask a previous ***g*** and verify the
Psalms
12:7 us, protecting us from this ***g*** forever.
14:5 because God is with the righteous ***g***.
24:6 are with the ***g*** that seeks him—
33:11 to do lasts from one ***g*** to the next.
45:17 name from one ***g*** to the next so
72:5 as long as the moon, ***g*** to generation.
78:4 tell the next ***g*** all about the
78:6 so that the next ***g*** and children not
78:8 stubborn ***g***, a generation
79:13 your praises from one ***g*** to the next.
85:5 your anger from one ***g*** to the next?
89:1 my own mouth from one ***g*** to the next.
89:4 throne from one ***g*** to the next.'"
90:1 have been our help, ***g*** after generation.
95:10 I despised that ***g***; I said, 'These
100:5 faithfulness lasts ***g*** after generation.
102:12 Your fame lasts from one ***g*** to the next!
102:18 down for the next ***g*** so that people
102:24 years go on from one ***g*** to the next!
106:31 righteous, ***g*** after generation,
109:13 their names be wiped out in just one ***g***!
119:90 extends from one ***g*** to the next! You
135:13 fame extends from one ***g*** to the next!
145:4 One ***g*** will praise your works to the
146:10 rule from one ***g*** to the next!
Proverbs
27:24 nor a crown ***g*** after generation.
Ecclesiastes
1:4 A ***g*** goes, and a generation comes, but
Isaiah
34:10 up forever. From ***g*** to generation it
34:17 will live in it from ***g*** to generation.
41:4 calling upon ***g*** after generation
Jeremiah
2:31 People of this ***g***, listen closely to
7:29 has cast off a ***g*** that provokes his
Lamentations
5:19 throne lasts from one ***g*** to the next.
Matthew
11:16 I compare this ***g***? It is like a
12:39 and unfaithful ***g*** searches for a
16:4 and unfaithful ***g*** searches for a
17:17 and crooked ***g***, how long will I
23:36 all these things will come upon this ***g***.

Mark
8:12 Why does this **g** look for a sign?
Acts
2:40 Be saved from this perverse **g**."
13:36 in his own **g**, then he died and

GENERATIONS → ALL GENERATIONS
Genesis
10:32 to their **g** and their
Exodus
6:16 names by their **g**: Gershon, Kohath,
16:33 it should be kept safe for future **g**."
Deuteronomy
5:9 third and fourth **g** of those who hate
Judges
3:2 teach war to the **g** of Israelites who
Job
42:16 years and saw four **g** of his children.
Psalms
22:30 will serve him; **g** to come will be
48:13 so that you may tell future **g**:
61:6 life! Let his years extend for many **g**!
71:18 Not until I tell **g** about your mighty
77:8 end? Is his promise over for future **g**?
79:8 of past **g**; let your
105:8 the word he commanded to a thousand **g**,
145:13 endures for all **g**. The LORD is
Isaiah
13:20 or live there for **g**. No Arab will
61:4 cities, places deserted in **g** past.
Matthew
1:17 were fourteen **g** from Abraham to
Ephesians
2:7 to show future **g** the greatness of
Colossians
1:26 for ages and **g** but which has now
Jude
1:14 who lived seven **g** after Adam,

GENTILE GOD-WORSHIPPERS
Ac 10:2; 13:16, 26, 50; 17:17

GENTILES → AMONG THE GENTILES
Matthew
4:15 across the Jordan, Galilee of the **G**,
5:47 doing? Don't even the **G** do the same?
6:7 words, as the **G** do. They think
12:18 and he'll announce judgment to the **G**.
20:19 him over to the **G** to be ridiculed,
Mark
10:33 to death and hand him over to the **G**.
10:42 the rulers by the **G** show off their
Acts
4:25 Why did the **G** rage, and the
4:27 Pilate, with **G** and Israelites,
9:15 my name before **G**, kings, and
10:45 had been poured out even on the **G**.
11:1 that even the **G** had welcomed
13:46 eternal life, we will turn to the **G**.
14:2 stirred up the **G**, poisoning their
15:5 and claimed, "The **G** must be
18:6 From now on I'll go to the **G**!"
21:11 and they will hand him over to the **G**.'"
26:17 people and from the **G**. I am sending you
28:28 been sent to the **G**. They will
Romans
1:6 Christ are also included among these **G**.
1:13 just as I have done among the other **G**.
2:14 **G** don't have the Law. But when they
2:24 is discredited by the **G** because of you.
9:24 the Jews but we also come from the **G**.
9:30 we going to say? **G** who weren't
11:11 has come to the **G** by their failure,
15:9 and so that the **G** could glorify God for
16:4 all the churches of the **G** do the same.
1 Corinthians
1:23 a scandal to Jews and foolishness to **G**.
2 Corinthians
11:26 my people, and **G**. I faced dangers
Galatians
1:16 about him to the **G**. I didn't
2:2 I preach to the **G** for them. But I
3:8 would make the **G** righteous on the
Ephesians
2:11 once you were **G** by physical
2:14 both Jews and **G** into one group.
3:1 am a prisoner of Christ for you **G**.
3:6 plan is that the **G** would be coheirs
3:8 immeasurable riches of Christ to the **G**.
4:17 life like the **G** anymore. They
1 Thessalonians
2:16 speaking to the **G** so they can be
1 Timothy
2:7 a teacher of the **G** in faith and
3 John
1:7 accepting any support from the **G**.

GEZER
Joshua
16:10 who lived in **G**. So today the
1 Chronicles
20:4 war broke out at **G** with the

GIBEAH
Judges
19:12 Israelites. We'll travel on to **G**.
Isaiah
10:29 Ramah trembles; **G** of Saul has fled.

GIBEON
Joshua
10:2 afraid, because **G** was a large city,
2 Samuel
2:13 at the pool of **G**. One group sat on
1 Kings
3:4 great shrine at **G** in order to

GIBEONITES
2 Samuel
21:2 called for the **G** and spoke to

GIDEON
Judges
6:24 So **G** built an altar there to the LORD
7:24 Then **G** sent messengers into all of the
Hebrews
11:32 I told you about **G**, Barak, Samson,

GIFT → FOOD GIFT, FOOD GIFT OF SOOTHING, GIFT FOR THE LORD, GIFT OFFERING, GIFT OFFERINGS, GIFT TO THE LORD
Acts
2:38 will receive the **g** of the Holy

3:3 to enter, he began to ask them for a ***g***.
8:20 you could buy God's ***g*** with money!
10:45 that the ***g*** of the Holy
Romans
1:11 some spiritual ***g*** to you so that
5:15 But the free ***g*** of Christ isn't like
5:16 The ***g*** isn't like the consequences of
5:17 grace and the ***g*** of righteousness
6:23 death, but God's ***g*** is eternal life
11:35 has given him a ***g*** and has been paid
12:6 to us. If your ***g*** is prophecy, you
1 Corinthians
1:7 any spiritual ***g*** while you wait
7:7 has a particular ***g*** from God: one has
13:2 If I have the ***g*** of prophecy and I know
14:39 to try to get the ***g*** of prophecy, but
16:3 of recommendation to bring your ***g***.
2 Corinthians
1:11 behalf for the ***g*** that was given to
8:12 A ***g*** is appreciated because of what a
9:5 the generous ***g*** you have already
9:15 Thank God for his ***g*** that words can't
Ephesians
2:8 is God's ***g***. It's not
4:7 out by the ***g*** that is given by
Philippians
4:17 not hoping for a ***g***, but I am hoping
1 Timothy
4:14 the spiritual ***g*** in you that was
2 Timothy
1:6 to revive God's ***g*** that is in you
Hebrews
6:4 the heavenly ***g***, become partners
11:4 to him for his ***g***. Though he died,
James
1:17 Every good ***g***, every perfect gift,
1 Peter
4:10 according to the ***g*** each person has
Revelation
22:17 receive life-giving water as a ***g***."

GIFT FOR THE LORD

Ex 29:18; 29:25; Lv 2:11; 2:16; 3:9, 11, 14; 7:5; 8:21, 28; 22:22, 27; 23:13; 24:7

GIFT OFFERING

Ex 29:27; 29:28, 41; 30:13, 14, 15; 35:24; Lv 10:14; Nm 5:9; 6:20; 15:19, 20, 21; 18:24, 26, 27, 28, 29; 31:29, 41, 52; Josh 22:23; 22:29

GIFT OFFERINGS

Ex 25:2; 25:3; 35:5, 21; 36:3, 6; Nm 18:11; 18:19; 2Ch 35:8

GIFT TO THE LORD

Ex 30:20; 35:29; Lv 7:14; 23:25, 27, 36; Nm 6:14; 15:3, 25; 28:13; 29:6; Ezr 3:5; 8:28; Eze 46:12

GIFTS → FOOD GIFTS

Matthew
2:11 him with ***g*** of gold,
7:11 how to give good ***g*** to your children,
Acts
24:17 to bring ***g*** for the poor of
Romans
11:29 God's ***g*** and calling can't be taken
12:6 We have different ***g*** that are consistent
1 Corinthians
12:1 you to be ignorant about spiritual ***g***.
14:1 to get spiritual ***g*** but especially so
Philippians
4:18 I received the ***g*** that you sent
1 Peter
4:10 as good managers of God's diverse ***g***.
Revelation
11:10 give each other ***g***, because these

GILEAD

Genesis
31:21 out directly for the mountains of ***G***.
Jeremiah
8:22 there no balm in ***G***? Is there no
Hosea
6:8 ***G*** is a city of wicked people, tracked
12:11 In ***G*** there is wickedness; they will

GILGAL

Joshua
10:7 went up from ***G*** with the entire
1 Samuel
11:14 Let's go to ***G***," Samuel told the
Hosea
12:11 to nothing. In ***G*** they sacrifice

GIVE → GIVE GLORY, GIVE PRIASE, GIVE THANKS

Genesis
1:29 God said, "I now ***g*** to you all the
1:30 that breathes—I ***g*** all the green
12:7 and said, "I ***g*** this land to your
15:2 can you possibly ***g*** me, since I still
17:8 I will ***g*** you and your descendants the
17:16 her and even ***g*** you a son from
21:24 Abraham said, "I ***g*** you my word
Exodus
1:16 the Hebrew women ***g*** birth and you see the baby being born
Deuteronomy
1:8 I promised to ***g*** to your ancestors
34:4 promised: 'I will ***g*** it to your
Joshua
1:2 that I am going to ***g*** to the Israelites.
Matthew
1:21 She will ***g*** birth to a son, and you will
5:31 his wife must ***g*** her a divorce
6:3 But when you ***g*** to the poor, don't let
6:11 ***G*** us the bread we need for today
7:6 Don't ***g*** holy things to dogs, and don't
7:10 Or ***g*** them a snake when they ask for
7:11 evil know how to ***g*** good gifts to
10:8 pay. Therefore, ***g*** without demanding
11:28 heavy loads, and I will ***g*** you rest.
14:8 the girl said, "***G*** me the head of
16:19 I'll ***g*** you the keys of the kingdom of
19:18 Don't steal. Don't ***g*** false testimony.
19:21 what you own, and ***g*** the money to the
20:8 the workers and ***g*** them their wages,
22:21 Then he said, "***G*** to Caesar what
23:23 Hypocrites! You ***g*** to God a tenth of
25:37 feed you, or thirsty and ***g*** you a drink?
25:43 and you didn't ***g*** me clothes to
Luke
15:12 father, 'Father, ***g*** me my share of
18:5 but I will ***g*** this widow justice because
21:15 I'll ***g*** you words and wisdom that none

GIVE [cont.]

John
1:22 you? We need to **g** an answer to
4:7 said to her, "**G** me some water to
5:21 too does the Son **g** life to whomever
6:27 Human One will **g** you. God the
11:22 whatever you ask God, God will **g** you."
13:34 I **g** you a new commandment: Love each
13:37 you now? I'll **g** up my life for
17:2 so that he could **g** eternal life to
18:40 Not this man! **G** us Barabbas!"
Acts
7:5 God didn't **g** him an inheritance here,
12:23 because he didn't **g** the honor to God.
13:34 God said, I will **g** to you the holy
Romans
2:7 one hand, he will **g** eternal life to
12:20 if he is thirsty, **g** him a drink. By
14:12 each of us will **g** an account of
1 Corinthians
7:6 saying this to **g** you permission;
7:25 married, but I'll **g** you my opinion as
2 Corinthians
4:6 in our hearts to **g** us the light of
6:3 We don't **g** anyone any reason to be
Galatians
6:9 we'll have a harvest if we don't **g** up.
2 Thessalonians
3:16 of peace himself **g** you peace always
1 Timothy
1:10 individuals who **g** false testimonies
2 Timothy
1:7 God didn't **g** us a spirit that is timid
2:7 the Lord will **g** you understanding
1 John
5:16 and God will **g** life to them—that
Revelation
2:10 death, and I will **g** you the crown of
10:9 and told him to **g** me the scroll. He
11:10 celebrate and **g** each other gifts,
12:4 who was about to **g** birth so that
21:6 I will freely **g** water from the

GIVE GLORY

Josh 7:19; Ps 115:1; Jn 9:24; Phi 1:11; Rev 4:9

GIVE PRAISE

Dt 32:3; 1Ch 16:10; Ps 63:11; 64:10; 105:3; Ro 14:11

GIVE THANKS

1Ki 8:33; 8:35; 1Ch 16:4; 16:7, 8, 34, 35, 41; 2Ch 6:24; 6:26; 20:21; 31:2; Neh 12:24; 12:31; Ps 30:4; 30:12; 33:2; 44:8; 52:9; 54:6; 57:9; 75:1; 86:12; 92:1; 97:12; 105:1; 106:1, 47; 107:1; 108:3; 118:1, 19, 28, 29; 119:7, 62; 122:4; 136:1, 2, 3, 4, 5, 6, 7, 10, 11, 13, 14, 16, 17, 26; 138:1, 4; 139:14; 140:13; 142:7; Jer 33:11; Eph 5:20; Col 1:3; 3:17; 1Th 5:18; Rev 11:17

GIVE TO THE LORD

Lv 23:38; Nm 18:12; 1Ch 16:28; 16:29; Ps 29:1; 29:2; 96:7, 8

GIVING → GIVING THANKS

Genesis
13:17 of the land because I am **g** it to you."
16:2 has kept me from **g** birth, so go to
Exodus
5:10 says, 'I'm not **g** you straw anymore.
Deuteronomy
1:20 which the LORD our God is **g** to us.
32:49 Canaan, which I'm **g** to the Israelites
Joshua
1:3 I am **g** you every place where you set
1:15 LORD your God is **g** them. Then you
Ecclesiastes
3:2 a time for **g** birth and a time for
Isaiah
40:29 **g** power to the tired and reviving the
41:2 him to serve—**g** him nations,
Jeremiah
8:14 has doomed us by **g** us poisoned water
Matthew
15:5 to you I'm **g** to God as a
Mark
7:11 corban (that is, a gift I'm **g** to God),"
Luke
12:32 Father delights in **g** you the kingdom.
Acts
14:17 blessed you by **g** you rain from
15:8 confirmed this by **g** them the Holy
22:20 I stood there **g** my approval, even
24:10 nodded at Paul, **g** him permission to
Romans
9:4 covenants, the **g** of the Law, the
1 Corinthians
12:24 body together, **g** greater honor to
2 Corinthians
5:12 Instead, we are **g** you an
1 Timothy
1:18 my child, I'm **g** you these
2 Timothy
4:1 I'm **g** you this commission in the
4:8 on that day. He's **g** it not only to me
Revelation
12:2 she was in labor, in pain from **g** birth.

GIVING THANKS

1Ch 25:3; 2Ch 7:3; 7:6; Lk 22:17; 22:19; 1Co 11:24; Eph 1:16; Phi 4:6; Col 1:12

GLAD

Exodus
18:9 Jethro was **g** about all the good things
Psalms
32:11 the LORD and be **g**! All you whose
48:11 Let Mount Zion be **g**; let the towns of
68:3 the righteous be **g** and celebrate
69:32 see it and be **g**! You who seek God-
70:4 rejoice and be **g** in you, and let
119:74 see me and be **g** because I have
Proverbs
10:1 makes a father **g**, but a foolish
24:17 stumble, don't let your heart be **g**,
27:9 make the heart **g**, and the
27:11 and make my heart **g**, so I can answer
Ecclesiastes
7:3 a sad face may lead to a **g** heart.
8:15 drink, and be **g**. This is what
Zechariah
2:10 Rejoice and be **g**, Daughter Zion,
10:7 They will be as **g** as if they were

Philippians
1:5 I'm **g** because of the way you have been
2:17 your faith, I am **g**. I'm glad with
3:1 and sisters, be **g** in the Lord. It's
4:4 Be **g** in the Lord always! Again I say,
1 Thessalonians
2:8 We were **g** to share not only God's good

GLORIFIED

Isaiah
9:1 but later he **g** the way of the
26:15 nation; you are **g**. You've expanded
55:5 the holy one of Israel, who has **g** you.
60:9 the holy one of Israel, who has **g** you.
66:5 Let the LORD be **g**; let's see your
Daniel
4:34 I worshipped and **g** the one who lives
Luke
5:26 with awe, they **g** God, saying,
John
7:39 yet since Jesus hadn't yet been **g**.
11:4 so that God's Son can be **g** through it."
12:16 After he was **g**, they remembered
12:23 has come for the Human One to be **g**.
12:28 heaven, "I have **g** it and I will
13:31 One has been **g**, and God has been
13:32 If God has been **g** in him, God will also
14:13 so that the Father can be **g** in the Son.
15:8 My Father is **g** when you produce much
17:4 I have **g** you on earth by finishing the
17:10 yours is mine; I have been **g** in them.
Acts
3:13 ancestors—has **g** his servant
Romans
8:17 him so that we can also be **g** with him.
8:30 whom he made righteous, he also **g**.
Revelation
18:7 extent that she **g** herself and

GLORIFY

Ezra
7:27 moved the king to **g** the LORD's house
Psalms
86:9 before you, Lord; they will **g** your name
86:12 heart, and I will **g** your name forever
91:15 times. I'll save you and **g** you.
Isaiah
10:15 Will the ax **g** itself over the one who
25:3 people will **g** you; the towns of
42:21 to expand and **g** the Instruction.
44:23 Jacob, and will **g** himself through
60:7 altar, and I will **g** my splendid house.
60:13 elm, and pine, to **g** the site of my
60:21 the work of my hands, to **g** myself.
61:3 planted by the LORD to **g** himself.
Ezekiel
39:13 on the day that I **g** myself. This is
39:21 When I **g** myself among the nations, all
Daniel
4:37 magnify, and **g** the king of
5:23 But you didn't **g** the true God who
Malachi
2:2 don't intend to **g** my name, says the
Luke
1:46 said, "With all my heart I **g** the Lord!
John
8:50 who is seeking to **g** me, and he's the
8:54 answered, "If I **g** myself, my glory
12:28 Father, **g** your name!" Then a voice came
13:32 God will also **g** the Human One in
16:14 He will **g** me, because he will take what
17:1 time has come. **G** your Son, so that
17:5 Now, Father, **g** me in your presence with
21:19 which Peter would **g** God. After saying
Romans
15:6 That way you can **g** the God and Father
15:9 Gentiles could **g** God for his
1 Peter
2:12 judge they will **g** him, because they
Revelation
15:4 you, Lord, and **g** your name? You

GLORIOUS

Exodus
16:7 see the LORD's **g** presence, because
16:10 and just then the **g** presence of the
24:16 The LORD's **g** presence settled on Mount
24:17 the LORD's **g** presence looked
29:43 it will be made holy by my **g** presence.
33:18 said, "Please show me your **g** presence."
33:22 As my **g** presence passes by, I'll set
40:34 and the LORD's **g** presence filled
40:35 and the LORD's **g** presence filled
Leviticus
9:6 that the LORD's **g** presence will
9:23 and the LORD's **g** presence appeared
10:3 will manifest my **g** presence,' this
Deuteronomy
28:58 the awesome and **g** name of the LORD
1 Chronicles
29:13 we thank you and praise your **g** name.
Nehemiah
9:5 bless your **g** name, which is
Psalms
24:7 rise up high! So the **g** king can enter!
24:8 Who is this **g** king? The LORD—strong
24:9 rise up high! So the **g** king can enter!
24:10 Who is this **g** king? The LORD of
29:3 the waters; the **g** God thunders; the
66:2 glory of God's name! Make **g** his praise!
72:19 Bless God's **g** name forever; let his
87:3 **G** things are said about you, the city
106:20 They traded their **g** God for an image of
111:3 are majestic and **g**. God's
145:5 all about the **g** splendor of your
Proverbs
4:9 head; she will give you a **g** crown."
Isaiah
4:2 beautiful and **g**. The earth's
11:10 him out, and his dwelling will be **g**.
12:5 who has done **g** things; proclaim
22:18 die, with your **g** chariots, you
24:23 and in Jerusalem, **g** before his elders.
63:12 hand with his **g** arm; who split
63:14 and made for yourself a **g** reputation.
63:15 your holy and **g** perch. Where are
64:11 Our holy, **g** house, where our ancestors
Jeremiah
13:18 because your **g** crowns will soon
14:21 don't scorn your **g** throne. Remember
Daniel
2:6 gifts and **g** honor from me. So
Micah
2:8 You strip off the **g** clothes from

Haggai
2:9 will be more **g** than its
Zechariah
2:5 the LORD, and I will be **g** inside it.
Acts
7:2 listen to me. Our **g** God appeared to
Romans
8:21 brought into the **g** freedom of God's
2 Corinthians
3:8 ministry of the Spirit be much more **g**?
3:9 how much more **g** is the ministry
3:10 In fact, what was **g** isn't glorious now,
3:11 fades away was **g**, how much more
Ephesians
1:6 and to honor his **g** grace that he has
1:18 richness of God's **g** inheritance among believers
Philippians
3:21 they are like his **g** body, by the
Colossians
1:11 through his **g** might so that you
1:27 to make the **g** riches of this
1 Timothy
1:11 agrees with the **g** gospel of the
Titus
2:13 hope and the **g** appearance of our
1 Peter
1:8 so rejoice with a **g** joy that is too
2 Peter
2:10 aren't afraid to insult the **g** ones,
Jude
1:24 and rejoicing before his **g** presence,

GLORY
→ GIVE GLORY, GLORY OF GOD, GLORY OF ISRAEL'S GOD, GOD'S GLORY

GLORY OF GOD
Prv 25:2; Jn 11:4; 1Co 11:7; 2Co 1:20; Phi 2:11

GLORY OF ISRAEL'S GOD
Eze 8:4; 9:3; 10:19; 11:22; 43:2

GOAL
Romans
10:4 Christ is the **g** of the Law, which leads
15:20 way, I have a **g** to preach the
1 Corinthians
9:26 without a clear **g** in sight. I fight
Philippians
3:11 perhaps reach the **g** of the
3:12 reached this **g** or have already
3:14 The **g** I pursue is the prize of God's
Colossians
1:29 struggle for this **g** with his energy,
2:2 My **g** is that their hearts would be
1 Timothy
1:5 The **g** of instruction is love from a
1:6 they missed this **g**, some people have
3:1 if anyone has a **g** to be a
6:10 pain because they made money their **g**.
6:21 they missed the **g** of faith. May
Hebrews
12:14 Pursue the **g** of peace along with
1 Peter
1:9 are receiving the **g** of your faith:

GOAT
Genesis
15:9 female **g**, a three-year-old
Exodus
23:19 boil a young **g** in its mother's
Leviticus
1:10 —whether sheep or **g**—you must present
3:12 the offering is a **g**, you must present
4:23 as his offering a flawless male **g**.
23:19 offer one male **g** as a purification
Deuteronomy
14:4 you are allowed to eat: ox, sheep, **g**,
14:5 roebuck, wild **g**, ibex, antelope,
1 Samuel
16:20 wine, and a young **g**, and he sent it
2 Chronicles
11:15 shrines and the **g** and calf idols he
Proverbs
30:31 rooster or a male **g**; and a king with
Isaiah
11:6 with the young **g**; the calf and the
13:21 live there, and **g** demons will dance
34:14 meet hyenas, the **g** demon will call
Ezekiel
43:22 a flawless male **g** as a purification
Luke
15:29 much as a young **g** so I could

GOATS
Genesis
27:9 two healthy young **g** so I can prepare
Exodus
12:5 take it from the sheep or from the **g**.
Leviticus
16:5 two male **g** for a
Numbers
7:17 rams, five male **g**, and five male
7:87 twelve male **g** for the
7:88 rams, sixty male **g**, and sixty male
1 Samuel
10:3 three young **g**, one carrying
24:2 soldiers near the rocks of the wild **g**.
25:2 and one thousand **g**. At that time, he
1 Kings
20:27 small flocks of **g**, but the Arameans
1 Chronicles
5:21 250,000 sheep and **g**, 2,000 donkeys,
27:31 of sheep and **g**—Jaziz the Hagrite
Ezra
6:17 twelve male **g**, according to the
8:35 and twelve male **g** as a purification
Job
39:1 when mountain **g** give birth; do
Psalms
50:9 from your house or **g** from your corrals
66:15 I will offer both bulls and **g**. Selah
104:18 to the mountain **g**; the ridges are
Proverbs
27:26 clothes, and the **g** will be the price
Song of Songs
1:8 graze your little **g** by the tents of
4:1 like a flock of **g** as they stream
6:5 like a flock of **g** as they stream
Isaiah
1:11 want the blood of bulls, lambs, and **g**.
5:17 pasture; young **g** will feed among
34:6 of lambs and **g**, from the kidney

Jeremiah
51:40 lambs for slaughter, like rams and ***g***.
Ezekiel
27:21 procured lambs, rams, and ***g*** for you.
34:17 the bucks among the sheep and the ***g***.
39:18 rams, lambs, ***g***, bulls, all
Zechariah
10:3 I will punish the ***g***. The LORD of
Matthew
25:32 separates the sheep from the ***g***.
25:33 side. But the ***g*** he will put on
Hebrews
9:12 by the blood of ***g*** or calves,
10:4 blood of bulls and ***g*** to take away sins.
11:37 of sheep and ***g***, needy,

GOD ALMIGHTY
Gn 28:3; 43:14; 48:3; Ex 6:3; Eze 10:5; Rev 4:8; 11:17; 15:3; 16:7; 21:22

GOD CREATED
Gn 1:21; 1:27; 5:1; Ac 17:26; 1Ti 4:3

GOD IS MY ROCK
2Sa 22:3; Ps 18:2; 62:2, 6; 94:22

GOD IS WITH YOU
Gn 21:22; Dt 7:21; Josh 1:9; 1Sa 10:7; 1Ch 17:2; 22:18; 28:20; Is 45:14; Zec 8:23

GOD OF HEAVEN
Gn 24:3; 24:7; 2Ch 36:23; Ezr 1:2; 5:11, 12; 6:9, 10; 7:12, 21, 23; Neh 1:4; 1:5; 2:4, 20; Ps 136:26; Dn 2:18; 2:19, 37, 44; Jon 1:9; Rev 11:13; 16:11

GOD OF HEAVENLY FORCES
1Ki 19:10; 19:14; Ps 59:5; 69:6; 80:4, 7, 14, 19; 84:8; 89:8; Is 1:24; 3:1, 15; 10:16, 23, 24, 33; 19:4; 22:5, 12, 14, 15; 28:22; Jer 5:14; 15:16; 46:10; 50:31; Hos 12:5; Am 3:13; 4:13; 5:14, 15, 16, 27; 6:8, 14; 9:5; Zec 12:5

GOD OF PEACE
Ro 15:33; 16:20; Phi 4:9; 1Th 5:23; Heb 13:20

GOD OUR FATHER
Ro 1:7; 1Co 1:3; 2Co 1:2; Eph 1:2; Phi 1:2; 4:20; Col 1:2; 2Th 1:1; 1:2; 2:16; Phm 1:3

GOD OUR SAVIOR
1Ch 16:35; 1Ti 1:1; 2:3; Ti 1:3; 2:10; Jud 1:25

GOD THE FATHER
Jn 6:27; 1Co 8:6; 15:24; Ga 1:1; 1:3; Eph 5:20; 6:23; Phi 2:11; Col 1:3; 3:17; 1Th 1:1; 1Ti 1:2; 2Ti 1:2; Ti 1:4; Jas 1:27; 1Pt 1:2; 2Pt 1:17; 2Jn 1:3; Jud 1:1

GOD'S ANGELS
Mk 12:25; Lk 12:8; 12:9; 15:10; Jn 1:51; Heb 1:6

GOD'S ANGER
Nm 1:53; Dt 6:15; 2Sa 22:8; Ps 18:7; 78:31; Is 5:25; 9:12, 17, 21; 10:4; Eph 5:6; Rev 15:1; 16:1

GOD'S CHEST
Dt 33:12; Josh 3:3; 4:5; 1Sa 3:3; 4:11, 13, 17, 18, 19, 21, 22; 5:1, 2, 10; 2Sa 6:2; 6:3, 4, 6, 7, 12; 7:2; 15:24, 25, 29; 1Ch 13:5; 13:7, 12, 14; 15:1, 2, 15, 24; 16:1; 2Ch 1:4

GOD'S CHURCH
Ac 20:28; 1Co 1:2; 10:32; 15:9; 2Co 1:1; Ga 1:13; 1Ti 3:5

GOD'S COVENANT
Lv 2:13; Dt 17:2; 29:12; 31:26; Jdg 20:27; 1Sa 4:4; 2Sa 15:24; 1Ch 16:6; Ps 78:10; Ac 7:51

GOD'S FAITHFUL LOVE
2Ch 5:13; 7:3, 6; Ps 52:1; 52:8; 103:11; 117:2; 118:2, 3, 4; 136:1, 2, 3, 4, 5, 6, 7, 8, 9, 10, 11, 12, 13, 14, 15, 16, 17, 18, 19, 20, 21, 22, 23, 24, 25, 26

GOD'S GLORY
1Ch 16:24; Ps 19:1; 96:3; 113:4; Is 6:3; 59:19; 60:2; Jn 11:40; 12:43; Ro 3:23; 5:2; 15:7; 1Co 10:31; 2Co 4:6; 4:15; Eph 1:12; 1:14; Heb 1:3; Rev 15:8; 21:11, 23

GOD'S GRACE
Ac 6:8; 11:23; 13:43; 14:26; 20:24; Ro 1:5; 4:16; 5:15; 11:5, 6; 12:6; 1Co 1:4; 3:10; 15:10; Eph 2:5; 2:8; 3:2; Phi 1:7; Col 1:6; Heb 2:9; 12:15; 1Pt 1:2

GOD'S HOUSE
Gn 28:17; 28:22; Josh 9:23; 1Ch 6:48; 9:11, 13, 26, 27; Ezr 1:4; 1:5; 2:68; 3:8, 9; 4:24; 5:2, 14, 15, 16; 6:3, 5, 12; 7:16, 17, 19, 20; 8:17, 30, 33, 36; 9:9; 10:1, 6, 9; Neh 6:10; 8:16; 10:32, 34, 36, 37, 38, 39; 11:11, 16, 22; 12:40; 13:4, 7, 11, 14; Ps 52:8; 55:14; 84:10; 122:9; Ecc 5:1; Dn 1:2; 5:3, 23; Hos 9:8; Jl 1:16; Mt 12:4; Mk 2:26; Lk 6:4; Heb 3:2; 3:5, 6; 10:21

GOD'S INSTRUCTION
Dt 1:26; Josh 24:26; Neh 8:18; 10:29; Ps 1:2

GOD'S KINGDOM
Ps 145:12; Mt 6:33; 12:28; 19:24; 21:31, 43; Mk 1:15; 4:11, 26, 30; 9:1, 47; 10:14, 15, 23, 24, 25; 12:34; 14:25; 15:43; Lk 4:43; 6:20; 7:28; 8:1, 10; 9:2, 11, 27, 60, 62; 10:9, 11; 11:20; 13:18, 20, 28, 29; 14:15; 16:16; 17:20, 21; 18:16, 17, 24, 25, 29; 19:11; 21:31; 22:16, 18; 23:51; Jn 3:3; 3:5; Ac 1:3; 8:12; 14:22; 19:8; 28:23, 31; Ro 14:17; 1Co 4:20; 6:9, 10; Ga 5:21; Col 4:11; 2Th 1:5

GOD'S MAJESTY
Ps 148:13; Is 2:10; 2:19, 21; Ac 7:55

GOD'S MESSENGER
Gn 21:17; 31:11; Ex 14:19; Jdg 6:20; 13:6, 9

GOD'S MOUNTAIN
Ex 3:1; 4:27; 18:5; 24:13; 1Ki 19:8; Eze 28:16

GOD'S NAME
Ex 3:13; 20:7; Lv 18:21; 19:12; 21:6; Dt 5:11; 18:7; 2Ch 36:13; Ps 66:2; 69:30, 36; 111:9; 135:3; 148:13; 149:3; Prv 30:9; Is 12:4; Dn 2:20; 1Ti 6:1; Rev 13:6

GOD'S PEOPLE
Ex 18:1; Jdg 20:2; 1Sa 2:24; 13:14; 2Sa 14:13; 2Ch 36:23; Ps 116:14; 116:18; Is 11:11; 11:16; 14:32; Ro 1:7; 12:13; 15:25, 26, 27, 31; 16:2; 1Co 1:2; 6:1, 2; 14:33; 16:1, 15; 2Co 1:1; 9:1, 12; 13:12; Eph 1:15; 2:19; 3:8; 4:12; Phi 1:1; 4:21, 22; Col 1:4; Phm 1:5; 1:7; Heb 4:9; 11:25; 1Pt 2:10

GOD'S POWER
2Ch 30:12; Ezr 7:6; 7:28; Job 27:11; Ps 78:42; 145:12; Eze 8:1; Mt 22:29; Mk 12:24; 1Co 1:24; 2Co 6:7; 13:4; Eph 1:19; 1:20; 2Ti 1:8; 3:5; 1Pt 1:5; 5:6

GOD'S PRAISE
Ps 106:12; 111:10; 149:1, 3; Is 42:12

GOD'S PRESENCE
Ex 18:12; Dt 12:7; 12:12, 18; 27:7; 1Ch 13:8; Job 33:26; Lk 1:19; 1Co 1:29; Eph 1:4; Heb 9:24; 1Jn 3:19

GOD'S PROMISE
1Ch 25:5; Ps 106:24; 130:5; Ro 4:20; Eph 2:12

GOD'S RIGHT SIDE
Ac 2:33; 7:55, 56; Ro 8:34; Eph 1:20; Col 3:1; 1Pt 3:22

GOD'S RIGHTEOUSNESS
Ps 22:31; 97:6; 103:17; 111:3; Mt 6:33; Ro 1:17; 3:21, 22; 5:21; 8:10; 10:3; Jas 1:20

GOD'S SANCTUARY
Lv 21:12; Jdg 18:31; 2Ch 30:8; Ps 73:17; 114:2

GOD'S SERVANT
2Ki 8:4; 1Ch 6:49; 2Ch 24:9; Neh 10:29; Dn 9:11; Ro 13:4; Rev 15:3

GOD'S SON
Mt 4:3; 4:6; 14:33; 26:63; 27:40, 43, 54; Mk 1:1; 3:11; 15:39; Lk 1:35; 4:3, 9, 41; 22:70; Jn 1:34; 1:49; 5:25; 10:36; 11:4, 27; 19:7; 20:31; Ac 9:20; Ro 1:4; 1:9; 2Co 1:19; Ga 2:20; Eph 4:13; Heb 4:14; 6:6; 7:3; 10:29; 1Jn 3:8; 4:15; 5:5, 10, 12, 13, 20; Rev 2:18

GOD'S SPIRIT
Nm 24:2; 1Sa 10:10; 11:6; 19:20, 23; 2Ch 15:1; Job 33:4; Is 61:1; Mt 12:28; Jn 3:8; Ro 8:9; 8:14; 15:19; 1Co 2:11; 2:12, 14; 3:16; 7:40; 12:3; Phi 3:3

GOD'S TEMPLE
Ex 23:19; 34:26; Dt 23:18; Jdg 9:27; 1Ch 10:10; 22:1, 2; 23:28; 25:6; 26:20; 28:12, 21; 29:2, 3, 7; 2Ch 4:11; 4:19; 5:1, 14; 7:5; 15:18; 22:12; 23:3, 9; 24:5, 7, 13, 16, 27; 25:24; 28:24; 31:13, 21; 33:7; 34:8, 9; 35:8; 36:18, 19; Ps 135:2; Dn 1:2; Mt 26:61; 1Co 3:16; 3:17; 2Co 6:16; 2Th 2:4; Rev 11:1; 11:19

GOD'S THRONE
Mt 5:34; 23:22; Heb 12:2; Rev 1:4; 7:15

GOD'S VOICE
Dt 4:33; 5:25, 26; 8:20; 9:23; 13:18; 15:5; 18:16; 26:14; 27:10; 28:1, 2, 15, 45, 62; 30:10; Jer 51:16; Ac 12:22

GOD'S WAY
2Ch 35:21; Mt 22:16; Mk 12:14; Lk 20:21; Ac 11:17; 18:26; 1Ti 1:4; 1Jn 2:2

GOD'S WISDOM
1Ki 3:28; Lk 11:49; 1Co 1:21; 1:24; 2:7

GOD'S WORD
1Sa 9:27; 1Ki 12:22; 1Ch 17:3; Ps 147:15; Is 40:8; Jer 23:18; Eze 6:3; 20:47; 25:3; 36:4; Mk 7:13; Lk 3:2; 5:1; 8:11, 21; 11:28; Jn 10:35; Ac 4:31; 6:2, 7; 8:14, 21; 11:1; 12:24; 13:5, 7, 46; 17:13; 18:11; Ro 9:6; 2Co 4:2; Eph 6:17; Col 1:25; 1Th 2:13; 1Ti 4:5; 2Ti 2:9; Ti 2:5; Heb 4:12; 13:7; 1Pt 4:11; 2Pt 3:5; Rev 20:4

GOD'S WORDS
2Ch 36:16; Ps 106:12; Prv 30:5; Jn 3:34; 8:47; Rev 17:17

GODS OF THE NATIONS
2Ki 19:12; 1Ch 16:26; 2Ch 32:17; Ps 96:5; Is 36:18; 37:12; Jer 14:22

GOLD
Exodus
3:22 silver and their ***g*** jewelry as well
25:3 from them: ***g***, silver, and
30:4 Make two ***g*** rings and attach them under the molding
Leviticus
8:9 head and put the ***g*** flower ornament,
Joshua
6:19 All silver and ***g***, along with bronze
Judges
8:24 had worn ***g*** earrings because
1 Kings
6:20 it with pure ***g*** and covered the
Ezra
1:4 with silver and ***g***, and with goods
8:33 silver and the ***g*** and the equipment
Psalms
19:10 desirable than ***g***—than tons of pur
21:3 you put a crown of pure ***g*** on his head.
45:9 your right, dressed in the ***g*** of Ophir.
45:13 in pearls, her robe embroidered with ***g***.
68:13 its pinions covered in precious ***g***."
72:15 long! Let Sheba's ***g*** be given to him!
105:37 with silver and ***g***; not one of its
115:4 just silver and ***g***—things made by
119:72 thousands of pieces of ***g*** and silver!
119:127 more than ***g***, even more than
135:15 just silver and ***g***—things made by
Proverbs
3:14 silver, and her gain better than ***g***.
8:10 silver, knowledge rather than choice ***g***.

8:19 is better than ***g***, even fine gold;
11:22 Like a ***g*** ring in a pig's nose is a
16:16 much better than ***g***, and acquiring
17:3 and a furnace for ***g***, but the LORD
20:15 Much ***g*** and many pearls exist, but wise
22:1 esteem is better than silver and ***g***.
25:11 time are like ***g*** apples in a
25:12 listens is like a ***g*** earring or
27:21 and a furnace for ***g***, so are people in
Ecclesiastes
2:8 silver and ***g*** for myself, the
12:6 snaps and the ***g*** bowl shatters;
Daniel
2:32 was made of pure ***g***; its chest and
3:1 made a ***g*** statue. It was
5:2 that the ***g*** and silver
10:5 had a brilliant ***g*** belt around his
11:8 their silver and ***g*** equipment. For
Matthew
2:11 him with gifts of ***g***, frankincense,
23:16 swear by the ***g*** in the temple,
1 Timothy
2:9 hairstyles, ***g***, pearls, or
Hebrews
9:4 It had the ***g*** altar for incense and the
James
2:2 One has a ***g*** ring and fine
5:3 Your ***g*** and silver have rusted, and
Revelation
1:12 lamps burning on top of seven ***g*** stands.
3:18 is that you buy ***g*** from me that has
4:4 clothing and had ***g*** crowns on their
5:8 held a harp and ***g*** bowls full of
8:3 and he held a ***g*** bowl for burning
9:7 what seemed to be ***g*** crowns. Their
14:14 One. He had a ***g*** crown on his head
15:6 linen and had ***g*** sashes around
17:4 glittered with ***g*** and jewels and
18:12 cargoes of ***g***, silver, jewels, and
18:16 glittered with ***g***, jewels, and
21:15 spoke to me had a ***g*** measuring rod

GOLIATH
1 Samuel
17:4 A champion named ***G*** from Gath came out
21:9 The sword of ***G***, the Philistine
2 Samuel
21:19 Bethlehem, killed ***G*** from Gath, whose
1 Chronicles
20:5 the brother of ***G*** the Gittite. The

GOMER
Genesis
10:2 Japheth's sons: ***G***, Magog, Madai,
1 Chronicles
1:5 Japheth's family: ***G***, Magog, Madai,
Ezekiel
38:6 ***G*** and all his troops, Beth-togarmah
Hosea
1:6 ***G*** became pregnant again and gave birth

GOMORRAH
Genesis
13:10 before the LORD destroyed Sodom and ***G***
18:20 from Sodom and ***G*** are countless,
19:24 from the skies onto Sodom and ***G***.
Deuteronomy
29:23 as Sodom and ***G***, Admah and
Isaiah
1:9 be like Sodom; we would resemble ***G***.
Jeremiah
23:14 than Sodom; its people are like ***G***.
Matthew
10:15 land of Sodom and ***G*** on Judgment Day
Romans
9:29 Sodom, and we would have become like ***G***.
2 Peter
2:6 of Sodom and ***G*** to total
Jude
1:7 way, Sodom and ***G*** and neighboring

GOOD → DO GOOD, DOING GOOD, GOOD AND EVIL, GOOD CONSCIENCE, GOOD FRUIT, GOOD NAME, GOOD NEWS, PREACHING THE GOOD NEWS, PROCLAIM THE GOOD NEWS, PROCLAIMING THE GOOD NEWS, PRODUCE GOOD FRUIT
Genesis
1:4 God saw how ***g*** the light was. God
Amos
5:14 Seek ***g*** and not evil, that you may live;
5:15 Hate evil, love ***g***, and establish
Malachi
2:17 doing evil is ***g*** in the LORD's
Matthew
5:13 salty again? It's ***g*** for nothing
5:45 the evil and the ***g*** and sends rain on
7:11 know how to give ***g*** gifts to your
7:17 same way, every ***g*** tree produces
12:12 person to do what is ***g*** on the Sabbath."
13:8 seed fell on ***g*** soil and bore
15:26 It is not ***g*** to take the
17:4 Lord, it's ***g*** that we're here.
19:16 Teacher, what ***g*** thing must I do
22:10 both evil and ***g***. The wedding
25:21 You are a ***g*** and faithful
Mark
10:17 him, and asked, "***G*** Teacher, what
John
1:46 from Nazareth be ***g***?" Philip said,
2:10 serves the ***g*** wine first. They
10:11 I am the ***g*** shepherd. The good shepherd
Romans
2:10 who does what is ***g***, for the Jew
2 Corinthians
9:8 than enough for every kind of ***g*** work.
Galatians
4:17 though not with ***g*** intentions.
Ephesians
6:6 yourself look ***g*** and try to
1 Timothy
1:5 a pure heart, a ***g*** conscience, and a
3:13 well gain a ***g*** standing and
2 Timothy
1:3 I serve with a ***g*** conscience as my
Titus
1:8 love what is ***g***, and be
Philemon
1:6 of all that is ***g*** among us in
James
1:17 Every ***g*** gift, every perfect gift, comes

GOOD [cont.]

2:7 who insult the ***g*** name spoken over
1 Peter
3:11 shun evil and do ***g***; seek peace and

GOOD AND EVIL
Gn 2:9; 2:17; 3:5, 22; 2Sa 14:17; Heb 5:14

GOOD CONSCIENCE
1Ti 1:5; 1:19; 2Ti 1:3; Heb 13:18; 1Pt 3:16; 3:21

GOOD FRUIT
Mt 3:10; 7:17, 18, 19; Lk 3:9; 6:43

GOOD NAME
Ps 23:3; 25:11; 31:3; 106:8; Ecc 7:1; Jas 2:7

GOOD NEWS
1Sa 31:9; 2Sa 4:10; 18:25, 26, 27, 31; 2Ki 7:9; Ps 40:9; 68:11; Prv 15:30; 25:25; Is 52:7; 61:1; Mt 4:23; 9:35; 11:5; 26:13; Mk 1:1; 1:14, 15; 8:35; 10:29; 13:10; 14:9; 16:15; Lk 1:19; 2:10; 3:18; 4:18, 43; 7:22; 8:1; 9:6; 16:16; 20:1; Ac 5:42; 8:4, 12, 25, 35, 40; 10:36; 11:20; 13:32; 14:7, 15, 21; 15:35; 16:10; 17:18; 20:24; Ro 1:1; 1:3, 9; 10:15, 16; 16:25; 1Co 1:17; 9:18; 15:1; Eph 1:13; 2:17; 3:8; 6:15; Col 1:5; 1:23; 1Th 1:5; 2:2, 4, 8, 9; 3:2, 6; 2Th 1:8; 2:14; 2Ti 1:8; 1:10, 11; 2:8; 4:5; Heb 4:2; 4:6; 1Pt 1:12; 1:25; 4:6, 17; Rev 10:7; 14:6

GOODNESS
Exodus
33:19 I'll make all my ***g*** pass in front of
2 Chronicles
7:10 because of the ***g*** the LORD had
Psalms
4:6 We can't find ***g*** anywhere. The
23:6 Yes, ***g*** and faithful love will pursue me
25:7 love for the sake of your ***g***, LORD.
27:13 the LORD's ***g*** in the land of
31:19 How great is the ***g*** that you've reserved
65:4 full by the ***g*** of your house, by
65:11 year with your ***g***; your paths
68:10 in it. In your ***g***, God, you
86:17 me a sign of your ***g*** so that those who hate me
128:5 Jerusalem's ***g*** your whole life
145:7 of your abundant ***g***; they will shout
Isaiah
16:5 based on ***g***, and someone will
Jeremiah
2:7 its gifts and ***g***, but you ruined
Hosea
3:5 and to the LORD's ***g*** in the latter
Zechariah
9:17 What is his ***g***, and what is his beauty?
Acts
2:47 God's ***g*** to everyone. The
Romans
15:14 are full of ***g***, filled with all
Galatians
5:22 patience, kindness, ***g***, faithfulness,
Ephesians
2:7 his grace by the ***g*** that God has
5:9 of every sort of ***g***, justice, and

GOSHEN
Genesis
45:10 in the land of ***G***, so you will be
47:27 in the land of ***G***. They settled in
50:8 and cattle remained in the land of ***G***.
Exodus
8:22 apart the land of ***G***, where my people
9:26 in the land of ***G*** where the

GOSPEL → PREACH THE GOSPEL
Matthew
24:14 This ***g*** of the kingdom will be
Acts
15:7 the word of the ***g*** and come to
Romans
1:15 to preach the ***g*** also to you who
1:16 ashamed of the ***g***: it is God's own
1 Corinthians
4:15 to you in Christ Jesus through the ***g***,
9:12 obstacle in the way of the ***g*** of Christ.
9:18 to which I'm entitled through the ***g***.
9:23 the sake of the ***g***, so I can be a
2 Corinthians
4:3 And even if our ***g*** is veiled, it is
4:4 the light of the ***g*** that reveals
8:18 of his work for the ***g*** along with him.
9:13 of Christ's ***g***. They will do
10:14 as far as Corinth with the ***g*** of Christ.
10:16 the point of the ***g*** being preached in
11:4 or a different ***g*** than the one you
11:7 I preached the ***g*** of God to you
Galatians
1:6 grace of Christ to follow another ***g***.
1:7 really another ***g***, but certain
1:11 to know that the ***g*** I preached isn't
2:14 the truth of the ***g***, I said to Cephas
Ephesians
3:6 of God in Christ Jesus through the ***g***.
3:7 a servant of the ***g*** because of the
6:19 makes this secret plan of the ***g*** known.
6:20 the sake of the ***g***. Pray so that the
Philippians
1:5 ministry of the ***g*** from the time you
1:7 in the defense and support of the ***g***.
1:12 to me have actually advanced the ***g***.
1:16 put here to give a defense of the ***g***;
1:27 of Christ's ***g***. Do this, whether
2:22 with me for the ***g*** like a son works
4:3 ministry of the ***g***, along with
1 Timothy
1:11 with the glorious ***g*** of the blessed
Philemon
1:13 my time in prison because of the ***g***.

GRACE → GOD'S GRACE, GRACE AND PEACE, GRACE OF GOD, GRACE OF OUR LORD, GRACE OF THE LORD

GRACE AND PEACE
Ga 1:3; Eph 1:2; Phi 1:2; Col 1:2; 1Th 1:1; 2Th 1:2; Ti 1:4; Phm 1:3; 1Pt 1:2; 2Pt 1:2; Rev 1:4

GRACE OF GOD
1Co 15:10; 2Co 1:12; 6:1; 8:1; Ga 2:21; Ti 2:11; 1Pt 5:12

GRACE OF OUR LORD
Ro 16:20; 2Co 8:9; Ga 6:18; 1Th 5:28; 2Th 3:18

GRACE OF THE LORD
Ac 15:11; 1Co 16:23; 2Co 13:13; Phi 4:23; Phm 1:25

GRACIOUS
Genesis
43:29 me about? God be ***g*** to you, my son."
Exodus
20:6 I am loyal and ***g*** to the thousandth
Numbers
6:25 his face shine on you and be ***g*** to you.
Psalms
37:26 They are always ***g*** and generous. Their
77:9 how to be ***g***? Has he angrily
Proverbs
11:16 A ***g*** woman gains honor; violent men gain only wealth
15:26 evil plans, but ***g*** words are pure.
19:17 Those who are ***g*** to the poor lend to the
22:11 —their speech is ***g***, and the king is
Isaiah
27:11 the one who formed them won't be ***g***.
Jeremiah
29:10 and fulfill my ***g*** promise to bring
33:14 I will fulfill my ***g*** promise with the
Amos
5:15 forces will be ***g*** to what is left
Malachi
1:9 now ask God to be ***g*** to us. After what
Luke
4:22 were they by the ***g*** words flowing
19:44 the time of your ***g*** visit from God."
Colossians
4:6 should always be ***g*** and sprinkled
1 Peter
3:7 a coheir of the ***g*** care of life. Do

GRAIN OFFERING
Ex 29:41; 30:9; 40:29; Lv 2:1; 2:3, 4, 6, 8, 9, 10, 11, 13, 14, 15; 5:13; 6:14, 15, 20, 21, 23; 7:9, 10, 37; 9:4, 17; 10:12; 14:10, 20, 21, 31; 23:13, 16; Nm 4:16; 5:15, 18, 25, 26; 6:15, 17; 7:13, 19, 25, 31, 37, 43, 49, 55, 61, 67, 73, 79, 87; 8:8; 15:4, 6, 9; 28:5, 8, 9, 12, 13, 20, 26, 28, 31; 29:3, 6, 9, 11, 14, 16, 18, 19, 21, 22, 24, 25, 27, 28, 30, 31, 33, 34, 37, 38; Jdg 13:19; 13:23; 2Ki 3:20; 16:13, 15; 1Ch 21:23; Neh 10:33; 13:5, 9; Is 57:6; 66:3; Eze 42:13; 45:17; 46:5, 7, 11, 14, 15; Jl 1:9; 1:13; 2:14; Mal 1:10; 1:11, 13

GRAIN OFFERINGS
Lv 2:13; 23:18, 37; Nm 18:9; 29:39; 2Sa 1:21; 1Ki 8:64; 1Ch 23:29; 2Ch 7:7; Ezr 7:17; Ps 20:3; Jer 14:12; 17:26; 33:18; 41:5; Eze 44:29; 45:15, 17, 24, 25; 46:20

GRANT
Leviticus
26:6 I will ***g*** peace in the land so that you
Numbers
6:26 up his face to you and ***g*** you peace.
Ruth
4:11 May the LORD ***g*** that the woman
Psalms
20:4 Let God ***g*** what is in your heart and
21:6 You ***g*** him blessings forever; you make
59:5 all the nations! ***G*** no mercy to any
67:1 A song.] Let God ***g*** us grace and
Isaiah
26:12 LORD, ***g*** us peace, because all that we
46:13 in Zion and ***g*** my splendor to
49:4 the LORD will ***g*** me justice; my
Ezekiel
37:26 forever. I will ***g*** it to them and

GRAPES
Genesis
40:10 and its clusters ripened into ***g***.
49:11 wine, his garments in the blood of ***g***.
Leviticus
19:10 gather up all the ***g*** that have fallen
25:5 or gather the ***g*** of your freely
Numbers
6:3 juice or eat ***g***, whether fresh or
13:20 It was the season of the first ripe ***g***.
Deuteronomy
23:24 can eat as many ***g*** as you like,
Nehemiah
13:15 as well as wine, ***g***, figs, and every
Job
15:33 will drop early ***g*** and cast off
Isaiah
5:2 it to grow good ***g***—but it grew rott
16:8 whose honored ***g*** overpowered
63:2 like those of one who stomps on ***g***?
Jeremiah
8:13 there are no ***g*** on the vine, no
25:30 who tread on ***g***, against everyone
31:29 longer say: Sour ***g*** eaten by parents
40:10 harvest the ***g***, the summer
48:32 to harvest your ***g*** and summer fruits.
Ezekiel
18:2 eat unripe ***g***, the children's
Hosea
9:10 Like ***g*** in the wilderness, I found
Joel
3:13 Go and crush ***g***, for the
Amos
9:13 one who crushes ***g*** will overtake the
Obadiah
1:5 those who gather ***g*** came to you,
Micah
6:15 oil; you tread ***g***, but don't drink
7:1 has no cluster of ***g*** to eat, no ripe
Matthew
7:16 get bunches of ***g*** from thorny
Revelation
14:18 of the earth, because its ***g*** are ripe."

GRASS
Numbers
22:4 an ox eats up the ***g*** in the field."
Deuteronomy
32:2 gentle rains on ***g***, like spring
2 Samuel
23:4 rain that brings ***g*** from the ground."
1 Kings
18:5 we can find some ***g*** to keep our
2 Kings
19:26 green shoots, the ***g*** on rooftops,

Job
5:25 will be like the ***g*** of the earth.
6:5 donkey bray over ***g*** or an ox bellow
8:12 it will wither before every other ***g***.
21:18 the wind, like dry ***g*** stolen by a storm.
38:27 dry wasteland and make ***g*** sprout?
40:15 along with you; he eats ***g*** like cattle.
Psalms
37:2 fade fast, like ***g***; they will wither
72:6 upon fresh-cut ***g***, like showers
72:16 Let it thrive like ***g*** on the land.
90:5 a dream, like ***g*** that is renewed
92:7 spring up like ***g*** and all evildoers
102:4 like dried-up ***g***. I even forget to
103:15 life are like ***g***: they bloom like
104:14 You make ***g*** grow for cattle; you make
106:20 God for an image of a bull that eats ***g***.
129:6 Let them be like ***g*** on a roof that dies
147:8 God makes the mountains sprout green ***g***.
Proverbs
19:12 his favor is like the dew on the ***g***.
27:25 When the ***g*** goes away, new growth
Isaiah
15:6 are used up. ***G*** has withered;
40:7 The ***g*** dries up and the flower withers
66:14 flourish like ***g***. The LORD's power
Jeremiah
12:4 mourn and the ***g*** in the fields dry
14:5 abandons her newborn, for there's no ***g***.
Matthew
6:30 If God dresses ***g*** in the field so
James
1:11 and dries up the ***g*** so that its
1 Peter
1:24 the earth is like ***g***, and all human
Revelation
8:7 up. All the green ***g*** was burned up.
9:4 not to hurt the ***g*** of the earth or

GRASSHOPPERS

Numbers
13:33 saw ourselves as ***g***, and that's how
2 Chronicles
6:28 locusts, or ***g***, or whenever
Psalms
105:34 the locusts came—countless ***g*** came!
Nahum
3:17 guards are like ***g***, your marshals

GRAVE

Genesis
35:20 a pillar on her ***g***. It's the pillar
Deuteronomy
32:22 the depths of the ***g***; it will destroy
34:6 now, no one knows where Moses' ***g*** is.
1 Samuel
2:6 takes down to the ***g***, and raises up!
2 Samuel
3:32 loudly at Abner's ***g***. All the troops
4:12 buried it in the ***g*** of Abner at
19:37 own town near the ***g*** of my parents.
22:6 The cords of the ***g*** surrounded me;
2 Chronicles
34:28 will go to your ***g*** in peace. You
Job
3:22 who are thrilled when they find a ***g***?
5:26 will come to your ***g*** in old age as
7:9 who descends to the ***g*** and won't rise,
10:19 existed, taken from the belly to the ***g***.
17:1 my days extinguished, the ***g***, mine.
21:13 go down to the ***g*** peacefully.
26:6 The ***g*** is naked before God; the
36:9 about their offenses and their ***g*** sins.
Psalms
6:5 dead. Who gives you thanks from the ***g***?
9:17 straight to the ***g***, the same for
16:10 my life to the ***g***; you won't let
18:5 The cords of the ***g*** surrounded me;
30:3 me up from the ***g***, brought me back
49:14 straight for the ***g***. Death will be
49:15 the power of the ***g***, because he will
55:15 them go to the ***g*** alive because
88:5 dead lying in the ***g***, like dead bodies-
88:11 proclaimed in the ***g***, your
89:48 rescued from the grip of the ***g***? Selah
116:3 distress of the ***g*** found me—I came
139:8 went down to the ***g***, you would be
141:7 the mouth of the ***g***, just like when
Proverbs
1:12 living like the ***g***—whole, like tho
5:5 down to death; her steps lead to the ***g***.
7:27 is a path to the ***g***, going down to
9:18 her guests are in the depths of the ***g***.
15:11 The ***g*** and the underworld lie open
15:24 an upward path, avoiding the ***g*** below.
23:14 you will save their lives from the ***g***.
27:20 The ***g*** and the underworld are never
28:18 on twisted paths will fall into the ***g***.
30:16 the ***g*** and a barren womb, a land never filled with water
Ecclesiastes
6:3 child with no ***g*** is better off
9:10 or wisdom in the ***g***, which is where
Isaiah
5:14 Therefore, the ***g*** opens wide its jaws,
7:11 it as deep as the ***g*** or as high as
53:9 His ***g*** was among the wicked, his tomb
Jeremiah
20:17 mother become my ***g***, her womb
30:12 injury is incurable; your illness is ***g***.
Ezekiel
32:22 round about his ***g***, all of them
39:15 to it until the ***g***-diggers bury it in
Hosea
13:14 the power of the ***g*** Heb Sheol Will I
Nahum
1:14 I will make your ***g***, for you are
Habakkuk
2:5 his jaws like the ***g***; like death, he
Matthew
27:64 order the ***g*** to be sealed
Acts
2:27 abandon me to the ***g***, nor permit your
Romans
3:13 Their throat is a ***g*** that has been
Revelation
1:18 I have the keys of Death and the ***G***.
6:8 Death, and the ***G*** was following
20:13 and Death and the ***G*** gave up the dead

GRAVES

Exodus
14:11 there enough ***g*** in Egypt that you

Psalms
5:9 throats are open ***g***; their tongues
49:11 Their ***g*** are their eternal homes, the
Ecclesiastes
8:10 brought to their ***g***, with people
Jeremiah
8:1 of Jerusalem will be taken from their ***g***
Ezekiel
32:23 who were assigned ***g*** in the deepest
32:26 around their ***g***, all of them
37:12 I'm opening your ***g***! I will raise you
37:13 when I open your ***g*** and raise you up
Matthew
23:29 and decorate the ***g*** of the righteous.
27:53 came out of their ***g*** and went into the
Luke
11:44 are like unmarked ***g*** and people walk
John
5:28 who are in their ***g*** will hear his

GREAT AND AWESOME
Dt 6:22; 7:21; 10:21; 2Sa 7:23; 1Ch 17:21; Neh 4:14; Ps 99:3; Dn 9:4

GREAT GOD
Ezr 5:8; Neh 8:6; Ps 35:27; 95:3; Dn 2:45; Ti 2:13

GREATER → GREATER THAN ALL
Genesis
39:9 No one is ***g*** than I am in this
Matthew
10:24 Disciples aren't ***g*** than their teacher,
11:11 ever been born is ***g*** than John the
12:6 that something ***g*** than the temple
12:41 And look, someone ***g*** than Jonah is
Mark
12:31 No other commandment is ***g*** than these.
John
1:15 comes after me is ***g*** than me because
1:50 tree? You will see ***g*** things than these!
8:53 Are you ***g*** than our father Abraham? He
14:28 because the Father is ***g*** than me.
15:20 Servants aren't ***g*** than their
Hebrews
3:3 But he deserves ***g*** glory than Moses in
1 John
3:20 us, God is ***g*** than our hearts
4:4 who is in you is ***g*** than the one who
5:9 testimony is ***g***, because this is

GREATER THAN ALL
Ex 18:11; Dt 7:7; 1Ki 4:30; 2Ch 2:5; Job 1:3; Ps 135:5; Ecc 2:9; Dn 11:37; Jn 10:29

GREATEST
Matthew
11:20 he had done his ***g*** miracles because
18:1 Who is the ***g*** in the kingdom of
22:36 what is the ***g*** commandment in
Acts
8:10 the least to the ***g***, gave him their

GREEK
Daniel
11:2 everyone, including the ***G*** kingdom.
Mark
7:26 The woman was ***G***, Syrophoenician by
John
19:20 was written in Aramaic, Latin, and ***G***.
Acts
6:1 complaint arose. ***G***-speaking disciples
9:29 debates with the ***G***-speaking Jews as w
11:20 Lord Jesus also to Jews who spoke ***G***.
16:1 believing Jewish woman and a ***G*** father.
17:4 larger number of ***G*** God-worshippers an
21:37 with you?" He answered, "Do you know ***G***?
Romans
1:14 who don't speak ***G***, both to the wise
1:16 to the Jew first and also to the ***G***.
10:12 between Jew and ***G***, because the same
1 Corinthians
12:13 whether Jew or ***G***, or slave or
Galatians
2:3 me and who was a ***G***, was required to
3:28 neither Jew nor ***G***; there is neither
Colossians
3:11 there is neither ***G*** nor Jew,
Revelation
9:11 Abaddon, and whose ***G*** name is Apollyon.

GREET
Matthew
5:47 And if you ***g*** only your brothers and
Luke
7:45 You didn't ***g*** me with a kiss, but she
1 Peter
5:14 ***G*** each other with the kiss of love.

GRIEF
Genesis
21:16 a distance, cried out in ***g***, and wept.
23:2 cried out in ***g*** and wept for
42:38 me—old as I am—to my grave in ***g***."
44:31 as he is—to his grave in ***g***.
50:11 the observance of ***g*** on Atad's
Exodus
2:24 their cry of ***g***, and God
6:5 heard the cry of ***g*** of the Israelites
1 Samuel
2:33 and be full of ***g***. Any new children
Job
6:2 Oh, that my ***g*** were actually weighed,
17:7 eye is weak from ***g***; my limbs like a
31:39 payment and caused its owners ***g***,
Psalms
6:7 because of my ***g***; it's weak
10:14 troublemaking and ***g***, and you do
31:9 because of my ***g***, as do my spirit
35:12 for good, leaving me stricken with ***g***.
102:1 and pouring out ***g*** to the LORD.]
107:39 down by oppression, trouble, and ***g***—
116:3 I came face-to-face with trouble and ***g***.
119:28 sags because of ***g***. Now raise me up
Proverbs
17:21 for a son brings ***g***; there's no joy
Ecclesiastes
5:17 with much aggravation, ***g***, and anger.
Isaiah
35:10 overwhelm them; ***g*** and groaning will
50:11 you by my hand: you will lie down in ***g***.

51:11 them; let **g** and groaning flee.
Jeremiah
8:18 No healing, only **g**; my heart is broken
16:6 themselves in **g** or shave their
47:5 How long will you gash yourselves in **g**?
Lamentations
1:5 LORD caused her **g** because of her
1:12 on me, the **g** that the LORD
3:15 saturated me with **g**, made me choke on
3:32 he has caused **g**, he will show
Luke
22:45 He found them asleep, overcome by **g**.
Revelation
18:7 give her pain and **g**. In her heart she
18:8 disease, **g**, and hunger. She

GRINDING → GRINDING THEIR TEETH
Deuteronomy
9:21 I smashed it, **g** it thoroughly
Judges
16:21 and he worked the **g** mill in the
2 Kings
23:15 the shrine, **g** it into dust.
2 Chronicles
34:4 and images, **g** them to dust and
Proverbs
27:22 in a mortar, even **g** them along with
Lamentations
2:16 they whistle, **g** their teeth. They
5:13 men have carried **g** stones; boys have
Matthew
24:41 Two women will be **g** at the mill. One

GRINDING THEIR TEETH
Ps 35:16; 37:12; Lam 2:16; Mt 8:12; 13:42, 50; 22:13; 24:51; 25:30

GROUND
Genesis
1:25 crawls on the **g**. God saw how good
Exodus
3:5 because you are standing on holy **g**."
14:29 walked on dry **g** through the sea.
16:14 thin flakes, as thin as frost on the **g**.
Ruth
2:10 down, face to the **g**, and replied to
Proverbs
24:31 weeds covered the **g**, and the stone
Matthew
10:29 will fall to the **g** without your
13:5 fell on rocky **g** where the soil
15:35 He told the crowd to sit on the **g**
25:18 dug a hole in the **g** and buried his
25:25 coin in the **g**. Here, you have
Luke
6:17 area of level **g**. A great company
24:5 faces toward the **g**, but the men said
John
8:6 and wrote on the **g** with his finger.
9:6 he spit on the **g**, made mud with
Acts
7:33 place where you are standing is holy **g**.
Romans
12:12 hope, stand your **g** when you're in
Hebrews
6:7 The **g** receives a blessing from God when
10:32 You stood your **g** while you were
11:38 mountains, caves, and holes in the **g**.

GROW
Genesis
1:11 Let the earth **g** plant life:
Numbers
6:5 letting his or her hair **g** untrimmed.
Job
8:11 Does papyrus **g** apart from a marsh?
11:20 the wicked will **g** faint; flight has
39:4 are healthy; they **g** up in the open
Psalms
69:23 Let their eyes **g** too dim to see; make
77:2 and don't **g** numb; my whole
92:12 tree. They will **g** strong like a
104:14 You make grass **g** for cattle; you make
144:12 that our sons can **g** up fully, in
Proverbs
1:5 hear them and **g** in wisdom; those
6:6 person; observe its ways and **g** wise.
11:24 with what is appropriate will **g** needy.
19:20 so you might **g** wise in the
22:6 go; when they **g** old, they won't
Ecclesiastes
12:2 sun and the light **g** dark, the moon
12:3 who look through the windows **g** dim;
Isaiah
5:2 He expected it to **g** good grapes—but
11:1 A shoot will **g** up from the stump of
14:29 root a viper will **g**, and it will
Jeremiah
4:28 and the heavens **g** dark because I
Nahum
2:10 in every groin; all the faces **g** pale.
Luke
12:27 how the lilies **g**. They don't wear
Acts
6:7 word continued to **g**. The number of
9:31 the church continued to **g** in numbers.
12:24 God's word continued to **g** and increase
1 Corinthians
3:6 Apollos watered, but God made it **g**.
James
1:19 slow to speak, and slow to **g** angry.
1 Peter
2:2 by it, you will **g** into salvation,
2 Peter
3:18 Instead, **g** in the grace and knowledge

GUARD
Genesis
3:24 flaming swords to **g** the way to the
Exodus
23:20 front of you to **g** you on your way
Leviticus
24:12 He was put under **g** until they could
Numbers
1:53 The Levites will **g** the covenant
Deuteronomy
4:9 But be on **g** and watch yourselves
23:9 your enemies, **g** yourself from
24:8 Be on **g** against outbreaks of skin
Joshua
6:9 The rear **g** was coming behind
1 Samuel
19:2 kill you. Be on **g** tomorrow morning.

Job
7:12 Sea Monster that you place me under ***g***?
21:32 someone keeps ***g*** over their tombs.
Psalms
86:2 ***G*** my life because I am faithful. Save
119:2 Those who ***g*** God's laws are truly happy!
127:1 the city, the ***g*** on duty is
140:1 people, LORD! ***G*** me from violent
141:3 Set a ***g*** over my mouth, LORD; keep close watch over the door
Daniel
1:11 spoke to the ***g*** whom the chief
Matthew
16:6 and be on your ***g*** for the yeast of
Mark
6:27 So he ordered a ***g*** to bring John's head.
John
10:3 The ***g*** at the gate opens the gate for
Acts
4:1 of the temple ***g***, and the
24:23 a centurion to ***g*** Paul. He was to
Philippians
1:13 whole Praetorian ***G*** and everyone else
1 John
5:18 born from God ***g*** themselves, and
5:21 Little children, ***g*** yourselves from

GUARDS

Mark
14:54 sitting with the ***g***, warming himself
14:65 Then the ***g*** took him and beat
Acts
5:22 However, the ***g*** didn't find them in the
12:10 first and second ***g*** and came to the

GUESTS

2 Samuel
15:11 hundred invited ***g*** went with Absalom
Matthew
9:15 The wedding ***g*** can't mourn while
22:10 good. The wedding party was full of ***g***.
John
2:10 only when the ***g*** are drinking
Hebrews
13:2 up your homes to ***g***, because by doing
James
2:25 messengers as her ***g*** and then sent

GUILT → BEAR THEIR GUILT

Exodus
28:38 on himself any ***g*** connected with
Deuteronomy
21:8 Don't put the ***g*** of innocent
25:2 blows in measure with the ***g*** determined.
Psalms
32:5 didn't conceal my ***g***. "I'll confess my
36:2 talk about their ***g*** ever being found
51:2 clean of my ***g***; purify me from
51:5 I was born in ***g***, in sin, from the
68:21 the very skulls of those who walk in ***g***.
69:27 Pile ***g*** on top of their guilt! Don't let
Proverbs
16:6 reconcile ***g***; the fear of the
Daniel
9:5 We have brought ***g*** on ourselves and
Hosea
5:5 because of their ***g***; Judah staggers
10:2 must bear their ***g***. The LORD will
Amos
8:14 who swear by the ***g*** of Samaria, and
Zechariah
3:4 have removed your ***g*** from you. Put on
3:9 I will remove the ***g*** of that land in

GUILTY → GUILTY OF SIN

Genesis
18:23 sweep away the innocent with the ***g***?
Leviticus
4:3 making the people ***g*** of sin, he must
26:39 account of their ***g*** deeds. And they
Numbers
5:6 with the LORD, that person becomes ***g***.
5:8 by which the ***g*** party himself is
35:31 a killer, who is ***g*** of a capital
Deuteronomy
25:2 If the ***g*** party is to be beaten, the
Ezra
6:11 the house of the ***g*** party, and the
Job
9:29 myself am thought ***g***; why have I tried
10:2 Don't declare me ***g***; tell me what you
10:7 know that I'm not ***g***, yet no one
10:15 If I were ***g***, doom to me; I'm innocent,
22:30 will deliver the ***g***; they will be
40:8 justice, deem me ***g*** so you can be
Psalms
32:2 doesn't consider ***g***—in whose spirit
37:33 be found ***g*** when they are
51:9 from my sins; wipe away all my ***g*** deeds!
109:7 let him be found ***g***—let his prayer
Ezekiel
25:12 The Judeans were ***g***, but Edom's
Daniel
6:4 He wasn't ***g*** of any negligence
Joel
3:21 not pardon the ***g***. The LORD dwells
Habakkuk
1:11 he will be held ***g***, the one whose
Matthew
12:37 judged innocent or condemned as ***g***."
Mark
3:29 That person is ***g*** of a sin with
2 Corinthians
7:3 to make you feel ***g***. I've already

GUILTY OF SIN

Lv 4:3; 4:13, 22, 27; 5:2, 3, 4, 5; 6:4; Dt 15:9; Jn 8:46

Hh

HADAD
Genesis
25:15 ***H***; Tema; Jetur; Naphish; and Kedemah
1 Kings
11:14 for Solomon: ***H*** the Edomite from
11:25 caused by ***H***. Rezon hated

HADADEZER
2 Samuel
8:3 Zobah's King ***H***, Rehob's son, as
8:12 plunder of Zobah's King ***H***, Rehob's son.
1 Kings
11:23 who had escaped from Zobah's King ***H***.
1 Chronicles
18:3 Zobah's King ***H*** at Hamath, as he
18:5 help Zobah's King ***H***, David killed

HAGAR
Genesis
16:3 Egyptian servant ***H*** and gave her to
16:15 ***H*** gave birth to a son for Abram, and
Galatians
4:25 ***H*** is Mount Sinai in Arabia, and she

HAGGAI
Ezra
5:1 Then the prophet ***H*** and the prophet
6:14 of the prophet ***H*** and Zechariah,
Haggai
1:1 word came through ***H*** the prophet in

HAIL
Exodus
9:18 the heaviest ***h*** to fall on Egypt
9:26 only place where ***h*** didn't fall was
10:5 left after the ***h***. They will eat
Job
38:22 storehouses, seen the storehouses of ***h***
Psalms
18:12 before him; ***h*** and coals of fire
18:13 voice heard with ***h*** and coals of fire.
78:47 their vines with ***h***, their sycamore
105:32 their rain into ***h*** along with
147:17 God throws his ***h*** down like crumbs—who
148:8 same, fire and ***h***, snow and smoke,
Isaiah
28:17 plumb line. But ***h*** will sweep away
30:30 consuming fire; in stormy rain and ***h***.
Haggai
2:17 and mildew and ***h***; but you didn't
Revelation
8:7 his trumpet, and ***h*** and fire mixed
11:19 thunder, an earthquake, and large ***h***.
16:21 for the plague of ***h***, because the

HAILSTONES
Joshua
10:11 died from the ***h*** than the
Ezekiel
13:11 appear and I send ***h***, it will
13:13 rains and ***h*** in consuming
38:22 flooding rain, ***h***, fire, and sulfur
Revelation
16:21 Huge ***h*** weighing about one hundred

HAIR
Genesis
25:25 clothed with ***h***, and she named
Leviticus
13:41 If the ***h*** is lost at the sides of the
19:27 not cut off the ***h*** on your foreheads
21:10 not dishevel his ***h*** or tear his
Numbers
5:18 the LORD, let the ***h*** of the woman hang
6:5 letting his or her ***h*** grow untrimmed.
Judges
16:22 But the ***h*** on his head began to grow
2 Samuel
14:26 year because his ***h*** was so heavy that
Proverbs
16:31 Gray ***h*** is a crown of glory; it is found
20:29 young men; gray ***h*** is the splendor
Daniel
3:27 to them: their ***h*** wasn't singed;
4:33 until he grew ***h*** like eagles'
7:9 like snow; his ***h*** was like a lamb's
Matthew
3:4 made of camel's ***h***, with a leather
5:36 you can't turn one ***h*** white or black.
Luke
7:44 with tears and wiped them with her ***h***.
21:18 Still, not a ***h*** on your heads will be
John
11:2 his feet with her ***h***. Her brother
12:3 feet dry with her ***h***. The house was
1 Corinthians
11:6 should have her ***h*** cut off. If it is
11:14 if a man has long ***h***, it is a disgrace
1 Peter
3:3 with stylish ***h*** or by wearing
Revelation
1:14 His head and ***h*** were white as white
9:8 their ***h*** was like women's hair, and

HAMAN
Esther
3:1 promoted ***H***, Hammedatha the

HAMATH
2 Kings
14:28 Damascus and ***H*** to Judah in

1 Chronicles
18:3 King Hadadezer at ***H***, as he continued
Amos
6:2 from there go to ***H*** the great; then
Zechariah
9:2 ***H*** also borders on it. Tyre and Sidon,

HANANIAH

1 Chronicles
8:24 ***H***, Omri, Elam, Anthothijah
2 Chronicles
26:11 the authority of ***H***, one of the
Ezra
10:28 Bebai: Jehohanan, ***H***, Zabbai, and
Jeremiah
28:10 Then the prophet ***H*** took hold of the
Daniel
1:6 were Daniel, ***H***, Mishael, and

HAND

Genesis
3:22 stretch out his ***h*** and take also
4:11 take your brother's blood from your ***h***.
47:29 so kind, lay your ***h*** under my thigh,
Exodus
8:5 Stretch out your ***h*** with your
Ezra
7:9 for the gracious ***h*** of his God was
Job
1:11 stretch out your ***h*** and strike all he
21:5 appalled; lay your ***h*** over your mouth.
26:13 became clear; his ***h*** split the fleeing
29:9 speech, put their ***h*** on their mouth;
Psalms
16:11 things are always in your right ***h***.
32:4 because your ***h*** was heavy upon me.
37:24 down, because the LORD holds their ***h***.
44:3 was your strong ***h***, your arm, and
74:11 do you pull your ***h*** back? Why do you
75:8 cup in the LORD's ***h*** full of foaming
80:17 Let your ***h*** be with the one on your
110:5 by your strong ***h***, God has crushed
137:5 I forget you, let my strong ***h*** wither!
138:7 wrath; you save me with your strong ***h***.
139:10 even there your ***h*** would guide me; even
145:16 opening your ***h*** and satisfying the
Proverbs
3:16 In her right ***h*** is a long life; in her
19:24 people bury their ***h*** in the bowl; they
21:1 of water in the ***h*** of the LORD; he
27:16 the wind or pick up oil in his ***h***.
Ecclesiastes
2:24 I also saw that this is from God's ***h***—
Ezekiel
2:9 and there in a ***h*** stretched out to
Daniel
5:5 of a human ***h*** appeared and
11:41 the Ammonites will escape from his ***h***.
Jonah
4:11 tell their right ***h*** from their left,
Matthew
5:30 And if your right ***h*** causes you to fall
6:3 let your left ***h*** know what your
18:8 If your ***h*** or your foot causes you to
20:19 They will ***h*** him over to the Gentiles to
26:23 one who dips his ***h*** with me into this
Luke
5:13 reached out his ***h***, touched him, and
John
20:25 nails, and put my ***h*** into his side, I
20:27 hands. Put your ***h*** into my side. No
Acts
2:25 he is at my right ***h*** I won't be shaken.
Romans
2:7 On the one ***h***, he will give eternal
1 Corinthians
5:5 time we need to ***h*** this man over to
13:3 that I have and ***h*** over my own body
2 Corinthians
6:7 in our right ***h*** and our left hand.
Galatians
3:19 through angels by the ***h*** of a mediator.
2 Thessalonians
3:17 with my own ***h***. This verifies
Philemon
1:19 this with my own ***h***). Of course, I
Hebrews
7:18 On the one ***h***, an earlier command is
7:19 On the other ***h***, a better hope is
8:9 took them by the ***h*** to lead them out
Revelation
1:16 in his right ***h***, and from his
5:1 in the right ***h*** of the one seated
13:16 on their right ***h*** or on their
20:4 their forehead or ***h***. They came to

HANDED

Judges
2:14 Israel, and he ***h*** them over to
Matthew
26:2 Human One will be ***h*** over to be
27:18 of the people had ***h*** him over because
27:26 whipped, then ***h*** him over to be
Acts
3:13 is the one you ***h*** over and denied
Romans
4:25 He was ***h*** over because of our mistakes,

HANDS

Genesis
5:29 the pain in our ***h***, because of the
Exodus
29:10 will lay their ***h*** on the bull's
32:15 tablets in his ***h***. The tablets were
1 Samuel
5:4 with both his ***h*** were cut off and
2 Samuel
24:14 into the LORD's ***h*** because his mercy
2 Kings
3:11 He used to pour water on Elijah's ***h***."
4:34 boy's eyes, his ***h*** on the boy's
Psalms
18:24 because my ***h*** are clean in his
22:16 like a lion—oh, my poor ***h*** and feet!
24:4 one with clean ***h*** and a pure heart;
47:1 Clap your ***h***, all you people!
63:4 I will lift up my ***h*** in your name.
90:17 the work of our ***h*** last. Make the
115:7 They have ***h***, but they can't feel. They
138:8 Don't let go of what your ***h*** have made.
Proverbs
21:25 because their ***h*** refuse to do
31:13 flax; she works joyfully with her ***h***.

31:20 she stretches out her ***h*** to the poor.
Ecclesiastes
4:5 Fools fold their ***h*** and eat their own
Isaiah
35:3 the weak ***h***, and support the
45:12 upon it. My own ***h*** stretched out the
55:12 trees of the field will clap their ***h***.
65:2 I extended my ***h*** all day to a rebellious
Jeremiah
1:16 and trusting in the works of their ***h***.
26:14 me? I'm in your ***h***. Do whatever you
Lamentations
3:41 up our hearts and ***h*** to God in heaven.
Ezekiel
1:8 Human ***h*** were under their wings on all
Daniel
2:45 but not by ***h***, shattered the
Hosea
14:3 the work of our ***h***. In you the
Micah
7:3 Their ***h*** are skilled at doing evil.
Malachi
1:13 accept such from your ***h***? says the LORD.
Mark
7:5 eat food with ritually unclean ***h***?"
14:41 to be betrayed into the ***h*** of sinners.
16:18 snakes with their ***h***. If they drink
Luke
23:46 into your ***h*** I entrust my
24:40 this, he showed them his ***h*** and feet.
Acts
6:6 who prayed and laid their ***h*** on them.
8:18 of the apostles' ***h***, he offered them
13:3 they laid their ***h*** on these two and
19:6 Paul placed his ***h*** on them, the Holy
Romans
10:21 stretched out my ***h*** to a disobedient
1 Corinthians
15:24 end, when Christ ***h*** over the kingdom
1 Timothy
2:8 by lifting up ***h*** that are holy,
4:14 prophecy when the elders laid ***h*** on you.
2 Timothy
1:6 in you through the laying on of my ***h***.
Hebrews
6:2 laying on of ***h***, the resurrection
10:31 to fall into the ***h*** of the living God!
1 John
1:1 have seen and our ***h*** handled, about

HANG
Genesis
40:19 audience and will ***h*** you from a tree

HANNAH
1 Samuel
1:2 wives, one named ***H*** and the other

HAPPINESS
Esther
8:16 was a day of light, ***h***, joy, and honor.
Psalms
68:6 free with ***h***, but the
Isaiah
16:10 Joy and ***h*** have been harvested from the
51:3 LORD's garden. ***H*** and joy will be
51:11 their heads. Let ***h*** and joy overwhelm
Matthew
3:17 whom I dearly love; I find ***h*** in him."
11:26 Indeed, Father, this brings you ***h***
Acts
2:28 your presence will fill me with ***h***.
13:52 the disciples were overflowing with ***h***.
14:17 and satisfying you with food and ***h***."
Romans
4:9 Is this state of ***h*** only for the
2 Corinthians
1:24 with you for your ***h***, because you
2:3 in you, that my ***h*** means your
7:4 overwhelmed with ***h*** while in the
8:2 extra amount of ***h*** and their extreme
2 Timothy
1:4 see you so that I can be filled with ***h***.

HAPPY
Deuteronomy
33:29 ***H*** are you, Israel! Who is like you? You
Judges
9:13 gods and humans ***h***, so that I can go
1 Samuel
18:20 reported to Saul, he was ***h*** about it.
19:5 saw it and were ***h*** about it. Why
Job
3:7 childless; may no ***h*** singing come in
5:17 Look, ***h*** is the person whom God
Psalms
1:1 The truly ***h*** person doesn't follow
2:12 take refuge in the LORD are truly ***h***!
32:1 whose sin is covered over, is truly ***h***!
34:8 one who takes refuge in him is truly ***h***!
41:1 poor are truly ***h***! The LORD rescues
41:2 the land as ***h*** people. You won't
65:4 How ***h*** is the one you choose to bring
72:17 be blessed through him and call him ***h***.
84:12 those who trust in you are truly ***h***!
86:4 servant's life ***h*** again because, my
89:15 shout are truly ***h***! They walk in the
90:15 Make us ***h*** for the same amount of time
106:3 always do what is right, are truly ***h***!
112:1 adore God's commandments, are truly ***h***!
119:1 in the LORD's Instruction—are truly ***h***!
127:5 them is truly ***h***! They won't be
128:1 who walks in God's ways, is truly ***h***!
Proverbs
3:13 ***H*** are those who find wisdom and those
8:32 listen to me: ***H*** are those who
8:34 ***H*** are those who listen to me, watching
29:18 but whoever obeys instruction is ***h***.
Ecclesiastes
4:16 came later aren't ***h*** with him. This
10:17 ***H*** is the land whose king is dignified
11:9 should make you ***h*** in your prime.
Isaiah
56:2 ***H*** is the one who does this, the person
Jonah
4:6 Jonah was very ***h*** about the shrub.
Matthew
5:3 ***H*** are people who are hopeless, because
13:16 ***H*** are your eyes because they see.
16:17 Jesus replied, "***H*** are you, Simon
24:46 ***H*** are those servants whom the master
John
8:29 because I always do what makes him ***h***."

13:17 things, you will be ***h*** if you do them.
14:28 me, you would be ***h*** that I am going
16:20 the world will be ***h***. You will be
20:29 you see me? ***H*** are those who
Romans
4:7 ***H*** are those whose actions outside the
4:8 ***H*** are those whose sin isn't counted
12:12 Be ***h*** in your hope, stand your ground
15:26 Achaia have been ***h*** to make a
16:19 everybody, so I'm ***h*** for you. But I
1 Corinthians
7:30 Those who are ***h*** should be like
13:6 it isn't ***h*** with injustice, but it is
16:17 I'm so ***h*** that Stephanas, Fortunatus,
2 Corinthians
2:3 ought to make me ***h***. I have
6:10 pain but always ***h***, as poor but
7:13 pleased at how ***h*** Titus was. His
11:19 are so wise, are ***h*** to put up with
13:9 We are ***h*** when we are weak but you are
Galatians
6:4 own work and be ***h*** with doing a good
Colossians
1:24 Now I'm ***h*** to be suffering for you. I'm
2:5 in spirit. I'm ***h*** to see the
2 Thessalonians
2:12 by the truth but is ***h*** with injustice.
1 Timothy
6:6 with being ***h*** with what you
James
5:13 If any of you are ***h***, they should sing.
1 Peter
3:14 But ***h*** are you, even if you suffer

HARAN

Genesis
11:26 the father of Abram, Nahor, and ***H***.
12:4 Abram was 75 years old when he left ***H***.
2 Kings
19:12 my fathers-Gozan, ***H***, Rezeph, or the
Isaiah
37:12 gods of Gozan, ***H***, Rezeph, or the
Acts
7:2 in Mesopotamia, before he settled in ***H***.
7:4 and settled in ***H***. After Abraham's

HARASS

Exodus
1:11 the Israelites to ***h*** them with hard
Numbers
33:55 side. They will ***h*** you in the land
Job
19:2 How long will you ***h*** me and crush me
Psalms
55:3 disaster on me and ***h*** me furiously.
119:86 true, but people ***h*** me for no reason.
Isaiah
11:13 of Judah, and Judah won't ***h*** Ephraim.
Jeremiah
17:15 See how they ***h*** me: "Where's the LORD's
Matthew
5:11 insult you and ***h*** you and speak all
5:44 enemies and pray for those who ***h*** you
10:23 Whenever they ***h*** you in one city, escape
Luke
3:14 Don't cheat or ***h*** anyone, and be
11:49 and they will ***h*** and kill some of
21:12 into custody and ***h*** you because of
John
15:20 me, it will ***h*** you too. If it
Acts
7:52 ancestors didn't ***h***? They even killed
12:1 Herod began to ***h*** some who belonged
13:50 others to ***h*** Paul and
Romans
12:14 Bless people who ***h*** you—bless and don't curse you
Galatians
1:23 man who used to ***h*** us now preaches

HARD

Exodus
1:14 miserable with ***h*** labor, making
18:26 would refer the ***h*** cases to Moses,
1 Kings
12:4 our workload very ***h*** for us. If you
14:6 yourself? I have ***h*** news for you.
Job
9:29 guilty; why have I tried so ***h*** in vain?
Proverbs
15:15 of the needy are ***h***, but a happy
Ecclesiastes
1:3 gain from all the ***h*** work that they
Jeremiah
32:17 arm; nothing is too ***h*** for you!
Matthew
19:23 it will be very ***h*** for a rich person
Acts
28:27 they've become ***h*** of hearing, and
Romans
16:12 Persis, who has worked ***h*** in the Lord.
2 Peter
3:16 his remarks are ***h*** to understand,

HARM

Genesis
31:7 ten times. Yet God didn't let him ***h*** me.
31:52 this mound and this pillar to do ***h***.
37:27 Let's not ***h*** him because he's
48:16 me from all ***h***, bless the young
1 Samuel
26:21 today, I won't ***h*** you again. I have
1 Chronicles
16:22 my anointed ones; don't ***h*** my prophets!"
Nehemiah
6:2 plain of Ono." But they wanted to ***h*** me,
Psalms
105:15 my anointed ones; don't ***h*** my prophets!"
Proverbs
3:29 Don't plan to ***h*** your neighbor who
12:21 No ***h*** happens to the righteous, but the
Amos
9:4 my eyes on them for ***h*** and not for good.
Luke
10:19 power of the enemy. Nothing will ***h*** you.
Acts
16:28 loudly, "Don't ***h*** yourself! We're
18:10 attacks you will ***h*** you, for I have
28:5 snake into the fire and suffered no ***h***.

HARP

Psalms
33:2 praises to him with the ten-stringed ***h***!
57:8 glory! Wake up, ***h*** and lyre! I will
81:2 the drum! Sweet lyre along with ***h***!
92:3 the ten-stringed ***h***, with the melody
108:2 Wake up, ***h*** and lyre! I will wake the
144:9 praises to you on a ten-stringed ***h***,
Isaiah
5:12 with lyre and ***h***, tambourine,
23:16 Take a ***h***, go around the city,
Amos
6:5 the sound of the ***h***, and, like David,
1 Corinthians
14:7 alive like a ***h*** or a lyre can
Revelation
5:8 Lamb. Each held a ***h*** and gold bowls

HARPS

1 Chronicles
15:16 including ***h***, lyres, and
25:1 by lyres, ***h***, and cymbals.
Nehemiah
12:27 and with cymbals, ***h***, and lyres.
Isaiah
14:11 the sound of your ***h***. Under you is a
Amos
5:23 I won't listen to the melody of your ***h***.
Revelation
14:2 like that of harpists playing their ***h***.
15:2 by the glass sea, holding ***h*** from God.

HARSHLY

Genesis
16:6 Sarai treated her ***h***, and she ran away
41:52 in the land where I've been treated ***h***."
1 Samuel
3:17 May God deal ***h*** with you and
20:10 father responds ***h***?" David asked
20:13 may the LORD deal ***h*** with me,
2 Samuel
3:9 May God deal ***h*** with me, Abner, and
3:35 May God deal ***h*** with me and worse
19:13 too? May God deal ***h*** with me and worse
2 Chronicles
10:13 the people ***h***. He ignored the
Job
39:16 treats her young ***h*** as if they were
Proverbs
18:23 for help, but the wealthy answer ***h***.
Matthew
17:18 Then Jesus spoke ***h*** to the demon. And it came out
Luke
3:19 been criticized ***h*** by John because
4:39 her and spoke ***h*** to the fever, and
20:47 prayers. They will be judged most ***h***."
23:40 criminal spoke ***h*** to him, "Don't
2 Corinthians
13:10 won't need to act ***h*** when I'm with you

HARVEST

Genesis
8:22 seedtime and ***h***, cold and hot,
30:14 During the wheat ***h***, Reuben found some
Exodus
23:16 Observe the ***H*** Festival for the early
34:22 of the wheat ***h***, and the
Leviticus
19:9 When you ***h*** your land's produce, you
23:22 When you ***h*** your land's produce, you
25:5 You must not ***h*** the secondary growth of
Numbers
18:12 the grain's first ***h*** that they give to
Deuteronomy
16:9 from the beginning of the grain ***h***.
24:19 are reaping the ***h*** of your field and
28:39 drink any wine or ***h*** the grapes
Joshua
3:15 way it does during the entire ***h*** season.
Ruth
1:22 at the beginning of the barley ***h***.
Job
4:8 who plow sin and sow trouble will ***h*** it.
31:12 to the underworld, uprooting all my ***h***.
Psalms
67:6 has yielded its ***h***. God blesses us—
107:37 and vineyards and obtain a fruitful ***h***.
126:5 tears reap the ***h*** with joyful
Proverbs
6:8 in summer; gathers its provisions at ***h***.
10:5 son sleeps right through the ***h***.
20:4 during winter; at ***h*** they look but
22:8 injustice will ***h*** evil; the rod of
25:13 of snow on a ***h*** day are reliable
26:1 summer or rain at ***h***, so honor isn't
Jeremiah
8:20 The ***h*** is past, the summer has ended,
51:33 In a little while her ***h*** will come.
Joel
3:13 sickle, for the ***h*** is ripe. Go and
Matthew
6:26 don't sow seed or ***h*** grain or gather
9:37 The size of the ***h*** is bigger than
13:39 is the devil. The ***h*** is the end of the
Luke
10:2 to them, "The ***h*** is bigger than
John
4:35 the fields are already ripe for the ***h***.
Galatians
6:7 A person will ***h*** what they plant.
Revelation
14:15 to reap the ***h***, for the time to

HASHABIAH

1 Chronicles
6:45 son of ***H*** son of Amaziah son of Hilkia
2 Chronicles
35:9 along with ***H***, Jeiel, and
Ezra
8:19 also brought us ***H*** and with him
Nehemiah
3:17 and next to him ***H***, ruler of half

HATE

Genesis
37:5 which made them ***h*** him even more.
Exodus
20:5 fourth generations of those who ***h*** me.
Leviticus
19:17 You must not ***h*** your fellow Israelite in
26:17 those who ***h*** you will rule

Numbers
10:35 scatter, and those who ***h*** you flee."
Deuteronomy
5:9 fourth generations of those who ***h*** me.
7:15 but will inflict them on all who ***h*** you.
19:11 if someone does ***h*** a neighbor and
30:7 and on those who ***h*** you and chase you.
32:43 in kind those who ***h*** him; he will
33:11 so that those who ***h*** him can't fight
Judges
14:16 and said, "You ***h*** me! You don't
2 Samuel
19:6 loving those who ***h*** you and hating
1 Kings
22:8 but I ***h*** him because he
2 Chronicles
1:11 over those who ***h*** you, or even a
18:7 but I ***h*** him because he
19:2 loved those who ***h*** the LORD? This is
Job
8:22 Those who ***h*** you will be clothed with
Psalms
5:5 in your sight; you ***h*** all evildoers;
45:7 righteousness and ***h*** wickedness. No
97:10 love the LORD, ***h*** evil! God guards
119:104 that's why I ***h*** every false path.
119:163 I ***h***, I absolutely despise, what is
139:21 Don't I ***h*** everyone who hates you? Don't
Proverbs
1:22 mocking dear, and fools ***h*** knowledge?
8:13 the LORD is to ***h*** evil. I hate
9:8 or they will ***h*** you; correct the
13:5 The righteous ***h*** false words, but the
25:17 they'll get fed up with you and ***h*** you.
29:10 Murderous people ***h*** the innocent, and
Ecclesiastes
9:1 both love and ***h***. People don't
Isaiah
61:8 love justice; I ***h*** robbery and
Jeremiah
44:4 do these detestable things that I ***h***."
Ezekiel
23:28 to those whom you ***h*** and from whom you recoil
35:6 Because you don't ***h*** bloodshed,
Amos
5:15 ***H*** evil, love good, and establish
Matthew
5:43 love your neighbor and ***h*** your enemy.
Luke
6:22 you when people ***h*** you, reject you,
6:27 enemies. Do good to those who ***h*** you.
14:26 to me and doesn't ***h*** father and
16:13 Either you will ***h*** the one and love
John
7:7 The world can't ***h*** you. It hates me
Romans
7:15 do. Instead, I do the thing that I ***h***.
12:9 pretending. ***H*** evil, and hold on

HATED
Genesis
37:4 brothers, they ***h*** him and couldn't
Proverbs
1:29 because they ***h*** knowledge and didn't
Ecclesiastes
2:17 So I ***h*** life, because the things that
John
15:18 hates you, know that it ***h*** me first.
17:14 and the world ***h*** them, because
Romans
9:13 written, I loved Jacob, but I ***h*** Esau.
Hebrews
1:9 righteousness and ***h*** lawless behavior.

HATES
Deuteronomy
16:22 the LORD your God ***h*** such things.
32:41 I'll punish in kind everyone who ***h*** me.
Proverbs
6:16 that the LORD ***h***, seven things
26:28 A lying tongue ***h*** those it crushes; a
John
15:19 the world. This is why the world ***h*** you.
15:23 Whoever ***h*** me also hates the Father
Ephesians
5:29 No one ever ***h*** his own body, but feeds

HAZAEL
1 Kings
19:15 Damascus and anoint ***H*** as king of Aram.
19:17 from the sword of ***H***, Jehu will kill.
2 Kings
8:8 the king said to ***H***, "Take a gift
8:9 So ***H*** went out to meet Elisha. He took
2 Chronicles
22:5 Aram's King ***H*** at Ramoth-gilead,
22:6 with Aram's King ***H***. Then Judah's
Amos
1:4 on the house of ***H***; it will devour

HAZOR
Joshua
11:10 time. He captured ***H*** and struck down

HEAD
Genesis
3:15 will strike your ***h***, but you will
28:18 had put near his ***h***, set it up as a
48:18 son. Put your right hand on his ***h***."
Numbers
6:5 be used on the ***h*** until the period
6:9 defiling the ***h*** of the nazirite,
Deuteronomy
28:13 will make you the ***h*** of things, not
Judges
16:17 ever touched my ***h***, because I've
1 Samuel
1:11 life. No razor will ever touch his ***h***."
9:2 and he stood ***h*** and shoulders
17:51 the Philistine's ***h*** with the sword.
31:9 cut off Saul's ***h*** and stripped off
2 Samuel
18:9 tree. Absalom's ***h*** got caught in the
20:22 they cut off the ***h*** of Sheba,
Psalms
23:5 You bathe my ***h*** in oil; my cup is
133:2 poured over the ***h***, running down
Proverbs
1:9 wreath on your ***h***, and beads for
4:9 wreath on your ***h***; she will give

HEAD [cont.]

10:6 cover the ***h*** of the righteous,
Isaiah
59:17 salvation on his ***h***, putting on
Jeremiah
9:1 If only my ***h*** were a spring of water
48:37 Every ***h*** is shaved, every beard is cut
Ezekiel
8:3 by the hair of my ***h***. A wind lifted me
Daniel
2:32 The statue's ***h*** was made of pure gold;
7:20 ten horns on its ***h***, and the other
Matthew
8:20 Human One has no place to lay his ***h***."
10:30 the hairs of your ***h*** are all counted.
14:8 Give me the ***h*** of John the
27:29 and put it on his ***h***. They put a stick
John
19:2 and put it on his ***h***, and dressed him
Romans
12:20 pile burning coals of fire upon his ***h***.
1 Corinthians
11:3 to know that the ***h*** of every man is
11:4 with his ***h*** covered shames
11:5 with her ***h*** uncovered
11:6 doesn't cover her ***h***, then she should
Ephesians
1:22 feet and made him ***h*** of everything in
5:23 A husband is the ***h*** of his wife like
Colossians
1:18 He is the ***h*** of the body, the church,
Revelation
1:14 His ***h*** and hair were white as white
10:1 rainbow over his ***h***. His face was
12:1 and a crown of twelve stars on her ***h***.
14:14 gold crown on his ***h*** and a sharp
19:12 flame, and on his ***h*** were many royal

HEADS

Psalms
22:7 fun of me—they gape, shaking their ***h***:
24:7 lift up your ***h***! Ancient doors:
74:14 Leviathan's ***h***. You gave it to
140:9 Let the ***h*** of the people surrounding me
Proverbs
25:22 coals on their ***h***, and the LORD
Isaiah
35:10 joy upon their ***h***. Happiness and
51:11 joy upon their ***h***. Let happiness
Daniel
7:6 beast had four ***h***. Authority was
Matthew
27:39 by insulted Jesus, shaking their ***h***
Luke
21:28 and raise your ***h*** because your
Revelation
4:4 and had gold crowns on their ***h***.
12:3 with seven ***h*** and ten horns,
17:9 mind. The seven ***h*** are seven

HEAL → HEAL THE SICK, I WILL HEAL

Numbers
12:13 cried to the LORD, "God, please ***h*** her!"
Deuteronomy
32:39 but now I will ***h***. There's no
2 Kings
20:5 now I'm going to ***h*** you. Three days
20:8 the LORD will ***h*** me and that I'll
2 Chronicles
7:14 forgive their sin, and ***h*** their land.
Job
5:18 binds up; he strikes, but his hands ***h***.
Psalms
6:2 I'm frail. ***H*** me, LORD, because
41:4 have mercy on me! ***H*** me because I have
Isaiah
19:22 who will hear their pleas and ***h*** them.
57:18 ways, but I will ***h*** them. I will
57:19 near, and I will ***h*** them, says the
Jeremiah
3:22 and I will ***h*** your rebellion.
17:14 ***H*** me, LORD, and I'll be healed. Save me
30:17 and I will ***h*** your wounds,
33:6 but now I will ***h*** and mend them. I will
Lamentations
2:13 is as vast as the sea. Who can ***h*** you?
Ezekiel
30:21 so that it might ***h***, nor has it been
34:4 the weak, ***h*** the sick, bind up
Hosea
5:13 But he could not ***h*** them; nor could
6:1 us and will ***h*** us; he has struck
7:1 When I would ***h*** Israel, the evil acts of
14:4 I will ***h*** their faithlessness; I will
Zechariah
11:16 seek the young or ***h*** the broken. He
Matthew
8:7 Jesus responded, "I'll come and ***h*** him.
10:1 them out and to ***h*** every disease and
10:8 ***H*** the sick, raise the dead, cleanse
12:10 allow a person to ***h*** on the Sabbath?"
13:15 hearts and lives that I may ***h*** them.
17:16 disciples, but they couldn't ***h*** him."
Mark
3:2 to see if he would ***h*** on the Sabbath.
8:22 and begged him to touch and ***h*** him.
Luke
4:23 to me. 'Doctor, ***h*** yourself. Do here
5:17 power of the Lord was with Jesus to ***h***.
6:7 see if he would ***h*** on the Sabbath.
7:3 to ask him to come and ***h*** his servant.
8:43 on doctors, but no one could ***h*** her.
9:1 over all demons and to ***h*** sicknesses.
9:2 God's kingdom and to ***h*** the sick.
10:9 ***H*** the sick who are there, and say to
John
4:47 he would come and ***h*** his son, for his
9:26 he do to you? How did he ***h*** your eyes?"
10:21 Can a demon ***h*** the eyes of
12:40 lives around—and I would ***h*** them.
Acts
28:27 hearts and lives that I may ***h*** them.
James
5:15 from faith will ***h*** the sick, for the

HEALED → HEALED YOU

Leviticus
13:37 the scabies has ***h***. The person is
14:3 disease has been ***h*** of the infection,
14:48 clean because the infection has been ***h***.
1 Samuel
6:3 Then you will be ***h***, and it will
2 Chronicles
30:20 LORD heard Hezekiah and ***h*** the people.

Psalms
30:2 out to you for help, and you ***h*** me.
107:20 the order and ***h*** them; he rescued
Isaiah
6:10 with their minds, and turn, and be ***h***."
53:5 made us whole; by his wounds we are ***h***.
58:8 and you will be ***h*** quickly. Your own
Jeremiah
17:14 LORD, and I'll be ***h***. Save me and I'll
Hosea
11:3 but they did not know that I ***h*** them.
Matthew
4:23 the kingdom and ***h*** every disease and
8:8 say the word and my servant will be ***h***.
8:13 And his servant was ***h*** that very moment.
9:21 If I only touch his robe I'll be ***h***.
12:15 crowds followed him, and he ***h*** them all.
12:22 to speak. Jesus ***h*** him so that he
14:14 for them and ***h*** those who were
15:28 And right then her daughter was ***h***.
19:2 crowds followed him, and he ***h*** them.
21:14 to Jesus in the temple, and he ***h*** them.
Mark
6:5 hands on a few sick people and ***h*** them.
6:56 Everyone who touched him was ***h***.
10:52 your faith has ***h*** you." At once, he
Luke
4:40 his hands on each of them, he ***h*** them.
5:15 listen and to be ***h*** from their
6:18 him and to be ***h*** from their
7:7 say the word and my servant will be ***h***.
7:21 Right then, Jesus ***h*** many of their
8:2 who had been ***h*** of evil spirits
8:47 him and how she had been immediately ***h***.
8:48 your faith has ***h*** you," Jesus said.
8:50 just keep trusting, and she will be ***h***."
9:11 kingdom, and ***h*** those who were
9:42 unclean spirit, ***h*** the child, and
13:14 that Jesus had ***h*** on the Sabbath,
17:15 that he had been ***h***, returned and
17:19 Get up and go. Your faith has ***h*** you."
18:42 your sight! Your faith has ***h*** you."
22:51 He touched the slave's ear and ***h*** him.
John
5:10 man who had been ***h***, "It's the
9:17 him, since he ***h*** your eyes?" He
11:37 of them said, "He ***h*** the eyes of the
Acts
4:9 a sick person, a good deed that ***h*** him?
14:9 and saw that he believed he could be ***h***.
28:8 He placed his hand on him and ***h*** him.
Hebrews
12:13 lame, it will be ***h*** rather than
James
5:16 that you may be ***h***. The prayer of
1 Peter
2:24 do with sin. By his wounds you were ***h***.
Revelation
13:3 deadly wound was ***h***. So the whole
13:12 first beast, whose fatal wound was ***h***.

HEALED YOU

Mt 9:22; Mk 5:34; 10:52; Lk 8:48; 17:19; 18:42

HEALING

Proverbs
4:22 find them, and ***h*** for their entire
13:17 trouble, but a reliable one brings ***h***.
16:24 sweet to the taste and ***h*** to the bones.
17:22 heart helps ***h***, but a broken
29:1 will be suddenly broken, beyond ***h***.
Ecclesiastes
3:3 and a time for ***h***, a time for
Isaiah
19:22 striking and then ***h***. They will return
Jeremiah
8:15 for a time of ***h***, but found only
8:18 No ***h***, only grief; my heart is broken
14:19 it; for a time of ***h***, only to be
15:18 so far beyond ***h***? You have become
Ezekiel
47:12 be for eating, their leaves for ***h***."
Malachi
4:2 revering my name; ***h*** will be in its
Acts
4:22 this sign of ***h*** was over 40 years
10:38 doing good and ***h*** everyone
1 Corinthians
12:9 Spirit, gifts of ***h*** to another in the
Revelation
22:2 leaves are for the ***h*** of the nations.

HEALTHY

Matthew
6:22 if your eye is ***h***, your whole body
9:12 it, he said, "***H*** people don't need

HEAR → HEAR HIS VOICE, HEAR THE LORD'S WORD

Numbers
7:89 LORD, he would ***h*** the voice
Joshua
6:5 As soon as you ***h*** that trumpet
7:9 of the land will ***h*** of it. They will
2 Kings
7:1 Elisha said, "***H*** the LORD's word! This
Psalms
39:12 ***H*** my prayer, LORD! Listen closely to my
51:8 Let me ***h*** joy and celebration again; let
54:2 God! ***H*** my prayer; listen to the words
94:9 the ear, can't he ***h***? The one who
Ecclesiastes
7:21 say, so you don't ***h*** your servant
Isaiah
1:10 ***H*** the LORD's word. Listen to our God's
21:3 too bent over to ***h***, too dismayed to
29:18 The deaf will ***h*** the words of a
30:21 left, you will ***h*** a word that comes
59:1 save, nor are his ears too dull to ***h***,
65:24 they are still speaking, I will ***h***.
Jeremiah
5:21 but don't see and ears but don't ***h***.
Ezekiel
33:7 Whenever you ***h*** me speaking, you
34:7 So now shepherds, ***h*** the LORD's word
Daniel
3:5 When you ***h*** the sound of the horn, pipe,
Hosea
4:1 ***H*** the LORD's word, people of Israel;

Joel
1:2 ***H*** this, elders, pay attention, everyone
Amos
3:1 ***H*** this word that the LORD has spoken
Matthew
11:5 who were deaf now ***h***. Those who were
11:15 Let the person who has ears, ***h***
13:17 what you see and ***h*** what you hear,
Mark
13:7 When you ***h*** of wars and reports of wars,
Luke
7:22 who were deaf now ***h***. Those who were
John
5:25 the dead will ***h*** the voice of
8:43 because you can't really ***h*** my words.
Romans
10:14 And how can they ***h*** without a
James
1:23 Those who ***h*** but don't do the word are
Revelation
3:20 knocking. If any ***h*** my voice and open

HEAR HIS VOICE

Dt 4:36; Mt 12:19; Jn 5:28; Ac 22:14; Heb 3:7; 3:15; 4:7

HEAR THE LORD'S WORD

2Ki 7:1; Is 1:10; Jer 9:20; 22:29; 34:4; Eze 13:2; 16:35; 34:7, 9; 36:1; 37:4; Hos 4:1; Am 7:16; Ac 13:44

HEARD → HEARD YOUR PRAYER

Genesis
3:8 breeze, they ***h*** the sound of the
21:17 God ***h*** the boy's cries, and God's
Exodus
2:24 God ***h*** their cry of grief, and God
6:5 I've also ***h*** the cry of grief of the
16:7 LORD have been ***h***. Who are we? Why
Numbers
12:2 also spoken through us?" The LORD ***h*** it.
14:27 against me? I've ***h*** the Israelites'
Deuteronomy
4:32 anything like it ever been ***h*** of before?
Psalms
18:6 God for help. God ***h*** my voice from his
62:11 I myself have ***h***: that strength
78:59 God ***h*** and became enraged; he rejected
141:6 my words will be ***h*** because they are
Isaiah
40:21 know? Haven't you ***h***? Wasn't it
40:28 know? Haven't you ***h***? The LORD is the
66:8 Whoever ***h*** of such a thing? Whoever saw
Jeremiah
18:13 Have you ever ***h*** anything like
Ezekiel
10:5 wings could be ***h*** as far as the
33:5 They ***h*** the sound of the trumpet but
Daniel
8:13 I then ***h*** a certain holy one speaking. A
10:9 Then I ***h*** the sound of the man's words.
12:8 I ***h*** it, but I didn't understand it. "My
Matthew
5:21 You have ***h*** that it was said to those
Luke
2:18 Everyone who ***h*** it was amazed at what
Acts
2:6 When they ***h*** this sound, a crowd
10:44 Spirit fell on everyone who ***h*** the word.
Romans
10:14 they haven't ***h*** of? And how can
15:21 and those who hadn't ***h*** will understand.
1 Corinthians
2:9 seen, or ear has ***h***, or that haven't
2 Corinthians
12:4 and that he ***h*** unspeakable words
1 Thessalonians
2:13 word that you ***h*** from us, you
Hebrews
4:2 the message they ***h*** didn't help them
2 Peter
1:18 We ourselves ***h*** this voice from heaven
2:8 of the immoral actions he saw and ***h***.)
1 John
1:3 we have seen and ***h***, we also announce
3:11 message that you ***h*** from the
4:3 which you have ***h*** is coming and is
2 John
1:6 command that you ***h*** from the
Revelation
1:10 Lord's day, and I ***h*** behind me a loud
21:3 I ***h*** a loud voice from the throne say,
22:8 am the one who ***h*** and saw these

HEARD YOUR PRAYER

1Ki 9:3; 2Ki 19:20; 20:5; 2Ch 7:12; Is 38:5

HEARING

Numbers
11:1 in the LORD's ***h***, the LORD heard
Deuteronomy
31:11 aloud, in the ***h*** of all the people.
Amos
8:11 for water, but of ***h*** the LORD 's words.
Matthew
13:15 become hard of ***h***, and they've shut
17:6 ***H*** this, the disciples fell on their
27:47 After ***h*** him, some standing there said,

HEARS

Psalms
116:1 LORD because he ***h*** my requests for
Matthew
7:24 Everybody who ***h*** these words of mine
28:14 if the governor ***h*** about this, we
Revelation
22:17 Let the one who ***h*** say, 'Come!' And
22:18 to everyone who ***h*** the words of the

HEART → ALL MY HEART, HEART IS RIGHT, WHOSE HEART IS RIGHT

Deuteronomy
6:5 God with all your ***h***, all your being,
8:5 Know then in your ***h*** that the LORD your
Joshua
22:5 serve him with all your ***h*** and being."
23:14 with all your ***h*** and being that
1 Samuel
10:9 him a different ***h***, and all these
12:20 LORD. Serve the LORD with all your ***h***.
16:7 eyes, but the LORD sees into the ***h***."

25:37 Nabal's ***h*** failed inside
1 Chronicles
22:13 and brave. Don't be afraid or lose ***h***!
2 Chronicles
6:38 with all their ***h*** and all their
7:16 My eyes and my ***h*** will always be
Psalms
16:9 That's why my ***h*** celebrates and my mood is joyous
17:3 have examined my ***h***, testing me at
19:14 meditations of my ***h*** be pleasing to
20:4 what is in your ***h*** and fulfill all
21:2 him what his ***h*** desires; you
24:4 hands and a pure ***h***; the one who
26:2 to the test! Purify my mind and my ***h***.
27:3 against me, my ***h*** won't be afraid.
31:24 be strong and let your ***h*** take courage.
33:21 Our ***h*** rejoices in God because we trust
37:4 and he will give what your ***h*** asks.
38:8 I groan because of my miserable ***h***.
51:10 Create a clean ***h*** for me, God; put a
55:4 My ***h*** pounds in my chest because death's terrors
55:21 war is in his ***h***; though his words
61:2 When my ***h*** is weak, I cry out to you
66:18 evil in my ***h***, my Lord would
73:1 to Israel, to those who are pure of ***h***.
73:13 I've kept my ***h*** pure for no good
73:21 When my ***h*** was bitter, when I was all
73:26 My body and my ***h*** fail, but God is my
74:12 salvation happen in the ***h*** of the earth!
77:6 meditate with my ***h*** at night; I
78:8 generation whose ***h*** wasn't set firm
78:72 them with a ***h*** of integrity; he
83:5 a single-minded ***h***; they make a
84:2 courtyards. My ***h*** and my body will
86:11 truth. Make my ***h*** focused only on
89:50 how I bear in my ***h*** all the insults
90:12 our days so we can have a wise ***h***.
97:11 joy too for those whose ***h*** is right.
101:2 will walk with a ***h*** of integrity in
101:4 A corrupt ***h*** will be far from me. I
111:1 LORD with all my ***h*** in the company of
119:7 to you with a ***h*** that does right
119:10 you with all my ***h***. Don't let me
119:11 word close, in my ***h***, so that I won't
119:32 because you give my ***h*** insight.
119:34 Instruction and keep it with all my ***h***.
119:36 Turn my ***h*** to your laws, not to greedy
119:80 Let my ***h*** be blameless in your statutes
119:145 out with all my ***h***: "Lord, answer me
138:1 you with all my ***h***, LORD. I sing
139:23 God! Look at my ***h***! Put me to the
141:4 Don't let my ***h*** turn aside to evil
Proverbs
3:1 Let your ***h*** guard my commands
3:3 write them on the tablet of your ***h***.
3:5 with all your ***h***; don't rely on
4:4 to me: "Let your ***h*** hold on to my
5:12 How my ***h*** despised
6:18 a ***h*** set on wicked plans, feet that run
6:21 Bind them on your ***h*** for all time;
7:3 write them on the tablet of your ***h***.
7:25 Don't turn your ***h*** to her ways; don't
8:5 are naive. Take this to ***h***, you fools.
10:20 silver, but the ***h*** of the wicked
11:20 detests a crooked ***h***, but he favors
12:20 Deceit is in the ***h*** of those who plan
12:23 but the ***h*** of fools
13:12 delayed makes the ***h*** sick; longing
14:10 The ***h*** knows its own distress; another
14:13 The ***h*** feels pain even in laughter, and
14:33 an understanding ***h***, but it's not
15:13 A joyful ***h*** brightens one's face, but a
15:14 An understanding ***h*** seeks knowledge; but
15:15 hard, but a happy ***h*** has a continual
15:28 The righteous ***h*** reflects before
16:1 the plans of the ***h***, but the answer
17:3 for gold, but the LORD tests the ***h***.
17:22 A joyful ***h*** helps healing, but a broken
20:5 waters of the ***h***; those with
21:1 The king's ***h*** is like channels of water
21:2 own eyes, but the LORD weighs the ***h***.
21:4 eyes, an arrogant ***h***, and the lamp of
22:11 who love a pure ***h***—their speech is
22:15 up in a child's ***h***; the rod of
23:15 My child, if your ***h*** is wise, then my
23:17 Don't let your ***h*** envy sinners, but fear the LORD
23:33 things, and your ***h*** will speak
24:17 they stumble, don't let your ***h*** be glad,
24:32 and took it to ***h***; I saw it and
25:20 to a troubled ***h*** is like taking
26:23 lips and an evil ***h*** are like silver
26:25 seven horrible things are in their ***h***.
27:9 incense make the ***h*** glad, and the
27:11 and make my ***h*** glad, so I can
27:19 the face, so the ***h*** reflects one
31:11 entrusts his ***h*** to her, and with
Ecclesiastes
2:10 I refused my ***h*** no pleasure.
7:2 and the living should take it to ***h***.
8:5 and the wise ***h*** knows the right
9:3 the human ***h*** is full of evil;
11:9 are young! Your ***h*** should make you
Song of Songs
4:9 have captured my ***h***, my sister, my
8:6 a seal over your ***h***, as a seal upon
Isaiah
57:15 reviving the ***h*** of those who have
66:14 see this, your ***h*** will rejoice;
Jeremiah
3:10 me with all her ***h*** but only
4:14 Cleanse your ***h*** of evil, Jerusalem, that
9:26 of Israel are uncircumcised in ***h***.
17:9 The most cunning ***h***—it's beyond help.
24:7 will give them a ***h*** to know me, for I
29:13 me with all your ***h***, you will find me.
32:39 give them one ***h*** and one mind so
Nahum
2:10 laid waste! The ***h*** grows faint and
Matthew
5:28 already committed adultery in his ***h***.
6:21 treasure is, there your ***h*** will be also.
18:35 your brother or sister from your ***h***."
22:37 God with all your ***h***, with all your
Mark
7:21 from the human ***h***, that evil
Luke
15:10 sinner who changes both ***h*** and life."
Acts
2:26 Therefore, my ***h*** was glad and my tongue
5:31 to change its ***h*** and life and to

Romans
10:8 mouth and in your ***h*** (that is, the
10:10 Trusting with the ***h*** leads to
1 Corinthians
7:37 in his own ***h*** not to marry the
2 Timothy
2:22 who confess the Lord with a clean ***h***.
4:8 have set their ***h*** on waiting for
Revelation
2:21 to change her ***h*** and life, but she
18:7 and grief. In her ***h*** she says, 'I sit

HEART IS RIGHT

Ps 7:10; 11:2, 7; 36:10; 37:37; 94:15; 97:11

HEARTS → CHANGE THEIR HEARTS AND LIVES, CHANGE YOUR HEARTS AND LIVES, CHANGED THEIR HEARTS AND LIVES

Leviticus
26:36 despair into the ***h*** of those of you
26:41 uncircumcised ***h*** are humbled and
Deuteronomy
10:16 circumcise your ***h*** and stop being so
30:6 circumcise your ***h*** and the hearts of
Joshua
2:11 this and our ***h*** turned to water.
5:1 over. Then their ***h*** melted. They lost
2 Samuel
15:6 Absalom stole the ***h*** of the Israelites.
19:14 he won over the ***h*** of everyone in
Job
1:5 God in their ***h***. Job did this
8:10 will words not proceed from their ***h***?
Psalms
7:9 are the one who examines ***h*** and minds.
32:11 All you whose ***h*** are right, sing
33:15 made all their ***h***, the one who
81:12 their wilful ***h***; they followed
95:10 have twisted ***h***. They don't know
105:25 whose ***h*** God changed so they hated his
Proverbs
14:14 Rebellious ***h*** receive satisfaction from
15:7 but the ***h*** of fools have
17:20 with crooked ***h*** won't prosper,
19:3 way, but their ***h*** rage against the
24:2 Their ***h*** are focused on violence, and
28:14 but those whose ***h*** are hard fall
31:6 and wine to those whose ***h*** are bitter.
Jeremiah
31:33 them on their ***h***. I will be their
Lamentations
3:41 lift up our ***h*** and hands to God
Ezekiel
11:19 remove the stony ***h*** from their bodies
32:9 will trouble the ***h*** of many peoples
Hosea
4:8 they set their ***h*** on evil things.
Matthew
5:8 who have pure ***h***, because they
15:8 lips, but their ***h*** are far away from
19:8 because your ***h*** are unyielding.
Luke
1:17 He will turn the ***h*** of fathers back
12:1 the mismatch between their ***h*** and lives.
16:15 God knows your ***h***. What is highly
24:32 Weren't our ***h*** on fire when he
Romans
1:21 and their foolish ***h*** were darkened.
2:15 written on their ***h***, and their
5:5 poured out in our ***h*** through the Holy
8:27 one who searches ***h*** knows how the
16:18 They deceive the ***h*** of innocent
Galatians
4:6 his Son into our ***h***, crying, "Abba,
Ephesians
3:17 will live in your ***h*** through faith. As
4:18 of their ignorance and their closed ***h***.
5:19 and make music to the Lord in your ***h***;
Hebrews
3:8 have stubborn ***h*** as they did in
3:10 I said, "Their ***h*** always go off
8:10 them on their ***h***. I will be their
10:16 my laws in their ***h*** and write them on
10:22 us, since our ***h*** are sprinkled
James
4:8 Purify your ***h***, you double-minded
5:5 have stuffed your ***h*** in preparation
2 Peter
1:19 and the morning star rises in your ***h***.
2:14 weak. They have ***h*** trained in greed.

HEAT

Psalms
19:6 at the other. Nothing escapes its ***h***.
Revelation
7:16 sun or scorching ***h*** will beat down on
16:9 burned by intense ***h***, and they cursed

HEAVEN → DOWN FROM HEAVEN, GOD OF HEAVEN, HEAVEN AND EARTH, HEAVEN AND ON EARTH, KINGDOM OF HEAVEN, VOICE FROM HEAVEN

2 Samuel
22:14 thundered from ***h***; the Most High
2 Kings
2:11 Then Elijah went to ***h*** in a windstorm.
Job
16:19 witness stands in ***h***; my advocate is
Psalms
2:4 one who rules in ***h*** laughs; my Lord
8:1 You made your glory higher than ***h***!
11:4 His throne is in ***h***. His eyes see
18:13 LORD thundered in ***h***; the Most High
57:3 sends orders from ***h*** and saves me,
57:5 God, higher than ***h***! Let your glory
57:10 is as high as ***h***; your
57:11 God, higher than ***h***! Let your glory
68:8 earth shook! Yes, ***h*** poured down
68:33 who rides through ***h***, the most ancient
73:9 to speak against ***h***! Their tongues
78:69 like the highest ***h*** and like the
89:2 You establish your faithfulness in ***h***."
89:5 ***H*** thanks you for your wondrous acts,
89:11 ***H*** is yours! The earth too! The world
89:29 His throne will last as long as ***h*** does.
96:5 but it is the LORD who created ***h***!
96:11 Let ***h*** celebrate! Let the earth rejoice!
97:6 ***H*** has proclaimed God's righteousness,
103:11 as high as ***h*** is above the
103:19 his throne in ***h***, and his kingdom
105:40 God filled them full with food from ***h***.
108:4 is higher than ***h***; your
108:5 God, higher than ***h***! Let your glory

115:16 The highest ***h*** belongs to the LORD, but
119:89 word, LORD, stands firm in ***h*** forever!
123:1 raise my eyes to you—you who rule ***h***.
148:1 the LORD from ***h***! Praise God on
148:4 You highest ***h***, praise God! Do the
148:13 Only God's majesty is over earth and ***h***.
Proverbs
30:4 has gone up to ***h*** and come down?
Ecclesiastes
2:3 days that human beings have under ***h***.
5:2 because God is in ***h***, but you are on
Jeremiah
7:18 for the Queen of ***H***. And to offend me
44:17 to the Queen of ***H*** and pour out
44:18 to the Queen of ***H*** and pouring drink
Daniel
7:2 the four winds of ***h*** churning the
8:8 came up toward the four winds of ***h***.
12:7 both hands to ***h***: "For one set
Zechariah
2:6 the four winds of ***h***, says the LORD.
Matthew
3:2 lives! Here comes the kingdom of ***h***!"
3:17 A voice from ***h*** said, "This is my Son
5:3 because the kingdom of ***h*** is theirs.
5:20 you will never enter the kingdom of ***h***.
6:9 Father who is in ***h***, uphold the
10:33 will deny before my Father who is in ***h***.
13:11 of the kingdom of ***h***, but you have.
19:23 rich person to enter the kingdom of ***h***.
23:22 who swear by ***h*** swear by God's
28:18 all authority in ***h*** and on earth.
Mark
1:10 water, Jesus saw ***h*** splitting open
1:11 was a voice from ***h***: "You are my Son,
7:34 Looking into ***h***, Jesus sighed deeply
8:11 test him, they asked for a sign from ***h***.
13:32 not the angels in ***h*** and not the Son.
16:19 lifted up into ***h*** and sat down on
Luke
9:54 call fire down from ***h*** to consume them?"
10:18 saw Satan fall from ***h*** like lightning.
10:20 that your names are written in ***h***."
John
1:32 coming down from ***h*** like a dove, and
3:13 has gone up to ***h*** except the one
6:41 I am the bread that came down from ***h***."
12:28 a voice came from ***h***, "I have
17:1 he looked up to ***h*** and said,
Acts
1:2 was taken up into ***h***. Before he was
1:10 staring toward ***h***, suddenly two men
7:56 Look! I can see ***h*** on display and
11:9 The voice from ***h*** spoke a second time,
2 Corinthians
12:2 up into the third ***h*** fourteen years
Hebrews
12:23 are registered in ***h***, to God the judge
12:26 shake not only the earth but ***h*** also.
James
5:12 by ***h*** nor earth, nor by
2 Peter
1:18 this voice from ***h*** while we were
3:5 by God's word, ***h*** and earth were
3:7 by the same word, ***h*** and earth are now
3:13 waiting for a new ***h*** and a new earth,
Revelation
4:1 been opened in ***h***. The first voice
5:13 every creature in ***h*** and on earth and
11:19 God's temple in ***h*** was opened, and
12:1 sign appeared in ***h***: a woman clothed
12:7 there was war in ***h***: Michael and his
15:5 and the temple in ***h***—that is, the tent
19:1 a huge crowd in ***h***. They said,
19:11 Then I saw ***h*** opened, and there was a
20:1 coming down from ***h***, holding in his
21:1 Then I saw a new ***h*** and a new earth, for
21:2 down out of ***h*** from God, made
21:10 coming down out of ***h*** from God.

HEAVEN AND EARTH
Gn 14:19; 14:22; 24:3; Dt 4:26; 30:19; 31:28; 2Ki 19:15; 2Ch 2:12; Ezr 5:11; Ps 69:34; 113:6; 115:15; 121:2; 124:8; 134:3; 146:6; Is 37:16; Jer 23:24; 32:17; 33:25; Mt 5:18; 11:25; 24:35; Mk 13:31; Lk 10:21; 16:17; 21:33; Ac 17:24; 2Pt 3:5; 3:7; Rev 14:7

HEAVEN AND ON EARTH
1Ch 29:11; Dn 6:27; Mt 28:18; Lk 2:14; Rev 5:13

HEAVENLY → GOD OF HEAVENLY FORCES, HEAVENLY BODIES, HEAVENLY CREATURES, HEAVENLY FATHER, HEAVENLY FORCES, LORD OF HEAVENLY FORCES, YOUR HEAVENLY FATHER
1 Chronicles
21:1 A ***h*** Adversary arose against Israel and
Psalms
20:6 one from his ***h*** sanctuary,
Daniel
7:13 coming with the ***h*** clouds. He came
Matthew
24:30 One coming in the ***h*** clouds with power
24:36 come, not the ***h*** angels and not
Mark
11:30 John's baptism of ***h*** or of human
11:31 we say, 'It's of ***h*** origin,' he'll
14:62 Almighty and coming on the ***h*** clouds."
John
3:12 believe if I tell you about ***h*** things?
Acts
26:19 I wasn't disobedient to that ***h*** vision.
Hebrews
3:1 partners in the ***h*** calling, think
8:5 and shadow of the ***h*** meeting tent.
12:22 the living God, ***h*** Jerusalem, to
James
1:17 creator of the ***h*** lights, in whose

HEAVENLY BODIES
Dt 4:19; 17:3; 2Ki 17:16; 23:4, 5; Mt 24:29; Mk 13:25; Lk 21:26; 1Co 15:40

HEAVENLY CREATURES
Ex 25:18; 25:19, 20, 22; 26:1, 31; 36:8, 35; 37:7, 8, 9; 1Sa 4:4; 2Sa 22:11; Ps 18:10; 80:1; 99:1

HEAVENLY FATHER
Mt 5:48; 6:14, 26, 32; 7:11; 15:13; 18:35; Lk 11:13

HEAVENLY FORCES
1Sa 1:3; 1:11; 4:4; 15:2; 17:45; 2Sa 5:10; 6:2, 18; 7:8, 26, 27; 1Ki 18:15; 19:10, 14; 22:19; 2Ki 3:14; 19:31; 1Ch 11:9; 17:7, 24; 2Ch 18:18; Neh 9:6; Ps 24:10; 46:7, 11; 48:8; 59:5; 69:6; 80:4, 7, 14, 19; 84:1, 3, 8, 12; 89:8; 103:21; 148:2; Is 1:9; 1:24; 2:12; 3:1, 15; 5:7, 9, 16, 24; 6:3, 5; 8:13, 18; 9:7, 13, 19; 10:16, 23, 24, 26, 33; 13:4, 13; 14:22, 23, 24, 27; 17:3; 18:7; 19:4, 12, 16, 17, 18, 20, 25; 21:10; 22:5, 12, 14, 15, 25; 23:9; 24:23; 25:6; 28:5, 22, 29; 29:6; 31:4, 5; 37:16, 32; 39:5; 44:6; 45:13; 47:4; 48:2; 51:15; 54:5; Jer 2:19; 5:14; 6:6, 9; 7:3, 21; 8:2, 3; 9:7, 15, 17; 10:16; 11:17, 20, 22; 15:16; 16:9; 19:3, 11, 15; 20:12; 23:15, 36; 25:8, 27, 28, 29, 32; 26:18; 27:4, 18, 19, 21; 28:2, 14; 29:4, 8, 17, 21, 25; 30:8; 31:23, 35; 32:14, 15, 18; 33:11, 12; 35:13, 17, 18, 19; 38:17; 39:16; 42:15, 18; 43:10; 44:2, 7, 11, 25; 46:10, 18, 25; 48:1, 15; 49:5, 7, 26, 35; 50:18, 25, 31, 33, 34; 51:5, 14, 19, 33, 57, 58; Dn 8:10; Hos 12:5; Am 3:13; 4:13; 5:14, 15, 16, 27; 6:8, 14; 9:5; Mi 4:4; Na 2:13; 3:5; Hab 2:13; Zep 2:9; 2:10; Hg 1:2; 1:5, 7, 9, 14; 2:4, 6, 7, 8, 9, 11, 23; Zec 1:3; 1:4, 6, 12, 14, 16, 17; 2:8, 9, 11; 3:7, 9, 10; 4:6, 9; 5:4; 6:12, 15; 7:3, 4, 9, 12, 13; 8:1, 2, 3, 4, 6, 7, 9, 11, 14, 18, 19, 20, 21, 22, 23; 9:15; 10:3; 12:5; 13:2, 7; 14:16, 17, 21; Mal 1:4; 1:6, 8, 9, 10, 11, 13, 14; 2:2, 4, 7, 8, 12, 16; 3:1, 5, 7, 10, 11, 12, 14, 17; 4:1, 3; Lk 2:13; Ro 9:29; Jas 5:4

HEAVENS → HEAVENS AND EARTH
Ezra
9:6 and our guilt has grown to the ***h***.
Nehemiah
9:6 the heaven of ***h***, with all their
Job
9:8 stretched out the ***h*** alone and trod on
11:8 higher than the ***h***—what can you do?
14:12 rise until the ***h*** cease; they don't
15:15 holy ones and the ***h*** aren't pure in
28:24 and surveys everything beneath the ***h***.
35:5 Look at the ***h*** and see; scan the clouds
Proverbs
3:19 establishing the ***h*** with
8:27 established the ***h***, when he marked
25:3 Like the high ***h*** and the depths of the
Ecclesiastes
3:1 a time for every matter under the ***h***:
Isaiah
1:2 Hear you ***h***, and listen earth, for the
13:5 from the faraway ***h***, the LORD and the
13:13 I will rattle the ***h***; the earth will
24:4 and wilts; the ***h*** wither away with
42:5 who created the ***h***, the one who
45:8 Pour down, you ***h*** above, and let the
45:12 stretched out the ***h***. I commanded all
48:13 spread out the ***h***. When I call to
51:6 Look up to the ***h***, and gaze at the
51:13 stretched out the ***h*** and founded the
55:9 Just as the ***h*** are higher than the
66:22 As the new ***h*** and the new earth that I'm
Jeremiah
2:12 such a thing, you ***h***; shudder and
4:23 or form; at the ***h*** and there was no
4:28 grieve and the ***h*** grow dark because
31:37 proclaims: If the ***h*** above could be
Ezekiel
1:1 River when the ***h*** opened and I saw
32:8 lights of the ***h***, I will make them
Hosea
2:21 I will answer the ***h*** and they will
Malachi
3:10 windows of the ***h*** for you and empty
Luke
19:38 in heaven and glory in the highest ***h***."
Acts
2:19 to occur in the ***h*** above and signs
Ephesians
1:20 sat him at God's right side in the ***h***,
2:6 seated us in the ***h*** with Christ Jesus.
3:10 and powers in the ***h*** the many
4:10 up above all the ***h*** so that he might
6:12 and spiritual powers of evil in the ***h***.
Hebrews
1:10 and the ***h*** are made by your
4:14 through the ***h***, who is Jesus,
7:26 sinners, and raised high above the ***h***.
8:1 of the throne of the majesty in the ***h***.
2 Peter
3:10 On that day the ***h*** will pass away
3:12 of that day, the ***h*** will be destroyed
Revelation
12:12 rejoice, you ***h*** and you who dwell

HEAVENS AND THE EARTH
Gn 2:1; 2:4; Ex 20:11; 31:17; Jer 10:11; Jl 3:16; Hg 2:21

HEAVY
Psalms
32:4 your hand was ***h*** upon me. My
38:4 are a weight that's way too ***h*** for me.
Proverbs
27:3 A stone is ***h*** and sand weighs much, but
29:4 one who imposes ***h*** taxes tears it
Isaiah
24:20 rebellion weighs ***h*** upon it; it will
47:6 made your yoke ***h*** even on the
Matthew
11:28 hard and carrying ***h*** loads, and I will
23:4 they tie together ***h*** packs that are

HEBREW
Genesis
14:13 he told Abram the ***H***, who lived near
41:12 A young ***H*** man, a servant of the
Exodus
1:19 Pharaoh, "Because ***H*** women aren't like
2:11 beating a ***H***, one of his own
21:2 you buy a male ***H*** slave, he will
2 Kings
18:26 speak with us in ***H*** because the
18:28 up and shouted in ***H*** at the top of his
Isaiah
36:11 speak with us in ***H***, because the
36:13 up and shouted in ***H*** at the top of his
Jeremiah
34:9 male and female ***H*** slaves and no
Jonah
1:9 to them, "I'm a ***H***. I worship the
Philippians
3:5 Benjamin. I am a ***H*** of the Hebrews.

Revelation
9:11 the abyss, whose ***H*** name is Abaddon,
16:16 place that is called in ***H***, Harmagedon.

HEBREWS

Genesis
40:15 the land of the ***H***, and here too
43:32 to eat with ***H***; the Egyptians
Exodus
1:22 boy born to the ***H*** into the Nile
9:13 the God of the ***H***, says: Let my
Deuteronomy
15:12 of your fellow ***H***, male or female,
1 Samuel
4:9 you'll serve the ***H*** like they've been
13:3 the land and said, "***H***! Listen up!"
13:7 Some ***H*** even crossed the Jordan River,
14:11 said, "Look, the ***H*** are coming out of
29:3 Who are these ***H***?" the Philistine
Jeremiah
34:14 you must free any ***H*** who have been
2 Corinthians
11:22 Are they ***H***? So am I. Are they
Philippians
3:5 a Hebrew of the ***H***. With respect to

HEBRON

Genesis
13:18 oaks of Mamre in ***H***. There he built
23:2 that is, in ***H***, in the land of
Joshua
14:13 him. He gave ***H*** to Caleb,
20:7 (that is, ***H***) in the highlands
21:13 priest they gave: ***H***, the refuge city
Judges
16:3 the top of the hill that is beside ***H***.
2 Samuel
2:1 David asked. "To ***H***," the LORD
3:2 sons were born in ***H***. His oldest son
1 Chronicles
11:1 around David at ***H***. "We're your own

HELL

Psalms
86:13 my life from the lowest part of ***h***.
88:3 my life is at the very brink of ***h***.
Matthew
5:22 they will be in danger of fiery ***h***.
5:29 that your whole body be thrown into ***h***.
5:30 than that your whole body go into ***h***.
10:28 can destroy both body and soul in ***h***.
18:9 be cast into a burning ***h*** with two eyes.
23:15 become twice the child of ***h*** you are.
23:33 be able to escape the judgment of ***h***?
Mark
9:43 into the fire of ***h***, which can't be
9:45 than to be thrown into ***h*** with two feet.
9:47 eye than to be thrown into ***h*** with two.
Luke
12:5 to throw you into ***h***. Indeed, I tell
Acts
8:20 be condemned to ***h*** along with you
James
3:6 is set on fire by the flames of ***h***.

HELP

Deuteronomy
1:38 the one who will ***h*** Israel inherit
22:4 it. You must ***h*** your fellow
23:4 they didn't ***h*** you with food or
26:7 we cried out for ***h*** to the LORD, our
30:9 your God will ***h*** you succeed in
Joshua
1:6 the one who will ***h*** this people take
10:6 Rescue us! ***H*** us! All the
24:7 they cried for ***h*** to the LORD. So
1 Samuel
12:21 idols that can't ***h*** you or save you.
19:17 David told me, '***H*** me get away or
Psalms
9:12 hasn't forgotten their cries for ***h***.
12:5 will provide the ***h*** they are gasping
18:6 to my God for ***h***. God heard my
18:35 supported me; your ***h*** has made me great.
18:41 They cried for ***h***, but there was no one
20:2 Let God send ***h*** to you from the
21:1 how happy he is about your saving ***h***!
21:5 of your saving ***h***; you've conferred
22:19 are my strength! Come quick and ***h*** me!
22:24 listened when I cried out to him for ***h***.
27:9 - you have been my ***h***! God who saves
30:2 out to you for ***h***, and you healed
31:22 mercy when I cried out to you for ***h***.
33:20 the LORD. He is our ***h*** and our shield.
34:15 his ears listen to their cries for ***h***.
35:2 a shield and armor; stand up and ***h*** me!
37:40 The LORD will ***h*** them and rescue them
38:22 Come quickly and ***h*** me, my Lord, my
39:12 to my cry for ***h***! Please don't
40:1 to me; he listened to my cry for ***h***.
44:5 foes away by your ***h***; we've trampled
63:7 you've been a ***h*** to me and I shout
70:1 to deliver me; hurry, LORD, to ***h*** me!
70:4 love your saving ***h*** say again and
71:16 LORD, I will ***h*** others remember
79:9 of our salvation, ***h*** us for the glory
90:1 you have been our ***h***, generation after
107:12 and there was no one to ***h*** them.
109:26 ***H*** me, LORD, my God! Save me according
115:11 in the LORD! God is their ***h*** and shield.
118:14 and protection; he was my saving ***h***!
119:27 ***H*** me understand what your precepts are
121:1 mountains. Where will my ***h*** come from?
124:8 Our ***h*** is in the name of the LORD, the
140:7 my strong saving ***h***—you've protected
142:1 cry out loud for ***h*** from the LORD. I
144:10 who gives saving ***h*** to rulers, and
146:3 beings—there's no saving ***h*** with them!
Proverbs
1:2 discipline, to ***h*** one understand
1:6 They ***h*** one understand proverbs and
3:2 because they will ***h*** you live a long
11:4 Riches don't ***h*** in the day of wrath, but
18:23 poor plead for ***h***, but the wealthy
Isaiah
1:17 Seek justice: ***h*** the oppressed;
50:7 The LORD God will ***h*** me; therefore, I

Jeremiah
2:37 those you rely on; they won't ***h*** you.
14:7 against us, ***h*** us, LORD, for
17:9 it's beyond ***h***. Who can figure
29:6 children; then ***h*** your sons find
48:3 to the cries for ***h*** from Horonaim:
48:4 Moab is shattered; its young cry for ***h***
50:32 and no one will ***h*** her up. I'll set
51:9 she was beyond ***h***. Let's depart
51:54 to the cries for ***h*** from Babylon,
Ezekiel
16:49 but she didn't ***h*** the poor and the
17:17 Pharaoh won't ***h*** him. There will be no
Hosea
13:9 you didn't realize that I could ***h*** you.
Amos
5:12 side, turning away the poor who seek ***h***.
Jonah
2:2 I cried out for ***h***; you have heard
Micah
2:7 Don't my words ***h*** the one who
Nahum
3:9 limit; Put and the Libyans were her ***h***.
Habakkuk
1:2 will I call for ***h*** and you not
Matthew
15:25 before him and said, "Lord, ***h*** me."
25:44 and didn't do anything to ***h*** you?'
John
6:63 the flesh doesn't ***h*** at all. The words
Acts
16:9 Come over to Macedonia and ***h*** us!"
Romans
8:26 Spirit comes to ***h*** our weakness. We
Galatians
5:2 circumcised, having Christ won't ***h*** you.
Hebrews
2:16 isn't trying to ***h*** angels, but
4:2 they heard didn't ***h*** them because they
13:9 Food doesn't ***h*** those who live in
13:17 about you, because that wouldn't ***h*** you.

HEMAN

Genesis
36:22 sons are Hori and ***H***, and Lotan's
1 Kings
4:31 or Mahol's sons: ***H***, Calcol, and
Psalms
88:1 A maskil of ***H*** the Ezrahite.

HERD

Leviticus
1:2 it from either the ***h*** or the flock.
23:18 one bull from the ***h***, and two rams.
Deuteronomy
12:21 animal from your ***h*** or flock that the
16:2 from the flock or ***h*** to the LORD your
Ezekiel
43:23 bull from the ***h*** and a flawless
Matthew
8:30 distance a large ***h*** of pigs was
8:31 us out, send us into the ***h*** of pigs."
8:32 pigs. The whole ***h*** rushed down the

HERMON

Deuteronomy
3:8 way from the Arnon ravine to Mount ***H***
Psalms
42:6 land of Jordan and ***H***, from Mount Mizar.
133:3 the dew on Mount ***H*** streaming down

HEROD

Matthew
2:1 the rule of King ***H***, magi came from
Mark
3:6 the supporters of ***H*** to plan how to
6:14 ***H*** the king heard about these things,
Luke
3:1 over Judea and ***H*** was ruler over
Acts
4:27 Indeed, both ***H*** and Pontius Pilate, with
12:20 ***H*** had been furious with the people of

HERODIAS

Matthew
14:3 prison because of ***H***, the wife of
Mark
6:17 prison because of ***H***, the wife of
Luke
3:19 John because of ***H***, Herod's

HESHBON

Numbers
21:26 Now ***H*** was the city of Sihon the Amorite
Deuteronomy
3:2 Sihon, the Amorite king who ruled in ***H***.

HEZEKIAH

2 Kings
18:1 ***H***, Ahaz's son, became king of Judah in
20:16 Isaiah said to ***H***, "Listen to the
1 Chronicles
3:13 son Ahaz, his son ***H***, his son Manasseh,
4:41 of Judah's King ***H***, attacked their
2 Chronicles
28:27 kings. His son ***H*** succeeded him as
29:1 ***H*** became king when he was 25 years old,
Ezra
2:16 of Ater, namely of ***H*** 9
Nehemiah
7:21 that is, of the descendants of ***H*** 98
10:17 Ater, ***H***, Azzur
Proverbs
25:1 copied by the men of ***H***, king of Judah:
Isaiah
1:1 kings Uzziah, Jotham, Ahaz, and ***H***.
36:1 them in the fourteenth year of King ***H***.
Jeremiah
26:18 rule of Judah's ***H***, said to all the
Hosea
1:1 Jotham, Ahaz, and ***H***, and in the days
Micah
1:1 Jotham, Ahaz, and ***H***, which he saw
Matthew
1:9 of Ahaz. Ahaz was the father of ***H***.
1:10 ***H*** was the father of Manasseh. Manasseh was the father of

HEZRON

Genesis
46:9 sons were Hanoch, Pallu, ***H***, and Carmi.

46:12 Canaan. Perez's sons were ***H*** and Hamul.

Exodus

6:14 Hanoch, Pallu, ***H***, and Carmi. These

Ruth

4:18 of Perez: Perez became the father of ***H***,
4:19 ***H*** the father of Ram, Ram the father of

Matthew

1:3 was the father of ***H***. Hezron was the

HID

Genesis

3:8 man and his wife ***h*** themselves from
3:10 because I was naked, and I ***h*** myself."

Exodus

2:2 beautiful, so she ***h*** him for three
2:12 the Egyptian and ***h*** him in the sand.
3:6 God." Moses ***h*** his face because

Joshua

6:17 is because she ***h*** the messengers we
6:25 because she ***h*** the spies whom

Judges

4:18 the tent, and she ***h*** him under a
4:19 gave him a drink, and ***h*** him again.

Job

10:13 These things you ***h*** in your heart; I
26:9 ***h*** the face of the full moon, spreading

Psalms

9:15 in the very net they themselves ***h***!
30:7 But then you ***h*** your presence. I
35:7 Because they ***h*** their net for me for no
35:8 Let the net they ***h*** catch them

Jeremiah

33:5 fierce anger. I ***h*** my face from the
36:26 prophet Jeremiah. But the LORD ***h*** them.

Ezekiel

39:23 against me, I ***h*** my face from
39:24 transgressions and ***h*** my face from them.

Matthew

13:33 a woman took and ***h*** in a bushel of
13:44 that somebody ***h*** in a field, which
25:25 was afraid. And I ***h*** my valuable coin

John

8:59 at him, but Jesus ***h*** himself and left
12:36 things, he went away and ***h*** from them.

HIDDEN

Joshua

2:4 the two men and ***h*** them. Then she
7:21 Now they are ***h*** in the ground
10:17 have been found, ***h*** in the cave at

Job

3:23 whose way is ***h***, whom God has
31:33 If I have ***h*** my transgressions like

Psalms

10:11 God has ***h*** his face. God
38:9 my Lord; my sighs aren't ***h*** from you.
51:6 truth in the most ***h*** places; you teach
69:5 my wrongdoings aren't ***h*** from you.

Daniel

2:22 what lies deeply ***h***; he knows what
11:43 of Egypt's ***h*** treasures of

Matthew

5:14 A city on top of a hill can't be ***h***.
10:26 nothing is ***h*** that won't be
11:25 because you've ***h*** these things from
13:35 what has been ***h*** since the

Mark

4:22 Everything ***h*** will be revealed, and

Romans

2:16 will judge the ***h*** truth about human

1 Corinthians

2:7 which has been ***h*** as a secret. God
4:5 things that are ***h*** in the dark to

Ephesians

1:9 God revealed his ***h*** design to us, which
3:5 didn't know this ***h*** plan that God has
3:9 that had been ***h*** since the

Colossians

1:26 that has been ***h*** for ages and
2:3 of wisdom and knowledge are ***h*** in him.
3:3 and your life is ***h*** with Christ in

2 Thessalonians

2:7 The ***h*** plan to live without any law is

1 Timothy

5:25 do is also obvious and can't be ***h***.

Hebrews

4:13 No creature is ***h*** from it, but rather
11:23 faith Moses was ***h*** by his parents

Revelation

2:17 some of the ***h*** manna to eat.

HIDE

Genesis

37:26 if we kill our brother and ***h*** his blood?

Deuteronomy

31:17 them! I'll ***h*** my face from
32:20 He said: I will ***h*** my face from them—

Job

3:10 womb, didn't ***h*** trouble from my
13:20 to me, then I won't ***h*** from your face.
13:24 Why ***h*** your face from me and consider me your enemy
14:13 I wish you would ***h*** me in the
20:12 mouths, they ***h*** it under their
24:4 way, make the land's needy ***h*** together.
27:11 God's power, not ***h*** what pertains to
34:22 where evildoers can ***h*** themselves;
40:13 ***H*** them together in the dust; bind their
41:7 Can you fill his ***h*** with darts, his head

Psalms

13:1 How long will you ***h*** your face from me?
17:8 of your eye! ***H*** me in the
22:24 he didn't ***h*** his face from me.
27:5 times; he will ***h*** me in a secret
27:9 Please don't ***h*** it from me! Don't push
31:20 You ***h*** them in the shelter of your
40:10 I didn't ***h*** your loyal love
51:9 ***H*** your face from my sins; wipe away all
55:12 exalted over me—I could ***h*** from them.
64:2 ***H*** me from the secret plots of wicked
69:17 Don't ***h*** your face from me, your
78:4 We won't ***h*** them from their descendants;
102:2 Don't ***h*** your face from me in my time of
104:29 But when you ***h*** your face, they are
119:19 the land. Don't ***h*** your commandments
139:11 will definitely ***h*** me; the light
143:7 is fading. Don't ***h*** your face from me

Proverbs

22:3 see trouble and ***h***, while the
25:2 glory of God to ***h*** something and the

HIDE [cont.]

28:12 but people ***h*** when the wicked
28:13 Those who ***h*** their sins won't succeed,
28:28 rise up, people ***h***, but when they
Isaiah
2:10 the rocks, and ***h*** yourself in the
Ezekiel
5:3 a few strands and ***h*** them in your
39:29 Israel, I won't ***h*** my face from them

HIGH PRIEST

Lv 21:10; 21:13; Nm 35:25; Josh 20:6; 2Ki 12:10; 22:4, 8; 23:4; 2Ch 24:11; 34:9; Neh 3:1; 3:20; 13:28; Jer 52:24; Hg 1:1; 1:12, 14; 2:4; Zec 3:1; 3:8; 6:11; Mt 26:3; 26:57, 62, 63, 65; Mk 2:26; 14:53, 60, 61, 63; Jn 11:49; 11:51; 18:13, 15, 16, 22, 24, 26; Ac 4:6; 5:17, 21, 27; 7:1; 9:1; 22:5; 23:2, 4, 5; 24:1; Heb 2:17; 3:1; 4:14, 15; 5:1, 2, 5, 10; 6:20; 7:26; 8:1, 3; 9:7, 11, 25; 10:21; 13:11

HILKIAH

2 Kings
22:4 the high priest ***H***. Have him
23:24 that the priest ***H*** found in the
1 Chronicles
6:13 Shallum of ***H***, Hilkiah of Azariah
6:45 of Hashabiah son of Amaziah son of ***H***
9:11 Azariah son of ***H*** son of Meshullam
26:11 ***H*** the second, Tebaliah the third, and
2 Chronicles
34:9 the high priest ***H***, they delivered
34:14 LORD's temple, ***H*** the priest found
35:8 and the Levites. ***H***, Zechariah, and
Ezra
7:1 son of Seraiah son of Azariah son of ***H***
Nehemiah
8:4 Anaiah, Uriah, ***H***, and Maaseiah on
11:11 Seraiah son of ***H*** son of Meshullam son
12:7 Sallu, Amok, ***H***, Jedaiah. These were
12:21 of ***H***, Hashabiah; of Jedaiah, Nethanel

HILL

Psalms
148:9 every single ***h***, fruit trees, and
Song of Songs
4:6 of myrrh, to the ***h*** of frankincense.
Isaiah
40:4 mountain and ***h*** will be
Matthew
5:14 A city on top of a ***h*** can't be hidden.
Acts
17:19 council on Mars ***H***. "What is this

HIRAM

2 Samuel
5:11 Tyre's King ***H*** sent messengers to David
1 Kings
5:10 So ***H*** gave Solomon all the cedar and
1 Chronicles
14:1 Tyre's King ***H*** sent messengers to David

HIRED

Exodus
22:15 If the animal was ***h***, only the fee for
Leviticus
19:13 Do not withhold a ***h*** laborer's pay
25:50 owner, as in the case of a ***h*** laborer.
Job
7:1 our days like those of a ***h*** worker?
7:2 shadow, await our task like a ***h*** worker.
Isaiah
7:20 with a razor ***h*** from beyond the
16:14 the years of a ***h*** worker, the glory
21:16 a laborer is ***h***, all the glory of
Matthew
20:12 These who were ***h*** last worked one hour,
Luke
15:17 of my father's ***h*** hands have more
John
10:12 When the ***h*** hand sees the wolf coming,
10:13 He's only a ***h*** hand and the sheep don't

HITTITE

Genesis
23:10 was a native ***H***. So Ephron the
25:9 Zohar's son Ephron the ***H***, near Mamre.
26:34 of Beeri the ***H***, and Basemath
27:46 loathe these ***H*** women. If Jacob
36:2 daughter of the ***H*** Elon; Oholibamah
49:29 that's in the field of Ephron the ***H***;
49:30 from Ephron the ***H*** as a burial
50:13 as burial property from Ephron the ***H***.
Joshua
1:4 including all ***H*** land, up to the
1 Samuel
26:6 Ahimelech the ***H*** and Joab's
2 Samuel
11:3 Bathsheba, the wife of Uriah the ***H***?"
11:6 me Uriah the ***H***." So Joab sent
11:17 army fell. Uriah the ***H*** was also killed.
11:21 servant Uriah the ***H*** is dead too.'"
11:24 your servant Uriah the ***H*** is dead too."
12:9 down Uriah the ***H*** with the sword
12:10 wife of Uriah the ***H*** as your own, the
23:39 and Uriah the ***H***—thirty-seven in all
24:6 on to Kadesh in ***H*** territory. They
1 Kings
10:29 them to all the ***H*** and Aramean kings.
15:5 in the matter of Uriah the ***H***.
2 Kings
7:6 has hired the ***H*** and Egyptian
1 Chronicles
11:41 Uriah the ***H***; Zabad, Ahlai's son
2 Chronicles
1:17 them to all the ***H*** and Aramean kings.
Ezekiel
16:3 father was an Amorite, your mother a ***H***.
16:45 Your mother was a ***H***, and your father

HITTITES

Genesis
15:20 the ***H***, the Perizzites, the Rephaim
23:3 his deceased wife, he spoke with the ***H***:
23:5 The ***H*** responded to Abraham
23:7 bowed to the local citizens the ***H***,
23:10 in order that the ***H*** and everyone at
23:16 before the ***H***: four hundred
23:18 presence of the ***H*** and of everyone
23:20 from the ***H*** to Abraham as his
25:10 field Abraham had purchased from the ***H***.
49:32 the cave in it that belonged to the ***H***."

Exodus
3:8 Canaanites, the ***H***, the Amorites,
3:17 Canaanites, the ***H***, the Amorites,
13:5 Canaanites, the ***H***, the Amorites,
23:23 the Amorites, the ***H***, the Perizzites,
23:28 the Canaanites, and the ***H*** before you.
33:2 the Amorites, the ***H***, the Perizzites,
34:11 Canaanites, the ***H***, the Perizzites,
Numbers
13:29 plain; the ***H***, Jebusites, and
Deuteronomy
7:1 before you—the ***H***, the Girgashites,
20:17 under the ban: ***H***, Amorites,
Joshua
3:10 the Canaanites, ***H***, Hivites,
9:1 They were ***H*** and Amorites,
11:3 to the Amorites, ***H***, Perizzites, and
12:8 land belonged to ***H***, Amorites,
24:11 Canaanites, ***H***, Girgashites,
Judges
1:26 the land of the ***H*** and built a city.
3:5 the Canaanites, ***H***, Amorites,
1 Kings
9:20 of the Amorites, ***H***, Perizzites,
11:1 Ammonites, Edomites, Sidonians, and ***H***.
2 Chronicles
8:7 remained of the ***H***, Amorites,
Ezra
9:1 Canaanites, the ***H***, the Perizzites,
Nehemiah
9:8 Canaanites, the ***H***, the Amorites,

HIVITES

Exodus
23:28 and drive out the ***H***, the Canaanites,
Joshua
9:7 said to the ***H***, "Perhaps you

HOLD

Psalms
40:9 I didn't ***h*** anything back—as
40:11 you, LORD—don't ***h*** back any of your
74:11 back? Why do you ***h*** your strong hand close to your chest?
82:8 earth because you ***h*** all nations in
139:10 your strong hand would ***h*** me tight!
Proverbs
1:22 naïvete, mockers ***h*** their mocking
3:18 her; those who ***h*** her tight are
3:21 from your eyes; ***h*** on to sound
4:4 Let your heart ***h*** on to my words:
4:13 ***H*** on to instruction; don't slack off;
24:11 to the slaughter, don't ***h*** back.
28:17 murder, don't ***h*** them back from
29:11 their anger, but the wise ***h*** it back.
Matthew
16:22 Then Peter took ***h*** of Jesus and,
Luke
14:4 Jesus took ***h*** of the sick man,
Romans
12:9 Hate evil, and ***h*** on to what is
Philippians
2:16 because you ***h*** on to the word of life.
3:12 that I may grab ***h*** of it because
2 Thessalonians
2:15 stand firm and ***h*** on to the
1 Timothy
3:9 They should ***h*** on to the faith that has
Revelation
3:11 I'm coming soon. ***H*** on to what you have
12:17 commandments and ***h*** firmly to the

HOLINESS

Exodus
15:11 you, foremost in ***h***, worthy of
Numbers
20:12 me to show my ***h*** before the
20:13 and he showed his ***h*** to them.
27:14 to show them my ***h*** by means of the
2 Chronicles
20:21 his majestic ***h***. They were to
Psalms
65:4 of your house, by the ***h*** of your temple.
77:13 God, your way is ***h***! Who is as great a
89:35 By my own ***h*** I've sworn one thing: I
93:5 are so faithful. ***H*** decorates your
Isaiah
57:15 live on high, in ***h***, and also with
Ezekiel
28:22 manifested my ***h***, they will know
28:25 I demonstrate my ***h*** through them in
38:16 through you I show my ***h*** in their sight!
38:23 show my ***h***, and make myself
44:19 must not transfer ***h*** to the people
46:20 and transferring ***h*** to the people,
Amos
4:2 promised by his ***h***: The days are
Matthew
6:9 in heaven, uphold the ***h*** of your name.
Luke
1:75 in ***h*** and righteousness in God's eyes,
11:2 uphold the ***h*** of your name.
Romans
1:4 on the Spirit of ***h***. This Son is
2 Corinthians
7:1 that we make our ***h*** complete in the
Ephesians
4:24 to God's image in justice and true ***h***.
1 Thessalonians
3:13 be blameless in ***h*** before our God
1 Timothy
2:15 faith, love, and ***h***, together with
Hebrews
12:10 our benefit so that we can share his ***h***.
12:14 everyone—and ***h*** as well, because

HOLY → HOLY ONE, HOLY ONE OF ISRAEL, HOLY ONES, HOLY PEOPLE, HOLY PLACE, HOLY SPIRIT, HOLY TEMPLE, HOLY TO THE LORD, YOU MUST BE HOLY

Genesis
2:3 day and made it ***h***, because on it
Exodus
12:16 day will be a ***h*** occasion for you.
16:23 a day of rest, a ***h*** Sabbath to the
19:6 for me and a ***h*** nation. These are
20:8 the Sabbath day and treat it as ***h***.
26:33 for you the ***h*** from the holiest
Leviticus
11:44 keep yourselves ***h*** and be holy,
19:2 You must be ***h***, because I, the
Numbers
4:4 in the meeting tent: the most ***h*** things.

16:7 that one is ***h***. You Levites have

Deuteronomy

5:12 and treat it as ***h***, exactly as the

26:15 down from your ***h*** home, from heaven

Joshua

5:15 are standing is ***h***." So Joshua did

24:19 because he is a ***h*** God. He is a

1 Samuel

2:2 No one is ***h*** like the LORD—no, no one

Nehemiah

11:1 to live in the ***h*** city of

Psalms

2:6 my king on Zion, my ***h*** mountain!"

24:3 Who can stand in his ***h*** sanctuary?

30:4 to him; give thanks to his ***h*** name!

43:3 bring me to your ***h*** mountain, to your

47:8 the nations. God sits on his ***h*** throne.

96:9 the LORD in his ***h*** splendor! Tremble

98:1 hand and his own ***h*** arm have won the

103:1 everything inside me bless his ***h*** name!

111:9 last forever. ***H*** and awesome is

145:21 will bless God's ***h*** name forever and

Isaiah

6:3 other, saying: "***H***, holy, holy is

11:9 anywhere on my ***h*** mountain. The

35:8 be called The ***H*** Way. The unclean

52:1 Jerusalem, you ***h*** city; for the

Jeremiah

17:22 the Sabbath day ***h*** as I commanded

31:23 righteous dwelling place, ***h*** mountain.

Joel

2:1 a shout on my ***h*** mountain! Let all

2:16 people; prepare a ***h*** meeting; assemble

3:9 Prepare a ***h*** war, wake up the

3:17 down in Zion, my ***h*** mountain.

Zechariah

8:3 heavenly forces will be the ***h*** mountain.

14:20 On that day, ***H*** to the LORD will be

Matthew

1:18 she became pregnant by the ***H*** Spirit.

4:5 him into the ***h*** city and stood

7:6 Don't give ***h*** things to dogs, and don't

12:31 But insulting the ***H*** Spirit won't be

23:19 or the altar that makes the gift ***h***?

28:19 and of the Son and of the ***H*** Spirit,

Mark

6:20 a righteous and ***h*** person, so he

8:38 the Father's glory with the ***h*** angels."

13:11 doing the speaking but the ***H*** Spirit is.

John

10:36 Father has made ***h*** and sent into the

14:26 Companion, the ***H*** Spirit, whom the

Acts

2:4 filled with the ***H*** Spirit and began

3:21 spoke long ago through his ***h*** prophets.

10:22 Jewish people. A ***h*** angel directed

Romans

1:3 prophets in the ***h*** scriptures. His

6:22 consequence of a ***h*** life, and the

12:1 sacrifice that is ***h*** and pleasing to

15:16 and made ***h*** by the Holy

1 Corinthians

1:2 have been made ***h*** to God in Christ

3:17 God's temple is ***h***, which is what

6:11 you were made ***h*** to God, and you

16:20 should greet each other with a ***h*** kiss.

1 Timothy

2:8 up hands that are ***h***, without anger or

4:7 women. Train yourself for a ***h*** life!

4:8 training in ***h*** living is useful

2 Timothy

1:9 called us with a ***h*** calling. This

3:15 have known the ***h*** scriptures that

Hebrews

10:19 we can enter the ***h*** of holies by

13:12 make the people ***h*** with his own

1 Peter

1:15 you must be ***h*** in every aspect of your

1:16 You will be ***h***, because I am

2:5 being made into a ***h*** priesthood to

3:5 in this way that ***h*** women who trusted

3:15 regard Christ as ***h*** in your hearts.

Revelation

4:8 keep on saying, "***H***, holy, holy is

6:10 a loud voice, "***H*** and true Master,

21:2 I saw the ***h*** city, New Jerusalem, coming

22:11 Let those who are ***h*** still be holy.

22:19 of life and the ***h*** city, which are

HOLY ONE

2Ki 19:22; Job 5:1; 6:10; Ps 22:3; 71:22; 78:41; 89:18; 106:16; Prv 9:10; 30:3; Is 1:4; 5:19, 24; 10:17, 20; 12:6; 17:7; 29:19, 23; 30:11, 12, 15; 31:1; 37:23; 40:25; 41:14, 16, 20; 43:3, 14, 15; 45:11; 47:4; 48:17; 49:7; 54:5; 55:5; 60:9, 14; Jer 50:29; 51:5; Dn 8:13; Hos 11:9; 11:12; Hab 1:12; 3:3; Mk 1:24; Lk 4:34; Jn 6:69; Ac 2:27; 13:35; 1Jn 2:20; Rev 16:5

HOLY ONE OF ISRAEL

2Ki 19:22; Ps 71:22; 78:41; 89:18; Is 1:4; 10:20; 12:6; 17:7; 29:19; 30:11, 12, 15; 31:1; 37:23; 41:14, 16, 20; 43:3, 14; 45:11; 47:4; 48:17; 49:7; 54:5; 55:5; 60:9, 14; Jer 50:29; 51:5

HOLY ONES

Dt 33:2; 33:3; Job 15:15; 36:14; Ps 16:3; 34:9; 89:5, 7; Is 13:3; Dn 7:18; 7:21, 22, 25, 27; 8:24; Zec 14:5; Jud 1:14

HOLY PEOPLE

Ex 22:31; Is 62:12; Mt 27:52; Ac 9:13; 9:32, 41; 26:10; Col 1:12; 1:26; 2Th 1:10; Heb 6:10; 13:24; Jud 1:3

HOLY PLACE

Ex 29:31; Lv 6:16; 6:26, 27, 30; 7:6; 10:13; 16:24; 24:9; 1Ki 6:5; 6:16; 7:50; 8:6, 8, 10; 2Ch 3:8; 3:10; 4:22; 5:7, 9, 11; 26:18; Ezr 9:8; Ecc 8:10; Is 63:18; Jer 25:30; Eze 41:4; 41:21, 23; 44:13, 27; 45:3, 4; 48:12; Dn 8:11; 9:24; Am 7:13; Mal 2:11; Mt 24:15; Lk 11:51; Ac 6:13; 21:28; Heb 8:2; 9:1, 2, 8, 24, 25

HOLY SPIRIT

Ps 51:11; Is 63:10; 63:11; Mt 1:18; 1:20; 3:11; 12:31, 32; 22:43; 28:19; Mk 1:8; 3:29; 12:36; 13:11; Lk 1:15; 1:35, 41, 67; 2:25, 26; 3:16, 22; 4:1; 10:21; 11:13; 12:10, 12; Jn 1:33; 14:26; 20:22; Ac 1:2; 1:5, 8, 16; 2:4, 33, 38; 4:8, 25, 31; 5:3, 32; 6:5; 7:51, 55; 8:15, 16, 17, 19; 9:17, 31; 10:38, 44, 45, 47; 11:15, 16, 24;

13:2, 4, 9, 52; 15:8, 28; 16:6; 19:2, 6; 20:23, 28; 21:11; 28:25; Ro 5:5; 9:1; 14:17; 15:13, 16; 1Co 6:19; 12:3; 2Co 6:6; 13:13; Eph 1:13; 1:14; 4:30; 1Th 1:5; 1:6; 4:8; 2Ti 1:14; Ti 3:5; Heb 2:4; 3:7; 6:4; 9:8; 10:15; 1Pt 1:12; 2Pt 1:21; Jud 1:20

HOLY TEMPLE
1Ch 29:3; Ps 5:7; 11:4; 79:1; 138:2; Jon 2:4; 2:7; Mi 1:2; Hab 2:20

HOLY TO THE LORD
Ex 28:36; 30:10, 37; 31:15; 39:30; Lv 19:8; 27:21, 28, 30, 32; Nm 6:8; Dt 14:2; 14:21; 26:19; Josh 6:19; 2Ch 30:17; 35:3; Ezr 8:28; Neh 8:9; Eze 48:14; Zec 14:20; 14:21

HOME
Genesis
27:39 you will make a ***h*** far away from the
1 Chronicles
28:2 as the permanent ***h*** for the chest
Psalms
16:6 for me; yes, I have a lovely ***h***.
84:3 too has found a ***h*** there; the
104:12 sky make their ***h***, chirping loudly
104:17 the stork has a ***h*** in the cypresses.
132:13 chose Zion; he wanted it for his ***h***.
Proverbs
3:33 but he blesses the ***h*** of the righteous.
7:19 my husband isn't ***h***; he's gone far
7:20 him; he won't come ***h*** till full moon."
21:20 oil stay in the ***h*** of the wise, but
24:15 secretly at the ***h*** of the righteous.
27:8 its nest, so is one who wanders from ***h***.
Ezekiel
36:8 because they will come ***h*** very soon.
Haggai
1:9 You bring it ***h***, and I blow it
Matthew
8:6 on his back at ***h***, paralyzed, and
8:14 Jesus went ***h*** with Peter and
9:6 up, take your cot, and go ***h***."
9:7 The man got up and went ***h***
12:45 in and make their ***h*** there. That
Luke
5:24 you, get up, take your cot, and go ***h***."
7:44 I entered your ***h***, you didn't give
8:39 Return ***h*** and tell the story of what
12:36 master to come ***h*** from a wedding
12:39 have allowed his ***h*** to be broken into.
John
12:1 came to Bethany, ***h*** of Lazarus, whom
19:27 on, this disciple took her into his ***h***.
Romans
12:13 and welcome strangers into your ***h***.
2 Corinthians
5:8 the body and to be at ***h*** with the Lord.

HOMES
Numbers
32:18 return to our ***h*** until each one of
Psalms
49:11 are their eternal ***h***, the place they
68:6 lonely in their ***h***; he sets
109:10 begging, driven out of their ruined ***h***.
Proverbs
30:26 but they make their ***h*** in the rocks.
Luke
16:9 will be welcomed into the eternal ***h***.
1 Timothy
5:14 and manage their ***h*** so that they
1 Peter
4:9 Open your ***h*** to each other without

HONEY
Exodus
3:8 full of milk and ***h***, a place where
33:3 full of milk and ***h***. But I won't go
Deuteronomy
6:3 you, in a land full of milk and ***h***.
8:8 a land of olive oil and ***h***;
Judges
14:8 of bees with ***h*** inside the lion's
14:9 He scooped the ***h*** into his hands, eating
14:18 sweeter than ***h***? What's stronger
Psalms
19:10 are sweeter than ***h***—even dripping of
81:16 satisfy you with ***h*** from the rock."
119:103 buds—it's sweeter than ***h*** in my mouth!
Proverbs
5:3 woman drip ***h***, and her tongue
16:24 words are flowing ***h***, sweet to the
24:13 My child, eat ***h***, for it is good. The
25:16 If you find ***h***, eat just the right
25:27 Eating too much ***h*** isn't good, nor is it
27:7 is full refuses ***h***, but anything
Matthew
3:4 his waist. He ate locusts and wild ***h***.
Revelation
10:9 stomach, but sweet as ***h*** in your mouth."
10:10 it was sweet as ***h*** in my mouth, but

HONOR → HONOR THE LORD
Exodus
20:12 ***H*** your father and your mother so that
Deuteronomy
5:16 ***H*** your father and your mother, exactly
1 Samuel
2:8 them the seat of ***h***! The pillars of
2:30 such thing! No. I ***h*** those who honor
1 Chronicles
29:12 of wealth and ***h***, and you rule
Esther
6:6 really wants to ***h***?" Haman thought
Psalms
22:23 descendants—***h*** him! All of you
25:14 those who ***h*** him; he makes his
34:9 LORD's holy ones, ***h*** him because those
50:15 will deliver you, then you will ***h*** me."
67:7 let the far ends of the earth ***h*** him.
119:38 that is for all those who ***h*** you.
145:19 to those who ***h*** him, listening to
149:9 That will be an ***h*** for all God's
Proverbs
3:16 life; in her left are wealth and ***h***.
4:8 you. She will ***h*** you if you
8:18 Riches and ***h*** are with me, as well as
11:16 woman gains ***h***; violent men gain
13:18 instruction; ***h*** belongs to those
14:31 those who are kind to the poor ***h*** God.
21:21 will find life, righteousness, and ***h***.
22:4 of the LORD is wealth, ***h***, and life.

25:27 good, nor is it appropriate to seek ***h***.
26:1 at harvest, so ***h*** isn't appropriate
29:23 low, but those of humble spirit gain ***h***.
31:25 Strength and ***h*** are her clothing; she is
Ecclesiastes
10:1 a little folly outweighs wisdom and ***h***.
Isaiah
29:13 their mouths, and ***h*** me with lip
Matthew
2:2 in the east, and we've come to ***h*** him."
2:8 to me so that I too may go and ***h*** him."
15:4 For God said, ***H*** your father and your
23:6 love to sit in places of ***h*** at banquets.
John
4:44 prophets have no ***h*** in their own
5:23 everyone will ***h*** the Son just as
8:49 replied. "But I ***h*** my Father and you
12:26 be. My Father will ***h*** whoever serves me.
Romans
12:10 Be the best at showing ***h*** to each other.
1 Corinthians
12:23 are the ones we ***h*** the most. The
Ephesians
6:2 The commandment ***H*** your father and
Hebrews
2:7 the human being with glory and ***h***.
3:3 deserves more ***h*** than the house
1 Peter
1:7 glory, and ***h*** for you when
2 Peter
1:17 He received ***h*** and glory from God the
Revelation
4:9 give glory, ***h***, and thanks to
4:11 receive glory and ***h*** and power,
5:12 and might, and ***h***, glory, and
7:12 thanksgiving and ***h*** and power and

HONOR THE LORD

Ex 12:42; Ps 15:4; 25:12; 34:11; 112:1; 115:11, 13; 118:4; 135:20; Prv 3:9; Is 24:15; Jer 13:16

HONORED

Proverbs
11:11 A city is ***h*** by the blessing of the
27:18 who look after their master will be ***h***.
Isaiah
23:9 to shame all the ***h*** of the earth.
45:4 I gave you an ***h*** title, though you
49:5 Moreover, I'm ***h*** in the LORD's
58:13 to the LORD, ***h***, and honor it
Lamentations
1:8 a joke. All who ***h*** her now detest
Daniel
2:46 bowed low and ***h*** Daniel. The king
Matthew
13:57 Prophets are ***h*** everywhere except
Luke
10:15 will you be ***h*** by being raised
12:37 at the table as ***h*** guests, and wait
14:10 Then you will be ***h*** in the presence
Philippians
2:9 God highly ***h*** him and gave him
2 Thessalonians
1:12 Jesus will be ***h*** by you, and you
3:1 quickly and be ***h***, just like it
Hebrews
13:4 Marriage must be ***h*** in every respect,
1 Peter
4:11 God may be ***h*** through Jesus

HOPE

→ HOPE IN GOD, HOPE IN THE LORD

Ruth
1:12 say that I have ***h***, even if I had a
Ezra
10:2 now, there is ***h*** for Israel in
Job
4:6 of your conduct, the source of your ***h***?
8:13 who forget God. ***H*** perishes for the
13:15 me; I'm without ***h***; I will surely
17:15 Where then is my ***h***? My hope—who can see it?
Psalms
9:18 forever, the ***h*** of those who
39:7 I be waiting for? My ***h*** is set on you.
62:5 God only because my ***h*** comes from him!
71:14 But me? I will ***h***. Always. I will add
119:116 let me be put to shame because of ***h***.
146:5 the person whose ***h*** rests on the LORD
Proverbs
11:7 wicked die, their ***h*** perishes. Yes,
13:12 ***H*** delayed makes the heart sick; longing
23:18 a future, and your ***h*** won't be cut off.
24:14 is a future. Your ***h*** won't be cut off.
26:12 There is more ***h*** for a fool than
29:20 There is more ***h*** for fools than
Jeremiah
14:8 You are the ***h*** of Israel, its savior in
29:11 to give you a future filled with ***h***.
30:10 LORD, Don't lose ***h***, Israel. I will
Lamentations
3:18 is gone, as well as my ***h*** from the LORD.
3:25 good to those who ***h*** in him, to the
3:29 mouth in the dirt—perhaps there is ***h***.
Ezekiel
19:5 in vain, her ***h*** faded. So she
37:11 dried up, and our ***h*** has perished. We
Zechariah
9:12 prisoners of ***h***. Moreover,
Matthew
12:21 Gentiles will put their ***h*** in his name.
John
5:45 is Moses, the one in whom your ***h*** rests.
Acts
2:26 Moreover, my body will live in ***h***,
23:6 because of my ***h*** in the
Romans
4:18 it was beyond ***h***, he had faith in
5:4 character, and character produces ***h***.
5:5 This ***h*** doesn't put us to shame, because
8:20 the one who subjected it—but in the ***h***
8:24 We were saved in ***h***. If we see what we
12:12 Be happy in your ***h***, stand your ground
15:4 we could have ***h*** through endurance
15:12 The Gentiles will place their ***h*** in him.
15:13 May the God of ***h*** fill you with all joy
1 Corinthians
13:13 Now faith, ***h***, and love remain—these
2 Corinthians
1:7 Our ***h*** for you is certain, because we
1:10 We have set our ***h*** on him that he
3:12 we have such a ***h***, we act with
Ephesians
1:12 we were the first to ***h*** in Christ.

2:12 In this world you had no ***h*** and no God.
4:4 just as God also called you in one ***h***.
Colossians
1:5 because of the ***h*** reserved for you
1:23 away from the ***h*** given in the good
1:27 Christ living in you, the ***h*** of glory.
1 Thessalonians
1:3 that comes from ***h*** in our Lord Jesus
2:19 What is our ***h***, joy, or crown that we
4:13 mourn like others who don't have any ***h***.
5:8 our body and the ***h*** of salvation as a
2 Thessalonians
2:16 gave us eternal comfort and a good ***h***.
1 Timothy
1:1 our savior and of Christ Jesus our ***h***.
3:14 I ***h*** to come to you quickly. But I'm
4:10 for this: "Our ***h*** is set on the
6:17 to place their ***h*** on their
2 Timothy
4:16 deserted me. I ***h*** that God doesn't
Titus
1:2 are based on the ***h*** of eternal life
2:13 for the blessed ***h*** and the glorious
3:7 we can inherit the ***h*** for eternal life."
Philemon
1:22 room for me. I ***h*** that I will be
Hebrews
3:6 and the pride that our ***h*** gives us.
6:11 to make your ***h*** sure until the
6:18 to grasp the ***h*** that is lying in
6:19 This ***h***, which is a safe and secure
7:19 hand, a better ***h*** is introduced,
10:23 confession of our ***h*** without wavering,
11:1 of what we ***h*** for, the proof of
1 Peter
1:3 into a living ***h*** through the
1:6 rejoice in this ***h***, even if it's
1:13 place your ***h*** completely on the
1:21 your faith and ***h*** should rest in
3:15 to speak of your ***h***, be ready to
1 John
3:3 who has this ***h*** in him purifies
2 John
1:12 and ink, but I ***h*** to visit you and
3 John
1:14 I ***h*** to see you soon, and we will speak

HOPE IN GOD
Ps 42:5; 42:11; 43:5; 78:7; Is 8:17; 1Ti 5:5; 6:17

HOPE IN THE LORD
Ps 27:14; 33:20; 37:9, 34; 40:1; Is 40:31; Phi 2:19

HOREB
Exodus
3:1 and he came to God's mountain called ***H***.
17:6 on the rock at ***H***. Hit the rock.
Deuteronomy
5:2 God made a covenant with us at Mount ***H***.
1 Kings
8:9 there while at ***H***, where the LORD
Psalms
106:19 made a calf at ***H***, bowing down to a
Malachi
4:4 and rules for all Israel at ***H***.

HORN
Exodus
19:13 when the ram's ***h*** sounds may they
Joshua
6:5 on the ram's ***h***. As soon as you
6:8 seven ram's ***h*** trumpets moved
1 Samuel
16:1 Israel. Fill your ***h*** with oil and get
Psalms
47:5 the LORD with the blast of the ram's ***h***.
81:3 Blow the ***h*** on the new moon, at the full
98:6 trumpets and a ***h*** blast, shout
150:3 of the ram's ***h***! Praise God with
Daniel
7:8 another small ***h*** came up between
8:5 goat's eyes was a ***h*** that was a sight
Joel
2:1 Blow the ***h*** in Zion; give a shout on my
Amos
2:2 war cry, with the sound of the ram's ***h***.
3:6 If a ram's ***h*** is blown in a city, won't
Micah
4:13 I will make your ***h*** out of iron; your
Zechariah
9:14 God will blow the ***h***; he will march

HORNS
Genesis
22:13 ram caught by its ***h*** in the dense
Exodus
27:2 Make ***h*** for the altar and attach them to
Jeremiah
17:1 hearts and on the ***h*** of their altars.
Daniel
7:7 beasts before it, and it had ten ***h***.
8:3 a ram with two ***h*** standing in front
Amos
3:14 of Bethel; the ***h*** of the altar will
Zechariah
1:18 Then I looked up and saw four ***h***
Revelation
5:6 It had seven ***h*** and seven eyes,
9:13 from the four ***h*** of the gold altar
12:3 heads and ten ***h***, and seven royal
13:1 sea. It had ten ***h*** and seven heads.
17:3 names. It had seven heads and ten ***h***.

HORROR
Exodus
15:14 shook in terror; ***h*** grabbed hold of
Deuteronomy
28:37 You will become a ***h***, fit only for use
Job
24:17 they recognize the ***h*** of darkness.
Isaiah
31:9 In ***h*** they will flee from their
66:24 They will be a ***h*** to everyone.
Jeremiah
15:4 them an object of ***h*** to all nations on
Ezekiel
6:11 feet, and cry "***H***" over all the
Revelation
8:13 a loud voice, "***H***, horror, oh! The
9:12 The first ***h*** has passed. Look! Two
11:14 The second ***h*** is over. The third horror
12:12 them. But oh! The ***h*** for the earth and
18:10 say, 'Oh, the ***h***! Babylon, you

HORSE

Exodus
15:1 victory! ***H*** and rider he
Esther
6:8 has worn and a ***h*** on which the king
Psalms
32:9 some senseless ***h*** or mule, whose
76:6 both chariot and ***h*** were stopped dead
147:10 the strength of a ***h***; God doesn't
Proverbs
21:31 A ***h*** is made ready for the day of
26:3 A whip for a ***h***, a bridle for a donkey,
Jeremiah
51:21 you I will crush ***h*** and rider. With
Zechariah
1:8 riding on a red ***h***, which was
James
3:2 Like a bridled ***h***, they can control
Revelation
6:2 there was a white ***h***. Its rider held a
19:11 there was a white ***h***. Its rider was

HORSEMEN

Genesis
50:9 Even chariots and ***h*** went with him; it
2 Samuel
1:6 with chariots and ***h*** closing in on him.
10:18 forty thousand ***h***. David wounded
2 Chronicles
9:25 twelve thousand ***h*** that he kept in
16:8 with chariots and ***h*** to spare? Still,
Isaiah
21:7 pairs of ***h***, donkey riders,
Jeremiah
4:29 As the ***h*** and archers approach, the
6:23 no mercy. Their ***h*** sound like the
Hosea
1:7 or by war, or by horses, or by ***h***."
Habakkuk
1:8 the evening. His ***h*** charge forward;
Acts
23:23 soldiers, seventy ***h***, and two hundred

HORSES

Genesis
47:17 them food for the ***h***, flocks, cattle,
Exodus
14:23 all of Pharaoh's ***h***, chariots, and
Deuteronomy
17:16 acquire too many ***h***, and he must not
Joshua
11:6 Cripple their ***h***! Burn their
1 Kings
4:26 and twelve thousand additional ***h***.
10:26 more chariots and ***h*** until he had
2 Kings
2:11 chariot and fiery ***h*** appeared and
6:17 was full of ***h*** and fiery
Psalms
20:7 others in ***h***; but we praise
Isaiah
31:3 not divine; their ***h*** are flesh and not
66:20 to the LORD—on ***h***, in chariots, in
Ezekiel
23:20 whose ejaculation was like that of ***h***.
27:14 traded ***h***, warhorses, and
38:15 of them riding ***h***, a great
39:20 at my table with ***h*** and riders,
Joel
2:4 They resemble ***h***, and like warhorses
Amos
2:15 those who ride ***h*** won't save
4:10 carried away your ***h***. I made the stink
6:12 Do ***h*** run on rocks? Does one plow the
Micah
1:13 Harness the ***h*** to the chariot,
5:10 cut down your ***h*** in your midst; I
Nahum
2:3 the day he has prepared; the ***h*** quiver.
Habakkuk
1:8 His ***h*** are faster than leopards; they
3:8 you rode on your ***h*** or rode your
3:15 You make your ***h*** tread on the sea;
Haggai
2:22 and rider; ***h*** and riders will
Zechariah
1:8 him were red, sorrel, and white ***h***.
6:2 chariot had red ***h***, and the second
6:3 chariot had white ***h***, and the fourth
6:6 with the black ***h*** is going to the
14:15 also affect the ***h***, mules, camels,
14:20 the bells of the ***h***, and the pots in
Acts
23:24 Have ***h*** ready for Paul to ride, so they
James
3:3 When we bridle ***h*** and put bits in their
Revelation
9:7 looked like ***h*** ready for battle.
18:13 cattle, sheep, ***h***, and carriages,
19:14 pure, were following him on white ***h***.

HOSANNA

Matthew
21:9 him shouted, "***H*** to the Son of
21:15 in the temple, "***H*** to the Son of
Mark
11:9 were shouting, "***H***! Blessings on the
11:10 our ancestor David! ***H*** in the highest!"
John
12:13 They shouted, "***H***! Blessings on the

HOSHEA

Numbers
13:8 the tribe of Ephraim, ***H***, Nun's son;
13:16 the name of ***H***, Nun's son, to
2 Kings
15:30 Then ***H***, Elah's son, plotted against
Nehemiah
10:23 ***H***, Hananiah, Hasshub

HOSPITALITY

Genesis
44:4 have you repaid ***h*** with ingratitude?
1 Timothy
3:2 They should show ***h*** and be skilled at
5:10 providing ***h*** to strangers,
Titus
1:8 they should show ***h***, love what is

HOUR

Psalms
119:148 encounter each ***h*** of the night as I

Matthew
20:12 last worked one ***h***, and they
24:36 when that day or ***h*** will come, not
25:13 you don't know the day or the ***h***.
26:40 Couldn't you stay alert one ***h*** with me?
Mark
13:32 when that day or ***h*** will come, not
14:37 Couldn't you stay alert for one ***h***?
Luke
1:10 during this ***h*** of incense
22:59 An ***h*** or so later, someone else
John
4:53 that this was the ***h*** when Jesus had
Romans
13:11 time it is. The ***h*** has already come
1 John
2:18 it is the last ***h***. Just as you have
Revelation
8:1 silence in heaven for about half an ***h***.
9:15 ready for that ***h***, day, month, and
11:13 At that ***h*** there was a great earthquake,
14:7 glory, for the ***h*** of his judgment
17:12 authority for an ***h***, along with the
18:10 city! In a single ***h*** your judgment has

HOUSE → GOD'S HOUSE
Genesis
19:2 to your servant's ***h***, spend the night,
24:23 in your father's ***h*** for us to spend
Exodus
12:22 out the door of your ***h*** until morning.
20:17 your neighbor's ***h***. Do not desire
Deuteronomy
5:21 your neighbor's ***h***, field, male or
Joshua
2:1 and entered the ***h*** of a prostitute
6:22 the prostitute's ***h***. Bring out the
2 Samuel
2:10 two years. The ***h*** of Judah,
3:1 between Saul's ***h*** and David's house
23:5 Yes, my ***h*** is this way with God! He has
2 Kings
15:5 in a separate ***h***. The king's son
Psalms
5:7 I will enter your ***h*** because of your
23:6 live in the LORD's ***h*** as long as I live.
26:8 beauty of your ***h***, LORD; I love the
45:10 Forget your people and your father's ***h***.
50:9 bulls from your ***h*** or goats from
66:13 I'll enter your ***h*** with entirely
98:3 to the ***h*** of Israel; every
115:12 will bless the ***h*** of Israel; God
127:1 who builds the ***h***, the builders'
128:3 In your ***h***, your wife will be like a
135:19 ***H*** of Israel, bless the LORD! House of
Proverbs
7:27 Her ***h*** is a path to the grave, going
9:1 Wisdom built her ***h***; she has carved out
14:1 woman builds her ***h***, while a foolish
14:11 The ***h*** of the wicked is destroyed, but
21:9 with a contentious woman in a large ***h***.
27:10 your relative's ***h*** when disaster
Ecclesiastes
10:18 sags; through idle hands, the ***h*** leaks.
Isaiah
5:8 those who acquire ***h*** after house, who
7:13 said, "Listen, ***h*** of David! Isn't
56:7 them joy in my ***h*** of prayer. I will
Jeremiah
18:2 to the potter's ***h***, and I'll give
Ezekiel
33:7 a lookout for the ***h*** of Israel.
39:29 Spirit upon the ***h*** of Israel, I
43:10 the temple to the ***h*** of Israel. Let
Obadiah
1:17 be holy; and the ***h*** of Jacob will
1:18 The ***h*** of Jacob will be a fire, the
Nahum
1:14 image from the ***h*** of your gods; I
Haggai
1:4 houses while this ***h*** lies in ruins?
2:7 I will fill this ***h*** with glory, says
Zechariah
8:9 for the ***h*** of the LORD of
14:21 merchants in the ***h*** of the LORD of
Matthew
7:24 wise builder who built a ***h*** on bedrock.
12:29 people go into a ***h*** that belongs to a
21:13 It's written, My ***h*** will be called a
Mark
3:25 And a ***h*** torn apart by divisions will
Luke
6:48 person building a ***h*** by digging deep
10:7 Remain in this ***h***, eating and drinking
11:17 wasteland, and a ***h*** torn apart by
11:24 says, 'I'll go back to the ***h*** I left.'
15:8 and sweep the ***h***, searching her
John
2:16 make my Father's ***h*** a place of
2:17 Passion for your ***h*** consumes me.
12:3 her hair. The ***h*** was filled with
14:2 My Father's ***h*** has room to spare. If
Romans
16:5 meets in their ***h***. Say hello to
2 Corinthians
5:1 from God. It's a ***h*** that isn't
Philemon
1:2 and the church that meets in your ***h***.
Hebrews
8:8 covenant with the ***h*** of Israel, and I

HOUSEHOLD
Genesis
7:1 with your whole ***h***, because among
50:8 Joseph's entire ***h***, his brothers, and
Exodus
12:3 a lamb for each ***h***, a lamb per house.
Proverbs
31:15 food for her ***h***, even some for
Ezekiel
2:5 since they are a ***h*** of rebels, they
44:30 a blessing may come to rest on your ***h***.
Matthew
10:25 members of his ***h*** by even worse
13:52 the head of a ***h*** who brings old
John
4:53 he and his entire ***h*** believed in Jesus.
8:35 member of the ***h***, but a son is.
Acts
11:14 you and your entire ***h*** can be saved.'
16:15 Once she and her ***h*** were baptized, she
16:31 will be saved—you and your entire ***h***."
18:8 and his entire ***h*** came to believe

1 Timothy
3:4 manage their own ***h*** well—they should
3:15 behave in God's ***h***. It is the church
1 Peter
2:18 ***H*** slaves, submit by accepting the
4:17 with God's own ***h***. But if judgment

HOUSEHOLDS
Numbers
16:32 them and their ***h***, including every
Matthew
10:36 enemies are members of their own ***h***.
13:57 own hometowns and in their own ***h***."
Mark
6:4 their relatives, and in their own ***h***."
1 Timothy
3:12 their children and their own ***h*** well.
2 Timothy
3:6 will slither into ***h*** and control
Titus
1:11 they upset entire ***h***. They teach what

HOUSES
Exodus
12:7 the door of the ***h*** in which they are
12:27 passed over the ***h*** of the Israelites
Ecclesiastes
2:4 projects: I built ***h*** for myself,
Isaiah
65:21 They will build ***h*** and live in them;
Jeremiah
29:28 time, so build ***h*** and settle down,
Ezekiel
11:3 aren't building ***h***. The city is the
Matthew
19:29 all who have left ***h***, brothers,
24:17 come down to grab things from their ***h***.
Mark
13:15 down or enter their ***h*** to grab anything.
Luke
16:4 people will welcome me into their ***h***.
Acts
4:34 properties or ***h*** would sell them,
5:42 Christ, both in the temple and in ***h***.
7:48 doesn't live in ***h*** built by human
1 Corinthians
11:22 Don't you have ***h*** to eat and drink in?

HUMAN → HUMAN ONE
Genesis
2:5 was still no ***h*** being to farm the
2:7 God formed the ***h*** from the topsoil
3:22 God said, "The ***h*** being has now
3:24 He drove out the ***h***. To the east of the
6:4 divine beings and ***h*** daughters had
9:6 Whoever sheds ***h*** blood, by a human his
Leviticus
24:21 whoever kills a ***h*** being must be
27:29 No ***h*** beings that have been devoted can
Deuteronomy
4:32 God first created ***h*** beings on earth,
5:24 can speak to a ***h*** being and they
Job
4:17 Can a ***h*** be more righteous than God, a
7:17 What are ***h*** beings, that you exalt them,
25:6 how much less a ***h***, a worm, a person's
Psalms
8:4 what are ***h*** beings that you think about
22:6 a worm, less than ***h***; insulted by one
104:15 and bread, which sustains the ***h*** heart.
146:3 don't trust any ***h*** beings
Proverbs
8:31 earth and delighting in the ***h*** race.
15:11 how much more the hearts of ***h*** beings!
18:14 The ***h*** spirit sustains a sick person,
30:2 too stupid to be ***h***, a man without
Ecclesiastes
6:12 what's good for ***h*** beings during
7:29 I found: God made ***h*** beings
9:3 Moreover, the ***h*** heart is full of
12:5 nothing; when the ***h*** goes to the
Ezekiel
1:5 like: Each had the form of a ***h*** being,
1:8 ***H*** hands were under their wings on all
Daniel
2:38 into your care ***h*** beings, wild
7:4 two feet, like a ***h*** being, and it
8:16 I then heard a ***h*** voice coming out of
8:25 will be broken—and not by a ***h*** hand.
10:16 who looked like a ***h*** being touched my
Matthew
9:8 had given such authority to ***h*** beings.
16:23 God's thoughts but ***h*** thoughts."
19:26 impossible for ***h*** beings. But all
Luke
7:28 that no greater ***h*** being has ever
20:4 baptism of heavenly or of ***h*** origin?"
John
1:13 blood nor from ***h*** desire or
5:34 I don't accept ***h*** testimony, I say
8:15 according to ***h*** standards, but I
10:33 God. You are ***h*** yet you make
12:43 but they loved ***h*** praise more than
Acts
5:38 or activity is of ***h*** origin, it will
7:48 houses built by ***h*** hands. As the
14:11 gods have taken ***h*** form and come
17:29 image made by ***h*** skill and thought.
19:26 that gods made by ***h*** hands aren't
Romans
1:18 the injustice of ***h*** beings who
2:9 for every ***h*** being who does
3:4 even if every ***h*** being is a liar,
9:20 You are only a ***h*** being. Who do you
14:18 way pleases God and gets ***h*** approval.
1 Corinthians
1:25 God is wiser than ***h*** wisdom, and the
3:21 should brag about ***h*** beings.
15:21 came through a ***h*** being, the
Colossians
2:22 Such rules are ***h*** commandments and
3:9 Take off the old ***h*** nature with its
Hebrews
2:6 Or what is the ***h*** being that you
9:11 isn't made by ***h*** hands (that is,
James
3:9 Father and curse ***h*** beings made in
1 Peter
3:18 put to death as a ***h***, but made alive
4:1 suffered as a ***h***, you should also
1 John
4:2 Christ has come as a ***h*** is from God,
5:9 If we receive ***h*** testimony, God's

Revelation
4:7 had a face like a ***h*** being. And the
9:7 crowns. Their faces were like ***h*** faces,
13:18 for it's a ***h*** being's number.
18:13 carriages, and slaves, even ***h*** lives.

HUMAN ONE

Eze 2:1; 2:3, 6, 8; 3:1, 3, 4, 10, 17, 25; 4:1, 16; 5:1; 6:2; 7:2; 8:5, 6, 8, 12, 15, 17; 11:2, 4, 15; 12:2, 3, 9, 18, 22, 27; 13:2, 17; 14:3, 13; 15:2; 16:2; 17:2; 20:3, 4, 27, 46; 21:2, 6, 9, 12, 14, 19, 28; 22:2, 18, 24; 23:2, 36; 24:2, 16, 25; 25:2; 26:2; 27:2; 28:2, 12, 21; 29:2, 18; 30:2, 21; 31:2; 32:2, 18; 33:2, 7, 10, 12, 24, 30; 34:2; 35:2; 36:1, 17; 37:3, 9, 11, 16; 38:2, 14; 39:1, 17; 40:4; 43:7, 10, 18; 44:5; 47:6; Dn 8:17; Mi 6:8; Mt 8:20; 9:6; 10:23; 11:19; 12:8, 32, 40; 13:37, 41; 16:13, 27, 28; 17:9, 12, 22; 19:28; 20:18, 28; 24:27, 30, 33, 37, 39, 44; 25:31; 26:2, 24, 45, 64; Mk 2:10; 2:28; 8:31, 38; 9:9, 12, 31; 10:33, 45; 13:26; 14:21, 41, 62; Lk 5:24; 6:5, 22; 7:34; 9:22, 26, 44, 58; 11:30; 12:8, 10, 40; 17:22, 24, 26, 30; 18:8, 31; 19:10; 21:27, 36; 22:22, 48, 69; 24:7; Jn 1:51; 3:13, 14; 5:27; 6:27, 53, 62; 8:28; 9:35; 12:23, 34; 13:31, 32; Ac 7:56; Rev 1:13; 14:14

HUMANITY → ALL HUMANITY

Genesis
1:26 Let us make ***h*** in our image to
5:1 day God created ***h***, he made them to
5:2 and called them ***h*** on the day they
6:5 The LORD saw that ***h*** had become
Ecclesiastes
6:1 the sun, and it weighs heavily upon ***h***.
Haggai
1:11 ground, on ***h***, on beasts, and
Zechariah
11:6 to bring upon ***h***, upon each of
12:1 who fashions the spirit of ***h*** within it:
Luke
3:6 All ***h*** will see God's salvation.
Acts
15:17 that the rest of ***h*** will seek the
1 Timothy
2:5 between God and ***h***, the human Christ
Hebrews
2:6 What is ***h*** that you think

HUMANS

Genesis
6:3 not remain in ***h*** forever, because
Job
5:7 Surely ***h*** are born to distress, just as
15:14 What are ***h*** that they might be pure, and
33:15 sleep falls upon ***h***, during their
34:15 die together, and ***h*** would return to
Psalms
14:2 from heaven on ***h*** to see if anyone
36:6 sea. LORD, you save both ***h*** and animals.
53:2 from heaven on ***h*** to see if anyone
57:4 those who devour ***h***. Their teeth are
58:1 you gods? Do you really judge ***h*** fairly?
78:60 the tent where he had lived with ***h***.
89:47 Have you created ***h*** for no good
90:3 people to dust, saying, "Go back, ***h***,"
94:10 The one who teaches ***h***, doesn't he know?
144:4 ***H*** are like a puff of air; their days go
Ecclesiastes
3:19 same life-breath. ***H*** are no better off
6:7 the hard work of ***h*** is for the mouth,
Micah
5:7 does not hope for ***h*** or wait for human ones
Mark
2:27 was created for ***h***; humans weren't
Romans
1:20 God has made. So ***h*** are without
1 Peter
2:4 was rejected by ***h***, from God's

HUMBLE

Numbers
12:3 the man Moses was ***h***, more so than
Deuteronomy
8:2 so he could ***h*** you, testing you
8:16 in order to ***h*** and test you, but
1 Kings
11:39 I will ***h*** David's descendants by means
Job
40:11 look on all the proud and ***h*** them.
Psalms
55:19 will hear and ***h*** them Selah
Proverbs
3:34 mockers, but he shows favor to the ***h***.
6:3 neighbor. So go, ***h*** yourself, and
16:19 Better to be ***h*** with the needy than to
29:23 low, but those of ***h*** spirit gain honor.
Isaiah
66:2 will look: to the ***h*** and contrite in
Daniel
4:37 and he is able to ***h*** all who walk in
10:12 things and to ***h*** yourself before
Zephaniah
2:3 the LORD, all you ***h*** of the land who
3:12 I will cause a ***h*** and powerless
Zechariah
9:9 victorious. He is ***h*** and riding on an
Matthew
5:5 people who are ***h***, because they
11:29 I'm gentle and ***h***. And you will
18:4 Those who ***h*** themselves like this little
21:5 is coming to you, ***h*** and riding on a
Philippians
3:21 transform our ***h*** bodies so that
James
3:13 are good with a ***h*** lifestyle that
4:6 against the proud, but favors the ***h***.
4:10 ***H*** yourselves before the Lord, and he
1 Peter
5:5 the proud, but he gives favor to the ***h***.
5:6 Therefore, ***h*** yourselves under God's
Malachi
2:9 you despised and ***h*** in the view of

HUNGER

Proverbs
16:26 for them, for their ***h*** presses them on.
Hosea
9:4 will be for their ***h*** alone; it will
Amos
8:11 when I will send ***h*** and thirst on the

HUNGER [cont.]

Luke
6:21 Happy are you who ***h*** now, because you
2 Corinthians
6:5 hard work, sleepless nights, and ***h***.
11:27 sleepless nights, ***h*** and thirst, often
Revelation
7:16 They won't ***h*** or thirst anymore. No sun
18:8 grief, and ***h***. She will be

HUNGRY

Genesis
25:29 stew, Esau came in from the field ***h***
Nehemiah
9:15 When they were ***h***, you gave them bread
Psalms
34:10 without and get ***h***, but those who
50:12 Even if I were ***h***, I wouldn't tell you
107:5 They were ***h*** and thirsty; their lives
107:9 he filled up the ***h*** with good things!
107:36 he settles the ***h***. They even build
Proverbs
19:15 brings on deep sleep; a slacker goes ***h***.
27:7 bitter tastes sweet to a ***h*** person.
Isaiah
8:21 dejected and ***h***, and when they
Ezekiel
18:7 give food to the ***h*** and clothes to
Matthew
5:6 people who are ***h*** and thirsty for
15:32 to send them away ***h*** for fear they
25:35 I was ***h*** and you gave me food to eat. I
25:42 I was ***h*** and you didn't give me food to
Mark
11:12 after leaving Bethany, Jesus was ***h***.
John
6:35 me will never go ***h***, and whoever
Acts
10:10 He became ***h*** and wanted to eat. While
Romans
12:20 If your enemy is ***h***, feed him; if he
1 Corinthians
4:11 moment we are ***h***, thirsty, wearing
11:21 One person goes ***h*** while another is
11:34 some of you are ***h***, they should eat
Philippians
4:12 whether full or ***h*** or whether having

HURRY

Genesis
19:22 ***H***! Escape to it! I can't do anything
Psalms
55:8 I'd ***h*** to my hideout, far from the
71:12 far from me, God! My God, ***h*** to help me!
79:8 your compassion ***h*** to meet us
119:60 I ***h*** to keep your commandments—I never put if off.
Proverbs
1:16 run to evil; they ***h*** to spill blood.
21:5 but those who ***h*** end up with loss.
Matthew
28:7 Now ***h***, go and tell his disciples,
Acts
22:18 speaking to me. '***H***!' he said. 'Leave

HURT

Proverbs
9:7 whoever corrects the wicked gets ***h***.
Isaiah
65:25 dust. They won't ***h*** or destroy at any
Matthew
5:39 those who want to ***h*** you. If people
1 Corinthians
8:12 and sisters and ***h*** their weak
Revelation
2:11 won't be ***h*** by the second
9:4 were told not to ***h*** the grass of the
9:10 is their power to ***h*** people for five
11:5 anyone wants to ***h*** them, fire comes

HUSBAND

Genesis
3:6 gave some to her ***h***, who was with
16:3 gave her to her ***h*** Abram as his wife.
Numbers
30:8 the day that her ***h*** hears it, he
30:16 concerning a ***h*** and his wife and
Deuteronomy
24:4 case, the first ***h*** who originally
Ruth
1:3 Naomi's ***h***, died. Then only
2:1 through her ***h*** from the family
Esther
1:22 It said that each ***h*** should rule over
Proverbs
7:19 For my ***h*** isn't home; he's gone far
12:4 is a crown to her ***h***, but a
31:11 Her ***h*** entrusts his heart to her, and
Jeremiah
3:14 for I'm your ***h***. I'll gather you—
31:32 I was their ***h***, declares the
Ezekiel
16:45 She loathed her ***h*** and also her
Hosea
2:16 will call me, "My ***h***," and no longer
Matthew
1:16 of Joseph, the ***h*** of Mary—of whom
Luke
2:36 she lived with her ***h*** for seven years.
16:18 divorced from her ***h*** commits adultery.
John
4:17 I don't have a ***h***." "You are right
1 Corinthians
7:2 have her own ***h*** because of sexual
7:3 The ***h*** should meet his wife's sexual
7:10 married: a wife shouldn't leave her ***h***,
7:11 reconciled to her ***h***. And a man
7:14 The ***h*** who doesn't believe belongs to
7:39 as long as her ***h*** is alive. But if
2 Corinthians
11:2 marriage to one ***h***. I promised to
Ephesians
5:23 A ***h*** is the head of his wife like Christ
Revelation
21:2 a bride beautifully dressed for her ***h***.

HUSBANDS

Ephesians
5:22 submit to their ***h*** as if to the Lord.
5:25 As for ***h***, love your wives just like

Colossians
3:18 submit to your ***h*** in a way that is
3:19 ***H***, love your wives and don't be harsh
Titus
2:4 women to love their ***h*** and children,
2:5 to their own ***h***, so that God's
1 Peter
3:1 to your own ***h***. Do this so that

HYSSOP

Exodus
12:22 Take a bunch of ***h***, dip it into the
Psalms
51:7 Purify me with ***h*** and I will be clean;
John
19:29 placed it on a ***h*** branch, and held
Hebrews
9:19 scarlet wool, and ***h***, and sprinkled

Ii

I AM GOD

Ps 46:10; 50:7; Is 43:12; 45:22; 46:9; Eze 28:2; Hos 11:9

I AM THE LORD

Gn 15:7; 28:13; Ex 6:2; 6:6, 8, 29; 7:5, 17; 10:2; 12:12; 14:4, 18; 15:26; 16:12; 20:2; Lv 11:44; 11:45; 18:2, 4, 5, 6, 21, 30; 19:3, 4, 10, 12, 14, 16, 18, 25, 28, 30, 31, 32, 36, 37; 20:7, 8; 21:12, 15, 23; 22:2, 3, 8, 9, 16, 30, 31, 32, 33; 23:22, 43; 24:22; 25:17, 38, 55; 26:1, 2, 13, 44, 45; Nm 3:13; 3:41, 45; 10:10; 15:41; Dt 5:6; 29:6; Jdg 6:10; 1Ki 20:13; 20:28; Ps 81:10; Is 41:13; 42:8; 43:3, 11, 15; 44:24; 45:3, 5, 6, 7, 19; 48:17; 49:23; 51:15; 60:16, 22; Jer 9:24; 16:21; 24:7; 32:27; Eze 6:7; 6:10, 13, 14; 7:4, 27; 11:10, 12; 12:15, 16, 20, 25; 13:9, 14, 21, 23; 14:8; 15:7; 16:62; 20:5, 7, 19, 20, 26, 38, 42, 44; 22:14, 16; 23:49; 24:24, 27; 25:5, 7, 11, 17; 26:6; 28:22, 23, 24; 29:6, 9, 16, 21; 30:8, 19, 25, 26; 32:15; 33:29; 34:27; 35:4, 9, 12, 15; 36:11, 23, 38; 37:6, 13, 14; 38:23; 39:6, 28; Hos 12:9; Jl 2:27; 3:17; Zec 10:6; Mal 3:6

I AM WITH YOU

Gn 26:24; 28:15; 1Ki 22:4; Is 41:10; 43:5; Jer 1:19; 15:20; 30:11; Hg 1:13; 2:4; Jn 14:25; Ro 1:12

I WILL BLESS YOU

Gn 22:17; 26:24; 27:7; Ps 63:4; 145:2; Hg 2:19

I WILL DELIVER

Ex 25:22; 2Ch 12:7; Ps 50:15; Jer 15:9; 15:13; 21:7; 30:10; 46:27; Eze 37:23; Zep 3:19; Zec 8:13

I WILL FORGIVE

Nm 14:20; Jer 31:34; 33:8; 36:3; 50:20; Jl 3:21

I WILL HEAL

Dt 32:39; Is 57:18; 57:19; Jer 3:22; 30:17; 33:6; Hos 14:4

I WILL RESCUE YOU

Jdg 7:7; 2Ki 20:6; Is 38:6; Jer 15:21; 39:17; Ac 26:17

IDOL

Exodus
20:4 Do not make an ***i*** for yourself—no form
Deuteronomy
5:8 Do not make an ***i*** for yourself—no form
9:16 a calf, an ***i*** made of cast
1 Samuel
19:16 they found the ***i*** in the bed with
Psalms
106:19 at Horeb, bowing down to a metal ***i***.
Isaiah
44:9 ***I***-makers are all as nothing; their
48:5 wouldn't say, "My ***i*** did them; my wood
Nahum
1:14 remove carved ***i*** and cast image
Habakkuk
2:18 what value is an ***i***, when its potter
Acts
7:41 when they made an ***i*** in the shape of a
1 Corinthians
8:7 to a real ***i***, because they

IDOLATRY

1 Samuel
15:23 like the evil of ***i***. Because you have
Zechariah
10:2 images speak ***i***, and diviners see
Galatians
5:20 ***i***, drug use and casting spells, hate,
Colossians
3:5 evil desire, and greed (which is ***i***).

IDOLS

Leviticus
19:4 Do not turn to ***i*** or make gods of cast
Deuteronomy
7:5 their sacred poles, and burn their ***i***
12:3 Hack their gods' ***i*** into pieces. Wipe
29:17 the filthy ***i*** of wood and
2 Kings
17:16 two metal ***i*** cast in the shape
21:21 same worthless ***i*** his father had
2 Chronicles
11:15 and the goat and calf ***i*** he had made.
24:18 sacred poles and ***i***. Anger came upon
33:19 sacred poles, and ***i*** he set up before
34:4 the sacred poles, ***i***, and images,
Psalms
78:58 shrines; they angered him with their ***i***.
96:5 nations are just ***i***, but it is the
97:7 who are proud of ***i***, are put to
115:4 Their ***i*** are just silver and gold—
135:15 The nations' ***i*** are just silver and
Jeremiah
32:34 their disgusting ***i*** in the temple
51:17 is shamed by his ***i***, for their images
51:47 with Babylon's ***i***; the whole land
Hosea
4:17 is associated with ***i***—let him alone!
8:4 gold they crafted ***i*** for their own
11:2 Baals, and they burned incense to ***i***.
13:2 metal images, ***i*** of silver, as a
14:8 Ephraim, what do ***i*** have to do with me?

Micah
1:7 will make all her ***i*** worthless. Since
Zechariah
13:2 the names of the ***i*** from the land;
Acts
15:20 associated with ***i***, sexual
15:29 food offered to ***i***, blood, the meat
17:16 find that the city was flooded with ***i***.
21:25 food offered to ***i***, blood, the meat
Romans
2:22 If you hate ***i***, do you rob
2 Corinthians
6:16 God's temple and ***i***? Because we are
1 Thessalonians
1:9 to God from ***i***. As a result, you
1 Peter
4:3 and their forbidden worship of ***i***.
1 John
5:21 children, guard yourselves from ***i***!
Revelation
2:14 sacrificed to ***i*** and commit sexual
9:20 demons and ***i*** made of gold,

IMAGE

Genesis
1:26 humanity in our ***i*** to resemble us so
5:3 of a son in his ***i***, resembling him,
9:6 for in the divine ***i*** God made human
Exodus
32:4 he made a metal ***i*** of a bull calf,
Judges
6:28 with the asherah ***i*** that had been
18:14 a sculpted ***i***, and a molded
Nehemiah
9:18 they had cast an ***i*** of a calf for
Psalms
17:15 I will be filled full by seeing your ***i***.
106:20 God for an ***i*** of a bull that
Mark
4:30 What's a good ***i*** for God's
12:16 to them, "Whose ***i*** and inscription
Acts
17:29 silver, or stone ***i*** made by human
19:35 and of her ***i***, which fell from
Romans
8:29 conformed to the ***i*** of his Son. That
1 Corinthians
11:7 because he is the ***i*** and glory of God;
2 Corinthians
3:18 into that same ***i*** from one degree
4:4 Christ's glory. Christ is the ***i*** of God.
Ephesians
4:24 to God's ***i*** in justice and
Colossians
1:15 The Son is the ***i*** of the invisible God,
3:10 conforming to the ***i*** of the one who
3:11 In this ***i*** there is neither Greek nor
Revelation
13:14 earth to make an ***i*** for the beast who
13:15 to the beast's ***i*** so that the
20:4 the beast or its ***i***, who hadn't

IMAGES → DIVINE IMAGES

Numbers
33:52 all their cast ***i***. You will
Deuteronomy
7:25 Burn the ***i*** of their gods. Don't desire
1 Samuel
6:5 You must make ***i*** of your tumors and the
1 Kings
14:9 gods and metal ***i*** to anger me. You
2 Kings
11:18 its altars and ***i*** into pieces. They
17:12 They worshipped ***i*** about which the LORD
17:15 worthless ***i*** so that they too
21:11 He has caused Judah to sin with his ***i***.
2 Chronicles
3:7 gold, and carved ***i*** of winged
23:17 its altars and ***i*** into pieces. They
28:2 Israel's kings, making ***i*** of the Baals
34:3 the sacred poles, idols, and ***i***.
Psalms
97:7 those who worship ***i***, those who are
Isaiah
10:10 with more ***i*** than Jerusalem
21:9 and all the ***i*** of her gods are
41:29 to nothing; their ***i*** are a total
Jeremiah
8:19 me with their ***i***, with pointless
10:14 idols, for their ***i*** are shams; they
50:2 Her ***i*** are shamed; her
51:17 idols, for their ***i*** are shams; they
Ezekiel
7:20 detestable ***i***! Therefore, I've
8:12 of sculptured ***i***? They say, "The
16:17 and you made male ***i*** for yourself and
21:21 the divine ***i***, and inspects the
23:14 in wall reliefs, ***i*** of Chaldeans
30:13 an end to the ***i*** in Memphis. Never
Hosea
3:4 a priestly vest or household divine ***i***.
13:2 have made metal ***i***, idols of silver,
Amos
5:26 star-god, your ***i***, which you made
Micah
1:7 All her ***i*** will be beaten to pieces; all
5:13 cut down your ***i*** and your sacred
Acts
7:43 god Rephan, the ***i*** that you made in
Romans
1:23 immortal God for ***i*** that look like

IMMIGRANT

Genesis
12:10 to live as an ***i*** since the famine
19:9 Does this ***i*** want to judge us?
20:1 he settled as an ***i*** in Gerar, between
21:23 me and the land in which you are an ***i***."
21:34 lived as an ***i*** in the
23:4 I am an ***i*** and a temporary resident
26:3 this land as an ***i***, and I will be
32:4 I've lived as an ***i*** with Laban, where
37:1 of Canaan where his father was an ***i***.
Exodus
2:22 I've been an ***i*** living in a
3:22 along with the ***i*** in her household
12:19 the person is an ***i*** or a native of
12:48 If an ***i*** who lives with you wants to
12:49 and for the ***i*** who lives with
18:3 I have been an ***i*** living in a
20:10 animals, or the ***i*** who is living
22:21 or oppress an ***i***, because you were
23:9 Don't oppress an ***i***. You know what it's

23:12 slave and the ***i*** may be refreshed.
Leviticus
16:29 citizen or the ***i*** who lives among
17:12 nor can the ***i*** who lives with
18:26 citizen nor ***i*** who lives with
19:10 the poor and the ***i***; I am the LORD
19:34 Any ***i*** who lives with you must be
20:2 Israelite or any ***i*** living in Israel
23:22 the poor and the ***i***; I am the LORD
24:16 will stone him. ***I*** and citizen
25:35 as you would an ***i*** or foreign guest
Numbers
9:14 If an ***i*** resides among you and wishes to
15:14 If an ***i*** lives with you or has settled
15:30 a citizen or an ***i***, and insults the
19:10 and for the ***i*** who lives among
Deuteronomy
1:16 or between a tribe member and an ***i***.
5:14 animals, or the ***i*** who is living
24:17 rights of an ***i*** or orphan. Don't
26:5 living as an ***i*** there with few
Judges
17:7 He was a Levite residing there as an ***i***.
19:1 living as an ***i*** in the far
Ruth
2:10 eyes, that you notice me? I'm an ***i***."
2 Samuel
1:13 the son of an ***i***," he answered.
1 Kings
8:41 also to the ***i*** who isn't from
8:42 arm. When the ***i*** comes and prays
8:43 do everything the ***i*** asks. Do this so
Psalms
39:12 a foreigner—an ***i*** staying with you,
69:8 own brothers, an ***i*** to my mother's
105:23 Jacob became an ***i*** in the land of
119:19 I'm an ***i*** in the land. Don't hide your
119:54 of praise wherever I lived as an ***i***.
120:5 I have been an ***i*** in Meshech,
Isaiah
56:3 Don't let the ***i*** who has joined with the
Jeremiah
7:6 advantage of the ***i***, orphan, or
Ezekiel
14:7 of Israel or any ***i*** in Israel who
22:29 mistreated the ***i***. They've
Acts
7:29 he lived as an ***i*** and had two sons.

IMMIGRANTS

Genesis
15:13 will live as ***i*** in a land that
17:8 in which you are ***i***, the whole land
28:4 which you are now ***i***, the land God
35:27 where Abraham and Isaac lived as ***i***.
36:7 they lived as ***i*** couldn't support
47:4 to the land as ***i*** because the
Exodus
6:4 land of Canaan where they lived as ***i***.
22:21 you were once ***i*** in the land of
23:9 because you were ***i*** in the land of
Leviticus
17:8 house or from the ***i*** who live with you
17:10 house or from the ***i*** who live with you
19:34 because you were ***i*** in the land of
22:18 house or from the ***i*** in Israel
Numbers
35:15 for Israelites, ***i***, and temporary
Deuteronomy
10:19 must also love ***i*** because you were
14:21 flesh to the ***i*** who live in your
14:29 along with the ***i***, orphans, and
16:11 your cities, the ***i***, the orphans, and
16:14 the Levites, the ***i***, the orphans, and
23:7 because you were ***i*** in their land.
24:14 Israelites or ***i*** who live in your
26:11 Levites and the ***i*** who are among you.
27:19 legal rights of ***i***, orphans, or
28:43 The ***i*** who live among you will be
29:11 wives, and the ***i*** who live with you
31:12 children, and the ***i*** who live in your
Joshua
8:33 included both ***i*** and full
20:9 and for ***i*** residing among
2 Samuel
4:3 Gittaim and even now live there as ***i***.
1 Chronicles
16:19 few in number—insignificant, just ***i***—
22:2 to gather the ***i*** living in the
29:15 our ancestors, ***i*** without permanent
Psalms
94:6 kill widows and ***i***; they murder
105:12 few in number—insignificant, just ***i***—
146:9 who protects ***i***, who helps
Isaiah
14:1 their own land. ***I*** will join them,
56:6 The ***i*** who have joined me, serving me
Ezekiel
20:38 they lived as ***i***, but they won't
22:7 you they oppress ***i*** and deny the
47:22 inheritance, the ***i*** who reside with
Hebrews
11:13 they were strangers and ***i*** on earth.
1 Peter
2:11 since you are ***i*** and strangers in

IMMORALITY

Mark
7:22 unrestrained ***i***, envy, insults,
Acts
15:20 idols, sexual ***i***, eating meat from
21:25 from strangled animals, and sexual ***i***."
1 Corinthians
5:1 there is sexual ***i*** among you. This
6:13 isn't for sexual ***i*** but for the Lord,
7:2 her own husband because of sexual ***i***.
10:8 practice sexual ***i***, like some of
2 Corinthians
12:21 sexual ***i***, and doing
Galatians
5:19 include sexual ***i***, moral
Ephesians
5:3 Sexual ***i***, and any kind of impurity or
Colossians
3:5 such as sexual ***i***, moral
1 Thessalonians
4:3 means that you stay away from sexual ***i***
1 Peter
4:3 unrestrained ***i*** and lust, their
2 Peter
1:4 from the world's ***i*** that sinful
2:2 unrestrained ***i***, and because of

Jude
1:4 into unrestrained ***i*** and deny our only
Revelation
2:14 to idols and commit sexual ***i***.
2:20 committing sexual ***i*** and eating food
9:21 their sexual ***i***, or their
17:2 committed sexual ***i*** with her, and
18:3 committed sexual ***i*** with her, and the
21:8 who commit sexual ***i***, those who use

IMPURE

Exodus
20:25 chisel on the stone will make it ***i***.
Leviticus
21:6 their God's name ***i***. They must be
21:12 God's sanctuary ***i*** by doing so,
21:15 make his children ***i*** among his people,
22:2 not make my holy name ***i***: I am the LORD.
Numbers
18:32 of the Israelites ***i***, on penalty of
25:1 made themselves ***i*** by having illicit
2 Chronicles
29:5 from the sanctuary any ***i*** thing.
Nehemiah
13:17 I asked. "You are making the Sabbath ***i***!
Job
14:4 Who can make pure from ***i***? Nobody
Ecclesiastes
9:2 the pure and the ***i***, those who
Isaiah
1:22 silver has become ***i***; your beer is
43:28 holy officials ***i***, handed over
47:6 my inheritance ***i*** and put them
48:11 my name be made ***i***? I won't give my
56:2 not making it ***i***, and avoids doing
Jeremiah
34:16 and made my name ***i***; each of you
Ezekiel
14:11 make themselves ***i*** with any of their
20:39 make my holy name ***i*** with your gifts
22:26 my holy things ***i***. They have not
23:38 unclean and made my sabbaths ***i***.
24:21 make my sanctuary ***i***, the pride of
28:16 and you became ***i***. So I expelled
Daniel
11:31 fortress ***i***. They will stop
Malachi
1:12 you make my name ***i*** when you say,
2:10 make the covenant of our ancestors ***i***?
John
18:28 palace would have made them ritually ***i***.
Acts
10:14 never eaten anything ***i*** or unclean."
10:28 never call a person ***i*** or unclean.
11:8 Lord! Nothing ***i*** or unclean has
Ephesians
5:5 sexually immoral, ***i***, or greedy—which
Revelation
17:4 of the vile and ***i*** things that came

IN THE LORD'S EYES

Nm 32:13; Dt 12:25; 21:9; 31:29; 1Sa 12:17; 15:19; 2Sa 11:27; 1Ki 11:6; 14:22; 15:5, 11, 26, 34; 16:7, 19, 25, 30; 21:20, 25; 22:43, 52; 2Ki 3:2; 8:18, 27; 12:2; 13:2, 11; 14:3, 24; 15:3, 9, 18, 24, 28, 34; 16:2; 17:2, 17; 18:3; 21:2, 6, 16, 20; 22:2; 23:32, 37; 24:9, 19; 2Ch 20:32; 21:6; 22:4; 24:2; 25:2; 26:4; 27:2; 28:1; 29:2; 33:2, 6, 22; 34:2; 36:5, 9; Is 49:5; Jer 52:2; Mal 2:17; Lk 1:15; 2Co 8:21

INCENSE ALTAR

Ex 30:6; 30:7, 27; 31:8; 35:15; 37:25; 1Ch 28:18; 2Ch 26:16; 26:19

INCENSE ALTARS

Lv 26:30; 2Ch 14:5; 30:14; 34:4, 7; Is 27:9; Eze 6:4; 6:6

INCREASE

Genesis
6:1 people started to ***i*** throughout the
48:4 many children, to ***i*** your numbers, and
1 Chronicles
4:10 bless me and ***i*** my territory. May
21:3 May the LORD ***i*** his people a
Psalms
16:4 their suffering ***i*** because they
71:21 Please ***i*** my honor and comfort me all
Proverbs
9:9 righteous, and their learning will ***i***.
19:4 Riches ***i*** one's friends, but the poor
Ecclesiastes
6:11 the more words ***i***, the more
Jeremiah
29:6 have children. ***I*** in number there
33:22 so I will ***i*** the descendants
Ezekiel
36:11 and animals ***i*** on you, they will
36:37 for them: that I ***i*** them like a human
37:26 and allow them to ***i***. I will set my
Daniel
12:4 will stray far, but knowledge will ***i***."
Luke
17:5 said to the Lord, "***I*** our faith!"
John
3:30 He must ***i*** and I must decrease
Acts
6:1 continued to ***i***, a complaint
12:24 God's word continued to grow and ***i***
2 Corinthians
4:15 gratitude to ***i***, which results in
9:10 seed and will ***i*** your crop, which
Philippians
1:26 and to ***i*** your pride in Christ Jesus
1 Thessalonians
3:12 Lord cause you to ***i*** and enrich your

INFECTION

Leviticus
13:2 and it becomes an ***i*** of skin disease
14:3 skin disease has been healed of the ***i***,
2 Timothy
2:17 spread like an ***i***. This includes

INHABITANTS

Exodus
23:31 I'll hand the ***i*** of the land over
34:12 covenant with the ***i*** of the land to
Leviticus
18:25 and the land vomited out its ***i***.

25:10 land to all its ***i***. It will be a

Job

26:5 dead writhe, the ***i*** beneath the

Psalms

24:1 in it, the world and its ***i*** too.
33:8 all the earth's ***i*** stand in awe of
75:3 earth and all its ***i*** will melt, but I
98:7 it roar; the world and all its ***i*** too.
107:34 dirt, when its ***i*** are wicked.

Habakkuk

2:8 to every village, and to all its ***i***.
2:17 land, the villages, and all their ***i***.

Zephaniah

1:4 against all the ***i*** of Jerusalem. I
2:5 Doom, ***i*** of the seacoast, nation of

INHABITED

Psalms

90:2 the earth and the ***i*** world

Proverbs

8:31 with his ***i*** earth and

Jeremiah

17:25 And this city will always be ***i***.

Ezekiel

12:20 The ***i*** cities will be laid waste, the
29:11 it, and it won't be ***i*** for forty years.
34:13 the riverbeds, and in all the ***i*** places.
35:9 cities won't be ***i***, and you will
36:10 cities will be ***i***, the ruins

Joel

3:20 But Judah will be ***i*** forever, and

Zechariah

2:4 Jerusalem will be ***i*** like open fields
7:7 and the western foothills were ***i***?"
9:5 perish from Gaza; Ashkelon won't be ***i***.

Romans

10:18 gone out to the corners of the ***i*** world.

INHERIT

Numbers

18:23 But they will not ***i*** land among the
34:13 that you will ***i*** by lot, which the

Psalms

37:11 But the weak will ***i*** the land; they will
69:36 servants will ***i*** Zion, and those

Proverbs

11:29 their family will ***i*** the wind. The
28:10 but the blameless will ***i*** good things.

Isaiah

57:13 refuge in me will ***i*** the land and

Ezekiel

33:25 you shed blood. Should you ***i*** the land?
33:26 adultery. Should you ***i*** the land?

Matthew

5:5 humble, because they will ***i*** the earth.
19:29 times more and will ***i*** eternal life.
25:34 from my Father. ***I*** the kingdom that

Romans

4:13 that he would ***i*** the world, didn't
4:14 If they ***i*** because of the Law, then

1 Corinthians

6:9 are unjust won't ***i*** God's kingdom?
15:50 and blood can't ***i*** the kingdom of

Galatians

5:21 kinds of things won't ***i*** God's kingdom.

Ephesians

5:5 persons won't ***i*** the kingdom of

Titus

3:7 his grace, we can ***i*** the hope for

Hebrews

1:14 those who are going to ***i*** salvation?
6:12 of the ones who ***i*** the promises
12:17 when he wanted to ***i*** the blessing, he

1 Peter

3:9 do this so that you might ***i*** a blessing.

Revelation

21:7 victorious will ***i*** these things. I

INHERITANCE

Deuteronomy

10:9 have a stake or ***i*** with the rest of

Judges

11:2 You won't get an ***i*** in our father's

Psalms

47:4 He chooses our ***i*** for us: the heights of
68:9 God; when your ***i*** grew weary, you
78:71 Jacob, to shepherd his ***i***, Israel.
79:1 come into your ***i***, God! They've
105:11 the land of Canaan as your allotted ***i***."
135:12 land over as an ***i***—as an inheritanc
136:21 land over as an ***i***—God's faithful l
136:22 As an ***i*** to Israel, his servant—God's

Proverbs

13:22 grandchildren an ***i***, but the wealth
17:2 and will divide an ***i*** with the brothers.
19:14 and riches are an ***i*** from one's
20:21 ***I*** gained quickly at first won't bless

Ecclesiastes

7:11 is as good as an ***i***—an advantage for

Zechariah

2:12 Judah as his ***i*** upon the holy

Luke

12:13 my brother to divide the ***i*** with me."
15:12 my share of the ***i***.' Then the father
20:14 Let's kill him so the ***i*** will be ours.'

Romans

4:16 That's why the ***i*** comes through faith,

Galatians

3:18 If the ***i*** were based upon the Law, it
4:30 won't share the ***i*** with the free

Ephesians

1:11 also received an ***i*** in Christ. We
1:14 payment on our ***i***, which is applied

Colossians

1:12 take part in the ***i***, in light granted
3:24 will receive an ***i*** as a reward. You

Hebrews

9:15 of the eternal ***i*** on the basis of

1 Peter

1:4 pure and enduring ***i*** that cannot

INJUSTICE

Genesis

18:20 The cries of ***i*** from Sodom and

2 Chronicles

19:7 there can be no ***i***, playing

Job

11:14 and don't let ***i*** dwell in your
13:7 Will you speak ***i*** for God, speak deceit

Psalms

58:2 hearts you plan ***i***; your hands do

Proverbs

22:8 Those who sow ***i*** will harvest evil; the

Jeremiah
22:13 chambers with ***i***, working his
Ezekiel
9:9 city is full of ***i***. They have said,
28:15 created until ***i*** was found in you,
34:4 you use force to rule them with ***i***.
Micah
3:10 with bloodshed and Jerusalem with ***i***!
Habakkuk
1:3 do you show me ***i*** and look at
2:12 and founding a village with ***i***.
Zephaniah
3:13 won't commit ***i***; they won't tell
Malachi
2:6 was in his mouth; ***i*** wasn't found on
Acts
1:18 received for his ***i***. Falling
Romans
1:18 behavior and the ***i*** of human beings
1:29 filled with all ***i***, wicked behavior,
1 Corinthians
13:6 isn't happy with ***i***, but it is happy
2 Thessalonians
2:12 by the truth but is happy with ***i***.

INNOCENT

Genesis
18:26 If I find fifty ***i*** people in the
Exodus
23:7 Don't put an ***i*** person who is in
Deuteronomy
19:10 ***I*** blood must not be spilled in the land
Job
4:7 Think! What ***i*** person has ever perished?
Psalms
19:13 I'll be ***i*** of great
73:13 washed my hands to stay ***i*** for nothing.
94:21 of the righteous. They condemn ***i*** blood.
106:38 They shed ***i*** blood, the blood of their
Proverbs
6:17 lying tongue, hands that spill ***i*** blood,
18:17 to testify seems ***i***, until the other
20:9 Who can say, "I'm ***i*** to the core; I'm
29:10 people hate the ***i***, and they seek
Isaiah
59:7 they rush to shed ***i*** blood. Their
Matthew
10:16 be wise as snakes and ***i*** as doves
27:4 I betrayed an ***i*** man." But they
27:24 the crowd. "I'm ***i*** of this man's
Acts
18:6 own fates! I'm ***i***! From now on I'll
2 Corinthians
11:2 present you as an ***i*** virgin to Christ
Philippians
2:15 and pure, ***i*** children of God
Hebrews
7:26 priest: holy, ***i***, incorrupt,

INSIDE

Genesis
6:14 places and cover it ***i*** and out with tar.
Exodus
4:6 Put your hand ***i*** your coat." So
40:20 and placed it ***i*** the chest. He put
1 Samuel
25:37 heart failed ***i*** him, and he
Psalms
5:9 all they have ***i*** them is
22:14 My heart is like wax; it melts ***i*** me.
42:5 are you so upset ***i***? Hope in God!
51:10 put a new, faithful spirit deep ***i*** me!
62:4 they bless, but ***i*** they are cursing.
73:21 was bitter, when I was all cut up ***i***,
103:1 Let everything ***i*** me bless his holy
109:18 let them seep ***i*** him like water,
142:3 my spirit is weak ***i*** me, you still
Ecclesiastes
11:5 does in the fetus ***i*** a pregnant
Ezekiel
1:5 And ***i*** that were forms of four living
1:16 them, as if one wheel were ***i*** another.
Daniel
3:25 walking around ***i*** the fire, and
Matthew
7:15 like sheep, but ***i*** they are vicious
Mark
7:21 It's from the ***i***, from the human
10:10 ***I*** the house, the disciples asked him
John
20:8 first, also went ***i***. He saw and
Acts
5:23 we opened the doors we found no one ***i***!"
10:12 ***I*** the sheet were all kinds of
10:27 talk, Peter went ***i*** and found a large
Romans
2:29 who is a Jew ***i***, who is
8:23 also groan ***i*** as we wait to be
2 Corinthians
4:16 we are on the ***i*** is being renewed
2 Timothy
1:5 I'm sure that this faith is also ***i*** you.
James
1:21 word planted deep ***i*** you—the very word that is able to save
1 Peter
3:4 beautiful on the ***i***, in your hearts,
Revelation
4:8 around and on the ***i*** with eyes. They
5:3 could open the scroll or look ***i*** it.
5:4 to open the scroll or to look ***i*** it.

INSIGHT

Deuteronomy
4:6 your wisdom and ***i*** to the nations
29:4 hasn't given you ***i*** to understand,
32:28 a thoughtful nation; they lack any ***i***.
Job
11:6 wisdom; for sound ***i*** has two sides.
17:4 their mind to ***i***; therefore, you
26:3 lacking wisdom, informed many with ***i***!
Psalms
49:3 my heart's meditation is full of ***i***.
119:32 because you give my heart ***i***.
119:99 I have greater ***i*** than all my teachers
Proverbs
2:3 Call out for ***i***, and cry aloud for
12:8 praised for his ***i***, but a warped
13:15 Good ***i*** brings favor, but the way of the
15:24 For those with ***i***, life is an upward
16:20 Those with ***i*** find prosperity; those who
16:22 One who has ***i*** is a fountain of life,
21:16 from the path of ***i*** will rest in the

INSIGHT [cont.]

Isaiah
29:24 and those who grumble will gain ***i***.
Daniel
2:21 the wise and knowledge to those with ***i***.
5:11 illumination, ***i***, and wisdom like
5:12 knowledge, and ***i*** into the meaning
5:14 illumination, ***i***, and
9:22 come: to give you ***i*** and understanding.
Mark
4:12 see but have no ***i***, and they can
Ephesians
3:4 understand my ***i*** into the secret
Philippians
1:9 rich with knowledge and all kinds of ***i***.
Colossians
4:6 sprinkled with ***i*** so that you may

INSPIRED

Micah
2:11 were to go about ***i*** and say
Matthew
22:43 is it that David, ***i*** by the Holy
Mark
12:36 David himself, ***i*** by the Holy Spirit,
Acts
4:8 Then Peter, ***i*** by the Holy Spirit,
11:28 stood up and, ***i*** by the Spirit,
2 Corinthians
8:7 commitment, and the love we ***i*** in you.
2 Timothy
3:16 scripture is ***i*** by God and is

INSTRUCTED

Numbers
9:4 Moses ***i*** the Israelites to keep the
16:40 just as the LORD ***i*** him through Moses.
1 Samuel
16:4 did what the LORD ***i***. When he came to
Psalms
16:7 at night I am ***i*** in the depths of
Jeremiah
13:5 it at the Euphrates, as the LORD ***i***.
36:8 prophet Jeremiah ***i*** him: he read all
38:27 as the king had ***i*** him. So they
51:59 prophet Jeremiah ***i*** the staff officer
Ezekiel
10:6 When he ***i*** the man clothed in linen to
Daniel
1:3 Nebuchadnezzar ***i*** his highest official
Matthew
26:19 did just as Jesus ***i*** them. They
Mark
6:8 He ***i*** them to take nothing for the
Luke
5:14 as Moses ***i***. This will be a
Acts
1:2 Spirit, Jesus ***i*** the apostles he
7:44 as he had been ***i*** by the one who
9:11 The Lord ***i*** him, "Go to Judas' house on
16:4 the cities, they ***i*** Gentile believers
18:25 He had been ***i*** in the way of the Lord

INSTRUCTION → GOD'S INSTRUCTION

Exodus
12:49 There will be one ***I*** for the native and
13:9 the LORD's ***i***, for the LORD
16:4 to see whether or not they follow my ***I***.
Leviticus
6:9 sons: This is the ***I*** for the entirely
7:1 This is the ***I*** for the compensation
11:46 concludes the ***I*** concerning
12:7 flow. This is the ***I*** for any woman who
13:59 concludes the ***I*** about the
14:2 This will be the ***I*** for anyone with skin
15:32 concludes the ***I*** concerning those
Numbers
6:13 This is the ***I*** for the nazirite. When
19:2 regulation in the ***I*** that the LORD
31:21 regulation in the ***I*** that the LORD
Deuteronomy
1:5 to explain this ***I***. He said the
4:44 Now this is the ***I*** that Moses set before
17:18 a copy of this ***I*** on a scroll in
28:61 written in this ***I*** scroll until you
29:21 that are written in this ***I*** scroll.
30:10 written in this ***I*** scroll, and
31:9 Moses wrote this ***I*** down and gave it
32:46 carefully all the words of this ***I***.
33:4 Moses gave the ***I*** to us—it's the
Joshua
1:7 obey all of the ***I*** that Moses my
1:8 about this ***I*** scroll. Recite it
Ezra
3:2 prescribed in the ***I*** from Moses the
7:6 skilled in the ***I*** from Moses, which
10:3 God. Let it be done according to the ***I***.
Nehemiah
8:1 to bring out the ***I*** scroll from
9:3 and read the ***I*** scroll from the
9:34 haven't kept your ***I***. They haven't
10:28 to follow the ***I*** from God,
12:44 required by the ***I*** for the priests
Job
5:17 so don't reject the Almighty's ***i***.
22:22 Receive ***i*** from his mouth; put his words
Psalms
1:2 love the LORD's ***I***, and they recite
19:7 The LORD's ***I*** is perfect, reviving one's
89:30 ever abandon my ***I***, stop following
94:12 the ones you teach from your ***I***—
119:1 walk in the LORD's ***I***—are truly happy!
119:174 for your saving help! Your ***I*** is my joy!
Proverbs
1:3 insightful ***i***, which is
1:7 LORD, but fools despise wisdom and ***i***.
1:8 to your father's ***i***; don't neglect
3:1 don't forget my ***i***. Let your heart
3:11 Don't reject the ***i*** of the LORD, my son;
4:1 fatherly ***i***; pay attention to
4:2 teach you well. Don't abandon my ***i***.
4:13 Hold on to ***i***; don't slack off; protect
5:12 say, "How I hated ***i***! How my heart
5:23 Those without ***i*** will die, misled by
6:20 command; don't abandon your mother's ***i***.
6:23 is a lamp and ***i*** a light;
7:2 and live, and my ***i*** like the pupil of
8:10 Take my ***i*** rather than silver, knowledge
8:33 Listen to ***i***, and be wise; don't avoid
10:17 Those who heed ***i*** are on the way to
13:18 don't care about ***i***; honor belongs to
15:5 like a father's ***i***, but those who
15:33 the LORD is wise ***i***, and humility

16:22 of life, but the ***i*** of the foolish is
19:20 advice and accept ***i***, so you might
23:12 your mind to ***i***, your ear to
23:13 Don't withhold ***i*** from children; if you
23:23 it; buy wisdom, ***i***, and
28:4 Those who abandon ***I*** praise the wicked,
28:7 children follow ***i***, but those who
28:9 ears from hearing ***i***—even their praye
29:18 control, but whoever obeys ***i*** is happy.
Isaiah
2:3 in God's paths." ***I*** will come from
Jeremiah
2:8 for the ***I*** didn't know me;
44:23 follow the LORD's ***i***, laws, or
Lamentations
2:9 There is no ***I***! Even her
Ezekiel
7:26 from the prophet. ***I*** disappears from
Daniel
9:11 Israel broke your ***I*** and turned away,
9:13 written in the ***I*** of Moses, but we
Hosea
4:6 forgotten the ***I*** of your God, so
8:1 my covenant, and have not kept my ***I***.
Amos
2:4 have rejected the ***I*** of the LORD, and
Micah
4:2 in God's paths!" ***I*** will come from
Habakkuk
1:4 The ***I*** is ineffective; justice does not
Zephaniah
3:4 is holy; they do violence to the ***I***.
3:7 me; she will take ***i*** so that her
Zechariah
7:12 hearing the ***I*** and the words
Malachi
2:6 True ***I*** was in his mouth; injustice
4:4 Remember the ***I*** from Moses, my servant,
Luke
1:4 soundness of the ***i*** you have received.
15:29 disobeyed your ***i***. Yet you've never
Acts
22:3 Under Gamaliel's ***i***, I was trained in
Romans
15:4 written for our ***i*** so that we could
1 Corinthians
11:17 the following ***i*** because when you
Ephesians
6:4 with discipline and ***i*** about the Lord.
1 Timothy
1:5 The goal of ***i*** is love from a pure
2 Timothy
4:2 and encourage with patience and ***i***.
Titus
1:9 with healthy ***i*** and refute those

INSTRUCTIONS

Genesis
26:5 commandments, my statutes, and my ***i***."
Exodus
16:28 refuse to obey my commandments and ***i***?
24:12 tablets with the ***i*** and the
Psalms
105:45 and observe his ***i***. Praise the LORD!
107:11 disobeyed God's ***i*** and rejected the
Ezekiel
22:26 violence to my ***i*** and made my holy
43:12 These are the ***i*** for the temple: the top
Matthew
15:9 since they teach ***i*** that are human
Mark
7:7 since they teach ***i*** that are human
16:9 the young man's ***i*** to those who were
1 Corinthians
11:2 remember all my ***i***, and you hold on
1 Thessalonians
4:2 You know the ***i*** we gave you through the
4:8 rejects these ***i*** isn't rejecting a
1 Timothy
1:18 giving you these ***i*** based on the
Hebrews
11:22 life, and gave ***i*** about burying his

INSTRUMENTS

Genesis
4:21 of those who play stringed and wind ***i***.
1 Samuel
18:6 tambourines, rejoicing, and musical ***i***.
2 Chronicles
7:6 LORD's musical ***i***, which King David
23:13 by musical ***i*** were leading the
Nehemiah
12:36 the musical ***i*** of David the man
Isaiah
13:5 the LORD and the ***i*** of his fury, to

INSULT

Leviticus
19:14 You must not ***i*** a deaf person or put
1 Samuel
17:10 I ***i*** Israel's troops today!" the
25:39 regarding Nabal's ***i*** to me and who
2 Kings
19:16 He sent them to ***i*** the living God!
19:22 Whom did you ***i*** and ridicule? Against
Job
19:3 humiliated me; shamelessly you ***i*** me.
Psalms
15:3 harm to a friend, doesn't ***i*** a neighbor;
69:9 of those who ***i*** you have fallen
74:10 God, will foes ***i*** you? Are enemies
74:22 unbelieving fools ***i*** you all day long.
Proverbs
17:5 who mock the poor ***i*** their maker;
18:3 so does contempt; with shame comes ***i***.
27:11 glad, so I can answer those who ***i*** me.
Matthew
5:11 you when people ***i*** you and harass
12:31 for every sin and ***i*** to God. But
26:65 Look, you've heard his ***i*** against God.
Mark
14:64 You've heard his ***i*** against God. What do
Luke
6:22 you, reject you, ***i*** you, and condemn
Acts
6:11 claim, "We heard him ***i*** Moses and God."
23:4 You dare to ***i*** God's high
James
2:7 they the ones who ***i*** the good name
1 Peter
3:9 evil for evil or ***i*** for insult.

2 Peter
2:10 aren't afraid to ***i*** the glorious ones,

INSULTED
1 Samuel
17:36 because he has ***i*** the army of the
17:45 God of Israel's army, the one you've ***i***.
2 Samuel
21:21 When he ***i*** Israel, Jonathan, who was the son of David's
23:9 David when they ***i*** the Philistines
1 Kings
9:7 will become a joke, ***i*** by everyone.
2 Kings
19:4 king-how he ***i*** the living God-per
19:23 You've ***i*** the Lord with your messengers;
2 Chronicles
7:20 I will make it a joke, ***i*** by everyone.
Psalms
4:2 my reputation be ***i***? How long will
22:6 less than human; ***i*** by one person,
69:7 I am ***i*** because of you. Shame covers my
69:10 while I fasted—even for that I was ***i***.
74:18 how enemies have ***i*** you, how
Proverbs
9:7 the cynic gets ***i***; whoever corrects
Isaiah
37:4 king. He ***i*** the living God!
37:24 servants, you've ***i*** the Lord; you
50:7 I haven't been ***i***. Therefore, I set
Jeremiah
15:15 Consider how I'm ***i*** on your account.
24:9 be disgraced and ***i***, mocked and
Matthew
27:39 were walking by ***i*** Jesus, shaking
27:44 with him ***i*** him in the same
Mark
15:29 People walking by ***i*** him, shaking their
15:32 had been crucified with Jesus ***i*** him.
Luke
23:39 next to Jesus ***i*** him, "Aren't you
John
9:28 They ***i*** him: "You are his disciple, but
Romans
15:3 insults of those who ***i*** you fell on me.
1 Corinthians
4:12 When we are ***i***, we respond with
1 Thessalonians
2:2 and were publicly ***i***, as you know.
1 Peter
2:23 When he was ***i***, he did not reply with

INSULTS
Deuteronomy
28:37 proverbs and in ***i*** by all the
Nehemiah
4:4 Turn their ***i*** to us back on
Psalms
69:9 consumed me, the ***i*** of those who
71:13 downfall be dressed in ***i*** and disgrace!
79:12 it hurts, for the ***i*** they used on you,
89:50 in my heart all the ***i*** of the nations,
119:22 Take all their ***i*** and contempt away from
Isaiah
3:8 in word and deed ***i*** the LORD, defying
50:6 hide my face from ***i*** and spitting.
Mark
3:28 for all sins and ***i*** of every kind.
3:29 But whoever ***i*** the Holy Spirit will
7:22 immorality, envy, ***i***, arrogance, and
John
10:36 into the world ***i*** God because he
Romans
15:3 is written, The ***i*** of those who
2 Corinthians
12:10 with weaknesses, ***i***, disasters,
Hebrews
10:29 blood, and who ***i*** the Spirit of
10:33 were exposed to ***i*** and abuse in
James
4:11 other. Whoever ***i*** or criticizes a
1 Peter
2:23 not reply with ***i***. When he

INTEGRITY
2 Samuel
22:24 I have lived with ***i*** before him; I've
22:26 you show ***i*** toward the one
2 Chronicles
19:9 times, in truth, and with complete ***i***.
Job
1:1 of absolute ***i***; he feared God
2:3 is of absolute ***i***, who reveres God
2:9 clinging to your ***i***? Curse God, and
4:6 confidence; the ***i*** of your conduct,
8:20 God won't reject ***i***, won't strengthen
9:20 me; I have ***i***; but God declares
27:5 my dying day, I won't give up my ***i***.
31:6 on accurate scales; let God know my ***i***.
33:23 thousand to declare one's ***i*** to another
Psalms
7:8 my righteousness and according to my ***i***.
18:23 I have lived with ***i*** before him; I've
18:25 you show ***i*** toward the one
25:21 Let ***i*** and virtue guard me because I
26:1 have walked with ***i***. I've trusted the
37:37 those who have ***i*** and watch those
41:12 support me in my ***i***; you put me in
78:72 with a heart of ***i***; he led them with
84:11 things to those who walk with ***i***.
101:2 study the way of ***i***—how long before
Proverbs
1:3 is righteous, just, and full of ***i***.
2:7 for those with ***i***. He is a shield
2:9 as well as ***i***, every good
2:13 the way of ***i*** and go on obscure
2:21 Those who have ***i*** will dwell in the
11:3 ***I*** guides the virtuous, but dishonesty
14:2 who walk with ***i*** fear the LORD,
16:13 righteous lips; they love words of ***i***.
17:26 to strike the honorable for their ***i***.
20:7 live with ***i***; happy are their
23:16 rejoice when your lips speak with ***i***.
Jeremiah
5:3 you look for ***i***? You have struck
Titus
2:7 of good actions. Show ***i***, seriousness,

INTERPRET
Genesis
40:8 there's no one to ***i*** them." Joseph
41:8 but they couldn't ***i*** them for Pharaoh.

Daniel
4:7 dream, but they couldn't ***i*** it for me.
5:8 read the writing or ***i*** it for the king.
Zechariah
10:2 see lies. They ***i*** dreams falsely
Luke
10:26 written in the Law? How do you ***i*** it?"
12:56 You know how to ***i*** conditions on
1 Corinthians
12:30 tongues, do they? All don't ***i***, do they?
14:5 they are able to ***i*** them so that the
14:13 a tongue should pray to be able to ***i***.
14:27 one at a time, and someone must ***i***.

INVITE
Exodus
2:20 leave this man? ***I*** him to eat a meal
34:15 gods, they may ***i*** you and you may
Proverbs
17:19 who build a high doorway ***i*** a collapse.
Jeremiah
35:2 family and ***i*** them to come to
Zechariah
3:10 everyone will ***i*** their neighbors
Matthew
22:9 edge of town and ***i*** everyone you find
Luke
14:12 or dinner, don't ***i*** your friends,
14:13 give a banquet, ***i*** the poor,

INVITED
Proverbs
1:24 I ***i*** you, but you rejected me; I
Lamentations
2:22 You ***i***—as if to a festival!—terrors
Matthew
22:3 to call those ***i*** to the wedding
Luke
7:36 of the Pharisees ***i*** Jesus to eat with
11:37 a Pharisee ***i*** him to share a
14:12 person who had ***i*** him, "When you
Revelation
19:9 who have been ***i*** to the wedding

IRON
Genesis
4:22 of bronze and ***i***.
Judges
1:19 the plain because they had ***i*** chariots.
4:3 had nine hundred ***i*** chariots and had
Psalms
2:9 them with an ***i*** rod; you will
105:18 shackles; his neck was in an ***i*** collar,
107:16 bronze doors and split ***i*** bars in two!
149:8 and their officials in ***i*** shackles,
Proverbs
27:17 As ***i*** sharpens iron, so friends sharpen
Ecclesiastes
12:11 the wise are like ***i***-tipped prods; the
Isaiah
60:17 gold; instead of ***i*** I will bring
Daniel
2:33 Its legs were of ***i***, and its feet were
4:15 earth, bound with ***i*** and bronze in the
5:4 silver, bronze, ***i***, wood, and stone.
7:7 and with massive ***i*** teeth. As it ate
Joel
3:10 Beat the ***i*** tips of your plows into
Micah
4:3 their swords into ***i*** plows and their
4:13 your horn out of ***i***; your hooves I
Revelation
2:27 nations with an ***i*** rod and smash
12:5 nations with an ***i*** rod. Her child
19:15 rule them with an ***i*** rod. And he is

ISAAC → ABRAHAM, ISAAC, AND JACOB
Genesis
21:4 his son ***I*** when he was eight
21:12 descendants will be traced through ***I***.
22:9 tied up his son ***I*** and laid him on
24:4 and find a wife for my son ***I*** there."
Leviticus
26:42 my covenant with ***I***. And my covenant
Matthew
1:2 was the father of ***I***. Isaac was the
22:32 the God of ***I***, and the God of
Luke
3:34 of Jacob son of ***I*** son of Abraham
Acts
7:8 circumcised him. ***I*** did the same with
Romans
9:7 descendants will be named through ***I***.
Galatians
4:28 you are children of the promise like ***I***.
Hebrews
11:9 tents along with ***I*** and Jacob, who
11:17 Abraham offered ***I*** when he was
11:20 By faith ***I*** also blessed Jacob and Esau
James
2:21 when he offered his son ***I*** on the altar?

ISAIAH
2 Kings
19:2 to the prophet ***I***, Amoz's son. They
2 Chronicles
26:22 down by the prophet ***I***, Amoz's son.
32:20 and the prophet ***I***, Amoz's son,
32:32 of the prophet ***I***, Amoz's son, in
Isaiah
7:3 the LORD said to ***I***, "Go out to meet
Matthew
3:3 the one of whom ***I*** the prophet spoke
4:14 This fulfilled what ***I*** the prophet said
8:17 so that what ***I*** the prophet said
12:17 spoken through ***I*** the prophet might
13:14 What ***I*** prophesied has become completely true for them
15:7 Hypocrites! ***I*** really knew what he was
Mark
1:2 the prophecy of ***I***: Look, I am
7:6 He replied, "***I*** really knew what he was
Luke
3:4 of the words of ***I*** the prophet, A
4:17 from the prophet ***I***. He unrolled the
John
1:23 straight just as the prophet ***I*** said."
12:38 of the prophet ***I***. Lord, who has
12:39 ***I*** explains why they couldn't believe
12:41 ***I*** said these things because he saw
Acts
8:28 the prophet ***I*** while sitting in

8:30 the prophet ***I***. He asked, "Do
28:25 your ancesters through ***I*** the prophet,
Romans
9:27 But ***I*** cries out for Israel, Though the
9:29 As ***I*** prophesied, If the Lord of the
10:16 the good news. As ***I*** says, Lord, who
10:20 And ***I*** even dares to say, I was found by
15:12 And again, ***I*** says, There will be a root

ISHBOSHETH
2 Samuel
2:8 army had taken ***I***, Saul's son, and

ISHMAEL
Genesis
16:16 when Hagar gave birth to ***I*** for Abram.
2 Kings
25:23 The officers were ***I***, Nethaniah's son
1 Chronicles
1:28 Abraham's family: Isaac and ***I***
2 Chronicles
23:1 Jehohanan's son ***I***, Obed's son
Ezra
10:22 Maaseiah, ***I***, Nethanel,
Jeremiah
40:8 at Mizpah: ***I***, Nethaniah's son;

ISHMAELITES
Genesis
37:25 saw a caravan of ***I*** coming from
37:27 sell him to the ***I***. Let's not harm
37:28 sold him to the ***I*** for twenty pieces
39:1 him from the ***I*** who had brought
Judges
8:24 worn gold earrings because they were ***I***.
Psalms
83:6 of Edom and the ***I***, Moab and the

ISRAEL → ALL ISRAEL, ASSEMBLY OF ISRAEL, HOLY ONE OF ISRAEL
Genesis
32:28 any longer, but ***I***, because you
49:24 name of the shepherd, the rock of ***I***,
Numbers
19:13 be cut off from ***I*** because the water
24:17 arises from ***I***, smashing Moab's
Deuteronomy
6:4 ***I***, listen! Our God is the LORD! Only
10:12 of all that, ***I***, what does the
18:1 inheritance in ***I***. They can eat the
Joshua
4:22 children know: '***I*** crossed over the
24:2 LORD, the God of ***I***, says: Long ago
Judges
17:6 was no king in ***I***; each person did
21:3 LORD, God of ***I***," they said, "why has
Ruth
4:14 May his name be proclaimed in ***I***.
1 Samuel
3:20 All ***I*** from Dan to Beer-sheba knew that
4:21 glory has left ***I***," referring to
14:23 The LORD saved ***I*** that day, and the
15:26 rejected you from being king over ***I***."
17:26 this insult from ***I***? Who is that
2 Samuel
5:2 the one who led ***I*** out to war and
5:3 and they anointed David king over ***I***.
7:24 your people ***I*** as your own
1 Kings
1:35 him to become ruler over ***I*** and Judah."
8:23 said: LORD God of ***I***, there's no god
10:9 the LORD loved ***I*** with an eternal
12:19 ***I*** has been in rebellion against the
18:17 Is that you, the one who troubles ***I***?"
19:18 who remain in ***I***, totaling seven
2 Kings
5:8 know that there's a prophet in ***I***."
17:21 When ***I*** broke away from David's dynasty,
1 Chronicles
17:22 your people ***I*** as your own
21:1 arose against ***I*** and incited David
29:25 before all ***I***, giving him such
2 Chronicles
9:8 your God loved ***I*** and wanted to
Psalms
78:21 Jacob; wrath also burned against ***I***
81:8 you! If only you would listen to me, ***I***.
98:3 to the house of ***I***; every corner of
125:5 with other evildoers! Peace be on ***I***!
Jeremiah
2:3 ***I*** was devoted to the LORD, the early
23:6 will be saved and ***I*** will live in
31:2 wilderness. As ***I*** searched for a
31:10 one who scattered ***I*** will gather them
31:31 with the people of ***I*** and Judah.
33:17 sit on the throne of the house of ***I***.
Ezekiel
3:17 for the house of ***I***. When you hear a
33:7 for the house of ***I***. Whenever you
36:1 Hear the LORD's word, mountains of ***I***!
37:28 I, the LORD, make ***I*** holy, when my
39:23 that the house of ***I*** went into exile
Daniel
9:20 sins of my people ***I***—while I was still
Hosea
7:1 When I would heal ***I***, the evil acts of
11:1 When ***I*** was a child, I loved him, and
Amos
4:12 Truly, ***I***, I will act in this way
7:11 by the sword, and ***I*** will be forced
8:2 upon my people ***I***; I will never
9:14 of my people ***I***; they will
Micah
5:2 to be a ruler in ***I*** on my behalf will
Matthew
2:6 who will shepherd my people ***I***."
10:6 to the lost sheep, the people of ***I***.
15:24 to the lost sheep, the people of ***I***."
Mark
12:29 important one is ***I***, listen! Our God
15:32 the king of ***I***, come down from
Luke
1:54 of his servant ***I***, remembering his
2:34 rising of many in ***I*** and to be a sign
22:30 overseeing the twelve tribes of ***I***.
John
12:13 the Lord! Blessings on the king of ***I***!"
Acts
1:6 going to restore the kingdom to ***I*** now?"
Romans
9:6 descended from ***I*** are part of
9:27 cries out for ***I***, Though the
9:31 But though ***I*** was striving for a Law of

11:7 So what? ***I*** didn't find what it was
11:26 In this way, all ***I*** will be saved, as it
Ephesians
2:12 than citizens of ***I***, and strangers to
Hebrews
8:8 with the house of ***I***, and I will make

ISRAELITE

Exodus
35:29 All the ***I*** men and women who were eager to contribute
John
1:47 is a genuine ***I*** in whom there is
Romans
11:1 not! I'm an ***I***, a descendant of

ISRAELITES

Exodus
1:7 But the ***I*** were fertile and became
3:10 bring my people, the ***I***, out of Egypt."
12:35 The ***I*** did as Moses had told them and
14:22 The ***I*** walked into the sea on dry
16:12 complaints of the ***I***. Tell them, 'At
31:16 The ***I*** should keep the Sabbath. They
33:5 Moses, "Tell the ***I***, 'You are a
39:42 The ***I*** did all of the work just as the
Numbers
2:32 are the enlisted ***I*** by their
6:23 will bless the ***I*** as follows. Say
9:2 Let the ***I*** keep the Passover at its
9:17 the tent, the ***I*** would march. And
14:2 All the ***I*** criticized Moses and Aaron.
35:10 Speak to the ***I*** and say to them: When
Deuteronomy
4:44 that Moses set before the ***I***.
33:1 man of God gave the ***I*** before he died.
Joshua
1:2 land that I am going to give to the ***I***.
5:6 was because the ***I*** journeyed forty
7:1 The ***I*** did a disrespectful thing
Matthew
27:9 price had been set by some of the ***I***,
Luke
1:16 will bring many ***I*** back to the Lord
Romans
9:4 They are ***I***. The adoption as God's
2 Corinthians
11:22 So am I. Are they ***I***? So am I. Are
Hebrews
4:2 us, just as the ***I*** did. However, the
4:8 Joshua gave the ***I*** rest, God
11:22 the exodus of the ***I*** at the end of his
Revelation
2:14 to trip up the ***I*** so that they
7:4 sealed from every tribe of the ***I***:

ISSACHAR

Genesis
30:18 to my husband." So she named him ***I***.
35:23 Simeon, Levi, Judah, ***I***, and Zebulun.
49:14 ***I*** is a sturdy donkey, bedding down
Exodus
1:3 ***I***, Zebulun, and Benjamin
Numbers
1:8 from ***I***, Nethanel, Zuar's son
1:28 descendants of ***I***, registered by
1:29 from the tribe of ***I*** were 54,400.
Deuteronomy
27:12 Levi, Judah, ***I***, Joseph, and
33:18 out and about; ***I***: celebrate when
Joshua
17:10 Asher on the north and ***I*** on the east.
17:11 to Manasseh in ***I*** and in Asher were
19:17 lot went out fourth for the clans of ***I***.
19:23 legacy for the clans of the ***I*** tribe.
21:6 of the tribes of ***I***, Asher, Naphtali,
21:28 From the tribe of ***I***: Kishion and its
Judges
5:15 The leaders of ***I*** came along with
10:1 of Dodo, a man of ***I***, arose to rescue
1 Kings
4:17 Jehoshaphat, Paruah's son, in ***I***
15:27 from the house of ***I***, plotted against
Ezekiel
48:25 to the western border: ***I***, one portion.
Revelation
7:7 from the tribe of ***I***, twelve thousand;

ITHAMAR

Exodus
6:23 birth to Nadab, Abihu, Eleazar, and ***I***.
28:1 Nadab and Abihu, and Eleazar and ***I***.
38:21 the direction of ***I***, Aaron the
Leviticus
10:6 sons, Eleazar and ***I***, "Don't dishevel
Numbers
3:2 the oldest, and Abihu, Eleazar, and ***I***.
3:4 sons. Eleazar and ***I*** served as priests
4:28 will be under ***I*** son of Aaron the
4:33 supervision of ***I*** son of Aaron the
7:8 supervision of ***I***, Aaron the
26:60 were born Nadab, Abihu, Eleazar, and ***I***.
1 Chronicles
6:3 family: Nadab, Abihu, Eleazar, and ***I***.
24:1 family: Nadab, Abihu, Eleazar, and ***I***.
24:2 and so Eleazar and ***I*** served as priests.
24:6 from Eleazar followed by one from ***I***.
Ezra
8:2 Gershom; of ***I***, Daniel; of

Jj

JABESH-GILEAD
Judges
21:8 was! No one from ***J*** had come to the
1 Samuel
10:27 the Ammonites' power and fled to ***J***.

JACOB → ABRAHAM, ISAAC, AND JACOB
Genesis
25:26 and she named him ***J***. Isaac was 60
27:19 ***J*** said to his father, "I'm Esau your
29:11 ***J*** kissed Rachel and wept aloud
32:24 But ***J*** stayed apart by himself, and a
35:22 heard about it. ***J*** had twelve sons.
Exodus
1:1 to Egypt with ***J*** along with their
Leviticus
26:42 my covenant with ***J***. I will also
Numbers
23:7 Come, curse ***J*** for me; come,
32:11 Isaac, and ***J***, because they
Deuteronomy
33:10 your case laws to ***J***, your Instruction
34:4 Isaac, and ***J*** when I promised:
Joshua
24:4 To Isaac I gave ***J*** and Esau. I gave
24:32 of field that ***J*** had purchased for
1 Samuel
12:8 When ***J*** entered Egypt, the Egyptians
2 Kings
17:34 the children of ***J***, whom he renamed
1 Chronicles
16:13 and the children of ***J***, his chosen ones.
16:17 binding law for ***J***, as an eternal
Psalms
14:7 for the better, ***J*** will rejoice;
44:4 the one who orders salvation for ***J***.
46:7 us! The God of ***J*** is our place of
47:4 the heights of ***J***, which he loves.
53:6 for the better, ***J*** will rejoice;
59:13 the earth that God rules over ***J***. Selah
77:15 the children of ***J*** and Joseph. Selah
78:5 a law for ***J*** and set up
78:71 his people ***J***, to shepherd his
79:7 They've devoured ***J*** and demolished his
99:4 worked justice and righteousness in ***J***.
105:6 and the children of ***J***, his chosen ones.
114:1 when the house of ***J*** came out from a
132:2 how he promised the strong one of ***J***:
146:5 is the God of ***J***—the person whose
147:19 his word to ***J***; his statutes and
Isaiah
2:5 Come, house of ***J***, let's walk by the
65:9 offspring from ***J***, and from Judah,
Jeremiah
10:25 have devoured ***J***; they have
51:19 the portion of ***J*** is utterly
Lamentations
2:3 he burned against ***J*** like a flaming
Ezekiel
28:25 land, which I gave to my servant ***J***.
37:25 to my servant ***J***, where their
39:25 the captives of ***J***. I will have
Amos
3:13 the house of ***J***, says the LORD
6:8 the pride of ***J***. I hate his
7:2 forgive! How can ***J*** survive? He is so
8:7 by the pride of ***J***: Surely I will
Obadiah
1:10 to your brother ***J***, shame will cover
1:17 and the house of ***J*** will drive out
1:18 The house of ***J*** will be a fire, the
Micah
1:5 for the crime of ***J*** and the sins of
7:20 faithfulness to ***J***, faithful love to
Malachi
1:2 brother? says the LORD. I loved ***J***,
2:12 from the tents of ***J***, anyone awaking,
3:6 you, children of ***J***, have not
Matthew
1:2 was the father of ***J***. Jacob was the
1:15 Matthan. Matthan was the father of ***J***.
1:16 ***J*** was the father of Joseph, the husband
John
4:5 was near the land ***J*** had given to his
4:12 than our father ***J***, are you? He gave
Acts
7:8 did the same with ***J***, and Jacob with
7:12 When ***J*** heard there was grain in Egypt,
7:15 So ***J*** went down to Egypt, where he and
7:46 a dwelling place for the God of ***J***.
Romans
9:13 written, I loved ***J***, but I hated Esau.
11:26 He will remove ungodly behavior from ***J***.
Hebrews
11:20 also blessed ***J*** and Esau
11:21 By faith ***J*** blessed each of Joseph's

JAMES
Matthew
13:55 Mary? Aren't ***J***, Joseph, Simon,
17:1 Jesus took Peter, ***J***, and John his
27:56 the mother of ***J*** and Joseph, and
Mark
1:19 further, he saw ***J*** and John,
3:17 ***J*** and John, Zebedee's sons, whom he
5:37 him except Peter, ***J***, and John, James'
6:3 the brother of ***J***, Joses, Judas,
9:2 Jesus took Peter, ***J***, and John, and
10:35 ***J*** and John, Zebedee's sons, came to
10:41 they became angry with ***J*** and John.
14:33 He took Peter, ***J***, and John along with
15:40 the mother of ***J*** (the younger one)

16:1 the mother of ***J***, and Salome
Acts
1:13 Peter, John, ***J***, and Andrew;
12:2 He had ***J***, John's brother, killed with
15:13 also fell silent, ***J*** responded,
21:18 of us went to see ***J***. All of the
1 Corinthians
15:7 he appeared to ***J***, then to all the
Galatians
1:19 apostles except ***J*** the brother of
2:9 ***J***, Cephas, and John, who are
2:12 people came from ***J***. But when they
James
1:1 From ***J***, a slave of God and of the Lord
Jude
1:1 and brother of ***J***. To those who are

JAPHETH
Genesis
5:32 became the father of Shem, Ham, and ***J***.

JAR
Genesis
24:14 me your water ***j*** so I can drink,'
Exodus
16:33 to Aaron, "Take a ***j***, and put one full
1 Kings
17:14 LORD, says: The ***j*** of flour won't
Psalms
2:9 will shatter them like a pottery ***j***."
Ecclesiastes
12:6 shatters; the ***j*** is broken at the
Jeremiah
19:1 Go buy a clay ***j*** from a potter in
22:28 broken pottery ***j*** that no one
Mark
14:13 carrying a water ***j*** will meet you.
John
4:28 down her water ***j*** and went into the
19:29 A ***j*** full of sour wine was nearby, so
Hebrews
9:4 there was a gold ***j*** containing manna,

JAWBONE
Judges
15:15 a donkey's fresh ***j***, picked it up,

JEALOUS
Genesis
30:1 Rachel became ***j*** of her sister and
37:11 His brothers were ***j*** of him, but his
Numbers
5:14 him and he is ***j*** of his wife who
11:29 to him, "Are you ***j*** for my sake? If
Deuteronomy
32:16 They made God ***j*** with strange gods,
Joshua
24:19 holy God. He is a ***j*** God. He won't
Psalms
37:1 don't be ***j*** of those who do
106:16 then they were ***j*** of Moses in the
Isaiah
11:13 Ephraim won't be ***j*** of Judah, and
Nahum
1:2 The LORD is a ***j*** and vengeful God; the
Acts
7:9 patriarchs were ***j*** of Joseph, they
17:5 the Jews became ***j*** and brought along
Romans
10:19 I will make you ***j*** of those who
11:11 failure, in order to make Israel ***j***.
1 Corinthians
10:22 we make the Lord ***j***? We aren't
13:4 is kind, it isn't ***j***, it doesn't brag,
Galatians
5:26 other angry, or be ***j*** of each other.
Philippians
1:15 Christ with ***j*** and competitive
James
4:2 murder. You are ***j*** for something you

JEALOUSY
Proverbs
6:34 ***J*** makes a man rage; he'll show no mercy
14:30 life to the body, but ***j*** rots the bones.
27:4 is a flood, but who can withstand ***j***?
Matthew
27:18 had handed him over because of ***j***.
Acts
5:17 the Sadducees, was overcome with ***j***.
13:45 overcome with ***j***. They argued
Romans
1:29 They are full of ***j***, murder,
Galatians
5:21 ***j***, drunkenness, partying, and other
1 Timothy
6:4 This creates ***j***, conflict, verbal
Titus
3:3 evil behavior and ***j***. We were
James
3:14 you have bitter ***j*** and selfish

JEBUSITE
2 Chronicles
3:1 at the threshing floor of Ornan the ***J***.

JEBUSITES
Genesis
15:21 the Girgashites, and the ***J***."
Exodus
3:8 the Hivites, and the ***J*** all live.
Joshua
15:63 remove the ***J*** who lived in
2 Samuel
5:6 against the ***J***, who inhabited

JEDAIAH
1 Chronicles
4:37 of Allon son of ***J*** son of Shimri son
Ezra
2:36 The family of ***J***, namely the house
Nehemiah
3:10 Next to them ***J***, Harumaph's son, made
12:21 of Hilkiah, Hashabiah; of ***J***, Nethanel
Zechariah
6:10 Tobijah, and from ***J***. As for you, go
6:14 Helem, Tobijah, ***J***, and for Hen,

JEHOAHAZ
2 Kings
10:35 Samaria. His son ***J*** succeeded him as
23:31 ***J*** was 23 years old when he became king,
23:33 Pharaoh Neco made ***J*** a prisoner at

23:34 Neco took **J** away; he later
2 Chronicles
36:2 **J** was 23 years old when he became king,
36:4 took his brother **J** prisoner and

JEHOASH
2 Kings
11:2 Ahaziah's son **J** from the rest of
11:21 **J** was 7 years old when he became king
12:2 **J** always did what was right in the
14:3 He did everything his father **J** did.
2 Chronicles
22:11 Ahaziah's son **J** from the rest of
24:24 ancestor's God. **J** was justly

JEHOIACHIN
2 Kings
24:6 His son **J** succeeded him as
24:8 **J** was 18 years old when he became king,
25:29 So **J** took off his prisoner clothes and
2 Chronicles
36:8 kings. His son **J** succeeded him as
36:9 **J** was 18 years old when he became king,
Jeremiah
52:2 in the LORD's eyes just as **J** had done.
52:31 Judah's King **J** had been in exile for
52:32 treated **J** kindly and gave
52:33 So **J** discarded his prison clothes and

JEHOIADA
2 Kings
11:4 the seventh year **J** sent for the
12:9 Then the priest **J** took a box, made a
1 Chronicles
12:27 also **J**, leader of Aaron's line, and
27:34 Benaiah's son **J**, and Abiathar.
2 Chronicles
22:11 of the priest **J** and the sister of
24:25 son of the priest **J**. So they killed
Jeremiah
29:26 temple instead of **J**. You are

JEHOIAKIM
2 Kings
23:34 Eliakim's name to **J**. Neco took
23:36 **J** was 25 years old when he became king,
24:1 Babylon attacked. **J** had submitted to
24:19 in the LORD's eyes, just as **J** had done.
1 Chronicles
3:15 the second **J**, the third
2 Chronicles
36:4 his name to **J**. Neco took his
36:5 **J** was 25 years old when he became king,
Jeremiah
1:3 of Judah's King **J**, Josiah's son,
22:18 the LORD says to **J** son of Judah's
35:1 rule of Judah's King **J**, Josiah's son:
45:1 of Judah's King **J**, Josiah's son,
46:2 year of Judah's King **J**, Josiah's son:
Daniel
1:1 of Judah's King **J**, Babylon's King
1:2 Judah's King **J** over to

JEHORAM
1 Kings
22:50 City. His son **J** succeeded him as
2 Kings
1:17 of Judah's King **J**, who was
8:16 Ahab's son, **J**, the son of
12:18 Jehoshaphat, **J**, and Ahaziah-along
2 Chronicles
17:8 and by the priests Elishama and **J**.
21:5 **J** was 32 years old when he became king,
21:18 the LORD struck **J** with an incurable
22:11 daughter of King **J**, the wife of the

JEHOSHAPHAT
2 Samuel
8:16 the army; Ahilud's son **J** was recorder;
20:24 labor; Ahilud's son **J** was the recorder;
1 Kings
22:8 king told **J**, "but I hate him
22:50 **J** died and was buried with his
22:51 of Judah's King **J**, Ahaziah, Ahab's
2 Kings
3:1 year of **J**, Judah's king. He
8:16 the son of Judah's King **J**, became king.
12:18 kings **J**, Jehoram, and
1 Chronicles
3:10 his son Abijah, his son Asa, his son **J**,
18:15 the army; Ahilud's son **J** was recorder;
2 Chronicles
17:1 Asa's son **J** succeeded him as king
21:1 **J** died and was buried with his
21:2 the other sons of **J**, were Azariah,
21:12 of your father **J** or the ways of
22:9 the grandson of **J**, who sought the
Joel
3:2 bring them to the **J** Valley. There I
3:12 come up to the **J** Valley; for there
Matthew
1:8 was the father of **J**. Jehoshaphat was

JEHU
1 Kings
16:1 word came to **J**, Hanani's son,
19:17 sword of Hazael, **J** will kill.
2 Kings
9:16 Then **J** got on a chariot and drove to
14:8 of Israel's King **J**, saying, "Come
15:12 the LORD spoke to **J**: Your descendants
1 Chronicles
2:38 was the father of **J**, Jehu was the
4:35 Joel, **J** son of Joshibiah son of Seraiah
12:3 sons; Beracah; **J** of Anathoth;
2 Chronicles
19:2 **J** son of Hanani the seer came out to
20:34 in the records of **J**, Hanani's son,
22:7 Joram to meet **J**, Nimshi's son,
22:8 While **J** was executing judgment on
22:9 **J** went looking for Ahaziah, who was
Hosea
1:4 the house of **J** for the blood of

JEPHTHAH
Judges
11:1 Now **J** the Gileadite was a mighty
11:30 **J** made a solemn promise to the LORD:

1 Samuel
12:11 Jerubbaal, Barak, ***J***, and Samson, and
Hebrews
11:32 Barak, Samson, ***J***, David, Samuel,

JEREMIAH
1 Chronicles
5:24 Eliel, Azriel, ***J***, Hodaviah, and
12:4 over the Thirty; ***J***; Jahaziel;
2 Chronicles
35:25 ***J*** composed a funeral song for Josiah,
36:12 the prophet ***J***, who spoke for
Ezra
1:1 word spoken by ***J***, the LORD stirred
Nehemiah
10:2 Seraiah, Azariah, ***J***
12:1 Shealtiel and Jeshua: Seraiah, ***J***, Ezra,
12:12 of Seraiah, Meraiah; of ***J***, Hananiah;
12:34 Judah, Benjamin, Shemaiah, and ***J***
Jeremiah
1:1 are the words of ***J***, Hilkiah's son,
36:5 Then ***J*** told Baruch, "I'm confined here
37:12 ***J*** set out for the land of Benjamin to
38:7 they had thrown ***J*** into the cistern.
Daniel
9:2 to the prophet ***J***. It was seventy
Matthew
2:17 the word spoken through ***J*** the prophet:
16:14 and still others ***J*** or one of the
27:9 the words of ***J*** the prophet: And

JERICHO
Numbers
22:1 of Moab across the Jordan from ***J***.
Deuteronomy
34:1 which faces ***J***. The LORD showed
Joshua
3:16 The people crossed opposite ***J***.
5:10 day of the month on the plains of ***J***.
6:2 I have given ***J*** and its king into
6:26 this city of ***J*** will be cursed
1 Kings
16:34 Bethel rebuilt ***J***. He set up its
2 Kings
25:5 with him in the ***J*** plains. His
Luke
10:30 from Jerusalem to ***J***. He encountered
18:35 As Jesus came to ***J***, a certain blind
19:1 Jesus entered ***J*** and was passing through

JEROBOAM
1 Kings
11:26 Now Nebat's son ***J*** was an Ephraimite
14:2 ***J*** said to his wife, "Please go with a
2 Kings
3:3 to the sins that ***J***, Nebat's son, had
23:15 shrine made by ***J***, Nebat's son, who
23:16 man of God when ***J*** stood by the
1 Chronicles
5:17 King Jotham and Israel's King ***J***.
2 Chronicles
9:29 seer Iddo concerning ***J***, Nebat's son?
13:20 ***J*** failed to regain power during the
Hosea
1:1 days of Israel's King ***J*** Joash's son.
Amos
1:1 days of Israel's King ***J***, Joash's son.
7:9 against the house of ***J*** with the sword."
7:10 to Israel's King ***J***, "Amos has
7:11 Amos has said, '***J*** will die by the

JERUSALEM → ATTACKED JERUSALEM
Joshua
10:5 were the kings of ***J***, Hebron, Jarmuth,
15:8 Jebusite city, ***J***, on the south.
1 Samuel
17:54 and brought it to ***J***, but he put the
2 Samuel
11:1 of Rabbah. But David remained in ***J***.
15:29 God's chest back to ***J*** and stayed there.
1 Kings
10:27 In ***J***, the king made silver as common
11:7 the hill east of ***J***, Solomon built a
Ezra
1:2 me to build him a house at ***J*** in Judah.
2:1 They returned to ***J*** and Judah, all to
Nehemiah
1:3 The wall around ***J*** is broken down,
Psalms
79:1 They've made ***J*** a bunch of ruins.
122:2 our feet are standing in your gates, ***J***!
122:3 ***J*** is built like a city joined together
122:6 Pray that ***J*** has peace: "Let those who
137:5 ***J***! If I forget you, let my strong hand
147:2 The LORD rebuilds ***J***, gathering up
147:12 Worship the LORD, ***J***! Praise your God, Zion!
Isaiah
3:1 is removing from ***J*** and from Judah
62:6 Upon your walls, ***J***, I have appointed
Jeremiah
13:27 terrible for you, ***J***! How long will
23:14 the prophets of ***J*** I saw something
Zechariah
14:8 flow out from ***J***, half of it to
Matthew
16:21 he had to go to ***J*** and suffer many
20:18 are going up to ***J***. The Human One
21:10 Jesus entered ***J***, the whole city
23:37 ***J***, Jerusalem! You who kill the
Mark
10:33 going up to ***J***. The Human One
15:41 other women who had come to ***J*** with him.
John
1:19 Jewish leaders in ***J*** sent priests and
5:1 festival, and Jesus went up to ***J***.
10:22 of Dedication in ***J***. It was winter,
Acts
1:8 my witnesses in ***J***, in all Judea and
Romans
15:19 gospel from ***J*** all the way
Galatians
4:25 the present-day ***J***, because the city
Hebrews
12:22 God, heavenly ***J***, to countless
Revelation
3:12 my God, the New ***J*** that comes down
21:2 holy city, New ***J***, coming down out
21:10 me the holy city, ***J***, coming down out

JESHUA
1 Chronicles
24:11 the ninth to ***J***, the tenth to Shecaniah
2 Chronicles
31:15 Eden, Miniamin, ***J***, Shemaiah, Amariah,
Ezra
4:3 But Zerubbabel, ***J***, and the rest of the
10:18 —of the family of ***J***, Jozadak's son
Nehemiah
12:1 of Shealtiel and ***J***: Seraiah

JESSE
Ruth
4:22 the father of ***J***, and Jesse the
1 Samuel
16:1 sending you to ***J*** of Bethlehem
1 Chronicles
2:12 of Obed, and Obed was the father of ***J***.
Isaiah
11:1 from the stump of ***J***; a branch will
11:10 day, the root of ***J*** will stand as a
Matthew
1:5 was Ruth. Obed was the father of ***J***.
1:6 ***J*** was the father of David the king.
Luke
3:32 son of ***J*** son of Obed son of Boaz son of
Romans
15:12 will be a root of ***J***, who will also

JESUS → APOSTLE OF JESUS, APOSTLE OF JESUS CHRIST, CHRIST JESUS, CHRIST JESUS OUR LORD, FOLLOWED JESUS, JESUS AND HIS DISCIPLES, JESUS CHRIST OUR LORD, JESUS IS THE CHRIST, JESUS OF NAZARETH, JESUS OUR LORD, LOOKING FOR JESUS, LORD JESUS, LORD JESUS CHRIST, NAME OF JESUS, NAME OF JESUS CHRIST, SAVIOR JESUS, SAVIOR JESUS CHRIST, SON JESUS, SON JESUS CHRIST, THROUGH JESUS, THROUGH JESUS CHRIST, THROUGH OUR LORD JESUS, YOU IN CHRIST JESUS
Matthew
1:1 the ancestors of ***J*** Christ, son of
1:21 you will call him ***J***, because he will
26:71 man was with ***J***, the man from
27:37 It read, "This is ***J***, the king of the
Acts
17:3 declared, "This ***J*** whom I proclaim
19:15 replied, "I know ***J*** and I'm familiar
22:8 you, Lord?' 'I am ***J*** the Nazarene,
Romans
10:9 with your mouth "***J*** is Lord" and in
2 Corinthians
4:6 of God's glory in the face of ***J*** Christ.
4:14 raised the Lord ***J*** will also raise
Philippians
2:10 at the name of ***J*** everyone in

JESUS AND HIS DISCIPLES
Mt 9:10; 9:19; 20:29; Mk 2:15; 5:1; 6:53; 8:22, 27; 10:32; 11:19, 20, 27; 14:32; Lk 8:22; 8:26; 9:57; 10:38; Jn 2:2; 3:22; 13:2

JESUS CHRIST OUR LORD
Ro 1:4; 5:21; 7:25; 1Co 1:9; Jud 1:25

JESUS IS THE CHRIST
Jn 20:31; Ac 5:42; 9:22; 1Jn 2:22; 5:1

JESUS OF NAZARETH
Mk 1:24; 10:47; 16:6; Lk 4:34; 24:19; Ac 6:14; 10:38

JESUS OUR LORD
Ro 4:24; 6:23; 8:38; 1Co 9:1; 15:31; Eph 3:11; 1Ti 1:2; 1:12; 2Ti 1:2; 2Pt 1:2

JESUS' DISCIPLES
Mt 13:10; 28:13; Mk 8:14; Jn 4:2; 4:27; 6:16; 9:2; 16:17

JETHRO
Exodus
3:1 his father-in-law ***J***, Midian's priest.
4:18 his father-in-law ***J*** and said to him,
18:1 ***J***, Midian's priest and Moses'

JEW
Esther
2:5 Now there was a ***J*** in the fortified part of Susa
10:3 Mordecai the ***J*** was second only
John
3:25 and a certain ***J*** about cleansing
18:35 I'm not a ***J***, am I? Your
Acts
21:39 replied, "I'm a ***J*** from Tarsus in
Romans
1:16 in God, to the ***J*** first and also to
2:9 evil, for the ***J*** first and also
2:29 person who is a ***J*** inside, who is
10:12 between ***J*** and Greek,
1 Corinthians
9:20 I act like a ***J*** to the Jews, so I can
Galatians
2:14 though you're a ***J***, live like a
3:28 There is neither ***J*** nor Greek; there is
Colossians
3:11 neither Greek nor ***J***, circumcised nor

JEWELRY
Genesis
24:53 gold and silver ***j*** and clothing and
Exodus
3:22 and their gold ***j*** as well as their
11:2 for all their silver and gold ***j***."
12:35 silver and gold ***j*** as well as their
33:4 they were sorry. No one put on any ***j***,
2 Samuel
1:24 he decorated your clothes with gold ***j***.
Job
28:17 it; she can't be acquired with gold ***j***.
Proverbs
25:12 like a gold earring or ***j*** of fine gold.
Song of Songs
7:1 like fine ***j***, the work of an
Isaiah
61:10 crown, and like a bride adorned in ***j***.
Jeremiah
2:32 woman forget her ***j*** or a bride her
4:30 yourself in gold ***j***, and color your
Ezekiel
16:11 you with fine ***j***, and put
23:40 your eyes, and you put on your ***j***.
Hosea
2:13 up with rings and ***j***, and went after

1 Peter
3:3 or by wearing gold ***j*** or fine clothes.

JEWISH → JEWISH AUTHORITIES, JEWISH LEADERS, JEWISH OPPOSITION
Nehemiah
5:8 bought back our ***J*** kin who had been
Esther
6:13 If he is of ***J*** birth, you'll not
Luke
7:3 he sent some ***J*** elders to Jesus
23:51 He was from the ***J*** city of Arimathea
John
2:6 jars used for the ***J*** cleansing ritual,
Acts
13:5 God's word in the ***J*** synagogues. John
24:24 Drusilla, who was ***J***, and summoned
Romans
9:5 The ***J*** ancestors are theirs, and the
15:27 a share of the ***J*** people's
Colossians
4:11 kingdom who are ***J*** converts. They
Titus
1:10 some of those who are ***J*** believers.
1:14 pay attention to ***J*** myths and

JEWISH AUTHORITIES
Jn 7:1; 7:13; 9:22; 19:38; 20:19

JEWISH LEADERS
Jn 1:19; 2:18, 20; 5:10, 15, 16, 18, 19; 7:11, 15; 8:22; 9:18, 19; 11:54; 13:33; 18:12, 14, 28, 31, 36, 38; 19:4, 7, 12, 14, 15, 31; Ac 23:12; 23:20; 25:2; 28:17

JEWISH OPPOSITION
Jn 6:41; 7:35; 8:48, 52, 57; 10:24, 31, 33; 11:8

JEWS → BOTH JEWS AND GREEKS, JEWS AND GREEKS, KING OF THE JEWS
Ezra
5:5 the elders of the ***J***, and they didn't
Nehemiah
4:1 angry and raged. He mocked the ***J***,
13:23 those days I saw ***J*** who had married
Esther
3:13 destroy all the ***J***, both young and
4:14 appear for the ***J*** from another
10:3 importance. The ***J*** also admired him
Daniel
3:8 seizing a chance to attack the ***J***.
Matthew
2:2 king of the ***J***? We've seen his
27:37 This is Jesus, the king of the ***J***."
Luke
23:3 the king of the ***J***?" Jesus replied,
John
4:22 know because salvation is from the ***J***.
19:3 king of the ***J***!" And they
Acts
21:20 many thousands of ***J*** have become
Romans
3:29 is God the God of ***J*** only? Isn't God
9:24 only from the ***J*** but we also come
1 Corinthians
1:22 ***J*** ask for signs, and Greeks look for
9:20 like a Jew to the ***J***, so I can recruit
1 Thessalonians
2:14 your own people as they did from the ***J***.
Revelation
2:9 who say they are ***J*** (though they are

JEWS AND GREEKS
Ac 14:1; 18:4; 19:10, 17; 20:21; Ro 3:9; 1Co 1:24

JEZEBEL
1 Kings
19:1 Ahab told ***J*** all that Elijah had done,
21:25 that his wife ***J*** led him to do.
2 Kings
9:7 violence done by ***J*** to my servants
9:37 one will be able to say, This was ***J***."
Revelation
2:20 with that woman, ***J***, who calls

JEZREEL
Joshua
15:56 ***J***, Jokdeam, Zanoah
19:18 border ran toward ***J***. They also owned
1 Kings
21:23 will devour Jezebel in the area of ***J***.
2 Kings
9:36 Jezebel's flesh in the area of ***J***.
10:7 in baskets and sent them to Jehu at ***J***.
Hosea
1:4 to him, "Name him ***J***; for in a little
1:5 the bow of Israel in the ***J*** Valley."
1:11 The day will be a wonderful one for ***J***.
2:22 the fresh oil, and they will answer ***J***;

JOAB
2 Samuel
2:13 ***J***, Zeruiah's son, and David's soldiers
3:22 soldiers and ***J*** returned from a
1 Kings
1:7 took advice from ***J***, Zeruiah's son,
11:21 and that ***J*** the general was
Ezra
2:6 namely the family of Jeshua and ***J*** 2,812
8:9 of ***J***, Obadiah, Jehiel's son and with
Nehemiah
7:11 the descendants of Jeshua and ***J*** 2,818
Psalms
60:1 and when ***J*** returned and

JOASH
Judges
6:11 that belonged to ***J*** the Abiezrite.
6:30 said to ***J***, "Bring out your
1 Kings
22:26 city official and to ***J*** the king's son.
2 Kings
13:9 Samaria. His son ***J*** succeeded him as
14:16 ***J*** lay down with this ancestors. He was

JOB
Job
1:9 the LORD, "Does ***J*** revere God for
Ezekiel
14:14 Noah, Daniel, and ***J***, lived there,
James
5:11 the endurance of ***J***. And you have

JOEL

1 Samuel
8:2 oldest son was ***J***; the name of the
Ezra
10:43 Zabad, Zebina, Jaddai, ***J***, and Benaiah.
Nehemiah
11:9 ***J*** son of Zichri was their supervisor,
Joel
1:1 word that came to ***J***, Pethuel's son:
Acts
2:16 what was spoken through the prophet ***J***:

JOHANAN

2 Kings
25:23 Nethaniah's son ***J***, Kareah's son;
1 Chronicles
3:15 the oldest ***J***, the second
Ezra
8:12 of Azgad, ***J***, Hakkatan's son and with
Nehemiah
12:22 Eliashib, Joiada, ***J***, and Jaddua, the
12:23 until the time of ***J***, Eliashib's son.
Jeremiah
40:8 Nethaniah's son; ***J*** and Jonathan,

JOHN → JOHN THE BAPTIST

Matthew
3:1 In those days ***J*** the Baptist appeared in
4:12 Jesus heard that ***J*** was arrested, he
10:2 the son of Zebedee; and ***J*** his brother;
11:4 Go, report to ***J*** what you hear and
11:12 From the days of ***J*** the Baptist until
14:10 Then he had ***J*** beheaded in prison
16:14 Some say ***J*** the Baptist,
John
1:6 A man named ***J*** was sent from God
Acts
3:1 Peter and ***J*** were going up to the temple
Galatians
2:9 Cephas, and ***J***, who are
Revelation
1:1 it through his angel to his servant ***J***,
22:8 I, ***J***, am the one who heard and saw

JOHN THE BAPTIST

Mt 3:1; 11:11, 12; 14:2, 8; 16:14; 17:13; Mk 6:14; 8:28; Lk 7:20; 7:33; 9:19

JOHN'S DISCIPLES

Mt 9:14; 11:7; 14:12; Mk 2:18; 6:29; Lk 7:18; 7:22; Jn 3:25

JONAH

2 Kings
14:25 the prophet ***J***, Amittai's son,
Jonah
1:3 So ***J*** got up—to flee to Tarshish from
1:17 fish to swallow ***J***. Jonah was in the
Matthew
12:40 Just as ***J*** was in the whale's belly for
Luke
11:30 Just as ***J*** became a sign to the people

JONATHAN

Judges
18:30 themselves, and ***J*** son of Gershom
1 Samuel
13:16 Saul, his son ***J***, and the people who
14:45 Saul, "Why should ***J*** die when he has
18:3 And ***J*** and David made a covenant
19:4 So ***J*** spoke highly about David to his
2 Samuel
1:25 midst of battle! ***J*** lies dead on your

JOPPA

Joshua
19:46 along with the territory opposite ***J***.
Acts
9:36 In ***J*** there was a disciple named Tabitha
9:38 Lydda was near ***J***, when the
11:13 saying, 'Send to ***J*** and summon Simon,

JORAM

2 Samuel
8:10 he sent his son ***J*** to King David to wish
2 Kings
8:16 of Israel's King ***J***, Ahab's son,
8:25 year of Israel's King ***J***, Ahab's son.
9:14 plotted against ***J***. Now Joram along
2 Chronicles
22:5 Israel's King ***J***, Ahab's son, to
22:6 ***J*** returned to Jezreel to recover from
22:7 this visit to ***J*** to bring about
Matthew
1:8 was the father of ***J***. Joram was the

JORDAN → ACROSS THE JORDAN, ACROSS THE JORDAN RIVER

Genesis
13:10 saw the entire ***J*** Valley. All of it
Numbers
22:1 of Moab across the ***J*** from Jericho.
34:12 descend to the ***J***. Its limit will
Deuteronomy
1:1 Israel across the ***J*** River, in the
3:27 but you will not cross the ***J*** River.
Joshua
1:2 to cross over the ***J*** with this entire
3:11 to cross over in front of you in the ***J***.
3:17 the middle of the ***J***. Meanwhile, all
4:8 the middle of the ***J***, matching the
4:22 crossed over the ***J*** here on dry
23:4 stretch from the ***J*** to the
2 Kings
2:7 and Elisha stood beside the ***J*** River.
5:10 times in the ***J*** River. Then your
6:4 They came to the ***J*** River and began
Psalms
114:3 and ran away; the ***J*** River retreated!
114:5 did you run away? ***J***, why did you
Isaiah
9:1 far side of the ***J***, and the Galilee
Jeremiah
12:5 you survive in the forest along the ***J***?
Matthew
3:6 sins, he baptized them in the ***J*** River.
4:15 sea, across the ***J***, Galilee of the
Mark
1:9 and John baptized him in the ***J*** River.
John
1:28 place across the ***J*** in Bethany where

JOSEPH

Genesis

35:24 The sons of Rachel were ***J*** and Benjamin

37:3 Now Israel loved ***J*** more than any of his

37:23 When ***J*** reached his brothers, they

39:6 he had to ***J*** and didn't pay

41:49 ***J*** amassed grain like the sand of the

50:7 So ***J*** left to bury his father. All of

Exodus

1:5 was seventy. ***J*** was already in

Numbers

13:11 from the tribe of ***J***: from the tribe of

27:1 and son of ***J***, came forward.

Deuteronomy

27:12 Levi, Judah, Issachar, ***J***, and Benjamin.

33:13 Then he told ***J***: "I pray that his land

Matthew

1:16 was the father of ***J***, the husband of

1:18 was engaged to ***J***, before they were

27:59 ***J*** took the body, wrapped it in a clean

Hebrews

11:22 By faith ***J*** recalled the exodus of the

Revelation

7:8 from the tribe of ***J***, twelve thousand;

JOSHUA

Exodus

17:9 Moses said to ***J***, "Choose some men for

Joshua

5:13 When ***J*** was near Jericho, he looked up.

6:27 The LORD was with ***J***. News about him

24:1 ***J*** gathered all the tribes of Israel at

Luke

3:29 son of ***J*** son of Eliezer son of Jorim

Hebrews

4:8 If ***J*** gave the Israelites rest, God

JOSIAH

1 Kings

13:2 His name will be ***J***. He will

2 Kings

21:24 Amon and made his son ***J*** the next king.

23:24 ***J*** burned those who consulted dead

Jeremiah

1:2 year of Judah's King ***J***, Amon's son,

Zephaniah

1:1 the days of Judah's King ***J***, Amon's son.

Zechariah

6:10 day to the house of ***J*** son of Zephaniah

Matthew

1:10 of Amos. Amos was the father of ***J***.

1:11 ***J*** was the father of Jechoniah and his

JOTHAM

Judges

9:5 stone. Only ***J*** the youngest of

2 Kings

15:32 ***J***, Uzziah's son, became king of Judah

15:38 ***J*** died and was buried with his

2 Chronicles

26:21 temple. His son ***J*** supervised the

Matthew

1:9 was the father of ***J***. Jotham was the

JOURNEY

Exodus

3:18 go on a three-day ***j*** into the desert

Ezra

7:9 The ***j*** from Babylon began on the first

8:21 ask of him a safe ***j*** for ourselves,

Psalms

119:105 before my feet and a light for my ***j***.

Matthew

25:15 ability. Then he left on his ***j***.

Luke

9:3 nothing for the ***j***—no walking stick,

John

4:6 tired from his ***j***, so he sat down

Acts

1:12 near Jerusalem—a sabbath day's ***j*** away.

JOY

Leviticus

9:24 They shouted for ***j*** and fell facedown.

Deuteronomy

24:5 so he can bring ***j*** to his new wife.

1 Chronicles

15:28 with shouts of ***j***, accompanied by

16:27 him; strength and ***j*** are in his place.

29:22 drank with great ***j*** before the LORD

2 Chronicles

15:14 voice, shouts of ***j***, and blasts from

30:26 There was great ***j*** in Jerusalem. Nothing

Ezra

3:12 many others shouted loudly with ***j***.

Nehemiah

8:10 sad, because the ***j*** from the LORD is

12:27 dedication with ***j***, with thanks and

12:43 with great ***j***. The women and

Esther

8:15 of Susa greeted him with shouts of ***j***.

8:16 day of light, happiness, ***j***, and honor.

8:17 of happiness and ***j***. For them it

9:22 from sadness to ***j***, and from sad,

Job

8:19 its way is a ***j***, for from the

8:21 your mouth with ***j***, your lips with a

20:5 is short, the ***j*** of the godless,

Psalms

4:7 heart with more ***j*** than when their

21:6 him happy with the ***j*** of your presence.

27:6 with shouts of ***j***! I will sing and

30:5 may stay all night, but by morning, ***j***!

30:11 funeral clothes and dressed me up in ***j***

32:11 whose hearts are right, sing out in ***j***!

35:27 for me shout for ***j*** and celebrate!

36:8 them drink from your river of pure ***j***.

43:4 come to God, my ***j***, my delight—then

45:7 with the oil of ***j*** more than all

45:15 they are led in with celebration and ***j***.

48:2 summit, the ***j*** of the whole

51:8 Let me hear ***j*** and celebration again;

51:12 Return the ***j*** of your salvation to me

63:5 mouth speaks praise with ***j*** on my lips—

63:7 and I shout for ***j*** in the protection

65:8 of morning and evening sing for ***j***.

65:12 and the hills are dressed in pure ***j***.

65:13 they shout for ***j***; they break out

67:4 and shout with ***j*** because you judge

78:51 tents, he struck their pride and ***j***.

81:1 strength! Shout for ***j*** to Jacob's God!

92:4 acts. I sing with ***j*** because of your

95:2 thanks! Let's shout songs of ***j*** to him!

97:11 righteous person; ***j*** too for those

100:2 Come before him with shouts of ***j***!
105:36 struck down their very pride and ***j***.
105:43 his chosen ones with songs of ***j***.
106:5 rejoice in the ***j*** of your nation,
107:22 what God has done in songs of ***j***!
119:24 your laws are my ***j***—they are my most
119:77 because your Instruction is my ***j***!
119:111 forever because they are my heart's ***j***.
119:143 me, but your commandments are my ***j***!
119:174 saving help! Your Instruction is my ***j***!
132:9 let your faithful shout out with ***j***!
132:16 faithful will shout out loud with ***j***!
137:3 songs of ***j***: "Sing us a song
137:6 I don't make Jerusalem my greatest ***j***.
149:5 let them shout for ***j*** on their beds.

Proverbs
10:28 result in ***j***, but the hopes of
11:10 wicked perish, there are shouts of ***j***.
12:20 but there is ***j*** for those who
14:10 another person can't share its ***j***.
14:13 and in the end, ***j*** turns to sorrow.
15:20 wise child brings ***j*** to a father, but
15:21 Folly is ***j*** to those who lack sense, but
15:23 answer is a ***j***; how good is a
15:30 Bright eyes give ***j*** to the heart
17:21 grief; there's no ***j*** for a scoundrel's
21:15 justly is a ***j*** to the righteous,

Ecclesiastes
2:26 knowledge, and ***j*** to those who
5:20 God gives an answer in their hearts' ***j***.

Song of Songs
3:11 wedding, on the day of his heart's ***j***.

Isaiah
9:3 increased its ***j***. They rejoiced
12:3 draw water with ***j*** from the springs
12:6 and sing for ***j***, city of Zion,
16:10 ***J*** and happiness have been harvested
24:11 the streets. All ***j*** has reached its
26:19 will shout for ***j***. Your shadow is a
29:19 will again find ***j*** in the LORD, and
35:2 and rejoice with ***j*** and singing. They
35:10 with everlasting ***j*** upon their heads.
51:3 Happiness and ***j*** will be found in
51:11 with everlasting ***j*** upon their heads.
56:7 and bring them ***j*** in my house of
60:15 forever, a ***j*** for all
61:3 of ashes, oil of ***j*** in place of
61:7 land; everlasting ***j*** will be theirs.
62:5 you. With the ***j*** of a bridegroom
65:18 Jerusalem as a ***j*** and her people as
66:5 let's see your ***j***." But they will
66:10 with her in ***j***, all you who

Jeremiah
7:34 the sound of ***j*** and delight as
15:16 they became my ***j***, the delight of
16:9 the sounds of ***j*** and gladness and
20:15 You have a son!"—filling him with ***j***.
25:10 the sounds of ***j*** and laughter and
31:4 play your tambourines and dance with ***j***.
31:9 With tears of ***j*** they will come; while
31:12 come shouting for ***j*** on the hills of
31:13 will dance for ***j***; the young and
33:9 bring me great ***j***, praise, and
33:11 the sounds of ***j*** and laughter and the
48:33 ***J*** and gladness have been taken from the

Lamentations
2:15 Beauty, the ***J*** of All the Earth?"
5:15 ***J*** has left our heart; our dancing has

Ezekiel
24:25 crowning ***j***, the delight of

Hosea
7:3 glad, and give ***j*** to the officials

Joel
1:12 are dried up. ***J*** fades away from
1:16 our eyes? Aren't ***j*** and gladness also

Zechariah
8:19 become times of ***j*** and gladness,

Matthew
2:10 saw the star, they were filled with ***j***.
5:12 Be full of ***j*** and be glad, because you
13:44 up. Full of ***j***, the finder sold

Luke
1:14 He will be a ***j*** and delight to you, and
1:44 the baby in my womb jumped for ***j***.
6:23 happens! Leap for ***j*** because you have
8:56 themselves with ***j***, but he ordered
10:21 overflowed with ***j*** from the Holy
15:7 will be more ***j*** in heaven over
15:10 way, I tell you, ***j*** breaks out in the
24:52 to Jerusalem overwhelmed with ***j***.

John
3:29 voice. Therefore, my ***j*** is now complete.
15:11 to you so that my ***j*** will be in you
16:20 but your sorrow will turn into ***j***.
16:21 because of her ***j*** that a child has
16:22 be overjoyed. No one takes away your ***j***.
16:24 so that your ***j*** will be complete.
17:13 that they can share completely in my ***j***.
20:20 saw the Lord, they were filled with ***j***.

Acts
12:14 so overcome with ***j*** when she

Romans
14:17 peace, and ***j*** in the Holy
15:13 fill you with all ***j*** and peace in
15:32 come to you with ***j*** by God's will and

Galatians
5:22 Spirit is love, ***j***, peace, patience,

Philippians
1:4 and it's always a prayer full of ***j***.
1:25 your progress and the ***j*** of your faith,
2:2 complete my ***j*** by thinking the same way,
2:29 Lord with great ***j*** and show great
4:1 miss, who are my ***j*** and crown, stand

Colossians
1:12 thanks with ***j*** to the Father. He

1 Thessalonians
1:6 Holy Spirit with ***j*** in spite of great
2:19 What is our hope, ***j***, or crown that we
2:20 You are our glory and ***j***
3:9 given all the ***j*** we have because

Philemon
1:7 I have great ***j*** and encouragement

Hebrews
10:34 possessions with ***j***, since you knew
12:2 the sake of the ***j*** that was laid out

James
1:2 tests you encounter as occasions for ***j***.
4:9 mourning and your ***j*** become sadness.

1 Peter
1:8 with a glorious ***j*** that is too much
4:13 have overwhelming ***j*** when his glory is

1 John
1:4 things so that our ***j*** can be complete.
2 John
1:12 so that our ***j*** can be complete.
3 John
1:4 I have no greater ***j*** than this: to hear

JOYFULLY

Deuteronomy
28:47 the LORD your God ***j*** and gladly above
Ezra
6:16 returned exiles, ***j*** celebrated the
6:22 They also ***j*** celebrated the Festival of
Psalms
33:1 righteous, shout ***j*** to the LORD! It's
47:1 you people! Shout ***j*** to God with a
66:1 A psalm.] Shout ***j*** to God, all the
96:12 of the forest too will shout out ***j***
145:7 they will shout ***j*** about your
Proverbs
31:13 and flax; she works ***j*** with her hands.
Ecclesiastes
9:7 Go, eat your food ***j*** and drink your wine
Matthew
13:20 the word and immediately receive it ***j***.
Luke
8:13 receive the word ***j*** when they hear

JUBILEE

Leviticus
25:10 It will be a ***J*** year for you:
Numbers
36:4 At the Israelite ***J***, their inheritance

JUDAH

Genesis
29:35 So she named him ***J***. Then she stopped
35:23 and Simeon, Levi, ***J***, Issachar, and
37:26 ***J*** said to his brothers, "What do we
38:1 At that time, ***J*** moved away from his
49:8 ***J***, you are the one your brothers will
Deuteronomy
33:7 said this to ***J***: "LORD, listen to
Joshua
15:63 But the people of ***J*** couldn't remove the
Judges
1:2 The tribe of ***J*** will go up. I've
Ruth
1:7 the road to return to the land of ***J***.
2 Samuel
2:4 the people of ***J*** came to Hebron
2:7 but the house of ***J*** has anointed me
5:5 He ruled over ***J*** for seven and a half
24:1 and count the people of Israel and ***J***.
1 Chronicles
28:4 forever. He chose ***J*** as leader, and
Nehemiah
6:7 is a king in ***J***! Now, the king
Psalms
48:11 let the towns of ***J*** rejoice because
60:7 Ephraim is my helmet; ***J*** is my scepter.
Isaiah
1:1 The vision about ***J*** and Jerusalem that
3:8 has stumbled and ***J*** has fallen,
Jeremiah
2:28 as many gods, ***J***, as you have
13:9 the brazen pride of ***J*** and Jerusalem!
30:3 people Israel and ***J*** from captivity,
31:31 with the people of Israel and ***J***.
Lamentations
1:3 ***J*** was exiled after suffering and hard
Hosea
1:7 on the house of ***J***. I, the LORD
Joel
3:1 bring back to ***J*** and Jerusalem
Micah
1:5 the shrines of ***J***? Isn't it
1:9 come as far as ***J***; he has struck as
Zechariah
1:19 that scattered ***J***, Israel, and
8:15 and the house of ***J***. Don't be afraid.
11:14 the alliance between ***J*** and Israel.
Malachi
2:11 ***J*** cheated—a detestable thing was done
Matthew
2:6 land of ***J***, by no means are
Hebrews
7:14 from the tribe of ***J***, but Moses never
8:8 a new covenant with the house of ***J***.
Revelation
5:5 of the tribe of ***J***, the Root of

JUDAS

Matthew
10:4 Cananaean; and ***J***, who betrayed
13:55 Joseph, Simon, and ***J*** his brothers?
26:14 who was called ***J*** Iscariot, went to
26:25 Now ***J***, who would betray him, replied,
26:47 still speaking, ***J***, one of the
27:3 When ***J***, who betrayed Jesus, saw that
27:5 ***J*** threw the silver pieces into the
Mark
3:19 and ***J*** Iscariot, who betrayed Jesus
6:3 of James, Joses, ***J***, and Simon?
14:10 ***J*** Iscariot, one of the Twelve, went to
14:43 still speaking, ***J***, one of the
14:45 as he got there, ***J*** said to Jesus,
Luke
6:16 ***J*** the son of James; and Judas Iscariot,
22:3 Satan entered ***J***, called Iscariot,
22:47 the one called ***J***, one of the
22:48 said to him, "***J***, would you betray
John
6:71 was speaking of ***J***, Simon Iscariot's
12:4 ***J*** Iscariot, one of his disciples (the
13:2 already provoked ***J***, Simon Iscariot's
13:26 and gave it to ***J***, Simon Iscariot's
13:27 After ***J*** took the bread, Satan entered
13:29 that, since ***J*** kept the money
13:30 So when ***J*** took the bread, he left
13:31 When ***J*** was gone, Jesus said, "Now the
14:22 ***J***(not Judas Iscariot) asked, "Lord,
18:2 ***J***, his betrayer, also knew the place
18:3 ***J*** brought a company of soldiers and
18:5 to them, "I Am." (***J***, his betrayer,
Acts
1:13 Simon the zealot; and ***J***, James' son—
1:16 concerning ***J***, who became a
1:25 from which ***J*** turned away to go
5:37 of the census, ***J*** the Galilean
15:22 They selected ***J*** Barsabbas and
15:27 we are sending ***J*** and Silas. They
15:32 ***J*** and Silas were prophets, and they
15:33 ***J*** and Silas stayed there awhile, then

JUDEA

Ezra
9:9 to give us a wall in ***J*** and Jerusalem.
Matthew
2:1 the territory of ***J*** during the rule
3:1 appeared in the desert of ***J*** announcing,
28:15 throughout all ***J*** to this very day.
Mark
3:8 ***J***, Jerusalem, Idumea, beyond the
Luke
1:5 of King Herod of ***J*** there was a
3:1 was governor over ***J*** and Herod was
7:17 spread throughout ***J*** and the
Acts
1:8 Jerusalem, in all ***J*** and Samaria, and
8:1 the regions of ***J*** and Samaria.
9:31 church throughout ***J***, Galilee, and
1 Thessalonians
2:14 of God in ***J***, which are in

JUDEANS

2 Kings
16:6 driving the ***J*** out of Elath. The
25:25 also killed the ***J*** and the Chaldeans
1 Chronicles
2:10 of Nahshon, tribal chief of the ***J***.
4:27 clans became as numerous as the ***J***.
2 Chronicles
14:8 hundred thousand ***J*** armed with body-sized shields
Ezekiel
25:12 of Judah. The ***J*** were guilty, but
Daniel
1:6 men from the ***J*** were Daniel,
Acts
2:14 and declared, "***J*** and everyone
15:2 against these ***J*** and argued

JUDGE

Genesis
18:25 you! Will the ***j*** of all the earth
19:9 immigrant want to ***j*** us? Now we will
Exodus
2:14 you a boss or ***j*** over us? Are you
18:13 Moses sat as a ***j*** for the people,
Deuteronomy
1:16 tribe members and ***j*** fairly, whether
17:9 and to the head ***j*** in office at that
Judges
11:27 LORD, who is the ***j***, decide today
1 Samuel
24:12 May the LORD ***j*** between me and you!
Psalms
7:8 The LORD will ***j*** the peoples. Establish
7:11 is a righteous ***j***, a God who is
9:8 rightly; he will ***j*** all people fairly.
50:4 to the earth in order to ***j*** his people:
50:6 because God himself is the ***j***. Selah
58:1 gods? Do you really ***j*** humans fairly?
67:4 joy because you ***j*** the nations
72:2 Let him ***j*** your people with
75:7 is God who is the ***j***. He brings this
82:2 long will you ***j*** unjustly by
82:8 Rise up, God! ***J*** the earth because you
94:2 Rise up, ***j*** of the earth! Pay back the
96:10 shaken. He will ***j*** all people
103:9 always play the ***j***; he won't be
Proverbs
8:16 govern, and officials ***j*** righteously.
31:9 out in order to ***j*** with
Ecclesiastes
3:17 myself, God will ***j*** both righteous
Isaiah
2:4 God will ***j*** between the nations, and
3:13 to accuse; he stands to ***j*** the peoples.
11:3 LORD. He won't ***j*** by appearances,
33:22 The LORD is our ***j***; the LORD is our
Jeremiah
11:20 forces, righteous ***j***, who tests the
Ezekiel
7:3 against you, I'll ***j*** you according to
7:27 have done and ***j*** them by their own
18:30 Therefore, I will ***j*** each of you
22:2 one, will you ***j***? Will you judge
33:20 measure up." I ***j*** each one of you
34:17 proclaims: I will ***j*** between the rams
Hosea
4:9 their ways, and ***j*** them for their
7:12 them down; I will ***j*** them according to
Joel
3:12 I will sit to ***j*** all the
Amos
2:3 will remove their ***j*** from them and
Micah
4:3 God will ***j*** between the nations and
Matthew
7:1 Don't ***j***, so that you won't be judged
Luke
6:37 Don't ***j***, and you won't be judged.
12:14 appointed me as ***j*** or referee
18:2 city there was a ***j*** who neither
19:22 replied, 'I will ***j*** you by the words
John
5:30 I hear, I ***j***, and my judgment
7:24 Don't ***j*** according to appearances. Judge
8:15 You ***j*** according to human standards, but
8:16 Even if I do ***j***, my judgment is
12:47 them, I don't ***j*** them. I didn't
18:31 yourselves and ***j*** him according to
Acts
7:27 Who appointed you as our leader and ***j***?
10:42 God appointed as ***j*** of the living and
Romans
2:1 one of you who ***j*** others is without
2:16 gospel, God will ***j*** the hidden truth
3:6 weren't just, how could he ***j*** the world?
14:3 eat must not ***j*** the ones who do,
1 Corinthians
4:3 any human court; I don't even ***j*** myself.
5:12 Isn't it your job to ***j*** insiders?
6:2 God's people will ***j*** the world? If the
Colossians
2:16 don't let anyone ***j*** you about eating
2 Timothy
4:1 who is coming to ***j*** the living and
4:8 is the righteous ***j***, is going to give
Hebrews
10:30 also said, The Lord will ***j*** his people.
12:23 to God the ***j*** of all, to the
13:4 because God will ***j*** the sexually
James
4:12 one lawgiver and ***j***, and he is able

5:9 judged. Look! The ***j*** is standing at
1 Peter
2:12 God visits to ***j*** they will glorify
4:5 who is ready to ***j*** the living and

JUDGED

1 Samuel
4:18 Eli had ***j*** Israel for forty
Psalms
9:19 Let the nations be ***j*** before you.
37:33 be found guilty when they are ***j***.
Matthew
7:1 Don't judge, so that you won't be ***j***
John
12:48 my words will be ***j*** at the last day
Romans
2:12 under the Law will be ***j*** by the Law.
3:4 and you will triumph when you are ***j***.
1 Corinthians
4:3 care less if I'm ***j*** by you or by any
11:31 But if we had ***j*** ourselves, we wouldn't
James
2:12 who will be ***j*** by the law of
3:1 we teachers will be ***j*** more strictly.
5:9 that you won't be ***j***. Look! The judge
Revelation
11:18 the dead to be ***j***; The time came to
19:2 just, because he ***j*** the great
20:12 And the dead were ***j*** on the basis of

JUDGES

Exodus
18:22 Let them sit as ***j*** for the people at all
Ruth
1:1 the days when the ***j*** ruled, there was
1 Samuel
8:1 his sons to serve as Israel's ***j***.
Job
9:24 the faces of its ***j***. If not God, then
Psalms
58:11 is a God who ***j*** people on the
Proverbs
29:14 If a king ***j*** the poor honestly, his
Luke
11:19 out? Therefore, they will be your ***j***.
1 Corinthians
4:4 because the Lord is the one who ***j*** me.
6:4 appoint people as ***j*** who aren't
James
2:4 yourselves and become evil-minded ***j***?
1 Peter
1:17 upon a Father who ***j*** all people
2:23 himself to the one who ***j*** justly.
Revelation
18:8 the Lord God who ***j*** her is powerful.
19:11 and True, and he ***j*** and makes war

JUDGMENT → JUDGMENT DAY

Ezra
7:26 Let ***j*** be strictly carried out upon
Psalms
51:4 correct when you issue your ***j***.
76:8 have announced ***j*** from heaven. The
82:1 council; he gives ***j*** among the gods:
119:66 and good ***j*** because I've put
143:2 your servant to ***j*** because no living
Proverbs
3:21 hold on to sound ***j*** and discretion.
16:10 an oracle; in a ***j***, one can't go
20:8 who sits on his ***j*** throne sifts out
22:10 disappears; ***j*** and shame also
24:23 the wise: Partiality in ***j*** isn't good.
Ecclesiastes
12:14 every deed to ***j***, including every
Isaiah
3:14 will enter into ***j*** with the elders
28:6 one who sits in ***j***, and a strength
Jeremiah
2:35 have sinned, I will pass ***j*** against you.
25:31 entering into ***j*** with all people,
Daniel
7:22 One came. Then ***j*** was given in
Joel
3:2 I will enter into ***j*** with them in
Habakkuk
1:12 Chaldean here for ***j***. Rock, you
Zephaniah
3:15 has removed your ***j***; he has turned
Malachi
3:5 near to you for ***j***. I will be quick
Matthew
5:21 commit murder will be in danger of ***j***.
5:22 be in danger of ***j***. If they say to
7:2 receive the same ***j*** you give.
8:29 to torture us before the time of ***j***?"
12:18 and he'll announce ***j*** to the Gentiles.
12:41 stand up at the ***j*** with this
23:33 you be able to escape the ***j*** of hell?
John
5:22 but he has given all ***j*** to the Son
5:30 I judge, and my ***j*** is just. I don't
7:24 to appearances. Judge with right ***j***."
9:39 world to exercise ***j*** so that those who
12:31 is the time for ***j*** of this world.
16:8 wrong about sin, righteousness, and ***j***.
16:11 was wrong about ***j*** because this
Acts
24:25 and the coming ***j***, Felix became
Romans
2:2 know that God's ***j*** agrees with the
5:16 person's sin. The ***j*** that came from
5:18 person, just as ***j*** fell on everyone
14:10 stand in front of the ***j*** seat of God.
1 Corinthians
11:29 are eating and drinking their own ***j***.
2 Thessalonians
1:5 shows that God's ***j*** is right, and
Hebrews
6:2 dead, and eternal ***j***—all over again.
9:27 destined to die once and then face ***j***.
10:30 the one who said, ***J*** is mine; I will
James
2:13 be no mercy in ***j*** for anyone who
5:12 or "No," or else you may fall under ***j***.
1 Peter
4:17 it's time for ***j*** to begin with
2 Peter
2:3 with lies. The ***j*** pronounced
2:4 keeping them there until the ***j***.
2:11 when pronouncing the Lord's ***j*** on them.
Jude
1:4 Jesus Christ. ***J*** was passed
1:6 until the ***j*** of the great day.

1:15 to execute ***j*** on everyone and to convict
Revelation
6:10 before you pass ***j***? How long before
14:7 the hour of his ***j*** has come. Worship
17:1 will show you the ***j*** upon the great
18:10 In a single hour your ***j*** has come.'
20:4 on them, and ***j*** was given in

JUDGMENT DAY
Hos 5:9; Mt 7:22; 10:15; 11:22, 24; 12:36; Lk 10:12; 2Pt 2:9; 3:7; 1Jn 4:17

JUDGMENTS
Psalms
19:9 The LORD's ***j*** are true. All of
72:1 God, give your ***j*** to the king. Give
John
8:16 I'm not alone. My ***j*** come from me and
Romans
11:33 mysterious as his ***j***, and they are as
Revelation
16:5 was, because you have given these ***j***.
16:7 Almighty, your ***j*** are true and
19:2 His ***j*** are true and just, because he

JUST
Nehemiah
9:33 You have been ***j*** in all that has
Job
34:5 innocent; God has denied my ***j*** cause;
35:2 right? You say, "I'm more ***j*** than God."
Psalms
119:121 I've done what is ***j*** and right. Don't
Proverbs
1:3 is righteous, ***j***, and full of
12:5 the righteous are ***j***, but the guidance
Ezekiel
33:14 from sin and do what is ***j*** and right—
Zechariah
7:9 proclaims: Make ***j*** and faithful
8:16 make truthful, ***j***, and peaceable
John
5:30 my judgment is ***j***. I don't seek my
1 Corinthians
6:1 people who aren't ***j***, instead of by
1 John
1:9 is faithful and ***j*** to forgive us our
Revelation
19:2 are true and ***j***, because he

JUSTICE → RIGHTEOUSNESS AND JUSTICE
Exodus
23:6 undermine the ***j*** that your poor
Deuteronomy
16:19 Don't delay ***j***; don't show favoritism.
33:21 the LORD's ***j*** and the Lord's
1 Samuel
8:3 accepted bribes, and they perverted ***j***.
2 Samuel
15:4 come to me, and I would give them ***j***."
1 Kings
3:28 was in him so he could execute ***j***.
7:7 room the Hall of ***J***, where he would
10:9 king to uphold ***j*** and
2 Chronicles
9:8 king to uphold ***j*** and
Ezra
7:10 and to teach law and ***j*** in Israel.
Job
8:3 Does God pervert ***j***, or does the
9:19 behold power! If ***j***—who calls God to
19:7 answered; I shout—but there is no ***j***.
29:14 I put on ***j***, and it clothed me,
34:12 the Almighty doesn't distort ***j***.
34:17 one who hates ***j*** rule; will you
36:17 of the wicked; ***j*** will be upheld in
Psalms
1:5 in the court of ***j***—neither will sin
7:6 up, my God; you command that ***j*** be done!
7:8 Establish ***j*** for me, LORD,
9:4 have established ***j*** for me and my
10:18 to establish ***j*** for the orphan and the
17:2 My ***j*** comes from you; let your eyes see
25:9 the weak to ***j***, teaching them
26:1 David.] Establish ***j*** for me, LORD,
35:23 up! Get up and do ***j*** for me; argue my
35:24 Establish ***j*** for me according to your
36:6 mountains; your ***j*** is like the
37:6 like the dawn, your ***j*** like high noon.
43:1 Establish ***j*** for me, God! Argue my case
45:6 Your royal scepter is a scepter of ***j***.
48:11 rejoice because of your acts of ***j***!
72:2 and your poor ones with ***j***.
75:2 is right, I will establish ***j*** just so.
76:9 up to establish ***j***, when God rose up
82:3 Give ***j*** to the lowly and the orphan;
94:15 No, but ***j*** will once again meet up with
96:13 to establish ***j*** on the earth! He
97:8 of your acts of ***j***, LORD,
98:9 to establish ***j*** on the earth! He
99:4 king who loves ***j***, you are the one
101:1 faithful love and ***j***! I want to sing
103:6 does ***j*** for all who are
105:5 works, and the ***j*** he declared—
106:3 people who uphold ***j***, who always do
110:6 the nations to ***j***, piling the dead
111:7 is honesty and ***j***; all God's rules
112:5 those who conduct their affairs with ***j***.
119:84 When will you bring my oppressors to ***j***?
122:5 the thrones of ***j*** are there—the th
135:14 The LORD gives ***j*** to his people and has
146:7 who gives ***j*** to people who are
149:9 achieving the ***j*** written against them.
Proverbs
2:8 the paths of ***j*** and guards the
8:20 of righteousness, on the paths of ***j***,
16:8 than great profits without ***j***.
17:23 secret bribes to twist the way of ***j***.
18:5 good; it denies ***j*** to the righteous.
19:28 witness mocks ***j***; the wicked mouth
21:7 away, for they refuse to act with ***j***.
28:5 don't understand ***j***, but those who
29:4 to the land by ***j***, but one who
29:26 to the ruler, but ***j*** comes from the
Isaiah
1:17 to do good. Seek ***j***: help the
1:21 She was full of ***j***; righteousness
1:27 be redeemed by ***j***, and those who
5:7 God expected ***j***, but there was
5:16 be exalted in ***j***, and the holy God
9:7 it with ***j*** and righteousness
10:2 my people of ***j***; to make widows

10:22 end is announced, overflowing with ***j***.
16:5 a judge who seeks ***j*** and timely
26:8 the path of your ***j***, LORD, we wait
28:6 and a spirit of ***j*** for the one who sits
29:21 postpone ***j*** for the innocent.
30:18 LORD is a God of ***j***; happy are all
32:1 rulers govern to promote ***j***,
33:5 filling Zion with ***j*** and righteousness.
40:14 him the path of ***j*** and knowledge and
42:1 him; he will bring ***j*** to the nations.
49:4 will grant me ***j***; my reward is
51:4 out from me, my ***j***, as a light to
59:8 peace; there's no ***j*** in their paths.
61:8 I, the LORD, love ***j***; I hate robbery

Jeremiah
4:2 God in truth, ***j***, and
5:4 the LORD's way or the ***j*** of their God.
9:24 with kindness, ***j***, and
10:24 LORD, but with ***j***, not in your
12:1 about your ***j***. Why do guilty
21:12 by administering ***j***, rescue those who

Lamentations
3:35 denying someone ***j*** before the Most High

Ezekiel
7:23 full of perverted ***j***, the city full of
22:29 They've oppressed and denied ***j***.
34:16 because I will tend my sheep with ***j***.
45:9 Establish ***j*** and

Daniel
4:37 all his paths are ***j***, and he is able

Hosea
2:19 and in ***j***, in devoted love,
12:6 faithful love and ***j***, and wait

Amos
5:7 to you who turn ***j*** into poison, and
6:12 you have turned ***j*** into poison and

Micah
3:1 Israel! Isn't it your job to know ***j***?—
6:8 from you: to do ***j***, embrace faithful
7:9 case and provides ***j*** for me. He will

Habakkuk
1:4 is ineffective; ***j*** does not endure
1:7 He makes his own ***j*** and dignity.

Zephaniah
2:3 who practice his ***j***; seek
3:5 he renders ***j***, but the

Malachi
2:17 doing evil" or "Where is the God of ***j***?"

Matthew
12:20 smoldering wick, until he makes ***j*** win.
23:23 of the Law: ***j***, peace, and

Luke
7:29 God's ***j*** because they had
11:42 while neglecting ***j*** and love for God.
18:3 asking, 'Give me ***j*** in this case

Acts
8:33 his humiliation ***j*** was taken away
28:4 but the goddess ***J*** hasn't let him

Romans
3:5 confirms God's ***j***, what will we

2 Corinthians
7:11 concern, what ***j***! In everything

Ephesians
4:24 to God's image in ***j*** and true holiness.
5:9 every sort of goodness, ***j***, and truth.
6:14 your waist, ***j*** as your

2 Thessalonians
1:8 He will give ***j*** with blazing fire to

Hebrews
1:8 your kingdom's scepter is a rod of ***j***.
11:33 brought about ***j***, realized

James
3:18 sow the seeds of ***j*** by their peaceful

2 Peter
1:1 ours through the ***j*** of our God and

Revelation
6:10 you require ***j*** for our blood,
15:4 for your acts of ***j*** have been
19:8 fine linen is the saints' acts of ***j***."

Kk

KADESH
Numbers
20:1 people stayed at ***K***. Miriam died and
Deuteronomy
1:46 so you stayed in ***K***-barnea for quite
Psalms
29:8 the LORD shakes the wilderness of ***K***.

KADESH-BARNEA
Numbers
32:8 I sent them from ***K*** to inspect the

KEEPING
Genesis
30:40 Laban's flock but ***k*** his flock
Deuteronomy
10:13 and by ***k*** the LORD's commandments and his regulations
13:18 your God's voice, ***k*** all his
1 Samuel
11:5 coming back from ***k*** the cattle in the
16:11 but he's out ***k*** the sheep." "Send
26:19 driven me off, ***k*** me from sharing
2 Samuel
21:5 to destroy us, ***k*** us from having a
1 Kings
1:2 our master the king and ***k*** him warm."
11:11 this instead of ***k*** my covenant and
11:38 right in my eyes, ***k*** my laws and my
2 Kings
7:9 news, but we're ***k*** quiet about it.
23:3 the LORD by ***k*** his commandments,
1 Chronicles
28:7 committed to ***k*** my commands and
2 Chronicles
7:17 commanded you and ***k*** my regulations
34:31 the LORD by ***k*** his commandments,
Ezra
8:26 out into their ***k*** six hundred fifty
Nehemiah
9:29 life comes by ***k*** them. They turned
Psalms
19:11 them; there is great reward in ***k*** them.
78:7 God's deeds, but ***k*** God's
89:31 like dirt, stop ***k*** my commandments—
119:5 when it comes to ***k*** your statutes!
119:17 so I can go on living and ***k*** your word.
Proverbs
15:3 are everywhere, ***k*** watch on evil and
26:24 with their lips, ***k*** their deception
Ecclesiastes
3:6 a time for ***k*** and a time for
3:7 a time for ***k*** silent and a time
Jeremiah
17:27 don't obey me by ***k*** the Sabbath day
Malachi
3:14 do we gain by ***k*** his obligation or
Matthew
15:3 command of God by ***k*** the rules handed
Luke
2:24 a sacrifice in ***k*** with what's
17:12 approached him. ***K*** their distance
23:56 on the Sabbath in ***k*** with the
Acts
9:24 scheme. They were ***k*** watch at the city
21:24 you too live a life in ***k*** with the Law.
25:4 responded by ***k*** Paul in Caesarea,
Romans
4:18 many nations, in ***k*** with the promise
1 Corinthians
7:19 What matters is ***k*** God's
Philemon
1:13 I considered ***k*** him with me so that he
James
1:5 thought, without ***k*** score. Wisdom
2 Peter
2:4 of darkness, ***k*** them there until
1 John
2:4 him," while not ***k*** his commandments,
Revelation
2:26 victorious, ***k*** my practices

KEILAH
1 Samuel
23:5 soldiers went to ***K*** and fought the

KEPT
Genesis
16:2 The LORD has ***k*** me from giving
20:6 this. In fact, I ***k*** you from sinning
26:5 obeyed me and ***k*** my orders, my
30:2 God alone has ***k*** you from giving
39:16 She ***k*** his garment with her until
48:16 may my name be ***k*** alive and the
Exodus
16:33 it should be ***k*** safe for future
36:3 sanctuary. They ***k*** bringing him
Deuteronomy
7:8 and because he ***k*** the solemn pledge
2 Samuel
22:22 because I have ***k*** the LORD's ways. I
2 Kings
18:6 from him. He ***k*** the commandments
Job
23:11 tracks. I have ***k*** his way and not
23:12 ***k*** the commandments from his lips and
Psalms
18:23 before him; I've ***k*** myself from
32:3 When I ***k*** quiet, my bones wore out; I
35:13 grieving, and I ***k*** a strict fast.
39:2 quiet, silent. I ***k*** my peace, but it

65:1 is praise. Promises made to you are ***k***—
73:13 Meanwhile, I've ***k*** my heart pure for no
99:7 of cloud. They ***k*** the laws and the
119:4 decrees should be ***k*** most carefully.
130:3 If you ***k*** track of sins, LORD—my Lord,
Proverbs
28:26 who walk in wisdom will be ***k*** safe.
Matthew
19:20 replied, "I've ***k*** all these. What
John
17:6 them to me, and they have ***k*** your word.
2 Timothy
4:7 finished the race, and ***k*** the faith.
1 Peter
1:4 that is presently ***k*** safe in heaven
2 Peter
3:7 reserve for fire, ***k*** for the Judgment
Jude
1:1 the Father and ***k*** safe by Jesus
1:6 The Lord has ***k*** them in eternal
Revelation
3:8 and yet you have ***k*** my word and
3:10 Because you ***k*** my command to endure, I will keep you safe

KIDNEYS
Exodus
29:13 and the two ***k*** along with the
Leviticus
3:4 the two ***k*** and the fat around them at
Job
16:13 me; he cuts my ***k*** open without pity

KIDRON
2 Samuel
15:23 king crossed the ***K*** Valley, and all
John
18:1 other side of the ***K*** Valley. He and

KILL
Genesis
4:14 and anyone who finds me will ***k*** me."
12:12 and they will ***k*** me but let you
20:11 here and they will ***k*** me to get my wife.
22:10 took the knife to ***k*** his son as a
26:7 live there will ***k*** me for Rebekah
37:18 to them, and they plotted to ***k*** him.
Exodus
2:15 it, he tried to ***k*** Moses. But Moses
4:23 now I'm going to ***k*** your oldest son.'
Leviticus
20:16 with it, you must ***k*** the woman and the
26:22 and they will ***k*** your children and
Deuteronomy
5:17 Do not ***k***
19:6 catch and ***k*** him even though a
20:13 to you; you must ***k*** all the city's
27:25 accepts money to ***k*** an innocent
Joshua
9:26 the Israelites, and they didn't ***k*** them.
Matthew
10:28 of those who ***k*** the body but
17:23 They will ***k*** him. But he will be raised
Mark
9:31 hands. They will ***k*** him. Three days
14:1 for a way to arrest Jesus and ***k*** him.
John
7:19 keep the Law. Why do you want to ***k*** me?"
10:10 only to steal, ***k***, and destroy. I
Revelation
11:7 gain victory over them, and ***k*** them.

KILLED
Genesis
4:8 attacked his brother Abel and ***k*** him.
Exodus
2:12 there. Then he ***k*** the Egyptian and
13:15 us go, the LORD ***k*** all the oldest
Nehemiah
9:26 Instruction. They ***k*** your prophets who
Psalms
44:22 we are getting ***k*** every day—it's b
78:31 against them: he ***k*** the most hearty
78:34 But whenever God ***k*** them, they went
78:47 God ***k*** their vines with hail, their
78:64 priests were ***k*** by the sword, and
105:29 waters into blood and ***k*** their fish.
135:10 down many nations and ***k*** mighty kings:
136:18 And ***k*** powerful kings—God's faithful
Hosea
6:5 prophets, I have ***k*** them by the words
Mark
8:31 experts, and be ***k***, and then, after
9:31 days after he is ***k*** he will rise up."
Luke
11:48 deeds. They ***k*** the prophets, and
Acts
3:15 You ***k*** the author of life, the very one
23:12 eat or drink until they had ***k*** Paul.
Romans
7:11 the commandment, deceived me, and ***k*** me.
11:3 Lord, they have ***k*** your prophets, and
Revelation
11:5 them, they have to be ***k*** in this way.

KILLER
Exodus
21:13 a place to which the ***k*** can run away.
21:14 should remove the ***k*** from my altar and
Numbers
35:24 between the ***k*** and the close
35:25 will protect the ***k*** from the hand of
35:26 But if the ***k*** ever goes outside the
35:28 The ***k*** must live in his refuge city
35:31 for the life of a ***k***, who is guilty of
Deuteronomy
19:6 chase after the ***k*** out of rage and—
19:12 word, and the ***k*** will be sent back
21:1 and the identity of the ***k*** is unknown,
Joshua
20:4 The ***k*** will flee to one of these cities,
20:5 won't hand the ***k*** over. This is
20:6 The ***k*** will live in that city until
21:13 refuge city for a ***k***, and its

KILLING
Genesis
18:25 you to do this, ***k*** the innocent with
Exodus
21:13 If the ***k*** wasn't on purpose but an
21:29 the ox ends up ***k*** a man or a woman,

Joshua
8:24 Israel finished **k** the entire population
Judges
4:16 **k** Sisera's entire
9:56 to his father by **k** his seventy
1 Samuel
15:8 under the ban, **k** them with the
17:50 down and **k** him—and David did
17:57 came back from **k** the Philistine,
18:6 came back from **k** the Philistine,
19:5 person by **k** David for no
22:18 the priests, **k** eighty-five men wh
2 Samuel
2:26 the sword keep **k** forever? Don't
2:31 the Benjaminites, **k** three hundred
21:16 planned on **k** David. The weight
21:17 down and **k** him. Then David's
23:8 eight hundred, **k** them on a single
1 Kings
11:24 when David was **k** them. They went
13:26 tore him apart, **k** him in agreement
17:20 that I am staying with by **k** her son?"
2 Kings
17:26 and the lions are **k** them because none
25:21 struck them down, **k** them in Riblah in
1 Chronicles
11:11 eight hundred, **k** them on a single
2 Chronicles
21:4 his rule by **k** all his brothers,
25:13 to Beth-horon, **k** three thousand
36:20 who survived the **k** so that they
Esther
9:5 with sword blows, **k**, and destruction.
Job
1:17 and took them, **k** the young men
Psalms
60:1 defeated Edom, **k** twelve thousand
Ecclesiastes
3:3 a time for **k** and a time for healing,
Isaiah
22:13 and frivolity, **k** of cattle and
Jeremiah
26:15 will be guilty of **k** an innocent man.
41:16 at Mizpah after **k** Gedaliah,
Daniel
5:19 he wanted: **k** or sparing,
Matthew
23:30 have joined them in **k** the prophets.'
Acts
7:24 and evened the score by **k** the Egyptian.
22:20 that belonged to those who were **k** him.'

KILLS

Genesis
4:15 anyone who **k** Cain will be paid
Exodus
21:12 who hits and **k** someone should be
21:14 someone plots and **k** another person on
Leviticus
24:17 If anyone **k** another person, they must
24:18 Someone who **k** an animal may make amends
24:21 Someone who **k** an animal must make
Numbers
35:6 the person who **k** someone to flee
35:11 a person who **k** someone by
35:15 for anyone who **k** a person by
35:27 refuge city and **k** him, he will not
35:30 Anyone who **k** another will be executed
Deuteronomy
22:26 someone attacks his neighbor and **k** him.
27:24 is anyone who **k** his neighbor in
Joshua
20:3 Anyone who **k** by striking down someone unintentionally
1 Samuel
17:25 riches whoever **k** that man. The
17:26 the person who **k** that Philistine
17:27 done for the man who **k** him," they said.
Job
9:23 calamity suddenly **k**, he mocks at the
20:16 poison; a viper's tongue **k** them.
24:14 at twilight, **k** the poor and
Isaiah
66:3 slaughters an ox **k** a person; the one
Lamentations
1:20 streets the sword **k**; in the house it
2 Corinthians
3:6 what is written **k**, but the Spirit

KINDNESS

Genesis
33:8 Jacob said, "To ask for my master's **k**."
33:10 please, do me the **k** of accepting my
1 Samuel
15:6 you showed **k** to the Israelites
23:21 have shown this **k** to me!" Saul said.
2 Samuel
9:3 could show God's **k** to?" "Yes," Ziba
1 Kings
2:7 Gilead, show them **k**. Let them eat
3:6 showed so much **k** to your servant
2 Chronicles
1:8 showed so much **k** to my father
32:25 to the **k** he had received,
Esther
2:9 him and won his **k**. He quickly began
4:8 king to seek his **k** and his help for
Job
10:12 Life and **k** you gave me, and you oversaw
37:13 his world, or for **k**, God makes it all
Psalms
90:17 Let the **k** of the Lord our God be over
Proverbs
20:28 **K** and faithfulness protect the king; he
21:21 righteousness and **k** will find life,
Jeremiah
9:24 who acts with **k**, justice, and
16:5 away my blessing, **k**, and mercy from
33:11 is good and his **k** lasts forever." I
Hosea
11:4 bands of human **k**, with cords of
Zechariah
7:9 decisions; show **k** and compassion to
Acts
15:14 how, in his **k**, God came to the
28:2 us extraordinary **k**. Because it was
Romans
2:4 that God's **k** is supposed to
3:12 no one who shows **k**. There is not
11:22 So look at God's **k** and harshness. It's

2 Corinthians
10:1 gentleness and ***k*** of Christ. I'm
Galatians
5:22 peace, patience, ***k***, goodness,
Colossians
3:12 on compassion, ***k***, humility,
Titus
3:4 God our savior's ***k*** and love appeared,
Philemon
1:14 that your act of ***k*** would occur

KINDS
Leviticus
19:19 field with two ***k*** of seed, and do
Matthew
4:24 who had various ***k*** of diseases,
Acts
10:12 sheet were all ***k*** of four-legged
1 Corinthians
12:10 different ***k*** of tongues to
12:28 skills, different ***k*** of tongues.
Hebrews
13:16 is pleased with these ***k*** of sacrifices.

KING → KING OF THE JEWS
Genesis
14:18 Melchizedek the ***k*** of Salem and the
26:8 the Philistine's ***K*** Abimelech looked
Exodus
1:8 Now a new ***k*** came to power in Egypt who
Numbers
21:26 Sihon the Amorite ***k*** who had fought
21:33 Og, Bashan's ***k***, came out at
22:10 to God, "Moab's ***K*** Balak, Zippor's
32:33 of Sihon the ***k*** of the Amorites,
Deuteronomy
17:14 Let's appoint a ***k*** over us, as all
Judges
9:8 out to anoint a ***k*** over themselves.
17:6 days there was no ***k*** in Israel; each
21:25 days there was no ***k*** in Israel; each
1 Samuel
8:5 So appoint us a ***k*** to judge us like
8:7 No, they've rejected me as ***k*** over them.
11:15 they made Saul ***k*** in the LORD's
12:12 the Ammonite ***k*** was coming
15:11 making Saul ***k*** because he has
16:1 rejected him as ***k*** over Israel.
2 Samuel
2:4 anointed David ***k*** over the house of
1 Kings
1:28 ***K*** David answered, "Bring me Bathsheba."
1:38 put Solomon on ***K*** David's mule.
1:39 the people said, "Long live ***K*** Solomon!"
Psalms
2:6 hereby appoint my ***k*** on Zion, my holy
5:2 of my cries, my ***k*** and my God,
18:50 victories to your ***k***, who shows
20:9 LORD, save the ***k***! Let him answer us
21:7 Because the ***k*** trusts the LORD, and
24:7 up high! So the glorious ***k*** can enter!
24:8 is this glorious ***k***? The LORD—strong
44:4 You who are my ***k***, the one who
45:1 my works to the ***k***. My tongue is the
47:2 he is the great ***k*** of the whole
48:2 far north, is the city of the great ***k***.
63:11 But the ***k*** should rejoice in God;
68:24 of my God, my ***k***, into the
72:1 judgments to the ***k***. Give your
74:12 God has been my ***k*** from ancient days-
84:3 LORD of heavenly forces, my ***k***, my God!
89:27 make him the high ***k*** of all earth's
95:3 God, the great ***k*** over all other
98:6 triumphantly before the LORD, the ***k***!
99:4 Strong ***k*** who loves justice, you are the
105:20 The ***k*** sent for Joseph and set him free;
105:21 The ***k*** made Joseph master of his house
135:11 the Amorite ***k***, Og, the king of
136:19 the Amorite ***k***—God's faithful l
145:1 my God, the true ***k***. I will bless
149:2 let Zion's children rejoice in their ***k***!
Proverbs
14:35 The ***k*** favors an insightful servant, but
19:12 A raging ***k*** roars like a lion; his favor
20:2 A ***k*** is as terrifying as a lion's growl.
20:8 A ***k*** who sits on his judgment throne
20:26 A wise ***k*** sifts out the wicked, and runs
20:28 protect the ***k***; he supports his
22:11 is gracious, and the ***k*** is their friend.
24:21 as well as the ***k***. Don't associate
25:3 so the mind of a ***k*** is unsearchable.
25:6 presence of the ***k***, or stand in the
29:4 A ***k*** gives stability to the land by
29:14 If a ***k*** judges the poor honestly, his
30:22 when he becomes ***k*** and fools when
30:27 don't have a ***k***, but they march
Ecclesiastes
1:12 Teacher. I was ***k*** over Israel in
4:13 old and foolish ***k***, who no longer
4:14 prison to become ***k***, even though
9:14 A mighty ***k*** came against it,
10:16 you, land, whose ***k*** is a boy and
10:20 Don't curse a ***k*** even in private; don't
Isaiah
6:5 Yet I've seen the ***k***, the LORD of
32:1 See here: A ***k*** rules to promote
43:15 holy one, Israel's creator, your ***k***!
44:6 LORD, Israel's ***k*** and redeemer, the
Jeremiah
10:10 the everlasting ***k***! When he's angry,
30:9 their God and the ***k*** whom I will raise
Ezekiel
37:24 David will be ***k*** over them. There
Daniel
1:19 When the ***k*** spoke with them, he found no one as good
2:2 The ***k*** summoned the dream interpreters,
3:1 ***K*** Nebuchadnezzar made a gold statue.
5:1 ***K*** Belshazzar threw a huge party for a
Hosea
3:5 and David their ***k***; they will come
10:15 At dawn, the ***k*** of Israel will be
Amos
1:1 days of Judah's ***K*** Uzziah and in the
2:1 to lime the bones of the ***k*** of Edom.
Haggai
1:1 second year of ***K*** Darius, in the
Malachi
1:14 am truly a great ***k***, says the LORD of

KING [cont.]

Matthew
1:6 of David the **k**. David was the
2:3 When **K** Herod heard this, he was
21:5 Zion, "Look, your **k** is coming to you,
22:2 heaven is like a **k** who prepared a
27:42 himself. He's the **k** of Israel, so let
Luke
19:14 We don't want this man to be our **k**.'
23:2 claiming that he is the Christ, a **k**."
John
1:49 God's Son. You are the **k** of Israel."
6:15 him to be their **k**, so he took
12:13 Lord! Blessings on the **k** of Israel!"
12:15 Zion. Look! Your **k** is coming,
19:14 to the Jewish leaders, "Here's your **k**."
Acts
17:7 by naming someone else as **k**: Jesus."
1 Timothy
1:17 Now to the **k** of the ages, to the
6:15 only master, the **K** of kings and Lord
Hebrews
7:1 who was **k** of Salem and
7:2 name means first "**k** of
Revelation
9:11 Their **k** is an angel from the abyss,
15:3 true are your ways, **k** of the nations.
17:10 come. When that **k** comes, he must
17:11 itself an eighth **k** that belongs to
17:14 Lord of lords and **K** of kings. Those
19:16 and on his thigh: **K** of kings and Lord

KING OF THE JEWS

Mt 2:2; 27:11, 29, 37; Mk 15:2; 15:9, 12, 18, 26; Lk 23:3; 23:37, 38; Jn 18:33; 18:39; 19:3, 19, 21

KINGDOM → ENTER GOD'S KINGDOM, GOD'S KINGDOM, KINGDOM OF HEAVEN

Exodus
19:6 You will be a **k** of priests for me and a
Numbers
24:7 than Agag, and his **k** will be lifted up.
32:33 Joseph's son—the **k** of Sihon the king
1 Samuel
15:28 has ripped the **k** of Israel from
18:8 What's next for him?—the **k** itself?"
24:20 and Israel's **k** will flourish in
28:17 has ripped the **k** out of your hands
2 Samuel
7:12 you, and I will establish his **k**.
1 Kings
11:31 about to tear the **k** from Solomon's
18:10 no nation or **k** where my master
Isaiah
9:7 and for his **k**, establishing and
Jeremiah
18:7 pull down, and destroy a nation or **k**;
Ezekiel
17:14 would be a lowly **k**, not asserting
29:14 origin. Egypt will be a lowly **k** there.
Daniel
2:39 place, another **k** will arise, one
2:44 up an everlasting **k** that will be
4:3 so powerful! His **k** is everlasting.
5:29 appointed as third in command in the **k**.
Hosea
1:4 will destroy the **k** of the house of
Amos
9:8 eyeing the sinful **k**, and I will
Obadiah
1:21 Esau, and the **k** will be the
Matthew
4:23 good news of the **k** and healed every
6:10 Bring in your **k** so that your will is
8:12 children of the **k** will be thrown
9:35 good news of the **k**, and healing
12:25 replied, "Every **k** involved in civil
12:26 himself. How then can his **k** endure?
13:19 word about the **k** and don't
13:38 followers of the **k**. But the weeds
13:41 gather out of his **k** all things that
13:43 in their Father's **k**. Those who have
16:28 see the Human One coming in his **k**."
20:1 The **k** of heaven is like a landowner
20:21 hand and one on your left, in your **k**."
24:14 gospel of the **k** will be
25:34 Inherit the **k** that was prepared
26:29 a new way with you in my Father's **k**."
Mark
3:24 A **k** involved in civil war will
6:23 to you, even as much as half of my **k**."
11:10 on the coming **k** of our ancestor
Luke
1:33 and there will be no end to his **k**."
11:2 holiness of your name. Bring in your **k**.
11:17 to them, "Every **k** involved in civil
11:18 how will his **k** endure? I ask
12:31 desire his **k** and these things
12:32 Father delights in giving you the **k**.
19:12 land to receive his **k** and then return.
19:15 receiving his **k**, he returned and
22:30 at my table in my **k**, and you will sit
23:42 remember me when you come into your **k**."
John
18:36 replied, "My **k** doesn't originate
Acts
1:6 going to restore the **k** to Israel now?"
20:25 whom I traveled and proclaimed the **k**.
1 Corinthians
15:24 hands over the **k** to God the
Ephesians
5:5 won't inherit the **k** of Christ and God.
Colossians
1:13 us into the **k** of the Son he
1 Thessalonians
2:12 calling you into his own **k** and glory.
2 Timothy
4:1 dead, and by his appearance and his **k**.
4:18 for his heavenly **k**. To him be the
Hebrews
12:28 are receiving a **k** that can't be
James
2:5 as heirs of the **k** he has promised
2 Peter
1:11 the everlasting **k** of our Lord and
Revelation
1:6 who made us a **k**, priests to his God
1:9 in the hardship, **k**, and endurance
5:10 You made them a **k** and priests to our
11:15 saying, "The **k** of the world has
12:10 and power and **k** of our God, and
16:10 covered its **k**. People bit their

KINGDOM OF HEAVEN

Mt 3:2; 4:17; 5:3, 10, 19, 20; 7:21; 8:11; 10:7; 11:11, 12; 13:11, 24, 31, 33, 44, 45, 47, 52; 16:19; 18:1, 3, 4, 23; 19:12, 14, 23; 20:1; 22:2; 23:13; 25:1, 14; 1Co 15:50

KINGDOMS

Deuteronomy
3:21 do to all the ***k*** where you're
28:25 All the earth's ***k*** will be horrified
Joshua
11:10 the head of all those ***k*** in the past.
1 Samuel
10:18 power of all the ***k*** that oppressed
2 Kings
19:15 all the earth's ***k***. You made both
19:19 all the earth's ***k*** will know that
1 Chronicles
29:30 and to all the ***k*** in other lands.
2 Chronicles
17:10 All the ***k*** surrounding Judah were afraid
20:6 You rule all the ***k*** of the nations.
20:29 the surrounding ***k*** when they heard
36:23 all the earth's ***k*** and has
Ezra
1:2 given me all the ***k*** of the earth. He
Nehemiah
9:22 You gave them ***k*** and peoples, and
Psalms
46:6 Nations roar; ***k*** crumble. God utters his
68:32 Sing to God, all ***k*** of the earth! Sing
79:6 know you, on the ***k*** that haven't
102:22 together—all ***k***—to serve the LORD
Isaiah
10:10 of idolatrous ***k*** with more images
13:4 An uproar of ***k***, of nations
13:19 a jewel among ***k***, the Chaldeans'
14:16 man who rattled the earth, who shook ***k***,
23:17 herself with all the ***k*** on the earth.
37:16 all the earth's ***k***. You made both
37:20 all the earth's ***k*** will know that
47:5 will no longer call you Queen of ***K***.
Jeremiah
24:9 evil to all the ***k*** of the earth.
28:8 disease against many lands and great ***k***.
49:28 Kedar and the ***k*** of Hazor, which
51:20 the nations. With you I will destroy ***k***.
51:27 her; summon ***k*** against her—
Ezekiel
29:15 Out of all the ***k***, it will be the
37:22 will no longer be divided into two ***k***.
Daniel
2:44 shatter other ***k***. It will put an
7:27 and power of all ***k*** under heaven will
8:22 means that four ***k*** will come from
Amos
6:2 better than these ***k***? Or is your
Nahum
3:5 your nakedness and ***k*** your dishonor.
Zephaniah
3:8 to collect ***k***, to pour out my
Haggai
2:22 thrones of the ***k***; I will destroy
Matthew
4:8 him all the ***k*** of the world and
24:7 Nations and ***k*** will fight against each
Mark
13:8 Nations and ***k*** will fight against each
Luke
4:5 single instant all the ***k*** of the world.
4:6 of all these ***k***. It's been
21:10 Nations and ***k*** will fight
Hebrews
11:33 they conquered ***k***, brought about

KINGS

Genesis
14:3 These latter ***k*** formed an alliance in
14:9 Arioch of Ellasar, four ***k*** against five.
17:6 from you, and ***k*** will come from
36:31 These are the ***k*** who ruled in the land
Joshua
12:1 struck down these ***k*** of the land and
1 Kings
10:23 all the earth's ***k*** in wealth and
Job
3:14 with ***k*** and earth's advisors, who
12:18 the belt of ***k***, binds a garment
36:7 he seats ***k*** on thrones
Psalms
2:10 So ***k***, wise up! Be warned, you rulers
33:16 ***K*** aren't saved by the strength of their
48:4 Look: the ***k*** assembled themselves,
68:29 Jerusalem, where ***k*** bring you gifts.
72:11 Let all the ***k*** bow down before him; let
76:12 terrifying to all the ***k*** of the earth.
89:27 him the high king of all earth's ***k***.
105:14 them. God punished ***k*** for their sake:
110:5 God has crushed ***k*** on his day of
135:10 down many nations and killed mighty ***k***:
136:17 struck down great ***k***—God's faithful
148:11 Do the same, you ***k*** of the earth and
Proverbs
8:15 By me ***k*** rule, and princes issue
16:12 ***K*** detest wicked deeds, for their
31:4 It isn't for ***k***, Lemuel, it isn't for
Isaiah
24:21 heaven, and the ***k*** of the earth on
52:15 many nations. ***K*** will be silenced
60:11 nations, and their ***k*** led in procession.
Daniel
2:47 of gods, Lord of ***k***, and a revealer
7:17 beasts are four ***k*** that will rise up
7:24 will rise ten ***k***, and after them
8:20 represents the ***k*** of Media and
11:2 have three more ***k***, but the fourth
Habakkuk
1:10 He makes fun of ***k***; rulers are
Matthew
10:18 and even ***k*** because of me so
17:25 whom do earthly ***k*** collect taxes,
Luke
10:24 many prophets and ***k*** wanted to see
21:12 be brought before ***k*** and governors
22:25 to them, "The ***k*** of the Gentiles
Acts
4:26 The ***k*** of the earth took their stand and
9:15 before Gentiles, ***k***, and Israelites.
1 Corinthians
4:8 You rule like ***k*** without us! I
1 Timothy
2:2 Pray for ***k*** and everyone who is in
6:15 the King of ***k*** and Lord of lords.

KINGS [cont.]

Hebrews
7:1 the defeat of the ***k***, and Melchizedek
Revelation
1:5 the ruler of the ***k*** of the earth. To
6:15 Then the ***k*** of the earth, the officials
17:2 The ***k*** of the earth have committed
17:9 woman is seated. They are also seven ***k***.
17:18 that rules over the ***k*** of the earth.
18:9 The ***k*** of the earth, who committed
19:18 eat the flesh of ***k***, the flesh of
21:24 light, and the ***k*** of the earth will

KINGSHIP

1 Samuel
10:16 uncle what Samuel had said about the ***k***.
14:47 Saul secured his ***k*** over Israel. He
2 Samuel
5:12 and that his ***k*** was held in great
2 Kings
15:31 rest of Pekah's ***k*** and all that he
1 Chronicles
14:2 and that his ***k*** was held in great
17:11 you, and I will establish his ***k***.
29:11 LORD, is the ***k***, and you are
Psalms
145:13 Your kingdom is a ***k*** that lasts forever;
Daniel
2:37 heaven has given ***k***, power, might,
4:17 dominates human ***k***. The Most High
5:18 High God gave ***k***, power, glory,
6:26 firm forever. His ***k*** is
7:14 Rule, glory, and ***k*** were given to him;
8:23 When their ***k*** nears its end and their

KISH

1 Samuel
9:1 of Benjamin named ***K***. He was the son
9:3 to Saul's father ***K*** were lost, Kish
14:51 ***K***, Saul's father, and Ner, Abner's
2 Samuel
21:14 of Saul's father ***K***. Once everything
1 Chronicles
8:30 Abdon, then Zur, ***K***, Baal, Ner, Nadab,
8:33 was the father of ***K***, Kish was the
9:36 followed by Zur, ***K***, Baal, Ner, Nadab,
9:39 was the father of ***K***, Kish of Saul,
23:21 Mushi. Mahli's family: Eleazar and ***K***.
24:29 from ***K*** and his family: Jerahmeel
2 Chronicles
29:12 of Merari: ***K***, Abdi's son, and
Esther
2:5 of Shimei and ***K***; he was a

KISS

Genesis
27:26 to him, "Come here and ***k*** me, my son."
31:28 even let me ***k*** my sons and my
Exodus
4:27 mountain and greeted him with a ***k***.
2 Samuel
15:5 his hand out, grab them, and ***k*** them.
20:9 hold of Amasa's beard as if to ***k*** him.
1 Kings
19:20 Elijah. "Let me ***k*** my father and my
Job
31:27 enticed, and threw a ***k*** with my hand,
Psalms
2:12 ***k*** his feet or else he will become
Proverbs
24:26 are like those who ***k*** on the lips.
Song of Songs
8:1 in the street and ***k*** you, and no one
Matthew
26:48 them a sign: "Arrest the man I ***k***."
Mark
14:44 Arrest the man I ***k***, and take him
Luke
7:45 greet me with a ***k***, but she hasn't
22:47 them. He approached Jesus to ***k*** him.
22:48 you betray the Human One with a ***k***?"
Romans
16:16 other with a holy ***k***. All the churches
1 Corinthians
16:20 should greet each other with a holy ***k***.
2 Corinthians
13:12 other with a holy ***k***. All of God's
1 Thessalonians
5:26 the brothers and sisters with a holy ***k***.
1 Peter
5:14 other with the ***k*** of love. Peace to

KISSED

Genesis
27:27 he came close and ***k*** him. When Isaac
29:11 Jacob ***k*** Rachel and wept aloud
31:55 in the morning, ***k*** his sons and
45:15 He ***k*** all of his brothers and wept,
50:1 body, wept over him, and ***k*** him.
Exodus
18:7 he bowed down and ***k*** him. They asked
Ruth
1:9 Then she ***k*** them, and they
1:14 wept again. Orpah ***k*** her mother-in-law,
1 Samuel
10:1 Saul's head and ***k*** him. "The LORD
20:41 The friends ***k*** each other, and
2 Samuel
14:33 the king. Then the king ***k*** Absalom.
19:39 behind. The king ***k*** Barzillai and
1 Kings
19:18 Baal and whose mouths haven't ***k*** him."
Psalms
85:10 met; righteousness and peace have ***k***.
Matthew
26:49 said, "Hello, Rabbi." Then he ***k*** him.
Mark
14:45 said to Jesus, "Rabbi!" Then he ***k*** him.
Luke
7:38 with her hair, ***k*** them, and poured
15:20 ran to him, hugged him, and ***k*** him.
Acts
20:37 as everyone embraced and ***k*** Paul.

KNEES

Genesis
48:12 from Israel's ***k***, and he bowed low
50:23 son, were also born on Joseph's ***k***.
Deuteronomy
9:25 But I fell on my ***k*** in the LORD's
28:35 in your ***k*** and legs, from
33:29 crawling on their ***k*** to you, but you
Judges
7:5 who bend down on their ***k*** to drink."

7:6 down on their ***k*** to drink water,
11:35 brought me to my ***k***! You are my
1 Kings
18:42 ground and put his face between his ***k***.
19:18 those whose ***k*** haven't bowed
Ezra
9:5 I fell upon my ***k***, spread out my
Job
3:12 Why did ***k*** receive me and breasts let me nurse?
4:4 the falling; you've steadied failing ***k***.
Isaiah
35:3 weak hands, and support the unsteady ***k***.
Ezekiel
21:6 sight; groan bitterly with trembling ***k***.
29:7 would break, bringing them to their ***k***—
Daniel
5:6 He felt weak, and his ***k*** were shaking.
10:10 me, lifting me up to my hands and ***k***.
Nahum
2:10 grows faint and ***k*** buckle; there is
Matthew
2:11 Falling to their ***k***, they honored
Mark
1:40 fell to his ***k***, and begged, "If
Luke
5:8 he fell at Jesus' ***k*** and said, "Leave
Acts
7:60 Falling to his ***k***, he shouted, "Lord,
Romans
11:4 who haven't bowed their ***k*** to Baal.
Hebrews
12:12 your drooping hands and weak ***k***!

KNEW

Genesis
4:1 The man Adam ***k*** his wife Eve intimately.
4:17 Cain ***k*** his wife intimately. She became
4:25 Adam ***k*** his wife intimately again, and
38:26 Judah never ***k*** her intimately
Deuteronomy
34:10 in Israel; Moses ***k*** the LORD face-to-f
Jeremiah
1:5 you in the womb I ***k*** you; before you
Hosea
13:5 I ***k*** you in the wilderness, in the land
Matthew
9:4 But Jesus ***k*** what they were thinking and
12:15 Jesus ***k*** what they intended to do, so he
25:26 lazy servant! You ***k*** that I harvest
26:10 But Jesus ***k*** what they were thinking. He
27:18 He ***k*** that the leaders of the people had
John
2:9 drawn the water ***k***. The headwaiter
6:6 for he already ***k*** what he was going
8:19 my Father. If you ***k*** me, you would
13:1 Passover, Jesus ***k*** that his time had
13:3 Jesus ***k*** the Father had given everything
13:11 He ***k*** who would betray him. That's why
18:4 Jesus ***k*** everything that was to happen
Acts
2:30 was a prophet, he ***k*** that God promised
16:3 for they all ***k*** Timothy's father
Romans
1:21 Although they ***k*** God, they didn't honor
8:29 this because God ***k*** them in advance,
11:2 people, who he ***k*** in advance. Or
Hebrews
10:34 joy, since you ***k*** that you had
1 Peter
1:2 of what he ***k*** beforehand. He

KNOW → KNOW GOD, KNOW THE LORD, KNOW THE TRUTH, KNOW THE WAY

Exodus
1:8 to power in Egypt who didn't ***k*** Joseph.
6:7 God. You will ***k*** that I, the LORD,
7:5 will come to ***k*** that I am the
14:4 Egyptians will ***k*** that I am the
18:11 Now I ***k*** that the LORD is greater than
33:12 assured me, 'I ***k*** you by name and
33:13 so that I may ***k*** you and so that
Numbers
16:28 By this you will ***k*** that the LORD
Deuteronomy
7:9 ***K*** now then that the LORD your God is
9:3 ***K*** right now that the LORD your God, who is crossing over
31:13 who don't yet ***k*** the Instruction,
Joshua
3:7 Then they will ***k*** that I will be
4:24 peoples might ***k*** that the LORD's
23:14 must take. You ***k*** with all your
Job
11:6 has two sides. ***K*** that God lets
19:25 But I ***k*** that my redeemer is alive and
42:2 I ***k*** you can do anything; no plan of
Psalms
9:10 Those who ***k*** your name trust you because
36:10 love to those who ***k*** you; extend your
46:10 enough! Now ***k*** that I am God! I
94:11 LORD does indeed ***k*** human thoughts,
95:10 twisted hearts. They don't ***k*** my ways.'
100:3 ***K*** that the LORD is God—he made us; we
139:2 You ***k*** when I sit down and when I stand
139:23 me to the test! ***K*** my anxious
140:12 I ***k*** that the LORD will take up the case
144:3 LORD, that you ***k*** them at all? What
Proverbs
27:1 for you don't ***k*** what a day will
29:7 The righteous ***k*** the rights of the poor,
Ecclesiastes
8:16 I set my mind to ***k*** wisdom and to
10:15 they don't even ***k*** the way to town!
11:6 because you don't ***k*** which will
11:9 eyes see, but ***k*** this: God will
Isaiah
1:3 Israel doesn't ***k***; my people don't
44:8 There is no other rock; I ***k*** of none.
49:26 all flesh will ***k*** that I, the LORD,
Jeremiah
4:22 They don't even ***k*** me! They are
22:16 what it means to ***k*** me? declares the
24:7 them a heart to ***k*** me, for I am the
48:30 I myself ***k*** about its arrogance,
Ezekiel
2:5 rebels, they will ***k*** that a prophet
6:10 and they will ***k*** that I am the LORD. Not

Daniel
2:3 and I'm anxious to ***k*** its meaning."
10:20 he said: "Do you ***k*** why I have come
Matthew
6:3 your left hand ***k*** what your right
7:11 you who are evil ***k*** how to give good
9:6 But so you will ***k*** that the Human One
22:29 because you don't ***k*** either the
24:42 alert! You don't ***k*** what day the Lord
26:74 swore, "I don't ***k*** the man!" At that
Mark
12:24 because you don't ***k*** either the
Luke
11:13 you who are evil ***k*** how to give good
12:48 one who didn't ***k*** the master's will
12:56 Hypocrites! You ***k*** how to interpret
13:25 reply, 'I don't ***k*** you or where you
18:20 You ***k*** the commandments. Don't commit adultery.
21:31 happening, you ***k*** that God's
23:34 for they don't ***k*** what they're
24:4 They didn't ***k*** what to make of this.
John
1:48 him, "How do you ***k*** me?" Jesus
2:9 wine. He didn't ***k*** where it came
3:2 him, "Rabbi, we ***k*** that you are a
3:8 but you don't ***k*** where it comes
3:10 of Israel and you don't ***k*** these things?
3:11 about what we ***k*** and testify about
4:22 what you don't ***k***; we worship what
4:25 woman said, "I ***k*** that the Messiah
4:32 food to eat that you don't ***k*** about."
4:42 for ourselves and ***k*** that this one is
5:13 been cured didn't ***k*** who it was,
5:32 about me, and I ***k*** his testimony
5:42 but I ***k*** you, that you don't have God's
6:42 and father we ***k***? How can he now
6:69 We believe and ***k*** that you are God's
7:27 We ***k*** where he is from, but when the
7:28 exclaimed, "You ***k*** me and where I am
7:29 I ***k*** him because I am from him and he
7:49 which doesn't ***k*** the Law. And they
8:14 is true, since I ***k*** where I came from
8:19 You don't ***k*** me and you don't
8:27 They didn't ***k*** he was speaking about his
8:28 up, then you will ***k*** that I Am. Then
8:37 I ***k*** that you are Abraham's children,
8:52 to Jesus, "Now we ***k*** that you have a
8:55 You don't ***k*** him, but I do. If I said I
9:12 is this man?" He replied, "I don't ***k***."
9:20 answered, "We ***k*** he is our son. We
9:21 But we don't ***k*** how he now sees, and we
9:24 glory to God. We ***k*** this man is a
9:25 I don't ***k*** whether he's a
9:29 We ***k*** that God spoke to Moses, but we
9:30 You don't ***k*** where he is from,
9:31 We ***k*** that God doesn't listen to
10:4 follow him, because they ***k*** his voice.
10:5 they don't ***k*** the stranger's
10:14 good shepherd. I ***k*** my own sheep and
10:15 knows me and I ***k*** the Father. I
10:27 to my voice. I ***k*** them and they
10:38 so that you can ***k*** and recognize
11:24 replied, "I ***k*** that he will rise
11:42 I ***k*** you always hear me. I say this for
11:49 year, told them, "You don't ***k*** anything!
12:35 darkness don't ***k*** where they are
12:50 I ***k*** that his commandment is eternal
13:12 to them, "Do you ***k*** what I've done
13:17 Since you ***k*** these things, you will be
13:18 all of you. I ***k*** those whom I've
13:35 how everyone will ***k*** that you are my
14:4 You ***k*** the way to the place I'm going.
14:5 Lord, we don't ***k*** where you are
14:7 me, you will also ***k*** the Father. From
14:9 Don't you ***k*** me, Philip, even
14:17 him. You ***k*** him, because he
14:20 that day you will ***k*** that I am in my
14:31 the world will ***k*** that I love the
15:15 servants don't ***k*** what their master
15:18 world hates you, ***k*** that it hated me
15:21 it doesn't ***k*** the one who sent
16:3 because they don't ***k*** the Father or me.
16:30 Now we ***k*** that you know everything and
17:3 eternal life: to ***k*** you, the only
17:7 Now they ***k*** that everything you have
17:23 the world will ***k*** that you sent me
17:25 the world didn't ***k*** you, but I've
18:21 what I told them. They ***k*** what I said."
19:4 to you to let you ***k*** that I find no
19:10 to me? Don't you ***k*** that I have
20:2 and we don't ***k*** where they've put
20:13 Lord, and I don't ***k*** where they've put
20:14 there, but she didn't ***k*** it was Jesus.
21:15 Yes, Lord, you ***k*** I love you."
21:16 Yes, Lord, you ***k*** I love you."
21:17 Lord, you ***k*** everything; you
21:24 them down. We ***k*** that his
Acts
1:7 isn't for you to ***k*** the times or
1:24 Lord, you ***k*** everyone's
Romans
1:13 I want you to ***k***, brothers and sisters,
6:6 This is what we ***k***: the person that we
6:16 Don't you ***k*** that if you offer
7:14 We ***k*** that the Law is spiritual, but I'm
7:18 I ***k*** that good doesn't live in me—that
8:26 We don't ***k*** what we should
8:28 We ***k*** that God works all things together
15:29 And I ***k*** that when I come to you I will
1 Corinthians
1:21 wouldn't come to ***k*** him through its
2:12 so that we can ***k*** the things given
3:16 Don't you ***k*** that you are God's temple
5:6 good! Don't you ***k*** that a tiny grain
6:2 Or don't you ***k*** that God's people will
6:3 Don't you ***k*** that we will judge angels?
7:16 How do you ***k*** as a wife if you will save
8:1 a false god: we ***k*** that we all have
8:4 to false gods, we ***k*** that a false god
9:13 Don't you ***k*** that those who serve in the
12:2 You ***k*** that when you were Gentiles you
13:2 of prophecy and I ***k*** all the mysteries
13:12 Now I ***k*** partially, but
2 Corinthians
4:14 this because we ***k*** that the one who
5:1 We ***k*** that if the tent that we live in
5:6 because we ***k*** that while we are
8:9 You ***k*** the grace of our Lord Jesus
12:2 I ***k*** a man in Christ who was caught up
Galatians
1:11 I want you to ***k*** that the gospel I
2:16 However, we ***k*** that a person isn't made

3:2 I just want to ***k*** this from you: Did you
4:13 You ***k*** that I first preached the gospel

Ephesians
3:5 didn't ***k*** this hidden plan
3:19 I ask that you'll ***k*** the love of Christ
5:5 Because you ***k*** for sure that persons who
6:8 You ***k*** that the Lord will reward every
6:9 them, because you ***k*** that both you and
6:22 —so that you will ***k*** about us. He can

Philippians
1:12 I want you to ***k*** that the things
1:16 because they ***k*** that I'm put here
1:19 glad because I ***k*** that this will
1:23 But I don't ***k*** what I prefer. I'm torn
2:22 You ***k*** his character, how he labors with
4:12 I ***k*** the experience of being in need and
4:15 You Philippians ***k*** from the time of my

Colossians
2:1 I want you to ***k*** how much I struggle for
3:24 You ***k*** that you will receive an
4:6 so that you may ***k*** how to respond to
4:8 so that you'll ***k*** all about us and
4:9 They will let you ***k*** about everything

1 Thessalonians
1:4 by God, and we ***k*** that he has
1:5 We ***k*** this because our good news didn't
2:1 As you yourselves ***k***, brothers and
2:2 and were publicly insulted, as you ***k***.
2:5 As you ***k***, we never used flattery, and
2:11 Likewise, you ***k*** how we treated each of
3:3 problems. You ***k*** very well that we
3:4 exactly like what happened, as you ***k***.
4:2 You ***k*** the instructions we gave you
4:13 we want you to ***k*** about people who
5:2 You ***k*** very well that the day of the

2 Thessalonians
2:6 Now you ***k*** what holds him back so that
3:7 You yourselves ***k*** how you need to

1 Timothy
1:8 Now we ***k*** that the Law is good if used
3:5 if they don't ***k*** how to manage
3:15 delayed, you'll ***k*** how you should

2 Timothy
1:12 not ashamed. I ***k*** the one in whom
1:15 You ***k*** that everyone in Asia has turned
1:18 that day (and you ***k*** very well how
2:23 since you ***k*** that they produce
3:14 found convincing. You ***k*** who taught you.

Titus
3:11 because you ***k*** that someone like this is

Hebrews
3:10 off course, and they don't ***k*** my ways."
8:11 sister, saying, "***K*** the Lord,"
10:30 We ***k*** the one who said, Judgment is
12:17 You ***k*** that afterward, when he wanted to inherit the blessing
13:23 You should ***k*** that our brother Timothy

James
1:3 After all, you ***k*** that the testing of
1:19 ***K*** this, my dear brothers and sisters:
3:1 because we ***k*** that we teachers
4:4 people! Don't you ***k*** that friendship
4:14 You don't really ***k*** about tomorrow. What

2 Peter
1:12 you already ***k*** them and stand
1:20 you must ***k*** that no prophecy
2:21 having come to ***k*** it, to turn back
3:3 Most important, ***k*** this: in the last

1 John
2:3 This is how we ***k*** that we know him: if
3:2 we will be. We ***k*** that when he
4:2 This is how you ***k*** if a spirit comes
4:13 This is how we ***k*** we remain in him and
5:2 This is how we ***k*** that we love the
5:20 We ***k*** that God's Son has come and has

3 John
1:12 of him, and you ***k*** that what we say

Jude
1:5 you already ***k*** very well. The
1:10 by what they ***k*** instinctively, as

Revelation
2:2 I ***k*** your works, your labor, and your
2:13 I ***k*** that you are living right where
3:1 seven stars: I ***k*** your works. You
3:3 and you won't ***k*** what time I will
7:14 to him, "Sir, you ***k***." Then he said to

KNOWING

Genesis
3:5 you will be like God, ***k*** good and evil."
19:35 him, without him ***k*** when she lay down

Leviticus
5:1 are a witness, ***k*** something, or

Job
4:20 they perish forever without anyone ***k***.
21:14 us; we take no pleasure in ***k*** your ways;

Ecclesiastes
6:8 the poor gain by ***k*** how to conduct
8:17 who are set on ***k*** are unable to

Matthew
10:29 without your Father ***k*** about it already.
22:18 ***K*** their evil motives, Jesus replied,

Mark
5:33 came forward. ***K*** what had happened

John
5:6 him lying there, ***k*** that he had
19:28 After this, ***k*** that everything was

Acts
23:6 ***K*** that some of them were Sadducees and

Philippians
3:8 superior value of ***k*** Christ Jesus my
3:10 I have comes from ***k*** Christ, the power

Colossians
4:1 to your slaves, ***k*** that you

Philemon
1:21 obedience and ***k*** that you will do

Hebrews
11:8 went out without ***k*** where he was
13:2 have been hosts to angels without ***k*** it.

1 Peter
1:18 Live in this way, ***k*** that you were not
3:7 that honor her, ***k*** that she is the

Jude
1:8 Yet, even ***k*** this, these dreamers in the

KNOWLEDGE → KNOWLEDGE OF GOD

Genesis
2:9 and the tree of the ***k*** of good and evil.
2:17 the tree of the ***k*** of good and evil,

KNOWLEDGE [cont.]

Numbers
15:24 without the ***k*** of the community,
24:16 the Most High's ***k***, who perceives
Deuteronomy
32:17 which they had no ***k***—new gods only
2 Chronicles
1:10 me wisdom and ***k*** so I can lead
Nehemiah
10:28 and all who have ***k*** and understanding.
Job
15:2 with windy ***k*** and fill their
33:3 heart; my lips speak ***k*** clearly.
34:35 speaks without ***k***; his words aren't
36:3 from my broad ***k***, attribute
37:16 amazing deeds of one with perfect ***k***,
42:3 counsel without ***k***?" I have indeed
Psalms
111:10 begins; sure ***k*** is for all who
119:66 Teach me ***k*** and good judgment because
139:6 That kind of ***k*** is too much for me; it's
147:5 so strong! God's ***k*** can't be grasped!
147:20 nations have no ***k*** of God's rules.
Proverbs
1:22 their mocking dear, and fools hate ***k***?
1:29 they hated ***k*** and didn't choose
2:5 of the LORD, and discover the ***k*** of God.
2:6 his mouth come ***k*** and understanding.
2:10 your mind, and ***k*** will fill you
3:20 With his ***k***, the watery depths burst
5:2 discrete, and your lips might guard ***k***.
8:10 than silver, ***k*** rather than
8:12 I have found ***k*** and discretion.
9:10 of the LORD; the ***k*** of the holy one
10:14 The wise store up ***k***, but the mouth of
11:9 but the righteous are saved by their ***k***.
12:1 discipline love ***k***, and those who
12:23 conceal their ***k***, but the heart of
14:6 gets none, but ***k*** comes quickly to
14:18 but the prudent are crowned with ***k***.
15:2 the wise enhances ***k***, but the mouth of
15:7 the wise spread ***k***, but the hearts
15:14 heart seeks ***k***; but fools feed
18:15 mind gains ***k***; the ear of the
19:25 understanding, and they will gain ***k***.
19:27 you will wander away from words of ***k***.
21:11 insight comes to the wise, ***k*** increases.
22:12 eyes protect ***k***, but he
22:17 of the wise; focus your mind on my ***k***.
22:20 thirty sayings full of advice and ***k***?
24:4 By ***k*** rooms are filled with all precious
30:3 nor do I have ***k*** of the holy one.
Ecclesiastes
1:16 mind has absorbed great wisdom and ***k***.
1:18 aggravation; the more ***k***, the more pain.
2:26 God gives wisdom, ***k***, and joy to those
7:12 the advantage of ***k*** is that wisdom
9:10 no work, thought, ***k***, or wisdom in the
12:9 taught the people ***k***. He listened and
Isaiah
11:2 a spirit of ***k*** and fear of the
11:9 filled with the ***k*** of the LORD, just
28:9 will God teach ***k***? To whom will he
33:6 wisdom, and ***k***—fear of the LORD
40:14 of justice and ***k*** and explained to
44:25 the wise and turns their ***k*** into folly.
47:10 Your wisdom and ***k*** spun you around.
53:11 Through his ***k***, the righteous
58:2 day, desiring ***k*** of my ways like a
Jeremiah
3:15 will lead you with ***k*** and understanding.
9:23 boast of their ***k***, nor warriors
10:12 his wisdom, crafted the skies by his ***k***.
11:19 so that even any ***k*** of him will be
51:15 wisdom, and crafted the skies by his ***k***.
Daniel
1:4 possessing ***k***, conversant with
1:17 And God gave ***k***, mastery of all
2:21 to the wise and ***k*** to those with
5:12 spirit, ***k***, and insight into
12:4 will stray far, but ***k*** will increase."
Hosea
4:6 from lack of ***k***. Since you have
Habakkuk
2:14 be full of the ***k*** of the LORD's
Malachi
2:7 should guard ***k***; everyone should
Luke
11:52 away the key of ***k***. You didn't enter
Acts
5:2 With his wife's ***k***, he withheld some of
Romans
2:20 full content of ***k*** and truth in the
3:20 says, because the ***k*** of sin comes
10:2 God. However, it isn't informed by ***k***.
11:33 wisdom, and ***k*** are so deep! They
15:14 filled with all ***k***, and are able to
1 Corinthians
1:5 your communication and every kind of ***k***,
8:1 that we all have ***k***. Knowledge makes
8:10 person who has ***k***) eating in an
8:11 Christ died is destroyed by your ***k***.
12:8 person, a word of ***k*** to another
13:8 will stop. As for ***k***, it will be
14:6 revelation, some ***k***, a prophecy, or a
2 Corinthians
2:14 fragrance of the ***k*** of him everywhere
4:6 the light of the ***k*** of God's glory in
6:6 displayed purity, ***k***, patience, and
8:7 as faith, speech, ***k***, total
10:5 up to oppose the ***k*** of God. They
11:6 not uneducated in ***k***. We have shown
Ephesians
3:19 that is beyond ***k*** so that you will
4:13 of faith and ***k*** of God's Son.
Philippians
1:9 more rich with ***k*** and all kinds of
Colossians
1:9 filled with the ***k*** of God's will,
1:10 good work and growing in the ***k*** of God;
2:2 might have the ***k*** of the secret
2:3 of wisdom and ***k*** are hidden in him.
3:10 is renewed in ***k*** by conforming to
1 Timothy
2:4 saved and to come to a ***k*** of the truth.
6:20 contradictory claims of so-called "***k***."
6:21 this false ***k***, they missed the
2 Timothy
2:25 mind and give them a ***k*** of the truth.
Titus
1:1 people and a ***k*** of the truth that
1:2 faith and this ***k*** are based on the
Hebrews
10:26 we receive the ***k*** of the truth,
1 Peter
5:9 Do so in the ***k*** that your fellow

2 Peter
1:2 peace through the ***k*** of God and Jesus
1:3 through the ***k*** of the one who
1:5 your faith; and to moral excellence, ***k***;
1:6 and to ***k***, self-control; and to
1:8 unfruitful in the ***k*** of our Lord Jesus
2:20 world through the ***k*** of our Lord and
3:18 in the grace and ***k*** of our Lord and

KNOWS

Genesis
3:5 God ***k*** that on the day you eat from it,
33:13 him, "My master ***k*** that the children
Deuteronomy
34:6 Even now, no one ***k*** where Moses'
Job
23:10 Surely he ***k*** my way; when he tests me, I
Psalms
33:15 the one who ***k*** everything they
37:13 them because he ***k*** that their day is
44:21 After all, God ***k*** every secret of
49:10 Everyone ***k*** that the wise die too, just
94:11 human thoughts, ***k*** that they are
103:14 Because God ***k*** how we're made, God
104:19 and the sun too, which ***k*** when to set.
Proverbs
10:32 of the wicked ***k*** only what is
14:10 The heart ***k*** its own distress; another
24:12 your life—he ***k***. He makes people
Ecclesiastes
2:19 And who ***k*** whether that one will be wise
3:21 Who ***k*** if a human being's life-breath
6:12 Because who ***k*** what's good for human
8:1 is wise? And who ***k*** the meaning of
8:5 the wise heart ***k*** the right time
8:7 because no one ***k*** what will happen, and
10:14 too much! No one ***k*** what will happen;
Isaiah
1:3 An ox ***k*** its owner, and a donkey its
8:4 Before the boy ***k*** how to say 'my father'
29:15 dark, who say, "Who sees us? Who ***k*** us?"
31:2 But God also ***k*** how to bring disaster;
59:8 no one who walks in them ***k*** peace.
Jeremiah
8:7 stork in the sky ***k*** the seasons, and
40:15 no one needs to ***k*** about this
Ezekiel
28:19 the peoples who ***k*** you will be
Daniel
2:22 deeply hidden; he ***k*** what hides in
Hosea
14:9 carefully ***k*** them. Truly, the
Joel
2:14 Who ***k*** whether he will have a change of
Jonah
3:9 He thought, Who ***k***? God may see this
Nahum
3:17 flight; no one ***k*** where they have
Zephaniah
3:5 but the unrighteous one ***k*** no shame.
Matthew
6:8 your Father ***k*** what you need
6:32 heavenly Father ***k*** that you need
9:30 them, "Make sure nobody ***k*** about this."
11:27 to me. No one ***k*** the Son except
24:36 But nobody ***k*** when that day or hour
Mark
13:32 But nobody ***k*** when that day or hour
Luke
10:22 to me. No one ***k*** who the Son is
12:30 Your Father ***k*** that you need
16:15 people, but God ***k*** your hearts. What
John
10:15 as the Father ***k*** me and I know the
19:35 is true. He ***k*** that he speaks
Acts
15:8 God, who ***k*** people's deepest thoughts
26:26 King Agrippa ***k*** about these things, and
Romans
8:27 searches hearts ***k*** how the Spirit
1 Corinthians
2:11 Who ***k*** a person's depths except their
3:20 also, The Lord ***k*** that the thoughts
7:36 woman whom he ***k***, and if he has
8:7 But not everybody ***k*** this. Some are
2 Corinthians
11:11 I don't love you? God ***k*** that I do!
11:31 blessed forever, ***k*** that I'm not
12:2 in the body or out of the body. God ***k***.
12:4 the body or apart from the body. God ***k***.
Philippians
1:13 and everyone else ***k*** that I'm in
2 Timothy
2:19 sign, The Lord ***k*** the people who
James
4:17 sin when someone ***k*** the right thing
2 Peter
2:9 that the Lord ***k*** how to rescue the
1 John
3:20 than our hearts and ***k*** all things.
4:6 The person who ***k*** God listens to
4:7 who loves is born from God and ***k*** God.
Revelation
2:17 it, which no one ***k*** except the one
12:12 rage, for he ***k*** that he only has
19:12 on him that no one ***k*** but he himself.

KOHATH

Genesis
46:11 sons were Gershon, ***K***, and Merari.
Exodus
6:16 Gershon, ***K***, and Merari. Levi
6:18 Hebron, and Uzziel. ***K*** lived 133 years.
Numbers
3:17 sons by name: Gershon, ***K***, and Merari.
2 Chronicles
20:19 from the lines of ***K*** and Korah stood

KOHATHITES

Numbers
4:15 After that the ***K*** will enter to

KORAH

Genesis
36:5 Jeush, Jalam, and ***K***. These are Esau's
Exodus
6:21 The Izharites: ***K***, Nepheg, and Zichri
Numbers
16:1 ***K***—Izhar's son, Kohath's grandson, and
26:9 the community of ***K***, when they fought
26:10 them, along with ***K***, when the
Jude
1:11 are destroyed in the uprising of ***K***.

Ll

LABAN
Genesis
24:29 a brother named ***L***, and Laban ran to
27:43 up and escape to my brother ***L*** in Haran.
31:24 God appeared to ***L*** the Aramean in a
31:55 ***L*** got up early in the morning, kissed
Deuteronomy
1:1 Paran and Tophel, ***L***, Hazeroth, and

LABOR
Exodus
1:14 with hard ***l***, making mortar
2:11 saw their forced ***l***. He saw an
6:6 Egyptian forced ***l***. I'll rescue you
6:7 has freed you from Egyptian forced ***l***.
6:9 complete exhaustion and their hard ***l***.
Deuteronomy
26:6 oppressing us and forcing hard ***l*** on us.
Joshua
16:10 used for forced ***l***, still live
17:13 to hard ***l*** but didn't remove
1 Samuel
4:19 birth because her ***l*** pains overwhelmed
1 Kings
9:15 the story of the ***l*** gang that King
Job
20:18 reward for their ***l***; they won't enjoy
39:16 worrying that her ***l*** might be in vain;
Psalms
127:2 the bread of hard ***l*** because God gives
Proverbs
12:24 a lazy one will be sentenced to hard ***l***.
Isaiah
13:8 woman writhing in ***l***, they will be
54:1 who were never in ***l***, for the children
65:23 They won't ***l*** in vain, nor bear children
66:7 Before she was in ***l***, she gave birth.
Jeremiah
6:24 us, pain like that of a woman in ***l***.
Romans
8:22 and suffering ***l*** pains up until
1 Corinthians
3:8 their own reward for their own ***l***.
15:58 know that your ***l*** isn't going to be
1 Thessalonians
5:3 attack them, like ***l*** pains start with
Revelation
2:2 your works, your ***l***, and your
12:2 she was in ***l***, in pain from

LACHISH
Joshua
10:32 The LORD gave ***L*** into the power of
2 Chronicles
25:27 Amaziah fled to ***L***, they sent men

LACK
Deuteronomy
8:9 won't ***l*** a thing there—
Psalms
23:1 The LORD is my shepherd. I ***l*** nothing.
34:9 those who honor him don't ***l*** a thing.
34:10 who seek the LORD ***l*** no good thing.
Proverbs
9:4 here," she says to those who ***l*** sense.
9:16 here," she says to those who ***l*** sense.
10:21 people, but fools who ***l*** sense will die.
12:9 than to be conceited and ***l*** food.
15:21 joy to those who ***l*** sense, but those
28:27 to the poor will ***l*** nothing, but
Ecclesiastes
6:2 so that they ***l*** nothing they
10:3 Fools ***l*** all sense even when they walk
Song of Songs
7:2 may it never ***l*** spiced wine! Your
Isaiah
34:16 none will ***l*** its mate. God's
50:2 fish stink from ***l*** of water; they
59:1 The LORD does not ***l*** the power to
Hosea
4:6 destroyed from ***l*** of knowledge.
Mark
9:24 I have faith; help my ***l*** of faith!"
Luke
22:35 you didn't ***l*** anything, did
1 Corinthians
7:5 you because of your ***l*** of self-control.
Hebrews
3:19 enter because of their ***l*** of faith.

LAKE
Matthew
8:18 to go over to the other side of the ***l***.
8:27 Even the winds and the ***l*** obey him!"
Mark
2:13 out beside the ***l*** again. The whole
3:7 and went to the ***l***. A large crowd
4:1 teach beside the ***l*** again. Such a
4:39 he said to the ***l***, "Silence! Be
5:13 down the cliff into the ***l*** and drowned.
6:48 walking on the ***l***. He intended to
Revelation
19:20 into the fiery ***l*** that burns with
20:10 thrown into the ***l*** of fire and
21:8 will be in the ***l*** that burns with

LAMB
Genesis
22:8 said, "The ***l*** for the entirely
30:33 and every male ***l*** with me that
Exodus
12:21 families, and slaughter the Passover ***l***.

2 Samuel
12:6 restore the ewe ***l*** seven times over
Isaiah
11:6 live with the ***l***, and the leopard
53:7 his mouth. Like a ***l*** being brought to
65:25 Wolf and ***l*** will graze together, and the
Jeremiah
11:19 was like a young ***l*** led to the
Ezekiel
46:11 to give for each ***l***, with one hin of
46:13 flawless year-old ***l***. You will make
46:15 So the ***l***, the grain offering, and the
Hosea
4:16 as the LORD tends a ***l*** in a pasture.
Mark
14:12 when the Passover ***l*** was sacrificed,
John
1:29 said, "Look! The ***L*** of God who takes
1:36 along he said, "Look! The ***L*** of God!"
Acts
8:32 and like a ***l*** before its
1 Corinthians
5:7 our Passover ***l*** has been
1 Peter
1:19 like that of a flawless, spotless ***l***.
Revelation
5:6 elders, I saw a ***L***, standing as if
5:8 down before the ***L***. Each held a harp
5:12 the slaughtered ***L*** to receive power,
5:13 throne and to the ***L*** forever and
6:1 looked on as the ***L*** opened one of the
6:3 When the ***L*** opened the second seal, I
7:9 and before the ***L***. They wore white
7:10 who sits on the throne, and to the ***L***."
7:17 because the ***L*** who is in the midst of
8:1 Then, when the ***L*** opened the seventh seal
12:11 the blood of the ***L*** and the word of
13:8 scroll of life of the ***l*** who was slain.
13:11 two horns like a ***l***, but it was
14:1 and there was the ***L***, standing on
14:10 presence of the holy angels and the ***L***.
15:3 the song of the ***L***, saying, "Great
17:14 make war on the ***L***, but the Lamb
19:7 day of the ***L*** has come, and his
19:9 banquet of the ***L***." He said to me,
21:22 is the Lord God Almighty and the ***L***.
21:23 is its light, and its lamp is the ***L***.
22:1 from the throne of God and the ***L***
22:3 of God and the ***L*** will be in it,

LAMBS
Luke
10:3 I'm sending you out as ***l*** among wolves.
John
21:15 you." Jesus said to him, "Feed my ***l***."

LAME
2 Samuel
5:6 the blind and the ***l*** will beat you
5:8 David hates the ***l*** and the blind."
19:26 your servant is ***l***, I asked my
Job
29:15 I was eyes to the blind, feet to the ***l***
Isaiah
33:23 divided; even the ***l*** will seize spoil.
35:6 Then the ***l*** will leap like the deer, and
Micah
4:6 I will gather the ***l***; I will assemble
4:7 I will make the ***l*** into survivors, those
Zephaniah
3:19 will deliver the ***l***; I will gather
Malachi
1:8 If you bring a ***l*** or sick one,
1:13 what is stolen, ***l***, or sick to be
Matthew
18:8 life crippled or ***l*** than to be thrown
21:14 were blind and ***l*** came to Jesus in
Mark
9:45 you to enter life ***l*** than to be thrown
Luke
14:13 the poor, crippled, ***l***, and blind.
14:21 the poor, crippled, blind, and ***l***.'
John
5:3 were sick, blind, ***l***, and paralyzed
Hebrews
12:13 if any part is ***l***, it will be

LAMECH
Genesis
4:18 Methushael, and Methushael fathered ***L***.
5:31 In all, ***L*** lived 777 years, and he died
1 Chronicles
1:3 Enoch, Methuselah, ***L***
Luke
3:36 son of Shem son of Noah son of ***L***

LAMENT
Job
9:27 I'll forget my ***l***, put on a
Isaiah
3:26 Her gates will ***l*** and mourn; desolate,
19:8 who fish will ***l***; all who cast
43:14 the Chaldeans' singing into a ***l***.
Jeremiah
9:10 mountains, and ***l*** for the grazing
16:5 don't grieve or ***l*** for them, for I
22:10 Don't weep or ***l*** for the dead king. Weep
Ezekiel
8:14 sitting and performing the Tammuz ***l***.
19:1 You, raise a ***l*** for Israel's princes
26:17 They will sing a ***l*** for you, and they
27:2 You, human one, sing a ***l*** for Tyre
27:32 they raise a ***l*** for you; they
28:12 Human one, sing a ***l*** for the king of
32:2 Human one, sing a ***l*** for Pharaoh,
32:16 This is a ***l***, and it will be sung as a
Joel
1:8 ***L*** like a woman dressed in funeral
1:13 you priests; ***l***, ministers of the
Amos
5:16 and those skilled in mourning to ***l***.
Nahum
3:7 Who will ***l*** for her?" Where
John
16:20 you will cry and ***l***, and the world

LAMP
Exodus
27:20 light so that the ***l*** may be set up to
27:21 will tend the ***l*** from evening to
Leviticus
24:2 to you for the ***l***, to keep a light

24:3 will tend the *l*, which will be
1 Samuel
3:3 God's *l* hadn't gone out yet, and Samuel
2 Samuel
21:17 You must not snuff out Israel's *l*!"
22:29 You are my *l*, LORD; the LORD illumines
1 Kings
11:36 always have a *l* before me in
15:4 God gave Abijam a *l* in Jerusalem by
2 Kings
4:10 a chair, and a *l* for him there.
8:19 to preserve a *l* for David and his
2 Chronicles
21:7 to preserve a *l* for David and his
Job
18:6 dark, and their *l* above doesn't
21:17 often does the *l* of the wicked
29:3 when his *l* shone on my head, I walked
Psalms
18:28 one who lights my *l*—the LORD my God
119:105 Your word is a *l* before my feet and a
132:17 I will prepare a *l* for my anointed
Proverbs
6:23 commandment is a *l* and instruction a
13:9 rejoices, but the *l* of the wicked
20:20 or mother—their *l* will be snuffed
20:27 a person is the *l* of the LORD,
21:4 heart, and the *l* of the wicked are
24:20 for the evil; the *l* of the wicked
31:18 she doesn't put out her *l* at night.
Daniel
5:5 the light of the *l*. The king saw the
Matthew
5:15 do people light a *l* and put it under
6:22 The eye is the *l* of the body.
Mark
4:21 anyone bring in a *l* in order to put
Luke
8:16 No one lights a *l* and then covers it
11:33 don't light a *l* and then put it
11:34 Your eye is the *l* of your body. When
11:36 light as when a *l* shines brightly
15:8 won't light a *l* and sweep the
John
5:35 and shining *l*, and, at least
2 Peter
1:19 as you would to a *l* shining in a dark
Revelation
18:23 The light of a *l* will never shine among
21:23 is its light, and its *l* is the Lamb.
22:5 the light of a *l* or the light of

LAMPS

Exodus
25:37 Make its seven *l* and set up its lamps
40:4 in the lampstand and set up its *l*.
Numbers
8:2 up, the seven *l* will give light
Zephaniah
1:12 Jerusalem with *l*; I will punish
Zechariah
4:2 bowl has seven *l* on top and seven
Matthew
25:1 who took their *l* and went out to
Luke
12:35 for service and keep your *l* lit.
Acts
20:8 There were many *l* in the upstairs room
Revelation
1:12 I saw seven oil *l* burning on top of

LAMPSTAND

Exodus
25:31 Make a *l* of pure hammered gold. The
40:24 He put the *l* in the meeting tent,
Numbers
3:31 the table, the *l*, the altars, the
4:9 and cover the *l* used for light,
8:2 will give light in front of the *l*.
Zechariah
4:2 I said, "I see a *l* made entirely of
4:3 trees beside the *l*, one to the right
4:11 on the right and left sides of the *l*?"
Matthew
5:15 it on top of a *l*, and it shines on
Mark
4:21 a bed? Shouldn't it be placed on a *l*?
Luke
8:16 it on top of a *l* so that those who
11:33 the lamp on a *l* so that those who
Hebrews
9:2 It contained the *l*, the table, and
Revelation
2:5 I will move your *l* from its place if

LAND

Genesis
1:9 so that the dry *l* can appear." And
1:10 God named the dry *l* Earth, and he named
7:22 Everything on dry *l* with life's breath
8:21 curse the fertile *l* anymore because
12:1 Leave your *l*, your family, and
12:7 I give this *l* to your
12:10 famine struck the *l*, Abram went down
13:15 because all the *l* that you see I give
15:13 immigrants in a *l* that isn't their
15:18 I give this *l*, from Egypt's
24:7 from my family's *l*, who spoke with
26:1 famine gripped the *l*
28:15 you back to this *l*. I will not leave
31:13 go back to the *l* of your
40:15 stolen from the *l* of the Hebrews,
41:30 abundance in the *l* of Egypt will be
42:7 said, "From the *l* of Canaan to buy
50:24 you out of this *l* to the land he
Exodus
1:7 grew dramatically, filling the whole *l*.
3:8 them out of that *l* and bring them to
6:8 you into the *l* that I promised
8:22 set apart the *l* of Goshen, where
20:12 on the fertile *l* that the LORD
22:21 were once immigrants in the *l* of Egypt.
32:11 out of the *l* of Egypt with
Numbers
13:2 to explore the *l* of Canaan, which
14:9 afraid of the people of the *l*. They are our prey
14:30 will enter the *l* in which I promised to
26:55 The *l*, however, will be apportioned by
35:33 not pollute the *l* in which you
36:9 An inheritance of *l* may not be

Deuteronomy
1:8 I have laid the ***l*** before you. Go
8:7 to a wonderful ***l***, a land with
10:11 possession of the ***l*** that I promised
11:10 The ***l*** you are about to enter and
28:21 off the fertile ***l*** you are entering
29:24 do this to this ***l***? What led to this
34:1 him the whole ***l***: the Gilead
Joshua
1:6 possession of the ***l***, which I pledged
2:1 Look over the ***l***, especially
5:12 produced in the ***l***. There was no
11:23 took the whole ***l***, exactly as the
13:2 This is the ***l*** that remains: All the
14:4 portion of the ***l***, except cities to
14:9 on that day, 'The ***l*** on which you have
Judges
1:27 were determined to live in that ***l***.
2:6 in order to take possession of the ***l***.
18:2 to spy on the ***l*** and explore it.
Ruth
1:1 a famine in the ***l***. A man with his
2 Samuel
21:14 God responded to prayers for the ***l***.
1 Kings
8:34 them to the ***l*** you gave their
17:7 up because there was no rain in the ***l***.
22:46 purged the ***l*** of the
2 Chronicles
7:14 forgive their sin, and heal their ***l***.
7:20 you from my ***l*** that I gave you,
32:31 occurred in the ***l***, when God had
36:21 carried out. The ***l*** finally enjoyed
Ezra
6:21 nations of the ***l*** to worship the
9:11 saying: 'The ***l*** which you are
Nehemiah
4:4 make them like plunder in a captive ***l***.
9:24 and possessed the ***l***. Before them, you
9:36 slaves in the ***l*** that you gave to
Esther
8:17 people in the ***l*** became Jews
Psalms
25:13 their descendants will possess the ***l***.
37:11 will inherit the ***l***; they will enjoy
37:29 will possess the ***l***; they will live
44:3 possession of the ***l***—their own arms
68:6 the rebellious dwell in a parched ***l***.
136:21 Handing their ***l*** over as an
140:11 be safe in the ***l***. Let calamity
142:5 are all I have in the ***l*** of the living."
Proverbs
2:21 will dwell in the ***l***; the innocent
12:11 who work their ***l*** will have plenty
13:23 A poor person's ***l*** might produce much
31:23 when he sits with the elders of the ***l***.
Ecclesiastes
10:16 Too bad for you, ***l***, whose king is a
10:17 Happy is the ***l*** whose king is dignified
11:2 know what disaster may come upon the ***l***.
Song of Songs
2:12 appeared in the ***l***; the season of
Isaiah
2:8 Their ***l*** is filled with idols; they
9:2 in a pitch-dark ***l***, light has dawned.
36:17 to take you to a ***l*** just like your
53:8 from the ***l*** of the living,
Jeremiah
2:7 you into a ***l*** of plenty, to
22:29 ***L***, land, land, hear the LORD's word
Lamentations
4:21 who live in the ***l*** of Uz. But this
Ezekiel
36:24 I will bring you to your own fertile ***l***.
39:28 them to their ***l***. I won't leave
48:21 the prince. The ***l*** from the edge of
48:29 This is the ***l*** that you will distribute
Daniel
11:9 king, but will return to his own ***l***.
12:2 in the dusty ***l*** will wake up—some
Hosea
2:23 for myself in the ***l***; and I will have
Jonah
2:10 and it vomited Jonah onto the dry ***l***.
Zechariah
3:9 remove the guilt of that ***l*** in one day.
14:10 The entire ***l*** will become like the
Malachi
3:11 of your fertile ***l***, and so that the
3:12 be a desirable ***l***, says the LORD of
4:6 come and strike the ***l*** with a curse.
Hebrews
8:9 them out of the ***l*** of Egypt, because
11:9 he lived in the ***l*** he had been
James
1:1 outside the ***l*** of Israel.
1 Peter
1:17 time of your dwelling in a strange ***l***.
Revelation
10:2 on the sea and his left foot on the ***l***.
10:5 sea and on the ***l*** raised his right
10:8 who stands on the sea and on the ***l***."

LANDS

Genesis
26:3 give all of these ***l*** to you and your
Ezra
9:1 the neighboring ***l*** with their
Psalms
105:44 God gave them the ***l*** of other nations;
106:27 nations, casting them across many ***l***.
Ezekiel
20:6 and honey, the most splendid of all ***l***.
39:27 them from the ***l*** of their enemies,
Acts
17:26 times and the boundaries of their ***l***.

LANGUAGE

Genesis
11:1 the earth had one ***l*** and the same
Deuteronomy
28:49 that speaks a ***l*** you can't
Esther
1:22 it in its own ***l***. It said that
3:12 and in the ***l*** of each people.
8:9 province and in the ***l*** of each people.
Psalms
55:9 Confuse their ***l*** because I see
81:5 when I heard a ***l*** I did not yet
114:1 from a people who spoke a different ***l***
Isaiah
19:18 that speak the ***l*** of Canaan and
33:19 who stammer in an incomprehensible ***l***.

Jeremiah
5:15 a nation whose ***l*** you don't know,
Ezekiel
3:5 to a people whose ***l*** and speech are
Daniel
1:4 them the Chaldean ***l*** and its
3:29 nation, and ***l***: whoever speaks
Acts
2:8 us hear them speaking in our native ***l***?
14:11 in the Lycaonian ***l***, "The gods have
1 Corinthians
14:9 If you don't use ***l*** that is easy to
14:10 are probably many ***l*** families in the
14:11 meaning of the ***l***, then I will be
14:16 trained in that ***l*** say "Amen!" to
Ephesians
5:4 Obscene ***l***, silly talk, or vulgar jokes
Colossians
3:8 rage, malice, slander, and obscene ***l***.
Revelation
5:9 from every tribe, ***l***, people, and
7:9 people, and ***l***. They were
13:7 every tribe, people, ***l***, and nation.
14:6 to every nation, tribe, ***l***, and people.

LANGUAGES
Genesis
10:5 to their ***l*** and their clans
10:20 clans, their ***l***, their lands, and
10:31 clans, their ***l***, their lands, and
Ezekiel
3:6 and obscure ***l***, whose words you
Daniel
3:4 nations, and ***l***! This is what you
Zechariah
8:23 different ***l*** will grab hold of
Mark
16:17 in my name. They will speak in new ***l***.
Acts
2:4 to speak in other ***l*** as the Spirit
2:6 heard them speaking in their native ***l***.
2:11 the mighty works of God in our own ***l***!"
10:46 speaking in other ***l*** and praising God.
19:6 speaking in other ***l*** and prophesying.
1 Corinthians
14:21 with foreign ***l*** and foreigners'
Revelation
10:11 many peoples, nations, ***l***, and kings."
11:9 peoples, tribes, ***l***, and nations will
17:15 are peoples, crowds, nations, and ***l***.

LARGE
Numbers
26:54 To a ***l*** clan you will give a large
33:54 clans. To the ***l*** you will make its
Deuteronomy
9:2 These people are ***l*** and tall—they are
Psalms
103:11 earth, that's how ***l*** God's faithful
104:25 living things both small and ***l***.
Proverbs
6:35 he'll refuse even a ***l*** bribe.
14:28 king's glory is a ***l*** population, but a
21:9 with a contentious woman in a ***l*** house.
Ezekiel
16:26 with the ***l*** sexual organs,
37:10 feet, an extraordinarily ***l*** company.

Galatians
6:11 Look at the ***l*** letters I'm making with

LAST
2 Samuel
23:1 These are David's ***l*** words: This is the
Ecclesiastes
3:14 God does will ***l*** forever; it's
Isaiah
41:4 LORD, was first, and I will be the ***l***!
44:6 and I am the ***l***, and besides me
48:12 the one; I am the first and I am the ***l***.
Matthew
19:30 are first will be ***l***. And many who are
20:8 with the ***l*** ones hired and
27:64 the dead.' This ***l*** deception will be
Mark
10:31 are first will be ***l***. And many who are
12:6 He sent him ***l***, thinking, They
John
6:40 and I will raise them up at the ***l*** day."
7:37 On the ***l*** and most important day of the
11:24 rise in the resurrection on the ***l*** day."
12:48 be judged at the ***l*** day by the word I
15:16 your fruit could ***l***. As a result,
Acts
2:17 In the ***l*** days, God says, I will pour
1 Corinthians
15:8 and ***l*** of all he appeared to me, as if I
15:26 Death is the ***l*** enemy to be brought to
15:45 person, and the ***l*** Adam became a
2 Timothy
3:1 that the ***l*** days will be
4:8 At ***l*** the champion's wreath that is
James
5:3 you have hoarded in the ***l*** days.
1 Peter
1:5 he is ready to reveal in the ***l*** time.
5:6 that he may raise you up in the ***l*** day.
2 Peter
3:3 know this: in the ***l*** days scoffers
1 John
2:18 it is the ***l*** hour. Just as you
Revelation
1:17 be afraid. I'm the first and the ***l***,
2:8 the first and the ***l***, who died and
15:1 and these are the ***l***, for with them
15:8 of the seven ***l*** angels were
21:9 full of the seven ***l*** plagues spoke
22:13 the first and the ***l***, the beginning

LATER
John
13:7 doing now, but you will understand ***l***."
13:36 follow me now, but you will follow ***l***."
Acts
7:30 Forty years ***l***, an angel appeared to
1 Timothy
5:24 but the sins of other people show up ***l***.

LAW → UNDER THE LAW
Genesis
47:26 So Joseph made a ***l*** that still exists
Exodus
21:31 this same case ***l*** applies to the
Leviticus
20:12 his daughter-in-***l***, both of them

24:22 There is but one ***l*** on this matter for
Numbers
27:11 and a case ***l*** for the
1 Samuel
30:25 regulation and a ***l*** in Israel, which
2 Kings
11:12 him the royal ***l***, and made him
1 Chronicles
2:7 by disobeying the ***l*** dedicating war
16:17 it up as binding ***l*** for Jacob, as an
2 Chronicles
23:11 him the royal ***l***, and made him
Ezra
7:10 and to teach ***l*** and justice in
7:26 your God and the ***l*** of your king,
Nehemiah
13:3 people heard this ***l***, they separated
Esther
1:15 According to the ***l***, what should I do
2:8 order and his new ***l*** became public,
3:14 was to become ***l*** in each province
3:15 Susa just as the ***l*** became public in
4:2 was against the ***l*** for anyone to
4:3 order and his new ***l*** arrived, a very
4:8 a copy of the ***l*** made public in
4:11 there's a single ***l*** in a case like
4:16 it's against the ***l***, I will go to the
8:13 was to become ***l*** in each province
8:14 order, and the ***l*** also became
8:17 order and his ***l*** arrived—for the J
9:1 order and his ***l*** were to be
9:13 to do what the ***l*** allows for today.
9:14 be done, and the ***l*** became public in
9:32 Purim part of the ***l***, so it was
Psalms
78:5 He established a ***l*** for Jacob and set up
81:4 this is the ***l*** for Israel; this
94:20 one who wreaks havoc by means of the ***l***?
105:10 it up as binding ***l*** for Jacob, as an
119:88 love so I can keep the ***l*** you've given!
122:4 tribes! It is the ***l*** for Israel to
148:6 God made a ***l*** that will not be
Proverbs
31:5 and forget the ***l***, and violate the
Isaiah
24:5 swept aside ***l***, and broken the
Jeremiah
32:7 Anathoth, for by ***l*** you are next in
Ezekiel
5:8 impose the case ***l*** penalties on you
Daniel
6:7 and enforce a ***l***, that for thirty
6:8 issue the ***l*** and sign the
6:9 signed the document containing the ***l***.
6:12 king about the ***l***: "Your Majesty!
6:13 as well as the ***l*** you signed. He
6:15 Majesty, that the ***l*** of Media and
7:25 times set by ***l***. And for a period
Matthew
5:17 do away with the ***L*** and the Prophets.
5:18 erased from the ***L*** until everything
7:12 you; this is the ***L*** and the Prophets.
11:13 Prophets and the ***L*** prophesied until
12:2 disciples are breaking the Sabbath ***l***."
12:4 and broke the ***l*** by eating the
12:5 you read in the ***L*** that on the
12:10 asked, "Does the ***L*** allow a person to
12:12 a sheep! So the ***L*** allows a person
14:4 It's against the ***l*** for you to marry
15:6 away with God's ***L*** for the sake of
19:3 said, "Does the ***L*** allow a man to
22:17 think: Does the ***L*** allow people to
22:36 is the greatest commandment in the ***L***?"
22:40 All the ***L*** and the Prophets depend on
23:23 matters of the ***L***: justice, peace,
27:6 According to the ***L*** it's not right to
Mark
2:24 Why are they breaking the Sabbath ***l***?"
6:18 It's against the ***l*** for you to marry
10:2 asked, "Does the ***L*** allow a man to
12:14 is. Does the ***L*** allow people to
Luke
2:22 with the ***L*** of Moses, they
2:23 written in the ***L*** of the Lord,
2:24 stated in the ***L*** of the Lord, A
2:27 do what was customary under the ***L***.
2:39 required by the ***L*** of the Lord, they
6:2 Why are you breaking the Sabbath ***l***?"
6:4 He broke the ***L*** by going into God's
10:26 is written in the ***L***? How do you
14:3 Does the ***L*** allow healing on
16:16 was only the ***L*** and the Prophets.
16:17 stroke of a pen in the ***L*** to drop out.
20:22 Does the ***L*** allow people to pay taxes to
24:44 about me in the ***L*** of Moses, the
John
1:17 as the ***L*** was given through Moses, so
1:45 about in the ***L*** and the Prophets:
7:15 taught! How has he mastered the ***L***?"
7:19 give you the ***L***? Yet none of you
7:23 breaking Moses' ***L***, why are you
7:49 doesn't know the ***L***. And they are
7:51 Our ***L*** doesn't judge someone without
8:5 In the ***L***, Moses commanded us to stone
8:17 In your ***L*** it is written that the
9:16 the sabbath ***l***." Others said,
10:34 written in your ***L***, I have said, you
12:34 heard from the ***L*** that the Christ
15:25 written in their ***L***, They hated me
18:31 according to your ***L***." The Jewish
19:7 We have a ***L***, and according to
Acts
5:34 teacher of the ***L*** named Gamaliel,
6:13 against this holy place and the ***L***.
7:53 You received the ***L*** given by angels, but
13:15 reading of the ***L*** and the Prophets,
13:38 relationship with God through Moses' ***L***,
15:5 be required to keep the ***L*** of Moses."
18:15 and your own ***L***, deal with them
21:20 all of them keep the ***L*** passionately.
21:24 too live a life in keeping with the ***L***.
21:28 our people, the ***L***, and this place.
22:3 of our ancestral ***L***. I am
22:12 standards of the ***L***, he was a pious
23:3 according to the ***L***, yet disobey the
23:29 related to their ***L***. I found no
24:14 set out in the ***L*** and written in
25:8 the Jewish ***L***, against the
28:23 appealing to the ***L*** of Moses and the
Romans
2:12 outside the ***L*** will also die
2:13 ones who hear the ***L*** who are righteous

2:14 don't have the ***L***. But when they
2:15 the proof of the ***L*** written on their
2:17 you rely on the ***L***; if you brag
2:18 are taught by the ***L*** so that you can
2:20 of knowledge and truth in the ***L***);
2:23 brag about the ***L***, do you shame God
2:25 you do what the ***L*** says. But if you
2:26 keeps the ***L***, won't his status
2:27 but keeps the ***L*** will judge you.
3:19 that whatever the ***L*** says, it speaks
3:20 by doing what the ***L*** says, because the
3:21 apart from the ***L***, which is
3:27 out. With which ***l***? With what we
3:28 but through the ***l*** of faith. We
3:31 then cancel the ***L*** through this
4:7 outside the ***L*** are forgiven, and
4:13 come through the ***L*** but through the
4:14 because of the ***L***, then faith has
4:15 The ***L*** brings about wrath. But when
4:16 are related by ***L*** but also for
5:13 there was no ***L***, it wasn't taken
5:20 The ***L*** stepped in to amplify the
6:14 you aren't under ***L*** but under grace.
6:15 we aren't under ***L*** but under grace?
7:1 who know the ***L***. Don't you know
7:2 husband under the ***L*** while he is
7:3 free from the ***L***, so she won't be
7:4 respect to the ***L*** through the body
7:5 through the ***L*** were at work in
7:6 released from the ***L***. We have died
7:7 to say? That the ***L*** is sin?
7:8 in me. Sin is dead without the ***L***.
7:9 alive without the ***L***, but when the
7:12 So the ***L*** itself is holy, and the
7:14 We know that the ***L*** is spiritual, but
7:16 do, I'm agreeing that the ***L*** is right.
7:22 gladly agree with the ***L*** on the inside,
7:23 I see a different ***l*** at work in my
7:25 a slave to God's ***L*** in my mind, but
8:2 The ***l*** of the Spirit of life in Christ
8:3 for the ***L***, since it was
8:4 of the ***L*** might be
8:7 submit to God's ***L***, because it can't.
9:4 the giving of the ***L***, the worship, and
9:31 striving for a ***L*** of righteousness,
10:4 the goal of the ***L***, which leads to
10:5 comes from the ***L***: The person who
13:4 to enforce the ***l*** for nothing. It
13:8 another person has fulfilled the ***L***.
13:10 therefore love is what fulfills the ***L***.

1 Corinthians
9:8 am I? Doesn't the ***L*** itself say these
9:9 In Moses' ***L*** it's written: You will not
9:20 I'm under the ***L*** to those under
9:21 I'm outside the ***L*** to those who are
14:21 In the ***L*** it is written: I will speak to
14:34 get under control, just as the ***L*** says.
15:56 is sin, and the power of sin is the ***L***.)

2 Corinthians
6:14 is outside the ***L***? What

Galatians
2:16 the works of the ***L*** but rather
2:18 I show that I myself am breaking the ***L***.
2:19 I died to the ***L*** through the Law, so
2:21 through the ***L***, then Christ died
3:2 the works of the ***L*** or by believing
3:5 the works of the ***L*** or by you
3:10 the works of the ***L*** are under a
3:11 righteous by the ***L*** as far as God is
3:12 The ***L*** isn't based on faith; rather, the
3:13 the curse of the ***L*** by becoming a
3:17 saying this: the ***L***, which came four
3:18 based upon the ***L***, it would no
3:19 So why was the ***L*** given? It was added
3:21 So, is the ***L*** against the promises of
3:23 guarded under the ***L***, locked up until
3:24 so that the ***L*** became our custodian
4:4 through a woman, and born under the ***L***.
4:5 those under the ***L*** so that we could
4:21 to be under the ***L***—don't you listen
5:3 that he is required to do the whole ***L***.
5:4 righteous by the ***L*** have been
5:14 All the ***L*** has been fulfilled in a
5:18 by the Spirit, you aren't under the ***L***.
5:23 There is no ***l*** against things
6:2 so you will fulfill the ***l*** of Christ.
6:13 don't observe the ***L*** themselves, but

Ephesians
2:15 rules of the ***L*** so that he could

Philippians
3:5 to observing the ***L***, I'm a Pharisee.
3:6 under the ***L***, I'm blameless.
3:9 not come from the ***L*** but rather from

2 Thessalonians
2:7 live without any ***l*** is at work now,

1 Timothy
1:7 to be teachers of ***L*** without
1:8 we know that the ***L*** is good if used
1:9 this: the ***L*** isn't established

Titus
3:9 fights about the ***L***, because they are

Hebrews
7:5 under the ***L*** to collect a
7:11 received the ***L*** under the
7:12 has to be a change in the ***L*** as well.
7:19 (because the ***L*** made nothing perfect).
7:28 The ***L*** appoints people who are prone to
8:4 others who offer gifts based on the ***L***.
9:19 both the ***L*** scroll itself and
10:1 The ***L*** is a shadow of the good things
10:8 offered because the ***L*** requires them.
10:28 rejected the ***L*** from Moses, they

James
1:25 study the perfect ***l***, the law of
2:8 fulfill the royal ***l*** found in
2:9 and by that same ***l*** you are exposed
2:10 keep all of the ***L*** but fails at one
2:12 who will be judged by the ***l*** of freedom.
4:11 criticizes the ***L***. If you find

LAWS → CASE LAWS

Deuteronomy
4:45 These are the ***l*** and the regulations and
6:17 along with the ***l*** and regulations
6:20 meaning of the ***l***, the regulations,

2 Samuel
22:23 haven't turned away from any of his ***l***.

1 Kings
2:3 and observing his ***l***, his commands,
3:3 to walk in the ***l*** of his father
3:14 ways and obey my ***l*** and commands,
6:12 If you follow my ***l***, enact my
8:58 his commands, his ***l***, and his

8:61 by following his **l** and observing his
9:4 and keep my regulations and case **l**,
11:11 covenant and my **l** that I commanded
11:33 eyes—keeping my **l** and judgments—as
11:34 who did keep my commands and my **l**.
11:38 eyes, keeping my **l** and my commands
Ezra
7:25 who know the **l** of your God. You
Esther
1:13 kingdom's written **l** and what judges
1:19 written into the **l** of Persia and
3:8 kingdom. Their **l** are different
Job
38:33 you know heaven's **l**, or can you
Psalms
18:22 haven't turned away from any of his **l**.
19:7 being. The LORD's **l** are faithful,
25:10 for those who keep his covenant and **l**.
50:16 you talk about my **l**? Why do you even mention my covenant
93:5 Your **l** are so faithful. Holiness
99:7 They kept the **l** and the rules God
105:45 would keep his **l** and observe his
111:10 who keep God's **l**. God's praise
119:2 who guard God's **l** are truly happy!
119:14 content of your **l** as if I were
119:22 away from me because I've kept your **l**!
119:24 Yes, your **l** are my joy—they are my
119:31 tight to your **l**, LORD. Please
119:36 my heart to your **l**, not to greedy
119:46 talk about your **l** before rulers
119:59 ways and turned my feet back to your **l**.
119:95 to kill me, but I'm studying your **l**.
119:99 teachers because I contemplate your **l**.
119:111 Your **l** are my possession forever
119:119 like waste—that's why I love your **l**.
119:125 me understand so I can know your **l**.
119:129 Your **l** are wonderful! That's why I
119:138 The **l** you commanded are righteous,
119:144 Your **l** are righteous forever. Help me
119:146 to you, "Save me so I can keep your **l**!"
119:152 learned from your **l** that you had
119:157 but I haven't turned away from your **l**.
119:167 I keep your **l**; I love them so much
119:168 precepts and your **l** because all my
132:12 covenant and the **l** that I will teach
Isaiah
10:1 decrees, and keep writing harmful **l**
Jeremiah
33:25 and night or the **l** of heaven and
44:10 and my **l** that I set before
44:23 LORD's instruction, **l**, or warnings."
23:24 will judge you according to their **l**.
Daniel
9:5 ignoring your commands and your **l**.
Amos
2:4 haven't kept his **l**. They have been
Zechariah
1:6 my words and **l**, which I gave to
Malachi
3:7 deviated from my **l** and have not kept
1 Timothy
1:9 who live without **l** and without
Hebrews
8:10 I will place my **l** in their minds,
10:16 I will place my **l** in their hearts

LAZARUS

Luke
16:20 poor man named **L** who was covered
John
11:11 Our friend **L** is sleeping, but
11:43 with a loud voice, "**L**, come out!"
12:1 Bethany, home of **L**, whom Jesus had

LAZY

Exodus
5:8 They are weak and **l**, and that's why
5:17 replied, "You are **l** bums, nothing but
Proverbs
6:6 to the ant, you **l** person; observe
6:9 How long, **l** person, will you lie down?
10:26 the eyes, so are **l** people to those
12:24 charge, while a **l** one will be
12:27 The **l** don't roast their prey, but hard
13:4 The **l** have strong desires but receive
15:19 The path of the **l** is like a hedge of
18:9 Those who are **l** in their work are
19:24 **L** people bury their hand in the bowl;
20:4 The **l** don't plow during winter; at
21:25 desires of the **l** will kill them
21:26 The **l** desire things constantly, but the
22:13 A **l** person says, "There's a lion in the
24:30 the field of a **l** person, by the
26:13 A **l** person says,"There's a lion in the
26:14 its hinge, so do **l** people in their
26:15 **L** people bury their hand into the bowl,
26:16 **L** people think they are wiser than
Matthew
25:26 You evil and **l** servant! You knew
1 Timothy
5:13 they learn to be **l** by going from
Titus
1:12 liars, wild animals, and **l** gluttons."
Hebrews
5:11 you have been **l** and you have't
6:12 so you won't be **l** but follow the

LEAD

Exodus
13:17 go, God didn't **l** them by way of
23:33 or else they will **l** you to sin
32:1 us gods who can **l** us. As for this
32:34 Now go and **l** the people to the place I
33:12 been telling me, '**L** these people
Numbers
27:17 someone who will **l** them out and
31:22 silver, copper, iron, tin, and **l**
Deuteronomy
10:11 me: Get going. **L** the people so
13:5 they tried to **l** you away from the
13:10 they desired to **l** you away from the
15:10 thing that will **l** to the LORD your
31:7 the one who will **l** this people to
1 Samuel
8:20 will judge us and **l** us and fight our
12:2 The king will **l** you now. I am old and
2 Kings
6:19 me, and I'll **l** you to the man
1 Chronicles
15:21 Azaziah were to **l** with lyres tuned
2 Chronicles
1:10 so I can **l** this people,

Esther
2:3 provinces to ***l*** the search. Have
6:9 to honor and ***l*** him on the horse
Job
19:24 instrument and ***l***, forever engraved
38:32 proper times, ***l*** the Bear with her
Psalms
5:8 enemies, please ***l*** me in your
25:5 ***L*** me in your truth—teach it to me—
27:11 of my opponents, ***l*** me on a good path.
31:3 Guide me and ***l*** me for the sake
37:8 get upset—it will only ***l*** to evil.
48:14 the one who will ***l*** us even to the
49:13 who follow their ***l***, pleased with
60:9 I wish someone would ***l*** me to Edom!"
61:2 of the earth. ***L*** me to the rock
108:10 I wish someone would ***l*** me to Edom!"
118:27 a light on us! So ***l*** the festival
119:35 ***L*** me on the trail of your commandments
139:24 way in me, then ***l*** me on the eternal
Proverbs
4:11 path of wisdom. I ***l*** you in straight
5:5 to death; her steps ***l*** to the grave.
6:22 around, they will ***l*** you; when you lie
10:16 of the righteous ***l*** to life; the
29:15 and correction ***l*** to wisdom, but
Ecclesiastes
7:3 a sad face may ***l*** to a glad heart.
Song of Songs
8:2 I would ***l*** you, I would bring you to my
Isaiah
11:6 and a little child will ***l*** them.
20:4 king of Assyria ***l*** the captives of
42:7 blind eyes, to ***l*** the prisoners
49:10 for them will ***l*** them and will
60:9 are in the ***l*** to bring your
63:17 Why do you ***l*** us astray, LORD, from your ways
Jeremiah
3:15 and they will ***l*** you with
6:29 bellows roar; the ***l*** is consumed. Yet
23:32 lies, they ***l*** my people astray.
27:10 their lies will ***l*** to banishment
31:9 them back. I will ***l*** them by quiet
31:32 by the hand to ***l*** them out of the
50:8 Like rams of the flock, ***l*** the way home.
51:40 I'll ***l*** them off like lambs for
Ezekiel
11:9 I will ***l*** you out of the city, hand you
12:12 the wall to ***l*** him out through
20:6 that I would ***l*** them out of the
22:18 tin, iron, and ***l***. In the furnace,
22:20 copper, iron, ***l***, and tin are
26:20 I will ***l*** you down into the pit, to the
27:12 exchanged silver, iron, tin, and ***l***.
34:13 I will gather and ***l*** them out from the
36:6 my passion and fury ***l*** me to speak.
38:4 in your jaws, and ***l*** you out, you and
Hosea
9:13 now Ephraim must ***l*** out his children
Micah
3:5 those who ***l*** my people astray,
Zechariah
3:7 then you will ***l*** my house and
5:7 Then a ***l*** cover was lifted, showing a
5:8 and he put the ***l*** stone over its
Matthew
6:13 And don't ***l*** us into temptation, but
Mark
10:32 with Jesus in the ***l***. The disciples
Luke
6:39 person can't ***l*** another blind
11:4 us. And don't ***l*** us into
13:15 its stall and ***l*** it out to get a
19:42 the things that ***l*** to peace. But now
John
10:16 sheep pen. I must ***l*** them too. They
21:18 tie your belt and ***l*** you where you
Acts
7:40 us gods that will ***l*** us. As for this
13:11 for someone to ***l*** him around by the
Romans
2:4 is supposed to ***l*** you to change
8:15 of slavery to ***l*** you back again
12:8 The leader should ***l*** with passion. The
16:26 in order to ***l*** to their faithful
1 Corinthians
11:34 together doesn't ***l*** to judgment. I
2 Thessalonians
3:5 May the Lord ***l*** your hearts to express
1 Timothy
5:17 Elders who ***l*** well should be paid
2 Timothy
2:16 because they will ***l*** many people into
Hebrews
8:9 by the hand to ***l*** them out of the
James
3:3 their mouths to ***l*** them wherever we
Revelation
7:17 them. He will ***l*** them to the

LEADER

Leviticus
4:22 If a ***l*** sins by unintentionally breaking
4:26 for the ***l*** to remove his
Numbers
14:4 Let's pick a ***l*** and let's go back
Joshua
22:14 ten leaders, one ***l*** from each
1 Samuel
9:16 anoint him as ***l*** of my people
12:2 I've been your ***l*** since I was young
13:14 commission him as ***l*** over God's
15:17 aren't you the ***l*** of Israel's
19:20 there as their ***l***. God's spirit
22:2 he became their ***l***. Approximately
25:30 and has installed you as Israel's ***l***,
2 Samuel
5:2 Israel, and you will be Israel's ***l***.
6:21 who appointed me ***l*** over the LORD's
7:8 the flock, to be ***l*** over my people
22:44 appointed me the ***l*** of many nations.
1 Kings
11:24 men and became ***l*** of a band when
12:18 them (he was the ***l*** of the work
14:7 you as a ***l*** over my people
16:2 and made you a ***l*** over my people
2 Kings
20:5 my people's ***l***: This is what the
1 Chronicles
5:2 brothers and a ***l*** came from him,
9:11 son of Ahitub the ***l*** of God's house;
9:17 Their brother Shallum was the ***l***,

9:20 with him, was their **l** in former times.
11:2 you will become a **l** over my people
11:42 the Reubenite, a **l** of the
12:3 Ahiezer was the **l**, then Joash, both
12:4 the Thirty and a **l** over the Thirty;
12:9 Ezer the **l**, Obadiah second, Eliab
12:18 of Amasai, the **l** of the Thirty:
12:27 also Jehoiada, **l** of Aaron's line, and
13:1 and a hundred, in fact with every **l**,
15:5 Uriel, the **l** of Kohath's family, and
15:6 Asaiah, the **l** of Merari's family, and
15:7 Joel, the **l** of Gershom's family, and
15:8 Shemaiah, the **l** of Elizaphan's family,
15:9 Eliel, the **l** of Hebron's family, and 80
15:10 Amminadab, the **l** of Uzziel's
15:22 Chenaniah was **l** of the Levites who
15:27 Chenaniah, the **l** of
16:5 Asaph was the **l**, and Zechariah his
17:7 the flock, to be **l** over my people
27:16 Reubenites—the **l** was Eliezer,
28:4 He chose Judah as **l**, and within

2 Chronicles
1:2 every Israelite **l** who was the head
10:18 them (he was the **l** of the work
19:11 son, the **l** of Judah's house,
32:21 every warrior, **l**, and officer in

Ezra
8:17 them to Iddo, the **l** at the place

Nehemiah
11:17 son of Asaph the **l** who began the
12:42 singers sang with Jezrahiah as their **l**.
12:46 there was a **l** of the singers,

Isaiah
3:6 You be our **l**! This mess will
3:7 Don't make me the **l** of the people!"
33:22 the LORD is our **l**; the LORD is our
66:17 following their **l** into the gardens,

Jeremiah
30:21 have their own **l**; their ruler will
48:45 including the **l** of this

Daniel
8:11 high as the very **l** of those forces,
8:25 even the supreme **l**. But he will be
9:25 Jerusalem until a **l** is anointed. And
9:26 army of a future **l** will destroy the
10:13 days the **l** of the Persian
10:20 back to fight the **l** of Persia. As I
10:21 these leaders except your **l** Michael.
11:22 same is true for the **l** of the covenant.
12:1 Michael the great **l** who guards your

Mark
5:36 to the synagogue **l**, "Don't be

Luke
8:41 was a synagogue **l**, came and fell at
13:14 The synagogue **l**, incensed that Jesus
22:26 lower status and the **l** like a servant.

John
3:1 a Pharisee named Nicodemus, a Jewish **l**.

Acts
5:31 his right side as **l** and savior so
7:27 Who appointed you as our **l** and judge?
7:35 you as our **l** and judge?' This
18:8 the synagogue **l**, and his entire
18:17 the synagogue **l**, and gave him a

Romans
12:8 attached. The **l** should lead with

LEADERS → JEWISH LEADERS

Genesis
17:20 of twelve tribal **l**, and I will make
25:16 twelve tribal **l** according to

Exodus
6:14 These were the **l** of their households.
6:25 These were the **l** of Levite
18:25 and set them as **l** over the people,
24:11 the Israelite **l**, though they
34:31 Aaron and all the **l** of the community

Numbers
1:16 tribes and **l** of the divisions
7:2 of Israel, the **l** of their
10:4 the chiefs, the **l** of Israel's
13:3 All the men were **l** among the
16:2 Israelite men, **l** of the community,
25:4 Take all the **l** of the people and
30:1 spoke to the **l** of the tribes of
31:26 priest, and the **l** of the
32:28 son, and to the **l** of the households
36:1 The **l** of the households of the clans of

Deuteronomy
1:13 I will appoint them as your **l**.
1:15 them up as your **l**. There were
29:10 your God—the **l** of your tribes,
33:5 when the people's **l** gathered
33:21 portion was, the **l** of the people

Joshua
9:15 their lives. The **l** of the community
9:18 was because the **l** of the community
9:19 Then all the **l** said to the whole
9:21 The **l** went on to say to them, "Let them
13:21 and Reba, the **l** of Midian. They
17:4 son, and the **l**. They said, "The
22:14 sent with him ten **l**, one leader from
22:30 the priest, the **l** of the community,
22:32 priest and the **l** left the people
24:1 of Israel, its **l**, judges, and

Judges
2:16 LORD raised up **l** to rescue them
2:17 obey their own **l** because they were
2:18 would raise up **l** for them, and the
5:15 The **l** of Issachar came along with
9:2 Ask all the **l** of Shechem, 'Which do

2 Samuel
7:7 Israel's tribal **l** I appointed to

1 Kings
8:1 all the tribal **l**, and the chiefs
9:22 his servants, his **l**, his officers,

2 Kings
10:6 with the city **l** who were raising
10:11 not one of his **l**, close
24:14 all the military **l**-ten thousand exile
24:15 the land's elite **l** from Jerusalem to

1 Chronicles
4:38 by name were **l** in their clans,
7:3 in all, and all of them **l**.
8:28 They were **l** who lived in
11:22 two of Moab's **l**, and on a snowy
12:20 and Zillethai, **l** of units of a
15:16 David told the **l** of the Levites to
17:6 Israel's tribal **l**, whom I appointed
19:3 the Ammonite **l** asked Hanun, "Do you
21:2 told Joab and the **l** of the people,
22:17 all of Israel's **l** to help his son
23:2 all Israel's **l** along with the
24:5 there were holy **l**, even outstanding

LEADERS [cont.]

24:6 of the king; the **l**; Zadok the
26:12 with their **l**, who were
26:26 by the household **l**, by the
27:22 These were the **l** of the tribes of
28:1 all of Israel's **l** in Jerusalem, the
29:6 Then the **l** of the households, the

2 Chronicles
5:2 all the tribal **l**, and the clan
12:5 Rehoboam and the **l** of Judah who had
12:6 Then the **l** of Israel and the king
21:4 along with some other **l** of Israel.
24:10 pleased all the **l** and all the
24:17 however, the **l** of Judah came and
24:23 all the people's **l**, and sent all the
28:12 of the Ephraimite **l**—Johanan's son Aza
29:20 gathered the city **l** and went to the
29:30 Hezekiah and the **l** ordered the
35:9 and Jozabad, the **l** of the Levites,
36:14 All the **l** of the priests and the people

Ezra
5:10 the names of the **l** for your
7:28 me. I gathered **l** from Israel to go
8:16 Meshullam, all **l**, together with
9:2 the officials and **l** have led the way
10:14 Let our **l** represent the entire

Nehemiah
4:16 Meanwhile, the **l** positioned
10:14 The **l** of the people: Parosh,
11:1 The **l** of the people lived in Jerusalem.
11:3 These are the **l** of the province who
11:16 were some of the **l** of the Levites in
12:7 These were the **l** of the priests
12:24 These were the **l** of the Levites:
12:31 I brought the **l** of Judah up onto

Esther
1:3 courtiers. The **l** of Persia and
1:14 kingdom's highest **l**, were in the
9:3 All the **l** of the provinces, rulers,

Job
12:24 from earth's **l**, making them

Psalms
2:2 their stand; the **l** scheme together
47:9 The **l** of all people are gathered with
107:40 contempt on their **l**, making them
113:8 to seat them with **l**—with the leaders
141:6 Their **l** will fall from jagged cliffs,
146:3 Don't trust **l**; don't trust any human

Proverbs
28:2 there are many **l**; but a person

Isaiah
3:12 My people—your **l** mislead you and
9:16 But this people's **l** were misleading,
14:9 ghosts, all the **l** of earth; it
22:3 All your **l** escaped together but were

Jeremiah
2:8 know me; the **l** rebelled against
29:2 the government **l** of Judah and
51:57 I'll make her **l** and sages drunk, her

Ezekiel
31:14 Nor would their **l** achieve the

Daniel
9:6 to our kings, our **l**, our parents, and
9:8 our kings, our **l**, and our parents
10:13 of the highest **l**, came to help me.
10:21 me against these **l** except your

Micah
3:1 But I said: Hear, **l** of Jacob, rulers of
3:9 Hear this, **l** of the house of Jacob,

Matthew
27:18 He knew that the **l** of the people had

Mark
5:22 of the synagogue **l**, came forward.

Luke
14:1 of one of the **l** of the Pharisees,
19:47 and the foremost **l** among the people
23:35 watching, but the **l** sneered at him,
24:20 priests and our **l** handed him over

John
7:26 it be that our **l** actually think he
7:48 Have any of the **l** believed in him? Has
12:42 Even so, many **l** believed in him, but

Acts
4:5 The next day the **l**, elders, and legal
4:8 answered, "**L** of the people and
13:15 the synagogue **l** invited them,
13:27 and their **l** didn't recognize
13:50 as the city's **l**. They instigated
14:5 including their **l**, hatched a plot
15:22 Silas, who were **l** among the
25:5 Some of your **l** can come down with me,"

1 Corinthians
2:6 or from today's **l** who are being

Galatians
2:2 the influential **l** to make sure that
2:6 The influential **l** didn't add anything
2:9 to be key **l**, shook hands with

Hebrews
13:7 Remember your **l** who spoke God's word to you
13:17 Rely on your **l** and defer to them,
13:24 Greet your **l** and all of God's holy

LEADS

Job
12:17 He **l** advisors away barefoot; makes
12:19 **l** priests away barefoot; overthrows the
12:23 expands nations and **l** them astray;

Psalms
23:2 meadows; he **l** me to restful
80:1 You, the one who **l** Joseph as if he

Proverbs
12:8 but a warped mind **l** to contempt.
12:25 Anxiety **l** to depression, but a good
12:28 of the righteous **l** to life, but the
14:23 hard work, but mere talk **l** to poverty.
14:29 Patience **l** to abundant understanding,
19:23 fear of the LORD **l** to life; then one
20:1 Those it **l** astray won't
22:16 to the wealthy **l** only to poverty.

Isaiah
48:17 own good, who **l** you in the way

Matthew
7:13 The gate that **l** to destruction is
7:14 But the gate that **l** to life is narrow
15:14 if a blind person **l** another blind

John
10:3 his own sheep by name and **l** them out.

Acts
8:26 the road that **l** from Jerusalem to

Romans
6:16 of sin, which **l** to death, or as
6:19 behavior that **l** to still more
8:6 from selfishness **l** to death, but the

10:4 of the Law, which *l* to righteousness
10:10 with the heart *l* to righteousness,
2 Corinthians
7:10 and life that *l* to salvation and
2 Timothy
3:15 in a way that *l* to salvation

LEAH
Genesis
29:16 older was named ***L*** and the younger
29:30 Rachel more than ***L***. He worked for
Ruth
4:11 Rachel and like ***L***, both of whom

LEARN
Deuteronomy
4:10 so that they will *l* to fear me every
14:23 so that you *l* to fear the LORD
31:12 they hear it, *l* it, and revere
1 Samuel
20:3 must not *l* about this or
2 Samuel
1:18 in Judah to *l* the Song of the
3:25 and go, and to *l* everything you
2 Chronicles
12:8 him so that they *l* the difference
Esther
2:11 women's house to *l* how Esther was
Psalms
40:3 Many people will *l* of this and be
94:8 people better *l* quickly. You
119:7 does right as I *l* your righteous
119:73 so I can *l* your commandments.
Proverbs
14:7 for you won't *l* wise speech there.
22:25 you will *l* their ways and
Isaiah
1:17 *l* to do good. Seek justice: help the
2:4 they will no longer *l* how to make war.
7:15 and honey, and *l* to reject evil
26:9 living in the world *l* righteousness.
26:10 they don't *l* righteousness;
Jeremiah
12:16 if they will *l* the ways of my
35:13 Can't you *l* a lesson about
Jonah
1:7 so that we might *l* who is to blame
Micah
4:3 they will no longer *l* how to make war.
6:5 that you might *l* to recognize the
Matthew
9:13 Go and *l* what this means: I want mercy
11:29 on my yoke, and *l* from me. I'm
24:32 ***L*** this parable from the fig tree.
Mark
13:28 ***L*** this parable from the fig tree.
Acts
16:38 were alarmed to *l* that Paul and
17:19 teaching? Can we *l* what you are
21:34 he couldn't *l* the truth, so he
1 Corinthians
4:6 so that you can *l* what it means not
14:31 that everyone can *l* and be encouraged.
14:35 If they want to *l* something, they
Galatians
1:12 receive it or *l* it from a human.
Ephesians
4:20 But you didn't *l* that sort of thing
1 Thessalonians
4:4 and *l* how to control your own body in a
1 Timothy
2:11 A wife should *l* quietly with complete
5:4 they should first *l* to respect their
5:13 Also, they *l* to be lazy by going from
Titus
3:14 should also *l* to devote
Revelation
14:3 And no one could *l* the song except

LEARNED
Psalms
78:3 we've heard and *l* about, ones that
119:71 because through it I *l* your statutes.
119:152 Long ago I *l* from your laws that you
Proverbs
24:32 it to heart; I saw it and *l* a lesson.
30:3 I haven't *l* wisdom, nor do I have
Matthew
2:16 the time that he had *l* from the magi.
14:13 When the crowds *l* this, they
Mark
15:45 When he *l* from the centurion that Jesus was dead
Luke
23:7 When he *l* that Jesus was from Herod's
John
6:45 to the Father and *l* from him comes to
Acts
7:22 Moses *l* everything Egyptian wisdom had to offer
9:30 of believers *l* about this, they
Romans
16:17 teaching that you *l*. Keep away from
Philippians
4:9 whatever you *l*, received, heard,
4:11 for I have *l* how to be content
4:12 enough; I have *l* the secret to
1 Thessalonians
4:1 and please God—just as you *l* from us.
2 Timothy
3:14 things you have *l* and found
Hebrews
5:8 he was a Son, he *l* obedience from

LEAST
2 Kings
18:24 back even the *l* important
1 Chronicles
12:14 officers, the *l* of them ready to
Esther
5:9 up nor seemed the *l* bit nervous
Isaiah
36:9 back even the *l* important
60:22 The *l* will become a thousand, and the
Jeremiah
6:13 From the *l* to the greatest, each is
50:12 will become the *l* of the nations: a
Jonah
3:5 greatest of them to the *l* significant.
Micah
5:2 you are the *l* significant of
Matthew
2:6 no means are you *l* among the rulers

LEAST [cont.]

5:19 one of the **l** of these commands
11:11 Yet whoever is **l** in the kingdom of
25:40 it for one of the **l** of these brothers
25:45 it for one of the **l** of these, you

Mark
9:35 be first must be **l** of all and the

Luke
7:28 Yet whoever is **l** in God's kingdom
9:48 me. Whoever is **l** among you all is
14:9 your seat in the **l** important place.
14:10 go and sit in the **l** important place.

Acts
8:10 from the **l** to the greatest,

1 Corinthians
15:9 I'm the **l** important of the apostles.

Ephesians
3:8 grace to me, the **l** of all God's

Hebrews
8:11 know me, from the **l** important of them

LEATHER

Genesis
3:21 man and his wife **l** clothes and

Exodus
25:5 skins dyed red; beaded **l**; acacia wood;
26:14 red and an outer covering of beaded **l**.
35:7 skins dyed red; beaded **l**; acacia wood;
36:19 red and an outer covering of beaded **l**.
39:34 of beaded **l**, and the veil for

Numbers
4:6 covering of fine **l** on it. They will
31:20 made of **l**, goat's hair, or

2 Kings
1:8 of hair with a **l** belt around his

Matthew
3:4 hair, with a **l** belt around his

Mark
1:6 hair, with a **l** belt around his
2:22 new wine into old **l** wineskins;

Acts
18:3 with them. They all worked with **l**.

LEAVE

Genesis
12:1 said to Abram, "**L** your land, your

Exodus
11:8 After that I'll **l**." Then Moses,
33:15 go yourself, don't make us **l** here.

Numbers
9:12 They must not **l** any of it until
11:20 him, saying, "Why did we **l** Egypt?" '

Joshua
1:5 Moses. I won't desert you or **l** you.
24:16 that we ever **l** the LORD to serve
24:20 If you **l** the LORD and serve foreign

Ruth
2:16 bales for her and **l** them behind for

Ezra
6:7 **L** the work on this house of God alone.
9:12 of the land, and **l** it for an

Nehemiah
6:3 work stop while I **l** it to come down

Psalms
27:9 don't neglect me! Don't **l** me all alone!
37:28 He will never **l** his faithful all
38:21 Don't **l** me all alone, LORD! Please, my
119:8 statutes. Please don't **l** me all alone!

Proverbs
3:3 and faithfulness **l** you. Bind them on
13:22 Good people **l** their grandchildren an

Ecclesiastes
2:18 I will have to **l** them to someone
2:21 and skill must **l** the results of
8:3 be dismayed; **l** his presence.
10:4 you, don't **l** your post,

Isaiah
65:15 You will **l** your name behind for my

Jeremiah
3:18 and Israel will **l** the north
9:19 We have to **l** the land and
51:50 survivors of war, **l** now; don't delay!

Ezekiel
5:17 and they will **l** you childless.
36:20 people, yet they had to **l** his land."
39:28 land. I won't **l** any of them

Hosea
5:15 I will **l** so that I can return to my
9:12 Doom to them indeed when I **l** them!

Joel
2:3 garden, but they **l** behind them a

Obadiah
1:5 to you, wouldn't they **l** some grapes?

Matthew
5:24 **l** your gift at the altar and go. First
10:14 your feet as you **l** that house or
18:12 off, wouldn't he **l** the ninety-nine on
19:5 this a man should **l** his father and

Mark
5:17 pleaded with Jesus to **l** their region.
6:11 to you, as you **l**, shake the dust
10:7 a man should **l** his father and
14:6 Jesus said, "**L** her alone. Why do you

Luke
5:8 knees and said, "**L** me, Lord, for I'm
8:37 asked Jesus to **l** their area
19:44 you. They won't **l** one stone on top

John
6:67 the Twelve, "Do you also want to **l**?"
12:7 Then Jesus said, "**L** her alone. This
14:27 Peace I **l** with you. My peace I give

Acts
1:4 them not to **l** Jerusalem but to
7:3 God told him, '**L** your homeland and kin,
7:7 they will **l** that land and
16:10 we prepared to **l** for the province
18:2 all Jews to **l** Rome. Paul
22:18 he said. '**L** Jerusalem at once
28:25 were starting to **l** when Paul made

Romans
12:19 dear friends, but **l** room for God's
15:28 to them, I will **l** for Spain,

1 Corinthians
5:10 you would have to **l** the world
7:10 a wife shouldn't **l** her husband,

2 Corinthians
5:8 would prefer to **l** the body and to
12:8 Lord three times for it to **l** me alone.

Ephesians
5:31 is why a man will **l** his father and

Philippians
1:23 because I want to **l** this life and be

Hebrews
2:8 he doesn't **l** anything out of

13:5 I will never ***l*** you or abandon
Revelation
3:12 they will never ***l*** it. I will write
11:2 the temple. ***L*** that out, because

LEAVES
Genesis
2:24 reason that a man ***l*** his father and
3:7 So they sewed fig ***l*** together and made
Exodus
21:33 When someone ***l*** a pit open or digs a pit
Psalms
1:3 time and whose ***l*** don't fade.
40:12 hairs on my head—my courage ***l*** me.
146:4 Their breath ***l*** them, then they go back
Proverbs
2:17 She ***l*** behind the partner of her youth;
Daniel
4:12 Its ***l*** were beautiful, its fruit
Matthew
12:43 an unclean spirit ***l*** a person, it
21:19 nothing except ***l***. Then he said to
24:32 it sprouts new ***l***, you know that
Mark
11:13 nothing except ***l***, since it wasn't
13:28 it sprouts new ***l***, you know that
John
10:12 wolf coming, he ***l*** the sheep and
1 Corinthians
9:25 to get a crown of ***l*** that shrivel up
2 Corinthians
7:10 to salvation and ***l*** no regrets, but
Revelation
22:2 The tree's ***l*** are for the

LEAVING
Genesis
9:10 of the earth, ***l*** the ark with you.
17:22 to him, God ascended, ***l*** Abraham alone.
31:20 not sending word to him that he was ***l***.
35:13 God ascended, ***l*** him alone in the
45:24 and as they were ***l***, he told them,
Exodus
14:8 the Israelites, who were ***l*** confidently.
19:1 the Israelites' ***l*** the land of
33:6 So after ***l*** Mount Horeb the Israelites
Deuteronomy
2:8 descendants, ***l*** the desert road
Judges
6:4 as far as Gaza, ***l*** nothing to keep
2 Samuel
14:7 I have left, ***l*** my husband
2 Kings
2:1 and Elijah and Elisha were ***l*** Gilgal.
7:7 in the evening, ***l*** their tents,
Ezra
9:8 shown favor in ***l*** us survivors and
Job
22:6 stripped the naked, ***l*** no clothes;
Psalms
35:12 evil for good, ***l*** me stricken with
49:10 do, all of them ***l*** their fortunes to
Isaiah
32:6 of the LORD, ***l*** the hungry empty,
Jeremiah
36:20 After ***l*** the scroll in the room of
Ezekiel
19:14 and fruit, ***l*** her no strong
Zephaniah
2:5 will exterminate you, ***l*** no inhabitant.
Zechariah
7:14 them, with no one ***l*** or returning.
Malachi
4:1 heavenly forces, ***l*** them neither root
Matthew
9:32 As they were ***l***, people brought to him
25:14 a man who was ***l*** on a trip. He
Mark
1:20 followed him, ***l*** their father
1:29 After ***l*** the synagogue, Jesus, James,
6:33 people saw them ***l*** and recognized
7:17 After ***l*** the crowd, he entered a house
7:31 After ***l*** the region of Tyre, Jesus went
8:13 ***L*** them, he got back in the boat and
10:46 As Jesus was ***l*** Jericho, together
11:12 next day, after ***l*** Bethany, Jesus
12:19 brother dies, ***l*** a widow but no
12:21 and died without ***l*** any children. The
Luke
4:38 After ***l*** the synagogue, Jesus went home
4:42 they tried to keep him from ***l*** them.
20:28 brother dies ***l*** a widow but no
20:31 they all died without ***l*** any children.
John
14:31 me. Get up. We're ***l*** this place.
16:28 you again: I am ***l*** the world and
Acts
12:10 by itself. After ***l*** the prison, they
13:42 and Barnabas were ***l*** the synagogue,
20:7 Since he was ***l*** the next day, he
2 Peter
2:15 ***L*** the straight path, they have gone off

LEBANON
Deuteronomy
11:24 the way to the ***L*** range, and from
1 Kings
4:33 the cedar in ***L*** or the hyssop
5:6 the cedars of ***L*** cut down for me.
2 Kings
14:9 a thistle in ***L*** sent a message to
Psalms
29:5 yes, the LORD shatters the cedars of ***L***.
72:16 flourish like ***L***. Let it thrive
92:12 will grow strong like a cedar of ***L***.
104:16 the cedars of ***L***, which God
Isaiah
40:16 ***L*** doesn't have enough fuel; its animals
Habakkuk
2:17 violence done to ***L***, he will
Zechariah
10:10 of Gilead and ***L*** until there is no

LED
Genesis
20:13 When God ***l*** me away from my father's
24:48 Abraham, who ***l*** me in the right
27:20 The LORD your God ***l*** me right to it."
Exodus
3:1 priest. He ***l*** his flock out to
13:18 So God ***l*** the people by the roundabout
32:21 to you that you ***l*** them to commit

Numbers
20:5 Why have you ***l*** us up from Egypt to
Deuteronomy
4:19 bodies, and be ***l*** astray,
8:2 the LORD your God ***l*** you during these
8:15 the one who ***l*** you through this vast and
29:24 this land? What ***l*** to this terrible
32:12 The LORD alone ***l*** Israel; no foreign god
Judges
2:1 up from Egypt and ***l*** you into the land
1 Samuel
18:13 men. David ***l*** the men out to
30:16 So the boy ***l*** David to them, and he
1 Kings
1:38 King David's mule. They ***l*** him to Gihon.
10:19 Six steps ***l*** up to the throne, and the
16:9 his officer who ***l*** half the
21:25 that his wife Jezebel ***l*** him to do.
2 Kings
11:19 land, and they ***l*** the king down
21:9 listen. Manasseh ***l*** them into doing
Ezra
9:2 and leaders have ***l*** the way in this
Nehemiah
9:12 of cloud you ***l*** them by day and
Psalms
45:14 colors, she is ***l*** to the king. Her
45:15 palace, they are ***l*** in with
77:20 You ***l*** your people like sheep under the
78:13 split the sea and ***l*** them through,
78:14 God ***l*** them with the cloud by day; by
78:52 God ***l*** his own people out like sheep,
78:53 God ***l*** them in safety—they were not
78:72 of integrity; he ***l*** them with the
106:9 right up; he ***l*** them through the
107:7 God ***l*** them straight to human
107:30 down; then God ***l*** them to the
136:16 to the one who ***l*** his people
Isaiah
9:16 and those being ***l*** were confused.
19:13 the tribal chiefs have ***l*** Egypt astray.
44:20 deluded mind has ***l*** him astray. He
48:21 thirsty when he ***l*** them through the
60:11 and their kings ***l*** in procession.
63:14 In this way you ***l*** your people and
Jeremiah
2:6 of Egypt, who ***l*** us through the
11:19 like a young lamb ***l*** to the slaughter;
13:19 into exile; everyone will be ***l*** away.
23:13 by Baal and ***l*** astray my people
38:22 of Judah will be ***l*** out to the
38:23 children will be ***l*** out to the
50:6 their shepherds ***l*** them astray; they
Ezekiel
12:4 out like those who are ***l*** out to exile.
13:10 a doubt, they ***l*** my people astray,
20:10 So I ***l*** them out of the land of Egypt
37:1 LORD's spirit, he ***l*** me out and set me
37:2 He ***l*** me through them all around, and I
40:22 Gate. Seven steps ***l*** up to the
40:49 feet wide. Steps ***l*** up into the
42:1 Then he ***l*** me north to the outer
42:15 of the temple, he ***l*** me out toward the
43:1 Then he ***l*** me to the East Gate
47:2 He ***l*** me out through the North Gate and
47:6 you see?" Then he ***l*** me back to the
Hosea
4:12 prostitution has ***l*** them astray; they
11:4 I ***l*** them with bands of human kindness,
Amos
2:4 They have been ***l*** off the right
2:10 of Egypt, and ***l*** you forty years
Matthew
4:1 Then the Spirit ***l*** Jesus up into the
26:57 arrested Jesus ***l*** him to Caiaphas
27:2 They bound him, ***l*** him away, and turned
27:31 back on him. They ***l*** him away to
Mark
8:23 man's hand, Jesus ***l*** him out of the
14:53 They ***l*** Jesus away to the high priest,
15:1 They bound Jesus, ***l*** him away, and
15:16 The soldiers ***l*** Jesus away into the
15:20 on him. Then they ***l*** him out to
Luke
2:27 ***L*** by the Spirit, he went into the
4:1 Spirit, and was ***l*** by the Spirit
4:5 Next the devil ***l*** him to a high place
4:29 out of town. They ***l*** him to the crest
22:54 Jesus, they ***l*** him away and
23:1 got up and ***l*** Jesus to Pilate
23:26 As they ***l*** Jesus away, they grabbed
23:32 They also ***l*** two other criminals to be
24:50 He ***l*** them out as far as Bethany, where
John
1:42 He ***l*** him to Jesus. Jesus looked at him
9:13 Then they ***l*** the man who had been born
18:13 and ***l*** him first to Annas. He was the
18:28 Jewish leaders ***l*** Jesus from
19:13 these words, he ***l*** Jesus out and
Acts
5:19 the night and ***l*** them out. The
7:36 This man ***l*** them out after he performed
7:40 this Moses who ***l*** us out of Egypt,
8:32 a sheep he was ***l*** to the slaughter
13:17 great power, he ***l*** them out of that
15:28 Holy Spirit has ***l*** us to the
16:30 He ***l*** them outside and asked, "Honorable masters
17:15 who escorted Paul ***l*** him as far as
21:38 a revolt and ***l*** four thousand
22:11 so my companions ***l*** me by the hand
Romans
1:24 desires, which ***l*** to the moral
5:16 one person's sin ***l*** to punishment,
8:14 All who are ***l*** by God's Spirit are God's
2 Corinthians
11:29 weak? Who is ***l*** astray without me
Galatians
5:18 if you are being ***l*** by the Spirit,
2 Peter
1:21 men and women ***l*** by the Holy
3:17 that you aren't ***l*** off course into

LEFT

Genesis
4:16 Cain ***l*** the LORD's presence, and he
11:31 They ***l*** Ur of the
12:4 Abram ***l*** just as the LORD told him, and
39:18 and screamed, he ***l*** his garment with
50:7 So Joseph ***l*** to bury his father. All of
Exodus
5:20 When they ***l*** Pharaoh, they met Moses and Aaron

16:1 after they had ***l*** the land of Egypt.
35:20 The whole Israelite community ***l*** Moses
36:4 the sanctuary ***l*** their work that

Deuteronomy
2:27 road. We won't step off it, right or ***l***.

Joshua
1:7 to the right or ***l***. Then you will
10:28 for God. He ***l*** no survivors. He

Judges
2:21 nations that Joshua ***l*** when he died."
2:23 the LORD ***l*** these nations instead of
3:15 who was ***l***-handed. The Israel
3:21 reached with his ***l*** hand and grabbed
16:29 right hand and the other with his ***l***.
19:2 secondary wife ***l*** him and went back
20:16 chosen men were ***l***-handed, and every

Ruth
1:3 Then only she was ***l***, along with her
2:11 to me: how you ***l*** behind your
4:14 who today hasn't ***l*** you without a

1 Samuel
4:22 The glory has ***l*** Israel because God's
17:22 David ***l*** his things with an attendant

Ezra
4:12 that the Jews who ***l*** you and came to
8:31 Then we ***l*** the Ahava River on the

Job
1:12 So the Adversary ***l*** the LORD's
20:26 them; what's ***l*** in their tent is
22:20 off; fire will devour what's ***l*** of them.
23:11 I have kept his way and not ***l*** it,

Psalms
4:6 The light of your face has ***l*** us, LORD!"
13:2 long will I be ***l*** to my own wits,
22:1 God, why have you ***l*** me all alone? Why
27:10 father and mother ***l*** me all alone, the
34:1 him so that he ***l***.] I will bless
37:25 the righteous ***l*** all alone, have
39:4 days do I have ***l***? I want to know
74:9 No prophet is ***l***. And none of us
77:19 waters. But your footprints ***l*** no trace!
79:2 They've ***l*** your servants' bodies as food
79:3 and there's no one ***l*** to bury them.
105:38 when they ***l*** because the dread

Proverbs
3:16 long life; in her ***l*** are wealth and
4:27 the right or the ***l***; turn your feet

Ecclesiastes
5:14 have children, they are ***l*** with nothing.
10:2 but the mind of the fool toward the ***l***.

Song of Songs
2:6 His ***l*** arm is beneath my head, his right

Isaiah
1:8 Daughter Zion is ***l*** like a small shelter
30:21 the right or the ***l***, you will hear a
54:3 right and to the ***l*** you will burst

Jeremiah
11:23 No one will be ***l*** because I will bring

Ezekiel
1:10 face on the ***l***, and also an

Hosea
4:12 astray; they have ***l*** God to follow
9:12 until no one is ***l***. Doom to them

Obadiah
1:18 will be no one ***l*** of the house of
1:20 and those ***l*** from Jerusalem

Jonah
4:11 hand from their ***l***, and also many

Haggai
2:3 Who among you is ***l*** who saw this house

Zechariah
4:3 right of its bowl and one to the ***l***."
11:9 Let those who are ***l*** devour the flesh
14:16 All those ***l*** from all the nations who

Matthew
4:11 The devil ***l*** him, and angels came and
4:13 He ***l*** Nazareth and settled in Capernaum,
4:20 Right away, they ***l*** their nets and
4:22 immediately they ***l*** the boat and their
5:39 you must turn the ***l*** cheek to them as
6:3 don't let your ***l*** hand know what
12:9 Jesus ***l*** that place and went into their
20:23 at my right or ***l*** hand isn't mine
24:2 no stone will be ***l*** on another.
24:40 One will be taken and the other ***l***.
25:33 But the goats he will put on his ***l***.
26:56 all the disciples ***l*** Jesus and ran
27:38 one on his right side and one on his ***l***.
27:46 My God, my God, why have you ***l*** me?"

Mark
1:18 Right away, they ***l*** their nets and
5:13 unclean spirits ***l*** the man and went
6:24 She ***l*** the banquet hall and said to her
7:29 The demon has already ***l*** your daughter."
10:1 Jesus ***l*** that place and went beyond the
13:2 one stone will be ***l*** upon another. All
14:52 but he ***l*** the linen cloth behind and ran
15:34 My God, my God, why have you ***l*** me?"

Luke
1:38 you have said." Then the angel ***l*** her.
10:30 beat him up, and ***l*** him near death.
18:29 anyone who has ***l*** house, husband,

John
13:30 the bread, he ***l*** immediately. And
16:28 I ***l*** the Father and came into the world.
20:3 the other disciple ***l*** to go to the tomb.
20:25 in the wounds ***l*** by the nails, and

Acts
5:41 The apostles ***l*** the council rejoicing
7:4 So Abraham ***l*** the land of the Chaldeans
12:9 the angel, Peter ***l*** the prison.

2 Corinthians
6:7 in our right hand and our ***l*** hand.

Revelation
10:2 on the sea and his ***l*** foot on the land.

LEGACY

Deuteronomy
25:6 his brother's ***l*** will not be
25:7 his brother's ***l*** in Israel. He's

Joshua
11:23 gave it as a ***l*** to Israel
13:6 it to Israel as a ***l*** exactly as I
13:7 up this land as a ***l*** for the nine
13:8 taken their ***l*** that Moses had
13:14 that he gave no ***l***. Their legacy
13:23 it. This was the ***l*** of the people of
13:28 This was the ***l*** of the Gadites—for
13:33 But Moses gave no ***l*** to the tribe of
14:2 Their ***l*** was assigned by lot, exactly as
14:3 had given out the ***l*** of the two and a
14:9 will forever be a ***l*** for you and your

14:13 to Caleb, Jephunneh's son, as a ***l***.
14:14 Kenizzite as a ***l*** today. This was
15:20 This is the ***l*** for the clans of the
16:4 Manasseh and Ephraim, received their ***l***.
16:5 border of their ***l*** ran from Ataroth-a
16:8 sea. This is the ***l*** for the clans of
16:9 within the ***l*** of the people of
17:4 to give us a ***l*** along with our
17:6 received a ***l*** along with his
17:14 parcel for a ***l***? We are a
18:2 left that had not yet received their ***l***.
18:4 determining their ***l***. Then they will
18:7 because their ***l*** is the priesthood
18:20 side. This is the ***l*** of the
18:28 This is the ***l*** of the
19:1 to Simeon. The ***l*** of the clans of
19:2 They had in their ***l***: Beer-sheba,
19:8 This is the ***l*** of the clans of
19:9 belonged to the ***l*** of the people of
19:10 border of their ***l*** ran as far as
19:16 areas are the ***l*** of Zebulun's
19:48 areas are the ***l*** for the clans of
19:49 to Joshua, Nun's son, a ***l*** among them.
21:3 out of their own ***l***. This was in
23:4 nations as a ***l*** for your tribes,
24:28 sent the people away to each one's ***l***.
24:32 They became a ***l*** of the

LEGAL → PHARISEES AND LEGAL EXPERTS, PRIESTS AND LEGAL EXPERTS

Exodus
24:14 Whoever has a ***l*** dispute may go to
Leviticus
19:15 act unjustly in a ***l*** case. Do not show
Numbers
15:16 and one ***l*** norm for the
Deuteronomy
17:8 If some ***l*** dispute in your cities is too
19:17 who have a ***l*** suit must stand
21:5 and because every ***l*** dispute and case
24:17 obstruct the ***l*** rights of an
27:19 who obstructs the ***l*** rights of
Job
27:2 who rejected my ***l*** claim, the
Proverbs
29:9 the wise make a ***l*** charge against
Matthew
7:29 authority and not like their ***l*** experts.
8:19 A ***l*** expert came and said to him,
9:3 Some ***l*** experts said among themselves,
12:38 time some of the ***l*** experts and the
13:52 Therefore, every ***l*** expert who has
17:10 Then why do the ***l*** experts say that
22:35 One of them, a ***l*** expert, tested him
23:2 The ***l*** experts and the Pharisees sit on
23:13 will be for you ***l*** experts and
23:34 wise people, and ***l*** experts. Some of
26:57 high priest. The ***l*** experts and the
27:41 along with the ***l*** experts and the
Mark
1:22 with authority, not like the ***l*** experts.
2:6 Some ***l*** experts were sitting there,
2:16 When some of the ***l*** experts from among the Pharisees
3:4 to them, "Is it ***l*** on the Sabbath to
3:22 The ***l*** experts came down from Jerusalem.
3:30 this because the ***l*** experts were
7:1 and some ***l*** experts from
8:31 priests, and the ***l*** experts, and be
9:11 Why do the ***l*** experts say that
9:14 them and ***l*** experts arguing
10:33 priests and the ***l*** experts. They
12:28 One of the ***l*** experts heard their
12:35 said, "Why do the ***l*** experts say that
14:1 chief priests and ***l*** experts through
14:53 elders, and ***l*** experts gathered.
15:1 —with the elders, ***l*** experts, and the
15:31 together with the ***l*** experts. "He
Luke
5:21 The ***l*** experts and Pharisees began to
5:30 and their ***l*** experts grumbled
6:7 The ***l*** experts and the Pharisees were
6:9 Jesus said to the ***l*** experts and
9:22 priests, and the ***l*** experts—and be
10:25 A ***l*** expert stood up to test Jesus.
10:29 But the ***l*** expert wanted to prove that
10:37 Then the ***l*** expert said, "The one who
11:45 One of the ***l*** experts responded,
11:46 terrible for you ***l*** experts too! You
11:52 terrible for you ***l*** experts! You
11:53 left there, the ***l*** experts and
19:47 priests, the ***l*** experts, and the
20:1 chief priests, ***l*** experts, and
20:19 The ***l*** experts and chief priests wanted
20:39 Some of the ***l*** experts responded,
20:46 out for the ***l*** experts. They
22:2 priests and the ***l*** experts were
22:66 chief priests and ***l*** experts, came
23:4 I find no ***l*** basis for action
23:22 I've found no ***l*** basis for the
John
8:3 The ***l*** experts and Pharisees brought a
Acts
4:5 elders, and ***l*** experts gathered
6:12 elders, and the ***l*** experts. They
13:28 find a single ***l*** basis for the
16:20 approached the ***l*** authorities, they
16:35 next morning the ***l*** authorities sent
16:38 this to the ***l*** authorities, who
19:39 can be resolved in a ***l*** assembly.
23:9 who were ***l*** experts stood up
1 Corinthians
1:20 Where are the ***l*** experts? Where
6:1 assembly has a ***l*** case against
Hebrews
7:16 rather than a ***l*** requirement about

LEGS

Exodus
12:9 with its head, ***l***, and internal
25:26 to the four corners at its four ***l***.
29:17 inner organs and ***l***, and put them
37:13 to the four corners at its four ***l***.
Leviticus
1:9 insides and lower ***l*** must be washed
4:11 its head, lower ***l***, entrails, and
8:21 insides and lower ***l*** with water, Moses
9:14 insides and lower ***l*** and completely
11:21 that have jointed ***l*** above their feet
Deuteronomy
28:35 in your knees and ***l***, from the sole of
Judges
15:8 taking their ***l*** right out from

Ruth
3:7 uncovered his ***l***, and lay down.
1 Kings
7:28 were panels connected between the ***l***.
7:29 between the ***l***. On the legs
Psalms
40:2 feet on solid rock. He steadied my ***l***.
109:24 My ***l*** are weak from fasting; my body is
147:10 God doesn't treasure the ***l*** of a runner.
Proverbs
26:7 As ***l*** dangle from a disabled person, so
Ezekiel
16:25 by spreading your ***l*** to all comers.
Daniel
2:33 Its ***l*** were of iron, and its feet were a
Amos
3:12 rescues two ***l*** or the piece of
John
19:31 to have the ***l*** of those
19:32 and broke the ***l*** of the two men
19:33 dead so they didn't break his ***l***.
Acts
14:8 strength in his ***l***. He had been

LENGTH

Genesis
13:17 through the ***l*** and breadth of
Exodus
12:40 The ***l*** of time that the Israelites had
26:13 of the leftover ***l*** of the tent's
Leviticus
19:35 measures of ***l***, weight, or
1 Samuel
28:20 fell full ***l*** on the ground,
2 Samuel
8:2 and one rope ***l*** for those who
1 Kings
6:20 thirty feet in ***l***, width, and
7:2 fifty feet in ***l***, seventy-five feet
2 Chronicles
3:3 of God. The ***l*** according to the
Job
41:3 he beg you at ***l*** or speak gentle
Ezekiel
4:4 on it. For the ***l*** of time that you
40:11 and the gate's ***l***, which was
40:18 their entire ***l***. That was the
40:20 courtyard. He measured its ***l*** and width,
41:2 he measured its ***l***, it was sixty
42:2 The ***l*** of the facade at the north
45:7 eastward. Its ***l*** will equal one
48:8 wide and the ***l*** of a tribal
Luke
23:9 Jesus at ***l***, but Jesus didn't
Acts
12:10 proceeded the ***l*** of one street,
Ephesians
3:18 love's width and ***l***, height and
Revelation
21:16 as a square. Its ***l*** was the same as

LET

Genesis
1:3 God said, "***L*** there be light." And so
Exodus
5:1 God, says: '***L*** my people go so
5:2 and I certainly won't ***l*** Israel go."
13:17 When Pharaoh ***l*** the people go, God
Psalms
22:8 to the LORD, so ***l*** God rescue him;
22:26 ***L*** all those who are suffering eat and
25:2 you. Please don't ***l*** me be put to
48:11 ***L*** Mount Zion be glad; let the towns of
118:25 save us! LORD, please ***l*** us succeed!
150:6 ***L*** every living thing praise the LORD!
Ecclesiastes
5:2 earth. Therefore, ***l*** your words be few.
5:6 Don't ***l*** your mouth make a sinner of
5:12 of the wealthy won't ***l*** them sleep.
9:8 ***L*** your garments always be white; don't
Joel
3:10 into spears; ***l*** the weakling say,
Matthew
5:16 In the same way, ***l*** your light shine
5:37 ***L*** your yes mean yes, and your no mean no
5:40 take your shirt, ***l*** them have your
6:3 the poor, don't ***l*** your left hand
7:4 or sister, '***L*** me take the
8:22 Follow me, and ***l*** the dead bury
11:15 ***L*** the person who has ears, hear
27:43 trusts in God, so ***l*** God deliver him
John
11:16 other disciples, "***L*** us go too so that
11:44 said to them, "Untie him and ***l*** him go."
11:48 If we ***l*** him go on like this, everyone
18:8 for me, then ***l*** these people go."
19:4 him out to you to ***l*** you know that I
Romans
6:12 So then, don't ***l*** sin rule your body, so
14:15 in love. Don't ***l*** your food destroy
14:16 And don't ***l*** something you consider to
Ephesians
4:26 sinning. Don't ***l*** the sun set on
4:29 Don't ***l*** any foul words come out of your
Philippians
4:5 ***L*** your gentleness show in your
4:20 ***L*** glory be given to God our Father
Colossians
2:16 So don't ***l*** anyone judge you about
Titus
2:15 authority. Don't ***l*** anyone disrespect
James
1:4 ***L*** this endurance complete its work so
4:9 mourn, and weep! ***L*** your laughter
Revelation
2:4 you: you have ***l*** go of the love
11:9 but they won't ***l*** their dead bodies
13:18 calls for wisdom. ***L*** the one who
19:7 ***L*** us rejoice and celebrate, and give
22:11 ***L*** those who do wrong keep doing what is wrong.
22:17 say, 'Come!' ***L*** the one who hears

LETTER

2 Samuel
11:14 David wrote a ***l*** to Joab and sent
11:15 He wrote in the ***l***, "Place Uriah at the
2 Kings
5:5 I will send a ***l*** to Israel's
10:2 weapons. Now when this ***l*** reaches you,
2 Chronicles
2:11 replied in a ***l*** that he sent to
21:12 A ***l*** from the prophet Elijah came to

LETTER [cont.]

Ezra
4:7 Artaxerxes. The **l** was written in
4:11 is a copy of the **l** they sent to
5:5 Darius and a **l** with his response
7:11 is a copy of the **l** that Artaxerxes
Nehemiah
2:8 king also issue a **l** to Asaph the
6:5 except that now he carried an open **l**.
Esther
9:26 with what this **l** said, with what
9:29 that this second **l** about Purim was
Jeremiah
29:1 Jeremiah sent a **l** from Jerusalem to
29:2 The **l** was sent after King Jeconiah, the
29:28 He has sent a **l** telling those of us in
29:29 read this **l** to the prophet
Matthew
5:18 the smallest **l** nor even the
Acts
15:20 we should write a **l**, telling them to
15:23 to carry this **l**: The apostles and
15:30 the believers and delivered the **l**.
21:25 we wrote a **l** about what we
23:25 He wrote the following **l**
Romans
16:22 I'm writing this **l** to you in the
1 Corinthians
5:9 you in my earlier **l** not to associate
2 Corinthians
3:2 You are our **l**, written on our hearts,
3:3 you are Christ's **l**, delivered by us.
7:8 Even though my **l** hurt you, I don't
Colossians
4:16 After this **l** has been read to you
1 Thessalonians
5:27 you to have this **l** read aloud to all
2 Thessalonians
2:2 a message, or a **l** supposedly from
2:15 taught you in person or through our **l**.
3:14 have said in this **l**. Don't associate
3:17 verifies that the **l** is from me, as in
Hebrews
13:22 I've only written a short **l** to you!
2 Peter
3:1 is now my second **l** to you. I have

LETTERS

1 Kings
21:8 So she wrote **l** in Ahab's name, putting
2 Kings
10:1 So Jehu wrote **l** and sent them to
10:2 The **l** said: "Your master's sons are in
19:14 Hezekiah took the **l** from the messengers
20:12 to Hezekiah with **l** and a gift. This
2 Chronicles
30:1 Judah, and wrote **l** to Ephraim and
30:6 runners took **l** from the king and
32:17 He wrote other **l** insulting the LORD God
Nehemiah
2:7 the king, may **l** be given me
2:9 them the king's **l**. The king had
6:17 Judah sent many **l** to Tobiah, and
6:19 Tobiah sent **l** to intimidate me.
Esther
8:8 king and seal the **l** with the king's
8:10 ring. He sent **l** with riders
9:20 down and sent **l** to all the Jews
9:30 **L** conveying good wishes and words of
Isaiah
8:1 on it in ordinary **l**, For Maher-shalal-
37:14 Hezekiah took the **l** from the messengers and read them.
39:1 son, sent **l** and a gift to
Jeremiah
29:25 You sent **l** on your own
Acts
9:2 seeking **l** to the synagogues in
22:5 me. I received **l** from them,
28:21 received any **l** about you from
1 Corinthians
16:3 to Jerusalem with **l** of recommendation
2 Corinthians
3:1 We don't need **l** of introduction
3:7 was carved in **l** on stone tablets.
10:9 I'm trying to intimidate you with my **l**.
10:10 are saying: "His **l** are severe and
Galatians
6:11 Look at the large **l** I'm making with my
2 Peter
3:1 have written both **l** to stir up your
3:16 things in all his **l**. Some of his

LEVI

Genesis
29:34 sons for him." So she named him **L**.
49:5 Simeon and **L** are brothers, weapons of violence
Exodus
6:16 Kohath, and Merari. **L** lived 137 years.
Joshua
13:14 to the tribe of **L** that he gave no
Mark
2:14 along, he saw **L**, Alphaeus' son,
Luke
3:24 of Matthat son of **L** son of Melchi son
3:29 son of Jorim son of Matthat son of **L**
5:27 collector named **L** sitting at a
5:28 **L** got up, left everything behind, and
5:29 Then **L** threw a great banquet for Jesus
Hebrews
7:5 descendants of **L** who receive the
Revelation
7:7 from the tribe of **L**, twelve thousand;

LEVIATHAN

Job
3:8 those with enough skill to awaken **L**.
41:1 Can you draw out **L** with a hook,
Psalms
104:26 ships on it, and **L**, which you made,
Isaiah
27:1 and will punish **L** the fleeing

LEVITE

Exodus
4:14 brother Aaron the **L**? I know he can
Judges
19:1 was a certain **L**, living as an
Acts
4:36 who encourages"), was a **L** from Cyprus.

LEVITES → PRIESTS AND LEVITES, PRIESTS AND THE LEVITES

Numbers
1:53 But the ***L*** will camp around the covenant dwelling
3:12 I claim the ***L*** from the Israelites in
8:6 Separate the ***L*** from the Israelites and
16:7 one is holy. You ***L*** have gone too
18:21 in Israel to the ***L*** as an
35:7 you give to the ***L*** will total forty
35:8 inheritance will give cities to the ***L***.
Joshua
14:4 and Ephraim. The ***L*** weren't given any
1 Chronicles
15:2 said, "Only the ***L*** may carry God's
2 Chronicles
31:2 priests and the ***L***, each to their
Ezra
6:18 divisions and the ***L*** in their sections
Nehemiah
8:9 scribe, and the ***L*** who taught the

LEVITICAL

Leviticus
25:32 back homes in the ***l*** cities that are
Deuteronomy
17:9 Go to the ***l*** priests and to the head
18:1 Neither the ***l*** priests nor any Levite
24:8 do everything the ***l*** priests teach
27:9 Moses and the ***l*** priests said to
Joshua
3:3 covenant and the ***l*** priests carrying
8:33 were facing the ***l*** priests who carry
21:1 The heads of the ***l*** families approached
21:20 clans from the ***l*** descendants of
1 Chronicles
24:6 son, the ***l*** scribe, recorded
24:31 heads of the priestly and ***l*** households.
2 Chronicles
5:12 All the ***l*** musicians—Asaph, Heman,
30:27 Then the ***l*** priests blessed the people,
34:9 temple by the ***l*** gatekeepers from
Jeremiah
33:18 And the ***l*** priests will always have
33:21 covenant with the ***l*** priests who
Ezekiel
43:19 offering to the ***l*** priests who are
44:15 priests of the ***l*** family of Zadok
48:22 from both the ***l*** property and the
Hebrews
7:11 came through the ***l*** office of priest

LIAR

Deuteronomy
19:18 the witness is a ***l***—that the witness
Job
24:25 can prove me a ***l*** and make my words
34:6 I'm thought a ***l***; my wound from an
Psalms
116:11 I said, out of fear, "Everyone is a ***l***!"
Proverbs
17:4 to guilty lips; a ***l*** listens to a
19:5 go unpunished, and a ***l*** won't escape.
19:22 it is better to be poor than a ***l***.
30:6 correct you and show you to be a ***l***.
John
8:44 Whenever that ***l*** speaks, he speaks
8:55 be like you, a ***l***. But I do know
Romans
3:4 human being is a ***l***, as it is
1 John
1:10 we make him a ***l*** and his word is
2:4 is a ***l***, and the truth is
2:22 Who is the ***l***? Isn't it the person who
4:20 sister, he is a ***l***, because the
5:10 has made God a ***l***, because that one

LIBNAH

Numbers
33:20 from Rimmon-perez and camped at ***L***.

LIE

Genesis
19:32 wine to drink, ***l*** down with him,
19:34 and you go in and ***l*** down with him so
39:12 garment, saying, "***L*** down with me."
39:14 He came to me to ***l*** down with me, but
47:30 When I ***l*** down with my fathers, carry me from Egypt
Exodus
8:29 don't let Pharaoh ***l*** to us again and
Leviticus
6:3 property, you ***l*** about it; or by
19:11 steal nor deceive nor ***l*** to each other.
26:6 so that you can ***l*** down without
Numbers
21:15 of Ar and ***l*** along the border
23:19 man that he would ***l***, or a human being
23:24 up. It doesn't ***l*** down until it
Deuteronomy
25:2 have that person ***l*** down and be
Joshua
7:10 up! Why do you ***l*** flat on your face
Ruth
3:4 his feet, and ***l*** down. And he will
3:7 He went over to ***l*** down by the edge
3:13 will redeem you. ***L*** down until the
1 Samuel
3:5 Eli replied. "Go ***l*** down." So he did.
3:9 Samuel, "Go and ***l*** down. If he calls
2 Samuel
7:12 to die and you ***l*** down with your
8:2 and made them ***l*** on the ground,
13:5 ***L*** down on your bed and pretend to be
2 Kings
4:16 of God, sir; don't ***l*** to your servant."
9:12 That's a ***l***!" they said. "Come on,
18:29 let Hezekiah ***l*** to you. He won't
Job
6:28 look at me—would I ***l*** to your face?
7:21 Then I would ***l*** down in the dust;
11:19 You will ***l*** down without anyone to scare
21:26 They ***l*** together in the dust and worms
27:19 They ***l*** down rich, but no longer; open
38:40 They ***l*** in their den, lie in ambush in
39:30 where carcasses ***l***, there they are.
Psalms
3:5 I ***l*** down, sleep, and wake up because
4:8 I will ***l*** down and fall asleep in peace
10:7 their tongues ***l*** troublemaking and
10:9 They ***l*** in ambush in secret places, like
17:1 it's spoken by lips that don't ***l***!
41:3 transform the place where they ***l*** ill.
57:4 pack of lions. I ***l*** down among those

59:3 Look at how they ***l*** in ambush for my
68:13 Even if you ***l*** down among the
76:5 The bravehearted ***l*** plundered. They sank
89:35 sworn one thing: I will not ***l*** to David.
102:7 I ***l*** awake all night. I'm all alone like
104:22 together and ***l*** down in their

Proverbs
1:18 ambush; they ***l*** in wait for their
3:24 If you ***l*** down, you won't be terrified.
6:9 person, will you ***l*** down? When will
6:10 little folding of the arms to ***l*** down—
6:22 you; when you ***l*** down, they will
14:5 witness doesn't ***l***, but a false
15:11 the underworld ***l*** open before the

Ecclesiastes
4:11 Also, if two ***l*** down together, they can
11:3 wherever it falls, there it will ***l***.

Isaiah
6:11 Until cities ***l*** ruined with no
11:6 the leopard will ***l*** down with the
11:7 Their young will ***l*** down together,
14:18 of the nations ***l*** down honored, all
14:30 their needy will ***l*** down secure. But
17:2 flocks, which will ***l*** down undisturbed.
27:10 graze there; they ***l*** down there and
34:10 it will ***l*** waste; no one
36:14 let Hezekiah ***l*** to you. He won't
43:17 they will ***l*** down together and
44:20 say, "Isn't this thing in my hand a ***l***?"
50:11 by my hand: you will ***l*** down in grief.
51:23 who said to you, "***L*** down so that we

Jeremiah
3:25 Let's ***l*** down in our shame. Let our
9:5 themselves to ***l***; they wear
9:22 Dead bodies will ***l*** like dung on the
18:15 sacrifices to a ***l***. And so they have
27:16 They are prophesying a ***l*** to you.
28:15 persuading these people to believe a ***l***.
29:31 he convinced you to believe a ***l***,
37:14 That's a ***l***," Jeremiah replied. "I'm
48:9 because its towns ***l*** in ruins, with no

Lamentations
2:21 and old alike ***l*** on the ground in

Ezekiel
4:4 Now, ***l*** on your left side, and set the
4:6 these days, ***l*** on your right
4:9 ninety days that you ***l*** on your side.
23:17 came to her to ***l*** down and make
31:12 and left it to ***l*** among the hills.
31:13 and on its boughs ***l*** all the beasts of
31:18 below. You will ***l*** among the
32:27 They don't ***l*** with the mighty men fallen
34:14 they will ***l*** down in a secure
45:3 the most holy place, will ***l*** on it.

Hosea
2:18 land; I will make you ***l*** down in safety.
6:9 As robbers ***l*** in wait for someone, so

Amos
6:4 who ***l*** on beds of ivory, stretch out on

Jonah
1:5 of the vessel to ***l*** down and was deep

Micah
7:2 All of them ***l*** in wait for

Zephaniah
2:7 they will ***l*** down in the
2:14 Flocks will ***l*** down in its midst, every
3:13 will graze and ***l*** down; no one will

Zechariah
13:3 you have told a ***l*** in the name of

Acts
5:3 influenced you to ***l*** to the Holy

Romans
1:25 God's truth for a ***l***, and they
3:7 by my ***l*** and it increases

Colossians
3:9 Don't ***l*** to each other. Take off the old

2 Thessalonians
2:11 them so that they will believe the ***l***.

Titus
1:2 God, who doesn't ***l***, promised before

Hebrews
6:18 for God to ***l***. He did this so

1 John
2:21 You know that no ***l*** comes from the

Revelation
11:8 dead bodies will ***l*** on the street of
14:5 No ***l*** came from their mouths; they are

LIES

Genesis
36:9 of Edom, which ***l*** in the mountains
49:9 you rise up. He ***l*** down and crouches

Exodus
5:9 and they can't focus on these empty ***l***."

Leviticus
14:47 Anyone who ***l*** down in the house must
15:4 with an emission ***l*** will be unclean,
15:18 If a man ***l*** with a woman and has an
15:20 on which she ***l*** or sits during
15:24 days. Any bed he ***l*** on will be
15:26 Any bed she ***l*** on during the discharge

Deuteronomy
3:25 land that ***l*** beyond it: those

Joshua
22:11 of Canaan. It ***l*** in the districts

Ruth
3:4 When he ***l*** down, notice the place where

2 Samuel
1:19 Your prince ***l*** dead on your
1:25 battle! Jonathan ***l*** dead on your

1 Kings
1:21 master the king ***l*** down with his

Job
8:18 its place, it ***l***, saying, "I can't
13:4 are plasterers of ***l***; ineffective
14:10 a human dies and ***l*** there; a person
14:12 But a human ***l*** down and doesn't rise
37:8 enters its lair, ***l*** down in its den.
40:21 He ***l*** under the lotuses, under the cover

Psalms
4:2 what is worthless and go after ***l***? Selah
7:14 conceive trouble, give birth to ***l***!
12:2 Everyone tells ***l*** to everyone else; they
34:13 and keep your lips from speaking ***l***!
38:12 threats, muttering ***l*** all day long.
40:4 to those who follow ***l***, are truly happy!
41:8 the next time he ***l*** down, he won't
50:19 then harness your tongue to tell ***l***.
59:12 For the curses and ***l*** they repeat,
62:9 are nothing but ***l***. They don't even
101:5 secretly tells ***l*** about a neighbor.
101:7 person who tells ***l*** won't last for
119:69 me with their ***l***, but I guard your

119:78 oppressed me with ***l***—meanwhile, I wil
144:8 mouths speak ***l***, and whose strong
Proverbs
6:19 who breathes ***l***, and one who
7:12 square. She ***l*** in wait at every
14:5 lie, but a false witness spews ***l***.
14:25 lives, but a deceiver proclaims ***l***.
21:6 treasure with ***l*** are like a
23:34 be like one who ***l*** down while out on
29:12 ruler listens to ***l***, those who serve
30:8 Fraud and ***l***—keep far from me! Don't
Isaiah
9:15 prophets who teach ***l*** are the tail.)
24:5 The earth ***l*** polluted under its
27:10 fortified city ***l*** alone, a hut
28:15 for we have made ***l*** our hiding place,
28:17 hiding place of ***l***, and water will
57:4 children of rebellion, offspring of ***l***,
59:3 Your lips speak ***l***; your tongues
Jeremiah
7:4 Don't trust in ***l***: "This is the LORD's
7:8 yet you trust in ***l*** that will only
9:3 bows to spew out ***l***; they are
13:25 you have forgotten me and trusted in ***l***.
14:14 are telling ***l*** in my name. I
16:19 inherited utter ***l***, things that are
23:14 adultery and tell ***l***. They encourage
23:25 prophesying ***l*** in my name. They
23:32 who dream up ***l*** and then proclaim
27:10 to you, and their ***l*** will lead to
29:9 are prophesying ***l*** to you in my
40:4 the whole land ***l*** before you; go
48:1 for Nebo; it ***l*** in ruins.
Ezekiel
13:9 and diviners of ***l***. They won't be
26:2 is broken, she ***l*** open before me,
35:12 I've heard the ***l*** and libels that
Daniel
2:22 who uncovers what ***l*** deeply hidden; he
11:27 table, telling ***l***, but with no
Hosea
7:3 give joy to the officials with their ***l***.
7:13 them, but they speak ***l*** against me.
10:13 the fruit of ***l***, because you have
11:12 me with ***l***, the house of
12:1 they multiply ***l*** and violence;
Amos
2:4 path by the same ***l*** after which their
Micah
7:5 mouth from her who ***l*** in your embrace.
Habakkuk
2:18 is a teacher of ***l***, for the potter
Zephaniah
3:13 they won't tell ***l***; a deceitful
Haggai
1:4 houses while this house ***l*** in ruins?
1:9 because my house ***l*** in ruins. But all
Zechariah
5:3 anyone swearing ***l*** will be purged
5:4 the one swearing ***l*** in my name. It
10:2 and diviners see ***l***. They interpret
Matthew
4:13 Capernaum, which ***l*** alongside the sea
2 Corinthians
3:15 is read, a veil ***l*** over their hearts.
1 Peter
3:10 and their lips from speaking ***l***.
2 Peter
2:3 of you with ***l***. The judgment
1 John
5:19 the whole world ***l*** in the power of

LIFE → FOUNTAIN OF LIFE, WAY OF LIFE

Genesis
2:7 into his nostrils. The human came to ***l***.
2:9 grew the tree of ***l*** in the middle of
3:24 to guard the way to the tree of ***l***.
4:1 I have given ***l*** to a man with the
Exodus
20:12 so that your ***l*** will be long on
21:6 he will serve him as his slave for ***l***.
21:23 then you will give a ***l*** for a life,
Leviticus
17:11 A creature's ***l*** is in the blood. I have
Numbers
35:31 a ransom for the ***l*** of a killer, who
Deuteronomy
5:16 so that your ***l*** will be long and
6:2 the days of your ***l*** and so that you
12:23 because blood is ***l***. You must not
30:19 now: I have set ***l*** and death,
Joshua
4:14 had revered Moses during all of his ***l***.
Judges
2:7 rest of Joshua's ***l*** and throughout
16:30 in his death than he did during his ***l***.
Ruth
4:15 will restore your ***l*** and sustain you
1 Samuel
1:11 for his entire ***l***. No razor will
2:6 death, gives ***l***, takes down to
7:13 the Philistines throughout Samuel's ***l***.
7:15 served as Israel's judge his whole ***l***.
18:1 Saul, Jonathan's ***l*** became bound up
20:21 make a pledge on the LORD's ***l***.
2 Samuel
11:11 on your very ***l***, I will not do
15:34 Please spare my ***l***! I was your
18:13 taken Absalom's ***l*** behind the king's
Esther
7:3 give me my ***l***—that's my wish
7:7 Esther for his ***l***. He saw clearly
Job
2:6 your power; only preserve his ***l***."
7:11 groan in the bitterness of my ***l***.
7:16 I reject ***l***; I don't want to live long;
10:1 I loathe my ***l***; I will let loose my
33:18 from the pit, a ***l*** from perishing by
33:22 A ***l*** approaches the pit; its very being
Psalms
16:10 won't abandon my ***l*** to the grave; you
16:11 me the way of ***l***. In your presence
17:13 down! Rescue my ***l*** from the wicked—
21:4 He asked you for ***l***, and you gave it to
22:20 sword. Deliver my ***l*** from the power of
23:6 the days of my ***l***, and I will live
25:1 [Of David.] I offer my ***l*** to you, LORD
26:9 taking my ***l*** along with
27:1 protecting my ***l***. Should I be
30:3 me back to ***l*** from among those
31:10 My ***l*** is consumed with sadness; my years
34:12 Do you love ***l***; do you relish the
35:17 my precious ***l*** from these

36:9 is the spring of **l**. In your light,
39:5 Yes, a human **l** is nothing but a
39:11 Yes, a human **l** is just a puff of
40:14 those who seek my **l**, who want me
42:8 with me—a prayer to the God of my **l**.
49:8 to save someone's **l** is too high—weal
49:15 God will save my **l** from the power of
54:4 is my helper; my Lord sustains my **l**.
56:13 you have saved my **l** from death, saved
57:4 My **l** is in the middle of a pack of
59:3 in ambush for my **l**! Powerful people
61:6 to the king's **l**! Let his years
63:3 faithful love is better than **l** itself!
64:1 God! Protect my **l** from the enemy's
69:28 of the scroll of **l**! Let them not be
70:2 those who seek my **l** be ashamed and
71:3 commanded that my **l** be saved because
74:19 Don't deliver the **l** of your dove to
85:6 bring us back to **l** again so that
86:2 Guard my **l** because I am faithful. Save
86:4 your servant's **l** happy again
86:13 you've rescued my **l** from the lowest
87:7 The source of my **l** comes from you."
88:3 with distress; my **l** is at the very
89:45 the prime of his **l**. You've wrapped
89:47 how short my **l** is! Have you
89:48 Who lives their **l** without seeing death?
90:14 rejoice and celebrate our whole **l** long.
102:24 in the prime of **l**—your years go on
103:4 saves your **l** from the pit, crowns you
103:15 days of a human **l** are like grass:
119:25 My **l** is stuck in the dirt. Now make me
121:7 all evil; God will protect your very **l**.
128:5 Jerusalem's goodness your whole **l** long.
133:3 commanded the blessing: everlasting **l**.
142:4 escape for me. No one cares about my **l**.
143:8 go because I offer my **l** up to you.
146:2 LORD with all my **l**; I will sing

Proverbs

2:7 for those who live a blameless **l**.
3:16 hand is a long **l**; in her left are
3:18 She is a tree of **l** to those who embrace
3:22 They will be **l** for your whole being,
4:10 then the years of your **l** will be many.
4:13 off; protect it, for it is your **l**.
4:22 They are **l** to those who find them, and
4:23 protect your mind, for **l** flows from it.
5:6 on the way of **l**. Her paths
6:23 corrective teaching is the path of **l**.
6:26 married woman hunts for a man's very **l**.
7:23 not aware that it will cost him his **l**.
8:35 who find me find **l**; they gain favor
9:11 be many; years will be added to your **l**.
10:11 is a fountain of **l**, but the mouth of
10:16 righteous lead to **l**; the earnings of
10:17 are on the way to **l**, but those who
10:27 increases one's **l**, but the years of
11:19 are headed toward **l**, but those who
11:30 is a tree of **l**, and the wise
12:28 leads to **l**, but the
13:8 ransom a person's **l**, but the poor
13:12 sick; longing fulfilled is a tree of **l**.
13:14 is a fountain of **l**, turning a person
14:27 is a fountain of **l**, turning people
14:30 mind gives **l** to the body, but
15:4 is a tree of **l**, but dishonest
15:24 with insight, **l** is an upward
15:31 that listens to **l**-giving correction
16:15 There's **l** in the light of the king's
18:21 Death and **l** are in the power of the
19:23 the LORD leads to **l**; then one rests
20:2 Those who anger him may lose their **l**.
21:21 will find **l**, righteousness,
22:4 of the LORD is wealth, honor, and **l**.
22:23 and press the **l** out of those who
23:22 who gave you **l**; don't despise
23:24 the one who gives **l** to the wise will
24:12 who protects your **l**—he knows.
25:13 they restore the **l** of their master.
29:17 of mind and bring delight into your **l**.
31:12 and not trouble all the days of her **l**.

Ecclesiastes

2:17 So I hated **l**, because the things that
5:18 them because that's their lot in **l**.
6:3 and live a long **l**. But no matter
6:12 beings during **l**, during their
8:8 control over the **l**-breath, to retain
9:9 Enjoy **l** with your dearly loved spouse
11:5 what the **l**-breath does in the
11:10 and the dawn of **l** are pointless too.
12:7 before and the **l**-breath returns to

Isaiah

38:5 I will add fifteen years to your **l**.
38:10 the prime of my **l**; I have been
53:10 suffer. If his **l** is offered as
66:9 I, who create **l**, close the womb?

Jeremiah

4:30 have rejected you and now seek your **l**.
8:3 prefer death to **l**, wherever I have
11:21 who seek your **l** and say, "Don't
15:15 mercy, spare my **l**. Consider how I'm
21:8 you the way of **l** and the way of
36:29 and eliminate every sign of **l** from it.
38:16 has given us this **l**, I won't put you
39:18 escape with your **l**, because you have
45:5 escape with your **l**."ORACLES
52:33 the king's table for the rest of his **l**.
52:34 the rest of his **l**, right up until

Lamentations

2:19 up to him for the **l** of your children—
3:58 Plead my desperate case; redeem my **l**.

Ezekiel

3:19 their guilt, but you will save your **l**.
3:21 the warning, and you will save your **l**.
18:4 are mine; the **l** of the parent and
20:11 laws, which bring **l** to all who
33:9 their guilt, but you will save your **l**.
33:15 and walk in **l**-giving regulations
37:6 and you come to **l**, you will know
37:10 they came to **l** and stood on

Daniel

4:2 the Most High God has worked in my **l**.
12:2 to eternal **l**, others to shame

Habakkuk

2:10 peoples and sinning against your own **l**.

Malachi

2:5 with him involved **l** and peace, which
2:16 Guard your own **l**, and don't cheat.

Matthew

6:25 worry about your **l**, what you'll eat
6:27 can add a single moment to your **l**?
7:14 that leads to **l** is narrow and the
13:22 worries of this **l** and the false

18:8 to enter into *l* crippled or lame
19:16 thing must I do to have eternal *l*?"
19:29 times more and will inherit eternal *l*.
20:28 and to give his *l* to liberate many
25:46 righteous ones will go into eternal *l*."
27:6 to pay for someone's *l*, it's unclean."
Mark
3:4 do evil, to save *l* or to kill?" But
4:19 worries of this *l*, the false appeal
6:16 whom I beheaded, has been raised to *l*."
9:43 you to enter into *l* crippled than to
9:45 for you to enter *l* lame than to be
10:17 what must I do to obtain eternal *l*?"
10:30 much now in this *l*—houses, brothers,
10:45 and to give his *l* to liberate many
Luke
6:9 do evil, to save *l* or to destroy it?"
8:14 and pleasures of *l*, and their fruit
8:55 Her *l* returned and she got up at once.
9:8 ancient prophets had come back to *l*.
9:19 ancient prophets has come back to *l*."
10:25 what must I do to gain eternal *l*?"
12:15 After all, one's *l* isn't determined
12:22 worry about your *l*, what you will
12:23 There is more to *l* than food and more
12:25 can add a single moment to your *l*?
14:26 even one's own *l*—cannot be my
15:7 both heart and *l* than over ninety
15:10 sinner who changes both heart and *l*."
15:24 has come back to *l*! He was lost and
17:33 to preserve their *l* will lose it, but
18:18 what must I do to obtain eternal *l*?"
18:30 age and eternal *l* in the coming
21:34 of day-to-day *l*. Don't let that
23:46 I entrust my *l*." After he said
24:47 of heart and *l* for the
John
1:4 the Word was *l*, and the life was
3:16 won't perish but will have eternal *l*.
3:36 Son has eternal *l*. Whoever doesn't
4:14 water that bubbles up into eternal *l*."
4:36 fruit for eternal *l* so that those who
5:21 dead and gives *l*, so too does the
5:24 me has eternal *l* and won't come
5:26 as the Father has *l* in himself, so he
5:29 resurrection of *l*, and those who
5:39 you have eternal *l*. They also
5:40 to come to me so that you can have *l*.
6:27 for eternal *l*, which the Human
6:33 from heaven and gives *l* to the world."
6:35 am the bread of *l*. Whoever comes to
6:40 will have eternal *l*, and I will raise
6:47 you, whoever believes has eternal *l*.
6:48 I am the bread of *l*
6:51 will give for the *l* of the world is
6:53 drink his blood, you have no *l* in you.
6:54 blood has eternal *l*, and I will raise
6:63 the one who gives *l* and the flesh
6:68 we go? You have the words of eternal *l*.
8:12 darkness but will have the light of *l*."
10:10 they could have *l*—indeed, so that t
10:11 shepherd lays down his *l* for the sheep.
10:15 Father. I give up my *l* for the sheep.
10:17 me: I give up my *l* so that I can
10:28 give them eternal *l*. They will never
11:25 and the *l*. Whoever believes
12:50 is eternal *l*. Therefore
13:37 you now? I'll give up my *l* for you."
13:38 you give up your *l* for me? I assure
14:6 truth, and the *l*. No one comes to
15:13 to give up one's *l* for one's friends.
17:2 give eternal *l* to everyone you
17:3 This is eternal *l*: to know you, the
19:30 Bowing his head, he gave up his *l*.
20:31 believing, you will have *l* in his name.
Acts
2:28 me the paths of *l*; your presence
3:15 the author of *l*, the very one
5:20 people everything about this new *l*."
5:31 its heart and *l* and to find
6:8 at work in his *l* and for his
7:38 one who received *l*-giving words to
7:59 prayed, "Lord Jesus, accept my *l*!"
8:22 your heart and *l*! Turn from your
8:33 because his *l* was taken from
9:31 church, and its *l* was marked by
9:36 is Dorcas). Her *l* overflowed with
11:18 lives so that they might have new *l*."
13:46 receive eternal *l*, we will turn to
13:48 was appointed for eternal *l* believed,
17:25 the one who gives *l*, breath, and
20:24 not even my *l*, is more
21:24 you too live a *l* in keeping with
23:1 I have lived my *l* with an
23:30 against his *l*, I sent him to
26:4 knows the way of *l* I have followed
26:5 the way of *l* set out by the
Romans
2:4 to lead you to change your heart and *l*?
2:7 will give eternal *l* to those who look
4:17 the God who gives *l* to the dead and
5:10 is it that we will be saved by his *l*?
5:17 certainly rule in *l* through the one
5:18 necessary for *l* are met for
5:21 to eternal *l* through Jesus
6:4 we too can walk in newness of *l*.
6:10 death, but he lives for God with his *l*.
6:13 brought back to *l* from the dead,
6:22 of a holy *l*, and the outcome
6:23 gift is eternal *l* in Christ Jesus
7:6 slaves in the new *l* under the Spirit,
7:9 the commandment came, sin sprang to *l*,
7:10 was intended to give *l* brought death.
8:2 of the Spirit of *l* in Christ Jesus
8:6 from the Spirit leads to *l* and peace.
8:10 Spirit is your *l* because of God's
8:11 dead will give *l* to your human
8:38 not death or *l*, not angels or
11:3 left, and they are trying to take my *l*.
11:15 anything less than *l* from the dead?
16:4 own necks for my *l*. I'm not the only
1 Corinthians
3:22 the world, *l*, death, things in
4:17 about my way of *l* in Christ Jesus.
7:17 live the kind of *l* that the Lord
15:19 only in this *l*, then we deserve
15:22 everyone will be given *l* in Christ.
15:36 doesn't come back to *l* unless it dies.
15:45 last Adam became a spirit that gives *l*.
2 Corinthians
2:16 the fountain of *l* to those who are
3:6 written kills, but the Spirit gives *l*.
4:10 so that Jesus' *l* can also be seen

4:12 at work in us, but ***l*** is at work in you.
5:4 what is dying can be swallowed up by ***l***.
7:10 changed heart and ***l*** that leads to

Galatians
1:13 about my previous ***l*** in Judaism, how
2:20 in me. And the ***l*** that I now live
3:21 was able to give ***l***, then
6:8 will harvest eternal ***l*** from the Spirit.

Ephesians
2:5 He brought us to ***l*** with Christ while
4:17 live your ***l*** like the Gentiles
4:18 from God's ***l*** because of their
4:22 the former way of ***l*** that was part of
5:2 Live your ***l*** with love, following the
5:8 so live your ***l*** as children of
5:15 to live your ***l*** wisely, not

Philippians
1:23 to leave this ***l*** and be with
2:16 on to the word of ***l***. This will allow
2:30 He risked his ***l*** and almost died for the
4:3 whose names are in the scroll of ***l***.

Colossians
3:3 died, and your ***l*** is hidden with
3:4 who is your ***l***, is revealed,
3:5 the parts of your ***l*** that belong to

2 Thessalonians
3:6 an undisciplined ***l*** that is not in

1 Timothy
1:16 going to believe in him for eternal ***l***.
2:2 and peaceful ***l*** in complete
4:7 women. Train yourself for a holy ***l***!
4:8 promise for this ***l*** now and the life
5:6 tries to live a ***l*** of luxury is dead
6:12 hold of eternal ***l***—you were called
6:13 of God, who gives ***l*** to all things,
6:19 they can take hold of what is truly ***l***.

2 Timothy
1:1 the promise of ***l*** that is in Christ
1:10 death and brought ***l*** and immortality
3:12 to live a holy ***l*** in Christ Jesus

Titus
1:2 hope of eternal ***l*** that God, who
3:7 we can inherit the hope for eternal ***l***."

Philemon
1:19 I won't mention that you owe me your ***l***.

Hebrews
1:12 the years of your ***l*** won't come to an
7:3 or end of ***l***, but he's like
7:16 by the power of a ***l*** that can't be
11:22 at the end of his ***l***, and gave
12:17 his heart and ***l***, though he looked

James
1:12 will receive the ***l*** God has promised
2:6 the wealthy make ***l*** difficult for
3:6 it, the circle of ***l*** is set on fire.
4:5 in the ***l*** he has given to
4:14 What is your ***l***? You are a mist
5:5 a self-satisfying ***l*** on this earth, a

1 Peter
1:23 seed is God's ***l***-giving and enduring
1:24 Thus, All human ***l*** on the earth is like
3:7 gracious care of ***l***. Do this so that
3:10 who want to love ***l*** and see good days

2 Peter
1:3 we need for ***l*** and godliness
1:14 that I am about to depart from this ***l***.
2:18 only just escaped ***l*** with those who

1 John
1:1 our hands handled, about the word of ***l***.
1:2 The ***l*** was revealed, and we have seen,
2:25 that he himself gave us: eternal ***l***.
3:14 from death to ***l***, because we love
3:15 murderer has eternal ***l*** residing in him.
3:16 laid down his ***l*** for us, and we
5:11 God gave eternal ***l*** to us, and this
5:12 has the Son has ***l***. The one who
5:13 you can know that you have eternal ***l***.
5:16 and God will give ***l*** to them—that is,
5:20 This is the true God and eternal ***l***.

Jude
1:21 Christ, who will give you eternal ***l***.

Revelation
2:7 from the tree of ***l***, which is in
2:8 the last, who died and came back to ***l***:
2:10 and I will give you the crown of ***l***.
2:21 her heart and ***l***, but she refuses
3:5 the scroll of ***l***, but will declare
7:17 to the springs of ***l***-giving water, and
11:11 the breath of ***l*** from God entered
13:8 —in the scroll of ***l*** of the lamb who
13:14 by the sword and yet came to ***l*** again.
17:8 in the scroll of ***l*** from the time the
20:4 They came to ***l*** and ruled with
20:5 didn't come to ***l*** until the
20:12 is the scroll of ***l***. And the dead
20:15 in the scroll of ***l*** was thrown into
21:6 give water from the ***l***-giving spring.
21:27 registered in the Lamb's scroll of ***l***.
22:1 me the river of ***l***-giving water, shin
22:2 is the tree of ***l***, which produces

LIFT

Exodus
14:16 As for you, ***l*** your shepherd's rod,
29:26 ordination and ***l*** it as an uplifted

Leviticus
14:12 of oil, and will ***l*** them up as an
23:11 The priest will ***l*** up the bundle before

Numbers
6:26 The LORD ***l*** up his face to you and grant

Joshua
3:6 to the priests, "***L*** up the covenant
4:5 Each of you, ***l*** up a stone on his
6:6 He said to them, "***L*** up the covenant

2 Samuel
12:17 approached him to ***l*** him up off the

Job
10:15 but can't ***l*** my head, full of
11:15 then you will ***l*** up your face without
22:26 in the Almighty; ***l*** up your face to
30:22 You ***l*** me to the wind and make me ride;

Psalms
24:7 Mighty gates: ***l*** up your heads! Ancient
28:2 to you, when I ***l*** up my hands to
34:3 me! Together let us ***l*** his name up high!
37:34 his way! He will ***l*** you up so you can
41:10 mercy on me and ***l*** me up so I can
63:4 I'm alive; I will ***l*** up my hands in
76:5 troops couldn't even ***l*** their hands!
116:13 I'll ***l*** up the cup of salvation. I'll
118:28 You are my God—I will ***l*** you up high!
119:48 I will ***l*** up my hands to your
134:2 ***L*** up your hands to the sanctuary and

Isaiah
2:9 each person laid low—don't ***l*** them up!
10:15 if a staff could ***l*** up the one not
40:11 in his arms and ***l*** them onto his
52:8 Your lookouts ***l*** their voice; they
60:4 ***L*** up your eyes and look all around:
Jeremiah
13:20 ***L*** up your eyes and see who is
22:20 and cry out, ***l*** up your voice in
23:39 I will ***l*** you up and cast you out of my
Lamentations
2:19 Lord like water. ***L*** your hands up to
3:41 We should ***l*** up our hearts and hands to
Ezekiel
33:25 the blood, you ***l*** your eyes to the
Hosea
11:4 like those who ***l*** infants to their
Nahum
3:5 I will ***l*** your skirts over
Matthew
23:4 are unwilling to ***l*** a finger to move
23:12 All who ***l*** themselves up will be brought
Luke
11:46 and you refuse to ***l*** a single finger
14:11 All who ***l*** themselves up will be brought
18:13 He wouldn't even ***l*** his eyes to look
18:14 Pharisee. All who ***l*** themselves up
James
4:10 before the Lord, and he will ***l*** you up.

LIFTED

Genesis
7:17 The waters rose, ***l*** the ark, and it
Exodus
10:19 west wind that ***l*** the locusts and
16:14 the layer of dew ***l***, there on the
19:4 and how I ***l*** you up on eagles'
Leviticus
8:27 sons' hands, then ***l*** them as an
8:29 offering and ***l*** it as an uplifted
23:12 day the bundle is ***l*** up for you, you
Ruth
1:9 them, and they ***l*** up their voices
1:14 Then they ***l*** up their voices and wept
2 Samuel
22:47 the rock of my salvation, be ***l*** high!
Job
6:2 weighed, all of it were ***l*** up in scales;
31:21 if I have ***l*** my hand against the
36:7 on thrones forever, and they are ***l*** up.
Psalms
18:46 Let the God of my salvation be ***l*** high!
18:48 enemies. Yes, you ***l*** me high above my
40:2 He ***l*** me out of the pit of death, out of
75:10 of the righteous will be ***l*** up."
81:6 I ***l*** the burden off your shoulders;
89:42 You ***l*** high his foes' strong hand. You
Isaiah
2:2 It will be ***l*** above the hills;
26:11 your hand is ***l*** up, but they
52:13 He will be exalted and ***l*** very high.
57:15 who is high and ***l*** up, who lives
Ezekiel
3:12 Then a wind ***l*** me up, and I heard behind
8:3 my head. A wind ***l*** me up between
10:16 winged creatures ***l*** their wings to
11:1 A wind ***l*** me up and brought me to the
Daniel
6:23 and Daniel was ***l*** out. Not a
8:3 When I ***l*** my eyes, I suddenly saw a ram
Micah
4:1 it will be ***l*** above the hills;
5:9 Your hand will be ***l*** over your foes; all
Zechariah
5:7 a lead cover was ***l***, showing a woman
Matthew
23:12 who make themselves low will be ***l*** up.
Mark
9:27 took his hand, ***l*** him up, and he
11:23 mountain, 'Be ***l*** up and thrown
16:19 to them, he was ***l*** up into heaven
Luke
1:52 from their thrones and ***l*** up the lowly.
14:11 who make themselves low will be ***l*** up."
18:14 who make themselves low will be ***l*** up."
24:50 Bethany, where he ***l*** his hands and
John
3:14 Just as Moses ***l*** up the snake in the
8:28 the Human One is ***l*** up, then you will
12:32 When I am ***l*** up from the earth, I will
12:34 Human One must be ***l*** up? Who is this
Acts
1:9 watching, he was ***l*** up and a cloud
4:24 listened, then ***l*** their voices in
10:26 But Peter ***l*** him up, saying, "Get up!

LIGHT → SEE THE LIGHT

Genesis
1:3 Let there be ***l***." And so light
Exodus
10:23 Israelites all had ***l*** where they lived.
13:21 to give them ***l***. This way they
25:37 they direct their ***l*** in front of the
27:20 olives for the ***l*** so that the lamp
35:8 the oil for the ***l***; spices for the
35:14 the lampstand for ***l*** with its equipment
35:28 and oil for ***l*** and for the
39:37 its equipment, and the oil for the ***l***,
Leviticus
1:7 the priest will ***l*** the altar and lay
24:2 lamp, to keep a ***l*** burning
Numbers
4:9 used for ***l***, its lamps, its
8:2 lamps will give ***l*** in front of the
Deuteronomy
4:1 Now, Israel, in ***l*** of all that, listen
10:12 Now in ***l*** of all that, Israel, what does
25:13 in your bag, a heavy one and a ***l*** one.
31:19 So in ***l*** of all that, you must write
Judges
16:2 kill him at the first ***l*** in the morning.
1 Samuel
29:10 morning and leave as soon as it is ***l***."
2 Samuel
12:12 before all Israel in the ***l*** of day."
23:4 is like the ***l*** of sunrise on a morning
2 Chronicles
13:11 At night they ***l*** the lamps on the
Esther
8:16 it was a day of ***l***, happiness, joy,
Job
3:4 above ignore it, and ***l*** not shine on it.
3:9 wait in vain for ***l***; may it not see
3:16 infant, like babies who never see ***l***?

3:20 Why is **l** given to the hard worker, life
3:23 Why is **l** given to the person whose way
10:22 a land whose **l** is like gloom, utter
12:22 makes utter darkness enter the **l**;
12:25 the dark without **l**; he makes them
17:12 night into day; **l** is near because
18:5 To be sure, the **l** of the wicked goes
18:6 The **l** in their tent becomes dark, and
18:18 are thrust from **l** into darkness,
22:28 it will stand; **l** will shine on
24:13 rebel against **l**, don't
24:16 in by day; they don't know the **l**.
25:3 counted? On whom does his **l** not rise?
26:10 at the limit of **l** and darkness.
28:11 of rivers; hidden things come to **l**.
29:3 my head, I walked by his **l** in the dark;
30:26 came; I expected **l**, but gloom
33:28 into the pit; my life beholds **l**."
33:30 from the pit, to shine with life's **l**.
37:22 comes golden **l**, the awesome
38:15 **L** is withheld from the wicked, the
38:19 the place where **l** dwells; darkness,
38:24 the place where **l** is divided up;
41:18 emit flashes of **l**; his eyes are

Psalms
4:6 anywhere. The **l** of your face has
19:8 are pure, giving **l** to the eyes.
21:9 LORD, you will **l** them up like an
27:1 The LORD is my **l** and my salvation.
36:9 of life. In your **l**, we see light.
38:10 me. Even the **l** of my eyes is
43:3 Send your **l** and truth—those will
44:3 your arm, and the **l** of your face
56:13 I can walk before God in the **l** of life.
76:4 are ablaze with **l**, mightier than
89:15 They walk in the **l** of your presence,
90:8 hidden faults in the **l** from your face.
97:11 **L** is planted like seed for the
104:2 You wear **l** like a robe; you open the
105:39 gave lightning to provide **l** at night.
118:27 He has shined a **l** on us! So lead
119:105 before my feet and a **l** for my journey.
119:130 your words gives **l**, giving simple
119:147 meet the predawn **l** and cry for help.
139:11 hide me; the **l** will become night
139:12 darkness is the same as **l** to you!

Proverbs
4:18 is like morning **l** that gets
6:23 and instruction a **l**; corrective
13:9 The **l** of the righteous rejoices, but
16:15 life in the **l** of the king's
29:13 the LORD gives **l** to the eyes of

Ecclesiastes
2:13 than folly, as **l** is more
11:7 Sweet is the **l**, and it's pleasant for
12:2 the sun and the **l** grow dark, the

Isaiah
2:5 of Jacob, let's walk by the LORD's **l**.
4:5 and smoke and the **l** of a blazing fire
5:20 darkness as **l** and light as
9:2 have seen a great **l**. On those living
10:17 The **l** of Israel will become a fire, its
13:10 won't show their **l**. The sun will be
26:19 is a shadow of **l**, but you will
30:26 The **l** of the moon will be like the
42:6 to the people, as a **l** to the nations,
42:16 before them into **l** and rough places
45:7 I form **l** and create darkness, make
49:6 appoint you as **l** to the nations so
50:10 and has no **l**? They will trust
50:11 Walk by the **l** of your fire, by
51:4 me, my justice, as a **l** to the nations.
53:11 he will see **l**, and he will be
58:8 Then your **l** will break out like the
58:10 afflicted, your **l** will shine in the
59:9 reach. We expect **l**, and there is
60:1 Shine! Your **l** has come; the
60:3 will come to your **l** and kings to your dawning radiance
60:19 no longer be your **l** by day, nor will
60:20 be an everlasting **l** for you, and your
62:1 shines out like a **l**, and her

Jeremiah
4:23 at the heavens and there was no **l**.
7:18 wood, the fathers **l** the fire, and the
13:16 you will hope for **l**, only to find
31:35 the sun to **l** up the day and

Lamentations
3:2 forced me to walk in darkness not **l**.

Ezekiel
21:24 your guilt to **l**, you will be
24:10 Pile on the wood, **l** the fire, and cook
32:7 and the moon won't radiate its **l**.

Daniel
2:22 hides in darkness; **l** lives with him!
2:31 with dazzling **l**, and was awesome
5:5 wall in the **l** of the lamp. The
5:12 mysteries. Now in **l** of all that,
6:19 the first sign of **l**, the king rose

Hosea
6:5 and my judgment goes forth like a **l**.

Joel
2:2 darkness and no **l**, a day of clouds

Amos
5:18 day of the LORD? It is darkness, not **l**;
5:20 darkness, not **l**; all dark with no

Micah
2:1 in bed. By the **l** of morning they
7:8 if I sit in darkness, the LORD is my **l**.
7:9 me out into the **l**; I will see by

Habakkuk
3:11 above. With the **l**, your arrows

Zechariah
14:6 there will be no **l**. Splendid things
14:7 but at evening time there will be **l**.

Matthew
4:16 have seen a great **l**, and a light has
5:14 You are the **l** of the world. A city on
5:15 Neither do people **l** a lamp and put it
5:16 way, let your **l** shine before
6:22 your whole body will be full of **l**.
6:23 If then the **l** in you is
10:27 tell in the **l**; and what you
11:30 is easy to bear, and my burden is **l**."
17:2 and his clothes became as white as **l**.
24:29 won't give its **l**. The stars will

Mark
13:24 dark,and the moon won't give its **l**.

Luke
1:79 to give **l** to those who are sitting in
2:32 It's a **l** for revelation to the Gentiles
8:17 be made known and brought to the **l**.
11:33 People don't **l** a lamp and then put it

11:34 body is full of ***l***. But when your
11:35 to it that the ***l*** in you isn't
11:36 body is full of ***l***—with no part dark
12:3 be heard in the ***l***, and whatever you
15:8 of them, won't ***l*** a lamp and sweep
16:8 than are people who belong to the ***l***.

John

1:4 and the life was the ***l*** for all people.
1:5 The ***l*** shines in the darkness, and the
1:7 concerning the ***l***, so that through
1:8 wasn't the ***l***, but his mission
1:9 The true ***l*** that shines on all people
1:10 The ***l*** was in the world, and the world
1:11 The ***l*** came to his own people, and his
3:19 for judgment: The ***l*** came into the
3:20 things hate the ***l*** and don't come to
3:21 comes to the ***l*** so that it can be
5:35 you were willing to celebrate in his ***l***.
8:12 saying, "I am the ***l*** of the world.
9:5 in the world, I am the ***l*** of the world."
11:10 stumble because the ***l*** isn't in them."
12:35 replied, "The ***l*** is with you for
12:36 as you have the ***l***, believe in the
12:46 I have come as a ***l*** into the world so

Acts

9:3 suddenly a ***l*** from heaven
12:7 appeared and a ***l*** shone in the
13:47 I have made you a ***l*** for the Gentiles,
22:6 suddenly a bright ***l*** from heaven
22:9 saw the ***l***, but they didn't
22:11 of that ***l***, so my companions
26:13 Agrippa, I saw a ***l*** from heaven
26:18 from darkness to ***l*** and from the
26:23 he would proclaim ***l*** both to my people
27:39 In the morning ***l*** they saw a bay with a

Romans

2:19 for the blind; a ***l*** to those who are
13:12 darkness and put on the weapons of ***l***.

1 Corinthians

4:5 in the dark to ***l***, and he will make
14:25 are brought to ***l***. When that

2 Corinthians

4:6 God said that ***l*** should shine out of the
6:14 relationship does ***l*** have with
11:14 disguises himself as an angel of ***l***.

Ephesians

1:18 will have enough ***l*** to see what is
5:8 but now you are ***l*** in the Lord, so
5:9 ***L*** produces fruit that consists of every
5:13 exposed to the ***l*** is revealed by
5:14 revealed by the ***l*** is light.

Colossians

1:12 inheritance, in ***l*** granted to God's

1 Thessalonians

5:5 are children of ***l*** and children of

1 Timothy

6:16 and lives in ***l*** that no one can

Hebrews

1:3 The Son is the ***l*** of God's glory and the
6:4 have seen the ***l***, tasted the
10:32 after you saw the ***l***. You stood your
12:5 child, don't make ***l*** of the Lord's

1 Peter

2:9 you out of darkness into his amazing ***l***.

1 John

1:5 to you: "God is ***l*** and there is no
1:7 if we live in the ***l*** in the same way
2:8 away and the true ***l*** already shines.
2:9 to be in the ***l*** while hating a
2:10 stays in the ***l***, and there is

Revelation

8:12 a third of its ***l***, and the night
18:1 was filled with ***l*** because of his
18:23 The ***l*** of a lamp will never shine among you again.
21:23 glory is its ***l***, and its lamp is
21:24 will walk by its ***l***, and the kings of
22:5 won't need the ***l*** of a lamp or the

LIGHTNING → COLUMN OF LIGHTNING

Exodus

9:23 and hail, and ***l*** struck the earth.
9:24 The hail and the ***l*** flashing in the
19:16 was thunder, ***l***, and a thick
19:18 down on it with ***l***. The smoke went
20:18 the thunder and ***l***, the sound of the
40:38 the day, with ***l*** in it at night,

Numbers

9:15 appeared with ***l*** over the dwelling.
9:16 it by day, appearing with ***l*** at night.

2 Samuel

22:15 he sent the ***l*** and whipped them

Job

36:30 how he spreads ***l*** across it and
36:32 He conceals ***l*** in his palms and orders
37:3 the whole sky, his ***l*** on earth's edges.
38:35 Can you send ***l*** so that it goes and then

Psalms

18:14 he sent the ***l*** and threw them
77:18 swirling storm; ***l*** lit up the whole
78:14 by day; by the ***l*** all through the
97:4 His ***l*** lights up the world; the earth
105:32 hail along with ***l*** flashes
105:39 a covering; gave ***l*** to provide light
135:7 earth. God makes ***l*** for the rain. God
144:6 Flash ***l*** and scatter the enemy! Shoot

Jeremiah

10:13 He sends the ***l*** with the rain,
51:16 earth. He makes ***l*** for the rain and

Ezekiel

1:13 them, and ***l*** flashed from the
1:14 looked like ***l*** streaking back
21:10 to flash like ***l***. Let's not
21:28 battle-ready, flashing like ***l***:

Daniel

10:6 like a flash of ***l***, and his eyes

Nahum

2:4 torches; they dart like bolts of ***l***.

Habakkuk

3:11 shoot, your spear at the flash of ***l***.

Zechariah

9:14 go forth like ***l***. The LORD God

Matthew

24:27 Just as the ***l*** flashes from the east to
28:3 his face was like ***l*** and his clothes

Luke

9:29 and his clothes flashed white like ***l***.
10:18 I saw Satan fall from heaven like ***l***.
17:24 that a flash of ***l*** lights up the sky

Revelation

4:5 the throne came ***l***, voices, and
8:5 thunder, voices, ***l***, and an
11:19 There were ***l***, voices, thunder,
16:18 There were ***l*** strikes, voices, and

LINEN

Genesis
41:42 he dressed him in ***l*** clothes, and he
Exodus
25:4 deep red yarns; fine ***l***; goats' hair;
26:1 of fine twisted ***l*** and blue, purple,
27:9 of fine twisted ***l*** stretching one
28:5 purple, and deep red yarns and fine ***l***.
35:6 deep red yarns; fine ***l***; goats' hair;
36:8 of fine twisted ***l*** and blue, purple,
38:9 of fine twisted ***l*** stretching one
38:23 and deep red yarns and in fine ***l***.
39:2 deep red yarns, and of fine twisted ***l***.
Leviticus
6:10 will dress in his ***l*** robe, with linen
13:47 on clothing—on wool or ***l*** clothing,
16:4 dress in a holy ***l*** tunic and wear
Deuteronomy
22:11 clothes that mix wool and ***l*** together.
Judges
14:12 give you thirty ***l*** robes and thirty
15:14 like burned-up ***l***, and the ties
1 Samuel
2:18 boy, clothed in a ***l*** priestly vest.
22:18 men who wore the ***l*** priestly vest
2 Samuel
6:14 dressed in a ***l*** priestly vest,
1 Chronicles
4:21 the clans of the ***l*** workers at Beth-as
15:27 David also wore a ***l*** priestly vest.
2 Chronicles
2:14 yarn, and fine ***l***. He can do any
3:14 out of fine ***l*** and violet,
5:12 dressed in fine ***l*** and stood east of
Esther
1:6 White ***l*** curtains and purple hangings
Proverbs
31:22 for herself; fine ***l*** and purple are
Isaiah
3:23 the mirrors and ***l*** garments; the turbans
Jeremiah
13:2 So I bought a ***l*** undergarment, as the
13:7 and I dug up the ***l*** undergarment from
Ezekiel
9:2 was dressed in ***l*** and had a writing
10:2 man clothed in ***l***: Go in between
16:10 your head in ***l***, and covered you
27:7 Fine embroidered ***l*** from Egypt was your
40:3 and he had a ***l*** cord and a
44:17 they will wear ***l*** garments. They
Daniel
10:5 a man clothed in ***l*** in front of me.
12:6 clothed in white ***l***, who was farther
Hosea
2:5 my wool and my ***l*** cloth, my oil and
2:9 my wool and my ***l*** cloth, which were
Matthew
27:59 body, wrapped it in a clean ***l*** cloth,
Mark
14:51 nothing but a ***l*** cloth. They
14:52 but he left the ***l*** cloth behind and ran
15:46 He bought a ***l*** cloth, took Jesus down
Luke
16:19 purple and fine ***l***, and who feasted
23:53 wrapped it in a ***l*** cloth and laid it
24:12 he saw only the ***l*** cloth. Then he
John
13:4 Picking up a ***l*** towel, he tied it
19:40 it, with the spices, in ***l*** cloths.
20:6 tomb and saw the ***l*** cloths lying
Acts
10:11 like a large ***l*** sheet being
Revelation
15:6 in pure bright ***l*** and had gold
18:12 and pearls; fine ***l***, purple, silk,
18:16 that wore fine ***l***, purple, and
19:8 fine, pure white ***l*** to wear, for the
19:14 wearing fine ***l*** that was white

LION

Genesis
49:9 crouches like a ***l***; like a lioness—
Numbers
23:24 a lioness, like a ***l*** it stands up. It
24:9 lay down like a ***l***; like a lioness,
Deuteronomy
33:20 He lives like a ***l***: he rips an arm,
33:22 Dan: "Dan is a ***l*** cub. He jumps up
Judges
14:5 a lone young ***l*** came roaring to
14:6 and he tore the ***l*** apart with his
14:18 stronger than a ***l***?" He replied to
1 Samuel
17:34 and if ever a ***l*** or a bear came
2 Samuel
23:20 a pit and killed a ***l*** on a snowy day.
1 Kings
13:24 departed, and a ***l*** found him on the
20:36 LORD's voice, a ***l*** will attack you
1 Chronicles
11:22 down into a pit where he killed a ***l***.
Job
4:10 The roar of a ***l*** and snarl of the king
4:11 the ***l*** perishes without prey, and its
10:16 boast like a ***l***, and you would
28:8 trodden on it; a ***l*** hasn't crossed
38:39 hunt prey for the ***l*** or fill the
Psalms
10:9 places, like a ***l*** in its lair. They
17:12 They are like a ***l*** eager to rip its
22:13 at me like a ***l*** ripping and
22:16 circle me like a ***l***—oh, my poor hand
22:21 the mouth of the ***l***. From the horns
Proverbs
19:12 king roars like a ***l***; his favor is
22:13 says, "There's a ***l*** in the street!
26:13 says,"There's a ***l*** in the path! A
28:1 the righteous are as confident as a ***l***.
28:15 like a growling ***l*** or a prowling
30:30 a ***l***, a warrior among beasts, which
Ecclesiastes
9:4 is definitely better off than a dead ***l***,
Isaiah
5:29 is like the ***l***; they roar like
11:6 and the young ***l*** will feed
15:9 upon Dibon: a ***l*** for Moab's
30:6 and roaring ***l***, viper and flying
31:4 to me: When the ***l*** growls, the young
35:9 no ***l*** will be there, and no predator
38:13 morning: "Like a ***l*** God crushes all
65:25 together, and the ***l*** will eat straw
Jeremiah
2:30 devoured your prophets like a hungry ***l***.

4:7 A *l* bursts out of the thicket; a
5:6 Therefore, a *l* from the forest will
12:8 against me like a *l* in the forest;
25:38 The *l* is on the prowl, and the land is
49:19 Like a *l* coming up from the jungle of
50:44 Like a *l* coming up from the jungle of
Lamentations
3:10 a bear lurking for me, a *l* in hiding.
Ezekiel
10:14 third that of a *l*, and the fourth
19:3 a strong young *l*; he learned to
19:5 and set him up as a strong young *l*.
19:6 a strong young *l*. He learned to
22:25 is like a roaring *l* ripping up prey.
32:2 yourself a young *l* among the
41:19 and the face of a *l* turned toward
Daniel
7:4 first was like a *l* with eagle's
Hosea
5:14 I am like a *l* to Ephraim, like a young
11:10 who roars like a *l*. When he roars,
13:7 become like a *l* to them; like a
Amos
3:4 Does a *l* roar in the forest, when it
3:8 A *l* has roared; who will not fear? The
3:12 the mouth of the *l*, so will the
5:19 fled from a *l*, and was met by a
Micah
5:8 peoples, like a *l* among the
Nahum
2:11 lions, where *l*, lioness, even
2:12 The *l* has torn enough prey for his cubs
1 Peter
5:8 like a roaring *l*, seeking someone
Revelation
4:7 was like a *l*. The second
5:5 weep. Look! The *L* of the tribe of
10:3 loud voice like a *l* roaring, and when

LIONS

1 Samuel
17:36 has fought both *l* and bears. This
2 Samuel
1:23 faster than eagles, stronger than *l*!
1 Kings
7:29 *L*, bulls, and winged otherworldly
10:20 Another twelve *l* stood on both sides of
2 Kings
17:25 so the LORD sent *l* against them, and
17:26 god. He's sent *l* against them, and
1 Chronicles
12:8 who looked like *l* and who were
2 Chronicles
9:19 Another twelve *l* stood on both sides of
Job
4:10 yet the teeth of *l* are shattered;
Psalms
34:10 Even strong young *l* go without and get
35:17 precious life from these predatory *l*!
57:4 of a pack of *l*. I lie down among
91:13 march on top of *l* and vipers;
104:21 The young *l* roar for their prey,
Isaiah
5:29 roar like young *l*; they growl,
Jeremiah
2:15 *L* roar at him; they growl. They destroy
50:17 driven away by *l*. First the king
51:38 Like *l* they will roar together; they
Ezekiel
19:2 the strong young *l* and reared her
19:6 with the other *l* and became a
Daniel
6:7 will be thrown into a pit of *l*.
Nahum
2:11 of the young *l*, where lion,
2:13 devour your young *l*; I will cut off
Zephaniah
3:3 midst are roaring *l*. Her judges are
Zechariah
11:3 among the young *l* because the pride
Hebrews
11:33 promises, shut the mouths of *l*,

LIPS

1 Samuel
1:13 in her heart; her *l* were moving, but
Job
2:10 In all this, Job didn't sin with his *l*.
8:21 with joy, your *l* with a victorious
11:5 God would speak, open his *l* against you
13:6 pay attention to the arguments of my *l*.
15:6 you, not I; your *l* argue against you.
16:5 my trembling *l* would be held in
23:12 from his *l* and not departed,
27:4 my *l* will utter no wickedness; my
32:20 relief; I will open my *l* and respond.
33:3 heart; my *l* speak knowledge
Psalms
12:3 all slick-talking *l* and every tongue
12:4 get the best of us with *l* like ours?"
16:4 I won't let their names cross my *l*.
17:1 it's spoken by *l* that don't lie!
17:4 ways by the command from your *l*.
21:2 denied what his *l* requested. Selah
31:18 Let their lying *l* be shut up whenever
34:13 and keep your *l* from speaking
45:2 out on your *l*. No wonder God
51:15 Lord, open my *l*, and my mouth will
59:7 are between their *l*! Who can listen
63:3 My *l* praise you because your faithful
63:5 mouth speaks praise with joy on my *l*—
66:14 the ones my *l* uttered, the ones my
71:23 My *l* will rejoice aloud when I make
89:34 I won't renege on what crossed my *l*.
106:33 so that he spoke rashly with his *l*.
119:171 Let my *l* overflow with praise because
120:2 me from lying *l* and a dishonest
140:3 spider poison is on their *l*. Selah
140:9 with the trouble their own *l* caused!
141:3 close watch over the door that is my *l*.
Proverbs
4:24 mouth; keep devious *l* far from you.
5:2 and your *l* might guard
5:3 The *l* of a mysterious woman drip honey,
8:6 correct; from my *l* come what is
8:7 the truth; my *l* despise
10:13 is found on the *l* of those who have
10:18 Lying *l* conceal hate, and those who
10:19 but the wise restrain their *l*.
10:21 The *l* of the righteous nourish many
12:13 of their *l*, but the
12:19 Truthful *l* endure forever, but a lying
12:22 detests false *l*; he favors those

13:3 but those who open their ***l*** are ruined.
14:3 a fool, but the ***l*** of the wise
15:7 The ***l*** of the wise spread knowledge, but
16:13 with righteous ***l***; they love words
16:23 and enhances the teaching of their ***l***.
16:27 up trouble; their ***l*** are like a
16:30 those who purse their ***l*** plan evil.
17:4 to guilty ***l***; a liar listens
17:28 wise; those who shut their ***l*** are smart.
18:6 The ***l*** of fools make accusations; their
18:7 their ruin; their ***l*** are a trap for
18:20 the mouth; one's ***l*** can earn a
19:1 than to have dishonest ***l*** and be a fool.
22:18 you, if you have them ready on your ***l***.
23:16 rejoice when your ***l*** speak with
24:2 violence, and their ***l*** speak of trouble.
24:26 are like those who kiss on the ***l***.
24:28 reason; don't deceive with your ***l***.
26:23 Smooth ***l*** and an evil heart are like
26:24 with their ***l***, keeping their
27:2 mouth; a stranger, and not your own ***l***.

Ecclesiastes
10:12 but fools are devoured by their own ***l***.

Song of Songs
4:3 ribbon are your ***l***; when you smile,
4:11 drops from your ***l***, my bride; honey
5:13 of spices. His ***l*** are lilies
7:9 love, gliding through the ***l*** and teeth.

Isaiah
6:5 man with unclean ***l***, and I live among
6:7 has touched your ***l***. Your guilt has
11:4 the breath of his ***l*** he will kill the
30:27 thick. His ***l*** are full of fury;
59:3 with guilt. Your ***l*** speak lies; your

Jeremiah
7:28 it has vanished from their ***l***.
12:2 always on their ***l*** but far from

Daniel
10:3 wine passed my ***l***, and I didn't
10:16 being touched my ***l***. Then I opened my

Hosea
8:1 a trumpet to your ***l***! It's as if a

Micah
3:7 cover their upper ***l***, for there will

Habakkuk
3:16 tremble. My ***l*** quiver at the

Zephaniah
3:13 be found on their ***l***. They will graze

Malachi
2:6 found on his ***l***. He walked with
2:7 The ***l*** of the priest should guard

Matthew
15:8 me with their ***l***, but their hearts

Mark
7:6 me with their ***l***, but their hearts

Luke
4:22 flowing from his ***l***. They said, "This
22:71 We've heard it from his own ***l***."

John
19:29 hyssop branch, and held it up to his ***l***.

Romans
3:13 the poison of vipers is under their ***l***.

1 Corinthians
14:21 and foreigners' ***l***, but they will

Hebrews
13:15 fruit from our ***l*** that confess his

1 Peter
3:10 and their ***l*** from speaking

LISTEN

Exodus
6:9 But they didn't ***l*** to Moses, because
6:30 How is Pharaoh ever going to ***l*** to me?"
9:12 Pharaoh wouldn't ***l*** to them, just as
16:20 But they didn't ***l*** to Moses. Some kept
23:22 But if you ***l*** carefully to what he says

Numbers
9:8 Wait while I ***l*** for what the LORD
12:6 He said, "***L*** to my words: If there is a
16:8 Moses said to Korah, "***L***, you Levites
20:10 He said to them, "***L***, you rebels!
23:18 Balak, and ***l***; hear me out,

Deuteronomy
1:43 but you wouldn't ***l***. You disobeyed
5:1 to them: "Israel! ***L*** to the
6:4 Israel, ***l***! Our God is the LORD! Only

Joshua
3:9 Come close. ***L*** to the words of
24:10 wasn't willing to ***l*** to Balaam, so he

Judges
5:3 Hear, kings! ***L***, rulers! I, to the
9:7 and called out, "***L*** to me, you
11:28 king refused to ***l*** to the message
19:25 men refused to ***l*** to him. So the

1 Samuel
8:5 said to him, "***L***. You are old now,
8:19 people refused to ***l*** to Samuel and
9:6 boy said to him, "***L***, there's a man of
12:1 to all Israel: "***L***: I have done
13:3 the land and said, "Hebrews! ***L*** up!"
15:1 people Israel. ***L*** now to the LORD's
28:22 it's your turn to ***l*** to me, your

2 Samuel
12:18 David wouldn't ***l*** to us when we

1 Kings
3:17 Your Majesty, ***l***: This woman and I
8:30 ***L*** to the request of your servant and
8:32 then ***l*** from heaven, act, and decide
10:8 you and get to ***l*** to your wisdom
11:38 If you ***l*** to all that I command and walk

Nehemiah
4:4 ***L***, God; we are despised! Turn their
9:30 But they wouldn't ***l***, so you handed
13:27 Should we then ***l*** to you and do all this

Job
5:27 and so it is; ***l*** and find out for
13:17 ***L*** closely to my words so that my
15:8 Did you ***l*** in God's council; is wisdom
21:2 ***L*** carefully to my remarks and let that
32:10 I say: "***L*** to me; I'll state
33:1 But now, ***l*** to me, Job; pay attention to
36:11 If they ***l*** and serve, they spend their
36:12 But if they don't ***l***, they perish by
37:2 ***L*** closely to the rumble of his voice,
42:4 You said, "***L*** and I will speak; I will

Psalms
4:1 Have mercy on me! ***L*** to my prayer!
10:17 LORD, you ***l*** to the desires of those who
17:1 prayer of David.] ***L*** to what's right,
17:6 toward me now—***l*** to what I'm
27:7 LORD, ***l*** to my voice when I cry out—
28:2 ***L*** to my request for mercy when I cry

30:10 LORD, ***l*** and have mercy on me! LORD, be
31:2 ***L*** closely to me! Deliver me quickly; be
34:2 LORD—let the suffering ***l*** and rejoice.
34:11 Come, children, ***l*** to me. Let me teach
34:15 his ears ***l*** to their cries
39:12 my prayer, LORD! ***L*** closely to my cry
45:10 ***L***, daughter; pay attention, and listen
49:1 the Korahites.] ***L*** to this, all you
50:7 ***L***, my people, I will now speak;
54:2 Hear my prayer; ***l*** to the words of
55:1 of David.] God, ***l*** to my prayer;
59:7 between their lips! Who can ***l*** to them?
61:1 Of David.] God, ***l*** to my cry; pay
64:1 psalm of David.] ***L*** to me when I
65:2 you ***l*** to prayer—and all living things
66:16 Come close and ***l***, all you who honor
78:1 maskil of Asaph.] ***L***, my people, to my
80:1 of Israel, ***l***! You, the one who
81:8 ***L***, my people, I'm warning you! If only
81:11 people wouldn't ***l*** to my voice.
81:13 my people would ***l*** to me! How I wish
84:8 hear my prayer; ***l*** closely, Jacob's
86:1 of David.] LORD, ***l*** closely to me and
86:6 ***L*** closely to my prayer, LORD; pay close
95:7 If only you would ***l*** to his voice
102:2 time of trouble! ***L*** to me! Answer me
106:25 and wouldn't ***l*** to the LORD's
119:149 ***L*** to my voice, according to your
130:2 my Lord, ***l*** to my voice! Let your ears
135:17 but they can't ***l***. No, there's no
140:6 You are my God! ***L*** to my request for
141:1 to me—quickly! ***L*** to my voice when
143:1 psalm of David.] ***L*** to my prayer,

Proverbs

1:8 ***L***, my son, to your father's
4:10 ***L***, my son, and take in my speech, then
5:7 Now children ***l*** to me, and don't deviate
5:13 I didn't ***l*** to the voice of my
7:24 Now, children, ***l*** to me, and pay
8:6 ***L***, for I speak things that are
8:32 Now children, ***l*** to me: Happy are those
8:33 ***L*** to instruction, and be wise; don't
8:34 are those who ***l*** to me, watching
12:15 way as right, but the wise ***l*** to advice.
13:1 but a mocker doesn't ***l*** to correction.
15:32 but those who ***l*** to correction
18:13 before they ***l*** are foolish and
19:20 ***L*** to advice and accept instruction, so
23:19 ***L***, my child, and be wise! Keep your
23:22 ***L*** to your father, who gave you life;

Ecclesiastes

5:1 acceptable to ***l*** than to offer the
7:5 the wise than to ***l*** to the song of

Song of Songs

2:8 ***L***! It's my lover: here he comes now,

Isaiah

1:2 you heavens, and ***l*** earth, for the
7:13 Isaiah said, "***L***, house of David!
13:4 ***L***! A roar on the mountains like that
46:12 ***L*** to me, you bullheaded people who are
66:5 ***L*** to the LORD's word, you who tremble

Jeremiah

2:4 ***L*** to the LORD's word, people of Judah,
2:31 this generation, ***l*** closely to the
5:21 ***L***, you foolish and senseless people

Lamentations

1:18 his word. ***L***, all you people;

Ezekiel

2:8 you, human one, ***l*** to what I say to
3:10 to me: Human one, ***l*** closely, and take
33:31 my people. They ***l*** to your words,
44:5 eyes and ears and ***l*** to all that I say

Daniel

5:18 ***L***, Your Majesty: The Most High God
9:10 We didn't ***l*** to the voice of the LORD
9:19 My Lord, ***l***! My Lord, forgive! My Lord,

Hosea

4:4 no one complain. ***L***, priest, I am
5:1 house of Israel! ***L***, house of the

Amos

5:23 songs; I won't ***l*** to the melody of

Micah

1:2 ***L***, all you peoples! Pay attention,

Habakkuk

1:2 help and you not ***l***? I cry out to

Zechariah

1:4 But they didn't ***l***; they didn't draw
3:8 Now ***l***, High Priest Joshua, you and
7:13 and they didn't ***l***, when they

Malachi

2:2 If you don't ***l***, or don't intend to

Matthew

10:14 to welcome you or ***l*** to your words,
15:10 and said to them, "***L*** and understand.
17:5 I am very pleased with him. ***L*** to him!"
18:15 together. If they ***l*** to you, then
18:16 But if they won't ***l***, take with you one
21:33 ***L*** to another parable. There was a

Mark

4:9 has ears to ***l*** should pay
4:24 He said to them, "***L*** carefully! God will
6:11 welcome you or ***l*** to you, as you
7:14 again and said, "***L*** to me, all of
9:7 my Son, whom I dearly love. ***L*** to him!"
12:29 one is Israel, ***l***! Our God is the

Luke

2:48 us like this? ***L***! Your father and
5:15 gathered to ***l*** and to be healed
8:18 Therefore, ***l*** carefully. Those who have
8:21 are those who ***l*** to God's word and
9:35 is my Son, my chosen one. ***L*** to him!"
15:1 gathering around Jesus to ***l*** to him.
16:29 and the Prophets. They must ***l*** to them.'
16:31 If they don't ***l*** to Moses and the
18:6 The Lord said, "***L*** to what the unjust

John

8:47 God's children ***l*** to God's words. You
9:27 and you didn't ***l***. Why do you want
9:31 that God doesn't ***l*** to sinners. God
10:3 and the sheep ***l*** to his voice. He

Acts

2:14 Know this! ***L*** carefully to my
2:22 Israelites, ***l*** to these words!
3:22 prophet like me. ***L*** to whatever he
3:23 Whoever doesn't ***l*** to that prophet will
7:2 and fathers, ***l*** to me. Our
10:33 of God to ***l*** to everything the
13:11 ***L***! The Lord's power is set against
13:16 God-worshippers, please ***l*** to me.
15:13 responded, "Fellow believers, ***l*** to me.
22:1 and fathers, ***l*** now to my

24:4 so I ask that you ***l*** with your usual
26:3 I ask you to ***l*** to me patiently.
28:28 sent to the Gentiles. They will ***l***!"
1 Corinthians
14:21 will not even ***l*** to me this way,
15:51 ***L***, I'm telling you a secret: all of us
Galatians
4:21 under the Law—don't you ***l*** to the Law?
1 Timothy
1:19 they refused to ***l*** to their
Hebrews
12:25 they refused to ***l*** to the one who
James
1:19 be quick to ***l***, slow to speak,
1:25 do it. They don't ***l*** and then forget,
2:5 and sisters, ***l***! Hasn't God
5:4 ***L***! Hear the cries of the wages of your
1 John
4:6 from God doesn't ***l*** to us. This is
Revelation
1:3 are those who ***l*** to it being read,
2:7 If you can hear, ***l*** to what the Spirit
13:9 Whoever has ears must ***l***
Malachi
3:16 attention and ***l*** to them. Then a
Mark
12:37 The large crowd ***l*** to him with
Luke
10:39 the Lord's feet and ***l*** to his message.
19:11 As they ***l*** to this, Jesus told them
John
6:45 Everyone who has ***l*** to the Father and
Acts
4:24 They ***l***, then lifted their voices in
15:12 quiet as they ***l*** to Barnabas and
16:14 cloth. As she ***l***, the Lord enabled
19:5 After they ***l*** to Paul, they were
22:22 The crowd ***l*** to Paul until he said this.
24:24 summoned Paul. He ***l*** to him talk about
2 Corinthians
6:2 He says, I ***l*** to you at the right time,
Ephesians
4:21 Since you really ***l*** to him and you were
Hebrews
4:2 in faith with the ones who ***l*** to it.

LISTENED

Genesis
3:17 Because you ***l*** to your wife's
Exodus
6:12 haven't even ***l*** to me. How can I
7:16 desert. Up to now you still haven't ***l***.
18:24 Moses ***l*** to his father-in-law's
Numbers
14:22 ten times and haven't ***l*** to my voice,
Deuteronomy
9:19 However, the LORD ***l*** to me again in
10:10 And the LORD ***l*** to me again in
1 Samuel
8:21 Samuel ***l*** to everything the people said
1 Kings
17:22 The LORD, ***l*** to Elijah's voice and gave
Nehemiah
8:3 and everyone ***l*** attentively to
Job
29:21 People ***l*** to me and waited, were silent
32:11 while you spoke, ***l*** while you
Psalms
6:9 The LORD has ***l*** to my request. The LORD
22:24 from me. No, he ***l*** when I cried out
28:6 because he has ***l*** to my request for
34:6 out: the LORD ***l*** and saved him
40:1 down to me; he ***l*** to my cry for
66:18 in my heart, my Lord would not have ***l***.
66:19 God definitely ***l***. He heard the
Ecclesiastes
12:9 knowledge. He ***l*** and investigated.
Jeremiah
7:13 you haven't ***l*** when I spoke to
8:6 I have ***l*** carefully but haven't heard a
25:8 because you haven't ***l*** to my words,
35:16 but this people have not ***l*** to me.
Hosea
9:17 they haven't ***l*** to him, my God
Zephaniah
3:2 She ***l*** to no voice; she accepted no
Haggai
1:12 among the people, ***l*** to the voice of

LISTENING

1 Samuel
3:9 Your servant is ***l***.'" So Samuel went
3:10 said, "Speak. Your servant is ***l***."
Psalms
145:19 who honor him, ***l*** to their cries
Proverbs
19:27 child, you stop ***l*** to discipline,
Song of Songs
8:13 my companions are ***l*** for your voice.
Jeremiah
13:10 Instead of ***l*** to me, this wicked people
22:21 your youth: not ***l*** to a word I say.
Zechariah
7:11 turned a cold shoulder and stopped ***l***.
Mark
6:20 Herod, yet he enjoyed ***l*** to him.
Luke
2:46 the teachers, ***l*** to them and
Acts
16:25 and the other prisoners were ***l*** to them.
17:21 talking about or ***l*** to the newest
18:8 and were baptized after ***l*** to Paul.
26:29 also all who are ***l*** to me today will
Romans
10:17 faith comes from ***l***, but it's
Hebrews
5:11 have been lazy and you have't been ***l***.

LISTENS

Psalms
34:17 cry out, the LORD ***l***; he delivers them
69:33 because the LORD ***l*** to the needy and
116:2 as I live because he ***l*** closely to me.
Proverbs
13:1 A wise son ***l*** to the discipline of his
15:29 wicked, but he ***l*** to the prayers of
15:31 The ear that ***l*** to life-giving
17:4 lips; a liar ***l*** to a destructive
21:28 but one who ***l*** will testify
25:12 to an ear that ***l*** is like a gold
29:12 If a ruler ***l*** to lies, those who serve
Ecclesiastes
4:13 king, who no longer ***l*** to advice.

Isaiah
50:10 the LORD? Who ***l*** to the voice of
Luke
10:16 Whoever ***l*** to you listens to me.
John
9:31 to sinners. God ***l*** to anyone who is
18:37 accepts the truth ***l*** to my voice."
1 John
4:5 point of view and the world ***l*** to them.
4:6 who knows God ***l*** to us. Whoever is
5:15 we know that he ***l*** to whatever we

LITTLE

Psalms
37:16 Better is the ***l*** that the righteous have
68:27 them, though he's ***l***; then the princes
Proverbs
6:10 A ***l*** sleep, a little slumber, a little
15:16 Better a ***l*** with fear of the LORD than a
16:8 Better a ***l*** with righteousness than
24:33 A ***l*** sleep, a little slumber,a little
Ecclesiastes
5:12 there's a lot or ***l*** to eat; but the
10:1 oil, so a ***l*** folly outweighs
Song of Songs
1:8 and graze your ***l*** goats by the
2:15 for us—those ***l*** foxes that spoil
Isaiah
11:6 together, and a ***l*** child will lead
28:10 qav leqav," a ***l*** of this, a little
Obadiah
1:2 will make you of ***l*** importance among
Zechariah
4:10 despise a time of ***l*** things will
13:7 I will turn my hand against the ***l*** ones.
Matthew
9:24 away, because the ***l*** girl isn't dead
10:42 water to these ***l*** ones because they
17:20 Because you have ***l*** faith," he said. "I
18:2 Then he called a ***l*** child over to sit
18:14 want to lose one of these ***l*** ones.
25:21 faithful over a ***l***. I'll put you in
Mark
9:36 reached for a ***l*** child, placed him
9:42 causes these ***l*** ones who believe
Luke
7:47 one who is forgiven ***l*** loves little."
9:47 Jesus took a ***l*** child and had the
12:32 Don't be afraid, ***l*** flock, because your
16:10 is faithful with ***l*** is also faithful
17:2 one of these ***l*** ones to trip and
John
6:7 for each person to have even a ***l*** bit."
7:33 with you for a ***l*** while before I go
12:35 you for only a ***l*** while. Walk while
13:33 ***L*** children, I'm with you for a little
2 Corinthians
8:15 who gathered less didn't have too ***l***.
Galatians
4:19 My ***l*** children, I'm going through labor
5:9 A ***l*** yeast works through the whole lump
1 Timothy
5:23 anymore but use a ***l*** wine because of
James
3:4 wherever they want with a ***l*** rudder.
1 John
2:1 My ***l*** children, I'm writing these things
3:7 ***L*** children, make sure no one deceives
4:4 You are from God, ***l*** children, and you
5:21 ***L*** children, guard yourselves from
Revelation
3:8 shut. You have so ***l*** power, and yet
6:11 told to rest a ***l*** longer, until
20:3 this he must be released for a ***l*** while.

LIVE → LIVE FOREVER

Genesis
2:1 earth and all who ***l*** in them were
3:22 tree of life and eat and ***l*** forever,"
12:10 toward Egypt to ***l*** as an immigrant
27:40 You will ***l*** by your sword; you will
47:6 Let them ***l*** in the land of
Exodus
1:16 But if it's a girl, you can let her ***l***."
2:21 to come and ***l*** with the man, who
22:18 Don't allow a female sorcerer to ***l***
34:15 with those who ***l*** in the land. When
Leviticus
3:17 wherever you ***l***: you must not eat
7:26 or animal blood—wherever you may ***l***.
11:46 creatures that ***l*** in water, and all
13:46 They must ***l*** alone outside the
14:8 but they must ***l*** outside their
16:20 he will bring forward the ***l*** goat.
17:8 immigrants who ***l*** with you who
20:22 where you will ***l***, won't vomit you
Numbers
21:8 is bitten can look at it and ***l***."
21:9 could look at the bronze snake and ***l***.
Deuteronomy
4:1 so that you may ***l***, enter, and
8:3 that people don't ***l*** on bread alone.
30:6 all your being in order that you may ***l***.
Judges
1:27 were determined to ***l*** in that land.
1 Samuel
10:24 the people shouted, "Long ***l*** the king!"
2 Samuel
7:5 one to build the temple for me to ***l*** in.
Esther
4:11 gold scepter may ***l***. In my case, I
9:19 is why Jews who ***l*** in villages make
Job
7:16 I don't want to ***l*** long; leave me
21:7 Why do the wicked ***l***, grow old, and
36:6 let the wicked ***l***, but grants
Psalms
4:8 you alone, LORD, let me ***l*** in safety.
5:4 wickedness; evil doesn't ***l*** with you.
15:1 David.] Who can ***l*** in your tent,
22:26 him! I pray your hearts ***l*** forever!
23:6 life, and I will ***l*** in the LORD's
25:13 They will ***l*** a good life, and their
27:4 all I seek—to ***l*** in the LORD's
33:14 place God observes all who ***l*** on earth.
37:3 LORD and do good; ***l*** in the land, and
37:27 Then you will ***l*** in the land
37:29 the land; they will ***l*** on it forever.
44:19 where jackals ***l***, covering us with
49:9 no one can ***l*** forever without
49:11 the place they ***l*** for all
49:12 People won't ***l*** any longer because of

55:7 so far away! I'd ***l*** in the desert.
55:10 walls, and evil and misery ***l*** inside it.
55:23 people not ***l*** out even half
61:4 Please let me ***l*** in your tent forever!
69:35 servants can ***l*** there and possess
72:5 Let the king ***l*** as long as the sun, as
74:21 let the oppressed ***l*** in shame. No, let
84:4 Those who ***l*** in your house are truly
85:9 so that his glory can ***l*** in our land.
90:10 We ***l*** at best to be seventy years old,
94:17 me, I would ***l*** instantly in
102:28 children ***l*** safe; let your
104:33 LORD as long as I ***l***; I will sing
107:36 They even build a city and ***l*** there!
116:2 him as long as I ***l*** because he
118:17 die—no, I will ***l*** and declare what
119:25 dirt. Now make me ***l*** again according
132:14 forever. I will ***l*** here because I
133:1 it is when families ***l*** together as one!
138:7 you make me ***l*** again; you send
140:13 who do right will ***l*** in your presence.
143:11 Make me ***l*** again, LORD, for your name's
146:2 sing praises to my God as long as I ***l***.

Proverbs
2:7 for those who ***l*** a blameless life.
3:2 will help you ***l*** a long time and
4:4 on to my words: Keep my commands and ***l***.
7:2 my commands and ***l***, and my
9:6 ways and ***l***; walk in the way
15:27 but those who hate bribes will ***l***.
20:7 The righteous ***l*** with integrity; happy
21:9 Better to ***l*** on the edge of a roof than
21:19 Better to ***l*** in a wilderness than in a
25:24 Better to ***l*** on the edge of a roof than
28:16 one who hates unjust gain will ***l*** long.

Ecclesiastes
3:12 and do what's good while they ***l***.
4:15 I saw all who ***l*** and walk under the sun
6:3 children and ***l*** a long life. But
6:6 who ***l*** a thousand years twice over but
7:15 the wicked may ***l*** long in spite of
8:12 crimes but still ***l*** long lives. But I
11:8 Even those who ***l*** many years should take pleasure

Isaiah
6:5 lips, and I ***l*** among a people
11:6 The wolf will ***l*** with the lamb, and the
26:19 Your dead will ***l***, their corpses will
55:3 and you will ***l***. I will make an

Lamentations
3:6 He made me ***l*** in dark places like those
4:20 we will ***l*** among the
4:21 Edom, you who ***l*** in the land of

Ezekiel
18:9 and they will ***l***, proclaims the
18:32 LORD God says. Change your ways, and ***l***!
37:3 can these bones ***l*** again?" I said,

Jonah
4:3 be better for me to die than to ***l***."

Habakkuk
2:4 the righteous person will ***l*** honestly.

Matthew
4:4 People won't ***l*** only by bread,
9:18 place your hand on her, and she'll ***l***."
24:45 right time to those who ***l*** in his house?

Mark
5:23 her so that she can be healed and ***l***."
12:44 she had, even what she needed to ***l*** on."

Luke
1:75 in God's eyes, for as long as we ***l***.
4:4 written, People won't ***l*** only by bread."
7:25 clothes and ***l*** in luxury are in
10:28 correctly. Do this and you will ***l***."
21:4 has given everything she had to ***l*** on."

John
5:25 Son, and those who hear it will ***l***.
6:51 this bread will ***l*** forever, and the
6:57 sent me, and I ***l*** because of the
6:58 eats this bread will ***l*** forever."
10:10 that they could ***l*** life to the
11:25 in me will ***l***, even though they
12:46 who believes in me won't ***l*** in darkness.
14:19 see me. Because I ***l***, you will live

Acts
2:26 Moreover, my body will ***l*** in hope,
7:4 resettle in this land where you now ***l***.
7:14 in all—and invited them to ***l*** with him.
7:48 Most High doesn't ***l*** in houses built
17:21 foreigners who ***l*** in Athens used to
17:24 earth. He doesn't ***l*** in temples made
17:26 human nation to ***l*** on the whole
17:28 In God we ***l***, move, and exist. As some
21:21 all the Jews who ***l*** among the
21:24 but that you too ***l*** a life in keeping
22:22 with this man! He's not fit to ***l***!"
28:4 the goddess Justice hasn't let him ***l***!"
28:16 was permitted to ***l*** by himself, with

Romans
1:17 The righteous person will ***l*** by faith.
6:8 faith that we will also ***l*** with him.
7:18 that good doesn't ***l*** in me—that is, in
8:4 Now the way we ***l*** is based on the
8:12 to ourselves to ***l*** our lives on the
8:13 If you ***l*** on the basis of selfishness,
10:5 who does these things will ***l*** by them.
12:18 of your ability, ***l*** at peace with all
13:13 as people who ***l*** in the day, not
14:7 We don't ***l*** for ourselves and we don't
14:8 If we ***l***, we live for the Lord, and if
14:11 is written, As I ***l***, says the Lord,

1 Corinthians
7:12 and she agrees to ***l*** with him, then he
8:6 through him, and we ***l*** through him.

2 Corinthians
5:2 We groan while we ***l*** in this residence.
5:7 We ***l*** by faith and not by sight
10:2 who think we ***l*** by human
10:3 Although we ***l*** in the world, we don't
12:18 did he? Didn't we ***l*** by the same
13:4 him, but we will ***l*** together with

Galatians
2:14 you're a Jew, ***l*** like a Gentile
2:19 so that I could ***l*** for God. I have
2:20 and I no longer ***l***, but Christ lives in
3:11 one will ***l*** on the basis of
3:12 one doing these things will ***l*** by them.
5:25 If we ***l*** by the Spirit, let's follow the

Ephesians
2:10 to be the way that we ***l*** our lives.
3:17 that Christ will ***l*** in your hearts
4:1 encourage you to ***l*** as people worthy
4:17 you shouldn't ***l*** your life like

5:2 **L** your life with love, following the
5:8 in the Lord, so **l** your life as
5:15 So be careful to **l** your life wisely,
6:3 you, and you will **l** for a long time

Philippians
1:20 now as always, whether I **l** or die.
1:22 If I continue to **l** in this world, I get
1:27 Most important, **l** together in a manner
2:13 and to actually **l** out his good
3:16 Only let's **l** in a way that is
3:17 watch those who **l** this way—you can
3:18 many people **l** as enemies of the

Colossians
1:10 so that you can **l** lives that are
1:19 of God was pleased to **l** in him,
2:6 So **l** in Christ Jesus the Lord in the
3:7 You used to **l** this way, when you were
3:16 of Christ must **l** in you richly.

1 Thessalonians
2:12 with you to **l** lives worthy of
4:1 better in how you **l** and please God—
4:11 Aim to **l** quietly, mind your own
5:10 or asleep, we will **l** together with him.
5:13 of their work. **L** in peace with

2 Thessalonians
2:7 hidden plan to **l** without any law

1 Timothy
1:9 for people who **l** without laws and
2:2 so that we can **l** a quiet and
4:15 these things, and **l** by them so that
5:6 who tries to **l** a life of luxury

2 Timothy
2:11 died together, we will also **l** together.
3:12 who wants to **l** a holy life in

Titus
2:12 us so that we can **l** sensible,

Hebrews
7:8 who continues to **l**, according to the
10:38 one will **l** by faith, and my
12:9 submit to the Father of spirits and **l**?
13:9 help those who **l** in this context.

James
4:15 wills, we will **l** and do this or

1 Peter
1:1 the diaspora, who **l** in Pontus,
1:18 **L** in this way, knowing that you were
2:12 **L** honorably among the unbelievers.
2:24 so that we might **l** in righteousness,
4:2 they don't **l** the rest of their
4:6 they could **l** by the Spirit

2 Peter
3:11 to be? You must **l** holy and godly

1 John
1:6 with him," and **l** in the darkness,
1:7 But if we **l** in the light in the same
2:6 in him ought to **l** in the same way
4:9 the world so that we can **l** through him.

2 John
1:3 will be ours who **l** in truth and love.
1:6 is love: that we **l** according to his

3 John
1:3 shown by how you **l** according to the

Revelation
3:10 world, to test those who **l** on earth.
6:10 was shed by those who **l** on earth?"
8:13 for those who **l** on earth because
11:10 Those who **l** on earth will rejoice over
13:8 All who **l** on earth worshipped it, all
13:12 and those who **l** in it worship the
13:14 those who **l** on earth by the
14:6 to those who **l** on earth, and to
17:2 and those who **l** on earth have
17:8 Those who **l** on earth, whose

LIVED

Joshua
24:7 Egyptians. You **l** in the desert for

Judges
3:5 So the Israelites **l** among the

Ruth
1:4 Ruth. And they **l** there for about
2:23 harvests. And she **l** with her mother-in

Ezra
4:6 against those who **l** in Judah and

Nehemiah
8:17 made booths and **l** in them. This was

Job
15:28 They **l** in ruined cities, unoccupied
29:25 sat as chief. I **l** like a king with
38:21 born then; you have **l** such a long time!
42:16 After this, Job **l** 140 years and saw

Psalms
18:23 I have **l** with integrity before him;
78:60 the tent where he had **l** with humans.
119:54 of praise wherever I **l** as an immigrant.
120:6 I've **l** far too long with people who

Ecclesiastes
8:10 those who had **l** honestly were
9:15 Now there **l** in that town a poor but

Isaiah
1:21 righteousness **l** in her—but now m

Jeremiah
35:10 We have **l** in tents and done everything

Daniel
4:12 All living things **l** off that tree.
5:21 an animal's. He **l** with wild

Matthew
4:16 the people who **l** in the dark have seen
5:21 said to those who **l** long ago, Don't
5:33 said to those who **l** long ago: Don't
14:35 the people who **l** in that place
23:30 say, 'If we had **l** in our ancestors'

Mark
5:3 This man **l** among the tombs, and no one

Luke
2:36 she married, she **l** with her husband
8:27 long time, he had **l** among the tombs,

Acts
1:21 whole time the Lord Jesus **l** among us,

Romans
14:9 Christ died and **l**: so that he might

2 Timothy
1:5 which first **l** in your

Hebrews
11:9 By faith he **l** in the land he had been

James
5:5 You have **l** a self-satisfying life on

2 Peter
2:8 righteous man **l** among them he

1 John
2:6 ought to live in the same way as he **l**.

Jude
1:14 Enoch, who **l** seven generations after

LIVES → CHANGE THEIR HEARTS AND LIVES, CHANGE YOUR HEARTS AND LIVES, CHANGED THEIR HEARTS AND LIVES, SAVE THEIR LIVES

Genesis
3:20 she is the mother of everyone who ***l***.
9:3 Everything that ***l*** and moves will be
19:17 said, "Save your ***l***! Don't look back!

Exodus
1:14 They made their ***l*** miserable with hard

Leviticus
16:29 or the immigrant who ***l*** among you.
17:11 for your ***l*** on the altar,
18:26 citizen nor immigrant who ***l*** with you
19:34 Any immigrant who ***l*** with you must be

Numbers
11:6 Now our ***l*** are wasting away. There is
15:14 If an immigrant ***l*** with you or has
16:38 and lost their ***l*** into thin plates
19:10 and for the immigrant who ***l*** among them.

Deuteronomy
4:10 day of their ***l*** on the fertile
4:18 the earth, or a fish that ***l*** in the sea.
12:18 the Levite who ***l*** in your city.

Ruth
3:13 then—as the LORD ***l***—I myself will red

Job
2:4 they have in exchange for their ***l***.
27:2 As God ***l***, who rejected my legal claim,

Psalms
9:11 to the LORD, who ***l*** in Zion! Proclaim
15:2 The person who ***l*** free of blame, does
18:46 The LORD ***l***! Bless God, my rock! Let
22:29 before him; my being also ***l*** for him.
33:19 to deliver their ***l*** from death and keep
34:22 his servants' ***l***; all those who
37:18 with the ***l*** of the blameless;
49:18 during their ***l***, and even thank
55:11 Disaster ***l*** inside it; oppression and
72:13 he saves the ***l*** of those who are
74:19 Don't forget the ***l*** of your afflicted
78:50 but delivered their ***l*** over to disease.
89:48 Who ***l*** their life without seeing death?
94:21 up against the ***l*** of the righteous.
97:10 God guards the ***l*** of his faithful
107:5 thirsty; their ***l*** were slipping
135:21 bless the one who ***l*** in Jerusalem!

Proverbs
1:18 they lie in wait for their own ***l***.
1:19 unjust gain; it costs them their ***l***.
3:29 neighbor who trusts and ***l*** near you.
11:30 a tree of life, and the wise gather ***l***.
13:3 guard their ***l***, but those who
14:25 witness saves ***l***, but a deceiver
16:17 who protect their path guard their ***l***.
18:7 their lips are a trap for their ***l***.
19:16 preserve their ***l***; those who
22:5 who guard their ***l*** keep their
29:10 and they seek the ***l*** of the virtuous.

Ecclesiastes
5:20 the days of their ***l*** because God gives
7:9 because anger ***l*** in the fool's
7:12 preserves the ***l*** of its possessors.
8:12 still live long ***l***. But I also know

Isaiah
1:27 who change their ***l*** by righteousness.
8:18 heavenly forces, who ***l*** on Mount Zion.
33:5 is exalted; he ***l*** on high, filling
38:20 the LORD's house all the days of our ***l***.
57:15 lifted up, who ***l*** forever, whose

Jeremiah
10:23 LORD, that our ***l*** are not our own,
12:16 As the LORD ***l***," just as they
51:45 Run for your ***l*** from the LORD's

Hosea
4:15 and don't swear, "As the LORD ***l***."

Amos
8:14 say, "As your god ***l***, Dan," and, "As

Matthew
5:10 are people whose ***l*** are harassed
10:39 who find their ***l*** will lose them,
16:25 to save their ***l*** will lose them.
16:26 but lose their ***l***? What will people
18:3 don't turn your ***l*** around and become

Mark
4:12 might turn their ***l*** around and be
8:36 gain the whole world but lose their ***l***?
8:37 people give in exchange for their ***l***?

Luke
8:14 go about their ***l***, are choked by
9:25 themselves yet perish or lose their ***l***?
12:1 mismatch between their hearts and ***l***.
13:4 than everyone else who ***l*** in Jerusalem?
21:19 By holding fast, you will gain your ***l***
21:35 upon everyone who ***l*** on the face of

John
4:50 home. Your son ***l***." The man
4:51 to meet him. They said, "Your son ***l***!"
4:53 to him, "Your son ***l***." And he and his
6:57 so whoever eats me ***l*** because of me.
11:26 Everyone who ***l*** and believes in me will
12:25 who love their ***l*** will lose them,
12:36 people whose ***l*** are determined by
12:40 and turn their ***l*** around
14:17 him, because he ***l*** with you and will

Acts
13:24 they were changing their hearts and ***l***.
13:52 Spirit in their ***l***, the disciples
15:26 devoted their ***l*** to the name of
27:22 Not one of your ***l*** will be lost,

Romans
6:10 his death, but he ***l*** for God with his
6:19 righteousness, which makes your ***l*** holy.
7:1 someone only as long as he or she ***l***?
7:17 Instead, it's sin that ***l*** in me.
8:5 People whose ***l*** are based on selfishness
8:11 from the dead ***l*** in you, the one
8:12 to live our ***l*** on the basis of

1 Corinthians
2:11 own spirit that ***l*** in them? In the
3:16 God's temple and God's Spirit ***l*** in you?

2 Corinthians
12:21 their hearts and ***l*** from what they
13:4 weakness, but he ***l*** by the power of

Galatians
2:20 live, but Christ ***l*** in me. And the

Ephesians
2:2 in persons whose ***l*** are characterized
2:10 to be the way that we live our ***l***.
2:22 a place where God ***l*** through the
4:17 They base their ***l*** on pointless

Philippians
3:19 Their ***l*** end with destruction. Their god

Colossians
1:10 that you can live ***l*** that are worthy
2:9 fullness of deity ***l*** in Christ's body.
1 Thessalonians
2:8 but also our very ***l*** because we cared
2:12 with you to live ***l*** worthy of the God
4:3 will is that your ***l*** are dedicated to
2 Thessalonians
3:6 or sister who ***l*** an undisciplined
1 Timothy
6:16 immortality and ***l*** in light that no
2 Timothy
1:14 through the Holy Spirit who ***l*** in us.
Titus
2:12 and godly ***l*** right now by
3:3 were spending our ***l*** in evil behavior
Hebrews
2:15 their entire ***l*** by their fear of
5:13 Everyone who ***l*** on milk is not used to the word of
7:25 because he always ***l*** to speak with God
13:7 consider the way their ***l*** turned out.
James
1:11 of their daily ***l***, the wealthy will
1:25 practice in their ***l***. They will be
3:6 our entire ***l***. Because of it,
4:1 cravings that are at war in your own ***l***?
1 Peter
1:15 aspect of your ***l***, just as the one
2:11 desires that wage war against your ***l***.
2:25 to the shepherd and guardian of your ***l***.
3:2 the reverent and holy manner of your ***l***.
4:2 of their human ***l*** in ways
4:19 commit their ***l*** to a trustworthy
2 Peter
3:11 You must live holy and godly ***l***,
1 John
2:11 the darkness and ***l*** in the darkness,
3:16 to lay down our ***l*** for our brothers
Revelation
2:13 was killed among you, where Satan ***l***.
4:9 the throne, who ***l*** forever and
4:10 the one who ***l*** forever and
10:6 by the one who ***l*** forever and
12:11 for their own ***l*** didn't make them
15:7 of the God who ***l*** forever and
18:13 carriages, and slaves, even human ***l***.

LIVESTOCK

Genesis
1:24 of living thing: ***l***, crawling things,
Exodus
9:3 disease on your ***l*** in the field: on
9:6 of the Egyptian ***l*** died, but not one
34:19 all your male ***l***, the oldest
Leviticus
1:2 of you present a ***l*** offering to the
5:2 animal, unclean ***l***, or unclean
Deuteronomy
11:15 lush for your ***l***, and you will eat
Judges
18:21 the children, the ***l***, and the prized
1 Samuel
30:20 of the other ***l***. The troops said,
John
4:12 it himself, as did his sons and his ***l***."

LIVING → ALL LIVING THINGS, LIVING GOD, LIVING WATER

Genesis
1:20 waters swarm with ***l*** things, and let
2:19 The human gave each ***l*** being its name.
8:21 destroy every ***l*** thing as I have
Numbers
16:22 the God of all ***l*** things. If one
Deuteronomy
5:14 immigrant who is ***l*** among you—so that
20:16 must not spare any ***l*** thing.
26:5 down to Egypt, ***l*** as an immigrant
Job
28:13 it isn't found in the land of the ***l***.
28:21 eyes of all the ***l***, concealed from
30:23 the house appointed for all the ***l***.
Psalms
27:13 LORD's goodness in the land of the ***l***!
52:5 you from the land of the ***l***! Selah
65:2 prayer—and all ***l*** things come to
66:9 us among the ***l***; he didn't let
91:1 ***L*** in the Most High's shelter, camping
104:25 creatures—***l*** things both small
107:23 ships, making their ***l*** on the high seas.
116:9 before the LORD in the land of the ***l***.
119:17 so I can go on ***l*** and keeping your
142:5 are all I have in the land of the ***l***."
145:16 satisfying the desire of every ***l*** thing.
145:21 praise, and every ***l*** thing will bless
150:6 Let every ***l*** thing praise the LORD!
Proverbs
1:12 swallow up the ***l*** like the grave
2:19 never again reach the ways of the ***l***.
Ecclesiastes
4:2 than the ***l***, who are still
6:8 how to conduct themselves before the ***l***?
7:2 destiny; and the ***l*** should take it to
9:4 is among the ***l*** can be certain
9:5 because the ***l*** know that they will die.
10:19 wine cheers the ***l***, and money
Isaiah
53:8 the land of the ***l***, struck dead
Lamentations
3:39 Why then does any ***l*** person complain; why
Ezekiel
1:5 forms of four ***l*** creatures. This
10:17 the spirit of the ***l*** creatures was in
Matthew
22:32 the God of the dead but of the ***l***."
Mark
7:5 disciples not ***l*** according to the
12:27 dead but of the ***l***. You are
Luke
2:8 shepherds were ***l*** in the fields,
15:13 his wealth through extravagant ***l***.
20:38 dead but of the ***l***. To him they are
24:5 do you look for the ***l*** among the dead?
John
6:51 I am the ***l*** bread that came down from
6:57 As the ***l*** Father sent me, and I live
7:35 scattered and are ***l*** among the Greeks!
Acts
1:19 known to everyone ***l*** in Jerusalem, so
10:42 as judge of the ***l*** and the dead.
Romans
12:1 your bodies as a ***l*** sacrifice that is

14:9 be Lord of both the dead and the ***l***.
1 Corinthians
3:3 unspiritual and ***l*** by human
9:6 have the right to not work for our ***l***?
9:14 should get their ***l*** from the gospel.
15:45 Adam, became a ***l*** person, and the
2 Corinthians
5:6 that while we are ***l*** in the body, we
Philippians
1:21 Because for me, ***l*** serves Christ and
Colossians
1:27 which is Christ ***l*** in you, the hope
2:20 as though you were ***l*** in the world?
1 Thessalonians
1:9 you are serving the ***l*** and true God,
4:1 Jesus to keep ***l*** the way you
4:11 and earn your own ***l***, just as I told
4:17 Then, we who are ***l*** and still around
2 Thessalonians
3:11 some of you are ***l*** an undisciplined
1 Timothy
4:8 training in holy ***l*** is useful for
6:11 holy ***l***, faithfulness,
2 Timothy
4:1 to judge the ***l*** and the dead, and
Hebrews
4:12 God's word is ***l***, active, and
10:20 through a new and ***l*** way that he opened
James
3:14 stop bragging and ***l*** in ways that deny
1 Peter
1:3 born anew into a ***l*** hope through the
2:4 to him as to a ***l*** stone. Even
2:5 being built like ***l*** stones into a
3:7 submit by ***l*** with your wife in
4:5 is ready to judge the ***l*** and the dead.
2 Peter
3:3 come, jeering, ***l*** by their own
2 John
1:4 of your children ***l*** in the truth,
3 John
1:4 my children are ***l*** according to the
Jude
1:16 grumblers, ***l*** according to
1:18 will come ***l*** according to
Revelation
1:18 and the ***l*** one. I was dead, but look!
2:13 know that you are ***l*** right where
4:6 throne, were four ***l*** creatures
16:3 corpse, and every ***l*** thing in the sea
19:4 and the four ***l*** creatures fell

LIVING GOD

Josh 3:10; 1Sa 17:26; 17:36; 2Ki 19:16; Ps 42:2; 84:2; Is 37:4; 37:17; Jer 4:2; 10:10; 23:36; Dn 6:20; 6:26; Hos 1:10; Mt 16:16; 26:63; Ac 14:15; 2Co 3:3; 6:16; 1Ti 3:15; 4:10; Heb 3:12; 9:14; 10:31; 12:22; Rev 7:2

LIVING WATER

Jer 2:13; 17:13; Jn 4:10; 4:11; 7:38

LOAVES

Numbers
6:15 and a basket of ***l*** of unleavened bread
Matthew
14:17 here except five ***l*** of bread and two
15:34 responded, "Seven ***l*** and a few fish."
16:9 remember the five ***l*** that fed the five
16:10 And the seven ***l*** that fed the four
Mark
6:38 they said, "Five ***l*** of bread and two
8:5 do you have?" They said, "Seven ***l***."
Luke
9:13 no more than five ***l*** of bread and two fish
11:5 Friend, loan me three ***l*** of bread
John
6:9 has five barley ***l*** and two fish. But

LOCUST

Exodus
10:19 Sea. Not a single ***l*** was left in the
Leviticus
11:22 kind of migrating ***l***, any kind of bald
1 Kings
8:37 blight, mildew, ***l***, or grasshopper;
Job
39:20 to leap like a ***l***, his majestic
Psalms
109:23 away; I'm shaken off, like some ***l***.
Ecclesiastes
12:5 blanches, the ***l*** droops, and the
Joel
1:4 What the cutting ***l*** left, the swarming
2:25 that the cutting ***l***, the swarming
Amos
4:9 vineyards. The ***l*** devoured your fig
Nahum
3:15 down; like the ***l*** it will consume
3:16 have stars. The ***l*** sheds its skin

LOCUSTS

Exodus
10:4 going to bring ***l*** into your country
10:14 The ***l*** swarmed over the whole land of Egypt
Deuteronomy
28:38 nothing because the ***l*** will eat it all.
Judges
6:5 like a swarm of ***l***, so that no one
2 Chronicles
6:28 blight, mildew, ***l***, or grasshoppers,
7:13 or I order the ***l*** to consume the
Psalms
78:46 their land's produce to ***l***.
105:34 spoke, and the ***l*** came—countless
Proverbs
30:27 ***L*** don't have a king, but they march
Isaiah
33:4 they rushed upon it like a swarm of ***l***.
Jeremiah
46:23 they outnumber ***l*** and can't be
51:14 like a swarm of ***l***; they will
51:27 call up the troops, like swarms of ***l***!
Amos
7:1 God was forming ***l*** at the time the
Matthew
3:4 He ate ***l*** and wild honey.
Revelation
9:3 Then ***l*** came forth from the smoke and

LOOK

Genesis
15:5 and said, "***L*** up at the sky and
19:17 your lives! Don't ***l*** back! And don't
Deuteronomy
1:8 ***L***, I have laid the land before you. Go
4:19 Don't ***l*** to the skies, to the sun or the
Joshua
2:1 He said, "Go. ***L*** over the land,
1 Samuel
16:7 him. God doesn't ***l*** at things like
Esther
2:7 and was lovely to ***l*** at. When her
Job
31:1 my eyes; how could I ***l*** at a virgin?
37:21 now, no one can ***l*** at the sun; it is
Psalms
8:3 When I ***l*** up at your skies, at what your
34:5 Those who ***l*** to God will shine; their
68:16 Why do you ***l*** with envy at the
77:2 I'm in trouble I ***l*** for my Lord. At
91:8 Just ***l*** with your eyes, and you will see
104:32 He has only to ***l*** at the earth, and it
145:15 All eyes ***l*** to you, hoping, and you give
Proverbs
11:27 Those who ***l*** for good find favor, but
23:31 Don't ***l*** at wine when it is red
23:35 When I wake up, I'll ***l*** for wine again!"
27:18 and those who ***l*** after their
Isaiah
17:7 their eyes will ***l*** to the holy one
31:1 But they don't ***l*** to the holy one
42:18 deaf ones, and blind ones, ***l*** and see!
51:2 ***L*** to Abraham your ancestor, and to
51:6 ***L*** up to the heavens, and gaze at the
Jeremiah
2:10 ***L*** to the west as far as the shores of
6:16 crossroads and ***l*** around; ask for
50:20 Judah, they will ***l*** in vain. I will
Ezekiel
3:25 ***L*** at you, human one! They've now put
34:6 was no one to ***l*** for them or find
Nahum
1:15 ***L***, on the mountains: the feet of a
3:7 Then all who ***l*** at you will recoil from
Habakkuk
1:13 are too pure to ***l*** on evil; you are
Zechariah
12:10 They will ***l*** to me concerning
Malachi
3:1 ***L***, I am sending my messenger who will
4:1 ***L***, the day is coming, burning like an
4:5 ***L***, I am sending Elijah the prophet to
Matthew
1:23 ***L***! A virgin will become pregnant and
6:26 ***L*** at the birds in the sky. They don't
11:10 it is written: ***L***, I'm sending my
21:5 Daughter Zion, "***L***, your king is
23:27 tombs. They ***l*** beautiful on the
Mark
1:2 of Isaiah: ***L***, I am sending my
8:12 this generation ***l*** for a sign? I
8:24 see people. They ***l*** like trees, only
Luke
7:25 refined clothes? ***L***, those who dress
24:39 ***L*** at my hands and my feet. It's really
John
1:36 along he said, "***L***! The Lamb of God!"
4:35 for harvest'? ***L***, I tell you: open
13:33 longer. You will ***l*** for me—but, just
19:37 says, They will ***l*** at him whom they
20:27 your finger here. ***L*** at my hands. Put
1 Corinthians
1:22 ask for signs, and Greeks ***l*** for wisdom,
Philippians
3:20 is in heaven. We ***l*** forward to a
1 Timothy
4:12 Don't let anyone ***l*** down on you because
1 Peter
2:6 in scripture, ***L***! I am laying a
Revelation
1:7 ***L***, he is coming with the clouds! Every
3:20 ***L***! I'm standing at the door and
5:4 to open the scroll or to ***l*** inside it.
22:12 ***L***! I'm coming soon. My reward is with

LOOKED

Genesis
19:26 When Lot's wife ***l*** back, she turned into
Exodus
2:25 God ***l*** at the Israelites, and God
Jeremiah
4:23 I ***l*** at the earth, and it was without
Daniel
8:15 of me was someone who ***l*** like a man.
10:5 I ***l*** up and suddenly saw a man clothed
10:6 His arms and feet ***l*** like polished
12:5 I, Daniel, ***l*** and suddenly saw two other
Zechariah
1:8 Tonight I ***l*** and saw a man riding on a
2:1 Then I ***l*** up and saw a man. In his hand
5:1 I ***l*** up again and saw a flying scroll
6:1 I ***l*** up again and saw four chariots
Matthew
14:19 and the two fish, ***l*** up to heaven,
17:8 When they ***l*** up, they saw no one except
19:26 Jesus ***l*** at them carefully and said,
Mark
8:24 The man ***l*** up and said, "I see people.
16:4 When they ***l*** up, they saw that the stone
Revelation
1:13 I saw someone who ***l*** like the Human
5:11 Then I ***l***, and I heard the sound of
6:2 So I ***l***, and there was a white horse.
6:12 I ***l*** on as he opened the sixth seal, and
7:9 After this I ***l***, and there was a great
8:13 Then I ***l*** and I heard an eagle flying
9:7 The locusts ***l*** like horses ready for
14:1 Then I ***l***, and there was the Lamb,
15:5 After this I ***l***, and the temple in

LORD GOD

Gn 2:4; 2:5, 7, 8, 9, 15, 16, 18, 19, 21, 22; 3:1, 8, 9, 13, 14, 21, 22, 23; 15:2, 8; 24:3, 7, 12, 27, 42; 32:9; Ex 9:30; 23:17; 34:23; Nm 12:13; Dt 3:24; Josh 7:7; 13:33; 14:14; Jdg 6:22; 16:28; 21:3; 1Sa 10:18; 14:41; 20:12; 23:10, 11; 25:32, 34; 2Sa 5:23; 7:18, 19, 20, 22, 25, 28, 29; 12:7; 1Ki 8:23; 19:10, 14; 2Ki 10:31; 19:15; 1Ch 17:16; 17:17, 27; 22:19; 24:19; 28:20; 29:1, 10, 18; 2Ch 1:9; 6:14, 16, 17, 41, 42; 26:5; 28:6; 29:5; 30:1, 5; 32:16, 17; Ezr 9:15; Neh 1:5; 9:7; Ps 25:12; 31:5; 50:1; 59:5;

69:6; 72:18; 73:28; 80:4, 19; 84:8; 85:8; 88:1; 89:8; 115:9, 11; 141:8; Is 1:24; 3:1, 15; 7:7; 10:16, 23, 24, 33; 17:6; 19:4; 21:17; 22:5, 12, 14, 15; 24:15; 25:8; 28:16, 22; 30:15; 37:21; 38:1; 40:10; 48:16; 49:22; 50:4, 5, 7, 9; 52:4; 56:8; 61:11; 65:13, 15; Jer 2:22; 4:10; 5:14; 7:20; 14:13; 15:16; 25:15; 32:17, 25; 44:26; 46:10; 50:31; Eze 2:4; 3:11, 27; 4:14; 5:5, 7, 8, 11; 6:3, 11; 7:2, 5; 9:8; 11:5, 7, 8, 13, 16, 17, 21; 12:10, 19, 23, 25, 28; 13:3, 8, 13, 16, 18, 20; 14:4, 6, 11, 14, 16, 18, 20, 21, 23; 15:6, 8; 16:3, 8, 14, 19, 23, 30, 36, 43, 48, 59, 63; 17:3, 9, 16, 19, 22; 18:3, 9, 23, 30, 32; 20:3, 5, 27, 30, 31, 33, 36, 39, 40, 44, 47, 49; 21:7, 13, 24, 26, 28; 22:3, 12, 19, 28, 31; 23:22, 28, 32, 34, 35, 46, 49; 24:3, 6, 9, 14, 21, 24; 25:3, 6, 8, 12, 13, 14, 15, 16; 26:3, 5, 7, 14, 15, 19, 21; 27:3; 28:2, 6, 10, 12, 22, 24, 25; 29:3, 8, 13, 16, 19, 20; 30:2, 6, 10, 13, 22; 31:10, 15, 18; 32:3, 8, 11, 14, 16, 31, 32; 33:11, 25, 27; 34:2, 8, 10, 11, 15, 17, 20, 30, 31; 35:3, 6, 11, 14; 36:2, 3, 4, 5, 6, 7, 13, 14, 15, 22, 23, 32, 33, 37; 37:3, 5, 9, 12, 19, 21; 38:3, 10, 14, 17, 18, 21; 39:1, 5, 8, 13, 17, 20, 25, 29; 43:18, 19, 27; 44:6, 9, 12, 15, 27; 45:9, 15, 18; 46:1, 16; 47:13, 23; 48:29; Dn 9:3; Hos 12:5; Am 1:8; 3:7, 8, 13; 4:2, 5; 5:3, 15; 6:8, 14; 7:1, 2, 4, 5, 6; 8:1, 3, 9, 11; 9:5, 8; Obad 1:1; Jon 4:6; Mi 1:2; Hab 3:19; Zep 1:7; Hg 1:12; Zec 9:14; Mal 2:16; Lk 1:32; 1:68; Rev 1:8; 4:8; 11:17; 15:3; 16:7; 18:8; 21:22; 22:5

LORD GOD ALMIGHTY

Rev 4:8; 11:17; 15:3; 16:7; 21:22

LORD JESUS

Mk 16:19; Lk 17:37; 24:3; Ac 1:21; 4:33; 7:59; 8:16; 11:17, 20; 15:11, 26; 16:31; 19:5, 13, 17; 20:21, 24; 21:13; 28:31; Ro 1:7; 5:1, 11; 13:14; 14:14; 15:6, 30; 16:20; 1Co 1:2; 1:3, 7, 8, 10; 5:4; 6:11; 8:6; 11:23; 15:57; 16:23; 2Co 1:2; 1:3, 14; 4:14; 8:9; 11:31; 13:13; Ga 1:3; 6:14, 18; Eph 1:2; 1:3, 15, 17; 5:20; 6:23, 24; Phi 1:2; 2:19; 3:20; 4:23; Col 1:3; 3:17; 1Th 1:1; 1:3; 2:15, 19; 3:13; 4:1, 2; 5:9, 23, 28; 2Th 1:1; 1:2, 7, 8, 12; 2:1, 8, 14, 16; 3:6, 12, 18; 1Ti 6:3; 6:14; Phm 1:3; 1:5, 25; Heb 13:20; Jas 1:1; 2:1; 1Pt 1:3; 2Pt 1:8; 1:14, 16; Jud 1:4; 1:17, 21; Rev 22:20

LORD JESUS CHRIST

Ac 11:17; 15:26; 28:31; Ro 1:7; 5:1, 11; 13:14; 15:6, 30; 16:20; 1Co 1:2; 1:3, 7, 8, 10; 6:11; 8:6; 15:57; 2Co 1:2; 1:3; 8:9; 13:13; Ga 1:3; 6:14, 18; Eph 1:2; 1:3, 17; 5:20; 6:23, 24; Phi 1:2; 3:20; 4:23; Col 1:3; 1Th 1:1; 1:3; 5:9, 28; 2Th 1:1; 1:2, 12; 2:14, 16; 3:6, 12, 18; 1Ti 6:3; 6:14; Phm 1:3; 1:25; Jas 1:1; 2:1; 1Pt 1:3; 2Pt 1:8; 1:14, 16; Jud 1:4; 1:17, 21

LORD MY GOD

Nm 22:18; Dt 4:5; 26:3; Josh 14:8; 14:9; 2Sa 24:24; 1Ki 3:7; 5:3, 4, 5; 8:28; 17:20, 21; 1Ch 21:17; 22:7; 2Ch 2:4; 6:19; Ps 7:1; 7:3; 13:3; 18:28; 30:2, 12; 35:24; 38:15; 40:5; 86:12; 104:1; 109:26; Is 40:27; Jer 31:18; Dn 9:4; 9:20; Am 3:11; Zec 11:4; 14:5

LORD OF HEAVENLY FORCES

1Sa 1:3; 1:11; 4:4; 15:2; 17:45; 2Sa 5:10; 6:2, 18; 7:8, 26, 27; 1Ki 18:15; 2Ki 3:14; 19:31; 1Ch 11:9; 17:7, 24; Ps 24:10; 46:7, 11; 48:8; 84:1, 3, 12; Is 1:9; 2:12; 5:7, 9, 16, 24; 6:3, 5; 8:13, 18; 9:7, 13, 19; 10:26; 13:4, 13; 14:22, 23, 24, 27; 17:3; 18:7; 19:12, 16, 17, 18, 20, 25; 21:10; 22:14, 25; 23:9; 24:23; 25:6; 28:5, 29; 29:6; 31:4, 5; 37:16, 32; 39:5; 44:6; 45:13; 47:4; 48:2; 51:15; 54:5; Jer 2:19; 6:6, 9; 7:3, 21; 8:3; 9:7, 15, 17; 10:16; 11:17, 20, 22; 16:9; 19:3, 11, 15; 20:12; 23:15, 36; 25:8, 27, 28, 29, 32; 26:18; 27:4, 18, 19, 21; 28:2, 14; 29:4, 8, 17, 21, 25; 30:8; 31:23, 35; 32:14, 15, 18; 33:11, 12; 35:13, 17, 18, 19; 38:17; 39:16; 42:15, 18; 43:10; 44:2, 7, 11, 25; 46:18, 25; 48:15; 49:5, 7, 26, 35; 50:18, 33, 34; 51:5, 14, 19, 33, 57, 58; Mi 4:4; Na 2:13; 3:5; Hab 2:13; Zep 2:9; 2:10; Hg 1:2; 1:5, 7, 9, 14; 2:4, 6, 7, 8, 9, 11, 23; Zec 1:3; 1:4, 6, 12, 14, 16, 17; 2:8, 9, 11; 3:7, 9, 10; 4:6, 9; 5:4; 6:12, 15; 7:3, 4, 9, 12, 13; 8:1, 2, 3, 4, 6, 7, 9, 11, 14, 18, 19, 20, 21, 22, 23; 9:15; 10:3; 13:2, 7; 14:16, 17, 21; Mal 1:4; 1:6, 8, 9, 10, 11, 13, 14; 2:2, 4, 7, 8, 12, 16; 3:1, 5, 7, 10, 11, 12, 14, 17; 4:1, 3; Jas 5:4

LORD OUR GOD

Ex 8:10; 8:26, 27; 10:25, 26; Dt 1:6; 1:19, 20, 25; 2:33, 36, 37; 3:3; 4:7; 5:24, 27; 6:20, 24, 25; 29:15, 18; Josh 18:6; 22:19, 29; 24:24; Jdg 11:24; 1Sa 7:8; 1Ki 8:57; 8:59, 61, 65; 2Ki 18:22; 19:19; 1Ch 13:2; 15:13; 29:16; 2Ch 2:4; 13:11; 14:7, 11; 19:7; 32:8, 11; Ps 90:17; 94:23; 99:5, 8, 9; 106:47; 113:5; 123:2; Is 26:13; 36:7; 37:20; Jer 3:22; 3:23, 25; 5:19, 24; 8:14; 14:22; 16:10; 26:16; 31:6; 37:3; 42:6, 20; 43:2; 50:28; 51:10; Dn 9:9; 9:10, 13, 14, 15; Mi 4:5; 7:17; Ac 2:39; Rev 19:6

LORD THEIR GOD

Ex 10:7; Lv 26:44; Jdg 3:7; 8:34; 1Sa 12:9; 1Ki 9:9; 2Ki 17:7; 17:9, 14, 16, 19; 18:12; 2Ch 31:6; Neh 9:3; 9:4; Ps 146:5; Jer 3:21; 22:9; 30:9; 43:1; 50:4; Eze 34:30; 39:28; Hos 1:7; 3:5; 7:10; Zep 2:7; Hg 1:12; Zec 9:16; 10:6; 12:5; Lk 1:16

LORD YOUR GOD

Gn 27:20; Ex 8:28; 10:8, 16, 17; 15:26; 16:12; 20:2, 5, 10, 12; 34:24; Lv 11:44; 18:2, 4, 30; 19:2, 3, 4, 10, 25, 31, 36; 20:7; 23:22, 28, 40, 43; 24:22; 25:17, 38, 55; 26:1, 13; Nm 10:9; 10:10; 15:41; Dt 1:10; 1:21, 30, 31; 2:7, 30; 3:20, 21, 22; 4:2, 3, 10, 19, 23, 24, 29, 30, 31, 40; 5:6, 9, 12, 15, 16, 32; 6:1, 2, 5, 10, 13, 15, 16; 7:1, 2, 6, 12, 18, 19, 20, 21, 22, 23, 25; 8:2, 7, 10, 11, 18; 9:4, 5, 6, 7, 16; 10:9, 12, 17, 20, 22; 11:1, 13, 22, 25, 29, 31; 12:4, 5, 9, 10, 11, 15, 18, 20, 29, 31; 13:3, 5, 10, 12, 16; 14:2, 21, 23, 24, 25, 29; 15:4, 6, 7, 14, 15, 19, 20, 21; 16:1, 5, 6, 7, 8, 10, 11, 15, 16, 17, 18, 20, 21, 22; 17:1, 2, 8, 12, 15; 18:5, 12, 13, 14, 15, 16; 19:1, 2, 3, 8, 9, 10; 20:1, 13, 16, 17, 18; 21:1, 5, 23; 22:5; 23:5, 18, 20, 21, 23; 24:4, 13, 18, 19; 25:15, 16, 19; 26:1, 2, 10, 19; 27:2, 3, 9; 28:1, 52, 53, 58; 29:6, 10, 12; 30:1, 2, 3, 4, 5, 6, 7, 9, 10, 16, 20; 31:3, 6, 11, 12, 13; Josh 1:9;

1:11, 13, 15, 17; 2:11; 3:9; 4:23, 24; 8:7; 9:9, 24; 10:19; 22:3, 4, 5; 23:3, 5, 8, 10, 11, 13, 14, 15, 16; Jdg 6:10; 6:26; 1Sa 12:12; 12:14, 19; 13:13; 15:15, 21, 30; 25:29; 2Sa 14:11; 14:17; 18:28; 24:3, 23; 1Ki 1:17; 2:3; 10:9; 13:6, 21; 17:12; 18:10; 2Ki 17:39; 19:4; 23:21; 1Ch 11:2; 22:11, 12, 18, 19; 28:8; 29:20; 2Ch 9:8; 16:7; 20:20; 30:8, 9; Neh 8:9; Ps 76:11; 81:10; Is 7:11; 37:4; 41:13; 43:3; 48:17; 51:15; 55:5; 60:9; Jer 2:17; 2:19; 3:13; 13:16; 26:13; 40:2; 42:2, 3, 4, 5, 13, 20, 21; Eze 20:5; 20:7, 19, 20; Hos 12:9; 13:4; 14:1; Jl 1:14; 2:13, 14, 23, 26, 27; 3:17; Am 9:15; Mi 7:10; Zep 3:17; Zec 6:15; Mt 4:7; 4:10; 22:37; Mk 12:30; Lk 4:8; 4:12; 10:27; Ac 3:22

LORD'S ANOINTED

1Sa 16:6; 24:6, 10; 26:9, 11, 16, 23; 2Sa 1:14; 1:16; 19:21

LORD'S MESSENGER

Gn 16:7; 16:9, 10, 11; 22:11, 15; Ex 3:2; Nm 22:22; 22:23, 24, 25, 26, 27, 31, 32, 34, 35; Jdg 2:1; 2:4; 5:23; 6:11, 12, 21, 22; 13:13, 15, 16, 17, 18, 20, 21; 2Sa 24:16; 1Ki 19:7; 2Ki 1:3; 1:15; 19:35; 1Ch 21:12; 21:15, 16, 18, 30; Ps 34:7; 35:5, 6; Is 37:36; Hg 1:13; Zec 1:11; 1:12; 3:5, 6; 12:8

LORD'S SPIRIT

Jdg 3:10; 6:34; 11:29; 13:25; 14:6, 19; 15:14; 1Sa 10:6; 16:13, 14; 2Sa 23:2; 1Ki 18:12; 22:24; 2Ki 2:16; 2Ch 18:23; 20:14; Is 11:2; 40:13; 63:14; Eze 11:5; 37:1; Ac 5:9; 8:39; 2Co 3:17

LOSE

Psalms
18:45 Foreigners **l** their nerve; they come
Proverbs
5:20 son, should you **l** your senses with
10:17 who ignore correction **l** their way.
19:4 friends, but the poor **l** their friends.
20:2 Those who anger him may **l** their life.
Amos
2:14 the strong will **l** their strength;
Matthew
5:29 better that you **l** a part of your
10:39 their lives will **l** them, and those
16:25 their lives will **l** them. But all who
18:14 doesn't want to **l** one of these
Mark
8:35 their lives will **l** them. But all who
8:36 gain the whole world but **l** their lives?
Luke
9:24 their lives will **l** them. But all who
9:25 themselves yet perish or **l** their lives?
17:33 their life will **l** it, but whoever
John
6:39 me, that I won't **l** anything he has
12:25 their lives will **l** them, and those
18:9 I didn't **l** anyone of those
Acts
27:34 None of you will **l** a single hair
1 Corinthians
3:15 flames, they'll **l** it. However, they
9:15 me to die than to **l** my right to brag
2 Peter
3:17 people, and **l** your own safe

LOST

Psalms
9:18 who suffer won't be **l** for all time.
119:176 off like a sheep, **l**.
Proverbs
2:15 are confused; they get **l** on their way.
Ecclesiastes
5:14 that wealth is **l** in a bad business
9:5 for them; even the memory of them is **l**.
Jeremiah
3:21 Israel, who have **l** their way and
50:6 My people were **l** sheep; their shepherds
Lamentations
1:6 Daughter Zion **l** all her glory. Her
Ezekiel
34:4 or seek out the **l**; but instead you
34:16 will seek out the **l**, bring back the
Joel
1:8 one who has **l** the husband of
Matthew
10:6 Go instead to the **l** sheep, the people
15:24 sent only to the **l** sheep, the people
Mark
2:22 the wine would be **l** and the wineskins
Luke
15:4 hundred sheep and **l** one of them.
19:10 Human One came to seek and save the **l**."
21:18 not a hair on your heads will be **l**.
John
10:20 a demon and has **l** his mind. Why
17:12 None of them were **l**, except the one
2 Peter
1:10 Do this and you will never ever be **l**.

LOT

Genesis
11:27 Haran. Haran became the father of ***L***.
13:10 ***L*** looked up and saw the entire Jordan
Numbers
26:55 be apportioned by **l**. They will
33:54 up the land by **l** according to your
Joshua
14:2 was assigned by **l**, exactly as the
Jonah
1:7 cast lots, and the **l** fell on Jonah.
Micah
2:5 boundary lines by **l** in the LORD's
Acts
1:26 cast lots, the **l** fell on Matthias.

LOTS → CAST LOTS

Joshua
18:10 Then Joshua cast **l** for them in Shiloh
1 Chronicles
24:5 both groups by **l** because there
Nehemiah
10:34 We have also cast **l** among the priests,
11:1 the people cast **l** to bring one out
Psalms
22:18 themselves; they cast **l** for my clothes.
119:165 enjoy peace—and **l** of it. There's no
Joel
3:3 and have cast **l** for my people. They

Obadiah
1:11 gates and cast ***l*** for Jerusalem;
Jonah
1:7 on, let's cast ***l*** so that we might
Matthew
27:35 up his clothes among them by drawing ***l***.
Mark
15:24 clothes, drawing ***l*** for them to
Luke
23:34 doing." They drew ***l*** as a way of
John
19:24 it. Let's cast ***l*** to see who will
Acts
1:26 When they cast ***l***, the lot fell on

LOUD

Psalms
3:4 I cry out ***l*** to the LORD, and he answers
106:44 distress when he heard their ***l*** cries.
150:5 Praise God with ***l*** cymbals! Praise God
Proverbs
27:14 a neighbor with a ***l*** voice early in
Matthew
27:46 cried out with a ***l*** shout, "Eli, Eli,
Mark
15:34 cried out with a ***l*** shout, "Eloi,
John
11:43 shouted with a ***l*** voice, "Lazarus,
Acts
8:7 With ***l*** shrieks, unclean spirits came
26:24 declared with a ***l*** voice, "You've
Revelation
1:10 heard behind me a ***l*** voice that
5:2 proclaimed in a ***l*** voice, "Who is
6:10 cried out with a ***l*** voice, "Holy and
7:2 cried out with a ***l*** voice to the four
8:13 It said with a ***l*** voice, "Horror,
10:3 called out with a ***l*** voice like a lion
11:12 Then they heard a ***l*** voice from heaven
12:10 Then I heard a ***l*** voice in heaven say,
14:2 rushing water and ***l*** thunder. The
16:1 Then I heard a ***l*** voice from the temple
18:2 called out with a ***l*** voice, saying,
19:17 called out with a ***l*** voice and said to
21:3 I heard a ***l*** voice from the throne say,

LOVE

→ FAITHFUL LOVE, FAITHFUL LOVE LASTS FOREVER, GOD'S FAITHFUL LOVE, LOVE AND FAITHFULNESS, LOVE EACH OTHER, LOVE GOD, LOVE LASTS FOREVER, LOVE OF GOD, LOVE THE LORD, LOVE YOUR NEIGHBOR, LOYAL LOVE, LOYAL LOVE AND FAITHFULNESS

Genesis
22:2 only son whom you ***l***, Isaac, and go to
27:4 food that I ***l*** and bring it to
29:32 and now my husband will ***l*** me."
Exodus
20:6 of those who ***l*** me and keep my
21:5 states, "I ***l*** my master, my
Leviticus
19:34 You must ***l*** them as yourself,
Deuteronomy
5:10 of those who ***l*** me and keep my
7:13 He will ***l*** you, bless you, and multiply
10:19 you must also ***l*** immigrants
21:11 and you fall in ***l*** with her and take
33:3 Yes, those who ***l*** the nations—all his
Judges
14:16 me! You don't ***l*** me! You told a
16:4 Samson fell in ***l*** with a woman
16:15 can you say, 'I ***l*** you,' when you
1 Samuel
18:22 all his servants ***l*** you. You should
2 Samuel
1:26 dear to me! Your ***l*** was more amazing
13:1 son Amnon fell in ***l*** with Tamar the
13:4 told him, "I'm in ***l*** with Tamar, the
13:15 greater than the ***l*** he had felt for
19:6 hating those who ***l*** you! Today you
1 Kings
3:26 for she had great ***l*** for her son. But
10:9 with an eternal ***l***, the LORD made
11:2 Solomon clung to these women in ***l***.
2 Chronicles
2:11 The LORD must ***l*** his people Israel
5:13 God's faithful ***l*** lasts forever!
Nehemiah
1:5 to those who ***l*** you and keep your
Esther
2:17 she had won his ***l*** and his favor
Psalms
1:2 these persons ***l*** the LORD's
4:2 you continue to ***l*** what is worthless
5:11 so that all who ***l*** your name can
6:4 me for the sake of your faithful ***l***!
18:1 Saul.] He said: I ***l*** you, LORD, my
26:8 I ***l*** the beauty of your house, LORD; I
34:12 Do you ***l*** life; do you relish the chance
40:16 Let those who ***l*** your salvation
45:1 A maskil. A ***l*** song.] A
45:7 You ***l*** righteousness and hate
52:3 You ***l*** evil more than good; you love
52:4 You ***l*** all destructive words; you love
60:5 that the people you ***l*** might be rescued.
70:4 and let those who ***l*** your saving help
108:6 that the people you ***l*** might be rescued.
109:4 of returning my ***l***, they accuse me—
109:5 for good, hatred in return for my ***l***.
119:47 in your commandments because I ***l*** them.
119:48 because I ***l*** them, and I will
119:97 I ***l*** your Instruction! I think about it
119:113 people, but I ***l*** your Instruction.
119:119 like waste—that's why I ***l*** your laws.
119:127 But I ***l*** your commandments more than
119:132 only right for those who ***l*** your name.
119:150 The people who ***l*** to plot wicked schemes
119:159 at how much I ***l*** your precepts.
119:163 false, but I'm in ***l*** with your
119:165 The people who ***l*** your Instruction enjoy
119:167 I keep your laws; I ***l*** them so much
122:6 peace: "Let those who ***l*** you have rest.
145:20 protects all who ***l*** him, but he
Proverbs
1:22 clueless people ***l*** your naïvete,
4:6 will guard you. ***L*** her, and she will
5:19 all the time; always be drunk on her ***l***.
7:18 drink deep of ***l*** until morning;
8:17 I ***l*** those who love me; those who seek
8:21 for those who ***l*** me and to fill up
8:36 all those who hate me ***l*** death.
9:8 correct the wise, and they will ***l*** you.
10:12 up conflict, but ***l*** covers all

12:1 Those who ***l*** discipline love knowledge,
14:20 hate the poor, but many ***l*** the wealthy.
15:17 of greens with ***l*** than a plump calf
16:13 lips; they ***l*** words of
17:9 One who seeks ***l*** conceals an offense,
17:17 Friends ***l*** all the time, and kinsfolk
17:19 Those who ***l*** an offense love a quarrel;
18:21 tongue; those who ***l*** it will eat its
19:8 good sense ***l*** themselves; those
20:13 Don't ***l*** sleep or you will be poor; stay
21:17 Those who ***l*** pleasure end up poor;
22:11 Those who ***l*** a pure heart—their speech
27:5 correction is better than hidden ***l***.

Ecclesiastes
9:1 along with both ***l*** and hate. People
9:6 Their ***l*** and their hate, as well as

Song of Songs
1:3 That's why the young women ***l*** you.
1:4 than wine. No wonder they all ***l*** you!"
1:7 me, you whom I ***l*** with all my heart-
1:13 of myrrh is my ***l*** to me, lying all
1:14 flowers is my ***l*** to me in the
1:16 —so beautiful, my ***l***! Yes, delightful!
2:4 wine; his banner raised over me is ***l***.
2:5 me with apples, for I'm weak with ***l***!
2:7 rouse, don't arouse ***l*** until it desires.
2:17 turn about, my ***l***; be like a
3:1 the one whom I ***l*** with all my
3:2 the one whom I ***l*** with all my
3:3 The one whom I ***l*** with all my heart-
3:4 the one whom I ***l*** with all my
3:5 rouse, don't arouse ***l*** until it desires.
3:10 inlaid with ***l***. Daughters of
4:16 flow! Let my ***l*** come to his
5:1 dear friends! Drink and get drunk on ***l***!
5:2 A sound! My ***l*** is knocking: Open
5:4 My ***l*** put his hand in through the latch
5:5 to open for my ***l***, and my hands
5:6 and opened for my ***l***, but my love had
5:8 If you find my ***l***, what should you
5:16 This is my ***l***, this my dearest,
7:6 so lovely—my ***l***, delightful one!
7:9 smoothly for my ***l***, gliding through
7:11 Come, my ***l***: Let's go out to the field
7:13 or ripened—my ***l***, I have kept them
8:4 never to arouse ***l*** until it desires.
8:6 your arm, for ***l*** is as strong as
8:7 can't quench ***l***; rivers can't
8:14 Take flight, my ***l***, and be like a

Isaiah
5:1 my loved one a ***l*** song for his
41:8 chosen, offspring of Abraham, whom I ***l***,
43:4 honored, and I ***l*** you. I give
54:8 with everlasting ***l*** I have consoled
61:8 I, the LORD, ***l*** justice; I hate robbery
63:9 saved them. In ***l*** and mercy God
66:10 her, all you who ***l*** her! Rejoice with

Jeremiah
2:2 your first ***l***, your devotion as
2:25 I have fallen in ***l*** with foreign
5:31 and my people ***l*** it this way! But
12:3 can tell that I ***l*** you. So drag them
12:7 given the one I ***l*** into the power of
31:3 loved you with a ***l*** that lasts
31:20 yearn for him and ***l*** him deeply,

Ezekiel
16:8 were ready for ***l***. So I spread my
23:17 lie down and make ***l*** with her,
33:32 like a singer of ***l*** songs with a

Daniel
9:4 to all who ***l*** him and keep his

Hosea
2:19 in justice, in devoted ***l***, and in mercy.
3:1 again, "Go, make ***l*** to a woman who
4:18 indeed, they "***l***"; shame is their
6:4 do with you? Your ***l*** is like a morning
9:15 my house. I will ***l*** them no more; all
11:4 with cords of ***l***. I treated them
14:4 I will ***l*** them freely, for

Amos
4:5 LORD; for so you ***l*** to do, people of
5:15 Hate evil, ***l*** good, and establish

Micah
3:2 who hate good and ***l*** evil, who tear

Zephaniah
3:17 calm with his ***l***; he will rejoice

Zechariah
8:19 the house of Judah. ***L*** truth and peace!

Matthew
3:17 Son whom I dearly ***l***; I find happiness
5:44 But I say to you, ***l*** your enemies and
5:46 If you ***l*** only those who love you, what
5:48 in showing ***l*** to everyone, so
6:5 hypocrites. They ***l*** to pray standing
6:24 hate the one and ***l*** the other, or you
10:37 Those who ***l*** father or mother more than
12:18 chose, the one I ***l***, in whom I find
17:5 Son whom I dearly ***l***. I am very
23:6 They ***l*** to sit in places of honor at
23:7 They ***l*** to be greeted with honor in the
24:12 will expand, the ***l*** of many will grow

Mark
1:11 whom I dearly ***l***; in you I find
9:7 Son, whom I dearly ***l***. Listen to him!"

Luke
3:22 whom I dearly ***l***; in you I find
6:27 willing to hear: ***L*** your enemies. Do
6:32 If you ***l*** those who love you, why
6:35 Instead, ***l*** your enemies, do good, and
7:42 both. Which of them will ***l*** him more?"
7:47 has shown great ***l***. The one who is
11:42 justice and ***l*** for God. These
11:43 Pharisees! You ***l*** the most
16:13 hate the one and ***l*** the other, or you
20:13 my son, whom I ***l*** dearly. Perhaps
20:46 long robes. They ***l*** being greeted

John
5:42 that you don't have God's ***l*** in you.
8:42 Father, you would ***l*** me, for I came
11:3 Lord, the one whom you ***l*** is ill."
12:25 Those who ***l*** their lives will lose them,
14:15 If you ***l*** me, you will keep my
14:21 and I will ***l*** them and reveal
14:23 My Father will ***l*** them, and we will
14:24 Whoever doesn't ***l*** me doesn't keep my
14:31 will know that I ***l*** the Father and do
15:9 I too have loved you. Remain in my ***l***.
15:10 will remain in my ***l***, just as I kept
15:13 one has greater ***l*** than to give up
15:19 the world would ***l*** you as its own.
17:26 so that your ***l*** for me will be in
21:15 of John, do you ***l*** me more than
21:16 of John, do you ***l*** me?" Simon
21:17 of John, do you ***l*** me?" Peter was

Romans
5:8 But God shows his ***l*** for us, because
8:35 us from Christ's ***l***? Will we be
8:38 us from God's ***l*** in Christ Jesus
12:9 ***L*** should be shown without pretending.
13:10 ***L*** doesn't do anything wrong to a
14:15 longer walking in ***l***. Don't let your
15:30 and through the ***l*** of the Spirit, to
1 Corinthians
2:9 for those who ***l*** him that no eye
4:21 you, or with ***l*** and a gentle
8:1 arrogant, but ***l*** builds people up.
13:1 but I don't have ***l***, I'm a clanging
13:2 but I don't have ***l***, I'm nothing.
13:3 but I don't have ***l***, I receive no
13:4 ***L*** is patient, love is kind, it isn't
13:7 ***L*** puts up with all things, trusts in
13:8 ***L*** never fails. As for prophecies, they
13:13 faith, hope, and ***l*** remain—these thre
14:1 Pursue ***l***, and use your ambition to try
16:14 Everything should be done in ***l***
16:24 My ***l*** is with all of you in Christ
2 Corinthians
2:4 the overwhelming ***l*** that I have for
2:8 you to show your ***l*** for this person.
5:14 The ***l*** of Christ controls us, because we
6:6 served with the Holy Spirit, genuine ***l***,
8:7 and the ***l*** we inspired in
8:8 prove the authenticity of your ***l*** also.
8:24 the proof of your ***l*** and the reason we
11:11 because I don't ***l*** you? God knows
12:15 your sake. If I ***l*** you more, will
13:11 the God of ***l*** and peace will be
Galatians
5:6 faith working through ***l*** does matter.
5:13 but serve each other through ***l***.
5:22 of the Spirit is ***l***, joy, peace,
Ephesians
1:5 because of his ***l***. This was
1:15 Jesus and your ***l*** for all God's
2:5 of the great ***l*** that he has for
3:17 a result of having strong roots in ***l***,
3:19 you'll know the ***l*** of Christ that is
4:2 and patience. Accept each other with ***l***,
4:15 the truth with ***l***, let's grow in
4:16 itself up with ***l*** as each one does
5:2 your life with ***l***, following the
5:25 As for husbands, ***l*** your wives just like
5:28 husbands ought to ***l*** their wives—in th
5:33 one of you should ***l*** his wife as
6:23 as well as ***l*** with the faith
6:24 all those who ***l*** our Lord Jesus
Philippians
1:9 prayer: that your ***l*** might become even
1:16 are motivated by ***l***, because they
2:1 any comfort in ***l***, any sharing in
2:2 having the same ***l***, being united,
4:1 sisters whom I ***l*** and miss, who are
Colossians
1:4 Jesus and your ***l*** for all God's
1:5 this faith and ***l*** because of the
1:7 fellow slave we ***l*** and Christ's
1:8 He informed us of your ***l*** in the Spirit
2:2 together in ***l*** so that they
3:14 things put on ***l***, which is the
3:19 Husbands, ***l*** your wives and don't be
1 Thessalonians
1:3 that comes from ***l***, and your
3:6 faithfulness and ***l***! He says that you
3:12 and enrich your ***l*** for each other
3:13 May the ***l*** cause your hearts to be
5:8 faithfulness and ***l*** as a piece of
5:13 them highly with ***l*** because of their
2 Thessalonians
1:3 bounds, and the ***l*** that all of you
2:10 have refused to ***l*** the truth that
3:5 to express God's ***l*** and Christ's
1 Timothy
1:5 of instruction is ***l*** from a pure
1:14 faithfulness and ***l*** that are in
2:15 in faith, ***l***, and holiness,
4:12 speech, behavior, ***l***, faith, and by
6:10 The ***l*** of money is the root of all kinds
6:11 faithfulness, ***l***, endurance, and
2 Timothy
1:13 the faith and ***l*** that are in
2:22 faith, ***l***, and peace
3:2 be selfish and ***l*** money. They will
3:3 brutal, and they won't ***l*** what is good.
3:4 They will ***l*** pleasure instead
3:10 patience, ***l***, and endurance.
4:10 has fallen in ***l*** with the present
Titus
1:8 show hospitality, ***l*** what is good, and
2:2 to their faith, ***l***, and patience.
2:4 young women to ***l*** their husbands
3:4 our savior's kindness and ***l*** appeared,
3:15 greet those who ***l*** us faithfully.
Philemon
1:7 because of your ***l***, since the hearts
1:9 to you through ***l***. I, Paul—an old
Hebrews
6:10 efforts and the ***l*** you have shown
10:24 other to show ***l*** and to do good
13:5 be free from the ***l*** of money, and you
James
1:12 to those who ***l*** him as their
2:5 he has promised to those who ***l*** him?
1 Peter
1:8 seen him, you ***l*** him. Even though
2:17 Honor everyone. ***L*** the family of
3:10 those who want to ***l*** life and see good
5:14 with the kiss of ***l***. Peace to you all
2 Peter
1:7 others; and to affection for others, ***l***.
1 John
2:15 Don't ***l*** the world or the things in the
3:1 See what kind of ***l*** the Father has given
3:10 who doesn't ***l*** a brother or
3:14 life, because we ***l*** the brothers and
3:16 is how we know ***l***: Jesus laid down
3:18 let's not ***l*** with words or
4:8 who doesn't ***l*** does not know
4:10 This is ***l***: it is not that we loved God
4:16 have believed the ***l*** that God has for
4:17 This is how ***l*** has been perfected in us,
4:18 is no fear in ***l***, but perfect love
4:19 We ***l*** because God first loved us
5:2 we know that we ***l*** the children of
2 John
1:1 whom I truly ***l*** (and I am not the
1:3 will be ours who live in truth and ***l***.
1:6 This is ***l***: that we live according to

3 John
1:1 my dear friend Gaius, whom I truly ***l***.
1:6 highly of your ***l*** in front of the
Jude
1:2 have more and more mercy, peace, and ***l***.
1:12 who join your ***l*** feasts are
Revelation
2:4 have let go of the ***l*** you had at first.
3:19 those whom I ***l***. So be earnest
12:11 of their witness. ***L*** for their own
22:15 and all who ***l*** and practice

LOVE AND FAITHFULNESS
2Sa 2:6; 15:20; Ps 40:11; 57:3; 61:7; 89:14; 98:3; 115:1; 138:2; Prv 16:6; Phm 1:5; Rev 2:19

LOVE EACH OTHER
Jn 13:34; 13:35; 15:12, 17; Ro 12:10; 13:8; 1Th 4:9; 1Pt 1:22; 1Jn 3:11; 3:23; 4:7, 11, 12; 2Jn 1:5

LOVE GOD
Ps 48:9; Mk 12:33; Ro 8:28; 1Jn 4:20; 4:21; 5:2

LOVE LASTS FOREVER
2Ch 5:13; 7:3, 6; 20:21; Ps 100:5; 107:1; 118:1, 2, 3, 4, 29; 136:1, 2, 3, 4, 5, 6, 7, 8, 9, 10, 11, 12, 13, 14, 15, 16, 17, 18, 19, 20, 21, 22, 23, 24, 25, 26; 138:8

LOVE OF GOD
Ro 5:5; 2Co 13:13; 1Jn 2:5; 3:17; 4:9; 5:3; Jud 1:21

LOVE THE LORD
Dt 6:5; 11:1; 30:6; Josh 22:5; 23:11; 1Ki 10:9; Ps 31:23; 97:10; 116:1; Hos 10:3; Mt 22:37; Mk 12:30; Lk 10:27; 1Co 16:22

LOVE YOUR NEIGHBOR
Lv 19:18; Mt 5:43; 19:19; 22:39; Mk 12:31; Lk 10:27; Ro 13:9; Ga 5:14; Jas 2:8

LOVED
Genesis
25:28 Isaac ***l*** Esau because he enjoyed eating
29:18 Jacob ***l*** Rachel and said, "I will work
37:3 Now Israel ***l*** Joseph more than any of
2 Samuel
1:23 Jonathan! So well ***l***, so dearly
Esther
2:17 The king ***l*** Esther more than all the
Ecclesiastes
9:9 with your dearly ***l*** spouse all the
Isaiah
5:1 me sing for my ***l*** one a love song
22:4 the destruction of my dearly ***l*** people."
Jeremiah
8:2 which they have ***l*** and served and
11:15 What are my ***l*** ones doing in my temple
14:10 Since they have ***l*** to wander off and
31:3 distance: I have ***l*** you with a love
Ezekiel
16:37 the ones you ***l*** and the ones you
Hosea
9:1 God. You have ***l*** a prostitute's
9:16 put to death their much ***l*** little ones.
Amos
3:2 You only have I ***l*** so deeply of all the
Malachi
1:2 I have ***l*** you, says the LORD; but you
2:11 impure, which God ***l***, and married the
Mark
10:21 him carefully and ***l*** him. He said,
12:6 one son whom he ***l*** dearly. He sent
John
3:16 God so ***l*** the world that he gave his
3:19 world, and people ***l*** darkness more
11:5 Jesus ***l*** Martha, her sister, and
11:36 The Jews said, "See how much he ***l*** him!
12:43 but they ***l*** human praise more
13:1 Father. Having ***l*** his own who were
13:23 one whom Jesus ***l***, was at Jesus'
13:34 Just as I have ***l*** you, so you also
14:21 loves me will be ***l*** by my Father, and
14:28 to you.' If you ***l*** me, you would be
15:9 As the Father ***l*** me, I too have loved
15:12 love each other just as I have ***l*** you.
16:27 because you have ***l*** me and believed
17:23 and that you have ***l*** them just as you
17:24 me because you ***l*** me before the
19:26 disciple whom he ***l*** standing nearby,
20:2 one whom Jesus ***l***, and said, "They
21:7 whom Jesus ***l*** said to Peter,
21:20 whom Jesus ***l*** following them.
Romans
1:7 who are dearly ***l*** by God and called
8:37 victory through the one who ***l*** us.
9:13 it is written, I ***l*** Jacob, but I
9:25 who isn't well ***l***, I will call
11:28 choice, they are ***l*** for the sake of
1 Corinthians
4:14 warn you, since you are my ***l*** children.
4:17 to you; he's my ***l*** and trusted child
15:58 of all this, my ***l*** brothers and
Galatians
2:20 of God's Son, who ***l*** me and gave
Ephesians
5:1 imitate God like dearly ***l*** children.
5:25 just like Christ ***l*** the church and
Philippians
2:12 Therefore, my ***l*** ones, just as you
4:1 crown, stand firm in the Lord. ***L*** ones,
Colossians
3:12 choice, holy and ***l***, put on
4:7 our dearly ***l*** brother, faithful
4:9 and dearly ***l*** brother, who is
4:14 Luke, the dearly ***l*** physician, and Demas
1 Thessalonians
1:4 sisters, you are ***l*** by God, and we
2 Thessalonians
2:13 sisters who are ***l*** by God. This is
2:16 God our Father ***l*** us and through
1 Timothy
6:2 believers who are ***l***. Teach and
Philemon
1:1 To Philemon our dearly ***l*** coworker,
1:16 is, as a dearly ***l*** brother. He is
Hebrews
1:9 You ***l*** righteousness and hated lawless

LOVED [cont.]

2 Peter
1:17 is my dearly **l** Son, with whom I
2:15 son of Bosor, who **l** the payment of
1 John
4:10 it is not that we **l** God but that he
4:11 friends, if God **l** us this way, we
4:19 We love because God first **l** us
Jude
1:1 who are called, **l** by God the Father
Revelation
3:9 feet and realize that I have **l** you.

LOVING THE LORD

Dt 11:13; 11:22; 19:9; 30:16, 20

LOVER

Ecclesiastes
5:10 The money **l** isn't satisfied with money;
Song of Songs
2:3 trees, so is my **l** among the young
2:8 Listen! It's my **l**: here he comes now,
2:9 My **l** is like a gazelle or a young stag.
2:10 My **l** spoke and said to me, "Rise up, my
2:16 I belong to my **l** and he belongs to me—
5:9 How is your **l** different from any other
5:10 My **l** is radiant and ruddy; he stands
6:1 way did your **l** go, you who are
6:2 My **l** has gone down to his garden, to
6:3 I belong to my **l** and my lover belongs
7:10 I belong to my **l**, and his longing is
8:5 against her **l**? Under the apple
Jeremiah
3:20 woman betrays her **l**, so you, people
Hosea
3:1 a woman who has a **l** and is involved

LOVERS

Proverbs
21:17 end up poor; **l** of wine and oil
Jeremiah
2:33 you at pursuing **l** that you instruct
3:1 with many **l**. Would you return
3:2 sit in wait for **l**, like a nomad in
3:6 about looking for **l** on top of every
4:30 decked out; your **l** have rejected you
22:20 because all your **l** have been
22:22 to the wind, your **l** taken off to
30:14 All your **l** disregard you; they write
Lamentations
1:2 None of her **l** comfort her. All
1:19 I called to my **l**, but they deceived
Ezekiel
16:33 gifts to all your **l**. From every
16:36 with your **l** and with the
16:37 all of your **l** whom you pleased,
23:5 and lusted after her **l** the Assyrians:
23:9 her over to her **l**, to the Assyrians
23:22 now inciting your **l** against you, all
Hosea
2:5 will seek out my **l**; they give me my
2:7 will go after her **l**, but she won't
2:10 plain view of her **l**, and no one will
2:12 my pay, which my **l** have given to
2:13 went after her **l**, and forgot me,
8:9 wandering alone; Ephraim has hired **l**.
1 Peter
3:8 sympathetic, **l** of your fellow

LOVES

Genesis
27:9 as the delicious food your father **l**.
44:20 only child. But his father **l** him.'
Deuteronomy
7:9 to everyone who **l** him and keeps his
10:18 widows, and he **l** immigrants,
15:16 because he **l** you and your
23:5 because the LORD your God **l** you.
Ruth
4:15 who **l** you has given
Psalms
11:5 very being hates anyone who **l** violence.
11:7 is righteous! He **l** righteous deeds.
33:5 He **l** righteousness and justice; the
37:28 The LORD **l** justice. He will never leave
47:4 the heights of Jacob, which he **l**. Selah
78:68 the mountain of Zion, which he **l**.
87:2 The LORD **l** Zion's gates more than all
99:4 Strong king who **l** justice, you are the
119:140 and tested; your servant **l** your word!
127:2 because God gives sleep to those he **l**.
146:8 low. The LORD: who **l** the righteous.
Proverbs
3:12 The LORD **l** those he corrects, just like
13:24 but the one who **l** them applies
15:9 the wicked, but **l** those who pursue
29:3 A man who **l** wisdom makes his father rejoice
Isaiah
1:23 thieves. Everyone **l** a bribe and
48:14 things? "The LORD **l** him. He will do
Hosea
3:1 just as the LORD **l** the people of
12:7 in his hands; he **l** to take advantage
Luke
7:5 He **l** our people and he built our
7:47 one who is forgiven little **l** little."
John
3:35 The Father **l** the Son and gives
5:20 The Father **l** the Son and shows him
10:17 is why the Father **l** me: I give up my
14:21 and keeps them **l** me. Whoever loves
14:23 Whoever **l** me will keep my
16:27 Father himself **l** you, because you
Romans
13:8 other. Whoever **l** another person
1 Corinthians
8:3 But if someone **l** God, then they are
2 Corinthians
9:7 of pressure. God **l** a cheerful giver.
Ephesians
1:6 to us freely through the Son whom he **l**.
5:28 Anyone who **l** his wife loves
Colossians
1:13 us into the kingdom of the Son he **l**.
Hebrews
12:6 whomever he **l**, and he punishes
1 John
2:15 world. If anyone **l** the world, the
4:7 and everyone who **l** is born from God
5:1 from God. Whoever **l** someone who is a
Revelation
1:5 To the one who **l** us and freed us
20:9 the city that God **l**. But fire came

LOVING

Deuteronomy
10:12 all his ways, by ***l*** him, by serving
10:15 your ancestors, ***l*** them and choosing
2 Samuel
19:6 by ***l*** those who hate you and hating
Psalms
25:10 LORD's paths are ***l*** and faithful for
59:10 My ***l*** God will come to meet me.
59:17 because God is my stronghold, my ***l*** God.
89:49 now are your ***l*** acts from long
Ecclesiastes
3:8 a time for ***l*** and a time for hating, a
Song of Songs
1:2 Oh, your ***l*** is sweeter than
1:4 Let's savor your ***l*** more than wine.
4:10 beautiful is your ***l***, my sister, my
7:12 bloomed. There I'll give my ***l*** to you.
Isaiah
56:6 serving me and ***l*** my name, becoming
56:10 bark, dreamers, loungers, ***l*** to sleep.
Lamentations
4:10 The hands of ***l*** women boiled their own children
2 Timothy
1:7 that is powerful, ***l***, and
3:4 will love pleasure instead of ***l*** God.
Hebrews
13:1 Keep ***l*** each other like family
1 John
2:10 The person ***l*** a brother and sister stays

LOW

1 Samuel
2:7 wealth, brings ***l***, but also lifts
28:14 and he bowed ***l*** out of respect,
Psalms
62:4 bring others down ***l***; they delight in
72:9 dwellers bow ***l*** before him; let
79:8 us because we've been brought so ***l***.
99:5 our God! Bow ***l*** at his footstool!
99:9 LORD our God! Bow ***l*** at his holy
142:6 brought down so ***l***! Deliver me from
145:14 straightens up all who are bent ***l***.
146:8 who are bent ***l***. The LORD: who
Proverbs
12:9 to be held in ***l*** regard and have a
29:23 Pride lays people ***l***, but those of
Isaiah
2:9 each person laid ***l***—don't lift them
2:12 that is lofty, and it will be laid ***l***;
5:15 each person laid ***l***, the eyes of the
10:33 to be cut down and the exalted laid ***l***.
13:11 the conceit of tyrants I will lay ***l***.
14:8 you were laid ***l***, no logger comes
25:11 God will lay ***l*** their pride, even
29:4 will speak; from ***l*** in the dust your
32:19 falls and the humbled city is laid ***l***,
60:14 will come bending ***l*** to you; all who
Ezekiel
17:6 grew and became a ***l*** spreading vine.
Daniel
2:46 bowed ***l*** and honored
Matthew
23:12 will be brought ***l***. But all who make
Luke
1:48 with favor on the ***l*** status of his
14:11 will be brought ***l***, and those who
18:14 will be brought ***l***, and those who
1 Corinthians
1:28 world considers ***l***-class and low-life
James
1:10 in their ***l*** status, because

LOWER

Hebrews
2:7 you made them ***l*** than angels. You
2:9 one who was made ***l*** in order than the

LOYAL → LOYAL LOVE, LOYAL LOVE AND FAITHFULNESS

Genesis
14:14 took all of the ***l*** men born in his
24:12 me today and be ***l*** to my master
24:14 know that you've been ***l*** to my master."
24:49 Now if you're ***l*** and faithful to my
32:10 don't deserve how ***l*** and truthful
39:21 and remained ***l*** to him. He caused
40:14 doing well and be ***l*** to me. Put in a
47:29 my thigh, and be ***l*** and true to me.
Exodus
20:6 But I am ***l*** and gracious to the
Numbers
14:18 and absolutely ***l***, forgiving wrongs
Deuteronomy
5:10 But I am ***l*** and gracious to the
7:9 and proves ***l*** to everyone who
Joshua
2:12 Now, I have been ***l*** to you. So pledge to
14:8 But I remained ***l*** to the LORD my
14:9 you remained ***l*** to the LORD my
14:14 he remained ***l*** to the LORD God
Judges
1:24 city, and we'll be ***l*** to you in return."
1 Samuel
20:8 So be ***l*** to your servant, because you've
20:14 remain alive, be ***l*** to me. But if I
20:15 ever stop being ***l*** to my household.
2 Samuel
2:5 for doing this ***l*** deed for your
3:8 been nothing but ***l*** to the house of
10:2 said, "I'll be ***l*** to Nahash's son
1 Kings
5:1 Hiram of Tyre was ***l*** to David
12:27 will again become ***l*** to their master
2 Kings
10:6 If you are ***l*** to me and ready
1 Chronicles
12:29 of whom had been ***l*** to Saul's
19:2 I'll be ***l*** to Nahash's son Hanun,"
2 Chronicles
6:41 may those ***l*** to you rejoice in
Job
6:14 Are friends ***l*** to the one who despairs,
Psalms
31:23 those who are ***l***, but he pays the
144:2 God is my ***l*** one, my fortress, my place
Proverbs
2:8 the way of those who are ***l*** to him.
18:24 are friends who are more ***l*** than family.
20:6 say that they are ***l***, but who can find

Isaiah
56:4 I desire, and remain **l** to my covenant,
57:1 it to heart. **L** people are
Matthew
6:24 or you will be **l** to the one and
Luke
16:13 or you will be **l** to the one and
Acts
22:3 I am passionately **l** to God, just like
Philippians
4:3 also asking you, **l** friend, to help

LOYAL LOVE
2Sa 2:6; 15:20; 16:17; Ps 36:5; 40:10, 11; 57:3; 89:1, 2, 14, 24, 28, 33; 92:2; 98:3; 100:5; 115:1; 138:2

LOYAL LOVE AND FAITHFULNESS
2Sa 2:6; 15:20; Ps 40:11; 57:3; 89:14; 98:3; 115:1; 138:2

LOYALTY
Genesis
20:13 her, 'This is the **l** I expect from
24:27 given up his **l** and his
Exodus
15:13 With your great **l** you led the people
34:6 full of great **l** and faithfulness,
34:7 showing great **l** to a thousand
Numbers
14:19 of your absolute **l**, just as you've
Deuteronomy
7:12 and display the **l** that he promised
32:20 they are children lacking **l**.
1 Samuel
26:23 righteousness and **l**, and I wasn't
1 Kings
3:6 kept this great **l** and kindness for
8:23 covenant and show **l** to your servants
1 Chronicles
12:33 of war, to help with undivided **l**;
2 Chronicles
6:14 covenant and show **l** to your servants
6:42 your faithful **l** to your servant
24:22 to remember the **l** that Jehoiada,
Proverbs
3:3 Don't let **l** and faithfulness leave you.
14:22 plan good receive **l** and faithfulness.
Isaiah
19:18 Canaan and swear **l** to the LORD of
40:6 is grass; all its **l** is like the
55:3 with you, my faithful **l** to David.
Lamentations
3:32 in measure with his covenant **l**.
Ezekiel
17:13 solemn pledge of **l**. He also took
Daniel
1:9 faithful **l** between Daniel
Hosea
4:1 faithful love or **l**, and no knowledge

LYING
Genesis
28:13 the land on which you are **l**.
29:2 of sheep were **l** down. That well
Exodus
23:1 with evil people to act as a **l** witness.
Deuteronomy
6:7 when you are **l** down and when you
9:25 and forty nights, **l** flat out, because
Ruth
3:4 place where he is **l**. Then go, uncover
1 Kings
13:18 But the old prophet was **l** to him.
22:23 LORD has placed a **l** spirit in the
Psalms
17:12 are like a strong young lion **l** in wait.
31:18 Let their **l** lips be shut up whenever
41:3 when they are **l** in bed, sick. You
52:3 good; you love **l** more than
78:36 They were **l** to him with their
88:5 among the dead **l** in the grave,
109:2 me, talking about me with **l** tongues.
120:2 deliver me from **l** lips and a
Proverbs
6:17 snobbish eyes, a **l** tongue, hands that
10:18 **L** lips conceal hate, and those who
12:19 forever, but a **l** tongue lasts only
21:28 A **l** witness will perish, but one who
24:33 slumber,a little **l** down with folded
26:28 A **l** tongue hates those it crushes; a
Song of Songs
1:13 is my love to me, **l** all night between
Isaiah
30:9 people, **l** children,
32:7 the poor with **l** words, even when
58:5 a reed and of **l** down in mourning
59:13 revolt, muttering **l** words conceived
Jeremiah
5:26 catch people, like hunters **l** in wait.
8:2 become like refuse **l** on the ground.
8:8 when the **l** pen of the
43:2 Jeremiah, "You're **l** to us! The LORD
Ezekiel
21:23 to them like a **l** divination,
21:29 False visions and **l** divinations set you
Daniel
2:9 to make false and **l** speeches before
4:5 while I was **l** in bed and the
Hosea
4:2 Swearing, **l**, murder, together with
Micah
6:12 falsehood with **l** tongues in their
Matthew
8:14 mother-in-law **l** in bed with a
9:2 was paralyzed, **l** on a cot. When
Mark
2:4 mat on which the paralyzed man was **l**.
Luke
2:12 baby wrapped snugly and **l** in a manger."
John
5:6 Jesus saw him **l** there, knowing
20:5 the linen cloths **l** there, but he
20:6 tomb and saw the linen cloths **l** there.
Romans
9:1 Christ—I'm not **l**, as my conscience
2 Corinthians
11:31 blessed forever, knows that I'm not **l**.
Galatians
1:20 God, I'm not **l** about the things
Ephesians
4:25 gotten rid of **l**, Each of you must
1 Timothy
2:7 truth and I'm not **l**! I'm a teacher of

4:2 the pretense of ***l***, and their own
Hebrews
6:18 the hope that is ***l*** in front of us.
1 John
1:6 darkness, we are ***l*** and do not act

LYRE
1 Samuel
16:16 how to play the ***l***. The musician can
18:10 David played the ***l*** as he usually
1 Chronicles
25:3 with the ***l*** and giving thanks
Job
21:12 raise drum and ***l***, rejoice at the
30:31 My ***l*** is for mourning, my flute, a
Psalms
33:2 the LORD with the ***l***! Sing praises to
43:4 you thanks with the ***l***, God, my God!
49:4 I will explain my riddle on the ***l***.
57:8 Wake up, harp and ***l***! I will wake the
71:22 for you with the ***l***, holy one of
81:2 the drum! Sweet ***l*** along with harp!
92:3 harp, with the melody of the ***l***
98:5 the LORD with the ***l***—with the lyre an
108:2 Wake up, harp and ***l***! I will wake the
147:7 sing praises to our God with a ***l***!
149:3 sing God's praise with the drum and ***l***!
150:3 ram's horn! Praise God with lute and ***l***!
Isaiah
5:12 They party with ***l*** and harp, tambourine,
Daniel
3:5 pipe, zither, ***l***, harp, flute, and
1 Corinthians
14:7 like a harp or a ***l*** can make a sound,

LYSTRA
Acts
14:6 cities of ***L*** and Derbe and the
16:1 Derbe, and then ***L***, where there was
2 Timothy
3:11 Iconium, and ***L***. I put up with

Mm

MAACAH

Genesis
22:24 birth to Tebah, Gaham, Tahash, and ***M***.
2 Samuel
3:3 was Absalom, by ***M***, who was the
10:6 the king of ***M*** with one thousand
10:8 from Tob and ***M*** remained in the
23:34 son from ***M***; Eliam,
1 Kings
15:2 mother's name was ***M***, and she was
15:10 name was ***M***; she was
15:13 his grandmother ***M*** from the position
1 Chronicles
2:48 ***M***, Caleb's secondary wife, gave birth
3:2 Absalom son of ***M***, the daughter of
7:15 sister's name was ***M***. The second
8:29 lived in Gibeon. His wife's name was ***M***;
19:7 as well as King ***M*** and his army, who
2 Chronicles
11:20 Later he married ***M***, Absalom's
11:21 daughter ***M*** more than all his
15:16 his grandmother ***M*** from the position

MAASEIAH

1 Chronicles
15:18 Eliab, Benaiah, ***M***, Mattithiah,
Ezra
10:18 and his brothers: ***M***, Eliezer, Jarib,
Nehemiah
8:4 Hilkiah, and ***M*** on his righthand
Jeremiah
35:4 above the room of ***M***, Shallum's son,

MACEDONIA

Acts
16:9 of a man from ***M*** came to Paul
18:5 arrived from ***M***, Paul devoted
20:3 he decided instead to return through ***M***.

MACHIR

Genesis
50:23 The children of ***M***, Manasseh's son,
Numbers
26:29 descendants: from ***M***, the Machirite
Deuteronomy
3:15 I also gave Gilead to ***M***
Joshua
13:31 to the people of ***M*** son of Manasseh.
17:1 belonged to ***M***, who was

MADE

Genesis
1:7 God ***m*** the dome and separated the waters
2:4 the day the LORD God ***m*** earth and sky—
3:7 together and ***m*** garments for them-
3:21 The LORD God ***m*** the man and his wife
Exodus
1:14 They ***m*** their lives miserable with hard
9:12 But the LORD ***m*** Pharaoh stubborn, and
31:17 six days the LORD ***m*** the heavens and
32:8 They have ***m*** a metal bull calf
36:8 skilled workers ***m*** the dwelling out
37:1 Bezalel ***m*** the chest of acacia wood. It
Numbers
21:9 Moses ***m*** a bronze snake and placed it on a pole.
Deuteronomy
1:28 Our brothers have ***m*** our hearts sick
5:2 The LORD our God ***m*** a covenant with us
32:15 up on the God who ***m*** him, thought the
Joshua
24:25 that day Joshua ***m*** a covenant for
1 Samuel
20:17 So Jonathan again ***m*** a pledge to David
2 Samuel
2:9 There he ***m*** him king over Gilead, the
5:3 King David ***m*** a covenant with
23:5 with God! He has ***m*** an eternal
1 Kings
5:12 Now the LORD ***m*** Solomon wise, just as he had promised.
12:28 advice and then ***m*** two gold calves.
2 Kings
1:8 He wore clothes ***m*** of hair with a
17:38 covenant that I ***m*** with you. Don't
18:4 snake that Moses ***m***, because up to
19:15 kingdoms. You ***m*** both heaven and
2 Chronicles
4:19 Solomon also ***m*** all the equipment for
Ezra
6:1 Then King Darius ***m*** a decree, and they
6:3 rule, King Cyrus ***m*** a decree:
Nehemiah
9:6 LORD. You alone ***m*** heaven, even the
13:26 his God, and God ***m*** him king over all
Job
7:20 Why have you ***m*** me your target so
31:1 I've ***m*** a covenant with my eyes; how
31:15 the one who ***m*** me in the belly
Psalms
8:5 You've ***m*** them only slightly less than
9:15 they themselves ***m***! Their feet are
18:11 God ***m*** darkness cloak him; his covering
19:4 earth. God has ***m*** a tent in heaven
33:6 The skies were ***m*** by the LORD's word,
95:5 the sea, which he ***m***, is his along with
100:3 LORD is God—he ***m*** us; we belong to
120:5 because I've ***m*** my home among
136:5 to the one who ***m*** the skies with
136:7 to the one who ***m*** the great lights—

148:6 and forever. God ***m*** a law that will
Proverbs
8:26 before God ***m*** the earth and the fields
16:4 The LORD ***m*** everything for a purpose,
Ecclesiastes
3:11 God has ***m*** everything fitting in its
7:13 can straighten what God has ***m*** crooked?
10:19 Feasts are ***m*** for laughter, wine cheers
Song of Songs
1:6 with me. They ***m*** me a caretaker of
3:9 King Solomon ***m*** a canopied couch for
3:10 Its pillars he ***m*** of silver, its
Isaiah
43:7 for my glory, whom I have formed and ***m***.
45:12 I myself ***m*** the earth, and created
54:5 is the one who ***m*** you—the LORD of
63:14 your people and ***m*** for yourself a
66:2 My hand ***m*** all these things and brought
Jeremiah
10:12 But God ***m*** the earth by his might; he
27:5 arm, I have ***m*** the earth and the
31:32 the covenant I ***m*** with their
33:2 the LORD who ***m*** the earth, who
51:15 God ***m*** the earth by his might, shaped
52:20 which Solomon had ***m*** for the LORD's
Lamentations
4:2 no more than clay pots ***m*** by a potter.
Ezekiel
3:17 Human one, I've ***m*** you a lookout for the house of Israel.
33:7 human one, I've ***m*** you a lookout for
Daniel
3:1 Nebuchadnezzar ***m*** a gold statue. It
Amos
5:8 The one who ***m*** the Pleiades and Orion,
Jonah
1:9 of heaven—who ***m*** the sea and the
4:5 city. There he ***m*** himself a hut and
Habakkuk
1:14 You ***m*** humans like the fish of the sea,
Zechariah
4:2 see a lampstand ***m*** entirely of gold.
6:1 the mountains were ***m*** of bronze.
Matthew
3:4 John wore clothes ***m*** of camel's hair,
19:4 the creator ***m*** them male and
19:12 who have been ***m*** eunuchs by other
19:28 everything is ***m*** new, when the
21:13 But you've ***m*** it a hideout for
Mark
1:6 John wore clothes ***m*** of camel's hair,
2:4 When they had ***m*** an opening, they
14:58 build another, one not ***m*** by humans.'"
Luke
3:5 crooked will be ***m*** straight and the
6:10 So he did and his hand was ***m*** healthy.
8:17 that won't be ***m*** known and brought
11:40 the one who ***m*** the outside also
John
2:15 He ***m*** a whip from ropes and chased them
9:6 on the ground, ***m*** mud with the
12:3 expensive perfume ***m*** of pure nard. She
17:19 I ***m*** myself holy on their behalf so that
Acts
2:36 that God has ***m*** this Jesus, whom
10:15 consider unclean what God has ***m*** pure."
17:24 God, who ***m*** the world and everything in
Romans
4:2 if Abraham was ***m*** righteous because
5:1 we have been ***m*** righteous through
1 Corinthians
1:2 who have been ***m*** holy to God in
1:20 Hasn't God ***m*** the wisdom of the
Galatians
2:16 a person isn't ***m*** righteous by the
3:11 since no one is ***m*** righteous by the
3:16 The promises were ***m*** to Abraham and to
5:4 are trying to be ***m*** righteous by the
Ephesians
1:22 Christ's feet and ***m*** him head of
2:14 is our peace. He ***m*** both Jews and
Colossians
1:12 to the Father. He ***m*** it so you could
2:13 circumcised, God ***m*** you alive with
1 Thessalonians
2:17 in our hearts. We ***m*** every effort in
Hebrews
2:7 For a while you ***m*** them lower than
8:9 covenant that I ***m*** with their
12:23 the righteous who have been ***m*** perfect,
James
2:22 his faith was ***m*** complete by his
3:9 curse human beings ***m*** in God's likeness.
1 Peter
2:5 You are being ***m*** into a holy
3:18 as a human, but ***m*** alive by the
1 John
4:12 in us and his love is ***m*** perfect in us.
4:18 afraid has not been ***m*** perfect in love.
5:10 believe God has ***m*** God a liar,
Revelation
7:14 their robes and ***m*** them white in the
14:7 the one who ***m*** heaven and earth,
19:7 and his bride has ***m*** herself ready.
21:21 of the gates was ***m*** from a single

MAGDALENE

Matthew
27:56 them were Mary ***M***, Mary the mother
27:61 Mary ***M*** and the other Mary were there,
28:1 of the week, Mary ***M*** and the other
Mark
15:40 including Mary ***M*** and Mary the
15:47 Mary ***M*** and Mary the mother of Joses saw
16:1 was over, Mary ***M***, Mary the mother
16:9 first to Mary ***M***, from whom he had
Luke
8:2 them were Mary ***M*** (from whom seven
24:10 It was Mary ***M***, Joanna, Mary the mother
John
19:25 Clopas, and Mary ***M*** stood near the
20:1 still dark, Mary ***M*** came to the tomb
20:18 Mary ***M*** left and announced to the

MAGOG

Genesis
10:2 sons: Gomer, ***M***, Madai, Javan,

MAGOG [cont.]

1 Chronicles
1:5 family: Gomer, ***M***, Madai, Javan,
Ezekiel
38:2 in the land of ***M***, chief prince of
39:6 will send fire on ***M*** and on those who
Revelation
20:8 earth—Gog and ***M***. He will gather

MAHANAIM

Genesis
32:2 and he named that sacred place ***M***.
2 Samuel
17:24 David had reached ***M*** by the time Absalom

MAJESTIC

Psalms
8:1 our Lord, how ***m*** is your name
8:9 our Lord, how ***m*** is your name
29:4 voice is strong; the LORD's voice is ***m***.
111:3 God's deeds are ***m*** and glorious. God's
145:12 power and the ***m*** glory of God's
Isaiah
28:1 Oh, the ***m*** garland of Ephraim's drunks
28:3 The ***m*** garland of Ephraim's drunks will
30:30 will unleash his ***m*** voice and display
33:21 no boat will go, no ***m*** ship will cross.
60:15 I will make you ***m*** forever, a joy
Daniel
4:30 strength and for my own ***m*** glory?"
Zechariah
6:13 He will be ***m***; he will sit and
10:3 make them like his ***m*** horse in battle.
11:2 has fallen; those ***m*** ones have been
Matthew
25:31 with him, he will sit on his ***m*** throne.

MAJESTY → GOD'S MAJESTY

2 Samuel
19:19 Please forget about it, Your ***M***,
1 Kings
1:17 to him, "Your ***M***, you swore by the
1 Chronicles
29:11 splendor, and ***m***, because
29:25 him such royal ***m*** as no king before
Job
13:11 Wouldn't his ***m*** scare you and dread of
40:10 with splendor and ***m***; clothe yourself
Psalms
68:34 God is! His ***m*** extends over
93:1 He is robed in ***m***—the LORD is robe
145:5 splendor of your ***m***; I will
148:13 all. Only God's ***m*** is over earth and
Isaiah
14:11 Your ***m*** has been brought down to the
24:14 they will shout about the LORD's ***m***.
26:10 and they fail to see the LORD's ***m***.
33:21 The LORD's ***m*** will be there for us: as a
Jeremiah
22:18 for him, saying, "My master, my ***m***!"
Daniel
2:29 lay in bed, Your ***M***, your thoughts
Micah
5:4 the LORD, in the ***m*** of the name of
Zechariah
11:3 because their ***m*** has been
Matthew
16:27 to come with the ***m*** of his Father
25:31 One comes in his ***m*** and all his
Acts
25:21 decision from His ***M*** the emperor, so I
25:25 appealed to His ***M***, I decided to
Hebrews
1:3 at the right side of the highest ***m***.
8:1 of the throne of the ***m*** in the heavens.
2 Peter
1:16 we witnessed his ***m*** with our own eyes.
Jude
1:25 belong glory, ***m***, power, and

MAKE

Genesis
1:26 God said, "Let us ***m*** humanity in our
2:18 is alone. I will ***m*** him a helper that
3:16 he said, "I will ***m*** your pregnancy
6:14 so ***m*** a wooden ark. Make the ark with
12:2 I will ***m*** of you a great nation and will
Exodus
5:7 they need to ***m*** bricks like you
5:9 ***M*** the men's work so hard that it's all
7:3 But I'll ***m*** Pharaoh stubborn, and I'll
23:32 Don't ***m*** any covenants with them or
25:8 They should ***m*** me a sanctuary so I can
25:10 Have them ***m*** an acacia-wood chest. It
Leviticus
1:4 for you, to ***m*** reconciliation
4:20 the priest will ***m*** reconciliation
26:1 You must not ***m*** any idols, and do not
Numbers
6:25 The LORD ***m*** his face shine on you and be
16:5 the LORD will ***m*** known who is his,
35:34 You will not ***m*** the land in which you
Deuteronomy
5:3 The LORD didn't ***m*** this covenant with
5:8 Do not ***m*** an idol for yourself—no form
Joshua
3:7 I will begin to ***m*** you great in the
2 Samuel
7:9 you. Now I will ***m*** your name great—
Ezra
10:3 Let's now ***m*** a covenant with our God to
10:11 But now, ***m*** a confession to the LORD God
Job
5:23 for you will ***m*** an agreement with the
Psalms
2:8 me, and I will ***m*** the nations your
71:22 my God. I will ***m*** music for you
73:18 path; you will ***m*** them fall into
108:1 I will sing and ***m*** music—yes, with
110:1 beside me until I ***m*** your enemies a
119:88 ***M*** me live again according to your
137:6 you, if I don't ***m*** Jerusalem my
143:11 ***M*** me live again, LORD, for your name's
147:1 it is a pleasure to ***m*** beautiful praise!
Proverbs
1:4 They ***m*** the naive mature, the young
14:17 people ***m*** stupid mistakes,
18:6 The lips of fools ***m*** accusations; their
27:11 my child, and ***m*** my heart glad, so
29:9 When the wise ***m*** a legal charge against

Ecclesiastes
5:4 When you ***m*** a promise to God, fulfill it
5:5 Better not to ***m*** a promise than to make
5:6 let your mouth ***m*** a sinner of you,
7:20 to do good only and never ***m*** a mistake.
9:2 for those who ***m*** solemn pledges
11:9 Your heart should ***m*** you happy in your
Isaiah
6:10 ***M*** the minds of this people dull. Make
14:23 I will ***m*** it the home of herons, a
29:16 maker, "He didn't ***m*** me? Should what
40:3 in the desert! ***M*** a level highway
55:3 will live. I will ***m*** an everlasting
61:8 their wage, and ***m*** with them an
Jeremiah
10:11 gods who didn't ***m*** the heavens and
16:20 Can humans ***m*** their own gods? If so,
31:31 LORD, when I will ***m*** a new covenant
32:40 I will ***m*** an everlasting covenant with
Ezekiel
34:25 I will ***m*** a covenant of peace for them,
37:26 I will ***m*** a covenant of peace for them.
39:7 I will ***m*** known my holy name among my people
46:13 lamb. You will ***m*** the offering
Hosea
2:18 that day, I will ***m*** a covenant for
12:9 of Egypt; I will ***m*** you live in tents
Joel
2:17 people, and don't ***m*** your inheritance
2:19 I will no longer ***m*** you a disgrace
Amos
8:9 LORD God, I will ***m*** the sun go down
Micah
4:3 they will no longer learn how to ***m*** war.
6:16 Therefore, I will ***m*** you a sign of
Haggai
2:6 while, I will ***m*** the heavens, the
2:7 I will ***m*** all the nations quake. The
2:21 I am about to ***m*** the heavens and
2:23 the LORD; I will ***m*** you like a signet
Matthew
3:3 way for the Lord; ***m*** his paths
28:19 Therefore, go and ***m*** disciples of all
Mark
1:3 way for the Lord; ***m*** his paths
1:40 If you want, you can ***m*** me clean."
Luke
3:4 way for the Lord; ***m*** his paths
5:12 if you want, you can ***m*** me clean."
20:43 until I ***m*** your enemies a footstool for
John
1:23 the wilderness, ***M*** the Lord's path
2:16 of here! Don't ***m*** my Father's house
Acts
2:35 until I ***m*** your enemies a footstool for
Romans
14:4 Lord has the power to ***m*** them stand).
2 Corinthians
7:2 ***M*** room in your hearts for us. We didn't
1 Timothy
2:10 They should ***m*** themselves attractive by
Hebrews
2:10 of suffering to ***m*** perfect the
8:8 Lord, when I will ***m*** a covenant with
8:10 that I will ***m*** with the house of
James
2:6 Don't the wealthy ***m*** life difficult
3:2 We all ***m*** mistakes often, but those who
3:18 Those who ***m*** peace sow the seeds of
5:12 sisters, never ***m*** a solemn pledge—
1 John
1:10 never sinned," we ***m*** him a liar and
3:7 Little children, ***m*** sure no one deceives
Revelation
17:14 They will ***m*** war on the Lamb, but the
19:19 had gathered to ***m*** war against the

MAKER
Psalms
95:6 Let's kneel before the LORD, our ***m***!
115:15 by the LORD, the ***m*** of heaven and
121:2 the LORD, the ***m*** of heaven and
124:8 of the LORD, the ***m*** of heaven and
134:3 May the LORD, the ***m*** of heaven and
146:6 God: the ***m*** of heaven and earth, the
149:2 celebrate its ***m***; let Zion's
Proverbs
14:31 anger their ***m***, while those who
17:5 poor insult their ***m***; those who
Isaiah
44:2 The LORD your ***m***, who formed you in the
51:13 the LORD your ***m***, the one who
Ezekiel
22:3 blood-letter, self-defiling idol ***m***:
Hosea
8:14 has forgotten his ***m***, and built

MALE
Genesis
1:27 God created them, ***m*** and female God
5:2 and created them ***m*** and female. He
6:19 to bring a pair, ***m*** and female, into
7:2 seven pairs, a ***m*** and his mate; and
17:10 must keep: Circumcise every ***m***.
1 Kings
11:15 and he had killed every ***m*** in Edom.
Proverbs
30:31 of a rooster or a ***m*** goat; and a king
Ezekiel
43:22 a flawless ***m*** goat as a
Matthew
2:16 to kill all the ***m*** children in
19:4 the creator made them ***m*** and female?
Mark
10:6 creation, God made them ***m*** and female.
Luke
2:23 Every firstborn ***m*** will be dedicated
Galatians
3:28 nor is there ***m*** and female, for
Revelation
12:5 birth to a son, a ***m*** child who is to
12:13 who had given birth to the ***m*** child.

MALES
Exodus
13:12 All of the first ***m*** born to your
23:17 All your ***m*** should appear three times a
Leviticus
6:18 Only the ***m*** from Aaron's descendants can eat it

MALES [cont.]

Numbers
3:12 of all the oldest ***m*** who open an
8:17 all the oldest ***m*** in the land of
18:15 redeem the oldest ***m*** of humans and of
33:4 their oldest ***m***, whom the LORD
Deuteronomy
20:13 kill all the city's ***m*** with the sword.
29:10 your officials, all the Israelite ***m***,
2 Chronicles
31:16 rations to those ***m***, registered by
Nehemiah
10:36 and the oldest ***m*** of our herds and
Psalms
78:51 of Egypt's oldest ***m***; in Ham's tents,
Romans
1:27 the same way, the ***m*** traded natural

MAN → BLIND MAN, RIGHTEOUS MAN
Genesis
2:23 woman because from a ***m*** she was taken."
2:24 the reason that a ***m*** leaves his father
2:25 were naked, the ***m*** and his wife, but
3:8 garden; and the ***m*** and his wife hid
3:9 God called to the ***m*** and said to him,
3:21 LORD God made the ***m*** and his wife
4:1 The ***m*** Adam knew his wife Eve
6:9 and exemplary ***m***; he walked with
32:24 by himself, and a ***m*** wrestled with him
Exodus
2:1 Now a ***m*** from Levi's household married a
2:19 An Egyptian ***m*** rescued us from a
11:3 as a great and important ***m*** in the land.
21:7 When a ***m*** sells his daughter as a slave,
Leviticus
19:20 If a ***m*** has sexual relations with a
20:10 If a ***m*** commits adultery with a married
Numbers
1:20 households. Every ***m*** 20 years old and
Deuteronomy
22:13 Suppose a ***m*** gets married and
23:1 No ***m*** whose testicles are crushed or
Judges
8:21 as they say, 'A ***m*** is measured by
13:6 her husband, "A ***m*** of God came to
Ruth
1:1 in the land. A ***m*** with his wife and
2:20 said to her, "The ***m*** is one of our
1 Samuel
2:27 Now a ***m*** of God came to Eli and said,
2 Samuel
1:2 the third day, a ***m*** showed up from
3:38 and a great ***m*** in Israel has
1 Kings
13:1 A ***m*** of God came from Judah by God's
17:18 wrong between us, ***m*** of God? Have you
20:35 command a certain ***m*** who belonged to a prophetic group
2 Kings
1:6 said to him, "A ***m*** met us and said,
1:11 said to Elijah, "***M*** of God, this is
1 Chronicles
12:28 Zadok, a young ***m***, a mighty
16:3 cake to every Israelite ***m*** and woman.
20:6 there was a huge ***m*** with six fingers
22:9 you. He'll be a ***m*** of peace, and
23:14 As for Moses the ***m*** of God, his sons
27:32 a counselor, a ***m*** of understanding,
28:3 are a military ***m*** and you've shed
2 Chronicles
8:14 what David the ***m*** of God had
Psalms
89:19 crown on a strong ***m***. I raised up
105:17 he sent a ***m*** ahead of them, who was sold
Proverbs
6:27 Can a ***m*** scoop fire into his lap and his
6:28 If a ***m*** walks on hot coals, don't his
6:29 So is the ***m*** who approaches his
6:34 Jealousy makes a ***m*** rage; he'll show no
24:34 deprivation like a ***m*** with a shield.
29:3 A ***m*** who loves wisdom makes his father rejoice
30:2 to be human, a ***m*** without
30:19 and the way of a ***m*** with a young
Ecclesiastes
7:28 find: I found one ***m*** among a thousand,
9:15 a poor but wise ***m*** who saved
Isaiah
4:1 will grab one ***m*** on that day,
6:5 I'm ruined! I'm a ***m*** with unclean
Jeremiah
3:1 If a ***m*** divorces his wife, and after she
Lamentations
3:27 It's good for a ***m*** to carry a yoke in
Ezekiel
9:2 them was another ***m*** who was dressed
10:2 He said to the ***m*** clothed in linen: Go
40:4 The ***m*** spoke to me, "Human one, look and listen well
Daniel
10:5 suddenly saw a ***m*** clothed in linen
12:7 I heard the ***m*** clothed in white linen,
Zechariah
1:8 looked and saw a ***m*** riding on a red
Matthew
5:28 to you that every ***m*** who looks at a
12:10 A ***m*** with a withered hand was there.
Mark
10:2 the Law allow a ***m*** to divorce his
16:5 they saw a young ***m*** in a white robe
Luke
6:8 so he said to the ***m*** with the withered
7:12 city gate, a dead ***m*** was being carried
13:6 this parable: "A ***m*** owned a fig tree
14:16 A certain ***m*** hosted a large
15:11 Jesus said, "A certain ***m*** had two sons
16:1 A certain rich ***m*** heard that his
16:18 Any ***m*** who divorces his wife and marries
16:20 a certain poor ***m*** named Lazarus who
20:9 A certain ***m*** planted a
John
4:29 Come and see a ***m*** who has told me
7:40 they said, "This ***m*** is truly the
Romans
7:3 with another ***m*** while her husband
9:10 children with one ***m***, our ancestor
1 Corinthians
5:1 the Gentiles—a ***m*** is having sex
7:2 Each ***m*** should have his own wife, and
11:3 the head of every ***m*** is Christ, and
11:14 you that if a ***m*** has long hair, it

Ephesians
5:31 This is why a ***m*** will leave his father
1 Timothy
5:1 correct an older ***m*** but encourage him
6:11 But as for you, ***m*** of God, run away from

MANAGER
Genesis
43:16 he said to the ***m*** of his household,
44:4 to his household ***m***, "Get ready, go
Matthew
20:8 said to his ***m***, 'Call the
Luke
16:1 his household ***m*** was wasting his
16:2 He called the ***m*** in and said to him,
Acts
19:35 The city ***m*** brought order to the crowd
1 Corinthians
4:2 is expected of a ***m*** is that they

MANASSEH
Genesis
41:51 the oldest son ***M***, "because," he
Numbers
1:35 from the tribe of ***M*** were 32,200.
2 Kings
21:1 ***M*** was 12 years old when he became king,
Ezra
10:30 Mattaniah, Bezalel, Binnui, and ***M***.
Jeremiah
15:4 what Judah's King ***M***, Hezekiah's son,
Matthew
1:10 was the father of ***M***. Manasseh was the
Revelation
7:6 from the tribe of ***M***, twelve thousand;

MANNA
Exodus
16:31 people called it ***m***. It was like
16:35 Israelites ate ***m*** for forty years,
Numbers
11:6 There is nothing but ***m*** in front of us."
11:7 The ***m*** was like coriander seed and its
11:9 the night, the ***m*** would fall with
Deuteronomy
8:3 feeding you the ***m*** that neither you
8:16 one who fed you ***m*** in the
Joshua
5:12 The ***m*** stopped on that next day, when
Nehemiah
9:20 withhold your ***m*** from them, and
Psalms
78:24 and rained ***m*** on them so they could eat.
John
6:31 Our ancestors ate ***m*** in the wilderness,
6:49 ancestors ate ***m*** in the wilderness
Hebrews
9:4 jar containing ***m***, Aaron's rod that
Revelation
2:17 of the hidden ***m*** to eat. I will

MANOAH
Judges
13:2 whose name was ***M***. His wife was
16:31 of his father ***M***. He had led

MARCH
Numbers
12:15 the people didn't ***m*** until Miriam was
Deuteronomy
20:1 When you ***m*** out to battle your enemies
24:5 doesn't have to ***m*** in battle.
Joshua
3:3 it, you are to ***m*** out from your
Psalms
74:3 ***M*** to the unending ruins, to all that
91:13 You'll ***m*** on top of lions and vipers;
125:5 may the LORD ***m*** them off with
Proverbs
30:27 a king, but they ***m*** together in ranks.
Isaiah
7:6 Let's ***m*** up against Judah, tear it
27:4 for me, I will ***m*** to battle against
36:10 who told me, '***M*** against this land
Jeremiah
12:12 roads destroyers ***m***; for the sword of
Ezekiel
20:35 I will ***m*** you out to the wilderness
Zechariah
9:14 the horn; he will ***m*** forth on the

MARK
Acts
12:12 was also known as ***M***.) Many believers
12:25 them John, who was also known as ***M***.
15:37 wanted to take John ***M*** with them.
15:39 Barnabas took ***M*** and sailed to
Colossians
4:10 to you. So does ***M***, Barnabas' cousin
2 Timothy
4:11 is with me. Get ***M***, and bring him
Philemon
1:24 as my coworkers ***M***, Aristarchus,
1 Peter
5:13 greets you, and so does my son ***M***.
Revelation
13:16 slaves—to have a ***m*** put on their
13:17 person has the ***m*** with the beast's
14:9 and receive a ***m*** on their
14:11 those who receive the ***m*** of its name."
16:2 had the beast's ***m*** and worshipped
19:20 the beast's ***m*** and into
20:4 received the ***m*** on their forehead

MARRIAGE
Genesis
34:12 bride price and ***m*** gifts as large as
Deuteronomy
21:13 consummate the ***m***. You will be her
22:13 consummates the ***m*** but subsequently
25:5 consummate the ***m*** according to the
Joshua
15:16 my daughter in ***m*** to whoever
15:17 gave him Achsah his daughter in ***m***.
Judges
15:2 I gave her in ***m*** to one of your
15:6 gave his wife in ***m*** to one of his
1 Samuel
18:17 her to you in ***m*** on this
18:27 gave his daughter Michal to him in ***m***.
1 Kings
11:19 sisters for ***m***, a sister of

1 Chronicles
2:35 his daughter in ***m*** to Jarha his
2 Chronicles
18:1 he allied himself with Ahab through ***m***.
Ezra
9:12 to their sons in ***m***, do not take
Nehemiah
10:30 our daughters in ***m*** to the
13:25 to their sons in ***m***, or take their
Matthew
22:30 they be given in ***m***. Instead, they
24:38 and giving in ***m***, until the day
Mark
12:25 they be given in ***m***. Instead, they
Luke
2:5 to him in ***m*** and who was
17:27 being given in ***m*** until the day
20:34 to this age marry and are given in ***m***.
20:35 marry nor will they be given in ***m***.
1 Corinthians
7:39 to stay in her ***m*** as long as her
2 Corinthians
11:2 I promised you in ***m*** to one husband. I
Ephesians
5:32 ***M*** is a significant allegory, and I'm
1 Timothy
4:3 will prohibit ***m*** and eating foods
Hebrews
13:4 ***M*** must be honored in every respect,

MARRIED

Genesis
6:2 were, so they ***m*** the ones they
20:3 you have taken. She is a ***m*** woman."
Leviticus
20:10 adultery with a ***m*** woman, committing
Numbers
5:19 defiled while ***m*** to your husband,
36:3 If they are ***m*** to someone from another
36:11 daughters, ***m*** their cousins.
Deuteronomy
20:7 but not yet ***m***? He may leave and
24:5 A newly ***m*** man doesn't have to march in battle.
Ezra
10:17 of all the men who had ***m*** foreign women.
Nehemiah
13:23 saw Jews who had ***m*** women of Ashdod,
Esther
2:2 young women who haven't yet ***m***.
Proverbs
6:26 of bread, but a ***m*** woman hunts for a
30:23 when she gets ***m*** and a female
Isaiah
62:4 and your land, ***M***. Because the LORD
Jeremiah
29:6 Get ***m*** and have children; then help your
Malachi
2:11 God loved, and ***m*** the daughter of a
Matthew
1:18 before they were ***m***, she became
22:25 us. The first one ***m***, then died.
22:28 her husband? They were all ***m*** to her."
Mark
6:17 brother Philip. Herod had ***m*** her,
12:20 The first one ***m*** a woman; when he
12:21 The second ***m*** her and died without
12:23 will she be? All seven were ***m*** to her."
John
3:29 who is getting ***m***. The friend of
1 Corinthians
7:9 they should get ***m***, because it's
7:32 A man who isn't ***m*** is concerned
7:34 A woman who isn't ***m*** or who is a
1 Timothy
5:11 from Christ, they will want to get ***m***.

MARRIES

Genesis
27:46 women. If Jacob ***m*** one of the
Leviticus
20:14 If a man ***m*** a woman and her mother as
20:17 If a man ***m*** his sister—his father's
20:21 If a man ***m*** his brother's wife, it is
22:12 priest's daughter ***m*** a layman, she is
Numbers
30:6 If she ***m*** while her solemn promise is in
Deuteronomy
24:1 Let's say a man ***m*** a woman, but she
Isaiah
62:5 As a young man ***m*** a young woman, so your
Jeremiah
3:1 she leaves him ***m*** another, can he
Matthew
5:32 And whoever ***m*** a divorced woman
19:9 and ***m*** another woman
Mark
10:11 his wife and ***m*** another commits
10:12 her husband and ***m*** another, she
Luke
16:18 his wife and ***m*** another commits
Romans
7:3 adultery if she ***m*** someone else.
1 Corinthians
7:38 the one who ***m*** the unmarried

MARRY

Genesis
28:1 orders: "Don't ***m*** a Canaanite woman.
Exodus
22:16 with her, he must ***m*** her and pay the
22:17 to let them ***m***, he must still
Leviticus
18:18 You must not ***m*** your wife's sister as a
21:7 Priests must not ***m*** a woman who is
21:13 high priest must ***m*** a woman who is a
Deuteronomy
7:3 of their sons to ***m***, and don't take
20:7 and someone else would ***m*** his fiancée."
22:30 A man cannot ***m*** his father's former
24:4 take her back and ***m*** her again after
25:5 the family and ***m*** a stranger.
25:7 does not want to ***m*** his sister-in-law,
25:8 insisting, "I don't want to ***m*** her,"
Jeremiah
16:2 Don't ***m*** or have children in this place
Ezekiel
44:22 They must not ***m*** widows or divorced
Hosea
1:2 said to him,"Go, ***m*** a prostitute and
Matthew
14:4 against the law for you to ***m*** her."

19:10 his wife, then it's better not to ***m***."
22:24 his brother must ***m*** his wife and
Luke
20:28 the brother must ***m*** the widow and
20:34 to this age ***m*** and are given in
20:35 the dead, won't ***m*** nor will they be
1 Corinthians
7:9 it's better to ***m*** than to burn with
7:28 But if you do ***m***, you haven't sinned;
7:37 in his own heart not to ***m*** the woman.
7:39 she is free to ***m*** whomever she
1 Timothy
5:14 younger widows to ***m***, have children,

MARTHA

Luke
10:38 a woman named ***M*** welcomed him as a
John
11:1 the village of Mary and her sister ***M***.

MARY

Matthew
1:16 the husband of ***M***—of whom Jesus was
27:56 Among them were ***M*** Magdalene, Mary the
27:61 ***M*** Magdalene and the other Mary were
28:1 day of the week, ***M*** Magdalene and the
Mark
15:40 including ***M*** Magdalene and
15:47 ***M*** Magdalene and Mary the mother of
16:1 Sabbath was over, ***M*** Magdalene, Mary
16:9 appeared first to ***M*** Magdalene, from
16:11 was alive and that ***M*** had seen him.
Luke
1:27 David's house. The virgin's name was ***M***.
2:5 together with ***M***, who was promised
2:6 the time came for ***M*** to have her baby.
2:16 quickly and found ***M*** and Joseph, and
2:19 ***M*** committed these things to memory and
2:34 them and said to ***M*** his mother, "This
2:39 When ***M*** and Joseph had completed
8:2 Among them were ***M*** Magdalene (from
10:39 a sister named ***M***, who sat at the
24:10 It was ***M*** Magdalene, Joanna, Mary the
John
11:1 the village of ***M*** and her sister
19:25 mother's sister, ***M*** the wife of
20:1 was still dark, ***M*** Magdalene came to
Acts
1:14 women, including ***M*** the mother of
12:12 to Mary's house. (***M*** was John's
Romans
16:6 Say hello to ***M***, who has worked very

MASTER

Genesis
1:28 the earth and ***m*** it. Take charge
24:12 LORD, God of my ***m*** Abraham, make
Exodus
21:5 I love my ***m***, my wife, and my
Job
15:24 scare them, ***m*** them like a king
Psalms
45:11 he is your ***m***, bow down to him
105:21 king made Joseph ***m*** of his house and
110:1 LORD says to my ***m***: "Sit right
110:5 My ***m***, by your strong hand, God has
Proverbs
8:30 beside him as a ***m*** of crafts. I was
24:8 plot evil will be called ***m*** schemers.
25:13 them; they restore the life of their ***m***.
27:18 who look after their ***m*** will be honored.
30:10 a servant to his ***m***; otherwise, the
Isaiah
19:4 over to a harsh ***m***; a strong king
37:6 Say this to your ***m***: The LORD says
Ezekiel
7:11 up as a wicked ***m***. It isn't from
Matthew
10:24 and slaves aren't greater than their ***m***.
24:46 servants whom the ***m*** finds fulfilling
25:21 His ***m*** replied, 'Excellent! You are a
25:23 His ***m*** replied, 'Well done! You are a
Mark
11:3 this?' say, 'Its ***m*** needs it, and he
Luke
8:24 Jesus, shouting "***M***, Master, we're
12:36 waiting for their ***m*** to come home from
14:21 excuses to his ***m***. The master of
16:8 The ***m*** commended the dishonest manager
19:31 it?' just say, 'Its ***m*** needs it.'"
John
13:16 than their ***m***, nor are those
15:15 know what their ***m*** is doing.
15:20 than their ***m***.' If the world
Acts
4:24 unison to God, "***M***, you are the one
1 Corinthians
3:10 like a wise ***m*** builder according
Ephesians
6:9 slaves have a ***m*** in heaven. He
Colossians
4:1 that you yourselves have a ***m*** in heaven.
1 Timothy
6:15 blessed and only ***m***, the King of
1 Peter
3:6 she called him ***m***. You have become
2 Peter
2:1 and deny the ***m*** who bought them,
Jude
1:4 and deny our only ***m*** and Lord, Jesus
Revelation
6:10 Holy and true ***M***, how long will

MASTERS

Exodus
3:7 of their slave ***m***. I know about
5:6 the people's slave ***m*** and supervisors,
Job
3:19 there; a servant is free from his ***m***.
Ecclesiastes
12:11 sayings of the ***m*** are like nails
Matthew
6:24 one can serve two ***m***. Either you will
Luke
16:13 can serve two ***m***. Either you will
Acts
16:30 asked, "Honorable ***m***, what must I do
Ephesians
6:5 obey your human ***m*** with fear and
6:9 As for ***m***, treat your slaves in the

Colossians
3:22 Slaves, obey your ***m*** on earth in
4:1 ***M***, be just and fair to your slaves,
1 Timothy
6:1 their own ***m*** as worthy of full
6:2 those who have ***m*** who are believers
Titus
2:9 to their own ***m*** and please them
1 Peter
2:18 authority of your ***m*** with all respect.

MATTANIAH
2 Kings
24:17 king made ***M***, Jehoiachin's

MEAL → EAT THE PASSOVER MEAL, PASSOVER MEAL
Genesis
19:3 He made a big ***m*** for them, even
24:33 and set out a ***m*** for him. But the man
31:54 relatives to a ***m***. They ate
43:25 heard that they would have a ***m*** there.
Exodus
2:20 man? Invite him to eat a ***m*** with us."
12:11 should eat the ***m*** in a hurry. It is
18:12 elders to eat a ***m*** with Moses'
Numbers
25:2 the people ate a ***m***, and they
Proverbs
15:17 Better a ***m*** of greens with love than a
Jeremiah
41:1 While they were eating a ***m*** together,
Hosea
8:7 it will yield no ***m***; if it were to
Matthew
22:4 Look, the ***m*** is all prepared.
Luke
10:40 ready for their ***m***. So Martha came
11:37 him to share a ***m*** with him, so
11:38 before the ***m***, he was
14:1 went to share a ***m*** in the home of
John
13:2 the evening ***m***. The devil had
21:20 Jesus at the ***m*** and asked him,
Acts
10:10 preparing the ***m***, he had a
16:34 and gave them a ***m***. He was overjoyed
20:7 together for a ***m***, Paul was holding
1 Corinthians
11:20 place, it isn't to eat the Lord's ***m***.
11:21 eats a private ***m***. One person goes
Hebrews
12:16 as the oldest son for one ***m***.
James
2:16 warm! Have a nice ***m***!"? What good is

MEANING
Genesis
33:8 said, "What's the ***m*** of this entire
40:5 and each man's dream had its own ***m***.
Deuteronomy
6:20 you, "What is the ***m*** of the laws, the
Ecclesiastes
8:1 And who knows the ***m*** of anything? A
Daniel
2:3 dream, and I'm anxious to know its ***m***."
4:6 so they might tell me the dream's ***m***.
5:7 and tell me its ***m*** will wear royal
5:12 insight into the ***m*** of dreams. He can
5:26 This is the ***m*** of the word mene: God
7:16 explained to me the ***m*** of these things.
9:23 word and grasp the ***m*** of this vision!
10:1 having discerned the ***m*** of the vision.
10:11 Now grasp the ***m*** of what I'm
Mark
4:15 This is the ***m*** of the seed that fell on
4:16 Here's the ***m*** of the seed that fell on
Luke
9:45 statement. Its ***m*** was hidden from
18:34 these words. The ***m*** of this message
20:17 Then what is the ***m*** of this text of
Acts
10:17 about the ***m*** of the vision.
1 Corinthians
1:17 cross won't be emptied of its ***m***.
14:10 world, and none of them are without ***m***.
14:11 I don't know the ***m*** of the language,

MEASURE
Genesis
41:49 stopped trying to ***m*** it because it was
Numbers
35:5 You will ***m*** outside the city on the east
Ezekiel
45:3 you will ***m*** out an area 7.1
Daniel
5:27 on the scales, and you don't ***m*** up.
Zechariah
2:2 said to me, "To ***m*** Jerusalem to see
Revelation
11:1 told, "Get up and ***m*** God's temple, the
11:2 But don't ***m*** the court outside the
21:15 rod with which to ***m*** the city, its

MEASURED
Judges
8:21 say, 'A man is ***m*** by his
Job
7:3 nights of toil have been ***m*** out for me.
28:15 gold; its price can't be ***m*** in silver,
Isaiah
40:12 Who has ***m*** the waters in the palm of a hand
Jeremiah
31:37 above could be ***m*** and the
Ezekiel
40:5 When he ***m*** the wall's height
41:1 main hall, and he ***m*** the arches. They
42:15 East Gate, and he ***m*** all the way
47:3 the east. When he ***m*** off fifteen
48:30 The north side is ***m*** at 1.28 miles.
Hosea
1:10 can be neither ***m*** nor numbered; and
Amos
7:17 your land will be ***m*** and divided up;
Romans
12:3 since God has ***m*** out a portion of
Ephesians
4:7 to each one of us ***m*** out by the gift
4:13 be fully grown, ***m*** by the standard
Revelation
21:16 as its width. He ***m*** the city with the
21:17 He also ***m*** the thickness of its wall. It

MEAT
Genesis
9:4 you must not eat ***m*** with its life,
Exodus
16:12 you will eat ***m***. And in the
Numbers
11:13 Where am I to get ***m*** for all these
18:18 But their ***m*** is yours. It will be yours
Deuteronomy
12:23 not consume the life along with the ***m***.
14:8 these animals' ***m***, and you must not
16:4 none of the ***m*** that you
Psalms
50:13 Do I eat bulls' ***m***? Do I drink goats'
78:20 too? Can he provide ***m*** for his people?"
78:27 He rained ***m*** on them as if it were dust
Proverbs
23:20 on wine or those who eat too much ***m***,
Ezekiel
4:14 and no unclean ***m*** has ever entered
11:3 is the cooking pot, and we are the ***m***."
Acts
15:20 eating ***m*** from strangled
21:25 idols, blood, the ***m*** from strangled
Romans
14:21 thing not to eat ***m*** or drink wine or
1 Corinthians
8:13 I won't eat ***m*** ever again, or
10:28 to you, "This ***m*** was sacrificed in

MEDIATOR
Job
9:33 that there were a ***m*** between us; he
33:23 this person, a ***m***, one out of a
Galatians
3:19 through angels by the hand of a ***m***.
3:20 Now the ***m*** does not take one side; but
1 Timothy
2:5 one God and one ***m*** between God and
Hebrews
9:15 is why he's the ***m*** of a new covenant
12:24 to Jesus the ***m*** of the new covenant, and

MEDITERRANEAN
Numbers
34:5 ravine. Its limit will be at the ***M*** Sea.
34:6 will be the ***M*** Sea. This will be
34:7 border: From the ***M*** Sea you will mark
Deuteronomy
11:24 River all the way to the ***M*** Sea.
34:2 entirety of Judah as far as the ***M*** Sea;
Joshua
1:4 land, up to the ***M*** Sea on the west.
9:1 coast of the ***M*** Sea toward
13:7 the Jordan to the ***M*** Sea in the west.
15:12 border was the ***M*** Sea and its
15:47 of Egypt and the ***M*** Sea and its
23:4 stretch from the Jordan to the ***M*** Sea.
Esther
10:1 including the islands of the ***M***.
Ezekiel
47:10 will be like the ***M*** Sea, having all
47:15 begins at the ***M*** Sea and goes in
47:17 boundary from the ***M*** Sea to Hazar-enon
47:19 of Egypt to the ***M*** Sea. This is the
47:20 limit, the ***M*** Sea is the
48:28 the border of Egypt and to the ***M*** Sea.
Zechariah
14:8 half of it to the ***M***; this will happen

MEET
Genesis
33:4 But Esau ran to ***m*** him, threw his arms
46:29 and went to ***m*** his father Israel
Exodus
18:7 Moses went out to ***m*** his father-in-law,
19:17 of the camp to ***m*** God, and they
Job
9:19 If justice—who calls God to ***m*** me?
21:15 him, and what can we gain if we ***m*** him?"
Psalms
79:8 hurry to ***m*** us because we've
94:15 will once again ***m*** up with
119:147 I ***m*** the predawn light and cry for help.
Proverbs
7:15 I've come out to ***m*** you, seeking you,
17:12 Safer to ***m*** a bear robbed of her cubs
Amos
4:12 to you. Prepare to ***m*** your God, Israel!
9:10 who say, "Evil won't overtake or ***m*** us."
Matthew
25:1 lamps and went out to ***m*** the groom.
1 Thessalonians
4:17 in the clouds to ***m*** with the Lord in

MEETING
Exodus
27:21 In the ***m*** tent, outside the veil that
40:35 enter the ***m*** tent because the
Leviticus
1:1 Moses and said to him from the ***m*** tent,
3:2 it at the ***m*** tent's entrance.
4:18 the LORD in the ***m*** tent. But he will
24:3 be inside the ***m*** tent but outside
Numbers
1:1 desert in the ***m*** tent on the first
31:54 brought it to the ***m*** tent as a
Deuteronomy
31:14 yourselves at the ***m*** tent so I can
Joshua
18:1 and set up the ***m*** tent there. The
19:51 entrance of the ***m*** tent and finished
1 Kings
8:4 LORD's chest, the ***m*** tent, and all the
1 Chronicles
9:21 gatekeeper at the ***m*** tent's entrance.
Psalms
74:4 in your own ***m*** place; they set
74:8 all of God's ***m*** places in the
Amos
9:11 will raise up the ***m*** tent of David
Acts
6:2 Twelve called a ***m*** of all the
11:26 for a whole year, ***m*** with the church
19:25 He called a ***m*** with these craftspeople
24:22 adjourned the ***m***. He said, "When
1 Corinthians
14:23 whole church is ***m*** and everyone is
14:28 keep quiet in the ***m***. They should
14:35 for a woman to talk during the ***m***.
Hebrews
8:2 which is the true ***m*** tent that God,

9:11 and more perfect ***m*** tent, which isn't
9:21 he sprinkled the ***m*** tent and also all
13:10 as priests in the ***m*** tent don't have
James
2:2 coming into your ***m***. One has a gold

MEGIDDO
Joshua
12:21 king of Taanach one the king of ***M*** one
17:11 the population of ***M*** and its dependent
Judges
1:27 Dor, Ibleam, ***M***, or any of their
1 Kings
4:12 son, in Taanach, ***M***, and all Beth-shea
9:15 of Jerusalem, Hazor, ***M***, and Gezer:
2 Kings
9:27 Ahaziah fled to ***M*** and died there.
23:29 Josiah in ***M***, he killed the
23:30 his body from ***M*** in a chariot.
1 Chronicles
7:29 and its towns, ***M*** and its towns,
2 Chronicles
35:22 went to fight Neco on the plain of ***M***.
Zechariah
12:11 of Hadad-Rimmon in the ***M*** Valley.

MELCHIZEDEK
Genesis
14:18 Now ***M*** the king of Salem and the priest
Psalms
110:4 are a priest forever in line with ***M***."
Hebrews
5:6 forever, according to the order of ***M***.
6:20 priest according to the order of ***M***.
7:1 This ***M***, who was king of Salem and

MEMBERS
Matthew
10:25 will call the ***m*** of his household
10:36 enemies are ***m*** of their own
Acts
4:15 the council ***m*** began to confer
5:33 When the council ***m*** heard this, they
7:54 Once the council ***m*** heard these words,
23:9 Council ***m*** were shouting loudly. Some

MEMORY
Deuteronomy
32:26 them down, erased them from human ***m***,
Job
18:17 The ***m*** of them will perish from the
Psalms
9:6 cities—even the ***m*** of them is dead.
34:16 even the ***m*** of them from the
109:15 the very ***m*** of them from the
Proverbs
10:7 The ***m*** of the righteous is a blessing,
Ecclesiastes
2:16 is no eternal ***m*** of the wise any
9:5 for them; even the ***m*** of them is lost.
Isaiah
26:14 them, and abolished all ***m*** of them.
Lamentations
3:19 The ***m*** of my suffering and homelessness
Matthew
26:13 done will also be told in ***m*** of her."
Luke
2:19 these things to ***m*** and considered
2 Peter
1:13 stirring up your ***m***, as long as I'm

MEN
Genesis
6:4 were the ancient heroes, famous ***m***.
18:2 saw three ***m*** standing near
Numbers
1:5 the names of the ***m*** who will assist
1:24 households. The ***m*** 20 years old and
13:2 Send out ***m*** to explore the land of
13:32 All the people we saw in it are huge ***m***.
Deuteronomy
1:23 I selected twelve ***m***, one from each
Joshua
2:1 secretly sent two ***m*** as spies from
Judges
1:4 They defeated ten thousand ***m*** at Bezek.
15:16 jawbone, I've killed one thousand ***m***."
1 Samuel
14:6 uncircumcised ***m***. Maybe the LORD
15:3 no one. Kill ***m*** and women,
Psalms
45:2 most handsome of ***m***; grace has been
59:1 when Saul sent ***m*** to watch the
78:63 his young ***m***, and his young
148:12 same, you young ***m***—young women too!
Proverbs
7:7 the naive young ***m*** and noticed among
11:16 honor; violent ***m*** gain only wealth.
20:29 glory of young ***m***; gray hair is the
25:1 copied by the ***m*** of Hezekiah, king
Ecclesiastes
12:3 and the strong ***m*** stoop; when the
Song of Songs
2:3 among the young ***m***. In his shade I
3:7 sixty heroic ***m*** round about it,
Isaiah
3:25 Your ***m*** will fall by the sword, your
Jeremiah
30:6 Ask and see: Can ***m*** bear children? Then
31:13 the young and old ***m*** will join in. I
Daniel
1:17 to these four ***m***. Daniel himself
3:25 Look! I see four ***m***, unbound, walking
Matthew
8:33 had happened to the demon-possessed ***m***.
14:21 five thousand ***m*** plus women and
15:38 Four thousand ***m*** ate, plus women and
20:30 When two blind ***m*** sitting along the road
24:40 there will be two ***m*** in the field. One
28:4 shook with fear and became like dead ***m***.
Luke
24:4 Suddenly, two ***m*** were standing
John
19:32 legs of the two ***m*** who were
Galatians
1:17 to see the ***m*** who were apostles
1 Timothy
2:8 Therefore I want ***m*** to pray everywhere

5:1 treat younger ***m*** like your
Titus
2:2 Tell the older ***m*** to be sober,
2:6 encourage the younger ***m*** to be sensible
2 Peter
1:21 will. Instead, ***m*** and women led by

MEPHIBOSHETH
2 Samuel
4:4 fell and was injured. His name was ***M***.
9:6 ***M***, Jonathan's son and Saul's grandson,
16:4 that belonged to ***M*** now belongs to
19:24 ***M***, Saul's grandson, also came down to
21:7 the king spared ***M***, Jonathan's son

MERARI
Genesis
46:11 sons were Gershon, Kohath, and ***M***.
1 Chronicles
6:16 Levi's family: Gershom, Kohath, and ***M***
2 Chronicles
34:12 descended from ***M***, and Zechariah

MERCHANTS
1 Kings
10:15 the traders, the ***m*** and their
2 Chronicles
9:14 the traders and ***m***. All the Arabian
Nehemiah
3:31 servants and the ***m***, opposite the
3:32 the goldsmiths and the ***m*** made repairs.
Job
6:19 from Tema look; ***m*** from Sheba hope
41:6 Will ***m*** sell him; will they divide him
Isaiah
23:8 crowns, whose ***m*** were princes,
Ezekiel
17:4 and set it down in a city of ***m***.
27:27 your leaks, your ***m***, all your
27:36 The ***m*** for the peoples hiss because of
38:13 and Dedan and the ***m*** and officials of
Zephaniah
1:11 wail; all the ***m*** will be silenced.
Zechariah
14:21 no longer be any ***m*** in the house of
Revelation
18:3 with her, and the ***m*** of the earth
18:11 The ***m*** of the earth will weep and mourn
18:15 The ***m*** who sold these things, and got
18:23 because your ***m*** ran the world,

MERCIFUL → MERCIFUL AND COMPASSIONATE
Deuteronomy
7:2 with them, and don't be ***m*** to them.
1 Kings
20:31 of Israel are ***m*** kings. Allow us
1 Chronicles
21:13 LORD, who is very ***m***; don't let me
2 Chronicles
30:9 LORD your God is ***m*** and
Nehemiah
9:17 ready to forgive, ***m*** and
9:27 Because you are ***m***, you gave them
Isaiah
30:18 is waiting to be ***m*** to you, and will
Jeremiah
18:20 begging you to be ***m*** and not to punish
42:12 I will be ***m*** to you, and he will be
Joel
2:13 God, for he is ***m*** and
Hebrews
2:17 he could become a ***m*** and faithful high

MERCIFUL AND COMPASSIONATE
2Ch 30:9; Neh 9:17; 9:31; Ps 145:8; Jl 2:13; Jon 4:2

MERCY → RECEIVE MERCY, SHOW ME MERCY, SHOW MERCY
Genesis
42:21 he begged us for ***m***, but we didn't
Deuteronomy
13:8 Don't have any ***m*** on them! Don't
13:17 you, showing you ***m*** and multiplying
19:13 Show no ***m*** to such killers. Remove
19:21 Show no ***m*** on this point: life for life,
25:12 you must cut off her hand. Show no ***m***
Joshua
6:21 Without ***m***, they wiped out everything
8:24 off without ***m***. Then all Israel
10:28 its king without ***m***. He wiped them
11:11 there without ***m***, wiping them out
11:20 showing them any ***m***. This was exactly
19:47 it down without ***m***. They took it
2 Samuel
12:22 The LORD may have ***m*** on me and let the
24:14 hands because his ***m*** is great, but
1 Kings
8:33 name, and ask for ***m*** before you at
8:47 begging for your ***m***, saying, "We have
8:50 those who captured them show them ***m***.
2 Kings
10:25 without ***m***. The guards and
2 Chronicles
6:24 name, and ask for ***m*** in your presence
6:37 begging for your ***m***, saying,"We have
30:9 will receive ***m*** from their
Nehemiah
9:19 in your great ***m***, didn't abandon
9:28 many times because of your great ***m***.
9:31 In your great ***m***, however, you didn't
13:22 according to the greatness of your ***m***.
Job
27:22 on them without ***m***; they flee
Psalms
4:1 my troubles! Have ***m*** on me! Listen to
6:2 Have ***m*** on me, LORD, because I'm frail.
9:13 Have ***m*** on me, LORD! Just look how I
25:16 me, God, and have ***m*** on me because I'm
26:11 with integrity. Save me! Have ***m*** on me!
27:7 I cry out—have ***m*** on me and answer
28:2 to my request for ***m*** when I cry out to
28:6 he has listened to my request for ***m***!
30:8 to you, LORD. I begged my Lord for ***m***:
30:10 listen and have ***m*** on me! LORD, be
31:9 Have ***m*** on me, LORD, because I'm
31:22 my request for ***m*** when I cried out
41:4 said, "LORD, have ***m*** on me! Heal me
41:10 LORD, please have ***m*** on me and lift me
51:1 Bathsheba.] Have ***m*** on me, God,
56:1 Gath.] God, have ***m*** on me because I'm
57:1 the cave.] Have ***m*** on me, God; have

59:5 nations! Grant no ***m*** to any wicked
86:3 Have ***m*** on me, Lord, because I cry out
86:6 to the sound of my requests for ***m***.
86:15 of compassion and ***m***; you are very
86:16 back to me! Have ***m*** on me! Give your
102:13 is time to have ***m*** on her—the time
102:14 stones; they show ***m*** even to her dirt.
109:12 him; let no one have ***m*** on his orphans.
111:4 The LORD is full of ***m*** and compassion.
116:1 because he hears my requests for ***m***.
119:29 from me; show ***m*** to me by means of
119:58 my heart; have ***m*** on me according
119:132 to me and have ***m*** on me; that's
123:2 the LORD our God until he has ***m*** on us.
123:3 Have ***m*** on us, LORD! Have mercy because
130:2 close attention to my request for ***m***!
140:6 God! Listen to my request for ***m***, LORD!"
142:1 I beg out loud for ***m*** from the LORD.
143:1 my requests for ***m***! Because of your

Proverbs
6:34 he'll show no ***m*** on his day of
21:10 their neighbors receive no ***m*** from them.
28:13 and give them up will receive ***m***.

Isaiah
9:17 and widows no ***m***; for everyone was
54:7 but with great ***m*** I will bring you
55:7 that he may have ***m*** on them, to our
63:9 them. In love and ***m*** God redeemed

Jeremiah
6:23 they show no ***m***. Their horsemen
13:14 I will show no ***m*** when I destroy
15:15 me. In your ***m***, spare my life.
16:5 kindness, and ***m*** from this people,
16:13 and night, for I will show you no ***m***.
20:16 destroyed without ***m***. May he hear
21:7 sword without pity, ***m***, or compassion.
26:19 and plead for his ***m***? Then the LORD
32:18 You act with ***m*** toward thousands upon
50:42 cruel and show no ***m***. Their horsemen
51:3 armor. Show no ***m*** to her young men;

Daniel
4:27 by showing ***m*** to the poor. Then
6:11 praying and seeking ***m*** from his God.

Hosea
2:19 in justice, in devoted love, and in ***m***.

Joel
2:17 them say, "Have ***m***, LORD, on your

Jonah
2:8 things lose their chance for ***m***.

Zechariah
12:10 of grace and ***m*** on David's house

Matthew
5:7 people who show ***m***, because they
9:13 means: I want ***m*** and not
12:7 means, I want ***m*** and not
15:22 shouted, "Show me ***m***, Son of David. My
17:15 Lord, show ***m*** to my son. He is
18:33 you also have ***m*** on your fellow
20:30 shouted, "Show us ***m***, Lord, Son of

Mark
5:19 for you and how he has shown you ***m***."
10:47 Jesus, Son of David, show me ***m***!"
10:48 even louder, "Son of David, show me ***m***!"

Luke
1:50 He shows ***m*** to everyone, from one
1:54 his servant Israel, remembering his ***m***,
1:58 that the Lord had shown her great ***m***.
1:72 He has shown the ***m*** promised to our
10:37 who demonstrated ***m*** toward him."
16:24 Abraham, have ***m*** on me. Send
17:13 and said, "Jesus, Master, show us ***m***!"
18:13 said, 'God, show ***m*** to me, a sinner.'

Romans
1:31 without affection, and without ***m***.
3:25 sacrifice where ***m*** is found by means
9:15 Moses, I'll have ***m*** on whomever I
9:16 depends entirely on God, who shows ***m***.
9:18 So then, God has ***m*** on whomever he wants
9:23 pots made for ***m***, which he
11:30 but now you have ***m*** because they were
11:31 because of the ***m*** that you
11:32 in order to have ***m*** on all of them.
12:8 The one showing ***m*** should be
15:9 God for his ***m***. As it is

1 Corinthians
7:25 you can trust because of the Lord's ***m***.

2 Corinthians
4:1 the same way that we received God's ***m***.

Galatians
6:16 May peace and ***m*** be on whoever follows this rule

Ephesians
2:5 God is rich in ***m***. He brought us to

Philippians
2:27 died. But God had ***m*** on him—and not just on him

1 Timothy
1:2 the faith. Grace, ***m***, and peace from
1:13 But I was shown ***m*** because I acted
1:16 why I was shown ***m***, so that Christ

2 Timothy
1:2 child. Grace, ***m***, and peace from
1:16 May the Lord show ***m*** to Onesiphorus'
1:18 him to find his ***m*** on that day (and

Titus
3:5 us because of his ***m***, not because of

Hebrews
4:16 we can receive ***m*** and find grace
10:28 to death without ***m*** on the basis of

James
2:13 There will be no ***m*** in judgment for
3:17 filled with ***m*** and good actions,
5:11 the Lord is full of compassion and ***m***.

1 Peter
1:3 of his vast ***m***, he has given us
2:10 hadn't received ***m***, but now you have

2 John
1:3 Grace, ***m***, and peace from God the

Jude
1:2 have more and more ***m***, peace, and love.
1:21 God, wait for the ***m*** of our Lord Jesus
1:22 Have ***m*** on those who doubt
1:23 Fearing God, have ***m*** on some, hating

MESHACH

Daniel
1:7 Mishael "***M***," and Azariah
2:49 Shadrach, ***M***, and Abednego to
3:12 Shadrach, ***M***, and Abednego—who

MESHULLAM

1 Chronicles
3:19 family: ***M***, Han-aniah, and th
Ezra
8:16 Zechariah, and ***M***, all leaders,
Nehemiah
3:4 made repairs. ***M***, Berechiah's son

MESSAGE

Genesis
32:4 Esau. This is the ***m*** of your servant
32:5 I'm sending this ***m*** to my master now
38:25 she sent this ***m*** to her father-in-l
45:16 heard the ***m*** "Joseph's
50:4 my request, give Pharaoh this ***m***:
Exodus
7:16 to you with this ***m***: Let my people go
Numbers
22:10 son, sent them to me with the ***m***,
23:16 and gave him a ***m***. He said, "Return
1 Samuel
16:22 Saul sent a ***m*** to Jesse: "Please allow
2 Samuel
11:6 Then David sent a ***m*** to Joab: "Send me
14:32 I sent you a ***m***: Come here so I
15:10 Israel with this ***m***: "When you hear
19:11 David sent a ***m*** to the priests
1 Kings
1:27 If this ***m*** was from my master the king,
5:2 Solomon sent the following ***m*** to Hiram
15:18 the following ***m*** to Aram's King
18:20 Ahab sent the ***m*** to all the Israelites.
Ezra
5:7 In the ***m*** they sent him, the following
Isaiah
28:9 he explain the ***m***? To those just
28:19 nothing but terror to understand the ***m***.
36:13 Listen to the ***m*** of the great
37:21 son, sent a ***m*** to Hezekiah: The
Jeremiah
7:2 there this ***m***: Listen to the
22:1 the king of Judah and declare this ***m***:
23:17 who scorn God's ***m***, "All will go
27:12 the same ***m*** to Judah's King
28:9 when that prophet's ***m*** is fulfilled."
34:6 delivered this ***m*** to Judah's King
38:20 the LORD, whose ***m*** I bring. You will
46:2 About Egypt! A ***m*** for the army of
Ezekiel
33:30 hear what sort of ***m*** has come from the
Daniel
4:1 Nebuchadnezzar's ***m*** to all the
5:24 God and why this ***m*** was written down.
10:1 King Cyrus, a ***m*** was revealed to
Obadiah
1:1 We have heard a ***m*** from the LORD—a
Haggai
1:13 gave the LORD's ***m*** to the people: I
Matthew
27:19 wife sent this ***m*** to him, "Leave
28:7 him there.' I've given the ***m*** to you."
Mark
16:9 and undying ***m*** of eternal
16:20 proclaimed the ***m*** everywhere. The
Luke
4:32 he delivered his ***m*** with authority.
10:39 the Lord's feet and listened to his ***m***.
18:34 meaning of this ***m*** was hidden from
John
6:60 this said, "This ***m*** is harsh. Who can
12:38 through our ***m***? To whom is the
Acts
2:41 accepted Peter's ***m*** were baptized.
10:36 This is the ***m*** of peace he sent to the
13:26 the ***m*** about this
15:31 it, delighted with its encouraging ***m***.
16:14 Lord enabled her to embrace Paul's ***m***.
18:15 squabbles about a ***m***, names, and your
20:2 region with a ***m*** of encouragement.
Romans
10:16 says, Lord, who has had faith in our ***m***?
10:17 it's listening by means of Christ's ***m***.
10:18 earth, and their ***m*** has gone out to
16:25 good news and the ***m*** that I preach
1 Corinthians
1:18 The ***m*** of the cross is foolishness to
2:4 My ***m*** and my preaching weren't presented
15:2 hold on to the ***m*** I preached to
2 Corinthians
1:18 is faithful, our ***m*** to you isn't both
5:19 us with this ***m*** of reconciliation.
Ephesians
6:19 mouth, I'll get a ***m*** that confidently
Colossians
1:5 hope through the true ***m***, the good news,
1:6 come to you. This ***m*** has been bearing
1:23 you heard. This ***m*** has been preached
1 Thessalonians
1:6 you accepted the ***m*** that came from
1:8 The ***m*** about the Lord rang out from you,
2:13 it as a human ***m***, you accepted it
4:15 are saying is a ***m*** from the Lord: we
2 Thessalonians
2:2 some spirit, a ***m***, or a letter
3:1 that the Lord's ***m*** will spread
2 Timothy
2:15 interprets the ***m*** of truth
4:17 that the entire ***m*** would be preached
Titus
1:3 God revealed his ***m*** at the appropriate
1:9 to the reliable ***m*** as it has been
2:8 and a sound ***m*** that is above criticism
Hebrews
1:3 with his powerful ***m***. After he carried
2:2 If the ***m*** that was spoken by angels was
4:2 did. However, the ***m*** they heard didn't
5:12 about God's ***m***. You have come to
13:22 put up with this ***m*** of encouragement,
1 John
1:5 This is the ***m*** that we have heard from
2:7 The old commandment is the ***m*** you heard.
3:11 This is the ***m*** that you heard from the

MESSENGER → GOD'S MESSENGER

Genesis
16:7 The LORD's ***m*** found Hagar at a spring in
22:11 But the LORD's ***m*** called out to Abraham
48:16 may the divine ***m*** who protected me from

MESSENGER [cont.]

Exodus
3:2 The LORD's ***m*** appeared to him in a flame
23:20 about to send a ***m*** in front of you
23:23 When my ***m*** goes in front of you and
32:34 to you. My ***m*** here will go in
33:2 I'll send a ***m*** before you. I'll drive
Numbers
20:16 our voice, sent a ***m***, and brought us
22:22 the LORD's ***m*** stood in the road
Judges
2:1 The LORD's ***m*** came up from Gilgal to
5:23 says the LORD's ***m***, "curse its
6:11 Then the LORD's ***m*** came and sat under
13:3 The LORD's ***m*** appeared to the woman and
13:6 looked like God's ***m***—very scary! I did
1 Samuel
4:17 The ***m*** answered, "Israel has fled from
23:27 But a ***m*** suddenly came to Saul. "Come
2 Samuel
11:19 to the king," Joab instructed the ***m***,
11:22 So the ***m*** set off, and when he arrived
15:13 A ***m*** came to David, reporting, "The
19:27 and king is a ***m*** of God. So do
24:16 when the divine ***m*** stretched out his
1 Kings
13:18 like you. A ***m*** spoke to me with
19:2 Jezebel sent a ***m*** to Elijah with this
22:13 Meanwhile, the ***m*** who had gone to summon Micaiah
2 Kings
1:3 But the LORD's ***m*** said to Elijah from
5:10 Elisha sent out a ***m*** who said, "Go and
6:32 The king sent a ***m*** on ahead, but
9:18 reported, "The ***m*** met them, but he
10:8 A ***m*** came and told Jehu, "They have
19:35 night the LORD's ***m*** went out and
1 Chronicles
21:12 and the LORD's ***m*** bringing disaster
2 Chronicles
18:12 Meanwhile, the ***m*** who had gone to summon Micaiah
32:21 the LORD sent a ***m*** who destroyed
Job
1:14 A ***m*** came to Job and said: "The oxen
33:23 Surely there's a ***m*** for this person, a
Psalms
34:7 side, the LORD's ***m*** protects those
35:5 let the LORD's ***m*** be the one who
35:6 let the LORD's ***m*** be the one who
Proverbs
16:14 king's anger is a ***m*** of death; the
17:11 a cruel ***m*** will be sent
Ecclesiastes
5:6 don't say to the ***m***: "It was a
Isaiah
37:36 The LORD's ***m*** went out and struck down
40:9 a high mountain, ***m*** Zion! Raise your
42:19 and deaf like my ***m*** whom I send? Who
52:7 are the feet of a ***m*** who proclaims
63:9 distressed, so a ***m*** who served him
Jeremiah
49:14 the LORD that a ***m*** is sent among the
51:31 joins courier, ***m*** joins messenger
Ezekiel
23:40 No sooner than a ***m*** was sent, they
Daniel
3:28 He sent his ***m*** to rescue his
6:22 My God sent his ***m***, who shut the lions'
Hosea
12:4 with the ***m*** and survived; he
Obadiah
1:1 from the LORD—a ***m*** has been sent
Nahum
1:15 the feet of a ***m*** who announces
Haggai
1:13 the LORD's ***m***, gave the LORD's
Zechariah
1:9 these, sir?" The ***m*** speaking with me
1:11 to the LORD's ***m***, who was standing
2:3 As I watched, the ***m*** speaking with me
3:1 before the ***m*** from the LORD,
4:1 The ***m*** speaking with me returned and
5:5 Then the ***m*** speaking with me came
6:4 and said to the ***m*** speaking with me,
12:8 like the LORD's ***m*** in front of them.
Malachi
2:7 for he is the ***m*** from the LORD of
3:1 I am sending my ***m*** who will clear
Matthew
11:10 I'm sending my ***m*** before you, who
Mark
1:2 I am sending my ***m*** before you. He
Luke
7:27 I'm sending my ***m*** before you, who
2 Corinthians
12:7 conceited. It's a ***m*** from Satan sent
2 Timothy
1:11 I was appointed a ***m***, apostle, and

MESSENGERS

Genesis
19:1 The two ***m*** entered Sodom in the evening.
28:12 sky, and God's ***m*** were ascending
32:1 on his way, and God's ***m*** approached him.
Numbers
20:14 Moses sent ***m*** from Kadesh to the king of Edom
21:21 Israelites sent ***m*** to Sihon the
22:5 He sent ***m*** to Balaam, Beor's son, at
24:12 I tell your ***m***, whom you sent to
Deuteronomy
2:26 I then sent ***m*** from the Kedemoth desert
Joshua
6:17 This is because she hid the ***m*** we sent.
7:22 Then Joshua sent ***m***. They ran to the
9:4 pretending to be ***m***.
Judges
6:35 He sent ***m*** into all of Manasseh, and
7:24 Then Gideon sent ***m*** into all of the
9:31 He sent ***m*** to Abimelech at Arumah to
11:12 Jephthah sent ***m*** to the Ammonite
1 Samuel
6:21 They sent ***m*** to the inhabitants of
11:3 so we can send ***m*** thoughout
16:19 So Saul sent ***m*** to Jesse to say, "Send
19:11 Saul sent ***m*** to David's house to keep
25:14 David sent ***m*** from the
29:9 one of God's own ***m***. Despite that,

2 Samuel
2:5 he sent ***m*** to the people of
3:12 Abner sent ***m*** to represent him to David
5:11 King Hiram sent ***m*** to David with
11:4 So David sent ***m*** to get her. When she
12:27 Joab then sent ***m*** to David, saying, "I
14:17 like one of God's ***m***, understanding
1 Kings
20:2 He sent ***m*** to Ahab, Israel's king,
2 Kings
1:2 was hurt. He sent ***m***, telling them,
7:15 their rush. The ***m*** returned and
14:8 Then Amaziah sent ***m*** to Israel's King
16:7 Ahaz sent ***m*** to Assyria's King
17:4 Hoshea sent ***m*** to Egypt's King
19:9 him. So he sent ***m*** to Hezekiah
20:12 Baladan, sent ***m*** to Hezekiah with
1 Chronicles
10:9 armor, and sent ***m*** throughout the
14:1 King Hiram sent ***m*** to David with
19:2 So David sent ***m*** with condolences
2 Chronicles
35:21 But Neco sent ***m*** to Josiah. "What do you want with me
36:15 them through his ***m*** because he had
Nehemiah
6:3 so I sent ***m*** to tell them, "I'm doing
Psalms
68:11 command—many ***m*** are bringing good news
78:49 distress, a troop of evil ***m***.
91:11 he will order his ***m*** to help you, to
103:20 You divine ***m***, bless the LORD! You who
104:4 the winds your ***m***; you make fire
148:2 you who are his ***m***! Praise God, all
Proverbs
13:17 Wicked ***m*** fall into trouble, but a
25:13 day are reliable ***m*** to those who send
Isaiah
14:32 to that nation's ***m***? The LORD has
18:2 that sends ***m*** by sea, reed vessels on
23:2 of Sidon, whose ***m*** crossed over the
33:7 in the streets; ***m*** of peace wept
37:14 letters from the ***m*** and read them.
Nahum
2:13 the voice of your ***m*** will never again
Mark
5:35 with her, ***m*** came from the
Luke
7:24 After John's ***m*** were gone, Jesus spoke
9:52 He sent ***m*** on ahead of him. Along the
Hebrews
1:4 than the other ***m***, such as angels,
James
2:25 she received the ***m*** as her guests and

MESSIAH
John
1:41 have found the ***M***"
4:25 I know that the ***M*** is coming, the

MICAH
Judges
17:1 was a man named ***M*** who lived in the
Jeremiah
26:18 ***M*** of Moresheth, who prophesied during
Micah
1:1 word that came to ***M*** of Moresheth in

MICAIAH
1 Kings
22:8 bad. His name is ***M***, Imlah's son."
2 Chronicles
13:2 mother's name was ***M***; she was Uriel's
18:7 bad. His name is ***M***, Imlah's son."
Jeremiah
36:11 When ***M***, Gemariah's son and Shaphan's
36:13 ***M*** told them all the words he heard

MICHAEL
1 Chronicles
5:13 their households: ***M***, Meshullam,
2 Chronicles
21:2 Azariah, ***M***, and Shephatiah.
Daniel
10:13 my way. But then ***M***, one of the
10:21 these leaders except your leader ***M***.
12:1 At that time, ***M*** the great leader who
Jude
1:9 The archangel ***M***, when he argued with
Revelation
12:7 war in heaven: ***M*** and his angels

MICHAL
1 Samuel
14:49 the oldest, and ***M***, the younger
18:20 younger daughter ***M*** loved David. When
19:11 David's wife ***M*** warned him, "If
25:44 his daughter ***M***, David's wife, to
2 Samuel
6:16 Saul's daughter ***M*** was watching from
1 Chronicles
15:29 David's City, ***M***, Saul's daughter,

MIDDLE
Genesis
3:3 the tree in the ***m*** of the garden.
Exodus
3:2 of fire in the ***m*** of a bush. Moses
38:4 halfway up to the ***m*** of the altar.
Joshua
3:17 dry land in the ***m*** of the Jordan.
4:3 right here in the ***m*** of the Jordan,
Nehemiah
8:3 morning until the ***m*** of the day. He
Job
34:20 In the ***m*** of the night they suddenly
Psalms
57:4 My life is in the ***m*** of a pack of lions.
63:6 meditate on you in the ***m*** of the night—
119:62 I get up in the ***m*** of the night to give
Isaiah
5:25 lay in the ***m*** of the streets
Ezekiel
1:4 center, in the ***m*** of the fire,
Mark
6:47 boat was in the ***m*** of the lake, but
14:60 stood up in the ***m*** of the gathering
Luke
11:5 friend in the ***m*** of the night.
23:45 in the sanctuary tore down the ***m***.
John
8:9 woman were left in the ***m*** of the crowd.

19:18 one on each side and Jesus in the ***m***.
Acts
1:18 burst open in the ***m*** and all his
16:33 then, in the ***m*** of the night, the
17:22 stood up in the ***m*** of the council on
Hebrews
2:12 praise you in the ***m*** of the assembly.
Revelation
1:13 In the ***m*** of the lampstands I saw
22:2 through the ***m*** of the city's main

MIDIAN

Exodus
2:15 in the land of ***M***. One day Moses
Psalms
83:9 what you did to ***M***, to Sisera, and
Habakkuk
3:7 curtains of the land of ***M*** were quaking.
Acts
7:29 this, he fled to ***M***, where he lived

MIDIANITE

Genesis
37:28 When some ***M*** traders passed by, they
Numbers
25:6 man brought a ***M*** woman to his

MIDIANITES

Genesis
37:36 Meanwhile the ***M*** had sold Joseph to the
Numbers
31:2 from the ***M***. Afterward you
Judges
6:16 you'll defeat the ***M*** as if they were

MIGHTY

Deuteronomy
3:24 and your ***m*** hand. What god in
6:21 brought us out of Egypt with a ***m*** hand.
10:17 lords, the great, ***m***, and awesome God
11:2 his power, his ***m*** hand and
26:5 became a great nation, ***m*** and numerous.
Joshua
6:2 your power, along with its ***m*** warriors.
24:17 He has done these ***m*** signs in our
Judges
6:12 The LORD is with you, ***m*** warrior!"
11:1 Gileadite was a ***m*** warrior. Gilead
1 Samuel
2:4 The bows of ***m*** warriors are shattered,
2 Samuel
1:19 Look how the ***m*** warriors have
22:33 Only God! My ***m*** fortress, who makes my
2 Kings
5:1 This man was a ***m*** warrior, but he
8:13 a dog, do such ***m*** things?" Elisha
2 Chronicles
6:41 you and your ***m*** chest. May your
30:21 by the LORD's ***m*** instruments.
Job
34:20 pass away. The ***m*** are removed, not
34:24 He shatters the ***m*** without examining
35:9 shout under the power of the ***m***.
36:5 Look, God is ***m*** and doesn't reject
37:4 thunders with a ***m*** voice, and no one
37:6 the downpour of rain, "Be a ***m*** shower."
37:14 Job; stop and ponder God's ***m*** deeds.
Psalms
9:11 Proclaim his ***m*** acts among all
20:6 answering with ***m*** acts of salvation
22:12 surround me; ***m*** bulls from Bashan
24:7 ***M*** gates: lift up your heads! Ancient
24:9 ***M*** gates: lift up your heads! Ancient
29:3 the LORD is over the ***m*** waters.
42:4 my way to the ***m*** one's abode, to
68:15 ***M*** mountain, Mount Bashan; many-peaked
68:33 God sends forth his voice, his ***m*** voice.
71:16 dwell on your ***m*** acts, my Lord.
71:18 about your ***m*** arm, tell all who
77:15 With your ***m*** arm you redeemed your
77:19 right through the ***m*** waters. But your
80:10 by its shade; the ***m*** cedars were
89:8 heavenly forces? ***M*** LORD, your
93:4 the sea's waves, ***m*** on high is the
103:20 LORD! You who are ***m*** in power and keep his word
106:2 all of the LORD's ***m*** acts or publicly
106:8 good name, to make known his ***m*** power.
110:2 LORD make your ***m*** scepter reach far
135:10 down many nations and killed ***m*** kings:
145:4 the next one, proclaiming your ***m*** acts.
150:2 Praise God in his ***m*** acts! Praise God as
Ecclesiastes
9:11 the battle to the ***m***, nor food to the
9:14 few residents. A ***m*** king came against
Isaiah
1:24 forces, the ***m*** one of Israel:
5:22 warriors, ***m*** at mixing drinks,
22:17 to hurl you down, ***m*** man! He is surely
29:6 earthquake, and a ***m*** voice, with
34:7 them, steers with ***m*** bulls, and their
40:26 strength and ***m*** power, not one is
43:16 in the sea and a path in the ***m*** waters,
49:26 savior, and the ***m*** one of Jacob is
60:16 and your redeemer, the ***m*** one of Jacob.
Jeremiah
10:6 are great, and great is your ***m*** name.
32:19 purposes, and ***m*** are your deeds.
48:17 Proclaim how its ***m*** scepter and
Ezekiel
1:24 like the sound of ***m*** waters, like the
32:12 by the swords of ***m*** men, the most
43:2 the sound of a ***m*** flood, and the
Zechariah
8:22 Many peoples and ***m*** nations will come to see the LORD
Luke
1:49 because the ***m*** one has done great things
19:37 of all the ***m*** things they had
John
9:3 so that God's ***m*** works might be
Acts
2:11 declaring the ***m*** works of God in
2 Thessalonians
1:9 presence and away from his ***m*** glory.
Hebrews
11:34 in weakness, were ***m*** in war, and

MILCAH

Genesis
11:29 Nahor's wife was ***M*** the daughter of
Numbers
26:33 Mahlah, Noah, Hoglah, ***M***, and Tirzah.
Joshua
17:3 Mahlah, Noah, Hoglah, ***M***, and Tirzah.

MILITARY

Numbers
1:3 is eligible for ***m*** service in
2:3 camp with its ***m*** units. The chief
10:14 first with its ***m*** units. Nahshon,
26:2 Israel who is eligible for ***m*** service.
33:1 to their ***m*** units under the
Joshua
10:24 He said to the ***m*** commanders who
22:14 family among the ***m*** units of Israel.
Jeremiah
46:13 about the ***m*** offensive of
49:35 of Elam, the backbone of its ***m*** might.
52:25 army in charge of ***m*** conscription and
Matthew
27:28 him and put a red ***m*** coat on him.
27:31 him of the ***m*** coat and put his
Mark
6:21 officials and ***m*** officers and
Acts
21:34 Paul be taken to the ***m*** headquarters.
2 Timothy
2:4 who serves in the ***m*** gets tied up with

MILK

Exodus
3:8 that's full of ***m*** and honey, a
23:19 boil a young goat in its mother's ***m***.
Leviticus
20:24 is a land full of ***m*** and honey." I am
Numbers
13:27 actually full of ***m*** and honey, and
Deuteronomy
6:3 you, in a land full of ***m*** and honey.
14:21 cook a lamb in its own mother's ***m***.
Joshua
5:6 us. It is a land full of ***m*** and honey.
Judges
4:19 opened a jug of ***m***, gave him a
5:25 and she provided ***m***; she presented
Job
10:10 pour me out like ***m***, curdle me like
21:24 buckets full of ***m***, their bones
Proverbs
27:27 be enough goat's ***m*** for your food,
30:33 because churning ***m*** makes curds,
Song of Songs
4:11 bride; honey and ***m*** are under your
5:1 my wine and my ***m***. Eat, dear
5:12 are bathing in ***m***, sitting by
Isaiah
7:22 the abundance of ***m***, for all who
28:9 just weaned from ***m***? To those who
55:1 money, at no cost, buy wine and ***m***!
60:16 You will suck the ***m*** of nations, and
Jeremiah
11:5 a land full of ***m*** and honey, as is
32:22 ancestors, a land full of ***m*** and honey.
Lamentations
4:7 dazzling than ***m***. Their limbs were
Ezekiel
20:6 a land full of ***m*** and honey, the
25:4 devour your fruit, and drink your ***m***.
34:3 You drink the ***m***, you wear the wool,
Joel
3:18 will flow with ***m***, and all the
1 Corinthians
3:2 I gave you ***m*** to drink instead of solid
9:7 a flock and doesn't drink its ***m***?
Hebrews
5:12 where you need ***m*** instead of solid
1 Peter
2:2 desire the pure ***m*** of the word.

MIND → CHANGED HIS MIND

Genesis
8:21 of the human ***m*** are evil from
Exodus
32:12 Change your ***m*** about doing
Numbers
23:19 would change his ***m***. Has he ever
Deuteronomy
4:9 never leave your ***m*** as long as you
13:3 God with all your ***m*** and all your
26:16 with all your ***m*** and with your
32:46 them: Set your ***m*** on all these
2 Chronicles
9:1 Solomon everything that was on her ***m***.
19:3 the land and set your ***m*** to seek God."
Job
11:13 If you make your ***m*** resolute and spread
15:12 Why has your ***m*** seized you, why have
17:4 closed their ***m*** to insight;
22:22 his mouth; put his words in your ***m***.
23:13 He is of one ***m***; who can reverse it?
31:27 and my ***m*** has been secretly enticed, and
36:5 anyone; he is mighty in strength and ***m***.
37:1 Oh, my ***m*** is disturbed by this and is
Psalms
16:7 I am instructed in the depths of my ***m***.
26:2 to the test! Purify my ***m*** and my heart.
31:12 completely out of ***m***; I am like a
64:6 deep within the human ***m*** and heart. "
106:45 love he has, God changed his ***m***.
110:4 won't change his ***m***: "You are a
143:4 weak inside me—inside, my ***m*** is numb.
Proverbs
2:2 and stretch your ***m*** toward
2:10 will enter your ***m***, and knowledge
4:21 from your sight. Guard them in your ***m***.
4:23 protect your ***m***, for life flows
7:10 like a prostitute and with a cunning ***m***.
10:8 The skilled ***m*** accepts commands, but a
12:8 but a warped ***m*** leads to contempt.
14:30 A peaceful ***m*** gives life to the body,
16:21 The skilled ***m*** is called discerning, and
16:23 The ***m*** of the wise makes their speech
17:16 money to pay for wisdom? He has no ***m***.
18:15 An understanding ***m*** gains knowledge;
19:21 are in a person's ***m***, but the LORD's
22:17 the wise; focus your ***m*** on my knowledge.
23:12 Bring your ***m*** to instruction, your ear
23:19 wise! Keep your ***m*** straight on the

23:26 child, give your ***m*** to me and let
25:3 the earth, so the ***m*** of a king is
29:17 give you peace of ***m*** and bring delight

Ecclesiastes
1:13 I applied my ***m*** to investigate and to
1:16 before me. My ***m*** has absorbed
1:17 But when I set my ***m*** to understand
7:25 I turned my ***m*** to know, to investigate,
8:16 Then I set my ***m*** to know wisdom and to
10:2 The ***m*** of the wise tends toward the

Isaiah
10:7 is on his ***m***, extermination of
13:17 the Medes pay no ***m*** to silver, no
44:20 his deluded ***m*** has led him
65:17 be remembered; they won't come to ***m***.

Jeremiah
4:28 neither change my ***m*** nor cancel the
7:31 a thing, nor did it ever cross my ***m***.
11:20 the heart and ***m***, let me see your
15:1 change my ***m*** about these
19:5 a thing, nor did it ever cross my ***m***.
20:12 the heart and the ***m***. Let me see your
26:3 harm I have in ***m*** for them because
29:11 plans I have in ***m*** for you, declares
32:35 it even cross my ***m***—that they should
32:39 one heart and one ***m*** so that they may

Ezekiel
23:19 bringing to ***m*** her youthful days
28:2 claim to have the ***m*** of a god, you are
38:10 come into your ***m***, and you will

Daniel
2:30 might know the thoughts of your own ***m***.
4:5 and the vision in my ***m*** overwhelmed me.
5:21 humans, and his ***m*** became like an
7:4 human being, and it received a human ***m***.
8:25 In his own ***m***, he will be
10:12 first set your ***m*** to understand
11:28 and set his ***m*** against a holy

Matthew
21:29 But later he changed his ***m*** and went.
22:37 all your being, and with all your ***m***.

Mark
3:21 They were saying, "He's out of his ***m***!"
12:30 with all your ***m***, and with all

Luke
10:27 and with all your ***m***, and love your

John
10:20 and has lost his ***m***. Why listen to

Acts
4:32 one in heart and ***m***. None of them
12:15 You've lost your ***m***!" they responded.
26:24 You've lost your ***m***, Paul! Too much

Romans
1:28 to a defective ***m*** to do
7:23 the law of my ***m*** and takes me
11:34 known the Lord's ***m***? Or who has been

1 Corinthians
1:10 with the same ***m*** and the same
2:2 I had made up my ***m*** not to think about
2:9 crossed the ***m*** of any human
2:16 Who has known the ***m*** of the Lord, who
14:14 spirit prays but my ***m*** isn't productive.
14:15 I'll pray with my ***m*** too; I'll sing a
14:19 words in my right ***m*** than speak

2 Corinthians
7:13 Titus was. His ***m*** has been put at

Ephesians
4:23 the thinking in your ***m*** by the Spirit

Philippians
1:27 in one spirit and ***m*** as you struggle

1 Thessalonians
4:11 to live quietly, ***m*** your own

2 Thessalonians
2:2 confused in your ***m*** or upset if you

2 Timothy
2:25 will change their ***m*** and give them a

Titus
1:15 Instead, their ***m*** and conscience

1 Peter
3:8 of you be of one ***m***, sympathetic,

Revelation
17:9 an understanding ***m***. The seven heads
17:13 will be of one ***m***, and they will

MINDS

Genesis
6:5 every idea their ***m*** thought up was

Exodus
14:5 changed their ***m*** about the people.

Deuteronomy
5:29 If only their ***m*** were like this: always
6:6 you today must always be on your ***m***.

2 Chronicles
11:16 had made up their ***m*** to seek the LORD,

Psalms
7:9 are the one who examines hearts and ***m***.

Ecclesiastes
9:3 of evil; people's ***m*** are full of

Isaiah
6:10 Make the ***m*** of this people dull. Make
32:4 the ***m*** of the rash will know and
32:6 folly; their ***m*** devise
44:18 can't see and their ***m*** can't comprehend.
59:13 lying words conceived in our ***m***.

Jeremiah
23:26 dominate the ***m*** of the prophets?

Ezekiel
20:32 What is in your ***m*** will never happen!

Daniel
11:27 kings, with their ***m*** set on evil, will

Matthew
9:4 do you fill your ***m*** with evil things?
13:15 with their ***m***, and change their

Mark
2:8 do you fill your ***m*** with these

Luke
5:22 do you fill your ***m*** with these
21:14 Make up your ***m*** not to prepare your
24:25 people! Your dull ***m*** keep you from
24:45 he opened their ***m*** to understand the

John
12:40 and closed their ***m*** so that they

Acts
14:2 poisoning their ***m*** against the
19:9 had closed their ***m***, though. They
28:6 changed their ***m*** and began to
28:27 with their ***m***, and change their

Romans
12:2 renewing of your ***m*** so that you can

1 Corinthians
14:23 they say that you are out of your ***m***?

2 Corinthians
3:14 But their ***m*** were closed. Right up to
4:4 has blinded the ***m*** of those who
11:3 afraid that your ***m*** might be seduced
Philippians
4:7 your hearts and ***m*** safe in Christ
Colossians
1:21 with him in your ***m***, which was shown
1 Timothy
6:5 people whose ***m*** are ruined and
2 Timothy
3:8 Moses. Their ***m*** are corrupt and
Hebrews
8:10 my laws in their ***m***, and write them
10:16 their hearts and write them on their ***m***.
1 Peter
1:13 you have your ***m*** ready for action
Revelation
2:23 one who examines ***m*** and hearts, and

MINISTER

Exodus
28:43 the altar to ***m*** as priests in the
29:30 the meeting tent to ***m*** in the sanctuary.
30:20 the altar to ***m*** and to offer a
Numbers
3:31 which they would ***m***, and the screen—a
Deuteronomy
10:8 covenant, to ***m*** before the LORD,
18:5 to stand and ***m*** in the LORD's
21:5 selected them to ***m*** for him and to
1 Chronicles
15:2 LORD's chest and to ***m*** to him forever."
16:37 his relatives, to ***m*** there continually
26:12 responsible to ***m*** in the LORD's
Psalms
134:1 now! All you who ***m*** in the LORD's
Jeremiah
33:21 priests who ***m*** before me be
33:22 David and the Levites who ***m*** before me.
Ezekiel
44:11 will stand before them to ***m*** to them.
45:4 who draw near to ***m*** in the LORD's
46:24 where those who ***m*** in the temple
Daniel
2:48 Babylon and chief ***m*** over all
Romans
15:16 helps me to be a ***m*** of Christ Jesus
15:27 they ought to ***m*** to them with
Colossians
1:7 and Christ's faithful ***m*** for your sake.
4:7 brother, faithful ***m***, and fellow slave

MINISTERS

Exodus
28:35 the robe when he ***m*** as a priest. Its
Deuteronomy
18:7 and ***m*** in the LORD his God's name, just
Ezra
8:17 namely, to send us ***m*** for God's house.
Psalms
104:4 you make fire and flame your ***m***.
Isaiah
61:6 of the LORD; ***M*** of Our God, they
Jeremiah
49:3 exile, together with his priests and ***m***.
Joel
1:9 The priests and the LORD's ***m*** mourn.
1:13 priests; lament, ***m*** of the altar.
2:17 the LORD's ***m***, weep. Let them
2 Corinthians
3:6 qualified us as ***m*** of a new
6:4 ourselves as ***m*** of God in every
11:23 Are they ***m*** of Christ? I'm speaking like
Hebrews
1:7 and who uses flames of fire as ***m***.

MINISTRY

Nehemiah
12:44 with the ***m*** of the priests
Luke
1:80 until he began his public ***m*** to Israel.
3:23 when he began his ***m***. People supposed
John
11:54 active in public ***m*** among the Jewish
Acts
1:17 us and received a share of this ***m***."
1:25 the place of this ***m*** and apostleship,
11:29 to this ***m*** according to each
20:24 other than the ***m*** I received from
21:19 done among the Gentiles through his ***m***.
Romans
11:13 to the Gentiles, I publicize my own ***m***
2 Corinthians
2:16 Who is qualified for this kind of ***m***?
3:7 The ***m*** that brought death was carved in
4:1 we received this ***m*** in the same way
5:18 who gave us the ***m*** of reconciliation.
6:3 so that our ***m*** won't be
9:12 Your ***m*** of this service to God's people
Philippians
1:5 partners in the ***m*** of the gospel
4:3 with me in the ***m*** of the gospel,
Colossians
4:17 you complete the ***m*** that you received
1 Timothy
1:12 me faithful. So he appointed me to ***m***
2 Timothy
4:11 He has been a big help to me in the ***m***.

MIRACLES

Deuteronomy
4:34 using tests, ***m***, wonders, war, a
Daniel
4:2 the signs and ***m*** that the Most
4:3 are superb! His ***m*** so powerful! His
6:27 signs and ***m*** in heaven and on
Matthew
7:22 name and do lots of ***m*** in your name?'
11:20 done his greatest ***m*** because they
11:21 For if the ***m*** done among you
11:23 After all, if the ***m*** that were done
13:54 Where did he get the power to work ***m***?
13:58 unable to do many ***m*** there because of
Mark
6:5 unable to do any ***m*** there, except
Luke
10:13 Bethsaida. If the ***m*** done among you
Acts
2:22 to you through ***m***, wonders, and
8:13 signs and great ***m*** that were
19:11 God was doing unusual ***m*** through Paul

MIRACLES [cont.]

1 Corinthians
12:10 performance of ***m*** to another, prophecy
12:28 teachers, then ***m***, then gifts of
12:29 are they? All don't perform ***m***, do they?
2 Corinthians
12:12 through signs, wonders, and ***m***.
Galatians
3:5 and working ***m*** among you do this
Hebrews
2:4 things, various ***m***, and gifts from

MIRACULOUS → MIRACULOUS SIGN, MIRACULOUS SIGNS

Matthew
14:2 This is why these ***m*** powers are at
Mark
6:14 and this is why ***m*** powers are at

MIRACULOUS SIGN

2Ch 32:24; 32:31; Jn 2:11; 2:18; 4:54; 6:14, 30; 12:18

MIRACULOUS SIGNS

Jn 2:23; 3:2; 4:48; 6:2, 26; 7:31; 9:16; 10:41; 11:47; 12:37; 20:30

MIRIAM

Exodus
15:20 Then the prophet ***M***, Aaron's sister,
26:59 to Aaron, Moses, and ***M*** their sister.
Deuteronomy
24:9 your God did to ***M*** on your departure
1 Chronicles
4:17 was the father of ***M***, Shammai, and
6:3 Aaron, Moses, and ***M***. Aaron's family:
Micah
6:4 I sent Moses, Aaron, and ***M*** before you.

MISSION

John
1:8 light, but his ***m*** was to testify
Acts
12:25 completing their ***m***, bringing with
1 Corinthians
16:9 has opened up for my ***m*** here.
16:15 to come from the ***m*** to Achaia. They
Philippians
4:15 time of my first ***m*** work in Macedonia

MIXED

Genesis
11:9 there the LORD ***m*** up the language
Nehemiah
13:3 out from Israel all those of ***m*** descent.
Daniel
2:41 so, you saw the iron ***m*** with earthy clay
Matthew
27:34 gave Jesus wine ***m*** with vinegar to

MIZPAH

Genesis
31:49 He also named it ***M***, because he said,
1 Samuel
7:6 they assembled at ***M***, and they drew
Jeremiah
41:1 Ahikam's son, at ***M***. While they were

MOAB

Genesis
19:37 son and named him ***M***. He is the
Numbers
22:4 son, was king of ***M*** at that time.
Deuteronomy
34:5 in the land of ***M***, according to the
Ruth
1:1 Judah to dwell in the territory of ***M***.
1 Samuel
22:3 went to Mizpeh in ***M***. He said to the
2 Kings
1:1 After Ahab died, ***M*** rebelled against
Isaiah
15:1 An oracle about ***M***. Ar was devastated
Jeremiah
48:1 Concerning ***M***: The LORD of heavenly
48:17 you neighbors of ***M***, all you who know
Ezekiel
25:11 judgments in ***M***, and they will
Amos
2:1 three crimes of ***M***, and for four, I
Zephaniah
2:9 God of Israel—***M*** will become like

MOABITE

Deuteronomy
34:1 hiked up from the ***M*** plains to Mount
Ruth
1:22 And Ruth the ***M***, her daughter-in-law
4:5 also buy Ruth the ***M***, the wife of the
Nehemiah
13:1 no Ammonite or ***M*** should ever enter

MOABITES

Genesis
19:37 Moab. He is the ancestor of today's ***M***.
Deuteronomy
23:3 Ammonites and ***M*** can't belong to the

MOLECH

Leviticus
18:21 them over to ***M*** so that you do
20:2 their children to ***M*** must be executed.
1 Kings
11:7 of Moab, and to ***M***, the detestable
2 Kings
23:10 child alive in honor of the god ***M***.
Isaiah
57:9 You went down to ***M*** with oil, and you
Jeremiah
32:35 and daughters to ***M***, though I never

MONEY

Exodus
22:25 If you lend ***m*** to my people who are poor
2 Kings
12:4 available ***m*** relating to holy
Psalms
15:5 who doesn't lend ***m*** with interest,
68:30 who delight in ***m***; scatter the
Proverbs
1:14 your lot with us; we'll share our ***m***."
7:20 took a pouch of ***m*** with him; he
11:7 Yes, any hope based on ***m*** perishes.
17:16 a fool have ***m*** to pay for
28:8 rates gather ***m*** for those who are

Ecclesiastes
5:10 The ***m*** lover isn't satisfied with money;
7:12 the protection of ***m***; the advantage of
10:19 the living, and ***m*** answers
Isaiah
55:1 Whoever has no ***m***, come, buy food
55:2 Why spend ***m*** for what isn't food, and
Amos
5:12 righteous, taking ***m*** on the side,
Matthew
10:9 coins for your ***m*** belts to take on
19:21 own, and give the ***m*** to the poor. Then
25:18 the ground and buried his master's ***m***.
26:9 sold for a lot of ***m*** and given to the
27:6 right to put this ***m*** in the treasury.
28:12 give a large sum of ***m*** to the soldiers.
Mark
12:43 who's been putting ***m*** in the treasury.
14:11 to give him ***m***. So he started
Luke
7:41 One owed enough ***m*** to pay five
9:3 bag, no bread, no ***m***, not even an
1 Corinthians
16:1 the collection of ***m*** for God's people:
1 Timothy
3:8 heavy drinkers, or greedy for ***m***.
6:5 that godliness is a way to make ***m***!
6:10 The love of ***m*** is the root of all kinds
2 Timothy
3:2 selfish and love ***m***. They will be the
Titus
1:11 they shouldn't to make ***m*** dishonestly.
Philemon
1:18 way or owes you ***m***, charge it to my
Hebrews
13:5 from the love of ***m***, and you should

MONTH

Exodus
12:2 This ***m*** will be the first month; it
40:2 on the first day of the first ***m***.
Numbers
3:15 enroll all the males over one ***m*** old.
11:21 them meat, and they will eat for a ***m***.'
29:1 of the seventh ***m*** will be a holy
Ezra
6:19 day of the first ***m***, the returned
Isaiah
66:23 From ***m*** to month and from Sabbath to
Ezekiel
47:12 fruit in every ***m***, because their
Daniel
10:4 day of the first ***m***, as I was on the
Revelation
9:15 that hour, day, ***m***, and year were
22:2 its fruit each ***m***. The tree's

MONTHS

Exodus
2:2 beautiful, so she hid him for three ***m***.
Judges
11:37 hold off for two ***m*** and let me and my
19:2 in Judah. She stayed there four full ***m***.
20:47 at the rock of Rimmon for four ***m***.
1 Samuel
6:1 in Philistine territory for seven ***m***.
Esther
1:4 a long time—six whole ***m***, to be exact!
2:12 the end of twelve ***m***. (She had six
Job
3:6 of a year; may it not appear in the ***m***.
7:3 I have inherited ***m*** of emptiness;
14:5 the number of our ***m*** with you, you set
39:2 Can you count the ***m*** of pregnancy; do
Ezekiel
39:12 For seven ***m***, the house of Israel will
39:14 their search at the end of seven ***m***.
Daniel
4:29 Twelve ***m*** later, he was walking on the
Amos
4:7 were still three ***m*** to the harvest. I
Zechariah
8:19 and tenth ***m*** will become times
Luke
1:24 She kept to herself for five ***m***, saying,
1:26 Elizabeth was six ***m*** pregnant, God
John
4:35 Four more ***m*** and then it's
Acts
7:20 and for three ***m*** his parents cared
18:11 for eighteen ***m***, teaching God's
19:8 the next three ***m***. He interacted
20:3 stayed for three ***m***. Because the Jews
28:11 After three ***m*** we put out to sea in a
Galatians
4:10 days and ***m*** and seasons and
Hebrews
11:23 parents for three ***m*** when he was born,
Revelation
9:5 suffer for five ***m***—and the suffering
9:10 their power to hurt people for five ***m***.
11:2 holy city underfoot for forty-two ***m***.
13:5 given authority to act for forty-two ***m***.

MOON

Genesis
37:9 the sun and the ***m*** and eleven stars
Numbers
29:6 of the new ***m*** with its grain
Deuteronomy
4:19 to the sun or the ***m*** or the stars, all
17:3 to the sun or the ***m*** or any of the
33:14 sun, with the gifts generated by the ***m***;
Joshua
10:12 at Gibeon! and ***M***, at the Aijalon
10:13 still and the ***m*** stood motionless
1 Samuel
20:5 is the new ***m***, and I'm supposed
2 Kings
4:23 It's not a new ***m*** or sabbath." She
23:5 the sun, to the ***m***, to the
2 Chronicles
8:13 for sabbaths, new ***m*** festivals, and
Job
25:5 If even the ***m*** is not bright and the
26:9 face of the full ***m***, spreading his
31:26 it shone, the ***m***, splendid as it
Psalms
8:3 made—the ***m*** and the stars
72:5 as long as the ***m***, generation to
72:7 peace prosper until the ***m*** is no more.
74:16 You established both the ***m*** and the sun.
81:3 horn on the new ***m***, at the full

MOON [cont.]

89:37 forever; like the ***m***, a faithful
104:19 God made the ***m*** for the seasons, and the sun too
121:6 the day; neither will the ***m*** at night.
136:9 The ***m*** and the stars to rule the night—
148:3 Sun and ***m***, praise God! All of you

Proverbs
7:20 him; he won't come home till full ***m***."

Ecclesiastes
12:2 grow dark, the ***m*** and the stars

Song of Songs
6:10 as the full ***m***, radiant as the
7:2 like the full ***m***—may it never

Isaiah
1:13 repulses me. New ***m***, sabbath, and the
3:18 headbands and ***m***-shaped pendants;
13:10 it rises; the ***m*** will no longer
24:23 The ***m*** will be diminished, and the sun
30:26 The light of the ***m*** will be like the
47:13 what will happen to you at each new ***m***.
60:19 day, nor will the ***m*** shine for

Jeremiah
8:2 to the sun, the ***m***, and the whole
31:35 and ordered the ***m*** and stars to

Ezekiel
32:7 a cloud, and the ***m*** won't radiate its
46:1 the day of the new ***m*** it will be opened,

Hosea
5:7 Now the new ***m*** will devour them

Joel
2:10 The sun and the ***m*** are darkened; the
2:31 darkness, and the ***m*** to blood before
3:15 The sun and the ***m*** are darkened; the

Amos
8:5 will the new ***m*** be over so that

Habakkuk
3:11 Sun and ***m*** stand still high above. With

Matthew
24:29 dark, and the ***m*** won't give its

Mark
13:24 dark,and the ***m*** won't give its

Luke
21:25 signs in the sun, ***m***, and stars. On

Acts
2:20 darkness, and the ***m*** will be changed
27:20 the sun nor the ***m*** appeared for many

1 Corinthians
15:41 of glory, the ***m*** has another kind

Colossians
2:16 a festival, a new ***m*** observance, or

Revelation
6:12 and the entire ***m*** turned red as
8:12 a third of the ***m***, and a third of
12:1 the sun, with the ***m*** under her feet
21:23 the sun or the ***m*** to shine on it,

MORDECAI

Ezra
2:2 Reelaiah, ***M***, Bilshan, Mispar,

Esther
2:5 whose name was ***M***, Jair's son. He

MORNING → MORNING STAR

Genesis
1:5 evening and there was ***m***: the first day.
22:3 up early in the ***m***, harnessed his
24:54 got up in the ***m***, the servant

Exodus
7:15 to Pharaoh in the ***m***. As he is going
8:20 up early in the ***m*** and confront
14:24 As ***m*** approached, the LORD looked down
16:13 camp. And in the ***m*** there was a layer
16:21 Every ***m*** they gathered it, as much as

Deuteronomy
28:67 In the ***m*** you will say: "I wish it was

Ruth
2:7 her feet from the ***m*** until now, and
3:14 at his feet until ***m***. Then she got up

2 Samuel
23:4 of sunrise on a ***m*** with no clouds,

Ezra
3:3 LORD, both the ***m*** and the evening

Job
38:7 while the ***m*** stars sang in unison and

Psalms
5:3 LORD, in the ***m*** you hear my voice. In
30:5 may stay all night, but by ***m***, joy!
46:5 crumble. God will help it when ***m*** dawns.
49:14 over them come ***m***!—their forms was
55:17 At evening, ***m***, and midday I complain
59:16 strength! In the ***m*** I will shout out
65:8 the gateways of ***m*** and evening sing
73:14 all day long. I'm punished every ***m***.
88:13 prayer meets you first thing in the ***m***!
90:5 like grass that is renewed in the ***m***.
90:6 True, in the ***m*** it thrives, renewed, but
90:14 us full every ***m*** with your
92:2 loyal love in the ***m***, your
101:8 Every ***m*** I will destroy all those who
130:6 watch waits for ***m***; yes, more than
143:8 love come ***m*** time because I

Proverbs
4:18 righteous is like ***m*** light that gets
7:18 of love until ***m***; let's savor our
27:14 early in the ***m*** will be viewed as

Ecclesiastes
10:16 a boy and whose princes feast in the ***m***.
11:6 your seed in the ***m***, and in the

Isaiah
50:4 them in the ***m***. God awakens my

Lamentations
3:23 are renewed every ***m***. Great is your

Zephaniah
3:3 evening; they leave nothing for the ***m***.
3:5 nothing unjust. ***M*** by morning he

Matthew
20:3 nine in the ***m*** and saw others

Luke
21:38 rose early in the ***m*** to hear him in
24:22 They went to the tomb early this ***m***

Acts
2:15 all, it's only nine o'clock in the ***m***!

MORNING STAR

Song 6:10; Is 14:12; 2Pt 1:19; Rev 2:28; 22:16

MOSES

Exodus
2:10 She named him ***M***, "because," she
2:15 he tried to kill ***M***. But Moses ran
3:1 ***M*** was taking care of the flock for his
3:14 God said to ***M***, "I Am Who I Am. So say

7:10 So ***M*** and Aaron went to Pharaoh and did just as the LORD
9:23 Then ***M*** raised his shepherd's rod toward
15:22 Then ***M*** had Israel leave the Reed Sea
19:3 while ***M*** went up to God. The LORD called to him
24:18 ***M*** entered the cloud and went up the
40:18 ***M*** set up the dwelling. He laid out its

Deuteronomy
34:7 ***M*** was 120 years old when he died. His
34:10 No prophet like ***M*** has yet emerged in

Joshua
1:1 After ***M*** the LORD's servant died, the
1:2 My servant ***M*** is dead. Now get ready to
1:3 you set foot, exactly as I promised ***M***.

Psalms
77:20 sheep under the care of ***M*** and Aaron.
90:1 [A prayer of ***M***, the man of God.] Lord,
99:6 ***M*** and Aaron were among his priests,
103:7 his ways known to ***M***; made his deeds
105:26 God sent ***M*** his servant and the one he chose
106:16 were jealous of ***M*** in the camp,
106:23 for the fact that ***M***, his chosen one,
106:32 went badly for ***M*** because of them,

Jeremiah
15:1 to me: Even if ***M*** and Samuel stood

Matthew
8:4 the gift that ***M*** commanded. This
17:3 ***M*** and Elijah appeared to them, talking
19:7 Then why did ***M*** command us to
22:24 asked, "Teacher, ***M*** said, If a man

John
1:17 was given through ***M***, so grace and

Romans
5:14 from Adam until ***M***, even over those

1 Corinthians
10:2 baptized into ***M*** in the cloud and

Hebrews
3:2 him just like ***M*** was faithful in
3:5 ***M*** was faithful in all God's house as a

Revelation
15:3 sing the song of ***M***, God's servant,

MOST HIGH GOD

Ps 78:56; Dn 3:26; 4:2; 5:18, 21; Mk 5:7; Lk 8:28; Ac 16:17; Heb 7:1

MOTHER

Genesis
2:24 his father and ***m*** and embraces his
3:20 she is the ***m*** of everyone who

Exodus
2:8 the girl went and called the child's ***m***.
20:12 father and your ***m*** so that your life
22:30 stay with their ***m*** for seven days.

Numbers
6:7 whether father, ***m***, brother, or sister.

Deuteronomy
5:16 father and your ***m***, exactly as the
21:19 the father and ***m*** will take the son
22:6 or eggs, and the ***m*** is sitting on the
27:16 their father or ***m***." All the people

Judges
5:7 until you arose as a ***m*** in Israel.

Ruth
1:8 household of your ***m***. May the LORD

1 Samuel
2:5 children, but the ***m*** with many sons
15:33 now your ***m*** will be childless

Job
17:14 father," the worm, "my ***m*** and sister."

Psalms
27:10 if my father and ***m*** left me all
35:14 down, sad, like I was a ***m*** in mourning.
50:20 with the children of your very own ***m***.
51:5 sin, from the moment my ***m*** conceived me.
113:9 now a joyful ***m*** with children!
131:2 child on its ***m***; I'm like the

Proverbs
10:1 a foolish child brings sorrow to his ***m***.
19:26 drive out their ***m*** are disgraceful
20:20 their father or ***m***—their lamp will
23:22 you life; don't despise your elderly ***m***.
28:24 their father and ***m***, and say, "It's
30:11 their father and don't bless their ***m***.
31:1 of Massa, which his ***m*** taught him:

Song of Songs
3:11 with which his ***m*** crowned him on
6:9 of a kind. To her ***m*** she's the only
8:5 there, where your ***m*** labored with you,

Isaiah
8:4 father' and 'my ***m***,' the wealth of
66:13 As a ***m*** comforts her child, so I will

Jeremiah
20:17 womb and let my ***m*** become my grave,
50:12 But ***M*** Babylon will be humiliated, the

Hosea
2:2 against your ***m***; plead with her!
4:5 prophet, and I will destroy your ***m***.

Micah
7:6 up against her ***m***, a daughter-in-law

Matthew
2:11 with Mary his ***m***. Falling to their
10:35 against her ***m***, and a daughter-in
10:37 love father or ***m*** more than me
12:48 Who is my ***m***? Who are my
13:55 son? Isn't his ***m*** named Mary?
19:5 his father and ***m*** and be joined
27:56 Mary the ***m*** of James and

Mark
7:10 father and your ***m***, and The person

Luke
12:53 against father; ***m*** against daughter
14:26 hate father and ***m***, spouse and
18:20 testimony. Honor your father and ***m***."
24:10 Joanna, Mary the ***m*** of James, and the

John
19:27 Here is your ***m***." And from that

Ephesians
5:31 his father and ***m*** and be united
6:2 your father and ***m*** is the first one

1 Thessalonians
2:7 like a nursing ***m*** caring for her

1 Timothy
5:2 women like your ***m***, and treat

2 Timothy
1:5 Lois and your ***m*** Eunice. I'm sure

Hebrews
7:3 without father or ***m*** or any family. He

Revelation
17:5 the great, the ***m*** of prostitutes

MOTHER-IN-LAW

Deuteronomy
27:23 has sex with his ***m***." All the people
Ruth
1:14 Orpah kissed her ***m***, but Ruth stayed
2:11 you did for your ***m*** after your
3:1 Naomi her ***m*** said to her, "My daughter,
Micah
7:6 against her ***m***; the enemies of a
Matthew
8:14 and saw Peter's ***m*** lying in bed with
10:35 and a daughter-in-law against her ***m***.
Mark
1:30 Simon's ***m*** was in bed, sick with a
Luke
4:38 Simon. Simon's ***m*** was sick with a
12:53 mother; and ***m*** against daughter-i

MOUNT → MOUNT OF OLIVES, MOUNT SINAI, MOUNT ZION

Exodus
33:6 So after leaving ***M*** Horeb the Israelites
Numbers
20:22 Israelite community came to ***M*** Hor.
21:4 They marched from ***M*** Hor on the Reed Sea
33:23 Kehelathah and camped at ***M*** Shepher.
34:7 will mark out your boundary to ***M*** Hor.
Deuteronomy
1:2 Kadesh-barnea along the ***M*** Seir route.
3:8 way from the Arnon ravine to ***M*** Hermon
3:17 the slopes of ***M*** Pisgah on the
11:29 the blessing on ***M*** Gerizim and the
27:4 right now on ***M*** Ebal. Cover them
32:49 mountains, to ***M*** Nebo, which is in
Joshua
8:30 built an altar on ***M*** Ebal to the LORD,
8:33 Half stood facing ***M*** Gerizim and half
11:17 stretching from ***M*** Halak, which goes
12:1 Valley as far as ***M*** Hermon and
12:7 Valley as far as ***M*** Halak, which goes
15:9 to the cities of ***M*** Ephron. The
15:10 from Baalah to ***M*** Seir. It passed
15:11 passed on to ***M*** Baalah, and went
24:4 and Esau. I gave ***M*** Seir to Esau to
Judges
2:9 highlands of Ephraim north of ***M*** Gaash.
3:3 of Lebanon from ***M*** Baal-hermon to
4:6 and assemble at ***M*** Tabor, taking ten
9:7 on the top of ***M*** Gerizim. He
9:48 him went up on ***M*** Zalmon. He
1 Samuel
31:1 and many fell dead on ***M*** Gilboa.
2 Samuel
1:6 happened to be on ***M*** Gilboa and Saul
1 Kings
12:25 Shechem at ***M*** Ephraim and lived
18:20 He gathered the prophets at ***M*** Carmel.
2 Kings
2:25 Elisha went to ***M*** Carmel and then
4:25 the man of God at ***M*** Carmel. As soon
1 Chronicles
4:42 went to ***M*** Seir, led by
5:23 Senir, and ***M*** Hermon. They were
10:1 and many fell dead on ***M*** Gilboa.
10:8 and his sons lying dead on ***M*** Gilboa.
2 Chronicles
3:1 in Jerusalem on ***M*** Moriah, where the
13:4 on the heights of ***M*** Zemaraim in
20:10 and those from ***M*** Seir—the people
Psalms
42:6 of Jordan and Hermon, from ***M*** Mizar.
68:14 the kings there, snow fell on ***M*** Zalmon.
68:15 Mighty mountain, ***M*** Bashan; many-peaked
133:3 like the dew on ***M*** Hermon streaming
Song of Songs
4:1 of goats as they stream down ***M*** Gilead.
7:5 crowns you like ***M*** Carmel, and your
Isaiah
14:13 I'll sit on the ***m*** of assembly, on
28:21 Just as on ***M*** Perazim, the LORD will
Jeremiah
26:18 and the temple ***m*** will become an
46:4 the horses; ***m*** the stallions!
Ezekiel
35:2 Human one, face ***M*** Seir, and prophesy
Amos
3:9 yourselves on ***M*** Samaria, and see
4:1 who are on ***M*** Samaria, who
6:1 those trusting in ***M*** Samaria, the
Obadiah
1:8 Edom and understanding from ***M*** Esau?
1:19 will possess ***M*** Esau, and those
Micah
3:12 and the temple ***m*** will become an

MOUNT OF OLIVES

2Sa 15:30; Zec 14:4; Mt 21:1; 24:3; 26:30; Mk 11:1; 13:3; 14:26; Lk 19:29; 19:37; 21:37; 22:39; Jn 8:1; Ac 1:12

MOUNT SINAI

Ex 19:11; 19:18, 20, 23; 24:16; 31:18; 34:2, 4, 29, 32; Lv 7:38; 25:1; 26:46; 27:34; Nm 3:1; 28:6; Neh 9:13; Ac 7:30; 7:38; Ga 4:24; 4:25

MOUNT ZION

2Ki 19:31; Ps 48:2; 48:11; 74:2; 125:1; Is 4:5; 8:18; 10:12; 18:7; 24:23; 29:8; 31:4; 37:32; Lam 5:18; Jl 2:32; Obad 1:17; 1:21; Mi 4:7; Heb 12:22; Rev 14:1

MOUNTAIN → GOD'S MOUNTAIN

Genesis
8:5 the tenth month the ***m*** peaks appeared.
22:14 say, "On this ***m*** the LORD is seen."
Exodus
3:1 and he came to God's ***m*** called Horeb.
19:2 Israel camped there in front of the ***m***
19:20 to the top of the ***m***. The LORD called
24:18 and went up the ***m***. Moses stayed on
32:19 them in pieces at the foot of the ***m***.
Deuteronomy
5:4 on the ***m*** from the very
32:50 will die on the ***m*** you have hiked
Joshua
15:8 to the top of the ***m*** that is opposite
18:13 on the ***m*** that is south of
Job
14:18 But an eroding ***m*** breaks up, and rock is
24:8 wet from ***m*** rains, with no refuge,

Psalms
2:6 appoint my king on Zion, my holy ***m***!"
3:4 he answers me from his holy ***m***. Selah
15:1 LORD? Who can dwell on your holy ***m***?
24:3 ascend the LORD's ***m***? Who can stand in
30:7 made me a strong ***m***. But then you hid
43:3 me to your holy ***m***, to your dwelling
48:1 and so worthy of praise! His holy ***m***
50:11 I know every ***m*** bird; even the insects
68:15 Mighty ***m***, Mount Bashan; many-peaked
68:16 You many-peaked ***m***: Why do you look
78:54 territory, to the ***m*** that his own
78:68 of Judah, the ***m*** of Zion, which he
95:4 in his hands; the ***m*** heights belong to
99:9 low at his holy ***m*** because the LORD
104:18 belong to the ***m*** goats; the ridges
Song of Songs
4:6 be off to the ***m*** of myrrh, to the
4:8 dens, from the ***m*** lairs of leopards.
Isaiah
2:2 days to come the ***m*** of the LORD's
11:9 on my holy ***m***. The earth will
40:4 up, and every ***m*** and hill will be
Daniel
2:45 was cut from the ***m***, but not by
Micah
4:1 days to come, the ***m*** of the LORD's
Zephaniah
3:11 will you be haughty on my holy ***m***,
Zechariah
14:4 west. Half of the ***m*** will move north,
Matthew
4:8 to a very high ***m*** and showed him
17:20 could say to this ***m***, 'Go from here to
21:21 even say to this ***m***, 'Be lifted up
Mark
9:2 of a very high ***m*** where they were
Luke
3:5 filled, and every ***m*** and hill will be
John
4:21 neither on this ***m*** nor in Jerusalem.
6:15 so he took refuge again, alone on a ***m***.
2 Peter
1:18 while we were with him on the holy ***m***.
Revelation
6:14 up, and every ***m*** and island was
8:8 like a huge ***m*** burning with fire
21:10 to a great, high ***m***, and he showed me

MOUNTAINS

Genesis
7:20 twenty-three feet high, covering the ***m***.
8:4 the ark came to rest on the Ararat ***m***.
Judges
5:5 The ***m*** quaked before the LORD, the one
6:2 and caves in the ***m*** as hidden
1 Kings
20:23 is a god of the ***m***. That's why they
Job
9:5 Who removes ***m***, and they are unaware;
28:9 into flint, pull up ***m*** from their roots,
Psalms
18:7 the bases of the ***m*** trembled and
36:6 the strongest ***m***; your justice is
46:2 apart, when the ***m*** crumble into the
65:6 you establish the ***m*** by your strength;
72:3 Let the ***m*** bring peace to the people;
76:4 mightier than the ***m*** that give food.
80:10 The ***m*** were covered by its shade; the
83:14 forest, just like flames set ***m*** ablaze,
87:1 God's foundation is set on the holy ***m***.
89:12 created them! The ***m*** Tabor and Hermon
90:2 Before the ***m*** were born, before you
97:5 The ***m*** melt like wax before the LORD,
98:8 hands; let the ***m*** rejoice out loud
104:6 the waters were higher than the ***m***!
114:4 The ***m*** leaped away like rams; the hills
121:1 eyes toward the ***m***. Where will my
125:2 ***M*** surround Jerusalem. That's how the
133:3 down onto the ***m*** of Zion because
144:5 come down! Touch the ***m*** so they smoke!
147:8 God makes the ***m*** sprout green
148:9 Do the same, you ***m***, every single hill,
Proverbs
8:25 Before the ***m*** were settled, before the
Song of Songs
2:8 leaping upon the ***m***, bounding over
2:17 or a young stag upon the jagged ***m***.
8:14 or a young stag on the ***m*** of spice!"
Isaiah
2:2 highest of the ***m***. It will be
52:7 upon the ***m*** are the feet of a
54:10 The ***m*** may shift, and the hills may be
55:12 peace. Even the ***m*** and the hills
Ezekiel
34:6 on all the ***m*** and on every high
39:4 fall on Israel's ***m***, you, all your
Hosea
10:8 will say to the ***m***, "Cover us," to
Joel
2:2 out upon the ***m***, a great and
3:18 In that day the ***m*** will drip sweet wine,
Amos
4:13 one who forms the ***m***, creates the
9:13 the seed. The ***m*** will drip wine,
Jonah
2:6 of the undersea ***m***. I have sunk down
Micah
1:4 Then the ***m*** will melt under him; the
4:1 highest of the ***m***; it will be
6:1 before the ***m***; let the hills
Nahum
1:5 The ***m*** quake because of him; the hills
1:15 Look, on the ***m***: the feet of a
3:18 across the ***m***; there is no one
Habakkuk
3:6 The everlasting ***m*** collapse; the
3:10 The ***m*** see you and writhe. A flood of
Haggai
1:11 the earth, on the ***m***, on the grain, on
Zechariah
6:1 from between two ***m***; the mountains
14:5 the valley of the ***m*** will reach to
Malachi
1:3 I turned Esau's ***m*** into desolation,
Matthew
24:16 those in Judea must escape to the ***m***.
Mark
13:14 those in Judea must escape to the ***m***.
Luke
21:21 must flee to the ***m***, those in the
23:30 will say to the ***m***, 'Fall on us,'

MOUNTAINS [cont.]

1 Corinthians
13:2 that I can move ***m*** but I don't have
Hebrews
11:38 in deserts, ***m***, caves, and holes
Revelation
6:15 in caves and in the rocks of the ***m***.
16:20 island fled, and the ***m*** disappeared.
17:9 heads are seven ***m*** on which the

MOURN

Nehemiah
8:9 your God. Don't ***m*** or weep." They
Job
14:22 their body, and they ***m*** for themselves.
Isaiah
3:26 will lament and ***m***; desolate, she
6:5 I said, "***M*** for me; I'm ruined! I'm a
19:8 in the Nile will ***m***, and those who
57:18 them with comfort. And for those who ***m***,
61:2 for our God, to comfort all who ***m***,
66:10 her in joy, all you who ***m*** over her,
Jeremiah
9:17 the women who ***m***, let them come;
9:20 your daughters to ***m***; teach each other to grieve.
12:4 will the land ***m*** and the grass in
16:4 No one will ***m*** for them or bury
25:33 And no one will ***m*** for them or
34:5 you as people ***m***, "Oh, master!" I
Lamentations
2:10 on the ground and ***m***. They throw dust
Ezekiel
7:12 no seller should ***m***, because wrath
24:16 stroke. Don't ***m*** or weep. Don't
24:23 feet. You won't ***m*** or weep. You will
32:18 Human one, ***m*** for Egypt's hordes. Send
Hosea
10:5 Its people will ***m*** over it, just as
Joel
1:9 The priests and the LORD's ministers ***m***.
Amos
8:8 who live in it ***m***, as it rises and
Micah
1:8 the jackals, and ***m*** like the
Zechariah
12:10 they will ***m*** over him like the
12:12 The land will ***m***, each of the clans by
Matthew
9:15 guests can't ***m*** while the groom
11:17 sang a funeral song and you didn't ***m***.'
Luke
6:25 laugh now, because you will ***m*** and weep.
John
11:31 assumed she was going to ***m*** at the tomb.
1 Thessalonians
4:13 so that you won't ***m*** like others who
James
4:9 out in sorrow, ***m***, and weep! Let
Revelation
1:7 of the earth will ***m*** because of him.
18:9 will weep and ***m*** over her when

MOURNING

Genesis
27:41 the period of ***m*** for the death of
37:34 put a simple ***m*** cloth around his
38:12 after a period of ***m***, he and his
50:4 the period of ***m*** had passed,
Deuteronomy
21:13 in your house, ***m*** her father and
26:14 portion while ***m***, nor did I remove
34:8 for weeping and for ***m*** Moses was over.
2 Samuel
11:27 After the time of ***m*** was over, David
14:2 Pretend to be in ***m***. Dress in
19:1 that the king was crying and ***m*** Absalom.
19:2 was turned into ***m*** for all the
1 Kings
20:31 Allow us to put ***m*** clothes on our
20:32 So they put ***m*** clothes on their bodies
21:27 clothes and put ***m*** clothes on his
2 Kings
6:30 he was wearing ***m*** clothes
19:1 himself with ***m*** clothes, and went
19:2 son. They were all wearing ***m*** clothes.
1 Chronicles
21:16 dressed in ***m*** clothes, fell on
Ezra
10:6 water, for he was ***m*** because of the
Esther
4:1 dressed in ***m*** clothes, and put
4:2 to pass through it wearing ***m*** clothes.
4:3 on the ground in ***m*** clothes and ashes.
4:4 wear instead of ***m*** clothes, but he
Job
30:31 My lyre is for ***m***, my flute, a weeping
Psalms
30:11 You changed my ***m*** into dancing. You took
35:14 down, sad, like I was a mother in ***m***.
Ecclesiastes
3:4 a time for ***m*** and a time for
7:2 go to a house in ***m*** than to a house
Isaiah
3:24 clothes, rags as ***m*** clothes; instead
15:3 streets they wear ***m*** clothes; on its
20:2 Go, take off the ***m*** clothes from your
22:12 for weeping and ***m***, and shaven
29:2 There will be ***m*** and lamentation;
32:11 skin, and tie ***m*** clothes around
37:1 himself with ***m*** clothes, and went
58:5 of lying down in ***m*** clothing and
60:20 you, and your days of ***m*** will be ended.
61:3 joy in place of ***m***, a mantle of
Jeremiah
16:5 where there is ***m***; don't grieve or
16:6 or time of ***m***. No one will gash
31:13 I will turn their ***m*** into laughter and
47:5 ***M*** will come upon Gaza; silence will
48:37 slashed, and everyone wears ***m*** clothes.
48:38 nothing but ***m***. I have shattered
Lamentations
1:4 roads are in ***m***; no one comes to
2:5 he multiplied ***m*** along with more
2:10 they put on ***m*** clothes.
Ezekiel
2:10 sides, songs of ***m***, lamentation, and
7:18 They will put on ***m*** clothes, and horror

7:27 king will go into ***m***, the prince will
24:17 Don't perform ***m*** rites, but bind
27:31 hair and put on ***m*** clothes. In
31:15 I caused ***m***. I blocked off

Daniel
9:3 and with fasting, ***m*** clothes, and
10:2 I, Daniel, had been ***m*** for three weeks.

Amos
5:16 wail, and those skilled in ***m*** to lament.
8:10 make people wear ***m*** clothes and shave

Jonah
3:5 a fast and put on ***m*** clothes, from the
3:6 himself with ***m*** clothes, and sat
3:8 alike put on ***m*** clothes, and let

Zechariah
12:10 over him like the ***m*** for an only
12:11 On that day, the ***m*** in Jerusalem will be

Mark
16:10 been with him, who were ***m*** and weeping.

Luke
8:52 all crying and ***m*** for her, but
23:27 women, who were ***m*** and wailing for

2 Corinthians
12:21 have to go into ***m*** over all the

James
4:9 laughter become ***m*** and your joy

Revelation
11:3 hundred sixty days, wearing ***m*** clothes.
18:19 out, weeping and ***m***. They said, 'Oh,
21:4 There will be no ***m***, crying, or pain

MOUTH

Genesis
4:11 that opened its ***m*** to take your

Exodus
4:10 I have a slow ***m*** and a thick

Numbers
16:30 ground opens its ***m*** and swallows them
16:32 earth opened its ***m*** and swallowed
22:28 the donkey's ***m*** and it said to
26:10 earth opened its ***m*** and swallowed

Deuteronomy
11:6 opened up its ***m*** and swallowed
18:18 my words in his ***m***, and he will tell
23:23 you promised it with your own ***m***.
30:14 you. It's in your ***m*** and in your
32:1 Earth! Listen to the words of my ***m***.

Joshua
6:10 come out of your ***m*** until the day I
10:18 stones over the ***m*** of the cave.
10:22 Open up the ***m*** of the cave.
10:27 stones over the ***m*** of the cave. The
15:5 Sea as far as the ***m*** of the Jordan.
18:19 at the southern ***m*** of the Jordan.

Judges
11:35 For I opened my ***m*** to the LORD, and
11:36 opened your ***m*** to the LORD, so
18:19 hand over your ***m***! Come with us and

1 Samuel
1:12 before the LORD, Eli watched her ***m***.
2:1 in the LORD! My ***m*** mocks my enemies
2:3 from your ***m*** because the LORD
17:35 animal from its ***m***. If it turned on

2 Samuel
1:16 because your own ***m*** testified against
22:9 out of his ***m*** came a devouring

1 Kings
17:24 the LORD's word is truly in your ***m***."
22:22 spirit in the ***m*** of all his

2 Kings
4:34 putting his ***m*** on the boy's
19:28 my bit in your ***m***. I will make you

2 Chronicles
35:22 from God's own ***m***, and went to

Esther
7:8 left the king's ***m*** before covering

Job
5:15 sword of their ***m***, the needy from
23:12 the words from his ***m*** more than my food.
40:4 answer you? I'll put my hand over my ***m***.
41:21 coals; a flame shoots from his ***m***.

Psalms
17:3 found anything wrong. My ***m*** doesn't sin.
19:14 the words of my ***m*** and the
40:3 a new song in my ***m***, a song of praise
71:8 My ***m*** is filled with your praise,
78:2 I will open my ***m*** with a proverb. I'll
119:103 buds—it's sweeter than honey in my ***m***!
145:21 My ***m*** will proclaim the LORD's praise,

Proverbs
2:6 wisdom; from his ***m*** come knowledge
8:7 My ***m*** utters the truth; my lips despise
10:11 The ***m*** of the righteous is a fountain of
10:31 The ***m*** of the righteous flows with
26:28 a flattering ***m*** causes
27:2 and not your own ***m***; a stranger, and

Ecclesiastes
5:2 quick with your ***m*** or say anything
6:7 humans is for the ***m***, but the appetite
10:12 a wise person's ***m*** are beneficial,

Song of Songs
5:16 His ***m*** is everything sweet, every bit of

Isaiah
40:5 the LORD's ***m*** has commanded it."
45:23 word has left my ***m***; it is reliable
48:3 long ago; from my ***m*** I proclaimed
49:2 He made my ***m*** like a sharp sword, and
51:16 my words in your ***m*** and hid you in
53:7 didn't open his ***m***. Like a lamb
55:11 comes from my ***m***; it does not
57:4 do you open your ***m*** wide and stick
58:14 Jacob. The ***m*** of the LORD has
59:21 placed in your ***m*** won't depart from
62:2 which the LORD's own ***m*** will determine.

Jeremiah
1:9 hand, touched my ***m***, and said to me,
5:14 my words in your ***m*** as a fire; it
23:16 own hearts, not from the LORD's ***m***.

Lamentations
3:29 He should put his ***m*** in the
3:38 From the ***m*** of the Most High evil things don't come
4:4 the roof of its ***m***, thirsty.

Ezekiel
3:2 So I opened my ***m***, and he fed me the
3:26 the roof of your ***m*** and take away

Daniel
7:8 human eyes and a ***m*** that bragged and

Hosea
6:5 the words of my ***m***, and my judgment

Joel
1:5 because it is snatched from your ***m***,
Amos
3:12 an ear from the ***m*** of the lion, so
Micah
4:4 them; for the ***m*** of the LORD of
7:5 the doors of your ***m*** from her who lies
Nahum
3:12 fruit falls into the ***m*** of the eater.
Zechariah
8:9 words from the ***m*** of the prophets
9:7 food from his ***m*** and pieces of
Malachi
2:6 was in his ***m***; injustice wasn't
2:7 from his ***m***, for he is the
Matthew
12:34 fills the heart comes out of the ***m***.
15:11 goes into the ***m*** that contaminates
17:27 When you open its ***m***, you will find a
18:16 by the ***m*** of two or three
Mark
9:18 He foams at the ***m***, grinds his
9:20 and rolled around, foaming at the ***m***.
Luke
9:39 to foam at the ***m***. It tortures him
19:22 words of your own ***m***, you worthless
Acts
8:32 is silent so he didn't open his ***m***.
11:8 or unclean has ever entered my ***m***.'
23:2 beside Paul to strike him in the ***m***.
Romans
3:19 to shut every ***m*** and make it so
10:9 confess with your ***m*** "Jesus is Lord"
Ephesians
4:29 come out of your ***m***. Only say what is
6:19 when I open my ***m***, I'll get a
2 Thessalonians
2:8 breath from his ***m***. When the Lord
2 Timothy
4:17 I was also rescued from the lion's ***m***!
James
3:10 from the same ***m***. My brothers and
Revelation
1:16 and from his ***m*** came a sharp, two-
2:16 with the sword that comes from my ***m***.
3:16 I'm about to spit you out of my ***m***.
12:15 Then from his ***m*** the snake poured a
13:2 a bear's, and its ***m*** was like a lion's
13:6 It opened its ***m*** to speak blasphemies
16:13 from the dragon's ***m***, the beast's
19:15 From his ***m*** comes a sharp sword that he
19:21 comes from the ***m*** of the rider on

MOUTHS

Psalms
8:2 From the ***m*** of nursing babies you have
36:3 words of their ***m*** are evil and
73:9 Their ***m*** dare to speak against heaven!
78:30 even with the food still in their ***m***!
115:5 They have ***m***, but they can't speak.
135:16 They have ***m***, but they can't speak.
144:8 whose ***m*** speak lies, and whose strong
149:6 God be in their ***m*** and a double-edged
Proverbs
13:3 who watch their ***m*** guard their
18:6 accusations; their ***m*** elicit beatings.
21:23 who guard their ***m*** and their tongues
24:7 They don't open their ***m*** in the gate.
Jeremiah
31:29 taste in the ***m*** of their children.
31:30 have a bitter taste in their own ***m***.
Daniel
6:22 shut the lions' ***m***. They haven't
Zechariah
14:12 and their tongues will rot in their ***m***.
Matthew
21:16 read, From the ***m*** of babies and
Luke
1:70 said through the ***m*** of his holy
Romans
3:14 Their ***m*** are full of cursing and
Hebrews
11:33 realized promises, shut the ***m*** of lions,
James
3:3 put bits in their ***m*** to lead them
Revelation
9:17 and out of their ***m*** came fire, smoke,
14:5 came from their ***m***; they are

MOVE

Job
24:2 People ***m*** boundary stones, herd flocks
Zechariah
14:4 the mountain will ***m*** north, and the
1 Corinthians
13:2 faith that I can ***m*** mountains but I

MULTIPLY

Genesis
1:22 Be fertile and ***m*** and fill the
8:17 earth, be fertile, and ***m*** on the earth."
9:1 Be fertile, ***m***, and fill the
35:11 Be fertile and ***m***. A nation, even a
Exodus
23:29 the wild animals won't ***m*** around you.
Deuteronomy
1:11 God, continue to ***m*** you
6:3 will continue to ***m*** exactly as the
7:13 bless you, and ***m*** you. He will
8:1 you can live and ***m*** and enter and
30:5 for you and ***m*** you—making you mo
Job
29:18 I'll die in my nest, ***m*** days like sand,
Psalms
94:19 When my anxieties ***m***, your comforting
Proverbs
28:28 they are destroyed, the righteous ***m***.
Ecclesiastes
5:7 When dreams ***m***, so do pointless
Jeremiah
23:3 and they will be fruitful and ***m***.
Ezekiel
36:11 on you, they will ***m*** and be fruitful.
Hosea
12:1 day long; they ***m*** lies and
Amos
4:4 commit a crime; ***m*** crimes at Gilgal.
Nahum
3:15 will consume you. ***M*** like the locust;
Romans
6:1 we continue sinning so grace will ***m***?
2 Corinthians
9:10 will supply and ***m*** your seed and
Hebrews
6:14 bless you and ***m*** your descendants.

MURDER → COMMIT MURDER

2 Chronicles
22:11 from Athaliah so she couldn't ***m*** him.
Psalms
94:6 widows and immigrants; they ***m*** orphans,
Proverbs
28:17 guilty about ***m***, don't hold them
Isaiah
14:30 to death, and ***m*** all who remain.
Jeremiah
7:9 you steal and ***m***, commit adultery
Ezekiel
11:6 to commit ***m*** in this city, and
16:38 of adultery and ***m***, and I will hand
Hosea
4:2 Swearing, lying, ***m***, together with
6:9 each other; they ***m*** on the road to
Luke
11:50 charged with the ***m*** of all the
18:20 adultery. Don't ***m***. Don't steal.
23:19 had occurred in the city, and for ***m***.
23:25 of a riot and ***m***. But he handed
Acts
8:1 with Stephen's ***m***. At that time,
26:21 me in the temple and tried to ***m*** me.
Romans
1:29 full of jealousy, ***m***, fighting,
13:9 adultery, don't ***m***, don't steal,
1 Timothy
1:9 fathers and mothers, and ***m*** others.

MURDERED

Judges
20:4 husband of the ***m*** woman, answered,
2 Samuel
3:30 brother Abishai ***m*** Abner, because he
1 Kings
2:5 Jether's son. He ***m*** them, spilling
19:10 and they have ***m*** your prophets
21:19 says: So, you've ***m*** and are now
2 Kings
11:2 were about to be ***m*** and hid him in a
14:19 him to Lachish, and they ***m*** him there.
15:25 with him. He ***m*** Pekahiah and
2 Chronicles
21:13 you have even ***m*** your own
22:11 were about to be ***m***, and hid him in a
24:22 had shown him and ***m*** Jehoida's son,
25:27 after him, and they ***m*** him in Lachish.
Jeremiah
41:2 the sword. They ***m*** him because he
41:3 Ishmael also ***m*** all the Judeans who had
Ezekiel
28:8 and you will die, ***m***, on the high seas.
Matthew
23:31 children of those who ***m*** the prophets.
Acts
7:52 one, and you've betrayed and ***m*** him!
Hebrews
11:37 died by being ***m*** with swords. They
James
5:6 condemned and ***m*** the righteous
1 John
3:12 the evil one and ***m*** his brother. And

MURDERER

Numbers
35:16 he dies, he is a ***m***. The murderer
2 Samuel
16:7 here! You are a ***m***! You are
16:8 in this trouble because you are a ***m***!"
2 Kings
6:32 you see that this ***m*** has sent someone
9:31 come in peace, Zimri, you master ***m***?"
Job
24:14 The ***m*** rises at twilight, kills the poor
John
8:44 wants. He was a ***m*** from the
Acts
3:14 and asked that a ***m*** be released to
28:4 man must be a ***m***! He was rescued
1 Peter
4:15 suffer as a ***m*** or thief or
1 John
3:15 or sister is a ***m***, and you know

MUSIC

Judges
5:3 sing. I will make ***m*** to the LORD,
5:16 listening to the ***m*** for the flocks?"
1 Samuel
19:9 in hand while David was playing ***m***.
1 Chronicles
6:31 in charge of the ***m*** in the LORD's
15:19 were to make ***m*** with bronze
Psalms
57:7 is unwavering. I will sing and make ***m***.
57:9 I will make ***m*** to you among the
71:22 God. I will make ***m*** for you with the
71:23 aloud when I make ***m*** for you; my whole
98:5 with the lyre and the sound of ***m***.
108:1 sing and make ***m***—yes, with my who
108:3 I will make ***m*** to you among the
Isaiah
38:20 and we will make ***m*** at the LORD's
Lamentations
5:14 city gate; young people stop their ***m***.
Luke
15:25 the house and heard ***m*** and dancing.
Ephesians
5:19 sing and make ***m*** to the Lord in

MY GOD

Gn 28:21; Ex 15:2; Nm 22:18; Dt 4:5; 26:3; Josh 14:8; 14:9; Ru 1:16; 2Sa 22:3; 22:7, 22, 30, 47; 24:24; 1Ki 3:7; 5:3, 4, 5; 8:28; 17:20, 21; 1Ch 17:25; 21:17; 22:7; 28:20; 29:17; 2Ch 2:4; 6:19, 40; Ezr 9:6; Neh 2:8; 2:12, 18; 5:19; 6:14; 7:5; 13:14, 22, 29, 31; Ps 3:7; 5:2; 7:1, 3, 6; 13:3; 18:2, 6, 21, 28, 29; 22:1, 2, 10; 25:2; 30:2, 12; 31:14; 35:23, 24; 38:15, 21; 40:5, 8, 17; 42:6, 11; 43:2, 4, 5; 59:1; 63:1; 68:24; 69:3; 71:4, 12, 22; 83:13; 84:3; 86:2, 12; 89:26; 91:2; 94:22; 102:24; 104:1, 33; 109:26; 118:28; 140:6; 143:10; 145:1; 146:2; Is 7:13; 25:1; 40:27; 44:17; 49:4, 5; 57:21; 61:10; Jer 31:18; Dn 4:8; 6:22; 9:4, 18, 19, 20; Hos 2:23; 8:2; 9:17; Jl 1:13; Am 3:11; Mi 7:7; Hab 1:12; Zec 11:4; 14:5; Mt 27:46; Mk 15:34; Jn 20:17; 20:28; Ro 1:8; 1Co 1:4; 2Co 12:21; Phi 1:3; 4:19; Phm 1:4; Rev 3:2; 3:12

Nn

NAAMAN
Genesis
46:21 Ashbel, Gera, ***N***, Ehi, Rosh,
Numbers
26:40 were Ard and ***N***: from Ard, the
2 Kings
5:1 ***N***, a general for the king of Aram, was
1 Chronicles
8:4 Abishua, ***N***, Ahoah
Luke
4:27 Instead, ***N*** the Syrian was

NABAL
1 Samuel
25:3 man's name was ***N***, and his wife's

NABOTH
1 Kings
21:2 Ahab ordered ***N***, "Give me your vineyard
2 Kings
9:21 that belonged to ***N*** the Jezreelite.

NADAB
Exodus
6:23 She gave birth to ***N***, Abihu, Eleazar,
Leviticus
10:1 Now ***N*** and Abihu, two of Aaron's sons,
Numbers
3:4 ***N*** and Abihu died before the LORD when
1 Kings
15:25 Jeroboam's son ***N*** became king of Israel

NAHOR
Genesis
11:26 the father of Abram, ***N***, and Haran.
22:23 Milcah bore for ***N***, Abraham's
24:15 of Milcah wife of ***N***, Abraham's
Joshua
24:2 was Terah, the father of Abraham and ***N***.
1 Chronicles
1:26 Serug, ***N***, Terah
Luke
3:34 son of Abraham son of Terah son of ***N***

NAKED
Genesis
2:25 two of them were ***n***, the man and his
3:7 that they were ***n***. So they sewed
3:11 you that you were ***n***? Did you eat from
9:22 saw his father ***n*** and told his two
Exodus
28:42 to cover their ***n*** skin from their
1 Samuel
19:24 of Samuel. He lay ***n*** that whole day
2 Chronicles
28:15 everyone who was ***n*** with items taken
Job
1:21 He said: "***N*** I came from my mother's
22:6 stripped the ***n***, leaving no
24:7 spend the night ***n***, unclothed, in the
24:10 poor go around ***n***, without clothes,
26:6 The grave is ***n*** before God; the
31:19 dying without clothes, the needy ***n***;
Ecclesiastes
5:15 mother's womb ***n***, naked they'll
Isaiah
20:2 did this, walking ***n*** and barefoot.
58:7 covering the ***n*** when you see
Lamentations
1:8 they've seen her ***n***. Even she groans
4:21 drunk on it. You will be stripped ***n***.
Ezekiel
16:7 thick. And you were completely ***n***.
16:22 lay completely ***n***, flailing about
18:7 to the hungry and clothes to the ***n***.
23:10 They stripped her ***n***, took her sons and
Hosea
2:3 I will strip her ***n*** and expose her as
Amos
2:16 will flee away ***n*** in that day,says
Habakkuk
2:15 out your wrath in order to see them ***n***.
Matthew
25:36 I was ***n*** and you gave me clothes to
Mark
14:52 the linen cloth behind and ran away ***n***.
Luke
8:27 lived among the tombs, ***n*** and homeless.
10:30 who stripped him ***n***, beat him up, and
John
21:7 (for he was ***n***) and jumped into
Acts
19:16 ran out of that house ***n*** and wounded.
2 Corinthians
5:3 tent, we won't find out that we are ***n***.
Hebrews
4:13 everything is ***n*** and exposed to
James
2:15 or sister who is ***n*** and never has
Revelation
3:17 pathetic, poor, blind, and ***n***.
16:15 don't go around ***n*** and exposed to

NAKEDNESS
Leviticus
18:7 your father's ***n***, which is your
18:8 not uncover the ***n*** of your father's
20:11 his father's ***n***. Both of them
Deuteronomy
28:48 famine, drought, ***n***, and total

Isaiah
47:3 Your ***n*** will be exposed, and your
57:8 You loved their bed; you saw their ***n***.
Ezekiel
16:8 and covered your ***n***. I made a solemn
22:10 In you a father's ***n*** is uncovered. In
23:18 known and her ***n*** exposed, I
Hosea
2:9 linen cloth, which were to cover her ***n***.
2:10 will uncover her ***n*** in plain view of
Micah
1:11 of Shaphir! In ***n*** and shame she
Nahum
3:5 show nations your ***n*** and kingdoms your
Romans
8:35 or famine, or ***n***, or danger, or
Revelation
3:18 wear so that your ***n*** won't be

NAME → GOD'S NAME, GOOD NAME, NAME OF JESUS, NAME OF JESUS CHRIST, NAME OF OUR LORD, NAME OF THE LORD, PRAISE THE LORD'S NAME, THANKS TO YOUR NAME
Genesis
11:4 and let's make a ***n*** for ourselves so
16:11 a son. You will ***n*** him Ishmael
17:5 nations, your ***n*** will no longer be
17:15 her Sarai. Her ***n*** will now be Sarah.
17:19 you, and you will ***n*** him Isaac. I will
19:22 That is why the ***n*** of the city is
21:31 Therefore, the ***n*** of that place is
21:33 there in the ***n*** of the LORD, El
25:30 red stuff." That's why his ***n*** is Edom.
32:28 he said, "Your ***n*** won't be Jacob
Exodus
3:15 you.' This is my ***n*** forever; this is
33:17 special approval, and I know you by ***n***."
33:19 before you the ***n***, 'The LORD.' I
39:14 each with its ***n*** for the twelve
Leviticus
22:2 not make my holy ***n*** impure: I am the
Numbers
1:2 recording the ***n*** of every male,
13:16 Moses changed the ***n*** of Hoshea, Nun's
17:2 Write each person's ***n*** on his staff.
Deuteronomy
6:13 him, and take your oaths in his ***n***!
9:14 will erase their ***n*** from under
25:6 will ***n*** the oldest male
Ezra
2:61 Gileadite and was called by their ***n***).
6:12 established his ***n*** there overthrow
8:20 Levites. These were all recorded by ***n***.
10:16 was designated by ***n***. On the first day
Nehemiah
1:9 I have chosen as a dwelling for my ***n***.'
1:11 in honoring your ***n***. Please give
9:5 your glorious ***n***, which is high
13:25 pledge in the ***n*** of God, saying,
Psalms
5:11 all who love your ***n*** can rejoice in
8:1 majestic is your ***n*** throughout the
8:9 majestic is your ***n*** throughout the
9:2 will sing praises to your ***n***, Most High.
9:10 who know your ***n*** trust you because
18:49 That's why I sing praises to your ***n***.
20:1 trouble. Let the ***n*** of Jacob's God
20:5 our flags in the ***n*** of our God. Let
22:22 will declare your ***n*** to my brothers
29:2 the glory due his ***n***! Bow down to the
30:4 to him; give thanks to his holy ***n***!
33:21 in God because we trust his holy ***n***.
34:3 me! Together let us lift his ***n*** up high!
41:5 When will he die and his ***n*** disappear?"
44:5 we've trampled our enemies by your ***n***.
44:8 give thanks to your ***n*** forever. Selah
45:17 perpetuate your ***n*** from one
52:9 will hope in your ***n*** because it's so
54:1 Save me by your ***n***; defend me by
54:6 thanks to your ***n***, LORD, because
61:5 possession as those who honor your ***n***.
61:8 praises to your ***n*** forever, and I
63:4 I will lift up my hands in your ***n***.
66:4 to you, sings praises to your ***n***!" Selah
68:4 praises to his ***n***! Exalt the one
72:17 Let the king's ***n*** last forever. Let his
72:19 God's glorious ***n*** forever; let his
74:7 defiled the dwelling place of your ***n***.
74:10 enemies going to abuse your ***n*** forever?
74:18 unbelieving fools have abused your ***n***.
74:21 let the poor and needy praise your ***n***!
75:1 give thanks! Your ***n*** is near. Your
76:1 in Judah; his ***n*** is great in
79:6 kingdoms that haven't called on your ***n***.
79:9 the glory of your ***n***! Deliver us and
80:18 us so that we can call on your ***n***.
83:4 a nation! Let the ***n*** Israel be
83:16 LORD, so that they might seek your ***n***.
83:18 that you—your ***n*** is the LORD!—you
86:9 you, Lord; they will glorify your ***n***
86:11 heart focused only on honoring your ***n***.
86:12 and I will glorify your ***n*** forever
89:12 and Hermon shout praises to your ***n***.
89:16 rejoice in your ***n*** all day long and
89:24 him. He will be strengthened by my ***n***.
91:14 I'll protect you because you know my ***n***.
92:1 to sing praises to your ***n***, Most High;
96:2 LORD! Bless his ***n***! Share the news
96:8 the glory due his ***n***! Bring gifts!
99:3 your great and awesome ***n***. He is holy!
99:6 who called on his ***n***. They cried out
100:4 with praise! Thank him! Bless his ***n***!
102:8 me; those who mock me curse using my ***n***!
105:1 call upon his ***n***; make his deeds
109:21 the sake of your ***n***; deliver me
115:1 but to your own ***n*** give glory
119:55 I remember you ***n*** at nighttime, and
119:132 only right for those who love your ***n***.
124:8 help is in the ***n*** of the LORD, the
135:13 LORD, your ***n*** is forever! LORD, your
138:2 and thank your ***n*** for your loyal
139:20 who use your ***n*** as if it were of
145:1 I will bless your ***n*** forever and
145:2 will praise your ***n*** forever and
147:4 stars by number, giving each one a ***n***.
Proverbs
10:7 blessing, but the ***n*** of the wicked
18:10 The LORD's ***n*** is a strong tower; the
21:24 mockers are their ***n***! Their conduct
30:4 is this person's ***n*** and the name of
Ecclesiastes
6:4 in darkness. Darkness covers its ***n***.

NAME [cont.]

7:1 A good ***n*** is better than fine oil, and

Song of Songs

1:3 sweet; your very ***n*** is perfume.

Isaiah

7:14 to a son, and she will ***n*** him Immanuel.

8:3 LORD said to me, "***N*** him Maher-shalal-hash-baz.

41:25 one who calls my ***n***. He tramples

43:1 I have called you by ***n***; you are mine.

48:2 the LORD of heavenly forces is his ***n***.

Jeremiah

10:6 are great, and great is your mighty ***n***.

10:16 the LORD of heavenly forces is his ***n***!

14:14 lies in my ***n***. I haven't sent

Ezekiel

20:9 the sake of my ***n***, so that it

Daniel

2:20 God's ***n*** be praised from age to eternal

2:26 to Daniel (whose ***n*** was

Hosea

1:4 said to him, "***N*** him Jezreel; for

1:6 said to Hosea, "***N*** her No

1:9 the LORD said, "***N*** him Not My People

Micah

4:5 walks in the ***n*** of their own god;

6:9 one fears your ***n***. Hear, tribe, and

Zechariah

5:4 lies in my ***n***. It will lodge in

6:12 is a man. His ***n*** is Branch, and he

Malachi

1:11 to sunset, my ***n*** will be great

Matthew

6:9 heaven, uphold the holiness of your ***n***.

7:22 prophesy in your ***n*** and expel demons

10:22 on account of my ***n***. But whoever

12:21 Gentiles will put their hope in his ***n***.

18:5 one such child in my ***n*** welcomes me.

18:20 gathered in my ***n***, I'm there with

19:29 because of my ***n*** will receive one

24:5 will come in my ***n***, saying, 'I'm the

24:9 will hate you on account of my ***n***.

28:19 them in the ***n*** of the Father and

Mark

3:16 twelve: Peter, a ***n*** he gave Simon;

Luke

1:13 to your son and you must ***n*** him John.

1:31 to a son, and you will ***n*** him Jesus.

1:60 replied, "No, his ***n*** will be John."

8:30 What is your ***n***?" "Legion," he

John

1:12 believed in his ***n***, he authorized to

10:3 his own sheep by ***n*** and leads them

Romans

9:17 and so that my ***n*** can be spread

15:9 and I will sing praises to your ***n***.

1 Corinthians

1:13 you, or were you baptized in Paul's ***n***?

Philippians

2:9 him and gave him a ***n*** above all names,

2:10 so that at the ***n*** of Jesus everyone in

3 John

1:15 you. Greet our friends there by ***n***.

Revelation

2:17 stone with a new ***n*** written on it,

6:8 Its rider's ***n*** was Death, and

8:11 The star's ***n*** is Wormwood, and a third

9:11 whose Hebrew ***n*** is Abaddon, and

13:17 with the beast's ***n*** or the number of

14:1 who had his ***n*** and his Father's

15:2 the number of its ***n*** were standing by

16:9 they cursed the ***n*** of the God who

17:5 A ***n***—a mystery—was written on her

19:12 crowns. He has a ***n*** written on him

20:15 Then anyone whose ***n*** wasn't found

22:4 his face, and his ***n*** will be on their

NAME OF JESUS

Mk 6:14; Ac 2:38; 3:6; 4:10, 18, 30; 5:40; 8:12; 9:27; 10:48; 16:18; 26:9; Phi 2:10

NAME OF JESUS CHRIST

Ac 2:38; 3:6; 4:10; 8:12; 10:48; 16:18

NAME OF OUR LORD

Ac 15:26; 1Co 1:2; 1:10; 5:4; Eph 5:20; 2Th 1:12; 3:6

NAME OF THE LORD

Gn 21:33; Dt 28:58; 1Sa 17:45; 2Sa 6:2; 6:18; 1Ki 5:3; 5:5; 8:17, 20; 18:24; 22:16; 2Ki 5:11; 1Ch 22:7; 2Ch 2:4; 6:7, 10; 33:18; Ps 7:17; 124:8; Is 18:7; 24:15; 60:9; Jer 26:16; Jl 2:26; Am 6:10; Mi 4:5; 5:4; Zep 3:9; 3:12; Zec 13:3; Mt 21:9; Mk 11:9; Lk 19:38; Jn 12:13; Ac 2:21; 8:16; 9:28; 19:5, 13, 17; 21:13; 1Co 6:11; Col 3:17; Jas 5:10; 5:14

NAMES

Genesis

25:13 These are the ***n*** of Ishmael's sons, by

25:16 These are their ***n*** by their villages

26:18 them the same ***n*** his father had

36:10 These are the ***n*** of Edom's sons: Eliphaz

36:40 These are the ***n*** of Esau's tribal chiefs

46:8 These are the ***n*** of the Israelites who

48:6 be determined under their brothers' ***n***.

48:16 alive and the ***n*** of my fathers

Exodus

1:1 These are the ***n*** of the Israelites who

6:16 were the Levites' ***n*** by their

23:13 Don't call on the ***n*** of other gods.

28:9 engrave on them the ***n*** of Israel's sons,

28:10 six ***n*** on one stone and the other six

28:11 stones with the ***n*** of Israel's sons.

28:12 presence their ***n*** on his two

28:21 stones with ***n*** corresponding to

28:29 will carry the ***n*** of Israel's sons

39:6 on them the ***n*** of Israel's sons,

39:14 stones with ***n*** corresponding to

Numbers

1:5 These are the ***n*** of the men who will

3:2 These are the ***n*** of Aaron's sons: Nadab

3:3 These are the ***n*** of Aaron's sons, who

3:18 These were the ***n*** of Gershon's sons by

3:40 one month of age and record their ***n***.

13:4 These are their ***n***: from the tribe of

13:16 These are the ***n*** of the men whom Moses

26:33 daughters. The ***n*** of Zelophehad's

26:53 according to the number of ***n***.

26:55 according to the ***n*** of their

27:1 His daughters' ***n*** were Mahlah,

32:38 Baal-meon (whose ***n*** were changed),

34:17 These are the ***n*** of the men who will

34:19 These are the ***n*** of the men: from the

Deuteronomy
7:24 will wipe their ***n*** out from under
12:3 Wipe out their ***n*** from that place.
Joshua
23:7 Don't invoke the ***n*** of their gods or
Ruth
1:2 Naomi, and the ***n*** of his two sons
1 Samuel
14:49 Malchishua. The ***n*** of his two
17:13 to war. Their ***n*** were Eliab the
2 Samuel
5:14 The ***n*** of his children in Jerusalem were
23:8 These are the ***n*** of David's warriors:
1 Kings
4:8 Here are their ***n***: Ben-hur in the
1 Chronicles
4:41 These whose ***n*** were recorded , however,
6:17 These are the ***n*** of Gershom's family:
9:44 six sons whose ***n*** were: Azrikam,
14:4 The ***n*** of his children in Jerusalem were
23:24 a listing of the ***n*** of each person 20
24:6 recorded their ***n*** in the presence
Ezra
5:4 What are the ***n*** of the people who
5:10 asked them their ***n*** so that we could
Nehemiah
9:38 writing, with the ***n*** of our officials,
10:1 the seals are the ***n*** of Governor
Psalms
9:5 You've erased their ***n*** for all time.
16:4 I won't let their ***n*** cross my lips.
109:13 let their ***n*** be wiped out in
Ezekiel
48:1 are the tribes' ***n***: Beginning at the
48:31 city go by the ***n*** of the tribes of
Daniel
1:7 gave them new ***n***. He named Daniel
Hosea
2:17 take away the ***n*** of the Baals from
Zephaniah
1:4 place and the ***n*** of the priestsof
Zechariah
13:2 eliminate the ***n*** of the idols from
Matthew
10:2 Here are the ***n*** of the twelve apostles:
10:25 of his household by even worse ***n***.
Luke
10:20 instead that your ***n*** are written in
Acts
18:15 about a message, ***n***, and your own
Philippians
2:9 him and gave him a name above all ***n***,
4:3 coworkers whose ***n*** are in the scroll
Revelation
3:5 scratch out their ***n*** from the scroll
13:1 and on its heads were blasphemous ***n***.
13:8 it, all whose ***n*** hadn't been
17:3 with blasphemous ***n***. It had seven
17:8 on earth, whose ***n*** haven't been
21:12 were written the ***n*** of the twelve
21:14 were the twelve ***n*** of the Lamb's

NAOMI
Ruth
1:2 of his wife was ***N***, and the names of

NAPHTALI
Genesis
30:8 and now I've won." So she named him ***N***.
35:25 Rachel's servant, were Dan and ***N***.
Exodus
1:4 Dan and ***N***, Gad and Asher
Numbers
1:43 from the tribe of ***N*** were 53,400.
Deuteronomy
27:13 Gad, Asher, Zebulun, Dan, and ***N***.
Joshua
19:32 For the people of ***N***, the lot went out
Ezekiel
48:3 to the western border: ***N***, one portion.
Matthew
4:13 the sea in the area of Zebulun and ***N***.
4:15 and land of ***N***, alongside the
Revelation
7:6 from the tribe of ***N***, twelve thousand;

NATHAN
2 Samuel
12:1 So the LORD sent ***N*** to David. When
1 Kings
1:8 the prophet ***N***, Shimei and his
1 Chronicles
2:36 was the father of ***N***, Nathan was the
29:29 Samuel the seer, ***N*** the prophet, and
2 Chronicles
9:29 of the prophet ***N***, the prophecies
29:25 the king's seer Gad, and the prophet ***N***.
Ezra
8:16 Jarib, Elnathan, ***N***, Zechariah, and
10:39 Shelemiah, ***N***, Adaiah
Psalms
51:1 when the prophet ***N*** came to him just
Luke
3:31 son of Mattatha son of ***N*** son of David

NATHANAEL
John
1:47 Jesus saw ***N*** coming toward him and said
21:2 (called Didymus), ***N*** from Cana in

NATION
Genesis
12:2 of you a great ***n*** and will bless
15:14 I punish the ***n*** they serve, they
17:20 and I will make a great ***n*** of him.
18:18 a great populous ***n***, and all the
20:4 you really put an innocent ***n*** to death?
21:13 son a great ***n*** too, because he
21:18 because I will make of him a great ***n***."
35:11 and multiply. A ***n***, even a large
46:3 I will make a great ***n*** of you there.
Exodus
9:24 of Egypt since it first became a ***n***.
19:6 for me and a holy ***n***. These are the
32:10 Then I'll make a great ***n*** out of you."
33:13 too that this ***n*** is your people."
34:10 earth or in any ***n***. All the people
Numbers
14:12 you into a great ***n***, stronger than
Deuteronomy
4:6 this great ***n*** wise and

4:7 there any great ***n*** that has gods as
4:8 Or does any great ***n*** have regulations
4:34 tried to take one ***n*** out of another
9:14 I will make a ***n*** out of you—one st
26:5 he became a great ***n***, mighty and
28:9 his own, a holy ***n***, just as he swore
28:32 given to another ***n*** while you watch;
28:36 you far away to a ***n*** that neither you
28:49 bring a distant ***n***—one from the far
28:50 a stern ***n*** that doesn't go easy on the
28:51 That ***n*** will devour your livestock's
28:52 That ***n*** will attack you in all your
28:64 you among every ***n***, from one end of
32:21 aggravate them with a ***n*** of fools.
32:28 not a thoughtful ***n***; they lack any
Joshua
3:17 until the entire ***n*** finished crossing
4:1 When the entire ***n*** had finished crossing
5:6 until the whole ***n*** died off. These
5:8 After the whole ***n*** had undergone
10:13 until a ***n*** took revenge on
Judges
2:20 Because this ***n*** has violated my
2 Samuel
7:23 They are the one ***n*** on earth that God
1 Kings
18:10 lives, there's no ***n*** or kingdom where
2 Kings
6:18 Strike this ***n*** with blindness."
1 Chronicles
16:20 wandering from ***n*** to nation, from one
17:21 Israel, a unique ***n*** on the earth,
2 Chronicles
9:23 kings of every ***n*** wanted an
15:6 ***N*** was crushed by nation and city by
32:15 god of any other ***n*** or kingdom has
Psalms
9:17 the same for every ***n*** that forgets God.
33:12 The ***n*** whose God is the LORD, the people whom God
83:4 them out as a ***n***! Let the name
105:13 wandering from ***n*** to nation, from one
106:5 the joy of your ***n***, so I can praise
147:20 with any other ***n***; those nations
Proverbs
14:34 dignifies a ***n***, but sin
Isaiah
1:4 Doom! Sinful ***n***, people weighed down
2:4 pruning tools. ***N*** will not take up
5:26 a signal to a ***n*** from far away and
7:8 Ephraim will be shattered as a ***n***);
9:3 You have made the ***n*** great; you have
10:6 Against a godless ***n*** I send him; against
10:7 mind, extermination of ***n*** after nation.
18:2 messengers, to a ***n*** tall and clean-sha
18:7 near and far, a ***n*** barbaric and
26:2 let a righteous ***n*** enter, a nation
26:15 enlarged the ***n***, LORD. You've
51:4 listen to me, my ***n***, for teaching
55:5 you will call a ***n*** you don't know, a
58:2 of my ways like a ***n*** that acted
60:12 The ***n*** and the dynasty that won't serve
65:1 I'm here!" to a ***n*** that didn't call
66:8 in one day? Can a ***n*** be born all at
Jeremiah
2:11 Has a ***n*** switched gods, though they
5:9 Shouldn't I take revenge on such a ***n***?
6:22 regions; a great ***n*** is roused from
7:28 say to them: This ***n*** neither obeys the
8:3 of this evil ***n*** will prefer death
9:9 the LORD; shouldn't I avenge such a ***n***?
12:17 will dig up that ***n***; yes, I will dig
18:7 pull down, and destroy a ***n*** or kingdom;
25:12 Babylon and his ***n*** for their
27:8 As for the ***n*** or country that won't
31:7 for the leading ***n***. Raise your
48:2 bring down the ***n***!" You too,
49:31 ready to attack a ***n*** that feels safe
50:3 A ***n*** from the north has risen up against
Lamentations
4:17 we watched for a ***n*** that doesn't save.
Ezekiel
31:6 and in its shade, every great ***n*** lived.
36:13 beings" and "You are depriving your ***n***,"
37:22 into a single ***n*** in the land on
Daniel
3:29 to every people, ***n***, and language:
8:22 come from one ***n***, but these four
11:23 gain power at the expense of a small ***n***.
Joel
1:6 because a ***n***, powerful and beyond
3:8 the Sabeans, to a ***n*** far away; for the
Amos
6:14 up against you a ***n***, house of Israel,
Micah
4:3 pruning tools. ***N*** will not take up
4:7 into a mighty ***n***. The LORD will
Habakkuk
1:6 and impetuous ***n***, which travels
Zephaniah
2:1 and assemble yourselves, shameless ***n***,
Haggai
2:14 people and this ***n*** become to me,
Malachi
3:9 and you, the entire ***n***, are robbing me.
John
11:50 rather than the whole ***n*** be destroyed."
18:35 a Jew, am I? Your ***n*** and its chief
Acts
2:5 Jews from every ***n*** under heaven
7:7 will condemn the ***n*** they serve as
10:35 Rather, in every ***n***, whoever worships
14:16 he permitted every ***n*** to go its own way.
17:26 every human ***n*** to live on the
24:2 has brought reforms to our ***n***.
24:10 judge over this ***n*** for many years,
24:17 the poor of my ***n*** and to offer
28:19 reason to bring charges against my ***n***.
1 Peter
2:9 a holy ***n***, a people who are
Revelation
5:9 every tribe, language, people, and ***n***.
7:9 were from every ***n***, tribe, people,
13:7 every tribe, people, language, and ***n***.
14:6 and to every ***n***, tribe, language,

NATIONS → ALL NATIONS, ALL NATIONS ON EARTH, AMONG THE NATIONS, GODS OF THE NATIONS

Genesis
10:5 and their clans within their ***n***.
10:20 languages, their lands, and their ***n***.
10:31 languages, their lands, and their ***n***.
10:32 and their ***n***. From them the

17:4 you will be the ancestor of many ***n***.
17:5 ancestor of many ***n***, your name will
17:6 I will produce ***n*** from you, and
17:16 she will become ***n***, and kings of
18:18 all the earth's ***n*** will be blessed
25:23 said to her, "Two ***n*** are in your womb;
27:29 May the ***n*** serve you, may peoples bow
35:11 a large group of ***n***, will come from
48:19 his descendants will become many ***n***."

Exodus
34:24 I will drive out ***n*** before you and

Leviticus
18:24 that is how the ***n*** that I am
18:28 vomited out the ***n*** that were before
20:23 practices of the ***n*** that I am

Numbers
14:15 one of them, the ***n*** who heard about
23:9 it doesn't consider itself among the ***n***.
24:8 will devour enemy ***n*** and break their

Deuteronomy
4:6 insight to the ***n*** who will hear
4:38 and stronger ***n*** from before you
7:1 out numerous ***n*** before you—the
7:5 do with these ***n***: rip down their
7:17 to yourself, These ***n*** are greater than
7:21 Don't dread these ***n*** because the LORD
7:22 drive out these ***n*** before you bit by
7:23 will lay these ***n*** before you,
8:20 Just like the ***n*** that the LORD is
9:1 possession of ***n*** larger and more
9:5 is because these ***n*** are wicked—that's
11:23 out all these ***n*** before you. You
12:2 place where the ***n*** that you are
17:14 as all our neighboring ***n*** have done."
18:9 the detestable things those ***n*** do.
20:15 that don't belong to these ***n*** here.
26:19 all the other ***n*** that he made in
28:12 will lend to many ***n***, but you won't
28:37 by all the ***n*** where the LORD
28:65 Among those ***n*** you will have no rest and
29:16 right through the ***n*** that you passed
30:1 among the various ***n*** where the LORD
31:3 destroy these ***n*** before you so you
32:8 divided up the ***n***—when he divided
33:3 who love the ***n***—all his holy one

Joshua
23:3 done to all these ***n*** because of you.

Judges
2:21 them any of the ***n*** that Joshua left
2:23 LORD left these ***n*** instead of
3:1 These are the ***n*** that the LORD left to

1 Samuel
8:5 to judge us like all the other ***n*** have."
8:20 all the other ***n***. Our king will

2 Samuel
7:23 by driving out ***n*** and their gods
22:44 leader of many ***n***. Strangers come
22:50 presence of the ***n***. That's why I

1 Kings
11:2 came from the ***n*** that the LORD had
14:24 just like those ***n*** that the LORD had

2 Kings
16:3 practices of the ***n*** that the LORD had
17:8 practices of the ***n*** that the LORD had
18:33 gods of the other ***n*** able to rescue
21:2 practices of the ***n*** that the LORD had

1 Chronicles
14:17 and the LORD made all the ***n*** fear him.
16:28 families of the ***n***—give to the LORD
16:31 rejoice! Let the ***n*** say, "The LORD
17:21 by driving out ***n*** before your
18:11 from all these ***n***: Edom, Moab, the

2 Chronicles
12:8 between serving me and serving other ***n***.
20:6 kingdoms of the ***n***. You are so
28:3 practices of the ***n*** the LORD had

Ezra
4:10 the rest of the ***n*** whom the great
6:21 pollutions of the ***n*** of the land to

Nehemiah
5:8 sold to other ***n***. But now you are
5:9 the taunts of the ***n*** that are our
5:17 the surrounding ***n***, gathered around
13:26 Among the many ***n*** there was no king

Job
12:23 makes ***n*** prominent and destroys them,

Psalms
2:1 Why do the ***n*** rant? Why do the peoples
2:8 I will make the ***n*** your possession;
9:5 denounced the ***n***, destroyed the
9:15 The ***n*** have fallen into the hole they
9:19 prevail! Let the ***n*** be judged before
9:20 LORD. Let the ***n*** know they are
10:16 and always! The ***n*** will vanish from
18:43 leader of many ***n***. Strangers come
18:49 presence of the ***n***. That's why I
33:10 what the ***n*** plan; he
44:14 a bad joke to the ***n***, something to be
46:6 ***N*** roar; kingdoms crumble. God utters
47:3 He subdues the ***n*** under us, subdues all
47:8 is king over the ***n***. God sits on his
65:7 roaring waves, calm the noise of the ***n***.
66:7 a good eye on the ***n***. So don't let the
66:8 All you ***n***, bless our God! Let the
67:4 you judge the ***n*** fairly and guide
78:55 God drove out the ***n*** before them and
79:6 your wrath on the ***n*** who don't know
79:10 Why should the ***n*** say, "Where's their
80:8 You drove out the ***n*** and planted it.
89:50 in my heart all the insults of the ***n***,
94:10 who disciplines ***n***, can't he punish?
96:7 families of the ***n***—give to the LORD
96:10 Tell the ***n***, "The LORD rules! Yes, he
99:1 LORD rules—the ***n*** shake! He sits
102:15 The ***n*** will honor the LORD's name; all
105:44 lands of other ***n***; they inherited
106:34 destroy the ***n*** as the LORD had
106:35 mixed up with the ***n***, learning what
106:41 them over to the ***n***; people who hated
111:6 gave them what had belonged to other ***n***.
115:2 Why do the ***n*** say, "Where's their God
117:1 the LORD, all you ***n***! Worship him, all
118:10 All the ***n*** surrounded me, but I cut them
135:10 struck down many ***n*** and killed mighty
147:20 nation; those ***n*** have no knowledge
149:7 against the ***n*** and punishment on

Proverbs
24:24 will curse them. ***N*** will condemn them.

Isaiah
2:3 Many ***n*** will go and say, "Come, let's go
9:1 the Jordan, and the Galilee of the ***n***.

11:10 the peoples. The ***n*** will seek him
13:4 of kingdoms, of ***n*** coming together.
14:6 blows, that ruled ***n*** with anger, with
16:8 masters of ***n***, had reached as
17:12 to the roar of ***n***, like the roaring
23:3 income; she was the marketplace of ***n***.
25:3 the towns of tyrant ***n*** will fear you.
29:7 The horde of ***n*** fighting against Ariel,
30:28 to shake the ***n*** with a sieve of
33:3 on account of your roar, ***n*** scattered.
34:1 Draw near, you ***n***, to hear; and listen,
34:2 against all the ***n***, and is angry
36:18 other gods of the ***n*** save their lands
37:12 the gods of the ***n*** that my ancestors
40:15 Look, the ***n*** are like a drop in a
41:1 Let the ***n*** renew their
42:1 him; he will bring justice to the ***n***.
43:4 your place, and ***n*** in exchange for
49:6 as light to the ***n*** so that my
51:4 me, my justice, as a light to the ***n***.
60:2 and gloom the ***n***, the LORD will
61:6 on the wealth of ***n***, and fatten
62:2 ***N*** will see your righteousness, all
63:6 I trampled down ***n*** in my anger and made
64:2 your enemies, the ***n*** would tremble in
66:12 and the wealth of ***n*** like an

Jeremiah
1:5 apart; I made you a prophet to the ***n***."
4:2 then the ***n*** will enjoy God's
6:18 pay attention, ***n***; take notice,
10:2 the ways of the ***n*** or be troubled by
10:3 rituals of the ***n*** are hollow: a
10:7 you, king of the ***n***? That is your
10:10 earth quakes; the ***n*** can't endure his
10:25 your wrath on the ***n*** that ignore you
12:14 The evil ***n*** have seized the
14:22 false gods of the ***n*** make it rain? Can
15:4 an object of horror to all ***n*** on earth.
16:19 of trouble. The ***n*** will flock to you
22:8 People from many ***n*** will pass by this
25:9 the surrounding ***n***. I will
25:11 and these ***n*** will serve the
25:14 Yes, many great ***n*** and powerful kings
31:10 LORD's word, you ***n***, and announce it
46:1 the prophet Jeremiah concerning the ***n***.
50:2 Tell the ***n***; proclaim it far and wide!
51:7 earth drunk. The ***n*** drank her wine

Lamentations
1:10 She watched ***n*** enter her
4:15 around. The ***n*** said, "They can't

Ezekiel
5:5 the middle of the ***n*** and surrounding
5:6 than these ***n*** and surrounding
6:9 me in the ***n*** to which they've
7:24 up the cruelest ***n***, and they will
11:12 the case laws of the ***n*** around you.
19:4 When the ***n*** heard about him, they caught him in their trap
20:9 the sight of the ***n*** among whom they
22:4 the ridicule of ***n*** and the derision
26:3 I will bring many ***n*** up against you.
29:15 itself over the ***n***, and I will make
30:11 terrible of the ***n***, will be brought
32:2 lion among the ***n***, but you are like
32:16 daughters of the ***n*** will lament for
36:3 the surviving ***n*** pressed in and
36:6 ridicule of the ***n***, my passion and
37:22 no longer be two ***n***, and they will no
38:12 gathered from the ***n***, who are
39:23 The ***n*** will know that the house of

Hosea
9:1 as other ***n*** do; for as whores

Joel
3:2 gather all the ***n***, and I will bring
3:12 Let the ***n*** prepare themselves, and come

Amos
6:1 the chiefs of the ***n***, to whom the
9:12 well as all the ***n*** who are called by

Obadiah
1:15 against all the ***n***. As you have

Micah
4:2 Many ***n*** will go and say: "Come, let's go
4:3 judge between the ***n*** and settle
4:11 Now many ***n*** may gather against you; they
5:15 and in wrath on the ***n*** that don't obey!
7:16 ***N*** will see and be ashamed of all their

Nahum
3:4 the one who sells ***n*** by means of her
3:5 face; I will show ***n*** your nakedness

Habakkuk
1:17 continue to slay ***n*** without sparing
2:13 just enough fire; ***n*** become tired for
3:6 out against the ***n***. The everlasting
3:12 the earth; in anger you tread the ***n***.

Zephaniah
2:11 coastlands of the ***n*** will bow down to
3:6 I will cut off ***n***; their towers will be
3:8 decide to gather ***n***, to collect

Haggai
2:22 strength of the ***n***. I will overthrow

Zechariah
1:15 those carefree ***n***. Though I was
2:8 concerning the ***n*** plundering you:
8:22 and mighty ***n*** will come to seek
9:10 peace to the ***n***. His rule will
12:2 the surrounding ***n***. There will be a

Matthew
24:7 ***N*** and kingdoms will fight against each

Acts
7:45 the land from the ***n*** whom God
13:19 conquered seven ***n*** in the land of
17:27 God made the ***n*** so they would seek him,

Romans
4:17 father of many ***n***. So Abraham is

1 Timothy
3:16 to throughout the ***n***, believed in

Revelation
2:26 end, I will give authority over the ***n***
10:11 many peoples, ***n***, languages, and
11:2 been given to the ***n***, and they will
12:5 to rule all the ***n*** with an iron rod.
14:8 She made all the ***n*** drink the wine of
15:3 and true are your ways, king of the ***n***.
16:19 the cities of the ***n*** fell. God
17:15 are peoples, crowds, ***n***, and languages.
19:15 strike down the ***n***. He is the one
20:3 to deceive the ***n*** until the
21:26 the glory and honor of the ***n*** into it.
22:2 leaves are for the healing of the ***n***.

NAZARENE
Matthew
2:23 be fulfilled: He will be called a ***N***.
Mark
14:67 You were also with the ***N***, Jesus."
Luke
18:37 told him, "Jesus the ***N*** is passing by."
John
18:5 Jesus the ***N***." He said to
18:7 looking for?" They said, "Jesus the ***N***."
19:19 read "Jesus the ***N***, the king of the
Acts
2:22 words! Jesus the ***N*** was a man whose
3:6 Jesus Christ the ***N***, rise up and
4:10 Jesus Christ the ***N***—whom you crucified
22:8 I am Jesus the ***N***, whom you are
24:5 He's a ringleader of the ***N*** faction
26:9 name of Jesus the ***N*** in every way

NAZARETH → JESUS OF NAZARETH
Matthew
2:23 in a city called ***N*** so that what was
Luke
1:26 angel Gabriel to ***N***, a city in
4:16 Jesus went to ***N***, where he had been
John
1:46 anything from ***N*** be good?" Philip

NAZIRITE
Numbers
6:2 promise to be a ***n*** in order to be
Judges
13:5 is going to be a ***n*** for God from

NEAR
Psalms
22:11 trouble is ***n*** and there's no
38:11 those who were ***n*** me now stay far
46:1 a help always ***n*** in times of great
73:28 good for me to be ***n*** God. I have taken
75:1 Your name is ***n***. Your marvelous
Proverbs
3:29 neighbor who trusts and lives ***n*** you.
Isaiah
13:6 of the LORD is ***n***. Like destruction
55:6 be found; call him while he is yet ***n***.
57:19 to those far and ***n***, and I will heal
Ezekiel
7:7 the day draws ***n***. On the hills
Joel
1:15 of the LORD is ***n***; it comes like
Obadiah
1:15 of the LORD is ***n*** against all the
Zephaniah
1:7 of the LORD is ***n***! The LORD has
1:14 of the LORD is ***n***; it is near and
Malachi
3:5 I will draw ***n*** to you for judgment. I
Matthew
10:7 The kingdom of heaven has come ***n***.'
26:18 says, "My time is ***n***. I'm going to
Luke
21:31 you know that God's kingdom is ***n***.
Romans
10:8 say? The word is ***n*** you, in your
Philippians
4:5 treatment of all people. The Lord is ***n***.
James
4:8 Come ***n*** to God, and he will come near to
5:8 because the coming of the Lord is ***n***.
Revelation
1:3 is written in it, for the time is ***n***.
22:10 in this scroll, because the time is ***n***.

NEBO
Deuteronomy
34:1 plains to Mount ***N***, the peak of the
Isaiah
46:1 crouches down; ***N*** cowers. Their
Jeremiah
48:1 How awful for ***N***; it lies in

NEBUCHADNEZZAR
2 Kings
24:1 days, King ***N*** of Babylon
1 Chronicles
6:15 Judah and Jerusalem to be exiled by ***N***.
2 Chronicles
36:6 Babylon's King ***N*** attacked him, bound
Ezra
2:1 Babylon's King ***N*** had deported to
Nehemiah
7:6 Babylon's King ***N*** had taken into
Esther
2:6 Babylon's King ***N*** exiled to
Jeremiah
21:2 Babylon's King ***N*** is attacking us.
Ezekiel
29:19 to Babylon's King ***N***. He will carry
Daniel
1:1 Babylon's King ***N*** came to Jerusalem
3:1 King ***N*** made a gold statue. It was
4:4 "While I, ***N***, was safe in my house,
5:2 that his father ***N*** had taken from
5:11 Your father King ***N*** appointed this
5:18 glory, and majesty to your father ***N***.
5:19 power God gave ***N***, all peoples,

NEBUZARADAN
2 Kings
25:8 Nebuchadnezzar, ***N*** arrived at
Jeremiah
52:12 Nebuchadnezzar, ***N*** commander of the

NECK
Genesis
27:16 arms and smooth ***n*** she put the hide
27:40 tear away his harness from your ***n***."
33:4 arms around his ***n***, kissed him, and
41:42 he put a gold necklace around his ***n***.
45:14 Benjamin's ***n*** and wept, and
46:29 arms around his ***n*** and wept,
49:8 will be on the ***n*** of your enemies;
Exodus
13:13 must break its ***n***. You should
34:20 must break its ***n***. You should
Leviticus
5:8 the back of its ***n*** without splitting
Deuteronomy
21:4 break the cow's ***n*** right there in

21:6 the cow whose ***n*** was broken in the
28:48 iron yoke on your ***n*** until he has
Judges
5:30 cloths as loot for every ***n***."
1 Samuel
4:18 the gate. His ***n*** broke, and he
Job
16:12 by the back of my ***n***, dashed me into
30:18 it binds me like the ***n*** of my shirt.
39:19 to the horse, clothe his ***n*** with a mane,
41:22 resides in his ***n***; violence dances
Psalms
69:1 because the waters have reached my ***n***!
105:18 his shackles; his ***n*** was in an iron
Proverbs
1:9 on your head, and beads for your ***n***.
3:3 Bind them on your ***n***; write them on
3:22 being, and an ornament for your ***n***.
6:21 all time; fasten them around your ***n***.
Song of Songs
1:10 with ear hoops; your ***n***, with beads.
4:4 tower is your ***n***, splendidly
7:4 your ***n***, like a tower of ivory; your
Isaiah
8:8 up to the ***n***. But God is with
10:27 the yoke on your ***n***. He has gone up
30:28 reaches up to the ***n***, to shake the
48:4 stubborn, your ***n*** is made of iron,
52:2 bonds from your ***n***, captive Daughter
66:3 breaks a dog's ***n***; the one who
Jeremiah
27:2 straps and bars and wear it on your ***n***.
28:10 the prophet Jeremiah's ***n*** and broke it.
29:26 who prophesies into stocks and ***n*** irons.
Lamentations
1:14 His yoke is on my ***n***; he makes my
Ezekiel
16:11 wrists and a necklace around your ***n***.
Daniel
5:7 chain around his ***n***, and will rule
Hosea
10:11 I spared her fair ***n***; but I will make
Habakkuk
3:13 bare the foundation up to the ***n***. Selah

NECO

2 Kings
23:29 king Pharaoh ***N*** marched against
2 Chronicles
35:20 Egypt's King ***N*** marched against
Jeremiah
46:2 army of Pharaoh ***N***, Egypt's king,

NEED

Genesis
33:11 have everything I ***n***." So Jacob
Exodus
5:7 the straw they ***n*** to make bricks
5:18 but you still ***n*** to make the same
8:27 We ***n*** to go for a three-day journey into
9:28 you go. You don't ***n*** to stay here any
10:24 flocks and herds ***n*** to stay behind.
10:25 Moses said, "You ***n*** to let us have
10:26 behind. We'll ***n*** some of them for
Leviticus
13:36 priest does not ***n*** to look for the
Deuteronomy
15:6 peoples but won't ***n*** to borrow a
15:8 generously lend them whatever they ***n***.
16:13 and drink you ***n***, perform the
28:12 but you won't have any ***n*** to borrow.
Joshua
7:3 him, "There is no ***n*** for all of the
Judges
19:19 servant with us. We don't ***n*** anything."
1 Samuel
26:8 stroke is all I ***n***! I won't need a
2 Samuel
19:29 You don't ***n*** to talk any more about
1 Kings
2:9 But you don't ***n*** to excuse him. You are
8:59 and his people Israel for each day's ***n***,
20:24 This is what you ***n*** to do: Remove the
2 Kings
12:5 wherever such a ***n*** for repair is
22:7 But there's no ***n*** to check on them
1 Chronicles
23:26 the Levites ***n*** no longer carry the
2 Chronicles
2:16 timber as you ***n*** from Lebanon and
20:17 You don't ***n*** to fight this battle. Just
35:3 son. You don't ***n*** to carry it
35:15 They didn't ***n*** to leave their
Nehemiah
2:4 is it that you ***n***?" I prayed to the
5:2 many, and we all ***n*** grain to eat and
Esther
1:13 Now, when a ***n*** arose, the king would
Psalms
72:13 saves the lives of those who are in ***n***.
86:1 answer me because I am poor and in ***n***.
112:9 to those in ***n***. Their
Proverbs
30:8 or wealth; give me just the food I ***n***.
Jeremiah
2:24 who desire her ***n*** not give up; with
31:34 will no longer ***n*** to teach each
46:19 Get what you ***n*** for deportation, you
Lamentations
3:56 your ear to my ***n*** for relief, to my
Ezekiel
17:9 and no one will ***n*** a strong arm or a
Daniel
3:16 We don't ***n*** to answer your
Hosea
7:4 baker doesn't ***n*** to stoke the
Amos
2:6 and those in ***n*** for a pair of
Micah
1:10 tell it not; no ***n*** to weep there! In
Matthew
3:14 him and said, "I ***n*** to be baptized by
6:8 Father knows what you ***n*** before you ask.
6:11 Give us the bread we ***n*** for today
6:32 heavenly Father knows that you ***n*** them.
9:12 people don't ***n*** a doctor, but
14:16 them, "There's no ***n*** to send them
25:29 more than they ***n***. But as for those
26:65 God! Why do we ***n*** any more
Mark
2:17 people don't ***n*** a doctor, but
2:25 when he was in ***n***, when he and

14:63 said, "Why do we ***n*** any more
Luke
5:31 people don't ***n*** a doctor, but
11:3 Give us the bread we ***n*** for today
11:41 give to those in ***n*** from the core of
12:30 Your Father knows that you ***n*** them.
12:33 give to those in ***n***. Make for
15:7 who have no ***n*** to change their
15:14 that country and he began to be in ***n***.
18:1 about their ***n*** to pray
22:71 said, "Why do we ***n*** further
John
1:22 Who are you? We ***n*** to give an answer
2:25 He didn't ***n*** anyone to tell him about
4:15 and will never ***n*** to come here to
13:10 who have bathed ***n*** only to have
13:29 Go, buy what we ***n*** for the feast,"
16:30 and you don't ***n*** anyone to ask
Acts
4:10 people of Israel ***n*** to know that this
4:17 the people, we ***n*** to warn them not
4:35 was distributed to anyone who was in ***n***.
Romans
15:1 who are powerful ***n*** to be patient
1 Corinthians
5:5 At that time we ***n*** to hand this man over
10:12 they are standing ***n*** to watch out or
12:21 hand, "I don't ***n*** you," or in turn,
14:34 Instead, they ***n*** to get under
2 Corinthians
3:1 again? We don't ***n*** letters of
9:8 everything you ***n*** always and in
10:11 These people ***n*** to think about
13:10 so that I won't ***n*** to act harshly
Ephesians
4:28 to share with whoever is in ***n***.
Philippians
4:11 this because I ***n*** anything, for I
4:12 of being in ***n*** and of having
4:19 meet your every ***n*** out of his riches
Colossians
1:23 But you ***n*** to remain well established
1 Thessalonians
1:8 so that we don't even ***n*** to mention it.
3:10 whatever you still ***n*** for your faith.
4:9 You don't ***n*** us to write about loving
4:12 outsiders, and you won't be in ***n***.
5:1 We don't ***n*** to write to you about the
2 Thessalonians
3:7 know how you ***n*** to imitate us
1 Timothy
6:17 Instead, they ***n*** to hope in God,
2 Timothy
2:15 who doesn't ***n*** to be ashamed but
Titus
3:13 so that they won't ***n*** anything.
Hebrews
4:16 mercy and find grace when we ***n*** help.
5:12 by now, you ***n*** someone to teach
7:11 was there still a ***n*** to speak about
9:16 is a will, you ***n*** to confirm the
10:36 You ***n*** to endure so that you can receive
13:17 for you. They ***n*** to be able to do
James
2:20 so slow? Do you ***n*** to be shown that
2 Peter
1:3 us everything we ***n*** for life and
1 John
2:27 and you don't ***n*** anyone to teach
3:17 or sister in ***n*** and that person
Revelation
3:17 and I don't ***n*** a thing.' You
21:23 The city doesn't ***n*** the sun or the moon
22:5 more. They won't ***n*** the light of a

NEEDS

Leviticus
14:4 for the person who ***n*** purification.
Numbers
4:26 everything that ***n*** to be done with
Judges
17:10 a set of clothes, and your basic ***n***."
19:20 care of all your ***n***. Just don't spend
Psalms
19:2 informs another what ***n*** to be known.
Proverbs
12:10 their livestock's ***n***, but even the
31:11 and with her he will have all he ***n***.
Jeremiah
23:2 attended to their ***n***, so I will take
40:15 son; no one ***n*** to knows about
Matthew
21:3 say that the Lord ***n*** it." He sent them
Mark
11:3 say, 'Its master ***n*** it, and he will
Luke
11:8 whatever he ***n*** because of his
19:31 it?' just say, 'Its master ***n*** it.'"
19:34 They replied, "Its master ***n*** it.
Acts
20:34 for my own ***n*** and for those of
Romans
12:13 Contribute to the ***n*** of God's people,
16:2 her whatever she ***n*** from you, because
1 Corinthians
3:10 it. Each person ***n*** to pay attention
7:3 his wife's sexual ***n***, and the wife
7:5 meet each other's ***n*** unless you both
2 Corinthians
9:12 meeting their ***n*** but it is also
Philippians
2:25 is your representative who serves my ***n***.
4:16 take care of my ***n*** even while I was
Titus
1:5 organize whatever ***n*** to be done and to
3:14 to meet pressing ***n*** so they aren't
James
1:5 But anyone who ***n*** wisdom should ask God,
2:16 actually give them what their body ***n***?

NEEDY

Deuteronomy
15:10 generously to ***n*** persons. Don't
24:14 of poor or ***n*** workers, whether
1 Samuel
2:8 lifts up the ***n*** from the garbage
Job
5:15 their mouth, the ***n*** from the grip of
24:4 way, make the land's ***n*** hide together.
29:16 a father to the ***n***; the case I
30:25 day or my soul grieve for the ***n***;
31:19 dying without clothes, the ***n*** naked;

Psalms
12:5 the groans of the ***n***, I'm now standing
35:10 the weak and the ***n*** from those who
37:14 the weak and the ***n***, to slaughter
40:17 me? I'm weak and ***n***. Let my Lord
69:33 listens to the ***n*** and doesn't
70:5 me? I'm poor and ***n***. Hurry to me,
72:4 of those who are ***n***, but let him
72:12 he delivers the ***n*** who cry out, the
72:13 the weak and the ***n***; he saves the
74:21 let the poor and ***n*** praise your name!
82:4 the lowly and the ***n***. Deliver them
107:41 God raises the ***n*** from their
109:16 the poor and ***n***—even the brokenh
109:22 I am poor and ***n***, and my heart is
109:31 right next to the ***n***, to save them
113:7 and raises up the ***n*** from the garbage
132:15 supply; I will fill its ***n*** full of food!
140:12 and will do what is right for the ***n***.
Proverbs
11:24 with what is appropriate will grow ***n***.
14:21 happy are those who are kind to the ***n***.
15:15 the days of the ***n*** are hard, but a
16:19 humble with the ***n*** than to divide
22:22 poor. Don't oppress the ***n*** in the gate.
28:3 who oppress the ***n*** are rain that
30:14 to devour the ***n*** from the earth,
31:5 law, and violate the rights of the ***n***.
31:9 and to defend the ***n*** and the poor.
31:20 out to the ***n***; she stretches
Isaiah
10:2 to deprive the ***n*** of their rights and to
11:4 He will judge the ***n*** with righteousness,
14:30 will graze; their ***n*** will lie down
25:4 a refuge for the ***n*** in distress, a
26:6 feet of the poor, the steps of the ***n***.
32:7 words, even when the ***n*** speak justly.
41:17 The poor and the ***n*** seek water, and
Jeremiah
20:13 has rescued the ***n*** from the clutches
22:16 of the poor and ***n***; then it went
Ezekiel
16:49 but she didn't help the poor and the ***n***.
18:12 the poor and ***n***, robs others and
Amos
4:1 who crush the ***n***, who say to their
8:4 trample on the ***n*** and destroy the
8:6 order to buy the ***n*** for silver and
Acts
4:34 There were no ***n*** persons among them.
2 Corinthians
9:9 he gave to the ***n***; his
1 Timothy
5:3 Take care of widows who are truly ***n***
5:5 who is truly ***n*** and all alone
5:16 can help other widows who are truly ***n***.
Hebrews
11:37 sheep and goats, ***n***, oppressed, and

NEIGHBOR → LOVE YOUR NEIGHBOR, YOUR NEIGHBOR AS YOURSELF

Genesis
38:12 he and his ***n*** Hirah the
38:20 kid goat with his ***n*** the Adullamite so
Exodus
3:22 will ask her ***n*** along with the
11:2 man to ask his ***n*** and every woman
12:4 share one with a ***n*** nearby. You
20:16 Do not testify falsely against your ***n***
20:17 anything else that belongs to your ***n***.
32:27 your brother, your friend, and your ***n***!"
Leviticus
19:18 must love your ***n*** as yourself; I am
Deuteronomy
5:20 Do not testify falsely against your ***n***
5:21 anything else that belongs to your ***n***.
19:4 who killed his ***n*** accidentally,
19:11 does hate a ***n*** and ambushes him,
22:26 someone attacks his ***n*** and kills him.
24:10 of loan to your ***n***, don't enter
27:24 who kills his ***n*** in secret." All
Joshua
20:5 struck down the ***n*** by accident and
Psalms
15:3 harm to a friend, doesn't insult a ***n***;
101:5 lies about a ***n***. I can't stomach
Proverbs
3:28 Don't say to your ***n***, "Go and come
3:29 plan to harm your ***n*** who trusts and
6:1 a loan for your ***n*** or shake hands in
6:3 control of your ***n***. So go, humble
11:12 despises their ***n*** lacks sense; a
24:28 against your ***n*** without reason;
25:8 in the future when your ***n*** shames you?
25:9 it out with your ***n***, and don't give
26:19 who deceive their ***n*** and say, "Hey, I
27:10 strikes. Better a ***n*** nearby than a
27:14 Greeting a ***n*** with a loud voice early in
Isaiah
3:5 the other, ***n*** against neighbor.
19:2 against another, ***n*** against neighbor,
Jeremiah
6:21 over them; ***n*** and friend alike
Ezekiel
22:12 by extorting your ***n***, and you neglect
Zechariah
8:10 I set everyone against their own ***n***.
11:9 are left devour the flesh of their ***n***."
Luke
10:29 so he said to Jesus, "And who is my ***n***?"
Acts
7:27 fight against his ***n*** pushed Moses
Ephesians
4:25 the truth to your ***n*** because we are
Hebrews
8:11 ever teach a ***n*** or their brother
James
4:12 But you who judge your ***n***, who are you?

NEIGHBORS

Leviticus
19:13 not oppress your ***n*** or rob them. Do
Deuteronomy
15:2 from their ***n*** or their
Joshua
9:16 actually their ***n*** and were living
2 Kings
4:3 from all your ***n***. Get as many
1 Chronicles
12:40 Even their ***n*** from as far away as
Ezra
1:6 All their ***n*** assisted them with silver
Psalms
31:11 still worse to my ***n***. I scare my

44:13 a joke to all our ***n***; we're mocked and
79:4 a joke to our ***n***, nothing but
79:12 Pay back our ***n*** seven times over, right
80:6 at odds with our ***n***; our enemies make
89:41 him. He's nothing but a joke to his ***n***.

Proverbs

11:9 destroy their ***n*** by their words,
12:26 guidance to their ***n***, but the path of
14:20 Even their ***n*** hate the poor, but many
14:21 who despise their ***n*** are sinners, but
16:29 entice their ***n*** and walk them
21:10 evil; their ***n*** receive no mercy
25:18 against their ***n*** are like a club,

Jeremiah

9:8 They wish their ***n*** well, but in
19:9 and to devouring the flesh of their ***n***.
48:17 this nation, you ***n*** of Moab, all you
48:39 of every joke, horrific to all its ***n***.
50:40 and their ***n***, declares the

Ezekiel

16:26 Egyptians, your ***n*** with the large
18:6 wives of their ***n*** or approach
28:24 of any of its ***n*** who hold it in

Daniel

9:16 have become a disgrace to all our ***n***.

Zechariah

3:10 will invite their ***n*** to sit beneath
14:13 the hand of their ***n***; neighbors will

Luke

1:58 Her ***n*** and relatives celebrated with her
1:65 All their ***n*** were filled with awe, and
14:12 or rich ***n***. If you do, they
15:6 his friends and ***n***, saying to them,
15:9 her friends and ***n***, saying,

John

9:8 The man's ***n*** and those who used to see

Romans

15:2 should please our ***n*** for their good in

NET

Job

18:8 their feet in a ***n***; they walk on
19:6 wronged me and enclosed his ***n*** over me.

Psalms

9:15 in the very ***n*** they themselves
25:15 he will free my feet from the ***n***.
31:4 me out of this ***n*** that's been set
35:7 they hid their ***n*** for me for no
35:8 it. Let the ***n*** they hid catch
57:6 They laid a ***n*** for my feet to bring me
66:11 trapped us in a ***n***, laid burdens on our
140:5 spread out a ***n*** alongside the

Proverbs

1:17 useless to cast a ***n*** in the sight of a
29:5 friends spread out a ***n*** for their feet.

Ecclesiastes

9:12 caught in a ***n*** or like birds

Isaiah

51:20 antelope in a ***n***, filled with the

Lamentations

1:13 them. He spread a ***n*** for my feet; he

Ezekiel

12:13 I will spread my ***n*** over him, catch
17:20 I will spread my ***n*** over him, and he
32:3 I will spread my ***n*** over you, and I

Hosea

5:1 at Mizpah, and a ***n*** spread out upon
7:12 I will spread my ***n*** over them; like

Habakkuk

1:15 them away with a ***n***; he collects them
1:16 sacrifices to his ***n***; he burns incense
1:17 to empty his ***n*** and continue to

Matthew

13:47 heaven is like a ***n*** that people threw

John

21:6 said, "Cast your ***n*** on the right side
21:8 dragging the ***n*** full of fish, for
21:11 up and pulled the ***n*** to shore. It was

NETHANEL

Numbers

1:8 from Issachar, ***N***, Zuar's son
10:15 ***N***, Zuar's son, commanded the military

1 Chronicles

2:14 ***N*** his fourth, Raddai his fifth
15:24 Joshaphat, ***N***, Amasai,
26:4 third, Sachar the fourth, ***N*** the fifth,

2 Chronicles

17:7 Zechariah, ***N***, and Micaiah to
35:9 Shemaiah and ***N***, along with

Ezra

10:22 Ishmael, ***N***, Jozabad, and

Nehemiah

12:21 of Hilkiah, Hashabiah; of Jedaiah, ***N***

NETS

Psalms

10:9 all right, dragging them off in their ***n***.
141:10 into their own ***n***—all together!—

Proverbs

22:5 Thorns and ***n*** are in the path of the

Isaiah

19:8 those who spread ***n*** on the water will

Ezekiel

19:8 They cast their ***n*** over him and
19:9 brought him with ***n*** to the king of
26:5 place for drying ***n*** in the middle of
47:10 for spreading ***n***. It will be like

Micah

7:2 bloodshed; they hunt each other with ***n***.

Habakkuk

1:16 to his fishing ***n***, because due to

Matthew

4:18 throwing fishing ***n*** into the sea,

Mark

1:16 throwing fishing ***n*** into the sea, for

Luke

5:4 water, and drop your ***n*** for a catch."

NEW → NEW COVENANT, NEW WINE

Leviticus

2:16 of the crushed ***n*** grain and oil
14:42 first ones, and ***n*** coating will be
23:16 must present a ***n*** grain offering to
26:10 to clear it out to make room for the ***n***!

Numbers

28:26 you present your ***n*** grain offering to
29:6 offering of the ***n*** moon with its

Deuteronomy

10:4 God wrote on the ***n*** tablets what had
20:5 has just built a ***n*** house but hasn't
22:8 you build a ***n*** house, you must

24:3 But this ***n*** husband also dislikes her,
24:5 so he can bring joy to his ***n*** wife.
32:17 no knowledge—***n*** gods only
Joshua
9:13 wineskins were ***n*** when we filled
Judges
5:8 When they chose ***n*** gods, then war came
15:13 him up with two ***n*** ropes, and
16:11 ties me up with ***n*** ropes that
1 Samuel
2:33 of grief. Any ***n*** children in your
6:7 So get a ***n*** cart ready along with two
20:5 Tomorrow is the ***n*** moon, and I'm
20:18 festival of the ***n*** moon," Jonathan
20:24 field. When the ***n*** moon came, the
20:27 the second of the ***n*** moon, David's
20:34 second day of the ***n*** moon because he
2 Samuel
6:3 God's chest on a ***n*** cart and carried
21:16 of bronze, and he was wearing ***n*** armor.
1 Kings
11:29 was wearing a ***n*** garment. The two
20:9 comply with this ***n*** command.'" The
2 Kings
2:20 said, "Bring me a ***n*** bowl, and put
16:14 it on the north side of the ***n*** altar.
1 Chronicles
13:7 God's chest on a ***n*** cart from
23:31 the sabbaths, the ***n*** moons, and
2 Chronicles
8:13 for sabbaths, ***n*** moon festivals,
20:5 temple in front of the ***n*** courtyard.
31:3 for the sabbaths, ***n*** moons, and
Ezra
3:5 offerings at the ***n*** moons, and at all
Nehemiah
10:33 sabbaths and the ***n*** moons and the
Esther
2:8 order and his ***n*** law became
4:3 order and his ***n*** law arrived, a
Job
32:19 wine; like ***n*** wineskins it will
Psalms
33:3 Sing to him a ***n*** song! Play your best
40:3 He put a ***n*** song in my mouth, a song of
51:10 me, God; put a ***n***, faithful spirit
81:3 the horn on the ***n*** moon, at the full
96:1 to the LORD a ***n*** song! Sing to the
98:1 to the LORD a ***n*** song because he
119:50 is this: your word gives me ***n*** life.
144:9 I will sing a ***n*** song to you, God. I
149:1 to the LORD a ***n*** song; sing God's
Proverbs
27:25 grass goes away, ***n*** growth appears,
Ecclesiastes
1:9 again. There's nothing ***n*** under the sun.
1:10 at this! It's ***n***!" But it was
Isaiah
1:13 repulses me. ***N*** moon, sabbath,
1:14 I hate your ***n*** moons and your festivals.
41:15 made you into a ***n*** threshing tool
42:9 but I'm declaring ***n*** things. Before
42:10 to the LORD a ***n*** song! Sing his
43:19 Look! I'm doing a ***n*** thing; now it
47:13 what will happen to you at each ***n*** moon.
48:6 on I'll tell you ***n*** things, guarded
57:10 You found ***n*** strength;
62:2 be called by a ***n*** name, which the
65:17 I'm creating a ***n*** heaven and a new
66:22 As the ***n*** heavens and the new earth that
Jeremiah
26:10 entrance of the ***N*** Gate of the
31:22 created something ***n*** on earth: Virgin
36:10 entrance of the ***N*** Gate of the
Lamentations
5:21 return! Give us ***n*** days, like those
Ezekiel
11:19 and I will put a ***n*** spirit in them. I
18:31 Make yourselves a ***n*** heart and a new
29:21 day I will give ***n*** strength to the
36:26 I will give you a ***n*** heart and put a new
45:17 the festivals, ***n*** moons, and
46:1 on the day of the ***n*** moon it will be
46:3 on sabbaths and ***n*** moons at the
46:6 the day of the ***n*** moon, the
Daniel
1:7 gave them ***n*** names. He named
7:8 for it. On this ***n*** horn were eyes
Hosea
2:11 festivals, her ***n*** moons, her
5:7 children. Now the ***n*** moon will devour
Amos
8:5 When will the ***n*** moon be over so
Matthew
9:16 sews a piece of ***n***, unshrunk cloth
13:52 brings old and ***n*** things out of
19:28 is made ***n***, when the Human
24:32 and it sprouts ***n*** leaves, you know
26:29 I drink it in a ***n*** way with you in
27:60 it in his own ***n*** tomb, which he
Mark
1:27 What's this? A ***n*** teaching with
2:21 sews a piece of ***n***, unshrunk cloth
13:28 and it sprouts ***n*** leaves, you know
14:25 I drink it in a ***n*** way in God's
16:17 name. They will speak in ***n*** languages.
Luke
5:36 a patch from a ***n*** garment to patch
John
13:34 I give you a ***n*** commandment: Love each
19:41 the garden was a ***n*** tomb in which no
Acts
5:20 people everything about this ***n*** life."
8:15 prayed that the ***n*** believers would
11:18 lives so that they might have ***n*** life."
17:19 What is this ***n*** teaching? Can we
Romans
7:6 be slaves in the ***n*** life under the
1 Corinthians
5:7 so you can be a ***n*** batch of dough,
2 Corinthians
5:17 is part of the ***n*** creation. The old
5:18 All of these ***n*** things are from God, who
Galatians
6:15 anything. What matters is a ***n*** creation.
Ephesians
2:15 could create one ***n*** person out of the
4:24 yourself with the ***n*** person created
Colossians
2:16 a festival, a ***n*** moon observance,
3:10 and put on the ***n*** nature, which is
1 Timothy
3:6 They shouldn't be ***n*** believers so that

Titus
3:5 the washing of ***n*** birth and the
Hebrews
8:13 When it says ***n***, it makes the first
9:10 imposed until the time of the ***n*** order.
10:20 through a ***n*** and living way that he
1 Peter
1:3 he has given us ***n*** birth. You have
1:23 have been given ***n*** birth—not from th
2 Peter
3:13 are waiting for a ***n*** heaven and a new
1 John
2:7 I'm not writing a ***n*** commandment to
2:8 I am writing a ***n*** commandment to
2 John
1:5 I'm writing a ***n*** command to you,
Revelation
2:17 stone with a ***n*** name written on
3:12 of my God, the ***N*** Jerusalem that
5:9 They took up a ***n*** song, saying, "You are
14:3 They sing a ***n*** song in front of the
21:1 Then I saw a ***n*** heaven and a new earth,
21:2 the holy city, ***N*** Jerusalem, coming
21:5 making all things ***n***." He also said,

NEW COVENANT

Jer 31:31; Lk 22:20; 1Co 11:25; 2Co 3:6; Heb 8:8; 9:15; 12:24

NEW WINE

Gn 27:28; Nm 18:12; 2Ki 18:32; 2Ch 31:5; Is 36:17; 65:8; Hos 2:8; 2:22; 4:11; 9:2; Jl 1:10; 2:19, 24; Mt 9:17; Mk 2:22; Lk 5:37; 5:38, 39; Ac 2:13

NEWS → GOOD NEWS, PREACHING THE GOOD NEWS, PROCLAIM THE GOOD NEWS, PROCLAIMING THE GOOD NEWS

Exodus
33:4 heard the bad ***n***, they were sorry.
Deuteronomy
2:25 Once they hear ***n*** of you, they will
17:4 and you hear ***n*** about it, then you must
Joshua
6:27 was with Joshua. ***N*** about him spread
1 Samuel
4:13 and gave the ***n*** to the city, and
4:14 hurriedly went and told Eli the ***n***.
4:19 she heard the ***n*** that God's chest
11:4 they reported the ***n*** directly to the
31:9 carrying the good ***n*** to their gods'
2 Samuel
1:5 who brought the ***n***, "that Saul and
1:6 who brought the ***n*** replied, "I just
1:13 brought him the ***n***. "I'm the son of
1:20 Gath; don't bring ***n*** of it to
4:4 old when the ***n*** about Saul and
11:19 reporting all the ***n*** of the battle to
18:19 run and take the ***n*** to the king that
18:20 one to bring the ***n*** today. You can
18:26 That one must be bringing good ***n*** too."
1 Kings
2:28 Now the ***n*** reached Joab because he had
12:2 son, heard the ***n***, he returned from
14:6 yourself? I have hard ***n*** for you.
16:16 They heard the ***n***: "Zimri has plotted
2 Kings
7:11 shouted out the ***n***, and it was
1 Chronicles
10:9 to spread the ***n*** to their idols
16:23 earth! Share the ***n*** of his saving
2 Chronicles
10:2 son, heard the ***n***, he returned from
Nehemiah
1:4 When I heard this ***n***, I sat down and
Esther
1:17 is the reason: ***N*** of what the queen
9:4 in the palace, ***n*** about him was
Psalms
19:2 day gushes the ***n*** to the next, and
40:9 told the good ***n*** of your
68:11 many messengers are bringing good ***n***:
96:2 name! Share the ***n*** of his saving
112:7 frightened at bad ***n***. Their hearts are
Proverbs
25:25 Good ***n*** from a distant land is like cold water
Isaiah
23:5 will be in anguish at the ***n*** about Tyre.
52:7 who brings good ***n***, who proclaims
Jeremiah
20:15 who delivered the ***n*** to my father,
20:16 bearer of that ***n*** be like the
49:23 they hear the bad ***n***. They are
51:31 to relate the ***n*** to the king of
Ezekiel
21:7 Because of the ***n***." When it comes,
24:26 so that you yourself will hear the ***n***.
26:15 quake at the ***n*** of your downfall,
Nahum
3:19 All who hear the ***n*** about you clap
Matthew
4:24 ***N*** about him spread throughout Syria.
9:26 ***N*** about this spread throughout that
14:1 the ruler heard the ***n*** about Jesus.
Mark
1:28 Right away the ***n*** about him spread
1:45 and spreading the ***n*** so that Jesus
7:36 the more eagerly they shared the ***n***.
16:11 they heard the ***n***, they didn't
Luke
4:14 to Galilee, and ***n*** about him spread
5:15 ***N*** of him spread even more and huge
7:17 This ***n*** about Jesus spread throughout
9:60 go and spread the ***n*** of God's kingdom."
Acts
5:24 received this ***n***, the captain of
9:42 The ***n*** spread throughout Joppa, and many
Romans
1:8 you, because the ***n*** about your
16:19 The ***n*** of your obedience has reached
1 Thessalonians
1:8 every place. The ***n*** about your

NICODEMUS

John
3:1 a Pharisee named ***N***, a Jewish leader.
7:50 ***N***, who was one of them and had come to Jesus earlier
19:39 ***N***, the one who at first had come to

NIGHT

Genesis
1:5 and the darkness ***N***. There was
1:16 the smaller light to rule over the ***n***.
8:22 and autumn, day and ***n*** will not cease.
14:15 During the ***n***, he and his servants
19:2 house, spend the ***n***, and wash your
20:3 to Abimelech that ***n*** in a dream and
24:23 father's house for us to spend the ***n***?"
26:24 to him that ***n*** and said, "I am
31:24 That ***n***, God appeared to Laban the
32:13 Jacob spent that ***n*** there. From what he
32:22 got up during the ***n***, took his two
41:11 both dreamed one ***n***, he and I, and
46:2 in a vision at ***n***, "Jacob! Jacob!"
Exodus
12:30 got up that ***n***, a terrible cry
13:21 guide them and at ***n*** in a column of
13:22 of lightning at ***n*** never left its
14:20 it lit up the ***n***. They didn't come
40:38 in it at ***n***, clearly visible
Numbers
9:15 covenant tent. At ***n*** until morning,
9:16 by day, appearing with lightning at ***n***.
9:21 it was day or ***n***, they would march
11:9 camp during the ***n***, the manna would
11:32 all that day, all ***n***, and all the next
14:1 their voice and the people wept that ***n***.
14:14 day and in a column of lightning by ***n***.
22:8 them, "Spend the ***n*** here and I'll
Deuteronomy
1:33 camp, in fire by ***n***, so you could see
16:4 on the first ***n*** should remain
28:62 the stars in the ***n*** sky, only a few
28:66 will be afraid ***n*** and day. You
Joshua
1:8 Recite it day and ***n*** so you can
8:9 Joshua spent that ***n*** among the people.
8:13 west side. That ***n***, Joshua went into
Judges
6:25 That ***n*** the LORD said to him, "Take your father's bull
7:9 That ***n*** the LORD said to him, "Get up
7:19 watch of the ***n***, when they had
9:34 him got up that ***n*** and set an ambush
16:2 for him all ***n*** at the city gate.
18:2 house, and they spent the ***n*** there.
19:4 drinking, and spending the ***n*** there.
19:6 not spend the ***n*** and enjoy
19:7 him, and he spent the ***n*** there again.
19:9 so spend the ***n***. Seriously, the
19:25 abused her all ***n*** long until
20:4 to Gibeah of Benjamin to spend the ***n***,
20:5 in the house at ***n*** and were
Ruth
3:8 the middle of the ***n***, the man
3:13 Stay the ***n***. And in the morning, if
1 Samuel
15:11 and he prayed to the LORD all ***n*** long.
15:16 said to me last ***n***." "Tell me," Saul
19:10 David fled and got away safely. That ***n***
19:24 whole day and ***n***. That's why
25:16 wall around us both ***n*** and day.
26:7 the troops at ***n*** and found Saul
28:20 he hadn't eaten anything all day or ***n***.
28:25 ate. They got up and left that very ***n***.
31:12 out, traveled all ***n*** long, and took
2 Samuel
2:29 then marched all ***n*** through the
2:32 men marched all ***n***. When daylight
4:7 and traveled all ***n*** through the
7:4 But that very ***n*** the LORD's word came to Nathan
12:16 and spent the ***n*** sleeping on the
17:8 He won't spend the ***n*** with his troops.
17:16 Don't spend the ***n*** in the desert
1 Kings
3:5 in a dream at ***n***. God said, "Ask
3:19 son died one ***n*** when she rolled
3:20 the middle of the ***n*** and took my son
8:59 our God day and ***n*** so that he may do
19:9 and spent the ***n***. The LORD's word
2 Kings
6:14 They came at ***n*** and surrounded
7:12 got up in the ***n***. He said to his
8:21 He got up at ***n*** to attack the
19:35 That ***n*** the LORD's messenger went out
25:4 soldiers fled by ***n*** using the gate
1 Chronicles
9:27 would spend the ***n*** patrolling God's
9:33 because they were on duty day and ***n***.
17:3 But that very ***n*** God's word came to
2 Chronicles
1:7 That ***n*** God appeared to Solomon and
7:12 to Solomon at ***n*** and said to him:
13:11 a clean table. At ***n*** they light the
21:9 him, attacked at ***n***, defeating him
Ezra
10:6 he spent the ***n***. He didn't eat
Nehemiah
1:6 pray before you ***n*** and day for your
2:12 I set out at ***n***, taking only a few
4:9 as protection against them day and ***n***.
4:22 servant spend the ***n*** in Jerusalem so
9:12 of lightning by ***n***; they lit the way
9:19 lightning lit their path during the ***n***.
13:20 spent the ***n*** outside Jerusalem.
13:21 you spending the ***n*** by the wall? If
Esther
6:1 That same ***n***, the king simply couldn't
Job
3:3 I was born, the ***n*** someone said, "A
3:6 gloom seize that ***n***; may it not be
3:7 May that ***n*** be childless; may no happy
4:13 visions of ***n***, when deep sleep
5:14 and at noon they fumble about as at ***n***.
7:4 will I get up?—***n*** drags on, and
17:12 They turn ***n*** into day; light is near
24:7 spend the ***n*** naked, unclothed, in the
24:14 and needy; at ***n***, they are like a
27:20 waters; a tempest snatches them by ***n***;
30:17 At ***n*** he bores my bones; my gnawing pain
31:32 didn't spend the ***n*** in the street; I
33:15 a vision of the ***n***, when deep sleep
34:20 the middle of the ***n*** they suddenly
34:25 overturns them at ***n***, and they are
35:10 God my maker; who gives songs in the ***n***;
36:20 wish for the ***n*** when people
39:9 or will it spend the ***n*** in your crib?
Psalms
1:2 recite God's Instruction day and ***n***!
6:6 groaning. Every ***n***, I drench my bed

16:7 me; even at ***n*** I am instructed
17:3 testing me at ***n***. You've looked me
19:2 the next, and one ***n*** informs another
30:5 may stay all ***n***, but by morning,
32:3 all day long—every day, every ***n***!—
42:3 food both day and ***n***, as people
42:8 faithful love; by ***n*** his song is with
55:10 Day and ***n*** they make their rounds on its
59:15 don't get their fill, they stay all ***n***.
63:6 on you in the middle of the ***n***—
74:16 to you! The ***n*** too! You
77:2 for my Lord. At ***n*** my hands are
77:6 with my heart at ***n***; I complain, and
78:14 by the lightning all through the ***n***.
88:1 day I cry out, even at ***n***, before you—
90:4 like a short period during the ***n*** watch.
91:5 of terrors at ***n***, arrows that fly
102:7 I lie awake all ***n***. I'm all alone like
104:20 and it is ***n***, when every
105:39 gave lightning to provide light at ***n***.
119:62 the middle of the ***n*** to give thanks to
119:148 each hour of the ***n*** as I think about
121:6 the day; neither will the moon at ***n***.
130:6 more than the ***n*** watch waits for
134:1 in the LORD's house at ***n***: bless God!
136:9 stars to rule the ***n***—God's faithful l
139:11 me; the light will become ***n*** around me,"

Proverbs

7:9 at the onset of ***n*** and darkness.
31:15 while it is still ***n***, providing food
31:18 she doesn't put out her lamp at ***n***.

Ecclesiastes

2:23 even at ***n***, their hearts
8:16 even going without sleep day and ***n***

Song of Songs

1:13 to me, lying all ***n*** between my
3:1 Upon my bed, ***n*** after night, I looked
3:8 thigh against terrors that come by ***n***.
5:2 with dew, my hair, with the ***n*** mists.
7:11 and rest all ***n*** among the

Isaiah

4:5 a blazing fire by ***n***. Over all the
15:1 devastated in a ***n***; Moab is ruined!
16:3 your shade like ***n***. Hide the
21:8 post I'm stationed throughout the ***n***.
21:11 how long is the ***n***? Guard, how long
21:12 but it is still ***n***. If you must
26:9 At ***n*** I long for you with my whole
27:3 I water it; ***n*** and day I guard
28:19 by day and by ***n***. It will be
29:7 be like a dream, a vision of the ***n***.
30:29 for you as on the ***n*** that people
34:10 ***N*** and day won't be extinguished; its
60:11 day and ***n*** they won't close,
60:19 illumination by ***n***. The LORD will be
62:6 all day and all ***n***, they won't keep
65:4 and spend the ***n*** among rocks; who

Jeremiah

6:5 let's attack by ***n*** and destroy her
9:1 weep day and ***n*** for the wounds of
14:8 like a tourist spending only the ***n***?
14:17 weeping—day and ***n***, because my
16:13 gods day and ***n***, for I will show
31:35 to light up the ***n***, who stirs up the
33:20 covenant with the ***n*** so that they
33:25 with day and ***n*** or the laws of
36:30 heat of the day and the frost of the ***n***.
39:4 to escape at ***n*** through the royal
49:9 would come in the ***n***, they would take
52:7 soldiers fled by ***n*** along the gate

Lamentations

1:2 bitterly in the ***n***, her tears on her
2:18 flood all day and ***n***. Don't relax at
2:19 the start of the ***n*** shift; pour out

Ezekiel

12:7 the daytime. At ***n*** I dug a hole
12:12 his backpack at ***n*** and go out. They

Daniel

2:19 in a vision by ***n***, the mystery was
5:30 That very same ***n***, Belshazzar the
6:18 through the ***n***. No pleasures
7:2 I had during the ***n*** I saw the four
7:7 to watch this ***n*** vision, I saw a
7:13 to watch this ***n*** vision of mine, I

Hosea

7:6 Throughout the ***n***, their anger

Joel

1:13 Come, spend the ***n*** in funeral

Amos

5:8 the day into ***n***; who summons the

Obadiah

1:5 if robbers by ***n***—how you've been

Jonah

4:10 it grew in a ***n*** and perished in a

Micah

3:6 it will become ***n*** for you, without

Zephaniah

2:14 will spend the ***n*** on its columns. A

Zechariah

14:7 neither day nor ***n***, but at evening

Matthew

2:14 and, during the ***n***, took the child
21:17 city to Bethany and spent the ***n*** there.
26:45 and rest all ***n***? Look, the time
28:13 disciples came at ***n*** and stole his

Mark

4:27 sleeps and wakes ***n*** and day. The seed
5:5 ***N*** and day in the tombs and the hills,
14:30 that on this very ***n***, before the
14:41 and rest all ***n***? That's enough!

Luke

2:8 the fields, guarding their sheep at ***n***.
2:37 God with fasting and prayer ***n*** and day.
5:5 worked hard all ***n*** and caught
6:12 pray, and he prayed to God all ***n*** long.
11:5 the middle of the ***n***. Imagine saying,
17:34 tell you, on that ***n*** two people will
18:7 to him day and ***n***? Will he be slow
21:37 but he spent each ***n*** on the Mount of

John

3:2 came to Jesus at ***n*** and said to him,
9:4 him who sent me. ***N*** is coming when no
11:10 walks in the ***n*** does stumble
13:30 he left immediately. And it was ***n***.
19:39 come to Jesus at ***n***, was there too.
21:3 throughout the ***n*** they caught

Acts

5:19 doors during the ***n*** and led them out.
9:25 took him by ***n*** and lowered him
12:6 The ***n*** before Herod was going to bring
16:9 Paul during the ***n***. He stood urging
16:33 the middle of the ***n***, the jailer
18:9 One ***n*** the Lord said to Paul in a
23:11 The following ***n*** the Lord stood near

23:31 Paul during the ***n*** and brought him
26:7 earnestly worship ***n*** and day. The Jews
27:23 Last ***n*** an angel from the God to whom I
27:27 On the fourteenth ***n***, we were being
Romans
13:12 The ***n*** is almost over, and the day is
1 Corinthians
11:23 on to you: on the ***n*** on which he was
2 Corinthians
11:25 I spent a day and a ***n*** on the open sea.
1 Thessalonians
2:9 while we worked ***n*** and day so we
3:10 ***N*** and day, we pray more than ever to
5:2 is going to come like a thief in the ***n***.
5:5 day. We don't belong to ***n*** or darkness.
5:7 sleep sleep at ***n***, and people who
2 Thessalonians
3:8 we worked ***n*** and day with
1 Timothy
5:5 with requests and prayers, ***n*** and day.
2 Timothy
1:3 remember you in my prayers day and ***n***.
Revelation
4:8 never rest day or ***n***, but keep on
7:15 him day and ***n*** in his temple,
8:12 light, and the ***n*** lost a third of
12:10 them day and ***n*** before our God,
14:11 is no rest day or ***n*** for those who
20:10 upon them day and ***n***, forever and
21:25 by day, and there will be no ***n*** there.
22:5 ***N*** will be no more. They won't need the

NIGHTS
Genesis
7:4 days and forty ***n***. I will wipe off
7:12 upon the earth forty days and forty ***n***.
Exodus
24:18 mountain for forty days and forty ***n***.
34:28 days and forty ***n***. He didn't eat
Deuteronomy
9:9 days and forty ***n***. I ate no bread,
9:25 days and forty ***n***, lying flat out,
10:10 forty days and ***n***. And the LORD
1 Samuel
30:12 drunk any water for three days and ***n***.
1 Kings
19:8 forty days and ***n*** until he arrived
Job
2:13 days and seven ***n***, not speaking a
7:3 of emptiness; ***n*** of toil have been
Jonah
1:17 of the fish for three days and three ***n***.
Matthew
4:2 days and forty ***n***, he was starving.
12:40 days and three ***n***, so the Human One
2 Corinthians
6:5 hard work, sleepless ***n***, and hunger.
11:27 many sleepless ***n***, hunger and

NILE
Genesis
41:2 up out of the ***N*** and grazed on the
Exodus
1:22 Hebrews into the ***N*** River, but you
7:15 the bank of the ***N*** River so you will
8:3 The ***N*** will overflow with frogs. They'll

NIMROD
Genesis
10:8 Cush fathered ***N***, the first great
Micah
5:6 the land of ***N*** with the drawn

NINE
Matthew
20:3 went out around ***n*** in the morning
Mark
15:25 It was ***n*** in the morning when they
Luke
16:6 He said, '***N*** hundred gallons of olive
17:17 ten cleansed? Where are the other ***n***?
Acts
2:15 all, it's only ***n*** o'clock in the
23:23 for Caesarea at ***n*** o'clock tonight.

NINEVEH
Jonah
1:2 Get up and go to ***N***, that great city,
Nahum
1:1 An oracle about ***N***: the scroll
Matthew
12:41 The citizens of ***N*** will stand up at the

NINTH
Leviticus
23:32 Sabbath on the ***n*** day of the month
25:22 produce until the ***n*** year. Until its
Numbers
7:60 On the ***n*** day Benjamin's Chief Abidan,
2 Kings
17:6 In Hoshea's ***n*** year, the Assyrian king
18:10 sixth year, which was Hoshea's ***n*** year.
25:1 So in the ***n*** year of Zedekiah's rule, on
25:3 On the ***n*** day of the month, the famine
1 Chronicles
12:12 Johanan eighth, Elzabad ***n***
24:11 the ***n*** to Jeshua, the tenth to
25:16 the ***n*** to Mattaniah, his family, and his
27:12 The ***n*** for the ninth month was Abiezer
Ezra
10:9 day of the ***n*** month. All of the
Jeremiah
36:9 In the ***n*** month of the fifth year of
36:22 Now it was the ***n*** month, and the king
39:1 In the ***n*** year and the tenth month of
39:2 Zedekiah, on the ***n*** day of the fourth
52:4 In the ***n*** year, the tenth month, and the
52:6 On the ***n*** day of the fourth month, the
Ezekiel
24:1 In the ***n*** year, on the tenth day of the
Zechariah
7:1 the fourth day of the ***n*** month, Kislev.
Revelation
21:20 was beryl. The ***n*** was topaz, the

NO OTHER GOD
Dt 4:35; 1Ki 8:60; Is 45:14; 45:21; Dn 3:29

NOAH
Genesis
5:29 and named him ***N***, saying, "This one
7:15 they came to ***N*** and entered the ark, two
8:1 God remembered ***N***, all those alive, and
9:28 After the flood, ***N*** lived 350 years

9:29 In all, ***N*** lived 950 years; then he
Numbers
26:33 were Mahlah, ***N***, Hoglah, Milcah,
27:1 were Mahlah, ***N***, Hoglah, Milcah,
36:11 Milcah, and ***N***, Zelophehad's
Joshua
17:3 named Mahlah, ***N***, Hoglah, Milcah,
1 Chronicles
1:4 ***N***; Noah's family: Shem, Ham, and
Isaiah
54:9 like the days of ***N*** for me, when I
Ezekiel
14:14 these three men, ***N***, Daniel, and Job,
Matthew
24:37 in the time of ***N***, so it will be at
24:38 until the day ***N*** entered the ark.
Luke
3:36 son of Shem son of ***N*** son of Lamech
17:26 in the days of ***N***, so it will be
17:27 until the day ***N*** entered the ark
Hebrews
11:7 By faith ***N*** responded with godly fear
1 Peter
3:20 the time of ***N***. Noah built an
2 Peter
2:5 he protected ***N***, a preacher of

NOON

Genesis
43:16 the men will have dinner with me at ***n***."
43:25 arrival at ***n***, since they had
Deuteronomy
28:29 around at high ***n*** as blind people
1 Kings
18:27 Around ***n***, Elijah started making fun of
2 Kings
4:20 sat on her lap until ***n***. Then he died.
Job
5:14 the day, and at ***n*** they fumble about
11:17 brighter than ***n***; darkness will be
Psalms
37:6 the dawn, your justice like high ***n***.
Song of Songs
1:7 you rest them at ***n***?—so I don't wand
Isaiah
16:3 justly; at high ***n*** provide your
58:10 and your gloom will be like the ***n***.
Jeremiah
6:4 let's attack by ***n***! Oh, no! Daylight
20:16 the morning, and the battle cries at ***n***,
Amos
8:9 sun go down at ***n***, and I will
Zephaniah
2:4 be driven out at ***n***; Ekron will be
Matthew
20:5 Again around ***n*** and then at three
27:45 From ***n*** until three in the afternoon the
Mark
15:33 From ***n*** until three in the afternoon the
Luke
23:44 It was now about ***n***, and darkness
John
4:6 sat down at the well. It was about ***n***.
19:14 It was about ***n*** on the Preparation Day
Acts
8:26 to Philip, "At ***n***, take the road
10:9 At ***n*** on the following day, as their
22:6 journey, about ***n***, as I approached

NORTH

Genesis
13:9 If you go ***n***, I will go south;
13:14 and gaze to the ***n***, south, east, and
14:15 chased them to Hobah, ***n*** of Damascus.
28:14 the west, east, ***n***, and south. Every
Exodus
26:20 other side on the ***n***, make twenty
26:35 Place the table by the ***n*** wall.
27:11 along the ***n*** side the drapes
36:25 other side on the ***n***, they made twenty
38:11 Likewise the ***n*** side stretched one
40:22 tent, on the ***n*** side of the
Leviticus
1:11 it on the ***n*** side of the altar
Numbers
2:25 On the ***n*** will be the banner of Dan's
3:35 to camp on the ***n*** side of the
35:5 feet, and on the ***n*** side three
Deuteronomy
2:3 this mountain long enough. Head ***n***.
3:27 Look west, ***n***, south, and east.
Joshua
8:11 Then they camped ***n*** of Ai, with the
8:13 main camp on the ***n*** side of the city
11:2 kings from the ***n*** part of the
15:5 The border on the ***n*** side ran from the
16:6 is on the ***n***. The border turns
17:9 lay on the ***n*** side of the
17:10 and what lay ***n*** of it belonged to
18:5 will stay on their territory to the ***n***.
19:14 The border turned ***n*** of Hannathon and
24:30 highlands of Ephraim ***n*** of Mount Gaash.
Judges
2:9 highlands of Ephraim ***n*** of Mount Gaash.
7:1 Midian's camp was ***n*** of theirs, in the
21:19 Shiloh, which is ***n*** of Bethel, east
1 Samuel
14:5 was on the ***n*** side, in front of
1 Kings
7:21 Jachin. The ***n*** column he named
7:25 three facing ***n***, three facing
7:39 and five on the ***n*** of the temple. He
2 Kings
11:11 the temple to the ***n*** side to protect
16:14 He put it on the ***n*** side of the new
1 Chronicles
9:24 four sides: east, west, ***n***, and south.
26:14 and his lot indicated the ***N*** Gate.
26:17 East had six, the ***N*** four, and the
2 Chronicles
3:17 the other on the ***n***. The one on the
4:4 three facing ***n***, three facing
4:6 and five on the ***n***. The items used
4:7 five on the south and five on the ***n***.
4:8 and five on the ***n***, as well as a
14:10 for battle in a valley ***n*** of Mareshah.
23:10 the temple to the ***n*** side, so as to
Job
23:9 ***n*** in his activity, and I don't grasp
26:7 He stretched the ***N*** over chaos, hung
37:9 its chamber, the cold from the ***n*** wind.
37:22 From the ***n*** comes golden light, the

NORTH [cont.]

Psalms
48:2 Zion, in the far ***n***, is the city of
89:12 ***N*** and south—you created them! The
107:3 from east and west, ***n*** and south.
Proverbs
25:23 The ***n*** wind stirs up rain, and a person
Ecclesiastes
1:6 around to the ***n***; around and
11:3 the south or the ***n***, wherever it
Song of Songs
4:16 Stir, ***n*** wind, and come, south wind!
Isaiah
14:31 coming from the ***n***; there is no
41:25 up one from the ***n*** and he came; from
43:6 I'll say to the ***n***, "Give them back!"
49:12 These from the ***n*** and west, and
Jeremiah
1:13 said, "A pot boiling over from the ***n***."
1:14 erupt from the ***n*** against the
1:15 nations from the ***n***, says the LORD,
3:12 words to the ***n*** and say: Return,
3:18 will leave the ***n*** together for the
4:6 disaster from the ***n***, massive
6:1 looms from the ***n***, massive
10:22 the land of the ***n***; it will reduce
13:20 from the ***n***. Where is the
15:12 iron, iron from the ***n***, or bronze?
16:15 the land of the ***n*** and from all the
23:8 the land of the ***n*** and from all the
25:9 the tribes of the ***n*** and my servant
25:26 the kings of the ***n***, those nearby and
31:8 back from the ***n***; I will gather
46:6 can't escape. Up ***n*** by the Euphrates
46:10 sacrifice in the ***n*** by the Euphrates
46:20 horsefly from the ***n*** is coming to bite
46:24 handed over to people from the ***n***.
47:2 rising from the ***n*** and turning into
50:3 A nation from the ***n*** has risen up
50:9 mobilize in the ***n***, and from there
51:48 out of the ***n*** destroying armies
Ezekiel
1:4 came out of the ***n***, a great cloud
8:3 Jerusalem, to the ***n***-facing entrance of
8:5 look toward the ***n***. So I looked
8:14 entrance of the ***N*** Gate of the
9:2 Gate that faces ***n***. All of them were
16:46 daughters in the ***n***. Your younger
20:47 from south to ***n*** will be scorched.
21:4 against everyone from south to ***n***.
26:7 Babylon from the ***n***, the greatest of
32:30 princes of the ***n*** are there, and
38:6 from the far ***n*** and all his
38:15 from the far ***n***, you and many
39:2 out of the far ***n***, and I will bring
40:19 the East Gate, he measured the ***N*** Gate,
41:11 space, one facing ***n***, the other facing
42:1 Then he led me ***n*** to the outer courtyard
44:4 me by way of the ***N*** Gate to the front
46:9 enter through the ***N*** Gate to worship
47:2 out through the ***N*** Gate and around
48:1 Beginning at the ***n***, along the
48:31 gates on the ***n*** side: one gate
Daniel
8:4 ram goring west, ***n***, and south. No
11:44 from the east and ***n*** will alarm him,
Amos
8:12 to sea, and from ***n*** to east; they
Zephaniah
2:13 hand against the ***n*** and will cause
Zechariah
2:6 the land of the ***n***, says the LORD,
6:6 is going to the ***n*** country; the
6:8 the ones going ***n*** have provided
14:4 will move ***n***, and the other
Luke
13:29 east and west, ***n*** and south, and
John
5:2 Sheep Gate in the ***n*** city wall is a
Revelation
21:13 gates on the ***n***, three gates on

NUMBER

Genesis
6:1 When the ***n*** of people started to
47:12 in proportion to the ***n*** of children.
Exodus
1:5 The total ***n*** in Jacob's family was
Leviticus
25:15 according to the ***n*** of years since
Numbers
3:22 according to the ***n*** of males over one
9:20 dwelling for a ***n*** of days, so they
23:10 dust of Jacob, or ***n*** a fourth of
26:53 according to the ***n*** of names.
26:54 according to the ***n*** of its enrollment.
29:18 will be as prescribed for their ***n***.
Deuteronomy
1:10 multiplied your ***n***—you are now as co
3:5 there were also a great ***n*** of villages.
11:21 as many as the ***n*** of days that the
25:2 his presence—the ***n*** of blows in
32:8 boundaries based on the ***n*** of the gods.
Joshua
4:5 to match the ***n*** of the tribes of
Judges
7:6 The ***n*** of men who lapped was three
20:46 in all, the total ***n*** of Benjaminites
1 Samuel
6:4 matching the ***n*** of the Philistine
6:18 mice matched the ***n*** of Philistine
2 Samuel
24:3 God increase the ***n*** of people a
24:9 to the king the ***n*** of the people who
1 Kings
7:47 to the very large ***n*** of objects,
18:22 Baal's prophets ***n*** four hundred
2 Kings
7:13 as the large ***n*** of Israelites who
1 Chronicles
16:19 they were few in ***n***—insignificant,
21:5 David the total ***n***: there were
23:31 a designated ***n*** were to serve in
25:7 the ***n*** of themselves and their
27:24 of this, the ***n*** wasn't entered
2 Chronicles
4:18 to the very large ***n*** of objects,
26:11 according to the ***n*** determined by the
Ezra
3:4 presented the ***n*** of entirely
6:17 according to the ***n*** of the tribes of
8:26 a certain ***n*** of kikkars, one
Nehemiah
7:7 and Baanah. The ***n*** of the people of
7:67 This ***n*** doesn't include their 7,337 male

Esther
9:11 concerning the ***n*** killed in the
Job
1:3 and a vast ***n*** of servants, so
5:9 wonderful things without ***n***;
9:10 unsearchable things, wonders beyond ***n***?
14:5 are fixed, the ***n*** of our months
14:16 Though you now ***n*** my steps, you would
15:20 are painful; the ***n*** of years reserved
16:22 A ***n*** of years will surely pass, and then
36:26 unknowable; the ***n*** of his years is
Psalms
90:12 Teach us to ***n*** our days so we can have a
90:15 us—for the same ***n*** of years that we
105:12 they were few in ***n***—insignificant,
139:17 to me! Their total ***n*** is countless!
147:4 the stars by ***n***, giving each one
Proverbs
23:28 and increases the ***n*** of the faithless.
Ecclesiastes
4:16 no counting the ***n*** of people he
Isaiah
21:16 according to the ***n*** of years for
Jeremiah
29:6 Increase in ***n*** there so that you
52:28 This is the ***n*** of people whom
Ezekiel
12:16 a few of their ***n*** from the sword,
Daniel
9:2 specifically the ***n*** of years that it
Hosea
1:10 Yet the ***n*** of the people of Israel will
8:12 for him a large ***n*** of my
Joel
1:6 and beyond ***n***, has invaded my
Zechariah
7:3 as I have done for a ***n*** of years?"
Luke
5:9 because of the ***n*** of fish they
5:29 his home. A large ***n*** of tax collectors
7:21 he gave sight to a ***n*** of blind people.
Acts
4:4 and their ***n*** grew to about
6:1 time, while the ***n*** of disciples
6:7 to grow. The ***n*** of disciples in
7:17 to Abraham, the ***n*** of our people in
11:21 them, and a large ***n*** came to believe
11:24 A considerable ***n*** of people were
14:1 a result, a huge ***n*** of Jews and
15:24 that some of our ***n*** have disturbed
17:4 a larger ***n*** of Greek God-worsh
17:12 including a ***n*** of reputable
19:19 This included a ***n*** of people who
Romans
9:27 Though the ***n*** of Israel's
11:12 come from the completion of their ***n***!
11:25 until the full ***n*** of the Gentiles
2 Corinthians
9:6 who sows a small ***n*** of seeds will
Hebrews
11:12 as many as the ***n*** of the stars in
Revelation
7:4 Then I heard the ***n*** of those who were
7:9 that no one could ***n***. They were from
9:16 The ***n*** of cavalry troops was two hundred
13:17 the beast's name or the ***n*** of its name.
13:18 the beast's ***n***, for it's a human
15:2 image, and the ***n*** of its name were
20:8 for battle. Their ***n*** is like the sand

NUMBERED

1 Kings
3:8 that can't be ***n*** or counted due to
1 Chronicles
7:2 In David's time they ***n*** 22,600.
7:40 battle listed in the records ***n*** 26,000.
26:9 and relatives, valiant men, ***n*** 18.
26:11 of Hosah's family and relatives ***n*** 13.
27:1 of the year. Each division ***n*** 24,000.
Ezra
1:11 silver objects ***n*** five thousand
Job
21:21 die, when their ***n*** days are cut off?
Isaiah
53:12 death and being ***n*** with rebels,
Jeremiah
33:22 the sky can't be ***n*** and the sand on
Daniel
5:26 mene: God has ***n*** the days of your
Hosea
1:10 measured nor ***n***; and in the place
Revelation
5:11 the elders. They ***n*** in the millions—

NURSING

Genesis
21:8 grew and stopped ***n***. On the day he
32:15 thirty ***n*** camels with their young, forty
33:13 for the ***n*** flocks and
Deuteronomy
32:25 men and women, ***n*** baby and senior
1 Samuel
6:7 along with two ***n*** cows that have
6:10 They took two ***n*** cows and
Psalms
8:2 the mouths of ***n*** babies you have
78:71 from shepherding ***n*** ewes to shepherd
Isaiah
11:8 A ***n*** child will play over the snake's
40:11 lap. He will gently guide the ***n*** ewes.
49:15 woman forget her ***n*** child, fail to
Hosea
1:8 Gomer finished ***n*** No Compassion,
Joel
2:16 children, even ***n*** infants. Let the
Matthew
24:19 and for women who are ***n*** their children.
Mark
13:17 and for women who are ***n*** their children.
Luke
21:23 for women who are ***n*** their children.
1 Thessalonians
2:7 with you like a ***n*** mother caring for

Oo

OAK

Genesis
12:6 Shechem, at the ***o*** of Moreh. The
35:8 Bethel under the ***o***, and Jacob named
Deuteronomy
11:30 Gilgal, next to the Moreh ***O*** Grove?
Joshua
19:33 Heleph, from the ***o*** in Zaanannim and
24:26 there under the ***o*** in the sanctuary
Judges
6:11 and sat under the ***o*** at Ophrah that
6:19 to him under the ***o*** and presented
9:6 king by the ***o*** at the stone
1 Samuel
10:3 will come to the ***o*** at Tabor. Three
2 Samuel
18:9 of a large ***o*** tree. Absalom's
18:10 saw Absalom hanging from an ***o*** tree."
18:14 while he was still alive in the ***o***.
1 Chronicles
10:12 bones under the ***o*** in Jabesh, and
Isaiah
1:30 will be like an ***o*** with withering
6:13 a terebinth or an ***o***, which when it is
44:14 a cypress or ***o***, selecting from
Ezekiel
6:13 and under every lofty tree and leafy ***o***.
Amos
2:9 was as strong as ***o*** trees. I

OBADIAH

1 Kings
18:4 LORD's prophets, ***O*** took one hundred
1 Chronicles
7:3 family—Michael, ***O***, Joel, and
2 Chronicles
17:7 Ben-hail, ***O***, Zechariah,
34:12 of Jahath and ***O***, who were Levites
Ezra
8:9 of Joab, ***O***, Jehiel's son and with him
Nehemiah
10:5 Harim, Meremoth, ***O***
12:25 Bakbukiah, ***O***. Meshullam,
Obadiah
1:1 The vision of ***O***. The LORD God

OBEY → OBEY THE LORD

Genesis
41:40 my people will ***o*** your command.
49:10 be brought to him; people will ***o*** him.
Exodus
1:17 so they didn't ***o*** the Egyptian
5:2 I'm supposed to ***o*** by letting Israel
16:28 you refuse to ***o*** my commandments
19:5 if you faithfully ***o*** me and stay true
23:13 Be careful to ***o*** everything that I have
24:7 has said we will do, and we will ***o***."
34:11 Be sure to ***o*** what I command you today.
Leviticus
26:14 But if you do not ***o*** me and do not carry
26:18 you still do not ***o*** me, I will punish
26:21 are unwilling to ***o*** me, I will strike
26:27 you still do not ***o*** me and continue
Numbers
15:22 you don't ***o*** all these
27:20 the entire Israelite community may ***o***.
Deuteronomy
4:30 LORD your God and you will ***o*** his voice,
9:23 trust him. You didn't ***o*** God's voice.
11:13 if you completely ***o*** God's
12:28 Observe and ***o*** all these words that I am
13:4 his commandments! ***O*** his voice!
13:8 in to them! Don't ***o*** them! Don't have
26:17 laws, and that you will ***o*** his voice.
27:10 So ***o*** the LORD your God's voice. Do his
Joshua
1:7 as you carefully ***o*** all of the
1:16 Joshua, "We will ***o*** everything you
22:5 all his ways and ***o*** his commandments.
23:6 strong. Carefully ***o*** everything
24:24 serve the LORD our God and will ***o*** him."
Judges
2:2 But you didn't ***o*** me. What have you
2:17 wouldn't even ***o*** their own leaders
1 Samuel
2:25 But they wouldn't ***o*** their father
12:14 worship him, ***o*** him, and not
2 Samuel
22:45 me; after hearing about me, they ***o*** me.
1 Kings
3:14 in my ways and ***o*** my laws and
20:8 to him, "Don't ***o*** and don't give
20:36 you didn't ***o*** the LORD's voice,
2 Kings
10:6 me and ready to ***o*** me, take the
22:13 failed to ***o*** the words of this
Ezra
7:26 who does not ***o*** the Instruction
Nehemiah
9:16 and wouldn't ***o*** your commandments.
9:17 They refused to ***o***, and didn't remember
9:29 and didn't ***o*** your commands.
Psalms
18:44 about me, they ***o*** me; foreigners
103:20 his word, who ***o*** everything he
Proverbs
1:33 Those who ***o*** me will dwell securely,
5:13 my instructor. I didn't ***o*** my teacher.
Ecclesiastes
7:5 It is better to ***o*** the reprimand of the
Isaiah
1:19 If you agree and ***o***, you will eat the

Jeremiah
7:23 required of them: ***O*** me so that I may
11:4 crucible, saying, ***O*** me and observe
11:6 of Jerusalem: ***O*** the terms of this
11:7 Egypt to this very day, saying, ***O*** me.
11:8 this covenant—for refusing to ***o***.
11:10 who refused to ***o*** my words. They
13:11 and grandeur. But they wouldn't ***o***.
17:23 and wouldn't ***o*** or accept
17:24 are careful to ***o*** me, declares the
17:27 But if you don't ***o*** me by keeping the
19:15 been stubborn and wouldn't ***o*** my words.
22:4 If you ***o*** this command, then through the
32:23 but they didn't ***o*** you or follow
34:14 ancestors didn't ***o*** or pay any
35:13 what it means to ***o*** me, declares the
42:6 or not, we will ***o*** all that the LORD
Daniel
7:27 every authority will serve them and ***o***."
Joel
2:11 are those who ***o*** his word. The day
Micah
5:15 in wrath on the nations that don't ***o***!
Zechariah
6:15 if you truly ***o*** the voice of the
Matthew
8:27 Even the winds and the lake ***o*** him!"
28:20 teaching them to ***o*** everything that I've
Mark
1:27 unclean spirits and they ***o*** him!"
4:41 this? Even the wind and the sea ***o*** him!"
Luke
8:25 winds and the water, and they ***o*** him!"
17:6 in the sea,' and it would ***o*** you.
Acts
4:19 before God to ***o*** you rather than
5:29 replied, "We must ***o*** God rather than
5:32 whom God has given to those who ***o*** him."
7:39 refused to ***o***. Instead, they
Romans
2:8 for those who ***o*** wickedness
6:16 the one whom you ***o***? That's true
Ephesians
6:1 As for children, ***o*** your parents in the
6:5 As for slaves, ***o*** your human masters
Philippians
2:12 as you always ***o*** me, not just when
Colossians
3:20 Children, ***o*** your parents in everything,
3:22 Slaves, ***o*** your masters on earth in
2 Thessalonians
1:8 God and don't ***o*** the good news of
3:14 who doesn't ***o*** what we have said
1 Timothy
6:14 ***O*** this order without fault or failure

OBEY THE LORD

Ex 15:26; Dt 8:20; 11:28; 27:10; 28:1, 2, 13, 45, 62; 30:16; 1Sa 12:15; 15:19, 20; Jer 26:13; 38:20; 42:6; 43:7; 44:23

OBEYED

Genesis
22:18 of your descendants, because you ***o*** me."
26:5 because Abraham ***o*** me and kept my
Deuteronomy
26:14 to the dead. I've ***o*** the LORD my God's
33:9 them'—but who ***o*** your words and
Joshua
1:17 same way that we ***o*** Moses. Just let
5:6 and who hadn't ***o*** the LORD. The
22:2 to them, "You ***o*** everything that
22:3 You faithfully ***o*** the command of
Judges
2:17 who had ***o*** the LORD's
2:20 of their ancestors and hasn't ***o*** me,
6:10 are living.' But you have not ***o*** me."
1 Samuel
15:24 I was afraid of the troops and ***o*** them.
28:21 your servant has ***o*** you. I risked my
1 Chronicles
29:23 and he prospered. All Israel ***o*** him,
Jeremiah
3:13 tree and haven't ***o*** me, declares the
9:13 them, and haven't ***o*** or followed it.
34:10 in bondage; they ***o*** the king's
35:8 We have ***o*** everything our ancestor
35:16 have thoroughly ***o*** their ancestor,
35:18 Because you have ***o*** all Jonadab's
40:3 LORD and haven't ***o*** him. That's why
42:21 you still haven't ***o*** all that the LORD
Ezekiel
5:7 you haven't ***o*** my regulations or
Romans
10:16 everyone hasn't ***o*** the good news. As
Hebrews
11:8 By faith Abraham ***o*** when he was called

OBJECT

Leviticus
15:4 unclean, and any ***o*** on which that
15:26 and any ***o*** she sits on will
Numbers
35:16 with an iron ***o*** and he dies, he
35:18 with a wood ***o*** in hand that
35:22 or throws any ***o*** at him without
Judges
21:22 come to us to ***o***, we'll tell them,
2 Kings
12:13 gold or silver ***o*** for the LORD's
2 Chronicles
29:8 and Jerusalem an ***o*** of terror and
30:7 he made them an ***o*** of horror as you
Jeremiah
15:4 will make them an ***o*** of horror to all
23:40 will make you an ***o*** of disgrace and
24:9 will make them an ***o*** of horror and
25:9 will make them an ***o*** of horror, shock,
25:18 a wasteland, an ***o*** of horror, shock,
29:18 will make them an ***o*** of horror to all
34:17 will make you an ***o*** of horror for all
42:18 will become an ***o*** of cursing,
44:8 and become an ***o*** of cursing and
44:12 will become an ***o*** of cursing,
49:13 will become an ***o*** of horror and
Lamentations
3:14 my people, the ***o*** of their song of
3:63 at how I am the ***o*** of their song of

Ezekiel
5:15 will become an ***o*** of ridicule, a
14:8 as a sign and an ***o*** lesson, and I
36:3 you became an ***o*** of the people's
Micah
6:16 inhabitants an ***o*** of hissing! You
Acts
10:16 times, then the ***o*** was suddenly
2 Thessalonians
2:4 so-called god or ***o*** of worship and

OBJECTS
Exodus
35:22 all sorts of gold ***o***. Everyone raised
Numbers
4:15 These are the ***o*** in the dwelling
4:26 that needs to be done with these ***o***.
4:32 list by name the ***o*** they are required
2 Samuel
8:10 silver, gold, and bronze ***o*** with him.
1 Kings
7:47 large number of ***o***, Solomon didn't
7:51 gold, and all the ***o*** his father David
10:25 with tribute: ***o*** of silver and
2 Kings
12:18 took all the holy ***o*** that had been
14:14 and all the ***o*** he could find in
23:4 all the religious ***o*** made for Baal,
24:13 all the gold ***o*** that Israel's
25:16 in all these ***o***-the two pillars,
1 Chronicles
9:28 for the worship ***o***; they counted
18:10 kinds of gold, silver, and bronze ***o***.
23:13 make the holiest ***o*** holy, to make
26:27 of the valuable ***o*** won in battle to
29:2 gold for gold ***o***, silver for
2 Chronicles
4:18 large number of ***o***, Solomon didn't
5:1 gold, and all the ***o*** his father David
5:5 and all the holy ***o*** that were in the
9:24 with tribute: ***o*** of silver and
15:18 silver and gold ***o*** that he and his
24:7 used all the holy ***o*** of the LORD's
24:14 pans, and other ***o*** made of gold and
25:24 and all the ***o*** he could find in
28:24 Ahaz gathered the ***o*** from God's temple,
Ezra
1:10 silver bowls, and one thousand other ***o***.
1:11 gold and silver ***o*** numbered five
Psalms
79:4 nothing but ***o*** of ridicule and
Isaiah
46:1 on beasts. The ***o*** you once carried
Ezekiel
15:3 make a peg from it and hang ***o*** on it?
Nahum
2:9 supplies, an abundance of precious ***o***!
Acts
17:23 observing your ***o*** of worship, I

OBSERVE
Genesis
31:49 The LORD will ***o*** both of us when
Exodus
10:9 we all must ***o*** the LORD's
12:14 for you. You will ***o*** it as a festival
12:17 You should ***o*** the Festival of Unleavened
12:24 You should ***o*** this ritual as a
12:25 you, be sure that you ***o*** this ritual.
12:47 whole Israelite community should ***o*** it.
12:48 with you wants to ***o*** the Passover to
23:14 You should ***o*** a festival for me three
23:15 ***O*** the Festival of Unleavened Bread, as
23:16 ***O*** the Harvest Festival for the early
31:16 They should ***o*** the Sabbath in
34:18 ***O*** the Festival of Unleavened Bread. You
34:22 You should ***o*** the Festival of Weeks, for
Leviticus
23:32 You will ***o*** your Sabbath on
25:18 You will ***o*** my rules, and you will keep
Numbers
9:19 Israelites would ***o*** the LORD's
Deuteronomy
12:28 ***O*** and obey all these words that I am
1 Kings
8:58 all his ways and ***o*** his commands, his
9:6 me and don't ***o*** the commands and
1 Chronicles
22:12 Israel, you will ***o*** the Instruction
23:32 way they were to ***o*** the instructions
28:8 carefully ***o*** all the commands
Nehemiah
10:29 servant, and to ***o*** faithfully all
Job
10:14 If I sin and you ***o*** me, you won't
36:25 him; people can ***o*** at great distance.
39:1 birth; do you ***o*** the birthing of
Psalms
37:37 ***O*** those who have integrity and watch
105:45 keep his laws and ***o*** his instructions.
Proverbs
6:6 you lazy person; ***o*** its ways and grow
Ecclesiastes
8:16 wisdom and to ***o*** the business that
11:4 and those who ***o*** the clouds will
Isaiah
41:20 see and know and ***o*** and comprehend
Jeremiah
11:4 Obey me and ***o*** all that I
Ezekiel
11:12 you didn't ***o*** and whose case
11:20 and carefully ***o*** my case laws.
20:11 which bring life to all who ***o*** them.
20:13 life to all who ***o*** them. They
20:18 regulations or ***o*** their case laws
20:19 my regulations! ***O*** my case laws and
20:21 my regulations or ***o*** my case laws,
20:24 they didn't ***o*** my case laws,
33:26 by the sword, you ***o*** detestable
36:27 and carefully ***o*** my case laws.
37:24 laws and carefully ***o*** my regulations.
43:11 so that they may ***o*** all of its entire
44:24 They must ***o*** my instructions
Mark
7:4 themselves. They ***o*** many other rules
Galatians
4:10 You ***o*** religious days and months and
6:13 circumcised don't ***o*** the Law

OFFER
Genesis
22:2 land of Moriah. ***O*** him up as an
Exodus
3:18 so that we can ***o*** sacrifices to the

8:25 and said, “Go, ***o*** sacrifices to
29:39 ***O*** one lamb in the morning and offer the
30:9 Don't ***o*** the wrong incense on the altar
30:20 minister and to ***o*** a food gift to

Leviticus
2:13 You must ***o*** salt with all
3:3 Then you can ***o*** a food gift to the LORD
7:11 that someone may ***o*** to the LORD:
7:12 you must ***o*** the following
14:20 The priest will ***o*** up the entirely
15:15 The priest will ***o*** them, one as a
16:6 Aaron will ***o*** the bull as a purification
17:9 in order to ***o*** it to the LORD
18:21 your children to ***o*** them over to
19:5 to the LORD, ***o*** it so that it
21:6 holy because they ***o*** the LORD's food

Deuteronomy
10:8 serve him, and to ***o*** blessings in his
12:14 where you must ***o*** up your entirely
16:2 ***O*** a Passover sacrifice from the flock
16:10 LORD your God. ***O*** a spontaneous
27:7 ***O*** up well-being sacrifices and eat them
33:19 where they ***o*** right sacrifices.

Joshua
22:23 the LORD or to ***o*** on it an entirely

Judges
5:2 people willingly ***o*** themselves—bless
6:26 second bull and ***o*** it as an entirely
13:16 burned offering, ***o*** it to the LORD.”

1 Samuel
1:22 I will ***o*** him as a nazirite

2 Samuel
24:24 price. I won't ***o*** up to the LORD my

1 Kings
3:4 there. He used to ***o*** a thousand
8:64 temple. He had to ***o*** the entirely
9:25 Solomon would ***o*** entirely burned
13:2 the shrines who ***o*** incense on you.
22:43 to sacrifice and ***o*** incense at them.

2 Kings
3:20 at the time to ***o*** the grain
5:17 will never again ***o*** entirely burned
10:24 they went in to ***o*** sacrifices and
12:4 temple that people ***o*** voluntarily.

1 Chronicles
16:40 They were to ***o*** continually, both
21:24 price. I won't ***o*** to the LORD what
29:14 should be able to ***o*** so willingly?

2 Chronicles
2:4 displayed, and to ***o*** entirely burned
7:7 temple. He had to ***o*** the entirely
13:11 evening they ***o*** entirely burned
23:18 LORD's temple to ***o*** entirely burned
29:21 Aaron's sons, to ***o*** them up on the
29:27 As they began to ***o*** the entirely
31:2 thanks, and to ***o*** praise in the

Ezra
3:2 that they might ***o*** entirely burned
6:10 so that they may ***o*** pleasing sacrifices
7:17 And you will ***o*** them on the altar

Nehemiah
4:2 Will they ***o*** sacrifices? Will
5:8 were silent, unable to ***o*** a response.

Esther
1:8 in the palace to ***o*** as much as each

Job
6:22 me something? ***O*** a bribe from your

Psalms
22:25 I ***o*** praise in the great congregation
25:1 [Of David.] I ***o*** my life to you, LORD
27:6 me, and I will ***o*** sacrifices in
50:14 ***O*** God a sacrifice of thanksgiving!
66:15 I will ***o*** the best burned offerings to
86:4 because, my Lord, I ***o*** my life to you,
107:22 Let them ***o*** thanksgiving sacrifices and
116:17 So I'll ***o*** a sacrifice of thanksgiving
143:8 go because I ***o*** my life up to you.

Proverbs
12:26 The righteous ***o*** guidance to their

Ecclesiastes
5:1 to listen than to ***o*** the fools'

Isaiah
37:4 God has heard. ***O*** up a prayer for
57:7 You went up there to ***o*** a sacrifice.
65:12 I will ***o*** you to the sword. You will all

Jeremiah
10:8 and silly; they ***o*** nothing because
14:12 and when they ***o*** entirely burned
16:7 dead. No one will ***o*** a cup of
35:2 When they arrive, ***o*** them some wine to

Lamentations
3:30 He should ***o*** his cheek for a blow; he
4:3 Even jackals ***o*** the breast; they nurse

Ezekiel
20:31 When you ***o*** up your gifts and make your
43:24 salt on them and ***o*** them as entirely
43:27 the priests will ***o*** your entirely
45:17 Israel. He will ***o*** the purification
46:4 the prince will ***o*** to the LORD an

Hosea
4:13 They ***o*** sacrifices on mountaintops, and
4:14 prostitutes, and ***o*** sacrifices with
8:13 Though they ***o*** choice sacrifices, though
14:2 of bulls, let us ***o*** what we can say:

Amos
4:5 ***O*** a thanksgiving sacrifice of leavened
8:5 so that we may ***o*** wheat for sale,

Jonah
2:9 But me, I will ***o*** a sacrifice to you

Micah
3:11 Her prophets ***o*** divination for

Haggai
2:14 hands. Whatever they ***o*** is unclean.

Matthew
5:24 and then come back and ***o*** your gift.
8:4 to the priest and ***o*** the gift that
24:24 and they will ***o*** great signs and

Mark
1:44 to the priest and ***o*** the sacrifice for
13:22 and they will ***o*** signs and wonders
14:57 Some stood to ***o*** false witness against

Luke
6:29 you on the cheek, ***o*** the other one as

Acts
14:13 he wanted to ***o*** sacrifices to
19:33 that he wanted to ***o*** a defense before
24:17 poor of my nation and to ***o*** sacrifices.
24:26 that Paul would ***o*** him some money,

Romans
6:13 Don't ***o*** parts of your body to sin, to
6:16 know that if you ***o*** yourselves to

OFFER [cont.]

1 Corinthians
9:18 when I preach, I ***o*** the good news
14:17 You may ***o*** a beautiful prayer of
2 Corinthians
1:4 of trouble. We ***o*** the same comfort
Ephesians
6:18 ***O*** prayers and petitions in the Spirit
Titus
2:7 in every way. ***O*** yourself as a role
Hebrews
5:1 sake, in order to ***o*** gifts and
5:3 weakness, he must ***o*** sacrifices for
7:27 doesn't need to ***o*** sacrifices every
8:3 is appointed to ***o*** gifts and
9:25 didn't enter to ***o*** himself over and
13:15 let's continually ***o*** up a sacrifice of
1 Peter
2:5 priesthood to ***o*** up spiritual
Revelation
8:3 in order to ***o*** it on behalf of

OFFERED

Genesis
22:13 took the ram, and ***o*** it as an entirely
31:54 Jacob ***o*** a sacrifice on the mountain,
46:1 There he ***o*** sacrifices to his
Exodus
29:41 the second lamb ***o*** at twilight,
40:29 tent dwelling. He ***o*** the entirely
Numbers
6:21 person may have ***o***. The person must
23:2 Balak and Balaam ***o*** a bull and a ram
28:24 LORD. It will be ***o*** in addition to
Deuteronomy
18:1 the sacrifices ***o*** to the LORD,
Joshua
8:31 On it they ***o*** entirely burned
Judges
2:5 Bochim, and they ***o*** a sacrifice to
5:9 who willingly ***o*** themselves among
6:28 the second bull ***o*** on the newly
13:19 offering and ***o*** them on a rock to
20:26 Then they ***o*** entirely burned
21:4 altar there. They ***o*** entirely burned
21:13 the rock of Rimmon and ***o*** them a truce.
1 Samuel
6:14 of the cart and ***o*** the cows as an
6:15 of Beth-shemesh ***o*** entirely burned
7:9 suckling lamb and ***o*** it as an entirely
11:15 presence. They ***o*** well-being sacrifi
13:9 Then he ***o*** the entirely
13:12 of myself and ***o*** the entirely
2 Samuel
6:17 it. Then David ***o*** entirely burned
15:24 and Abiathar ***o*** sacrifices until
24:25 for the LORD and ***o*** entirely burned
1 Kings
3:15 covenant. Then he ***o*** entirely burned
8:63 Solomon ***o*** well-being sacrifices to the
10:5 offerings that he ***o*** at the LORD's
12:33 Israelites and ***o*** sacrifices on the
2 Kings
3:27 as king, and he ***o*** him on the wall
1 Chronicles
21:26 for the LORD and ***o*** entirely burned
21:28 the Jebusite, he ***o*** sacrifices there.
23:31 offerings were ***o*** to the LORD for
29:21 next day they ***o*** sacrifices and
2 Chronicles
1:6 meeting tent and ***o*** a thousand
7:15 to the prayers ***o*** in this place,
8:12 Then Solomon ***o*** entirely burned
9:4 offerings he ***o*** at the LORD's
24:14 were regularly ***o*** in the LORD's
29:27 offering to be ***o*** up on the altar.
33:16 the LORD's altar, ***o*** well-being sacrifi
Ezra
1:6 in addition to all that was freely ***o***.
3:3 peoples, and they ***o*** entirely burned
6:3 place where they ***o*** sacrifices be
7:15 have freely ***o*** to the God of
8:25 and all Israel present there had ***o***.
Nehemiah
12:43 They ***o*** great sacrifices on that day and
Job
32:12 to you, but you ***o*** no rebuke to Job,
Psalms
106:28 and ate sacrifices ***o*** to the dead.
Isaiah
53:10 If his life is ***o*** as restitution,
Jeremiah
18:15 me; they have ***o*** sacrifices to a
Ezekiel
6:13 wherever they ***o*** up pleasing
20:26 gifts when they ***o*** up all their
23:37 borne to me and ***o*** them up to be
44:7 When you ***o*** my food of fat
Hosea
2:13 Baals, when she ***o*** sweet-smelling
Jonah
1:16 reverence; they ***o*** a sacrifice to
Malachi
1:11 offering will be ***o*** everywhere in my
Matthew
27:48 it on a pole. He ***o*** it to Jesus to
Mark
15:36 it on a pole. He ***o*** it to Jesus to
Luke
2:24 They ***o*** a sacrifice in keeping with
Acts
7:41 shape of a calf, ***o*** a sacrifice to
8:18 the apostles' hands, he ***o*** them money.
12:5 the church ***o*** earnest prayer to
15:29 refuse food ***o*** to idols, blood, the meat
19:8 those present and ***o*** convincing
21:25 they avoid food ***o*** to idols, blood,
Romans
6:19 Once, you ***o*** the parts of your
11:16 batch of dough is ***o*** to God as holy,
Hebrews
5:7 on earth, Christ ***o*** prayers and
7:27 this once for all when he ***o*** himself.
9:9 that are being ***o*** can't perfect the
9:14 living God? He ***o*** himself to God
9:28 Christ was also ***o*** once to take on
10:1 that are ***o*** continually every
11:4 By faith Abel ***o*** a better sacrifice to
James
2:21 actions when he ***o*** his son Isaac on
Revelation
8:4 of the incense ***o*** for the prayers

OFFERING → BURNED OFFERING, COMPENSATION OFFERING, DRINK OFFERING, GIFT OFFERING, GRAIN OFFERING

Genesis
4:3 Cain presented an ***o*** to the LORD from
35:14 him. He poured an ***o*** of wine on it and
Exodus
22:29 Don't delay ***o*** the produce of your
29:14 the camp. It is a purification ***o***.
29:24 as an uplifted ***o*** in the LORD's
30:8 a regular incense ***o*** in the LORD's
30:10 the purification ***o*** for
35:22 an uplifted ***o*** of gold to the
38:29 from the uplifted ***o*** was seventy
Leviticus
1:2 a livestock ***o*** to the LORD, you
1:14 If the ***o*** for the LORD is an entirely
2:7 If your ***o*** is grain prepared in a pan,
3:1 If the ***o*** is a communal sacrifice of
3:2 the head of the ***o*** and slaughter it
3:6 If the ***o*** for a communal sacrifice of
3:7 a sheep as the ***o***, you must present
3:8 the head of the ***o*** and slaughter it
3:12 If the ***o*** is a goat, you must present it
3:14 present as your ***o***—a food gift for
4:3 as a purification ***o*** for the sin he
4:8 the purification ***o***: the fat that
4:14 as a purification ***o***. They will bring
5:11 can bring as the ***o*** for your sin a
6:17 the purification ***o*** and the
6:20 This is the ***o*** that Aaron and his sons
6:25 the purification ***o***: The purification
7:12 If you are ***o*** it for thanksgiving, you
7:13 must present this ***o***, plus the
8:27 them as an uplifted ***o*** before the LORD.
8:29 the ordination ***o*** and lifted it as
8:31 of the ordination ***o***, just as I was
9:2 as a purification ***o*** and a ram as an
10:14 for the uplifted ***o*** and the thigh for
10:16 the purification ***o***, and discovered
14:13 the purification ***o*** and the entirely
15:15 as a purification ***o*** and the other as
21:18 to make an ***o***: this includes
22:14 eats a holy ***o*** unintentionally,
23:14 bring your God's ***o***. This is a
23:15 for the uplifted ***o***; these must be
Numbers
3:4 an unauthorized ***o*** to the LORD in
5:15 He will bring the ***o*** required for her,
6:11 a purification ***o*** and the other as
7:11 present their ***o*** for the
7:23 old. This was the ***o*** of Nethanel,
Deuteronomy
12:27 ***o*** up your entirely burned
Judges
6:18 bring out my ***o***, and set it in
1 Samuel
2:15 say to the person ***o*** the sacrifice,
2:17 were disrespecting the Lord's own ***o***.
6:3 to return a guilt ***o*** to him. Then you
7:10 While Samuel was ***o*** the entirely burned
2 Samuel
6:18 David finished ***o*** the entirely
15:12 While Absalom was ***o*** the sacrifices, he
24:12 LORD says: I'm ***o*** you three
1 Kings
18:29 for the evening ***o***. Still there was
18:36 of the evening ***o***, the prophet
1 Chronicles
21:10 LORD says: I'm ***o*** you three
23:5 with instruments made for ***o*** praise.
23:29 the griddle, the ***o*** mixed with oil,
29:17 your people here ***o*** so willingly to
2 Chronicles
8:14 their posts for ***o*** praise and
35:16 Passover and ***o*** up entirely
Ezra
6:17 as a purification ***o*** for all Israel,
8:25 equipment, the ***o*** for the house of
Nehemiah
10:34 we bring the wood ***o*** into our God's
13:31 for the wood ***o*** at appointed
Psalms
38:1 For the memorial ***o***.] Please, LORD,
70:1 For the memorial ***o***.] Hurry, God, to
118:27 lead the festival ***o*** with ropes all
141:2 uplifted hands be like the evening ***o***.
Isaiah
66:20 all nations as an ***o*** to the LORD
Jeremiah
52:19 the basins, and the ***o*** bowls.
Ezekiel
43:19 as a purification ***o*** to the levitical
46:6 the new moon, the ***o*** will be a
Daniel
9:21 of the evening ***o***. This was the
Hosea
9:4 pour wine as an ***o*** to the LORD;
Malachi
2:12 and making an ***o*** to the LORD of
3:3 to the LORD, presenting a righteous ***o***.
Luke
1:10 outside during this hour of incense ***o***.
5:14 and make an ***o*** for your
13:1 killed while they were ***o*** sacrifices.
23:36 They came up to him ***o*** him sour wine
Acts
10:4 acts are like a memorial ***o*** to God.
10:31 acts are like a memorial ***o*** to him.
21:26 when the ***o*** would be
Romans
15:16 so that the ***o*** of the Gentiles
15:28 of the Gentiles' ***o*** to them, I will
2 Corinthians
2:15 aroma of Christ's ***o*** to God, both to
Ephesians
5:2 was a sacrificial ***o*** that smelled
Philippians
2:17 out like a drink ***o*** upon the altar of
Hebrews
10:5 a sacrifice or an ***o***, but you prepared
10:8 a sacrifice or an ***o*** or with entirely
10:10 will through the ***o*** of Jesus Christ's
10:11 day serving and ***o*** the same
10:14 made holy with one ***o*** for all time.
10:18 there is no longer an ***o*** for sin.
11:17 the promises was ***o*** his only son.

13:11 high priest as an ***o*** for sin, and

OFFERINGS → BURNED OFFERINGS, COMPENSATION OFFERINGS, DRINK OFFERINGS, GIFT OFFERINGS, GRAIN OFFERINGS

Exodus
28:38 with the holy ***o*** that the
38:24 from the uplifted ***o***, was twenty-nine
Leviticus
2:12 as first-choice ***o*** to the LORD, but
7:38 to present their ***o*** to the LORD, in
10:19 purification ***o*** and their
16:27 the purification ***o***, whose blood was
22:10 to eat the holy ***o***. No foreign guest
26:31 smell the soothing smells of your ***o***.
Numbers
7:3 brought their ***o*** before the LORD:
7:10 presented their ***o*** before the altar.
18:8 sacred ***o***. I have given
18:9 the most holy ***o***, from the
Deuteronomy
12:26 bring your sacred ***o*** and your payments
Joshua
13:14 of the fire ***o*** for the LORD, the
1 Samuel
2:28 Israelites' food ***o*** to your father's
2:29 sacrifices and my ***o***—the very ones I
2 Samuel
1:21 yielding grain ***o***. Because it was
2 Kings
12:16 and purification ***o***, it wasn't
1 Chronicles
23:13 holy, to make ***o*** before the LORD,
29:9 presented their ***o*** to the LORD so
2 Chronicles
29:31 sacrificial thank ***o*** to the LORD's
29:33 and three thousand sheep as holy ***o***.
30:22 well-being ***o*** and praising the
32:23 people brought ***o*** to the LORD in
33:16 and thank ***o*** on it, and
35:7 thousand bulls, all for the Passover ***o***.
Ezra
3:5 continual burned ***o***, the offerings at
Psalms
4:5 Bring righteous ***o***, and trust the LORD
16:4 in their blood ***o***; I won't let
40:6 sacrifices or ***o***; you don't
56:12 I will present thanksgiving ***o*** to you
69:22 them become a trap, their ***o*** a snare.
Isaiah
1:13 worthless ***o***. Your incense
19:21 sacrifices and ***o***, making solemn
43:23 you worship with ***o***; I didn't weary
60:7 will be your ***o***; they will be
Jeremiah
11:15 Can sacred ***o*** cancel your sin
19:13 roofs they made ***o*** to the heavenly
32:29 on whose roofs ***o*** have been made to
33:11 who say, as thank ***o*** are brought to
44:3 me by making ***o*** and worshipping
44:5 They continued making ***o*** to other gods.
44:15 wives had made ***o*** to other gods,
44:21 were making ***o*** to other gods—
48:35 LORD, for making ***o*** on the shrines,
Ezekiel
20:28 irksome ***o*** here, pleasing
20:40 ask for their ***o***, their finest
40:41 in all, for preparing the animal ***o***.
40:43 The tables were for the flesh of the ***o***.
42:13 priests eat the ***o*** that have been
45:25 the purification ***o***, entirely burned
46:20 than taking these ***o*** out into the
Daniel
2:46 grain and incense ***o*** be made to Daniel.
9:27 sacrifices and ***o***. In their place
Hosea
4:13 entirely burned ***o*** on hills; they
Amos
5:25 me sacrifices and ***o*** during the forty
Zephaniah
3:10 my dispersed ones, will bring me ***o***.
Malachi
3:8 you?" With your tenth-part gifts and ***o***.
Acts
7:42 sacrifices and ***o*** to me for forty

OFFICER

Genesis
37:36 Pharaoh's chief ***o***, commander of the
1 Kings
4:19 was a single ***o*** who was in the
16:9 Zimri, his ***o*** who led half the chariots,
22:9 king called an ***o*** and ordered,
2 Kings
7:2 Then the ***o***, the one the king leaned on
7:19 the ***o*** had answered the man of God,
9:25 his chariot ***o***, "Pick him up,
15:25 and Pekahiah's ***o***, plotted against
18:17 his chief ***o***, and his field
22:12 and Asaiah the royal ***o*** as follows:
25:19 took away an ***o*** who was in charge
1 Chronicles
26:24 was the chief ***o*** in charge of the
2 Chronicles
18:8 king called an ***o*** and ordered,
26:11 and Maaseiah, an ***o*** under the
32:21 leader, and ***o*** in the camp of
34:20 and the royal ***o*** Asaiah as follows:
Nehemiah
11:11 son of Ahitub the ***o*** of God's house,
Proverbs
6:7 The ant has no commander, ***o***, or ruler
Jeremiah
20:1 Immer's son, the ***o*** in charge of the
39:3 the chief ***o***, Nergal-sharezer
51:59 the staff ***o*** Seraiah, Neriah's
Daniel
2:15 the king's royal ***o***, "Why is the
Jonah
1:6 The ship's ***o*** came and said to him, "How
Matthew
5:25 you over to the ***o*** of the court, and
Luke
12:58 you over to the ***o***, and the officer

OFFICERS

Genesis
40:2 with his two ***o***, the chief wine
40:7 He asked the ***o*** of Pharaoh who were
Exodus
18:21 the people as ***o*** of groups of
Numbers
11:16 as elders and ***o*** of the people.

31:14 of the army, the **o** of thousands and
Joshua
1:10 Joshua gave orders to the people's **o**:
3:2 of three days the **o** went through the
8:33 —with its elders, **o**, and judges—were
23:2 judges, and their **o**. He said to them,
24:1 judges, and **o**. They presented
Judges
7:25 two Midianite **o**, Oreb and Zeeb.
8:3 you the Midianite **o** Oreb and Zeeb.
1 Samuel
14:38 said, "All you **o** in the army, come
18:30 rest of Saul's **o**, so his fame
1 Kings
4:7 had twelve **o** over all Israel.
9:22 his leaders, his **o**, and those in
14:27 them to the **o** of the guard who
20:6 I will send my **o** to you, and they
22:31 chariot **o**, "Don't bother
2 Kings
6:8 counsel with his **o**, saying, "I'll
6:11 He called his **o** and said to them,
9:11 to his master's **o**. They said to
10:1 to the senior **o** of the city, the
19:6 heard, which the **o** of Assyria's king
24:10 At that time, the **o** of Babylon's King
25:23 All the army **o** and their soldiers heard
1 Chronicles
12:14 were military **o**, the least of
23:4 the LORD's temple, 6,000 **o** and judges,
27:1 and their **o**. They served the
28:1 as well as the **o**, warriors, and
2 Chronicles
1:2 including the **o** of the army, the
8:10 fifty chief **o** who were in
12:10 them to the **o** of the guard who
17:14 follows: Judah's **o** over units of a
18:30 his chariot **o**, "Don't bother
19:11 serve as your **o** of the court.
21:9 night, defeating him and his chariot **o**.
28:14 loot before the **o** and the whole
32:6 military **o** over the troops,
Ezra
7:28 the king's mighty **o**. I took courage
Nehemiah
2:9 The king had sent **o** of the army and
4:14 officials, the **o**, and the rest of
5:7 officials and the **o**. I told them,
7:5 officials, the **o**, and the people
Esther
1:3 with his provincial officials and **o**.
Isaiah
31:9 stronghold; their **o** will be terrified
37:6 heard, which the **o** of Assyria's king
Jeremiah
8:1 of Judah and its **o**, the bones of the
17:25 David and their **o**, all riding on
35:4 used by the chief **o** and right above
38:17 surrender to the **o** of the king of
39:3 the commanding **o** of the king of
40:7 Some of the army **o** and their troops
41:1 one of the chief **o** of the king, came
42:1 Then all the army **o**, including
52:10 he slaughtered all Judah's **o** at Riblah.
Ezekiel
17:12 its king and its **o** away with him to
23:6 governors and **o**, charioteers and
Daniel
6:2 them three main **o** to whom they
Nahum
2:5 He musters his **o**; they stumble as they
Matthew
26:58 outside with the **o** to see how it
Mark
6:21 and military **o** and Galilee's
Luke
22:4 priests and the **o** of the temple
Acts
21:32 some soldiers and **o** and ran down to

OFFICIAL
Exodus
28:11 who engraves **o** seals, you will
30:13 according to the **o** shekel of the
39:6 sons, like an **o** seal is engraved.
39:14 engraved like **o** seals, each with
39:30 engraving on an **o** seal, they
1 Kings
11:41 written in the **o** records of
22:26 to Amon the city **o** and to Joash the
2 Kings
1:18 written in the **o** records of
8:6 king appointed an **o** to help her,
8:23 written in the **o** records of
18:24 least important **o** among my master's
1 Chronicles
9:1 was listed in the **o** records of
2 Chronicles
16:11 written in the **o** records of
31:18 The **o** genealogy included all their
Nehemiah
2:10 the Ammonite **o** heard this, they
12:23 recorded in the **o** records until the
Esther
6:1 sleep. He had the **o** royal records
10:2 written in the **o** records of the
Ecclesiastes
5:8 because a high **o** watches over
Isaiah
36:9 least important **o** among my master's
Ezekiel
13:9 house of Israel's **o** records, or enter
Daniel
1:3 his highest **o** Ashpenaz to
1:7 But the chief **o** gave them new names. He
1:8 to the chief **o** in hopes that he
1:9 loyalty between Daniel and the chief **o**;
1:10 but the chief **o** said to Daniel, "I'm
Micah
7:3 at doing evil. **O** and judge alike
John
4:46 a certain royal **o** whose son was
4:49 The royal **o** said to him, "Lord, come
Acts
8:27 a eunuch and an **o** responsible for

OFFICIALS
Exodus
7:10 Pharaoh and his **o**, and it turned
8:4 on you, your people, and all your **o**."
9:14 on you, your **o**, and your people
9:20 Some of Pharaoh's **o** who took the LORD's word seriously

10:7 Pharaoh's ***o*** said to him, "How long will
14:5 Pharaoh and his ***o*** changed their

Numbers
21:18 The well that the ***o*** dug, that the
22:8 to me." So the ***o*** of Moab stayed
22:21 donkey, and went with the ***o*** of Moab.
25:5 said to Israel's ***o***, "Each of you:

Deuteronomy
1:15 tens, as well as ***o*** for each of your
16:18 judges and ***o*** for each of your
20:5 The ***o*** will also say to the troops: "Is
29:10 elders, and your ***o***, all the

Judges
8:6 But the ***o*** of Succoth replied, "Haven't
8:14 the seventy-seven ***o*** and elders of

1 Samuel
2:8 sits them with ***o***, gives them the
8:15 your vineyards to his ***o*** and servants.

2 Samuel
10:3 the Ammonite ***o*** asked their master

1 Kings
4:2 These were his ***o***: the priest Azariah,
10:15 Arabian kings, and the ***o*** of the land.
11:26 of Solomon's own ***o***, Jeroboam fought
15:18 gave them to his ***o***. Then King Asa
20:14 of the district ***o*** will do it." "Who
21:8 to the elders and ***o*** who lived in the

2 Kings
9:32 Two or three high ***o*** looked down at
12:20 Jehoash's ***o*** plotted a conspiracy and
14:5 he executed the ***o*** who had
21:23 Amon's ***o*** plotted against him and
22:9 to him: "Your ***o*** have released the
24:12 officers, and his ***o***, came out to
25:24 of the Chaldean ***o***. Stay in the land

1 Chronicles
26:29 outside the temple as ***o*** and judges.
28:1 a hundred, the ***o*** in charge of all
28:21 you to do it. The ***o*** and all the

2 Chronicles
17:7 sent his ***o*** Ben-hail, Obadiah,
23:20 commanders, the ***o***, the rulers of
24:25 but his own ***o*** plotted against
25:3 he executed the ***o*** who had
26:11 of Hananiah, one of the king's ***o***.
28:21 palace, and the ***o*** to buy off the
30:2 The king, his ***o***, and the entire
31:8 Hezekiah and the ***o*** saw the piles,
32:3 with his ***o*** and soldiers
33:24 His own ***o*** plotted against him and
34:13 served as scribes, ***o***, and guards.
34:22 and the royal ***o*** went to the
35:8 His ***o*** also provided spontaneous gift
36:18 temple and those of the king and his ***o***.

Ezra
4:5 and bribed ***o*** to frustrate their plan.
5:6 colleagues the ***o*** who were in the
6:6 colleagues, the ***o*** in the province
8:25 counselors, his ***o***, and all Israel
9:1 finished, the ***o*** approached me and
10:8 mandated by the ***o*** and elders, would

Nehemiah
2:16 The ***o*** didn't know where I had gone or
3:5 but their ***o*** wouldn't help
4:14 and said to the ***o***, the officers,
5:7 against the ***o*** and the officers.
5:17 fifty Jews and ***o***, along with those
6:17 in those days the ***o*** of Judah sent
7:5 to assemble the ***o***, the officers,
9:32 our kings, our ***o***, our priests, our
10:29 join with their ***o*** and relatives,
12:32 went Hoshaiah and half the ***o*** of Judah,
13:11 So I scolded the ***o***, asking, "Why is

Esther
1:3 feast for all his ***o*** and courtiers.
1:16 the king and the ***o***. "Queen Vashti,"
2:18 for all his ***o*** and courtiers. He
3:1 him above all the ***o*** who worked with
3:12 well as for the ***o*** of each people.
4:11 All the king's ***o*** and the people in his
5:11 him over the ***o*** and high royal
6:9 one of the king's ***o***. Have him
8:9 governors, and ***o*** of the provinces

Job
29:10 the voices of ***o*** were hushed, their

Psalms
83:11 Make their ***o*** like Oreb and Zeeb, all
149:8 in chains and their ***o*** in iron shackles,

Proverbs
8:16 rulers govern, and ***o*** judge righteously.

Isaiah
5:13 their ***o*** are dying of
10:16 and among his ***o***, a blaze will
19:13 The ***o*** of Tanis have become fools; the
30:4 Though their ***o*** are in Zoan, and their
34:11 plummet stone of emptiness over its ***o***.
43:27 sinned, and your ***o*** rebelled against
43:28 I made the holy ***o*** impure, handed

Jeremiah
2:26 their kings, ***o***, priests, and
24:1 and the Judean ***o***, as well as the
24:8 Zedekiah and his ***o***, as well as the
25:18 its kings and ***o***. This was to make
26:10 When the ***o*** of Judah heard these things,
27:20 with all the ***o*** of Judah and
29:2 mother, the court ***o***, the government
32:32 their kings and ***o***, their priests
34:10 So all the ***o*** and people who entered
36:12 he found all the ***o*** meeting together:
37:14 Jeremiah and brought him to the ***o***,
38:4 Then the ***o*** said to the king: "This man
39:3 the rest of the ***o*** of the king of
44:17 our kings and our ***o***, have done in the
48:7 exile, together with his priests and ***o***.
49:38 of its king and ***o***, declares the
50:35 the LORD, along with its ***o*** and sages.
51:23 With you I will crush governors and ***o***.

Lamentations
1:6 her glory. Her ***o*** are like deer
2:2 kingdom and its ***o***, he forced to the
2:9 her king and her ***o*** are now among the
5:12 ***O*** have been hung up by their hands;

Ezekiel
11:1 I saw that two ***o*** of the people,
17:13 He also took away the land's ***o***.
22:27 The ***o*** in her are like wolves ripping up
38:13 the merchants and ***o*** of Tarshish will

Daniel
3:2 the provincial ***o*** to assemble and

Hosea
7:3 and give joy to the ***o*** with their lies.
7:5 of our king, the ***o*** became sick with
7:16 bow; their ***o*** will fall by the

9:15 them no more; all their ***o*** are rebels.
Amos
1:15 away, he and his ***o*** together, says the
2:3 slay all their ***o*** with him, says the
Jonah
3:7 the king and his ***o***: Neither human
Micah
3:11 Her ***o*** give justice for a bribe, and her
Nahum
3:10 cast lots for her ***o***; all of her
3:18 of Assyria! Your ***o*** are lying down.
Matthew
20:25 their high-ranking ***o*** order them around.
Mark
6:21 his high-ranking ***o*** and military
10:42 their high-ranking ***o*** order them around.
Acts
16:19 them before the ***o*** in the city
17:6 before the city ***o***. They were
17:8 the crowd and the city ***o*** even more.
19:31 Even some ***o*** of the province of Asia,
Revelation
6:15 of the earth, the ***o*** and the generals,

OFFSPRING

Genesis
3:15 between your ***o*** and hers. They
4:4 flock's oldest ***o*** with their fat.
7:3 so that their ***o*** will survive
Exodus
11:5 and all the first ***o*** of the animals.
12:29 all the first ***o*** in the land of
13:2 Each first ***o*** from any
13:15 all the oldest ***o*** in the land of
34:19 Every first ***o*** is mine. That includes
34:20 a donkey's oldest ***o*** you may ransom
Leviticus
22:28 ox or sheep and its ***o*** on the same day.
27:26 any oldest ***o*** from livestock,
Numbers
18:17 But the oldest ***o*** of a cow, sheep, or
Deuteronomy
7:13 your oil, and the ***o*** of your cattle
12:6 and the oldest ***o*** of your herds and
12:17 oil; the oldest ***o*** of your herds and
14:23 wine, oil, oldest ***o*** of your herds and
28:4 your livestock's ***o***—the young of both
30:9 your livestock's ***o***, and your land's
Joshua
15:14 and Talmai. They were the ***o*** of Anak.
2 Samuel
19:43 we are the oldest ***o***, not you! So why
1 Kings
14:15 and their ***o***, and he will
2 Kings
20:18 your very own ***o***, will be taken
1 Chronicles
16:13 you who are the ***o*** of Israel, his
Nehemiah
10:36 bring the oldest ***o*** of our children
Job
5:25 children. Your ***o*** will be like the
18:12 Their ***o*** hunger; calamity is ready for
18:19 They have no ***o*** or descendants among
21:8 with them, their ***o*** in their sight,
27:14 the sword; their ***o*** won't have enough
31:8 and another reap; let my ***o*** be uprooted.
39:3 for their young, send forth their ***o***.
Psalms
21:10 destroy their ***o*** from the land;
22:23 are all Israel's ***o***—stand in awe of
69:36 The ***o*** of God's servants will inherit
89:4 establish your ***o*** forever; I will
105:6 you who are the ***o*** of Abraham, his
106:27 scattering their ***o*** among the nations,
112:2 the land. The ***o*** of those who do
135:8 Egyptians' oldest ***o***—both human and a
136:10 Egyptians' oldest ***o***—God's faithful
Isaiah
1:4 crimes, evildoing ***o***, corrupt
14:20 people. Such evil ***o*** will never be
22:24 hang on him, the ***o*** and the
34:1 all who fill it, world and all its ***o***.
41:8 I have chosen, ***o*** of Abraham, whom
42:5 the earth and its ***o***, the one who gave
44:3 and my blessing upon your ***o***.
45:19 didn't say to the ***o*** of Jacob, "Seek
48:19 Your ***o*** would be like the sand, and your
53:10 he will see his ***o***; he will enjoy
57:3 of sorcery, ***o*** of adultery and
57:4 you children of rebellion, ***o*** of lies,
61:9 Their ***o*** will be known among the
65:9 I will bring out ***o*** from Jacob, and from
Jeremiah
49:10 take cover. His ***o***, family, and
Lamentations
2:20 eat their own ***o***, their own
Zechariah
9:9 an ass, on a colt, the ***o*** of a donkey.
Malachi
2:3 to denounce your ***o***; I will scatter
2:15 one seeking godly ***o***. You should guard
Matthew
21:5 donkey, and on a colt the donkey's ***o***."
Acts
17:28 of your own poets said, 'We are his ***o***.'
17:29 as God's ***o***, we have no need

OIL → ANOINTING OIL

Genesis
27:28 the sky, olive ***o*** from the earth,
28:18 pillar, and poured ***o*** on the top of it.
35:14 wine on it and then poured ***o*** over it.
Exodus
25:6 ***o*** for the lamps; spices for the
27:20 to bring you pure ***o*** of crushed olives
28:41 Anoint them with ***o***, ordain them, and
29:2 made with ***o***, and unleavened
29:23 made with ***o***, and one wafer
29:40 of a hin of ***o*** from crushed
30:24 sanctuary shekel—and a hin of olive ***o***.
30:32 else to use this ***o***. Don't make
30:33 Whoever blends an ***o*** like it or whoever
35:8 the ***o*** for the light; spices for the
35:14 and its lamps, the ***o*** for the light,
35:28 spices and ***o*** for light and for the
39:37 its equipment, and the ***o*** for the light,
Leviticus
2:1 They must pour ***o*** on it and put
5:11 must not put any ***o*** on it, nor any
6:15 choice flour and ***o*** from the grain
7:10 mixed with ***o*** or dry, will
7:12 mixed with ***o***, unleavened thin
8:11 some of the ***o*** on the altar

8:26 made with **o**, and one
9:4 mixed with **o**, because today
14:10 flour mixed with **o**, and one log of
14:12 with the log of **o**, and will lift
14:15 of the log of **o** and pour it into
14:16 finger into the **o** and sprinkle some
14:17 put some of the **o** that is left in
14:18 is left of the **o** in his hand on
14:21 flour mixed with **o**; a log of oil;
14:24 and the log of **o**, and will lift
14:26 pour some of the **o** into his left
14:27 some of the **o** seven times
14:28 put some of the **o** that is in his
14:29 is left of the **o** in his hand on
23:13 flour mixed with **o**, as a food gift
24:2 pressed olive **o** to you for the
Numbers
4:9 containers for **o** that are used in
4:16 oversight of the **o** for lighting, the
5:15 He will not pour **o** on it, nor offer
6:15 and mixed with **o**, and unleavened
7:13 flour mixed with **o** for a grain
11:8 It tasted like cakes baked in olive **o**.
15:4 mixed with one-fourth of a hin of **o**.
18:12 All the choice **o**, new wine, and the
28:5 with a fourth of a hin of beaten **o**.
28:9 mixed with **o**, and its drink
35:25 priest who was anointed with holy **o**.
Deuteronomy
7:13 your wine, your **o**, and the
8:8 a land of olive **o** and honey;
11:14 can stock up your grain, wine, and **o**.
12:17 grain, wine, and **o**; the oldest
14:23 your grain, wine, **o**, oldest offspring
18:4 grain, wine, and **o**, and the first of
28:40 with their **o** because your
28:51 grain, wine, or **o** left—nor any youn
32:13 a boulder, with **o** from a hard rock:
33:24 one who dips his foot in fine **o**.
Judges
9:9 stop producing my **o**, which is how
1 Samuel
10:1 a small jar of **o** and poured it
16:1 your horn with **o** and get going.
16:13 took the horn of **o** and anointed him
2 Samuel
1:21 of Saul!—never again anointed with **o**.
14:2 yourself with **o**. Act like a woman
1 Kings
1:39 took the horn of **o** from the tent and
5:11 kors of pure **o** for his palace
17:12 jar and a bit of **o** in a bottle. Look
17:14 and the bottle of **o** won't run out
17:16 did the bottle of **o** run out, just as
2 Kings
4:2 in the house except a small jar of **o**."
4:4 your sons. Pour **o** into all those
4:6 any more." Then the **o** stopped flowing,
4:7 Go! Sell the **o** and pay your
9:1 take this jug of **o** with you, and go
9:3 Take the jug of **o** and pour it on his
9:6 then poured **o** on his head and
18:32 a land of olive **o** and honey. Then
20:13 and the fine **o**. He also showed
1 Chronicles
9:29 the flour, wine, **o**, incense, and
12:40 of raisins, wine, **o**, oxen, and sheep,
23:29 mixed with **o**, as well as all
27:28 in charge of the stores of **o**—Joash;
2 Chronicles
2:10 and twenty thousand baths of olive **o**.
2:15 barley, olive **o**, and wine he has
11:11 supplied them with food, **o**, and wine.
31:5 grain, new wine, **o**, honey, and all
32:28 wine, and olive **o**; stalls for all
Ezra
3:7 food, drink, and **o** to the Sidonians
6:9 salt, wine, or **o**, as requested by
7:22 hundred baths of **o**, and unlimited
Nehemiah
5:11 grain, wine, and **o** that you are
10:37 the wine, and the **o** to the priests at
10:39 grain, wine, and **o** to the storerooms
13:5 grain, wine, and **o**. These items were
13:12 grain, wine, and **o** into the
Job
29:6 a rock poured out pools of **o** for me.
Psalms
23:5 bathe my head in **o**; my cup is so
45:7 you with the **o** of joy more than
55:21 more silky than **o**, they are really
89:20 David. I anointed him with my holy **o**.
104:15 along with **o**, which makes the
109:18 like water, seep into his bones like **o**!
133:2 is like expensive **o** poured over the
141:5 that kind of fine **o** because my
Proverbs
5:3 and her tongue is smoother than **o**,
21:17 lovers of wine and **o** won't get rich.
21:20 treasure and **o** stay in the home
27:9 **O** and incense make the heart glad, and
27:16 the wind or pick up **o** in his hand.
Ecclesiastes
7:1 better than fine **o**, and the day of
9:8 don't run short of **o** for your head.
10:1 the perfumer's **o**, so a little
Isaiah
1:6 not bandaged, not soothed with **o**.
39:2 spices and fine **o**—and everything in
57:9 to Molech with **o**, and you
61:3 place of ashes, **o** of joy in place
Jeremiah
31:12 grain, wine, **o**, flocks, and
41:8 wheat, barley, **o**, and honey hidden
Ezekiel
16:9 off your blood, and poured **o** on you.
16:13 flour, honey, and **o**. You became very
16:18 them. You set my **o** and incense
16:19 eat—fine wheat, **o**, and honey—before
23:41 and you set my incense and my **o** on it.
27:17 millet, honey, **o**, and balm for
32:14 rivers flow like **o**. This is what the
45:14 regular amount of **o**, one-tenth of a
46:5 with one hin of **o** for each ephah.
Hosea
2:5 and my linen cloth, my **o** and my drink."
2:8 and the fresh **o**, and that I gave
2:22 and the fresh **o**, and they will
12:1 with Assyria, and **o** is carried to
Joel
1:10 new wine dries up, the olive **o** fails.
2:19 wine, and fresh **o**, and you will be
2:24 overflow with new wine and fresh **o**.

Micah
6:7 many torrents of ***o***? Should I give my
6:15 don't anoint with ***o***; you tread
Haggai
1:11 on the olive ***o***, on that which
2:12 stew, wine, ***o***, or any kind of
Zechariah
4:12 empty out golden ***o*** through the two
Matthew
25:3 lamps but didn't bring ***o*** for them.
Mark
6:13 people with olive ***o*** and healed them.
Luke
7:37 brought perfumed ***o*** in a vase made of
7:38 kissed them, and poured the ***o*** on them.
7:46 my head with ***o***, but she has
10:34 tending them with ***o*** and wine. Then he
16:6 gallons of olive ***o***.' The manager
John
11:2 with fragrant ***o*** and wiped his
Romans
11:17 produces the rich ***o*** of the olive tree,
Hebrews
1:9 anointed you with ***o*** instead of your
James
5:14 them with ***o*** in the name of
Revelation
1:12 I saw seven ***o*** lamps burning on
6:6 don't damage the olive ***o*** and the wine."
18:13 wine, ***o***, fine flour, and

OLD

Genesis
18:11 were both very ***o***. Sarah was no
18:12 to have children and my husband's ***o***.
21:7 given birth to a son when he was ***o***!"
Numbers
1:3 20 years ***o*** and above, who is eligible
14:29 from 20 years ***o*** and above, who
Psalms
71:9 cast me off in ***o*** age. Don't
90:10 be seventy years ***o***, maybe eighty, if
91:16 you full with ***o*** age. I'll show
92:14 fruit even when ***o*** and gray; they
148:12 you who are ***o*** together with you
Proverbs
20:29 gray hair is the splendor of ***o*** age.
22:6 when they grow ***o***, they won't
Ecclesiastes
4:13 is better than an ***o*** and foolish king,
Joel
2:28 prophesy, your ***o*** men will dream
Matthew
9:17 new wine into ***o*** wineskins. If
Mark
2:21 unshrunk cloth on ***o*** clothes;
2:22 new wine into ***o*** leather
5:42 was twelve years ***o***. They were
Luke
1:7 pregnant and they both were very ***o***.
1:18 of this? My wife and I are very ***o***."
2:42 was twelve years ***o***, they went up to
3:23 about 30 years ***o*** when he began his
5:36 to patch an ***o*** garment.
5:37 new wine into ***o*** wineskins. If
Romans
4:19 nearly 100 years ***o***, took into
1 Corinthians
5:7 Clean out the ***o*** yeast so you can be a
2 Corinthians
5:17 new creation. The ***o*** things have gone
1 John
2:7 to you, but an ***o*** commandment that
Revelation
12:9 thrown down. The ***o*** snake, who is
20:2 the dragon, the ***o*** snake, who is the

OLDER

Genesis
10:21 children and Japheth's ***o*** brother.
19:31 The ***o*** daughter said to the younger,
24:1 Abraham became ***o***, the LORD blessed
25:23 the other; the ***o*** will serve the
27:1 he summoned his ***o*** son Esau and said
29:16 daughters: the ***o*** was named Leah
Exodus
2:4 The baby's ***o*** sister stood watch nearby
1 Samuel
17:14 These three ***o*** sons followed
1 Kings
2:22 all, he is my ***o*** brother and has
1 Chronicles
23:3 of every male 30 and ***o*** totaled 38,000.
2 Chronicles
22:1 killed all the ***o*** sons. So Ahaziah,
25:5 20 years old and ***o*** and found that
31:16 years old and ***o***, all who entered
31:17 0 years of age and ***o*** according to
Ezra
3:12 But many of the ***o*** priests and Levites
Job
15:10 with us; those much ***o*** than your father.
32:4 Job spoke, for they were ***o*** than he.
Ezekiel
16:46 Your ***o*** sister is Samaria, who lives
23:4 The ***o*** sister was named Oholah, and the
Luke
15:25 Now his ***o*** son was in the field. Coming
15:28 Then the ***o*** son was furious and didn't
Romans
9:12 said to her: The ***o*** child will be a
1 Timothy
4:7 down from the ***o*** women. Train
5:1 Don't correct an ***o*** man but encourage
5:2 treat ***o*** women like your mother, and
5:9 the list who is ***o*** than 60 years old
Titus
2:2 Tell the ***o*** men to be sober, dignified,
2:3 tell the ***o*** women to be

OLDEST

Genesis
4:4 his flock's ***o*** offspring with
10:15 fathered Sidon his ***o*** son, and Heth,
19:4 youngest to the ***o***—surrounded the
22:21 They are Uz his ***o*** son, Buz his brother,
24:2 said to the ***o*** servant of his
25:13 Ishmael's ***o*** son; Kedar;
27:19 I'm Esau your ***o*** son. I've made
27:32 said, "I'm your son, your ***o*** son, Esau."
29:26 give the younger woman before the ***o***.
35:23 Reuben, Jacob's ***o*** son, and Simeon,
36:15 Eliphaz, Esau's ***o*** son: Chief Teman,
38:6 Judah married his ***o*** son Er to a woman

38:7 Judah's ***o*** son Er immoral,
41:51 Joseph named the ***o*** son Manasseh,
43:33 of him from the ***o*** to the youngest
44:12 He searched the ***o*** first and the
46:8 and his sons. Jacob's ***o*** son was Reuben.
48:14 hands because Manasseh was the ***o*** son.
48:18 This is the ***o*** son. Put your
49:3 you are my ***o*** son, my strength

Exodus
4:22 what the LORD says: Israel is my ***o*** son.
4:23 now I'm going to kill your ***o*** son.'
6:14 Reuben, Israel's ***o*** son: Hanoch,
11:5 Every ***o*** child in the land of Egypt will
12:12 strike down every ***o*** child in the land
12:29 Egypt, from the ***o*** child of Pharaoh
13:2 to me all your ***o*** children. Each
13:13 ransom every ***o*** male among your
13:15 killed all the ***o*** offspring in the
22:29 and winepresses. Give me your ***o*** son.
34:19 livestock, the ***o*** offspring of cows
34:20 But a donkey's ***o*** offspring you may

Leviticus
27:26 dedicate any ***o*** offspring from

Numbers
1:20 Reuben, Israel's ***o***, registered by
3:12 place of all the ***o*** males who open an
8:16 the newborn, the ***o*** of all the
18:15 Any ***o*** male from the womb of any living
18:17 But the ***o*** offspring of a cow, sheep, or
26:5 Reuben, Israel's ***o*** son. Reuben's
33:4 burying their ***o*** males, whom the

Deuteronomy
12:6 gifts, and the ***o*** offspring of your
12:17 and oil; the ***o*** offspring of your
14:23 grain, wine, oil, ***o*** offspring of your
15:19 must devote every ***o*** male animal from
21:15 children, but the ***o*** male is the
21:16 wife's son as the ***o*** male rather than
21:17 wife's son as the ***o*** male, giving to
25:6 -law will name the ***o*** male son that she

Joshua
6:26 cost them their ***o*** child. Setting up
17:1 actually Joseph's ***o*** son. Gilead and

Judges
8:20 So he ordered his ***o*** son Jether, "Stand

1 Samuel
8:2 The name of his ***o*** son was Joel; the
14:49 were Merab, the ***o***, and Michal, the
17:13 Jesse's three ***o*** sons had gone with Saul
17:28 When David's ***o*** brother Eliab heard him
18:17 Look, here is my ***o*** daughter Merab. I

2 Samuel
3:2 in Hebron. His ***o*** son was Amnon, by
13:21 because he loved him as his ***o*** child.
19:43 more, we are the ***o*** offspring, not

1 Kings
16:34 the cost of his ***o*** son Abiram. He

2 Kings
3:27 Then he took his ***o*** son, who was to

Job
1:13 wine in their ***o*** brother's house.
1:18 wine in their ***o*** brother's house,

Psalms
78:51 all of Egypt's ***o*** males; in Ham's
105:36 down all the ***o*** sons throughout
135:8 the Egyptians' ***o*** offspring—both
136:10 the Egyptians' ***o*** offspring—God's

Isaiah
14:30 The ***o*** offspring of the poor will graze;

Jeremiah
31:9 father, Ephraim will be my ***o*** child.

Ezekiel
20:26 up all their ***o*** children. They

Hosea
12:3 tried to be the ***o*** of twin brothers;

Micah
6:7 Should I give my ***o*** child for my

Zechariah
12:10 mourning over the death of an ***o*** child.

Hebrews
12:16 inheritance as the ***o*** son for one meal.

OLIVE

Genesis
8:11 grasping a torn ***o*** leaf in its beak.
27:28 from the sky, ***o*** oil from the
27:39 far away from the ***o*** groves of the

Exodus
23:11 with your vineyard and your ***o*** trees.
30:24 sanctuary shekel—and a hin of ***o*** oil.

Leviticus
24:2 pure, pressed ***o*** oil to you for

Numbers
11:8 It tasted like cakes baked in ***o*** oil.

Deuteronomy
6:11 vineyards and ***o*** trees that you
8:8 a land of ***o*** oil and honey;
24:20 olives off your ***o*** trees, don't go
28:40 might have many ***o*** trees throughout

Joshua
24:13 vineyards and ***o*** groves that you

Judges
9:8 they said to the ***o*** tree, 'Be our
9:9 But the ***o*** tree replied to them,
15:5 grain, vineyards, and ***o*** orchards.

1 Samuel
8:14 vineyards, and ***o*** groves and give

2 Samuel
15:23 passed by on the ***O*** road into the

1 Kings
6:23 creatures of ***o*** wood for the
6:31 sanctuary from ***o*** wood and carved
6:32 overlaid the two ***o***-wood doors with go
6:33 doorframes of ***o*** wood with four

2 Kings
5:26 silver, clothes, ***o*** trees, vineyards,
18:32 a land of ***o*** oil and honey.

1 Chronicles
27:28 in charge of the ***o*** and sycamore trees

2 Chronicles
2:10 and twenty thousand baths of ***o*** oil.
2:15 wheat, barley, ***o*** oil, and wine he
32:28 grain, wine, and ***o*** oil; stalls for

Nehemiah
5:11 vineyards, their ***o*** orchards, and
8:15 bring branches of ***o***, wild olive,
9:25 vineyards, ***o*** orchards, and a

Job
15:33 and cast off their blossoms like the ***o***.

Psalms
52:8 I am like a green ***o*** tree in God's
128:3 will be like ***o*** trees, freshly

Isaiah
17:6 like a stripped ***o*** tree: two or

24:13 like a smashed *o* tree, like
41:19 myrtle, and *o* trees; I will put
Jeremiah
11:16 A blossoming *o* tree, fair and
Hosea
14:6 will be like the *o* tree, and his
Joel
1:10 the new wine dries up, the *o* oil fails.
Amos
4:9 fig treesand your *o* trees; yet you
Habakkuk
3:17 vine; though the *o* crop withers, and
Haggai
1:11 the wine, on the *o* oil, on that
2:19 or has the *o* tree not borne
Zechariah
4:3 It has two *o* trees beside the
4:11 are these two *o* trees on the
4:12 are these two *o* branches that
Mark
6:13 sick people with *o* oil and healed
Luke
16:6 gallons of *o* oil.' The manager
Romans
11:17 you were a wild *o* branch, and you
11:24 part of a wild *o* tree and you were
Revelation
6:6 don't damage the *o* oil and the wine."
11:4 These are the two *o* trees and the two

OLIVES → MOUNT OF OLIVES
Exodus
27:20 oil of crushed *o* for the light so
29:40 oil from crushed *o* and a quarter of
Deuteronomy
24:20 when you beat the *o* off your olive
Job
24:11 crush *o* between millstones, tread
Isaiah
17:6 two or three *o* on the highest
Micah
6:15 You tread down *o*, but you don't
James
3:12 fig tree produce *o*? Can a grapevine

OMRI
1 Kings
16:16 made their general ***O*** king of Israel.
16:25 ***O*** did evil in the LORD's eyes, more
Micah
6:16 the policies of ***O***, all the

ONE GOD
Ps 20:6; Mal 2:10; Mk 2:7; 10:18; Lk 18:19; 1Co 8:4; 8:6; Eph 4:6; 1Ti 2:5

ONLY GOD
Ex 8:19; Dt 4:35; 4:39; 2Sa 22:33; Ps 18:32; 62:2, 6; 139:19; Lk 5:21; Jn 5:44; 1Ti 1:17; Jud 1:25

OPENED
Genesis
4:11 the ground that *o* its mouth to take
7:11 and the windows in the skies *o*.
8:6 forty days, Noah *o* the window of the
21:19 Then God *o* her eyes, and she saw a
29:31 was unloved, he *o* her womb; but
41:56 land, and Joseph *o* all of the
42:27 one of them *o* his sack to feed
42:35 When they *o* their sacks, each man found a pouch
43:21 the night and *o* our sacks, there
44:11 down to the ground and each *o* his sack.
Exodus
2:6 When she *o* it, she saw the child. The
Numbers
16:32 The earth *o* its mouth and swallowed
22:28 Then the LORD *o* the donkey's mouth and
26:10 The earth *o* its mouth and swallowed
Deuteronomy
11:6 when the ground *o* up its mouth and
Judges
3:25 but he never *o* the doors of the
4:19 thirsty." So she *o* a jug of milk,
11:35 my agony! For I *o* my mouth to the
11:36 father, you've *o* your mouth to the
19:27 the morning, he *o* the doors of the
1 Samuel
3:15 morning, then *o* the doors of the
1 Kings
19:6 Elijah *o* his eyes and saw flatbread
2 Kings
4:35 boy sneezed seven times and *o* his eyes.
6:17 Then the LORD *o* the servant's
6:20 see." The LORD *o* their eyes, and
9:10 the young prophet *o* the door and ran.
Nehemiah
7:3 aren't to be *o* during the
8:5 Ezra the scribe *o* the scroll in the
Job
29:23 me as for rain, *o* their mouth as
31:32 in the street; I *o* my doors to the
Psalms
78:23 to the skies above, *o* heaven's doors,
105:41 God *o* the rock and out gushed water—
106:17 So the earth *o* up, swallowing Dathan,
109:2 wicked liars have *o* up against me,
Song of Songs
5:6 I went and *o* for my love, but my love
7:12 and the blossoms *o*, see if the
Isaiah
10:14 a wing or *o* a mouth to chirp."
35:5 the blind will be *o*, and the ears of
50:5 The LORD God *o* my ear; I didn't rebel;
Jeremiah
50:25 The LORD has *o* his arsenal and brought
Lamentations
3:46 our enemies have *o* their mouths
Ezekiel
1:1 when the heavens *o* and I saw visions
3:2 So I *o* my mouth, and he fed me the
24:27 mouth will be *o* to the refugee,
33:22 the morning, God *o* my mouth. So my
44:2 It shouldn't be *o*. No one should
46:1 the day of the new moon it will be *o*,
46:12 east will be *o* for him, and he
Daniel
7:10 sat in session; the scrolls were *o*.
10:16 my lips. Then I *o* my mouth and
Nahum
2:6 of the rivers are *o*; the palace melts.

Matthew
2:11 him. Then they ***o*** their treasure
3:16 water. Heaven was ***o*** to him, and he
7:7 Knock, and the door will be ***o*** to you.
7:8 to everyone who knocks, the door is ***o***.
9:30 Their eyes were ***o***. Then Jesus sternly
Mark
7:35 At once, his ears ***o***, his twisted
Luke
3:21 While he was praying, heaven was ***o***
11:9 Knock and the door will be ***o*** to you.
11:10 To everyone who knocks, the door is ***o***.
24:31 Their eyes were ***o*** and they recognized
24:45 Then he ***o*** their minds to understand the
Acts
5:19 from the Lord ***o*** the prison doors
5:23 but when we ***o*** the doors we
9:8 the ground, he ***o*** his eyes but he
9:40 get up!" She ***o*** her eyes, saw
10:11 He saw heaven ***o*** up and something like a large linen sheet
12:10 to the city. It ***o*** for them by
12:16 They finally ***o*** the gate and saw
14:27 and how God had ***o*** a door of faith
Romans
3:13 that has been ***o***. They are
1 Corinthians
16:9 opportunity has ***o*** up for my mission
Hebrews
10:20 way that he ***o*** up for us through
Revelation
4:1 that had been ***o*** in heaven. The
6:1 on as the Lamb ***o*** one of the seven
6:3 When the Lamb ***o*** the second seal, I
9:2 He ***o*** the shaft of the abyss; and smoke
10:8 Go, take the ***o*** scroll from the
11:19 in heaven was ***o***, and the chest
12:16 woman. The earth ***o*** its mouth and
13:6 It ***o*** its mouth to speak blasphemies
15:5 is, the tent of witness—was ***o***.
19:11 Then I saw heaven ***o***, and there was a
20:12 and scrolls were ***o***. Another scroll

OPPORTUNITY

Ezekiel
16:15 fame. At every ***o***, you seduced all
Matthew
26:16 he was looking for an ***o*** to turn him in.
Mark
14:11 looking for an ***o*** to turn him in.
Luke
4:13 departed from him until the next ***o***.
21:13 will provide you with an ***o*** to testify.
22:6 looking for an ***o*** to hand Jesus
Acts
25:16 accusers and had ***o*** to offer a
Romans
7:8 sin seized the ***o*** and used this
7:11 Sin seized the ***o*** through the
1 Corinthians
7:21 to be free, take advantage of the ***o***.
16:9 and productive ***o*** has opened up for
16:12 to go now. He'll come when he has an ***o***.
2 Corinthians
1:15 you could have a second ***o*** to see me.
2:12 the Lord gave me an ***o*** to preach.
5:12 are giving you an ***o*** to be proud of us
Galatians
5:13 freedom be an ***o*** to indulge your
6:10 we have an ***o***, and especially
Ephesians
4:27 Don't provide an ***o*** for the devil
5:16 of every ***o*** because these are
Colossians
4:5 outsiders, making the most of the ***o***.
Hebrews
11:15 would have had the ***o*** to return to it.

OPPOSE

Leviticus
17:10 I will ***o*** the person who consumes
20:6 I will also ***o*** anyone who resorts to
26:21 you continue to ***o*** me and are
26:41 which made me ***o*** them, so I took them
2 Chronicles
20:6 are so powerful that no one can ***o*** you.
Ezra
4:23 to Jerusalem to ***o*** the Jews and made
Job
16:4 words together to ***o*** you, shake my
Psalms
38:20 with evil; they ***o*** me for pursuing
Isaiah
49:25 I myself will ***o*** those who oppose
Daniel
11:14 times, many will ***o*** the southern
11:16 will be able to ***o*** him. He will take
Matthew
5:39 that you must not ***o*** those who want to
Acts
26:9 that I ought to ***o*** the name of Jesus
2 Corinthians
10:5 is raised up to ***o*** the knowledge of
2 Timothy
3:8 These people ***o*** the truth in the same
James
5:6 the righteous one, who doesn't ***o*** you.

OPPOSITE

Exodus
26:5 set. The loops should be ***o*** each other.
26:35 set the lampstand ***o*** the table by the
30:4 molding on two ***o*** sides of the
36:12 set. The loops were ***o*** each other.
37:27 molding on two ***o*** sides of the
40:24 the meeting tent, ***o*** the table on the
Numbers
26:3 plains of Moab by the Jordan ***o*** Jericho:
Deuteronomy
4:46 in the valley ***o*** Beth-peor, in the
32:49 the land of Moab ***o*** Jericho. Take a
Joshua
3:16 The people crossed ***o*** Jericho.
15:7 Gilgal was ***o*** the ascent of
15:8 mountain that is ***o*** the Hinnom Valley
17:7 which is ***o*** Shechem. The
18:14 mountain that is ***o*** Beth-horon on the
19:11 touched the ravine that is ***o*** Jokneam.
1 Samuel
14:1 fort on the ***o*** side." But he
17:3 positions on the ***o*** hill. There was a
17:21 their battle formations ***o*** each other.
20:25 Jonathan sat ***o*** him while Abner

26:3 Hachilah's hill ***o*** Jeshimon beside
2 Samuel
2:13 other sat on the ***o*** side of the pool.
1 Kings
4:12 and over to the region ***o*** Jokmeam;
20:29 two armies camped ***o*** each other for
1 Chronicles
5:11 family lived ***o*** them in the land
Nehemiah
3:10 son, made repairs ***o*** his house, and
3:16 from the point ***o*** David's tombs as
3:19 another section ***o*** the ascent to the
3:23 made repairs ***o*** their house.
3:25 from the point ***o*** the Angle and the
3:26 up to the point ***o*** the Water Gate to
3:27 another section ***o*** the great
3:28 made repairs, each one ***o*** his own house.
3:29 son, made repairs ***o*** his own house.
3:30 son, made repairs ***o*** his own room.
3:31 the merchants, ***o*** the Parade Gate,
12:9 associates stood ***o*** them in the
12:24 who stood ***o*** them to praise
Ezekiel
40:7 porch at the gate ***o*** the temple was
40:23 inner courtyard ***o*** the North and
42:1 set of chambers ***o*** the yard and the
46:9 Instead, they should go out the ***o*** gate.
Acts
20:15 there and arrived ***o*** Chios. On the day

OPPOSITION → JEWISH OPPOSITION

Leviticus
26:40 me, and for their continued ***o*** to me—
Job
27:7 like the wicked, my ***o*** like the vicious.
Luke
2:34 and to be a sign that generates ***o***
Acts
6:9 ***O*** arose from some who belonged to the
18:12 united in their ***o*** against Paul and
2 Corinthians
12:20 competitive ***o***, backstabbing,
Galatians
5:20 competitive ***o***, conflict,
1 Thessalonians
2:2 spite of a lot of ***o***, although we had
Hebrews
12:3 who endured such ***o*** from sinners so

OPPRESS

Exodus
22:21 Don't mistreat or ***o*** an immigrant,
23:9 Don't ***o*** an immigrant. You know what
Leviticus
19:13 You must not ***o*** your neighbors or rob
Deuteronomy
23:16 seems good to them. Don't ***o*** them.
1 Chronicles
16:21 didn't let anyone ***o*** them. God
Job
10:3 to you that you ***o*** me, that you
Psalms
89:22 No enemy will ***o*** him; no wicked person
105:14 didn't let anyone ***o*** them. God
119:122 Please don't let the arrogant ***o*** me.
119:134 the people who ***o*** me so I can keep
Proverbs
22:22 are poor. Don't ***o*** the needy in the
22:23 press the life out of those who ***o*** them.
28:3 Poor people who ***o*** the needy are rain
Isaiah
3:5 The people will ***o*** each other, each one
29:2 but I will ***o*** Ariel. There will be
58:3 you want, and ***o*** all your workers.
Jeremiah
22:17 practice cruelty; you ***o*** your subjects.
30:16 ravaged; all who ***o*** you will go into
Ezekiel
22:7 In you they ***o*** immigrants and
45:8 will no longer ***o*** my people. They
Amos
2:13 So now I will ***o*** you, just like a cart
6:14 and they will ***o*** you from Lebo-hama
Micah
2:2 them away. They ***o*** a householder and
Zechariah
7:10 Don't ***o*** the widow, the orphan, the
Malachi
3:5 wages as well as ***o*** the widow and the

OPPRESSED

Genesis
15:13 they will be ***o*** slaves for four
Exodus
1:12 more they were ***o***, the more they
3:7 seen my people ***o*** in Egypt. I've
Numbers
20:15 The Egyptians ***o*** us as they had
Deuteronomy
28:29 be constantly ***o*** and taken
Judges
2:18 under those who ***o*** and crushed them.
4:3 chariots and had ***o*** the Israelites
10:12 and Maonites ***o*** you and you cried
1 Samuel
10:18 power of all the kingdoms that ***o*** you.
12:3 Have I ever ***o*** or mistreated
12:4 You haven't ***o*** or mistreated us, and
12:8 the Egyptians ***o*** them. So your
2 Samuel
21:5 who opposed and ***o*** us, who planned
2 Kings
13:22 King Hazael had ***o*** Israel throughout
Nehemiah
5:15 their servants ***o*** the people. But
Psalms
7:4 with evil or ***o*** a foe for no
9:9 place for the ***o***—a safe place in
10:18 orphan and the ***o***, so that people
12:5 the poor are ***o***, because of the
42:9 to walk around, sad, ***o*** by enemies?"
43:2 have to walk around, sad, ***o*** by enemies?
74:21 Don't let the ***o*** live in shame. No, let
102:1 [A prayer of an ***o*** person, when weak and
103:6 does justice for all who are ***o***.
106:42 Their enemies ***o*** them, and they were
119:78 because they ***o*** me with lies—
146:7 to people who are ***o***, who gives bread
Ecclesiastes
4:1 the tears of the ***o***—and they have no
5:8 the poor being ***o*** or the violation

OPPRESSED [cont.]

Isaiah
1:17 justice: help the ***o***; defend the
14:32 founded Zion; the ***o*** among God's
52:4 Assyria has ***o*** them without
53:7 He was ***o*** and tormented, but didn't open
Jeremiah
22:3 right; rescue the ***o*** from the power of
50:33 of Israel were ***o***, together with
Ezekiel
22:29 robbery. They've ***o*** the poor and
Zechariah
10:2 but they are ***o*** because there is
Luke
4:18 sight to the blind, to liberate the ***o***,
Acts
10:38 healing everyone ***o*** by the devil
Hebrews
11:37 and goats, needy, ***o***, and mistreated.

OPPRESSION

Exodus
4:31 had seen their ***o***, they bowed down
Deuteronomy
26:7 saw our misery, our trouble, and our ***o***.
Job
35:9 because of heavy ***o***; shout under the
36:15 affliction, opens their ears through ***o***.
Psalms
44:24 face, forgetting our suffering and ***o***?
55:11 lives inside it; ***o*** and fraud never
72:14 their lives from ***o*** and violence;
73:8 their privileged positions they plan ***o***.
107:39 brought down by ***o***, trouble, and
Proverbs
1:27 when distress and ***o*** overcome you.
Ecclesiastes
7:7 ***O*** turns the wise into fools; a bribe
Isaiah
30:12 word and trust in ***o*** and cunning and
54:14 stay far from ***o*** because you won't
59:13 our God, planning ***o*** and revolt,
Jeremiah
6:6 for there's nothing but ***o*** in her midst.
Ezekiel
45:9 from violence and ***o***. Establish
Acts
7:34 clearly seen the ***o*** my people ave

ORACLE

Numbers
24:3 his address: "The ***o*** of Balaam, Beor's
Proverbs
16:10 speech is like an ***o***; in a judgment,
Isaiah
13:1 An ***o*** about Babylon, which Isaiah,
14:28 This ***o*** came in the year of King Ahaz's
15:1 An ***o*** about Moab. Ar was devastated in a
17:1 An ***o*** about Damascus. Look! Damascus is
19:1 An ***o*** about Egypt. Look! The LORD is
21:1 An ***o*** about the wilderness near the sea.
21:11 An ***o*** about Dumah. Someone is calling to
21:13 An ***o*** about the desert. In the woods, in
22:1 An ***o*** about the Valley of Vision. What
23:1 An ***o*** about Tyre. Wail, ships of
30:6 An ***o*** about the beasts in the arid
Nahum
1:1 An ***o*** about Nineveh: the scroll
Habakkuk
1:1 The ***o*** that Habakkuk the prophet saw

ORDER

Genesis
23:10 publicly in ***o*** that the Hittites
25:13 to their birth ***o***: Nebaioth,
31:18 in Paddan-aram in ***o*** to return to his
31:53 Nahor will keep ***o*** between us." So
43:33 their exact birth ***o***, and the men
50:20 good from it, in ***o*** to save the lives
Exodus
1:17 Egyptian king's ***o***. Instead, they
1:22 Pharaoh gave an ***o*** to all his
3:8 the Egyptians in ***o*** to take them out
9:16 this reason: in ***o*** to show you my
19:9 a thick cloud in ***o*** that the people
24:12 that I've written in ***o*** to teach them."
28:10 other stone, in the ***o*** of their birth.
29:1 make them holy in ***o*** to serve me as
Leviticus
9:7 offering in ***o*** to make
11:47 in ***o*** to distinguish between the unclean
13:54 the priest will ***o*** that the infected
13:59 any skin item, in ***o*** to declare
14:4 the priest will ***o*** that two birds—wild
16:10 the LORD in ***o*** to make
17:9 entrance in ***o*** to offer it to
26:45 the nations, in ***o*** to be their God;
Numbers
2:17 march in the same ***o*** as they camp:
5:15 recognition in ***o*** to recognize
6:2 be a nazirite in ***o*** to be dedicated
8:12 to the LORD in ***o*** to seek
8:21 for them in ***o*** to cleanse them.
10:28 This was the ***o*** of departure of the
22:23 the donkey in ***o*** to turn him back
Deuteronomy
4:36 hear his voice in ***o*** to discipline
4:38 in ***o*** to remove larger and stronger
8:16 experienced, in ***o*** to humble and
8:18 be prosperous in ***o*** to establish the
17:16 to Egypt in ***o*** to acquire more
19:6 was not in ***o*** because the
26:19 in ***o*** to set you high above all the
30:6 all your being in ***o*** that you may live.
31:12 your cities—in ***o*** that they hear
Joshua
8:8 word. Indeed, I have given you an ***o***!"
8:29 Joshua gave an ***o***, and they took
10:27 Joshua gave an ***o***, and they took
Judges
2:6 property in ***o*** to take
Ruth
4:5 the dead man, in ***o*** to preserve the
1 Samuel
5:10 God to us? In ***o*** to kill us and
15:15 and cattle in ***o*** to sacrifice them
15:21 the ban—but in ***o*** to sacrifice them
23:26 and his soldiers in ***o*** to capture them.
2 Samuel
2:26 long before you ***o*** the troops to
4:12 So David gave the ***o*** to his servants,

13:28 am giving you the ***o***. Be brave and
14:8 and I will issue an ***o*** in your behalf."
19:29 said to him. "I ***o*** you and Ziba to

1 Kings
2:27 priesthood in ***o*** to fulfill the
3:4 at Gibeon in ***o*** to sacrifice
3:9 mind in ***o*** to govern your
5:6 Now give the ***o*** and have the cedars of
5:17 finest quality in ***o*** to lay the
10:24 with Solomon in ***o*** to hear his God-
15:22 Asa issued an ***o*** to every Judean
18:33 put the wood in ***o***, butchered the

2 Kings
15:19 silver kikkars in ***o*** to become his
20:1 your affairs in ***o*** because you are
23:3 all his being in ***o*** to fulfill the
23:35 taxed the land in ***o*** to meet Pharaoh's
24:2 against Judah in ***o*** to destroy it.

1 Chronicles
12:17 intentions in ***o*** to help me, then
13:5 to Lebo-hamath in ***o*** to bring up God's
16:4 LORD's chest in ***o*** to remember, to
17:19 great thing in ***o*** to make all these
21:6 Joab disagreed with the king's ***o***.
21:18 the Jebusite in ***o*** to set up an
22:5 beyond compare in ***o*** to win fame and
25:2 and prophesied by ***o*** of the king.
25:6 God's temple, by ***o*** of the king. As

2 Chronicles
3:3 structures in ***o*** to build the
7:13 is no rain or I ***o*** the locusts to
9:23 with Solomon in ***o*** to hear his God-
11:22 as his successor in ***o*** to make him king.
18:2 were with him in ***o*** to persuade him
31:5 As soon as the ***o*** was issued, the
31:21 the commands, in ***o*** to seek his God,
32:18 them, in ***o*** to capture the
32:31 abandoned him in ***o*** to test him and
34:31 all his being, in ***o*** to fulfill the
35:6 your relatives in ***o*** to celebrate

Ezra
4:19 I issued an ***o***; they searched and
4:21 issue an ***o*** to stop these
4:22 to carry out this ***o***! Why should
6:12 to change this ***o*** or to destroy
8:30 weighed out, in ***o*** to bring them to
10:7 An ***o*** was then circulated throughout
10:9 because of this ***o*** and because of

Nehemiah
5:3 and our houses in ***o*** to get grain
5:4 and vineyards in ***o*** to pay the king's
5:7 large assembly in ***o*** to deal with them.
8:13 the scribe in ***o*** to study the
12:27 they lived in ***o*** to bring them to
13:22 the gates in ***o*** to keep the

Esther
1:10 he gave an ***o*** to Mehuman,
1:19 send out a royal ***o*** and have it
1:20 When the ***o*** becomes public through the
2:8 When the king's ***o*** and his new law
3:3 Why don't you obey the king's ***o***?"
4:3 where the king's ***o*** and his new law
8:5 to call back the ***o***—the order that pu
8:10 and sealed the ***o*** with the king's
8:17 the king's ***o*** and his law
9:1 that the king's ***o*** and his law were

Job
28:25 In ***o*** to weigh the wind, to prepare a
38:34 Can you issue an ***o*** to the clouds so

Psalms
8:2 of your foes, in ***o*** to stop vengeful
50:4 to the earth in ***o*** to judge his
59:1 the house in ***o*** to kill him.] Oh,
91:11 Because he will ***o*** his messengers to
92:15 in ***o*** to proclaim: "The LORD is
101:8 in the land in ***o*** to eliminate all
104:14 human farming in ***o*** to get food from
107:20 God gave the ***o*** and healed them; he

Proverbs
28:2 a person with understanding brings ***o***.
31:9 Speak out in ***o*** to judge with

Isaiah
38:1 your affairs in ***o*** because you are

Jeremiah
29:6 find husbands in ***o*** that they too may
31:36 If the created ***o*** should vanish from my

Lamentations
1:15 feast for me—in ***o*** to crush my young

Ezekiel
21:4 In ***o*** to cut off the righteous and
24:8 In ***o*** to arouse wrath, to guarantee
33:15 regulations in ***o*** not to sin—they w
39:12 will bury them in ***o*** to cleanse the
43:26 the altar in ***o*** to purify it and
44:25 In ***o*** to avoid uncleanness, they must

Daniel
3:7 because of this ***o*** as soon as they
3:28 the king's ***o***, sacrificing
6:16 the king gave the ***o***, and they brought
11:35 too will fall in ***o*** that they might

Amos
1:13 in Gilead in ***o*** to possess more
6:11 LORD is giving an ***o***; he will shatter
8:6 in ***o*** to buy the needy for silver and
9:3 I will give an ***o*** to the sea
9:4 I will give an ***o*** to the sword, and

Habakkuk
2:15 out your wrath in ***o*** to see them naked.

Zechariah
11:10 chopped it up in ***o*** to break my
13:4 put on a shaggy coat in ***o*** to deceive.
13:7 the shepherd in ***o*** to scatter the

Matthew
2:13 search for the child in ***o*** to kill him."
12:14 out and met in ***o*** to find a way to
14:28 if it's you, ***o*** me to come to you
16:1 came to Jesus. In ***o*** to test him they
19:3 came to him. In ***o*** to test him, they
20:25 high-ranking officials ***o*** them around.
24:24 and wonders in ***o*** to deceive, if
27:64 Therefore, ***o*** the grave to be sealed

Mark
4:21 in a lamp in ***o*** to put it under a
7:9 commandment in ***o*** to establish
10:42 high-ranking officials ***o*** them around.
13:22 and wonders in ***o*** to deceive, if
14:55 against Jesus in ***o*** to put him to

Luke
8:31 with him not to ***o*** them to go back

John
6:28 must we do in ***o*** to accomplish
10:31 picked up stones in ***o*** to stone him.
11:11 but I am going in ***o*** to wake him up."

ORDER [cont.]

19:28 completed, in ***o*** to fulfill the
Acts
6:2 of God's word in ***o*** to serve tables.
7:43 that you made in ***o*** to worship them.
10:25 and fell at his feet in ***o*** to honor him.
12:19 left Judea in ***o*** to spend some
16:35 jailer with the ***o*** "Release those
19:35 manager brought ***o*** to the crowd and
20:30 the word in ***o*** to lure followers
21:35 the soldiers in ***o*** to protect him
Romans
3:19 under the Law, in ***o*** to shut every
6:6 with him in ***o*** to get rid of the
11:11 their failure, in ***o*** to make Israel
11:32 disobedience, in ***o*** to have mercy on
14:1 faith—but not in ***o*** to argue about
15:2 for their good in ***o*** to build them up.
15:8 God's truth, in ***o*** to confirm the
16:26 the Gentiles in ***o*** to lead to their
1 Corinthians
14:40 be done with dignity and in proper ***o***.
15:23 in the right ***o***: Christ, the
2 Corinthians
8:8 I'm not giving an ***o***, but by mentioning
11:8 a salary from them in ***o*** to serve you!
11:32 city of Damascus in ***o*** to capture me,
13:11 Put things in ***o***, respond to my
Philippians
1:11 Jesus Christ, in ***o*** to give glory and
Colossians
1:25 to me for you, in ***o*** to complete God's
1 Thessalonians
5:27 authority, I ***o*** all of you to
1 Timothy
6:14 Obey this ***o*** without fault or failure
Titus
2:14 himself for us in ***o*** to rescue us from
3:14 to doing good in ***o*** to meet pressing
Hebrews
2:9 was made lower in ***o*** than the angels
2:17 to God, in ***o*** to wipe away the
3:5 as a servant in ***o*** to affirm the
5:1 their sake, in ***o*** to offer gifts
5:6 according to the ***o*** of Melchizedek.
6:20 according to the ***o*** of Melchizedek.
7:11 according to the ***o*** of Melchizedek
7:17 according to the ***o*** of Melchizedek.
9:10 imposed until the time of the new ***o***.
9:14 dead works in ***o*** to serve the
11:28 of blood, in ***o*** that the
1 Peter
3:18 He did this in ***o*** to bring you into
Revelation
2:10 into prison in ***o*** to test you. You
8:3 of incense, in ***o*** to offer it on

ORDERED

Matthew
8:18 saw the crowd, he ***o*** his disciples to
12:16 But he ***o*** them not to spread the word
14:19 He ***o*** the crowds to sit down on the
16:20 Then he ***o*** the disciples not to tell
18:25 back, the master ***o*** that he should be
21:6 went and did just as Jesus had ***o*** them.
Mark
3:12 But he strictly ***o*** them not to reveal
6:27 So he ***o*** a guard to bring John's head.
8:30 Jesus ***o*** them not to tell anyone about
9:9 the mountain, he ***o*** them not to tell
Luke
1:3 write a carefully ***o*** account for you,
5:14 Jesus ***o*** him not to tell anyone.
8:56 with joy, but he ***o*** them to tell no

ORDERS

Genesis
12:20 gave his men ***o*** concerning Abram,
42:25 Then Joseph gave ***o*** to fill their bags
50:16 Your father gave ***o*** before he died,
Exodus
6:13 king, giving them ***o*** to let the
Numbers
3:39 Aaron enrolled by ***o*** from the LORD,
Joshua
1:10 Then Joshua gave ***o*** to the people's
1:11 the camp and give ***o*** to the people.
18:8 go, Joshua gave ***o*** to those going to
Judges
21:10 there with these ***o***: "Go kill all the
1 Samuel
21:2 king has given me ***o***, but he
2 Samuel
5:25 followed God's ***o*** exactly, and they
18:5 The king gave ***o*** to Joab, Abishai, and
2 Kings
22:3 the LORD's temple with the following ***o***:
1 Chronicles
14:16 followed God's ***o*** exactly, and they
22:2 David gave ***o*** to gather the immigrants
2 Chronicles
2:1 Solomon gave ***o*** to build a temple for
Ezra
8:36 the king's ***o*** to the royal
Nehemiah
13:9 Then I gave ***o*** that the rooms be
13:19 Sabbath, I gave ***o*** that the doors
Esther
1:22 He sent written ***o*** to all the king's
3:12 ordered. The ***o*** were for the
Job
36:32 in his palms and ***o*** it to its target.
Psalms
44:4 king, the one who ***o*** salvation for
57:3 He sends ***o*** from heaven and saves me,
78:23 God gave ***o*** to the skies above, opened
Jeremiah
34:22 about to issue ***o***, declares the
37:21 Zedekiah gave ***o*** that Jeremiah be
39:11 gave ***o*** concerning
Amos
9:9 Look, I am giving ***o***, and I will shake
Matthew
8:26 got up and gave ***o*** to the winds and
Mark
4:39 got up and gave ***o*** to the wind, and
5:43 gave them strict ***o*** that no one
7:36 the people strict ***o*** not to tell
8:15 gave them strict ***o***: "Watch out and
Luke
8:24 got up and gave ***o*** to the wind and
9:21 gave them strict ***o*** not to tell this
John
11:57 had given ***o*** that anyone who

Acts
23:31 Following their *o*, the soldiers took
Hebrews
11:23 they weren't afraid of the king's *o*.

ORPHAN

Exodus
22:22 Don't treat any widow or *o* badly
Deuteronomy
24:17 an immigrant or *o*. Don't take a
Job
5:15 he rescues the *o* from the sword of
6:27 gamble over an *o*, barter away your
24:9 The *o* is stolen from the breast; the
31:17 alone, and not shared any with an *o*
31:18 I raised the *o* as a father, and
Psalms
10:18 justice for the *o* and the
82:3 the lowly and the *o*; maintain the
Isaiah
1:17 defend the *o*; plead for the
1:23 don't defend the *o*, and the widow's
Jeremiah
5:28 the plight of the *o*, reluctant to
7:6 of the immigrant, *o*, or widow; if you
22:3 the refugee, the *o*, and the widow.
Hosea
14:3 hands. In you the *o* finds compassion."
Zechariah
7:10 the widow, the *o*, the stranger,
Malachi
3:5 the widow and the *o*, and against

ORPHANS

→ ORPHANS AND THE WIDOWS, ORPHANS AND WIDOWS

Exodus
22:24 be widows, and your children will be *o*.
Deuteronomy
26:13 immigrants, the *o*, and the widows—
27:19 of immigrants, *o*, or widows." All
Job
29:12 who cried out, the *o* who lacked help.
31:21 hand against the *o*, when I saw that
Psalms
68:5 Father of *o* and defender of widows is
94:6 widows and immigrants; they murder *o*,
109:9 children become *o*; let his wife
109:12 to him; let no one have mercy on his *o*.
Proverbs
23:10 marker; don't invade the fields of *o*,
Isaiah
10:2 widows their loot; to steal from *o*!
John
14:18 leave you as *o*. I will come to

ORPHANS AND THE WIDOWS

Dt 16:11; 16:14; 24:19, 20, 21; 26:12, 13

ORPHANS AND WIDOWS

Dt 10:18; 14:29; Ps 146:9; Is 9:17; Eze 22:7; Jas 1:27

OSTRICHES

Job
30:29 to jackals, a companion to young *o*.
Isaiah
13:21 filled with owls. ***O*** will live there,
34:13 a dwelling for jackals, a home for *o*.
43:20 the jackals and *o*, will honor me,
Lamentations
4:3 people has become cruel, like desert *o*.
Micah
1:8 like the jackals, and mourn like the *o*.

OTHNIEL

Joshua
15:17 So ***O*** son of Kenaz, Caleb's brother

OUTER

Exodus
26:4 the edge of the *o* curtain in the
36:11 the edge of the *o* curtain of the
36:12 loops on the *o* curtain that was
36:19 dyed red and an *o* covering of
Numbers
4:25 its covering, the *o* covering of fine
Joshua
2:15 house was on the *o* side of the city
2 Samuel
20:15 stood against the *o* wall. All of
1 Kings
6:29 temple—inner and *o* rooms
7:9 and from the *o* boundary to the
2 Chronicles
33:14 rebuilt the *o* wall of David's
Esther
6:4 just entered the *o* courtyard of the
Job
26:14 are only the *o* fringe of his
41:13 can remove his *o* garment; who can
Ezekiel
10:5 as far as the *o* courtyard. It was
40:5 Now there was an *o* wall that went all
41:9 The width of the *o* wall of the side
42:1 me north to the *o* courtyard and
43:13 wide, with an *o* curb measuring
44:1 me back to the *o* sanctuary gate
46:21 he took me to the *o* courtyard, and he
47:2 outside to the *o* East Gate, where
Mark
14:68 outside into the *o* courtyard. A
Acts
12:13 knocked at the *o* gate, a female

OTHER GODS

Ex 20:3; 23:13; Dt 4:28; 5:7; 6:14; 7:4; 8:19; 11:16, 28; 13:2, 6, 13; 17:3; 18:20; 28:14, 36, 64; 29:26; 30:17; 31:18, 20; 32:39; Josh 23:16; 24:2, 16; Jdg 2:12; 2:17, 19; 10:13; 1Sa 8:8; 26:19; 1Ki 9:6; 9:9; 11:4, 10; 14:9; 2Ki 5:17; 17:7, 35, 37, 38; 22:17; 1Ch 16:25; 2Ch 2:5; 7:19, 22; 28:25; 34:25; Ps 95:3; 96:4; 97:9; 135:5; 138:1; Is 36:18; Jer 1:16; 7:6, 9; 11:10; 13:10; 16:11, 13; 19:4, 13; 22:9; 25:6; 32:29; 35:15; 44:3, 5, 8, 15, 21, 23; Hos 3:1; 4:12; 13:4

OUTSIDE

Genesis
15:5 he brought Abram *o* and said, "Look
19:16 took him out, and left him *o* the city.
39:12 his garment in her hands and ran *o*.
Exodus
12:46 any of the meat *o* the house, and

21:19 to walk around ***o*** with a cane, then
26:35 Place the table ***o*** the veil, and set the
27:21 the meeting tent, ***o*** the veil that
29:14 with a fire ***o*** the camp. It is a
33:7 and pitched it ***o*** the camp, far
40:22 north side of the dwelling, ***o*** the veil.

Leviticus
4:12 a clean location ***o*** the camp, to the
4:21 take the bull ***o*** the camp and burn
6:11 take the ashes ***o*** the camp to a
8:17 burned with fire ***o*** the camp just as
9:11 flesh and hide with fire ***o*** the camp.
10:4 the sanctuary to a place ***o*** the camp."
10:5 tunics to a place ***o*** the camp, just as
13:46 They must live alone ***o*** the camp.
14:3 he will go ***o*** the camp. If the priest
16:27 will be taken ***o*** the camp. Their
17:3 ox, sheep, or goat inside or ***o*** the camp
18:9 into the same household as you or ***o*** it.
24:3 meeting tent but ***o*** the inner curtain

Numbers
5:3 must send them ***o*** the camp so that
15:35 community should stone him ***o*** the camp.
19:3 he will take it ***o*** the camp and
31:13 community went to meet them ***o*** the camp.
31:19 You will remain ***o*** the camp for seven
35:26 killer ever goes ***o*** the boundaries of

Deuteronomy
3:5 and crossbars. ***O*** the towns there
23:12 latrines must be ***o*** the camp. You
24:11 You must wait ***o***. The person to whom
25:5 wife must not go ***o*** the family and
32:25 ***O***, in the streets, the sword will

Joshua
2:19 Those who go ***o*** the doors of your house
6:23 out and let them stay ***o*** Israel's camp.
7:5 chased them from ***o*** the gate as far

Judges
12:9 to those ***o*** his clan, and
19:23 of the house went ***o*** and said to them,
19:25 wife and sent her ***o*** to them. They
19:27 house and went ***o*** to set out on his

1 Samuel
9:26 the two of them, he and Samuel, went ***o***.

1 Kings
6:6 niches around the ***o*** of the temple so
8:8 visible from ***o***. They are still
21:10 Then take Naboth ***o*** and stone him so
21:13 took Naboth ***o*** the town and

2 Kings
10:24 eighty soldiers ***o*** and told them,
16:18 royal entrance ***o*** the LORD's
23:4 king burned them ***o*** Jerusalem in the
23:6 the Kidron Valley ***o*** Jerusalem. There

1 Chronicles
26:29 over Israel ***o*** the temple as

2 Chronicles
5:9 visible from ***o***. They are still
24:8 made and placed ***o*** the gate of the
32:3 up the springs ***o*** the city, and
32:5 another wall ***o*** the first,
33:15 in Jerusalem, dumping them ***o*** the city.

Ezra
10:13 continue to stand ***o***. Nor can this

Nehemiah
11:16 in charge of the ***o*** work on God's
13:20 spent the night ***o*** Jerusalem.

Job
31:34 me; I was quiet and didn't venture ***o***.

Psalms
84:10 prefer to stand ***o*** the entrance of

Proverbs
5:16 fountains flood ***o***, streams of water
24:27 Get your ***o*** work done; make preparations

Song of Songs
2:9 he stands now, ***o*** our wall, peering

Jeremiah
22:19 dragging him ***o*** the gates of

Ezekiel
7:15 ***O***, the sword! Inside, plague and
40:40 ***O***, two pairs of tables flanked the
41:25 tree stood ***o***, in front of the
43:21 place of the temple ***o*** of the sanctuary.
46:2 will come in from ***o*** by way of the
47:2 and around the ***o*** to the outer East

Hosea
7:1 breaks in; a group of bandits raid ***o***.

Matthew
8:12 will be thrown ***o*** into the
23:25 You clean the ***o*** of the cup and
23:27 beautiful on the ***o***. But inside they

Mark
1:45 He remained ***o*** in deserted
3:31 They stood ***o*** and sent word to
3:32 and sisters are ***o*** looking for you."
4:11 to those who are ***o*** everything comes
7:15 Nothing ***o*** of a person can enter and
11:4 tied to a gate ***o*** on the street,
11:19 and his disciples went ***o*** the city.
14:68 And he went ***o*** into the outer

Luke
1:10 were praying ***o*** during this hour
8:20 are standing ***o***, wanting to see
11:39 clean the ***o*** of the cup and
11:40 one who made the ***o*** also make the
13:25 you will stand ***o*** and knock on the
13:33 a prophet to be killed ***o*** of Jerusalem.'

John
18:16 Peter stood ***o*** near the gate.
20:11 Mary stood ***o*** near the tomb, crying. As

Acts
4:15 them to wait ***o***, the council
5:13 No one from ***o*** the church dared to join
5:34 the men be taken ***o*** for a few moments.
12:16 Peter remained ***o***, knocking at the
14:13 was located just ***o*** the city, brought
16:13 Sabbath we went ***o*** the city gate to
16:30 He led them ***o*** and asked, "Honorable

Romans
2:12 who have sinned ***o*** the Law will also
4:7 whose actions ***o*** the Law are

1 Corinthians
5:10 people in the ***o*** world by any
6:18 do is committed ***o*** the body, except
9:21 I act like I'm ***o*** the Law to those who

2 Corinthians
4:16 down on the ***o***, the person that
6:14 that which is ***o*** the Law? What
10:15 other people do ***o*** of our

1 Timothy
3:7 with those ***o*** the church so
Hebrews
13:11 and their bodies are burned ***o*** the camp.
13:12 also suffered ***o*** the city gate to
13:13 let's go to him ***o*** the camp, bearing
James
1:1 who are scattered ***o*** the land of
1 Peter
3:3 beautiful on the ***o***, with stylish
Revelation
11:2 measure the court ***o*** the temple. Leave
14:20 was trampled ***o*** the city, and the
22:15 ***O*** are the dogs, the drug users and

OVERCOME

1 Samuel
17:9 slaves, but if I ***o*** him and kill him,
Psalms
106:14 They were ***o*** with craving in the desert;
Proverbs
1:27 when distress and oppression ***o*** you.
Jeremiah
22:23 you when you are ***o*** in pain, like
Ezekiel
30:4 trembling will ***o*** Cush, when the
30:9 Anguish will ***o*** them on Egypt's
Mark
4:41 ***O*** with awe, they said to each other,
7:37 People were ***o*** with wonder, saying, "He
9:15 ran to greet him, ***o*** with excitement.
12:17 His reply left them ***o*** with wonder.
16:8 ***O*** with terror and dread, they fled from
Luke
1:12 angel, he was startled and ***o*** with fear.
5:9 with him were ***o*** with amazement
8:37 because they were ***o*** with fear. So he
9:32 him were almost ***o*** by sleep, but
9:34 the cloud, they were ***o*** with awe.
22:45 He found them asleep, ***o*** by grief.
Acts
5:17 the Sadducees, was ***o*** with jealousy.
12:14 She was so ***o*** with joy when she
13:45 crowds, they were ***o*** with jealousy.
2 Peter
2:20 it again and are ***o*** by it, they are

OWNED

Genesis
14:12 and everything he ***o***, and took off.
24:2 of everything he ***o***, "Put your hand
25:5 Abraham gave everything he ***o*** to Isaac
30:43 very rich: he ***o*** large flocks,
31:1 our father ***o*** and from it he
46:1 up everything he ***o*** and traveled to
46:34 servants have ***o*** livestock since
1 Samuel
25:2 important man and ***o*** three thousand
1 Chronicles
2:22 of Jair, who ***o*** twenty-three towns
Esther
8:1 enemy of the Jews ***o***. Mordecai himself
9:10 lay a hand on anything their enemies ***o***.
Job
1:3 and ***o*** seven thousand sheep, three
Psalms
105:21 house and ruler over everything he ***o***,
Matthew
13:46 and sold all that he ***o*** and bought it.
Luke
13:6 parable: "A man ***o*** a fig tree
Acts
4:34 them. Those who ***o*** properties or
4:37 He ***o*** a field, sold it, brought the
28:7 prominent person, ***o*** a large estate in

OWNER

Exodus
21:20 When a slave ***o*** hits a male or female
22:5 of its crop, the ***o*** must pay them
22:15 If the ***o*** was present, no payment needs
Leviticus
6:5 give it to the ***o*** on the day you
25:50 with their ***o*** the time from the
27:24 is the original ***o*** of the family
Deuteronomy
22:1 You must return the animal to its ***o***.
22:2 If the ***o*** doesn't live nearby, or you
Judges
19:22 the old man, the ***o*** of the house,
19:23 The ***o*** of the house went outside and
1 Kings
16:24 the previous ***o*** of the hill of
Isaiah
1:3 An ox knows its ***o***, and a donkey its
Matthew
20:8 evening came, the ***o*** of the vineyard
21:40 When the ***o*** of the vineyard comes, what
Mark
12:9 So what will the ***o*** of the vineyard do?
14:14 say to the ***o*** of the house,
Luke
13:25 Once the ***o*** of the house gets up and
20:13 The ***o*** of the vineyard said, 'What
20:15 What will the ***o*** of the vineyard
22:11 Say to the ***o*** of the house, 'The teacher
2 Timothy
2:21 be useful to the ***o*** of the mansion

OX

Exodus
20:17 female servant, ***o***, donkey, or
21:28 When an ***o*** gores a man or a woman to
22:1 someone steals an ***o*** or a sheep and
23:4 upon your enemy's ***o*** or donkey that
Leviticus
4:10 removed from the ***o*** for the communal
7:23 eat the fat of an ***o***, sheep, or goat.
9:4 an ***o*** and a ram as a well-being
17:3 who slaughters an ***o***, sheep, or goat
22:23 however, offer an ***o*** or sheep that is
27:26 oldest. Whether ***o*** or sheep, it
Numbers
7:3 chiefs, and an ***o*** for every chief.
15:11 be done with each ***o***, each ram, or for
22:4 around us, as an ***o*** eats up the grass
Deuteronomy
5:21 female servant, ***o***, donkey, or
14:4 you are allowed to eat: ***o***, sheep, goat,
15:19 your oldest male ***o*** and don't shear
22:1 Israelite's ***o*** or sheep
25:4 Don't muzzle an ***o*** while it is threshing
1 Samuel
12:3 stolen someone's ***o***? Have I ever

14:34 must bring their ***o*** or sheep, and
2 Samuel
6:13 sacrificed an ***o*** and a fatling
Nehemiah
5:18 One ***o***, six choice sheep, and birds
Job
6:5 over grass or an ***o*** bellow over its
24:3 donkey, take a widow's ***o*** as collateral,
39:9 Will the wild ***o*** agree to be your slave,
Psalms
29:6 Sirion jump around like a young wild ***o***.
69:31 the LORD than an ***o***, more pleasing
92:10 strong as a wild ***o***. I'm soaked in
Proverbs
7:22 her, like an ***o*** to the slaughter,
Isaiah
1:3 An ***o*** knows its owner, and a donkey its
11:7 and a lion will eat straw like an ***o***.
32:20 sending out ***o*** and donkey to
65:25 straw like the ***o***, but the snake—it
66:3 who slaughters an ***o*** kills a person;
Luke
13:15 untie your ***o*** or donkey from
14:5 your child or ***o*** fell into a ditch
1 Corinthians
9:9 not muzzle the ***o*** when it is
1 Timothy
5:18 a muzzle on an ***o*** while it treads
Revelation
4:7 was like an ***o***. The third living

OXEN

Genesis
49:6 whenever they wished, they maimed ***o***.
49:22 bull by a spring, who strides with ***o***.
Exodus
20:24 sheep, and your ***o***. I will come to
22:1 pay back five ***o*** for the one ox or
24:5 and slaughter ***o*** as well-being
Numbers
7:3 wagons and twelve ***o***—a wagon for every
22:40 Balak sacrificed ***o*** and sheep and sent
31:28 whether human, ***o***, donkeys, or
Deuteronomy
5:14 servants, your ***o*** or donkeys or any
17:1 LORD your God any ***o*** or sheep that
18:3 sacrifices of ***o*** or sheep: they
Judges
6:4 alive, not even sheep, ***o***, or donkeys.
1 Samuel
11:7 He took two ***o***, cut them into pieces,
15:3 and infants, ***o*** and sheep, camels
22:19 and infants, even ***o***, donkeys, and
2 Samuel
6:6 grabbed it because the ***o*** had stumbled.
24:22 is best. Here are ***o*** for the entirely
24:24 floor and the ***o*** for fifty shekels
1 Kings
1:9 prepared lamb, ***o***, and fattened
1:19 quantities of ***o***, fattened cattle,
1:25 down and prepared ***o***, fattened cattle,
7:25 rested on twelve ***o*** with their backs
8:5 chest sacrificed countless sheep and ***o***.
8:63 thousand ***o*** and one hundred
19:19 twelve yoke of ***o*** before him.
1 Chronicles
12:40 mules, and ***o***. There was an
13:9 grabbed it because the ***o*** had stumbled.
21:23 even provide the ***o*** for the entirely
2 Chronicles
4:4 rested on twelve ***o*** with their backs
5:6 chest sacrificed countless sheep and ***o***.
7:5 thousand ***o*** and one hundred
15:11 seven hundred ***o*** and seven
18:2 many sheep and ***o*** for Jehoshaphat
Job
1:3 hundred pairs of ***o***, five hundred
1:14 and said: "The ***o*** were plowing, and
42:12 thousand yoke of ***o***, and one thousand
Psalms
22:21 horns of the wild ***o*** you have answered
Proverbs
14:4 When there are no ***o***, the stall is
Isaiah
30:24 The ***o*** and donkeys that are working the
34:7 Wild ***o*** will fall with them, steers with
Jeremiah
51:23 crush farmers and ***o***. With you I will
Amos
6:12 plow the sea with ***o***? But you have
Matthew
22:4 butchered the ***o*** and the fattened
Luke
14:19 five teams of ***o***, and I'm going to
1 Corinthians
9:9 is threshing. Is God worried about ***o***,

Pp

PADDAN-ARAM

Genesis
25:20 sister of Laban the Aramean, from ***P***.

PAID

Genesis
4:15 Cain will be ***p*** back seven times.
29:15 Tell me what you would like to be ***p***."
30:16 me because I've ***p*** for you with my
Exodus
30:16 of the compensation ***p*** for your lives.
Deuteronomy
15:18 double that of a ***p*** worker. The LORD
Judges
1:7 table, so God has ***p*** me back exactly
9:56 Thus God ***p*** back Abimelech for the evil
9:57 God also ***p*** back the people of Shechem
2 Samuel
16:8 The LORD has ***p*** you back for all the
2 Kings
12:11 supervisors then ***p*** money to those
12:15 the money and ***p*** the workers,
2 Chronicles
25:9 hundred kikkars I ***p*** for the Israelite
26:8 The Meunites ***p*** taxes to Uzziah whose
27:5 Ammonites. They ***p*** him one hundred
34:10 who in turn ***p*** it to those
Ezra
4:20 and taxes and dues were ***p*** to them.
6:4 The cost will be ***p*** from the royal
6:8 cost is to be ***p*** to these people,
Isaiah
40:2 penalty has been ***p***, that she has
Ezekiel
16:31 in every square, you refused to be ***p***.
Jonah
1:3 for Tarshish. He ***p*** the fare and went
Matthew
5:26 until you've ***p*** the very last
18:30 into prison until he ***p*** back his debt.
18:34 until he had ***p*** the whole debt.
26:15 to you?" They ***p*** him thirty pieces
Luke
6:34 sinners expecting to be ***p*** back in full.
12:59 until you have ***p*** the very last
Romans
1:27 and they were ***p*** back with the
3:24 of a ransom that was ***p*** by Christ Jesus.
11:35 him a gift and has been ***p*** back by him?
1 Corinthians
6:20 been bought and ***p*** for, so honor God
7:23 were bought and ***p*** for. Don't become
2 Corinthians
5:10 person can be ***p*** back for the
1 Timothy
5:17 well should be ***p*** double,
Hebrews
7:9 received a tenth, ***p*** a tenth through
7:10 body when Abraham ***p*** the tenth to

PAIN

Genesis
3:16 very painful; in ***p*** you will bear
3:17 of you; in ***p*** you will eat from
5:29 work, from the ***p*** in our hands,
34:25 were still in ***p***, two of Jacob's
1 Kings
8:38 their own ***p*** and spread out
1 Chronicles
4:9 him Jabez, saying, "I bore him in ***p***."
4:10 not to cause me ***p***." And God granted
2 Chronicles
6:29 their own ***p*** and suffering and
21:19 die in horrible ***p***. His people
Job
2:13 they saw that he was in excruciating ***p***.
6:10 in persistent ***p***; for I've not
14:22 only feel the ***p*** of their body,
16:6 If I speak, my ***p*** is not eased; if I
21:17 with its fury inflicting ***p*** on them?
30:17 my bones; my gnawing ***p*** won't rest.
33:19 be disciplined by ***p*** while in bed,
Psalms
32:10 The ***p*** of the wicked is severe, but
38:17 to falling, and my ***p*** is always with me.
39:2 but it did no good. My ***p*** got worse.
69:26 talk about the ***p*** of those you've
69:29 I'm full of ***p***. Let your
73:4 They suffer no ***p***; their bodies are fit
Proverbs
14:13 The heart feels ***p*** even in laughter, and
23:35 hit, I feel no ***p***; though beaten
Ecclesiastes
1:18 the more knowledge, the more ***p***.
2:23 their days are ***p***, and their work
11:10 heart, banish ***p*** from your body,
Isaiah
14:3 you rest from ***p*** and trouble and
17:11 on a day of sickness and incurable ***p***.
Jeremiah
4:19 my suffering! My ***p*** is unbearable; my
6:24 overwhelms us, ***p*** like that of a
13:21 allies? Won't ***p*** grip you like
15:18 am I always in ***p***? Why is my wound
19:8 pass by it will be shocked at its ***p***.
22:23 are overcome in ***p***, like that of
30:6 man bent over in ***p***, as if he's in
30:7 of unspeakable ***p*** for my people
30:15 relief from your ***p***? Your wound is
45:3 sorrow to my ***p***. I'm worn out
49:24 by anguish and ***p***, like a woman in
50:43 overwhelms him, ***p*** like that of a

51:8 medicine for her ***p***; perhaps she will
Micah
4:9 perished, so that ***p*** has seized you
Matthew
4:24 those in ***p***, those possessed
Luke
16:25 being comforted and you are in great ***p***.
John
16:21 birth, she has ***p*** because her time
Romans
9:2 sadness and constant ***p*** in my heart.
2 Corinthians
6:10 as going through ***p*** but always happy, as
Philippians
1:17 to cause me more ***p*** while I'm in
1 Timothy
6:10 with a lot of ***p*** because they made
1 Peter
2:19 should endure ***p*** through suffering
Revelation
11:10 had brought such ***p*** to those who live
12:2 was in labor, in ***p*** from giving birth.
14:10 will suffer the ***p*** of fire and
16:10 bit their tongues because of their ***p***,
18:7 ways, give her ***p*** and grief. In her
18:10 are afraid of the ***p*** she suffers, and
18:15 they fear the ***p*** she suffers. They
21:4 crying, or ***p*** anymore, for the

PALACE

Exodus
7:23 went back to his ***p***. He wasn't
8:3 get into your ***p***, into your
2 Samuel
5:11 and carpenters to build David a ***p***.
7:2 living in a cedar ***p***, but God's chest
20:3 arrived at his ***p*** in Jerusalem, the
1 Kings
3:1 his royal ***p***, the LORD's
7:1 as for Solomon's ***p***, it took thirteen
9:10 the LORD's temple and the royal ***p***.
10:4 wise Solomon was, the ***p*** he had built,
10:12 and for the royal ***p*** as well as lyres
10:17 these in the Forest of Lebanon ***P***.
10:21 Forest of Lebanon ***P*** were made of pure
13:7 with me to the ***p*** and refresh
13:8 gave me half your ***p***, I wouldn't go
14:26 and the royal ***p***. He took
14:27 protected the entrance to the royal ***p***.
15:18 and the royal ***p***, and he gave them
16:9 who had charge over the ***p*** at Tirzah.
16:18 fort of the royal ***p*** and burned it
18:3 in charge of the ***p*** affairs. (Obadiah
20:6 will search your ***p*** and the houses of
20:43 king went to his ***p*** at Samaria,
21:1 was next to the ***p*** of King Ahab of
21:2 right next to my ***p***. In exchange for
21:4 Ahab went to his ***p***, irritated and
22:39 the ivory ***p*** he built and all
2 Kings
14:14 treasuries of the ***p***, along with some
18:15 LORD's temple and in the ***p*** treasuries.
18:18 who was the ***p*** administrator,
20:15 they seen in your ***p***?" Isaiah asked.
1 Chronicles
14:1 and carpenters to build David a ***p***.
17:1 settled into his ***p***, he said to the
2 Chronicles
2:1 and to build a royal ***p*** for himself.
8:11 David's City to a ***p*** he had built for
9:3 wise Solomon was, the ***p*** he had built,
25:24 treasuries of the ***p***, along with some
33:24 against him and killed him in his ***p***.
Ezra
4:14 salary from the ***p***, and since it is
Esther
1:5 in the walled garden of the royal ***p***.
2:13 her from the women's house to the ***p***.
Psalms
45:15 enter the king's ***p***, they are led in
144:12 be like pillars carved to decorate a ***p***;
Song of Songs
1:5 like the curtains of Solomon's ***p***.
Isaiah
32:14 The ***p*** will be deserted, the crowded
36:3 who was the ***p*** administrator,
36:22 who was the ***p*** administrator,
37:2 sent Eliakim the ***p*** administrator,
39:7 eunuchs in the king of Babylon's ***p***."
Jeremiah
22:1 Go down to the ***p*** of the king of
22:4 the gates of this ***p*** will come kings
26:10 up from the royal ***p*** to the LORD's
27:18 and in the royal ***p*** of Judah and
30:18 its ruins and the ***p*** in its rightful
32:2 quarters in the ***p*** of Judah's king.
36:12 in the royal ***p***. There he found
37:17 secretly in the ***p***: "Is there a word
38:7 in the royal ***p***, got word that
39:8 down the royal ***p*** and the houses of
43:9 of Pharaoh's ***p*** in Tahpanhes
52:13 temple, the royal ***p***, all the houses
Lamentations
2:7 he handed Zion's ***p*** walls over to
Daniel
1:4 in the king's ***p***. Ashpenaz was to
4:4 was safe in my house, content in my ***p***,
4:29 on the roof of the royal ***p*** in Babylon.
5:5 of the king's ***p*** wall in the light
6:18 went home to his ***p*** and fasted
Nahum
2:6 of the rivers are opened; the ***p*** melts.
Mark
15:16 courtyard of the ***p*** known as the
Luke
11:21 guards his own ***p***, his possessions
John
18:28 Roman governor's ***p***. It was early in
18:33 back into the ***p***. He summoned
19:4 came out of the ***p*** again and said to
Acts
7:10 ruler over Egypt and over his whole ***p***.
23:35 Paul be kept in custody in Herod's ***p***.

PALACES

2 Chronicles
36:19 fire to all its ***p***, destroying
Psalms
45:8 coming from ivory ***p*** entertains you.
Proverbs
30:28 in your hand, but they are in kings' ***p***.
Isaiah
13:22 in its luxurious ***p***. Babylon's time
23:13 stripped its ***p***, and made it a

34:13 grow up in its ***p***, weeds and
Jeremiah
33:4 this city and the ***p*** of the kings of
Lamentations
2:5 devoured all her ***p***; he made ruins of
Hosea
8:14 maker, and built ***p***; and Judah has
Amos
1:4 it will devour the ***p*** of Ben-hadad.
1:7 wall of Gaza; it will devour Gaza's ***p***.
1:10 wall of Tyre; it will devour their ***p***.
1:14 will devour its ***p***, with a war cry
2:2 will devour the ***p*** of Kerioth. Moab
2:5 and it will devour the ***p*** of Jerusalem.
3:9 it to the ***p*** of Ashdod and to
3:10 up violence and robbery in their ***p***.
3:11 places, and your ***p*** will be robbed.
Matthew
11:8 wear refined clothes are in royal ***p***.
Luke
7:25 and live in luxury are in royal ***p***.

PALM
Exodus
15:27 water and seventy ***p*** trees. They
Leviticus
14:15 log of oil and pour it into his left ***p***.
23:40 majestic trees, ***p*** branches,
Numbers
24:6 Like ***p*** groves that stretch out, like
33:9 water and seventy ***p*** trees and they
Deuteronomy
34:3 Jericho Valley, ***P*** City
Judges
1:16 of Judah from ***P*** City into the
3:13 Israel, and took possession of ***P*** City.
4:5 under Deborah's ***p*** tree between
1 Kings
6:29 winged creatures, ***p*** trees, and
7:36 lions, and ***p*** trees with
2 Chronicles
3:5 decorated them with ***p*** trees and chains.
28:15 them to Jericho, ***P*** City, near their
Nehemiah
8:15 olive, myrtle, ***p***, and other leafy
Psalms
92:12 spring up like a ***p*** tree. They will
Song of Songs
7:7 resembles a date ***p*** and your breasts
7:8 I will climb the ***p*** tree; I will hold
Isaiah
9:14 head and tail, ***p*** branch and reed
19:15 head nor tail, ***p*** branch nor reed
40:12 the waters in the ***p*** of a hand or
62:3 a royal turban in the ***p*** of God's hand.
Ezekiel
10:7 and set it in the ***p*** of the one
40:16 The arches were decorated with ***p*** trees.
40:22 porch, and ***p*** decorations had
41:18 creatures and ***p*** trees. The palm
Joel
1:12 Pomegranate, ***p***, and apple
Matthew
21:8 road. Others cut ***p*** branches off the
John
12:13 They took ***p*** branches and went out to
Revelation
7:9 robes and held ***p*** branches in their

PANIC
Exodus
14:24 and threw the Egyptian camp into a ***p***.
15:15 were terrified; ***p*** grabbed hold of
23:27 you meet into a ***p***. I'll make all
Deuteronomy
7:23 them into a huge ***p*** until they are
20:3 be afraid! Don't ***p***! Don't shake in
Joshua
10:10 threw them into a ***p*** before Israel.
Judges
4:15 and army into a ***p*** before Barak;
8:12 and threw the entire army into ***p***.
1 Samuel
5:9 causing a huge ***p***. God struck the
5:11 was a deadly ***p*** throughout the
7:10 into such a ***p*** that they were
14:15 ***P*** broke out in the camp, in the field,
2 Samuel
17:2 throw him into a ***p***. All the troops
Job
22:10 you; sudden dread brings ***p*** to you
Psalms
14:5 will be in utter ***p*** because God is
53:5 will be in utter ***p*** because God will
Jeremiah
6:24 of them and are ***p***-stricken; distress
20:3 from Pashhur to ***P*** Lurks Everywhere.
20:4 going to strike ***p*** into your heart
20:10 whispering—"***P*** Lurks Everywhere!-
30:5 I hear screams of ***p*** and terror; no
46:5 don't turn back. ***P*** lurks at every
49:24 to flee, but ***p*** overwhelms her.
49:29 shout as you go: "***P*** Lurks Everywhere!"
50:2 shamed, Marduk is ***p***-stricken. Her
50:43 of them and is ***p***-stricken; distress
Ezekiel
7:7 draws near. On the hills ***p***, not glory.
Zechariah
14:13 that day, a great ***p*** brought on by the

PARABLE
Ezekiel
17:2 a riddle and a ***p*** about the house
24:3 Compose a ***p*** for the rebels' household
Matthew
13:18 Consider then the ***p*** of the farmer
13:24 told them another ***p***: "The kingdom of
13:31 He told another ***p*** to them: "The kingdom of heaven
13:33 told them another ***p***: "The kingdom of
13:36 to us the ***p*** of the weeds in
21:33 to another ***p***. There was a
21:45 heard the ***p***, they knew Jesus
24:32 Learn this ***p*** from the fig tree. After
Mark
3:23 to them in a ***p***: "How can Satan
4:13 understand this ***p***? Then how will
4:30 kingdom? What ***p*** can I use to
12:12 he had told the ***p*** against them. But
13:28 Learn this ***p*** from the fig tree. After
Luke
5:36 he told them a ***p***. "No one tears a
8:4 after another, he spoke to them in a ***p***:

8:9 disciples asked him what this **p** meant.
8:11 The **p** means this: the seed is God's
12:16 he told them a **p**: "A certain rich
12:41 you telling this **p** for us or for
13:6 Jesus told this **p**: "A man owned a fig
14:7 seats at the table, he told them a **p**.
15:3 Jesus told them this **p**
18:1 telling them a **p** about their need
18:9 Jesus told this **p** to certain people who
19:11 told them another **p** because he was
20:9 the people this **p**. "A certain man
20:19 he had told this **p** against them. But
21:29 Jesus told them a **p**. "Look at the fig

PARABLES

Hosea
12:10 visions, and through them I uttered **p**.
Habakkuk
2:6 everyone tell **p** about him or
Matthew
13:3 things to them in **p**: "A farmer went
13:10 Why do you use **p** when you speak to
13:13 to the crowds in **p**: although they
13:34 to the crowds in **p**, and he spoke to
13:35 I'll speak in **p**; I'll declare
13:53 Jesus finished these **p**, he departed.
22:1 Jesus responded by speaking again in **p**
Mark
4:2 things to them in **p**. While teaching
4:10 with the Twelve, asked him about the **p**.
4:11 who are outside everything comes in **p**.
4:13 Then how will you understand all the **p**?
4:33 With many such **p** he continued to give
4:34 to them only in **p**, then explained
12:1 spoke to them in **p**. "A man planted a
Luke
8:10 everyone else in **p** so that when they

PARALYZED

Psalms
90:7 wrath; we are **p** with fear on
Jeremiah
47:3 children, so **p** are they with
Matthew
4:24 those who were **p**, and he healed
8:6 his back at home, **p**, and his
9:2 him a man who was **p**, lying on a cot.
9:6 the man who was **p**—"Get up, take you
15:30 those who were **p**, blind, injured,
15:31 talking, and the **p** cured, and the
Mark
2:3 were bringing to him a man who was **p**.
2:4 the mat on which the **p** man was lying.
2:9 say to a **p** person, 'Your
2:10 sins"—he said to the man who was **p**,
Luke
5:18 a man who was **p**, lying on a cot.
5:24 the man who was **p**, "I say to you,
John
5:3 sick, blind, lame, and **p** sat there.
Acts
8:7 and many who were **p** or crippled were
9:33 Aeneas who was **p** and had been

PARENTS

Exodus
10:6 houses. Your **p** and even your
Deuteronomy
21:18 when the **p** discipline him,
24:16 **P** shouldn't be executed because of what
Joshua
4:21 will ask their **p**, 'What about
1 Samuel
22:4 So David left his **p** with the Moabite
2 Samuel
19:37 the grave of my **p**. But here is your
2 Kings
14:6 LORD commanded, **P** shouldn't be
17:41 same thing their **p** did. And that's
2 Chronicles
25:4 LORD commanded, **P** shouldn't be
Esther
2:7 look at. When her **p** died, Mordecai
Proverbs
17:6 and the glory of children is their **p**.
28:7 who befriend gluttons shame their **p**.
Isaiah
38:19 as I do today. **P** will tell
Jeremiah
6:21 people, and both **p** and children will
13:14 one of them, even **p** and children,
31:29 grapes eaten by **p** leave a bitter
47:3 chariots' wheels, **p** abandon children,
Ezekiel
5:10 Therefore, **p** among you will eat their
18:2 of Israel: "When **p** eat unripe
18:11 even though his **p** didn't do any of
Daniel
9:6 our leaders, our **p**, and to all the
9:8 leaders, and our **p** who sinned
9:16 wrongdoing of our **p**, both Jerusalem
Malachi
3:17 them just as **p** spare a child who
4:6 the hearts of the **p** to the children
Matthew
10:21 will defy their **p** and have them
Mark
5:40 the child's **p** and his disciples
13:12 up against their **p** and have them
Luke
2:21 passed, Jesus' **p** circumcised him
2:27 Meanwhile, Jesus' **p** brought the child
2:41 Each year his **p** went to Jerusalem for
2:43 in Jerusalem. His **p** didn't know it.
2:48 When his **p** saw him, they were shocked.
8:56 Her **p** were beside themselves with joy,
18:29 sisters, **p**, or children
21:16 betrayed by your **p**, brothers and
John
9:2 he was born blind, this man or his **p**?"
9:3 he nor his **p**. This happened so
9:18 his sight until they called for his **p**.
9:20 His **p** answered, "We know he is our son.
9:22 His **p** said this because they feared the
9:23 That's why his **p** said, "He's old
Acts
7:20 three months his **p** cared for him in
Romans
1:30 and they are disobedient to their **p**.
2 Corinthians
12:14 save up for their **p** but parents for
Galatians
4:2 guardians until the date set by the **p**.

Ephesians
6:1 obey your ***p*** in the Lord,
6:4 As for ***p***, don't provoke your children
Colossians
3:20 obey your ***p*** in everything,
3:21 ***P***, don't provoke your children in a
1 Timothy
5:4 and repay their ***p***, because this
2 Timothy
3:2 to their ***p***. They will be
Hebrews
11:23 was hidden by his ***p*** for three months
12:9 we had human ***p*** who disciplined
12:10 Our human ***p*** disciplined us for a little
1 John
2:13 ***P***, I'm writing to you because you have
2:14 know the Father. ***P***, I write to you

PARTS

Psalms
139:13 my innermost ***p***; you knit me
139:15 together in the deep ***p*** of the earth.
Proverbs
20:27 the LORD, searching all the inmost ***p***.
20:30 evil; beatings cleanse the inner ***p***.
Romans
12:4 We have many ***p*** in one body, but the
1 Corinthians
6:15 your bodies are ***p*** of Christ? So
12:12 unit and has many ***p***; and all the
12:18 each one of the ***p*** in the body just
12:27 the body of Christ and ***p*** of each other.
Ephesians
3:6 be coheirs and ***p*** of the same body,
4:25 because we are ***p*** of each other in
5:30 because we are ***p*** of his body
Colossians
3:5 put to death the ***p*** of your life that
Revelation
16:19 split into three ***p***, and the cities

PARTY

Genesis
40:20 and he gave a ***p*** for all of his
Exodus
21:22 then the guilty ***p*** will be fined
32:18 The sound of ***p*** songs is what I
Leviticus
20:5 the guilty ***p*** and anyone with
Numbers
5:7 more, and give it to the injured ***p***.
5:8 which the guilty ***p*** himself is
Deuteronomy
25:2 If the guilty ***p*** is to be beaten, the
1 Samuel
25:36 he was throwing a ***p*** fit for a king in
30:8 this raiding ***p***? Will I catch
1 Kings
8:32 the guilty ***p***, repaying them
2 Kings
13:21 saw a raiding ***p***. They threw the
2 Chronicles
6:23 the guilty ***p***, repaying them
22:1 the raiding ***p*** that had invaded
Ezra
6:11 of the guilty ***p***, and the guilty
Ecclesiastes
7:2 than to a house ***p***, because that is
Isaiah
5:12 They ***p*** with lyre and harp, tambourine,
22:2 roaring city, you ***p*** town? Your dead
Jeremiah
16:16 I will send a ***p*** of hunters to
Daniel
5:1 threw a huge ***p*** for a thousand of
5:2 be brought to the ***p*** so that the king,
Matthew
14:6 Herod's birthday ***p*** Herodias'
22:2 who prepared a wedding ***p*** for his son.
22:10 good. The wedding ***p*** was full of

PASS

Genesis
18:3 so kind, don't just ***p*** by your servant.
Exodus
12:12 I'll ***p*** through the land of Egypt that
12:13 the blood, I'll ***p*** over you. No
12:23 the LORD will ***p*** over that door.
33:19 all my goodness ***p*** in front of you,
Leviticus
25:46 You can ***p*** them on to your children as
26:6 land, and no sword will ***p*** through it.
Numbers
20:17 land. We won't ***p*** through any field
21:22 Let us ***p*** through your land. We won't
Deuteronomy
2:27 Please let us ***p*** through your land. We
2:28 can drink. Let us ***p*** through on foot—
2:30 willing to let us ***p*** through his land
Judges
1:36 from the Akrabbim ***p***, from Sela, and
8:13 from the battle by the Heres ***P***.
11:17 allow us to ***p*** through your
1 Samuel
1:23 the LORD bring to ***p*** what you've
3:12 I will bring to ***p*** against Eli
13:23 had marched out to the ***p*** at Michmash.
14:4 in the ***p*** where Jonathan
2 Samuel
23:5 and brings my every desire to ***p***.
1 Chronicles
28:8 good land and ***p*** it on to your
2 Chronicles
19:6 careful when you ***p*** judgment. You
20:16 through the Ziz ***p***, meet them at the
Nehemiah
2:14 the animal on which I was riding to ***p***,
Esther
4:2 law for anyone to ***p*** through it
Job
16:22 years will surely ***p***, and then I'll
19:8 path so I can't ***p*** and put darkness
34:20 are shaken and ***p*** away. The mighty
Psalms
39:13 again before I ***p*** away and am gone.
49:12 just like the animals that ***p*** away.
49:20 just like the animals that ***p*** away.
84:6 As they ***p*** through the Baca Valley, they
89:41 All those who ***p*** by plunder him. He's
102:26 These things will ***p*** away, but you will
Proverbs
9:15 invites those who ***p*** by on the path,

Ecclesiastes
5:16 they must ***p*** on just as they
6:12 life, which will ***p*** away like a
Isaiah
2:18 the idols will completely ***p*** away
8:21 They will ***p*** through the land, dejected
10:29 crossed at the ***p***: "We'll camp at
28:19 morning it will ***p***, by day and by
34:10 no one will ever ***p*** through it again.
43:2 When you ***p*** through the waters, I will
44:12 If he didn't drink water, he'd ***p*** out.
51:10 the sea, a road for the redeemed to ***p***?
62:10 ***P*** through, pass through the gates;
Jeremiah
2:35 sinned, I will ***p*** judgment against
5:22 that it can't ***p***? Though its waves
18:16 on it. All who ***p*** by are shocked
19:8 horrible; all who ***p*** by it will be
22:8 many nations will ***p*** by this city and
35:7 in the fertile land you ***p*** through.'
49:17 All who ***p*** by will be
50:13 ruin. All who ***p*** by Babylon will
51:43 no one lives or dares to ***p*** through.
Lamentations
1:12 to all you who ***p*** by? Look around:
2:15 All who ***p*** by on the road clap their
2:16 waiting for. We've seen it come to ***p***."
4:21 But this cup will ***p*** over to you too.
Ezekiel
5:14 you, in the sight of all who ***p*** by.
14:17 the sword to ***p*** through and
20:31 your children ***p*** through the fire,
46:21 and he had me ***p*** through its four
Daniel
2:44 rule will never ***p*** to another
4:16 Seven periods of time will ***p*** over it.
7:14 it will never ***p*** away!
11:4 heaven. It won't ***p*** to his
Joel
3:17 again will strangers ***p*** through it.
Amos
5:17 because I will ***p*** through your
6:7 who lounged at the table will ***p*** away.
Micah
1:11 ***P*** by (for your sake), inhabitants of
2:13 break out and ***p*** through the gate;
Zephaniah
2:15 All those who ***p*** through her hiss
3:6 No one will ***p*** through. Their
Zechariah
9:8 will no longer ***p*** through against
10:11 They will ***p*** through the sea of distress
Matthew
24:34 generation won't ***p*** away until all
24:35 and earth will ***p*** away, but my
Mark
6:48 on the lake. He intended to ***p*** by them.
7:13 to you, which you ***p*** on to others. And
13:30 generation won't ***p*** away until all
13:31 and earth will ***p*** away, but my
Luke
16:17 and earth to ***p*** away than for the
19:4 see Jesus, who was about to ***p*** that way.
21:32 generation won't ***p*** away until
21:33 and earth will ***p*** away, but my
Acts
14:22 kingdom, we must ***p*** through many
Romans
1:11 to see you to ***p*** along some
1 Corinthians
6:5 is wise enough to ***p*** judgment between
2 Corinthians
13:7 want to appear to ***p*** the test but so
2 Timothy
2:2 witnesses and ***p*** them on to
Hebrews
1:11 They will ***p*** away, but you remain. They
2 Peter
3:10 the heavens will ***p*** away with a
Revelation
6:10 wait before you ***p*** judgment? How

PASSED

Genesis
15:17 a fiery flame ***p*** between the
Exodus
2:23 A long time ***p***, and the Egyptian king
12:27 for the LORD ***p*** over the houses
34:6 The LORD ***p*** in front of him and
Leviticus
25:30 a full year has ***p***, the house in the
Deuteronomy
2:8 So we ***p*** through the territory of our
29:16 Egypt and how we ***p*** right through the
Joshua
15:3 of Akrabbim, ***p*** on to Zin, and
18:9 the men went and ***p*** through the land
19:13 From there it ***p*** on the east side,
23:1 A long time ***p***. The LORD had given rest to Israel
24:17 all the nations through which we've ***p***.
Judges
2:10 generation had ***p*** away, another
3:26 waiting and had ***p*** the carved stones
8:3 said this, their anger against him ***p***.
9:25 everyone who ***p*** by them on the
11:29 on Jephthah. He ***p*** through Gilead
11:39 two months had ***p***, she returned to
1 Samuel
7:2 Now a long time ***p***—a total of twenty
2 Samuel
2:15 counted as they ***p*** by: twelve for
15:23 all the troops ***p*** by on the Olive
16:1 When David had ***p*** a short distance
18:23 by way of the plain, and ***p*** the Cushite.
1 Kings
18:29 As noon ***p*** they went crazy with their
20:39 When the king ***p*** by, the prophet called
2 Kings
4:8 so whenever he ***p*** by, he would stop
6:30 And as he ***p*** by along the
8:3 seven years had ***p***, the woman
Job
15:19 given and no stranger ***p*** in their midst.
17:11 My days have ***p***; my goals are
37:21 sky; the wind has ***p*** and cleared away
Psalms
109:7 the sentence is ***p***, let him be found
Isaiah
10:28 against Aiath, ***p*** to Migron. At
51:20 Your children ***p*** out; they lay at the
57:1 of evil the righteous one ***p*** away.
Jeremiah
34:19 the people who ***p*** through the

Ezekiel
16:8 When I ***p*** by you, I realized that you
36:34 it seemed a wasteland to all who ***p*** by.
Daniel
10:3 meat nor wine ***p*** my lips, and I
11:13 some years have ***p***, he will attack
Jonah
2:3 waves and rushing water ***p*** over me.
Mark
1:16 As Jesus ***p*** alongside the Galilee Sea,
Luke
2:21 eight days had ***p***, Jesus' parents
4:30 But he ***p*** through the crowd and went on
John
5:24 judgment but has ***p*** from death into
Acts
5:15 could fall on some of them as he ***p*** by.
12:10 They ***p*** the first and second guards and
21:3 Cyprus, but ***p*** by it on our
24:27 two years had ***p***, Felix was
25:13 several days had ***p***, King Agrippa and
27:4 we sailed off. We ***p*** Cyprus, using the
27:9 had already ***p***. Paul warned them,
1 Corinthians
15:3 I ***p*** on to you as most important what I
1 Timothy
4:7 myths that are ***p*** down from the
Hebrews
4:14 high priest who ***p*** through the
9:11 have happened. He ***p*** through the
Jude
1:4 Judgment was ***p*** against them a
Revelation
9:12 first horror has ***p***. Look! Two
21:1 former earth had ***p*** away, and the sea
21:4 for the former things have ***p*** away."

PASSOVER → EAT THE PASSOVER, EAT THE PASSOVER MEAL, FESTIVAL OF UNLEAVENED BREAD, PASSOVER MEAL
Exodus
12:11 in a hurry. It is the ***P*** of the LORD.
12:21 families, and slaughter the ***P*** lamb.
12:27 say, 'It is the ***P*** sacrifice to the
12:43 for the ***P***. No foreigner may
12:48 to observe the ***P*** to the LORD, then
34:25 sacrifice of the ***P*** Festival
Leviticus
23:5 The LORD's ***P*** is on the fourteenth day
Numbers
9:2 keep the ***P*** at its appointed
9:4 the Israelites to keep the ***P***.
9:5 they kept the ***P*** in the Sinai
9:6 to keep the ***P*** on that day. They
9:10 they may still keep the ***P*** to the LORD.
9:11 They will eat the ***P*** lamb with
9:12 will keep the ***P*** according to all
9:13 don't keep the ***P***, those persons
9:14 to keep the ***P*** to the LORD, that
28:16 there will be a ***P*** offering to the
33:3 the day after the ***P*** the Israelites
Deuteronomy
16:1 must perform the ***P*** for the LORD your
Joshua
5:10 They celebrated ***P*** on the evening of
5:11 next day after ***P***, they ate food
2 Kings
23:21 Celebrate a ***P*** to the LORD your
23:22 A ***P*** like this hadn't been celebrated
23:23 rule, this ***P*** was celebrated to
2 Chronicles
30:1 to celebrate the ***P*** of the LORD God
35:1 the LORD's ***P*** in Jerusalem.
35:6 Slaughter the ***P*** lambs and prepare the
Ezra
6:19 the returned exiles celebrated the ***P***.
6:20 slaughtered the ***P*** animals for all
Ezekiel
45:21 Your ***P*** will be on the fourteenth day of
Matthew
26:2 know that the ***P*** is two days from
26:18 to celebrate the ***P*** with my disciples
26:19 instructed them. They prepared the ***P***.
Mark
14:1 two days before ***P*** and the Festival
14:12 Bread, when the ***P*** lamb was
Luke
2:41 went to Jerusalem for the ***P*** Festival.
22:1 which is called ***P***, was approaching.
22:7 arrived, when the ***P*** had to be
22:15 to eat this ***P*** with you before I
John
2:13 for the Jewish ***P***, and Jesus went
2:23 Jerusalem for the ***P*** Festival, many
6:4 nearly time for ***P***, the Jewish
11:55 for the Jewish ***P***, and many people
12:1 Six days before ***P***, Jesus came to
13:1 the Festival of ***P***, Jesus knew that
18:28 could eat the ***P***, the Jewish
18:39 for you at ***P***. Do you want me
19:14 Day for the ***P***. Pilate said to
Acts
12:4 to charge him publicly after the ***P***.
1 Corinthians
5:7 bread. Christ our ***P*** lamb has been
Hebrews
11:28 faith he kept the ***P*** and the

PASSOVER MEAL
2Ch 30:18; Ezr 6:21; Mt 26:17; Mk 14:12; 14:14, 16; Lk 22:8; 22:11, 13

PAST
Exodus
21:29 people in the ***p*** and its owner had
21:36 for goring in the ***p*** and its owner
Deuteronomy
4:32 into days long ***p***, before your time-
32:7 the days long ***p***; consider the
Joshua
11:10 head of all those kingdoms in the ***p***.
20:5 and hadn't been an enemy in the ***p***.
24:20 of having done you good in the ***p***."
1 Samuel
20:22 The arrow is ***p*** you,' then run
20:37 yelled to him, "Isn't the arrow ***p*** you?"
2 Samuel
5:2 In the ***p***, when Saul ruled over us, you
15:18 servants marched ***p*** him, as did all
20:13 Joab marched ***p*** in pursuit of
2 Kings
13:5 at home, just as they had in the ***p***.
19:25 it in the distant ***p***! Now I have made

1 Chronicles
11:2 In the **p**, even when Saul ruled over
16:36 forever in the **p** to forever
Nehemiah
2:13 the Valley Gate **p** the Dragon's
12:37 to the wall, **p** the house of
12:38 along the wall **p** the Tower of the
12:39 **p** the Gate of Ephraim and over the
Esther
1:13 had decided about cases in the **p**.
4:11 to the king for the **p** thirty days."
Job
9:11 him; he glides **p**, and I can't
11:16 will remember it as water that flows **p**.
Psalms
44:1 you did in their days, in days long **p**.
77:5 about days long **p**; I remember years
77:11 your wondrous acts from times long **p**.
79:8 the iniquities of **p** generations; let
90:2 forever in the **p** to forever in the
90:4 like yesterday **p**, like a short
143:5 the days long **p**; I meditate on
Proverbs
8:22 way, before his deeds long in the **p**.
Ecclesiastes
1:11 of things in the **p**, nor of things to
Song of Songs
2:11 the winter is **p**; the rains have
Isaiah
37:26 it in the distant **p**! Now I have made
42:9 announced in the **p**—look—they've
43:9 to us the **p** events? Let them
48:3 **P** things I announced long ago; from my
48:8 known; as in ages **p** your ears are
51:9 Awake as in times **p**, generations long
58:12 of generations **p** you will restore.
61:4 places deserted in generations **p**.
65:16 God called Amen. **P** troubles will be
65:17 and a new earth: **p** events won't be
Jeremiah
8:20 The harvest is **p**, the summer has
Lamentations
1:7 from days long **p**. When her people
Zechariah
7:5 month for these **p** seventy years,
Luke
13:7 fig tree for the **p** three years, and
Acts
14:16 In the **p**, he permitted every nation to
17:30 things in times **p**, but now directs
19:18 came, confessing their **p** practices.
20:16 decided to sail **p** Ephesus so that
Romans
15:4 written in the **p** was written for
Hebrews
1:1 In the **p**, God spoke through the
11:2 The elders in the **p** were approved
11:11 was barren and **p** the age for
1 Peter
3:20 In the **p**, these spirits were
2 Peter
1:9 they were cleansed from their **p** sins.

PASTURE

Genesis
24:63 to inspect the **p**, and while
29:7 flock, and then go, put them out to **p**."
2 Samuel
7:8 took you from the **p**, from following
1 Chronicles
4:39 the valley, to find **p** for their flocks.
4:40 found fertile **p**, and the land was
4:41 because there was **p** there for their
13:2 their cities with **p** lands. Let's ask
17:7 took you from the **p**, from following
Psalms
74:1 smolder at the sheep of your own **p**?
79:7 devoured Jacob and demolished his **p**.
79:13 of your very own **p**. We will give you
95:7 the people of his **p**, the sheep in his
100:3 are his people, the sheep of his own **p**.
Song of Songs
1:7 where do you **p** your flock, where
Isaiah
5:17 as if in their **p**; young goats will
32:14 of wild donkeys, and a **p** for flocks—
35:7 habitat, a **p**; grass will
49:9 will graze; their **p** will be on every
65:10 will become a **p** for sheep, and
Jeremiah
6:2 You are like a lovely **p**, Daughter Zion
23:1 the sheep of my **p**, declares the
23:3 back to their **p**, and they will be
25:36 because the LORD is ravaging their **p**.
49:20 off, as their **p** watches in utter
50:7 LORD, the true **p**, the hope of
50:19 Israel to their **p**; theywill graze
50:45 off, as their **p** watches in utter
Lamentations
1:6 that can't find **p**. They have gone
Ezekiel
34:14 feed them in good **p**, and their
34:18 feeding in good **p** or drinking clear
34:31 the flock of my **p**. You are human,
Hosea
4:16 them, as the LORD tends a lamb in a **p**.
Joel
1:18 there is no **p** for them; even
Zephaniah
2:7 Judah; they will **p** beside the sea;
Luke
15:4 in the **p** and search for
John
10:9 will come in and go out and find **p**.

PASTURES

Genesis
47:4 there are no more **p** for your
Numbers
35:2 give the Levites **p** around their
Joshua
21:11 of Judah and the **p** around it.
2 Chronicles
11:14 left their **p** and property to
Psalms
65:12 Even the desert **p** drip with it, and the
83:12 Let's take God's **p** for ourselves."
Isaiah
17:2 They will be **p** for flocks, which
30:23 day, your cattle will graze in large **p**.
Jeremiah
33:12 -will again become **p** for shepherds to
Ezekiel
34:14 in a secure fold and feed on green **p**.

48:15 and for ***p***. The city will be
48:17 There will be ***p*** for the city, three
Joel
1:19 destroyed the ***p*** of the
Amos
1:2 Jerusalem; the ***p*** of the shepherds

PATH

Genesis
18:19 to the LORD's ***p***, being moral and
49:17 a serpent on the ***p***, biting a horse's
Exodus
32:8 abandoned the ***p*** that I commanded.
Numbers
22:24 in the narrow ***p*** between vineyards
Deuteronomy
5:33 walk the precise ***p*** that the LORD
9:12 to turn from the ***p*** I commanded them!
11:28 stray from the ***p*** that I am giving
13:5 you away from the ***p*** the LORD your God
31:29 from the ***p*** I've commanded
Judges
4:9 you. However, the ***p*** you're taking
1 Kings
2:2 following the ***p*** that the whole
Nehemiah
9:19 lightning lit their ***p*** during the night.
Job
16:22 then I'll walk a ***p*** that I won't
18:10 for them; a trap for them along the ***p***.
19:8 He walled up my ***p*** so I can't pass and
24:18 no one walks down a ***p*** in the vineyards.
28:7 A ***p***—no bird of prey knows it; a
28:26 for the rain, a ***p*** for thunderbolts,
29:25 I decided their ***p***, sat as chief. I
34:8 and travels a ***p*** with wrongdoers,
Psalms
25:12 God will teach them which ***p*** to take.
27:11 of my opponents, lead me on a good ***p***.
35:6 Let their ***p*** be dark and slippery—and
36:4 themselves to a ***p*** that is no good.
50:23 the correct ***p*** that I will show
73:18 on a slippery ***p***; you will make
78:50 God blazed a ***p*** for his wrath. He didn't
119:32 I run the same ***p*** as your commandments
139:24 in me, then lead me on the eternal ***p***!
142:3 a trap for me in the ***p*** I'm taking.
Proverbs
1:15 don't go on the ***p*** with them; keep
2:12 you from the evil ***p***, from people who
2:20 stay on the ***p*** of good people,
3:23 safely on your ***p***, and your foot
4:11 I teach you the ***p*** of wisdom. I lead you
4:14 don't walk on the ***p*** of evil people.
4:19 The ***p*** of the wicked is like deep
5:8 Stay on a ***p*** that is far from her; don't
5:21 every person's ***p***, observing all
6:23 corrective teaching is the ***p*** of life.
7:8 and walked down the ***p*** to her house
7:27 Her house is a ***p*** to the grave, going
8:2 heights along the ***p***, at the
8:13 arrogance, the ***p*** of evil and
9:15 pass by on the ***p***, those going
10:29 The ***p*** of the LORD is a refuge for the
11:5 makes their ***p*** straight, but the
11:20 he favors those whose ***p*** is innocent.
12:26 but the ***p*** of the wicked
12:28 but the detestable ***p*** leads to death.
13:6 innocent on the ***p***, but wickedness
14:2 those who take a crooked ***p*** despise him.
14:12 There is a ***p*** that may seem straight to
15:9 LORD detests the ***p*** of the wicked,
15:19 The ***p*** of the lazy is like a hedge of
15:24 life is an upward ***p***, avoiding the
16:7 When a person's ***p*** draws favor from the
16:9 People plan their ***p***, but the LORD
16:17 who protect their ***p*** guard their lives.
16:25 There is a ***p*** that may seem straight to
16:29 and walk them down a ***p*** that isn't good.
16:31 it is found on the ***p*** of righteousness.
20:24 how then can people understand their ***p***?
21:2 Everyone's ***p*** is straight in their own
21:16 wander from the ***p*** of insight will
21:29 the virtuous think about the ***p*** ahead.
22:5 nets are in the ***p*** of the crooked;
23:19 wise! Keep your mind straight on the ***p***.
23:26 to me and let your eyes keep to my ***p***.
26:13 a lion in the ***p***! A lion in the
28:10 onto an evil ***p*** will fall into
29:27 the straight ***p*** is disgusting to
Isaiah
26:7 level; you clear a ***p*** for the righteous.
26:8 In the ***p*** of your justice, LORD, we wait
30:11 way; step off the ***p***; let's have no
40:14 taught him the ***p*** of justice and
41:3 untouched, needing no ***p*** for his feet.
43:16 in the sea and a ***p*** in the mighty
Jeremiah
2:18 So why take the ***p*** to Egypt to drink
7:23 Follow the ***p*** I mark out for
31:21 traveled, the ***p*** you have taken.
Lamentations
3:11 took me from my ***p*** and tore me
Ezekiel
23:31 in your sister's ***p***, so I have put
Hosea
2:6 I will line her ***p*** with thorns; and
Joel
2:7 to their own ***p***; they didn't
2:8 to their own ***p***. Even if they
Amos
2:4 led off the right ***p*** by the same lies
Malachi
2:8 turned from the ***p***. You have caused
3:1 will clear the ***p*** before me;
Matthew
13:4 some fell on the ***p***, and birds came
13:19 is the seed that was sown on the ***p***.
Mark
4:4 some fell on the ***p***; and the birds
4:15 that fell on the ***p***: When the word is
Luke
1:79 death, to guide us on the ***p*** of peace."
8:5 some fell on the ***p*** where it was
8:12 The seed on the ***p*** are those who hear,
John
1:23 Make the Lord's ***p*** straight just as
Romans
4:12 also walk in the ***p*** of faith, like
James
5:20 from the wrong ***p*** will save them

PATH [cont.]

2 Peter
2:15 the straight **p**, they have gone

PATHS

Job
8:13 So are the **p** of all who forget God.
Psalms
17:5 firmly on your **p**; my feet haven't
23:3 me in proper **p** for the sake of
25:4 known to me, LORD; teach me your **p**.
25:10 All the LORD's **p** are loving and
65:11 goodness; your **p** overflow with
119:9 people keep their **p** pure? By guarding
119:15 your precepts and examine all your **p**.
Proverbs
2:8 He protects the **p** of justice and guards
2:13 way of integrity and go on obscure **p**.
2:15 Their **p** are confused; they get lost on
2:18 to death, and her **p** go down to the
3:6 him in all your **p**, and he will keep
3:17 are pleasant; all her **p** are peaceful.
4:26 the way, and all your **p** will be secure.
5:6 way of life. Her **p** wander, but she
7:25 to her ways; don't wander down her **p**.
8:20 of righteousness, on the **p** of justice,
10:9 those on crooked **p** will be found out.
28:6 than to be on crooked **p** and wealthy.
28:18 who go on twisted **p** will fall into
Isaiah
2:3 may walk in God's **p**." Instruction
3:12 leaders mislead you and confuse your **p**.
42:16 guide them in **p** they don't know.
43:19 way in the desert, **p** in the wilderness.
45:13 smooth all his **p**. He will build my
57:2 walk in straight **p** will find rest on
59:8 justice in their **p**. They make their
Jeremiah
2:17 LORD your God, who has directed your **p**?
3:2 the well-traveled **p** and see! Where
3:21 the well-traveled **p**; it's the crying
6:16 for the ancient **p**. Where is the
7:29 the well-traveled **p**. The LORD has
10:23 that we're not able to direct our **p**.
13:16 on the mountain **p** in the evening
14:6 the well-traveled **p**, panting like
18:15 along the ancient **p**. They have taken
31:9 and on smooth **p** so they don't
Lamentations
3:9 He walled in my **p** with stonework; he
Daniel
4:37 truth, all his **p** are justice, and
Hosea
2:6 her, so that she can't find her **p**.
Micah
4:2 may walk in God's **p**!" Instruction
Habakkuk
3:6 bow down; the eternal **p** belong to him.
Zechariah
3:7 will walk in my **p**, if you will keep
Matthew
3:3 way for the Lord; make his **p** straight."
Mark
1:3 way for the Lord; make his **p** straight."
Luke
3:4 way for the Lord; make his **p** straight.
Acts
2:28 have shown me the **p** of life; your
13:10 ways of the Lord into crooked **p**?
Romans
11:33 and they are as hard to track as his **p**!
Hebrews
12:13 Make straight **p** for your feet so that

PATIENCE

Job
21:4 another human; why is my **p** short?
Proverbs
14:29 **P** leads to abundant understanding, but
25:15 be persuaded with **p**, and a tender
Ecclesiastes
7:8 its beginning. **P** is better than
Micah
2:7 Is the LORD's **p** cut short? Are
John
10:24 will you test our **p**? If you are the
Romans
2:4 tolerance, and **p**? Don't you
8:25 we don't see, we wait for it with **p**.
2 Corinthians
6:6 knowledge, **p**, and generosity.
Galatians
5:22 love, joy, peace, **p**, kindness,
Ephesians
4:2 gentleness, and **p**. Accept each
Colossians
1:11 that you endure everything and have **p**;
3:12 kindness, humility, gentleness, and **p**.
1 Timothy
1:16 show his endless **p** to me first of
2 Timothy
3:10 faithfulness, **p**, love, and
4:2 and encourage with **p** and instruction.
Titus
2:2 in respect to their faith, love, and **p**.
Hebrews
6:12 the promises through faith and **p**.
6:15 obtained the promise by showing **p**.
2 Peter
3:15 Consider the **p** of our Lord to be

PATIENT

Exodus
34:6 merciful, very **p**, full of great
Numbers
14:18 The LORD is very **p** and absolutely
Nehemiah
9:17 very **p**, and truly
9:30 You were **p** with them for many years and
Psalms
86:15 you are very **p** and full of
103:8 merciful, very **p**, and full of
145:8 very **p**, and full of
Proverbs
15:18 up conflict, but **p** people calm down
16:32 Better to be **p** than a warrior, and
Joel
2:13 very **p**, full of faithful
Jonah
4:2 God, very **p**, full of faithful
Nahum
1:3 The LORD is very **p** but great in power;

Matthew
18:26 said, 'Please, be ***p*** with me, and I'll
Romans
2:7 immortality based on their ***p*** good work.
3:26 the time of God's ***p*** tolerance. He
15:1 need to be ***p*** with the weakness
1 Corinthians
13:4 Love is ***p***, love is kind, it isn't
1 Thessalonians
5:14 Help the weak. Be ***p*** with everyone.
2 Timothy
2:24 toward all people, able to teach, ***p***,
James
5:7 you must be ***p*** as you wait for
5:10 as an example of ***p*** resolve and
2 Peter
3:9 but he is ***p*** toward you, not

PAUL
Acts
13:9 also known as ***P***
14:19 over. They stoned ***P*** and dragged him
17:22 ***P*** stood up in the middle of the council
18:9 the Lord said to ***P*** in a vision,
24:27 favor to the Jews, he left ***P*** in prison.
28:15 to meet us. When ***P*** saw them, he gave
Romans
1:1 From ***P***, a slave of Christ Jesus,
1 Corinthians
3:5 Apollos? What is ***P***? They are
2 Peter
3:15 and brother ***P*** wrote to you

PAY
Genesis
30:28 so name your price and I will ***p*** it.
30:31 What will I ***p*** you?" Jacob said,
31:41 flock, and you changed my ***p*** ten times.
34:12 like, and I will ***p*** whatever you tell
50:15 us, and wants to ***p*** us back seriously
Exodus
2:9 for me, and I'll ***p*** you for your
21:19 except to ***p*** for the loss of
21:30 the owner has to ***p*** compensation
21:32 the owner will ***p*** thirty silver
21:34 loss. He should ***p*** money to the ox's
22:1 the thief must ***p*** back five oxen
23:21 ***P*** attention to him and do as he says.
30:12 of them should ***p*** compensation for
30:13 is counted should ***p*** a half shekel
30:15 to the LORD to ***p*** compensation for
Leviticus
19:13 withhold a hired laborer's ***p*** overnight.
25:51 Israelite will ***p*** for their
25:52 that and ***p*** for their
27:23 The person must ***p*** the value on that
Numbers
16:15 to the LORD, "***P*** no attention to
20:19 livestock, we'll ***p*** for it. It's a
Deuteronomy
23:18 God's temple to ***p*** a solemn promise
24:15 ***P*** them their salary the same day,
32:41 of justice, I'll ***p*** my enemies back;
32:43 blood; he will ***p*** back his enemies;
Judges
16:5 Then we'll each ***p*** you eleven
20:10 who are going to ***p*** back Gibeah of
2 Samuel
20:17 he answered. "***P*** close attention
1 Kings
5:6 servants. I'll ***p*** your servants
21:2 you prefer, I'll ***p*** you the price in
22:28 Then he added, "***P*** attention, every
2 Kings
3:4 sheep. He would ***p*** Israel's king one
4:7 Sell the oil and ***p*** your debts. You
9:26 swear that I will ***p*** you back on this
10:24 them escape will ***p*** for it with his
12:4 is money people ***p*** to redeem persons
18:14 King Hezekiah to ***p*** him three hundred
22:5 in turn should ***p*** it to those who
22:6 should be used to ***p*** for lumber and
2 Chronicles
2:10 I will ***p*** the woodcutters twenty
7:15 and my ears will ***p*** attention to the
20:15 ***P*** attention, all of Judah, every
34:11 the builders to ***p*** for quarried
Ezra
4:13 they will not ***p*** tribute or tax or
Nehemiah
5:4 in order to ***p*** the king's tax."
10:32 commandment and ***p*** one-third of a shekel each year
Esther
4:7 Haman promised to ***p*** into the royal
Job
13:6 my teaching and ***p*** attention to the
33:1 to me, Job; ***p*** attention to all
34:16 hear this; ***p*** attention to the
35:13 the Almighty doesn't ***p*** attention to it.
Psalms
28:4 ***P*** them back for what they've done! Pay
35:12 They ***p*** me back evil for good, leaving
37:21 borrow and don't ***p*** it back, but the
41:10 me and lift me up so I can ***p*** them back!
49:7 person! It can't ***p*** a life's ransom-pr
79:12 ***P*** back our neighbors seven times over,
94:2 of the earth! ***P*** back the arrogant
Proverbs
6:31 caught, he must ***p*** sevenfold; he
17:16 have money to ***p*** for wisdom? He
19:19 Angry people must ***p*** the penalty; if you
24:12 He makes people ***p*** for their actions.
24:29 did to me. I'll ***p*** them back for
Hosea
2:12 These are my ***p***, which my lovers
5:15 place until they ***p*** for their deeds,
9:1 a prostitute's ***p*** on all threshing
12:14 down on him and ***p*** him back for his
Jonah
2:9 promised, I will ***p***. Deliverance
Zechariah
14:16 go up annually to ***p*** homage to the
14:17 to Jerusalem to ***p*** homage to the
Matthew
10:8 without having to ***p***. Therefore, give
13:9 who has ears should ***p*** attention."
17:24 your teacher ***p*** the temple tax?"
18:17 they still won't ***p*** attention, report
18:28 throat and said, '***P*** me back what you
20:2 the workers to ***p*** them a denarion,
22:17 allow people to ***p*** taxes to Caesar
22:19 the coin used to ***p*** the tax." And

PAY [cont.]

Mark
4:9 has ears to listen should **p** attention!"
6:37 eight months' **p** and give it to
12:14 allow people to **p** taxes to Caesar
14:5 almost a year's **p** and the money
Luke
3:14 anyone, and be satisfied with your **p**."
7:41 enough money to **p** five hundred
8:8 who has ears should **p** attention."
10:7 deserve their **p**. Don't move from
10:35 I return, I will **p** you back for any
14:35 has ears to hear should **p** attention."
20:22 allow people to **p** taxes to Caesar
John
4:36 receiving their **p** and gathering
Acts
21:24 with them, and **p** the cost of
Romans
12:17 Don't **p** back anyone for their evil
12:19 to me; I will **p** it back, says the
13:6 You should also **p** taxes for the same
13:7 So **p** everyone what you owe them.
1 Corinthians
3:10 person needs to **p** attention to the
Galatians
5:10 you will **p** the penalty,
2 Thessalonians
1:6 right for God to **p** back the ones
1:7 and to **p** back you who are having
1:9 They will **p** the penalty of eternal
1 Timothy
5:18 grain, and Workers deserve their **p**.
2 Timothy
4:14 me. The Lord will **p** him back for what
1 Peter
3:9 Don't **p** back evil for evil or insult

PAYMENT

Genesis
31:7 me and changed my **p** ten times. Yet
Exodus
21:2 year, he will go free without any **p**.
22:11 accept that, and no **p** needs to be made.
Leviticus
7:16 of well-being is **p** for a solemn
22:18 it is **p** for a solemn
22:23 be acceptable as **p** for a solemn
Numbers
5:7 Each will make **p** for his guilt,
5:8 to whom the **p** can be made, then
18:31 because it is **p** for your service
22:7 went with the **p** for divination in
Deuteronomy
15:3 allowed to demand **p** from foreigners,
23:18 male prostitute's **p** to the LORD your
1 Chronicles
18:2 Moab, enslaving them and requiring **p**.
18:6 and required **p**. The LORD gave
Job
31:39 its yield without **p** and caused its
Isaiah
40:10 reward with him and his **p** before him.
62:11 arrives, bringing reward and **p**!"
65:7 out to them full **p** for their actions.
Jeremiah
4:18 you. This is your **p** and how bitter it
Ezekiel
16:41 indeed, you will never again give **p**.
29:20 land of Egypt as **p** for his laboring
Matthew
10:8 Therefore, give without demanding **p**.
18:25 that the proceeds should be used as **p**.
Luke
22:5 were delighted and arranged **p** for him.
23:2 opposing the **p** of taxes to
Acts
1:18 a field with the **p** he received for
2 Corinthians
1:22 the Spirit as a down **p** in our hearts.
5:5 us the Spirit as a down **p** for our home.
Ephesians
1:14 is the down **p** on our
1 Timothy
2:6 gave himself as a **p** to set all people
2 Peter
2:13 they will receive **p** for their
2:15 Bosor, who loved the **p** of doing wrong.

PEACE → GOD OF PEACE, GRACE AND PEACE, PEACE FROM GOD, PEACE TO YOU

Genesis
15:15 your ancestors in **p** and be buried
34:21 These men want **p** with us. Let them
Exodus
4:18 Jethro said to Moses, "Go in **p**."
Leviticus
26:6 I will grant **p** in the land so that you
Numbers
6:26 up his face to you and grant you **p**.
Deuteronomy
2:26 Sihon, Heshbon's king, with words of **p**:
Joshua
9:15 Joshua made **p** with them. He made a
10:1 Gibeon had made **p** with Israel and
10:4 it has made **p** with Joshua and
11:19 city that made **p** with the
Judges
3:30 and there was **p** in the land for
4:17 because there was **p** between Hazor's
6:23 said to him, "**P**! Don't be afraid!
6:24 The LORD makes **p**." It still stands
18:6 to them, "Go in **p**. The LORD is
1 Samuel
1:17 Then go in **p**. And may the God
7:14 And there was **p** between Israel
16:4 fear. "Do you come in **p**?" they asked.
20:42 to David, "Go in **p** because the two
24:19 the enemy away in **p**? May the LORD
25:35 Return home in **p**," he told her.
29:7 now, and go in **p**. Don't do
2 Samuel
3:21 At that, David sent Abner off in **p**.
10:19 Israel, they made **p** with Israel and
15:9 Go in **p**," the king said. So Absalom
17:3 seeking; everyone else can be at **p**."
18:28 out to the king, "**P**!" then bowed low
1 Kings
2:13 Are you coming in **p**?" He said, "Yes.
2:33 may the LORD's **p** be on David, his
4:24 the Euphrates. He had **p** on all sides.
5:4 God has given me **p** on every side,
5:12 and Hiram made a covenant and had **p**.
20:18 have come out in **p**, take them alive;

22:44 Jehoshaphat made ***p*** with Israel's king
2 Kings
5:19 to him, "Go in ***p***." But when Naaman
9:17 meet them to ask, 'Do you come in ***p***?'"
20:19 There will be ***p*** and security in
22:20 to your grave in ***p***. You won't
1 Chronicles
19:19 Israel, they made ***p*** with David and
22:9 He'll be a man of ***p***, and I'll give
22:18 He's given you ***p*** on every side.
23:25 given his people ***p*** and has made his
2 Chronicles
14:1 time, the land had ***p*** for ten years.
14:5 so that the kingdom was at ***p*** under him.
14:6 the land was at ***p***, he built
15:15 and the LORD gave them ***p*** on every side.
23:21 the city was at ***p*** now that Athaliah
33:12 Manasseh made ***p*** with the LORD his
34:28 to your grave in ***p***. You won't
Ezra
5:7 was written: To King Darius, all ***p***!
7:12 from the God of heaven. ***P***! And now
9:12 never seek their ***p*** or prosperity.
Job
5:23 of the field will be at ***p*** with you.
22:21 God and be at ***p***; from this
25:2 God; he establishes ***p*** on his heights.
Psalms
4:8 fall asleep in ***p*** because you
29:11 Let the LORD bless his people with ***p***!
34:14 evil! Do good! Seek ***p*** and go after it!
35:27 God wants his servant to be at ***p***."
37:11 land; they will enjoy a surplus of ***p***.
37:37 the future belongs to persons of ***p***.
39:2 silent. I kept my ***p***, but it did no
72:3 mountains bring ***p*** to the people;
72:7 lives, and let ***p*** prosper until the
85:8 because he speaks ***p*** to his people and
85:10 met; righteousness and ***p*** have kissed.
116:7 You can be at ***p*** again because the
119:165 Instruction enjoy ***p***—and lots of it.
120:6 far too long with people who hate ***p***.
120:7 I'm for ***p***, but when I speak, they are
122:6 Jerusalem has ***p***: "Let those who
122:7 Let there be ***p*** on your walls; let there
122:8 friends, I say, "***P*** be with you,
125:5 with other evildoers! ***P*** be on Israel!
128:6 see your grandchildren. ***P*** be on Israel!
Proverbs
12:20 there is joy for those who advise ***p***.
16:7 even their enemies are at ***p*** with them.
29:17 will give you ***p*** of mind and bring
Ecclesiastes
3:8 a time for war and a time for ***p***.
6:5 anything. But it has more ***p*** than those
Song of Songs
8:10 I'm in his eyes as one who brings ***p***.
Isaiah
9:6 God, Eternal Father, Prince of ***P***.
9:7 and endless ***p*** for David's
26:3 you will keep in ***p***, in peace because
26:12 LORD, grant us ***p***, because all that we
27:5 let them make ***p*** with me; let them
32:17 will be ***p***, and the outcome
33:7 streets; messengers of ***p*** wept bitterly.
39:8 there will be ***p*** and security in
52:7 who proclaims ***p***, who brings good
54:10 my covenant of ***p*** won't be shaken,
54:13 I will make ***p*** abound for your
55:12 brought back in ***p***. Even the
57:2 They will find ***p***; those who walk in
57:21 There is no ***p***, says my God, for the
59:8 know the way of ***p***; there's no
60:17 iron. I will make ***p*** your governor and
Jeremiah
4:10 by promising them ***p*** even though the
14:13 give you lasting ***p*** in this place.'"
14:19 us? We look for ***p***, but nothing good
28:9 who prophesies ***p*** is recognized as
29:11 are plans for ***p***, not disaster, to
33:6 with an abundance of ***p*** and security.
Lamentations
3:17 I've rejected ***p***; I've forgotten what
Ezekiel
7:25 come! They seek ***p***, but there is
13:10 astray, saying "***P***" when there was
13:16 and envisioned ***p*** when there was no
16:49 eat, and enjoyed ***p*** and prosperity;
34:25 a covenant of ***p*** for them, and I
37:26 a covenant of ***p*** for them. It will
Daniel
4:1 the entire earth: "I wish you much ***p***.
6:25 the entire earth: I wish you much ***p***.
8:25 In a time of ***p***, he will bring
Micah
3:5 then proclaim "***P***!" but stir up war
5:5 become one of ***p***. When Assyria
Nahum
1:15 who announces ***p***! Celebrate your
Zechariah
8:19 the house of Judah. Love truth and ***p***!
9:10 he will speak ***p*** to the nations.
Malachi
2:5 involved life and ***p***, which I gave
2:6 walked with me in ***p*** and did the right
Matthew
5:9 people who make ***p***, because they
10:12 When you go into a house, say, '***P***!
10:13 your blessing of ***p***. But if the house
10:34 come to bring ***p*** to the earth. I
23:23 the Law: justice, ***p***, and faith. You
Mark
5:34 healed you; go in ***p***, healed from your
9:50 yourselves and keep ***p*** with each other."
Luke
1:79 death, to guide us on the path of ***p***."
2:14 and on earth ***p*** among those whom
2:29 servant go in ***p*** according to your
7:50 Your faith has saved you. Go in ***p***."
8:48 has healed you," Jesus said. "Go in ***p***."
10:5 first say, 'May ***p*** be on this house.'
10:6 shares God's ***p***, then your peace
12:51 come to bring ***p*** to the earth? No,
14:32 discuss terms of ***p*** while his enemy
19:38 name of the Lord. ***P*** in heaven and
19:42 that lead to ***p***. But now they are
24:36 among them and said, "***P*** be with you!"
John
14:27 ***P*** I leave with you. My peace I give
16:33 you will have ***p*** in me. In the
20:19 among them. He said, "***P*** be with you."
20:21 to them again, "***P*** be with you. As

20:26 among them. He said, "***P*** be with you."
Acts
7:26 He tried to make ***p*** between them by
9:31 enjoyed a time of ***p***. God strengthened
10:36 is the message of ***p*** he sent to the
15:33 a blessing of ***p*** from the brothers
16:36 released. You can leave now. Go in ***p***."
17:6 disturbing the ***p*** throughout the
24:2 substantial ***p***, and your
Romans
2:10 glory, honor, and ***p*** for everyone who
3:17 and they don't know the way of ***p***
5:1 faith, we have ***p*** with God through
8:6 from the Spirit leads to life and ***p***.
12:18 ability, live at ***p*** with all people.
14:17 righteousness, ***p***, and joy in the
14:19 things that bring ***p*** and the things
15:13 with all joy and ***p*** in faith so that
15:33 May the God of ***p*** be with you all. Amen
16:20 The God of ***p*** will soon crush Satan
1 Corinthians
1:3 Grace to you and ***p*** from God our Father
7:15 circumstances. God has called you to ***p***.
14:33 disorder but of ***p***. Like in all the
16:11 send him on in ***p*** so he can join
2 Corinthians
13:11 and live in ***p***—and the God of lo
Galatians
5:22 is love, joy, ***p***, patience,
6:16 May ***p*** and mercy be on whoever follows this rule
Ephesians
2:14 Christ is our ***p***. He made both Jews and
2:15 person out of the two groups, making ***p***.
4:3 Spirit with the ***p*** that ties you
6:15 are ready to spread the good news of ***p***.
6:23 May there be ***p*** with the brothers and
Philippians
4:7 Then the ***p*** of God that exceeds all
Colossians
1:20 He brought ***p*** through the blood
3:15 The ***p*** of Christ must control your
1 Thessalonians
5:3 saying, "There is ***p*** and security," at
5:13 their work. Live in ***p*** with each other.
2 Thessalonians
3:16 May the Lord of ***p*** himself give you
2 Timothy
2:22 faith, love, and ***p*** together with
Hebrews
7:2 king of Salem," that is, "king of ***p***."
11:31 because she welcomed the spies in ***p***.
12:14 the goal of ***p*** along with
James
2:16 you said, "Go in ***p***! Stay warm! Have
3:18 Those who make ***p*** sow the seeds of
1 Peter
3:11 and do good; seek ***p*** and chase after
2 Peter
1:2 more grace and ***p*** through the
3:14 found by him in ***p***—pure and faultles
3 John
1:15 ***P*** be with you. Your friends here greet
Jude
1:2 have more and more mercy, ***p***, and love.
Revelation
6:4 allowed to take ***p*** from the earth so

PEACE FROM GOD

Ro 1:7; 1Co 1:3; 2Co 1:2; Phi 1:2; 1Ti 1:2; 2Ti 1:2; Ti 1:4; Phm 1:3; 2Jn 1:3

PEACE TO YOU

1Sa 25:6; Ga 1:3; Eph 1:2; 2:17; Col 1:2; 1Pt 5:14; Rev 1:4

PEACEFUL

Deuteronomy
20:10 you should first extend ***p*** terms to it.
20:11 responds with ***p*** terms and
Judges
3:11 and the land was ***p*** for forty years,
5:31 And the land was ***p*** for forty years.
8:28 The land was ***p*** for forty years
2 Samuel
20:19 I am one of the ***p*** and faithful in
1 Kings
2:6 Don't allow him to die a ***p*** death.
1 Chronicles
4:40 quiet, and ***p***; the people of
2 Chronicles
20:30 rule was ***p*** because his God
Proverbs
3:17 ways are pleasant; all her paths are ***p***.
14:30 A ***p*** mind gives life to the body, but
Isaiah
32:18 will live in a ***p*** dwelling, in
Jeremiah
25:37 silence in the ***p*** meadows, because
34:5 you will die a ***p*** death. As burial
Zechariah
1:11 earth. The whole earth is ***p*** and quiet."
1 Timothy
2:2 live a quiet and ***p*** life in complete
Titus
3:2 they should be ***p***, kind, and show
Hebrews
12:11 it yields the ***p*** fruit of
James
3:17 is pure, and then ***p***, gentle,
3:18 the seeds of justice by their ***p*** acts.
1 Peter
3:4 of a gentle, ***p*** spirit. This type

PEKAH

2 Kings
15:25 ***P***, Remaliah's son and Pekahiah's
2 Chronicles
28:6 In Judah, ***P***, Remaliah's son, killed
Isaiah
7:1 and Israel's King ***P*** (Remaliah's son)

PENDANT

Exodus
28:4 make: a chest ***p***, a vest, a robe,
29:5 and the chest ***p***. Put the vest on
35:9 vest and in the priest's chest ***p***.
39:8 embroidered chest ***p*** in the style of

PEOPLE → ALL GOD'S PEOPLE, ALL OF THE PEOPLE, ALL PEOPLE, AMONG THE PEOPLE, BLIND PEOPLE, EVIL PEOPLE, GOD'S PEOPLE, HOLY PEOPLE, RIGHTEOUS PEOPLE, SHEPHERD MY PEOPLE, SICK PEOPLE, UNGODLY PEOPLE
Genesis
4:26 At that time, ***p*** began to worship
11:6 There is now one ***p*** and they all have
18:24 fifty innocent ***p*** in the city? Will
34:16 We will live with you and be one ***p***.
Exodus
3:12 you bring the ***p*** out of Egypt, you
13:17 Pharaoh let the ***p*** go, God didn't
15:24 The ***p*** complained against Moses, "What
19:11 on Mount Sinai for all the ***p*** to see.
20:20 Moses said to the ***p***, "Don't be afraid,
32:1 The ***p*** saw that Moses was taking a long
32:3 So all the ***p*** took out the gold rings
32:9 watching these ***p***, and I've seen
32:12 plan to take the ***p*** out and kill them
33:5 are a stubborn ***p***. If I were to go
Leviticus
18:27 because the ***p*** who had the land before
Numbers
11:1 When the ***p*** complained intensely in the
11:11 placed the burden of all these ***p*** on me?
14:11 long will these ***p*** disrespect me?
14:19 wrongs of these ***p*** because of your
21:7 The ***p*** went to Moses and said, "We've
22:5 the land of his ***p***, to summon him:
22:12 Don't curse the ***p***, because they are
25:1 at Shittim, the ***p*** made themselves
32:15 Then you will destroy this entire ***p***."
Deuteronomy
4:6 great nation wise and insightful ***p***!"
4:20 his own treasured ***p***, which is what
5:28 I heard what the ***p*** said when they
7:6 because you are a ***p*** holy to the LORD
26:18 be his treasured ***p***, just like he
31:7 will lead this ***p*** to the land the
31:16 and the ***p*** will rise up and
32:6 stupid, senseless ***p***? Isn't he your
32:9 property was his ***p***; Jacob was his
32:30 How could two ***p*** make ten thousand
33:29 you? You are a ***p*** saved by the
Joshua
1:2 with this entire ***p*** to the land that
1:6 will help this ***p*** take possession
3:16 completely. The ***p*** crossed opposite
17:14 We are a numerous ***p*** whom the LORD has
24:25 covenant for the ***p*** and established
24:28 Joshua sent the ***p*** away to each
Judges
2:7 The ***p*** served the LORD throughout the
21:15 Since the ***p*** had a change of heart
Ruth
1:16 I will stay. Your ***p*** will be my
1 Samuel
10:24 asked all the ***p***. "He has no equal
12:22 won't abandon his ***p***, because the LORD
29:5 is the same David ***p*** sing about in
2 Samuel
24:16 destroying the ***p***, "That's enough!
1 Kings
3:8 the middle of the ***p*** you have chosen,
8:30 servant and your ***p*** Israel when they
8:56 given rest to his ***p*** Israel just as he
18:39 All the ***p*** saw this and fell on their
22:37 king had died, ***p*** came from Samaria
2 Kings
23:3 All of the ***p*** accepted the
25:11 guard exiled the ***p*** who were left in
25:19 the land's ***p*** to fight, as well
25:26 Then all the ***p***, young and old, along
1 Chronicles
29:18 the mind of your ***p*** forever, and
2 Chronicles
2:11 must love his ***p*** Israel because he
7:5 king and all the ***p*** dedicated God's
11:16 ***P*** from every tribe of Israel who had
Ezra
2:1 These were the ***p*** of the province who
3:1 their towns, the ***p*** gathered together
Nehemiah
1:10 servants and your ***p***. They are the
4:6 because the ***p*** were eager to
7:4 large, only a few ***p*** were living
8:1 came and the ***p*** of Israel were
Esther
3:6 Mordecai, for ***p*** had told him
10:3 for his Jewish ***p*** and to speak up
Job
12:2 you are the ***p***, and wisdom will
34:11 for he repays ***p*** based on what they do,
37:24 Therefore, ***p*** fear him; none of the wise
Psalms
3:8 May your blessing be on your ***p***! Selah
5:6 The LORD despises ***p*** who are violent
29:11 strength to his ***p***! Let the LORD
33:12 is the LORD, the ***p*** that God has
50:4 to the earth in order to judge his ***p***:
94:8 You ignorant ***p*** better learn quickly.
94:14 not reject his ***p***; he will not
95:7 and we are the ***p*** of his pasture,
95:10 I said, 'These ***p*** have twisted
119:9 How can young ***p*** keep their paths pure?
125:2 surrounds his ***p*** from now until
135:14 justice to his ***p*** and has
144:15 The ***p*** who have it like this are truly
146:7 gives justice to ***p*** who are
147:11 treasures the ***p*** who honor him,
149:9 all God's faithful ***p***. Praise the LORD!
Proverbs
1:22 will you clueless ***p*** love your
2:12 evil path, from ***p*** who twist their
2:20 the path of good ***p***, guarding the
3:31 envy violent ***p*** or choose any of
3:32 Devious ***p*** are detestable to the LORD,
6:12 Worthless ***p*** and guilty people go around
6:30 ***P*** don't despise a thief if he steals to
7:26 corpses to fall; she has killed many ***p***.
8:4 cry out to you, ***p***; my voice goes
10:2 but righteousness rescues ***p*** from death.
10:21 nourish many ***p***, but fools who
10:26 eyes, so are lazy ***p*** to those who
11:14 guidance, a ***p*** will fall, but
11:17 but cruel ***p*** harm themselves.
11:26 ***P*** curse those who hoard grain, but they
12:2 LORD favors good ***p***, but he condemns
12:14 of their speech, ***p*** are well
13:2 ***P*** eat well from the fruit of their

13:3 ***P*** who watch their mouths guard their
13:20 Walk with wise ***p*** and become wise;
13:22 Good ***p*** leave their grandchildren an
14:17 Short-tempered ***p*** make stupid mistakes,
14:27 of life, turning ***p*** away from
14:28 but a dwindling ***p*** is a ruler's ruin.
14:34 a nation, but sin disgraces a ***p***.
15:3 keeping watch on evil and good ***p***.
15:18 but patient ***p*** calm down strife.
16:1 To ***p*** belong the plans of the heart, but
16:2 All the ways of ***p*** are pure in their
16:9 ***P*** plan their path, but the LORD secures
16:27 Worthless ***p*** dig up trouble; their lips
16:28 Destructive ***p*** produce conflict; gossips
16:29 Violent ***p*** entice their neighbors and
17:27 their talking; ***p*** with
18:1 Unfriendly ***p*** look out for themselves;
18:16 the way for access to important ***p***.
19:11 Insightful ***p*** restrain their anger;
19:19 Angry ***p*** must pay the penalty; if you
19:22 ***P*** long for trustworthiness; it is
19:24 Lazy ***p*** bury their hand in the bowl;
20:6 Many ***p*** will say that they are loyal,
20:11 Even young ***p*** are known by their
20:24 how then can ***p*** understand their
21:8 The ways of some ***p*** are twisted and
21:10 Wicked ***p*** desire evil; their neighbors
21:16 ***P*** who wander from the path of insight
22:3 Prudent ***p*** see trouble and hide, while
22:9 are generous ***p***, because they
22:24 Don't befriend ***p*** controlled by anger;
22:29 Do you see ***p*** who work skillfully? They
23:6 food with stingy ***p***; don't long for
24:7 is beyond foolish ***p***. They don't open
24:9 of fools is sin; ***p*** detest mockers.
24:12 knows. He makes ***p*** pay for their
24:24 innocent"—the ***p*** will curse them.
25:6 or stand in the place of important ***p***,
25:14 ***P*** who brag about a gift never given are
25:18 ***P*** who testify falsely against their
26:12 Do you see ***p*** who consider themselves
26:14 its hinge, so do lazy ***p*** in their beds.
26:15 Lazy ***p*** bury their hand into the bowl,
26:16 Lazy ***p*** think they are wiser than seven
26:21 to fire, quarrelsome ***p*** kindle strife.
26:24 Hateful ***p*** mislead with their lips,
27:12 Prudent ***p*** see evil and hide; the
27:21 for gold, so are ***p*** in the presence
28:3 Poor ***p*** who oppress the needy are rain
28:11 Rich ***p*** think they are wise, but an
28:12 respect, but ***p*** hide when the
28:20 Reliable ***p*** will have abundant
28:21 aren't good; ***p*** do wrong for a
28:25 Greedy ***p*** stir up conflict, but those
28:28 wicked rise up, ***p*** hide, but when
29:2 numerous, the ***p*** rejoice, but when
29:5 ***P*** who flatter their friends spread out
29:10 Murderous ***p*** hate the innocent, and they
29:18 no vision, the ***p*** get out of
29:20 Do you see ***p*** who are quick to speak?
29:22 Angry ***p*** stir up conflict; hotheads
29:23 Pride lays ***p*** low, but those of humble
29:25 ***P*** are trapped by their fear of others;

Ecclesiastes

1:3 What do ***p*** gain from all the hard work
1:10 ***P*** may say about something: "Look at
2:22 I mean, What do ***p*** get for all their
3:14 done this so that ***p*** are reverent
3:17 and wicked ***p***, because there's
4:4 observed that ***p*** work hard and
4:8 There are ***p*** who are utterly alone, with
4:16 the number of ***p*** he ruled, but
5:13 under the sun: ***p*** hoard their
5:18 appropriate for ***p*** to eat, drink,
5:19 God gives ***p*** wealth and riches
5:20 Indeed, ***p*** shouldn't brood too much over
6:2 God may give some ***p*** plenty of wealth,
6:3 Some ***p*** may have one hundred children
6:11 is pointless. What do ***p*** gain by it?
6:12 the future holds for ***p*** under the sun?
7:14 latter so that ***p*** can't discover
7:21 all the things ***p*** say, so you don't
8:9 sun. Sometimes ***p*** exercise power
8:10 graves, with ***p*** processing from a
8:11 quickly; that's why ***p*** dare to do evil.
8:15 better for ***p*** to do under the
9:1 love and hate. ***P*** don't know
9:12 ***P*** most definitely don't know when their time will come
10:5 of mistake that comes from ***p*** in power.
11:2 portion to seven ***p***, even to eight:
12:5 when ***p*** are afraid of things above and
12:9 taught the ***p*** knowledge. He

Isaiah

1:4 Sinful nation, ***p*** weighed down with
6:10 the minds of this ***p*** dull. Make their
9:2 The ***p*** walking in darkness have seen a
29:13 says: Since these ***p*** turn toward me
40:7 blows on it. Surely the ***p*** are grass.
42:6 a covenant to the ***p***, as a light to
49:8 a covenant to the ***p***, to restore the
49:13 has comforted his ***p***, and taken pity
52:9 has comforted his ***p*** and has redeemed
60:21 Your ***p*** will all be righteous; they will
65:2 to a rebellious ***p*** walking in a way

Jeremiah

2:31 ***P*** of this generation, listen closely to
5:14 will consume the ***p***, who are but
7:16 pray for these ***p***, don't cry out or
31:33 make with the ***p*** of Israel after
50:6 My ***p*** were lost sheep; their shepherds

Lamentations

1:1 was once full of ***p***. Once great among
5:14 city gate; young ***p*** stop their music.

Ezekiel

46:20 holiness to the ***p***, this is the

Daniel

7:27 be given to the ***p***, the holy ones of
8:24 the mighty and the ***p*** of the holy ones.
9:19 city and your ***p*** are called by
9:24 for your ***p*** and for your holy
10:14 happen to your ***p*** in the future,
11:32 covenant, but the ***p*** who acknowledge

Hosea

1:10 the number of the ***p*** of Israel will be
4:14 so now the ***p*** without sense

Joel

2:18 about this land, and had pity on his ***p***.
3:16 a refuge for his ***p***, a shelter for

Obadiah

1:12 rejoiced over the ***p*** of Judah on the

Micah
6:2 against his ***p***; with Israel he
7:14 Shepherd your ***p*** with your staff, the
Zephaniah
3:12 and powerless ***p*** to remain in your
Matthew
1:21 he will save his ***p*** from their sins."
4:4 It's written, ***P*** won't live only
4:16 the ***p*** who lived in the dark have seen a
4:19 and I'll show you how to fish for ***p***."
4:24 throughout Syria. ***P*** brought to him
5:3 Happy are ***p*** who are hopeless, because
5:39 to hurt you. If ***p*** slap you on your
6:16 their faces so ***p*** will know they
9:12 he said, "Healthy ***p*** don't need a
10:33 denies me before ***p***, I also will deny
13:47 like a net that ***p*** threw into the
15:8 This ***p*** honors me with their lips, but
16:8 and said, "You ***p*** of weak faith!
16:13 Who do ***p*** say the Human One
16:26 Why would ***p*** gain the whole world but
21:23 and elders of the ***p*** came to him as he
24:5 the Christ.' They will deceive many ***p***.
24:51 the hypocrites. ***P*** there will be
27:25 All the ***p*** replied, "Let his blood be on
Mark
7:6 He wrote, This ***p*** honors me with
8:27 disciples, "Who do ***p*** say that I am?"
15:29 ***P*** walking by insulted him, shaking
Luke
1:17 will make ready a ***p*** prepared for the
1:68 come to help and has delivered his ***p***.
21:23 the earth and angry judgment on this ***p***.
23:27 A huge crowd of ***p*** followed Jesus,
24:25 You foolish ***p***! Your dull minds
John
11:50 man die for the ***p*** rather than the
18:14 for one person to die for the ***p***.)
Acts
2:7 aren't all the ***p*** who are speaking
2:15 These ***p*** aren't drunk, as you suspect;
2:41 three thousand ***p*** into the
5:13 even though the ***p*** spoke highly of
15:14 to raise up from them a ***p*** of God.
18:10 you, for I have many ***p*** in this city."
Romans
11:1 God rejected his ***p***? Absolutely not!
15:10 it says, Rejoice, Gentiles, with his ***p***.
1 Thessalonians
3:13 Lord Jesus comes with all his ***p***. Amen.
1 Timothy
6:9 But ***p*** who are trying to get rich fall
Titus
1:10 are rebellious ***p***, loudmouths, and
2:14 cleanse a special ***p*** for himself who
Hebrews
2:17 order to wipe away the sins of the ***p***.
5:3 for his own sins as well as for the ***p***.
10:30 mine; I will pay ***p*** back. And he also
13:12 gate to make the ***p*** holy with his own
James
3:7 ***P*** can tame and already have tamed every kind of animal
4:4 You unfaithful ***p***! Don't you know that
5:1 you wealthy ***p***! Weep and moan
1 Peter
2:9 a holy nation, a ***p*** who are God's own
2:10 you weren't a ***p***, but now you are
2:16 yet also as free ***p***, not using your
Jude
1:4 Godless ***p*** have slipped in among you.

PEOPLES → ALL PEOPLES, AMONG THE PEOPLES

Genesis
17:16 and kings of ***p*** will come from
25:23 two different ***p*** will emerge from
27:29 serve you, may ***p*** bow down to you.
28:3 you will become a large group of ***p***.
48:4 a large group of ***p***. I will give this
Exodus
15:14 The ***p*** heard, they shook in terror;
Leviticus
20:24 who has separated you from all other ***p***.
20:26 you from all other ***p*** to be my own.
Deuteronomy
7:7 In fact, you were the smallest of ***p***!
13:7 the neighboring ***p***, whether nearby
15:6 to many different ***p*** but won't need to
20:16 cities of these ***p***—the ones the LORD
28:10 All the earth's ***p*** will see that you are
Joshua
4:24 all the earth's ***p*** might know that
Judges
2:12 the surrounding ***p***, they worshipped
2 Samuel
22:48 on my behalf, who subdues ***p*** before me,
1 Kings
8:53 all the earth's ***p*** as your own
1 Chronicles
5:25 the gods of the ***p*** of the land, whom
2 Chronicles
32:19 the gods of the other ***p*** of the earth.
Ezra
3:3 the neighboring ***p***, and they offered
4:4 The neighboring ***p*** discouraged the
9:1 separate from the ***p*** of the
10:2 the neighboring ***p***. But even now,
Nehemiah
9:22 them kingdoms and ***p***, and assigned to
10:28 the neighboring ***p*** to follow the
13:24 of various ***p***; they couldn't
Esther
1:16 officials and the ***p*** in all the
8:13 for all its ***p*** to read. The Jews
Job
36:31 water he judges ***p*** and gives food in
Psalms
2:1 rant? Why do the ***p*** rave uselessly?
7:7 Let the assembled ***p*** surround you. Rule
7:8 will judge the ***p***. Establish
33:10 he frustrates what the ***p*** intend to do.
44:2 crushed all the ***p***, but you set our
45:5 Let the ***p*** fall beneath you. May your
45:17 the next so the ***p*** will praise you
57:9 among all the ***p***; I will make
68:30 the calves of the ***p***. Trample those
87:6 he registers the ***p***: "Each one was
105:44 they inherited the wealth of many ***p***—
108:3 among all the ***p***; I will make
117:1 you nations! Worship him, all you ***p***!
149:7 the nations and punishment on the ***p***,

Isaiah
2:2 above the hills; ***p*** will stream to it.
3:13 to accuse; he stands to judge the ***p***.
8:9 Unite yourselves, ***p***, and be shattered!
10:14 the wealth of the ***p*** as if it were in
11:10 a signal to the ***p***. The nations will
14:2 The ***p*** will take them and will bring
17:12 raging of many ***p***; like the
33:3 At the noise, ***p*** fled; on account of
34:1 and listen, you ***p***. Hear, earth and
43:9 together; the ***p*** are assembled.
49:22 and to the ***p*** I will lift up my
51:5 will judge the ***p***. The coastlands
55:4 a witness to the ***p***, a prince and
62:10 stones! Raise up a signal for the ***p***.
63:3 myself—from the ***p***, no one was with
Ezekiel
3:6 No, not to many ***p*** who speak difficult
20:34 you out from the ***p*** and gather you
25:7 you off from the ***p***, remove you from
26:2 The gate of the ***p*** is broken, she
27:36 merchants for the ***p*** hiss because of
28:25 Israel from the ***p*** among whom
31:12 All the earth's ***p*** departed from its
32:3 company of many ***p*** I will spread my
32:9 hearts of many ***p*** when I bring
32:10 I will make many ***p*** appalled because of
34:13 the countries and ***p***, and I will bring
36:15 the scorn of the ***p***. And you will no
38:6 all his troops; many ***p*** are with you.
39:4 troops, and the ***p*** who are with you.
Daniel
3:7 all the ***p***, nations, and
4:1 to all the ***p***, nations, and
6:25 To all the ***p***, nations, and
Joel
2:6 their presence, ***p*** shake with fear;
Micah
1:2 Listen, all you ***p***! Pay attention,
4:1 above the hills; ***p*** will stream to it.
4:5 Each of the ***p*** walks in the name of
4:13 will crush many ***p***; you will
5:7 will be amid many ***p*** like dew from the
5:8 amid many ***p***, like a lion
Nahum
3:4 her whorings and ***p*** by means of her
Habakkuk
2:8 the rest of the ***p*** will plunder you
2:10 cutting off many ***p*** and sinning
2:13 heavenly forces? ***P*** grow weary from
Zephaniah
3:9 the speech of the ***p*** into pure speech,
3:20 the neighboring ***p*** when I restore
Zechariah
8:20 forces proclaims: ***P*** will still come,
8:22 Many ***p*** and mighty nations will come to
11:10 that I had made with all the ***p***.
12:3 stone for all the ***p***. All who carry it
12:4 will strike blind every horse of the ***p***.
14:12 strike all the ***p*** who swarmed
Acts
4:25 Gentiles rage, and the ***p*** plot in vain?
Revelation
10:11 again about many ***p***, nations,
11:9 members of the ***p***, tribes,
17:15 is seated, are ***p***, crowds, nations,
21:3 they will be his ***p***. God himself will

PEOR

Numbers
25:3 to the Baal of ***P***, and the LORD was
Deuteronomy
4:3 the Baal of ***P***. The LORD your
Joshua
22:17 the offense of ***P*** enough for us?

PEREZ

Genesis
38:29 out on your own." So he was named ***P***.
Ruth
4:12 the household of ***P***, whom Tamar bore
Matthew
1:3 was the father of ***P*** and Zerah, whose
Luke
3:33 son of Herzon son of ***P*** son of Judah

PERFECT

Genesis
2:18 make him a helper that is ***p*** for him."
2:20 But a helper ***p*** for him was
Deuteronomy
18:13 you must be ***p*** before the LORD
2 Samuel
22:31 God! His way is ***p***; the LORD's word is
22:33 My mighty fortress, who makes my way ***p***,
Job
22:3 Does he gain when you ***p*** your ways?
37:16 amazing deeds of one with ***p*** knowledge,
Psalms
10:8 wait in a place ***p*** for ambush; from
18:30 God! His way is ***p***; the LORD's word is
18:32 me with strength and makes my way ***p***,
19:7 Instruction is ***p***, reviving one's
50:2 From Zion, ***p*** in beauty, God shines
64:6 We've devised a ***p*** plot! It's deep
119:96 no matter how ***p***, has a limit, but
Song of Songs
5:2 my dove, my ***p*** one! My head is
6:9 but my dove, my ***p*** one, is one of a
Lamentations
2:15 the city called ***P*** Beauty, the Joy
Ezekiel
16:14 beauty. It was ***p*** because of the
1 Corinthians
13:10 but when the ***p*** comes, what is partial
2 Corinthians
12:9 power is made ***p*** in weakness." So
Colossians
3:14 on love, which is the ***p*** bond of unity.
Hebrews
2:10 suffering to make ***p*** the pioneer of
5:9 he had been made ***p***, he became the
7:19 Law made nothing ***p***). On the other
7:28 a Son who has been made ***p*** forever.
9:9 offered can't ***p*** the conscience of
9:11 greater and more ***p*** meeting tent,
10:1 It never can ***p*** the ones who are
11:40 so they wouldn't be made ***p*** without us.
12:23 of the righteous who have been made ***p***,
James
1:17 good gift, every ***p*** gift, comes from
1:25 who study the ***p*** law, the law of
1 John
4:12 in us and his love is made ***p*** in us.

4:18 fear in love, but *p* love drives out

PERFORM

Exodus
7:3 and I'll *p* many of my signs
11:9 you so that I can *p* even more amazing
13:5 honey. You should *p* this ritual in
29:37 days you should *p* the ritual of
30:10 year Aaron should *p* a ritual of
34:10 your people, I'll *p* dramatic displays
Leviticus
5:10 the priest will *p* an entirely
9:7 to the altar and *p* your purification
14:19 priest will then *p* the purification
15:30 The priest will *p* a purification
16:9 LORD's lot and *p* a purification
Numbers
1:50 its equipment, *p* its religious
3:7 They will *p* duties for him and for the
3:28 old, who would *p* duties for the
8:19 and his sons to *p* the service of
15:13 citizen will *p* these rituals in
16:9 approach him, to *p* the service of
18:3 They will *p* their duties for you and
18:23 The Levites will *p* the service of the
Deuteronomy
3:24 as you do or can *p* your deeds and
6:24 commanded us to *p* all these
8:1 must carefully *p* all of the
12:14 where you must *p* everything I'm
16:1 time you must *p* the Passover for
16:10 At that point, *p* the Festival of Weeks
16:13 drink you need, *p* the Festival of
16:15 days you must *p* the festival for
25:7 not willing to *p* the brother-in-law
32:46 your children to *p* carefully all the
Joshua
22:27 that we too *p* the service of
Judges
16:25 Samson so he can *p* for us!" So they
1 Chronicles
28:21 Levites who will *p* all the service
Ezra
7:10 to study and *p* the LORD's
Psalms
45:4 Let your strong hand *p* awesome deeds.
Isaiah
14:3 and from the hard labor that you *p*,
Jeremiah
11:6 the terms of this covenant and *p* them.
21:2 the LORD will *p* one of his mighty
Ezekiel
13:23 empty visions or *p* divinations. I
24:17 still. Don't *p* mourning rites,
27:31 you, and bitterly *p* the mourning
43:11 and all its regulations and *p* them.
Micah
5:12 the sorceries you *p*; you will have no
Luke
23:8 He was hoping to see Jesus *p* some sign.
Acts
8:6 they saw him *p*, and they gave
14:3 signs and wonders he enabled them to *p*.
1 Corinthians
12:29 they? All don't *p* miracles, do they?
Hebrews
9:6 all the time as they *p* their service.

PERFORMED

Exodus
4:30 to Moses, and he *p* the signs in
Leviticus
8:15 that reconciliation could be *p* on it.
Numbers
3:38 and his sons, who *p* the duties of the
14:11 all the signs that I *p* among them?
Deuteronomy
6:22 eyes, the LORD *p* great and awesome
10:21 God—the one who *p* these great and
11:3 the acts that he *p* in the heart of
11:7 each of these powerful acts the LORD *p*.
Judges
16:25 prison, and he *p* in front of them.
16:27 were on the roof watching as Samson *p*.
2 Samuel
23:20 from Kabzeel who *p* great deeds. He
1 Kings
18:26 or answer. They *p* a hopping dance
1 Chronicles
11:22 was a hero who *p* great deeds. He
25:1 list of those who *p* this special
2 Chronicles
30:22 Levites who had *p* so skillfully for
Nehemiah
9:10 You *p* signs and wonders against
12:45 They *p* the service of their God and the
Psalms
78:12 But God *p* wonders in their ancestors'
78:43 how God *p* his signs in Egypt, his
Jeremiah
32:20 You have *p* signs and wonders in the
Ezekiel
13:6 visions and *p* deceptive
Acts
2:22 signs, which God *p* through him among
2:43 everyone. God *p* many wonders and
4:16 aware of the sign *p* through them.
4:30 and wonders to be *p* through the name
5:12 The apostles *p* many signs and wonders
7:36 them out after he *p* wonders and signs
Romans
1:27 each other. Males *p* shameful actions
2 Corinthians
12:12 an apostle were *p* among you with
Philippians
3:3 confidence in rituals *p* on the body,
Colossians
2:11 him. This wasn't *p* by human hands

PERFUME

Ruth
3:3 put on some *p*, wear nice
Song of Songs
1:3 your very name is *p*. That's why the
Matthew
26:7 very expensive *p*. She poured it on
John
12:3 of very expensive *p* made of pure

PERIOD

Genesis
27:41 himself, When the *p* of mourning for

31:35 I'm having my **p**." He searched but
38:12 Then, after a **p** of mourning, he
50:3 that is the **p** required for
Leviticus
8:33 days, until the **p** of your
12:2 as she is during her menstrual **p**.
12:5 her menstrual **p**—and will be in a
14:46 during the entire **p** when it is
15:25 her menstrual **p**, or whenever she
20:18 her menstrual **p** and has sexual
25:29 its sale. The **p** for buying it
Numbers
6:5 head until the **p** of dedication to
6:6 The **p** of dedication to the LORD also
6:12 The previous **p** will be invalid,
2 Samuel
11:4 after her monthly **p**.) Then she
1 Chronicles
9:25 to assist them for a **p** of seven days.
Ezra
4:15 over a long **p** of time. As a
4:19 kings over a long **p** of time. There
Psalms
37:19 times, and in a **p** of famine they
90:4 like a short **p** during the night
Daniel
7:25 by law. And for a **p** of time, periods
Acts
1:3 to them over a **p** of forty days,
13:20 happened over a **p** of about four
1 Corinthians
7:5 agree for a short **p** of time to devote

PERISH

Numbers
17:13 dwelling will die. Are we doomed to **p**?"
24:20 nations, but its end is to **p** forever."
24:24 Eber, and even he will **p** forever."
Judges
5:31 all your enemies **p** like this, LORD!
Job
3:3 **P** the day I was born, the night someone
4:9 deeply, they **p**; by a breath of
4:20 and evening; they **p** forever without
6:18 they go up into untamed areas and **p**.
18:17 of them will **p** from the earth;
20:7 they will **p** forever like their dung;
36:12 listen, they **p** by the sword,
Psalms
68:2 fire, let the wicked **p** before God!
Proverbs
10:28 but the hopes of the wicked will **p**.
11:10 when the wicked **p**, there are shouts
19:9 won't go unpunished, and liars will **p**.
21:28 witness will **p**, but one who
Isaiah
29:14 their wise will **p**, and the
29:20 the mocker will **p**, and all who plot
41:11 with you will be as nothing and will **p**.
60:12 serve you will **p**; such nations
Jeremiah
6:21 them; neighbor and friend alike will **p**.
10:11 the earth will **p** from the earth
27:10 I will drive you out, and you will **p**.
27:15 out, and you will **p**, both you and
40:15 and the few who are left will **p**."
44:12 They will all **p** there. They will
49:10 will **p**, and there will
51:6 your lives! Don't **p** because of her
Amos
1:8 who remain will **p**,says the LORD God.
3:15 of ivory will **p**; the great houses
Jonah
1:6 some thought to us so that we won't **p**."
1:14 don't let us **p** on account of
3:9 from his wrath, so that we might not **p**.
Zephaniah
2:13 cause Assyria to **p**. Let him make
Zechariah
9:5 up. The king will **p** from Gaza;
Luke
9:25 themselves yet **p** or lose their
John
3:16 in him won't **p** but will have
1 Peter
1:4 that cannot **p**—an inheritance
2 Peter
3:9 wanting anyone to **p** but all to change

PERIZZITES

Genesis
13:7 Canaanites and the **P** lived in the land.
Exodus
3:8 the Amorites, the **P**, the Hivites, and
Joshua
24:11 were Amorites, **P**, Canaanites,

PERMANENT

Exodus
27:21 It will be a **p** regulation for
29:28 Israelites as a **p** provision,
30:21 This will be a **p** regulation for
Leviticus
3:17 This is a **p** rule for your future
6:18 can eat it as a **p** portion from the
6:22 the offering as a **p** portion for the
7:34 to his sons as a **p** portion from the
10:9 die—this is a **p** rule throughout
10:15 children as a **p** portion, just as
16:29 This will be a **p** rule for you: On the
17:7 This will be a **p** rule for them
23:14 This is a **p** rule throughout
24:3 LORD. This is a **p** rule throughout
25:34 that is their **p** family property.
Numbers
10:8 This will be a **p** regulation for
15:15 will be **p** for all time. You
18:8 an allowance. This is a **p** regulation.
19:10 This will be a **p** regulation for
25:13 a covenant of **p** priesthood,
Deuteronomy
15:17 he will be your **p** servant. Do the
Judges
18:1 live in, since no **p** territory had
1 Samuel
28:2 I will make you my **p** bodyguard."
1 Chronicles
28:2 a temple as the **p** home for the
29:15 without **p** homes. Our days
Job
41:4 so that you will take him as a **p** slave?
Ezekiel
46:14 flour. This is a **p** and perpetual

John
8:35 A slave isn't a ***p*** member of the
Hebrews
13:14 We don't have a ***p*** city here, but rather

PERSIA
Ezra
6:14 Darius, and King Artaxerxes of ***P***.
Daniel
8:20 represents the kings of Media and ***P***.
10:20 the leader of ***P***. As I leave, the

PERSIAN
Nehemiah
12:22 families in the rule of Darius the ***P***.

PERSON → RIGHTEOUS PERSON
Exodus
9:19 the open. Every ***p*** or animal that is
12:19 whether the ***p*** is an immigrant
12:48 But no uncircumcised ***p*** may eat it.
21:14 and kills another ***p*** on purpose, you
23:7 put an innocent ***p*** who is in the
Leviticus
4:27 If any ordinary ***p*** sins unintentionally
7:19 fire. Any clean ***p*** may eat the flesh,
13:6 will declare the ***p*** clean; it is just
13:8 will declare the ***p*** unclean; it is a
19:14 not insult a deaf ***p*** or put some
Numbers
6:12 The ***p*** will be rededicated to the LORD
19:20 Any ***p*** who is unclean and didn't cleanse
Deuteronomy
1:17 out, whether the ***p*** is important or
17:7 the guilty ***p*** from the start;
19:3 places to which a ***p*** who has killed
24:11 wait outside. The ***p*** to whom you are
25:1 declaring one ***p*** legally right and
27:18 misleads a blind ***p*** on a road." All
29:19 When that kind of ***p*** hears the words of
32:30 How could one ***p*** chase off a thousand in
Judges
17:6 in Israel; each ***p*** did what they
1 Samuel
2:31 won't be an old ***p*** left in your
19:5 to an innocent ***p*** by killing David
26:23 rewards every ***p*** for their
Nehemiah
13:30 with specific duties for each ***p***.
Job
1:1 man was honest, a ***p*** of absolute
3:23 given to the ***p*** whose way is
4:7 What innocent ***p*** has ever
4:17 than God, a ***p*** purer than their
5:17 happy is the ***p*** whom God
11:12 A stupid ***p*** becomes intelligent when a
25:4 How can a ***p*** be innocent before God;
Psalms
1:1 The truly happy ***p*** doesn't follow wicked
14:3 No one does good—not even one ***p***!
15:2 The ***p*** who lives free of blame, does
15:5 any innocent ***p***. Whoever does
22:6 insulted by one ***p***, despised by
24:5 That kind of ***p*** receives blessings from
34:6 This suffering ***p*** cried out: the LORD
38:14 become like a ***p*** who doesn't hear
49:7 save a single ***p***! It can't pay a
52:1 Hey, powerful ***p***! Why do you brag
53:3 No one does good—not even one ***p***!
64:4 shoot an innocent ***p***. They shoot
75:7 He brings this ***p*** down, but that
78:25 Each ***p*** ate the bread of the powerful
87:5 it is said: "Each ***p*** was born in it,
89:22 him; no wicked ***p*** will make him
101:6 close to me. The ***p*** who walks without
101:7 But the ***p*** who acts deceitfully won't
102:1 of an oppressed ***p***, when weak and
107:42 but every wicked ***p*** shuts their mouth.
109:6 Appoint a wicked ***p*** to be against this
109:16 All because this ***p*** didn't remember to
127:5 The ***p*** who fills a quiver full with them
145:20 him, but he destroys every wicked ***p***.
146:5 The ***p*** whose help is the God of Jacob—
148:11 and every single ***p***, you princes and
Proverbs
5:9 to others, your years to a cruel ***p***.
6:6 the ant, you lazy ***p***; observe its ways
6:9 How long, lazy ***p***, will you lie down?
10:22 blessing makes a ***p*** rich, and no
11:12 lacks sense; a sensible ***p*** keeps quiet.
11:13 but a trustworthy ***p*** keeps a
12:8 A ***p*** is praised for his insight, but a
13:14 life, turning a ***p*** away from
14:10 distress; another ***p*** can't share its
17:7 so false speech for an honorable ***p***.
17:10 an understanding ***p*** than a hundred
18:17 The first ***p*** to testify seems innocent,
19:25 and a naive ***p*** will become
20:6 loyal, but who can find a reliable ***p***?
20:16 garment of the ***p*** who secures a
20:27 The breath of a ***p*** is the lamp of the
21:11 the naive ***p*** gains wisdom;
21:22 A wise ***p*** fought a city of warriors and
21:29 The wicked ***p*** appears brash, but the
22:13 A lazy ***p*** says, "There's a lion in the
24:5 A wise ***p*** is mightier than a strong one;
24:30 field of a lazy ***p***, by the vineyard
25:19 a treacherous ***p*** at a difficult
25:23 up rain, and a ***p*** who plots quietly
25:25 land is like cold water for a weary ***p***.
25:28 A ***p*** without self-control is like a
26:7 from a disabled ***p***, so does a
26:13 A lazy ***p*** says,"There's a lion in the
26:18 Like a crazy ***p*** shooting deadly flaming
27:2 Let another ***p*** praise you, and not your
27:7 bitter tastes sweet to a hungry ***p***.
27:13 garment of the ***p*** who secures a
27:19 so the heart reflects one ***p*** to another.
28:2 leaders; but a ***p*** with
28:11 an insightful poor ***p*** sees through them.
29:27 The unjust ***p*** is disgusting to the
Ecclesiastes
2:19 Either way, that ***p*** will have control
7:19 makes a wise ***p*** stronger than ten
9:2 The good ***p*** is like the
9:18 one incompetent ***p*** destroys much
11:9 Rejoice, young ***p***, while you are young
Isaiah
2:9 down; each ***p*** laid low—don't
5:15 humiliated; each ***p*** laid low, the
9:19 for the fire. Not one ***p*** pitied another:
19:11 I'm a wise ***p***, one of the
29:8 when a hungry ***p*** dreams of eating

PERSON [cont.]

32:8 But an honorable ***p*** plans honorable
56:2 does this, the ***p*** who holds it
65:20 be like a young ***p***, and the one
66:3 an ox kills a ***p***; the one who

Jeremiah
5:1 and wide for one ***p***, even one who
15:12 Can a ***p*** shatter iron, iron from the

Lamentations
3:25 hope in him, to the ***p*** who seeks him.
3:39 any living ***p*** complain; why

Ezekiel
17:15 army. Can such a ***p*** succeed? Can one
33:2 take a certain ***p*** from their

Daniel
2:30 any other living ***p*** but so that the
6:12 thirty days any ***p*** who prays to any
8:16 help this ***p*** understand what
10:16 saying to the ***p*** standing in front
11:21 A worthless ***p*** will arise in his place.

Hosea
8:6 is from Israel, a ***p*** made it; it is

Zephaniah
3:6 There will be no ***p***, no inhabitant

Haggai
2:13 If an unclean ***p*** touches any of

Malachi
3:8 Should a ***p*** deceive God? Yet you deceive

Matthew
8:27 What kind of ***p*** is this? Even the
11:15 Let the ***p*** who has ears, hear
12:10 the Law allow a ***p*** to heal on the
12:12 valuable is a ***p*** than a sheep! So
12:43 spirit leaves a ***p***, it wanders
12:45 home there. That ***p*** is worse off at
15:4 mother, and The ***p*** who speaks
15:11 contaminates a ***p*** in God's sight.
15:14 But if a blind ***p*** leads another
15:18 what contaminates a ***p*** in God's sight.
15:20 contaminate a ***p*** in God's sight.
16:27 each one for what that ***p*** has done.
18:7 it is for the ***p*** who causes those
19:23 hard for a rich ***p*** to enter the
19:24 than for a rich ***p*** to enter God's
21:44 stone will crush the ***p*** it falls on."
26:24 it is for that ***p*** who betrays the

Luke
6:39 riddle. "A blind ***p*** can't lead
6:45 A good ***p*** produces good from the good
6:48 It's like a ***p*** building a house by
14:9 to this other ***p***.' Embarrassed,
14:12 Jesus said to the ***p*** who had invited
14:30 say, 'Here's the ***p*** who began
16:5 sent for each ***p*** who owed his
17:1 it is for the ***p*** through whom they
17:4 my ways,' you must forgive that ***p***."
18:14 I tell you, this ***p*** went down to his
18:25 than for a rich ***p*** to enter God's
20:18 stone will crush the ***p*** it falls on."
22:22 it is for that ***p*** who betrays him."
22:26 become like a ***p*** of lower status

John
6:7 enough for each ***p*** to have even a
18:14 better for one ***p*** to die for the

Acts
1:22 from us. This ***p*** must become along
8:9 of Samaria. He claimed to be a great ***p***.
10:28 never call a ***p*** impure or unclean.
17:26 From one ***p*** God created every human
19:16 The ***p*** who had an evil spirit jumped on
28:7 most prominent ***p***, owned a large

Romans
2:1 you judge another ***p*** because the one
2:26 So if the ***p*** who isn't circumcised keeps
2:29 it is the ***p*** who is a Jew
3:28 consider that a ***p*** is treated as
4:6 a blessing on the ***p*** to whom God
5:12 world through one ***p***, and death came
6:6 what we know: the ***p*** that we used to
6:7 because a ***p*** who has died has been freed
10:5 from the Law: The ***p*** who does these
13:1 Every ***p*** should place themselves under
14:1 Welcome the ***p*** who is weak in faith—but

1 Corinthians
3:10 top of it. Each ***p*** needs to pay
3:17 will destroy that ***p***, because God's
5:11 gods, an abusive ***p***, a drunk, or a
6:5 Isn't there one ***p*** among you who is
7:17 each ***p*** should live the
11:21 private meal. One ***p*** goes hungry while
12:7 is given to each ***p*** for the common
12:8 the Spirit to one ***p***, a word of
12:11 who gives what he wants to each ***p***.
14:17 but the other ***p*** is not being
15:45 became a living ***p***, and the last

2 Corinthians
2:5 anyone sad, that ***p*** hasn't hurt me
4:16 the outside, the ***p*** that we are on
5:10 so that each ***p*** can be paid back
5:17 in Christ, that ***p*** is part of the
8:12 because of what a ***p*** can afford, not
10:7 to Christ, that ***p*** should think
10:10 powerful, but in ***p*** he is weak and
10:18 It isn't the ***p*** who promotes himself or
11:4 If a ***p*** comes and preaches some other
11:23 like a crazy ***p***. What I've done

Galatians
2:16 we know that a ***p*** isn't made
6:1 and sisters, if a ***p*** is caught doing
6:4 Each ***p*** should test their own work and
6:5 Each ***p*** will have to carry their own
6:7 is not mocked. A ***p*** will harvest what

Ephesians
2:1 were like a dead ***p*** because of the
2:15 create one new ***p*** out of the two
4:22 was part of the ***p*** you once were,
4:24 with the new ***p*** created according
6:8 will reward every ***p*** who does what is

Philippians
2:4 Instead of each ***p*** watching out for
2:20 like him. He is a ***p*** who genuinely

Colossians
1:28 and teach every ***p*** with all wisdom
4:6 you may know how to respond to every ***p***.

1 Thessalonians
3:10 see all of you in ***p*** and to complete

2 Thessalonians
2:3 first and the ***p*** who is lawless is
2:8 Then the ***p*** who is lawless will be
2:9 When the ***p*** who is lawless comes, it
2:15 we taught you in ***p*** or through our

1 Timothy
6:4 that ***p*** is conceited. They don't

2 Timothy
3:17 so that the ***p*** who belongs to God can be
Titus
3:10 more to do with a ***p*** who causes
Hebrews
1:12 be changed like a ***p*** changes clothes,
7:7 less important ***p*** is blessed by the
7:13 The ***p*** we are talking about belongs to
8:11 and each ***p*** won't ever teach a neighbor
10:29 deserved by the ***p*** who walks all
13:4 sexually immoral ***p*** and the person
James
1:20 because an angry ***p*** doesn't produce
2:3 But to the poor ***p*** you say, "Stand
2:24 So you see that a ***p*** is shown to be
5:17 Elijah was a ***p*** just like us. When he
1 Peter
1:11 what sort of ***p*** or what sort of
2:6 valuable. The ***p*** who believes in
4:10 to the gift each ***p*** has received, as
1 John
2:4 a liar, and the truth is not in this ***p***.
2:10 The ***p*** loving a brother and sister stays
2:11 But the ***p*** who hates a brother or sister
3:4 Every ***p*** who practices sin commits an
3:14 and sisters. The ***p*** who does not love
3:17 But if a ***p*** has material possessions and
3:24 The ***p*** who keeps his commandments
4:6 are from God. The ***p*** who knows God
2 John
1:7 This kind of ***p*** is the deceiver
Revelation
9:5 that of a scorpion when it strikes a ***p***.
13:17 unless the ***p*** has the mark with
22:18 will add to that ***p*** the plagues that

PERSONS

Genesis
46:15 All of these ***p***, including his
Exodus
18:21 for capable ***p*** who respect God.
18:25 chose capable ***p*** from all Israel
Leviticus
13:11 quarantine such ***p***, because they are
Numbers
5:7 Such ***p*** will confess the sin they have
9:6 But there were ***p*** who were unclean from contact
19:13 dwelling. Such ***p*** must be cut off
26:10 fire devoured 250 ***p***. They became a
31:40 of which the LORD's tribute was 32 ***p***.
32:11 None of the ***p*** that went up from Egypt,
Deuteronomy
15:4 won't be any poor ***p*** among you because
15:11 Poor ***p*** will never disappear from the
Judges
9:36 on the hills just look like ***p*** to you."
2 Kings
12:4 pay to redeem ***p*** according to
1 Chronicles
12:1 The following ***p*** came to David at Ziklag
Job
22:15 the ancient way traveled by sinful ***p***,
33:29 all this, twice, three times with ***p***
34:8 with wrongdoers, walking with evil ***p***.
Psalms
1:2 things, these ***p*** love the LORD's
37:37 the future belongs to ***p*** of peace.
Proverbs
11:17 Kind ***p*** benefit themselves, but cruel
11:25 Generous ***p*** will prosper; those who
18:24 There are ***p*** for companionship, but then
Jeremiah
12:1 Why do guilty ***p*** enjoy success?
Daniel
11:14 king. Violent ***p*** from among your
Jonah
3:8 And let all ***p*** stop their evil
Luke
4:27 were also many ***p*** with skin
Acts
1:15 hundred twenty ***p***. Peter stood
4:34 were no needy ***p*** among them. Those
5:16 large numbers of ***p*** from towns around
9:2 If he found ***p*** who belonged to
Ephesians
2:2 is now at work in ***p*** whose lives are
5:3 among you, which is right for holy ***p***.
Revelation
5:9 purchased for God ***p*** from every tribe,

PETER

Matthew
4:18 who is called ***P***, and Andrew,
16:18 you that you are ***P***. And I'll build
26:69 Meanwhile, ***P*** was sitting outside in the
Mark
8:33 sternly corrected ***P***: "Get behind me,
Luke
22:61 straight at ***P***, and Peter
22:62 And ***P*** went out and cried
24:12 But ***P*** ran to the tomb. When he bent
John
1:42 called Cephas" (which is translated ***P***).
21:15 Jesus asked Simon ***P***, "Simon son of
Acts
4:8 Then ***P***, inspired by the Holy Spirit,
12:6 case forward, ***P*** was asleep
Galatians
2:7 just as ***P*** had been to the
2:8 one who empowered ***P*** to become an
1 Peter
1:1 ***P***, an apostle of Jesus Christ, To
2 Peter
1:1 From Simon ***P***, a slave and apostle of

PHARAOH

Genesis
12:17 the LORD struck ***P*** and his household
41:25 Joseph said to ***P***, "Pharaoh has
47:5 ***P*** said to Joseph, "Since your father
Exodus
6:11 Go and tell ***P***, Egypt's king, to let
13:17 When ***P*** let the people go, God didn't
14:17 at the expense of ***P***, all his army,
Deuteronomy
7:8 from the power of ***P***, Egypt's king.
Isaiah
36:6 That's all that ***P***, Egypt's king, is
Acts
7:10 recognized by ***P***, king of Egypt,
7:13 who he was, and ***P*** learned about
Romans
9:17 Scripture says to ***P***, I have put you in

PHARISEE
Matthew
23:26 Blind ***P***! First clean the inside of the
Luke
7:39 When the ***P*** who had invited Jesus saw
11:37 was speaking, a ***P*** invited him to
11:38 When the ***P*** saw that Jesus didn't
18:10 pray. One was a ***P*** and the other a
18:11 The ***P*** stood and prayed about himself
18:14 rather than the ***P***. All who lift
John
3:1 There was a ***P*** named Nicodemus, a Jewish
7:48 the leaders believed in him? Has any ***P***?
Acts
5:34 council member, a ***P*** and teacher of
23:6 Brothers, I'm a ***P*** and a descendant
26:5 group of our religion. I am a ***P***.
Philippians
3:5 respect to observing the Law, I'm a ***P***.

PHARISEES → CHIEF PRIESTS AND PHARISEES, PHARISEES AND LEGAL EXPERTS, PHARISEES AND SADDUCEES, PRIESTS AND PHARISEES
Matthew
3:7 Many ***P*** and Sadducees came to be
5:20 experts and the ***P***, you will never
9:11 But when the ***P*** saw this, they said to
9:14 do we and the ***P*** frequently fast,
9:34 But the ***P*** said, "He throws out demons
12:2 When the ***P*** saw this, they said to him,
12:14 The ***P*** went out and met in order to find
12:24 When the ***P*** heard, they said, "This man
12:38 experts and the ***P*** requested of
15:1 Then ***P*** and legal experts came to Jesus
15:12 you know that the ***P*** were offended by
15:14 Leave the ***P*** alone. They are blind
16:1 The ***P*** and Sadducees came to Jesus. In
16:6 for the yeast of the ***P*** and Sadducees."
16:11 for the yeast of the ***P*** and Sadducees."
16:12 the teaching of the ***P*** and Sadducees.
19:3 Some ***P*** came to him. In order to test
19:7 The ***P*** said to him, "Then why did Moses
21:45 priests and the ***P*** heard the
22:15 Then the ***P*** met together to find a way
22:34 When the ***P*** heard that Jesus had left
22:41 Now as the ***P*** were gathering, Jesus
23:2 experts and the ***P*** sit on Moses'
23:13 legal experts and ***P***! Hypocrites! You
27:62 priests and the ***P*** gathered before
Mark
2:16 from among the ***P*** saw that he was
2:18 disciples and the ***P*** had a habit of
2:24 The ***P*** said to Jesus, "Look! Why are
3:6 At that, the ***P*** got together with the
7:1 The ***P*** and some legal experts from
7:3 The ***P*** and all the Jews don't eat
7:5 So the ***P*** and legal experts asked Jesus,
8:11 The ***P*** showed up and began to argue with
8:15 the yeast of the ***P*** as well as the
10:2 Some ***P*** came and, trying to test him,
12:13 sent some of the ***P*** and supporters of
Luke
5:17 was teaching, ***P*** and legal experts
5:21 legal experts and ***P*** began to mutter
5:30 The ***P*** and their legal experts grumbled
5:33 disciples of the ***P*** do the same, but
6:2 Some ***P*** said, "Why are you breaking the
6:7 experts and the ***P*** were watching him
6:9 legal experts and ***P***, "Here's a
7:30 But the ***P*** and legal experts rejected
7:36 One of the ***P*** invited Jesus to eat with
11:39 to him, "Now, you ***P*** clean the outside
11:42 terrible for you ***P***! You give a tenth
11:53 legal experts and ***P*** began to resent
12:1 the yeast of the ***P***—I mean, the misma
13:31 that time, some ***P*** approached Jesus
14:1 leaders of the ***P***, they were
14:3 the lawyers and ***P***, "Does the Law
15:2 The ***P*** and legal experts were grumbling,
16:14 The ***P***, who were money-lovers, heard
17:20 ***P*** asked Jesus when God's kingdom was
19:39 Some of the ***P*** from the crowd said to
John
1:24 Those sent by the ***P***
4:1 learned that the ***P*** had heard that he
7:32 The ***P*** heard the crowd whispering such
8:3 legal experts and ***P*** brought a woman
8:13 Then the ***P*** said to him, "Because you
9:13 man who had been born blind to the ***P***.
11:46 them went to the ***P*** and told them
12:19 Therefore, the ***P*** said to each other,
Acts
15:5 from among the ***P*** stood up and
23:6 and the others ***P***, Paul exclaimed
23:7 between the ***P*** and Sadducees,
23:8 or spirit, but ***P*** affirm them all.
23:9 loudly. Some ***P*** who were legal

PHARISEES AND LEGAL EXPERTS
Mt 15:1; Mk 7:5; Lk 5:17; 7:30; 15:2

PHARISEES AND SADDUCEES
Mt 3:7; 16:1, 6, 11, 12; Ac 23:7

PHILIP
Matthew
10:3 ***P***; and Bartholomew; Thomas; and
Mark
3:18 and Andrew; ***P***; Bartholomew; Matthew;
Luke
6:14 Andrew; James; John; ***P***; Bartholomew;
John
1:43 and he found ***P***. Jesus said to
Acts
1:13 and Andrew; ***P*** and Thomas;
6:5 faith, ***P***, Prochorus,
8:5 ***P*** went down to a city in Samaria and
8:26 the Lord spoke to ***P***, "At noon, take

PHILIPPI
Matthew
16:13 area of Caesarea ***P***, he asked his
Acts
16:12 there we went to ***P***, a city of
Philippians
1:1 To all those in ***P*** who are God's

PHILISTINE
Exodus
23:31 Reed Sea to the ***P*** Sea and from the

1 Samuel
14:1 go over to the ***P*** fort on the
17:23 Goliath, the ***P*** champion from
17:37 the power of this ***P***." "Go!" Saul

PHILISTINES

Genesis
21:32 forces, returned to the land of the ***P***.
26:1 and toward King Abimelech of the ***P***.
Exodus
13:17 the land of the ***P***, even though that
Judges
10:7 them over to the ***P*** and the Ammonites.
13:1 them over to the ***P*** for forty years.
16:5 The rulers of the ***P*** confronted her and
1 Samuel
4:1 In those days the ***P*** gathered for war
5:1 After the ***P*** took God's chest, they
31:1 When the ***P*** attacked the Israelites, the
2 Samuel
5:17 When the ***P*** heard that David had been
8:1 defeated the ***P*** and subdued them.
8:12 Ammonites, the ***P***, and Amalek,
21:15 out between the ***P*** and Israel. David
2 Kings
18:8 struck down the ***P*** as far as Gaza
Jeremiah
47:4 will destroy the ***P***, the few left
Ezekiel
25:16 overpower the ***P***, eliminate the
Amos
1:8 Ekron, and the ***P*** who remain will

PHINEHAS

Exodus
6:25 She gave birth to ***P***. These were the
Numbers
25:7 When ***P***(Eleazar's son and Aaron the
Joshua
22:13 Israelites sent ***P*** son of Eleazar
1 Samuel
1:3 sons Hophni and ***P*** were the LORD's
Ezra
7:5 of Abishua son of ***P*** son of Eleazar
8:2 of the family of ***P***, Gershom; of
Psalms
106:30 Then ***P*** stood up and prayed, and the

PICK

Genesis
21:18 Get up, ***p*** up the boy, and take him by
45:19 and wives, and ***p*** up your father
Exodus
12:21 said to them, "Go ***p*** out one of the
Leviticus
19:10 Also do not ***p*** your vineyard clean or
27:33 gift must not ***p*** out the good from
Numbers
14:4 other, "Let's ***p*** a leader and
Deuteronomy
24:21 Again, when you ***p*** the grapes of your
Joshua
3:12 Now ***p*** twelve men from the tribes of
4:2 ***P*** twelve men from the people, one man
4:3 Command them, '***P*** up twelve stones from
18:4 ***P*** out three men for each tribe. I will
Judges
1:7 big toes used to ***p*** up scraps under
2 Samuel
17:1 Absalom, "Let me ***p*** twelve thousand
2 Kings
4:36 Elisha. He told her, "***P*** up your son."
9:25 chariot officer, "***P*** him up, and throw
9:26 the LORD. Now ***p*** him up, and throw
Psalms
74:6 they hacked down with hatchet and ***p***.
140:2 their hearts, who ***p*** fights every
Proverbs
27:16 the wind or ***p*** up oil in his
Ecclesiastes
4:10 fall, one can ***p*** up the other. But
Jeremiah
6:9 few in Israel. ***P*** clean every last
9:22 the harvest, with no one to ***p*** them up.
49:9 come to you to ***p*** grapes, they
Jonah
1:12 He said to them, "***P*** me up and hurl me
Matthew
10:38 Those who don't ***p*** up their crosses and
Mark
16:18 They will ***p*** up snakes with their hands.
Luke
6:44 nor do they ***p*** grapes from
John
5:8 to him, "Get up! ***P*** up your mat and
Ephesians
6:13 Therefore ***p*** up the full armor of God so

PIECE

Exodus
25:7 in the priest's vest and chest ***p***.
37:22 lampstand was one ***p*** of pure hammered
Leviticus
8:8 placed the chest ***p*** on Aaron and set
27:24 Jubilee year the ***p*** of land will
Judges
1:14 for a certain ***p*** of land. As she
8:25 they spread out a ***p*** of cloth, and
2 Kings
3:25 a stone on every ***p*** of good land
6:6 Elisha then cut a ***p*** of wood, threw it
1 Chronicles
16:3 loaf of bread, a ***p*** of meat, and a
Job
2:8 Job took a ***p*** of broken pottery to
32:17 I will state my ***p***; I too will
Psalms
22:15 dried up like a ***p*** of broken
31:12 mind; I am like a ***p*** of pottery,
104:6 deep like a ***p*** of clothing; the
Jeremiah
2:27 they say to a ***p*** of wood, "You are
18:4 But the ***p*** he was making was flawed
19:11 the potter's ***p*** beyond repair, so
Lamentations
1:17 is just a ***p*** of garbage to
Ezekiel
24:4 to it, every good ***p***. With shoulder
24:6 removed! Empty it ***p*** by piece. She is
Hosea
4:12 advice from a ***p*** of wood, and
Amos
3:12 two legs or the ***p*** of an ear from

Matthew
9:16 No one sews a ***p*** of new, unshrunk cloth
Mark
2:21 No one sews a ***p*** of new, unshrunk cloth
Luke
24:42 They gave him a ***p*** of baked fish
John
13:26 I will give this ***p*** of bread once I
19:23 woven as one ***p*** from the top to
Acts
5:1 wife Sapphira, sold a ***p*** of property.
1 Thessalonians
5:8 and love as a ***p*** of armor that

PIECES

Genesis
37:33 him. Joseph must have been torn to ***p***!"
Exodus
28:7 have two shoulder ***p*** attached to its
34:1 first tablets, which you broke into ***p***.
Deuteronomy
12:3 gods' idols into ***p***. Wipe out their
32:21 me with their ***p*** of junk. So I am
Judges
19:29 limb, into twelve ***p***. Then he sent
20:6 up, and sent her ***p*** into every part
1 Samuel
11:7 cut them into ***p***, and sent them by
15:33 cut Agag to ***p*** in the LORD's
Job
16:12 dashed me into ***p***; he raised me up
Psalms
35:15 know tore me to ***p*** and wouldn't quit.
50:22 I'll rip you to ***p*** with no one to
119:72 than thousands of ***p*** of gold and
Song of Songs
8:11 for its fruit a thousand ***p*** of silver.
Isaiah
7:4 over these two ***p*** of smoking
Ezekiel
23:34 break it into ***p***, and tear off
Hosea
3:2 her for fifteen ***p*** of silver, a
10:14 were dashed into ***p*** with their
Amos
6:11 into bits and the little house into ***p***.
Micah
1:7 will be beaten to ***p***; all her wages
3:3 their bones in ***p***, and spread them
5:8 and tears to ***p*** with no one to
Nahum
3:10 were dashed to ***p*** at the head of
Zechariah
9:7 his mouth and ***p*** of unclean food
11:6 beat the land to ***p***, but I won't
Matthew
15:36 broke them into ***p*** and gave them to
24:51 will cut them in ***p*** and put them in a
26:15 you?" They paid him thirty ***p*** of silver.
27:3 the thirty ***p*** of silver to the
Mark
6:41 the loaves into ***p***, and gave them to
6:43 with the leftover ***p*** of bread and fish.
Luke
12:46 cut them into ***p*** and assign them a
John
6:12 up the leftover ***p***, so that nothing
6:13 baskets with the ***p*** of the five
Acts
2:45 They would sell ***p*** of property and
23:10 tear Paul to ***p***. He ordered
27:41 was broken into ***p*** by the force of

PIGS

Matthew
7:6 in front of ***p***. They will stomp
8:30 distance a large herd of ***p*** was feeding.
8:32 and went into the ***p***. The whole herd
Mark
5:11 A large herd of ***p*** was feeding on the
5:12 Send us into the ***p***!" they begged.
Luke
8:32 A large herd of ***p*** was feeding on the
15:16 from what the ***p*** ate, but no one

PILATE

Matthew
27:2 and turned him over to ***P*** the governor.
27:58 He came to ***P*** and asked for Jesus' body.
John
19:22 ***P*** answered, "What I've written, I've
Acts
13:28 they asked ***P*** to have him
1 Timothy
6:13 when testifying before Pontius ***P***.

PILLAR

Genesis
19:26 back, she turned into a ***p*** of salt.
28:18 it up as a sacred ***p***, and poured oil
28:22 up as a sacred ***p*** will be God's
31:13 anointed a sacred ***p*** and where you
31:45 took a stone, set it up as a sacred ***p***,
31:51 is the sacred ***p*** that I've set up
31:52 and the sacred ***p*** are witnesses
35:14 set up a sacred ***p***, a stone pillar,
35:20 Jacob set up a ***p*** on her grave. It's the
Leviticus
26:1 image or sacred ***p***. You must not
Deuteronomy
31:15 in the tent in a ***p*** of cloud; the
Judges
9:6 by the oak at the stone ***p*** in Shechem.
2 Samuel
18:18 raised a large ***p*** for himself in
2 Kings
3:2 the sacred ***p*** of Baal that his
10:26 the sacred ***p*** out of Baal's
10:27 Baal's sacred ***p*** and destroyed
11:14 by the royal ***p***, as was the
23:3 stood beside the ***p*** and made a
25:17 Each ***p*** was twenty-seven feet high. The
2 Chronicles
23:13 by the royal ***p*** at the entrance,
Nehemiah
9:12 With a ***p*** of cloud you led them by day
Psalms
99:7 to them from a ***p*** of cloud. They
Jeremiah
1:18 city, an iron ***p***, and a bronze

PILLARS

Exodus
23:24 and smash their sacred stone ***p*** to bits.

24:4 sacred stone ***p*** for the twelve
34:13 sacred stone ***p***, and cut down

Numbers
3:36 its bars, ***p***, bases, and all
3:37 and the ***p*** of the courtyard all around,
4:31 meeting tent, its bars, ***p***, and bases;
4:32 the ***p*** of the courtyard all around, with

Judges
16:25 Then they had him stand between the ***p***.

1 Samuel
2:8 of honor! The ***p*** of the earth

1 Kings
7:15 cast two bronze ***p***. Each one was
7:18 He made the ***p*** and two rows of

2 Kings
17:10 set up sacred ***p*** and sacred poles
18:4 the sacred ***p*** and cut down the
23:14 the sacred ***p*** and cut down the
25:16 objects-the two ***p***, the Sea, and the

1 Chronicles
18:8 bronze basin, the ***p***, and the bronze

2 Chronicles
3:17 he set up the ***p*** in front of the
14:3 the sacred ***p***, cut down the
31:1 the sacred ***p***, cut down the

Job
9:6 from its place, and its ***p*** shudder?
26:11 Heaven's ***p*** shook, terrified by his

Psalms
75:3 but I will keep its ***p*** steady." Selah
144:12 can be like ***p*** carved to

Proverbs
9:1 house; she has carved out her seven ***p***.

Song of Songs
3:6 wilderness, like ***p*** of smoke? She is
3:10 Its ***p*** he made of silver, its covering,
5:15 His thighs are ***p*** of whitest stone set

Jeremiah
27:19 about the ***p***, the Sea, the
43:13 the sacred ***p*** in the temple of

Amos
9:1 said: Strike the ***p*** until the

Micah
5:13 and your sacred ***p*** in your midst.

Revelation
3:12 I will make them ***p*** in the temple of
10:1 sun, and his feet were like fiery ***p***.

PIT

Exodus
21:33 someone leaves a ***p*** open or digs a

2 Samuel
18:17 him into a big ***p*** in the forest.
23:20 went down into a ***p*** and killed a lion

1 Chronicles
11:22 went down into a ***p*** where he killed a

Job
9:31 me into a slimy ***p*** so that my
33:18 one from the ***p***, a life from
33:22 approaches the ***p***; its very being
33:24 going down to the ***p***; I have found a
33:28 crossing into the ***p***; my life beholds
33:30 back from the ***p***, to shine with

Psalms
7:15 They make a ***p***, dig it all out, and
16:10 let your faithful follower see the ***p***.
28:1 be just like those going down to the ***p***.
30:3 from among those going down to the ***p***.
30:9 down into the ***p***? Does dust thank
35:7 they dug a ***p*** for me for no
40:2 me out of the ***p*** of death, out of
49:9 forever without experiencing the ***p***.
55:23 to the deepest ***p***. Let bloodthirsty
57:6 down; they dug a ***p*** for me, but they
69:15 up! Don't let the ***p*** close its mouth
88:4 into the ***p***. I am like those
88:6 in the deepest ***p***, in places dark
94:13 times until a ***p*** is dug for the
103:4 life from the ***p***, crowns you with
107:20 them; he rescued them from their ***p***.
143:7 I'll be like those going down to the ***p***!

Proverbs
1:12 like those who go down into the ***p***.
22:14 woman is a deep ***p***; those under the
23:27 is a deep ***p***, and a foreign
26:27 Those who dig a ***p*** will fall in it;
28:10 into their own ***p***, but the
28:17 hold them back from fleeing to the ***p***.

Ecclesiastes
10:8 Whoever digs a ***p*** may fall into it, and
12:6 and the wheel is crushed at the ***p***;

Isaiah
14:15 are brought, to the depths of the ***p***.
14:19 down to the stony ***p***—like a trampled
24:22 prisoners in a ***p***, shut into a
38:17 being from the ***p*** of destruction,
38:18 go down to the ***p*** can't hope for
51:14 won't die in the ***p*** nor even lack

Jeremiah
18:22 They have dug a ***p*** to capture me,
48:44 will fall into a ***p***; those who escape

Lamentations
3:53 me alive in a ***p*** and threw stones
3:55 name, LORD, from the depths of the ***p***.

Ezekiel
26:20 you down into the ***p***, to the
31:14 human beings who go down to the ***p***.
31:16 go down to the ***p***, all the trees of
32:18 among those who go down to the ***p***.
32:23 region of the ***p***. His assembly
32:24 shame like those who go down to the ***p***.
32:25 go down to the ***p***; in the midst of
32:29 like those who go down to the ***p***.
32:30 shame like those who go down to the ***p***.

Daniel
6:7 will be thrown into a ***p*** of lions.

Jonah
2:6 But you brought me out of the ***p***.'

Zechariah
9:11 your prisoners from the waterless ***p***.

Matthew
12:11 that falls into a ***p*** on the Sabbath

Mark
12:1 around it, dug a ***p*** for the

PITY

Deuteronomy
7:16 you. Show them no ***p***. And don't serve
28:50 very old or show ***p*** to the very young.

2 Chronicles
36:17 and showed no ***p*** for young men or

Job
16:13 open without ***p*** and doesn't care,
19:21 ***P*** me. Pity me. You're my friends. God's

PITY [cont.]

Psalms
17:10 They have no ***p***; their mouths speak
Isaiah
9:17 their youth no ***p***, and showed their
47:6 You took no ***p*** on them. You made
49:13 people, and taken ***p*** on those who
49:15 child, fail to ***p*** the child of her
63:15 concern and your ***p***? Don't hold back!
Jeremiah
13:14 I won't take ***p***; I won't have
15:5 Who will ***p*** you, Jerusalem? Who will
21:7 the sword without ***p***, mercy, or
22:23 cedar, who will ***p*** you when you are
30:18 tents and have ***p*** on their
Ezekiel
7:4 you or show any ***p***. Instead, I'll
7:9 tear or show any ***p*** when I turn your
8:18 I won't spare or ***p*** anyone. Even
9:10 won't spare or ***p*** anyone! I will
16:5 No one took ***p*** or cared enough to do any
24:14 or have any ***p*** or compassion.
Joel
2:18 this land, and had ***p*** on his people.
Jonah
4:11 my part, can't I ***p*** Nineveh, that
Habakkuk
2:12 ***P*** the one building a city with

PLACE → HOLY PLACE

Psalms
7:9 firmly in ***p*** because you, the
8:3 the stars that you set firmly in ***p***—
9:9 LORD is a safe ***p*** for the oppressed-
10:8 They wait in a ***p*** perfect for ambush;
12:8 roam all over the ***p***, while depravity
18:2 salvation's strength, my ***p*** of safety.
26:8 LORD; I love the ***p*** where your glory
27:5 me in a secret ***p*** in his own tent;
33:14 From his dwelling ***p*** God observes all
37:10 around their ***p***, they won't be
41:3 transform the ***p*** where they lie
43:3 your holy mountain, to your dwelling ***p***.
44:19 crushed us in the ***p*** where jackals
46:7 God of Jacob is our ***p*** of safety. Selah
46:11 God of Jacob is our ***p*** of safety. Selah
48:3 revealing himself as a ***p*** of safety.
49:11 homes, the ***p*** they live for all
64:10 heart is in the right ***p*** give praise!
69:4 what I didn't steal in the first ***p***?
74:4 your own meeting ***p***; they set up
74:7 defiled the dwelling ***p*** of your name.
74:17 of the earth in ***p***. Summer and
76:2 His dwelling ***p*** became Salem; his
84:1 is your dwelling ***p***, LORD of heavenly
91:9 the Most High, your ***p*** of residence—
93:1 world firmly in ***p***; it won't be
95:11 They will never enter my ***p*** of rest!'"
96:10 world firmly in ***p***; it won't be
104:8 valleys to the ***p*** you established
119:73 me and set me in ***p***. Help me
119:90 earth firmly in ***p***, and it is still
132:5 until I find a ***p*** for the LORD, a
132:7 God's dwelling ***p***; let's worship at
139:15 in a secret ***p***, when I was being
144:2 my fortress, my ***p*** of safety, my
148:6 God set them in ***p*** always and forever.
Proverbs
4:9 She will ***p*** a graceful wreath on your
11:8 distress, and the wicked take their ***p***.
21:18 be punished in the ***p*** of the virtuous.
23:2 ***P*** a knife at your throat to control
25:6 or stand in the ***p*** of important
Ecclesiastes
1:5 panting to the ***p*** where it dawns.
1:7 full; to the ***p*** where the rivers
3:16 the sun: in the ***p*** of justice, there
3:20 go to the same ***p***: all are from the
4:1 that take ***p*** under the sun, I
4:15 youth who would rise to take his ***p***.
5:19 to accept their ***p*** in the world and
8:10 from a holy ***p***, while those who
Romans
3:25 Jesus as the ***p*** of sacrifice

PLACES

Genesis
6:14 ark with nesting ***p*** and cover it
Job
18:21 the dwelling ***p*** of the evil; this
27:21 are gone, removes them from their ***p***,
28:4 any inhabitant, ***p*** forgotten by
38:36 wisdom in remote ***p***, or who gave
40:20 him tribute, ***p*** where all the
Psalms
10:8 from their hiding ***p*** they kill
10:9 ambush in secret ***p***, like a lion in
51:6 the most hidden ***p***; you teach me
56:1 Dove of Distant ***P***. A miktam of
64:4 from their hiding ***p*** so as to shoot an
74:8 all of God's meeting ***p*** in the land.
74:20 the land's dark ***p*** are full of
88:6 in the deepest pit, in ***p*** dark and deep.
Matthew
12:43 through dry ***p*** looking for a
23:6 love to sit in ***p*** of honor at
24:7 and earthquakes in all sorts of ***p***.
Mark
1:45 in deserted ***p***, but people came
12:39 They long for ***p*** of honor in the
13:8 in all sorts of ***p***. These things are
Luke
3:5 straight and the rough ***p*** made smooth.
5:16 withdraw to deserted ***p*** for prayer.
11:24 through dry ***p*** looking for a
15:5 is thrilled and ***p*** it on his
20:46 They long for the ***p*** of honor in the

PLAGUE

Exodus
8:2 then I'll send a ***p*** of frogs over
12:13 pass over you. No ***p*** will destroy you
30:12 counted. Then no ***p*** will descend on
32:35 the LORD sent a ***p*** on the people
Leviticus
26:25 I will send a ***p*** on you, and you
Numbers
8:19 will not be a ***p*** when the
14:12 them down with a ***p*** and disown them.
14:37 men died by a ***p*** in the LORD's
16:46 anger has gone out. The ***p*** has begun."
16:50 of the meeting tent once the ***p*** stopped.
25:8 stomach. Then the ***p*** stopped spreading
26:1 After the ***p*** the LORD said to Moses

31:16 so there was a **p** among the LORD's
Deuteronomy
28:21 LORD will make a **p** stick to you
32:24 hunger, consuming **p**, bitter sickness.
Joshua
22:17 when there was a **p** on the LORD's
1 Samuel
6:4 because the same **p** came on all of
2 Samuel
24:13 be three days of **p** in your land?
24:15 the LORD sent a **p** on Israel from
1 Kings
8:37 is a famine or **p** in the land; or
1 Chronicles
21:12 sword, that is, **p** in the land and
21:14 the LORD sent a **p** throughout
21:17 but spare your people from the **p**."
21:22 the LORD, and the **p** among the people
2 Chronicles
6:28 is a famine or **p** in the land, or
7:13 land or I send a **p** against my people,
20:9 sword, flood, **p**, or famine comes
Psalms
39:10 Get this **p** of yours off me! I'm being
106:29 they did, so a **p** broke out against
106:30 up and prayed, and the **p** was contained.
Jeremiah
21:6 they will die of a terrible **p**.
21:7 who have survived **p**, war, and famine
Ezekiel
5:12 you will die of **p** and waste away by
6:11 will fall by the sword, famine, and **p**.
7:15 sword! Inside, **p** and famine!
12:16 famine, and **p**, so that they may
14:19 suppose I send a **p** against that land
28:23 I will hurl **p** against it, and blood
33:27 strongholds and caves will die of **p**.
38:22 with him, with **p** and blood. I will
Amos
4:10 I sent a **p** against you like the one in
Habakkuk
3:5 in front of him. **P** marches at his
Zechariah
14:12 This will be the **p** with which the LORD
Revelation
11:6 earth with any **p**, as often as they
16:21 God for the **p** of hail, because

PLAGUES
Genesis
12:17 with severe **p** because of
Exodus
9:14 to send all my **p** on you, your
Deuteronomy
28:61 diseases and **p** that aren't
29:22 all that land's **p** and the
Psalms
78:48 over to disease, their herds to **p**.
Revelation
9:18 By these three **p** a third of humankind
15:1 angels with seven **p**—and these are the
16:9 power over these **p**. But they didn't
18:4 sins and don't receive any of her **p**.
18:8 This is why her **p** will come in a single
21:9 of the seven last **p** spoke with me.
22:18 that person the **p** that are written

PLAIN
Genesis
12:9 the arid southern **p**, making and
Deuteronomy
1:1 desert, on the **p** across from Suph,
3:17 Also the desert **p**, with the Jordan
11:30 in the desert **p**, across from
34:3 the arid southern **p**, and the plain—in
Joshua
11:2 in the desert **p** south of
11:16 arid southern **p**, the whole land
12:1 the whole eastern part of the desert **p**.
12:8 in the desert **p**, in the slopes,
15:19 the arid southern **p**, you should also
18:18 north and went down into the desert **p**.
19:8 the arid southern **p**. This is the
2 Samuel
6:20 himself in **p** view of the
16:22 wives in **p** sight before all
24:7 in the arid southern **p** of Judah.
2 Kings
25:4 the soldiers ran toward the desert **p**.
2 Chronicles
26:10 lowlands and the **p**. He had many
28:18 the arid southern **p** of Judah,
35:22 went to fight Neco on the **p** of Megiddo.
Nehemiah
6:2 villages in the **p** of Ono." But they
Song of Songs
2:1 of the Sharon **p**, a lily of the
Isaiah
1:7 devouring it in **p** sight. It's a
21:1 the arid southern **p**, it comes from
40:4 level, and rough terrain a valley **p**.
Jeremiah
13:19 the arid southern **p** will be
52:7 the soldiers fled toward the desert **p**.
Ezekiel
20:46 the thicket in the arid southern **p**.
20:47 the arid southern **p**: Hear the LORD
Hosea
2:10 her nakedness in **p** view of her
Obadiah
1:19 the arid southern **p** will possess
1:20 the cities of the arid southern **p**.
Habakkuk
2:2 and make it **p** upon a tablet so
Zechariah
4:7 you will become a **p**. He will present
7:7 the arid southern **p** and the western
Romans
1:19 God should be **p** to them because

PLAINS
Numbers
22:1 and camped in the **p** of Moab across
26:3 the people on the **p** of Moab by the
33:50 to Moses on the **p** of Moab by the
Joshua
4:13 presence to the **p** of Jericho, ready
5:10 day of the month on the **p** of Jericho.
10:40 the arid southern **p**, the lowlands,
13:32 was in the Moab **p** on the other side
Jeremiah
39:5 Zedekiah in the **p** of Jericho. They
52:8 caught him in the **p** of Jericho. (His

PLAN

Genesis
11:6 now all that they ***p*** to do will be
Exodus
26:30 according to the ***p*** for it that you
32:12 He had an evil ***p*** to take the
Judges
20:38 The ***p*** between the main force of the
1 Samuel
17:28 and your devious ***p***: you came down
30:24 with you on this ***p***? The share of
2 Samuel
13:32 been Absalom's ***p*** ever since the
17:4 This ***p*** seemed excellent to Absalom and
1 Kings
12:24 this is my ***p***.'" When they
2 Kings
16:10 sent the altar's ***p*** and details for
1 Chronicles
28:11 son Solomon the ***p*** for the entrance
28:19 including the ***p*** for all of the
2 Chronicles
11:4 this is my ***p***. When they heard
28:13 told them. "Your ***p*** will only add to
30:4 Since the ***p*** seemed good to the king and
Ezra
4:5 frustrate their ***p***. They did this
Esther
1:21 king liked the ***p***, as did the other
2:4 king liked the ***p*** and implemented
3:7 best day for his ***p***. They tried every
8:3 secret ***p*** directed against
8:5 into effect the ***p*** of Haman,
9:25 said: The wicked ***p*** that Haman made
Job
42:2 do anything; no ***p*** of yours can be
Psalms
21:11 devised a wicked ***p***—but they will
31:13 against me, they ***p*** to take my life!
33:10 what the nations ***p***; he frustrates
33:11 But the LORD's ***p*** stands forever; what
58:2 your hearts you ***p*** injustice; your
64:5 evil words. They ***p*** on laying traps
73:8 privileged positions they ***p*** oppression.
Proverbs
3:29 Don't ***p*** to harm your neighbor who
12:20 of those who ***p*** evil, but there
14:22 Don't those who ***p*** evil go astray? Those
16:9 People ***p*** their path, but the LORD
16:30 those who purse their lips ***p*** evil.
19:18 is hope, but don't ***p*** to kill them.
Isaiah
5:19 can see; let the ***p*** of Israel's holy
8:10 Create a ***p***, but be frustrated! Speak a
14:26 This is the ***p*** that has been made for
14:27 has created a ***p***; who can stop it?
29:15 who hide their ***p*** deep, away from
30:1 LORD, who make a ***p***, which is not
46:10 done, saying, "My ***p*** will stand; all
46:11 land for my ***p***. As surely as I
Jeremiah
4:28 have declared my ***p*** and will neither
18:11 I'm working out a ***p*** against you. So
49:30 counsel and devised a ***p*** against you.
51:12 the LORD has a ***p*** against the
Ezekiel
38:10 mind, and you will devise an evil ***p***.
43:11 its entire ***p*** and all of its
Daniel
1:14 along with their ***p*** and tested them
Micah
2:1 to those who ***p*** evil when they
Habakkuk
2:10 You ***p*** shame for your own house, cutting
Zechariah
6:13 two of them will share a peaceable ***p***.
7:10 the poor; don't ***p*** evil against each
8:15 course and again ***p*** to do good to
8:17 Don't ***p*** evil for each other. Don't
Mark
3:6 of Herod to ***p*** how to destroy
15:1 a ***p***. They bound
Luke
23:51 agreed with the ***p*** and actions of
Acts
2:23 God's established ***p*** and
4:28 your power and ***p*** had already
5:38 them go! If their ***p*** or activity is of
20:27 proclaiming the entire ***p*** of God to you.
27:12 supported a ***p*** to put out to sea
27:13 carry out their ***p***. They pulled up
27:43 out their ***p***. He ordered those
Romans
13:14 Christ, and don't ***p*** to indulge your
Ephesians
1:5 was according to his goodwill and ***p***
1:9 goodwill and the ***p*** that he intended
1:11 destined by the ***p*** of God, who
3:3 me his secret ***p*** in a revelation,
6:19 makes this secret ***p*** of the gospel
Colossians
1:26 it with a secret ***p*** that has been
2:2 of the secret ***p*** of God, namely
4:3 preach the secret ***p*** of Christ—which
2 Thessalonians
2:7 The hidden ***p*** to live without any law is

PLANNED

Genesis
50:20 You ***p*** something bad for me, but God
Deuteronomy
9:25 because the LORD ***p*** on wiping you out.
19:19 him what he had ***p*** to do to his
Judges
20:32 Israelites had ***p***, We'll retreat
1 Samuel
14:4 where Jonathan ***p*** on crossing over
2 Samuel
14:13 Why have you ***p*** the very same
21:5 oppressed us, who ***p*** to destroy us,
21:16 of the Raphah, ***p*** on killing David.
2 Kings
10:19 a great sacrifice ***p*** for Baal. Anyone
19:25 up long ago; I ***p*** it in the distant
2 Chronicles
32:2 Sennacherib also ***p*** on fighting
Esther
2:21 king, but they secretly ***p*** to kill him.
3:6 race. Instead, he ***p*** to wipe out all
6:2 who secretly ***p*** to kill King
8:7 pole because he ***p*** to attack the
9:24 all the Jews, had ***p*** to destroy the

Isaiah
2:12 forces has ***p*** a day: against
7:5 Aram has ***p*** evil against you with
14:24 be; and as I have ***p***, so it will
19:12 heavenly forces has ***p*** concerning Egypt.
22:11 consider the one who ***p*** it long ago.
23:8 Who ***p*** this concerning Tyre, the one who
23:9 heavenly forces ***p*** it, to defile the
25:1 wonderful things, ***p*** long ago,
37:26 up long ago; I ***p*** it in the distant
46:11 it happen; I have ***p***, and yes, I'll do
Jeremiah
23:20 all that he has ***p***. In the days to
Lamentations
2:8 The LORD ***p*** to destroy Daughter Zion's
2:17 did what he had ***p***. He accomplished
Micah
6:5 King Balak had ***p***, and how Balaam,
Zechariah
1:6 to what we have done, exactly as he ***p***.
8:14 Just as I ***p*** evil against you
Acts
12:4 guarded him. He ***p*** to charge him
Romans
1:13 sisters, that I ***p*** to visit you many
2 Corinthians
1:17 unreliable when I ***p*** to do this, was
Ephesians
1:10 This is what God ***p*** for the climax of
2:10 good things. God ***p*** for these good

PLANS

Genesis
27:42 is planning revenge. He ***p*** to kill you.
Deuteronomy
28:29 in darkness. Your ***p*** won't prosper.
1 Samuel
23:10 heard that Saul ***p*** on coming to
2 Samuel
14:14 instead, he makes ***p*** so those banished
17:21 Ahithophel has made ***p*** against you!"
2 Kings
16:11 following the ***p*** that King Ahaz
1 Chronicles
28:12 all of the ***p*** he had in mind:
2 Chronicles
25:16 said, "I know God ***p*** to destroy you
Nehemiah
4:15 had spoiled their ***p***. So we all
Job
5:13 so that the ***p*** of the devious
18:7 slow down; their ***p*** trip themselves.
21:27 I know your thoughts; your ***p*** harm me.
Psalms
5:10 fail by their own ***p***. Throw them out
14:6 may humiliate the ***p*** of those who
17:11 They make their ***p*** to put me in the
20:4 in your heart and fulfill all your ***p***.
40:5 deeds and your ***p*** for us—no one
83:3 concoct crafty ***p*** against your own
107:11 and rejected the Most High's ***p***.
139:2 from far away, you comprehend my ***p***.
139:17 God, your ***p*** are incomprehensible to me!
140:8 Don't allow their ***p*** to succeed, or
146:4 On that very same day, their ***p*** die too.
Proverbs
6:18 set on wicked ***p***, feet that run
12:5 The ***p*** of the righteous are just, but
15:22 ***P*** fail with no counsel, but with many
15:26 LORD detests evil ***p***, but gracious
16:1 people belong the ***p*** of the heart, but
16:3 to the LORD, and your ***p*** will succeed.
19:21 Many ***p*** are in a person's mind, but the
20:18 ***P*** are firmed up by advice; wage wars
21:5 The ***p*** of the diligent end up in profit,
Isaiah
10:7 But he has other ***p***; he schemes in
19:3 frustrate their ***p***. They will
32:7 are evil. He ***p*** schemes to
53:10 life. The LORD's ***p*** will come to
65:2 that isn't good, following their own ***p***;
Jeremiah
18:12 follow our own ***p*** and act according
19:7 I will foil the ***p*** of Judah and
29:11 I know the ***p*** I have in mind for you,
49:20 for Edom and the ***p*** he's devised
50:45 Babylon and the ***p*** he's devised
51:29 the LORD's ***p*** against Babylon
Ezekiel
11:2 men devise evil ***p*** and give wicked
Daniel
6:3 that the king had ***p*** to set him over
11:24 He will make ***p*** against
Micah
4:12 don't know the ***p*** of the LORD; they

PLANT

Genesis
1:11 the earth grow ***p*** life: plants
47:23 seed for you. ***P*** the seed on the
Exodus
23:10 years you should ***p*** crops on your
Leviticus
19:19 livestock, do not ***p*** your field with
19:23 the land and ***p*** any fruit tree,
25:3 You will ***p*** your fields for six years,
26:16 away. You will ***p*** seed for no
27:16 seed needed to ***p*** it: fifty silver
Deuteronomy
6:11 that you didn't ***p***—and you eat and
16:21 Don't ***p*** any tree to serve as a sacred
22:9 Don't ***p*** your vineyards with two types
28:30 in it. You might ***p*** a vineyard, but
28:39 You might ***p*** lots of vineyards and work
Joshua
24:13 and olive groves that you didn't ***p***.
2 Samuel
7:10 Israel, and ***p*** them so that they
2 Kings
19:29 and harvest it; ***p*** vineyards and eat
1 Chronicles
17:9 Israel, and ***p*** them so that they
Nehemiah
10:31 year we won't ***p*** crops, and we
Job
8:16 a well-watered ***p*** in the sun; its
14:9 will bud and produce sprouts like a ***p***.
Psalms
107:37 They ***p*** fields and vineyards and obtain
126:5 Let those who ***p*** with tears reap the
Isaiah
17:10 you. Therefore, ***p*** your pleasant

17:11 grow the day you ***p*** them, and make
28:25 sow cumin, and ***p*** wheat and barley
37:30 the third year, ***p*** seed and harvest
41:19 I will ***p*** in the desert cedar, acacia,
53:2 up like a young ***p*** before us, like a
65:21 them; they will ***p*** vineyards and eat
65:22 to live in, nor ***p*** for others to

Jeremiah
1:10 destroy and demolish, to build and ***p***."
4:3 rocky soil; don't ***p*** among the thorns.
12:2 You ***p*** them, and they take root; they
18:9 I will build and ***p*** a nation or
24:6 them down; I will ***p*** them and not dig
29:28 and settle down, ***p*** gardens and eat
31:5 Again, you will ***p*** vineyards on the
32:41 and I will ***p*** them in this land
35:7 or own houses or ***p*** gardens and
42:10 you down. I will ***p*** you and not dig
50:16 from those who ***p*** and those who

Ezekiel
16:7 like a young ***p*** in the field, and
17:22 and I myself will ***p*** it on a very high
17:23 highlands I will ***p*** it, and it will
28:26 build houses, ***p*** vineyards, and
37:14 will live. I will ***p*** you on your

Amos
9:14 them. They will ***p*** vineyards and
9:15 I will ***p*** them upon their land, and they

Zephaniah
1:13 them; they will ***p*** vineyards, but

Matthew
13:27 didn't you ***p*** good seed in your
15:13 replied, "Every ***p*** that my heavenly

Luke
12:24 they neither ***p*** nor harvest, they
19:22 and harvesting what I didn't ***p***?

Galatians
6:7 A person will harvest what they ***p***.
6:8 Those who ***p*** only for their own benefit

Revelation
9:4 or any green ***p*** or any tree. They

PLANTED

Genesis
2:8 The LORD God ***p*** a garden in Eden in the
9:20 made a new start and ***p*** a vineyard.
21:33 Abraham ***p*** a tamarisk tree in
26:12 Isaac ***p*** grain in that land and reaped

Exodus
15:17 them in and ***p*** them on your own
23:16 crops that you ***p*** in the field, and

Leviticus
11:37 that is to be ***p***, the seed is

Numbers
24:6 that the LORD has ***p***, like cedar trees

Deuteronomy
20:6 here who has ***p*** a vineyard but
21:4 been plowed or ***p***—and they will bre
22:9 that you have ***p*** and the produce

Joshua
4:3 had been firmly ***p***. Bring them

Judges
6:3 the Israelites ***p*** seeds, the

Psalms
44:2 nations, but you ***p*** our ancestors.
80:8 You drove out the nations and ***p*** it.
80:9 for it; then it ***p*** its roots deep,
80:15 root that you ***p*** with your strong
97:11 Light is ***p*** like seed for the righteous
104:16 the cedars of Lebanon, which God ***p***,
128:3 will be like olive trees, freshly ***p***.

Ecclesiastes
2:4 for myself, ***p*** vineyards for
3:2 and a time for uprooting what was ***p***,

Isaiah
5:2 away its stones, ***p*** it with excellent
40:24 Scarcely are they ***p***, scarcely sown,
60:21 the shoot that I ***p***, the work of my
61:3 of Righteousness, ***p*** by the LORD to

Jeremiah
2:21 Yet it was I who ***p*** you, a precious vine
11:17 forces who ***p*** you has announced
17:8 be like trees ***p*** by the streams,
45:4 that which I have ***p***—the entire land.

Ezekiel
17:5 a native seed and ***p*** it in a prepared
17:8 where it was ***p*** to grow branches,
17:10 Though it is ***p***, will it thrive? When
19:10 in a vineyard ***p*** beside the
19:13 So now she is ***p*** in the desert, in a
31:4 where it was ***p***. From there,
36:36 down and have ***p*** what was made

Hosea
9:13 Tyre, Ephraim was ***p*** in a lovely

Amos
5:11 in them; you have ***p*** pleasant

Matthew
13:19 off what was ***p*** in their hearts.
13:24 like someone who ***p*** good seed in his
13:25 an enemy came and ***p*** weeds among the
21:33 a landowner who ***p*** a vineyard. He

Mark
4:15 and steals the word that was ***p*** in them.
4:32 but when it's ***p***, it grows and becomes
12:1 parables. "A man ***p*** a vineyard, put a

Luke
13:6 owned a fig tree ***p*** in his vineyard.
13:19 someone took and ***p*** in a garden. It
17:6 Be uprooted and ***p*** in the sea,' and
19:21 and you harvest what you haven't ***p***.'
20:9 A certain man ***p*** a vineyard,

1 Corinthians
3:6 I ***p***, Apollos watered, but God made it

James
1:21 welcome the word ***p*** deep inside you—

PLANTS

Genesis
1:11 grow plant life: ***p*** yielding seeds
1:29 to you all the ***p*** on the earth that
2:5 before any wild ***p*** appeared on the
3:18 for you, even as you eat the field's ***p***;

2 Kings
4:39 field to gather ***p***; he found a wild
19:26 become like ***p*** in a field,

Job
8:19 joy, for from the dust other ***p*** sprout.

Psalms
104:14 cattle; you make ***p*** for human farming
105:35 devoured all the ***p*** in their land;
144:12 their youth, like ***p***; so that our

Proverbs
27:25 appears, and the ***p*** of the hills are
31:16 her own resources, she ***p*** a vineyard.

Isaiah
17:10 your pleasant ***p***, and set out
37:27 become like ***p*** in a field,
44:14 of the forest. He ***p*** a pine, and the
55:10 and yield ***p*** and providing
Amos
7:2 eating the green ***p*** of the land, I
Matthew
13:6 it scorched the ***p***, and they dried
13:37 The one who ***p*** the good seed is
Mark
4:6 it scorched the ***p***; and they dried
4:32 of all vegetable ***p***. It produces such
Luke
6:44 figs from thorny ***p***, nor do they pick
8:7 fell among thorny ***p***. The thorns grew
1 Corinthians
3:7 the one who ***p*** nor the one who
3:8 The one who ***p*** and the one who waters
9:7 own way? Who ***p*** a vineyard and
Hebrews
6:7 and yields useful ***p*** for those who

PLEADED

Genesis
19:3 He ***p*** earnestly with them, so they went
41:55 and the people ***p*** to Pharaoh for
Exodus
5:15 came and ***p*** to Pharaoh, "Why
32:11 But Moses ***p*** with the LORD his God,
1 Kings
13:6 So the man of God ***p*** before the LORD,
Isaiah
53:12 sin of many and ***p*** on behalf of
Matthew
8:31 The demons ***p*** with him, "If you throw us out
8:34 saw him, they ***p*** with him to leave
Mark
5:10 They ***p*** with Jesus not to send them out
5:17 Then they ***p*** with Jesus to leave their
5:18 demon-possessed ***p*** with Jesus to let
5:23 and ***p*** with him, "My daughter is about
Luke
7:4 they earnestly ***p*** with Jesus. "He
8:31 They ***p*** with him not to order them to go
8:41 Jesus' feet. He ***p*** with Jesus to
2 Corinthians
12:8 I ***p*** with the Lord three times for it to
1 Thessalonians
2:12 you, and ***p*** with you to live

PLEASANT

Genesis
49:15 that the land was ***p***. He lowered his
Esther
2:12 of treatment with ***p***-smelling creams an
Psalms
55:14 It was so ***p*** when together we entered
Proverbs
3:17 Her ways are ***p***; all her paths are
3:24 you lie down, your sleep will be ***p***.
9:17 is sweet; food eaten in secret is ***p***."
13:19 fulfilled is ***p***, but fools find
16:21 discerning, and ***p*** speech enhances
16:24 ***P*** words are flowing honey, sweet to the
22:18 It will be ***p*** if you keep the words in
23:8 them out. You will waste your ***p*** words.
24:4 filled with all precious and ***p*** wealth.
Ecclesiastes
11:7 light, and it's ***p*** for the eyes to
Isaiah
17:10 plant your ***p*** plants, and set
32:12 breasts for the ***p*** fields, for the
Jeremiah
31:26 looked around. What a ***p*** sleep I had!
48:11 taste is still ***p***, and its aroma is
Hosea
4:13 their shade is ***p***. Therefore, your
Amos
5:11 you have planted ***p*** vineyards, but
Zechariah
8:19 joy and gladness, ***p*** feasts for the

PLEASE

Exodus
21:8 If she doesn't ***p*** her master who chose
Deuteronomy
2:27 ***P*** let us pass through your land. We
21:8 LORD, ***p*** forgive your people Israel,
26:15 ***P*** look down from your holy home, from
Ruth
2:7 She said, '***P*** let me glean so that I
Psalms
5:8 of many enemies, ***p*** lead me in your
6:1 psalm of David.] ***P***, LORD, don't
7:9 ***P*** let the evil of the wicked be over,
22:11 ***P*** don't be far from me because trouble
25:2 God, I trust you. ***P*** don't let me be
25:11 ***P***, for the sake of your good name,
25:20 ***P*** protect my life! Deliver me! Don't
25:22 ***P***, God, save Israel from all its
27:9 ***P*** don't hide it from me! Don't push
31:1 in you, LORD. ***P*** never let me be
35:22 quiet about it. ***P*** don't be far from
38:1 offering.] ***P***, LORD, don't
38:21 all alone, LORD! ***P***, my God, don't be
39:12 my cry for help! ***P*** don't ignore my
41:10 But you, LORD, ***p*** have mercy on me and
51:11 ***P*** don't throw me out of your presence;
61:4 ***P*** let me live in your tent forever!
71:21 ***P*** increase my honor and comfort me all
80:14 ***P*** come back, God of heavenly forces!
90:13 back to us, LORD! ***P***, quick! Have some
116:4 on the LORD's name: "LORD, ***p*** save me!"
118:25 LORD, ***p*** save us! LORD, please let us
119:8 your statutes. ***P*** don't leave me
119:31 your laws, LORD. ***P*** don't let me be
119:43 ***P*** don't take your true word out of my
119:76 ***P*** let your faithful love comfort me,
119:108 ***P***, LORD, accept my spontaneous gifts
119:122 for your servant. ***P*** don't let the
143:2 ***P*** don't bring your servant to judgment
Ecclesiastes
2:26 joy to those who ***p*** God. But to those
Isaiah
36:11 field commander, "***P*** speak to your
37:20 now LORD our God, ***p*** save us from
38:3 ***P***, LORD, remember how I've walked
Jeremiah
27:5 are on it. I can give it to anyone I ***p***.
37:3 with this plea: "***P*** pray for us to
42:2 to ask you: ***P*** pray to the LORD

Lamentations
5:21 to yourself. ***P*** let us return!
Hosea
9:4 sacrifices won't ***p*** him. Such
Romans
8:8 are self-centered aren't able to ***p*** God.
15:1 don't have power, and not ***p*** ourselves.
15:2 Each of us should ***p*** our neighbors for
15:3 Christ didn't ***p*** himself, but, as it is
1 Corinthians
7:32 Lord's concerns—how he can ***p*** the Lord.
7:33 concerns—how he can ***p*** his wife.
7:34 concerns—how she can ***p*** her husband.
10:33 that I do. I ***p*** everyone in
Galatians
1:10 Or am I trying to ***p*** people? If I were
1 Thessalonians
2:4 aren't trying to ***p*** people, but we
2:15 out. They don't ***p*** God, and they are
4:1 how you live and ***p*** God—just as you l
2 Timothy
2:4 so that they can ***p*** the one who
Titus
2:9 own masters and ***p*** them in
Hebrews
11:6 impossible to ***p*** God without faith

PLEASED
Genesis
45:16 both Pharaoh and his servants were ***p***.
Numbers
14:8 If the LORD is ***p*** with us, he'll bring
24:1 saw that it ***p*** the LORD to bless
Deuteronomy
21:14 But if you aren't ***p*** with her, you must
1 Samuel
16:22 in my service because I am ***p*** with him."
18:5 and this ***p*** all the troops as
2 Samuel
3:36 of this and were ***p*** by it. Indeed,
15:26 says, 'I'm not ***p*** with you,' then I
19:18 to do whatever ***p*** him. Gera's son
22:20 pulled me out, because he is ***p*** with me.
1 Kings
3:10 It ***p*** the LORD that Solomon had made
8:66 tents happy and ***p*** about all the
10:9 because he was ***p*** to place you on
1 Chronicles
28:4 family he was ***p*** with me, making
2 Chronicles
9:8 because he was ***p*** to put you on the
24:10 This so ***p*** all the leaders and all the
Ezra
5:17 may the king be ***p*** to send us his
Nehemiah
2:6 return?" So it ***p*** the king to send
Esther
2:9 The young woman ***p*** him and won his
2:14 unless he was so ***p*** that he called
5:2 court, he was ***p***. The king held
Job
33:26 God, and God is ***p*** with them; they
Psalms
18:19 me out safe because he is ***p*** with me.
30:7 Because it ***p*** you, LORD, you made me a
41:11 I'll know you are ***p*** with me because
44:3 your face because you were ***p*** with them.
49:13 their lead, ***p*** with their talk.
51:16 burned offering, you wouldn't be ***p***.
77:7 me forever? Will he never be ***p*** again?
149:4 the LORD is ***p*** with his people,
Isaiah
39:2 Hezekiah was ***p***, and he showed them his
Jeremiah
3:15 with whom I'm ***p***, and they will
Ezekiel
16:37 lovers whom you ***p***, the ones you
Daniel
8:4 did whatever it ***p***. It became
Amos
5:22 food—I won't be ***p***; I won't even
Micah
6:7 Will the LORD be ***p*** with thousands of
Malachi
1:8 Would he be ***p*** with it or accept
Matthew
17:5 love. I am very ***p*** with him. Listen
Acts
6:5 This proposal ***p*** the entire community.
12:3 he saw that this ***p*** the Jews, he
1 Corinthians
1:21 Instead, God was ***p*** to save those who
2 Corinthians
7:13 we were even more ***p*** at how happy
Galatians
1:15 called me through his grace. He was ***p***
Colossians
1:19 fullness of God was ***p*** to live in him,
Hebrews
10:6 you weren't ***p*** with entirely burned
10:8 and you weren't ***p*** with a sacrifice
10:38 being won't be ***p*** with anyone who
11:5 for having ***p*** God before he was
13:16 because God is ***p*** with these kinds

PLEASING
Genesis
8:21 LORD smelled the ***p*** scent, and the
Deuteronomy
24:1 but she isn't ***p*** to him because
Ezra
6:10 they may offer ***p*** sacrifices to the
Psalms
19:14 of my heart be ***p*** to you, LORD, my
45:8 clothes have the ***p*** scent of myrrh,
69:31 that is more ***p*** to the LORD than
104:34 Let my praise be ***p*** to him; I'm
119:103 Your word is so ***p*** to my taste buds—
133:1 at how good and ***p*** it is when
141:6 words will be heard because they are ***p***.
Ecclesiastes
12:10 searched for ***p*** words, and he
Ezekiel
6:13 they offered up ***p*** aromas for all
16:19 before them as a ***p*** aroma. This is
20:28 offerings here, ***p*** aromas there, and
20:41 accept you as a ***p*** aroma. Through
Malachi
3:4 Jerusalem will be ***p*** to the LORD as in
Romans
12:1 that is holy and ***p*** to God. This is
12:2 will is—what is good and ***p*** and mature.

Ephesians
5:10 everything to see what's ***p*** to the Lord,
Colossians
1:10 of the Lord and ***p*** to him in every
Hebrews
12:28 in a way that is ***p*** to God with

PLEASURE

Job
7:7 is wind; my eyes won't see ***p*** again.
21:14 us; we take no ***p*** in knowing your
22:26 you will take ***p*** in the Almighty;
Psalms
68:30 the peoples who take ***p*** in battles.
147:1 Because it is a ***p*** to make beautiful
Proverbs
10:23 with understanding take ***p*** in wisdom.
18:2 Fools find no ***p*** in understanding, but
21:17 Those who love ***p*** end up poor; lovers of
Ecclesiastes
2:1 you experience ***p***; enjoy what is
2:2 is madness; ***p***, of no use at all.
2:10 my heart no ***p***. Indeed, my heart
2:24 and experience ***p*** in their hard
5:4 God has no ***p*** in fools. Fulfill
5:19 world and to find ***p*** in their hard
11:8 years should take ***p*** in them all. But
12:1 you'll say, "I take no ***p*** in these"—
Song of Songs
2:3 his shade I take ***p*** in sitting, and
Isaiah
21:4 has turned my evening of ***p*** into dread—
32:14 suited for the ***p*** of wild donkeys,
Jeremiah
6:10 of the LORD's word and take no ***p*** in it.
Ezekiel
18:23 Do I take ***p*** in the death of the wicked?
33:11 I live, do I take ***p*** in the death of
43:27 accept you with ***p***. This is what the
Obadiah
1:12 have taken no ***p*** over your brother
Habakkuk
3:14 those who take ***p*** in secretly
Matthew
12:18 whom I find great ***p***. I'll put my
23:25 are full of violence and ***p*** seeking.
2 Timothy
3:4 They will love ***p*** instead of loving
Hebrews
13:17 to do this with ***p*** and not with

PLEDGE

Exodus
22:11 swear a solemn ***p*** before the LORD
Leviticus
5:1 a public solemn ***p*** even though you
Numbers
5:19 swear a solemn ***p***, saying to the
30:2 swears a solemn ***p*** of binding
Deuteronomy
7:8 kept the solemn ***p*** he swore to your
24:17 take a widow's coat as ***p*** for a loan.
Joshua
2:12 loyal to you. So ***p*** to me by the LORD
2:20 for this ***p*** you made us
9:15 the community made a solemn ***p*** to them.
Judges
21:1 had made a ***p*** at Mizpah
1 Samuel
14:24 by a solemn ***p***: "Anyone who eats
20:12 told David, "I ***p*** by the LORD God
24:21 make a solemn ***p*** to me by the LORD
25:26 I ***p***, my master, as surely as the LORD
30:15 him. "Make a ***p*** to me by God that
2 Samuel
21:2 sworn a solemn ***p*** to spare them,
1 Kings
1:29 made a solemn ***p*** and said, "As
2:42 swear a solemn ***p*** by the LORD? And
8:31 make a solemn ***p*** asserting
2 Kings
11:4 swear a solemn ***p*** in the LORD's
25:24 made a solemn ***p*** to them and their
1 Chronicles
16:16 the solemn ***p*** he swore to Isaac.
2 Chronicles
6:22 take a solemn ***p*** asserting his
15:15 with the solemn ***p*** because they had
36:13 the solemn ***p*** Nebuchadnezzar
Ezra
10:5 take a solemn ***p*** that they would
Nehemiah
6:18 to him by solemn ***p*** because he was
10:29 and make a solemn ***p*** to live by God's
10:32 We ***p*** ourselves to keep the commandment
13:25 swear a solemn ***p*** in the name of
Psalms
105:9 the solemn ***p*** he swore to Isaac.
110:4 sworn a solemn ***p*** and won't change
Proverbs
20:16 a stranger; take his ***p*** for a foreigner.
27:13 a stranger; take his ***p*** for a foreigner.
Ecclesiastes
8:2 command as you would keep a solemn ***p***.
Song of Songs
2:7 Make a solemn ***p***, daughters of
5:9 that you make us swear a solemn ***p***?
8:4 Make a solemn ***p***, daughters of
Isaiah
45:23 sworn a solemn ***p***; a word has left
65:16 who make a solemn ***p*** in the land will
Jeremiah
5:2 when making a ***p***—"As the LORD liv
11:5 fulfill my solemn ***p*** that I made to
12:16 to make a solemn ***p*** in my name, "As
44:26 in the solemn ***p***: "As surely as
Ezekiel
17:13 him take a solemn ***p*** of loyalty. He
20:5 I swore a solemn ***p*** to the
44:12 I made a solemn ***p*** against them—this
Matthew
5:33 a false solemn ***p***, but you should
5:34 that you must not ***p*** at all. You must
5:35 You must not ***p*** by the earth, because
5:36 And you must not ***p*** by your head,
14:9 of his solemn ***p*** and his guests he
26:72 With a solemn ***p***, he denied it again,
Mark
6:26 of his solemn ***p*** and his guests,

Luke
1:73 the solemn ***p*** he made to our ancestor
Acts
2:30 him with a solemn ***p*** to seat one of
Hebrews
6:16 People ***p*** by something greater than
6:17 he guaranteed it with a solemn ***p***.
7:20 without a solemn ***p***! The others have
7:21 with a solemn ***p*** by the one who
7:28 of the solemn ***p***, which came after
James
5:12 make a solemn ***p***—neither by heaven

PLENTY

Genesis
24:25 We have ***p*** of straw and feed
27:28 from the earth, ***p*** of grain and new
33:9 I already have ***p***, my brother. Keep
34:21 it; there's ***p*** of land for them.
Numbers
24:7 seed will have ***p*** of water; his
2 Chronicles
2:9 to prepare ***p*** of timber for me, because
11:23 and gave them ***p*** of food and
31:10 to eat with ***p*** to spare. The
32:4 come and find ***p*** of water?" they
Esther
1:7 made sure there was ***p*** of royal wine.
Job
20:22 Even in their ***p***, they are
31:25 wealth was great, when my hand found ***p***;
36:11 their days in ***p***, their years
Psalms
78:15 gave them ***p*** to drink—as if
103:5 you with ***p*** of good things so
Proverbs
3:10 be filled with ***p***, and your vats
12:11 land will have ***p*** to eat, but those
20:13 stay alert and you will have ***p*** to eat.
28:19 land will have ***p*** to eat, but those
Ecclesiastes
6:2 give some people ***p*** of wealth,
Jeremiah
2:7 into a land of ***p***, to enjoy its
44:17 Then we had ***p*** to eat and we
Ezekiel
16:49 were proud, had ***p*** to eat, and
Luke
6:25 for you who have ***p*** now, because you
12:19 have stored up ***p*** of goods, enough
John
6:10 down." There was ***p*** of grass there.
6:12 When they had ***p*** to eat, he said to his
Romans
3:2 ***P*** in every way. First of all, the Jews
Philippians
4:12 or whether having ***p*** or being poor.
4:18 I now have ***p*** and it is more than

PLOT

Genesis
23:4 for a burial ***p*** among you so that
Exodus
23:1 rumors. Don't ***p*** with evil people
2 Samuel
23:11 where there was a ***p*** of land full of
23:12 the middle of the ***p***, defended it, and
1 Kings
16:20 deeds and the ***p*** he carried out,
2 Kings
9:21 meet him at the ***p*** of ground that
9:37 a field in that ***p*** of land in
Esther
8:3 overturn the evil ***p*** of Haman the
Psalms
35:20 instead, they ***p*** false accusations
36:4 They ***p*** evil even while resting in bed!
37:12 The wicked ***p*** against the righteous,
64:6 devised a perfect ***p***! It's deep within
71:10 me; those who stalk me ***p*** together:
83:3 own people; they ***p*** against the
83:5 They ***p*** with a single-minded heart; they
119:150 who love to ***p*** wicked schemes
140:2 who ***p*** evil things in their hearts, who
140:4 violent people who ***p*** to trip me up!
Proverbs
16:30 wink their eye ***p*** destruction;
24:8 Those who ***p*** evil will be called master
Isaiah
29:20 and all who ***p*** evil will be
30:1 mine; who weave a ***p***, but not by my
Jeremiah
9:8 well, but in their hearts ***p*** their ruin.
48:2 are hatching a ***p*** against her:
Hosea
7:15 strength, yet they ***p*** evil against me.
Zephaniah
2:9 like Gomorrah: a ***p*** of weeds, salt
Acts
4:25 rage, and the peoples ***p*** in vain?
9:23 the Jews hatched a ***p*** to kill Saul.
14:5 hatched a ***p*** to mistreat and
20:3 Jews hatched a ***p*** against Paul as
23:12 formulated a ***p*** and solemnly

PLOTTED

Genesis
37:18 close to them, and they ***p*** to kill him.
Exodus
18:11 when the Egyptians ***p*** against them."
1 Kings
15:27 of Issachar, ***p*** against him and
16:9 the chariots, ***p*** against him. Elah
16:16 news: "Zimri has ***p*** against the king
2 Kings
9:14 grandson, ***p*** against Joram.
10:9 I'm the one who ***p*** against my master
12:20 officials ***p*** a conspiracy and
14:19 in Jerusalem ***p*** against him. When
15:10 Jabesh's son, ***p*** against
21:23 Amon's officials ***p*** against him and
21:24 all those who had ***p*** against King Amon
2 Chronicles
24:21 But the people ***p*** against Zechariah, and
24:25 his own officials ***p*** against him for
24:26 Those who ***p*** against him were the
33:24 His own officials ***p*** against him and
33:25 all those who had ***p*** against King Amon
Nehemiah
4:8 They ***p*** together to come and fight
Amos
7:10 Amos has ***p*** against you

Luke
11:54 They **p** against him, trying to trap him
John
11:53 From that day on they **p** to kill him

PLUNDER

Genesis
49:27 prey; in the evening he divides the **p**."
Deuteronomy
2:35 animals and the **p** from the towns we
3:7 the animals and the **p** from the towns.
13:16 Gather all the **p** into the middle of the
20:14 the city—all its **p**. You can then
Joshua
8:2 and cattle as **p**. Set your ambush
8:27 of that city as **p** for themselves,
11:14 and the cattle as **p** for themselves.
1 Samuel
14:30 of their enemies' **p** today when they
15:19 LORD's eyes when you tore into the **p**!"
15:21 cattle from the **p**—the very best ite
30:16 large amount of **p** they had taken
2 Samuel
8:12 including the **p** of Zobah's King
23:10 to Eleazar, but only to **p** the dead.
2 Kings
3:23 themselves! Now get the **p**, Moab!"
21:14 be nothing but **p** and loot for
2 Chronicles
28:8 amounts of **p**, which they took
Nehemiah
4:4 and make them like **p** in a captive land.
Psalms
35:10 and the needy from those who **p** them."
44:10 from the enemy; our adversaries **p** us.
89:41 those who pass by **p** him. He's nothing
109:11 he owns; let strangers **p** his wealth.
Proverbs
1:13 wealth; we'll fill our houses with **p**.
16:19 needy than to divide **p** with the proud.
29:24 Those who share **p** with thieves hate
Isaiah
9:3 harvest, as those who divide **p** rejoice.
10:6 spoil, to steal **p**, and to trample
11:14 they will **p** the people to the
42:22 They have become **p** with no one to
Jeremiah
15:13 I will deliver as **p**, without a fee,
27:20 didn't **p** when he deported
30:16 and all who **p** you will be
49:32 will become **p**; their many
Ezekiel
7:21 wicked ones as **p**—they will defile
23:46 them, and decree terror and **p** for them.
25:7 you. Nations will **p** you. I will cut
26:12 your wealth, **p** your goods, tear
29:19 wealth, he will **p** and loot it, and
36:5 themselves as a possession only for **p**.
38:12 to take **p** and seize loot, to use my
39:10 So they will take **p** and seize loot.
Daniel
11:24 He will hand out **p**, spoil, and
11:33 and by flame, by captivity and by **p**.
Nahum
2:9 **P** silver! Plunder gold! There is no end
3:1 deceit, full of **p**: prey cannot get
Habakkuk
2:7 awaken; you will become **p** for them.
2:8 the peoples will **p** you because of
Zephaniah
2:9 my people will **p** them; the rest of

POINT

Leviticus
5:5 at that **p**, when you have become guilty
6:4 at that **p**, once you have sinned and
13:17 clean; at that **p**, the person is
14:8 in water; at that **p**, they will be
25:28 year, at which **p** it will return to
25:41 at which **p** the poor Israelite along
26:44 them to the **p** of totally
Deuteronomy
2:14 It was at that **p** that the last of
12:9 up to this **p** you haven't yet
12:11 At that **p**, you must bring all that I
13:14 at that **p** you must look into this
15:17 From that **p** on, he will be
16:10 At that **p**, perform the Festival of
19:21 no mercy on this **p**: life for life,
22:2 for it, at which **p** you must return
Joshua
8:18 said to Joshua, "**P** the dagger in
Judges
16:16 he became worn out to the **p** of death.
18:1 the tribes of Israel up to that **p**.
1 Samuel
18:9 a close eye on David from that **p** on.
2 Kings
4:35 the boy, at which **p** the boy sneezed
4:41 can eat." At that **p**, there was
18:4 up to that **p** the Israelites
20:7 at which **p** Hezekiah started
2 Chronicles
20:24 arrived at the **p** overlooking the
Nehemiah
3:16 repaired from the **p** opposite David's
13:21 on you!" At that **p**, they stopped
Job
12:5 is idle, a fixed **p** for slipping feet.
Proverbs
6:13 their feet, and **p** with their
Jeremiah
17:1 with a diamond **p** on the tablets of
44:22 it was at that **p** that your land
52:6 city reached a **p** that no food
Ezekiel
21:20 and **p** out the way for the sword to
Daniel
5:9 At that **p** King Belshazzar was really
Matthew
4:5 at the highest **p** of the temple. He
16:3 the signs that **p** to what the time
24:1 disciples came to **p** out to him the
Mark
14:59 didn't agree even on this **p**.
Luke
4:9 at the highest **p** of the temple. He
Acts
26:24 At this **p** in Paul's defense, Festus
1 Corinthians
15:32 From a human **p** of view, what good does it do me

2 Corinthians
1:16 at which ***p*** I was hoping you
5:16 then, from this ***p*** on we won't
10:16 grows even to the ***p*** of the gospel
Philippians
2:8 obedient to the ***p*** of death, even
1 Timothy
4:6 If you ***p*** these things out to the
2 Timothy
2:9 suffering to the ***p*** that I'm in
Hebrews
4:12 penetrates to the ***p*** that it separates
8:1 Now the main ***p*** of what we are saying is
11:16 But at this ***p*** in time, they are longing
12:4 yet to the ***p*** of shedding blood,
James
2:10 but fails at one ***p*** is guilty of
1 John
4:5 from the world's ***p*** of view and the
Revelation
2:5 remember the high ***p*** from which you
2:10 even to the ***p*** of death, and I

POINTLESS

Psalms
127:1 builders' work is ***p***. Unless it is the
127:2 It is ***p*** that you get up early and stay
Ecclesiastes
1:2 Perfectly ***p***, says the Teacher,
1:14 everything is ***p***, a chasing after
2:1 enjoy what is good! But this too was ***p***!
2:11 that it was ***p***—a chasing after w
2:15 wise? I said to myself, This too is ***p***.
2:17 everything is ***p***—just wind chasing
2:19 here under the sun. That too is ***p***.
2:21 it. This too is ***p***—it's a terrible w
2:23 hearts don't find rest. This too is ***p***.
2:26 God. This too is ***p*** and a chasing
3:19 than animals because everything is ***p***.
4:4 envy. This too is ***p***, just wind
4:7 the sun something else that was ***p***:
4:8 This too is ***p*** and a terrible
4:16 him. This too is ***p*** and a chasing
5:7 multiply, so do ***p*** thoughts and
5:10 satisfied with income. This too is ***p***.
6:2 it. This is ***p*** and a sickening
6:9 This too is ***p***, just wind
6:11 everything is ***p***. What do people
6:12 their brief ***p*** life, which will
7:6 under a kettle. That too is ***p***.
7:15 everything in my ***p*** lifetime: the
8:10 neglected in the city. This too is ***p***.
8:14 on earth that is ***p***: the righteous
9:9 the days of your ***p*** life that God
11:8 days. Everything that happens is ***p***.
11:10 youth and the dawn of life are ***p*** too.
12:8 Perfectly ***p***, says the Teacher,
Jeremiah
8:19 with their images, with ***p*** foreign gods?
Romans
1:21 reasoning became ***p***, and their
Ephesians
4:17 They base their lives on ***p*** thinking,
1 Timothy
6:20 Avoid godless and ***p*** discussions and

POLES

Exodus
25:13 Make acacia-wood ***p*** and cover them with
27:6 Make acacia-wood ***p*** for the altar and
27:7 Put the ***p*** through the rings so that the
30:4 will house the ***p*** used to carry the
34:13 pillars, and cut down their sacred ***p***.
35:12 chest with its ***p*** and its cover,
37:4 made acacia wood ***p*** and covered them
38:5 of the copper grate to house the ***p***.
39:35 the covenant with its ***p*** and the cover,
39:39 copper grate, its ***p***, and all its
40:20 chest. He put the ***p*** on the chest, and
Numbers
4:6 it, and they will set its ***p*** in place.
Deuteronomy
7:5 down their sacred ***p***, and burn their
12:3 Burn their sacred ***p*** with fire. Hack
1 Kings
8:7 covering the chest and its carrying ***p***.
8:8 The carrying ***p*** were so long that their
14:15 LORD angry by making their sacred ***p***.
14:23 and sacred ***p*** on top of every
2 Kings
17:10 and sacred ***p*** on every high
23:14 down the sacred ***p***, filling the
1 Chronicles
15:15 God's chest with ***p*** on their
2 Chronicles
5:8 covering the chest and its carrying ***p***.
14:3 sacred pillars, cut down the sacred ***p***,
17:6 shrines and the sacred ***p*** from Judah.
19:3 the sacred ***p*** from the land and
24:18 worshipped sacred ***p*** and idols. Anger
31:1 down the sacred ***p***, and completely
33:3 and made sacred ***p***. He bowed down to
33:19 shrines, sacred ***p***, and idols he set
34:3 the sacred ***p***, idols, and
34:4 up the sacred ***p***, idols, and
34:7 altars and sacred ***p***, ground the idols
Esther
2:23 on pointed ***p***. A report about
9:13 the ten sons of Haman on pointed ***p***."
9:25 impaled him and his sons on pointed ***p***.
Isaiah
17:8 made: sacred ***p*** and incense
27:9 chalk, sacred ***p*** and incense
Jeremiah
17:2 altars and sacred ***p*** by the lush trees
Micah
5:14 down your sacred ***p*** in your midst; I

POLLUTED

Leviticus
21:3 married—you may be ***p*** for her sake.
Deuteronomy
12:15 People who are ***p*** and people who
15:22 whether you are ***p*** or purified, just
23:10 the camp becomes ***p*** due to a
24:4 she has been ***p*** in this way
26:14 it while I was ***p***, nor have I
2 Chronicles
36:14 the nations. They ***p*** the LORD's temple
Ezra
9:11 possess is a land ***p*** by the impurity

Proverbs
25:26 a contaminated spring or a ***p*** fountain.
Isaiah
24:5 The earth lies ***p*** under its inhabitants,
Lamentations
4:14 in the streets, ***p*** with blood. No
Ezekiel
36:17 land, they ***p*** it with their
Malachi
1:7 my altar with ***p*** food. But you
1:12 of the LORD is ***p***. Its fruit, its

POMEGRANATES
Exodus
28:33 its lower hem add ***p*** made of blue,
39:24 hem, they added ***p*** made of blue,
39:25 bells between the ***p***, all around the
Numbers
13:23 them. They also took ***p*** and figs.
20:5 figs, vines, or ***p***? And there's no
Deuteronomy
8:8 fig trees, and ***p***; a land of olive
1 Kings
7:18 and two rows of ***p*** for each network
2 Kings
25:17 lattices and ***p***, all made from
2 Chronicles
3:16 He made a hundred ***p*** and placed them
4:13 four hundred ***p*** for the two networks,
Song of Songs
4:13 are an orchard of ***p*** with all kinds of
6:11 in flower, whether the ***p*** had bloomed.
7:12 see if the ***p*** have bloomed.
Jeremiah
52:22 design of bronze ***p*** around it. The
52:23 were ninety-six ***p*** on the sides, a

POOL
2 Samuel
2:13 them at the ***p*** of Gibeon. One
4:12 them up by the ***p*** at Hebron. But
1 Kings
22:38 chariot at the ***p*** of Samaria. The
2 Kings
18:17 of the Upper ***P***, which is on the
20:20 he made the ***p*** and the channel
Nehemiah
2:14 and to the King's ***P***. Since there was
3:15 the wall of the ***P*** of Shelah of the
3:16 as the artificial ***p*** and the Warriors
Psalms
114:8 that rock into a ***p*** of water, that
Song of Songs
4:2 from the washing ***p***—all of them perf
4:12 bride; an enclosed ***p***, a sealed spring.
6:6 from the washing ***p***—all of them perf
Isaiah
7:3 of the Upper ***P***, by the road to
22:9 collected the waters of the lower ***p***.
35:7 will become a ***p***, and the thirsty
36:2 of the Upper ***P***, which is on the
Jeremiah
41:12 son, at the great ***p*** in Gibeon.
Nahum
2:8 has been like a ***p*** of water. Such
John
5:2 city wall is a ***p*** with the Aramaic
9:7 Go, wash in the ***p*** of Siloam" (this
9:11 said, 'Go to the ***P*** of Siloam and

POOR
Exodus
22:25 my people who are ***p*** among you, don't
23:6 justice that your ***p*** deserve in their
23:11 so that the ***p*** among your people
30:15 give more and the ***p*** shouldn't give
Leviticus
14:21 if the person is ***p*** and cannot afford
19:10 items for the ***p*** and the
19:15 favoritism to the ***p*** or deference to
23:22 items for the ***p*** and the
25:37 Do not lend a ***p*** Israelite money with
25:41 which point the ***p*** Israelite along
Numbers
13:20 the land rich or ***p***? Are there trees
Deuteronomy
15:4 won't be any ***p*** persons among you
15:7 if there are some ***p*** persons among
15:9 you resent your ***p*** fellow Israelites
15:11 ***P*** persons will never disappear from the
24:12 if the person is ***p***, you are not
24:14 take advantage of ***p*** or needy workers,
24:15 because they are ***p***, and their very
Judges
14:15 Were we invited here just to become ***p***?"
Ruth
3:10 haven't gone after rich or ***p*** young men.
1 Samuel
2:7 LORD! He makes ***p***, gives wealth,
2:8 God raises the ***p*** from the dust, lifts
18:23 -law? I don't! I'm ***p*** and
2 Samuel
12:1 men in the same city, one rich, one ***p***.
2 Kings
25:12 of the land's ***p*** people behind to
Esther
9:22 to each other and money gifts to the ***p***.
Job
5:16 so the ***p*** have hope and violence shuts
20:10 will repay the ***p***; their hands will
20:19 and abandoned the ***p***; stole a house
24:4 thrust the ***p*** out of the way, make the
24:9 the infant of the ***p*** is taken as
24:10 The ***p*** go around naked, without clothes,
24:14 kills the ***p*** and needy; at
31:16 denied what the ***p*** wanted, made a
34:19 the rich over the ***p***, for they are all
34:28 the cry of the ***p*** to reach him, he
36:6 live, but grants justice to the ***p***.
Psalms
9:18 Because the ***p*** won't be forgotten
10:9 They seize the ***p*** all right,
12:5 Because the ***p*** are oppressed,
22:16 like a lion—oh, my ***p*** hands and feet!
41:1 attention to the ***p*** are truly happy!
49:2 people of every kind, rich and ***p*** alike
68:10 goodness, God, you provided for the ***p***.
70:5 But me? I'm ***p*** and needy. Hurry to me,
72:2 and your ***p*** ones with justice.
72:4 to people who are ***p***; let him save the
72:12 who cry out, the ***p***, and those who

74:21 No, let the **p** and needy praise
76:9 up to save all of the earth's **p**. Selah
82:3 the right of the **p** and the destitute!
86:1 answer me because I am **p** and in need.
109:16 chased after the **p** and needy—even
109:22 because I am **p** and needy, and my heart
113:7 God lifts up the **p** from the dirt and
140:12 the case of the **p** and will do what
147:6 LORD helps the **p**, but throws the
149:4 will beautify the **p** with saving help.
Proverbs
10:15 the ruin of the **p** is their poverty.
13:7 pretend to be **p**, but have great
13:8 life, but the **p** don't even
13:23 A **p** person's land might produce much
14:20 hate the **p**, but many love
14:31 those who are kind to the **p** honor God.
17:5 who mock the **p** insult their
18:23 The **p** plead for help, but the wealthy
19:1 Better to be **p** and walk in innocence
19:4 friends, but the **p** lose their
19:7 relatives of the **p** hate them; even
19:17 gracious to the **p** lend to the LORD,
19:22 it is better to be **p** than a liar.
20:13 or you will be **p**; stay alert and
21:13 the cries of the **p** will themselves
21:17 pleasure end up **p**; lovers of wine
22:2 The rich and the **p** have this in common:
22:7 rule over the **p**; a borrower is a
22:9 they give some of their food to the **p**.
22:16 Oppressing the **p** to get rich and giving
22:22 steal from the **p**, because they are
28:3 **P** people who oppress the needy are rain
28:6 Better to be **p** and walk in innocence
28:8 for those who are generous to the **p**.
28:11 but an insightful **p** person sees
28:15 ruler over the **p** is like a
28:27 who give to the **p** will lack
29:7 the rights of the **p**, but the wicked
29:13 The **p** and their oppressors have a
29:14 a king judges the **p** honestly, his
30:9 LORD?" Or I'll be **p** and steal, and
30:14 the earth, and the **p** from humanity.
31:9 and to defend the needy and the **p**.
31:20 she stretches out her hands to the **p**.
Ecclesiastes
4:13 A **p** but wise youth is better than an
4:14 during his rule a **p** child is born.
5:8 you witness the **p** being oppressed
6:8 Or what do the **p** gain by knowing
9:15 in that town a **p** but wise man who
Isaiah
3:14 stolen from the **p** are in your
3:15 the faces of the **p**? says the LORD
10:2 and to rob the **p** among my people
14:30 offspring of the **p** will graze; their
25:4 a refuge for the **p**, a refuge for the
26:6 the feet of the **p**, the steps of the
29:19 The **p** will again find joy in the LORD,
32:7 to destroy the **p** with lying words,
41:17 The **p** and the needy seek water, and
58:7 the homeless **p** into your house,
61:1 good news to the **p**, to bind up the
Jeremiah
2:34 of the innocent **p**, even though you
5:4 These are the **p** who don't know
5:28 to defend the rights of the **p**.
22:16 the rights of the **p** and needy; then
52:16 left some of the **p** to tend the
Ezekiel
16:49 she didn't help the **p** and the needy.
18:12 oppresses the **p** and needy, robs others
18:17 oppressing the **p** by taking neither
22:29 oppressed the **p** and mistreated
Daniel
4:27 mercy to the **p**. Then your safety
Amos
2:7 the head of the **p** into the dust of
5:12 side, turning away the **p** who seek help.
8:4 needy and destroy the **p** of the land,
Habakkuk
3:14 pleasure in secretly devouring the **p**.
Zechariah
7:10 stranger, and the **p**; don't plan evil
Matthew
6:2 you give to the **p**, don't blow your
6:3 you give to the **p**, don't let your
6:4 may give to the **p** in secret. Your
11:5 raised up. The **p** have good news
19:21 the money to the **p**. Then you will
26:9 for a lot of money and given to the **p**."
26:11 always have the **p** with you, but you
Mark
10:21 the money to the **p**. Then you will
12:42 One **p** widow came forward and put in two small copper coins
12:43 you that this **p** widow has put in
14:5 given to the **p**." And they
14:7 always have the **p** with you; and
Luke
4:18 good news to the **p**, to proclaim
6:20 are you who are **p**, because God's
7:22 up. And good news is preached to the **p**.
14:13 invite the **p**, crippled, lame,
14:21 and bring the **p**, crippled, blind,
16:20 lay a certain **p** man named Lazarus
16:22 The **p** man died and was carried by
18:22 the money to the **p**. Then you will
19:8 to the **p**. And if I have
21:2 He also saw a **p** widow throw in two
21:3 you that this **p** widow has put in
John
12:5 it sold and the money given to the **p**?"
12:6 cared about the **p** but because he
12:8 always have the **p** among you, but
13:29 that he should give something to the **p**.
Acts
24:17 gifts for the **p** of my nation and
Romans
15:26 for the **p** among God's
2 Corinthians
6:10 always happy, as **p** but making many
8:9 rich, he became **p** for our sakes, so
Galatians
2:10 remember the **p**, which was
4:14 Though my **p** health burdened you, you
Philippians
4:12 or whether having plenty or being **p**.
James
1:9 sisters who are **p** should find
2:2 the other is **p**, dressed in
2:3 here." But to the **p** person you say,
2:5 those who are **p** by worldly
2:6 dishonored the **p**. Don't the

Revelation
3:17 pathetic, ***p***, blind, and naked.
13:16 the rich and ***p***, the free and

POPULATION

Joshua
2:9 us. The entire ***p*** of the land has
1 Kings
3:8 chosen, a large ***p*** that can't be
2 Kings
17:32 from their whole ***p***. These priests
25:11 Babylon's king, and the rest of the ***p***.
Proverbs
14:28 glory is a large ***p***, but a dwindling

PORCH

Judges
3:23 out to the ***p***, and closed and
1 Kings
6:3 The ***p*** in front of the temple's main
7:6 He made a ***p*** with columns seventy-five
7:12 of the LORD's temple and its ***p***.
7:19 columns in the ***p*** were made like
7:21 at the temple's ***p***. He named the
2 Chronicles
3:4 the temple was a ***p*** as long as the
8:12 Solomon had built in front of the ***p***,
Ezekiel
8:16 between the ***p*** and the altar,
40:7 plaza next to the ***p*** at the gate
41:25 tree stood outside, in front of the ***p***,
41:26 the facade of the ***p***, the temple's
44:3 in and go out by way of the gate's ***p***.
46:2 by way of the ***p*** of the gate and
46:8 in by way of the ***p*** of the gate and
Joel
2:17 Between the ***p*** and the altar let the
John
10:23 in the covered ***p*** named for Solomon.
Acts
3:11 them at Solomon's ***P***, completely
5:12 come together regularly at Solomon's ***P***.

PORTION

Genesis
30:31 care of your flock again, and keep a ***p***.
43:34 but Benjamin's ***p*** was five times as
48:22 giving you one ***p*** more than to your
Exodus
29:26 the LORD's presence. It will be your ***p***.
Leviticus
2:2 burn this token ***p*** on the altar as a
5:12 it—the token ***p***—and will burn it
6:15 burn this token ***p*** completely on the
7:34 as a permanent ***p*** from the
7:36 their permanent ***p*** throughout their
8:29 to Moses as his ***p***, just as the LORD
10:13 it is your ***p*** and your sons'
24:7 stack, as a token ***p*** for the bread; it
24:9 the LORD's food gifts, a permanent ***p***.
Numbers
18:24 one-tenth ***p***, which they have
Deuteronomy
18:1 to the LORD, which are the LORD's ***p***,
26:13 removed the holy ***p*** from my house,
33:21 the commander's ***p*** was, the leaders
Joshua
14:4 weren't given any ***p*** of the land,
15:13 Joshua gave a ***p*** among the
18:7 there won't be a ***p*** among you for the
19:9 Some of the ***p*** of the people of Judah
22:25 Gad. You have no ***p*** in the LORD!' So
24:32 at Shechem in the ***p*** of field that
Ruth
2:3 to be the ***p*** of the field that
4:3 is selling the ***p*** of the field that
1 Samuel
9:23 cook, "Serve the ***p*** I gave you—
2 Chronicles
29:16 purify the inner ***p*** of the LORD's
31:3 As his ***p***, the king personally
31:4 the required ***p*** for the priests
Nehemiah
12:47 set aside the ***p*** for the Levites,
Job
24:18 surface; their ***p*** of the land is
27:13 is the wicked's ***p*** with God, the
Psalms
16:5 You, LORD, are my ***p***, my cup; you
60:6 up Shechem and ***p*** out the Succoth
108:7 up Shechem and ***p*** out the Succoth
Ecclesiastes
11:2 Give a ***p*** to seven people, even to
Isaiah
61:7 of shame, their ***p*** will be double;
Jeremiah
10:16 Jacob's ***p*** is utterly different because
51:19 But the ***p*** of Jacob is utterly
Lamentations
3:24 The LORD is my ***p***! Therefore, I'll
Ezekiel
45:1 set aside a holy ***p*** of land for the
48:1 to the western border: Dan, one ***p***.
Hosea
3:2 amount of barley, and a ***p*** of wine.
Micah
2:4 He exchanges the ***p*** of my people; he
Habakkuk
1:16 due to them his ***p*** grows fat and his
Luke
6:38 to you. A good ***p***—packed down, firm
Romans
12:3 measured out a ***p*** of faith to each

POSSESS

Genesis
15:8 do I know that I will actually ***p*** it?"
24:60 may your children ***p*** their enemies'
Exodus
23:30 grow and you eventually ***p*** the land.
32:13 this whole land to ***p*** for all time.'"
Leviticus
14:34 disease on a house in the land you ***p***,
20:24 will certainly ***p*** their fertile
25:24 land that you ***p***, you must allow
Numbers
14:24 descendants will ***p*** it because he has
33:53 I've given the land to you to ***p***.
Deuteronomy
1:8 you. Go and ***p*** the land that I
32:47 you are crossing the Jordan River to ***p***.
33:23 blessing—go ***p*** the west and the

Joshua
17:17 people and ***p*** great strength.
Judges
11:24 Shouldn't you ***p*** what Chemosh your god
Ezra
9:11 about to enter to ***p*** is a land
Nehemiah
9:15 them to go in to ***p*** the land that you
9:23 told their ancestors to enter and ***p***.
Psalms
25:13 and their descendants will ***p*** the land.
37:9 in the LORD—they will ***p*** the land.
37:22 by God will ***p*** the land, but
37:29 righteous will ***p*** the land; they
37:34 you up so you can ***p*** the land. When
69:35 God's servants can live there and ***p*** it.
Isaiah
14:2 of Israel will ***p*** them as male and
34:11 and crows will ***p*** it; owls and
34:17 line. They will ***p*** it forever; they
54:3 children will ***p*** the nations' land
57:13 the land and ***p*** my holy mountain.
60:21 they will ***p*** the land forever.
61:7 share. They will ***p*** a double portion
Jeremiah
8:8 We are wise; we ***p*** the LORD's
30:3 to their ancestors, and they will ***p*** it.
Ezekiel
2:6 be afraid! You ***p*** thistles and
Daniel
2:41 but it will ***p*** some of the
5:11 man was shown to ***p*** illumination,
5:14 you and that you ***p*** illumination,
Hosea
9:6 them. Briars will ***p*** their precious
Amos
1:13 in Gilead in order to ***p*** more land.
9:12 so that they may ***p*** what is left of
Obadiah
1:19 plain will ***p*** Mount Esau, and
1:20 Israelites will ***p*** the land of the
Habakkuk
1:6 the earth to ***p*** dwelling places
Zephaniah
2:9 the rest of my nation will ***p*** them.
Zechariah
2:12 The LORD will ***p*** Judah as his
1 Corinthians
4:19 but I'll find out what power they ***p***.
1 Thessalonians
5:9 but rather to ***p*** salvation through
2 Thessalonians
2:14 news so you could ***p*** the honor of our

POSSESSION

Genesis
15:7 to give you this land as your ***p***."
17:8 as an enduring ***p***. And I will be
48:4 following you as an enduring ***p***.'
Exodus
6:8 it to you as your ***p***. I am the LORD.'"
19:5 my most precious ***p*** out of all the
22:4 in the thief's ***p***, he must pay back
34:9 and our sin and take us as your own ***p***."
Leviticus
14:34 to you as a ***p***, and I put an
25:28 remain in the ***p*** of the buyer
Numbers
13:30 go up and take ***p*** of it, because we
21:24 swords and took ***p*** of his land from
24:18 will become a ***p***, Seir a
27:11 He will take ***p*** of it. This will
32:18 the Israelites takes ***p*** of his property.
33:53 You will take ***p*** of the land and live in
Deuteronomy
2:12 descendants took ***p*** of their area,
3:14 of Manasseh, took ***p*** of the entire
4:22 and you will take ***p*** of that wonderful
4:47 They took ***p*** of his land and the land of
6:18 enter and take ***p*** of the wonderful
7:1 entering to take ***p*** of, and he drives
8:1 enter and take ***p*** of the land that
9:1 to enter and take ***p*** of nations larger
10:11 enter and take ***p*** of the land that
11:8 to enter and take ***p*** of the land that
12:29 and taking ***p*** of, and you have
16:20 long and take ***p*** of the land that
17:14 you have taken ***p*** of it and settled
26:1 and you take ***p*** of it and are
29:8 We took ***p*** of their land and gave it as
33:4 —it's the prized ***p*** of Jacob's
Joshua
1:6 this people take ***p*** of the land,
1:11 is going to give it to you as your ***p***.'"
1:15 and they too take ***p*** of the land that
Judges
1:19 and they took ***p*** of the highlands.
2:6 in order to take ***p*** of the land.
3:13 Israel, and took ***p*** of Palm City.
11:21 Israelites took ***p*** of all the land
18:9 from going and taking ***p*** of the land.
1 Samuel
10:1 you as leader of his very own ***p***:
12:5 anything in my ***p***." "Agreed," they
13:22 be found in the ***p*** of any of the
2 Kings
10:2 sons are in your ***p***, along with
2 Chronicles
20:11 us out of your ***p*** that you gave to
Ezra
4:16 will then have no ***p*** in the province
Nehemiah
9:22 side. They took ***p*** of the land of
9:25 land, and took ***p*** of houses filled
Job
22:24 Lay your prized ***p*** in the dust, your
22:25 be your prized ***p***, silver piled up
Psalms
2:8 the nations your ***p***; the far corners
17:14 people whose only ***p*** is their fleeting
28:9 God! Bless your ***p***! Shepherd them
33:12 has chosen as his ***p***, is truly happy!
44:3 did they take ***p*** of the land—
61:5 given me the same ***p*** as those who
74:2 tribe of your own ***p***—remember Mount Zion
78:62 the sword; he was enraged at his own ***p***.
82:8 because you hold all nations in your ***p***!
94:5 LORD! They abuse your very own ***p***.
94:14 he will not abandon his very own ***p***.
106:5 so I can praise along with your ***p***.
106:40 his people; he despised his own ***p***.
119:57 The LORD is my ***p***. I promise to do what

119:111 Your laws are my ***p*** forever because they
135:4 God chose Israel as his treasured ***p***.
Ecclesiastes
2:21 hard work as a ***p*** to those who
Isaiah
65:9 ones will take ***p***; my servants will
Jeremiah
32:23 entered and took ***p*** of it, but they
32:43 and in the ***p*** of the
50:11 plunderers of my ***p***. Sure, you dance
Ezekiel
25:4 for them to take ***p***. They will set up
35:10 We will take ***p*** of them even if
36:5 for themselves as a ***p*** only for plunder.
Hosea
13:15 his household of every cherished ***p***.
Joel
3:2 my people and my ***p***, Israel, which
3:8 daughters as a ***p*** of the people of
Malachi
3:17 be my special ***p***. I will spare
Matthew
15:22 is suffering terribly from demon ***p***."
Luke
8:29 it had taken ***p*** of him, so he
Acts
7:5 the land as his ***p*** to him and to his
7:45 they took ***p*** of the land from
1 Peter
2:9 who are God's own ***p***. You have become

POSSESSIONS

Genesis
12:5 Lot, all of their ***p***, and those who
45:20 worry about your ***p*** because you will
Leviticus
27:28 LORD from their ***p***—whether humans, a
Judges
18:21 and the prized ***p*** in front of them.
Ezra
8:21 ourselves, our children, and all our ***p***.
Job
1:10 hands so that his ***p*** extend throughout
20:26 their treasured ***p***; fire that no one
42:10 the LORD doubled all Job's earlier ***p***.
Obadiah
1:13 have stolen his ***p*** on the day of his
Zephaniah
2:7 will visit them and restore their ***p***.
3:20 I restore your ***p*** and you can see
Zechariah
9:4 will take her ***p*** away and knock
Matthew
12:29 man and steal his ***p***, unless they
19:22 away saddened, because he had many ***p***.
24:47 will put them in charge of all his ***p***.
25:14 servants and handed his ***p*** over to them.
Mark
10:22 away saddened, because he had many ***p***.
Luke
11:21 his own palace, his ***p*** are secure.
12:15 by one's ***p***, even when
12:33 Sell your ***p*** and give to those in need.
12:44 will put them in charge of all his ***p***.
14:33 up all of your ***p*** can be my
17:31 the roof, whose ***p*** are in the house,
19:8 I give half of my ***p*** to the poor. And
Acts
2:45 of property and ***p*** and distribute
4:32 any of their ***p***, but held
1 Corinthians
7:30 should be like people who don't have ***p***.
Hebrews
10:34 of your ***p*** with joy, since
1 John
2:16 pride in one's ***p***—is not of the
3:17 has material ***p*** and sees a

POSTS

Exodus
26:32 four acacia-wood ***p*** covered in gold.
27:10 with twenty ***p***, twenty copper bases,
35:11 boards, its bars, its ***p***, and its bases,
36:36 four acacia-wood ***p*** covered in gold
38:10 with twenty ***p***, twenty copper bases,
39:33 boards, its bars, its ***p***, and its bases,
40:18 inserted its bars, and raised up its ***p***.
1 Kings
20:24 their military ***p*** and appoint
2 Chronicles
7:6 stood at their ***p***, as did the
8:14 Levites to their ***p*** for offering
35:2 priests to their ***p***, encouraging them
Nehemiah
7:3 at their watch ***p*** and some in front
Esther
1:6 rings and marble ***p***. Gold and silver
Ecclesiastes
10:6 appointed to high ***p***, while the rich
Ezekiel
27:29 oars desert their ***p***. All sailors and

POUR → POUR OUT MY SPIRIT

Exodus
4:9 Nile River and ***p*** it out on dry
29:7 anointing oil and ***p*** it on his head to
29:12 with your finger. ***P*** out the rest of
30:9 offering. Don't ***p*** a drink offering
Leviticus
2:1 flour. They must ***p*** oil on it and put
14:26 The priest will ***p*** some of the oil into
Numbers
5:15 He will not ***p*** oil on it, nor
Deuteronomy
12:16 animals' blood. ***P*** it out on the
12:24 any of it. ***P*** it out on the
15:23 any blood. ***P*** it out on the
Judges
6:20 this rock, then ***p*** out the broth."
1 Kings
18:33 with water and ***p*** it on the
2 Kings
3:11 here. He used to ***p*** water on Elijah's
4:4 and your sons. ***P*** oil into all
9:3 jug of oil and ***p*** it on his head.
Job
3:24 my bread; my roars ***p*** out like water.
10:10 Didn't you ***p*** me out like milk, curdle
36:28 the clouds ***p*** moisture and drip
Psalms
62:8 him at all times! ***P*** out your hearts
69:24 ***P*** out your anger on them—let your
75:8 spice. He will ***p*** it out, and all
79:6 ***P*** out your wrath on the nations who

POUR [cont.]

142:2 I ***p*** out my concerns before God; I
Isaiah
44:3 I will ***p*** out water upon thirsty ground
45:8 ***P*** down, you heavens above, and let the
46:6 Those who ***p*** out gold from a bag and
Jeremiah
6:11 of holding it in. ***P*** it out on the
7:18 the more, they ***p*** out drink
7:20 I'm going to ***p*** out my fierce
10:25 ***P*** out your wrath on the nations that
14:16 children. I will ***p*** out on them their
44:17 of Heaven and ***p*** out drink
48:12 to spill it—to ***p*** out his wine and
Lamentations
1:16 eyes, my own eyes ***p*** water because a
2:19 the night shift; ***p*** out your heart
3:48 Streams of water ***p*** from my eyes because
Ezekiel
7:8 you I will ***p*** out my wrath, and
9:8 God! When you ***p*** out your wrath on
14:19 that land and ***p*** out my fury on
20:8 that I would ***p*** out my wrath on
20:13 that I would ***p*** out my anger
20:21 that I would ***p*** out my wrath on
21:31 I will ***p*** out my wrath against you.
24:7 her. She didn't ***p*** it out on the
30:15 I will ***p*** out my anger on Pelusium, the
38:22 and blood. I will ***p*** out flooding
39:29 When I ***p*** my Spirit upon the house of
Hosea
5:10 the land; I will ***p*** out my anger like
9:4 They won't ***p*** wine as an offering to the
Joel
2:23 he will ***p*** down abundant
Micah
1:6 vineyards. I will ***p*** her stones into
Zephaniah
3:8 kingdoms, to ***p*** out my
Zechariah
12:10 but I will ***p*** out a spirit of grace and
Matthew
6:7 you pray, don't ***p*** out a flood of
9:17 Instead, people ***p*** new wine into new
Revelation
16:1 angels, "Go and ***p*** out the seven
18:6 she has poured, ***p*** her twice as much.

POUR OUT MY SPIRIT

Prv 1:23; Is 44:3; Jl 2:28; 2:29; Ac 2:17; 2:18

POURED → ANGEL POURED HIS BOWL

Genesis
28:18 pillar, and ***p*** oil on the top of
35:14 spoke to him. He ***p*** an offering of
Leviticus
8:12 He ***p*** some of the anointing oil on
8:15 the altar. He ***p*** the rest of the
9:9 altar's horns. He ***p*** the rest of the
11:38 But if water is ***p*** on some seed and part
Numbers
28:7 of brandy will be ***p*** out for the LORD.
Deuteronomy
12:27 must be ***p*** out on the LORD
Judges
5:4 shook, the sky ***p*** down, the clouds
1 Samuel
7:6 drew water and ***p*** it out in the
10:1 jar of oil and ***p*** it over Saul's
2 Samuel
21:10 until the rains ***p*** down on the
23:16 to drink it and ***p*** it out to the
1 Kings
22:35 his blood had ***p*** from his wound
2 Kings
9:6 The prophet then ***p*** oil on his head
1 Chronicles
11:18 to drink it and ***p*** it out to the
Job
29:6 cream and a rock ***p*** out pools of oil
30:16 Now my life is ***p*** out on me; days of
Psalms
22:14 I'm ***p*** out like water. All my bones have
41:8 thing has been ***p*** into him; the
45:2 grace has been ***p*** out on your lips.
68:8 Yes, heaven ***p*** down before God,
77:17 The clouds ***p*** water, the skies cracked
79:3 They've ***p*** out the blood of the faithful
133:2 expensive oil ***p*** over the head,
Isaiah
19:14 The LORD has ***p*** into them a spirit of
26:16 you out; they ***p*** out prayers to
29:10 The LORD has ***p*** on you a spirit of deep
32:15 from on high is ***p*** out on us, and
42:25 So God ***p*** out on Jacob the heat of his
57:6 lot. For them you ***p*** out a drink
Jeremiah
19:13 force and ***p*** out drink
42:18 fierce anger was ***p*** out on the people
44:6 my fierce anger ***p*** out and blazed
48:11 It hasn't been ***p*** into jars; nor
Lamentations
2:4 in sight; he ***p*** out his wrath
2:11 My insides are ***p*** on the ground
4:11 his fury; he ***p*** out his fierce
Ezekiel
16:9 off your blood, and ***p*** oil on you.
20:33 and with wrath ***p*** out, I will be
20:34 outstretched arm and with wrath ***p*** out!
22:22 I, the LORD, have ***p*** out my rage on
22:31 So I've ***p*** out my anger on them. With my
36:18 and so I ***p*** out my fury on them for all
Micah
1:4 the fire, like waters ***p*** down a slope.
Zephaniah
1:17 blood will be ***p*** out like dust and
Matthew
23:35 that has been ***p*** out on the earth,
26:7 perfume. She ***p*** it on Jesus' head
26:28 which is ***p*** out for many so
Mark
14:3 open the vase and ***p*** the perfume on
14:24 the covenant, which is ***p*** out for many.
Luke
7:38 kissed them, and ***p*** the oil on them.
7:46 oil, but she has ***p*** perfumed oil on
22:20 by my blood, which is ***p*** out for you.
John
13:5 Then he ***p*** water into a washbasin and
Acts
2:33 Holy Spirit. He ***p*** out this Spirit,
10:45 Spirit had been ***p*** out even on the

Romans
5:5 of God has been ***p*** out in our hearts
Ephesians
1:8 which he ***p*** over us with wisdom and
Philippians
2:17 But even if I am ***p*** out like a drink
1 Timothy
1:14 Our Lord's favor ***p*** all over me along
2 Timothy
4:6 I'm already being ***p*** out like a
Titus
3:6 which God ***p*** out upon us generously
Revelation
12:15 mouth the snake ***p*** a river of water
12:16 that the dragon ***p*** out of his mouth.
14:10 passionate anger, ***p*** full strength
18:6 cup that she has ***p***, pour her twice

POWER → GOD'S POWER, POWER OF GOD
Genesis
9:2 of the sea's fish. They are in your ***p***.
31:29 and I have the ***p*** to punish you.
45:13 father about my ***p*** in Egypt and
Exodus
1:8 new king came to ***p*** in Egypt who
13:3 LORD acted with ***p*** to bring you out
13:9 brought you out of Egypt with great ***p***.
14:31 saw the amazing ***p*** of the LORD
17:16 He said, "The ***p*** of the LORD's banner!
34:10 displays of ***p*** that have never
Numbers
11:23 Is the LORD's ***p*** too weak? Now you
27:20 him some of your ***p*** so that the
Deuteronomy
2:15 fact, the LORD's ***p*** was against them,
34:12 the extraordinary ***p*** that Moses
Joshua
4:24 that the LORD's ***p*** is great and that
8:7 LORD your God will give it into your ***p***.
10:19 your God has given them into your ***p***."
22:31 the Israelites from the ***p*** of the LORD."
Judges
2:15 out, the LORD's ***p*** worked against
1 Samuel
2:4 stumbling now dress themselves in ***p***!
12:10 us from the ***p*** of our enemies,
17:37 me from the ***p*** of both lions and
27:1 by Saul's ***p***. The best thing
2 Samuel
3:6 Abner was gaining ***p*** in Saul's house.
18:19 vindicated him against his enemies' ***p***."
22:1 him from the ***p*** of all his
1 Kings
18:46 but the LORD's ***p*** strengthened Elijah.
2 Kings
3:15 played, the LORD's ***p*** came over Elisha.
2 Chronicles
32:13 able to rescue their lands from my ***p***?
Ezra
5:12 over into the ***p*** of Babylon's King
8:31 to Jerusalem. The ***p*** of our God was
Nehemiah
1:10 by your great ***p*** and your strong
2:8 for the gracious ***p*** of my God was
9:27 them over to the ***p*** of their enemies
9:28 them over to the ***p*** of their enemies
9:37 sins. They have ***p*** over our bodies
Esther
3:11 are under your ***p***. Do as you like
9:29 her full royal ***p*** to show that this
Job
1:12 is within your ***p***; only don't
5:20 death; in war, from the ***p*** of the sword.
10:7 yet no one delivers me from your ***p***.
25:2 Supreme ***p*** and awe belong to God; he
26:12 By his ***p*** he stilled the Sea; split
36:22 due to his ***p***; who is a teacher
Psalms
18:1 him from the ***p*** of all his
21:13 We will sing and praise your ***p***!
22:20 Deliver my life from the ***p*** of the dog.
29:1 LORD—give to the LORD glory and ***p***!
33:16 aren't rescued by how much ***p*** they have.
37:33 righteous to the ***p*** of the wicked,
49:15 my life from the ***p*** of the grave,
59:11 instead, by your ***p*** shake them up and
60:5 Save us by your ***p*** and answer us so that
63:2 sanctuary; I've seen your ***p*** and glory.
65:6 strength; you are dressed in raw ***p***;
66:7 God rules with ***p*** forever; keeps a good
68:35 strength and ***p*** to his people!
71:4 me from the ***p*** of the wicked;
74:13 the sea with your ***p***. You shattered
75:10 of the wicked's ***p***, but the strength
78:22 because they didn't trust his saving ***p***.
78:61 God let his ***p*** be held captive, let his
80:2 Wake up your ***p***! Come to save us!
82:4 Deliver them from the ***p*** of the wicked!"
88:5 those who are cut off from your ***p***.
90:11 comprehend the ***p*** of your anger?
96:7 nations—give to the LORD glory and ***p***!
97:10 them from the ***p*** of the wicked.
103:20 who are mighty in ***p*** and keep his
106:8 good name, to make known his mighty ***p***.
106:10 redeemed them from the ***p*** of the enemy.
106:42 and they were humbled under their ***p***.
107:2 redeemed from the ***p*** of their enemies,
108:6 Save me by your ***p*** and answer me so that
119:173 Let your ***p*** help me because I have
138:7 you send your ***p*** against my
140:4 me from the ***p*** of the wicked,
144:7 deep water, from the ***p*** of strangers,
144:11 me from the ***p*** of strangers,
145:6 will speak of the ***p*** of your awesome
145:11 kingdom; they talk all about your ***p***,
Proverbs
3:27 it, when it is in your ***p*** to do so.
18:21 life are in the ***p*** of the tongue;
Ecclesiastes
4:1 oppressors wield ***p***—but they have no
8:9 people exercise ***p*** over each other
10:5 of mistake that comes from people in ***p***.
Isaiah
10:33 with terrible ***p***. The loftiest
37:27 have lost their ***p***; they are
43:13 one can escape my ***p***. I act, and who
66:14 grass. The LORD's ***p*** will be known
Jeremiah
12:7 one I love into the ***p*** of her enemies.
15:9 the sword, to the ***p*** of their enemies,

32:21 and with awesome ***p***, yes, with signs
Lamentations
5:8 is no one to rescue us from their ***p***.
Ezekiel
1:3 There the LORD's ***p*** overcame him.)
3:14 With the LORD's ***p*** pressing down
6:14 I will direct my ***p*** against them. I
33:22 The LORD's ***p*** was with me in the evening
40:1 day, the LORD's ***p*** was on me, and he
Daniel
4:36 I received more ***p*** than ever before.
7:7 extraordinary ***p*** and with massive
7:25 they will be delivered into his ***p***.
7:27 authority, and ***p*** of all kingdoms
8:4 others from its ***p***. The ram did
11:23 He will gain ***p*** at the expense of
11:42 will extend his ***p*** into other
12:7 the holy people's ***p*** is over, all
Hosea
13:14 them from the ***p*** of the grave Heb
Micah
3:8 I am filled with ***p***, with the spirit
4:8 come, the royal ***p*** belonging to
4:10 redeem you from the ***p*** of your enemies.
Nahum
1:3 but great in ***p***; the LORD
Habakkuk
3:4 That is the hiding place of his ***p***.
Zechariah
4:6 Neither by ***p***, nor by strength,
Matthew
13:54 did he get the ***p*** to work miracles?
24:30 clouds with ***p*** and great
Mark
5:30 recognized that ***p*** had gone out from
7:18 a person has the ***p*** to contaminate?
9:1 they see God's kingdom arrive in ***p***."
13:26 the clouds with great ***p*** and splendor.
Luke
1:17 the spirit and ***p*** of Elijah. He
1:35 over you and the ***p*** of the Most High
1:66 be?" Indeed, the Lord's ***p*** was with him.
1:71 and from the ***p*** of all those who
1:74 rescued from the ***p*** of our enemies so
4:14 returned in the ***p*** of the Spirit to
4:36 with authority and ***p***, and they leave?"
5:17 Now the ***p*** of the Lord was
6:19 him, because ***p*** was going out
8:46 me. I know that ***p*** has gone out from
9:1 and he gave them ***p*** and authority
10:19 over all the ***p*** of the enemy.
21:27 on a cloud with ***p*** and great
22:29 I confer royal ***p*** on you just as my
24:49 have been furnished with heavenly ***p***."
Acts
1:2 working in the ***p*** of the Holy
1:8 you will receive ***p*** when the Holy
3:12 we made him walk by our own ***p*** or piety?
4:7 asked, "By what ***p*** or in what name
4:28 did what your ***p*** and plan had
6:8 with divine ***p***, was doing great
7:18 king rose to ***p*** over Egypt who
10:38 and endowed with ***p***. Jesus traveled
11:21 The Lord's ***p*** was with them, and a large
13:11 The Lord's ***p*** is set against
13:17 With his great ***p***, he led them out
19:13 tried to use the ***p*** of the name of
26:18 and from the ***p*** of Satan to God,
Romans
1:4 as God's Son with ***p*** through his
1:16 it is God's own ***p*** for salvation to
1:20 eternal ***p*** and divine nature-
3:9 and Greeks are all under the ***p*** of sin.
6:7 has died has been freed from sin's ***p***.
6:9 again. Death no longer has ***p*** over him.
6:14 Sin will have no ***p*** over you, because
7:1 that the Law has ***p*** over someone only
9:17 so I can show my ***p*** in you and so
9:21 potter have the ***p*** over the clay to
9:22 show his wrath and to make his ***p*** known?
14:4 the Lord has the ***p*** to make them
15:1 who don't have ***p***, and not please
15:13 with hope by the ***p*** of the Holy
15:19 by the ***p*** of signs and wonders, and by
1 Corinthians
2:4 a demonstration of the Spirit and of ***p***.
4:19 but I'll find out what ***p*** they possess.
4:20 kingdom isn't about words but about ***p***.
5:4 in spirit with the ***p*** of our Lord Jesus.
6:14 Lord and will raise us through his ***p***.
15:24 rule, every authority and ***p*** to an end.
15:43 into the ground, but it's raised in ***p***.
15:56 is sin, and the ***p*** of sin is the
2 Corinthians
4:7 that the awesome ***p*** belongs to God
9:8 God has the ***p*** to provide you with more
12:9 for you, because ***p*** is made perfect
13:3 with you but shows his ***p*** among you.
Ephesians
1:21 and authority and ***p*** and angelic
2:2 spiritual ***p***. This is the
3:7 me through the exercise of his ***p***.
3:18 you'll have the ***p*** to grasp love's
3:20 or imagine by his ***p*** at work within us;
Philippians
3:10 Christ, the ***p*** of his
3:21 body, by the ***p*** that also makes
4:13 through the ***p*** of the one who
1 Thessalonians
1:5 but also with ***p*** and the Holy
2 Thessalonians
1:11 good desire and faithful work by his ***p***.
2:9 all kinds of fake ***p***, signs, and
1 Timothy
6:16 Honor and eternal ***p*** belong to him.
Hebrews
2:14 one who holds the ***p*** over death
7:16 a priest by the ***p*** of a life that
1 Peter
1:12 did this in the ***p*** of the Holy
4:11 him be honor and ***p*** forever and
5:11 To him be ***p*** forever and always. Amen
2 Peter
1:3 By his divine ***p*** the Lord has given us
1 John
5:19 world lies in the ***p*** of the evil one.
Jude
1:25 glory, majesty, ***p***, and authority,
Revelation
1:6 him be glory and ***p*** forever and
1:16 like the sun shining with all its ***p***.

3:8 have so little **p**, and yet you have
4:11 and honor and **p**, because you
5:12 Lamb to receive **p**, wealth, wisdom,
5:13 honor, glory, and **p** belong to the one
7:2 been given the **p** to damage the
7:12 and honor and **p** and might be to
9:3 They were given **p** like the power
9:10 tails is their **p** to hurt people
9:19 The horses' **p** is in their mouths and
11:6 They have the **p** to close up the sky so
11:17 taken your great **p** and enforced your
12:10 the salvation and **p** and kingdom of
13:2 gave it his **p**, throne, and
14:18 angel, who has **p** over fire, came
15:8 God's glory and **p**, and no one could
16:9 the God who had **p** over these
17:12 received royal **p**. But they will
17:13 will give their **p** and authority to
17:17 give their royal **p** to the beast,
18:3 rich from the **p** of her loose and
19:1 salvation and glory and **p** of our God!
19:6 the Almighty, exercised his royal **p**!
20:6 death has no **p** over them, but

POWER OF GOD

Ezr 8:22; Lk 11:20; 22:69; Ac 8:10; 1Co 1:18; 2:5; 2Co 13:4; Col 2:12

POWERFUL

Genesis
26:16 you have become too **p** among us."
Numbers
13:28 are, however, **p** people who live
20:20 them with a **p** army and a strong
Deuteronomy
3:24 or can perform your deeds and **p** acts?
9:1 larger and more **p** than you, along
11:7 each of these **p** acts the LORD
2 Samuel
5:10 grew increasingly **p**, and the LORD of
22:18 saved me from my **p** enemy, saved me
Job
9:4 He is wise and **p**; who can resist him
21:22 God—he who judges the most **p**?
22:8 The **p** own land; the favored live in
37:23 find him—he is **p** and just,
Psalms
18:17 saved me from my **p** enemy, saved me
22:29 all the earth's **p** will worship him;
24:8 LORD—strong and **p**! The LORD—powerfu
37:35 have seen wicked **p** people, exalting
52:1 Hey, **p** person! Why do
59:3 for my life! **P** people are
78:25 the bread of the **p** ones; God sent
79:11 you. With your **p** arm spare those
89:13 You have a **p** arm; your hand is strong;
105:24 fruitful, more **p** than their
111:6 proclaimed his **p** deeds to his
132:8 you and your **p** covenant chest!
136:18 And killed **p** kings—God's faithful
Proverbs
24:5 a knowledgeable person than a **p** one.
30:26 creatures aren't **p**, but they make
31:17 works energetically; her arms are **p**.
Joel
1:6 because a nation, **p** and beyond number,
2:2 a great and **p** army comes,
2:5 stubble; like a **p** army ready for
Micah
2:1 they do it, for they are very **p**.
7:3 for a bribe; the **p** speak however
Nahum
3:10 all of her **p** citizens were
Zechariah
6:7 Then the **p** ones approached, intent on
Mark
6:2 What about the **p** acts accomplished
9:39 No one who does **p** acts in my name
Luke
1:52 He has pulled the **p** down from their
3:16 one who is more **p** than me is
24:19 Because of his **p** deeds and words,
Acts
4:33 continued to bear **p** witness to the
7:22 and he was a man of **p** words and deeds.
Romans
15:1 We who are **p** need to be patient with
1 Corinthians
1:26 not many were **p**, not many were
2 Corinthians
10:10 are severe and **p**, but in person he
Ephesians
6:10 by the Lord and his **p** strength.
2 Thessalonians
1:7 revealed from heaven with his **p** angels.
2 Timothy
1:7 but one that is **p**, loving, and
1:12 that God is **p** enough to protect
Hebrews
1:3 with his **p** message. After he
James
5:16 person is **p** in what it can
2 Peter
1:16 you about the **p** coming of our
2:11 stronger and more **p**, don't use
Revelation
5:2 I saw a **p** angel, who proclaimed in a
6:15 the rich and the **p**, and everyone,
10:1 I saw another **p** angel coming down
18:8 the Lord God who judges her is **p**.
18:10 great city, you **p** city! In a single
18:21 Then a **p** angel picked up a stone that
19:6 rushing water and **p** thunder. They
19:18 the flesh of the **p**, and the flesh of

PRACTICE

Leviticus
18:22 with a woman; it is a detestable **p**.
Ruth
4:7 this was the **p** regarding
1 Samuel
27:11 this was David's **p** during the entire
Ezra
9:14 the peoples who **p** these detestable
Psalms
119:56 This has been my **p** because I guard your
Ecclesiastes
8:8 won't deliver those who **p** it.
Jeremiah
22:17 the innocent; you **p** cruelty; you
Daniel
6:5 use against him from his religious **p**."

Zephaniah
2:3 of the land who ***p*** his justice; seek
Matthew
6:1 that you don't ***p*** your religion in
7:24 puts them into ***p*** is like a wise
7:26 put them into ***p*** will be like a
Luke
6:47 hears my words, and puts them into ***p***.
6:49 don't put into ***p*** what they hear
11:28 who hear God's word and put it into ***p***."
Acts
16:21 that we Romans can't accept or ***p***."
25:16 contrary to Roman ***p*** to hand someone
Romans
1:32 but also approve others who ***p*** them.
1 Corinthians
10:8 Let's not ***p*** sexual immorality, like
2 Corinthians
12:21 what they used to ***p***: moral
Philippians
4:9 ***P*** these things: whatever you learned,
Colossians
2:18 who wants to ***p*** harsh self-denial
1 Timothy
4:15 ***P*** these things, and live by them so
Hebrews
5:14 are trained by ***p*** to distinguish
James
1:25 they put it into ***p*** in their lives.
2:18 putting it into ***p*** in faithful
1 John
3:9 from God don't ***p*** sin because God's
3:10 who doesn't ***p*** righteousness is
Revelation
22:15 and all who love and ***p*** deception.

PRACTICES → YOUR DETESTABLE PRACTICES
Leviticus
18:3 must not follow the ***p*** of those places.
20:23 not follow the ***p*** of the nations
Numbers
9:3 its regulations and its customary ***p***.
9:14 and its customary ***p***. There will be
Deuteronomy
12:30 following their ***p*** after they've
18:10 through fire; who ***p*** divination, is a
Judges
2:19 drop their bad ***p*** or hardheaded
2 Kings
17:19 either. They followed the ***p*** of Israel.
17:26 the religious ***p*** of the local god.
17:27 them the religious ***p*** of the local god."
17:33 to the religious ***p*** of the nations
17:34 former religious ***p*** to this very day.
17:40 doing their former religious ***p***.
2 Chronicles
27:2 the people continued their crooked ***p***.
Hosea
4:11 false religious ***p***. Wine and new wine
Micah
6:16 of Omri, all the ***p*** of the house of
Acts
6:14 alter the customary ***p*** Moses gave us."
19:18 believe came, confessing their past ***p***.
Romans
1:32 persist in such ***p*** deserve death,
1 Corinthians
9:25 who competes ***p*** self-discipline in
Colossians
2:17 These religious ***p*** are only a shadow of
3:9 off the old human nature with its ***p***
1 Timothy
5:21 to follow these ***p*** without bias, and
1 John
2:29 every person who ***p*** righteousness is
3:4 Every person who ***p*** sin commits an act
3:7 The person who ***p*** righteousness is
3:8 The person who ***p*** sin belongs to the
3 John
1:11 is good. Whoever ***p*** what is good
Revelation
2:22 their hearts from following her ***p***—
2:26 keeping my ***p*** until the end, I

PRAISE → GIVE PRIASE, GOD'S PRAISE, PRAISE GOD, PRAISE THE LORD, PRAISE THE LORD'S NAME, WORTHY OF PRAISE
Exodus
15:2 God, whom I will ***p***, the God of my
15:11 worthy of highest ***p***, doing awesome
Deuteronomy
10:21 He is your ***p***, and he is your God—the
26:19 that he made in ***p***, fame, and honor;
1 Chronicles
16:4 thanks, and to ***p*** the LORD,
16:25 and so worthy of ***p***. He is awesome
16:35 your holy name and rejoice in your ***p***."
23:5 with instruments made for offering ***p***.
29:13 we thank you and ***p*** your glorious
2 Chronicles
5:13 together to ***p*** and thank the
7:6 used when he gave ***p***. Across from
8:14 for offering ***p*** and ministering
23:13 were leading the ***p***. Athaliah ripped
31:2 and to offer ***p*** in the gates of
Ezra
3:11 shouted with ***p*** to the LORD
Nehemiah
9:5 which is high above all blessing and ***p***.
12:24 opposite them to ***p*** and give thanks
12:46 were songs of ***p*** and thanks to God.
Job
36:24 Remember to ***p*** his work that all of us
40:14 I, even I, will ***p*** you, for your
Psalms
6:5 one is going to ***p*** you when they are
21:13 We will sing and ***p*** your power!
22:3 one, enthroned. You are Israel's ***p***.
22:22 sisters; I will ***p*** you in the very
22:23 revere the LORD—***p*** him! All of you
22:25 I offer ***p*** in the great congregation
22:26 who seek the LORD ***p*** him! I pray your
34:1 at all times; his ***p*** will always be in
35:18 assembly; I will ***p*** you in a huge
35:28 it will talk about your ***p*** all day long.
40:3 mouth, a song of ***p*** for our God. Many
45:17 the peoples will ***p*** you forever and
48:1 and so worthy of ***p***! His holy mountain
48:10 Your ***p***, God, just like your
51:15 and my mouth will proclaim your ***p***.
56:4 God, whose word I ***p***. I trust in God;
56:10 God: whose word I ***p***. The LORD: whose
63:3 My lips ***p*** you because your faithful

63:5 My mouth speaks ***p*** with joy on my
65:1 even silence is ***p***. Promises made to
66:2 of God's name! Make glorious his ***p***!
66:8 God! Let the sound of his ***p*** be heard!
66:17 cried out to him with ***p*** on my tongue.
71:6 mother's womb. My ***p*** is always about
71:8 filled with your ***p***, glorifying you
71:14 hope. Always. I will add to all your ***p***.
74:21 No, let the poor and needy ***p*** your name!
76:10 will turn to your ***p*** when you dress
78:4 all about the ***p*** due the LORD and
84:4 truly happy; they ***p*** you constantly.
96:4 and so worthy of ***p***. He is awesome
100:4 courtyards with ***p***! Thank him! Bless
102:21 in Zion and his ***p*** declared in
104:34 Let my ***p*** be pleasing to him; I'm
106:2 acts or publicly recount all his ***p***?
106:5 nation, so I can ***p*** along with your
106:47 your holy name and rejoice in your ***p***!
119:54 been my songs of ***p*** wherever I lived
119:108 gifts of ***p***. Teach me your
119:164 I ***p*** you seven times a day for your
119:171 overflow with ***p*** because you've
119:175 again so I can ***p*** you! Let your
138:1 LORD. I sing your ***p*** before all other
145:2 every day. I will ***p*** your name forever
145:4 generation will ***p*** your works to the
145:21 the LORD's ***p***, and every living
147:12 the LORD, Jerusalem! ***P*** your God, Zion!
148:14 his people, the ***p*** of all his
149:3 Let them ***p*** God's name with dance; let

Proverbs
27:2 another person ***p*** you, and not your
28:4 Instruction ***p*** the wicked, but
31:31 let her deeds ***p*** her in the city

Song of Songs
6:9 queens and secondary wives ***p*** her.

Isaiah
25:1 exalt you; I will ***p*** your name, for
38:18 nor can death ***p*** you; those who go
42:8 my glory to others or my ***p*** to idols.
42:10 song! Sing his ***p*** from the ends of
43:21 for myself, who will recount my ***p***.
57:19 create reason for ***p***: utter prosperity
60:18 your walls Salvation, and your gates ***P***.
61:3 a mantle of ***p*** in place of
61:11 righteousness and ***p*** before all the
62:7 and makes it the ***p*** of the earth.
64:5 right; they will ***p*** you for your

Jeremiah
13:11 for my honor, ***p***, and grandeur.
31:7 your voices with ***p*** and call out:
33:9 me great joy, ***p***, and renown
48:2 one sings Moab's ***p*** any longer! In

Daniel
2:23 I acknowledge and ***p*** you, my fathers'

Joel
2:26 and you will ***p*** the name of the

Habakkuk
3:3 the heavens and his ***p*** fills the earth.

Zephaniah
3:19 their shame into ***p*** and fame
3:20 give you fame and ***p*** among all the

Matthew
5:16 things you do and ***p*** your Father who
6:2 that they may get ***p*** from people. I
11:25 Jesus said, "I ***p*** you, Father, Lord
21:16 you've arranged ***p*** for yourself? "
26:30 singing songs of ***p***, they went to the

Mark
14:26 singing songs of ***p***, they went out to

Luke
10:21 and said, "I ***p*** you, Father, Lord
17:10 no special ***p***. We have only

John
5:41 I don't accept ***p*** from people
5:44 when you receive ***p*** from each other
12:43 they loved human ***p*** more than God's

Romans
2:28 who will receive ***p*** from God, and it
2:29 That person's ***p*** doesn't come from

1 Corinthians
11:2 I ***p*** you because you remember all my
11:17 Now I don't ***p*** you as I give the
11:22 to you? Will I ***p*** you? No, I don't

Philippians
1:11 in order to give glory and ***p*** to God.
4:8 is lovely, and all that is worthy of ***p***.

Hebrews
2:12 sisters. I will ***p*** you in the middle
13:15 up a sacrifice of ***p*** through him,

1 Peter
1:7 will result in ***p***, glory, and honor
2:14 doing evil and to ***p*** those doing good.
2:20 But what ***p*** comes from enduring

Revelation
19:5 throne and said, "***P*** our God, all you

PRAISE GOD

Ps 33:1; 48:10; 69:34; 107:32; 109:30; 135:1; 148:1, 2, 3, 4; 150:1, 2, 3, 4, 5; Lk 2:38; 17:18; 1Co 14:16

PRAISE THE LORD

Gn 29:35; 1Ch 16:4; 23:30; 2Ch 20:19; 20:22; 29:30; Ps 27:6; 34:2; 56:10; 102:18; 104:35; 105:45; 106:1, 48; 111:1; 112:1; 113:1, 9; 115:17, 18; 116:19; 117:1, 2; 135:1, 3, 21; 146:1, 2, 10; 147:1, 20; 148:1, 7, 14; 149:1, 9; 150:1, 6; Is 62:9; Jer 20:13; Ro 15:11

PRAISE THE LORD'S NAME

Ps 20:7; 113:1; 135:1; 148:5, 13

PRAISED → PRAISED GOD

Genesis
12:15 saw her, they ***p*** her to Pharaoh;
24:26 The man bowed down and ***p*** the LORD

Judges
16:24 saw him, they ***p*** their god, for

2 Samuel
14:25 Israel was as ***p*** for his good

Ezra
3:11 They ***p*** and gave thanks to the LORD,

Nehemiah
5:13 said, "Amen," and ***p*** the LORD. And the

Psalms
12:8 while depravity is ***p*** by human beings.
113:3 to sunset, let the LORD's name be ***p***!

Proverbs
12:8 A person is ***p*** for his insight, but a
31:30 a woman who fears the LORD is to be ***p***.

Isaiah
64:11 our ancestors ***p*** you, has gone up

Ezekiel
26:17 sea, city once ***p***, who once
Daniel
2:19 to Daniel! Daniel ***p*** the God of heaven:
2:20 God's name be ***p*** from age to eternal
3:28 and Abednego be ***p***! He sent his
4:34 to me, and I ***p*** the Most High. I
5:4 of wine; and they ***p*** the gods of gold,
6:10 down, prayed, and ***p*** his God three
Hosea
13:1 he was ***p*** in Israel; but he
Matthew
15:31 seeing. And they ***p*** the God of Israel.
Luke
4:15 their synagogues and was ***p*** by everyone.

PRAISED GOD

Mt 9:8; Mk 2:12; Lk 2:28; 7:16; 13:13; 17:15; 18:43; 19:37; 23:47; Ac 2:47; 11:18; 21:20

PRAISES → SING PRAISES

Psalms
9:14 declare all your ***p***, so I can rejoice
79:13 proclaim your ***p*** from one
89:12 Tabor and Hermon shout ***p*** to your name.
98:4 happy! Rejoice out loud! Sing your ***p***!
98:5 Sing your ***p*** to the LORD with the lyre—
101:1 I want to sing my ***p*** to you, LORD!
Proverbs
27:21 in the presence of someone who ***p*** them.
31:28 children bless her; her husband ***p*** her:
Isaiah
60:6 and incense, proclaiming the LORD's ***p***.
63:7 sing the LORD's ***p***, because of all
Romans
15:11 and all the people should sing his ***p***.

PRAISING GOD

Lk 1:64; 2:13, 20; 5:25; 18:43; 24:53; Ac 3:8; 3:9; 4:21; 10:46

PRAY → PRAY FOR US, PRAY FOR YOU, PRAY TO THE LORD

Exodus
8:28 go too far away and you ***p*** for me."
1 Samuel
12:19 Samuel, "Please ***p*** for us, your
2 Samuel
7:27 the courage to ***p*** this prayer to
1 Kings
8:30 Israel when they ***p*** toward this
8:35 but they then ***p*** toward this
13:6 LORD your God and ***p*** for me so that I
1 Chronicles
17:25 the courage to ***p*** this prayer to
2 Chronicles
7:14 to me will humbly ***p***, seek my face,
Ezra
6:10 God of heaven and ***p*** for the lives of
Nehemiah
1:6 which I now ***p*** before you night
Job
22:27 You will ***p*** to him, and he will hear
33:26 They ***p*** to God, and God is pleased with
Psalms
20:1 of David.] I ***p*** that the LORD
22:26 praise him! I ***p*** your hearts live
32:6 faithful should ***p*** to you during
122:6 ***P*** that Jerusalem has peace: "Let those
122:9 our God's house I will ***p*** for your good.
Isaiah
1:15 Even when you ***p*** for a long time,
16:12 his sanctuary to ***p***, he won't prevail.
45:20 know; those who ***p*** to a god who
Jeremiah
7:16 As for you, don't ***p*** for these people,
11:14 As for you, don't ***p*** for these people,
14:11 said to me: Don't ***p*** for the safety of
29:12 me and come and ***p*** to me, I will
31:9 come; while they ***p***, I will bring
37:3 plea: "Please ***p*** for us to the
42:20 God, saying, "***P*** for us to the
Daniel
9:18 by your name! We ***p*** our prayers for
Matthew
5:44 your enemies and ***p*** for those who
6:5 When you ***p***, don't be like hypocrites.
6:6 But when you ***p***, go to your room, shut
6:7 When you ***p***, don't pour out a flood of
6:9 ***P*** like this: Our Father who is in
14:23 by himself to ***p***. Evening came and
19:13 hands on them and ***p***. But the
21:22 you will receive whatever you ***p*** for."
24:20 ***P*** that it doesn't happen in winter or
26:36 here while I go and ***p*** over there."
26:41 Stay alert and ***p*** so that you won't give
Mark
6:46 Jesus went up onto a mountain to ***p***.
11:24 you, whatever you ***p*** and ask for,
11:25 you stand up to ***p***, if you have
13:18 ***P*** that it doesn't happen in winter
14:32 said to them, "Sit here while I ***p***."
14:38 Stay alert and ***p*** so that you won't give
Luke
5:33 fast often and ***p*** frequently. The
6:12 the mountain to ***p***, and he prayed to
6:28 who curse you. ***P*** for those who
9:28 James, and went up on a mountain to ***p***.
11:1 teach us to ***p***, just as John
11:2 them, "When you ***p***, say: 'Father,
18:1 their need to ***p*** continuously and
18:10 to the temple to ***p***. One was a
22:40 he said to them, "***P*** that you won't
22:46 Get up and ***p*** so that you won't
John
17:21 I ***p*** they will be one, Father, just as
Acts
10:9 city, Peter went up on the roof to ***p***.
20:36 he knelt down with all of them to ***p***.
27:29 the stern and began to ***p*** for daylight.
Romans
8:26 what we should ***p***, but the Spirit
15:31 ***P*** that I will be rescued from the
1 Corinthians
14:13 a tongue should ***p*** to be able to
14:14 If I ***p*** in a tongue, my spirit prays but
14:15 should I do? I'll ***p*** in the Spirit,
2 Corinthians
13:7 We ***p*** to God that you don't do anything
13:9 are strong. We ***p*** for this: that

Ephesians
1:17 I ***p*** that the God of our Lord Jesus
1:18 I ***p*** that the eyes of your heart will
6:19 As for me, ***p*** that when I open my mouth,
6:20 of the gospel. ***P*** so that the Lord
Philippians
1:4 you every time I ***p***, and it's always
1:10 I ***p*** this so that you will be able to
1:11 I ***p*** that you will then be filled with
Colossians
4:4 ***P*** that I might be able to make it as
1 Thessalonians
3:10 Night and day, we ***p*** more than ever to
5:17 ***P*** continually
2 Thessalonians
3:2 ***P*** too that we will be rescued from
1 Timothy
2:2 ***P*** for kings and everyone who is in
2:8 I want men to ***p*** everywhere by
Philemon
1:6 I ***p*** that your partnership in the faith
James
5:13 they should ***p***. If any of you
5:14 the elders should ***p*** over them,
5:16 to each other and ***p*** for each other so
1 Peter
4:7 and clearheaded so you can ***p***.
1 John
5:16 they should ***p***, and God will
Jude
1:20 most holy faith, ***p*** in the Holy

PRAY FOR US

1Sa 12:19; Jer 37:3; 42:20; Col 4:3; 1Th 5:25; 2Th 3:1; Heb 13:18

PRAY FOR YOU

Gn 20:7; Ex 8:9; 1Sa 12:23; Job 42:8; 2Co 9:14; Col 1:3

PRAY TO THE LORD

Ex 8:8; 8:29; 9:28; 10:17; 1Sa 7:5; 1Ki 8:44; Jer 29:7; 42:2, 4

PRAYED → PRAYED TO THE LORD

Genesis
20:17 Abraham ***p*** to God; and God restored
Numbers
21:7 from us." So Moses ***p*** for the people.
Deuteronomy
9:20 out! So I also ***p*** hard for Aaron at
1 Samuel
1:27 I ***p*** for this boy, and the LORD gave me
2:1 Then Hannah ***p***: My heart rejoices in
8:6 king to judge us," so he ***p*** to the LORD.
2 Samuel
15:31 Absalom, so he ***p***, "Please, LORD,
1 Kings
18:36 drew near and ***p***: "LORD, the God
2 Chronicles
30:18 way. But Hezekiah ***p*** for them: "May
32:20 Amoz's son, ***p*** about this,
33:13 He ***p***, and God was moved by his
Ezra
8:23 So we fasted and ***p*** to our God for this,
Nehemiah
2:4 that you need?" I ***p*** to the God of
4:9 So we ***p*** to our God and set a guard as
Job
42:10 fortune when he ***p*** for his friends,
Psalms
38:16 Because I ***p***: "Don't let them celebrate
72:15 him! Let him be ***p*** for always! Let
106:30 stood up and ***p***, and the plague
Isaiah
37:21 this: Since you ***p*** to me about
Daniel
6:10 knelt down, ***p***, and praised his
Matthew
26:39 on his face and ***p***, "My Father, if
26:42 he went away and ***p***, "My Father, if
26:44 again went and ***p*** the same words
Mark
14:35 to the ground. He ***p*** that, if
14:39 he left them and ***p***, repeating the
Luke
6:12 to pray, and he ***p*** to God all night
18:11 stood and ***p*** about himself
22:32 However, I have ***p*** for you that your
22:41 a stone's throw, knelt down, and ***p***.
22:44 in anguish and ***p*** even more
Acts
1:24 They ***p***, "Lord, you know everyone's
4:31 After they ***p***, the place where they
6:6 the apostles, who ***p*** and laid their
7:59 stones, Stephen ***p***, "Lord Jesus,
8:15 where they ***p*** that the new
9:40 then knelt and ***p***. He turned to the
10:2 Jewish people and ***p*** to God constantly.
13:3 they fasted and ***p***, they laid their
21:5 town where we knelt on the beach and ***p***.
28:8 to see him and ***p***. He placed his
James
5:17 When he earnestly ***p*** that it wouldn't
5:18 He ***p*** again, God sent rain, and the

PRAYED TO THE LORD

Gn 25:21; Ex 8:30; 10:18; Nm 11:2; Dt 9:26; 1Sa 1:10; 8:6; 15:11; 2Ki 4:33; 6:18; 19:15; 20:2; 2Ch 32:24; Is 37:15; 38:2; Jer 32:16; Dn 9:4; Jon 2:1; 4:2

PRAYER → HEARD YOUR PRAYER

Genesis
25:21 was moved by his ***p***, and his wife
1 Samuel
7:9 cried out in ***p*** to the LORD for
2 Samuel
7:27 the courage to pray this ***p*** to you.
2 Kings
19:4 heard. Send up a ***p*** for those few
1 Chronicles
5:20 God granted their ***p*** because they
17:25 the courage to pray this ***p*** to you.
Nehemiah
1:6 open to hear the ***p*** of your servant,
1:11 attentive to the ***p*** of your servant
11:17 thanksgiving with ***p***, and Bakbukiah
Job
16:17 violence in my hands, and my ***p*** is pure.

Psalms
4:1 Have mercy on me! Listen to my ***p***!
6:9 to my request. The LORD accepts my ***p***.
17:1 [A ***p*** of David.] Listen to what's right,
35:13 fast. When my ***p*** came back
39:12 Hear my ***p***, LORD! Listen closely to my
42:8 is with me—a ***p*** to the God of my
54:2 God! Hear my ***p***; listen to the words of
55:1 God, listen to my ***p***; don't avoid my
61:1 to my cry; pay attention to my ***p***!
65:2 you listen to ***p***—and all living
66:19 listened. He heard the sound of my ***p***.
66:20 didn't reject my ***p***; he didn't
69:13 But me? My ***p*** reaches you, LORD, at just
80:4 will you fume against your people's ***p***?
84:8 forces, hear my ***p***; listen closely,
86:1 [A ***p*** of David.] LORD, listen closely to
86:6 closely to my ***p***, LORD; pay close
88:2 let my ***p*** reach you! Turn your ear to my
88:13 to you, LORD! My ***p*** meets you first
90:1 [A ***p*** of Moses, the man of God.] Lord,
102:1 [A ***p*** of an oppressed person, when weak
102:17 will turn to the ***p*** of the
109:4 love, they accuse me—but I am at ***p***.
109:7 guilty—let his ***p*** be found sinful!
141:2 Let my ***p*** stand before you like incense;
142:1 in the cave. A ***p***.] I cry out loud
143:1 Listen to my ***p***, LORD! Because of
Isaiah
37:4 heard. Offer up a ***p*** for those few
38:5 I have heard your ***p*** and have seen
56:7 in my house of ***p***. I will accept
Lamentations
3:8 out and cry for help, he silences my ***p***.
Daniel
9:3 an answer with ***p*** and pleading, and
9:17 to your servant's ***p*** and pleas for
9:20 still praying my ***p*** for help to the
9:21 speaking this ***p***, the man Gabriel
Jonah
2:7 the LORD, and my ***p*** came to you, to
Habakkuk
3:1 The ***p*** of Habakkuk the prophet,
Matthew
21:13 called a house of ***p***.. But you've made
23:5 make extra-wide ***p*** bands for their
Mark
1:35 place where he could be alone in ***p***.
9:29 this kind of spirit out requires ***p***."
11:17 called a house of ***p*** for all nations?
Luke
2:37 God with fasting and ***p*** night and day.
5:16 withdraw to deserted places for ***p***.
19:46 be a house of ***p***, but you have
Acts
1:14 their devotion to ***p***, along with some
3:1 the afternoon, the established ***p*** time.
6:4 ourselves to ***p*** and the service
12:5 offered earnest ***p*** to God for him.
14:23 each church. With ***p*** and fasting, they
16:13 be a place for ***p***. We sat down and
16:16 to the place for ***p***, we met a slave
Romans
10:1 salvation. That's my ***p*** to God for them.
12:12 in trouble, and devote yourselves to ***p***.
1 Corinthians
7:5 yourselves to ***p***. Then come back
14:17 offer a beautiful ***p*** of thanksgiving,
2 Corinthians
1:11 helping with your ***p*** for us. Then many
Philippians
1:4 pray, and it's always a ***p*** full of joy.
1:9 This is my ***p***: that your love might
1 Timothy
4:5 are made holy by God's word and ***p***.
James
5:15 ***P*** that comes from faith will heal the
5:16 be healed. The ***p*** of the righteous

PRAYERS

2 Samuel
21:14 done, God responded to ***p*** for the land.
24:25 responded to the ***p*** for the land, and
2 Chronicles
6:40 ears attentive to the ***p*** of this place.
7:15 attention to the ***p*** offered in this
Psalms
72:20 The ***p*** of David, Jesse's son, are ended
102:17 impoverished; he won't despise their ***p***.
141:5 oil because my ***p*** are always
Proverbs
15:8 but favors the ***p*** of those who do
15:29 he listens to the ***p*** of the righteous.
28:9 even their ***p*** will be detested.
Isaiah
26:16 they poured out ***p*** to you when you
Jeremiah
36:7 will hear their ***p***. The LORD has
Lamentations
3:44 up in a cloud; ***p*** can't make it
Daniel
6:7 anyone who says ***p*** to any god or
6:13 He says his ***p*** three times a
9:18 name! We pray our ***p*** for help to you,
Mark
12:40 off they say long ***p***. They will be
Luke
1:13 Zechariah. Your ***p*** have been heard.
20:47 off they say long ***p***. They will be
Acts
2:42 to their shared meals, and to their ***p***.
10:4 angel said, "Your ***p*** and your
10:31 has heard your ***p***, and your
Romans
1:10 in all my ***p***. I'm always asking that
15:30 my struggles in your ***p*** to God for me.
2 Corinthians
1:11 to us through the ***p*** of many people.
Ephesians
1:16 for you when I remember you in my ***p***.
6:18 Offer ***p*** and petitions in the Spirit all
Philippians
1:3 God every time I mention you in my ***p***.
1:19 through your ***p*** and the help of
4:6 to God in your ***p*** and petitions,
Colossians
4:2 and guard your ***p*** with thanksgiving.
4:12 for you in ***p*** so that you will
1 Thessalonians
1:2 we mention you constantly in our ***p***.
1 Timothy
2:1 that requests, ***p***, petitions, and
5:5 with requests and ***p***, night and day.

2 Timothy
1:3 remember you in my ***p*** day and night.
Philemon
1:4 my God every time I mention you in my ***p***
1:22 to be with you because of your ***p***.
Hebrews
5:7 Christ offered ***p*** and requests with
1 Peter
3:7 this so that your ***p*** won't be hindered.
3:12 are open to their ***p***. But the Lord
Revelation
5:8 incense, which are the ***p*** of the saints.
8:3 on behalf of the ***p*** of all the saints
8:4 offered for the ***p*** of the saints

PRAYING

1 Samuel
1:12 As she kept ***p*** before the LORD, Eli
1:13 Now Hannah was ***p*** in her heart; her lips
1:16 time I've been ***p*** out of my great
1:26 stood here next to you, ***p*** to the LORD.
7:8 don't stop ***p*** to the LORD our
1 Kings
8:29 your servant is ***p*** toward this place.
8:54 Solomon finished ***p*** and making these
2 Chronicles
6:20 your servant is ***p*** concerning this
7:1 Solomon finished ***p***, fire came down
Ezra
10:1 While Ezra was ***p*** and confessing,
Nehemiah
1:4 days, fasting and ***p*** before the God of
Psalms
5:2 king and my God, because I am ***p*** to you!
Daniel
6:11 came upon Daniel ***p*** and seeking mercy
9:20 still speaking, ***p***, and confessing
Luke
1:10 to worship were ***p*** outside during
3:21 While he was ***p***, heaven was opened
9:18 when Jesus was ***p*** by himself, the
9:29 As he was ***p***, the appearance of his
11:1 Jesus was ***p*** in a certain place. When he
21:36 at all times, ***p*** that you are
22:45 he got up from ***p***, he went to the
John
17:9 I'm ***p*** for them. I'm not praying for
17:20 I'm not ***p*** only for them but also for
Acts
9:11 a man from Tarsus named Saul. He is ***p***.
10:30 afternoon, I was ***p*** at home. Suddenly
11:5 the city of Joppa ***p*** when I had a
12:12 had gathered there and were ***p***.
16:25 and Silas were ***p*** and singing hymns
22:17 Jerusalem and was ***p*** in the temple, I
Ephesians
6:18 in there and ***p*** for all believers.
Colossians
1:9 haven't stopped ***p*** for you and
1:10 We're ***p*** this so that you can live lives
4:2 Keep on ***p*** and guard your prayers with
2 Thessalonians
1:11 We are constantly ***p*** for you for this:
3 John
1:2 Dear friend, I'm ***p*** that all is well

PREACH → PREACH THE GOSPEL

Ezekiel
20:46 one, face Teman, ***p*** against the
21:2 face Jerusalem, ***p*** against their
Amos
7:16 Israel, and don't ***p*** against the house
Micah
2:6 They mustn't ***p***!" so they preach.
2:11 I will ***p*** to you for wine
Matthew
11:1 there to teach and ***p*** in their cities.
Mark
1:38 so that I can ***p*** there too. That's
3:14 to be with him, to be sent out to ***p***,
Luke
4:18 He has sent me to ***p*** good news to the
4:43 to them, "I must ***p*** the good news of
Acts
8:5 Samaria and began to ***p*** Christ to them.
9:20 away, he began to ***p*** about Jesus in
10:42 commanded us to ***p*** to the people and
28:31 he continued to ***p*** God's kingdom and
Romans
2:21 yourself? If you ***p***, "No stealing,"
10:8 is, the message of faith that we ***p***).
10:15 And how can they ***p*** unless they are
16:25 message that I ***p*** about Jesus
1 Corinthians
1:17 to baptize but to ***p*** the good news.
1:23 but we ***p*** Christ crucified, which is a
2:2 Christ, and to ***p*** him as crucified.
9:18 get? That when I ***p***, I offer the good
15:11 this is what we ***p*** and this is what
2 Corinthians
2:12 came to Troas to ***p*** Christ's gospel,
4:5 We don't ***p*** about ourselves. Instead, we
Galatians
1:8 angel should ever ***p*** anything
1:16 so that I might ***p*** about him to the
2:2 the gospel that I ***p*** to the Gentiles
Philippians
1:15 Some certainly ***p*** Christ with jealous
1:17 the others ***p*** Christ because of their
Colossians
1:28 This is what we ***p*** as we warn and teach
4:3 word so we can ***p*** the secret plan
4:4 it as clear as I ought to when I ***p***.
2 Timothy
4:2 ***P*** the word. Be ready to do it whether
1 Peter
3:19 that he went to ***p*** to the spirits in

PREACH THE GOSPEL

Ro 1:15; 15:20; 1Co 9:14; 9:16; Ga 2:7

PREACHED

Zechariah
1:4 former prophets ***p***: The LORD of
Luke
7:22 up. And good news is ***p*** to the poor.
16:16 God's kingdom is ***p***, and everyone is
24:47 of sins must be ***p*** in his name to
Acts
8:12 Philip, who ***p*** the good news
9:27 which Saul had ***p*** in the name of
10:37 in Galilee after the baptism John ***p***.
15:36 city where we ***p*** the Lord's word.

PREACHED [cont.]

1 Corinthians
15:1 good news that I ***p*** to you, which you
2 Corinthians
1:19 the one who was ***p*** among you by us—
10:16 the gospel being ***p*** in places beyond
11:4 than the one we ***p***, or if you
Galatians
1:8 from what we ***p*** to you, they
1:11 that the gospel I ***p*** isn't human in
3:8 faith, scripture ***p*** the gospel in
4:13 know that I first ***p*** the gospel to you
Colossians
1:23 message has been ***p*** throughout all
1 Thessalonians
2:9 and hard work. We ***p*** God's good news
1 Timothy
3:16 seen by angels, ***p*** to throughout the
2 Timothy
4:17 message would be ***p*** through me and so
Hebrews
4:2 had the good news ***p*** to us, just as
1 Peter
4:6 news was also ***p*** to the dead. This

PREACHING → PREACHING THE GOOD NEWS

Matthew
12:41 to Jonah's ***p***. And look,
Mark
1:39 Galilee ***p*** in their
Luke
4:44 So he continued ***p*** in the Judean
8:1 and villages, ***p*** and proclaiming
11:32 to Jonah's ***p***—and one greater
Romans
15:19 the circuit of ***p*** Christ's gospel
1 Corinthians
1:21 believe through the foolishness of ***p***.
2:1 I didn't come ***p*** God's secrets to
2:4 My message and my ***p*** weren't presented
9:27 be disqualified after ***p*** to others.
15:14 raised, then our ***p*** is useless and
Galatians
2:6 to what I was ***p***—and whatever they
5:11 if I'm still ***p*** circumcision, why
1 Timothy
4:13 to public reading, ***p***, and teaching.
Titus
1:3 time through ***p***, and I was

PREACHING THE GOOD NEWS

Ac 8:4; 8:25, 40; 17:18; Ro 1:9

PRECEPTS

Psalms
119:15 think about your ***p*** and examine all

PRECIOUS

Exodus
19:5 will be my most ***p*** possession out of
1 Samuel
26:21 my life ***p*** today, I won't
1 Kings
10:2 of gold, and ***p*** stones. After she
1 Chronicles
29:2 every kind of ***p*** stone, and a
29:8 Anyone who had ***p*** stones donated them to
2 Chronicles
3:6 the room with ***p*** stones for
9:1 of gold, and ***p*** stones. After she
32:27 his silver, gold, ***p*** stones, spices,
Ezra
8:27 copper, which were as ***p*** as gold.
Job
28:10 rocks; their eyes see everything ***p***.
28:16 from Ophir, with ***p*** onyx or lapis
Psalms
35:17 rescue my ***p*** life from these
45:9 standing in your ***p*** jewels; the queen
68:13 silver; its pinions covered in ***p*** gold."
72:14 violence; their blood is ***p*** in his eyes.
92:10 as a wild ox. I'm soaked in ***p*** ointment.
Proverbs
1:13 find all sorts of ***p*** wealth; we'll
12:27 but hard workers receive ***p*** riches.
20:15 but wise speech is the most ***p*** jewel.
21:20 ***P*** treasure and oil stay in the home of
24:4 filled with all ***p*** and pleasant
Isaiah
43:4 Because you are ***p*** in my eyes, you are
54:12 beryl, and all your walls of ***p*** jewels.
Jeremiah
2:21 planted you, a ***p*** vine of fine
Lamentations
1:11 up their most ***p*** things for food
2:4 He killed every ***p*** thing in sight;
4:2 Zion's ***p*** children, once valued as pure
Ezekiel
22:25 up wealth and ***p*** goods and made
27:22 every kind of ***p*** stone, and gold.
28:13 gold and every ***p*** stone: carnelian,
Daniel
11:38 rare stones and ***p*** things, he will
11:43 and all its ***p*** things. Libyans
Hosea
9:6 possess their ***p*** things of silver;
Nahum
2:9 supplies, an abundance of ***p*** objects!
Matthew
13:46 he found one very ***p*** pearl, he went
1 Corinthians
3:12 gold, silver, ***p*** stones, wood,
James
5:7 forward to the ***p*** fruit of the
1 Peter
1:19 liberated by the ***p*** blood of Christ,
3:4 type of beauty is very ***p*** in God's eyes.
2 Peter
1:4 has given us his ***p*** and wonderful

PREGNANT

Genesis
4:1 She became ***p*** and gave birth to
16:4 and she became ***p***. But when she
19:36 daughters became ***p*** by their father.
21:2 She became ***p*** and gave birth to a son
25:21 prayer, and his wife Rebekah became ***p***.
29:32 Leah became ***p*** and gave birth to a son.
30:5 Bilhah became ***p*** and gave birth to a son
38:3 she became ***p*** and gave birth to a son,
38:4 She became ***p*** again, gave birth to a

Exodus
2:2 The woman became ***p*** and gave birth to a son
21:22 fighting injure a ***p*** woman so that she
Judges
13:2 unable to become ***p*** and had not given
Ruth
4:13 let her become ***p***, and she gave
1 Samuel
4:19 wife, was ***p*** and about to give
2 Samuel
11:5 sent word to David. "I'm ***p***," she said.
2 Kings
8:12 children and rip open their ***p*** women."
15:16 and ripped open all its ***p*** women.
Ecclesiastes
11:5 fetus inside a ***p*** woman's womb, so
Isaiah
7:14 young woman is ***p*** and is about to
8:3 and she became ***p*** and gave birth to
26:17 As a ***p*** woman close to childbirth is in
Jeremiah
20:17 become my grave, her womb ***p*** forever.
Hosea
1:3 and she became ***p*** and bore him a
1:6 Gomer became ***p*** again and gave birth to
1:8 she became ***p*** and gave birth to
13:16 dashed, and their ***p*** women ripped open.
Amos
1:13 have ripped open ***p*** women in Gilead
Matthew
1:18 she became ***p*** by the Holy
1:23 will become ***p*** and give birth to
24:19 for women who are ***p*** and for women who
Mark
13:17 for women who are ***p*** and for women who
Luke
1:7 unable to become ***p*** and they both
1:24 Elizabeth became ***p***. She kept to
2:5 to him in marriage and who was ***p***.
21:23 for women who are ***p*** or for women who
23:29 unable to become ***p***, the wombs that
1 Thessalonians
5:3 start with a ***p*** woman, and they
Revelation
12:2 She was ***p***, and she cried out because

PREPARE

Genesis
27:9 goats so I can ***p*** them as the
43:16 an animal and ***p*** it because the
Exodus
12:39 have time to ***p*** any food for
19:15 He told the men, "***P*** yourselves for
30:25 ***P*** a holy anointing oil, blending them
Leviticus
6:22 succeed him will ***p*** the offering as a
Numbers
23:1 altars here and ***p*** for me seven
Judges
13:15 to stay so we can ***p*** a young goat for
2 Samuel
12:4 flock or herd to ***p*** for the guest who
13:5 to eat. Let her ***p*** the food in my
13:7 Amnon's house and ***p*** some food for
1 Kings
18:23 add fire. I'll ***p*** the other bull,
18:25 of these bulls. ***P*** it first since
2 Kings
20:7 Isaiah said, "***P*** a bandage made of
1 Chronicles
22:5 so I myself will ***p*** things for him.
2 Chronicles
2:9 to ***p*** plenty of timber for me, because
31:11 ordered them to ***p*** storerooms in the
35:6 lambs and ***p*** the holy
Esther
5:8 feast that I will ***p*** for them.
5:14 him: "Have people ***p*** a pointed pole
Job
28:25 the wind, to ***p*** a measure for
38:3 ***P*** yourself like a man; I will
42:8 servant Job, and ***p*** an entirely
Psalms
132:17 thrive. I will ***p*** a lamp for my
Isaiah
8:9 of the earth! ***P*** to be shattered!
14:21 ***P*** a place to slaughter his sons for the
25:6 forces will ***p*** for all peoples a
38:21 Isaiah said, "***P*** a salve made from
62:10 the gates; ***p*** the way for the
Jeremiah
1:17 But you must ***p*** for battle and be ready
6:4 ***P*** for battle against her; get ready;
12:3 them like sheep. ***P*** them for the
25:33 mourn for them or ***p*** their bodies for
46:3 Grab your shields and ***p*** for war
49:14 forces and come against her; ***p*** for war!
50:27 all her bulls; ***p*** them for
51:3 bows; let them ***p*** their armor. Show
Ezekiel
4:2 ***P*** the siege: Build a wall, construct
12:3 you, human one, ***p*** a backpack for
35:6 as I live, I will ***p*** you for blood,
Daniel
11:25 army, will ***p*** for war, but he
Hosea
14:2 ***P*** to speak and return to the LORD; say
Joel
2:16 the people; ***p*** a holy meeting;
3:9 the nations: ***P*** a holy war, wake
3:12 Let the nations ***p*** themselves, and come
Amos
4:12 do this to you. ***P*** to meet your God,
Nahum
3:14 for yourself to ***p*** for siege!
Matthew
3:3 the wilderness, "***P*** the way for the
11:10 you, who will ***p*** your way before
26:17 do you want us to ***p*** for you to eat
Mark
1:2 before you. He will ***p*** your way,
1:3 the wilderness: "***P*** the way for the
14:12 do you want us to ***p*** for you to eat
Luke
1:76 will go before the Lord to ***p*** his way.
3:4 the wilderness: "***P*** the way for the
7:27 you, who will ***p*** your way before
9:52 Samaritan village to ***p*** for his arrival,
10:40 has left me to ***p*** the table all by
12:47 will but didn't ***p*** for it or act on
21:14 your minds not to ***p*** your defense in

22:8 task: "Go and ***p*** for us to eat the
John
14:2 that I'm going to ***p*** a place for you?
14:3 When I go to ***p*** a place for you, I will
Acts
23:23 and said, "***P*** two hundred
1 Corinthians
14:8 then who will ***p*** for battle?

PREPARED

Genesis
21:8 nursing, Abraham ***p*** a huge banquet.
26:30 Isaac ***p*** a banquet for them, and they
29:22 people of that place and ***p*** a banquet.
Joshua
7:7 only we had been ***p*** to live on the
18:8 When the men had ***p*** to go, Joshua gave
Judges
6:19 Gideon went and ***p*** a young goat and
2 Samuel
12:4 ewe lamb and ***p*** it for the
1 Chronicles
15:1 City, David ***p*** a place for God's
28:2 footrest. But when I ***p*** to build it,
29:19 to build the temple that I have ***p***.
2 Chronicles
1:4 the place he had ***p*** for it because he
3:1 place David had ***p*** at the threshing
16:14 the tomb he had ***p*** for himself in
35:14 Next they ***p*** food for themselves and for
35:15 their fellow Levites ***p*** food for them.
35:16 service was ***p*** for celebrating
Nehemiah
5:18 and birds were ***p*** each day. Every
13:5 ***p*** a large room for Tobiah to use. This
Esther
5:4 for the feast that I have ***p*** for him."
6:14 off to the feast that Esther had ***p***.
Job
1:5 the morning, he ***p*** entirely burned
Isaiah
34:2 them out and has ***p*** them for
Jeremiah
13:25 that I have ***p*** for you, declares
Ezekiel
17:5 planted it in a ***p*** field, placing it
28:13 crafted pendants and engravings were ***p***.
38:7 ready and be ***p***, you and all your
43:18 day when it is ***p*** for making
Nahum
2:3 on the day he has ***p***; the horses
Matthew
20:23 to those for whom my Father ***p*** it."
22:2 like a king who ***p*** a wedding party
22:4 the meal is all ***p***. I've butchered
22:8 wedding party is ***p***, but those who
24:44 also should be ***p***, because the
25:7 bridesmaids got up and ***p*** their lamps.
25:34 kingdom that was ***p*** for you before
25:41 that has been ***p*** for the devil and
26:12 over my body she's ***p*** me to be buried.
26:19 instructed them. They ***p*** the Passover.
Mark
6:21 when he had ***p*** a feast for his
10:40 to those for whom it has been ***p***."
14:16 them, and they ***p*** the Passover meal.
Luke
1:17 make ready a people ***p*** for the Lord."
2:31 You ***p*** this salvation in the presence of
6:40 whoever is fully ***p*** will be like
12:20 the things you have ***p*** for yourself?'
22:13 them, and they ***p*** the Passover meal.
23:56 went away and ***p*** fragrant spices
24:1 the fragrant spices they had ***p***.
Acts
16:10 the vision, we ***p*** to leave for the
23:15 closely. We're ***p*** to kill him
Romans
9:23 mercy, which he ***p*** in advance for
1 Corinthians
2:9 written: God has ***p*** things for those
2 Corinthians
5:5 Now the one who ***p*** us for this very
9:3 that you can be ***p***, just as I keep
Hebrews
9:6 things have been ***p*** in this way,
10:5 an offering, but you ***p*** a body for me;
11:16 their God—he has ***p*** a city for them.
Revelation
12:6 where God has ***p*** a place for her.

PRESENCE

→ BREAD OF THE PRESENCE, GOD'S PRESENCE, PRESENCE OF GOD, PRESENCE OF THE LORD
Genesis
4:14 hidden from your ***p***, I'm about to
27:7 you in the LORD's ***p*** before I die.'
47:10 blessed Pharaoh and left Pharaoh's ***p***.
Exodus
10:11 Pharaoh had them chased out of his ***p***.
33:18 said, "Please show me your glorious ***p***."
33:22 As my glorious ***p*** passes by, I'll set
40:35 LORD's glorious ***p*** filled the
Ruth
4:4 Buy it, in the ***p*** of those sitting
1 Kings
8:65 seven days in the ***p*** of the LORD our
2 Kings
5:27 left Elisha's ***p***, flaky like snow
1 Chronicles
12:1 banished from the ***p*** of Saul, Kish's
24:31 had done in the ***p*** of King David,
2 Chronicles
26:19 forehead in the ***p*** of the priests
Nehemiah
6:19 good deeds in my ***p*** and then reported
8:3 He read it in the ***p*** of the men and
Job
1:12 So the Adversary left the LORD's ***p***.
Psalms
16:11 of life. In your ***p*** is total
18:49 you, LORD, in the ***p*** of the nations.
21:6 make him happy with the joy of your ***p***.
22:25 promises in the ***p*** of those who
30:7 then you hid your ***p***. I was terrified.
39:1 as long as the wicked were in my ***p***.
41:12 you put me in your ***p*** forever.
42:5 again give him thanks, my saving ***p*** and
42:11 him thanks, my saving ***p*** and my God.
43:5 him thanks, my saving ***p*** and my God.
51:11 me out of your ***p***; please don't
52:9 acted. In the ***p*** of your faithful
78:12 their ancestors' ***p***—in the land of

89:15 They walk in the light of your ***p***, LORD!
102:28 descendants live secure in your ***p***."
116:14 the LORD in the ***p*** of all God's
116:18 the LORD in the ***p*** of all God's
139:7 Where could I go to escape your ***p***?
140:13 those who do right will live in your ***p***.

Proverbs
25:5 from the king's ***p***, and his throne
25:6 yourself in the ***p*** of the king, or
27:21 are people in the ***p*** of someone who

Ecclesiastes
8:3 leave his ***p***. Don't linger in

Isaiah
59:12 numerous in your ***p***; our sins testify
64:2 the nations would tremble in your ***p***.

Jeremiah
4:1 idols from my ***p*** and wander no
19:1 a potter in the ***p*** of the elders of
23:39 you out of my ***p***, together with
28:5 Hananiah in the ***p*** of the priests
33:18 someone in my ***p*** to make entirely
34:18 agreed to in my ***p***, such as the calf
52:3 them out of his ***p***. Zedekiah

Ezekiel
2:6 shrink from their ***p***, because they are
14:1 house of Israel came to sit in my ***p***,
30:24 will groan like a dying man in his ***p***.
38:20 will quake in my ***p***. Mountains will
44:15 will stand in my ***p*** to present fat
46:3 may bow in the ***p*** of the LORD on

Daniel
7:10 out from his ***p***; thousands upon

Hosea
2:2 from her ***p***, and adultery

Joel
2:6 In their ***p***, peoples shake with fear;

Luke
2:31 this salvation in the ***p*** of all peoples.
13:26 and drank in your ***p***, and you taught
14:10 be honored in the ***p*** of all your
15:10 breaks out in the ***p*** of God's angels
20:45 In the ***p*** of all the people, Jesus said
23:14 him in your ***p*** and found nothing

John
17:5 me in your ***p*** with the glory I
20:30 in his disciples' ***p***, signs that

Acts
2:28 of life; your ***p*** will fill me with
3:13 in Pilate's ***p***, even though he
13:52 of the abundant ***p*** of the Holy
18:17 a beating in the ***p*** of the governor.

Romans
3:20 righteous in his ***p*** by doing what the

2 Corinthians
2:10 I did it for you in the ***p*** of Christ.
4:14 bring us into his ***p*** along with you.

Philippians
1:26 Jesus through my ***p*** when I visit you

1 Thessalonians
1:3 Christ in the ***p*** of our God and

2 Thessalonians
1:9 from the Lord's ***p*** and away from his

1 Timothy
6:12 of it in the ***p*** of many witnesses.

Jude
1:24 and rejoicing before his glorious ***p***,

Revelation
3:5 names in the ***p*** of my Father and
13:12 beast in its ***p***. It also makes
13:13 heaven to earth in the ***p*** of the people.
13:14 to do in the ***p*** of the beast. It
14:10 and sulfur in the ***p*** of the holy
19:20 in the beast's ***p***. (He had used the

PRESENCE OF GOD

Ac 10:33; 2Co 2:17; 3:4; 1Ti 6:13; 2Ti 4:1; 1Pt 3:18

PRESENCE OF THE LORD

Ex 16:10; Dt 14:23; 15:20; 16:16; 29:10; 1Sa 12:3; 1Ki 8:65; Eze 46:3

PRESENT

Genesis
33:11 Take this ***p*** that I've brought because

Exodus
10:25 offerings to ***p*** to the LORD our
20:21 the thick darkness in which God was ***p***.
22:14 the owner isn't ***p***, full payment
25:8 a sanctuary so I can be ***p*** among them.
29:3 in one basket and ***p*** them in the
29:10 ***P*** the bull at the front of the meeting
30:14 and above, should ***p*** a gift offering

Numbers
7:11 per day will ***p*** their offering
8:11 Aaron will ***p*** the Levites as an uplifted
29:36 You will ***p*** an entirely burned offering,

Deuteronomy
31:14 two of you must ***p*** yourselves at the

Joshua
7:12 reserved for me that are ***p*** among you.
7:13 for me are ***p*** among you. You

1 Samuel
20:29 ordered me to be ***p***. Please do me a

2 Samuel
2:18 three sons were ***p*** at the battle:

1 Chronicles
23:30 They were to be ***p*** every morning to

2 Chronicles
5:11 priests who were ***p*** had sanctified
31:1 who were ***p*** went out to the
35:17 who were ***p*** celebrated the

Ezra
3:6 they began to ***p*** entirely burned
8:25 and all Israel ***p*** there had offered.

Esther
2:23 in the royal record with the king ***p***.

Job
1:6 beings came to ***p*** themselves before
2:1 beings came to ***p*** themselves before
13:3 I would gladly ***p*** my case to God.
36:4 one with total knowledge is ***p*** with you.
37:19 to him; we can't ***p*** our case due to

Psalms
56:12 you, God. I will ***p*** thanksgiving
72:10 the kings of Sheba and Seba ***p*** gifts.

Isaiah
5:20 good evil, who ***p*** darkness as light
41:21 ***P*** your case, says the LORD. Bring

Jeremiah
29:14 I will be ***p*** for you, declares the LORD,
32:12 Judeans who were ***p*** in the prison
33:18 grain offerings, and to ***p*** sacrifices.

41:5 and incense to ***p*** at the LORD's
42:9 have sent me to ***p*** your plea to the
44:15 of women who were ***p***, as well as the
Ezekiel
43:22 day, you will ***p*** a flawless male
43:23 you will ***p*** a flawless bull
44:15 in my presence to ***p*** fat and blood to
46:2 The priests will ***p*** the prince's
Hosea
13:13 time he doesn't ***p*** himself at the
Zechariah
4:7 a plain. He will ***p*** the capstone to
14:18 go up and doesn't ***p*** itself, then no
Matthew
6:6 Father who is ***p*** in that secret
13:39 is the end of the ***p*** age. The
Luke
2:22 up to Jerusalem to ***p*** him to the Lord.
12:56 don't know how to interpret the ***p*** time?
13:1 Some who were ***p*** on that occasion told
18:40 to him. When he was ***p*** Jesus asked,
Acts
19:8 with those ***p*** and offered
21:18 to see James. All of the elders were ***p***.
25:24 and everyone ***p*** with us: You see
Romans
3:26 righteous in the ***p*** time, and to
6:13 do wrong. Instead ***p*** yourselves to God
6:19 Now, you should ***p*** the parts of your
8:18 believe that the ***p*** suffering is
8:38 or rulers, not ***p*** things or future
11:5 So also in the ***p*** time there is a
11:8 not hear, right up until the ***p*** day.
12:1 encourage you to ***p*** your bodies as a
1 Corinthians
2:6 comes from the ***p*** day or from
2:8 that none of the ***p***-day rulers have un
3:22 things in the ***p***, things in the
4:13 runs off everything, up to the ***p*** time.
5:3 physically, I'm ***p*** in the spirit and
5:4 Jesus, I'll be ***p*** in spirit with
7:26 because of the ***p*** crisis: stay as
7:31 this world in its ***p*** form is passing
2 Corinthians
3:14 Right up to the ***p*** day the same veil
8:14 At the ***p*** moment, your surplus can fill
11:2 I promised to ***p*** you as an
Galatians
1:4 us from this ***p*** evil age,
4:25 to the ***p***-day Jerusalem,
Ephesians
5:27 He did this to ***p*** himself with a
Philippians
2:12 just when I am ***p*** but now even more
Colossians
1:22 through death, to ***p*** you before God as
1:28 so that we might ***p*** each one mature
2 Timothy
2:15 Make an effort to ***p*** yourself to God as
4:10 in love with the ***p*** world and has
Hebrews
9:9 a symbol for the ***p*** time. It shows
Jude
1:24 falling, and to ***p*** you blameless and
Revelation
17:8 it was and is not and will again be ***p***.

PRESENTED

Genesis
4:3 time later, Cain ***p*** an offering to
43:26 the house, they ***p*** him the gift they
47:2 five men and ***p*** them before
Exodus
29:23 bread that was ***p*** to the LORD.
Leviticus
7:35 they have been ***p*** to serve the LORD
8:18 Then Moses ***p*** the ram for the entirely
9:9 Then Aaron's sons ***p*** the blood to him,
Numbers
7:10 The chiefs ***p*** their offerings
8:15 cleansed them and ***p*** them as an
16:38 altar. Since they ***p*** them in the
31:52 offering that was ***p*** to the LORD from
Deuteronomy
31:14 Joshua went and ***p*** themselves at the
Joshua
24:1 officers. They ***p*** themselves before
Judges
3:17 Then he ***p*** the tribute payment to Moab's
5:25 milk; she ***p*** him cream in a
6:19 out to him under the oak and ***p*** them.
1 Samuel
1:9 Hannah got up and ***p*** herself before
16:10 Jesse ***p*** seven of his sons to Samuel,
17:57 sent for him and ***p*** him to Saul. The
1 Chronicles
29:9 because they had ***p*** their offerings
Ezra
3:4 Every day they ***p*** the number of
3:5 After this, they ***p*** the continual burned
Psalms
45:14 following her, are ***p*** to you as well.
Isaiah
57:6 offering, and ***p*** a grain offering.
Daniel
7:13 the ancient one and was ***p*** before him.
Matthew
2:11 chests and ***p*** him with gifts of
Acts
6:6 The community ***p*** these seven to the
6:13 the council, they ***p*** false witnesses
9:41 the widows, and ***p*** her alive to them.
21:26 offering would be ***p*** for each one of
25:2 Jewish leaders ***p*** their case
1 Corinthians
2:4 preaching weren't ***p*** with convincing
Hebrews
9:2 and the loaves of bread ***p*** to God.

PREY

Genesis
49:9 cub; from the ***p***, my son, you rise
49:27 he devours the ***p***; in the evening
Numbers
14:9 They are our ***p***. Their defense
23:24 until it eats the ***p*** and drinks the
Deuteronomy
14:13 black kite, and any kind of bird of ***p***,
2 Samuel
21:10 let any birds of ***p*** land on the
Job
4:11 perishes without ***p***, and its cubs are
9:26 made of reeds, as an eagle swoops on ***p***.

24:5 searching for ***p***; the wasteland is
24:21 They ***p*** on the barren, the childless, do
28:7 path—no bird of ***p*** knows it; a
29:17 the wicked, rescued ***p*** from their teeth.
38:39 Can you hunt ***p*** for the lion or fill the
Psalms
10:10 collapse, falling ***p*** to the strength
17:12 eager to rip its ***p***; they are like a
104:21 roar for their ***p***, seeking their
Proverbs
12:27 don't roast their ***p***, but hard workers
Isaiah
5:29 seize their ***p***, and carry it
31:4 lion, over its ***p***, though a band of
46:11 I call a bird of ***p*** from the east, a man
Jeremiah
2:14 If not, why then has he become ***p***?
12:9 like a bird of ***p***, surrounded and
Ezekiel
13:21 They will be ***p*** in your clutches
22:25 lion ripping up ***p***. They've piled up
22:27 wolves ripping up ***p***. They shed blood
26:5 says. It will become ***p*** for the nations,
34:8 my flock became ***p***. My flock became
34:22 never again be ***p***. I will even
34:28 will no longer ***p*** on them, and wild
39:4 to the birds of ***p***, to every kind of
39:17 to the birds of ***p***, to every kind of
44:31 dies naturally or is torn apart by ***p***.
Hosea
5:14 one who tears the ***p*** and goes forth;
8:1 as if a bird of ***p*** has flown over
Amos
3:4 when it has no ***p***? Does a young
Nahum
2:12 has torn enough ***p*** for his cubs and
2:13 will cut off your ***p*** from the earth,
3:1 full of plunder: ***p*** cannot get away.
Zechariah
2:9 they will become ***p*** to their own

PRICE

Genesis
23:9 me for the full ***p***, to be witnessed
23:13 will give you the ***p*** of the field.
30:28 so name your ***p*** and I will pay it.
30:32 female goats. That will be my ***p***.
34:12 Make the bride ***p*** and marriage gifts as
Exodus
21:35 ox and divide its ***p***. They should also
Leviticus
25:16 will raise the ***p*** if there are more
25:50 Jubilee year. The ***p*** of their release
27:15 to its valued ***p***, and it will be
Numbers
18:16 Their redemption ***p*** from one month of
2 Samuel
24:24 you at a fair ***p***. I won't offer up
1 Kings
5:6 servants whatever ***p*** you set, because
10:28 by the king's agents at the going ***p***.
21:2 prefer, I'll pay you the ***p*** in silver."
1 Chronicles
21:22 charging me full ***p***, so that I may
21:24 you at a fair ***p***. I won't offer to
2 Chronicles
1:16 by the king's agents at the going ***p***.
Job
28:15 with gold; its ***p*** can't be measured
28:18 be mentioned; the ***p*** of wisdom is more
Psalms
44:12 not even bothering to set a decent ***p***.
49:8 The ***p*** to save someone's life is too
Proverbs
27:26 the goats will be the ***p*** of your fields.
Isaiah
45:13 free, not for a ***p*** and not for a
Lamentations
5:4 water—but for a ***p***; we gather our
Daniel
11:39 many and dividing up the land for a ***p***.
Zechariah
11:13 too magnificent a ***p***." So I took the
Matthew
27:9 of silver, the ***p*** for the one whose
Acts
5:8 receive this ***p*** for the field?"

PRIDE

2 Kings
19:28 and because your ***p*** has reached my
2 Chronicles
17:6 Jehoshaphat took ***p*** in the LORD's ways
32:26 in their ***p***, and so they
Job
33:17 from a deed and to smother human ***p***.
35:12 answer, because of the ***p*** of the wicked.
41:15 scales are his ***p***, closely locked
Psalms
31:18 the righteous with ***p*** and contempt!
59:12 captured in their ***p***. For the curses
78:51 Ham's tents, he struck their ***p*** and joy.
105:36 land; struck down their very ***p*** and joy.
Proverbs
8:13 hate evil. I hate ***p*** and arrogance,
11:2 When ***p*** comes, so does shame, but wisdom
13:10 conflict out of ***p***; those who take
14:3 ***P*** sprouts in the mouth of a fool, but
16:18 ***P*** comes before disaster, and arrogance
18:12 ***P*** comes before a disaster, but humility
21:24 Their conduct involves excessive ***p***.
29:23 ***P*** lays people low, but those of humble
Isaiah
2:17 People's ***p*** will be brought down and
4:2 fruit will be the ***p*** and splendor of
13:11 I will end the ***p*** of the insolent,
16:6 heard of Moab's ***p***, his great pride,
23:9 it, to defile the ***p*** of all beauty, to
25:11 lay low their ***p***, even by the
37:29 and because your ***p*** has reached my
41:16 the LORD and take ***p*** in the holy one
Jeremiah
13:9 ruin the brazen ***p*** of Judah and
48:29 heard of Moab's ***p***: arrogant, puffed
49:16 as has your own ***p***. Though you live
51:41 defeated, the ***p*** of the whole
Ezekiel
7:10 The staff blossoms, and ***p*** springs up!
7:20 which they took ***p***, they have made
24:21 impure, the ***p*** of your strength,
32:12 an end to Egypt's ***p***, and all of its
Daniel
4:37 is able to humble all who walk in ***p***."

5:20 in stubborn ***p***, he was pulled
Hosea
4:18 indeed, they "love"; shame is their ***p***.
5:5 Israel's ***p*** is a witness against him;
Amos
6:8 I reject the ***p*** of Jacob. I hate
8:7 has sworn by the ***p*** of Jacob: Surely
Nahum
2:2 will restore the ***p*** of Jacob, indeed,
Zephaniah
2:10 account of their ***p***, because they
3:11 boasting with ***p***. No longer will
Zechariah
9:6 eliminate the ***p*** of the
10:11 will dry up. The ***p*** of Assyria will
11:3 lions because the ***p*** of the Jordan has
Romans
5:3 We even take ***p*** in our problems,
5:11 we even take ***p*** in God through
1 Corinthians
15:31 I swear by the ***p*** I have in you in
2 Corinthians
5:12 those who take ***p*** in superficial
10:13 We won't take ***p*** in anything more than
Philippians
1:26 to increase your ***p*** in Christ Jesus
3:19 and they take ***p*** in their disgrace
Hebrews
3:6 and the ***p*** that our hope
1 John
2:16 and the arrogant ***p*** in one's

PRIEST → AARON THE PRIEST, CHIEF PRIEST, HIGH PRIEST
Exodus
39:26 ministering as a ***p***, just as the LORD
39:41 clothes for the ***p*** Aaron and the
40:13 him holy so that he may serve me as ***p***.
Numbers
5:10 anyone gives to the ***p*** will be his.
Judges
17:10 be a father and a ***p*** to me, and I'll
18:27 as well as the ***p*** who had been with
1 Samuel
2:11 boy served the LORD under Eli the ***p***.
2:35 a trustworthy ***p*** who will act in
21:6 So the ***p*** gave David holy bread, because
2 Chronicles
13:9 rams can become a ***p*** of these phony
Ezra
2:63 holy food until a ***p*** arose who could
7:12 to Ezra the ***p***, the scribe of
10:10 Then Ezra the ***p*** stood up and said to
Nehemiah
8:9 Ezra the ***p*** and scribe, and
Psalms
110:4 mind: "You are a ***p*** forever in line
Jeremiah
23:11 Both prophet and ***p*** are godless; I even
Lamentations
2:6 rage, he scorned both monarch and ***p***.
2:20 babies? Should ***p*** and prophet be
Ezekiel
1:3 burst in on the ***p*** Ezekiel, Buzi's
45:19 The ***p*** will take some of the blood from
Hosea
4:9 The ***p*** will be just like the people; I
Amos
7:10 Then Amaziah, the ***p*** of Bethel, reported
Malachi
2:7 The lips of the ***p*** should guard
Matthew
8:4 yourself to the ***p*** and offer the
Mark
1:44 yourself to the ***p*** and offer the
Luke
1:5 Judea there was a ***p*** named Zechariah
1:8 was serving as a ***p*** before God
5:14 yourself to the ***p*** and make an
10:31 happened that a ***p*** was also going
Acts
14:13 The ***p*** of Zeus, whose temple was located
Romans
15:16 I'm working as a ***p*** of God's gospel
Hebrews
5:6 place, You are a ***p*** forever,
7:1 king of Salem and ***p*** of the Most High
7:3 God's Son and remains a ***p*** for all time.
7:5 the office of ***p*** have a
7:11 office of ***p*** (for the people
7:12 the order of the ***p*** changes, there
7:15 if another ***p*** appears who is
7:16 He has become a ***p*** by the power of a
7:17 You are a ***p*** forever,
7:21 but this ***p*** was affirmed with a solemn
7:24 the office of ***p*** permanently
8:2 He's serving as a ***p*** in the holy place,
8:4 he wouldn't be a ***p*** because there are
10:11 Every ***p*** stands every day serving and
10:12 But when this ***p*** offered one sacrifice

PRIESTLY
Exodus
29:5 Then take the ***p*** clothes and put them on
29:21 and all their ***p*** garments will be
Leviticus
6:23 Every ***p*** grain offering must be a
8:2 with him, the ***p*** clothing, the
16:24 and dress in his ***p*** clothing. Then he
21:10 to dress in the ***p*** clothing—must not
Numbers
18:7 I give you your ***p*** service as a
Deuteronomy
10:6 Eleazar succeeded him in the ***p*** role.
Judges
8:27 fashioned a ***p*** vest out of it,
17:5 He made a ***p*** vest and divine
2 Samuel
6:14 in a linen ***p*** vest, danced with
1 Chronicles
15:27 David also wore a linen ***p*** vest.
16:39 and his other ***p*** relatives at the
24:31 the heads of the ***p*** and levitical
Isaiah
30:22 your gold-covered ***p*** vest, and you
61:10 a bridegroom in a ***p*** crown, and like a
Ezekiel
42:14 will place the ***p*** vests that they
Hosea
3:4 stone, without a ***p*** vest or household
Zechariah
3:4 your guilt from you. Put on ***p*** robes."

Luke
1:5 belonged to the ***p*** division of
Romans
12:1 This is your appropriate ***p*** service.
Hebrews
8:6 a superior ***p*** service just as

PRIESTS → AARON'S SONS THE PRIESTS, CHIEF PRIESTS, CHIEF PRIESTS AND ELDERS, CHIEF PRIESTS AND PHARISEES, PRIESTS AND ELDERS, PRIESTS AND LEGAL EXPERTS, PRIESTS AND LEVITES, PRIESTS AND PHARISEES, PRIESTS AND THE LEVITES, PRIESTS AND THE PROPHETS

PRIESTS AND ELDERS
Mt 21:23; 26:3, 47; 27:3, 12; Ac 4:23; 23:14; 25:15

PRIESTS AND LEGAL EXPERTS
Mt 16:21; 20:18; 21:15; Mk 11:18; 14:1; Lk 22:66

PRIESTS AND LEVITES
1Ch 13:2; 24:6; 28:13; 2Ch 23:4; 23:18; 29:4; 31:9; Ezr 3:12; 7:24; Neh 13:30; Is 66:21; Jn 1:19

PRIESTS AND PHARISEES
Jn 7:32; 7:45; 11:47, 57; 18:3

PRIESTS AND THE LEVITES
1Ki 8:4; 1Ch 15:14; 23:2; 28:21; 2Ch 5:5; 11:13; 24:5; 30:15, 25; 31:2, 4; 34:30; 35:8, 10; Ezr 1:5; 3:8; 6:16, 20; 7:7; 8:30; 9:1; Neh 8:13; 11:20; 12:1, 30, 44; 13:29

PRIESTS AND THE PROPHETS
2Ki 23:2; Jer 8:1; 26:8, 11, 16; 29:1

PRINCE
Genesis
34:2 and the country's ***p*** saw her, he took
Deuteronomy
33:16 on the crown of that ***p*** among brothers.
2 Samuel
1:19 no, Israel! Your ***p*** lies dead on your
3:38 you know that a ***p*** and a great man
13:4 ***P***," Jonadab said to him, "why are you
1 Chronicles
29:22 presence as ***p***, and Zadok as
2 Chronicles
6:5 chosen anyone as ***p*** over my people
6:6 and David as ***p*** over my people
Ezra
1:8 them out to Sheshbazzar the ***p*** of Judah.
Job
31:37 of my steps, approach him like a ***p***.
Psalms
82:7 you will fall down like any ***p***."
Proverbs
28:16 A ***p*** without understanding is a cruel
Isaiah
9:6 Mighty God, Eternal Father, ***P*** of Peace.
55:4 to the peoples, a ***p*** and commander of
Jeremiah
38:6 of the royal ***p*** Malchiah, within
Ezekiel
7:27 mourning, the ***p*** will clothe
17:13 Then he took a ***p*** from the royal line,
21:25 you vile, wicked ***p*** of Israel whose
28:2 one, say to the ***p*** of Tyre, The LORD
30:13 will there be a ***p*** from the land of
34:24 will be their ***p***. I, the LORD,
37:25 servant David will be their ***p*** forever.
38:2 of Magog, chief ***p*** of Meshech and
39:1 you, Gog, chief ***p*** of Meshech and
44:3 As for the ***p***, he may sit in it to eat
45:7 territory for the ***p*** will be on both
46:2 and the ***p*** will come in from outside by
48:21 belongs to the ***p***. The land from
Hosea
3:4 without king or ***p***, without

PRINCES
Genesis
12:15 When Pharaoh's ***p*** saw her, they praised
Joshua
13:21 had lived in the land as ***p*** of Sihon.
2 Samuel
13:27 and all the other ***p***. Then Absalom
13:29 Then all the ***p*** got up, jumped
13:30 killed all of the ***p***! Not one remains."
13:32 all the young ***p*** have been killed—
13:33 that all the ***p*** are dead, because
13:35 king, "Look, the ***p*** are coming, just
13:36 speaking, the ***p*** arrived. They
1 Kings
1:9 (the royal ***p***) and all the
1:19 all the royal ***p*** as well as
1:25 all the royal ***p***, the generals,
1 Chronicles
7:40 the heads of the ***p***. Those ready for
2 Chronicles
22:8 he discovered the ***p*** of Judah,
Ezra
8:20 David and the ***p*** had appointed to
Job
3:15 or with ***p*** who have gold, who fill their
29:9 ***p*** restrained speech, put their hand on
34:19 shows no favor to ***p*** nor regards the
Psalms
45:16 appoint them as ***p*** throughout the
68:27 little; then the ***p*** of Judah, their
76:12 the spirit of ***p***. He is terrifying
83:11 Zeeb, all their ***p*** like Zebah and
105:22 to make sure his ***p*** acted according to
148:11 person, you ***p*** and every single
Proverbs
8:15 kings rule, and ***p*** issue righteous
19:10 less so for a servant to rule over ***p***.
Ecclesiastes
10:7 horseback, while ***p*** walk on foot like
10:16 a boy and whose ***p*** feast in the
10:17 and whose ***p*** feast at the
Isaiah
1:23 Your ***p*** are rebels, companions of
3:14 the elders and ***p*** of his people:
19:13 become fools; the ***p*** of Memphis are
23:8 merchants were ***p***, whose traders
34:12 call it, and all its ***p*** will disappear.
Jeremiah
1:18 of Judah, its ***p***, its priests, and
4:9 the king and his ***p*** will fail, the

Ezekiel
19:1 You, raise a lament for Israel's ***p***
21:12 all of Israel's ***p***, handed over to
22:6 Look, Israel's ***p***, every one of them,
22:25 The conspiracy of ***p*** in her is like a
26:16 All the ***p*** of the sea will come down
27:8 The ***p*** of Sidon and Arvad were your
27:21 and all the ***p*** of Kedar traded
32:29 kings and all its ***p***, who, though
32:30 All the ***p*** of the north are there, and
39:18 the blood of the ***p*** of the earth:
45:8 in Israel, and my ***p*** will no longer
45:9 Enough, ***p*** of Israel! Turn
Daniel
4:36 associates and my ***p*** wanted to be with
5:1 a thousand of his ***p***, and he drank a
5:2 the king, his ***p***, his consorts,
5:3 and the king, his ***p***, his consorts,
5:9 his face, and his ***p*** were also very
5:10 the king and his ***p***, the queen
5:23 and you, your ***p***, your consorts,
6:17 with those of his ***p*** so that Daniel's
11:5 but one of his ***p*** will overpower
Hosea
5:10 The ***p*** of Judah act like raiders who
8:4 me; they chose ***p***, but without my
8:10 due to the burden of kings and ***p***.
Micah
5:5 him seven shepherds and eight human ***p***.
Zephaniah
1:8 I will punish the ***p***, the king's sons,
3:3 The ***p*** in her midst are roaring lions.

PRISCILLA
Acts
18:2 with his wife ***P*** because Claudius

PRISON
Genesis
40:14 so he sets me free from this ***p***.
42:16 you will stay in ***p***. We will find out
42:17 He put them all in ***p*** for three days
42:19 brothers stay in ***p***, and the rest of
Judges
16:21 he worked the grinding mill in the ***p***.
16:25 Samson from the ***p***, and he performed
1 Kings
22:27 Put this man in ***p*** and feed him
2 Kings
17:4 king arrested him and put him in ***p***.
25:27 Jehoiachin from ***p***. This happened in
2 Chronicles
18:26 Put this man in ***p*** and feed him
Psalms
142:7 me out of this ***p*** so I can give
Ecclesiastes
4:14 He emerged from ***p*** to become king, even
Isaiah
24:22 pit, shut into a ***p***, and punished
42:7 prisoners from ***p***, and those who
Jeremiah
32:2 confined to the ***p*** quarters in the
32:8 showed up at the ***p*** quarters and told
32:12 who were present in the ***p*** quarters.
33:1 confined to the ***p*** quarters, the
37:15 which had been turned into a ***p***.
37:18 people that you should throw me into ***p***?
37:21 be held in the ***p*** quarters and that
38:6 within the ***p*** quarters, and
39:14 Jeremiah from the ***p*** quarters. They
39:15 was still confined to the ***p*** quarters:
52:11 and put him in ***p***, where he
52:31 released him from ***p*** on the twenty-fiftH
52:33 discarded his ***p*** clothes and ate
Matthew
5:25 court, and you will be thrown into ***p***.
11:2 John heard in ***p*** about the things
14:3 and put him in ***p*** because of
18:30 he threw him into ***p*** until he paid
25:36 of me. I was in ***p*** and you visited
Mark
6:17 and put in ***p*** because of
6:27 guard went to the ***p***, cut off John's
Luke
3:20 his evil deeds: he locked John up in ***p***.
12:58 and the officer throw you into ***p***.
22:33 go with you, both to ***p*** and to death!"
John
3:24 John hadn't yet been thrown into ***p***.
Acts
4:3 and put them in ***p*** until the next
5:19 Lord opened the ***p*** doors during the
5:21 sent word to the ***p*** to have the
5:25 people you put in ***p*** are standing in
8:3 men and women and throw them into ***p***.
12:4 He put Peter in ***p***, handing him over to
12:9 Peter left the ***p***. However, he
16:23 threw them into ***p*** and ordered the
16:40 Silas left the ***p*** and made their
22:4 delivering both men and women into ***p***.
24:27 a favor to the Jews, he left Paul in ***p***.
25:14 There is a man whom Felix left in ***p***.
26:10 holy people in ***p*** under the
Philippians
1:7 during my time in ***p*** and in the
1:13 else knows that I'm in ***p*** for Christ.
Colossians
4:18 that I'm in ***p***. Grace be with
2 Timothy
2:9 point that I'm in ***p*** like a common
Philemon
1:10 in the faith during my time in ***p***.
1:13 during my time in ***p*** because of the
1:22 be released from ***p*** to be with you
1:23 who is in ***p*** with me for the
Hebrews
10:34 toward people in ***p*** and accepted the
11:36 they were even put in chains and in ***p***.
13:3 as if you were in ***p*** with them, and
1 Peter
3:19 he went to preach to the spirits in ***p***.
Revelation
2:10 some of you into ***p*** in order to test
20:7 Satan will be released from his ***p***.

PRISONER
Exodus
12:29 child of the ***p*** in jail, and all
Judges
15:10 up to take Samson ***p***," they replied,

15:12 down to take you ***p*** so we can turn
15:13 only take you ***p*** so we can turn
1 Samuel
30:2 in the city ***p***, whether young or
30:3 sons, and their daughters taken ***p***,
1 Kings
20:39 someone brought a ***p***. 'Guard this
20:40 and that, and the ***p*** disappeared."
Matthew
27:15 to the crowd one ***p***, whomever they
27:16 was a well-known ***p*** named Jesus
Mark
15:6 released one ***p*** to them, whomever
John
18:39 I release one ***p*** for you at
19:16 crucified. The soldiers took Jesus ***p***.
Acts
23:18 and said, "The ***p*** Paul asked me to
25:27 foolish to send a ***p*** without
28:17 ancestors, I'm a ***p*** from Jerusalem.
Romans
7:23 mind and takes me ***p*** with the law of
Ephesians
3:1 why I, Paul, am a ***p*** of Christ for you
4:1 Therefore, as a ***p*** for the Lord, I
Colossians
4:10 my fellow ***p***, says hello to
2 Timothy
1:8 or of me, his ***p***. Instead, share
Philemon
1:1 Paul, who is a ***p*** for the cause of
1:9 and now also a ***p*** for Christ Jesus—

PRISONERS

Genesis
31:26 my daughters as if they were ***p*** of war.
Deuteronomy
21:10 hands them over to you and you take ***p***,
28:41 because they will be taken away as ***p***.
32:36 gone, that both ***p*** and free people
1 Kings
8:46 them away as ***p*** to enemy
2 Chronicles
6:36 them away as ***p*** to enemy
28:5 carried off many ***p***, bringing them to
Job
3:18 ***P*** are entirely at ease; they don't hear
Psalms
68:6 homes; he sets ***p*** free with
107:10 gloom; they were ***p*** suffering in
146:7 are starving! The LORD: who frees ***p***.
Isaiah
10:4 among the ***p*** and falling among
14:17 and wouldn't let his ***p*** go home?"
24:22 together like ***p*** in a pit, shut
42:7 eyes, to lead the ***p*** from prison, and
49:9 saying to the ***p***, "Come out," and to
61:1 for captives, and liberation for ***p***,
Lamentations
1:18 and young men have gone away as ***p***.
3:34 crushing underfoot all the earth's ***p***,
Zechariah
9:11 will release your ***p*** from the
9:12 the stronghold, ***p*** of hope.
Matthew
18:34 for punishing ***p***, until he had
Luke
4:18 release to the ***p*** and recovery of
Acts
9:2 him to take them as ***p*** to Jerusalem.
9:21 same people as ***p*** to the chief
16:25 and the other ***p*** were listening to
27:1 and some other ***p*** were placed in
Romans
16:7 and my fellow ***p***. They are
1 Corinthians
4:9 line. We are like ***p*** sentenced to
Ephesians
4:8 he captured ***p***, and he gave
Hebrews
13:3 Remember ***p*** as if you were in prison

PROCLAIM

→ PROCLAIM THE GOOD NEWS

Exodus
33:19 of you, and I'll ***p*** before you the
Leviticus
23:37 that you will ***p*** as holy
Deuteronomy
32:3 because I ***p*** the LORD's name: Give
Job
36:33 announces it; even cattle ***p*** its rising.
Psalms
9:11 lives in Zion! ***P*** his mighty acts
22:31 They will ***p*** God's righteousness to
30:9 thank you? Does it ***p*** your faithfulness?
40:5 you! If I were to ***p*** and talk about
50:6 The skies ***p*** his righteousness because
51:15 lips, and my mouth will ***p*** your praise.
79:13 forever; we will ***p*** your praises from
89:1 forever. I will ***p*** your faithfulness
92:2 to ***p*** your loyal love in the morning,
92:15 in order to ***p***: "The LORD is righteous.
145:21 My mouth will ***p*** the LORD's praise, and
Isaiah
12:4 on God's name; ***p*** God's deeds among
12:5 glorious things; ***p*** this throughout
40:2 to Jerusalem, and ***p*** to her that her
41:22 significance. Or ***p*** to us what is to
44:8 no fear! Didn't I ***p*** it? Didn't I
48:20 a loud shout, ***p*** it; broadcast it
61:1 brokenhearted, to ***p*** release for
61:2 to ***p*** the year of the LORD's favor and a
Jeremiah
2:2 Go and ***p*** to the people of Jerusalem,
3:12 Go ***p*** these words to the north and say:
4:5 in Jerusalem ***p***, sound the alarm
4:16 Warn the nations, ***p*** it to Jerusalem!
7:2 LORD's temple and ***p*** there this
11:2 this covenant and ***p*** them to the
16:10 When you ***p*** all these things to the
19:2 Broken Pots and ***p*** there the words I
20:10 Everywhere!—***p***, yes, let's
23:28 who has my word ***p*** it faithfully.
34:8 in Jerusalem to ***p*** liberty for their
48:17 know his name. ***P*** how its mighty
50:2 Tell the nations; ***p*** it far and wide!
Ezekiel
21:22 rams in place, to ***p*** war and raise the
Amos
3:9 ***P*** it to the palaces of Ashdod and to
Micah
3:5 teeth and then ***p*** "Peace!" but stir

Mark
5:20 away and began to ***p*** in the Ten Cities
Luke
4:18 to the poor, to ***p*** release to the
4:19 and to ***p*** the year of the Lord's favor
9:2 sent them out to ***p*** God's kingdom and
John
16:13 he hears and will ***p*** to you what is to
16:14 will take what is mine and ***p*** it to you.
16:15 what is mine and will ***p*** it to you.
Acts
13:38 Through Jesus we ***p*** forgiveness of
17:3 Jesus whom I ***p*** to you is the
17:23 you worship as unknown, I now ***p*** to you.
20:20 so that I could ***p*** to you and teach
26:23 dead, he would ***p*** light both to my
Revelation
14:6 good news to ***p*** to those who live

PROCLAIM THE GOOD NEWS

Mk 16:15; Ac 5:42; 11:20; 14:7; 16:10

PROCLAIMED

Exodus
34:5 with him, and ***p*** the name, "The
34:6 front of him and ***p***: "The LORD! The
36:6 command that was ***p*** throughout the
Numbers
23:21 his God is with him, ***p*** as his king.
Ruth
4:14 redeemer. May his name be ***p*** in Israel.
2 Chronicles
20:3 LORD's help and ***p*** a fast for all
Psalms
88:11 faithful love ***p*** in the grave,
97:6 Heaven has ***p*** God's righteousness, and
111:6 God ***p*** his powerful deeds to his people
Isaiah
21:2 harsh vision was ***p*** to me: The
41:26 it, no one ***p*** it, and no one
43:12 I saved, I ***p***, not some
45:21 together! Who ***p*** this from the
48:3 from my mouth I ***p*** them. I acted
48:5 they came about I ***p*** them to you so
Jeremiah
13:1 The LORD ***p*** to me: Go and buy a linen
17:19 The LORD ***p*** to me: Go and stand by the
23:22 they would have ***p*** my words to my
34:15 each of you ***p*** liberty for the
Daniel
3:4 The herald ***p*** loudly: "Peoples, nations,
4:14 He ***p*** loudly: 'Cut down the tree and
Jonah
3:5 God. They ***p*** a fast and put on
Zechariah
7:7 that the LORD ***p*** through the
Matthew
11:5 up. The poor have good news ***p*** to them.
24:14 kingdom will be ***p*** throughout the
Mark
6:12 they went out and ***p*** that people
13:10 good news must be ***p*** to all the
16:20 they went out and ***p*** the message
John
5:15 The man went and ***p*** to the Jewish
Acts
8:25 had testified and ***p*** the Lord's word,
8:35 passage, Philip ***p*** the good news
11:19 and Antioch. They ***p*** the word only to
13:24 appearance, John ***p*** to all the
14:21 Paul and Barnabas ***p*** the good news to
15:21 Moses has been ***p*** in every city for
17:13 that Paul also ***p*** God's word in
18:25 of the baptism John ***p*** and practiced.
20:25 whom I traveled and ***p*** the kingdom.
26:20 Instead, I ***p*** first to those in Damascus
Philippians
1:18 since Christ is ***p*** in every possible
Hebrews
9:19 after he had ***p*** every command of
1 Peter
1:12 have now been ***p*** to you by those
1:25 the word that was ***p*** to you as good
Revelation
5:2 angel, who ***p*** in a loud voice,

PROCLAIMS

Judges
6:8 Israel's God, ***p***: I myself brought
Psalms
147:19 God ***p*** his word to Jacob; his statutes
Proverbs
12:23 the heart of fools ***p*** their stupidity.
14:25 saves lives, but a deceiver ***p*** lies.
Isaiah
29:22 Therefore, ***p*** the LORD, the God of the
48:17 one of Israel, ***p***: I am the LORD
52:3 The LORD ***p***: You were sold for nothing,
65:8 The LORD ***p***: As new wine is found in
Jeremiah
2:2 The LORD ***p***: I remember your
5:14 heavenly forces ***p***: Because you have
17:5 The LORD ***p***: Cursed are those who trust in mere humans
19:1 The LORD ***p***: Go buy a clay jar from a
29:4 God of Israel, ***p*** to all the exiles
33:12 heavenly forces ***p***: This wasteland,
51:58 heavenly forces ***p***: Babylon's
Ezekiel
2:4 you will say to them: The LORD God ***p***.
6:3 The LORD God ***p*** to the mountains
7:5 The LORD God ***p***: Disaster! A singular
16:23 doom to you, ***p*** the LORD God—
29:13 The LORD God ***p***: At the end of forty
36:33 The LORD God ***p***: On the day that I
37:5 The LORD God ***p*** to these bones: I am
37:9 The LORD God ***p***: Come from the
Amos
1:3 The LORD ***p***: For three crimes of
7:17 the LORD ***p***: 'Your wife will
Obadiah
1:1 The LORD God ***p*** concerning Edom:
Micah
2:3 the LORD ***p***: I myself am
Nahum
1:12 The LORD ***p***: Though once they were a
2:13 I am against you, ***p*** the LORD of
Zechariah
1:3 heavenly forces ***p***: Return to me,
8:23 heavenly forces ***p***: In those days
Malachi
1:4 heavenly forces ***p***: They may build,

PROCLAIMING THE GOOD NEWS
Lk 8:1; 9:6; 20:1; Ac 10:36; 14:15

PRODUCE → PRODUCE FRUIT, PRODUCE GOOD FRUIT
Genesis
1:24 Let the earth ***p*** every kind of
17:6 fertile. I will ***p*** nations from you,
41:34 of all the ***p*** of the land of
43:11 the land's choice ***p***, and bring it
Exodus
5:8 sure that they ***p*** the same number
5:14 Why didn't you ***p*** the same number
8:18 experts tried to ***p*** lice by their
Numbers
18:13 The early ***p*** of everything in their
18:30 equivalent to the ***p*** of the grain and
20:8 water. You will ***p*** water from the
20:10 rebels! Should we ***p*** water from the
28:26 day of the early ***p***, when you present
Deuteronomy
14:22 of whatever your fields ***p*** each year.
Joshua
24:13 and are enjoying ***p*** from vineyards
Nehemiah
9:37 Its ***p*** profits the kings whom you have
10:35 bring the early ***p*** of our soil and
13:31 as for the early ***p***. Remember me, my
Job
14:9 it will bud and ***p*** sprouts like a
37:15 commands them, his clouds ***p*** lightning?
Psalms
78:46 their land's ***p*** to locusts.
85:12 is good, and our land yields its ***p***.
Proverbs
13:23 land might ***p*** much food, but it
14:4 is a strong bull, there is abundant ***p***.
16:28 people ***p*** conflict; gossips
25:14 like clouds and wind that ***p*** no rain.
Isaiah
5:10 of vineyard will ***p*** just one bath,
14:29 grow, and it will ***p*** a winged creature.
27:6 sprout and fill the whole world with ***p***.
Jeremiah
2:3 LORD, the early ***p*** of the harvest.
29:5 cultivate gardens and eat what they ***p***.
29:28 plant gardens and eat what they ***p***."
Ezekiel
36:30 and the fields' ***p*** so that you will
Habakkuk
3:17 and there's no ***p*** on the vine;
Haggai
1:10 has withheld its ***p*** because of you.
1:11 and upon everything that handles ***p***.
Zechariah
8:12 will give its ***p***; the heavens will
Matthew
7:18 A good tree can't ***p*** bad fruit. And a
13:23 bear fruit and ***p***—in one case a
21:43 be given to a people who ***p*** its fruit.
22:24 his wife and ***p*** children for his
Luke
6:43 good tree doesn't ***p*** bad fruit, nor
John
15:5 then you will ***p*** much fruit.
15:8 when you ***p*** much fruit and in
Romans
7:8 commandment to ***p*** all kinds of
1 Corinthians
9:10 do so with the hope of sharing the ***p***.
2 Timothy
2:23 since you know that they ***p*** conflicts.
James
1:20 person doesn't ***p*** God's
3:12 can a fig tree ***p*** olives? Can a
Revelation
14:4 as early ***p*** for God and the

PRODUCE FRUIT
Eze 47:12; Mt 3:8; Lk 3:8; 13:9; Jn 15:2; 15:4, 16

PRODUCE GOOD FRUIT
Mt 3:10; 7:18, 19; Lk 3:9; 6:43

PRODUCES
Genesis
1:29 trees whose fruit ***p*** its seeds within
Leviticus
25:6 Whatever the land ***p*** during its sabbath
Proverbs
30:33 blood, and stirring up anger ***p*** strife.
Ecclesiastes
5:15 their hard work ***p*** nothing—nothing
Isaiah
30:23 food the ground ***p*** will be rich and
54:16 of coal and who ***p*** a tool for his
Matthew
7:17 every good tree ***p*** good fruit, and
Mark
4:28 The earth ***p*** crops all by itself, first
4:32 plants. It ***p*** such large
Luke
6:45 A good person ***p*** good from the good
John
15:2 any branch that ***p*** fruit so that it
Romans
5:3 we know that trouble ***p*** endurance,
5:4 endurance ***p*** character, and character
11:17 the root that ***p*** the rich oil of
1 Corinthians
12:6 the same God who ***p*** all of them in
2 Corinthians
7:10 Godly sadness ***p*** a changed heart and
9:11 Such generosity ***p*** thanksgiving to
Ephesians
5:9 Light ***p*** fruit that consists of every
5:18 on wine, which ***p*** depravity.
Hebrews
6:8 But if it ***p*** thorns and thistles, it's
James
1:3 the testing of your faith ***p*** endurance.
2 Peter
1:4 immorality that sinful craving ***p***.
Revelation
22:2 of life, which ***p*** twelve crops of

PROFIT
Leviticus
25:36 or any kind of ***p*** from interest,
25:37 with interest or lend food at a ***p***.
1 Samuel
8:3 tried to turn a ***p***, they accepted

PROFIT [cont.]

Job
22:2 God? Can an intelligent person bring ***p***?
30:13 destroy my road, ***p*** from my fall, with
Proverbs
3:14 Her ***p*** is better than silver, and her
10:2 the wicked won't ***p*** them, but
14:23 There is ***p*** in hard work, but mere talk
21:5 end up in ***p***, but those who
Ecclesiastes
10:11 then there's no ***p*** for the snake
Isaiah
33:15 who rejects ***p*** from extortion,
56:11 own ways, every last one greedy for ***p***.
Jeremiah
6:13 each is eager to ***p***; from prophet to
8:10 all are eager to ***p***. From prophet to
Ezekiel
18:8 interest or take ***p***. They refrain
22:12 and fees, you ***p*** by extorting your
Acts
19:24 a lot of ***p*** for the
2 Corinthians
2:17 of God to make a ***p***. We are speaking
Philippians
4:17 I am hoping for a ***p*** that accumulates
1 Timothy
6:6 a great source of ***p*** when it is
James
4:13 buying and selling, and making a ***p***."
Jude
1:11 of Cain. For ***p*** they give

PROMISE → ACCORDING TO YOUR PROMISE, GOD'S PROMISE

Genesis
28:20 made a solemn ***p***: "If God is with
31:13 you made a solemn ***p*** to me. Now, get up and leave
46:4 with you, and I ***p*** to bring you out
50:5 My father made me ***p***, telling me, 'I'm
50:25 Israel's sons ***p***, "When God takes
Exodus
13:19 Israel's sons ***p*** when he said to
Leviticus
7:16 for a solemn ***p*** or if it is a
22:18 for a solemn ***p*** or a spontaneous
27:2 makes solemn ***p*** to the LORD
27:8 prevents the ***p*** maker from giving
Numbers
6:2 makes a binding ***p*** to be a nazirite
Deuteronomy
2:27 your land. We ***p*** to stay on the
9:5 to establish the ***p*** he made to your
23:18 to pay a solemn ***p*** because both of
Joshua
21:45 Israel failed. Every ***p*** was fulfilled.
Judges
8:19 the LORD lives, I ***p*** that if you had
11:30 made a solemn ***p*** to the LORD: "If
15:12 to them, "Just ***p*** that you won't
1 Samuel
1:11 she made this ***p***: "LORD of
2 Samuel
7:25 forever the ***p*** you have made
15:7 I can fulfill a ***p*** I made to the
15:8 servant made this ***p*** when I lived in
17:2 will run off. I ***p*** to kill the king
Nehemiah
5:13 don't keep this ***p***. So may they be
9:8 have kept your ***p*** because you are
Psalms
15:4 who keeps their ***p*** even when it
77:8 end? Is his ***p*** over for future
105:42 his holy ***p*** to Abraham his
119:38 Confirm your ***p*** to your servant—the
119:49 Remember your ***p*** to your servant, for
119:57 my possession. I ***p*** to do what you
119:65 well, LORD, according to your ***p***.
119:74 glad because I have waited for your ***p***.
119:81 your saving help! I wait for your ***p***.
119:114 and my shield—I wait for your ***p***.
119:147 and cry for help. I wait for your ***p***.
132:11 to David a true ***p*** that God won't
Proverbs
20:25 and only reflect after making the ***p***.
Ecclesiastes
5:4 When you make a ***p*** to God, fulfill it
5:5 not to make a ***p*** than to make a
Isaiah
54:9 earth. Likewise I ***p*** not to rage
Jeremiah
29:10 my gracious ***p*** to bring you back
44:25 fulfill our ***p*** to burn incense
Ezekiel
16:8 I made a solemn ***p*** and entered into
17:18 though he made a ***p***, he did all these
Acts
2:39 This ***p*** is for you, your children, and
7:5 However, God did ***p*** to give the land
7:17 God to keep the ***p*** he made to
18:18 had made a solemn ***p***. Then,
21:23 Four men among us have made a solemn ***p***.
26:6 the hope in the ***p*** God gave our
26:7 This is the ***p*** our twelve tribes hope to
Romans
4:13 The ***p*** to Abraham and to his
9:8 children from the ***p*** who are counted
9:9 The words in the ***p*** were: A year from
Galatians
3:14 would receive the ***p*** of the Spirit
3:17 by God so that it cancels the ***p***.
4:23 free woman was conceived through a ***p***.
4:28 you are children of the ***p*** like Isaac.
Ephesians
6:2 is the first one with a ***p*** attached:
1 Timothy
4:8 It has ***p*** for this life now
2 Timothy
1:1 to promote the ***p*** of life that is
Hebrews
4:1 since the ***p*** that we can enter
6:13 gave Abraham his ***p***, he swore by
6:15 obtained the ***p*** by showing
6:17 the heirs of the ***p*** that his purpose
9:15 might receive the ***p*** of the eternal
11:9 Jacob, who were coheirs of the same ***p***.
12:26 now he has made a ***p***: Still once more
2 Peter
2:19 false teachers ***p*** freedom, but they
3:4 Where is the ***p*** of his coming?
3:9 slow to keep his ***p***, as some think of
3:13 according to his ***p*** we are waiting

1 John
2:25 This is the ***p*** that he himself gave us:

PROMISED

Genesis
14:22 king of Sodom, "I ***p*** the LORD, El
21:1 carried out just what he had ***p*** her.
28:15 done everything that I have ***p*** you."
50:6 Go, bury your father as you ***p***."
50:24 to the land he ***p*** to Abraham, to
Exodus
6:8 the land that I ***p*** to give to
12:25 that the LORD has ***p*** to give you, be
13:5 that the LORD ***p*** your ancestors to
13:11 it to you as ***p*** to you and your
32:13 whom you yourself ***p***, 'I'll make your
33:1 Go to the land I ***p*** to Abraham,
Numbers
6:21 just as they have ***p***, in adherence
10:29 for the LORD has ***p*** to treat Israel
11:12 land that you ***p*** their ancestors?
14:16 that he solemnly ***p*** to give them. So
14:23 see the land I ***p*** to their
14:30 land in which I ***p*** to settle you,
23:19 not done it, or ***p*** and not fulfilled
32:10 LORD became angry on that day and ***p***,
32:11 ground that I ***p*** to Abraham,
32:24 your flocks, but do what you have ***p***."
Deuteronomy
1:8 the land that I ***p*** to give to your
1:11 And may God bless you, just as he ***p***.
1:21 God, has ***p*** you. Don't be
1:35 land that I ***p*** to give to your
6:3 ancestors' God, ***p*** you, in a land
6:19 enemies from before you, just as he ***p***.
7:12 the loyalty that he ***p*** your ancestors.
9:28 the land he'd ***p*** them. Because he
10:9 just as the LORD your God ***p*** them.)
10:11 the land that I ***p*** I'd give to their
11:25 you. Just as he ***p***, the LORD your
12:11 that you solemnly ***p*** to the LORD, to
12:17 you have solemnly ***p***; your spontaneous
12:20 territory, as he ***p*** you, and you
18:2 inheritance—just as God ***p*** them.
23:23 God because you ***p*** it with your own
26:15 honey—just like you ***p*** our ancestors."
26:18 just like he ***p***—by keeping his co
27:3 the LORD, your ancestor's God, ***p*** you.
28:68 by the route I ***p*** you would never
29:13 God just as he ***p*** you and just as
34:4 and Jacob when I ***p***: 'I will give it
Joshua
1:3 you set foot, exactly as I ***p*** Moses.
11:23 as the LORD had ***p*** Moses. Joshua
13:14 of Israel, exactly as he had ***p*** them.
13:33 is their legacy, exactly as he ***p*** them.
14:10 exactly as he ***p***. It is forty-five
14:12 that the LORD ***p*** me that day.
21:45 that the LORD had ***p*** to the house of
22:4 exactly as he ***p*** them. So turn
23:5 exactly as the LORD your God has ***p*** you.
23:10 fights for you, exactly as he ***p*** you.
23:14 the LORD your God ***p*** about you has
23:15 the LORD your God ***p*** about you has
Judges
2:1 land that I had ***p*** to your
11:36 just what you've ***p***. After all, the
11:39 her what he had ***p***. She had not
1 Samuel
1:23 pass what you've ***p***." So the woman
2:30 declares: I had ***p*** that your
20:3 David solemnly ***p*** in response,
24:4 spoke of when he ***p*** you, 'I will hand
25:30 things he has ***p*** you, and has
28:10 But Saul ***p*** to her by the LORD, "As
2 Samuel
7:25 and his dynasty. Do just as you have ***p***
7:28 and you have ***p*** this good thing
7:29 LORD God, have ***p***. Let your
15:8 in Aram. I ***p*** that if the LORD
1 Kings
2:24 me exactly as he ***p***—Adonijah will be
5:12 just as he had ***p***. Solomon and
8:24 father, which you ***p*** him. Today, you
8:25 keep what you ***p*** my father David,
8:53 LORD, just as you ***p*** through your
8:56 Israel just as he ***p***. He hasn't
9:5 just as I ***p*** your father
2 Kings
4:17 year. This was what Elisha had ***p*** her.
8:19 The LORD had ***p*** to preserve a
23:27 temple where I ***p*** my name would
1 Chronicles
11:3 just as the LORD had ***p*** through Samuel.
11:10 him king, as the LORD had ***p*** Israel.
17:23 and his dynasty. Do as you have ***p***
17:26 God, and you ***p*** this good thing
17:27 LORD God, have ***p***. Let your
22:11 of the LORD your God, as he ***p*** you.
27:23 the LORD had ***p*** to make Israel as
2 Chronicles
2:15 barley, olive oil, and wine he has ***p***,
6:15 father, which you ***p*** him. Today you
6:16 keep what you ***p*** my father David
6:20 place where you ***p*** to put your name,
7:18 throne, just as I ***p*** your father
21:7 dynasty. He had ***p*** to preserve a
23:3 just as the LORD ***p*** about David's
Ezra
10:19 They ***p*** to send their wives away, and
Nehemiah
5:12 made them swear to do what they had ***p***.
5:13 LORD. And the people did as they had ***p***.
9:8 with him. You ***p*** to give to his
Esther
4:7 silver that Haman ***p*** to pay into the
Psalms
39:1 of David.] I ***p*** I would watch my
61:8 I will do what I ***p*** every single day.
89:3 my chosen one; I ***p*** my servant David:
89:49 the same ones you ***p*** to David by your
132:2 the LORD, how he ***p*** the strong one of
Isaiah
14:24 forces has ***p***: As I intended,
38:7 the LORD that he will do what he ***p***:
54:9 for me, when I ***p*** that Noah's
62:8 The LORD has ***p*** with raised hand and
Jeremiah
32:22 land that you ***p*** to their
32:42 bring on them all the good I ***p*** them.
Joel
2:32 as the LORD has ***p***; and in

PROMISED [cont.]

Amos
4:2 God has solemnly **p** by his holiness:
Jonah
2:9 That which I have **p**, I will pay.
Mark
14:11 delighted and **p** to give him
Luke
1:55 just as he **p** to our ancestors, to
1:72 shown the mercy **p** to our ancestors,
2:5 Mary, who was **p** to him in
24:49 what my Father **p**, but you are to
Acts
1:4 the Father had **p**. He said, "This
2:30 he knew that God **p** him with a solemn
2:33 the Father the **p** Holy Spirit. He
13:23 Israel a savior, Jesus, just as he **p**.
13:32 good news. What God **p** to our ancestors,
23:12 plot and solemnly **p** that they
23:14 We have solemnly **p** to eat nothing
23:21 have solemnly **p** not to eat or
Romans
1:3 God **p** this good news about his Son
4:21 that God was able to do what he **p**.
2 Corinthians
9:5 you have already **p**. I want it to be
11:2 As your father, I **p** you in marriage
Ephesians
1:13 sealed with the **p** Holy Spirit
Titus
1:2 who doesn't lie, **p** before time began.
Hebrews
11:9 land he had been **p** as a stranger. He
11:11 that the one who **p** was faithful.
11:39 receive what was **p**, though they were
James
1:12 the life God has **p** to those who love
2:5 kingdom he has **p** to those who love

PROMISES

Leviticus
23:38 for solemn **p**, and all the
Numbers
29:39 for solemn **p**, your spontaneous
30:4 all her solemn **p** and any of her
30:5 of her solemn **p** nor any of her
30:7 solemn **p** will stand as
30:11 all her solemn **p** will stand and
30:12 to her solemn **p** or the binding
30:14 all her solemn **p**, or all her
Deuteronomy
12:6 for solemn **p**, your spontaneous
12:26 for solemn **p** to the location
23:22 don't make any **p**, you won't be
Job
22:27 you; you will fulfill your solemn **p**.
Psalms
12:6 The LORD's **p** are pure, like silver
22:25 I will fulfill my **p** in the presence
24:4 hasn't made false **p**, the one who
50:14 Fulfill the **p** you made to the
56:12 I will fulfill my **p** to you, God. I will
61:5 have heard my **p**; you've given me
65:1 is praise. **P** made to you are
66:13 I'll keep the **p** I made to you,
76:11 Make **p** to the LORD your God and keep
116:14 I'll keep the **p** I made to the LORD in
116:18 I'll keep the **p** I made to the LORD in
Proverbs
7:14 today I fulfilled my solemn **p**.
31:2 son of my womb! No, son of my solemn **p**!
Isaiah
19:21 making solemn **p** to the LORD and
52:6 day; I'm the one who **p** it; I'm here.
Jeremiah
44:25 to her." Go ahead and keep your **p**!
Jonah
1:16 to the LORD and made solemn **p**.
Nahum
1:15 your solemn **p**! The worthless
Malachi
1:14 flock, but who **p** and sacrifices to
Luke
1:45 would fulfill the **p** he made to her."
Acts
13:34 the holy and firm **p** I made to David.
Romans
9:4 the worship, and the **p** belong to them.
15:8 to confirm the **p** given to the
2 Corinthians
1:20 All of God's **p** have their yes in him.
7:1 we have these **p**, let's cleanse
Galatians
3:16 The **p** were made to Abraham and to his
3:21 Law against the **p** of God?
Ephesians
3:6 the Jews in the **p** of God in Christ
Hebrews
6:12 who inherit the **p** through faith and
7:6 blessed the one who had received the **p**.
8:6 covenant that is enacted with better **p**.
10:23 the one who made the **p** is reliable.
10:36 can receive the **p** after you do
11:13 receiving the **p**, but they saw the
11:17 who received the **p** was offering his
11:33 justice, realized **p**, shut the mouths
2 Peter
1:4 and wonderful **p**, that you may

PROPERTY

Genesis
14:16 all of the looted **p**, together with
14:21 people and take the **p** for yourself."
23:4 you. Give me some **p** for a burial plot
23:9 witnessed by you, as my own burial **p**."
23:18 to Abraham as his **p** in the presence of
23:20 Hittites to Abraham as his burial **p**.
34:10 travel through it, and buy **p** in it."
34:23 livestock, their **p**, and all of their
34:29 carried off their **p**, their children,
36:6 and all of the **p** he had acquired
47:11 and gave them **p** in the land of
49:30 from Ephron the Hittite as a burial **p**.
50:13 as burial **p** from Ephron the
Exodus
21:21 because the slave is the owner's **p**.
22:8 or not the owner stole the other's **p**.
22:11 touch the other's **p**. The owner must
Leviticus
6:2 or pledged **p**; by cheating a
6:3 you've found lost **p**, you lie about
6:4 must return the **p** you took by
25:10 to your family **p** and to your

25:13 to your family **p** in this year of
25:25 of their family **p**, the closest
25:27 Then it will go back to the family **p**.
25:28 point it will return to the family **p**.
25:32 cities that are part of their family **p**.
25:33 Levite **p** that can be bought
25:34 that is their permanent family **p**.
25:41 extended family and to their family **p**.
25:45 land. These can belong to you as **p**.
25:46 own as permanent **p**. You can make
27:16 from their family **p** to the LORD, the
27:21 land; it will be the priest's **p**.
27:22 that is not part of their family **p**—
27:24 is the original owner of the family **p**.
27:28 from their family **p**—cannot be sold or

Numbers
5:9 offer will be the **p** of the priest.
27:4 a son? Give us **p** among our
27:7 means, give them **p** as an inheritance
31:11 and the valuable **p**, both human and
31:12 the valuable **p**, and the spoils
31:26 of the valuable **p** and the captives,
31:27 the valuable **p** between the
31:32 The valuable **p** remaining from the
32:5 your servants as **p**. Don't make us
32:18 Israelites takes possession of his **p**.
32:19 received our **p** on the east side
32:22 land will be your **p** before the LORD.
32:30 possession of **p** with you in the
32:32 for war. But the **p** we inherit will
35:2 their inherited **p** to the Levites in
35:8 you give from the **p** of the

Deuteronomy
2:5 Mount Seir to Esau's family as their **p**.
2:9 Ar to Lot's descendants as their **p**.
2:19 it to Lot's descendants as their **p**.
3:20 can return to the **p** that I have given
19:14 in your allotted **p** that you will
27:17 their neighbor's **p** lines." All the
32:9 Surely the LORD's **p** was his people;
32:49 giving to the Israelites as their **p**.

Joshua
12:6 their land as **p** to the
12:7 to the tribes of Israel as shares of **p**.
21:12 to Caleb, Jephunneh's son, as his **p**.
21:41 within the **p** of the
22:4 where you hold **p**, which Moses the
22:19 If your own **p** is unclean land, then

Judges
2:6 their own family **p** in order to take
2:9 of his family **p** in Timnath-heres

2 Samuel
14:30 Look, Joab's **p** is next to mine.
14:31 have your servants set my **p** on fire?"
19:29 I order you and Ziba to divide the **p**."

1 Chronicles
9:2 to resettle their **p** in their towns
27:31 these were stewards of King David's **p**.
28:1 charge of all the **p** and livestock of

2 Chronicles
11:14 pastures and **p** to come to Judah

Ezra
7:26 confiscation of **p**, or imprisonment.
10:8 have all their **p** taken away. They

Nehemiah
5:13 their house and **p** if they don't
11:3 of Judah on their own **p** in their towns.
11:20 of Judah, each of them in their own **p**.

Esther
3:13 Adar). They were also to seize their **p**.

Job
15:29 won't last; their **p** won't extend over

Psalms
2:8 corners of the earth will be your **p**.
16:6 The **p** lines have fallen beautifully for
78:55 and apportioned **p** for them; he

Jeremiah
37:12 to secure his share of the family **p**.

Lamentations
5:2 Our **p** has been turned over to

Ezekiel
44:28 be given family **p** in Israel; I am
45:5 Twenty chambers are theirs as their **p**.
45:6 As the **p** for the city, you will set
45:7 and the city **p**, alongside the
45:8 land will be his **p** in Israel, and my
46:16 their family **p** as an inheritance.
46:18 from their family **p**. He will bequeath
48:20 holy portion in addition to the city **p**.
48:21 and the city **p** belongs to the
48:22 the levitical **p** and the city

Luke
16:12 someone else's **p**, who will give

Acts
2:45 sell pieces of **p** and possessions
5:1 his wife Sapphira, sold a piece of **p**.
5:4 Wasn't that **p** yours to keep? After you

PROPHECY

2 Kings
9:25 when the LORD spoke this **p** about him:

2 Chronicles
15:8 words and the **p** of Azariah,

Nehemiah
6:12 he spoke this **p** against me

Mark
1:2 about in the **p** of Isaiah: Look,

Acts
21:9 who were involved in the work of **p**.

Romans
12:6 If your gift is **p**, you should

1 Corinthians
12:10 to another, **p** to another, the
13:2 have the gift of **p** and I know all
14:6 some knowledge, a **p**, or a teaching?
14:22 who believe. But **p** is a sign for
14:39 get the gift of **p**, but don't

1 Timothy
4:14 was given through **p** when the elders

2 Peter
1:20 must know that no **p** of scripture
1:21 because no **p** ever came by human will.

Revelation
1:3 the words of this **p** out loud, and
19:10 witness of Jesus is the spirit of **p**!"
22:7 the words of the **p** contained in this
22:10 the words of the **p** contained in this
22:18 the words of the **p** contained in this
22:19 of this scroll of **p**, God will take

PROPHESIED

Numbers
11:25 on them, they **p**, but only this
11:26 out to the tent, so they **p** in the camp.

1 Chronicles
25:2 direction and ***p*** by order of the
2 Chronicles
20:37 from Mareshah, ***p*** against
Ezra
5:1 Iddo's son, ***p*** to the Jews who
Jeremiah
20:6 your friends to whom you ***p*** falsely."
23:13 shocking: They ***p*** by Baal and led
23:21 speak to them, yet they ***p*** anyway.
25:13 which Jeremiah ***p*** against all the
26:18 of Moresheth, who ***p*** during the rule
26:20 another man who ***p*** in the LORD's
28:6 that you have ***p*** and bring back
28:8 and me long ago ***p*** war, disaster,
29:31 Because Shemaiah ***p*** to you when I
37:19 prophets now who ***p*** that the king of
Ezekiel
13:16 of Israel who ***p*** to Jerusalem and
37:7 I ***p*** just as I was commanded. There was
37:10 I ***p*** just as he commanded me. When the
38:17 the ones who ***p*** for years in
Matthew
11:13 Prophets and the Law ***p*** until John came.
13:14 What Isaiah ***p*** has become completely
15:7 was talking about when he ***p*** about you,
Mark
7:6 about when he ***p*** about you
Luke
1:67 was filled with the Holy Spirit and ***p***,
John
11:51 that year, he ***p*** that Jesus would
Romans
9:29 As Isaiah ***p***, If the Lord of the
Jude
1:14 after Adam, ***p*** about these

PROPHESY

1 Kings
22:13 the same thing they say and ***p*** success."
1 Chronicles
25:1 for service to ***p*** accompanied by
2 Chronicles
18:12 the same thing they say and ***p*** success."
Jeremiah
5:31 The prophets ***p*** falsely, the priests
11:21 and say, "Don't ***p*** in the LORD's
19:14 had sent him to ***p***, he stood in the
25:30 Now ***p*** all these things and say to them:
26:9 Why do you ***p*** in the LORD's name that
26:12 LORD sent me to ***p*** to this temple
32:3 him: "Why do you ***p***, 'This is what
Ezekiel
4:7 of Jerusalem directly and ***p*** against it.
6:2 face Israel's mountains, and ***p*** to them.
11:4 Therefore, ***p*** against them, human one,
13:2 Human one, ***p*** to Israel's prophets who
13:17 those women who ***p*** from their
20:46 the south, and ***p*** against the
21:2 sanctuary, and ***p*** against Israel's
21:9 Human one, ***p***! Say, The Lord proclaims!
21:14 you, human one, ***p***! Strike hand to
21:28 You, human one, ***p*** and say, The LORD God
25:2 face the Ammonites and ***p*** against them.
28:21 Human one, face Sidon, ***p*** against it
29:2 Egypt's king, and ***p*** against him and
30:2 Human one, ***p*** and say, The LORD God
34:2 Human one, ***p*** against Israel's
35:2 one, face Mount Seir, and ***p*** against it.
36:1 You, human one, ***p*** to Israel's mountains
36:3 Therefore, ***p*** and say, The LORD God
36:6 ***P*** concerning Israel's fertile land, and
37:4 He said to me, "***P*** over these bones, and
37:9 He said to me, "***P*** to the breath;
37:12 So now, ***p*** and say to them, The LORD God
38:2 of Meshech and Tubal. ***P*** concerning him
38:14 So now, ***p***, human one, and say to Gog,
39:1 You, human one, ***p*** about Gog and say,
Joel
2:28 daughters will ***p***, your old men
Amos
2:12 the prophets, saying, "You won't ***p***."
3:8 The LORD God has spoken; who can but ***p***?
7:12 eat your bread there, and ***p*** there;
7:13 but never again ***p*** at Bethel, for it is
7:15 said to me, 'Go, ***p*** to my people
7:16 You say, 'Don't ***p*** against Israel,
Matthew
7:22 Lord, didn't we ***p*** in your name and
26:68 and said, "***P*** for us, Christ! Who hit
Mark
14:65 hit him, saying, "***P***!" Then the guards
Luke
22:64 asked him repeatedly, "***P***! Who hit you?"
Acts
2:17 daughters will ***p***. Your young will
2:18 Spirit in those days, and they will ***p***.
Romans
12:6 you should ***p*** in proportion to
1 Corinthians
13:9 We know in part and we ***p*** in part
14:1 but especially so that you might ***p***.
14:3 Those who ***p*** speak to people, building
14:4 those who ***p*** build up the
14:5 rather you could ***p***. Those who
14:31 You can all ***p*** one at a time so that
Revelation
10:11 told, "You must ***p*** again about many
11:3 two witnesses to ***p*** for one thousand
11:6 as long as they ***p***. They also have

PROPHESYING

Numbers
11:27 Eldad and Medad are ***p*** in the camp."
1 Samuel
10:11 Saul saw him ***p*** with the
1 Kings
22:10 the prophets were ***p*** in front of them.
1 Chronicles
25:3 direction, ***p*** with the lyre and
2 Chronicles
18:9 the prophets were ***p*** in front of them.
Ezra
6:14 because of the ***p*** of the prophet
Jeremiah
14:14 to them. They are ***p*** to you false
14:16 people they are ***p*** to will be thrown
20:1 temple, heard Jeremiah ***p*** these words,

23:25 the prophets ***p*** lies in my name.
26:11 to die for ***p*** against this city
27:15 LORD; they are ***p*** falsely in my
27:16 prophets who are ***p*** to you, "In a
29:9 They are ***p*** lies to you in my name. I
29:21 son, who are ***p*** lies to you in my
Ezekiel
11:13 While I was ***p***, Benaiah's son Pelatiah
37:7 noise as I was ***p***, then a great
Acts
19:6 speaking in other languages and ***p***.
1 Corinthians
14:24 if everyone is ***p*** when an

PROPHET

Genesis
20:7 wife. He's a ***p***; he will pray for
Exodus
7:1 and your brother Aaron will be your ***p***.
15:20 Then the ***p*** Miriam, Aaron's sister, took
Numbers
12:6 If there is a ***p*** of the LORD among
Deuteronomy
13:1 Now if a ***p*** or a dream interpreter
13:5 That ***p*** or dream interpreter must be
18:15 will raise up a ***p*** like me from your
18:18 I'll raise up a ***p*** for them from among
18:19 words, which that ***p*** will speak in my
18:20 However, any ***p*** who arrogantly speaks a
18:22 the answer: The ***p*** who speaks in the
34:10 No ***p*** like Moses has yet emerged in
Judges
4:4 Now Deborah, a ***p***, the wife of
6:8 LORD sent them a ***p***, who said to
1 Samuel
3:20 Samuel was trustworthy as the LORD's ***p***.
22:5 Then the ***p*** Gad told David, "Don't stay
2 Samuel
7:2 king said to the ***p*** Nathan, "Look!
12:25 sent word by the ***p*** Nathan to name
24:11 word came to the ***p*** Gad, David's seer:
1 Kings
18:36 offering, the ***p*** Elijah drew near
20:42 Then the ***p*** said to the king, "This is
22:7 there any other ***p*** of the Lord whom
2 Kings
3:11 Isn't there any ***p*** of the LORD
5:3 come before the ***p*** who lives in
6:12 the Israelite ***p*** who tells
9:1 The ***p*** Elisha called to a member of the
9:4 So the young ***p*** went to Ramoth-gilead
14:25 his servant the ***p*** Jonah, Amittai's
19:2 priests to the ***p*** Isaiah, Amoz's
20:1 deathly ill. The ***p*** Isaiah, Amoz's
23:18 the bones of the ***p*** who came from
1 Chronicles
17:1 he said to the ***p*** Nathan, "I'm
29:29 seer, Nathan the ***p***, and Gad the
Ezra
5:1 Then the ***p*** Haggai and the prophet
6:14 of the ***p*** Haggai and
Psalms
51:1 David, when the ***p*** Nathan came to
74:9 signs anymore. No ***p*** is left. And none
Isaiah
3:2 judge and ***p***; fortune-teller an
28:7 beer: priest and ***p*** stagger from
37:2 priests to the ***p*** Isaiah, Amoz's
38:1 deathly sick. The ***p*** Isaiah, Amoz's
39:3 Then Isaiah the ***p*** came to King Hezekiah
Jeremiah
1:5 apart; I made you a ***p*** to the nations."
6:13 to profit; from ***p*** to priest, each
8:10 to profit. From ***p*** to priest, all
23:11 Both ***p*** and priest are godless; I even
25:2 The ***p*** Jeremiah addressed all the people
28:1 fourth year, the ***p*** Hananiah, Azzur's
29:1 The ***p*** Jeremiah sent a letter from
32:2 and the ***p*** Jeremiah was
34:6 The ***p*** Jeremiah delivered this message
36:8 everything the ***p*** Jeremiah
37:2 LORD's words spoken by the ***p*** Jeremiah.
38:9 in treating the ***p*** Jeremiah the way
42:2 Jeremiah the ***p*** and said to him, "We
43:6 Jeremiah the ***p*** and Baruch,
45:1 him. Jeremiah the ***p*** told Baruch,
46:1 the LORD told the ***p*** Jeremiah
47:1 word to the ***p*** Jeremiah
49:34 the LORD told the ***p*** Jeremiah
50:1 the Babylonians through the ***p*** Jeremiah:
51:59 This is what the ***p*** Jeremiah instructed
Lamentations
2:20 Should priest and ***p*** be killed in my
Ezekiel
2:5 will know that a ***p*** has been among
7:26 a vision from the ***p***. Instruction
14:4 then comes to the ***p***, I, the LORD,
14:9 As for the ***p*** who was seduced into
14:10 The ***p*** and the inquirer alike will bear
33:33 will know that a ***p*** has been among
Daniel
9:2 word to the ***p*** Jeremiah. It was
Hosea
4:5 so will your ***p***, and I will
9:7 cries, "The ***p*** is a fool, the
9:8 The ***p*** is God's watchman looking over
12:13 By a ***p*** the LORD brought Israel up from
Amos
7:14 I am not a ***p***, nor am I a
Habakkuk
1:1 The oracle that Habakkuk the ***p*** saw
3:1 of Habakkuk the ***p***, according to
Haggai
1:1 Haggai the ***p*** in the second
1:3 LORD's word came through Haggai the ***p***:
1:12 of Haggai the ***p*** because the LORD
2:1 LORD's word came through Haggai the ***p***:
2:10 the LORD's word came to Haggai the ***p***:
Zechariah
1:1 to Zechariah the ***p***, Berechiah's son
13:5 say, "I'm not a ***p***. I'm a man who
Malachi
4:5 Elijah the ***p*** to you, before
Matthew
1:22 through the ***p*** would be
2:5 of Judea, for this is what the ***p*** wrote:
2:15 through the ***p***: I have called my
2:17 the word spoken through Jeremiah the ***p***:

3:3 whom Isaiah the ***p*** spoke when he
4:14 This fulfilled what Isaiah the ***p*** said
8:17 what Isaiah the ***p*** said would be
10:41 who receive a ***p*** as a prophet will
11:9 go out to see? A ***p***? Yes, I tell you,
12:17 Isaiah the ***p*** might be
13:35 fulfill what the ***p*** spoke: I'll speak
14:5 because they thought John was a ***p***.
21:4 happened to fulfill what the ***p*** said,
21:11 It's the ***p*** Jesus from
21:26 since everyone thinks John was a ***p***."
21:46 the crowds, who thought he was a ***p***.
27:9 of Jeremiah the ***p***: And I took the

Mark
6:15 saying, "He is a ***p*** like one of the
11:32 because they all thought John was a ***p***.

Luke
1:76 will be called a ***p*** of the Most High,
2:36 There was also a ***p***, Anna the daughter
3:4 of Isaiah the ***p***, A voice crying
4:17 scroll from the ***p*** Isaiah. He
4:24 you that no ***p*** is welcome in the
4:27 the time of the ***p*** Elisha, but none
7:16 God. "A great ***p*** has appeared
7:26 go out to see? A ***p***? Yes, I tell you,
7:39 this man were a ***p***, he would know
11:51 murder of every ***p***—from Abel to Zech
13:33 impossible for a ***p*** to be killed
20:6 they are convinced that John was a ***p***."
24:19 by God and all the people as a ***p***.

John
1:21 Are you the ***p***?" John answered,
1:23 straight just as the ***p*** Isaiah said."
1:25 the Christ, nor Elijah, nor the ***p***?"
4:19 said, "Sir, I see that you are a ***p***.
6:14 is truly the ***p*** who is coming
7:40 they said, "This man is truly the ***p***."
7:52 will see that the ***p*** doesn't come from
9:17 your eyes?" He replied, "He's a ***p***."
12:38 the word of the ***p*** Isaiah. Lord, who

Acts
2:16 is what was spoken through the ***p*** Joel:
2:30 Because he was a ***p***, he knew that God
3:22 your own people a ***p*** like me. Listen
3:23 listen to that ***p*** will be totally
7:37 up for you a ***p*** like me from your
7:48 built by human hands. As the ***p*** says,
7:52 there a single ***p*** your ancestors
8:28 was reading the ***p*** Isaiah while
8:30 man reading the ***p*** Isaiah. He asked,
8:34 whom does the ***p*** say this? Is he
13:6 who was a false ***p*** and practiced
13:20 judges until the time of the ***p*** Samuel.
21:10 several days, a ***p*** named Agabus came
28:25 to your ancesters through Isaiah the ***p***,

Revelation
2:20 calls herself a ***p***. You allow her to
16:13 mouth, and the mouth of the false ***p***.
19:20 with the false ***p*** who had done
20:10 and the false ***p*** also were. There

PROPHETS → FALSE PROPHETS, PRIESTS AND PROPHETS

Numbers
11:29 people were ***p*** with the LORD

1 Samuel
10:11 with the ***p***, they said to
19:24 say, "Is Saul also one of the ***p***?"
28:6 not by the Urim, and not by the ***p***.

1 Kings
18:4 killed the LORD's ***p***, Obadiah took one
18:40 Seize Baal's ***p***! Don't let any
19:10 murdered your ***p*** with the sword.

2 Kings
17:23 his servants the ***p***. So Israel was
24:2 had spoken through his servants the ***p***.

1 Chronicles
16:22 my anointed ones; don't harm my ***p***!"

2 Chronicles
18:22 mouths of these ***p*** of yours it is

Ezra
5:2 Jerusalem. God's ***p*** were with them,
9:11 your servants the ***p***, saying: 'The

Nehemiah
9:30 through the ***p***. But they

Psalms
105:15 my anointed ones; don't harm my ***p***!"

Isaiah
9:15 are the head; ***p*** who teach lies
29:10 your eyes, you ***p***, and covered your

Jeremiah
5:13 The ***p*** are so much wind; the word isn't
14:14 said to me: The ***p*** are telling lies
23:9 As for the ***p***: My heart inside me is
23:30 I'm against the ***p*** who steal my

Lamentations
2:9 Even her ***p*** couldn't find a
2:14 Your ***p*** gave you worthless and empty

Ezekiel
13:2 to Israel's ***p*** who prophesy from

Hosea
6:5 them by the ***p***, I have killed
12:10 I spoke to the ***p***; and I multiplied

Micah
3:6 will set on the ***p***; the day will be
3:11 for hire. Her ***p*** offer divination

Zephaniah
3:4 Her ***p*** are reckless, men of treachery.

Zechariah
1:5 your ancestors? Do the ***p*** live forever?
1:6 my servants, the ***p***, pursue your
13:4 day each of the ***p*** will be ashamed

Matthew
5:17 the Law and the ***P***. I haven't come
22:40 the Law and the ***P*** depend on these

Mark
6:4 said to them, "***P*** are honored
6:15 a prophet like one of the ancient ***p***."
8:28 Elijah, and still others one of the ***p***."

Luke
6:23 ancestors did the same things to the ***p***.
10:24 you that many ***p*** and kings wanted
11:49 I will send ***p*** and apostles to
16:29 Moses and the ***P***. They must listen
24:25 believing all that the ***p*** talked about.
24:44 Law of Moses, the ***P***, and the Psalms

Acts
3:24 All the ***p*** who spoke—from Samuel
10:43 All the ***p*** testify about him that
13:1 Antioch included ***p*** and teachers:
26:22 than what the ***P*** and Moses
28:23 to the Law of Moses and the ***P***.

Romans
1:3 time through his ***p*** in the holy

3:21 is confirmed by the Law and the ***P***.
11:3 have killed your ***p***, and they have
16:26 through what the ***p*** wrote. It is made
1 Corinthians
12:28 apostles, second ***p***, third teachers,
12:29 they? All aren't ***p***, are they? All
14:32 The spirits of ***p*** are under the control
Ephesians
2:20 the apostles and ***p*** with Christ Jesus
3:5 holy apostles and ***p*** through the
1 Thessalonians
2:15 Jesus and the ***p*** and drove us out.
Titus
1:12 one of their own ***p*** said, "People
Hebrews
1:1 spoke through the ***p*** to our ancestors
11:32 Jephthah, David, Samuel, and the ***p***.
James
5:10 sisters, take the ***p*** who spoke in the
1 Peter
1:10 The ***p***, who long ago foretold the grace
2 Peter
3:2 what the holy ***p*** foretold as well
Revelation
10:7 news he gave to his servants the ***p***."
11:10 because these two ***p*** had brought such
11:18 servants, the ***p*** and saints, and
16:6 of saints and ***p***, and you have
18:20 apostles, and ***p***—because God has c
18:24 the blood of ***p***, of saints, and of all
22:6 spirits of the ***p***, sent his angel
22:9 and sisters, the ***p***, and those who

PROSTITUTE

Genesis
34:31 didn't he treat our sister like a ***p***?"
38:15 thought she was a ***p*** because she had
Exodus
34:15 land. When they ***p*** themselves with
34:16 daughters who ***p*** themselves with
Joshua
2:1 the house of a ***p*** named Rahab. They
6:17 Only Rahab the ***p*** is to stay alive,
6:25 let Rahab the ***p*** live, her family,
Judges
16:1 there, he saw a ***p*** and had sex with
Proverbs
6:26 for a ***p*** costs a loaf of bread, but a
7:10 dressed like a ***p*** and with a
23:27 A ***p*** is a deep pit, and a foreign woman
Isaiah
1:21 town has become a ***p***! She was full of
23:15 will become like the ***p*** in the song:
23:16 city, forgotten ***p***. Play well, sing
23:17 trade and will ***p*** herself with all
Jeremiah
2:20 lush tree, you have acted like a ***p***.
3:3 act like a brazen ***p*** who refuses to
3:8 not afraid but kept on playing the ***p***.
Ezekiel
16:30 things, the deeds of a hardened ***p***.
16:31 like an ordinary ***p***! When you built
20:30 did, and will you ***p*** yourself after
23:3 they began to ***p*** themselves by
Hosea
1:2 him,"Go, marry a ***p*** and have children
2:5 has played the ***p***; she who
3:3 won't act like a ***p***; you won't have
4:15 you act like a ***p***, don't let Judah
5:3 have acted like a ***p***; Israel is
6:10 acts like a ***p***; Israel is
Amos
7:17 will become a ***p*** in the city, and
Micah
1:7 the wages of a ***p***, they will again
Hebrews
11:31 faith Rahab the ***p*** wasn't killed
James
2:25 wasn't Rahab the ***p*** shown to be
Revelation
17:1 upon the great ***p***, who is seated on
19:2 judged the great ***p***, who ruined the

PROTECT

Genesis
28:15 you now, I will ***p*** you everywhere
Numbers
35:25 community will ***p*** the killer from
Deuteronomy
13:8 compassion on them and don't ***p*** them!
32:38 up and help you! They should ***p*** you now!
Joshua
9:15 with them to ***p*** their lives. The
22:26 we said, 'Let's ***p*** ourselves by
2 Samuel
18:5 For my sake, ***p*** my boy Absalom."
2 Kings
11:7 guard the LORD's temple to ***p*** the king.
11:11 the north side to ***p*** the king.
2 Chronicles
23:10 to the north side, so as to ***p*** the king.
Psalms
5:11 out loud forever! ***P*** them so that all
16:1 miktam of David.] ***P*** me, God, because
20:1 Let the name of Jacob's God ***p*** you.
23:4 Your rod and your staff—they ***p*** me.
25:20 Please ***p*** my life! Deliver me! Don't let
32:7 hideout! You ***p*** me from trouble.
40:11 loyal love and faithfulness always ***p*** me
64:1 I complain, God! ***P*** my life from the
91:4 God will ***p*** you with his pinions; you'll
91:11 to help you, to ***p*** you wherever you
91:14 rescue you. I'll ***p*** you because you
121:7 The LORD will ***p*** you from all evil; God
121:8 The LORD will ***p*** you on your journeys—
140:4 ***P*** me from the power of the wicked,
141:9 ***P*** me from the trap they've set for me;
Proverbs
2:11 guard you; understanding will ***p*** you.
4:6 you. Love her, and she will ***p*** you.
4:13 don't slack off; ***p*** it, for it is
4:23 you guard, ***p*** your mind, for
6:22 down, they will ***p*** you; when you
14:3 fool, but the lips of the wise ***p*** them.
16:17 evil; those who ***p*** their path guard
20:28 and faithfulness ***p*** the king; he
22:12 The LORD's eyes ***p*** knowledge, but he
Jeremiah
15:20 I am with you to ***p*** and rescue you,
Ezekiel
33:12 sin, their righteousness won't ***p*** them.

PROTECT [cont.]

Daniel
11:1 took my stand to strengthen and ***p*** him."
Nahum
2:1 watch the road, ***p*** your groin, save
Zechariah
9:15 forces will ***p*** them. They will
12:8 day the LORD will ***p*** the inhabitants
Luke
4:10 his angels concerning you, to ***p*** you
Acts
21:35 in order to ***p*** him from the
2 Thessalonians
3:3 you strength and ***p*** you from the evil
1 Timothy
6:20 Timothy, ***p*** what has been given to you
2 Timothy
1:12 enough to ***p*** what he has
1:14 ***P*** this good thing that has been placed
Jude
1:24 who is able to ***p*** you from falling,

PROUD

2 Samuel
22:28 are against the ***p***. You bring them
2 Chronicles
32:25 Hezekiah was too ***p*** to respond
Esther
10:3 and sisters were ***p*** of him. He always
Job
28:8 ***p*** beasts haven't trodden on it; a lion
38:11 no farther; here your ***p*** waves stop"?
40:11 look on all the ***p*** and humble them.
Psalms
18:27 and brings down those with ***p*** eyes.
31:23 but he pays the ***p*** back to the
40:4 attention to the ***p*** or to those who
54:3 The ***p*** have come up against me; violent people want
97:7 those who are ***p*** of idols, are put
101:5 anyone who has ***p*** eyes or an
123:4 more than enough shame from the ***p***.
131:1 my heart isn't ***p***; my eyes aren't
Proverbs
16:19 than to divide plunder with the ***p***.
21:24 Incredibly ***p***—mockers are their name!
Isaiah
2:11 People's ***p*** gazing will be stopped and
9:9 But with a ***p*** and arrogant
13:3 my warriors, my ***p***, jubilant ones,
Jeremiah
13:17 If you are too ***p*** to listen, I will go
Ezekiel
7:24 I'll break their ***p*** strength, and
16:49 daughters were ***p***, had plenty to
24:25 from them their ***p*** stronghold—their
28:5 But then you became ***p*** of your riches.
30:6 helpers fall, its ***p*** strength will
30:18 an end to its ***p*** strength. A cloud
33:28 waste. Its ***p*** strength will
Hosea
13:6 hearts became ***p***; therefore, they
Obadiah
1:3 Your ***p*** heart has tricked you—you who
Luke
1:51 arrogant thoughts and ***p*** inclinations.
16:3 strong enough to dig and too ***p*** to beg.
Romans
1:30 They are rude and ***p***, and they brag.
11:20 don't think in a ***p*** way; instead be
1 Corinthians
5:2 And you're ***p*** of yourselves instead of
2 Corinthians
1:14 we will make you ***p*** as you will also
5:12 opportunity to be ***p*** of us so that you
7:4 you. I'm terribly ***p*** of you. I'm
8:24 reason we are so ***p*** of you, in such a
11:10 of Greece that I'm ***p*** of what I did.
Ephesians
2:9 something you did that you can be ***p*** of.
1 Timothy
1:13 people, and I was ***p***. But I was shown
3:6 they won't become ***p*** and fall under
2 Timothy
3:2 brag and who are ***p***. They will
James
4:6 against the ***p***, but favors the
1 Peter
5:5 against the ***p***, but he gives

PROVIDE

Genesis
3:6 the tree would ***p*** wisdom, so she
16:2 Maybe she will ***p*** me with
24:41 me. Even if they ***p*** no one for you,
38:8 and ***p*** children for your
45:18 to me. Let me ***p*** you with good
Leviticus
22:14 they must ***p*** the priest with
Numbers
18:28 You will ***p*** from it a gift
20:8 tell the rock to ***p*** water. You will
Deuteronomy
11:14 then he will ***p*** rain for your land at
15:14 Instead, ***p*** for them fully from your
Joshua
20:4 into the city and ***p*** a place of refuge
Judges
19:19 food and wine to ***p*** for me, the
21:7 What can we do to ***p*** wives for the ones
21:16 can we do to ***p*** wives for the
Ruth
1:9 May the LORD ***p*** for you so that you may
2 Samuel
7:10 I'm going to ***p*** a place for my people
19:33 with me. I will ***p*** for you at my
1 Kings
4:7 food. Each would ***p*** the supplies for
5:9 I ask you to ***p*** for my royal
17:4 ordered the ravens to ***p*** for you there.
1 Chronicles
17:9 I'm going to ***p*** a place for my people
21:23 best. I'll even ***p*** the oxen for the
25:6 and lyres to ***p*** service in God's
2 Chronicles
29:31 volunteering to ***p*** entirely burned
31:4 in Jerusalem to ***p*** the required
Ezra
7:20 responsible to ***p***, you may provide
Esther
2:3 so that he might ***p*** beauty treatments
Psalms
12:5 up. I will ***p*** the help they are
65:9 of water. You ***p*** people with grain

78:20 bread too? Can he ***p*** meat for his
105:39 gave lightning to ***p*** light at night.
Proverbs
1:3 They ***p*** insightful instruction, which is
3:2 a long time and ***p*** you with well-bein
8:21 to ***p*** for those who love me and to fill
27:26 the lambs will ***p*** your clothes, and
Isaiah
16:3 at high noon ***p*** your shade like
30:23 God will ***p*** rain for the seed you sow in
33:6 He will ***p*** security during a lifetime: a
58:10 the hungry, and ***p*** abundantly for
58:11 continually and ***p*** for you, even in
61:3 to ***p*** for Zion's mourners, to give them
Jeremiah
33:9 of all the good I ***p*** for them. They
Ezekiel
43:19 You will ***p*** a young bull as a
45:22 the prince will ***p*** a young bull as
45:23 festival, he will ***p*** seven flawless
45:24 He will also ***p*** the grain offerings, one
46:7 and he will ***p*** a grain offering of one
46:13 LORD, you will ***p*** a flawless year-old
46:14 You will ***p*** a grain offering along with
Micah
7:20 You will ***p*** faithfulness to Jacob,
Habakkuk
3:17 the fields don't ***p*** food; though the
Haggai
2:9 forces. I will ***p*** prosperity in
Zechariah
10:2 falsely and ***p*** empty comfort.
Luke
18:7 Won't God ***p*** justice to his chosen
21:13 This will ***p*** you with an opportunity to
Acts
3:20 the Lord will ***p*** a season of
7:46 that he might ***p*** a dwelling place
24:23 hindered in their efforts to ***p*** for him.
2 Corinthians
9:8 has the power to ***p*** you with more
Ephesians
4:27 Don't ***p*** an opportunity for the devil
1 Timothy
5:8 someone doesn't ***p*** for their own
3 John
1:6 would do well to ***p*** for their journey

PROVIDED
Genesis
24:32 the camels, ***p*** straw and feed
47:12 Joseph ***p*** food for his father, his
Exodus
8:28 in the desert, ***p*** you don't go too
Leviticus
17:11 the blood. I have ***p*** you the blood to
Numbers
7:84 Israelite chiefs ***p*** for the
Joshua
13:15 Moses ***p*** for the clans of the Reubenite
13:24 Moses ***p*** for the clans of the Gadite
13:29 Moses ***p*** for half the tribe of Manasseh.
22:7 Moses had ***p*** for half of the tribe of
Judges
5:25 water, and she ***p*** milk; she
2 Samuel
20:3 under guard. He ***p*** for them, but he
1 Kings
2:24 father David, and ***p*** a royal house for
4:27 The officials ***p*** King Solomon and all
2 Kings
21:8 their ancestors, ***p*** they carefully do
1 Chronicles
12:39 while their relatives ***p*** food for them.
15:22 the Levites who ***p*** transportation,
22:3 David also ***p*** a huge amount of iron for
22:14 effort I've now ***p*** for the LORD's
28:12 He ***p*** all of the plans he had in mind:
29:2 my disposal, I've ***p*** everything for my
29:3 to all that I've ***p*** for the holy
29:16 that we have ***p*** to build you a
2 Chronicles
2:7 who were ***p*** by my father
30:24 the officials ***p*** another thousand
33:8 your ancestors, ***p*** they carefully do
35:8 officials also ***p*** spontaneous gift
35:9 of the Levites, ***p*** the Levites with
Ezra
7:21 of you, it must be ***p*** precisely,
Nehemiah
13:31 I also ***p*** for the wood offering at
Psalms
68:10 your goodness, God, you ***p*** for the poor.
Isaiah
33:16 His food will be ***p***, his water
Jeremiah
52:34 Babylonian king ***p*** him daily
Ezekiel
11:16 the earth, I've ***p*** some sanctuary
46:15 and the oil are ***p*** every morning as
Amos
4:6 cities, and not ***p*** enough bread in
Jonah
1:17 the LORD ***p*** a great fish to
4:6 Then the LORD God ***p*** a shrub, and it
4:7 But God ***p*** a worm the next day at dawn,
4:8 the sun rose God ***p*** a dry east wind,
Zechariah
6:8 going north have ***p*** rest for my
Luke
8:3 many others who ***p*** for them out of
Acts
20:34 know that I have ***p*** for my own needs
Romans
11:22 kindness for you, ***p*** you continue in
1 Corinthians
16:18 Indeed they've ***p*** my spirit and yours
Hebrews
11:40 God ***p*** something better for us so they

PSALM
Acts
13:33 in the second ***p***, You are my son;
1 Corinthians
14:15 too; I'll sing a ***p*** in the Spirit,
14:26 each one has a ***p***, a teaching, a

PUBLIC
Leviticus
5:1 after hearing a ***p*** solemn pledge
2 Samuel
21:12 bones from the ***p*** square in
2 Kings
10:27 turning it into a ***p*** restroom, which

PUBLIC [cont.]

15:10 him down in ***p***, murdering him.
23:6 and threw the dust on the ***p*** graveyard.

Esther
1:11 to the general ***p*** and to his
1:20 the order becomes ***p*** through the whole
2:8 new law became ***p***, many young women
2:18 He declared a ***p*** holiday for the
3:14 to be posted in ***p*** for all peoples
3:15 as the law became ***p*** in the fortified
4:8 of the law made ***p*** in Susa
8:13 and be on ***p*** display for all
8:14 law also became ***p*** in the fortified
9:14 the law became ***p*** in Susa. They

Proverbs
1:20 street; in the ***p*** square she raises
5:16 streams of water in the ***p*** squares?
7:12 one foot in the ***p*** square. She lies
26:26 but their evil will be revealed in ***p***.
27:5 A ***p*** correction is better than hidden

Isaiah
3:9 their sins in ***p***. Doom to them,
42:2 aloud or make his voice heard in ***p***.
59:14 stumbled in the ***p*** square, and

Luke
1:80 he began his ***p*** ministry to

John
7:26 is, speaking in ***p***, yet they aren't
11:54 longer active in ***p*** ministry among
19:19 Pilate had a ***p*** notice written and

Acts
4:21 them. Because of ***p*** support for Peter
5:18 and made a ***p*** show of putting
18:28 arguments in ***p*** debate, using the

1 Corinthians
4:5 motivations ***p***. Then there will

2 Corinthians
4:2 of God by the ***p*** announcement of
11:6 I'm uneducated in ***p*** speaking, I'm not

Colossians
2:15 exposed them to ***p*** disgrace by

1 Timothy
4:13 pay attention to ***p*** reading,
5:17 who work with ***p*** speaking and

Hebrews
6:6 over again and exposing him to ***p*** shame.
10:33 and abuse in ***p***. Other times you
11:36 experienced ***p*** shame by being

PULLED

Genesis
19:10 reached out and ***p*** Lot back into the
37:28 passed by, they ***p*** Joseph up out of
38:29 As soon as he ***p*** his hand back, his
43:31 face, came back, ***p*** himself together,
48:2 is here now," he ***p*** himself together

Exodus
2:10 she said, "I ***p*** him out of the

Leviticus
14:40 is found to be ***p*** out and discarded
14:43 stones have been ***p*** out and the house

Deuteronomy
21:3 that hasn't been used or yet ***p*** a plow,

Judges
16:3 gateposts, and ***p*** them up with the
16:14 on a loom, and ***p*** it tight with a

2 Samuel
22:20 spaces; he ***p*** me out, because

2 Kings
3:27 Israel. So they ***p*** back from Moab's
10:15 hand, and Jehu ***p*** him up into the
12:18 Hazael then ***p*** back from

Ezra
6:11 a beam is to be ***p*** out of the house
9:3 and cloak, ***p*** out hair from my

Nehemiah
13:25 some of them, and ***p*** out their hair. I

Job
4:21 their tent cord ***p*** up? They die

Psalms
18:19 spaces; he ***p*** me out safe
22:9 are the one who ***p*** me from the womb,
30:1 LORD, because you ***p*** me up; you didn't
129:6 a roof that dies before it can be ***p*** up,

Isaiah
22:19 you will be ***p*** down from your
33:20 stakes are never ***p*** up, whose ropes

Jeremiah
38:13 they ***p*** him up by the ropes and got him

Daniel
5:20 pride, he was ***p*** off his royal
7:4 its wings were ***p*** off, and it was

Matthew
13:48 it was full, they ***p*** it to the shore,
15:13 Father didn't plant will be ***p*** up.

Luke
1:52 He has ***p*** the powerful down from their

John
21:11 Peter got up and ***p*** the net to shore.

Acts
10:16 object was suddenly ***p*** back into heaven.
11:10 then everything was ***p*** back into heaven.
27:13 their plan. They ***p*** up anchor and

PUNISH

Genesis
15:14 But after I ***p*** the nation they serve,
31:29 have the power to ***p*** you. However,

Exodus
20:5 passionate God. I ***p*** children for

Leviticus
26:18 obey me, I will ***p*** you for your sins
26:28 anger! I will ***p*** you for your sins

Numbers
12:11 please don't ***p*** us for the sin

Deuteronomy
5:9 passionate God. I ***p*** children for
22:18 must then take that husband and ***p*** him.
32:41 back; I'll ***p*** in kind everyone
32:43 enemies; he will ***p*** in kind those who

1 Samuel
3:13 him that I would ***p*** his family
15:2 I am going to ***p*** the Amalekites

2 Samuel
13:21 but he refused to ***p*** his son Amnon

2 Kings
19:4 God will ***p*** him for the the

1 Chronicles
12:17 our ancestors' God see it and ***p*** you."

2 Chronicles
20:12 God, won't you ***p*** them? We are

Psalms
6:1 LORD, don't ***p*** me when you are

38:1 LORD, don't ***p*** me, when you are
59:5 Wake up and ***p*** all the nations!
89:32 then I will ***p*** their sin with a stick,
94:10 nations, can't he ***p***? The one who
Proverbs
17:26 It isn't good to ***p*** the righteous, to
Isaiah
10:12 he will ***p*** the Assyrian
24:21 the LORD will ***p*** the forces of
27:1 mighty, and will ***p*** Leviathan the
37:4 Perhaps he will ***p*** him for the words
66:4 will choose to ***p*** them, to bring
Jeremiah
2:19 wrongdoing will ***p*** you. Your acts of
5:29 Shouldn't I ***p*** such acts? declares the
9:9 Shouldn't I ***p*** them for this? declares
11:22 I'm going to ***p*** them. Their young
14:10 their wrongdoing and ***p*** their sin.
18:20 you to be merciful and not to ***p*** them.
21:14 I will ***p*** you based on what you have
23:34 I will ***p*** anyone, including prophet or
25:12 are over, I will ***p*** the king of
27:8 his yoke, I will ***p*** it with sword,
29:32 I will ***p*** Shemaiah the Nehelamite and
30:20 before me. I will ***p*** their oppressors.
32:5 his days until I ***p*** him, declares the
36:31 I will ***p*** him and his family and his
44:13 I will ***p*** those who live in the land of
44:29 the LORD: I will ***p*** you here so that
46:25 I'm going to ***p*** Amon of Thebes,
50:18 I'm going to ***p*** the king of
51:44 I will ***p*** Bel in Babylon; I will force
Hosea
1:4 while I will ***p*** the house of Jehu
2:13 I will ***p*** her for the days dedicated to
4:9 people; I will ***p*** them for their
4:14 I will not ***p*** your daughters because
8:13 wickedness and ***p*** their sins; they
9:9 their wickedness; he will ***p*** their sins.
10:10 I will come and ***p*** them; nations will be
12:2 Judah, and will ***p*** Jacob according
Amos
3:2 Therefore, I will ***p*** you for all your
3:14 On the day I ***p*** the crimes of Israel, I
Zephaniah
1:8 sacrifice, I will ***p*** the princes, the
1:9 I will ***p*** the one leaping on the
1:12 lamps; I will ***p*** the men growing
Zechariah
10:3 shepherds; I will ***p*** the goats. The
Acts
4:21 find a way to ***p*** them. Everyone
1 Corinthians
4:21 a big stick to ***p*** you, or with love
2 Corinthians
10:6 we are ready to ***p*** any disobedience.
1 Peter
2:14 They are sent to ***p*** those doing evil

PUNISHED

Exodus
21:19 him shouldn't be ***p***, except to pay
21:20 immediately, the owner should be ***p***.
21:21 shouldn't be ***p*** because the slave
21:28 But the owner of the ox shouldn't be ***p***.
Deuteronomy
25:2 lie down and be ***p*** in his presence—
1 Kings
8:35 sin because you have ***p*** them for it,
2 Kings
17:20 descendants. He ***p*** them, and he
1 Chronicles
16:21 oppress them. God ***p*** kings for their
21:7 offended by this census and ***p*** Israel.
2 Chronicles
6:26 sin because you have ***p*** them for it,
24:24 ancestor's God. Jehoash was justly ***p***.
Ezra
9:13 our God, have ***p*** us less than our
Psalms
73:14 down all day long. I'm ***p*** every morning.
91:8 eyes, and you will see the wicked ***p***.
105:14 oppress them. God ***p*** kings for their
Proverbs
6:29 wife; anyone who touches her will be ***p***.
21:11 When a mocker is ***p***, the naive person
21:18 will be ***p*** in the place of
22:3 simpleminded go right to it and get ***p***.
27:12 simpleminded go right to it and get ***p***.
Isaiah
24:22 into a prison, and ***p*** after many days.
26:14 Indeed, you have ***p*** and destroyed
Jeremiah
44:13 Egypt, just as I ***p*** Jerusalem with
50:18 land, just as I ***p*** the king of
Ezekiel
6:6 altars will be ***p*** and then broken
23:45 and they will be ***p*** as adulterers and
Hosea
10:10 when they are ***p*** for their double
Acts
22:5 to Jerusalem so they could be ***p***.
Romans
13:2 who take this kind of stand will get ***p***.
2 Corinthians
6:9 We were seen as ***p*** but not killed,

PUNISHMENT

Genesis
4:13 to the LORD, "My ***p*** is more than I
Leviticus
5:1 so that you become liable to ***p***;
5:17 and then become guilty and liable to ***p***,
7:18 who eats of it will be liable to ***p***.
10:17 the community's ***p*** by making
17:16 their body, they will be liable to ***p***.
18:25 it liable for ***p***, and the land
19:8 will be liable to ***p***, because they
19:20 there must be a ***p***. But they will
20:17 his sister; he will be liable to ***p***.
20:19 both of you will be liable to ***p***.
20:20 will be liable to ***p***; they will die
22:9 become liable to ***p*** and die for
22:16 liable to ***p*** requiring
24:15 who curses his God will be liable to ***p***.
Numbers
11:33 struck the people with a very great ***p***.
14:18 doesn't forgo all ***p***, disciplining the
31:3 the LORD's just ***p*** against Midian.
Deuteronomy
17:6 Capital ***p*** must be decided by two or
32:35 my domain, so is ***p***-in-kind, at the ex
Joshua
22:23 on it, let the LORD himself seek ***p***.

PUNISHMENT [cont.]

Judges
11:36 carried out just ***p*** for you on your
2 Kings
19:3 day of distress, ***p***, and humiliation.
25:6 at Riblah. There his ***p*** was determined.
Job
19:29 for wrath brings ***p*** by the sword. You
21:19 God stores up his ***p*** for his children.
24:1 times for ***p***? Why can't those
34:31 I have borne ***p***; I won't sin
37:13 Whether for ***p***, for his world, or for
Psalms
149:7 the nations and ***p*** on the peoples,
Isaiah
10:3 do on the day of ***p*** when disaster
37:3 day of distress, ***p***, and humiliation.
53:5 He bore the ***p*** that made us
Jeremiah
46:21 to haunt them, the time of their ***p***.
46:28 let you avoid ***p***; I will
48:44 the year of its ***p***, declares the
49:12 expect to escape ***p***. You won't! You
51:9 each of you. Her ***p*** reaches to heaven
Lamentations
4:6 Greater was the ***p*** of the daughter of my
4:22 Your ***p*** is over, Daughter Zion; God
Ezekiel
4:4 on your side, you will bear their ***p***.
4:5 you will bear the ***p*** of the house of
21:25 day has come, the time of final ***p***,
21:29 day had come, the time of final ***p***.
22:4 shed is your ***p***, and all the
23:24 I will hand your ***p*** over to them, and
35:5 their distress, during their final ***p***.
Hosea
9:7 The days of ***p*** have come; the days of
Amos
1:3 hold back the ***p***, because they
2:1 hold back the ***p***, because he
Micah
7:4 lookouts! Your ***p*** has arrived. The
Matthew
25:46 away into eternal ***p***. But the
Luke
12:48 things deserving ***p*** will be beaten
21:22 are the days of ***p***, when everything
Romans
5:16 sin led to ***p***, but the free
13:4 to carry out his ***p*** on those who do
13:5 to avoid God's ***p*** but also for the
2 Corinthians
2:6 The ***p*** handed out by the majority is
Ephesians
2:3 headed for ***p*** just like
Hebrews
10:29 How much worse ***p*** do you think is
2 Peter
2:9 unrighteous for ***p*** on the Judgment
1 John
4:18 fear expects ***p***. The person who
Jude
1:7 By undergoing the ***p*** of eternal fire,

PURE

Genesis
2:12 land's gold is ***p***, and the land
20:5 intentions were ***p***, and I acted
20:6 intentions were ***p*** when you did
Numbers
5:28 and she is ***p***, then she will be
Deuteronomy
32:32 Their grapes are ***p*** poison; their
2 Samuel
22:27 You are ***p*** toward the pure, but toward
1 Kings
6:20 overlaid it with ***p*** gold and covered
6:21 interior with ***p*** gold. He placed
7:49 the lampstands of ***p*** gold, five on the
7:50 and censers of ***p*** gold; and the
10:18 throne and covered it with ***p*** gold.
10:21 were made of ***p*** gold, not silver,
2 Kings
2:22 water has stayed ***p*** right up to this
25:15 were made of ***p*** gold and pure
1 Chronicles
28:17 and cups of ***p*** gold; for the
2 Chronicles
3:4 covered the inside walls with ***p*** gold.
4:20 lamps, all of ***p*** gold, to burn
4:21 the lamps, and the tongs of ***p*** gold;
4:22 and censers of ***p*** gold. As for the
9:17 throne and covered it with ***p*** gold.
9:20 were made of ***p*** gold, not silver,
Job
8:6 If you are ***p*** and do the right thing,
11:4 My teaching is ***p***, and I'm clean in
14:4 Who can make ***p*** from impure? Nobody
15:14 they might be ***p***, and those born
15:15 and the heavens aren't ***p*** in his eyes,
16:17 in my hands, and my prayer is ***p***.
22:30 they will be saved by your ***p*** hands."
25:4 before God; one born of a woman be ***p***?
25:5 bright and the stars not ***p*** in his eyes,
28:19 her; she can't be set alongside ***p*** gold.
33:9 I'm ***p***, without sin; I'm innocent,
Psalms
12:6 promises are ***p***, like silver
18:26 You are ***p*** toward the pure, but toward
19:8 commands are ***p***, giving light to
19:10 than tons of ***p*** gold!—and they a
21:3 you put a crown of ***p*** gold on his head.
24:4 clean hands and a ***p*** heart; the one
36:8 them drink from your river of ***p*** joy.
65:12 it, and the hills are dressed in ***p*** joy.
73:1 to Israel, to those who are ***p*** of heart.
73:13 kept my heart ***p*** for no good
119:9 keep their paths ***p***? By guarding them
119:127 more than gold, even more than ***p*** gold.
Proverbs
15:26 evil plans, but gracious words are ***p***.
16:2 of people are ***p*** in their eyes,
20:11 whether their conduct is ***p*** and upright.
21:8 behavior of those who do right is ***p***.
22:11 Those who love a ***p*** heart—their speech
Ecclesiastes
9:2 and the bad, the ***p*** and the impure,
Lamentations
4:2 once valued as ***p*** gold—oh no!—now
Daniel
2:32 head was made of ***p*** gold; its chest
Habakkuk
1:13 Your eyes are too ***p*** to look on evil;
Zephaniah
3:9 the peoples into ***p*** speech, that all

Malachi
1:11 Incense and a ***p*** grain offering
Matthew
5:8 people who have ***p*** hearts, because
Mark
14:3 perfume of ***p*** nard. She broke
John
12:3 perfume made of ***p*** nard. She
Acts
10:15 consider unclean what God has made ***p***."
11:9 consider unclean what God has made ***p***.'
24:18 I was ritually ***p***. There was no
2 Corinthians
1:12 sincerity and ***p*** motives in the
Philippians
2:15 be blameless and ***p***, innocent
4:8 just, all that is ***p***, all that is
1 Thessalonians
4:4 own body in a ***p*** and respectable
1 Timothy
1:5 is love from a ***p*** heart, a good
4:12 love, faith, and by being sexually ***p***.
5:22 of others. Keep yourself morally ***p***.
Titus
2:5 sensible, morally ***p***, working at home,
Hebrews
10:22 and our bodies are washed with ***p*** water.
James
1:27 the kind that is ***p*** and faultless
3:17 First, it is ***p***, and then
1 Peter
1:4 You have a ***p*** and enduring inheritance
2:2 baby, desire the ***p*** milk of the word.
1 John
3:3 him purifies himself even as he is ***p***.
Revelation
15:6 were clothed in ***p*** bright linen and
19:8 was given fine, ***p*** white linen to
19:14 was white and ***p***, were following
21:18 and the city was ***p*** gold, like pure
21:21 main street was ***p*** gold, as

PURIFICATION

Exodus
29:14 outside the camp. It is a ***p*** offering.
29:36 offer a bull as a ***p*** offering for
30:10 the blood of the ***p*** offering for
Leviticus
4:3 the herd as a ***p*** offering for the
Numbers
6:11 offer one for a ***p*** offering and the
28:15 male goat for a ***p*** offering to the
31:23 with the water of ***p***. Anything that
2 Kings
12:16 compensation and ***p*** offerings, it
Ezra
6:17 lambs, and as a ***p*** offering for all
8:35 male goats as a ***p*** offering. All
Nehemiah
10:33 offerings and the ***p*** offerings to make
12:45 the service of ***p***, as did the
Ezekiel
40:39 offerings, the ***p*** offerings, and
42:13 offering, the ***p*** offering, and the
43:19 a young bull as a ***p*** offering to the
43:21 selected as the ***p*** offering, and the
43:22 male goat as a ***p*** offering. The
43:23 completed the ***p***, you will present
43:25 a male goat for a ***p*** offering. You
44:27 will present his ***p*** offering. This is
44:29 offerings, the ***p*** offerings, and
45:17 He will offer the ***p*** offering, the
45:19 blood from the ***p*** offering, and he
45:22 young bull as the ***p*** offering for
45:23 and, for the ***p*** offering, one
45:25 for the ***p*** offerings,
46:20 offerings and the ***p*** offerings, and
Acts
21:24 go through the ***p*** ritual with them,
21:26 went through the ***p*** ritual with them.
21:27 the seven days of ***p*** were almost over,
Hebrews
10:8 offerings or a ***p*** offering, which

PURIFIED

Numbers
8:21 The Levites ***p*** themselves and washed
19:19 that he will have ***p*** him on the
31:23 It will also be ***p*** with the water of
Deuteronomy
12:15 people who are ***p*** can join in the
15:22 are polluted or ***p***, just as you
2 Kings
2:21 has said: I have ***p*** this water. It
2 Chronicles
29:18 We have ***p*** the LORD's entire
30:18 people who hadn't ***p*** themselves and so
34:8 after he had ***p*** the land and the
Ezra
6:20 the Levites had ***p*** themselves; all
Nehemiah
12:30 and the Levites ***p*** themselves, they
13:9 that the rooms be ***p***, and I put back
13:30 So I ***p*** them of everything foreign and
Psalms
12:6 refined in an oven, ***p*** seven times over!
Isaiah
66:20 an offering in ***p*** containers to the
Ezekiel
43:22 just as they ***p*** the altar with
Daniel
11:35 might be refined, ***p***, and cleansed
Acts
15:9 us and them, but ***p*** their deepest
Revelation
1:15 that has been ***p*** in a furnace, and
3:18 me that has been ***p*** by fire so that

PURIFY

Exodus
29:33 that was used to ***p*** them, to ordain
Leviticus
16:19 this way, he will ***p*** it and make it
Numbers
31:19 a corpse must ***p*** themselves on the
31:20 You must also ***p*** every garment, and
2 Chronicles
29:15 and went in to ***p*** the LORD's temple
29:16 went in to ***p*** the inner portion
Nehemiah
13:22 the Levites to ***p*** themselves and to
Job
1:5 send word and ***p*** his children.
9:30 myself with snow, ***p*** my hands with

Psalms
26:2 me to the test! ***P*** my mind and my
51:2 clean of my guilt; ***p*** me from my sin!
51:7 ***P*** me with hyssop and I will be clean;
Isaiah
52:11 of that place; ***p*** yourselves,
66:17 became holy and ***p*** themselves,
Ezekiel
39:14 in order to ***p*** it. They will
39:16 is Hamonah). So they will ***p*** the land.
43:20 around. So you will ***p*** it and purge it.
43:22 The priests will ***p*** the altar just as
43:26 altar in order to ***p*** it and to
45:18 the herd, and you will ***p*** the sanctuary.
Daniel
12:10 Many will ***p***, cleanse, and refine
Malachi
3:3 silver. He will ***p*** the Levites and
Matthew
15:2 don't ritually ***p*** their hands by
Luke
11:38 didn't ritually ***p*** his hands by
John
11:55 to Jerusalem to ***p*** themselves
James
4:8 you sinners. ***P*** your hearts, you

PURPLE

Exodus
25:4 blue, ***p***, and deep red yarns; fine
Numbers
4:13 the altar and spread a ***p*** cloth on it.
Judges
8:26 pendants, and the ***p*** robes worn by the
2 Chronicles
2:7 as well as in ***p***, crimson, and
Esther
1:6 curtains and ***p*** hangings were
Proverbs
31:22 fine linen and ***p*** are her clothing.
Song of Songs
3:10 cushions, royal ***p***; its interior
7:5 braided in royal ***p***—a king is bound
Jeremiah
10:9 in blue and ***p***, all of them
Lamentations
4:5 wore the finest ***p*** clothes now cling
Ezekiel
27:7 made of blue and ***p*** cloth from the
27:16 traded turquoise, ***p*** cloth, colorful
27:24 you, garments of ***p*** and brocade, and
Daniel
5:29 be dressed in a ***p*** robe, have a gold
Mark
15:17 him up in a ***p*** robe and twisted
Luke
16:19 himself in ***p*** and fine linen,
John
19:2 his head, and dressed him in a ***p*** robe.
Acts
16:14 a dealer in ***p*** cloth. As she
Revelation
17:4 The woman wore ***p*** and scarlet clothing,
18:12 fine linen, ***p***, silk, and
18:16 wore fine linen, ***p***, and scarlet, who

PURPOSE

Exodus
21:13 killing wasn't on ***p*** but an accident
21:14 another person on ***p***, you should
Nehemiah
8:4 made for this ***p***. And standing
Job
10:3 and cause the ***p*** of sinners to
Proverbs
1:2 Their ***p*** is to teach wisdom and
16:4 everything for a ***p***, even the wicked
19:21 mind, but the LORD's ***p*** will succeed.
22:21 Their ***p*** is to teach you true, reliable
Ezekiel
20:12 the LORD, have set them apart for my ***p***.
Acts
13:36 served God's ***p*** in his own
26:16 to you for this ***p***: to appoint you
28:23 for this ***p***, many people came
Romans
8:28 who are called according to his ***p***.
9:11 shown that God's ***p*** would continue
1 Corinthians
1:10 with the same mind and the same ***p***.
2 Corinthians
7:11 what fear, what ***p***, such concern,
Galatians
2:21 the Law, then Christ died for no ***p***.
Ephesians
3:10 God's ***p*** is now to show the rulers and
4:12 His ***p*** was to equip God's people for the
Philippians
3:12 grabbed hold of me for just this ***p***.
2 Timothy
1:9 based on his own ***p*** and grace that he
3:10 conduct, ***p***, faithfulness,
Hebrews
6:17 promise that his ***p*** doesn't change,
1 John
3:8 appeared for this ***p***: to destroy the
Revelation
10:7 God's mysterious ***p*** will be

PURSUE → PURSUE RIGHTEOUSNESS

Genesis
35:5 so that they didn't ***p*** Jacob's sons.
Exodus
15:9 enemy said, "I'll ***p***, I'll overtake,
1 Samuel
27:4 fled to Gath, he didn't ***p*** him anymore.
2 Samuel
2:28 They didn't ***p*** Israel anymore,
20:7 of Jerusalem to ***p*** Bichri's son
1 Chronicles
16:11 ***P*** the LORD and his strength; seek his
Job
13:25 to tremble, or will you ***p*** dry straw?
19:22 Why do you ***p*** me like God does, always
19:28 say, "How will we ***p*** him so that the
Psalms
23:6 love will ***p*** me all the days
71:11 abandoned him! ***P*** him! Grab him
83:15 ***p*** them with your storm, terrify them
105:4 ***P*** the LORD and his strength; seek his
Proverbs
11:19 but those who ***p*** evil, toward
19:7 them. When they ***p*** them with words,

Jeremiah
2:25 with foreign gods, and I must ***p*** them."
9:16 heard. I will ***p*** them with the
13:10 hearts and ***p*** other gods,
29:18 I will ***p*** them with the sword, famine,
48:2 will be silenced; the sword will ***p*** you.
Ezekiel
5:12 winds, letting loose a sword to ***p*** them.
35:6 and blood will ***p*** you. Because you
Hosea
5:11 Ephraim chose to ***p*** worthless things.
8:3 from the good; the enemy will ***p*** him.
Nahum
1:8 her place and ***p*** his enemies into
Zephaniah
1:6 don't seek the LORD and don't ***p*** him.
Zechariah
1:6 the prophets, ***p*** your ancestors?
1 Corinthians
14:1 ***P*** love, and use your ambition to try to
Philippians
3:12 perfected, but I ***p*** it, so that I may
3:14 The goal I ***p*** is the prize of God's
1 Thessalonians
5:15 wrong, but always ***p*** the good for each
Hebrews
12:14 ***P*** the goal of peace along with

PURSUE RIGHTEOUSNESS

Dt 16:20; Prv 15:9; 21:21; 1Ti 6:11; 2Ti 2:22

Qq

QUEEN

1 Kings

2:19 set up for the ***q*** mother. She sat
10:1 When the ***q*** of Sheba heard reports about
11:19 for marriage, a sister of ***Q*** Tahpenes.
15:13 the position of ***q*** mother because

2 Kings

10:13 king's sons and the ***q*** mother's sons."
24:15 also exiled the ***q*** mother, the

2 Chronicles

9:1 When the ***q*** of Sheba heard reports about
9:12 Solomon gave the ***q*** of Sheba
15:16 the position of ***q*** mother because

Nehemiah

2:6 With the ***q*** sitting beside him, the king asked me

Esther

1:9 At the same time, ***Q*** Vashti held a feast
2:4 Vashti's place as ***q***." The king liked
2:22 he reported it to ***Q*** Esther. She spoke
5:2 the king noticed ***Q*** Esther standing
7:1 came in for the banquet with ***Q*** Esther,
7:5 Ahasuerus said to ***Q*** Esther, "Who is
8:1 Ahasuerus gave ***Q*** Esther what Haman
8:7 Ahasuerus said to ***Q*** Esther and to
9:12 the king said to ***Q*** Esther in the
9:31 the Jew and ***Q*** Esther had made.

Psalms

45:9 jewels; the ***q*** stands at your

Isaiah

47:5 will no longer call you ***Q*** of Kingdoms.

Jeremiah

7:18 cakes for the ***q*** of heaven. And to
13:18 the king and the ***q*** mother: Come down
29:2 Jeconiah, the ***q*** mother, the court
44:17 incense to the ***q*** of heaven and
44:18 incense to the ***q*** of heaven and
44:19 incense to the ***q*** of heaven and
44:25 incense to the ***q*** of heaven and

Lamentations

1:1 a widow. Once a ***q*** over provinces,

Ezekiel

26:17 have perished, ***q*** of the sea, city

Daniel

5:10 his princes, the ***q*** entered the

Matthew

12:42 The ***q*** of the South will be raised up by

Luke

11:31 The ***q*** of the South will rise up at the

Acts

8:27 is the title given to the Ethiopian ***q***.

Revelation

18:7 I sit like a ***q***! I'm not a widow.

QUESTION

1 Samuel

10:22 asked another ***q*** of the LORD: "Has
17:29 David replied. "It was just a ***q***!"
20:12 that I will ***q*** my father by this

2 Samuel

16:10 then who is to ***q***, 'Why are you
20:18 ago: 'Ask your ***q*** at Abel, and that

2 Kings

1:3 you are going to ***q*** Ekron's god Baal-
3:11 so we could ***q*** the LORD through
8:8 the man of God. ***Q*** the LORD through
22:18 who sent you to ***q*** the LORD: This is

2 Chronicles

34:26 who sent you to ***q*** the LORD: This is

Job

40:8 Would you ***q*** my justice, deem me guilty
42:4 speak; I will ***q*** you and you will

Psalms

35:11 stand up. They ***q*** me about things I

Jeremiah

38:27 Jeremiah to ***q*** him. And he

Daniel

3:16 We don't need to answer your ***q***.

Matthew

21:24 I have a ***q*** for you. If you

Mark

11:29 them, "I have a ***q*** for you. Give me

Luke

6:9 Here's a ***q*** for you: Is it
20:3 replied, "I have a ***q*** for you. Tell me:
22:68 And if I ask you a ***q***, you won't answer

John

8:7 They continued to ***q*** him, so he stood up
8:41 ancestry isn't in ***q***! The only Father

Acts

2:36 know beyond ***q*** that God has made
15:2 to set this ***q*** before the

2 Corinthians

8:23 If there is any ***q*** about Titus, he is my

1 Timothy

3:16 Without ***q***, the mystery of godliness is

Hebrews

7:7 Without ***q***, the less important person

QUESTIONED

1 Samuel

14:37 So Saul ***q*** God: "Should I go after the
22:10 Ahimelech ***q*** the LORD for David, and
22:15 the first time I ***q*** God for him? Of
23:2 David ***q*** the LORD, "Should I go and
23:4 So David ***q*** the LORD again, and the LORD
28:6 When Saul ***q*** the LORD, the LORD didn't

2 Samuel
2:1 time later, David ***q*** the LORD, "Should
1 Kings
1:6 he never ***q*** why Adonijah did
2 Kings
8:6 The king ***q*** the woman, and she told him
Esther
3:4 after day they ***q*** him, but he paid
Psalms
42:3 people constantly ***q*** me, "Where's your
Jeremiah
37:17 sent for him and ***q*** Jeremiah secretly
Mark
1:27 was shaken and ***q*** among themselves,
15:2 Pilate ***q*** him, "Are you the king of the
Luke
23:9 Herod ***q*** Jesus at length, but Jesus
23:14 people. I have ***q*** him in your
John
9:17 of the Pharisees ***q*** the man who had
9:26 They ***q*** him, "What did he do to you?
18:19 the chief priest ***q*** Jesus about his
Acts
9:21 was baffled. They ***q*** each other,
22:24 that Paul be ***q*** under the whip so

QUIET

Genesis
25:27 Jacob became a ***q*** man who stayed at
34:5 decided to keep ***q*** until they got
Deuteronomy
27:9 to all Israel: ***Q*** down and listen,
Judges
16:2 gate. They kept ***q*** all night long,
2 Samuel
13:20 with you? Keep ***q*** about it for now,
1 Kings
19:12 the fire, there was a sound. Thin. ***Q***.
2 Kings
7:9 but we're keeping ***q*** about it. If we
18:36 the people kept ***q*** and didn't answer
1 Chronicles
4:40 was spacious, ***q***, and peaceful;
22:9 Israel peace and ***q*** during his reign.
Nehemiah
8:11 saying, "Be ***q***, for this day is
Job
3:26 I had no ease, ***q***, or rest, and
6:24 me and I'll be ***q***; inform me how
7:11 But I won't keep ***q***; I will speak in
13:5 were completely ***q***; that would be
13:13 Be ***q*** and I will speak, come what may
13:19 with me, for then I would be ***q*** and die.
30:27 are never ***q***; days of
31:34 me; I was ***q*** and didn't
33:31 Job; hear me; be ***q***, and I will speak.
33:33 must hear me; be ***q***, and I will teach
34:29 if he remains ***q***, who can condemn;
Psalms
32:3 When I kept ***q***, my bones wore out; I
35:22 LORD. Don't keep ***q*** about it. Please
39:2 I was completely ***q***, silent. I kept
50:3 he won't keep ***q***. A devouring fire
50:21 and I've kept ***q***. You thought I
83:1 silent! Don't be ***q*** or sit still, God,
109:1 psalm.] God of my praise, don't keep ***q***
Proverbs
11:12 lacks sense; a sensible person keeps ***q***.
17:1 a dry crust with ***q*** than a house full
17:28 Fools who keep ***q*** are deemed wise;
Isaiah
36:21 But they kept ***q*** and didn't answer him
41:1 Be ***q*** before me, coastlands. Let the
Jeremiah
31:9 will lead them by ***q*** streams and on
49:23 the raging sea, which can't become ***q***.
Ezekiel
38:11 come against a ***q*** people who all
Daniel
10:15 my face to the ground and kept ***q***.
Zechariah
1:11 The whole earth is peaceful and ***q***."
Matthew
20:31 told them to be ***q***. But they shouted
Mark
10:48 telling him to be ***q***, but he shouted
Luke
18:39 telling him to be ***q***, but he shouted
Acts
12:17 with his hand to ***q*** them down, then
15:12 assembly fell ***q*** as they listened
21:40 When they were ***q***, he addressed
22:2 in Aramaic, they became even more ***q***.
Romans
16:25 secret that was kept ***q*** for a long time.
1 Corinthians
14:28 they should keep ***q*** in the meeting.
14:30 down, the first one should be ***q***.
14:34 women should be ***q*** during the
1 Timothy
2:2 we can live a ***q*** and peaceful life
2:12 Instead, she should be a ***q*** listener.

Rr

RABBAH

Deuteronomy
3:11 Ammonite town of ***R***? By standard
Joshua
13:25 the Ammonites as far as Aroer near ***R***.
15:60 and ***R***. In total: two
2 Samuel
11:1 the city of ***R***. But David
12:26 the Ammonites at ***R*** and captured the
12:27 fought against ***R*** and captured the
12:29 marched to ***R***, fought against
17:27 who was from ***R*** of the Ammonites;
1 Chronicles
20:1 and besieged ***R***. David stayed in
Jeremiah
49:2 alarm against ***R***, the capital city
49:3 you daughters of ***R***; put on funeral
Ezekiel
21:20 to come: "To ***R*** of the Ammonites"
25:5 I'll make ***R*** into pastureland for camels
Amos
1:14 at the wall of ***R***; the fire will

RABBI

Matthew
23:7 the markets and to be addressed as '***R***.'
26:25 not me, is it, ***R***?" Jesus answered,
Mark
9:5 saying to Jesus, "***R***, it's good that
11:21 said to Jesus, "***R***, look how the fig
14:45 said to Jesus, "***R***!" Then he kissed
John
1:49 replied, "***R***, you are God's
3:2 and said to him, "***R***, we know that you
4:31 spoke to Jesus, saying, "***R***, eat."
6:25 they asked him, "***R***, when did you get
9:2 disciples asked, "***R***, who sinned so
11:8 replied, "***R***, the Jewish

RACHEL

Genesis
29:20 Jacob worked for ***R*** for seven years, but
30:2 was angry at ***R*** and said, "Do you
31:34 Now ***R*** had taken the divine images and
Ruth
4:11 household be like ***R*** and like Leah,
Jeremiah
31:15 and wailing. It's ***R*** crying for her
Matthew
2:18 much grieving. ***R*** weeping for her

RAGE

Genesis
27:44 while until your brother's ***r*** subsides,
49:7 is violent, their ***r***; it is
Numbers
25:11 turned back my ***r*** toward the
Deuteronomy
9:19 massive anger and ***r*** the LORD had for
19:6 the killer out of ***r*** and—especially if
32:27 their enemies' ***r*** concerned me;
1 Samuel
20:34 the table in a ***r***. He didn't eat
2 Kings
19:27 and come in, and how you ***r*** against me.
19:28 And because you ***r*** against me and
23:26 from the great ***r*** that burned
2 Chronicles
25:10 against Judah, and they left in a ***r***.
Esther
5:9 suddenly felt great ***r*** toward Mordecai.
Job
3:17 There the wicked ***r*** no more; there the
18:4 tear yourself in ***r***—will earth be
Psalms
37:8 anger and leave ***r*** behind! Don't get
38:3 because of your ***r***; there's no
46:3 waters roar and ***r***, when the
76:10 Even human ***r*** will turn to your praise
79:5 How long will you ***r***, LORD? Forever?
90:7 with fear on account of your ***r***.
124:3 whole with their ***r*** burning against
Proverbs
6:34 makes a man ***r***; he'll show no
19:3 but their hearts ***r*** against the LORD.
Isaiah
9:19 scorched by the ***r*** of the LORD of
13:9 coming with cruel ***r*** and burning
13:13 of the ***r*** of the LORD of
14:6 struck peoples in ***r*** with ceaseless
28:21 Valley he will ***r*** to do his deed
37:28 and come in, and how you ***r*** against me.
37:29 Because you ***r*** against me and because
41:11 All who ***r*** against you will be shamed
42:13 God will stir up ***r***. God will shout,
54:8 In an outburst of ***r***, I hid my face
54:9 I promise not to ***r*** against you or
57:17 I struck them; in ***r*** I withdrew from
60:10 you. Though in my ***r*** I struck you
64:9 Don't ***r*** so fiercely, LORD; don't hold
Jeremiah
6:11 with the LORD's ***r*** and am tired of
10:10 quakes; the nations can't endure his ***r***.
21:5 and strong arm in fierce anger and ***r***.
32:37 fierce anger and ***r***. I will bring
Lamentations
2:3 In his burning ***r***, he cut off each of
2:6 in his fierce ***r***, he scorned both
Ezekiel
16:42 my anger, and my ***r*** has turned away
22:20 in my anger and ***r*** I will collect

22:22 the LORD, have poured out my ***r*** on you.
Daniel
2:12 in a furious ***r*** and ordered that
3:13 In a violent ***r*** Nebuchadnezzar ordered
3:19 was filled with ***r***, and his face
11:11 king, in a bitter ***r***, will come out to
11:30 in fear. He will ***r*** against a holy
11:44 and in a great ***r*** he will set off
Hosea
7:16 because of the ***r*** of their tongues;
Jonah
1:11 us?" (The sea was continuing to ***r***.)
1:13 the sea continued to ***r*** against them.
Acts
4:25 did the Gentiles ***r***, and the peoples
26:11 slander God. My ***r*** bordered on the
Colossians
3:8 such as anger, ***r***, malice, slander,
Revelation
12:12 to you with great ***r***, for he knows

RAHAB
Joshua
6:17 the LORD. Only ***R*** the prostitute is
Job
9:13 the helpers of ***R*** bow beneath him.
26:12 the Sea; split ***R*** with his
Psalms
87:4 I count ***R*** and Babel among those who
89:10 you who crushed ***R*** like a dead body;
Isaiah
30:7 Therefore, I call her ***R*** Who Sits Still.
51:9 one who crushed ***R***, who pierced the
Matthew
1:5 whose mother was ***R***. Boaz was the
Hebrews
11:31 By faith ***R*** the prostitute wasn't killed
James
2:25 same way, wasn't ***R*** the prostitute

RAIN
Genesis
2:5 hadn't yet sent ***r*** on the earth and
7:4 now I will send ***r*** on the earth for
Exodus
16:4 to make bread ***r*** down from the sky
Deuteronomy
11:14 he will provide ***r*** for your land at
1 Kings
17:1 neither dew nor ***r*** these years
18:1 Ahab. I will then send ***r*** on the earth.
2 Chronicles
6:26 holds back its ***r*** because Israel
Job
28:26 a decree for the ***r***, a path for
Psalms
11:6 God will ***r*** fiery coals and sulfur on
147:8 clouds; God makes ***r*** for the earth;
Jeremiah
14:22 nations make it ***r***? Can the sky by
Zechariah
14:17 forces, upon them no ***r*** will fall.
Matthew
5:45 good and sends ***r*** on both the
7:25 The ***r*** fell, the floods came, and the
Revelation
11:6 sky so that no ***r*** will fall for as

RAISE
Genesis
39:15 When he heard me ***r*** my voice and scream,
Exodus
9:22 said to Moses, "***R*** your hand toward
10:21 said to Moses, "***R*** your hand toward
Leviticus
25:16 You will ***r*** the price if there are more
Numbers
6:20 the priest will ***r*** them as an
16:37 priest's son, to ***r*** the censers from
18:19 the Israelites ***r*** to the LORD I
Deuteronomy
18:15 your God will ***r*** up a prophet like
18:18 I'll ***r*** up a prophet for them from among
Judges
2:18 So the LORD would ***r*** up leaders for
1 Samuel
2:10 to his king and ***r*** high the strength
18:17 battles." I won't ***r*** my hand against
2 Samuel
1:14 weren't afraid to ***r*** your hand and
7:12 ancestors, I will ***r*** up your
1 Kings
14:14 the LORD will ***r*** up a king over
20:25 Then ***r*** another army like the one that
2 Kings
4:28 sir? Didn't I say, 'Don't ***r*** my hopes'?"
19:22 whom did you ***r*** your voice and
1 Chronicles
15:16 as singers to ***r*** their voices
17:11 to die, I will ***r*** up a descendant
Job
15:25 for they ***r*** a fist against God and try
21:12 They ***r*** drum and lyre, rejoice at the
Psalms
71:20 earth, you will ***r*** me up one more
93:3 their voices; the floods ***r*** up a roar!
95:1 the LORD! Let's ***r*** a joyful shout to
119:28 of grief. Now ***r*** me up according
121:1 song.] I ***r*** my eyes toward
123:1 song.] I ***r*** my eyes to you
Isaiah
5:26 God will ***r*** a signal to a nation from
7:21 day, one will ***r*** a young cow and
10:26 of Oreb. He will ***r*** a rod over the
11:12 God will ***r*** a signal for the nations and
13:2 a bare mountain ***r*** a signal; cry
14:13 stars, I will ***r*** my throne. I'll
15:5 Horonaim, they will ***r*** a piercing cry.
19:16 of heavenly forces will ***r*** against them.
24:14 They ***r*** their voice; they sing with joy;
29:3 and I will ***r*** up siegeworks
30:32 The LORD will ***r*** his arm and fight
37:23 whom did you ***r*** your voice and
40:9 messenger Zion! ***R*** your voice and
49:6 my servant, to ***r*** up the tribes of
49:22 Look, I will ***r*** my hand to the
58:1 don't hold back; ***r*** your voice like a
62:10 away the stones! ***R*** up a signal for
Jeremiah
23:5 LORD, when I will ***r*** up a righteous

30:9 king whom I will ***r*** up for them from
31:7 leading nation. ***R*** your voices with
33:15 that time, I will ***r*** up a righteous
50:15 ***R*** a victory shout against her on every
Ezekiel
17:24 the tall tree and ***r*** up the lowly
19:1 You, ***r*** a lament for Israel's princes
21:22 proclaim war and ***r*** the alarm, to
27:32 lamentation they ***r*** a lament for you;
37:12 graves! I will ***r*** you up from your
37:13 your graves and ***r*** you up from your
47:22 with you and ***r*** families among
Daniel
2:44 of heaven will ***r*** up an everlasting
Hosea
6:2 third day he will ***r*** us up, so that we
11:7 the Most High, he will not ***r*** them up.
Amos
5:2 on her land, with no one to ***r*** her up.
6:14 Indeed, I will ***r*** up against you a
9:11 that day I will ***r*** up the meeting
Jonah
4:10 which you didn't ***r***; it grew in a
Micah
5:5 then we will ***r*** up against him
Habakkuk
3:9 You ***r*** up your empty bow, uttering
Zechariah
1:21 that no one could ***r*** his head. The
2:9 I am about to ***r*** my hand against
Matthew
3:9 God is able to ***r*** up Abraham's
10:8 Heal the sick, ***r*** the dead, cleanse
Mark
12:19 the widow and ***r*** up children for
Luke
3:8 God is able to ***r*** up Abraham's
20:28 the widow and ***r*** up children for
21:28 up straight and ***r*** your heads
John
2:19 temple and in three days I'll ***r*** it up."
2:20 and you will ***r*** it up in three
6:39 me, but I will ***r*** it up at the last
Acts
3:22 your God will ***r*** up from your own
7:37 God will ***r*** up for you a
15:14 first place, to ***r*** up from them a
1 Corinthians
6:14 the Lord and will ***r*** us through his
15:15 when he didn't ***r*** him if it's the
2 Corinthians
4:14 Jesus will also ***r*** us with Jesus,
Ephesians
6:4 to anger, but ***r*** them with
Hebrews
11:19 God could even ***r*** him from the
1 Peter
5:6 so that he may ***r*** you up in the

RAISED

Genesis
28:12 dreamed and saw a ***r*** staircase, its
39:18 but when I ***r*** my voice and screamed, he
Exodus
7:20 commanded. He ***r*** the shepherd's
9:23 Then Moses ***r*** his shepherd's rod toward
10:22 So Moses ***r*** his hand toward the sky, and
15:12 You ***r*** your strong hand; earth swallowed
29:27 thigh that was ***r*** for the gift
35:22 objects. Everyone ***r*** an uplifted
40:18 inserted its bars, and ***r*** up its posts.
Leviticus
9:22 Aaron then ***r*** his hands toward the
Numbers
14:1 entire community ***r*** their voice and
18:24 which they have ***r*** to the LORD as a
20:11 Then Moses ***r*** his hand and struck the
23:7 Then he ***r*** his voice and made his
23:18 Then Balaam ***r*** his voice and made his
24:3 He ***r*** his voice and made his address:
Joshua
7:26 They ***r*** over him a great pile of stones
8:29 gate. Then they ***r*** over it a great
Judges
2:4 Israelites, they ***r*** their voices and
2:16 Then the LORD ***r*** up leaders to rescue
3:15 LORD. So the LORD ***r*** up a deliverer
8:28 and no longer ***r*** its head. The
9:7 Mount Gerizim. He ***r*** his voice and
2 Samuel
12:3 he had bought. He ***r*** that lamb, and it
18:18 Absalom had ***r*** a large pillar
23:1 of a man ***r*** high, a man
23:8 of the Three. He ***r*** his spear against
1 Kings
11:14 So the LORD ***r*** up an opponent for
11:20 that Genubath was ***r*** in Pharaoh's
11:23 God ***r*** up another opponent for Solomon:
16:2 I ***r*** you up from the dust and made you a
Job
4:4 Your words have ***r*** up the falling;
16:12 into pieces; he ***r*** me up for his
31:18 from my youth I ***r*** the orphan as a
Psalms
74:5 looked like axes ***r*** against a thicket
89:13 is strong; your strong hand is ***r*** high!
89:19 a strong man. I ***r*** up someone
93:3 the floods have ***r*** up—the floods
106:26 So God ***r*** his hand against them, making
148:14 God ***r*** the strength of his people
Proverbs
30:13 their eyes; how their eyebrows are ***r***!
Song of Songs
2:4 of wine; his banner ***r*** over me is love.
Isaiah
1:2 children; I ***r*** them, and they
9:11 So the LORD ***r*** up their foes against
18:3 when a signal is ***r*** on the mountains,
23:4 birth; I never ***r*** young men or
23:13 animals: they ***r*** up their siege
40:4 valley will be ***r*** up, and every
49:21 sent off. So who ***r*** these? I was left
51:18 the hand among all the children she ***r***.
62:8 has promised with ***r*** hand and strong
Jeremiah
29:15 say, the LORD has ***r*** up prophets for
Lamentations
2:17 over you; he ***r*** up your
2:22 nurtured, that I ***r*** myself, my enemy
Ezekiel
10:19 winged creatures ***r*** their wings and
11:22 winged creatures ***r*** their wings. The

31:4 it; the deep ***r*** it up, because
41:8 chambers. Each ***r*** section was ten
Daniel
4:34 Nebuchadnezzar, ***r*** my eyes to
7:5 a bear. It was ***r*** on one side. It
7:9 thrones were ***r*** up. The ancient
12:7 forever as he ***r*** both hands to
Amos
2:11 I ***r*** up some of your children to be
Micah
2:4 a taunt will be ***r*** against you;
Matthew
11:5 who were dead are ***r*** up. The poor have
11:23 honored by being ***r*** up to heaven? No,
12:42 the South will be ***r*** up by God at the
14:2 He's been ***r*** from the dead.
16:21 to be killed and ***r*** on the third day.
17:9 the Human One is ***r*** from the dead."
17:23 But he will be ***r*** on the third
20:19 But he will be ***r*** on the third day."
26:32 But after I'm ***r*** up, I'll go before you
27:52 many holy people who had died were ***r***.
27:64 He's been ***r*** from the dead.'
28:6 because he's been ***r*** from the dead,
28:7 He's been ***r*** from the dead.
Mark
1:31 by the hand, and ***r*** her up. The fever
2:12 Jesus ***r*** him up, and right away he
6:14 Baptist has been ***r*** from the dead,
6:16 whom I beheaded, has been ***r*** to life."
14:28 But after I'm ***r*** up, I will go before
16:6 He has been ***r***. He isn't here.
16:14 those who saw him after he was ***r*** up.
Luke
1:69 He has ***r*** up a mighty savior for us in
4:16 where he had been ***r***. On the Sabbath
6:20 Jesus ***r*** his eyes to his disciples and
7:22 who were dead are ***r*** up. And good news
9:7 that John had been ***r*** from the dead,
9:22 be killed and be ***r*** on the third day."
10:15 honored by being ***r*** up to heaven? No,
17:13 they ***r*** their voices and said, "Jesus,
20:37 that the dead are ***r***—in the passage ab
24:6 but has been ***r***. Remember what he
John
2:22 After he was ***r*** from the dead, his
12:1 whom Jesus had ***r*** from the dead.
12:9 Lazarus, whom he had ***r*** from the dead.
12:17 of the tomb and ***r*** him from the dead
21:14 disciples after he was ***r*** from the dead.
Acts
2:14 apostles. He ***r*** his voice and
2:24 God ***r*** him up! God freed him from
2:32 This Jesus, God ***r*** up. We are all
3:7 right hand and ***r*** him up. At once
3:15 very one whom God ***r*** from the dead.
3:26 After God ***r*** his servant, he sent him to
4:10 crucified but whom God ***r*** from the dead.
5:30 of our ancestors ***r*** Jesus from the
9:41 her his hand and ***r*** her up. Then he
10:40 but God ***r*** him up on the third day and
10:41 with him after God ***r*** him from the dead.
12:7 him, the angel ***r*** him up and said,
13:22 removed him, he ***r*** up David to be
13:30 But God ***r*** him from the dead
13:34 God ***r*** Jesus from the dead, never again
13:37 one whom God has ***r*** up didn't
22:3 in Cilicia but ***r*** in this city.
27:40 the rudders. They ***r*** the foresail to
Romans
4:24 in the one who ***r*** Jesus our Lord
6:4 as Christ was ***r*** from the dead
6:9 Christ has been ***r*** from the dead and
7:4 the one who was ***r*** from the dead so
8:11 of the one who ***r*** Jesus from the
8:34 more, who was ***r***, and who also is
10:9 faith that God ***r*** him from the
1 Corinthians
6:14 God has ***r*** the Lord and will raise us
15:12 Christ has been ***r*** from the dead,
15:52 the dead will be ***r*** with bodies that
2 Corinthians
4:14 that the one who ***r*** the Lord Jesus
5:15 the one who died for them and was ***r***.
10:5 defense that is ***r*** up to oppose the
Galatians
1:1 God the Father who ***r*** him from the dead;
Ephesians
1:20 Christ when God ***r*** him from the dead
2:6 And God ***r*** us up and seated us in the
Colossians
2:12 baptism and ***r*** with him through
3:1 if you were ***r*** with Christ, look
1 Thessalonians
1:10 who is the one he ***r*** from the dead and
2 Timothy
2:8 Christ, who was ***r*** from the dead and
Hebrews
7:26 from sinners, and ***r*** high above the
1 Peter
1:21 to the God who ***r*** him from the dead
Revelation
10:3 out, the seven thunders ***r*** their voices.
10:5 and on the land ***r*** his right hand to

RAM

Genesis
22:13 and saw a single ***r*** caught by its
Daniel
8:3 I suddenly saw a ***r*** with two horns

RAMAH

Jeremiah
31:15 voice is heard in ***R***, weeping and
Matthew
2:18 was heard in ***R***, weeping and much

RAMOTH-GILEAD

1 Kings
22:3 don't you, that ***R*** is ours? But we
22:29 Judah's King Jehoshaphat attacked ***R***.

RAMS

1 Samuel
15:22 attention is better than fat from ***r***,
Psalms
114:4 leaped away like ***r***; the hills leaped
Micah
6:7 with thousands of ***r***, with many

RAN
Genesis
39:12 his garment in her hands and ***r*** outside.
1 Kings
18:46 his clothes and ***r*** in front of Ahab
Matthew
28:8 from the tomb and ***r*** to tell his
Luke
24:12 But Peter ***r*** to the tomb. When he bent

RANSOM
Exodus
13:13 donkey you should ***r*** with a sheep.
13:15 of the womb. But I ***r*** my oldest sons.'
34:20 offspring you may ***r*** with a sheep. Or
Numbers
35:31 may not accept a ***r*** for the life of a
35:32 may not accept a ***r*** for someone who
Job
5:20 In famine he will ***r*** you from death; in
6:23 hand of my enemy? ***R*** me from the grip
33:24 down to the pit; I have found a ***r***."
Psalms
49:7 It can't pay a life's ***r***-price to God.
Proverbs
13:8 Wealth can ***r*** a person's life, but the
21:18 The wicked are a ***r*** for the righteous;
Isaiah
43:3 Egypt as your ***r***, Cush and Seba in
Hosea
13:14 Will I ***r*** them from the power of the
Romans
3:24 because of a ***r*** that was paid by

RAVENS
1 Kings
17:4 also ordered the ***r*** to provide for
17:6 The ***r*** brought bread and meat in the
Psalms
147:9 even to the baby ***r*** when they cry out.
Proverbs
30:17 a mother, may the ***r*** of the river
Isaiah
34:11 it; owls and ***r*** will live there.
Luke
12:24 Consider the ***r***: they neither plant nor

RAVINE
Numbers
13:23 the Cluster ***r***, cut down from
21:12 they marched and camped in the Zered ***r***.
34:5 to the Egypt ***r***. Its limit will
Deuteronomy
1:24 as the Cluster ***r***. They walked all
2:13 Cross the Zered ***r***." So we crossed
2:24 Cross the Arnon ***r***. I have handed
21:4 the cow down to a ***r*** with a flowing
Joshua
13:16 the middle of the ***r***, and the whole
15:7 was south of the ***r***. The border
17:9 South of the ***r*** are those cities
19:11 and touched the ***r*** that is opposite
1 Samuel
30:9 came to the Besor ***r***, where some
Amos
6:14 you from Lebo-hamath to the desert ***r***.

REACH
Exodus
4:4 said to Moses, "***R*** out and grab the
Deuteronomy
9:1 with fortifications that ***r*** to the sky.
Judges
19:13 servant, "let's ***r*** Gibeah or Ramah
2 Samuel
15:5 respect, he would ***r*** his hand out,
1 Kings
7:15 a cord of eighteen feet to ***r*** around it.
Esther
1:17 queen did will ***r*** all women, making
Job
7:6 shuttle; they ***r*** their end without
34:28 of the poor to ***r*** him, he hears the
Psalms
19:4 their words ***r*** the ends of the
32:6 a great flood of water won't ***r*** them.
59:1 put me out of ***r*** from those who
79:11 groaning ***r*** you. With your
88:2 let my prayer ***r*** you! Turn your ear to
102:1 LORD, hear my prayer! Let my cry ***r*** you!
110:2 mighty scepter ***r*** far from Zion!
119:169 Let my cry ***r*** you, LORD; help me
Proverbs
2:19 will never again ***r*** the ways of the
Isaiah
11:8 toddlers will ***r*** right over the
28:15 through, it won't ***r*** us; for we have
30:4 in Zoan, and their messengers ***r*** Hanes,
40:28 His understanding is beyond human ***r***,
49:6 my salvation may ***r*** to the end of the
59:9 beyond our ***r***. We expect light,
Jeremiah
17:8 whose roots ***r*** down to the
51:25 earth! I will ***r*** out against you;
Ezekiel
31:10 its branches to ***r*** up among the
Jonah
1:13 The men rowed to ***r*** dry land, but they
Zechariah
14:5 mountains will ***r*** to Azal. You will
Luke
5:19 but they couldn't ***r*** him because of the
8:19 were unable to ***r*** him because of
Acts
17:27 him, perhaps even ***r*** out to him and
20:16 was hurrying to ***r*** Jerusalem, if
27:12 they might ***r*** Phoenix in Crete
Ephesians
4:13 until we all ***r*** the unity of faith and
Philippians
3:11 I may perhaps ***r*** the goal of the
3:13 behind me and ***r*** out for the
Revelation
12:14 of the snake's ***r***—for a time

READ
Exodus
17:14 on the scroll and ***r*** it to Joshua: I
24:7 scroll and ***r*** it out loud for
Deuteronomy
17:19 him, and he must ***r*** in it every day
31:11 selects, you must ***r*** this Instruction
Joshua
8:34 Afterward, Joshua ***r*** aloud all the words

8:35 Joshua failed to ***r*** aloud in the
2 Kings
5:6 Israel's king. It ***r***, "Along with this
5:7 king of Israel ***r*** the letter, he
10:5 back to Jehu that ***r***, "We are your
19:14 messengers and ***r*** them. Then he
22:8 the scroll over to Shaphan, who ***r*** it.
22:10 a scroll," and he ***r*** it out loud
22:16 in the scroll that Judah's king has ***r***!
23:2 There the king ***r*** out loud all the
2 Chronicles
21:12 to Jehoram that ***r***, "This is what
30:6 and Judah, which ***r***: People of
34:18 a scroll," and he ***r*** it out loud
34:24 that they have ***r*** to Judah's king.
34:30 There the king ***r*** out loud all the
Ezra
4:18 to us has been ***r*** in translation
4:23 letter was ***r*** before Rehum and
Nehemiah
8:3 Water Gate, he ***r*** it aloud, from
8:18 He ***r*** from God's Instruction scroll
9:3 their place and ***r*** the Instruction
13:1 Moses was being ***r*** to the people,
Esther
3:14 all peoples to ***r***. The people were
8:13 its peoples to ***r***. The Jews were to
Isaiah
29:11 it to one who can ***r***, saying, "Read
34:16 LORD's scroll and ***r***: Not one of these
37:14 messengers and ***r*** them. Then he
Jeremiah
29:29 priest Zephaniah ***r*** this letter to
36:6 of fasting, and ***r*** the LORD's words
36:8 him: he ***r*** all the LORD's
36:10 Then Baruch ***r*** Jeremiah's words from the
51:61 see to it that you ***r*** all these words.
Daniel
5:7 Anyone who can ***r*** this writing and
5:8 but they couldn't ***r*** the writing or
Habakkuk
2:2 a tablet so that a runner can ***r*** it.
Matthew
12:3 Haven't you ***r*** what David did
12:5 Or haven't you ***r*** in the Law that on the
19:4 Haven't you ***r*** that at the
21:16 Haven't you ever ***r***, From the mouths
21:42 Haven't you ever ***r*** in the
22:31 dead, haven't you ***r*** what God told you,
27:37 against him. It ***r***, "This is Jesus,
Mark
2:25 Haven't you ever ***r*** what David did
12:10 Haven't you ***r*** this scripture, The stone
12:26 dead, haven't you ***r*** in the scroll
Luke
4:16 as he normally did and stood up to ***r***.
6:3 Haven't you ***r*** what David and
23:38 against him. It ***r*** "This is the king
John
19:19 on the cross. It ***r*** "Jesus the
19:20 Many of the Jews ***r*** this sign, for the
Acts
13:27 the prophets that are ***r*** every Sabbath.
15:21 long time, and is ***r*** aloud every
15:31 The people ***r*** it, delighted with its
23:34 After he ***r*** the letter, he asked Paul
2 Corinthians
1:13 what you can ***r*** and also
3:2 on our hearts, known and ***r*** by everyone.
3:14 old covenant is ***r***. The veil is not
3:15 whenever Moses is ***r***, a veil lies over
Ephesians
3:4 (when you ***r*** this, you'll understand my
Colossians
4:16 letter has been ***r*** to you publicly,
1 Thessalonians
5:27 have this letter ***r*** aloud to all the
Revelation
1:3 to it being ***r***, and keep what is

REALIZED

Genesis
16:4 But when she ***r*** that she was
16:5 but when she ***r*** she was pregnant,
28:8 Esau ***r*** that his father Isaac considered
30:1 When Rachel ***r*** that she could bear Jacob
30:9 When Leah ***r*** that she had stopped
38:14 Timnah, since she ***r*** that although
39:13 When she ***r*** that he had left his garment
41:7 Pharaoh woke up and ***r*** it was a dream.
50:15 Joseph's brothers ***r*** that their father
Exodus
2:14 afraid when he ***r***: They obviously
Judges
6:22 Then Gideon ***r*** that it had been the
13:21 and Manoah then ***r*** that it had been
16:18 When Delilah ***r*** that he had told her his
18:26 way. When Micah ***r*** that they were
1 Samuel
3:8 me?" Then Eli ***r*** that it was the
20:33 him, and Jonathan ***r*** that his father
2 Samuel
10:6 the Ammonites ***r*** that they had
12:19 whispering, he ***r*** the child had
1 Kings
3:15 Solomon awoke and ***r*** it was a dream.
22:33 chariot officers ***r*** that he wasn't
1 Chronicles
19:6 the Ammonites ***r*** that they had
2 Chronicles
13:14 and suddenly ***r*** that they were
18:32 chariot officers ***r*** that he wasn't
32:2 When Hezekiah ***r*** that Sennacherib also
Nehemiah
6:12 Then I ***r*** that God hadn't sent him at
Ecclesiastes
1:14 under the sun, I ***r*** that everything
1:17 and folly, I ***r*** that this too was
2:11 to achieve, I ***r*** that it was
2:14 But I also ***r*** that the same
Jeremiah
31:19 I regretted it; I ***r*** what I had done,
Ezekiel
10:20 River, and I ***r*** that they were
16:8 passed by you, I ***r*** that you were
19:5 When she ***r*** that she waited in vain, her
Daniel
5:21 his body until he ***r*** that the Most
Matthew
17:13 the disciples ***r*** he was telling

REALIZED [cont.]

Luke
1:22 to them. They ***r*** he had seen a
John
4:53 Then the father ***r*** that this was the
6:22 side of the lake ***r*** that only one
Acts
16:19 Her owners ***r*** that their hope for making
19:34 but when they ***r*** he was a Jew, they all
22:29 alarmed when he ***r*** he had bound a
Hebrews
11:33 about justice, ***r*** promises, shut

REASON

Genesis
2:24 This is the ***r*** that a man leaves his
22:14 sees. That is the ***r*** people today say,
Exodus
5:21 You've given them a ***r*** to kill us."
9:16 standing for this ***r***: in order to show
Leviticus
26:16 plant seed for no ***r*** because your
26:20 be spent for no ***r***: your land will
26:43 for no other ***r*** than the fact
Numbers
21:14 For this ***r*** the scroll of the LORD's
Deuteronomy
1:36 children for this ***r***: he was
23:14 to you. For this ***r*** your camp must be
Joshua
5:4 This is the ***r*** Joshua did so: All the
1 Samuel
19:5 person by killing David for no ***r***?"
1 Kings
14:14 For this ***r*** the LORD will raise up a
2 Kings
4:27 has hidden the ***r*** from me and
2 Chronicles
20:27 had given them ***r*** to rejoice over
Esther
1:17 This is the ***r***: News of what the queen
3:8 There's no good ***r*** for the king to
Job
2:3 you incited me to ruin him for no ***r***."
9:17 and multiplies my wounds for no ***r***?
13:14 For what ***r*** will I take my flesh in my
22:6 family for no ***r***; stripped the
22:10 For this ***r***, snares surround you;
Psalms
7:4 with evil or oppressed a foe for no ***r***—
35:7 net for me for no ***r***, they dug a pit
35:19 who hate me for no ***r*** wink at my demise.
38:19 who hate me for no ***r*** seem countless.
56:7 them for any ***r***! In wrath bring
69:4 hate me for no ***r***. My treacherous
73:13 pure for no good ***r***; I've washed my
89:42 gave all his enemies ***r*** to celebrate.
89:47 Have you created humans for no good ***r***?
109:3 surround me; they attack me for no ***r***.
119:86 but people harass me for no ***r***. Help me!
Proverbs
3:30 anyone without ***r***, when they
24:28 neighbor without ***r***; don't deceive
Isaiah
42:6 you for a good ***r***. I will grasp
57:19 I will create ***r*** for praise: utter
Lamentations
3:52 like a bird, relentlessly, for no ***r***.
Ezekiel
22:4 years! For this ***r*** I've given you
33:19 right, it is for that ***r*** they will live.
42:6 For this ***r***, the top story
44:12 Israel. For that ***r*** I made a solemn
Daniel
4:34 to heaven. My ***r*** returned to me,
4:36 at that moment my ***r*** returned to me.
Matthew
19:3 to divorce his wife for just any ***r***?"
Mark
12:24 Isn't this the ***r*** you are wrong,
Luke
6:7 looking for a ***r*** to bring charges
John
5:18 For this ***r*** the Jewish leaders wanted
6:65 said, "For this ***r*** I said to you
8:6 they wanted a ***r*** to bring an
12:27 for this is the ***r*** I have come to
15:25 their Law, They hated me without a ***r***.
18:37 world for this ***r***: to testify to
Acts
10:29 For this ***r***, when you sent for me, I
18:14 I would have ***r*** to accept your
28:18 couldn't find any ***r*** for putting me to
28:19 because I had any ***r*** to bring charges
Romans
4:2 would have had a ***r*** to brag, but not
13:6 for the same ***r***, because the
1 Corinthians
9:16 gospel, I have no ***r*** to brag, since
13:11 like a child, ***r*** like a child,
16:10 that he has no ***r*** to be afraid
2 Corinthians
2:9 This is another ***r*** why I wrote you. I
6:3 give anyone any ***r*** to be offended
8:24 your love and the ***r*** we are so proud
Ephesians
1:15 all God's people, this is the ***r*** that
6:22 sent him for this ***r***—so that you will
Philippians
1:7 I have good ***r*** to think this way about
3:4 I have good ***r*** to have this kind
1 Timothy
5:14 give the enemy any ***r*** to slander us.
2 Timothy
2:9 This is the ***r*** I'm suffering to the
Titus
1:5 The ***r*** I left you behind in Crete was to
Philemon
1:15 Maybe this is the ***r*** that Onesimus was
James
5:16 For this ***r***, confess your sins to each
1 Peter
4:6 this is the ***r*** the good news was
Revelation
7:15 This is the ***r*** they are before God's

REBEKAH

Genesis
24:29 ***R*** had a brother named Laban, and Laban
25:21 prayer, and his wife ***R*** became pregnant.
49:31 and his wife ***R*** are buried, and

REBEL

Exodus
23:21 as he says. Don't **r** against him. He
Numbers
14:9 Only don't **r** against the LORD and don't
Joshua
22:18 the LORD. If you **r** against the LORD
1 Samuel
12:14 obey him, and not **r** against the
12:15 obey the LORD and **r** against the
2 Kings
18:20 trusting in that you now **r** against me?
Nehemiah
6:6 Jews intend to **r**. This is why you
Job
24:13 They **r** against light, don't acknowledge
34:6 is incurable, even though I didn't **r**."
Psalms
68:18 from those who **r** against the LORD
106:43 determined to **r**, and so they were
Isaiah
1:5 Why continue to **r**? Everyone's head
1:20 if you refuse and **r**, you will be
36:5 you trusting that you now **r** against me?
48:8 were; you were known as a **r** from birth.
50:5 my ear; I didn't **r**; I didn't turn my
Ezekiel
20:38 you those who **r** and transgress
Micah
2:4 me; he gives away our fields to a **r**."
1 Peter
4:15 a murderer or thief or evildoer or **r**.

REBELLED

Numbers
20:24 because you **r** against my
27:14 you, you **r** against my
2 Samuel
20:21 highlands, has **r** against King
1 Kings
13:21 says this: You **r** against the
13:26 man of God who **r** against the
2 Kings
1:1 After Ahab died, Moab **r** against Israel
3:5 died, Moab's king **r** against Israel's
8:20 rule Edom **r** against Judah's
8:22 to this day. Libnah **r** at the same time.
18:7 he tried. He **r** against Assyria's
24:1 changed his mind and **r** against him.
24:20 Now Zedekiah **r** against the
2 Chronicles
13:6 David's son, who **r** against his
21:8 rule, Edom **r** against Judah's
21:10 this day. Libnah **r** against Jehoram's
36:13 Moreover, he **r** against King
Nehemiah
9:26 were disobedient, **r** against you, and
Psalms
5:10 sins because they've **r** against you.
78:40 How often they **r** against God in the
106:7 you have. So they **r** by the sea—at
Isaiah
43:27 and your officials **r** against me.
53:12 and pleaded on behalf of those who **r**.
63:10 But they **r**, and made God's holy spirit
66:24 of the people who **r** against me, where
Jeremiah
2:8 me; the leaders **r** against me; the
2:29 me? You have all **r** against me,
3:13 how you have **r** against the LORD
4:17 because she has **r** against me,
52:3 Zedekiah **r** against the king
Lamentations
3:42 who did wrong; we **r**. But you, God,
Ezekiel
5:6 But she **r** against my case laws and my
17:15 But the prince **r** against him and sent
20:8 But they **r** against me and refused to
20:21 But the children **r** against me. They
39:23 Because they **r** against me, I hid
Daniel
9:5 on ourselves and **r**, ignoring your
9:9 our God, because we **r** against him.
Hosea
7:13 because they have **r** against me. I
13:16 because she has **r** against her God;
Hebrews
3:16 Who was it who **r** when they heard his

REBELLION

Exodus
34:7 kind of sin and **r**, yet by no means
Joshua
22:16 altar as an act of **r** against the LORD.
24:19 He won't forgive your **r** and your sins.
1 Samuel
15:23 because **r** is as bad as the sin of
24:11 of wrongdoing or **r**. I haven't
1 Kings
12:19 has been in **r** against the house
2 Chronicles
10:19 has been in **r** against David's
Ezra
4:19 There has been much **r** and revolt there.
Job
8:4 them into the power of their **r**.
14:17 My **r** is sealed in a bag; you would
17:2 with me, and my eye looks on their **r**.
34:37 He adds **r** to his sin; mocks us openly
Proverbs
17:11 people seek only **r**; a cruel
Isaiah
24:20 like a hut; its **r** weighs heavy upon
53:8 struck dead because of my people's **r**.
57:4 you children of **r**, offspring of
Jeremiah
3:22 I will heal your **r**. "Here we are; we
28:16 you have incited **r** against the LORD."
29:32 for he incited **r** against me.
33:8 them for all of their guilt and **r**.
Daniel
8:12 In an act of **r**, another force will
8:13 the desolating **r**, and the handing
9:24 to complete the **r**, to end sins, to
Matthew
23:28 inside you are full of pretense and **r**.
2 Thessalonians
2:3 come unless the **r** comes first and
Hebrews
3:8 they did in the **r**, on the day when
3:15 stubborn hearts as they did in the **r**.
1 John
3:4 commits an act of **r**, and sin is

REBELLIOUS

Leviticus
16:16 because of their **r** sins, as well as
16:21 and all their **r** sins, as well as
Deuteronomy
9:24 You've been **r** toward the LORD from the
21:18 stubborn and **r** child, who
31:27 I know how **r** and hardheaded
32:15 got fat, then **r**. It was you who
1 Samuel
20:30 of a stubborn, **r** woman!" he said.
Ezra
4:12 rebuilding the **r** and wicked city;
4:15 that this is a **r** city, harmful to
Psalms
66:7 So don't let the **r** exalt themselves.
68:6 but the **r** dwell in a
78:8 ancestors: a **r**, stubborn
Proverbs
14:14 **R** hearts receive satisfaction from
24:21 Don't associate with those who are **r**.
Isaiah
30:1 Doom to you, **r** children, says the LORD,
30:9 These are **r** people, lying children,
43:25 wipes out your **r** behavior for my
65:2 all day to a **r** people walking in
Jeremiah
3:14 Return, **r** children, declares the LORD,
3:22 Return, **r** children, and I will heal
5:23 have stubborn and **r** hearts; they turn
6:28 headstrong and **r**. They live to
8:5 does this people, **r** Jerusalem,
31:22 hem and haw, my **r** daughter? The
48:45 including the leader of this **r** nation.
49:4 is exhausted, you **r** daughter. You
Ezekiel
2:3 a traitorous and **r** people. They and
17:12 Say now to the **r** household: Don't you
Titus
1:10 are many who are **r** people,

REBELS

Numbers
17:10 as a sign to the **r** so that their
20:10 Listen, you **r**! Should we
Deuteronomy
9:7 you have been **r** against the LORD.
Proverbs
28:2 When a land **r**, there are many leaders;
Isaiah
1:28 God will shatter **r** and sinners
46:8 take courage; take it to heart, you **r**.
53:12 numbered with **r**, though he
Ezekiel
2:5 a household of **r**, they will know
3:9 because they are a household of **r**.
12:2 in a household of **r**. They have eyes
44:6 Speak to the **r**, to the house of
Hosea
9:15 no more; all their officials are **r**.
Mark
3:26 If Satan **r** against himself and is
15:7 up with the **r** who had committed

REBUILD

Joshua
6:26 who starts to **r** this city of
Ezra
3:2 kin, started to **r** the altar of
5:2 son, began to **r** God's house in
6:7 of the Jews **r** this house of God
Nehemiah
2:5 my family's graves so that I may **r** it."
2:17 fire! Come, let's **r** the wall of
4:10 rubble. We are unable to **r** the wall!"
Job
3:14 advisors, who **r** ruins for
Psalms
28:5 God will tear them down and never **r**!
51:18 by your favor. **R** Jerusalem's walls.
69:35 Zion and will **r** Judah's cities so
102:16 the LORD will **r** Zion; he will be
Isaiah
9:10 fallen, but let's **r** with stones.
58:12 They will **r** ancient ruins on your
60:10 Foreigners will **r** your walls, and their
61:4 They will **r** the ancient ruins; they
Jeremiah
33:7 and I will **r** them as they were
Daniel
9:25 to restore and **r** Jerusalem until a
Amos
9:11 ruins, and I will **r** it like a long
9:14 Israel; they will **r** the ruined cities
Zephaniah
1:13 They will **r** houses, but not
Haggai
1:2 come, the time to **r** the LORD's house."
1:8 bring back wood. **R** the temple so
Malachi
1:4 down, but we will **r** the ruins"; but
Matthew
26:61 God's temple and **r** it in three
27:40 the temple and **r** it in three days,
Mark
15:29 the temple and **r** it in three days,
Acts
15:16 and I will **r** David's fallen
Galatians
2:18 If I **r** the very things that I tore

REBUILT

Deuteronomy
13:16 of rubble forever. It must not be **r**.
Judges
18:28 Valley. They **r** the city and
21:23 their territory, **r** the cities, and
1 Kings
16:34 Hiel from Bethel **r** Jericho. He set
2 Kings
14:22 He **r** Elath, restoring it to Judah after
15:35 at them. Jotham **r** the Upper Gate of
21:3 He **r** the shrines that his father
2 Chronicles
8:2 Solomon next **r** the cities Huram had
26:2 He **r** Eloth, restoring it to Judah after
27:3 Jotham **r** the Upper Gate of the LORD's
32:5 vigorously **r** all the broken
33:3 He **r** the shrines that his father
33:14 this, Manasseh **r** the outer wall of
Ezra
4:13 if this city is **r** and the walls
5:15 God's house be **r** on its original
6:3 sacrifices be **r** and let its

Nehemiah
3:14 the Dung Gate. He ***r*** it and set up its
6:1 heard that I had ***r*** the wall and that
7:4 within it, and no houses had been ***r***.
Job
12:14 down, it can't be ***r***; if he ties a
Isaiah
25:2 into a city no more, never to be ***r***.
44:26 They will be ***r***, and I will
Jeremiah
30:18 city will be ***r*** on its ruins and
31:38 the city will be ***r*** for the LORD from
Ezekiel
26:14 you will never be ***r***. I, the LORD,
36:10 cities will be inhabited, the ruins ***r***.
Daniel
9:25 the city will be ***r*** with a courtyard

REBUKE
Leviticus
19:17 in your heart. ***R*** your fellow
2 Samuel
22:16 at the LORD's ***r***, at the angry
Job
22:4 Does he ***r*** you for your piety, bring you
32:12 you offered no ***r*** to Job, no answer
Psalms
18:15 laid bare at your ***r***, LORD, at the
68:30 ***R*** the wild animals of the marshland,
76:6 At your ***r***, Jacob's God, both chariot
80:16 They die at the ***r*** coming from you.
104:7 But at your ***r*** they ran away; they fled
119:21 You ***r*** the arrogant, accursed people who
Proverbs
17:10 A ***r*** goes deeper to an understanding
24:25 for those who ***r*** them. A rich
Isaiah
17:13 But God will ***r*** them, and they
50:2 to save? With my ***r*** I dry up the sea
51:20 LORD's wrath, with the ***r*** of your God.
54:9 not to rage against you or ***r*** you.
66:15 in hot anger, to ***r*** with fiery flames.
Habakkuk
1:12 Rock, you established him as a ***r***.
Jude
1:9 Instead, he said, "The Lord ***r*** you!"

RECEIVE → RECEIVE MERCY
Exodus
25:2 offerings for me. ***R*** my gift offerings
25:3 that you should ***r*** from them: gold,
Numbers
3:47 you will ***r*** five shekels each. You will
18:26 to them: When you ***r*** from the
Deuteronomy
19:14 that you will ***r*** there, you must
24:10 enter their house to ***r*** the collateral.
Ruth
2:12 deed. May you ***r*** a rich reward
1 Samuel
25:8 same. So please ***r*** these young men
2 Kings
22:7 the money they ***r***, because they are
Ezra
4:14 Since we ***r*** our salary from the palace,
Job
2:10 woman. Will we ***r*** good from God but
3:12 Why did knees ***r*** me and breasts let me
20:18 They won't ***r*** the reward for their
22:22 ***R*** instruction from his mouth; put his
27:13 that the ruthless ***r*** from the Almighty.
35:7 him? Or what does he ***r*** from your hand?
Psalms
73:24 advice; later you will ***r*** me with glory.
106:46 allowed them to ***r*** compassion from
Proverbs
3:35 wise gain respect, but fools ***r*** shame.
11:24 give generously ***r*** more, but those
12:21 but the wicked ***r*** their fill of
13:4 desires but ***r*** nothing; the
14:14 Rebellious hearts ***r*** satisfaction from
21:10 their neighbors ***r*** no mercy from
21:13 themselves call out but ***r*** no answer.
Isaiah
35:2 They will ***r*** the glory of
Jeremiah
37:21 and that he ***r*** a loaf of bread
Ezekiel
47:13 of Israel. Joseph will ***r*** two portions.
47:22 They will ***r*** an inheritance
Daniel
2:6 meaning, you'll ***r*** generous gifts
7:18 Most High will ***r*** the kingship.
11:34 fall, they will ***r*** a little help,
12:13 and will stand to ***r*** your reward at
Hosea
14:2 wickedness; and ***r*** the good. Instead
Matthew
7:2 You'll ***r*** the same judgment you give.
10:40 Those who ***r*** you are also receiving me,
12:39 but it won't ***r*** any sign except
13:12 who have will ***r*** more and they
13:20 the word and immediately ***r*** it joyfully.
16:4 But it won't ***r*** any sign except
19:29 of my name will ***r*** one hundred times
20:10 they would ***r*** more. But each of
21:22 faith, you will ***r*** whatever you pray
25:41 me, you who will ***r*** terrible things.
Mark
4:16 word, they immediately ***r*** it joyfully.
10:30 will ***r*** one hundred times as much now in
10:38 cup I drink or ***r*** the baptism I
11:24 that you will ***r*** it, and it will
Luke
6:38 determine the portion you ***r*** in return."
8:13 are those who ***r*** the word joyfully
8:18 who have will ***r*** more, but as for
11:9 Ask and you will ***r***. Seek and you
14:10 Instead, when you ***r*** an invitation, go
18:42 said to him, "***R*** your sight! Your
19:12 a distant land to ***r*** his kingdom and
John
3:11 seen, but you don't ***r*** our testimony.
3:27 No one can ***r*** anything unless
5:43 and you don't ***r*** me. If others
5:44 believe when you ***r*** praise from each
7:39 in him would soon ***r*** the Spirit, but
12:48 me and doesn't ***r*** my words will be
14:17 the world can't ***r*** because it
16:24 Ask and you will ***r***, so that your joy
20:22 on them and said, "***R*** the Holy Spirit.

RECEIVE [cont.]

Acts
1:8 Rather, you will ***r*** power when the Holy
2:38 Then you will ***r*** the gift of the
3:5 expecting to ***r*** something from
5:8 and your husband ***r*** this price for
8:15 believers would ***r*** the Holy Spirit.
13:46 are unworthy to ***r*** eternal life, we
19:2 them, "Did you ***r*** the Holy Spirit
20:35 is more blessed to give than to ***r***.'"
22:13 Brother Saul, ***r*** your sight!' he
26:7 tribes hope to ***r*** as they earnestly
26:18 Satan to God, and ***r*** forgiveness of
Romans
2:28 who will ***r*** praise from God,
5:17 those who ***r*** the multiplied
8:15 You didn't ***r*** a spirit of slavery to
13:3 right, and you will ***r*** its approval.
1 Corinthians
3:8 but each one will ***r*** their own reward
4:7 that you didn't ***r***? And if you
9:25 but we do it to ***r*** a crown that
13:3 have love, I ***r*** no benefit
2 Corinthians
1:5 is because we ***r*** so much comfort
6:1 you not to ***r*** the grace of God
11:4 or if you ***r*** a different
Galatians
1:12 I didn't ***r*** it or learn it from a human.
3:2 from you: Did you ***r*** the Spirit by
3:14 and that we would ***r*** the promise of
Colossians
3:24 that you will ***r*** an inheritance as
3:25 evildoers will ***r*** their reward for
2 Thessalonians
1:10 on that day to ***r*** honor from his
Hebrews
7:5 of Levi who ***r*** the office of
9:15 are called might ***r*** the promise of
10:26 to sin after we ***r*** the knowledge of
11:39 people didn't ***r*** what was
James
1:7 that they will ***r*** anything from the
1:12 true. They will ***r*** the life God has
1 Peter
1:5 so that you can ***r*** the salvation he
5:4 appears, you will ***r*** an unfading crown
2 Peter
1:11 this way you will ***r*** a rich welcome
2:13 way, they will ***r*** payment for their
1 John
3:22 We ***r*** whatever we ask from him because
5:9 If we ***r*** human testimony, God's
2 John
1:8 worked for but instead ***r*** a full reward.
Revelation
4:11 Lord and God, to ***r*** glory and honor
5:12 Lamb to ***r*** power, wealth,
14:9 its image, and ***r*** a mark on their
14:11 and those who ***r*** the mark of its
17:12 But they will ***r*** royal authority
18:4 sins and don't ***r*** any of her
22:17 one who wishes ***r*** life-giving water

RECEIVE MERCY

2Ch 30:9; Prv 28:13; Mt 5:7; Ro 11:31; Heb 4:16

RECEIVED

2 Chronicles
9:13 Solomon ***r*** an annual income of six
Jeremiah
7:1 Jeremiah ***r*** the LORD's word
44:1 Jeremiah ***r*** the LORD's word for the
Matthew
10:8 out demons. You ***r*** without having to
13:11 they haven't ***r*** the secrets of
19:11 those who have ***r*** the ability to
20:9 afternoon came, each one ***r*** a denarion.
25:18 servant who had ***r*** the one valuable
28:18 to them, "I've ***r*** all authority in
Luke
1:4 of the instruction you have ***r***.
6:24 you have already ***r*** your comfort.
John
1:16 we have all ***r*** grace upon grace;
10:18 it up again. I ***r*** this commandment
19:30 When he had ***r*** the sour wine, Jesus
Acts
1:17 was one of us and ***r*** a share of this
7:53 You ***r*** the Law given by angels, but you
8:17 on them, and they ***r*** the Holy Spirit.
22:5 about me. I ***r*** letters from
28:21 We haven't ***r*** any letters about
Romans
1:5 him we have ***r*** God's grace and
4:11 He ***r*** the sign of circumcision as a seal
8:15 fear, but you ***r*** a Spirit that
11:31 mercy that you ***r***, so now they can
1 Corinthians
2:12 We haven't ***r*** the world's spirit but
4:7 And if you ***r*** it, then why are
11:23 I ***r*** a tradition from the Lord, which I
15:1 which you also ***r*** and in which you
15:3 what I also ***r***: Christ died for
2 Corinthians
1:4 comfort that we ourselves ***r*** from God.
4:1 given that we ***r*** this ministry in
7:7 comfort he had ***r*** from you. He told
11:4 the one you had ***r***, or a different
11:24 I ***r*** the "forty lashes minus one" from
12:7 revelations I've ***r*** so that I
Galatians
1:9 from what you ***r***, they should be
Ephesians
1:11 We have also ***r*** an inheritance in
4:1 worthy of the call you ***r*** from God.
Philippians
4:9 you learned, ***r***, heard, or saw in
4:18 because I ***r*** the gifts that
2 Thessalonians
3:6 with the traditions that you ***r*** from us.
1 Timothy
4:4 nothing that is ***r*** with thanksgiving
Hebrews
1:4 angels, that he ***r*** a more important
2:2 of disobedience ***r*** an appropriate
7:6 related to them, ***r*** a tenth of
8:6 now, Jesus has ***r*** a superior
11:11 faith even Sarah ***r*** the ability to
11:35 Women ***r*** back their dead by
James
2:25 when she ***r*** the messengers as
1 Peter
1:10 grace that you've ***r***, searched and

2:10 Once you hadn't ***r*** mercy, but now
4:10 each person has ***r***, as good managers

2 Peter
1:1 To those who ***r*** a faith equal to
1:17 He ***r*** honor and glory from God the

1 John
2:27 that you ***r*** from him remains
5:15 know that we have ***r*** what we asked

2 John
1:10 should neither be ***r*** nor welcomed into

Revelation
2:28 just as I ***r*** authority from my Father. I
3:3 remember what you ***r*** and heard. Hold on to it
17:12 who haven't yet ***r*** royal power. But
20:4 image, who hadn't ***r*** the mark on their

RECOGNIZE

Genesis
27:23 Isaac didn't ***r*** him because his arms
38:25 See if you ***r*** whose seal, cord,
42:8 his brothers, but they didn't ***r*** him.

Job
2:12 and didn't ***r*** him, they wept

Isaiah
43:19 up; don't you ***r*** it? I'm making a
61:9 who see them will ***r*** that they are a
63:16 nd Israel doesn't ***r*** us. You, LORD,

Micah
6:5 might learn to ***r*** the righteous

Matthew
13:14 see but never ***r*** what you are
16:3 you are unable to ***r*** the signs that

Luke
19:44 you didn't ***r*** the time of your

John
1:10 but the world didn't ***r*** the light.
1:26 stands among you, whom you don't ***r***.
10:38 you can know and ***r*** that the Father

Acts
13:27 leaders didn't ***r*** Jesus. By
28:26 see but never ***r*** what you are

1 Corinthians
14:37 then let them ***r*** that what I'm
14:38 someone doesn't ***r*** this, they aren't

2 Corinthians
5:16 point on we won't ***r*** people by human

2 Thessalonians
1:8 those who don't ***r*** God and don't

James
5:20 ***r*** that whoever brings a sinner back

1 John
3:1 the world didn't ***r*** him, it doesn't
4:6 This is how we ***r*** the Spirit of

RECOGNIZED

Genesis
15:6 and the LORD ***r*** Abram's high
28:6 from there. He ***r*** that, when Isaac
37:33 He ***r*** it and said, "It's my son's robe!
38:26 Judah ***r*** them and said, "She's more
42:7 his brothers, he ***r*** them, but he
42:8 Joseph ***r*** his brothers, but they didn't

Judges
18:3 house, they ***r*** the accent of the

1 Samuel
26:17 Saul ***r*** David's voice and said, "David,

Matthew
14:35 in that place ***r*** him, they sent

Mark
1:34 the demons speak, because they ***r*** him.
2:8 Jesus immediately ***r*** what they were
5:30 moment, Jesus ***r*** that power had
6:33 them leaving and ***r*** them, so they ran
6:54 came ashore. People immediately ***r*** Jesus
12:15 Since Jesus ***r*** their deceit, he said to

Luke
4:41 because they ***r*** that he was the
5:22 Jesus ***r*** what they were discussing and
20:23 Since Jesus ***r*** their deception, he said
22:49 those around him ***r*** what was about to
24:19 and words, he was ***r*** by God and all
24:31 opened and they ***r*** him, but he

John
4:10 If you ***r*** God's gift and

Acts
3:10 They ***r*** him as the same one who used to
4:13 They also ***r*** that they had
7:10 gave Joseph were ***r*** by Pharaoh, king
12:14 with joy when she ***r*** Peter's voice

1 Corinthians
14:7 tune from the harp or the lyre be ***r***?
14:38 doesn't recognize this, they aren't ***r***.

Galatians
2:9 equals when they ***r*** the grace that

Ephesians
3:15 in heaven or on earth is ***r*** by him.

RECONCILIATION

Exodus
29:36 offering for ***r***. You should
29:37 the ritual of ***r*** for the altar and
30:10 a ritual of ***r*** on its horns with
32:30 I can arrange ***r*** on account of

Leviticus
1:4 be accepted for you, to make ***r*** for you.
4:20 priest will make ***r*** for them, and
23:27 is the Day of ***R***. It will be a
25:9 throughout your land on the Day of ***R***.

Numbers
5:8 to the ram of ***r*** by which the
6:11 He will seek ***r*** for the person on
8:12 in order to seek ***r*** for the Levites.
15:25 priest will seek ***r*** for the entire
16:46 and seek ***r*** for them. Indeed,
25:13 God and sought ***r*** for the
28:22 offering to seek ***r*** for yourselves.
29:5 offering to seek ***r*** for yourselves.
31:50 seek ***r*** for ourselves

1 Chronicles
6:49 place, to make ***r*** for Israel, just

Ezekiel
45:15 to make ***r*** for them. This is
45:17 sacrifice to make ***r*** on behalf of the

Acts
27:9 since the Day of ***R*** had already

2 Corinthians
5:18 and who gave us the ministry of ***r***.
5:19 has trusted us with this message of ***r***.

RECORDED

Exodus
38:21 that were ***r*** at Moses'

RECORDED [cont.]

Numbers
1:20 service was individually ***r*** by name.
3:43 one month old, ***r*** by name according
33:2 Moses ***r*** the points of departure for
1 Chronicles
4:41 whose names were ***r***, however, came in
24:6 levitical scribe, ***r*** their names in
Ezra
8:20 the Levites. These were all ***r*** by name.
8:34 weighed, and the total weight was ***r***.
Nehemiah
12:22 the priests were ***r*** as heads of
12:23 of families were ***r*** in the official
Psalms
69:28 Let them not be ***r*** along with the
Ezekiel
13:9 council, or ***r*** in the house of
John
20:30 signs that aren't ***r*** in this scroll.
21:25 all of them were ***r***, I imagine the

RED

Genesis
25:25 first came out ***r*** all over, clothed
Exodus
25:4 purple, and deep ***r*** yarns; fine
Numbers
19:2 must bring you a ***r*** cow without
Deuteronomy
14:13 the ***r*** kite, the black kite, and any
Joshua
2:18 you tie this ***r*** woven cord in the
2:21 Then she tied the ***r*** cord in the
2 Kings
3:22 a distance. It looked as ***r*** as blood.
Zechariah
1:8 a man riding on a ***r*** horse, which was
Matthew
16:2 weather because the sky is bright ***r***.'
Acts
7:36 in Egypt at the ***R*** Sea and for forty
Hebrews
11:29 they crossed the ***R*** Sea as if they
Revelation
6:4 horse, fiery ***r***. Its rider was
6:12 and the entire moon turned ***r*** as blood.
9:17 that were fiery ***r***, dark blue, and
12:3 was a great fiery ***r*** dragon, with

REDEEM

Numbers
18:15 However, you will ***r*** the oldest males
Ruth
3:13 morning, if he'll ***r*** you—good, let him
4:4 If you will ***r*** it, redeem it;
4:6 Then I can't ***r*** it for myself,
2 Kings
12:4 people pay to ***r*** persons according
Psalms
69:18 Come close to me! ***R*** me! Save me because
119:134 ***R*** me from the people who oppress me so
119:154 Argue my case and ***r*** me. Make me live
130:8 the one who will ***r*** Israel from all
Isaiah
50:2 hand too small to ***r*** you? Don't I have
Jeremiah
15:21 wicked; I will ***r*** you from the
Lamentations
3:58 Plead my desperate case; ***r*** my life.
Hosea
7:13 me. I would ***r*** them, but they
13:14 Heb Sheol Will I ***r*** them from death's
Micah
4:10 the LORD will ***r*** you from the
Luke
24:21 the one who would ***r*** Israel. All these
Galatians
4:5 was so he could ***r*** those under the

REDEEMED

Deuteronomy
13:5 out of Egypt, who ***r*** you from the
2 Samuel
7:23 on earth that God ***r*** as his own
1 Chronicles
17:21 earth, that God ***r*** as his own
Nehemiah
1:10 whom you have ***r*** by your great
Psalms
74:2 ago, that you ***r*** to be the tribe
77:15 mighty arm you ***r*** your people;
106:10 powers; he ***r*** them from the
107:2 those who are ***r*** by the LORD say,
107:4 Some of the ***r*** had wandered into the
Isaiah
1:27 Zion will be ***r*** by justice, and those
29:22 of Jacob, who ***r*** Abraham: Jacob
35:9 be there; only the ***r*** will walk on it.
43:1 fear, for I have ***r*** you; I have
44:22 Return to me, because I have ***r*** you.
44:23 it. The LORD has ***r*** Jacob, and will
48:20 The LORD has ***r*** his servant
51:10 you make the ***r*** a road to cross
52:3 and you will be ***r*** without money.
52:9 his people and has ***r*** Jerusalem.
62:12 The Holy People, ***R*** By the LORD. And
63:9 and mercy God ***r*** them, lifting and
Micah
6:4 land of Egypt; I ***r*** you from the
Galatians
3:13 Christ ***r*** us from the curse of the Law
3:14 He ***r*** us so that the blessing of Abraham

REDEEMER

Ruth
3:9 your servant, because you are a ***r***."
3:12 true that I'm a ***r***, there's a
4:1 Just then, the ***r*** about whom Boaz
4:3 Boaz said to the ***r***, "Naomi, who has
4:6 But the ***r*** replied, "Then I can't redeem
4:8 Then the ***r*** said to Boaz, "Buy it for
4:14 you without a ***r***. May his name be
Job
19:25 I know that my ***r*** is alive and
Psalms
19:14 to you, LORD, my rock and my ***r***.
78:35 rock, that the Most High was their ***r***.
Proverbs
23:11 for their ***r*** is strong. He will bring
Isaiah
41:14 LORD. The holy one of Israel is your ***r***.
43:14 The LORD your ***r***, the holy one of

44:6 Israel's king and ***r***, the LORD of
44:24 The LORD your ***r*** who formed you in the
47:4 Our ***r*** has spoken; the LORD of heavenly
48:17 The LORD your ***r***, the holy one of
49:7 The LORD, ***r*** of Israel and its holy one,
49:26 and the mighty one of Jacob is your ***r***.
54:8 consoled you, says your ***r***, the LORD.
59:20 A ***r*** will come to Zion and to those in
60:16 savior and your ***r***, the mighty one
63:16 since long ago is that of our ***r***.
Jeremiah
50:34 Yet their ***r*** is strong; the LORD of

REED → REED SEA
Exodus
2:3 she took a ***r*** basket and sealed
1 Kings
14:15 it shakes like a ***r*** in water. He will
2 Kings
18:21 but a broken ***r***! It will stab the
Job
8:11 a marsh? Does a ***r*** flourish without
40:21 under the cover of ***r*** and marsh.
Isaiah
9:14 palm branch and ***r*** from Israel in
18:2 by sea, ***r*** vessels on the
19:15 palm branch nor ***r*** will be able to
36:6 but a broken ***r***! It will stab the
42:3 break a bruised ***r***; he won't
58:5 one's head like a ***r*** and of lying down

REED SEA
Ex 10:19; 13:18; 15:4, 22; 23:31; Nm 14:25; 21:4; 33:10, 11; Dt 1:40; 2:1; 11:4; Josh 2:10; 4:23; 24:6; Jdg 11:16; 1Ki 9:26; Neh 9:9; Ps 106:7; 106:9, 22; 136:13, 15; Jer 49:21

REFUGE → REFUGE CITIES, REFUGE CITY
Numbers
35:12 you a place of ***r*** from the close
35:15 cities will be ***r*** for Israelites,
Joshua
20:3 places will be a ***r*** for you from any
20:4 a place of ***r*** for the killer to
Ruth
2:12 whose wings you've come to seek ***r***."
2 Samuel
22:3 my rock—I take ***r*** in him!—he's my
22:31 is a shield for all who take ***r*** in him.
Job
24:8 rains, with no ***r***, huddled against
Psalms
2:12 But all who take ***r*** in the LORD are
5:11 let all who take ***r*** in you celebrate.
7:1 I take ***r*** in you, LORD, my
11:1 I have taken ***r*** in the LORD. So
14:6 who suffer, but the LORD is their ***r***.
16:1 me, God, because I take ***r*** in you.
17:7 those who take ***r*** in you, saving
18:2 my rock—I take ***r*** in him!—he's my
18:30 is a shield for all who take ***r*** in him.
25:20 put to shame because I take ***r*** in you.
31:1 of David.] I take ***r*** in you, LORD.
31:19 to those who take ***r*** in you—in the
34:8 The one who takes ***r*** in him is truly
34:22 those who take ***r*** in him won't be
36:7 Humanity finds ***r*** in the shadow of
37:39 LORD; he is their ***r*** in times of
37:40 them because they have taken ***r*** in him.
46:1 song.] God is our ***r*** and strength, a
52:7 make God their ***r***. Instead they
57:1 I have taken ***r*** in you. I take
61:3 you have been my ***r***, a tower of
61:4 let me take ***r*** in the shelter of
62:7 God is my strong rock. My ***r*** is in God.
62:8 hearts before him! God is our ***r***! Selah
64:10 let them take ***r*** in him; let
71:1 I've taken ***r*** in you, LORD. Don't let me
73:28 I have taken my ***r*** in you, my LORD
91:2 LORD, "You are my ***r***, my stronghold!
94:22 is my fortress; my God is my rock of ***r***.
104:18 goats; the ridges are the ***r*** of badgers.
118:8 better to take ***r*** in the LORD than
141:8 LORD God. I take ***r*** in you; don't let
142:5 help. "You are my ***r***," I say. "You are
144:2 in whom I take ***r***, and the one who
Proverbs
10:29 of the LORD is a ***r*** for the innocent
14:26 confidence and ***r*** for one's
14:32 but the righteous find ***r*** even in death.
18:10 the righteous run to it and find ***r***.
30:5 a shield for those who take ***r*** in him.
Isaiah
10:31 flown. Gebim's inhabitants sought ***r***.
14:32 among God's people will find ***r*** there.
25:4 You have been a ***r*** for the poor, a
27:5 cling to me for ***r***; let them make
30:3 Pharaoh's ***r*** will become your shame,
32:2 the wind and a ***r*** from a storm,
33:16 will be his ***r***. His food will be
57:13 But those taking ***r*** in me will
Jeremiah
16:19 you are my ***r*** in time of
17:17 me; you are my ***r*** in time of
Ezekiel
6:12 and whoever finds ***r*** will die of
Joel
3:16 But the LORD is a ***r*** for his people, a
Amos
2:14 will find no ***r***; the strong will
5:19 a bear; or sought ***r*** in a house,
Nahum
1:7 acknowledges those who take ***r*** in him.
3:11 you will have to seek ***r*** from the enemy!
Zephaniah
3:12 they will seek ***r*** in the name of
John
6:15 king, so he took ***r*** again, alone on a
Hebrews
6:18 who have taken ***r*** in him, can be

REFUGE CITIES
Nm 35:6; 35:11, 13, 14; Josh 20:2; 1Ch 6:57; 6:67

REFUGE CITY
Nm 35:25; 35:26, 27, 28, 32; Josh 21:13; 21:21, 27, 32, 38

REFUSE
Exodus
8:2 If you ***r*** to let them go, then I'll send
9:2 If you ***r*** to let them go and you
10:3 How long will you ***r*** to respect me?

16:28 long will you *r* to obey my
Deuteronomy
30:17 away and you *r* to listen, and so
Esther
3:8 else, and they *r* to obey the
Job
6:7 I *r* to touch them; they resemble food
13:28 wastes away like *r*, like clothing
Psalms
28:1 my rock; don't *r* to hear me. If
Proverbs
6:35 he'll *r* even a large
15:32 Those who *r* discipline despise
21:7 away, for they *r* to act with
21:25 because their hands *r* to do anything.
Isaiah
1:20 But if you *r* and rebel, you will be
Jeremiah
5:3 faces harder than rock and *r* to return.
8:2 will become like *r* lying on the
8:5 They cling to deceit and *r* to return.
9:6 their deceit they *r* to know me,
16:4 They will be like *r* lying on the
25:28 If they *r* to take the cup in your hand
25:33 will become like *r* lying on the
38:21 But if you *r* to surrender, this is what
Ezekiel
2:5 or whether they *r*, since they are a
3:7 Israel—they will *r* to listen to you
33:31 words, but they *r* to do them.
Matthew
5:42 ask, and don't *r* those who wish to
Mark
6:26 his guests, he didn't want to *r* her.
Luke
11:46 burdens and you *r* to lift a single
Acts
15:29 *r* food offered to idols, blood, the
1 Corinthians
7:5 Don't *r* to meet each other's needs
1 Peter
2:7 For those who *r* to believe,
2:8 Because they *r* to believe in the
3:1 if some of them *r* to believe the
4:17 to those who *r* to believe God's

REFUSED
Genesis
37:35 him, but he *r* to be comforted,
39:8 He *r* and said to his master's wife,
48:19 But his father *r* and said, "I know, my
Exodus
4:23 me." But you *r* to let him go. As
9:35 Pharaoh *r* to let the
13:15 When Pharaoh *r* to let us go, the LORD
Numbers
22:13 for the LORD has *r* to allow me to go
22:14 they said, "Balaam *r* to come with us."
1 Samuel
8:19 But the people *r* to listen to Samuel
Nehemiah
9:17 They *r* to obey, and didn't remember the
Esther
1:12 But Queen Vashti *r* to come as the king
1:17 Vashti before him, but she *r* to come.'
Job
30:1 whose fathers I *r* to put beside my
Psalms
78:10 covenant; they *r* to walk in his
Ecclesiastes
2:10 eyes desired. I *r* my heart no
Isaiah
28:12 place of repose"; but they *r* to listen.
30:15 will be your strength—but you *r*.
Jeremiah
11:10 ancestors who *r* to obey my words.
35:6 But they *r*: "We don't drink wine
50:33 captors held them and *r* to let them go.
Ezekiel
16:31 in every square, you *r* to be paid.
20:8 against me and *r* to listen to me.
Hosea
11:5 because they have *r* to return to me.
Zechariah
7:11 But they *r* to pay attention. They
Matthew
18:30 But he *r*. Instead, he threw him into
Luke
9:53 villagers *r* to welcome him
18:4 For a while he *r* but finally said to
Acts
7:39 our ancestors *r* to obey. Instead,
19:9 though. They *r* to believe and
28:24 what he said, but others *r* to believe.
2 Thessalonians
2:10 because they have *r* to love the truth
1 Timothy
1:19 because they *r* to listen to
Hebrews
11:24 By faith Moses *r* to be called the son
11:35 were tortured and *r* to be released so
12:25 escape when they *r* to listen to the

REGISTERED
Numbers
1:18 month. They *r* them by their
11:26 were among those *r*, but they hadn't
14:29 enlisted and were *r* from 20 years old
1 Chronicles
23:24 heads were *r*, along with a
2 Chronicles
17:14 *r* by their clans as follows: Judah's
31:16 to those males, *r* by genealogy,
31:17 to those priests *r* by their
Ezra
8:3 Zechariah and with him were *r* 150 men;
Nehemiah
7:5 they could be *r* by families. I
Hebrews
12:23 children who are *r* in heaven, to God
Revelation
21:27 those who are *r* in the Lamb's

REGULATION
Exodus
12:14 every generation as a *r* for all time.
12:43 This is the *r* for the Passover.
13:10 follow this *r* at its appointed
15:25 The LORD made a *r* and a ruling
Leviticus
5:10 according to the *r*. In this way, the
9:16 and did with it according to the *r*.

Numbers
10:8 be a permanent ***r*** for you
18:8 as an allowance. This is a permanent ***r***.
19:2 This is the ***r*** in the Instruction that
27:11 This will be a ***r*** and a case law
31:21 war, "This is the ***r*** in the
1 Samuel
30:25 David made that a ***r*** and a law in
Ezekiel
46:14 and perpetual ***r*** for the grain

REGULATIONS

Exodus
15:26 keep all of his ***r***, then I won't
18:20 Explain the ***r*** and instructions to them.
Leviticus
18:4 No, my ***r*** and my rules are the ones you
26:46 are the rules, ***r***, and instructions
Numbers
9:12 the Passover according to all its ***r***.
35:29 These will be the ***r*** and case laws for
Deuteronomy
4:1 listen to the ***r*** and the case laws
30:16 commandments, his ***r***, and his case
Psalms
19:8 The LORD's ***r*** are right, gladdening the
Ezekiel
5:6 case laws and my ***r*** with greater
20:11 I gave them my ***r*** and made known to them
33:15 in life-giving ***r*** in order not to
44:5 concerning the ***r*** of the LORD's
Luke
1:6 of all the Lord's commandments and ***r***.
Acts
16:4 to keep the ***r*** put into place by
Colossians
2:20 to rules and ***r*** as though you
Hebrews
9:1 covenant had ***r*** for the priests'
9:10 are superficial ***r*** that are only
9:22 to the Law's ***r***, and there is no

REHOBOAM

1 Kings
11:43 David's City, and ***R*** his son succeeded
12:1 ***R*** went to Shechem where all Israel had
14:21 ***R***, Solomon's son, ruled over Judah.
1 Chronicles
3:10 of Solomon: ***R***, his son Abijah,
2 Chronicles
10:1 ***R*** went to Shechem, where all Israel had
Matthew
1:7 was the father of ***R***. Rehoboam was the

REJECT

Leviticus
26:15 if you ***r*** my rules and despise my
26:44 I will not ***r*** them or despise
1 Kings
9:7 them and I will ***r*** the temple that I
2 Kings
23:27 Israel. I will ***r*** this city,
1 Chronicles
28:9 you abandon him, he will ***r*** you forever.
2 Chronicles
6:42 LORD God, don't ***r*** your anointed one.
7:20 you, and I will ***r*** this temple that
Job
5:17 so don't ***r*** the Almighty's
7:16 I ***r*** life; I don't want to live long;
8:20 Surely God won't ***r*** integrity, won't
9:21 yet don't know myself; I ***r*** my life.
10:3 me, that you ***r*** the work of your
34:33 you because you ***r*** sin, for you must
36:5 and doesn't ***r*** anyone; he is
Psalms
10:3 the greedy ***r*** the LORD, cursing.
10:13 Why do the wicked ***r*** God? Why do they
36:4 is no good. They don't ***r*** what is evil.
44:23 Lord? Get up! Don't ***r*** us forever!
66:20 God! He didn't ***r*** my prayer; he
77:7 Will my Lord ***r*** me forever? Will he
88:14 Why do you ***r*** my very being, LORD? Why
94:14 The LORD will not ***r*** his people; he will
132:10 David, do not ***r*** your anointed one.
141:5 Let my head never ***r*** that kind of fine
Proverbs
3:11 Don't ***r*** the instruction of the LORD, my son
Isaiah
7:15 and learn to ***r*** evil and choose
7:16 the boy learns to ***r*** evil and choose
30:12 says: Because you ***r*** this word and
31:7 you will each ***r*** the idols of
41:9 servant; I chose you and didn't ***r*** you":
Jeremiah
3:12 the LORD. I won't ***r*** you, for I'm
14:21 sake, don't ***r*** us, don't scorn
31:37 only then would I ***r*** Israel's
33:26 than I would ***r*** the descendants of Jacob
Lamentations
3:31 My Lord definitely won't ***r*** forever
Ezekiel
20:3 as I live, I ***r*** your petitions.
Hosea
4:6 so I will ***r*** you from serving
9:17 him, my God will ***r*** them; they will
Amos
5:10 gate, and they ***r*** the one who
5:21 I hate, I ***r*** your festivals; I don't
6:8 forces: I ***r*** the pride of
Micah
2:8 trusting passersby, those who ***r*** war.
3:9 Israel, you who ***r*** justice and make
Luke
6:22 people hate you, ***r*** you, insult you,
Acts
13:46 first. Since you ***r*** it and show that
21:21 the Gentiles to ***r*** Moses, telling
1 Corinthians
1:19 wise, and I will ***r*** the intelligence
2 Corinthians
4:2 Instead, we ***r*** secrecy and shameful
Galatians
4:14 down on me or ***r*** me, but you
Titus
1:14 commands from people who ***r*** the truth.
Hebrews
12:25 we escape if we ***r*** the one who is
Jude
1:8 themselves, ***r*** authority, and

REJECTED

Leviticus
26:43 fact that they ***r*** my regulations
Numbers
11:20 you. You've ***r*** the LORD who's
14:31 and they will know the land that you ***r***.
Deuteronomy
1:26 to go up. You ***r*** the LORD your
32:19 LORD saw this and ***r*** out of
Judges
15:2 had completely ***r*** her that I gave
1 Samuel
8:7 they haven't ***r*** you. No, they've
10:19 But today you've ***r*** your God who saved
15:23 Because you have ***r*** what the LORD
16:1 over Saul? I have ***r*** him as king over
2 Kings
17:15 They ***r*** his regulations and the covenant
17:20 So the LORD ***r*** all of Israel's
Esther
4:4 of mourning clothes, but he ***r*** them.
Job
27:2 As God lives, who ***r*** my legal claim, the
31:13 If I've ***r*** the just cause of my male or
Psalms
43:2 Why have you ***r*** me? Why do I have
44:9 But now you've ***r*** and humiliated us. You no longer
53:5 them to shame because God has ***r*** them.
60:1 God, you have ***r*** us—shattered us.
60:10 But you have ***r*** us, God, haven't you?
78:59 became enraged; he ***r*** Israel utterly.
78:67 God ***r*** the tent of Joseph and didn't
89:38 you, God, have ***r*** and despised him.
105:28 dark, but the Egyptians ***r*** his word.
106:24 But then they ***r*** the land that was so
107:11 instructions and ***r*** the Most High's
108:11 But you have ***r*** us, God, haven't you?
118:22 The stone ***r*** by the builders is now the
Proverbs
1:24 you, but you ***r*** me; I stretched
1:30 my advice; they ***r*** all my
Isaiah
5:24 for they have ***r*** the teaching of
8:6 this people has ***r*** the waters of
14:19 own grave like a ***r*** branch, covered
33:8 pledges were ***r***; no one cared for
49:7 to one despised, ***r*** by nations, to
54:6 wife when she is ***r***, says your God.
Jeremiah
2:30 vain; they have ***r*** my correction.
4:30 your lovers have ***r*** you and now seek
6:19 my words and they have ***r*** my teaching.
7:29 The LORD has ***r*** you and has cast
8:9 Look, they have ***r*** the LORD's word;
12:8 growls at me; therefore, I have ***r*** her.
14:19 you completely ***r*** Judah? Do you
33:24 The LORD has ***r*** the two families
Lamentations
2:7 My Lord ***r*** his altar, he abandoned his
3:17 I've ***r*** peace; I've forgotten what is
5:22 have completely ***r*** us, or have
Ezekiel
5:6 who also ***r*** my case laws and
16:27 by your infamous ways and had ***r*** you.
16:37 and the ones you ***r***. I will gather
20:13 regulations and ***r*** my case laws,
24:6 Empty it piece by piece. She is ***r***
Hosea
4:10 because they have ***r*** the LORD to
8:5 Your calf is ***r***, Samaria. My anger
Amos
2:4 because they have ***r*** the Instruction
Zechariah
10:6 though I hadn't ***r*** them, for I am
Malachi
1:3 but I ***r*** Esau. I turned Esau's mountains
Matthew
21:42 that the builders ***r*** has become the
Mark
8:31 things and be ***r*** by the elders,
9:12 One would suffer many things and be ***r***?
12:10 that the builders ***r*** has become the
Luke
7:30 and legal experts ***r*** God's will for
9:22 things and be ***r***—by the elders,
12:9 others will be ***r*** before God's
17:25 things and be ***r*** by this
20:17 that the builders ***r*** has become the
Acts
3:14 You ***r*** the holy and righteous one, and
4:11 you builders ***r***; he has become
7:35 Moses whom they ***r*** when they asked,
14:2 the Jews who ***r*** the faith stirred
Romans
11:1 ask you, has God ***r*** his people?
11:2 God hasn't ***r*** his people, who he knew in
1 Timothy
4:4 received with thanksgiving should be ***r***.
Hebrews
10:28 When someone ***r*** the Law from Moses, they were put
12:17 blessing, he was ***r*** because he
1 Peter
2:4 this stone was ***r*** by humans, from

REJOICE

Leviticus
23:40 the streams, and ***r*** before the LORD
Deuteronomy
12:12 Then you will ***r*** in the LORD your God's
32:43 Heavens: ***R*** with God! All you gods: bow
1 Samuel
2:1 enemies because I ***r*** in your
2 Samuel
1:20 daughters will ***r***; the daughters of
1 Chronicles
16:10 Let the hearts ***r*** of all those
16:31 Let the earth ***r***! Let the nations
16:35 your holy name and ***r*** in your praise."
2 Chronicles
6:41 those loyal to you ***r*** in what is good.
20:27 them reason to ***r*** over their
Nehemiah
12:43 God had made them ***r*** with great joy.
Job
3:22 who ***r*** excitedly, who are thrilled when
21:12 drum and lyre, ***r*** at the sound of a
22:19 righteous see and ***r***; the innocent
Psalms
5:11 all who love your name can ***r*** in you.
9:2 celebrate and ***r*** in you; I will
9:14 praises, so I can ***r*** in your salvation
13:4 won!" My foes will ***r*** over my downfall.

13:5 My heart will ***r*** in your salvation.
14:7 Jacob will ***r***; Israel will
20:5 Then we will ***r*** that you've been helped.
25:2 shame! Don't let my enemies ***r*** over me!
31:7 I ***r*** and celebrate in your faithful love
32:11 are righteous, ***r*** in the LORD and
34:2 LORD—let the suffering listen and ***r***.
35:9 But I will ***r*** in the LORD; I will
40:16 you celebrate and ***r*** in you. Let those
48:11 towns of Judah ***r*** because of your
51:8 let the bones you crushed ***r*** once more.
53:6 Jacob will ***r***; Israel will
58:10 righteous will ***r*** when they see
63:11 the king should ***r*** in God; everyone
64:10 Let the righteous ***r*** in the LORD; let
68:3 before God. Let them ***r*** with gladness!
70:4 all who seek you ***r*** and be glad in
71:23 My lips will ***r*** aloud when I make music
75:9 But I will ***r*** always; I will sing
81:1 Of Asaph.] ***R*** out loud to God,
84:2 and my body will ***r*** out loud to the
85:6 again so that your people can ***r*** in you?
89:16 They ***r*** in your name all day long and
90:14 love so we can ***r*** and celebrate our
96:11 Let the earth ***r***! Let the sea and
97:1 Let the earth ***r***! Let all the
97:8 towns of Judah ***r***,because of your
97:12 ***R*** in the LORD, righteous ones! Give
98:4 earth! Be happy! ***R*** out loud! Sing
98:8 let the mountains ***r*** out loud
104:31 Let the LORD ***r*** in all he has
105:3 Let the hearts ***r*** of all those
106:5 so I can ***r*** in the joy of
106:47 to your holy name and ***r*** in your praise!
118:24 acted; we will ***r*** and celebrate in
119:14 I ***r*** in the content of your laws as if I
119:47 I will ***r*** in your commandments because I
119:70 blubber, but I ***r*** in your
149:2 let Zion's children ***r*** in their king!

Proverbs
5:18 be blessed. ***R*** in the wife of
17:5 maker; those who ***r*** in disaster won't
23:16 inner being will ***r*** when your lips
23:24 one who gives life to the wise will ***r***.
23:25 your mother will ***r***; she who gave you
24:17 fall, don't ***r***. When they
28:12 the righteous ***r***, there is great
29:2 the people ***r***, but when the
29:3 makes his father ***r***, but one who
29:6 own sin; the righteous sing and ***r***.

Ecclesiastes
11:9 ***R***, young person, while you are young!

Song of Songs
1:4 Let's exult and ***r*** in you. Let's

Isaiah
9:3 harvest, as those who divide plunder ***r***.
14:8 the cypresses ***r*** over you, the
14:29 Don't ***r***, all you Philistines, that the
25:9 let's be glad and ***r*** in his salvation!"
29:19 of people will ***r*** in the holy one
35:1 wilderness will ***r*** and blossom like
41:16 them. You will ***r*** in the LORD and
45:25 Israelites will be victorious and ***r***."
49:13 Sing, heavens! ***R***, earth! Break out,
61:7 they will ***r*** over their share.
62:5 so your God will ***r*** because of you.
65:13 My servants will ***r***, but you will be
66:14 your heart will ***r***; your entire

Jeremiah
32:41 I will ***r*** in treating them graciously,
50:11 you gloat and ***r***, you plunderers
51:48 all creation will ***r*** over Babylon,

Lamentations
2:17 He made the enemy ***r*** over you; he
4:21 ***R*** and be happy, Daughter Edom, you who

Ezekiel
7:12 No buyer should ***r***, and no seller
21:10 Let's not ***r***, because no one

Hosea
9:1 Don't ***r***, Israel! Don't celebrate as

Joel
2:21 fertile land; ***r*** and be glad, for
2:23 Children of Zion, ***r*** and be glad in the

Amos
6:13 you who ***r*** in Lo-debar, who say,

Micah
7:8 Do not ***r*** over me, my enemy, because

Habakkuk
3:18 I will ***r*** in the LORD. I will rejoice in

Zephaniah
3:14 ***R***, Daughter Zion! Shout, Israel!
3:17 his love; he will ***r*** over you with

Zechariah
2:10 ***R*** and be glad, Daughter Zion, because I
4:10 things will ***r*** when they see the
9:9 ***R*** greatly, Daughter Zion. Sing aloud,
10:7 glad. Their hearts will ***r*** in the LORD.

Luke
1:14 and many people will ***r*** at his birth,
1:28 to her, he said, "***R***, favored one! The
1:47 of who I am I ***r*** in God my savior.
6:23 ***R*** when that happens! Leap for joy
10:20 don't ***r*** because the

Romans
15:10 again, it says, ***R***, Gentiles, with

Galatians
4:27 It's written: ***R***, barren woman, you who

1 Thessalonians
5:16 ***R*** always

1 Peter
1:6 You now ***r*** in this hope, even if it's
1:8 trust him and so ***r*** with a glorious
4:13 Instead, ***r*** as you share Christ's

Revelation
11:10 on earth will ***r*** over them. They
12:12 Therefore, ***r***, you heavens and you who
18:20 ***R*** over her, heaven—you saints,
19:7 Let us ***r*** and celebrate, and give him

REJOICED

2 Kings
11:20 of the land ***r***, and the city was

1 Chronicles
29:9 The people ***r*** at this response, because

2 Chronicles
23:21 of the land ***r***, and the city was
29:36 all the people ***r*** at what God had
30:25 of Judah ***r***, as did the

Ezra
3:13 the people ***r*** very loudly. The

Nehemiah
12:43 on that day and ***r***, for God had made

Job
31:25 if I've ***r*** because my wealth was great,
31:29 If I have ***r*** over my foes' ruin or was
Psalms
28:7 helped, my heart ***r***, and I thank him
66:6 river on foot. Right there we ***r*** in him!
107:30 So they ***r*** because the waves had calmed
122:1 Of David.] I ***r*** with those who
Isaiah
9:3 its joy. They ***r*** before you as
Ezekiel
25:6 feet when you ***r*** with utter
35:15 Just as you ***r*** over the house of
Hosea
10:5 priests who ***r*** over its glory
Obadiah
1:12 shouldn't have ***r*** over the people
Luke
13:17 in the crowd ***r*** at all the
Acts
2:26 and my tongue ***r***. Moreover, my
13:48 heard this, they ***r*** and honored the

REJOICING
1 Samuel
18:6 with tambourines, ***r***, and musical
2 Kings
11:14 of the land were ***r*** and blowing
1 Chronicles
15:25 went with ***r*** to bring up the
2 Chronicles
23:13 of the land were ***r*** and blowing
23:18 from Moses, with ***r*** and singing, just
Nehemiah
8:17 Nun's son, and there was very great ***r***.
Esther
9:17 making it a day of feasts and ***r***.
9:19 of Adar a day of ***r*** and feasts, a
Job
20:5 that the ***r*** of the wicked is short, the
Psalms
104:34 be pleasing to him; I'm ***r*** in the LORD!
105:43 people out with ***r***, his chosen ones
119:14 laws as if I were ***r*** over great wealth.
Proverbs
2:14 enjoy doing evil, ***r*** in their twisted
Luke
19:37 disciples began ***r***. They praised God
Acts
5:41 left the council ***r*** because they had
8:8 There was great ***r*** in that city
8:39 saw him again but went on his way ***r***.
Jude
1:24 you blameless and ***r*** before his

RELATIVE
Genesis
29:15 you are my ***r***. Tell me what you
Leviticus
18:6 any blood ***r*** for sexual
20:19 your own close ***r***; both of you will
25:25 the closest ***r*** will come and buy
Numbers
5:8 has no close ***r*** to whom the
27:11 to his nearest ***r*** from his clan. He
35:12 from the close ***r*** of the dead. The
Ruth
2:1 had a respected ***r***, a man of worth,
3:2 were with, our ***r***? Tonight he will
3:12 a redeemer who is a closer ***r*** than I am.
2 Samuel
19:42 the king is our ***r***! Why are you
1 Kings
16:11 on a wall, whether ***r*** or friend.
1 Chronicles
6:39 His ***r*** was Asaph, who stood on his
Proverbs
27:10 a neighbor nearby than a ***r*** far away.
Amos
6:10 If a ***r***, someone who burns the dead,
Luke
1:36 her old age, your ***r*** Elizabeth has
John
18:26 high priest, a ***r*** of the one whose
Romans
16:11 Say hello to my ***r*** Herodion. Say hello

RELATIVES
Genesis
13:8 and between our herders since we are ***r***.
16:12 He will live at odds with all his ***r***."
24:38 and to my ***r*** and choose a wife
31:3 and to your ***r***, and I will be
32:9 country and your ***r***, and I'll make
Leviticus
10:4 Go carry your ***r*** out from the
18:17 They are her blood ***r***; it is shameful.
21:2 for your closest ***r***: for your mother,
25:48 One of their ***r*** can buy them back:
25:49 of their blood ***r*** from their family
Deuteronomy
2:4 territory of your ***r*** who live in Seir:
3:18 of your Israelite ***r*** as a fighting
10:9 the rest of their ***r***. The LORD is the
13:6 if one of your ***r***—even one of your
15:2 or their ***r*** because the
18:7 just like his ***r***—the other Levites
23:7 they are your ***r***. Don't detest
Joshua
17:4 with our male ***r***." So in agreement
Judges
1:25 but they let that man and all his ***r*** go.
9:26 son, and his ***r*** came passing
14:3 among your own ***r*** or among all our
18:8 back to their ***r*** at Zorah and
20:13 demand of their own ***r*** the Israelites.
21:6 concerning their ***r*** the Benjaminites.
Ruth
2:20 one of our close ***r***; he's one of our
2 Samuel
15:20 and take your ***r*** with you. May the
19:12 You are my ***r***! You are my flesh and
1 Kings
12:24 war against your ***r*** the Israelites.
Ezra
8:18 with his sons and ***r*** so that there
8:19 together with his ***r*** and their sons so
8:24 Hashabiah and ten of their ***r*** with them.
Nehemiah
3:18 After him, their ***r*** made repairs:
4:23 Neither I nor my ***r***, nor my servants,
10:29 officials and ***r***, and make a

Proverbs
6:19 and one who causes conflicts among ***r***.
19:7 All the ***r*** of the poor hate them; even
Jeremiah
12:6 Even your ***r***, your very family, are
Ezekiel
11:3 say, "The nearest ***r*** aren't building
11:15 your nearest ***r***, the whole house
Mark
6:4 among their ***r***, and in their own
Luke
1:58 Her neighbors and ***r*** celebrated with her
1:61 her, "None of your ***r*** have that name."
4:40 brought to Jesus ***r*** and acquaintances
14:12 and sisters, your ***r***, or rich
21:16 and sisters, ***r***, and friends.
Acts
7:14 Jacob and all his ***r***—seventy-five in a
10:24 had gathered his ***r*** and close friends.
Romans
9:3 sisters, who are my flesh-and-blood ***r***.
16:7 and Junia, my ***r*** and my fellow
16:21 and Lucius, Jason, and Sosipater, my ***r***.

RELEASE

Leviticus
14:7 the priest will ***r*** the wild bird
25:50 price of their ***r*** will be based on
Job
6:9 to crush me, ***r*** his hand and cut
Ecclesiastes
8:8 death. There's no ***r*** from war, and
Isaiah
61:1 to proclaim ***r*** for captives, and
Jeremiah
39:14 sent orders to ***r*** Jeremiah from the
Ezekiel
46:17 until the year of ***r***, and then it will
Zechariah
9:11 covenant, I will ***r*** your prisoners
Matthew
27:15 the governor to ***r*** to the crowd one
27:17 you like me to ***r*** to you, Jesus
27:21 do you want me to ***r*** to you?"
Mark
15:8 asked Pilate to ***r*** someone, as he
15:9 you want me to ***r*** to you the king
15:11 crowd to have him ***r*** Barabbas to them
Luke
4:18 poor, to proclaim ***r*** to the prisoners
23:18 Away with this man! ***R*** Barabbas to us."
23:20 again because he wanted to ***r*** Jesus.
John
18:39 a custom that I ***r*** one prisoner for
19:10 have authority to ***r*** you and also to
19:12 Pilate wanted to ***r*** Jesus. However,
Acts
3:13 though he had already decided to ***r*** him.
4:23 After their ***r***, Peter and John returned
16:35 jailer with the order "***R*** those people."
28:18 who intended to ***r*** me after they
Philippians
1:19 will result in my ***r*** through your
Revelation
9:14 had the trumpet, "***R*** the four angels

RELEASED

Leviticus
16:22 then the goat will be ***r*** into the wild.
19:20 hasn't yet been ***r*** or given her
25:28 year. It will be ***r*** in the Jubilee
27:21 piece of land is ***r*** in the Jubilee
Judges
15:5 the torches and ***r*** the foxes into
15:9 in Judah, and ***r*** their forces on
2 Kings
22:9 officials have ***r*** the money that
25:27 of Babylon, he ***r*** Judah's King
Psalms
105:20 free; the ruler of many people ***r*** him.
Isaiah
51:14 ones will soon be ***r***; they won't die
Jeremiah
20:3 day, when Pashhur ***r*** Jeremiah from
40:1 special guard had ***r*** him from Ramah.
52:31 plight and ***r*** him from prison
Ezekiel
5:16 you, I have ***r*** them for your
Matthew
18:27 on that servant, ***r*** him, and forgave
27:26 Then he ***r*** Barabbas to them. He had
Mark
7:35 tongue was ***r***, and he began to
15:6 festival, Pilate ***r*** one prisoner to
15:15 the crowd, so he ***r*** Barabbas to them.
Luke
23:25 He ***r*** the one they asked for, who had
Acts
3:14 that a murderer be ***r*** to you instead.
4:21 further, then ***r*** them. Because of
16:36 both are to be ***r***. You can leave
17:9 the others posted bail, they ***r*** them.
26:32 could have been ***r*** if he hadn't
Romans
7:2 dies, she is ***r*** from the Law
7:6 now we have been ***r*** from the Law. We
Philemon
1:22 that I will be ***r*** from prison to be
Hebrews
11:35 and refused to be ***r*** so they could
Revelation
9:15 and year were ***r*** to kill a third
20:3 this he must be ***r*** for a little
20:7 over, Satan will be ***r*** from his prison.

RELIABLE

Numbers
12:7 has proved to be ***r*** with all my
Proverbs
13:17 trouble, but a ***r*** one brings
20:6 are loyal, but who can find a ***r*** person?
22:21 teach you true, ***r*** words so you can
25:13 a harvest day are ***r*** messengers to
28:20 ***R*** people will have abundant blessings,
Isaiah
45:23 my mouth; it is ***r*** and won't fail.
1 Timothy
1:15 This saying is ***r*** and deserves full
3:1 This saying is ***r***: if anyone has a goal
4:9 This saying is ***r*** and deserves complete
2 Timothy
2:11 This saying is ***r***: "If we have died

Titus
1:9 attention to the ***r*** message as it has
2:10 are completely ***r*** in everything so
3:8 This saying is ***r***. And I want you to
Hebrews
2:2 by angels was ***r***, and every
10:23 the one who made the promises is ***r***.
2 Peter
1:19 we have a most ***r*** prophetic word,

RELIGIOUS → RELIGIOUS EXPERTS
Numbers
1:50 perform its ***r*** ceremonies, and
2 Kings
17:26 don't know the ***r*** practices of the
23:4 temple all the ***r*** objects made for
1 Chronicles
9:13 men for the ***r*** work of God's
2 Chronicles
19:11 in charge of all ***r*** matters, and
Daniel
6:5 use against him from his ***r*** practice."
Hosea
2:11 will end all her ***r*** celebrations, her
4:11 false ***r*** practices. Wine and new wine
Acts
17:22 I see that you are very ***r*** in every way.
Galatians
4:10 You observe ***r*** days and months and
Colossians
2:17 These ***r*** practices are only a shadow of
2 Timothy
3:5 like they are ***r*** but deny God's
Hebrews
10:2 out their ***r*** duties had been

RELIGIOUS EXPERTS
Gn 41:8; 41:24; Ex 7:11; 7:22; 8:7, 18, 19; 9:11

REMAIN
Genesis
6:3 breath will not ***r*** in humans
Exodus
12:10 let any of it ***r*** until morning,
Leviticus
6:9 that must ***r*** on the altar
11:11 and must ***r*** so. You must not eat their
22:27 is born, it must ***r*** with its mother
25:28 was sold will ***r*** in the possession
Ezra
1:4 for all those who ***r*** in the various
9:15 and a few ***r*** until now. Here
Job
8:15 grasps it, and it can't ***r*** in place.
24:11 tread winepresses, but ***r*** thirsty.
Psalms
92:14 and gray; they will ***r*** lush and fresh
125:3 wicked rod won't ***r*** in the land given
Proverbs
2:21 in the land; the innocent will ***r*** in it.
5:2 so you might ***r*** discrete, and your lips
Isaiah
6:13 Even if one-tenth ***r*** there, they will be
7:22 milk, for all who ***r*** in the land will
14:30 to death, and murder all who ***r***.
37:32 Those who ***r*** will go out from Jerusalem,
56:4 I desire, and ***r*** loyal to my
Jeremiah
13:27 Jerusalem! How long will you ***r*** dirty?
17:8 their leaves will ***r*** green. They won't
27:22 where they will ***r*** until the day I
Daniel
12:9 these words must ***r*** secret and sealed
Hosea
3:4 Israelites will ***r*** many days without
8:5 them. How long will they ***r*** guilty?
9:3 They won't ***r*** in the land of the LORD;
Amos
6:9 If ten people ***r*** in one house, then they
Obadiah
1:20 Those who ***r*** of the Israelites will
Zephaniah
3:12 people to ***r*** in your midst;
Mark
6:10 house you enter, ***r*** there until you
Luke
1:20 believe, you will ***r*** silent, unable to
9:4 house you enter, ***r*** there until you
10:7 ***R*** in this house, eating and drinking
John
8:31 disciples if you ***r*** faithful to my
15:4 ***R*** in me, and I will remain in you. A
19:31 the bodies to ***r*** on the cross on
21:22 If I want him to ***r*** until I come,
Acts
3:21 Jesus must ***r*** in heaven until the
14:22 and urged them to ***r*** firm in the
1 Corinthians
13:13 hope, and love ***r***—these three thing
1 John
2:6 one who claims to ***r*** in him ought to
2:28 little children, ***r*** in relationship
3:17 care—how can the love of God ***r*** in him?
4:15 Son, God remains in us and we ***r*** in God.
Revelation
17:10 comes, he must ***r*** for only a short

REMAINED
Genesis
7:17 The flood ***r*** on the earth for forty
18:22 but Abraham ***r*** standing in front
21:20 God ***r*** with the boy; he grew up, lived
39:21 with Joseph and ***r*** loyal to him. He
Exodus
7:13 However, Pharaoh ***r*** stubborn. He
14:20 camp. The cloud ***r*** there, and when
Numbers
11:26 Two men had ***r*** in the camp, one named
Deuteronomy
10:10 the first time, I ***r*** on the mountain
Ezra
9:4 exiles while I ***r*** sitting in shock
Nehemiah
8:7 while the people ***r*** in their places.
Psalms
116:10 I have ***r*** faithful, even when I said, "I
Jeremiah
37:10 in their tents ***r***, they would rise
38:28 Jeremiah ***r*** in the prison quarters until
40:6 him and the people who ***r*** in the land.
52:25 advisors who ***r*** in the city. He
Daniel
2:35 no trace of them ***r***. But the stone

Haggai
1:12 with all who ***r*** among the people,
John
1:39 staying, and they ***r*** with him that
6:22 the crowd that ***r*** on the other side
11:20 to meet him, while Mary ***r*** in the house.
Acts
7:45 This tent ***r*** in the land until
12:16 Meanwhile, Peter ***r*** outside, knocking at
17:14 but Silas and Timothy ***r*** at Beroea.
19:22 while he ***r*** awhile in the

REMAINS

Genesis
17:14 of his foreskin ***r*** uncircumcised
Exodus
26:12 half curtain that ***r***, should hang over
Leviticus
4:12 all that ***r*** of the bull—will be taken
13:23 if the shiny spot ***r*** where it was and
Joshua
13:1 much of the land ***r*** to be taken over.
13:2 is the land that ***r***: All the
Judges
14:8 at the lion's ***r***, and there was a
1 Samuel
30:25 in Israel, which ***r*** in place even now.
2 Samuel
13:30 killed all of the princes! Not one ***r***."
2 Kings
4:7 You and your sons can live on what ***r***."
6:31 Shaphat's son, ***r*** on his shoulders
1 Chronicles
28:7 forever if he ***r*** committed to
Job
18:15 Nothing they own ***r*** in their tent;
19:4 If so, my error ***r*** hidden inside me.
21:34 to me; only deceit ***r*** in your responses.
34:29 Still, if he ***r*** quiet, who can condemn;
Psalms
76:10 yourself with whatever ***r*** of your wrath.
Ecclesiastes
1:4 but the earth ***r*** as it always has.
Isaiah
4:3 Whoever ***r*** in Zion and is left in
24:12 Ruin ***r*** in the city, and the gate is
24:13 olive tree, like ***r*** from the grape
46:3 Jacob, all that ***r*** from the house of
Jeremiah
4:29 Every city is deserted; no one ***r***.
Ezekiel
39:14 bury the human ***r*** that are left on
44:2 to me, This gate ***r*** closed. It
John
3:36 the angry judgment of God ***r*** on them."
6:56 drinks my blood ***r*** in me and I in
9:41 now that you say, 'We see,' your sin ***r***.
12:34 that the Christ ***r*** forever. How can
2 Corinthians
3:14 day the same veil ***r*** when the old
9:9 the needy; his righteousness ***r*** forever.
Hebrews
7:3 God's Son and ***r*** a priest for all
1 John
2:14 the word of God ***r*** in you, and you
2:27 received from him ***r*** on you, and you
3:6 Every person who ***r*** in relationship to
3:24 his commandments ***r*** in God and God
4:12 each other, God ***r*** in us and his
4:16 love remain in God and God ***r*** in them.
2 John
1:2 of the truth that ***r*** with us and will

REMEMBER → REMEMBER THE LORD

Genesis
9:15 I will ***r*** the covenant between me and
9:16 seeing it I will ***r*** the enduring
40:14 But please, ***r*** me when you are doing
40:23 steward didn't ***r*** Joseph; he forgot
41:31 No one will ***r*** the abundance in the land
Exodus
3:15 this is how all generations will ***r*** me.
13:3 to the people, "***R*** this day which is
20:8 ***R*** the Sabbath day and treat it as holy
33:13 approve of me. ***R*** too that this
Leviticus
26:42 then I will ***r*** my covenant with Jacob. I
26:45 their sake I will ***r*** the covenant with
Numbers
11:5 We ***r*** the fish we ate in Egypt for free,
15:39 will see it and ***r*** all the LORD's
15:40 this way you'll ***r*** to do all my
Deuteronomy
4:10 ***R*** that day when you stood before the
5:15 ***R*** that you were a slave in Egypt, but
7:18 afraid of them! ***R***, instead, what
8:2 ***R*** the long road on which the LORD your
9:27 ***R*** your servants: Abraham, Isaac, and
15:15 ***R*** how each of you were slaves in Egypt
16:3 Do this so you ***r*** the day you fled
16:12 ***R*** how each of you were slaves in Egypt,
24:22 ***R*** how you were a slave in Egypt. That's
32:7 ***R*** the days long past; consider the
Joshua
1:13 ***R*** the command that Moses the LORD's
Judges
16:28 LORD God, please ***r*** me! Make me
1 Samuel
1:11 pain and ***r*** me! Don't forget
25:31 for my master, please ***r*** your servant."
2 Samuel
19:19 hold me guilty or ***r*** your servant's
2 Kings
9:25 the Jezreelite. ***R*** how you and I
20:3 Please, LORD, ***r*** how I have walked
1 Chronicles
16:4 chest in order to ***r***, to give thanks,
16:12 ***R*** the wondrous works he has done, all
2 Chronicles
6:42 anointed one. ***R*** your faithful
24:22 Jehoash failed to ***r*** the loyalty that
35:25 continues to ***r*** Josiah in their
Nehemiah
1:8 ***R*** the word that you gave to your
4:14 afraid of them! ***R*** that the LORD is
5:19 ***R*** in my favor, my God, all that I've
6:14 My God, ***r*** these deeds of Tobiah and
9:17 obey, and didn't ***r*** the wonders that
13:14 ***R*** me, my God, concerning this. Don't
13:22 Sabbath day holy. ***R*** this also in my
13:29 ***R*** them, my God, because they have
13:31 early produce. ***R*** me, my God, for
Esther
9:28 Jews. They will ***r*** to keep them

REMEMBER [cont.]

Job
7:7 ***R*** that my life is wind; my eyes won't
10:9 ***R*** that you made me from clay, and you
11:16 trouble; you will ***r*** it as water that
14:13 passes, set a time for me, and ***r*** me.
36:24 ***R*** to praise his work that all of us
41:8 on him, you would never ***r*** the battle.
Psalms
22:27 of the earth will ***r*** and come back to
25:6 LORD, ***r*** your compassion and faithful
25:7 But don't ***r*** the sins of my youth or my
42:4 But I ***r*** these things as I bare my soul:
42:6 That's why I ***r*** you from the land
71:16 will help others ***r*** nothing but your
74:2 ***R*** your congregation that you took as
74:18 So ***r*** this, LORD: how enemies have
74:22 Make your case! ***R*** how unbelieving
77:3 I ***r*** God and I moan. I complain, and my spirit grows
77:5 days long past; I ***r*** years that seem
77:11 But I will ***r*** the LORD's deeds; yes, I
78:35 They would ***r*** that God was their rock,
78:42 They didn't ***r*** God's power—the day
79:8 Don't ***r*** the iniquities of past
88:5 —those you don't ***r*** anymore, those
89:47 ***R*** how short my life is! Have you
89:50 ***R*** your servant's abuse, my Lord!
103:16 the ground where it stood doesn't ***r*** it.
103:18 his covenant and ***r*** to keep his
105:5 ***R*** the wondrous works he has done, all
106:4 ***R*** me, LORD, with the favor you show
106:7 They didn't ***r*** how much faithful
109:16 person didn't ***r*** to demonstrate
119:49 ***R*** your promise to your servant, for
119:52 When I ***r*** your ancient rules, I'm
119:55 LORD, I ***r*** you name at nighttime, and I
137:6 mouth if I don't ***r*** you, if I don't
137:7 LORD, ***r*** what the Edomites did on
143:5 I ***r*** the days long past; I meditate on
Proverbs
31:7 poverty and no longer ***r*** their toil.
Ecclesiastes
1:18 ***R***: In much wisdom is much aggravation;
5:3 ***R***: Dreams come with many cares, and
5:7 ***R***: When dreams multiply, so do
7:20 ***R***: there's no one on earth so
12:1 ***R*** your creator in your prime, before
Isaiah
17:10 you, and didn't ***r*** the rock who
23:16 sing many songs, so they'll ***r*** you.
38:3 Please, LORD, ***r*** how I've walked before
43:18 Don't ***r*** the prior things; don't ponder
43:25 for my sake. I won't ***r*** your sin.
44:21 ***R*** these things, Jacob; Israel, for you
46:8 ***R*** this and take courage; take it to
46:9 ***R*** the prior things—from long ago; I
54:4 you'll no longer ***r*** the disgrace of
57:11 you lied, didn't ***r*** me or give me a
Jeremiah
2:2 LORD proclaims: I ***r*** your first love,
3:16 won't recall or ***r*** it; they won't
14:21 glorious throne. ***R*** your covenant
15:15 understand, LORD! ***R*** me and act on my
17:2 Their children ***r*** their altars and
18:20 set traps for me. ***R*** that I stood
31:34 and never again ***r*** their sins.
Lamentations
3:20 I can't help but ***r*** and am depressed
Ezekiel
6:9 fugitives will ***r*** me in the nations
16:22 you didn't ***r*** the days of your
16:43 you didn't ***r*** your youthful
16:60 I will ***r*** my covenant with
20:43 There you will ***r*** how your ways and all
23:27 at them, and you won't ***r*** Egypt anymore.
36:31 Then you will ***r*** your evil ways and
Hosea
7:2 hearts that I ***r*** all their
8:13 them. Now he will ***r*** their wickedness
9:9 Gibeah; he will ***r*** their wickedness;
Micah
6:5 My people, ***r*** what Moab's King Balak had
Habakkuk
3:2 it known. Though angry, ***r*** compassion.
Zechariah
10:9 they will ***r*** me in the distant
Malachi
4:4 ***R*** the Instruction from Moses, my
Matthew
5:23 altar and there ***r*** that your brother
16:9 yet? Don't you ***r*** the five loaves
27:63 said, "Sir, we ***r*** that while that
Mark
8:18 ears? Why can't you hear? Don't you ***r***?
Luke
16:25 said, 'Child, ***r*** that during your
17:32 ***R*** Lot's wife
23:42 he said, "Jesus, ***r*** me when you come
24:6 has been raised. ***R*** what he told you
John
15:20 ***R*** what I told you, 'Servants aren't
16:4 comes, you will ***r*** that I told you
Acts
20:31 Stay alert! ***R*** that for three years I
1 Corinthians
11:2 you because you ***r*** all my
11:24 which is for you; do this to ***r*** me."
11:25 time you drink it, do this to ***r*** me."
Galatians
2:10 that we would ***r*** the poor, which
Ephesians
1:16 God for you when I ***r*** you in my prayers.
2:11 So ***r*** that once you were Gentiles by
Colossians
4:18 personally. ***R*** that I'm in
1 Thessalonians
1:3 is because we ***r*** your work that
2:9 You ***r***, brothers and sisters, our
2 Thessalonians
2:5 You ***r*** that I used to tell you these
2 Timothy
1:3 did. I constantly ***r*** you in my prayers
1:4 When I ***r*** your tears, I long to see you
2:8 ***R*** Jesus Christ, who was raised from the
Hebrews
8:12 and I won't ***r*** their sins
10:17 And I won't ***r*** their sins and their
10:32 But ***r*** the earlier days, after you saw
13:3 ***R*** prisoners as if you were in prison
13:7 ***R*** your leaders who spoke God's word to

2 Peter
1:15 for you always to ***r*** these things
Jude
1:17 dear friends, ***r*** the words spoken
Revelation
2:5 So ***r*** the high point from which you have fallen
3:3 So ***r*** what you received and heard. Hold

REMEMBER THE LORD

Dt 8:18; Jdg 8:34; 1Sa 26:23; 2Sa 14:11; Jer 51:50; Ac 20:35

REMEMBERED

Genesis
8:1 God ***r*** Noah, all those alive, and all
19:29 the valley, God ***r*** Abraham and sent
30:22 Then God ***r*** Rachel, responded to her,
41:9 Pharaoh: "Today I've just ***r*** my mistake.
42:9 Joseph ***r*** the dreams he had dreamed
Exodus
2:24 of grief, and God ***r*** his covenant with
6:5 into slaves, and I've ***r*** my covenant.
20:24 place where I make sure my name is ***r***.
28:38 the people may be ***r*** favorably in the
Numbers
10:9 that you may be ***r*** by the LORD your
1 Samuel
1:19 his wife Hannah, and the LORD ***r*** her.
Esther
2:1 less angry, he ***r*** Vashti, what she
Job
24:20 them; they aren't ***r***, and so
Psalms
83:4 Let the name Israel be ***r*** no more!"
98:3 God has ***r*** his loyal love and
105:42 Because God ***r*** his holy promise to
106:45 God ***r*** his covenant for their sake, and
109:14 wrongdoing be ***r*** before the LORD;
112:6 the righteous will be ***r*** forever!
136:23 God ***r*** us when we were humiliated—
137:1 we sat down, crying because we ***r*** Zion.
Ecclesiastes
9:15 his wisdom. But no one ***r*** that poor man.
Isaiah
63:11 Then they ***r*** earlier times, when he
65:17 events won't be ***r***; they won't come
Ezekiel
3:20 deeds won't be ***r***, and I will hold
18:24 deeds will be ***r***. They will die
21:24 Now that you have ***r*** your guilt and
25:10 will no longer be ***r*** among the nations.
33:16 committed will be ***r*** against them.
Jonah
2:7 was weakening, I ***r*** the LORD, and my
Zechariah
13:2 will no longer be ***r***. Moreover, I will
Matthew
26:75 Peter ***r*** Jesus' words, "Before the
Mark
11:21 Peter ***r*** and said to Jesus, "Rabbi, look
14:72 time. Peter ***r*** what Jesus told
Luke
1:72 our ancestors, and ***r*** his holy covenant,
22:61 Peter, and Peter ***r*** the Lord's words,
24:8 Then they ***r*** his words
John
2:17 His disciples ***r*** that it is written,
12:16 glorified, they ***r*** that these things
Acts
11:16 I ***r*** the Lord's words: 'John will
Revelation
16:19 nations fell. God ***r*** Babylon the great
18:5 as heaven, and God ***r*** her unjust acts.

REMOVE

Exodus
8:9 your people to ***r*** the frogs from
12:15 day you must ***r*** yeast from your
21:14 you should ***r*** the killer from
29:36 You should ***r*** the sin from the
Leviticus
1:16 the priest will ***r*** its throat along
Numbers
4:13 They will ***r*** the ashes from the altar
Deuteronomy
7:15 The LORD will ***r*** all sickness from you.
17:7 at the end. ***R*** such evil from
19:13 to such killers. ***R*** innocent
22:21 father's house. ***R*** such evil from
24:7 must die. ***R*** such evil from
26:14 nor did I ***r*** it while I was
Judges
20:13 execute them and ***r*** the evil from
1 Kings
22:43 that he didn't ***r*** the shrines. The
Job
9:34 ***r*** his rod from me, so his fury wouldn't
13:21 ***R*** your hand far from me and don't
41:13 Who can ***r*** his outer garment; who can
Psalms
119:29 ***R*** all false ways from me; show mercy to
119:39 ***R*** the insults that I dread because your
Proverbs
20:30 Blows and bruises ***r*** evil; beatings
22:10 ***R*** the mocker and conflict disappears;
22:28 Don't ***r*** an ancient boundary marker that your ancestors
25:4 ***R*** the dross from the silver, and a
25:5 ***R*** the wicked from the king's presence,
Ecclesiastes
11:10 ***R*** anxiety from your heart, banish pain
Isaiah
1:16 Wash! Be clean! ***R*** your ugly deeds from
1:25 as with lye, and ***r*** all your cinders.
3:18 the LORD will ***r***: the splendid
10:27 day, God will ***r*** the burden from
14:25 trample it and ***r*** its yoke from my
20:2 your waist, and ***r*** the shoes from
25:8 face; he will ***r*** his people's
47:2 and grind flour! ***R*** your veil, strip
57:14 build a road! ***R*** barriers from my
58:9 here." If you ***r*** the yoke from
Jeremiah
22:24 hand, I would still ***r*** you from there.
30:8 their necks and ***r*** their shackles.
51:26 They will never ***r*** a cornerstone or a
Ezekiel
11:18 and they will ***r*** from it all its
11:19 in them. I will ***r*** the stony hearts
20:38 I will ***r*** from among you those who rebel
21:26 LORD God says: ***R*** the turban, take
22:15 and so I will ***r*** your uncleanness

23:26 from you and ***r*** your beautiful
25:7 from the peoples, ***r*** you from the
26:16 their thrones, ***r*** their royal
32:13 I will ***r*** all its livestock from beside
36:26 in you. I will ***r*** your stony heart
43:9 Now let them ***r*** their disloyalties and
44:19 people, they will ***r*** the garments in
Daniel
4:27 accept my advice: ***r*** your sins by
Hosea
2:2 husband. Let her ***r*** prostitution from
Joel
2:20 I will ***r*** the northern army far from you
Amos
2:3 I will ***r*** their judge from them and slay
9:3 them there and ***r*** them. If they
Micah
2:3 not be able to ***r*** your necks! You
Nahum
1:14 your name. I will ***r*** carved idol and
Zephaniah
3:11 me; then I will ***r*** from your midst
3:18 I will ***r*** from you those worried about
Zechariah
3:9 forces. I will ***r*** the guilt of that
9:7 I will ***r*** bloody food from his mouth and
13:2 Moreover, I will ***r*** the prophets and
John
11:39 Jesus said, "***R*** the stone." Martha, the
Acts
7:33 Lord continued, '***R*** the sandals from
23:10 to go down and ***r*** him by force from
Romans
11:26 Zion. He will ***r*** ungodly behavior

REMOVED
Genesis
8:13 the earth. Noah ***r*** the ark's hatch
Exodus
8:31 Moses asked and ***r*** the swarms of
Deuteronomy
12:29 LORD your God has ***r*** from before you
25:10 Israel as "the house of the ***r*** sandal."
26:13 your God: "I have ***r*** the holy portion
Psalms
32:5 I said. Then you ***r*** the guilt of my
44:2 by your own hand, ***r*** all the nations,
103:12 how far God has ***r*** our sin from us.
Isaiah
56:5 them an enduring name that won't be ***r***.
Jeremiah
13:18 crowns will soon be ***r*** from your heads.
Ezekiel
28:16 God's mountain. I ***r*** you, winged
Zephaniah
3:15 The LORD has ***r*** your judgment; he has
Zechariah
3:4 Look, I have ***r*** your guilt from
11:16 who have been ***r***. He won't seek
Luke
16:4 that, when I am ***r*** from my
John
11:41 So they ***r*** the stone. Jesus looked up
Acts
13:22 After God ***r*** him, he raised up David to
2 Corinthians
3:14 The veil is not ***r*** because it is
3:16 turns back to the Lord, the veil is ***r***.
Colossians
2:11 whole body was ***r*** through this

REPAIRED
1 Kings
11:27 structure and ***r*** the broken wall
18:30 closed in, and he ***r*** the LORD's altar
2 Kings
12:6 the priests still hadn't ***r*** the temple.
12:7 Why haven't you ***r*** the temple?" he
2 Chronicles
15:8 highlands, and he ***r*** the LORD's altar
29:3 of the LORD's temple, having ***r*** them.
Nehemiah
3:6 Besodeiah's son, ***r*** the Mishneh Gate;
3:30 sixth son, ***r*** another section.

REPAY
Exodus
22:6 started the fire must fully ***r*** the loss.
1 Samuel
24:19 May the LORD ***r*** you with good for
2 Samuel
3:39 me. May the LORD ***r*** the one who does
16:12 the LORD will ***r*** me with good for
1 Kings
8:39 Forgive, act, and ***r*** each person
2 Chronicles
6:30 Forgive, act, and ***r*** each person
Job
20:10 children will ***r*** the poor; their
34:33 Will he ***r*** you because you reject sin,
41:11 me that I must ***r***? Everything under
Psalms
38:20 Those who give, ***r*** good with evil; they
62:12 and that you will ***r*** everyone
94:23 He will ***r*** them for their wickedness,
103:10 to our sin or ***r*** us according to
109:5 They ***r*** me evil for good, hatred in
Proverbs
19:17 LORD, and the Lord will fully ***r*** them.
20:22 Don't say, "I'll ***r*** the evildoer!" Wait
22:27 If you can't ***r***, why should they be
Isaiah
59:18 God will ***r*** according to their actions:
65:6 but I will ***r***; I will repay in
66:15 a windstorm, to ***r*** in hot anger, to
Jeremiah
5:29 LORD. Shouldn't I ***r*** that nation for
51:24 I will ***r*** Babylon and all its
Daniel
11:18 even though he won't ***r*** that disgrace.
Joel
2:25 I will ***r*** you for the years that the
3:7 them, and I will ***r*** you for your
Matthew
16:27 And then he will ***r*** each one for what
Luke
14:14 they can't ***r*** you. Instead, you
19:8 cheated anyone, I ***r*** them four times
Romans
2:6 God will ***r*** everyone based on their
1 Timothy
5:4 own family and ***r*** their parents,
Revelation
22:12 is with me, to ***r*** all people as

REPHAIM
Genesis
14:5 and attacked the ***R*** in Ashteroth-karna
15:20 the Hittites, the Perizzites, the ***R***
Deuteronomy
2:11 the Emim were ***R***, like the Anakim
2:20 that land was ***R*** territory as
3:11 the last of the ***R***. His bed was made
3:13 of Bashan, was often called ***R*** Country.
Joshua
12:4 the last of the ***R***. He lived in
13:12 the last of the ***R***. Moses had struck
15:8 is at the north end of the ***R*** Valley.
17:15 Perizzites and ***R***, because the
18:16 north part of the ***R*** Valley. It went
2 Samuel
5:18 and spread out over the ***R*** Valley.
5:22 up and spread out across the ***R*** Valley.
23:13 were camped in the ***R*** Valley.
1 Chronicles
11:15 the Philistines camped in the ***R*** Valley.
14:9 and were plundering the ***R*** Valley.
Isaiah
17:5 one who gathers grain in the ***R*** Valley.

REPLY
Deuteronomy
27:15 All the people will ***r***: "We agree!"
1 Samuel
2:16 assistant would ***r***, "No, hand it
17:30 the people said the same thing in ***r***.
2 Samuel
3:11 a single word in ***r*** to Abner because
1 Kings
20:10 sent back this ***r***: "May the gods do
2 Kings
4:29 greets you, don't ***r***. Put my staff on
2 Chronicles
25:18 the following ***r*** to Judah's King
Ezra
5:11 This was their ***r*** to us: "We are the
10:12 shouted in ***r***, "Yes. We must do
Nehemiah
6:4 and every time I gave them a similar ***r***.
6:8 I sent him this ***r***: "Nothing that
Esther
4:10 In ***r*** Esther ordered Hathach to tell
Job
13:22 answer, or I'll speak and you can ***r***.
21:3 I myself; and after my ***r*** you can mock.
Jeremiah
5:19 to us?" you must ***r***, "Just as you
Daniel
2:26 In ***r*** the king said to Daniel (whose
Matthew
25:37 righteous will ***r*** to him, 'Lord,
Mark
12:17 to God." His ***r*** left them
Luke
13:25 for us.' He will ***r***, 'I don't know
Acts
9:5 whom you are harassing," came the ***r***.
Romans
11:4 But what is God's ***r*** to him? I have kept
1 Peter
2:23 he did not ***r*** with insults.

REPORT
Genesis
37:14 the flock is, and ***r*** back to me." So
Numbers
13:26 brought back a ***r*** to them and to
13:27 they gave their ***r***: "We entered the
Deuteronomy
1:22 use and bring a ***r*** about the cities
Joshua
9:9 We have heard a ***r*** about him and
14:7 I brought back a ***r*** to him of what I
18:6 you will write a ***r*** in seven parts
22:11 heard a ***r***: "Look. The
1 Samuel
2:24 do this. The ***r*** I hear spreading
4:16 What's the ***r***, my son?" Eli
29:10 this negative ***r***, because you've
2 Samuel
1:4 What's the ***r***?" David asked him. "Tell
13:30 on the way, the ***r*** came to David:
15:35 you there. So ***r*** everything you
15:36 Use them to ***r*** to me everything
17:17 would come and ***r*** to them, and they
1 Kings
1:42 an honest man and will bring a good ***r***."
2:30 Benaiah sent a ***r*** back to the king:
10:6 The ***r*** I heard about your deeds and
18:12 where—then I'll ***r*** to Ahab, but he
2 Chronicles
9:5 The ***r*** I heard about your deeds and
34:16 king with this ***r***: "Your servants
Ezra
5:5 stop them until a ***r*** reached Darius
Esther
2:23 pointed poles. A ***r*** about the event
4:8 it to Esther and ***r*** it to her.
6:2 They came to the ***r*** about Mordecai
9:11 That same day, a ***r*** concerning the
10:2 also want a full ***r*** about how
Job
28:22 have said, "We've heard a ***r*** of her."
Proverbs
22:21 words so you can ***r*** back reliably to
Ecclesiastes
10:20 winged creature could ***r*** what you said!
Isaiah
21:6 Go, post a lookout to ***r*** what he sees.
30:10 Don't ***r*** truthful visions;
41:23 ***R*** things that will happen in the
48:20 the Chaldeans! ***R*** this with a loud
Jeremiah
36:16 We must at once ***r*** all this to the
49:14 I have heard a ***r*** from the LORD that a
Ezekiel
13:7 And didn't you ***r*** deceptive
Daniel
6:2 whom they would ***r*** so that the king
6:14 king heard this ***r***, he was very
Hosea
7:12 according to the ***r*** made to their
Matthew
2:8 you've found him, ***r*** to me so that I
11:4 responded, "Go, ***r*** to John what you
18:17 pay attention, ***r*** it to the church.
28:15 told. And this ***r*** has spread
Mark
5:36 overheard their ***r*** and said to the

Luke
7:22 disciples, "Go, ***r*** to John what you
16:2 you? Give me a ***r*** of your
John
11:57 he was should ***r*** it, so they could
Acts
15:4 They gave a full ***r*** of what God had
21:19 them a detailed ***r*** of what God had
21:31 to kill him, a ***r*** reached the
23:17 because he has something to ***r*** to him."
23:19 asked, "What do you have to ***r*** to me?"
Galatians
1:23 They only heard a ***r*** about me: "The man

REPORTED
Exodus
19:8 will do." Moses ***r*** to the LORD what
Leviticus
14:2 When it has been ***r*** to the priest,
Deuteronomy
1:25 down to us. They ***r*** to us: "The land
1:43 I ***r*** this to you but you wouldn't
Joshua
10:17 It was ***r*** to Joshua, "The five kings
1 Samuel
11:4 Saul lived, they ***r*** the news directly
18:24 Saul's servants ***r*** what David said
2 Samuel
7:17 Nathan ***r*** all of these words and this
1 Kings
21:14 It was then ***r*** to Jezebel, "Naboth was
Nehemiah
6:6 It stated: It is ***r*** among the nations
6:19 presence and then ***r*** back to him what
Esther
2:22 wind of it, he ***r*** it to Queen
Isaiah
21:10 forces, the God of Israel, I ***r*** to you.
Ezekiel
33:21 came to me and ***r***, "The city has
Amos
7:10 priest of Bethel, ***r*** to Israel's King
Mark
16:9 They promptly ***r*** all of the young
16:10 She went and ***r*** to the ones who had been with him
16:13 returned, they ***r*** it to the others,
Luke
2:17 saw this, they ***r*** what they had
14:21 the servant ***r*** these excuses to
24:9 the tomb, they ***r*** all these things
Acts
4:23 and sisters and ***r*** everything the
5:22 in the prison. They returned and ***r***,
11:13 He ***r*** to us how he had seen an angel
14:27 together and ***r*** everything that
15:14 Simon ***r*** how, in his kindness, God came
16:36 So the jailer ***r*** this to Paul, informing
16:38 The police ***r*** this to the legal
22:26 the commander and ***r*** it. He asked,
23:16 military headquarters and ***r*** it to Paul.
28:21 brothers come and ***r*** or said anything

REPUTATION
Exodus
23:27 My terrifying ***r*** will precede you, and
Numbers
16:2 chosen by the assembly, men of ***r***.
Deuteronomy
22:14 she has a bad ***r***, because he said
22:19 daughters a bad ***r***. Moreover, she
Joshua
9:9 because of the ***r*** of the LORD your
1 Samuel
12:22 the sake of his ***r***, the LORD won't
1 Kings
4:31 and Darda. His ***r*** was known
8:41 a distant country because of your ***r***—
8:42 of your great ***r***, your great
8:43 may know your ***r*** and revere you,
2 Chronicles
6:32 of your great ***r***, your great
6:33 may know your ***r*** and revere you,
Psalms
4:2 people, will my ***r*** be insulted? How
7:5 ground, laying my ***r*** in the dirt. Selah
21:5 The king's ***r*** is great because of your
48:10 just like your ***r***, extends to the
Proverbs
22:1 A good ***r*** is better than much wealth;
Isaiah
48:9 the sake of my ***r*** I control my
48:11 the sake of my ***r***, for my own sake,
63:12 to create an enduring ***r*** for himself,
63:14 and made for yourself a glorious ***r***.
63:16 our father; your ***r*** since long ago is
Ezekiel
16:43 you not added bad ***r*** to all your
16:58 bear your bad ***r*** and your
Habakkuk
3:2 I have heard your ***r***. I have seen your
1 Corinthians
4:13 when our ***r*** is attacked, we are
1 Timothy
3:7 also have a good ***r*** with those
5:10 She should have a ***r*** for doing good:
6:1 and our teaching won't get a bad ***r***.
Revelation
3:1 You have the ***r*** of being alive,

REQUEST
Genesis
17:20 I've heard your ***r***. I will bless him
50:4 you approve my ***r***, give Pharaoh
Numbers
32:5 you approve our ***r***, give this land
Judges
8:8 and made the same ***r***. And the people
8:24 May I make one ***r*** of you? Everyone
11:17 sent the same ***r*** to the king of
1 Samuel
8:7 with the people's ***r***—everything they a
8:9 comply with their ***r***, but give them a
8:22 with their ***r***. Give them a
25:35 I've heard your ***r*** and have agreed
2 Samuel
14:15 king will act on the ***r*** of his servant,
1 Kings
2:16 I have just one ***r*** of you. Don't
3:10 the LORD that Solomon had made this ***r***.
8:28 prayer and ***r***, and hear the cry

2 Kings
2:10 made a difficult ***r***. If you can see
16:9 king heard the ***r*** and marched
1 Chronicles
4:10 cause me pain." And God granted his ***r***.
2 Chronicles
1:12 your ***r*** for wisdom and knowledge is
6:19 prayer and ***r***, and hear the cry
33:13 was moved by his ***r***. God listened to
Psalms
6:9 listened to my ***r***. The LORD accepts
28:2 Listen to my ***r*** for mercy when I cry out
31:22 But you heard my ***r*** for mercy when I
55:1 listen to my prayer; don't avoid my ***r***!
119:170 Let my ***r*** for grace come before you;
130:2 pay close attention to my ***r*** for mercy!
140:6 God! Listen to my ***r*** for mercy, LORD!"
Joel
1:14 Demand a fast, ***r*** a special assembly.
2:15 demand a fast; ***r*** a special
Mark
6:25 she made her ***r***: "I want you to
Luke
23:24 issued his decision to grant their ***r***.
John
12:21 and made a ***r***, "Sir, we want to
2 Corinthians
10:1 make a personal ***r*** to you with the
2 Thessalonians
2:1 we have a ***r*** for you
1 Peter
5:1 I have a ***r*** for the elders

REQUIRED
Ezra
3:4 burned offerings ***r*** by ordinance for
7:20 anything else is ***r*** for God's house
Nehemiah
8:18 eighth day, just as the Instruction ***r***.
12:44 them the portions ***r*** by the
Jeremiah
7:23 this is what I ***r*** of them: Obey me
Mark
7:12 you are no longer ***r*** to care for your
Luke
2:39 everything ***r*** by the Law of the
17:10 done everything ***r*** of you, you
Acts
15:5 They must be ***r*** to keep the Law
Galatians
2:3 was a Greek, was ***r*** to be circumcised.
5:3 that he is ***r*** to do the whole

RESCUE → ABLE TO RESCUE, I WILL RESCUE YOU
Genesis
45:7 survive and to ***r*** your lives in
Exodus
14:13 watch the LORD ***r*** you today. The
Deuteronomy
7:19 your God used to ***r*** you. That's what
22:27 help, but there was no one to ***r*** her.
2 Chronicles
32:17 couldn't ***r*** their people from
Job
6:23 ***R*** me from the hand of my enemy? Ransom
22:29 say: "Cheer up; God will ***r*** the lowly.
33:24 person and says, "***R*** this one from
36:19 he arrange your ***r*** from distress or
Psalms
3:8 ***R*** comes from the LORD! May your
7:1 Save me from all who chase me! ***R*** me!
7:2 dragging me off with no chance of ***r***.
17:13 Bring them down! ***R*** my life from the
17:14 ***R*** me from these people—your own
22:8 LORD, so let God ***r*** him; let God
31:1 be put to shame. ***R*** me by your
32:7 You surround me with songs of ***r***! Selah
35:10 to you? You ***r*** the weak from
35:17 this happen? ***R*** me from their
37:40 help them and ***r*** them—rescue them
55:16 out to God, and the LORD will ***r*** me.
56:7 Don't ***r*** them for any reason! In wrath
71:2 Deliver me and ***r*** me by your
71:4 My God, ***r*** me from the power of the
82:4 ***R*** the lowly and the needy. Deliver them
91:14 to me, I'll ***r*** you. I'll protect
140:1 psalm of David.] ***R*** me from evil
144:7 hand from above! ***R*** me and deliver me
144:11 ***R*** me and deliver me from the power of
Proverbs
2:12 Wisdom will ***r*** you from the evil path,
19:19 penalty; if you ***r*** them, then you
24:11 ***R*** those being taken off to death; and
Isaiah
19:20 them a savior and defender to ***r*** them.
58:11 places. He will ***r*** your bones. You
Jeremiah
1:8 I'm with you to ***r*** you," declares
22:3 just and right; ***r*** the oppressed
31:11 The LORD will ***r*** the people of Jacob and
42:11 to save you and ***r*** you from his hand.
Ezekiel
34:10 because I will ***r*** my flock from
Matthew
6:13 temptation, but ***r*** us from the evil
2 Corinthians
1:10 and he will ***r*** us. We have set
1 Thessalonians
1:10 the one who will ***r*** us from the
2 Timothy
4:18 The Lord will ***r*** me from every evil
Titus
2:14 us in order to ***r*** us from every
2 Peter
2:9 Lord knows how to ***r*** the godly from

RESCUED
Exodus
14:30 The LORD ***r*** Israel from the Egyptians
Nehemiah
9:28 from heaven and ***r*** them many times
Job
21:30 spared; on the day of fury they are ***r***.
29:12 because I ***r*** the weak who cried out, the
29:17 of the wicked, ***r*** prey from their
Psalms
22:4 you—they trusted you and you ***r*** them;
33:16 warriors aren't ***r*** by how much power
60:5 so that the people you love might be ***r***.
81:7 cried out, so I ***r*** you. I answered
86:13 because you've ***r*** my life from the
89:48 Who is ever ***r*** from the grip of

107:20 healed them; he **r** them from their
108:6 so that the people you love might be **r**.
136:24 God **r** us from our enemies—God's
Isaiah
36:20 countries has **r** their land from
63:11 times, when he **r** his people. Where
Jeremiah
20:13 LORD, for he has **r** the needy from
41:16 group they had **r** in Gibeon,
Ezekiel
14:16 alone would be **r**, but the land
14:18 or daughters. They alone would be **r**.
Daniel
6:27 the proof: He **r** Daniel from the
12:1 found written in the scroll will be **r**.
Amos
3:12 of Israel be **r**. Those who live
Micah
4:10 There you will be **r**; there the LORD
Matthew
24:22 nobody would be **r**. But for the sake
Mark
13:20 no one would be **r**. But for the sake
Luke
1:74 that we would be **r** from the power of
Acts
7:10 and **r** him from all his troubles. The
12:11 his angel and **r** me from Herod and
16:30 masters, what must I do to be **r**?"
23:27 soldiers, and I **r** him when I
28:4 murderer! He was **r** from the sea, but
Romans
15:31 that I will be **r** from the people
2 Corinthians
1:10 God **r** us from a terrible death, and he
Colossians
1:13 He **r** us from the control of darkness
2 Thessalonians
3:2 that we will be **r** from
2 Timothy
3:11 abuse, and the Lord **r** me from it all!
4:17 it. I was also **r** from the lion's
1 Peter
3:20 is, eight) lives were **r** through water.
4:18 are barely **r**, what will happen
2 Peter
2:7 And he **r** righteous Lot, who was made

RESERVED → RESERVED FOR GOD

2 Peter
2:17 The underworld has been **r** for them.
Jude
1:13 of the underworld is **r** forever.

RESERVED FOR GOD

Josh 6:21; 7:1, 15; 8:26; 10:1, 28, 35, 37, 39, 40; 11:11, 12, 20, 21; 22:20

RESIDENTS

Numbers
13:32 that devours its **r**. All the people
35:15 and temporary **r**, as a place to
1 Samuel
23:5 that's how David saved the **r** of Keilah.
2 Chronicles
33:9 led Judah and the **r** of Jerusalem into
34:9 Benjamin, and the **r** of Jerusalem.
35:18 were present, and the **r** of Jerusalem.
Ecclesiastes
9:14 with only a few **r**. A mighty king
Isaiah
42:10 fills it, the coastlands and their **r**.
48:2 They are known as **r** of the holy city,
Jeremiah
4:3 Judah and to the **r** of Jerusalem:
4:4 of Judah and **r** of Jerusalem, or
11:9 the people of Judah and **r** of Jerusalem.
19:12 place and its **r**, declares the
25:9 country and its **r** as well as
36:31 as well as the **r** of Jerusalem and
Mark
6:21 officers and Galilee's leading **r**.
Acts
2:9 as well as **r** of Mesopotamia,

RESPECT

Genesis
16:5 I lost her **r**. Let the LORD
43:28 And they bowed down again with deep **r**.
Exodus
10:3 you refuse to **r** me? Let my people
18:21 persons who **r** God. They should
Leviticus
19:3 Each of you must **r** your mother and
19:30 my sanctuary with **r**; I am the LORD.
19:32 an old person and **r** the elderly. You
26:2 my sabbaths and **r** my sanctuary; I
Deuteronomy
32:51 me with proper **r** before the
1 Samuel
2:29 place? Why do you **r** your sons more
28:14 bowed low out of **r**, nose to the
2 Samuel
1:2 to the ground, bowing low out of **r**.
6:16 the LORD, and she lost all **r** for him.
9:6 bowing low out of **r**. "Mephibosheth?"
9:8 bowed low out of **r** and said, "Who am
14:4 bowing low out of **r**. "King, help me!"
15:5 bowing low out of **r**, he would reach
16:4 I bow out of **r**! Please think
1 Kings
3:28 king made. Their **r** for the king grew
1 Chronicles
15:29 and dancing, she lost all **r** for him.
2 Chronicles
19:7 Therefore, **r** the LORD and act
19:9 them, "You must **r** the LORD at all
Proverbs
3:35 The wise gain **r**, but fools receive
13:13 but those who **r** the commandment
15:33 and humility comes before **r**.
18:12 disaster, but humility comes before **r**.
26:8 in a sling, so is giving **r** to a fool.
28:12 there is great **r**, but people hide
Lamentations
5:12 hands; elders have been shown no **r**.
Malachi
1:6 where is my **r**? says the LORD of
2:9 keep my ways or show **r** for Instruction.
Matthew
21:37 to them. 'They will **r** my son,' he said.
Mark
12:6 him last, thinking, They will **r** my son.

Luke
18:4 himself, I don't fear God or ***r*** people,
20:13 love dearly. Perhaps they will ***r*** him.'
Acts
22:12 who enjoyed the ***r*** of all the Jews
Romans
7:4 also died with ***r*** to the Law
7:6 We have died with ***r*** to the thing that
12:17 actions, but show ***r*** for what everyone
13:7 are charged, give ***r*** to those you
Ephesians
5:21 to each other out of ***r*** for Christ.
5:33 and wives should ***r*** their husbands.
Philippians
2:29 and show great ***r*** for people like
3:5 the Hebrews. With ***r*** to observing the
3:6 With ***r*** to devotion to the faith, I
1 Thessalonians
5:12 we ask you to ***r*** those who are
1 Timothy
3:4 children are obedient with complete ***r***,
5:2 like your sisters with appropriate ***r***.
5:4 first learn to ***r*** their own family
6:1 as worthy of full ***r*** so that God's
Titus
2:2 and healthy in ***r*** to their faith,
Hebrews
12:28 that is pleasing to God with ***r*** and awe,
13:4 honored in every ***r***, with no cheating
1 Peter
2:18 masters with all ***r***. Do this not only

RESPOND

Job
15:2 Will the wise ***r*** with windy knowledge
29:22 they didn't ***r***. My words fell
31:35 let the Almighty ***r***, and let my
32:20 get relief; I will open my lips and ***r***.
35:13 certainly doesn't ***r*** to a deceitful
37:23 abundantly righteous—he won't ***r***.
38:3 interrogate you, and you will ***r*** to me.
40:1 The LORD continued to ***r*** to Job
40:7 interrogate you, and you will ***r*** to me.
Proverbs
1:23 You should ***r*** when I correct you. Look,
29:19 might understand, but they don't ***r***.
Isaiah
41:17 I, the LORD, will ***r*** to them; I, the
42:23 will pay attention and ***r*** from now on?
50:4 to know how to ***r*** to the weary with
65:1 I was ready to ***r*** to those who didn't
Jeremiah
7:27 When you call to them, they won't ***r***.
35:17 listen to me or ***r*** when I called.
Ezekiel
8:18 I will certainly ***r*** with wrath. I won't
Hosea
2:15 There she will ***r*** to me as in the
12:2 to his ways, and ***r*** to him according
Habakkuk
2:1 me and how he will ***r*** to my complaint.
2:11 village wall, and a tree branch will ***r***.
Zechariah
10:6 the LORD their God; I will ***r*** to them.
13:9 name, and I will ***r*** to them. I will
Matthew
15:23 But he didn't ***r*** to her at all. His
26:62 you going to ***r*** to the testimony
Mark
9:6 know how to ***r***, for the three of
9:34 They didn't ***r***, since on the way they
14:40 and they didn't know how to ***r*** to him.
14:60 you going to ***r*** to the testimony
Luke
13:27 He will ***r***, 'I don't know you or where
23:9 at length, but Jesus didn't ***r*** to him.
1 Corinthians
4:12 are insulted, we ***r*** with a blessing;
2 Corinthians
13:11 things in order, ***r*** to my
Colossians
4:6 you may know how to ***r*** to every person.
2 Thessalonians
3:2 that we meet won't ***r*** with faith.
1 Peter
3:6 do good and don't ***r*** to threats with

RESPONSIBLE

Leviticus
19:17 so you don't become ***r*** for his sin.
Numbers
3:8 They will be ***r*** for all the equipment of
4:31 is what they are ***r*** to carry as their
18:22 or they will be ***r*** for their sin and
35:19 close relative ***r*** for the blood of
35:27 him, he will not be ***r*** for his blood.
Psalms
34:21 who hate the righteous will be held ***r***.
34:22 in him won't be held ***r*** for anything.
Ezekiel
18:26 turn from their ***r*** ways and act
33:4 taken away, they are ***r*** for their blood.
33:8 but I will hold you ***r*** for their blood.
45:17 prince will be ***r*** for the entirely
Matthew
18:34 over to the guard ***r*** for punishing
Acts
5:28 to hold us ***r*** for this man's
8:27 and an official ***r*** for the entire
18:6 to them, "You are ***r*** for your own
20:26 you that I'm not ***r*** for anyone's fate.
Hebrews
13:17 going to be held ***r*** for you. They

REST

Genesis
8:4 the ark came to ***r*** on the Ararat
Exodus
16:23 is a day of ***r***, a holy Sabbath
31:15 of complete ***r*** that is holy to
Leviticus
25:4 a special sabbath ***r***, a Sabbath to the
Numbers
9:7 time with the ***r*** of the
Deuteronomy
12:10 he will give you ***r*** from all your
Joshua
1:13 God will give you ***r*** and give you this
11:23 shares. Then the land had a ***r*** from war.
21:44 LORD gave them ***r*** from surrounding
Ruth
3:18 The man won't ***r*** until he resolves
2 Samuel
7:11 I will give you ***r*** from all your

Job
3:17 wicked rage no more; there the weak ***r***.
30:17 my bones; my gnawing pain won't ***r***.
Psalms
16:9 yes, my whole body will ***r*** in safety
23:2 He lets me ***r*** in grassy meadows; he
95:11 They will never enter my place of ***r***!'"
Ecclesiastes
2:23 hearts don't find ***r***. This too is
Isaiah
11:2 spirit will ***r*** upon him, a
30:15 In return and ***r*** you will be
44:17 And the ***r*** of it he makes into a god,
Jeremiah
47:6 Return to your sheath; ***r*** and be still!
Matthew
11:28 heavy loads, and I will give you ***r***.
Mark
6:31 to a secluded place and ***r*** for a while."
Hebrews
3:11 I swore: "They will never enter my ***r***!"
4:3 are entering the ***r***. As God said, And
4:10 who entered God's ***r*** also rested from
Revelation
14:11 There is no ***r*** day or night for
14:13 so they can ***r*** from their

RESTED

Genesis
2:2 seventh day God ***r*** from all the work
2:3 because on it God ***r*** from all the work
Exodus
16:30 So the people ***r*** on the seventh day
20:11 in six days, but ***r*** on the seventh
31:17 day the LORD ***r*** and was
39:21 the chest pendant ***r*** on the vest's
Numbers
10:36 When it ***r***, he would say, "Return, LORD
11:25 When the spirit ***r*** on them, they
11:26 and the spirit ***r*** on them. They
1 Kings
7:25 The Sea ***r*** on twelve oxen with their
8:7 where the chest ***r***, covering the
2 Chronicles
4:4 The Sea ***r*** on twelve oxen with their
5:8 where the chest ***r***, covering the
36:21 it lay empty, it ***r***, until seventy
Ezra
8:32 in Jerusalem, we ***r*** there three days.
Esther
9:17 day they ***r***, making it a day
9:18 month. But they ***r*** on the fifteenth
Ezekiel
41:8 roof all around ***r*** on the side
Luke
2:25 Israel, and the Holy Spirit ***r*** on him.
23:56 oils. They ***r*** on the Sabbath in
John
1:32 heaven like a dove, and it ***r*** on him.
Hebrews
4:4 of creation: God ***r*** on the seventh
4:10 God's rest also ***r*** from his works,

RESTING

Psalms
36:4 evil even while ***r*** in bed! They
139:3 my traveling and ***r***. You are
Ecclesiastes
4:6 But better is ***r*** with one handful than
Isaiah
34:14 Lilith will lurk and find her ***r*** place.
65:10 Achor Valley a ***r*** place for cattle,
66:1 for me, and where could my ***r*** place be?
Amos
6:1 Doom to those ***r*** comfortably in Zion and those trusting
Matthew
3:16 coming down like a dove and ***r*** on him.
John
1:33 coming down and ***r*** is the one who
Acts
7:49 says the Lord, 'or where is my ***r*** place?

RESTORE

Deuteronomy
30:3 your God will ***r*** you as you were
Ruth
4:15 He will ***r*** your life and sustain you in
2 Samuel
9:7 Jonathan. I will ***r*** to you all the
12:6 He must ***r*** the ewe lamb seven times over
1 Kings
12:21 of Israel and ***r*** the kingdom for
2 Chronicles
11:1 Israel and to ***r*** the kingdom to
Nehemiah
4:2 doing? Will they ***r*** things
Psalms
13:3 me, LORD my God! ***R*** sight to my eyes!
60:1 us. You've been so angry. Now ***r*** us!
80:3 ***R*** us, God! Make your face shine so that
80:7 ***R*** us, God of heavenly forces! Make your face shine
80:19 ***R*** us, LORD God of heavenly forces! Make your face shine
85:4 who can save us, ***r*** us! Stop being
Proverbs
25:13 send them; they ***r*** the life of their
Isaiah
1:26 Then I will ***r*** your judges as in earlier
44:26 be rebuilt, and I will ***r*** their ruins";
49:5 his servant—to ***r*** Jacob to God, so
49:8 to the people, to ***r*** the land, and to
58:12 past you will ***r***. You will be
61:4 ruins; they will ***r*** formerly deserted
Jeremiah
12:15 on them and ***r*** their inheritance
27:22 them back and ***r*** them to this
28:3 two years I will ***r*** to this place all
30:17 I will ***r*** your health, and I will heal
33:26 and Jacob. I will ***r*** the captives and
50:19 But I will ***r*** Israel to their pasture;
Daniel
9:25 word went out to ***r*** and rebuild
Nahum
2:2 The LORD will ***r*** the pride of Jacob,
Zephaniah
2:7 visit them and ***r*** their possessions.
3:20 peoples when I ***r*** your possessions
Matthew
17:11 does come first and will ***r*** all things.
Mark
9:12 come first to ***r*** all things. Why

Acts
1:6 are you going to ***r*** the kingdom to
9:12 put his hands on him to ***r*** his sight."
15:16 what has been torn down. I will ***r*** it
Galatians
6:1 spiritual should ***r*** someone like this
Hebrews
6:4 impossible to ***r*** people to changed
James
5:15 for the Lord will ***r*** them to health.
1 Peter
5:10 will himself ***r***,empower,

RESTORED

2 Kings
5:10 your skin will be ***r*** and become clean."
5:14 His skin was ***r*** like that of a
2 Chronicles
33:16 He ***r*** the LORD's altar, offered
Nehemiah
3:8 next to him. They ***r*** Jerusalem as far
Job
22:23 you will be ***r***; if you keep
Psalms
18:20 righteousness; he ***r*** me because my
18:24 And so the LORD ***r*** me for my
68:9 grew weary, you ***r*** it yourself,
Isaiah
42:19 is blind like the ***r*** one, blind like
Jeremiah
8:22 have my people not been ***r*** to health?
Daniel
8:14 Then the sanctuary will be ***r***."
Mark
8:25 his sight was ***r***, and he could see
Luke
7:10 they found the servant ***r*** to health.
Romans
5:11 we now have a ***r*** relationship with
1 Corinthians
1:10 Instead be ***r*** with the same

RESURRECTION → RESURRECTION FROM THE DEAD, RESURRECTION OF THE DEAD

Matthew
22:23 deny that there is a ***r***, came to Jesus.
22:28 At the ***r***, which of the seven brothers
22:30 At the ***r*** people won't marry nor will
27:53 After Jesus' ***r*** they came out of their
Mark
12:18 that there is a ***r***, came to Jesus
12:23 At the ***r***, when they all rise up, whose
12:26 As for the ***r*** from the dead, haven't you
Luke
20:27 that there's a ***r***, came to Jesus
20:33 In the ***r***, whose wife will she be? All
20:36 children since they share in the ***r***.
John
5:29 come out into the ***r*** of life, and
11:24 he will rise in the ***r*** on the last day."
11:25 to her, "I am the ***r*** and the life.
Acts
1:22 along with us a witness to his ***r***."
2:31 spoke about the ***r*** of Christ, that
4:33 witness to the ***r*** of the Lord
17:18 the good news about Jesus and the ***r***.)
23:8 that there's no ***r***, angel, or
24:15 there will be a ***r*** of both the
Romans
6:5 be united together in a ***r*** like his.
Philippians
3:10 the power of his ***r***, and the
2 Timothy
2:18 claiming that the ***r*** has already
Hebrews
11:35 their dead by ***r***. Others were
1 Peter
1:3 hope through the ***r*** of Jesus Christ
3:21 comes through the ***r*** of Jesus Christ,
Revelation
20:5 years were over. This is the first ***r***.
20:6 in the first ***r***. The second death

RESURRECTION FROM THE DEAD

Mk 12:26; Lk 20:35; Ac 17:32; Ro 1:4; Heb 6:2

RESURRECTION OF THE DEAD

Mt 22:31; Ac 4:2; 23:6; 24:21; 1Co 15:12; 15:13, 21, 42; Phi 3:11

RETURN → RETURN TO THE LORD

Genesis
15:16 generation will ***r*** here since the
Leviticus
6:4 of sin, you must ***r*** the property you
27:24 of land will ***r*** to the seller, to
Numbers
10:36 he would say, "***R***, LORD of the ten
14:3 it be better for us to ***r*** to Egypt?"
17:10 said to Moses, "***R*** Aaron's staff in
Deuteronomy
23:15 Don't ***r*** slaves to owners if they've
Ruth
1:6 to ***r*** from the field of
1:7 along the road to ***r*** to the land of
1:10 instead we will ***r*** with you, to your
1 Kings
2:44 May the LORD ***r*** your evil on your
13:9 water! Don't ***r*** by the way you
1 Chronicles
21:27 the messenger to ***r*** his sword to its
Esther
2:14 morning she would ***r*** to the second
Job
1:21 naked I will ***r*** there. The LORD
7:10 won't ***r*** home again, won't be recognized
10:9 from clay, and you will ***r*** me to dust.
10:21 I go and don't ***r*** to a land of
15:13 so that you ***r*** your breath to God and
16:22 then I'll walk a path that I won't ***r***.
22:23 If you ***r*** to the Almighty, you will be
30:23 I know you will ***r*** me to death, the
34:15 together, and humans would ***r*** to dust.
39:4 in the open country, leave and never ***r***.
Psalms
51:12 ***R*** the joy of your salvation to me and
85:8 ones. Don't let them ***r*** to foolish ways.
90:3 You ***r*** people to dust, saying, "Go back,
104:29 their breath, they die and ***r*** to dust.
109:5 evil for good, hatred in ***r*** for my love.
119:79 those who know your precepts ***r*** to me.
Proverbs
2:19 to her will never ***r***; they will never
17:13 the house of those who ***r*** evil for good.

26:15 bowl, too tired to ***r*** it to their mouth.
Ecclesiastes
3:20 are from the dust; all ***r*** to the dust.
4:9 they have a good ***r*** for their hard
5:15 naked they'll ***r***, ending up just
12:2 before the clouds ***r*** after the rain;
Hosea
2:7 will say, "I will ***r*** to my first
12:6 But you! ***R*** to your God with faithful
Joel
2:12 says the LORD, ***r*** to me with all
2:13 your clothing. ***R*** to the LORD your
Amos
4:6 yet you didn't ***r*** to me,says the
Zechariah
1:3 forces proclaims: ***R*** to me, says the
Malachi
3:7 not kept them. ***R*** to me and I will
Matthew
2:12 in a dream not to ***r*** to Herod, they
Luke
6:35 nothing in ***r***. If you do, you
6:38 the portion you receive in ***r***."
8:39 ***R*** home and tell the story of what God
10:6 If not, your blessing will ***r*** to you.
10:35 him, and when I ***r***, I will pay you
14:12 invite you in ***r*** and that will be
19:12 land to receive his kingdom and then ***r***.
19:13 Do business with this until I ***r***.'
19:16 has earned a ***r*** of one thousand
19:18 money has made a ***r*** of five hundred
John
11:7 disciples, "Let's ***r*** to Judea again."
14:3 for you, I will ***r*** and take you to
Acts
15:16 After this I will ***r***, and I will
18:21 willing, I will ***r***." Then he sailed
19:21 decided to ***r*** to Jerusalem,
20:3 decided instead to ***r*** through Macedonia.
25:4 since he was to ***r*** there very soon
Romans
9:9 from now I will ***r***, and Sarah will
Hebrews
11:15 have had the opportunity to ***r*** to it.
1 Peter
3:9 give blessing in ***r***. You were called
Jude
1:16 to people when they want a favor in ***r***.

RETURN TO THE LORD

Dt 4:30; 30:2; 2Ch 19:4; 30:6, 9; Is 19:22; 55:7; Lam 3:40; Hos 6:1; 7:10; 14:2; Jl 2:13

RETURNED

Genesis
8:9 set its foot. It ***r*** to him in the ark
50:14 Then Joseph ***r*** to Egypt, he, his
Exodus
4:7 the skin of his hand had ***r*** to normal.
14:27 daybreak, the sea ***r*** to its normal
14:28 The waters ***r*** and covered the chariots
Numbers
13:25 They ***r*** from exploring the land after
Ruth
1:21 but the LORD has ***r*** me empty. Why
4:3 Naomi, who has ***r*** from the field of
Ezra
2:1 Babylonia. They ***r*** to Jerusalem and
4:1 heard that the ***r*** exiles were
6:16 the rest of the ***r*** exiles, joyfully
8:35 captivity, the ***r*** exiles, offered
9:4 of the ***r*** exiles while I
10:7 that all the ***r*** exiles should
10:16 Then the ***r*** exiles did so. Ezra the
Nehemiah
2:15 I turned back and ***r*** by entering
4:15 plans. So we all ***r*** to doing our own
7:6 the province who ***r*** from the
8:17 of those who had ***r*** from captivity
13:7 and ***r*** to Jerusalem. That was when I saw
Esther
6:12 Mordecai ***r*** to the King's
7:8 The king ***r*** from the palace garden to
Psalms
60:1 and when Joab ***r*** and defeated
Jeremiah
11:10 They have ***r*** to the sins of their
Zechariah
1:16 LORD says: I have ***r*** to Jerusalem with
4:1 speaking with me ***r*** and woke me like
8:3 proclaims: I have ***r*** to Zion; I will
Matthew
27:3 deep regret. He ***r*** the thirty pieces
Luke
2:15 When the angels ***r*** to heaven, the
2:20 The shepherds ***r*** home, glorifying and
17:18 No one ***r*** to praise God except this
24:9 When they ***r*** from the tomb, they
24:12 cloth. Then he ***r*** home, wondering
24:52 him and ***r*** to Jerusalem
Hebrews
7:1 met Abraham as he ***r*** from the defeat
13:19 this so that I can be ***r*** to you quickly.
1 Peter
2:25 you have now ***r*** to the shepherd

REUBEN

Genesis
29:32 She named him ***R*** because she said,
37:22 ***R*** said to them, "Don't spill his blood!
49:3 ***R***, you are my oldest son, my strength
Joshua
13:23 of the people of ***R*** was the Jordan
18:7 of the LORD. Gad, ***R***, and half the
Ezekiel
48:6 to the western border: ***R***, one portion.
Revelation
7:5 from the tribe of ***R***, twelve thousand;

REUBENITES

Numbers
32:1 owned by the ***R*** and the Gadites
Deuteronomy
29:8 to the ***R***, Gadites, and
Joshua
13:8 of Manasseh, the ***R*** and Gadites

REVEAL

Exodus
6:3 but I didn't ***r*** myself to them by
Joshua
2:14 If you don't ***r*** our mission, we
2:20 But if you ***r*** our mission, we won't be

Proverbs
1:23 spirit on you. I'll ***r*** my words to you.
12:16 Fools ***r*** their anger right away, but the
20:19 Gossips ***r*** secrets; don't associate with
Jeremiah
33:3 I will answer and ***r*** to you wondrous
Lamentations
2:14 They didn't ***r*** your sin so as to
Daniel
2:47 you were able to ***r*** this mystery!"
Matthew
11:27 anyone to whom the Son wants to ***r*** him.
Mark
3:12 ordered them not to ***r*** who he was.
Luke
10:22 anyone to whom the Son wants to ***r*** him."
John
14:21 I will love them and ***r*** myself to them."
14:22 are you about to ***r*** yourself to us
Galatians
1:16 to ***r*** his Son to me, so that I might
Ephesians
3:9 God sent me to ***r*** the secret plan that
5:11 you should ***r*** the truth about
Philippians
3:15 God will ***r*** it to him or her.
Hebrews
12:27 still once more" ***r*** the removal of
1 Peter
1:5 he is ready to ***r*** in the last time.

REVEALED

Genesis
35:7 because God had ***r*** himself to him
45:1 with him when he ***r*** his identity to
Deuteronomy
29:29 LORD our God. The ***r*** things belong to
1 Samuel
2:27 the LORD says: I ***r*** myself very
3:7 LORD's word hadn't yet been ***r*** to him.)
3:21 because the LORD ***r*** himself to Samuel
9:15 the LORD had ***r*** the following to
2 Samuel
7:27 God, have ***r*** to your servant
1 Chronicles
17:25 You, my God, have ***r*** to your servant
Job
38:17 gates been ***r*** to you; can you
Psalms
31:21 he has wondrously ***r*** his faithful love
98:2 known; he has ***r*** his righteousness
Proverbs
26:26 but their evil will be ***r*** in public.
Isaiah
22:14 forces has ***r*** in my hearing:
53:1 whose sake has the LORD's arm been ***r***?
56:1 soon, and my righteousness will be ***r***.
Ezekiel
40:4 things could be ***r*** to you. Describe
Daniel
2:19 the mystery was ***r*** to Daniel! Daniel
2:29 of mysteries has ***r*** to you what will
2:30 this mystery was ***r*** to me, not
2:45 A great God has ***r*** to the king what
10:1 a message was ***r*** to Daniel, who
Matthew
10:26 that won't be ***r***, and nothing
Mark
4:22 hidden will be ***r***, and everything
Luke
2:15 confirm what the Lord has ***r*** to us."
2:26 The Holy Spirit ***r*** to him that he
2:35 of many will be ***r***. And a sword will
12:2 that won't be ***r***, and nothing is
17:30 will be on the day the Human One is ***r***.
John
2:11 of Galilee. He ***r*** his glory, and
12:38 To whom is the arm of the Lord fully ***r***?
17:6 I have ***r*** your name to the people you
Romans
1:17 is being ***r*** in the gospel,
1:18 wrath is being ***r*** from heaven
2:5 judgment will be ***r*** on the day of
3:21 has been ***r*** apart from the
8:18 glory that is going to be ***r*** to us.
10:20 look for me; I ***r*** myself to those
16:26 that secret is ***r*** through what the
1 Corinthians
1:7 wait for our Lord Jesus Christ to be ***r***.
2:10 God has ***r*** these things to us through
3:13 it will be ***r*** with fire
Galatians
3:23 until faith that was coming would be ***r***,
Ephesians
1:9 God ***r*** his hidden design to us, which is
3:5 that God has now ***r*** to his holy
5:13 exposed to the light is ***r*** by the light.
5:14 that is ***r*** by the light is
Colossians
1:26 has now been ***r*** to his holy
3:4 is your life, is ***r***, then you also
2 Thessalonians
1:7 the Lord Jesus is ***r*** from heaven with
2:3 who is lawless is ***r***, who is headed
2:6 so that he can be ***r*** when his time
2:8 lawless will be ***r***. The Lord Jesus
1 Timothy
3:9 that has been ***r*** with a clear
3:16 is great: he was ***r*** as a human,
6:15 appearance is ***r*** by God alone, who
2 Timothy
1:10 Now his grace is ***r*** through the
Titus
1:3 God ***r*** his message at the appropriate
Hebrews
9:8 place hadn't been ***r*** yet while the
1 Peter
1:7 honor for you when Jesus Christ is ***r***.
1:12 It was ***r*** to them that in their search
1:13 brought to you when Jesus Christ is ***r***.
1:20 but was only ***r*** at the end of
4:13 overwhelming joy when his glory is ***r***.
5:1 is about to be ***r***.) I urge the
1 John
1:2 The life was ***r***, and we have seen, and
4:9 love of God is ***r*** to us: God has
Revelation
15:4 for your acts of justice have been ***r***."

REVENGE

Genesis
27:42 is planning ***r***. He plans to kill

REVENGE [cont.]

Leviticus
19:18 You must not take ***r*** nor hold a grudge
Deuteronomy
32:35 ***R*** is my domain, so is
Joshua
10:13 a nation took ***r*** on its enemies."
20:3 of the victim's family seeking ***r***.
20:5 follows, seeking ***r***, they won't hand
20:9 family seeking ***r***, until there
Judges
15:7 I won't stop until I get ***r*** on you!"
16:28 so I can have ***r*** on the
1 Samuel
14:24 when I have taken ***r*** on my enemies is
2 Samuel
14:11 the one seeking ***r*** doesn't add to
2 Kings
9:7 way I will take ***r*** for the violence
Psalms
44:16 because of the enemy who is out for ***r***.
149:7 to get ***r*** against the nations and
Proverbs
6:34 he'll show no mercy on his day of ***r***.
Jeremiah
5:9 Shouldn't I take ***r*** on such a nation?
11:20 let me see your ***r*** upon them,
20:10 against him and get our ***r*** on him!"
23:2 so I will take ***r*** on you for the
Ezekiel
5:13 them and take my ***r***. Then they will
25:15 they enacted ***r*** with utter
Romans
12:19 Don't try to get ***r*** for yourselves, my
1 Peter
2:23 did not threaten ***r***. Instead, he

REVERE → REVERE THE LORD

Genesis
22:12 now know that you ***r*** God and didn't
1 Kings
8:40 so that they may ***r*** you all the days
8:43 reputation and ***r*** you, as your
2 Chronicles
6:31 that they may ***r*** you by following
6:33 reputation and ***r*** you, as your
Job
1:9 the LORD, "Does Job ***r*** God for nothing?
Daniel
6:26 must fear and ***r*** Daniel's God
Malachi
3:5 and do not ***r*** me, says the LORD

REVERE THE LORD

Dt 6:13; 10:12, 20; 17:19; 31:12, 13; Josh 4:24; 24:14; Ps 22:23

REWARD

Genesis
15:1 protector. Your ***r*** will be very
Numbers
18:21 They are a ***r*** for performing
Ruth
2:12 May the LORD ***r*** you for your deed. May
1 Samuel
17:25 The king will ***r*** with great riches
2 Samuel
2:6 myself will also ***r*** you because you
4:10 him. That was the ***r*** I gave him for
18:22 asked. "You'll get no ***r*** for going."
19:36 why should the king give me such a ***r***?
Esther
6:3 done to honor and ***r*** Mordecai for
Job
8:6 your behalf and ***r*** your innocent
15:31 worth, for their ***r*** will be worthless.
20:18 won't receive the ***r*** for their labor;
Psalms
19:11 them; there is great ***r*** in keeping them.
58:11 Yes, there is a ***r*** for the
109:20 all that be the ***r*** my accusers get
127:3 the fruit of the womb is a divine ***r***.
Proverbs
11:18 who sow righteousness receive a true ***r***.
12:14 satisfied; their work results in ***r***.
13:21 but good things ***r*** the righteous.
14:14 good receive the due ***r*** for their deeds.
22:4 The ***r*** of humility and the fear of the
25:22 their heads, and the LORD will ***r*** you.
Ecclesiastes
2:10 that was the ***r*** from all my hard
9:5 There is no more ***r*** for them; even
Isaiah
40:10 arm, bringing his ***r*** with him and his
49:4 grant me justice; my ***r*** is with my God.
57:18 guide them, and ***r*** them with
62:11 arrives, bringing ***r*** and payment!"
Jeremiah
32:19 humanity, and you ***r*** us for how we
Daniel
12:13 to receive your ***r*** at the end of
Matthew
5:12 you have a great ***r*** in heaven. In the
5:46 love you, what ***r*** do you have?
6:1 you will have no ***r*** from your Father
6:18 Father who sees in secret will ***r*** you.
10:41 a prophet's ***r***. Those who
Luke
6:23 you have a great ***r*** in heaven. Their
14:12 you in return and that will be your ***r***.
1 Corinthians
3:8 receive their own ***r*** for their own
3:14 work survives, they'll get a ***r***.
9:18 What ***r*** do I get? That when I preach, I
Ephesians
6:8 the Lord will ***r*** every person who
Colossians
3:24 inheritance as a ***r***. You serve the
3:25 receive their ***r*** for their evil
Hebrews
10:35 your confidence—it brings a great ***r***.
11:26 since he was looking forward to the ***r***.
James
1:12 to those who love him as their ***r***.
2 John
1:8 for but instead receive a full ***r***.
Revelation
11:18 The time came to ***r*** your servants,
22:12 coming soon. My ***r*** is with me, to

RICH

Genesis
14:23 say, 'I'm the one who made Abram ***r***.'
30:43 became very, very ***r***: he owned large

Exodus
30:15 your lives, the ***r*** shouldn't give
Numbers
13:20 Is the land ***r*** or poor? Are there trees
Ruth
2:12 May you receive a ***r*** reward from the
3:10 haven't gone after ***r*** or poor young men.
2 Samuel
12:1 men in the same city, one ***r***, one poor.
2 Kings
4:8 went to Shunem. A ***r*** woman lived
Nehemiah
8:10 Go, eat ***r*** food, and drink something
9:35 in the wide and ***r*** land that you
Job
15:29 They won't get ***r***; their wealth won't
27:19 They lie down ***r***, but no longer; open
34:19 nor regards the ***r*** over the poor,
36:16 your table is set with ***r*** food.
Psalms
21:3 You bring ***r*** blessings right to him; you
49:2 people of every kind, ***r*** and poor alike
49:16 someone becomes ***r***, their house
63:5 as with a ***r*** dinner. My mouth
65:11 your paths overflow with ***r*** food.
Proverbs
10:4 brings poverty; hard work makes one ***r***.
10:22 makes a person ***r***, and no trouble
13:7 pretend to be ***r*** but have nothing,
21:17 lovers of wine and oil won't get ***r***.
22:2 The ***r*** and the poor have this in common:
22:16 the poor to get ***r*** and giving to the
23:4 out trying to get ***r***; be smart enough
24:25 rebuke them. A ***r*** blessing will
28:8 Those who become ***r*** through high
28:11 ***R*** people think they are wise, but an
28:22 stingy try to get ***r*** fast, unaware
Ecclesiastes
10:6 posts, while the ***r*** sit in lowly
10:20 don't curse the ***r*** in your bedroom,
Isaiah
5:17 will feed among the ruins of the ***r***.
25:6 for all peoples a ***r*** feast, a feast of
30:23 produces will be ***r*** and abundant. On
Jeremiah
5:27 loot. No wonder they are ***r*** and powerful
9:23 might, nor the ***r*** boast of their
14:3 The ***r*** send their servants for water,
22:14 cedar paneling, and ***r*** red decor."
51:13 and you are ***r*** in treasures. But
Ezekiel
28:4 you made yourself ***r***, and you filled
Daniel
10:3 I didn't eat any ***r*** foods. Neither meat
Hosea
12:8 has said, "I'm ***r***, I've gained
Joel
3:5 have carried my ***r*** treasures into
Zechariah
11:5 for I have become ***r***." And their own
Matthew
19:23 very hard for a ***r*** person to enter
19:24 needle than for a ***r*** person to enter
27:57 came. He was a ***r*** man from
Mark
10:25 needle than for a ***r*** person to enter
12:41 their money. Many ***r*** people were
Luke
1:53 and sent the ***r*** away empty-handed.
6:24 for you who are ***r***, because you have
12:16 A certain ***r*** man's land
14:12 relatives, or ***r*** neighbors. If you
16:1 A certain ***r*** man heard that
18:23 became sad because he was extremely ***r***.
18:25 needle than for a ***r*** person to enter
19:2 a ruler among tax collectors, was ***r***.
21:1 up, Jesus saw ***r*** people throwing
Romans
11:17 that produces the ***r*** oil of the olive
1 Corinthians
1:5 is, you were made ***r*** through him in
4:8 You've become ***r*** already! You rule
2 Corinthians
6:10 but making many ***r***, and as having
8:2 resulted in a surplus of ***r*** generosity.
8:9 Although he was ***r***, he became poor
9:11 You will be made ***r*** in every way so that
Ephesians
2:5 However, God is ***r*** in mercy. He brought
Philippians
1:9 more and more ***r*** with knowledge
1 Timothy
6:9 are trying to get ***r*** fall into
6:17 people who are ***r*** at this time not
6:18 to do good, to be ***r*** in the good
James
2:5 standards to be ***r*** in terms of
2 Peter
1:11 will receive a ***r*** welcome into the
Revelation
2:9 you are actually ***r***). I also know the
3:17 you say, 'I'm ***r***, and I've grown
3:18 that you may be ***r***, and white
6:15 the generals, the ***r*** and the powerful,
13:16 and great, the ***r*** and poor, the
18:3 the earth became ***r*** from the power of
18:15 and got so ***r*** by her, will
18:19 at sea became so ***r*** by her prosperity

RICHES

1 Samuel
17:25 reward with great ***r*** whoever kills
2 Chronicles
1:11 for wealth, ***r***, fame, victory
1:12 give you wealth, ***r***, and fame beyond
17:5 so that he had abundant ***r*** and honor.
Esther
1:4 off the awesome ***r*** of his kingdom
Job
20:21 their food, so their ***r*** will not endure.
Psalms
45:13 with ***r*** of every sort for the royal
112:3 wealth and ***r*** will be in their houses.
Proverbs
6:31 he must give all the ***r*** of his house.
8:18 ***R*** and honor are with me, as well as
10:15 The ***r*** of the wealthy are their strong
11:4 ***R*** don't help in the day of wrath, but
12:27 but hard workers receive precious ***r***.
13:7 pretend to be poor, but have great ***r***.
13:11 ***R*** gotten quickly will dwindle, but
18:11 The ***r*** of the wealthy are a strong city
19:4 ***R*** increase one's friends, but the poor

RICHES [cont.]

19:14 House and ***r*** are an inheritance from
29:3 time with prostitutes destroys ***r***.
Ecclesiastes
5:19 people wealth and ***r*** and enables them
6:2 plenty of wealth, ***r***, and glory so
Isaiah
45:3 of secret ***r***, so you will know
61:6 and fatten yourself on their ***r***.
Ezekiel
22:27 blood and destroy lives for unjust ***r***.
28:5 multiplied your ***r***. But then you
Daniel
11:2 through his great ***r***, he will disturb
Luke
8:14 by the concerns, ***r***, and pleasures of
16:11 wealth, who will trust you with true ***r***?
Romans
2:4 contempt for the ***r*** of God's
11:12 failure brings ***r*** to the world, and
11:33 God's ***r***, wisdom, and knowledge are so
Ephesians
3:8 the immeasurable ***r*** of Christ to the
3:16 selves from the ***r*** of his glory
Philippians
4:19 need out of his ***r*** in the glory that
Colossians
1:27 make the glorious ***r*** of this secret
2:2 have all the ***r*** of assurance that
James
5:2 Your ***r*** have rotted. Moths have

RIDERS

2 Kings
2:12 chariots and its ***r***!" When he could
13:7 fifty chariot ***r***, ten chariots,
18:23 horses if you can supply the ***r***!
Esther
8:10 sent letters with ***r*** mounted on royal
8:14 The ***r*** mounted on royal horses left
Isaiah
21:7 horsemen, donkey ***r***, camel riders, he
31:1 are many, and on ***r*** because they are
36:8 horses if you can supply the ***r***!
36:9 relying on Egypt for chariots and ***r***?
Ezekiel
38:4 army, horses and ***r***, handsomely
39:20 with horses and ***r***, mighty men and
Haggai
2:22 rider; horses and ***r*** will fall. Each
Revelation
9:17 horses and their ***r*** in the vision:
19:18 horses and their ***r***. Come and eat the

RIGHT → DO RIGHT, DO THE RIGHT THING, DOING WHAT IS RIGHT, GOD'S RIGHT SIDE, HEART IS RIGHT, WHOSE HEART IS RIGHT

Genesis
48:13 Ephraim in his ***r*** hand at Israel's
Exodus
14:22 for them on their ***r*** hand and on their
15:26 God thinks is ***r***, pay attention to
Joshua
1:7 it, either to the ***r*** or left. Then you
1 Kings
15:5 David did the ***r*** thing in the
Esther
8:5 if the idea seems ***r*** to the king, and
Psalms
16:8 not stumble because he is on my ***r*** side.
16:11 things are always in your ***r*** hand.
17:2 from you; let your eyes see what is ***r***!
19:8 regulations are ***r***, gladdening the
22:28 Because the ***r*** to rule belongs to the
33:1 to the LORD! It's ***r*** for those who do
33:4 LORD's word is ***r***, his every act is
37:14 to slaughter those whose way is ***r***.
45:9 stands at your ***r***, dressed in the
52:3 more than speaking what is ***r***. Selah
58:1 speak what is ***r***, you gods? Do you
69:13 LORD, at just the ***r*** time. God, in
75:2 the time is ***r***, I will establish
80:17 the one on your ***r*** side—with the
106:3 always do what is ***r***, are truly happy!
111:8 are fulfilled with truth and ***r*** doing.
125:4 are good, to people whose hearts are ***r***.
140:12 and will do what is ***r*** for the needy.
Proverbs
3:16 In her ***r*** hand is a long life; in her
4:27 a bit to the ***r*** or the left; turn
8:6 correct; from my lips come what is ***r***.
12:15 their own way as ***r***, but the wise
15:19 way of those who do ***r*** is a clear road.
15:23 joy; how good is a word at the ***r*** time!
16:17 of those who do ***r*** turns away from
17:7 talking isn't ***r*** for a fool; even
20:3 off from a fight, but fools jump ***r*** in.
25:11 spoken at the ***r*** time are like
28:10 those who do ***r*** onto an evil path
Ecclesiastes
3:16 place of what was ***r***, there was
5:8 what is just and ***r*** in some
8:6 because there's a ***r*** time and right way
10:2 tends toward the ***r***, but the mind of
10:17 feast at the ***r*** time for energy,
Song of Songs
2:6 is beneath my head, his ***r*** embraces me.
8:3 beneath my head, and his ***r*** embraces me!
Isaiah
30:21 you stray to the ***r*** or the left, you
54:3 To the ***r*** and to the left you will burst
Jeremiah
Ezekiel
1:10 face on the ***r*** and a bull's face
4:6 days, lie on your ***r*** side to bear the
10:3 standing to the ***r*** of the temple
21:22 On his ***r*** side appeared the omen for
Jonah
4:11 can't tell their ***r*** hand from their
Zechariah
11:17 his arm and his ***r*** eye. His arm will
Matthew
5:24 First make things ***r*** with your brother
5:29 And if your ***r*** eye causes you to fall
5:30 And if your ***r*** hand causes you to fall
5:39 slap you on your ***r*** cheek, you must
6:3 hand know what your ***r*** hand is doing
20:21 sit, one on your ***r*** hand and one on
27:38 one on his ***r*** side and one on
Luke
1:11 standing to the ***r*** of the altar of
6:6 was there whose ***r*** hand was withered.
22:50 servant, cutting off his ***r*** ear.
22:69 be seated on the ***r*** side of the power

John
4:17 You are ***r*** to say, 'I don't
18:10 cutting off his ***r*** ear. (The
21:6 your net on the ***r*** side of the boat
Acts
2:25 he is at my ***r*** hand I won't be
2:34 said to my Lord, 'Sit at my ***r*** side,
3:7 grasped the man's ***r*** hand and raised
8:21 because your heart isn't ***r*** with God.
Romans
3:4 show that you are ***r*** in your words;
1 Corinthians
9:4 Don't we have the ***r*** to eat and drink
9:12 made use of this ***r***, but we put up
Ephesians
3:2 grace, which God gave to me for you, ***r***?
4:19 lack all sense of ***r*** and wrong, and
Revelation
1:16 stars in his ***r*** hand, and from
5:1 a scroll in the ***r*** hand of the one
10:2 hand. He put his ***r*** foot on the sea
13:16 mark put on their ***r*** hand or on their

RIGHTEOUS → RIGHTEOUS ACTS, RIGHTEOUS DEEDS, RIGHTEOUS MAN, RIGHTEOUS ONE, RIGHTEOUS PEOPLE, RIGHTEOUS PERSON, YOU ARE RIGHTEOUS
Genesis
38:26 said, "She's more ***r*** than I am,
Deuteronomy
4:8 and case laws as ***r*** as all this
6:25 be considered ***r*** if we are careful
9:4 It's because I'm ***r*** that the LORD
16:19 the wise and twists the words of the ***r***.
24:13 be considered ***r*** before the LORD
32:4 deceiving; altogether ***r*** and true is he.
1 Samuel
24:17 You are more ***r*** than I am because
1 Kings
2:32 better and more ***r*** than he was. He
Job
4:17 a human be more ***r*** than God, a
6:29 Don't be faithless. Turn now! I am ***r***.
22:19 The ***r*** see and rejoice; the innocent
27:17 amass, but the ***r*** will wear it; the
32:1 Job because he thought he was ***r***.
32:2 he considered himself more ***r*** than God.
36:7 his eyes from the ***r***; he seats kings
37:23 just, abundantly ***r***—he won't respond
Psalms
1:5 will sinners in the assembly of the ***r***.
1:6 the way of the ***r***, but the way of
4:1 I cry out, my ***r*** God! Set me free
4:5 Bring ***r*** offerings, and trust the LORD
5:12 LORD, bless the ***r***. You cover them
7:9 over, but set the ***r*** firmly in place
7:11 God is a ***r*** judge, a God who is angry at
11:5 examines both the ***r*** and the wicked;
11:7 the LORD is ***r***! He loves
14:5 because God is with the ***r*** generation.
19:9 judgments are true. All of these are ***r***!
31:18 against the ***r*** with pride and
32:11 You who are ***r***, rejoice in the LORD and
33:1 All you who are ***r***, shout joyfully to
34:15 eyes watch the ***r***, his ears listen
34:17 When the ***r*** cry out, the LORD listens;
34:19 The ***r*** have many problems, but the LORD
34:21 who hate the ***r*** will be held
37:12 plot against the ***r***, grinding their
37:16 little that the ***r*** have than the
37:17 be broken, but the LORD supports the ***r***.
37:21 it back, but the ***r*** are generous and
37:25 never seen the ***r*** left all alone,
37:29 The ***r*** will possess the land; they will
37:30 The mouths of the ***r*** recite wisdom;
37:32 hand, target the ***r***, seeking to kill
37:33 won't leave the ***r*** to the power of
37:39 salvation of the ***r*** comes from the
52:6 The ***r*** will see and be in awe; they will
55:22 God will never let the ***r*** be shaken!"
58:10 But the ***r*** will rejoice when they see
58:11 a reward for the ***r***! Yes, there is a
64:10 Let the ***r*** rejoice in the LORD; let them
68:3 But let the ***r*** be glad and celebrate
69:28 them not be recorded along with the ***r***!
72:7 Let the ***r*** flourish throughout their
75:10 strength of the ***r*** will be lifted
92:12 The ***r*** will spring up like a palm tree.
92:15 The LORD is ***r***. He's my rock.
94:21 the lives of the ***r***. They condemn
106:31 is considered ***r***, generation after
112:4 are merciful, compassionate, and ***r***.
112:6 be shaken; the ***r*** will be
116:5 is mericful and ***r***; our God is
118:15 the tents of the ***r***: "The LORD's
118:20 gate; those who are ***r*** enter through it.
119:7 does right as I learn your ***r*** rules.
119:172 because all your commandments are ***r***.
125:3 land given to the ***r*** so that they
129:4 But the LORD is ***r***—God cut me free
140:13 Yes, the ***r*** will give thanks to your
141:5 Instead, let the ***r*** discipline me; let
142:7 name. Then the ***r*** will gather all
143:2 no living thing is ***r*** before you.
145:17 The LORD is ***r*** in all his ways, faithful
146:8 bent low. The LORD: who loves the ***r***.
Proverbs
1:3 which is ***r***, just, and full
2:20 people, guarding the road of the ***r***.
3:33 but he blesses the home of the ***r***.
4:18 The way of the ***r*** is like morning light
8:8 of my mouth are ***r***; nothing in them
8:15 rule, and princes issue ***r*** decrees.
9:9 wiser; inform the ***r***, and their
10:3 doesn't let the ***r*** starve, but he
10:6 the head of the ***r***, but the mouth of
10:7 The memory of the ***r*** is a blessing, but
10:11 The mouth of the ***r*** is a fountain of
10:16 The wages of the ***r*** lead to life; the
10:20 The tongue of the ***r*** is choice silver,
10:21 The lips of the ***r*** nourish many people,
10:24 but what the ***r*** desire will be
10:25 no more, but the ***r*** stand firm
10:28 of the ***r*** result in joy,
10:30 The ***r*** will never be shaken, but the
10:31 The mouth of the ***r*** flows with wisdom,
11:8 The ***r*** are saved from distress, and the
11:9 words, but the ***r*** are saved by
11:10 When the ***r*** succeed, a city rejoices;
11:19 The ***r*** are headed toward life, but those
11:21 but the children of the ***r*** will escape.
11:23 desires of the ***r*** end up well, but

11:28 wither, but the ***r*** will thrive like
11:30 The fruit of the ***r*** is a tree of life,
11:31 If the ***r*** receive their due on earth,
12:3 the roots of the ***r*** can't be
12:5 The plans of the ***r*** are just, but the
12:7 but the family of the ***r*** will endure.
12:10 The ***r*** care about their livestock's
12:12 wicked, but the root of the ***r*** endures.
12:13 lips, but the ***r*** escape from
12:21 happens to the ***r***, but the wicked
12:26 The ***r*** offer guidance to their
12:28 The way of the ***r*** leads to life, but the
13:5 The ***r*** hate false words, but the wicked
13:9 The light of the ***r*** rejoices, but the
13:21 sinners, but good things reward the ***r***.
13:22 of sinners is stored up for the ***r***.
13:25 The ***r*** eat their fill, but the wicked
14:19 people are at the gates of the ***r***.
14:32 own evil, but the ***r*** find refuge even
15:6 the house of the ***r***, but the gain of
15:28 The ***r*** heart reflects before answering,
15:29 but he listens to the prayers of the ***r***.
16:13 favor those with ***r*** lips; they love
17:15 Judging the ***r*** wicked and the wicked
17:26 to punish the ***r***, to strike the
18:5 isn't good; it denies justice to the ***r***.
18:10 strong tower; the ***r*** run to it and
20:7 The ***r*** live with integrity; happy are
21:15 is a joy to the ***r***, but dreaded by
21:18 a ransom for the ***r***; the treacherous
21:26 but the ***r*** give without
23:24 The father of the ***r*** will be very happy;
24:15 the home of the ***r***. Don't destroy
24:16 The ***r*** may fall seven times but still
28:1 them, but the ***r*** are as confident
28:12 When the ***r*** rejoice, there is great
28:28 they are destroyed, the ***r*** multiply.
29:2 When the ***r*** become numerous, the people
29:6 their own sin; the ***r*** sing and rejoice.
29:7 The ***r*** know the rights of the poor, but
29:16 so do crimes; the ***r*** will see their
29:27 disgusting to the ***r***; the straight

Ecclesiastes

3:17 will judge both ***r*** and wicked
7:16 Don't be too ***r*** or too wise, or you may
7:20 one on earth so ***r*** as to do good
8:14 is pointless: the ***r*** get what the
9:1 all of it: The ***r*** and the wise and
9:2 fate awaits the ***r*** and the wicked,

Isaiah

1:26 will be called ***R*** City, Faithful
3:10 Tell the ***r*** how blessed they are; they
26:2 gates and let a ***r*** nation enter, a
26:7 The way of the ***r*** is level; you clear a
41:10 I will hold you with my ***r*** strong hand.
45:21 God except me, a ***r*** God and a savior;
56:1 and do what is ***r***, because my
58:2 They ask me for ***r*** judgments,
60:21 will all be ***r***; they will

Jeremiah

11:20 heavenly forces, ***r*** judge, who tests
20:12 forces tests the ***r*** and discerns the
23:5 I will raise up a ***r*** descendant from
31:23 LORD bless you, ***r*** dwelling place,
33:15 I will raise up a ***r*** branch from

Lamentations

4:13 those who shed ***r*** blood in the

Ezekiel

3:21 you do warn the ***r*** not to sin, and
13:22 You hurt the ***r*** with slander—I didn't
14:14 because they were ***r***. This is what the
14:20 save their lives because they were ***r***.
16:52 they are now more ***r*** than you. Be
21:3 cut off both the ***r*** and the wicked
21:4 to cut off the ***r*** and wicked from
33:12 of the ***r*** doesn't rescue
33:13 if I've told the ***r*** they will live,
33:18 When the ***r*** turn from their

Hosea

14:9 right, and the ***r*** will walk in

Amos

5:12 afflicting the ***r***, taking money on

Habakkuk

1:4 surround the ***r***. Justice becomes
1:13 the wicked swallows one who is more ***r***?

Zephaniah

3:5 The LORD is ***r*** in her midst. He does

Zechariah

9:9 to you. He is ***r*** and victorious.

Malachi

3:3 to the LORD, presenting a ***r*** offering.
3:18 between the ***r*** and the wicked,

Matthew

5:10 because they are ***r***, because the
5:45 rain on both the ***r*** and the
13:43 Then the ***r*** will shine like the sun in
21:32 to you on the ***r*** road, and you
23:28 same way you look ***r*** to people. But
23:29 and decorate the graves of the ***r***.
23:35 will come all the ***r*** blood that has
25:37 those who are ***r*** will reply to

Mark

6:20 regarded him as a ***r*** and holy person,

Luke

1:6 They were both ***r*** before God, blameless
1:17 disobedient to ***r*** patterns of
2:25 Jerusalem. He was ***r*** and devout. He
18:9 that they were ***r*** and who looked on
23:47 It's really true: this man was ***r***."

John

17:25 ***R*** Father, even the world didn't know

Acts

24:15 of both the ***r*** and the

Romans

2:13 the Law who are ***r*** in God's eyes. It
3:20 be treated as ***r*** in his presence
3:24 are treated as ***r*** freely by his
3:26 that he is ***r*** in the present
3:28 is treated as ***r*** by faith, apart
3:30 the circumcised ***r*** by faith will
4:2 Abraham was made ***r*** because of his
4:5 faith in God who makes the ungodly ***r***.
4:11 faith in God, and so are counted as ***r***.
5:1 we have been made ***r*** through his
5:9 we have been made ***r*** by his blood, we
5:18 So now the ***r*** requirements necessary for
5:19 people were made ***r*** through the
7:12 the commandment is holy, ***r***, and good.
8:4 this so that the ***r*** requirement of
8:30 he also made ***r***. Those whom he

1 Corinthians
1:30 that he made us ***r*** and holy, and he
Galatians
2:16 person isn't made ***r*** by the works of
2:17 trying to be made ***r*** in Christ, then
2:21 if we become ***r*** through the Law,
3:8 make the Gentiles ***r*** on the basis of
3:11 no one is made ***r*** by the Law as far
3:24 so that we might be made ***r*** by faith.
5:4 trying to be made ***r*** by the Law have
1 Timothy
3:16 a human, declared ***r*** by the Spirit,
2 Timothy
4:8 Lord, who is the ***r*** judge, is going
Titus
3:5 not because of ***r*** things we had
3:7 we have been made ***r*** by his grace, we can inherit
Hebrews
11:4 that he was ***r***, since God gave
12:23 spirits of the ***r*** who have been
James
2:21 he shown to be ***r*** through his
2:23 regarded him as ***r***. What is more,
2:24 is shown to be ***r*** through faithful
2:25 shown to be ***r*** when she received
1 Peter
3:12 eyes are on the ***r*** and his ears are
4:18 If the ***r*** are barely rescued, what will
2 Peter
2:7 And he rescued ***r*** Lot, who was made
1 John
2:29 know that he is ***r***, you also know
3:7 righteousness is ***r***, in the same way
3:12 but the works of his brother were ***r***.
Revelation
22:11 Let those who are ***r*** keep doing what

RIGHTEOUS ACTS
1Sa 12:7; Ps 71:15; Dn 9:16; 9:18; Mi 6:5

RIGHTEOUS DEEDS
Ps 11:7; 71:16; Is 64:6; Eze 3:20; 18:24; 33:13

RIGHTEOUS MAN
Mt 1:19; 23:35; 27:19; Lk 23:50; Ac 10:22; 2Pt 2:8

RIGHTEOUS ONE
Job 34:17; Prv 21:12; Is 24:16; 53:11; 57:1; Mi 7:2; Ac 3:14; 7:52; 22:14; Ga 3:11; Heb 10:38; Jas 5:6; 1Pt 3:18; 1Jn 2:1

RIGHTEOUS PEOPLE
Eze 3:20; Mt 9:13; 13:17, 49; Mk 2:17; Lk 5:32; 15:7

RIGHTEOUS PERSON
2Sa 4:11; Ps 11:3; 97:11; Prv 25:26; Ecc 7:15; Is 57:1; Hab 2:4; Mt 10:41; Ro 1:17; 3:10; 5:7; 1Ti 1:9; Jas 5:16

RIGHTEOUSNESS → GOD'S RIGHTEOUSNESS, PURSUE RIGHTEOUSNESS, RIGHTEOUSNESS AND JUSTICE
1 Samuel
26:23 person for their ***r*** and loyalty, and
2 Samuel
8:15 justice and ***r*** for all his
22:21 me for my ***r***; he restored me
22:25 me for my ***r***, because I am
1 Kings
3:6 you in truth, ***r***, and with a heart
8:32 person, repaying them for their ***r***.
10:9 made you king to uphold justice and ***r***."
1 Chronicles
18:14 justice and ***r*** for all his
2 Chronicles
6:23 person, repaying them for their ***r***.
9:8 their king to uphold justice and ***r***."
Job
29:14 it clothed me, ***r*** as my coat and
33:26 joyful shout. God rewards a person's ***r***.
35:8 you, and your ***r*** affects fellow
Psalms
5:8 lead me in your ***r***. Make your way
7:8 according to my ***r*** and according to
7:17 the LORD for his ***r***; I will sing
17:15 see your face in ***r***; when I awake, I
18:20 me for my ***r***; he restored me
18:24 me for my ***r*** because my hands
24:5 from the LORD and ***r*** from the God who
31:1 be put to shame. Rescue me by your ***r***!
35:24 according to your ***r***, LORD, my God.
35:28 all about your ***r***; it will talk
36:6 Your ***r*** is like the strongest mountains;
36:10 you; extend your ***r*** to those whose
37:6 will make your ***r*** shine like the
40:9 good news of your ***r*** in the great
40:10 didn't keep your ***r*** only to myself. I
45:4 humility, and ***r***! Let your strong
45:7 You love ***r*** and hate wickedness. No
48:10 Your strong hand is filled with ***r***.
50:6 proclaim his ***r*** because God
51:14 so that my tongue can sing of your ***r***.
51:19 sacrifices of ***r***—entirely burned
65:5 In ***r*** you answer us, by your awesome
69:27 guilt! Don't let them come into your ***r***!
71:2 rescue me by your ***r***! Bend your ear
71:19 your ultimate ***r***, God, because
71:24 will tell of your ***r*** all day long
72:1 king. Give your ***r*** to the king's son.
72:2 your people with ***r*** and your poor
72:3 to the people; let the hills bring ***r***.
85:10 truth have met; ***r*** and peace have
85:11 from the ground; ***r*** gazes down from
85:13 ***R*** walks before God, making a road for
88:12 of darkness, your ***r*** in the land of
89:16 all day long and are uplifted by your ***r***
94:15 meet up with ***r***, and all whose
98:2 has revealed his ***r*** in the eyes of
99:4 You worked justice and ***r*** in Jacob.
103:6 The LORD works ***r***; does justice for all
112:3 their houses. Their ***r*** stands forever.
112:9 in need. Their ***r*** stands forever.
118:19 Open the gates of ***r*** for me so I can
119:40 your precepts! Make me live by your ***r***.
119:142 Your ***r*** lasts forever! Your Instruction
132:9 be dressed in ***r***; let your
143:1 mercy! Because of your ***r***, answer me!
143:11 me out of distress because of your ***r***.
145:7 they will shout joyfully about your ***r***:
Proverbs
8:18 me, as well as enduring wealth and ***r***.

8:20 on the way of ***r***, on the paths of
10:2 profit them, but ***r*** rescues people
11:4 day of wrath, but ***r*** rescues from
11:5 The ***r*** of the innocent makes their path
11:6 saved by their ***r***, but the
11:18 but those who sow ***r*** receive a true
13:6 ***R*** guards the innocent on the path, but
14:34 ***R*** dignifies a nation, but sin disgraces
16:8 a little with ***r*** than great
16:12 for their thrones are founded on ***r***.
16:31 of glory; it is found on the path of ***r***.
25:5 his throne will be established in ***r***.
31:9 to judge with ***r*** and to defend the

Ecclesiastes
7:15 in spite of their ***r***; then again, the

Isaiah
1:21 full of justice; ***r*** lived in her—but
1:27 and those who change their lives by ***r***.
5:7 was bloodshed; ***r***, but there was a
5:16 holy God will show himself holy in ***r***.
9:7 with justice and ***r*** now and forever.
11:4 the needy with ***r***, and decide with
11:5 ***R*** will be the belt around his hips, and faithfulness
16:5 a judge who seeks justice and timely ***r***.
26:9 those living in the world learn ***r***.
26:10 they don't learn ***r***; even among those
28:17 line and ***r*** the plumb line.
32:1 rules to promote ***r***; rulers govern to
32:16 wild lands, and ***r*** will abide in
32:17 The fruit of ***r*** will be peace, and the
33:5 high, filling Zion with justice and ***r***.
42:21 the sake of his ***r*** to expand and
45:8 clouds flow with ***r***. Let the earth
45:24 they will say, "***R*** and strength come
48:18 a river, and your ***r*** like the waves of
51:1 you who look for ***r***, you who seek the
51:6 forever, and my ***r*** will be unbroken.
51:8 like wool, but my ***r*** is forever, and
54:14 firmly founded in ***r***. You will stay
54:17 servants, whose ***r*** comes from me,
56:1 coming soon, and my ***r*** will be revealed.
57:12 about your ***r*** and your actions;
58:8 quickly. Your own ***r*** will walk before
59:9 far from us, and ***r*** beyond our reach.
59:14 is pushed aside; ***r*** stands far off,
59:16 God's arm brought victory, upheld by ***r***,
59:17 putting on ***r*** as armor and a helmet of
60:17 your governor and ***r*** your taskmaster.
61:3 be called Oaks of ***R***, planted by the
61:10 me in a robe of ***r*** like a bridegroom
61:11 God will grow ***r*** and praise before
62:1 still until her ***r*** shines out like a
62:2 will see your ***r***, all kings your
63:1 is I, proclaiming ***r***, powerful to save!

Jeremiah
4:2 justice, and ***r***, then the nations
9:24 justice, and ***r*** in the world, and
23:6 And his name will be The LORD is Our ***R***.
33:16 he will be called, The LORD Is Our ***R***.

Ezekiel
18:24 thing turn from ***r*** and engage in the
33:12 your people: The ***r*** of the righteous
33:13 trust in their ***r*** and do wrong.
33:18 turn from their ***r*** to do wrong, they
45:9 justice and ***r***. Cease your

Daniel
9:7 ***R*** belongs to you, my Lord! But we are
9:24 to bring eternal ***r***, to seal up
12:3 who lead many to ***r*** will shine like

Hosea
2:19 for my wife in ***r*** and in justice,
10:12 for yourselves ***r***; reap faithful

Joel
2:23 rain as a sign of ***r***; he will pour

Amos
5:7 into poison, and throw ***r*** to the ground!
5:24 like waters, and ***r*** like an ever-flowing
6:12 and the fruit of ***r*** into bitterness—

Micah
7:9 light; I will see by means of his ***r***.

Zephaniah
2:3 his justice; seek ***r***; seek humility.

Zechariah
8:8 I will be their God—in truth and in ***r***.

Malachi
4:2 But the sun of ***r*** will rise on those

Matthew
3:15 to fulfill all ***r***." So John agreed
5:6 and thirsty for ***r***, because they
5:20 that unless your ***r*** is greater than

Luke
1:75 in holiness and ***r*** in God's eyes, for as

John
16:8 was wrong about sin, ***r***, and judgment.
16:10 was wrong about ***r*** because I'm going

Romans
3:5 if our lack of ***r*** confirms God's
3:25 demonstrate his ***r*** in passing over
4:3 God, and it was credited to him as ***r***.
4:5 is credited as ***r*** to those who
4:6 whom God credits ***r*** apart from
4:9 Faith was credited to Abraham as ***r***."
4:11 as a seal of the ***r*** that comes from
4:13 but through the ***r*** that comes from
4:22 Therefore it was credited to him as ***r***
4:25 to meet the requirements of ***r*** for us.
5:17 and the gift of ***r*** will even more
6:16 the kind of obedience that leads to ***r***.
6:18 from sin, you have become slaves of ***r***.
6:19 body as slaves to ***r***, which makes your
6:20 you were free from the control of ***r***.
9:30 striving for ***r*** achieved
9:31 for a Law of ***r***, they didn't
10:4 which leads to ***r*** for all who have
10:5 writes about the ***r*** that comes from
10:6 But the ***r*** that comes from faith talks
10:10 heart leads to ***r***, and confessing
14:17 but about ***r***, peace, and joy

2 Corinthians
3:9 glorious is the ministry that brings ***r***?
5:21 him we could become the ***r*** of God.
6:7 the weapons of ***r*** in our right hand
6:14 What does ***r*** share with that
9:9 to the needy; his ***r*** remains forever.
9:10 will increase your crop, which is ***r***.
11:15 as servants of ***r***. Their end will

Galatians
3:6 God and it was credited to him as ***r***,"
3:21 give life, then ***r*** would in fact
5:5 for the hope of ***r*** through the

Philippians
1:11 with the fruit of ***r***, which comes from

3:6 With respect to **r** under the Law,
3:9 Christ I have a **r** that is not my
3:10 The **r** that I have comes from knowing
2 Timothy
4:8 is awarded for **r** is waiting for
Hebrews
1:9 You loved **r** and hated lawless behavior.
5:13 to the word of **r**, because they are
7:2 first "king of **r**," and then "king
11:7 an heir of the **r** that comes from
12:11 peaceful fruit of **r** for those who
1 Peter
2:24 we might live in **r**, having nothing
3:14 suffer because of **r**! Don't be
2 Peter
2:5 a preacher of **r**, along with seven
2:21 known the way of **r** than, having come
3:13 and a new earth, where **r** is at home.
1 John
2:29 who practices **r** is born from him.
3:7 who practices **r** is righteous, in
3:10 doesn't practice **r** is not from God,

RIGHTEOUSNESS AND JUSTICE

Ps 33:5; 89:14; 97:2; Prv 2:9; 21:3

RING

Genesis
24:22 took out a gold **r**, weighing a half
24:30 he had seen the **r** and the bracelets
24:47 him.' I put a **r** in her nose and
41:42 took his signet **r** from his hand and
Exodus
26:24 the top with one **r**. In this way,
36:29 the top with one **r**. In this way,
2 Kings
21:12 of anyone who hears about it will **r**.
Esther
3:10 removed his royal **r** from his finger
3:12 the order with the king's royal **r**.
8:2 off his royal **r**, the one he had
8:8 the king's royal **r**. Anything written
8:10 the king's royal **r**. He sent letters
Job
42:11 one gave him a qesitah and a gold **r**.
Proverbs
11:22 Like a gold **r** in a pig's nose is a
Jeremiah
22:24 were a signet **r** on my right hand,
Ezekiel
16:12 I put a **r** in your nose, earrings in
Daniel
6:17 it with his own **r** and with those of
Haggai
2:23 you like a signet **r** because I have
Luke
15:22 it on him! Put a **r** on his finger and
1 Corinthians
9:26 a boxer in the **r**, not like someone
James
2:2 One has a gold **r** and fine clothes,

RINGS

Genesis
35:4 as well as the **r** in their ears,
Exodus
25:12 Cast four gold **r** for it and put them on
Numbers
31:50 bracelets, signet **r**, earrings, and
Esther
1:6 tied to silver **r** and marble posts.
Isaiah
3:21 the signet **r** and nose rings
Hosea
2:13 herself up with **r** and jewelry, and

RISE → RISE FROM THE DEAD

Exodus
12:34 the yeast made it **r**, with their bread
40:37 the cloud didn't **r**, then they didn't
Deuteronomy
31:16 the people will **r** up and act
Job
5:7 born to distress, just as sparks **r** up.
7:9 who descends to the grave and won't **r**,
9:7 and it does not **r**, even seals up
11:17 A life span will **r** brighter than noon;
14:12 down and doesn't **r** until the heavens
19:25 and afterward he'll **r** upon the dust.
25:3 counted? On whom does his light not **r**?
30:12 right, upstarts **r** and target my
30:28 sunshine; I **r** in the assembly
Psalms
24:7 Ancient doors: **r** up high! So the
59:1 reach from those who **r** up against me.
68:1 Let God **r** up; let his
74:22 God, **r** up! Make your case! Remember how unbelieving fools
78:6 and so they can **r** up and tell their
82:8 ***R*** up, God! Judge the earth because you
86:14 The arrogant **r** up against me, God. A
88:10 dead? Do ghosts **r** up and give you
89:9 When its waves **r** up, it's you who
94:2 ***R*** up, judge of the earth! Pay back the
109:28 bless me! If they **r** up, let them be
Proverbs
6:9 down? When will you **r** from your sleep?
28:28 When the wicked **r** up, people hide, but
Ecclesiastes
4:15 youth who would **r** to take his place.
Song of Songs
2:10 and said to me, "***R*** up, my dearest,
2:13 are fragrant. ***R*** up, my dearest,
3:2 I will **r** now and go all around the
Isaiah
14:9 of the nations **r** from their
28:21 the LORD will **r** up; as in the
Lamentations
3:62 of those who **r** up against me,
Daniel
7:17 kings that will **r** up from the earth,
11:7 her roots will **r** up in his place.
Joel
2:20 Its stench will **r** up; its stink
Malachi
4:2 will **r** on those revering
Matthew
5:45 He makes the sun **r** on both the evil
Mark
13:12 Children will **r** up against their
Acts
3:6 Christ the Nazarene, **r** up and walk!"

1 Corinthians
5:6 yeast makes a whole batch of dough ***r***?
1 Thessalonians
4:16 those who are dead in Christ will ***r***.

RISE FROM THE DEAD

Mk 8:31; 12:25; Lk 24:46; Jn 20:9; Ac 17:3; 26:23

RITUAL

Exodus
12:24 observe this ***r*** as a regulation
13:5 should perform this ***r*** in this month.
29:36 altar through a ***r*** of
30:10 should perform a ***r*** of reconciliation
1 Kings
18:29 crazy with their ***r*** until it was time
Ezekiel
40:42 used in the ***r*** slaughter was set
Luke
2:22 came for their ***r*** cleansing, in
John
2:6 Jewish cleansing ***r***, each able to
11:55 through ***r*** washing before
Acts
21:24 the purification ***r*** with them, and
21:26 the purification ***r*** with them. He
Hebrews
6:2 of teaching about ***r*** ways to wash with
9:10 and various ***r*** ways to wash with

RIVER → ACROSS THE JORDAN RIVER, BEYOND THE RIVER

Genesis
2:10 A ***r*** flows from Eden to water the
2:11 name of the first ***r*** is the Pishon. It
2:13 of the second ***r*** is the Gihon. It
2:14 name of the third ***r*** is the Tigris,
15:18 from Egypt's ***r*** to the great
50:10 of the Jordan ***R***, they observed a
Exodus
7:25 after the LORD had struck the Nile ***R***.
17:5 you used to strike the Nile ***R***, and go.
23:31 the desert to the ***R***. I'll hand the
Deuteronomy
1:7 all the way to the great Euphrates ***R***.
2:29 cross the Jordan ***R*** into the land
2:37 the Jabbok ***R***, in compliance
3:12 beside the Arnon ***R***, up through half
4:21 cross the Jordan ***R*** or enter the
11:24 the Euphrates ***R*** all the way to
21:4 cow's neck right there in the ***r*** valley.
Joshua
1:4 great Euphrates ***R***, including all
Judges
4:7 you at the Kishon ***R***, and then I'll
4:13 Harosheth-ha-goiim to the Kishon ***R***.
Job
14:11 from the sea; a ***r*** dries up
22:16 when a ***r*** flooded their
40:23 If the ***r*** surges, he doesn't hurry; he
Psalms
36:8 let them drink from your ***r*** of pure joy.
46:4 There is a ***r*** whose streams gladden
66:6 could cross the ***r*** on foot. Right
72:8 to sea, from the ***r*** to the ends of
80:11 went all the way to the Euphrates ***R***.
83:9 Sisera, and to Jabin at the Kishon ***R***.
105:41 flowing like a ***r*** through the
114:3 and ran away; the Jordan ***R*** retreated!
Proverbs
30:17 the ravens of the ***r*** valley peck it
Isaiah
19:5 will dry up; the ***r*** will be parched
30:28 is like a raging ***r*** that reaches up
48:18 would be like a ***r***, and your
59:19 like a rushing ***r*** that the LORD's
66:12 to her like a ***r***, and the wealth
Jeremiah
46:2 the Euphrates ***R*** in the fourth
46:6 by the Euphrates ***R***, they stagger and
46:10 in the north by the Euphrates ***R***.
48:20 it by the Arnon ***R***: Moab's been
51:13 beside a great ***r***, and you are rich
51:32 The ***r*** crossings are blocked; the
51:63 it and throw it into the Euphrates ***R***.
Ezekiel
1:1 at the Chebar ***R*** when the heavens
1:3 at the Chebar ***R***. There the LORD's
3:15 beside the Chebar ***R*** at Tel-abib. I sta
10:15 that I had seen at the Chebar ***R***.
43:3 saw at the Chebar ***R***, and I fell on my
47:18 along the Jordan ***R*** as far as the
Daniel
7:10 A ***r*** of fire flowed out from his
10:4 was on the bank of the great Tigris ***R***,
Amos
8:8 then falls again, like the ***R*** of Egypt?
Micah
7:12 from Egypt to the ***R***, from sea to sea,
Zechariah
9:10 sea, and from the ***r*** to the ends of
10:11 the depths of the ***r*** will dry up. The
Matthew
3:5 all around the Jordan ***R*** came to him.
3:6 sins, he baptized them in the Jordan ***R***.
3:13 to the Jordan ***R*** so that John
4:25 and from the areas beyond the Jordan ***R***.
Mark
1:5 out to the Jordan ***R*** and were being
1:9 and John baptized him in the Jordan ***R***.
Luke
3:3 of the Jordan ***R***, calling for
4:1 from the Jordan ***R*** full of the Holy
Revelation
9:14 are bound at the great ***r*** Euphrates."
12:15 snake poured a ***r*** of water after
12:16 and swallowed the ***r*** that the dragon
16:12 bowl on the great ***r*** Euphrates. Its
22:1 showed me the ***r*** of life-giving wat
22:2 each side of the ***r*** is the tree of

RIVERS

Exodus
7:19 their ***r***, their canals,
8:5 rod over the ***r***, the canals, and
2 Samuel
22:5 all around me; ***r*** of wickedness
2 Kings
5:12 Aren't the ***r*** in Damascus, the Abana and
Job
20:17 streams, ***r*** of honey, and

28:11 the sources of ***r***; hidden things
Psalms
18:4 around me; ***r*** of wickedness
74:15 you made strong-flowing ***r*** dry right up.
78:16 from the rock, made water run like ***r***.
78:44 God turned their ***r*** into blood; they
89:25 I will set his strong hand on the ***r***.
98:8 Let all the ***r*** clap their hands; let the
107:33 God turns ***r*** into desert, watery springs
119:136 ***R*** of tears stream from my eyes because
Ecclesiastes
1:7 place where the ***r*** flow, there they
Song of Songs
8:7 quench love; ***r*** can't wash it
Isaiah
18:1 of winged ships, beyond the ***r*** of Cush
18:2 oppressive, whose land the ***r*** divide.
18:7 whose land the ***r*** divide, to the
19:6 The ***r*** will stink; the streams will
33:21 us: as a place of ***r***, broad streams
42:15 I will turn ***r*** into deserts, and
43:2 when through the ***r***, they won't sweep
47:2 expose your thighs, wade through the ***r***!
50:2 sea and make the ***r*** into wilderness.
Ezekiel
31:15 I dried up its ***r*** and restrained
32:2 about in your ***r***, you roil the
32:14 and make its ***r*** flow like oil.
Nahum
1:4 dry up all the ***r***. Bashan and
2:6 The gates of the ***r*** are opened; the
Habakkuk
3:8 against the ***r***? Or was your
3:9 Selah With ***r*** you split open
Zephaniah
3:10 From beyond the ***r*** of Cush, my daughter,
John
7:38 concerning me, ***R*** of living water
2 Corinthians
11:26 dangers from ***r***, robbers, my
Revelation
8:10 on a third of the ***r*** and springs of
16:4 his bowl into the ***r*** and springs of

ROAD

Numbers
22:23 standing in the ***r*** with his sword
Deuteronomy
2:1 the Reed Sea ***r***, exactly as the
Joshua
2:22 all along the ***r*** but never found
23:14 walking on the ***r*** to death that all
Ruth
1:7 went along the ***r*** to return to the
Psalms
1:1 stand on the ***r*** of sinners, and
85:13 before God, making a ***r*** for his steps.
140:5 net alongside the ***r***. They've set
Proverbs
2:20 guarding the ***r*** of the righteous.
Isaiah
42:16 the blind walk a ***r*** they don't know,
51:10 the redeemed a ***r*** to cross through
Jeremiah
6:25 Don't walk on the ***r***! The enemies'
31:21 think about the ***r*** you have
Lamentations
2:15 pass by on the ***r*** clap their hands
Ezekiel
21:19 Where the ***r*** to the city
21:21 the fork in the ***r*** where the two
48:1 along the Hethlon ***r*** from Lebo-hamath the boundary
Daniel
5:23 his hand and who owns every ***r*** you take.
Hosea
6:9 murder on the ***r*** to Shechem; they
13:7 a leopard I will lurk beside the ***r***.
Nahum
2:1 watch the ***r***, protect your
Matthew
7:13 is broad and the ***r*** wide, so many
7:14 is narrow and the ***r*** difficult, so few
8:28 that nobody could travel on that ***r***.
10:10 backpack for the ***r*** or two shirts or
20:17 by themselves on the ***r***. He told them,
20:30 sitting along the ***r*** heard that Jesus
21:8 clothes on the ***r***. Others cut palm
21:19 tree along the ***r***, but when he came
21:32 on the righteous ***r***, and you didn't
Mark
10:17 down the ***r***, a man ran up,
10:32 were on the ***r***, going up to
10:46 Timaeus' son, was sitting beside the ***r***.
11:8 clothes on the ***r*** while others
Luke
9:57 along the ***r***, someone said to
10:31 down the same ***r***. When he saw the
10:32 other side of the ***r*** and went on his
18:35 man was sitting beside the ***r*** begging.
19:36 they spread their clothes on the ***r***.
19:37 approached the ***r*** leading down from
24:32 to us along the ***r*** and when he
24:35 along the ***r*** and how Jesus was
Acts
8:26 noon, take the ***r*** that leads from
8:36 went down the ***r***, they came to
26:13 While on the ***r*** at midday, King Agrippa,
2 Corinthians
2:15 those who are on the ***r*** to destruction.
4:3 those who are on the ***r*** to destruction.
James
2:25 and then sent them on by another ***r***?

ROADS

Leviticus
26:22 number that your ***r*** will seem
Deuteronomy
19:3 Mark out the ***r*** to them and divide the
Judges
20:31 along the main ***r***, one of which
20:32 away from the city toward the main ***r***.
20:45 men on the main ***r***. And when they
Isaiah
49:9 Along the ***r*** animals will
49:11 my mountains into ***r***; my highways will
59:8 They make their ***r*** crooked; no one
Jeremiah
12:12 all the desert ***r*** destroyers march;
18:15 have taken side ***r***, not the main
48:19 Stand by the ***r*** and watch, you

ROADS [cont.]

Lamentations
1:4 Zion's **r** are in mourning; no one comes
Ezekiel
21:19 one, mark two **r** for the coming of
21:21 where the two **r** begin and
Obadiah
1:14 waited on the **r** to destroy his
Matthew
22:9 go to the **r** on the edge of
22:10 went to the **r** and gathered

ROAR

1 Chronicles
16:32 everything in it **r**! Let the
Job
4:10 The **r** of a lion and snarl of the king
30:22 and make me ride; you melt me in its **r**.
37:2 of his voice, the **r** issuing from his
Psalms
46:3 when its waters **r** and rage, when the
46:6 Nations **r**; kingdoms crumble. God
93:3 their voices; the floods raise up a **r**!
96:11 Let the sea and everything in it **r**!
98:7 everything in it **r**; the world and
104:21 The young lions **r** for their prey,
Isaiah
5:29 the lion; they **r** like young lions;
5:30 day, they will **r** over it like the
13:4 Listen! A **r** on the mountains like that
17:12 Doom to the **r** of nations, like
17:13 Nations **r** like the roaring of rushing
24:8 have ceased; the **r** of partyers has
25:5 you subdue the **r** of foreigners.
31:4 by their **r**. So the LORD of
33:3 account of your **r**, nations
42:13 will shout, will **r**; over enemies he
51:15 so that its waves **r**—the LORD of heavenly forces
Jeremiah
2:15 Lions **r** at him; they growl. They
4:19 trumpet and the **r** of the battle cry!
5:22 may rise and **r**, they can't pass
6:29 The bellows **r**; the lead is consumed.
10:13 heavenly waters **r**. He raises the
47:3 at the deafening **r** of the chariots'
51:16 heavenly waters **r**. God raises the
51:38 lions they will **r** together; they
51:55 her outcry, whose **r** is like the
Daniel
10:6 it sounded like the **r** of a crowd.
Amos
3:4 Does a lion **r** in the forest, when it

ROBE

Genesis
37:3 old. Jacob had made for him a long **r**.
37:33 It's my son's **r**! A wild animal
Exodus
28:4 a vest, a **r**, a woven tunic, a
28:31 You will make the **r** for the vest all of
39:26 lower hem of the **r** that is used for
Leviticus
6:10 in his linen **r**, with linen
8:7 him in the **r**. Moses then put
Joshua
7:21 single beautiful **r** in the Babylonian
7:24 the silver, the **r**, the gold bar,
Ruth
3:9 Spread out your **r** over your
1 Samuel
2:19 make a small **r** for him and take
15:27 at the edge of his **r**, and it ripped.
18:4 took off the **r** he was wearing
24:4 up and cut off a corner of Saul's **r**.
28:14 wrapped in a **r**." Then Saul knew
2 Samuel
13:18 a long-sleeved **r** because that was
13:19 the long-sleeved **r** she was wearing.
20:12 into a field and threw a **r** over him.
1 Chronicles
15:27 wore a fine-linen **r**, as did the
Nehemiah
5:13 the fold of my **r**, saying, "So may
Esther
6:8 bring out a royal **r** that the king
6:9 hand over the **r** and the horse to
6:10 Hurry, take the **r** and the horse
6:11 So Haman took the **r** and the horse and put the robe
8:15 and white royal **r** wearing a large
Psalms
45:13 in pearls, her **r** embroidered with
104:2 wear light like a **r**; you open the
Isaiah
6:1 the edges of his **r** filling the
22:21 give him your **r** and wrap him in
47:2 strip off your **r**, expose your
61:10 wrapped me in a **r** of righteousness
Daniel
5:29 in a purple **r**, have a gold
Jonah
3:6 himself of his **r**, covered himself
Matthew
9:21 If I only touch his **r** I'll be healed.
Mark
15:17 up in a purple **r** and twisted
15:20 him of the purple **r** and put his own
16:5 man in a white **r** seated on the
Luke
15:22 out the best **r** and put it on
John
19:2 head, and dressed him in a purple **r**.
19:5 and the purple **r**, Pilate said to
Revelation
1:13 One. He wore a **r** that stretched
6:11 was given a white **r**, and they were
19:13 He wore a **r** dyed with blood, and his
19:16 written on his **r** and on his thigh:

ROBES

Exodus
12:34 wrapped in their **r** on their
Judges
8:26 and the purple **r** worn by the
14:12 you thirty linen **r** and thirty sets
14:13 me thirty linen **r** and thirty sets
1 Kings
22:10 in their royal **r** at the threshing
2 Kings
10:22 So he brought out **r** for them.
2 Chronicles
18:9 in their royal **r** at the threshing
Ezra
2:69 manehs of silver, and 100 priestly **r**.

Nehemiah
7:70 of gold, 50 bowls, and 530 priestly **r**.
7:72 manehs of silver, and 67 priestly **r**.
Psalms
45:14 In **r** of many colors, she is led to the
133:2 extended over the collar of his **r**.
Isaiah
3:22 the **r** and capes; the shawls and
Ezekiel
26:16 their royal **r**, and strip off
Daniel
5:7 will wear royal **r**, will have a gold
5:16 will wear royal **r**, have a gold
Zechariah
3:4 guilt from you. Put on priestly **r**."
Mark
12:38 around in long **r**. They want to be
Luke
20:46 around in long **r**. They love being
John
13:4 and took off his **r**. Picking up a
13:12 he put on his **r** and returned to
Acts
1:10 two men in white **r** stood next to
Revelation
7:9 They wore white **r** and held palm
7:13 wearing white **r**, and where did
7:14 have washed their **r** and made them
22:14 who wash their **r** so that they may

ROCK → GOD IS MY ROCK
Genesis
49:24 name of the shepherd, the **r** of Israel,
Exodus
17:6 of you on the **r** at Horeb. Hit the
33:21 me where you will stand beside the **r**.
33:22 in a gap in the **r**, and I'll cover
Leviticus
11:5 the **r** badger—though it rechews food,
Numbers
20:8 tell the **r** to provide water.
20:11 and struck the **r** with his staff
Deuteronomy
8:15 water flow for you out of a hard **r**;
14:7 the hare, and the **r** badger—because
32:4 The **r**: his acts are perfection! No
32:13 from a boulder, with oil from a hard **r**:
32:31 compare to our **r**! Our enemies are
1 Samuel
2:2 except you! There is no **r** like our God!
23:25 down to a certain **r** there and stayed
23:28 why that place is called Escape **R**.
2 Samuel
21:10 by herself on a **r**. She stayed there
22:2 LORD is my solid **r**, my fortress, my
22:32 LORD? And who is a **r** except our God?
22:47 Bless God, my **r**! Let my God, the
23:3 spoken, Israel's **r** said to me:
1 Chronicles
11:15 down from the **r** to David at the
Nehemiah
9:15 water out of the **r** for them. You
Job
14:18 mountain breaks up, and **r** is displaced.
18:4 for your sake, a **r** be dislodged from
22:24 from Ophir on a **r** in a desert
24:8 with no refuge, huddled against a **r**.
28:2 from the earth; **r** is smelted into
29:6 with cream and a **r** poured out pools
39:28 an outcropping of **r**, their fortress
41:24 is solid like a **r**, hard like a
Psalms
18:2 LORD is my solid **r**, my fortress, my
18:31 the LORD? And who is a **r** but our God?
18:46 Bless God, my **r**! Let the God of
19:14 to you, LORD, my **r** and my redeemer.
27:5 he will set me up high, safe on a **r**.
28:1 LORD. You are my **r**; don't refuse to
31:2 me quickly; be a **r** that protects me;
31:3 are definitely my **r** and my fortress.
40:2 my feet on solid **r**. He steadied my
42:9 to God, my solid **r**, "Why have you
61:2 Lead me to the **r** that is higher
62:7 God is my strong **r**. My refuge is in
71:3 Be my **r** of refuge where I can always
73:26 God is my heart's **r** and my share
75:5 speak so arrogantly against the **r**."
78:16 flow from the **r**, made water run
78:20 God struck the **r** and water gushed
78:35 God was their **r**, that the Most
81:16 satisfy you with honey from the **r**."
89:26 father, my God, the **r** of my salvation."
92:15 He's my **r**. There's nothing
95:1 joyful shout to the **r** of our salvation!
105:41 God opened the **r** and out gushed water—
114:8 who turned that **r** into a pool of
137:9 and smashes them against the **r**!
144:1 the LORD, my **r**, who taught my
Proverbs
30:19 of a snake on the **r**, the way of a
Song of Songs
2:14 My dove—in the **r** crevices, hidden in
Isaiah
8:14 trip over and a **r** to stumble on for
10:26 Midian at the **r** of Oreb. He will
17:10 remember the **r** who shelters you.
26:4 for the LORD is a **r** for all ages.
30:29 LORD's mountain, to the **r** of Israel.
44:8 There is no other **r**; I know of none.
48:21 flow from the **r** for them; split
51:1 LORD: Look to the **r** from which you
Jeremiah
5:3 faces harder than **r** and refuse to
13:4 to the Euphrates and put it under a **r**.
21:13 valley, like a **r** of the plain,
23:29 that shatters **r**? declares the LORD
Ezekiel
24:7 but she spread it out on a bare **r**.
24:8 blood on a bare **r**, never to be
26:4 all its dirt and make it into a bare **r**,
26:14 you into a bare **r**, a place for
Obadiah
1:3 the cracks of the **r**, whose dwelling
Habakkuk
1:12 for judgment. **R**, you established
Matthew
16:18 my church on this **r**. The gates of the
27:60 carved out of the **r**. After he rolled
Mark
15:46 carved out of **r**. He rolled a
Luke
8:6 seed fell on **r**. As it grew, it
8:13 The seed on the **r** are those who receive

23:53 carved out of the ***r***, in which no one
Romans
9:33 Zion, which is a ***r*** that offends
1 Corinthians
10:4 from a spiritual ***r*** that followed
1 Peter
2:8 stumble and a ***r*** that makes them

ROCKS
Numbers
23:9 the top of the ***r*** I see him; from
Deuteronomy
32:31 But, no, their ***r*** can't compare to our
32:37 their gods—the ***r*** they trusted in—
1 Samuel
13:6 thickets, among ***r***, in tunnels, and
24:2 soldiers near the ***r*** of the wild goats.
2 Samuel
16:6 He threw ***r*** at David and at all of King
16:13 as he went, throwing ***r*** and dirt at him.
Job
6:12 my strength that of ***r***, my flesh bronze?
8:17 over a pile of ***r***, for it sees a
28:6 Its ***r*** are the source for lapis lazuli;
28:10 cut channels into ***r***; their eyes see
30:6 ravines, holes in the ground and ***r***.
Psalms
78:15 God split ***r*** open in the wilderness,
Proverbs
30:26 but they make their homes in the ***r***.
Isaiah
2:10 Go into the ***r***, and hide yourself in
2:19 into caves in the ***r*** and holes in the
2:21 in fissures of ***r*** and in crevices
65:4 the night among ***r***; who eat swine's
Amos
6:12 Do horses run on ***r***? Does one plow the
Nahum
1:6 like fire; the ***r*** are shattered
Matthew
27:51 bottom. The earth shook, the ***r*** split,
Acts
27:29 somewhere on the ***r***, they hurled out
Revelation
6:15 in caves and in the ***r*** of the mountains.
6:16 mountains and the ***r***, "Fall on us and

ROD
Exodus
4:2 hand?" Moses replied, "A shepherd's ***r***."
4:4 it turned back into a ***r*** in his hand.
Numbers
22:27 angry and beat the donkey with the ***r***.
2 Samuel
7:14 him with a human ***r***, with blows from
Job
9:34 remove his ***r*** from me, so his fury
Psalms
2:9 them with an iron ***r***; you will shatter
23:4 are with me. Your ***r*** and your staff—
125:3 The wicked ***r*** won't remain in the land
Proverbs
10:13 but there is a ***r*** for the back of
13:24 who withhold the ***r*** hate their
22:8 harvest evil; the ***r*** of their fury
22:15 heart; the ***r*** of discipline
23:13 strike them with a ***r***, they won't die.
23:14 them with a ***r***, and you will
26:3 a donkey, and a ***r*** for the back of
29:15 The ***r*** and correction lead to wisdom,
Isaiah
9:4 and the ***r*** of their
10:5 Doom to Assyria, ***r*** of my anger, in
11:4 violent with the ***r*** of his mouth; by
14:5 staff of the wicked, the ***r*** of tyrants
14:29 that the ***r*** that struck you
28:27 with a staff, and cumin with a ***r***.
30:31 Assyria; with a ***r*** he will smite it.
Lamentations
3:1 the suffering caused by God's angry ***r***.
Ezekiel
20:37 walk under the ***r***, and I will bring
21:13 When even the ***r*** rejects, will it
40:3 cord and a measuring ***r*** in his hand.
40:5 The measuring ***r*** in the man's hand
42:16 same measuring ***r*** on all four
Hosea
4:12 their divining ***r*** gives them
Micah
5:1 us; with a ***r*** they will strike
Acts
16:22 of their clothes and beaten with a ***r***.
Hebrews
1:8 kingdom's scepter is a ***r*** of justice.
9:4 manna, Aaron's ***r*** that budded, and
Revelation
2:27 with an iron ***r*** and smash them
11:1 given a measuring ***r***, which was like a
12:5 with an iron ***r***. Her child was
19:15 them with an iron ***r***. And he is the
21:15 a gold measuring ***r*** with which to
21:16 the city with the ***r***, and it was

ROOF
Genesis
6:16 Make a ***r*** for the ark and complete it
19:8 are now under the protection of my ***r***."
Deuteronomy
22:8 a railing for the ***r*** so that you don't
Joshua
2:6 them up to the ***r*** and hidden them
2:8 down, Rahab went up to them on the ***r***.
Judges
9:51 inside, and climbed to the tower's ***r***.
16:27 women were on the ***r*** watching as
1 Samuel
9:25 made for Saul on the ***r***, and he slept.
9:26 to Saul on the ***r***, "Wake up! I will
2 Samuel
11:2 and forth on the ***r*** of the palace.
16:22 Absalom on the ***r***, and he had sex
18:24 went up on the ***r*** of the gate by
1 Kings
6:9 the temple with a ***r*** of cedar beams
7:3 palace's cedar ***r*** stood above forty-
2 Kings
4:10 small room on the ***r***. We'll set up a
4:11 to the room on the ***r***, and lay down.
23:12 that were on the ***r*** of Ahaz's upper
Psalms
22:15 sticks to the ***r*** of my mouth;
102:7 I'm all alone like a bird on a ***r***.
129:6 like grass on a ***r*** that dies before
137:6 stick to the ***r*** of my mouth if I

Proverbs
21:9 on the edge of a ***r*** than with a
25:24 on the edge of a ***r*** than to share a
Ecclesiastes
10:18 laziness, the ***r*** sags; through
Lamentations
4:4 sticks to the ***r*** of its mouth,
Ezekiel
3:26 stick to the ***r*** of your mouth and
41:8 the temple: Its ***r*** all around rested
Daniel
4:29 walking on the ***r*** of the royal
Matthew
8:8 you come under my ***r***. Just say the
24:17 Those on the ***r*** shouldn't come down to grab things
Mark
2:4 off part of the ***r*** above where Jesus
13:15 Those on the ***r*** shouldn't come down or
Luke
5:19 him up on the ***r*** and lowered him—
7:6 deserve to have you come under my ***r***.
17:31 day, those on the ***r***, whose
Acts
10:9 city, Peter went up on the ***r*** to pray.

ROOM

Daniel
6:10 Now his upper ***r*** had open windows
7:8 out to make ***r*** for it. On this
Matthew
6:6 pray, go to your ***r***, shut the door,
Mark
5:40 he went to the ***r*** where the child
14:14 is my guest ***r*** where I can eat
14:15 show you a large ***r*** upstairs already
Luke
5:19 into the crowded ***r*** in front of Jesus.
14:22 been followed and there is still ***r***.'
22:12 a large upstairs ***r***, already
John
14:2 house has ***r*** to spare. If that
21:25 have enough ***r*** for the scrolls
Acts
1:13 to the upstairs ***r*** where they were
9:37 body, they laid her in an upstairs ***r***.
20:8 in the upstairs ***r*** where we had
Romans
12:19 but leave ***r*** for God's wrath.
2 Corinthians
7:2 Make ***r*** in your hearts for us. We didn't
Philemon
1:22 a guest ***r*** for me. I hope

ROOT

Deuteronomy
29:18 there isn't any ***r*** among you that is
2 Kings
19:30 escaped will take ***r*** below and bear
Job
5:3 the foolish take ***r*** and promptly
19:28 him so that the ***r*** of the matter can
30:4 on a bush, the ***r*** of the broom—a
Psalms
80:15 this ***r*** that you planted with your
Proverbs
12:12 wicked, but the ***r*** of the righteous
Isaiah
11:10 On that day, the ***r*** of Jesse will stand
14:29 from the snake's ***r*** a viper will
27:6 Jacob will take ***r***; Israel will
53:2 before us, like a ***r*** from dry ground.
Jeremiah
12:2 and they take ***r***; they flourish
Ezekiel
31:7 because it took ***r*** in plentiful
Daniel
4:15 leave its deepest ***r*** in the earth,
Hosea
9:16 is sick, their ***r*** is dried up, they
Malachi
4:1 leaving them neither ***r*** nor branch.
Matthew
3:10 is already at the ***r*** of the trees.
Mark
11:20 the fig tree withered from the ***r*** up.
Luke
3:9 is already at the ***r*** of the trees.
8:13 but they have no ***r***. They believe for
Romans
11:16 is holy too. If a ***r*** is holy, the
11:17 and shared the ***r*** that produces the
11:18 that sustains the ***r***, but it's the
15:12 There will be a ***r*** of Jesse, who
1 Timothy
6:10 of money is the ***r*** of all kinds of
Hebrews
12:15 Make sure that no ***r*** of bitterness
Revelation
5:5 of Judah, the ***R*** of David, has
22:16 churches. I'm the ***r*** and descendant of

ROPES

Judges
15:13 up with two new ***r***, and brought him
15:14 over him, the ***r*** on his arms
16:12 Delilah took new ***r*** and tied him up
2 Samuel
17:13 Israel will bring ***r*** to that city, and
Esther
1:6 and red-purple ***r*** tied to silver
Job
36:8 are tied with ***r***, caught in cords
39:5 wild donkey, loosed the ***r*** of the onager
Psalms
2:3 tear off their ***r*** and throw off
116:3 Death's ***r*** bound me; the distress of the
118:27 offering with ***r*** all the way to
119:61 me with their ***r***, I haven't
129:4 cut me free from the ***r*** of the wicked!
140:5 trap for me with ***r***. They've spread
Proverbs
5:22 grabbed by the ***r*** of their own sin.
Isaiah
5:18 fraud, and haul sin as if with cart ***r***,
33:20 never pulled up, whose ***r*** won't snap.
33:23 Your ***r*** are loosened; they can't hold
54:2 your tent ***r*** and strengthen
58:6 untying the ***r*** of a yoke,
Jeremiah
10:20 l its ***r*** are cut, and my
38:6 him down by ***r***. Now there wasn't
38:11 lowered them down the cistern by the ***r***
38:12 hold on to the ***r***." When Jeremiah

38:13 him up by the ***r*** and got him out
Ezekiel
27:24 tied with ***r***, among your
John
2:15 made a whip from ***r*** and chased them
Acts
27:32 then cut the ***r*** to the lifeboat
27:40 they untied the ***r*** that ran back to

ROSE

Song of Songs
2:1 I'm a ***r*** of the Sharon plain, a lily of

ROYAL

Deuteronomy
17:18 he sits on his ***r*** throne, he
Joshua
10:2 like one of the ***r*** cities. It was
2 Samuel
7:13 I will establish his ***r*** throne forever.
12:26 at Rabbah and captured the ***r*** city.
14:26 two hundred shekels by the ***r*** weight.
16:2 are for the ***r*** family to ride,"
1 Kings
3:1 building his ***r*** palace, the
22:10 dressed in their ***r*** robes at the
2 Kings
11:1 destroyed the entire ***r*** family.
Psalms
45:6 everlasting. Your ***r*** scepter is a
45:9 The ***r*** princess is standing in your
45:13 sort for the ***r*** princess, dressed
Song of Songs
3:10 its cushions, ***r*** purple; its
7:5 hair, braided in ***r*** purple—a king is
Isaiah
60:13 and I will honor my ***r*** footstool.
60:16 and nurse at ***r*** breasts. You will
62:3 LORD's hand, a ***r*** turban in the
Jeremiah
26:10 went up from the ***r*** palace to the
36:12 chamber in the ***r*** palace. There he
52:25 and the seven ***r*** advisors who
Ezekiel
17:13 a prince from the ***r*** line, made an
26:16 remove their ***r*** robes, and strip
Daniel
1:3 to choose ***r*** descendants and
2:15 Arioch the king's ***r*** officer, "Why is
2:49 Daniel himself remained at the ***r*** court.
4:29 on the roof of the ***r*** palace in Babylon.
4:30 I built as the ***r*** house by my own
5:7 meaning will wear ***r*** robes, will have
5:16 me, you will wear ***r*** robes, have a
5:20 pulled off his ***r*** throne and the
6:7 the ***r*** associates, and
11:21 in his place. ***R*** majesty will not
11:45 He will pitch his ***r*** tents between the
Amos
7:13 the king's holy place and his ***r*** house."
Micah
4:8 will come, the ***r*** power belonging
Matthew
11:8 wear refined clothes are in ***r*** palaces.
Luke
7:25 and live in luxury are in ***r*** palaces.
22:29 And I confer ***r*** power on you just as my
John
4:46 was a certain ***r*** official whose
4:49 The ***r*** official said to him, "Lord, come
Acts
12:21 himself in ***r*** attire, seated
James
2:8 fulfill the ***r*** law found in
1 Peter
2:9 a chosen race, a ***r*** priesthood, a
Revelation
12:3 horns, and seven ***r*** crowns on his
13:1 decorated with a ***r*** crown, and on its
17:12 yet received ***r*** power. But they
17:17 and give their ***r*** power to the
19:6 the Almighty, exercised his ***r*** power!
19:12 head were many ***r*** crowns. He has a

RUIN

Deuteronomy
4:16 Don't ***r*** everything and make an idol for yourself
4:25 the land, if you ***r*** things by making
31:29 dead, you will ***r*** everything,
1 Samuel
24:9 people say, 'David wants to ***r*** you'?
2 Chronicles
28:23 they became the ***r*** of both him and
Job
2:3 you incited me to ***r*** him for no
30:14 wall; they roll along beneath the ***r***.
31:29 over my foes' ***r*** or was excited
Psalms
39:11 like a moth, you ***r*** what they
73:18 path; you will make them fall into ***r***!
78:33 of air, and their years in total ***r***.
Proverbs
3:25 terror or the ***r*** that comes to the
5:14 brink of utter ***r*** in the assembled
10:14 but the mouth of a fool brings on ***r***.
10:15 strong city; the ***r*** of the poor is
10:29 the innocent and ***r*** for those who do
13:15 the way of the faithless is their ***r***.
14:28 but a dwindling people is a ruler's ***r***.
18:7 of fools is their ***r***; their lips are a
24:22 Who can know the ***r*** that both can
Isaiah
5:6 turn it into a ***r***; it won't be
13:9 the earth a ***r***, and wiping out
17:1 as a city; it will become a fallen ***r***.
23:13 stripped its palaces, and made it a ***r***.
24:12 ***R*** remains in the city, and the gate is
25:2 town into a ***r***, the fortress of
64:11 all that we treasured has become a ***r***.
Jeremiah
7:6 or go after other gods to your own ***r***,
22:5 LORD, that this palace will become a ***r***.
26:6 this temple a ***r*** like Shiloh, and
50:13 reduced to total ***r***. All who pass by
Ezekiel
6:6 turned into utter ***r***. Your altars will
14:16 rescued, but the land would become a ***r***.
15:8 the land into a ***r*** because they
21:27 A ***r***, ruin, ruin, I'll make it! Such a
29:10 into an utter ***r***, a wasteland,
38:8 a perpetual ***r***. This country was
Hosea
4:14 people without sense must come to ***r***.

Joel
1:17 granaries are in ***r*** because the grain
Amos
6:6 aren't grieved over the ***r*** of Joseph!
Micah
7:10 eyes will see her ***r***; now she will
Acts
5:38 is of human origin, it will end in ***r***.
2 Corinthians
7:2 anyone. We didn't ***r*** anyone. We didn't
1 Timothy
6:9 plunge people into ***r*** and destruction.

RUINED

Exodus
8:24 Egypt. The land was ***r*** by the insects.
9:32 wheat weren't ***r***, because they
Deuteronomy
9:12 of Egypt, have ***r*** everything! They
Job
15:28 They lived in ***r*** cities, unoccupied
20:26 them; what's left in their tent is ***r***.
Psalms
9:6 like something ***r*** forever. You've
109:10 begging, driven out of their ***r*** homes.
Proverbs
10:8 commands, but a foolish talker is ***r***.
10:10 those who speak foolishly are ***r***.
13:3 but those who open their lips are ***r***.
Isaiah
6:5 for me; I'm ***r***! I'm a man with
6:11 Until cities lie ***r*** with no one
15:1 a night; Moab is ***r***! Kir was
61:4 they will renew ***r*** cities, places
Jeremiah
2:7 goodness, but you ***r*** my land; you
4:20 the whole land is ***r***. Suddenly, my
10:25 him completely and ***r*** his country.
13:7 it. But it was ***r*** and good for
18:16 They have ***r*** their country and brought
51:18 at the appointed timethey will be ***r***!
Ezekiel
29:12 devastated of ***r*** cities. It will
30:7 desolate; of all cities, the most ***r***.
36:35 cities that were ***r***, ravaged, and
36:38 festivals, the ***r*** cities will be
Daniel
7:26 be taken away—***r*** and wiped out for
9:17 your face on your ***r*** sanctuary, for
Amos
9:14 will rebuild the ***r*** cities and
Matthew
9:17 would be ***r***. Instead, people
Luke
5:36 garment would be ***r***, and the new
5:37 spill, and the wineskins would be ***r***.
1 Timothy
1:19 Some people have ***r*** their faith
6:5 whose minds are ***r*** and who have been
Revelation
19:2 prostitute, who ***r*** the earth by her

RULE

Genesis
1:16 larger light to ***r*** over the day and
1:18 to ***r*** over the day and over the night,
3:16 your husband, but he will ***r*** over you."
4:7 entice you, but you must ***r*** over it."
37:8 be our king and ***r*** over us?" So they
Exodus
15:18 The LORD will ***r*** forever and always
Leviticus
3:17 is a permanent ***r*** for your future
26:17 who hate you will ***r*** over you; and you
Deuteronomy
17:20 ensure lasting ***r*** in Israel for
19:4 Here is the ***r*** concerning a person who
23:3 belong to the LORD's assembly, as a ***r***,
33:5 A king came to ***r*** in Jeshurun, when the
Joshua
24:25 established just ***r*** for them at
Judges
8:22 said to Gideon, "***R*** over us, you and
15:11 the Philistines ***r*** over us? What
1 Samuel
8:9 how the king will ***r*** over them and
10:1 said. "You will ***r*** the LORD's people
13:14 but now your ***r*** won't last. The LORD
2 Samuel
21:1 during David's ***r***. David asked the
1 Kings
1:5 and said, "I'll ***r*** as king myself."
6:1 year of Solomon's ***r*** over Israel, he
11:37 you, and you will ***r*** over all that you
Job
34:17 who hates justice ***r***; will you condemn
38:33 laws, or can you impose its ***r*** on earth?
Psalms
7:7 surround you. ***R*** them from on high!
8:6 You've let them ***r*** over your handiwork,
9:4 because you ***r*** from the throne,
19:13 Don't let them ***r*** me. Then I'll be
22:28 the right to ***r*** belongs to the
49:14 their hearts will ***r*** over them come
72:8 Let the king ***r*** from sea to sea, from
81:4 for Israel; this is a ***r*** of Jacob's God.
89:9 You ***r*** over the surging sea: When its
102:12 But you, LORD, ***r*** forever! Your fame
110:2 far from Zion! ***R*** over your enemies!
119:133 by your word; don't let any sin ***r*** me.
123:1 my eyes to you—you who ***r*** heaven.
132:12 children too will ***r*** on your throne
136:8 The sun to ***r*** the day—God's faithful
136:9 and the stars to ***r*** the night—God's
145:13 forever; your ***r*** endures for all
146:10 The LORD will ***r*** forever! Zion, your God
Proverbs
8:15 By me kings ***r***, and princes issue
19:10 so for a servant to ***r*** over princes.
22:7 The wealthy ***r*** over the poor; a borrower
Ecclesiastes
4:14 though during his ***r*** a poor child is
Isaiah
3:4 mischief makers will ***r*** over them.
3:12 and swindlers ***r*** them. My people—
17:3 will Damascus's ***r***. What's left of
19:4 strong king will ***r*** them, says the
24:23 forces will ***r*** on Mount Zion and
28:14 you scoffers who ***r*** this people in
63:19 those you don't ***r***, like those not
Jeremiah
1:3 throughout the ***r*** of Judah's King
3:6 During the ***r*** of King Josiah, the LORD
5:31 the priests ***r*** at their sides,

22:30 on David's throne and ***r*** again in Judah.
23:5 line, and he will ***r*** as a wise king.
26:1 Early in the ***r*** of Judah's King
26:18 during the ***r*** of Judah's
27:1 Early in the ***r*** of Judah's King
28:1 early in the ***r*** of Judah's King
32:1 eighteenth year of Nebuchadnezzar's ***r***.
33:21 have a descendant to ***r*** on his throne.
35:1 word during the ***r*** of Judah's King
49:34 beginning of the ***r*** of Judah's King
49:38 will establish my ***r*** in Elam and
51:28 and all the countries they ***r***.
51:59 Zedekiah in the fourth year of his ***r***.

Lamentations
5:8 Slaves ***r*** over us; there is no one to
5:19 you, LORD, will ***r*** forever; your

Ezekiel
17:16 the authority to ***r***, whose solemn
26:20 you will neither ***r*** nor radiate
28:2 God, and as God I ***r*** the seas!" Though
34:4 you use force to ***r*** them with

Daniel
1:1 third year of the ***r*** of Judah's King
2:44 Its ***r*** will never pass
4:3 is everlasting. His ***r*** is for all time.
5:7 neck, and will ***r*** the kingdom as
6:26 God's ***r*** will last until
11:4 No one will ***r*** like he did

Amos
6:3 evil day and make violent ***r*** draw near:

Obadiah
1:21 to Mount Zion to ***r*** Mount Esau, and

Micah
4:7 The LORD will ***r*** over them on

Habakkuk
1:14 things with no one to ***r*** over them.

Zechariah
6:13 he will sit and ***r*** on his throne.
9:10 the nations. His ***r*** will stretch from

Matthew
2:1 Judea during the ***r*** of King Herod,
20:25 that those who ***r*** the Gentiles show

Luke
1:5 During the ***r*** of King Herod of Judea
1:33 He will ***r*** over Jacob's house forever,
3:1 year of the ***r*** of the emperor
22:25 of the Gentiles ***r*** over their

Acts
11:28 (This occurred during Claudius' ***r***.)

Romans
5:17 more certainly ***r*** in life through
5:21 that grace will ***r*** through God's
6:12 don't let sin ***r*** your body, so
7:21 I find that, as a ***r***, when I want to
15:12 will also rise to ***r*** the Gentiles. The

1 Corinthians
4:8 rich already! You ***r*** like kings
15:24 every form of ***r***, every authority
15:25 for him to ***r*** until he puts all

Galatians
6:16 follows this ***r*** and on God's

Ephesians
2:2 You followed the ***r*** of a destructive

2 Timothy
2:12 we will also ***r*** together. If we

Revelation
2:27 to ***r*** the nations with an iron rod and
5:10 to our God, and they will ***r*** on earth."
11:15 and he will ***r*** forever and
12:5 child who is to ***r*** all the nations
19:15 the one who will ***r*** them with an iron
20:6 Christ, and will ***r*** with him for one
22:5 and they will ***r*** forever and

RULED

Psalms
106:41 people who hated them ***r*** over them.

Ecclesiastes
1:16 than any who ***r*** over Jerusalem
4:16 of people he ***r***, but those who

Isaiah
14:6 blows, that ***r*** nations with
26:13 besides you have ***r*** us, but we will
37:38 Ararat. His son Esarhaddon ***r*** after him.

Jeremiah
34:1 and people he ***r***, were attacking
52:1 king, and he ***r*** for eleven years

Daniel
9:1 by birth and who ***r*** the Chaldean

Matthew
2:22 that Archelaus ***r*** over Judea in

Romans
5:14 But death ***r*** from Adam until Moses, even over those
5:17 If death ***r*** because of one person's
5:21 our Lord, just as sin ***r*** in death.

Revelation
20:4 came to life and ***r*** with Christ for

RULER

Genesis
45:8 household, and ***r*** of the whole land
45:26 He's actually ***r*** of all the land

Joshua
3:11 chest of the ***r*** of the entire
3:13 of the LORD, ***r*** of the whole

Judges
9:30 Zebul the city's ***r*** heard the words

1 Kings
1:35 him to become ***r*** over Israel and
11:34 will keep him as ***r*** throughout his
22:47 Edom had no king; only a deputy was ***r***.

Esther
2:17 head and made her ***r*** in place of

Psalms
94:20 Can a wicked ***r*** be your ally; one who
105:20 set him free; the ***r*** of many people
105:21 of his house and ***r*** over everything
148:11 princes and every single ***r*** on earth!

Proverbs
6:7 ant has no commander, officer, or ***r***.
23:1 to dine with a ***r***, carefully
25:7 demoted before a ***r***. What your eyes
28:15 A wicked ***r*** over the poor is like a
29:12 If a ***r*** listens to lies, those who serve
29:26 access to the ***r***, but justice

Ecclesiastes
9:17 the racket caused by a ***r*** among fools.

Isaiah
16:1 Send lambs to the ***r*** of the land, from
24:17 and trap are upon you, ***r*** of the earth!
26:21 iniquity of the ***r*** of the earth down
40:12 heavens with a ***r*** or scooped the

Jeremiah
30:21 own leader; their ***r*** will come from
Daniel
2:10 No king or ***r***, no matter how
2:38 and has made you ***r*** of all of them.
2:48 him, making him ***r*** over all the
Micah
5:2 who is to be a ***r*** in Israel on my
Matthew
9:18 to them, a ***r*** came and knelt in
9:34 with the authority of the ***r*** of demons."
12:24 of Beelzebul, the ***r*** of the demons."
14:1 time Herod the ***r*** heard the news
Mark
3:22 with the authority of the ***r*** of demons."
6:25 back to the ***r***, she made her
Luke
3:1 and Herod was ***r*** over Galilee, his
3:19 But Herod the ***r*** had been criticized
9:7 Herod the ***r*** heard about everything that was happening
11:15 of Beelzebul, the ***r*** of demons."
18:18 A certain ***r*** asked Jesus, "Good Teacher,
18:21 Then the ***r*** said, "I've kept all of
19:2 Zacchaeus, a ***r*** among tax
John
12:31 Now this world' ***r*** will be thrown
14:30 this world's ***r*** is coming. He has
16:11 this world's ***r*** stands condemned.
Acts
7:10 who appointed him ***r*** over Egypt and
23:5 speak evil about a ***r*** of your people."
Ephesians
1:21 far above every ***r*** and authority and
Colossians
2:10 is the head of every ***r*** and authority.
1 Peter
2:13 submitting to the emperor as supreme ***r***,
Revelation
1:5 the dead, and the ***r*** of the kings of
3:14 true witness, the ***r*** of God's creation.

RULERS

Judges
3:3 the five ***r*** of the Philistines, and all
Psalms
2:2 The earth's ***r*** take their stand; the
2:10 wise up! Be warned, you ***r*** of the earth!
102:15 all the earth's ***r*** will honor your
119:23 Even if ***r*** gather and scheme against me,
119:46 your laws before ***r*** with no shame
119:161 ***R*** persecute me without cause, but my
138:4 all the earth's ***r*** give thanks to
144:10 saving help to ***r***, and who rescues
149:8 binding their ***r*** in chains and their
Proverbs
8:16 By me ***r*** govern, and officials judge
19:6 seek favor from ***r***; everyone
31:4 drink wine, for ***r*** to crave strong
Ecclesiastes
7:19 stronger than ten ***r*** who are in a city.
Isaiah
10:13 I knocked down their ***r*** like a bull.
32:1 righteousness; ***r*** govern to promote
49:7 to the slave of ***r***: Kings will see
52:5 nothing. Their ***r*** wail, says the
Jeremiah
1:15 will set up their ***r*** by the entrances
33:26 descendants as ***r*** for the children
Lamentations
1:5 have become ***r***; her enemies
4:12 The earth's ***r*** didn't believe it—
Ezekiel
26:17 sea, she and her ***r***, who spread their
Daniel
9:12 and against our ***r***, bringing great
Hosea
7:7 they devour their ***r***. All their kings
13:10 whom you said, "Give me a king and ***r***"?
Micah
3:1 leaders of Jacob, ***r*** of the house of
3:9 house of Jacob, ***r*** of the house of
Habakkuk
1:10 fun of kings; ***r*** are ridiculous to
Matthew
2:6 least among the ***r*** of Judah, because
Mark
10:42 considered the ***r*** by the Gentiles
Luke
12:11 the synagogues, ***r***,and authorities,
23:13 chief priests and the ***r*** of the people.
Acts
3:17 you acted in ignorance. So did your ***r***.
4:26 stand and the ***r*** gathered together
Romans
8:38 not angels or ***r***, not present
1 Corinthians
2:8 the present-day ***r*** have understood,
Ephesians
3:10 now to show the ***r*** and powers in the
6:12 but against ***r***, authorities,
Colossians
1:16 or powers, or ***r*** or authorities,
2:15 he disarmed the ***r*** and authorities,
Titus
3:1 them to submit to ***r*** and authorities.

RULES

Leviticus
10:11 all the ***r*** that the LORD
18:4 and my ***r*** are the ones you
19:19 You must keep my ***r***. Do not crossbreed
20:8 You will keep my ***r*** and do them; I am
25:18 will observe my ***r***, and you will
26:3 according to my ***r***, keep my
Psalms
2:4 The one who ***r*** in heaven laughs; my Lord
9:7 But the LORD ***r*** forever! He assumes his
10:5 twisted. Your ***r*** are too lofty for
10:16 The LORD ***r*** forever and always! The
18:22 All his ***r*** are right in front of me; I
22:28 belongs to the LORD, he ***r*** all nations.
59:13 the earth that God ***r*** over Jacob. Selah
66:7 God ***r*** with power forever; keeps a good
89:30 my Instruction, stop following my ***r***—
93:1 The LORD ***r***! He is robed in majesty—
96:10 The LORD ***r***! Yes, he set the
97:1 The LORD ***r***! Let the earth rejoice! Let
99:1 The LORD ***r***—the nations shake! He
99:7 the laws and the ***r*** God gave to them.
103:19 in heaven, and his kingdom ***r*** over all.
111:7 justice; all God's ***r*** are trustworthy—

RULES [cont.]

113:5 the LORD our God? God ***r*** from on high;
119:7 does right as I learn your righteous ***r***.
147:20 knowledge of God's ***r***. Praise the LORD!
Proverbs
17:2 servant ***r*** over a
Isaiah
9:9 and the one who ***r*** in Samaria. But
32:1 See here: A king ***r*** to promote
52:7 who says to Zion, "Your God ***r***!"
Jeremiah
40:5 and the people he ***r*** or go wherever
Daniel
4:26 once you acknowledge that heaven ***r*** all.
Amos
1:5 the one who ***r*** from Beth-eden;
1:8 the one who ***r*** from Ashkelon. I
Malachi
4:4 Instruction and ***r*** for all Israel at
Matthew
15:2 the elders' ***r*** handed down to
15:3 by keeping the ***r*** handed down to
15:6 the sake of the ***r*** that have been
15:9 teach instructions that are human ***r***."
Mark
7:3 of observing the ***r*** handed down by
7:4 many other ***r*** that have been
7:5 according to the ***r*** handed down by
7:8 holding on to ***r*** created by humans
7:9 in order to establish these ***r***.
7:13 in favor of the ***r*** handed down to
Luke
22:53 this is your time, when darkness ***r***."
Romans
9:5 He is the one who ***r*** over all things,
Ephesians
2:15 the detailed ***r*** of the Law so
Colossians
2:20 do you submit to ***r*** and regulations
2:22 are used. Such ***r*** are human
2 Timothy
2:5 don't win unless they follow the ***r***.
1 Peter
3:22 into heaven, he ***r*** over all angels,
Revelation
17:18 great city that ***r*** over the kings of

RULING

Exodus
15:25 regulation and a ***r*** there, and there
Deuteronomy
1:17 because the ***r*** belongs to God.
17:8 kinds of legal ***r***, or different
17:11 give you and the ***r*** they announce to
Judges
9:2 is better to have ***r*** over you: seventy
14:4 because they were ***r*** over Israel at
2 Chronicles
7:18 fail to have a successor ***r*** in Israel.'
Job
34:30 person from ***r***, from capturing
Isaiah
14:2 their captors and ***r*** their oppressors.
53:8 Due to an unjust ***r*** he was taken away,
Ezekiel
29:15 it small to keep it from ***r*** the nations.
Daniel
1:3 members of the ***r*** class from the
11:5 overpower him, ***r*** in his place. His
Haggai
2:11 Go ahead and ask the priests for a ***r***:
1 Peter
5:3 Don't shepherd by ***r*** over those

RUN

Genesis
39:13 his garment in her hands and ***r*** outside,
2 Samuel
18:19 Please let me ***r*** and take the news
Esther
8:10 horses born from mares known to ***r*** fast.
Job
15:26 They ***r*** toward him aggressively, with a
Psalms
21:12 them turn and ***r*** when you aim your
55:7 I'd ***r*** so far away! I'd live in the
59:4 They ***r*** and take their stand—but not
66:12 let other people ***r*** right over our
68:1 those who hate him ***r*** scared before him!
68:12 armies are on the ***r***! The women back
78:16 the rock, made water ***r*** like rivers.
114:5 Sea, why did you ***r*** away? Jordan, why
119:32 I ***r*** the same path as your commandments
Proverbs
1:16 their feet ***r*** to evil; they
4:12 when you ***r***, you won't
6:18 plans, feet that ***r*** quickly to evil,
18:10 the righteous ***r*** to it and find
28:1 The wicked ***r*** away even though no one
Song of Songs
1:4 with you; let's ***r***! My king has
Isaiah
40:31 eagles; they will ***r*** and not be tired;
Ezekiel
7:17 hang limp; urine will ***r*** down every leg.
28:23 and blood will ***r*** in its streets.
1 Corinthians
9:24 in the stadium ***r***, but only one
9:26 now this is how I ***r***
10:14 my dear friends, ***r*** away from the
Galatians
4:17 you out so that you would ***r*** after them.
Philippians
2:16 that I haven't ***r*** for nothing or
1 Timothy
6:11 you, man of God, ***r*** away from all
2 Timothy
2:22 ***R*** away from adolescent cravings.
Hebrews
12:1 then let's also ***r*** the race that is
James
4:7 the devil, and he will ***r*** away from you.
Revelation
9:6 die, but death will ***r*** away from them.

Ss

SABBATH → SABBATH DAY, SABBATH TO THE LORD

Exodus
16:26 seventh day, the ***S***, there will be
20:8 Remember the ***S*** day and treat it as
20:11 LORD blessed the ***S*** day and made it
31:13 because the ***S*** is a sign between
Numbers
28:10 for every ***S***, in addition to
2 Kings
4:23 not a new moon or ***s***." She said,
11:5 of you coming on ***s*** duty will guard
16:18 took away the ***s*** canopy that had
1 Chronicles
9:32 the stacks of bread for each ***S***.
Nehemiah
10:31 to sell on the ***S***, we won't buy it
13:15 on the ***S***. They were also
Isaiah
1:13 me. New moon, ***s***, and the calling
56:2 who keeps the ***S***, not making it
58:13 trampling the ***S***, stop doing
66:23 to month and from ***S*** to Sabbath, all
Lamentations
2:6 both festival and ***s***; in his fierce
Ezekiel
46:1 But on the ***S*** and on the day of
Amos
8:5 grain, and the ***S*** so that we may
Matthew
12:1 fields on the ***S***. His disciples
12:2 your disciples are breaking the ***S*** law."
12:5 Law that on the ***S*** the priests in
12:8 The Human One is Lord of the ***S***.
12:10 Law allow a person to heal on the ***S***?"
28:1 After the ***S***, at dawn on the first day
Mark
1:21 on the ***S*** Jesus entered the
2:23 fields on the ***S***. As the disciples
2:24 Why are they breaking the ***S*** law?"
2:27 he said, "The ***S*** was created for
2:28 the Human One is Lord even over the ***S***."
3:2 to see if he would heal on the ***S***.
3:4 it legal on the ***S*** to do good or to
6:2 On the ***S***, he began to teach in the
15:42 on Preparation Day, just before the ***S***,
16:1 When the ***S*** was over, Mary Magdalene,
Luke
4:16 raised. On the ***S*** he went to the
4:31 Galilee and taught the people each ***S***.
6:1 One ***S***, as Jesus was going through the
6:2 said, "Why are you breaking the ***S*** law?"
6:5 them, "The Human One is Lord of the ***S***."
6:6 On another ***S***, Jesus entered a
6:7 would heal on the ***S***. They were
6:9 it legal on the ***S*** to do good or to
13:10 in one of the synagogues on the ***S***.
13:15 of you on the ***S*** untie your ox or
14:1 One ***S***, when Jesus went to share a meal
14:3 the Law allow healing on the ***S*** or not?"
23:54 Day for the ***S***, and the Sabbath
23:56 rested on the ***S*** in keeping with
John
5:9 mat and walked. Now that day was the ***S***.
5:10 healed, "It's the ***S***; you aren't
5:16 he had done these things on the ***S***.
5:18 away with the ***S*** but also because
7:22 you circumcise a man on the ***S***.
7:23 on the ***S*** without breaking
9:16 he breaks the ***s*** law." Others
19:31 the cross on the ***S***, especially since
Acts
1:12 near Jerusalem—a ***s*** day's journey
Hebrews
4:9 So you see that a ***s*** rest is left open

SABBATH DAY
Ex 20:8; 20:11; 31:15; 35:3; Nm 15:32; 28:9; Dt 5:12; 5:15; Neh 13:22; Ps 92:1; Jer 17:21; 17:22, 24, 27; Eze 46:4; 46:12; Mt 24:20; Lk 13:14; 13:16; 14:5; Jn 9:14

SABBATH TO THE LORD
Ex 16:23; 16:25; 20:10; Lv 23:3; 25:4

SABBATHS
Exodus
31:13 sure to keep my ***s***, because the
Leviticus
19:3 you must keep my ***s***; I am the LORD
19:30 You must keep my ***s*** and treat my
23:38 to the LORD's ***s*** and in addition
26:2 You must keep my ***s*** and respect my
1 Chronicles
23:31 the LORD for the ***s***, the new moons,
2 Chronicles
2:4 evening, on the ***s***, the first of
8:13 of Moses for ***s***, new moon
31:3 offerings for the ***s***, new moons, and
Nehemiah
10:33 offering, for the ***s*** and the new moons
Isaiah
56:4 who keep my ***s***, choose what I
Ezekiel
20:12 also gave them my ***s*** as a sign between
22:8 my holy things and degrade my ***s***.
23:38 sanctuary unclean and made my ***s*** impure.
44:24 my festivals. They must keep my ***s*** holy.

45:17 new moons, and **s**, all the
46:3 of the LORD on **s** and new moons at
Acts
17:2 and for three **S** interacted with
Colossians
2:16 festival, a new moon observance, or **s**.

SACRED

Genesis
1:14 will mark events, **s** seasons, days,
12:6 as far as the **s** place at Shechem,
13:3 Bethel and to the **s** place there,
28:17 and thought, This **s** place is awesome.
28:18 set it up as a **s** pillar, and
28:19 He named that **s** place Bethel, though
28:22 I've set up as a **s** pillar will be
31:13 you anointed a **s** pillar and where
31:45 took a stone, set it up as a **s** pillar,
31:51 and here is the **s** pillar that I've
31:52 mound and the **s** pillar are
32:2 and he named that **s** place Mahanaim.
35:14 So Jacob set up a **s** pillar, a stone
Exodus
23:24 and smash their **s** stone pillars to
24:4 He set up twelve **s** stone pillars for
28:38 give as their **s** donations. It
34:13 smash their **s** stone pillars,
Leviticus
12:4 holy or enter the **s** area until her
26:1 divine image or **s** pillar. You must
Numbers
5:9 from all the **s** donations that
5:10 The **s** donations belong to each person
15:3 gift, or at your **s** seasons—
18:8 the Israelites' **s** offerings. I have
18:32 must not make the **s** gifts of the
Deuteronomy
7:5 smash their **s** stones, cut down
12:3 and shatter their **s** stones. Burn
12:26 must bring your **s** offerings and
16:21 to serve as a **s** pole next to the
16:22 Don't set up any **s** stone either,
32:38 who drank their **s** wine? They should
1 Samuel
20:8 servant into a **s** covenant with
1 Kings
14:15 the LORD angry by making their **s** poles.
14:23 stones, and **s** poles on top of
16:33 Ahab also made a **s** pole and did more to
2 Kings
3:2 He removed the **s** pillar of Baal
10:26 They brought the **s** pillar out of Baal's
10:27 tore down Baal's **s** pillar and
13:6 them! Moreover, a **s** pole stood in
17:10 They set up **s** pillars and sacred poles
17:16 calves and made a **s** pole. They bowed
18:4 He smashed the **s** pillars and cut
21:3 Baal, and made a **s** pole, just as
23:14 He smashed the **s** pillars and cut down
23:15 into dust. Then he burned its **s** pole.
2 Chronicles
14:3 smashed the **s** pillars, cut down
17:6 the shrines and the **s** poles from Judah.
19:3 have removed the **s** poles from the
24:18 and worshipped **s** poles and idols.
31:1 smashed the **s** pillars, cut down
33:3 Baals, and made **s** poles. He bowed
33:19 of the shrines, **s** poles, and idols
34:3 the shrines, the **s** poles, idols, and
34:4 He broke up the **s** poles, idols, and
34:7 the altars and **s** poles, ground the
Ezra
3:5 and at all the **s** feasts of the
Isaiah
8:13 you should hold **s**, whom you should
17:8 fingers made: **s** poles and incense
23:18 and wages will be **s** to the LORD. They
27:9 shattered chalk, **s** poles and incense
58:13 a delight, **s** to the LORD,
Jeremiah
11:15 evil schemes? Can **s** offerings cancel
17:2 their altars and **s** poles by the lush
43:13 will shatter the **s** pillars in the
51:51 have violated the **s** places of the
Lamentations
4:1 gold is changed. **S** jewels are
Hosea
2:11 Sabbath days, and all her **s** seasons.
3:4 sacrifice or **s** standing stone,
10:1 the more he set up **s** standing stones.
Micah
5:13 images and your **s** pillars in your
5:14 tear down your **s** poles in your
Mark
16:9 to the west, the **s** and undying
Romans
14:5 days to be more **s** than others,
14:6 that a day is **s**, thinks that way
1 Timothy
1:9 and nothing is **s** to them. They

SACRIFICE → COMMUNAL SACRIFICE, DAILY SACRIFICE

Genesis
4:4 LORD looked favorably on Abel and his **s**
4:5 on Cain and his **s**. Cain became very
22:10 took the knife to kill his son as a **s**.
31:54 Jacob offered a **s** on the mountain, and
Exodus
12:27 is the Passover **s** to the LORD, for
13:15 to the LORD as a **s** every male that
20:24 soil on which to **s** your entirely
23:18 the blood of my **s** with anything
34:15 their gods and **s** to their gods,
34:25 the blood of my **s** with anything
Leviticus
7:15 thanksgiving **s** of well-being must
9:4 as a well-being **s** before the LORD;
9:22 and the well-being **s**, he came down.
19:6 the day of your **s** or the following
Numbers
6:14 one flawless ram as a well-being **s**,
6:17 as a well-being **s** to the LORD with
7:17 the well-being **s** two oxen, five
15:3 offering, or a **s** to fulfill a
Deuteronomy
15:21 you must not **s** it to the LORD
16:2 Offer a Passover **s** from the flock or
17:1 Don't **s** to the LORD your God any oxen
Joshua
22:26 an entirely burned offering or for **s**.'
22:29 gift offering, or **s**, other than the
Judges
2:5 and they offered a **s** to the LORD there.

11:31 the LORD. I will ***s*** it as an entirely
16:23 to make a great ***s*** to their god
1 Samuel
1:3 to worship and ***s*** to the LORD of
1:4 give parts of the ***s*** to his wife
1:21 make the annual ***s*** and keep his
3:14 be reconciled by ***s*** or by offering."
9:12 there is a ***s*** today for the
15:15 in order to ***s*** them to the LORD
16:2 I have come to make a ***s*** to the LORD.'
20:6 is an annual ***s*** there for his
1 Kings
3:4 in order to ***s*** there. He used to
12:27 continue to ***s*** at the LORD's
13:2 Josiah. He will ***s*** on you, Altar,
18:33 pour it on the ***s*** and on the wood,"
22:43 continued to ***s*** and offer incense
2 Kings
10:19 I have a great ***s*** planned for Baal.
15:35 continued to ***s*** and burn incense
17:36 arm. Bow down to him! ***S*** to him!
2 Chronicles
7:12 chosen this place as my house of ***s***.
11:16 to Jerusalem to ***s*** to the LORD, the
28:23 he said, "I'll ***s*** to them too, so
29:24 entirely burned ***s*** and the
35:12 their families to ***s*** to the LORD as
Ezra
9:4 sitting in shock until the evening ***s***.
9:5 of the evening ***s***, I ended my
Psalms
50:5 who made a covenant with me by ***s***."
50:14 Offer God a ***s*** of thanksgiving! Fulfill
50:23 one who offers a ***s*** of thanksgiving
51:17 spirit is my ***s***, God. You won't
54:6 I will ***s*** to you freely; I will give
116:17 So I'll offer a ***s*** of thanksgiving to
Proverbs
7:14 I've made a ***s*** of well-being; today I
21:3 is more valued by the LORD than ***s***.
Ecclesiastes
5:1 offer the fools' ***s***—they have no idea
9:2 impure, those who ***s*** and those who
Isaiah
34:6 the LORD has a ***s*** in Bozrah, a
57:7 bed. You went up there to offer a ***s***.
Jeremiah
7:9 and perjury, ***s*** to Baal and go
32:35 where they ***s*** their sons and
46:10 is preparing a ***s*** in the north by
Ezekiel
39:17 around for the ***s*** that I make for
39:19 blood, from the ***s*** that I have made
45:17 the well-being ***s*** to make
46:12 or a well-being ***s***, the gate facing
Hosea
3:4 prince, without ***s*** or sacred
6:6 love and not ***s***, the knowledge of
12:11 In Gilgal they ***s*** bulls, so their
13:2 of craftsmen. "***S*** to these," they
Amos
4:5 a thanksgiving ***s*** of leavened
Jonah
1:16 they offered a ***s*** to the LORD and
2:9 I will offer a ***s*** to you with a
Zephaniah
1:7 has established a ***s***; he has made holy
1:8 day of the LORD's ***s***, I will punish
Zechariah
14:21 All those who ***s*** will come. They
Malachi
1:8 a blind animal to ***s***, isn't that evil?
1:13 be brought for a ***s***, And you bring
Matthew
9:13 mercy and not ***s***. I didn't come to
12:7 mercy and not ***s***, you wouldn't
Mark
1:44 and offer the ***s*** for your
Luke
2:24 They offered a ***s*** in keeping with what's
Acts
7:41 a calf, offered a ***s*** to it, and began
Romans
3:25 as the place of ***s*** where mercy is
12:1 as a living ***s*** that is holy and
1 Corinthians
10:20 but this kind of ***s*** is sacrificed to
Philippians
4:18 an acceptable ***s*** that pleases God.
2 Timothy
4:6 poured out like a ***s*** to God, and the
Hebrews
9:14 eternal Spirit as a ***s*** without any flaw.
10:5 You didn't want a ***s*** or an offering,
10:8 pleased with a ***s*** or an offering or
10:12 offered one ***s*** for sins for all
10:26 there isn't a ***s*** for sins left any
11:4 offered a better ***s*** to God than Cain,
13:15 offer up a ***s*** of praise through
1 Peter
1:2 obedience and ***s*** of Jesus Christ.
1 John
4:10 his Son as the ***s*** that deals with

SACRIFICED

Numbers
22:40 Balak ***s*** oxen and sheep and sent them to Balaam
23:4 altars and I have ***s*** a bull and a ram
Deuteronomy
16:4 the meat that you ***s*** on the first
32:17 They ***s*** to demons, not to God, to
Joshua
8:31 to the LORD and ***s*** well-being offerin
1 Samuel
1:4 Whenever he ***s***, Elkanah would give
2 Samuel
6:13 six steps, David ***s*** an ox and a
1 Kings
3:3 that he also ***s*** and burned
8:5 before the chest ***s*** countless sheep
8:62 and all Israel with him ***s*** to the LORD.
11:8 who burned incense and ***s*** to their gods.
12:32 in Judah. He ***s*** on the altar. At
2 Kings
16:4 He also ***s*** and burned incense at the
1 Chronicles
6:49 and his sons ***s*** on the altar for
15:26 covenant, they ***s*** seven bulls and
2 Chronicles
5:6 before the chest ***s*** countless sheep
7:4 king and all the people ***s*** to the LORD.
7:5 King Solomon ***s*** twenty-two thousand oxen

15:11 On that day they **s** to the LORD part of
28:4 He also **s** and burned incense at the
33:17 however, still **s** at the shrines,
33:22 had done. He **s** to all the idols
34:4 the graves of those who had **s** to them.
Psalms
51:19 bulls will again be **s** on your altar.
66:15 with the smoke of **s** rams. I will
106:37 They **s** their own sons and daughters to
106:38 the ones they **s** to Canaan's false
Ezekiel
16:20 to me, and you **s** these to them so
Mark
14:12 Passover lamb was **s**, the disciples
Luke
22:7 arrived, when the Passover had to be **s**.
1 Corinthians
5:7 Christ our Passover lamb has been **s**,
8:1 that has been **s** to a false god:
8:7 it really is food **s** to a real idol,
8:10 to eat the meat **s** to false gods?
9:13 share part of what is **s** on the altar?
10:19 then? That food **s** to a false god is
10:20 of sacrifice is **s** to demons and not
10:28 This meat was **s** in a temple,"
Revelation
2:14 would eat food **s** to idols and
2:20 immorality and eating food **s** to idols.

SACRIFICES → COMMUNAL SACRIFICES

Genesis
46:1 There he offered **s** to his father
Exodus
3:18 that we can offer **s** to the LORD our
5:3 so we can offer **s** to the LORD our
5:8 Let us go and offer **s** to our God.'
5:17 Let us go and offer **s** to the LORD.'
8:8 so that they can offer **s** to the LORD."
10:25 to let us have **s** and entirely
18:12 offering and **s** to God. Aaron
20:24 your well-being **s**, your sheep, and
22:20 Anyone who offers **s** to any god, other
24:5 oxen as well-being **s** to the LORD.
29:28 to the LORD from their well-being **s**.
32:6 well-being **s**. The people sat
32:8 to it and offered **s** to it and
Numbers
10:10 your well-being **s**. They will serve
25:2 the people to the **s** for their god. So
29:39 drink offerings, and your well-being **s**.
Deuteronomy
12:6 offerings, your **s**, your tenth-part g
12:11 offerings, your **s**, your tenth-part g
18:1 They can eat the **s** offered to the
18:3 from the people's **s** of oxen or sheep:
27:7 up well-being **s** and eat them
32:38 the fat of their **s**, who drank their
33:19 they offer right **s**. It's true:
Joshua
22:23 well-being **s** on it, let the
22:27 burned offerings, **s**, and well-being of
Judges
20:26 offerings and well-being **s** to the LORD.
21:4 burned offerings and well-being **s**.
1 Samuel
2:29 do you kick my **s** and my offerings—
6:15 offerings and made **s** to the LORD.
10:8 make well-being **s**. Wait seven days
15:22 offerings and **s** as much as
2 Samuel
6:17 presence in addition to well-being **s**.
6:18 the well-being **s**, he blessed the
15:12 was offering the **s**, he summoned
15:24 Abiathar offered **s** until all the
24:25 and well-being **s**. The LORD
1 Kings
3:15 and well-being **s**, and held a
8:63 well-being **s** to the LORD:
8:64 fat of well-being **s** there, because
9:25 and well-being **s** on the altar that
12:33 and offered **s** on the altar by
2 Kings
5:17 offerings or **s** to any other gods
10:24 went in to offer **s** and entirely
16:13 blood of his well-being **s** on the altar.
16:15 the following **s** on the main
Ezra
6:3 they offered **s** be rebuilt and
6:10 offer pleasing **s** to the God of
Nehemiah
4:2 Will they offer **s**? Will they finish
12:43 offered great **s** on that day and
Psalms
27:6 and I will offer **s** in God's tent—
40:6 You don't relish **s** or offerings; you
50:8 you for your **s** or for your
51:16 You don't want **s**. If I gave an
51:19 will again want **s** of righteousness—
106:28 Baal-peor and ate **s** offered to the
107:22 thanksgiving **s** and declare what
Proverbs
15:8 LORD detests the **s** of the wicked,
21:27 LORD detests the **s** of the wicked,
Isaiah
1:11 about all your **s**? says the LORD.
19:21 will worship with **s** and offerings,
43:23 me with your **s**. I didn't make
43:24 the fat of your **s**. Instead, you
56:7 offerings and **s** on my altar. My
66:3 the one who **s** a sheep breaks a
Jeremiah
6:20 your pardon; your **s** won't appease me.
7:21 offerings to your **s** and eat them
7:22 entirely burned offerings or **s**.
17:26 burned offerings, **s**, grain offerings,
18:15 they have offered **s** to a lie. And so
33:18 and grain offerings, and to present **s**.
Ezekiel
20:28 they made their **s**: irksome
43:27 your well-being **s** on the altar from
44:11 offerings and the **s** for the people,
45:15 for well-being **s** to make
46:2 and well-being **s**, and then he will
Daniel
9:27 he will stop both **s** and offerings. In
Hosea
2:13 sweet-smelling **s** to them and
4:13 They offer **s** on mountaintops, and make entirely burned
4:14 and offer **s** with consecrated
4:19 wings, they will be ashamed of their **s**.
8:13 they offer choice **s**, though they eat
9:4 the LORD; their **s** won't please him.

Amos
4:4 Bring your **s** every morning,
5:25 Did you bring me **s** and offerings during
Habakkuk
1:16 Therefore, he **s** to his net; he burns
Malachi
1:14 who promises and **s** to the LORD that
Mark
12:33 of entirely burned offerings and **s**."
Luke
13:1 had killed while they were offering **s**.
Acts
7:42 Did you bring **s** and offerings to
14:13 crowds, he wanted to offer **s** to them.
24:17 the poor of my nation and to offer **s**.
1 Corinthians
8:4 involved in these **s** to false gods, we
10:18 those who eat the **s** share from the
Hebrews
5:1 in order to offer gifts and **s** for sins.
5:3 he must offer **s** for his own sins
5:7 and tears as his **s** to the one who
7:27 need to offer **s** every day like
8:3 offer gifts and **s**. So it's
9:9 the gifts and **s** that are being
9:23 with these **s**, but the heavenly
10:1 through the same **s** that are offered
10:3 Instead, these **s** are a reminder of sin
10:11 offering the same **s** over and over,
13:16 God is pleased with these kinds of **s**.
1 Peter
2:5 up spiritual **s** that are

SAD

1 Samuel
1:8 Why are you so **s**? Aren't I worth
1:15 I'm just a very **s** woman. I haven't
1:18 ate some food, and wasn't **s** any longer.
Nehemiah
2:1 I had never seemed **s** in his presence,
2:2 Why do you seem **s**? Since you aren't
2:3 shouldn't I seem **s** when the city,
8:10 LORD. Don't be **s**, because the joy
8:11 for this day is holy. Don't be **s**!"
Esther
9:22 to joy, and from **s**, loud crying to a
Psalms
35:14 was weighed down, **s**, like I was a
38:6 down; I wander around all day long, **s**.
42:9 to walk around, **s**, oppressed by
43:2 to walk around, **s**, oppressed by
Ecclesiastes
7:3 because a **s** face may lead to
9:3 This is the **s** thing about all that
Isaiah
63:10 spirit terribly **s**, so that he
Amos
8:10 your feasts into **s** affairs and all
Matthew
6:16 don't put on a **s** face like the
26:37 sons, he began to feel **s** and anxious.
26:38 them, "I'm very **s**. It's as if I'm
Mark
14:34 them, "I'm very **s**. It's as if I'm
Luke
18:23 the man became **s** because he was
John
21:17 me?" Peter was **s** that Jesus asked
1 Corinthians
7:30 Those who are **s** should be like people
2 Corinthians
2:2 If I make you **s**, who will be there to
7:8 letter made you **s**, though only for

SAFE

Psalms
9:9 The LORD is a **s** place for the
18:19 he pulled me out **s** because he is
18:36 me walk fast and **s**, without even
27:5 he will set me up high, **s** on a rock.
31:20 of your wings, **s** from human
60:4 rally around it, **s** from attack. Selah
69:29 Let your salvation keep me **s**, God!
102:28 children live **s**; let your
107:28 brought them out **s** from their
140:11 no slanderer be **s** in the land. Let
Proverbs
21:22 the stronghold in which they felt **s**.
28:26 who walk in wisdom will be kept **s**.

SAFELY

Genesis
28:21 and I return **s** to my father's
33:18 Jacob arrived **s** at the city of Shechem
Deuteronomy
12:10 side so that you live **s** and securely.
33:12 dearest one rests **s** on him. The Lord
Joshua
10:21 people came back **s** to Joshua in the
1 Samuel
19:10 David fled and got away **s**. That night
20:13 you can escape **s**. May the LORD be
2 Samuel
19:24 king left until the day he returned **s**.
19:30 my master and king has come home **s**."
1 Kings
22:17 Let them return **s** to their own
22:27 of bread and water until I return **s**.'"
22:28 you ever return **s**," Micaiah
2 Chronicles
18:16 Let them return **s** to their own
18:26 of bread and water until I return **s**.'"
18:27 you ever return **s**," Micaiah
Job
11:18 hope; you will look around and rest **s**.
Psalms
22:9 womb, placing me **s** at my mother's
141:10 but let me make it through **s**.
Proverbs
3:23 you will walk **s** on your path, and
Ezekiel
34:25 Then they will **s** live in the
Acts
23:24 they may take him **s** to Governor
27:44 In this way, everyone reached land **s**.
28:1 reaching land **s**, we learned that
Romans
15:28 this job and have **s** delivered the
1 Timothy
2:15 will be brought **s** through giving

SAFETY

Genesis
43:9 guarantee his **s**; you can hold me
44:32 the young man's **s** to my father,
Deuteronomy
33:27 God is a place of **s**; the eternal arms
33:28 now lives in **s**—Jacob's
2 Samuel
15:27 to the city in **s**—you and Abiathar
22:3 my place of **s** and my shelter.
Job
5:4 are far from **s**, crushed in the
18:14 snatched from the **s** of their tent; it
30:15 like wind; my **s** disappears like a
Psalms
4:8 you alone, LORD, let me live in **s**.
16:9 yes, my whole body will rest in **s**
18:2 my salvation's strength, my place of **s**.
46:7 God of Jacob is our place of **s**. Selah
46:11 God of Jacob is our place of **s**. Selah
48:3 revealing himself as a place of **s**.
78:53 God led them in **s**—they were not
144:2 my place of **s**, my rescuer, my
Jeremiah
14:11 Don't pray for the **s** of these people.
23:6 will live in **s**. And his name
33:16 will live in **s**. And this is what
Ezekiel
28:26 live on it in **s**. They will build
34:28 They will live in **s**, with no one to
Daniel
4:27 poor. Then your **s** will be long
Hosea
2:18 land; I will make you lie down in **s**.

SAINTS

Romans
8:27 it pleads for the **s**, consistent with
16:15 and all the **s** who are with them.
2 Corinthians
8:4 of sharing in this service for the **s**.
1 Timothy
5:10 the feet of the **s**, helping those in
Revelation
5:8 which are the prayers of the **s**.
8:3 of all the **s** on the gold altar
8:4 prayers of the **s** rose up before
11:18 the prophets and **s**, and those who
13:7 make war on the **s** and to gain
13:10 and faithfulness on the part of the **s**.
14:12 endurance of the **s**, who keep God's
16:6 out the blood of **s** and prophets, and
17:6 the blood of the **s** and the blood of
18:20 her, heaven—you **s**, apostles, and
18:24 of prophets, of **s**, and of all who

SAKE

Genesis
18:24 the place for the **s** of the fifty
26:24 children for my servant Abraham's **s**."
Psalms
6:4 Save me for the **s** of your faithful
9:7 his throne for the **s** of justice.
23:3 paths for the **s** of his good name.
25:7 love for the **s** of your goodness,
25:11 Please, for the **s** of your good name,
31:3 lead me for the **s** of your good name!
44:26 Save us for the **s** of your faithful
79:9 cover our sins for the **s** of your name!
105:14 them. God punished kings for their **s**:
106:8 them for the **s** of his good name,
106:45 for their **s**, and because of
109:21 my behalf for the **s** of your name;
122:8 For the **s** of my family and friends, I
132:10 And for the **s** of your servant David, do
138:8 all this for my **s**. Your faithful
143:11 for your name's **s**. Bring me out of
Jeremiah
14:7 for your name's **s**. We have turned
Ezekiel
20:9 I acted for the **s** of my name, so
36:32 Not for your **s** do I act. This is what
Micah
1:11 Pass by (for your **s**), inhabitants of
Matthew
15:6 God's Law for the **s** of the rules that
24:22 But for the **s** of the ones whom
Mark
13:20 But for the **s** of the chosen
Acts
9:16 he must suffer for the **s** of my name."
21:13 Jerusalem for the **s** of the name of
Romans
1:5 to faithful obedience for his name's **s**.
4:23 wasn't written only for Abraham's **s**.
8:36 day long for your **s**. We are treated
11:28 enemies for your **s**, but according to
13:5 but also for the **s** of your
15:8 for the **s** of God's truth,
1 Corinthians
9:10 entirely for our **s**? It was written
9:23 I do are for the **s** of the gospel, so
10:28 eat it for the **s** of the one who
11:9 created for the **s** of the woman, but
2 Corinthians
2:1 that, for my own **s**, I wouldn't visit
4:5 ourselves as your slaves for Jesus' **s**.
4:11 death for Jesus' **s** so that Jesus'
5:13 it's for God's **s**. If we are
5:14 one died for the **s** of all;
5:15 He died for the **s** of all so that those
5:21 to be sin for our **s** so that through
7:12 it wasn't for the **s** of the one who
8:19 care of for the **s** of the glory of
12:10 for the **s** of Christ,
12:15 be spent for your **s**. If I love you
Ephesians
6:20 in chains for the **s** of the gospel.
Philippians
1:24 me to stay in this world for your **s**.
1:29 but also of suffering for Christ's **s**.
3:7 them off as a loss for the **s** of Christ.
Colossians
1:7 Christ's faithful minister for your **s**.
1:24 this for the **s** of his body,
1 Thessalonians
1:5 we were with you, which was for your **s**.
2 Timothy
2:10 for the **s** of those who are
Hebrews
5:1 to God for their **s**, in order to
6:10 for his name's **s** when you served
12:2 shame, for the **s** of the joy that
12:7 hardship for the **s** of discipline.

1 Peter
2:13 For the ***s*** of the Lord submit to every
3 John
1:7 journey for the ***s*** of Jesus Christ
Revelation
2:3 lot for my name's ***s***, and you haven't

SALEM
Genesis
14:18 the king of ***S*** and the priest of
Psalms
76:2 place became ***S***; his habitation
John
3:23 at Aenon near ***S*** because there was
Hebrews
7:1 who was king of ***S*** and priest of the
7:2 and then "king of ***S***," that is, "king

SALT
Genesis
19:26 back, she turned into a pillar of ***s***.
Exodus
30:35 seasoned with ***s***, pure and holy.
Leviticus
2:13 offerings with ***s***. Do not omit the
Numbers
18:19 is a covenant of ***s*** forever in the
Deuteronomy
29:23 by sulfur and ***s***, unsuitable for
Joshua
15:62 Nibshan (the ***S*** City), and En-gedi. In total
Judges
9:45 the city and scattered ***s*** over it.
2 Samuel
8:13 thousand Edomites in the ***S*** Valley.
2 Kings
2:20 and put some ***s*** in it." They did
2:21 out and threw ***s*** into the spring.
14:7 Edomites in the ***S*** Valley and
1 Chronicles
18:12 thousand Edomites in the ***S*** Valley.
2 Chronicles
25:11 his people to the ***S*** Valley, where
Ezra
6:9 of heaven, wheat, ***s***, wine, or oil, as
7:22 hundred baths of oil, and unlimited ***s***.
Job
6:6 eaten without ***s***, or does egg
39:6 his dwelling place in the ***s*** flats?
Psalms
60:1 thousand in the ***S*** Valley.] God, you
Ezekiel
16:4 or rubbed with ***s***, and you weren't
43:24 will throw ***s*** on them and offer
47:11 be made fresh (they are left for ***s***),
Zephaniah
2:9 a plot of weeds, ***s*** pits, and
Matthew
5:13 You are the ***s*** of the earth. But if
Mark
9:50 ***S*** is good; but if salt loses its
Luke
14:34 ***S*** is good. But if salt loses its
James
3:11 fresh water and ***s*** water don't come

SALVATION
Exodus
15:2 he has become my ***s***. This is my God,
Deuteronomy
32:15 the rock of his ***s*** was worthless.
2 Samuel
22:36 shield of your ***s***; your help has
22:47 God, the rock of my ***s***, be lifted high!
2 Chronicles
6:41 be clothed with ***s***; may those loyal
Psalms
9:14 rejoice in your ***s*** in the gates of
13:5 love. My heart will rejoice in your ***s***.
14:7 Let Israel's ***s*** come out of Zion! When
18:35 shield of your ***s***; your strong hand
18:46 Let the God of my ***s*** be lifted high!
20:6 mighty acts of ***s*** achieved by his
27:1 my light and my ***s***. Should I fear
35:3 out to get me! Say to me: "I'm your ***s***!"
35:9 in the LORD; I will celebrate his ***s***.
37:39 The ***s*** of the righteous comes from the
38:22 quickly and help me, my Lord, my ***s***!
40:10 and your ***s***. I didn't hide
40:16 who love your ***s*** always say, "The
44:4 king, the one who orders ***s*** for Jacob.
50:23 path that I will show divine ***s***."
51:12 the joy of your ***s*** to me and sustain
51:14 God, God of my ***s***, so that my
53:6 Let Israel's ***s*** come out of Zion! When
62:1 do I find rest; my ***s*** comes from him.
62:2 is my rock and my ***s***—my stronghold!—
62:6 is my rock and my ***s***—my stronghold!—
65:5 deeds, God of our ***s***—you, who are the
67:2 so that your ***s*** becomes known
68:19 The God of our ***s*** supports us day
68:20 God is the God of ***s***, and escape from
69:13 love, answer me with your certain ***s***!
69:29 of pain. Let your ***s*** keep me safe, God!
74:12 God, who makes ***s*** happen in the
79:9 God of our ***s***, help us for the glory of
85:7 faithful love, LORD! Give us your ***s***!
85:9 God's ***s*** is very close to those who
88:1] LORD, God of my ***s***, by day I cry
89:26 my father, my God, the rock of my ***s***."
91:16 full with old age. I'll show you my ***s***."
95:1 a joyful shout to the rock of our ***s***!
98:2 LORD has made his ***s*** widely known; he
98:3 of the earth has seen our God's ***s***.
116:13 up the cup of ***s***. I'll call on the
119:41 to me—let your ***s*** come to me
119:155 ***S*** is far from the wicked because they
132:16 its priests in ***s***, and its faithful
Isaiah
12:2 God is indeed my ***s***; I will trust and
12:3 water with joy from the springs of ***s***.
25:9 let's be glad and rejoice in his ***s***!"
26:1 city! God makes ***s*** its walls and
33:2 morning, our ***s*** in times of
33:6 a source of ***s***, wisdom, and
45:8 earth open for ***s*** to bear fruit;
45:17 of everlasting ***s***. You won't be
46:13 isn't far, and my ***s***—it won't delay. I
49:6 so that my ***s*** may reach to the
49:8 you; on a day of ***s***, I helped you. I
51:5 my victory. My ***s*** is on its way,
51:6 gnats. But my ***s*** will endure
51:8 forever, and my ***s*** for all

52:7 who proclaims **s**, who says to
56:1 because my **s** is coming soon,
59:11 is none; we await **s**, but it is far
59:17 and a helmet of **s** on his head,
60:18 call your walls **S**, and your gates
62:1 a light, and her **s** blazes like a
Jeremiah
3:23 in the LORD our God is the **s** of Israel.
Micah
7:7 for the God of my **s**; my God will hear
Habakkuk
3:13 people. For the **s** of your anointed
Mark
16:9 of eternal **s**. Amen.
Luke
1:71 He has brought **s** from our enemies and
2:30 because my eyes have seen your **s**
2:31 You prepared this **s** in the presence of
3:6 All humanity will see God's **s**.
19:9 to him, "Today, **s** has come to this
John
4:22 we know because **s** is from the Jews.
Acts
4:12 **S** can be found in no one else.
13:26 about this **s** has been sent to
13:47 you could bring **s** to the end of the
16:17 are proclaiming a way of **s** to you!"
28:28 of this: God's **s** has been sent to
Romans
1:16 own power for **s** to all who have
10:1 is for Israel's **s**. That's my prayer
10:10 confessing with the mouth leads to **s**.
11:11 not! But **s** has come to the
13:11 sleep. Now our **s** is nearer than
2 Corinthians
1:6 you comfort and **s**. If we are
6:2 you on the day of **s**. Look, now is the
7:10 that leads to **s** and leaves no
Ephesians
1:13 good news of your **s**. You were sealed
2:8 your faith. This **s** is God's gift.
6:17 the helmet of **s** and the sword of
Philippians
1:28 and your **s**, which is from
2:12 out your own **s** with fear and
1 Thessalonians
5:8 our body and the hope of **s** as a helmet.
5:9 rather to possess **s** through our Lord
2 Thessalonians
2:13 This brought **s**, through your
2 Timothy
2:10 may experience **s** in Christ Jesus
3:15 way that leads to **s** through faith
Titus
2:11 has appeared, bringing **s** to all people.
Hebrews
1:14 serve those who are going to inherit **s**?
2:3 such a great **s**? It was first
2:10 the pioneer of **s**. This salvation
5:9 the source of **s** for everyone who
6:9 way—things that go together with **s**.
1 Peter
1:5 can receive the **s** he is ready to
1:9 the goal of your faith: your **s**.
1:10 inquiring carefully about this **s**.
2:2 Nourished by it, you will grow into **s**,
3:21 toward God. Your **s** comes through the
2 Peter
3:15 of our Lord to be **s**, just as our dear
Jude
1:3 concerning the **s** we share.
Revelation
12:10 say, "Now the **s** and power and
19:1 Hallelujah! The **s** and glory and

SAMARIA

1 Kings
16:24 the hill of **S** from Shemer for
16:32 Baal temple he had constructed in **S**.
20:43 to his palace at **S**, irritated and
21:1 next to the palace of King Ahab of **S**.
2 Kings
17:6 king captured **S**. He sent Israel
Isaiah
7:9 of Ephraim is **S**; and the chief of
Ezekiel
23:4 Now Oholah is **S**, and Oholibah is
Hosea
8:5 calf is rejected, **S**. My anger burns
Amos
6:1 trusting in Mount **S**, the chiefs of
Micah
1:6 So I will make **S** a pile of rubble in
John
4:4 Jesus had to go through **S**
Acts
1:8 in all Judea and **S**, and to the end
8:1 throughout the regions of Judea and **S**.
9:31 Galilee, and **S** enjoyed a time of

SAMARITAN

Luke
10:33 A **S**, who was on a journey, came to
17:16 feet and thanked him. He was a **S**.
John
4:7 A **S** woman came to the well to draw
8:48 that you are a **S** and have a demon,

SAMSON

Judges
13:24 son and named him **S**. The boy grew up,
15:16 **S** said, "With a donkey's jawbone,
16:6 Delilah said to **S**, "Please tell me
16:29 **S** grabbed the two central pillars that
1 Samuel
12:11 Jephthah, and **S**, and he delivered
Hebrews
11:32 Gideon, Barak, **S**, Jephthah, David,

SAMUEL

1 Samuel
2:18 Now **S** was serving the LORD. He was a
3:10 just as before, "**S**, Samuel!" Samuel
3:19 So **S** grew up, and the LORD was with
10:1 **S** took a small jar of oil and poured it
12:1 **S** said to all Israel: "Listen: I have
16:13 So **S** took the horn of oil and anointed
25:1 Now **S** died, and all Israel gathered to
1 Chronicles
6:33 Heman the singer, son of Joel son of **S**
9:22 David and **S** the seer assigned
11:3 as the LORD had promised through **S**.
26:28 was dedicated by **S** the seer, as well
29:29 in the records of **S** the seer, Nathan

2 Chronicles
35:18 of the prophet ***S*** had such a
Psalms
99:6 his priests, ***S*** too among those
Jeremiah
15:1 Even if Moses and ***S*** stood before me,
Acts
3:24 who spoke—from ***S*** forward—announced
13:20 judges until the time of the prophet ***S***.
Hebrews
11:32 Jephthah, David, ***S***, and the prophets.

SANBALLAT
Nehemiah
2:10 When ***S*** the Horonite and Tobiah the
13:28 a son-in-law of ***S*** the Horonite. So

SANCTUARY → GOD'S SANCTUARY
Exodus
15:13 your power you guided them to your ***s***.
15:17 your home, the ***s***, LORD, that your
25:8 should make me a ***s*** so I can be
28:29 he goes into the ***s*** as a reminder
29:30 the meeting tent to minister in the ***s***.
30:13 shekel of the ***s*** (the shekel is
31:11 incense for the ***s***. They will do
35:19 in the ***s***, and the holy
36:1 of building the ***s*** do all that the
38:24 of the whole ***s***, gold from the
39:1 as priests in the ***s***. They made the
Leviticus
10:4 the front of the ***s*** to a place
16:33 part of the ***s*** and will do the
19:30 and treat my ***s*** with respect; I
20:3 Molech, making my ***s*** unclean and
21:12 must not exit the ***s***, making his God's
21:23 these parts of my ***s*** impure by doing
26:2 and respect my ***s***; I am the LORD.
Joshua
24:26 under the oak in the ***s*** of the LORD.
1 Kings
6:16 built the inner ***s***, the most holy
7:49 of the inner ***s***; the flowers, the
8:8 of the inner ***s***, though they
1 Chronicles
22:19 and build the ***s*** of the LORD God,
23:32 for the ***s***, and the
28:10 a temple for him as the ***s***, work hard.
Nehemiah
10:39 where the ***s*** equipment is
Psalms
20:2 to you from the ***s*** and support you
20:6 from his heavenly ***s***, answering with
24:3 mountain? Who can stand in his holy ***s***?
28:2 lift up my hands to your holy inner ***s***.
60:6 has spoken in his ***s***: "I will
63:2 seen you in the ***s***; I've seen your
68:17 My Lord came from Sinai into the ***s***.
68:24 of my God, my king, into the ***s***.
74:3 all that the enemy destroyed in the ***s***.
74:7 set fire to your ***s***, burned it to the
78:60 God abandoned the ***s*** at Shiloh, the tent
78:69 God built his ***s*** like the highest heaven
96:6 him; strength and beauty are in his ***s***.
108:7 has spoken in his ***s***: "I will
134:2 your hands to the ***s*** and bless the
150:1 Praise God in his ***s***! Praise God in
Isaiah
8:14 God will become a ***s***—but he will be a
16:12 and comes to his ***s*** to pray, he won't
60:13 the site of my ***s***, and I will honor
63:18 Why did our enemies trample your ***s***?
Jeremiah
7:12 Just go to my ***s*** in Shiloh, where I let
17:12 the place of our ***s*** from the
Lamentations
1:10 nations enter her ***s***—nations that you
2:7 he abandoned his ***s***; he handed Zion's
2:20 prophet be killed in my Lord's own ***s***?
Ezekiel
5:11 you made my ***s*** unclean with all
8:6 me far from my ***s***? Yet you will see
9:6 mark. Begin at my ***s***. So they began
11:16 provided some ***s*** for them in the
21:2 against their ***s***, and prophesy
23:38 day, they made my ***s*** unclean and made
23:39 they came into my ***s*** and made it
24:21 about to make my ***s*** impure, the pride
25:3 laughed when my ***s*** was degraded,
37:26 I will set my ***s*** among them
37:28 holy, when my ***s*** is among them
42:14 go out of the ***s*** to the outer
43:21 place of the temple outside of the ***s***.
44:1 back to the outer ***s*** gate that faces
44:5 the temple through all the ***s*** portals.
45:2 will be for the ***s***. All around it
47:12 comes from the ***s***. Their fruit will
48:21 and the temple ***s*** are in the middle
Daniel
8:13 over of the ***s*** and its forces to
8:14 mornings. Then the ***s*** will be restored."
9:17 on your ruined ***s***, for your own
9:26 the city and the ***s***. His end will
11:31 come and make the ***s*** fortress impure.
Matthew
27:51 curtain of the ***s*** was torn in two
Mark
15:38 curtain of the ***s*** was torn in two
Luke
1:9 go into the Lord's ***s*** and burn incense.
1:21 why he was in the ***s*** for such a long
23:45 curtain in the ***s*** tore down the
Hebrews
6:19 being, enters the ***s*** behind the

SANDALS
Exodus
3:5 Take off your ***s***, because you are
12:11 with your ***s*** on your feet and
Deuteronomy
29:5 your back nor the ***s*** on your feet have
Joshua
5:15 Take your ***s*** off your feet
9:5 worn-out, patched ***s*** on their feet and
9:13 These clothes and ***s*** of ours are worn
1 Kings
2:5 his waist and on the ***s*** on his feet.
2 Chronicles
28:15 them clothing, ***s***, food and drink,
Isaiah
11:15 streams so that it can be crossed in ***s***.
Ezekiel
16:10 put fine ***s*** on you, wrapped

24:23 your heads, your **s** on your feet. You
Amos
2:6 and those in need for a pair of **s**.
8:6 the helpless for **s**, and sell garbage
Matthew
3:11 to carry his **s**. He will baptize
10:10 or two shirts or **s** or a walking
Mark
1:7 over and loosen the strap of his **s**.
6:9 told them to wear **s** but not to put on
Luke
3:16 the strap of his **s**. He will baptize
10:4 no bag, and no **s**. Don't even greet
15:22 a ring on his finger and **s** on his feet!
22:35 a wallet, bag, or **s**, you didn't lack
John
19:23 clothes and his **s**, and divided them
Acts
7:33 Remove the **s** from your feet,
12:8 Put on your **s**." Peter did as he
13:25 me. I'm not worthy to loosen his **s**.'

SARAH
Genesis
17:15 call her Sarai. Her name will now be **S**.
21:1 was attentive to **S** just as he had
49:31 and his wife **S** are buried, and
Isaiah
51:2 ancestor, and to **S**, who gave you
Romans
9:9 I will return, and **S** will have a son.
Hebrews
11:11 By faith even **S** received the ability to
1 Peter
3:6 For example, **S** accepted Abraham's

SARAI
Genesis
17:15 As for your wife **S**, you will no

SAT
Judges
6:11 came and **s** under the oak at
19:6 the two of them **s** down and ate and
21:2 to Bethel and **s** there until
Ruth
2:7 now, and has **s** down for only a
2:14 the vinegar." She **s** alongside the
4:1 to the gate and **s** down there. Just
4:2 said, "Sit down here." And they **s** down.
1 Samuel
20:24 came, the king **s** at the feast to
20:25 wall. Jonathan **s** opposite him
28:23 got up off the ground and **s** on a couch.
2 Samuel
2:13 Gibeon. One group **s** on one side of
7:18 David went and **s** in the LORD's
19:8 the king went and **s** down in the city
1 Kings
2:12 Solomon **s** on the throne of his father
2:19 the queen mother. She **s** to his right.
16:11 became king and **s** on the throne, he
19:4 He finally **s** down under a
21:13 liars came and **s** in front of him.
2 Kings
4:20 mother. The boy **s** on her lap until
11:19 where the king **s** upon the royal
2 Chronicles
23:20 where the king **s** upon the royal
Ezra
9:3 my head and beard, and **s** down in shock.
10:9 All of the people **s** in the area in
10:16 tenth month they **s** down to examine
Nehemiah
1:4 this news, I **s** down and wept. I
Esther
1:6 silver couches **s** on a mosaic floor
3:15 king and Haman **s** down to have a
Job
2:8 himself and **s** down on a mound
2:13 They **s** with Job on the ground seven
29:25 their path, **s** as chief. I lived
Psalms
137:1 streams, there we **s** down, crying
Jeremiah
15:17 in them. I **s** alone because
Daniel
7:10 him! The court **s** in session; the
Jonah
3:6 with mourning clothes, and **s** in ashes.
4:5 from the city and **s** down east of the
Matthew
5:1 up a mountain. He **s** down and his
9:10 As Jesus **s** down to eat in Matthew's
13:1 of the house and **s** down beside the
13:2 into a boat and **s** down. The whole
13:48 shore, where they **s** down and put the
15:29 Sea. He went up a mountain and **s** down.
21:7 clothes on them. Then he **s** on them.
26:55 Day after day, I **s** in the temple
26:58 that area and **s** outside with the
27:36 They **s** there, guarding him
28:2 stone, he rolled it away and **s** on it.
Mark
2:15 Jesus **s** down to eat at Levi's house.
4:1 on the lake. He **s** in the boat while
6:40 They **s** down in groups of hundreds and fifties
9:35 He **s** down, called the Twelve, and said
11:7 their clothes upon it, and he **s** on it.
12:41 Jesus **s** across from the collection box
16:19 into heaven and **s** down on the right
Luke
4:20 assistant, and **s** down. Every eye
5:3 the shore. Jesus **s** down and taught
5:29 and others **s** down to eat with
7:15 The dead man **s** up and began to speak,
10:13 They would have **s** around in funeral
10:39 named Mary, who **s** at the Lord's
22:55 the courtyard and **s** down together,
John
4:6 journey, so he **s** down at the well.
5:3 blind, lame, and paralyzed **s** there.
6:3 up a mountain and **s** there with his
6:10 grass there. They **s** down, about five
8:2 him, and he **s** down and taught
12:14 young donkey and **s** on it, just as it
Acts
9:40 opened her eyes, saw Peter, and **s** up.
16:13 for prayer. We **s** down and began to
1 Corinthians
10:7 The people **s** down to eat and

Ephesians
1:20 from the dead and ***s*** him at God's
Hebrews
1:3 their sins, he ***s*** down at the right
8:1 high priest. He ***s*** down at the right
10:12 for all time, he ***s*** down at the right
12:2 front of him, and ***s*** down at the right
Revelation
3:21 victorious and ***s*** down with my

SATAN
Matthew
4:10 Go away, ***S***, because it's
12:26 If ***S*** throws out Satan, he is at war
16:23 Get behind me, ***S***. You are a stone
Mark
4:15 it, right away ***S*** comes and steals
8:33 Get behind me, ***S***. You are not
Luke
10:18 replied, "I saw ***S*** fall from heaven
22:3 Then ***S*** entered Judas, called Iscariot,
John
13:27 took the bread, ***S*** entered into him.
Acts
5:3 how is it that ***S*** has influenced
26:18 from the power of ***S*** to God, and
Romans
16:20 will soon crush ***S*** under your feet.
1 Corinthians
5:5 this man over to ***S*** to destroy his
7:5 again so that ***S*** might not tempt
2 Corinthians
2:11 advantage of by ***S***, because we are
6:15 Christ have with ***S***? What does a
11:14 no wonder! Even ***S*** disguises himself
12:7 a messenger from ***S*** sent to torment
1 Thessalonians
2:18 over and over again—and ***S*** stopped us.
1 Timothy
1:20 them over to ***S*** so that they can
5:15 have already turned away to follow ***S***.)
Revelation
2:13 was killed among you, where ***S*** lives.
2:24 deep secrets" of ***S***—I won't burden yo
12:9 the devil and ***S***, the deceiver of
20:2 is the devil and ***S***, and bound him
20:7 years are over, ***S*** will be released

SATISFIED
Deuteronomy
8:10 eat, you will be ***s***, and you will
11:15 livestock, and you will eat and be ***s***.
Ruth
2:14 her. She ate, was ***s***, and had
Nehemiah
9:25 until they were ***s*** and grew fat, and
Job
14:6 until we are ***s*** like a worker at
42:17 Then Job died, old and ***s***
Psalms
63:5 I'm fully ***s***—as with a rich dinner.
78:29 were completely ***s***; God gave them
107:9 because God ***s*** the one who was parched
Proverbs
12:14 people are well ***s***; their work
13:4 the appetite of the diligent is ***s***.
18:20 The stomach is ***s*** by the fruit of the
27:20 are never ***s***; and people's
30:15 that are never ***s***; four that never
Ecclesiastes
1:8 The eye isn't ***s*** with seeing,
4:8 end, never ***s*** with their
5:10 money lover isn't ***s*** with money;
Isaiah
9:20 left, and weren't ***s***. They devoured
44:16 meat, and he is ***s***. He warms himself
53:11 and he will be ***s***. Through his
66:11 may nurse and be ***s*** from her
Jeremiah
5:7 I could have ***s*** them, they
Ezekiel
7:8 my anger will be ***s***. I'll judge you
16:28 Still not ***s***, you prostituted yourself
16:29 of traders, but again you weren't ***s***.
16:42 When I've ***s*** my anger, and my rage has
27:33 the seas, you ***s*** many people. Your
Hosea
4:10 eat but not be ***s***; they will have
13:6 them, they were ***s***; and their hearts
Joel
2:19 you will be fully ***s*** by it; and I will
2:26 abundantly and be ***s***, and you will
Amos
4:8 and weren't ***s***; yet you didn't
Micah
6:14 but you aren't ***s***; a gnawing
Habakkuk
2:5 he is never ***s***. He gathers all
Luke
3:14 harass anyone, and be ***s*** with your pay."
6:21 you will be ***s***. Happy are you

SAUL
1 Samuel
9:2 had a son named ***S***, who was a
11:15 Gilgal they made ***S*** king in the
15:11 I regret making ***S*** king because he has
16:21 how David came to ***S*** and entered his
18:7 in celebration: "***S*** has killed his
18:12 ***S*** was afraid of David because the LORD
19:24 people say, "Is ***S*** also one of the
26:7 night and found ***S*** lying there,
31:4 ***S*** said to his armor-bearer, "Draw your
Psalms
18:1 enemies and from ***S***.] He said: I love
52:1 came and told ***S***
54:1 came and said to ***S***
57:1 when he fled from ***S*** into the cave.
59:1 of David, when ***S*** sent men to watch
Acts
8:1 ***S*** was in full agreement with Stephen's
9:4 asking him, "***S***, Saul, why are
13:9 the Holy Spirit, ***S***, also known as

SAVE → SAVE THEIR LIVES, SAVE US, SAVE YOU, SAVE YOURSELF
Genesis
18:24 it away and not ***s*** the place for the
18:26 of Sodom, I will ***s*** it because of
19:16 LORD intended to ***s*** him, the men
19:17 the men said, "***S*** your lives! Don't
19:19 been so kind to ***s*** my life. But I
32:11 ***S*** me from my brother Esau! I'm afraid
37:22 He intended to ***s*** Joseph from them

45:5 God sent me before you to **s** lives.
50:20 it, in order to **s** the lives of many
Exodus
21:30 pay the agreed amount to **s** his life.
Leviticus
7:15 it; you cannot **s** any of it until
Deuteronomy
25:11 fight, trying to **s** her husband from
1 Samuel
9:16 Israel. He will **s** my people from
10:1 LORD's people and **s** them from the
17:47 the LORD doesn't **s** by means of sword
23:2 Fight the Philistines and **s** Keilah!"
2 Samuel
22:3 shelter. My savior! **S** me from violence!
22:42 was no one to **s** them. They looked
2 Kings
16:7 son. Come up and **s** me from the power
19:34 this city and **s** it for my sake!
Nehemiah
6:11 the temple to **s** his life? I won't
Psalms
3:7 Stand up, LORD! **S** me, my God! In fact, hit all my
6:4 LORD! Deliver me! **S** me for the sake
7:1 LORD, my God. **S** me from all who
18:41 was no one to **s** them. They cried
20:9 LORD, **s** the king! Let him answer us
22:21 **S** me from the mouth of the lion. From
25:22 Please, God, **s** Israel from all its
26:11 with integrity. **S** me! Have mercy on
31:16 on your servant; **s** me by your
33:17 victory; it can't **s** despite its great
36:6 sea. LORD, you **s** both humans and
37:40 and he will **s** them because they
44:3 own arms didn't **s** them—no, it was
44:6 trust in my bow; my sword won't **s** me
49:7 Wealth? It can't **s** a single person! It
49:8 The price to **s** someone's life is too
49:15 But God will **s** my life from the power
54:1 us? God! **S** me by your name;
59:2 from evildoers; **s** me from the
69:1 Of David.] **S** me, God, because
69:14 **S** me from the mud! Don't let me drown!
69:18 to me! Redeem me! **S** me because of my enemies
69:35 most certainly **s** Zion and will
71:2 Bend your ear toward me and **s** me!
72:4 are poor; let him **s** the children of
76:9 God rose up to **s** all of the
78:50 wrath. He didn't **s** them from death,
86:16 your strength; **s** this child of
108:6 **S** me by your power and answer me so
109:26 me, LORD, my God! **S** me according to
109:31 to the needy, to **s** them from any who
116:4 the LORD's name: "LORD, please **s** me!"
119:146 cry out to you, "**S** me so I can keep
138:7 wrath; you **s** me with your
Isaiah
36:18 of the nations **s** their lands from
36:20 Will the LORD **s** Jerusalem from my
37:12 destroyed **s** them, the gods of
37:35 this city and **s** it for my sake
44:17 to it, saying, "**S** me, for you are
44:20 astray. He can't **s** himself and say,
45:20 those who pray to a god who won't **s**.
46:7 answer. It can't **s** people from their
47:14 them. They won't **s** themselves from
49:25 you, and I myself will **s** your children.
50:2 enough power to **s**? With my rebuke I
59:1 lack the power to **s**, nor are his ears
63:1 righteousness, powerful to **s**!
Jeremiah
11:12 but they won't **s** them when
17:14 I'll be healed. **S** me and I'll be
47:4 who might try to **s** Gaza, because the
50:14 now shoot at her; **s** none of your
Lamentations
4:17 we watched for a nation that doesn't **s**.
Ezekiel
3:19 their guilt, but you will **s** your life.
3:21 the warning, and you will **s** your life.
33:9 their guilt, but you will **s** your life.
Daniel
6:14 he could do to **s** Daniel before the
Hosea
1:7 their God, will **s** them; I will not
Amos
2:15 who ride horses won't **s** themselves.
Nahum
2:1 protect your groin, **s** your strength!
Habakkuk
3:13 You go out to **s** your people. For the
Matthew
1:21 because he will **s** his people from
27:42 but he can't **s** himself. He's the
27:49 see if Elijah will come and **s** him."
Mark
3:4 or to do evil, to **s** life or to kill?"
15:31 they said, "but he can't **s** himself.
Luke
6:9 or to do evil, to **s** life or to
19:10 Human One came to seek and **s** the lost."
23:35 others. Let him **s** himself if he
John
12:27 I say? 'Father, **s** me from this
12:47 come to judge the world but to **s** it.
Acts
27:43 wanted to **s** Paul, so he
Romans
11:14 own people jealous and **s** some of them.
1 Corinthians
1:21 was pleased to **s** those who believe
7:16 wife if you will **s** your husband? Or
9:22 so I could **s** some by all
2 Corinthians
12:14 responsibility to **s** up for their
1 Timothy
1:15 into the world to **s** sinners"—and I'm
6:19 things, they will **s** a treasure for
2 Timothy
4:18 action and will **s** me for his
Hebrews
5:7 who was able to **s** him from death.
7:25 he can completely **s** those who are
9:28 away sin but to **s** those who are
James
2:14 to have faith can't **s** anyone, can it?
4:12 and he is able to **s** and to destroy.
5:20 wrong path will **s** them from death
Jude
1:23 **S** some by snatching them from the fire.

SAVE THEIR LIVES
Prv 23:14; Eze 14:20; Am 2:14; Mt 16:25; Mk 8:35; Lk 9:24

SAVE US
Jdg 10:15; 1Sa 4:3; 7:8; 10:27; 11:3; 2Ki 19:19; 1Ch 16:35; 2Ch 20:9; Ps 44:26; 60:5; 80:2; 85:4; 106:47; 118:25; Is 37:20; Jer 2:27; Hos 14:3

SAVE YOU
Dt 20:4; 23:14; 28:31; 1Sa 12:21; Ps 91:3; 91:15; Prv 20:22; Is 35:4; 47:13, 15; 57:13; Jer 42:11; Eze 36:29; Hos 13:10; Jas 1:21

SAVE YOURSELF
Mt 27:40; Mk 15:30; Lk 23:37; 23:39; 1Ti 4:16

SAVED → SAVED YOU, YOU WILL BE SAVED

Genesis
19:20 escape there, and my life will be ***s***."
27:36 Haven't you ***s*** a blessing for
32:30 face-to-face, and my life has been ***s***."
37:21 they said, he ***s*** him from them,
47:25 said, "You've ***s*** our lives. If you

Numbers
10:9 your God and be ***s*** from your enemies.

Deuteronomy
9:26 whom you ***s*** by your own
21:8 Israel, whom you ***s***. Don't put the
33:29 You are a people ***s*** by the LORD! He's

Judges
7:2 than for me, thinking, We ***s*** ourselves.

1 Samuel
11:13 because today the LORD has ***s*** Israel."
14:23 The LORD ***s*** Israel that day, and the
14:39 one who has ***s*** Israel—even if it
23:5 that's how David ***s*** the residents of

2 Samuel
19:5 servants who have ***s*** your life today,
22:4 the LORD, and I was ***s*** from my enemies.
22:18 God ***s*** me from my powerful enemy, saved me from

2 Kings
14:27 heaven, so he ***s*** them through

1 Chronicles
17:21 your people whom you ***s*** from Egypt?

Ezra
8:31 was with us; he ***s*** us from the power

Nehemiah
9:27 them saviors who ***s*** them from the

Job
22:30 they will be ***s*** by your pure
26:2 helped the weak, ***s*** those with frail

Psalms
18:3 the LORD, and I was ***s*** from my enemies.
18:17 God ***s*** me from my powerful enemy, saved me from
22:5 you and they were ***s***; they trusted you
31:5 God of faithfulness—you have ***s*** me.
33:16 Kings aren't ***s*** by the strength of their
34:6 LORD listened and ***s*** him from every
56:13 because you have ***s*** my life from death,
69:14 drown! Let me be ***s*** from those who
71:3 that my life be ***s*** because you are
71:23 being, which you ***s***, will do the same.
78:42 —the day when he ***s*** them from the
80:3 your face shine so that we can be ***s***!
80:7 your face shine so that we can be ***s***!
80:19 your face shine so that we can be ***s***!
106:8 But God ***s*** them for the sake of his good
106:10 God ***s*** them from hostile powers; he
106:21 the God who ***s*** them—the one who
107:13 distress, and God ***s*** them from their
107:19 distress, and God ***s*** them from their
119:117 me so I can be ***s*** and so I can

Proverbs
11:8 The righteous are ***s*** from distress, and
11:9 the righteous are ***s*** by their
28:18 innocence will be ***s***, but those who go

Ecclesiastes
9:15 but wise man who ***s*** everyone by his

Isaiah
23:18 be stored or ***s***. Her profits will
25:9 and he has ***s*** us! This is the
38:20 LORD has truly ***s*** me, and we will
43:12 I announced, I ***s***, I proclaimed, not
45:17 Israel has been ***s*** by the LORD of
45:22 Turn to me and be ***s***, all you ends of
63:9 who served him ***s*** them. In love and

Jeremiah
4:14 that you may be ***s***. How long will
8:20 the summer has ended, yet we aren't ***s***."
17:14 me and I'll be ***s***, for you are my
23:6 Judah will be ***s*** and Israel will
31:7 The LORD has ***s*** his people, the
33:16 Judah will be ***s*** and Jerusalem

Ezekiel
14:14 alone would be ***s*** because they were
33:5 warning, they would have ***s*** their lives.

Joel
2:32 name will be ***s***; for on Mount

Matthew
10:22 stands firm until the end will be ***s***.
19:25 Then who can be ***s***?" they asked.
27:42 He ***s*** others, but he can't save

Mark
10:26 to each other, "Then who can be ***s***?"
13:13 stands firm until the end will be ***s***.
15:31 experts. "He ***s*** others," they
16:16 baptized will be ***s***, but whoever

Luke
1:77 people how to be ***s*** through the
8:12 so that they won't believe and be ***s***.
13:23 only a few be ***s***?" Jesus said to
18:26 heard this said, "Then who can be ***s***?"
23:35 him, saying, "He ***s*** others. Let him

John
3:17 that the world might be ***s*** through him.
5:34 say these things so that you can be ***s***.
10:9 me will be ***s***. They will come

Acts
2:21 on the name of the Lord will be ***s***.
2:40 them, saying, "Be ***s*** from this
2:47 the community those who were being ***s***.
4:12 humans through which we must be ***s***."
11:14 and your entire household can be ***s***.'
15:1 received from Moses, you can't be ***s***."
15:11 we and they are ***s*** in the same way,
27:20 hope of our being ***s*** from this peril
27:31 the ship, you can't be ***s*** from peril."

Romans
5:9 that we will be ***s*** from God's wrath
5:10 is it that we will be ***s*** by his life?

8:24 We were **s** in hope. If we see what we
9:27 sea, only a remaining part will be **s**,
10:13 who call on the Lord's name will be **s**.
11:26 Israel will be **s**, as it is
1 Corinthians
1:18 of God for those of us who are being **s**.
3:15 will be **s** as if they had
5:5 spirit might be **s** on the day of the
10:33 for many people so that they can be **s**.
15:2 You are being **s** through it if you hold
2 Corinthians
2:15 who are being **s** and to those who
2:16 who are being **s**. Who is qualified
Ephesians
2:5 has for us. You are **s** by God's grace!
2:8 You are **s** by God's grace because of
1 Thessalonians
2:16 so they can be **s**. Their sins are
2 Thessalonians
2:10 truth that would allow them to be **s**.
1 Timothy
2:4 all people to be **s** and to come to a
2 Timothy
1:9 is the one who **s** and called us
Titus
3:5 he **s** us because of his mercy, not
Jude
1:5 Lord, who once **s** a people out of

SAVED YOU

Dt 7:8; 15:15; 24:18; 1Sa 10:19; Lk 7:50; Ac 16:31

SAVES

2 Samuel
22:28 are the one who **s** people who
Job
36:15 He **s** the weak in their affliction,
Psalms
7:10 is my shield; he **s** those whose heart
17:7 are the one who **s** those who take
18:27 are the one who **s** people who suffer
20:6 that the LORD **s** his anointed one;
24:5 and righteousness from the God who **s**.
25:5 are the God who **s** me. I put my hope
27:9 my help! God who **s** me, don't neglect
31:2 me; be a strong fortress that **s** me!
34:18 brokenhearted; he **s** those whose
34:22 The LORD **s** his servants' lives; all
55:18 He **s** me, unharmed, from my struggle,
57:3 from heaven and **s** me, rebukes the
72:13 and the needy; he **s** the lives of
103:4 **s** your life from the pit, crowns you
116:6 simple folk; he **s** me whenever I am
Proverbs
14:25 truthful witness **s** lives, but a
Isaiah
17:10 the God who **s** you, and didn't
1 Peter
3:21 is like that. It **s** you now—not

SAVING

Exodus
18:9 for Israel in **s** them from the
1 Samuel
14:6 the LORD from **s**, whether there
1 Chronicles
16:23 the news of his **s** work every single
Psalms
17:7 refuge in you, **s** them from their
21:1 look how happy he is about your **s** help!
21:5 because of your **s** help; you've
22:1 you so far from **s** me—so far from m
42:5 give him thanks, my **s** presence and
42:11 him thanks, my **s** presence and my
43:5 him thanks, my **s** presence and my
70:4 who love your **s** help say again
71:15 acts and your **s** deeds all day
78:22 because they didn't trust his **s** power.
96:2 the news of his **s** work every single
106:4 your people. Visit me with your **s** help
118:14 and protection; he was my **s** help!
118:21 me, because you were my **s** help.
119:81 yearns for your **s** help! I wait for
119:123 looking for your **s** help—looking for
119:166 I wait for your **s** help. I do what
119:174 I long for your **s** help! Your
140:7 God, my strong **s** help—you've prot
144:10 -the one who gives **s** help to rulers,
145:19 to their cries for help and **s** them.
146:3 beings—there's no **s** help with them!
149:4 God will beautify the poor with **s** help.
Isaiah
31:5 shielding and **s**, sparing and
Jonah
4:6 for his head and **s** him from his

SAVIOR → GOD OUR SAVIOR, SAVIOR JESUS, SAVIOR JESUS CHRIST

Deuteronomy
28:29 and taken advantage of without any **s**.
2 Samuel
22:3 my shelter. My **s**! Save me from
2 Kings
13:5 sent Israel a **s**, and they escaped
1 Chronicles
16:35 us, God, our **s**! Gather us!
Isaiah
19:20 will send them a **s** and defender to
43:3 of Israel, your **s**. I have given
43:11 the LORD, and there is no **s** besides me.
45:15 who hides himself, Israel's God and **s**.
45:21 God and a **s**; there's none
49:26 the LORD, am your **s**, and the mighty
60:16 am the LORD, your **s** and your
63:8 do what is wrong." God became their **s**.
Jeremiah
14:8 of Israel, its **s** in times of
Daniel
6:27 He is rescuer and **s**; God performs
Hosea
13:4 gods but me; there is no **s** besides me.
Luke
1:47 of who I am I rejoice in God my **s**.
1:69 up a mighty **s** for us in his
2:11 Your **s** is born today in David's city.
John
4:42 this one is truly the **s** of the world."
Acts
5:31 as leader and **s** so that he could
13:23 to Israel a **s**, Jesus, just as
Ephesians
5:23 the church, that is, the **s** of the body.

Philippians
3:20 look forward to a **s** that comes from
1 Timothy
4:10 God, who is the **s** of all people,
2 Timothy
1:10 appearance of our **s**, Christ Jesus. He
Titus
1:4 God the Father and Christ Jesus our **s**.
3:6 generously through Jesus Christ our **s**.
2 Peter
3:2 what the Lord and **s** commanded through
1 John
4:14 sent the Son to be the **s** of the world.
Jude

SAVIOR JESUS
Ac 13:23; Ti 2:13; 2Pt 1:1; 1:11; 2:20; 3:18

SAVIOR JESUS CHRIST
Ti 2:13; 2Pt 1:1; 1:11; 2:20; 3:18

SCALES
Leviticus
11:9 that has fins and **s**, whether in sea
19:36 have accurate **s** and accurate
Deuteronomy
14:9 can eat anything that has fins and **s**.
14:10 that lacks **s** or fins. These
Job
6:2 weighed, all of it were lifted up in **s**;
31:6 me on accurate **s**; let God know my
41:15 His matching **s** are his pride, closely
Proverbs
11:1 detests dishonest **s**, but delights in
16:11 balances and **s** are the LORD's;
20:23 weights; deceptive **s** aren't right.
Jeremiah
32:10 and weighed out the silver on the **s**.
51:53 Even if Babylon **s** the heavens and
Ezekiel
5:1 beard. Then use **s** to divide the
29:4 cling to your **s**. I will drag you
45:10 You must use fair **s**, a fair ephah, and
Daniel
5:27 weighed on the **s**, and you don't
Micah
6:11 I approve wicked **s** and a bag of

SCATTER
Leviticus
26:33 I will **s** you among the nations. I will
Numbers
10:35 let your enemies **s**, and those who
16:37 from the fire and **s** the ashes about,
Deuteronomy
4:27 The LORD will **s** you among the nations.
28:38 You might **s** a lot of seed on the field,
28:64 The LORD will **s** you among every nation,
1 Kings
14:15 and he will **s** them across the
Nehemiah
1:8 I will **s** you among the
Psalms
53:5 because God will **s** the bones of
68:1 let his enemies **s**; let those who
68:30 delight in money; **s** the peoples who
144:6 lightning and **s** the enemy! Shoot
Ecclesiastes
11:6 **S** your seed in the morning, and in the
Isaiah
24:1 twist its face and **s** its inhabitants.
28:25 doesn't he **s** fennel, and sow
30:22 and you will **s** them like
41:16 the tempest will **s** them. You will
Jeremiah
9:16 I will **s** them among nations about whom
13:24 So I will **s** you like straw that is
18:17 east wind, I will **s** them before their
23:1 who destroy and **s** the sheep of my
24:9 earth. Wherever I **s** them, they will
49:32 pillaged. I will **s** to the winds
49:36 and I will **s** them to the
Ezekiel
5:2 and right. Then **s** one-third to the
5:10 laws on you and **s** all that is left
5:12 one-third I will **s** to all the winds,
6:5 idols, and I'll **s** your bones all
10:2 creatures, and **s** them over the
11:16 caused them to **s** throughout the
12:14 with him, I will **s** his helpers and
12:15 the nations and **s** them throughout
20:23 the nations and **s** them throughout
22:15 I will **s** you among the nations and
30:23 I will **s** the Egyptians among the
30:26 When I **s** the Egyptians among the
Daniel
4:14 its leaves and **s** its fruit! The
Zechariah
1:21 of Judah with their horns to **s** it."
2:6 LORD, for I will **s** you like the four
13:7 in order to **s** the flock! I will
Malachi
2:3 offspring; I will **s** feces on your
Matthew
13:3 parables: "A farmer went out to **s** seed.
Mark
4:3 to this! A farmer went out to **s** seed.
Luke
8:5 went out to **s** his seed. As he

SCATTERED
Exodus
32:20 crushed powder, **s** it on the water,
Deuteronomy
30:3 peoples where the LORD your God **s** you.
Judges
9:45 he leveled the city and **s** salt over it.
1 Samuel
11:11 survivors were so **s** that not even two
30:16 and he found them **s** all over the
2 Samuel
17:19 opening, then **s** grain over it so
1 Kings
22:17 I saw all Israel **s** on the hills like
2 Chronicles
18:16 I saw all Israel **s** on the hills like
Job
2:12 his garment and **s** dust above his
4:11 without prey, and its cubs are **s**.
18:15 tent; sulfur is **s** over their home.
38:24 divided up; the east wind **s** over earth?

Psalms
44:11 you've **s** us among the
68:14 When the Almighty **s** the kings there,
89:10 a dead body; you **s** your enemies with
92:9 die, how all evildoers are **s** abroad!
141:7 bones have been **s** at the mouth of
Isaiah
27:13 those who were **s** in the land of
33:3 on account of your roar, nations **s**.
41:2 his sword, like **s** straw with his
Jeremiah
8:3 wherever I have **s** them, declares
10:21 they have failed and their flock is **s**.
50:17 Israelites are **s** sheep, driven away by
Lamentations
4:1 Sacred jewels are **s** on every street
4:16 presence that **s** them; he no
Ezekiel
6:8 when you are **s** throughout the
34:6 My flock was **s**, and there was no
Joel
3:2 which they have **s** among the
Nahum
3:18 Your people are **s** across the
Zechariah
1:19 the horns that **s** Judah, Israel,
1:21 the horns that **s** Judah so that no
7:14 I **s** them throughout the nations whom
Mark
4:15 When the word is **s** and people hear
4:18 are like the seed **s** among the thorny
4:20 The seed **s** on good soil are those who
4:31 seed. When **s** on the ground,
Luke
1:51 his arm. He has **s** those with
8:8 grain than was **s**." As he said
John
2:15 and the sheep. He **s** the coins and
7:35 people have been **s** and are living
11:52 God's children **s** everywhere would
16:32 of you will be **s** to your own homes
Acts
5:36 of his followers **s**, and nothing came
5:37 and all his followers **s** far and wide.
8:1 the apostles was **s** throughout the
8:4 who had been **s** moved on,
11:19 those who were **s** as a result of
2 Corinthians
9:9 it is written, He **s** everywhere; he
James
1:1 tribes who are **s** outside the land

SCHEMES
Job
5:12 frustrates the **s** of the clever so
Psalms
10:2 in the very same **s** they've thought
26:10 hands are evil **s**, whose strong
37:7 ahead—someone who invents evil **s**.
64:2 people; hide me from the **s** of evildoers
119:150 to plot wicked **s** are nearby, but
139:20 only for wicked **s**; the people who
Proverbs
1:31 and they'll be full of their own **s**.
28:20 get-rich-quick **s** won't go
Isaiah
10:7 other plans; he **s** in secret;
32:7 evil. He plans **s** to destroy the
55:7 the sinful their **s**. Let them return
Jeremiah
11:15 their many evil **s**? Can sacred
11:19 planning their **s** against me:
Hosea
11:6 take everything because of their **s**.
Acts
20:19 came upon me because of the Jews' **s**.
2 Corinthians
2:11 because we are well aware of his **s**.

SCRIBE
2 Kings
12:10 box, the royal **s** and the high
1 Chronicles
24:6 the levitical **s**, recorded their
27:32 and a **s**. Jehiel,
2 Chronicles
24:11 box, the royal **s** and the
26:11 determined by the **s** Jeiel and
Ezra
4:8 and Shimshai the **s** wrote a letter
7:6 Babylon. He was a **s** skilled in the
Nehemiah
8:1 asked Ezra the **s** to bring out the
12:26 Nehemiah and of Ezra the priest and **s**.
12:36 of God. Ezra the **s** went in front of
13:13 Shelemiah, the **s** Zadok, and
Psalms
45:1 My tongue is the pen of a skillful **s**.
Jeremiah
36:12 Elishama the **s**; Delaiah,
37:15 the house of the **s** Jonathan, which
52:25 He also took the **s** of the commander

SCRIPTURE
Mark
12:10 you read this **s**, The stone that
Luke
4:21 Today, this **s** has been
20:17 of this text of **s**, The stone that
22:37 you that this **s** must be fulfilled
John
2:22 they believed the **s** and the word that
7:42 Didn't the **s** say that the Christ comes
10:35 **S** calls those to whom God's word came,
13:18 is to fulfill the **s**, The one who eats
17:12 so that **s** would be
19:24 to fulfill the **s**, They divided my
19:28 to fulfill the **s**, Jesus said, "I
19:36 to fulfill the **s**, They won't break
19:37 And another **s** says, They will look at
20:9 understand the **s** that Jesus must
Acts
1:16 and sisters, the **s** that the Holy
8:32 the passage of **s** he was reading:
Romans
4:3 What does the **s** say? Abraham had faith
4:23 But the **s** that says it was credited to
9:17 **S** says to Pharaoh, I have put you in
10:11 The **s** says, All who have faith in him
11:2 you know what the **s** says in the case
1 Corinthians
1:19 It is written in **s**: I will destroy the
6:16 that person? The **s** says, The two
15:54 this statement in **s** will happen:

2 Corinthians
4:13 is written in **s**, I had faith, and
Galatians
3:8 basis of faith, **s** preached the
3:22 But **s** locked up all things under sin,
4:30 But what does the **s** say? Throw out the
Ephesians
4:8 That's why **s** says, When he climbed up
1 Timothy
5:18 The **s** says, Don't put a muzzle on an ox
2 Timothy
3:16 Every **s** is inspired by God and is
James
2:8 law found in **s**, Love your
2:23 So the **s** was fulfilled that says,
4:5 you suppose that **s** is meaningless?
1 Peter
2:6 it is written in **s**, Look! I am
2 Peter
1:20 no prophecy of **s** represents the

SCRIPTURES

Matthew
21:42 ever read in the **s**, The stone that
22:29 don't know either the **s** or God's power.
26:54 how would the **s** be fulfilled that
26:56 said in the **s** might be
Mark
12:24 don't know either the **s** or God's power?
14:49 arrest me. But let the **s** be fulfilled."
Luke
24:27 in all the **s**, starting with
24:32 and when he explained the **s** for us?"
24:45 opened their minds to understand the **s**.
John
5:39 Examine the **s**, since you think that in
7:38 drink! As the **s** said concerning
Acts
17:2 with them on the basis of the **s**.
17:3 of the **s**, he demonstrated
17:11 and examined the **s** each day to see
18:24 and effective in his use of the **s**.
18:28 debate, using the **s** to prove that
Romans
1:3 in the holy **s**. His Son was
15:4 and through the encouragement of the **s**.
1 Corinthians
15:3 died for our sins in line with the **s**,
15:4 on the third day in line with the **s**.
2 Timothy
3:15 known the holy **s** that help you to
2 Peter
3:16 just as they do the other **s**.

SCROLL → SCROLL OF LIFE

Exodus
17:14 a reminder on the **s** and read it to
24:7 took the covenant **s** and read it out
32:32 me out of your **s** that you've
32:33 wipe out of my **s** are those who
Numbers
5:23 curses in the **s** and wipe them off
21:14 this reason the **s** of the LORD's
Deuteronomy
17:18 Instruction on a **s** in the presence
28:61 this Instruction **s** until you are
29:20 written in this **s** will stretch out
30:10 this Instruction **s**, and because you
31:26 this Instruction **s** and put it next
Joshua
1:8 this Instruction **s**. Recite it day
23:6 the Instruction **s** from Moses. Don't
24:26 God's Instruction **s**. Then he took a
1 Samuel
10:25 and wrote it in a **s** and placed it in
2 Samuel
1:18 it is written in the **s** from Jashar.)
2 Kings
14:6 the Instruction **s** from Moses, where
22:8 the Instruction **s** in the LORD's
23:2 of the covenant **s** that had been
23:24 written in the **s** that the priest
2 Chronicles
17:9 Instruction **s** as they made
25:4 the Instruction **s** from Moses, where
34:14 the Instruction **s** that the LORD had
35:12 as written in the **s** from Moses, and
Ezra
6:2 But a **s** was found in Ecbatana, the
6:18 as it is written in the **s** from Moses.
Nehemiah
8:1 the Instruction **s** from Moses,
8:18 God's Instruction **s** every day, from
9:3 the Instruction **s** from the LORD
13:1 day, when the **s** from Moses was
Job
19:23 were written down, inscribed on a **s**
Psalms
40:7 I come! I'm inscribed in the written **s**.
56:8 bottle—aren't they on your **s** already?
139:16 and on your **s** every day was
Isaiah
29:11 words of a sealed **s**. When they give
29:12 And when the **s** is given to one who
29:18 the words of a **s** and, freed from
30:8 inscribe it on a **s**, so in the future
34:4 roll up like a **s**, and all the
34:16 the LORD's **s** and read: Not one
Jeremiah
25:13 written in this **s**, which Jeremiah
30:2 Write down in a **s** all the words I
36:2 Take a **s** and write in it all the words
36:32 took another **s** and gave it to
45:1 was writing in a **s** the words that
51:60 down in a single **s** all the disasters
51:63 reading the **s**, tie a stone to
Ezekiel
2:9 in a hand stretched out to me was a **s**.
3:1 found. Eat this **s** and go, speak to
Daniel
10:21 is written in the **S** of Truth. No one
12:1 found written in the **s** will be rescued.
12:4 secret! Seal the **s** until the end
Nahum
1:1 Nineveh: the **s** containing the
Zechariah
5:1 I looked up again and saw a flying **s**
5:2 I see a flying **s**, thirty feet long
5:3 one side of the **s**, and anyone
Malachi
3:16 to them. Then a **s** of remembrance
Mark
12:26 you read in the **s** from Moses, in

SCROLL [cont.]

Luke
3:4 written in the **s** of the words of
4:17 gave him the **s** from the prophet
4:20 He rolled up the **s**, gave it back to
20:42 says in the **s** of Psalms, The
John
20:30 signs that aren't recorded in this **s**.
Acts
1:1 the first **s** I wrote concerned
1:20 in the Psalms **s**, Let his home
7:42 is written in the **s** of the Prophets:
Galatians
3:10 that have been written in the Law **s**.
Hebrews
9:19 both the Law **s** itself and all
10:7 has been written about me in the **s**."
Revelation
1:11 Write down on a **s** whatever you see,
5:1 Then I saw a **s** in the right hand of the
5:9 to take the **s** and open its
6:14 like a **s** being rolled up,
10:2 He held an open **s** in his hand. He put
10:10 So I took the **s** from the angel's hand
22:7 of the prophecy contained in this **s**."
22:9 keep the words of this **s**. Worship God!"
22:10 contained in this **s**, because the time
22:18 contained in this **s**: If anyone adds
22:19 the words of this **s** of prophecy, God

SCROLL OF LIFE

Ps 69:28; Phi 4:3; Rev 3:5; 13:8; 17:8; 20:12, 15; 21:27

SEA → DEAD SEA, REED SEA

Genesis
1:2 over the deep **s**, and God's wind
1:21 created the great **s** animals and all
1:26 the fish of the **s**, the birds of the
32:12 the sand of the **s**, so many you
Exodus
14:22 walked into the **s** on dry ground.
15:1 Horse and rider he threw into the **s**!
Leviticus
11:9 and scales, whether in **s** or stream.
Numbers
11:22 the fish in the **s** be found and
34:5 limit will be at the Mediterranean ***S***.
34:11 the eastern slope of the Galilee ***S***.
Joshua
1:4 up to the Mediterranean ***S*** on the west.
5:1 kings near the **s** heard that the
9:1 the Mediterranean ***S*** toward Lebanon.
12:3 of the Chinneroth ***S***. This ran
13:7 the Mediterranean ***S*** in the west. The
13:27 of the Chinnereth ***S*** on the east side
15:11 to Jabneel. The border ended at the **s**.
15:12 the Mediterranean ***S*** and its
15:46 Ekron toward the **s**, everything that
16:3 and as far as Gezer. It ends at the **s**.
16:6 goes to the **s**. Michmethath is
17:10 to Manasseh. The **s** was its border.
19:29 and ended at the **s**. They also owned
23:4 from the Jordan to the Mediterranean ***S***.
24:6 you came to the **s**. The Egyptians
24:7 He brought the **s** down on them, and
1 Kings
4:20 alongside the **s**. They ate, drank,
5:9 Mountains to the **s**. I'll make rafts
7:39 He placed the ***S*** at the southeast
7:44 one ***S***; twelve oxen beneath the Sea
10:22 ships was at **s** with Hiram's
18:44 up from the **s**." Elijah said,
2 Kings
25:13 and the bronze ***S*** that were in the
1 Chronicles
16:32 Let the **s** and everything in it roar!
Ezra
3:7 cedarwood by **s** from Lebanon to
Nehemiah
9:11 You divided the **s** before them so that
Job
6:3 the sands of the **s**; therefore, my
7:12 Am I ***S*** or the Sea Monster that you
9:8 alone and trod on the waves of the ***S***;
11:9 than the earth and broader than the **s**.
12:8 the fish of the **s** will recount it
14:11 vanishes from the **s**; a river dries up
26:12 he stilled the ***S***; split Rahab with
28:14 not with me"; the ***S*** says, "Not
38:8 Who enclosed the ***S*** behind doors when it burst forth
41:31 pot, stirs up the **s** like a pot of
Psalms
8:8 that travels the pathways of the **s**.
36:6 like the deepest **s**. LORD, you save
46:2 crumble into the center of the **s**,
66:6 He turned the **s** into dry land so they
72:8 king rule from **s** to sea, from the
74:13 You split the **s** with your power. You
77:19 through the **s**; your pathways
78:13 God split the **s** and led them through,
78:53 afraid! But the **s** engulfed their
80:11 the way to the **s**; its shoots went
89:9 over the surging **s**: When its waves
89:25 his hand on the **s**. I will set his
95:5 the **s**, which he made, is his along
96:11 rejoice! Let the **s** and everything in
98:7 Let the **s** and everything in it roar;
104:25 then there's the **s**, wide and deep,
107:24 wondrous works in the depths of the **s**.
114:3 The **s** saw it happen and ran away; the
114:5 ***S***, why did you run away? Jordan, why
146:6 and earth, the **s**, and all that is
148:7 the earth, you **s** monsters and all
Proverbs
8:27 marked out the horizon on the deep **s**,
8:29 a limit for the **s**, so the water
23:34 while out on the **s** or one who lies
30:19 out on the open **s**, and the way of a
Ecclesiastes
1:7 flow to the **s**, but the sea is
Isaiah
5:30 roaring of the **s**. And if one looks
10:22 the sand of the **s**, only a few
10:26 a rod over the **s**, as he did in
11:9 LORD, just as the water covers the **s**.
27:1 will kill the dragon that is in the **s**.
42:10 You who sail the **s** and all that
57:20 like the churning **s** that can't keep
Jeremiah
5:22 shoreline for the **s**, an ancient
6:23 like the roaring **s**, arrayed in

46:18 the mountains and Carmel is by the **s**.
49:23 like the raging **s**, which can't
50:42 like the roaring **s**, arrayed in
51:34 up like a great **s** monster; he's
52:17 and the bronze **S** in the LORD's

Lamentations
2:13 is as vast as the **s**. Who can heal you?

Ezekiel
26:3 you! Just as the **s** hurls up its
27:3 entrance to the **s**, the people's
31:15 off the deep **s** against it. I
32:2 you are like the **s** monster! You
38:20 The fish of the **s**, the birds in the
39:11 east of the **s**. It will block

Daniel
7:2 winds of heaven churning the great **s**.
7:3 emerged from the **s**, each different
11:45 tents between the **s** and the beautiful

Hosea
1:10 the sand of the **s**, which can be
4:3 sky, even the fish of the **s** are dying.

Joel
2:20 into the eastern **s**, and its rear

Amos
5:8 the waters of the **s**, and pours them
6:12 Does one plow the **s** with oxen? But
8:12 will wander from **s** to sea, and from
9:3 the bottom of the **s**, I will give an
9:6 the waters of the **s**, and pours them

Jonah
1:4 wind upon the **s**, so that there
1:5 the ship into the **s** to make it
1:9 made the **s** and the dry land."
1:11 you so that the **s** will become calm
1:12 hurl me into the **s**! Then the sea
1:13 it because the **s** continued to rage
1:15 him into the **s**, and the sea

Micah
7:12 the River, from **s** to sea, and from
7:19 all our sins into the depths of the **s**.

Nahum
1:4 He can blast the **s** and make it dry up;
3:8 whose fortress is **s** and whose city-wal

Habakkuk
1:14 the fish of the **s**, like creeping
2:14 glory, just as water covers the **s**.
3:8 against the **s** when you rode on
3:15 tread on the **s**; turbulent waters

Zephaniah
1:3 the fish in the **s**. I will make the
2:7 beside the **s**; in the houses of

Haggai
2:6 the earth, the **s**, and the dry land

Zechariah
9:4 wealth into the **s**. She will be
9:10 will stretch from **s** to sea, and from
10:11 pass through the **s** of distress and

Matthew
4:13 alongside the **s** in the area of
4:18 the Galilee **S**, he saw two
15:29 of the Galilee **S**. He went up a
23:15 You travel over **s** and land to make

Mark
1:16 the Galilee **S**, he saw two
4:41 Even the wind and the **s** obey him!"
7:31 the Galilee **S** through the

Luke
17:6 planted in the **s**,' and it would
21:25 the roaring of the **s** and surging waves.

John
6:1 the Galilee **S** (that is, the
21:1 disciples at the **S** of Tiberius. This

Acts
4:24 the earth, the **s**, and everything
7:36 Egypt at the Red **S** and for forty
14:15 the earth, the **s**, and everything
21:2 Phoenicia, boarded, and put out to **s**.
27:2 So we put out to **s**. Aristarchus, a
27:5 across the open **s** off the coast of
27:12 to put out to **s** from there. They
27:19 ship's gear and hurled it into the **s**.
27:27 the Adriatic **S**. Around midnight
27:30 lifeboat into the **s**, pretending they
27:38 ship by throwing the grain into the **s**.
27:40 left them in the **s**. At the same
28:4 rescued from the **s**, but the goddess
28:11 we put out to **s** in a ship that

Romans
9:27 the sand of the **s**, only a remaining

1 Corinthians
10:1 cloud and they all went through the **s**.
10:2 into Moses in the cloud and in the **s**.

2 Corinthians
11:25 spent a day and a night on the open **s**.
11:26 desert, on the **s**, and from false

Hebrews
11:29 crossed the Red **S** as if they wee on

James
1:6 the surf of the **s**, tossed and

Jude
1:13 wild waves of the **s** foaming up their

Revelation
4:6 like a glass **s**, like crystal,
5:13 earth and in the **s**
7:1 against the earth, the **s**, or any tree.
7:2 the power to damage the earth and **s**.
7:3 the earth, the **s**, or the trees
8:8 down into the **s**. A third of the
8:9 living in the **s** died, and a third
10:2 right foot on the **s** and his left foot
10:5 standing on the **s** and on the land
10:6 is in it, and the **s** and what is in
10:8 who stands on the **s** and on the land."
12:12 for the earth and **s**! The devil has
13:1 up out of the **s**. It had ten horns
14:7 and earth, the **s** and springs of
15:2 appeared to be a **s** of glass mixed
16:3 his bowl into the **s**, and the sea
18:17 Every **s** captain, every
18:19 who have ships at **s** became so rich by
18:21 threw it into the **s**, saying, "With
20:8 Their number is like the sand of the **s**.
20:13 The **s** gave up the dead that were in it,
21:1 had passed away, and the **s** was no more.

SEAL

Genesis
38:18 she said, "Your **s**, its cord, and
38:25 recognize whose **s**, cord, and staff

Exodus
28:36 like an official **s**: "Holy to the
39:6 sons, like an official **s** is engraved.

SEAL [cont.]

39:30 on an official **s**, they engraved on
1 Kings
21:8 name, putting his **s** on them. She sent
Nehemiah
9:38 our Levites, and our priests on the **s**.
Esther
8:8 of the king and **s** the letters with
Job
38:14 like clay for a **s**, so it stands out
Song of Songs
8:6 Set me as a **s** over your heart, as a
Isaiah
8:16 up the testimony; **s** up the teaching
Daniel
8:26 But you must **s** it up, because it
9:24 righteousness, to **s** up prophetic
12:4 words secret! **S** the scroll until
Romans
4:11 circumcision as a **s** of the
1 Corinthians
9:2 you! You are the **s** that shows I'm an
Revelation
6:3 opened the second **s**, I heard the
7:2 east, holding the **s** of the living
7:3 we have put a **s** on the foreheads
8:1 the seventh **s**, there was
9:4 didn't have the **s** of God on their
10:4 from heaven say, "**S** up what the seven
22:10 to me, "Don't **s** up the words of

SEALED

Exodus
2:3 a reed basket and **s** it up with black
Numbers
19:15 jar without a **s** cover on it is
Deuteronomy
32:34 I have this stored up, **s** in my vaults?
Esther
3:12 Ahasuerus and **s** the order with
8:8 of the king and **s** with the king's
8:10 Ahasuerus and **s** the order with
Job
14:17 My rebellion is **s** in a bag; you would
41:15 are his pride, closely locked and **s**.
Song of Songs
4:12 my bride; an enclosed pool, a **s** spring.
Isaiah
29:11 the words of a **s** scroll. When they
Jeremiah
32:10 signed the deed, **s** it, had it
32:11 of purchase—the **s** copy, with its
32:14 documents—this **s** deed of purchase
32:44 will be signed, **s**, and witnessed in
Daniel
6:17 the pit. The king **s** it with his own
12:9 remain secret and **s** up until the end
Matthew
27:64 the grave to be **s** until the third
2 Corinthians
1:22 God also **s** us and gave the Spirit as a
Ephesians
1:13 You were **s** with the promised
4:30 unhappy—you were **s** by him for the
Revelation
5:1 back, and it was **s** with seven seals.
7:4 of those who were **s**: one hundred
7:5 thousand were **s**; from the tribe
7:8 of Benjamin, twelve thousand were **s**.
20:3 then locked and **s** it over him. This

SEARCH

Deuteronomy
12:5 Instead, you must **s** for the location
1 Samuel
13:14 The LORD will **s** for a man of his
16:16 servants will **s** for someone who
2 Samuel
10:3 to you to **s** the city, spy it
1 Kings
18:6 To **s**, they divided the land between
20:6 and they will **s** your palace and
2 Kings
2:16 let them go and **s** for your master.
1 Chronicles
19:3 have come to **s** the city, spy it
26:31 David's rule, a **s** was made and
Ezra
4:15 so that you may **s** the records of your
5:17 the king, may a **s** be made in the
Esther
2:2 the king have a **s** made for
2:3 to lead the **s**. Have them bring
Job
3:21 for death, who **s** for it more than
7:21 dust; you would **s** hard for me, and
8:5 If you will **s** eagerly for God, plead
10:6 that you **s** for my wrongdoing and seek my sin
39:29 From there they **s** for food; their eyes
Psalms
63:1 God! It's you—I **s** for you! My whole
78:34 would turn and earnestly **s** for God.
Proverbs
2:4 it like silver; **s** for it like
Ecclesiastes
7:29 but they **s** for many
Jeremiah
5:1 **S** every street in Jerusalem, comb the
29:13 When you **s** for me, yes, search for me
46:11 Egypt. You **s** out remedies in
50:5 They will **s** for Zion, turning their
Lamentations
3:40 We must **s** and examine our ways; we must return
Ezekiel
34:11 I myself will **s** for my flock and
39:14 will begin their **s** at the end of
Amos
9:3 of Carmel, I will **s** for them there
Zephaniah
1:12 that time, I will **s** Jerusalem with
Matthew
2:8 saying, "Go and **s** carefully for the
2:13 Herod will soon **s** for the child in
7:7 you will receive. **S**, and you will
13:45 is like a merchant in **s** of fine pearls.
18:12 and go in **s** for the one that
Luke
15:4 the pasture and **s** for the lost one
Acts
11:25 Barnabas went to Tarsus in **s** of Saul
12:19 for a thorough **s**. When Peter
1 Peter
1:12 that in their **s** they were not

SEAS
Genesis
1:10 gathered waters **S**. God saw how good
1:22 the waters in the **s**, and let the
Leviticus
11:10 anything in the **s** or streams that
Nehemiah
9:6 is on it, and the **s** and all that is
Psalms
24:2 it on the **s**; God set it
33:7 he put the deep **s** into storerooms.
65:5 edges of the earth, even the distant **s**;
65:7 calm the roaring **s**; calm the roaring
107:23 making their living on the high **s**.
135:6 on earth, in the **s** and in every
Isaiah
17:12 the thundering **s** they thunder.
Ezekiel
26:19 over you and the raging **s** cover you,
27:26 out onto the high **s**; an east wind
28:2 as God I rule the **s**!" Though you
Jonah
2:3 the heart of the **s**, and the flood

SEATED
Genesis
43:33 They were **s** in front of him from the
2 Kings
25:28 to Jehoiachin and **s** him above the
Mark
3:32 A crowd was **s** around him, and those
3:34 around at those **s** around him in a
16:5 in a white robe **s** on the right
Luke
9:15 They did so, and everyone was **s**
22:27 the one who is **s** at the table or
22:69 Human One will be **s** on the right side
John
19:13 led Jesus out and **s** him on the
20:12 dressed in white, **s** where the body of
Acts
6:15 Everyone **s** in the council stared at
12:21 in royal attire, **s** himself on the
Ephesians
2:6 raised us up and **s** us in the heavens
Revelation
4:2 and someone was **s** on the throne.
5:1 hand of the one **s** on the throne. It
6:16 face of the one **s** on the throne and
7:15 and the one **s** on the throne
11:16 elders, who were **s** on their thrones
14:14 On the cloud was **s** someone who
17:1 prostitute, who is **s** on deep waters.
19:4 God, who is **s** on the throne,
20:11 the one who is **s** on it. Before his
21:5 Then the one **s** on the throne said,

SECOND
Genesis
1:8 and there was morning: the **s** day.
4:2 She gave birth a **s** time to Cain's
Jeremiah
33:1 LORD's word came to Jeremiah a **s** time:
Daniel
7:5 another beast, a **s** one, like a bear.
8:13 one speaking. A **s** holy one said to
Jonah
3:1 The LORD's word came to Jonah a **s** time
Zephaniah
1:10 wailing from the **s** quarter, a loud
Haggai
2:20 came to Haggai a **s** time on the
Matthew
22:26 happened with the **s** brother and the
25:22 The **s** servant also came forward and
26:42 A **s** time he went away and prayed, "My
Mark
12:21 The **s** married her and died without
12:31 The **s** is this, You will love your
14:69 him and began a **s** time to say to
14:72 rooster crowed a **s** time. Peter
Luke
19:18 The **s** servant came and said, 'Master,
John
3:4 womb for a **s** time and be born,
4:54 This was the **s** miraculous sign Jesus
Acts
10:15 The voice spoke a **s** time, "Never
11:9 heaven spoke a **s** time, 'Never
12:10 the first and **s** guards and came
13:33 written in the **s** psalm, You are my
1 Corinthians
12:28 first apostles, **s** prophets, third
2 Corinthians
1:15 you could have a **s** opportunity to
11:5 myself as **s**-rate in any way co
13:2 with you on my **s** visit, I already
Titus
3:10 After a first and **s** warning, have
Hebrews
8:7 wouldn't have made sense to expect a **s**.
9:3 a tent behind the **s** curtain called
9:7 priest enters the **s** tent once a year.
9:28 He will appear a **s** time, not to take
10:9 an end to the first to establish the **s**.
James
1:5 without a **s** thought, without
2 Peter
3:1 this is now my **s** letter to you. I
Revelation
2:11 won't be hurt by the **s** death.
4:7 like a lion. The **s** living creature
6:3 Lamb opened the **s** seal, I heard the
8:8 Then the **s** angel blew his trumpet, and
11:14 The **s** horror is over. The third horror
14:8 Another angel, a **s** one, followed and
16:3 The **s** angel poured his bowl into the
19:3 Then they said a **s** time, "Hallelujah!
20:6 resurrection. The **s** death has no
20:14 This, the fiery lake, is the **s** death.
21:8 fire and sulfur. This is the **s** death."
21:19 was jasper, the **s** was sapphire, the

SECRET
Exodus
7:11 same thing by using their **s** knowledge.
7:22 thing with their **s** knowledge. As a
8:7 thing by their **s** knowledge. They
8:18 lice by their **s** knowledge, but
Numbers
5:13 herself in **s**—even though there
Deuteronomy
27:24 his neighbor in **s**." All the people

29:29 The **s** things belong to the LORD our
Joshua
7:11 They have stolen and kept it a **s**.
Judges
3:19 said, "I have a **s** message for you,
16:9 a flame. So the **s** of his strength
16:17 her his whole **s**. He said to her,
16:18 her his whole **s**, she sent word to
2 Samuel
15:10 But Absalom sent **s** agents throughout
Esther
8:3 the Agagite—his **s** plan directed
Job
11:7 Can you find the **s** of God or find the
Psalms
10:9 lie in ambush in **s** places, like a
27:5 will hide me in a **s** place in his own
32:7 You are my **s** hideout! You protect me
44:21 all, God knows every **s** of the heart.
51:6 teach me wisdom in the most **s** space.
64:2 Hide me from the **s** plots of wicked
64:5 laying traps in **s**. "Who will be
81:7 you in the **s** of thunder. I
139:15 put together in a **s** place, when I was
Proverbs
6:25 her beauty in **s**; don't let her
9:17 is sweet; food eaten in **s** is pleasant."
17:23 The wicked take **s** bribes to twist the
21:14 A **s** gift calms anger, and a hidden
25:9 and don't give away someone's **s**.
Isaiah
10:7 he schemes in **s**; destruction is
45:3 treasures of **s** riches, so you
45:19 I didn't speak in **s** or in some land of
48:16 haven't spoken in **s**. Whenever
Jeremiah
23:24 themselves in **s** places so I might
Daniel
12:4 keep these words **s**! Seal the scroll
12:9 words must remain **s** and sealed up
Amos
3:7 revealing his **s** to his servants
Matthew
6:4 to the poor in **s**. Your Father who
6:6 present in that **s** place. Your
6:18 present in that **s** place. Your
10:26 and nothing **s** that won't be
Mark
4:11 to them, "The **s** of God's kingdom
4:22 and everything **s** will come out
Luke
12:2 and nothing is **s** that won't be
John
7:10 he went too—not openly but in **s**.
19:38 of Jesus, but a **s** one because he
Romans
11:25 unaware of this **s**, brothers and
16:25 of the **s** that was kept
16:26 Now that **s** is revealed through what the
1 Corinthians
2:7 been hidden as a **s**. God determined
15:51 I'm telling you a **s**: all of us won't
Ephesians
3:3 God showed me his **s** plan in a
3:4 insight into the **s** plan about
3:9 me to reveal the **s** plan that had
5:12 about what certain persons do in **s**.
6:19 makes this **s** plan of the
Philippians
4:12 have learned the **s** to being content
Colossians
1:26 it with a **s** plan that has
1:27 riches of this **s** plan known among
2:2 knowledge of the **s** plan of God,
4:3 we can preach the **s** plan of Christ—
2 Thessalonians
2:7 but it will be **s** only until the

SECURE

Numbers
24:21 Your dwelling is **s**; your nest is set
Deuteronomy
33:28 residence is **s**—in a land full o
Joshua
2:14 our own lives to **s** yours. If you
Judges
18:7 undisturbed and **s**. Nobody held back
18:10 come upon a **s** people and a wide
18:27 undisturbed and **s**. They killed the
1 Samuel
12:11 every side. And you lived safe and **s**.
20:31 dynasty will be **s**. Now have him
2 Samuel
23:5 me, laid out and **s** in every detail.
1 Kings
2:45 David's throne be **s** before the LORD
Job
5:24 that your tent is **s**. You will examine
11:15 blemish; you will be **s** and not fear.
11:18 You will be **s**, for there is hope; you
12:6 God's provokers **s**, who carry God in
24:23 make themselves **s**; they are at
Psalms
37:23 steps are made **s** by the LORD when
48:8 God. May God make it **s** forever! Selah
102:28 descendants live **s** in your presence."
Proverbs
4:26 the way, and all your paths will be **s**.
11:15 who refuses to shake hands will be **s**.
29:25 others; those who trust the LORD are **s**.
Isaiah
14:30 will lie down **s**. But he will
32:11 of you who are **s**! Strip
32:18 dwelling, in **s** homes, in
47:8 one who sits **s**, who says in her
47:10 You felt **s** in your evil; you said, "No
Jeremiah
22:21 you felt safe and **s**, but you said, "I
37:12 of Benjamin to **s** his share of the
49:31 feels safe and **s**, declares the
Ezekiel
34:14 lie down in a **s** fold and feed on
Micah
5:4 They will dwell **s**, because he will
Matthew
27:65 Go and make it as **s** as you know how."
Luke
11:21 his own palace, his possessions are **s**.
Acts
16:23 the jailer to **s** them with great
Romans
4:16 the promise is **s** for all of
Hebrews
6:19 is a safe and **s** anchor for our

2 Peter
1:12 them and stand **s** in the truth you

SECURELY

Leviticus
25:18 so that you can live **s** on the land.
25:19 you can eat your fill and live **s** on it.
26:5 fill of food and live **s** in your land.
Deuteronomy
12:10 side so that you live safely and **s**.
1 Samuel
25:29 will be bound up **s** in the bundle of
2 Samuel
22:34 who lets me stand **s** on the heights,
1 Kings
4:25 Beer-sheba lived **s** under their vines
2 Chronicles
1:1 David's son, was **s** established over
12:13 King Rehoboam was **s** established in
27:6 Jotham was **s** established because he
Psalms
18:33 who lets me stand **s** on the heights,
89:37 It will be **s** established forever; like
Proverbs
1:33 me will dwell **s**, untroubled by
Isaiah
22:23 I will fasten him **s** like a tent peg,
22:25 that is fastened **s** will give way; it
Jeremiah
10:4 and fastened **s** with hammer and
32:37 them back to this place to live **s**.
Ezekiel
27:24 rolled up and **s** tied with ropes,
38:8 the peoples, and all of them live **s**.
38:11 who all live **s** without walls,
38:14 that day, when my people Israel live **s**?
39:6 on those who live **s** in the
39:26 me when they live **s** on their fertile
40:43 inches wide, were **s** fixed all the way
Daniel
7:18 hold the kingship **s** forever and
7:22 and the holy ones held the kingship **s**.
Zephaniah
2:15 the one dwelling **s**, the one saying
Zechariah
14:11 be destroyed. Jerusalem will dwell **s**.

SEE THE LORD

Ex 19:21; Josh 3:3; 2Ki 6:20; Ps 146:8; Prv 20:12; Is 38:11; 52:8; Heb 12:14; Jud 1:14

SEED

Genesis
47:19 control. Give us **s** so that we can
47:23 Pharaoh, here's **s** for you. Plant
Exodus
16:31 like coriander **s**, white, and
Leviticus
11:37 bodies falls on **s** that is to be
11:38 is poured on some **s** and part of their
19:19 with two kinds of **s**, and do not wear
26:16 You will plant **s** for no reason
27:16 according to the **s** needed to plant
27:30 land, whether of **s** from the ground
Numbers
11:7 like coriander **s** and its color was
24:7 his branches; his **s** will have plenty
Deuteronomy
11:10 you sowed your **s** and irrigated it
22:9 with two types of **s**; otherwise, the
28:38 scatter a lot of **s** on the field, but
2 Kings
19:29 third year, sow **s** and harvest it;
Psalms
97:11 is planted like **s** for the righteous
126:6 carrying their **s**, come home with
Ecclesiastes
11:6 Scatter your **s** in the morning, and in
Isaiah
5:10 and a homer of **s** will produce only
6:13 leaves a stump. Its stump is a holy **s**.
30:23 rain for the **s** you sow in the
37:30 third year, plant **s** and harvest it;
55:10 and providing **s** to the sower and
Ezekiel
17:5 He took a native **s** and planted it in a
Amos
9:13 one who sows the **s**. The mountains
Haggai
2:19 Is the **s** yet in the granary—or the
Zechariah
8:12 The **s** is healthy: the vine will give
Matthew
6:26 They don't sow **s** or harvest grain
13:3 A farmer went out to scatter **s**.
13:31 is like a mustard **s** that someone took and planted
13:37 who plants the good **s** is the Human One.
17:20 size of a mustard **s**, you could say to
25:24 crops where you haven't spread **s**.
25:26 gather crops where I haven't spread **s**?
Mark
4:3 this! A farmer went out to scatter **s**.
4:15 meaning of the **s** that fell on the
4:16 meaning of the **s** that fell on
4:18 are like the **s** scattered among
4:20 The **s** scattered on good soil are those
4:26 someone scatters **s** on the ground,
4:27 and day. The **s** sprouts and
4:31 a mustard **s**. When scattered
Luke
8:5 to scatter his **s**. As he was
13:19 like a mustard **s** that someone took
17:6 size of a mustard **s**, you could say to
John
12:24 only be a single **s**. But if it dies,
1 Corinthians
15:36 When you put a **s** into the ground,
15:37 a bare grain of wheat or some other **s**.
2 Corinthians
9:10 one who supplies **s** for planting and
1 Peter
1:23 from the type of **s** that decays but

SEEDS

Genesis
1:11 plants yielding **s** and fruit trees
Numbers
6:4 the grapevine, not even its **s** or skin.
Judges
6:3 planted **s**, the Midianites,
Isaiah
61:11 garden grows its **s**, so the LORD God

Jeremiah
31:27 when I will plant **s** in Israel and
Matthew
13:32 smallest of all **s**. But when it's
13:38 And the good **s** are the followers
Mark
4:7 and choked the **s**, and they
4:31 the smallest of all the **s** on the earth;
1 Corinthians
15:38 he gives each of the **s** its own shape.
2 Corinthians
9:6 a small number of **s** will also reap a
James
3:18 peace sow the **s** of justice by

SEEING

Genesis
9:16 clouds, and upon **s** it I will
33:10 my gift. **S** your face is like
46:30 can die now after **s** your face. You
Exodus
4:14 now, and he's looking forward to **s** you.
Judges
21:16 who are left, **s** that the
1 Samuel
28:21 Saul, and after **s** how scared he
2 Samuel
14:28 years without ever **s** the king's face.
Job
10:18 I wish I had died without any eye **s** me.
Psalms
17:15 I will be filled full by **s** your image.
27:4 days of my life, **s** the LORD's beauty
89:48 life without **s** death? Who is
Ecclesiastes
1:8 satisfied with **s**, neither is the
Isaiah
59:16 **S** that there was no one, and astonished
Ezekiel
14:23 **S** their ways and their deeds will bring
22:28 for them, **s** false visions and
Micah
3:7 Those **s** visions will be ashamed, and
Matthew
13:14 see but never recognize what you are **s**.
15:31 and the blind **s**. And they praised
Mark
6:50 **S** him was terrifying to all of them.
Luke
23:40 you fear God, **s** that you've also
23:48 their chests after **s** what had happened.
24:37 They thought they were **s** a ghost.
Acts
2:33 and you are **s** and hearing the
3:12 **S** this, Peter addressed the people:
12:9 all this. He thought he was **s** a vision.
14:11 **S** what Paul had done, the crowd shouted
28:6 a long time and **s** nothing unusual
28:26 see but never recognize what you are **s**.

SEEK → SEEK GOD, SEEK THE LORD

Numbers
6:11 offering. He will **s** reconciliation
Joshua
22:23 it, let the LORD himself **s** punishment.
Ruth
2:12 whose wings you've come to **s** refuge."
3:1 shouldn't I **s** security for you,
1 Samuel
20:16 the LORD will **s** retribution from
25:26 and those who **s** to harm my master
2 Kings
1:16 word you could **s**? Because of this
1 Chronicles
16:11 and his strength; **s** his face always!
28:9 thought. If you **s** him, he will be
2 Chronicles
7:14 will humbly pray, **s** my face, and turn
15:2 with him. If you **s** him, he will be
20:3 decided to **s** the LORD's help
25:15 him. "Why do you **s** the gods of this
30:19 has decided to **s** the true God, the
34:3 boy, he began to **s** the God of his
Ezra
8:22 favors all who **s** him, but his
9:12 marry, and never **s** their peace or
Nehemiah
2:10 had come to **s** the welfare of
Esther
4:8 go to the king to **s** his kindness and
Job
10:6 search for my wrongdoing and **s** my sin?
Psalms
9:10 have not abandoned any who **s** you, LORD.
10:15 wicked and evil. **S** out their
27:4 LORD—it's all I **s**—to live in the
34:14 evil! Do good! **S** peace and go
40:14 Let those who **s** my life, who want me
40:16 But let all who **s** you celebrate and
45:12 of all, will **s** your favor with
69:6 let those who **s** you be disgraced
69:32 be glad! You who **s** God—let your
70:2 Let those who **s** my life be ashamed and humiliated
70:4 But let all who **s** you rejoice and be
71:13 Let those who **s** my downfall be
71:24 because those who **s** my downfall have
83:16 LORD, so that they might **s** your name.
105:4 and his strength; **s** his face always!
143:9 enemies, LORD! I **s** protection from
Proverbs
1:19 ways of all who **s** unjust gain; it
1:28 answer; they will **s** me, but won't
2:4 **S** it like silver; search for it like
8:17 love me; those who **s** me will find me.
11:27 but those who **s** evil—it will come
17:11 Evil people **s** only rebellion; a cruel
19:6 Many **s** favor from rulers; everyone
25:27 good, nor is it appropriate to **s** honor.
29:10 and they **s** the lives of the
29:26 Many **s** access to the ruler, but justice
Ecclesiastes
7:25 and to **s** wisdom, along
Isaiah
1:17 learn to do good. **S** justice: help the
11:10 The nations will **s** him out, and his
41:17 and the needy **s** water, and there
45:19 of Jacob, "**S** me in chaos." I
58:2 They **s** me day after day, desiring
65:10 for cattle, for my people who **s** me.

Jeremiah
4:30 have rejected you and now **s** your life.
10:21 senses and don't **s** answers from the
11:21 from Anathoth who **s** your life and
19:7 before those who **s** their lives. I
21:7 their enemies who **s** to do them harm.
22:25 over to those who **s** to kill you,
34:20 their enemies who **s** to kill them. And
34:21 their enemies who **s** to kill them:
37:7 his emissaries to **s** advice from me:
38:4 This man doesn't **s** their welfare but
38:16 you over to those who **s** to kill you."
44:30 his enemies who **s** to kill him, just
45:5 You **s** great things for yourself, but
46:11 up to Gilead and **s** balm, virgin
46:26 over to those who **s** to kill them,
48:45 tired refugees **s** shelter. But fire
49:37 before those who **s** to kill them. I
Ezekiel
7:25 It has come! They **s** peace, but there
7:26 rumor. They **s** a vision from the
20:31 Should I let you **s** me out, house of
27:29 and helmsmen **s** footing on the
34:4 the strays, or **s** out the lost; but
34:8 shepherds didn't **s** out my flock.
34:11 search for my flock and **s** them out.
34:12 so will I **s** out my flock. I
34:16 I will **s** out the lost, bring back the
Hosea
2:5 She said, "I will **s** out my lovers;
2:7 them; she will **s** them, but she
5:15 deeds, until they **s** me. In their
7:10 their God, or **s** him because of
Amos
5:4 to the house of Israel: **S** me and live.
5:5 But don't **s** Bethel, don't enter into
5:12 side, turning away the poor who **s** help.
5:14 **S** good and not evil, that you may live;
Nahum
3:7 could I possibly **s** comforters for
3:11 you will have to **s** refuge from the
Zephaniah
3:12 midst; they will **s** refuge in the
Zechariah
8:21 Let's go and **s** the favor of the
11:16 removed. He won't **s** the young or heal
Malachi
2:7 everyone should **s** Instruction from
Luke
11:9 you will receive. **S** and you will
19:10 Human One came to **s** and save the
John
5:30 is just. I don't **s** my own will but
5:44 other but don't **s** the praise that
7:18 on their own **s** glory for
Acts
17:27 so they would **s** him, perhaps even
1 Corinthians
13:5 rude, it doesn't **s** its own
1 Peter
3:11 evil and do good; **s** peace and chase
Revelation
9:6 days people will **s** death, but they

SEEK GOD

1Ch 21:30; 2Ch 19:3; Job 5:8; Ps 10:4; 69:32; 119:2

SEEK THE LORD

Dt 4:29; 2Ch 11:16; 14:4; 15:12, 13; 16:12; Ps 22:26; 34:10; Prv 28:5; Is 9:13; 31:1; 51:1; 55:6; Jer 50:4; Hos 3:5; 5:6; 10:12; Am 5:6; Zep 1:6; 2:3; Zec 8:22; Ac 15:17

SEEKING

Numbers
15:28 is an accident, **s** reconciliation so
Joshua
20:3 of the victim's family **s** revenge.
2 Samuel
14:11 so that the one **s** revenge doesn't
15:6 came to the king **s** justice. This is
1 Kings
14:5 wife has come **s** a word from you
2 Kings
16:15 use the bronze altar for **s** guidance."
1 Chronicles
16:10 hearts rejoice of all those **s** the LORD!
22:19 yourselves to **s** the LORD your
2 Chronicles
12:14 he didn't set his heart on **s** the LORD.
17:3 ways of his father by not **s** Baal.
Psalms
37:32 target the righteous, **s** to kill them.
104:21 for their prey, **s** their food from
105:3 hearts rejoice of all those **s** the LORD!
Proverbs
7:15 out to meet you, **s** you, and I have
Isaiah
58:13 things your way, **s** what you want and
Jeremiah
19:9 to the city, **s** their lives, they
Lamentations
1:11 are groaning, **s** bread. They give
Daniel
6:11 praying and **s** mercy from his
Amos
8:12 roam all around, **s** the LORD's word,
Malachi
2:15 the one? The one **s** godly offspring.
3:1 LORD whom you are **s** will come to his
Matthew
23:25 are full of violence and pleasure **s**.
Luke
11:16 were testing him, **s** a sign from
19:47 among the people were **s** to kill him.
John
8:50 one who is **s** to glorify me,
Acts
9:2 **s** letters to the synagogues in
1 Peter
5:8 a roaring lion, **s** someone to devour.

SEEKS

1 Samuel
22:23 The one who **s** my life now seeks
Job
39:8 hills for food and **s** any green sprout.
Psalms
14:2 anyone is wise, to see if anyone **s** God,
24:6 generation that **s** him—that seeks
53:2 anyone is wise, to see if anyone **s** God.
Proverbs
15:14 heart **s** knowledge; but
17:9 One who **s** love conceals an offense, but

18:15 the ear of the wise **s** knowledge.
31:13 She **s** out wool and flax; she works
Isaiah
16:5 —a judge who **s** justice and
40:20 rot and then **s** a skilled artisan
Jeremiah
5:1 acts justly and **s** truth that I may
50:20 nothing; if one **s** out the
Lamentations
3:25 hope in him, to the person who **s** him.
Ezekiel
34:12 As a shepherd **s** out the flock when some in the flock
Daniel
2:27 explain to the king the mystery he **s**.
Matthew
7:8 receives. Whoever **s**, finds. And to
Luke
11:10 receives. Whoever **s**, finds. To

SEER
1 Samuel
9:9 Let's go to the **s**," because the
9:11 water. "Is the **s** here?" they asked
9:19 I'm the **s**," Samuel told Saul. "Go on
2 Samuel
24:11 came to the prophet Gad, David's **s**:
1 Chronicles
9:22 and Samuel the **s** assigned them to
21:9 The LORD told Gad, David's **s**
25:5 Heman the king's **s**, according to
26:28 by Samuel the **s**, as well as by
29:29 of Samuel the **s**, Nathan the
2 Chronicles
9:29 visions of the **s** Iddo concerning
12:15 Shemaiah and the **s** Iddo, including
16:7 time Hanani the **s** came to Judah's
16:10 angry with the **s**. Asa was so mad
19:2 son of Hanani the **s** came out to meet
29:25 David, the king's **s** Gad, and the
29:30 of David and the **s** Asaph. They did
35:15 and the king's **s** Jeduthun, as did
Isaiah
21:8 Then the **s** called out: "Upon a

SEES
Genesis
22:14 place "the LORD **s**. That is the
44:31 and when he **s** that the young man isn't
Exodus
12:23 the Egyptians and **s** the blood on the
Numbers
12:8 in riddles. He **s** the LORD's form.
Deuteronomy
12:15 the LORD your God **s** fit to bless you
32:36 him, once he **s** that their
1 Samuel
16:7 eyes, but the LORD **s** into the heart."
Esther
8:5 and if he still **s** me as a good
Job
7:8 The eye that **s** me now will no longer
8:17 of rocks, for it **s** a home among
11:11 worthless people, **s** sin, and
34:21 human ways, and he **s** all their steps.
Psalms
10:11 hidden his face. God never **s** anything!
31:11 and whoever **s** me in the street,
33:13 from heaven; he **s** every human being.
64:8 everyone who **s** them will just
97:4 the world; the earth **s** it and trembles!
Proverbs
28:11 insightful poor person **s** through them.
Daniel
1:10 will happen if he **s** your faces
Matthew
6:4 Your Father who **s** what you do in
6:18 Your Father who **s** in secret will
John
5:19 except what he **s** the Father doing.
9:21 know how he now **s**, and we don't
10:12 the hired hand **s** the wolf coming,
12:45 Whoever **s** me sees the one who sent me
14:17 it neither **s** him nor
1 Corinthians
8:10 Suppose someone **s** you (the person who has knowledge
2 Corinthians
12:6 than what anyone **s** or hears about me.
1 John
3:17 possessions and **s** a brother or
5:16 If anyone **s** a brother or sister

SEIR
Genesis
14:6 the mountains of **S** as far as El-paran
32:3 the land of **S**, the open country
33:14 are able to go, until I meet you in **S**."
33:16 day Esau returned on the road to **S**,
36:8 is Edom, lived in the mountains of **S**.
36:9 Edom, which lies in the mountains of **S**.
36:20 are the sons of **S**, the Horite, who
36:30 to their chiefs in the land of **S**.
Numbers
24:18 a possession, **S** a possession of
Deuteronomy
1:2 Kadesh-barnea along the Mount **S** route.)
1:44 a beating from **S** all the way to
2:1 all around Mount **S** for a long time.
2:4 who live in **S**: Esau's
2:5 have given Mount **S** to Esau's family
2:8 who live in **S**, Esau's
2:12 had lived in **S** previously, but
2:22 who live in **S**, when he
2:29 who live in **S** and the Moabites
33:2 from Sinai: from **S** he shone like the
Joshua
11:17 goes up toward **S**, as far as Baal
12:7 goes up toward **S**. Joshua gave it
15:10 Baalah to Mount **S**. It passed on to
24:4 I gave Mount **S** to Esau to take
Judges
5:4 you set out from **S**, when you marched
1 Chronicles
4:42 went to Mount **S**, led by Pelatiah,
2 Chronicles
20:10 those from Mount **S**—the people you wouldn't let
25:11 they killed ten thousand people from **S**.
25:14 of the people of **S**. He set them up
Isaiah
21:11 to me from **S**: "Guard, how long

Ezekiel
25:8 Because Moab and ***S*** say, "Aha! The
35:2 one, face Mount ***S***, and prophesy
35:3 you, Mount ***S***! I will use my
35:7 I will turn Mount ***S*** into a desolate
35:15 with you. Mount ***S***, you will become

SEIZE

Joshua
8:8 As soon as you ***s*** the city, set it on
Judges
11:15 Israel didn't ***s*** the land of the
12:6 So they would ***s*** him and kill him
1 Kings
13:4 altar and said, "***S*** him!" But the
18:40 said to them, "***S*** Baal's prophets!
20:6 valuable they will ***s*** and take away.'"
Esther
3:13 They were also to ***s*** their property.
Job
3:6 May gloom ***s*** that night; may it not be counted
Psalms
10:9 so they can ***s*** those who suffer!
109:11 Let a creditor ***s*** everything he owns;
Isaiah
3:6 Someone will ***s*** a family member, saying,
5:29 they growl, ***s*** their prey, and
10:6 I direct him to ***s*** spoil, to steal
33:23 be divided; even the lame will ***s*** spoil.
Jeremiah
42:16 war you fear will ***s*** you in the land
49:29 ***S*** their tents and their flocks, their
Ezekiel
7:24 and they will ***s*** their houses.
14:5 So I'll ***s*** the hearts of the house of
21:11 for polishing, to ***s*** in the hand. The
23:25 sword. They will ***s*** your sons and
23:29 you: They will ***s*** your pay and
38:12 take plunder and ***s*** loot, to use my
39:10 take plunder and ***s*** loot. This is
Daniel
11:21 of security and ***s*** the kingdom by
Micah
2:2 covet fields and ***s*** them, houses and
Matthew
11:12 attacked as violent people ***s*** it.
John
7:30 So they wanted to ***s*** Jesus, but they

SEIZED

Genesis
21:25 a well that Abimelech's servants had ***s***.
Joshua
7:24 Then Joshua ***s*** Achan, Zerah's son, along
8:23 But they ***s*** the king of Ai alive and
Judges
8:16 Then he ***s*** the city's elders, and he
11:13 from Egypt, they ***s*** my land from the
2 Samuel
10:4 So Hanun ***s*** David's servants and shaved
1 Kings
14:26 He ***s*** the treasures of the LORD's temple
18:40 The people ***s*** the prophets, and
1 Chronicles
5:21 They ***s*** their livestock: 50,000 of their
2 Chronicles
8:3 Solomon went to Hamath-zobah and ***s*** it
12:9 Jerusalem and ***s*** the treasures of
28:8 relatives and ***s*** enormous amounts
Job
15:12 Why has your mind ***s*** you, why have your eyes flashed
16:8 ***s*** me, which became grounds for an
16:12 he shattered me, ***s*** me by the back of
30:16 out on me; days of misery have ***s*** me.
40:24 Can he be ***s*** by his eyes? Can anyone
Psalms
56:1 the Philistines ***s*** him in Gath.
119:53 But I'm ***s*** with anger because of the
Isaiah
13:8 they will be ***s*** by spasms and
21:3 Pains have ***s*** me like the pains
33:14 Zion; trembling ***s*** the godless: "Who
Jeremiah
12:14 evil nations have ***s*** the land that I
26:8 all the people ***s*** him and said,
38:6 So they ***s*** Jeremiah, threw him into the
48:41 will be ***s***. On that day, the
49:2 the land ***s*** by its captors,
Micah
4:9 so that pain has ***s*** you like that of
Acts
4:3 They ***s*** Peter and John and put them in
5:11 and dread ***s*** the whole church
5:18 They ***s*** the apostles and made a public
18:17 but everyone ***s*** Sosthenes, the synagogue
19:17 Everyone was ***s*** with fear and
19:29 the theater. They ***s*** Gaius and
21:30 came rushing, ***s*** Paul, and dragged
23:27 This man was ***s*** by the Jews and was
26:21 of this,some Jews ***s*** me in the temple
Romans
7:8 But sin ***s*** the opportunity and used this
7:11 Sin ***s*** the opportunity through the
1 Corinthians
10:13 No temptation has ***s*** you that isn't
Revelation
19:20 But the beast was ***s***, along with the
20:2 He ***s*** the dragon, the old snake, who is

SELECTED

Genesis
24:14 be the one you've ***s*** for your servant
24:44 the LORD has ***s*** for my master's
47:2 his brothers, he ***s*** five men and
Leviticus
16:9 present the goat ***s*** by the LORD's lot
16:10 But the goat ***s*** by Azazel's lot will be
Numbers
1:17 Aaron took these men who were ***s*** by name
8:19 I have ***s*** the Levites from the
31:5 each tribe were ***s***. Twelve thousand
Deuteronomy
1:23 good to me, so I ***s*** twelve men, one
14:2 whom the LORD ***s*** to be his own, to
Joshua
7:15 The person ***s***, who has the things
Judges
14:11 saw him, they ***s*** thirty companions

SELECTED [cont.]

Ezra
8:24 Then I **s** twelve of the leading priests,
Esther
2:9 seven servants **s** from among the
Song of Songs
3:6 and frankincense, **s** from all the
Ezekiel
43:21 take the bull **s** as the
Acts
6:5 community. They **s** Stephen, a man
15:22 Barnabas. They **s** Judas Barsabbas
22:14 our ancestors has **s** you to know his

SELL

Genesis
25:31 Jacob said, "**S** me your birthright
47:22 they didn't have to **s** their farmland.
1 Kings
21:6 Naboth. I said, '**S** me your vineyard.
Nehemiah
10:31 or any grain to **s** on the Sabbath,
Job
41:6 Will merchants **s** him; will they divide
Proverbs
11:26 grain, but they bless those who **s** it.
23:23 truth and don't **s** it; buy wisdom,
Isaiah
50:1 lender did I **s** you? On account
Ezekiel
30:12 canals; I will **s** the land to
Joel
3:8 I will **s** your sons and your daughters
Amos
8:5 so that we may **s** grain, and the
8:6 for sandals, and **s** garbage as grain?"
Zechariah
11:5 Those who **s** them will say,
Matthew
19:21 be complete, go, **s** what you own, and
25:9 go to those who **s** oil and buy some
Mark
10:21 one thing. Go, **s** what you own, and
Luke
12:33 **S** your possessions and give to those in
18:22 one more thing. **S** everything you
22:36 own a sword must **s** their clothes and
Acts
2:45 They would **s** pieces of property and
4:34 or houses would **s** them, bring the
Revelation
13:17 a purchase or **s** anything unless

SEND

Genesis
7:4 from now I will **s** rain on the earth
Exodus
4:13 Please, my Lord, just **s** someone else."
8:2 go, then I'll **s** a plague of frogs
33:12 me whom you will **s** with me. Yet
Numbers
21:7 so that he will **s** the snakes away
Deuteronomy
1:22 saying, "Let's **s** spies ahead of
Joshua
1:16 commanded us and go anywhere you **s** us.
2:3 word to Rahab: "**S** out the men who
18:4 tribe. I will **s** them out, and
Ezra
4:14 dishonor, we now **s** this letter and
10:19 They promised to **s** their wives away,
Nehemiah
2:5 with you, please **s** me to Judah, to
8:12 and to drink, to **s** portions, and to
Job
38:35 Can you **s** lightning so that it goes and
Psalms
20:2 Let God **s** help to you from the
43:3 **S** your light and truth—those will
138:7 live again; you **s** your power
Proverbs
25:13 to those who **s** them; they
Ecclesiastes
11:1 **S** your bread out on the water because,
Isaiah
6:8 Whom should I **s**, and who will go
Jeremiah
1:7 a child.' Where I **s** you, you must go;
Daniel
11:20 arise who will **s** his agent to
Hosea
8:14 but I will **s** a fire upon his
Amos
1:4 I will **s** down fire on the house of
Malachi
2:2 then I will **s** a curse among
Matthew
8:31 you throw us out, **s** us into the herd
9:38 of the harvest to **s** out workers for
13:41 Human One will **s** his angels, and
14:15 getting late. **S** the crowds away
24:31 He will **s** his angels with the sound of
26:53 and he will **s** to me more than
Luke
16:24 have mercy on me. **S** Lazarus to dip
20:13 should I do? I'll **s** my son, whom I
John
3:17 God didn't **s** his Son into the world to
6:37 me, and I won't **s** away anyone who
13:20 someone I **s** receives me, and
14:16 and he will **s** another
14:26 the Father will **s** in my name, will
15:26 whom I will **s** from the Father
16:7 you. But if I go, I will **s** him to you.
Acts
3:20 age and he will **s** Jesus, whom he
7:43 Therefore, I will **s** you far away,
10:5 **S** messengers to Joppa at once and
10:32 Therefore, **s** someone to Joppa and
11:13 and saying, '**S** to Joppa and
11:29 they would **s** support to the
15:22 church, agreed to **s** some delegates
15:25 delegates and **s** them to you along
16:37 now they want to **s** us away secretly?
22:21 me, 'Go! I will **s** you far away to
24:25 now! When I have time, I'll **s** for you."
25:21 be held until I could **s** him to Caesar."
25:25 Majesty, I decided to **s** him to Rome.
25:27 be foolish to **s** a prisoner
Romans
15:24 I hope you will **s** me on my way
1 Corinthians
1:17 Christ didn't **s** me to baptize but to
16:3 I get there, I'll **s** whomever you

16:6 so that you can **s** me on my way to
16:11 him, but **s** him on in peace
Philippians
2:19 the Lord Jesus to **s** Timothy to see
2:23 that I hope to **s** as soon as I find
2:25 also necessary to **s** Epaphroditus to
4:21 sisters with me **s** you their
4:22 household, **s** you their
2 Thessalonians
2:11 is why God will **s** them an influence
Titus
3:12 When I **s** Artemas or Tychicus to you,
Revelation
1:11 you see, and **s** it to the seven

SENDING
Proverbs
26:6 **S** messages with a fool is like cutting
Jeremiah
8:17 See, I'm **s** serpents against you, vipers
43:10 proclaims: I'm **s** for my servant
Ezekiel
2:3 Human one, I'm **s** you to the
2:4 I'm **s** you to their hardheaded and
34:26 a blessing by **s** the rain in its
Joel
2:19 people: See, I am **s** you the corn, new
Malachi
3:1 Look, I am **s** my messenger who will
4:5 Look, I am **s** Elijah the prophet to you,
Matthew
10:16 Look, I'm **s** you as sheep among wolves.
11:10 Look, I'm **s** my messenger
23:34 look, I'm **s** you prophets,
Mark
1:2 Look, I am **s** my messenger
Luke
7:27 Look, I'm **s** my messenger
10:3 though, that I'm **s** you out as lambs
24:49 Look, I'm **s** to you what my Father
John
20:21 As the Father sent me, so I am **s** you."
Acts
7:34 them. Come! I am **s** you to Egypt.'
15:27 Therefore, we are **s** Judas and Silas.
26:17 and from the Gentiles. I am **s** you
Romans
8:3 in the body by **s** his own Son to
2 Corinthians
8:18 We are **s** the brother who is famous in
9:3 But I'm **s** the brothers so that our

SENNACHERIB
2 Kings
18:13 Assyria's King **S** marched against all of
2 Chronicles
32:1 Assyria's King **S** invaded Judah and
Isaiah
36:1 Assyria's King **S** marched against all of

SENSE
Job
39:17 endow her with **s**, didn't give her
Psalms
94:8 You fools—when will you get some **s**?
Proverbs
7:7 among the youth, one who had no **s**.
9:4 here," she says to those who lack **s**.
9:16 in here," she says to those who lack **s**.
10:13 a rod for the back of those with no **s**.
10:21 people, but fools who lack **s** will die.
11:12 neighbor lacks **s**; a sensible
12:11 who engage in empty pursuits have no **s**.
15:21 to those who lack **s**, but those with
17:18 One with no **s** shakes hands on a deal,
19:8 who acquire good **s** love themselves;
24:30 by the vineyard of one with no **s**.
Ecclesiastes
10:3 Fools lack all **s** even when they walk
Isaiah
56:10 they all lack **s**. They are all
Hosea
4:14 the people without **s** must come to ruin.
7:11 without common **s**; they call upon
Matthew
16:3 know how to make **s** of the sky's

SENT → SENT FROM GOD
Genesis
8:8 Then he **s** out a dove to see if the
45:5 Actually, God **s** me before you to
Exodus
3:14 Israelites, 'I Am has **s** me to you.'"
32:35 Then the LORD **s** a plague on the people
Numbers
13:17 When Moses **s** them out to explore the
16:29 all humans, then the LORD hasn't **s** me.
21:6 So the LORD **s** poisonous snakes among
Joshua
2:1 son, secretly **s** two men as spies
24:12 I **s** the hornet before you. It drove
24:28 Then Joshua **s** the people away to each
2 Samuel
22:15 the enemy; he **s** the lightning and
2 Kings
14:9 in Lebanon **s** a message to a
Isaiah
61:1 me. He has **s** me to bring good
Jeremiah
3:8 also saw that I **s** unfaithful Israel
28:9 who is actually **s** by the LORD only
44:4 time and again I **s** you all my
Daniel
3:28 be praised! He **s** his messenger to
6:22 My God **s** his messenger, who shut the
Matthew
10:40 me are receiving the one who **s** me.
Luke
1:26 pregnant, God **s** the angel Gabriel
4:18 me. He has **s** me to preach good
9:2 He **s** them out to proclaim God's kingdom
10:16 rejects me rejects the one who **s** me."
13:34 those who were **s** to you! How often
John
1:6 A man named John was **s** from God
3:28 but that I'm the one **s** before him.
4:34 of the one who **s** me and by
5:24 in the one who **s** me has eternal
8:16 from me and from the Father who **s** me.
9:4 works of him who **s** me. Night is
16:5 to the one who **s** me. None of you
17:3 true God, and Jesus Christ whom you **s**.

SENT [cont.]

17:18 As you **s** me into the world, so I have
20:21 As the Father **s** me, so I am
Romans
10:15 unless they are **s**? As it is
Galatians
4:4 time came, God **s** his Son, born
4:6 daughters, God **s** the Spirit of his
1 John
4:10 he loved us and **s** his Son as the
4:14 the Father has **s** the Son to be the
Revelation
22:16 I, Jesus, have **s** my angel to bear

SENT FROM GOD

Dn 5:24; Lk 9:20; 23:35; Jn 1:6; 2Co 2:17

SEPARATED

Genesis
1:4 light was. God **s** the light from
1:7 made the dome and **s** the waters under
13:11 the east, and they **s** from each other.
13:14 After Lot **s** from him, the LORD said to
Job
41:17 to its pair; joined, they can't be **s**.
Isaiah
59:2 misdeeds have **s** you from your
Ezekiel
22:26 have not clearly **s** the holy from the
Romans
8:35 love? Will we be **s** by trouble, or
2 Corinthians
6:17 among them and be **s**, says the Lord.
1 Thessalonians
2:17 sisters, we were **s** from you for a
Philemon
1:15 that Onesimus was **s** from you for a

SERAIAH

2 Samuel
8:17 Abiathar were priests; **S** was secretary;
2 Kings
25:18 also took away **S** the chief priest,
Ezra
2:2 Jeshua, Nehemiah, **S**, Reelaiah,
Jeremiah
36:26 son, along with **S**, Azriel's son,
40:8 Kareah's sons; **S** son of Tanhumeth;
52:24 guard also took **S** the high priest,

SERVANT → GOD'S SERVANT

Leviticus
22:11 purchases a **s**, that person can
Numbers
11:11 you treated your **s** so badly? And why
Deuteronomy
3:24 to show your **s** your greatness
5:21 male or female **s**, ox, donkey, or
12:18 male and female **s**, and the Levite
15:16 Now if your male **s** says to you: "I
15:17 be your permanent **s**. Do the same
34:5 Moses, the LORD's **s**, died—right there
Joshua
1:1 Moses the LORD's **s** died, the LORD
Judges
2:8 and the LORD's **s**, died when he was
Ruth
2:13 to your female **s**—even though I'm
3:9 I'm Ruth your **s**. Spread out your
1 Samuel
1:11 Don't forget your **s**! Give her a boy!
1:18 well of me, your **s**," Hannah said.
3:9 LORD. Your **s** is listening.'"
17:32 Saul. "I, your **s**, will go out and
1 Kings
3:7 made me, your **s**, king in my
8:56 promise he made through his **s** Moses.
8:66 had done for his **s** David and for his
20:40 Your **s** got busy doing this and that,
Job
1:8 thought about my **s** Job; surely there
2:3 thought about my **s** Job, for there is
42:8 rams, go to my **s** Job, and prepare
Psalms
19:11 about it: your **s** is enlightened by
19:13 and save your **s** from willful sins.
31:16 your face on your **s**; save me by your
78:70 chose David, his **s**, taking him from
89:3 my chosen one; I promised my **s** David:
105:26 sent Moses his **s** and the one he
119:135 your face on your **s**, and teach me
136:22 to Israel, his **s**—God's faithful
Proverbs
11:29 wind. The fool will be **s** to the wise.
14:35 an insightful **s**, but is furious
Ecclesiastes
7:21 so you don't hear your **s** cursing you.
Isaiah
41:8 you, Israel my **s**, Jacob, whom I
42:1 But here is my **s**, the one I uphold; my
43:10 says the LORD, my **s**, whom I chose, so
44:1 this, Jacob my **s**, and Israel, whom
45:4 the sake of my **s** Jacob and Israel
48:20 The LORD has redeemed his **s** Jacob!"
49:3 me, "You are my **s**, Israel, in whom
52:13 Look, my **s** will succeed. He will be
Jeremiah
30:10 be afraid, my **s** Jacob, declares
33:21 covenant with my **s** David and my
Ezekiel
34:24 their God, and my **s** David will be
Zechariah
3:8 look, I am about to bring my **s**, Branch.
Matthew
8:13 And his **s** was healed that
20:26 to be great among you will be your **s**.
Luke
1:38 I am the Lord's **s**. Let it be with
1:54 to the aid of his **s** Israel,
1:69 savior for us in his **s** David's house,
John
12:26 I am, there my **s** will also be. My
18:26 A **s** of the high priest, a relative of
Acts
3:13 -has glorified his **s** Jesus. This is
Romans
13:4 It is God's **s** given for your benefit.
15:8 Christ became a **s** of those who are
Galatians
2:17 then is Christ a **s** of sin?
Ephesians
3:7 I became a **s** of the gospel because of
6:21 and faithful **s** of the Lord, can
Colossians
1:23 I, Paul, became a **s** of this good news.

1:25 I became a **s** of the church by God's
1 Timothy
4:6 will be a good **s** of Christ Jesus
Hebrews
3:5 God's house as a **s** in order to
Revelation
1:1 it through his angel to his **s** John,
15:3 of Moses, God's **s**, and the song of
22:9 do that! I'm a **s** just like you and

SERVANTS

Genesis
12:16 male donkeys, men **s**, women servants,
Deuteronomy
5:14 male or female **s**, your oxen or
16:11 male and female **s**, the Levites who
34:11 to all his **s**, and to his
Judges
3:24 out, the king's **s** came and found
6:27 took ten of his **s** and did just as
Ruth
2:13 though I'm not one of your female **s**."
2 Kings
17:23 through all his **s** the prophets. So
Ezra
5:11 us: "We are the **s** of the God of
Job
1:3 a vast number of **s**, so that he was
4:18 doesn't trust his **s** and levels a
19:15 guests and female **s** think me a
Psalms
90:13 quick! Have some compassion for your **s**!
135:9 Egypt—against Pharaoh and all his **s**.
Proverbs
9:3 out her female **s**; she issues an
29:19 **S** aren't disciplined by words; they
29:21 Pamper **s** from a young age, and later on
31:15 household, even some for her female **s**.
Ecclesiastes
2:7 I acquired male **s** and female servants;
Isaiah
65:8 the sake of my **s** and not destroy
Jeremiah
7:25 sent you all my **s** the prophets—day
Ezekiel
38:17 times through my **s**, Israel's
46:17 gives one of his **s** a gift from his
Daniel
9:6 listened to your **s**, the prophets,
Joel
1:13 funeral clothing, **s** of my God,
Amos
3:7 his secret to his **s** the prophets.
Nahum
2:7 while her female **s** moan like doves,
Zechariah
1:6 I gave to my **s**, the prophets,
Matthew
13:27 The **s** of the landowner came and said
Mark
12:5 sent many other **s**, but the tenants
13:34 and put the **s** in charge, giving
14:66 one of the high priest's **s**, approached
John
15:15 I don't call you **s** any longer, because
15:20 what I told you, '**S** aren't greater
18:18 The **s** and the guards had made a fire
Acts
4:29 and enable your **s** to speak your
Romans
14:4 someone else's **s**? They stand or
1 Corinthians
3:5 is Paul? They are **s** who helped you to
Revelation
19:2 for the blood of his **s** from her hand."
22:3 be in it, and his **s** will worship him.

SERVE → SERVE OTHER GODS, SERVE THE LORD

Genesis
25:23 other; the older will **s** the younger."
41:46 when he began to **s** Pharaoh, Egypt's
Exodus
21:2 slave, he will **s** you for six
28:1 the Israelites to **s** me as priests—
30:16 tent. It will **s** for the
40:15 so that they may **s** me as priests.
Leviticus
16:32 and ordained to **s** as priest after
Numbers
8:15 will enter to **s** the meeting tent,
18:2 assist you and **s** you and your sons
Deuteronomy
6:13 LORD your God, **s** him, and take
7:16 pity. And don't **s** their gods
10:8 the LORD, to **s** him, and to offer
28:48 you will **s** your enemies—the ones the
29:18 favor of going to **s** these nations'
32:36 on those who **s** him, once he sees
Joshua
22:5 on to him and **s** him with all your
24:14 revere the LORD. **S** him honestly and
24:20 the LORD and **s** foreign gods,
24:21 No! The LORD is the one we will **s**."
24:27 This stone will **s** here as a witness
Judges
2:19 other gods, to **s** them and to
9:28 that we ought to **s** him? Didn't this
9:38 that we ought to **s** him?' Aren't
10:6 away from the LORD and didn't **s** him.
1 Samuel
2:35 him, and he will **s** before my
4:9 Otherwise, you'll **s** the Hebrews like
8:1 his sons to **s** as Israel's
9:23 to the cook, "**S** the portion I
12:24 fear the LORD and **s** him faithfully
17:9 become our slaves and you will **s** us.
25:41 servant, ready to **s** and wash the feet
27:12 in Israel that he'll **s** me forever.
29:6 much like you to **s** with me in the
2 Samuel
16:19 whom should I **s** if not David's
22:44 many nations. Strangers come to **s** me.
1 Kings
1:2 king. She will **s** the king and take
10:8 who continually **s** you and get to
12:4 demanded from us, then we will **s** you."
17:1 God, the one I **s**, there will be
18:15 lives, the one I **s**, I will appear
2 Kings
3:14 stand before and **s**, if I didn't care
4:41 pot and said, "**S** the people so
5:16 of the LORD. I **s** that I won't

17:35 down to them or **s** them. Don't
17:41 but they also **s** their idols. The
18:7 Assyria's king and wouldn't **s** him.
25:24 in the land and **s** the Babylonian

1 Chronicles
16:4 of the Levites to **s** before the LORD's
23:13 the LORD, to **s** him, and to give
23:28 the Aaronites to **s** in the LORD's
23:31 number were to **s** in the LORD's
28:9 father's God and **s** him with

2 Chronicles
9:7 who continually **s** you and get to
10:4 demanded from us, then we will **s** you."
13:10 descendants **s** as the LORD's
19:11 The Levites will **s** as your officers
29:11 his presence to **s** him, so that you
31:2 sacrifices, to **s**, to give thanks,

Ezra
8:20 had appointed to **s** the Levites.

Nehemiah
9:35 them, they didn't **s** you or turn from
10:36 the priests who **s** in our God's

Job
21:15 that we should **s** him, and what can
36:11 they listen and **s**, they spend their

Psalms
18:43 many nations. Strangers come to **s** me.
22:30 descendants will **s** him; generations
72:11 before him; let all the nations **s** him.
103:21 LORD! All you who **s** him and do his
135:14 and has compassion on those who **s** him.

Proverbs
29:12 lies, those who **s** him will be

Isaiah
41:2 to summon him to **s**—giving him natio
59:6 Their webs can't **s** as clothing; they
60:10 their kings will **s** you. Though in my
60:12 that won't **s** you will perish;

Jeremiah
2:20 said, "I won't **s** you." On every
5:19 land, so you will **s** strangers in a
15:14 I will make you **s** your enemies in a
25:11 nations will **s** the king of
27:7 All nations will **s** him, his son and
27:8 that won't **s** Babylon's King
27:9 to you, "Don't **s** the king of
27:12 of Babylon and **s** him and his
27:13 nation that won't **s** the king of
27:14 you not to **s** the king of
27:17 listen to them; **s** the king of
28:14 and they will **s** Babylon's King
40:9 in the land, **s** the king of

Ezekiel
19:14 and it will **s** as a lamentation.
20:39 Go ahead and **s** your idols, all
20:40 of Israel will **s** me there—every
41:6 the way around to **s** as supports, but
44:15 near to me to **s** me. They will

Daniel
1:5 that time they could **s** before the king.
3:12 They don't **s** your gods, and
6:16 God—the one you **s** so consistently—
7:10 stood ready to **s** him! The court

Zephaniah
3:9 name of the LORD and will **s** him as one.

Matthew
4:10 the Lord your God and **s** only him."
6:24 No one can **s** two masters. Either you
20:28 but rather to **s** and to give his
27:55 followed Jesus from Galilee to **s** him.

Mark
10:45 but rather to **s** and to give his

Luke
1:74 so that we could **s** him without fear,
4:8 the Lord your God and **s** only him."
12:37 dress himself to **s**, seat them at the
16:2 you can no longer **s** as my manager.'
16:13 servant can **s** two masters.

Acts
6:2 of God's word in order to **s** tables.
7:7 the nation they **s** as slaves, God

Romans
1:9 I **s** God in my spirit by preaching the
6:16 true whether you **s** as slaves of sin,
15:25 going to Jerusalem, to **s** God's people.

1 Corinthians
9:13 that those who **s** in the temple get

2 Corinthians
11:8 a salary from them in order to **s** you!

Galatians
5:13 impulses, but **s** each other

Ephesians
6:7 **S** your owners enthusiastically, as

Philippians
3:3 are the ones who **s** by God's Spirit

1 Timothy
3:10 tested and then **s** if they are
6:2 they should **s** them more

2 Timothy
1:3 to God, whom I **s** with a good

Philemon
1:13 so that he might **s** me in your place

Hebrews
1:14 who are sent to **s** those who are
6:10 and continue to **s** God's holy people.
7:23 prevented them from continuing to **s**.
7:24 because he continues to **s** forever.
8:5 They **s** in a place that is a copy and
9:14 works in order to **s** the living God?
12:28 gratitude, let's **s** in a way that is
13:10 and those who **s** as priests in the

1 Peter
4:10 And **s** each other according to the gift

Jude
1:7 of eternal fire, they **s** as a warning.

Revelation
7:3 the foreheads of those who **s** our God."

SERVE OTHER GODS

Dt 28:64; Josh 23:16; 24:16; 1Ki 9:6; 2Ch 7:19; Jer 16:13; 35:15

SERVE THE LORD

Lv 7:35; Josh 24:14; 24:15, 18, 19, 22, 24; 1Sa 12:20; 2Ch 30:8; Ps 2:11; 100:2; 102:22; 113:1; 134:1; 135:1; Jer 30:9; Eze 40:46; Ro 12:11; Col 3:24

SERVED → SERVED THE LORD

Genesis
19:33 That night they **s** their father wine,
39:2 man and **s** in his Egyptian

Numbers
3:4 and Ithamar **s** as priests during
Joshua
24:2 Euphrates. They **s** other gods. Among
24:14 your ancestors **s** beyond the
24:15 your ancestors **s** beyond the
Judges
2:11 the LORD saw as evil: They **s** the Baals;
2:13 from the LORD and **s** Baal and the
3:6 with them and **s** their gods.
3:7 their God. They **s** the Baals and the
3:14 So the Israelites **s** Moab's King Eglon
10:6 saw as evil. They **s** the Baals and the
10:13 away from me and **s** other gods, so I
Ruth
2:14 and he **s** roasted grain to
1 Samuel
2:22 the women who **s** at the meeting
7:6 the LORD." Samuel **s** as judge of the
7:15 Samuel **s** as Israel's judge his whole
7:17 In Ramah too he **s** as Israel's
8:2 was Abijah. They **s** as judges in Beer-
19:7 Saul, and David **s** Saul as he had
28:25 She **s** this to Saul and his servants,
2 Samuel
10:19 all the kings who **s** Hadadezer saw
13:9 took the pan and **s** Amnon, but he
13:11 When she **s** him the food, he grabbed her
16:19 David's son? I **s** your father, and
1 Kings
1:4 for the king and **s** him, but the king
4:21 to Solomon and **s** him all the days
12:6 elders who had **s** his father
12:8 had grown up with him and now **s** him.
16:31 the Sidonians. He **s** and worshipped
19:21 he got up, followed Elijah, and **s** him.
22:53 Ahaziah **s** Baal and worshipped him. He
2 Kings
4:40 The stew was **s** to the men, but as they
5:2 land of Israel. She **s** Naaman's wife.
10:18 to them, "Ahab **s** Baal a little.
17:16 all the heavenly bodies. They **s** Baal.
17:33 but they also **s** their own gods
Nehemiah
2:1 was about to be **s** wine. I took the
Esther
1:7 They **s** the drinks in cups made of gold,
1:10 seven eunuchs who **s** King Ahasuerus
Isaiah
63:9 a messenger who **s** him saved them.
Jeremiah
5:19 abandoned me and **s** foreign gods in
8:2 have loved and **s** and which they
16:11 LORD. They have **s** and worshipped
22:9 God and worshipped and **s** other gods."
34:14 After they have **s** you for six
Daniel
7:10 upon thousands **s** him; ten thousand
Hosea
12:12 there Israel **s** for a wife, and
Matthew
8:15 left her. Then she got up and **s** them.
20:28 didn't come to be **s** but rather to
Mark
1:31 up. The fever left her, and she **s** them.
10:45 didn't come to be **s** but rather to
Luke
4:39 her. She got up at once and **s** them.
15:29 Look, I've **s** you all these
John
12:2 for him. Martha **s** and Lazarus was
Acts
13:21 Benjamin, and he **s** as their king for
13:36 David **s** God's purpose in his own
17:25 Nor is God **s** by human hands, as though he needed
Romans
1:25 worshipped and **s** the creation
1 Corinthians
10:27 eat whatever is **s**, without asking
2 Corinthians
6:6 generosity. We **s** with the Holy
1 Timothy
3:13 Those who have **s** well gain a good
Hebrews
6:10 sake when you **s** and continue to
7:13 and no one ever **s** at the altar from

SERVED THE LORD

Josh 24:31; Jdg 2:7; 10:16; 1Sa 2:11; Ac 20:19

SERVICE

Genesis
50:2 physicians in his **s** to embalm his
Exodus
30:16 it to support the **s** of the meeting
31:10 for his sons for their **s** as priests,
35:19 and his sons for their **s** as priests.
39:40 equipment for the **s** of the dwelling,
Leviticus
25:52 purchase according to the years of **s**.
Numbers
8:25 will retire from **s**. They will
1 Samuel
2:21 the boy Samuel grew up in the LORD's **s**.
Job
14:14 the days of my **s** I would wait
Psalms
78:36 him with lip **s**. They were lying
Luke
1:9 of priestly **s**, he was chosen by
12:35 Be dressed for **s** and keep your lamps
1 Corinthians
16:15 themselves to the **s** of God's people.
Revelation
2:19 your **s** and endurance. I

SERVING → SERVING THE LORD

Deuteronomy
4:19 worshipping and **s** them. The LORD
7:4 that they end up **s** other gods. That
8:19 other gods, **s** and bowing down
11:13 your God and by **s** him with all your
11:16 you stray away, **s** other gods and
17:3 by following and **s** other gods, and by
18:7 -the other Levites **s** there in the
28:14 now by following other gods and **s** them.
29:26 other gods, **s** them, and
30:17 worshipping other gods and **s** them,
31:20 other gods, **s** them and
1 Samuel
2:33 eliminate from **s** at my altar will

4:9 like they've been ***s*** you. Act like men
7:16 and Mizpah, ***s*** as Israel's judge
1 Kings
1:15 and Abishag from Shunem was ***s*** the king.
9:9 worshipping and ***s*** them. That is why
2 Chronicles
7:22 worshipping and ***s*** them. This is why
12:8 between ***s*** me and serving
22:8 nephews, ***s*** Ahaziah, and Jehu
Esther
1:8 ordered everyone ***s*** wine in the
7:9 of the eunuchs ***s*** the king, said,
Psalms
106:36 and ***s*** those false gods, which became a
Isaiah
56:6 have joined me, ***s*** me and loving my
Jeremiah
11:10 other gods and ***s*** them. The people
13:10 worshipping and ***s*** them. They will
40:9 be afraid of ***s*** the Babylonians.
Daniel
1:4 and capable of ***s*** in the king's
Hosea
4:6 reject you from ***s*** me as a priest.
Malachi
3:14 You said, "***S*** God is useless. What do we gain
3:18 between those ***s*** God and those not
Matthew
27:19 While he was ***s*** as judge, his wife sent
Luke
1:8 day Zechariah was ***s*** as a priest
Romans
12:7 yourself to ***s***. If your gift is
Ephesians
4:12 for the work of ***s*** and building up
1 Thessalonians
1:9 a result, you are ***s*** the living and
Hebrews
8:2 He's ***s*** as a priest in the holy place,
9:9 the conscience of the one who is ***s***.
10:11 stands every day ***s*** and offering the
1 Peter
1:12 they were not ***s*** themselves but

SERVING THE LORD

Dt 10:12; 17:12; 1Sa 2:18; 3:1; Ro 16:18; Eph 6:7

SET APART

Gn 21:29; 49:26; Ex 8:22; Josh 16:9; 20:7; 1Sa 9:24; 1Ki 9:3; 1Ch 23:13; 25:1; Ps 139:14; Jer 31:40; Eze 45:4; Ro 1:1; 1Co 7:14; 2Ti 2:21

SETH

Genesis
4:25 She named him ***S*** "because God has
5:8 In all, ***S*** lived 912 years, and he died
1 Chronicles
1:1 Adam, ***S***, Enosh
Luke
3:38 of Enos son of ***S*** son of Adam son

SETTING

Numbers
7:1 Moses finished ***s*** up the dwelling,
Deuteronomy
4:8 that I am ***s*** before you today?
2 Samuel
2:24 The sun was ***s*** when they came to
Proverbs
25:11 are like gold apples in a silver ***s***.
Isaiah
45:6 of the sun to its ***s***, that there is
54:11 look, I am ***s*** your gemstones in
Jeremiah
21:8 LORD says: I'm ***s*** before you the
40:4 But I'm ***s*** you free from the chains on
Daniel
12:11 is stopped to the ***s*** up of the
Amos
7:8 said, "See, I am ***s*** a plumb line in
Obadiah
1:7 you. They are ***s*** your own bread as
Luke
4:40 When the sun was ***s***, everyone brought to Jesus
1 Timothy
5:12 be judged for ***s*** aside their

SETTLE

Genesis
46:34 will be able to ***s*** in the land of
Numbers
9:21 the cloud would ***s*** only overnight,
Deuteronomy
8:12 full, build nice houses, and ***s*** down,
12:10 River and will ***s*** in the land the
Joshua
22:19 property and ***s*** among us. That's
Judges
2:6 each went to ***s*** on their own
4:5 would come to her to ***s*** disputes.
17:8 in Judah to ***s*** as an immigrant
17:9 I'm looking to ***s*** as an immigrant
2 Chronicles
19:8 and to ***s*** disputes among
Isaiah
1:18 now, and let's ***s*** this, says the
2:4 the nations, and ***s*** disputes of
7:19 will come and ***s*** in the steep
23:7 whose feet carried her to ***s*** far away?
49:20 crowded for me; make room for me to ***s***."
54:3 nations' land and ***s*** their desolate
Jeremiah
29:5 Build houses and ***s*** down; cultivate
29:28 build houses and ***s*** down, plant
40:10 arrive. But you? ***S*** down in the towns
48:11 like wine left to ***s*** on its sediment.
50:40 will live in Babylon or ***s*** there again.
Ezekiel
18:8 from evil and ***s*** cases between
32:4 in the sky to ***s*** on you, and all
Joel
3:17 LORD your God, ***s*** down in Zion, my
Micah
4:3 the nations and ***s*** disputes of
Zechariah
8:3 to Zion; I will ***s*** in Jerusalem.
Matthew
18:23 who wanted to ***s*** accounts with his
18:24 When he began to ***s*** accounts, they

SETTLED

Genesis
2:15 the human and **s** him in the garden
13:12 Abram **s** in the land of Canaan, and Lot
47:11 Joseph **s** his father and brothers and
Exodus
2:15 from Pharaoh and **s** down in the land
24:16 glorious presence **s** on Mount Sinai,
40:35 the cloud had **s** on it, and the
Numbers
9:17 would camp wherever the cloud **s**.
21:25 the Israelites **s** in all the cities
21:31 Israel **s** in the land of the Amorites
22:5 the land. They have **s** next to me.
Deuteronomy
3:20 as you have been **s**, and they also
17:14 of it and **s** down in it, you
26:1 take possession of it and are **s** there,
Joshua
19:47 took it over and **s** it. Then they
21:43 They took it over and **s** there.
22:9 owned. They had **s** there at the
24:13 hadn't built. You **s** in them and are
Judges
1:32 people of Asher **s** among the
1:33 or Beth-anath but **s** among the
4:11 and had **s** as far away as
18:28 They rebuilt the city and **s** in it.
Ruth
1:2 the territory of Moab and **s** there.
1 Samuel
12:8 ancestors out of Egypt and **s** them here.
2 Samuel
7:1 When the king was **s** in his palace, and
20:18 at Abel, and that **s** the matter.
2 Kings
2:15 spirit has **s** on Elisha!" So
16:6 came to Elath and **s** there, and that's
17:24 control of Samaria and **s** in its cities.
18:11 to Assyria. He **s** them in Halah, in
1 Chronicles
4:41 seen today. They **s** in their place,
5:9 They also **s** in the east as far as the
17:1 When David was **s** into his palace, he
2 Chronicles
8:2 given him, and he **s** Israelites there.
Ezra
2:70 temple servants **s** in their own
4:10 deported and **s** in the cities of
Nehemiah
7:73 and all Israel **s** in their towns.
11:4 and Benjamin **s** in Jerusalem.
11:30 villages. So they **s** from Beer-sheba to
Psalms
68:10 your creatures **s** in it. In your
78:55 for them; he **s** Israel's tribes
Proverbs
8:25 mountains were **s**, before the
Jeremiah
49:1 Why have his people **s** in its towns?
Matthew
2:23 He **s** in a city called Nazareth so that
4:13 left Nazareth and **s** in Capernaum,
14:32 got into the boat, the wind **s** down.
25:19 returned and **s** accounts with
Mark
4:39 still!" The wind **s** down and there
6:51 and the wind **s** down. His
Acts
7:2 in Mesopotamia, before he **s** in Haran.
7:4 the Chaldeans and **s** in Haran. After
2 Corinthians
13:1 Every matter is **s** on the evidence

SEVEN

Genesis
4:15 will be paid back **s** times. The LORD
7:2 animal, take **s** pairs, a male and
7:10 After **s** days, the floodwaters arrived
8:10 He waited **s** more days and sent the dove
21:28 by themselves, **s** female lambs from
29:18 work for you for **s** years for Rachel,
29:30 Leah. He worked for Laban **s** more years.
31:23 chased Jacob for **s** days, and caught
33:3 to the ground **s** times as he was
41:2 In front of him, **s** healthy-looking,
41:53 The **s** years of abundance in the land of
41:54 and the **s** years of famine began, just
50:10 He grieved **s** days for his
Exodus
2:16 priest who had **s** daughters. The
7:25 **S** days went by after the LORD had
12:15 bread for **s** days. On the
12:19 For **s** days no yeast should be found in
13:6 bread for **s** days. The seventh
22:30 their mother for **s** days. On the
23:15 bread for **s** days at the
25:37 Make its **s** lamps and set up its lamps
29:30 should wear them **s** days when he
29:35 commanded you. Ordain them for **s** days.
29:37 **S** days you should perform the ritual of
34:18 bread for **s** days, as I
37:23 He made its **s** lamps and its tongs and
Leviticus
4:6 some of it **s** times before the
8:11 oil on the altar **s** times, and
8:33 entrance for **s** days, until the
12:2 be unclean for **s** days—just as she
13:4 the infected person for **s** days.
13:5 quarantine the person for **s** more days.
14:7 from skin disease **s** times and declare
15:13 he will count off **s** days for his
16:14 with his finger **s** times in front of
22:27 its mother for **s** days. From the
23:6 must eat unleavened bread for **s** days.
25:8 Count off **s** weeks of years—that is,
26:18 punish you for your sins **s** more times:
Numbers
8:2 set them up, the **s** lamps will give
12:14 not be shamed for **s** days? Let her be
19:4 and sprinkle it **s** times in front of
23:1 Balak, "Build me **s** altars here and
28:11 one ram, and **s** one-year-old male
29:2 one ram, and **s** male lambs one
29:12 a festival to the LORD for **s** days.
31:19 the camp for **s** days. Everyone
31:52 sixteen thousand **s** hundred fifty
Deuteronomy
7:1 the Jebusites: **s** nations that are
16:3 it. Instead, for **s** days you must eat
16:9 Count out **s** weeks, starting the count

16:13 the Festival of Booths for **s** days.
16:15 **S** days you must perform the festival
28:7 away from you in **s** different
31:10 At the end of **s** years, at the
Joshua
6:4 Have **s** priests carry seven trumpets
6:15 city in this way **s** times. It was
18:2 the Israelites, **s** tribes were left
18:9 city by city, in **s** sections. They
Judges
6:1 over to the Midianites for **s** years.
6:25 and a second bull **s** years old. Break
8:26 was one thousand **s** hundred shekels
12:9 his sons. He led Israel for **s** years.
14:12 answer within the **s** days of the
16:7 ties me up with **s** fresh bowstrings
16:8 brought her **s** fresh bowstrings
16:13 If you weave the **s** braids of my hair
16:14 asleep, wove the **s** braids of his
16:19 him shave off the **s** braids of
20:16 this entire army, **s** hundred specially
Ruth
4:15 him. She's better for you than **s** sons."
1 Samuel
2:5 has birthed **s** children, but the
6:1 in Philistine territory for **s** months.
10:8 sacrifices. Wait **s** days until I get
16:10 Jesse presented **s** of his sons to
31:13 tree at Jabesh, and they fasted **s** days.
2 Samuel
2:11 of Judah totaled **s** and a half years.
5:5 over Judah for **s** and a half years
8:4 chariots, **s** hundred
10:18 David destroyed **s** hundred of their
12:6 the ewe lamb **s** times over
21:6 hand over **s** of his sons to us, and we
21:9 the LORD. The **s** of them died at
1 Kings
18:43 see anything." **S** times Elijah
19:18 Israel, totaling **s** thousand
20:29 each other for **s** days. On the
2 Kings
3:9 around for **s** days until there
3:26 So he took **s** hundred soldiers
4:35 the boy sneezed **s** times and opened
5:10 Go and wash **s** times in the
5:14 in the Jordan **s** times, just as
8:1 to the land and will last **s** years."
8:2 away, living in Philistia **s** years.
8:3 When **s** years had passed, the woman
24:16 king also exiled **s** thousand warriors-
1 Chronicles
3:4 he reigned for **s** and a half years.
9:25 to assist them for a period of **s** days.
10:12 oak in Jabesh, and fasted for **s** days.
11:23 an Egyptian **s** and a half feet
15:26 they sacrificed **s** bulls and seven
18:4 from him, **s** thousand cavalry,
19:18 and David killed **s** thousand Aramean
29:4 gold of Ophir, **s** thousand kikkars
29:27 for forty years: **s** years in Hebron
2 Chronicles
3:11 wings was **s** and a half feet
3:12 creature was **s** and a half feet
3:15 feet high, with a **s**-and-a-half-foot ca
4:2 from rim to rim, **s** and a half feet
6:13 a bronze platform **s** and a half feet
7:8 the festival for **s** days. It was a
7:9 the altar for **s** days and
9:16 gold, using **s** and a half pounds
13:9 a young bull and **s** rams can become a
15:11 they had taken: **s** hundred oxen and
26:13 of three hundred **s** thousand five
29:21 They brought **s** bulls, seven rams, and
30:21 Bread for **s** days, with the
35:17 of Unleavened Bread for **s** days.
Ezra
6:22 Bread for **s** days, because the
7:14 the king and his **s** counselors to
Nehemiah
8:18 the festival for **s** days and held a
Esther
1:5 the king held a **s**-day feast for ever
1:10 and Carcas, the **s** eunuchs who
1:14 They were **s** very important
2:9 He also gave her **s** servants selected
Job
1:2 He had **s** sons and three daughters
1:3 and owned **s** thousand sheep, three
2:13 Job on the ground **s** days and seven
5:19 deliver you; from **s** harm won't touch
42:8 So now, take **s** bulls and seven rams, go
42:13 He also had **s** sons and three daughters
Psalms
12:6 in an oven, purified **s** times over!
79:12 our neighbors **s** times over, right
119:164 I praise you **s** times a day for your
Proverbs
6:16 the LORD hates, **s** things detestable
9:1 she has carved out her **s** pillars.
24:16 may fall **s** times but still
26:16 are wiser than **s** people who answer
26:25 believe them, for **s** horrible things
Ecclesiastes
11:2 Give a portion to **s** people, even to
Isaiah
4:1 **S** women will grab one man on that day,
11:15 and break it into **s** streams so that
30:26 the sun will be **s** times brighter—
Jeremiah
15:9 The mother of **s** will grow weak and gasp
52:22 it that towered **s** and a half feet
52:25 the army and the **s** royal advisors
Ezekiel
3:15 there among them for **s** desolate days.
3:16 At the end of the **s** days, the LORD's
39:9 will burn them with fire for **s** years.
40:7 with a space of **s** and a half feet
40:22 of the East Gate. **S** steps led up to
43:14 upper ledge is **s** feet; the upper
43:26 For **s** days the priests will purge the
44:26 clean again, he must count off **s** days.
45:2 portion, an area **s** hundred fifty
45:23 For the **s** days of the festival, he will
45:25 and oil, for all **s** days of the
Daniel
3:19 be heated to **s** times its normal
4:16 of an animal. **S** periods of time
4:32 like cattle, and **s** periods of time
9:25 There will be **s** weeks from the
Micah
5:5 up against him **s** shepherds and
Zechariah
3:9 stone, there are **s** facets. I am

4:2 top. The bowl has ***s*** lamps on top and
4:10 These are the ***s*** eyes of the LORD,

Matthew
12:45 brings with it ***s*** other spirits
15:34 They responded, "***S*** loaves and a few
15:36 He took the ***s*** loaves of bread and the
15:37 collected ***s*** baskets full of
16:10 And the ***s*** loaves that fed the four
18:21 Should I forgive as many as ***s*** times?"
18:22 said, "Not just ***s*** times, but rather
22:25 Now there were ***s*** brothers among us. The first one married
22:26 third, and in fact with all ***s*** brothers.
22:28 which of the ***s*** brothers will be

Mark
8:5 do you have?" They said, "***S*** loaves."
8:6 He took the ***s*** loaves, gave
8:8 They collected ***s*** baskets full of
8:20 And when I broke ***s*** loaves of bread for those four
12:20 Now there were ***s*** brothers. The first
12:22 None of the ***s*** left any children.
12:23 will she be? All ***s*** were married to
16:9 from whom he had cast out ***s*** demons.

Luke
2:36 she lived with her husband for ***s*** years.
8:2 (from whom ***s*** demons had been
11:26 brings with it ***s*** other spirits
17:4 sins against you ***s*** times in one day
20:29 Now there were ***s*** brothers. The first
20:31 Eventually all ***s*** married her, and
20:33 will she be? All ***s*** were married to
24:13 Emmaus, about ***s*** miles from

Acts
6:3 carefully choose ***s*** well-respected men
6:6 presented these ***s*** to the apostles,
13:19 God conquered ***s*** nations in the land of
19:14 The ***s*** sons of Sceva, a Jewish chief
21:8 one of the ***S***, and stayed with
21:27 When the ***s*** days of purification were

Romans
11:4 kept for myself ***s*** thousand people

Hebrews
11:30 people marched around them for ***s*** days.

2 Peter
2:5 of righteousness, along with ***s*** others.

Jude
1:14 Enoch, who lived ***s*** generations after

Revelation
1:4 John, to the ***s*** churches that are in
1:20 mystery of the ***s*** stars that you
2:1 one who holds the ***s*** stars in his
3:1 who holds God's ***s*** spirits and the
4:5 the throne were ***s*** flaming torches,
5:1 back, and it was sealed with ***s*** seals.
5:6 slain. It had ***s*** horns and seven
6:1 opened one of the ***s*** seals. I heard
8:2 Then I saw the ***s*** angels who stand
10:3 called out, the ***s*** thunders raised
11:13 of the city fell. ***S*** thousand people
12:3 red dragon, with ***s*** heads and ten
13:1 had ten horns and ***s*** heads. Each of
15:1 There were ***s*** angels with seven
15:8 temple until the ***s*** plagues of the
16:1 temple say to the ***s*** angels, "Go and
17:1 Then one of the ***s*** angels who had the
17:3 names. It had ***s*** heads and ten
17:7 the woman and the ***s***-headed, ten-horned
17:9 mind. The ***s*** heads are seven
17:11 belongs to the ***s***, and it is going
21:9 Then one of the ***s*** angels who had the

SEVENTH

Genesis
2:2 done, and on the ***s*** day God rested
2:3 God blessed the ***s*** day and made it holy,
8:4 and in the ***s*** month, on the seventeenth

Exodus
12:16 first day and the ***s*** day will be a
16:30 So the people rested on the ***s*** day
23:11 But in the ***s*** year you should leave it
23:12 days. But on the ***s*** day you should

Leviticus
13:5 On the ***s*** day the priest will again
25:20 we eat in the ***s*** year if we don't

Deuteronomy
5:14 but the ***s*** day is a Sabbath to the LORD
15:12 years, but in the ***s*** year you must set

Joshua
6:16 The ***s*** time, the priests blew the

2 Samuel
12:18 On the ***s*** day, the child died. David's

Ezra
3:6 first day of the ***s*** month, they began

Esther
1:10 On the ***s*** day, when wine had put the

Haggai
2:1 day of the ***s*** month, the LORD's

Zechariah
7:5 month and the ***s*** month for these
8:19 fourth, fifth, ***s***, and tenth months

Hebrews
4:4 this about the ***s*** day of creation

Revelation
8:1 Lamb opened the ***s*** seal, there was
10:7 the days when the ***s*** angel blows his
11:15 Then the ***s*** angel blew his trumpet, and
16:17 Then the ***s*** angel poured his bowl into
21:20 carnelian, the ***s*** was chrysolite,

SEVENTY

Genesis
50:3 the Egyptians mourned him for ***s*** days.

Exodus
24:1 and Abihu, and ***s*** of Israel's

Numbers
11:25 placed it on the ***s*** elders. When the

Judges
1:7 He said, "***S*** kings with severed thumbs
9:5 and killed all ***s*** of his brothers,
9:18 killed his ***s*** sons on a single
12:14 mounted on ***s*** donkeys. He led

1 Samuel
6:19 chest. God struck ***s*** people, and the

2 Chronicles
29:32 brought ***s*** bulls, a hundred
36:21 it rested, until ***s*** years were

Psalms
90:10 at best to be ***s*** years old, maybe

Isaiah
23:17 At the end of ***s*** years, the LORD will

Jeremiah
25:12 When the ***s*** years are over, I will

SEVENTY [cont.]

29:10 When Babylon's **s** years are up, I
Daniel
9:2 the prophet Jeremiah. It was **s** years.
9:24 **S** weeks are appointed for your people
Zechariah
1:12 you have been angry these **s** years?"
7:5 for these past **s** years, did you
Matthew
18:22 but rather as many as **s**-seven times.
Luke
10:1 Lord commissioned **s**-two others
10:17 The **s**-two returned joyously, saying,
Acts
23:23 hundred soldiers, **s** horsemen, and two
27:37 were two hundred **s**-six of us on the s

SEVENTY-FIVE

Genesis
6:15 fifty feet long, **s** feet wide, and
Exodus
27:12 should consist of **s** feet of drapes
38:12 drapes stretched **s** feet, with their
38:28 seven hundred **s** shekels of silver
1 Kings
7:2 feet in length, **s** feet in width,
7:6 with columns **s** feet long and
Esther
5:14 a pointed pole **s** feet high. In the
9:16 The total was **s** thousand dead,
Ezekiel
40:15 It was **s** feet from the front of the
42:2 hundred fifty feet, its depth **s** feet.
45:2 it will be an open space **s** feet wide.
48:17 three hundred **s** feet on the north
John
19:39 myrrh and aloe, nearly **s** pounds in all.

SEVERE

Genesis
12:10 since the famine was so **s** in the land.
12:17 household with **s** plagues because
41:31 famine that follows will be so very **s**.
41:56 the famine became more and more **s**.
41:57 the famine had also become more **s**.
43:1 The famine was **s** in the land
47:4 the famine is so **s** in the land of
47:13 the famine was so **s**. The land of
Exodus
9:24 the hail were so **s** that there had
Deuteronomy
28:59 descendants with **s** and chronic
1 Kings
15:23 old, Asa developed a **s** foot disease.
2 Chronicles
16:12 Asa developed a **s** foot disease. But
28:5 who defeated him with a **s** beating.
Job
2:7 struck Job with **s** sores from the
Psalms
32:10 of the wicked is **s**, but faithful
89:32 their wrongdoing with a **s** beating.
Proverbs
15:10 Discipline is **s** for those who abandon
Luke
15:14 his resources, a **s** food shortage
Acts
11:28 predicted that a **s** famine would
2 Corinthians
10:10 His letters are **s** and powerful, but

SEX

Leviticus
18:14 his wife for **s**; she is your aunt.
Numbers
25:1 by having illicit **s** with Moabite
Deuteronomy
22:14 I went to have **s** with her, I
22:21 extramarital **s** while still in
22:22 is found having **s** with a woman who
22:23 with her in a town and has **s** with her,
22:25 her and having **s** with her there,
22:28 grabs her and has **s** with her, and
22:29 the man who had **s** with her must give
27:20 is anyone who has **s** with his father's
27:21 is anyone who has **s** with any kind of
27:22 is anyone who has **s** with his sister,
27:23 is anyone who has **s** with his mother-in
28:30 man will have **s** with her. You
Judges
16:1 he saw a prostitute and had **s** with her.
1 Samuel
1:19 Elkanah had **s** with his wife
2:22 and how they had **s** with the women
2 Samuel
3:7 Why have you had **s** with my father's
11:4 to him, he had **s** with her. (Now
11:11 drink, and have **s** with my wife? I
12:11 and he will have **s** with your wives
12:24 to her and had **s** with her. She
13:11 said, "Come have **s** with me, my
16:21 Have **s** with your father's secondary
16:22 roof, and he had **s** with his father's
20:3 he didn't have **s** with them. They
1 Kings
1:4 but the king didn't have **s** with her.
1 Chronicles
7:23 Ephraim had **s** with his wife, and she
Isaiah
8:3 I then had **s** with the prophetess, and
Hosea
3:3 you won't have **s** with a man, nor I
4:10 they will have **s** like prostitutes,
1 Corinthians
5:1 man is having **s** with his father's
7:1 for a man not to have **s** with a woman."
1 Timothy
1:10 with the same **s**. They are

SEXUAL

Genesis
6:4 daughters had **s** relations and
Exodus
22:19 Anyone who has **s** relations with an
Leviticus
15:24 If a man has **s** intercourse with her and
15:33 men who have had **s** intercourse with
18:6 relative for **s** contact: I am the
19:20 If a man has **s** relations with a woman
20:11 If a man has **s** intercourse with his
20:12 If a man has **s** intercourse with his
20:13 If a man has **s** intercourse with a man
20:15 If a man has **s** relations with an
20:17 they have **s** contact with each
20:18 period and has **s** contact with her,

20:19 You must not have **s** contact with your
20:20 If a man has **s** intercourse with his
1 Samuel
21:4 troops have abstained from **s** activity."
1 Chronicles
2:21 Later, Hezron had **s** relations with the
Ezekiel
16:26 with the large **s** organs, and as
16:33 them to come to you for your **s** favors.
16:34 you for **s** favors, but you
23:20 consorts, whose **s** organs were like
Matthew
1:25 he didn't have **s** relations with
5:32 wife except for **s** unfaithfulness
15:19 adultery, **s** sins, thefts,
19:9 wife, except for **s** unfaithfulness,
Mark
7:21 thoughts come: **s** sins, thefts,
Luke
1:34 I haven't had **s** relations with a
Acts
15:20 with idols, **s** immorality,
15:29 animals, and **s** immorality. You
21:25 strangled animals, and **s** immorality."
Romans
1:26 traded natural **s** relations for
1:27 traded natural **s** relations with
1 Corinthians
5:1 that there is **s** immorality among
6:13 body isn't for **s** immorality but
6:18 Avoid **s** immorality! Every sin that a
7:2 own husband because of **s** immorality.
7:3 meet his wife's **s** needs, and the
10:8 not practice **s** immorality, like
2 Corinthians
12:21 moral corruption, **s** immorality, and
Galatians
5:19 they include **s** immorality, moral
Ephesians
5:3 **S** immorality, and any kind of impurity
Colossians
3:5 earth, such as **s** immorality, moral
1 Thessalonians
4:3 that you stay away from **s** immorality
4:5 by your **s** urges like the
Jude
1:7 practiced immoral **s** relations and
Revelation
2:14 to idols and commit **s** immorality.
2:20 into committing **s** immorality and
9:21 and drugs, their **s** immorality, or
17:2 have committed **s** immorality with
18:3 earth committed **s** immorality with
18:9 who committed **s** immorality with
21:8 those who commit **s** immorality, those
22:15 those who commit **s** immorality, the

SHADE

Job
40:22 screen him with **s**; poplars of the
Psalms
80:10 covered by its **s**; the mighty
91:1 shelter, camping in the Almighty's **s**,
121:5 the LORD is your **s** right beside you.
Song of Songs
2:3 young men. In his **s** I take pleasure
Isaiah
4:6 booth by day for **s** from the heat and
16:3 noon provide your **s** like night. Hide
18:4 like a cloud's **s** in the harvest
25:4 from the storm, a **s** from the heat.
32:2 like the **s** of a massive
Ezekiel
17:23 find shelter in the **s** of its boughs.
31:3 branches, dense **s**, towering height;
31:6 and in its **s**, every great
31:12 departed from its **s** and abandoned it.
31:17 lived under his **s**, these also went
Daniel
4:12 Wild animals took **s** under it; birds
Hosea
4:13 because their **s** is pleasant.
Jonah
4:5 under it, in the **s**, to see what
4:6 Jonah, providing **s** for his head and
Mark
4:32 in the sky are able to nest in its **s**."

SHADOW

2 Kings
9:30 put on her eye **s** and arranged her
20:9 true: Should the **s** go forward ten
20:10 easy for the **s** to go forward ten
20:11 who made the **s** go back ten
1 Chronicles
29:15 days are like a **s** on the ground,
Job
7:2 we pant for a **s**, await our task
8:9 know because our days on earth are a **s**.
14:2 flee like a **s**, and don't last.
17:7 grief; my limbs like a **s**—all of them.
Psalms
36:7 finds refuge in the **s** of your wings.
57:1 refuge in the **s** of your wings
102:11 days are like a **s** soon gone. I'm
109:23 a lengthening **s**, I'm passing
144:4 puff of air; their days go by like a **s**.
Ecclesiastes
6:12 pass away like a **s**? Who can say what
Isaiah
26:19 for joy. Your **s** is a shadow of
30:2 refuge and hiding in Egypt's **s**.
30:3 hiding in Egypt's **s** your disgrace.
34:15 and hatch in its **s**. There too
38:8 once the **s** cast by the sun descends on
49:2 and hid me in the **s** of God's own
51:16 hid you in the **s** of my hand,
Hosea
14:7 live beneath my **s**, they will
Matthew
4:16 lived in the region and in **s** of death.
Luke
1:79 and in the **s** of death, to
Acts
5:15 at least Peter's **s** could fall on
Colossians
2:17 are only a **s** of what was
Hebrews
8:5 is a copy and **s** of the heavenly
9:5 casting their **s** over the seat of
10:1 The Law is a **s** of the good things that
12:18 burning fire, darkness, **s**, a whirlwind,

SHADRACH

Daniel
3:23 these three men, ***S***, Meshach, and

SHAKE

Psalms
46:3 the mountains ***s*** because of its
59:11 by your power ***s*** them up and bring
64:8 who sees them will just ***s*** their heads.
82:5 dark. All the earth's foundations ***s***.
99:1 the nations ***s***! He sits
109:25 they see me, they just ***s*** their heads.
Proverbs
6:1 your neighbor or ***s*** hands in
11:15 who refuses to ***s*** hands will be
22:26 Don't ***s*** hands to guarantee a loan
Isaiah
7:2 trees of a forest ***s*** when there is a
10:32 stand at Nob and ***s*** his fist at
13:13 the earth will ***s*** loose from its
30:28 to the neck, to ***s*** the nations with
52:2 ***S*** the dust off yourself; rise up; sit
Jeremiah
18:16 pass by are shocked and ***s*** their heads.
48:27 jokes? Didn't you ***s*** your head as if
Hosea
10:5 of Samaria ***s*** because of the
Joel
2:6 presence, peoples ***s*** with fear; all
2:10 them; the heavens ***s***. The sun and the
Amos
9:1 the foundations ***s***, shatter them on
9:9 and I will ***s*** the house of
Zephaniah
2:15 pass through her hiss and ***s*** their fist.
Matthew
10:14 to your words, ***s*** the dust off your
Mark
6:11 as you leave, ***s*** the dust off your
Luke
6:48 water couldn't ***s*** the house because
9:5 leave that city, ***s*** the dust off your
Hebrews
12:26 once more I will ***s*** not only the

SHAKEN

1 Chronicles
16:30 world firmly in place; it won't be ***s***.
Job
34:20 die; people are ***s*** and pass away.
Psalms
55:22 God will never let the righteous be ***s***!"
62:2 my stronghold!—I won't be ***s*** anymore.
62:6 my stronghold!—I will not be ***s***.
93:1 world firmly in place; it won't be ***s***.
96:10 it won't be ***s***. He will judge
109:23 passing away; I'm ***s*** off, like some
112:6 will never be ***s***; the righteous
125:1 Mount Zion: never ***s***, lasting forever.
Proverbs
10:30 will never be ***s***, but the wicked
Isaiah
21:3 Therefore, I'm ***s*** to my core in anguish.
54:10 the hills may be ***s***, but my faithful
Nahum
3:12 the trees are ***s***, the fruit falls
Matthew
24:29 and other heavenly bodies will be ***s***.
Mark
1:27 Everyone was ***s*** and questioned among
13:25 and other heavenly bodies will be ***s***.
Luke
4:36 They were all ***s*** and said to each other,
6:38 down, firmly ***s***, and overflowing—
21:26 bodies will be ***s***, causing people
Acts
2:25 he is at my right hand I won't be ***s***.
4:31 were gathered was ***s***. They were all
1 Thessalonians
3:3 any of you to be ***s*** by these
Hebrews
12:27 of what is ***s***—the things that a
12:28 that can't be ***s***, let's continue
Revelation
6:13 its fruit when ***s*** by a strong wind.

SHAME

Genesis
30:23 and said, "God has taken away my ***s***."
Leviticus
19:29 will become promiscuous and full of ***s***.
1 Samuel
20:30 with Jesse's son? ***S*** on you and on the
2 Samuel
13:13 could I hide my ***s***?
Ezra
9:7 and to utter ***s***, as is now the
Nehemiah
1:3 great trouble and ***s***! The wall around
Esther
6:12 home feeling great ***s***, his head covered.
Job
8:22 be clothed with ***s***, and the tent of
10:15 my head, full of ***s*** and facing my
11:3 will you mock and not be put to ***s***?
Psalms
25:2 let me be put to ***s***! Don't let my
25:20 let me be put to ***s*** because I take
31:1 let me be put to ***s***. Rescue me by
35:4 and put to ***s***. Let those who
40:14 and put to ***s***. Let those who
44:7 you who put those who hate us to ***s***.
53:5 will put them to ***s*** because God has
69:6 in you be put to ***s*** because of me.
71:1 LORD. Don't let me ever be put to ***s***!
74:21 oppressed live in ***s***. No, let the poor
83:16 their faces with ***s***, LORD, so that
86:17 it and be put to ***s***—show a sign that
89:45 life. You've wrapped him up in ***s***. Selah
97:7 idols, are put to ***s***. All gods bow
109:29 be dressed in ***s***; let them wear
119:31 LORD. Please don't let me be put to ***s***.
123:3 because we've had more than enough ***s***.
132:18 his enemies in ***s***, but the crown he
Proverbs
3:35 wise gain respect, but fools receive ***s***.
6:33 disgraced. His ***s*** will never be
11:2 comes, so does ***s***, but wisdom
13:18 Poverty and ***s*** come to those who don't
18:3 so does contempt; with ***s*** comes insult.
22:10 disappears; judgment and ***s*** also stop.
28:7 who befriend gluttons ***s*** their parents.
29:15 out of control ***s*** their mothers.

Song of Songs
8:1 kiss you, and no one would **s** me for it.
8:7 love, he would be laughed to utter **s**.
Isaiah
3:24 mourning clothes; instead of beauty, **s**.
23:9 of all beauty, to **s** all the honored
30:3 will become your **s**, hiding in
30:5 are no profit; rather, **s** and disgrace.
45:24 who are angry with him will come to **s**.
54:4 will forget the **s** of your youth;
61:7 Instead of **s**, their portion will be
Jeremiah
2:36 But Egypt will **s** you no less than
3:24 From our youth, **s** has devoured the
3:25 lie down in our **s**. Let our dishonor
6:15 but they have no **s**; they don't even
8:12 but they have no **s**; they don't even
13:26 skirt over your face and expose your **s**.
18:16 and brought utter **s** on it. All who
20:18 misery, and my days are filled with **s**?
23:40 and enduring **s** that no one will
46:12 hear of your **s**; the earth is
48:13 will be put to **s** on account of
48:39 turns away! What **s**! Moab has become
Lamentations
3:30 for a blow; he should be filled with **s**.
Ezekiel
7:18 On every face, **s**; on all their
16:63 because of your **s**, after I've
32:24 They bore their **s** like those who go
36:30 again endure the **s** of famine among
Daniel
12:2 life, others to **s** and eternal
Hosea
4:7 me; they exchanged their glory for **s**.
4:18 indeed, they "love"; **s** is their pride.
9:10 a thing of **s**; they became
10:6 will be put to **s**; Israel will be
Joel
2:26 my people will never again be put to **s**.
2:27 never again will my people be put to **s**.
Obadiah
1:10 brother Jacob, **s** will cover you,
Micah
1:11 In nakedness and **s** she will not go
7:10 enemy will see; **s** will cover her
Habakkuk
2:10 You plan **s** for your own house, cutting
Zephaniah
3:5 but the unrighteous one knows no **s**.
3:19 will change their **s** into praise and
Luke
13:17 were put to **s**, but all those in
Romans
2:23 the Law, do you **s** God by breaking
5:5 doesn't put us to **s**, because the love
9:33 has faith in him will not be put to **s**.
10:11 have faith in him won't be put to **s**.
1 Corinthians
1:27 foolish to **s** the wise. God
Philippians
1:20 I won't be put to **s** in anything.
Hebrews
6:6 again and exposing him to public **s**.
11:36 public **s** by being taunted
12:2 ignoring the **s**, for the sake of
13:13 to him outside the camp, bearing his **s**.
Jude
1:13 up their own **s**; wandering stars
Revelation
16:15 go around naked and exposed to **s**.

SHARE

Genesis
21:10 son won't **s** the inheritance
Exodus
12:4 a lamb, it should **s** one with a
18:22 for you, and they will **s** your load.
Leviticus
6:17 it the priests' **s** from my food
7:7 offering—they **s** the same
24:9 part of their **s** of the LORD's
Numbers
18:20 will you have a **s** among them. I am
Deuteronomy
18:2 but they won't **s** an inheritance with
1 Samuel
30:22 said, "We won't **s** any of the
30:24 on this plan? The **s** of those who went
1 Kings
4:28 brought their **s** of barley and
1 Chronicles
16:23 all the earth! **S** the news of his
Nehemiah
2:20 you will have no **s**, right, or claim
Psalms
68:23 can lap up their **s** of your enemies."
73:26 is my heart's rock and my **s** forever.
96:2 Bless his name! **S** the news of his
Proverbs
1:14 your lot with us; we'll **s** our money."
14:10 another person can't **s** its joy.
25:24 of a roof than to **s** a house with a
29:24 Those who **s** plunder with thieves hate
31:31 Let her **s** in the results of her work;
Ecclesiastes
3:19 and animals **s** the same fate.
Isaiah
53:12 I will give him a **s** with the great,
61:7 over their **s**. They will
Jeremiah
37:12 to secure his **s** of the family
Daniel
4:2 I'm delighted to **s** the signs and
Zechariah
6:13 two of them will **s** a peaceable plan.
Matthew
25:9 because if we **s** with you, there
Mark
12:2 the tenants his **s** of the fruit of
Luke
3:11 two shirts must **s** with the one who
11:37 invited him to **s** a meal with him,
14:1 Jesus went to **s** a meal in the
15:12 give me my **s** of the
20:10 the tenants his **s** of the fruit of
20:36 since they **s** in the
22:17 Take this and **s** it among
John
4:38 and you will **s** in their hard
17:13 so that they can **s** completely in my
Acts
1:17 us and received a **s** of this
8:21 have no part or **s** in God's word

SHARE [cont.]

24:15 in God I also **s** with my accusers,
Romans
15:27 Gentiles got a **s** of the Jewish
1 Corinthians
9:13 at the altar **s** part of what is
10:17 because we all **s** the one loaf of
10:18 eat the sacrifices **s** from the altar?
2 Corinthians
1:5 same way that we **s** so many of
6:14 righteousness **s** with that which
Galatians
4:30 woman's son won't **s** the inheritance
6:6 the word should **s** all good things
Ephesians
3:6 that they would **s** with the Jews in
4:28 have something to **s** with whoever is
Philippians
4:14 you have done well to **s** my distress.
1 Thessalonians
2:8 We were glad to **s** not only God's good
1 Timothy
6:18 to be generous, and to **s** with others.
2 Timothy
1:8 Instead, **s** the suffering for
2:3 Accept your **s** of suffering like a good
2:6 should get the first **s** of the crop.
Hebrews
2:14 the children **s** in flesh and
12:10 benefit so that we can **s** his holiness.
13:16 to do good and to **s** what you have
1 Peter
4:13 rejoice as you **s** Christ's
2 Peter
1:4 that you may **s** the divine nature
Jude
1:3 the salvation we **s**. Instead, I must
Revelation
20:6 those who have a **s** in the first
21:8 all liars—their **s** will be in the
22:19 that person's **s** in the tree of

SHARON

1 Chronicles
5:16 boundaries of all the open lands of **S**.
27:29 that grazed in **S**—Shitrai
Song of Songs
2:1 I'm a rose of the **S** plain, a lily of
Isaiah
33:9 it withered. **S** became like the
35:2 of Carmel and **S**. They will see
65:10 **S** will become a pasture for sheep, and
Acts
9:35 in Lydda and **S** saw him and

SHATTERED

Exodus
9:25 fields, and it **s** every tree out in
32:19 tablets down and **s** them in pieces at
Judges
5:26 his head; she **s** and pierced his
1 Samuel
2:4 warriors are **s**, but those who
2 Kings
25:13 The Chaldeans **s** the bronze columns, the
Job
4:10 beasts—yet the teeth of lions are **s**
16:12 at rest, but he **s** me, seized me by
24:20 and so wickedness is **s** like a tree.
29:17 I **s** the fangs of the wicked, rescued
Psalms
60:1 rejected us—**s** us. You've been
74:13 your power. You **s** the heads of the
105:33 their fig trees; **s** the trees of
107:14 and deep gloom; he **s** their chains.
107:16 because God has **s** bronze doors and
Isaiah
7:8 years Ephraim will be **s** as a nation
8:9 peoples, and be **s**! Listen, all
9:4 of Midian, you've **s** the yoke that
20:5 They will be **s** and shamed because of
21:9 of her gods are **s** on the ground!"
27:9 altar stones like **s** chalk, sacred
30:14 that is totally **s**. No piece from
Jeremiah
2:20 your yoke; I **s** your chains. But
5:5 broken their yoke and **s** the chains.
48:4 Moab is **s**; its young cry for help
48:17 scepter and magnificent staff are **s**!
48:38 mourning. I have **s** Moab like a
48:39 How it's **s**! Go wail! How Moab turns
50:23 been broken and **s** into pieces! How
51:8 Babylon fell and **s** into pieces. Wail
Lamentations
2:9 he broke and **s** her bars; her
2:11 of my people is **s**, because children
Ezekiel
6:6 incense altars **s**, and all your
27:34 Now you are **s** by the seas; your
Daniel
2:34 feet of iron and clay and **s** them.
2:35 all the parts **s** simultaneously
2:45 but not by hands, **s** the iron, bronze,
Obadiah
1:9 warriors will be **s**, Teman, and
Nahum
1:6 fire; the rocks are **s** because of him.

SHAVE

Leviticus
13:33 the person must **s** the area, without
14:8 their clothes, **s** off all of their
21:5 Priests must not **s** bald patches on
Numbers
6:9 he or she will **s** the head on the
6:18 The nazirite will **s** his ordained head
8:7 them, have them **s** their bodies,
Deuteronomy
14:1 and don't **s** your foreheads
21:12 home, she must **s** her head, cut her
Judges
13:5 allow a razor to **s** his head, because
16:19 a man and had him **s** off the seven
2 Samuel
14:26 head—he had to **s** his head at the
Isaiah
3:17 the Lord will **s** the heads of Zion's
7:20 the Lord will **s** with a razor
Jeremiah
16:6 in grief or **s** their heads in
Ezekiel
5:1 like a razor and **s** your head and
5:11 I myself will **s** you. I will not
44:20 They must neither **s** their heads nor let

Amos
8:10 clothes and **s** their heads

SHEBA
2 Samuel
20:1 man named **S**, Bichri's son,
1 Kings
10:1 When the queen of **S** heard reports about Solomon

SHECHEM
Genesis
34:2 When **S** the son of the Hivite Hamor and the country's
Joshua
24:1 of Israel at **S**. He summoned the
Judges
9:2 the leaders of **S**, 'Which do you

SHED
Genesis
9:6 his blood will be **s**; for in the
Leviticus
19:16 neighbor's blood is **s**; I am the LORD.
Numbers
35:33 the blood that is **s** in it, except by
Deuteronomy
21:7 hands did not **s** this blood. Our
1 Samuel
25:31 that you **s** blood needlessly
1 Kings
2:31 over the innocent blood that Joab **s**.
1 Chronicles
22:8 told me: You've **s** much blood and
28:3 are a military man and you've **s** blood.
Psalms
106:38 They **s** innocent blood, the blood of
Isaiah
59:7 they rush to **s** innocent blood.
Jeremiah
7:6 if you don't **s** the blood of the
15:5 Who will **s** tears over you?
Lamentations
4:13 those who **s** righteous blood
Ezekiel
5:11 you. I will not **s** a tear. You will
7:4 I won't **s** a tear for you or show any
22:4 blood that you've **s** is your
33:25 idols, and you **s** blood. Should you
Joel
3:19 whose land they have **s** innocent blood.
Romans
3:15 Their feet are quick to **s** blood
Hebrews
9:22 no forgiveness without blood being **s**.
Revelation
6:10 blood, which was **s** by those who live

SHEEP → SHEEP WITHOUT A SHEPHERD
Genesis
29:2 three flocks of **s** were lying down.
30:32 and spotted **s**, all of the black
31:19 out shearing his **s**, Rachel stole the
37:13 tending the **s** near Shechem?
38:12 to those who were shearing his **s**.
Exodus
12:5 take it from the **s** or from the goats.
13:13 ransom with a **s**. If you don't
20:24 sacrifices, your **s**, and your oxen. I
34:3 Don't even let **s** and cattle graze
34:19 the oldest offspring of cows and **s**.
34:20 may ransom with a **s**. Or if you don't
Leviticus
1:10 flock—whether **s** or goat—you must
3:7 If you present a **s** as the offering, you
4:32 If you offer a **s** as a purification
5:6 flock, either a **s** or goat, as a
7:23 not eat the fat of an ox, **s**, or goat.
9:3 young bull and a **s**—both one-year-old
12:8 cannot afford a **s**, she can bring
14:10 two flawless male **s**, one flawless one-
17:3 slaughters an ox, **s**, or goat inside
22:19 from the herd, the **s**, or the goats.
23:20 lift up the two **s**, along with the
27:26 Whether ox or **s**, it belongs to
Numbers
27:17 won't be like **s** without their
Deuteronomy
17:1 God any oxen or **s** that have defects
22:1 Israelite's ox or **s** wandering around
Joshua
6:21 young and old, cattle, **s**, and donkeys.
Judges
5:16 back among the **s** pens, listening
6:4 alive, not even **s**, oxen, or donkeys.
1 Samuel
15:14 this bleating of **s** in my ears and
2 Samuel
12:2 The rich man had a lot of **s** and cattle
24:17 wrong. But these **s**—what have they do
1 Kings
4:23 one hundred **s**; as well as deer,
8:5 chest sacrificed countless **s** and oxen.
8:63 twenty thousand **s** when the king and
2 Kings
3:4 King Mesha kept **s**. He would pay
5:26 trees, vineyards, **s**, cattle, or male
Ezra
6:9 bulls, rams, or **s** for entirely
Nehemiah
3:1 and built the **S** Gate. They
12:39 as far as the **S** Gate. They came
Psalms
8:7 all **s** and all cattle, the wild animals
44:11 us over like **s** for butchering;
44:22 we are considered **s** ready for
49:14 Like **s**, they're headed straight for
74:1 smolder at the **s** of your own
77:20 your people like **s** under the care of
78:52 people out like **s**, guiding them
79:13 people and the **s** of your very own
80:1 as if he were a **s**. You, who are
95:7 his pasture, the **s** in his hands. If
100:3 his people, the **s** of his own
107:41 makes their families as numerous as **s**!
119:176 off like a **s**, lost. Find your
Ecclesiastes
2:7 of cattle and **s**, more than any
Isaiah
7:21 one will raise a young cow and two **s**
53:6 Like **s** we had all wandered away, each
66:3 who sacrifices a **s** breaks a dog's
Jeremiah
23:1 and scatter the **s** of my pasture,

50:6 people were lost **s**; their shepherds
Ezekiel
34:21 ram all the weak **s** until you've
45:15 and one **s** from the flock for every two
Micah
7:14 your staff, the **s** of your
Zechariah
10:2 they wander like **s**, but they are
Matthew
7:15 you dressed like **s**, but inside they
10:6 to the lost **s**, the people of
10:16 sending you as **s** among wolves.
12:11 among you has a **s** that falls into a
12:12 a person than a **s**! So the Law
15:24 only to the lost **s**, the people of
18:12 had one hundred **s** and one of them
18:13 having that one **s** than about the
25:32 separates the **s** from the goats.
25:33 He will put the **s** on his right side.
26:31 shepherd, and the **s** of the flock will
Mark
14:27 shepherd, and the **s** will go off in
Luke
2:8 the fields, guarding their **s** at night.
15:4 had one hundred **s** and lost one of
15:6 with me because I've found my lost **s**.'
17:7 or tending **s**, 'Come! Sit down
John
5:2 near the **S** Gate in the north
10:3 for him, and the **s** listen to his
10:11 shepherd lays down his life for the **s**.
10:12 he leaves the **s** and runs away.
10:13 hand and the **s** don't matter to
10:14 I know my own **s** and they know me,
10:15 Father. I give up my life for the **s**.
10:16 I have other **s** that don't belong to
10:26 because you don't belong to my **s**.
10:27 My **s** listen to my voice. I know them
21:16 Jesus said to him, "Take care of my **s**."
21:17 you." Jesus said to him, "Feed my **s**.
Acts
8:32 reading: Like a **s** he was led to the
Romans
8:36 We are treated like **s** for slaughter.
Hebrews
11:37 the skins of **s** and goats, needy,
13:20 shepherd of the **s**, our Lord Jesus,
1 Peter
2:25 like straying **s**, you have now
Revelation
18:13 wheat; cattle, **s**, horses, and

SHEEP WITHOUT A SHEPHERD

1Ki 22:17; 2Ch 18:16; Is 13:14; Mt 9:36; Mk 6:34

SHEKEL

Genesis
24:22 weighing a half **s**, and two gold
Exodus
30:13 should pay a half **s** according to the
Leviticus
5:15 the sanctuary's **s**, as a
Numbers
3:47 to the sanctuary **s** of twenty gerahs
3:50 shekels, according to the sanctuary **s**.
7:13 to the sanctuary **s**, both of them
18:16 to the sanctuary **s**, which is twenty
1 Samuel
13:21 two-thirds of a **s** for plowshares
2 Kings
7:1 will sell for a **s** at Samaria's
7:16 did sell for a **s**, and two seahs of
7:18 will sell for a **s** at Samaria's
Nehemiah
10:32 one-third of a **s** each year for the
Ezekiel
45:12 The **s** must weigh twenty gerahs. Twenty shekels
Amos
8:5 enlarge the **s**, and deceive with
Matthew
17:27 you will find a **s** coin. Take it and

SHEKELS

Genesis
23:15 is four hundred **s** of silver between
24:22 bracelets for her arms, weighing ten **s**.
Exodus
21:32 pay thirty silver **s** to the slave's
Leviticus
5:15 in silver **s** according to the
27:3 is fifty silver **s** according to the
27:6 is five silver **s**, for a female
27:16 it: fifty silver **s** per homer of
Numbers
3:47 will receive five **s** each. You will
7:13 hundred thirty **s**, one silver basin
7:14 bowl weighing ten **s** full of incense;
31:52 sixteen thousand seven hundred fifty **s**.
Deuteronomy
22:19 hundred silver **s**, giving that to
22:29 give fifty silver **s** to the young
Joshua
7:21 two hundred **s** of silver, and a
Judges
8:26 seven hundred **s** of gold, not
2 Samuel
14:26 was two hundred **s** by the royal
21:16 was three hundred **s** of bronze, and he
24:24 and the oxen for fifty **s** of silver.
2 Kings
5:5 six thousand **s** of gold, and ten
6:25 sold for eighty **s** of silver and a
15:20 give fifty silver **s** each to Assyria's
1 Chronicles
21:25 Ornan six hundred **s** of gold by weight
2 Chronicles
3:9 weighed fifty **s**. He also covered
Nehemiah
5:15 as well as forty **s** of silver. Even
Isaiah
7:23 worth a thousand silver **s** once grew.
Jeremiah
32:9 out for him seventeen **s** of silver.
Ezekiel
45:12 gerahs. Twenty **s**, twenty-five sheke
Zechariah
11:12 out my wages, thirty **s** of silver.
11:13 I took the thirty **s** of silver and put

SHELAH

Genesis
10:24 fathered **S**, and Shelah

38:5 son and named him **S**. She was in
46:12 were Er, Onan, **S**, Perez, and
Numbers
26:20 their clans: from **S**, the Shelanite
1 Chronicles
1:18 father, and **S** was Eber's father.
Nehemiah
3:15 of the Pool of **S** of the King's
Luke
3:35 Reu son of Peleg son of Eber son of **S**

SHELTER

Exodus
9:19 So bring under **s** your livestock and all
9:20 servants and livestock inside for **s**.
Judges
9:15 come and take **s** in my shade; but
2 Samuel
22:3 of safety and my **s**. My savior! Save
Psalms
27:5 Because he will **s** me in his own
31:20 hide them in the **s** of your wings,
59:16 my stronghold, my **s** when I was
61:4 refuge in the **s** of your wings!
91:1 the Most High's **s**, camping in the
119:114 You are my **s** and my shield—I wait for
Isaiah
1:8 left like a small **s** in a vineyard,
4:6 hiding place and **s** from a stormy
28:15 place, and in falsehood we take **s**."
28:17 of lies, and water will overflow the **s**.
32:2 each like a **s** from the wind and a
Jeremiah
4:20 tents are destroyed, my **s** in a moment.
9:2 I could flee for **s** in the desert, to
48:45 refugees seek **s**. But fire is
49:3 eyes out, run for **s**. Milcom will
Ezekiel
17:23 in it and find **s** in the shade of
Daniel
4:14 flee from its **s**; the birds should
Joel
3:16 for his people, a **s** for the people of
Acts
27:4 the island to **s** us from the
27:7 sailed under the **s** of Crete off
27:16 sailing under the **s** of an island
Revelation
7:15 one seated on the throne will **s** them.

SHEMAIAH

1 Kings
12:22 God's word came to **S** the man of God,
2 Chronicles
12:5 Then the prophet **S** went to Rehoboam and the leaders
Jeremiah
29:24 Tell **S** the Nehelamite

SHEPHERD → SHEEP WITHOUT A SHEPHERD, SHEPHERD MY PEOPLE

Genesis
29:9 her father's flock since she was its **s**.
48:15 God who was my **s** from the
49:24 the name of the **s**, the rock of
Numbers
27:17 won't be like sheep without their **s**."
1 Samuel
17:15 Saul's side to **s** his father's
21:7 He was an Edomite and Saul's head **s**.
Psalms
23:1 The LORD is my **s**. I lack nothing.
28:9 your possession! **S** them and carry
49:14 will be their **s**—but those who do
78:71 nursing ewes to **s** his people Jacob,
80:1 Asaph. A psalm.] **S** of Israel,
Ecclesiastes
12:11 are like nails fixed firmly by a **s**.
Isaiah
40:11 Like a **s**, God will tend the flock; he
44:28 about Cyrus, "My **s**—he will do all t
61:5 will stay and **s** your sheep, and
63:11 from the sea, the **s** of the flock?
Jeremiah
10:21 The **s** kings have lost their senses and
31:10 and keep them safe, as a **s** his flock.
43:12 just as a **s** wraps his garment
49:19 can direct me? What **s** can withstand me?
50:44 can direct me? What **s** can withstand me?
Ezekiel
34:5 Without a **s**, my flock was scattered;
34:8 I live, without a **s**, my flock became
34:12 As a **s** seeks out the flock when some in
34:23 for them a single **s**, and he will feed
37:24 will be just one **s** for all of them.
Amos
3:12 Just as the **s** rescues two legs
7:14 son; but I am a **s**, and a trimmer of
Micah
5:4 He will stand and **s** his flock in the
5:6 They will **s** the land of Assyria with
7:14 **S** your people with your staff, the
Zechariah
10:2 are oppressed because there is no **s**.
11:4 LORD my God says: **S** the flock
11:9 I said, "I won't **s** you. Let the
11:15 again the equipment of a foolish **s**
11:16 to appoint a **s** in the land. He
11:17 Doom, foolish **s** who forsakes the flock.
13:7 arise against my **s**, against the man
Matthew
25:32 other, just as a **s** separates the
26:31 I will hit the **s**, and the sheep of
Mark
14:27 I will hit the **s**, and the sheep
John
10:2 through the gate is the **s** of the sheep.
10:11 I am the good **s**. The good shepherd
10:12 he isn't the **s**; the sheep aren't
10:14 I am the good **s**. I know my own sheep
10:16 there will be one flock, with one **s**.
Acts
20:28 supervisors, to **s** God's church,
Hebrews
13:20 back the great **s** of the sheep, our
1 Peter
2:25 returned to the **s** and guardian of
5:2 over it. Don't **s** because you must,
5:3 Don't **s** by ruling over those entrusted
5:4 when the chief **s** appears, you will
Revelation
7:17 the throne will **s** them. He will

SHEPHERD MY PEOPLE

2Sa 5:2; 7:7; 1Ch 11:2; 17:6; Mt 2:6

SHEPHERDS

Genesis
26:20 Isaac's **s** argued with Gerar's
29:3 there, the **s** would roll the
46:32 The men are **s**, because they own
46:34 think all **s** are beneath their
47:3 servants are **s**, both we and our
Exodus
2:17 But some **s** came along and rudely chased
2:19 from a bunch of **s**. Afterward, he
Numbers
14:33 children will be **s** in the desert for
1 Samuel
25:7 As you know, your **s** were with us in
2 Kings
10:12 Beth-eked of the **S** was on his way.
Song of Songs
1:8 little goats by the tents of the **s**.
Isaiah
13:20 camp there; no **s** will rest flocks
31:4 though a band of **s** is summoned
56:11 enough. They are **s** who don't
Jeremiah
3:15 I will appoint **s** with whom I'm pleased,
12:10 Many **s** have destroyed my vineyard; they have trampled
51:23 you I will crush **s** and flocks. With
Ezekiel
34:7 So now **s**, hear the LORD's word
34:10 I'm against the **s**! I will hold them
Amos
1:1 Amos, one of the **s** of Tekoa. He
1:2 pastures of the **s** wither, and the
Micah
5:5 against him seven **s** and eight human
Nahum
3:18 Your **s** have fallen asleep, king of
Zephaniah
2:6 with wells for **s** and pens for the
Zechariah
10:3 hot against the **s**; I will punish
11:3 appears among the **s** because their
11:5 And their own **s** won't spare them.
11:8 I removed three **s** in one month when I
Luke
2:8 Nearby **s** were living in the fields,
2:15 to heaven, the **s** said to each
2:18 it was amazed at what the **s** told them.
2:20 The **s** returned home, glorifying and
1 Corinthians
9:7 its fruit? Who **s** a flock and
1 Peter
5:2 Like **s**, tend the flock of God among

SHIELD

Deuteronomy
33:29 LORD! He's the **s** that helps you,
Judges
5:8 there wasn't a **s** or spear to be
1 Samuel
17:7 pounds. His **s**-bearer walked in f
17:41 to David, and his **s**-bearer
2 Samuel
1:21 mighty warrior's **s** was defiled—the
22:3 in him!—he's my **s** and my
22:31 and true. He is a **s** for all who take
22:36 given me the **s** of your
1 Kings
10:16 using fifteen pounds of gold in each **s**,
10:17 of gold in each **s**. The king placed
2 Kings
19:32 the city with a **s**. He won't build a
1 Chronicles
5:18 who carried **s** and sword, drew
12:8 armed with **s** and spear, who
12:24 Judah, carrying **s** and spear, 6,800
12:34 well as 37,000 armed with **s** and spear;
2 Chronicles
9:15 pounds of hammered gold in each **s**;
9:16 gold in each **s**. The king placed
17:17 hundred thousand armed with bow and **s**;
Job
15:26 with a massive and strong **s**.
Psalms
3:3 you, LORD, are my **s**! You are my
5:12 You cover them with favor like a **s**.
7:10 God is my **s**; he saves those whose
18:2 in him!—he's my **s**, my salvation's
18:30 and true. He is a **s** for all who take
18:35 given me the **s** of your
28:7 strength and my **s**. My heart trusts
33:20 in the LORD. He is our help and our **s**.
35:2 Grab a **s** and armor; stand up and help
59:11 down, you who are our **s** and my Lord.
76:3 of the bow, the **s**, the sword—even
84:9 Look at our **s**, God; pay close
84:11 LORD is a sun and **s**; God is favor and
89:18 because our **s** is the LORD's own; our
91:4 His faithfulness is a protective **s**.
115:9 in the LORD! God is their help and **s**.
115:10 of Aaron! God is their help and **s**.
115:11 in the LORD! God is their help and **s**.
119:114 my shelter and my **s**—I wait for your
144:2 my rescuer, my **s**, in whom I take
Proverbs
2:7 He is a **s** for those who
24:34 deprivation like a man with a **s**.
30:5 tried and true; a **s** for those who
Isaiah
12:2 strength and my **s**; he has become my
22:6 and horsemen, and Kir uncovered the **s**.
31:5 forces will **s** Jerusalem:
37:33 the city with a **s**. He won't build a
Jeremiah
46:9 with your **s** in hand, you
Ezekiel
23:24 great army, with **s**, buckler, and
38:4 with buckler and **s**, all of them
38:5 all of them equipped with **s** and helmet.
Nahum
2:5 wall, and the portable **s** is set up.
Ephesians
6:16 all, carry the **s** of faith so that

SHIELDS

Deuteronomy
33:12 The Lord always **s** him; he rests on

2 Samuel
8:7 took the gold **s** carried by
1 Kings
10:16 body-sized **s** of hammered gold,
10:17 hundred small **s** of hammered gold,
14:26 even all the gold **s** that Solomon had
14:27 them with bronze **s** and assigned them
14:28 would carry the **s** and then return
2 Kings
11:10 spears and **s**, which were kept
1 Chronicles
18:7 took the gold **s** carried by
Nehemiah
4:16 held the spears, **s**, bows, and body
Song of Songs
4:4 built! A thousand **s** are hung upon it—
Isaiah
21:5 Arise, captains! Polish the **s**."
Jeremiah
46:3 Grab your **s** and prepare for war
51:11 prepare your **s**. The LORD is
Ezekiel
26:8 siege ramps against you, and set up **s**.
27:10 By hanging their **s** and helmets on
32:27 heads and their **s** over their bones.
Nahum
2:3 The **s** of his warriors are red; his

SHILOH
Joshua
18:1 assembled at **S** and set up the
1 Samuel
1:24 brought him to the LORD's house at **S**.
3:21 to appear at **S** because the LORD
Psalms
78:60 the sanctuary at **S**, the tent where

SHIMEI
Exodus
6:17 Libni and **S** and their clans.
2 Samuel
16:5 His name was **S**; he was Gera's

SHINE
Genesis
1:15 of the sky to **s** on the earth."
1:17 the dome of the sky to **s** on the earth,
Numbers
6:25 make his face **s** on you and be
Psalms
31:16 **S** your face on your servant; save me by
34:5 look to God will **s**; their faces are
37:6 righteousness **s** like the dawn,
67:1 let God make his face **s** on us, Selah
80:3 Make your face **s** so that we can be
80:7 Make your face **s** so that we can be
80:19 Make your face **s** so that we can be
104:15 makes the face **s**, and bread, which
112:4 They **s** in the dark for others who do
119:135 **S** your face on your servant, and teach
132:18 shame, but the crown he wears will **s**."
139:12 Nighttime would **s** bright as day
Isaiah
13:10 it rises; the moon will no longer **s**.
58:10 your light will **s** in the darkness,
60:1 Arise! **S**! Your light has come; the
60:2 the LORD will **s** upon you; God's
60:19 nor will the moon **s** for illumination
Daniel
9:17 pleas for help. **S** your face on your
12:3 in wisdom will **s** like the sky.
Matthew
5:16 let your light **s** before people, so
13:43 righteous will **s** like the sun in
2 Corinthians
4:6 that light should **s** out of the
Ephesians
5:14 the dead, and Christ will **s** on you.
Philippians
2:15 these people you **s** like stars in the
Revelation
18:23 a lamp will never **s** among you again.
21:23 or the moon to **s** on it, because
22:5 the Lord God will **s** on them, and they

SHIP
Proverbs
30:19 the way of a **s** out on the open
Isaiah
33:21 boat will go, no majestic **s** will cross.
Ezekiel
27:9 Every seagoing **s** and its sailors
Jonah
1:3 Jaffa and found a **s** headed for
1:4 on the sea; the **s** looked like it
1:5 that was in the **s** into the sea to
Acts
20:13 We went on to the **s** and sailed for
21:2 We found a **s** crossing over to
27:2 We boarded a **s** from Adramyttium that
27:30 to abandon the **s** by lowering the
27:44 debris from the **s**. In this way,
28:11 out to sea in a **s** that had spent

SHIPS
Genesis
49:13 at the harbor of **s**, his border will
Numbers
24:24 **S** from Kittim will attack Asshur; they
Deuteronomy
28:68 back to Egypt in **s**, by the route I
Judges
5:17 remain with the **s**? Asher stayed by
1 Kings
10:22 of Tarshish-style **s** was at sea with
22:48 Tarshish-styled **s** to go to Ophir
22:49 sailors on the **s**." But Jehoshaphat
2 Chronicles
8:18 servants bring **s** to Solomon, along
20:36 Tarshish-styled **s**, and they built
20:37 have made." The **s** were wrecked and
Job
9:26 sweep by like **s** made of reeds, as
Psalms
48:7 wind when it smashes the **s** of Tarshish.
104:26 There go the **s** on it, and Leviathan,
107:23 on the ocean in **s**, making their
Proverbs
31:14 fleet of merchant **s**, bringing food
Isaiah
2:16 against all the **s** of Tarshish; against
18:1 land of winged **s**, beyond the
23:1 about Tyre. Wail, **s** of Tarshish,
23:14 Wail, **s** of Tarshish, for your fortress

60:9 the coastlands. **S** from Tarshish are
Ezekiel
27:25 The **s** of Tarshish carried your goods.
30:9 messengers in **s** will go out from me to
Daniel
11:30 Kittim **s** will fight against him, and he
11:40 horses and many **s**. He will invade
James
3:4 Consider **s**: they are so large that
Revelation
8:9 and a third of the **s** were destroyed.
18:19 all who have **s** at sea became so

SHOCKED

Genesis
27:33 Isaac was so **s** that he trembled
1 Kings
9:8 now, will be **s** and will whistle,
2 Chronicles
7:21 now—will be **s** and will wonder,
Isaiah
29:9 Be **s** and stunned; blind yourselves; be
Jeremiah
4:9 be stunned, and the prophets will be **s**.
8:9 be shamed and **s** when they are
18:16 who pass by are **s** and shake their
19:8 who pass by it will be **s** at its pain.
48:20 is shamed and **s**; weep and wail!
49:17 who pass by will be **s** by its injuries.
50:13 Babylon will be **s**; they will gasp
Daniel
4:19 Belteshazzar, was **s** for a bit. What
Joel
1:11 Be **s**, you farmers; howl, you
Mark
5:42 She was twelve years old. They were **s**!
10:26 They were **s** even more and said to each
Luke
2:48 him, they were **s**. His mother said,
John
4:27 arrived and were **s** that he was

SHOOK

Exodus
15:14 heard, they **s** in terror; horror
19:16 All the people in the camp **s** with fear.
19:18 while the whole mountain **s** violently.
20:18 the people **s** with fear and
Judges
5:4 fields, the land **s**, the sky poured
1 Samuel
4:5 such a loud shout that the ground **s**.
14:15 and the raiders **s** with fear. The
2 Samuel
22:8 earth rocked and **s**; the sky's
1 Kings
1:40 The ground **s** at their noise.
Nehemiah
5:13 I also **s** out the fold of my robe,
Job
4:14 and dread struck me; all of my bones **s**.
26:11 Heaven's pillars **s**, terrified by his
Psalms
18:7 earth rocked and **s**; the bases of the
68:8 the earth **s**! Yes, heaven poured down
77:16 you and reeled! Even the deep depths **s**!
77:18 whole world; the earth **s** and quaked.
Isaiah
6:4 The doorframe **s** at the sound of their
7:2 of their people **s** as the trees of a
14:16 who rattled the earth, who **s** kingdoms,
Matthew
27:51 bottom. The earth **s**, the rocks split,
28:4 of him that they **s** with fear and
Mark
1:26 unclean spirit **s** him and screamed,
Luke
9:42 him down and **s** him violently.
Acts
13:51 Paul and Barnabas **s** the dust from their
16:26 that it **s** the prison's
18:6 slandered him, he **s** the dust from his
28:5 Paul **s** the snake into the fire and
Galatians
2:9 be key leaders, **s** hands with me and
Hebrews
12:26 His voice **s** the earth then, but now he

SHOOT

1 Samuel
20:20 third day I will **s** an arrow to the
20:36 the arrow that I **s**." So the boy ran
2 Samuel
11:20 you know they would **s** from the wall?
2 Kings
13:17 king did so. "Now **s**!" Elisha told
19:32 city. He won't **s** a single arrow
1 Chronicles
12:2 either hand to **s** arrows or sling
2 Chronicles
26:15 wall designed to **s** arrows and large
Job
41:19 Shafts of fire **s** from his mouth; like
Psalms
11:2 ready to secretly **s** those whose heart
64:4 places so as to **s** an innocent
64:7 But God will **s** them with an arrow!
144:6 the enemy! **S** your arrows and
Isaiah
11:1 A **s** will grow up from the stump of
37:33 city. He won't **s** a single arrow
40:24 scarcely is their **s** rooted in the
60:21 They are the **s** that I planted,
Jeremiah
50:14 you archers; now **s** at her; save none
Ezekiel
17:22 pluck a tender **s** from its crown,
Amos
2:15 Those who **s** the bow won't survive. Fast
Habakkuk
3:11 your arrows **s**, your spear at

SHORT

1 Samuel
21:15 Am I **s** on insane people that you've
Job
20:5 of the wicked is **s**, the joy of the
21:4 another human; why is my patience **s**?
24:24 are exalted for a **s** time, but no
Psalms
37:38 the future of the wicked will be cut **s**.
39:5 made my days so **s**; my lifetime is
89:47 Remember how **s** my life is! Have you
90:4 past, like a **s** period during the

102:23 in midstride, cutting my days **s**.
Proverbs
10:27 the years of the wicked will be cut **s**.
14:17 **S**-tempered people make stupid
Ecclesiastes
9:8 white; don't run **s** of oil for your
Isaiah
28:20 The bed is too **s** to stretch out, and
65:20 the one falling **s** of a hundred will
Jeremiah
27:16 to you, "In a **s** while, the temple
Micah
2:7 patience cut **s**? Are these his
Matthew
24:22 whom God chose that time will be cut **s**.
26:39 Then he went a **s** distance farther and
26:73 A **s** time later those standing there
Luke
19:3 was, but, being a **s** man, he couldn't
Acts
26:28 that, in such a **s** time, you've made
26:29 Whether it is a **s** or a long time, I
Romans
3:23 have sinned and fall **s** of God's glory,
1 Corinthians
7:5 both agree for a **s** period of time to
7:29 time has drawn **s**. From now on,
11:6 a woman to have **s** hair or to be
2 Corinthians
7:8 made you sad, though only for a **s** time.
Hebrews
13:22 I've only written a **s** letter to you!
James
4:14 for only a **s** while before it
1 Peter
1:6 distressed for a **s** time by various
Revelation
12:12 he knows that he only has a **s** time."
17:10 he must remain for only a **s** time.

SHOULDER

Genesis
21:14 the boy in her **s** sling and sent
24:15 coming out with a water jar on her **s**.
45:14 and wept, and Benjamin wept on his **s**.
49:15 He lowered his **s** to haul loads and
Exodus
28:7 will have two **s** pieces attached
39:4 They made **s** pieces for it attached to
Numbers
6:19 will take the **s** from the ram
Deuteronomy
18:3 the priest the **s**, the jaws, and
Joshua
4:5 up a stone on his **s** to match the
Judges
9:48 them onto his **s**. Then he ordered
14:16 wife cried on his **s** and said, "You
Nehemiah
9:29 turned a stubborn **s**, became
Job
31:22 arm fall from my **s**, my forearm be
31:36 bear it on my **s**, tie it around me
Isaiah
10:27 burden from your **s** and destroy the
22:22 house on his **s**; what he opens no
Ezekiel
12:6 While they watch, **s** your backpack and
12:12 Their prince will **s** his backpack at
24:4 good piece. With **s** and thigh, the
29:18 bald, and every **s** was rubbed raw,
34:21 You shove with **s** and flank, and with
Zechariah
7:11 turned a cold **s** and stopped

SHOULDERS

Genesis
9:23 it over their **s**, walked backward,
Exodus
12:34 pans wrapped in their robes on their **s**.
28:12 their names on his two **s** as a reminder.
Numbers
7:9 things that had to be carried on the **s**.
Judges
16:3 put them on his **s** and carried them
1 Samuel
9:2 he stood head and **s** above everyone
10:23 he was head and **s** taller than
2 Kings
6:31 Shaphat's son, remains on his **s** today!"
1 Chronicles
15:15 poles on their **s**, just as Moses
2 Chronicles
35:3 it around on your **s** anymore. Now
Psalms
81:6 burden off your **s**; your hands are
Isaiah
9:4 staff on their **s**, and the rod of
9:6 will be on his **s**. He will be named
14:25 his burden will be taken from their **s**.
30:6 on donkeys' **s** and their
46:7 the idol on their **s** and support it;
49:22 will carry your daughters on their **s**.
Ezekiel
29:7 and make their **s** sore; when they
Daniel
1:20 them head and **s** above all the
Matthew
23:4 put them on the **s** of others, but
Luke
15:5 he is thrilled and places it on his **s**.
Acts
15:10 a burden on the **s** of these

SHOUT

Leviticus
13:45 upper lip, and **s** out, "Unclean!
Joshua
6:5 all the people **s** out a loud war
6:10 people, "Don't **s**. Don't let your
6:16 to the people, "**S**, because the LORD
Judges
7:18 camp. And then **s**, 'For the LORD
1 Samuel
4:5 out such a loud **s** that the ground
4:6 the sound of that **s**, they asked,
17:52 jumped up with a **s** and chased the
26:14 Who are you to **s** to the king?"
1 Kings
18:27 fun of them: "**S** louder! Certainly
22:36 the sun set, a **s** spread throughout
1 Chronicles
16:33 the forest will **s** out joyfully

SHOUT [cont.]

Ezra
3:13 of the joyful ***s*** from the sound of
Esther
6:9 he goes, have him ***s***, 'This is what
Job
8:21 joy, your lips with a victorious ***s***.
19:7 not answered; I ***s***—but there is no
30:5 from society, ***s*** at them as if to
33:26 with a joyful ***s***. God rewards a
35:9 heavy oppression; ***s*** under the power
39:7 the town, doesn't hear the driver's ***s***,
Psalms
33:1 are righteous, ***s*** joyfully to the
35:27 set right for me ***s*** for joy and
47:1 all you people! ***S*** joyfully to God
47:5 up with a joyous ***s***—the LORD with
59:16 morning I will ***s*** out loud about
60:8 shoe at Edom. I ***s*** in triumph over
63:7 help to me and I ***s*** for joy in the
65:13 in grain—they ***s*** for joy; they
66:1 A song. A psalm.] ***S*** joyfully to God,
67:4 celebrate and ***s*** with joy because
81:1 our strength! ***S*** for joy to
89:12 Tabor and Hermon ***s*** praises to your
89:15 the celebratory ***s*** are truly happy!
95:1 raise a joyful ***s*** to the rock of
95:2 thanks! Let's ***s*** songs of joy to
96:12 of the forest too will ***s*** out joyfully
98:4 ***S*** triumphantly to the LORD, all the
98:6 and a horn blast, ***s*** triumphantly
100:1 psalm of thanks.] ***S*** triumphantly to
108:9 shoe at Edom. I ***s*** in triumph over
132:9 let your faithful ***s*** out with joy!
132:16 its faithful will ***s*** out loud with joy!
145:7 they will ***s*** joyfully about
149:5 glory; let them ***s*** for joy on their
Proverbs
8:1 Wisdom cry out and Understanding ***s***?
29:9 the fools ***s***, they laugh
Isaiah
12:6 ***S*** and sing for joy, city of Zion,
15:4 armed men of Moab ***s***, spirits
24:14 west they will ***s*** about the LORD's
26:19 in the dust will ***s*** for joy. Your
40:9 your voice and ***s***, messenger
42:2 won't cry out or ***s*** aloud or make his
42:11 and its towns ***s*** aloud, the
42:13 up rage. God will ***s***, will roar; over
44:23 LORD has acted; ***s***, depths of the
48:20 this with a loud ***s***, proclaim it;
58:1 ***S*** loudly; don't hold back; raise your
Jeremiah
31:6 when the watchmen ***s*** from the
31:7 people of Jacob; ***s*** for the leading
49:29 their camels and ***s*** as you go: "Panic
50:2 back; just ***s*** it: "Babylon is
50:15 Raise a victory ***s*** against her on every
Joel
2:1 in Zion; give a ***s*** on my holy
Zephaniah
3:14 Daughter Zion! ***S***, Israel! Rejoice
Matthew
12:19 He won't argue or ***s***, and nobody will
27:46 out with a loud ***s***, "Eli, Eli, lama
27:50 cried out with a loud ***s***. Then he died.
Mark
10:47 he began to ***s***, "Jesus, Son of
15:34 out with a loud ***s***, "Eloi, eloi,
Luke
19:40 they were silent, the stones would ***s***."
Acts
19:28 and began to ***s***, "Great is
Galatians
4:27 Break out with a ***s***, you who have not
1 Thessalonians
4:16 the signal of a ***s*** by the head angel

SHOUTED

Joshua
6:20 Then the people ***s***. They blew the
1 Samuel
10:24 Then the people ***s***, "Long live the
Ezra
3:11 All of the people ***s*** with praise to
3:12 although many others ***s*** loudly with joy.
10:12 whole assembly ***s*** in reply, "Yes.
Job
38:7 in unison and all the divine beings ***s***?
Isaiah
6:3 They ***s*** to each other, saying: "Holy,
36:13 stood up and ***s*** in Hebrew at the
Lamentations
2:7 to enemies. They ***s*** in the LORD's own
4:15 Unclean!" was ***s*** at them, "Go
Matthew
14:30 began to sink, he ***s***, "Lord, rescue
15:22 came out and ***s***, "Show me mercy,
20:30 passing by, they ***s***, "Show us mercy,
20:31 quiet. But they ***s*** even louder,
21:9 and behind him ***s***, "Hosanna to the
27:23 he done?" They ***s*** even louder,
Mark
3:11 at his feet and ***s***, "You are God's
10:48 be quiet, but he ***s*** even louder, "Son
15:13 They ***s*** back, "Crucify him!
15:14 he done?" They ***s*** even louder,
Luke
8:28 him. Then he ***s***, "What have you
9:38 from the crowd ***s***, "Teacher, I beg
16:24 He ***s***, 'Father Abraham, have mercy on
18:38 The blind man ***s***, "Jesus, Son of David,
18:39 be quiet, but he ***s*** even louder, "Son
23:18 one voice they ***s***, "Away with this
John
7:37 stood up and ***s***, "All who are
11:43 said this Jesus ***s*** with a loud
12:13 to meet him. They ***s***, "Hosanna!
12:44 Jesus ***s***, "Whoever believes in me
18:40 They ***s***, "Not this man! Give us
19:6 saw him, they ***s*** out, "Crucify,
Acts
7:60 to his knees, he ***s***, "Lord, don't
14:11 done, the crowd ***s*** in the Lycaonian
14:14 and rushed out into the crowd. They ***s***,
16:28 But Paul ***s*** loudly, "Don't harm
19:32 confusion. Some ***s*** one thing, others
19:34 a Jew, they all ***s*** in unison, "Great
21:34 Some in the crowd ***s*** one thing, others
22:22 this. Then they ***s***, "Away with this

SHOUTS

2 Samuel
6:15 LORD's chest with ***s*** and trumpet

1 Chronicles
15:28 covenant with **s** of joy,
2 Chronicles
15:14 a loud voice, **s** of joy, and
Esther
8:15 city of Susa greeted him with **s** of joy.
Psalms
27:6 sacrifices with **s** of joy! I will
29:9 but in his temple everyone **s**, "Glory!"
33:3 new song! Play your best with joyful **s**!
42:4 with joyous **s** and thanksgiving
100:2 Come before him with **s** of joy!
126:2 with joyful **s**. It was even
126:5 tears reap the harvest with joyful **s**.
126:6 home with joyful **s**, carrying bales
Proverbs
1:20 Wisdom **s** in the street; in the public
8:3 the city, at the entrances she **s**:
11:10 the wicked perish, there are **s** of joy.
Isaiah
16:10 one sings, no one **s**. No treader
Jeremiah
48:33 presses. No one **s** with joy while
Amos
1:2 from Zion. He **s** from Jerusalem;
Zechariah
4:7 the capstone to **s** of great

SHOW → SHOW ME MERCY, SHOW MERCY

Genesis
12:1 for the land that I will **s** you.
26:2 in the land that I will **s** you.
Exodus
9:16 in order to **s** you my power and
25:9 that I will **s** you for the
33:18 said, "Please **s** me your glorious
Leviticus
19:15 case. Do not **s** favoritism to the
Numbers
20:12 trust me to **s** my holiness
27:14 my command to **s** them my holiness
Deuteronomy
4:6 because that will **s** your wisdom and
16:19 justice; don't **s** favoritism. Don't
19:13 **S** no mercy to such killers. Remove
25:12 you must cut off her hand. **S** no mercy
Joshua
5:6 to them never to **s** them the land
Judges
1:24 said to him, "**S** us the way into
4:22 Come and I'll **s** you the man
6:17 approval, please **s** me a sign that
1 Samuel
14:8 go over to the men and **s** ourselves.
2 Samuel
9:1 that I could **s** faithful love for
22:26 the faithful; you **s** integrity toward
Psalms
18:25 the faithful; you **s** integrity toward
50:23 path that I will **s** divine salvation."
68:28 strength, God! **S** how strong you
80:1 winged heavenly creatures. **S** yourself
85:7 **S** us your faithful love, LORD! Give us
86:17 **S** me a sign of your goodness so that
91:16 with old age. I'll **s** you my salvation."
94:1 God—avenging God, **s** yourself!
106:4 the favor you **s** your people.
143:8 I trust you. **S** me the way I
Proverbs
6:34 a man rage; he'll **s** no mercy on his
24:10 If you **s** yourself weak on a day of
28:21 Those who **s** favoritism aren't good;
29:11 Fools **s** all their anger, but the wise
30:6 correct you and **s** you to be a liar.
Ecclesiastes
3:18 God tests them to **s** them that they
10:3 the street; they **s** everyone that
Isaiah
30:18 will rise up to **s** you compassion.
Jeremiah
6:23 are cruel; they **s** no mercy. Their
18:17 them, I will **s** them my back, not
42:3 the LORD your God **s** us where we
50:42 are cruel and **s** no mercy. Their
51:3 their armor. **S** no mercy to her
Lamentations
3:32 grief, he will **s** compassion in
Hosea
7:2 Now their deeds **s** who they are,
Micah
7:15 of Egypt, I will **s** Israel wonderful
Nahum
3:5 your face; I will **s** nations your
Habakkuk
1:3 Why do you **s** me injustice and look at
Zechariah
1:9 me said, "I will **s** you what they
1:17 LORD will again **s** compassion to
7:9 decisions; **s** kindness and
Malachi
2:9 keep my ways or **s** respect for
Matthew
4:19 said, "and I'll **s** you how to fish
16:1 they asked him to **s** them a sign from
20:30 they shouted, "**S** us mercy, Lord,
22:19 **S** me the coin used to pay the tax." And
John
2:18 What miraculous sign will you **s** us?"
14:8 said, "Lord, **s** us the Father;
16:8 he comes, he will **s** the world it was
21:19 He said this to **s** the kind of death by
Romans
2:15 They **s** the proof of the Law written on
3:4 So that it can **s** that you are
9:15 mercy, and I'll **s** compassion to
9:22 he wanted to **s** his wrath and to
12:17 evil actions, but **s** respect for what
1 Corinthians
12:31 And I'm going to **s** you an even
2 Corinthians
10:11 our actions will **s** that we are the
Ephesians
2:7 God did this to **s** future generations
2 Thessalonians
2:4 displaying himself to **s** that he is God.
1 Timothy
1:16 Jesus could **s** his endless
3:2 They should **s** hospitality and
5:24 the sins of other people **s** up later.
Titus
1:8 they should **s** hospitality, love
2:7 of good actions. **S** integrity,
2:10 they should **s** that they are
3:2 kind, and **s** complete courtesy

SHOW [cont.]

Hebrews
6:11 each of you to ***s*** the same effort
10:24 each other to ***s*** love and to do
James
2:18 Instead, I'll ***s*** you my faith by
3:13 understanding? ***S*** that your actions
1 Peter
4:8 Above all, ***s*** sincere love to each
Revelation
1:1 God gave him to ***s*** his servants what
4:1 here, and I will ***s*** you what must
17:1 he said, I will ***s*** you the judgment
21:9 he said, "I will ***s*** you the bride,
22:6 sent his angel to ***s*** his servants what

SHOW ME MERCY

Mt 15:22; Mk 10:47; 10:48; Lk 18:38; 18:39

SHOW MERCY

Ps 102:14; 119:29; Mt 5:7; 17:15; Lk 18:13; 2Ti 1:16

SHOWED

Deuteronomy
4:36 you. On earth he ***s*** you his great
34:1 Jericho. The LORD ***s*** him the whole
Matthew
4:8 high mountain and ***s*** him all the
Luke
4:5 a high place and ***s*** him in a single
24:40 he said this, he ***s*** them his hands
John
20:20 he said this, he ***s*** them his hands
Revelation
21:10 mountain, and he ***s*** me the holy city,
22:1 Then the angel ***s*** me the river of

SHRINE

1 Samuel
9:12 today for the people at the ***s***.
10:5 down from the ***s*** preceded by
1 Kings
3:4 went to the great ***s*** at Gibeon in
11:7 Solomon built a ***s*** to Chemosh the
2 Kings
17:11 At every ***s*** they burned incense, just as
23:15 That was the ***s*** made by Jeroboam,
1 Chronicles
16:39 the LORD's dwelling at the ***s*** in Gibeon.
21:29 offerings were then at the ***s*** in Gibeon,
2 Chronicles
1:3 went to the ***s*** at Gibeon because
1:13 went from the ***s*** in Gibeon, from
Isaiah
16:12 out going to the ***s***, and comes to his
Jeremiah
19:4 this place into a ***s*** for other gods,
Ezekiel
20:29 to them, What ***s*** are you going to

SHRINES → BUILT SHRINES

Leviticus
26:30 eliminate your ***s***, chop down your
Numbers
21:28 and swallowed up the ***s*** of the Arnon.
33:52 images. You will eliminate all their ***s***.
1 Kings
3:2 at the ***s*** because a temple
3:3 sacrificed and burned incense at the ***s***.
12:31 Jeroboam made ***s*** on the high places and appointed priests
13:2 priests of the ***s*** who offer incense
15:14 Though the ***s*** weren't eliminated,
22:43 didn't remove the ***s***. The people
2 Kings
12:3 However, the ***s*** were not removed. People kept sacrificing
15:35 didn't remove the ***s***. The people
18:4 He removed the ***s***. He smashed the
23:8 he defiled the ***s*** where the priests
23:19 removed all the ***s*** on the high hills
23:20 priests of the ***s*** who were there,
2 Chronicles
11:15 priests for the ***s*** and the goat and
14:5 also removed the ***s*** and incense
15:17 Although the ***s*** weren't removed from
17:6 again removed the ***s*** and the sacred
20:33 didn't remove the ***s***. The people were
21:11 constructed ***s*** throughout
34:3 Jerusalem of the ***s***, the sacred
Psalms
78:58 with their many ***s***; they angered him
Isaiah
15:2 temple, to the ***s*** to weep. Moab
36:7 he the one whose ***s*** and altars
Ezekiel
6:3 a sword against you and destroy your ***s***.
16:16 to make colorful ***s*** and prostituted
43:7 and with their kings' corpses at the ***s***.
Hosea
10:8 of Israel, the ***s*** of Aven will be
Amos
7:9 The ***s*** of Isaac will be made desolate,
Micah
1:3 down and tread on the ***s*** of the earth.
1:5 for the ***s*** of Judah? Isn't
Matthew
17:4 I'll make three ***s***: one for you, one
Mark
9:5 Let's make three ***s***—one for you, one
Luke
9:33 construct three ***s***: one for you, one

SHUT

Numbers
12:14 days? Let her be ***s*** out of the camp
12:15 So they ***s*** Miriam out of the camp seven
Joshua
2:7 went out, the gate was ***s*** behind them.
Judges
9:51 had fled there, ***s*** themselves
18:19 ***S*** up!" they said to him. "Put your
2 Kings
6:32 door and hold it ***s*** against him. The
2 Chronicles
28:24 cut them up, ***s*** the doors of the
Nehemiah
6:10 itself. Let's ***s*** the doors of the
7:3 duty, have them ***s*** and bar the
13:19 doors should be ***s***. I also ordered
Job
24:16 into houses; they ***s*** themselves in by

Psalms
31:18 lying lips be **s** up whenever they
39:1 to keep my mouth **s** as long as the
63:11 the mouths of liars are **s** for good.
Proverbs
17:28 wise; those who **s** their lips are
Ecclesiastes
12:4 to the street are **s**, when the sound
Isaiah
24:10 every house is **s**, without entrance.
24:22 in a pit, **s** into a prison,
26:20 your rooms and **s** your doors behind
29:10 sleep, and has **s** your eyes, you
45:1 before him, so no gates will be **s**:
Jeremiah
6:10 Their ears are **s** tight, so they
51:36 dry up her sea; I'll **s** up her springs.
Ezekiel
3:24 me and said: Go, **s** yourself up
Daniel
6:22 messenger, who **s** the lions'
Malachi
1:10 among you will **s** the doors of the
Matthew
6:6 go to your room, **s** the door, and
13:15 and they've **s** their eyes so
23:13 Hypocrites! You **s** people out of the
25:10 into the wedding. Then the door was **s**.
Acts
28:27 and they've **s** their eyes so
Romans
3:19 Law, in order to **s** every mouth and
Galatians
4:17 they want to **s** you out so that
Hebrews
11:33 promises, **s** the mouths of
Revelation
3:7 no one will **s**; and whatever he
3:8 that no one can **s**. You have so
21:25 will never be **s** by day, and there

SICK → HEAL THE SICK, SICK PEOPLE
Deuteronomy
1:28 made our hearts **s** by saying,
1 Samuel
19:14 arrest David, but she said, "He's **s**."
30:13 me when I got **s** three days ago.
2 Samuel
12:15 borne for David, and he became very **s**.
13:2 he made himself **s**. She was a
13:5 and pretend to be **s**," Jonadab said to
13:6 pretended to be **s**. The king came to
1 Kings
14:1 time, Jeroboam's son Abijah became **s**.
14:5 her son. He is **s**. Say this and
2 Kings
8:7 Ben-hadad became **s**. The king was
13:14 Now Elisha became **s** with the illness
20:12 he had heard that Hezekiah was **s**.
Nehemiah
2:2 Since you aren't **s**, you must have a
Job
6:7 them; they resemble food for the **s**.
Psalms
35:13 when they were **s**, I wore clothes
41:3 are lying in bed, **s**. You will
69:20 my heart. I'm **s** about it. I hoped
Proverbs
13:12 makes the heart **s**; longing
18:14 spirit sustains a **s** person, but who
Isaiah
10:18 as when a **s** person wastes
33:24 will say, "I'm **s**." The people
38:1 became deathly **s**. The prophet
38:9 when he was **s** and then
Lamentations
1:13 He left me devastated, constantly **s**.
1:22 my groans are many, my heart is **s**.
5:17 this our heart is **s**; because of these
Ezekiel
16:30 How **s** was your heart—the LORD God
Daniel
8:27 and felt **s** for days. When I
Hosea
4:3 itself becomes **s**, and all who live
7:5 officials became **s** with the heat of
9:16 Ephraim is **s**, their root is dried up,
Amos
9:5 live in it are **s** to death. All of
Micah
6:13 I have made you **s** by striking you!
Malachi
1:8 bring a lame or **s** one, isn't that
1:13 stolen, lame, or **s** to be brought for
Matthew
8:16 a word. He healed everyone who was **s**.
14:14 for them and healed those who were **s**.
14:35 they brought to him everyone who was **s**.
25:36 to wear. I was **s** and you took care
25:39 did we see you **s** or in prison and
25:43 to wear. I was **s** and in prison,
25:44 or naked or **s** or in prison and
Mark
1:30 was in bed, **s** with a fever, and
1:32 those who were **s** or demon-possessed
1:34 many who were **s** with all kinds of
3:10 everyone who was **s** pushed forward so
6:56 would place the **s** in the
16:18 hands on the **s**, and they will
Luke
4:38 mother-in-law was **s** with a high
9:11 kingdom, and healed those who were **s**.
14:4 took hold of the **s** man, cured him,
John
4:46 certain royal official whose son was **s**.
5:3 people who were **s**, blind, lame, and
5:5 who had been **s** for thirty-eight y
5:7 The **s** man answered him, "Sir, I don't
6:2 signs he had done among the **s**.
Acts
4:9 was done for a **s** person, a good
5:15 even bring the **s** out into the main
5:16 bringing the **s** and those
19:12 were taken to the **s**, and their
28:8 was bedridden, **s** with a fever and
28:9 the rest of the **s** on the island
1 Corinthians
11:30 you are weak and **s**, and quite a few
Philippians
2:26 was upset because you heard he was **s**.
2:27 fact, he was so **s** that he nearly

SICK [cont.]

1 Timothy
6:4 but have a **s** obsession with
James
5:14 If any of you are **s**, they should call
Revelation
10:9 It will make you **s** to your stomach,

SICK PEOPLE

Mt 9:12; Mk 2:17; 6:5, 13, 55; Lk 5:31

SICKNESS

Exodus
23:25 your water. I'll take **s** away from you,
Deuteronomy
7:15 will remove all **s** from you. As for
32:24 plague, bitter **s**. I'll send animal
1 Kings
17:17 became ill. His **s** got steadily
2 Kings
8:8 him: 'Will I recover from this **s**?'"
8:9 to ask, 'Will I recover from this **s**?'"
Psalms
38:11 from me in my **s**; those who were
91:3 the hunter's trap and from deadly **s**.
91:6 or **s** that prowls in the dark,
103:3 all your sins, heals all your **s**,
Isaiah
17:11 on a day of **s** and incurable
38:9 was sick and then recovered from his **s**:
53:3 who knew **s** well. Like
53:4 was certainly our **s** that he carried,
Jeremiah
10:19 This is my **s**, and I must bear
Hosea
5:13 Ephraim saw his **s**, and Judah his
Matthew
4:23 every disease and **s** among the people.
9:35 and healing every disease and every **s**.
10:1 and to heal every disease and every **s**.
Luke
13:12 Woman, you are set free from your **s**."

SIDON

Judges
1:31 living in Acco, **S**, Ahlab, Achzib,
1 Kings
17:9 to Zarephath near **S** and stay there. I
Ezekiel
28:21 Human one, face **S**, prophesy against it
Matthew
11:21 done in Tyre and **S**, they would have
Mark
7:31 went through **S** toward the
Luke
4:26 city of Zarephath in the region of **S**.
Acts
12:20 of Tyre and **S** for some time.

SIEGE

Deuteronomy
20:20 using it in the **s** against the city
1 Samuel
11:1 went up and laid **s** to Jabesh-gilead.
1 Kings
15:27 Israel were laying **s** against Gibbethon.
16:17 up from Gibbethon and laid **s** to Tirzah.
2 Kings
6:25 The **s** lasted so long that there was a
24:10 Jerusalem and laid **s** to the city.
25:1 city and built a **s** wall all around
Job
19:12 construct their **s** ramp against me;
30:12 feet, build their **s** ramps against me,
Psalms
31:21 to me when I was like a city under **s**!
Isaiah
21:2 Go up, Elam! Lay **s**, Media! Put an
23:13 raised up their **s** towers, stripped
29:3 and I will lay a **s** against you with
Jeremiah
6:6 trees, and build **s** ramps against
10:17 ready to leave, you who live under **s**.
19:9 their enemies lay **s** to the city,
32:24 Now the **s** ramps are in place to take
33:4 defend against the **s** ramps and weapons
52:5 city was under **s** until the
Ezekiel
4:2 Prepare the **s**: Build a wall, construct
5:2 At the end of the **s**, burn one-third of
17:17 in battle when **s** ramps are set up
21:22 and to set up **s** ramps and build
26:8 you, erect **s** ramps against
Daniel
11:15 will throw up a **s** ramp and occupy a
Micah
5:1 They have laid **s** against us; with
Nahum
3:14 to prepare for **s**! Strengthen your
Zechariah
12:2 There will be a **s** against Judah and

SIGHT

Genesis
6:11 In God's **s**, the earth had become
Exodus
3:3 out this amazing **s** and find out why
Leviticus
20:17 be cut off in the **s** of their people.
25:53 not harshly rule over them in your **s**.
26:45 land in the **s** of all the
Numbers
20:27 Mount Hor in the **s** of the entire
25:6 brothers in the **s** of Moses and the
33:3 defiantly in the **s** of all the
Deuteronomy
6:18 in the LORD's **s** so that things
9:18 evil in the LORD's **s**, infuriating him.
Joshua
5:13 up. He caught **s** of a man standing
8:20 They caught **s** of the smoke of
24:17 signs in our **s**. He has protected
1 Samuel
2:17 in the LORD's **s** because they were
6:13 chest, they were overjoyed at the **s**.
2 Samuel
13:5 the food in my **s** so I can watch
16:22 wives in plain **s** before all
2 Kings
17:20 he finally threw them out of his **s**.
Nehemiah
4:5 sins from your **s**. They have thrown
8:5 the scroll in the **s** of all of the

Job
18:3 considered beasts, ignorant in your ***s***?
19:15 a stranger; I'm a foreigner in their ***s***.
21:8 with them, their offspring in their ***s***,
41:9 surely the ***s*** of him makes one
Psalms
5:5 last long in your ***s***; you hate all
13:3 my God! Restore ***s*** to my eyes!
31:19 refuge in you—in the ***s*** of everyone!
51:4 evil in your ***s***. That's why you
118:23 of the LORD; it is astounding in our ***s***!
Proverbs
1:17 to cast a net in the ***s*** of a bird.
4:21 slip from your ***s***. Guard them in
Song of Songs
2:14 let me catch ***s*** of you; let me
Isaiah
1:7 it in plain ***s***. It's a
1:16 deeds from my ***s***. Put an end to
65:16 will be forgotten and hidden from my ***s***.
Jeremiah
7:15 you out of my ***s***, just as I cast
16:17 Nor is their sin concealed from my ***s***.
19:10 clay jar in the ***s*** of the people who
31:36 vanish from my ***s***, declares the
32:31 and so it must be removed from my ***s***—
34:15 was right in my ***s***; each of you
51:24 to Zion in your ***s***, declares the
Lamentations
2:4 precious thing in ***s***; he poured out
Ezekiel
5:8 on you in the ***s*** of the nations.
39:27 them in the ***s*** of the many
43:11 down in their ***s*** so that they may
Daniel
8:5 eyes was a horn that was a ***s*** to see.
8:8 horns, each a ***s*** to see, came up
Amos
9:3 they hide from my ***s*** at the bottom of
Jonah
2:4 away from your ***s***. Will I ever
2:6 me with no end in ***s***. But you brought
Matthew
15:11 a person in God's ***s***. It's what comes
15:18 what contaminates a person in God's ***s***.
15:20 a person in God's ***s***. But eating
Mark
7:15 a person in God's ***s***; rather, the
7:19 could contaminate a person in God's ***s***.
7:20 someone in God's ***s***," he said.
7:23 and contaminate a person in God's ***s***."
8:25 wide open, his ***s*** was restored, and
9:15 crowd caught ***s*** of Jesus. They
Luke
4:18 and recovery of ***s*** to the blind, to
7:21 and he gave ***s*** to a number of
18:42 Receive your ***s***! Your faith has
24:31 him, but he disappeared from their ***s***.
John
9:18 and received his ***s*** until they called
Acts
1:9 up and a cloud took him out of their ***s***.
7:31 Enthralled by the ***s***, Moses approached
9:12 put his hands on him to restore his ***s***."
22:13 receive your ***s***!' he said.
1 Corinthians
9:26 a clear goal in ***s***. I fight like a
2 Corinthians
4:2 conscience in the ***s*** of God by the
5:7 We live by faith and not by ***s***
7:12 own enthusiasm for us in the ***s*** of God.
12:19 speaking in the ***s*** of God and in
2 Timothy
2:14 warn them in the ***s*** of God not to
Hebrews
12:21 The ***s*** was so frightening that Moses

SIGN → MIRACULOUS SIGN
Genesis
4:15 The LORD put a ***s*** on Cain so that
30:27 by a divine ***s*** that the LORD has
Exodus
4:8 to the first ***s***, they may believe
8:23 your people. This ***s*** will happen
12:13 will be your ***s*** on the houses
13:9 It will be a ***s*** on your hand and a
31:13 the Sabbath is a ***s*** between me and
31:17 It is a ***s*** forever between me and the
Numbers
6:7 they bear the ***s*** of their
16:38 They will be a ***s*** for the
17:10 to serve as a ***s*** to the rebels so
26:10 250 persons. They became a warning ***s***.
Deuteronomy
6:8 on your hand as a ***s***. They should be
11:18 on your hand as a ***s***. They should be
13:1 you and performs a ***s*** or wonder for you,
13:2 and the ***s*** or wonder that was spoken
18:10 divination, is a ***s*** reader, fortune
18:14 listened to ***s*** readers and
28:46 things will be a ***s*** and a wonder on
Joshua
2:12 my family. Give me a ***s*** of good faith.
Judges
6:17 please show me a ***s*** that it's really
1 Samuel
2:34 will be a ***s*** for you: they
10:1 this will be the ***s*** for you that the
14:10 that will be the ***s*** that the LORD has
17:18 bring back some ***s*** that they are
1 Kings
13:3 man of God gave a ***s***: "This is the
13:5 just like the ***s*** that the man of
20:33 this as a good ***s***, Ben-hadad's men
2 Kings
19:29 this will be the ***s*** for you,
20:8 What is the ***s*** that the LORD
20:9 will be your ***s*** from the LORD
21:6 alive, consulted ***s*** readers and
2 Chronicles
33:6 Valley, consulted ***s*** readers, fortune
Psalms
86:17 Show me a ***s*** of your goodness so that
Isaiah
7:11 Ask a ***s*** from the LORD your God. Make
7:14 will give you a ***s***. The young woman
19:20 It will be a ***s*** and a witness to the
20:3 three years, as a ***s*** and omen against
37:30 this will be the ***s*** for you,
38:7 This will be your ***s*** from the LORD that
38:22 What's the ***s*** that I'll be able
66:19 I will put a ***s*** on them, by sending out
Jeremiah
9:10 is heard; no ***s*** of birds or

36:29 and eliminate every **s** of life from it.
44:29 this will be a **s** for you, declares
Ezekiel
4:3 it. This is a **s** for the house of
12:6 I'm making you a **s** for the house of Israel
12:11 Say: I'm your **s**. Just as I have done,
14:8 set them up as a **s** and an object
20:12 my sabbaths as a **s** between us that
20:20 and let them be a **s** between us that I
21:19 road to the city begins, set up a **s**,
24:24 Ezekiel is your **s**. You will do
24:27 You will be their **s**, and they will
Daniel
6:8 issue the law and **s** the document so
6:12 Didn't you **s** a law, that for
6:19 at the first **s** of light, the
Joel
2:23 early rain as a **s** of righteousness;
Micah
6:16 I will make you a **s** of destruction,
Zechariah
3:8 these men are a **s**—look, I am about
Matthew
12:38 we would like to see a **s** from you."
12:39 searches for a **s**, but it won't
16:1 asked him to show them a **s** from heaven.
16:4 searches for a **s**. But it won't
24:3 What will be the **s** of your coming
24:30 Then the **s** of the Human One will appear
26:48 had given them a **s**: "Arrest the man
Mark
8:11 him, they asked for a **s** from heaven.
8:12 look for a **s**? I assure you
13:4 happen? What **s** will show that
14:44 had given them a **s**: "Arrest the man
Luke
2:12 This is a **s** for you: you will find a
2:34 and to be a **s** that generates
11:16 testing him, seeking a **s** from heaven.
11:29 It looks for a **s**, but no sign will
11:30 as Jonah became a **s** to the people of Nineveh
21:7 happen? What **s** will show that
23:8 was hoping to see Jesus perform some **s**.
John
19:20 Jews read this **s**, for the place
Acts
4:16 is aware of the **s** performed through
4:22 experienced this **s** of healing was
Romans
4:11 He received the **s** of circumcision as a
1 Corinthians
14:22 tongues are a **s** for those who
Philippians
1:28 and courage are a **s** of their coming
2 Timothy
2:19 with this **s**, The Lord knows
Revelation
12:1 Then a great **s** appeared in heaven: a
12:3 Then another **s** appeared in heaven: it
15:1 and awe-inspiring **s** in heaven. There

SIGNS → MIRACULOUS SIGNS, SIGNS AND WONDERS

Exodus
4:9 even these two **s** or pay attention
4:17 with you too so that you can do the **s**."
4:28 and all the **s** that the LORD had
4:30 he performed the **s** in front of the
7:3 many of my **s** and amazing acts
10:1 stubborn so that I can show them my **s**
10:2 with the **s** I did among them.
Numbers
14:11 me after all the **s** that I performed
14:22 my glory and the **s** I did in Egypt
Deuteronomy
11:3 the **s** and the acts that he performed in the heart of
Joshua
24:17 done these mighty **s** in our sight. He
1 Samuel
10:7 Once these **s** have happened to you, do
10:9 and all these **s** happened that
Psalms
74:4 place; they set up their own **s** there!
74:9 don't see our own **s** anymore. No
78:43 God performed his **s** in Egypt, his
105:27 They put God's **s** on Egypt, his
Jeremiah
10:2 or be troubled by **s** in the sky, even
31:21 markers, put up **s**; think about the
51:54 from Babylon, **s** of massive
Daniel
4:2 to share the **s** and miracles that
4:3 His **s** are superb! His miracles so
6:27 God performs **s** and miracles in
Joel
2:30 I will give **s** in the heavens and on the
Matthew
16:3 to recognize the **s** that point to
Mark
16:17 These **s** will be associated with those
16:20 the word by the **s** associated with
Luke
17:20 isn't coming with **s** that are easily
21:11 sights and great **s** in the sky.
21:25 There will be **s** in the sun, moon, and
Acts
2:19 heavens above and **s** on the earth
2:22 wonders, and **s**, which God
2:43 many wonders and **s** through the
6:8 great wonders and **s** among the people.
7:36 wonders and **s** in Egypt at the
8:6 say and the **s** they saw him
8:13 saw firsthand the **s** and great
1 Corinthians
1:22 Jews ask for **s**, and Greeks look for
2 Corinthians
12:12 The **s** of an apostle were performed
Hebrews
2:4 message with **s**, amazing things,
Revelation
13:13 It does great **s** so that it even makes
13:14 on earth by the **s** that it was
16:14 spirits that do **s**. They go out to
19:20 who had done **s** in the beast's

SIGNS AND WONDERS

Dt 7:19; 26:8; 29:3; 34:11; Neh 9:10; Ps 135:9; Is 8:18; Jer 32:20; 32:21; Mt 24:24; Mk 13:22; Jn 4:48; Ac 4:30; 5:12; 14:3; 15:12; Ro 15:19; 2Th 2:9

SIHON

Numbers
21:21 sent messengers to ***S*** the Amorite king:
Deuteronomy
4:46 in the land of ***S*** the Amorite king
Psalms
135:11 ***S***, the Amorite king, Og, the king of

SILAS

Acts
15:22 Barsabbas and ***S***, who were leaders
16:19 grabbed Paul and ***S*** and dragged them
18:5 Once ***S*** and Timothy arrived from

SILENCE

Job
4:16 front of my eyes. ***S***! Then I heard a
11:3 your idle talk ***s*** everyone; will
Psalms
65:1 Zion, to you even ***s*** is praise.
94:17 me, I would live instantly in total ***s***.
115:17 LORD, nor do those who go down to ***s***.
Jeremiah
7:34 I will ***s*** the sound of joy and delight
16:9 lifetime, I will ***s*** in this place the
18:18 word. Come, let's ***s*** him and pay no
25:10 I will ***s*** the sounds of joy and laughter
25:37 There's an eerie ***s*** in the peaceful
47:5 come upon Gaza; ***s*** will cover
Lamentations
3:26 good to wait in ***s*** for the LORD's
Amos
8:3 corpses, thrown about everywhere. ***S***."
Mark
1:25 ***S***!" Jesus said, speaking harshly to
4:39 to the lake, "***S***! Be still!" The
7:36 more he tried to ***s*** them, the more
Luke
4:35 ***S***!" Jesus said, speaking harshly to
Romans
1:18 human beings who ***s*** the truth with
1 Peter
2:15 good you will ***s*** the ignorant talk
Revelation
8:1 seal, there was ***s*** in heaven for

SILENT

Leviticus
10:3 is what he meant!" But Aaron was ***s***.
Numbers
30:4 herself and keeps ***s***—then all her sol
30:11 hears, keeps ***s***, and doesn't
1 Samuel
1:13 but her voice was ***s***, so Eli thought
Nehemiah
5:8 At this they were ***s***, unable to offer
Job
29:21 to me and waited, were ***s*** for my advice.
Psalms
39:2 completely quiet, ***s***. I kept my peace,
39:9 I am completely ***s***; I won't open my
56:1 ***S*** Dove of Distant
76:8 The earth grew afraid and fell ***s***
83:1 God, don't be ***s***! Don't be quiet
Ecclesiastes
3:7 time for keeping ***s*** and a time for
Isaiah
16:9 have fallen ***s*** concerning your
25:5 by a cloud, the tyrants' song falls ***s***.
42:14 time. I've been ***s*** and restrained
47:5 Sit ***s*** and go into darkness, Daughter
53:7 like a ewe ***s*** before her
57:11 it because I was ***s*** and closed my
62:1 sake I won't keep ***s***, and for
62:6 they won't keep ***s***. You who call on
64:12 Will you keep ***s*** and torment us so
65:6 me. I won't be ***s***, but I will
Jeremiah
4:19 I can't be ***s***, because I hear
47:6 until you are ***s***? Return to your
47:7 How can you be ***s*** when the LORD has directed you
49:26 soldiers will be ***s*** on that day,
Lamentations
3:28 sit alone and be ***s*** when God lays it
Ezekiel
24:27 and no longer be ***s***. You will be
Amos
5:13 is wise will keep ***s*** in that time; it
Habakkuk
1:13 or keep ***s*** when the wicked
2:19 Get up" to the ***s*** stone. Does it
2:20 Let all the earth be ***s*** before him.
Zechariah
2:13 Be ***s***, everyone, in the LORD's
Matthew
26:63 But Jesus was ***s***. The high priest said,
Mark
14:61 But Jesus was ***s*** and didn't answer.
Luke
1:20 you will remain ***s***, unable to speak
19:40 you, if they were ***s***, the stones would
Acts
8:32 its shearer is ***s*** so he didn't open
15:13 Paul also fell ***s***, James responded,
18:9 afraid. Continue speaking. Don't be ***s***.

SILVANUS

2 Corinthians
1:19 us—through me, ***S***, and Timothy—he
1 Thessalonians
1:1 From Paul, ***S***, and Timothy. To the
2 Thessalonians
1:1 From Paul, ***S***, and Timothy: To the
1 Peter
5:12 lines to you by ***S***. I consider him

SILVER

Genesis
37:28 twenty pieces of ***s***, and they brought
Exodus
11:2 for all their ***s*** and gold jewelry."
20:23 me gods of ***s*** or gold for
25:3 receive from them: gold, ***s***, and copper;
Numbers
7:13 offering was one ***s*** dish weighing one

10:2 Make two **s** trumpets and make them from
22:18 his house full of **s** and gold, I
31:22 Gold, **s**, copper, iron, tin, and lead-

Deuteronomy
17:17 the king acquire too much **s** and gold.

Joshua
7:21 shekels of **s**, and a single

Judges
5:19 but they captured no spoils of **s**.
17:4 So he gave the **s** back to his mother,
17:10 you ten pieces of **s** a year, a set of

1 Samuel
2:36 him for a bit of **s** or a loaf of
9:8 quarter-shekel of **s**. I'll give that

Ezra
1:4 supply them with **s** and gold, and
1:11 of the gold and **s** objects numbered
6:5 the gold and **s** equipment from

Nehemiah
5:15 forty shekels of **s**. Even their

Job
3:15 gold, who fill their houses with **s**.
27:17 it; the innocent will divide the **s**.
28:15 gold; its price can't be measured in **s**,

Psalms
12:6 are pure, like **s** that's been
66:10 tested us—you've refined us like **s**,
68:13 dove covered with **s**; its pinions
105:37 out, filled with **s** and gold; not one
115:4 idols are just **s** and gold—things
119:72 than thousands of pieces of gold and **s**!
135:15 idols are just **s** and gold—things

Proverbs
2:4 Seek it like **s**; search for it like
3:14 is better than **s**, and her gain
8:10 rather than **s**, knowledge rather
8:19 my crops are better than choice **s**.
10:20 is choice **s**, but the heart of
16:16 understanding is better than **s**.
17:3 A crucible is for **s** and a furnace for
22:1 high esteem is better than **s** and gold.
25:4 dross from the **s**, and a vessel
25:11 are like gold apples in a **s** setting.
26:23 evil heart are like **s** coating on clay.
27:21 A crucible is for **s** and a furnace for

Ecclesiastes
2:8 I amassed **s** and gold for myself, the
12:6 before the **s** cord snaps and the gold

Song of Songs
1:11 hoops of gold beaded with **s** for you!
3:10 he made of **s**, its covering,
8:9 build a turret of **s** on her. And if
8:11 for its fruit a thousand pieces of **s**.

Isaiah
48:10 you, but not like **s**; I have tested

Ezekiel
22:18 they've become the waste product of **s**.

Daniel
2:32 were made from **s**; its abdomen and
5:4 the gods of gold, **s**, bronze, iron,

Haggai
2:8 The **s** and the gold belong to me, says

Zechariah
11:12 out my wages, thirty shekels of **s**.
13:9 like one refines **s**; I will test them

Malachi
3:3 and a purifier of **s**. He will purify

Matthew
27:3 thirty pieces of **s** to the chief
27:5 Judas threw the **s** pieces into the

Luke
15:8 if she owns ten **s** coins and loses

Acts
17:29 is like a gold, **s**, or stone image
19:24 He made **s** models of
20:33 craved anyone's **s**, gold, or

1 Corinthians
3:12 with gold, **s**, precious stones,

2 Timothy
2:20 just gold and **s** bowls but also

James
5:3 Your gold and **s** have rusted, and their

1 Peter
1:18 things like **s** or gold from the

Revelation
9:20 made of gold, **s**, bronze, stone,
18:12 cargoes of gold, **s**, jewels, and

SIMEON

Genesis
29:33 me this son too," and she named him **S**.

Luke
2:34 **S** blessed them and said to Mary his

Acts
13:1 Barnabas, **S** (nicknamed

Revelation
7:7 from the tribe of **S**, twelve thousand;

SIMON

Matthew
4:18 saw two brothers, **S**, who is called
16:17 Happy are you, **S** son of Jonah,
26:6 the house of **S**, who had a skin
27:32 out, they found **S**, a man from

Acts
8:18 When **S** perceived that the Spirit was

2 Peter
1:1 From **S** Peter, a slave and apostle of

SIN → FALL INTO SIN, GUILTY OF SIN

Genesis
4:7 the right thing, **s** will be waiting
18:20 countless, and their **s** is very serious!
20:9 done to us? What **s** did I commit
39:9 this terrible thing and **s** against God?"

Exodus
10:17 Please forgive my **s** this time. Pray to
16:1 and came to the **S** desert, which is
17:1 set out from the **S** desert to
20:20 in awe of God so that you don't **s**."
23:33 will lead you to **s** against me. If
29:36 should remove the **s** from the altar
32:21 led them to commit such a terrible **s**?"
32:30 a terrible **s**. So now I will go
32:31 what a terrible **s** these people have
32:32 forgive their **s**! And if not, then
32:34 I'll count their **s** against them."
34:7 every kind of **s** and rebellion,
34:9 our guilt and our **s** and take us as

Leviticus
4:14 once the **s** that they committed becomes known

4:23 once the **s** that he committed is made
4:26 to remove his **s**, and he will be
4:28 once the **s** they committed is made known
4:35 for you for the **s** you committed,
5:1 If you **s**: by not providing information
5:6 for the **s** that was
5:7 for your **s** two doves or two
5:10 because of the **s** you committed,
5:11 offering for your **s** a tenth of an
5:17 If you **s** by breaking any of the LORD's
6:2 If you **s**: by acting unfaithfully
6:3 that someone might do and so **s**,
19:17 you don't become responsible for his **s**.
19:22 on account of the **s** he committed.

Numbers
5:6 woman commits any **s** against anyone
5:7 will confess the **s** they have done.
9:13 time. Those persons will bear their **s**.
12:11 punish us for the **s** that we foolishly
15:28 when the **s** is an accident,
15:29 anyone who commits an unintentional **s**.
18:22 be responsible for their **s** and die.
27:3 died for his own **s**, but he had no
32:23 LORD. Know that your **s** will find you.
33:11 Reed Sea and camped in the **S** desert.
33:12 marched from the **S** desert and camped

Deuteronomy
9:18 because of the **s** that you had
9:27 stubbornness, wickedness, and **s**.

Joshua
22:17 from that **s**, when there was a

1 Samuel
2:17 The **s** of these priestly assistants was
12:23 me? I would never **s** against the LORD
14:34 with me. Don't **s** against the LORD
14:38 find out what **s** was committed
15:23 is as bad as the **s** of divination;
15:25 please forgive my **s**! Come back with

2 Samuel
12:13 has removed your **s**," Nathan replied

1 Kings
8:34 and forgive the **s** of your people
8:35 away from their **s** because you have
8:36 and forgive the **s** of your servants,
8:46 When they **s** against you (for there is
14:16 he made Israel **s** too, God will
15:26 Jeroboam and the **s** Jeroboam had
15:34 ways and the **s** he had caused
16:2 my people Israel **s**, making me angry
16:13 caused Israel to **s**. They angered
16:19 ways and the **s** he had done by
16:26 caused Israel to **s**. They angered
17:18 attention to my **s** and kill my son?"
21:22 me and because you've made Israel **s**.
22:52 son, who had caused Israel to **s**.

2 Kings
17:21 LORD. He caused them to commit great **s**.
21:11 has caused Judah to **s** with his images.
21:17 and the **s** he committed,
23:15 caused Israel to **s**. Josiah tore down

2 Chronicles
6:25 and forgive the **s** of your people
6:26 away from their **s** because you have
6:27 and forgive the **s** of your servants,
6:36 When they **s** against you, for there is
7:14 forgive their **s**, and heal their
19:10 warn them not to **s** against the LORD,
20:35 King Ahaziah, which caused him to **s**.
24:18 Jerusalem as a consequence of their **s**,
28:13 only add to our **s** and guilt before
29:24 to take away the **s** of all Israel,
33:19 answer, all his **s** and

Nehemiah
6:13 me and to make me **s** by acting in this
13:26 King Solomon **s** on account of

Job
1:22 In all this, Job didn't **s** or blame God
2:10 all this, Job didn't **s** with his lips.
4:8 those who plow **s** and sow trouble
7:21 not forgive my **s**, overlook my
10:6 search for my wrongdoing and seek my **s**?
10:14 If I **s** and you observe me, you won't
11:6 God lets some of your **s** be forgotten.
11:11 people, sees **s**, and certainly
11:14 you throw out the **s** in your hands and don't let injustice
14:16 you would not keep a record of my **s**.
14:17 sealed in a bag; you would cover my **s**.
15:16 corrupt, for they drink **s** like water.
31:30 let my mouth **s** by asking for
33:9 pure, without **s**; I'm innocent,
34:10 God to do evil and the Almighty to **s**,
34:31 have borne punishment; I won't **s** again?
34:33 you reject **s**, for you must
34:37 rebellion to his **s**; mocks us openly
35:3 you? What have I gained by avoiding **s**?"

Psalms
4:4 afraid, and don't **s**! Think hard about
17:3 anything wrong. My mouth doesn't **s**.
19:12 done wrong? Clear me of any unknown **s**
32:1 forgiven, whose **s** is covered over,
32:5 So I admitted my **s** to you; I didn't
38:3 no health in my bones because of my **s**.
38:18 my wrongdoing; I'm worried about my **s**.
39:1 so as not to **s** with my tongue;
39:11 people for their **s**, punishing them;
51:2 clean of my guilt; purify me from my **s**!
51:3 wrongdoings, my **s** is always right
51:5 born in guilt, in **s**, from the moment
59:3 not because of any error or **s** of mine.
59:12 For the **s** of their mouths, the words
78:17 they continued to **s** against God,
89:32 will punish their **s** with a stick, and
103:10 according to our **s** or repay us
103:12 how far God has removed our **s** from us.
106:43 they were brought down by their own **s**.
109:14 let his mother's **s** never be wiped
119:11 heart, so that I won't **s** against you.
119:133 by your word; don't let any **s** rule me.
130:8 who will redeem Israel from all its **s**.

Proverbs
5:22 grabbed by the ropes of their own **s**.
10:16 the earnings of the wicked lead to **s**.
14:34 a nation, but **s** disgraces a
20:9 to the core; I'm cleansed from my **s**"?
24:9 of fools is **s**; people detest
29:6 by their own **s**; the righteous

Isaiah
5:18 fraud, and haul **s** as if with cart
6:7 has departed, and your **s** is removed."
13:11 bring their own **s** upon the wicked.
30:1 not by my spirit, piling up **s** on sin;
30:13 your **s** will be like a crack in a high
33:24 living there will be forgiven their **s**.
43:25 for my sake. I won't remember your **s**.
53:12 he carried the **s** of many and
64:7 us, and have handed us over to our **s**.
Jeremiah
2:22 the stain of your **s** is still before
5:25 away. Your **s** has robbed you of
11:15 cancel your **s** so that you revel
14:10 their wrongdoing and punish their **s**.
14:20 acknowledge our **s**, LORD, the
16:17 me. Nor is their **s** concealed from my
16:18 their evil and **s**, because they
17:1 Judah's **s** is engraved with an iron pen.
18:23 cleanse their **s** from before you.
32:35 detestable thing, leading Judah to **s**.
50:20 searches for the **s** of Israel, they
Lamentations
2:14 reveal your **s** so as to prevent
Ezekiel
3:20 them of their **s**. Their righteous
3:21 righteous not to **s**, and they don't
16:49 This is the **s** of your sister Sodom: She
16:51 Samaria didn't **s** even half as much as
33:6 away in their **s**, but I'll hold
33:12 they begin to **s**. Nor does the
33:14 if they turn from **s** and do what is
33:15 in order not to **s**—they will live an
Daniel
9:20 and confessing my **s** and the sins of
Hosea
4:8 They feed on the **s** of my people; they
8:11 to take away **s**, they became
10:8 The **s** of Israel, the shrines of Aven
12:8 has been found in me that would be **s**."
13:12 is bound up; his **s** is kept in store.
Micah
1:13 the beginning of **s** for Daughter
3:8 his wrongdoing and to Israel his **s**!
6:7 of my body for the **s** of my spirit?
7:18 overlooking the **s** of the few
Zechariah
13:1 to cleanse the **s** and impurity of
14:19 This would be the **s** of Egypt and the
Matthew
12:31 for every **s** and insult to
13:41 to fall away and all people who **s**.
13:57 him and fell into **s**. But Jesus said
Mark
3:29 is guilty of a **s** with consequences
6:3 were repulsed by him and fell into **s**.
John
1:29 God who takes away the **s** of the world!
5:14 made well. Don't **s** anymore in case
8:11 Go, and from now on, don't **s** anymore."
8:21 will die in your **s**. Where I'm going,
8:34 that everyone who sins is a slave to **s**.
9:34 completely in **s**! How is it that
9:41 wouldn't have any **s**, but now that you
15:22 now they have no excuse for their **s**.
16:8 was wrong about **s**, righteousness,
16:9 was wrong about **s** because they
19:11 me over to you has the greater **s**."
Acts
7:60 don't hold this **s** against them!"
Romans
3:9 Greeks are all under the power of **s**.
3:20 the knowledge of **s** comes through the
4:8 are those whose **s** isn't counted
5:12 the same way that **s** entered the world
5:13 Although **s** was in the world, since
5:14 those who didn't **s** in the same way
5:16 of one person's **s**. The judgment
5:20 but where **s** increased, grace
5:21 our Lord, just as **s** ruled in death.
6:2 All of us died to **s**. How can we still
6:6 controlled by **s**. That way we
6:10 He died to **s** once and for all with his
6:11 dead to **s** but alive for God
6:12 then, don't let **s** rule your body,
6:13 of your body to **s**, to be used as
6:14 **S** will have no power over you, because
6:15 what? Should we **s** because we aren't
6:16 as slaves of **s**, which leads to
6:17 to be slaves of **s**, you gave
6:18 set free from **s**, you have become
6:20 were slaves of **s**, you were free
6:22 set free from **s** and become slaves
6:23 The wages that **s** pays are death, but
7:7 That the Law is **s**? Absolutely not!
7:8 But **s** seized the opportunity and used
7:9 the commandment came, **s** sprang to life,
7:11 **S** seized the opportunity through the
7:13 not! But **s** caused my death
7:14 blood, and I'm sold as a slave to **s**.
7:17 Instead, it's **s** that lives in me.
7:20 Instead, it is **s** that lives in me
7:23 with the law of **s** that is in my
8:2 you free from the law of **s** and death.
8:3 God condemned **s** in the body by
8:10 but the body is dead because of **s**.
14:23 that isn't based on faith is **s**.
1 Corinthians
6:18 immorality! Every **s** that a person can
8:12 You **s** against Christ if you sin against
15:34 should and don't **s**. Some of you are
15:56 (Death's sting is **s**, and the power of
2 Corinthians
5:21 who didn't know **s** to be sin for our
11:7 Did I commit a **s** by humbling myself to
13:2 who continued to **s**. Now I'm
Galatians
2:17 Christ a servant of **s**? Absolutely not!
3:22 all things under **s**, so that the
Hebrews
4:15 way that we are, except without **s**.
9:5 the chest, where **s** is taken care of.
9:26 to get rid of **s** by sacrificing
9:28 not to take away **s** but to save those
10:2 one would have been aware of **s** anymore.
10:3 are a reminder of **s** every year,
10:6 burned offerings or a **s** offering.
10:18 there is no longer an offering for **s**.
10:26 the decision to **s** after we receive
11:25 of having the temporary pleasures of **s**.
12:1 get rid of the **s** that trips us up,

12:4 struggle against **s**, you haven't
13:11 an offering for **s**, and their bodies

James
1:15 give birth to **s**; and when sin
2:9 are committing a **s**, and by that same
4:17 It is a **s** when someone knows the right

1 Peter
2:22 He committed no **s** nor did he ever speak
2:24 to do with **s**. By his wounds
4:1 whoever suffers is finished with **s**.

2 Peter
2:14 opportunities to **s**. They ensnare

1 John
1:7 his Son, cleanses us from every **s**.
1:8 don't have any **s**," we deceive
2:1 so that you don't **s**. But if you do
3:4 who practices **s** commits an act of
3:5 away sins, and there is no **s** in him.
3:6 to him does not **s**. Any person who
3:8 who practices **s** belongs to the
3:9 don't practice **s** because God's DNA
5:16 committing a **s** that does not
5:17 action is **s**, but there is a
5:18 from God does not **s**, but the ones

SINAI → MOUNT SINAI

Exodus
19:1 of Egypt, they came into the ***S*** desert.

Numbers
1:19 them in the ***S*** desert just as

Psalms
68:17 My Lord came from ***S*** into the

SINFUL

Genesis
13:13 were very evil and **s** against the LORD.

Numbers
32:14 a group of **s** men, to intensify

Deuteronomy
9:21 And as for that **s** thing you made, that

1 Samuel
15:18 Go, and put the **s** Amalekites under

1 Kings
12:30 This act was **s**. The people went to
15:3 followed all the **s** ways of his

Job
22:15 the ancient way traveled by **s** persons,

Psalms
36:1 I know the **s** utterance of the
107:17 because of their **s** ways. They
109:7 guilty—let his prayer be found **s**!

Proverbs
21:4 and the lamp of the wicked are all **s**.

Isaiah
1:4 Doom! ***S*** nation, people weighed down
55:7 ways and the **s** their schemes.

Ezekiel
18:30 Don't let them be **s** obstacles for you.
36:31 because of your **s** and detestable

Amos
9:8 God is eyeing the **s** kingdom, and I

Zechariah
13:2 prophets and the **s** spirit from the

Mark
8:38 unfaithful and **s** generation, the

Luke
13:2 they were more **s** than all the

Romans
7:5 the **s** passions aroused
7:13 more thoroughly **s** through the

Titus
3:11 is twisted and **s**—so they condemn

1 Peter
4:18 what will happen to the godless and **s**?

2 Peter
1:4 immorality that **s** craving produces.
2:10 cravings of the **s** nature and defy
2:18 speech, they use **s** cravings and
3:17 into the error of **s** people, and lose

Jude
1:15 harsh things that **s** ungodly people
1:23 clothing contaminated by their **s** urges.

SING → SING PRAISES, SING TO GOD, SING TO THE LORD

Numbers
21:17 this song: "Well, flow up! ***S*** about it!

Judges
5:3 the LORD, I will **s**. I will make
5:12 Wake up, wake up, **s** a song! Arise,

1 Samuel
21:11 the one people **s** about in their
29:5 same David people **s** about in their

2 Chronicles
5:13 they began to **s**, praising the

Job
29:13 reached me; I made the widow's heart **s**;
33:27 They **s** before people and say: "I have

Psalms
5:11 Let them **s** out loud forever!
21:13 strength! We will **s** and praise your
27:6 of joy! I will **s** and praise the
32:11 whose hearts are right, **s** out in joy!
33:3 ***S*** to him a new song! Play your best
51:14 my tongue can **s** of your
57:7 is unwavering. I will **s** and make music.
59:16 But me? I will **s** of your strength! In
65:8 of morning and evening **s** for joy.
68:33 ***S*** to the one who rides through heaven,
87:7 dance, people **s**: "The source of
89:1 Ezrahite.] I will **s** of the LORD's
92:4 by your acts. I **s** with joy because
95:1 Come, let's **s** out loud to the LORD!
98:4 Rejoice out loud! ***S*** your praises!
101:1 Oh, let me **s** about faithful
108:1 God. I will **s** and make music—
137:3 asked us to **s**; our tormentors
137:4 could we possibly **s** the LORD's song
138:1 my heart, LORD. I **s** your praise
138:5 Let them **s** about the LORD's ways
144:9 I will **s** a new song to you, God. I will
147:1 it is good to **s** praise to our
149:3 dance; let them **s** God's praise with

Proverbs
29:6 own sin; the righteous **s** and rejoice.

Isaiah
5:1 Let me **s** for my loved one a love song
12:6 Shout and **s** for joy, city of Zion,
23:16 Play well, **s** many songs, so
24:14 their voice; they **s** with joy; from
27:2 On that day: ***S*** about a delightful
35:6 speechless will **s**. Waters will

42:11 cliff dwellers ***s***; from the top of
44:23 **S**, heavens, for the LORD has acted;
49:13 **S**, heavens! Rejoice, earth! Break out,
52:8 their voice; they ***s*** out together!
54:1 **S**, barren woman who has borne no
63:7 acts; I will ***s*** the LORD's
65:14 My servants will ***s*** with contented
Jeremiah
31:7 LORD proclaims: **S** joyfully for the
Ezekiel
26:17 They will ***s*** a lament for you, and they
27:2 You, human one, ***s*** a lament for Tyre
27:32 for you; they ***s*** lamentions over
28:12 Human one, ***s*** a lament for the king of
32:2 Human one, ***s*** a lament for Pharaoh,
Amos
6:5 who ***s*** idle songs to the sound of the
Zechariah
9:9 Daughter Zion. **S** aloud, Daughter
1 Corinthians
14:15 my mind too; I'll ***s*** a psalm in the
Ephesians
5:19 spiritual songs; ***s*** and make music to
James
5:13 If any of you are happy, they should ***s***.
Revelation
14:3 They ***s*** a new song in front of the
15:3 They ***s*** the song of Moses, God's

SING PRAISES
2Sa 22:50; 1Ch 16:9; Ps 7:17; 9:2, 11; 18:49; 30:4, 12; 33:2; 47:6, 7; 59:17; 61:8; 66:2; 68:4, 32; 75:9; 92:1; 104:33; 105:2; 135:3; 144:9; 146:2; 147:7; Ro 15:9

SING TO GOD
1Ch 16:9; Ps 68:4; 68:32; 105:2; Col 3:16

SING TO THE LORD
Ex 15:1; 15:21; 1Ch 16:23; Ps 13:6; 96:1, 2; 98:1; 104:33; 147:7; 149:1; Is 12:5; 42:10; Jer 20:13

SINGERS
2 Samuel
19:35 of men or women ***s***? Why should your
1 Chronicles
9:33 The ***s*** were the heads of the households
15:16 relatives as ***s*** to raise their
15:19 The ***s*** Heman, Asaph, and Ethan were to
15:27 robe, as did the ***s***, all the Levites
2 Chronicles
5:13 trumpeters and ***s*** joined together
23:13 trumpets, and ***s*** accompanied by
35:15 The Asaphite ***s*** also remained at their
Ezra
2:41 The ***s***: The family of Asaph 1
2:65 they also had 200 male and female ***s***,
2:70 the people, the ***s***, the gatekeepers,
7:7 the Levites, the ***s*** and gatekeepers
7:24 and Levites, the ***s***, the doorkeepers,
10:24 Of the ***s***: Eliashib. Of the
Nehemiah
7:1 the gatekeepers, ***s***, and Levites were
7:44 The ***s***: the descendants of Asaph 14
7:67 they also had 245 male and female ***s***,
7:73 gatekeepers, the ***s***, some of the
10:28 gatekeepers, the ***s***, the temple
10:39 and the ***s*** reside. We won't
11:22 who were the ***s*** in charge of the
11:23 out the daily requirements of the ***s***.
12:28 The ***s*** also gathered together both from
12:29 because the ***s*** had built
12:42 and Ezer. The ***s*** sang with
12:45 as did the ***s*** and the
12:46 a leader of the ***s***, and there were
12:47 portions for the ***s*** and the
13:5 for the Levites, ***s***, and gatekeepers
13:10 so they and the ***s*** who did the work
Psalms
68:25 First came the ***s***, then the musicians;
Ecclesiastes
2:8 male and female ***s*** for myself, along
12:4 rises, and all the ***s*** come down low;

SINGING
1 Samuel
18:6 King Saul with ***s*** and dancing, with
1 Chronicles
25:6 direction when ***s*** in the LORD's
25:7 were trained in ***s*** to the LORD and
2 Chronicles
23:18 rejoicing and ***s***, just as David
29:28 worshipped with ***s*** choirs and
Ezra
3:11 to the LORD, ***s*** responsively, "He
Nehemiah
12:27 with thanks and ***s***, and with
Job
3:7 childless; may no happy ***s*** come in it.
Proverbs
25:20 **S** a song to a troubled heart is like
Song of Songs
2:12 the season of ***s*** has arrived, and
Isaiah
30:29 There will be ***s*** for you as on the night
35:2 with joy and ***s***. They will
35:10 enter Zion with ***s***, with everlasting
43:14 turning the Chaldeans' ***s*** into a lament.
51:3 in her—thanks and the sound of ***s***.
51:11 come to Zion with ***s*** and with
54:1 break forth into ***s*** and cry out, you
Amos
8:10 and all your ***s*** into a funeral
Zephaniah
3:17 love; he will rejoice over you with ***s***.
Matthew
26:30 Then, after ***s*** songs of praise, they
Mark
14:26 After ***s*** songs of praise, they went out
Acts
16:25 were praying and ***s*** hymns to God, and
Colossians
3:16 all wisdom by ***s*** psalms, hymns,

SINGLE
Genesis
22:13 up and saw a ***s*** ram caught by its
Exodus
10:19 Reed Sea. Not a ***s*** locust was left
33:5 you even for a ***s*** moment, I would
Deuteronomy
3:4 There wasn't a ***s*** city that we
29:21 the LORD will ***s*** them out for

Psalms
84:10 Better is a **s** day in your courtyards
148:9 mountains, every **s** hill, fruit
Song of Songs
4:7 dearest; there's not a **s** flaw in you.
Ezekiel
11:19 will give them a **s** heart, and I will
Daniel
6:17 A **s** stone was brought and placed over
8:9 A **s**, very small horn came out of one
Matthew
6:27 can add a **s** moment to your
27:14 not even a **s** word. So the
John
12:24 it can only be a **s** seed. But if it
Acts
7:52 Was there a **s** prophet your ancestors
27:34 you will lose a **s** hair from his
2 Peter
3:8 with the Lord a **s** day is like a
Revelation
18:8 will come in a **s** day—deadly
18:10 city! In a **s** hour your
21:21 was made from a **s** pearl. And the

SINNED → SINNED AGAINST GOD, SINNED AGAINST YOU, YOU HAVE SINNED
Exodus
9:27 This time I've **s**. The LORD is
9:34 had stopped, he **s** again. Pharaoh
10:16 and said, "I've **s** against the LORD
32:33 my scroll are those who **s** against me.
Leviticus
4:3 priest who has **s**, making the
Numbers
14:40 the LORD told us to, for we have **s**."
15:28 the person who **s** unintentionally,
16:38 of those who **s** and lost their
21:7 and said, "We've **s**, for we spoke
22:34 messenger, "I've **s**, because I didn't
32:23 do this, you've **s** against the LORD.
Deuteronomy
1:41 to me: "We've **s** against the LORD!
9:16 I saw how you **s** against the LORD
32:5 weren't his own **s** against him with
Joshua
7:11 Israel has **s**. They have violated my
7:20 It's true. I've **s** against the LORD,
Judges
10:15 the LORD, "We've **s**. Do to us
1 Samuel
7:6 We have **s** against the
12:10 said: 'We have **s** because we have
15:24 Samuel, "I have **s** because I
15:30 I have **s**," Saul said, "but please
26:21 said, "I have **s**! David, my son,
2 Samuel
12:13 I've **s** against the LORD!" David said
19:20 knows that I have **s**. But look, I am
24:10 the LORD, "I have **s** greatly in what I
24:17 I'm the one who **s**! I'm the one who
1 Kings
8:47 saying, "We have **s**, we have done
18:9 said, "How have I **s** that you are
2 Kings
17:7 the Israelites **s** against the LORD
1 Chronicles
21:8 to God, "I have **s** greatly in what I
2 Chronicles
6:37 saying,"We have **s**, we have done
Ezra
10:13 many of us have **s** in this matter.
Nehemiah
1:6 you. Both I and my family have **s**.
Job
1:5 my children have **s** and then cursed
7:20 If I **s**, what did I do to you, guardian
8:4 If your children **s** against him, then he delivered them
33:27 and say: "I have **s**, perverted
34:32 see; if I've **s**, I won't do it
35:6 If you've **s**, how have you affected
Psalms
106:6 We have **s**—right along with our
Isaiah
42:24 LORD, the one we **s** against? They
43:27 first ancestor **s**, and your
64:5 angry when we **s**; you hid yourself
Jeremiah
2:35 claim not to have **s**, I will pass
3:25 us, for we have **s** against the LORD
8:14 because we have **s** against the LORD!
16:10 How have we **s** against the LORD
44:23 to other gods and **s** against the LORD—
50:7 because they have **s** against the LORD,
50:14 because she's **s** against the LORD.
Lamentations
1:8 Jerusalem has **s** greatly; therefore,
5:7 Our fathers have **s** and are gone, but we
5:16 head. We are doomed because we have **s**.
Ezekiel
37:23 places where they **s**, and I will
Daniel
9:5 We have **s** and done wrong. We have
9:15 this day: We have **s** and done the
Hosea
4:7 the more they **s** against me; they
Micah
7:9 LORD, for I have **s** against him,
Zephaniah
1:17 because they **s** against the LORD.
3:11 with which you **s** against me; then
Luke
15:18 Father, I have **s** against heaven
15:21 Father, I have **s** against heaven
John
8:7 Whoever hasn't **s** should throw the
9:2 Rabbi, who **s** so that he was
Romans
2:12 Those who have **s** outside the Law will
3:23 All have **s** and fall short of God's
5:12 beings with the result that all **s**.
1 Corinthians
7:28 you haven't **s**; and if someone
2 Corinthians
12:21 people who have **s** before and
Hebrews
3:17 with the ones who **s**, whose bodies
James
5:15 And if they have **s**, they will be
2 Peter
2:4 angels when they **s** but cast them

SINNED [cont.]

1 John
1:10 We have never **s**," we make him a

SINNED AGAINST THE LORD

Ex 10:16; Nm 32:23; Dt 1:41; 9:16; Josh 7:20; 1Sa 7:6; 2Sa 12:13; 2Ki 17:7; Jer 3:25; 8:14; 16:10; 40:3; 44:23; 50:7, 14; Zep 1:17

SINNED AGAINST YOU

Jdg 10:10; 11:27; 1Ki 8:33; 8:35, 50; 2Ch 6:24; 6:26, 39; Ps 41:4; 51:4; Jer 14:7; 14:20; Dn 9:8

SINNERS → TAX COLLECTORS AND SINNERS

Job
9:22 God destroys the blameless and the **s**.
10:3 and cause the purpose of **s** to shine?
24:19 snow, just as the underworld steals **s**.
Psalms
1:1 on the road of **s**, and doesn't sit
1:5 neither will **s** in the assembly
25:8 thing; he teaches **s** which way they
26:9 me up with the **s**, taking my life
51:13 your ways, and **s** will come back to
104:35 Let **s** be wiped clean from the earth;
Proverbs
1:10 My son, don't let **s** entice you. Don't
1:18 But these **s** set up a deadly ambush;
11:31 earth, how much more the wicked and **s**?
13:6 on the path, but wickedness misleads **s**.
13:21 Trouble pursues **s**, but good things
13:22 but the wealth of **s** is stored up for
14:21 neighbors are **s**, but happy are
23:17 your heart envy **s**, but fear the
Isaiah
1:28 rebels and **s** alike; those who
13:9 the earth a ruin, and wiping out its **s**.
33:14 **S** became terrified in Zion; trembling
Amos
9:10 All the **s** of my people will die by the
Matthew
9:10 collectors and **s** joined Jesus and
9:13 come to call righteous people, but **s**."
11:19 collectors and **s**.' But wisdom is
26:45 One to be betrayed into the hands of **s**.
Mark
2:15 collectors and **s** were eating with
2:16 was eating with **s** and tax
2:17 come to call righteous people, but **s**."
14:41 One to be betrayed into the hands of **s**.
Luke
5:32 people but **s** to change their
6:32 commended? Even **s** love those who
6:33 you be commended? Even **s** do that.
6:34 commended? Even **s** lend to sinners
15:1 collectors and **s** were gathering
15:2 man welcomes **s** and eats with
24:7 be handed over to **s**, be crucified,
John
9:31 doesn't listen to **s**. God listens to
15:22 they wouldn't be **s**. But now they
15:24 they wouldn't be **s**. But now they
Romans
5:8 we were still **s** Christ died for
5:19 people were made **s** through the
Galatians
2:15 We are born Jews—we're not Gentile **s**
2:17 we ourselves are **s** while we are
1 Timothy
1:9 ungodly and the **s**. They are people
1:15 the world to save **s**"—and I'm the bigg
Hebrews
7:26 separate from **s**, and raised high
12:3 opposition from **s** so that you won't
James
4:8 your hands, you **s**. Purify your

SINS → FORGIVE SINS, SINS ARE FORGIVEN, YOUR SINS, YOUR SINS ARE FORGIVEN

Genesis
50:17 your brothers' **s** and misdeeds, for
Exodus
20:5 their parents' **s** even to the third
34:7 their parents' **s** their children
Leviticus
4:2 whenever someone **s** unintentionally
4:22 If a leader **s** by unintentionally
4:27 ordinary person **s** unintentionally
5:13 one of the **s** you committed,
16:16 their rebellious **s**, as well as for
16:21 their rebellious **s**, as well as all
16:34 from all their **s** once a year.It
Numbers
15:27 If an individual **s** unintentionally,
16:22 If one person **s**, should you
16:26 you too be wiped out for all their **s**."
18:23 for their own **s**. This is a
Deuteronomy
5:9 their parents' **s**—even to the third
1 Samuel
2:25 If someone **s** against someone else, God
12:19 added to our many **s** the evil of
1 Kings
14:16 Because of the **s** Jeroboam committed,
14:22 LORD's eyes. The **s** they committed
16:31 to walk in the **s** of Jeroboam,
2 Kings
3:3 clung to the **s** that Jeroboam,
10:29 deviate from the **s** that Jeroboam,
21:16 include the **s** he caused Judah
24:3 of all the **s** that Manasseh had
Nehemiah
1:6 I confess the **s** of the people of
4:5 or blot out their **s** from your sight.
9:2 to confess their **s** and the terrible
9:37 us because of our **s**. They have power
Job
13:23 my offenses and **s**? Inform me about
36:9 about their offenses and their grave **s**.
Psalms
5:10 for their many **s** because they've
19:13 from willful **s**. Don't let them
25:7 remember the **s** of my youth or my
25:11 LORD, forgive my **s**, which are many!
25:18 and trouble—forgive all my **s**!
32:5 I'll confess my **s** to the LORD," is
39:8 me from all my **s**; don't make me
51:9 your face from my **s**; wipe away all my
65:3 too much for me, you forgive our **s**.
78:38 forgiving their **s**, kept avoiding
79:9 us and cover our **s** for the sake of
85:2 you've covered all their **s**. Selah

90:8 You put our **s** right in front of you,
130:3 you kept track of **s**, LORD—my Lord,
Proverbs
28:13 who hide their **s** won't succeed,
Isaiah
3:9 display their **s** in public. Doom
27:9 this was how his **s** were finally
38:17 have cast all my **s** behind your back.
40:2 the LORD's hand double for all her **s**!
58:1 crime, to the house of Jacob their **s**.
59:12 presence; our **s** testify against
64:6 like a leaf; our **s**, like the wind,
64:9 don't hold our **s** against us
Jeremiah
11:10 returned to the **s** of their
13:22 of your many **s** that you have
14:7 Even though our **s** testify against us,
17:3 committed such **s** throughout your
31:30 die for their own **s**: whoever eats
31:34 and never again remember their **s**.
32:18 of the fathers' **s** on their children
36:3 I will forgive their wrongdoing and **s**.
44:9 you forgotten the **s** of your ancestors
Lamentations
3:39 should anyone complain about their **s**?
4:13 of her prophets' **s**, her priests'
Ezekiel
14:11 with any of their **s**. They will be my
14:13 suppose a land **s** against me by
18:4 to me. Only the one who **s** will die.
18:14 who sees all the **s** that his father
18:20 Only the one who **s** will die. A child
18:21 away from all the **s** that they have
18:22 None of the **s** that they committed will
18:24 die because of their treacheries and **s**.
18:28 from all their **s**, they will surely
18:31 of your repeated **s**. Make yourselves
23:49 you will bear the **s** of your idols.
28:18 your many other **s**, you made your
33:10 and our **s** weigh on us! We
33:16 None of the **s** they've committed will be
45:20 for anyone who **s** through
Daniel
8:23 its end and their **s** are almost
9:16 Because of our **s** and the
9:20 my sin and the **s** of my people
9:24 rebellion, to end **s**, to cover over
Hosea
8:13 and punish their **s**; they will return
9:9 wickedness; he will punish their **s**.
Micah
1:5 of Jacob and the **s** of the house of
7:19 will hurl all our **s** into the depths
Matthew
1:21 he will save his people from their **s**."
3:6 confessed their **s**, he baptized them
6:14 others their **s**, your heavenly
15:19 adultery, sexual **s**, thefts, false
18:15 brother or sister **s** against you, go
18:21 or sister who **s** against me?
26:28 many so that their **s** may be forgiven.
Mark
1:4 and wanted God to forgive their **s**.
1:5 by John as they confessed their **s**.
3:28 for all **s** and insults of
7:21 come: sexual **s**, thefts, murders,
Luke
1:77 through the forgiveness of their **s**.
3:3 and wanted God to forgive their **s**.
7:47 you that her many **s** have been
7:49 is this person that even forgives **s**?"
11:4 Forgive us our **s**, for we also forgive
17:3 brother or sister **s**, warn them to
17:4 Even if someone **s** against you seven
24:47 forgiveness of **s** must be preached
John
8:34 that everyone who **s** is a slave to sin.
20:23 forgive anyone's **s**, they are
Acts
5:31 and life and to find forgiveness for **s**.
10:43 forgiveness of **s** through his name."
13:38 forgiveness of **s** to you. From all
26:18 forgiveness of **s** and a place among
Romans
3:25 in passing over **s** that happened
4:7 are forgiven, and whose **s** are covered.
11:27 with them, when I take away their **s**.
1 Corinthians
15:3 died for our **s** in line with the
2 Corinthians
5:19 counting people's **s** against them. He
Galatians
1:4 himself for our **s**, so he could
Colossians
1:14 free through the Son and forgave our **s**.
1 Thessalonians
2:16 be saved. Their **s** are constantly
1 Timothy
5:22 in the **s** of others. Keep
5:24 The **s** of some people are obvious, and
2 Timothy
3:6 are burdened with **s** and driven by all
Hebrews
1:3 people from their **s**, he sat down at
2:17 order to wipe away the **s** of the people.
5:1 to offer gifts and sacrifices for **s**.
5:3 for his own **s** as well as for
7:27 for their own **s** and then for the
8:12 and I won't remember their **s** anymore.
9:7 and for the **s** the people
9:28 on himself the **s** of many people.
10:4 of bulls and goats to take away **s**.
10:11 sacrifices that can never take away **s**.
10:12 one sacrifice for **s** for all time, he
10:17 remember their **s** and their lawless
10:26 a sacrifice for **s** left any longer.
James
5:20 bring about the forgiveness of many **s**.
1 Peter
2:24 on the cross the **s** we committed. He
3:18 on account of **s**, once for all,
4:8 brings about the forgiveness of many **s**.
2 Peter
1:9 they were cleansed from their past **s**.
1 John
1:9 if we confess our **s**, he is faithful
2:2 dealing with our **s**, not only ours
3:5 to take away **s**, and there is no
3:6 Any person who **s** has not seen him
4:10 as the sacrifice that deals with our **s**.
5:16 those who commit **s** that don't result
Revelation
1:5 and freed us from our **s** by his blood,

18:4 take part in her *s* and don't receive
18:5 Her *s* have piled up as high as heaven,

SINS ARE FORGIVEN
Mt 9:2; 9:5; Mk 2:5; 2:9; Lk 5:20; 5:23; 7:48

SISERA
Judges
4:2 of his army was **S**, and he was
4:13 **S** summoned all of his nine hundred iron chariots
4:22 after chasing **S**. Jael went out to
1 Samuel
12:9 them over to **S**, the commander of
Ezra
2:53 Barkos, **S**, Temah
Psalms
83:9 did to Midian, to **S**, and to Jabin at

SISTER → BROTHER OR SISTER
Genesis
12:13 them you are my *s* so that they will
20:2 Sarah, "She's my *s*." So King
26:7 said, "She's my *s*," because he was
34:13 because Shechem defiled their *s* Dinah.
Exodus
15:20 Miriam, Aaron's *s*, took a
Leviticus
18:9 contact with your *s*—regardless
20:17 a man marries his *s*—his father's
21:3 your unmarried *s*, who is close to
Deuteronomy
27:22 has sex with his *s*, whether his
2 Samuel
13:1 the beautiful *s* of Absalom, who
13:4 with Tamar, the *s* of my brother
13:11 said, "Come have sex with me, my *s*."
13:32 since the day Amnon raped his *s* Tamar.
Proverbs
7:4 You are my *s*"; call
Song of Songs
4:9 my heart, my *s*, my bride! You
4:10 your loving, my *s*, my bride! Your
4:12 garden is my *s*, my bride; an
5:1 to my garden, my *s*, my bride! I have
5:2 Open for me, my *s*, my dearest, my
8:8 Our *s* is small; she has no breasts.
Jeremiah
3:7 didn't. Her disloyal *s* Judah saw this.
Ezekiel
16:46 Your older *s* is Samaria, who lives with
16:55 Then your *s* Sodom and her daughters
Hosea
2:1 My People, and to your *s*, Compassion:
Matthew
12:50 heaven is my brother, *s*, and mother."
Mark
3:35 will is my brother, *s*, and mother."
John
11:1 the village of Mary and her *s* Martha.
11:5 Jesus loved Martha, her *s*, and Lazarus
11:28 privately to her *s* Mary, "The
11:39 Martha, the *s* of the dead man,
19:25 and his mother's *s*, Mary the wife of
Acts
23:16 Paul's *s* had a son who heard about the
Romans
16:1 introducing our *s* Phoebe to you,

SISTERS → BROTHERS AND SISTERS
Genesis
34:14 allowing our *s* to marry
Matthew
13:56 And his *s*, aren't they here with us?
19:29 houses, brothers, *s*, father, mother,
John
11:3 So the *s* sent word to Jesus, saying,
12:2 Lazarus and his *s* hosted a dinner for him
1 Timothy
5:2 women like your *s* with appropriate

SIT
Exodus
18:14 Why do you *s* alone, while all
Judges
4:5 She would *s* under Deborah's palm tree
Psalms
1:1 and doesn't *s* with the
26:5 and I don't *s* with wicked
50:20 You *s* around, talking about your own
55:2 me! I can't *s* still while
69:12 Those who *s* at the city gate muttered
83:1 silent! Don't be quiet or *s* still, God,
110:1 to my master: "**S** right beside me
139:2 You know when I *s* down and when I stand
Proverbs
23:1 When you *s* down to dine with a ruler,
Ecclesiastes
10:6 while the rich *s* in lowly
Song of Songs
8:13 You who *s* in the gardens, my companions
Isaiah
14:13 my throne. I'll *s* on the mount of
16:5 and someone will *s* faithfully on it
Jeremiah
33:17 his descendants *s* on the throne of
Zechariah
3:10 neighbors to *s* beneath their
6:13 majestic; he will *s* and rule on his
Malachi
3:3 He will *s* as a refiner and a purifier
Matthew
19:28 you also will *s* on twelve thrones
20:23 my cup, but to *s* at my right or
22:44 said to my lord, '**S** at my right side
23:2 and the Pharisees *s* on Moses' seat.
23:6 They love to *s* in places of honor at
25:31 with him, he will *s* on his majestic
Mark
14:32 said to them, "**S** here while I
Luke
22:30 and you will *s* on thrones
John
6:10 Have the people *s* down." There was
9:8 this the man who used to *s* and beg?"
Acts
2:34 said to my Lord, '**S** at my right side,
Hebrews
1:13 of the angels, **S** at my right side

SITTING
Genesis
19:1 Lot, who was **s** at the gate of
Deuteronomy
6:7 them when you are **s** around your house
11:19 them when you are **s** around your house
22:6 and the mother is **s** on the baby birds
1 Samuel
4:13 there, Eli was **s** in a chair beside
2 Chronicles
6:16 have a successor **s** on Israel's
18:9 Jehoshaphat were **s** on their thrones
Esther
5:1 king was inside **s** on his royal
5:13 Mordecai the Jew **s** at the King's
Psalms
107:10 redeemed had been **s** in darkness and
Song of Songs
2:3 take pleasure in **s**, and his fruit is
5:12 bathing in milk, **s** by brimming pools.
Isaiah
6:1 I saw the Lord **s** on a high and
Jeremiah
8:14 Why are we **s** here? Come, let's go to
29:16 the king **s** on David's throne
38:7 the king was **s** at the Benjamin
Lamentations
3:63 Whether **s** or standing, look at how I am
Matthew
9:9 man named Matthew **s** at a kiosk for
24:3 while Jesus was **s** on the Mount of
26:7 Jesus' head while he was **s** at dinner.
26:64 see the Human One **s** on the right side
26:69 Peter was **s** outside in the
27:61 Mary were there, **s** in front of the
Mark
2:6 experts were **s** there, muttering
2:14 Alphaeus' son, **s** at a kiosk for
5:15 with many demons **s** there fully
10:46 Timaeus' son, was **s** beside the road.
13:3 Jesus was **s** on the Mount of Olives
14:54 courtyard. He was **s** with the guards,
14:62 see the Human One **s** on the right side
Luke
1:79 to those who are **s** in darkness and
2:46 temple. He was **s** among the
5:2 saw two boats **s** by the lake. The
5:17 experts were **s** nearby. They had
5:27 named Levi **s** at a kiosk for
7:32 are like children **s** in the
8:35 had gone. He was **s** at Jesus' feet,
14:31 without first **s** down to consider
18:35 blind man was **s** beside the road
22:56 woman saw him **s** in the firelight.
John
2:14 in exchanging currency **s** there.
6:11 to those who were **s** there. He did the
12:15 king is coming, **s** on a donkey's
13:28 No one **s** at the table understood why
Acts
2:2 the entire house where they were **s**.
8:28 prophet Isaiah while **s** in his carriage.
14:8 birth and had never walked. **S** there, he
20:9 Eutychus was **s** in the window. He
26:30 Bernice, and those **s** with them.
1 Corinthians
14:30 else who is **s** down, the first
Colossians
3:1 where Christ is **s** at God's right

SIX
Exodus
20:9 **S** days you may work and do all your
37:19 A total of **s** branches grew out
Numbers
35:6 **S** of the cities that you give to the
35:13 will establish **s** refuge cities for
Deuteronomy
16:8 For **s** days you will eat unleavened
1 Chronicles
20:6 a huge man with **s** fingers on each
Proverbs
6:16 There are **s** things that the LORD hates,
Isaiah
6:2 him. Each had **s** wings: with two
Revelation
4:8 creatures had **s** wings, and each
13:18 Its number is **s** hundred sixty-six.

SIXTH
Genesis
1:31 and there was morning: the **s** day.
2:2 On the **s** day God completed all the
Revelation
6:12 as he opened the **s** seal, and there
9:13 Then the **s** angel blew his trumpet, and
9:14 It said to the **s** angel, who had the
16:12 Then the **s** angel poured his bowl on the
21:20 was sardonyx, the **s** was carnelian,

SIXTY
Numbers
7:88 bulls, **s** rams, sixty male
Song of Songs
3:7 Solomon's bed—**s** heroic men round
6:8 There may be **s** queens and eighty
Matthew
13:8 case a yield of **s** to one, and in
13:23 case a yield of **s** to one, and in

SKIES
Genesis
6:7 the birds in the **s**, because I regret
7:11 and the windows in the **s** opened.
8:2 deep sea and the **s** closed up. The
9:2 the birds in the **s**, everything
19:24 asphalt from the **s** onto Sodom and
49:25 from the **s** above and
Deuteronomy
4:19 Don't look to the **s**, to the sun or the
7:24 from under the **s**. No one will be
2 Samuel
22:10 God parted the **s** and came down; thick
Nehemiah
1:9 under distant **s**, I will gather
Psalms
8:3 I look up at your **s**, at what your
18:9 God parted the **s** and came down; thick
33:6 The **s** were made by the LORD's word, all
36:5 extends to the **s**; your
50:4 calls out to the **s** above and to the
50:6 The **s** proclaim his righteousness
77:17 poured water, the **s** cracked thunder;
78:23 orders to the **s** above, opened

SKIES [cont.]

78:26 moving across the **s** and drove the
102:25 long ago; the **s** are your
104:2 a robe; you open the **s** like a curtain.
113:4 God's glory is higher than the **s**!
136:5 one who made the **s** with skill—God's
144:5 LORD, part your **s** and come down! Touch the mountains
147:8 God covers the **s** with clouds; God makes rain

Proverbs
3:20 depths burst open, and the **s** drop dew.

Isaiah
34:4 dissolve, the **s** will roll up like
40:22 stretches out the **s** like a curtain

Jeremiah
10:12 wisdom, crafted the **s** by his knowledge.
51:15 and crafted the **s** by his knowledge.

Haggai
1:10 Therefore, the **s** above you have

SKILLED → SKILLED WORKERS

Exodus
28:3 Tell all who are **s**, to whom I have
30:25 them like a **s** perfume maker to
30:35 Like a **s** perfume maker, carefully blend
35:10 of you who are **s** in crafts should
35:25 All the **s** women spun cloth with their
36:1 and every other **s** worker whom the
36:2 and every **s** person whom the
37:29 incense like a **s** perfume maker.

1 Kings
5:6 one here who is **s** in cutting wood
7:14 was a Tyrian **s** in bronze work.

1 Chronicles
15:22 transportation, because he was **s** at it.

2 Chronicles
2:7 me a craftsman **s** in gold, silver,
2:13 I'm sending you a **s** and experienced
2:14 from Tyre. He's **s** in working with

Ezra
7:6 He was a scribe **s** in the

Proverbs
10:8 The **s** mind accepts commands, but a
16:21 The **s** mind is called discerning, and

Song of Songs
3:8 all of them **s** with the sword, expert in

Isaiah
40:20 and then seeks a **s** artisan to set up

Jeremiah
2:33 So **s** are you at pursuing lovers that
4:22 they are **s** at doing wrong,

Ezekiel
33:32 lovely voice and **s** technique. They

Daniel
1:4 without defects, **s** in all wisdom,
12:3 Those **s** in wisdom will shine like the
12:10 but those **s** in wisdom will

Amos
5:16 wail, and those **s** in mourning to

Micah
7:3 Their hands are **s** at doing evil.

1 Timothy
3:2 show hospitality and be **s** at teaching.

SKILLED WORKERS

Ex 36:4; 36:8; 2Ki 24:14; 24:16; 1Ch 4:14; 29:5; Jer 52:15

SKIN

Genesis
27:11 is a hairy man, but I have smooth **s**.

Exodus
4:6 his hand had a **s** disease flaky
4:7 out again, the **s** of his hand had
9:9 It will cause **s** sores that will
9:10 and it caused **s** sores and
9:11 because of the **s** sores, because
28:42 cover their naked **s** from their hips
34:29 realize that the **s** of his face shown
34:30 saw the **s** of Moses' face
34:35 see that the **s** of Moses' face

Leviticus
11:32 is wood, cloth, **s**, or funeral
13:2 spot on their **s**, and it becomes
14:2 for anyone with **s** disease at the
15:17 Any clothing or **s** on which there is an
22:4 is afflicted with **s** disease or has a

Numbers
5:2 anyone with a **s** disease, an
6:4 the grapevine, not even its seeds or **s**.
12:10 developed a **s** disease flaky
19:5 front of him, its **s**, flesh, and

Deuteronomy
24:8 outbreaks of **s** disease by being

Judges
8:7 to beat your **s** with desert

2 Samuel
3:29 a discharge or a **s** disease, someone

2 Kings
4:34 bent over him, the child's **s** grew warm.
5:1 mighty warrior, but he had a **s** disease.
5:27 Naaman's **s** disease will now cling to
7:3 four men with **s** disease at the
15:5 the king with a **s** disease that he

2 Chronicles
26:19 at the priests, **s** disease erupted
26:20 and saw the **s** disease on his
26:21 King Uzziah had **s** disease until the day he died
26:23 said, "He had **s** disease." His son
29:34 enough priests to **s** all these

Job
2:4 to the LORD, "**S** for skin—people
4:15 by my face; the hair of my **s** bristled.
7:5 crusted earth; my **s** hardens and oozes.
10:11 clothed me with **s** and flesh, wove
16:15 cloth over my **s** and buried my
18:13 some of their **s**. Death's firsborn
19:20 bones cling to my **s** and flesh; I have
19:26 After my **s** has been torn apart this
30:30 My **s** is charred; my bones are scorched

Psalms
102:5 My bones are protruding from my **s**.
109:24 from fasting; my body is **s** and bones.

Isaiah
32:11 bare your **s**, and tie mourning

Jeremiah
13:23 change his **s** or a leopard its

Lamentations
3:4 my flesh and my **s**; he broke my
4:8 streets. Their **s** shriveled on
5:10 Our **s** is as hot as an oven because of

Ezekiel
37:6 cover you with **s**. When I put
37:8 covered over with **s**. But there was

Micah
3:2 who tear the **s** off them, and the
3:3 tear off their **s**, break their
Nahum
3:16 The locust sheds its **s** and flies away.
Matthew
8:2 A man with a **s** disease came, kneeled
8:3 Instantly his **s** disease was
10:8 those with **s** diseases, and
11:5 People with **s** diseases are
26:6 house of Simon, who had a **s** disease,
Mark
1:40 A man with a **s** disease approached
1:42 Instantly, the **s** disease left him, and
14:3 Simon, who had a **s** disease. During
Luke
4:27 many persons with **s** diseases in
5:12 covered with a **s** disease. When he
5:13 Instantly, the **s** disease left him.
7:22 walk. People with **s** diseases are
17:12 ten men with **s** diseases
Acts
19:12 had touched his **s** were taken to the

SKY

Genesis
1:8 named the dome ***S***. There was
1:9 waters under the **s** come together
2:4 the day the LORD God made earth and **s**—
6:17 under the **s** that breathes.
7:3 the birds in the **s** as well, take
11:4 its top in the **s**, and let's make a
15:5 Look up at the **s** and count the
22:17 the stars in the **s** and as the grains
26:4 the stars in the **s**, and I will give
27:28 showers from the **s**, olive oil from
27:39 away from the showers of the **s** above.
28:12 top touching the **s**, and God's
Exodus
9:22 hand toward the **s** so that hail will
9:23 rod toward the **s**, and the LORD
10:21 hand toward the **s** so that darkness
10:22 hand toward the **s**, and an intense
16:4 down from the **s** for you. The
17:14 out the memory of Amalek under the **s**."
20:4 anything in the **s** above or on the
24:10 tiles, dazzlingly pure like the **s**.
32:13 the stars in the **s**. And I've
Leviticus
26:19 I will turn your **s** to iron and your
Deuteronomy
1:10 now as countless as the stars in the **s**.
1:28 huge, with walls **s**-high! Worse still,
4:11 fire up to the **s**, with darkness,
4:17 animal, a bird that flies in the **s**,
5:8 anything in the **s** above or on the
9:1 fortifications that reach to the **s**.
10:14 the LORD owns the **s**, the highest
10:22 as the stars in the nighttime **s**!
11:17 He will close the **s** up tight. There
28:23 The **s** over your head will be as hard as
28:24 on you from the **s** until you are
28:26 every bird in the **s** and animal on
28:62 in the night **s**, only a few of
Joshua
8:20 rising toward the **s**. They had no
10:11 stones from the **s** all the way to
10:13 the middle of the **s**. For a whole day,
Judges
5:4 land shook, the **s** poured down, the
5:20 fought from the **s**; from their
13:20 up toward the **s**, the LORD's
20:40 entire city going up in smoke to the **s**.
2 Samuel
21:10 bodies from the **s**, and she wouldn't
1 Kings
8:22 spreading out his hands toward the **s**,
8:35 When the **s** holds back its rain because
18:45 little while, the **s** became dark with
2 Kings
1:10 down from the **s** and burn up you
1:12 down from the **s** and burn up you
1:14 came from the **s** and burned up the
7:2 windows in the **s**, how could that
7:19 windows in the **s**, how could that
21:3 the stars in the **s** and worshipped
21:5 the stars in the **s** in both
1 Chronicles
21:16 the earth and the **s** with a drawn
27:23 as numerous as the stars in the **s**.
2 Chronicles
6:13 and spreading his hands toward the **s**,
6:26 When the **s** holds back its rain because
7:13 When I close the **s** so that there is no
33:3 the stars in the **s** and worshipped
33:5 the stars in the **s** in both
Job
1:16 fell from the **s** and burned up the
2:12 dust above his head toward the **s**.
12:7 the birds in the **s**, and they will
28:21 living, concealed from birds of the **s**.
35:11 us wiser than the birds in the **s**?"
37:3 under the whole **s**, his lightning on
37:18 Can you form the **s** with him, hard like
37:21 is bright in the **s**; the wind has
Psalms
8:8 the birds in the **s**, the fish of the
19:1 God's glory; the **s** is proclaiming
19:6 in one end of the **s**; its circuit is
89:6 there any in the **s** who could compare
89:37 a faithful witness in the **s**. Selah
104:12 the birds in the **s** make their home,
107:26 as high as the **s**; they crashed
148:4 same, you waters that are above the **s**!
150:1 Praise God in his fortress, the **s**!
Proverbs
30:19 an eagle in the **s**, the way of a
Isaiah
40:26 Look up at the **s** and consider: Who
55:10 down from the **s** and don't return
Jeremiah
4:25 every bird in the **s** had taken flight.
8:7 the stork in the **s** knows the
10:2 by signs in the **s**, even though the
14:22 it rain? Can the **s** by itself bring
33:22 the stars in the **s** can't be numbered
Ezekiel
29:5 earth and the birds in the **s** for food.
31:6 the birds in the **s** made nests in its
31:13 the birds in the **s**, and on its
32:4 the birds in the **s** to settle on you,
32:7 I will cover the **s**, and I will
38:20 the birds in the **s**, the beasts of

SKY [cont.]

Daniel
2:38 and birds in the **s**—wherever they liv
4:11 as high as the **s**; it could be seen
4:20 as high as the **s**, that could be
4:22 is as high as the **s**; your rule
12:3 shine like the **s**. Those who lead
Hosea
2:18 the birds in the **s**, and the creeping
4:3 the birds in the **s**, even the fish of
7:12 like birds in the **s**, I will bring
Zephaniah
1:3 the birds in the **s** and the fish in
Zechariah
5:9 the basket between the earth and the **s**.
Matthew
6:26 the birds in the **s**. They don't sow
8:20 the birds in the **s** have nests, but
13:32 the birds in the **s** come and nest in
16:2 weather because the **s** is bright red.'
16:3 today because the **s** is cloudy.' You
24:29 fall from the **s** and the planets
24:30 appear in the **s**. At that time all
24:31 from one end of the **s** to the other.
Mark
4:32 the birds in the **s** are able to nest
13:25 fall from the **s**, and the planets
Luke
8:5 and the birds in the **s** came and ate it.
9:58 the birds in the **s** have nests, but
12:56 earth and in the **s**. How is it that
13:19 the birds in the **s** nested in its
17:24 lights up the **s** from one end to
21:11 sights and great signs in the **s**.
Acts
7:42 the stars in the **s**, just as it is
Hebrews
11:12 the stars in the **s** and as countless
Revelation
6:13 The stars of the **s** fell to the earth as
6:14 The **s** disappeared like a scroll being
11:6 to close up the **s** so that no rain

SLAIN

Numbers
19:16 touches a person **s** by the sword, or
23:24 prey and drinks the blood of the **s**."
25:14 The name of the **s** Israelite man who was killed with
31:8 along with others **s**. They also killed
Joshua
13:22 to those others **s**, the Israelites
2 Samuel
1:22 the blood of the **s**, from the gore of
1 Chronicles
11:20 men he had **s**, but he wasn't
Isaiah
10:4 falling among the **s**? Even so, God's
26:21 blood and will conceal its **s** no longer.
66:16 humanity; many will be **s** by the LORD.
Jeremiah
14:18 I see only the **s** in battle. If I
33:5 corpses of those **s** in my fierce
Nahum
3:3 spear; countless **s**, masses of
Revelation
5:6 as if it had been **s**. It had seven
5:9 because you were **s**, and by your
13:3 to have been **s** and killed, but
13:8 scroll of life of the lamb who was **s**.

SLANDER

Proverbs
10:18 hate, and those who spread **s** are fools.
25:10 vilify you; the **s** against you will
30:10 Don't **s** a servant to his master;
Jeremiah
6:28 They live to **s**. They act
9:4 and every friend traffics in **s**.
Ezekiel
13:22 righteous with **s**—I didn't wound th
36:3 object of the people's **s** and derision.
Acts
26:11 them to **s** God. My rage
Romans
1:30 they **s** people, and they hate God. They
3:8 (Some people who **s** us accuse us of
Ephesians
4:31 shouting, and **s**, along with every
Colossians
3:8 rage, malice, **s**, and obscene
1 Timothy
5:14 give the enemy any reason to **s** us.
2 Timothy
3:2 proud. They will **s** others, and they
1 Peter
2:1 and all deceit, pretense, envy, and **s**.
3:16 Christ may be ashamed when they **s** you.
4:4 unrestrained wickedness. So they **s** you.
2 Peter
2:12 destroyed. They **s** what they don't
Jude
1:8 reject authority, and **s** the angels.
1:9 charge him with **s**. Instead, he
1:10 But these people **s** whatever they don't

SLAUGHTER

Genesis
43:16 to the house and **s** an animal and
Exodus
12:6 community should **s** their lambs.
12:21 your families, and **s** the Passover lamb.
24:5 offerings and **s** oxen as well-being
29:11 Then **s** the bull in the LORD's presence
34:25 Don't **s** the blood of my sacrifice with
Leviticus
1:5 Then you will **s** the bull before the
1:11 You must **s** it on the north side of the
3:2 the offering and **s** it at the meeting
4:4 Then he will **s** the bull before
14:13 The priest will **s** the sheep at the same
16:11 He will **s** the bull for his
22:28 But you will not **s** an ox or sheep and
Numbers
19:3 the camp and **s** it in front of
Deuteronomy
12:15 you wish, you may **s** and eat meat, as
12:21 you live, then **s** an animal from
1 Samuel
14:34 ox or sheep, and **s** them here with
2 Samuel
18:7 soldiers. A great **s** of twenty
2 Chronicles
28:9 Your merciless **s** of them stinks to

35:6 ***S*** the Passover lambs and prepare the
Psalms
37:14 and the needy, to ***s*** those whose way
44:22 we are considered sheep ready for ***s***.
Proverbs
7:22 like an ox to the ***s***, like a deer
24:11 staggering to the ***s***, don't hold back.
Isaiah
14:21 a place to ***s*** his sons for the
34:2 them out and has prepared them for ***s***.
53:7 being brought to ***s***, like a ewe
57:5 green tree, who ***s*** children in the
65:12 all bow down for ***s***, because I called
Jeremiah
11:19 lamb led to the ***s***; I didn't realize
20:4 exile some to Babylon and ***s*** others.
25:34 The day of your ***s*** has arrived. You
50:27 prepare them for ***s***. How terrible for
51:40 like lambs for ***s***, like rams and
Ezekiel
16:40 with stones, and ***s*** you with their
21:10 For utter ***s*** it is sharpened, polished
34:3 the wool, and you ***s*** the fat animals,
40:42 used in the ritual ***s*** was set on them.
44:11 temple. They will ***s*** the entirely
Hosea
9:13 must lead out his children for ***s***.
Obadiah
1:10 Because of the ***s*** and violence done to
Zechariah
11:4 Shepherd the flock intended for ***s***.
11:7 intended for ***s***, the afflicted of
Luke
15:23 fattened calf and ***s*** it. We must
19:27 bring them here and ***s*** them before me.'"
Acts
8:32 he was led to the ***s*** and like a lamb
Romans
8:36 sake. We are treated like sheep for ***s***.
James
5:5 hearts in preparation for the day of ***s***.

SLAUGHTERED

Genesis
37:31 Joseph's robe, ***s*** a male goat, and
Leviticus
4:24 head. It will be ***s*** at the place
6:25 offering must be ***s*** before the LORD
7:2 offering must be ***s*** at the same place
8:15 Moses ***s*** it, then took the blood and,
9:8 to the altar and ***s*** the young bull
9:12 Then Aaron ***s*** the entirely burned
14:5 that one bird be ***s*** over fresh water
14:6 the bird that was ***s*** over the fresh
14:13 offering are ***s***: in the holy
14:19 the entirely burned offering will be ***s***.
14:51 the bird that was ***s***. He will then
Numbers
11:22 be found and ***s*** for them? Or can
14:16 give them. So he ***s*** them in the
21:35 They ***s*** Og, his sons, and all his people
Deuteronomy
28:31 Your ox will be ***s*** while you watch, but
Judges
20:35 The Israelites ***s*** twenty-five thousand
1 Samuel
1:25 They ***s*** the bull, then brought the boy
11:11 morning watch and ***s*** them until the
14:32 and calves. They ***s*** them right on the
14:34 whatever they had and ***s*** it there.
22:21 that Saul had ***s*** the LORD's
1 Kings
19:21 pair of oxen, and ***s*** them. Then with
2 Kings
10:7 king's sons and ***s*** all seventy of
10:14 them alive, then ***s*** them at the well
23:20 He actually ***s*** on those altars all the
25:7 sons were ***s*** right before his
2 Chronicles
18:2 in Samaria, Ahab ***s*** many sheep and
29:22 When they ***s*** the bulls, the priests took
30:15 They ***s*** the Passover lambs on the
35:1 Jerusalem. They ***s*** the Passover
35:11 Then they ***s*** the Passover lambs, and the
Ezra
6:20 were clean. They ***s*** the Passover
Proverbs
9:2 She ***s*** her animals, mixed her wine, and
Isaiah
22:2 Your dead weren't ***s*** by the sword;
Jeremiah
18:21 let their men be ***s*** and their youth
39:6 king of Babylon ***s*** Zedekiah's
41:7 the men with him ***s*** them and threw
52:10 king of Babylon ***s*** Zedekiah's
Lamentations
2:21 you killed; you ***s***, showing no
Ezekiel
4:14 wasn't properly ***s***, and no unclean
16:21 You ***s*** my sons and placed them in the
23:39 When they ***s*** their children for their
40:39 and the compensation offerings were ***s***.
Luke
15:27 your father has ***s*** the fattened calf
15:30 prostitutes, you ***s*** the fattened calf
Revelation
5:12 Worthy is the ***s*** Lamb to receive
6:9 who had been ***s*** on account of the
18:24 all who have been ***s*** on the earth was

SLAVE

Genesis
39:17 The Hebrew ***s*** whom you brought
44:10 it will be my ***s***, and the rest of
44:17 cup will be my ***s***. As for the rest
44:33 stay as your ***s*** instead of the
Exodus
3:7 because of their ***s*** masters. I know
5:6 the people's ***s*** masters and
12:44 However, any ***s*** who has been bought may eat it
21:2 buy a male Hebrew ***s***, he will serve
23:12 of your female ***s*** and the immigrant
Leviticus
19:20 a woman who is a ***s*** engaged to
25:39 you, you must not make him work as a ***s***.
25:44 male or a female ***s*** from the nations
Deuteronomy
5:15 that you were a ***s*** in Egypt, but the
21:14 or treat her as a ***s*** because you have
24:18 how you were a ***s*** in Egypt but how

24:22 how you were a **s** in Egypt. That's
1 Samuel
30:13 asked him, "Whose **s** are you? Where do
1 Kings
14:10 a wall, whether **s** or free. Then I
20:32 is your **s**. He begs, 'Please
21:21 belongs to Ahab, whether **s** or free.
2 Kings
9:8 a wall, whether **s** or free, in
14:26 suffered, whether **s** or free, with no
Job
7:2 Like a **s** we pant for a shadow, await
39:9 agree to be your **s**, or will it spend
41:4 you will take him as a permanent **s**?
Psalms
105:17 who was sold as a **s**: it was Joseph.
Proverbs
22:7 poor; a borrower is a **s** to a lender.
Isaiah
24:2 priest; for the **s** and for his
49:7 nations, to the **s** of rulers: Kings
Jeremiah
2:14 Is Israel a **s**, a servant by birth? If
Lamentations
1:1 over provinces, she has become a **s**.
Zechariah
9:8 or returning. A **s** driver will no
Matthew
20:27 to be first among you will be your **s**—
26:51 the high priest's **s**, he cut off his
Mark
10:44 first among you will be the **s** of all,
14:47 the high priest's **s** and cut off his
John
8:34 that everyone who sins is a **s** to sin.
8:35 A **s** isn't a permanent member of the
Acts
16:16 prayer, we met a **s** woman. She had a
Romans
1:1 From Paul, a **s** of Christ Jesus, called
7:14 and blood, and I'm sold as a **s** to sin.
7:25 So then I'm a **s** to God's Law in
9:12 child will be a **s** to the younger
1 Corinthians
7:21 If you were a **s** when you were called,
7:22 Anyone who was a **s** when they were
9:19 I make myself a **s** to all people, to
9:27 it like a **s**. I do this to be
12:13 Jew or Greek, or **s** or free, and we
Galatians
1:10 people, I wouldn't be Christ's **s**.
3:28 there is neither **s** nor free; nor is
4:7 are no longer a **s** but a son or
Ephesians
6:8 that person is a **s** or a free person.
Philippians
2:7 the form of a **s** and by becoming
Colossians
1:7 who is the fellow **s** we love and
3:11 Scythian, **s** nor free, but
4:7 and fellow **s** in the Lord, will
2 Timothy
2:24 God's **s** shouldn't be argumentative but
Titus
1:1 From Paul, a **s** of God and an apostle of
Philemon
1:16 no longer as a **s** but more than a
James
1:1 From James, a **s** of God and of the Lord
2 Peter
1:1 Simon Peter, a **s** and apostle of
Jude
1:1 Jude, a **s** of Jesus Christ and brother
Revelation
6:15 and everyone, **s** and free, hid
19:18 both free and **s**, both small and

SLAVERY

Exodus
6:6 you from your **s** to them. I'll set
14:5 Israel go free from their **s** to us?"
20:2 out of Egypt, out of the house of **s**.
Deuteronomy
5:6 out of Egypt, out of the house of **s**.
6:12 out of Egypt, out of the house of **s**.
13:10 out of Egypt, out of the house of **s**.
Judges
6:8 and I led you out of the house of **s**.
Ezra
9:8 revived us for a little while in our **s**.
9:9 us in our **s**. Instead, he's
Nehemiah
5:5 daughters into **s**, and some of our
9:17 return to their **s** in Egypt. But you
Job
7:1 Isn't **s** everyone's condition on earth,
Jeremiah
34:13 land of Egypt, out of the house of **s**.
Micah
6:4 from the house of **s**. I sent Moses,
Acts
7:9 sold him into **s** in Egypt. God was
Romans
8:15 a spirit of **s** to lead you back
8:21 be set free from **s** to decay and
Galatians
4:25 the city is in **s** with her children.
5:1 don't submit to the bondage of **s** again.
1 Timothy
6:1 the bondage of **s** should consider
Hebrews
2:15 who were held in **s** their entire

SLAVES

Genesis
15:13 will be oppressed **s** for four hundred
43:18 capture us, make **s** of us, and take
44:9 to death, and we'll be my master's **s**."
47:25 If you wish, we will be Pharaoh's **s**."
50:18 him, and said, "We're here as your **s**."
Exodus
6:5 have turned into **s**, and I've
13:3 place you were **s**, because the LORD
13:14 of Egypt, out of the place we were **s**.
21:7 in the same way as male **s** are set free.
Leviticus
25:42 land. They must not be sold as **s**.
26:13 being Egypt's **s**. I broke your
Deuteronomy
6:21 We were Pharaoh's **s** in Egypt. But the
15:15 each of you were **s** in Egypt and how
16:12 each of you were **s** in Egypt, so
23:15 Don't return **s** to owners if they've
28:68 yourselves as **s**—both male and fem

1 Samuel
2:27 when they were **s** in Egypt to the
8:17 then you yourselves will become his **s**!
17:9 will become your **s**, but if I
25:10 are all sorts of **s** running away from
1 Kings
9:22 to work as **s**; instead, they
2 Kings
4:1 to take my two children away as **s**."
1 Chronicles
18:13 became David's **s**. The LORD gave
2 Chronicles
8:9 to work as **s**; instead, they
36:20 they could be his **s** and the slaves of
Ezra
9:9 though we are **s**, our God hasn't
Nehemiah
5:5 are already **s**! There is nothing
9:36 now today we are **s**, slaves in the
Esther
7:4 male and female **s**, I would have
Ecclesiastes
2:7 I even had **s** born in my house.
10:7 I have seen **s** on horseback, while
Isaiah
14:2 male and female **s** in the LORD's
Jeremiah
17:4 I will make you **s** of your enemies
34:8 to proclaim liberty for their **s**:
34:9 and female Hebrew **s** and no longer
34:10 male and female **s** and no longer
34:16 and forced them to be your **s** again.
Lamentations
5:8 **S** rule over us; there is no one to
Joel
2:29 out my spirit on the male and female **s**.
Zechariah
2:9 prey to their own **s**, so you will know
Matthew
10:24 teacher, and **s** aren't greater
10:25 their teacher and **s** like their
John
8:33 been anyone's **s**. How can you say
Acts
6:9 of Former **S**. Members from
7:7 they serve as **s**, God said, and
Romans
6:6 way we wouldn't be **s** to sin anymore,
7:6 so that we can be **s** in the new life
1 Corinthians
7:23 and paid for. Don't become **s** of people.
2 Corinthians
4:5 ourselves as your **s** for Jesus' sake.
Galatians
2:4 have in Christ Jesus, and to make us **s**.
4:9 Do you want to be **s** to it again?
Ephesians
6:5 As for **s**, obey your human masters with
6:6 but act like **s** of Christ
6:9 treat your **s** in the same way.
Philippians
1:1 Paul and Timothy, **s** of Christ Jesus.
Colossians
3:22 **S**, obey your masters on earth in
4:1 and fair to your **s**, knowing that you
Titus
2:9 Tell **s** to submit to their own masters
3:3 deceived, and **s** to our desires
1 Peter
2:16 Do this as God's **s**, and yet also as
2:18 Household **s**, submit by accepting the
2 Peter
2:19 themselves are **s** of immorality;
Revelation
13:16 the free and **s**—to have a mark
18:13 and carriages, and **s**, even human lives.

SLEEP

Genesis
2:21 a deep and heavy **s**, and took one of
41:22 I went to **s** again and saw in my dream
Exodus
22:27 person have to **s** in? And if he
Deuteronomy
24:13 so they can **s** in their own
1 Samuel
26:12 because a deep **s** from the LORD had
2 Samuel
11:13 Uriah went out to **s** in the same
1 Kings
19:6 ate and drank, and then went back to **s**.
Esther
6:1 simply couldn't **s**. He had the
Job
3:13 down quietly; I'd **s**; rest would be
4:13 of night, when deep **s** falls on people,
14:12 they don't get up and awaken from **s**.
33:15 night, when deep **s** falls upon
Psalms
3:5 I lie down, **s**, and wake up because the
13:3 Otherwise, I'll **s** the sleep of
127:2 because God gives **s** to those he loves.
132:4 my eyes close, won't let my eyelids **s**,
Proverbs
3:24 you lie down, your **s** will be pleasant.
4:16 They don't **s** unless they do evil; they
6:4 Don't give **s** to your eyes or slumber to
6:9 down? When will you rise from your **s**?
6:10 A little **s**, a little slumber, a little
19:15 brings on deep **s**; a slacker goes
20:13 Don't love **s** or you will be poor; stay
24:33 A little **s**, a little slumber, a little
Ecclesiastes
5:12 is the worker's **s**, whether there's
8:16 even going without **s** day and night
Isaiah
5:27 don't rest or **s**; no belt is
29:10 a spirit of deep **s**, and has shut
56:10 bark, dreamers, loungers, loving to **s**.
Jeremiah
31:26 looked around. What a pleasant **s** I had!
51:39 asleep. They will **s** forever, never to
51:57 well. They will **s** forever, never to
Ezekiel
34:25 live in the desert and **s** in the forest.
Daniel
6:18 were brought to him, and he couldn't **s**.
12:2 Many of those who **s** in the dusty land
Jonah
1:5 vessel to lie down and was deep in **s**.
Matthew
25:5 they all became drowsy and went to **s**.
26:43 sleeping. Their eyes were heavy with **s**.
26:45 them, "Will you **s** and rest all

Mark
14:41 them, "Will you **s** and rest all
Luke
9:32 overcome by **s**, but they managed
John
11:13 was in a deep **s**, but Jesus had
Acts
20:9 into a deep **s** as Paul talked on
Romans
13:11 wake up from your **s**. Now our
1 Thessalonians
5:6 then, let's not **s** like the others,
5:7 People who **s** sleep at night, and people

SLEEPING

Genesis
34:7 Israel by **s** with Jacob's
38:16 What will you give me for **s** with you?"
Numbers
31:17 known a man intimately by **s** with him.
31:18 man intimately by **s** with him, spare
31:35 known a man intimately by **s** with him.
1 Samuel
26:5 general, were **s**. Saul was
26:7 and the army were **s** all around him.
2 Samuel
12:16 and spent the night **s** on the ground.
Psalms
44:23 up! Why are you **s**, Lord? Get up!
78:65 —as if he'd been **s**! Like a warrior
Song of Songs
5:2 I was **s**, but my heart was awake. A
Daniel
2:1 dreams made him anxious, but he kept **s**.
Jonah
1:6 you possibly be **s** so deeply? Get
Matthew
13:25 While people were **s**, an enemy came and planted weeds
26:40 and found them **s**. He said to
26:43 and found them **s**. Their eyes were
28:13 and stole his body while you were **s**.
Mark
4:38 rear of the boat, **s** on a pillow. They
5:39 The child isn't dead. She's only **s**."
7:4 of cups, jugs, pans, and **s** mats.
13:36 you weren't expecting and find you **s**.
14:37 and found them **s**. He said to
14:40 he found them **s**, for they
Luke
8:52 cry. She isn't dead. She's only **s**."
22:46 Why are you **s**? Get up and pray
John
11:11 friend Lazarus is **s**, but I am going
11:12 Lord, if he's **s**, he will get
Romans
13:13 drunk, not in **s** around and
1 Corinthians
6:15 of someone who is **s** around? No way!
6:16 to someone who is **s** around is one
2 Peter
2:3 idle, nor is their destruction **s**.

SLEPT

Genesis
15:12 sun set, Abram **s** deeply. A
16:4 He **s** with Hagar, and she became
26:10 people would have **s** with your wife;
29:23 her to Jacob, and he **s** with her.
29:30 Jacob **s** with Rachel, and he loved
30:4 Jacob as his wife, and he **s** with her.
30:16 herbs." So he **s** with her that
34:2 her, he took her, **s** with her, and
35:22 Reuben went and **s** with Bilhah his
38:2 he married her. After he **s** with her,
38:9 be his so when he **s** with his
38:18 these to her, **s** with her, and she
Numbers
5:19 If no man has **s** with you and if
Judges
16:3 But Samson **s** only half the night. He
21:11 and every woman who has **s** with a man."
21:12 man intimately or **s** with one, and
1 Samuel
9:25 made for Saul on the roof, and he **s**.
2 Samuel
11:9 However, Uriah **s** at the palace entrance
1 Kings
19:5 He lay down and **s** under the solitary
21:27 He fasted, even **s** in mourning
Ezekiel
23:8 who had **s** with her in her

SMALL

Genesis
19:20 flee to, and it's **s**. It's small,
Exodus
12:4 household is too **s** for a lamb, it
Leviticus
11:29 for you among the **s** creatures that
11:31 Of all **s** moving creatures, these are
21:20 hunchback or too **s**; anyone who has
Numbers
20:19 for it. It's a **s** matter. We would
22:18 to do anything, **s** or great, to
26:54 and to a **s** clan you will
26:56 they are large or **s**, each tribe will
33:54 large, and to the **s** you will make its
Deuteronomy
14:16 the **s** owl and the large owl, the water
25:14 in your house, a large one and a **s** one.
Joshua
8:35 the women and **s** children, along
17:15 Ephraimite highland is too **s** for you."
1 Samuel
2:19 would make a **s** robe for him and
10:1 Samuel took a **s** jar of oil and poured
14:43 only took a very **s** taste of honey on
20:2 anything big or **s** without telling
2 Samuel
7:19 even this was too **s** in your eyes,
12:3 nothing—just one **s** ewe lamb that he
1 Kings
2:20 I have just one **s** request for you.
8:64 presence was too **s** to contain the
10:17 and three hundred **s** shields of hammered
18:44 said, "I see a **s** cloud the size of
20:27 them like two **s** flocks of goats,
22:31 anyone big or **s**. Fight only with
2 Kings
4:2 in the house except a **s** jar of oil."

4:10 Let's make a **s** room on the roof. We'll
6:1 under your authority is too **s** for us.
1 Chronicles
17:17 even this was too **s** in your eyes,
25:8 assigned duties, **s** as well as great,
26:13 whether their household was **s** or large.
2 Chronicles
7:7 had made was too **s** to contain the
9:16 and three hundred **s** shields of hammered
14:8 armed with **s** shields and bows.
18:30 anyone big or **s**. Fight only with
23:9 and large and **s** shields that were
24:24 were relatively **s**, the LORD handed
31:18 all their **s** children, their
36:18 both large and **s**, including the
Job
3:19 Both **s** and great are there; a servant
Psalms
104:25 living things both **s** and large.
Proverbs
24:10 of distress, your strength is too **s**.
Ecclesiastes
9:14 There was a **s** town with only a few
Song of Songs
8:8 Our sister is **s**; she has no breasts.
Isaiah
1:8 is left like a **s** shelter in a
16:14 will dwindle. The **s** remnant will be
50:2 Is my hand too **s** to redeem you?
Jeremiah
41:16 with him took the **s** group they had
42:2 God for us, this **s** group, for as you
52:19 find as well: the **s** bowls, the fire
Ezekiel
16:20 this promiscuity of yours a **s** thing?
16:47 practices in any **s** way. You were far
29:15 I will make it **s** to keep it from
Daniel
7:8 suddenly, another **s** horn came up
8:9 A single, very **s** horn came out of one
11:23 power at the expense of a **s** nation.
Amos
7:2 How can Jacob survive? He is so **s**!"
7:5 How can Jacob survive? He is so **s**!"
Matthew
10:29 sold for a **s** coin? But not one
Mark
3:9 to get a **s** boat ready for
12:42 and put in two **s** copper coins
Luke
12:6 sold for two **s** coins? Yet not
12:26 can't do such a **s** thing, why worry
19:17 faithful in a **s** matter, you will
21:2 throw in two **s** copper coins
Acts
19:12 Even the **s** towels and aprons that had
2 Corinthians
9:6 one who sows a **s** number of seeds
James
3:5 the tongue is a **s** part of the body,
3:6 The tongue is a **s** flame of fire, a
Revelation
11:18 your name, both **s** and great, and to
13:16 everyone—the **s** and great, the
19:5 you who fear him, both **s** and great."
19:18 both free and slave, both **s** and great."
20:12 the great and the **s**, standing before

SMELL
Exodus
29:18 LORD, a soothing **s**, a food gift for
29:25 as a soothing **s** in the LORD's
29:41 as a soothing **s**, a gift offering
Leviticus
1:9 a food gift of soothing **s** to the LORD.
Numbers
15:3 as a soothing **s** for the LORD from
29:36 as a soothing **s** to the LORD: one
Deuteronomy
4:28 that cannot see, listen, eat, or **s**.
Psalms
115:6 They have noses, but they can't **s**.
Daniel
3:27 before; they didn't even **s** like fire!
John
11:39 said, "Lord, the **s** will be awful!
1 Corinthians
12:17 what would happen to the sense of **s**?
2 Corinthians
2:15 We **s** like the aroma of Christ's
2:16 We **s** like a contagious dead person to

SMOKE
Genesis
19:28 He saw the **s** from the land
Exodus
19:18 Sinai was all in **s** because the LORD
29:13 and burn them up in **s** on the altar.
Numbers
5:26 and turn it into **s** on the altar. And
18:17 their fat into **s** for a soothing
Deuteronomy
4:11 sky, with darkness, cloud, and thick **s**!
5:22 and the thick **s**. He added no
Joshua
8:20 sight of the **s** of the city
8:21 city and that the **s** of the city was
Judges
20:38 sent up a big cloud of **s** from the city,
20:40 the column of **s** began to rise
2 Samuel
22:9 **S** went up from God's nostrils; out of
Job
41:20 **S** pours from his nostrils like a
Psalms
18:8 **S** went up from God's nostrils; out of
37:20 like the beauty of a meadow—in **s**.
66:15 along with the **s** of sacrificed
68:2 Like **s** is driven away, drive them away!
102:3 disappear like **s**, my bones are
104:32 the mountains, and they erupt in **s**.
119:83 dried up by **s**, though I haven't
144:5 down! Touch the mountains so they **s**!
148:8 hail, snow and **s**, stormy wind that
Proverbs
10:26 to the teeth and **s** to the eyes, so
Song of Songs
3:6 like pillars of **s**? She is perfumed
Isaiah
4:5 cloud by day and **s** and the light of
6:4 and the house was filled with **s**.
9:18 the forest; they swirled in rising **s**.
14:31 you Philistines! **S** is coming from

30:27 blazing, his **s**-cloud thick. His
34:10 extinguished; its **s** will go up
51:6 disappear like **s**, the earth will
Ezekiel
46:22 to handle **s**. All four were
Hosea
13:3 floor, or like **s** from a window.
Joel
2:30 earth—blood and fire and columns of **s**.
Nahum
2:13 your chariots in **s**; the sword will
Acts
2:19 below, blood and fire and a cloud of **s**.
Revelation
8:4 The **s** of the incense offered for the
9:2 of the abyss; and **s** rose up from the
14:11 The **s** of their painful suffering goes
15:8 was filled with **s** from God's glory
18:9 when they see the **s** from her burning.
18:18 as they saw the **s** from her burning
19:3 Hallelujah! **S** goes up from her

SNAKE

Genesis
3:1 The **s** was the most intelligent of all
49:17 Dan will be a **s** on the road, a serpent
Exodus
4:3 it turned into a **s**. Moses jumped
4:4 out and grab the **s** by the tail." So
7:15 shepherd's rod that turned into a **s**.
Numbers
21:8 Make a poisonous **s** and place it on a
21:9 made a bronze **s** and placed it on
Deuteronomy
32:33 their wine is **s** poison, venom from a
2 Kings
18:4 the bronze **s** that Moses made,
Psalms
58:5 it can't hear the **s** charmer's voice
Proverbs
23:32 it bites like a **s** and poisons like
30:19 sky, the way of a **s** on the rock, the
Ecclesiastes
10:8 through a wall may be bitten by a **s**.
10:11 If a **s** bites before it's charmed, then
Isaiah
34:15 There the **s** will nest and lay eggs and
65:25 the ox, but the **s**—its food will be
Jeremiah
46:22 the sound of a **s** hissing as it
Amos
5:19 the wall, and was bitten by a **s**.
Micah
7:17 dust like the **s**, like things that
Matthew
7:10 Or give them a **s** when they ask for
Luke
11:11 you would give a **s** to your child if
John
3:14 lifted up the **s** in the
Acts
28:5 Paul shook the **s** into the fire and
2 Corinthians
11:3 same way as the **s** deceived Eve with
Revelation
12:9 down. The old **s**, who is called
12:15 his mouth the **s** poured a river of
20:2 dragon, the old **s**, who is the devil

SODOM

Genesis
13:13 The citizens of **S** were very evil and
18:20 of injustice from **S** and Gomorrah are
19:24 from the skies onto **S** and Gomorrah.
Isaiah
1:9 we would be like **S**; we would
Ezekiel
16:46 younger sister is **S**, who lives with
Luke
10:12 I assure that **S** will be better off on
Romans
9:29 have been like **S**, and we would
Jude
1:7 In the same way, **S** and Gomorrah and
Revelation
11:8 called **S** and Egypt, where

SOIL

Genesis
3:19 taken; you are **s**, to the soil you
18:27 Lord, even though I'm just **s** and ash,
Exodus
20:24 from fertile **s** on which to
2 Chronicles
26:10 and vineyards, because he loved the **s**.
Nehemiah
10:35 produce of our **s** and the early
10:37 produce of our **s** to the Levites,
Job
14:19 floods carry away **s**; you destroy a
21:33 The **s** near the desert streambed is
Psalms
105:35 they devoured the fruit of their **s**.
137:4 sing the LORD's song on foreign **s**?
Isaiah
32:13 for my people's **s** growing barbs and
34:7 with blood; its **s** soaked with fat.
Jeremiah
4:3 your hard rocky **s**; don't plant
22:10 will never return to see his native **s**.
22:26 from your native **s**, and there the
Hosea
10:11 Jacob will turn the **s** for himself.
Zechariah
13:5 ground, for the **s** has been my
Matthew
13:5 ground where the **s** was shallow. They
13:8 seed fell on good **s** and bore fruit,
13:23 planted on good **s**, this refers to
Mark
4:5 ground where the **s** was shallow. They
4:8 fell into good **s** and bore fruit.
4:20 scattered on good **s** are those who
Luke
8:8 landed on good **s**. When it grew, it
8:15 that fell on good **s** are those who
14:35 neither for the **s** nor for the

SOLD

Genesis
25:33 And he did. He **s** his birthright to
45:4 brother Joseph! The one you **s** to Egypt.
45:5 that you **s** me here.
47:20 every Egyptian **s** his field when

Exodus
21:16 they have been ***s*** or are still
22:3 he must be ***s*** to pay for his
Leviticus
25:16 of harvests that are being ***s*** to you.
Deuteronomy
32:30 their rock ***s*** them off, only
1 Kings
21:25 like Ahab who ***s*** out by doing evil
2 Kings
6:25 A donkey's head ***s*** for eighty
7:16 seahs of barley ***s*** for a shekel, in
Nehemiah
5:8 kin who had been ***s*** to other nations.
Esther
7:4 We have been ***s***—I and my people—to be wiped out
Psalms
44:12 You've ***s*** your people for nothing, not
105:17 of them, who was ***s*** as a slave: it
Isaiah
45:14 Cush will be ***s***, and the tall
50:1 sins you were ***s***; on account of
52:3 You were ***s*** for nothing, and
Jeremiah
34:14 who have been ***s*** to you. After
Ezekiel
7:13 get back what was ***s***, even if both of
23:30 you because you ***s*** yourself to the
48:14 of it will be ***s***, exchanged, or
Joel
3:3 prostitutes, and ***s*** girls for wine,
3:6 You have ***s*** the people of Judah and
3:7 where you have ***s*** them, and I will
Amos
2:6 because they have ***s*** the innocent for
Matthew
10:29 two sparrows ***s*** for a small coin?
13:44 joy, the finder ***s*** everything and
13:46 he went and ***s*** all that he owned
18:25 that he should be ***s***, along with his
21:12 and the chairs of those who ***s*** doves.
26:9 could have been ***s*** for a lot of
Mark
11:15 and the chairs of those who ***s*** doves.
14:5 could have been ***s*** for almost a
Luke
12:6 five sparrows ***s*** for two small
John
12:5 Why wasn't it ***s*** and the money
Acts
4:37 He owned a field, ***s*** it, brought the
5:1 wife Sapphira, ***s*** a piece of
5:4 keep? After you ***s*** it, wasn't the
7:9 of Joseph, they ***s*** him into slavery
Romans
7:14 and blood, and I'm ***s*** as a slave to sin.
1 Corinthians
10:25 that is ***s*** in the
Hebrews
12:16 like Esau. He ***s*** his inheritance
Revelation
18:15 merchants who ***s*** these things, and

SOLDIERS

Joshua
5:4 the men who were ***s***, had died in the
6:3 city with all the ***s***, going around the
7:14 will come forward by individual ***s***.
7:17 as individual ***s***. Zabdi was
8:3 thousand brave ***s***. He sent them out
10:2 was larger than Ai. All its men were ***s***.
10:7 the entire army and all the bravest ***s***.
Judges
4:13 and all of the ***s*** who were with him
7:22 swords of fellow ***s*** against each
20:2 thousand foot ***s*** armed with swords.
1 Samuel
4:10 thirty thousand Israelite foot ***s*** fell,
Ezra
8:22 for a group of ***s*** and cavalry to
Isaiah
37:36 thousand ***s*** in the Assyrian
Jeremiah
48:14 you claim, "We're ***s***; we're war
50:30 Therefore, her ***s*** will fall in the
51:14 your cities with ***s*** like a swarm of
Matthew
27:27 The governor's ***s*** took Jesus into the
28:12 to give a large sum of money to the ***s***.
Mark
15:16 The ***s*** led Jesus away into the courtyard
Luke
3:14 ***S*** asked, "What about us? What should we do?
23:36 The ***s*** also mocked him. They came up to
John
19:23 When the ***s*** crucified Jesus, they took

SOLEMN PLEDGE

Ex 22:11; Lv 5:1; Nm 5:19; 30:2, 10; Dt 7:8; Josh 9:15; 9:18, 19, 20; Jdg 21:5; 1Sa 14:24; 14:26, 28; 20:42; 24:21, 22; 2Sa 21:2; 21:7, 17; 1Ki 1:29; 2:42; 8:31; 2Ki 11:4; 25:24; 1Ch 16:16; 2Ch 6:22; 15:15; 36:13; Ezr 10:5; Neh 6:18; 10:29; 13:25; Ps 105:9; 110:4; Ecc 8:2; Song 2:7; 5:9; 8:4; Is 45:23; 65:16; Jer 11:5; 12:16; 44:26; Eze 17:13; 17:16, 18, 19; 20:5, 15, 23; 44:12; Mt 5:33; 14:9; 26:72; Mk 6:26; Lk 1:73; Ac 2:30; Heb 6:16; 6:17; 7:20, 21, 28; Jas 5:12

SOLEMN PROMISE

Gn 28:20; 31:13; Lv 7:16; 22:18, 21, 23; 27:2, 9, 11; Nm 6:21; 15:3, 8; 21:2; 30:2, 3, 4, 6, 8, 9, 10, 13; Dt 23:18; Jdg 11:30; 1Sa 1:21; 1Ki 2:43; Eze 16:8; Ac 18:18; 21:23

SOLEMN PROMISES

Lv 23:38; Nm 29:39; 30:4, 5, 7, 11, 12, 14; Dt 12:6; 12:26; Job 22:27; Prv 7:14; 31:2; Is 19:21; Jon 1:16; Na 1:15

SOLEMNLY PROMISED

Nm 14:16; Dt 12:11; 12:17; 1Sa 20:3; Am 4:2; Ac 23:12; 23:14, 21

SOLOMON

2 Samuel
12:24 son and named him ***S***. The LORD loved
1 Kings
1:10 David's veterans, or his brother ***S***.
2:12 ***S*** sat on the throne of his father
3:5 LORD appeared to ***S*** at Gibeon in a

5:1 his servants to ***S*** when he heard
8:1 Then ***S*** assembled Israel's elders, all
10:10 of Sheba gave this gift to King ***S***.
11:5 ***S*** followed Astarte the goddess of the
11:43 Then ***S*** lay down with his ancestors. He
Matthew
1:6 was the father of ***S***, whose mother had
John
10:23 in the covered porch named for ***S***.
Acts
7:47 But it was ***S*** who actually built a house

SON → BIRTH TO A SON, GOD'S SON, SON JESUS, SON JESUS CHRIST, SON OF DAVID, YOU ARE GOD'S SON, YOU ARE MY SON
Genesis
5:3 the father of a ***s*** in his image,
17:23 Abraham took his ***s*** Ishmael, all those
21:4 circumcised his ***s*** Isaac when he was
22:2 said, "Take your ***s***, your only son
22:12 hold back your ***s***, your only son,
25:11 God blessed his ***s*** Isaac, and Isaac
Exodus
4:23 to you, "Let my ***s*** go so he could
Deuteronomy
18:10 who passes his ***s*** or daughter
21:19 will take the ***s*** before the elders
34:9 Joshua, Nun's ***s***, was filled with
Ruth
4:17 name, saying, "A ***s*** has been born to
1 Samuel
1:23 and nursed her ***s*** until she had
9:2 He had a ***s*** named Saul, who was a
13:16 Saul, his ***s*** Jonathan, and the people
16:19 Send me your ***s*** David, the one
2 Samuel
7:14 and he will be a ***s*** to me. Whenever
1 Kings
3:23 one says, 'My ***s*** is alive and your
8:19 your very own ***s*** will build the
2 Kings
6:29 cooked and ate my ***s***. The next day I
1 Chronicles
22:10 He'll become my ***s***, and I'll become
Job
32:2 Elihu ***s*** of Barachel the Buzite from the
32:6 Elihu ***s*** of Barachel the Buzite, said:
Psalms
3:1 he fled from his ***s*** Absalom.] LORD, I
72:1 your righteousness to the king's ***s***.
72:20 prayers of David, Jesse's ***s***, are ended.
80:15 strong hand, this ***s*** whom you secured
116:16 servant and the ***s*** of your female
Proverbs
1:1 Solomon, King David's ***s***, from Israel:
1:8 Listen, my ***s***, to your father's
1:10 My ***s***, don't let sinners entice you.
1:15 My ***s***, don't go on the path with them;
2:1 My ***s***, accept my words and store up my
3:1 My ***s***, don't forget my instruction. Let
3:11 of the LORD, my ***s***; don't despise
3:12 a father who treats his ***s*** with favor.
3:21 My ***s***, don't let them slip from your
4:3 When I was a ***s*** to my father, tender and
4:10 Listen, my ***s***, and take in my speech,
4:20 My ***s***, pay attention to my words. Bend
5:1 My ***s***, pay attention to my wisdom. Bend
5:20 Why, my ***s***, should you lose your senses
6:1 My ***s***, if you guarantee a loan for your
6:3 Do this, my ***s***, to get out of it, for
6:20 My ***s***, keep your father's command;
7:1 My ***s***, keep my words; store up my
10:5 A wise ***s*** harvests in the summer; a
13:1 A wise ***s*** listens to the discipline of
17:2 a disgraceful ***s*** and will divide
17:21 a fool for a ***s*** brings grief;
17:25 A foolish ***s*** is irritating to his father
19:13 A foolish ***s*** is a disaster to his
30:1 of Agur, Jakeh's ***s***, from Massa. The
31:2 No, my ***s***! No, son of my womb! No, son
Isaiah
9:6 is born to us, a ***s*** is given to us,
Ezekiel
44:25 father or mother, ***s*** or daughter,
Hosea
11:1 him, and out of Egypt I called my ***s***.
Amos
7:14 am I a prophet's ***s***; but I am a
Malachi
1:6 A ***s*** honors a father, and a servant
Matthew
2:15 I have called my ***s*** out of Egypt.
3:17 said, "This is my ***S*** whom I dearly
11:27 No one knows the ***S*** except the
13:55 the carpenter's ***s***? Isn't his mother
16:16 the Christ, the ***S*** of the living
17:5 said, "This is my ***S*** whom I dearly
22:42 the Christ? Whose ***s*** is he?""David's
24:36 and not the ***S***. Only the Father
28:19 Father and of the ***S*** and of the Holy
Mark
9:7 This is my ***S***, whom I dearly
13:32 and not the ***S***. Only the Father
14:61 the Christ, the ***S*** of the blessed
Luke
1:32 be called the ***S*** of the Most High.
2:7 child, a ***s***, wrapped him
9:35 said, "This is my ***S***, my chosen one.
15:21 Then his ***s*** said, 'Father, I have sinned
19:9 because he too is a ***s*** of Abraham.
20:44 him 'Lord,' how can he be David's ***s***?"
John
3:16 he gave his only ***S***, so that everyone
3:36 believes in the ***S*** has eternal life.
5:19 you that the ***S*** can't do anything
6:40 all who see the ***S*** and believe in
17:1 Glorify your ***S***, so that the Son
Romans
5:10 the death of his ***S*** while we were
8:3 sending his own ***S*** to deal with sin
8:29 the image of his ***S***. That way his Son
8:32 spare his own ***S*** but gave him up
1 Corinthians
15:28 control, then the ***S*** himself will also
Colossians
1:13 us into the kingdom of the ***S*** he loves.
1 Thessalonians
1:10 waiting for his ***S*** from heaven. His
Hebrews
1:2 to us through a ***S***. God made his Son
7:28 Law, appointed a ***S*** who has been made
James
2:21 he offered his ***s*** Isaac on the

2 Peter
1:17 my dearly loved ***S***, with whom I am
1 John
1:3 Father and with his ***S***, Jesus Christ.
1:7 of Jesus, his ***S***, cleanses us from
2:23 who denies the ***S*** does not have the
4:9 has sent his only ***S*** into the world so
4:14 has sent the ***S*** to be the savior
5:11 life to us, and this life is in his ***S***.

SON OF DAVID

Mt 1:1; 1:20; 9:27; 12:23; 15:22; 20:30, 31; 21:9, 15; Mk 10:47; 10:48; Lk 3:31; 18:38, 39

SON OF MAN → HUMAN ONE

SONG

Exodus
15:1 sang this ***s*** to the LORD: I
32:18 of a victory ***s***. It isn't the
Numbers
21:17 sang this ***s***: "Well, flow up!
Judges
5:12 wake up, sing a ***s***! Arise, Barak!
1 Samuel
18:8 with anger. This ***s*** annoyed him.
2 Samuel
1:17 sang this funeral ***s*** for Saul and his
1:18 to learn the ***S*** of the Bow.
3:33 sang this funeral ***s*** for Abner:
22:1 the words of this ***s*** to the LORD after
1 Chronicles
6:32 ministered with ***s*** before the
2 Chronicles
20:22 broke into joyful ***s*** and praise, the
29:27 the LORD's ***s*** also began,
35:25 a funeral ***s*** for Josiah, and
Job
30:9 And now I'm their ***s***; I'm their cliché
Psalms
28:7 rejoiced, and I thank him with my ***s***.
33:3 Sing to him a new ***s***! Play your best
40:3 He put a new ***s*** in my mouth, a song of
42:8 by night his ***s*** is with me
47:7 Sing praises with a ***s*** of instruction!
65:13 shout for joy; they break out in ***s***!
69:30 God's name with ***s***; I will magnify
81:2 Take up a ***s*** and strike the drum! Sweet
137:3 joy: "Sing us a ***s*** about Zion!" they
137:4 sing the LORD's ***s*** on foreign soil?
144:9 I will sing a new ***s*** to you, God. I will
Proverbs
25:20 Singing a ***s*** to a troubled heart is like
Ecclesiastes
7:5 wise than to listen to the ***s*** of fools,
Song of Songs
1:1 The ***S*** of Songs, which is for Solomon
Isaiah
5:1 loved one a love ***s*** for his vineyard.
14:7 rests quietly, then it breaks into ***s***.
23:15 become like the prostitute in the ***s***:
25:5 a cloud, the tyrants' ***s*** falls silent.
26:1 On that day, this ***s*** will be sung in the
42:10 to the LORD a new ***s***! Sing his praise
49:13 mountains, with a ***s***. The LORD has
52:9 Break into ***s*** together, you ruins of
55:12 will burst into ***s*** before you; all
Lamentations
3:14 object of their ***s*** of ridicule all
3:63 I am the object of their ***s*** of ridicule.
Amos
5:1 word—a funeral ***s***—that I am lifting
8:10 into a funeral ***s***; I will make
Matthew
11:17 We sang a funeral ***s*** and you didn't
Luke
7:32 We sang a funeral ***s*** and you didn't
Revelation
5:9 took up a new ***s***, saying, "You are
14:3 They sing a new ***s*** in front of the
15:3 They sing the ***s*** of Moses, God's

SONGS

Genesis
31:27 celebration, with ***s*** and tambourines
Exodus
32:18 The sound of party ***s*** is what I hear."
2 Samuel
6:5 strength, with ***s***, zithers, harps,
1 Kings
4:32 proverbs and one thousand five ***s***.
1 Chronicles
13:8 accompanied by ***s***, zithers, harps,
16:42 for God's ***s***. Jeduthun's
2 Chronicles
35:25 in their funeral ***s***. They are now
Nehemiah
12:8 the thanksgiving ***s*** along with his
12:46 and there were ***s*** of praise and
Job
35:10 God my maker; who gives ***s*** in the night;
Psalms
32:7 You surround me with ***s*** of rescue! Selah
42:4 and thanksgiving ***s***—a huge crowd
69:12 about me; drunkards made up rude ***s***.
78:63 and his young women had no wedding ***s***.
95:2 thanks! Let's shout ***s*** of joy to him!
105:43 his chosen ones with ***s*** of joy.
107:22 declare what God has done in ***s*** of joy!
118:15 sounds of joyful ***s*** and deliverance
119:54 have been my ***s*** of praise
137:3 requested ***s*** of joy: "Sing us
Song of Songs
1:1 The Song of ***S***, which is for Solomon
Isaiah
23:16 well, sing many ***s***, so they'll
24:16 we have heard ***s***: "Glory to the
Jeremiah
30:19 be laughter and ***s*** of thanks. I will
Ezekiel
2:10 on both sides, ***s*** of mourning,
26:13 your cacophonous ***s***; the sound of
33:32 a singer of love ***s*** with a lovely
Amos
5:23 the noise of your ***s***; I won't listen
6:5 who sing idle ***s*** to the sound of the
8:3 wail the temple ***s***," says the LORD
Matthew
26:30 after singing ***s*** of praise, they
Mark
14:26 After singing ***s*** of praise, they went
Ephesians
5:19 and spiritual ***s***; sing and make

Colossians
3:16 and spiritual **s**. Sing to God with

SONS → AARON AND HIS SONS, AARON'S SONS, AARON'S SONS THE PRIESTS

Genesis
9:1 Noah and his **s** and said to them,
10:32 clans of Noah's **s** according to
35:22 heard about it. Jacob had twelve **s**.
Exodus
13:15 from the oldest **s** to the oldest
28:9 on them the names of Israel's **s**,
Numbers
18:8 to you and your **s** as an allowance.
Deuteronomy
7:3 to one of their **s** to marry, and
Ruth
4:15 She's better for you than seven **s**."
1 Samuel
1:8 Aren't I worth more to you than ten **s**?"
Joel
2:28 everyone; your **s** and your
Acts
2:17 all people. Your **s** and daughters
2 Corinthians
6:18 you will be my **s** and daughters,

SOON

Isaiah
13:22 time is coming **s**; its days won't
56:1 is coming **s**, and my
Ezekiel
12:23 days are coming **s** for the
Romans
16:20 God of peace will **s** crush Satan under
Revelation
1:1 what must **s** take place.
2:16 am coming to you **s**, and I will make
3:11 I'm coming **s**. Hold on to what you have
11:14 is over. The third horror is coming **s**.
22:6 his servants what must **s** take place.
22:7 Look! I'm coming **s**. Favored is the
22:12 Look! I'm coming **s**. My reward is with
22:20 Yes, I'm coming **s**." Amen. Come,

SOOTHING → FOOD GIFT OF SOOTHING

Exodus
29:18 for the LORD, a **s** smell, a food
Leviticus
1:9 a food gift of **s** smell to the LORD.
Numbers
15:3 to the LORD as a **s** smell for the
18:17 into smoke for a **s** smell to the LORD.
28:2 my food gift as a **s** smell to me at
29:2 offering as a **s** smell to the
29:36 a food gift as a **s** smell to the

SOUL

Judges
5:15 of Reuben there was deep **s**-searching.
5:16 of Reuben there was deep **s**-searching.
Job
3:20 hard worker, life to those bitter of **s**,
30:25 day or my **s** grieve for the
Psalms
42:4 as I bare my **s**: how I made my
Matthew
10:28 can't kill the **s**. Instead, be
1 Thessalonians
5:23 may your spirit, **s**, and body be kept
Hebrews
4:12 it separates the **s** from the spirit

SOUND

Genesis
3:8 they heard the **s** of the LORD God
3:10 I heard your **s** in the garden; I
Exodus
20:18 lightning, the **s** of the horn, and
28:35 as a priest. Its **s** will be heard
32:18 It isn't the **s** of a victory
Leviticus
26:36 Just the **s** of a windblown
Numbers
29:1 be for you a day of the trumpet's **s**.
Deuteronomy
4:12 You heard the **s** of words, but you
Judges
4:21 While Sisera was **s** asleep from
5:11 To the **s** of instruments at the watering
1 Samuel
4:6 heard the **s** of that shout,
4:14 Eli heard the **s** of the cry and said,
2 Samuel
5:24 as you hear the **s** of marching in
15:10 you hear the **s** of the trumpet,
1 Kings
1:41 Joab heard the **s** of the ram's
1:45 a commotion. That is the **s** you heard.
14:6 Ahijah heard the **s** of her feet
18:26 But there was no **s** or answer. They
18:29 there was no **s** or answer, no
18:41 I hear the **s** of a rainstorm
19:12 the fire, there was a **s**. Thin. Quiet.
2 Kings
4:31 but there was no **s** or response. So
6:32 against him. The **s** of his master's
7:6 camp hear the **s** of chariots,
7:10 not even the **s** of anyone! The
1 Chronicles
14:15 as you hear the **s** of marching in
2 Chronicles
13:12 who are ready to **s** the battle
Ezra
3:13 distinguish the **s** of the joyful
Nehemiah
4:20 hear the trumpet **s**, come and gather
12:43 rejoiced, and the **s** of the joy in
Job
11:6 of wisdom; for **s** insight has two
15:21 a **s** of terror pierces their ears; when
21:12 and lyre, rejoice at the **s** of a flute.
21:24 milk, their bones marrow-filled and **s**.
30:31 is for mourning, my flute, a weeping **s**.
33:8 hearing; I heard the **s** of your words:
34:16 pay attention to the **s** of my words.
39:25 At a trumpet's **s**, he says, "Aha!"
Psalms
5:2 attention to the **s** of my cries, my
19:4 but their **s** extends throughout the
66:8 our God! Let the **s** of his praise be
66:19 listened. He heard the **s** of my prayer.
86:6 attention to the **s** of my requests

93:4 mightier than the **s** of much water,
98:5 with the lyre and the **s** of music.
104:7 fled in fear at the **s** of your thunder.
Proverbs
3:21 eyes; hold on to **s** judgment and
Ecclesiastes
12:4 shut, when the **s** of the mill
Song of Songs
2:12 arrived, and the **s** of the turtledove
2:14 your voice! The **s** of your voice is
5:2 was awake. A **s**! My love is
Isaiah
6:4 shook at the **s** of their
14:11 along with the **s** of your harps.
24:18 flees from the **s** of terror will
26:3 Those with **s** thoughts you will keep in
30:19 you. Hearing the **s** of your outcry,
51:3 in her—thanks and the **s** of singing.
65:19 ever hear the **s** of weeping or
66:6 The **s** of an uproar from the city! A
Jeremiah
4:5 proclaim, **s** the alarm
6:1 trumpet in Tekoa, **s** the alarm in Beth-
6:23 Their horsemen **s** like the roaring
7:34 will silence the **s** of joy and
9:10 and deserted; no **s** of the flocks is
9:19 The **s** of sobbing is heard from Zion:
10:13 At the **s** of his voice, the heavenly
10:22 Listen! The **s** is getting louder, a
30:10 again be safe and **s**, with no one
46:22 Like the **s** of a snake hissing as it
46:27 again be safe and **s**, with no one
49:2 LORD, when I will **s** the battle alarm
50:22 There's the **s** of war in the land and
50:42 Their horsemen **s** like the roaring
50:46 quakes at the **s** of Babylon's
51:16 At the **s** of God's voice, the heavenly
51:27 flag in the land; **s** the alarm among
Ezekiel
1:24 Then I heard the **s** of their wings when
1:25 Then there was a **s** from above the dome
1:28 face. I heard the **s** of someone
3:12 a great quaking **s** from his place.
3:13 The **s** was the creatures' wings beating
10:5 The **s** of the winged creatures' wings
19:7 horrified by the **s** of his raging,
23:42 The **s** of a noisy crowd was around her.
26:13 songs; the **s** of your lyres
30:22 arms, both the **s** one and the
31:16 quaked at the **s**. When I cast it
33:4 If they hear the **s** of the trumpet but
33:5 They heard the **s** of the trumpet but
43:2 the east. Its **s** was like the
Daniel
2:14 with wisdom and **s** judgment,
3:5 When you hear the **s** of the horn, pipe,
3:7 as they heard the **s** of the horn,
3:10 who hears the **s** of the horn,
3:15 when you hear the **s** of horn, pipe,
10:9 Then I heard the **s** of the man's words.
Hosea
5:8 trumpet in Ramah. **S** the warning at
Amos
2:2 war cry, with the **s** of the ram's horn.
6:5 idle songs to the **s** of the harp, and,
Habakkuk
3:16 quiver at the **s**. Rottenness
Zephaniah
1:14 very quickly. The **s** of the day of the
Zechariah
11:3 The **s** of screaming appears among the
Matthew
24:31 angels with the **s** of a great
Luke
15:27 he received his son back safe and **s**.'
John
3:8 You hear its **s**, but you don't
Acts
2:2 Suddenly a **s** from heaven like the
2:6 they heard this **s**, a crowd
20:9 on. When he was **s** asleep, he fell
26:25 I'm speaking what is **s** and true.
1 Corinthians
14:7 a lyre can make a **s**, but if there
Galatians
4:20 and change how I **s**, because I'm at a
1 Timothy
1:10 else that is opposed to **s** teaching.
1:11 **S** teaching agrees with the glorious
6:3 agree with **s** teaching about
2 Timothy
1:13 to the pattern of **s** teaching that you
4:3 will not tolerate **s** teaching. They
Titus
2:1 way that is consistent with **s** teaching.
2:8 and a **s** message that is above criticism
Hebrews
12:19 a trumpet, and a **s** of words that
Revelation
5:11 and I heard the **s** of many angels
9:9 chests, and the **s** of their wings
14:2 I heard a **s** from heaven that was like
18:22 The **s** of harpists and musicians, of
18:23 you again. The **s** of a bridegroom

SOUTH

Genesis
13:9 north, I will go **s**; and if you go
28:14 east, north, and **s**. Every family of
Exodus
26:35 the table by the **s** wall of the
27:9 The courtyard's **s** side should have
38:9 The courtyard's **s** side had drapes
40:24 the table on the **s** side of the
Numbers
2:10 On the **s** side will be the banner of
3:29 to camp on the **s** side of the
10:6 the camp on the **s** side will march.
34:4 border will turn **s** of the ascent of
35:5 feet, on the **s** side three
Deuteronomy
3:27 Look west, north, **s**, and east. Have a
33:23 go possess the west and the **s**!"
Joshua
11:2 the desert plain **s** of Chinneroth, in
13:4 in the **s**. The whole land of the
15:2 Their **s** border ran from the end of the
17:7 The border went **s** to the population
18:5 territory to the **s**. The house of
19:34 Zebulun on the **s**, Asher on the
Judges
21:19 Bethel to Shechem, and **s** of Lebonah."
Job
23:9 grasp him; he turns **s**, and I don't see.

37:17 hot when earth is calmed by the ***s*** wind?
39:26 flys, spreading its wings to the ***s***?

Psalms
75:6 or west; it's not from the ***s*** either.
78:26 and drove the ***s*** wind by his
89:12 North and ***s***—you created them! The
107:3 from east and west, north and ***s***.

Ecclesiastes
1:6 wind blows to the ***s***, goes around to
11:3 whether to the ***s*** or the north,

Song of Songs
4:16 wind, and come, ***s*** wind! Blow upon

Isaiah
43:6 back!" and to the ***s***, "Don't detain

Ezekiel
16:46 who lives with her daughters in the ***s***.
20:46 against the ***s***, and prophesy
20:47 everything from ***s*** to north will be
21:4 against everyone from ***s*** to north.
40:2 there was a city structure to the ***s***.

Daniel
8:4 west, north, and ***s***. No animal could
8:9 toward the ***s***, the east, and
11:29 against the ***s***, but the second

Zechariah
6:6 and the spotted ones are going ***s***."
9:14 forth on the stormy winds of the ***s***.
14:4 north, and the other half will move ***s***.
14:10 Geba to Rimmon, ***s*** of Jerusalem.

Matthew
12:42 The queen of the ***S*** will be raised up by

Luke
11:31 The queen of the ***S*** will rise up at the
12:55 And when a ***s*** wind blows, you say, 'A
13:29 west, north and ***s***, and sit down to

Acts
27:13 When a gentle ***s*** wind began to blow,
28:13 After one day a ***s*** wind came up, and

Revelation
21:13 gates on the ***s***, and three gates

SOUTHERN

Job
9:9 Pleiades and the ***s*** constellations;

Daniel
11:5 Then the ***s*** king will gain power, but
11:40 the end time, the ***s*** king will attack

SOW

2 Kings
19:29 the third year, ***s*** seed and harvest

Job
4:8 who plow sin and ***s*** trouble will
31:8 then let me ***s*** and another reap; let my

Proverbs
11:18 but those who ***s*** righteousness
22:8 Those who ***s*** injustice will harvest

Ecclesiastes
11:4 blow will never ***s***, and those who

Hosea
2:23 I will ***s*** him for myself in the land;
8:7 Because they ***s*** the wind, they will get
10:12 ***S*** for yourselves righteousness; reap

Micah
6:15 You ***s***, but you don't gather. You tread

Matthew
6:26 sky. They don't ***s*** seed or harvest

John
4:36 so that those who ***s*** and those who

James
3:18 who make peace ***s*** the seeds of

2 Peter
2:22 and a washed ***s*** wallows in the

SPARED

Exodus
12:27 the Egyptians, he ***s*** our houses.'" The

Joshua
9:26 in this way. He ***s*** them from the

1 Samuel
15:9 and the troops ***s*** Agag along with
15:15 the troops ***s*** the best sheep
24:10 to kill you. I ***s*** you, saying, 'I
27:11 David never ***s*** a man or woman so they

2 Samuel
8:2 who were to be ***s***. The Moabites
21:7 But the king ***s*** Mephibosheth, Jonathan's

2 Kings
17:18 Only the tribe of Judah was ***s***.

2 Chronicles
21:17 Jehoram's youngest son, was ***s***.

Job
21:30 the wicked are ***s***; on the day of

Isaiah
1:9 forces had not ***s*** a few of us, we
38:17 You yourself have ***s*** my whole being

Jeremiah
21:9 will live; yes, their lives will be ***s***.
38:2 will live; yes, their lives will be ***s***.
50:20 in vain. I will forgive those I have ***s***.

Hosea
10:11 to pull a plow; I ***s*** her fair neck;

Mark
14:35 he might be ***s*** the time of

SPEAK

Genesis
18:27 decided to ***s*** with my Lord,
18:32 Lord, but let me ***s*** just once more.
19:14 Lot went to ***s*** to his sons-in-law,
34:6 went out to Jacob to ***s*** with him.

Exodus
4:10 been able to ***s*** well, not
4:16 Aaron will ***s*** for you to the people.
19:19 Moses would ***s***, and God would
33:11 the LORD used to ***s*** to Moses face-to-f

Deuteronomy
5:24 that God can ***s*** to a human being
18:19 which that prophet will ***s*** in my name.
32:1 and I will ***s***; Earth! Listen to

1 Samuel
3:9 calls you, say '***S***, LORD. Your

Nehemiah
13:24 they couldn't ***s*** the language of

Esther
4:14 if you don't ***s*** up at this very
10:3 people and to ***s*** up for all his

Job
7:11 quiet; I will ***s*** in the adversity
9:35 Then I would ***s***—unafraid—for I'm not
10:1 complaint; I will ***s*** out of my own
11:5 that God would ***s***, open his lips
13:3 But I want to ***s*** to the Almighty; I

16:6 If I **s**, my pain is not eased; if I
42:8 you didn't **s** correctly, as did
Psalms
17:10 no pity; their mouths **s** arrogantly.
31:18 up whenever they **s** arrogantly
35:20 They don't **s** the truth; instead, they
35:21 They **s** out against me, saying, "Yes!
38:13 someone who can't **s**, whose mouth
41:5 My enemies **s** maliciously about me:
50:7 I will now **s**; Israel, I will
58:1 Do you really **s** what is right,
59:12 words that they **s**, let them be
73:9 mouths dare to **s** against heaven!
75:5 so highly. Don't **s** so arrogantly
77:4 closing. I'm so upset I can't even **s**.
109:20 reward for those who **s** evil against me!
115:5 but they can't **s**. They have eyes,
120:7 peace, but when I **s**, they are for war.
135:16 but they can't **s**. They have eyes,
144:8 whose mouths **s** lies, and whose strong
144:11 whose mouths **s** lies, and whose
145:6 They will **s** of the power of your
145:11 They **s** of the glory of your kingdom;
Proverbs
8:6 Listen, for I **s** things that are
10:10 those who **s** foolishly are
12:17 state the truth **s** justly, but a
23:9 Don't **s** in the ears of fools, for they
23:16 when your lips **s** with integrity.
23:33 and your heart will **s** distorted words.
24:2 violence, and their lips **s** of trouble.
24:26 Those who **s** honestly are like those who kiss
26:25 Though they **s** graciously, don't believe
29:20 who are quick to **s**? There is more
31:8 **S** out on behalf of the voiceless, and
31:9 **S** out in order to judge with
Ecclesiastes
1:8 no one is able to **s**. The eye isn't
Isaiah
32:6 Fools **s** folly; their minds devise
59:3 guilt. Your lips **s** lies; your
Jeremiah
1:6 don't know how to **s** because I'm only
Ezekiel
2:1 stand on your feet, and I'll **s** to you.
2:7 You'll **s** my words to them whether they
20:3 Human one, **s** to Israel's elders and say
44:6 **S** to the rebels, to the house of
Matthew
5:11 harass you and **s** all kinds of bad
9:32 was demon-possessed and unable to **s**.
9:33 man who couldn't **s** began to talk.
10:19 about how to **s** or what you will
12:22 and unable to **s**. Jesus healed him
12:34 How can you **s** good things while
12:36 Day for every useless word they **s**.
13:10 use parables when you **s** to the crowds?"
13:13 This is why I **s** to the crowds in
15:31 been unable to **s** talking, and the
Mark
1:34 let the demons **s**, because they
2:7 Why does he **s** this way? He's insulting
7:32 and could hardly **s**, and they begged
7:37 and gives speech to those who can't **s**."
9:17 a spirit that doesn't allow him to **s**.
16:17 my name. They will **s** in new languages.
Luke
1:19 I was sent to **s** to you and to
1:20 silent, unable to **s** until the day
1:22 he was unable to **s** to them. They
1:64 was able to **s** again, and he
2:38 praise God and to **s** about Jesus to
4:41 allow them to **s** because they
6:26 for you when all **s** well of you.
7:15 up and began to **s**, and Jesus gave
7:40 to say to you." "Teacher, **s**," he said.
11:14 man who couldn't **s** began to talk.
12:1 Jesus began to **s** first to his
John
3:11 you that we **s** about what we
7:17 is from God or whether I **s** on my own.
7:18 Those who **s** on their own seek glory for themselves
8:45 Because I **s** the truth, you don't
8:46 of sin? Since I **s** the truth, why
9:21 him. He's old enough to **s** for himself."
12:49 I don't **s** on my own, but the Father who
13:13 Lord,' and you **s** correctly,
14:10 to you I don't **s** on my own. The
16:13 truth. He won't **s** on his own, but
16:25 I will no longer **s** to you in such
16:29 See! Now you **s** plainly; you
18:23 replied, "If I **s** wrongly, testify
19:10 said, "You won't **s** to me? Don't you
Acts
2:4 and began to **s** in other
11:15 When I began to **s**, the Holy Spirit
Romans
1:14 those who don't **s** Greek, both to
15:18 I don't dare **s** about anything except
1 Corinthians
12:30 they? All don't **s** in different
13:1 If I **s** in tongues of human beings and
13:11 child, I used to **s** like a child,
14:13 those who **s** in a tongue
14:19 church I'd rather **s** five words in my
2 Corinthians
4:13 We also have faith, and so we also **s**.
Ephesians
5:19 **s** to each other with psalms, hymns, and
Philippians
1:14 the Lord to **s** the word boldly
1 Thessalonians
2:2 through God to **s** God's good news
2:4 exactly how we **s**. We aren't trying
1 Timothy
1:13 though I used to **s** against him,
1:20 can be taught not to **s** against God.
Titus
1:9 and refute those who **s** against it.
3:2 They shouldn't **s** disrespectfully about
Hebrews
7:11 still a need to **s** about raising up
7:25 he always lives to **s** with God for them.
James
1:19 listen, slow to **s**, and slow to grow
1 Peter
2:9 so that you may **s** of the wonderful
2:22 nor did he ever **s** in ways meant to
3:15 asks you to **s** of your hope, be
4:11 so as those who **s** God's word.
1 John
4:5 world. So they **s** from the world's

3 John
1:12 itself. We also **s** highly of him,
1:14 you soon, and we will **s** face-to-face.
Jude
1:16 own desires. They **s** arrogant words
Revelation
13:6 its mouth to **s** blasphemies
13:15 image would even **s** and cause anyone

SPEAKING
Exodus
31:18 When God finished **s** with Moses on Mount
34:33 Moses finished **s** with them, he put
Deuteronomy
5:26 God's voice **s** out of the very
Joshua
1:8 Never stop **s** about this Instruction
Psalms
34:13 evil and keep your lips from **s** lies!
52:3 lying more than **s** what is right.
Ecclesiastes
3:7 for keeping silent and a time for **s**,
10:13 and end up **s** awful nonsense.
Isaiah
32:6 irreverently, **s** falsely of the
59:4 in emptiness and **s** deceit, they
65:24 while they are still **s**, I will hear.
Matthew
9:18 While Jesus was **s** to them, a ruler came
22:1 Jesus responded by **s** again in parables
Mark
13:11 aren't doing the **s** but the Holy
Acts
1:3 of forty days, **s** to them about
2:6 heard them **s** in their native
10:46 They heard them **s** in other languages
Romans
3:5 us, isn't just (I'm **s** rhetorically)?
6:19 (I'm **s** with ordinary metaphors because
1 Corinthians
14:39 but don't prevent **s** in tongues.
Revelation
13:11 a lamb, but it was **s** like a dragon.

SPEAKS
Numbers
22:8 as the LORD **s** to me." So the
Deuteronomy
5:27 the LORD our God **s** to you. We'll
18:20 who arrogantly **s** a word in my name
18:22 The prophet who **s** in the LORD's
28:49 a nation that **s** a language you
1 Samuel
16:18 a warrior who **s** well and is good-l
2 Samuel
14:10 If anyone **s** against you, bring him to
23:2 The LORD's spirit **s** through me; his
Job
33:14 God **s** in one way, in two ways, but no
34:35 Job **s** without knowledge; his words
Psalms
2:5 But then God **s** to them angrily; then he
15:2 is right, and **s** the truth
49:3 My mouth **s** wisdom; my heart's
50:1 the LORD God, **s**, calling out to
63:5 dinner. My mouth **s** praise with joy
85:8 says, because he **s** peace to his
Proverbs
7:13 Her face is brazen as she **s** to him:
Isaiah
33:15 righteously and **s** truthfully, who
45:19 LORD, the one who **s** truth, who
Ezekiel
10:5 the sound of God Almighty when he **s**.
16:44 Now everyone who **s** in proverbs will say this about you
Daniel
3:29 language: whoever **s** disrespectfully
Amos
5:10 they reject the one who **s** the truth.
Matthew
12:32 And whoever **s** a word against the Human
15:4 The person who **s** against father or
Mark
7:10 The person who **s** against father or
Luke
12:10 Anyone who **s** a word against the Human
20:37 bush, when he **s** of the Lord as
John
3:31 to the earth and **s** as one from the
3:34 one whom God sent **s** God's words
4:26 to her, "I Am—the one who **s** with you."
8:44 that liar **s**, he speaks
19:35 He knows that he **s** the truth, and he
Romans
3:19 the Law says, it **s** to those who are
2 Corinthians
13:3 proof that Christ **s** through me,
Hebrews
12:24 blood that **s** better than
1 Peter
4:11 Whoever **s** should do so as those who
3 John
1:12 Everyone **s** highly of Demetrius, even

SPEAR
Numbers
25:7 of the community, took a **s** in his hand,
Judges
5:8 a shield or **s** to be seen among
1 Samuel
17:7 His **s** shaft was as strong as the bar on
19:10 the wall with his **s**, but David
Psalms
35:3 Use your **s** and ax against those who are
46:9 shattering the **s**, burning chariots
John
19:34 his side with a **s**, and immediately
Acts
26:14 It's hard for you to kick against a **s**.'

SPEECH
Numbers
24:4 who hears God's **s**, who perceives
24:16 who hears God's **s**, and understands
Deuteronomy
20:9 completed their **s** to the troops,
32:2 raindrops; my **s** will settle like
Job
16:5 you with my **s**; my trembling
29:9 restrained **s**, put their hand

29:22 After my ***s***, they didn't respond. My
Psalms
12:2 talk with slick ***s*** and divided
19:3 there's no ***s***, no words—their
Proverbs
4:10 and take in my ***s***, then the years
4:20 to my words. Bend your ear to my ***s***.
7:24 to me, and pay attention to my ***s***.
8:13 the path of evil and corrupt ***s***.
12:6 but the ***s*** of those who do
12:14 fruit of their ***s***, people are well
14:7 for you won't learn wise ***s*** there.
15:4 Wholesome ***s*** is a tree of life, but
16:10 A king's ***s*** is like an oracle; in a
16:21 and pleasant ***s*** enhances teaching.
16:23 wise makes their ***s*** insightful and
17:7 less so false ***s*** for an honorable
20:15 exist, but wise ***s*** is the most
22:11 heart—their ***s*** is gracious, and
Ecclesiastes
5:7 and excessive ***s***. Therefore, fear
Isaiah
28:11 With derisive ***s*** and a foreign tongue,
29:4 in the dust your ***s*** will come. Your
33:19 the people of ***s*** too obscure to
58:9 you, the finger-pointing, the wicked ***s***;
Jeremiah
5:15 don't know, whose ***s*** you won't
Lamentations
3:62 the ***s*** of those who rise up against me,
Ezekiel
3:5 language and ***s*** are difficult and
Zephaniah
3:9 I will change the ***s*** of the peoples
Mark
7:37 to hear and gives ***s*** to those who
John
16:25 using figures of ***s*** with you. The
16:29 plainly; you aren't using figures of ***s***.
Acts
12:21 the throne, and gave a ***s*** to the people.
1 Corinthians
2:1 like I was an expert in ***s*** or wisdom.
2 Corinthians
8:7 such as faith, ***s***, knowledge, total
10:10 he is weak and his ***s*** is worth nothing."
Colossians
3:17 do, whether in ***s*** or action, do it
4:6 Your ***s*** should always be gracious and
1 Thessalonians
1:5 to you just in ***s*** but also with
1 Timothy
4:12 through your ***s***, behavior, love,
2 Peter
2:18 self-important ***s***, they use sinful
1 John
3:18 with words or ***s*** but with action

SPEND

Genesis
19:2 servant's house, ***s*** the night, and
24:23 father's house for us to ***s*** the night?"
42:27 they stopped to ***s*** the night, one of
43:21 we stopped to ***s*** the night and
Numbers
22:8 He said to them, "***S*** the night here and
Judges
19:6 the man, "Why not ***s*** the night and
20:4 to Gibeah of Benjamin to ***s*** the night,
2 Samuel
17:8 fighter. He won't ***s*** the night with
17:16 tell him, 'Don't ***s*** the night in the
1 Kings
5:14 Then they would ***s*** two months at
1 Chronicles
9:27 They would ***s*** the night patrolling God's
Nehemiah
4:22 and his servant ***s*** the night in
Job
21:13 They ***s*** their days contentedly, go down
24:7 ***s*** the night naked, unclothed, in the
31:32 A stranger didn't ***s*** the night in the
36:11 and serve, they ***s*** their days in
39:9 slave, or will it ***s*** the night in your
Psalms
26:4 I don't ***s*** time with people up to no
50:18 you see one; you ***s*** your time with
Proverbs
25:17 Don't ***s*** too much time in your
Isaiah
55:2 Why ***s*** money for what isn't food, and your earnings
65:4 sit in tombs and ***s*** the night among
Joel
1:13 the altar. Come, ***s*** the night in
Zephaniah
2:14 porcupine will ***s*** the night on its
Acts
12:19 Judea in order to ***s*** some time in
17:21 in Athens used to ***s*** their time doing
20:16 wouldn't need to ***s*** too much time in
27:12 in Crete and ***s*** the winter in its
1 Corinthians
16:6 with you or even ***s*** the winter there
16:7 since I hope to ***s*** some time with
2 Corinthians
12:9 So I'll gladly ***s*** my time bragging
12:15 will very gladly ***s*** and be spent for
Titus
3:12 I've decided to ***s*** the winter there.

SPENT

Genesis
24:54 ate and drank and ***s*** the night. When
47:18 the silver is ***s*** and that we've
Leviticus
26:20 strength will be ***s*** for no reason:
Joshua
8:9 of Ai. Joshua ***s*** that night among
Judges
18:2 house, and they ***s*** the night there.
19:7 him, and he ***s*** the night there
1 Samuel
30:31 David and his soldiers had ***s*** time.
2 Samuel
12:16 He fasted and ***s*** the night
14:2 a woman who has ***s*** a long time
1 Kings
19:9 into a cave and ***s*** the night. The
Ezra
10:6 son, where he ***s*** the night. He
Nehemiah
13:20 of merchandise ***s*** the night outside

Esther
4:3 up eating and **s** whole days
Matthew
21:17 city to Bethany and **s** the night there.
Mark
5:26 doctors, and had **s** everything she
Luke
8:43 years. She had **s** her entire
21:37 temple, but he **s** each night on the
John
3:22 Judea, where he **s** some time with
Acts
21:7 sisters there and **s** a day with them.
28:11 a ship that had **s** the winter at the
2 Corinthians
11:25 three times. I **s** a day and a night
12:15 spend and be **s** for your sake. If

SPICES
Exodus
25:6 for the lamps; **s** for the anointing
30:23 high-quality **s**: five hundred
30:34 of each of these **s**: gum resin,
35:8 for the light; **s** for the anointing
35:28 **s** and oil for light and for the
1 Kings
10:2 camels carrying **s**, a large amount
10:25 weapons, **s**, horses, and
2 Kings
20:13 the gold, the **s**, and the fine
1 Chronicles
9:29 the flour, wine, oil, incense, and **s**.
9:30 priests blended the ointment for the **s**;
2 Chronicles
9:1 camels carrying **s**, large amounts of
9:9 great quantity of **s**, and precious
9:24 weapons, **s**, horses, and
16:14 filled with sweet **s** and various kinds
32:27 precious stones, **s**, shields, and
Song of Songs
4:13 kinds of luscious fruit, henna, and **s**:
5:1 my myrrh and my **s**. I have eaten my
5:13 towers of **s**. His lips are
Isaiah
39:2 and the gold, the **s** and fine oil—and
43:24 You didn't buy **s** for me with your
Ezekiel
27:19 iron, cinnamon, and **s** for your wares.
27:22 the finest **s**, every kind of
Mark
16:1 and Salome bought **s** so that they
Luke
23:56 prepared fragrant **s** and perfumed
24:1 the fragrant **s** they had prepared.
John
19:40 it, with the **s**, in linen cloths.

SPIES
Genesis
42:9 to them, "You are **s**. You've come to
42:34 that you are not **s** but honest men. I
Numbers
21:32 Moses sent **s** to Jazer. They captured
Deuteronomy
1:22 Let's send **s** ahead of us—they
Joshua
2:1 sent two men as **s** from Shittim. He
2:15 she lowered the **s** on a rope through
6:23 men who had been **s** went and brought
6:25 she hid the **s** whom Joshua had
Judges
1:24 the **s** saw a man coming out of the city,
1 Samuel
26:4 he sent **s** and discovered that Saul had
Luke
20:20 closely and sent **s** who pretended to
Hebrews
11:31 because she welcomed the **s** in peace.

SPIRIT → EVIL SPIRIT, GOD'S SPIRIT, HOLY SPIRIT, LORD'S SPIRIT, POUR OUT MY SPIRIT, SPIRIT FROM GOD, THROUGH THE SPIRIT, UNCLEAN SPIRIT
Exodus
31:3 with the divine **s**, with skill,
Numbers
11:25 took some of the **s** that was on him
11:26 Medad, and the **s** rested on them.
11:29 with the LORD placing his **s** on them!"
14:24 has a different **s**, and he has
27:18 a man who has the **s**, and lay your
Deuteronomy
2:30 God had made his **s** hard and his
28:65 mind, failing eyes, and a depressed **s**.
1 Kings
22:21 one particular **s** approached the
22:22 will be a lying **s** in the mouth of
22:23 placed a lying **s** in the mouths of
2 Kings
2:9 said, "Let me have twice your **s**."
2:15 said, "Elijah's **s** has settled on
19:7 about to put a **s** in him, so when
1 Chronicles
5:26 stirred up the **s** of Assyria's King
12:18 Then a **s** took hold of Amasai, the
2 Chronicles
18:20 one particular **s** approached the
18:21 will be a lying **s** in the mouths of
18:22 placed a lying **s** in the mouths of
24:20 Then the **s** of God enwrapped Zechariah
Ezra
1:1 stirred up the **s** of Persia's King
1:5 whose **s** God had stirred
Nehemiah
9:20 gave your good **s** to teach them.
9:30 them by your **s** through the
Job
6:4 are in me; my **s** drinks their
7:11 adversity of my **s**, groan in the
17:1 My **s** is broken, my days extinguished,
21:25 dies in bitter **s**, never having
32:8 But the **s** in a person, the Almighty's
32:18 of words. The **s** in my belly
34:14 to gather his **s** and breath back
Psalms
31:5 I entrust my **s** into your hands; you,
31:9 of my grief, as do my **s** and my body.
32:2 guilty—in whose **s** there is no
51:10 put a new, faithful **s** deep inside me!
51:12 to me and sustain me with a willing **s**.
51:17 A broken **s** is my sacrifice, God. You
76:12 He breaks the **s** of princes. He is
77:3 I complain, and my **s** grows tired. Selah
77:6 I complain, and my **s** keeps searching:

78:8 firm and whose ***s*** wasn't faithful
119:28 My ***s*** sags because of grief. Now raise
139:7 away from your ***s***? Where could I go
142:3 When my ***s*** is weak inside me, you still
143:4 My ***s*** is weak inside me—inside, my
143:10 Guide me by your good ***s*** into good land.
Proverbs
15:4 life, but dishonest talk breaks the ***s***.
15:13 but a troubled heart breaks the ***s***.
17:22 but a broken ***s*** dries up the
18:14 The human ***s*** sustains a sick person, but
29:23 low, but those of humble ***s*** gain honor.
Isaiah
32:15 until a ***s*** from on high is poured out on
42:1 I've put my ***s*** upon him; he will
48:16 the LORD God has sent me with his ***s***.)
57:15 reviving the ***s*** of the lowly,
59:21 says the LORD. My ***s***, which is upon
66:2 and contrite in ***s***, who tremble at
Jeremiah
51:11 stirring up the ***s*** of kings from
Ezekiel
11:19 I will put a new ***s*** in them. I will
39:29 When I pour my ***S*** upon the house of
Hosea
4:12 predictions. A ***s*** of prostitution
5:4 God, because the ***s*** of prostitution
Micah
3:8 power, with the ***s*** of the LORD, with
6:7 fruit of my body for the sin of my ***s***?
Haggai
1:14 LORD moved the ***s*** of Judah's
2:5 out of Egypt, my ***s*** stands in your
Zechariah
4:6 but by my ***s***, says the LORD of
6:8 provided rest for my ***s*** in the north."
7:12 sent by his ***s*** through the
12:1 who fashions the ***s*** of humanity
12:10 I will pour out a ***s*** of grace and
13:2 and the sinful ***s*** from the land.
Malachi
2:15 remnant of his ***s***? What is the one?
Matthew
3:16 and he saw the ***S*** of God coming
4:1 Then the ***S*** led Jesus up into the
10:20 talking, but the ***S*** of my Father is
12:18 I'll put my ***S*** upon him, and
26:41 temptation. The ***s*** is eager, but the
Mark
1:10 open and the ***S***, like a dove,
1:12 At once the ***S*** forced Jesus out into the
9:17 since he has a ***s*** that doesn't
9:20 him. When the ***s*** saw Jesus, it
9:26 boy horribly, the ***s*** came out. The boy
9:28 Why couldn't we throw this ***s*** out?"
9:29 this kind of ***s*** out requires
14:38 temptation. The ***s*** is eager, but the
Luke
1:17 equipped with the ***s*** and power of
2:27 Led by the ***S***, he went into the temple
4:14 the power of the ***S*** to Galilee, and
4:18 The ***S*** of the Lord is upon me, because
4:33 synagogue had the ***s*** of an unclean
9:39 Look, a ***s*** seizes him and, without any
13:11 disabled by a ***s*** for eighteen
John
1:32 I saw the ***S*** coming down from
1:33 whom you see the ***S*** coming down and
3:5 of water and the ***S***, it's not
3:6 whatever is born of the ***S*** is spirit.
3:34 because God gives the ***S*** generously.
4:23 will worship in ***s*** and truth. The
4:24 God is ***s***, and it is necessary to
6:63 The ***S*** is the one who gives life and the
7:39 concerning the ***S***. Those who
14:17 Companion is the ***S*** of Truth, whom
15:26 the Father—the ***S*** of Truth who
16:13 However, when the ***S*** of Truth comes, he will guide you
16:15 I said that the ***S*** takes what is
Acts
6:3 endowed by the ***S*** with exceptional
6:10 the wisdom the ***S*** gave him as he
8:18 that the ***S*** was given through
8:29 The ***S*** told Philip, "Approach this
10:19 the vision, the ***S*** interrupted him,
11:12 The ***S*** told me to go with them even
11:28 inspired by the ***S***, predicted that a
16:7 Bithynia, but the ***S*** of Jesus wouldn't
16:16 woman. She had a ***s*** that enabled her
16:18 and said to the ***s***, "In the name of
18:25 stirred up by the ***S***. He taught
19:21 guided by the ***S***, decided to
20:22 compelled by the ***S***, I'm going to
21:4 Compelled by the ***S***, they kept
23:8 angel, or ***s***, but Pharisees
23:9 man! What if a ***s*** or angel has
Romans
1:4 was based on the ***S*** of holiness. This
1:9 I serve God in my ***s*** by preaching the
2:29 is circumcised in ***s***, not literally.
7:6 life under the ***S***, not in the old
8:2 The law of the ***S*** of life in Christ
8:4 is based on the ***S***, not based on
8:5 are based on the ***S*** think about
8:6 comes from the ***S*** leads to life and
8:9 you are in the ***S***, if in fact God's
8:10 is in you, the ***S*** is your life
8:11 If the ***S*** of the one who raised Jesus
8:13 of the body with the ***S***, you will live.
8:15 didn't receive a ***s*** of slavery to
8:16 The same ***S*** agrees with our spirit, that
8:23 who have the ***S*** as the first crop
8:26 the same way, the ***S*** comes to help our
8:27 knows how the ***S*** thinks, because
11:8 gave them a dull ***s***, so that their
12:11 -be on fire in the ***S*** as you serve the
15:30 the love of the ***S***, to join me in my
1 Corinthians
2:4 a demonstration of the ***S*** and of power.
2:11 except their own ***s*** that lives in
2:13 taught by the ***S***—we are interpreting
3:4 you acting like people without the ***S***?
4:21 you, or with love and a gentle ***s***?
5:3 present in the ***s*** and I've already
5:4 be present in ***s*** with the power of
5:5 so that his ***s*** might be saved on
6:11 Jesus Christ and in the ***S*** of our God.
6:17 joined to the Lord is one ***s*** with him.
7:34 in both body and ***s***. But a married
12:4 spiritual gifts but the same ***S***;
12:7 of the ***S*** is given to each
12:8 is given by the ***S*** to one person, a
12:9 by the same ***S***, gifts of healing

12:11 the one and same **S** who gives what he
12:13 baptized by one **S** into one body,
14:2 it—they speak mysteries by the **S**.
14:14 in a tongue, my ***s*** prays but my mind
14:15 I'll pray in the **S**, but I'll pray
14:16 praise God in the **S**, how will the
15:45 last Adam became a ***s*** that gives life.
16:18 provided my ***s*** and yours with a

2 Corinthians
1:22 us and gave the **S** as a down payment
3:3 ink but with the **S** of the living
3:6 but on the **S**, because what is
3:8 ministry of the **S** be much more
3:17 The Lord is the **S**, and where the
3:18 This comes from the Lord, who is the **S**.
4:13 the same faithful ***s*** as what is
5:5 God gave us the **S** as a down payment
7:1 our body or ***s*** so that we make
11:4 a different **S** than the one you
12:18 live by the same **S**? Didn't we walk

Galatians
3:2 you receive the **S** by doing the
3:3 started with the **S**, are you now
3:5 you with the **S** and working
3:14 the promise of the **S** through faith.
4:6 God sent the **S** of his Son into
4:29 the one who was conceived by the **S**.
5:16 be guided by the **S** and you won't
5:17 set against the **S**, and the Spirit
5:18 being led by the **S**, you aren't under
5:22 the fruit of the **S** is love, joy,
5:25 If we live by the **S**, let's follow the
6:1 like this with a ***s*** of gentleness.
6:8 benefit of the **S** will harvest
6:18 Lord Jesus Christ be with your ***s***. Amen.

Ephesians
1:17 will give you a ***s*** of wisdom and
2:2 This is the ***s*** of disobedience
2:18 the Father through Christ by the one **S**.
4:3 the unity of the **S** with the peace
4:4 one body and one ***s*** just as God also
4:23 the thinking in your mind by the **S**
5:18 filled with the **S** in the following
6:17 the sword of the **S**, which is God's
6:18 petitions in the **S** all the time.

Philippians
1:19 and the help of the **S** of Jesus Christ.
1:27 united in one ***s*** and mind as you
2:1 any sharing in the **S**, any sympathy,

Colossians
1:8 He informed us of your love in the **S**
2:5 I'm with you in ***s***. I'm happy to see

1 Thessalonians
5:19 Don't suppress the **S**
5:20 Don't brush off **S**-inspired messages
5:23 him; and may your ***s***, soul, and body

2 Thessalonians
2:2 it through some ***s***, a message, or a
2:13 to God by the **S** and through your

1 Timothy
3:16 righteous by the **S**, seen by angels,
4:1 The **S** clearly says that in latter times

2 Timothy
1:7 didn't give us a ***s*** that is timid but
4:22 Lord be with your ***s***. Grace be with

Philemon
1:25 the Lord Jesus Christ be with your ***s***.

Hebrews
4:12 the soul from the ***s*** and the joints
9:14 the eternal **S** as a sacrifice
10:29 blood, and who insults the **S** of grace?

1 Peter
1:11 wondered what the **S** of Christ within
3:4 gentle, peaceful ***s***. This type of

1 John
3:24 because of the **S** that he has given
4:1 believe every ***s***. Test the spirits
4:13 he has given us a measure of his **S**.
5:6 blood. And the **S** is the one who
5:8 the **S**, the water, and the blood—and

Jude
1:19 don't have the **S**, they are worldly.

Revelation
1:10 I was in a **S**-inspired trance on the
2:7 to what the **S** is saying to the
4:2 once I was in a **S**-inspired trance an
14:13 Yes," says the **S**, "so they can
17:3 brought me in a **S**-inspired trance to
19:10 witness of Jesus is the ***s*** of prophecy!"
21:10 He took me in a **S**-inspired trance to a
22:17 The **S** and the bride say, 'Come!' Let

SPIRIT FROM GOD

1Sa 16:15; 16:16, 23; 18:10; 1Co 6:19

SPIRITS → EVIL SPIRITS, UNCLEAN SPIRITS

Leviticus
19:31 resort to dead ***s*** or inquire of
20:6 resorts to dead ***s*** or spirits of

Deuteronomy
18:11 with ghosts or ***s*** or communicates

2 Kings
23:24 consulted dead ***s*** and the mediums,

Esther
1:10 the king in high ***s***, he gave an order
5:9 place happy, his ***s*** high, but then he

Psalms
34:18 he saves those whose ***s*** are crushed.

Isaiah
8:19 ghosts and the ***s*** that chirp and
15:4 armed men of Moab shout, ***s*** trembling.
19:3 the idols and ***s*** and ghosts and
65:14 heartache; with broken ***s*** you will wail.

Matthew
8:16 He threw the ***s*** out with just a
12:45 it seven other ***s*** more evil than

Luke
10:20 because the ***s*** submit to you.
11:26 it seven other ***s*** more evil than

1 Corinthians
12:10 ability to tell ***s*** apart to another,
14:32 The ***s*** of prophets are under the control

Philippians
4:23 the Lord Jesus Christ be with your ***s***.

1 Timothy
4:1 pay attention to ***s*** that deceive and

Hebrews
1:7 one who uses the ***s*** for his
1:14 ministering ***s*** who are sent to
12:9 we submit to the Father of ***s*** and live?
12:23 of all, to the ***s*** of the righteous

1 Peter
3:19 he went to preach to the ***s*** in prison.
3:20 the past, these ***s*** were disobedient—

1 John
4:1 spirit. Test the **s** to see if they
Revelation
1:4 from the seven **s** that are before
3:1 holds God's seven **s** and the seven
4:5 torches, which are the seven **s** of God.
5:6 are God's seven **s**, sent out into
16:14 These are demonic **s** that do signs. They
22:6 the God of the **s** of the prophets,

SPIRITUAL
Hosea
9:7 is a fool, the **s** man is mad!"
Romans
1:11 pass along some **s** gift to you so
7:14 that the Law is **s**, but I'm made of
15:27 Jewish people's **s** resources, they
1 Corinthians
1:7 missing any **s** gift while you
2:13 are interpreting **s** things to
2:14 can only be comprehended in a **s** way.
2:15 **S** people comprehend everything, but
3:1 talk to you like **s** people but like
9:11 If we sowed **s** things in you, is it so
10:3 All ate the same **s** food
10:4 drank the same **s** drink. They drank
12:1 want you to be ignorant about **s** gifts.
12:4 are different **s** gifts but the
14:1 to try to get **s** gifts but
14:12 are ambitious for **s** gifts, use your
14:37 are prophets or "**s** people," then let
15:44 it's raised as a **s** body. If there's
15:46 first, not the **s** one—the spiritual
Galatians
6:1 you who are **s** should restore
Ephesians
1:3 Christ with every **s** blessing that
2:2 of a destructive **s** power. This is
5:19 hymns, and **s** songs; sing and
6:12 darkness, and **s** powers of evil in
Colossians
1:9 with all wisdom and **s** understanding.
3:16 hymns, and **s** songs. Sing to
1 Timothy
1:9 who are not **s**, and nothing is
4:14 Don't neglect the **s** gift in you that
1 Peter
2:5 stones into a **s** temple. You are

SPLENDOR
1 Chronicles
16:29 Bow down to the LORD in his holy **s**!
29:11 and power, honor, **s**, and majesty,
Job
31:23 terror to me; I couldn't endure his **s**.
37:22 golden light, the awesome **s** of God.
40:10 yourself with **s** and majesty;
Psalms
29:2 name! Bow down to the LORD in holy **s**!
89:17 you are the **s** of their
89:44 put an end to his **s**. You've thrown
96:9 LORD in his holy **s**! Tremble before
145:5 the glorious **s** of your majesty;
Proverbs
20:29 men; gray hair is the **s** of old age.
Isaiah
2:10 the LORD, from the **s** of God's majesty!
4:2 be the pride and **s** of Israel's
46:13 in Zion and grant my **s** to Israel.
Ezekiel
16:14 because of the **s** that I had given
26:20 rule nor radiate **s** in the land of
28:7 wisdom, and they will degrade your **s**.
28:17 the sake of your **s**. I will cast you
Daniel
4:36 me. My honor and **s** came back to me
Micah
2:9 children you take away my **s** forever.
Zechariah
10:3 take care of his **s**, the house of
12:7 Judah so that the **s** of David's house
Matthew
6:29 in all of his **s** wasn't dressed
24:30 heavenly clouds with power and great **s**.
Mark
13:26 in the clouds with great power and **s**.
Luke
9:31 with heavenly **s** and spoke about
12:27 in all his **s** wasn't dressed
21:27 on a cloud with power and great **s**.
Acts
19:27 her, but her **s** will soon be

SPLIT
Genesis
15:10 of these animals, **s** them in half, and
15:17 passed between the **s**-open animals.
22:3 his son Isaac. He **s** the wood for the
Exodus
14:16 over the sea, and **s** it in two so that
14:21 dry land. The waters were **s** into two.
Leviticus
11:3 hoofs, completely **s**, and that rechews
11:26 not completely **s**, and that do not
Numbers
16:31 words, the ground under them **s** open.
Joshua
9:4 wineskins that were **s** and mended.
9:13 here they are, **s** open. These
Judges
15:19 So God **s** open the hollow rock in Lehi,
1 Kings
16:21 of Israel were **s** in two. One half
Job
26:12 stilled the Sea; **s** Rahab with his
26:13 clear; his hand **s** the fleeing
39:3 They crouch, **s** open for their young,
Psalms
74:13 You **s** the sea with your power. You
78:13 God **s** the sea and led them through,
107:16 bronze doors and **s** iron bars in two!
136:13 to the one who **s** the Reed Sea in
Isaiah
11:15 The LORD will **s** the tongue of the
48:21 rock for them; **s** the rock, and
63:12 glorious arm; who **s** the water for
Ezekiel
30:16 Thebes will be **s** open, Memphis
Micah
1:4 the valleys will **s** apart, like wax
Habakkuk
3:9 Selah With rivers you **s** open the earth.
Zechariah
14:4 of Olives will be **s** in half by a very

Matthew
27:51 bottom. The earth shook, the rocks **s**,
Revelation
16:19 The great city **s** into three parts, and

SPOKE
Genesis
8:15 God **s** to Noah
16:13 the LORD who **s** to her, "You are
18:29 again Abraham **s**, "What if forty
Exodus
20:1 Then God **s** all these words
30:11 The LORD **s** to Moses
Leviticus
10:11 that the LORD **s** to them through
16:1 the LORD and died, the LORD **s** to Moses:
Numbers
1:1 The LORD **s** to Moses in the Sinai desert
2:1 The LORD **s** to Moses and Aaron
Deuteronomy
1:1 words that Moses **s** to all Israel
18:22 That prophet **s** arrogantly. Don't
32:48 The LORD **s** to Moses that very same day
Joshua
1:1 died, the LORD **s** to Joshua, Nun's
Judges
2:4 LORD's messenger **s** these words to
9:1 in Shechem. He **s** to them and to
1 Kings
17:16 out, just as the LORD **s** through Elijah.
2 Kings
2:22 agreement with the word that Elisha **s**.
Job
3:1 Afterward, Job **s** up and cursed the day
Psalms
18:1 servant, who **s** the words of this
33:9 Because when he **s**, it happened! When
39:3 burned. Then I **s** out with my
66:14 the ones my mouth **s** when I was in
78:19 They **s** against God! "Can God set a
89:19 Once you **s** in a vision to your faithful
99:7 he **s** to them from a pillar of cloud.
105:31 God **s**, and the insects came—gnats
106:33 bitter so that he **s** rashly with his
107:25 God **s** and stirred up a storm that
114:1 from a people who **s** a different
Song of Songs
2:10 My lover **s** and said to me, "Rise up, my
Isaiah
7:10 Again the LORD **s** to Ahaz
8:11 The LORD **s** to me, taking hold of me and warning
Jeremiah
2:8 me; the prophets **s** in the name of
13:3 The LORD **s** to me again
46:13 that the LORD **s** to the prophet
Ezekiel
2:2 As he **s** to me, a wind came to me and
3:24 me on my feet, he **s** to me and said:
40:4 The man **s** to me, "Human one, look and
Daniel
10:6 bronze. When he **s**, it sounded like
10:16 my mouth and **s**, saying to the
Hosea
1:2 the LORD first **s** through Hosea,
Jonah
2:10 Then the LORD **s** to the fish, and it
Malachi
3:16 and every one, **s** among themselves.
Mark
4:34 He **s** to them only in parables, then
9:7 them, and a voice **s** from the cloud,
1 Corinthians
14:5 that all of you **s** in tongues, but
Hebrews
1:1 In the past, God **s** through the prophets
1:2 days, though, he **s** to us through a
13:7 your leaders who **s** God's word to
James
5:10 the prophets who **s** in the name of
2 Peter
1:21 led by the Holy Spirit **s** from God.
2:16 has no voice, **s** with a human
Revelation
10:4 seven thunders **s**, I was about to
10:8 heard from heaven **s** to me again and
13:5 a mouth that **s** boastful and
17:1 the seven bowls **s** with me. "Come,"
21:9 last plagues **s** with me. "Come,"
21:15 The angel who **s** to me had a gold

SPOKEN
Exodus
34:32 that the LORD had **s** with him on Mount
Numbers
12:2 Has the LORD **s** only through
32:31 as the LORD has **s** to your servants.
Deuteronomy
18:22 the LORD hasn't **s**. That prophet
1 Kings
2:27 word that was **s** against Eli's
13:26 with the LORD's word that was **s** to him.
14:11 who die in the field. The LORD has **s**!
15:29 the LORD's word **s** by the LORD's
16:12 that had been **s** by the prophet
16:34 the LORD's word **s** through Joshua,
22:38 bathed in it, just as the LORD had **s**.
2 Kings
1:17 that Elijah had **s**. Because Ahaziah
9:36 the LORD's word **s** through his
10:17 the LORD's word that was **s** to Elijah.
21:7 the LORD had **s** about to David
1 Chronicles
17:17 God. You have **s** about the future
2 Chronicles
33:7 temple God had **s** about to David
36:21 the LORD's word **s** by Jeremiah was
Ezra
1:1 the LORD's word **s** by Jeremiah, the
Job
42:7 the LORD had **s** these words to
Psalms
17:1 my prayer; it's **s** by lips that
60:6 God has **s** in his sanctuary: "I will
62:11 God has **s** one thing—make it two
68:22 My Lord has **s**: "From Bashan I will
108:7 God has **s** in his sanctuary: "I will
119:13 out loud all the rules you have **s**.
Proverbs
25:11 Words **s** at the right time are like gold
Song of Songs
8:8 sister on the day that she is **s** for?

Jeremiah
29:23 wives and deceit **s** in my name, with
30:2 a scroll all the words I have **s** to you.
Matthew
1:22 what the Lord had **s** through the
12:17 so that what was **s** through Isaiah the
Acts
2:16 this is what was **s** through the
9:27 that the Lord had **s** to Saul. He also
23:9 if a spirit or angel has **s** to him?"
2 Corinthians
6:11 we have **s** openly to you,
Hebrews
2:2 message that was **s** by angels was
3:5 the things that would be **s** later.
4:8 God wouldn't have **s** about another day
Jude
1:17 the words **s** beforehand by the

SPRING

Genesis
16:7 found Hagar at a **s** in the desert,
24:13 stand here by the **s** while the
49:22 a young bull by a **s**, who strides with
Nehemiah
2:13 past the Dragon's **S** to the Dung Gate
2:14 I went on to the **S** Gate and to the
3:15 repaired the **S** Gate. He rebuilt
Job
29:23 rain, opened their mouth as for **s** rain.
Psalms
36:9 Within you is the **s** of life. In your
84:6 they make it a **s** of water. Yes,
92:7 though the wicked **s** up like grass and
92:12 righteous will **s** up like a palm
92:13 LORD's house will **s** up in the
114:8 that flint stone into a **s** of water!
Proverbs
5:18 May your **s** be blessed. Rejoice in the
16:15 is like a cloud that brings **s** rain.
25:26 a contaminated **s** or a polluted
Ecclesiastes
12:6 is broken at the **s** and the wheel is
Song of Songs
4:12 my bride; an enclosed pool, a sealed **s**.
4:15 You are a garden **s**, a well of fresh
Isaiah
35:6 sing. Waters will **s** up in the desert,
Jeremiah
2:13 forsaken me, the **s** of living water.
3:3 failed and the **s** rains have
5:24 in autumn and **s** and who assures
9:1 my head were a **s** of water and my
15:18 for me as unreliable as a **s** gone dry!
31:27 and both people and animals will **s** up.
Hosea
6:3 showers, like the **s** rains that give
13:15 and his **s** will dry up; his
Joel
3:18 with water; a **s** will come forth
Amos
3:5 it? Will a trap **s** up from the
Micah
5:7 the LORD, like **s** showers upon the
Zechariah
10:1 is time for the **s** rain. The LORD is
John
4:14 who drink it a **s** of water that
James
3:11 don't come from the same **s**, do they?
3:12 doesn't flow from a saltwater **s** either.
5:7 in the fall and **s**, looking forward
Revelation
21:6 give water from the life-giving **s**.

SPRINGS

Genesis
7:11 that day all the **s** of the deep sea
8:2 The **s** of the deep sea and the skies
Exodus
15:27 there were twelve **s** of water and
Numbers
33:9 there were twelve **s** of water and
Deuteronomy
8:7 streams of water, **s**, and wells that
Joshua
15:19 also give me **s** of water." So he
Judges
1:15 plain, give me **s** of water."So
2 Kings
3:19 up all the **s**, and ruining the
2 Chronicles
32:3 stopping up the **s** outside the city,
32:4 stop up all the **s** and the streams
Psalms
74:15 You split open **s** and streams; you made
85:11 Truth **s** up from the ground;
104:10 You put gushing **s** into dry riverbeds.
107:33 desert, watery **s** into thirsty
107:35 pools, thirsty ground into watery **s**,
Proverbs
8:24 there were no **s** flowing with
Isaiah
12:3 water with joy from the **s** of salvation.
41:18 hilltops and **s** in valleys. I
49:10 them and will guide them by **s** of water.
Jeremiah
51:36 dry up her sea; I'll shut up her **s**.
Ezekiel
7:10 The staff blossoms, and pride **s** up!
Hosea
10:4 so judgment **s** up like poisonous
2 Peter
2:17 teachers are **s** without water,
Revelation
7:17 lead them to the **s** of life-giving
8:10 a third of the rivers and **s** of water.
14:7 and earth, the sea and **s** of water."
16:4 the rivers and **s** of water, and

SPRINKLE

Exodus
29:21 anointing oil and **s** them on Aaron and
Leviticus
4:6 the blood and **s** some of it seven
5:9 Then he will **s** some of the blood of the
14:7 He will **s** the person who needs
16:14 bull's blood and **s** it with his
Numbers
8:7 to cleanse them: **s** water of
19:4 his finger and **s** it seven times in
2 Kings
16:15 drink offerings. "**S** all the blood of

SPRINKLE [cont.]

Ezekiel
36:25 I will **s** clean water on you, and you

SPRINKLING

2 Kings
12:13 wick trimmers, **s** bowls, trumpets,
16:13 offering, and **s** the blood of his
25:15 fire pans and the **s** bowls, which were
Jeremiah
52:18 trimmers, the **s** bowls, the
52:19 fire pans, the **s** bowls, the pots,
Hebrews
11:28 Passover and the **s** of blood, in

SQUARE

Exodus
27:1 altar should be **s**, seven and a half
28:16 It will be **s** and doubled, nine inches
30:2 altar should be **s**, eighteen inches
37:25 The altar was **s**, eighteen inches
38:1 The altar was **s**, seven and a half
39:9 the chest pendant **s** and doubled, nine
1 Kings
7:31 of the stands were **s** rather than round.
Ezekiel
40:12 and each of the rooms was nine feet **s**.
40:42 inches **s** and eighteen
40:47 courtyard. It was **s**, one hundred
41:21 there were **s** doorposts in
43:16 twenty-one feet **s**; each side is
43:17 half feet wide, a **s**. Its outer rim is
45:2 fifty feet **s** will be for the
48:20 by 7.1 miles, a **s**; it includes the
Acts
7:5 here, not even a **s** foot of land.
Revelation
21:16 was laid out as a **s**. Its length was

STAFF

Genesis
32:10 with just my **s**, but now I've
38:18 its cord, and the **s** in your hand." He
38:25 whose seal, cord, and **s** these are."
49:10 nor the ruler's **s** from among his
Leviticus
27:32 the shepherd's **s**—will be holy to
Numbers
17:2 take from them a **s** from each
20:8 brother, take the **s** and assemble the
Judges
5:14 those carrying the official's **s**.
6:21 the tip of the **s** that was in his
1 Samuel
14:27 the end of the **s** he was carrying
14:43 on the end of my **s**," he said. "And
17:40 then grabbed his **s** and chose five
2 Samuel
23:21 him armed with a **s**. He grabbed the
2 Kings
4:29 ready, take my **s**, and go! If you
4:31 them. He set the **s** on the young
18:21 are trusting in a **s**—Egypt—that's
Psalms
23:4 Your rod and your **s**—they protect me.
Isaiah
9:4 them, the **s** on their
10:5 in whose hand is the **s** of my fury!
10:15 lifts it! As if a **s** could lift up the
10:24 and raises its **s** against you as
14:5 has broken the **s** of the wicked,
28:27 is beaten with a **s**, and cumin with a
36:6 are trusting in a **s**—Egypt—that's not
Jeremiah
48:17 and magnificent **s** are shattered!
51:59 instructed the **s** officer Seraiah,
Ezekiel
7:10 has arrived! The **s** blossoms, and
Micah
7:14 people with your **s**, the sheep of
Zechariah
8:4 them will have a **s** in their hand
11:10 Then I took the **s** Delight, and I
11:14 up my second **s** Harmony, to break
Acts
10:7 a pious soldier from his personal **s**.
Hebrews
11:21 in worship over the head of his **s**.

STAND → ABLE TO STAND, STAND BEFORE THE LORD, STAND FIRM

Exodus
9:11 experts couldn't **s** up to Moses
14:13 Don't be afraid. **S** your ground, and
Leviticus
26:13 your bonds and made you **s** up straight.
26:37 have no power to **s** before your
Numbers
30:4 binding obligations for herself will **s**.
30:5 for herself will **s**. The LORD will
Deuteronomy
9:2 say: "Who can **s** up to the Anakim?"
Joshua
3:8 of the Jordan, **s** still in the
10:12 Israelites: "Sun, **s** still at Gibeon!
2 Chronicles
20:17 take your places, **s** ready, and watch
35:5 **S** in the sanctuary, according to the
Psalms
10:1 Why do you **s** so far away, LORD, hiding
24:3 mountain? Who can **s** in his holy
76:7 awesome! Who can **s** before you when
130:3 LORD—my Lord, who would **s** a chance?
141:2 Let my prayer **s** before you like
Isaiah
11:10 of Jesse will **s** as a signal to
29:23 one of Jacob, and **s** in awe of
Jeremiah
7:2 **S** near the gate of the LORD's temple
14:6 The wild donkeys **s** on the well-traveled
26:2 LORD proclaims: **S** in the temple
Ezekiel
2:1 to me: Human one, **s** on your feet, and
22:30 the wall and **s** in the gap for me
46:2 of the gate and **s** at the gate's
47:10 People will **s** fishing beside it, from
Micah
5:4 He will **s** and shepherd his flock in the
Habakkuk
3:11 Sun and moon **s** still high above. With
3:16 I tremble while I **s**, while I wait for
Zechariah
14:4 that day he will **s** upon the Mount of
Matthew
12:41 of Nineveh will **s** up at the

Acts
14:10 Paul said, "***S*** up straight on
22:30 of prison and had him ***s*** before them.
26:16 Get up! ***S*** on your feet! I have appeared
27:24 Paul! You must ***s*** before Caesar!
Romans
5:2 grace in which we ***s*** through him, and
14:4 servants? They ***s*** or fall before
14:10 We all will ***s*** in front of the
Ephesians
6:11 you can make a ***s*** against the
Revelation
8:2 seven angels who ***s*** before God, and
18:10 They will ***s*** a long way off because they
18:15 rich by her, will ***s*** a long way off

STAND BEFORE THE LORD
Nm 5:16; 5:18, 30; Dt 19:17; 1Sa 6:20; 2Ki 16:14; Rev 11:4

STAND FIRM
2Ch 20:20; Prv 10:25; Dn 2:44; 1Co 15:58; 16:13; 2Co 1:24; Ga 5:1; Phi 1:27; 4:1; Col 4:12; 2Th 2:15; Jas 1:12; 1Pt 5:12

STANDING
Genesis
18:22 Abraham remained ***s*** in front of the
Exodus
3:5 because you are ***s*** on holy ground."
Leviticus
16:10 lot will be left ***s*** alive before the
Numbers
22:23 LORD's messenger ***s*** in the road with
Joshua
4:10 the chest were ***s*** in the middle of
Judges
15:5 stacked grain, ***s*** grain, vineyards,
18:17 The priest was ***s*** at the entrance
1 Samuel
4:20 to die, the women ***s*** by helping her
17:26 the soldiers ***s*** by him, "What
19:20 with Samuel ***s*** there as their
22:9 Edomite, who was ***s*** with Saul's
2 Samuel
17:17 and Ahimaaz were ***s*** by at En-rogel. A
1 Kings
8:14 of Israel was ***s*** there, he blessed
13:1 Jeroboam was ***s*** at the altar
13:25 road and the lion ***s*** beside it. They
13:28 lion were still ***s*** beside the body.
14:23 built shrines, ***s*** stones, and
2 Kings
9:17 The guard ***s*** on the tower at Jezreel saw
11:14 and saw the king ***s*** by the royal pillar,
1 Chronicles
21:15 messenger was ***s*** near the
Psalms
1:5 will have no ***s*** in the court of
3:1 many enemies! So many are ***s*** against me.
12:5 needy, I'm now ***s*** up. I will
45:9 royal princess is ***s*** in your precious
122:2 Now our feet are ***s*** in your gates,
Isaiah
19:19 of Egypt, and a ***s*** stone for the
21:8 Lord, I'm ***s*** all day; and upon
Jeremiah
28:5 people who were ***s*** in the LORD's
34:7 only fortified towns still ***s*** in Judah.
36:21 officials who were ***s*** next to the king.
Lamentations
3:63 sitting or ***s***, look at how I am
Ezekiel
8:11 of Israel were ***s*** in front of them,
10:3 creatures were ***s*** to the right of
40:3 I saw a man ***s*** in the gate. He
43:6 A man was ***s*** next to me, but the voice
Daniel
8:3 with two horns ***s*** in front of the
10:16 to the person ***s*** in front of me:
12:5 figures—one ***s*** on each side of
Amos
7:7 me: The LORD was ***s*** by a wall, with a
9:1 I saw the LORD ***s*** beside the altar, and
Zechariah
1:8 horse, which was ***s*** among the myrtle
1:10 The man ***s*** among the myrtles responded,
1:11 who was ***s*** among the
3:1 Priest Joshua, ***s*** before the
Matthew
6:5 They love to pray ***s*** in the synagogues
Acts
7:55 majesty and Jesus ***s*** at God's right
7:56 and the Human One ***s*** at God's right
1 Corinthians
10:12 think they are ***s*** need to watch out
1 Timothy
3:13 well gain a good ***s*** and considerable
James
5:9 Look! The judge is ***s*** at the door!
Revelation
3:20 Look! I'm ***s*** at the door and knocking.
7:9 They were ***s*** before the throne
20:12 and the small, ***s*** before the

STANDS
Numbers
14:14 Your cloud ***s*** over them. You go
23:24 like a lion it ***s*** up. It doesn't
35:12 to death until he ***s*** before the
Joshua
22:19 of the LORD ***s***. But don't rebel
22:29 LORD our God that ***s*** before his
Judges
6:24 peace." It still ***s*** today in Ophrah
12:4 Ephraim! Gilead ***s*** within Ephraim
1 Kings
7:27 made ten bronze ***s***. Each was six
2 Kings
25:13 columns, the ***s***, and the bronze
25:16 the Sea, and the ***s*** that Solomon had
Job
16:19 now my witness ***s*** in heaven; my
38:14 for a seal, so it ***s*** out like a
Psalms
33:11 the LORD's plan ***s*** forever; what he
45:9 jewels; the queen ***s*** at your right,
109:31 Because God ***s*** right next to the needy,
111:3 God's righteousness ***s*** forever.
112:3 houses. Their righteousness ***s*** forever.
112:9 righteousness ***s*** forever. Their
119:89 Your word, LORD, ***s*** firm in heaven

Song of Songs
2:9 stag. Here he ***s*** now, outside our
5:10 and ruddy; he ***s*** out among ten
Isaiah
3:13 to accuse; he ***s*** to judge the
Jeremiah
27:19 the Sea, the ***s***, and the rest of
52:17 columns, the ***s***, and the bronze
52:20 it up, and the ***s***, all of which
Ezekiel
21:21 king of Babylon ***s*** at the fork in
27:35 kings, their hair ***s*** on end; their
41:22 is the table that ***s*** before the LORD."
Mark
13:13 name. But whoever ***s*** firm until the
John
1:26 Someone greater ***s*** among you, whom
Revelation
1:12 lamps burning on top of seven gold ***s***.
10:8 of the angel who ***s*** on the sea and on

STARS

Genesis
1:16 God made the ***s*** and two great lights:
15:5 sky and count the ***s*** if you think you
22:17 as many as the ***s*** in the sky and as
26:4 as the ***s*** in the sky, and I
37:9 moon and eleven ***s*** were bowing down
Exodus
32:13 as many as the ***s*** in the sky. And
Deuteronomy
1:10 now as countless as the ***s*** in the sky.
4:19 the moon or the ***s***, all the heavenly
10:22 numerous as the ***s*** in the nighttime
28:62 countless as the ***s*** in the night sky,
Judges
5:20 The ***s*** fought from the sky; from their
2 Kings
21:3 down to all the ***s*** in the sky and
21:5 for all the ***s*** in the sky in
1 Chronicles
27:23 Israel as numerous as the ***s*** in the sky.
2 Chronicles
33:3 down to all the ***s*** in the sky and
33:5 for all the ***s*** in the sky in
Nehemiah
9:23 as the ***s*** of heaven. You
Job
3:9 May its evening ***s*** stay dark; may it
9:7 it does not rise, even seals up the ***s***;
22:12 heaven; see how high the topmost ***s*** are?
25:5 bright and the ***s*** not pure in his
38:7 while the morning ***s*** sang in unison and
38:32 Can you guide the ***s*** at their proper
Psalms
8:3 - the moon and the ***s*** that you set
136:9 The moon and the ***s*** to rule the night—
147:4 God counts the ***s*** by number, giving each
148:3 God! All of you bright ***s***, praise God!
Ecclesiastes
12:2 the moon and the ***s*** too, before the
Isaiah
13:10 Heaven's ***s*** and constellations won't
14:13 above God's ***s***, I will raise my
34:4 All the ***s*** of heaven will dissolve, the
47:13 who gaze at the ***s***, and predict what
Jeremiah
31:35 the moon and ***s*** to light up the
33:22 And just as the ***s*** in the sky can't be
Ezekiel
32:7 I will darken the ***s***. I will cover the
Daniel
8:10 and some of the ***s*** down to the
12:3 shine like the ***s*** forever and
Joel
2:10 are darkened; the ***s*** have stopped
3:15 are darkened; the ***s*** have ceased
Obadiah
1:4 is set among the ***s***, I will bring you
Nahum
3:16 the heavens have ***s***. The locust sheds
Matthew
24:29 its light. The ***s*** will fall from
Mark
13:25 The ***s*** will fall from the sky, and the
Luke
21:25 sun, moon, and ***s***. On the earth,
Acts
7:42 to worship the ***s*** in the sky, just
1 Corinthians
15:41 of glory, and the ***s*** have another kind
Philippians
2:15 people you shine like ***s*** in the world
Hebrews
11:12 the number of the ***s*** in the sky and as
Jude
1:13 shame; wandering ***s*** for whom the
Revelation
1:16 He held seven ***s*** in his right hand, and
1:20 of the seven ***s*** that you saw in
2:1 holds the seven ***s*** in his right hand
3:1 and the seven ***s***: I know your
6:13 The ***s*** of the sky fell to the earth as a
8:12 a third of the ***s*** so that a third
12:1 and a crown of twelve ***s*** on her head.
12:4 third of heaven's ***s*** and threw them to

STATIONED

Genesis
3:24 of Eden, he ***s*** winged creatures
Judges
4:2 and he was ***s*** in Harosheth-ha-go
1 Kings
22:19 heavenly forces ***s*** beside him, at
2 Kings
10:24 But Jehu had ***s*** eighty soldiers
1 Chronicles
9:18 ***s*** until now in the King's Gate on the
18:6 David ***s*** soldiers in Aram of Damascus,
18:13 He ***s*** soldiers in Edom, and all the
21:16 LORD's messenger ***s*** between the earth
2 Chronicles
1:14 horses, which he ***s*** in chariot cities
18:18 heavenly forces ***s*** at his right and
Nehemiah
4:13 open area. Then I ***s*** the people by
13:19 on the Sabbath, I ***s*** some of my own
Isaiah
6:2 creatures were ***s*** around him. Each
21:8 post I'm ***s*** throughout the
Ezekiel
27:11 and Helech were ***s*** on your walls all

John
18:16 to the woman **s** at the gate, and
18:17 The servant woman **s** at the gate asked

STATUTES → TEACH ME YOUR STATUTES
Genesis
26:5 commandments, my **s**, and my
Nehemiah
1:7 commandments, the **s**, and the
9:13 Instruction, good **s** and commandments.
9:14 commandments, **s**, and Instruction
10:29 judgments, and **s** of our LORD God.
Psalms
89:31 if they treat my **s** like dirt, stop
119:5 strong when it comes to keeping your **s**!
119:8 I will keep your **s**. Please don't leave
119:16 delight in your **s**; I will not
119:23 your servant will contemplate your **s**!
119:33 me what your **s** are about, and I
119:48 and I will contemplate all your **s**.
119:54 Your **s** have been my songs of praise
119:71 me because through it I learned your **s**.
119:80 blameless in your **s** so that I am not
119:83 though I haven't forgotten your **s**.
119:112 to keep your **s** forever, every
119:117 so I can focus constantly on your **s**.
119:118 strays from your **s** because they are
119:145 answer me so I can guard your **s**!"
119:155 because they haven't pursued your **s**.
119:171 praise because you've taught me your **s**.
147:19 to Jacob; his **s** and rules to

STEAL
Genesis
31:30 so much, but why did you **s** my gods?"
44:8 Canaan. We didn't **s** silver or gold
Exodus
20:15 Do not **s**
Leviticus
19:11 You must not **s** nor deceive nor lie to
Deuteronomy
5:19 Do not **s**
2 Samuel
19:41 people of Judah **s** you away, and
Job
24:19 Drought and heat **s** melted snow, just as
Psalms
69:4 what I didn't **s** in the first
Proverbs
22:22 Don't **s** from the poor, because they are
28:24 Those who **s** from their father and
30:9 I'll be poor and **s**, and dishonor my
Isaiah
10:2 widows their loot; to **s** from orphans!
10:6 seize spoil, to **s** plunder, and to
Jeremiah
7:9 Will you **s** and murder, commit adultery
23:30 the prophets who **s** my words from
Hosea
5:10 like raiders who **s** the land; I will
7:1 they deceive and **s**, a thief breaks
Obadiah
1:5 wouldn't they **s** only what they
Matthew
6:19 and where thieves break in and **s** them.
12:29 a strong man and **s** his possessions,
19:18 adultery. Don't **s**. Don't give false
27:64 may come and **s** the body and tell
Mark
10:19 adultery. Don't **s**. Don't give false
Luke
18:20 murder. Don't **s**. Don't give false
John
10:10 enters only to **s**, kill, and
Romans
2:21 If you preach, "No stealing," do you **s**?
13:9 murder, don't **s**, don't desire
Ephesians
4:28 should no longer **s**. Instead they
Titus
2:10 or **s**. Instead they should show that

STEPS
Exodus
20:26 my altar using **s**: then your
2 Samuel
6:13 advanced six **s**, David sacrificed
1 Kings
10:19 Six **s** led up to the throne, and the
10:20 sides of the six **s**. No other kingdom
2 Kings
9:13 Jehu on the paved **s**. They blew a
20:9 go forward ten **s** or back ten
2 Chronicles
9:11 The king made **s** for the LORD's temple
9:18 Six **s** led up to the throne, which had a
9:19 sides of the six **s**. No other kingdom
Job
14:16 you now number my **s**, you would not
34:21 on human ways, and he sees all their **s**.
Psalms
17:5 My **s** are set firmly on your paths; my
37:23 A person's **s** are made secure by the
39:1 I would watch my **s** so as not to sin
44:18 neither have our **s** strayed from your
56:6 are watching my **s**, hoping for my
73:2 stumbled; my **s** had nearly slipped
85:13 before God, making a road for his **s**.
119:133 Keep my **s** steady by your word; don't
Proverbs
5:5 down to death; her **s** lead to the grave.
14:15 the prudent give thought to their **s**.
16:9 path, but the LORD secures their **s**.
20:24 A person's **s** are from the LORD; how
Ecclesiastes
5:1 Watch your **s** when you go to God's
Isaiah
26:6 feet of the poor, the **s** of the needy.
38:8 descends on the **s** of Ahaz, I will
Lamentations
1:14 My **s** are being watched; by his hand
4:18 Our **s** were tracked; we could no longer
Ezekiel
40:6 He went up its **s**, and he measured
40:49 feet wide. **S** led up into the
Acts
21:35 Paul reached the **s**, he had to be
21:40 Paul stood on the **s** and gestured to

STICK
Exodus
12:11 and your walking **s** in your hand. You

Deuteronomy
28:21 make a plague **s** to you until he
28:60 you were so afraid; they will **s** to you!
2 Samuel
19:7 not one man will **s** with you tonight—
Job
21:9 dread, God's punishing **s** not upon them.
41:23 of his flesh **s** together; on him
Psalms
89:32 their sin with a **s**, and I will
101:3 wrongdoing; none of that will **s** to me.
137:6 Let my tongue **s** to the roof of my mouth
Isaiah
57:4 mouth wide and **s** out your tongue?
Ezekiel
3:26 make your tongue **s** to the roof of
37:16 human one, take a **s**, and write on it,
37:17 to make a single **s** so that they
37:19 taking Joseph's **s**, which has been
Matthew
10:10 two shirts or sandals or a walking **s**.
27:29 head. They put a **s** in his right
27:30 they took the **s** and struck his
Mark
6:8 except a walking **s**—no bread, no bags
15:19 his head with a **s**. They spit on him
Luke
9:3 walking **s**, no bag, no
1 Corinthians
4:21 to you with a big **s** to punish you, or

STOLEN

Genesis
30:33 that isn't black will be considered **s**."
31:32 didn't know that Rachel had **s** them.
40:15 I was **s** from the land of the Hebrews,
Exodus
22:7 safe and they are **s** from the other
22:12 if the animal was **s**, the person must
Deuteronomy
28:31 donkey will be **s** right out from
Joshua
7:11 things. They have **s** and kept it a
1 Samuel
12:3 Have I ever **s** someone's ox?
2 Samuel
21:12 who had **s** the bones from
Job
21:18 the wind, like dry grass **s** by a storm.
24:2 boundary stones, herd flocks they've **s**,
24:9 The orphan is **s** from the breast; the
Proverbs
9:17 ***S*** water is sweet; food eaten in secret
20:17 ***S*** bread is sweet, but afterward the
Isaiah
3:14 the goods **s** from the poor are
Obadiah
1:13 shouldn't have **s** his possessions
Malachi
1:13 permit what is **s**, lame, or sick to
Luke
11:22 he had trusted and divides the **s** goods.

STOMACH

Numbers
5:22 curses enter your **s** and make your
25:8 through the **s**. Then the plague
Deuteronomy
18:3 the shoulder, the jaws, and the **s**.
Judges
3:21 thigh. He stabbed it into Eglon's **s**,
3:22 sword out of his **s**, the fat closed
2 Samuel
2:23 hit him in the **s** with the back end
3:27 Abner in the **s**, and he died for
4:6 him in the **s**. Then Rechab and
20:10 struck him in the **s** with it so that
Job
40:16 in his thighs, his power in **s** muscles.
Psalms
101:5 neighbor. I can't **s** anyone who has
Proverbs
6:30 if he steals to fill his starving **s**.
18:20 The **s** is satisfied by the fruit of the
Lamentations
1:20 am in trouble. My **s** is churning; my
2:11 from weeping; my **s** is churning. My
Ezekiel
3:3 and fill your **s** with this scroll
Matthew
15:17 mouth enters the **s** and goes out into
Mark
7:19 but into the **s**, and it goes out
1 Corinthians
6:13 Food is for the **s** and the stomach is
Philippians
3:19 god is their **s**, and they take
1 Timothy
5:23 because of your **s** problems and your
Revelation
10:9 you sick to your **s**, but sweet as
10:10 I swallowed it, it made my **s** churn.

STONE

Genesis
28:18 he took the **s** that he had put
28:22 This **s** that I've set up as a sacred
29:2 that well. A huge **s** covered the
29:10 up, rolled the **s** from the well's
31:45 So Jacob took a **s**, set it up as a
35:14 sacred pillar, a **s** pillar, at the
Exodus
17:4 They are getting ready to **s** me."
24:12 I'll give you the **s** tablets with the
28:10 six names on one **s** and the other six
31:18 tablets, the **s** tablets written
34:1 Moses, "Cut two **s** tablets like the
34:13 their sacred **s** pillars, and cut
Deuteronomy
4:13 and wrote them on two **s** tablets.
16:22 set up any sacred **s** either, because
28:36 worship other gods made of wood and **s**.
29:17 idols of wood and **s**, silver and gold,
Joshua
4:5 of you, lift up a **s** on his shoulder
24:26 he took a large **s** and put it up
24:27 the people, "This **s** will serve here
1 Samuel
7:12 Samuel took a **s** and set it up
17:50 a sling and a **s**, striking the
25:37 inside him, and he became like a **s**.
Ezra
5:8 with dressed **s** and with timber

Nehemiah
9:11 the depths, as a **s** into the mighty
Psalms
91:12 so you don't bruise your foot on a **s**.
114:8 water, that flint **s** into a spring of
118:22 The **s** rejected by the builders is now
Proverbs
24:31 ground, and the **s** wall was falling
26:8 Like tying a **s** in a sling, so is giving
26:27 those who roll a **s** will have it turn
27:3 A **s** is heavy and sand weighs much, but the nuisance of fools
Song of Songs
5:15 of whitest **s** set on pedestals
Isaiah
8:14 - but he will be a **s** to trip over and
28:16 laying in Zion a **s**, a tested stone,
Jeremiah
3:9 committing adultery with **s** and tree.
Ezekiel
3:9 harder than **s**. Don't be afraid
46:23 All four had **s** masonry all the way
Daniel
5:4 silver, bronze, iron, wood, and **s**.
6:17 A single **s** was brought and placed over
Zechariah
3:9 See this **s** that I have put before
Matthew
4:6 that you won't hit your foot on a **s**."
7:9 your children a **s** when they ask for
24:2 I assure that no **s** will be left on
28:2 Coming to the **s**, he rolled it
Mark
12:10 scripture, The **s** that the builders
16:3 going to roll the **s** away from the
16:4 they saw that the **s** had been rolled
Luke
4:3 Son, command this **s** to become a loaf
20:18 who falls on that **s** will be crushed.
John
8:7 sinned should throw the first **s**."
10:32 For which of those works do you **s** me?"
19:13 the place called **S** Pavement (in
Acts
4:11 This Jesus is the **s** you builders
2 Corinthians
3:3 on tablets of **s** but on tablets of
Hebrews
9:4 budded, and the **s** tablets of the
1 Peter
2:4 as to a living **s**. Even though this
2:7 though, the **s** the builders
2:8 This is a **s** that makes people stumble
Revelation
2:17 of them a white **s** with a new name
9:20 silver, bronze, **s**, and wood—idols
18:21 angel picked up a **s** that was like a

STONED

Exodus
19:13 must be either **s** to death or shot
21:28 the ox should be **s** to death, and the
Leviticus
20:27 They will be **s**; their blood is
24:23 the camp and **s** him. The
Numbers
15:36 the camp and **s** him. He died as
Joshua
7:25 Then all Israel **s** him. They burned
1 Kings
12:18 all Israel **s** him to death.
21:13 the town and **s** him so that he
21:14 to Jezebel, "Naboth was **s**. He's dead."
21:15 Naboth had been **s** to death, she
2 Chronicles
10:18 the Israelites **s** him to death.
24:21 king's command **s** him to death in
Matthew
21:35 killed. Some of them they **s** to death.
Acts
14:19 crowds over. They **s** Paul and dragged
2 Corinthians
11:25 times. I was **s** once. I was
Hebrews
11:37 They were **s** to death, they were cut in
12:20 touches the mountain, it must be **s**.

STONES

Exodus
28:21 will be twelve **s** with names
39:14 There were twelve **s** with names
Deuteronomy
27:2 you, set up large **s** and cover them
27:5 God—an altar of **s** that haven't been
Joshua
4:3 Pick up twelve **s** from right here
1 Samuel
17:40 chose five smooth **s** from the
1 Kings
18:31 took twelve **s**, according to the
Job
5:23 with the **s** of the field; and
8:17 of rocks, for it sees a home among **s**.
24:2 move boundary **s**, herd flocks
Psalms
102:14 cherish Zion's **s**; they show mercy
Ecclesiastes
3:5 time for throwing **s** and a time for
10:9 Whoever quarries **s** may be injured by
Hosea
10:1 the more he set up sacred standing **s**.
10:2 altars and destroy their standing **s**.
12:11 be like piles of **s** on the rows of
Micah
1:6 I will pour her **s** into the valley;
Zechariah
5:4 destroy the wood and **s** of that house."
9:15 subdue like sling **s**. They will drink,
Matthew
3:9 up Abraham's children from these **s**.
4:3 Son, command these **s** to become bread."
Mark
5:5 he would howl and cut himself with **s**.
13:1 look! What awesome **s** and buildings!"
Luke
3:8 up Abraham's children from these **s**.
19:40 they were silent, the **s** would shout."
21:5 with beautiful **s** and ornaments
John
8:59 So they picked up **s** to throw at him,
10:31 picked up **s** in order to stone
Acts
7:59 battered him with **s**, Stephen prayed,

1 Corinthians
3:12 silver, precious **s**, wood, grass, or
1 Peter
2:5 built like living **s** into a spiritual

STOOD

Genesis
19:27 the place where he had **s** with the LORD,
24:21 The man **s** gazing at her, wondering
Leviticus
9:5 came forward and **s** before the LORD.
Deuteronomy
4:10 that day when you **s** before the LORD
4:11 came close and **s** at the foot of
31:15 the cloud pillar **s** at the tent's
Joshua
3:17 covenant chest **s** firmly on dry
10:13 The sun **s** still and the moon stood
Psalms
103:16 ground where it **s** doesn't remember
106:23 his chosen one, **s** in the way, right
106:30 Then Phinehas **s** up and prayed, and the
Luke
2:9 The Lord's angel **s** before them, the
10:25 A legal expert **s** up to test Jesus.
23:49 him from Galilee, **s** at a distance
24:36 Jesus himself **s** among them and
John
20:19 Jesus came and **s** among them. He
21:4 morning, Jesus **s** on the shore, but
Acts
1:10 two men in white robes **s** next to them.
2 Timothy
4:17 But the Lord **s** by me and gave me
Hebrews
10:32 the light. You **s** your ground while
Revelation
7:11 All the angels **s** in a circle around the
8:3 angel came and **s** at the altar, and
11:11 them, and they **s** on their feet.
12:4 earth. The dragon **s** in front of the
12:18 Then the dragon **s** on the seashore
18:17 living on the sea **s** a long way off.

STOP

Matthew
6:34 Therefore, **s** worrying about tomorrow,
Mark
9:39 replied, "Don't **s** him. No one who
Romans
14:13 So **s** judging each other. Instead, this
Hebrews
10:25 Don't **s** meeting together with other
Revelation
9:20 They didn't **s** worshipping

STOPPED

Numbers
16:48 dead and the living, and the plague **s**.
Joshua
5:12 The manna **s** on that next day, when they ate
2 Kings
4:6 any more." Then the oil **s** flowing,
Job
32:1 These three men **s** answering Job because
Psalms
36:3 They have **s** being wise and
76:6 chariot and horse were **s** dead still.
77:9 Has he angrily **s** up his
85:3 You've **s** being furious; you've turned
Ezekiel
10:19 beside them. They **s** at the entrance
11:23 the city, and it **s** at the mountain
Hosea
4:18 Though they have **s** drinking, they
Joel
2:10 are darkened; the stars have **s** shining,
Mark
5:29 Her bleeding **s** immediately, and she
10:49 Jesus **s** and said, "Call him forward."

STORM

Psalms
50:3 is before him; a **s** rages all around
55:8 far from the rushing wind and **s**.
77:18 in the swirling **s**; lightning lit up
83:15 them with your **s**, terrify them
107:25 and stirred up a **s** that brought the
107:29 God quieted the **s** to a whisper; the
Isaiah
17:13 mountains, like tumbleweeds before a **s**.
25:4 place from the **s**, a shade from the
32:2 a refuge from a **s**, like streams of
54:11 Suffering one, **s**-tossed, uncomforted,
Jeremiah
11:16 of a powerful **s** he will set it
23:19 The LORD's angry **s** breaks out; it
25:32 A terrible **s** comes from the
30:23 like a violent **s**, a fierce wind
Ezekiel
1:4 a driving **s** came out of the
13:11 collapse, and the **s** winds will break
13:13 I will make a **s** wind break out,
38:9 like a sudden **s**. You and all your
Daniel
11:40 king will **s** against him with
Amos
1:14 with strong wind on the day of the **s**.
Jonah
1:4 there was a great **s** on the sea; the
1:12 that this great **s** has come upon
Nahum
1:3 in whirlwind and **s**; clouds are the
Matthew
8:24 A huge **s** arose on the lake so that
Luke
8:24 waves. The **s** died down and it
Acts
27:15 was caught in the **s** and couldn't be
27:18 by the violent **s** that the next day
27:20 and the raging **s** continued to

STRAIGHT

Leviticus
26:13 your bonds and made you stand up **s**.
Deuteronomy
32:32 Their roots run **s** from Sodom—from the fields of
Joshua
6:5 will rise up, attacking **s** ahead."
6:20 city, attacking **s** ahead. They

1 Samuel
4:15 his eyes stared **s** ahead, unable to
6:12 The cows went **s** ahead following the
6:16 this, they went **s** back to Ekron.
17:16 For forty days **s** the Philistine came
2 Samuel
4:6 They went **s** into his house, as if
14:24 said, "He must go **s** to his own house.
14:31 So Joab went **s** to Absalom's house and
2 Kings
8:11 Elisha stared **s** at Hazael until he felt
Psalms
9:17 Let the wicked go **s** to the grave, the
20:8 but we will stand up **s** and strong.
21:12 when you aim your bow **s** at their faces!
49:14 they're headed **s** for the grave.
77:19 Your way went **s** through the sea; your
107:7 God led them **s** to human habitation
119:128 That's why I walk **s** by every single one
Proverbs
3:6 paths, and he will keep your ways **s**.
4:11 of wisdom. I lead you in **s** courses.
4:25 Focus your eyes **s** ahead; keep your gaze
9:15 the path, those going **s** on their way.
11:5 makes their path **s**, but the wicked
14:12 that may seem **s** to someone, but
15:21 those with understanding walk **s** ahead.
16:25 that may seem **s** to someone, but
21:2 path is **s** in their own
23:19 be wise! Keep your mind **s** on the path.
29:27 righteous; the **s** path is
Isaiah
57:2 those who walk in **s** paths will find
Ezekiel
1:9 they each went **s** ahead without
1:12 Each moved **s** ahead wherever the wind
10:22 same. All four of them moved **s** ahead.
Daniel
3:15 will be thrown **s** into the furnace
Micah
3:9 justice and make crooked all that is **s**,
Matthew
3:3 way for the Lord; make his paths **s**."
Mark
1:3 way for the Lord; make his paths **s**."
Luke
3:4 the way for the Lord; make his paths **s**.
3:5 will be made **s** and the rough
13:11 was bent over and couldn't stand up **s**.
21:28 happen, stand up **s** and raise your
22:61 turned and looked **s** at Peter, and
John
1:23 the Lord's path **s** just as the
Acts
9:11 Judas' house on **S** Street and ask
13:10 stop twisting the **s** ways of the Lord
14:10 said, "Stand up **s** on your feet!" He
16:11 sailed from Troas **s** for Samothrace
21:1 we set sail on a **s** course to Cos,
Hebrews
12:13 Make **s** paths for your feet so that if
2 Peter
2:15 Leaving the **s** path, they have gone off

STRANGER

Deuteronomy
25:5 and marry a **s**. Instead, her
Job
15:19 was given and no **s** passed in their
19:15 think me a **s**; I'm a foreigner
31:32 A **s** didn't spend the night in the
Psalms
69:8 I have become a **s** to my own brothers,
Proverbs
6:1 or shake hands in agreement with a **s**,
11:15 the debt of a **s** brings big
20:16 a loan for a **s**; take his pledge
27:2 your own mouth; a **s**, and not your own
27:13 a loan for a **s**; take his pledge
Ecclesiastes
6:2 it; instead, a **s** enjoys it. This
Isaiah
43:12 not some **s** among you. You
Jeremiah
14:8 are you like a **s** in the land, like
Zechariah
7:10 the orphan, the **s**, and the poor;
Matthew
25:35 a drink. I was a **s** and you welcomed
25:43 I was a **s** and you didn't welcome me. I
John
10:5 won't follow a **s** but will run away
Hebrews
11:9 promised as a **s**. He lived in

STRANGERS

2 Samuel
22:44 of many nations. **S** come to serve me.
Psalms
18:43 of many nations. **S** come to serve me.
35:15 against me! **S** I didn't know
109:11 he owns; let **s** plunder his
144:7 from deep water, from the power of **s**,
144:11 from the power of **s**, whose mouths
Proverbs
5:10 Otherwise, **s** will sap your strength,
5:17 yours alone, not for you as well as **s**.
Isaiah
61:5 your sheep, and **s** will be your
Jeremiah
5:19 so you will serve **s** in a land not
51:51 disgraced that **s** have violated the
Lamentations
5:2 turned over to **s**; our houses
Ezekiel
14:5 whose idols have made them all **s** to me.
16:32 wife: you take in **s** instead of your
Hosea
7:9 **S** have eaten up his strength, yet he
8:7 if it were to yield, **s** would devour it.
Joel
3:17 and never again will **s** pass through it.
Obadiah
1:11 You stood nearby, **s** carried off his
Matthew
17:25 taxes, from their children or from **s**?"
17:26 From **s**," he said. Jesus said to him,
27:7 potter's field where **s** could be buried.
Acts
7:6 will be **s** in a land that
13:17 they lived as **s** in the land of
Romans
12:13 people, and welcome **s** into your home.

Ephesians
2:12 of Israel, and **s** to the covenants
2:19 you are no longer **s** and aliens.
1 Timothy
5:10 hospitality to **s**, washing the feet
Hebrews
11:13 that they were **s** and immigrants on
1 Peter
1:1 To God's chosen **s** in the world of
2:11 immigrants and **s** in the world, I
3 John
1:5 and sisters, even though they are **s**.

STRAW

Genesis
24:25 have plenty of **s** and feed for the
24:32 camels, provided **s** and feed for them
Exodus
5:7 people with the **s** they need to make
5:10 says, 'I'm not giving you **s** anymore.
15:7 hot anger; it burns them up like **s**.
Judges
19:19 We've got our own **s** and feed for our
1 Kings
4:28 of barley and **s** for the horses
Job
13:25 to tremble, or will you pursue dry **s**?
21:18 Let them be like **s** in the wind, like
41:27 He treats iron as **s**, bronze as rotten
41:28 him flee; slingstones he turns to **s**.
41:29 a club like **s**; he laughs at the
Isaiah
11:7 and a lion will eat **s** like an ox.
25:10 trampled down as **s** is trampled into
33:11 You conceive **s**, give birth to stubble;
40:24 the windstorm carries them off like **s**.
41:2 sword, like scattered **s** with his bow?
41:15 them; you will reduce hills to **s**.
65:25 the lion will eat **s** like the ox, but
Jeremiah
13:24 scatter you like **s** that is blown
23:28 between **s** and wheat!
Obadiah
1:18 the house of Esau **s**; they will burn
Malachi
4:1 evil will become **s**. The coming day

STREAM

Genesis
2:6 though a **s** rose from the earth and
Leviticus
11:9 fins and scales, whether in sea or **s**.
Deuteronomy
9:21 the dust into the **s** that ran down the
21:4 with a flowing **s**—one that has not
2 Samuel
17:20 crossed over the **s**." They looked for
Job
6:15 like a **s** in the desert,
40:22 shade; poplars of the **s** surround him.
Psalms
65:9 greatly by God's **s**, full of water.
110:7 God drinks from a **s** along the way, then holds his head
119:136 Rivers of tears **s** from my eyes because
Proverbs
18:4 a bubbling **s**, a fountain of
Song of Songs
4:1 of goats as they **s** down Mount Gilead.
6:5 of goats as they **s** down from Gilead.
Isaiah
2:2 above the hills; peoples will **s** to it.
30:33 the LORD, like a **s** of brimstone,
32:20 sow beside any **s** will be happy,
66:12 an overflowing **s**. You will nurse
Jeremiah
51:44 will no longer **s** to him, and
Daniel
12:5 standing on each side of the **s**.
Amos
5:24 righteousness like an ever-flowing **s**.
Micah
4:1 above the hills; peoples will **s** to it.

STREAMS

Leviticus
11:10 in the seas or **s** that does not
23:40 willows of the **s**, and rejoice
Deuteronomy
8:7 land, a land with **s** of water,
10:7 which is a land with flowing **s**.
2 Kings
19:24 own feet, I dried up all of Egypt's **s**.'
2 Chronicles
32:4 springs and the **s** that flowed
Job
20:17 won't experience **s**, rivers of honey,
20:28 off by rushing **s** on the day of his
Psalms
1:3 tree replanted by **s** of water, which
42:1 deer that craves **s** of water, my
46:4 is a river whose **s** gladden God's
74:15 open springs and **s**; you made strong-
78:16 God made **s** flow from the rock, made
78:20 water gushed and **s** flowed, but can
78:44 they couldn't drink from their own **s**.
126:4 better, like dry **s** in the desert
137:1 Babylon's **s**, there we sat
Proverbs
5:16 flood outside, **s** of water in the
Ecclesiastes
1:7 All **s** flow to the sea, but the sea is
Song of Songs
4:15 a well of fresh water, **s** from Lebanon.
Isaiah
7:18 from the remotest **s** of Egypt and for
11:15 it into seven **s** so that it can be
19:6 will stink; the **s** will shrink and
30:25 every high hill, **s** will run with
32:2 a storm, like **s** of water in a
33:21 of rivers, broad **s** where no boat
34:9 Edom's **s** will be turned into pitch, its
35:6 in the desert, and **s** in the wilderness.
37:25 own feet, I dried up all of Egypt's **s**."
41:18 I will open **s** on treeless hilltops and
43:20 in the desert and **s** in the wilderness
44:3 ground and **s** upon dry land. I
44:4 the reeds like willows by flowing **s**.
44:27 depths, "Dry up; I will dry your **s**";
Jeremiah
9:18 fill up with tears and water **s** down.
17:8 planted by the **s**, whose roots
18:14 Do the cool mountain **s** ever dry up?
31:9 them by quiet **s** and on smooth

Lamentations
3:48 **S** of water pour from my eyes because of
Ezekiel
31:4 up, because its **s** flowed around the
Joel
1:20 you because the **s** have dried up;

STREET

Joshua
2:19 house into the **s** will have only
Job
31:32 the night in the **s**; I opened my
Psalms
31:11 whoever sees me in the **s**, runs away!
Proverbs
1:20 shouts in the **s**; in the public
7:8 was crossing the **s** at her corner and
7:12 one foot in the **s**, one foot in the
22:13 a lion in the **s**! I'll be killed
Ecclesiastes
10:3 walk down the **s**; they show
12:4 the doors to the **s** are shut, when
12:5 with mourners all around in the **s**;
Song of Songs
8:1 find you in the **s** and kiss you, and
Isaiah
51:20 the head of every **s** like antelope in
51:23 ground, like a **s** for those walking
Jeremiah
5:1 Search every **s** in Jerusalem, comb the
37:21 daily from the **s** vendors—until
Lamentations
2:19 fainting from hunger on every **s** corner.
4:1 jewels are scattered on every **s** corner.
Ezekiel
7:19 silver into the **s**, and their gold
16:31 the head of every **s** and made your
Nahum
3:10 the head of every **s**. They cast lots
Matthew
6:5 and on the **s** corners so that
Mark
11:4 outside on the **s**, and they untied
Acts
9:11 house on Straight **S** and ask for a man
12:10 the length of one **s**, when abruptly
Revelation
11:8 will lie on the **s** of the great city
21:21 the city's main **s** was pure gold, as
22:2 the city's main **s**. On each side of

STREETS

Deuteronomy
32:25 Outside, in the **s**, the sword will
Psalms
18:42 them out like mud dumped in the **s**.
144:14 walls, no exile, no outcries in our **s**!
Song of Songs
3:2 city, through the **s** and the squares.
Isaiah
5:25 the middle of the **s** like dung. Even
58:12 of Broken Walls, Restorer of Livable **S**.
Jeremiah
6:11 children in the **s** and on the youths
7:17 of Judah and in the **s** of Jerusalem?
14:16 thrown into the **s** of Jerusalem,
51:4 land of Babylon, struck down in her **s**.
Lamentations
1:20 so bitter. In the **s** the sword kills;
2:11 and babies are fainting in the city **s**.
4:5 tremble in the **s**. Those who wore
Amos
5:16 In all the **s** they will say,
Micah
7:10 to be trampled, like mud in the **s**.
Nahum
2:4 through the **s**; they rush back
Zephaniah
3:6 devastate their **s**. No one will pass
Zechariah
9:3 like dust and gold like mud in the **s**,
10:5 through the muddy **s** during battle.
Matthew
6:2 and in the **s** so that they may
12:19 nobody will hear his voice in the **s**.
Luke
10:10 welcome you, go out into the **s** and say,
13:26 presence, and you taught in our **s**.'
14:21 to the city's **s**, the busy ones
Acts
5:15 out into the main **s** and lay them on

STRENGTH

Genesis
49:3 my oldest son, my **s** and my first
Exodus
3:20 So I'll use my **s** and hit Egypt with
15:2 The LORD is my **s** and my power; he has
Leviticus
26:20 so that your **s** will be spent for no
Deuteronomy
33:25 and that your **s** lasts all your
Joshua
14:11 sent me out. My **s** then was as my
17:17 and possess great **s**. You will have
Judges
16:5 him such great **s** and what we can
1 Samuel
2:1 in the LORD. My **s** rises up in the
2 Samuel
22:3 my salvation's **s**, my place of
22:40 equipped me with **s** for war; you
1 Chronicles
16:11 the LORD and his **s**; seek his face
29:12 In your hand are **s** and might, and it
2 Chronicles
32:8 he has is human **s**, but we have the
Nehemiah
4:10 The carrier's **s** is failing, for
8:10 the joy from the LORD is your **s**!"
Job
4:3 many and given **s** to drooping hands.
39:19 Did you give **s** to the horse, clothe his
Psalms
10:10 falling prey to the **s** of the wicked.
18:1 He said: I love you, LORD, my **s**.
18:2 my salvation's **s**, my place of
18:32 equips me with **s** and makes my way
18:39 equipped me with **s** for war; you
21:1 celebrates your **s**, LORD; look how
21:13 LORD, in your **s**! We will sing and
22:15 My **s** is dried up like a piece of broken
22:19 away! You are my **s**! Come quick and
28:7 The LORD is my **s** and my shield. My

28:8 is his people's **s**; he is a fortress
29:11 Let the LORD give **s** to his people! Let
31:10 with groaning. **S** fails me because
33:16 saved by the **s** of their armies;
33:17 it can't save despite its great **s**.
38:10 heart pounds; my **s** abandons me. Even
46:1 is our refuge and **s**, a help always
59:9 for you, my **s**, because God is
59:16 will sing of your **s**! In the morning I
59:17 to you, my **s**, because God is
61:3 a tower of **s** in the face of
62:11 have heard: that **s** belongs to God,
65:6 mountains by your **s**; you are dressed
66:3 of your great **s**, your enemies
68:28 Summon your **s**, God! Show how strong
68:34 over Israel; his **s** is in the clouds.
68:35 Israel who gives **s** and power to his
71:9 Don't abandon me when my **s** is used up!
71:18 all who are yet to come about your **s**,
75:4 the wicked I said, "Don't exalt your **s**!
75:5 Don't exalt your **s** so highly. Don't
75:10 power, but the **s** of the righteous
77:14 demonstrated your **s** among all peoples.
78:4 the LORD and his **s**—the wondrous wor
78:26 and drove the south wind by his **s**.
81:1 loud to God, our **s**! Shout for joy to
84:5 who put their **s** in you are truly
84:7 They go from **s** to strength, until they
86:16 your servant your **s**; save this child
89:17 splendor of their **s**. By your favor
93:1 clothed with **s**. Yes, he set the
96:6 in front of him; **s** and beauty are in
102:23 God broke my **s** in midstride, cutting my
105:4 the LORD and his **s**; seek his face
110:3 Your youthful **s** is like the dew
112:9 forever. Their **s** increases
118:14 The LORD was my **s** and protection; he
132:17 will make David's **s** thrive. I will
138:3 me. You encouraged me with inner **s**.
147:10 doesn't prize the **s** of a horse; God
148:14 God raised the **s** of his people, the

Proverbs
5:9 will give your **s** to others, your
5:10 will sap your **s**, and your hard
8:14 as well as understanding and **s**.
20:29 **S** is the glory of young men; gray hair
24:10 a day of distress, your **s** is too small.
31:3 Don't give your **s** to women, your ways
31:25 **S** and honor are her clothing; she is

Isaiah
12:2 the LORD, is my **s** and my shield; he
40:26 of God's great **s** and mighty power,
40:31 will renew their **s**; they will fly up

Micah
5:4 his flock in the **s** of the LORD, in
7:16 of all their **s**; they will cover

Nahum
2:1 road, protect your groin, save your **s**!

Matthew
15:32 they won't have enough **s** to travel."

Mark
8:3 won't have enough **s** to travel, for
12:30 all your mind, and with all your **s**.
12:33 and all of one's **s**, and to love

Luke
1:51 He has shown **s** with his arm. He has
10:27 with all your **s**, and with all

Acts
9:19 he regained his **s**. He stayed with
14:8 man who lacked **s** in his legs. He

1 Corinthians
1:25 of God is stronger than human **s**.

2 Corinthians
1:8 so far beyond our **s** that we were

Ephesians
1:19 by the energy of God's powerful **s**.
6:10 by the Lord and his powerful **s**.

Philippians
4:13 the power of the one who gives me **s**.

2 Thessalonians
2:17 and give you **s** in every good
3:3 and will give you **s** and protect you

1 Timothy
1:12 who has given me **s** because he

2 Timothy
2:1 child, draw your **s** from the grace
4:17 by me and gave me **s**, so that the

Hebrews
11:34 the sword, found **s** in weakness, were

1 Peter
4:11 do so from the **s** that God

Revelation
14:10 poured full **s** into the cup of

STRENGTHEN

Deuteronomy
1:38 will enter it. **S** him because he's
3:28 command Joshua, **s** him, and
33:7 his own people, **s** his hands; be his

2 Kings
15:19 his ally and to **s** his hold on the

1 Chronicles
29:12 is in your power to magnify and **s** all.

2 Chronicles
16:9 whole world to **s** those who are

Nehemiah
6:9 get finished." But now, God, **s** me!

Job
8:20 integrity, won't **s** the hand of the
16:5 heap up words, **s** you with my

Psalms
41:3 The LORD will **s** them when they are
89:21 sustain him—yes, my arm will **s** him!

Song of Songs
2:5 raisin cakes, **s** me with apples,

Isaiah
35:3 **S** the weak hands, and support the
41:10 your God. I will **s** you, I will
45:5 is no God. I **s** you—though you
54:2 your tent ropes and **s** your stakes.

Jeremiah
31:25 I will **s** the weary and renew those who

Ezekiel
30:24 I will **s** the arms of the king of
30:25 I will **s** the arms of the king of
34:4 You don't **s** the weak, heal the sick,
34:16 the wounded, and **s** the weak. But the

Daniel
11:1 I took my stand to **s** and protect him."

Nahum
3:14 for siege! **S** your

Zechariah
10:6 I will **s** the house of Judah and deliver

10:12 I will **s** them in the LORD, and they
Luke
22:32 have returned, **s** your brothers and
Romans
16:25 be to God who can **s** you with my good
Ephesians
3:16 ask that he will **s** you in your inner
1 Thessalonians
3:2 We sent him to **s** and encourage you
Hebrews
12:12 So **s** your drooping hands and weak
1 Peter
5:10 restore,empower, **s**, and establish
Revelation
3:2 Wake up and **s** whatever you have left,

STRENGTHENED

1 Kings
18:46 the LORD's power **s** Elijah. He
2 Chronicles
11:17 They **s** the kingdom of Judah and
17:1 king. Jehoshaphat **s** his position
Psalms
89:24 be with him. He will be **s** by my name.
Proverbs
3:8 body will be healthy and your bones **s**.
Ezekiel
13:22 them!—and you **s** the hands of the
Daniel
11:6 fathered her, and the one who **s** her.
Luke
22:43 angel appeared to him and **s** him.
Acts
3:16 name, God has **s** this man whom you
9:31 of peace. God **s** the church, and
14:22 they **s** the disciples and urged them to
15:32 encouraged and **s** the brothers and
16:5 the churches were **s** in the faith and
19:20 word grew abundantly and **s** powerfully.
Romans
1:11 gift to you so that you can be **s**.
Ephesians
6:10 Finally, be **s** by the Lord and his
Colossians
1:11 by being **s** through his glorious might
1 Thessalonians
3:13 your hearts to be **s**, to be blameless
Hebrews
13:9 the heart to be **s** by grace rather

STRETCH

Genesis
3:22 Now so he doesn't **s** out his hand and take
22:12 said, "Don't **s** out your hand
Exodus
7:19 rod and **s** out your hand
14:16 shepherd's rod, **s** out your hand
Numbers
24:6 palm groves that **s** out, like gardens
Deuteronomy
29:20 this scroll will **s** out over them,
Joshua
1:4 territory will **s** from the desert
23:4 destroyed. They **s** from the Jordan
2 Kings
21:13 I will **s** out over Jerusalem the same
Job
1:11 But **s** out your hand and strike all he
1:12 power; only don't **s** out your hand
2:5 But **s** out your hand and strike his
Psalms
68:31 Egypt; let Cush **s** out its hands to
143:6 I **s** out my hands to you; my whole being
144:7 **S** out your hand from above! Rescue me
Proverbs
2:2 wisdom, and **s** your mind toward
Jeremiah
6:12 as well. I will **s** out my hand
Amos
2:8 They **s** out beside every altar on
6:4 on beds of ivory, **s** out on their
Zephaniah
1:4 I will **s** out my hand against Judah and
2:13 He will **s** out his hand against the
Zechariah
9:10 His rule will **s** from sea to sea,
Matthew
12:13 said to the man, "**S** out your hand."
Mark
3:5 said to the man, "**S** out your hand."
Luke
6:10 said to the man, "**S** out your hand."
John
21:18 old, you will **s** out your hands
Acts
4:30 **S** out your hand to bring healing and

STRETCHED

Genesis
8:9 earth. Noah **s** out his hand,
22:10 Then Abraham **s** out his hand and took
Exodus
8:6 So Aaron **s** out his hand over the waters
8:17 did this. Aaron **s** out his hand with
10:13 So Moses **s** out his shepherd's rod over
14:21 Then Moses **s** out his hand over the sea.
Joshua
8:26 the hand that was **s** out holding a
2 Samuel
24:16 divine messenger **s** out his hand to
1 Kings
13:4 Bethel, Jeroboam **s** his hand from the
17:21 Then he **s** himself over the boy three
1 Chronicles
21:16 sword in his hand **s** out against
Job
9:8 **s** out the heavens alone and trod on the
26:7 He **s** the North over chaos, hung earth
38:5 you know. Who **s** a measuring tape
Proverbs
1:24 rejected me; I **s** out my hand to
Isaiah
42:5 the one who **s** them out, the one
44:24 of all, who alone **s** out the heavens,
45:12 it. My own hands **s** out the heavens.
51:13 the one who **s** out the heavens
Jeremiah
1:9 Then the LORD **s** out his hand, touched
4:31 breath, her arms **s** out, and moaning,
Lamentations
2:8 Zion's wall. He **s** out a measuring
Ezekiel
1:11 of wings that **s** out overhead

8:3 He **s** out the form of a hand and picked
10:7 winged creatures **s** a hand between
Hosea
7:5 heat of wine; he **s** out his hand to
Zechariah
1:16 a measuring line be **s** over Jerusalem.
Matthew
12:49 He **s** out his hand toward his disciples
Romans
10:21 All day long I **s** out my hands to a
Revelation
1:13 wore a robe that **s** down to his feet,

STRIKE

Genesis
3:15 hers. They will **s** your head, but
Exodus
12:12 night, and I'll **s** down every oldest
17:5 that you used to **s** the Nile River,
Leviticus
26:21 obey me, I will **s** you for your sins
26:24 you. I will **s** you for your sins
Numbers
1:53 anger will not **s** the Israelite
14:12 I'll **s** them down with a plague and
24:8 their bones; he will **s** with his arrows.
Deuteronomy
7:2 you, you must **s** them down,
13:15 must completely **s** down the
28:22 The LORD will **s** you with consumption,
Joshua
7:3 could go up and **s** Ai. Don't make
9:18 Israelites didn't **s** at them. This was
10:4 help me. We will **s** at Gibeon,
Judges
8:21 You stand up and **s** us yourself,
20:31 They began to **s** down some of the
1 Samuel
17:35 go after it, **s** it, and rescue
17:46 to me. I will **s** you down and cut
20:33 at Jonathan to **s** him, and Jonathan
26:10 the LORD who will **s** him down, or his
2 Samuel
1:15 here!" he said. "**S** him down!" So the
5:8 Jebusites should **s** the windpipe
13:28 and I tell you to **s** Amnon down, then
1 Kings
14:15 The LORD will **s** Israel so that it
20:35 friend: "Please **s** me." But his
20:37 and said, "Please **s** me." He hit the
2 Kings
6:18 to the LORD, "**S** this nation with
9:7 You will **s** down your master Ahab's
2 Chronicles
21:14 the LORD will now **s** your family, your
Job
1:11 out your hand and **s** all he has. He
2:5 out your hand and **s** his bones and
15:24 master them like a king ready to **s**;
16:10 mouths at me and **s** my cheek in a
30:24 Surely he won't **s** someone in ruins if
Psalms
9:20 **S** them with fear, LORD. Let the nations
81:2 up a song and **s** the drum! Sweet
89:23 of him. I will **s** down all those
118:16 hand is ready to **s**! The LORD's
121:6 The sun won't **s** you during the day;
Proverbs
17:26 the righteous, to **s** the honorable for
19:25 **S** someone who scoffs, and a naive
23:13 children; if you **s** them with a rod,
23:14 **S** them with a rod, and you will save
Isaiah
11:4 the land. He will **s** the violent with
Ezekiel
21:12 my people. Therefore, **s** your thigh.
22:13 I now **s** my hands over your ill-gotten
39:3 I will **s** your bow from your left hand,
Hosea
11:6 The sword will **s** wildly in their
Amos
9:1 the LORD said: **S** the pillars until
Micah
5:1 a rod they will **s** the cheek of the
Zechariah
13:7 heavenly forces! **S** the shepherd in
Malachi
4:6 I will come and **s** the land with a
John
18:23 if I speak correctly, why do you **s** me?"
Acts
23:2 beside Paul to **s** him in the mouth.
23:3 God is about to **s** you, you
Revelation
11:6 blood, and to **s** the earth with
19:15 he will use to **s** down the nations.

STRONG

Exodus
15:6 Your **s** hand, LORD, is dominant in
Deuteronomy
31:6 Be **s**! Be fearless! Don't be afraid and
Joshua
1:6 Be brave and **s**, because you are the
10:25 Be brave and **s**, because this is
2 Samuel
10:11 prove too **s** for me, you must
24:9 hundred thousand **s** men who could
1 Kings
2:2 whole earth takes. Be **s** and be a man.
2 Chronicles
32:7 Be brave and be **s**! Don't let the king
Job
1:19 when a **s** wind came from the desert and
5:15 the needy from the grip of the **s**;
8:2 that your utterances become a **s** wind?
12:21 on royalty; loosens the belt of the **s**;
15:26 with a massive and **s** shield.
16:14 and over, runs against me like a **s** man.
18:7 Their **s** strides slow down; their plans
21:7 live, grow old, and even become **s**?
24:22 drag away the **s** by force; they
40:14 you, for your **s** hand has
Psalms
8:2 you have laid a **s** foundation
17:7 from their attackers by your **s** hand.
17:12 they are like a **s** young lion lying
18:35 salvation; your **s** hand has
20:6 of salvation achieved by his **s** hand.
20:8 but we will stand up straight and **s**.
21:8 enemies; your **s** hand will catch
26:10 schemes, whose **s** hands are full of
27:14 in the LORD! Be **s**! Let your heart
29:4 LORD's voice is **s**; the LORD's voice

30:7 you made me a ***s*** mountain. But
31:2 protects me; be a ***s*** fortress that
34:10 Even ***s*** young lions go without and get
38:19 enemies are so ***s***; those who hate
44:3 —no, it was your ***s*** hand, your arm,
45:4 Let your ***s*** hand perform
48:10 the earth. Your ***s*** hand is filled
62:7 on God. God is my ***s*** rock. My refuge
68:28 God! Show how ***s*** you are, God,
69:32 seek God—let your hearts beat ***s*** again
71:7 people because you are my ***s*** refuge.
73:4 no pain; their bodies are fit and ***s***.
74:11 do you hold your ***s*** hand close to
76:5 lethargy. All the ***s*** troops couldn't
77:10 thought, that the ***s*** hand of the Most
78:54 that his own ***s*** hand had acquired.
80:15 planted with your ***s*** hand, this son
83:8 they are the ***s*** arm for Lot's
89:10 scattered your enemies with your ***s*** arm.
90:10 eighty, if we're ***s***. But their
92:10 you've made me as ***s*** as a wild ox. I'm
98:1 things! His own ***s*** hand and his own
99:4 ***S*** king who loves justice, you are the
110:5 master, by your ***s*** hand, God has
112:2 will be ***s*** throughout the
117:2 love toward us is ***s***, the LORD's
118:15 The LORD's ***s*** hand is
119:5 wish my ways were ***s*** when it comes to
132:2 how he promised the ***s*** one of Jacob:
132:5 dwelling place for the ***s*** one of Jacob."
136:12 With a ***s*** hand and outstretched arm—
137:5 If I forget you, let my ***s*** hand wither!
138:7 wrath; you save me with your ***s*** hand.
139:10 even there your ***s*** hand would hold
140:7 My LORD God, my ***s*** saving help—you've protected
144:8 lies, and whose ***s*** hand is a strong
144:11 lies, and whose ***s*** hand is a strong
147:5 is great and so ***s***! God's knowledge

Proverbs
10:15 wealthy are their ***s*** city; the ruin of
12:4 A ***s*** woman is a crown to her husband,
13:4 The lazy have ***s*** desires but receive
14:4 when there is a ***s*** bull, there is
14:26 of the LORD is ***s*** confidence and
18:10 LORD's name is a ***s*** tower; the
18:11 the wealthy are a ***s*** city and like a
18:18 conflicts and keep ***s*** opponents apart.
23:11 their redeemer is ***s***. He will bring
24:5 mightier than a ***s*** one; a
30:25 creatures aren't ***s***, but they store
31:4 wine, for rulers to crave ***s*** drink.
31:6 Give ***s*** drink to those who are perishing

Ecclesiastes
12:3 tremble and the ***s*** men stoop; when

Song of Songs
8:6 for love is as ***s*** as death,

Isaiah
35:4 panicking: "Be ***s***! Don't fear!

Jeremiah
50:34 their redeemer is ***s***; the LORD of

Zechariah
8:9 proclaims: Be ***s***, you who are now

Matthew
12:29 that belongs to a ***s*** man and steal his

Mark
3:27 the house of a ***s*** person and steals
5:3 no one was ever ***s*** enough to

Romans
4:20 but he grew ***s*** in faith and gave

1 Corinthians
1:27 world considers weak to shame the ***s***.
16:13 firm in your faith, be brave, be ***s***.

2 Corinthians
12:10 because when I'm weak, then I'm ***s***.

1 John
2:14 because you are ***s***, the word of God

Revelation
6:13 its fruit when shaken by a ***s*** wind.

STRONGER

Deuteronomy
1:28 People far ***s*** and much taller
11:23 that are larger and ***s*** than you are.

2 Samuel
3:1 kept getting ***s***, while Saul's

Psalms
142:6 persecutors because they're ***s*** than me.

Ecclesiastes
6:10 with the one who is ***s*** than they are.
7:19 a wise person ***s*** than ten rulers

Jeremiah
31:11 the power of those ***s*** than they are.

Matthew
3:11 after me is ***s*** than I am. I'm

Mark
1:7 announced, "One ***s*** than I am is

Luke
11:22 But as soon as a ***s*** one attacks and

Acts
9:22 But Saul grew ***s*** and stronger. He

1 Corinthians
1:25 of God is ***s*** than human
10:22 We aren't ***s*** than he is, are

2 Peter
2:11 angels, who are ***s*** and more

STRONGHOLDS

Judges
6:2 and caves in the mountains as hidden ***s***.

Psalms
89:40 You've made his ***s*** a pile of ruins.

Isaiah
13:22 will howl in its ***s***, and jackals in

Jeremiah
48:41 be captured; the ***s*** will be seized.

Ezekiel
33:27 and those in the ***s*** and caves will

Micah
7:17 from their ***s*** to the LORD our

STRUCK

Exodus
7:25 by after the LORD had ***s*** the Nile River.
9:23 and lightning ***s*** the earth. The
12:27 in Egypt. When he ***s*** down the
12:29 midnight the LORD ***s*** down all the

Numbers
20:11 his hand and ***s*** the rock with his

2 Samuel
1:15 So the servant ***s*** the Amalekite

Psalms
18:38 I ***s*** them down; they couldn't get up
69:26 you've already ***s***; they talk about

78:20 True, God **s** the rock and water gushed
78:51 God **s** down all of Egypt's oldest males;
105:36 God **s** down all the oldest sons
135:8 God **s** down the Egyptians' oldest
136:10 to the one who **s** down the
Amos
4:9 I **s** you with disease and mildew. I
Matthew
27:30 the stick and **s** his head again
Mark
12:4 to them, but they **s** him on the head
14:47 drew a sword and **s** the high priest's
15:19 and again, they **s** his head with a
Luke
18:13 Rather, he **s** his chest and
22:50 One of them **s** the high priest's
24:11 Their words **s** the apostles as nonsense,
John
18:10 drew it and **s** the high priest's

STUBBORN

Exodus
4:21 But I'll make him **s** so that he won't
7:3 I'll make Pharaoh **s**, and I'll perform
33:5 You are a **s** people. If I were
Deuteronomy
9:6 you are a **s** people!
Joshua
11:20 Their **s** resistance came from the LORD
1 Samuel
6:6 Why be **s** like the Egyptians and
20:30 You son of a **s**, rebellious
2 Kings
17:14 listen. They were **s** like their
2 Chronicles
30:8 So don't be **s** like your ancestors.
36:13 name. He became **s** and refused to
Nehemiah
9:16 They were **s** and wouldn't obey
9:29 They turned a **s** shoulder, became
Psalms
78:8 a rebellious, **s** generation, a
Proverbs
29:1 One who stays **s** after many corrections
Isaiah
48:4 know that you are **s**, your neck is
Jeremiah
5:23 the people have **s** and rebellious
7:26 they were **s** and did more harm
17:23 They were **s** and wouldn't obey
19:15 they have been **s** and wouldn't obey
31:18 though I was as **s** as a mule. Bring
Daniel
5:20 acting in **s** pride, he was
Hosea
4:16 Like a **s** cow Israel is stubborn. Now
Acts
7:51 You **s** people! In your thoughts and
Titus
1:7 they shouldn't be **s**, irritable,
Hebrews
3:8 don't have **s** hearts as they did in the
3:15 voice, don't have **s** hearts as they
4:7 hear his voice, don't have **s** hearts.

STUMBLE

Leviticus
26:37 They will **s** over each other as they
2 Chronicles
25:8 God will make you **s** before the enemy,
Job
12:25 light; he makes them **s** like drunks.
41:9 surely the sight of him makes one **s**.
Psalms
10:6 We'll never **s**. We'll never
15:5 Whoever does these things will never **s**.
16:8 of me; I will not **s** because he is on
21:7 High's faithful love, he will not **s**.
27:2 my foes and my enemies, who **s** and fall!
30:6 comfortable, I said, "I will never **s**."
Proverbs
3:23 on your path, and your foot won't **s**.
4:12 be hindered; when you run, you won't **s**.
4:16 of sleep unless they make someone **s**.
4:19 they don't know where they will **s**.
24:16 up, but the wicked will **s** into trouble.
24:17 When they **s**, don't let your
Isaiah
8:14 and a rock to **s** on for the two
63:13 a horse in the desert, they didn't **s**.
Jeremiah
13:16 late, before you **s** on the mountain
31:9 so they don't **s**. I will be
Ezekiel
3:20 and I make them **s** because of it,
21:15 to make many **s** and fall. I've
33:12 wicked make them **s** if they turn from
Daniel
11:19 country but will **s**, fall, and
Hosea
4:5 You will **s** by day; and at nighttime so
14:9 in them, but evildoers will **s** in them.
Nahum
2:5 officers; they **s** as they press
3:3 dead bodies—they **s** over their dead
Malachi
2:8 caused many to **s** by your
Matthew
11:6 those who don't **s** and fall because
16:23 could make me **s**, for you are not
26:33 stumbles because of you, I'll never **s**."
Luke
7:23 who doesn't **s** along the way
John
11:9 the day doesn't **s** because they see
11:10 in the night does **s** because the light
1 Peter
2:8 that makes people **s** and a rock that
1 John
2:10 in the light that causes a person to **s**.

SUBMIT

Ezra
8:21 so that we might **s** before our God
Luke
10:17 even the demons **s** themselves to us
10:20 the spirits **s** to you. Rejoice
Romans
8:7 God. It doesn't **s** to God's Law,
10:3 They don't **s** to God's righteousness
Galatians
2:5 give in and **s** to them for a

5:1 firm and don't **s** to the bondage of
Ephesians
5:21 and **s** to each other out of respect for
5:22 wives should **s** to their husbands
5:24 So wives **s** to their husbands in
Colossians
2:20 acts, why do you **s** to rules and
3:18 Wives, **s** to your husbands in a way that
Titus
2:9 Tell slaves to **s** to their own masters
3:1 Remind them to **s** to rulers and
Hebrews
12:9 more should we **s** to the Father of
James
4:7 Therefore, **s** to God. Resist the devil,
1 Peter
2:13 sake of the Lord **s** to every human
2:15 **S** to them because it's God's will that
2:18 Household slaves, **s** by accepting the
3:1 Wives, likewise, **s** to your own
3:7 likewise, **s** by living with

SUCCEED
Leviticus
6:22 Aaron's sons to **s** him will prepare
Numbers
14:41 disobey the LORD's command? It won't **s**.
Deuteronomy
29:9 and do them so you can **s** in all you do.
30:9 God will help you **s** in everything you
Joshua
1:8 your objectives and you will **s**.
1 Samuel
26:25 will certainly **s**." Then David went
30:8 catch them and will **s** in the rescue!"
2 Samuel
7:12 own children—to **s** you, and I will
1 Kings
1:30 will certainly **s** me; he will sit
2:3 this way you will **s** in whatever you
19:16 Shaphat's son, to **s** you as prophet.
22:13 the king will **s**. You should say
2 Kings
3:27 son, who was to **s** him as king, and
24:17 uncle, **s** Jehoiachin as
1 Chronicles
17:11 your own sons, to **s** you, and I will
2 Chronicles
13:12 of your ancestors, for you won't **s**!"
18:12 the king will **s**. You should say
18:21 agreed: 'You will **s** in persuading
20:20 stand firm; trust his prophets and **s**!"
22:1 son Ahaziah **s** him as king
Job
5:13 that the plans of the devious don't **s**.
Psalms
45:4 Go and **s** in your grandeur! Ride out on
45:16 great king, will **s** your fathers; you
118:25 please save us! LORD, please let us **s**!
140:8 their plans to **s**, or they'll exalt
Proverbs
11:10 the righteous **s**, a city rejoices;
15:22 but with many counselors they **s**.
16:3 to the LORD, and your plans will **s**.
19:21 mind, but the LORD's purpose will **s**.
28:13 their sins won't **s**, but those who
Ecclesiastes
11:6 know which will **s**, this one or
Isaiah
47:12 will be able to **s**. Maybe you will
48:15 will happen to him; I will make him **s**.
52:13 my servant will **s**. He will be
54:17 against you will **s**, and you may
Jeremiah
37:1 Josiah's son, to **s** Coniah,
Ezekiel
17:15 Can such a person **s**? Can one who does
26:2 me, she is destroyed, but I will **s**!"
Daniel
8:12 ground and will **s** in everything it
8:24 He will **s** in all he does.
8:25 cunning, he will **s** by using deceit.
11:17 him, but it won't **s** and it won't
11:36 of gods. He will **s** until the doom is
Romans
1:10 will, I might **s** in visiting you

SUCCOTH
Genesis
33:17 Jacob traveled to **S**. He built a house
Judges
8:16 the people of **S** with desert

SUFFER
Genesis
27:45 Why should I **s** the loss of both
Leviticus
24:19 they will **s** the same injury
Numbers
14:33 years. They will **s** for your
Judges
10:16 could no longer stand to see Israel **s**.
2 Samuel
22:28 saves people who **s**, but your eyes
Nehemiah
9:27 who made them **s**. But when they
Psalms
9:12 those who **s**; the LORD hasn't
9:13 Just look how I **s** because of those
9:18 hope of those who **s** won't be lost for
10:2 of those who **s**. Let them get
10:9 seize those who **s**! They seize the
10:12 God! Don't forget the ones who **s**!
10:17 of those who **s**. You steady their
14:6 of those who **s**, but the LORD is
18:27 saves people who **s** and brings down
60:3 made your people **s** hardship; you've
73:4 They **s** no pain; their bodies are fit
89:22 him; no wicked person will make him **s**.
119:75 right and that you rightly made me **s**.
Isaiah
11:4 for those who **s** in the land. He
24:6 its inhabitants **s** for their guilt.
49:13 people, and taken pity on those who **s**.
53:10 and to make him **s**. If his life is
Jeremiah
17:13 forsake you will **s** disgrace; those
Lamentations
3:33 enjoy affliction, making humans **s**.
Ezekiel
18:2 unripe grapes, the children's teeth **s**"?
28:24 will no longer **s** from the pricking
36:7 about you will themselves **s** ridicule.

Obadiah
1:15 to you; your actions will make you ***s***!
Zephaniah
1:17 make humanity ***s***; they will walk
Matthew
16:21 to Jerusalem and ***s*** many things from
17:12 One is also going to ***s*** at their hands."
Mark
8:31 Human One must ***s*** many things and
9:12 Human One would ***s*** many things and
Luke
9:22 Human One must ***s*** many things and
17:25 first he must ***s*** many things and
22:15 eat this Passover with you before I ***s***.
24:26 for the Christ to ***s*** these things and
24:46 the Christ will ***s*** and rise from the
Acts
3:18 the prophets: that his Christ would ***s***.
5:41 as worthy to ***s*** disgrace for the
9:16 how much he must ***s*** for the sake of
17:3 the Christ had to ***s*** and rise from the
26:23 the Christ would ***s*** and that, as the
27:10 our voyage will ***s*** damage and great
Romans
8:17 if we really ***s*** with him so that
1 Corinthians
12:26 all the parts ***s*** with it; if one
2 Corinthians
1:6 the same sufferings that we also ***s***.
1 Thessalonians
5:9 intend for us to ***s*** his wrath but
Hebrews
9:26 would have to ***s*** many times since
1 Peter
2:20 done good and ***s*** for it, this is
3:14 you, even if you ***s*** because of
3:17 It is better to ***s*** for doing good (if
4:15 of you should ***s*** as a murderer or
4:16 be ashamed if you ***s*** as one who
4:19 then, those who ***s*** because they
Revelation
2:10 you are going to ***s***. Look! The devil
9:5 only to make them ***s*** for five months—
14:10 wrath. They will ***s*** the pain of fire

SUFFERED

1 Samuel
4:17 The army has ***s*** a massive defeat.
2 Kings
14:26 brutally Israel ***s***, whether slave or
2 Chronicles
22:6 the wounds he ***s*** at Ramah in his
Psalms
22:24 of the one who ***s***—he didn't hide h
107:17 sinful ways. They ***s*** because of their
119:67 Before I ***s***, I took the wrong way, but
132:1 remember David—all the ways he ***s***
Isaiah
53:3 others; a man who ***s***, who knew
Jeremiah
14:17 my people, have ***s*** a crushing blow
Nahum
3:19 you. Who has not ***s*** from your
Matthew
27:19 man alone. I've ***s*** much today in a
Mark
5:26 She had ***s*** a lot under the care of many
Acts
28:5 the snake into the fire and ***s*** no harm.
Galatians
4:27 you who have not ***s*** labor pains;
1 Thessalonians
2:2 we had already ***s*** and were publicly
2:14 because you also ***s*** the same things
Hebrews
2:9 of his death. He ***s*** death so that he
5:8 he learned obedience from what he ***s***.
11:26 the abuses he ***s*** for Christ were
13:12 And so Jesus also ***s*** outside the city
1 Peter
2:21 because Christ ***s*** on your behalf.
2:23 insults. When he ***s***, he did not
3:18 Christ himself ***s*** on account of sins,
4:1 since Christ ***s*** as a human, you
5:10 After you have ***s*** for a little while,

SUFFERING

1 Samuel
9:16 I have seen the ***s*** of my people, and
2 Chronicles
6:29 own pain and ***s*** and spread out
Nehemiah
9:27 to you in their ***s***, you heard them
Job
9:28 afraid of all my ***s***; I know that you
Psalms
16:4 let their ***s*** increase because they
22:24 or detest the ***s*** of the one who
22:26 all those who are ***s*** eat and be full!
25:16 mercy on me because I'm alone and ***s***.
25:18 Look at my ***s*** and trouble—forgive all
31:7 you saw my ***s***—you were intimat
31:10 me because of my ***s***; my bones dry up.
34:2 LORD—let the ***s*** listen and
34:6 This ***s*** person cried out: the LORD
44:24 face, forgetting our ***s*** and oppression?
88:9 of looking at my ***s***. I've been
107:10 gloom; they were prisoners ***s*** in chains
107:41 needy from their ***s***; he makes their
116:10 even when I said, "I am ***s*** so badly!"
119:50 comfort during my ***s*** is this: your
119:71 My ***s*** was good for me because through it I learned
119:92 I would have died because of my ***s***.
119:107 I have been ***s*** so much—LORD, make me
119:153 Look at my ***s*** and deliver me because I
Proverbs
23:29 Who is ***s***? Who is uneasy? Who has
Isaiah
51:21 hear this, ***s*** one, who is
54:11 ***S*** one, storm-tossed, uncomforted, look,
Jeremiah
4:19 Oh, my ***s***, my suffering! My pain is
14:18 I see only those ***s*** from famine. Even
20:18 when all I see is ***s*** and misery, and
Lamentations
1:3 was exiled after ***s*** and hard service.
1:7 While ***s*** and homeless, Jerusalem
1:9 Lord, look at my ***s***—the enemy has
1:12 Is there any ***s*** like the
1:18 look at my ***s***. My young women
3:1 who saw the ***s*** caused by God's
3:19 The memory of my ***s*** and homelessness is bitterness

Obadiah
1:13 looked on his **s** on the day of his
Matthew
8:6 home, paralyzed, and his **s** is awful."
15:22 My daughter is **s** terribly from
24:21 will be great **s** such as the world
24:29 after the **s** of that time the
26:39 take this cup of **s** away from me.
Mark
13:19 will be great **s** such as the world
13:24 days, after the **s** of that time, the
14:35 he might be spared the time of **s**.
14:36 Take this cup of **s** away from me.
Luke
13:2 Do you think the **s** of these
14:2 A man **s** from an abnormal swelling of
16:24 my tongue because I'm **s** in this flame.'
22:42 take this cup of **s** away from me.
Acts
1:3 After his **s**, he showed them that he
Romans
8:18 that the present **s** is nothing
8:22 together and **s** labor pains up
2 Corinthians
1:7 are partners in **s** so also you are
1:8 with a load of **s** that was so far
Ephesians
3:13 by what I'm **s** for you, which is
Philippians
1:29 Christ but also of **s** for Christ's sake.
Colossians
1:24 I'm happy to be **s** for you. I'm
1 Thessalonians
1:6 Spirit with joy in spite of great **s**.
2 Thessalonians
1:5 of God's kingdom for which you are **s**.
2 Timothy
1:8 share the **s** for the good
1:12 is also why I'm **s** the way I do, but
2:3 your share of **s** like a good
2:9 is the reason I'm **s** to the point that
4:5 Endure **s**, do the work of a
Hebrews
2:9 because of the **s** of his death. He
2:10 experiences of **s** to make perfect
2:18 experienced **s** when he was
10:32 while you were **s** from an enormous
James
5:13 If any of you are **s**, they should pray.
1 Peter
1:11 about the **s** that would happen
2:19 should endure pain through **s** unjustly.
4:13 share Christ's **s**. You share his
5:9 enduring the same **s** throughout the
Revelation
9:5 months—and the **s** they inflict is
14:11 of their painful **s** goes up forever
20:10 There painful **s** will be inflicted

SUMMER

Genesis
8:22 cold and hot, **s** and autumn, day
2 Samuel
16:2 The bread and **s** fruit are for the
Psalms
32:4 was sapped as if in a **s** drought. Selah
74:17 earth in place. **S** and winter? You
Proverbs
6:8 gets its food in **s**; gathers its
10:5 harvests in the **s**; a disgraceful
26:1 Like snow in the **s** or rain at harvest,
30:25 they store away their food in the **s**.
Isaiah
16:9 concerning your **s** fruit and your
18:6 will eat them in **s**, all the beasts
28:4 fig before the **s** harvest: whoever
Jeremiah
8:20 is past, the **s** has ended, yet we
40:10 the grapes, the **s** fruits and figs,
40:12 large amounts of grapes and **s** fruits.
48:32 to harvest your grapes and **s** fruits.
Daniel
2:35 chaff, left on **s** threshing floors.
Amos
3:15 as well as the **s** house; the houses
8:1 God showed me: a basket of **s** fruit.
8:2 A basket of **s** fruit." Then the
Micah
7:1 even after the **s** fruit has been
Zechariah
14:8 will happen during the **s** and the fall.
Matthew
24:32 new leaves, you know that **s** is near.

SUN

Genesis
15:12 After the **s** set, Abram slept deeply. A
19:23 As the **s** rose over the earth, Lot
28:11 there. When the **s** had set, he took
32:31 The **s** rose as Jacob passed Penuel,
37:9 and this time the **s** and the moon and
Exodus
16:21 eat. But when the **s** grew hot, it
22:26 return it before the **s** goes down.
Leviticus
22:7 Once the **s** has set and he has become
Deuteronomy
4:19 the skies, to the **s** or the moon or
16:6 time, when the **s** sets, which was
17:3 to them, to the **s** or the moon or
23:11 and when the **s** sets, he can come
24:15 day, before the **s** sets, because
33:14 produced by the **s**, with the gifts
Joshua
10:12 the Israelites: "**S**, stand still at
10:13 The **s** stood still and the moon stood
Judges
5:31 be like the **s**, rising in its
14:18 day, before the **s** set, the
19:14 on, and the **s** set when they
1 Samuel
11:9 by the time the **s** is hot, you will
2 Samuel
2:24 after Abner. The **s** was setting when
3:35 anything else before the **s** goes down."
1 Kings
22:36 When the **s** set, a shout spread
2 Kings
23:5 to Baal, to the **s**, to the moon, to
23:11 dedicated to the **s**. They were kept
2 Chronicles
18:34 he died, just as the **s** was going down.
Job
8:16 plant in the **s**; its runners

9:7 Who commands the **s**, and it does not
31:26 looked at the **s** when it shone,
37:21 can look at the **s**; it is bright in
Psalms
19:4 has made a tent in heaven for the **s**.
19:5 The **s** is like a groom coming out of his
50:1 the rising of the **s** to where it sets,
58:8 child, let them never see the **s**.
72:5 as long as the **s**, as long as the
72:17 as long as the **s**. Let all the
74:16 established both the moon and the **s**.
84:11 The LORD is a **s** and shield; God is
89:36 will be like the **s**, always before me.
104:19 seasons, and the **s** too, which knows
104:22 When the **s** rises, they gather together
121:6 The **s** won't strike you during the day;
136:8 The **s** to rule the day—God's faithful
148:3 **S** and moon, praise God! All of you
Ecclesiastes
1:3 that they work so hard at under the **s**?
1:5 The **s** rises, the sun sets; it returns
1:9 again. There's nothing new under the **s**.
1:14 happens under the **s**, I realized that
2:11 Nothing is to be gained under the **s**.
2:17 happen under the **s** were troublesome
2:18 here under the **s**, because I will
2:19 here under the **s**. That too is
2:20 all my laborious hard work under the **s**,
2:22 hard work and struggles under the **s**?
3:16 else under the **s**: in the place of
4:1 place under the **s**, I saw the tears
4:3 things that happen under the **s**.
4:7 I saw under the **s** something else
4:15 walk under the **s** following the
5:13 tragedy under the **s**: people hoard
5:18 work under the **s** during the brief
6:1 tragedy under the **s**, and it weighs
6:5 hasn't seen the **s** or experienced
6:12 future holds for people under the **s**?
7:11 an advantage for those who see the **s**.
8:9 happens under the **s**. Sometimes people
8:15 to do under the **s** but to eat,
8:17 happens under the **s**. Those who strive
9:3 happens under the **s**: the same fate
9:6 stake in all that happens under the **s**.
9:9 you under the **s**—all the days of y
9:11 under the **s** that the race
9:13 wisdom under the **s**—it impressed me
10:5 seen under the **s**: the kind of
11:7 pleasant for the eyes to see the **s**.
12:2 before the **s** and the light grow dark,
Song of Songs
6:10 radiant as the **s**, formidable as
Isaiah
13:10 their light. The **s** will be dark when
19:18 will be called "the city of the **s**."
24:23 and the **s** will fade, since
30:26 the light of the **s**, and the light of
38:8 cast by the **s** descends on the
45:6 the rising of the **s** to its setting,
49:10 burning heat and **s** won't strike
60:19 The **s** will no longer be your light by
60:20 Your **s** will no longer set; your moon
Jeremiah
8:2 exposed to the **s**, the moon, and
15:9 gasp for air; her **s** will set while it
31:35 established the **s** to light up the
43:13 the temple of the **s** in Egypt and burn
Ezekiel
8:16 They were bowing to the **s** in the east.
32:7 I will cover the **s** with a cloud, and
Daniel
6:14 to save Daniel before the **s** went down.
Joel
2:10 shake. The **s** and the moon are
2:31 The **s** will be turned to darkness, and
3:15 The **s** and the moon are darkened; the
Amos
8:9 I will make the **s** go down at noon,
Jonah
4:8 Then as the **s** rose God provided a dry
Micah
3:6 divination! The **s** will set on the
Nahum
3:17 day; when the **s** rises, they take
Habakkuk
3:11 **S** and moon stand still high above. With
Malachi
4:2 But the **s** of righteousness will rise on
Matthew
5:45 He makes the **s** rise on both the
13:6 But when the **s** came up, it scorched the
13:43 shine like the **s** in their Father's
17:2 shone like the **s**, and his clothes
20:12 to work the whole day in the hot **s**.'
24:29 of that time the **s** will become dark,
Mark
4:6 When the **s** came up, it scorched the
13:24 of that time, the **s** will become
Luke
4:40 When the **s** was setting, everyone
21:25 be signs in the **s**, moon, and stars.
23:45 while the **s** stopped shining. Then the
Acts
2:20 The **s** will be changed into darkness,
26:13 That light was brighter than the **s**.
27:20 When neither the **s** nor the moon
1 Corinthians
15:41 The **s** has one kind of glory, the moon
Ephesians
4:26 Don't let the **s** set on your anger.
James
1:11 The **s** rises with its scorching heat and
Revelation
1:16 was like the **s** shining with all
6:12 earthquake. The **s** became black as
7:16 anymore. No **s** or scorching heat
8:12 a third of the **s** was struck, and a
9:2 huge furnace. The **s** and air were
10:1 face was like the **s**, and his feet
12:1 clothed with the **s**, with the moon
16:8 his bowl on the **s**, and it was
19:17 standing in the **s**, and he called
21:23 doesn't need the **s** or the moon to
22:5 the light of the **s**, for the Lord God

SUPERVISORS

Exodus
5:6 the people's slave masters and **s**,
1 Kings
5:16 hundred **s** in charge of the
2 Kings
12:11 the temple. These **s** then paid money
22:5 be given to the **s** in charge of the

Ezra
7:25 you have, appoint **s** and judges to
Nehemiah
3:5 wouldn't help with the work of their **s**.
Acts
20:28 has placed you as **s**, to shepherd
Philippians
1:1 Jesus, along with your **s** and servants .
Titus
1:7 This is because **s** should be without

SUPPLIES

Genesis
14:11 including its food **s**, and left.
Joshua
1:11 people. Say, 'Get **s** ready for
9:5 bread in their **s** was dry and
Judges
7:8 gathered their **s** and trumpets, and
20:10 thousand to take **s** for the troops
1 Samuel
10:22 said, "Yes, he's hiding among the **s**."
25:13 hundred men remained back with the **s**.
30:24 stayed with the **s** will be divided
1 Kings
4:7 would provide the **s** for one month per
2 Chronicles
17:13 and had many **s** in the cities of Judah.
Proverbs
31:24 sells them; she **s** sashes to traders.
Jeremiah
50:38 against the water **s** so that they dry
Nahum
2:9 is no end to the **s**, an abundance of
2 Corinthians
9:10 The one who **s** seed for planting and

SUPPORT

Genesis
13:6 the land couldn't **s** both of them.
36:7 couldn't **s** all of their
45:11 I will **s** you there, so you, your
Exodus
30:16 and use it to **s** the service of
Deuteronomy
27:26 who doesn't **s** the words of this
33:27 arms are a **s**. He drove out the
2 Samuel
18:3 much better if you **s** us from the city."
22:19 of my distress, but the LORD was my **s**.
1 Kings
1:14 I'll come along and **s** your words."
1:44 To **s** him, the king sent along Zadok the
2:22 and has the **s** of Abiathar the
2 Kings
7:2 leaned on for **s**, spoke to the man
7:17 he leaned on for **s** in charge of the
18:25 the LORD's **s**? It was the LORD
1 Chronicles
11:10 who continued to **s** him while he was
2 Chronicles
26:13 force that could **s** the king against
28:20 to Ahaz, but he brought trouble, not **s**.
Ezra
10:4 matter; we will **s** you. Be strong
Psalms
18:18 of my distress, but the LORD was my **s**.
20:2 from the sanctuary and **s** you from
Zion.
41:12 You **s** me in my integrity; you put me in
55:22 LORD—he will **s** you! God will
89:43 his sword and didn't **s** him in battle.
119:117 **S** me so I can be saved and so I can
Isaiah
3:1 every form of **s**: all rations of
35:3 weak hands, and **s** the unsteady
36:10 the LORD's **s**? It was the LORD
38:14 heaven. Lord, I'm overwhelmed; **s** me!"
46:4 turn gray I will **s** you. I have done
46:7 shoulders and **s** it; they set it
Jeremiah
44:19 our husbands' **s** when we make
Daniel
9:26 No one will **s** him. The army of
11:14 will rise up to **s** the vision, but
11:39 on those who **s** him, making them
Joel
3:2 with them in **s** of my people and
Acts
4:21 Because of public **s** for Peter and
11:29 they would send **s** to the brothers
Philippians
1:7 and in the defense and **s** of the gospel.
2 Thessalonians
3:9 have a right to insist on financial **s**.
1 Timothy
3:15 and the backbone and **s** of the truth.
3 John
1:7 accepting any **s** from the Gentiles.

SURROUND

Deuteronomy
25:19 the enemies that **s** you in the land
Joshua
7:9 of it. They will **s** us and make our
19:8 the areas that **s** these cities as
1 Samuel
10:1 the enemies who **s** them. And this
23:26 were trying to **s** David and his
2 Kings
11:8 **S** the king completely, each of you
with your weapons
2 Chronicles
14:7 Judah. "We'll **s** them with walls,
23:7 The Levites must **s** the king, each with
Job
16:13 His archers **s** me; he cuts my kidneys
22:10 reason, snares **s** you; sudden dread
40:22 shade; poplars of the stream **s** him.
Psalms
7:7 assembled peoples **s** you. Rule them
17:11 suddenly, they **s** me! They make
22:12 Many bulls **s** me; mighty bulls from
22:16 Dogs **s** me; a pack of evil people circle
32:7 from trouble. You **s** me with songs of
33:22 faithful love **s** us, because we
40:12 countless evils **s** me. My
88:17 They **s** me all day long like water; they
97:2 thick darkness **s** God. His throne
109:3 Hateful words **s** me; they attack me for
125:2 Mountains **s** Jerusalem. That's how the
139:5 You **s** me—front and back. You put your
Isaiah
29:3 I will **s** you like a wall, and I will

Jeremiah
50:29 who draw the bow! **S** her and let no
51:2 land. They will **s** her on the day of
Lamentations
1:17 enemies to **s** him. Jerusalem is
Ezekiel
23:24 and they will **s** you. I will hand
Amos
3:11 An enemy will **s** the land; he will
Habakkuk
1:4 the wicked **s** the righteous.

SURROUNDED

Judges
19:22 a perverse bunch, **s** the house and
20:5 attack me. They **s** me in the house
2 Samuel
18:15 of Joab **s** Absalom, struck
22:6 of the grave **s** me; death's traps
1 Kings
20:1 He went up, **s** Samaria, and made
2 Kings
3:25 stone throwers **s** it and attacked
6:14 They came at night and **s** the city.
8:21 Edomites who had **s** him and his
16:5 to fight. They **s** Ahaz, but they
2 Chronicles
13:14 that they were **s**, they cried out
14:7 he sought us and **s** us with rest." As
21:9 Edomites, who had **s** him, attacked at
Nehemiah
9:35 own kingdom, **s** by the great
Job
41:14 of his mouth, **s** by frightening
Psalms
18:5 of the grave **s** me; death's traps
118:10 All the nations **s** me, but I cut them
118:11 Yes, they **s** me on every single side,
118:12 They **s** me like bees, but they were
119:61 the wicked have **s** me with their
Ecclesiastes
9:14 came against it, **s** it, and waged a
Jeremiah
12:9 a bird of prey, **s** and attacked. Go,
13:19 plain will be **s**; no one will get
21:4 who have **s** you! I will round
32:2 king had **s** Jerusalem, and
39:1 army came against Jerusalem and **s** it.
52:7 the Babylonians **s** the city while
Ezekiel
32:23 pit. His assembly **s** his grave, all of
Hosea
11:12 Ephraim has **s** me with lies, the house
Luke
21:20 you see Jerusalem **s** by armies, then
Acts
14:20 the disciples **s** him, he got up
25:7 from Jerusalem **s** him. They brought
2 Corinthians
7:5 We were **s** by problems.
Philippians
2:15 children of God **s** by people who are
Revelation
4:4 seated upon them, **s** the throne. The
20:9 whole earth and **s** the saints' camp,

SURVIVE

Joshua
11:14 didn't let anything that breathed **s**.
Joel
2:32 the LORD will summon those who **s**.
2 Corinthians
1:8 that we were afraid we might not **s**.

SURVIVORS

Numbers
21:35 there were no **s**. Then they took
24:19 will rule and destroy the **s** from Ir."
Deuteronomy
2:34 children—under the ban. We left no **s**.
7:20 until even the **s** and those hiding
Isaiah
4:2 the pride and splendor of Israel's **s**.
49:6 to bring back the **s** of Israel. Hence,
66:19 out some of the **s** to the nations,
Jeremiah
8:3 The **s** of this evil nation will prefer
15:9 will deliver the **s** to the sword, to
51:50 You **s** of war, leave now; don't delay!
Ezekiel
14:22 Yet a few **s** will be left. Sons and
Obadiah
1:14 handed over his **s** on the day of
Micah
4:7 the lame into **s**, those driven
Zephaniah
2:7 belong to the **s** from the house of

SUSA

Ezra
4:9 the people of **S**
Nehemiah
1:1 while I was in the fortress city of **S**,
Esther
1:2 throne in the fortified part of **S**.

SWEAR

Exodus
22:11 the person should **s** a solemn pledge
Leviticus
5:4 one might **s** carelessly—and
19:12 You must not **s** falsely by my name,
Numbers
5:19 will make her **s** a solemn pledge,
Deuteronomy
8:19 down to them, I **s** to you right now
10:20 him, cling to him, **s** by his name alone!
32:40 to heaven—I **s** by my own
Joshua
2:14 said to her, "We **s** by our own lives
1 Samuel
14:27 make the people **s** the pledge, so he
2 Samuel
11:11 with my wife? I **s** on your very
19:7 your followers! I **s** to the LORD that
1 Kings
1:13 master the king **s** to your servant,
1:51 Solomon must **s** to me first that
2:42 I make you **s** a solemn pledge
18:10 would make them **s** that they
2 Kings
3:14 Elisha said, "I **s** by the life of the

4:30 mother said, "I **s** by your life and
5:16 Elisha said, "I **s** by the life of
9:26 the LORD. I **s** that I will pay
11:4 and made them **s** a solemn pledge
2 Chronicles
36:13 had forced him to **s** in God's name. He
Nehemiah
5:12 and made them **s** to do what they
13:25 I also made them **s** a solemn pledge
Ecclesiastes
9:2 pledges and those who are afraid to **s**.
Song of Songs
5:9 that you make us **s** a solemn pledge?
Isaiah
19:18 of Canaan and **s** loyalty to the
48:1 of Judah, who **s** by the LORD's
Jeremiah
4:2 and if you **s** by the living God in
5:2 As the LORD lives"—they **s** falsely.
5:7 forsaken me and **s** by gods that are
12:16 my people to **s** to Baal, then
22:5 these words, I **s** by myself,
44:26 land of Egypt. I **s** by my great name,
49:13 I myself **s**, declares the LORD, that
Ezekiel
36:7 I myself **s** that the nations
Daniel
12:7 farther upstream, **s** by the one who
Hosea
4:15 and don't **s**, "As the LORD
Amos
8:14 Those who **s** by the guilt of Samaria,
Matthew
23:16 say, 'If people **s** by the temple,
Mark
5:7 Most High God? **S** to God that you
1 Corinthians
15:31 and sisters, I **s** by the pride I
Galatians
4:15 that you had? I **s** that, if
5:3 Again I **s** to every man who has himself
Hebrews
3:18 whom did he **s** that they would
6:13 since he couldn't **s** by anyone greater.

SWEET

Genesis
2:12 the land also has **s**-smelling resins an
37:25 camels carrying **s** resin, medicinal
Exodus
15:25 the water became **s**. The LORD made a
Deuteronomy
33:10 Israel. They hold **s** incense to your
Judges
14:14 came something **s**." For three days
2 Chronicles
16:14 a bed filled with **s** spices and
Nehemiah
8:10 drink something **s**," he said to
Job
20:12 wickedness is **s** in their mouths,
21:33 streambed is **s** to them; everyone
Psalms
81:2 strike the drum! **S** lyre along with
Proverbs
9:17 Stolen water is **s**; food eaten in
16:24 flowing honey, **s** to the taste and
20:17 Stolen bread is **s**, but afterward the
24:13 good. The honeycomb is **s** in your mouth.
27:7 bitter tastes **s** to a hungry
Ecclesiastes
5:12 **S** is the worker's sleep, whether
11:7 **S** is the light, and it's pleasant for
Song of Songs
1:3 Your fragrance is **s**; your very name is
2:3 and his fruit is **s** to my taste.
2:14 of your voice is **s**, and the sight of
4:14 nard and saffron, **s** cane and cinnamon,
5:16 is everything **s**, every bit of him
Isaiah
5:20 make bitterness **s** and sweetness
Jeremiah
6:20 from Sheba or **s** cane from a
Ezekiel
3:3 in my mouth it became as **s** as honey.
Hosea
2:13 when she offered **s**-smelling sacrifice
Joel
1:5 Scream over the **s** wine, all you
3:18 will drip **s** wine, the hills
Ephesians
5:2 offering that smelled **s** to God.
Revelation
10:9 your stomach, but **s** as honey in your
10:10 it. And it was **s** as honey in my

SWORD

Genesis
27:40 will live by your **s**; you will serve
48:22 the Amorites with my **s** and my bow."
Exodus
15:9 I'll draw my **s**; my hand will
17:13 Amalek and his army with the **s**.
18:4 who rescued me from Pharaoh's **s**."
22:24 kill you with the **s**. Then your wives
32:27 strap on your **s**! Go back and
Leviticus
26:6 the land, and no **s** will pass through
Numbers
14:3 to fall by the **s**? Our wives and
Deuteronomy
32:41 my blazing **s** and my hand grabs
Joshua
5:13 of him with his **s** drawn. Joshua
13:22 Balaam, Beor's son, with the **s**.
1 Samuel
17:45 against me with **s**, spear, and
17:47 save by means of **s** and spear. The
31:4 Draw your **s** and kill me with
2 Samuel
12:10 as your own, the **s** will never leave
1 Chronicles
21:30 he feared the **s** of the LORD's
Ezra
9:7 the lands, to the **s**, to captivity, to
Esther
9:5 enemies with **s** blows, killing,
Job
5:15 orphan from the **s** of their mouth,
15:22 darkness; they are destined for a **s**.
41:26 The **s** that touches him won't prevail;

SWORD [cont.]

Psalms
22:20 me from the **s**. Deliver my life
37:15 But the **s** of the wicked will enter
44:6 trust in my bow; my **s** won't save me
45:3 Strap on your **s**, great warrior, with
63:10 blood flow by the **s**! Let them be food
76:3 the shield, the **s**—even the battle
78:62 people up to the **s**; he was enraged
89:43 the edge of his **s** and didn't
144:10 his servant David from the evil **s**.
149:6 and a double-edged **s** in their hands,
Proverbs
5:4 as gall, sharp as a double-edged **s**.
12:18 like a stabbing **s**, but a wise
25:18 are like a club, **s**, and sharpened
Song of Songs
3:8 skilled with the **s**, expert in
Isaiah
2:4 will not take up **s** against nation;
49:2 like a sharp **s**, and hid me in
Jeremiah
4:10 even though the **s** is at their
18:21 them die by the **s**. Let their wives
21:7 put them to the **s** without pity,
21:9 will die by the **s**, famine, and
24:10 I will send the **s**, famine, and disease
25:16 because of the **s** that I am sending
27:8 punish it with **s**, famine, and
29:17 going to send the **s**, famine, and
29:18 them with the **s**, famine, and
31:2 who survived the **s** found grace in
32:36 Babylon through **s**, famine, and
34:17 to die by the **s**, disease, and
38:2 will die by the **s**, famine, and
41:2 with the **s**. They murdered
42:17 will die by the **s**, famine, and
44:12 will fall by the **s** and perish due to
46:10 with enemies. The **s** will devour until
47:6 You **s** of the LORD, how long until you
48:2 be silenced; the **s** will pursue you.
49:37 I will send the **s** to attack them
50:16 of its ruthless **s**. Now return, all
50:35 A **s** against Babylon and its people,
Lamentations
1:20 the streets the **s** kills; in the
2:21 fall dead by the **s**. On the day of
4:9 stabbed by the **s** than for those
Ezekiel
5:2 third with the **s** left and right.
6:3 about to bring a **s** against you and
7:15 Outside, the **s**! Inside, plague and
11:8 You fear the **s**, so I will bring the
11:10 will fall by the **s**! At Israel's
12:14 winds and let the **s** loose after them.
12:16 number from the **s**, famine, and
14:17 suppose I bring a **s** against that land
17:21 will fall by the **s**, and those who
21:3 I will draw my **s** from its sheath
23:10 her with the **s**. And she became
24:21 you left behind, will fall by the **s**.
25:13 to Dedan. They will fall by the **s**.
26:6 be put to the **s**. Then they will
28:23 streets. When the **s** comes against it
29:8 I'm bringing a **s** against you, and
30:4 A **s** will come into Egypt, and trembling
31:17 to those who are slain by the **s**.
32:10 I brandish my **s** before them. They
33:2 Suppose I bring a **s** against a
35:5 over to the **s** in the time of
38:8 freed from the **s**, a gathering from
Daniel
11:33 they will fall by **s** and by flame, by
Hosea
2:18 with the bow, the **s**, and war from the
Amos
7:9 the house of Jeroboam with the **s**."
7:11 will die by the **s**, and Israel will
9:10 will die by the **s**, those who say,
Micah
4:3 will not take up **s** against nation;
Zephaniah
2:12 too, Cushites, will be pierced by my **s**.
Haggai
2:22 will fall by the **s** of his companion.
Zechariah
9:13 I will make you like a warrior's **s**.
11:17 the flock. A **s** will strike his
13:7 **S**, arise against my shepherd, against
Matthew
10:34 I haven't come to bring peace but a **s**.
26:51 reached for his **s**. Striking the
26:52 to him, "Put the **s** back into its
Mark
14:47 bystanders drew a **s** and struck the
Luke
2:35 revealed. And a **s** will pierce your
21:24 the edge of the **s** and be taken away
22:36 who don't own a **s** must sell their
John
18:10 Peter, who had a **s**, drew it and
18:11 Peter, "Put your **s** away! Am I not to
Acts
12:2 James, John's brother, killed with a **s**.
16:27 so he drew his **s** and was about to
Romans
8:35 famine, or nakedness, or danger, or **s**?
Ephesians
6:17 salvation and the **s** of the Spirit,
Hebrews
4:12 any two-edged **s**. It penetrates to
11:34 the edge of the **s**, found strength
Revelation
1:16 sharp, two-edged **s**. His appearance
2:12 the one who has the sharp, two-edged **s**:
2:16 on them with the **s** that comes from
6:4 each other. He was given a large **s**.
6:8 earth, to kill by **s**, famine, disease,
13:10 be killed by the **s**, then by the
13:14 wounded by the **s** and yet came to
19:15 comes a sharp **s** that he will use
19:21 killed by the **s** that comes from

SWORDS

Genesis
3:24 wielding flaming **s** to guard the way
34:25 Levi took their **s**, came into the
34:26 with their **s**, took Dinah from
Numbers
21:24 down with their **s** and took
1 Samuel
13:19 Hebrews must not make **s** and spears."
13:22 of the battle, no **s** or spears were to
21:9 are no other **s** here." David
25:13 strap on your **s**!" So each of them

1 Kings
18:28 themselves with **s** and knives as was
Nehemiah
4:13 and they had their **s**, spears, and bows.
4:18 built with **s** fastened in their
Job
1:15 young men with **s**. I alone escaped
Psalms
37:14 wicked draw their **s** and bend their
44:3 not by their own **s** did they take
55:21 than oil, they are really drawn **s**:
57:4 arrows; their tongues are sharpened **s**.
59:7 their mouths: **s** are between their
64:3 tongues like **s**. They aim their
Proverbs
30:14 whose teeth are **s**; their jaw is a
Isaiah
2:4 will beat their **s** into iron plows
21:15 have fled from **s**, from the drawn
Ezekiel
6:8 the nations' **s** when you are
16:40 stones, and slaughter you with their **s**.
23:47 up with their **s**, slay their sons
28:7 let loose their **s** against your fine
30:11 will draw their **s** against Egypt and
32:12 fall by the **s** of mighty men,
32:27 they put their **s** under their heads
38:4 and shield, all of them wielding **s**.
38:21 God says! The **s** of the warriors
Joel
3:10 your plows into **s** and your pruning
Micah
4:3 will beat their **s** into iron plows
Matthew
26:47 crowd carrying **s** and clubs. They
26:55 you come with **s** and clubs to
Mark
14:43 a mob carrying **s** and clubs. They
14:48 you come with **s** and clubs to
Luke
22:38 here are two **s**." He replied,
22:49 Lord, should we fight with our **s**?"
22:52 you come with **s** and clubs to
Hebrews
11:37 murdered with **s**. They went around

SWORE

Leviticus
6:5 it was that you **s** falsely about.
Deuteronomy
6:18 land that the LORD **s** to your ancestors,
34:4 the land that I **s** to Abraham,
1 Samuel
3:14 Because of that I **s** about Eli's
14:44 still if you don't die today!" Saul **s**.
19:6 Jonathan and then **s**, "As surely as
2 Samuel
3:9 David exactly what the LORD **s** to him—
19:23 not die." And the king **s** this to him.
21:17 Then David's men **s** a solemn pledge
1 Kings
1:17 Majesty, you **s** by the LORD your
1:30 regarding what I **s** to you by the LORD,
2:8 at the Jordan, I **s** to him by the
2:23 King Solomon **s** by the LORD, "May God do to me as
1 Chronicles
16:16 the solemn pledge he **s** to Isaac.
2 Chronicles
15:14 They **s** this to the LORD with a loud
Psalms
95:11 So in anger I **s**: 'They will never
105:9 the solemn pledge he **s** to Isaac.
132:2 and how he **s** to the LORD, how he
132:11 The LORD **s** to David a true promise that
Jeremiah
38:16 So King Zedekiah **s** to Jeremiah behind
Ezekiel
20:5 I chose Israel, I **s** a solemn pledge
47:14 What I **s** to give to your ancestors, you
Micah
7:20 Abraham, as you **s** to our ancestors
Matthew
14:7 Then he **s** to give her anything she
23:16 they are obligated to do what they **s**.'
26:74 he cursed and **s**, "I don't know
Mark
6:23 Then he **s** to her, "Whatever you ask I
14:71 But he cursed and **s**, "I don't know
Hebrews
3:11 of my anger I **s**: "They will never
6:13 his promise, he **s** by himself since
Revelation
10:6 He **s** by the one who lives forever and

SYCAMORE

1 Kings
10:27 as plentiful as **s** trees that grow
1 Chronicles
27:28 of the olive and **s** trees in the
2 Chronicles
1:15 as plentiful as **s** trees that grow
9:27 as common as **s** trees that grow
Psalms
78:47 with hail, their **s** trees with frost.
Amos
7:14 a shepherd, and a trimmer of **s** trees.
Luke
19:4 and climbed up a **s** tree so he could

SYNAGOGUE

Matthew
12:9 left that place and went into their **s**.
13:54 people in their **s**. They were
Mark
1:21 Jesus entered the **s** and started
1:23 there in the **s**, a person with an
1:29 After leaving the **s**, Jesus, James, and
3:1 returned to the **s**. A man with a
5:22 one of the **s** leaders, came
5:35 came from the **s** leader's house
5:36 and said to the **s** leader, "Don't be
5:38 They came to the **s** leader's house, and
6:2 to teach in the **s**. Many who heard
Luke
4:16 he went to the **s** as he normally
4:17 The **s** assistant gave him the scroll
4:20 it back to the **s** assistant, and
4:28 everyone in the **s** was filled with
4:33 A man in the **s** had the spirit of an
4:38 After leaving the **s**, Jesus went home
6:6 Jesus entered a **s** to teach. A man
7:5 our people and he built our **s** for us."

8:41 Jairus, who was a **s** leader, came and
8:49 came from the **s** leader's house,
13:14 The **s** leader, incensed that Jesus had
John
6:59 he was teaching in the **s** in Capernaum.
9:22 Christ would be expelled from the **s**.
12:42 Pharisees would expel them from the **s**.
16:2 you from the **s**. The time is
Acts
6:9 to the so-called **S** of Former Slaves.
13:14 entered and found seats in the **s** there.
13:15 the Prophets, the **s** leaders invited
13:42 were leaving the **s**, the people urged
13:43 the people in the **s** were dismissed,
14:1 the Jewish **s** and spoke as they
15:21 read aloud every Sabbath in every **s**."
17:1 where there was a Jewish **s**.
17:2 he entered the **s** and for three
17:10 arrived, they went to the Jewish **s**.
17:17 in the **s**. He also
18:4 people in the **s**, trying to
18:7 He left the **s** and went next door to the
18:8 Crispus, the **s** leader, and his entire
18:17 Sosthenes, the **s** leader, and gave
18:19 and entered the **s** and interacted
18:26 confidence in the **s**. When Priscilla
19:8 Paul went to the **s** and spoke
22:19 to go from one **s** to the next,
24:12 whether in the **s** or anywhere else
26:11 In one **s** after another—indeed, in all
Revelation
2:9 are not, but are really Satan's **s**
3:9 from Satan's **s** (who say they are

SYNAGOGUES

Matthew
4:23 teaching in their **s**. He announced the
6:2 do in the **s** and in the
6:5 standing in the **s** and on the street
9:35 teaching in their **s**, announcing the
10:17 and they will beat you in their **s**.
23:34 will beat in your **s** and chase from
Mark
1:39 in their **s** and throwing out
12:39 of honor in the **s** and at banquets.
13:9 be beaten in the **s**. You will stand
Luke
4:15 taught in their **s** and was praised
4:44 he continued preaching in the Judean **s**.
11:43 seats in the **s** and respectful
12:11 you before the **s**, rulers,and
13:10 in one of the **s** on the Sabbath.
20:46 of honor in the **s** and at banquets.
21:12 hand you over to **s** and prisons, and
John
18:20 always taught in **s** and in the
Acts
9:2 letters to the **s** in Damascus. If
9:20 Jesus in the **s**. "He is God's
13:5 in the Jewish **s**. John was with
26:11 in all the **s**—I would often tor

SYRIA

Matthew
4:24 spread throughout **S**. People brought

Tt

TABLE

Genesis
43:34 from Joseph's ***t*** were brought to
Exodus
25:23 an acacia-wood ***t***, three feet long,
Leviticus
24:6 a stack, on the pure ***t*** before the LORD.
Numbers
3:31 the chest, the ***t***, the lampstand,
4:7 the presentation ***t*** and place on it
Judges
1:7 scraps under my ***t***, so God has paid
1 Samuel
20:27 son come to the ***t***, either yesterday
20:29 why David hasn't been at the king's ***t***."
20:34 got up from the ***t*** in a rage. He
2 Samuel
9:7 Saul, and you will eat at my ***t*** always."
19:28 who eat at your ***t***. So what right do
1 Kings
4:27 him at the royal ***t*** with monthly food
7:48 altar; the golden ***t*** for the bread of
10:5 the food on his ***t***, the servants'
13:20 sitting at the ***t***, the LORD's word
18:19 of Asherah who eat at Jezebel's ***t***."
2 Kings
4:10 set up a bed, a ***t***, a chair, and a
1 Chronicles
28:16 of gold for each ***t*** with the stacks
2 Chronicles
9:4 the food on his ***t***, his servants'
13:11 upon a clean ***t***. At night they
29:18 and the ***t*** for the stacks of
Nehemiah
5:17 nations, gathered around my ***t***.
Job
36:16 distress; your ***t*** is set with rich
Psalms
23:5 You set a ***t*** for me right in front of my
69:22 Let the ***t*** before them become a trap,
78:19 God set a dinner ***t*** in the
128:3 All around your ***t***, your children
Proverbs
9:2 animals, mixed her wine, and set her ***t***.
Isaiah
21:5 setting the ***t***, spreading the cloth,
65:11 who set a ***t*** for a god of good
Jeremiah
52:33 at the king's ***t*** for the rest of
Ezekiel
23:41 with a richly set ***t*** in front of it,
39:20 yourselves at my ***t*** with horses and
41:22 me, "This is the ***t*** that stands
44:16 will approach my ***t*** to minister to
Daniel
11:27 will sit at one ***t***, telling lies,
Amos
6:7 who lounged at the ***t*** will pass away.
Malachi
1:7 you say, "The ***t*** of the LORD can
1:12 you say, "The ***t*** of the LORD is
Matthew
9:10 Jesus and his disciples at the ***t***.
15:27 crumbs that fall off their masters' ***t***."
26:20 his place at the ***t*** with the twelve
Mark
7:28 dogs under the ***t*** eat the
Luke
7:36 home, he took his place at the ***t***.
7:49 The other ***t*** guests began to say among
10:40 me to prepare the ***t*** all by myself?
11:37 Jesus went and took his place at the ***t***.
12:37 seat them at the ***t*** as honored
14:7 best seats at the ***t***, he told them a
16:21 the rich man's ***t***. Instead, dogs
17:8 the clothes of a ***t*** servant and wait
22:14 his place at the ***t***, and the apostles
22:21 is with me; his hand is on this ***t***.
22:27 is seated at the ***t*** or the one who
22:30 and drink at my ***t*** in my kingdom,
24:30 his seat at the ***t*** with them, he
John
12:2 among those who joined him at the ***t***.
13:4 got up from the ***t*** and took off his
13:12 his place at the ***t***. He said to them,
13:28 sitting at the ***t*** understood why
Romans
11:9 David says, Their ***t*** should become a
1 Corinthians
10:21 in the ***t*** of the Lord and
2 Thessalonians
3:12 and put their own food on the ***t***.
Hebrews
9:2 lampstand, the ***t***, and the loaves

TABLETS → COVENANT TABLETS

Exodus
24:12 you the stone ***t*** with the
31:18 the two covenant ***t***, the stone
32:15 the two covenant ***t*** in his hands. The
34:1 Cut two stone ***t*** like the first
Deuteronomy
4:13 and wrote them on two stone ***t***.
5:22 them on two stone ***t***, then gave them
9:9 to get the stone ***t***, the covenant
9:17 I grabbed the two ***t*** and threw them down
10:1 Carve two stone ***t***, just like the
1 Kings
8:9 the two stone ***t*** Moses had placed
2 Chronicles
5:10 the two stone ***t*** Moses placed

Jeremiah
17:1 point on the ***t*** of their hearts
2 Corinthians
3:3 written on ***t*** of stone but on
3:7 letters on stone ***t***. It came with
Hebrews
9:4 and the stone ***t*** of the covenant.

TAIL
Exodus
4:4 the snake by the ***t***." So Moses
29:22 the ram: the fat ***t***, the fat around
Leviticus
3:9 the whole fat ***t***, which should be
7:3 offered: the fat ***t***; the fat that
Deuteronomy
28:13 things, not the ***t***; you will be at
28:44 the head of things; you will be the ***t***.
Judges
15:4 turned the foxes ***t*** to tail, and put
2 Samuel
22:41 my enemies turn ***t*** from me; I
Job
40:17 He stiffens his ***t*** like a cedar; the
Psalms
18:40 my enemies turn ***t*** from me; I
Isaiah
9:14 cut off head and ***t***, palm branch and
9:15 prophets who teach lies are the ***t***.)
19:15 Neither head nor ***t***, palm branch nor
Revelation
12:4 His ***t*** swept down a third of heaven's

TAKES
Genesis
50:25 When God ***t*** care of you, you
Exodus
21:10 If he ***t*** another woman for himself, he
Psalms
4:3 this: the LORD ***t*** personal care of
34:8 is! The one who ***t*** refuge in him is
82:1 of Asaph.] God ***t*** his stand in the
89:51 abuse every step your anointed one ***t***.
Isaiah
44:15 for humans, so he ***t*** some of the wood
Luke
6:29 well. If someone ***t*** your coat, don't
11:22 the stronger one ***t*** away the armor he
John
1:29 Lamb of God who ***t*** away the sin of
2 Corinthians
11:20 you, if someone ***t*** advantage of you,
Revelation
22:19 If anyone ***t*** away from the words of this

TALK
Genesis
37:4 him and couldn't even ***t*** nicely to him.
44:7 does my master ***t*** to us like this?
45:15 brothers were finally able to ***t*** to him.
Deuteronomy
6:7 to your children. ***T*** about them when
25:8 summon him and ***t*** to him about
Judges
9:38 Where's all your ***t*** now, you who
1 Samuel
19:3 you'll be. I'll ***t*** to my father
27:11 said, "they might ***t*** about us, and
2 Samuel
1:20 Don't ***t*** about it in Gath; don't bring
13:13 Please, just ***t*** to the king! He
14:15 the king to ***t*** about this
19:29 don't need to ***t*** any more about
19:43 we the first to ***t*** about bringing
20:16 to come over here, so I can ***t*** to him."
1 Kings
2:19 King Solomon to ***t*** with him about
2 Kings
2:3 said, "Yes, I know. Don't ***t*** about it!"
2:5 said, "Yes, I know. Don't ***t*** about it!"
9:15 from the city to ***t*** about it in
Nehemiah
6:7 reports, so come; let's ***t*** together.
Esther
1:13 king would often ***t*** with certain very
Job
11:3 Will your idle ***t*** silence everyone; will
12:8 or ***t*** to earth, and it will teach you;
12:20 silences the ***t*** of trusted people; takes
16:3 Will windy ***t*** ever cease; what bothers
27:12 recognize this—why then this empty ***t***?
Psalms
5:9 graves; their tongues slick with ***t***.
9:1 my heart; I will ***t*** about all your
12:2 else; they ***t*** with slick speech
15:3 damage with their ***t***, does no harm to
28:1 me. If you won't ***t*** to me, I'll be
28:3 the type who ***t*** nice to their
35:28 my tongue will ***t*** all about your
36:2 are slick with ***t*** about their guilt
40:5 to proclaim and ***t*** about all of
41:7 those who hate me ***t*** about me,
49:13 their lead, pleased with their ***t***. Selah
50:16 says, "Why do you ***t*** about my laws?
55:21 Though his ***t*** is smoother than butter,
69:26 struck; they ***t*** about the pain of
73:8 They scoff and ***t*** so cruel; from their
73:15 I said, "I will ***t*** about all this,"
73:28 God, so I can ***t*** all about your
119:46 I will ***t*** about your laws before rulers
139:20 the people who ***t*** about you, but only
145:5 They will ***t*** all about the glorious
145:11 kingdom; they ***t*** all about your
Proverbs
6:12 guilty people go around with crooked ***t***.
7:21 him with all her ***t***. She entices him
14:23 hard work, but mere ***t*** leads to poverty.
15:4 but dishonest ***t*** breaks the spirit.
20:19 associate with those who ***t*** too much.
Ecclesiastes
5:6 angry at such ***t*** and destroy what
10:14 Fools ***t*** too much! No one knows what
Isaiah
3:8 the way they ***t*** and act in word
Jeremiah
3:16 will no longer ***t*** about the LORD's
48:30 the LORD, the idle ***t***, the empty deeds.
Lamentations
4:20 one we used to ***t*** about, saying,
Ezekiel
16:56 will no longer ***t*** about your sister
33:30 one, your people ***t*** about you beside
Matthew
9:33 speak began to ***t***. The crowds were

26:73 of them. The way you ***t*** gives you away."
Mark
9:32 this kind of ***t***, and they were
Luke
11:14 speak began to ***t***. The crowds were
Acts
10:27 they continued to ***t***, Peter went
16:13 down and began to ***t*** with the women
21:14 Since we couldn't ***t*** him out of it, the
24:24 listened to him ***t*** about faith in
Romans
9:20 think you are to ***t*** back to God? Does
16:18 people with smooth ***t*** and flattery.
1 Corinthians
2:7 We ***t*** about God's wisdom, which has been
3:1 I couldn't ***t*** to you like
14:34 not allowed to ***t***. Instead, they
14:35 for a woman to ***t*** during the
Ephesians
5:4 language, silly ***t***, or vulgar jokes
5:12 to even ***t*** about what
1 Timothy
1:6 distracted by ***t*** that doesn't mean
Titus
2:1 But you should ***t*** in a way that is
2:9 they do. They shouldn't ***t*** back
2:15 ***T*** about these things. Encourage and
Hebrews
9:5 now we can't ***t*** about these
1 Peter
2:15 the ignorant ***t*** of foolish people.
2 John
1:12 to visit you and ***t*** with you face-to-f

TALKING
Genesis
29:9 he was still ***t*** to them, Rachel
Exodus
4:10 since you've been ***t*** to your servant.
19:9 will hear me ***t*** with you so that
33:11 like two people ***t*** to each other.
34:29 because he had been ***t*** with God.
Deuteronomy
11:19 your children, by ***t*** about them when
1 Samuel
2:3 go on and on, ***t*** so proudly,
14:19 As Saul was ***t*** to the priest, the
17:28 Eliab heard him ***t*** to the soldiers,
18:1 had finished ***t*** with Saul,
30:6 the troops were ***t*** about stoning
2 Samuel
6:22 the female servants you are ***t*** about!"
1 Kings
13:25 old prophet lived and were ***t*** about it.
21:6 her, "I was ***t*** to Naboth. I
2 Kings
2:11 walking along, ***t***, when suddenly a
Nehemiah
6:19 They also kept ***t*** about his good deeds
Job
2:10 to her, "You're ***t*** like a foolish
18:2 you all stop ***t***. Try to
Psalms
3:2 So many are ***t*** about me: "Even God won't help him.
50:20 You sit around, ***t*** about your own
71:10 enemies have been ***t*** about me; those
109:2 up against me, ***t*** about me with
Proverbs
17:7 Too much ***t*** isn't right for a fool; even
17:27 restrain their ***t***; people with
Ecclesiastes
10:13 Fools start out ***t*** foolishness and end
Ezekiel
11:15 they were ***t*** about your
Matthew
10:20 aren't doing the ***t***, but the Spirit
15:7 knew what he was ***t*** about when he
15:31 unable to speak ***t***, and the
16:11 that I wasn't ***t*** about bread? But
17:3 Elijah appeared to them, ***t*** with Jesus.
21:45 they knew Jesus was ***t*** about them.
26:70 I don't know what you are ***t*** about."
Mark
1:45 out and started ***t*** freely and
7:6 knew what he was ***t*** about when he
8:17 Why are you ***t*** about the fact
9:4 Moses appeared and were ***t*** with Jesus.
14:68 know what you're ***t*** about. I don't
14:71 I don't know this man you're ***t*** about."
Luke
6:11 furious and began ***t*** with each other
9:30 men, Moses and Elijah, were ***t*** with him.
21:5 Some people were ***t*** about the temple,
22:60 know what you are ***t*** about!" At that
24:14 They were ***t*** to each other about
24:17 What are you ***t*** about as you walk
John
2:21 temple Jesus was ***t*** about was his
4:27 that he was ***t*** with a woman. But
13:22 about which of them he was ***t*** about.
13:24 him to ask Jesus who he was ***t*** about.
16:18 We don't understand what he's ***t*** about."
Acts
8:34 say this? Is he ***t*** about himself or
17:19 Can we learn what you are ***t*** about?
17:21 doing nothing but ***t*** about or
20:7 day, he continued ***t*** until midnight.
Romans
7:1 and sisters, I'm ***t*** to you as people
1 Corinthians
2:13 the things we are ***t*** about—not with wo
5:10 But I wasn't ***t*** about the sexually
10:15 I'm ***t*** to you like you are sensible
2 Corinthians
6:13 a fair trade—I'm ***t*** to you like you
1 Timothy
1:7 or what they are ***t*** about with such
5:13 and busybodies, ***t*** about things they
Hebrews
2:5 (the world we are ***t*** about) under the
6:9 though we are ***t*** this way—things
7:13 The person we are ***t*** about belongs to

TAMAR
Genesis
38:6 his oldest son Er to a woman named ***T***.
Ruth
4:12 of Perez, whom ***T*** bore to Judah
2 Samuel
13:1 fell in love with ***T*** the beautiful
1 Kings
9:18 Baalath, and ***T*** in the wilderness

Matthew
1:3 whose mother was ***T***. Perez was the

TARSHISH
Psalms
48:7 wind when it smashes the ships of ***T***.
Isaiah
60:9 Ships from ***T*** are in the lead
Jonah
1:3 up—to flee to ***T*** from the LORD !
4:2 is why I fled to ***T*** earlier! I know

TARSUS
Acts
9:11 for a man from ***T*** named Saul. He is
11:25 Barnabas went to ***T*** in search of Saul

TAUGHT
Deuteronomy
31:22 very day, and he ***t*** it to the
2 Kings
17:28 in Bethel and ***t*** the people how to
2 Chronicles
17:9 They ***t*** throughout Judah. They brought
Nehemiah
8:9 the Levites who ***t*** the people said
Psalms
71:17 You've ***t*** me since my youth, God, and
119:102 because you are the one who has ***t*** me.
119:171 because you've ***t*** me your statutes.
144:1 my rock, who ***t*** my hands how to
Proverbs
4:4 he ***t*** me and said to me: "Let your heart
31:1 of Massa, which his mother ***t*** him:
Ecclesiastes
12:9 he constantly ***t*** the people
Isaiah
40:14 Who ***t*** him the path of
Jeremiah
9:12 Who has been ***t*** by the LORD and
9:14 the Baals, as their ancestors ***t*** them.
12:16 just as they once ***t*** my people to
32:33 and though I ***t*** them over and
Ezekiel
22:26 and they have not ***t*** the difference
Hosea
11:3 Yet it was I who ***t*** Ephraim to walk; I
Matthew
5:2 He ***t*** them, saying
13:54 his hometown, he ***t*** the people in
Mark
6:30 him everything they had done and ***t***.
10:1 him again and, as usual, he ***t*** them.
11:17 He ***t*** them, "Hasn't it been written, My
Luke
4:15 He ***t*** in their synagogues and was
4:31 in Galilee and ***t*** the people each
5:3 sat down and ***t*** the crowds from
11:1 to pray, just as John ***t*** his disciples."
13:26 presence, and you ***t*** in our streets.'
John
6:45 they will all be ***t*** by God. Everyone
7:15 He's never been ***t***! How has he
8:2 around him, and he sat down and ***t*** them.
8:28 I say just what the Father has ***t*** me.
18:20 I've always ***t*** in synagogues and
Acts
1:1 Jesus did and ***t*** from the
15:35 many others, they ***t*** and proclaimed
18:25 by the Spirit. He ***t*** accurately the
Romans
2:18 God; if you are ***t*** by the Law so
1 Corinthians
2:13 with words ***t*** by human wisdom
Galatians
6:6 Those who are ***t*** the word should share
Ephesians
4:21 him and you were ***t*** how the truth is
Colossians
2:7 with thanksgiving just as you were ***t***.
1 Thessalonians
4:9 God has already ***t*** you to love each
2 Thessalonians
2:15 the traditions we ***t*** you, whether we
1 Timothy
1:20 that they can be ***t*** not to speak
2 Timothy
3:14 found convincing. You know who ***t*** you.
Titus
1:9 as it has been ***t*** to them so that
1 John
2:27 relationship to him just as he ***t*** you.
Revelation
2:14 Balaam had ***t*** Balak to trip up

TAX → TAX COLLECTOR, TAX COLLECTORS, TAX COLLECTORS AND SINNERS
2 Chronicles
24:5 the annual ***t*** of silver due
24:6 and Jerusalem the ***t*** imposed by the
24:9 to the LORD the ***t*** that God's
Ezra
4:13 pay tribute or ***t*** or dues, and the
Nehemiah
5:4 in order to pay the king's ***t***."
Amos
5:11 and because you ***t*** their grain, you
Matthew
17:24 temple ***t*** came to Peter and
17:27 Take it and pay the ***t*** for both of us."
22:19 used to pay the ***t***." And they
Luke
2:1 should be enrolled in the ***t*** lists.

TAX COLLECTOR
Mt 10:3; 18:17; Lk 5:27; 18:10, 11, 13

TAX COLLECTORS
Mt 5:46; 9:10, 11; 11:19; 21:31, 32; Mk 2:15; 2:16; Lk 3:12; 5:29, 30; 7:29, 34; 15:1; 19:2

TAX COLLECTORS AND SINNERS
Mt 9:10; 9:11; 11:19; Mk 2:15; Lk 5:30; 7:34; 15:1

TEACH → TEACH ME YOUR STATUTES
Exodus
4:12 speak, and I'll ***t*** you what you
18:16 of them. I also ***t*** them God's
24:12 that I've written in order to ***t*** them."
35:34 the ability to ***t*** others. Both he
Leviticus
10:11 so that you can ***t*** the Israelites

Deuteronomy
4:9 long as you live. ***T*** them to your
4:10 fertile land, and ***t*** their children to
5:31 that you must ***t*** the Israelites to
6:1 commanded me to ***t*** you to follow in
8:3 so he could ***t*** you that people
11:19 ***T*** them to your children, by talking
20:18 Then they can't ***t*** you to do all the
24:8 levitical priests ***t*** you, just as I
31:19 this poem and ***t*** it to the
33:10 They ***t*** your case laws to Jacob, your
Judges
3:2 survived only to ***t*** war to the
13:8 more, so he can ***t*** us how we should
1 Samuel
12:23 for you. I will ***t*** you what is good
14:12 on up! We'll ***t*** you a lesson!" So
1 Kings
8:36 people Israel. ***T*** them the best way
2 Kings
17:27 there. He should ***t*** them the
2 Chronicles
6:27 people Israel. ***T*** them the best way
15:3 a priest to ***t*** them, and without
17:7 and Micaiah to ***t*** in the cities of
Ezra
7:10 and to ***t*** law and justice
7:25 You will also ***t*** those who do not
Nehemiah
9:20 good spirit to ***t*** them. You didn't
Job
12:7 and he will ***t*** you, the birds in
12:8 and it will ***t*** you; the fish of
27:11 I will ***t*** you God's power, not hide what pertains
33:33 me; be quiet, and I will ***t*** you wisdom.
34:32 You ***t*** me what I can't see; if I've
Psalms
16:11 You ***t*** me the way of life. In your
25:4 known to me, LORD; ***t*** me your paths.
25:5 in your truth—***t*** it to me—because
25:12 LORD? God will ***t*** them which path
27:11 LORD, ***t*** me your way; because of my
32:8 instruct you and ***t*** you about the
34:11 to me. Let me ***t*** you how to honor
51:6 places; you ***t*** me wisdom in the
51:13 Then I will ***t*** wrongdoers your ways, and
78:5 our ancestors to ***t*** them to their
86:11 ***T*** me your way, LORD, so that I can walk
90:12 ***T*** us to number our days so we can have
94:12 the ones you ***t*** from your
105:22 his will, and to ***t*** wisdom to his
119:66 ***T*** me knowledge and good judgment
119:108 gifts of praise. ***T*** me your rules!
132:12 laws that I will ***t*** them, then their
143:10 ***T*** me to do what pleases you, because
Proverbs
1:2 purpose is to ***t*** wisdom and
4:2 I'll ***t*** you well. Don't abandon my
4:11 I ***t*** you the path of wisdom. I lead you
9:9 ***T*** the wise, and they will become wiser;
22:21 purpose is to ***t*** you true,
Song of Songs
8:2 house; she would ***t*** me what to do. I
Isaiah
2:3 so that he may ***t*** us his ways and
9:15 prophets who ***t*** lies are the
28:9 To whom will God ***t*** knowledge? To whom will he explain
Jeremiah
9:20 from his mouth: ***t*** your daughters to
16:21 Therefore, I will ***t*** them; this time I
31:34 no longer need to ***t*** each other to
Ezekiel
44:23 They must ***t*** my people the difference
Daniel
1:4 Ashpenaz was to ***t*** them the Chaldean
1:5 Ashpenaz was to ***t*** them for three
Micah
3:11 and her priests ***t*** for hire. Her
4:2 so that he may ***t*** us his ways and
Habakkuk
2:19 stone. Does it ***t***? Look, it is
Matthew
11:1 on from there to ***t*** and preach in
15:9 empty since they ***t*** instructions that
22:16 and that you ***t*** God's way as it
Mark
2:13 came to him, and he began to ***t*** them.
4:1 Jesus began to ***t*** beside the lake again.
6:2 he began to ***t*** in the synagogue.
6:34 Then he began to ***t*** them many things.
7:7 empty since they ***t*** instructions that
8:31 Jesus began to ***t*** his disciples:
12:14 favoritism but ***t*** God's way as it
Luke
6:6 a synagogue to ***t***. A man was there
11:1 said, "Lord, ***t*** us to pray, just
20:21 what you say and ***t***. You don't show
John
4:25 he comes, he will ***t*** everything to us."
7:14 went up to the temple and started to ***t***.
7:35 He isn't going to ***t*** the Greeks, is he?
9:34 that you dare to ***t*** us?" Then they
14:26 in my name, will ***t*** you everything
Acts
5:21 told and began to ***t***. When the high
5:28 that you not ***t*** in this name. And
5:42 they continued to ***t*** and proclaim the
20:20 to you and ***t*** you both publicly
21:21 informed that you ***t*** all the Jews who
28:31 kingdom and to ***t*** about the Lord
Romans
2:21 teaching others ***t*** yourself? If you
15:14 and are able to ***t*** each other.
1 Corinthians
4:17 Jesus. He'll ***t*** the same way as I
7:17 This is what I ***t*** in all the
11:14 nature itself ***t*** you that if a man
14:19 in a tongue so that I can ***t*** others.
Colossians
1:28 as we warn and ***t*** every person with
3:16 in you richly. ***T*** and warn each
1 Timothy
2:12 allow a wife to ***t*** or to control her
4:11 Command these things. ***T*** them
4:16 and on what you ***t***. If you do this,
5:7 ***T*** these things so that the families
6:2 who are loved. ***T*** and encourage
2 Timothy
2:24 toward all people, able to ***t***, patient,
Titus
1:11 households. They ***t*** what they
2:8 when you ***t***, so that any

Hebrews
5:12 need someone to ***t*** you an
8:11 person won't ever ***t*** a neighbor or
1 John
2:27 need anyone to ***t*** you the truth.
Revelation
2:20 You allow her to ***t*** and to mislead my

TEACH ME YOUR STATUTES
Ps 119:12; 119:26, 64, 68, 124, 135

TEACHER
2 Kings
12:2 because the priest Jehoiada was his ***t***.
1 Chronicles
25:8 as well as great, ***t*** and pupil alike.
Job
36:22 due to his power; who is a ***t*** like him?
Proverbs
5:13 of my instructor. I didn't obey my ***t***.
Ecclesiastes
1:1 The words of the ***T*** of the Assembly,
7:27 I found, says the ***T***, examining one
12:8 says the ***T***, everything is
Isaiah
30:20 oppression, your ***t*** will no longer
Habakkuk
2:18 shaped? It is a ***t*** of lies, for the
Matthew
8:19 and said to him, "***T***, I'll follow you
9:11 Why does your ***t*** eat with tax
10:24 than their ***t***, and slaves
12:38 of Jesus, "***T***, we would like to
17:24 Doesn't your ***t*** pay the temple
19:16 him and said, "***T***, what good thing
22:16 Herod, to him. "***T***," they said, "we
23:8 you have one ***t***, and all of you
23:10 Don't be called ***t***, because Christ is
26:18 and say, 'The ***t*** says, "My time is
Mark
4:38 him up and said, "***T***, don't you care
5:35 has died. Why bother the ***t*** any longer?"
9:17 crowd responded, "***T***, I brought my son
9:38 said to Jesus, "***T***, we saw someone
10:17 and asked, "Good ***T***, what must I do
12:14 to him and said, "***T***, we know that
13:1 said to him, "***T***, look! What
14:14 the house, 'The ***t*** asks, "Where is
Luke
3:12 said to him, "***T***, what should we
6:40 than their ***t***, but whoever is
7:40 to say to you." "***T***, speak," he said.
8:49 died. Don't bother the ***t*** any longer."
9:38 crowd shouted, "***T***, I beg you to
10:25 to test Jesus. "***T***," he said, "what
11:45 responded, "***T***, when you say
12:13 said to him, "***T***, tell my brother
18:18 Jesus, "Good ***T***, what must I do
19:39 said to Jesus, "***T***, scold your
20:21 They asked him, "***T***, we know that you
21:7 They asked him, "***T***, when will these
22:11 the house, 'The ***t*** says to you,
John
1:38 is translated ***T***), where are you
3:2 that you are a ***t*** who has come from
3:10 You are a ***t*** of Israel and you
8:4 said to Jesus, "***T***, this woman was
11:28 sister Mary, "The ***t*** is here and he's
13:14 I, your Lord and ***t***, have washed your
20:16 in Aramaic, "Rabbouni" (which means ***T***).
Acts
5:34 a Pharisee and ***t*** of the Law named
Romans
2:20 of the foolish; a ***t*** of infants (since
Galatians
6:6 share all good things with their ***t***.
1 Timothy
2:7 not lying! I'm a ***t*** of the Gentiles
2 Timothy
1:11 apostle, and ***t*** of this good news.

TEACHERS → FALSE TEACHERS
Psalms
119:99 than all my ***t*** because I
Daniel
11:33 The people's ***t*** will help many
11:35 Some of the ***t*** too will fall in order
Luke
2:46 sitting among the ***t***, listening to
Acts
13:1 prophets and ***t***: Barnabas, Simeon
1 Corinthians
12:28 prophets, third ***t***, then miracles,
12:29 they? All aren't ***t***, are they? All
Ephesians
4:11 evangelists, and some pastors and ***t***.
1 Timothy
1:7 They want to be ***t*** of Law without
2 Timothy
4:3 They will collect ***t*** who say what they
Hebrews
5:12 should have been ***t*** by now, you need
James
3:1 you should become ***t***, because we know

TEACHING
Deuteronomy
4:1 laws that I am ***t*** you to follow, so
4:5 attention! I am ***t*** all of you the
32:2 My ***t*** will fall like raindrops; my
2 Chronicles
17:9 all the cities of Judah, ***t*** the people.
Job
11:4 You've said, "My ***t*** is pure, and I'm
13:6 Hear my ***t*** and pay attention to the
20:3 I hear ***t*** that insults me, but I am
Psalms
25:9 the weak to justice, ***t*** them his way.
78:1 my people, to my ***t***; tilt your ears
Proverbs
1:8 don't neglect your mother's ***t***;
6:23 light; corrective ***t*** is the path of
13:14 The ***t*** of the wise is a fountain of
16:21 and pleasant speech enhances ***t***.
16:23 and enhances the ***t*** of their lips.
22:19 in the LORD, I'm ***t*** you today—yes,
31:26 of wisdom; kindly ***t*** is on her tongue.
Isaiah
1:10 to our God's ***t***, people of
5:24 have rejected the ***t*** of the LORD of
8:16 seal up the ***t*** among my
30:9 unwilling to hear the LORD's ***t***,
42:4 the land. The coastlands await his ***t***.

42:24 ways, and wouldn't listen to his **t**.
51:4 my nation, for **t** will go out from
51:7 who carry my **t** in your heart:
Jeremiah
6:19 my words and they have rejected my **t**.
Matthew
4:23 Galilee, **t** in their
7:28 words, the crowds were amazed at his **t**
7:29 because he was **t** them like someone with authority
9:35 and villages, **t** in their
11:1 Jesus finished **t** his twelve
16:12 watch out for the **t** of the Pharisees
19:11 can accept this **t**, but only those
21:23 to him as he was **t**. They asked,
22:33 this, they were astonished at his **t**.
26:55 sat in the temple **t**, but you didn't
28:20 **t** them to obey everything that I've
Mark
1:21 entered the synagogue and started **t**.
1:22 amazed by his **t**, for he was
1:27 this? A new **t** with authority!
4:2 in parables. While **t** them, he said,
6:6 through the surrounding villages **t**.
9:31 because he was **t** his disciples,
11:18 whole crowd was enthralled at his **t**.
12:35 While Jesus was **t** in the temple, he
12:38 As he was **t**, he said, "Watch out for
14:49 I was with you, **t** in the temple,
Luke
4:32 amazed by his **t** because he
5:17 when Jesus was **t**, Pharisees and
13:10 Jesus was **t** in one of the synagogues on
13:22 and villages **t** and making his
19:47 Jesus was **t** daily in the temple. The
20:1 when Jesus was **t** the people in the
21:37 day Jesus was **t** in the temple,
23:5 people with his **t** throughout Judea—
John
6:59 while he was **t** in the synagogue
7:16 responded, "My **t** isn't mine but
7:17 tell whether my **t** is from God or
7:28 While Jesus was **t** in the temple, he
8:20 while he was **t** in the temple
8:31 if you remain faithful to my **t**.
8:37 kill me because you don't welcome my **t**.
18:19 Jesus about his disciples and his **t**.
Acts
2:42 to the apostles' **t**, to the
4:2 the apostles were **t** the people and
4:18 all speaking and **t** in the name of
5:25 in the temple and **t** the people!"
5:28 with your **t**. And you are
11:26 the church and **t** large numbers of
13:12 was astonished by the **t** about the Lord.
15:1 down from Judea **t** the family of
17:11 whether Paul and Silas's **t** was true.
17:19 What is this new **t**? Can we learn
18:11 eighteen months, **t** God's word among
Romans
2:21 don't you who are **t** others teach
6:17 obedience to the **t** that was handed
12:7 If your gift is **t**, devote yourself
16:17 against the **t** that you learned.
1 Corinthians
14:6 some knowledge, a prophecy, or a **t**?
14:26 has a psalm, a **t**, a revelation, a
Ephesians
4:14 that comes from **t** with deceitful
1 Timothy
1:3 individuals not to spread wrong **t**.
1:4 Their **t** only causes
1:10 else that is opposed to sound **t**.
1:11 Sound **t** agrees with the glorious gospel
3:2 show hospitality and be skilled at **t**.
4:1 that deceive and to the **t** of demons.
4:6 and the good **t** that you've
4:13 to public reading, preaching, and **t**.
5:17 who work with public speaking and **t**.
6:1 name and our **t** won't get a bad
6:3 agree with sound **t** about our Lord
2 Timothy
1:13 pattern of sound **t** that you heard
2:2 who are also capable of **t** others.
3:10 attention to my **t**, conduct,
3:16 and is useful for **t**, for showing
4:3 tolerate sound **t**. They will
4:15 out for him, because he opposes our **t**.
Titus
2:1 a way that is consistent with sound **t**.
2:3 their behavior, **t** what is good,
2:10 might make the **t** about God our
Hebrews
6:2 of **t** about ritual ways to wash with
2 John
1:9 continue in the **t** about Christ does
1:10 not affirm this **t** should neither be
Revelation
2:14 follow Balaam's **t**. Balaam had
2:15 some who follow the Nicolaitans' **t**.
2:24 don't follow this **t** and haven't

TEAR

Exodus
34:13 You must **t** down their altars, smash
Leviticus
1:15 altar. He will **t** off its head and
1:17 He will then **t** the bird open by its
21:10 dishevel his hair or **t** his clothing.
Judges
14:6 as one might **t** apart a young
2 Samuel
3:31 were with him, "***T*** your clothes and
Job
18:4 To you who **t** yourself in rage—will
Psalms
2:3 say. "We will **t** off their ropes
28:5 God will **t** them down and
52:5 snatch you up, **t** you out of your
58:6 of their mouths! ***T*** out the lions'
62:3 how long will you **t** them down as if
80:13 the forest can **t** it up, so that
Jeremiah
5:6 their towns will **t** to pieces anyone
Ezekiel
5:11 I will not shed a **t**. You will have no
13:14 I will **t** down the wall on which you
16:39 and they will **t** down your
17:9 thrive? Won't he **t** out its roots,
19:3 he learned to **t** flesh and devour
19:6 He learned to **t** flesh and devour
23:34 into pieces, and **t** off your breasts,
26:9 crowbars he will **t** down your towers.
26:12 your goods, **t** down your walls,

TEAR [cont.]

Hosea
13:8 cubs, and I will **t** open the covering
Joel
2:13 **t** your hearts and not your clothing.
Amos
3:15 I will **t** down the winter house as well
Micah
3:2 love evil, who **t** the skin off
3:3 of my people, **t** off their skin,
5:11 your land; I will **t** down your
5:14 I will **t** down your sacred poles in your
Nahum
1:13 yoke from you and **t** off your chains.
Malachi
1:4 build, but I will **t** them down. They
Matthew
5:29 to fall into sin, **t** it out and throw
9:16 away the cloth and makes a worse **t**.
18:9 to fall into sin, **t** it out and throw
Mark
2:21 new from the old, and makes a worse **t**.
9:47 to fall into sin, **t** it out. It's
Luke
12:18 I'll do. I'll **t** down my barns and
John
19:24 other, "Let's not **t** it. Let's cast
Acts
23:10 feared they might **t** Paul to pieces.
2 Corinthians
13:10 I could build you up, not **t** you down.
Revelation
7:17 wipe away every **t** from their eyes."
21:4 wipe away every **t** from their eyes.

TEARS

Deuteronomy
1:45 respond to your **t** or give you a
1 Samuel
24:16 your voice?" Then he broke down in **t**,
30:4 him broke into **t** and cried until
2 Kings
20:5 have seen your **t**. So now I'm going
Job
12:14 If he **t** down, it can't be rebuilt; if
16:9 His anger **t** me and afflicts me; he
16:20 my friend. While my eyes drip **t** to God,
Psalms
6:6 my bed with **t**; I soak my couch
39:12 don't ignore my **t**! I'm just a
42:3 My **t** have been my food both day and
56:8 my misery. Put my **t** into your bottle—
80:5 bread made of **t**; you've given
102:9 I've been mixing **t** into my drinks
116:8 my eyes from **t**, and my foot from
119:136 Rivers of **t** stream from my eyes because
126:5 who plant with **t** reap the harvest
Proverbs
14:1 a foolish woman **t** hers down with
29:4 one who imposes heavy taxes **t** it down.
Ecclesiastes
4:1 sun, I saw the **t** of the oppressed—
Isaiah
25:8 God will wipe **t** from every face;
Jeremiah
9:1 a fountain of **t**, I would weep day
15:5 Who will shed **t** over you? Who
31:9 With **t** of joy they will come; while
Lamentations
1:2 in the night, her **t** on her cheek.
2:18 Zion; make your **t** run down like a
Ezekiel
24:16 or weep. Don't even let your **t** well up.
Hosea
5:14 I am the one who **t** the prey and goes
Micah
5:8 by, tramples and **t** to pieces with no
Malachi
2:13 of the Lord with **t**, weeping, and
Matthew
9:16 because the patch **t** away the cloth
Mark
2:21 the patch **t** away from it, the
Luke
5:36 parable. "No one **t** a patch from a
7:38 his feet with her **t**. She wiped them
7:44 wet my feet with **t** and wiped them
Acts
20:19 humility and with **t** in the midst of
2 Corinthians
2:4 I wrote to you in **t**, with a very
2 Timothy
1:4 I remember your **t**, I long to see
Hebrews
5:7 loud cries and **t** as his sacrifices
12:17 life, though he looked for it with **t**.

TEETH → GRINDING THEIR TEETH

Genesis
49:12 than wine, and his **t** whiter than milk.
Numbers
11:33 between their **t** and not yet
Job
4:10 beasts—yet the **t** of lions are
13:14 my flesh in my **t**, put my life in
16:9 at me with his **t**. My enemy pierces
19:20 I have escaped by the skin of my **t**.
29:17 the wicked, rescued prey from their **t**.
41:14 his mouth, surrounded by frightening **t**?
Psalms
3:7 the jaw; shatter the **t** of the wicked!
57:4 humans. Their **t** are spears and
58:6 God, break their **t** out of their mouths!
112:10 they grind their **t**, but disappear to
124:6 us over like food for our enemies' **t**!
Proverbs
10:26 vinegar to the **t** and smoke to the
30:14 are those whose **t** are swords; their
Song of Songs
4:2 Your **t** are like newly shorn ewes as
6:6 Your **t** are like a flock of ewes as they
7:9 love, gliding through the lips and **t**.
Isaiah
41:15 tool with sharp **t**. You will thresh
Lamentations
3:16 He crushed my **t** into the gravel; he
Ezekiel
18:2 grapes, the children's **t** suffer"?
Daniel
7:5 mouth between its **t**. It was told:
7:7 with massive iron **t**. As it ate and
7:19 with its iron **t** and bronze claws.
Joel
1:6 my land. Its **t** are like lions'

Micah
3:5 chew with their **t** and then proclaim
Zechariah
9:7 from between his **t**. He will be a
Mark
9:18 mouth, grinds his **t**, and stiffens up.
Luke
13:28 and grinding of **t** when you see
Acts
7:54 and began to grind their **t** at Stephen.
Revelation
9:8 hair, and their **t** were like lions'

TEKOA

2 Samuel
14:4 the woman from **T** came to the king,
Amos
1:1 the shepherds of **T**. He perceived

TEMPLE

→ BUILD A TEMPLE, BUILD THE LORD'S TEMPLE, BUILD THE TEMPLE, GOD'S TEMPLE, HOLY TEMPLE

Judges
9:4 silver from the **t** of Baal-berith,
16:26 that hold up the **t**, so I can lean on
16:27 Now the **t** was filled with men and
1 Samuel
3:3 in the LORD's **t**, where God's
5:2 it into Dagon's **t** and set it next
5:5 who enters his **t** in Ashdod doesn't
31:10 armor in the **t** of Astarte, and
2 Samuel
5:8 and the lame will not enter the **t**."
7:6 lived in a **t** from the day I
7:7 Why haven't you built me a cedar **t**?
22:7 my voice from his **t**; my cry for help
1 Kings
3:1 the LORD's **t**, and the wall
5:18 stones for the construction of the **t**.
6:1 over Israel, he built the LORD's **t**.
7:12 of the LORD's **t** and its porch.
8:6 sanctuary of the **t**, the most holy
9:1 the LORD's **t**, the royal
10:5 at the LORD's **t**, it took her
12:27 at the LORD's **t** in Jerusalem,
14:26 of the LORD's **t** and the royal
15:15 into the LORD's **t** the silver and
16:32 Baal in the Baal **t** he had
2 Kings
5:18 into Rimmon's **t** to bow down there
10:21 entered Baal's **t** until it was
11:3 in the LORD's **t** for six years
12:4 is brought to the **t**-some is money peop
14:14 in the LORD's **t** and the
15:35 rebuilt the Upper Gate of the LORD's **t**.
16:8 was in the LORD's **t** and in the palace
18:15 was in the LORD's **t** and in the palace
19:1 clothes, and went to the LORD's **t**.
20:5 will be able to go up to the LORD's **t**.
21:4 of the LORD's **t**-the very place the
22:3 to the LORD's **t** with the
23:2 up to the LORD's **t**, together with
24:13 of the LORD's **t** and of the royal
25:9 down the LORD's **t**, the royal
1 Chronicles
6:10 as priest in the **t** that Solomon
9:2 the Levites, and the **t** servants.
9:33 They lived in **t** rooms and were
17:5 lived in a **t** from the day I
22:14 for the LORD's **t** one hundred
23:4 on the LORD's **t**, 6,000 officers
24:19 enter the LORD's **t** according to
25:6 in the LORD's **t** with cymbals,
26:12 in the LORD's **t**, along with their
28:6 will build my **t** and my
29:1 task, since this **t** won't be for
29:16 to build you a **t** for your holy
2 Chronicles
2:5 The **t** I am about to build must be
3:4 the front of the **t** was a porch as
4:16 for the LORD's **t** were made of
36:14 the LORD's **t** that God had
Ezra
3:10 of the LORD's **t**, the priests
7:24 doorkeepers, the **t** servants, or
Nehemiah
2:8 the beams of the **t** fortress' gates,
11:12 the work in the **t**: 822. There was
13:9 I put back the **t** equipment, along
Psalms
18:6 my voice from his **t**; I called to him
27:4 beauty and constantly adoring his **t**.
29:9 bare, but in his **t** everyone shouts,
30:1 A song for the **t** dedication. Of
48:9 on your faithful love, God, in your **t**.
65:4 your house, by the holiness of your **t**.
68:29 from your **t** above Jerusalem, where
Isaiah
6:1 the edges of his robe filling the **t**.
56:5 in my **t** and courts, I will give them a
Jeremiah
7:4 is the LORD's **t**! The LORD's
26:2 Stand in the **t** courtyard and
52:20 Solomon had made for the LORD's **t**.
Ezekiel
8:14 North Gate of the **t**, where women were
8:16 of the LORD's **t**. There, at the
43:4 came into the **t** by way of the
Daniel
5:2 from Jerusalem's **t** be brought to the
5:3 out of the **t**, God's house in
Joel
1:9 from the LORD's **t**. The priests and
1:13 have gone from the **t** of your God.
1:14 people to the **t** of the LORD your
Amos
8:3 will wail the **t** songs," says the
Micah
3:12 rubble, and the **t** mount will become
Haggai
2:15 was placed on stone in the LORD's **t**,
2:18 foundation for the LORD's **t** was laid.
Zechariah
6:14 in the LORD's **t** for Helem,
Malachi
1:10 the doors of the **t** so that you don't
3:1 will come to his **t**. The messenger of
Matthew
4:5 highest point of the **t**. He said to him,
12:5 priests in the **t** treat the Sabbath
12:6 something greater than the **t** is here.
17:24 the half-shekel **t** tax came to Peter
21:12 went into the **t** and threw out all

23:16 swear by the ***t***, it's nothing.
24:1 Jesus left the ***t*** and was going
26:55 day, I sat in the ***t*** teaching, but you
27:5 pieces into the ***t*** and left. Then he
27:40 to destroy the ***t*** and rebuild it in

Mark
11:11 and went into the ***t***. After he looked
11:15 entering the ***t***, he threw out
12:35 teaching in the ***t***, he said, "Why do
12:41 box for the ***t*** treasury and
13:1 As Jesus left the ***t***, one of his
13:3 across from the ***t***. Peter, James,
14:49 teaching in the ***t***, but you didn't
14:58 will destroy this ***t***, constructed by
15:29 to destroy the ***t*** and rebuild it in

Luke
1:22 a vision in the ***t***, for he gestured
2:27 he went into the ***t*** area. Meanwhile,
2:37 never left the ***t*** area but
2:46 found him in the ***t***. He was sitting
4:9 point of the ***t***. He said to him,
18:10 went up to the ***t*** to pray. One was
19:45 Jesus entered the ***t***, he threw out
19:47 daily in the ***t***. The chief
20:1 the people in the ***t*** and proclaiming
21:1 the collection box for the ***t*** treasury.
22:4 officers of the ***t*** guard how he
24:53 continuously in the ***t*** praising God.

John
2:14 He found in the ***t*** those who were
2:15 all out of the ***t***, including the
2:19 Destroy this ***t*** and in three days
2:20 to build this ***t***, and you will
2:21 But the ***t*** Jesus was talking about was
5:14 found him in the ***t*** and said, "See!
7:14 went up to the ***t*** and started to
7:28 teaching in the ***t***, he exclaimed,
8:2 returned to the ***t***. All the people
8:20 teaching in the ***t*** area known as the
8:59 but Jesus hid himself and left the ***t***.
10:23 Jesus was in the ***t***, walking in the
11:48 take away both our ***t*** and our people."
11:56 each other in the ***t***, they said, "What
18:20 and in the ***t***, where all the

Acts
2:46 together in the ***t*** and ate in their
5:42 Christ, both in the ***t*** and in houses.

1 Corinthians
6:19 your body is a ***t*** of the Holy
8:10 in an idol's ***t***. Won't the person
9:13 who serve in the ***t*** get to eat food
10:28 sacrificed in a ***t***," then don't eat

Ephesians
2:21 grows up into a ***t*** that is dedicated

1 Peter
2:5 into a spiritual ***t***. You are being

Revelation
3:12 pillars in the ***t*** of my God, and
7:15 and night in his ***t***, and the one
11:2 court outside the ***t***. Leave that out,
14:15 came out of the ***t***, calling in a
14:17 came out of the ***t*** in heaven, and he
15:5 I looked, and the ***t*** in heaven—that is
15:6 came out of the ***t***. They were
15:8 The ***t*** was filled with smoke from God's
16:1 voice from the ***t*** say to the seven
16:17 came out from the ***t***, from the throne,
21:22 I didn't see a ***t*** in the city, because

TEN

Genesis
18:32 What if there are ***t***?" And the LORD
42:3 So Joseph's ***t*** brothers went down to buy grain
45:23 father he sent ***t*** male donkeys

Exodus
34:28 the words of the covenant, the ***t*** words.

Deuteronomy
4:13 you to do—the ***T*** Commandments—and wrote them
10:4 first set: the ***T*** Commandments that
32:30 two people make ***t*** thousand flee for

1 Samuel
1:8 I worth more to you than ***t*** sons?"

1 Kings
14:3 Take ***t*** loaves of bread, cakes, and a

Esther
9:14 They impaled the ***t*** sons of Haman

Psalms
33:2 to him with the ***t***-stringed harp!

Ecclesiastes
7:19 stronger than ***t*** rulers who are in

Isaiah
38:8 make it back up ***t*** steps." And the

Daniel
1:12 your servants for ***t*** days? You could
7:7 beasts before it, and it had ***t*** horns.
7:24 The ***t*** horns mean that from this

Amos
5:3 hundred will have ***t*** left in the house
6:9 If ***t*** people remain in one house, then

Matthew
25:1 will be like ***t*** young bridesmaids
25:28 and give it to the one who has ***t*** coins.

Mark
5:20 proclaim in the ***T*** Cities all that
10:41 when the other ***t*** disciples heard

Luke
15:8 if she owns ***t*** silver coins and
17:12 a village, ***t*** men with skin
19:13 called together ***t*** servants and gave

Revelation
12:3 seven heads and ***t*** horns, and seven
13:1 the sea. It had ***t*** horns and seven
17:3 names. It had seven heads and ***t*** horns.
17:16 As for the ***t*** horns that you saw, they

TENT

Genesis
9:21 and took off his clothes in his ***t***.
12:8 and pitched his ***t*** with Bethel on
13:3 first pitched his ***t*** between Bethel
13:18 Abram packed his ***t*** and went and
24:67 mother Sarah's ***t***. He married

Exodus
18:7 doing, and then they went into the ***t***.
26:7 goats' hair for a ***t*** over the
27:19 use and all its ***t*** pegs and all the
28:43 into the meeting ***t*** or when they
29:4 to the meeting ***t*** and wash them
30:16 of the meeting ***t***. It will serve
31:7 the meeting ***t***, the chest containing
33:7 Moses took the ***t*** and pitched it outside
35:11 the dwelling, its ***t*** and its covering,

36:14 goats' hair for a **t** over the
38:20 All the **t** pegs for the dwelling and for
39:33 the dwelling, the **t**, and all its
40:2 up the meeting **t** dwelling on the
Leviticus
1:1 and said to him from the meeting **t**,
4:16 of the bull's blood into the meeting **t**.
Deuteronomy
31:14 at the meeting **t** so I can command
31:15 appeared in the **t** in a pillar of
Joshua
7:21 ground inside my **t**, with the silver
13:30 all sixty of the **t** villages of Jair
18:1 up the meeting **t** there. The
19:51 of the meeting **t** and finished
Judges
4:21 wife, picked up a **t** stake and a
5:24 be blessed above all **t**-dwelling women.
1 Samuel
17:54 the Philistine's weapons in his own **t**.
2 Samuel
7:2 but God's chest is housed in a **t**!"
1 Kings
1:39 of oil from the **t** and anointed
2:28 ran to the LORD's **t** and grabbed the
8:4 the meeting **t**, and all the holy
2 Kings
7:8 They entered a **t** where they ate
1 Chronicles
6:32 of the meeting **t**, until Solomon
9:23 the LORD's house, that is, the **t**.
15:1 for God's chest and pitched a **t** for it.
16:1 it inside the **t** David had pitched
17:5 traveling from **t** to tent and from
23:32 for the meeting **t**, the instructions
2 Chronicles
1:3 God's meeting **t** was, the tent
5:5 the meeting **t**, and all the holy
24:6 assembly for the covenant **t**?"
Job
4:21 Isn't their **t** cord pulled up? They die
5:24 know that your **t** is secure. You
8:22 shame, and the **t** of the wicked
18:6 light in their **t** becomes dark, and
18:14 safety of their **t**; it parades them
18:15 remains in their **t**; sulfur is
19:12 ramp against me; they camp around my **t**.
20:26 them; what's left in their **t** is ruined.
21:28 Where is the **t**, the dwelling of
22:23 if you keep wrongdoing out of your **t**.
29:4 prime; when God's counsel was in my **t**;
31:31 those in my **t** never said: "Who
Psalms
15:1 can live in your **t**, LORD? Who can
19:4 God has made a **t** in heaven for the
27:5 place in his own **t**; he will set me
27:6 in God's **t**—sacrifices with
52:5 you out of your **t**, and uproot you
61:4 me live in your **t** forever! Please
78:60 at Shiloh, the **t** where he had
78:67 God rejected the **t** of Joseph and didn't
91:10 no disease will come close to your **t**.
Proverbs
14:11 but the **t** flourishes for
Isaiah
22:23 securely like a **t** peg, and he will
33:20 dwelling, a **t** that is not
38:12 like a shepherd's **t**. My life is
40:22 spreads it out like a **t** for dwelling.
54:2 the site of your **t**, and stretch out
Jeremiah
10:20 But now my **t** is destroyed
Lamentations
2:4 wrath like fire on Daughter Zion's **t**.
Ezekiel
41:1 so that was also the depth of the **t**.
Amos
9:11 up the meeting **t** of David that has
Zechariah
10:4 cornerstone, the **t** peg, and the bow
Acts
7:43 you took the **t** of Moloch with
7:44 The **t** of testimony was with our
7:45 had received the **t**, our ancestors
15:16 David's fallen **t**; I will rebuild
2 Corinthians
5:1 know that if the **t** that we live in
Hebrews
8:2 the true meeting **t** that God, not any
9:2 pitched the first **t** called the holy
9:11 perfect meeting **t**, which isn't made
13:10 in the meeting **t** don't have the
Revelation
15:5 is, the **t** of witness—was

TENTH

Genesis
8:5 until the **t** month, and on the
28:22 give me I will give a **t** back to you."
Exodus
12:3 community: On the **t** day of this month
Leviticus
27:30 All **t**-part gifts from the land,
27:33 one bringing the **t**-part gift must not
Deuteronomy
12:6 sacrifices, your **t**-part gifts, your
14:22 must reserve a **t**-part of whatever y
26:12 paying the entire **t**-part
Nehemiah
10:37 also bring one **t** of the produce of
12:44 produce, and the **t**-part gifts. They
13:5 together with the **t**-part gifts of
Amos
4:4 morning, your **t**-part gifts every
Malachi
3:8 you?" With your **t**-part gifts and off
3:10 Bring the whole **t**-part to the storage
Luke
11:42 You give a **t** of your mint,
18:12 a week. I give a **t** of everything I
Hebrews
7:2 Abraham gave a **t** of everything to him.
7:10 when Abraham paid the **t** to Melchizedek.
Revelation
11:13 earthquake, and a **t** of the city fell.
21:20 was topaz, the **t** was chrysoprase,

TENTS

Genesis
4:20 those who live in **t** and own livestock.
Job
11:14 don't let injustice dwell in your **t**,

15:34 and fire consumes the ***t*** of bribers.
Psalms
69:25 let no one dwell in their ***t***.
78:51 males; in Ham's ***t***, he struck their
78:55 he settled Israel's tribes in their ***t***.
84:10 comfortably in the ***t*** of the wicked!
106:25 muttered in their ***t*** and wouldn't
118:15 are heard in the ***t*** of the righteous:
120:5 I've made my home among Kedar's ***t***.
Song of Songs
1:5 like the black ***t*** of the Kedar
1:8 little goats by the ***t*** of the shepherds.
Jeremiah
4:20 Suddenly, my ***t*** are destroyed, my
6:3 They pitch their ***t*** around her and
30:18 restore Jacob's ***t*** and have pity on
35:7 to dwell in ***t*** so you may live a
35:10 We have lived in ***t*** and done everything
37:10 wounded in their ***t*** remained, they
49:29 Seize their ***t*** and their flocks, their
Daniel
11:45 pitch his royal ***t*** between the sea
Hosea
9:6 of silver; thorns will be in their ***t***.
12:9 make you live in ***t*** again, as in
Habakkuk
3:7 I saw the ***t*** of Cushan under duress. The curtains of the
Zechariah
12:7 first deliver the ***t*** of Judah so that
Malachi
2:12 does so from the ***t*** of Jacob, anyone
Hebrews
11:9 He lived in ***t*** along with Isaac

TERAH

Genesis
11:24 years old, he became the father of ***T***.
Numbers
33:27 marched from Tahath and camped at ***T***.
Joshua
24:2 Among them was ***T***, the father of
1 Chronicles
1:26 Serug, Nahor, ***T***
Luke
3:34 son of Abraham son of ***T*** son of Nahor

TERRIFIED

Genesis
20:8 that had happened, the men were ***t***.
28:17 He was ***t*** and thought, This sacred place
32:7 Jacob was ***t*** and felt trapped, so he
42:28 hearts stopped. ***T***, they said to
45:3 respond because they were ***t*** before him.
Exodus
14:10 Israelites were ***t*** and cried out to
15:15 chiefs were ***t***; panic grabbed
Numbers
22:3 The Moabites were ***t*** of the Israelites.
Deuteronomy
1:29 to you: Don't be ***t***! Don't be afraid
5:5 because you were ***t*** of the fire and
28:67 which will be ***t***, and because of
Joshua
1:9 be alarmed or ***t***, because the LORD
8:1 be afraid or ***t***. Take the entire
10:25 be afraid or ***t***. Be brave and
1 Samuel
2:10 His enemies are ***t***! God thunders
5:6 of Ashdod: God ***t*** them and struck
17:11 said, they were distressed and ***t***.
17:24 every one of them ran away ***t*** of him.
28:20 ground, utterly ***t*** at what Samuel
31:4 because he was ***t***. So Saul took the
2 Samuel
22:5 around me; rivers of wickedness ***t*** me.
1 Kings
19:3 Elijah was ***t***. He got up and ran for
1 Chronicles
10:4 because he was ***t***. So Saul took the
2 Chronicles
14:14 Gerar who were ***t*** of the LORD. They
Job
26:11 Heaven's pillars shook, ***t*** by his blast
Psalms
6:3 is completely ***t***! But you, LORD!
6:10 and completely ***t***; they will be
10:18 of the land will never again be ***t***.
18:4 around me; rivers of wickedness ***t*** me.
30:7 then you hid your presence. I was ***t***.
83:17 be shamed and ***t*** forever. Let them
104:29 face, they are ***t***; when you take
Proverbs
3:24 you won't be ***t***. When you lie
Isaiah
8:12 fear what they fear, and don't be ***t***.
13:8 and they will be ***t***. Like a woman
19:17 it, they will be ***t*** because of the
31:9 officers will be ***t*** at the signal,
33:14 Sinners became ***t*** in Zion; trembling
Jeremiah
46:5 Why do I see them ***t***, retreating in
50:36 its warriors so that they are ***t***.
51:32 are on fire; the soldiers are ***t***.
Ezekiel
26:16 They will be so ***t***, they won't stop
Daniel
5:19 languages were ***t*** of him. He did
8:17 me, and I was ***t*** when he came. I
10:7 that, they were ***t*** and ran away to
Jonah
1:5 The sailors were ***t***, and each one cried
1:10 Then the men were ***t*** and said to him,
Matthew
14:26 lake, they were ***t*** and said, "It's a
28:4 guards were so ***t*** of him that they
Mark
9:6 respond, for the three of them were ***t***.
Luke
2:9 shone around them, and they were ***t***.
12:4 friends, don't be ***t*** by those who can
24:37 They were ***t*** and afraid. They thought
Acts
5:5 who heard this conversation was ***t***.
Hebrews
12:21 that Moses said, "I'm ***t*** and shaking!"
1 Peter
3:14 Don't be ***t*** or upset by them.

TERRITORY

Genesis
14:7 and attacked the ***t*** of the
Leviticus
26:34 you are in enemy ***t***, the land will

Numbers
32:33 cities, and the ***t*** surrounding the
33:44 camped at Iye- abarim in the ***t*** of Moab.
Deuteronomy
2:4 to enter into the ***t*** of your relatives
19:8 God enlarges your ***t***, as he swore to
34:1 the Gilead region as far as Dan's ***t***;
Joshua
1:4 Your ***t*** will stretch from the desert and
Job
38:20 take it to its ***t***; do you know the
Psalms
78:54 them to his holy ***t***, to the mountain
114:2 God's sanctuary; Israel was God's ***t***.
Ecclesiastes
5:8 and right in some ***t***, don't be
Jeremiah
15:13 of all your sins throughout your ***t***.
Ezekiel
27:4 But your ***t*** is in the depths of the sea,
45:7 The ***t*** for the prince will be on both
48:22 The prince's ***t*** will be between
Amos
6:2 Or is your ***t*** greater than
Micah
5:6 our land and treads within our ***t***.
Malachi
1:4 a wicked ***t***, the people
Matthew
2:1 Bethlehem in the ***t*** of Judea during
2:16 the surrounding ***t*** who were two

TERROR

Exodus
15:14 they shook in ***t***; horror grabbed
15:16 ***T*** and fear came over them; because of
Deuteronomy
7:20 God will send ***t*** on them until
32:25 there will be ***t*** for young men and
Joshua
2:9 you the land. ***T*** over you has
1 Samuel
14:15 very ground shook! It was a ***t*** from God.
2 Chronicles
29:8 an object of ***t*** and horror,
Esther
7:6 was overcome with ***t*** in the presence
Job
15:21 a sound of ***t*** pierces their ears; when
20:25 its shaft in their liver brings ***t***.
31:23 God's calamity is ***t*** to me; I couldn't
Psalms
6:2 because my bones are shaking in ***t***!
31:13 the gossiping, ***t*** all around; so
64:1 Protect my life from the enemy's ***t***!
Proverbs
1:27 when ***t*** hits you like a hurricane, and
3:25 Don't fear sudden ***t*** or the ruin that
Isaiah
2:10 the dust from the ***t*** of the LORD, from
2:19 dust before the ***t*** of the LORD and
2:21 cliffs before the ***t*** of the LORD and
14:31 city! Melt in ***t***, all you
17:14 evening, there is ***t***; but before
19:16 will tremble with ***t*** before the hand
24:17 ***T***, trench, and trap are upon you,
24:18 from the sound of ***t*** will fall into
28:19 be nothing but ***t*** to understand the
47:12 to succeed. Maybe you will inspire ***t***.
54:14 fear, far from ***t*** because it won't
Jeremiah
8:15 a time of healing, but found only ***t***.
15:8 I will bring distress and ***t*** upon them.
30:5 screams of panic and ***t***; no one is safe.
48:43 ***T***, traps, and trackers are upon you,
48:44 who flee from ***t*** will fall into a
49:16 The ***t*** you have inflicted on others has
Lamentations
3:47 ***T*** and trap have come upon us,
Ezekiel
23:46 them, and decree ***t*** and plunder for
26:16 clothed only in ***t*** as they sit on
26:17 who spread their ***t*** abroad, every one
27:36 You have become a ***t***; from now on you
28:19 You will become a ***t***. From that time
32:23 sword, who caused ***t*** in the land of
32:24 below, who caused ***t*** in the land of
32:25 for they caused ***t*** in the land of
32:26 for they caused ***t*** in the land of
32:27 their bones. The ***t*** of the mighty men
32:30 in spite of the ***t*** of their
32:32 was I who put his ***t*** in the land of
Mark
16:8 Overcome with ***t*** and dread, they fled

TEST

Exodus
16:4 In this way, I'll ***t*** them to see
20:20 has come only to ***t*** you and to make
Deuteronomy
6:16 Don't ***t*** the LORD your God the way you
8:16 to humble and ***t*** you, but in order
Judges
2:22 As a ***t*** for Israel, to see whether they
3:1 the LORD left to ***t*** all those
3:4 were to be the ***t*** for Israel, to
6:39 just one more ***t*** with the fleece:
1 Kings
10:1 name, she came to ***t*** him with riddles.
2 Chronicles
9:1 to Jerusalem to ***t*** Solomon with
32:31 him in order to ***t*** him and to
Job
7:18 them each morning, ***t*** them every moment?
12:11 Doesn't the ear ***t*** words and the palate
Psalms
26:2 put me to the ***t***! Purify my mind
139:23 Put me to the ***t***! Know my anxious
Isaiah
7:12 I won't ask; I won't ***t*** the LORD."
Jeremiah
9:7 to refine and ***t*** them, for what
Daniel
1:12 Why not ***t*** your servants for ten days?
Zechariah
13:9 silver; I will ***t*** them like one
Malachi
3:10 my house. Please ***t*** me in this, says
3:15 are built up; they ***t*** God and escape."
Matthew
4:7 written, Don't ***t*** the Lord your
16:1 In order to ***t*** him they asked
19:3 him. In order to ***t*** him, they said,

TEST [cont.]

22:18 Why do you **t** me, you

Mark

8:11 with Jesus. To **t** him, they asked
10:2 and, trying to **t** him, they asked,

Luke

4:12 been said, Don't **t** the Lord your
10:25 stood up to **t** Jesus. "Teacher,"

John

6:6 said this to **t** him, for he
8:6 They said this to **t** him, because they
10:24 long will you **t** our patience? If

1 Corinthians

3:13 fire will **t** the quality of
10:9 Let's not **t** Christ, like some of them
11:28 individual should **t** himself or

2 Corinthians

2:9 you. I wanted to **t** you and see if
13:5 are in the faith. ***T*** yourselves. Don't
13:6 will realize that we don't fail the **t**.
13:7 to pass the **t** but so that you

Galatians

6:4 person should **t** their own work

Ephesians

5:10 Therefore **t** everything to see what's

1 Peter

4:12 come among you to **t** you. These are

1 John

4:1 every spirit. ***T*** the spirits to

Revelation

2:10 in order to **t** you. You will
3:10 whole world, to **t** those who live on

TESTED

Genesis

22:1 these events, God **t** Abraham and said

Exodus

15:25 a ruling there, and there he **t** them.
17:7 argued with and **t** the LORD, asking,

Numbers

14:22 the desert, but **t** me these ten

Deuteronomy

33:8 one—the one you **t** at Massah, the

Job

34:36 wish Job would be **t** to the limit

Psalms

66:10 you, God, have **t** us—you've refine
78:18 They **t** God in their hearts, demanded
78:41 time again they **t** God, provoking
78:56 But they **t** and defied the Most High
81:7 of thunder. I **t** you at the waters
95:9 your ancestors **t** me and
106:14 the desert; they **t** God in the
119:140 been tried and **t**; your servant

Ecclesiastes

7:23 I **t** all of this by wisdom. I thought, I

Isaiah

28:16 Zion a stone, a **t** stone, a valuable
48:10 silver; I have **t** you in the

Daniel

1:14 their plan and **t** them for ten days.

Matthew

22:35 One of them, a legal expert, **t** him

1 Corinthians

14:24 in, they are **t** by all and called

2 Corinthians

8:2 they were being **t** by many problems,
8:22 them. We have **t** his commitment in

1 Timothy

3:10 should also be **t** and then serve if

Hebrews

3:8 the day when they **t** me in the desert.
3:9 challenged and **t** me, though they
11:17 Isaac when he was **t**. The one who

James

1:13 No one who is **t** should say, "God is

1 Peter

1:7 it is itself **t** by fire.) Your

Revelation

2:2 evil. You have **t** those who say

TESTIFIED

Ruth

1:21 when the LORD has **t** against me, and

2 Samuel

1:16 your own mouth **t** against you when

1 Kings

21:13 of him. They **t** against Naboth in

John

1:15 John **t** about him, crying out, "This is
1:32 John **t**, "I saw the Spirit coming down
1:34 I have seen and **t** that this one is
3:26 about whom you **t**, is baptizing and
4:39 word when she **t**, "He told me
4:44 (Jesus himself had **t** that prophets
5:33 to John, and he **t** to the truth.
13:21 disturbed and **t**, "I assure you,
19:35 who saw this has **t**, and his

Acts

2:40 other words he **t** to them and
6:13 witnesses who **t**, "This man never
8:25 the apostles had **t** and proclaimed
13:22 their king. God **t** concerning him,
20:21 You know I have **t** to both Jews and
23:11 Just as you have **t** about me in
28:23 he explained and **t** concerning God's

1 Corinthians

15:15 God, because we **t** against God that

1 John

5:9 this is what God **t**: he has testified

TESTIFY

Exodus

20:16 Do not **t** falsely against your neighbor

Numbers

35:30 alone cannot **t** against a person

Deuteronomy

5:20 Do not **t** falsely against your neighbor
19:16 someone, so as to **t** against them

1 Kings

21:10 him and have them **t** as follows: 'You

Psalms

50:7 I will now **t** against you. I am

Proverbs

18:17 first person to **t** seems innocent,
21:28 one who listens will **t** successfully.
25:18 People who **t** falsely against their
29:24 even under oath, they don't **t**.

Isaiah

59:12 our sins **t** against us. Our

Jeremiah

14:7 though our sins **t** against us, help

Lamentations

2:13 What can I **t** about you, Daughter

Malachi
3:5 will be quick to ***t*** against the
Matthew
23:31 You ***t*** against yourselves that you are
Mark
13:9 of me so that you can ***t*** before them.
Luke
11:48 In this way, you ***t*** that you approve of
21:13 provide you with an opportunity to ***t***.
John
1:7 as a witness to ***t*** concerning the
1:8 mission was to ***t*** concerning the
3:11 what we know and ***t*** about what we
3:28 yourselves can ***t*** that I said that
5:31 If I ***t*** about myself, my testimony
5:36 These works I do ***t*** about me that the
5:39 eternal life. They also ***t*** about me,
7:7 though, because I ***t*** that its works
8:14 Even if I ***t*** about myself, my
10:25 I do in my Father's name ***t*** about me,
15:26 from the Father—he will ***t*** about me.
15:27 You will ***t*** too, because you have been
18:23 I speak wrongly, ***t*** about what was
18:37 this reason: to ***t*** to the truth.
Acts
10:42 the people and to ***t*** that he is the
10:43 All the prophets ***t*** about him that
20:24 Lord Jesus: to ***t*** about the good
20:26 today I ***t*** to you that I'm
22:5 Council can ***t*** about me. I
23:11 Jerusalem, so too you must ***t*** in Rome."
26:5 to, they could ***t*** that I followed
1 John
1:2 have seen, and we ***t*** and announce to
4:14 We have seen and ***t*** that the Father has

TESTIMONY → FALSE TESTIMONY
Deuteronomy
17:6 be executed on the basis of only one ***t***.
31:21 them, giving its ***t***, because it won't
Joshua
4:16 containing the ***t*** to come up out of
Psalms
60:1 A ***t***. A miktam of
80:1 A ***t*** of Asaph.
Isaiah
8:16 Bind up the ***t***; seal up the teaching
8:20 and for ***t***"—they will surely
Matthew
8:4 commanded. This will be a ***t*** to them."
10:18 you may give your ***t*** to them and to
19:18 Don't steal. Don't give false ***t***.
24:14 the world as a ***t*** to all the
26:62 to respond to the ***t*** these people have
27:13 you hear the ***t*** they bring
Mark
1:44 commanded. This will be a ***t*** to them."
14:55 were looking for ***t*** against Jesus in
14:60 to respond to the ***t*** these people have
Luke
5:14 instructed. This will be a ***t*** to them."
22:71 we need further ***t***? We've heard it
John
1:19 This is John's ***t*** when the Jewish
3:11 have seen, but you don't receive our ***t***.
3:32 and heard, but no one accepts his ***t***.
3:33 accepts his ***t*** confirms that God
5:31 testify about myself, my ***t*** isn't true.
5:32 me, and I know his ***t*** about me is true.
5:34 accept human ***t***, I say these
5:36 than John's ***t***. The Father has
8:13 about yourself, your ***t*** isn't valid."
8:14 about myself, my ***t*** is true, since I
19:35 and his ***t*** is true. He knows
21:24 them down. We know that his ***t*** is true.
Acts
7:44 The tent of ***t*** was with our ancestors
22:18 they won't accept your ***t*** about me.'
1 Corinthians
1:6 same way that the ***t*** about Christ was
2 Thessalonians
1:10 believed—and our ***t*** to you was
1 Timothy
2:6 free. This was a ***t*** that was given at
2:7 apostle of this ***t***—I'm telling the
2 Timothy
1:8 be ashamed of the ***t*** about the Lord or
Hebrews
10:28 the basis of the ***t*** of two or three
1 John
5:9 we receive human ***t***, God's testimony
5:10 God's Son has the ***t*** within; the one
5:11 And this is the ***t***: God gave eternal

THANK → THANK GOD, THANK THE LORD
2 Samuel
22:50 That's why I ***t*** you, LORD, in the
1 Chronicles
23:30 every morning to ***t*** and praise the
29:13 now, our God, we ***t*** you and praise
2 Chronicles
29:31 sacrificial ***t*** offerings to the
33:16 sacrifices and ***t*** offerings on it,
Psalms
9:1 of David.] I will ***t*** you, LORD, with
18:49 That's why I ***t*** you, LORD, in the
28:7 rejoiced, and I ***t*** him with my song.
30:9 pit? Does dust ***t*** you? Does it
35:18 Then I will ***t*** you in the great
49:18 lives, and even ***t*** you when you deal
67:3 Let the people ***t*** you, God! Let all the
67:5 Let the people ***t*** you, God! Let all the
71:22 a harp—I will ***t*** you for your
99:3 Let them ***t*** your great and awesome name.
100:4 with praise! ***T*** him! Bless his
118:21 I ***t*** you because you answered me,
138:2 holy temple and ***t*** your name for
Isaiah
12:1 on that day: "I ***t*** you, LORD. Though
38:18 underworld can't ***t*** you, nor can
38:19 the living can ***t*** you, as I do
Jeremiah
33:11 those who say, as ***t*** offerings are
Luke
17:9 You won't ***t*** the servant because the
18:11 words, 'God, I ***t*** you that I'm not
John
11:41 said, "Father, ***t*** you for hearing
Romans
1:8 First of all, I ***t*** my God through Jesus
1:21 God as God or ***t*** him. Instead,
Philippians
1:3 I ***t*** my God every time I mention you in

THANK [cont.]

1 Timothy
1:12 I ***t*** Christ Jesus our Lord, who has
Philemon
1:4 Philemon, I ***t*** my God every time I

THANK GOD
Ro 6:17; 7:25; 14:6; 1Co 1:14; 10:30; 14:18; 2Co 1:11; 2:14; 8:16; 9:15; 1Th 1:2; 2:13; 3:9; 2Th 1:3; 2:13

THANK THE LORD
Dt 32:6; 2Ch 5:13; Ps 7:17; 107:8, 15, 21, 31; 111:1; Is 12:4; Ro 14:6

THANKS → GIVE THANKS, GIVING THANKS, THANKS TO GOD, THANKS TO THE LORD, THANKS TO YOUR NAME
Jonah
2:9 with a voice of ***t***. That which I
Matthew
15:36 After he gave ***t***, he broke them
26:27 took a cup, gave ***t***, and gave it to
Mark
8:6 loaves, gave ***t***, broke them
14:23 took a cup, gave ***t***, and gave it to
John
6:11 When he had given ***t***, he distributed
6:23 bread over which the Lord had given ***t***.
Acts
27:35 took bread, gave ***t*** to God in front
28:15 saw them, he gave ***t*** to God and was
Romans
16:4 the only one who ***t*** God for them, but
1 Corinthians
15:57 ***T*** be to God, who gives us this victory
Revelation
4:9 glory, honor, and ***t*** to the one seated
11:17 said, "We give ***t*** to you, Lord God

THANKS TO GOD
Neh 12:46; Ac 27:35; 28:15; Eph 1:16; 5:20; Col 1:3; 3:17

THANKS TO THE LORD
1Ch 16:7; 16:8, 34, 41; 2Ch 7:3; 7:6; 20:21; Ezr 3:11; Ps 33:2; 92:1; 105:1; 106:1; 107:1; 109:30; 118:1, 19, 29; 136:1, 3; Jer 33:11

THANKS TO YOUR NAME
1Ki 8:33; 8:35; 2Ch 6:24; 6:26; Ps 44:8; 54:6; 140:13; 142:7

THANKSGIVING
Leviticus
7:12 offering it for ***t***, you must offer
7:13 with the communal ***t*** sacrifice of well-
22:29 sacrifice of ***t*** for the LORD, you
Nehemiah
11:17 who began the ***t*** with prayer, and
12:8 in charge of the ***t*** songs along with
Psalms
42:4 joyous shouts and ***t*** songs
50:14 a sacrifice of ***t***! Fulfill the
50:23 a sacrifice of ***t*** is the one who
56:12 God. I will present ***t*** offerings to you
107:22 Let them offer ***t*** sacrifices and declare
116:17 a sacrifice of ***t*** to you, and I'll
Jeremiah
17:26 incense, and ***t*** offerings to the
Amos
4:5 Offer a ***t*** sacrifice of leavened bread,
1 Corinthians
14:16 Amen!" to your ***t***, when they don't
14:17 prayer of ***t***, but the other
2 Corinthians
9:11 produces ***t*** to God through us.
9:12 in many expressions of ***t*** to God.
Ephesians
5:4 believers. Instead, there should be ***t***.
Colossians
2:7 and overflow with ***t*** just as you were
4:2 praying and guard your prayers with ***t***.
1 Timothy
2:1 petitions, and ***t*** be made for all
4:3 be accepted with ***t*** by those who are
4:4 is received with ***t*** should be
Revelation
7:12 and wisdom and ***t*** and honor and

THESSALONICA
Acts
17:1 then came to ***T***, where there was
Philippians
4:16 care of my needs even while I was in ***T***.

THIEF
Exodus
22:1 or sells it, the ***t*** must pay back
22:2 If the ***t*** is caught breaking in and is
22:3 For his part, the ***t*** must make good on
22:7 house and the ***t*** is caught, the
22:8 If the ***t*** isn't caught, the owner of the
Job
24:14 and needy; at night, they are like a ***t***.
30:5 society, shout at them as if to a ***t***;
Proverbs
6:30 don't despise a ***t*** if he steals to
Jeremiah
2:26 As a ***t*** is ashamedwhen caught in his
Hosea
7:1 and steal, a ***t*** breaks in; a
Zechariah
5:4 the house of the ***t*** and the one
Matthew
24:43 at what time the ***t*** would come, he
26:55 arrest me, like a ***t***? Day after day, I
Luke
12:33 runs out. No ***t*** comes near there,
12:39 what time the ***t*** was coming, he
22:52 to arrest me, as though I were a ***t***?
John
10:1 over the wall is a ***t*** and an outlaw.
10:10 The ***t*** enters only to steal, kill, and
12:6 because he was a ***t***. He carried the
1 Thessalonians
5:2 is going to come like a ***t*** in the night.
5:4 won't catch you by surprise like a ***t***.
1 Peter
4:15 as a murderer or ***t*** or evildoer or
2 Peter
3:10 will come like a ***t***. On that day the
Revelation
3:3 will come like a ***t***, and you won't
16:15 I'm coming like a ***t***! Favored are

THIGH

Genesis
24:2 he owned, "Put your hand under my ***t***.
24:9 master Abraham's ***t*** and gave him his
32:25 grabbed Jacob's ***t*** and tore a muscle
47:29 hand under my ***t***, and be loyal and
Exodus
29:22 and the right ***t*** (because it is a
29:27 offering and the ***t*** that was raised
Leviticus
7:32 give the right ***t*** of your communal
8:25 and their fat—as well as the right ***t***.
8:26 on the fat pieces and on the right ***t***.
9:21 and the right ***t*** as an uplifted
10:14 offering and the ***t*** for the gift
Numbers
6:20 offering and the ***t*** of the gift
18:18 offering and the right ***t*** are yours.
Judges
3:16 it on his right ***t*** under his clothes.
3:21 from his right ***t***. He stabbed it
1 Samuel
9:24 the cook took the ***t*** and what was on
Song of Songs
3:8 ready at his ***t*** against terrors
Ezekiel
21:12 my people. Therefore, strike your ***t***.
24:4 With shoulder and ***t***, the meatiest
Revelation
19:16 robe and on his ***t***: King of kings

THINK

Genesis
15:5 the stars if you ***t*** you can count
30:2 and said, "Do you ***t*** I'm God? God
31:15 Doesn't he ***t*** of us as foreigners since
39:21 jail's commander to ***t*** highly of Joseph.
43:32 the Egyptians ***t*** it beneath their
46:34 since Egyptians ***t*** all shepherds are
Exodus
14:3 Pharaoh will ***t*** to himself, The
33:12 know you by name and ***t*** highly of you.'
33:13 Now if you do ***t*** highly of me, show me
Leviticus
14:35 the priest, "I ***t*** some sort of
Numbers
22:34 road. Now, if you ***t*** it's wrong, I'll
Deuteronomy
7:17 If you happen to ***t*** to yourself, These
8:17 Don't ***t*** to yourself, My own strength
9:4 before you, don't ***t*** to yourself, It's
12:20 you, and you ***t*** to yourself, I'd
20:19 them down! Do you ***t*** a tree of the
Joshua
8:6 city. They will ***t***, They are fleeing
Judges
9:2 Which do you ***t*** is better to have
15:2 Don't you ***t*** her younger
18:14 buildings? Now ***t*** about what you
19:30 until today? ***T*** about it, decide
20:7 say what you ***t*** should be done
1 Samuel
1:16 Don't ***t*** your servant is some
1:18 Please ***t*** well of me, your servant,"
14:36 Do whatever you ***t*** is best," the
14:40 Do whatever you ***t*** is best," the
15:17 Even if you ***t*** you are
18:23 said, "Do you ***t*** it's a simple
20:30 he said. "Do you ***t*** I don't know how
21:15 me? Do you really ***t*** I'm going to let
24:4 him whatever you ***t*** best.'" So David
25:17 ***T*** about that and see what you can do,
29:9 David. "I ***t*** you're as good as
2 Samuel
4:11 What do you ***t*** I'll do when evil people
13:13 ***T*** about me—where could I hide my
13:32 master shouldn't ***t*** that all the
13:33 my master; don't ***t*** that all the
14:22 knows that you ***t*** well of me, my
16:4 respect! Please ***t*** well of me, my
18:4 do whatever you ***t*** is best." So the
19:37 and king, and treat him as you ***t*** best."
19:38 treat him as I ***t*** best. And I will
2 Kings
18:20 Do you ***t*** that empty words are the same as good strategy
18:25 more, do you ***t*** I've marched
2 Chronicles
25:19 Do you ***t*** that because you've defeated
28:10 And now you ***t*** you can enslave the men
Ezra
7:18 may do what you ***t*** best with the
Esther
4:13 to Esther: "Don't ***t*** for one minute
Job
4:7 ***T***! What innocent person has ever
7:4 If I lie down and ***t***—When will I get
12:24 away the power to ***t*** from earth's
19:15 female servants ***t*** me a stranger;
23:15 his presence; I ***t*** and become afraid
35:2 Do you ***t*** it right? You say, "I'm more
Psalms
4:4 and don't sin! ***T*** hard about it in
8:4 beings that you ***t*** about them; what
10:6 They ***t*** to themselves, We'll never
10:11 The wicked ***t*** to themselves: God has
10:13 God? Why do they ***t*** to themselves
40:17 Let my Lord ***t*** of me. You are my
77:5 I ***t*** about days long past; I remember
119:15 I will ***t*** about your precepts and
119:97 Instruction! I ***t*** about it
119:148 of the night as I ***t*** about your word.
Proverbs
21:29 but the virtuous ***t*** about the path
26:16 Lazy people ***t*** they are wiser than seven
28:11 Rich people ***t*** they are wise, but an
30:12 are those who ***t*** they are clean,
Isaiah
1:11 What should I ***t*** about all your
5:21 wise, who ***t*** of themselves as
33:18 dismay you will ***t***: Where is the one
36:5 Do you ***t*** that empty words are the same
36:10 more, do you ***t*** I've marched
41:22 them, and we'll ***t*** about them and
44:19 He doesn't ***t***, and has no knowledge or
47:7 didn't stop and ***t***; you didn't
49:21 And you will ***t*** to yourself, Who bore me
53:3 despised, and we didn't ***t*** about him.
53:8 fate—who will ***t*** about it? He was
Jeremiah
3:9 She didn't ***t*** twice about corrupting the
31:21 put up signs; ***t*** about the road
44:19 added, "Do you ***t*** that we burn
44:21 Do you really ***t*** the LORD was unaware

THINK [cont.]

Lamentations
3:24 I **t**: The LORD is my portion!
Ezekiel
43:10 guilt when they **t** about its design.
Daniel
4:35 to him, 'What do you **t** you are doing?'
Matthew
3:9 And don't even **t** about saying to
5:17 even begin to **t** that I have come
6:7 Gentiles do. They **t** that by saying
10:34 Don't **t** that I've come to bring peace
17:25 do you **t**, Simon? From whom
18:12 What do you **t**? If someone had one
21:28 What do you **t**? A man had two sons.
22:17 tell us what you **t**: Does the Law
22:42 What do you **t** about the Christ? Whose
26:53 Or do you **t** that I'm not able to ask my
26:66 What do you **t**?" And they answered, "He deserves to die
Mark
12:14 about what people **t**. You don't show
14:64 God. What do you **t**?" They all
Luke
3:8 And don't even **t** about saying to
10:36 What do you **t**? Which one of these
12:51 Do you **t** that I have come to bring
13:2 replied, "Do you **t** the suffering of
13:4 on them? Do you **t** that they were
14:32 And if he didn't **t** he could win, he
John
5:39 since you **t** that in them you
5:45 Don't **t** that I will accuse you before
7:26 leaders actually **t** he is the Christ?
11:56 What do you **t**? He won't come to
16:2 who kill you will **t** that they are
Acts
5:4 What made you **t** of such a thing?
13:25 said, 'Who do you **t** I am? I'm not the
28:19 to Caesar. Don't **t** I appealed to
28:22 But we **t** it's important to hear what
Romans
1:28 Since they didn't **t** it was worthwhile
2:3 things yourself, **t** about this: Do
8:5 on selfishness **t** about selfish
9:20 being. Who do you **t** you are to talk
11:20 So don't **t** in a proud way;
11:25 way you won't **t** too highly of
12:3 one of you: don't **t** of yourself more
12:16 equal, and don't **t** that you're
1 Corinthians
2:2 up my mind not to **t** about anything
3:18 If some of you **t** they are worldly-
4:1 a person should **t** about us this way-
7:26 So I **t** this advice is good because of
7:40 way she is. And I **t** that I have God's
10:12 So those who **t** they are standing need
10:15 sensible people. ***T*** about what I'm
12:22 body that people **t** are the weakest
12:23 the body that we **t** are less
13:11 like a child, **t** like a child. But
14:20 in the way you **t**. Well, be babies
2 Corinthians
10:2 those people who **t** we live by human
10:7 person should **t** again. We belong
10:11 people need to **t** about this—that
12:16 spite of that you **t** I'm a con artist
Galatians
5:10 that you won't **t** any other way.
Philippians
1:7 good reason to **t** this way about
1:18 What do I **t** about this? Just this:
2:3 but with humility **t** of others as
2:25 I **t** it is also necessary to send
3:8 but what I lost I **t** of as sewer
3:13 I myself don't **t** I've reached it,
3:15 mature should **t** this way and if
Colossians
3:2 ***T*** about the things above and not things on earth.
1 Thessalonians
5:13 ***T*** of them highly with love because of
1 Timothy
6:5 the truth. They **t** that godliness is
2 Timothy
2:7 ***T*** about what I'm saying; the Lord will
Hebrews
2:6 humanity that you **t** about them? Or
3:1 heavenly calling, **t** about Jesus, the
10:24 Let's also **t** about how to motivate each
10:29 punishment do you **t** is deserved by
12:3 ***T*** about the one who endured such
James
1:2 and sisters, **t** of the various
3:5 it boasts wildly. ***T*** about this: a
1 Peter
4:4 They **t** it's strange that you don't join
2 Peter
1:13 I **t** it's right that I keep stirring up
3:9 promise, as some **t** of slowness, but

THINKING

Genesis
20:10 What were you **t** when you did this
Job
24:15 for twilight, **t**, No eye can see
Psalms
10:4 no God—that's what they are always **t**.
Matthew
12:25 what they were **t**, he replied,
Ephesians
4:17 They base their lives on pointless **t**,
4:23 Instead renew the **t** in your mind by the
Colossians
2:18 arrogant by their selfish way of **t**.
Hebrews
11:15 If they had been **t** about the country
1 Peter
1:13 and you are **t** clearly, place
4:1 with his way of **t**. This is because

THINKS

Genesis
27:12 touches me and **t** I'm making fun of
Exodus
15:26 God, do what God **t** is right, pay
2 Samuel
15:25 city. If the LORD **t** well of me, then
16:3 king, "because he **t** that the
24:22 king do what he **t** is best. Here are
1 Chronicles
21:23 king do what he **t** is best. I'll
Jeremiah
23:36 because everyone **t** they have

Matthew
21:26 since everyone ***t*** John was a
Romans
8:27 how the Spirit ***t***, because it
14:6 Someone who ***t*** that a day is sacred,
14:14 But if someone ***t*** something is
1 Corinthians
7:36 If someone ***t*** he is acting
8:2 If anyone ***t*** they know something, they
14:37 If anyone ***t*** that they are prophets or
Galatians
6:3 If anyone ***t*** they are important when
Philippians
3:15 way and if anyone ***t*** differently, God
Colossians
2:8 the way the world ***t*** and acts rather
2:20 the way the world ***t*** and acts, why do

THIRD

Genesis
1:13 and there was morning: the ***t*** day.
Leviticus
7:17 sacrifice on the ***t*** day must be
1 Samuel
3:8 A ***t*** time the LORD called Samuel. He got
20:20 On the ***t*** day I will shoot an arrow to
Hosea
6:2 revive us; on the ***t*** day he will raise
Matthew
16:21 to be killed and raised on the ***t*** day.
17:23 be raised on the ***t*** day." And they
20:19 But he will be raised on the ***t*** day."
22:26 brother and the ***t***, and in fact with
26:44 prayed the same words for the ***t*** time.
27:64 sealed until the ***t*** day. Otherwise,
Luke
9:22 be killed and be raised on the ***t*** day."
13:32 and on the ***t*** day I will
18:33 kill him. On the ***t*** day, he will rise
20:12 He sent a ***t*** servant. They wounded this
20:31 and then the ***t*** brother married her.
23:22 For the ***t*** time, Pilate said to them,
24:7 and on the ***t*** day rise again."
24:46 and rise from the dead on the ***t*** day,
John
2:1 On the ***t*** day there was a wedding in
21:14 This was now the ***t*** time Jesus appeared
21:17 He asked a ***t*** time, "Simon son of John,
Acts
10:40 him up on the ***t*** day and allowed
20:9 he fell from the ***t*** floor and died.
27:19 On the ***t*** day, they picked up the ship's
1 Corinthians
12:28 second prophets, ***t*** teachers, then
15:4 he rose on the ***t*** day in line with
2 Corinthians
12:2 up into the ***t*** heaven fourteen
12:14 to visit you a ***t*** time, and I won't
13:1 This is the ***t*** time that I'm coming to
Revelation
4:7 like an ox. The ***t*** living creature
6:5 he opened the ***t*** seal, I heard the
8:7 to the earth. A ***t*** of the earth was
9:15 were released to kill a ***t*** of humankind.
11:14 is over. The ***t*** horror is coming
12:4 tail swept down a ***t*** of heaven's stars
14:9 another angel, a ***t*** one, followed
16:4 The ***t*** angel poured his bowl into the
21:19 was sapphire, the ***t*** was chalcedony,

THIRST

Exodus
17:3 children, and our livestock with ***t***?"
Judges
15:18 going to die of ***t*** and fall into the
2 Chronicles
32:11 by hunger and ***t*** when he says,
Nehemiah
9:20 and you gave them water for their ***t***.
Psalms
69:21 To quench my ***t*** they gave me
104:11 the wild donkeys quench their ***t***.
107:9 was parched with ***t***, and he filled up
Isaiah
5:13 so many of them are dried up with ***t***.
41:17 are parched with ***t***. I, the LORD,
49:10 won't hunger or ***t***; the burning heat
50:2 from lack of water; they die of ***t***.
65:13 but you will ***t***. My servants will
Hosea
2:3 into a dry land, and make her die of ***t***.
Amos
8:11 send hunger and ***t*** on the land;
8:13 and the young men will faint with ***t***.
2 Corinthians
11:27 hunger and ***t***, often without
Revelation
7:16 won't hunger or ***t*** anymore. No sun

THIRSTY

Exodus
17:3 people were very ***t*** for water there,
Judges
4:19 to drink. I'm ***t***." So she opened a
15:18 Samson was very ***t***, so he called out
Ruth
2:9 Whenever you are ***t***, go to the jugs
2 Samuel
17:29 tired, and ***t*** in the
Nehemiah
9:15 when they were ***t***, you brought
Job
5:5 thorns, and the ***t*** pant after their
22:7 water to the ***t***, withheld bread
24:11 tread winepresses, but remain ***t***.
Psalms
107:5 were hungry and ***t***; their lives were
107:33 desert, watery springs into ***t*** ground,
107:35 watery pools, ***t*** ground into
Proverbs
25:21 if they are ***t***, give them water
Isaiah
21:14 meet the ***t*** with water; inhabitants of
29:8 empty. Or when a ***t*** person dreams of
32:6 empty, and depriving the ***t*** of drink.
35:7 a pool, and the ***t*** ground, fountains
44:3 out water upon ***t*** ground and
48:21 They weren't ***t*** when he led them
through the deserts
55:1 of you who are ***t***, come to the
Jeremiah
14:6 panting like ***t*** dogs; they go
Lamentations
4:4 of its mouth, ***t***. Children ask for

Ezekiel
19:13 in the desert, in a parched and ***t*** land,
Amos
4:8 So two or three ***t*** towns went to one
Matthew
5:6 are hungry and ***t*** for
25:35 to eat. I was ***t*** and you gave me a
25:37 and feed you, or ***t*** and give you a
25:42 to eat. I was ***t*** and you didn't
25:44 see you hungry or ***t*** or a stranger or
John
4:13 who drinks this water will be ***t*** again,
4:14 will never be ***t*** again. The water
4:15 I will never be ***t*** and will never
6:35 whoever believes in me will never be ***t***.
7:37 All who are ***t*** should come to me!
19:28 the scripture, Jesus said, "I am ***t***."
Romans
12:20 him; if he is ***t***, give him a
1 Corinthians
4:11 we are hungry, ***t***, wearing rags,
Revelation
21:6 the end. To the ***t*** I will freely
22:17 the one who is ***t*** come! Let the one

THIRTY

Genesis
18:30 me speak. What if ***t*** are there?" The
Leviticus
12:4 For ***t***-three days the mother will be in
27:4 is a female, her value is ***t*** shekels.
Deuteronomy
34:8 Moses' death for ***t*** days. At that
2 Samuel
23:18 was chief of the ***T***. He raised his
Ezra
1:9 was the count: ***t*** gold dishes, one
Proverbs
22:20 I written for you ***t*** sayings full of
Ezekiel
40:17 the way around. ***T*** chambers came up
Daniel
6:7 a law, that for ***t*** days anyone who
Zechariah
5:2 a flying scroll, ***t*** feet long and
11:12 out my wages, ***t*** shekels of silver.
11:13 So I took the ***t*** shekels of silver
Matthew
13:8 in another case a yield of ***t*** to one.
26:15 you?" They paid him ***t*** pieces of silver.

THORNS

Exodus
22:6 and it catches in ***t*** and then spreads
Numbers
33:55 your eyes and be ***t*** in your side.
Joshua
23:13 on your sides and ***t*** in your eyes,
Judges
8:7 your skin with desert ***t*** and briars!"
8:16 of Succoth with desert ***t*** and briars.
2 Samuel
23:6 people are like ***t***, all of them good
Job
5:5 even from the ***t***, and the thirsty
Psalms
58:9 pots feel the ***t***, whether green or
118:12 like burning ***t***. I cut them down
Proverbs
15:19 like a hedge of ***t***, but the way of
22:5 ***T*** and nets are in the path of the
24:31 ***T*** grew all over it; weeds covered the
Isaiah
5:6 or hoed, and ***t*** and thistles will
7:23 there will be ***t*** and thistles in
10:17 and devour its ***t*** and thistles in a
27:4 but if it yields ***t*** and thistles for
32:13 growing barbs and ***t***, for all the
33:12 burned to lime, ***t*** cut up and set
34:13 ***T*** will grow up in its palaces, weeds
Jeremiah
4:3 rocky soil; don't plant among the ***t***.
Ezekiel
2:6 thistles and ***t*** that subdue
Hosea
2:6 her path with ***t***; and I will build
9:6 things of silver; ***t*** will be in their
Nahum
1:10 tangled up like ***t***, like drunkards
Matthew
27:29 a crown of ***t*** and put it on his
Mark
15:17 a crown of ***t*** and put it on him.
Luke
8:7 plants. The ***t*** grew with the
John
19:2 a crown of ***t*** and put it on his
19:5 the crown of ***t*** and the purple
Hebrews
6:8 if it produces ***t*** and thistles,

THOSE WHO DO RIGHT

Nm 23:10; Ps 33:1; 49:14; 107:42; 111:1; 112:2; 140:13; Prv 11:6; 12:6; 14:9, 11; 15:8, 19; 16:17; 21:8; 28:10; Is 26:10; Eze 18:20

THOSE WHO DO THE RIGHT THING

Job 4:7; 17:8; Eze 18:24; 18:26; Mi 7:4

THOSE WHOSE HEART IS RIGHT

Ps 7:10; 11:2, 7; 36:10; 37:37; 97:11

THOUGHT

1 Samuel
1:13 was silent, so Eli ***t*** she was drunk.
1 Kings
12:26 Jeroboam ***t*** to himself, The kingdom is
Job
1:8 Have you ***t*** about my servant
32:1 Job because he ***t*** he was righteous.
34:6 of my cause I'm ***t*** a liar; my wound
Psalms
10:2 in the very same schemes they've ***t*** up!
50:21 kept quiet. You ***t*** I was just like
77:10 my misfortune, I ***t***, that the strong
86:14 me dead. They don't give a ***t*** for you.
Proverbs
14:15 but the prudent give ***t*** to their steps.
Isaiah
29:16 the potter be ***t*** of as clay?
Matthew
9:21 She ***t***, If I only touch his robe I'll
14:5 because they ***t*** John was a
20:10 first came, they ***t*** they would

21:46 the crowds, who *t* he was a prophet.
Mark
6:49 on the lake, they *t* he was a ghost
11:32 because they all *t* John was a
Luke
12:18 Then he *t*, Here's what I'll do. I'll
19:11 and they *t* God's kingdom
24:37 and afraid. They *t* they were seeing
John
11:13 They *t* Jesus meant that Lazarus was in
13:29 Some *t* that, since Judas kept the money

THOUGHTS

Psalms
28:3 while evil *t* are in their
56:5 all their *t* are evil against
92:5 your works, LORD! Your *t* are so deep!
94:11 indeed know human *t*, knows that they are nothing
139:23 Put me to the test! Know my anxious *t*!
Ezekiel
38:10 On that day, *t* will come into
Daniel
2:30 you might know the *t* of your own mind.
4:5 dream. My *t* while I was lying
7:28 about this: My *t* disturbed me
Matthew
15:19 heart come evil *t*, murders,
16:23 thinking God's *t* but human
Mark
7:21 heart, that evil *t* come: sexual
8:33 thinking God's *t* but human
Luke
1:51 with arrogant *t* and proud
2:35 so that the inner *t* of many will be
6:8 Jesus knew their *t*, so he said to the
9:47 of their deepest *t*, Jesus took a
Acts
1:24 deepest *t* and desires. Show
7:39 and, in their *t* and desires,
7:51 people! In your *t* and hearing, you
15:8 people's deepest *t* and desires,
15:9 their deepest *t* and desires
Romans
2:15 Their conflicting *t* will accuse them,
1 Corinthians
3:20 knows that the *t* of the wise are
Philippians
3:19 because their *t* focus on earthly
4:8 focus your *t* on these things:
Hebrews
4:12 to judge the heart's *t* and intentions.

THOUSAND

Genesis
20:16 your brother one *t* pieces of silver.
24:60 thousands of ten *t*; may your
Exodus
34:7 loyalty to a *t* generations,
Deuteronomy
1:11 multiply you—a *t* times more! And
Joshua
23:10 one of you puts a *t* to flight. This
Judges
15:16 jawbone, I've killed one *t* men."
Job
1:3 and owned seven *t* sheep, three thousand
9:3 with him, he won't answer one in a *t*.
15:5 your sins a *t* times; you opt
33:23 one out of a *t* to declare one's
42:12 He had fourteen *t* sheep, six
Psalms
50:10 to me, as do the cattle on a *t* hills.
60:1 killing twelve *t* in the Salt
68:17 are twice ten *t*—countless
84:10 courtyards than a *t* days anywhere
90:4 perspective a *t* years are like
91:7 Even if one *t* people fall dead next to
105:8 word he commanded to a *t* generations,
Song of Songs
4:4 built! A *t* shields are hung
5:10 and ruddy; he stands out among ten *t*!
8:11 for its fruit a *t* pieces of silver.
8:12 You can have the *t*, Solomon
Matthew
14:21 About five *t* men plus women and
15:38 Four *t* men ate, plus women and
16:9 that fed the five *t* and how many
18:24 who owed him ten *t* bags of gold.
Mark
5:13 herd of about two *t* pigs rushed down
John
6:10 They sat down, about five *t* of them.
Acts
4:4 and their number grew to about five *t*.
21:38 and led four *t* terrorists into
1 Corinthians
4:15 You may have ten *t* mentors in Christ,
10:8 and twenty-three *t* died in one day.
2 Peter
3:8 day is like a *t* years and a
Revelation
7:4 forty-four *t*, sealed from
20:2 and Satan, and bound him for a *t* years.
20:7 When the *t* years are over, Satan will

THOUSANDS

1 Samuel
18:7 has killed his *t*, but David has
21:11 has killed his *t*, but David has
Psalms
3:6 be afraid of *t* of people
68:17 countless *t*! My Lord came
119:72 me is better than *t* of pieces of gold
144:13 can be in the *t*—even tens of
Jeremiah
32:18 with mercy toward *t* upon thousands,
Daniel
7:10 his presence; *t* upon thousands
11:12 will kill tens of *t*, but he will not
11:41 and tens of *t* will die. But
Micah
6:7 be pleased with *t* of rams, with
Luke
12:1 When a crowd of *t* upon thousands had
Acts
21:20 you see how many *t* of Jews have
1 Corinthians
14:19 mind than speak *t* of words in a
Revelation
5:11 in the millions—*t* upon *t*.

THREE

Genesis
6:10 Noah had ***t*** sons: Shem, Ham, and
18:2 and suddenly saw ***t*** men standing near
40:13 After ***t*** days, Pharaoh will give you an
40:16 dream, there were ***t*** baskets of white
42:17 He put them all in prison for ***t*** days
Exodus
23:14 a festival for me ***t*** times a year.
Deuteronomy
4:41 Moses set aside ***t*** cities on the
16:16 ***T*** times a year every male among you
19:15 must stand by two or ***t*** witnesses.
Job
2:11 When Job's ***t*** friends heard about all
Psalms
80:5 given them tears to drink ***t*** times over!
Proverbs
30:15 give!" There are ***t*** things that are
30:18 ***T*** things are too wonderful for me, four
30:21 At ***t*** things the earth trembles, at four
30:29 There are ***t*** things that are excellent
Ecclesiastes
4:12 up resistance. A ***t***-ply cord doesn't e
Daniel
3:24 Didn't we throw ***t*** men, bound, into
7:5 one side. It had ***t*** ribs in its mouth
Amos
1:3 proclaims: For ***t*** crimes of
Jonah
1:17 of the fish for ***t*** days and three
Zechariah
11:8 I removed ***t*** shepherds in one month when I grew impatient
Matthew
12:40 whale's belly for ***t*** days and three
15:32 been with me for ***t*** days and have
17:4 want, I'll make ***t*** shrines: one for
18:16 by the mouth of two or ***t*** witnesses.
18:20 For where two or ***t*** are gathered in my
20:5 noon and then at ***t*** in the afternoon,
26:34 tonight, you will deny me ***t*** times."
26:61 temple and rebuild it in ***t*** days.'"
26:75 you will deny me ***t*** times." And Peter
27:40 and rebuild it in ***t*** days, were you?
27:45 From noon until ***t*** in the afternoon the
27:46 At about ***t*** Jesus cried out with a loud
27:63 he said, 'After ***t*** days I will
Mark
8:31 and then, after ***t*** days, rise from
14:30 crows twice, you will deny me ***t*** times."
John
2:19 temple and in ***t*** days I'll raise
13:38 you will deny me ***t*** times before the
Acts
3:1 to the temple at ***t*** o'clock in the
1 Corinthians
13:13 remain—these ***t*** things—and
14:27 two or at most ***t*** speak, one at a
2 Corinthians
11:25 beaten with rods ***t*** times. I was
12:8 with the Lord ***t*** times for it to
13:1 on the evidence of two or ***t*** witnesses.
1 John
5:7 The ***t*** are testifying
Revelation
16:13 Then I saw ***t*** unclean spirits, like
16:19 city split into ***t*** parts, and the
21:13 There were ***t*** gates on the east, three

THRESHING

Genesis
50:10 arrived at the ***t*** floor of Atad on
50:11 grief on Atad's ***t*** floor, they said,
Leviticus
26:5 Your ***t*** season will last until the grape
Numbers
15:20 a gift offering from the ***t*** floor.
18:27 the grain of the ***t*** floor and what
Deuteronomy
25:4 Don't muzzle an ox while it is ***t*** grain
Judges
6:11 son Gideon was ***t*** wheat in a
6:37 fleece on the ***t*** floor. If there
Ruth
3:2 be winnowing barley at the ***t*** floor.
1 Samuel
19:22 the well at the ***t*** floor that was on
23:1 Keilah and looting the ***t*** floors!"
2 Samuel
6:6 Nacon's ***t*** floor, Uzzah
24:16 was by the ***t*** floor of Araunah
1 Kings
22:10 robes at the ***t*** floor beside the
2 Kings
6:27 for you? From the ***t*** floor or the
1 Chronicles
13:9 came to Chidon's ***t*** floor, Uzzah
21:15 standing near the ***t*** floor of Ornan
2 Chronicles
3:1 prepared at the ***t*** floor of Ornan
18:9 robes at the ***t*** floor beside the
Job
39:12 your grain to gather into your ***t*** floor?
Isaiah
21:10 threshed on my ***t*** floor, what I
28:27 threshed with a ***t*** sledge, nor is a
41:15 you into a new ***t*** tool with sharp
Daniel
2:35 left on summer ***t*** floors. The wind
Hosea
9:1 pay on all ***t*** floors of grain.
9:2 ***T*** floor and wine vat won't feed them;
13:3 swirl from the ***t*** floor, or like
Joel
2:24 The ***t*** floors will be full of grain; the
Micah
4:12 bring them like grain to the ***t*** floor!
Matthew
3:12 clean out his ***t*** area and bring
Luke
3:17 clean out his ***t*** area and bring
1 Corinthians
9:9 the ox when it is ***t***. Is God worried

THRONE → GOD'S THRONE

Exodus
11:5 who sits on his ***t*** to the oldest
12:29 sitting on his ***t*** to the oldest
Deuteronomy
17:18 sits on his royal ***t***, he himself must
2 Samuel
3:10 securing David's ***t*** over Israel and
7:13 I will establish his royal ***t*** forever.

1 Chronicles
17:12 and I will establish his ***t*** forever.
29:23 sat on the LORD's ***t*** as king,
Esther
1:2 from his royal ***t*** in the fortified
5:1 on his royal ***t*** and facing the
Psalms
9:4 you rule from the ***t***, establishing
9:7 He assumes his ***t*** for the sake of
11:4 The LORD! His ***t*** is in heaven. His
45:6 Your divine ***t*** is eternal and
47:8 the nations. God sits on his holy ***t***.
89:4 build up your ***t*** from one
93:2 Your ***t*** is set firm for a very long
97:2 surround God. His ***t*** is built on
103:19 established his ***t*** in heaven, and
132:11 put one of your own children on your ***t***.
Proverbs
20:8 on his judgment ***t*** sifts out all
20:28 king; he supports his ***t*** by kindness.
25:5 presence, and his ***t*** will be
29:14 honestly, his ***t*** will be
Isaiah
6:1 high and exalted ***t***, the edges of his
66:1 Heaven is my ***t***, and earth is my
Jeremiah
33:21 have a descendant to rule on his ***t***.
Lamentations
5:19 forever; your ***t*** lasts from one
Ezekiel
1:26 in the form of a ***t***. Above the form
Daniel
5:20 off his royal ***t*** and the glory was
7:9 lamb's wool. His ***t*** was made of
Jonah
3:6 got up from his ***t***, stripped himself
Zechariah
6:13 and rule on his ***t***. There will be a
Matthew
19:28 his magnificent ***t***, you also will
25:31 him, he will sit on his majestic ***t***.
Luke
1:32 will give him the ***t*** of David his
Acts
7:49 Heaven is my ***t***, and the earth is my
Hebrews
1:8 Son, God, your ***t*** is forever and
4:16 draw near to the ***t*** of favor with
8:1 right side of the ***t*** of the majesty in
Revelation
2:13 where Satan's ***t*** is. You are
3:21 sit with me on my ***t***, just as I
4:2 and I saw a ***t*** in heaven, and
4:10 one seated on the ***t***. They worship the
5:13 one seated on the ***t*** and to the Lamb
20:11 saw a great white ***t*** and the one who
22:1 flowing from the ***t*** of God and the
22:3 be any curse. The ***t*** of God and the

THRONES

1 Kings
22:10 sitting on their ***t***, dressed in their
2 Chronicles
18:9 sitting on their ***t*** dressed in their
Job
36:7 he seats kings on ***t*** forever, and they
Psalms
122:5 because the ***t*** of justice are there—
Proverbs
16:12 deeds, for their ***t*** are founded on
Isaiah
14:9 kings of the nations rise from their ***t***.
Ezekiel
26:16 down from their ***t***, remove their
Daniel
7:9 I was watching, ***t*** were raised up.
Haggai
2:22 overthrow the ***t*** of the kingdoms;
Matthew
19:28 sit on twelve ***t*** overseeing the
Luke
1:52 down from their ***t*** and lifted up the
22:30 you will sit on ***t*** overseeing the
Colossians
1:16 Whether they are ***t*** or powers, or
Revelation
4:4 Twenty-four ***t***, with twenty-four elders
11:16 seated on their ***t*** before God, fell
20:4 Then I saw ***t***, and people took their

THROUGH CHRIST

Ro 2:16; 1Co 4:10; 2Co 1:5; 2:14, 17; 3:4; 5:18, 19; Ga 3:14; Eph 2:18; 3:11; 1Pt 1:21

THROUGH FAITH

Ac 15:9; Ro 3:30; 4:16; Ga 3:14; 3:26; Eph 3:12; 3:17; Col 2:12; 2Ti 3:15; Heb 6:12; 11:4, 33; Jas 2:24

THROUGH JESUS

Jn 1:17; Ac 3:16; 10:36; 13:38, 39; Ro 1:8; 5:21; 7:25; 16:27; Ga 1:1; Eph 1:5; Ti 3:6; Heb 13:21; 1Pt 2:5; 4:11; Jud 1:25

THROUGH JESUS CHRIST

Jn 1:17; Ac 10:36; Ro 1:8; 5:21; 7:25; 16:27; Ga 1:1; Eph 1:5; Ti 3:6; Heb 13:21; 1Pt 2:5; 4:11; Jud 1:25

THROUGH OUR LORD JESUS

Ro 5:1; 5:11; 15:30; 1Co 15:57; 1Th 5:9

THROUGH THE SPIRIT

1Co 2:10; Ga 5:5; Eph 2:22; 3:5, 16

THROW OUT DEMONS

Mt 10:8; 12:27, 28; Mk 3:15; 16:17; Lk 11:18; 11:19, 20

THROWN

2 Samuel
20:21 His head will be ***t*** over the wall to
1 Kings
13:24 him. His body was ***t*** down on the road.
Nehemiah
4:5 sight. They have ***t*** insults at the
Psalms
22:10 I was ***t*** on you from birth; you've been
37:24 up, they won't be ***t*** down, because the
89:39 servant. You've ***t*** his crown in the
89:44 splendor. You've ***t*** his throne to the
Proverbs
14:32 The wicked are ***t*** down by their own

THROWN [cont.]

Isaiah
25:12 walls will be ***t*** down, will be
26:5 He has ***t*** down those living on high, and he will level
Jeremiah
14:16 to will be ***t*** into the streets
26:23 and his body was ***t*** into the common
38:7 that they had ***t*** Jeremiah into the
38:9 have; they have ***t*** him into the
Ezekiel
16:5 of your birth and ***t*** out on the open
19:12 down in anger, ***t*** down to the
38:20 Mountains will be ***t*** down and cliffs
Daniel
3:6 be immediately ***t*** into a furnace of
6:7 Majesty, will be ***t*** into a pit of
Joel
1:7 their bark and ***t*** it down; their
Amos
8:3 be many corpses, ***t*** about everywhere.
Matthew
5:29 that your whole body be ***t*** into hell.
6:30 and tomorrow it's ***t*** into the furnace,
7:19 is chopped down and ***t*** into the fire.
8:12 kingdom will be ***t*** outside into the
9:33 When Jesus had ***t*** out the demon, the man
11:23 No, you will be ***t*** down to the place
18:8 lame than to be ***t*** into the eternal
21:21 Be lifted up and ***t*** into the lake.'
Mark
9:22 It has often ***t*** him into a fire or into
9:45 lame than to be ***t*** into hell with
11:23 Be lifted up and ***t*** into the sea'—and
Luke
8:2 whom seven demons had been ***t*** out),
12:28 and tomorrow it's ***t*** into the furnace,
13:28 but you yourselves will be ***t*** out.
17:2 for them to be ***t*** into a lake with
23:19 (Barabbas had been ***t*** into prison
23:25 for, who had been ***t*** into prison
John
3:24 John hadn't yet been ***t*** into prison.
12:31 Now this world' ruler will be ***t*** out.
15:6 a branch that is ***t*** out and dries up.
Revelation
8:7 appeared, and was ***t*** down to the
12:9 great dragon was ***t*** down. The old
18:21 Babylon will be ***t*** down, and it
19:20 two of them were ***t*** alive into the
20:15 of life was ***t*** into the fiery

THUMMIM

Exodus
28:30 the Urim and the ***T***, so they will be
Leviticus
8:8 set the Urim and ***T*** into the chest
Deuteronomy
33:8 Levi: "Give your ***T*** to Levi, your
1 Samuel
14:41 respond with ***T***." Jonathan and
Ezra
2:63 arose who could consult Urim and ***T***.
Nehemiah
7:65 arose who could consult Urim and ***T***.

THUNDER

Exodus
9:23 and the LORD sent ***t*** and hail, and
19:16 day, there was ***t***, lightning, and a
19:19 speak, and God would answer him with ***t***.
20:18 witnessed the ***t*** and lightning,
1 Samuel
12:17 the LORD to send ***t*** and rain. Then
12:18 and God sent ***t*** and rain on that
Job
36:29 cloud and the ***t*** of his pavilion,
36:33 His ***t*** announces it; even cattle
38:25 the downpours and a way for blasts of ***t***
40:9 like God; can you ***t*** with a voice like
Psalms
77:17 the skies cracked ***t***; your arrows were
77:18 The crash of your ***t*** was in the swirling
81:7 in the secret of ***t***. I tested you at
104:7 fled in fear at the sound of your ***t***.
Isaiah
17:12 seas they ***t***. Doom to the roar
29:6 come to you with ***t***, earthquake, and
Mark
3:17 Boanerges, which means "sons of ***T***";
John
12:29 and said, "It's ***t***." Others said,
Revelation
4:5 voices, and ***t***. In front of the
6:1 say in a voice like ***t***, "Come!"
8:5 and there were ***t***, voices,
11:19 voices, ***t***, an earthquake,
14:2 water and loud ***t***. The sound I
16:18 voices, and ***t***, and a great
19:6 and powerful ***t***. They said,

THYATIRA

Acts
16:14 from the city of ***T***, a dealer in
Revelation
2:18 of the church in ***T***: These are the

TIED

Joshua
2:21 off. Then she ***t*** the red cord in
Esther
1:6 red-purple ropes ***t*** to silver rings
Job
36:8 If they are ***t*** with ropes, caught in
Ezekiel
27:24 up and securely ***t*** with ropes, among
Matthew
21:2 find a donkey ***t*** up and a colt
John
11:44 and his hands ***t***, and his face
13:4 a linen towel, he ***t*** it around his
21:18 were younger you ***t*** your own belt and
Acts
21:11 took Paul's belt, ***t*** his own feet and
1 Corinthians
7:15 or sister isn't ***t*** down in these
2 Corinthians
6:14 Don't be ***t*** up as equal partners with

TIGLATH-PILESER

2 Kings
15:19 Assyria's King ***T*** marched against

2 Chronicles
28:20 Assyria's King ***T*** came to Ahaz, but he

TIME

Genesis
4:26 Enosh. At that ***t***, people began to
Numbers
15:23 of the LORD's command onward for all ***t***,
Joshua
6:3 the city one ***t***. Do this for six
6:16 The seventh ***t***, the priests blew the
Esther
4:14 very important ***t***, relief and
9:31 at the proper ***t***, following the
Psalms
1:3 at just the right ***t*** and whose leaves
69:13 at just the right ***t***. God, in your
78:41 ***T*** and time again they tested God,
89:29 dynasty for all ***t***. His throne will
119:126 It is ***t*** for the LORD to do something!
Proverbs
3:2 you live a long ***t*** and provide you
5:19 you all the ***t***; always be drunk
6:14 they create controversies all the ***t***.
6:21 heart for all ***t***; fasten them
8:30 fun, smiling before him all the ***t***,
15:23 joy; how good is a word at the right ***t***!
17:17 love all the ***t***, and kinsfolk are
25:11 at the right ***t*** are like gold
25:17 spend too much ***t*** in your
25:19 at a difficult ***t*** is like having a
29:3 one who spends ***t*** with prostitutes
Ecclesiastes
3:1 everything and a ***t*** for every matter
7:17 a fool, or you may die before your ***t***.
8:5 knows the right ***t*** and the right way
9:12 know when their ***t*** will come. Like
10:17 at the right ***t*** for energy, not
11:1 in the course of ***t***, you may find it
Daniel
7:25 for a period of ***t***, periods of time,
11:27 because the end will come at the set ***t***.
12:9 secret and sealed up until the end ***t***.
Hosea
10:12 ground, for it is ***t*** to seek the LORD,
13:13 not aware of the ***t*** to be born; for
Joel
3:1 days and in that ***t***, I will bring
Micah
2:3 arrogantly, for it will be an evil ***t***.
Habakkuk
2:3 for the appointed ***t***; it testifies to
3:2 your work. Over ***t***, revive it. Over
Zephaniah
1:12 At that ***t***, I will search Jerusalem
Zechariah
4:10 who despise a ***t*** of little things
10:1 rain when it is ***t*** for the spring
14:7 but at evening ***t*** there will be
Malachi
3:7 Ever since the ***t*** of your ancestors, you
Matthew
8:29 torture us before the ***t*** of judgment?"
24:29 suffering of that ***t*** the sun will
24:37 As it was in the ***t*** of Noah, so it will
24:40 At that ***t*** there will be two men in the
24:43 knew at what ***t*** the thief would
26:18 teacher says, "My ***t*** is near. I'm
26:45 night? Look, the ***t*** has come for the
Mark
6:21 Finally, the ***t*** was right. It was on one
13:33 You don't know when the ***t*** is coming.
Luke
1:20 at the proper ***t***. But because you
4:25 during Elijah's ***t***, when it didn't
12:39 had known what ***t*** the thief was
12:40 is coming at a ***t*** when you don't
12:56 know how to interpret the present ***t***?
22:53 But this is your ***t***, when darkness
23:29 The ***t*** will come when they will say,
John
2:4 to do with me? My ***t*** hasn't come yet."
3:4 womb for a second ***t*** and be born,
4:23 But the ***t*** is coming—and is here!—when true worshippers
7:6 is fine. But my ***t*** hasn't come yet.
12:31 Now is the ***t*** for judgment of this
21:17 He asked a third ***t***, "Simon son of
Romans
1:3 his Son ahead of ***t*** through his
3:26 during the ***t*** of God's patient
11:5 in the present ***t*** there is a
13:11 you know what ***t*** it is. The hour
1 Corinthians
4:5 before the right ***t***—wait until the
7:29 and sisters: the ***t*** has drawn short.
2 Corinthians
6:2 you at the right ***t***, and I helped you
13:1 This is the third ***t*** that I'm coming to
Galatians
4:4 of the ***t*** came, God sent
2 Timothy
1:9 gave us in Christ Jesus before ***t*** began.
4:3 There will come a ***t*** when people will
4:6 to God, and the ***t*** of my death is
Hebrews
7:3 Son and remains a priest for all ***t***.
9:9 for the present ***t***. It shows that
10:14 made holy with one offering for all ***t***.
11:32 would run out of ***t*** if I told you
1 Peter
1:5 he is ready to reveal in the last ***t***.
1:20 at the end of ***t***. This was done
3:20 waited during the ***t*** of Noah. Noah
4:17 because it's ***t*** for judgment to begin
2 Peter
3:6 the world of that ***t*** was flooded and
Jude
1:25 before all ***t***, now and forever.
Revelation
1:3 is written in it, for the ***t*** is near.
2:21 I gave her ***t*** to change her heart and
12:14 reach—for a ***t*** and times and
22:10 in this scroll, because the ***t*** is near.

TIMOTHY

Acts
16:1 a disciple named ***T***. He was the son
Romans
16:21 ***T*** my coworker says hello to you, and

1 Corinthians
4:17 is why I've sent ***T*** to you; he's my
2 Corinthians
1:1 God's will, and ***T*** our brother. To
Philippians
2:19 Jesus to send ***T*** to see you soon
Colossians
1:1 Jesus by God's will, and ***T*** our brother.
1 Thessalonians
3:5 That's why I sent ***T*** to find out about
2 Thessalonians
1:1 Silvanus, and ***T***: To the church of
1 Timothy
1:2 To ***T***, my true child in the faith.
1:18 ***T***, my child, I'm giving you these
6:20 ***T***, protect what has been given to you
2 Timothy
1:2 To ***T***, my dear child. Grace, mercy, and
Philemon
1:1 and our brother ***T***. To Philemon our
Hebrews
13:23 that our brother ***T*** has been set

TIRED

Exodus
17:12 Moses' hands grew ***t***. So they took a
Deuteronomy
25:18 you were weak and ***t***, and because he
2 Samuel
17:2 him while he is ***t*** and weak, and I
17:29 grown hungry, ***t***, and thirsty in
21:15 the Philistines. When David grew ***t***,
Job
31:16 the poor wanted, made a widow's eyes ***t***,
Psalms
63:1 you in a dry and ***t*** land, no water
69:3 I am ***t*** of crying. My throat is hoarse.
77:3 complain, and my spirit grows ***t***. Selah
88:9 My eyes are ***t*** of looking at my
Proverbs
26:15 the bowl, too ***t*** to return it to
30:1 man declares: I'm ***t***, God; I'm tired,
Isaiah
1:14 become a burden that I'm ***t*** of bearing.
5:27 Not one is ***t***; not one stumbles; they
40:28 He doesn't grow ***t*** or weary. His
40:29 power to the ***t*** and reviving the
40:30 will become ***t*** and weary, young
40:31 run and not be ***t***; they will walk
43:22 to me, Jacob; you were ***t*** of me, Israel.
57:10 new strength; therefore, you weren't ***t***.
Jeremiah
6:11 rage and am ***t*** of holding it in.
15:6 and destroy you. I'm ***t*** of holding back.
48:45 In Heshbon ***t*** refugees seek shelter. But
Habakkuk
2:13 fire; nations become ***t*** for nothing.
Malachi
2:17 made the LORD ***t*** with your words.
John
4:6 there. Jesus was ***t*** from his journey,
Galatians
6:9 Let's not get ***t*** of doing good, because
Revelation
2:3 name's sake, and you haven't gotten ***t***.

TIRZAH

1 Kings
15:33 He ruled in ***T*** for twenty-four ye

TITUS

2 Corinthians
2:13 find my brother ***T*** there. So I said
8:23 question about ***T***, he is my partner
Galatians
2:1 with Barnabas, and I took ***T*** along also.
2 Timothy
4:10 to Galatia, and ***T*** has gone to
Titus
1:4 To ***T***, my true child in a common faith.

TOBIAH

Ezra
2:60 family of Delaiah, ***T***, and Nekoda, 652
Nehemiah
2:10 the Horonite and ***T*** the Ammonite

TODAY

Deuteronomy
2:18 ***T*** you are crossing through the
30:15 Look here! ***T*** I've set before you life
Joshua
24:15 LORD, then choose ***t*** whom you will
Psalms
2:7 You are my son, ***t*** I have become
Proverbs
7:14 of well-being; ***t*** I fulfilled my
22:19 the LORD, I'm teaching you ***t***—yes, you.
Isaiah
37:3 says this: ***T*** is a day of
Matthew
6:11 Give us the bread we need for ***t***
6:30 though it's alive ***t*** and tomorrow it's
11:23 in Sodom, it would still be here ***t***.
16:3 be bad weather ***t*** because the sky
21:28 Son, go and work in the vineyard ***t***.'
27:19 suffered much ***t*** in a dream
Luke
2:11 savior is born ***t*** in David's city.
4:21 explain to them, "***T***, this scripture
13:32 healing people ***t*** and tomorrow, and
19:9 said to him, "***T***, salvation has
22:61 a rooster crows ***t***, you will deny me
23:43 assure you that ***t*** you will be with
2 Corinthians
3:15 Even ***t***, whenever Moses is read, a veil
Hebrews
13:8 is the same yesterday, ***t***, and forever!
James
4:13 you who say, "***T*** or tomorrow we
1 Peter
2:12 the unbelievers. ***T***, they defame you,

TOMB

Genesis
35:20 on Rachel's ***t*** that's still
50:5 bury me in the ***t*** I dug for myself
Judges
8:32 was buried in the ***t*** of his father
16:31 Eshtaol in the ***t*** of his father
1 Samuel
10:2 men near Rachel's ***t*** at Zelzah on the

2 Samuel
2:32 in his father's ***t*** in Bethlehem.
17:23 died. He was buried in his father's ***t***.
21:14 territory, in the ***t*** of Saul's father
1 Kings
14:13 alone will have a ***t***, because only in
2 Kings
9:28 was buried in his ***t*** with his
13:21 into Elisha's ***t*** and ran off. When
21:26 was buried in his ***t*** in the Uzza
23:16 and saw the ***t*** of the man of God
23:17 replied, "That ***t*** belongs to the
23:30 him in his own ***t***. The people of
2 Chronicles
16:14 was buried in the ***t*** he had prepared
Isaiah
14:18 all of them, each in his own ***t***.
22:16 have hewed out a ***t*** for yourself, you
53:9 the wicked, his ***t*** with evildoers,
Matthew
27:60 it in his own new ***t***, which he had
28:1 the other Mary came to look at the ***t***.
28:8 away from the ***t*** and ran to tell
Mark
6:29 took his dead body and laid it in a ***t***.
16:5 Going into the ***t***, they saw a young man
Luke
23:53 and laid it in a ***t*** carved out of the
24:1 women went to the ***t***, bringing the
24:24 us went to the ***t*** and found things
John
11:17 already been in the ***t*** for four days.
12:17 out of the ***t*** and raised him
19:41 garden was a new ***t*** in which no one
19:42 Day and the ***t*** was nearby, they
20:1 came to the ***t*** and saw that the
20:11 outside near the ***t***, crying. As she
Acts
2:29 buried, and his ***t*** is with us to
7:16 and placed in the ***t*** that Abraham had
13:29 from the cross and laid him in a ***t***.
Revelation
11:9 let their dead bodies be put in a ***t***.

TOMORROW

Proverbs
3:28 give it to you ***t***," when you have
27:1 Don't brag about ***t***, for you don't know
Isaiah
22:13 wine: "Eat and drink! ***T*** we will die!"
56:12 Let's drink beer! ***T*** will be like
Matthew
6:30 alive today and ***t*** it's thrown into
6:34 worrying about ***t***, because tomorrow
Luke
12:28 alive today and ***t*** it's thrown into
13:32 people today and ***t***, and on the third
13:33 to travel today, ***t***, and the next day
Acts
23:20 to the council ***t***. They will
25:22 the man myself." "***T***," Festus replied,
1 Corinthians
15:32 eat and drink because ***t*** we'll die.
James
4:13 say, "Today or ***t*** we will go to
4:14 really know about ***t***. What is your

TONGUE

Exodus
4:10 I have a slow mouth and a thick ***t***."
2 Samuel
23:2 speaks through me; his word is on my ***t***.
Job
6:30 there wrong on my ***t***, or can my mouth
15:5 thousand times; you opt for a clever ***t***.
20:16 cobra's poison; a viper's ***t*** kills them.
27:4 no wickedness; my ***t*** will mumble no
29:10 hushed, their ***t*** stuck to their
33:2 my mouth; my ***t*** is speaking in my
41:1 a hook, restrain his ***t*** with a rope?
Psalms
12:3 lips and every ***t*** that brags and
22:15 pottery. My ***t*** sticks to the
34:13 must keep your ***t*** from evil and
35:28 Then my ***t*** will talk all about your
39:1 to sin with my ***t***; promised to keep
39:3 burned. Then I spoke out with my ***t***:
45:1 to the king. My ***t*** is the pen of a
50:19 evil, then harness your ***t*** to tell lies.
51:14 so that my ***t*** can sing of your
52:2 Your ***t*** devises destruction: it's like a
52:4 words; you love the deceiving ***t***.
66:17 cried out to him with praise on my ***t***.
71:24 My ***t***, also, will tell of your
119:172 Let my ***t*** declare your word because all your commandments
120:2 me from lying lips and a dishonest ***t***!"
120:3 will be done to you, you dishonest ***t***?
137:6 Let my ***t*** stick to the roof of my mouth
139:4 a word on my ***t***, LORD, that you
Proverbs
5:3 honey, and her ***t*** is smoother than
6:17 eyes, a lying ***t***, hands that spill
6:24 the flattering ***t*** of the foreign
10:20 The ***t*** of the righteous is choice
10:31 but the twisted ***t*** will be cut off.
12:18 a stabbing sword, but a wise ***t*** heals.
12:19 but a lying ***t*** lasts only for a
15:2 The ***t*** of the wise enhances knowledge,
16:1 the answer of the ***t*** comes from the
17:4 a liar listens to a destructive ***t***.
18:21 the power of the ***t***; those who love
25:15 and a tender ***t*** can break a bone.
26:28 A lying ***t*** hates those it crushes; a
31:26 of wisdom; kindly teaching is on her ***t***.
Song of Songs
4:11 are under your ***t***, and the
Isaiah
5:24 Therefore, as a ***t*** of fire devours
11:15 will split the ***t*** of the Egyptian
28:11 and a foreign ***t***, he will speak to
30:27 full of fury; his ***t*** is like a
35:6 the deer, and the ***t*** of the speechless
45:23 knee will bow and every ***t*** will confess;
50:4 me an educated ***t*** to know how to
54:17 may condemn every ***t*** that disputes
57:4 stick out your ***t***? Aren't you
Jeremiah
9:8 Their ***t*** is a lethal arrow; their words
Lamentations
4:4 The baby's ***t*** sticks to the roof of its
Ezekiel
3:26 I'll make your ***t*** stick to the roof of

Zephaniah
3:13 lies; a deceitful **t** won't be found on
Mark
7:33 Then he spit and touched the man's **t**.
7:35 his twisted **t** was released, and
Luke
16:24 water and cool my **t** because I'm
Acts
2:26 was glad and my **t** rejoiced.
Romans
14:11 to me, and every **t** will give praise
1 Corinthians
14:2 who speak in a **t** don't speak to
14:27 some speak in a **t**, then let two or
Philippians
2:11 and every **t** confess that Jesus Christ
James
3:5 even though the **t** is a small part
3:6 The **t** is a small flame of fire, a world
3:8 one can tame the **t**, though. It is a
1 Peter
3:10 should keep their **t** from evil

TONGUES

Judges
7:5 water with their **t**, as a dog laps,
Job
20:12 mouths, they hide it under their **t**;
Psalms
5:9 open graves; their **t** slick with talk.
10:7 Under their **t** lie troublemaking
12:4 with our **t**! Who could get
31:20 in a shelter, safe from accusing **t**.
37:30 recite wisdom; their **t** discuss justice.
57:4 and arrows; their **t** are sharpened
64:3 who sharpen their **t** like swords. They
64:8 over their own **t**; everyone who
68:23 that your dogs' **t** can lap up their
73:9 against heaven! Their **t** roam the earth!
78:36 They were lying to him with their **t**.
109:2 me, talking about me with lying **t**.
126:2 laughter; our **t** were filled with
140:3 sharpen their **t** like a snake's;
Proverbs
17:20 with twisted **t** will fall into
21:23 mouths and their **t** guard themselves
28:23 favor than those with flattering **t**.
Isaiah
32:4 and the **t** of those who
41:17 is none; their **t** are parched with
59:3 lips speak lies; your **t** mutter malice.
Jeremiah
9:3 They bend their **t** like bows to spew out
Hosea
7:16 the rage of their **t**; in Egypt they
Micah
6:12 falsehood with lying **t** in their mouths?
Zechariah
14:12 and their **t** will rot in their
Romans
3:13 with their **t**, and the poison
1 Corinthians
12:10 kinds of **t** to another, and
13:1 If I speak in **t** of human beings and of
14:5 of you spoke in **t**, but I'd rather
14:39 but don't prevent speaking in **t**.

Revelation
16:10 People bit their **t** because of their

TOP

Genesis
28:18 pillar, and poured oil on the **t** of it.
Exodus
19:20 Sinai to the **t** of the mountain.
25:21 the gold cover on **t** of the chest and
40:20 and he set the cover on **t** of the chest.
Numbers
20:28 died there at the **t** of the mountain.
Deuteronomy
3:27 Go up to the **t** of Mount Pisgah. Look
28:35 your foot to the **t** of your head. You
Joshua
15:8 went up to the **t** of the mountain
15:9 turned from the **t** of the mountain
Judges
6:26 the proper way on **t** of this high
9:7 and stood on the **t** of Mount Gerizim.
16:3 them up to the **t** of the hill that
1 Samuel
2:8 LORD; he set the world on **t** of them!
26:13 side and stood on **t** of a hill with
2 Samuel
2:25 their positions on the **t** of a hill.
11:21 millstone on **t** of him from the
1 Kings
7:17 the capitals on **t** of the columns,
10:19 rounded at the **t**. Two lions stood
14:23 sacred poles on **t** of every high
18:42 went up to the **t** of Mount Carmel.
2 Kings
4:34 and lay down on **t** of the child,
2 Chronicles
3:15 seven-and-a-half-foot cap on **t** of each.
Job
2:7 sole of his foot to the **t** of his head.
Psalms
69:27 Pile guilt on **t** of their guilt! Don't
91:13 You'll march on **t** of lions and vipers;
Proverbs
9:3 from the **t** of the city
23:34 the sea or one who lies on **t** of a mast.
Isaiah
36:13 in Hebrew at the **t** of his voice:
42:11 sing; from the **t** of the mountains
Jeremiah
3:6 for lovers on **t** of every high
6:9 forces says: From **t** to bottom, let
Ezekiel
17:3 and took the **t** branch of the
43:12 the temple: the **t** of the mountain,
Amos
1:2 wither, and the **t** of Carmel dries
9:3 themselves on the **t** of Carmel, I will
Zechariah
4:2 It has a bowl on **t**. The bowl has
Matthew
5:14 world. A city on **t** of a hill can't
5:15 they put it on **t** of a lampstand,
17:1 them to the **t** of a very high
27:51 torn in two from **t** to bottom. The
Mark
9:2 them to the **t** of a very high
15:38 was torn in two from **t** to bottom.

Luke
8:16 they put it on **t** of a lampstand so
19:44 one stone on **t** of another within
John
19:23 as one piece from the **t** to the bottom.
1 Corinthians
3:10 is building on **t** of it. Each
3:12 someone builds on **t** of the foundation
Revelation
1:12 lamps burning on **t** of seven gold

TORE

Genesis
32:25 Jacob's thigh and **t** a muscle in
37:29 Joseph wasn't in it, he **t** his clothes.
37:34 Then Jacob **t** his clothes, put a simple
44:13 At this, they **t** their clothing. Then
Numbers
14:6 had explored the land, **t** their clothes
Judges
6:30 because he **t** down the altar to
6:32 with him," because he **t** down his altar.
11:35 he saw her, he **t** his clothes and
14:6 over him, and he **t** the lion apart
1 Samuel
14:32 So the troops **t** into the plunder,
15:19 eyes when you **t** into the plunder!"
2 Samuel
13:19 on her head and **t** the long-sleeved
13:31 The king got up, **t** his garments, and
1 Kings
11:30 Ahijah **t** his new garment into twelve
13:26 to that lion that **t** him apart,
14:8 I **t** the kingdom from David's house and gave it to you
19:11 very strong wind **t** through the
20:41 prophet quickly **t** the bandage from
21:27 these words, he **t** his clothes and
2 Kings
10:27 They **t** down Baal's sacred pillar and
11:18 Baal's temple and **t** it down, smashing
23:7 The king **t** down the shrines for the
23:8 incense. He also **t** down the shrines
23:12 The king also **t** down the altars that
23:15 Josiah also **t** down the altar that was
25:10 of the guard **t** down the walls
2 Chronicles
23:17 Baal's temple and **t** it down, smashing
34:7 **t** down the altars and sacred poles,
Ezra
9:3 I heard this, I **t** my clothes and
Esther
4:1 had been done, he **t** his clothes,
Job
1:20 Job arose, **t** his clothes, shaved his
2:12 loudly. Each one **t** his garment and
19:10 **t** me down completely so that I'll die,
Psalms
35:15 I didn't know **t** me to pieces and
Isaiah
14:17 a wasteland and **t** down its cities,
22:10 houses, and you **t** down houses to
Jeremiah
36:24 words were alarmed or **t** their clothes.
Lamentations
2:2 in his wrath he **t** down the walled
3:11 from my path and **t** me apart; he made
Matthew
26:65 the high priest **t** his clothes and
Mark
2:4 crowd, so they **t** off part of the
14:63 the high priest **t** his clothes and
Luke
23:45 in the sanctuary **t** down the middle.
Acts
14:14 about this, they **t** their clothes in
21:1 After we **t** ourselves away from them, we
Galatians
2:18 things that I **t** down, I show that

TORN

Genesis
8:11 grasping a **t** olive leaf in its
37:33 Joseph must have been **t** to pieces!"
44:28 must have been **t** up by a wild
Exodus
22:13 apart and its **t** body is brought
Leviticus
13:45 disease must wear **t** clothes, dishevel
22:24 bruised, crushed, **t**, or cut off
Deuteronomy
28:63 you. You will be **t** off the very
Judges
6:31 it was his altar that was **t** down."
1 Samuel
4:12 His clothes were **t**, and dirt was on
2 Samuel
1:2 with his clothes **t** and dirt on his
13:31 near him, their garments **t** as well.
14:30 their clothes **t**. "Absalom's
1 Kings
13:28 body, nor had it **t** the donkey apart.
19:10 They have **t** down your altars,
19:14 They have **t** down your altars,
2 Chronicles
34:4 the Baals were **t** down, and the
Ezra
9:5 still wearing my **t** clothes and
Job
19:26 my skin has been **t** apart this way—
Psalms
9:6 forever. You've **t** down their cities-
80:12 why have you now **t** down its walls so
Jeremiah
33:4 Judah that were **t** down to defend
41:5 shaved beards, **t** clothes, and
Ezekiel
36:36 rebuilt what was **t** down and have
44:31 dies naturally or is **t** apart by prey.
Daniel
2:5 you will be **t** limb from limb,
3:29 God will be **t** limb from limb
Hosea
10:8 of Aven will be **t** down. Thorn and
Nahum
2:12 The lion has **t** enough prey for his cubs
Matthew
12:25 city or house **t** apart by
27:51 the sanctuary was **t** in two from top
Mark
3:25 And a house **t** apart by divisions will
15:38 the sanctuary was **t** in two from top

Luke
11:17 and a house ***t*** apart by
John
21:11 the net hadn't ***t***, even with so
Acts
15:16 what has been ***t*** down. I will
Romans
11:3 and they have ***t*** down your altars.
2 Corinthians
5:1 in on earth is ***t*** down, we have a
Philippians
1:23 I prefer. I'm ***t*** between the two

TOUCH
Genesis
3:3 it, and don't ***t*** it, or you will
20:6 That's why I didn't allow you to ***t*** her.
27:21 here and let me ***t*** you, my son. Are
Exodus
12:22 in the bowl, and ***t*** the beam above
19:12 mountain or to ***t*** any part of it.'
19:13 No one should ***t*** anyone who has touched
22:11 that he didn't ***t*** the other's
Leviticus
11:8 these animals or ***t*** their dead
12:4 She must not ***t*** anything holy or
Numbers
4:15 but they will not ***t*** the sanctuary,
16:26 men and don't ***t*** anything of
Deuteronomy
14:8 and you must not ***t*** their carcasses.
Joshua
9:19 God of Israel. So we can't ***t*** them now.
1 Samuel
1:11 life. No razor will ever ***t*** his head."
23:17 Saul's hand won't ***t*** you. You will be
2 Samuel
18:12 hand, I wouldn't ***t*** the king's son!
23:7 No one can ***t*** them, except with iron bar
1 Chronicles
16:22 Don't ***t*** my anointed ones; don't harm
Esther
1:20 The rule should ***t*** everyone, whether
Job
5:19 you; from seven harm won't ***t*** you.
6:7 I refuse to ***t*** them; they resemble food
20:6 heaven and their heads ***t*** the clouds,
Psalms
69:2 My feet can't ***t*** the bottom! I
105:15 Don't ***t*** my anointed ones; don't harm
144:5 and come down! ***T*** the mountains so
Isaiah
52:11 Unclean! Don't ***t***! Get out of that
Lamentations
4:14 No one would even ***t*** their clothing.
4:15 Away!" "Don't ***t***!" So they fled
Ezekiel
9:6 Only don't ***t*** anyone who has
Hosea
9:4 for those who ***t*** the dead; all who
Matthew
9:21 If I only ***t*** his robe I'll be
14:36 they might just ***t*** the edge of his
Mark
3:10 forward so that they could ***t*** him.
5:28 If I can just ***t*** his clothes, I'll
6:56 to allow them to ***t*** even the hem of
8:22 Jesus and begged him to ***t*** and heal him.
Luke
6:19 crowd wanted to ***t*** him, because
24:39 It's really me! ***T*** me and see, for a
2 Corinthians
6:17 the Lord. Don't ***t*** what is unclean.
Colossians
2:21 handle!" "Don't taste!" "Don't ***t***!"
Hebrews
11:28 could not ***t*** their firstborn
1 John
5:18 and the evil one cannot ***t*** them.

TOUCHED
Genesis
27:22 Isaac, and Isaac ***t*** him and said,
Exodus
4:25 Then she ***t*** Moses' genitals
19:13 anyone who has ***t*** it, or they must
Numbers
19:18 and on anyone who ***t*** bone, the slain,
31:19 a person or ***t*** a corpse must
Joshua
3:15 their feet ***t*** the edge of the
4:18 of their feet ***t*** dry ground. At
Judges
6:21 in his hand and ***t*** the meat and the
16:17 razor has ever ***t*** my head, because
1 Samuel
10:26 courageous men whose hearts God had ***t***.
1 Kings
6:27 wing of the one ***t*** one wall and the
2 Kings
13:21 When the body ***t*** Elisha's bones,
2 Chronicles
3:11 feet long and ***t*** the temple wall,
Esther
5:2 came forward and ***t*** the scepter's tip.
Isaiah
6:7 He ***t*** my mouth and said, "See, this has
Jeremiah
1:9 out his hand, ***t*** my mouth, and
Ezekiel
1:9 their wings ***t*** each other's wings. When
23:3 and nubile breasts to be ***t*** and fondled.
23:21 the Egyptians ***t*** and fondled her
Daniel
6:22 They haven't ***t*** me because I was
8:18 Then Gabriel ***t*** me and set me up
10:10 But then a hand ***t*** me, lifting me up to
Matthew
8:3 out his hand and ***t*** him, saying, "I
8:15 He ***t*** her hand, and the fever left her.
9:20 behind Jesus and ***t*** the hem of his
9:25 Jesus went in and ***t*** her hand, and the
9:29 Then Jesus ***t*** their eyes and said, "It
14:36 clothes. Everyone who ***t*** him was cured.
17:7 Jesus came and ***t*** them. "Get up,"
20:34 on them and ***t*** their eyes.
Mark
1:41 out his hand, ***t*** him, and said, "I
5:27 him in the crowd and ***t*** his clothes.
5:30 the crowd and said, "Who ***t*** my clothes?"
5:31 against you? Yet you ask, 'Who ***t*** me?'"
6:56 Everyone who ***t*** him was healed.

7:33 Then he spit and ***t*** the man's tongue.
Luke
5:13 out his hand, ***t*** him, and said, "I
7:14 forward and ***t*** the stretcher on
8:44 up behind him and ***t*** the hem of his
8:45 Who ***t*** me?" Jesus asked. When everyone
8:46 said, "Someone ***t*** me. I know that
8:47 why she had ***t*** him and how she
22:51 more of this!" He ***t*** the slave's ear
Acts
19:12 aprons that had ***t*** his skin were
Hebrews
12:18 that can be ***t***: a burning fire,

TOUCHES

Genesis
26:11 Anyone who ***t*** this man or his
27:12 What if my father ***t*** me and thinks I'm
Exodus
19:12 Anyone who even ***t*** the mountain must
29:37 and whatever ***t*** the altar will
30:29 holy. Whatever ***t*** them will become
Leviticus
6:18 Anything that ***t*** these food gifts
Numbers
19:11 The person who ***t*** the dead body of any
Job
41:16 One ***t*** another; even air can't come
41:26 The sword that ***t*** him won't prevail;
Psalms
104:32 shakes. God just ***t*** the mountains,
Proverbs
6:29 wife; anyone who ***t*** her will be
Ezekiel
17:10 the east wind ***t*** it, won't it
Amos
9:5 heavenly forces, ***t*** the earth and it
Haggai
2:12 and that hem ***t*** bread, stew,
2:13 an unclean person ***t*** any of these
Hebrews
12:20 a wild animal ***t*** the mountain, it

TOWER

Genesis
11:4 a city and a ***t*** with its top in
11:5 the city and the ***t*** that the humans
35:21 his tent farther on near the ***t*** of Eder.
Judges
8:9 in victory, I'll break down this ***t***!"
8:17 down Penuel's ***t***, and killed the
9:46 leaders in the ***T*** of Shechem heard
9:47 leaders from the ***T*** of Shechem had
9:49 the people in the ***T*** of Shechem died
9:51 was a strong ***t*** inside the city.
9:52 came to the ***t*** to storm it. But
2 Kings
9:17 standing on the ***t*** at Jezreel saw a
9:18 Meanwhile, the ***t*** guard reported,
9:20 The ***t*** guard reported, "The messenger
Nehemiah
3:1 it as far as the ***T*** of the Hundred
3:11 another section and the ***T*** of the Ovens.
3:25 the Angle and the ***t*** projecting from
3:26 Gate to the east and the projecting ***t***.
3:27 great projecting ***t*** as far as the
12:38 the wall past the ***T*** of the Ovens to
12:39 Fish Gate, the ***T*** of Hananel, and
Psalms
61:3 been my refuge, a ***t*** of strength in
Proverbs
18:10 name is a strong ***t***; the righteous
Song of Songs
4:4 Like David's ***t*** is your neck, splendidly
7:4 your neck, like a ***t*** of ivory; your
Isaiah
2:15 every tall ***t***; against every
5:2 vines, built a ***t*** inside it, and
Jeremiah
31:38 the LORD from the ***T*** of Hananel to the
Ezekiel
31:10 fate of those who ***t*** high! When it
31:14 tree would ***t*** high or allow its
Micah
4:8 As for you, ***T*** of Eder, hill of Daughter
Zechariah
14:10 from the Hananel ***T*** to the king's
Matthew
21:33 it, and built a ***t***. Then he rented
Mark
12:1 and built a ***t***. Then he rented
Luke
13:4 killed when the ***t*** of Siloam fell on
14:28 wanted to build a ***t***, wouldn't you
14:29 finish the ***t***, all who see it

TOWERS

1 Chronicles
27:25 villages, and ***t***—Jonathan, Uzziah
2 Chronicles
14:7 them with walls, ***t***, gates, and
26:9 He built ***t*** in Jerusalem, at the Corner
26:10 He also built ***t*** in the wilderness and
26:15 Jerusalem on the ***t*** and corners of
27:4 fortresses and ***t*** in the wooded
32:5 the wall, erected ***t***, constructed
Psalms
48:12 go all the way around it; count its ***t***.
Song of Songs
5:13 plantings, ***t*** of spices. His
8:10 breasts are the ***t***. So now I'm in
Isaiah
23:13 up their siege ***t***, stripped its
25:12 The fortified ***t*** of their walls will be
29:3 you with assault ***t***, and I will raise
30:25 of the great massacre, when the ***t*** fall.
33:18 weighs? Where is the one who counts ***t***?
54:12 I will make your ***t*** of rubies, and your
Jeremiah
50:15 surrendered; her ***t*** have collapsed;
Ezekiel
17:17 are set up and ***t*** are built to
21:22 and to set up siege ramps and build ***t***.
26:4 throw down its ***t***, I will scrape
26:8 he will build ***t*** against you,
26:9 with crowbars he will tear down your ***t***.
27:11 were in your ***t***. They hung their
Zephaniah
1:16 cities and against their high ***t***.
3:6 nations; their ***t*** will be

TOWN
Nehemiah
7:6 and Judah, everyone to their own ***t***.
Matthew
22:9 on the edge of ***t*** and invite
Mark
1:33 The whole ***t*** gathered near the door
1:45 able to enter a ***t*** openly. He

TOWNS
Numbers
32:24 So build ***t*** for your children and walled
Joshua
10:37 its king, all its ***t***, and everyone in
Psalms
48:11 be glad; let the ***t*** of Judah rejoice
97:8 celebrates, the ***t*** of Judah
Isaiah
25:3 glorify you; the ***t*** of tyrant nations
42:11 desert and its ***t*** shout aloud, the
Jeremiah
11:13 gods as you have ***t***, Judah, and you
51:43 Her ***t*** are devastated; her land is
Ezekiel
26:6 and its ***t*** around it will be put to the
26:8 The ***t*** around you he will destroy with
30:18 cover it, and the ***t*** around it will go
Amos
4:8 or three thirsty ***t*** went to one city
Luke
5:12 was in one of the ***t*** where there was
Acts
5:16 of persons from ***t*** around Jerusalem
Jude
1:7 and neighboring ***t*** practiced immoral

TRAMPLED
Judges
9:27 their vineyards, ***t*** them out, and had
20:43 from Nohah, and ***t*** them to the east
2 Samuel
22:43 stomped on them, ***t*** them like mud
2 Kings
7:17 gate. The people ***t*** the officer at
7:20 him. The people ***t*** him at the city
9:33 wall and on the horses, and they ***t*** her.
14:9 Lebanon came along and ***t*** the thistle.
2 Chronicles
25:18 Lebanon came along and ***t*** the thistle.
Psalms
44:5 your help; we've ***t*** our enemies by
56:1 because I'm being ***t***. All day long the
Isaiah
5:5 down its walls, so it will be ***t***.
14:19 to the stony pit—like a ***t*** corpse.
25:10 Moab will be ***t*** down as straw is
28:3 Ephraim's drunks will be ***t*** underfoot.
63:3 them in my anger, ***t*** them in my wrath.
63:6 I ***t*** down nations in my anger and made them drunk
Jeremiah
12:10 they have ***t*** down my field;
51:33 floor ready to be ***t*** down. In a little
Lamentations
1:13 into my bones; he ***t*** them. He spread a
Ezekiel
34:19 your feet have ***t*** and drink water
Daniel
8:7 on the ground and ***t*** on it. No one
8:10 down to the earth. Then it ***t*** on them.
8:13 the sanctuary and its forces to be ***t***?"
Micah
7:10 something to be ***t***, like mud in the
Matthew
5:13 thrown away and ***t*** under people's
Revelation
14:20 the winepress was ***t*** outside the city,

TRAP
Exodus
10:7 will this man ***t*** us in a corner
23:33 it will become a dangerous ***t*** for you.
34:12 it will become a dangerous ***t*** for you.
Deuteronomy
7:16 gods because that would be a ***t*** for you.
Joshua
23:13 be a snare and a ***t*** for you. They
Judges
2:3 and their gods will be a ***t*** for you."
8:27 and it became a ***t*** for Gideon and
2 Kings
9:23 to Ahaziah, "It's a ***t***, Ahaziah!"
Job
18:9 A ***t*** grabs them by the heel; a snare
18:10 for them; a ***t*** for them along
Psalms
69:22 them become a ***t***, their offerings
91:3 from the hunter's ***t*** and from deadly
106:36 false gods, which became a ***t*** for them.
119:110 wicked have set a ***t*** for me, I won't
124:7 from the hunters' ***t***; the trap was
140:5 have laid a ***t*** for me with
141:9 me from the ***t*** they've set for
142:3 they've hidden a ***t*** for me in the
Proverbs
7:22 like a deer leaping into a ***t***,
12:12 evil is a ***t*** for the wicked,
18:7 their lips are a ***t*** for their lives.
Ecclesiastes
7:26 she who is a ***t***, her heart a
Isaiah
8:14 of Israel; a ***t*** and a snare for
24:17 trench, and ***t*** are upon you,
24:18 be caught in the ***t***. Heaven's windows
Jeremiah
12:6 are planning to ***t*** you. They are out
48:44 captured by the ***t***. I will bring
50:24 You set a ***t*** for others, Babylon, but
Lamentations
3:47 Terror and ***t*** have come upon us,
Ezekiel
7:7 in your own ***t***! The time has
12:13 catch him in my ***t***, and bring him to
13:20 that you use to ***t*** human lives. I
17:20 be caught in my ***t***. I will bring him
19:4 him in their ***t*** and carried him
19:8 over him and caught him in their ***t***.
Hosea
5:1 you have been a ***t*** at Mizpah, and a
9:8 yet a hunter's ***t*** is set, covering
Amos
3:5 bird fall into a ***t*** on the ground
Obadiah
1:7 own bread as a ***t*** under you, but

Matthew
22:15 to find a way to ***t*** Jesus in his
Mark
12:13 of Herod to ***t*** him in his words.
Luke
11:54 him, trying to ***t*** him in his words.
20:20 They wanted to ***t*** him in his words
20:26 They couldn't ***t*** him in his words in
21:35 like a ***t***. It will come upon everyone
Romans
11:9 a pitfall and a ***t***, a stumbling
1 Timothy
3:7 and fall into the devil's ***t***.
2 Timothy
2:26 from the devil's ***t*** that holds them

TRAPPED
Genesis
32:7 and felt ***t***, so he divided
Exodus
14:3 in the land. The desert has ***t*** them.
Deuteronomy
7:25 or you will be ***t*** by it. That is
12:30 Don't be ***t*** by following
1 Samuel
23:7 because he has ***t*** himself by
Psalms
9:16 that the wicked are ***t***. Higgayon. Selah
66:11 ***t*** us in a net, laid burdens on our
88:8 to them. I can't escape. I'm ***t***!
Proverbs
6:2 you will be ***t*** by your words; you will
12:13 The wicked are ***t*** by the transgressions
22:25 you will learn their ways and become ***t***.
29:25 People are ***t*** by their fear of others;
Ecclesiastes
7:26 escapes her, but a sinner is ***t*** by her.
9:12 net or like birds ***t*** in a snare, so
Isaiah
42:22 looted, everyone ***t*** in holes and
Jeremiah
6:11 with wife will be ***t***, as will those
20:9 fire in my heart, ***t*** in my bones. I'm
Ezekiel
13:20 the lives that you've ***t*** like birds.
1 Timothy
6:9 They are ***t*** by many stupid

TRAVEL
Genesis
31:52 that I won't ***t*** beyond this mound
34:10 you: settle down, ***t*** through it, and
34:21 in the land and ***t*** through it;
42:34 you, and you may ***t*** throughout the
Exodus
13:21 way they could ***t*** during the day
Joshua
18:4 will go up and ***t*** throughout the
18:8 the land. "Go and ***t*** around the land,
Judges
19:12 Israelites. We'll ***t*** on to Gibeah.
2 Samuel
17:17 they would then ***t*** and report to
2 Chronicles
15:5 it wasn't safe to ***t*** because great
Nehemiah
2:7 the River to allow me to ***t*** to Judah.
Isaiah
35:8 The unclean won't ***t*** on it, but it
Jeremiah
2:18 the Nile? Why ***t*** the path to
Ezekiel
14:15 there or even ***t*** through it on
Matthew
8:28 that nobody could ***t*** on that road.
15:32 they won't have enough strength to ***t***."
23:15 Hypocrites! You ***t*** over sea and land
Mark
8:3 strength to ***t***, for some have
Luke
13:33 for me to ***t*** today, tomorrow,
John
7:1 He didn't want to ***t*** in Judea, because
Acts
18:27 When he wanted to ***t*** to Achaia, the
1 Corinthians
9:5 have the right to ***t*** with a wife who
16:4 for me to go too, they'll ***t*** with me.
2 Corinthians
10:14 the first ones to ***t*** as far as Corinth
Hebrews
13:23 soon, we will ***t*** together to see

TRAVELED
Exodus
12:37 The Israelites ***t*** from Rameses to
15:22 Shur desert. They ***t*** for three days in
19:2 They ***t*** from Rephidim, came into the
Numbers
33:8 desert. Then they ***t*** three days in the
Deuteronomy
2:1 instructed me. We ***t*** all around Mount
10:7 the Israelites ***t*** to Gudgodah, then
Job
22:15 the ancient way ***t*** by sinful persons,
Jeremiah
31:21 the road you have ***t***, the path you
Matthew
4:23 Jesus ***t*** throughout Galilee, teaching in
9:35 Jesus ***t*** among all the cities and
Mark
1:39 He ***t*** throughout Galilee preaching in
6:6 Then Jesus ***t*** through the
Luke
7:11 disciples and a great crowd ***t*** with him.
8:1 afterward, Jesus ***t*** through the
9:57 and his disciples ***t*** along the road,
13:22 Jesus ***t*** through cities and villages
17:11 Jerusalem, Jesus ***t*** along the border
John
7:1 After this Jesus ***t*** throughout Galilee.
Acts
8:40 in Azotus. He ***t*** through that
10:38 with power. Jesus ***t*** around doing good
11:19 of Stephen ***t*** as far as
13:6 They ***t*** throughout the island until they
13:31 to those who had ***t*** with him from
14:24 Paul and Barnabas ***t*** through Pisidia,
15:3 their way. They ***t*** through Phoenicia
15:41 He ***t*** through Syria and Cilicia,
16:4 his companions ***t*** through the
16:6 his companions ***t*** throughout the
18:23 there he left and ***t*** from place to
19:13 some Jews who ***t*** around throwing

20:2 He ***t*** through that region with a message
20:25 —you among whom I ***t*** and proclaimed

TREASURE

Genesis
43:23 have hidden a ***t*** in your sacks. I
2 Kings
12:18 the gold in the ***t*** rooms of the
1 Chronicles
29:3 my own private ***t*** of gold and
Job
3:21 who search for it more than for ***t***,
20:20 belly; couldn't escape with their ***t***.
Psalms
39:11 ruin what they ***t***. Yes, a human
119:162 word, like someone who finds great ***t***.
147:10 God doesn't ***t*** the legs of a
Proverbs
2:4 silver; search for it like hidden ***t***.
10:2 The ***t*** of the wicked won't profit them,
15:6 Great ***t*** is in the house of the
15:16 the LORD than a great ***t*** with turmoil.
21:6 Those who gain ***t*** with lies are like a
21:20 Precious ***t*** and oil stay in the home of
27:24 for no ***t*** lasts forever, nor a crown
Ecclesiastes
2:8 every human luxury, ***t*** chests galore!
Isaiah
33:6 fear of the LORD will be Zion's ***t***.
Jeremiah
17:3 well as your wealth and all that you ***t***.
Matthew
2:11 they opened their ***t*** chests and
6:21 Where your ***t*** is, there your heart will be
12:35 from their good ***t***. But evil people
13:44 heaven is like a ***t*** that somebody hid
13:52 and new things out of their ***t*** chest."
19:21 you will have ***t*** in heaven. And
Mark
10:21 you will have ***t*** in heaven. And
Luke
12:33 don't wear out—a ***t*** in heaven that
12:34 Where your ***t*** is, there your heart will
18:22 you will have ***t*** in heaven. And
2 Corinthians
4:7 But we have this ***t*** in clay pots so that
1 Timothy
6:19 they will save a ***t*** for themselves
James
5:3 Consider the ***t*** you have hoarded

TREASURES

Deuteronomy
33:19 are nourished on buried ***t*** in the sand."
1 Samuel
9:20 all of Israel's ***t***, anyway? Isn't it
1 Kings
14:26 He seized the ***t*** of the LORD's temple
2 Kings
24:13 took away all the ***t*** of the LORD's
1 Chronicles
28:12 rooms where the ***t*** of God's temple
2 Chronicles
12:9 and seized the ***t*** of the LORD's
36:18 including the ***t*** of the LORD's
Esther
1:4 and beautiful ***t*** as mirrors of how
Psalms
147:11 No. The LORD ***t*** the people who honor
Ecclesiastes
2:8 for myself, the ***t*** of kings and
Isaiah
2:7 have countless ***t***. Their land is
10:13 I raided their ***t***; I knocked down
30:6 and their ***t*** on camels' humps
45:3 give you hidden ***t*** of secret riches,
Jeremiah
20:5 including the ***t*** of the kings of
48:7 own strength and ***t***, you also will be
49:4 You trust in your ***t***, never imagining
50:37 sword against its ***t*** so that they are
51:13 you are rich in ***t***. But your time
51:34 belly with our ***t***; and he's spit us
Lamentations
1:7 remembers all her ***t*** from days long
1:10 grabbed all her ***t***. She watched
Daniel
11:43 of Egypt's hidden ***t*** of gold, silver,
Joel
3:5 carried my rich ***t*** into your temples.
Obadiah
1:6 Esau has been looted, his ***t*** taken away!
Micah
6:10 Are the ***t*** of wickedness still in the
Matthew
6:19 Stop collecting ***t*** for your own benefit
6:20 Instead, collect ***t*** for yourselves in
Colossians
2:3 All the ***t*** of wisdom and knowledge are hidden in him
Hebrews
11:26 valuable than the ***t*** of Egypt, since

TREASURIES

1 Kings
7:51 put them in the ***t*** of the LORD's
15:18 remained in the ***t*** of the LORD's
2 Kings
14:14 temple and the ***t*** of the palace,
16:8 and in the palace ***t***, and sent a gift
18:15 the LORD's temple and in the palace ***t***.
1 Chronicles
9:26 of the rooms and the ***t*** of God's house.
26:20 in charge of the ***t*** of God's temple
27:25 of the king's ***t***—Azmaveth, Adiel's
28:11 its buildings, ***t***, upper and inner
2 Chronicles
5:1 and put them in the ***t*** of God's temple.
8:15 the priests, the Levites, or the ***t***.
16:2 and gold from the ***t*** of the LORD's
25:24 and in the ***t*** of the palace,
Esther
3:9 The silver can go into the king's ***t***."
Proverbs
8:21 who love me and to fill up their ***t***.
Jeremiah
10:13 with the rain, the wind from his ***t***.
51:16 the rain and sends the wind from his ***t***.

TREASURY

Genesis
47:14 and he deposited it in Pharaoh's ***t***.

Joshua
6:19 LORD. They must go into the LORD's ***t***."
6:24 into the ***t*** of the LORD's
2 Kings
20:13 everything in his ***t***-the silver, the
1 Chronicles
29:8 them to the ***t*** of the LORD's
Ezra
6:4 The cost will be paid from the royal ***t***.
7:20 you may provide it from the royal ***t***.
Nehemiah
7:70 gave to the ***t*** 1,000 darics of
7:71 manehs of silver to the ***t*** for the work.
10:38 house, to the storerooms of the ***t***.
Esther
4:7 into the royal ***t***. It was in
Isaiah
39:2 showed them his ***t***—the silver and
Daniel
1:2 temple, putting them in his god's ***t***.
Zechariah
11:13 Put it in the ***t***. They value me at
Matthew
27:6 this money in the ***t***. Since it was
Mark
12:41 for the temple ***t*** and observed how
12:43 who's been putting money in the ***t***.
Luke
6:45 from the good ***t*** of the inner
21:1 the collection box for the temple ***t***.
John
8:20 area known as the ***t***. No one arrested
Acts
8:27 for the entire ***t*** of Candace.

TREAT
Exodus
5:15 Why do you ***t*** your servants
22:22 Don't ***t*** any widow or orphan badly
Leviticus
19:30 my sabbaths and ***t*** my sanctuary with
21:8 You will ***t*** the priests as holy, because
22:2 careful how they ***t*** the holy things
Deuteronomy
5:12 Sabbath day and ***t*** it as holy,
Psalms
89:31 if they ***t*** my statutes like dirt, stop
Jeremiah
3:19 it would be to ***t*** you like children
6:14 They ***t*** the wound of my people as if it
7:5 actions; if you ***t*** each other justly;
8:11 They ***t*** the wound of my people as if it
24:5 good figs, I will ***t*** kindly the Judean
Ezekiel
22:7 In you they ***t*** father and mother with
Hosea
11:8 Admah? How can I ***t*** you like Zeboiim?
Nahum
3:6 at you; I will ***t*** you with contempt
Matthew
7:12 you should ***t*** people in the
12:5 in the temple ***t*** the Sabbath as
18:17 to the church, ***t*** them as you would
Luke
6:31 ***T*** people in the same way that you want
Romans
3:26 time, and to ***t*** the one who has
Ephesians
6:9 As for masters, ***t*** your slaves in the
2 Thessalonians
3:15 Don't ***t*** them like enemies, but warn
1 Timothy
5:1 he's your father; ***t*** younger men like
5:2 ***t*** older women like your mother, and

TREATED
Genesis
16:6 to her." So Sarai ***t*** her harshly, and
Numbers
11:11 Why have you ***t*** your servant so
Deuteronomy
26:6 The Egyptians ***t*** us terribly, oppressing
Joshua
9:26 So Joshua ***t*** them in this way. He spared
Judges
9:16 and have ***t*** him as his
1 Samuel
24:17 because you have ***t*** me generously,
2 Samuel
15:6 is how Absalom ***t*** every Israelite
Psalms
119:65 You have ***t*** your servant well, LORD,
Isaiah
1:6 raw wounds, not ***t***, not bandaged,
51:12 will die, mortals who are ***t*** like grass?
63:7 of Israel. God ***t*** them
Jeremiah
22:8 Why has the LORD ***t*** that great city
52:32 Awil-merodach ***t*** Jehoiachin kindly and
Ezekiel
16:4 is how you were ***t*** on the day you
Hosea
11:4 cords of love. I ***t*** them like those
Zechariah
1:6 forces has ***t*** us according to
Matthew
21:36 first group. They ***t*** them in the same
Mark
12:4 on the head and ***t*** him disgracefully.
Luke
2:48 why have you ***t*** us like this?
20:11 they beat him, ***t*** him
23:11 and his soldiers ***t*** Jesus with
Acts
27:3 in Sidon. Julius ***t*** Paul kindly and
Romans
2:13 Law says who will be ***t*** as righteous.
3:20 being will be ***t*** as righteous in
3:24 but all are ***t*** as righteous freely by
3:28 that a person is ***t*** as righteous by
8:36 your sake. We are ***t*** like sheep for
2 Corinthians
6:8 We were ***t*** with honor and dishonor and
11:12 who want to be ***t*** like they are the
12:13 How were you ***t*** worse than the other
1 Thessalonians
2:11 you know how we ***t*** each of you like
Hebrews
10:33 with those who were ***t*** that way.

TREE
Genesis
2:9 every beautiful ***t*** with edible
2:17 eat from the ***t*** of the knowledge

TREE [cont.]

3:1 eat from any ***t*** in the garden?"
18:4 and refresh yourselves under the ***t***.
18:8 stood under the ***t*** near them as they
21:33 a tamarisk ***t*** in Beer-sheba, and
40:19 hang you from a ***t*** where birds will

Exodus
9:25 it shattered every ***t*** out in the field.
15:25 pointed out a ***t*** to him. He threw

Leviticus
19:23 plant any fruit ***t***, you must

Deuteronomy
16:21 Don't plant any ***t*** to serve as a sacred
19:5 to cut down the ***t***, the axhead flies
20:19 Do you think a ***t*** of the field is
20:20 you know that a ***t*** is not a food-
21:22 and you then hang them on a ***t***,
21:23 hanging on the ***t*** but must bury it
22:6 way, whether in a ***t*** or on the ground,

Joshua
8:29 king of Ai on a ***t*** until evening. At

Judges
4:5 Deborah's palm ***t*** between Ramah and
9:8 said to the olive ***t***, 'Be our king!'
9:9 But the olive ***t*** replied to them,
9:10 said to the fig ***t***, 'You come and be
9:11 The fig ***t*** replied to them, 'Should I

1 Samuel
2:31 be an old person left in your family ***t***.
2:32 be an old person in your family ***t***.
14:2 the pomegranate ***t*** at Migron. He had
22:6 the tamarisk ***t*** on the hill at
31:13 the tamarisk ***t*** at Jabesh, and

2 Samuel
3:29 his entire family ***t***! May Joab's
18:9 of a large oak ***t***. Absalom's head
18:10 saw Absalom hanging from an oak ***t***."

1 Kings
13:14 a terebinth ***t***. He said to him,
14:23 high hill and under every green ***t***.

2 Kings
3:25 down every good ***t***. Only Kir-hareseth
6:5 cutting down a ***t*** when his ax head
16:4 every hill and beneath every shady ***t***.
17:10 high hill and beneath every green ***t***.
18:31 own vine and fig ***t***, and drink water

2 Chronicles
28:4 every hill and beneath every shady ***t***.

Nehemiah
10:37 fruit of every ***t***, the wine, and

Job
14:7 is hope for a ***t***. If it's cut down
19:10 die, and uprooted my hope like a ***t***.
24:20 so wickedness is shattered like a ***t***.

Psalms
1:3 They are like a ***t*** replanted by streams
52:8 a green olive ***t*** in God's house; I
92:12 up like a palm ***t***. They will grow

Proverbs
3:18 She is a ***t*** of life to those who embrace
11:30 righteous is a ***t*** of life, and the
13:12 sick; longing fulfilled is a ***t*** of life.
15:4 speech is a ***t*** of life, but
27:18 who tend a fig ***t*** will eat its

Ecclesiastes
2:5 planting every kind of fruit ***t*** in them.
11:3 the earth. If a ***t*** falls, whether to
12:5 when the almond ***t*** blanches, the

Song of Songs
2:3 Like an apple ***t*** among the wild trees,
2:13 is on the fig ***t***, and the
7:8 climb the palm ***t***; I will hold its
8:5 Under the apple ***t*** I aroused you—

Isaiah
17:6 a stripped olive ***t***: two or three
24:13 a smashed olive ***t***, like remains
34:4 from a vine, like fruit from a fig ***t***.
36:16 own vine and fig ***t*** and drink water
44:23 forest, and every ***t*** in it. The LORD
56:3 let the eunuch say, "I'm just a dry ***t***."
57:5 under every green ***t***, who slaughter
65:22 the days of a ***t*** will be the days

Jeremiah
1:11 I said, "A branch of an almond ***t***."
2:20 under every lush ***t***, you have acted
3:6 every high hill and under every lush ***t***.
3:9 committing adultery with stone and ***t***.
3:13 every lush ***t*** and haven't
8:13 no figs on the ***t***, only withered
10:3 are hollow: a ***t*** from the forest
11:16 blossoming olive ***t***, fair and
11:19 destroy the ***t*** with its fruit;

Ezekiel
6:13 and under every lofty ***t*** and leafy oak.
17:24 down the tall ***t*** and raise up the
20:47 and every dry ***t*** in you. Its
31:14 well-watered ***t*** would tower high
41:19 toward one palm ***t***, and the face of
41:25 single luxuriant ***t*** stood outside, in

Daniel
4:10 center of the earth was a towering ***t***.
4:11 The ***t*** grew in size and strength; it was
4:12 All living things lived off that ***t***.
4:14 Cut down the ***t*** and shear off its
4:20 The ***t*** you saw that grew in size and
4:22 Majesty, that ***t*** is you! You have
4:23 Cut down the ***t*** and destroy it,
4:26 root of the ***t***—that means your

Hosea
9:10 fruit on the fig ***t***, I saw your
14:6 be like the olive ***t***, and his
14:8 a green cypress ***t***; your fruit comes

Joel
1:12 dried up; the fig ***t*** withers.
2:22 turn green; the ***t*** will bear its

Habakkuk
2:11 wall, and a ***t*** branch will
2:19 one saying to the ***t***, "Wake up!" or
3:17 Though the fig ***t*** doesn't bloom, and

Haggai
2:19 the vine, the fig ***t***, or the

Matthew
3:10 Therefore, every ***t*** that doesn't
7:17 way, every good ***t*** produces good
7:18 A good ***t*** can't produce bad fruit. And a
7:19 Every ***t*** that doesn't produce good fruit
12:33 consider the ***t*** good and its
13:32 It becomes a ***t*** so that the birds
21:19 He saw a fig ***t*** along the road, but when
21:20 How did the fig ***t*** dry up so fast?"
21:21 done to the fig ***t***. You will even
24:32 from the fig ***t***. After its branch

Mark
11:13 he noticed a fig ***t*** in leaf, so he
11:20 they saw the fig ***t*** withered from the

11:21 look how the fig ***t*** you cursed has
13:28 from the fig ***t***. After its branch
Luke
3:9 Therefore, every ***t*** that doesn't
6:43 A good ***t*** doesn't produce bad fruit,
6:44 Each ***t*** is known by its own fruit.
13:6 man owned a fig ***t*** planted in his
13:7 fruit on this fig ***t*** for the past
13:19 developed into a ***t*** and the birds in
17:6 to this mulberry ***t***, 'Be uprooted and
19:4 up a sycamore ***t*** so he could see
21:29 Look at the fig ***t*** and all the trees.
23:31 things when the ***t*** is green, what
John
1:48 called you, I saw you under the fig ***t***."
1:50 you under the fig ***t***? You will see
Acts
5:30 you killed by hanging him on a ***t***.
10:39 They killed him by hanging him on a ***t***,
Romans
11:17 produces the rich oil of the olive ***t***,
11:24 of a wild olive ***t*** and you were cut
Galatians
3:13 Everyone who is hung on a ***t*** is cursed.
James
3:12 can a fig ***t*** produce olives?
Revelation
2:7 to eat from the ***t*** of life, which is
6:13 earth as a fig ***t*** drops its fruit
7:1 against the earth, the sea, or any ***t***.
9:4 plant or any ***t***. They could only
22:2 the river is the ***t*** of life, which
22:14 of access to the ***t*** of life and may
22:19 share in the ***t*** of life and the

TREES

Genesis
1:11 seeds and fruit ***t*** bearing fruit
2:16 your fill from all of the garden's ***t***;
3:2 We may eat the fruit of the garden's ***t***
3:8 God in the middle of the garden's ***t***.
23:17 it, and all the ***t*** within the
30:37 almond, and plane ***t***; and he peeled
Exodus
10:5 will eat all your ***t*** growing in the
15:27 and seventy palm ***t***. They camped
23:11 with your vineyard and your olive ***t***.
Leviticus
23:40 from majestic ***t***, palm branches,
26:4 yield, and the ***t*** of the field will
26:20 yield, and the ***t*** of the land won't
27:30 or fruit from the ***t***, belong to the
Numbers
13:20 poor? Are there ***t*** in it or not? Be
24:6 like eaglewood ***t*** that the LORD has
33:9 and seventy palm ***t*** and they camped
Deuteronomy
6:11 and olive ***t*** that you didn't
8:8 vines, fig ***t***, and
12:2 or hills or under leafy green ***t***.
20:19 don't destroy its ***t*** by cutting them
24:20 off your olive ***t***, don't go back
28:40 have many olive ***t*** throughout your
28:42 over all your ***t*** and your soil's
Joshua
10:26 them on five ***t***. They were
10:27 down from the ***t***. They threw them
Judges
9:8 Once the ***t*** went out to anoint a king
9:15 replied to the ***t***, 'If you're
2 Samuel
5:23 at them from in front of the balsam ***t***.
5:24 the tops of the ***t***, then attack, for
1 Kings
4:25 vines and fig ***t*** throughout the
4:33 the botany of ***t***, whether the
6:29 creatures, palm ***t***, and blossoming
7:36 lions, and palm ***t*** with wreaths
10:27 as sycamore ***t*** that grow in the
2 Kings
3:19 down all the good ***t***, stopping up all
5:26 clothes, olive ***t***, vineyards,
6:4 Jordan River and began cutting down ***t***.
19:23 best of its pine ***t***. I have reached
1 Chronicles
14:14 at them from in front of the balsam ***t***.
16:33 Then the ***t*** of the forest will shout out
27:28 and sycamore ***t*** in the western
2 Chronicles
1:15 as sycamore ***t*** that grow in the
3:5 decorated them with palm ***t*** and chains.
9:27 as sycamore ***t*** that grow in the
Nehemiah
8:15 and other leafy ***t*** to make booths,
9:25 great many fruit ***t***. They ate until
10:35 fruit from all ***t*** every year to the
Psalms
29:5 breaks cedar ***t***—yes, the LORD
74:5 axes raised against a thicket of ***t***.
78:47 with hail, their sycamore ***t*** with frost.
96:12 Then all the ***t*** of the forest too
104:12 their home, chirping loudly in the ***t***.
104:16 The LORD's ***t*** are well watered—the
105:33 and their fig ***t***; shattered the
128:3 will be like olive ***t***, freshly planted.
137:2 We hung our lyres up in the ***t*** ther
148:9 hill, fruit ***t***, and every single
Proverbs
11:28 the righteous will thrive like leafy ***t***.
Song of Songs
2:3 among the wild ***t***, so is my lover
3:9 for himself from the ***t*** of Lebanon.
Isaiah
7:2 shook as the ***t*** of a forest shake
10:19 remaining ***t*** will be no more
37:24 best of its pine ***t***. I have reached
41:19 myrtle, and olive ***t***; I will put in
44:14 from all the ***t*** of the forest. He
55:12 you; all the ***t*** of the field will
Jeremiah
5:17 vines and fig ***t***; it will shatter
6:6 Cut down her ***t***, and build siege
7:20 beasts, on the ***t*** of the field and
17:2 poles by the lush ***t*** and high hills.
17:8 They will be like ***t*** planted by the
Ezekiel
15:2 the wood of all the ***t*** in the forest?
15:6 Of all the ***t*** in the forest, I
17:24 Then all the ***t*** in the countryside will
20:28 hills and lofty ***t***, there they made
31:4 down to all the other ***t*** of the field.
34:27 The ***t*** in the field will bear fruit, and
39:10 or chop down ***t*** from the forest,
40:16 The arches were decorated with palm ***t***.

41:18 and palm **t**. The palm trees
47:7 I saw very many **t** on both banks of
Hosea
2:12 vines and her fig **t**, of which she
4:13 various green **t**, because their
Joel
1:7 splintered my fig **t**, stripped off
1:12 apple—all the **t** of the field are
1:19 have burned all the **t** of the field.
Amos
2:9 as tall as cedar **t**, and whose
4:9 your olive **t**; yet you didn't
7:14 shepherd, and a trimmer of sycamore **t**.
Micah
4:4 their own fig **t**. There will be no
Nahum
3:12 are fig **t** with ripe fruit;
Zechariah
1:8 among the myrtle **t** in the valley;
3:10 sit beneath their vines and the fig **t**."
4:3 It has two olive **t** beside the
4:11 these two olive **t** on the right and
Matthew
3:10 the root of the **t**. Therefore, every
21:8 branches off the **t** and spread them
Mark
8:24 They look like **t**, only they are
Luke
3:9 the root of the **t**. Therefore, every
21:29 Look at the fig tree and all the **t**.
Jude
1:12 fruitless autumn **t**, twice dead,
Revelation
7:3 the sea, or the **t** until we have put
8:7 A third of the **t** were burned up.
11:4 are the two olive **t** and the two

TREMBLE

1 Chronicles
16:30 ***T*** before him, all the earth! Yes, he
Ezra
10:3 and of those who **t** at the
Job
13:25 leaf to **t**, or will you
Psalms
69:23 see; make their insides **t** constantly.
96:9 holy splendor! ***T*** before him, all
114:7 Earth: **t** before the Lord! Tremble
Ecclesiastes
12:3 the housekeepers **t** and the strong
Isaiah
19:1 idols will **t** before God; the
19:16 women and will **t** with terror
28:16 foundation: the one who trusts won't **t**.
32:11 ***T***, all of you who are at ease;
41:5 ends of the earth **t**; they draw near
44:8 Don't **t**; have no fear! Didn't I
44:11 gather and stand, **t** and be ashamed
60:5 your heart will **t** and open wide,
64:2 the nations would **t** in your presence.
66:2 contrite in spirit, who **t** at my word.
66:5 word, you who **t** at his word: Your
Jeremiah
5:22 the LORD, and **t** before me, the
8:16 the whole land **t**. They come to
Lamentations
4:5 gourmet food now **t** in the streets.
Ezekiel
7:27 people will **t**. When I do to
26:18 the wastelands **t** on the day of
32:10 them. They will **t** for their lives
Joel
2:1 of the land **t**, for the day of
Amos
3:6 won't people **t**? If disaster
8:8 Will not the land **t** on this account,
Habakkuk
3:16 and my insides **t**. My lips quiver
James
2:19 believe this, and they **t** with fear.

TRIBE

Numbers
1:4 one man from each **t** who is the head
Deuteronomy
1:16 to your fellow **t** members and judge
1:23 I selected twelve men, one from each **t**.
Judges
21:6 said, "Today one **t** has been cut off
1 Kings
11:13 I will give one **t** to your son on
Psalms
74:2 to be the **t** of your own
78:67 and didn't choose the **t** of Ephraim.
78:68 he chose the **t** of Judah, the
Hebrews
7:13 to another **t**, and no one ever
7:14 came from the **t** of Judah, but
Revelation
5:5 The Lion of the **t** of Judah, the
5:9 from every **t**, language,
14:6 to every nation, **t**, language, and

TRIBES

Genesis
49:28 are the twelve **t** of Israel, and
Exodus
24:4 pillars for the twelve **t** of Israel.
39:14 each with its name for the twelve **t**.
Numbers
33:54 land according to your ancestral **t**.
2 Samuel
5:1 All the Israelite **t** came to David at
1 Kings
11:31 Solomon's hand. I will give you ten **t**.
14:21 among all the **t** of Israel to set
18:31 the number of the **t** of the sons of
2 Kings
21:7 of all Israel's **t**, I will put my
Ezra
6:17 to the number of the **t** of Israel.
Psalms
78:55 he settled Israel's **t** in their tents.
105:37 and gold; not one of its **t** stumbled.
122:4 That is where the **t** go up—the LORD's
Isaiah
49:6 to raise up the **t** of Jacob and to
63:17 your servants the **t** that are your
Jeremiah
1:15 for all the **t** of great nations
25:9 to muster all the **t** of the north and
25:24 the kings of Arabia and the nomadic **t**,
Ezekiel
37:19 hand, and the **t** of Israel

47:21 according to the ***t*** of Israel.
48:31 the names of the ***t*** of Israel. There
Hosea
5:9 Day. Against the ***t*** of Israel I will
Zechariah
9:1 Aram and all the ***t*** of Israel belong
Matthew
19:28 overseeing the twelve ***t*** of Israel.
24:30 that time all the ***t*** of the earth will
Luke
22:30 overseeing the twelve ***t*** of Israel.
Acts
26:7 our twelve ***t*** hope to receive
James
1:1 To the twelve ***t*** who are scattered
Revelation
1:7 him, and all the ***t*** of the earth will
11:9 of the peoples, ***t***, languages, and
21:12 names of the twelve ***t*** of Israel's sons.

TRIBUTE
Numbers
31:28 You will offer as ***t*** to the LORD from
31:37 of which the LORD's ***t*** was 675
31:38 36,000, of which the LORD's ***t*** was 72.
31:39 30,500, of which the LORD's ***t*** was 61.
31:40 of which the LORD's ***t*** was 32 persons.
31:41 Moses gave the ***t***, a gift offering for
Judges
3:15 him to take their ***t*** payment to Moab's
3:17 he presented the ***t*** payment to Moab's
3:18 delivering the ***t*** payment, Ehud
2 Samuel
8:2 David's subjects and brought him ***t***.
8:6 and brought him ***t***. The LORD gave
1 Kings
4:21 areas brought ***t*** to Solomon and
10:25 they came with ***t***: objects of
2 Kings
17:3 Shalmaneser's servant, paying him ***t***.
17:4 stopped paying ***t*** to the Assyrian
2 Chronicles
9:24 they came with ***t***: objects of
17:5 Jehoshaphat ***t***, so that he had
17:11 load of silver as ***t*** to Jehoshaphat.
Ezra
4:13 they will not pay ***t*** or tax or dues,
4:20 Beyond the River. ***T*** and taxes and
6:8 is made up of the ***t*** of the province
7:24 for you to charge ***t***, custom, or dues
Job
40:20 hills bring him ***t***, places where all
Psalms
68:18 receiving ***t*** from people, even
72:10 the islands bring ***t***; let the kings of

TRIP
Leviticus
19:14 cause them to ***t***. Instead, fear
Job
18:7 slow down; their plans ***t*** themselves.
Psalms
37:24 Though they ***t*** up, they won't be thrown
64:8 will make them ***t*** over their own
140:4 violent people who plot to ***t*** me up!
Isaiah
8:14 be a stone to ***t*** over and a rock
Matthew
18:6 believe in me to ***t*** and fall into
18:7 cause people to ***t*** and fall into
21:33 it to tenant farmers and took a ***t***.
25:14 was leaving on a ***t***. He called his
Mark
9:42 believe in me to ***t*** and fall into
12:1 it to tenant farmers and took a ***t***.
13:34 if someone took a ***t***, left the
Luke
15:13 and took a ***t*** to a land far
17:1 cause people to ***t*** and fall into sin
17:2 little ones to ***t*** and fall into sin.
20:9 and went on a ***t*** for a long time.
Revelation
2:14 taught Balak to ***t*** up the Israelites

TROOPS
Deuteronomy
20:2 come forward and will address the ***t***.
Joshua
8:14 he and all his ***t***, the men of the
Judges
4:7 his chariots and ***t*** against you at
20:10 supplies for the ***t*** who are going to
1 Kings
22:4 with you, and my ***t*** and my horses are
2 Kings
1:14 and their ***t*** of fifty
3:7 one: you and I, our ***t*** and our horses."
Job
19:12 His ***t*** come as one and construct their
25:3 Can his ***t*** be counted? On whom does his light not rise?
29:25 a king with his ***t***, like one who
Psalms
76:5 All the strong ***t*** couldn't even
Jeremiah
38:4 the few remaining ***t*** left in the city,
40:7 and their ***t*** were still hiding
Ezekiel
12:14 and all his ***t*** to the winds and
17:21 with all his ***t*** will fall by the
30:17 The elite ***t*** of On and Pi-beseth will
31:2 king, and his ***t***: With whom do you
38:6 Gomer and all his ***t***, Beth-togarmah
39:4 you, all your ***t***, and the peoples
Joel
2:11 numerous are his ***t***! Mighty are those
Micah
5:1 Now muster your ***t***, Daughter Troop!
Revelation
9:16 number of cavalry ***t*** was two hundred

TROUBLE
Genesis
35:3 me when I was in ***t*** and who has been
Numbers
23:21 nor has he seen ***t*** for Israel. The
Deuteronomy
26:7 our misery, our ***t***, and our
Judges
11:7 you coming to me now when you're in ***t***?"
15:3 to bring down ***t*** on the
1 Samuel
1:16 praying out of my great worry and ***t***!"

TROUBLE [cont.]

2:32 You'll see **t** in my dwelling place,
13:6 that they were in **t** and that their
14:29 has brought **t** to the land. Look
20:21 won't be any **t**—I make a pledge
22:2 who was in **t**, in debt, or in
25:17 can do, because **t** is coming for our
26:24 and may he deliver me from all **t**."
28:10 lives, you won't get into **t** for this."
28:15 I'm in deep **t**!" Saul replied.
30:6 David was in deep **t** because the troops

2 Samuel
4:9 me from all kinds of **t**," he told them,
7:10 will no longer **t** them, as they had
12:11 says: I am making **t** come against you
14:10 and he will never **t** you again," the
16:8 You are in this **t** because you are a
19:7 that will be more **t** for you than all
20:6 will cause more **t** for us than
24:14 I'm in deep **t**," David said to Gad.

1 Kings
1:29 lives, who rescued me from every **t**,

2 Kings
4:13 gone to all this **t** for us. What can

1 Chronicles
2:7 Achar, who made **t** for Israel by
4:10 to keep me from **t**, so as not to
17:9 will no longer **t** them as they did
21:13 I'm in deep **t**," David said to Gad.

2 Chronicles
15:4 in their time of **t** they turned to
28:20 to Ahaz, but he brought **t**, not support.

Nehemiah
1:3 are in great **t** and shame! The
2:17 You see the **t** that we're in:

Esther
9:24 month and day to **t** greatly and

Job
3:10 womb, didn't hide **t** from my eyes.
4:8 who plow sin and sow **t** will harvest it.
5:6 Surely **t** doesn't come from dust, nor
11:16 You will forget **t**; you will remember
20:22 all sorts of **t** come on them.
36:16 from the brink of **t** to a wide place

Psalms
7:14 evil, conceive **t**, give birth to
7:16 The **t** they cause will come back on
20:1 you are in **t**. Let the name of
22:11 from me because **t** is near and
25:18 my suffering and **t**—forgive all my
32:7 protect me from **t**. You surround me
34:6 listened and saved him from every **t**.
37:39 LORD; he is their refuge in times of **t**.
46:1 a help always near in times of great **t**.
49:5 in times of **t**, when the
50:15 you are in **t**; I will deliver
66:14 my mouth spoke when I was in deep **t**.
69:17 I'm in deep **t**. Answer me
73:5 They are never in **t**; they aren't
77:2 day when I'm in **t** I look for my
86:7 Whenever I am in **t**, I cry out to you
90:10 hard work and **t** because they go
90:15 number of years that we saw only **t**.
102:2 me in my time of **t**! Listen to me!
107:39 down by oppression, **t**, and grief—
116:3 I came face-to-face with **t** and grief.
120:1 when I was in **t** (and he answered
138:7 I am in deep **t**, you make me live
140:9 covered with the **t** their own lips

Proverbs
10:10 wink an eye bring **t**; those who speak
10:22 a person rich, and no **t** is added to it.
11:15 brings big **t**, but the one who
11:29 Those who **t** their family will inherit
12:21 but the wicked receive their fill of **t**.
13:13 ***T*** will come on those who despise a
13:17 fall into **t**, but a reliable
13:20 wise; befriend fools and get in **t**.
13:21 ***T*** pursues sinners, but good things
15:6 but the gain of the wicked brings **t**.
15:27 unjustly gain **t** for their house,
16:27 people dig up **t**; their lips are
17:17 and kinsfolk are born for times of **t**.
17:20 with twisted tongues will fall into **t**.
19:28 justice; the wicked mouth gulps down **t**.
21:12 wicked, turning the wicked toward **t**.
21:23 their tongues guard themselves from **t**.
22:3 people see **t** and hide, while
24:2 on violence, and their lips speak of **t**.
24:16 up, but the wicked will stumble into **t**.
28:14 whose hearts are hard fall into **t**.
29:21 age, and later on there will be **t**.
31:12 him good and not **t** all the days of

Ecclesiastes
12:1 the days of **t** arrive, and those

Isaiah
14:3 from pain and **t** and from the hard

Jeremiah
1:14 LORD said to me, "***T*** will erupt from
2:27 in their time of **t** they say, "Arise
2:28 in your time of **t**. You have as many
14:8 in times of **t**. Why are you like
15:11 your enemies in time of **t** and distress?
16:19 refuge in time of **t**. The nations will

Lamentations
1:20 LORD, for I am in **t**. My stomach is

Ezekiel
32:9 I will **t** the hearts of many peoples
32:13 nor livestock's hoof will **t** it again.
34:28 live in safety, with no one to **t** them.

Daniel
9:12 bringing great **t** on us. What
9:13 All this **t** came upon us, exactly as it
9:14 oversaw the great **t** and brought it on

Matthew
6:34 Each day has enough **t** of its own.
26:10 Why do you make **t** for the woman?

Mark
14:6 Why do you make **t** for her? She has

Acts
11:19 a result of the **t** that occurred

Romans
2:9 There will be **t** and distress for every
5:3 we know that **t** produces
8:35 be separated by **t**, or distress, or
12:12 when you're in **t**, and devote

1 Corinthians
9:16 to do it. I'm in **t** if I don't preach

2 Corinthians
1:4 us in all our **t** so that we can
1:6 So if we have **t**, it is to bring you
4:8 all kinds of **t**, but we aren't

Philippians
3:1 the Lord. It's no **t** for me to repeat

1 Thessalonians
3:7 our distress and ***t*** through your
2 Thessalonians
1:4 harassments and ***t*** that you have put
1:6 the ones making ***t*** for you with
1:7 who are having ***t*** with relief along
Hebrews
12:15 that might cause ***t*** and pollute many

TROUBLED

1 Kings
18:18 I haven't ***t*** Israel; you and
2 Chronicles
15:6 by city, as God ***t*** them with every
28:22 was during this ***t*** time that King
Job
17:8 guiltless become ***t*** about the godless.
20:2 Therefore my ***t*** thoughts make me turn
32:15 They are ***t***, no longer answer; words
37:1 by this and is more ***t*** than usual.
Psalms
32:6 to you during ***t*** times, so that a
Proverbs
15:13 one's face, but a ***t*** heart breaks the
25:20 a song to a ***t*** heart is like
Jeremiah
10:2 the nations or be ***t*** by signs in the
Ezekiel
27:28 cries for help, the ***t*** waters seethe.
Daniel
8:27 I remained ***t*** by the vision and
Matthew
2:3 this, he was ***t***, and everyone in
9:36 because they were ***t*** and helpless,
John
11:33 also, he was deeply disturbed and ***t***.
12:27 Now I am deeply ***t***. What should I say?
14:1 Don't be ***t***. Trust in God. Trust also
14:27 the world gives. Don't be ***t*** or afraid.
Acts
2:37 they were deeply ***t***. They said to
2 Corinthians
2:4 with a very ***t*** and anxious

TROUBLES

Genesis
41:51 forget all of my ***t*** and everyone in
Deuteronomy
1:12 I handle all your ***t***, burdens, and
1 Samuel
10:19 you from all your ***t*** and difficulties
1 Kings
18:17 Is that you, the one who ***t*** Israel?"
Esther
9:16 put to rest the ***t*** with their
9:22 put to rest the ***t*** with their
Psalms
4:1 me free from my ***t***! Have mercy on
25:17 My heart's ***t*** keep getting bigger—set
25:22 God, save Israel from all its ***t***!
34:17 he delivers them from all their ***t***.
71:20 shown me many ***t*** and calamities,
Isaiah
65:16 called Amen. Past ***t*** will be forgotten
Jeremiah
44:17 we were thriving; we didn't have any ***t***.
Acts
7:10 him from all his ***t***. The grace and
14:22 kingdom, we must pass through many ***t***."
20:23 to city that prisons and ***t*** await me.
2 Corinthians
1:8 be unaware of the ***t*** that we went

TRUE → TRUE GOD

Genesis
41:13 came ***t*** exactly: Pharaoh
42:16 if your words are ***t***. If not, as
Exodus
19:5 obey me and stay ***t*** to my covenant,
Numbers
11:23 my word will come ***t*** for you or not."
32:12 because they remained ***t*** to the LORD.'
Deuteronomy
4:4 of you who stayed ***t*** to the LORD your
22:20 if the claim is ***t*** and proof of the
1 Samuel
20:2 father hide this from me? It isn't ***t***!"
21:5 That's even more ***t*** today, with the
2 Samuel
22:31 word is tried and ***t***. He is a shield
1 Kings
3:6 and with a heart ***t*** to you. You've
8:26 your servant David, my father, come ***t***.
10:6 still at home is ***t***," she said to the
13:32 of Samaria will most certainly come ***t***."
2 Kings
10:10 will fail to come ***t***. The LORD has
19:17 It's ***t***, LORD, that the Assyrian kings
20:9 his promise come ***t***: Should the
2 Chronicles
6:17 promise to your servant David come ***t***.
9:5 still at home is ***t***," she said to the
31:20 his God considered good, right, and ***t***.
Nehemiah
9:13 judgments and ***t*** Instruction, good
Esther
2:23 and found to be ***t***, so the two men
3:4 words would hold ***t***. (He had told
Psalms
1:4 That's not ***t*** for the wicked! They are
18:30 word is tried and ***t***. He is a shield
19:9 judgments are ***t***. All of these are
78:20 ***T***, God struck the rock and water
90:6 ***T***, in the morning it thrives, renewed,
105:19 what the LORD had said proved him ***t***.
119:43 don't take your ***t*** word out of my
119:86 commandments are ***t***, but people
119:142 lasts forever! Your Instruction is ***t***!
119:151 too, and all your commandments are ***t***.
119:160 is that it is ***t*** and that all your
145:1 high, my God, the ***t*** king. I will
Proverbs
11:18 sow righteousness receive a ***t*** reward.
12:22 lips; he favors those who do what is ***t***.
22:21 is to teach you ***t***, reliable words
30:5 are tried and ***t***; a shield for
Isaiah
37:18 It's ***t***, LORD, that the Assyrian kings
43:9 let them hear and say, "It's ***t***!"
Jeremiah
42:5 the LORD be a ***t*** and faithful
44:28 whose word is ***t***—mine or theirs!

50:7 the LORD, the ***t*** pasture, the hope
Daniel
3:14 Abednego: Is it ***t*** that you don't
8:26 announced, is ***t***. But you must
10:1 The message was ***t***: there would be a
11:22 him. The same is ***t*** for the leader of
Malachi
2:6 ***T*** Instruction was in his mouth;
Matthew
13:14 become completely ***t*** for them: You
Luke
1:20 spoken will come ***t*** at the proper
16:11 who will trust you with ***t*** riches?
23:47 It's really ***t***: this man was
John
1:9 The ***t*** light that shines on all people
4:23 is here!—when ***t*** worshippers will
4:37 This is a ***t*** saying, that one sows and
5:31 about myself, my testimony isn't ***t***.
5:32 and I know his testimony about me is ***t***.
6:32 gives you the ***t*** bread from heaven.
6:55 My flesh is ***t*** food and my blood is true
7:28 who sent me is ***t***, and you don't
8:14 my testimony is ***t***, since I know
8:17 that the witness of two people is ***t***.
8:26 who sent me is ***t***, and what I have
10:41 John said about this man was ***t***."
15:1 I am the ***t*** vine, and my Father is the
19:35 his testimony is ***t***. He knows that he
21:24 down. We know that his testimony is ***t***.
Acts
7:1 asked, "Are these accusations ***t***?"
17:11 Paul and Silas's teaching was ***t***.
26:25 I'm speaking what is sound and ***t***.
Romans
3:4 not! God must be ***t***, even if every
6:16 you obey? That's ***t*** whether you serve
16:10 who is tried and ***t*** in Christ. Say
1 Corinthians
14:12 The same holds ***t*** for you: since you are
2 Corinthians
7:14 been proven to be ***t***, just like
Ephesians
4:24 God's image in justice and ***t*** holiness.
Philippians
1:18 from dishonest or ***t*** motives, I'm glad
4:8 all that is ***t***, all that is
Colossians
1:5 hope through the ***t*** message, the good
1 Timothy
1:2 To Timothy, my ***t*** child in the faith.
Titus
1:4 To Titus, my ***t*** child in a common faith.
1:13 This statement is ***t***. Because of this,
Hebrews
8:2 which is the ***t*** meeting tent that
9:24 is a copy of the ***t*** holy place) so
James
1:12 are tried and ***t***. They will
1:18 us birth by his ***t*** word, and here is
1:27 ***T*** devotion, the kind that is pure and
2 Peter
2:10 is especially ***t*** for those who
1 John
2:8 to you, which is ***t*** in him and in
2:27 all things (it's ***t*** and not a lie),
5:20 the one who is ***t***. We are in the
3 John
1:12 and you know that what we say is ***t***.
Revelation
3:7 who is holy and ***t***, who has the key
3:14 the faithful and ***t*** witness, the
6:10 voice, "Holy and ***t*** Master, how long
15:3 Just and ***t*** are your ways,
16:7 your judgments are ***t*** and just."
19:2 His judgments are ***t*** and just, because
19:9 to me, "These are the ***t*** words of God."
19:11 Faithful and ***T***, and he judges
21:5 for these words are trustworthy and ***t***."
22:6 trustworthy and ***t***. The Lord, the

TRUE GOD

Dt 7:9; 2Ki 19:19; 2Ch 15:3; 30:19; 33:13; Ps 78:20; Jer 10:10; Dn 5:23; Jn 17:3; 1Th 1:9; 1Jn 5:20

TRULY

2 Samuel
7:28 LORD God, you are ***t*** God! Your words are trustworthy
1 Kings
10:8 to listen to your wisdom are ***t*** happy!
17:24 the LORD's word is ***t*** in your mouth."
21:25 ***T*** there has never been anyone like Ahab
1 Chronicles
17:26 LORD, you are ***t*** God, and you promised
26:5 the eighth. God ***t*** blessed him.
2 Chronicles
9:7 to listen to your wisdom are ***t*** happy!
33:12 the LORD his God, ***t*** submitting
Nehemiah
1:5 covenant and is ***t*** faithful to those
9:17 very patient, and ***t*** faithful. You
Job
15:4 You are ***t*** making religion ineffective
19:21 my friends. God's hand has ***t*** struck me.
Psalms
1:1 The ***t*** happy person doesn't follow
2:12 take refuge in the LORD are ***t*** happy!
32:1 whose sin is covered over, is ***t*** happy!
32:2 is no dishonesty—that one is ***t*** happy!
33:12 chosen as his possession, is ***t*** happy!
34:8 one who takes refuge in him is ***t*** happy!
40:4 to those who follow lies, are ***t*** happy!
41:1 to the poor are ***t*** happy! The LORD
73:1 psalm of Asaph.] ***T*** God is good to
84:4 in your house are ***t*** happy; they
84:5 in you are ***t*** happy; pilgrimage
84:12 those who trust in you are ***t*** happy!
89:15 shout are ***t*** happy! They walk
94:12 LORD, are ***t*** happy—the ones y
106:3 always do what is right, are ***t*** happy!
112:1 adore God's commandments, are ***t*** happy!
119:1 in the LORD's Instruction—are ***t*** happy!
119:2 God's laws are ***t*** happy! They seek
127:5 full with them is ***t*** happy! They won't
128:1 who walks in God's ways, is ***t*** happy!
144:15 it like this are ***t*** happy! The people
146:5 on the LORD their God—is ***t*** happy!
Isaiah
38:20 The LORD has ***t*** saved me, and we will
41:26 That's right"? ***T***, no one announced

45:14 plead with you: "***T*** God is with you;
63:8 God said, "***T***, they are my people,
Jeremiah
7:5 No, if you ***t*** reform your ways and your
50:38 dry up. It is ***t*** the land of
Daniel
9:4 the covenant, and ***t*** faithful to all
Hosea
14:9 knows them. ***T***, the LORD's ways
Joel
3:1 ***T***, in those days and in that time, I
Amos
4:12 ***T***, Israel, I will act in this way
5:11 ***T***, because you crush the weak, and
5:16 ***T***, the LORD proclaims, the God of
Habakkuk
2:4 desires are ***t*** audacious; they
Zephaniah
1:18 make an end, a ***t*** horrible one, for
Zechariah
6:15 happen if you ***t*** obey the voice of
Malachi
1:14 is corrupt. I am ***t*** a great king,
John
4:42 that this one is ***t*** the savior of the
6:14 said, "This is ***t*** the prophet who
7:40 they said, "This man is ***t*** the prophet."
8:31 in him, "You are ***t*** my disciples if
17:8 them. They ***t*** understood that I
1 Corinthians
14:25 out loud that ***t*** God is among you!
Colossians
1:6 day you heard and ***t*** understood God's
1 Thessalonians
2:13 it for what it ***t*** is. Instead of
1 Timothy
5:3 Take care of widows who are ***t*** needy
5:5 A widow who is ***t*** needy and all alone
5:16 can help other widows who are ***t*** needy.
6:19 they can take hold of what is ***t*** life.
1 John
2:5 love of God is ***t*** perfected in
2 John
1:1 children, whom I ***t*** love (and I am
3 John
1:1 To my dear friend Gaius, whom I ***t*** love.

TRUMPET → ANGEL BLEW HIS TRUMPET
Leviticus
23:24 a holy occasion marked by a ***t*** signal.
25:9 Then have the ***t*** blown on the tenth day
Joshua
6:5 as you hear that ***t*** blast, have all
6:20 people heard the ***t*** blast, they
Judges
7:16 every man with a ***t*** and an empty jar,
7:18 When I blow the ***t***, along with all who
2 Samuel
2:28 Joab blew the ***t***, and all the soldiers
6:15 LORD's chest with shouts and ***t*** blasts.
15:10 the sound of the ***t***, then say
18:16 Joab sounded the ***t***, and the troops
20:1 He sounded the ***t*** and said: "We
20:22 Joab sounded the ***t***, and his troops
2 Kings
9:13 They blew a ***t*** and said, "Jehu
Nehemiah
4:20 When you hear the ***t*** sound, come and
Isaiah
18:3 see! When the ***t*** blasts, you will
27:13 that day, a great ***t*** will be played.
58:1 your voice like a ***t***! Announce to my
Jeremiah
4:19 the blast of the ***t*** and the roar of
4:21 flags and hear the blast of the ***t***?
6:1 Blow the ***t*** in Tekoa, sound
Ezekiel
33:3 he blows the ***t*** and warns the
33:4 the sound of the ***t*** but don't heed
33:5 the sound of the ***t*** but didn't heed
33:6 doesn't blow the ***t*** to warn the
Hosea
5:8 in Gibeah; blow a ***t*** in Ramah. Sound
8:1 Put a ***t*** to your lips! It's as if a bird
Zephaniah
1:16 for blowing the ***t*** and alarm against
Matthew
6:2 don't blow your ***t*** as the hypocrites
24:31 sound of a great ***t***, and they will
1 Corinthians
14:8 And if a ***t*** call is unrecognizable, then
15:52 eye, at the final ***t***. The trumpet will
1 Thessalonians
4:16 a blast on God's ***t***. First, those who
Hebrews
12:19 a blast of a ***t***, and a sound of words
Revelation
1:10 me a loud voice that sounded like a ***t***.
4:1 sounded like a ***t***, said to me,
9:14 who had the ***t***, "Release the

TRUMPETS
Numbers
10:2 Make two silver ***t*** and make them from
10:8 will blow the ***t***. This will be a
10:9 blasts with the ***t*** so that you may
10:10 you will blow the ***t*** over your
31:6 equipment and the ***t*** for sounding the
Joshua
6:4 carry seven ***t*** made from rams'
Judges
7:8 supplies and ***t***, and Gideon sent
2 Kings
11:14 and blowing ***t***. Athalaiah ripped
12:13 sprinkling bowls, ***t***, or any gold or
1 Chronicles
13:8 harps, tambourines, cymbals, and ***t***.
15:24 were to blow the ***t*** before God's
15:28 ram's horn, by ***t*** and cymbals, and
16:6 Jahaziel blowing ***t*** regularly before
16:42 were also the ***t*** and the cymbals
2 Chronicles
5:12 one hundred twenty priests blowing ***t***.
5:13 Accompanied by ***t***, cymbals, and
7:6 were blowing ***t*** while all Israel
13:12 sound the battle ***t*** against you. So,
13:14 LORD while the priests sounded the ***t***
15:14 of joy, and blasts from ***t*** and horns.
20:28 harps, lutes, and ***t***, and they went to
23:13 and blowing ***t***, and singers
29:26 instruments, and the priests their ***t***,
29:27 by the ***t*** and the other
29:28 and blaring ***t*** until the end of

Ezra
3:10 carrying their ***t***, and the Levites
Nehemiah
12:35 priests with ***t***—Zechariah son of
12:41 Zechariah, and Hananiah with ***t***.
Psalms
98:6 With ***t*** and a horn blast, shout
Revelation
8:2 God, and seven ***t*** were given to
8:6 held the seven ***t*** got ready to blow
8:13 of the remaining ***t*** that the three

TRUST → TRUST IN THE LORD, TRUST THE LORD
Exodus
19:9 they will always ***t*** you." Moses told
Numbers
20:12 you didn't ***t*** me to show my
Deuteronomy
9:23 You didn't ***t*** him. You didn't
Judges
11:20 Yet Sihon didn't ***t*** the Israelites to
16:15 when you won't ***t*** me? Three times
2 Kings
19:10 let the God you ***t*** in persuade you
Job
4:18 If he doesn't ***t*** his servants and levels
8:14 fragile thing, their ***t***, a spider's web.
15:15 If he doesn't ***t*** his holy ones and the
15:31 They shouldn't ***t*** in what has no worth,
31:24 I've made gold my ***t***, said to fine
39:11 Will you ***t*** it because its strength is
Psalms
9:10 know your name ***t*** you because you
20:7 Some people ***t*** in chariots, others in
25:2 My God, I ***t*** you. Please don't let me be
27:3 me, I will continue to ***t*** in this:
31:14 But me? I ***t*** you, LORD! I affirm, "You
33:21 in God because we ***t*** his holy name.
37:5 way to the LORD! ***T*** him! He will act
44:6 No, I won't ***t*** in my bow; my sword won't save me
49:6 those people who ***t*** in their fortunes
52:8 in God's house; I ***t*** in God's faithful
55:23 half their days. But me? I ***t*** in you!
56:3 I'm afraid, I put my ***t*** in you—
56:4 word I praise. I ***t*** in God; I won't
56:11 I ***t*** in God; I won't be afraid. What can
62:8 All you people: ***T*** in him at all times!
62:10 Don't ***t*** in violence; don't set false
78:22 because they didn't ***t*** his saving power.
84:12 forces, those who ***t*** in you are truly
91:2 You are my God—the one I ***t***!"
106:24 desirable. They didn't ***t*** God's promise.
115:8 idols and all who ***t*** in them become
118:8 refuge in the LORD than to ***t*** any human.
118:9 in the LORD than to ***t*** any human leader.
119:66 I've put my ***t*** in your
135:18 idols and all who ***t*** in them become
143:8 time because I ***t*** you. Show me the
146:3 Don't ***t*** leaders; don't trust any human
Proverbs
11:28 Those who ***t*** in their wealth will
22:19 So that your ***t*** will be in the LORD, I'm
28:26 Those who ***t*** in their own reasoning are
Isaiah
12:2 salvation; I will ***t*** and won't be
22:11 But you didn't ***t*** its maker; you
26:3 peace, in peace because they ***t*** in you.
30:12 this word and ***t*** in oppression and
30:15 quietness and ***t*** will be your
31:1 rely on horses, ***t*** in chariots
37:10 let the God you ***t*** deceive you by
42:17 are those who ***t*** in idols, who say
Jeremiah
5:17 towns in which you ***t***—with the sword!
7:4 Don't ***t*** in lies: "This is the LORD's
7:8 And yet you ***t*** in lies that will only
9:4 friends! Don't ***t*** your sibling!
12:6 get you. So don't ***t*** them, even if
17:5 are those who ***t*** in mere humans,
49:4 daughter. You ***t*** in your
49:11 look after them; ***t*** your widows into
Ezekiel
33:13 if they ***t*** in their
Micah
7:5 a friend; put no ***t*** in a companion;
Mark
1:15 and lives, and ***t*** this good news!"
Luke
16:11 wealth, who will ***t*** you with true
John
2:24 But Jesus didn't ***t*** himself to them
14:1 be troubled. ***T*** in God. Trust
14:11 ***T*** me when I say that I am in the Father
Acts
14:23 Lord, in whom they had placed their ***t***.
1 Corinthians
7:25 someone you can ***t*** because of the
1 Timothy
6:20 given to you in ***t***. Avoid godless
2 Timothy
1:12 I've placed my ***t***. I'm convinced
1:14 placed in your ***t*** through the Holy
1 Peter
1:8 see him now, you ***t*** him and so

TRUST IN THE LORD
2Ki 18:22; Ps 40:4; 115:9, 10, 11; 125:1; Is 26:4; 36:7; Jer 17:7; Zep 3:2; Phi 2:24

TRUST THE LORD
2Ki 6:33; 17:14; 18:30; 2Ch 20:20; Ps 4:5; 31:6; 37:3; 40:3; Prv 16:20; 28:25; 29:25; Is 36:15

TRUSTED
Genesis
15:6 Abram ***t*** the LORD, and the LORD
Deuteronomy
32:37 are their gods—the rocks they ***t*** in—
1 Samuel
27:12 Achish ***t*** David, thinking, David has
2 Kings
18:5 Hezekiah ***t*** in the LORD, Israel's God.
1 Chronicles
5:20 their prayer because they ***t*** in him.
9:22 seer assigned them to their ***t*** position.
2 Chronicles
32:8 The troops ***t*** Judah's King
Job
6:20 ashamed that they ***t***; they arrive and

12:20 the talk of ***t*** people; takes
Psalms
13:5 But I have ***t*** in your faithful love. My
22:4 Our ancestors ***t*** you—they trusted you
22:5 were saved; they ***t*** you and they
26:1 integrity. I've ***t*** the LORD without
41:9 friend, the one I ***t***, who shared my
52:7 Instead they ***t*** in their own
71:5 are the one I've ***t*** since childhood.
106:12 So our ancestors ***t*** God's words; they
119:24 my joy—they are my most ***t*** advisors!
119:42 mock me, because I have ***t*** in your word!
Isaiah
7:9 don't believe this, you can't be ***t***.'"
8:2 Summon ***t*** people, Uriah the priest and
22:8 On that day, you ***t*** the weapons in
Jeremiah
13:21 defenders, your ***t*** allies? Won't
13:25 you have forgotten me and ***t*** in lies.
38:22 will say: Your ***t*** friends have
39:18 because you have ***t*** in me, declares
48:13 on account of Bethel, in which they ***t***.
Ezekiel
16:15 But you ***t*** in your beauty and traded on
Daniel
2:45 is certain. Its meaning can be ***t***."
3:28 his servants who ***t*** him. They ignored
6:23 found on him, because he ***t*** in his God.
Hosea
10:13 because you have ***t*** in your way and
Luke
11:22 the armor he had ***t*** and divides the
Romans
3:2 the Jews were ***t*** with God's
1 Corinthians
4:17 he's my loved and ***t*** child in the
2 Corinthians
5:19 them. He has ***t*** us with this
1 Thessalonians
2:4 by God to be ***t*** with the good
1 Timothy
1:11 the blessed God that has been ***t*** to me.
Titus
1:3 and I was ***t*** with preaching
1 Peter
3:5 holy women who ***t*** in God used to

TRUSTWORTHY

Genesis
17:1 am El Shaddai. Walk with me and be ***t***.
Exodus
18:21 They should be ***t*** and not corrupt.
1 Samuel
2:35 for myself a ***t*** priest who will
3:20 that Samuel was ***t*** as the LORD's
22:14 who is as ***t*** as David? He is
2 Samuel
7:28 Your words are ***t***, and you have
Nehemiah
13:13 were considered ***t***, and their task
Psalms
111:7 and justice; all God's rules are ***t***—
119:138 commanded are righteous, completely ***t***.
145:13 The LORD is ***t*** in all that he
Proverbs
11:13 secrets, but a ***t*** person keeps a
27:6 ***T*** are the bruises of a friend;
Daniel
6:4 Daniel was ***t***. He wasn't guilty
1 Peter
4:19 their lives to a ***t*** creator by doing
Revelation
21:5 down, for these words are ***t*** and true."
22:6 These words are ***t*** and true. The

TRUTH → KNOW THE TRUTH

Exodus
23:2 don't stretch the ***t*** to favor
Joshua
22:24 No! The ***t*** is we did this out of concern
1 Samuel
12:3 here: Tell the ***t*** about me in the
1 Kings
3:6 before you in ***t***, righteousness,
22:16 you tell me the ***t*** when you speak in
2 Kings
20:3 before you in ***t*** and sincerity. I
2 Chronicles
18:15 you tell me the ***t*** when you speak in
19:9 at all times, in ***t***, and with
Psalms
5:9 there's no ***t*** in my enemies'
15:2 is right, and speaks the ***t*** sincerely;
25:5 Lead me in your ***t***—teach it to me
26:3 in front of me—I walk in your ***t***!
35:20 don't speak the ***t***; instead, they
43:3 your light and ***t***—those will guide
45:4 out on behalf of ***t***, humility, and
51:6 And yes, you want ***t*** in the most hidden
85:10 Faithful love and ***t*** have met;
85:11 ***T*** springs up from the ground;
86:11 can walk in your ***t***. Make my heart
111:8 are fulfilled with ***t*** and right doing.
Proverbs
8:7 mouth utters the ***t***; my lips despise
12:17 who state the ***t*** speak justly, but
23:23 Buy ***t*** and don't sell it; buy wisdom,
Isaiah
38:3 before you in ***t*** and sincerity.
45:19 one who speaks ***t***, who announces
59:14 far off, because ***t*** has stumbled in
59:15 ***T*** is missing; anyone turning from evil
Jeremiah
4:2 the living God in ***t***, justice, and
5:1 justly and seeks ***t*** that I may pardon
7:28 correction; ***t*** has disappeared;
8:6 heard a word of ***t*** from them. No one
9:3 land, but not for ***t***. They go from bad
9:5 no one tells the ***t***; they train
Daniel
4:37 All his works are ***t***, all his paths
7:16 asked him for the ***t*** about all this.
8:12 It will throw ***t*** to the ground and
10:21 in the Scroll of ***T***. No one stands
11:2 now tell you the ***t***. Persia will have
Amos
5:10 they reject the one who speaks the ***t***.
Zechariah
8:3 the city of ***t***; the mountain of
8:8 be their God—in ***t*** and in
8:16 do: Speak the ***t*** to each other;
8:19 the house of Judah. Love ***t*** and peace!
Matthew
25:12 I tell you the ***t***, I don't know

TRUTH [cont.]

26:13 I tell you the **t** that wherever in the
Mark
5:33 of Jesus and told him the whole **t**.
14:9 I tell you the **t** that, wherever in the
John
1:14 father's only son, full of grace and **t**.
1:17 so grace and **t** came into being
3:21 Whoever does the **t** comes to the light
4:18 your husband. You've spoken the **t**."
4:23 in spirit and **t**. The Father looks
4:24 to worship God in spirit and **t**."
5:33 to John, and he testified to the **t**.
7:18 me are people of **t**; there's no
8:40 has spoken the **t** I heard from God.
8:44 stood for the **t**, because there's
8:45 I speak the **t**, you don't
8:46 Since I speak the **t**, why don't you
14:6 am the way, the **t**, and the life. No
14:17 is the Spirit of ***T***, whom the world
15:26 Spirit of ***T*** who proceeds from
16:13 the Spirit of ***T*** comes, he will
17:17 them holy in the **t**; your word is
17:19 they also would be made holy in the **t**.
18:37 to testify to the **t**. Whoever accepts
18:38 What is **t**?" Pilate asked. After
19:35 he speaks the **t**, and he has
Acts
21:34 learn the **t**, so he ordered
24:9 affirming the **t** of these
Romans
1:18 who silence the **t** with injustice.
1:25 They traded God's **t** for a lie, and they
2:2 agrees with the **t**, and his judgment
2:8 instead of the **t** because they are
2:16 judge the hidden **t** about human
2:20 content of knowledge and **t** in the Law);
3:7 But if God's **t** is demonstrated by my
9:1 I'm speaking the **t** in Christ—I'm not
15:8 the sake of God's **t**, in order to
1 Corinthians
5:8 of honesty and **t**, not with old
13:6 injustice, but it is happy with the **t**.
2 Corinthians
4:2 by the public announcement of the **t**.
6:7 telling the **t**, and God's power. We
11:10 Since Christ's **t** is in me, I won't stop
12:6 I'd tell the **t**. I'm holding back
13:8 against the **t** but only to help
Galatians
2:5 so that the **t** of the gospel
2:14 with the **t** of the gospel, I
4:16 become your enemy by telling you the **t**?
5:7 stopped you from obeying the **t**?
Ephesians
1:13 heard the word of **t** in Christ, which
4:15 by speaking the **t** with love, let's
4:21 you were taught how the **t** is in Jesus,
4:25 you must tell the **t** to your neighbor
5:9 every sort of goodness, justice, and **t**.
5:11 you should reveal the **t** about them.
6:14 with the belt of **t** around your
2 Thessalonians
2:10 to love the **t** that would allow
2:12 convinced by the **t** but is happy with
2:13 and through your belief in the **t**.
1 Timothy
2:4 and to come to a knowledge of the **t**.
2:7 telling the **t** and I'm not
3:15 and the backbone and support of the **t**.
6:5 robbed of the **t**. They think that
2 Timothy
2:15 interprets the message of **t** correctly.
2:18 deviated from the **t** by claiming that
2:25 and give them a knowledge of the **t**.
3:7 arrive at an understanding of the **t**.
3:8 people oppose the **t** in the same way
4:4 their back on the **t** and turn to myths.
Titus
1:1 knowledge of the **t** that agrees with
1:14 commands from people who reject the **t**.
Hebrews
10:26 knowledge of the **t**, there isn't a
James
3:14 and living in ways that deny the **t**.
5:19 wander from the **t** and someone turns
1 Peter
1:22 obedience to the **t** so that you might
2 Peter
1:12 and stand secure in the **t** you have.
2:2 the way of **t** will be slandered.
2:18 those who have wandered from the **t**.
2:22 demonstrate the **t** of the proverb:
1 John
1:8 ourselves and the **t** is not in us.
2:4 a liar, and the **t** is not in this
2:27 to teach you the **t**. But since his
3:18 words or speech but with action and **t**.
3:19 we belong to the **t** and reassure our
4:6 the Spirit of **t** and the spirit of
5:6 testifies, because the Spirit is the **t**.
2 John
1:2 because of the **t** that remains with us
1:3 will be ours who live in **t** and love.
1:4 living in the **t**, just as we had
3 John
1:3 to the **t**, shown by how you
1:4 children are living according to the **t**.
1:8 so that we can be coworkers with the **t**.
1:12 even the **t** itself. We also

TURN FROM YOUR EVIL

2Ki 17:13; Jer 18:11; 25:5; 35:15; Zec 1:4; Ac 3:26

TWELFTH

Numbers
7:78 On the **t** day Naphtali's Chief, Ahira,
1 Kings
19:19 was with the **t** yoke. Elijah met
2 Kings
8:25 king in the **t** year of Israel's
17:1 in Samaria in the **t** year of Judah's
25:27 the twenty-seventh day of the **t** month.
1 Chronicles
24:12 eleventh to Eliashib, the **t** to Jakim,
25:19 the **t** to Hashabiah, his family, and his
27:15 The **t** for the twelfth month was Heldai
2 Chronicles
34:3 David, and in the **t** year he began
Ezra
8:31 River on the **t** day of the first
Esther
3:7 of Nisan) in the **t** year of the rule

3:13 day of the ***t*** month (that is,
8:12 day of the ***t*** month (that is,
9:1 day of the ***t*** month (that is,
Jeremiah
52:31 day of the ***t*** month of that
Ezekiel
29:1 year, on the ***t*** day of the tenth
32:1 In the ***t*** year, on the first day of the
32:17 In the ***t*** year, on the fifteenth day of
33:21 In the ***t*** year, on the fifth day of the
Revelation
21:20 was jacinth, and the ***t*** was amethyst.

TWELVE

Genesis
35:22 heard about it. Jacob had ***t*** sons.
49:28 These are the ***t*** tribes of Israel, and
Exodus
24:4 He set up ***t*** sacred stone
28:21 There will be ***t*** stones with names
39:14 There were ***t*** stones with names
Leviticus
24:5 flour and bake ***t*** loaves of
Numbers
1:44 Aaron, and the ***t*** chiefs of Israel,
7:84 it was anointed: ***t*** silver dishes,
7:86 the ***t*** gold bowls full of incense
7:87 offering were ***t*** bulls, twelve
17:2 their households, ***t*** staffs. Write
29:17 the second day: ***t*** bulls from the
31:5 were selected. ***T*** thousand were
33:9 Elim there were ***t*** springs of water
Deuteronomy
1:23 me, so I selected ***t*** men, one from
Joshua
4:3 them, 'Pick up ***t*** stones from right
21:40 their total allotment was ***t*** cities.
Judges
19:29 by limb, into ***t*** pieces. Then he
21:10 dispatched ***t*** thousand warriors
1 Kings
4:7 Solomon had ***t*** officers over all Israel.
7:25 The Sea rested on ***t*** oxen with their
7:44 one Sea; ***t*** oxen beneath the Sea
10:20 Another ***t*** lions stood on both sides of
18:31 Elijah took ***t*** stones, according to the
Ezra
6:17 for all Israel, ***t*** male goats,
8:24 Then I selected ***t*** of the leading
8:35 the God of Israel ***t*** bulls for all
Esther
2:12 at the end of ***t*** months. (She had
Jeremiah
52:20 Sea and the ***t*** bronze bulls that
Ezekiel
40:9 the gate: it was ***t*** feet, and its
47:13 to the ***t*** tribes of Israel.
Daniel
4:29 ***T*** months later, he was walking on the
Matthew
10:1 He called his ***t*** disciples and gave them
14:20 and they filled ***t*** baskets with the
19:28 also will sit on ***t*** thrones
Mark
5:25 who had been bleeding for ***t*** years.
5:42 around. She was ***t*** years old. They
6:7 He called for the ***T*** and sent them out
6:43 They filled ***t*** baskets with the leftover
8:19 did you gather?" They answered, "***T***."
Luke
2:42 When he was ***t*** years old, they went up
John
6:13 them and filled ***t*** baskets with the
11:9 Aren't there ***t*** hours in the day?
Acts
6:2 The ***T*** called a meeting of all the
7:8 Jacob, and Jacob with the ***t*** patriarchs.
19:7 Altogether, there were about ***t*** people
24:11 in Jerusalem no more than ***t*** days ago.
26:7 the promise our ***t*** tribes hope to
Revelation
7:5 tribe of Judah, ***t*** thousand were
12:1 and a crown of ***t*** stars on her head.
21:12 high wall with ***t*** gates. By the
21:14 The city wall had ***t*** foundations, and on them were
21:21 The ***t*** gates were twelve pearls; each
22:2 which produces ***t*** crops of fruit,

TWENTY

Genesis
18:31 my Lord, what if ***t*** are there?" The
Numbers
18:16 sanctuary shekel, which is ***t*** gerahs.
Judges
4:3 the Israelites cruelly for ***t*** years.

TWICE

Exodus
16:5 it will be ***t*** as much as they
16:22 people collected ***t*** as much food as
Numbers
20:11 with his staff ***t***. Out flooded
Deuteronomy
24:20 go back over them ***t***. Let the
24:21 pick them over ***t***. Let the
1 Kings
11:9 of Israel, who had appeared to him ***t***.
2 Kings
2:9 said, "Let me have ***t*** your spirit."
Nehemiah
13:20 Once or ***t*** the traders and sellers of
Job
33:29 does all this, ***t***, three times with
40:5 I won't answer; ***t***, I won't do it
Psalms
68:17 chariots are ***t*** ten thousand—
Ecclesiastes
6:6 a thousand years ***t*** over but don't
Jeremiah
3:9 She didn't think ***t*** about corrupting the
Ezekiel
21:14 the sword strike ***t***, three times!
Nahum
1:9 annihilate! Distress will not arise ***t***.
Matthew
23:15 they become ***t*** the child of hell
Mark
14:30 the rooster crows ***t***, you will deny me
14:72 a rooster crows ***t***, you will deny me
Luke
18:12 I fast ***t*** a week. I give a tenth of
Jude
1:12 autumn trees, ***t*** dead, uprooted;

Revelation
18:6 Give her back ***t*** as much for what

TWISTED

Exodus
26:1 curtains of fine ***t*** linen and blue,
Deuteronomy
32:5 they are a ***t*** and perverse
Psalms
10:5 ways are always ***t***. Your rules are
78:57 ancestors; they ***t*** away like a
95:10 people have ***t*** hearts. They
125:5 turn to their own ***t*** ways—
Proverbs
2:14 doing evil, rejoicing in their ***t*** evil.
8:8 nothing in them is ***t*** or crooked.
10:31 wisdom, but the ***t*** tongue will be
17:20 and those with ***t*** tongues will fall
21:8 some people are ***t*** and strange, but
28:18 those who go on ***t*** paths will fall
Daniel
3:19 and his face ***t*** beyond
Matthew
27:29 They ***t*** together a crown of thorns and
Mark
7:35 ears opened, his ***t*** tongue was
15:17 a purple robe and ***t*** together a crown
John
19:2 The soldiers ***t*** together a crown of
Titus
3:11 like this is ***t*** and sinful—so the

TYRE

1 Kings
5:1 King Hiram of ***T*** was loyal to
Psalms
45:12 The city of ***T***, the wealthiest of all,
Matthew
11:21 had been done in ***T*** and Sidon, they
Acts
12:20 the people of ***T*** and Sidon for

Uu

UNCIRCUMCISED
Genesis
17:14 Any ***u*** male whose flesh of his foreskin
34:14 sisters to marry ***u*** men, because it's
Exodus
12:48 the land. But no ***u*** person may eat it.
Leviticus
26:41 if their ***u*** hearts are
Joshua
5:7 place. They were ***u*** because they
Judges
14:3 a wife from the ***u*** Philistines?" Yet
15:18 and fall into the hands of the ***u***?"
1 Samuel
14:6 the fort of these ***u*** men. Maybe the
17:26 Who is that ***u*** Philistine,
17:36 and bears. This ***u*** Philistine will
31:4 Otherwise, these ***u*** men will come and
2 Samuel
1:20 the daughters of the ***u*** will celebrate.
1 Chronicles
10:4 Otherwise, these ***u*** men will come and
Isaiah
52:1 city; for the ***u*** and unclean will
Jeremiah
9:26 are really ***u***; even the people
Ezekiel
28:10 will die as the ***u*** do, at the hands
31:18 lie among the ***u***, with those who
32:19 Go down and take your bed with the ***u***,
44:7 and spiritually ***u***. When you offered
44:9 and physically ***u*** must not enter my
Acts
11:3 the home of the ***u*** and ate with
Ephesians
2:11 who were called "***u***" by Jews who are
Colossians
3:11 circumcised nor ***u***, barbarian,

UNCLEAN SPIRIT
Mt 12:43; Mk 1:26; 5:8; 7:25; 9:25; Lk 8:29; 9:42; 11:24; Rev 18:2

UNCLEAN → UNCLEAN SPIRIT, UNCLEAN SPIRITS
Genesis
7:2 and from every ***u*** animal, take one
7:8 the clean and ***u*** animals, from the
Leviticus
5:2 by touching some ***u*** thing—the dead
Psalms
106:39 made themselves ***u*** by what they did;
Isaiah
6:5 I'm a man with ***u*** lips, and I live
52:11 out from there! ***U***! Don't touch! Get
Lamentations
4:15 Go away! ***U***!" was shouted at them, "Go
Ezekiel
4:13 will eat their ***u*** bread among the
9:7 Make the temple ***u***! Fill the courts
44:25 however, become ***u*** for their father
Amos
7:17 will die in an ***u*** land, and Israel
Haggai
2:13 said, "If an ***u*** person touches
2:14 their hands. Whatever they offer is ***u***.
Zechariah
9:7 and pieces of ***u*** food from between
Matthew
27:6 to pay for someone's life, it's ***u***."
Mark
7:2 eating food with ***u*** hands. (They were
7:5 eat food with ritually ***u*** hands?"
Luke
4:33 the spirit of an ***u*** demon. He
Acts
10:14 have never eaten anything impure or ***u***."
10:15 Never consider ***u*** what God has made
10:28 should never call a person impure or ***u***.
11:8 Nothing impure or ***u*** has ever entered
11:9 Never consider ***u*** what God has made
2 Corinthians
6:17 touch what is ***u***. Then I will
Revelation
21:27 Nothing ***u*** will ever enter it, nor

UNCLEAN SPIRITS
Mt 10:1; Mk 1:27; 5:13; 6:7; Lk 4:36; 6:18; Ac 5:16; 8:7; Rev 16:13

UNDER THE BAN
Dt 2:34; 3:6; 7:2, 26; 13:15; 20:17; 1Sa 15:3; 15:8, 9, 15, 18, 20, 21

UNDER THE LAW
Lk 2:27; Ro 2:12; 3:19, 27, 28; 7:2; 1Co 9:20; 9:21; Ga 3:23; 4:4, 5, 21; 5:18; Phi 3:6; Heb 7:5

UNDERSTAND
Genesis
11:7 so they won't ***u*** each other's
Numbers
14:34 This is how you will ***u*** my frustration."
Deuteronomy
28:49 that speaks a language you can't ***u***,
29:4 you insight to ***u***, eyes to see, or
32:29 they would ***u*** this; they would
Judges
13:18 do you ask my name? You couldn't ***u*** it."
2 Samuel
15:27 Do you ***u***?" the king said to the
1 Kings
20:7 Please know and ***u*** the evil this man
20:22 Know and ***u*** that at the turn

UNDERSTAND [cont.]

2 Kings
18:26 because we ***u*** it. Don't speak
Nehemiah
8:2 and anyone who could ***u*** what they heard.
8:3 those who could ***u***, and everyone
8:7 the people to ***u*** the Instruction
8:8 so the people could ***u*** what they heard.
Job
15:9 know; what do you ***u*** that isn't among
18:2 talking. Try to ***u*** and then we can
23:5 he would answer, ***u*** what he would say
26:14 him. Who can ***u*** his thunderous
32:9 wise; the old don't ***u*** what's right.
37:16 Do you ***u*** the positioning of the clouds,
42:3 things I didn't ***u***, wonders beyond
Psalms
49:20 They just don't ***u***; they're just
64:9 act of God, will ***u*** it was God's work.
73:16 when I tried to ***u*** these things, it
82:5 know; they don't ***u***; they wander
92:6 people don't know—fools don't ***u*** this:
106:7 in Egypt didn't ***u*** your wondrous
119:27 Help me ***u*** what your precepts are about
119:34 Help me ***u*** so I can guard your
119:73 in place. Help me ***u*** so I can learn
119:125 servant! Help me ***u*** so I can know
119:144 forever. Help me ***u*** so I can live!
119:169 LORD; help me ***u*** according to what
Proverbs
1:2 discipline, to help one ***u*** wise sayings.
1:6 They help one ***u*** proverbs and difficult
2:5 Then you will ***u*** the fear of the LORD,
2:9 Then you will ***u*** righteousness and
8:5 ***U*** skill, you who are naive. Take this
8:9 to those who ***u***, and upright for
14:8 the prudent ***u*** their way, but
20:24 LORD; how then can people ***u*** their path?
24:12 doesn't he ***u***? The one who
28:5 Evil people don't ***u*** justice, but those
29:7 of the poor, but the wicked don't ***u***.
29:19 words; they might ***u***, but they don't
Ecclesiastes
1:17 I set my mind to ***u*** wisdom, and also
11:5 Just as you don't ***u*** what the
Isaiah
5:13 since they didn't ***u***—their officials
5:19 holy one come quickly, so we can ***u*** it."
6:9 but don't ***u***; look carefully,
6:10 their ears, or ***u*** with their minds,
28:19 be nothing but terror to ***u*** the message.
29:16 the one who shaped it, "He doesn't ***u***"?
33:19 too obscure to ***u***, who stammer in
36:11 because we ***u*** it. Don't speak
43:10 believe me and ***u*** that I am the
56:11 who don't ***u***. All of them have
Jeremiah
2:19 out. Don't you ***u*** how terribly
5:4 They don't ***u*** the LORD's way or
5:15 don't know, whose speech you won't ***u***.
9:12 is wise enough to ***u*** this? Who has
9:24 this: that they ***u*** and know me. I am
10:14 is too foolish to ***u***; every goldsmith
15:15 You ***u***, LORD! Remember me and act on my behalf
16:21 might. They will ***u*** that I am the
23:20 to come, you will ***u*** what this means.
30:24 to come, you will ***u*** what this means.
51:17 is too foolish to ***u***; every smith is
Ezekiel
3:6 you wouldn't ***u***. If I did send
3:27 who hear will ***u***, but those who
12:3 of rebels, perhaps they will ***u***.
14:23 then you will ***u*** what I've done,
39:21 the nations will ***u*** the judgments
Daniel
8:5 I was trying to ***u*** this when suddenly a
8:16 help this person ***u*** what he has seen."
8:27 by the vision and couldn't ***u*** it.
9:23 treasured. So now ***u*** this word and
10:12 set your mind to ***u*** things and to
10:14 come to help you ***u*** what will happen
11:33 will help many ***u***, but for a time
12:8 it, but I didn't ***u*** it. "My lord," I
12:10 the wicked will ***u***, but those
Micah
4:12 LORD; they can't ***u*** his scheme,
Matthew
13:13 they hear, they don't really hear or ***u***.
13:23 who hear and ***u***, and bear fruit
15:10 near and said to them, "Listen and ***u***.
15:16 Jesus said, "Don't you ***u*** yet
16:9 Don't you ***u*** yet? Don't you remember the five loaves
24:15 holy place (the reader should ***u*** this),
24:43 But you ***u*** that if the head of the house
Mark
4:12 can hear but not ***u***. Otherwise, they
7:14 said, "Listen to me, all of you, and ***u***.
8:17 Don't you ***u***? Are your hearts
8:21 said to them, "And you still don't ***u***?"
9:32 But they didn't ***u*** this kind of talk,
13:14 (the reader should ***u*** this), then those
14:68 about. I don't ***u*** what you're
Luke
2:50 But they didn't ***u*** what he said to them
8:10 see, and when they hear, they can't ***u***.
9:45 They didn't ***u*** this statement. Its
24:45 opened their minds to ***u*** the scriptures.
John
8:43 Why don't you ***u*** what I'm saying? It's
10:6 analogy didn't ***u*** what he was
12:16 disciples didn't ***u*** these things at
12:40 with their eyes, ***u*** with their minds,
13:7 You don't ***u*** what I'm doing
16:18 soon'? We don't ***u*** what he's talking
20:9 They didn't yet ***u*** the scripture that
Acts
7:25 his own kin to ***u*** that God was
8:30 Do you really ***u*** what you are
26:3 is because you ***u*** well all the
28:26 sure, but never ***u***; and you will
28:27 their ears or ***u*** with their minds,
Romans
10:3 they don't ***u*** his
10:19 didn't Israel ***u***? First, Moses
15:21 see, and those who hadn't heard will ***u***.
1 Corinthians
2:8 if they did ***u*** it, they would
14:9 that is easy to ***u*** when you speak in
2 Corinthians
1:13 can read and also ***u***. I hope that you
1:14 us partly. ***U*** that in the day

13:5 Don't you ***u*** that Jesus Christ
Galatians
3:6 ***U*** that in the same way that Abraham
Ephesians
3:4 read this, you'll ***u*** my insight into
5:17 be ignorant, but ***u*** the Lord's will.
1 Timothy
1:9 We ***u*** this: the Law isn't established
6:4 They don't ***u*** anything but have
2 Timothy
3:1 ***U*** that the last days will be dangerous
Hebrews
11:3 By faith we ***u*** that the universe has
2 Peter
2:12 what they don't ***u*** and, like
3:16 are hard to ***u***, and people who
Jude
1:10 they don't ***u***. They are

UNDERSTANDING

2 Samuel
14:17 God's messengers, ***u*** good and evil.
1 Kings
3:12 you a wise and ***u*** mind. There has
4:29 and very great ***u***—insight as long a
1 Chronicles
22:12 you insight and ***u*** so that when he
27:32 a man of ***u***, and a scribe.
2 Chronicles
2:12 the knowledge and ***u*** to build a temple
Nehemiah
10:28 and all who have knowledge and ***u***.
Job
12:12 old age is wisdom; ***u*** in a long life."
12:13 and power; counsel and ***u*** are his.
20:3 am forced to answer based on my own ***u***.
28:12 it be found; where is the place of ***u***?
28:20 she come from? Where is the place of ***u***?
28:28 is wisdom; turning from evil is ***u***."
32:8 person, the Almighty's breath, gives ***u***.
34:16 But if you have ***u***, hear this; pay
36:12 sword, breathe their last without ***u***.
38:36 places, or who gave ***u*** to a rooster?
39:26 Is it due to your ***u*** that the hawk flys,
Psalms
119:100 I have more ***u*** than the elders because I
119:130 gives light, giving simple folk ***u***.
Proverbs
1:5 in wisdom; those with ***u*** gain guidance.
2:2 wisdom, and stretch your mind toward ***u***.
2:3 out for insight, and cry aloud for ***u***.
2:6 from his mouth come knowledge and ***u***.
2:11 will guard you; ***u*** will protect you.
3:13 who find wisdom and those who gain ***u***.
3:19 establishing the heavens with ***u***.
4:1 instruction; pay attention to gain ***u***.
4:5 Get wisdom; get ***u***. Don't forget and
4:7 Get wisdom! Get ***u*** before anything
7:4 You are my sister"; call ***u***"friend,"
8:1 Doesn't Wisdom cry out and ***U*** shout
8:14 and ability, as well as ***u*** and strength.
9:6 ways and live; walk in the way of ***u***."
9:10 the knowledge of the holy one is ***u***.
10:13 of those who have ***u***, but there is a
10:23 but those with ***u*** take pleasure in
14:29 leads to abundant ***u***, but impatience
14:33 resides in an ***u*** heart, but it's
15:14 An ***u*** heart seeks knowledge; but fools
15:21 but those with ***u*** walk straight
15:32 those who listen to correction gain ***u***.
16:16 and acquiring ***u*** is better than
17:10 goes deeper to an ***u*** person than a
17:24 of those with ***u***, but the eyes of
17:27 talking; people with ***u*** are coolheaded.
18:2 no pleasure in ***u***, but only in
18:15 An ***u*** mind gains knowledge; the ear of
19:8 those who keep ***u*** find success.
19:25 someone with ***u***, and they will
20:5 heart; those with ***u*** can draw it out.
21:30 No wisdom, ***u***, or advice can stand up
23:23 it; buy wisdom, instruction, and ***u***.
24:3 house is built; by ***u*** it is established.
28:2 but a person with ***u*** brings order.
28:16 A prince without ***u*** is a cruel
30:2 stupid to be human, a man without ***u***.
Isaiah
11:2 of wisdom and ***u***, a spirit of
27:11 people have no ***u***; therefore, their
29:24 spirit will have ***u***, and those who
40:14 and explained to him the way of ***u***?
40:28 or weary. His ***u*** is beyond human
44:19 no knowledge or ***u*** to think: Half of
Jeremiah
3:15 will lead you with knowledge and ***u***.
4:22 children without ***u***; they are skilled
Daniel
1:17 himself gained ***u*** of every type of
1:20 of wisdom and ***u***, he found them
8:15 needed help ***u*** the vision I saw.
9:22 I've come: to give you insight and ***u***.
Hosea
4:11 practices. Wine and new wine destroy ***u***.
Obadiah
1:8 wise from Edom and ***u*** from Mount Esau?
Mark
12:33 the heart, a full ***u***, and all of one's
Luke
2:47 was amazed by his ***u*** and his answers.
Acts
24:22 had an accurate ***u*** of the Way,
Romans
1:31 They are without ***u***, disloyal, without
10:19 aren't a people, of a people without ***u***.
1 Corinthians
11:29 without correctly ***u*** the body are
2 Corinthians
10:12 with themselves, they have no ***u***.
Ephesians
1:8 he poured over us with wisdom and ***u***.
Philippians
4:7 that exceeds all ***u*** will keep your
Colossians
1:9 will, with all wisdom and spiritual ***u***.
2:2 that come with ***u***, so that they
1 Timothy
1:7 of Law without ***u*** either what they
2 Timothy
2:7 Lord will give you ***u*** about everything.
3:7 can never arrive at an ***u*** of the truth.
Philemon
1:6 effective by an ***u*** of all that is

James
3:13 of you wise and ***u***? Show that your
1 Peter
2:19 because of one's ***u*** of God, someone
2 Peter
1:20 the prophet's own ***u*** of things,
3:1 stir up your sincere ***u*** with a reminder.
1 John
5:20 and has given us ***u*** to know the one
Revelation
17:9 This calls for an ***u*** mind. The seven

UNDERWORLD

Job
11:8 Deeper than the ***u***—what can you kn
14:13 hide me in the ***u***, conceal me until
17:13 If I hope for the ***u*** as my dwelling, lay
17:16 with me to the ***u***; will we descend
24:19 snow, just as the ***u*** steals sinners.
26:6 naked before God; the ***u*** lacks covering.
31:12 consumes to the ***u***, uprooting all my
Psalms
88:11 the grave, your faithfulness in the ***u***?
Proverbs
15:11 The grave and the ***u*** lie open before the
27:20 The grave and the ***u*** are never
Isaiah
14:9 The ***u*** beneath becomes restless to greet
14:11 down to the ***u***, along with the
14:15 But down to the ***u*** you are brought, to
26:19 will bring down the ghosts into the ***u***.
28:15 death; with the ***u*** we made a pact.
38:10 the gates of the ***u*** for the rest of
38:18 The ***u*** can't thank you, nor can death
57:9 far away, sent them down to the ***u***.
Ezekiel
31:15 went down to the ***u***, I caused
31:16 it down into the ***u***, with those who
31:17 with him to the ***u***, to those who are
32:21 the middle of the ***u***, for the
32:27 went down to the ***u*** with their
Amos
9:2 through into the ***u***, from there my
Jonah
2:2 the belly of the ***u*** I cried out for
2:6 sunk down to the ***u***; its bars held me
Matthew
16:18 The gates of the ***u*** won't be able to
2 Peter
2:4 level of the ***u*** and committed
2:17 by the wind. The ***u*** has been reserved
Jude
1:6 chains in the ***u*** until the
1:13 darkness of the ***u*** is reserved

UNFAITHFUL → UNFAITHFUL TO THE LORD

Deuteronomy
32:51 two of you were ***u*** toward me in
Judges
2:17 because they were ***u***, following other
8:27 All Israel became ***u*** there because of
1 Chronicles
5:25 But they were ***u*** to the God of their
2 Chronicles
21:11 citizens to be ***u***, and led Judah
21:13 citizens to be ***u***, just as the
26:18 you have been ***u***! The LORD God
29:6 ancestors were ***u*** and did what was
36:14 grew increasingly ***u***, following all
Ezra
10:2 Ezra, "We've been ***u*** to our God by
10:10 You have been ***u*** by marrying
Nehemiah
1:8 said, 'If you are ***u***, I will scatter
Psalms
73:15 I would have been ***u*** to your children.
73:27 annihilate all those who are ***u*** to you.
Jeremiah
3:6 you noticed what ***u*** Israel has done?
3:8 saw that I sent ***u*** Israel away with
3:11 LORD said to me: ***u*** Israel is less
3:12 and say: Return, ***u*** Israel, declares
Ezekiel
23:5 But Oholah became ***u*** to me and lusted
Matthew
12:39 An evil and ***u*** generation
16:4 An evil and ***u*** generation searches for a
Mark
8:38 my words in this ***u*** and sinful
Luke
12:46 and assign them a place with the ***u***.
Romans
11:23 continue to be ***u***, because God is
1 Timothy
1:10 who are sexually ***u***, and people who
Hebrews
3:12 you have an evil, ***u*** heart that
James
4:4 You ***u*** people! Don't you know that

UNFAITHFUL TO THE LORD

1Ch 10:13; 2Ch 12:2; 28:19, 22; 30:7

UNGODLY PEOPLE

Ps 43:1; Ro 5:6; 2Pt 2:5; 2:6; 3:7; Jud 1:15

UNITED

Judges
20:11 together and were ***u*** as one against
1 Kings
22:4 troops and my horses are ***u*** with yours.
2 Chronicles
18:3 my people will be ***u*** with you and your
Acts
1:14 all were ***u*** in their devotion to prayer,
2:44 believers were ***u*** and shared
8:6 The crowds were ***u*** by what they heard
15:25 We reached a ***u*** decision to select some
18:12 Achaia, the Jews ***u*** in their
Romans
6:5 If we were ***u*** together in a death like
7:2 married woman is ***u*** with her husband
7:4 that you could be ***u*** with someone
Ephesians
5:31 and mother and be ***u*** with his wife,
Philippians
1:27 you stand firm, ***u*** in one spirit and
2:2 same love, being ***u***, and agreeing
Colossians
2:2 be encouraged and ***u*** together in love
Hebrews
4:2 they weren't ***u*** in faith with the

1 John
5:8 the three are ***u*** in agreement.

UNLEAVENED → FESTIVAL OF UNLEAVENED BREAD

Genesis
19:3 them, even baking ***u*** bread, and they
Exodus
12:8 eat it along with ***u*** bread and bitter
12:15 You will eat ***u*** bread for seven days. On
12:18 day, you should eat ***u*** bread.
Deuteronomy
16:3 days you must eat ***u*** bread, bread
1 Corinthians
5:7 supposed to be ***u*** bread. Christ our
5:8 feast with the ***u*** bread of honesty

UPLIFTED

Exodus
29:24 lift them as an ***u*** offering in the
35:22 raised an ***u*** offering of gold
38:24 gold from the ***u*** offerings, was
38:29 copper from the ***u*** offering was
Leviticus
7:30 be lifted as an ***u*** offering before
Numbers
6:20 raise them as an ***u*** offering before
18:18 the breast of the ***u*** offering and the
Job
38:15 from the wicked, the ***u*** arm broken.
Psalms
89:16 day long and are ***u*** by your
141:2 incense; let my ***u*** hands be like the

UPPER

Leviticus
13:45 hair, cover their ***u*** lip, and shout
Deuteronomy
24:6 or even just the ***u*** millstone must
Joshua
15:19 he gave her the ***u*** springs and the
16:5 on the east as far as ***U*** Beth-horon.
Judges
1:15 Caleb gave her the ***u*** and lower springs.
9:53 woman dropped an ***u*** millstone on
2 Samuel
11:21 a woman throw an ***u*** millstone on top
1 Kings
7:7 cedar from the lower to the ***u*** levels.
17:19 him to the ***u*** room where he was
17:23 boy down from the ***u*** room of the house
2 Kings
15:35 rebuilt the ***U*** Gate of the
18:17 channel of the ***U*** Pool, which is on
23:12 roof of Ahaz's ***u*** story, which had
1 Chronicles
7:24 both Lower and ***U*** Beth-horon and Uzz
26:16 gate on the ***u*** road. The guards
28:11 treasuries, ***u*** and inner rooms,
2 Chronicles
3:9 He also covered the ***u*** rooms with gold.
8:5 also built ***U*** Beth-horon and Low
23:20 through the ***U*** Gate to the
27:3 rebuilt the ***U*** Gate of the
32:30 who blocked the ***u*** outlet of the
32:33 was buried in the ***u*** area of the tombs
Nehemiah
3:25 from the ***u*** house of the king
3:31 and as far as the ***u*** room at the
3:32 And between the ***u*** room of the corner
Isaiah
7:3 channel of the ***U*** Pool, by the road
36:2 channel of the ***U*** Pool, which is on
Jeremiah
20:2 at the ***u*** Benjamin Gate in
22:13 and his ***u*** chambers with
22:14 palace, with huge ***u*** chambers, ornate
36:10 son, in the ***u*** courtyard near
Ezekiel
9:2 men came from the ***U*** Gate that faces
24:17 don't cover your ***u*** lip or eat in
24:22 cover your ***u*** lip nor eat in
42:5 The ***u*** chambers were smaller, because
43:14 the lower to the ***u*** ledge is seven
Daniel
6:10 house. Now his ***u*** room had open
Amos
9:6 who builds his ***u*** rooms in the
Micah
3:7 all cover their ***u*** lips, for there
1 Corinthians
1:26 not many were from the ***u*** class.

UPSET

Genesis
21:11 This ***u*** Abraham terribly because the boy
21:12 Don't be ***u*** about the boy and
40:6 the morning, he saw that they were ***u***.
45:5 Now, don't be ***u*** and don't be angry with
48:17 head, he was ***u*** and grasped his
Numbers
11:10 The LORD was outraged, and Moses was ***u***.
1 Samuel
1:10 Hannah was very ***u*** and couldn't stop
15:11 said." Samuel was ***u*** at this, and he
20:3 this or he'll be ***u***.' But I promise
29:7 do anything to ***u*** the Philistine
2 Samuel
11:25 Joab: 'Don't be ***u*** about this
13:2 Amnon was so ***u*** over his half sister
1 Kings
20:43 his palace at Samaria, irritated and ***u***.
21:4 irritated and ***u*** at what Naboth
21:5 him. "Why are you ***u*** and not eating
2 Kings
6:11 was extremely ***u*** about this. He
Esther
4:4 body showed how ***u*** she was. She sent
Psalms
37:1 Don't get ***u*** over evildoers;
37:7 him. Don't get ***u*** when someone gets
37:8 behind! Don't get ***u***—it will only lead
42:5 Why are you so ***u*** inside? Hope in
42:11 Why are you so ***u*** inside? Hope in
43:5 Why are you so ***u*** inside? Hope in
77:4 closing. I'm so ***u*** I can't even
Isaiah
51:7 and don't be ***u*** when they abuse
59:15 looked and was ***u*** at the absence of
Matthew
14:9 the king was ***u***, because of his

UPSET [cont.]

Mark
6:26 the king was ***u***, because of his
Romans
14:15 or sister is ***u*** by your food, you
1 Corinthians
5:2 of being so ***u*** that the one who
2 Corinthians
2:1 wouldn't visit you again while I was ***u***.
Philippians
2:26 all, and he was ***u*** because you heard
2 Thessalonians
2:2 in your mind or ***u*** if you hear that
Titus
1:11 because they ***u*** entire
1 Peter
3:14 Don't be terrified or ***u*** by them.

UR

Genesis
11:28 his native land, in ***U*** of the Chaldeans.
Nehemiah
9:7 him out of ***U*** of the Chaldeans

URIAH

2 Samuel
11:7 When ***U*** came to him, David asked about the welfare of Joab
11:11 living in tents," ***U*** told David. "And
11:14 a letter to Joab and sent it with ***U***.
12:10 took the wife of ***U*** the Hittite as
Nehemiah
8:4 Shema, Anaiah, ***U***, Hilkiah, and
Isaiah
8:2 trusted people, ***U*** the priest and
Matthew
1:6 whose mother had been the wife of ***U***.

URIM

Exodus
28:30 decisions the ***U*** and the Thummim,
Leviticus
8:8 Aaron and set the ***U*** and Thummim into
Deuteronomy
33:8 to Levi, your ***U*** to your faithful
1 Samuel
14:41 respond with ***U***, but if the
28:6 not by the ***U***, and not by the
Ezra
2:63 arose who could consult ***U*** and Thummim.
Nehemiah
7:65 arose who could consult ***U*** and Thummim.

UZZIAH

2 Kings
15:13 of Judah's King ***U***. He ruled for one
Ezra
10:21 Elijah, Shemaiah, Jehiel, and ***U***.
Nehemiah
11:4 Athaiah son of ***U*** son of Zechariah
Isaiah
1:1 of Judah's kings ***U***, Jotham, Ahaz,
7:1 of Judah's King ***U***), Aram's King
Hosea
1:1 of Judah's Kings ***U***, Jotham, Ahaz,
Amos
1:1 of Judah's King ***U*** and in the days
Zechariah
14:5 of Judah's King ***U***. The LORD my God
Matthew
1:8 of Joram. Joram was the father of ***U***.

Vv

VALLEY

Nehemiah
2:13 night through the **V** Gate past the
11:30 from Beer-sheba to the Hinnom **V**.
11:35 Lod, and Ono, the **v** of artisans
Job
39:10 row; will it plow the **v** behind you?
39:21 He paws in the **v**, prances proudly,
Psalms
23:4 the darkest **v**, I fear no danger
60:6 Shechem and portion out the Succoth **V**.
84:6 through the Baca **V**, they make it a
108:7 Shechem and portion out the Succoth **V**.
Proverbs
30:17 of the river **v** peck it out, and
Song of Songs
6:11 growth in the **v**, to see whether
Isaiah
40:4 Every **v** will be raised up, and every
Jeremiah
31:40 The entire **v** defiled by corpses and
Ezekiel
3:22 up! Go out to the **v**, and I'll speak
39:11 in the Travelers' **V** east of the sea.
Micah
1:6 stones into the **v**; her foundations
Luke
3:5 Every **v** will be filled, and every

VALLEYS

Deuteronomy
8:7 that gush up in the **v** and on the hills;
11:11 land of hills and **v**, where your
1 Kings
20:28 not a god of the **v**, I am handing
1 Chronicles
12:15 living in the **v** to the east and
27:29 the cattle in the **v**—Shaphat, Adlai's
Psalms
65:13 with flocks, the **v** decked out in
104:8 down the **v** to the place you
Song of Songs
2:1 of the Sharon plain, a lily of the **v**.
Isaiah
22:7 Your finest **v** were filled with
41:18 and springs in **v**. I will make the
42:15 mountains and **v**, and I will dry
57:5 children in the **v**, under the rocky
Jeremiah
48:8 will escape. The **v** will be ravaged;
Ezekiel
6:3 and hills, to the **v** and their deepest
31:12 fell among the **v**, and its boughs
32:5 and I will fill the **v** with your gore.
35:8 hills and your **v**, and all your
36:4 and the **v**, the desolate
36:6 and to the **v**, The Lord God
Micah
1:4 under him; the **v** will split apart,

VALUABLE

Numbers
31:11 of war and the **v** property, both
31:32 The **v** property remaining from the
Joshua
11:14 took all the **v** things from those
1 Samuel
26:24 your life **v** today, may the
2 Samuel
12:30 was set with a **v** stone. It was
1 Kings
20:6 that you find **v** they will seize
1 Chronicles
20:2 was set with a **v** stone. It was
26:27 some of the **v** objects won in
2 Chronicles
36:10 along with **v** equipment from
Ezra
1:6 livestock, and **v** gifts, in
Isaiah
28:16 a tested stone, a **v** cornerstone, a
Matthew
12:12 How much more **v** is a person than a
25:15 one he gave five **v** coins, and to
25:28 take from him the **v** coin and give it
Hebrews
11:26 Christ were more **v** than the
1 Peter
1:7 faith is more **v** than gold, which
2:4 from God's perspective it is chosen, **v**.
2:6 in Zion, chosen, **v**. The person who

VALUE

Job
28:13 doesn't know its **v**; it isn't found
34:27 him and didn't **v** all his ways,
Psalms
41:6 say nothing of **v**. Their hearts
Proverbs
3:15 Her **v** exceeds pearls; all you desire
10:20 but the heart of the wicked lacks **v**.
31:10 one find her? Her **v** is far above
Habakkuk
2:18 Of what **v** is an idol, when its potter
Luke
14:35 It has no **v**, neither for the soil nor
Acts
19:19 publicly. The **v** of those
Philippians
3:8 with the superior **v** of knowing Christ

1 Timothy
4:8 training has some ***v***, training in holy
James
2:20 faith without actions has no ***v*** at all?

VASHTI
Esther
1:9 same time, Queen ***V*** held a feast for

VEIL
Genesis
38:14 herself with a ***v***, put on makeup,
38:19 and took off her ***v***, dressing once
Exodus
26:31 Make a ***v*** of blue, purple, and deep red
27:21 tent, outside the ***v*** that hangs in
30:6 in front of the ***v*** that hangs before
34:33 with them, he put a ***v*** over his face.
36:35 They made the ***v*** of blue, purple, and
38:27 the bases for the ***v***, one hundred
39:34 beaded leather, and the ***v*** for a screen,
40:3 Hide the chest from view with the ***v***.
40:26 in the meeting tent in front of the ***v***.
Song of Songs
4:1 doves behind the ***v*** of your hair!
4:3 of your face behind the ***v*** of your hair.
6:7 of your face behind the ***v*** of your hair.
Isaiah
25:7 this mountain the ***v*** that is veiling
47:2 Remove your ***v***, strip off your
2 Corinthians
3:13 who used to put a ***v*** over his face so
3:14 day the same ***v*** remains when the
3:15 Moses is read, a ***v*** lies over their
3:16 back to the Lord, the ***v*** is removed.

VENGEANCE
1 Samuel
18:25 foreskins as ***v*** on the king's
24:12 May the LORD take ***v*** on you for me,
25:26 and taking ***v*** into your own
25:33 blood and taking ***v*** into my own hands
2 Chronicles
24:22 dying, "May the LORD see and seek ***v***!"
Psalms
58:10 when they see ***v*** done, when they
79:10 God now?" Let ***v*** for the spilled
Isaiah
34:8 LORD has a day of ***v***, a year of
35:4 God, coming with ***v***; with divine
47:3 seen. I will take ***v***; no one will
59:17 on garments of ***v***, and wrapping
63:4 intended a day of ***v***; the year of my
Lamentations
3:60 of my enemies' ***v***, all of their
Ezekiel
24:8 to guarantee ***v***, I will spread
25:12 guilty, but Edom's ***v*** was excessive.
25:14 I will execute my ***v*** in Edom through my
25:17 them with great ***v*** and with wrathful
Micah
5:15 I will exact ***v*** in anger and in wrath on

VEST
Exodus
25:7 in the priest's ***v*** and chest piece.
28:4 chest pendant, a ***v***, a robe, a woven
29:5 vest's robe, the ***v*** itself, and the
35:9 in the priest's ***v*** and in the
39:2 They made the ***v*** of gold, of blue,
39:21 loose from the ***v***, just as the LORD
Leviticus
8:7 put the priestly ***v*** on Aaron, tied
Judges
8:27 a priestly ***v*** out of it, and
17:5 made a priestly ***v*** and divine images
18:14 is a priestly ***v***, divine images, a
1 Samuel
2:18 boy, clothed in a linen priestly ***v***.
2:28 wear the priestly ***v*** in my presence. I
14:3 a priestly ***v***. None of the
14:18 the priestly ***v***!" because at that
21:9 behind a priestly ***v***. If you want it,
22:18 who wore the linen priestly ***v*** that day.
23:6 Keilah, bringing a priestly ***v*** with him.
23:9 Abiathar, "Bring the priestly ***v*** now."
30:7 the priestly ***v*** to me." So
2 Samuel
6:14 a linen priestly ***v***, danced with all
1 Chronicles
15:27 David also wore a linen priestly ***v***.
Isaiah
30:22 priestly ***v***, and you will
Hosea
3:4 a priestly ***v*** or household

VICTORIOUS
Judges
11:31 me when I return ***v*** from the
1 Samuel
14:47 Wherever he turned, he was ***v***.
Job
8:21 with joy, your lips with a ***v*** shout.
Psalms
118:15 The LORD's strong hand is ***v***!
118:16 strike! The LORD's strong hand is ***v***!"
Isaiah
45:25 the Israelites will be ***v*** and rejoice."
Zechariah
9:9 is righteous and ***v***. He is humble and
Revelation
2:7 those who emerge ***v*** to eat from the
3:5 Those who emerge ***v*** will wear white
5:5 has emerged ***v*** so that he can
17:14 Lamb will emerge ***v***, for he is Lord
21:7 Those who emerge ***v*** will inherit these

VICTORY
Genesis
14:20 who gave you the ***v*** over your
49:18 I long for your ***v***, LORD
Exodus
15:1 an overflowing ***v***! Horse and rider
15:21 an overflowing ***v***! Horse and rider
32:18 the sound of a ***v*** song. It isn't
Judges
8:9 When I return in ***v***, I'll break down
15:18 this great ***v*** to be
1 Samuel
14:45 won this great ***v*** for Israel? No
19:5 LORD won a great ***v*** for all Israel.
2 Samuel
8:6 The LORD gave David ***v*** wherever he went.

19:2 So the **v** that day was turned into
23:10 a great **v** that day. The
23:12 The LORD accomplished a great **v**.
1 Kings
3:11 life, wealth, or **v** over your enemies
2 Kings
5:1 LORD had given **v** to Aram. This man
1 Chronicles
11:14 So the LORD achieved a great **v**.
18:6 The LORD gave David **v** wherever he went.
2 Chronicles
1:11 riches, fame, **v** over those who
13:16 before Judah, and God gave Judah the **v**.
Job
5:11 exalts the lowly, raises mourners to **v**
Psalms
33:17 is a bad bet for **v**; it can't save
98:1 and his own holy arm have won the **v**!
118:7 helper. I look in **v** on those who hate
Proverbs
11:14 but there is **v** with many
21:31 of battle, but **v** belongs to the
24:6 with guidance; **v** comes with many
Isaiah
46:12 bullheaded people who are far from **v**:
46:13 I'm bringing my **v** near—it isn't far,
51:5 quickly bring my **v**. My salvation is
52:10 of the earth have seen our God's **v**.
59:16 God's arm brought **v**, upheld by
61:10 with clothes of **v**, wrapped me in a
63:5 my arm brought **v** for me; my wrath
Jeremiah
50:15 Raise a **v** shout against her on every
51:14 they will celebrate their **v** over you.
Habakkuk
3:8 your horses or rode your chariots to **v**?
Zephaniah
3:17 warrior bringing **v**. He will create
Romans
8:37 we win a sweeping **v** through the one
1 Corinthians
15:54 Death has been swallowed up by a **v**.
15:55 Where is your **v**, Death? Where is your sting
15:57 who gives us this **v** through our Lord
1 John
5:4 And this is the **v** that has defeated
Revelation
6:2 And he went forth from **v** to victory.
7:10 a loud voice: "**V** belongs to our
11:7 war on them, gain **v** over them, and
12:11 They gained the **v** over him on account
13:7 and to gain **v** over them. It was
15:2 Those who gained **v** over the beast,

VILLAGE

Genesis
49:14 bedding down beside the **v** hearths.
Habakkuk
2:8 earth, to every **v**, and to all its
2:11 cry out from a **v** wall, and a tree
2:12 and founding a **v** with injustice.
Matthew
10:11 Whatever city or **v** you go into, find
21:2 Go into the **v** over there. As
Mark
8:23 him out of the **v**. After spitting
8:26 home, saying, "Don't go into the **v**!"
11:2 Go into the **v** over there. As
Luke
5:17 come from every **v** in Galilee and
9:52 a Samaritan **v** to prepare for
9:56 and they went on to another **v**
10:38 Jesus entered a **v** where a woman
17:12 As he entered a **v**, ten men with skin
19:30 Go into the **v** over there. When
24:13 traveling to a **v** called Emmaus,
John
7:42 family and from Bethlehem, David's **v**?"
11:1 from Bethany, the **v** of Mary and her
11:30 entered the **v** but was still in

VILLAGES

Genesis
25:16 names by their **v** and their
Numbers
21:25 the Amorites, in Heshbon and all its **v**.
21:32 They captured its **v** and took
32:41 captured their **v** and named them
32:42 its surrounding **v**. He renamed it
Deuteronomy
3:5 there were also a great number of **v**.
Joshua
13:30 sixty of the tent **v** of Jair that are
Judges
1:27 or any of their **v**. The Canaanites
11:26 Heshbon and its **v**, in Aroer and its
1 Samuel
6:18 cities to country **v**. And the large
1 Kings
4:13 controlled the **v** of Jair,
1 Chronicles
2:23 as Kenath and its **v**, sixty towns. All
4:32 Their **v** were Etam, Ain, Rimmon, Tochen,
4:33 well as all their **v** around these
18:1 took Gath and its **v** from Philistine
27:25 country, cities, **v**, and towers—
2 Chronicles
13:19 and Ephron, along with their **v**.
28:18 its surrounding **v**, Timnah and its
Nehemiah
6:2 in one of the **v** in the plain of
11:25 As for the **v** with their fields, some of
11:27 Hazar-shual, in Beer-sheba and its **v**,
11:28 in Ziklag, in Meconah and its **v**
11:30 and their **v**, Lachish and its
11:31 at Michmash, Aija, Bethel and its **v**,
12:28 and from the **v** of the
12:29 built themselves **v** around Jerusalem.
Esther
9:19 Jews who live in **v** make the
Isaiah
17:2 The **v** of Aroer are abandoned forever.
42:11 shout aloud, the **v** that Kedar
Jeremiah
49:2 its neighboring **v** will be burned to
Habakkuk
2:17 the land, the **v**, and all their
Matthew
9:35 the cities and **v**, teaching in
14:15 can go into the **v** and buy food for

Mark
1:38 to the nearby ***v***, so that I can
6:6 through the surrounding ***v*** teaching.
6:36 countryside and ***v*** and buy something
8:27 went into the ***v*** near Caesarea
Luke
8:1 the cities and ***v***, preaching and
9:6 went through the ***v*** proclaiming the
9:12 go to the nearby ***v*** and countryside
13:22 cities and ***v*** teaching and
Acts
8:25 news to many Samaritan ***v*** along the way.

VINE

Genesis
40:9 dream there was a ***v*** right in front of
49:11 donkey to the ***v***, the colt of his
Judges
9:12 trees said to the ***v***, 'You come and be
9:13 But the ***v*** replied to them, 'Should I
2 Kings
4:39 he found a wild ***v*** and gathered wild
18:31 eat from your own ***v*** and fig tree, and
Job
15:33 like the ***v***, they will drop early
Psalms
80:8 You brought a ***v*** out of Egypt. You drove out the nations
80:14 and perceive it! Attend to this ***v***,
128:3 will be like a ***v*** full of fruit.
Song of Songs
6:11 see whether the ***v*** was in flower,
Isaiah
24:7 dries up; the ***v*** withers; all the
32:12 pleasant fields, for the fruitful ***v***,
34:4 withering from a ***v***, like fruit from
36:16 eat from your own ***v*** and fig tree and
Jeremiah
2:21 you, a precious ***v*** of fine quality;
6:9 Pick clean every last grape on the ***v***!
8:13 no grapes on the ***v***, no figs on the
48:32 weep for you, ***v*** of Sibmah, more
49:9 a few on the ***v***. If thieves would
Ezekiel
17:6 a low spreading ***v***. Its foliage
17:7 plumage. This ***v*** bent its roots
17:8 bear fruit, and become a splendid ***v***.
19:10 mother was like a ***v*** in a vineyard
Hosea
10:1 is a growing ***v*** that yields its
14:7 blossom like the ***v***, their fragrance
Habakkuk
3:17 no produce on the ***v***; though the olive
Haggai
2:19 granary—or the ***v***, the fig tree, or
Zechariah
8:12 is healthy: the ***v*** will give its
Malachi
3:11 and so that the ***v*** doesn't abort its
Luke
22:18 the fruit of the ***v*** until God's
John
15:1 I am the true ***v***, and my Father is the
15:4 remain in the ***v***. Likewise, you
15:5 I am the ***v***; you are the branches. If

VINEYARD

Genesis
9:20 made a new start and planted a ***v***.
Exodus
22:5 the field or ***v*** to be stripped of
23:11 same with your ***v*** and your olive
Leviticus
19:10 do not pick your ***v*** clean or gather
Numbers
16:14 of field and ***v***. Would you also
20:17 any field or ***v***, or drink water
21:22 into a field or ***v***. We won't drink
Deuteronomy
20:6 who has planted a ***v*** but hasn't yet
22:9 the produce of the ***v*** will be unusable.
23:24 your neighbor's ***v***, you can eat as
24:21 grapes of your ***v***, don't pick them
28:30 You might plant a ***v***, but you won't
1 Kings
21:1 Jezreel had a ***v*** in Jezreel that
21:2 Give me your ***v*** so it can become
21:18 He is in Naboth's ***v***. He has gone down
Proverbs
24:30 person, by the ***v*** of one with no
31:16 from her own resources, she plants a ***v***.
Song of Songs
1:6 but I couldn't care for my own ***v***.
8:11 Solomon had a ***v*** in Baal-hamon. He gave charge of the
8:12 My ***v***, my very own, is before me. You
Isaiah
1:8 shelter in a ***v***, like a hut in a
3:14 have devoured the ***v***; the goods stolen
5:1 love song for his ***v***. My loved one had
5:3 of Judah, judge between me and my ***v***:
5:4 to do for my ***v*** that I haven't
5:5 I'm doing to my ***v***. I'm removing its
5:7 The ***v*** of the LORD of heavenly forces is
5:10 Ten acres of ***v*** will produce just one
27:2 On that day: Sing about a delightful ***v***
Jeremiah
12:10 have destroyed my ***v***; they have
Ezekiel
19:10 like a vine in a ***v*** planted beside
Matthew
20:1 the morning to hire workers for his ***v***.
21:28 Son, go and work in the ***v*** today.'
21:41 and rent the ***v*** to other tenant
Mark
12:1 A man planted a ***v***, put a fence
Luke
13:6 planted in his ***v***. He came looking
20:9 man planted a ***v***, rented it to
John
15:1 vine, and my Father is the ***v*** keeper.
1 Corinthians
9:7 way? Who plants a ***v*** and doesn't eat
Revelation
14:18 clusters in the ***v*** of the earth,
14:19 and cut the ***v*** of the earth, and

VINEYARDS

Exodus
22:29 produce of your ***v*** and winepresses.
Leviticus
25:3 and prune your ***v*** and gather their

25:4 not plant your fields or prune your ***v***.
Numbers
22:24 path between ***v*** with a stone wall
Deuteronomy
6:11 you didn't make, ***v*** and olive trees
22:9 Don't plant your ***v*** with two types of
28:39 plant lots of ***v*** and work hard in
Joshua
24:13 produce from ***v*** and olive groves
Judges
9:27 from their ***v***, trampled them
14:5 he came to the ***v*** in Timnah,
15:5 standing grain, ***v***, and olive
21:20 Go and hide like an ambush in the ***v***
21:21 rush out from the ***v***. Each one of you,
1 Samuel
8:14 your best fields, ***v***, and olive groves
8:15 grain and your ***v*** to his officials
22:7 give fields and ***v*** to each and every
2 Kings
5:26 olive trees, ***v***, sheep, cattle,
18:32 land of bread and ***v***, a land of olive
19:29 harvest it; plant ***v*** and eat their
25:12 behind to work the ***v*** and be farmers.
1 Chronicles
27:27 in charge of the ***v***—Shimei the
2 Chronicles
26:10 his farms and ***v***, because he loved
Nehemiah
5:3 our fields, our ***v***, and our houses
9:25 cisterns, ***v***, olive orchards,
Job
24:6 in the field, glean in unproductive ***v***,
24:18 no one walks down a path in the ***v***.
Psalms
107:37 plant fields and ***v*** and obtain a
Ecclesiastes
2:4 for myself, planted ***v*** for myself.
Song of Songs
1:6 caretaker of the ***v***—but I couldn't
2:15 foxes that spoil ***v***, now that our
7:12 out early for the ***v***. We will see if
Isaiah
16:10 and in the ***v*** no one sings, no
36:17 and new wine, a land of bread and ***v***.
37:30 harvest it; plant ***v*** and eat their
65:21 they will plant ***v*** and eat their
Jeremiah
5:10 Climb through her ***v*** and ravage them,
31:5 you will plant ***v*** on the hills of
32:15 fields, and ***v*** will again be
35:7 plant gardens and ***v***; rather, you are
35:9 to live in or had ***v***, fields, or crops.
39:10 He gave them ***v*** and fields at
52:16 poor to tend the ***v*** and till the land.
Ezekiel
28:26 houses, plant ***v***, and live in
Hosea
2:15 I will give her ***v***, and make the
Amos
4:9 gardens and your ***v***. The locust
5:11 planted pleasant ***v***, but you won't
5:17 In all the ***v*** there will be bitter
9:14 They will plant ***v*** and drink their
Micah
1:6 for planting ***v***. I will pour her
Zephaniah
1:13 they will plant ***v***, but not drink

VIOLENCE

Genesis
6:11 become corrupt and was filled with ***v***.
6:13 the earth with ***v***. I am now about
49:5 weapons of ***v*** their stock in
Exodus
5:3 will give us a deadly disease or ***v***."
Judges
9:24 because of the ***v*** done to
2 Samuel
22:3 my shelter. My savior! Save me from ***v***!
2 Kings
8:12 I know what ***v*** you will do to
9:7 revenge for the ***v*** done by Jezebel
Job
5:16 poor have hope and ***v*** shuts its mouth.
16:17 But there is no ***v*** in my hands, and my
19:7 If I cry "***V***!" I'm not answered; I
41:22 in his neck; ***v*** dances before him.
Psalms
7:16 own heads; the ***v*** they commit will
10:7 dishonesty, ***v***. Under their
11:5 very being hates anyone who loves ***v***.
51:14 Deliver me from ***v***, God, God of my
55:9 because I see ***v*** and conflict in
58:2 your hands do ***v*** on the earth.
62:10 Don't trust in ***v***; don't set false
72:14 oppression and ***v***; their blood is
73:6 a necklace, why ***v*** covers them like
74:20 the land's dark places are full of ***v***.
Proverbs
4:17 of evil, and they drink the wine of ***v***.
10:6 but the mouth of the wicked conceals ***v***.
10:11 but the mouth of the wicked conceals ***v***.
13:2 have an appetite only for ***v***.
21:7 The ***v*** of the wicked will sweep them
24:2 are focused on ***v***, and their lips
26:6 off one's feet or drinking down ***v***.
Isaiah
53:9 he had done no ***v***, and had spoken
59:6 and the work of ***v*** is in their hands.
60:18 ***V*** will no longer resound throughout
Jeremiah
6:7 forth evil. ***V*** and destruction
20:8 cry out and say, "***V*** and destruction!"
51:46 else: rumors of ***v*** and uprisings.
Ezekiel
7:11 ***V*** rises up as a wicked master. It isn't
7:23 perverted justice, the city full of ***v***.
8:17 the land with ***v***, and they
12:19 it because of the ***v*** of all who live
22:26 priests have done ***v*** to my
45:9 Turn aside from ***v*** and oppression.
Hosea
12:1 multiply lies and ***v***; they make a
Joel
3:19 is because of the ***v*** done to the
Amos
3:10 who store up ***v*** and robbery in
Obadiah
1:10 the slaughter and ***v*** done to your
Jonah
3:8 behavior and the ***v*** that's under

Micah
6:12 are full of ***v*** and whose
Habakkuk
1:2 cry out to you, "***V***!" but you don't
1:3 devastation and ***v*** are before me?
1:9 They come for ***v***, the horde with all
2:8 bloodshed and the ***v*** done to the
2:17 Because of the ***v*** done to Lebanon, he
Zephaniah
1:9 of their master with ***v*** and deceit.
3:4 is holy; they do ***v*** to the
Zechariah
1:15 somewhat angry, they added to the ***v***.
Malachi
2:16 his garment with ***v***, says the LORD of
Matthew
23:25 they are full of ***v*** and pleasure
Acts
21:35 to protect him from the ***v*** of the crowd.

VIOLENT

Genesis
49:7 anger; it is ***v***, their rage; it
2 Samuel
22:49 you delivered me from ***v*** people.
1 Kings
2:9 what to do to him. Give him a ***v*** death."
2 Chronicles
29:9 ancestors died ***v*** deaths, while our
Psalms
5:6 people who are ***v*** and dishonest.
17:4 have avoided such ***v*** ways by the
18:48 you delivered me from ***v*** people.
26:9 taking my life along with ***v*** people
27:12 witnesses and ***v*** accusers have
35:11 ***V*** witnesses stand up. They question me about things
54:3 up against me; ***v*** people want me
86:14 God. A gang of ***v*** people want me
140:1 people, LORD! Guard me from ***v*** people
140:4 Guard me from ***v*** people who plot
140:11 hunt down ***v*** people—and quick
Proverbs
3:31 Don't envy ***v*** people or choose any of
11:16 gains honor; ***v*** men gain only
16:29 ***V*** people entice their neighbors and
Isaiah
11:4 will strike the ***v*** with the rod of
Jeremiah
15:21 redeem you from the grasp of the ***v***.
30:23 breaks out like a ***v*** storm, a fierce
51:1 I'm stirring up a ***v*** wind against
Ezekiel
7:22 treasured place. ***V*** intruders will
18:10 one of them has a ***v*** child who sheds
Daniel
3:13 In a ***v*** rage Nebuchadnezzar ordered them
11:14 southern king. ***V*** persons from
Amos
3:9 city, and what ***v*** deeds are inside
6:3 the evil day and make ***v*** rule draw near:
Zephaniah
3:1 one, the defiled one, the ***v*** city.
Matthew
8:28 him. They were so ***v*** that nobody could
11:12 attacked as ***v*** people seize it.
Luke
8:24 the wind and the ***v*** waves. The storm
Acts
16:26 there was such a ***v*** earthquake that
27:18 battered by the ***v*** storm that the
Revelation
18:21 With such ***v*** force the great

VIRGIN

Leviticus
21:13 priest must marry a woman who is a ***v***.
21:14 can only marry a ***v*** from his own
Deuteronomy
22:14 find any proof that she was a ***v***."
22:28 woman, who is a ***v*** and not engaged,
2 Samuel
13:2 sick. She was a ***v***, and it seemed
13:18 that was what the ***v*** princesses wore
Job
31:1 with my eyes; how could I look at a ***v***?
Isaiah
23:12 violated ***v*** Daughter Sidon.
47:1 sit in the dust, ***v*** Daughter Babylon!
Jeremiah
14:17 night, because my ***v*** daughter, my
18:13 like this? ***V*** Israel has done
31:4 will be rebuilt, ***v*** Israel. Again,
31:21 taken. Return, ***v*** Israel; return to
31:22 new on earth: ***V*** Israel will once
46:11 and seek balm, ***v*** Daughter Egypt.
Amos
5:2 more to rise, is ***v*** Israel, deserted
Matthew
1:23 Look! A ***v*** will become pregnant and give
Luke
1:27 to a ***v*** who was engaged to a man named
1 Corinthians
7:34 or who is a ***v*** is concerned
2 Corinthians
11:2 you as an innocent ***v*** to Christ himself.

VISION

Genesis
15:1 to Abram in a ***v***, "Don't be
46:2 to Israel in a ***v*** at night, 'Jacob!
Numbers
8:4 according to the ***v*** that the LORD had
Deuteronomy
16:19 blinds the ***v*** of the wise and
1 Samuel
3:15 Samuel was afraid to tell the ***v*** to Eli.
2 Samuel
7:17 these words and this entire ***v*** to David.
2 Chronicles
32:32 written in the ***v*** of the prophet
Job
20:8 them, carried away like a nighttime ***v***.
33:15 In the dream, a ***v*** of the night, when
Psalms
6:7 My ***v*** fails because of my grief; it's
11:4 eyes see—his ***v*** examines all of
31:9 I'm depressed. My ***v*** fails because of
89:19 you spoke in a ***v*** to your faithful
Proverbs
29:18 When there's no ***v***, the people get out
Isaiah
1:1 The ***v*** about Judah and Jerusalem that

21:2 A harsh ***v*** was proclaimed to me: The
22:1 the Valley of ***V***. What is wrong
22:5 in the Valley of ***V***, a breaking down
29:7 will be like a dream, a ***v*** of the night.
29:11 This entire ***v*** has become for you like
Lamentations
2:9 couldn't find a ***v*** from the LORD.
Ezekiel
7:13 them survive. The ***v*** concerns the
7:26 They seek a ***v*** from the prophet.
8:3 and in a divine ***v*** it brought me to
11:24 through a ***v*** with a divine
12:22 The days go by, and every ***v*** vanishes."
12:23 soon for the fulfillment of every ***v***.
12:24 be any worthless ***v*** or deceptive
12:27 now saying, "The ***v*** that he sees is
Daniel
1:17 of every type of ***v*** and dream.
2:19 Then, in a ***v*** by night, the mystery was
2:28 was the ***v*** in your head as
4:5 in bed and the ***v*** in my mind
4:13 I saw another ***v***: A holy watcher
7:1 had a dream—a ***v*** in his head as he
8:1 rule, a ***v*** came to me,
8:27 troubled by the ***v*** and couldn't
9:21 in my earlier ***v***. He was weary
9:23 word and grasp the meaning of this ***v***!
9:24 seal up prophetic ***v***, and to anoint
10:1 having discerned the meaning of the ***v***.
10:7 Daniel, saw this ***v***. The other people
10:8 to see this great ***v*** all by myself.
10:14 there is another ***v*** concerning that
10:16 me: "My lord, the ***v*** bothered me
11:14 up to support the ***v***, but they will
Obadiah
1:1 The ***v*** of Obadiah. The LORD God
Micah
3:6 for you, without ***v***, only darkness
Nahum
1:1 containing the ***v*** of Nahum the
Habakkuk
2:2 and said, Write a ***v***, and make it
2:3 There is still a ***v*** for the appointed
Zechariah
13:4 be ashamed of his ***v*** when he
Matthew
17:9 anybody about the ***v*** until the Human
Luke
1:22 he had seen a ***v*** in the temple,
24:23 had even seen a ***v*** of angels who
Acts
9:10 spoke to him in a ***v***, "Ananias!" He
9:12 In a ***v*** he has seen a man named Ananias
10:3 from God in a ***v***. The angel came
10:17 meaning of the ***v***. Just then, the
10:19 brooding over the ***v***, the Spirit
11:5 experience. In my ***v***, I saw something
12:9 all this. He thought he was seeing a ***v***.
16:9 A ***v*** of a man from Macedonia came to
16:10 after he saw the ***v***, we prepared to
18:9 said to Paul in a ***v***, "Don't be
26:19 wasn't disobedient to that heavenly ***v***.
Revelation
9:17 riders in the ***v***: they had

VISIONS

Numbers
12:6 known to him in ***v***. I speak to him
24:4 the Almighty's ***v***, who falls down
24:16 the Almighty's ***v***, who falls down
1 Samuel
3:1 at that time, and ***v*** weren't widely
2 Chronicles
9:29 Shiloh, and the ***v*** of the seer Iddo
Job
4:13 thoughts, ***v*** of night, when
7:14 me with dreams, frighten me with ***v***.
Isaiah
28:7 when receiving ***v***; they stumble
30:10 report truthful ***v***; tell us
Jeremiah
14:14 to you false ***v***, worthless
23:16 you. Their ***v*** come from their
Lamentations
2:14 and empty ***v***. They didn't
Ezekiel
1:1 the heavens opened and I saw ***v*** of God.
13:6 saw worthless ***v*** and performed
13:7 you see worthless ***v***? And didn't you
13:8 and had false ***v***, I'm against you.
13:23 longer see empty ***v*** or perform
21:29 False ***v*** and lying divinations set you
22:28 seeing false ***v*** and making wrong
40:2 In God's ***v***, he brought me to the land
Daniel
4:9 the meaning of the ***v*** I had in my dream.
7:15 to worry. My ***v*** disturbed me
Hosea
12:10 and I multiplied ***v***, and through them
Joel
2:28 dreams, and your young men will see ***v***.
Micah
3:7 Those seeing ***v*** will be ashamed, and the
Acts
2:17 young will see ***v***. Your elders will
2 Corinthians
12:1 I'll move on to ***v*** and revelations
Colossians
2:18 they have seen in ***v*** and have become

VISIT

Genesis
20:13 in each place we ***v***, tell them, "He
Judges
15:1 Samson went to ***v*** his wife,
2 Samuel
12:4 traveler came to ***v*** the rich man, but
2 Kings
8:29 went down to ***v*** Joram, Ahab's
9:16 King Ahaziah had also come to ***v*** Joram.
10:13 come down for a ***v*** with the king's
2 Chronicles
22:6 son, went down to ***v*** Joram, Ahab's
22:7 But God used this ***v*** to Joram to bring
Job
7:18 ***v*** them each morning, test them every
Psalms
41:6 they come to ***v***, they say nothing
65:9 You ***v*** the earth and make it abundant,
106:4 show your people. ***V*** me with your
Isaiah
23:17 the LORD will ***v*** Tyre. She will

Hosea
4:14 men themselves ***v*** prostitutes, and
Amos
3:14 I will also ***v*** the altars of
Zephaniah
2:7 their God will ***v*** them and restore
Matthew
25:39 see you sick or in prison and ***v*** you?'
25:43 and in prison, and you didn't ***v*** me.'
Luke
19:44 the time of your gracious ***v*** from God."
Acts
7:13 their second ***v***, Joseph told his
7:23 he decided to ***v*** his family, the
9:32 he went to ***v*** God's holy people
10:28 to associate or ***v*** with outsiders.
14:11 human form and come down to ***v*** us!"
15:36 go back and ***v*** all the brothers
19:21 been there, I must ***v*** Rome as well."
Romans
1:13 that I planned to ***v*** you many times,
15:24 I'll ***v*** you when I go to Spain. I hope
1 Corinthians
16:7 to make a quick ***v*** to you, since I
16:12 encouraged him to ***v*** you with the
2 Corinthians
1:15 this, I wanted to ***v*** you first so that
1:16 I wanted to ***v*** you on my way to
2:1 sake, I wouldn't ***v*** you again while I
12:14 I'm ready to ***v*** you a third time,
13:1 I'm coming to ***v*** you. Every matter
13:2 you on my second ***v***, I already warned
Galatians
1:18 to Jerusalem to ***v*** Cephas and stayed
Philippians
1:26 through my presence when I ***v*** you again.
2:24 the Lord that I also will ***v*** you soon.
1 Thessalonians
2:1 and sisters, our ***v*** with you wasn't a
2 John
1:12 but I hope to ***v*** you and talk with

VOICE → GOD'S VOICE, HEAR HIS VOICE, VOICE FROM HEAVEN, VOICE OF THE LORD

Genesis
3:17 to your wife's ***v*** and you ate from
27:22 and said, "The ***v*** is Jacob's voice,
39:18 when I raised my ***v*** and screamed, he
Exodus
19:8 with one ***v***: "Everything that
Numbers
7:89 he would hear the ***v*** speaking to him
21:3 LORD heard the ***v*** of Israel and
23:18 Balaam raised his ***v*** and made his
Deuteronomy
4:12 see any form. There was only a ***v***.
4:30 LORD your God and you will obey his ***v***,
4:36 made you hear his ***v*** in order to
5:23 you heard the ***v*** from the darkness
5:24 We've heard his ***v*** come out of the
13:4 Obey his ***v***! Worship him!
30:8 obey the LORD's ***v*** and do all his
30:20 by obeying his ***v***, and by clinging
33:7 listen to Judah's ***v***! Bring him back
Joshua
6:10 Don't let your ***v*** be heard. Don't
10:14 to a human ***v***. The LORD fought
Judges
9:7 He raised his ***v*** and called out,
18:25 Don't raise your ***v*** with us or else
1 Samuel
1:13 moving, but her ***v*** was silent, so
24:16 son, is that your ***v***?" Then he broke
26:17 David's ***v*** and said, "David,
28:18 to the LORD's ***v*** and didn't carry
2 Samuel
19:4 out in a loud ***v***, "Oh, my son
22:7 God. God heard my ***v*** from his temple;
22:14 heaven; the Most High made his ***v*** heard.
1 Kings
17:22 to Elijah's ***v*** and gave the boy
20:36 obey the LORD's ***v***, a lion will
Nehemiah
9:4 out with a loud ***v*** to the LORD their
Job
40:9 God; can you thunder with a ***v*** like him?
Psalms
5:3 you hear my ***v***. In the morning I
18:6 God heard my ***v*** from his temple;
18:13 High made his ***v*** heard with hail
27:7 listen to my ***v*** when I cry out—
29:3 The LORD's ***v*** is over the waters; the
29:4 The LORD's ***v*** is strong; the LORD's
29:5 The LORD's ***v*** breaks cedar trees—yes,
29:7 The LORD's ***v*** unleashes fiery flames
29:8 the LORD's ***v*** shakes the wilderness—
29:9 The LORD's ***v*** convulses the oaks, strips
46:6 God utters his ***v***; the earth melts.
55:17 and moan so that God will hear my ***v***.
58:5 snake charmer's ***v*** or the spells of
68:33 sends forth his ***v***, his mighty voice.
81:11 listen to my ***v***. Israel simply
95:7 you would listen to his ***v*** right now!
106:25 and wouldn't listen to the LORD's ***v***.
119:149 Listen to my ***v***, according to your
130:2 listen to my ***v***! Let your ears
141:1 Listen to my ***v*** when I cry out to
Proverbs
1:20 in the public square she raises her ***v***.
5:13 listen to the ***v*** of my instructor.
8:4 you, people; my ***v*** goes out to all
27:14 with a loud ***v*** early in the
Ecclesiastes
5:3 cares, and the ***v*** of fools with
10:20 could carry your ***v***; some winged
Song of Songs
2:14 let me hear your ***v***! The sound of
8:13 listening for your ***v***. Let me hear it!
Isaiah
40:3 A ***v*** is crying out: "Clear the LORD's
Jeremiah
3:21 A ***v*** is heard on the well-traveled
31:16 Keep your ***v*** from crying and
Lamentations
3:56 Hear my ***v***. Don't close your ear to my
Daniel
4:31 mouth when a ***v*** came from heaven:
8:16 heard a human ***v*** coming out of the
9:14 made, but we haven't listened to his ***v***.
Joel
2:11 LORD utters his ***v*** at the head of
3:16 and utters his ***v*** from Jerusalem;

Jonah
2:2 out for help; you have heard my ***v***.
2:9 to you with a ***v*** of thanks. That
Micah
6:1 mountains; let the hills hear your ***v***!
Nahum
2:13 the earth, the ***v*** of your
Habakkuk
3:10 deep utters its ***v***; it raises its
Zephaniah
3:2 listened to no ***v***; she accepted no
Matthew
2:18 A ***v*** was heard in Ramah, weeping and
3:3 when he said: The ***v*** of one shouting
12:19 nobody will hear his ***v*** in the streets.
17:5 them. A ***v*** from the cloud
Mark
1:3 a ***v*** shouting in the wilderness:
9:7 them, and a ***v*** spoke from the
Luke
1:42 With a loud ***v*** she blurted out, "God has
3:4 the prophet, A ***v*** crying out in the
9:35 Then a ***v*** from the cloud said, "This is
9:36 Even as the ***v*** spoke, Jesus was found
17:15 returned and praised God with a loud ***v***.
19:37 God with a loud ***v*** because of all
23:18 But with one ***v*** they shouted, "Away with this man!
23:46 out in a loud ***v***, Jesus said,
John
1:23 replied, "I am a ***v*** crying out in the
5:25 will hear the ***v*** of God's Son, and
10:3 listen to his ***v***. He calls his own
12:28 name!" Then a ***v*** came from heaven,
Acts
9:7 they heard the ***v*** but saw no one.
10:13 A ***v*** told him, "Get up, Peter! Kill and
22:9 didn't hear the ***v*** of the one who
26:24 with a loud ***v***, "You've lost
Romans
10:18 Definitely! Their ***v*** has gone out into
15:6 Lord Jesus Christ together with one ***v***.
Hebrews
3:16 they heard his ***v***? Wasn't it all of
12:26 His ***v*** shook the earth then, but now he
2 Peter
1:17 the Father when a ***v*** came to him from
2:16 which has no ***v***, spoke with a
Revelation
3:20 If any hear my ***v*** and open the
4:1 heaven. The first ***v*** that I had heard,
6:10 out with a loud ***v***, "Holy and true
12:10 I heard a loud ***v*** in heaven say,
18:2 out with a loud ***v***, saying, "Fallen,
21:3 I heard a loud ***v*** from the throne say

VOICE FROM HEAVEN

Mt 3:17; Mk 1:11; Lk 3:22; Ac 11:9; 2Pt 1:18; Rev 10:4; 11:12; 14:13; 18:4

VOICE OF THE LORD

Jer 3:25; Dn 9:10; Mi 6:9; Hg 1:12; Zec 6:15

VOICES

Judges
2:4 they raised their ***v*** and cried out
21:2 raising their ***v*** and crying
Ruth
1:9 and they lifted up their ***v*** and wept.
1:14 lifted up their ***v*** and wept again.
2 Samuel
19:35 I even hear the ***v*** of men or women
1 Chronicles
15:16 to raise their ***v*** joyfully,
Job
29:10 the ***v*** of officials were hushed, their
Psalms
19:3 no words—their ***v*** can't be heard—
44:16 because of the ***v*** of those who make fun
74:23 Don't forget the ***v*** of your enemies, the
93:3 raised up their ***v***; the floods raise
Jeremiah
16:9 gladness and the ***v*** of the bridegroom
25:10 laughter and the ***v*** of the bride and
31:7 Raise your ***v*** with praise and
33:11 laughter and the ***v*** of the bride and
Luke
17:13 they raised their ***v*** and said, "Jesus,
23:23 Jesus be crucified. Their ***v*** won out.
Acts
4:24 then lifted their ***v*** in unison to God,
Revelation
4:5 came lightning, ***v***, and thunder. In
8:5 were thunder, ***v***, lightning, and
10:3 out, the seven thunders raised their ***v***.
11:15 there were loud ***v*** in heaven saying,
11:19 were lightning, ***v***, thunder, an
16:18 strikes, ***v***, and thunder, and

Ww

WAGES
Proverbs
10:16 The *w* of the righteous lead to life;
11:18 wicked earn false *w*, but those who
Isaiah
23:18 Her profits and *w* will be sacred to the
Jeremiah
22:13 nothing, refusing to give them their *w*.
Ezekiel
29:19 it, and it will be the *w* for his army.
Micah
1:7 pieces; all her *w* will be burned; I
Haggai
1:6 Anyone earning *w* puts those wages
Zechariah
8:10 there were no *w* for people or
11:12 you, give me my *w*; but if not, then
Malachi
3:5 out of their *w* as well as
Matthew
20:8 give them their *w*, beginning with
Luke
10:35 days' worth of *w* and gave them to
19:13 four months' *w*. He said, 'Do
John
12:5 worth a year's *w*! Why wasn't it
Romans
6:23 The *w* that sin pays are death, but
7:23 in my body. It *w* a war against the
James
5:4 the cries of the *w* of your field

WAIL
Isaiah
13:6 *W*, for the day of the LORD is near.
14:31 *W*, gate! Cry out, city! Melt in
16:7 let Moab *w*; let everyone
23:1 about Tyre. *W*, ships of
23:6 over to Tarshish; *w*, inhabitants of
23:14 *W*, ships of Tarshish, for your
52:5 Their rulers *w*, says the LORD,
65:14 with broken spirits you will *w*.
Jeremiah
4:8 Weep and *w*, for the LORD's
6:26 ashes; weep and *w* as for an only
9:10 I will weep and *w* for the mountains,
25:34 *W*, you shepherds, cry out. Roll in the
48:20 shocked; weep and *w*! Tell it by the
48:31 But I'll still *w* for Moab; I'll cry out
48:39 shattered! Go *w*! How Moab turns
49:3 been destroyed. *W*, you daughters of
51:8 into pieces. *W* for her! Bring
Ezekiel
21:12 cry aloud, and *w*, for it comes
27:30 bitterly they *w*, and they put
Amos
5:16 the farmers to *w*, and those
8:3 the people will *w* the temple
Micah
2:4 you; someone will *w* bitterly: "We are
Zephaniah
1:11 the grain will *w*; all the

WAIST
Genesis
37:34 cloth around his *w*, and mourned for
2 Samuel
20:8 the tunic at his *w* he wore a sword
1 Kings
2:5 belt around his *w* and on the
12:10 is thicker than my father's entire *w*!
2 Kings
1:8 belt around his *w*." Ahaziah said,
2 Chronicles
10:10 finger is thicker than my father's *w*!
Isaiah
11:5 and faithfulness the belt around his *w*.
20:2 clothes from your *w*, and remove the
32:11 and tie mourning clothes around your *w*,
Ezekiel
1:27 looked like his *w*, I saw something
8:2 looked like his *w* was fire, but
47:4 me cross the water, and it was *w*-high.
Daniel
10:5 had a brilliant gold belt around his *w*,
Matthew
3:4 belt around his *w*. He ate locusts
Mark
1:6 belt around his *w*. He ate locusts
John
13:4 a linen towel, he tied it around his *w*.
Ephesians
6:14 truth around your *w*, justice as your

WAIT → WAIT FOR THE LORD
Ruth
1:13 would you *w* until they grew up? Would
Job
36:2 *W* a little while so I demonstrate for
Psalms
5:3 out before you. Then I *w* expectantly.
10:8 They *w* in a place perfect for ambush;
17:12 like a strong young lion lying in *w*.
33:18 him, all who *w* for his faithful
33:22 love surround us, because we *w* for you.
37:7 the LORD, and *w* for him. Don't
38:15 But I *w* for you, LORD! You will answer,
40:17 my rescuer. My God, don't *w* any longer!
104:27 your creations *w* for you to give
106:13 done! They wouldn't *w* for his advice.
119:49 your servant, for which you made me *w*.
119:81 your saving help! I *w* for your promise.
119:95 The wicked *w* for me, wanting to kill

119:114 and my shield—I ***w*** for your promise.
119:147 and cry for help. I ***w*** for your promise.
119:166 LORD, I ***w*** for your saving help. I do
130:5 being hopes, and I ***w*** for God's promise.
147:11 the people who ***w*** for his faithful
Proverbs
1:11 Let's secretly ***w*** for the innocent
1:18 they lie in ***w*** for their own
7:12 square. She lies in ***w*** at every corner.
24:15 Wicked one, don't ***w*** secretly at the
Isaiah
30:18 justice; happy are all who ***w*** for him.
Jeremiah
3:2 you sit in ***w*** for lovers, like
5:26 catch people, like hunters lying in ***w***.
Lamentations
3:21 all this to mind—therefore, I will ***w***.
3:24 my portion! Therefore, I'll ***w*** for him.
3:26 It's good to ***w*** in silence for the
Hosea
6:9 As robbers lie in ***w*** for someone, so the
12:6 and justice, and ***w*** continually for
Micah
5:7 hope for humans or ***w*** for human ones.
7:2 of them lie in ***w*** for bloodshed;
7:7 the LORD; I will ***w*** for the God of my
Habakkuk
2:3 If it delays, ***w*** for it; for it is
3:16 I stand, while I ***w*** for the day of
Zephaniah
3:8 Therefore, ***w*** for me, says the LORD,
Luke
12:37 table as honored guests, and ***w*** on them.
17:8 table servant and ***w*** on me while I eat
Acts
1:4 Jerusalem but to ***w*** for what the
4:15 ordering them to ***w*** outside, the
Romans
8:23 inside as we ***w*** to be adopted and
8:25 we don't see, we ***w*** for it with
1 Corinthians
1:7 gift while you ***w*** for our Lord
11:33 get together to eat, ***w*** for each other.
Galatians
5:5 We eagerly ***w*** for the hope of
Titus
2:13 the same time we ***w*** for the blessed
James
5:7 be patient as you ***w*** for the coming of
5:8 You also must ***w*** patiently,
Jude
1:21 the love of God, ***w*** for the mercy of
Revelation
6:10 how long will you ***w*** before you pass

WAIT FOR THE LORD

Ps 31:24; 130:7; 131:3; Prv 20:22; Is 8:17

WAITED

Genesis
8:10 He ***w*** seven more days and sent the dove
1 Samuel
13:8 He ***w*** seven days, the time appointed by
Psalms
119:43 mouth because I have ***w*** for your rules.
119:74 glad because I have ***w*** for your promise.
Ezekiel
19:5 realized that she ***w*** in vain, her hope
Obadiah
1:14 shouldn't have ***w*** on the roads to
Acts
17:16 While Paul ***w*** for them in Athens, he was deeply distressed
20:5 went on ahead and ***w*** for us in Troas.
1 Peter
3:20 God patiently ***w*** during the time

WAITING

Genesis
4:7 sin will be ***w*** at the door ready
Exodus
5:20 Moses and Aaron who were ***w*** for them.
Deuteronomy
30:14 and in your heart, ***w*** for you to do it.
Judges
3:26 while they were ***w*** and had passed
16:9 an ambush was ***w*** for her signal in
16:12 an ambush was ***w*** in an inner room.
1 Samuel
4:13 beside the road, ***w*** because he was
22:6 hand, with all his servants ***w*** on him.
22:13 now against me, ***w*** in ambush, which
22:17 the guards ***w*** on him: "Go ahead
2 Samuel
15:28 I will be ***w*** in the desert plains until
Job
3:21 those ***w*** in vain for death, who search
Psalms
39:7 what should I be ***w*** for? My hope is
69:3 eyes are exhausted with ***w*** for my God.
Proverbs
8:34 daily at my doors, ***w*** at my doorposts.
Isaiah
30:18 the LORD is ***w*** to be merciful to
Jeremiah
20:10 my friends are ***w*** for me to
Lamentations
2:16 day we've been ***w*** for. We've seen
Luke
1:21 the people were ***w*** for Zechariah,
8:40 him, for they had been ***w*** for him.
12:36 Be like people ***w*** for their master to
12:37 the master finds ***w*** up when he
Acts
22:16 What are you ***w*** for? Get up, be
23:21 forty of them are ***w*** to ambush him.
28:6 drop dead. After ***w*** a long time and
1 Corinthians
16:11 can join me. I'm ***w*** for him along
1 Thessalonians
1:10 and you are ***w*** for his Son from heaven.
2 Timothy
4:8 righteousness is ***w*** for me. The Lord,
Hebrews
9:28 save those who are eagerly ***w*** for him.
10:13 Since then, he's ***w*** until his enemies
2 Peter
3:12 ***w*** for and hastening the coming day of
3:13 promise we are ***w*** for a new heaven
3:14 while you are ***w*** for these things

WAKE

Judges
5:12 ***W*** up, wake up, Deborah! Wake up, wake
1 Samuel
9:26 on the roof, "***W*** up! I will send
1 Kings
18:27 Or maybe he is asleep and must ***w*** up!"
2 Kings
4:31 and told him, "The boy didn't ***w*** up."
Job
41:32 leaves a bright ***w*** behind him; the
Psalms
3:5 down, sleep, and ***w*** up because the
7:6 fury of my foes! ***W*** up, my God; you
35:23 ***W*** up! Get up and do justice for me;
44:23 ***W*** up! Why are you sleeping, Lord? Get
57:8 ***W*** up, my glory! Wake up, harp and lyre!
59:5 God of Israel! ***W*** up and punish all
80:2 and Manasseh! ***W*** up your power!
108:2 ***W*** up, harp and lyre! I will wake the
Proverbs
23:35 about it. When I ***w*** up, I'll look for
Isaiah
5:11 Doom to those who ***w*** up early in the
51:17 ***W*** yourself, wake yourself! Rise up,
Daniel
12:2 dusty land will ***w*** up—some to eterna
Joel
1:5 ***W*** up, you who drink too much, and weep.
3:9 a holy war, ***w*** up the warriors;
Habakkuk
2:19 to the tree, "***W*** up!" or "Get up"
John
11:11 but I am going in order to ***w*** him up."
Romans
13:11 come for you to ***w*** up from your
Ephesians
5:14 it says, ***W*** up, sleeper! Get
Revelation
3:2 ***W*** up and strengthen whatever you have
3:3 If you don't ***w*** up, I will come

WALK

Genesis
13:17 Stand up and ***w*** around through the
17:1 I am El Shaddai. ***W*** with me and be
22:5 boy and I will ***w*** up there,
Exodus
21:19 and is able to ***w*** around outside
Leviticus
11:27 the animals that ***w*** on four feet, the
26:12 I will ***w*** around among you; I will be
Numbers
20:17 any well. We will ***w*** on the King's
21:22 a well. We will ***w*** on the King's
Deuteronomy
5:33 You must ***w*** the precise path that the
26:17 and that you will ***w*** in his ways and
28:9 God's commandments and ***w*** in his ways.
Joshua
22:5 LORD your God. ***W*** in all his ways
Judges
2:22 would carefully ***w*** in the LORD's
5:10 blankets, who ***w*** along the road:
1 Samuel
17:39 but he couldn't ***w*** around well
2 Samuel
22:37 You've let me ***w*** fast and safe, without
1 Kings
2:4 will take care to ***w*** before me
3:3 Solomon loved to ***w*** in the laws of
3:14 And if you ***w*** in my ways and obey my
8:23 your servants who ***w*** before you with
8:25 carefully ***w*** before me just as
8:58 hearts to him to ***w*** in all his ways
9:4 for you, if you ***w*** before me just as
11:38 I command and ***w*** in my ways, if
16:31 found it easy to ***w*** in the sins of
2 Kings
21:22 the LORD-he didn't ***w*** in the LORD's way.
2 Chronicles
6:14 your servants who ***w*** before you with
6:16 carefully ***w*** according to my
7:17 you, if you will ***w*** before me just as
28:15 who couldn't ***w*** they placed on
Nehemiah
5:9 Why don't you ***w*** in the fear of
Job
16:22 and then I'll ***w*** a path that I
18:8 by their feet in a net; they ***w*** on mesh.
30:28 I ***w*** in the dark, lacking sunshine; I
Psalms
18:36 You've let me ***w*** fast and safe, without
23:4 Even when I ***w*** through the darkest
26:3 in front of me—I ***w*** in your truth!
26:6 are innocent! I ***w*** all around your
26:11 But me? I ***w*** with integrity. Save me!
36:11 arrogant people ***w*** all over me;
42:9 Why do I have to ***w*** around, sad,
43:2 Why do I have to ***w*** around, sad,
48:12 ***W*** around Zion; go all the way around
56:13 so that I can ***w*** before God in the
68:21 very skulls of those who ***w*** in guilt.
78:10 they refused to ***w*** in his
81:13 How I wish Israel would ***w*** in my ways!
84:11 things to those who ***w*** with integrity.
86:11 so that I can ***w*** in your truth.
89:15 truly happy! They ***w*** in the light of
101:2 gets here? I will ***w*** with a heart of
115:7 but they can't ***w***. They can't even
116:9 so I'll ***w*** before the LORD in the land
119:1 blameless—who ***w*** in the LORD's
119:3 anything wrong! They ***w*** in God's ways.
119:45 I will ***w*** around in wide-open spaces
119:128 That's why I ***w*** straight by every single
Proverbs
3:23 Then you will ***w*** safely on your path,
4:12 When you ***w***, you won't be hindered;
4:14 the wicked; don't ***w*** on the path of
6:22 When you ***w*** around, they will lead you;
8:20 I ***w*** on the way of righteousness, on the
9:6 ways and live; ***w*** in the way of
10:9 Those who ***w*** in innocence walk with
13:20 ***W*** with wise people and become wise;
14:2 Those who ***w*** with integrity fear the
15:21 with understanding ***w*** straight ahead.
16:29 neighbors and ***w*** them down a path
19:1 to be poor and ***w*** in innocence than
28:6 to be poor and ***w*** in innocence than
28:18 Those who ***w*** in innocence will be saved,
28:26 but those who ***w*** in wisdom will be

30:29 four that are excellent as they ***w***:
Ecclesiastes
2:14 head, but fools ***w*** around in
4:15 all who live and ***w*** under the sun
10:3 even when they ***w*** down the street;
10:7 while princes ***w*** on foot like
Isaiah
2:3 ways and we may ***w*** in God's paths."
2:5 of Jacob, let's ***w*** by the LORD's
3:16 tiptoeing as they ***w***, feet jingling—
8:11 warning me not to ***w*** in the way of
30:21 behind you: "This is the way; ***w*** in it."
35:9 there; only the redeemed will ***w*** on it.
40:31 be tired; they will ***w*** and not be weary.
42:5 people and life to those who ***w*** on it—
42:16 make the blind ***w*** a road they don't
42:24 not willing to ***w*** in God's ways,
43:2 you. When you ***w*** through the fire,
50:11 igniting torches. ***W*** by the light of
51:23 so that we can ***w*** on you. Make your
57:2 peace; those who ***w*** in straight paths
58:8 will ***w*** before you, and
59:9 a gleam of light, but ***w*** about in gloom.
Jeremiah
6:16 good way? Then ***w*** in it and find a
6:25 the field! Don't ***w*** on the road! The
10:5 they can't ***w***. Don't be afraid
Lamentations
3:2 forced me to ***w*** in darkness not
4:18 could no longer ***w*** in our streets.
5:18 deserted—only jackals ***w*** on it now!
Ezekiel
20:37 I will make you ***w*** under the rod, and I
29:11 or human, will ***w*** across it, and it
33:15 for robbery, and ***w*** in life-giving reg
36:12 I will let people ***w*** through you, my
36:27 so that you may ***w*** according to my
40:24 Then he had me ***w*** toward the south,
Daniel
4:37 is able to humble all who ***w*** in pride."
Hosea
11:3 taught Ephraim to ***w***; I took them up
11:10 They will ***w*** after the LORD, who roars
14:9 righteous will ***w*** in them, but
Amos
3:3 Will two people ***w*** together unless they
Jonah
3:3 enormous city, a three days' ***w*** across.)
Micah
4:2 ways and we may ***w*** in God's paths!"
4:5 for us, we will ***w*** in the name of
6:8 love, and ***w*** humbly with your
Habakkuk
3:19 He will let me ***w*** upon the heights.
Zephaniah
1:17 suffer; they will ***w*** like the blind
Zechariah
3:7 If you will ***w*** in my paths, if
10:12 and they will ***w*** in his name, says
Mark
5:42 up and began to ***w*** around. She was
12:38 They like to ***w*** around in long
Luke
7:22 were crippled now ***w***. People with skin
11:44 graves and people ***w*** on them without
20:46 They like to ***w*** around in long
24:17 about as you ***w*** along?" They
John
5:8 him, "Get up! Pick up your mat and ***w***."
5:11 said to me, 'Pick up your mat and ***w***.'"
8:12 follows me won't ***w*** in darkness but
12:35 a little while. ***W*** while you have
Acts
3:6 Christ the Nazarene, rise up and ***w***!"
3:8 up, he began to ***w*** around. He
3:12 as if we made him ***w*** by our own power
14:10 feet!" He jumped up and began to ***w***.
Romans
4:12 but who also ***w*** in the path of
6:4 we too can ***w*** in newness of
2 Corinthians
12:18 Spirit? Didn't we ***w*** in the same
James
1:24 at themselves, ***w*** away, and
Revelation
3:4 They will ***w*** with me clothed
9:20 that can't see or hear or ***w***.
21:24 The nations will ***w*** by its light, and

WALKED

Genesis
5:22 Enoch ***w*** with God. After Methuselah's
6:9 moral and exemplary man; he ***w*** with God.
9:23 their shoulders, ***w*** backward, and
18:22 turned away and ***w*** toward Sodom, but
21:16 She ***w*** away from him about as far as a
22:6 and the two of them ***w*** on together.
48:15 Abraham and Isaac ***w***, may the God who
Exodus
2:5 women servants ***w*** along beside the
14:22 The Israelites ***w*** into the sea on dry
14:29 however, ***w*** on dry ground
15:19 the Israelites ***w*** through the sea
Deuteronomy
1:24 ravine. They ***w*** all around that
1:36 give the land he ***w*** on to him and his
Joshua
14:9 on which you have ***w*** will forever be a
Judges
11:38 and her friends ***w*** on the hills and
1 Samuel
17:7 His shield-bearer ***w*** in front of him.
2 Samuel
3:31 King David himself ***w*** behind the body.
13:19 on her head and ***w*** away, crying as
15:30 his head covered, ***w*** barefoot up the
1 Kings
3:6 David when he ***w*** before you in
8:25 before me just as you ***w*** before me."
11:33 They haven't ***w*** in my ways by
16:2 Israel, but you ***w*** in Jeroboam's
16:26 He ***w*** in all the ways and sins of
21:27 clothes, and ***w*** around depressed.
22:43 Jehoshapat ***w*** in all the ways of his
22:52 LORD's eyes. He ***w*** in his father's
2 Kings
8:18 He ***w*** in the ways of Israel's kings,
13:2 LORD's eyes. He ***w*** in the sins that
13:6 to commit; they ***w*** in them!
13:11 Israel to commit, but he ***w*** in them!
16:3 Instead, he ***w*** in the ways of Israel's
20:3 how I have ***w*** before you in
21:21 He ***w*** in all the ways his father had

22:2 LORD's eyes, and ***w*** in the ways of
2 Chronicles
6:16 just as you have ***w*** before me."
20:32 Jehoshaphat ***w*** in the way of his father
21:6 He ***w*** in the ways of Israel's kings,
21:12 you haven't ***w*** in the ways of
21:13 but have ***w*** in the ways of Israel's
22:3 Ahaziah ***w*** in the ways of Ahab's
28:2 Instead, he ***w*** in the ways of Israel's
34:2 LORD's eyes and ***w*** in the ways of
Job
29:3 on my head, I ***w*** by his light in
31:5 If I have ***w*** with frauds or my feet have
38:16 sea's sources, ***w*** in the chamber of
Psalms
26:1 because I have ***w*** with integrity.
Proverbs
7:8 at her corner and ***w*** down the path to
Isaiah
20:3 Isaiah has ***w*** naked and
38:3 remember how I've ***w*** before you in
Jeremiah
28:11 Then the prophet Jeremiah ***w*** away.
34:18 in two and then ***w*** between the
Ezekiel
28:14 where you ***w*** among the stones
Amos
2:4 lies after which their ancestors ***w***.
Malachi
2:6 on his lips. He ***w*** with me in peace
Matthew
4:18 As Jesus ***w*** alongside the Galilee Sea,
Mark
2:12 up his mat and ***w*** out in front of
John
5:9 up his mat and ***w***. Now that day was
9:1 As Jesus ***w*** along, he saw a man who was blind
21:18 your own belt and ***w*** around wherever
Acts
14:8 and had never ***w***. Sitting there, he

WALKING

Genesis
3:8 of the LORD God ***w*** in the garden;
18:16 Abraham was ***w*** along with them
24:65 Who is this man ***w*** through the
Exodus
12:11 feet and your ***w*** stick in your
Deuteronomy
8:6 LORD your God by ***w*** in his ways and
30:16 LORD your God, by ***w*** in his ways, and
Joshua
23:14 Look. I'm now ***w*** on the road to death
2 Samuel
6:4 chest while Ahio was ***w*** in front of it.
16:13 and his men kept ***w***, while Shimei
1 Kings
2:3 LORD your God, ***w*** in his ways and
16:19 eyes and by ***w*** in Jeroboam's
2 Kings
2:11 They were ***w*** along, talking, when
17:22 continued ***w*** in all the sins
Job
34:8 with wrongdoers, ***w*** with evil persons.
Isaiah
3:16 themselves, ***w*** with their chins
9:2 The people ***w*** in darkness have seen a
20:2 Isaiah did this, ***w*** naked and
35:8 will be for those ***w*** on that way. Even
51:23 like a street for those ***w*** on it."
65:2 rebellious people ***w*** in a way that
Daniel
3:25 men, unbound, ***w*** around inside the
4:29 later, he was ***w*** on the roof of
Jonah
3:4 into the city, ***w*** one day, and he
Malachi
3:14 obligation or by ***w*** around as
Matthew
10:10 or two shirts or sandals or a ***w*** stick.
11:5 were crippled are ***w***. People with skin
14:25 came to his disciples, ***w*** on the lake.
14:26 disciples saw him ***w*** on the lake, they
14:29 the boat and was ***w*** on the water
15:31 and the injured ***w***, and the blind
27:39 Those who were ***w*** by insulted Jesus,
Mark
6:8 journey except a ***w*** stick—no bread,
6:48 he came to them, ***w*** on the lake. He
6:49 When they saw him ***w*** on the lake, they
8:24 like trees, only they are ***w*** around."
11:20 disciples were ***w*** along, they saw
11:27 As Jesus was ***w*** around the
15:29 People ***w*** by insulted him, shaking their
16:12 of them who were ***w*** along in the
Luke
9:3 the journey—no ***w*** stick, no bag, no
John
1:36 When he saw Jesus ***w*** along he said,
6:19 they saw Jesus ***w*** on the water. He
10:23 in the temple, ***w*** in the covered
Acts
3:8 temple with them, ***w***, leaping, and
3:9 the people saw him ***w*** and praising God.
17:23 As I was ***w*** through town and carefully
Romans
14:15 you are no longer ***w*** in love. Don't

WALL

Exodus
14:22 waters formed a ***w*** for them on their
Leviticus
14:37 to be deeper than the surface of the ***w***,
Numbers
22:24 vineyards with a stone ***w*** on each side.
22:25 against the ***w*** and squeezed
35:4 extend from the ***w*** of the city
Joshua
2:15 side of the city ***w***, and she lived
6:5 Then the city ***w*** will collapse,
6:20 war cry. Then the ***w*** collapsed. The
1 Samuel
18:11 pin David to the ***w***. But David
19:10 pin David to the ***w*** with his spear,
20:25 seat by the ***w***. Jonathan sat
25:16 were a protective ***w*** around us both
31:10 hung his body on the ***w*** of Beth-shan.
31:12 his sons off the ***w*** of Beth-shan. Then
2 Samuel
11:20 you know they would shoot from the ***w***?
22:30 with my God I can leap over a ***w***.
1 Kings
3:1 temple, and the ***w*** around Jerusalem.

14:10 who urinates on a ***w***, whether slave or
21:21 who urinates on a ***w*** that belongs to
2 Kings
6:26 by on the city ***w*** when a woman
9:8 who urinates on a ***w***, whether slave or
18:26 the people on the ***w*** will hear it."
20:2 his face to the ***w*** and prayed to the
25:1 city and built a siege ***w*** all around it.
2 Chronicles
33:14 rebuilt the outer ***w*** of David's City,
Ezra
9:9 and to give us a ***w*** in Judea and
Nehemiah
1:3 and shame! The ***w*** around Jerusalem
2:17 let's rebuild the ***w*** of Jerusalem so
12:27 of Jerusalem's ***w***, they sought out
13:21 the night by the ***w***? If you do that
Job
30:14 a destroyed ***w***; they roll along
Psalms
18:29 with my God I can leap over a ***w***.
78:13 making the waters stand up like a ***w***.
Proverbs
18:11 and like a high ***w*** in their
24:31 and the stone ***w*** was falling down.
Ecclesiastes
10:8 breaks through a ***w*** may be bitten by
Song of Songs
2:9 now, outside our ***w***, peering through
8:9 If she is a city ***w***, then we will build
8:10 I'm a city ***w***, and my breasts are the
Jeremiah
1:18 and a bronze ***w*** against the
15:20 a sturdy bronze ***w*** against these
52:4 the city and built a siege ***w*** around it.
Lamentations
2:8 Daughter Zion's ***w***. He stretched out
2:18 the heart, you ***w*** of Daughter Zion;
Ezekiel
8:7 When I looked, I saw a hole in the ***w***.
8:8 dig through the ***w***. So I dug through
22:30 to repair the ***w*** and stand in the
Hosea
2:6 I will build a ***w*** against her, so
Joel
2:7 they climb the ***w***. Each keeps to
Amos
7:7 was standing by a ***w***, with a plumb
Habakkuk
2:11 from a village ***w***, and a tree
Zechariah
2:5 But I will be a ***w*** of fire around it,
John
5:2 in the north city ***w*** is a pool with
10:1 climbs over the ***w*** is a thief and an
Acts
9:25 through an opening in the city ***w***.
23:3 you whitewashed ***w***! You sit and
2 Corinthians
11:33 basket through a window in the city ***w***.
Revelation
21:12 had a great high ***w*** with twelve
21:18 The ***w*** was built of jasper, and the city

WALLED

Leviticus
25:29 sells a home in a ***w*** city, it may be
25:30 the house in the ***w*** city will belong
Numbers
32:16 We will build ***w*** enclosures here
32:24 your children and ***w*** enclosures for
32:36 cities and ***w*** enclosures for
1 Kings
4:13 large ***w*** cities with
Esther
1:5 all met in the ***w*** garden of the
Job
19:8 He ***w*** up my path so I can't pass and put
Lamentations
2:2 he tore down the ***w*** cities of
3:7 He ***w*** me in so I couldn't escape; he
3:9 He ***w*** in my paths with stonework; he
Daniel
8:2 it I was in the ***w*** city of Susa in
11:7 he will enter the ***w*** fortress of the
11:39 He will deal with ***w*** fortresses with the
Hosea
8:14 has multiplied ***w*** cities; but I

WALLS

Leviticus
14:37 infection in the ***w*** of the house
14:39 has spread over the ***w*** of the house,
Deuteronomy
1:28 are huge, with ***w*** sky-high! Worse
3:5 with high ***w***, double gates,
28:52 high, reinforced ***w*** that you thought
1 Kings
6:5 the temple ***w*** around both the
2 Kings
25:4 between the two ***w*** near the king's
25:10 tore down the ***w*** surrounding
1 Chronicles
29:4 silver for covering the ***w*** of the rooms,
2 Chronicles
3:4 He covered the inside ***w*** with pure gold.
8:5 cities with ***w***, gates, and
14:7 them with ***w***, towers, gates,
26:6 broke down the ***w*** of Gath, Jabneh,
36:19 demolished the ***w*** of Jerusalem, and
Ezra
4:12 completing the ***w*** and repairing the
5:8 set into the ***w***. This work makes
Nehemiah
2:13 could inspect the ***w*** of Jerusalem that
4:7 the work on the ***w*** was progressing
Psalms
51:18 by your favor. Rebuild Jerusalem's ***w***.
55:10 rounds on its ***w***, and evil and
62:3 they were leaning ***w*** or broken-down
80:12 now torn down its ***w*** so that all who
89:40 through all his ***w***. You've made his
122:7 be peace on your ***w***; let there be
144:14 any breach in the ***w***, no exile, no
Proverbs
25:28 is like a breached city, one with no ***w***.
Song of Songs
5:7 from me, those guards of the city ***w***!
Isaiah
5:5 breaking down its ***w***, so it will be
58:12 Mender of Broken ***W***, Restorer of
62:6 Upon your ***w***, Jerusalem, I have
Jeremiah
1:15 Jerusalem, on its ***w***, and in every

39:8 and they destroyed the Jerusalem ***w***.
49:27 set fire to the ***w*** of Damascus; it
51:58 Babylon's massive ***w*** will come down,
52:14 destroyed the ***w*** surrounding
Lamentations
2:5 ruins of her city ***w***. In Daughter
2:7 Zion's palace ***w*** over to enemies.
2:8 barricades and ***w*** wither—together
Ezekiel
8:10 of Israel engraved on the ***w*** all around.
26:12 tear down your ***w***, and raze your
Joel
2:9 they run upon the ***w***. They climb into
Micah
7:11 building of your ***w***! On that day, the
Hebrews
11:30 faith Jericho's ***w*** fell after the

WANDER
Numbers
32:13 and made them ***w*** in the desert for
Judges
11:37 me and my friends ***w*** the hills in
2 Samuel
15:20 should I make you ***w*** around with us
Job
12:24 making them ***w*** in untraveled
15:23 They ***w*** about for bread. "Where is it?"
Psalms
35:14 I would ***w*** around like I was grieving a
38:6 down; I ***w*** around all day
39:6 Yes, people ***w*** around like shadows; yes, they hustle
82:5 understand; they ***w*** around in the
107:40 making them ***w*** aimlessly in the
109:10 Let his children ***w*** aimlessly, begging,
Proverbs
5:6 life. Her paths ***w***, but she doesn't
7:25 to her ways; don't ***w*** down her paths.
12:26 the path of the wicked makes them ***w***.
19:27 you will ***w*** away from words
21:16 People who ***w*** from the path of insight
Song of Songs
1:7 so I don't ***w*** about among the
Isaiah
7:25 cattle are turned loose and sheep ***w***.
29:24 Those who ***w*** in spirit will have
38:15 has acted. I will ***w*** my whole life
Jeremiah
2:5 me that made them ***w*** so far? They
4:1 idols from my presence and ***w*** no more,
14:10 have loved to ***w*** off and haven't
14:18 and priest ***w*** about aimlessly
50:8 Now ***w*** far from Babylon. Get out of that country
Hosea
9:17 them; they will ***w*** among the nations.
Amos
8:12 They will ***w*** from sea to sea, and from
Zechariah
10:2 Therefore, they ***w*** like sheep, but
Matthew
18:13 about the ninety-nine who didn't ***w*** off.
James
5:19 if any of you ***w*** from the truth

WANTED
Exodus
4:19 there who ***w*** to kill you has
33:7 Everyone who ***w*** advice from the
Judges
13:23 him, "If the LORD ***w*** to kill us, he
14:7 the woman; she was the one Samson ***w***.
1 Samuel
2:25 father because the LORD ***w*** to kill them.
2 Samuel
3:17 elders. "You've ***w*** David to be your
4:8 your enemy, who ***w*** you dead. Today
1 Kings
8:17 My father David ***w*** to build a temple for
Esther
1:8 to offer as much as each guest ***w***.
1:11 gorgeous, and he ***w*** to show off her
8:3 her kindly. She ***w*** him to overturn
9:5 did whatever they ***w*** with those who
10:3 of him. He always ***w*** to do good things
Job
31:16 what the poor ***w***, made a widow's
Psalms
35:25 Exactly what we ***w***! Don't let them
132:13 LORD chose Zion; he ***w*** it for his home.
132:14 live here because I ***w*** it for myself.
Isaiah
53:10 But the LORD ***w*** to crush him and to make
57:17 they went on wandering wherever they ***w***.
Obadiah
1:5 only what they ***w***? If those who
Matthew
14:5 Although Herod ***w*** to kill him, he feared
23:37 you. How often I ***w*** to gather your
Luke
1:59 the child. They ***w*** to name him
23:20 again because he ***w*** to release Jesus.

WAR
Genesis
14:2 declared ***w*** on Sodom's King Bera,
31:26 as if they were prisoners of ***w***.
Exodus
1:10 in number. And if ***w*** breaks out, they
13:17 to fight and face ***w***, they will run
15:9 the spoils of ***w***. I'll be
17:16 The LORD is at ***w*** with Amalek in
32:17 Moses, "It sounds like ***w*** in the camp."
Numbers
10:9 When you go to ***w*** in your land against
31:11 all the spoils of ***w*** and the valuable
32:6 brothers go to ***w***, while you stay
32:32 equipped for ***w***. But the property
Deuteronomy
1:39 would be taken in ***w***, and your young
4:34 wonders, ***w***, a strong hand
20:2 toward the ***w***, the priest will
20:12 you but makes ***w*** against you, you
21:10 When you wage ***w*** against your enemies
Joshua
1:14 organized for ***w***, must cross over
4:13 armed for ***w*** crossed over in
11:18 Joshua waged ***w*** against all these kings

Judges
3:2 only to teach ***w*** to the
5:8 new gods, then ***w*** came to the city
1 Samuel
4:1 gathered for ***w*** against Israel,
18:13 David led the men out to ***w*** and back.
28:15 are at ***w*** with me, and God
2 Samuel
3:1 The ***w*** between Saul's house and David's
1 Kings
12:24 says: Don't make ***w*** against your
2 Kings
3:6 at once. He prepared all Israel for ***w***.
1 Chronicles
2:7 the law dedicating ***w*** spoils to God.
20:5 In another ***w*** with the Philistines,
20:6 At another ***w*** in Gath there was a huge
2 Chronicles
6:34 your people go to ***w*** against their
Job
5:20 from death; in ***w***, from the power
38:23 of distress, for a day of battle and ***w***?
Psalms
18:34 my hands for ***w*** so my arms can
18:39 with strength for ***w***; you brought my
27:3 be afraid. If ***w*** comes up against
55:21 than butter, ***w*** is in his heart;
60:1 when he went to ***w*** with Aram-naharaim
120:7 but when I speak, they are for ***w***.
Proverbs
24:6 You should make ***w*** with guidance;
Ecclesiastes
3:8 a time for ***w*** and a time for
8:8 no release from ***w***, and wickedness
9:14 it, and waged a terrible ***w*** against it.
9:18 than weapons of ***w***, but one
Isaiah
2:4 will no longer learn how to make ***w***.
29:7 and all who make ***w*** on her and her
Jeremiah
4:16 raising their ***w*** cries against the
11:22 men will die in ***w***, and their sons
32:5 LORD. If you make ***w*** against the
43:11 exile. and those marked for ***w***, to war.
51:20 my weapon of ***w***. With you I will
Ezekiel
7:21 as loot taken in ***w***, to the earth's
21:22 to proclaim ***w*** and raise the
32:27 their weapons of ***w***, they put their
Daniel
7:21 same horn waged ***w*** against the holy
9:26 will be decreed until the end of the ***w***.
11:10 get ready for ***w***, gathering
11:25 will prepare for ***w***, but he won't
Hosea
1:7 by sword, or by ***w***, or by horses, or
2:18 the sword, and ***w*** from the land; I
10:9 Will not ***w*** overtake them in
10:14 the noise of ***w*** will rise against
Joel
3:9 Prepare a holy ***w***, wake up the
Amos
1:14 palaces, with a ***w*** cry on the day of
2:2 uproar, with a ***w*** cry, with the
Micah
2:8 trusting passersby, those who reject ***w***.
3:5 but stir up ***w*** against the one
4:3 will no longer learn how to make ***w***.
Matthew
12:25 involved in civil ***w*** becomes a
12:26 Satan, he is at ***w*** with himself. How
Mark
3:24 involved in civil ***w*** will collapse.
Luke
11:17 involved in civil ***w*** becomes a
11:18 If Satan is at ***w*** with himself, how will
14:31 king would go to ***w*** against another
Romans
7:23 body. It wages a ***w*** against the law
1 Timothy
1:18 you follow them, you can wage a good ***w***
Hebrews
11:34 were mighty in ***w***, and routed
James
4:1 that are at ***w*** in your own lives?
1 Peter
2:11 desires that wage ***w*** against your
Revelation
2:16 and I will make ***w*** on them with the
11:7 abyss will make ***w*** on them, gain
12:7 Then there was ***w*** in heaven: Michael and his angels
13:7 allowed to make ***w*** on the saints and
17:14 They will make ***w*** on the Lamb, but the
19:11 True, and he judges and makes ***w*** justly.

WARN

Exodus
19:21 Go down and ***w*** the people not to
2 Chronicles
19:10 laws, you must ***w*** them not to sin
24:19 the LORD and to ***w*** them, they
Jeremiah
4:16 ***W*** the nations, proclaim it to
6:10 can I speak and ***w***? How can I get
6:17 watchmen to ***w*** you. But you
46:14 Tell Egypt, ***w*** Migdol, alert Memphis and
Ezekiel
3:18 die but you don't ***w*** them, if you say
3:19 If you do ***w*** the wicked and they don't
3:20 you didn't ***w*** them of their
3:21 But if you do ***w*** the righteous not to
33:6 the trumpet to ***w*** the people, when
33:8 and you don't ***w*** them to turn from
33:9 suppose you do ***w*** the wicked of
Luke
16:28 He needs to ***w*** them so that they
17:3 or sister sins, ***w*** them to stop. If
Acts
4:17 we need to ***w*** them not to speak
1 Corinthians
4:14 ashamed but to ***w*** you, since you
Galatians
5:21 like that. I ***w*** you as I have
Colossians
1:28 we preach as we ***w*** and teach every
3:16 richly. Teach and ***w*** each other with
1 Thessalonians
5:14 we urge you to ***w*** those who are

WARN [cont.]

2 Thessalonians
3:15 like enemies, but ***w*** them like you
2 Timothy
2:14 these things and ***w*** them in the sight

WARNED

Exodus
19:23 Sinai because you ***w*** us and said, 'Set
21:29 owner had been ***w*** but didn't watch
Judges
2:15 as the LORD had ***w*** them. And they
1 Samuel
19:2 So Jonathan ***w*** David, "My father Saul is
19:11 wife Michal ***w*** him, "If you
2 Kings
6:10 time, Elisha ***w*** the king, and the
17:13 The LORD ***w*** Israel and Judah through all the prophets
17:23 what he had ***w*** through all his
Nehemiah
9:26 prophets who had ***w*** them so that they
9:29 You also ***w*** them to return to your
9:30 many years and ***w*** them by your
13:15 on the Sabbath. I ***w*** them at that time
13:21 But I ***w*** them: "Why are you spending the night by the wall
Psalms
2:10 wise up! Be ***w***, you rulers of
Jeremiah
11:7 and tirelessly ***w*** your ancestors
18:8 if that nation I ***w*** turns from its
40:3 done just as he ***w*** because all of
42:19 a doubt that I have ***w*** you this day.
Matthew
2:12 Because they were ***w*** in a dream not to
2:22 Having been ***w*** in a dream, he
3:7 of snakes! Who ***w*** you to escape
9:30 Jesus sternly ***w*** them, "Make sure
Luke
3:7 of snakes! Who ***w*** you to escape
10:3 Go! Be ***w***, though, that I'm sending you
Acts
20:31 and tearfully ***w*** each one of you.
27:9 had already passed. Paul ***w*** them,
2 Corinthians
13:2 visit, I already ***w*** those who
Galatians
5:21 as I have already ***w*** you, that those
1 Thessalonians
4:6 we told you before and sternly ***w*** you.
Hebrews
8:5 when Moses was ***w*** by God when he
11:7 fear when he was ***w*** about events he
12:25 to the one who ***w*** them on earth,
2 Peter
3:17 you have been ***w*** in advance, be on

WARNING

Numbers
26:10 250 persons. They became a ***w*** sign.
1 Samuel
8:9 give them a clear ***w***, telling them how
Psalms
64:4 They shoot without ***w*** and without fear.
64:7 an arrow! Without ***w***, they will be
81:8 my people, I'm ***w*** you! If only you
Isaiah
8:11 hold of me and ***w*** me not to walk in
Ezekiel
3:17 you hear a word from me, deliver my ***w***.
3:21 they heeded the ***w***, and you will
23:48 the land. Taking ***w***, no woman will
33:4 don't heed the ***w***, when the sword
33:5 didn't heed the ***w***, so their blood
33:7 speaking, you must give them ***w*** from me.
Hosea
5:8 Ramah. Sound the ***w*** at Beth-aven:
Luke
9:39 and, without any ***w***, he screams. It
Acts
20:31 each one of you. I never stopped ***w*** you!
1 Corinthians
10:11 were written as a ***w*** for us to whom
2 Corinthians
13:2 repeating that ***w*** to all the rest
Titus
3:10 first and second ***w***, have nothing
Hebrews
12:25 we reject the one who is ***w*** from heaven?
2 Peter
2:6 them to ashes as a ***w*** to ungodly people.
Jude
1:7 of eternal fire, they serve as a ***w***.

WARRIOR

Genesis
10:8 Nimrod, the first great ***w*** on earth.
Exodus
15:3 The LORD is a ***w***; the LORD is his name
Numbers
31:28 LORD from each ***w*** who went into
Deuteronomy
20:19 is some sort of ***w*** to be attacked by
Joshua
17:1 father. This was because he was a ***w***.
Judges
5:30 or two for each ***w***; loot of colored
6:12 said, "The LORD is with you, mighty ***w***!"
11:1 was a mighty ***w***. Gilead was his
20:17 and every one of them was a trained ***w***.
1 Samuel
16:18 man and heroic, a ***w*** who speaks well
17:33 But he's been a ***w*** since he was a
18:17 you must be my ***w*** and fight the
2 Samuel
17:10 your father is a ***w*** and that those
2 Kings
5:1 man was a mighty ***w***, but he had a
1 Chronicles
1:10 of Nimrod, the first ***w*** in the land.
12:4 from Gibeon, a ***w*** in the Thirty and
12:28 man, a mighty ***w***, and 22 officers
27:6 Benaiah was a ***w*** of the Thirty and
2 Chronicles
17:17 came a valiant ***w***: Eliada, together
28:7 An Ephraimite ***w*** named Zichri killed the king's son
32:21 destroyed every ***w***, leader, and
Psalms
19:5 suite; like a ***w***, it thrills at
45:3 your sword, great ***w***, with your glory

78:65 sleeping! Like a **w** shaking off wine,
127:4 are like arrows in the hand of a **w**.
Proverbs
6:11 like a prowler, destitution like a **w**.
16:32 be patient than a **w**, and better to
30:30 a lion, a **w** among beasts, which doesn't
Isaiah
3:2 soldier and **w**; judge and prophet;
42:13 a soldier; like a **w** God will stir up
Jeremiah
14:9 surprise, like a **w** unable to act?
Ezekiel
39:20 men and every **w**. This is what the
Daniel
11:3 Then a **w**-king will come forward,
Amos
2:16 The bravest **w** will flee away naked in
Habakkuk
3:14 the head of his **w** with his own
Zephaniah
1:14 the LORD is bitter. A **w** screams there.
3:17 in your midst—a **w** bringing victory.
Zechariah
10:7 will be like a **w**. They will be as

WARRIORS

Numbers
31:27 between the **w** who went into
31:49 have counted the **w** in our charge and
Deuteronomy
33:2 with him; his **w** were next to him,
Joshua
6:2 your power, along with its mighty **w**.
Judges
5:13 LORD's people marched down against **w**.
5:23 aid, to the LORD's aid against the **w**."
20:44 fell, all of whom were strong **w**.
20:46 armed with swords and were strong **w**.
21:10 twelve thousand **w** there with these
1 Samuel
2:4 bows of mighty **w** are shattered,
2 Samuel
1:19 Look how the mighty **w** have fallen!
1 Kings
9:22 they became **w**, his servants,
12:21 thousand select **w**—to fight against
2 Kings
24:16 seven thousand **w**-each one a hero
1 Chronicles
11:11 list of David's **w**: Jashobeam, a
Nehemiah
3:16 as the artificial pool and the **W** House.
Psalms
33:16 of their armies; **w** aren't rescued by
Proverbs
21:22 fought a city of **w** and brought down
Song of Songs
4:4 upon it—all the weapons of the **w**.
Isaiah
3:25 fall by the sword, your **w** in battle!
5:22 the wine-swigging **w**, mighty at mixing
9:5 of the thundering **w**, and every
13:3 I have called my **w**, my proud,
49:24 be taken from **w**? Can a tyrant's
49:25 the captives of **w** will be taken,
Jeremiah
5:16 Its weapons are deadly; its **w** are many
9:23 knowledge, nor **w** boast of their
26:21 and all his **w** and officials
50:30 streets; all her **w** will be silenced
50:36 sword against its **w** so that they are
51:30 Babylon's **w** quit fighting; they hide in
51:56 Babylon. Her **w** are captured;
51:57 officials, and **w** as well. They
Lamentations
1:15 my mighty **w**. He called a
Ezekiel
23:6 **w** dressed in fine blue cloth, governors
23:12 and officers, **w** richly clothed,
23:15 the appearance of **w** of the third
27:10 and Put were the **w** in your army. By
27:27 all your **w** in you, and all
38:21 The swords of the **w** will be against
39:18 eat the flesh of **w** and drink the
Hosea
10:13 trusted in your way and in your many **w**.
Joel
2:7 Like **w** they charge; like soldiers they
3:9 war, wake up the **w**; let all the
Obadiah
1:9 Your **w** will be shattered, Teman, and
Nahum
2:3 shields of his **w** are red; his
Habakkuk
3:14 own spear. His **w** are driven off,
Zechariah
10:5 will be like **w**, trampling

WASH

Deuteronomy
21:6 the corpse will **w** their hands over
23:11 arrives, he must **w** with water; and
2 Kings
5:10 who said, "Go and **w** seven times in
Job
9:30 If I **w** myself with snow, purify my
Psalms
26:6 I **w** my hands—they are innocent! I walk around your altar
51:2 **W** me completely clean of my guilt;
51:7 I will be clean; **w** me and I will be
58:10 done, when they **w** their feet in the
68:23 so that you can **w** your feet in their
Song of Songs
8:7 rivers can't **w** it away. If
Isaiah
1:16 **W**! Be clean! Remove your ugly deeds
Daniel
4:15 from heaven is to **w** it, and it must
4:23 from heaven is to **w** it, and it must
Matthew
6:17 fast, brush your hair and **w** your face.
John
9:7 said to him, "Go, **w** in the pool of
9:11 of Siloam and **w**.' So I went and
13:5 and began to **w** the disciples'
13:14 feet, you too must **w** each other's feet.
Acts
22:16 be baptized, and **w** away your sins as
Hebrews
6:2 ritual ways to **w** with water,
9:14 blood of Jesus **w** our consciences

James
4:8 come near to you. ***W*** your hands, you
Revelation
22:14 are those who ***w*** their robes so

WASHED

Exodus
19:14 holy and that they ***w*** their clothes.
40:32 the altar, they ***w*** themselves, just
Leviticus
8:6 his sons forward and ***w*** them in water.
8:21 After he ***w*** the insides and lower legs
13:54 infected piece be ***w***, and he will
15:17 of semen must be ***w*** in water and will
Numbers
8:21 themselves and ***w*** their clothes.
Judges
19:21 donkeys, and they ***w*** their feet, ate,
2 Samuel
19:24 his beard, or ***w*** his clothes from
2 Kings
18:17 road to the field where clothes are ***w***.
2 Chronicles
4:6 in these. The priests ***w*** in the Sea.
Job
29:6 my steps were ***w*** with cream and a
Psalms
73:13 good reason; I've ***w*** my hands to stay
Proverbs
30:12 but haven't ***w*** off their own
Ezekiel
16:4 cut, you weren't ***w*** clean with water
16:9 Then I ***w*** you with water, rinsed off
Daniel
4:25 and will be ***w*** by dew from
4:33 Dew from heaven ***w*** his body until he
5:21 dew from heaven ***w*** his body until he
Matthew
27:24 he took water and ***w*** his hands in
John
9:7 man went away and ***w***. When he
9:11 So I went and ***w***, and then I could
9:15 mud on my eyes, I ***w***, and now I see."
13:10 have their feet ***w***, because they are
13:12 After he ***w*** the disciples' feet, he put
13:14 and teacher, have ***w*** your feet, you
Acts
9:37 died. After they ***w*** her body, they
16:33 welcomed them and ***w*** their wounds. He
1 Corinthians
6:11 be! But you were ***w*** clean, you were
Hebrews
10:22 and our bodies are ***w*** with pure water.
2 Peter
2:22 own vomit, and a ***w*** sow wallows in
Revelation
7:14 They have ***w*** their robes and

WASHING

Exodus
30:18 copper basin for ***w*** along with its
40:30 the altar, and put water in it for ***w***.
Song of Songs
4:2 come up from the ***w*** pool—all of them
6:6 come up from the ***w*** pool—all of them
Jeremiah
13:1 Wear it for a while without ***w*** it.
Ezekiel
40:38 in the arches for ***w*** the entirely
Matthew
15:2 their hands by ***w*** before they eat."
15:20 eating without ***w*** hands doesn't
Mark
7:2 purifying their hands through ***w***.
7:3 eat without first ***w*** their hands
7:4 down, such as the ***w*** of cups, jugs,
Luke
5:2 had gone ashore and were ***w*** their nets.
11:38 his hands by ***w*** before the meal,
John
11:55 through ritual ***w*** before the
Ephesians
5:26 make her holy by ***w*** her in a bath of
1 Timothy
5:10 to strangers, ***w*** the feet of the
Titus
3:5 it through the ***w*** of new birth and

WASTE

Genesis
34:19 young man didn't ***w*** any time doing
Deuteronomy
7:10 The LORD does not ***w*** time with anyone
1 Samuel
25:21 saying, "What a ***w*** of time—guarding
2 Samuel
18:14 said, "I won't ***w*** time like this
Ezra
4:15 As a result, this city was laid ***w***.
Job
30:3 dry ground, yesterday's desolate ***w***,
Psalms
119:119 on earth like ***w***—that's why I love
126:4 like dry streams in the desert ***w***!
Proverbs
23:8 out. You will ***w*** your pleasant
Isaiah
10:16 well-fed people ***w*** away; and among
17:4 dwindle; his sleek body will ***w*** away.
24:16 But I say, "I ***w*** away; I waste
34:10 it will lie ***w***; no one will ever
Jeremiah
3:23 on the hills is a ***w***, as is the uproar
9:12 rubble and laid ***w*** like a desert,
Ezekiel
4:17 and they will ***w*** away because of
5:12 die of plague and ***w*** away by famine
12:20 will be laid ***w***, the land left
19:7 widows and laid ***w*** to their cities.
22:18 has become a ***w*** product for me.
24:23 or weep. You will ***w*** away in your
25:3 land was laid ***w***, and when the
30:7 the lands laid ***w***, it will be the
33:10 weigh on us! We ***w*** away because of
38:12 the resettled ***w*** places, against a
Amos
7:9 will be laid ***w***, and I will rise
Nahum
2:10 the city is laid ***w***! The heart grows
Zephaniah
3:6 will be laid ***w***. There will be no
Matthew
26:8 they were angry and said, "Why this ***w***?

Mark
14:4 said to each other, "Why ***w*** the perfume?
1 Corinthians
4:13 of the earth, the ***w*** that runs off
1 Thessalonians
2:1 our visit with you wasn't a ***w*** of time.
3:5 our work would have been a ***w*** of time.
James
1:11 daily lives, the wealthy will ***w*** away.
4:3 intentions, to ***w*** it on your own

WASTELAND

Deuteronomy
32:10 a howling desert ***w***—he protected him
Joshua
8:24 out into the open ***w***. All of them were
15:1 of Edom. The Zin ***w*** was the southern
18:12 and ended at the ***w*** of Beth-aven.
20:8 up Bezer in the ***w*** on the plateau
Job
24:5 for prey; the ***w*** is food for their
38:27 to saturate dry ***w*** and make grass
Psalms
68:7 when you marched through the ***w***, Selah
107:4 desert, into the ***w***. They couldn't
Isaiah
1:7 sight. It's a ***w***, as when
14:17 made the world a ***w*** and tore down its
17:9 of the Israelites. They will be a ***w***,
32:2 of water in a ***w***, like the shade
45:18 create it a ***w*** but formed it as
64:10 has become a wilderness, Jerusalem a ***w***.
Jeremiah
2:31 Have I been a ***w*** to Israel or a
7:34 for the country will be reduced to a ***w***.
9:11 towns of Judah a ***w***, without
25:11 be reduced to a ***w***, and these
25:12 of the Babylonians to a ***w*** for all time.
25:18 to make them a ***w***, an object of
33:10 place, "It is a ***w***, without humans
33:12 proclaims: This ***w***, without humans
34:22 will make Judah a ***w***, without
44:2 They are now a ***w*** with no one left
44:6 to an utter ***w***, as they are
44:22 to an utter ***w*** and a curse, as
46:19 be reduced to a ***w***, a ruin with no
49:13 and scorn, a ***w*** and a curse. And
49:17 will become a ***w***. All who pass by
50:23 has become a ***w*** among the nations!
51:26 You will be a ***w*** forever, declares
51:29 Babylon to a ***w***, with no one left
51:37 of wild dogs, a ***w*** with no one left
51:41 has become a ***w*** among the nations!
51:62 animal; that it will forever be a ***w***!"
Ezekiel
6:14 into a greater ***w*** than the Riblah
25:13 and make it a ***w*** from Teman to
29:9 be turned into a ***w*** and ruins. Then
29:10 an utter ruin, a ***w***, from Migdol to
29:12 It will be a ***w*** for forty years,
32:15 of Egypt into a ***w*** and the land is
35:3 you. I will make you into a desolate ***w***,
35:7 into a desolate ***w***, when I cut off
36:34 when it seemed a ***w*** to all who passed
Joel
2:3 them a barren ***w***; nothing escapes
Zechariah
7:14 They turned a delightful land into a ***w***.
Matthew
12:25 war becomes a ***w***. Every city or
Luke
11:17 war becomes a ***w***, and a house torn

WATCH

Genesis
31:12 Look up and ***w*** all the striped,
Exodus
12:6 should keep close ***w*** over it until the
33:8 their tents and ***w*** Moses until he
Deuteronomy
4:15 So ***w*** your conduct closely, because you
Nehemiah
7:3 some at their ***w*** posts and some in
Esther
8:6 How can I bear to ***w*** the terrible evil
Psalms
17:8 ***W*** me with the very pupil of your eye!
33:18 the LORD's eyes ***w*** all who honor
34:15 The LORD's eyes ***w*** the righteous, his
35:17 my Lord, will you ***w*** this happen?
37:37 integrity and ***w*** those whose heart
39:1 promised I would ***w*** my steps so as
59:1 Saul sent men to ***w*** the house in
61:7 it so love and faithfulness ***w*** over him!
90:4 like a short period during the night ***w***.
130:6 than the night ***w*** waits for
141:3 LORD; keep close ***w*** over the door
Proverbs
4:26 ***W*** your feet on the way, and all your
5:21 The LORD's eyes ***w*** over every person's
13:3 People who ***w*** their mouths guard their
15:3 keeping ***w*** on evil and good
Ecclesiastes
5:1 ***W*** your steps when you go to God's
11:4 Those who ***w*** the wind blow will never
Isaiah
18:4 I will quietly ***w*** from my own
42:20 but don't keep ***w***. With ears open,
Jeremiah
20:4 friends. You will ***w*** as they fall in
23:1 ***W*** out, you shepherds who destroy and
31:28 harm, so I will ***w*** over them to
48:19 by the roads and ***w***, you inhabitants
Ezekiel
4:12 it on human excrement while they ***w***.
40:46 priests who keep ***w*** over the altar.
Daniel
7:7 as I continued to ***w*** this night
Micah
7:7 me! I will keep ***w*** for the LORD; I
Habakkuk
1:5 the nations and ***w***! Be astonished
2:1 I will keep ***w*** to see what the
Zephaniah
3:19 ***W*** what I am about to do to all your
Zechariah
10:7 children will ***w*** and be glad.
Matthew
7:15 ***W*** out for false prophets. They come to
10:17 ***W*** out for people—because they will
16:6 said to them, "***W*** out and be on

16:12 telling them to ***w*** out for the
24:4 Jesus replied, "***W*** out that no one
Mark
8:15 strict orders: "***W*** out and be on
12:38 he said, "***W*** out for the legal
13:5 Jesus said, "***W*** out that no one deceives
13:9 ***W*** out for yourselves. People will hand
13:23 But you, ***w*** out! I've told you
13:33 ***W*** out! Stay alert! You don't know when
Luke
12:1 his disciples. "***W*** out for the yeast
12:15 said to them, "***W*** out! Guard
17:3 ***W*** yourselves! If your brother or sister
20:46 ***W*** out for the legal experts. They like
21:8 Jesus said, "***W*** out that you aren't
John
17:11 you. Holy Father, ***w*** over them in your
Acts
9:24 They were keeping ***w*** at the city gates
20:28 ***W*** yourselves and the whole flock, in
Romans
16:17 I urge you to ***w*** out for people
1 Corinthians
8:9 But ***w*** out or else this freedom of yours
10:12 standing need to ***w*** out or else they
2 Corinthians
3:13 couldn't ***w*** the end of what
Galatians
6:1 of gentleness. ***W*** out for
Philippians
2:4 their own good, ***w*** out for what is
3:2 ***W*** out for the "dogs." Watch out for
3:17 of me and ***w*** those who live
2 Timothy
4:15 But ***w*** out for him, because he opposes
Hebrews
3:12 ***W*** out, brothers and sisters, so that
13:17 because they ***w*** over your whole
1 Peter
5:2 of God among you. ***W*** over it. Don't
2 John
1:8 ***W*** yourselves so that you don't lose

WATCHED

Exodus
17:6 Moses did so while Israel's elders ***w***.
21:36 its owner hadn't ***w*** out for it, the
Deuteronomy
1:30 he fought for you in Egypt while you ***w***,
2:7 you have done. He ***w*** over your journey
4:34 God did for you in Egypt while you ***w***?
9:17 own hands, shattering them while you ***w***.
32:10 cared for him, ***w*** over him with his
Judges
5:28 the window she ***w***, Sisera's mother
1 Samuel
1:12 before the LORD, Eli ***w*** her mouth.
Job
29:2 to be, like days when God ***w*** over me;
Jeremiah
31:28 Just as I ***w*** over them to dig up and
Lamentations
1:10 treasures. She ***w*** nations enter her
1:14 steps are being ***w***; by his hand they
4:17 our watchtower we ***w*** for a nation that
Ezekiel
1:4 As I ***w***, suddenly a driving storm came
10:2 them over the city. As I ***w***, he went in.
10:19 While I ***w***, the winged creatures raised
12:7 and carried it out while they ***w***.
Daniel
7:11 kept watching. I ***w*** from the moment
7:21 As I ***w***, this same horn waged war
Zechariah
2:3 As I ***w***, the messenger speaking with me
John
17:12 was with them, I ***w*** over them in your
Revelation
11:12 in a cloud, while their enemies ***w*** them.

WATCHING

Genesis
30:36 while Jacob was ***w*** the rest of
Exodus
12:42 a night of intent ***w***, to bring them
32:9 Moses, "I've been ***w*** these people, and
Deuteronomy
31:7 with all Israel ***w***, said to him: "Be
Judges
16:27 were on the roof ***w*** as Samson
18:6 The LORD is ***w*** over you on this
1 Samuel
17:28 he said. "Who is ***w*** those few sheep
25:16 were with them, ***w*** our sheep, they
2 Samuel
6:16 Michal was ***w*** from a window.
2 Kings
2:12 Elisha was ***w***, and he cried out, "Oh,
2 Chronicles
7:3 Israelites were ***w*** when the fire
Psalms
22:17 Meanwhile, they just stare at me, ***w*** me.
56:6 ambush—they are ***w*** my steps, hoping
Proverbs
8:34 who listen to me, ***w*** daily at my
Isaiah
44:16 and says, "Ah, I'm warm, ***w*** the fire!"
Jeremiah
1:12 right, for I'm ***w*** over my word
16:17 I am ***w*** their every move; not one is
43:9 while the people of Judah are ***w***.
44:27 I'm ***w*** over them for harm and not for
Daniel
7:6 I kept ***w***, and suddenly there was
7:9 As I was ***w***, thrones were raised up.
7:11 I kept ***w***. I watched from the moment
Matthew
27:55 Many women were ***w*** from a distance. They had followed Jesus
Mark
3:2 Jesus, they were ***w*** Jesus closely to
15:40 Some women were ***w*** from a distance,
Luke
6:7 Pharisees were ***w*** him closely to
14:1 the Pharisees, they were ***w*** him closely.
20:20 priests were ***w*** Jesus closely and
23:35 standing around ***w***, but the leaders
Acts
1:9 as they were ***w***, he was lifted up
22:20 my approval, even ***w*** the clothes that
Philippians
2:4 of each person ***w*** out for their own

Colossians
3:22 when they are ***w***. Instead obey

WATER → LIVING WATER
Genesis
2:10 from Eden to ***w*** the garden, and
18:4 Let a little ***w*** be brought so you may
21:14 and a flask of ***w***, and gave it to
24:11 evening, when women come out to draw ***w***.
24:46 lowered her ***w*** jar and said,
26:19 and found a well there with fresh ***w***.
29:2 their source for ***w*** because the
32:22 crossed the Jabbok River's shallow ***w***.
36:24 the one who found ***w*** in the desert
37:24 an empty cistern with no ***w*** in it.
43:24 and gave them ***w*** to wash their
Exodus
7:20 rod and hit the ***w*** in the Nile in
15:25 threw it into the ***w***, and the water
17:2 said, "Give us ***w*** to drink." Moses
17:6 Hit the rock. ***W*** will come out of
40:7 tent and the altar and put ***w*** in it.
40:30 the altar, and put ***w*** in it for washing.
Leviticus
1:9 be washed with ***w***. The priest will
11:9 from all ***w*** animals: You may
14:5 over fresh ***w*** in a pottery jar.
15:5 clothes, bathe in ***w***, and will be
16:4 bathe his body in ***w*** and then put them
17:15 clothes, bathe in ***w***, and will be
22:6 unless he has bathed his body in ***w***.
Numbers
5:19 immune from the ***w*** of bitterness
19:9 be kept for the ***w*** of purification
20:2 Now there was no ***w*** for the community,
21:5 is no food or ***w***. And we detest
Deuteronomy
11:4 he made the ***w*** of the Reed Sea
11:11 your drinking ***w*** will be rain from
12:16 Pour it out on the ground, just like ***w***.
23:11 he must wash with ***w***; and when the sun
Joshua
2:10 LORD dried up the ***w*** of the Reed Sea
2:11 hearts turned to ***w***. Because of you,
3:16 that moment the ***w*** of the Jordan
4:23 God dried up the ***w*** of the Jordan
Judges
5:4 poured down, the clouds poured down ***w***.
5:25 He asked for ***w***, and she provided milk;
15:19 rock in Lehi, and ***w*** flowed out of it.
2 Samuel
12:27 and captured the city's ***w*** supply.
1 Kings
13:8 I eat food or drink ***w*** in this place.
14:15 like a reed in ***w***. He will uproot
17:10 get a little ***w*** for me in this
18:4 He supplied them with food and ***w***.)
19:6 and a jar of ***w*** right by his
2 Kings
2:8 up, and hit the ***w***. Then the water
2:19 location, but the ***w*** is bad, and the
2:21 purified this ***w***. It will no
3:11 He used to pour ***w*** on Elijah's
6:5 fell into the ***w***. He cried out,
1 Chronicles
11:17 me a drink of ***w*** from the well by
11:18 camp and drew ***w*** from the well by
14:11 enemies, the way ***w*** bursts out."
2 Chronicles
18:26 of bread and ***w*** until I return
32:4 come and find plenty of ***w***?" they asked.
Ezra
10:6 eat food or drink ***w***, for he was
Nehemiah
3:26 opposite the ***W*** Gate to the east
4:23 our clothes, even when they sent for ***w***.
8:1 in front of the ***W*** Gate. They asked
9:15 you brought ***w*** out of the rock
13:2 with food and ***w*** but instead hired
Job
34:7 man like Job? He drinks mockery like ***w***
38:26 to bring ***w*** to uninhabited land, a
38:30 ***W*** hardens like stone; the surface of
38:37 and who can tilt heaven's ***w*** containers
Psalms
1:3 by streams of ***w***, which bears
18:11 covering was dark ***w*** and dense cloud.
18:16 me; he took me out of all that ***w***.
22:14 poured out like ***w***. All my bones
32:6 a great flood of ***w*** won't reach them.
42:1 craves streams of ***w***, my whole being
58:7 dissolve like ***w*** flowing away.
63:1 in a dry and tired land, no ***w*** anywhere.
65:9 stream, full of ***w***. You provide
66:12 through fire and ***w***. But you brought
69:2 have entered deep ***w***; the flood has
72:6 grass, like showers that ***w*** the earth.
74:13 the heads of the sea monsters on the ***w***.
77:17 The clouds poured ***w***, the skies cracked
78:16 from the rock, made ***w*** run like rivers.
78:20 the rock and ***w*** gushed and
79:3 the faithful like ***w*** all around
84:6 it a spring of ***w***. Yes, the early
88:17 all day long like ***w***; they engulf me
93:4 the sound of much ***w***, mightier than
104:11 providing ***w*** for every wild animal—the
104:13 lofty house, you ***w*** the mountains.
105:41 and out gushed ***w***—flowing like a
109:18 inside him like ***w***, seep into his
114:8 into a pool of ***w***, that flint stone
136:6 the earth on the ***w***—God's faithful
144:7 me from deep ***w***, from the power
147:18 his winds blow; the ***w*** flows again.
Proverbs
5:15 Drink ***w*** from your own cistern, gushing
5:16 streams of ***w*** in the public
8:24 there were no springs flowing with ***w***.
8:29 the sea, so the ***w*** couldn't go
9:17 Stolen ***w*** is sweet; food eaten in
17:14 like letting out ***w***, so drop the
21:1 like channels of ***w*** in the hand of
25:21 they are thirsty, give them ***w*** to drink.
25:25 land is like cold ***w*** for a weary
27:19 As ***w*** reflects the face, so the heart
30:16 never filled with ***w***, and fire that
Ecclesiastes
2:6 for myself to ***w*** my lush groves.
11:1 bread out on the ***w*** because, in the
Song of Songs
4:15 a well of fresh ***w***, streams from
5:12 by channels of ***w***. They are bathing

WATER [cont.]

Isaiah
12:3 You will draw ***w*** with joy from the
30:20 distress and the ***w*** of oppression,
32:2 like streams of ***w*** in a wasteland,
49:10 and will guide them by springs of ***w***.
Jeremiah
2:18 to Egypt to drink ***w*** from the Nile?
17:8 reach down to the ***w***. They won't fear
38:6 there wasn't any ***w*** in the cistern,
50:38 sword against the ***w*** supplies so that
Lamentations
1:16 my own eyes pour ***w*** because a
2:19 my Lord like ***w***. Lift your hands
3:48 Streams of ***w*** pour from my eyes because
3:54 ***w*** flowed over my head. I thought: I'm
5:4 We drink our own ***w***—but for a price;
Ezekiel
36:25 sprinkle clean ***w*** on you, and you
Joel
3:18 will flow with ***w***; a spring will
Amos
4:8 one city to drink ***w***, and weren't
8:11 nor a thirst for ***w***, but of hearing
Jonah
2:3 waves and rushing ***w*** passed over me.
3:7 anything! No grazing and no drinking ***w***!
Nahum
2:8 like a pool of ***w***. Such are its
3:14 Draw ***w*** for yourself to prepare for
Habakkuk
2:14 LORD's glory, just as ***w*** covers the sea.
3:10 A flood of ***w*** rushes through.
Zechariah
14:8 that day, running ***w*** will flow out
Matthew
3:11 I baptize with ***w*** those of you who have changed your
3:16 up out of the ***w***. Heaven was
10:42 a cup of cold ***w*** to these little
14:28 you, order me to come to you on the ***w***."
14:29 and was walking on the ***w*** toward Jesus.
17:15 he often falls into the fire or the ***w***.
27:24 So he took ***w*** and washed his
Mark
1:8 baptize you with ***w***, but he will
1:10 up out of the ***w***, Jesus saw heaven
9:22 a fire or into ***w*** trying to kill
9:41 you a cup of ***w*** to drink because
14:13 A man carrying a ***w*** jar will meet
Luke
3:16 baptize you with ***w***, but the one who
5:4 into the deep ***w***, and drop your
6:48 came, the rising ***w*** smashed against
7:44 didn't give me ***w*** for my feet, but
8:23 filling up with ***w*** and they were in
8:25 the winds and the ***w***, and they obey
16:24 of his finger in ***w*** and cool my
22:10 a man carrying a ***w*** jar will meet
John
2:9 tasted the ***w*** that had become
3:5 is born of ***w*** and the Spirit,
4:10 Give me some ***w*** to drink,' you
13:5 Then he poured ***w*** into a washbasin and
19:34 and immediately blood and ***w*** came out.
21:7 he was naked) and jumped into the ***w***.
Acts
1:5 baptized with ***w***, but in only a
8:36 they came to some ***w***. The eunuch said,
8:38 went down to the ***w***, where Philip
8:39 up out of the ***w***, the Lord's
10:47 from being baptized with ***w***, can they?"
11:16 will baptize with ***w***, but you will be
27:28 and found the ***w*** to be about one
Ephesians
5:26 her in a bath of ***w*** with the word.
1 Timothy
5:23 Don't drink ***w*** anymore but use a little
Hebrews
6:2 ways to wash with ***w***, laying on of
9:10 ways to wash with ***w***. They are
9:19 goats, along with ***w***, scarlet wool,
10:22 and our bodies are washed with pure ***w***.
James
3:11 Both fresh ***w*** and salt water don't come
3:12 not, and fresh ***w*** doesn't flow from
1 Peter
3:20 eight) lives were rescued through ***w***.
2 Peter
2:17 springs without ***w***, mists driven by
3:5 long ago out of ***w*** and by means of
1 John
5:6 one who came by ***w*** and blood: Jesus
5:8 the Spirit, the ***w***, and the blood—and
Revelation
1:15 and his voice sounded like rushing ***w***.
7:17 of life-giving ***w***, and God will
8:10 a third of the rivers and springs of ***w***.
8:11 died from the ***w***, because it
12:15 poured a river of ***w*** after the woman
14:2 sound of rushing ***w*** and loud thunder.
14:7 and earth, the sea and springs of ***w***."
16:4 and springs of ***w***, and they turned
16:12 Euphrates. Its ***w*** was dried up so
19:6 like rushing ***w*** and powerful
21:6 will freely give ***w*** from the life-giving
22:1 of life-giving ***w***, shining like
22:17 receive life-giving ***w*** as a gift."

WATERS

Genesis
1:2 sea, and God's wind swept over the ***w***
1:10 the gathered ***w*** Seas. God saw how
7:17 forty days. The ***w*** rose, lifted the
8:1 over the earth so that the ***w*** receded.
8:13 first month, the ***w*** dried up from the
49:4 As wild as the ***w***, you won't endure,
Exodus
7:19 hand over Egypt's ***w***—over their rivers
14:21 dry land. The ***w*** were split into
15:5 they sank into the deep ***w*** like a stone.
20:4 below or in the ***w*** under the earth.
Numbers
20:13 These were the ***w*** of Meribah, where the
Deuteronomy
5:8 below or in the ***w*** under the earth.
33:13 with the deep ***w*** stretching out
Joshua
11:5 together at the ***w*** of Merom to fight
15:7 passed on to the ***w*** of En-shemesh and
15:9 mountain to the ***w*** of Nephtoah
16:1 eastward to the ***w*** of Jericho. It
18:15 proceeded to the ***w*** of Nephtoah

Judges
5:19 by Megiddo's ***w***, but they
7:24 of the Jordan's ***w*** as far as Beth-bar
2 Samuel
22:17 grabbed me; he took me out of deep ***w***.
2 Kings
5:12 than all Israel's ***w***? Couldn't I wash
19:24 wells, have drunk ***w*** in foreign lands.
2 Chronicles
32:30 outlet of the ***w*** of the Gihon
Nehemiah
9:11 depths, as a stone into the mighty ***w***.
Job
26:5 the inhabitants beneath the ***w*** as well.
27:20 them like ***w***; a tempest
28:25 the wind, to prepare a measure for ***w***,
38:34 clouds so their abundant ***w*** cover you?
Psalms
23:2 meadows; he leads me to restful ***w***;
24:2 the seas; God set it firmly on the ***w***.
29:3 voice is over the ***w***; the glorious God
33:7 the ocean ***w*** into a heap; he
46:3 when its ***w*** roar and rage, when the
69:1 God, because the ***w*** have reached my
77:16 The ***w*** saw you, God—the waters saw you
77:19 the mighty ***w***. But your
78:13 making the ***w*** stand up like a
81:7 I tested you at the ***w*** of Meribah. Selah
104:3 house on the ***w***; you make the
104:6 of clothing; the ***w*** were higher than
105:29 God turned their ***w*** into blood and
106:11 But the ***w*** covered over their foes—not
106:32 God at Meribah's ***w***, and things went
124:4 Then the ***w*** would have drowned us; the
124:5 then the raging ***w*** would have come over our necks!
148:4 Do the same, you ***w*** that are above
Proverbs
18:4 mouth are deep ***w***, a bubbling
20:5 from the deep ***w*** of the heart;
30:4 has bound up the ***w*** in a garment? Who
Song of Songs
8:7 Rushing ***w*** can't quench love; rivers
Isaiah
43:2 pass through the ***w***, I will be with
54:9 that Noah's ***w*** would never again
57:20 churn up from their ***w*** muck and mud.
Jeremiah
10:13 the heavenly ***w*** roar. He raises
47:2 LORD proclaims: ***W*** are rising from
48:34 Even the ***w*** of Nimrim are
51:16 the heavenly ***w*** roar. God raises
Ezekiel
1:24 sound of mighty ***w***, like the sound
32:2 you roil the ***w*** with your feet,
Amos
5:8 who summons the ***w*** of the sea, and
5:24 roll down like ***w***, and
9:6 who summons the ***w*** of the sea, and
Jonah
2:5 ***W*** have grasped me to the point of
Micah
1:4 to the fire, like ***w*** poured down a
Nahum
2:8 Such are its ***w***, and others are
3:8 by the Nile, ***w*** surrounding her,
Habakkuk
3:15 tread on the sea; turbulent ***w*** foam.
1 Corinthians
3:7 nor the one who ***w*** is anything, but
3:8 and the one who ***w*** work together,
Revelation
8:11 a third of the ***w*** became wormwood,
11:6 power over the ***w***, to turn them
16:5 the angel of the ***w*** say, "You are
17:1 prostitute, who is seated on deep ***w***.
17:15 said to me, "The ***w*** that you saw,

WAVES
2 Samuel
22:5 Death's ***w*** were all around me; rivers of
Job
9:8 alone and trod on the ***w*** of the Sea;
38:11 no farther; here your proud ***w*** stop"?
Psalms
42:7 all your massive ***w*** surged over me.
46:3 shake because of its surging ***w***. Selah
65:7 calm the roaring ***w***, calm the noise
89:9 sea: When its ***w*** rise up, it's you
93:4 than the sea's ***w***, mighty on high
107:25 up a storm that brought the ***w*** up high.
107:26 The ***w*** went as high as the sky; they
107:29 to a whisper; the sea's ***w*** were hushed.
107:30 because the ***w*** had calmed down;
Isaiah
33:15 extortion, who ***w*** away a bribe
48:18 righteousness like the ***w*** of the sea.
51:15 sea so that its ***w*** roar—the LORD of
Jeremiah
5:22 pass? Though its ***w*** may rise and
31:35 sea into crashing ***w***, whose name is
51:42 Babylon; its pounding ***w*** overwhelm her.
51:55 like the crushing ***w***, a deafening
Ezekiel
26:3 sea hurls up its ***w***, I will bring
Jonah
2:3 All your strong ***w*** and rushing water
Zechariah
10:11 the sea with ***w***. All the depths
Matthew
8:24 the lake so that ***w*** were sloshing
14:24 battered by the ***w*** and was already
Mark
4:37 winds arose, and ***w*** crashed against
Luke
8:24 and the violent ***w***. The storm died
21:25 the roaring of the sea and surging ***w***.
Acts
27:41 into pieces by the force of the ***w***.
Jude
1:13 wild ***w*** of the sea foaming up their own

WAY → GOD'S WAY, KNOW THE WAY, WAY OF LIFE
Genesis
3:24 to guard the ***w*** to the tree of
32:1 Jacob went on his ***w***, and God's
Exodus
13:18 by the roundabout ***w*** of the Reed Sea
13:21 them light. This ***w*** they could travel
Leviticus
20:4 to look the other ***w*** when someone

WAY [cont.]

Joshua
6:15 the city in this **w** seven times. It
Judges
1:22 In the same **w**, Joseph's household went
1:25 showed them the **w** into the city.
1 Samuel
21:13 So he changed the **w** he acted with them,
26:25 David went on his **w**, but Saul went
30:23 Don't act that **w** with the things
2 Samuel
22:31 God! His **w** is perfect; the LORD's word
1 Kings
8:36 them the best **w** for them to
13:9 water! Don't return by the **w** you came!"
2 Kings
8:7 The man of God has come all this **w**."
21:22 LORD-he didn't walk in the LORD's **w**.
2 Chronicles
6:27 them the best **w** for them to
Nehemiah
5:15 God-fearing, I didn't behave in this **w**.
6:13 by acting in this **w**. Then they could
9:12 they lit the **w** in which the
Job
22:15 keep the ancient **w** traveled by
23:10 he knows my **w**; when he tests
33:14 God speaks in one **w**, in two ways, but
Psalms
1:6 with the **w** of the righteous,
2:12 angry, and your **w** will be destroyed
5:8 Make your **w** clear, right in
6:6 I soak my couch all the **w** through.
18:30 God! His **w** is perfect; the LORD's word
18:32 with strength and makes my **w** perfect,
25:8 teaches sinners which **w** they should go.
25:9 weak to justice, teaching them his **w**.
27:11 teach me your **w**; because of my
37:5 Commit your **w** to the LORD! Trust him!
37:14 to slaughter those whose **w** is right.
37:23 by the LORD when they delight in his **w**.
37:34 LORD and keep his **w**! He will lift you
38:4 are a weight that's **w** too heavy for me.
42:4 how I made my **w** to the mighty
44:18 have our steps strayed from your **w**.
48:12 Zion; go all the **w** around it; count
67:2 so that your **w** becomes known on earth,
77:13 God, your **w** is holiness! Who is as
77:19 Your **w** went straight through the sea;
80:11 branches all the **w** to the sea; its
86:11 Teach me your **w**, LORD, so that I can
101:2 want to study the **w** of integrity—how
106:23 one, stood in the **w**, right in front
107:4 find their **w** to a city or town.
110:7 stream along the **w**, then holds his
118:27 ropes all the **w** to the horns of
119:1 Those whose **w** is blameless—who walk
119:30 I've chosen the **w** of faithfulness; I'm
119:37 things. Make me live by your **w**.
119:67 I took the wrong **w**, but now I do
137:7 it down! All the **w** to its
139:24 is any idolatrous **w** in me, then lead
142:3 you still know my **w**. But they've
143:8 you. Show me the **w** I should go
146:9 but who makes the **w** of the wicked
Proverbs
1:15 with them; keep your feet from their **w**
1:31 fruit of their **w**, and they'll be
2:8 and guards the **w** of those who are
2:13 They forsake the **w** of integrity and go
2:15 are confused; they get lost on their **w**.
4:14 Don't go on the **w** of the wicked; don't
4:18 The **w** of the righteous is like morning
4:26 your feet on the **w**, and all your
8:20 I walk on the **w** of righteousness, on
8:22 beginning of his **w**, before his deeds
9:6 live; walk in the **w** of understanding."
9:15 path, those going straight on their **w**.
10:17 are on the **w** to life, but
12:15 see their own **w** as right, but the
12:28 The **w** of the righteous leads to life,
13:15 favor, but the **w** of the faithless
14:8 understand their **w**, but the
15:10 who abandon the **w**; those who hate
15:19 thorns, but the **w** of those who do
17:23 bribes to twist the **w** of justice.
18:16 A gift opens the **w** for access to
19:3 corrupts their **w**, but their hearts
22:6 children in the **w** they should go;
30:19 the **w** of an eagle in the sky, the way
30:20 This is the **w** of an adulterous woman:
Ecclesiastes
2:19 foolish? Either **w**, that person will
8:5 knows the right time and the right **w**
8:6 time and right **w** for every matter.
12:5 terrors along the **w**; when the almond
Song of Songs
1:8 don't know your **w**, most beautiful
6:1 Which **w** did your lover go, you who are
Isaiah
30:21 you: "This is the **w**; walk in it."
35:8 called The Holy **W**. The unclean
40:3 Clear the LORD's **w** in the desert!
48:17 who leads you in the **w** you should go.
53:6 going its own **w**, but the LORD let
65:2 walking in a **w** that isn't good,
Jeremiah
3:21 have lost their **w** and forgotten the
5:4 the LORD's **w** or the justice of
22:21 have been that **w** since your youth:
23:10 right and their **w** is evil, the land
Lamentations
2:10 their heads all the **w** to the ground.
Ezekiel
4:13 In this same **w** the Israelites
18:25 say, "My Lord's **w** doesn't measure
46:9 go out the same **w** they came in.
46:23 masonry all the **w** around, and
Daniel
10:13 blocked my **w**. But then
Hosea
10:13 trusted in your **w** and in your many
Amos
2:7 out of the **w**. Father and son
4:12 will act in this **w** toward you;
8:14 and, "As the **w** of Beer-sheba live
Nahum
1:3 punishes. His **w** is in whirlwind
Matthew
3:3 Prepare the **w** for the Lord;
10:11 and stay there until you go on your **w**.
11:10 who will prepare your **w** before you.

17:12 In the same ***w*** the Human One is
26:29 drink it in a new ***w*** with you in my
Mark
1:2 before you. He will prepare your ***w***,
1:3 Prepare the ***w*** for the Lord;
2:7 he speak this ***w***? He's insulting
14:25 drink it in a new ***w*** in God's kingdom."
Luke
7:27 who will prepare your ***w*** before you.
10:4 Don't even greet anyone along the ***w***.
10:31 side of the road and went on his ***w***.
14:33 In the same ***w***, none of you who are
22:20 In the same ***w***, he took the cup after
22:39 left and made his ***w*** to the Mount of
John
4:23 looks for those who worship him this ***w***.
7:46 No one has ever spoken the ***w*** he does."
14:6 I am the ***w***, the truth, and
16:22 In the same ***w***, you have sorrow now;
Acts
1:11 come in the same ***w*** that you saw him
9:2 belonged to the ***W***, whether men or
19:9 slandered the ***W***. As a result,
22:4 who followed this ***W*** to their death,
24:14 a follower of the ***W***, which they call
Romans
3:2 Plenty in every ***w***. First of all, the
15:28 leave for Spain, visiting you on the ***w***.
1 Corinthians
9:14 In the same ***w***, the Lord commanded that those who preach
10:13 also supply a ***w*** out so that you
12:31 I'm going to show you an even better ***w***.
Galatians
3:6 that in the same ***w*** that Abraham
Colossians
2:20 Christ to the ***w*** the world thinks
3:18 husbands in a ***w*** that is
3:21 children in a ***w*** that ends up
2 Timothy
1:12 I'm suffering the ***w*** I do, but I'm not
2:5 Also in the same ***w***, athletes don't win
3:8 truth in the same ***w*** that Jannes and
3:15 to be wise in a ***w*** that leads to
Titus
2:1 should talk in a ***w*** that is
2:4 That ***w*** they can mentor young women to love
2:7 in every ***w***. Offer yourself as a role
2:10 God our savior attractive in every ***w***.
Hebrews
9:8 showing that the ***w*** into the holy
10:20 a new and living ***w*** that he opened up
13:18 want to do the right thing in every ***w***.
James
2:12 In every ***w***, then, speak and act as
3:5 In the same ***w***, even though the tongue
3:10 sisters, it just shouldn't be this ***w***!
2 Peter
2:15 following the ***w*** of Balaam son of
2:21 to have known the ***w*** of righteousness

WAY OF LIFE

Ps 16:11; Prv 5:6; Jer 21:8; Ac 26:4; 26:5; 1Co 4:17; Eph 4:22; Heb 13:5; 1Pt 3:1

WAYS → ALL HIS WAYS, EVIL WAYS
Exodus
33:13 me, show me your ***w*** so that I may
Leviticus
2:8 in one of these ***w*** to the LORD,
Deuteronomy
8:6 by walking in his ***w*** and by fearing
10:12 in all his ***w***, by loving him,
11:22 in all his ***w***, and by clinging
19:9 walking in his ***w***—you can add three
26:17 will walk in his ***w*** and follow his
28:9 God's commandments and walk in his ***w***.
30:16 by walking in his ***w***, and by keeping
32:4 about it: all his ***w*** are right! He's
Joshua
22:5 Walk in all his ***w*** and obey his
Judges
2:19 once again act in ***w*** that weren't as
2:22 in the LORD's ***w*** just as their
2 Samuel
3:25 you know the evil ***w*** of Abner, Ner's
22:22 kept the LORD's ***w***. I haven't acted
1 Kings
8:58 walk in all his ***w*** and observe his
16:2 in Jeroboam's ***w***, making my people
2 Kings
17:13 from your evil ***w***. Keep my
Job
21:14 we take no pleasure in knowing your ***w***;
34:21 eyes are on human ***w***, and he sees all
Psalms
7:12 change their ***w***, God will sharpen
10:5 Their ***w*** are always twisted. Your rules
17:4 such violent ***w*** by the command
17:7 love in amazing ***w*** because you are
18:21 kept the LORD's ***w***. I haven't acted
25:4 Make your ***w*** known to me, LORD; teach me your paths
51:13 wrongdoers your ***w***, and sinners will
81:13 How I wish Israel would walk in my ***w***!
85:8 Don't let them return to foolish ***w***.
95:10 twisted hearts. They don't know my ***w***.'
103:7 God made his ***w*** known to Moses; made his deeds known
107:17 of their sinful ***w***. They suffered
119:3 anything wrong! They walk in God's ***w***.
119:168 laws because all my ***w*** are seen by you.
125:5 their own twisted ***w***—may the LORD march them off
128:1 who walks in God's ***w***, is truly happy!
132:1 remember David—all the ***w*** he suffered
138:5 about the LORD's ***w*** because the
139:3 are thoroughly familiar with all my ***w***.
145:17 in all his ***w***, faithful in all
Proverbs
1:19 These are the ***w*** of all who seek unjust
2:19 never again reach the ***w*** of the living.
3:6 and he will keep your ***w*** straight.
3:17 Her ***w*** are pleasant; all her paths are
3:31 people or choose any of their ***w***,
5:21 person's path, observing all their ***w***.
6:6 person; observe its ***w*** and grow wise.
7:25 your heart to her ***w***; don't wander
8:32 me: Happy are those who keep to my ***w***!
9:6 your simplistic ***w*** and live; walk in
14:14 from their ***w***; the good receive

WAYS [cont.]

16:2 All the ***w*** of people are pure in their
19:16 those who disregard their ***w*** will die.
21:8 The ***w*** of some people are twisted and
22:25 will learn their ***w*** and become
31:3 to women, your ***w*** to those who wipe

Isaiah
2:3 may teach us his ***w*** and we may walk
42:24 to walk in God's ***w***, and wouldn't
55:8 nor are your ***w*** my ways, says the
66:3 chosen their own ***w***, and prefer their

Jeremiah
18:11 from your evil ***w***; reform your ways

Lamentations
3:40 and examine our ***w***; we must return

Ezekiel
16:47 follow in their ***w*** or engage in
28:15 was found in you, your ***w*** were assured.
33:9 wicked of their ***w*** so that they
36:32 because of all your ***w***, house of Israel.

Hosea
14:9 Truly, the LORD's ***w*** are right, and

Micah
4:2 may teach us his ***w*** and we may walk

Zechariah
1:4 from your evil ***w*** and your evil

Malachi
2:9 of you keep my ***w*** or show respect

Matthew
6:12 us for the ***w*** we have wronged

Mark
6:52 changed so that they resisted God's ***w***.

Luke
17:4 I am changing my ***w***,' you must

Acts
3:26 each of you to turn from your evil ***w***."
13:10 the straight ***w*** of the Lord into
15:39 their separate ***w***. Barnabas took
28:10 us in many ***w***. When we were

Romans
1:30 brag. They invent ***w*** to be evil, and
3:16 destruction and misery are in their ***w***

2 Corinthians
8:22 in many ***w*** and many times.

Ephesians
5:18 with the Spirit in the following ***w***:

Hebrews
1:1 our ancestors in many times and many ***w***.
3:10 off course, and they don't know my ***w***."
6:2 about ritual ***w*** to wash with
9:10 various ritual ***w*** to wash with

James
1:8 double-minded, unstable in all their ***w***.
3:14 and living in ***w*** that deny the

1 Peter
2:22 he ever speak in ***w*** meant to deceive.
3:7 with your wife in ***w*** that honor her,
4:2 human lives in ***w*** determined by

Revelation
15:3 and true are your ***w***, king of the
18:3 power of her loose and extravagant ***w***."
18:7 and extravagant ***w***, give her pain
18:9 and extravagant ***w***, will weep and

WEAK

Genesis
41:19 seven other cows, ***w*** and frail and

Exodus
5:8 number! They are ***w*** and lazy, and

Numbers
11:23 LORD's power too ***w***? Now you will see
13:18 live in it strong or ***w***, few or many?

Deuteronomy
25:18 because you were ***w*** and tired, and

Judges
6:6 became very ***w*** on account of
16:5 up and make him ***w***. Then we'll each

1 Samuel
3:2 eyes had grown so ***w*** he was unable to
28:20 had said. He was ***w*** because he hadn't

2 Samuel
3:39 king, I am ***w***. These men,
17:2 he is tired and ***w***, and I will throw

2 Chronicles
14:11 you can help the ***w*** against the

Job
3:17 wicked rage no more; there the ***w*** rest.
17:7 My eye is ***w*** from grief; my limbs like a
26:2 have helped the ***w***, saved those with
29:12 I rescued the ***w*** who cried out,
36:15 He saves the ***w*** in their affliction,

Psalms
6:7 of my grief; it's ***w*** because of all my
25:9 God guides the ***w*** to justice, teaching
35:10 You rescue the ***w*** from those who
37:11 But the ***w*** will inherit the land; they
37:14 to bring down the ***w*** and the needy, to
40:17 But me? I'm ***w*** and needy. Let my Lord
61:2 When my heart is ***w***, I cry out to you
72:13 compassion on the ***w*** and the needy; he
102:1 person, when ***w*** and pouring out
109:24 My legs are ***w*** from fasting; my body is
142:3 When my spirit is ***w*** inside me, you
143:4 My spirit is ***w*** inside me—inside, my

Proverbs
24:10 you show yourself ***w*** on a day of

Song of Songs
2:5 me with apples, for I'm ***w*** with love!
5:8 you tell him? That I'm ***w*** with love!

Isaiah
14:10 you've become ***w*** like we are! You
35:3 Strengthen the ***w*** hands, and support the unsteady knees
44:12 hungry and ***w***. If he didn't

Jeremiah
15:9 seven will grow ***w*** and gasp for air;
31:25 the weary and renew those who are ***w***.

Ezekiel
18:18 he exploited the ***w*** or committed
34:4 strengthen the ***w***, heal the sick,
34:16 strengthen the ***w***. But the fat and
34:21 you ram all the ***w*** sheep until

Daniel
5:6 He felt ***w***, and his knees

Hosea
4:3 live on it grow ***w***; together with

Amos
4:1 who cheat the ***w***, who crush the
5:11 you crush the ***w***, and because you

Matthew
6:30 more for you, you people of ***w*** faith?
8:26 you people of ***w*** faith?" Then he
14:31 You man of ***w*** faith! Why did
16:8 You people of ***w*** faith! Why are

26:41 spirit is eager, but the flesh is ***w***."
Mark
14:38 spirit is eager, but the flesh is ***w***."
Luke
12:28 God do for you, you people of ***w*** faith!
Acts
20:35 we must help the ***w***. In this way we
Romans
5:6 we were still ***w***, at the right
8:3 Law, since it was ***w*** because of
14:1 the person who is ***w*** in faith—but not
14:2 while the ***w*** person eats only
1 Corinthians
1:27 world considers ***w*** to shame the
8:9 might be a problem for those who are ***w***.
9:22 I act ***w*** to the weak, so I can recruit
11:30 many of you are ***w*** and sick, and
2 Corinthians
12:10 because when I'm ***w***, then I'm strong.
Galatians
4:9 back again to the ***w*** and worthless
1 Thessalonians
5:14 Help the ***w***. Be patient with
Hebrews
7:18 set aside because it was ***w*** and useless
12:12 your drooping hands and ***w*** knees!
2 Peter
2:14 whose faith is ***w***. They have hearts
3:16 whose faith is ***w*** twist them to

WEALTH

Genesis
15:14 serve, they will leave it with great ***w***.
31:1 and from it he produced all of this ***w***."
31:16 All of the ***w*** God took from our father
49:26 mountains, the ***w*** of the
Joshua
22:8 home with great ***w*** and many cattle,
1 Samuel
2:7 makes poor, gives ***w***, brings low, but
1 Kings
3:11 long life, ***w***, or victory over
3:13 didn't ask for: ***w*** and fame. There
10:7 far more wisdom and ***w*** than I was told.
10:23 all the earth's kings in ***w*** and wisdom,
1 Chronicles
29:12 are the source of ***w*** and honor, and
29:28 a full life, ***w***, and honor; and
2 Chronicles
1:11 than asking for ***w***, riches, fame,
1:12 also give you ***w***, riches, and fame
9:22 all the earth's kings in ***w*** and wisdom,
18:1 already had great ***w*** and honor, he
29:35 addition to the ***w*** of entirely
32:29 because God had given him great ***w***.
Esther
5:11 about his great ***w*** and his many
Job
6:22 Offer a bribe from your ***w*** for me?
15:29 get rich; their ***w*** won't last; their
20:10 their hands will give back their ***w***.
20:15 They swallow ***w*** and vomit it; God
20:18 won't enjoy the ***w*** from their
20:28 Their household ***w*** will be carried off
31:25 because my ***w*** was great, when
36:18 lure you with ***w***; don't let a huge
Psalms
37:16 than the overabundant ***w*** of the wicked.
39:6 who will get the ***w*** they've amassed.
49:6 and boast of their fantastic ***w***?
49:7 ***W***? It can't save a single person! It
49:8 is too high—***w*** will never be
49:12 longer because of ***w***; they're just
52:7 their own great ***w***. They sought
62:10 in robbery. When ***w*** bears fruit,
73:12 ones, always relaxed, piling up the ***w***!
105:44 they inherited the ***w*** of many peoples—
109:11 he owns; let strangers plunder his ***w***.
112:3 ***w*** and riches will be in their houses.
119:14 as if I were rejoicing over great ***w***.
Proverbs
1:13 sorts of precious ***w***; we'll fill our
3:9 LORD with your ***w*** and with the
3:16 long life; in her left are ***w*** and honor.
8:18 well as enduring ***w*** and righteousness.
11:16 gains honor; violent men gain only ***w***.
11:28 trust in their ***w*** will wither, but
13:8 ***W*** can ransom a person's life, but the
13:22 but the ***w*** of sinners is
14:24 ***W*** is the crown of the wise, and the
22:1 better than much ***w***; high esteem is
22:4 fear of the LORD is ***w***, honor, and life.
23:5 your eyes fly to ***w*** it is gone; it
24:4 with all precious and pleasant ***w***.
30:8 either poverty or ***w***; give me just the
Ecclesiastes
4:8 with their ***w***. So for whom am I
5:10 is the lover of ***w*** satisfied with
5:13 hoard their ***w*** to their own
5:14 Then that ***w*** is lost in a bad business
5:19 God gives people ***w*** and riches and
6:2 people plenty of ***w***, riches, and
9:11 to the wise, nor ***w*** to the
Isaiah
8:4 my mother,' the ***w*** of Damascus and
10:3 for help; where will you stash your ***w***?
10:14 My hand found the ***w*** of the peoples as if it were
30:6 will carry their ***w*** on donkeys'
60:5 you; the nations' ***w*** will come to you.
60:11 bring to you the ***w*** of nations, and
61:6 will feed on the ***w*** of nations, and
66:12 a river, and the ***w*** of nations like
Jeremiah
9:23 might, nor the rich boast of their ***w***.
15:13 Your ***w*** and belongings I will deliver as
17:3 as well as your ***w*** and all that you
17:11 who acquire their ***w*** corruptly. By
20:5 hand over all the ***w*** of this city, all
Ezekiel
22:25 They've piled up ***w*** and precious
26:12 will destroy your ***w***, plunder your
27:12 procurer of great ***w***. For your wares,
27:18 out of its great ***w*** the wine of
27:27 your wares, your ***w***, your sailors,
27:33 Your abundant ***w*** and merchandise
29:19 carry off its ***w***, he will plunder
30:4 in Egypt, its ***w*** carried away, and
Daniel
11:24 spoil, and ***w*** to them. He will
11:28 with great ***w*** and set his mind
Hosea
12:8 rich, I've gained ***w*** for myself; in

Obadiah
1:11 carried off his ***w***, and foreigners
Micah
4:13 the LORD, their ***w*** to the LORD of
Zephaniah
1:13 Their ***w*** will be looted and their houses
Haggai
2:7 quake. The ***w*** of all the
Zechariah
9:4 and knock her ***w*** into the sea. She
14:14 in Jerusalem. The ***w*** of all the
Matthew
6:24 the other. You cannot serve God and ***w***.
13:22 false appeal of ***w*** choke the word,
Mark
4:19 false appeal of ***w***, and the desire
Luke
15:13 he wasted his ***w*** through
16:9 you, use worldly ***w*** to make friends
16:11 with worldly ***w***, who will trust
16:13 the other. You cannot serve God and ***w***."
Romans
9:23 this to make the ***w*** of his glory
Revelation
5:12 to receive power, ***w***, wisdom, and
18:17 hour such great ***w*** was destroyed.'

WEALTHY

Genesis
13:2 Abram was very ***w*** in livestock, silver,
26:13 and richer until he was extremely ***w***.
1 Samuel
9:1 There was a ***w*** man from the tribe of
2 Samuel
19:32 because Barzillai was a very ***w*** man.
2 Kings
15:20 money. All the ***w*** people had to
2 Chronicles
32:27 became very ***w*** and greatly
Psalms
49:20 ***W*** people? They just don't understand;
Proverbs
10:15 The riches of the ***w*** are their strong
13:11 who acquire them gradually become ***w***.
14:20 hate the poor, but many love the ***w***.
18:11 The riches of the ***w*** are a strong city
18:23 for help, but the ***w*** answer harshly.
22:7 The ***w*** rule over the poor; a borrower is
22:16 and giving to the ***w*** leads only to
28:6 than to be on crooked paths and ***w***.
Ecclesiastes
5:12 the excess of the ***w*** won't let them
Micah
6:12 in a city whose ***w*** are full of violence
Mark
10:23 very hard for the ***w*** to enter God's
Luke
12:15 even when someone is very ***w***."
18:24 very hard for the ***w*** to enter God's
James
1:10 Those who are ***w*** should find
1:11 daily lives, the ***w*** will waste away.
2:6 poor. Don't the ***w*** make life
5:1 attention, you ***w*** people! Weep and
Revelation
3:17 and I've grown ***w***, and I don't need

WEAPONS

Genesis
49:5 are brothers, ***w*** of violence their
Deuteronomy
1:41 you grabbed your ***w***. You thought it
1 Samuel
8:12 or to make his ***w*** or parts for his
17:54 put the Philistine's ***w*** in his own tent.
20:40 handed his ***w*** to the boy and
2 Samuel
1:27 Look how the ***w*** of war have been
1 Kings
10:25 gold, clothing, ***w***, spices, horses,
2 Kings
10:2 city, and ***w***. Now when this
11:8 of you with your ***w*** drawn. Whoever
11:11 each with their ***w*** drawn, then took
1 Chronicles
12:33 with all the ***w*** of war, to help
12:37 120,000 armed with all the ***w*** of war.
2 Chronicles
9:24 gold, clothing, ***w***, spices, horses,
23:7 each with his ***w*** drawn. Whoever
23:10 each with their ***w*** drawn, near the
32:5 made a large supply of ***w*** and shields.
Job
39:21 prances proudly, charges at battle ***w***,
Psalms
7:13 God has deadly ***w*** in store for those who won't change
Ecclesiastes
9:18 is better than ***w*** of war, but one
Song of Songs
4:4 upon it—all the ***w*** of the warriors.
Isaiah
22:8 you trusted the ***w*** in the Forest
Jeremiah
5:16 Its ***w*** are deadly; its warriors are
21:4 to turn your own ***w*** against you, yes,
22:7 will use their ***w*** to cut down your
33:4 to defend against the siege ramps and ***w***
50:25 out his brutal ***w***. The LORD God of
Ezekiel
9:1 city, and bring your ***w*** of destruction!
9:2 them were holding ***w*** of destruction.
23:24 against you with ***w***, chariots, and
27:11 They hung their ***w*** on your walls all
32:27 with their ***w*** of war, they put
39:9 a fire with the ***w***—shield and buckle
39:10 burning with the ***w***. So they will
Joel
2:8 they fall among the ***w***, they won't stop.
John
18:3 carrying lanterns, torches, and ***w***.
Romans
6:13 to be used as ***w*** to do wrong.
13:4 it doesn't have ***w*** to enforce the
13:12 the darkness and put on the ***w*** of light.
2 Corinthians
6:7 We carried the ***w*** of righteousness
10:4 Our ***w*** that we fight with aren't human,

WEAR

Genesis
28:20 gives me bread to eat and clothes to ***w***,
Deuteronomy
8:4 clothes didn't ***w*** out and your feet

22:5 Women must not ***w*** men's clothes, and men
Ruth
3:3 on some perfume, ***w*** nice clothes, and
Nehemiah
9:21 clothes didn't ***w*** out, and their
Job
27:17 righteous will ***w*** it; the innocent
Psalms
73:6 That's why they ***w*** arrogance like a
102:26 these things will ***w*** out like
104:2 You ***w*** light like a robe; you open the
109:29 shame; let them ***w*** their disgrace
Proverbs
23:4 Don't ***w*** yourself out trying to get
Isaiah
51:6 the earth will ***w*** out like
Jeremiah
9:5 to lie; they ***w*** themselves out by
13:1 undergarment. ***W*** it for a while
27:2 straps and bars and ***w*** it on your neck.
Ezekiel
34:3 the milk, you ***w*** the wool, and you
44:17 they will ***w*** linen garments.
44:18 They won't ***w*** anything that
44:19 holy chambers and ***w*** other clothing.
Amos
8:10 will make people ***w*** mourning clothes
Matthew
6:31 to drink?' or 'What are we going to ***w***?'
11:8 Look, those who ***w*** refined clothes
25:36 me clothes to ***w***. I was sick and
Mark
6:9 He told them to ***w*** sandals but not to
Luke
12:22 or about your body, what you will ***w***.
12:27 grow. They don't ***w*** themselves out
12:33 that don't ***w*** out—a treasure in
Hebrews
1:11 They will all ***w*** out like old
Revelation
3:5 victorious will ***w*** white clothing
3:18 white clothing to ***w*** so that your
19:8 white linen to ***w***, for the fine

WEARING

Exodus
18:18 end up totally ***w*** yourself out,
Leviticus
16:23 clothes he was ***w*** when he entered
16:32 reconciliation, ***w*** the holy linen
Joshua
9:5 feet and were ***w*** worn-out clothes.
1 Samuel
14:3 at Shiloh. He was ***w*** a priestly vest.
18:4 the robe he was ***w*** and gave it to
2 Samuel
13:18 She was ***w*** a long-sleeved robe because
13:19 robe she was ***w***. She put her hand
21:16 of bronze, and he was ***w*** new armor.
1 Kings
11:29 way. Ahijah was ***w*** a new garment.
2 Kings
6:30 see that he was ***w*** mourning clothes
19:2 son. They were all ***w*** mourning clothes.
Ezra
9:5 acts. While still ***w*** my torn clothes
Esther
1:11 Vashti before him ***w*** the royal crown.
4:2 to pass through it ***w*** mourning clothes.
8:15 white royal robe ***w*** a large gold
Song of Songs
3:11 —on King Solomon ***w*** the crown with
Isaiah
22:12 shaven heads, and ***w*** of mourning
37:2 son. They were all ***w*** mourning clothes.
Jeremiah
13:4 that you are ***w*** and go at once to
Ezekiel
23:15 ***w*** only loincloths around their hips and flowing headbands
Zephaniah
1:8 sons, and all those ***w*** foreign clothes.
Zechariah
3:3 Joshua was ***w*** filthy clothes and
Matthew
22:11 a man who wasn't ***w*** wedding clothes.
Mark
14:51 a disciple, was ***w*** nothing but a
John
13:5 drying them with the towel he was ***w***.
19:5 Jesus came out, ***w*** the crown of
1 Corinthians
4:11 hungry, thirsty, ***w*** rags, abused, and
1 Thessalonians
5:8 let's stay sober, ***w*** faithfulness and
Hebrews
11:37 They went around ***w*** the skins of
James
2:3 notice of the one ***w*** fine clothes,
1 Peter
3:3 hair or by ***w*** gold jewelry or
Revelation
7:13 are these people ***w*** white robes, and
11:3 hundred sixty days, ***w*** mourning clothes.
19:14 Heaven's armies, ***w*** fine linen that was

WEDDING

Psalms
78:63 and his young women had no ***w*** songs.
Song of Songs
3:11 on the day of his ***w***, on the day of
Jeremiah
2:32 or a bride her ***w*** dress? Yet you
Matthew
9:15 responded, "The ***w*** guests can't
22:2 who prepared a ***w*** party for his son.
25:10 with him into the ***w***. Then the door
Mark
2:19 Jesus said, "The ***w*** guests can't fast
Luke
5:34 can't make the ***w*** guests fast while
12:36 come home from a ***w*** celebration, who
14:8 invites you to a ***w*** celebration,
John
2:1 day there was a ***w*** in Cana of
Revelation
19:7 glory, for the ***w*** day of the Lamb
19:9 invited to the ***w*** banquet of the

WEEP

Genesis
43:30 he was about to ***w***, so he rushed to

2 Samuel
1:24 of Israel, ***w*** over Saul! He
Nehemiah
8:9 Don't mourn or ***w***." They said this
Job
27:15 with the dead; their widows won't ***w***.
30:25 if I didn't ***w*** for those who have a
Psalms
4:4 it in your bed and ***w*** over it! Selah
Isaiah
15:2 to the shrines to ***w***. Moab wails over
16:9 Therefore, I will ***w*** with Jazer's
22:4 at me; let me ***w*** bitterly. Don't
30:19 you will ***w*** no longer. God
Jeremiah
4:8 funeral clothing. ***W*** and wail, for the
6:26 roll in ashes; ***w*** and wail as for
9:1 of tears, I would ***w*** day and night for
9:10 I will ***w*** and wail for the mountains,
9:18 Hurry! Let them ***w*** for us so that our
13:17 eyes out. I will ***w*** uncontrollably
22:10 Don't ***w*** or lament for the dead king.
48:20 and shocked; ***w*** and wail! Tell it
48:32 I'll ***w*** for you, vine of Sibmah, more
49:3 ***W***, you people of Heshbon; Ai has been
Ezekiel
24:16 Don't mourn or ***w***. Don't even let
24:23 won't mourn or ***w***. You will waste
27:31 In despair they ***w*** for you, and
Joel
1:5 too much, and ***w***. Scream over the
2:17 LORD's ministers, ***w***. Let them say,
Micah
1:10 not; no need to ***w*** there!
Zechariah
7:3 Should I ***w*** in the fifth
Luke
6:21 Happy are you who ***w*** now, because you
6:25 now, because you will mourn and ***w***.
James
4:9 mourn, and ***w***! Let your
5:1 wealthy people! ***W*** and moan over the
Revelation
5:4 So I began to ***w*** and weep, because no
5:5 to me, "Don't ***w***. Look! The Lion
18:9 ways, will ***w*** and mourn over
18:11 of the earth will ***w*** and mourn over
18:15 They will ***w*** and mourn, and

WEEPING

Numbers
25:6 who were ***w*** at the entrance
Deuteronomy
34:8 the time for ***w*** and for mourning
Ezra
3:13 of the people's ***w***, because the
10:1 and confessing, ***w*** and bowing down
Esther
4:3 spent whole days ***w*** and crying out
Job
30:31 is for mourning, my flute, a ***w*** sound.
Psalms
30:5 lasts a lifetime. ***W*** may stay all
Isaiah
15:3 everyone wails and falls down ***w***.
15:5 will go up with ***w***. On the road to
16:9 weep with Jazer's ***w*** for the vines of
22:12 on that day for ***w*** and mourning, and
65:19 hear the sound of ***w*** or crying in it
Jeremiah
8:19 Listen to the ***w*** of my people all across
14:17 I can't stop ***w***—day and night, be
31:15 heard in Ramah, ***w*** and wailing. It's
31:16 your eyes from ***w***, because your
41:6 to meet them, ***w*** as he went. When
48:5 is uncontrollable ***w***. On the way down
50:4 together; with ***w*** they will leave
Lamentations
2:11 are worn out from ***w***; my stomach is
Joel
2:12 with fasting, with ***w***, and with sorrow;
Malachi
2:13 LORD with tears, ***w***, and groaning
Matthew
2:18 heard in Ramah, ***w*** and much
8:12 there will be ***w*** and grinding
13:42 there will be ***w*** and grinding
13:50 there will be ***w*** and grinding
22:13 there will be ***w*** and grinding
24:51 there will be ***w*** and grinding
25:30 there will be ***w*** and grinding
Mark
16:10 been with him, who were mourning and ***w***.
Luke
13:28 There will be ***w*** and grinding of teeth
Acts
21:13 this? Why are you ***w*** and breaking my
Revelation
18:19 they cried out, ***w*** and mourning.

WEIGHED

Ezra
8:25 I ***w*** out to them the silver and the gold
8:33 the equipment was ***w*** out in our God's
Job
6:2 were actually ***w***, all of it were
Psalms
35:14 a brother. I was ***w*** down, sad, like I
73:5 they aren't ***w*** down like other
73:14 I'm ***w*** down all day long. I'm punished
Isaiah
1:4 nation, people ***w*** down with crimes,
40:12 measuring cup or ***w*** the mountains on
Daniel
5:27 that you've been ***w*** on the scales,

WEIGHING

Genesis
24:22 out a gold ring, ***w*** a half shekel,
Exodus
25:39 be made from pure gold ***w*** one kikkar.
37:24 equipment from pure gold ***w*** one kikkar.
Numbers
7:13 one silver dish ***w*** one hundred
Joshua
7:21 a single gold bar ***w*** fifty shekels. I
1 Samuel
17:5 scale-armor ***w*** one hundred
Ezra
8:26 silver containers ***w*** a certain number
Zephaniah
1:11 will eliminate all those ***w*** out silver.

Revelation
6:5 rider held a balance for ***w*** in his hand.
16:21 Huge hailstones ***w*** about one hundred

WEIGHT

Exodus
30:23 five hundred ***w*** of solid myrrh;
38:24 thirty shekels in ***w***, measured by the
Leviticus
19:35 measures of length, ***w***, or volume.
26:26 out bread by ***w***. You will eat but
Deuteronomy
25:15 have only one ***w***, complete and
Judges
8:26 The ***w*** of the gold earrings that he
1 Samuel
6:5 will lighten the ***w*** of his hand on
2 Samuel
14:26 to shave it—the ***w*** of the hair from
21:16 David. The ***w*** of his spear was
1 Chronicles
21:25 shekels of gold by ***w*** for the site.
28:14 for the ***w*** of all the gold equipment
Ezra
8:34 weighed, and the total ***w*** was recorded.
Psalms
38:4 head; they are a ***w*** that's way too
Proverbs
11:1 scales, but delights in an accurate ***w***.
Ezekiel
4:10 eat your food by ***w***, fourteen ounces
1 Thessalonians
2:7 have thrown our ***w*** around as

WELCOME

Judges
19:3 father saw him, he was happy to ***w*** him.
19:20 answered, "You're ***w*** to stay with me,
1 Samuel
13:10 Saul went out to meet him and ***w*** him.
Matthew
10:14 anyone refuses to ***w*** you or listen to
25:38 as a stranger and ***w*** you, or naked and
25:43 and you didn't ***w*** me. I was naked
Mark
6:11 a place doesn't ***w*** you or listen to
10:15 whoever doesn't ***w*** God's kingdom
Luke
4:24 no prophet is ***w*** in the prophet's
9:5 they don't ***w*** you, as you leave
9:53 refused to ***w*** him because he
10:8 and its people ***w*** you, eat what
10:10 the people don't ***w*** you, go out into
16:4 people will ***w*** me into their
18:17 whoever doesn't ***w*** God's kingdom
19:6 came down at once, happy to ***w*** Jesus.
John
1:11 and his own people didn't ***w*** him.
1:12 But those who did ***w*** him, those who
8:37 me because you don't ***w*** my teaching.
Acts
25:13 arrived in Caesarea to ***w*** Festus.
Romans
12:13 God's people, and ***w*** strangers into
14:1 ***W*** the person who is weak in faith—but
15:7 So ***w*** each other, in the same way that
16:2 ***W*** her in the Lord in a way that is
2 Corinthians
6:17 what is unclean. Then I will ***w*** you.
Philippians
2:29 So ***w*** him in the Lord with great joy and
Colossians
4:10 about him; if he comes to you, ***w*** him).
1 Thessalonians
1:9 what sort of ***w*** we had from you
Philemon
1:17 me a partner, ***w*** Onesimus as if
James
1:21 wickedness, and ***w*** the word planted
2 Peter
1:11 receive a rich ***w*** into the
3 John
1:9 to put himself first, doesn't ***w*** us.
1:10 only refuses to ***w*** the brothers and

WELCOMED

Matthew
25:35 a drink. I was a stranger and you ***w*** me.
Luke
8:40 the crowd ***w*** him, for they had
9:11 followed him. He ***w*** them, spoke to
10:38 a woman named Martha ***w*** him as a guest.
16:9 gone, you will be ***w*** into the eternal
John
4:45 the Galileans ***w*** him because they
Acts
11:1 even the Gentiles had ***w*** God's word.
15:4 the elders all ***w*** them. They gave a
16:33 night, the jailer ***w*** them and washed
17:7 more, Jason has ***w*** them into his
21:17 the brothers and sisters ***w*** us warmly.
28:2 they built a fire and ***w*** all of us.
28:7 in that area. He ***w*** us warmly into
28:30 full years and ***w*** everyone who came
Romans
15:7 that Christ also ***w*** you, for God's
2 Corinthians
7:15 obedient when you ***w*** him with fear and
Galatians
4:14 me, but you ***w*** me as if I were
1 Thessalonians
2:13 from us, you ***w*** it for what it
Hebrews
11:13 a distance and ***w*** them. They
11:31 because she ***w*** the spies in
2 John
1:10 be received nor ***w*** into your home,

WEPT

Genesis
21:16 a distance, cried out in grief, and ***w***.
23:2 cried out in grief and ***w*** for Sarah.
27:34 agonizing cry and ***w*** bitterly. He said
27:38 me too, my father!" And Esau ***w*** loudly.
29:11 Jacob kissed Rachel and ***w*** aloud
33:4 his neck, kissed him, and they ***w***.
37:35 my son." And Joseph's father ***w*** for him.
42:24 from them and ***w***. When he
43:30 he rushed to another room and ***w*** there.
45:2 He ***w*** so loudly that the Egyptians and
45:14 neck and ***w***, and Benjamin
45:15 his brothers and ***w***, embracing them.
46:29 his neck and ***w***, embracing him

WEPT [cont.]

50:1 father's body, ***w*** over him, and
50:17 God."' Joseph ***w*** when they spoke
50:18 His brothers ***w*** too, fell down in front

Numbers
14:1 voice and the people ***w*** that night.
20:29 of Israel ***w*** thirty days for

Judges
20:23 went back up and ***w*** before the LORD
20:26 up to Bethel and ***w***, just sitting

Ruth
1:9 and they lifted up their voices and ***w***.
1:14 their voices and ***w*** again. Orpah

1 Samuel
11:4 people there. Then they all ***w*** aloud.

2 Samuel
3:32 Hebron. The king ***w*** loudly at Abner's
12:22 I fasted and ***w*** because I

Ezra
3:12 the first house, ***w*** aloud when they
10:1 him. The people also ***w*** in distress.

Nehemiah
1:4 I sat down and ***w***. I mourned for
8:9 all the people ***w*** when they heard

Esther
8:3 at his feet, ***w***, and begged him

Job
2:12 him, they ***w*** loudly. Each one
31:38 out against me, its rows ***w*** together;

Psalms
69:10 I ***w*** while I fasted—even for that I

Isaiah
33:7 messengers of peace ***w*** bitterly.

Hosea
12:4 and survived; he ***w*** and sought his

Luke
19:41 the city and observed it, he ***w*** over it.

WEST

Exodus
10:19 a very strong ***w*** wind that lifted

Joshua
1:4 up to the Mediterranean Sea on the ***w***.
15:12 The ***w*** border was the Mediterranean Sea

Psalms
75:6 from the east or ***w***; it's not from
103:12 as east is from ***w***—that's how far
107:3 from east and ***w***, north and south.

Isaiah
43:5 children; from the ***w*** I'll gather you.

Jeremiah
2:10 Look to the ***w*** as far as the shores of

Daniel
8:4 the ram goring ***w***, north, and
8:5 came from the ***w***, crossing the

Zechariah
14:4 from east to ***w***. Half of the

Matthew
8:11 from east and ***w*** and sit down to
24:27 the east to the ***w***, so it will be

Luke
12:54 forming in the ***w***, you immediately
13:29 from east and ***w***, north and south,

Revelation
21:13 on the south, and three gates on the ***w***.

WESTERN

Numbers
34:6 Your ***w*** border will be the Mediterranean

Deuteronomy
11:30 down along the ***w*** road in the

Joel
2:20 its rear into the ***w*** sea. Its stench

Obadiah
1:19 and those of the ***w*** foothills, the

Zechariah
7:7 plain and the ***w*** foothills were

WHEAT

Genesis
30:14 During the ***w*** harvest, Reuben found some erotic herbs

Exodus
34:22 produce of the ***w*** harvest, and the

Deuteronomy
8:8 a land of ***w*** and barley, vines, fig
32:14 with the finest ***w***—and for drink,

Judges
6:11 was threshing ***w*** in a winepress to
15:1 the time of the ***w*** harvest, Samson

Ruth
2:23 of the barley and ***w*** harvests. And she

1 Samuel
6:13 were harvesting ***w*** in the valley.
12:17 Isn't the ***w*** harvest today? I will call

2 Samuel
4:6 as if getting ***w***, and they stabbed
17:28 along with ***w***, barley, flour,

Ezra
6:9 God of heaven, ***w***, salt, wine, or
7:22 hundred kors of ***w***, one hundred

Job
31:40 grow instead of ***w***, poisonous weeds

Psalms
4:7 than when their ***w*** and wine are
81:16 with the finest ***w***. I would satisfy
147:14 fills you full with the very best ***w***.

Song of Songs
7:2 mound of winnowed ***w*** edged with lilies.

Isaiah
28:25 cumin, and plant ***w*** and barley in

Jeremiah
12:13 They have sown ***w*** and reaped weeds; they have worn
23:28 between straw and ***w***! declares the
41:8 kill us; we have ***w***, barley, oil, and

Ezekiel
4:9 You, gather some ***w*** and barley, beans
16:19 you to eat—fine ***w***, oil, and honey—
27:17 the finest ***w***, millet, honey,
45:13 for each homer of ***w***, and one-sixth of

Joel
1:11 over the ***w*** and the barley,

Amos
8:5 that we may offer ***w*** for sale, make

Matthew
3:12 uses to sift the ***w*** from the husks is
13:25 weeds among the ***w*** and went away.

Mark
2:23 went through the ***w*** fields on the

Luke
3:17 uses to sift the ***w*** from the husks is
22:31 the right to sift you all like ***w***.
John
12:24 unless a grain of ***w*** falls into the
1 Corinthians
15:37 a bare grain of ***w*** or some other
Revelation
6:6 said, "A quart of ***w*** for a denarion,
18:13 fine flour, and ***w***; cattle, sheep,

WHEELS
Exodus
14:25 their chariot ***w*** so that they
1 Kings
7:30 were four bronze ***w*** with bronze axles
7:32 There were four ***w*** beneath the panels.
7:33 of the ***w*** resembled chariot
Isaiah
5:28 like flint; their ***w*** like the
Jeremiah
47:3 of the chariots' ***w***, parents abandon
Ezekiel
1:16 of the ***w*** were like
10:2 Go in between the ***w*** under the winged
11:22 their wings. The ***w*** were next to
26:10 of the charioteers and chariot ***w***.
Daniel
7:9 made of flame; its ***w*** were blazing fire.

WHIRLWIND
Job
38:1 Then the LORD answered Job from the ***w***
40:6 The LORD answered Job from the ***w***
Proverbs
10:25 After a ***w*** passes by, the wicked are no
Isaiah
5:28 like flint; their wheels like the ***w***.
29:6 voice, with ***w***, tempest, and
Hosea
8:7 they will get the ***w***. Standing grain,
Nahum
1:3 His way is in ***w*** and storm; clouds
Hebrews
12:18 a burning fire, darkness, shadow, a ***w***,

WHITE
Leviticus
13:3 area has turned ***w*** and the infection
13:25 hair has turned ***w*** in the shiny
Judges
5:10 You who ride ***w*** donkeys, who sit on
Esther
1:6 ***W*** linen curtains and purple hangings
8:15 in a blue and ***w*** royal robe
Job
6:6 without salt, or does egg ***w*** have taste?
41:32 him; the frothy deep seems ***w***-haired.
Ecclesiastes
9:8 always be ***w***; don't run short
Isaiah
1:18 they will be ***w*** as snow. If they
Ezekiel
27:18 wealth the wine of Helbon and ***w*** wool.
Daniel
7:9 His clothes were ***w*** like snow; his
12:6 man clothed in ***w*** linen, who was
12:7 man clothed in ***w*** linen, who was
Joel
1:7 it down; their branches have turned ***w***.
Zechariah
1:8 him were red, sorrel, and ***w*** horses.
6:3 third chariot had ***w*** horses, and the
6:6 country; the ***w*** ones are going to
Matthew
5:36 you can't turn one hair ***w*** or black.
17:2 and his clothes became as ***w*** as light.
28:3 lightning and his clothes as ***w*** as snow.
Mark
9:3 than if they had been bleached ***w***.
16:5 a young man in a ***w*** robe seated on
Luke
9:29 his clothes flashed ***w*** like lightning.
John
20:12 angels dressed in ***w***, seated where the
Acts
1:10 two men in ***w*** robes stood next
Revelation
1:14 and hair were ***w*** as white wool—like
2:17 to each of them a ***w*** stone with a new
3:4 me clothed in ***w*** because they are
6:2 and there was a ***w*** horse. Its rider
7:13 people wearing ***w*** robes, and where
14:14 and there was a ***w*** cloud. On the
19:8 given fine, pure ***w*** linen to wear,
20:11 I saw a great ***w*** throne and the

WICKED
Numbers
14:27 long will this ***w*** community
16:26 tents of these ***w*** men and don't
Deuteronomy
1:35 people—this ***w*** generation!—will
9:5 these nations are ***w***
13:13 certain ***w*** people have gone out from
15:9 Make sure no ***w*** thought crosses
1 Samuel
2:9 ones, but the ***w*** die in darkness
2 Samuel
3:34 falls before the ***w***." Then the troops
1 Chronicles
2:3 considered him ***w*** and put him to
2 Chronicles
7:14 turn from their ***w*** ways, then I will
19:2 did you help the ***w***? Why have you
24:7 Now ***w*** Athaliah and her followers had
Ezra
4:12 rebellious and ***w*** city; they are
Nehemiah
9:35 serve you or turn from their ***w*** works.
Esther
7:6 an enemy—this ***w*** Haman!" Haman was
9:25 order said: The ***w*** plan that Haman
Job
3:17 There the ***w*** rage no more; there the
8:20 won't strengthen the hand of the ***w***.
8:22 and the tent of the ***w*** will vanish.
9:24 over to the ***w***; he covers the
11:20 The eyes of the ***w*** will grow faint;
15:20 the days of the ***w*** are painful; the

16:11 and forces me into the hands of the ***w***.
18:5 the light of the ***w*** goes out; the
20:5 rejoicing of the ***w*** is short, the joy
20:29 This is a ***w*** person's lot from God,
21:7 Why do the ***w*** live, grow old, and even
21:17 the lamp of the ***w*** flicker or
21:28 is the tent, the dwelling of the ***w***?"
21:30 of disaster the ***w*** are spared; on
27:7 enemy be like the ***w***, my opposition
29:17 the fangs of the ***w***, rescued prey
31:3 disaster for the ***w***, destruction for
32:3 answer but nevertheless thought Job ***w***.
35:12 answer, because of the pride of the ***w***.
36:6 doesn't let the ***w*** live, but grants
36:17 the case of the ***w***; justice will be
38:13 by its edges and shake the ***w*** out of it?
38:15 withheld from the ***w***, the uplifted arm
40:12 them; trample the ***w*** in their place.

Psalms

1:1 doesn't follow ***w*** advice, doesn't
1:6 but the way of the ***w*** is destroyed.
3:7 on the jaw; shatter the teeth of the ***w***!
7:9 the evil of the ***w*** be over, but set
7:14 But look how the ***w*** hatch evil, conceive
9:17 Let the ***w*** go straight to the grave, the
10:2 Meanwhile, the ***w*** are proudly in hot
10:11 The ***w*** think to themselves: God has
10:15 of those who are ***w*** and evil. Seek
11:2 because the ***w*** have already bent their
12:8 The ***w*** roam all over the place, while
17:9 away from the ***w*** who are out to get me,
17:13 my life from the ***w***—use your sword!
21:11 they devised a ***w*** plan
26:5 and I don't sit with ***w*** people.
28:3 me off with the ***w*** and those who do
31:17 to you. Let the ***w*** be put to shame;
32:10 The pain of the ***w*** is severe, but
34:21 will kill the ***w***, and those who
36:1 utterance of the ***w***: No fear of God
36:11 let the hands of the ***w*** drive me off.
37:10 little while the ***w*** won't exist! If
39:1 as long as the ***w*** were in my
50:16 But to the ***w*** God says, "Why do you talk
55:3 noise, at the ***w*** person's racket,
58:3 The ***w*** backslide from the womb; liars go
58:10 wash their feet in the blood of the ***w***.
59:5 Grant no mercy to any ***w*** traitor! Selah
64:2 secret plots of ***w*** people; hide me
68:2 fire, let the ***w*** perish before God!
71:4 the power of the ***w***; rescue me from
75:4 arrogant!" To the ***w*** I said, "Don't
75:8 of the earth's ***w*** people must drink
82:2 by granting favor to the ***w***? Selah
84:10 live comfortably in the tents of the ***w***!
89:22 oppress him; no ***w*** person will make
91:8 eyes, and you will see the ***w*** punished.
92:7 though the ***w*** spring up like grass and
94:3 How long will the ***w***—oh, LORD!—how
97:10 them from the power of the ***w***.
101:8 all those who are ***w*** in the land in
104:35 earth; let the ***w*** be no more. But
106:18 whole group; flames burned up the ***w***.
107:34 dirt, when its inhabitants are ***w***.
109:2 the mouths of ***w*** liars have opened
112:10 The ***w*** see all this and fume; they grind
119:53 because of the ***w***—because of those
125:3 The ***w*** rod won't remain in the land
129:4 cut me free from the ropes of the ***w***!
139:19 would kill the ***w***! If only
140:4 the power of the ***w***, LORD! Guard me
141:4 that I don't do ***w*** things with
145:20 him, but he destroys every ***w*** person.
146:9 makes the way of the ***w*** twist and turn!
147:6 but throws the ***w*** down on the dirt!

Proverbs

2:22 But the ***w*** will be cut off from the
3:25 terror or the ruin that comes to the ***w***.
3:33 the house of the ***w***, but he blesses
4:14 on the way of the ***w***; don't walk on
4:19 The path of the ***w*** is like deep
5:22 The ***w*** will be caught by their own evil
6:18 a heart set on ***w*** plans, feet that run
9:7 whoever corrects the ***w*** gets hurt.
10:2 treasure of the ***w*** won't profit
10:3 but he rejects the desires of the ***w***.
10:6 the mouth of the ***w*** conceals violence.
10:7 a blessing, but the name of the ***w*** rots.
10:11 the mouth of the ***w*** conceals violence.
10:16 the earnings of the ***w*** lead to sin.
10:20 but the heart of the ***w*** lacks value.
10:24 What the ***w*** dread will come on them, but what the righteous
10:25 passes by, the ***w*** are no more, but
10:27 the years of the ***w*** will be cut short.
10:28 but the hopes of the ***w*** will perish.
10:30 shaken, but the ***w*** won't dwell in
10:32 the mouth of the ***w*** knows only what
11:5 straight, but the ***w*** fall in their
11:7 When the ***w*** die, their hope perishes.
11:8 distress, and the ***w*** take their place.
11:10 when the ***w*** perish, there are
11:11 it is destroyed by the words of the ***w***.
11:18 The ***w*** earn false wages, but those who
11:23 the expectations of the ***w*** bring wrath.
11:31 earth, how much more the ***w*** and sinners?
12:3 is established by ***w*** acts, but the
12:5 but the guidance of the ***w*** is deceptive.
12:6 The words of the ***w*** are a deathtrap, but
12:7 The ***w*** are destroyed and are no more,
12:10 even the compassion of the ***w*** is cruel.
12:12 is a trap for the ***w***, but the root of
12:13 The ***w*** are trapped by the transgressions
12:21 but the ***w*** receive their
12:26 the path of the ***w*** makes them wander.
13:5 words, but the ***w*** create disgust
13:9 but the lamp of the ***w*** goes out.
13:17 ***W*** messengers fall into trouble, but a
13:25 fill, but the ***w*** have empty
14:11 The house of the ***w*** is destroyed, but
14:19 before the good, ***w*** people are at the
14:32 The ***w*** are thrown down by their own
15:6 but the gain of the ***w*** brings trouble.
15:8 sacrifices of the ***w***, but favors the
15:9 the path of the ***w***, but loves those
15:28 but the ***w*** mouth blurts out
15:29 is far from the ***w***, but he listens
16:4 a purpose, even the ***w*** for an evil day.
16:12 Kings detest ***w*** deeds, for their thrones
17:15 the righteous ***w*** and the wicked
17:23 The ***w*** take secret bribes to twist the
18:3 When the ***w*** arrive, so does contempt;
18:5 Favoring the ***w*** isn't good; it denies
19:28 justice; the ***w*** mouth gulps down

20:26 sifts out the ***w***, and runs them
21:4 and the lamp of the ***w*** are all sinful.
21:7 violence of the ***w*** will sweep them
21:10 ***W*** people desire evil; their neighbors
21:12 the house of the ***w***, turning the
21:18 The ***w*** are a ransom for the righteous;
21:27 sacrifices of the ***w***, especially when
21:29 The ***w*** person appears brash, but the
24:15 ***W*** one, don't wait secretly at the home
24:16 get up, but the ***w*** will stumble into
24:19 evil people; don't be envious of the ***w***.
24:20 the lamp of the ***w*** will be put out.
25:5 Remove the ***w*** from the king's presence,
25:26 giving in to the ***w*** is like a
28:1 The ***w*** run away even though no one
28:4 praise the ***w***, but those who
28:12 but people hide when the ***w*** prosper.
28:15 A ***w*** ruler over the poor is like a
28:28 When the ***w*** rise up, people hide, but
29:2 but when the ***w*** dominate, the
29:6 The ***w*** are snared by their own sin; the
29:7 the poor, but the ***w*** don't understand.
29:12 to lies, those who serve him will be ***w***.
29:16 When the ***w*** become numerous, so do
29:27 straight path is disgusting to the ***w***.

Ecclesiastes
3:17 righteous and ***w*** people, because
7:15 then again, the ***w*** may live long in
7:17 Don't be too ***w*** and don't be a fool, or
8:10 Then I saw the ***w*** brought to their
8:11 condemnation for ***w*** acts isn't
8:13 go well for the ***w***; they won't live
8:14 get what the ***w*** deserve, and the
9:2 righteous and the ***w***, the good and the

Isaiah
3:11 Doom to the ***w***; they are evil. What
10:1 who pronounce ***w*** decrees, and keep
11:4 breath of his lips he will kill the ***w***.
13:11 own sin upon the ***w***. I will end the
14:5 the staff of the ***w***, the rod of
26:10 When the ***w*** are favored, they don't
48:22 well-being, says the LORD, for the ***w***.
53:9 was among the ***w***, his tomb with
55:7 Let the ***w*** abandon their ways and the
57:20 But the ***w*** are like the churning sea
57:21 is no peace, says my God, for the ***w***.
58:6 choose: releasing ***w*** restraints,
58:9 you, the finger-pointing, the ***w*** speech;
63:18 Why did the ***w*** bring down your holy

Jeremiah
2:33 that you instruct even the most ***w***.
13:10 to me, this ***w*** people follow
15:21 the hand of the ***w***; I will redeem
23:19 it whirls around the heads of the ***w***.
30:23 wind that strikes the heads of the ***w***.

Ezekiel
3:18 declare that the ***w*** will die but you
13:22 the hands of the ***w*** so that they
18:21 But if the ***w*** turn away from all the
18:23 the death of the ***w***? says the LORD
21:25 But you vile, ***w*** prince of Israel whose
33:8 death sentence on ***w*** people, and you
33:11 the death of the ***w***? If the wicked
33:19 And when the ***w*** turn from their

Daniel
12:10 but the ***w*** will act

Hosea
5:2 In their ***w*** condition, they have sunk
6:8 is a city of ***w*** people, tracked
7:1 exposed, and the ***w*** deeds of Samaria;

Micah
6:11 Can I approve ***w*** scales and a bag of
7:4 The confusion of the ***w*** is nearby.)

Habakkuk
1:4 because the ***w*** surround the
1:13 silent when the ***w*** swallows one who

Zephaniah
1:3 I will make the ***w*** into a heap of

Malachi
1:4 call themselves a ***w*** territory, the
3:18 righteous and the ***w***, between those
4:3 will crush the ***w***; they will be

Matthew
18:32 and said, 'You ***w*** servant! I
21:41 destroy those ***w*** farmers and rent

Luke
6:35 he is kind to ungrateful and ***w*** people.

John
3:20 All who do ***w*** things hate the light and
5:29 and those who did ***w*** things into the

Acts
2:23 with the help of ***w*** men, had Jesus
8:22 hope that your ***w*** intent can be

Romans
1:29 all injustice, ***w*** behavior, greed,

2 Thessalonians
2:10 every sort of ***w*** deception of

3 John
1:10 unjustified and ***w*** accusations

WICKEDNESS

Deuteronomy
9:4 of these nations' ***w*** that the LORD is
9:27 this people's stubbornness, ***w***, and sin.

2 Samuel
22:5 around me; rivers of ***w*** terrified me.

2 Chronicles
22:3 encouraged in this ***w*** by his mother.

Job
20:12 Though ***w*** is sweet in their mouths, they
22:5 Isn't your ***w*** massive, your iniquity
24:20 and so ***w*** is shattered like
27:4 will utter no ***w***; my tongue will
34:26 because of their ***w*** at a place where

Psalms
5:4 a God who enjoys ***w***; evil doesn't
10:15 Seek out their ***w*** until there's no
18:4 around me; rivers of ***w*** terrified me.
45:7 and hate ***w***. No wonder God,
94:23 them for their ***w***, completely
107:17 ways. They suffered because of their ***w***.

Proverbs
8:7 utters the truth; my lips despise ***w***."
11:5 but the wicked fall in their ***w***.
13:6 on the path, but ***w*** misleads sinners.

Ecclesiastes
3:16 there was ***w***; and in the place
7:15 may live long in spite of their ***w***.
7:25 to know that ***w*** is foolishness
8:8 from war, and ***w*** won't deliver

Isaiah
1:13 I can't stand ***w*** with celebration!
9:18 ***W*** burned like fire, devouring thorn and

32:6 minds devise ***w***, acting
Jeremiah
14:16 I will pour out on them their own ***w***.
22:22 and humiliated by all your ***w***.
23:14 turns from their ***w***. In my eyes, they
23:15 poison to drink. ***W*** has spread from
Ezekiel
3:19 turn from their ***w*** or their wicked
16:23 After all your ***w***—doom, doom to you,
16:57 before your ***w*** was exposed. You are now
33:12 sin. Nor does the ***w*** of the wicked
33:19 turn from their ***w*** to do what is
Hosea
7:2 all their ***w***. Now their deeds
7:3 By their ***w*** they make the king glad, and give joy
8:13 remember their ***w*** and punish their
9:7 of your great ***w***, your rejection
9:9 remember their ***w***; he will punish
9:15 Every ***w*** of theirs began at Gilgal;
10:13 You have plowed ***w***, you have reaped
10:15 of your great ***w***. At dawn, the
12:11 Gilead there is ***w***; they will surely
13:12 Ephraim's ***w*** is bound up; his sin is
14:1 you have stumbled because of your ***w***.
14:2 Forgive all ***w***; and receive the
Joel
3:13 with wine, for their ***w*** is great.
Micah
2:1 those who devise ***w***, to those who
6:10 the treasures of ***w*** still in the
Habakkuk
3:13 of the house of ***w***, laying bare the
Zechariah
5:8 He said, "This is ***w***." He shoved her
Luke
11:39 insides are stuffed with greed and ***w***.
Acts
8:22 Turn from your ***w***! Plead with the
Romans
2:8 those who obey ***w*** instead of the
1 Corinthians
5:8 yeast or with the yeast of evil and ***w***.
2 Timothy
2:19 confesses the Lord's name must avoid ***w***.
James
1:21 and the growth of ***w***, and welcome the
1 Peter
4:4 of unrestrained ***w***. So they slander

WIDE

Deuteronomy
15:8 Open your hand ***w*** to them. You must
Job
36:16 of trouble to a ***w*** place without
Psalms
81:10 Open your mouth ***w***—I will fill it up
Isaiah
5:14 the grave opens ***w*** its jaws, opens
60:5 tremble and open ***w***, because the
Lamentations
2:16 your enemies open ***w*** their mouths
Ezekiel
23:32 Deep and ***w*** is your sister's
40:5 feet high and ten and a half feet ***w***.
Nahum
3:13 have been flung ***w*** open to your
Zechariah
2:2 to see how ***w*** and long it will
Matthew
7:13 and the road ***w***, so many people
Mark
8:25 with his eyes ***w*** open, his sight
Acts
5:37 all his followers scattered far and ***w***.
2 Corinthians
6:11 to you, and our hearts are ***w*** open.
6:13 are children—open your hearts ***w*** too.

WIDOW

Genesis
38:11 Stay as a ***w*** in your father's
38:14 she wore as a ***w***, covered herself
38:19 again in the clothing she wore as a ***w***.
Exodus
22:22 Don't treat any ***w*** or orphan badly
Leviticus
21:14 He cannot marry a ***w***, a divorced woman,
22:13 daughter is a ***w*** or divorced and
Numbers
30:9 promise of a ***w*** or a divorced
1 Kings
17:15 The ***w*** went and did what Elijah said. So the widow
17:20 evil upon the ***w*** that I am staying
Job
24:21 childless, do nothing good for the ***w***.
31:18 and from my mother's womb I led the ***w***
Psalms
109:9 orphans; let his wife turn into a ***w***.
Isaiah
1:17 defend the orphan; plead for the ***w***.
47:8 never sit as a ***w***; I'll never know
Jeremiah
7:6 orphan, or ***w***; if you don't
22:3 orphan, and the ***w***. Don't spill the
Lamentations
1:1 has become like a ***w***. Once a queen
Zechariah
7:10 Don't oppress the ***w***, the orphan, the
Malachi
3:5 as oppress the ***w*** and the orphan,
Matthew
22:25 children he left his ***w*** to his brother.
Mark
12:19 dies, leaving a ***w*** but no children,
12:42 One poor ***w*** came forward and put in two small copper
12:43 that this poor ***w*** has put in more
Luke
2:37 ***w***. She never left
18:3 city there was a ***w*** who kept coming
21:3 that this poor ***w*** has put in more
1 Timothy
5:4 if a particular ***w*** has children or
5:5 A ***w*** who is truly needy and all alone
5:6 But a ***w*** who tries to live a life of
5:9 Put a ***w*** on the list who is older than
Revelation
18:7 queen! I'm not a ***w***. I'll never see

IDOWS → ORPHANS AND THE WIDOWS,
PHANS AND WIDOWS

odus
2:24 wives will be ***w***, and your

amuel
20:3 the day they died, and lived like ***w***.

b
22:9 You have sent ***w*** away empty; crushed
7:15 with the dead; their ***w*** won't weep.

alms
68:5 and defender of ***w*** is God in his
8:64 the sword, and his ***w*** couldn't even cry.
94:6 They kill ***w*** and immigrants; they murder

iah
10:2 justice; to make ***w*** their loot; to

remiah
15:8 Their ***w*** will outnumber the sand on the shore
8:21 wives be barren ***w***; let their men be
9:11 after them; trust your ***w*** into my care."

mentations
5:3 no father; our mothers are like ***w***.

ekiel
19:7 he ravaged their ***w*** and laid waste to
2:25 precious goods and made many ***w*** in her.
4:22 must not marry ***w*** or divorced

ark
2:40 ones who cheat ***w*** out of their

ke
4:25 there were many ***w*** in Israel during
0:47 ones who cheat ***w*** out of their

ts
6:1 because their ***w*** were being
9:39 room. All the ***w*** stood beside him,
9:41 including the ***w***, and presented

Corinthians
7:8 are single and ***w*** that it's good

Timothy
5:3 Take care of ***w*** who are truly needy
5:11 accept younger ***w*** for the list.
5:14 So I want younger ***w*** to marry, have
5:16 is a believer has ***w*** in her family,

IDTH

odus
7:12 The courtyard's ***w*** on the west side
8:18 and, along the ***w*** of it, seven and

Kings
6:3 across the whole ***w*** of the temple and
6:20 feet in length, ***w***, and height.
7:26 as thick as the ***w*** of a hand. Its

Chronicles
3:3 was ninety feet and the ***w*** thirty feet.
4:5 as thick as the ***w*** of a hand. Its

ra
6:3 be ninety feet and its ***w*** ninety feet,

iah
8:8 his wings will cover the ***w*** of the land.

ekiel
40:5 wall's height and ***w*** it was ten and a

hesians
3:18 to grasp love's ***w*** and length,

velation
1:16 the same as its ***w***. He measured the

WIFE → ABRAM'S WIFE, DIVORCES HIS WIFE

Genesis
2:24 and embraces his ***w***, and they become
3:20 The man named his ***w*** Eve because she is the mother
12:18 Why didn't you tell me she was your ***w***?
19:26 When Lot's ***w*** looked back, she turned
20:11 here and they will kill me to get my ***w***.
24:37 Don't choose a ***w*** for my son from

Exodus
20:17 your neighbor's ***w***, male or female

Leviticus
18:8 of your father's ***w***; it is your
20:10 with a neighbor's ***w***, both the

Numbers
5:12 suspect that his ***w*** has had an affair

Deuteronomy
5:21 your neighbor's ***w***. Do not crave
24:5 year, so he can bring joy to his new ***w***.

Ruth
4:13 she became his ***w***. He was intimate

2 Samuel
12:10 me and took the ***w*** of Uriah the

Esther
5:10 friends and his ***w*** Zeresh should

Job
2:9 Job's ***w*** said to him, "Are you still
19:17 stinks to my ***w***; I am odious to
31:10 then may my ***w*** grind for another and

Psalms
109:9 orphans; let his ***w*** turn into a widow.
128:3 your house, your ***w*** will be like a

Proverbs
5:18 Rejoice in the ***w*** of your youth.
6:29 his neighbor's ***w***; anyone who
18:22 He who finds a ***w*** finds what is good,
19:13 a contentious ***w*** is like constant
19:14 but an insightful ***w*** is from the LORD.
31:10 A competent ***w***, how does one find her?

Isaiah
54:1 children of the ***w*** who has been
54:6 you; as a young ***w*** when she is

Jeremiah
5:8 roving about, snorting for another's ***w***.
6:11 husband with ***w*** will be trapped,

Ezekiel
16:32 an adulterous ***w***: you take in
18:11 mountains, defiles his neighbor's ***w***,
22:11 his neighbor's ***w***, every man
24:18 and by evening my ***w*** was dead. The

Daniel
11:17 will give him a ***w***, intending to

Hosea
2:2 She is not my ***w***, and I am not her
12:12 served for a ***w***, and for a wife

Amos
7:17 proclaims: 'Your ***w*** will become a

Malachi
2:14 about you and the ***w*** of your youth

Matthew
1:20 take Mary as your ***w***, because the
1:24 God commanded and took Mary as his ***w***.
14:3 of Herodias, the ***w*** of Herod's
18:25 along with his ***w*** and children and
19:3 to divorce his ***w*** for just any

19:5 together with his ***w***, and the two will
19:10 a man and his ***w***, then it's better
22:24 must marry his ***w*** and produce
27:19 as judge, his ***w*** sent this message

Mark
6:17 of Herodias, the ***w*** of Herod's
6:18 law for you to marry your brother's ***w***!"
10:2 the Law allow a man to divorce his ***w***?"
10:4 certificate and to divorce his ***w***."
10:7 and be joined together with his ***w***,
10:12 and if a ***w*** divorces her husband and
12:23 rise up, whose ***w*** will she be? All

Luke
1:5 of Abijah. His ***w*** Elizabeth was a
1:13 been heard. Your ***w*** Elizabeth will
1:18 sure of this? My ***w*** and I are very
1:24 Afterward, his ***w*** Elizabeth became
3:19 Herod's brother's ***w***, and because of
8:3 Joanna (the ***w*** of Herod's servant
17:32 Remember Lot's ***w***
18:29 house, husband, ***w***, brothers,
20:33 whose ***w*** will she be? All

Acts
5:1 along with his ***w*** Sapphira, sold a
5:7 hours later, his ***w*** entered, but she
18:2 Italy with his ***w*** Priscilla because
24:24 came with his ***w*** Drusilla, who was

1 Corinthians
5:1 man is having sex with his father's ***w***!
7:2 have his own ***w***, and each woman
7:3 needs, and the ***w*** should do the
7:4 The ***w*** doesn't have authority over her
7:10 are married: a ***w*** shouldn't leave
7:11 And a man shouldn't divorce his ***w***.
7:12 a believer has a ***w*** who doesn't
7:14 because of his ***w***, and the wife who
7:16 do you know as a ***w*** if you will save
7:33 concerns—how he can please his ***w***.
9:5 to travel with a ***w*** who believes like

Ephesians
5:23 the head of his ***w*** like Christ is
5:28 Anyone who loves his ***w*** loves himself.
5:31 united with his ***w***, and the two of
5:33 should love his ***w*** as himself, and

1 Timothy
2:11 A ***w*** should learn quietly with complete
2:12 I don't allow a ***w*** to teach or to
2:14 but rather his ***w*** became the one
2:15 But a ***w*** will be brought safely through

1 Peter
3:7 living with your ***w*** in ways that

Revelation
21:9 will show you the bride, the Lamb's ***w***."

WILDERNESS

Leviticus
16:10 sending it away into the ***w*** to Azazel.
16:21 it away into the ***w*** with someone

Deuteronomy
1:40 back toward the ***w*** along the route
2:1 back toward the ***w*** along the Reed
2:8 turned and went along the Moab ***w*** route.
4:43 Bezer in the ***w*** on the plateau for the
8:16 you manna in the ***w***, which your
9:7 furious in the ***w***. From the very
11:24 will run from the ***w*** all the way to
29:5 led you in the ***w*** forty years now;
32:51 in the Zin ***w***, because you

1 Samuel
17:28 for you in the ***w***? I know how
23:14 fortresses in the ***w*** and in the hills
23:15 in the Ziph ***w*** he learned that
23:24 were in the Maon ***w*** in the desert
23:25 in the Maon ***w***. When Saul heard
24:1 that David was in the En-gedi ***w***.
25:1 then left and went down to the Maon ***w***.
25:4 While in the ***w***, David heard that Naba
25:7 with us in the ***w***. We didn't
25:14 from the ***w*** to greet our
25:21 stuff in the ***w*** so that nothing
26:2 down to the Ziph ***w*** to look for David
26:3 stayed in the ***w***. When David

2 Samuel
2:24 faces Giah on the road to the Gibeon ***w***
2:29 night through the ***w***, crossing the
4:7 and traveled all night through the ***w***.
15:23 passed by on the Olive road into the ***w***
16:2 for those who get exhausted in the ***w***.'
17:29 hungry, tired, and thirsty in the ***w***."

1 Kings
2:34 Joab was buried at his home in the ***w***.
9:18 and Tamar in the ***w***(within the land),

2 Kings
3:8 road that goes through the Edomite ***w***

2 Chronicles
1:3 LORD's servant Moses had made in the ***w***.
8:4 Tadmor in the ***w***, along with all
20:16 valley that opens into the Jeruel ***w***.
20:20 into the Tekoa ***w***. When they were
20:24 overlooking the ***w***, all they could
24:9 Moses had imposed on Israel in the ***w***.
26:10 towers in the ***w*** and dug many

Nehemiah
9:19 them in the ***w***. The column of
9:21 nothing in the ***w***! Their clothes

Psalms
29:8 voice shakes the ***w***—yes, the LORD sh
78:15 rocks open in the ***w***, gave them plenty
78:19 a dinner table in the ***w***?" they asked.
78:40 God in the ***w*** and distressed
78:52 guiding them like a flock in the ***w***.
95:8 did when you were at Massah, in the ***w***

Proverbs
21:19 to live in a ***w*** than in a house

Song of Songs
3:6 up from the ***w***, like pillars of
8:5 up from the ***w*** leaning against

Isaiah
21:1 oracle about the ***w*** near the sea.
35:1 will be glad; the ***w*** will rejoice and
35:6 up in the desert, and streams in the ***w***.
40:3 a level highway in the ***w*** for our God!
41:19 I will put in the ***w*** cypress, elm, and
43:19 a way in the desert, paths in the ***w***.
43:20 streams in the ***w*** to give water to
50:2 the rivers into ***w***. Their fish stink
51:3 like Eden and her ***w*** like the LORD's
64:10 have become a ***w***; Zion has become

Jeremiah
2:2 me in the ***w***, in an unplanted
2:6 us through the ***w***, in a land of

2:24 donkey in the ***w***, lustfully
3:2 a nomad in the ***w***. You have
9:10 lands in the ***w***. They are dried
2:10 my treasured field to a desolate ***w***.
17:6 places of the ***w***, in a barren land
3:10 and the grazing areas in the ***w*** wither.
31:2 grace in the ***w***. As Israel
9:33 for wild dogs, a ***w*** forever. No one
0:12 of the nations: a ***w***, a desert, and
mentations
4:19 mountains; they ambushed us in the ***w***.
ekiel
0:35 you out to the ***w*** nations, and
sea
9:10 grapes in the ***w***, I found Israel.
13:5 I knew you in the ***w***, in the land of no
3:15 rising from the ***w***; and his spring
el
1:19 pastures of the ***w***; and flames have
1:20 destroyed the meadows of the ***w***.
2:22 meadows of the ***w*** will turn green;
3:19 Edom a desolate ***w***. This is because
mos
2:10 years in the ***w***, to lay claim to
5:25 forty years in the ***w***, house of Israel?
phaniah
2:13 a desolate place like the ***w***.
alachi
1:3 his inheritance into a ***w*** for jackals.
atthew
3:3 shouting in the ***w***, "Prepare the way
4:1 Jesus up into the ***w*** so that the devil
11:7 you go out to the ***w*** to see? A stalk
5:33 food in this ***w*** to satisfy such a
ark
1:3 shouting in the ***w***: "Prepare the way
1:4 John was in the ***w*** calling for people to
1:12 the Spirit forced Jesus out into the ***w***.
1:13 He was in the ***w*** for forty days, tempted
8:4 food in this ***w*** to satisfy these
ke
1:80 He was in the ***w*** until he began
3:2 came to John son of Zechariah in the ***w***.
3:4 crying out in the ***w***: "Prepare the way
4:1 and was led by the Spirit into the ***w***.
7:24 go out into the ***w*** to see? A stalk
8:29 the demon would force him into the ***w***.
hn
1:23 crying out in the ***w***, Make the Lord's
3:14 the snake in the ***w***, so must the
6:31 ate manna in the ***w***, just as it is
6:49 ate manna in the ***w*** and they died.
1:54 a place near the ***w***, to a city called
cts
7:30 burning bush in the ***w*** near Mount Sinai.
7:36 Red Sea and for forty years in the ***w***.
7:38 assembly in the ***w*** with our
7:42 forty years in the ***w***, house of Israel?
7:44 ancestors in the ***w***. Moses built it
3:18 years, God put up with them in the ***w***.
Corinthians
10:5 and they were struck down in the ***w***.

ILLING

xodus
10:27 so that he wasn't ***w*** to let them go.
Deuteronomy
1:26 But you weren't ***w*** to go up. You
2:30 king, wasn't ***w*** to let us pass
10:10 The LORD wasn't ***w*** to destroy you.
25:7 Israel. He's not ***w*** to perform the
29:20 The LORD won't be ***w*** to forgive that
Joshua
24:10 But I wasn't ***w*** to listen to Balaam, so
Judges
10:18 Whoever is ***w*** to launch the
1 Samuel
15:9 They weren't ***w*** to put them under
26:23 and I wasn't ***w*** to lift a hand
2 Samuel
3:19 and the house of Benjamin were ***w*** to do.
12:4 but he wasn't ***w*** to take anything
13:25 the king wasn't ***w*** to go, although
2 Kings
8:19 the LORD wasn't ***w*** to destroy Judah.
1 Chronicles
28:21 you will have ***w*** and able workers
2 Chronicles
21:7 the LORD wasn't ***w*** to destroy
Job
6:9 that God be ***w*** to crush me, release his
17:3 Who else is ***w*** to make an
Psalms
51:12 to me and sustain me with a ***w*** spirit.
Song of Songs
7:1 sandaled feet, ***w*** woman! The smooth
Isaiah
42:24 They were not ***w*** to walk in God's
Jonah
4:2 of faithful love, and ***w*** not to destroy.
Matthew
11:14 If you are ***w*** to accept it, he is Elijah
26:60 who were ***w*** to come forward.
Luke
6:27 to you who are ***w*** to hear: Love
John
5:35 a while, you were ***w*** to celebrate in
Acts
18:21 he added, "God ***w***, I will return."
25:9 Paul, "Are you ***w*** to go up to
25:20 if he would be ***w*** to go to
1 Corinthians
4:19 if the Lord is ***w***, I'll come to you
Galatians
2:10 was certainly something I was ***w*** to do.

WIND

Genesis
1:2 sea, and God's ***w*** swept over the
4:21 who play stringed and ***w*** instruments.
8:1 ark. God sent a ***w*** over the earth so
41:6 by the east ***w***, sprouted after
Exodus
10:13 LORD made an east ***w*** blow over the
10:19 LORD turned the ***w*** into a very
14:21 by a strong east ***w*** all night,
15:10 blew with your ***w***; the sea covered
Numbers
11:31 A ***w*** from the LORD blew up and brought quails
1 Kings
18:45 clouds, and a ***w*** came up with a

19:11 A very strong ***w*** tore through the
2 Kings
3:17 You won't see any ***w*** or rain, but that
Job
1:19 when a strong ***w*** came from the desert
6:26 treat the words of a hopeless man as ***w***?
7:7 that my life is ***w***; my eyes won't
8:2 that your utterances become a strong ***w***?
13:25 Will you cause a ***w***-tossed leaf to
15:2 and fill their belly with the east ***w***?
15:30 be taken away by the ***w*** from his mouth.
21:18 like straw in the ***w***, like dry grass
26:13 Due to his ***w***, heaven became clear; his
27:21 an east ***w*** lifts them, and they are
28:25 to weigh the ***w***, to prepare a
30:15 my honor like ***w***; my safety
30:22 lift me to the ***w*** and make me ride;
37:9 its chamber, the cold from the north ***w***.
37:17 when earth is calmed by the south ***w***?
37:21 in the sky; the ***w*** has passed and
38:24 up; the east ***w*** scattered over
Psalms
1:4 are like dust that the ***w*** blows away.
11:6 with nothing but a scorching hot ***w***
18:10 flew; he soared on the wings of the ***w***.
18:42 blown away by the ***w***; I threw them out
35:5 like dust on the ***w***—and let the LORD
48:7 or like the east ***w*** when it smashes the
55:8 far from the rushing ***w*** and storm.
78:26 God set the east ***w*** moving across the
83:13 tumbleweeds, like chaff blown by ***w***.
103:16 but when the ***w*** blows through it, it's
104:3 going around on the wings of the ***w***.
135:7 God releases the ***w*** from its
148:8 and smoke, stormy ***w*** that does what
Proverbs
11:29 will inherit the ***w***. The fool will be
25:14 like clouds and ***w*** that produce no
25:23 The north ***w*** stirs up rain, and a person
27:16 can control the ***w*** or pick up oil in
30:4 has gathered the ***w*** by the handful?
Ecclesiastes
1:6 The ***w*** blows to the south, goes around
1:14 is pointless, a chasing after ***w***.
1:17 that this too was just ***w*** chasing.
2:11 chasing after ***w***. Nothing is to be
2:17 is pointless—just ***w*** chasing.
2:26 too is pointless and a chasing after ***w***.
4:4 This too is pointless, just ***w*** chasing.
4:6 for two fistfuls and chasing after ***w***.
4:16 too is pointless and a chasing after ***w***.
5:16 they gain from working so hard for ***w***?
6:9 This too is pointless, just ***w*** chasing.
11:4 who watch the ***w*** blow will never
Song of Songs
4:16 Stir, north ***w***, and come, south wind!
Isaiah
4:4 it by means of a ***w*** of judgment and a
7:2 of a forest shake when there is a ***w***.
11:15 with a powerful ***w*** and break it into
17:13 like chaff by ***w*** in the mountains,
26:18 we gave birth to ***w***. We have achieved
27:8 fierce blast on the day of the east ***w***.
32:2 shelter from the ***w*** and a refuge from
37:27 on rooftops, blasted by the east ***w***.
41:16 winnow them, the ***w*** will carry them
57:13 save you! The ***w*** will lift them
59:19 river that the LORD's ***w*** drives on.
64:6 our sins, like the ***w***, carry us away.
Jeremiah
2:24 sniffing the ***w***. Who can restrain
4:11 A blistering ***w*** from the bare
4:12 This ***w*** is too devastating for that. Now
5:13 are so much ***w***; the word isn't
10:13 the rain, the ***w*** from his
18:17 a strong east ***w***, I will scatter
22:22 be tossed to the ***w***, your lovers
30:23 storm, a fierce ***w*** that strikes the
51:1 up a violent ***w*** against Babylon
51:16 and sends the ***w*** from his
Ezekiel
1:12 wherever the ***w*** propelled them;
1:20 Wherever the ***w*** would appear to go, the wind would make
2:2 he spoke to me, a ***w*** came to me and
3:12 Then a ***w*** lifted me up, and I heard
3:14 Then the ***w*** picked me up and took me
3:24 When a ***w*** came to me and stood me on my feet
5:2 one-third to the ***w*** and let loose the
8:3 of my head. A ***w*** lifted me up
11:1 A ***w*** lifted me up and brought me to th
11:24 And a ***w*** lifted me up and brought me t
13:13 will make a storm ***w*** break out, and in
17:10 When the east ***w*** touches it, won't
19:12 ground. The east ***w*** dried her out and
27:26 seas; an east ***w*** sank you into the
43:5 A ***w*** picked me up and brought me to the inner courtyard
Daniel
2:35 floors. The ***w*** lifted them away
Hosea
4:19 The ***w*** has wrapped her in its wings,
8:7 they sow the ***w***, they will get
12:1 Ephraim herds the ***w***, and pursues the
13:15 rushes, the east ***w*** will come—the
Amos
1:14 with strong ***w*** on the day of the
4:13 creates the ***w***, makes known his
Jonah
1:4 hurled a great ***w*** upon the sea, so
4:8 a dry east ***w***, and the sun beat
Habakkuk
1:11 through like the ***w*** and invades; but
Zechariah
5:9 out. There was a ***w*** in their wings;
Matthew
7:25 came, and the ***w*** blew and beat
11:7 to see? A stalk blowing in the ***w***?
14:30 saw the strong ***w***, he became
14:32 got into the boat, the ***w*** settled down.
Mark
4:39 orders to the ***w***, and he said to
4:41 is this? Even the ***w*** and the sea obey
6:48 forward, but the ***w*** was blowing
6:51 the boat, and the ***w*** settled down. His
Luke
7:24 to see? A stalk blowing in the ***w***?
8:24 orders to the ***w*** and the violent
12:55 And when a south ***w*** blows, you say, 'A
John
6:18 rough because a strong ***w*** was blowing.
6:19 When the ***w*** had driven them out for

cts
2:2 of a fierce ***w*** filled the entire
27:7 of Cnidus. The ***w*** wouldn't allow us
:7:13 a gentle south ***w*** began to blow,
:7:14 ***w*** known as a
7:15 turned into the ***w***. So we gave in to
:7:40 to catch the ***w*** and made for the
:8:13 one day a south ***w*** came up, and we
hesians
4:14 around by every ***w*** that comes from
mes
1:6 of the sea, tossed and turned by the ***w***.
Peter
2:17 driven by the ***w***. The underworld
evelation
6:13 its fruit when shaken by a strong ***w***.
7:1 winds so that no ***w*** would blow

INDOW

enesis
8:6 Noah opened the ***w*** of the ark that
26:8 looked out his ***w*** and saw Isaac
shua
2:15 rope through the ***w***. Her house was on
2:18 woven cord in the ***w*** through which you
2:21 Then she tied the red cord in the ***w***.
dges
5:28 Through the ***w*** she watched, Sisera's
Samuel
19:12 David through a ***w***. He took off and
Samuel
6:16 watching from a ***w***. She saw King
Kings
7:4 Three sets of ***w*** frames faced each
Kings
1:2 fell out the ***w***
9:30 her hair. She looked down out of the ***w***.
9:32 looked up to the ***w*** and said, "Who's
9:33 her out of the ***w***. Some of her
13:17 said, "Open the ***w*** to the east." The
Chronicles
15:29 looked out the ***w***. When she saw
roverbs
7:6 When from the ***w*** of my house, from
osea
13:3 floor, or like smoke from a ***w***.
ephaniah
2:14 resound from the ***w***. Desolation will
cts
20:9 sitting in the ***w***. He was sinking
Corinthians
11:33 a basket through a ***w*** in the city wall.

VINDOWS

enesis
7:11 erupted, and the ***w*** in the skies
Kings
6:4 recessed and latticed ***w*** for the temple
Kings
7:2 LORD should make ***w*** in the sky, how
cclesiastes
12:3 those who look through the ***w*** grow dim;
ong of Songs
2:9 through the ***w***, peeking through
saiah
24:18 trap. Heaven's ***w*** will open, and
Jeremiah
9:21 through our ***w***; it has entered
22:14 chambers, ornate ***w***, cedar paneling,
Ezekiel
40:16 arches had closed ***w***; there were also
41:26 while closed ***w*** and palm trees decorated
Daniel
6:10 room had open ***w*** that faced
Joel
2:9 they enter through the ***w*** like thieves.
Malachi
3:10 not open all the ***w*** of the heavens

WINDS

Psalms
104:4 You make the ***w*** your messengers; you
147:18 God makes his ***w*** blow; the water
Jeremiah
13:24 that is blown away by the desert ***w***.
49:32 scatter to the ***w*** those who are
49:36 against Elam four ***w*** from the four
Ezekiel
5:10 all that is left of you to the ***w***.
5:12 to all the ***w***, letting loose a
12:14 his troops to the ***w*** and let the sword
13:11 and the storm ***w*** will break it
17:21 scattered to the ***w***. Then you will
37:9 from the four ***w***, breath! Breathe
Daniel
7:2 I saw the four ***w*** of heaven
8:8 came up toward the four ***w*** of heaven.
11:4 to the four ***w*** of heaven. It
Zechariah
2:6 you like the four ***w*** of heaven, says
6:5 are the four ***w*** of heaven that
9:14 forth on the stormy ***w*** of the south.
Matthew
8:26 orders to the ***w*** and the lake, and
8:27 is this? Even the ***w*** and the lake obey
Mark
4:37 Gale-force ***w*** arose, and waves crashed
Luke
8:23 Gale-force ***w*** swept down on the
8:25 commands even the ***w*** and the water,
James
3:4 large that strong ***w*** are needed to
Jude
1:12 along by the ***w***; fruitless autumn
Revelation
7:1 the earth's four ***w*** so that no wind

WINE → NEW WINE

Genesis
9:21 drank some of the ***w***, became drunk,
19:32 give our father ***w*** to drink, lie
27:25 ate, and he brought him ***w*** and he drank.
35:14 an offering of ***w*** on it and then
49:12 are darker than ***w***, and his teeth
Exodus
29:40 of a hin of ***w*** for a drink
Leviticus
10:9 must not drink ***w*** or beer when you
23:13 must be a quarter of a hin of ***w***.
Numbers
6:3 must refrain from ***w*** and brandy. He or
6:20 After this the nazirite may drink ***w***.

15:5 of a hin of ***w*** as a drink
28:14 be half a hin of ***w*** for a bull, a

Deuteronomy
7:13 your grain, your ***w***, your oil, and
11:14 can stock up your grain, ***w***, and oil.
28:39 won't drink any ***w*** or harvest the
29:6 bread nor drunk ***w*** or beer during
32:14 and for drink, ***w*** from the juiciest
32:33 their ***w*** is snake poison, venom from a
32:38 their sacred ***w***? They should
33:28 full of grain and ***w***, where the

Judges
13:4 not to drink ***w*** or brandy or to

1 Samuel
1:15 I haven't had any ***w*** or beer but have

2 Samuel
13:28 is happy with ***w*** and I tell you to
16:2 to eat, and the ***w*** is for those who

1 Chronicles
9:29 the flour, ***w***, oil, incense,
12:40 of raisins, ***w***, oil, oxen, and
27:27 produce for the ***w*** cellars—Zabdi the

2 Chronicles
2:10 thousand baths of ***w***, and twenty
2:15 olive oil, and ***w*** he has promised,
11:11 supplied them with food, oil, and ***w***.
32:28 harvest of grain, ***w***, and olive oil;

Nehemiah
13:12 of the grain, ***w***, and oil into the

Esther
1:7 made sure there was plenty of royal ***w***.
5:6 As they sipped ***w***, the king asked, "Now
7:2 day we've met for ***w***. What is your

Job
1:13 and drinking ***w*** in their oldest
32:19 is like unopened ***w***; like new

Psalms
4:7 when their wheat and ***w*** are everywhere!
60:3 you've given us ***w*** and we stagger.
75:8 full of foaming ***w***, mixed with
78:65 sleeping! Like a warrior shaking off ***w***,
104:15 and ***w***, which cheers people's hearts,

Proverbs
3:10 and your vats will burst with ***w***.
4:17 evil, and they drink the ***w*** of violence.
9:2 mixed her ***w***, and set her
9:5 my food, and drink the ***w*** I have mixed.
20:1 ***W*** is a mocker; beer a carouser. Those
21:17 poor; lovers of ***w*** and oil won't get
23:20 who get drunk on ***w*** or those who eat
23:30 who linger over ***w***; those who go
23:31 Don't look at ***w*** when it is red
23:35 When I wake up, I'll look for ***w*** again!"
31:4 kings to drink ***w***, for rulers to
31:6 are perishing and ***w*** to those whose

Ecclesiastes
2:3 myself with ***w*** and by embracing
9:7 and drink your ***w*** happily because
10:19 for laughter, ***w*** cheers the

Song of Songs
1:2 Oh, your loving is sweeter than ***w***!
1:4 loving more than ***w***. No wonder they
2:4 to the house of ***w***; his banner
4:10 much better than ***w***, and your
5:1 I have drunk my ***w*** and my milk. Eat,
7:2 never lack spiced ***w***! Your belly is a
7:9 is like excellent ***w***
8:2 give you spiced ***w*** to drink, some of

Isaiah
5:22 Doom to the ***w***-swigging warriors,
28:7 also stagger from ***w*** and stumble from
29:9 drunk, but not on ***w***; stagger, but not
51:21 one, who is drunk, but not from ***w***.
55:1 money, at no cost, buy ***w*** and milk!
56:12 I'll get some ***w***! Let's drink
62:8 won't drink your ***w*** for which you
65:11 fill cups of mixed ***w*** for a god of fate:

Jeremiah
13:12 proclaims: Every ***w*** jug should be
23:9 has had too much ***w*** to drink, because
25:15 seething cup of ***w*** from my hand and
31:12 gifts: grain, ***w***, oil, flocks, and
35:2 arrive, offer them some ***w*** to drink.
35:14 not to drink ***w***, and to this very
48:11 at ease, like ***w*** left to settle on
51:7 The nations drank her ***w*** and went mad

Lamentations
2:12 are grain and ***w***?" while fainting

Ezekiel
23:42 drinkers of ***w***, were brought
27:18 great wealth the ***w*** of Helbon and
44:21 should drink ***w*** when they come

Daniel
1:8 or the royal ***w***, and he appealed
5:1 he drank a lot of ***w*** in front of them.
10:3 Neither meat nor ***w*** passed my lips,

Hosea
2:9 its time, and my ***w*** in its season;
7:5 with the heat of ***w***; he stretched out
7:14 fight over grain and ***w***; they resist me.
9:4 They won't pour ***w*** as an offering to the
14:7 will be like the ***w*** of Lebanon.

Joel
1:5 over the sweet ***w***, all you wine
3:3 sold girls for ***w***, which they drank
3:13 overflow with ***w***, for their
3:18 will drip sweet ***w***, the hills will

Amos
2:8 god they drink ***w*** bought with fines
2:12 nazirites drink ***w***, and commanded
5:11 vineyards, but you won't drink their ***w***.
6:6 drink bowls of ***w***, put the best of
9:13 will drip ***w***, and all the
9:14 and drink their ***w***; and they will

Micah
2:11 preach to you for ***w*** and liquor," such
6:15 you tread grapes, but don't drink ***w***.

Habakkuk
2:5 Moreover, ***w*** betrays an arrogant man. He doesn't rest

Zephaniah
1:12 sediment in their ***w***, those saying to
1:13 plant vineyards, but not drink the ***w***.

Haggai
1:11 the grain, on the ***w***, on the olive
2:12 bread, stew, ***w***, oil, or any kind
2:16 one came to the ***w*** vat for fifty

Zechariah
9:15 like one having ***w***. They will be
9:17 men flourish; so too ***w*** his young women.
10:7 were drinking ***w***. Their children
14:10 the Hananel Tower to the king's ***w*** vats

Matthew
26:29 I won't drink ***w*** again until that
27:34 they gave Jesus ***w*** mixed with vinegar to
Mark
14:25 I won't drink ***w*** again until that
15:23 tried to give him ***w*** mixed with myrrh,
15:36 sponge with sour ***w***, and put it on a
Luke
1:15 He must not drink ***w*** and liquor. He
7:33 nor drinking ***w***, and you say, 'He
10:34 them with oil and ***w***. Then he placed
23:36 They came up to him offering him sour ***w***
John
2:3 When the ***w*** ran out, Jesus' mother said
4:46 the water into ***w***. In Capernaum
19:29 jar full of sour ***w*** was nearby, so
19:30 received the sour ***w***, Jesus said, "It
Romans
14:21 eat meat or drink ***w*** or to do anything
Ephesians
5:18 get drunk on ***w***, which produces
1 Timothy
5:23 but use a little ***w*** because of your
Revelation
6:6 don't damage the olive oil and the ***w***."
14:8 nations drink the ***w*** of her lustful
14:10 also drink the ***w*** of God's
16:19 he gave her the ***w*** cup of his
17:2 drunk with the ***w*** of her whoring."
18:3 fallen due to the ***w*** of her lustful
18:13 and frankincense; ***w***, oil, fine flour,

WINGED → WINGED CREATURE, WINGED CREATURES, WINGED HEAVENLY CREATURES
Genesis
1:21 kind, and all the ***w*** birds, each
Deuteronomy
14:19 Also, all ***w*** insects are off-limits for
1 Kings
7:29 Lions, bulls, and ***w*** otherworldly
Isaiah
18:1 to the land of ***w*** ships, beyond the

WINGED CREATURE
Dt 14:20; 1Ki 6:24; 6:25; Ecc 10:20; Is 14:29; Eze 10:9; 10:14; 28:14, 16; 41:18

WINGED CREATURES
Gn 3:24; Nm 7:89; 2Sa 6:2; 1Ki 6:23; 6:25, 26, 27, 28, 29, 32, 35; 8:6, 7; 2Ki 19:15; 1Ch 13:6; 28:18; 2Ch 3:7; 3:10, 14; 5:7, 8; Is 6:2; 6:6; 37:16; Eze 9:3; 10:1, 2, 3, 4, 6, 7, 8, 9, 15, 16, 18, 19, 20; 11:22; 41:18, 20, 25; Heb 9:5

WINGED HEAVENLY CREATURES
Ex 25:18; 25:19, 20, 22; 26:1, 31; 36:8, 35; 37:7, 8, 9; 1Sa 4:4; Ps 80:1; 99:1

WINGS
Exodus
19:4 you up on eagles' ***w*** and brought you
25:20 should have their ***w*** spread out above,
37:9 spread out their ***w*** above, shielding
Leviticus
1:17 bird open by its ***w***, without
Deuteronomy
32:11 spread out his ***w***, took hold of
Ruth
2:12 under whose ***w*** you've come to
2 Samuel
22:11 and flew; he was seen on the wind's ***w***.
1 Kings
6:24 The ***w*** of the first winged creature were
6:27 the temple. Their ***w*** spread out so
8:6 spot beneath the ***w*** of the winged
8:7 spread their ***w*** over the place
1 Chronicles
28:18 spreading their ***w*** and covering the
2 Chronicles
3:11 first creature's ***w*** was seven and a
3:13 The ***w*** of these creatures extended
5:7 spot beneath the ***w*** of the winged
5:8 spread their ***w*** over the place
Job
39:13 The ostrich's ***w*** flap joyously, but her
39:18 she flaps her ***w*** high, she laughs
39:26 spreading its ***w*** to the south?
Psalms
17:8 Hide me in the protection of your ***w***
18:10 flew; he soared on the ***w*** of the wind.
31:20 shelter of your ***w***, safe from human
36:7 finds refuge in the shadow of your ***w***.
55:6 I wish I had ***w*** like a dove! I'd
57:1 shadow of your ***w*** until destruction
61:4 refuge in the shelter of your ***w***! Selah
63:7 for joy in the protection of your ***w***.
68:13 there are ***w*** of a dove covered
91:4 refuge under his ***w***. His faithfulness
104:3 going around on the ***w*** of the wind.
139:9 could fly on the ***w*** of dawn, stopping
Proverbs
23:5 is gone; it grows ***w*** like an eagle and
Isaiah
6:2 him. Each had six ***w***: with two they
8:8 the span of his ***w*** will cover the
40:31 will fly up on ***w*** like eagles; they
Jeremiah
48:9 Give ***w*** to Moab, and it would fly away
48:40 an eagle and spreads its ***w*** over Moab.
49:22 and spreads his ***w*** over Bozrah. On
Ezekiel
1:6 though each had four faces and four ***w***
3:13 the creatures' ***w*** beating against
10:5 winged creatures' ***w*** could be heard as
11:22 raised their ***w***. The wheels were
17:3 eagle with great ***w***, long feathers,
17:7 eagle with great ***w*** and much plumage.
Daniel
7:4 lion with eagle's ***w***. I observed it
7:6 back it had four ***w*** like bird wings.
Hosea
4:19 her in its ***w***, they will be
Zechariah
5:9 a wind in their ***w***; their wings were
Malachi
4:2 will be in its ***w*** so that you will
Matthew
23:37 chicks under her ***w***. But you didn't
Luke
13:34 chicks under her ***w***. But you didn't
Revelation
4:8 creatures had six ***w***, and each was

9:9 sound of their ***w*** was like the
12:14 was given the two ***w*** of the great

WIPE

Genesis
6:7 said, "I will ***w*** off of the land
7:4 nights. I will ***w*** off from the
Exodus
17:14 I will completely ***w*** out the memory of
23:23 and the Jebusites, and I ***w*** them out,
32:12 mountains and so ***w*** them off the
32:32 And if not, then ***w*** me out of your
32:33 The ones I'll ***w*** out of my scroll
Numbers
5:23 in the scroll and ***w*** them off into the
Deuteronomy
6:15 you, and he will ***w*** you off the
7:24 you, and you will ***w*** their names out
9:3 fire! He will ***w*** them out! He will
9:8 by you that he threatened to ***w*** you out.
9:14 I am going to ***w*** them out. I will
9:19 was going to ***w*** you out! However,
9:20 was going to ***w*** him out! So I
12:3 into pieces. ***W*** out their names
25:19 possess, you must ***w*** out Amalek's
29:20 and the LORD will ***w*** out their name
Joshua
9:24 land and to ***w*** out all its
11:20 was then able to ***w*** them out as
23:15 as well. He could ***w*** you out from this
1 Kings
9:21 weren't able to ***w*** them out—Solomon
2 Kings
10:19 so that he could ***w*** out Baal's
21:13 family. I will ***w*** Jerusalem clean
Esther
3:6 he planned to ***w*** out all the Jews,
3:13 people to ***w*** out, kill, and
8:11 Jews were free to ***w*** out, kill, and
Psalms
51:1 faithful love! ***W*** away my
51:9 from my sins; ***w*** away all my
83:4 they say, "let's ***w*** them out as a
143:12 ***W*** out my enemies because of your
Proverbs
31:3 your ways to those who ***w*** out kings.
Isaiah
25:8 The LORD God will ***w*** tears from every
34:2 God is about to ***w*** them out and has
Jeremiah
4:7 your land, to ***w*** out your towns,
51:3 to her young men; ***w*** out her entire
Lamentations
3:66 hunt them down; ***w*** them out from
Daniel
2:24 had appointed to ***w*** out Babylon's
Zephaniah
1:2 I will ***w*** out everything from the earth,
Hebrews
2:17 God, in order to ***w*** away the sins of
Revelation
7:17 and God will ***w*** away every tear
21:4 He will ***w*** away every tear from their

WIPED

Genesis
7:23 God ***w*** away every living thing that was
Numbers
16:26 lest you too be ***w*** out for all their
Deuteronomy
12:30 they've been ***w*** out before you.
28:20 until you are ***w*** out and until you
32:36 prisoners and free people are ***w*** out.
Joshua
2:10 of the Jordan. You utterly ***w*** them out.
6:17 is to be utterly ***w*** out as something
8:26 until he had ***w*** out the whole
10:1 Ai and had ***w*** it out as
11:12 without mercy. He ***w*** them out as
11:21 Joshua went and ***w*** out the Anakim
24:8 their land. I ***w*** them out before
Judges
20:32 They're being ***w*** out before us
20:35 The LORD ***w*** out the Benjaminites before
20:39 going to be ***w*** out before us, as
1 Samuel
15:18 against them until you've ***w*** them out.'
1 Kings
15:29 family; he ***w*** them out
2 Kings
10:17 were completely ***w*** out, in agreement
21:9 the LORD had ***w*** out before the
2 Chronicles
33:9 that the LORD had ***w*** out before the
Esther
7:4 my people—to be ***w*** out, killed, and
Psalms
9:6 Every enemy is ***w*** out, like something
69:28 Let them be ***w*** out of the scroll of
104:35 Let sinners be ***w*** clean from the earth;
109:13 their names be ***w*** out in just one
109:14 let his mother's sin never be ***w*** out.
119:87 They've almost ***w*** me off the face of the
Proverbs
6:33 His shame will never be ***w*** away.
Isaiah
48:19 eliminated, never ***w*** out from before
Jeremiah
11:19 any knowledge of him will be ***w*** out."
Ezekiel
6:6 shattered, and all your works ***w*** out.
Daniel
2:12 that all Babylon's sages be ***w*** out.
7:26 away—ruined and ***w*** out for all time.
Luke
7:38 her tears. She ***w*** them with her
7:44 with tears and ***w*** them with her
John
11:2 fragrant oil and ***w*** his feet with her
12:3 with it, then ***w*** his feet dry with
Acts
3:19 to God so that your sins may be ***w*** away.

WISDOM → GOD'S WISDOM

Genesis
3:6 would provide ***w***, so she took some
Deuteronomy
4:6 will show your ***w*** and insight to
32:29 If they had any ***w***, they would
34:9 was filled with ***w*** because Moses had
2 Samuel
14:20 But my master's ***w*** is like the

Kings

4:29 God gave Solomon ***w*** and very great

10:6 your deeds and ***w*** when I was still

10:24 in order to hear his God-given ***w***.

11:41 did and all his ***w***, aren't they

Chronicles

1:10 Give me ***w*** and knowledge so I can lead

9:22 all the earth's kings in wealth and ***w***,

zra

7:25 on the divine ***w*** that you have,

ob

11:6 you secrets of ***w***; for sound

12:13 With him are ***w*** and power; counsel and

28:12 But ***w***, where can it be found; where is

28:28 of the LORD is ***w***; turning from

33:33 me; be quiet, and I will teach you ***w***.

38:36 Who put ***w*** in remote places, or who gave understanding

salms

37:30 righteous recite ***w***; their tongues

49:3 My mouth speaks ***w***; my heart's

51:6 you teach me ***w*** in the most

05:22 will, and to teach ***w*** to his advisors.

11:10 the LORD is where ***w*** begins; sure

roverbs

1:2 is to teach ***w*** and discipline,

1:5 them and grow in ***w***; those with

1:7 ***W*** begins with the fear of the LORD, but

1:20 ***W*** shouts in the street; in the public

2:2 your ear toward ***w***, and stretch your

2:6 The LORD gives ***w***; from his mouth come knowledge

2:10 ***W*** will enter your mind, and knowledge

2:12 ***W*** will rescue you from the evil path,

2:16 ***W*** will rescue you from the mysterious

3:13 those who find ***w*** and those who

3:19 of the earth with ***w***, establishing the

4:5 Get ***w***; get understanding. Don't forget

4:7 The beginning of ***w***: Get wisdom! Get

4:11 you the path of ***w***. I lead you in

5:1 attention to my ***w***. Bend your ear to

7:4 Say to ***w***, "You are my sister"; call

8:1 Doesn't ***W*** cry out and Understanding

8:11 ***W*** is better than pearls; nothing is

8:12 I, ***W***, dwell with prudence; I have

9:1 ***W*** built her house; she has carved out

9:10 The beginning of ***w*** is the fear of the

10:13 ***W*** is found on the lips of those who

10:23 with understanding take pleasure in ***w***.

10:31 flows with ***w***, but the twisted

11:2 so does shame, but ***w*** brings humility.

14:6 searches for ***w*** and gets none,

14:8 By their ***w*** the prudent understand their

14:33 ***W*** resides in an understanding heart,

16:16 Acquiring ***w*** is much better than gold,

17:16 money to pay for ***w***? He has no mind.

17:24 ***W*** is right in front of those with

18:4 a bubbling stream, a fountain of ***w***.

21:11 person gains ***w***; when insight

21:30 No ***w***, understanding, or advice can

23:23 sell it; buy ***w***, instruction, and

24:3 By ***w*** a house is built; by understanding

24:7 ***W*** is beyond foolish people. They don't

24:14 Know that ***w*** is like that for your whole

28:26 those who walk in ***w*** will be kept safe.

29:3 A man who loves ***w*** makes his father

29:15 lead to ***w***, but children out

30:3 I haven't learned ***w***, nor do I have

31:26 mouth is full of ***w***; kindly teaching

Ecclesiastes

1:13 and to explore by ***w*** all that happens

1:16 has absorbed great ***w*** and knowledge.

1:17 to understand ***w***, and also to

1:18 Remember: In much ***w*** is much

2:3 folly—with ***w*** still guiding me—

2:9 Jerusalem. Moreover, my ***w*** stood by me.

2:12 then turned to ***w***, madness, and

2:13 I saw that ***w*** is more beneficial than

2:19 my hard work and ***w*** here under the

2:21 worked hard with ***w***, knowledge, and

2:26 because God gives ***w***, knowledge, and

7:11 ***W*** is as good as an inheritance—an

7:12 knowledge is that ***w*** preserves the

7:19 ***W*** makes a wise person stronger than ten

7:23 all of this by ***w***. I thought, I

7:25 and to seek ***w***, along with an

8:1 A person's ***w*** brightens the

8:16 my mind to know ***w*** and to observe

9:10 knowledge, or ***w*** in the grave,

9:13 example of ***w*** under the sun—it

9:15 everyone by his ***w***. But no one

9:16 So I thought, ***W*** is better than might,

9:18 ***W*** is better than weapons of war, but

10:1 a little folly outweighs ***w*** and honor.

Isaiah

11:2 him, a spirit of ***w*** and

28:29 gives wondrous counsel and increases ***w***.

Jeremiah

8:9 LORD's word; what kind of ***w*** is that?

10:12 the world by his ***w***, crafted the

49:7 proclaims: Is ***w*** no longer in

51:15 the world by his ***w***, and crafted the

Ezekiel

28:4 By your ***w*** and discernment, you made

28:7 against your fine ***w***, and they will

28:12 You were full of ***w*** and beauty, the

28:17 corrupted your ***w*** for the sake of

Daniel

1:4 skilled in all ***w***, possessing

5:14 insight, and extraordinary ***w***.

Micah

6:9 out to the city; ***w*** appears when one

Matthew

11:19 and sinners.' But ***w*** is proved to be

12:42 to hear Solomon's ***w***. And look,

13:54 did he get this ***w***? Where did he get

Mark

6:2 What's this ***w*** he's been given?

12:34 had answered with ***w***, he said to him,

Luke

2:40 was filled with ***w***, and God's favor

2:52 Jesus matured in ***w*** and years, and in

7:35 But ***w*** is proved to be right by all her

11:31 to hear Solomon's ***w***. And look,

21:15 you words and ***w*** that none of your

Acts

6:3 with exceptional ***w***. We will put them

6:10 resist the ***w*** the Spirit gave

7:10 The grace and ***w*** he gave Joseph

7:22 Egyptian ***w*** had to offer, and

WISDOM [cont.]

Romans
11:33 God's riches, ***w***, and knowledge are so
1 Corinthians
1:19 will destroy the ***w*** of the wise, and
1:20 God made the ***w*** of the world
1:22 ask for signs, and Greeks look for ***w***,
1:25 wiser than human ***w***, and the weakness
1:30 Jesus. He became ***w*** from God for us.
2:1 like I was an expert in speech or ***w***.
2:5 not depend on the ***w*** of people but on
2:6 What we say is ***w*** to people who are
2:8 It is a ***w*** that none of the present-day
2:13 taught by human ***w*** but with words
3:19 This world's ***w*** is foolishness to God.
12:8 A word of ***w*** is given by the Spirit to
2 Corinthians
1:12 act with human ***w*** but we relied on
Ephesians
1:8 over us with ***w*** and understanding.
1:17 you a spirit of ***w*** and revelation
3:10 varieties of his ***w*** through the
Colossians
1:9 will, with all ***w*** and spiritual
1:28 person with all ***w*** so that we might
2:3 the treasures of ***w*** and knowledge are
3:16 other with all ***w*** by singing
James
1:5 anyone who needs ***w*** should ask God,
3:13 a humble lifestyle that comes from ***w***.
3:15 This is not the ***w*** that comes down from above
3:17 What of the ***w*** from above? First, it is
2 Peter
3:15 to you according to the ***w*** given to him,
Revelation
5:12 power, wealth, ***w***, and might, and
7:12 and glory and ***w*** and thanksgiving
13:18 This calls for ***w***. Let the one who

WISE

Genesis
41:33 an intelligent, ***w*** man and give him
Exodus
7:11 together his ***w*** men and wizards,
Deuteronomy
1:13 tribes, choose ***w***, discerning, and
1:15 people who were ***w*** and well-regarded,
4:6 this great nation ***w*** and insightful
16:19 the vision of the ***w*** and twists the
2 Samuel
14:2 and brought a ***w*** woman from there.
20:16 Then a ***w*** woman called from the city,
20:22 everyone with her ***w*** counsel, they cut
1 Kings
2:9 him. You are ***w*** and know what to
3:12 hereby give you a ***w*** and understanding
4:31 than anyone, more ***w*** than Ethan the
5:7 has given David a ***w*** son who is in
5:12 LORD made Solomon ***w***, just as he had
10:4 of Sheba saw how ***w*** Solomon was, the
1 Chronicles
26:14 son Zechariah, a ***w*** counselor, and
2 Chronicles
2:12 gave King David a ***w*** son who possesses
9:3 of Sheba saw how ***w*** Solomon was, the
Ezra
8:16 with Joiarib and Elnathan, who were ***w***.
Job
5:13 trapping the ***w*** in their cleverness so
9:4 He is ***w*** and powerful; who can resist
15:2 Will the ***w*** respond with windy knowledge
15:18 what the ***w*** have told and have not
17:10 and I won't find a ***w*** one among you.
32:9 in days aren't ***w***; the old don't
34:2 Hear my words, ***w*** ones; knowledgeable
34:34 people say to me, the ***w*** who hear me,
37:24 fear him; none of the ***w*** can see him.
38:37 Who is ***w*** enough to count the clouds,
Psalms
2:10 So kings, ***w*** up! Be warned, you rulers
14:2 see if anyone is ***w***, to see if anyone
19:7 are faithful, making naive people ***w***.
36:3 stopped being ***w*** and stopped doing
49:10 knows that the ***w*** die too, just
53:2 see if anyone is ***w***, to see if anyone
90:12 our days so we can have a ***w*** heart.
107:43 Whoever is ***w*** will pay attention to
Proverbs
1:2 to help one understand ***w*** sayings.
1:5 The ***w*** hear them and grow in wisdom;
1:6 the words of the ***w***, and their
3:7 consider yourself ***w***. Fear the LORD
3:35 The ***w*** gain respect, but fools receive
6:6 person; observe its ways and grow ***w***.
8:33 instruction, and be ***w***; don't avoid it.
9:8 you; correct the ***w***, and they will
9:9 Teach the ***w***, and they will become
9:12 If you are ***w***, it is to your benefit;
10:1 of Solomon: A ***w*** child makes a
10:5 A ***w*** son harvests in the summer; a
10:14 The ***w*** store up knowledge, but the mouth of a fool
10:19 but the ***w*** restrain their
10:32 The lips of the ***w*** know what is
11:29 The fool will be servant to the ***w***.
11:30 a tree of life, and the ***w*** gather lives.
12:15 as right, but the ***w*** listen to advice.
12:18 a stabbing sword, but a ***w*** tongue heals.
13:1 A ***w*** son listens to the discipline of
13:10 of pride; those who take advice are ***w***.
13:14 teaching of the ***w*** is a fountain of
13:20 Walk with ***w*** people and become wise;
14:1 A ***w*** woman builds her house, while a
14:3 but the lips of the ***w*** protect them.
14:7 for you won't learn ***w*** speech there.
14:16 The ***w*** are careful and avoid evil, but
14:24 the crown of the ***w***, and the folly of
15:2 The tongue of the ***w*** enhances knowledge,
15:7 The lips of the ***w*** spread knowledge, but
15:12 correct them. They won't go to the ***w***.
15:20 A ***w*** child brings joy to a father, but
15:31 correction dwells among the ***w***.
15:33 of the LORD is ***w*** instruction, and
16:14 of death; the ***w*** will calm him.
16:23 The mind of the ***w*** makes their speech
17:27 ***W*** are those who restrain their talking;
17:28 quiet are deemed ***w***; those who shut
18:15 the ear of the ***w*** seeks knowledge.
19:20 so you might grow ***w*** in the future.
20:1 Those it leads astray won't become ***w***.
20:15 pearls exist, but ***w*** speech is the
20:26 A ***w*** king sifts out the wicked, and runs

21:11 comes to the ***w***, knowledge
21:20 the home of the ***w***, but fools
21:22 A ***w*** person fought a city of warriors
22:17 the words of the ***w***; focus your mind
23:15 if your heart is ***w***, then my heart
23:19 my child, and be ***w***! Keep your mind
23:24 who gives life to the ***w*** will rejoice.
24:5 A ***w*** person is mightier than a strong
24:23 sayings of the ***w***: Partiality in
25:12 ***W*** correction to an ear that listens is
26:5 folly, or they will deem themselves ***w***.
26:12 themselves ***w***? There is more
27:11 Be ***w***, my child, and make my heart
28:11 think they are ***w***, but an
29:8 on fire, but the ***w*** turn back anger.
29:9 When the ***w*** make a legal charge against
29:11 their anger, but the ***w*** hold it back.
30:24 on earth, but they are the extremely ***w***:

Ecclesiastes
2:14 The ***w*** have eyes in their head, but
7:19 Wisdom makes a ***w*** person stronger than ten rulers
9:17 calm words of the ***w*** are better heeded
12:11 The words of the ***w*** are like iron-tipped

Isaiah
29:14 wisdom of their ***w*** will perish, and

Jeremiah
8:9 The ***w*** will be shamed and shocked when
9:12 Who is ***w*** enough to understand this? Who has been taught
49:7 the perceptive? Are they no longer ***w***?

Daniel
2:21 wisdom to the ***w*** and knowledge to

Hosea
14:9 Whoever is ***w*** understands these things.

Amos
5:13 the one who is ***w*** will keep silent

Obadiah
1:8 LORD, destroy the ***w*** from Edom and

Zechariah
9:2 Sidon, indeed, each is exceedingly ***w***.

Matthew
7:24 is like a ***w*** builder who built
10:16 Therefore be ***w*** as snakes and
11:25 things from the ***w*** and intelligent
23:34 you prophets, ***w*** people, and legal
24:45 the faithful and ***w*** servants whom
25:2 five of them were ***w***, and the other
25:4 But the ***w*** ones took their lamps and
25:8 said to the ***w*** ones, 'Give us
25:9 But the ***w*** bridesmaids replied, 'No,

Luke
10:21 things from the ***w*** and intelligent
12:42 the faithful and ***w*** managers whom the

Romans
1:14 both to the ***w*** and to the
1:22 claiming to be ***w***, they made fools
16:19 I want you to be ***w*** about what's
16:27 God, who alone is ***w***! May the glory be

1 Corinthians
1:19 the wisdom of the ***w***, and I will
1:20 Where are the ***w***? Where are the legal
1:26 not many were ***w***, not many were
1:27 to shame the ***w***. God chose what
2:4 with convincing ***w*** words but with a
3:10 foundation like a ***w*** master builder
3:18 foolish so that they can become ***w***.
3:19 He catches the ***w*** in their
3:20 that the thoughts of the ***w*** are silly.
4:10 but you are ***w*** through Christ!
6:5 among you who is ***w*** enough to pass

2 Corinthians
11:19 you, who are so ***w***, are happy to put

Colossians
2:23 like they are ***w*** with this self-mad

2 Timothy
3:15 help you to be ***w*** in a way that

James
3:13 Are any of you ***w*** and understanding?

WISH

Genesis
16:6 do whatever you ***w*** to her." So Sarai

Exodus
16:3 them, "Oh, how we ***w*** that the LORD had just put us
33:19 to whomever I ***w*** to be kind, and I

Leviticus
7:29 If you ***w*** to offer a

Deuteronomy
12:15 whenever you ***w***, you may
12:21 eat it in your cities whenever you ***w***.
28:67 you will say: "I ***w*** it was

Judges
9:33 you, you can do to him whatever you ***w***."

2 Samuel
8:10 to King David to ***w*** him well and

1 Kings
3:5 Ask whatever you ***w***, and I'll give it
5:8 I will do as you ***w*** with the cedar

2 Kings
5:3 her mistress, "I ***w*** that my master

1 Chronicles
18:10 to King David to ***w*** him well and to

2 Chronicles
1:7 Ask whatever you ***w***, and I will give
1:11 this is what you ***w***, and because

Esther
5:6 what is it you ***w***? I'll give it to
7:2 What is your ***w***, Queen Esther?
9:12 What do you ***w*** now? I'll give it

Job
10:18 from the womb? I ***w*** I had died
14:13 I ***w*** you would hide me in the
34:36 I ***w*** Job would be tested to the limit
36:20 Don't ***w*** for the night when people
37:20 inform him that I ***w*** to speak, or

Psalms
55:6 say to myself, I ***w*** I had wings like
60:9 I ***w*** someone would bring me to a
81:13 How I ***w*** my people would listen to me!
108:10 I ***w*** someone would bring me to a
119:5 How I ***w*** my ways were strong when it

Jeremiah
9:8 deceitful. They ***w*** their neighbors
15:10 I ***w*** I had never been born! I have

Daniel
4:1 the entire earth: "I ***w*** you much peace.
6:25 the entire earth: I ***w*** you much peace.

Matthew
5:40 When they ***w*** to haul you to court and
5:42 refuse those who ***w*** to borrow from
15:28 be just as you ***w***." And right then

Mark
6:22 me whatever you ***w***, and I will give
Luke
12:49 the earth. How I ***w*** that it was
16:26 you. Those who ***w*** to cross over
Romans
9:3 I ***w*** I could be cursed, cut off from
1 Corinthians
4:8 without us! I ***w*** you did rule so
7:7 I ***w*** all people were like me, but each
14:5 I ***w*** that all of you spoke in tongues,
Galatians
4:20 But I ***w*** I could be with you now and
5:12 I ***w*** that the ones who are upsetting you
Revelation
3:15 cold nor hot. I ***w*** that you were
11:6 with any plague, as often as they ***w***.

WISHES
Leviticus
27:13 the promise maker ***w*** to buy it back,
27:15 the house ***w*** to buy it back,
27:19 the land ***w*** to buy it back,
27:31 If someone ***w*** to buy back part of their
Numbers
9:14 among you and ***w*** to keep the
Deuteronomy
9:5 and because he ***w*** to establish the
21:14 her away as she ***w***. You are not
Esther
1:19 Now, if the king ***w***, let him send out a
3:9 If the king ***w***, let a written order be
5:4 If the king ***w***, please come
5:8 and if the king ***w*** to grant my wish
7:3 and if the king ***w***, give me my life
8:5 If the king ***w***, and if I please
9:13 If the king ***w***, let the Jews who
9:30 conveying good ***w*** and words of
John
3:8 blows wherever it ***w***. You hear its
5:21 the Son give life to whomever he ***w***.
Revelation
22:17 Let the one who ***w*** receive

WITHER
Job
8:12 uncut, it will ***w*** before every
14:2 we bloom, then ***w***, flee like a
18:16 dry out below; their branches ***w*** above.
Psalms
37:2 grass; they will ***w*** like green
137:5 If I forget you, let my strong hand ***w***!
Proverbs
11:28 their wealth will ***w***, but the
Isaiah
24:4 the heavens ***w*** away with the
42:15 I will ***w*** mountains and valleys, and I
64:6 rag. All of us ***w*** like a leaf; our
Jeremiah
14:2 mourns; her gates ***w*** away. The people
23:10 the grazing areas in the wilderness ***w***.
Lamentations
2:8 and walls ***w***—together they was
Ezekiel
17:9 its branches to ***w***? It will dry up,
17:10 it completely ***w***? On the bed in
17:24 the green tree ***w*** and the dry tree
47:12 leaves won't ***w***, and their
Amos
1:2 of the shepherds ***w***, and the top of
Nahum
1:4 Bashan and Carmel ***w***; the bud of
Zechariah
11:17 eye. His arm will ***w*** completely; his

WITHIN
Judges
2:9 They buried him ***w*** the boundaries of his family
1 Kings
6:15 built the walls ***w*** the temple with
Psalms
36:9 ***W*** you is the spring of life. In your
40:8 my God. Your Instruction is deep ***w*** me."
64:6 plot! It's deep ***w*** the human mind
69:34 oceans too, and all that moves ***w*** them!
Proverbs
7:1 my words; store up my commands ***w*** you.
26:24 their lips, keeping their deception ***w***.
Jeremiah
31:33 my Instructions ***w*** them and engrave
Zechariah
8:16 and peaceable decisions ***w*** your gates.
12:1 fashions the spirit of humanity ***w*** it:
Mark
14:58 by humans, and ***w*** three days I will
John
7:38 living water will flow out from ***w*** him."
2 Corinthians
10:15 it expands fully (***w*** the boundaries,
Ephesians
3:20 or imagine by his power at work ***w*** us;
1 Peter
1:11 Spirit of Christ ***w*** them was saying
1 John
5:10 has the testimony ***w***; the one who

WITNESS → FALSE WITNESS
Exodus
23:1 with evil people to act as a lying ***w***.
23:2 When you act as a ***w***, don't stretch
Leviticus
5:1 though you are a ***w***, knowing
Numbers
35:30 But one ***w*** alone cannot
Deuteronomy
19:15 A solitary ***w*** against someone in any
31:21 this poem will ***w*** against them,
31:26 It must remain there as a ***w*** against you
Joshua
22:27 But it is to be a ***w*** between us and you
Judges
11:10 The LORD is our ***w***; we will surely
1 Samuel
6:18 chest on is a ***w*** even now in the
12:6 the people: "The ***w*** is indeed the
20:42 The LORD is ***w*** between us and
1 Chronicles
28:8 with God as our ***w***, carefully
Ezra
4:14 fitting for us to ***w*** the king's
Job
16:8 My leanness rises to bear ***w*** against me.

16:19 Surely now my ***w*** stands in heaven; my
21:20 their own eyes ***w*** their doom. Let
Psalms
89:37 moon, a faithful ***w*** in the sky. Selah
112:8 end, they will ***w*** their enemies'
Proverbs
14:5 A truthful ***w*** doesn't lie, but a false
14:25 A truthful ***w*** saves lives, but a
19:28 A worthless ***w*** mocks justice; the wicked
21:28 A lying ***w*** will perish, but one who
24:28 Don't be a ***w*** against your neighbor
Ecclesiastes
5:8 If you ***w*** the poor being oppressed or
Isaiah
19:20 be a sign and a ***w*** to the LORD of
30:8 so in the future it will endure as a ***w***.
55:4 I made him a ***w*** to the peoples, a
Jeremiah
29:23 of it and am ***w*** to it, declares
39:16 good. You will ***w*** it for yourself
42:5 true and faithful ***w*** against us if we
Hosea
5:5 pride is a ***w*** against him; both
Micah
1:2 the LORD God be a ***w*** against you, the
Zephaniah
3:8 I rise up as a ***w***, when I decide to
Mark
6:11 off your feet as a ***w*** against them."
Luke
9:5 off your feet as a ***w*** against them."
John
1:7 He came as a ***w*** to testify concerning
5:36 I have a ***w*** greater than John's
8:17 written that the ***w*** of two people is
8:18 I am one ***w*** concerning myself and the
Acts
1:22 along with us a ***w*** to his
4:33 to bear powerful ***w*** to the
14:17 himself without a ***w***. He has blessed
22:15 You will be his ***w*** to everyone
22:20 When Stephen your ***w*** was being killed, I stood there
26:16 as my servant and ***w*** of what you have
26:22 here and bear ***w*** to the lowly and
Romans
1:9 and God is my ***w*** that I
2 Corinthians
1:23 call on God as my ***w***
Philippians
1:8 God is my ***w*** that I feel affection for
1 Thessalonians
2:5 and God is our ***w*** that we didn't
1 Peter
1:11 when he bore ***w*** beforehand about
5:1 elder and a ***w*** of Christ's
Revelation
1:2 who bore ***w*** to the word of God and to
1:5 faithful ***w***, the firstborn
2:13 my faithful ***w***, was killed among
3:14 faithful and true ***w***, the ruler of
6:9 word of God and the ***w*** they had given.
12:11 the word of their ***w***. Love for their
12:17 and hold firmly to the ***w*** of Jesus.
15:5 is, the tent of ***w***—was opened.
19:10 firmly to the ***w*** of Jesus. Worship
20:4 for their ***w*** to Jesus and
22:16 my angel to bear ***w*** to all of you
22:18 Now I bear ***w*** to everyone who hears the
22:20 The one who bears ***w*** to these things

WITNESSES → FALSE WITNESSES

Genesis
23:11 of my people's ***w***, I will give it
31:52 sacred pillar are ***w*** that I won't
Numbers
5:13 there are no ***w*** and she isn't
35:30 the evidence of ***w***. But one witness
Deuteronomy
4:26 and earth as my ***w*** against you
17:6 by two or three ***w***. No one may be
19:15 decision must stand by two or three ***w***.
30:19 and earth as my ***w*** against you right
31:28 heaven and earth as my ***w*** against them,
Joshua
22:27 after us. It ***w*** that we too
24:22 people, "You are ***w*** against
Ruth
4:9 Today you are ***w*** that I've bought
4:10 gate of his hometown—today you are ***w***."
4:11 said, "We are ***w***. May the LORD
1 Samuel
12:5 anointed one are ***w*** against you today
Job
10:17 to send your ***w*** against me and
Psalms
35:11 Violent ***w*** stand up. They question me
Isaiah
43:9 them bring their ***w*** as a defense; let
Jeremiah
32:12 Hanamel and the ***w*** named in the
32:25 sure there are ***w***, when the city is
Matthew
18:16 by the mouth of two or three ***w***.
26:65 we need any more ***w***? Look, you've
Mark
14:63 and said, "Why do we need any more ***w***?
Luke
24:48 You are ***w*** of these things
Acts
1:8 you will be my ***w*** in Jerusalem, in
2:32 raised up. We are all ***w*** to that fact.
3:15 raised from the dead. We are ***w*** of this.
5:32 We are ***w*** of such things, as is the Holy
7:58 to stone him. The ***w*** placed their
10:39 We are ***w*** of everything he did, both in
10:41 but by us. We are ***w*** whom God chose
13:31 They are now his ***w*** to the people.
2 Corinthians
13:1 on the evidence of two or three ***w***.
1 Thessalonians
2:10. You and God are ***w*** of how holy, just,
1 Timothy
5:19 it is confirmed by two or three ***w***.
6:12 of it in the presence of many ***w***.
2 Timothy
2:2 of many other ***w*** and pass them on
Hebrews
10:28 of the testimony of two or three ***w***.
12:1 a great cloud of ***w*** surrounding us.
Revelation
11:3 will allow my two ***w*** to prophesy for

17:6 blood of Jesus' ***w***. I was completely

WIVES

Genesis
6:18 your sons, your wife, and your sons' ***w***.
25:6 secondary ***w***, Abraham gave
36:6 Esau took his ***w***, his sons, his
46:26 Jacob's sons' ***w***—totaled 66 person
Exodus
22:24 sword. Then your ***w*** will be widows,
32:2 the ears of your ***w***, your sons, and
34:16 daughters as ***w*** for your sons.
Numbers
14:3 by the sword? Our ***w*** and our children
16:27 tents with their ***w***, children, and
32:26 Our children, ***w***, livestock, and all of
Deuteronomy
17:17 not take numerous ***w*** so that his heart
21:15 a man has two ***w***—one of them loved
29:11 children, your ***w***, and the
Joshua
1:14 Your ***w***, children, and cattle may
Judges
8:30 sons of his own because he had many ***w***.
21:7 we do to provide ***w*** for the ones who
21:16 we do to provide ***w*** for the ones who
21:23 did. They took ***w*** for their whole
Ruth
1:4 They took ***w*** for themselves, Moabite
1 Kings
11:4 grew old, his ***w*** turned his heart
11:8 all his foreign ***w***, who burned
Ezra
10:11 peoples and from the foreign ***w***."
Esther
2:14 of the secondary ***w***. She would never
Song of Songs
6:8 eighty secondary ***w***, young women
6:9 queens and secondary ***w*** praise her.
Jeremiah
6:12 their fields and ***w*** as well. I will
38:23 All your ***w*** and children will be led
44:25 You and your ***w*** have done exactly
Ezekiel
18:6 don't defile the ***w*** of their
Daniel
5:2 and his secondary ***w*** could drink wine
6:24 their ***w*** and children.
Matthew
19:8 to divorce your ***w*** because your
1 Corinthians
7:29 those who have ***w*** should be like
Ephesians
5:22 For example, ***w*** should submit to their
5:25 love your ***w*** just like Christ
Colossians
3:18 ***W***, submit to your husbands in a way
1 Peter
3:1 ***W***, likewise, submit to your own

WOMAN

Genesis
2:22 God fashioned a ***w*** and brought her
2:23 will be called a ***w*** because from a
3:6 The ***w*** saw that the tree was beautiful
3:12 man said, "The ***w*** you gave me, she
3:15 you and the ***w***, between your
3:16 To the ***w*** he said, "I will make your
12:11 I know you are a good-looking ***w***.
20:3 because of this ***w*** you have taken.
24:44 may she be the ***w*** the LORD has
28:1 orders: "Don't marry a Canaanite ***w***.
Exodus
3:22 Every ***w*** will ask her neighbor along
21:22 injure a pregnant ***w*** so that she has a
Leviticus
15:33 sexual intercourse with an unclean ***w***.
18:23 by it. Nor will a ***w*** present herself
20:14 a man marries a ***w*** and her mother as
20:18 man sleeps with a ***w*** during her
21:13 priest must marry a ***w*** who is a virgin.
Numbers
5:18 will make the ***w*** stand before the
30:3 When a ***w*** makes a solemn promise to the LORD
30:9 or a divorced ***w*** who makes a
30:10 If a ***w*** makes a solemn promise in her
Deuteronomy
21:11 a beautiful ***w***, and you fall in
24:1 a man marries a ***w***, but she isn't
28:30 get engaged to a ***w***, but another man
28:56 and refined ***w*** among you, who is
Judges
4:9 over Sisera to a ***w***." Then Deborah
9:54 be said of me, 'A ***w*** killed him.'" So
14:2 A Philistine ***w*** in Timnah caught
16:4 in love with a ***w*** whose name was
Ruth
3:11 gate—know that you are a ***w*** of worth.
1 Samuel
1:15 just a very sad ***w***. I haven't had
25:3 and attractive ***w***, but her husband
28:7 Find me a ***w*** who communicates
28:24 The ***w*** had a fattened calf in the house,
2 Samuel
11:2 the roof he saw a ***w*** bathing; the
13:17 said, "Get this ***w*** out of my
14:2 brought a wise ***w*** from there. He
20:16 Then a wise ***w*** called from the city,
20:22 When the ***w*** went to everyone with her
1 Kings
1:2 to find a young ***w*** for our master
17:24 man of God," the ***w*** said to Elijah,
2 Kings
4:8 to Shunem. A rich ***w*** lived there. She
8:1 spoke to the ***w*** whose son he had
9:34 with this cursed ***w*** and bury her. She
19:21 him: The young ***w***, Daughter Zion,
Esther
2:4 Let the young ***w*** who pleases you the
Job
2:10 like a foolish ***w***. Will we receive
15:14 and those born of ***w*** that they might
25:4 before God; one born of a ***w*** be pure?
31:9 been drawn to a ***w*** and I have lurked
Psalms
48:6 right there—like a ***w*** giving birth,
113:9 the once barren ***w*** at home—now a
Proverbs
2:16 the mysterious ***w***, from the foreign
5:3 of a mysterious ***w*** drip honey, and
5:20 with a mysterious ***w*** and embrace the
6:24 you from the evil ***w***, from the
6:26 but a married ***w*** hunts for a man's

7:5 the mysterious ***w***, from the foreign
7:10 All of a sudden a ***w*** approaches him,
9:13 ***W*** Folly is noisy; she's stupid and
11:16 A gracious ***w*** gains honor; violent men
11:22 is a beautiful ***w*** who lacks
12:4 A strong ***w*** is a crown to her husband,
14:1 A wise ***w*** builds her house, while a
21:9 with a contentious ***w*** in a large house.
21:19 a house with a contentious and angry ***w***.
22:14 of a mysterious ***w*** is a deep pit;
23:27 pit, and a foreign ***w*** is a narrow well.
25:24 to share a house with a contentious ***w***.
27:15 day and a contentious ***w*** are alike;
30:19 and the way of a man with a young ***w***.
30:20 of an adulterous ***w***: she eats and
30:23 at a detested ***w*** when she gets married
31:30 fleeting, but a ***w*** who fears the

Ecclesiastes
7:26 I found one ***w*** more bitter than death:
7:28 I couldn't find a ***w*** among any of

Song of Songs
7:1 feet, willing ***w***! The smooth

Isaiah
7:14 a sign. The young ***w*** is pregnant and
54:1 Sing, barren ***w*** who has borne no child;
62:5 marries a young ***w***, so your sons

Jeremiah
2:32 Does a young ***w*** forget her jewelry or a
4:31 hear the cry of a ***w*** in labor, the
48:41 be like that of a ***w*** in the throes of
50:43 him, pain like that of a ***w*** in labor.

Lamentations
1:15 of the young ***w*** Daughter Judah.
2:13 you, young ***w*** Daughter Zion?

Ezekiel
23:2 were two women, daughters of one ***w***.
23:43 For a foolish ***w*** they become
23:48 warning, no ***w*** will betray as

Hosea
3:1 make love to a ***w*** who has a lover
13:13 The pangs of a ***w*** in childbirth come for

Joel
1:8 Lament like a ***w*** dressed in funeral

Amos
2:7 the same young ***w***, degrading my

Micah
4:9 seized you like that of a ***w*** in labor?
4:10 Zion, like a ***w*** in labor! Now you

Zechariah
5:7 lifted, showing a ***w*** sitting in the

Matthew
5:28 who looks at a ***w*** lustfully has
5:32 marries a divorced ***w*** commits adultery.
9:20 Then a ***w*** who had been bleeding for
9:22 you." And the ***w*** was healed from
13:33 yeast, which a ***w*** took and hid in a
14:11 it to the young ***w***, and she brought
15:22 A Canaanite ***w*** from those territories
15:28 Jesus answered, "***W***, you have great
19:9 marries another ***w*** commits adultery."
22:27 Finally, the ***w*** died
26:7 a ***w*** came to him with a vase made of
26:10 trouble for the ***w***? She's done a
26:69 A servant ***w*** came and said to
26:71 the gate, another ***w*** saw him and said

Mark
5:25 A ***w*** was there who had been bleeding for
5:33 The ***w***, full of fear and trembling,
5:41 koum," which means, "Young ***w***, get up."
5:42 the young ***w*** got up and began
6:22 said to the young ***w***, "Ask me whatever
6:28 it to the young ***w***, and she gave it
7:25 In fact, a ***w*** whose young daughter was
7:26 The ***w*** was Greek, Syrophoenician by
12:20 one married a ***w***; when he died, he
12:22 left any children. Finally, the ***w*** died.
14:3 During dinner, a ***w*** came in with a
14:66 the courtyard. A ***w***, one of the high

Luke
1:36 a son. This ***w*** who was labeled
7:37 Meanwhile, a ***w*** from the city, a sinner,
7:39 know what kind of ***w*** is touching him.
7:44 turned to the ***w*** and said to
7:50 Jesus said to the ***w***, "Your faith has
8:43 A ***w*** was there who had been bleeding for twelve years
8:47 When the ***w*** saw that she couldn't escape notice
10:38 a village where a ***w*** named Martha
11:27 things, a certain ***w*** in the crowd
13:11 A ***w*** was there who had been disabled by
13:12 to him and said, "***W***, you are set free
13:16 that this ***w***, a daughter of
13:21 yeast, which a ***w*** took and hid in a
15:8 Or what ***w***, if she owns ten silver
16:18 man who marries a ***w*** divorced from her
20:29 man married a ***w*** and then died
20:32 Finally, the ***w*** died too
22:56 Then a servant ***w*** saw him sitting in the
22:57 it, saying, "***W***, I don't know

John
2:4 Jesus replied, "***W***, what does that have
4:7 A Samaritan ***w*** came to the well to draw
4:9 The Samaritan ***w*** asked, "Why do you, a
4:11 The ***w*** said to him, "Sir, you don't have
4:15 The ***w*** said to him, "Sir, give me this
4:17 The ***w*** replied, "I don't have a
4:19 The ***w*** said, "Sir, I see that you are a
4:21 her, "Believe me, ***w***, the time is
4:25 The ***w*** said, "I know that the Messiah is
4:27 talking with a ***w***. But no one
4:28 The ***w*** put down her water jar and went
4:42 they said to the ***w***, "We no longer
8:3 brought a ***w*** caught in
8:4 Teacher, this ***w*** was caught in the
8:9 Jesus and the ***w*** were left in the
8:10 and said to her, "***W***, where are they?
16:21 When a ***w*** gives birth, she has pain
18:16 and spoke to the ***w*** stationed at the
18:17 The servant ***w*** stationed at the gate
19:26 to his mother, "***W***, here is your
20:13 asked her, "***W***, why are you
20:15 said to her, "***W***, why are you

Acts
16:1 believing Jewish ***w*** and a Greek
16:16 we met a slave ***w***. She had a spirit
17:34 on Mars Hill, a ***w*** named Damaris,

Romans
7:2 A married ***w*** is united with her husband

1 Corinthians
7:1 for a man not to have sex with a ***w***."

7:2 wife, and each ***w*** should have her
7:34 is divided. A ***w*** who isn't married
11:6 If a ***w*** doesn't cover her head, then she
11:7 glory of God; but the ***w*** is man's glory.
11:12 As ***w*** came from man so also man comes from woman
14:35 disgraceful for a ***w*** to talk during

Galatians
4:4 born through a ***w***, and born under

1 Thessalonians
5:3 with a pregnant ***w***, and they

1 Timothy
5:16 If any ***w*** who is a believer has widows

Revelation
2:20 put up with that ***w***, Jezebel, who
12:1 in heaven: a ***w*** clothed with the
12:4 in front of the ***w*** who was about to
12:13 he chased the ***w*** who had given
17:3 There I saw a ***w*** seated on a
17:18 The ***w*** whom you saw is the great city

WOMB

Genesis
25:23 are in your ***w***; two different
29:31 he opened her ***w***; but Rachel was
38:27 she discovered she had twins in her ***w***.
49:25 below, blessings from breasts and ***w***.

Exodus
13:2 any Israelite ***w*** belongs to me,
13:12 comes out of the ***w*** first. All of the
13:15 comes out of the ***w***. But I ransom my

Numbers
3:12 open an Israelite ***w***. The Levites are
5:21 a miscarriage and your ***w*** discharges.
5:22 and make your ***w*** discharge and
5:27 and her ***w*** will discharge
12:12 as it comes out of the mother's ***w***."
18:15 male from the ***w*** of any living

Deuteronomy
28:11 fertility of your ***w***, your livestock's
28:53 of your own ***w***—the flesh of your

Ruth
1:11 be sons in my ***w***, that they would

Job
1:21 from my mother's ***w***; naked I will
3:10 of my mother's ***w***, didn't hide
3:11 birth, come forth from the ***w*** and die?
10:18 emerge from the ***w***? I wish I had
24:20 The ***w*** forgets them; the worm consumes
31:15 the same one fashion us in the ***w***?
31:18 from my mother's ***w*** I led the widow),
38:8 doors when it burst forth from the ***w***,

Psalms
22:9 me from the ***w***, placing me
22:10 my God since I was in my mother's ***w***.
58:3 from the ***w***; liars go astray
71:6 from my mother's ***w***. My praise is
110:3 from the dawn's ***w***, fight! Your
127:3 the fruit of the ***w*** is a divine
139:13 while I was still in my mother's ***w***.

Proverbs
30:16 and a barren ***w***, a land never
31:2 No, son of my ***w***! No, son of my

Ecclesiastes
5:15 their mother's ***w*** naked, naked
11:5 pregnant woman's ***w***, so you can't

Isaiah
44:2 formed you in the ***w*** and will help
44:24 formed you in the ***w*** says: I am the
46:3 pregnancy, whom I carried from the ***w***
49:1 my name when I was in my mother's ***w***.
49:5 me from the ***w*** as his servant—
49:15 the child of her ***w***? Even these may
66:9 Will I open the ***w*** and not bring to

Jeremiah
1:5 you in the ***w*** I knew you;
20:17 kill me in the ***w*** and let my mother

Hosea
9:14 them? Give them a ***w*** that miscarries
12:3 From the ***w*** he tried to be the oldest of
13:13 present himself at the mouth of the ***w***.

Luke
1:41 leaped in her ***w***, and Elizabeth
1:44 the baby in my ***w*** jumped for joy.

John
3:4 the mother's ***w*** for a second time

Romans
4:19 as dead, and Sarah's ***w***, which was dead.

WOMEN

Exodus
1:16 the Hebrew ***w*** give birth and

Numbers
25:1 by having illicit sex with Moabite ***w***.
31:16 These very ***w***, on Balaam's advice, made

Deuteronomy
22:5 ***W*** must not wear men's clothes, and men must not wear

Judges
5:24 blessed above all ***w***; may the wife of
21:22 capture enough ***w*** for every man

1 Samuel
2:22 had sex with the ***w*** who served at the
18:7 The ***w*** sang in celebration: "Saul has

2 Samuel
1:26 more amazing to me than the love of ***w***.

1 Kings
11:1 many foreign ***w***, including
11:2 Solomon clung to these ***w*** in love.

2 Kings
8:12 and rip open their pregnant ***w***."
15:16 and ripped open all its pregnant ***w***.
23:7 temple, where ***w*** made woven

Ezra
10:2 marrying foreign ***w*** from the

Nehemiah
13:23 who had married ***w*** of Ashdod, Ammon,
13:27 toward our God by marrying foreign ***w***?"

Esther
2:2 beautiful young ***w*** who haven't yet

Job
14:1 of us are born of ***w***, have few days,
42:15 No ***w*** in all the land were as beautiful

Psalms
45:14 the young ***w*** servants
68:12 on the run! The ***w*** back home divide
68:25 them the young ***w*** were playing hand
78:63 and his young ***w*** had no wedding
148:12 young men—young ***w*** too!—you who are old together

Proverbs
27:27 house, and to nourish your young ***w***.

31:3 your strength to ***w***, your ways to
31:29 Many ***w*** act competently, but you
Ecclesiastes
12:3 stoop; when the ***w*** who grind stop
Song of Songs
1:3 That's why the young ***w*** love you.
1:8 most beautiful of ***w***, then follow the
2:2 so is my dearest among the young ***w***.
5:9 most beautiful of ***w***? How is your
6:1 most beautiful of ***w***? Which way did
6:8 wives, young ***w*** beyond counting,
6:9 bore her. Young ***w*** see her and
Isaiah
4:1 Seven ***w*** will grab one man on that day,
27:11 they are broken. ***W*** come and set fire
32:9 ***W*** of leisure, stand up! Hear my voice!
Jeremiah
9:20 ***W***, hear the LORD's word. Listen
31:13 Then the young ***w*** will dance for joy;
Lamentations
1:4 her young ***w*** grieving. She is
1:18 My young ***w*** and young men
2:10 Jerusalem's young ***w*** bow their heads
2:20 done this! Should ***w*** eat their own
2:21 streets; my young ***w*** and young men
4:10 hands of loving ***w*** boiled their own
5:11 ***W*** have been raped in Zion, young women
Ezekiel
8:14 the temple, where ***w*** were sitting and
13:18 Doom to the ***w*** who sew bands on
18:6 neighbors or approach menstruating ***w***.
44:22 or divorced ***w***, but only
Daniel
11:37 god cherished by ***w***. He will give no
Hosea
13:16 and their pregnant ***w*** ripped open.
Amos
1:13 open pregnant ***w*** in Gilead in
8:13 beautiful young ***w*** and the young men
Micah
2:9 You drive out the ***w*** of my people, each
Nahum
3:13 your people are ***w*** in your midst.
Zechariah
5:9 again and saw two ***w*** going out. There
14:2 and the ***w*** will be raped.
Matthew
24:41 Two ***w*** will be grinding at the mill. One
28:5 angel said to the ***w***, "Don't be
Mark
15:41 in Galilee, these ***w*** had followed and
Luke
1:42 you above all ***w***, and he has
8:2 along with some ***w*** who had been healed
23:27 Jesus, including ***w***, who were
23:55 The ***w*** who had come with Jesus from
John
8:5 us to stone ***w*** like this. What
Acts
1:14 along with some ***w***, including Mary
2:18 servants, men and ***w***, I will pour out
8:12 Christ, both men and ***w*** were baptized.
16:13 to talk with the ***w*** who had gathered.
17:4 and quite a few prominent ***w***.
1 Corinthians
14:34 the ***w*** should be quiet during the
Galatians
4:24 an allegory: the ***w*** are two
Philippians
4:3 to help these ***w*** who have
1 Timothy
2:9 same way, I want ***w*** to enhance their
5:2 treat older ***w*** like your mother, and
2 Timothy
3:6 control immature ***w*** who are burdened
Titus
2:3 tell the older ***w*** to be reverent in
2:4 can mentor young ***w*** to love their
Hebrews
11:35 ***W*** received back their dead by
1 Peter
3:5 way that holy ***w*** who trusted in
2 Peter
1:21 Instead, men and ***w*** led by the Holy
Revelation
14:4 defiled with ***w***, for these people

WONDERFUL
Genesis
30:20 has given me a ***w*** gift. Now my
Deuteronomy
1:25 the LORD our God is giving to us is ***w***!"
11:17 disappear off the ***w*** land the LORD is
Joshua
3:5 the LORD will do ***w*** things among you."
2 Chronicles
26:15 he had received ***w*** help until he
Job
5:9 comprehension, ***w*** things without
21:23 Someone dies in ***w*** health, completely
Psalms
9:1 I will talk about all your ***w*** acts.
26:7 my thanks, declaring all your ***w*** deeds!
40:5 things—your ***w*** deeds and your
98:1 he has done ***w*** things! His own
119:129 Your laws are ***w***! That's why I guard
131:1 with things too great or ***w*** for me.
139:14 Your works are ***w***—I know that very
Proverbs
30:18 things are too ***w*** for me, four that
Isaiah
9:6 He will be named ***W*** Counselor, Mighty
25:1 for you have done ***w*** things, planned
Jeremiah
3:19 to myself, How ***w*** it would be to
Hosea
1:11 The day will be a ***w*** one for Jezreel.
Micah
7:15 of Egypt, I will show Israel ***w*** things.
1 Peter
2:9 may speak of the ***w*** acts of the one
2 Peter
1:4 his precious and ***w*** promises, that

WONDERS → SIGNS AND WONDERS
Deuteronomy
4:34 tests, miracles, ***w***, war, a strong
Nehemiah
9:17 remember the ***w*** that you
Job
9:10 unsearchable things, ***w*** beyond number?
42:3 understand, ***w*** beyond my

Psalms
77:14 the God who works ***w***; you have
78:12 But God performed ***w*** in their ancestors'
88:10 Do you work ***w*** for the dead? Do ghosts
88:12 Are your ***w*** known in the land of
119:18 I can examine the ***w*** of your
136:4 who makes great ***w***—God's faithful
Isaiah
64:3 you accomplished ***w*** beyond all our
Joel
2:26 God, who has done ***w*** for you; and my
Acts
2:19 I will cause ***w*** to occur in the heavens
2:22 through miracles, ***w***, and signs, which
2:43 performed many ***w*** and signs through
6:8 was doing great ***w*** and signs among
7:36 he performed ***w*** and signs in
2 Corinthians
12:12 through signs, ***w***, and miracles.
2 Thessalonians
2:9 all kinds of fake power, signs, and ***w***.

WONDROUS

1 Chronicles
16:9 to him; dwell on all his ***w*** works!
16:12 Remember the ***w*** works he has done, all
16:24 declare his ***w*** works among all
Job
37:5 roars with his ***w*** voice; he does
Psalms
71:17 and I'm still proclaiming your ***w*** deeds!
72:18 the only one who does ***w*** things!
77:11 remember your ***w*** acts from times
78:4 strength—the ***w*** works God has
78:11 as well as the ***w*** works he showed
78:32 and had no faith in God's ***w*** works.
89:5 you for your ***w*** acts, LORD—for y
96:3 declare his ***w*** works among all
105:2 to the Lord; dwell on all his ***w*** works!
105:5 Remember the ***w*** works he has done, all his marvelous
106:7 understand your ***w*** works. They
106:22 ***w*** works in the land of Ham, awesome
107:8 love and his ***w*** works for all
107:15 love and his ***w*** works for all
107:21 love and his ***w*** works for all
107:24 they saw his ***w*** works in the
107:31 love and his ***w*** works for all
111:4 is famous for his ***w*** works. The LORD
119:27 so I can contemplate your ***w*** works!
145:5 I will contemplate your ***w*** works.
Isaiah
28:29 forces, who gives ***w*** counsel and
Jeremiah
33:3 and reveal to you ***w*** secrets that you

WOOD → ACACIA WOOD

Genesis
22:3 He split the ***w*** for the entirely
Exodus
31:5 setting; carve ***w***; and do every
35:33 setting, carve ***w***, do every kind of
Leviticus
1:7 light the altar and lay ***w*** on the fire.
11:32 whether it is ***w***, cloth, skin, or
14:45 stones, ***w***, and all the
Numbers
15:32 a man gathering ***w*** on the Sabbath
31:20 made of leather, goat's hair, or ***w***."
35:18 strikes with a ***w*** object in hand
Deuteronomy
28:64 have known—gods of ***w*** and stone.
Judges
6:26 offering with the ***w*** of the Asherah
1 Samuel
6:14 chopped up the ***w*** of the cart and
2 Samuel
24:22 threshing boards and oxen yokes for ***w***.
1 Kings
18:23 and set it on the ***w***, but don't add
Nehemiah
10:34 that we bring the ***w*** offering into our
13:31 provided for the ***w*** offering at
Job
41:27 iron as straw, bronze as rotten ***w***.
Psalms
120:4 with burning coals from a ***w*** fire!
Proverbs
26:20 Without ***w*** a fire goes out; without
26:21 to embers or ***w*** to fire,
Isaiah
44:19 Should I bow down to a block of ***w***?
60:17 instead of ***w***, bronze; and
Jeremiah
2:27 say to a piece of ***w***, "You are my
7:18 children gather ***w***, the fathers
10:8 offer nothing because they are mere ***w***.
Lamentations
4:8 on their bones; it became dry like ***w***.
5:4 we gather our own ***w***—but pay for it.
5:13 boys have stumbled under loads of ***w***.
Ezekiel
20:32 lands in the service of ***w*** and stone."
Daniel
5:4 silver, bronze, iron, ***w***, and stone.
5:23 bronze, iron, ***w***, and stone—gods
Hosea
4:12 from a piece of ***w***, and their
10:7 is like a chip of ***w*** on the surface of
Haggai
1:8 and bring back ***w***. Rebuild the
Zechariah
5:4 and destroy the ***w*** and stones of
12:6 like a pot on a ***w*** fire and like a
1 Corinthians
3:12 precious stones, ***w***, grass, or hay,
2 Timothy
2:20 that are made of ***w*** and clay. Some
Revelation
9:20 stone, and ***w***—idols that can't
18:12 made of scented ***w***, ivory, fine

WOOL

Deuteronomy
22:11 clothes that mix ***w*** and linen
2 Kings
3:4 lambs and the ***w*** from one hundred
Job
31:20 weren't warmed by the ***w*** from my sheep;
Psalms
147:16 snow like it was ***w***; God scatters

Proverbs
31:13 She seeks out ***w*** and flax; she works
Isaiah
1:18 as crimson, they will become like ***w***.
51:8 eat them like ***w***, but my
Ezekiel
27:18 wealth the wine of Helbon and white ***w***.
34:3 you wear the ***w***, and you
44:17 won't wear any ***w*** when they
Daniel
7:9 was like a lamb's ***w***. His throne was
Hosea
2:5 and my water, my ***w*** and my linen
2:9 will take away my ***w*** and my linen
Hebrews
9:19 water, scarlet ***w***, and hyssop, and
Revelation
1:14 white as white ***w***—like snow

WORD → GOD'S WORD, HEAR THE LORD'S WORD
Genesis
15:1 the LORD's ***w*** came to Abram in
Exodus
9:20 took the LORD's ***w*** seriously rushed
18:6 He sent ***w*** to Moses: "I, your
Numbers
30:2 cannot break his ***w***. He must do
36:5 to the LORD's ***w***: "The tribe of
36:6 This is the ***w*** that the LORD commands to Zelophehad's
Deuteronomy
30:14 Not at all! The ***w*** is very close to you.
Joshua
2:3 of Jericho sent ***w*** to Rahab: "Send
8:8 to the LORD's ***w***. Indeed, I have
22:32 of Canaan. They brought ***w*** back to them.
1 Samuel
3:1 Eli. The LORD's ***w*** was rare at that
3:21 at Shiloh through the LORD's own ***w***.
4:1 And Samuel's ***w*** went out to all Israel.
15:10 Then the LORD's ***w*** came to Samuel
1 Kings
17:2 Then the LORD's ***w*** came to Elijah
22:19 now to the LORD's ***w***: I saw the LORD
2 Kings
2:22 agreement with the ***w*** that Elisha spoke.
2 Chronicles
35:6 to the LORD's ***w*** through Moses."
36:15 ancestors, sent ***w*** to them through
36:21 is how the LORD's ***w*** spoken by
Ezra
1:1 the LORD's ***w*** spoken by
Nehemiah
1:8 Remember the ***w*** that you gave to your
Psalms
33:4 the LORD's ***w*** is right, his
56:4 in God, whose ***w*** I praise. I trust in
56:10 God: whose ***w*** I praise. The LORD: whose
119:11 I keep your ***w*** close, in my heart, so
119:42 me, because I have trusted in your ***w***!
119:89 Your ***w***, LORD, stands firm in heaven
119:105 Your ***w*** is a lamp before my feet and a
138:2 your name and ***w*** greater than
139:4 There isn't a ***w*** on my tongue, LORD,
Proverbs
12:25 to depression, but a good ***w*** encourages.
13:13 who despise a ***w***, but those who
15:1 but an offensive ***w*** stirs up anger.
15:23 joy; how good is a ***w*** at the right time!
Ecclesiastes
8:4 the king's ***w*** has authority, no
Isaiah
55:11 so is my ***w*** that comes from my mouth; it does not return
66:5 to the LORD's ***w***, you who tremble
Jeremiah
5:13 so much wind; the ***w*** isn't in them.
23:29 Isn't my ***w*** like fire and like a hammer
Lamentations
1:18 I disobeyed his ***w***. Listen, all you
2:17 accomplished the ***w*** that he had
Ezekiel
1:3 The LORD's ***w*** burst in on the priest
Daniel
9:2 to the LORD's ***w*** to the prophet
Hosea
1:1 The LORD's ***w*** that came to Hosea,
Joel
1:1 The LORD's ***w*** that came to Joel,
2:11 who obey his ***w***. The day of the
Amos
3:1 Hear this ***w*** that the LORD has spoken
4:1 Hear this ***w***, you cows of Bashan, who
5:1 Hear this ***w***—a funeral song—that I am lifting up
8:12 the LORD's ***w***, but they won't
Jonah
1:1 The LORD's ***w*** came to Jonah, Amittai's
Micah
1:1 The LORD's ***w*** that came to Micah of
4:2 Zion and the LORD's ***w*** from Jerusalem.
Zephaniah
1:1 The LORD's ***w*** that came to Zephaniah,
2:5 The LORD's ***w*** is against you,
Haggai
1:1 The LORD's ***w*** came through Haggai the
Zechariah
1:1 the LORD's ***w*** came to Zechariah
11:11 flock knew that it was the LORD's ***w***.
Malachi
1:1 The LORD's ***w*** to Israel through
Matthew
4:4 bread, but by every ***w*** spoken by God."
12:36 Day for every useless ***w*** they speak.
Mark
4:14 The farmer scatters the ***w***
16:20 confirming the ***w*** by the signs
Luke
1:2 servants of the ***w*** handed down to us.
12:10 who speaks a ***w*** against the Human
John
1:1 beginning was the ***W*** and the Word was
1:14 The ***W*** became flesh and made his home
8:51 whoever keeps my ***w*** will never die."
17:17 holy in the truth; your ***w*** is truth.
21:23 Therefore, the ***w*** spread among the
Acts
6:4 and the service of proclaiming the ***w***."
19:10 Jews and Greeks—heard the Lord's ***w***.
19:20 way the Lord's ***w*** grew abundantly
20:30 will distort the ***w*** in order to lure

WORD [cont.]

Romans
10:8 does it say? The ***w*** is near you, in
13:9 summed up in one ***w***: You must love
1 Corinthians
12:8 A ***w*** of wisdom is given by the Spirit to
14:36 Did the ***w*** of God originate with you?
2 Corinthians
2:17 who hustle the ***w*** of God to make a
Galatians
6:6 are taught the ***w*** should share all
Ephesians
1:13 You too heard the ***w*** of truth in Christ,
5:26 her in a bath of water with the ***w***.
Philippians
1:14 Lord to speak the ***w*** boldly and
2:16 hold on to the ***w*** of life. This
Colossians
3:16 The ***w*** of Christ must live in you
4:3 a door for the ***w*** so we can preach
2 Timothy
4:2 Preach the ***w***. Be ready to do it
Hebrews
5:13 not used to the ***w*** of righteousness,
6:1 about Christ's ***w***. Let's not lay a
6:5 tasted God's good ***w*** and the powers of
11:3 been created by a ***w*** from God so that
12:19 beg that there wouldn't be one more ***w***.
James
1:18 birth by his true ***w***, and here is the
1:21 and welcome the ***w*** planted deep
1:22 be doers of the ***w*** and not only
1:23 but don't do the ***w*** are like those
1 Peter
1:23 is God's life-giving and enduring ***w***.
1:25 but the Lord's ***w*** endures forever. This
2:2 pure milk of the ***w***. Nourished by it,
2:8 to believe in the ***w***, they stumble.
3:1 to believe the ***w***, they may be won
2 Peter
1:19 prophetic ***w***, and you would do
3:7 But by the same ***w***, heaven and earth
1 John
1:1 our hands handled, about the ***w*** of life.
1:10 make him a liar and his ***w*** is not in us.
2:5 whoever keeps his ***w***. This is how we
2:14 are strong, the ***w*** of God remains in
Revelation
1:2 witness to the ***w*** of God and to the
1:9 because of the ***w*** of God and my
3:8 you have kept my ***w*** and haven't
6:9 on account of the ***w*** of God and the
12:11 the Lamb and the ***w*** of their witness.
19:13 and his name was called the ***W*** of God.

WORDS → GOD'S WORDS

Genesis
4:23 attention to my ***w***: I killed a man
Exodus
20:1 Then God spoke all these ***w***
24:3 all the LORD's ***w*** and all the case
34:28 the tablets the ***w*** of the covenant,
Numbers
11:24 people the LORD's ***w***. He assembled
22:7 came to Balaam and told him Balak's ***w***.
Deuteronomy
11:18 Place these ***w*** I'm speaking on your
18:19 listen to my ***w***, which that
31:24 entirety all the ***w*** of this
32:45 speaking all these ***w*** to all Israel,
Joshua
8:34 aloud all the ***w*** of the
Judges
2:4 spoke these ***w*** to all the
13:17 may honor you when your ***w*** come true?"
16:16 him with her ***w*** day after day and
1 Samuel
3:19 him, not allowing any of his ***w*** to fail.
15:1 Israel. Listen now to the LORD's ***w***!
21:12 David took these ***w*** very seriously and
2 Samuel
7:28 truly God! Your ***w*** are trustworthy,
23:1 are David's last ***w***: This is the
1 Kings
1:14 I'll come along and support your ***w***."
12:7 and speaking good ***w*** today," they
12:24 heard the LORD's ***w***, they went back
13:11 their father the ***w*** that he spoke to
2 Kings
22:16 citizens-all the ***w*** in the scroll
23:2 out loud all the ***w*** of the covenant
23:3 to fulfill the ***w*** of this covenant
2 Chronicles
11:4 heard the LORD's ***w***, they abandoned
18:27 added, "Mark my ***w***, every last one
29:30 LORD by using the ***w*** of David and the
Ezra
9:4 trembled at the ***w*** of the God of
Nehemiah
1:1 These are the ***w*** of Nehemiah, Hacaliah's
8:9 they heard the ***w*** of the
8:13 to study the ***w*** of the
Esther
3:4 or not Mordecai's ***w*** would hold true.
9:30 good wishes and ***w*** of friendship
Job
4:2 be annoyed? But who can hold ***w*** back?
4:4 Your ***w*** have raised up the falling;
6:3 of the sea; therefore, my ***w*** are rash.
6:10 I've not denied the ***w*** of the holy one.
42:7 had spoken these ***w*** to Job, he said
Psalms
5:1 David.] Hear my ***w***, LORD! Consider
18:1 who spoke the ***w*** of this song to
19:3 no speech, no ***w***—their voices can
19:4 the world; their ***w*** reach the ends of
19:14 Let the ***w*** of my mouth and the
36:3 The ***w*** of their mouths are evil and
50:17 and you toss my ***w*** behind your back.
52:4 all destructive ***w***; you love the
54:2 my prayer; listen to the ***w*** of my mouth!
55:21 heart; though his ***w*** are more silky
59:12 their mouths, the ***w*** that they speak,
64:5 with evil ***w***. They plan on
78:1 your ears toward the ***w*** of my mouth.
94:4 spew arrogant ***w***; all the
109:3 Hateful ***w*** surround me; they attack me
119:130 Access to your ***w*** gives light, giving
141:6 cliffs, but my ***w*** will be heard
Proverbs
1:6 sayings, the ***w*** of the wise, and
1:23 spirit on you. I'll reveal my ***w*** to you.
2:1 My son, accept my ***w*** and store up my
2:12 path, from people who twist their ***w***.

2:16 the foreign woman with her slick ***w***.
4:4 hold on to my ***w***: Keep my commands
4:5 forget and don't turn away from my ***w***.
4:20 attention to my ***w***. Bend your ear to
5:7 don't deviate from the ***w*** of my mouth.
6:2 trapped by your ***w***; you will be
7:1 My son, keep my ***w***; store up my
8:8 All the ***w*** of my mouth are righteous;
10:19 With lots of ***w*** comes wrongdoing, but
11:9 by their ***w***, but the
11:11 it is destroyed by the ***w*** of the wicked.
12:6 The ***w*** of the wicked are a deathtrap,
13:2 fruit of their ***w***, but the
13:5 hate false ***w***, but the wicked
15:26 evil plans, but gracious ***w*** are pure.
16:10 a judgment, one can't go against his ***w***.
16:13 lips; they love ***w*** of integrity.
16:24 Pleasant ***w*** are flowing honey, sweet to
18:4 The ***w*** of a person's mouth are deep
18:8 The ***w*** of gossips are like choice
19:7 pursue them with ***w***, they aren't
19:27 will wander away from ***w*** of knowledge.
22:12 he frustrates the ***w*** of the
22:17 ear and hear the ***w*** of the wise;
22:18 if you keep the ***w*** in you, if you
22:21 true, reliable ***w*** so you can report
23:8 out. You will waste your pleasant ***w***.
23:9 for they will scorn your insightful ***w***.
23:33 and your heart will speak distorted ***w***.
25:11 ***W*** spoken at the right time are like
26:22 The ***w*** of gossips are like choice
29:19 disciplined by ***w***; they might
30:1 The ***w*** of Agur, Jakeh's son, from Massa.
30:6 Don't add to his ***w***, or he will correct
31:1 The ***w*** of King Lemuel of Massa, which

Ecclesiastes
1:1 The ***w*** of the Teacher of the Assembly,
5:2 on earth. Therefore, let your ***w*** be few.
5:3 and the voice of fools with many ***w***.
6:11 Because the more ***w*** increase, the more
12:11 The ***w*** of the wise are like iron-tipped

Isaiah
29:4 from the dust your ***w*** will whisper.
59:21 upon you, and my ***w***, which I have

Jeremiah
15:16 When your ***w*** turned up, I feasted on
30:2 a scroll all the ***w*** I have spoken to
51:64 against it." Jeremiah's ***w*** end here.

Ezekiel
2:6 of them or their ***w***. Don't be afraid!
35:13 me and spoke your ***w*** against me. I

Daniel
9:12 God confirmed the ***w*** he spoke against us
12:4 must keep these ***w*** secret! Seal the

Hosea
6:5 them by the ***w*** of my mouth, and
10:4 have spoken empty ***w***, swearing falsely

Amos
1:1 These are the ***w*** of Amos, one of the
8:11 water, but of hearing the LORD 's ***w***.

Micah
2:7 deeds?" Don't my ***w*** help the one who

Haggai
1:12 God and to the ***w*** of Haggai the

Zechariah
1:6 fact, didn't my ***w*** and laws, which I

Malachi
2:17 tired with your ***w***. You say, "How

Matthew
7:24 who hears these ***w*** of mine and puts
12:37 By your ***w*** you will be either judged
24:35 pass away, but my ***w*** will certainly

Mark
6:20 him. John's ***w*** greatly confused
12:13 of Herod to trap him in his ***w***.
13:31 pass away, but my ***w*** will certainly
14:39 them and prayed, repeating the same ***w***.

Luke
6:47 to me, hears my ***w***, and puts them
19:22 judge you by the ***w*** of your own
24:44 These are my ***w*** that I spoke to

John
6:68 we go? You have the ***w*** of eternal life.
15:7 in me and my ***w*** remain in you,

Acts
5:5 heard these ***w***, he dropped dead.
7:22 he was a man of powerful ***w*** and deeds.

Romans
3:4 are right in your ***w***; and you will
9:9 The ***w*** in the promise were: A year from

1 Corinthians
2:13 about—not with ***w*** taught by human
14:19 rather speak five ***w*** in my right mind

2 Corinthians
9:3 won't be empty ***w***, and so that you
9:15 God for his gift that ***w*** can't describe!
12:4 heard unspeakable ***w*** that were things

Ephesians
4:29 let any foul ***w*** come out of your

1 Thessalonians
4:18 So encourage each other with these ***w***

1 Timothy
4:6 trained by the ***w*** of faith and the

2 Timothy
2:14 in battles over ***w*** that aren't

Hebrews
12:19 and a sound of ***w*** that made the
12:27 The ***w*** "still once more" reveal the

James
3:2 with their ***w*** have reached full

1 Peter
1:8 a glorious joy that is too much for ***w***.

1 John
3:18 not love with ***w*** or speech but

Jude
1:16 speak arrogant ***w*** and they show
1:17 remember the ***w*** spoken beforehand

Revelation
1:3 one who reads the ***w*** of this prophecy
22:6 to me, "These ***w*** are trustworthy
22:19 away from the ***w*** of this scroll of

WORK

Genesis
2:2 completed all the ***w*** that he had done,

Exodus
20:10 Do not do any ***w*** on it—not you
23:12 Do your ***w*** in six days. But on the
32:16 were God's own ***w***. What was written
40:33 When Moses had finished all the ***w***,

Leviticus
11:32 can be used to do ***w***. It must be put
23:35 You must not do any job-related ***w***.

25:46 make these people ***w*** as slaves, but
Numbers
3:7 tent, doing the ***w*** of the dwelling.
4:49 through Moses to ***w*** and to carry his
28:18 You will not do any job-related ***w***.
Deuteronomy
5:13 Six days you may ***w*** and do all your
5:14 God. Don't do any ***w*** on it—not you
23:20 you in all your ***w*** on the land you
28:12 blessing all your ***w***. You will lend to
33:11 favors his hard ***w***, and crushes the
Ruth
2:19 Where did you ***w***? May the one who
1 Samuel
8:16 and donkeys, and make them do his ***w***.
2 Samuel
9:10 You will ***w*** the land for him—you, your
12:31 and put them to ***w*** making bricks.
19:18 to do the ***w*** of ferrying over the king's
1 Kings
7:40 finished his ***w*** on the LORD's
2 Kings
12:11 supervised the ***w*** on the temple.
25:12 people behind to ***w*** the vineyards and
1 Chronicles
22:16 iron. So get to ***w***, and may the LORD
2 Chronicles
2:7 engraver. He will ***w*** with my craftsmen
8:16 All Solomon's ***w*** was carried out from
32:19 he were the ***w*** of human hands,
Ezra
4:24 At that time the ***w*** on God's house in
6:7 Leave the ***w*** on this house of God alone.
6:22 them in the ***w*** on the house of
Esther
2:21 continued to ***w*** at the King's
Job
1:10 blessed the ***w*** of his hands so
Psalms
64:9 of God, will understand it was God's ***w***.
73:16 things, it just seemed like hard ***w***
88:10 Do you ***w*** wonders for the dead? Do
90:10 brings hard ***w*** and trouble
90:17 over us. Make the ***w*** of our hands
96:2 news of his saving ***w*** every single day!
101:6 who walks without blame will ***w*** for me.
104:23 go off to their ***w***, to do their work
107:12 them with hard ***w***. They stumbled,
127:1 the builders' ***w*** is pointless.
Proverbs
5:10 and your hard ***w*** will end up in a
10:4 brings poverty; hard ***w*** makes one rich.
12:11 Those who ***w*** their land will have plenty
12:14 satisfied; their ***w*** results in reward.
14:23 is profit in hard ***w***, but mere talk
16:3 Commit your ***w*** to the LORD, and your
18:9 are lazy in their ***w*** are brothers to
22:29 see people who ***w*** skillfully? They
24:27 Get your outside ***w*** done; make
28:19 Those who ***w*** the land will have plenty
31:31 results of her ***w***; let her deeds
Ecclesiastes
1:3 from all the hard ***w*** that they work so
3:13 and enjoy the results of their hard ***w***.
11:5 understand the ***w*** of God, who makes
Song of Songs
7:1 fine jewelry, the ***w*** of an artist's
Isaiah
64:8 All of us are the ***w*** of your hand.
Jeremiah
10:9 they are the ***w*** of a craftsman
48:10 doing the LORD's ***w***. Cursed is the
Ezekiel
44:14 temple, all its ***w***, and all that is
Daniel
6:4 with Daniel's ***w*** for the kingdom.
Hosea
13:2 all of them the ***w*** of craftsmen.
14:3 Our God,' to the ***w*** of our hands. In
Jonah
4:10 which you didn't ***w*** and which you
Habakkuk
3:2 I have seen your ***w***. Over time,
Haggai
1:14 they came and did ***w*** on the house of
2:4 says the LORD. ***W***, for I am with
Matthew
6:28 out with ***w***, and they don't
13:54 did he get the power to ***w*** miracles?
14:2 powers are at ***w*** through him."
20:12 though we had to ***w*** the whole day in
21:28 Son, go and ***w*** in the vineyard
25:16 them and went to ***w*** doing business
Mark
6:14 powers are at ***w*** through him."
16:9 through the ***w*** of his disciples,
Luke
7:41 for a day's ***w***. The other owed
12:27 out with ***w***, and they don't
13:14 days during which ***w*** is permitted.
13:32 on the third day I will complete my ***w***.
John
4:34 who sent me and by completing his ***w***.
4:38 what you didn't ***w*** hard for; others
6:27 Don't ***w*** for the food that doesn't last
7:21 I did one ***w***, and you were all
9:4 me. Night is coming when no one can ***w***.
10:33 you for a good ***w*** but for insulting
17:4 by finishing the ***w*** you gave me to do.
Acts
13:2 and Saul to the ***w*** I have called
21:9 who were involved in the ***w*** of prophecy.
Romans
2:7 based on their patient good ***w***.
4:5 those who don't ***w***, because they
7:5 the Law were at ***w*** in all the parts
7:23 different law at ***w*** in my body. It
15:23 have any place to ***w*** in these regions
1 Corinthians
3:8 one who waters ***w*** together, but
3:13 each one's ***w*** will be clearly shown. The
4:12 We ***w*** hard with our own hands. When we are insulted
16:10 he does the ***w*** of the Lord just
2 Corinthians
6:5 experienced hard ***w***, sleepless
8:18 because of his ***w*** for the gospel
8:19 companion in this ***w*** of grace, which
9:8 than enough for every kind of good ***w***.
10:13 boundaries of our ***w*** area that God has
11:27 dangers with hard ***w*** and heavy labor,
Galatians
4:11 Perhaps my hard ***w*** for you has been

6:4 test their own ***w*** and be happy with
6:10 So then, let's ***w*** for the good of all
Ephesians
3:20 or imagine by his power at ***w*** within us;
Philippians
1:6 started a good ***w*** in you will stay
Colossians
1:10 in every good ***w*** and growing in
1:29 I ***w*** hard and struggle for this goal
2 Thessalonians
2:7 any law is at ***w*** now, but it will
3:10 doesn't want to ***w***, they shouldn't
1 Timothy
4:10 We ***w*** and struggle for this: "Our hope
5:17 those who ***w*** with public
2 Timothy
2:21 the mansion for every sort of good ***w***.
4:5 suffering, do the ***w*** of a preacher of
Hebrews
3:9 they had seen my ***w*** for forty years.
James
1:4 complete its ***w*** so that you may
2:22 his faith was at ***w*** along with his
3:6 world of evil at ***w*** in us. It
1 Peter
1:2 the Holy Spirit's ***w*** of making you

WORKED
Genesis
29:20 Jacob ***w*** for Rachel for seven years, but
29:30 than Leah. He ***w*** for Laban seven
30:26 whom I've ***w*** for, and I will
30:29 know how I've ***w*** for you, and how
31:6 know that I've ***w*** for your father
31:41 your household. I ***w*** for fourteen
Exodus
36:8 heavenly creatures ***w*** into their design.
36:35 heavenly creatures ***w*** into its design.
Numbers
4:37 clans, all who ***w*** in the meeting
4:41 clans, all who ***w*** in the meeting
Deuteronomy
15:18 because they ***w*** for you for six
Judges
2:15 the LORD's power ***w*** against them,
16:21 chains, and he ***w*** the grinding mill
Ruth
2:19 with whom she had ***w*** and said, "The
2 Kings
12:11 to those who ***w*** on the LORD's
17:32 These priests ***w*** in the houses at
2 Chronicles
34:12 The men ***w*** conscientiously under the
Esther
3:1 above all the officials who ***w*** with him.
Psalms
99:4 what is fair. You ***w*** justice and
128:2 enjoy what you've ***w*** hard for—you'll
Ecclesiastes
2:11 and what I had ***w*** so hard to
2:18 the things I ***w*** so hard for here
2:21 those who have ***w*** hard with wisdom,
Daniel
4:2 the Most High God has ***w*** in my life.
Matthew
13:33 the yeast had ***w*** its way through
20:12 were hired last ***w*** one hour, and
Mark
16:20 The Lord ***w*** with them,
Luke
5:5 Master, we've ***w*** hard all night
13:21 the yeast had ***w*** its way through
John
4:38 hard for; others ***w*** hard, and you
Acts
18:3 he stayed and ***w*** with them. They
19:19 make if they ***w*** for one hundred
Romans
16:6 to Mary, who has ***w*** very hard for you.
16:12 Persis, who has ***w*** hard in the Lord.
1 Corinthians
15:10 In fact, I have ***w*** harder than all
2 Corinthians
11:23 done. I've ***w*** much harder. I've
Galatians
2:2 working or that I hadn't ***w*** for nothing.
Philippians
2:16 run for nothing or ***w*** for nothing.
Colossians
2:14 requirements that ***w*** against us. He
4:13 him that he has ***w*** hard for you and
1 Thessalonians
2:9 to you, while we ***w*** night and day so
2 Thessalonians
3:8 it. Instead, we ***w*** night and day
2 John
1:8 lose what we've ***w*** for but instead

WORKERS → SKILLED WORKERS
Deuteronomy
24:14 of poor or needy ***w***, whether they are
Ruth
2:21 me, 'Stay with my ***w*** until they've
1 Kings
5:13 thirty thousand ***w*** from all over
2 Chronicles
24:13 The ***w*** labored hard, and the restoration
26:10 He had many ***w*** who tended his
34:13 and all the ***w***, no matter what
34:17 it over to the supervisors and the ***w***."
Ezra
3:9 to supervise the ***w*** in God's house.
Nehemiah
4:16 only half of my ***w*** continued in the
Esther
3:2 All the royal ***w*** at the King's Gate
Job
31:3 wicked, destruction for ***w*** of iniquity?
Proverbs
12:27 prey, but hard ***w*** receive precious
16:26 The appetite of ***w*** labors for them, for
Ecclesiastes
3:9 What do ***w*** gain from all their hard
Isaiah
19:9 ***W*** with flax will be dismayed; carders
58:3 you want, and oppress all your ***w***.
Jeremiah
49:9 If ***w*** would come to you to pick grapes,
Ezekiel
48:18 will produce the food for the city's ***w***.
48:19 The city's ***w*** from every tribe of Israel
Hosea
4:14 with consecrated ***w*** at temples; so

Matthew
9:37 you can imagine, but there are few ***w***.
10:9 ***W*** deserve to be fed, so don't gather
20:1 the morning to hire ***w*** for his vineyard.
20:8 Call the ***w*** and give them
Mark
1:20 Zebedee in the boat with the hired ***w***.
Luke
10:2 but there are few ***w***. Therefore plead
10:7 before you, for ***w*** deserve their
Romans
16:12 Tryphosa, who are ***w*** for the Lord. Say
2 Corinthians
11:13 and dishonest ***w*** who disguise
Colossians
4:11 my only fellow ***w*** for God's kingdom
1 Timothy
5:18 treads grain, and ***W*** deserve their pay.

WORKING

Ecclesiastes
4:6 one handful than ***w*** hard for two
4:8 So for whom am I ***w*** so hard and
5:16 do they gain from ***w*** so hard for wind?
12:3 who grind stop ***w*** because they're
John
5:17 Father is still ***w*** and I am working
Acts
1:2 he was taken up, ***w*** in the power of
19:25 and others ***w*** in related trades
20:35 you that, by ***w*** hard, we must
Galatians
5:6 Jesus, but faith ***w*** through love does
Ephesians
1:19 power that is ***w*** among us

WORKS

Judges
6:13 all his amazing ***w*** that our
1 Chronicles
16:9 to him; dwell on all his wondrous ***w***!
16:12 the wondrous ***w*** he has done, all
16:24 declare his wondrous ***w*** among all people
Nehemiah
9:35 serve you or turn from their wicked ***w***.
Esther
6:10 the Jew, who ***w*** at the King's
Psalms
45:1 as I mention my ***w*** to the king. My
66:3 awesome are your ***w***! Because of your
66:5 God's deeds; his ***w*** for human beings
73:28 God, so I can talk all about your ***w***!
77:12 on all your ***w***; I will ponder
77:14 are the God who ***w*** wonders; you have
78:4 strength—the wondrous ***w*** God has done.
78:11 well as the wondrous ***w*** he showed them.
78:32 and had no faith in God's wondrous ***w***.
78:43 his marvelous ***w*** in the field of
86:8 is nothing that can compare to your ***w***!
92:5 awesome are your ***w***, LORD! Your
96:3 declare his wondrous ***w*** among all people
103:6 The LORD ***w*** righteousness; does justice
105:2 the Lord; dwell on all his wondrous ***w***!
105:5 the wondrous ***w*** he has done, all
105:27 his marvelous ***w*** on the land of
106:7 your wondrous ***w***. They didn't
106:22 wondrous ***w*** in the land of Ham, awesome deeds at the Reed
107:8 love and his wondrous ***w*** for all people
107:15 love and his wondrous ***w*** for all people
107:21 love and his wondrous ***w*** for all people.
107:24 saw his wondrous ***w*** in the depths of
107:31 love and his wondrous ***w*** for all people.
111:2 The ***w*** of the LORD are magnificent; they are treasured
111:4 for his wondrous ***w***. The LORD is full
119:27 so I can contemplate your wondrous ***w***!
139:14 set apart. Your ***w*** are wonderful—I
145:4 will praise your ***w*** to the next one,
145:5 I will contemplate your wondrous ***w***.
Proverbs
31:13 and flax; she ***w*** joyfully with her
31:17 She ***w*** energetically; her arms are
Isaiah
44:12 with his tools ***w*** it over coals,
Jeremiah
1:16 and trusting in the ***w*** of their hands.
Ezekiel
6:6 shattered, and all your ***w*** wiped out.
Daniel
4:37 heaven. All his ***w*** are truth, all
Micah
5:13 longer bow down to the ***w*** of your hands!
Zechariah
13:5 I'm a man who ***w*** the ground, for
Matthew
11:19 wisdom is proved to be right by her ***w***."
John
5:20 show him greater ***w*** than these so
7:3 can see the amazing ***w*** that you do.
7:7 because I testify that its ***w*** are evil.
8:39 children, you would do Abraham's ***w***.
9:3 that God's mighty ***w*** might be
9:4 we must do the ***w*** of him who sent
10:37 If I don't do the ***w*** of my Father, don't
14:10 The Father who dwells in me does his ***w***.
14:11 believe on account of the ***w*** themselves.
14:12 in me will do the ***w*** that I do. They
15:24 If I hadn't done ***w*** among them that no
Acts
2:11 the mighty ***w*** of God in our own
9:36 with good ***w*** and compassionate
Romans
2:6 will repay everyone based on their ***w***.
8:28 We know that God ***w*** all things together
1 Corinthians
16:16 of anyone who cooperates and ***w*** hard.
Galatians
2:16 righteous by the ***w*** of the Law but
3:2 by doing the ***w*** of the Law or by
3:5 by you doing the ***w*** of the Law or by
3:10 who rely on the ***w*** of the Law are
5:9 A little yeast ***w*** through the whole lump
Philippians
2:22 gospel like a son ***w*** with his father.
Colossians
1:29 his energy, which ***w*** in me powerfully.
2 Timothy
4:14 the craftsman who ***w*** with metal, has

Hebrews
4:3 And yet God's ***w*** were completed at
4:4 on the seventh day from all his ***w***.
4:10 rested from his ***w***, just as God
6:1 away from dead ***w***, of faith in God,
9:14 clean from dead ***w*** in order to serve
10:24 other to show love and to do good ***w***.
2 Peter
3:10 earth and all the ***w*** done on it will
1 John
3:8 purpose: to destroy the ***w*** of the devil.
3:12 because his own ***w*** were evil, but
Revelation
2:2 I know your ***w***, your labor, and your
15:3 are your ***w***, Lord God

WORLD

Exodus
9:14 there is no one like me in the whole ***w***.
9:16 to make my name known in the whole ***w***.
1 Samuel
2:8 the LORD; he set the ***w*** on top of them!
17:46 Then the whole ***w*** will know that
1 Chronicles
16:14 is everywhere throughout the whole ***w***.
16:30 Yes, he set the ***w*** firmly in place;
2 Chronicles
16:9 scan the whole ***w*** to strengthen
Job
18:18 into darkness, banished from the ***w***.
34:13 gave him dominion over the entire ***w***?
37:13 for his ***w***, or for kindness,
Psalms
9:8 justice in the ***w*** rightly; he will
19:4 throughout the ***w***; their words
24:1 in it, the ***w*** and its
46:2 afraid when the ***w*** falls apart, when
46:9 corner of the ***w***, breaking the bow
46:10 I am exalted throughout the ***w***!"
47:2 he is the great king of the whole ***w***.
47:7 king of the whole ***w***! Sing praises
48:2 joy of the whole ***w***. Mount Zion, in
49:1 closely, all you citizens of the ***w***
50:12 because the whole ***w*** and everything in
77:18 lit up the whole ***w***; the earth shook
89:11 earth too! The ***w*** and all that
90:2 and the inhabited ***w***—from forever in
93:1 Yes, he set the ***w*** firmly in place;
96:10 Yes, he set the ***w*** firmly in place;
96:13 justice in the ***w*** rightly. He will
97:4 lights up the ***w***; the earth sees
97:5 LORD, before the Lord of the whole ***w***!
98:7 in it roar; the ***w*** and all its
98:9 justice in the ***w*** rightly; he will
105:7 is everywhere throughout the whole ***w***.
119:64 LORD, the ***w*** is full of your faithful
Ecclesiastes
5:19 place in the ***w*** and to find
Isaiah
13:11 disaster upon the ***w*** for its evil, and
Jeremiah
10:12 he shaped the ***w*** by his wisdom,
Lamentations
4:12 who inhabit the ***w***—that either
Ezekiel
26:20 you in the ***w*** below, in the
35:14 As the whole ***w*** rejoices, I will
Daniel
9:12 happened anywhere else in the entire ***w***!
Nahum
1:5 before him—the ***w*** and all who dwell
Matthew
4:8 the kingdoms of the ***w*** and their glory.
5:14 the light of the ***w***. A city on top of
16:26 gain the whole ***w*** but lose their
26:13 in the whole ***w*** this good news is
Mark
8:36 gain the whole ***w*** but lose their
13:19 such as the ***w*** has never before
14:9 in the whole ***w*** the good news is
16:15 into the whole ***w*** and proclaim the
Luke
4:5 instant all the kingdoms of the ***w***.
9:25 gain the whole ***w*** for themselves
12:30 nations of the ***w*** long for these
16:8 belong to this ***w*** are more clever
21:26 of what is coming upon the ***w***.
John
1:10 light was in the ***w***, and the world
1:29 of God who takes away the sin of the ***w***!
3:16 God so loved the ***w*** that he gave his
3:17 his Son into the ***w*** to judge the
8:12 the light of the ***w***. Whoever follows
9:5 While I am in the ***w***, I am the light of
15:19 belonged to the ***w***, the world would
16:33 in me. In the ***w*** you have
17:18 sent me into the ***w***, so I have sent
18:36 from this ***w***. If it did, my
Acts
4:12 the whole ***w***, no other name
11:28 the entire Roman ***w***. (This occurred
17:24 God, who made the ***w*** and everything in
17:31 to judge the ***w*** justly by a man
19:27 entire civilized ***w***—worships her, but
Romans
3:19 it so the whole ***w*** has to answer to
5:12 sin entered the ***w*** through one
10:18 out to the corners of the inhabited ***w***.
1 Corinthians
1:27 chose what the ***w*** considers foolish
3:22 Cephas, the ***w***, life, death,
6:2 will judge the ***w***? If the world is
2 Corinthians
5:19 reconciling the ***w*** to himself
Galatians
4:9 and worthless ***w*** system? Do you
6:14 Jesus Christ. The ***w*** has been
Ephesians
1:4 presence before the creation of the ***w***.
2:2 people in our ***w*** do. You followed
2:12 promise. In this ***w*** you had no hope
Philippians
1:22 to live in this ***w***, I get results
1:24 for me to stay in this ***w*** for your sake.
2:15 people you shine like stars in the ***w***
Colossians
1:6 fruit and growing in the whole ***w***.
2:8 and the way the ***w*** thinks and acts
2:20 to the way the ***w*** thinks and acts,
1 Timothy
1:15 came into the ***w*** to save sinners"—
3:16 in around the ***w***, and taken up in

6:7 anything into the ***w*** and so we can't
2 Timothy
4:10 with the present ***w*** and has deserted
Titus
2:12 lives and the desires of this ***w***.
Hebrews
1:6 into the ***w***, he said, All of
11:7 he criticized the ***w*** and became an
11:38 The ***w*** didn't deserve them. They
James
1:27 and to keep the ***w*** from
3:6 flame of fire, a ***w*** of evil at work
4:4 with the ***w*** makes you an
1 Peter
1:20 creation of the ***w***, but was only
1 John
2:2 only ours but the sins of the whole ***w***.
2:15 Don't love the ***w*** or the things in the
5:4 God defeats the ***w***. And this is the
2 John
1:7 gone into the ***w*** who do not
Revelation
11:15 kingdom of the ***w*** has become the
12:9 of the whole ***w***, was thrown down
16:14 of the whole ***w***, to gather them
18:23 merchants ran the ***w***, because all the

WORN

Deuteronomy
29:5 the sandals on your feet have ***w*** out.
Joshua
9:5 They had ***w***-out, patched sandals on
9:13 of ours are ***w*** out from the very
Judges
8:24 Midianites had ***w*** gold earrings
8:26 the purple robes ***w*** by the Midianite
16:16 until he became ***w*** out to the point
Esther
6:8 king himself has ***w*** and a horse on
Job
16:7 God has surely ***w*** me out. You have
Psalms
6:6 I'm ***w*** out from groaning. Every night, I
38:8 I'm ***w*** out, completely crushed; I groan
119:20 I'm ***w*** out by longing every minute for
119:82 My eyes are ***w*** out looking for your
119:123 My eyes are ***w*** out looking for your
Isaiah
32:2 of a massive cliff in a ***w***-out land.
57:10 ***W*** out by all your efforts, yet you
Jeremiah
12:5 people and are ***w*** out, how will you
12:13 weeds; they have ***w*** themselves out
45:3 to my pain. I'm ***w*** out from groaning
51:30 Their strength is ***w*** out; their
Lamentations
2:11 My eyes are ***w*** out from weeping; my
5:5 our necks; we are ***w*** out, but have no

WORRY

Genesis
45:20 Don't ***w*** about your possessions because
Judges
18:7 living without ***w*** in the same way
1 Samuel
1:16 praying out of my great ***w*** and trouble!"
29:10 I gave you. Don't ***w*** about this
2 Kings
4:23 sabbath." She said, "Don't ***w*** about it."
Ecclesiastes
7:21 Don't ***w*** about all the things people
Daniel
7:15 me, Daniel, to ***w***. My visions
Joel
2:6 with fear; all faces turn red with ***w***.
Matthew
6:25 say to you, don't ***w*** about your life,
6:28 And why do you ***w*** about clothes? Notice how the lilies
6:31 Therefore, don't ***w*** and say, 'What are
6:34 tomorrow will ***w*** about itself.
10:19 you over, don't ***w*** about how to
28:14 so you will have nothing to ***w*** about."
Mark
12:14 and you don't ***w*** about what people
13:11 you over, don't ***w*** ahead of time
Luke
12:11 don't ***w*** about how to
12:22 say to you, don't ***w*** about your life,
12:26 a small thing, why ***w*** about the rest?
Philippians
2:28 again you can be glad and I won't ***w***.

WORSE

Deuteronomy
1:28 walls sky-high! ***W*** still, we saw the
31:27 it's bound to get ***w*** once I'm dead!
1 Samuel
3:17 with you and ***w*** still if you hide
14:44 with me and ***w*** still if you
20:13 me, Jonathan, and ***w*** still if I don't
23:3 Judah. It'll be ***w*** if we go to
25:22 me, David, and ***w*** still if I leave
2 Samuel
3:9 me, Abner, and ***w*** still if I don't
3:35 with me and ***w*** still if I eat
13:16 me away would be ***w*** than the wrong
19:13 with me and ***w*** still if you
1 Kings
17:17 got steadily ***w*** until he wasn't
2 Chronicles
21:19 he grew steadily ***w***, until two days
Psalms
31:11 my enemies, still ***w*** to my neighbors.
39:2 but it did no good. My pain got ***w***.
Jeremiah
9:3 go from bad to ***w***. They don't know
16:12 you have acted ***w*** than your
Matthew
9:16 away the cloth and makes a ***w*** tear.
10:25 of his household by even ***w*** names.
12:45 That person is ***w*** off at the end
27:64 deception will be ***w*** than the first."
Mark
2:21 new from the old, and makes a ***w*** tear.
5:26 any better. In fact, she had gotten ***w***.
Luke
11:26 That person is ***w*** off at the end
John
5:14 in case something ***w*** happens to you."
2 Corinthians
12:13 were you treated ***w*** than the other
1 Timothy
5:8 faith. They are ***w*** than those who

2 Timothy
3:13 will grow even ***w***, as they deceive
Hebrews
10:29 How much ***w*** punishment do you think is deserved
2 Peter
2:20 by it, they are ***w*** off than they

WORSHIP → BOW DOWN AND WORSHIP, WORSHIP GOD, WORSHIP HIM, WORSHIP OTHER GODS, WORSHIP THE LORD

Genesis
4:26 people began to ***w*** in the LORD's
22:5 walk up there, ***w***, and then come
Exodus
4:23 go so he could ***w*** me." But you
7:16 so that they can ***w*** me in the desert.
8:1 Let my people go so that they can ***w*** me.
20:5 down to them or ***w*** them, because I,
23:24 to their gods, ***w*** them, or do what
23:33 me. If you ***w*** their gods, it
24:1 Israel's elders, and ***w*** from a distance.
Deuteronomy
5:9 down to them or ***w*** them because I,
12:30 did these nations ***w*** their gods? I
13:2 experienced—"and we should ***w*** them,"
Joshua
23:7 by them. Don't serve them or ***w*** them.
23:16 other gods and ***w*** them, then the
Judges
2:19 serve them and to ***w*** them. They
6:10 God; you must not ***w*** the gods of the
1 Samuel
1:3 leave his town to ***w*** and sacrifice to
12:10 of our enemies, and we will ***w*** you.'
1 Kings
9:6 and go to serve other gods, and ***w*** them,
12:30 people went to ***w*** before the one
2 Kings
17:36 Instead, ***w*** only the LORD He's the one
17:39 Instead, ***w*** only the LORD your God. He
18:22 You must ***w*** before this altar
1 Chronicles
9:28 for the ***w*** objects; they
2 Chronicles
7:19 and go to serve other gods and ***w*** them,
20:18 of Jerusalem fell before the LORD in ***w***.
24:7 LORD's temple in their ***w*** of the Baals
29:29 all who were with him bowed down in ***w***.
29:30 then they bowed down in ***w*** too.
32:12 You must ***w*** and burn incense
Ezra
4:2 with you, for we ***w*** your God as you
Nehemiah
9:6 all, and the heavenly forces ***w*** you.
Psalms
22:27 among all the nations will ***w*** you.
95:6 Come, let's ***w*** and bow down! Let's kneel
97:7 All those who ***w*** images, those who are
132:7 place; let's ***w*** at the place God
Isaiah
2:8 with idols; they ***w*** their handiwork,
2:20 which they made for themselves to ***w***.
19:21 day. They will ***w*** with sacrifices
19:23 Egyptians will ***w*** with the
36:7 You must ***w*** only at this
43:23 I didn't make you ***w*** with offerings; I
46:6 he makes a god. They bow down; they ***w***
66:23 will come to ***w*** me, says the LORD.
Jeremiah
11:12 the gods they ***w***, but they won't
26:2 to the temple to ***w***. Tell them
32:39 so that they may ***w*** me all the days
35:15 actions; don't ***w*** or serve other
Ezekiel
46:9 the North Gate to ***w*** should go out
Daniel
3:11 wouldn't bow and ***w*** would be thrown
3:28 wouldn't serve or ***w*** any god but their
4:37 Nebuchadnezzar, ***w***, magnify, and
11:38 place, he will ***w*** a god of walled
Matthew
15:9 Their ***w*** of me is empty since they teach
Mark
7:7 Their ***w*** of me is empty since they teach
Luke
1:10 who gathered to ***w*** were praying
4:7 if you will ***w*** me, it will all
John
4:20 it is necessary to ***w*** in Jerusalem."
4:21 your people will ***w*** the Father
4:22 and your people ***w*** what you don't
4:23 worshippers will ***w*** in spirit and
12:20 who had come up to ***w*** at the festival.
Acts
7:42 them over to ***w*** the stars in the
7:43 made in order to ***w*** them. Therefore,
8:27 he had come to ***w***. He was a eunuch
17:23 your objects of ***w***, I even found an
24:11 that I went up to ***w*** in Jerusalem no
24:14 Accordingly, I ***w*** the God of our
26:7 as they earnestly ***w*** night and day.
27:23 I belong and whom I ***w*** stood beside me.
Romans
9:4 of the Law, the ***w***, and the promises
1 Corinthians
5:10 or people who ***w*** false gods—
6:9 those who ***w*** false gods,
8:7 were used to idol ***w*** until now. Their
10:7 Don't ***w*** false gods like some of them
10:14 run away from the ***w*** of false gods!
Colossians
2:18 self-denial and ***w*** angels rob you of
2 Thessalonians
2:4 god or object of ***w*** and promotes
Hebrews
11:21 and bowed in ***w*** over the head of
1 Peter
4:3 and their forbidden ***w*** of idols.
Revelation
4:10 the throne. They ***w*** the one who lives
11:1 the altar, and those who ***w*** there.
13:12 who live in it ***w*** the first beast,
13:15 anyone who didn't ***w*** the beast's image
14:7 has come. ***W*** the one who made
14:9 voice, "If any ***w*** the beast and its
14:11 for those who ***w*** the beast and its
15:4 and fall down in ***w*** before you, for
22:8 I fell down to ***w*** at the feet of

WORSHIP GOD
Ex 3:12; 2Sa 15:32; Ps 55:19; Ecc 12:13; Jn 4:24; Ac 18:13; 1Co 14:25; Rev 19:10; 22:9

WORSHIP HIM

Dt 13:4; 1Sa 7:3; 12:14; Ps 22:29; 117:1; Jn 4:23; Heb 1:6; Rev 7:15; 19:10; 22:3

WORSHIP OTHER GODS

Dt 4:28; 13:6, 13; 28:36; 1Sa 26:19; 2Ki 17:35; 17:37, 38; Jer 25:6

WORSHIP THE LORD

Ex 10:7; 10:8, 11, 24, 26; 12:31; 1Sa 15:25; 15:30; 2Sa 15:8; 2Ki 17:25; 17:28, 34, 41; 2Ch 33:16; Ezr 6:21; Ps 147:12; Jer 7:2; Jon 1:9; Mt 4:10; Lk 4:8

WORSHIPPED → BOWED DOWN AND WORSHIPPED, WORSHIPPED THE LORD

Genesis
12:8 to the LORD and ***w*** in the LORD's
13:4 altar. There he ***w*** in the LORD's
21:33 and he ***w*** there in the name
26:25 altar there and ***w*** in the LORD's
Exodus
34:8 once Moses bowed to the ground and ***w***.
Numbers
22:31 in his hand. Then he bowed low and ***w***.
25:2 ate a meal, and they ***w*** their god.
Deuteronomy
12:2 are displacing ***w*** their gods—whethe
Joshua
5:14 on his face and ***w***. Joshua said to
Judges
2:12 peoples, they ***w*** them, and they
7:15 its meaning, he ***w***. Then he returned
1 Samuel
1:28 LORD." Then they ***w*** there before the
12:10 the LORD and have ***w*** the Baals and the
1 Kings
1:47 throne.'" The king then ***w*** on his bed
11:33 abandoned me and ***w*** the Sidonian
16:31 of the Sidonians. He served and ***w*** Baal.
22:53 served Baal and ***w*** him. He angered
2 Kings
17:7 Egypt's king. They ***w*** other gods.
17:12 They ***w*** images about which the LORD had said, Don't
21:3 to all the stars in the sky and ***w*** them.
21:21 had walked. He ***w*** the same
1 Chronicles
29:20 bowed down, and ***w*** before the LORD
2 Chronicles
1:5 is where Solomon and the assembly ***w***.
24:18 God, and ***w*** sacred poles and
29:28 congregation ***w*** with singing
33:3 to all the stars in the sky and ***w*** them.
33:22 idols his father had made and ***w*** them.
Job
1:20 his head, fell to the ground, and ***w***.
Jeremiah
8:2 consulted, and ***w***. Their bones
16:11 have served and ***w*** them, while
22:9 their God and ***w*** and served other
Daniel
4:34 the Most High. I ***w*** and glorified the
Hosea
9:10 to Baal-peor, and ***w*** a thing of shame;
Matthew
14:33 those in the boat ***w*** Jesus and said,
28:9 came and grabbed his feet and ***w*** him.
28:17 saw him, they ***w*** him, but some
Luke
2:37 temple area but ***w*** God with fasting
24:52 They ***w*** him and returned to Jerusalem
John
4:20 Our ancestors ***w*** on this mountain, but
9:38 Lord, I believe." And he ***w*** Jesus.
Romans
1:25 a lie, and they ***w*** and served the
Revelation
5:14 Amen," and the elders fell down and ***w***.
7:11 facedown before the throne and ***w*** God,
11:16 God, fell on their faces and ***w*** God.
13:4 They ***w*** the dragon because it had given
13:8 who live on earth ***w*** it, all whose
16:2 had the beast's mark and ***w*** its image.
19:4 fell down and ***w*** God, who is
20:4 those who hadn't ***w*** the beast or its

WORSHIPPED THE LORD

Gn 24:48; 1Sa 1:19; 7:4; 15:31; 2Ki 17:32; 17:33; Neh 9:3; Jon 1:16

WORSHIPPING

Exodus
10:26 some of them for ***w*** the LORD our God.
Deuteronomy
4:19 be led astray, ***w*** and serving them.
11:16 away, serving other gods and ***w*** them.
29:26 serving them, and ***w*** them—other gods that they
30:17 so are misled, ***w*** other gods and
Joshua
22:25 make our children stop ***w*** the LORD.
Judges
2:17 other gods and ***w*** them. They
8:33 unfaithfully by ***w*** the Baals,
1 Samuel
8:8 minute, abandoning me and ***w*** other gods.
1 Kings
9:9 other gods, ***w*** and serving them.
2 Kings
19:37 while he was ***w*** in the temple of
2 Chronicles
7:3 to the ground, ***w*** and giving thanks
7:22 other gods, ***w*** and serving them.
Isaiah
37:38 while he was ***w*** in the temple of
Jeremiah
1:16 abandoning me, ***w*** other gods, and
11:13 altars for ***w*** Baal as you have
11:17 done evil and made me angry by ***w*** Baal.
13:10 other gods, ***w*** and serving them.
44:3 offerings and ***w*** other gods that
48:35 on the shrines, and ***w*** their gods.
Acts
13:2 As they were ***w*** the Lord and fasting,
Revelation
9:20 They didn't stop ***w*** demons and idols
19:20 mark and into ***w*** the beast's

WORTH

Ruth
2:1 a man of ***w***, through her
3:11 gate—know that you are a woman of ***w***.

1 Samuel
1:8 so sad? Aren't I ***w*** more to you than
2 Samuel
18:3 us. But you are ***w*** ten thousand of
Ezra
8:27 twenty gold bowls ***w*** one thousand
Job
15:31 in what has no ***w***, for their reward
40:4 I'm of little ***w***. What can I
Ecclesiastes
2:3 what is really ***w*** doing in the few
Isaiah
7:23 a thousand vines ***w*** a thousand silver
Lamentations
4:2 no!—now they are ***w*** no more than clay
Matthew
6:26 them. Aren't you ***w*** much more than
10:31 afraid. You are ***w*** more than many
Mark
6:37 off and buy bread ***w*** almost eight
12:42 in two small copper coins ***w*** a penny.
Luke
10:35 two full days' ***w*** of wages and gave
12:7 afraid. You are ***w*** more than many
12:24 them. You are ***w*** so much more than
19:13 of them money ***w*** four months'
21:2 in two small copper coins ***w*** a penny.
John
6:7 year's salary ***w*** of food wouldn't
12:5 This perfume was ***w*** a year's wages! Why
2 Corinthians
10:10 is weak and his speech is ***w*** nothing."

WORTHLESS

Deuteronomy
32:15 the rock of his salvation was ***w***.
Judges
9:4 Abimelech hired ***w*** and reckless men,
11:3 the land of Tob. ***W*** men gathered
1 Kings
15:12 away with all the ***w*** idols that his
16:26 God, the LORD, with their ***w*** idols.
21:26 after the ***w*** idols exactly
2 Kings
17:15 They followed ***w*** images so that
21:21 the same ***w*** idols his father
23:24 gods and the ***w*** idols-all the
2 Chronicles
13:7 some useless, ***w*** people joined his
Job
11:11 He knows ***w*** people, sees sin, and
15:31 no worth, for their reward will be ***w***.
34:18 say to a king, "***W***!" to royalty,
Psalms
4:2 to love what is ***w*** and go after
31:6 is completely ***w***. I myself trust
60:11 against the enemy; human help is ***w***.
101:3 eyes on anything ***w***. I hate
108:12 against the enemy—human help is ***w***.
119:37 from looking at ***w*** things. Make me
Proverbs
6:12 ***W*** people and guilty people go around
16:27 ***W*** people dig up trouble; their lips are
19:28 A ***w*** witness mocks justice; the wicked
28:19 but those with ***w*** pursuits will
Isaiah
1:13 Stop bringing ***w*** offerings. Your incense
30:7 help is utterly ***w***. Therefore, I
Jeremiah
2:5 pursued what was ***w*** and became
14:14 false visions, ***w*** predictions, and
15:19 not what is ***w***, you will be my
Lamentations
2:14 prophets gave you ***w*** and empty
Ezekiel
12:24 will there be any ***w*** vision or
13:6 They saw ***w*** visions and performed
13:7 Didn't you see ***w*** visions? And didn't
13:8 Because you spoke ***w*** things and had
15:5 was whole, it was ***w***. Now that the
24:12 It's a ***w*** task. Even by fire its great
37:23 idols or their ***w*** things or with
Daniel
11:21 A ***w*** person will arise in his place.
Hosea
5:11 Ephraim chose to pursue ***w*** things.
7:16 become like a ***w*** bow; their
Jonah
2:8 Those deceived by ***w*** things lose their
Micah
1:7 all her idols ***w***. Since she
Nahum
1:11 evil against the LORD—a ***w*** counselor!
1:14 I will make your grave, for you are ***w***.
1:15 promises! The ***w*** one will never
Matthew
25:30 Now take the ***w*** servant and throw him
Luke
19:22 own mouth, you ***w*** servant! You
Acts
14:15 away from such ***w*** things. He made
Romans
3:12 They have become ***w*** together. There
1 Corinthians
15:17 your faith is ***w***; you are still in
Galatians
4:9 to the weak and ***w*** world system? Do
Titus
3:9 Law, because they are useless and ***w***.
James
1:26 themselves. Their devotion is ***w***.

WORTHY → WORTHY OF PRAISE

Exodus
15:11 in holiness, ***w*** of highest
1 Samuel
15:28 yours, someone who is more ***w*** than you.
18:18 I'm not ***w***," David replied to Saul,
Proverbs
19:26 disgraceful children, ***w*** of reproach.
Matthew
3:11 I am. I'm not ***w*** to carry his
10:38 crosses and follow me aren't ***w*** of me.
22:8 but those who were invited weren't ***w***.
Mark
1:7 me. I'm not even ***w*** to bend over and
Luke
3:16 coming. I'm not ***w*** to loosen the
20:35 are considered ***w*** to participate in
John
1:27 me, but I'm not ***w*** to untie his
Acts
5:41 been regarded as ***w*** to suffer

13:25 after me. I'm not ***w*** to loosen his
Romans
16:2 in a way that is ***w*** of God's people,
Ephesians
4:1 to live as people ***w*** of the call you
Philippians
1:27 in a manner ***w*** of Christ's
Colossians
1:10 lives that are ***w*** of the Lord and
1 Thessalonians
2:12 you to live lives ***w*** of the God who is
2 Thessalonians
1:5 be considered ***w*** of God's kingdom
1:11 God will make you ***w*** of his calling
Revelation
3:4 me clothed in white because they are ***w***.
4:11 You are ***w***, our Lord and God, to
5:2 voice, "Who is ***w*** to open the
5:4 no one was found ***w*** to open the
5:9 saying, "You are ***w*** to take the
5:12 in a loud voice, "***W*** is the

WORTHY OF PRAISE
1Ch 16:25; Ps 48:1; 96:4; 145:3; Phi 4:8

WOUND
Exodus
21:25 a bruise for a bruise, a ***w*** for a wound.
Job
34:6 a liar; my ***w*** from an arrow is
Proverbs
25:20 a cold day or putting vinegar on a ***w***.
Jeremiah
10:19 to my injury; my ***w*** is terrible. Yet
30:15 your pain? Your ***w*** is incurable. I
Hosea
5:13 and Judah his ***w***, then Ephraim
Nahum
3:19 your injury; your ***w*** is grievous. All
Revelation
13:3 but its deadly ***w*** was healed. So
13:12 first beast, whose fatal ***w*** was healed.

WOUNDED
Deuteronomy
32:39 I'm the one who ***w***, but now I will
Judges
9:40 away. Many fell ***w***, all the way up
1 Samuel
31:3 archers located him, they ***w*** him badly.
2 Samuel
1:10 after being ***w*** like that. I took
10:18 horsemen. David ***w*** their army
2 Kings
8:28 where the Arameans ***w*** Joram.
8:29 son, at Jezreel because he had been ***w***.
2 Chronicles
22:5 where the Arameans ***w*** Joram.
22:6 son, at Jezreel because he had been ***w***.
24:25 left him badly ***w***, but his own
35:23 servants, "Take me away; I'm badly ***w***!"
Job
24:12 of the mortally ***w*** screams, but God
Psalms
64:7 arrow! Without warning, they will be ***w***!
Proverbs
6:33 He is ***w*** and disgraced. His shame will
Jeremiah
14:17 a crushing blow and are mortally ***w***.
37:10 you and only the ***w*** in their tents
51:52 idols, and the ***w*** in her land will
Lamentations
2:12 fainting like the ***w*** in the city
Ezekiel
26:15 when the ***w*** groan, and when
34:16 bind up the ***w***, and strengthen
Luke
10:34 he placed the ***w*** man on his own
20:12 servant. They ***w*** this servant and
Acts
19:16 they ran out of that house naked and ***w***.
Revelation
13:14 who had been ***w*** by the sword and

WOUNDS
Job
9:17 and multiplies my ***w*** for no reason?
Psalms
38:5 My ***w*** reek; they are all infected
147:3 the brokenhearted and bandages their ***w***.
Proverbs
23:29 has unnecessary ***w***? Who has glazed
26:10 an archer who ***w*** someone randomly,
Isaiah
1:6 cuts, and raw ***w***, not treated, not
30:26 and heals the ***w*** inflicted by his
53:5 made us whole; by his ***w*** we are healed.
Jeremiah
6:7 her; injury and ***w*** are ever before
9:1 day and night for the ***w*** of my people.
30:17 I will heal your ***w***, declares the
Micah
1:9 weakened by her ***w***! It has come as
Zechariah
13:6 What are these ***w*** between your
Luke
10:34 and bandaged his ***w***, tending them
John
20:25 my finger in the ***w*** left by the
Acts
16:33 and washed their ***w***. He and everyone
1 Peter
2:24 do with sin. By his ***w*** you were healed.

WRATH
Deuteronomy
29:23 the LORD devastated in anger and ***w***!
29:28 land in anger, ***w***, and great fury.
Joshua
9:20 them live so that ***w*** won't come down
22:20 reserved for God? ***W*** came on the
1 Chronicles
27:24 experienced ***w*** because of this,
Ezra
7:23 God of heaven, or ***w*** will come upon
8:22 but his fierce ***w*** is against all
Nehemiah
13:18 are bringing more ***w*** upon Israel by
Job
19:29 yourselves, for ***w*** brings punishment
21:20 Let them drink from the Almighty's ***w***.
Psalms
10:4 the peak of their ***w***, the wicked don't

56:7 any reason! In ***w*** bring down the
76:10 with whatever remains of your ***w***.
78:21 against Jacob; ***w*** also burned
78:38 many times, wouldn't stir up all his ***w***!
78:50 a path for his ***w***. He didn't save
79:6 Pour out your ***w*** on the nations who
89:46 How long will your ***w*** burn like fire?
90:7 because of your ***w***; we are paralyzed
90:11 that is due you corresponds to your ***w***.
102:10 of your anger and ***w***, because you
110:5 God has crushed kings on his day of ***w***.
138:7 my enemies' ***w***; you save me with

Proverbs
11:4 in the day of ***w***, but
11:23 the expectations of the wicked bring ***w***.
15:1 answer turns back ***w***, but an offensive
21:14 and a hidden bribe removes furious ***w***.
22:14 under the LORD's ***w*** will fall in it.
27:4 ***W*** is cruel and anger is a flood, but

Isaiah
13:3 proud, jubilant ones, to execute my ***w***.
51:17 drank the cup of ***w*** from the LORD's
63:6 them drunk on my ***w***; I spilled their

Jeremiah
10:25 Pour out your ***w*** on the nations that

Lamentations
2:1 On that day of ***w***, he didn't
2:2 meadows; in his ***w*** he tore down the
2:4 he poured out his ***w*** like fire on
3:43 yourself up in ***w*** and hunted us;

Ezekiel
20:8 would pour out my ***w*** on them and

Hosea
13:11 my anger, and I took him away in my ***w***.

Amos
1:11 anger alive, and fueled his ***w*** forever.

Jonah
3:9 and turn from his ***w***, so that we might

Micah
5:15 in anger and in ***w*** on the nations

Nahum
1:2 and strong in ***w***. The LORD is
1:6 of his fury? His ***w*** pours out like

Habakkuk
2:15 pouring out your ***w*** in order to see

Romans
1:18 God's ***w*** is being revealed from heaven
2:5 are storing up ***w*** for yourself
2:8 there will be ***w*** and anger for
3:5 God, who brings ***w*** upon us, isn't
4:15 Law brings about ***w***. But when there
5:9 will be saved from God's ***w*** through him.
9:22 pots made for ***w*** that were
12:19 room for God's ***w***. It is written,

Colossians
3:6 The ***w*** of God is coming upon disobedient

1 Thessalonians
1:10 who will rescue us from the coming ***w***.
2:16 the limit. God's ***w*** has caught up
5:9 us to suffer his ***w*** but rather to

Revelation
6:16 on the throne and from the Lamb's ***w***!
6:17 day of their ***w*** has come, and who
11:18 enraged, but your ***w*** came. The time
14:10 the cup of his ***w***. They will suffer

WRITE

Exodus
17:14 said to Moses, "***W*** this as a
34:27 said to Moses: "***W*** down these words

Numbers
5:23 The priest will ***w*** these curses in the
17:2 twelve staffs. ***W*** each person's
17:3 ***W*** Aaron's name on Levi's staff, for

Deuteronomy
6:9 ***W*** them on your house's doorframes and your city's
10:2 I will ***w*** on the tablets the words that
11:20 ***W*** them on your house's doorframes and your city's
17:18 he himself must ***w*** a copy of this
27:3 crossed over, ***w*** on the stones all
27:8 Make sure to ***w*** all the words of this
31:19 that, you must ***w*** down this poem

Joshua
18:4 land. They will ***w*** a description of
18:6 But you will ***w*** a report in seven parts
18:8 to those going to ***w*** a description of

Ezra
5:10 so that we could ***w*** down the names of

Job
13:26 You even ***w*** bitter things about me, make me inherit
31:35 and let my accuser ***w*** an indictment.

Proverbs
3:3 on your neck; ***w*** them on the
7:3 on your fingers; ***w*** them on the

Isaiah
8:1 large tablet, and ***w*** on it in ordinary
30:8 Now go, ***w*** it before them on a tablet,
44:5 Another will ***w*** on his hand, "The

Jeremiah
30:2 proclaims: ***W*** down in a scroll

Ezekiel
24:2 Human one, ***w*** down today's date, because today the king
37:16 take a stick, and ***w*** on it, "Belonging
43:11 its regulations. ***W*** them down in

Hosea
8:12 Even though I ***w*** out for him a large

Habakkuk
2:2 me and said, ***W*** a vision, and

Mark
10:4 allowed a man to ***w*** a divorce

Luke
1:3 also decided to ***w*** a carefully
16:6 down quickly, and ***w*** four hundred
16:7 your contract and ***w*** eight hundred.'

John
19:21 to Pilate, "Don't ***w***, 'The king of the

Acts
15:20 we should ***w*** a letter, telling
25:26 definite to ***w*** to our lord

2 Corinthians
1:13 We don't ***w*** anything to you except what you can read
2:4 heart. I didn't ***w*** to make you sad
9:1 for me to ***w*** to you about this

1 Thessalonians
4:9 don't need us to ***w*** about loving your
5:1 We don't need to ***w*** to you about the

2 Thessalonians
3:17 every letter of mine. This is how I ***w***.

Hebrews
8:10 their minds, and ***w*** them on their
Revelation
1:19 So ***w*** down what you have seen, both the scene now
3:12 leave it. I will ***w*** on them the name
21:5 He also said, "***W*** this down, for

WRITING
Exodus
32:16 was God's own ***w*** inscribed on the
Deuteronomy
31:24 had finished ***w*** in their entirety
Ezra
1:1 kingdom (it was also in ***w***) that stated:
Nehemiah
9:38 firm agreement in ***w***, with the names
Esther
8:13 A copy of the ***w*** was to become law in
Isaiah
10:1 wicked decrees, and keep ***w*** harmful laws
Jeremiah
45:1 son, Baruch was ***w*** in a scroll the
Ezekiel
2:10 was filled with ***w*** on both sides,
9:2 linen and had a ***w*** case at his side.
Daniel
5:7 who can read this ***w*** and tell me its
Luke
1:63 everyone by ***w***, "His name is
Romans
15:15 already know. I'm ***w*** to you in this
16:22 Tertius, and I'm ***w*** this letter to
1 Corinthians
14:37 that what I'm ***w*** to you is the
2 Corinthians
13:10 This is why I'm ***w*** these things while
1 John
2:7 friends, I'm not ***w*** a new commandment
2 John
1:5 not as though I'm ***w*** a new command to
Revelation
5:1 throne. It had ***w*** on the front and

WRITTEN
Exodus
24:12 that I've ***w*** in order to teach
32:32 me out of your scroll that you've ***w***."
Deuteronomy
28:58 that are ***w*** in this scroll,
Joshua
1:8 obey everything ***w*** in it. Then you
23:6 obey everything ***w*** in the
2 Samuel
1:18 (In fact, it is ***w*** in the scroll
1 Kings
2:3 just as it is ***w*** in the
22:45 aren't they ***w*** in the official
1 Chronicles
16:40 following the ***w*** requirements in
Ezra
4:7 The letter was ***w*** in Aramaic and
5:7 the following was ***w***: To King Darius,
6:18 as it is ***w*** in the scroll
Nehemiah
8:14 And they found ***w*** in the Instruction
Esther
1:13 the kingdom's ***w*** laws and what
10:2 him. Are they not ***w*** in the official
Psalms
40:7 I come! I'm inscribed in the ***w*** scroll.
102:18 Let this be ***w*** down for the next
139:16 every day was ***w*** what was being
149:9 the justice ***w*** against them.
Proverbs
22:20 Haven't I ***w*** for you thirty sayings full
Isaiah
65:6 Look, this stands ***w*** before me. I won't
Jeremiah
25:13 all that is ***w*** in this scroll,
36:27 the words ***w*** by Baruch at
Ezekiel
37:20 that you've ***w*** on are in your
Daniel
5:25 This is what was ***w*** down: mene, mene,
9:11 long ago—the one ***w*** in the
10:21 tell you what is ***w*** in the Scroll of
12:1 who is found ***w*** in the scroll
Malachi
3:16 remembrance was ***w*** before the LORD
Matthew
4:4 replied, "It's ***w***, People won't
4:6 down; for it is ***w***, I will command
4:7 Again it's ***w***, Don't test the
4:10 because it's ***w***, You will worship
11:10 one of whom it is ***w***: Look, I'm
21:13 to them, "It's ***w***, My house will be
26:24 just as it is ***w*** about him. But
26:31 is because it is ***w***, I will hit the
Mark
1:2 just as it was ***w*** about in the
9:12 Why was it ***w*** that the Human
9:13 wanted, just as it was ***w*** about him."
11:17 Hasn't it been ***w***, My house will be
14:27 to me. It is ***w***, I will hit the
15:26 against him was ***w***, "The king of the
Luke
10:20 that your names are ***w*** in heaven."
24:46 This is what is ***w***: the Christ will
John
20:31 these things are ***w*** so that you will
21:25 room for the scrolls that would be ***w***.
Acts
1:20 It is ***w*** in the Psalms scroll, Let his
7:42 just as it is ***w*** in the scroll of
13:29 that had been ***w*** about him, they
15:15 words agree with this; as it is ***w***,
23:5 priest. It is ***w***, You will not
24:14 out in the Law and ***w*** in the Prophets.
Romans
2:15 proof of the Law ***w*** on their hearts,
15:4 Whatever was ***w*** in the past was written
15:21 Instead, as it's ***w***, Those who hadn't
1 Corinthians
4:6 what has been ***w*** and so none of
10:11 example and were ***w*** as a warning for
2 Corinthians
3:3 us. You weren't ***w*** with ink but with
Hebrews
10:7 This has been ***w*** about me in the
2 Peter
3:1 to you. I have ***w*** both letters to

Revelation
2:17 with a new name ***w*** on it, which no
13:8 names hadn't been ***w***—from the time the earth was made
14:1 his Father's name ***w*** on their
17:5 mystery—was ***w*** on her forehead:
20:15 name wasn't found ***w*** in the scroll of
21:12 on the gates were ***w*** the names of the
22:18 the plagues that are ***w*** in this scroll.

WRONG → DO WRONG, DOING WRONG, DONE WRONG

Leviticus
4:13 done something ***w*** unintentionally
Deuteronomy
1:39 know right and ***w***—they will enter
30:15 what's good versus death and what's ***w***.
31:18 of the many ***w*** things they have
1 Samuel
19:5 you do something ***w*** to an innocent
29:3 found anything ***w*** with him from the
2 Samuel
3:8 of doing something ***w*** with this woman.
14:25 his head there was nothing ***w*** with him.
1 Kings
8:50 Forgive all their ***w*** that they have
17:18 What's gone ***w*** between us, man
1 Chronicles
12:17 I've done no ***w***, then may our
Esther
1:16 done something ***w*** not just to the
Job
6:30 Is there ***w*** on my tongue, or can my
33:12 Now you're ***w*** about this; I'll answer
36:10 and commands them to turn from ***w***.
Psalms
7:3 if my hands have done anything ***w***,
17:3 found anything ***w***. My mouth doesn't
99:8 also the one who avenged their ***w*** deeds.
119:3 even do anything ***w***! They walk in
119:67 I took the ***w*** way, but now I do
125:3 don't use their hands to do anything ***w***.
Proverbs
30:20 and she says, "I've done nothing ***w***!"
Ecclesiastes
2:21 too is pointless—it's a terrible ***w***.
Isaiah
22:1 Vision. What is ***w*** with you, that
63:8 won't do what is ***w***." God became
64:5 sinned; you hid yourself when we did ***w***.
Jeremiah
2:5 LORD says: What ***w*** did your
26:3 them because of the ***w*** they have done.
40:16 you are saying about Ishmael is ***w***."
Lamentations
1:5 of her many ***w*** acts. Her
1:22 because of all my ***w*** acts; my groans
3:42 the ones who did ***w***; we rebelled. But
Ezekiel
22:28 and making ***w*** predictions for
Daniel
9:15 We have sinned and done the ***w*** thing."
Matthew
20:13 I did you no ***w***. Didn't I agree
22:29 You are ***w*** because you don't
27:4 said, "I did ***w*** because I betrayed an
27:23 said, "Why? What ***w*** has he done?"
Luke
23:41 did. But this man has done nothing ***w***."
John
16:8 the world it was ***w*** about sin,
18:23 about what was ***w***. But if I speak
18:30 had done nothing ***w***, we wouldn't have
Acts
23:9 We find nothing ***w*** with this man!
Romans
13:4 if you do what's ***w***, be afraid
13:10 do anything ***w*** to a neighbor;
14:14 that nothing is ***w*** to eat in itself.
1 Corinthians
15:8 to me, as if I was born at the ***w*** time.
2 Corinthians
7:2 do anything ***w*** to anyone. We
12:13 burden on you? Forgive me for this ***w***!
13:7 don't do anything ***w***, not because we
Galatians
2:11 him to his face, because he was ***w***.
6:1 doing something ***w***, you who are
Ephesians
2:1 things you did ***w*** and your offenses
2:5 that we did ***w***. He did this
4:19 of right and ***w***, and who have
1 Thessalonians
5:15 no one repays a ***w*** with a wrong, but
1 Timothy
1:3 individuals not to spread ***w*** teaching.
James
5:20 back from the ***w*** path will save

WROTE

Exodus
24:4 Moses then ***w*** down all the LORD's words.
34:28 any water. He ***w*** on the tablets
Deuteronomy
4:13 and ***w*** them on two stone
5:22 no more. God ***w*** them on two stone
10:4 God ***w*** on the new tablets what had been written
31:9 Then Moses ***w*** this Instruction down and gave it
31:22 So Moses ***w*** this poem down that very
Joshua
8:32 Joshua ***w*** on the stones a
18:9 the land and ***w*** about it in a
24:26 Joshua ***w*** these words in God's
1 Samuel
10:25 operate and ***w*** it in a scroll
2 Samuel
11:14 morning David ***w*** a letter to Joab
11:15 He ***w*** in the letter, "Place Uriah at the
1 Kings
21:8 So she ***w*** letters in Ahab's name,
21:9 This is what she ***w*** in the letters:
2 Kings
10:1 Samaria. So Jehu ***w*** letters and sent
10:6 Jehu ***w*** them a second letter: "If you
17:37 that he ***w*** for you. Don't
2 Chronicles
30:1 and Judah, and ***w*** letters to
32:17 He ***w*** other letters insulting the LORD
Ezra
4:7 their associates ***w*** to Persia's King
4:8 the scribe ***w*** a letter

Esther
3:12 each people. They ***w*** in the alphabet
8:5 son, that he ***w*** to destroy the
9:20 Mordecai ***w*** these things down and sent
Ecclesiastes
12:10 words, and he ***w*** truthful words
Jeremiah
36:4 to him, Baruch ***w*** them in the
36:18 to me, and I ***w*** them with ink in
36:32 Neriah's son, who ***w*** at Jeremiah's
51:60 Jeremiah ***w*** down in a single scroll all
Daniel
5:5 hand appeared and ***w*** on the plaster of
6:25 Then King Darius ***w*** the following
7:1 on his bed. He ***w*** the dream down.
Matthew
2:5 Judea, for this is what the prophet ***w***:
Mark
7:6 hypocrites. He ***w***, This people
10:5 said to them, "He ***w*** this commandment
12:19 Teacher, Moses ***w*** for us that if a
Luke
20:28 Teacher, Moses ***w*** for us that if a
John
1:45 the one Moses ***w*** about in the Law
5:46 believe me, because Moses ***w*** about me.
8:6 bent down and ***w*** on the ground
8:8 Bending down again, he ***w*** on the ground
21:24 things and who ***w*** them down. We
Acts
1:1 first scroll I ***w*** concerned
18:27 him and ***w*** to the disciples
21:25 believers, we ***w*** a letter about
23:25 He ***w*** the following letter
Romans
16:26 what the prophets ***w***. It is made known
1 Corinthians
5:9 I ***w*** to you in my earlier letter not to
7:1 about what you ***w***: "It's good for a
2 Corinthians
2:3 That's why I ***w*** this very thing to you,
2:4 I ***w*** to you in tears, with a very
2:9 reason why I ***w*** you. I wanted to
7:12 So although I ***w*** to you, it wasn't for
10:11 as the words we ***w*** when we were away
Philippians
3:7 my assets, but I ***w*** them off as a
2 Peter
3:15 and brother Paul ***w*** to you according
3 John
1:9 I ***w*** something to the church, but

Yy

YEAR

Genesis
17:21 be born to Sarah at this time next **y**.
Exodus
12:2 be the first month of the **y** for you.
23:14 a festival for me three times a **y**.
30:10 Once a **y** Aaron should perform a ritual
34:24 the LORD your God three times a **y**.
Leviticus
16:34 their sins once a **y**.It was done just
25:11 The fiftieth **y** will be a Jubilee year
Deuteronomy
1:3 in the fortieth **y**, on the first day
Joshua
5:12 So that **y** they ate the
1 Samuel
1:3 Every **y** this man would leave his town
7:16 Each **y** he traveled between Bethel,
2 Samuel
14:26 the end of each **y** because his hair
Ezra
1:1 In the first **y** of King Cyrus of
Nehemiah
1:1 in the twentieth **y**, while I was in
10:31 Every seventh **y** we won't plant
Esther
9:21 Adar as special days each and every **y**.
Job
3:6 in the days of a **y**; may it not
Psalms
65:11 You crown the **y** with your goodness;
Isaiah
6:1 In the **y** of King Uzziah's death, I saw
34:8 of vengeance, a **y** of payback for
61:2 to proclaim the **y** of the LORD's favor
63:4 of vengeance; the **y** of my deliverance
Jeremiah
1:2 in the thirteenth **y** of Judah's King
34:14 every seventh **y** each of you must
Daniel
7:1 In the first **y** of Babylon's King
11:1 In the first **y** of Darius the Mede's
Haggai
1:1 in the second **y** of King Darius,
Luke
2:41 Each **y** his parents went to Jerusalem
4:19 to proclaim the **y** of the Lord's
13:9 fruit next **y**; if not, then you
John
11:49 high priest that **y**, told them, "You
18:13 of Caiaphas, the high priest that **y**.
Acts
11:26 there for a whole **y**, meeting with the
Romans
9:9 promise were: A **y** from now I will
2 Corinthians
8:10 to do it last **y** but you wanted to
9:2 ready since last **y**," and your
Hebrews
10:3 are a reminder of sin every **y**,
James
4:13 will stay there a **y**, buying and
Revelation
9:15 day, month, and **y** were released to

YEARS

Genesis
1:14 events, sacred seasons, days, and **y**.
5:3 When Adam was 130 **y** old, he became the father of
5:4 Adam lived 800 **y**; he had other
41:26 cows are seven **y**, and the seven
41:30 After them, seven **y** of famine will
47:9 traveler for 130 **y**. My years have
47:28 for seventeen **y**, and after he had
50:26 when he was 110 **y** old. They
Exodus
12:40 in Egypt was four hundred thirty **y**.
16:35 manna for forty **y**, until they came
30:14 counted, from 20 **y** old and above,
38:26 in the census, 20 **y** old and above,
Numbers
1:3 20 **y** old and above, who is eligible for
14:34 just as many **y** you'll bear your
32:13 desert for forty **y** until the entire
Deuteronomy
2:7 these forty **y** the LORD your God
8:4 these forty **y**, your clothes
34:7 Moses was 120 **y** old when he died. His eyesight wasn't
Joshua
5:6 journeyed forty **y** in the desert
14:7 I was 40 **y** old when Moses the LORD's
1 Samuel
4:15 Now Eli was 98 **y** old, and his eyes
13:1 Saul was 30 **y** old when he became king,
Ezra
3:8 Levites 20 **y** old and more to
5:11 was built many **y** ago, which a
Nehemiah
9:21 forty **y**—they lacked nothing
9:30 them for many **y** and warned them
Job
10:5 of a human, your **y** like years of a
15:20 the number of **y** reserved for the
16:22 A number of **y** will surely pass, and
32:7 let multiple **y** make wisdom known.
36:11 days in plenty, their **y** contentedly.
36:26 the number of his **y** is beyond
42:16 Job lived 140 **y** and saw four

Psalms
31:10 with sadness; my **y** are consumed with groaning
61:6 life! Let his **y** extend for many
77:5 past; I remember **y** that seem an
78:33 puff of air, and their **y** in total ruin.
90:4 a thousand **y** are like
90:9 we finish up our **y** with a whimper.
90:10 to be seventy **y** old, maybe
90:15 same number of **y** that we saw only
95:10 For forty **y** I despised that generation;
102:24 of life—your **y** go on from one
102:27 But you are the one! Your **y** never end
Proverbs
4:10 speech, then the **y** of your life will
5:9 to others, your **y** to a cruel person.
9:11 will be many; **y** will be added to
10:27 life, but the **y** of the wicked
Ecclesiastes
6:6 live a thousand **y** twice over but
11:8 who live many **y** should take
12:1 arrive, and those **y**, about which
Isaiah
20:3 barefoot three **y**, as a sign and
38:5 I will add fifteen **y** to your life.
Jeremiah
25:12 When the seventy **y** are over, I will
Ezekiel
29:11 and it won't be inhabited for forty **y**.
40:1 exactly fourteen **y** after the city
Daniel
9:2 the number of **y** that it would
11:6 After some **y**, they will make an
Joel
2:25 repay you for the **y** that the cutting
Amos
5:25 during the forty **y** in the
Zechariah
1:12 you have been angry these seventy **y**?"
7:5 past seventy **y**, did you fast for
Malachi
3:4 as in ancient days and in former **y**.
Matthew
2:16 who were two **y** old and younger,
9:20 for twelve **y** came up behind
Mark
5:25 who had been bleeding for twelve **y**.
5:42 She was twelve **y** old. They were
Luke
3:23 was about 30 **y** old when he began
4:25 three and a half **y** and there was a
John
2:20 took forty-six **y** to build this
Acts
4:22 this sign of healing was over 40 **y** old.
7:23 Moses was 40 **y** old, he decided
7:30 Forty **y** later, an angel appeared to
9:33 been confined to his bed for eight **y**.
13:18 For about forty **y**, God put up with
19:10 went on for two **y**, so that everyone
20:31 that for three **y** I constantly and
24:10 nation for many **y**, so I gladly
28:30 for two full **y** and welcomed
Galatians
4:10 days and months and seasons and **y**.
Hebrews
3:17 angry for forty **y**? Wasn't it with
James
5:17 no rain fell for three and a half **y**.
2 Peter
3:8 like a thousand **y** and a thousand
Revelation
20:2 Satan, and bound him for a thousand **y**.

YEAST

Exodus
12:15 you must remove **y** from your houses
13:7 bread and no **y** should be seen
Leviticus
2:11 can be made with **y**. You must not
Deuteronomy
16:3 containing **y** along with it.
16:4 No dough with **y** should appear in any of your territory
Matthew
13:33 of heaven is like **y**, which a woman
16:6 guard for the **y** of the Pharisees
Luke
13:21 It's like **y**, which a woman took and
1 Corinthians
5:6 a tiny grain of **y** makes a whole
5:7 Clean out the old **y** so you can be a new
5:8 not with old **y** or with the yeast
Galatians
5:9 A little **y** works through the whole lump

YOKE

Numbers
19:2 and on which no **y** has been laid.
Deuteronomy
28:48 will put an iron **y** on your neck
1 Kings
19:19 with twelve **y** of oxen before
Job
42:12 one thousand **y** of oxen, and one
Isaiah
9:4 shattered the **y** that burdened
10:27 and destroy the **y** on your neck. He
14:25 it and remove its **y** from my people;
47:6 You made your **y** heavy even on the
58:6 the ropes of a **y**, setting free the
58:9 If you remove the **y** from among you,
Jeremiah
2:20 ago I broke your **y**; I shattered your
5:5 have broken their **y** and shattered the
27:2 to me: Make a **y** of straps and
28:2 I have broken the **y** of the king of
30:8 I will break the **y** off their necks
Lamentations
1:14 tripped up. His **y** is on my neck; he
3:27 for a man to carry a **y** in his youth.
Ezekiel
30:18 I break Egypt's **y** and bring an end
34:27 the bars of their **y** and deliver them
Nahum
1:13 break off his **y** from you and tear
Matthew
11:29 Put on my **y**, and learn from me. I'm
11:30 My **y** is easy to bear, and my burden is

YOU ARE GOD'S SON

Mt 4:3; 4:6; 27:40; Mk 3:11; Lk 4:3; 4:9, 41; Jn 1:49

YOU ARE MY GOD
Ps 31:14; 43:2; 91:2; 118:28; 140:6; 143:10; Is 25:1; 44:17; Hos 2:23

YOU ARE MY SON
Ps 2:7; Mk 1:11; Lk 3:22; Ac 13:33; Heb 1:5; 5:5

YOU ARE RIGHTEOUS
Dt 9:5; Ezr 9:15; Neh 9:8; Job 35:7; Ps 119:137

YOU ARE THE CHRIST
Mt 16:16; 26:63; Mk 8:29; Lk 22:67; Jn 10:24; 11:27

YOU ARE THE ONE
Gn 3:14; 49:8; Dt 31:7; 31:23; Josh 1:6; Jdg 15:18; 2Sa 22:28; 22:51; Neh 1:5; 9:7, 32; Ps 3:3; 9:13; 17:7; 18:27, 28, 50; 22:9; 99:4; 102:27; 119:102; 139:13; Ac 4:24; 4:25

YOU MUST BE HOLY
Lv 11:45; 19:2; 20:7, 26; 1Pt 1:15

YOU WERE CALLED
1Co 1:9; 1:26; 7:21, 24; Ga 5:13; Col 3:15; 1Ti 6:12; 1Pt 2:21; 3:9

YOU WILL BE BLESSED
Gn 27:29; Nm 24:9; Dt 28:3; 28:6; Lk 14:14

YOU WILL BE FORGIVEN
Lv 4:35; 5:10, 13, 16, 18; 6:7; Lk 6:37

YOU WILL BE SAVED
1Sa 11:9; 2Ki 19:11; Is 30:15; 37:11; Ac 16:31; Ro 10:9

YOUNG

Exodus
22:16 a man seduces a **y** woman who isn't
33:11 the camp. But his **y** assistant Joshua,
34:26 Don't boil a **y** goat in its

Deuteronomy
22:6 do not remove the mother from her **y**.

Joshua
6:23 So the **y** men who had been spies went

Ruth
2:5 Boaz said to his **y** man, the one who was
4:12 LORD will give you from this **y** woman."

1 Samuel
1:24 was still very **y**, Hannah took him,
2:18 LORD. He was a **y** boy, clothed in a
9:2 was a handsome **y** man. No one in

Nehemiah
12:35 were also some **y** priests with

Esther
2:3 all the beautiful **y** women together to
3:13 the Jews, both **y** and old, even

Job
1:15 and killed the **y** men with swords.
19:18 Even the **y** despise me; I get up, and
39:30 and their **y** lap up blood; where

Psalms
17:12 are like a strong **y** lion lying in
29:6 around like a **y** bull, makes
34:10 Even strong **y** lions go without and get
37:25 I was **y** and now I'm old, but I have
45:14 attendants, the **y** women servants
68:25 between them the **y** women were
69:31 pleasing than a **y** bull with full
78:63 Fire devoured his **y** men, and his young
84:3 she can lay her **y** beside your
88:15 Since I was **y** I've been afflicted, I've
91:13 you'll trample **y** lions and
104:21 The **y** lions roar for their prey,
119:9 How can **y** people keep their paths pure?
127:4 born when one is **y** are like arrows
148:12 Do the same, you **y** men—young women

Proverbs
1:4 naive mature, the **y** knowledgeable and discreet.
7:7 among the naive **y** men and noticed
20:11 Even **y** people are known by their
20:29 is the glory of **y** men; gray hair is
27:27 house, and to nourish your **y** women.
29:21 servants from a **y** age, and later on
30:17 peck it out, and the eagle's **y** eat it.
30:19 and the way of a man with a **y** woman.

Ecclesiastes
11:9 Rejoice, **y** person, while you are young!

Song of Songs
1:3 That's why the **y** women love you.
2:2 so is my dearest among the **y** women.
2:3 lover among the **y** men. In his shade
2:9 a gazelle or a **y** stag. Here he
2:17 a gazelle or a **y** stag upon the
6:8 secondary wives, **y** women beyond
6:9 one who bore her. **Y** women see her and
8:14 a gazelle or a **y** stag on the

Isaiah
7:14 you a sign. The **y** woman is pregnant

Jeremiah
11:19 I was like a **y** lamb led to the
11:22 them. Their **y** men will die in

Lamentations
1:4 are groaning, her **y** women grieving.
2:10 Jerusalem's **y** women bow their
4:3 they nurse their **y**. But the daughter
5:14 the city gate; **y** people stop their

Ezekiel
46:6 be a flawless **y** bull from the

Daniel
1:4 good-looking **y** men without defects,
1:15 than all the **y** men who were
1:18 to review the **y** men as the king

Hosea
5:14 Ephraim, like a **y** lion to the house

Joel
2:28 dreams, and your **y** men will see

Amos
2:7 with the same **y** woman, degrading
3:4 no prey? Does a **y** lion cry out from
4:10 I killed your **y** men with the
8:13 day the beautiful **y** women and the

Micah
2:9 house; from their **y** children you take
5:8 forest, like a **y** lion among flocks

Nahum
2:11 the meadow of the **y** lions, where
2:13 will devour your **y** lions; I will cut

YOUNG [cont.]

Zechariah
2:4 Run! Say to this **y** man: Jerusalem
9:17 will make his **y** men flourish; so
11:3 heard among the **y** lions because the
11:16 He won't seek the **y** or heal the
13:5 has been my occupation since I was **y**."
Matthew
14:11 gave it to the **y** woman, and she
19:20 The **y** man replied, "I've kept all
19:22 But when the **y** man heard this, he went away saddened
25:1 will be like ten **y** bridesmaids who
Mark
5:41 koum," which means, "**Y** woman, get up."
7:25 a woman whose **y** daughter was
14:51 One **y** man, a disciple, was wearing
16:5 tomb, they saw a **y** man in a white
Luke
2:24 A pair of turtledoves or two **y** pigeons.
7:14 Jesus said, "**Y** man, I say to
15:29 me as much as a **y** goat so I could
John
12:14 Jesus found a **y** donkey and sat on it,
Acts
2:17 prophesy. Your **y** will see visions.
7:58 in the care of a **y** man named Saul.
20:9 A **y** man named Eutychus was sitting in
1 John
2:13 the beginning. **Y** people, I'm
2:14 the beginning. **Y** people, I write

YOUNGER

Genesis
19:35 also, and the **y** daughter lay down
27:42 she summoned her **y** son Jacob and
29:16 older was named Leah and the **y** Rachel.
48:19 be great. But his **y** brother will be
Job
30:1 But now those **y** than I mock me, whose
Ezekiel
16:46 the north. Your **y** sister is Sodom,
23:4 Oholah, and the **y** sister was named
Matthew
2:16 two years old and **y**, according to the
Mark
15:40 of James (the **y** one) and Joses,
Luke
15:12 The **y** son said to his father, 'Father,
15:13 afterward, the **y** son gathered
John
21:18 when you were **y** you tied your own
Romans
9:12 child will be a slave to the **y** one.
1 Timothy
5:1 father; treat **y** men like your
5:11 But don't accept **y** widows for the list.
5:14 So I want **y** widows to marry, have
Titus
2:6 encourage the **y** men to be sensible
1 Peter
5:5 urge you who are **y**: accept the

YOUNGEST

Genesis
9:24 what his **y** son had done to
42:20 But bring your **y** brother back to me so
Joshua
6:26 gates will cost them their **y** child."
1 Samuel
16:11 is still the **y** one," Jesse
17:14 (David was the **y**.) These three older

YOUR DETESTABLE PRACTICES

Eze 5:9; 7:3, 4, 8, 9; 14:6; 16:22, 51; 44:6, 7

YOUR FRUIT

Eze 25:4; 36:8; Hos 14:8; Mk 11:14; Jn 15:16

YOUR HEAVENLY FATHER

Mt 5:48; 6:14, 26, 32; 7:11

YOUR NEIGHBOR AS YOURSELF

Lv 19:18; Mk 12:31; Lk 10:27; Ro 13:9; Ga 5:14; Jas 2:8

YOUR SINS

Lv 16:30; 26:18, 21, 24, 28; Josh 24:19; Job 15:5; Ps 103:3; Is 1:18; 43:24; 44:22; 50:1; 59:2; 65:7; Jer 15:13; 30:14, 15; Lam 4:22; Eze 16:52; 18:30; 21:24; Dn 4:27; Am 5:12; Mi 6:13; Mt 6:15; 9:2, 5; Mk 2:5; 2:9; Lk 5:20; 5:23; 7:48; Jn 8:24; Ac 2:38; 3:19; 22:16; 1Co 15:17; Jas 5:16; 1Jn 2:12

YOUR SINS ARE FORGIVEN

Mt 9:2; 9:5; Mk 2:5; 2:9; Lk 5:20; 5:23; 7:48, 48, 48, 48, 48; Is 43:24; 44:22; 50:1; 59:2; 65:7; Jer 15:13; 30:14, 15; Lam 4:22; Eze 16:52; 18:30; 21:24; Dn 4:27; Am 5:12; Mi 6:13; 6:15; 9:2, 5; 2:5, 9; 5:20, 23; 7:48; Jn 8:24; Ac 2:38; 3:19; 22:16; 1Co 15:17; Jas 5:16; 1Jn 2:12

YOUTH

Genesis
8:21 evil from their **y**. I will never
Numbers
11:28 since his **y**, responded, "My
2 Samuel
19:7 you've faced from your **y** until now.
1 Kings
11:17 While still a **y**, Hadad escaped to
11:28 saw how well this **y** did his work. So
18:12 servant has feared the LORD from my **y**.
Job
31:18 for from my **y** I raised the orphan as a
33:25 like a child's; they regain their **y**.
Psalms
25:7 the sins of my **y** or my wrongdoing.
71:17 me since my **y**, God, and I'm
78:31 he cut down Israel's **y** in their prime.
103:5 so that your **y** is made fresh
129:1 song.] From **y**, people have
129:2 from **y** people have constantly attacked
144:12 fully, in their **y**, like plants; so
Proverbs
2:17 partner of her **y**; she even forgets
5:18 blessed. Rejoice in the wife of your **y**.
7:7 noticed among the **y**, one who had no
Ecclesiastes
4:13 A poor but wise **y** is better than an old
4:15 the next **y** who would rise to
11:10 body, because **y** and the dawn of

Isaiah
9:17 Lord showed their **y** no pity, and
47:15 from your **y**: each has
54:4 the shame of your **y**; you'll no longer
Jeremiah
3:4 to me, "My father, my friend since **y**,
3:24 From our **y**, shame has devoured the
3:25 from our **y** to this very day.
9:21 the streets, the **y** from the squares.
18:21 and their **y** struck down in
22:21 way since your **y**: not listening to
32:30 eyes since their **y**; the people of
Lamentations
3:27 for a man to carry a yoke in his **y**.
Ezekiel
23:21 days of her **y**, when the
Hosea
2:15 the days of her **y**, like the time
Joel
1:8 one who has lost the husband of her **y**.
Amos
2:11 and some of your **y** to be nazirites.
Malachi
2:14 the wife of your **y** against whom you
2:15 Don't cheat on the wife of your **y**
John
6:9 A **y** here has five barley loaves and
Acts
26:4 followed since my **y** because, from the

Zz

ZACCHAEUS
Luke
19:2 A man there named **Z**, a ruler among tax collectors

ZADOK
2 Samuel
8:17 Ahitub's son **Z** and Ahimelech's son
15:24 **Z** was there too, along with all the
17:15 told the priests **Z** and Abiathar,
19:11 to the priests **Z** and Abiathar:
20:25 was secretary; **Z** and Abiathar were
1 Kings
1:8 But **Z** the priest, Jehoiada's son
Ezra
7:2 son of Shallum son of **Z** son of Ahitu
Nehemiah
3:4 next to them, and **Z**, Baana's son,
Ezekiel
43:19 descendants of **Z**, the ones who may
44:15 family of **Z** who did keep
Matthew
1:14 was the father of **Z**. Zadok was the

ZEBEDEE
Matthew
4:21 James the son of **Z** and his brother
Mark
1:20 their father **Z** in the boat with

ZEBULUN
Genesis
30:20 him six sons." So she named him **Z**.
49:13 **Z** will live at the seashore; he'll live
Joshua
19:10 for the clans of **Z**. The border of
Matthew
4:13 the sea in the area of **Z** and Naphtali.
Revelation
7:8 from the tribe of **Z**, twelve thousand;

ZECHARIAH
2 Kings
14:29 Israel. His son **Z** succeeded him as
Ezra
5:1 and the prophet **Z**, Iddo's son,
Nehemiah
8:4 Hash-baddanah, **Z**, and Meshullam
Isaiah
8:2 the priest and **Z**, Jeberechiah's
Zechariah
1:1 word came to **Z** the prophet,
Matthew
23:35 to the blood of **Z** the son of
Luke
1:5 a priest named **Z** who belonged to
1:67 John's father **Z** was filled with the

ZEDEKIAH
2 Kings
24:17 changed Mattaniah's name to **Z**.
25:5 army chased King **Z** and caught up
1 Chronicles
3:15 the third **Z**, and the fourth
3:16 family: his son Jeconiah and his son **Z**.
Nehemiah
10:1 Nehemiah, Hacaliah's son, and **Z**;
Jeremiah
1:3 year of King **Z**, Josiah's son,
21:1 word when King **Z** sent Pashhur,
27:3 come to Jerusalem to Judah's King **Z**.
27:12 to Judah's King **Z**: If you want to
52:8 army chased down **Z** and caught him in the plains

ZEPHANIAH
2 Kings
25:18 the chief priest, **Z** the priest next
1 Chronicles
6:36 son of Joel son of Azariah son of **Z**
Jeremiah
21:1 and the priest **Z**, Maaseiah's son,
Zephaniah
1:1 word that came to **Z**, Cushi's son,
Zechariah
6:10 day to the house of Josiah son of **Z**

ZERAH
Genesis
36:13 sons: Nahath, **Z**, Shammah, and
Numbers
26:13 from **Z**, the Zerahite clan; from Shaul,
26:20 clan; from **Z**, the Zerahite
Nehemiah
11:24 son, from the family of **Z**, Judah's son.
Matthew
1:3 of Perez and **Z**, whose mother was

ZERUBBABEL
1 Chronicles
3:19 Pedaiah's family: **Z** and Shimei.
Ezra
2:2 They came with **Z**, Jeshua, Nehemiah,
Nehemiah
7:7 They came with **Z**, Jeshua, Nehemiah,
Zechariah
4:6 LORD's word to **Z**: Neither by
Matthew
1:12 Salathiel was the father of **Z**.
Luke
3:27 of Rhesa son of **Z** son of Shealtiel

ZIBA
2 Samuel
9:2 household named **Z**, and he was

ZIKLAG
Joshua
15:31 **Z**, Madmannah, Sansannah
1 Samuel
27:6 gave the town of **Z** to David at that
2 Samuel
1:1 Amalekites, he stayed in **Z** two days.
Nehemiah
11:28 in **Z**, in Meconah and its villages

ZILPAH
Genesis
29:24 given his servant **Z** to his daughter
46:18 are the sons of **Z**, whom Laban gave

ZIMRI
Numbers
25:14 woman was **Z** the son of Salu,
1 Kings
16:10 **Z** came, attacked, and killed Elah in
16:16 heard the news: "**Z** has plotted
16:19 of the sins **Z** had committed by
Jeremiah
25:25 all the kings of **Z**, Elam, and Media

ZION → DAUGHTER ZION, MOUNT ZION
2 Samuel
5:7 the fortress of **Z**—which became Davi
1 Kings
8:1 LORD's covenant from David's City **Z**.
1 Chronicles
11:5 fortress of **Z**, which became
2 Chronicles
5:2 LORD's covenant from **Z**, David's City.
Psalms
2:6 my king on **Z**, my holy
14:7 come out of **Z**! When the LORD
50:2 From **Z**, perfect in beauty, God shines
65:1 A song.] God of **Z**, to you even
78:68 the mountain of **Z**, which he loves.
102:13 compassion on **Z** because it is
137:3 Sing us a song about **Z**!" they said.
Song of Songs
3:11 daughters of **Z**—on King Solomon
Isaiah
1:27 **Z** will be redeemed by justice, and
14:32 LORD has founded **Z**; the oppressed
28:16 I'm laying in **Z** a stone, a tested
40:9 messenger **Z**! Raise your voice
51:3 LORD will comfort **Z**; he will comfort
51:11 and come to **Z** with singing and
52:1 on your strength, **Z**! Put on your
52:8 eyes they see the LORD returning to **Z**.
Jeremiah
50:5 will search for **Z**, turning their
Joel
2:1 Blow the horn in **Z**; give a shout on my
3:16 LORD roars from **Z**, and utters his
3:21 the guilty. The LORD dwells in **Z**.
Amos
1:2 LORD roars from **Z**. He shouts from
Micah
3:12 because of you, **Z** will be plowed
4:2 will come from **Z** and the LORD's
Zechariah
1:17 compassion to **Z** and will again
Romans
9:33 block in **Z**, which is a rock
11:26 will come from **Z**. He will remove
1 Peter
2:6 a cornerstone in **Z**, chosen,

ZOAR
Genesis
19:30 of living in **Z**, he and his two
Deuteronomy
34:3 Jericho Valley, Palm City—as far as **Z**.
Isaiah
15:5 fugitives flee to **Z**, to Eglath-shelish
Jeremiah
48:34 resound from **Z** to Horonaim and

Abbreviations

BOOKS OF THE BIBLE

Old Testament

Book	Abbreviation
Genesis	Gn
Exodus	Ex
Leviticus	Lv
Numbers	Nm
Deuteronomy	Dt
Joshua	Josh
Judges	Jdg
Ruth	Ru
1, 2 Samuel	1, 2Sa
1, 2 Kings	1, 2Ki
1, 2 Chronicles	1, 2Ch
Ezra	Ezr
Nehemiah	Neh
Esther	Est
Job	Job
Psalms	Ps
Proverbs	Prv
Ecclesiastes	Ecc
Song of Songs	Song
Isaiah	Is
Jeremiah	Jer
Lamentations	Lam
Ezekiel	Eze
Daniel	Dn
Hosea	Hos
Joel	Jl
Amos	Am
Obadiah	Obad
Jonah	Jon
Micah	Mi
Nahum	Na
Habakkuk	Hab
Zephaniah	Zep
Haggai	Hg
Zechariah	Zec
Malachi	Mal

New Testament

Book	Abbreviation
Matthew	Mt
Mark	Mk
Luke	Lk
John	Jn
Acts	Ac
Romans	Ro
1, 2 Corinthians	1, 2Co
Galatians	Ga
Ephesians	Eph
Philippians	Phi
Colossians	Col
1, 2 Thessalonians	1, 2Th
1, 2 Timothy	1, 2Ti
Titus	Ti
Philemon	Phm
Hebrews	Heb
James	Jas
1, 2 Peter	1, 2Pt
1, 2, 3 John	1, 2, 3Jn
Jude	Jud
Revelation	Rev